INSTITUTES

OF

THE CHRISTIAN RELIGION

By
JOHN CALVIN

Translated by
HENRY BEVERIDGE

WM. B. EERDMANS PUBLISHING COMPANY
Grand Rapids, Michigan

This one-volume edition first published 1989 by
Wm. B. Eerdmans Publishing Co., 255 Jefferson Ave. SE,
Grand Rapids, MI 49503.

Printed in the United States of America

Publisher's Note
The Henry Beveridge translation of Calvin's *Institutes of the
Christian Religion* was originally published in two volumes.
In this single volume edition we have retained the pagination of
the original two volumes. Thus, following page 582 in the first half
of this volume, the page numbers will resume at page 1.
The tables and indexes retain their designation of volumes i and ii,
now signifying the first or second half of this volume.

Reprinted, September 1993

Introduction

By THE REV. JOHN MURRAY, M.A., TH.M.

THE publication in English of another edition of the *opus magnum* of Christian theology is an event fraught with much encouragement. Notwithstanding the decadence so patent in our present-day world and particularly in the realm of Christian thought and life, the publishers have confidence that there is sufficient interest to warrant such an undertaking. If this faith is justified we have reason for thanksgiving to God. For what would be a better harbinger of another Reformation than widespread recourse to the earnest and sober study of the Word of God which would be evinced by the readiness carefully to peruse *The Institutes of the Christian Religion.*

Dr. B. B. Warfield in his admirable article, "On the Literary History of the *Institutes,*" has condensed for us the appraisal accorded Calvin's work by the critics who have been most competent to judge. Among these tributes none expresses more adequately, and none with comparable terseness, the appraisal which is Calvin's due than that of the learned Joseph Scaliger, "Solus inter theologos Calvinus."

It would be a presumptuous undertaking to try to set forth all the reasons why Calvin holds that position of eminence in the history of Christian theology. By the grace and in the overruling providence of God there was the convergence of multiple factors, and all of these it would be impossible to trace in their various interrelations and interactions. One of these, however, calls for special mention. Calvin was an exegete and biblical theologian of the first rank. No other one factor comparably served to equip Calvin for the successful prosecution of his greatest work which in 1559 received its definitive edition.

The attitude to Scripture entertained by Calvin and the principles which guided him in its exposition are nowhere stated with more simplicity and fervor than in the Epistle Dedicatory to his first commentary, the commentary on the epistle to the Romans. "Such veneration," he says, "we ought indeed to entertain for the Word of God, that we ought not to pervert it in the least degree by varying expositions; for its majesty is diminished, I know not how much, especially when not expounded with great discretion and with great sobriety. And if it be deemed a great wickedness to contaminate any thing that is dedicated to God, he surely cannot be endured, who, with impure, or even with unprepared hands, will handle that very thing, which of all things is the most sacred on earth. It is therefore an audacity, closely allied to a sacrilege, rashly to turn Scripture in any way we please, and to indulge our fancies as in sport; which has been done by many in former times" (English Translation, Grand Rapids, 1947, p. xxvii).

It was Calvin preeminently who set the pattern for the exercise of that sobriety which guards the science of exegesis against those distortions and perversions to which allegorizing methods are ever prone to subject the interpretation and application of Scripture. The debt we owe to Calvin in establishing sound canons of interpretation and in thus directing the future course of exegetical study is incalculable. It is only to be lamented that too frequently the preaching of Protestant and even Reformed communions has not been sufficiently grounded in the hermeneutical principles which Calvin so nobly exemplified.

One feature of Calvin's exegetical work is his concern for the analogy of Scripture. He is always careful to take account of the unity and harmony of Scripture teaching. His expositions are not therefore afflicted with the vice of expounding particular passages without respect to the teaching of Scripture elsewhere and without respect to the system of truth set forth in the Word of God. His exegesis, in a word, is theologically oriented. It is this quality that lies close to that which was *par excellence* his genius.

However highly we assess Calvin's exegetical talent and product, his eminence as an exegete must not be allowed to overshadow what was, after all, his greatest gift. He was *par excellence* a theologian. It was his systematizing genius preeminently that equipped him for the prosecution and completion of his masterpiece.

When we say that he was *par excellence* a theologian we must dissociate from our use of this word every notion that is suggestive of the purely speculative. No one has ever fulminated with more passion and eloquence against "vacuous and meteoric speculation" than has Calvin. And no one has ever been more keenly conscious that the theologian's task was the humble and, at the same time, truly noble one of being a disciple of the Scripture. "No man," he declares, "can have the least knowledge of true and sound doctrine, without having been a disciple of the Scripture. Hence originates all true wisdom, when we embrace with reverence the testimony which God hath been pleased therein to deliver concerning himself. For obedience is the source, not only of an absolutely perfect and complete faith, but of all right knowledge of God" (*Inst.* I, vi, 2). In the words of William Cunningham: "In theology there is, of course, no room for originality properly so called, for its whole materials are contained in the actual statements of God's word; and he is the greatest and best theologian who has most accurately apprehended the meaning of the statements of Scripture — who, by comparing and combining them, has most fully and correctly brought out the whole mind of God on all the topics on which the Scriptures give us information — who classifies and digests the truths of Scripture in the way best fitted to commend them to the apprehension and acceptance of men — and who can most clearly and forcibly bring out their scriptural evidence, and most skillfully and effectively defend them against the assaults of adversaries . . . Calvin was far above the weakness of aiming at the invention of novelties in theology, or of wishing to be regarded as the discoverer of new opinions" (*The Reformers and the Theology of the Reformation*, Edinburgh, 1866, p. 296). As we bring even elementary understanding to bear upon our reading of the *Institutes* we shall immediately discover the profound sense of the majesty of God, veneration for the Word of God, and the jealous care for faithful exposition and systematization which were marked features of the author. And because of this we shall find the *Institutes* to be suffused with the warmth of godly fear. The *Institutes* is not only the classic of Christian theology; it is also a model of Christian devotion. For what Calvin sought to foster was that "pure and genuine religion" which consists in "faith united with the serious fear of God, such fear as may embrace voluntary reverence and draw along with it legitimate worship such as is prescribed in the law" (*Inst.* I, ii, 2).

* * *

The present edition is from the translation made by Henry Beveridge in 1845 for the Calvin Translation Society. The reader may be assured that the translation faithfully reflects the teaching of Calvin but must also bear in mind that no translation can perfectly convey the thought of the original. It may also be added that a more adequate translation of Calvin's *Institutes* into English is a real *desideratum*. In fulfilling this need the translator or translators would perform the greatest service if the work of translation were supplemented by footnotes in which at crucial points, where translation is difficult or most accurate translation impossible, the Latin text would be reproduced and comment made on its more exact import. Furthermore, footnotes which would supply the reader with references to other places in Calvin's writings where he deals with the same subject would be an invaluable help to students of Calvin and to the cause of truth. Admittedly such work requires linguistic skill of the highest order, thorough knowledge of Calvin's writings, and deep sympathy with his theology. It would also involve prodigious labour. We may hope that the seed being sown by the present venture on the part of the Wm. B. Eerdmans Publishing Company may bear fruit some day in such a harvest.

JOHN MURRAY,
Professor of Systematic Theology,
Westminster Theological Seminary.

PHILADELPHIA, PENNA.

CONTENTS

** THE DIVISION AND ARRANGEMENT OF THE CHAPTERS OF THE INSTITUTES
* WILL BE FOUND UNDER No. VI.

THE SECTIONS ARE INTRODUCED AT THE COMMENCEMENT OF EACH CHAPTER.

---

* * THE DIVISION AND ARRANGEMENT OF THE CHAPTERS OF THE INSTITUTES
* WILL BE FOUND UNDER No. VI

THE SECTIONS ARE INTRODUCED AT THE COMMENCEMENT OF EACH CHAPTER.

TABLES

INSTITUTES OF THE CHRISTIAN RELIGION.

TABLE I.

OF PASSAGES FROM THE HOLY SCRIPTURES, AND FROM THE APOCRYPHA, WHICH ARE QUOTED, OR INCIDENTALLY ILLUSTRATED, IN THE INSTITUTES.

Chap.	GENESIS.	Vol.	Chap.	GENESIS.	Vol.	Chap.	GENESIS.	Vol.
i. 2,	...	i. 80	xviii. 23,	...	ii. 162	xlviii. 14,	...	ii. 326
i. 3,	...	i. 116	xx. 3,	...	i. 196	xlviii. 16,	i. 145 ;	ii. 172
i. 26,	...	i. 134, 163	xx. 3, 18,	...	i. 332	xlix. 5, 6,	...	i. 77
i. 27,	..	i. 102, 406	xx. 7,	...	i. 196	xlix. 18,	...	i. 379
i. 31,	...	ii. 570	xxi. 1,	...	ii. 18	l. 20.		i. 190
ii. 7,	...	i. 165, 423	xxi. 10,	...	ii. 307	l. 25,	...	i. 379
ii. 17,	...	i. 474	xxi. 12,	...	ii. 18			
ii. 18,	...	ii. 475	xxii 8,	...	i. 175		EXODUS.	
ii. 23,	i. 407 ;	ii. 648	xxii. 16. 18,	...	ii. 121	ii. 12,	...	ii. 660
iii. 9,	...	i. 537	xxiii. 4,	...	ii. 271	iii. 14,	...	i. 132
iii. 15,	...	i. 154, 412	xxiii. 19,	...	ii. 271	iii. 21,	...	i. 189
iii. 22,	...	ii. 499	xxiv. 7,	...	i. 150	iv. 11,	...	i. 123
iv. 4,	...	ii. 79	xxvii. 38, 39,	...	i. 589	iv. 21,	i. 201, 268 ;	ii. 252
iv. 7,	...	i. 288	xxviii. 12,	...	i. 150	iv. 25,	...	ii. 525
iv. 10,	...	i. 474	xxviii. 20,	...	ii. 476	vi. 7,	...	i. 374
vi. 5,	...	i. 244	xxx. 2,	...	i. 178	vii. 1,	...	i. 117
vi. 6,	...	i. 195	xxxi. 19,	...	i. 97	xi. 3,	...	i. 269
vi. 18,	...	ii. 494	xxxii. 10,	...	ii. 174	xii. 5,	...	ii. 553
viii. 21,	... i. 246 ;	ii. 74	xxxii. 29, 30,	...	i. 118	xii. 26,	...	ii. 550
ix. 9,	...	ii. 494	xxxiv. 25,	...	ii. 800	xii. 43,	...	ii. 575
xii. 17,	...	i. 332	xxxv. 22,	...	ii. 800	xiii. 12,	...	ii. 553
xiv. 18,	...	ii. 608	xxxvii. 18,	...	ii. 800	xiv. 31,	...	ii. 890
xv. 1,	i. 389 ;	ii. 273	xxxvii. 28,	...	ii. 800	xvi. 7,	...	i. 78
xv. 5,	...	ii. 121	xxxvii. 33,	...	i. 878	xvii. 6,	...	ii. 620
xv. 17,	...	ii. 505	xxxviii. 16,	..	ii. 800	xvii. 15,	...	i. 117
xvii. 2,	...	ii. 494	xxxviii. 18		i. 878	xviii. 16,	...	ii. 445
xvii. 7,	...	i. 333, 374	xliii. 14,	...	i. 270	xix. 5,	..	ii. 537
xvii. 10,	...	ii. 530	xlv. 5,	...	i. 190	xix. 6,	..	i. 301
xvii. 13,	...	ii. 575	xlvii. 9,	...	i. 878	xx. 2. 3,	..	i. 326
xvii. 15,	...	ii. 535	xlvii. 29, 80,	...	i. 879	xx. 3,	...	i. 328

Chap.	MATTHEW.	Vol.
xxiv. 45,	...	ii. 552
xxv. 21,	...	i. 261 ; ii. 93
xxv. 23,	...	i. 261
xxv. 29,	...	i. 261 ; ii. 93
xxv. 32,	...	ii. 272
xxv. 34,	...	ii. 121, 257
xxv. 34, 35,	..	ii. 120
xxv. 40,	...	ii. 125
xxv. 41,	...	i. 151, 155
xxvi. 11,	...	ii. 579
xxvi. 26,	ii. 411, 557, 572	
xxvi. 28,	...	i. 456
xxvi. 38,	...	ii. 22
xxvi. 39,	...	i. 445
xxvii. 46,	...	i. 416
xxviii. 6,	...	ii. 584
xxviii. 18,	...	ii. 94
xxviii. 19,	...	i. 124
	ii. 515, 526, 644	
xxviii. 19, 20,		ii. 391
xxviii. 20,	...	i. 14, 449
	ii. 394, 396, 530	

Chap.	MARK.	Vol.
i. 4,		i. 525 ; ii 635
i. 14,	...	i. 365
i. 15,	...	i. 525
vi. 13,	...	ii. 636
viii. 38,	...	il. 301
ix. 24,	...	ii. 496
ix. 43,	...	ii. 274
x. 9,	...	ii. 281
x. 30,	...	ii. 122
xi. 24,	...	ii. 156
xii. 18,	...	ii. 265
xiv. 22,	...	ii. 572
xv. 28,	...	i. 438
xv. 34,	...	i. 444
xvi. 15,	...	ii. 318, 644
xvi. 16,	..	ii. 513, 548
xvi. 19,	...	i. 449
xvi. 20,	...	i. 9

Chap.	LUKE.	Vol.
i. 6,	...	ii. 110
i. 15,	...	ii. 541
i. 32,	...	i. 419, 421
i. 33,	...	i. 427
i. 34,	...	ii. 579
i. 35,	...	i. 419
i. 43,	...	i. 419
i. 55,	...	i. 371
i. 72,	...	i. 371, 404
i. 74, 75,	..	ii. 99
i. 77,	...	ii. 57
i. 79,	...	i. 404
ii. 37,	...	ii. 463
iii. 3,	i. 525 ; ii. 516, 635	
iii. 14,	...	ii. 662
iii. 16,	. i. 465 ; ii. 516	
iii. 38,	...	i. 406

Chap.	LUKE.	Vol.
iv. 18,	...	i. 537
v. 17,	...	i. 538
v. 34,	...	ii. 464
vi. 13,	...	ii. 319
vi. 24,	...	ii. 136
vii. 29,	...	ii. 38
vii. 35,	...	ii. 38
vii. 36, 50	...	i 567
vii. 47,	...	i. 562
viii. 15,	...	ii. 498
ix. 23,	...	ii. 96
ix. 55,	...	ii. 162
x. 1,	...	ii. 319
x. 13,	...	i. 524
x. 16,	...	ii. 318, 391
x. 18,	..	i. 154
x. 20,	...	ii. 249
x. 21,	...	i. 108
x. 22,	i. 470 ; ii. 620	
x. 23,	...	i. 361
x. 25,	...	ii. 483
x. 27,	..	i. 324, 356
x. 32,	...	i. 290
xi. 21, 22,	...	i. 154
xi. 33,	...	i. 102
xi. 46,	...	ii. 414
xii. 10,	...	i. 528
xii. 14,	...	ii. 446
xv. 7,	...	i. 146
xv. 20,	...	ii. 185
xvi. 9,	...	ii. 124
xvi. 15,	...	ii. 38, 62
xvi. 16,	...	i. 312
xvii. 5,	...	ii. 496
xvii. 9,	...	ii. 84
xvii. 10,	...	ii. 83, 92
xvii. 21,	...	i. 429
xvii. 22,	...	i. 429
xviii. 13,	i. 549 ; ii. 66	
xviii. 14,	i. 567 ; ii. 39	
xviii. 19,	...	i. 132
xix. 26,	...	i. 261
xx. 27,	...	ii. 265
xx. 32,	...	i. 375
xxi. 28,	...	ii. 29
xxii. 17,	...	ii. 599
xxii. 19,	...	ii. 320
xxii. 20	i. 456 ; ii. 561, 572	
xxii. 25, 26,	...	ii. 446, 656
xxii. 32,	...	ii. 246, 385
xxii. 44,	..	ii. 22
xxii. 61,	...	i. 567
xxiii. 42,	...	ii. 250
xxiii. 43,	...	ii. 267
xxiv. 6,	...	ii. 263
xxiv. 26,	i. 459 ; ii. 587	
xxiv. 27,	...	i. 86, 500
xxiv. 31,	...	ii. 585
xxiv. 39,	...	ii. 583
xxiv. 44,	...	i. 578
xxiv. 45,	...	i. 500
xxiv. 46, 47,	...	i. 403, 525

Chap.	JOHN.	Vol.
i. 1,	...	i. 116, 130
i. 4,	...	i. 165, 293
i. 4, 5,	...	i. 238
i. 5,	..	i. 238
i. 12,	...	ii. 185, 222
i. 12, 13,	...	i. 465
i. 13.	...	i. 239
i. 14,	...	i. 119, 424
i. 16,	...	i. 410, 430
i. 17,	...	i. 312
i. 18,	i. 364 ; ii. 586	
i. 23,	...	i. 367
i. 29,	i. 367, 438, 456, 557	
		ii. 516
i. 40,	...	ii. 357
i. 42,	...	ii. 357
i. 51,	...	i. 150, 365
ii. 19,	i. 419 ; ii. 269	
ii. 24, 25,	...	i. 480
iii. 3,	...	ii. 541
iii. 5,	...	ii. 546
iii. 6,	...	i. 216, 249
iii. 13,	i. 417 ; ii. 586	
iii. 14,	...	i. 404
iii. 16,	i. 403, 436, 454 ; ii.	
		85, 245
iii. 27,	...	i. 239
iii. 33,	...	i. 476
iii. 34,	...	i. 429
iii. 36,	...	ii. 551
iv. 22,	i. 61, 67, 293	
iv. 23,	...	ii. 180, 423
iv. 24,	...	i. 134
iv. 25,	i. 426 ; ii. 394	
iv. 35,	...	ii. 552
iv. 42,	...	i. 473
iv. 53,	...	i. 472
v. 8,	...	ii. 644
v. 17,	i. 115, 120, 176	
v. 18,	...	i. 120
v. 22,	...	i. 451
v. 23,	...	i. 294
v. 24,	· ii. 95, 245, 260, 547	
v. 25,	i. 291, 404 ; ii. 76	
v. 26,	...	ii. 562
v. 28, 29,	...	ii. 264, 269
v. 29.	...	ii. 120
v. 32,	...	i. 125
v. 35,	...	i. 367
v. 46,	...	i. 364
vi. 27,	...	ii. 120
vi. 29,	...	ii. 128
vi. 35,	...	ii. 245
vi. 37,	...	ii. 219, 246
vi. 37, 39,	...	ii. 245
vi. 39,	ii. 219, 247, 271	
vi. 39, 40,	...	ii. 223
vi. 44,	i. 239, 261, 500, 501 ;	
		ii. 240
vi. 44, 45,	i. 277 ; ii. 219	
vi. 45,	i. 257, 260 ; ii. 253	
vi. 45, 46,	i. 500 ; ii. 219	

TABLE II.

OF HEBREW WORDS EXPLAINED.

TABLE III.

OF GREEK WORDS EXPLAINED.

INDEX

TO

THE AUTHORS QUOTED IN THE INSTITUTES.

INSTITUTIONS

OF

THE CHRISTIAN RELIGION.

PREFATORY ADDRESS

TO

HIS MOST CHRISTIAN MAJESTY,

THE MOST MIGHTY AND ILLUSTRIOUS MONARCH,

FRANCIS, KING OF THE FRENCH,

HIS SOVEREIGN ;[1]

JOHN CALVIN PRAYS PEACE AND SALVATION IN CHRIST.[2]

SIRE,—When I first engaged in this work, nothing was farther from my thoughts than to write what should afterwards be presented to your Majesty. My intention was only to furnish a kind of rudiments, by which those who feel some interest in religion might be trained to true godliness. And I toiled at the task chiefly for the sake of my countrymen the French, multitudes of whom I perceived to be hungering and thirsting after Christ, while very few seemed to have been duly imbued with even a slender knowledge of him. That this was the object which I had in view is apparent from the work itself, which is written in a simple and elementary form adapted for instruction.

But when I perceived that the fury of certain bad men had risen to such a height in your realm, that there was no place in it for sound doctrine, I thought it might be of service if I were in the same work both to give instruction to my countrymen, and also lay before your Majesty a Confession, from which you may learn what the doctrine is that so inflames the rage of those madmen who are this day, with fire and sword, troubling your kingdom. For I fear not to declare, that what I have here given may be regarded as a summary of the very doctrine which, they vociferate, ought to be punished

---

[1] In the last edition by Calvin, the words are, as here translated, simply, " Principi suo." In the edition published at Basle in 1536, the words are, " Principi ac Domino suo sibiobservando."

[2] Ed. 1536. " In Domino."

with confiscation, exile, imprisonment, and flames, as well as exterminated by land and sea.

I am aware, indeed, how, in order to render our cause as hateful to your Majesty as possible, they have filled your ears and mind with atrocious insinuations ; but you will be pleased, of your clemency, to reflect, that neither in word nor deed could there be any innocence, were it sufficient merely to accuse. When any one, with the view of exciting prejudice, observes that this doctrine, of which I am endeavouring to give your Majesty an account, has been condemned by the suffrages of all the estates, and was long ago stabbed again and again by partial sentences of courts of law, he undoubtedly says nothing more than that it has sometimes been violently oppressed by the power and faction of adversaries, and sometimes fraudulently and insidiously overwhelmed by lies, cavils, and calumny. While a cause is unheard, it is violence to pass sanguinary sentences against it ; it is fraud to charge it, contrary to its deserts, with sedition and mischief.

That no one may suppose we are unjust in thus complaining, you yourself, most illustrious Sovereign, can bear us witness with what lying calumnies it is daily traduced in your presence, as aiming at nothing else than to wrest the sceptres of kings out of their hands, to overturn all tribunals and seats of justice, to subvert all order and government, to disturb the peace and quiet of society, to abolish all laws, destroy the distinctions of rank and property, and, in short, turn all things upside down. And yet, that which you hear is but the smallest portion of what is said ; for among the common people are disseminated certain horrible insinuations—insinuations which, if well founded, would justify the whole world in condemning the doctrine with its authors to a thousand fires and gibbets. Who can wonder that the popular hatred is inflamed against it, when credit is given to those most iniquitous accusations ? See, why all ranks unite with one accord in condemning our persons and our doctrine !

Carried away by this feeling, those who sit in judgment merely give utterance to the prejudices which they have imbibed at home, and think they have duly performed their part if they do not order punishment to be inflicted on any one until convicted, either on his own confession, or on legal evidence. But of what crime convicted ? " Of that condemned doctrine," is the answer. But with what justice condemned ? The very essence of the defence was, not to abjure the doctrine itself, but to maintain its truth. On this subject, however, not a whisper is allowed !

Justice, then, most invincible Sovereign, entitles me to demand that you will undertake a thorough investigation of this cause, which has hitherto been tossed about in any kind of way, and handled in the most irregular manner, without any order of law, and with passionate heat rather than judicial gravity.

Let it not be imagined that I am here framing my own private defence, with the view of obtaining a safe return to my native land. Though I cherish towards it the feelings which become me as a man, still, as matters now are, I can be absent from it without regret. The cause which I plead is the common cause of all the godly, and therefore the very cause of Christ—a cause which, throughout your realm, now lies, as it were, in despair, torn and trampled upon in all kinds of ways, and that more through the tyranny of certain Pharisees than any sanction from yourself. But it matters not to inquire how the thing is done ; the fact that it is done cannot be denied. For so far have the wicked prevailed, that the truth of Christ, if not utterly routed and dispersed, lurks as if it were ignobly buried ; while the poor Church, either wasted by cruel slaughter or driven into exile, or intimidated and terror-struck, scarcely ventures to breathe. Still her enemies press on with their wonted rage and fury over the ruins which they have made, strenuously assaulting the wall, which is already giving way. Meanwhile, no man comes forth to offer his protection against such furies. Any who would be thought most favourable to the truth, merely talk of pardoning the error and imprudence of ignorant men. For so those modest personages[1] speak ; giving the name of *error and imprudence* to that which they know to be[2] the infallible truth of God, and of *ignorant men* to those whose intellect they see that Christ has not despised, seeing he has deigned to intrust them with the mysteries of his heavenly wisdom.[3] Thus all are ashamed of the Gospel.

Your duty, most serene Prince, is, not to shut either your ears or mind against a cause involving such mighty interests as these : how the glory of God is to be maintained on the earth inviolate, how the truth of God is to preserve its dignity, how the kingdom of Christ is to continue amongst us compact and secure. The cause is worthy of your ear, worthy of your investigation, worthy of your throne.

The characteristic of a true sovereign is, to acknowledge that, in the administration of his kingdom, he is a minister of God. He who does not make his reign subservient to the divine glory, acts the part not of a king, but a robber. He, moreover, deceives himself who anticipates long prosperity to any kingdom which is not ruled by the sceptre of God, that is, by his divine word. For the heavenly oracle is infallible which has declared, that " where there is no vision the people perish" (Prov. xxix. 18).

Let not a contemptuous idea of our insignificance dissuade you from the investigation of this cause. We, indeed, are perfectly conscious how poor and abject we are: in the presence of God we are miserable sinners, and in the sight of men most despised—we are (if you will) the mere dregs and off-scourings of the world, or worse, if

---

1 " Modesti homines," not in Ed. 1536.
2 " Quam norunt," not in Ed. 1536.
3 The words, " Quorum ingenium non adeo despicabile Christi fuisse vident," not in Ed. 1536.

worse can be named : so that before God there remains nothing of which we can glory save only his mercy, by which, without any merit of our own, we are admitted to the hope of eternal salvation :[1] and before men not even this much remains,[2] since we can glory only in our infirmity, a thing which, in the estimation of men, it is the greatest ignominy even tacitly[3] to confess.   But our doctrine must stand sublime above all the glory of the world, and invincible by all its power, because it is not ours, but that of the living God and his Anointed, whom the Father has appointed King, that he may rule from sea to sea, and from the rivers even to the ends of the earth ; and so rule as to smite the whole earth and its strength of iron and brass, its splendour of gold and silver, with the mere rod of his mouth, and break them in pieces like a potter's vessel ; according to the magnificent predictions of the prophets respecting his kingdom (Dan. ii. 34 ; Isaiah xi. 4 ; Psalm ii. 9.)

Our adversaries, indeed, clamorously maintain that our appeal to the word of God is a mere pretext,—that we are, in fact, its worst corrupters.   How far this is not only malicious calumny, but also shameless effrontery, you will be able to decide, of your own know-ledge, by reading our Confession.   Here, however, it may be necessary to make some observations which may dispose, or at least assist, you to read and study it with attention.

When Paul declared that all prophecy ought to be according to the analogy of faith (Rom. xii. 6), he laid down the surest rule for deter-mining the meaning of Scripture.   Let our doctrine be tested by this rule and our victory is secure.   For what accords better and more aptly with faith than to acknowledge ourselves divested of all virtue that we may be clothed by God, devoid of all goodness that we may be filled by Him, the slaves of sin that he may give us freedom, blind that he may enlighten, lame that he may cure, and feeble that he may sustain us ; to strip ourselves of all ground of glorying that he alone may shine forth glorious, and we be glorified in him ?   When these things, and others to the same effect, are said by us, they interpose, and querulously complain, that in this way we overturn some blind light of nature, fancied preparatives, free will, and works meritorious of eternal salvation, with their own supererogations also ;[4] because they cannot bear that the entire praise and glory of all goodness, virtue, justice, and wisdom, should remain with God.   But we read not of any having been blamed for drinking too much of the fountain of living water ; on the contrary, those are severely reprimanded who " have hewed them out cisterns, broken cisterns, that can hold no water " (Jer. ii. 13).   Again, what more agreeable to faith than to feel assured that God is a propitious Father when Christ is acknow-

---

1 The words stand thus in the Ed. 1536 : "Qua salvi nullo nostro merito facti sumus."
2 " Non ita multum," not in Ed. 1536.
3 " Cum nutu," not in Ed. 1536.
4 The only word in the Ed. 1536 after "free will," is "merita."

ledged as a brother and propitiator, than confidently to expect all prosperity and gladness from Him, whose ineffable love towards us was such that He " spared not his own Son, but delivered him up for us all" (Rom. viii. 32), than to rest in the sure hope of salvation and eternal life whenever Christ, in whom such treasures are hid, is conceived to have been given by the Father ? Here they attack us, and loudly maintain that this sure confidence is not free from arrogance and presumption. But as nothing is to be presumed of ourselves, so all things are to be presumed of God; nor are we stript of vainglory for any other reason than that we may learn to glory in the Lord. Why go farther ? Take but a cursory view, most valiant King, of all the parts of our cause, and count us of all wicked men the most iniquitous, if you do not discover plainly, that " therefore we both labour and suffer reproach because we trust in the living God" (1 Tim. iv. 10) ; because we believe it to be " life eternal" to know " the only true God, and Jesus Christ," whom he has sent (John xvii. 3). For this hope some of us are in bonds, some beaten with rods, some made a gazing-stock, some proscribed, some most cruelly tortured, some obliged to flee ; we are all pressed with straits, loaded with dire execrations, lacerated by slanders, and treated with the greatest indignity.

Look now to our adversaries (I mean the priesthood, at whose beck and pleasure others ply their enmity against us), and consider with me for a little by what zeal they are actuated. The true religion which is delivered in the Scriptures, and which all ought to hold, they readily permit both themselves and others to be ignorant of, to neglect and despise ; and they deem it of little moment what each man believes concerning God and Christ, or disbelieves, provided he submits to the judgment of the Church with what they call[1] implicit faith ; nor are they greatly concerned though they should see the glory of God dishonoured by open blasphemies, provided not a finger is raised against the primacy of the Apostolic See and the authority of holy mother Church.[2] Why, then, do they war for the mass, purgatory, pilgrimage, and similar follies, with such fierceness and acerbity, that though they cannot prove one of them from the word of God, they deny godliness can be safe without faith in these things—faith drawn out, if I may so express it, to its utmost stretch ? Why ? just because their belly is their God, and their kitchen their religion ; and they believe, that if these were away they would not only not be Christians, but not even men. For although some wallow in luxury, and others feed on slender crusts, still they all live by the same pot, which without that fuel might not only cool, but altogether freeze. He, accordingly, who is most anxious about his stomach, proves the fiercest champion of his faith. In short, the object on which all to a man are bent, is to

---

1 Ut aiunt," not in Ed. 1536.
2 No part of this sentence from " provided" is in the Ed. 1536.

keep their kingdom safe or their belly filled ; not one gives even the smallest sign of sincere zeal.

Nevertheless, they cease not to assail our doctrine, and to accuse and defame it in what terms they may, in order to render it either hated or suspected. They call it new, and of recent birth ; they carp at it as doubtful and uncertain ; they bid us tell by what miracles it has been confirmed ; they ask if it be fair to receive it against the consent of so many holy Fathers and the most ancient custom ; they urge us to confess either that it is schismatical in giving battle to the Church, or that the Church must have been without life during the many centuries in which nothing of the kind was heard. Lastly, they say there is little need of argument, for its quality may be known by its fruits, namely, the large number of sects, the many seditious disturbances, and the great licentiousness which it has produced. No doubt, it is a very easy matter for them, in presence of an ignorant and credulous multitude, to insult over an undefended cause ; but were an opportunity of mutual discussion afforded, that acrimony which they now pour out upon us in frothy torrents, with as much license as impunity,[1] would assuredly boil dry.

1. First, in calling it new, they are exceedingly injurious to God, whose sacred word deserved not to be charged with novelty. To them, indeed, I very little doubt it is new, as Christ is new, and the Gospel new ; but those who are acquainted with the old saying of Paul, that Christ Jesus " died for our sins, and rose again for our justification " (Rom. iv. 25), will not detect any novelty in us. That it long lay buried and unknown is the guilty consequence of man's impiety ; but now when, by the kindness of God, it is restored to us, it ought to resume its antiquity just as the returning citizen resumes his rights.

2. It is owing to the same ignorance that they hold it to be doubtful and uncertain ; for this is the very thing of which the Lord complains by his prophet, " The ox knoweth his owner, and the ass his master's crib ; but Israel doth not know, my people doth not consider " (Isaiah i. 3). But however they may sport with its uncertainty, had they to seal their own doctrine with their blood, and at the expense of life, it would be seen what value they put upon it. Very different is our confidence—a confidence which is not appalled by the terrors of death, and therefore not even by the judgment-seat of God.

3. In demanding miracles from us, they act dishonestly ; for we have not coined some new gospel, but retain the very one the truth of which is confirmed by all the miracles which Christ and the apostles ever wrought. But they have a peculiarity which we have not—they can confirm their faith by constant miracles down to the present day ! Nay rather, they allege miracles which might produce wavering in minds otherwise well disposed ; they are so frivolous and ridiculous,

---

[1] " Tam licenter quam impune," not in Ed. 1536.

so vain and false. But were they even exceedingly wonderful, they could have no effect against the truth of God, whose name ought to be hallowed always, and everywhere, whether by miracles, or by the natural course of events. The deception would perhaps be more specious if Scripture did not admonish us of the legitimate end and use of miracles. Mark tells us (Mark xvi. 20) that the signs which followed the preaching of the apostles were wrought in confirmation of it ; so Luke also relates that the Lord " gave testimony to the word of his grace, and granted signs and wonders to be done" by the hands of the apostles (Acts xiv. 3). Very much to the same effect are those words of the apostle, that salvation by a preached gospel was confirmed, " the Lord bearing witness with signs and wonders, and with divers miracles" (Heb. ii. 4). Those things which we are told are seals of the gospel, shall we pervert to the subversion of the gospel? what was destined only to confirm the truth, shall we misapply to the confirmation of lies? The proper course, therefore, is, in the first instance, to ascertain and examine the doctrine which is said by the Evangelist to precede ; then after it has been proved, but not till then, it may receive confirmation from miracles. But the mark of sound doctrine given by our Saviour himself is its tendency to promote the glory not of men, but of God (John vii. 18 ; viii. 50). Our Saviour having declared this to be test of doctrine, we are in error if we regard as miraculous, works which are used for any other purpose than to magnify the name of God.[1] And it becomes us to remember that Satan has his miracles, which, although they are tricks rather than true wonders, are still such as to delude the ignorant and unwary. Magicians and enchanters have always been famous for miracles, and miracles of an astonishing description have given support to idolatry : these, however, do not make us converts to the superstitions either of magicians or idolaters. In old times, too, the Donatists used their power of working miracles as a battering-ram, with which they shook the simplicity of the common people. We now give to our opponents the answer which Augustine then gave to the Donatists (in Joan. Tract. 23), " The Lord put us on our guard against those wonder-workers, when he foretold that false prophets would arise, who, by lying signs and divers wonders, would, if it were possible, deceive the very elect" (Matth. xxiv. 24). Paul, too, gave warning that the reign of antichrist would be " withall power, and signs, and lying wonders" (2 Thess. ii. 9).

But our opponents tell us that their miracles are wrought not by idols, not by sorcerers, not by false prophets, but by saints : as if we did not know it to be one of Satan's wiles to transform himself " into an angel of light" (2 Cor. xi. 14). The Egyptians, in whose neighbourhood Jeremiah was buried, anciently sacrificed and paid other divine honours to him (Hieron. in Præf. Jerem). Did they not

---

[1] No part of the passage, beginning above, " The deception," &c., is in Ed 1536.

make an idolatrous abuse of the holy prophet of God? and yet, in recompense for so venerating his tomb, they thought [1] that they were cured of the bite of serpents.   What, then, shall we say but that it has been, and always will be, a most just punishment of God, to send on those who do not receive the truth in the love of it, "strong delusion, that they should believe a lie"? (2 Thess. ii. 11).   We, then, have no lack of miracles, sure miracles, that cannot be gainsaid; but those to which our opponents lay claim are mere delusions of Satan, inasmuch as they draw off the people from the true worship of God to vanity.

4. It is a calumny to represent us as opposed to the Fathers (I mean the ancient writers of a purer age), as if the Fathers were supporters of their impiety.   Were the contest to be decided by such authority (to speak in the most moderate terms), the better part of the victory would be ours.[2]   While there is much that is admirable and wise in the writings of those Fathers, and while in some things it has fared with them as with ordinary men; these pious sons, forsooth, with the peculiar acuteness of intellect, and judgment, and soul, which belongs to them, adore only their slips and errors, while those things which are well said they either overlook, or disguise, or corrupt; so that it may be truly said their only care has been to gather dross among gold.   Then, with dishonest clamour, they assail us as enemies and despisers of the Fathers.   So far are we from despising them, that if this were the proper place, it would give us no trouble to support the greater part of the doctrines which we now hold by their suffrages.   Still, in studying their writings, we have endeavoured to remember (1 Cor. iii. 21–23; see also Augustin. Ep. 28), that all things are ours, to serve, not lord it over us, but that we are Christ's only, and must obey him in all things without exception. He who does not draw this distinction will not have any fixed principles in religion; for those holy men were ignorant of many things, are often opposed to each other, and are sometimes at variance with themselves.

It is not without cause (remark our opponents) we are thus warned by Solomon, "Remove not the ancient landmarks which thy fathers have set" (Prov. xxii. 28).   But the same rule applies not to the measuring of fields and the obedience of faith.   The rule applicable to the latter is, "Forget also thine own people, and thy father's house" (Ps. xlv. 10).   But if they are so fond of allegory, why do they not understand the apostles, rather than any other class of Fathers, to be meant by those whose landmarks it is unlawful to remove?   This is the interpretation of Jerome, whose words they have quoted in their canons.   But as regards those to whom they apply

---

[1] Instead of "thought they were cured," the Ed. 1536 says simply, "they were cured" (curarentur).

[2] "Ut modestissime etiam loquar," not in the Ed. 1536.

the passage, if they wish the landmarks to be fixed, why do they, whenever it suits their purpose, so freely overleap them?

Among the Fathers there were two, the one of whom said,[1] " Our God neither eats nor drinks, and therefore has no need of chalices and salvers;" and the other,[2] " Sacred rites do not require gold, and things which are not bought with gold, please not by gold." They step beyond the boundary, therefore, when in sacred matters they are so much delighted with gold, silver, ivory, marble, gems, and silks, that unless everything is overlaid with costly show, or rather insane luxury[3], they think God is not duly worshipped.

It was a Father who said,[4] " He ate flesh freely on the day on which others abstained from it, because he was a Christian." They overleap the boundaries, therefore, when they doom to perdition every soul that, during Lent, shall have tasted flesh.

There were two Fathers, the one of whom said,[5] " A monk not labouring with his own hands is no better than a violent man and a robber;" and the other,[6] " Monks, however assiduous they may be in study, meditation, and prayer, must not live by others." This boundary, too, they transgressed, when they placed lazy gormandising monks in dens and stews, to gorge themselves on other men's substance.

It was a Father who said,[7] " It is a horrid abomination to see in Christian temples a painted image either of Christ or of any saint." Nor was this pronounced by the voice of a single individual; but an Ecclesiastical Council also decreed,[8] " Let nought that is worshipped be depicted on walls."[9] Very far are they from keeping within these boundaries when they leave not a corner without images.

Another Father counselled,[10] " That after performing the office of humanity to the dead in their burial, we should leave them at rest." These limits they burst through when they keep up a perpetual anxiety about the dead.

It is a Father who testifies,[11] " That the substance of bread and wine in the Eucharist does not cease but remains, just as the nature and substance of man remains united to the Godhead in the Lord Jesus Christ." This boundary they pass in pretending that, as soon as the words of our Lord are pronounced, the substance of bread and wine ceases, and is transubstantiated into body and blood.

---

1 i. Acatius in lib. xi. cap 16, F. Triport. Hist.
2 ii. Ambr. lib. ii. De Officiis, cap. 28.
3 Instead of the words here translated—viz. " exquisito splendore vel potius insanc luxu," the Ed. 1536 has only the word "luxu."
4 iii. Spiridion. Trip. Hist. lib. i. cap. 10.
5 iv. Trip. Hist. lib. viii. cap 1.
6 August. De Opere Monach cap 7.
7 vi. Epiph. Epist. ab Hieron. versa.   8 vii. Conc. Elibert. can. 36.
9 No part of this sentence is in Ed 1536.
10 viii. Ambr de Abraha. lib. i. c. 7.
11 ix. Gelasius Papa in Conc. Rom.

They were Fathers, who, as they exhibited only one Eucharist to the whole Church,[1] and kept back from it the profane and flagitious; so they, in the severest terms, censured all those[2] who, being present, did not communicate How far have they removed these landmarks, in filling not churches only, but also private houses, with their masses, admitting all and sundry to be present, each the more willingly the more largely he pays, however wicked and impure he may be,—not inviting any one to faith in Christ and faithful communion in the sacraments, but rather vending their own work for the grace and merits of Christ![3]

There were two Fathers, the one of whom decided that those were to be excluded altogether from partaking of Christ's sacred supper,[4] who, contented with communion in one kind, abstained from the other; while the other Father strongly contends[5] that the blood of the Lord ought not to be denied to the Christian people, who, in confessing him, are enjoined to shed their own blood.   These landmarks, also, they removed, when, by an unalterable law, they ordered the very thing which the former Father punished with excommunication, and the latter condemned for a valid reason.

It was a Father who pronounced it rashness,[6] in an obscure question, to decide in either way without clear and evident authority from Scripture.   They forgot this landmark when they enacted so many constitutions, so many canons, and so many dogmatical decisions, without sanction from the word of God.

It was a Father who reproved Montanus, among other heresies,[7] for being the first who imposed laws of fasting.   They have gone far beyond this landmark also in enjoining fasting under the strictest laws.

It was a Father who denied[8] that the ministers of the Church should be interdicted from marrying, and pronounced married life to be a state of chastity; and there were other Fathers who assented to his decision.   These boundaries they overstepped in rigidly binding their priests to celibacy.

It was a Father who thought[9] that Christ only should be listened to, from its being said, "hear him;" and that regard is due not to what others before us have said or done, but only to what Christ, the

---

[1] x. Chrys. in 1. cap. Ephes.
[2] xi. Calixt. Papa, De Consecrat. dist. 2.
[3] Instead of the whole passage, beginning at bottom of p. 11, "It is a Father who testifies," &c., the Ed. 1536 has the following sentence: "Ex patribus erat qui negavit in sacramento cœnæ esse verum corpus sed mysterium duntaxat corporis; sic enim ad verbum loquitur."   On the margin, reference is made to the author of an unfinished Tract on Matthew, forming the 11th Homil. among the works of Chrysostom.
[4] xii. Gelas. can. Comperimus, De Consec. dist. 2.
[5] xiii. Cypr. Epist. 2, lib. i. De Lapsis.
[6] xiv. August. lib. ii. De Peccat. Mer. cap. uıt.
[7] xv. Apollon. De quo Eccles. Hist. lib. v. cap. 12.
[8] xvi. Paphnut. Tripart. Hist. lib. ii. cap 14.
[9] xvii. Cypr. Epist. 2, lib. ii.

head of all, has commanded. This landmark they neither observe themselves nor allow to be observed by others, while they subject themselves and others to any master whatever, rather than Christ.

There is a Father who contends[1] that the Church ought not to prefer herself to Christ, who always judges truly, whereas ecclesiastical judges, who are but men, are generally deceived. Having burst through this barrier also, they hesitate not to suspend the whole authority of Scripture on the judgment of the Church.[2]

All the Fathers with one heart execrated, and with one mouth protested[3] against, contaminating the word of God with the subtleties of sophists, and involving it in the brawls of dialecticians. Do they keep within these limits when the sole occupation of their lives is to entwine and entangle the simplicity of Scripture with endless disputes, and worse than sophistical jargon? So much so, that were the Fathers to rise from their graves, and listen to the brawling art which bears the name of speculative theology, there is nothing they would suppose it less to be than a discussion of a religious nature.

But my discourse would far exceed its just limits were I to show, in detail, how petulantly those men shake off the yoke of the Fathers, while they wish to be thought their most obedient sons. Months, nay, years would fail me; and yet so deplorable and desperate is their effrontery, that they presume to chastise us for overstepping the ancient landmarks!

5. Then, again, it is to no purpose they call us to the bar of custom. To make everything yield to custom would be to do the greatest injustice. Were the judgments of mankind correct, custom would be regulated by the good. But it is often far otherwise in point of fact; for, whatever the many are seen to do, forthwith obtains the force of custom. But human affairs have scarcely ever been so happily constituted as that the better course pleased the greater number. Hence the private vices of the multitude have generally resulted in public error, or rather that common consent in vice which these worthy men would have to be law. Any one with eyes may perceive that it is not one flood of evils which has deluged us; that many fatal plagues have invaded the globe; that all things rush headlong; so that either the affairs of men must be altogether despaired of, or we must not only resist, but boldly attack prevailing evils. The cure is prevented by no other cause than the length of time during which we have been accustomed to the disease. But be it so that public error must have a place in human society, still, in the kingdom of God, we must look and listen only to his eternal truth, against which no series of years, no custom, no conspiracy, can plead prescription. Thus Isaiah for-

---

[1] xviii Aug. cap. 2, Cont. Cresconium Grammat.
[2] No part of this passage is in Ed. 1536.
[3] xix. Calv. De Scholast. Doctor. Judicium. Vid. Book II. cap. ii. sec. 6; Book III. cap. iv. sec. 1, 2, 7, 13, 14, 26–29; Book III. cap. xi. sec. 14, 15; Book IV. cap xviii. sec. 1; and cap. xix. sec. 10, 11, 22, 23.

merly taught the people of God, "Say ye not, A confederacy, to all to whom this people shall say, A confederacy;" *i.e.* do not unite with the people in an impious consent; "neither fear ye their fear, nor be afraid. Sanctify the Lord of hosts himself; and let him be your fear, and let him be your dread" (Is. viii. 12). Now, therefore, let them, if they will, object to us both past ages and present examples; if we sanctify the Lord of hosts, we shall not be greatly afraid. Though many ages should have consented to like ungodliness, He is strong who taketh vengeance to the third and fourth generation; or the whole world should league together in the same iniquity. He taught experimentally what the end is of those who sin with the multitude, when He destroyed the whole human race with a flood, saving Noah with his little family, who, by putting his faith in Him alone, "condemned the world" (Heb. xi. 7). In short, depraved custom is just a kind of general pestilence in which men perish not the less that they fall in a crowd. It were well, moreover, to ponder the observation of Cyprian,[1] that those who sin in ignorance, though they cannot be entirely exculpated, seem, however, to be, in some sense, excusable; whereas those who obstinately reject the truth, when presented to them by the kindness of God, have no defence to offer.[2]

6. Their dilemma does not push us so violently as to oblige us to confess, either that the Church was a considerable time without life, or that we have now a quarrel with the Church. The Church of Christ assuredly has lived, and will live, as long as Christ shall reign at the right hand of the Father. By his hand it is sustained, by his protection defended, by his mighty power preserved in safety. For what he once undertook he will undoubtedly perform, he will be with his people always, "even to the end of the world" (Matth. xxviii. 20). With the Church we wage no war, since, with one consent, in common with the whole body of the faithful, we worship and adore one God, and Christ Jesus the Lord, as all the pious have always adored him. But they themselves err not a little from the truth in not recognising any church but that which they behold with the bodily eye, and in endeavouring to circumscribe it by limits, within which it cannot be confined.

The hinges on which the controversy turns are these: first, in their contending that the form of the Church is always visible and apparent; and, secondly, in their placing this form in the see of the Church of Rome and its hierarchy. We, on the contrary, maintain, both that the Church may exist without any apparent form, and, moreover, that the form is not ascertained by that external splendour which they foolishly admire, but by a very different mark, namely, by the pure preaching of the word of God, and the due administration of

---

1 Epist. 3, lib. ii.; et in Epist ad Julian. De Hæret. Baptiz.
2 No part of this sentence is in ed. 1536.

the sacraments. They make an outcry whenever the Church cannot be pointed to with the finger. But how oft was it the fate of the Church among the Jews to be so defaced that no comeliness appeared? What do we suppose to have been the splendid form when Elijah complained that he was left alone? (1 Kings xix. 14). How long after the advent of Christ did it lie hid without form? How often since has it been so oppressed by wars, seditions, and heresies, that it was nowhere seen in splendour? Had they lived at that time, would they have believed there was any Church? But Elijah learned that there remained seven thousand men who had not bowed the knee to Baal; nor ought we to doubt that Christ has always reigned on earth ever since he ascended to heaven. Had the faithful at that time required some discernible form, must they not have forthwith given way to despondency? And, indeed, Hilary accounted it a very great fault in his day, that men were so possessed with a foolish admiration of Episcopal dignity as not to perceive the deadly hydra lurking under that mask. His words are (Cont. Auxentium), " One advice I give : Beware of Antichrist; for, unhappily, a love of walls has seized you; unhappily, the Church of God which you venerate exists in houses and buildings; unhappily, under these you find the name of peace. Is it doubtful that in these Antichrist will have his seat? Safer to me are mountains, and woods, and lakes, and dungeons, and whirlpools; since in these prophets, dwelling or immersed, did prophesy."

And what is it at the present day that the world venerates in its horned bishops, unless that it imagines those who are seen presiding over celebrated cities to be holy prelates of religion? Away, then, with this absurd mode of judging![1] Let us rather reverently admit, that as God alone knows who are his, so he may sometimes withdraw the external manifestation of his Church from the view of men. This, I allow, is a fearful punishment which God sends on the earth; but if the wickedness of men so deserves, why do we strive to oppose the just vengeance of God?[2] It was thus that God, in past ages, punished the ingratitude of men ; for after they had refused to obey his truth, and had extinguished his light, he allowed them, when blinded by sense, both to be deluded by lying vanities and plunged in thick darkness, so that no face of a true Church appeared. Meanwhile, however, though his own people were dispersed and concealed amidst errors and darkness, he saved them from destruction. No wonder ; for he knew how to preserve them even in the confusion of Babylon and the flame of the fiery furnace.

But as to the wish that the form of the Church should be ascertained by some kind of vain pomp, how perilous it is I will briefly indicate, rather than explain, that I may not exceed all bounds.

---

1 No part of the passage beginning above is in the Ed. 1536.
2 In the last Ed., " justæ Dei ultionis;" in Ed. 1536, " divinæ zustitiæ."

What they say is, that the Pontiff,[1] who holds the apostolic see, and the priests who are anointed and consecrated by him,[2] provided they have the insignia of fillets and mitres, represent the Church, and ought to be considered as in the place of the Church, and therefore cannot err. Why so? because they are pastors of the Church, and consecrated to the Lord. And were not Aaron and other prefects of Israel pastors? But Aaron and his sons, though already set apart to the priesthood, erred notwithstanding when they made the calf (Exod. xxxii. 4). Why, according to this view, should not the four hundred prophets who lied to Ahab represent the Church? (1 Kings xxii. 11, &c.) The Church, however, stood on the side of Micaiah. He was alone, indeed, and despised, but from his mouth the truth proceeded. Did not the prophets also exhibit both the name and face of the Church, when, with one accord, they rose up against Jeremiah, and with menaces boasted of it as a thing impossible that the law should perish from the priest, or counsel from the wise, or the word from the prophet? (Jer. xviii. 18). In opposition to the whole body of the prophets, Jeremiah is sent alone to declare from the Lord (Jer. iv. 9), that a time would come when the law would perish from the priest, counsel from the wise, and the word from the prophet. Was not like splendour displayed in that council when the chief priests, scribes, and Pharisees assembled to consult how they might put Jesus to death? Let them go, then, and cling to the external mask, while they make Christ and all the prophets of God schismatics, and, on the other hand, make Satan's ministers the organs of the Holy Spirit!

But if they are sincere, let them answer me in good faith,—in what place, and among whom, do they think the Church resided, after the Council of Basle degraded and deposed Eugenius from the popedom, and substituted Amadeus in his place? Do their utmost, they cannot deny that that Council was legitimate as far as regards external forms, and was summoned not only by one Pontiff, but by two. Eugenius, with the whole herd of cardinals and bishops who had joined him in plotting the dissolution of the Council, was there condemned of con-tumacy, rebellion, and schism. Afterwards, however, aided by the favour of princes, he got back his popedom safe. The election of Amadeus, duly made by the authority of a general holy synod, went to smoke; only he himself was appeased with a cardinal's cap, like a piece of offal thrown to a barking dog. Out of the lap of these re-bellious and contumacious schismatics proceeded all future popes, cardinals, bishops, abbots, and presbyters. Here they are caught, and cannot escape. For, on which party will they bestow the name of Church? Will they deny it to have been a general Council, though it lacked nothing as regards external majesty, having been solemnly

---

[1] " Papa Romanus," in the Ed. 1536.

[2] Instead of the words, "qui ab eo instites inuncti et consecrati, infulis modo et lituis insigniti sunt," the Ed. 1536 has only " episcopi alii."

called by two bulls, consecrated by the legate of the Roman See as its president, constituted regularly in all respects, and continuing in possession of all its honours to the last ? Will they admit that Eugenius, and his whole train, through whom they have all been consecrated, were schismatical ? Let them, then, either define the form of the Church differently, or, however numerous they are, we will hold them all to be schismatics in having knowingly and willingly received ordination from heretics. But had it never been discovered before that the Church is not tied to external pomp, we are furnished with a lengthened proof in their own conduct, in proudly vending themselves to the world under the specious title of Church, notwithstanding that they are the deadly pests of the Church. I speak not of their manners and of those tragical atrocities with which their whole life teems, since it is said that they are Pharisees who should be heard, not imitated. By devoting some portion of your leisure to our writings, you will see, not obscurely, that their doctrine—the very doctrine to which they say it is owing that they are the Church—is a deadly murderer of souls, the firebrand, ruin, and destruction of the Church.

7. Lastly, they are far from candid when they invidiously number up the disturbances, tumults, and disputes, which the preaching of our doctrine has brought in its train, and the fruits which, in many instances, it now produces; for the doctrine itself is undeservedly charged with evils which ought to be ascribed to the malice of Satan. It is one of the characteristics of the divine word, that whenever it appears, Satan ceases to slumber and sleep. This is the surest and most unerring test for distinguishing it from false doctrines which readily betray themselves, while they are received by all with willing ears, and welcomed by an applauding world. Accordingly, for several ages, during which all things were immersed in profound darkness, almost all mankind[1] were mere jest and sport to the god of this world, who, like any Sardanapalus, idled and luxuriated undisturbed. For what else could he do but laugh and sport while in tranquil and undisputed possession of his kingdom ? But when light beaming from above somewhat dissipated the darkness—when the strong man arose and aimed a blow at his kingdom—then, indeed, he began to shake off his wonted torpor, and rush to arms. And first he stirred up the hands of men, that by them he might violently suppress the dawning truth; but when this availed him not, he turned to snares, exciting dissensions and disputes about doctrine by means of his Catabaptists, and other portentous miscreants, that he might thus obscure, and, at length, extinguish the truth. And now he persists in assailing it with both engines, endeavouring to pluck up the true seed by the violent hand of man, and striving, as much as in him lies, to choke it with his tares, that it may not grow and bear fruit. But it will be in vain, if we listen to the admonition of the Lord, who long ago disclosed his

---

1 For "cuncti fere mortales" the Ed. 1536 has only "homines."

wiles, that we might not be taken unawares, and armed us with full protection against all his machinations. But how malignant to throw upon the word of God itself the blame either of the seditions which wicked men and rebels, or of the sects which impostors stir up against it! The example, however, is not new. Elijah was interrogated whether it were not he that troubled Israel. Christ was seditious, according to the Jews; and the apostles were charged with the crime of popular commotion. What else do those who, in the present day, impute to us all the disturbances, tumults, and contentions which break out against us? Elijah, however, has taught us our answer (1 Kings xviii. 17, 18). It is not we who disseminate errors or stir up tumults, but they who resist the mighty power of God.

But while this single answer is sufficient to rebut the rash charges of these men, it is necessary, on the other hand, to consult for the weakness of those who take the alarm at such scandals, and not unfrequently waver in perplexity. But that they may not fall away in this perplexity, and forfeit their good degree, let them know that the apostles in their day experienced the very things which now befall us. There were then unlearned and unstable men who, as Peter tells us (2 Pet. iii. 16), wrested the inspired writings of Paul to their own destruction. There were despisers of God, who, when they heard that sin abounded in order that grace might more abound, immediately inferred, " We will continue in sin that grace may abound" (Rom. vi. 1); when they heard that believers were not under the law, but under grace, forthwith sung out, " We will sin because we are not under the law, but under grace" (Rom. vi. 15). There were some who charged the apostle with being the minister of sin. Many false prophets entered in privily to pull down the churches which he had reared. Some preached the gospel through envy and strife, not sincerely (Phil. i. 15)—maliciously even—thinking to add affliction to his bonds. Elsewhere the gospel made little progress. All sought their own, not the things which were Jesus Christ's. Others went back like the dog to his vomit, or the sow that was washed to her wallowing in the mire. Great numbers perverted their spiritual freedom to carnal licentiousness. False brethren crept in to the imminent danger of the faithful. Among the brethren themselves various quarrels arose. What, then, were the apostles to do? Were they either to dissemble for the time, or rather lay aside and abandon that gospel which they saw to be the seed-bed of so many strifes, the source of so many perils, the occasion of so many scandals? In straits of this kind, they remembered that " Christ was a stone of stumbling, and a rock of offence," " set up for the fall and rising again of many," and " for a sign to be spoken against" (Luke ii. 34); and, armed with this assurance, they proceeded boldly through all perils from tumults and scandals. It becomes us to be supported by the same consideration, since Paul declares that it is a never-failing characteristic of the gospel to be a " savour of death unto death in them that perish" (2 Cor. ii. 16), although rather destined to us for the purpose of being a savour of life unto life, and the power of God for the salvation of believers. This we should certainly experience it to be, did we not by our ingratitude corrupt this unspeakable gift of God, and turn to our destruction what ought to be our only saving defence.[1]

But to return, Sire.[2] Be not moved by the absurd insinuations with which our adversaries are striving to frighten you into the belief that nothing else is wished and aimed at by this new gospel (for so they term it), than opportunity for sedition and impunity for all kinds of vice. Our God[3] is not the author of division, but of peace; and the Son of God, who came to destroy the works of the devil, is not the minister of sin. We, too, are undeservedly charged with desires of a kind for which we have never given even the smallest suspicion. We, forsooth, meditate the subversion of kingdoms; we, whose voice was never heard in faction, and whose life, while passed under you, is known to have been always quiet and simple; even now, when exiled from our home, we nevertheless cease not to pray for all prosperity to your person and your kingdom. We, forsooth, are aiming after an unchecked indulgence in vice, in whose manners, though there is much to be blamed, there is nothing which deserves such an imputation; nor (thank God) have we profited so little in the gospel that our life may not be to these slanderers an example of chastity, kindness, pity, temperance, patience, moderation, or any other virtue. It is plain, indeed, that we fear God sincerely, and worship him in truth, since, whether by life or by death, we desire his name to be hallowed; and hatred herself has been forced to bear testimony to the innocence and civil integrity of some of our people on whom death was inflicted for the very thing which deserved the highest praise. But if any, under pretext of the gospel, excite tumults (none such have as yet been detected in your realm), if any use the liberty of the grace of God as a cloak for licentiousness (I know of numbers who do), there are laws and legal punishments by which they may be punished up to the measure of their deserts—only, in the mean time, let not the gospel of God be evil spoken of because of the iniquities of evil men.

Sire,[4] That you may not lend too credulous an ear to the accusations of our enemies, their virulent injustice has been set before you at sufficient length; I fear even more than sufficient, since this preface has grown almost to the bulk of a full apology. My object, however, was not to frame a defence, but only with a view to the hearing

---

1 Instead of the concluding part of the sentence beginning "though rather," &c., and stopping at the reference, the Ed. 1536 simply continues the quotation "odor vitæ in vitam iis qui salvi sunt."

2 Instead of " Rex" simply, the Ed. 1536 has "magnanime Rex.'

3 Instead of " Deus noster," the Ed. 1536 has only " Deus."

4 In Ed. 1536, " Rex magnificentissime "

of our cause, to mollify your mind, now indeed turned away and estranged from us—I add, even inflamed against us—but whose good will, we are confident, we should regain, would you but once, with calmness and composure, read this our Confession, which we desire your Majesty to accept instead of a defence. But if the whispers of the malevolent so possess your ear, that the accused are to have no opportunity of pleading their cause; if those vindictive furies, with your connivance, are always to rage with bonds, scourgings, tortures, maimings, and burnings, we, indeed, like sheep doomed to slaughter, shall be reduced to every extremity; yet so that, in our patience, we will possess our souls, and wait for the strong hand of the Lord, which, doubtless, will appear in its own time, and show itself armed, both to rescue the poor from affliction, and also take vengeance on the despisers, who are now exulting so securely.[1]

Most illustrious King, may the Lord, the King of kings, establish your throne in righteousness, and your sceptre in equity.

BASLE, 1st *August* 1536.

---

[1] The words, " qui tanta securitate nunc exsultant," not in Ed. 1536.

THE EPISTLE TO THE READER.

[PREFIXED TO THE SECOND EDITION, PUBLISHED AT STRASBURG IN 1539.]

In the First Edition of this work, having no expectation of the success which God has, in his goodness, been pleased to give it, I had, for the greater part, performed my office perfunctorily, as is usual in trivial undertakings. But when I perceived that almost all the godly had received it with a favour which I had never dared to wish, far less to hope for, being sincerely conscious that I had received much more than I deserved, I thought I should be very ungrateful if I did not endeavour, at least according to my humble ability, to respond to the great kindness which had been expressed towards me, and which spontaneously urged me to diligence. I therefore ask no other favour from the studious for my new work than that which they have already bestowed upon me beyond my merits. I feel so much obliged, that I shall be satisfied if I am thought not to have made a bad return for the gratitude I owe. This return I would have made much earlier, had not the Lord, for almost two whole years, exercised me in an extraordinary manner. But it is soon enough if well enough. I shall think it has appeared in good season when I perceive that it produces some fruit to the Church of God. I may add, that my object in this work was to prepare and train students of theology for the study of the sacred volume, so that they might both have an easy introduction to it, and be able to proceed in it, with unfaltering step, seeing I have endeavoured to give such a summary of religion in all its parts, and have digested it into such an order as may make it not difficult for any one, who is rightly acquainted with it, to ascertain both what he ought principally to look for in Scripture, and also to what head he ought to refer whatever is contained in it. Having thus, as it were, paved the way, I shall not feel it necessary, in any Commentaries on Scripture which I may afterwards publish, to enter into long discussions of doctrine, or dilate on common places, and will, therefore, always compress them. In this way the pious reader will be saved much trouble and weariness, provided he comes furnished with a knowledge of the present work as an essential prerequisite. As my Commentary on the Epistle to the Romans will give a specimen of this plan, I would much rather let it speak for itself than declare it in words. Farewell, dear reader, and if you derive any fruit from my labours, give me the benefit of your prayers to the Lord.

STRASBURG, 1st *August* 1539

SUBJECT OF THE PRESENT WORK.

[PREFIXED TO THE FRENCH EDITION, PUBLISHED AT GENEVA IN 1545.]

IN order that my readers may be the better able to profit by the present work, I am desirous briefly to point out the advantage which they may derive from it. For by so doing I will show them the end at which they ought to aim, and to which they ought to give their attention in reading it.

Although the Holy Scriptures contain a perfect doctrine, to which nothing can be added—our Lord having been pleased therein to unfold the infinite treasures of his wisdom—still every person, not intimately acquainted with them, stands in need of some guidance and direction, as to what he ought to look for in them, that he may not wander up and down, but pursue a certain path, and so attain the end to which the Holy Spirit invites him.

Hence it is the duty of those who have received from God more light than others to assist the simple in this matter, and, as it were, lend them their hand to guide and assist them in finding the sum of what God has been pleased to teach us in his word. Now, this cannot be better done in writing than by treating in succession of the principal matters which are comprised in Christian philosophy. For he who understands these will be prepared to make more progress in the school of God in one day than any other person in three months, inasmuch as he, in a great measure, knows to what he should refer each sentence, and has a rule by which to test whatever is presented to him.

Seeing, then, how necessary it was in this manner to aid those who desire to be instructed in the doctrine of salvation, I have endeavoured, according to the ability which God has given me, to employ myself in so doing, and with this view have composed the present book. And first I wrote it in Latin, that it might be serviceable to all studious persons, of what nation soever they might be; afterwards, desiring to communicate any fruit which might be in it to my French countrymen, I translated it into our own tongue. I dare not bear too strong a testimony in its favour, and declare how profitable the reading of it will be, lest I should seem to prize my own work too highly. However, I may promise this much, that it will be a kind of key opening up to all the children of God a right and ready access to the understanding of the sacred volume. Wherefore, should our Lord give me henceforth means and opportunity of composing some Commentaries, I will use the greatest possible brevity, as there will be no occasion to make long digressions, seeing that I have in a manner deduced at length all the articles which pertain to Christianity.

And since we are bound to acknowledge that all truth and sound doctrine proceed from God, I will venture boldly to declare what I think of this work, acknowledging it to be God's work rather than mine. To him, indeed, the praise due to it must be ascribed. My opinion of the work then is this: I exhort all who reverence the word of the Lord, to read it, and diligently imprint it on their memory, if they would, in the first place, have a summary of Christian doctrine, and, 'n the second place, an introduction to the profitable reading both of the Old and New Testament. When they shall have done so, they will know by experience that I have not wished to impose upon them with words. Should any one be unable to comprehend all that is contained in it, he must not, however, give it up in despair; but continue always to read on, hoping that one passage will give him a more familiar exposition of another. Above all things, I would recommend that recourse be had to Scripture in considering the proofs which I adduce from it.

EPISTLE TO THE READER.

[PREFIXED TO THE LAST EDITION, REVISED BY THE AUTHOR.]

In the first edition of this work, having not the least expectation of the success which God, in his boundless goodness, has been pleased to give it, I had, for the greater part, performed my task in a perfunctory manner (as is usual in trivial undertakings) ; but when I understood that it had been received, by almost all the pious, with a favour which I had never dared to ask, far less to hope for, the more I was sincerely conscious that the reception was beyond my deserts, the greater I thought my gratitude would be, if, to the very kind wishes which had been expressed towards me, and which seemed of their own accord to invite me to diligence, I did not endeavour to respond, at least according to my humble ability. This I attempted not only in the second edition, but in every subsequent one the work has received some improvement. But though I do not regret the labour previously expended, I never felt satisfied until the work was arranged in the order in which it now appears. Now I trust it will approve itself to the judgment of all my readers. As a clear proof of the diligence with which I have laboured to perform this service to the Church of God, I may be permitted to mention, that last winter, when I thought I was dying of quartan ague, the more the disorder increased, the less I spared myself, in order that I might leave this book behind me, and thus make some return to the pious for their kind urgency. I could have wished to give it sooner, but it is soon enough if good enough. I shall think it has appeared in good time when I see it more productive of benefit than formerly to the Church of God. This is my only wish.

And truly it would fare ill with me if, not contented with the approbation of God alone, I were unable to despise the foolish and perverse censures of ignorant, as well as the malicious and unjust censures of ungodly men. For although, by the blessing of God, my most ardent desire has been to advance his kingdom, and promote the public good,—although I feel perfectly conscious, and take

God and his angels to witness, that ever since I began to discharge the office of teacher in the Church, my only object has been to do good to the Church, by maintaining the pure doctrine of godliness; yet I believe there never was a man more assailed, stung, and torn by calumny—[as well by the declared enemies of the truth of God, as by many worthless persons who have crept into his Church—as well by monks who have brought forth their frocks from their cloisters to spread infection wherever they come, as by other miscreants not better than they[1]]. After this letter to the reader was in the press, I had undoubted information that, at Augsburg, where the Imperial Diet was held, a rumour of my defection to the papacy was circulated, and entertained in the courts of the princes more readily than might have been expected.[2] This, forsooth, is the return made me by those who certainly are not unaware of numerous proofs of my constancy— proofs which, while they rebut the foul charge, ought to have defended me against it, with all humane and impartial judges. But the devil, with all his crew, is mistaken if he imagines that, by assailing me with vile falsehoods, he can either cool my zeal or diminish my exertions. I trust that God, in his infinite goodness, will enable me to persevere with unruffled patience in the course of his holy vocation. Of this I give the pious reader a new proof in the present edition.

I may further observe, that my object in this work has been, so to prepare and train candidates for the sacred office, for the study of the sacred volume, that they may both have an easy introduction to it, and be able to prosecute it with unfaltering step; for, if I mistake not, I have given a summary of religion in all its parts, and digested it in an order which will make it easy for any one, who rightly comprehends it, to ascertain both what he ought chiefly to look for in Scripture, and also to what head he ought to refer whatever is contained in it. Having thus, as it were, paved the way, as it will be unnecessary, in any Commentaries on Scripture which I may afterwards publish, to enter into long discussions of doctrinal points, and enlarge on commonplaces, I will compress them into narrow compass. In this way much trouble and fatigue will be spared to the pious reader, provided he comes prepared with a knowledge of the present work as an indispensable prerequisite. The system here followed being set forth as in a mirror in all my Commentaries, I think it better to let it speak for itself than to give any verbal explanation of it.

---

1 The passage in brackets occurs only in the French original. The words are as follows: " Tant des ennemis manifestes de la vérité de Dieu, que de beaucoup de canailles qui se sont fourrez en son Eglise : tant des Moines qui ont apporté leurs frocs hors de leurs cloistres pour infecter le lieu où ils venoyent, que d'autres vilains qui ne valent pas mieux qu'eux."

2 The words in the French are, "Avec trop grande facilité; ce qui monstroit que beaucoup de meschans hypocrites, faisans profession de l'Evangile, eussent bien voulu qu'ainsi fust." With too great facility; showing that many wicked hypocrites, making profession of the gospel, would have been very glad it had been so.

Farewell, kind reader : if you derive any benefit from my labours, aid me with your prayers to our heavenly Father.

GENEVA, 1st *August* 1559.

> The zeal of those whose cause I undertook,
> Has swelled a short defence into a book.

"I profess to be one of those who, by profiting, write, and by writing profit."—*Augustine*, Epist. vii.

METHOD AND ARRANGEMENT,

OR SUBJECT OF THE WHOLE WORK.

[FROM AN EPITOME OF THE INSTITUTIONS, BY GASPAR OLEVIAN.]

THE subject handled by the author of these Christian Institutes is twofold: the former, the knowledge of God, which leads to a blessed immortality; and the latter (which is subordinate to the former), the knowledge of ourselves. With this view the author simply adopts the arrangement of the Apostles' Creed, as that with which all Christians are most familiar. For as the Creed consists of four parts, the first relating to God the Father, the second to the Son, the third to the Holy Spirit, and the fourth to the Church, so the author, in fulfilment of his task, divides his Institutes into four parts, corresponding to those of the Creed. Each of these parts it will now be proper to explain separately.

I. The first article of the Apostles' Creed is concerning *God the Father*, the creation, preservation, and government of the universe, as implied in his omnipotence. Accordingly, the First Book of the Institutes treats of the knowledge of God, considered as the Creator, Preserver, and Governor of the world, and of everything contained in it. It shows both wherein the true knowledge of the Creator consists, and what the end of this knowledge is, chap. i. and ii.; that it is not learned at school, but that every one is self-taught it from the womb, chap. iii. Such, however, is man's depravity, that he stifles and corrupts this knowledge, partly by ignorance, partly by wicked design; and hence does not by means of it either glorify God as he ought, or attain to happiness, chap. iv. This inward knowledge is aided from without, namely, by the creatures in which, as in a mirror, the perfections of God may be contemplated. But man does not properly avail himself of this assistance; and hence to those to whom God is pleased to make himself more intimately known for salvation, he communicates his written word. This leads to a consideration of the Holy Scriptures, in which God has revealed that not the Father only, but along with the Father, the Son, and Holy Spirit, is that Creator of heaven and earth whom, in consequence of our innate depravity, we were unable, either from innate natural knowledge or the beautiful mirror of the world, to know so as to glorify. Here the author treats of the manifestation of God in Scripture; and in connection with it, of the one divine essence in three persons. But, lest man should lay the blame of his voluntary blindness on God, the author shows in what state man was created at first, introducing dissertations on the image of God, free will, and original righteousness. The subject of Creation being thus disposed of, the preservation and government of the world is considered in the three last chapters, which contain a very full discussion of the doctrine of Divine Providence.

II. As man, by sinning, forfeited the privileges conferred on him at his creation, recourse must be had to Christ. Accordingly, the next article in the Creed is, *And in Jesus Christ his only Son, &c.* In like manner, the Second Book of the Institutes treats of the knowledge of God considered as a Redeemer in Christ, and, showing man his fall, conducts him to Christ the Mediator. Here the subject of original sin is considered, and it is shown that man has no means within himself by which he can escape from guilt and the impending curse: that, on the contrary, until he is reconciled and renewed, everything that proceeds from him is of the nature of sin. This subject is considered as far as the vi. chapter. Man being thus utterly undone in himself, and incapable of working out his own cure by thinking a good thought, or doing what is acceptable to God, must seek redemption without himself—viz. in Christ. The end for which the Law was given, was not to secure worshippers for itself, but to conduct them unto Christ. This leads to an exposition of the Moral Law. Christ was known to the Jews under the Law as the author of salvation, but is more fully revealed under the Gospel in which he was manifested to the world. Hence arises the doctrine concerning the similarity and difference of the two Testaments, the Old and the New, the Law and the Gospel. These topics occupy as far as the xii. chapter. It is next shown that, in order to secure a complete salvation, it was necessary that the eternal Son of God should become man, and assume a true human nature. It is also shown in what way these two natures constitute one person. In order to purchase a full salvation by his own merits, and effectually apply it, Christ was appointed to the offices of Prophet, Priest, and King. The mode in which Christ performs these offices is considered, and also whether in point of fact he did accomplish the work of redemption. Here an exposition is given of the articles relating to Christ's death, resurrection, and ascension into heaven. In conclusion, it is proved that Christ is rightly and properly said to have merited divine grace and salvation for us.

III. So long as Christ is separated from us we have no benefit from him. We must be ingrafted in him like branches in the vine. Hence the Creed, after treating of Christ, proceeds in its third article, *I believe in the Holy Spirit,*—the Holy Spirit being the bond of union between us and Christ. In like manner, the Third Book of the Institutes treats of the Holy Spirit which unites us to Christ, and, in connection with it, of faith, by which we embrace Christ with a double benefit—viz. that of gratuitous righteousness, which he imputes to us, and regeneration, which he begins in us by giving us repentance. In order to show the worthlessness of a faith which is not accompanied with a desire of repentance, the author, before proceeding to a full discussion of justification, treats at length from chapter iii.-x. of repentance, and the constant study of it—repentance which Christ, when apprehended by faith, begets in us by his Spirit. Chapter xi. treats of the primary and peculiar benefit of Christ when united to us by the Holy Spirit—viz. justification. This subject is continued to the xx. chapter, which treats of prayer, the hand, as it were, to receive the blessings which faith knows to be treasured up for it with God, according to the word of promise. But, as the Holy Spirit, who creates and preserves our faith, does not unite all men to Christ, who is the sole author of salvation, chapter xxi. treats of the eternal election of God, to which it is owing that we, in whom he foresaw no good which he had not previously bestowed, are given to Christ, and united to him by the effectual calling of the Gospel. This subject is continued to the xxv. chapter, which treats of complete regeneration and felicity, namely, the final resurrection to which we must raise our eyes, seeing that, in regard to fruition, the happiness of the godly is only begun in this world.

IV. Since the Holy Spirit does not ingraft all men into Christ, or endue them with faith, and those whom he does so endue he does not ordinarily endue without means, but uses for that purpose the preaching of the Gospel and the dispensation of the Sacraments, together with the administration of all kinds of discipline, the Creed contains the following article, *I believe in the Holy Catholic Church*, namely, that Church which, when lying in eternal death, the Father, by gratuitous election, freely reconciled to himself in Christ and endued with the Holy Spirit, that, being ingrafted into Christ, it might have communion with him as its proper head; whence flow perpetual remission of sins, and full restoration to eternal life. Accordingly, the Church is treated of in the first fourteen chapters of the Fourth Book, which thereafter treats of the means which the Holy Spirit employs in calling us effectually from spiritual death, and preserving the Church, in other words, Baptism and the Lord's Supper. These means are, as it were, the royal sceptre of Christ, by which, through the efficacy of his Spirit, he commences his spiritual reign in the Church, advances it from day to day, and after this life, without the use of means, finally perfects it. This subject is continued to the xx. chapter.

And because civil governments are, in this life, the hospitable entertainers (*hospitia*) of the Church (though civil government is distinct from the spiritual kingdom of Christ), the author shows how great blessings they are, blessings which the Church is bound gratefully to acknowledge, until we are called away from this tabernacle to the heavenly inheritance, where God will be all in all.

Such is the arrangement of the Institutes, which may be thus summed up : Man being at first created upright, but afterwards being not partially but totally ruined, finds his entire salvation out of himself in Christ, to whom being united by the Holy Spirit freely given, without any foresight of future works, he thereby obtains a double blessing—viz. full imputation of righteousness, which goes along with us even to the grave, and the commencement of sanctification, which daily advances till at length it is perfected in the day of regeneration or resurrection of the body, and this, in order that the great mercy of God may be celebrated in the heavenly mansions throughout eternity.

GENERAL INDEX OF CHAPTERS.

BOOK FIRST.

OF THE KNOWLEDGE OF GOD THE CREATOR.

Eighteen Chapters.

BOOK SECOND.

OF THE KNOWLEDGE OF GOD THE REDEEMER, IN CHRIST,
AS FIRST MANIFESTED TO THE FATHERS UNDER THE LAW,
AND THEREAFTER TO US UNDER THE GOSPEL.

Seventeen Chapters.

BOOK THIRD.

THE MODE OF OBTAINING THE GRACE OF CHRIST.
THE BENEFITS IT CONFERS, AND THE EFFECTS RESULTING FROM IT.

Twenty-Five Chapters.

INSTITUTES

OF

THE CHRISTIAN RELIGION.

BOOK FIRST.

OF THE KNOWLEDGE OF GOD THE CREATOR.

ARGUMENT.

THE First Book treats of the knowledge of God the Creator. But as it is in the creation of man that the divine perfections are best displayed, so man also is made the subject of discourse. Thus the whole book divides itself into two principal heads—the former relating to the knowledge of God, and the latter to the knowledge of man. In the first chapter, these are considered jointly; and in each of the following chapters, separately: occasionally, however, intermingled with other matters which refer to one or other of the heads; *e.g.*, the discussions concerning Scripture and images falling under the former head, and the other three, concerning the creation of the world, the holy angels, and devils, falling under the latter. The last point discussed—viz. the method of the divine government—relates to both.

With regard to the former head—viz. the knowledge of God—it is shown, in the first place, what the kind of knowledge is which God requires, Chap. II. And, in the second place (Chap. III.—IX.), where this knowledge must be sought, namely, not in man ; because, although naturally implanted in the human mind, it is stifled, partly by ignorance, partly by evil intent, Chap. III. and IV.; not in the frame of the world: because, although it shines most clearly there, we are so stupid that these manifestations, however perspicuous, pass away without any beneficial result, Chap. V.; but in Scripture (Chap. VI.), which is treated of, Chap. VII.—IX. In the third place, it is shown what the character of God is, Chap. X. In the fourth place, how impious it is to give a visible form to God (here images, the worship of them, and its origin, are considered), Chap. XI. In the fifth place, it is shown that God is to be solely and wholly worshipped, Chap. XII Lastly, Chap. XIII. treats of the unity of the divine essence, and the distinction of three persons.

With regard to the latter head—viz. the knowledge of man—first, Chap. XIV. treats of the creation of the world, and of good and bad angels (these all having reference to man). And then Chap. XV., taking up the subject of man himself, examines his nature and his powers.

The better to illustrate the nature both of God and man, the three remaining Chapters—viz. XVI.—XVIII.—proceed to treat of the general government of the world, and particularly of human actions, in opposition to fortune and fate, explaining both the doctrine and its use. In conclusion, it is shown, that though God employs the instrumentality of the wicked, he is pure from sin and from taint of every kind.

INSTITUTES

OF

THE CHRISTIAN RELIGION.

BOOK FIRST.

OF THE KNOWLEDGE OF GOD THE CREATOR:

CHAPTER I.

THE KNOWLEDGE OF GOD AND OF OURSELVES MUTUALLY CONNECTED. —NATURE OF THE CONNECTION.

Sections.

1. The sum of true wisdom—viz. the knowledge of God and of ourselves. Effects of the latter.
2. Effects of the knowledge of God, in humbling our pride, unveiling our hypocrisy, demonstrating the absolute perfections of God, and our own utter helplessness.
3. Effects of the knowledge of God illustrated by the examples, 1. of holy patriarchs; 2. of holy angels; 3. of the sun and moon.

1. OUR wisdom, in so far as it ought to be deemed true and solid wisdom, consists almost entirely of two parts: the knowledge of God and of ourselves. But as these are connected together by many ties, it is not easy to determine which of the two precedes, and gives birth to the other. For, in the first place, no man can survey himself without forthwith turning his thoughts towards the God in whom he lives and moves; because it is perfectly obvious, that the endowments which we possess cannot possibly be from ourselves; nay, that our very being is nothing else than subsistence in God alone. In the second place, those blessings which unceasingly distil to us from heaven, are like streams conducting us to the fountain. Here, again, the infinitude of good which resides in God becomes more apparent from our poverty. In particular, the miserable ruin into which the revolt of the first man has plunged us, compels us to turn our eyes upwards; not only that while hungry and famishing we may thence ask what we want, but being aroused by fear may learn

humility. For as there exists in man something like a world of misery, and ever since we were stript of the divine attire our naked shame discloses an immense series of disgraceful properties, every man, being stung by the consciousness of his own unhappiness, in this way necessarily obtains at least some knowledge of God. Thus, our feeling of ignorance, vanity, want, weakness, in short, depravity and corruption, reminds us (see Calvin on John iv. 10) that in the Lord, and none but He, dwell the true light of wisdom, solid virtue, exuberant goodness. We are accordingly urged by our own evil things to consider the good things of God; and, indeed, we cannot aspire to Him in earnest until we have begun to be displeased with ourselves. For what man is not disposed to rest in himself? Who, in fact, does not thus rest, so long as he is unknown to himself; that is, so long as he is contented with his own endowments, and unconscious or unmindful of his misery? Every person, therefore, on coming to the knowledge of himself, is not only urged to seek God, but is also led as by the hand to find him.

2. On the other hand, it is evident that man never attains to a true self-knowledge until he have previously contemplated the face of God, and come down after such contemplation to look into himself. For (such is our innate pride) we always seem to ourselves just, and upright, and wise, and holy, until we are convinced, by clear evidence, of our injustice, vileness, folly, and impurity. Convinced, however, we are not, if we look to ourselves only, and not to the Lord also— He being the only standard by the application of which this conviction can be produced. For, since we are all naturally prone to hypocrisy, any empty semblance of righteousness is quite enough to satisfy us instead of righteousness itself. And since nothing appears within us or around us that is not tainted with very great impurity, so long as we keep our mind within the confines of human pollution, anything which is in some small degree less defiled, delights us as if it were most pure: just as an eye, to which nothing but black had been previously presented, deems an object of a whitish, or even of a brownish hue, to be perfectly white. Nay, the bodily sense may furnish a still stronger illustration of the extent to which we are deluded in estimating the powers of the mind. If, at mid-day, we either look down to the ground, or on the surrounding objects which lie open to our view, we think ourselves endued with a very strong and piercing eyesight; but when we look up to the sun, and gaze at it unveiled, the sight which did excellently well for the earth, is instantly so dazzled and confounded by the refulgence, as to oblige us to confess that our acuteness in discerning terrestrial objects is mere dimness when applied to the sun. Thus, too, it happens in estimating our spiritual qualities. So long as we do not look beyond the earth, we are quite pleased with our own righteousness, wisdom, and virtue; we address ourselves in the most flattering terms, and seem only less than demigods. But should we once begin to raise our

thoughts to God, and reflect what kind of Being he is, and how absolute the perfection of that righteousness, and wisdom, and virtue, to which, as a standard, we are bound to be conformed, what formerly delighted us by its false show of righteousness, will become polluted with the greatest iniquity; what strangely imposed upon us under the name of wisdom, will disgust by its extreme folly; and what presented the appearance of virtuous energy, will be condemned as the most miserable impotence. So far are those qualities in us, which seem most perfect, from corresponding to the divine purity.

3. Hence that dread and amazement with which, as Scripture uniformly relates, holy men were struck and overwhelmed whenever they beheld the presence of God. When we see those who previously stood firm and secure so quaking with terror, that the fear of death takes hold of them, nay, they are, in a manner, swallowed up and annihilated, the inference to be drawn is, that men are never duly touched and impressed with a conviction of their insignificance, until they have contrasted themselves with the majesty of God. Frequent examples of this consternation occur both in the Book of Judges and the Prophetical Writings;[1] so much so, that it was a common expression among the people of God, "We shall die, for we have seen the Lord." Hence the Book of Job, also, in humbling men under a conviction of their folly, feebleness, and pollution, always derives its chief argument from descriptions of the divine wisdom, virtue, and purity. Nor without cause: for we see Abraham the readier to acknowledge himself but dust and ashes, the nearer he approaches to behold the glory of the Lord, and Elijah unable to wait with unveiled face for His approach, so dreadful is the sight. And what can man do, man who is but rottenness and a worm, when even the Cherubim themselves must veil their faces in very terror? To this, undoubtedly, the Prophet Isaiah refers, when he says (Isaiah xxiv. 23), "The moon shall be confounded, and the sun ashamed, when the Lord of Hosts shall reign;" i.e., when he shall exhibit his refulgence, and give a nearer view of it, the brightest objects will, in comparison, be covered with darkness.

But though the knowledge of God and the knowledge of ourselves are bound together by a mutual tie, due arrangement requires that we treat of the former in the first place, and then descend to the latter.

---

[1] Judges xiii. 22; Isaiah vi. 5; Ezek. i. 28, iii. 14; Job ix. 4, &c.; Gen. xviii. 27; 1 Kings xix. 13.

CHAPTER II.

WHAT IT IS TO KNOW GOD.—TENDENCY OF THIS KNOWLEDGE.

Sections.

1. The knowledge of God the Creator defined. The substance of this knowledge, and the use to be made of it.
2. Further illustration of the use, together with a necessary reproof of vain curiosity, and refutation of the Epicureans. The character of God as it appears to the pious mind, contrasted with the absurd views of the Epicureans. Religion defined.

1. By the knowledge of God, I understand that by which we not only conceive that there is some God, but also apprehend what it is for our interest, and conducive to his glory, what, in short, it is befitting to know concerning him. For, properly speaking, we cannot say that God is known where there is no religion or piety. I am not now referring to that species of knowledge by which men, in themselves lost and under curse, apprehend God as a Redeemer in Christ the Mediator. I speak only of that simple and primitive knowledge, to which the mere course of nature would have conducted us, had Adam stood upright. For although no man will now, in the present ruin of the human race, perceive God to be either a father, or the author of salvation, or propitious in any respect, until Christ interpose to make our peace; still it is one thing to perceive that God our Maker supports us by his power, rules us by his providence, fosters us by his goodness, and visits us with all kinds of blessings, and another thing to embrace the grace of reconciliation offered to us in Christ. Since, then, the Lord first appears, as well in the creation of the world as in the general doctrine of Scripture, simply as a Creator, and afterwards as a Redeemer in Christ,—a twofold knowledge of him hence arises: of these the former is now to be considered, the latter will afterwards follow in its order. But although our mind cannot conceive of God, without rendering some worship to him, it will not, however, be sufficient simply to hold that he is the only being whom all ought to worship and adore, unless we are also persuaded that he is the fountain of all goodness, and that we must seek everything in him, and in none but him. My meaning is: we must be persuaded not only that as he once formed the world, so he sustains it by his boundless power, governs it by his wisdom, preserves it by his goodness, in particular, rules the human race with justice and judgment, bears with them in mercy, shields them by his protection; but also that not a particle of light, or wisdom, or justice, or power, or rectitude, or genuine truth, will anywhere be found, which does not flow

from him, and of which he is not the cause; in this way we must learn to expect and ask all things from him, and thankfully ascribe to him whatever we receive. For this sense of the divine perfections is the proper master to teach us piety, out of which religion springs. By piety I mean that union of reverence and love to God which the knowledge of his benefits inspires. For, until men feel that they owe everything to God, that they are cherished by his paternal care, and that he is the author of all their blessings, so that nought is to be looked for away from him, they will never submit to him in voluntary obedience; nay, unless they place their entire happiness in him, they will never yield up their whole selves to him in truth and sincerity.

3. Those, therefore, who, in considering this question, propose to inquire what the essence of God is, only delude us with frigid speculations,—it being much more our interest to know what kind of being God is, and what things are agreeable to his nature. For, of what use is it to join Epicurus in acknowledging some God who has cast off the care of the world, and only delights himself in ease? What avails it, in short, to know a God with whom we have nothing to do? The effect of our knowledge rather ought to be, *first*, to teach us reverence and fear; and, *secondly*, to induce us, under its guidance and teaching, to ask every good thing from him, and, when it is received, ascribe it to him. For how can the idea of God enter your mind without instantly giving rise to the thought, that since you are his workmanship, you are bound, by the very law of creation, to submit to his authority?—that your life is due to him?—that whatever you do ought to have reference to him? If so, it undoubtedly follows that your life is sadly corrupted, if it is not framed in obedience to him, since his will ought to be the law of our lives. On the other hand, your idea of his nature is not clear unless you acknowledge him to be the origin and fountain of all goodness. Hence would arise both confidence in him, and a desire of cleaving to him, did not the depravity of the human mind lead it away from the proper course of investigation.

For, first of all, the pious mind does not devise for itself any kind of God, but looks alone to the one true God; nor does it feign for him any character it pleases, but is contented to have him in the character in which he manifests himself, always guarding, with the utmost diligence, against transgressing his will, and wandering, with daring presumption, from the right path. He by whom God is thus known, perceiving how he governs all things, confides in him as his guardian and protector, and casts himself entirely upon his faithfulness,—perceiving him to be the source of every blessing, if he is in any strait or feels any want, he instantly recurs to his protection and trusts to his aid,—persuaded that he is good and merciful, he reclines upon him with sure confidence, and doubts not that, in the divine clemency, a remedy will be provided for his every time of need,— acknowledging him as his Father and his Lord, he considers himself bound to have respect to his authority in all things, to reverence his majesty, aim at the advancement of his glory, and obey his commands, —regarding him as a just judge, armed with severity to punish crimes, he keeps the judgment-seat always in his view. Standing in awe of it, he curbs himself, and fears to provoke his anger. Nevertheless, he is not so terrified by an apprehension of judgment as to wish he could withdraw himself, even if the means of escape lay before him; nay, he embraces him not less as the avenger of wickedness than as the rewarder of the righteous; because he perceives that it equally appertains to his glory to store up punishment for the one, and eternal life for the other. Besides, it is not the mere fear of punishment that restrains him from sin. Loving and revering God as his father, honouring and obeying him as his master, although there were no hell, he would revolt at the very idea of offending him.

Such is pure and genuine religion, namely, confidence in God coupled with serious fear—fear, which both includes in it willing reverence, and brings along with it such legitimate worship as is prescribed by the law. And it ought to be more carefully considered, that all men promiscuously do homage to God, but very few truly reverence him. On all hands there is abundance of ostentatious ceremonies, but sincerity of heart is rare.

CHAPTER III.

THE KNOWLEDGE OF GOD NATURALLY IMPLANTED IN THE HUMAN MIND.

Sections.

1. The knowledge of God being manifested to all makes the reprobate without excuse· Universal belief and acknowledgment of the existence of God.
2. Objection — that religion and the belief of a Deity are the inventions of crafty politicians. Refutation of the objection. This universal belief confirmed by the examples of wicked men and Atheists.
3. Confirmed also by the vain endeavours of the wicked to banish all fear of God from their minds. Conclusion, that the knowledge of God is naturally implanted in the human mind.

1. THAT there exists in the human mind, and indeed by natural instinct, some sense of Deity, we hold to be beyond dispute, since God himself, to prevent any man from pretending ignorance, has endued all men with some idea of his Godhead, the memory of which he constantly renews and occasionally enlarges, that all to a man, being aware that there is a God, and that he is their Maker, may be condemned by their own conscience when they neither worship him nor consecrate their lives to his service. Certainly, if there is any quarter where it may be supposed that God is unknown, the most likely for such an instance to exist is among the dullest tribes farthest removed from civilisation. But, as a heathen tells us,[1] there is no nation so barbarous, no race so brutish, as not to be imbued with the conviction that there is a God. Even those who, in other respects, seem to differ least from the lower animals, constantly retain some sense of religion ; so thoroughly has this common conviction possessed the mind, so firmly is it stamped on the breasts of all men. Since, then, there never has been, from the very first, any quarter of the globe, any city, any household even, without religion, this amounts to a tacit confession, that a sense of Deity is inscribed on every heart. Nay, even idolatry is ample evidence of this fact. For we know how reluctant man is to lower himself, in order to set other creatures above him. Therefore, when he chooses to worship wood and stone rather than be thought to have no God, it is evident how very strong this impression of a Deity must be ; since it is more difficult to obliterate it from the

---

1 " Intelligi necesse est deos, quoniam insitas eorum vel potius innatas cognitiones habemus.—Quæ nobis natura informationem deorum ipsorum dedit, eadem insculpsit in mentibus ut eos æternos et beatos haberemus."—Cic. de Nat. Deor. lib. i. c. 17.— " Itaque inter omnes omnium gentium summa constat ; omnibus enim innatum est, et in animo quasi insculptum esse deos."—Lib. ii. c. 4. See also Lact. Inst. Div. lib. iii. c. 10.

mind of man, than to break down the feelings of his nature,—these certainly being broken down, when, in opposition to his natural haughtiness, he spontaneously humbles himself before the meanest object as an act of reverence to God.

2. It is most absurd, therefore, to maintain, as some do, that religion was devised by the cunning and craft of a few individuals, as a means of keeping the body of the people in due subjection, while there was nothing which those very individuals, while teaching others to worship God, less believed than the existence of a God. I readily acknowledge, that designing men have introduced a vast number of fictions into religion, with the view of inspiring the populace with reverence or striking them with terror, and thereby rendering them more obsequious ; but they never could have succeeded in this, had the minds of men not been previously imbued with that uniform belief in God, from which, as from its seed, the religious propensity springs. And it is altogether incredible that those who, in the matter of religion, cunningly imposed on their ruder neighbours, were altogether devoid of a knowledge of God. For though in old times there were some, and in the present day not a few are found[1] who deny the being of a God, yet, whether they will or not, they occasionally feel the truth which they are desirous not to know. We do not read of any man who broke out into more unbridled and audacious contempt of the Deity than C. Caligula,[2] and yet none showed greater dread when any indication of divine wrath was manifested. Thus, however unwilling, he shook with terror before the God whom he professedly studied to contemn. You may every day see the same thing happening to his modern imitators. The most audacious despiser of God is most easily disturbed, trembling at the sound of a falling leaf. How so, unless in vindication of the divine majesty, which smites their consciences the more strongly the more they endeavour to flee from it. They all, indeed, look out for hiding-places, where they may conceal themselves from the presence of the Lord, and again efface it from their mind ; but after all their efforts they remain caught within the net. Though the conviction may occasionally seem to vanish for a moment, it immediately returns, and rushes in with new impetuosity, so that any interval of relief from the gnawings of conscience is not unlike the slumber of the intoxicated or the insane, who have no quiet rest in sleep, but are continually haunted with dire horrific dreams. Even the wicked themselves, therefore, are an example of the fact that some idea of God always exists in every human mind.

3. All men of sound judgment will therefore hold, that a sense of Deity is indelibly engraven on the human heart. And that this belief is naturally engendered in all, and thoroughly fixed as it were

[1] As to some Atheists of the author's time, see Calvinus De Scandalis.
[2] Suet. Calig. c. 51.

in our very bones, is strikingly attested by the contumacy of the wicked, who, though they struggle furiously, are unable to extricate themselves from the fear of God. Though Diagoras,[1] and others of like stamp, make themselves merry with whatever has been believed in all ages concerning religion, and Dionysius scoffs at the judgment of heaven, it is but a Sardonian grin; for the worm of conscience, keener than burning steel, is gnawing them within. I do not say with Cicero, that errors wear out by age, and that religion increases and grows better day by day. For the world (as will be shortly seen) labours as much as it can to shake off all knowledge of God, and corrupts his worship in innumerable ways. I only say, that, when the stupid hardness of heart, which the wicked eagerly court as a means of despising God, becomes enfeebled, the sense of Deity, which of all things they wished most to be extinguished, is still in vigour, and now and then breaks forth. Whence we infer, that this is not a doctrine which is first learned at school, but one as to which every man is, from the womb, his own master; one which nature herself allows no individual to forget, though many, with all their might, strive to do so. Moreover, if all are born and live for the express purpose of learning to know God, and if the knowledge of God, in so far as it fails to produce this effect, is fleeting and vain, it is clear that all those who do not direct the whole thoughts and actions of their lives to this end fail to fulfil the law of their being. This did not escape the observation even of philosophers. For it is the very thing which Plato meant (in *Phæd. et Theact.*) when he taught, as he often does, that the chief good of the soul consists in resemblance to God; *i.e.*, when, by means of knowing him, she is wholly transformed into him. Thus Gryllus, also, in Plutarch (*lib. quod bruta anim. ratione utantur*), reasons most skilfully, when he affirms that, if once religion is banished from the lives of men, they not only in no respect excel, but are, in many respects, much more wretched than the brutes, since, being exposed to so many forms of evil, they continually drag on a troubled and restless existence: that the only thing, therefore, which makes them superior is the worship of God, through which alone they aspire to immortality.

[1] Cic. De Nat. Deor. lib. i. c. 23.   Valer. Max. lib. i. c. 1.

CHAPTER IV.

THE KNOWLEDGE OF GOD STIFLED OR CORRUPTED, IGNORANTLY OR MALICIOUSLY.

Sections.

1. The knowledge of God suppressed by ignorance, many falling away into superstition. Such persons, however, inexcusable, because their error is accompanied with pride and stubbornness.
2. Stubbornness the companion of impiety.
3. No pretext can justify superstition. This proved, first, from reason; and, secondly, from Scripture.
4. The wicked never willingly come into the presence of God. Hence their hypocrisy. Hence, too, their sense of Deity leads to no good result.

1. BUT though experience testifies that a seed of religion is divinely sown in all, scarcely one in a hundred is found who cherishes it in his heart, and not one in whom it grows to maturity, so far is it from yielding fruit in its season. Moreover, while some lose themselves in superstitious observances, and others, of set purpose, wickedly revolt from God, the result is that, in regard to the true knowledge of him, all are so degenerate, that in no part of the world can genuine godliness be found. In saying that some fall away into superstition, I mean not to insinuate that their excessive absurdity frees them from guilt; for the blindness under which they labour is almost invariably accompanied with vain pride and stubbornness. Mingled vanity and pride appear in this, that when miserable men do seek after God, instead of ascending higher than themselves, as they ought to do, they measure him by their own carnal stupidity, and, neglecting solid inquiry, fly off to indulge their curiosity in vain speculation. Hence, they do not conceive of him in the character in which he is manifested, but imagine him to be whatever their own rashness has devised. This abyss standing open, they cannot move one footstep without rushing headlong to destruction. With such an idea of God, nothing which they may attempt to offer in the way of worship or obedience can have any value in his sight, because it is not him they worship, but, instead of him, the dream and figment of their own heart. This corrupt procedure is admirably described by Paul, when he says, that "thinking to be wise, they became fools" (Rom. i. 22). He had previously said that "they became vain in their imaginations," but lest any should suppose them blameless, he afterwards adds, that they were deservedly blinded, because, not contented with sober inquiry, because, arrogating to themselves more than they have any title to

do, they of their own accord court darkness, nay, bewitch themselves with perverse, empty show. Hence it is that their folly, the result not only of vain curiosity, but of licentious desire and overweening confidence in the pursuit of forbidden knowledge, cannot be excused.

2. The expression of David (Psalm xiv 1, liii. 1), "The fool hath said in his heart, There is no God," is primarily applied to those who, as will shortly farther appear, stifle the light of nature, and intentionally stupifiy themselves. We see many, after they have become hardened in a daring course of sin, madly banishing all remembrance of God, though spontaneously suggested to them from within, by natural sense. To show how detestable this madness is, the Psalmist introduces them as distinctly denying that there is a God, because, although they do not disown his essence, they rob him of his justice and providence, and represent him as sitting idly in heaven. Nothing being less accordant with the nature of God than to cast off the government of the world, leaving it to chance, and so to wink at the crimes of men that they may wanton with impunity in evil courses; it follows, that every man who indulges in security, after extinguishing all fear of divine judgment, virtually denies that there is a God. As a just punishment of the wicked, after they have closed their own eyes, God makes their hearts dull and heavy, and hence, seeing, they see not. David, indeed, is the best interpreter of his own meaning, when he says elsewhere, the wicked has "no fear of God before his eyes" (Psalm xxxvi. 1); and, again, "He hath said in his heart, God hath forgotten; he hideth his face; he will never see it." Thus, although they are forced to acknowledge that there is some God, they however, rob him of his glory by denying his power. For, as Paul declares, "If we believe not, he abideth faithful, he cannot deny himself" (2 Tim. ii. 13) ; so those who feign to themselves a dead and dumb idol, are truly said to deny God It is, moreover, to be observed, that though they struggle with their own convictions, and would fain not only banish God from their minds, but from heaven also, there stupefaction is never so complete as to secure them from being occasionally dragged before the divine tribunal. Still, as no fear restrains them from rushing violently in the face of God, so long as they are hurried on by that blind impulse, it cannot be denied that their prevailing state of mind in regard to him is brutish oblivion.

3. In this way, the vain pretext which many employ to clothe their superstition is overthrown. They deem it enough that they have some kind of zeal for religion, how preposterous soever it may be, not observing that true religion must be conformable to the will of God as its unerring standard; that he can never deny himself, and is no spectre or phantom, to be metamorphosed at each individual's caprice. It is easy to see how superstition, with its false glosses, mocks God, while it tries to please him. Usually fastening merely on things on which he has declared he sets no value, it either contemptuously overlooks, or even undisguisedly rejects, the things which he expressly

enjoins, or in which we are assured that he takes pleasure. Those, therefore, who set up a fictitious worship, merely worship and adore their own delirious fancies; indeed, they would never dare so to trifle with God, had they not previously fashioned him after their own childish conceits. Hence that vague and wandering opinion of Deity is declared by an apostle to be ignorance of God: "Howbeit, then, when ye knew not God, ye did service unto them which by nature are no gods." And he elsewhere declares, that the Ephesians were "without God" (Eph. ii. 12) at the time when they wandered without any correct knowledge of him. It makes little difference, at least in this respect, whether you hold the existence of one God, or a plurality of gods, since, in both cases alike, by departing from the true God, you have nothing left but an execrable idol. It remains, therefore, to conclude with Lactantius (*Instit. Div.* lib. i. 2, 6), "No religion is genuine that is not in accordance with truth."

4. To this fault they add a second—viz. that when they do think of God it is against their will; never approaching him without being dragged into his presence, and when there, instead of the voluntary fear flowing from reverence of the divine majesty, feeling only that forced and servile fear which divine judgment extorts—judgment which, from the impossibility of escape, they are compelled to dread, but which, while they dread, they at the same time also hate. To impiety, and to it alone, the saying of Statius properly applies: "Fear first brought gods into the world" (*Theb.* lib. i.). Those whose inclinations are at variance with the justice of God, knowing that his tribunal has been erected for the punishment of transgression, earnestly wish that that tribunal were overthrown. Under the influence of this feeling they are actually warring against God, justice being one of his essential attributes. Perceiving that they are always within reach of his power, that resistance and evasion are alike impossible, they fear and tremble. Accordingly, to avoid the appearance of contemning a majesty by which all are overawed, they have recourse to some species of religious observance, never ceasing meanwhile to defile themselves with every kind of vice, and add crime to crime, until they have broken the holy law of the Lord in every one of its requirements, and set his whole righteousness at nought; at all events, they are not so restrained by their semblance of fear as not to luxuriate and take pleasure in iniquity, choosing rather to indulge their carnal propensities than to curb them with the bridle of the Holy Spirit. But since this shadow of religion (it scarcely even deserves to be called a shadow) is false and vain, it is easy to infer how much this confused knowledge of God differs from that piety which is instilled into the breasts of believers, and from which alone true religion springs. And yet hypocrites would fain, by means of tortuous windings, make a show of being near to God at the very time they are fleeing from him. For while the whole life ought to be one perpetual course of obedience, they rebel without fear in almost all their actions, and seek to appease

him with a few paltry sacrifices; while they ought to serve him with integrity of heart and holiness of life, they endeavour to procure his favour by means of frivolous devices and punctilios of no value. Nay, they take greater license in their grovelling indulgencies, because they imagine that they can fulfil their duty to him by preposterous expiations; in short, while their confidence ought to have been fixed upon him, they put him aside, and rest in themselves or the creatures. At length they bewilder themselves in such a maze of error, that the darkness of ignorance obscures, and ultimately extinguishes, those sparks which were designed to show them the glory of God. Still, however, the conviction that there is some Deity continues to exist, like a plant which can never be completely eradicated, though so corrupt that it is only capable of producing the worst of fruit. Nay, we have still stronger evidence of the proposition for which I now contend—viz. that a sense of Deity is naturally engraven on the human heart, in the fact, that the very reprobate are forced to acknowledge it. When at their ease, they can jest about God, and talk pertly and loquaciously in disparagement of his power; but should despair, from any cause, overtake them, it will stimulate them to seek him, and dictate ejaculatory prayers, proving that they were not entirely ignorant of God, but had perversely suppressed feelings which ought to have been earlier manifested.

CHAPTER V.

THE KNOWLEDGE OF GOD CONSPICUOUS IN THE CREATION AND CONTINUAL GOVERNMENT OF THE WORLD.

This chapter consists of two parts: 1. The former, which occupies the first ten sections, divides all the works of God into two great classes, and elucidates the knowledge of God as displayed in each class. The one class is treated of in the first six, and the other in the four following sections: 2. The latter part of the chapter shows, that, in consequence of the extreme stupidity of men, those manifestations of God, however perspicuous, lead to no useful result. This latter part, which commences at the eleventh section, is continued to the end of the chapter.

Sections.

1. The invisible and incomprehensible essence of God, to a certain extent, made visible in his works
2. This declared by the first class of works—viz. the admirable motions of the heavens and the earth, the symmetry of the human body, and the connection of its parts ; in short, the various objects which are presented to every eye.
3. This more especially manifested in the structure of the human body.
4. The shameful ingratitude of disregarding God, who, in such a variety of ways, is manifested within us. The still more shameful ingratitude of contemplating the endowments of the soul, without ascending to Him who gave them. No objection can be founded on any supposed organism in the soul.
5. The powers and actions of the soul, a proof of its separate existence from the body. Proofs of the soul's immortality. Objection that the whole world is quickened by one soul. Reply to the objection. Its impiety.
6. Conclusion from what has been said—viz. that the omnipotence, eternity, and goodness of God, may be learned from the first class of works, i.e., those which are in accordance with the ordinary course of nature.
7. The second class of works—viz. those above the ordinary course of nature—afford clear evidence of the perfections of God, especially his goodness, justice, and mercy.
8. Also his providence, power, and wisdom.
9. Proofs and illustrations of the divine Majesty. The use of them—viz. the acquisition of divine knowledge in combination with true piety.
10. The tendency of the knowledge of God to inspire the righteous with the hope of future life and remind the wicked of the punishments reserved for them. Its tendency, moreover, to keep alive in the hearts of the righteous a sense of the divine goodness.
11. The second part of the chapter, which describes the stupidity both of learned and unlearned, in ascribing the whole order of things, and the admirable arrangements of divine Providence, to fortune.
12. Hence Polytheism, with all its abominations, and the endless and irreconcilable opinions of the philosophers concerning God.
13. All guilty of revolt from God, corrupting pure religion, either by following general custom, or the impious consent of antiquity.
14. Though irradiated by the wondrous glories of creation, we cease not to follow our own ways.
15. Our conduct altogether inexcusable, the dulness of perception being attributable to ourselves, while we are fully reminded of the true path, both by the structure and the government of the world.

1. SINCE the perfection of blessedness consists in the knowledge of God, he has been pleased, in order that none might be excluded from the means of obtaining felicity, not only to deposit in our minds that seed of religion of which we have already spoken, but so to manifest his perfections in the whole structure of the universe, and daily place himself in our view, that we cannot open our eyes without being compelled to behold him. His essence, indeed, is incomprehensible, utterly transcending all human thought; but on each of his works his glory is engraven in characters so bright, so distinct, and so illustrious, that none, however dull and illiterate, can plead ignorance as their excuse. Hence, with perfect truth, the Psalmist exclaims, "He covereth himself with light as with a garment" (Psalm civ. 2); as if he had said, that God for the first time was arrayed in visible attire when, in the creation of the world, he displayed those glorious banners, on which, to whatever side we turn, we behold his perfections visibly portrayed. In the same place, the Psalmist aptly compares the expanded heavens to his royal tent, and says, "He layeth the beams of his chambers in the waters, maketh the clouds his chariot, and walketh upon the wings of the wind," sending forth the winds and lightnings as his swift messengers. And because the glory of his power and wisdom is more refulgent in the firmament, it is frequently designated as his palace. And, first, wherever you turn your eyes, there is no portion of the world, however minute, that does not exhibit at least some sparks of beauty; while it is impossible to contemplate the vast and beautiful fabric as it extends around, without being overwhelmed by the immense weight of glory. Hence, the author of the Epistle to the Hebrews elegantly describes the visible worlds as images of the invisible (Heb. xi. 3), the elegant structure of the world serving us as a kind of mirror, in which we may behold God, though otherwise invisible. For the same reason, the Psalmist attributes language to celestial objects, a language which all nations understand (Psalm xix. 1); the manifestation of the Godhead being too clear to escape the notice of any people, however obtuse. The apostle Paul, stating this still more clearly, says, "That which may be known of God is manifest in them, for God hath showed it unto them. For the invisible things of him from the creation of the world are clearly seen, being understood by the things that are made, even his eternal power and Godhead" (Rom. i. 20).

2. In attestation of his wondrous wisdom, both the heavens and the earth present us with innumerable proofs, not only those more recondite proofs which astronomy, medicine, and all the natural sciences, are designed to illustrate, but proofs which force themselves on the notice of the most illiterate peasant, who cannot open his eyes without beholding them. It is true, indeed, that those who are more or less intimately acquainted with those liberal studies are thereby assisted and enabled to obtain a deeper insight into the secret workings of divine wisdom. No man, however, though he be ignorant of these,

is incapacitated for discerning such proofs of creative wisdom as may well cause him to break forth in admiration of the Creator. To investigate the motions of the heavenly bodies, to determine their positions, measure their distances, and ascertain their properties, demands skill, and a more careful examination ; and where these are so employed, as the providence of God is thereby more fully unfolded, so it is reasonable to suppose that the mind takes a loftier flight, and obtains brighter views of his glory.[1] Still, none who have the use of their eyes can be ignorant of the divine skill manifested so conspicuously in the endless variety, yet distinct and well-ordered array, of the heavenly host ; and, therefore, it is plain that the Lord has furnished every man with abundant proofs of his wisdom. The same is true in regard to the structure of the human frame. To determine the connection of its parts, its symmetry and beauty, with the skill of a Galen (Lib. De Usu Partium), requires singular acuteness; and yet all men acknowledge that the human body bears on its face such proofs of ingenious contrivance as are sufficient to proclaim the admirable wisdom of its Maker.

3. Hence certain of the philosophers[2] have not improperly called man a *microcosm* (*miniature world*), as being a rare specimen of divine power, wisdom, and goodness, and containing within himself wonders sufficient to occupy our minds, if we are willing so to employ them. Paul, accordingly, after reminding the Athenians that they "might feel after God and find him," immediately adds, that "he is not far from every one of us" (Acts xvii. 27) ; every man having within himself undoubted evidence of the heavenly grace by which he lives, and moves, and has his being. But if, in order to apprehend God, it is unnecessary to go farther than ourselves, what excuse can there be for the sloth of any man who will not take the trouble of descending into himself that he may find Him ? For the same reason, too, David, after briefly celebrating the wonderful name and glory of God, as everywhere displayed, immediately exclaims, "What is man, that thou art mindful of him ?" and again, "Out of the mouths of babes and sucklings thou hast ordained strength" (Psalm viii. 2, 4). Thus he declares not only that the human race are a bright mirror of the Creator's works, but that infants hanging on their mothers' breasts have tongues eloquent enough to proclaim his glory without the aid of other orators. Accordingly, he hesitates not to bring them forward as fully instructed to refute the madness of those who, from devilish pride, would fain extinguish the name of God. Hence, too, the passage which Paul quotes from Aratus, "We are his offspring" (Acts xvii. 28), the excellent gifts with which he has endued us attesting that he is our Father. In the same way, also, from natural instinct, and, as it were, at the dictation of experience, heathen poets

[1] Augustinus : Astrologia magnum religiosis argumentum, tormentumque curiosis.
[2] See Aristot. Hist. Anim. lib. i. c. 17 ; Macrob. in Somn. Scip. lib. ii. c. 12 ; Boeth. De Definitione.

call him the father of men.   No one, indeed, will voluntarily and willingly devote himself to the service of God unless he has previously tasted his paternal love, and been thereby allured to love and reverence Him.

4. But herein appears the shameful ingratitude of men.   Though they have in their own persons a factory where innumerable operations of God are carried on, and a magazine stored with treasures of inestimable value—instead of bursting forth in his praise, as they are bound to do, they, on the contrary, are the more inflated and swelled with pride.   They feel how wonderfully God is working in them, and their own experience tells them of the vast variety of gifts which they owe to his liberality.   Whether they will or not, they cannot but know that these are proofs of his Godhead, and yet they inwardly suppress them.   They have no occasion to go farther than themselves, provided they do not, by appropriating as their own that which has been given them from heaven, put out the light intended to exhibit God clearly to their minds.   At this day, however, the earth sustains on her bosom many monster minds—minds which are not afraid to employ the seed of Deity deposited in human nature as a means of suppressing the name of God.   Can anything be more detestable than this madness in man, who, finding God a hundred times both in his body and his soul, makes his excellence in this respect a pretext for denying that there is a God?   He will not say that chance has made him differ from the brutes that perish; but, substituting nature as the architect of the universe, he suppresses the name of God.   The swift motions of the soul, its noble faculties and rare endowments, bespeak the agency of God in a manner which would make the suppression of it impossible, did not the Epicureans, like so many Cyclops, use it as a vantage-ground, from which to wage more audacious war with God.   Are so many treasures of heavenly wisdom employed in the guidance of such a worm as man, and shall the whole universe be denied the same privilege?   To hold that there are organs in the soul corresponding to each of its faculties, is so far from obscuring the glory of God, that it rather illustrates it.   Let Epicurus tell what concourse of atoms, cooking meat and drink, can form one portion into refuse and another portion into blood, and make all the members separately perform their office as carefully as if they were so many souls acting with common consent in the superintendence of one body.

5. But my business at present is not with that stye : I wish rather to deal with those who, led away by absurd subtleties, are inclined, by giving an indirect turn to the frigid doctrine of Aristotle, to employ it for the purpose both of disproving the immortality of the soul and robbing God of his rights.   Under the pretext that the faculties of the soul are organised, they chain it to the body as if it were incapable of a separate existence, while they endeavour as much as in them lies, by pronouncing eulogiums on nature, to suppress the

name of God. But there is no ground for maintaining that the powers of the soul are confined to the performance of bodily functions. What has the body to do with your measuring the heavens, counting the number of the stars, ascertaining their magnitudes, their relative distances, the rate at which they move, and the orbits which they describe? I deny not that Astronomy has its use; all I mean to show is, that these lofty investigations are not conducted by organised symmetry, but by the faculties of the soul itself apart altogether from the body. The single example I have given will suggest many others to the reader. The swift and versatile movements of the soul in glancing from heaven to earth, connecting the future with the past, retaining the remembrance of former years, nay, forming creations of its own—its skill, moreover, in making astonishing discoveries, and inventing so many wonderful arts, are sure indications of the agency of God in man. What shall we say of its activity when the body is asleep, its many revolving thoughts, its many useful suggestions, its many solid arguments, nay, its presentiment of things yet to come? What shall we say but that man bears about with him a stamp of immortality which can never be effaced? But how is it possible for man to be divine, and yet not acknowledge his Creator? Shall we, by means of a power of judging implanted in our breast, distinguish between justice and injustice, and yet there be no judge in heaven? Shall some remains of intelligence continue with us in sleep, and yet no God keep watch in heaven? Shall we be deemed the inventors of so many arts and useful properties that God may be defrauded of his praise, though experience tells us plainly enough, that whatever we possess is dispensed to us in unequal measures by another hand? The talk of certain persons concerning a secret inspiration quickening the whole world, is not only silly, but altogether profane. Such persons are delighted with the following celebrated passage of Virgil :[1]—

> " Know, first, that heaven, and earth's compacted frame,
> And flowing waters, and the starry flame,
> And both the radiant lights, one common soul
> Inspires and feeds—and animates the whole.
> This active mind, infused through all the space,
> Unites and mingles with the mighty mass :
> Hence, men and beasts the breath of life obtain,
> And birds of air, and monsters of the main.
> Th' ethereal vigour is in all the same,
> And every soul is filled with equal flame."[2]

The meaning of all this is, that the world, which was made to display the glory of God, is its own creator. For the same poet has in another place,[3] adopted a view common to both Greeks and Latins :—

---

[1] Æneid, vi. 724, sq. See Calvin on Acts xvii. 28. Manil. lib. i. Astron.
[2] Dryden's Virgil, Æneid, Book vi. 1. 980–990.
[3] Georgic iv. 220. Plat. in Tim. Arist. lib. i. De Animo. See also Metaph. lib. 1. Merc. Trismegr. in Pimandro.

"Hence to the bee some sages have assigned
  A portion of the God, and heavenly mind;
  For God goes forth, and spreads throughout the whole,
  Heaven, earth, and sea, the universal soul;
  Each, at its birth, from him all beings share,
  Both man and brute, the breath of vital air;
  To him return, and, loosed from earthly chain,
  Fly whence they sprang, and rest in God again
  Spurn at t'.3 grave, and, fearless of decay,
  Dwell in high heaven, and star th' ethereal way."[1]

Here we see how far that jejune speculation, of a universal mind animating and invigorating the world, is fitted to beget and foster piety in our minds. We have a still clearer proof of this in the profane verses which the licentious Lucretius has written as a deduction from the same principle.[2] The plain object is to form an unsubstantial deity, and thereby banish the true God whom we ought to fear and worship. I admit, indeed, that the expression, "Nature is God," may be piously used, if dictated by a pious mind; but as it is inaccurate and harsh (Nature being more properly the order which has been established by God), in matters which are so very important, and in regard to which special reverence is due, it does harm to confound the Deity with the inferior operations of his hands.

6. Let each of us, therefore, in contemplating his own nature, remember that there is one God who governs all natures, and, in governing, wishes us to have respect to himself, to make him the object of our faith, worship, and adoration. Nothing, indeed, can be more preposterous than to enjoy those noble endowments which bespeak the divine presence within us, and to neglect him who, of his own good pleasure, bestows them upon us. In regard to his power, how glorious the manifestations by which he urges us to the contemplation of himself; unless, indeed, we pretend not to know whose energy it is that by a word sustains the boundless fabric of the universe—at one time making heaven reverberate with thunder, sending forth the scorching lightning, and setting the whole atmosphere in a blaze; at another, causing the raging tempests to blow, and forthwith, in one moment, when it so pleases him, making a perfect calm; keeping the sea, which seems constantly threatening the earth with devastation, suspended as it were in air; at one time, lashing it into fury by the impetuosity of the winds; at another, appeasing its rage, and stilling all its waves. Here we might refer to those glowing descriptions of divine power, as illustrated by natural events, which occur throughout Scripture; but more especially in the book of Job and the prophecies of Isaiah. These, however, I purposely omit, because a better opportunity of introducing them will be found when

---

1 Dryden's Virgil, Book iv. l. 252–262.
2 He maintains, in the beginning of the First Book, that nothing is produced of nothing, but that all things are formed out of certain primitive materials. He also perverts the ordinary course of generation into an argument against the existence of God. In the Fifth Book, however, he admits that the world was born and will die.

I come to treat of the Scriptural account of the creation. (*Infra*, chap. xiv. s. 1, 2, 20, *sq.*) I only wish to observe here, that this method of investigating the divine perfections, by tracing the lineaments of his countenance as shadowed forth in the firmament and on the earth, is common both to those within and to those without the pale of the Church. From the power of God we are naturally led to consider his eternity, since that from which all other things derive their origin must necessarily be self-existent and eternal. Moreover, if it be asked what cause induced him to create all things at first, and now inclines him to preserve them, we shall find that there could be no other cause than his own goodness. But if this is the only cause, nothing more should be required to draw forth our love towards him; every creature, as the Psalmist reminds us, participating in his mercy. "His tender mercies are over all his works" (Ps. cxlv. 9).

7. In the second class of God's works, namely, those which are above the ordinary course of nature, the evidence of his perfections are in every respect equally clear. For in conducting the affairs of men, he so arranges the course of his providence, as daily to declare, by the clearest manifestations, that though all are in innumerable ways the partakers of his bounty, the righteous are the special objects of his favour, the wicked and profane the special objects of his severity. It is impossible to doubt his punishment of crimes; while at the same time he, in no unequivocal manner, declares that he is the protector, and even the avenger of innocence, by shedding blessings on the good, helping their necessities, soothing and solacing their griefs, relieving their sufferings, and in all ways providing for their safety. And though he often permits the guilty to exult for a time with impunity, and the innocent to be driven to and fro in adversity, nay, even to be wickedly and iniquitously oppressed, this ought not to produce any uncertainty as to the uniform justice of all his procedure. Nay, an opposite inference should be drawn. When any one crime calls forth visible manifestations of his anger, it must be because he hates all crimes; and, on the other hand, his leaving many crimes unpunished, only proves that there is a judgment in reserve, when the punishment now delayed shall be inflicted. In like manner, how richly does he supply us with the means of contemplating his mercy, when, as frequently happens, he continues to visit miserable sinners with unwearied kindness, until he subdues their depravity, and woos them back with more than a parent's fondness?

8. To this purpose the Psalmist (Ps. cvii.), mentioning how God, in a wondrous manner, often brings sudden and unexpected succour to the miserable when almost on the brink of despair, whether in protecting them when they stray in deserts, and at length leading them back into the right path, or supplying them with food when famishing for want, or delivering them when captive from iron fetters and foul dungeons, or conducting them safe into harbour after shipwreck, or bringing them back from the gates of death by curing

their diseases, or, after burning up the fields with heat and drought, fertilising them with the river of his grace, or exalting the meanest of the people, and casting down the mighty from their lofty seats :— the Psalmist, after bringing forward examples of this description, infers that those things which men call fortuitous events, are so many proofs of divine providence, and more especially of paternal clemency, furnishing ground of joy to the righteous, and at the same time stopping the mouths of the ungodly. But as the greater part of mankind, enslaved by error, walk blindfold in this glorious theatre, he exclaims that it is a rare and singular wisdom to meditate carefully on these works of God, which many, who seem most sharp-sighted in other respects, behold without profit. It is indeed true, that the brightest manifestation of divine glory finds not one genuine spectator among a hundred. Still, neither his power nor his wisdom is shrouded in darkness. His power is strikingly displayed when the rage of the wicked, to all appearance irresistible, is crushed in a single moment; their arrogance subdued, their strongest bulwarks overthrown, their armour dashed to pieces, their strength broken, their schemes defeated without an effort, and audacity which set itself above the heavens is precipitated to the lowest depths of the earth. On the other hand, the poor are raised up out of the dust, and the needy lifted out of the dunghill (Ps. cxiii. 7), the oppressed and afflicted are rescued in extremity, the despairing animated with hope, the unarmed defeat the armed, the few the many, the weak the strong. The excellence of the divine wisdom is manifested in distributing everything in due season, confounding the wisdom of the world, and taking the wise in their own craftiness (1 Cor. iii. 19); in short, conducting all things in perfect accordance with reason.

9. We see there is no need of a long and laborious train of argument in order to obtain proofs which illustrate and assert the Divine Majesty. The few which we have merely touched, show them to be so immediately within our reach in every quarter, that we can trace them with the eye, or point to them with the finger. And here we must observe again (see chap. ii. s. 2), that the knowledge of God which we are invited to cultivate is not that which, resting satisfied with empty speculation, only flutters in the brain, but a knowledge which will prove substantial and fruitful wherever it is duly perceived, and rooted in the heart. The Lord is manifested by his perfections. When we feel their power within us, and are conscious of their benefits, the knowledge must impress us much more vividly than if we merely imagined a God whose presence we never felt. Hence it is obvious that, in seeking God, the most direct path and the fittest method is, not to attempt with presumptuous curiosity to pry into his essence, which is rather to be adored than minutely discussed, but to contemplate him in his works, by which he draws near, becomes familiar, and in a manner communicates himself to us. To this the Apostle referred when he said, that we need not go far in

search of him (Acts xvii. 27), because, by the continual working of his power he dwells in every one of us. Accordingly, David (Psalm cxlv.), after acknowledging that his greatness is unsearchable, proceeds to enumerate his works, declaring that his greatness will thereby be unfolded. It therefore becomes us also diligently to prosecute that investigation of God which so enraptures the soul with admiration as, at the same time, to make an efficacious impression on it. And, as Augustine expresses it (in Psalm cxliv.), since we are unable to comprehend Him, and are, as it were, overpowered by his greatness, our proper course is to contemplate his works, and so refresh ourselves with his goodness.

10. By the knowledge thus acquired, we ought not only to be stimulated to worship God, but also aroused and elevated to the hope of future life. For, observing that the manifestations which the Lord gives both of his mercy and severity are only begun and incomplete, we ought to infer that these are doubtless only a prelude to higher manifestations, of which the full display is reserved for another state. Conversely, when we see the righteous brought into affliction by the ungodly, assailed with injuries, overwhelmed with calumnies, and lacerated by insult and contumely, while, on the contrary, the wicked flourish, prosper, acquire ease and honour, and all these with impunity, we ought forthwith to infer, that there will be a future life in which iniquity shall receive its punishment and righteousness its reward. Moreover, when we observe that the Lord often lays his chastening rod on the righteous, we may the more surely conclude, that far less will the unrighteous ultimately escape the scourges of his anger. There is a well-known passage in Augustine (De Civitat. Dei, lib. i. c. 8), "Were all sin now visited with open punishment, it might be thought that nothing was reserved for the final judgment; and, on the other hand, were no sin now openly punished, it might be supposed there was no divine providence." It must be acknowledged, therefore, that in each of the works of God, and more especially in the whole of them taken together, the divine perfections are delineated as in a picture, and the whole human race thereby invited and allured to acquire the knowledge of God, and, in consequence of this knowledge, true and complete felicity. Moreover, while his perfections are thus most vividly displayed, the only means of ascertaining their practical operation and tendency is to descend into ourselves, and consider how it is that the Lord there manifests his wisdom, power, and energy,—how he there displays his justice, goodness, and mercy. For although David (Psalm xcii. 6) justly complains of the extreme infatuation of the ungodly in not pondering the deep counsels of God, as exhibited in the government of the human race, what he elsewhere says (Psalm xl.) is most true, that the wonders of the divine wisdom in this respect are more in number than the hairs of our head. But I leave this topic at present, as it will be more fully considered afterwards in its own place (Book I. c. 16, sec. 6-9).

11. Bright, however, as is the manifestation which God gives both of himself and his immortal kingdom in the mirror of his works, so great is our stupidity, so dull are we in regard to these bright manifestations, that we derive no benefit from them. For in regard to the fabric and admirable arrangement of the universe, how few of us are there who, in lifting our eyes to the heavens, or looking abroad on the various regions of the earth, ever think of the Creator? Do we not rather overlook Him, and sluggishly content ourselves with a view of his works? And then in regard to supernatural events, though these are occurring every day, how few are there who ascribe them to the ruling providence of God—how many who imagine that they are casual results produced by the blind evolutions of the wheel of chance? Even when, under the guidance and direction of these events, we are in a manner forced to the contemplation of God (a circumstance which all must occasionally experience), and are thus led to form some impressions of Deity, we immediately fly off to carnal dreams and depraved fictions, and so by our vanity corrupt heavenly truth. This far, indeed, we differ from each other, in that every one appropriates to himself some peculiar error; but we are all alike in this, that we substitute monstrous fictions for the one living and true God —a disease not confined to obtuse and vulgar minds, but affecting the noblest, and those who, in other respects, are singularly acute. How lavishly in this respect have the whole body of philosophers betrayed their stupidity and want of sense? To say nothing of the others whose absurdities are of a still grosser description, how completely does Plato, the soberest and most religious of them all, lose himself in his round globe?[1] What must be the case with the rest, when the leaders, who ought to have set them an example, commit such blunders, and labour under such hallucinations? In like manner, while the government of the world places the doctrine of providence beyond dispute, the practical result is the same as if it were believed that all things were carried hither and thither at the caprice of chance; so prone are we to vanity and error. I am still referring to the most distinguished of the philosophers, and not to the common herd, whose madness in profaning the truth of God exceeds all bounds.

12. Hence that immense flood of error with which the whole world is overflowed. Every individual mind being a kind of labyrinth, it is not wonderful, not only that each nation has adopted a variety of fictions, but that almost every man has had his own god. To the darkness of ignorance have been added presumption and wantonness, and hence there is scarcely an individual to be found without some idol or phantom as a substitute for Deity. Like water gushing forth from a large and copious spring, immense crowds of gods have issued from the human mind, every man giving himself full license, and

---

[1] Plato in Timæos. See also Cic. De Nat. Deorum, lib. i ; Plut. De Philos Placitis, lib. i.

devising some peculiar form of divinity, to meet his own views. It
is unnecessary here to attempt a catalogue of the superstitions with
which the world was overspread. The thing were endless; and the
corruptions themselves, though not a word should be said, furnish
abundant evidence of the blindness of the human mind. I say nothing
of the rude and illiterate vulgar; but among the philosophers[1] who
attempted, by reason and learning, to pierce the heavens, what
shameful disagreement! The higher any one was endued with
genius, and the more he was polished by science and art, the more
specious was the colouring which he gave to his opinions. All these,
however, if examined more closely, will be found to be vain show.
The Stoics plumed themselves on their acuteness, when they said[2]
that the various names of God might be extracted from all the parts
of nature, and yet that his unity was not thereby divided: as if we
were not already too prone to vanity, and had no need of being presented with an endless multiplicity of gods, to lead us further and
more grossly into error. The mystic theology of the Egyptians shows
how sedulously they laboured to be thought rational on this subject.[3]
And, perhaps, at the first glance, some show of probability might
deceive the simple and unwary; but never did any mortal devise a
scheme by which religion was not foully corrupted. This endless
variety and confusion emboldened the Epicureans, and other gross
despisers of piety, to cut off all sense of God. For when they saw
that the wisest contradicted each other, they hesitated not to infer
from their dissensions, and from the frivolous and absurd doctrines of
each, that men foolishly, and to no purpose, brought torment upon
themselves by searching for a God, there being none: and they
thought this inference safe, because it was better at once to deny God
altogether than to feign uncertain gods, and thereafter engage in
quarrels without end. They, indeed, argue absurdly, or rather weave
a cloak for their impiety out of human ignorance; though ignorance
surely cannot derogate from the prerogatives of God. But since all
confess that there is no topic on which such difference exists, both
among learned and unlearned, the proper inference is, that the human
mind, which thus errs in inquiring after God, is dull and blind in
heavenly mysteries. Some praise the answer of Simonides, who being
asked by King Hiero what God was, asked a day to consider. When
the king next day repeated the question, he asked two days; and
after repeatedly doubling the number of days, at length replied,
"The longer I consider, the darker the subject appears."[4] He, no
doubt, wisely suspended his opinion, when he did not see clearly:

---

[1] Cicero: Qui deos esse dixerunt tanta sunt in varietate ac dissensione, ut eorum
molestum sit enumerare sententias.—Cicero, De Nat Deorum, lib. i. and ii. Lactant
Inst. Div. lib. i. &c.
[2] Seneca, De Benef., lib. iv. c. 7, et Natural. Quæst, lib. i. in Præf., et lib. ii, c 45.
[3] Plutarch. lib. De Iside et Osiride.
[4] Cicero. De Nat. Deor. lib. i.

still his answer shows, that if men are only naturally taught, instead of having any distinct, solid, or certain knowledge, they fasten only on contradictory principles, and, in consequence, worship an unknown God.

13. Hence we must hold, that whosoever adulterates pure religion (and this must be the case with all who cling to their own views), make a departure from the one God. No doubt, they will allege that they have a different intention; but it is of little consequence what they intend or persuade themselves to believe, since the Holy Spirit pronounces all to be apostates who, in the blindness of their minds, substitute demons in the place of God. For this reason Paul declares that the Ephesians were "without God" (Eph. ii. 12), until they had learned from the gospel what it is to worship the true God. Nor must this be restricted to one people only, since, in another place, he declares in general, that all men "became vain in their imaginations," after the majesty of the Creator was manifested to them in the structure of the world. Accordingly, in order to make way for the only true God, he condemns all the gods celebrated among the Gentiles as lying and false, leaving no Deity anywhere but in Mount Zion, where the special knowledge of God was professed (Hab. ii. 18, 20). Among the Gentiles in the time of Christ, the Samaritans undoubtedly made the nearest approach to true piety; yet we hear from his own mouth that they worshipped they knew not what (John iv. 22); whence it follows that they were deluded by vain errors. In short, though all did not give way to gross vice, or rush headlong into open idolatry, there was no pure and authentic religion founded merely on common belief. A few individuals may not have gone all insane lengths with the vulgar; still Paul's declaration remains true, that the wisdom of God was not apprehended by the princes of this world (1 Cor. ii. 8). But if the most distinguished wandered in darkness, what shall we say of the refuse? No wonder, therefore, that all worship of man's device is repudiated by the Holy Spirit as degenerate. Any opinion which man can form in heavenly mysteries, though it may not beget a long train of errors, is still the parent of error. And though nothing worse should happen, even this is no light sin—to worship an unknown God at random. Of this sin, however, we hear from our Saviour's own mouth (John iv. 22), that all are guilty who have not been taught out of the law who the God is whom they ought to worship. Nay, even Socrates in Xenophon (lib. i. Memorabilia) lauds the response of Apollo enjoining every man to worship the gods according to the rites of his country, and the particular practice of his own city. But what right have mortals thus to decide of their own authority in a matter which is far above the world; or who can so acquiesce in the will of his forefathers, or the decrees of the people, as unhesitatingly to receive a god at their hands? Every one will adhere to his own judgment sooner than submit to the dictation of others. Since, therefore, in regulating the worship of God, the custom of a city, or

the consent of antiquity, is a too feeble and fragile bond of piety:
it remains that God himself must bear witness to himself from
heaven.

14. In vain for us, therefore, does Creation exhibit so many bright
lamps lighted up to show forth the glory of its Author. Though they
beam upon us from every quarter, they are altogether insufficient of
themselves to lead us into the right path. Some sparks, undoubtedly, they do throw out; but these are quenched before they can give
forth a brighter effulgence. Wherefore, the apostle, in the very place
where he says that the worlds are images of invisible things, adds
that it is *by faith* we understand that they were framed by the word
of God (Heb. xi. 3); thereby intimating that the invisible Godhead
is indeed represented by such displays, but that we have no eyes to
perceive it until they are enlightened through faith by internal revelation from God. When Paul says that that which may be known
of God is manifested by the creation of the world, he does not mean
such a manifestation as may be comprehended by the wit of man (Rom.
i. 19); on the contrary, he shows that it has no further effect than to
render us inexcusable (Acts xvii. 27). And though he says, elsewhere, that we have not far to seek for God, inasmuch as he dwells
within us, he shows, in another passage, to what extent this nearness
to God is availing. God, says he, " in times past, suffered all nations
to walk in their own ways. Nevertheless, he left not himself without
witness, in that he did good, and gave us rain from heaven, and fruitful seasons, filling our hearts with food and gladness" (Acts xiv. 16,
17). But though God is not left without a witness, while, with
numberless varied acts of kindness, he woos men to the knowledge of
himself, yet they cease not to follow their own ways, in other words,
deadly errors.

15. But though we are deficient in natural powers which might
enable us to rise to a pure and clear knowledge of God, still, as the
dulness which prevents us is within, there is no room for excuse. We
cannot plead ignorance, without being at the same time convicted by
our own consciences both of sloth and ingratitude. It were, indeed, a
strange defence for man to pretend that he has no ears to hear the
truth, while dumb creatures have voices loud enough to declare it;
to allege that he is unable to see that which creatures without eyes
demonstrate; to excuse himself on the ground of weakness of mind,
while all creatures without reason are able to teach. Wherefore,
when we wander and go astray, we are justly shut out from every
species of excuse, because all things point to the right path. But
while man must bear the guilt of corrupting the seed of divine knowledge so wondrously deposited in his mind, and preventing it from
bearing good and genuine fruit, it is still most true that we are not
sufficiently instructed by that bare and simple, but magnificent testimony which the creatures bear to the glory of their Creator. For no
sooner do we, from a survey of the world, obtain some slight know-

ledge of Deity, than we pass by the true God, and set up in his stead the dream and phantom of our own brain, drawing away the praise of justice, wisdom, and goodness from the fountain-head, and transferring it to some other quarter. Moreover, by the erroneous estimate we form, we either so obscure or pervert his daily works, as at once to rob them of their glory, and the author of them of his just praise.

CHAPTER VI.

THE NEED OF SCRIPTURE, AS A GUIDE AND TEACHER, IN COMING TO GOD AS A CREATOR.

Sections.

1. God gives his elect a better help to the knowledge of himself—viz. the Holy Scriptures. This he did from the very first.
2. First. By oracles and visions, and the ministry of the Patriarchs. Secondly, By the promulgation of the Law, and the preaching of the Prophets. Why the doctrines of religion are committed to writing.
3. This view confirmed, 1. By the depravity of our nature making it necessary in every one who would know God to have recourse to the word; 2. From those passages of the Psalms in which God is introduced as reigning.
4. Another confirmation from certain direct statements in the Psalms. Lastly, From the words of our Saviour.

1. THEREFORE, though the effulgence which is presented to every eye, both in the heavens and on the earth, leaves the ingratitude of man without excuse, since God, in order to bring the whole human race under the same condemnation, holds forth to all, without exception, a mirror of his Deity in his works, another and better help must be given to guide us properly to God as a Creator. Not in vain, therefore, has he added the light of his Word in order that he might make himself known unto salvation, and bestowed the privilege on those whom he was pleased to bring into nearer and more familiar relation to himself. For, seeing how the minds of men were carried to and fro, and found no certain resting-place, he chose the Jews for a peculiar people, and then hedged them in that they might not, like others, go astray. And not in vain does he, by the same means, retain us in his knowledge, since but for this, even those who, in comparison of others, seem to stand strong, would quickly fall away. For as the aged, or those whose sight is defective, when any book, however fair, is set before them, though they perceive that there is something written, are scarcely able to make out two consecutive words, but, when aided by glasses, begin to read distinctly, so Scripture, gathering together the impressions of Deity, which, till then, lay confused in their minds, dissipates the darkness, and shows us the true God clearly. God therefore bestows a gift of singular value, when, for the instruction of the Church, he employs not dumb teachers merely, but opens his own sacred mouth; when he not only proclaims that some God must be worshipped, but at the same time declares that He is the God to whom worship is due; when he not

only teaches his elect to have respect to God, but manifests himself as the God to whom this respect should be paid.

The course which God followed towards his Church from the very first, was to supplement these common proofs by the addition of his Word, as a surer and more direct means of discovering himself. And there can be no doubt that it was by this help, Adam, Noah, Abraham, and the other patriarchs, attained to that familiar knowledge which, in a manner, distinguished them from unbelievers. I am not now speaking of the peculiar doctrines of faith by which they were elevated to the hope of eternal blessedness. It was necessary, in passing from death unto life, that they should know God, not only as a Creator, but as a Redeemer also; and both kinds of knowledge they certainly did obtain from the Word. In point of order, however, the knowledge first given was that which made them acquainted with the God by whom the world was made and is governed. To this first knowledge was afterwards added the more intimate knowledge which alone quickens dead souls, and by which God is known, not only as the Creator of the world, and the sole author and disposer of all events, but also as a Redeemer, in the person of the Mediator. But as the fall and the corruption of nature have not yet been considered, I now postpone the consideration of the remedy (for which, see Book II. c. vi., &c.). Let the reader then remember, that I am not now treating of the covenant by which God adopted the children of Abraham, or of that branch of doctrine by which, as founded in Christ, believers have, properly speaking, been in all ages separated from the profane heathen. I am only showing that it is necessary to apply to Scripture, in order to learn the sure marks which distinguish God, as the Creator of the world, from the whole herd of fictitious gods. We shall afterward, in due course, consider the work of Redemption. In the mean time, though we shall adduce many passages from the New Testament, and some also from the Law and the Prophets, in which express mention is made of Christ, the only object will be to show that God, the Maker of the world, is manifested to us in Scripture, and his true character expounded, so as to save us from wandering up and down, as in a labyrinth, in search of some doubtful deity.

2. Whether God revealed himself to the fathers by oracles and visions,[1] or, by the instrumentality and ministry of men, suggested what they were to hand down to posterity, there cannot be a doubt that the certainty of what he taught them was firmly engraven on their hearts, so that they felt assured and knew that the things which they learnt came forth from God, who invariably accompanied his word with a sure testimony, infinitely superior to mere opinion. At length, in order that, while doctrine was continually enlarged,

[1] The French adds, " C'est à dire, temoignages celestes;"—that is to say, messages from heaven.

its truth might subsist in the world during all ages, it was his pleasure that the same oracles which he had deposited with the fathers should be consigned, as it were, to public records. With this view the law was promulgated, and prophets were afterwards added to be its interpreters. For though the uses of the law were manifold (Book II. c. 7 and 8), and the special office assigned to Moses and all the prophets was to teach the method of reconciliation between God and man (whence Paul calls Christ "the end of the law," Rom. x. 4); still I repeat that, in addition to the proper doctrine of faith and repentance in which Christ is set forth as a Mediator, the Scriptures employ certain marks and tokens to distinguish the only wise and true God, considered as the Creator and Governor of the world, and thereby guard against his being confounded with the herd of false deities. Therefore, while it becomes man seriously to employ his eyes in considering the works of God, since a place has been assigned him in this most glorious theatre that he may be a spectator of them, his special duty is to give ear to the Word, that he may the better profit.[1] Hence it is not strange that those who are born in darkness become more and more hardened in their stupidity; because the vast majority, instead of confining themselves within due bounds by listening with docility to the Word, exult in their own vanity. If true religion is to beam upon us, our principle must be, that it is necessary to begin with heavenly teaching, and that it is impossible for any man to obtain even the minutest portion of right and sound doctrine without being a disciple of Scripture. Hence the first step in true knowledge is taken, when we reverently embrace the testimony which God has been pleased therein to give of himself. For not only does faith, full and perfect faith, but all correct knowledge of God, originate in obedience. And surely in this respect God has with singular Providence provided for mankind in all ages.

3. For if we reflect how prone the human mind is to lapse into forgetfulness of God, how readily inclined to every kind of error, how bent every now and then on devising new and fictitious religions, it will be easy to understand how necessary it was to make such a depository of doctrine as would secure it from either perishing by the neglect, vanishing away amid the errors, or being corrupted by the presumptuous audacity of men. It being thus manifest that God, foreseeing the inefficiency of his image imprinted on the fair form of the universe, has given the assistance of his Word to all whom he has ever been pleased to instruct effectually, we, too, must pursue this straight path, if we aspire in earnest to a genuine contemplation of God;—we must go, I say, to the Word, where the character of God, drawn from his works, is described accurately and to the life;

---

[1] Tertullian, Apologet. adv. Gentes: "Quæ plenius et impressius tam ipsum quam dispositiones ejus et voluntates adiremus, instrumentum adjecit literaturæ," &c.

these works being estimated, not by our depraved judgment, but by the standard of eternal truth. If, as I lately said, we turn aside from it, how great soever the speed with which we move, we shall never reach the goal, because we are off the course. We should consider that the brightness of the Divine countenance, which even an apostle declares to be inaccessible (1 Tim. vi. 16), is a kind of labyrinth,—a labyrinth to us inextricable, if the Word do not serve us as a thread to guide our path; and that it is better to limp in the way, than run with the greatest swiftness out of it. Hence the Psalmist, after repeatedly declaring (Psalm xciii. xcvi. xcvii. xcix. &c.) that superstition should be banished from the world in order that pure religion may flourish, introduces God as *reigning;* meaning by the term, not the power which he possesses and which he exerts in the government of universal nature, but the doctrine by which he maintains his due supremacy: because error never can be eradicated from the heart of man until the true knowledge of God has been implanted in it.

4. Accordingly, the same prophet, after mentioning that the heavens declare the glory of God, that the firmament showeth forth the works of his hands, that the regular succession of day and night proclaim his Majesty, proceeds to make mention of the Word:—"The law of the Lord," says he, "is perfect, converting the soul; the testimony of the Lord is sure, making wise the simple. The statutes of the Lord are right, rejoicing the heart; the commandment of the Lord is pure, enlightening the eyes" (Psalm xix. 1—9). For though the law has other uses besides (as to which, see Book II. c. 7, sec. 6, 10, 12), the general meaning is, that it is the proper school for training the children of God; the invitation given to all nations, to behold him in the heavens and earth, proving of no avail. The same view is taken in the xxix. Psalm, where the Psalmist, after discoursing on the dreadful voice of God, which, in thunder, wind, rain, whirlwind, and tempest, shakes the earth, makes the mountains tremble, and breaks the cedars, concludes by saying, "that in his temple doth every one speak of his glory," unbelievers being deaf to all God's words when they echo in the air. In like manner another Psalm, after describing the raging billows of the sea, thus concludes, "Thy testimonies are very sure; holiness becometh thine house for ever" (Psalm xciii. 5). To the same effect are the words of our Saviour to the Samaritan woman, when he told her that her nation and all other nations worshipped they knew not what; and that the Jews alone gave worship to the true God (John iv. 22). Since the human mind, through its weakness, was altogether unable to come to God if not aided and upheld by his sacred word, it necessarily followed that all mankind, the Jews excepted, inasmuch as they sought God without the Word, were labouring under vanity and error.

CHAPTER VII.

THE TESTIMONY OF THE SPIRIT NECESSARY TO GIVE FULL AUTHOR-
ITY TO SCRIPTURE.   THE IMPIETY OF PRETENDING THAT THE
CREDIBILITY OF SCRIPTURE DEPENDS ON THE JUDGMENT
OF THE CHURCH.

Sections.

1. The authority of Scripture derived not from men, but from the Spirit of God.   Objection, That Scripture depends on the decision of the Church.   Refutation, I.
The truth of God would thus be subjected to the will of man.   II. It is insulting
to the Holy Spirit.   III. It establishes a tyranny in the Church.   IV. It forms a
mass of errors.   V. It subverts conscience.   VI. It exposes our faith to the scoffs
of the profane.

2. Another reply to the objection drawn from the words of the Apostle Paul.   Solution
of the difficulties started by opponents.   A second objection refuted.

3 A third objection founded on a sentiment of Augustine considered.

4. Conclusion, That the authority of Scripture is founded on its being spoken by God.
This confirmed by the conscience of the godly, and the consent of all men of the
least candour.   A fourth objection common in the mouths of the profane.   Refu
tation.

5. Last and necessary conclusion, That the authority of Scripture is sealed on the
hearts of believers by the testimony of the Holy Spirit.   The certainty of this testimony.   Confirmation of it from a passage of Isaiah, and the experience of believers.
Also, from another passage of Isaiah.

1. BEFORE proceeding farther, it seems proper to make some observations on the authority of Scripture, in order that our minds may
not only be prepared to receive it with reference, but be divested of
all doubt.

When that which professes to be the Word of God is acknowledged
to be so, no person, unless devoid of common sense and the feelings
of a man, will have the desperate hardihood to refuse credit to the
speaker.   But since no daily responses are given from heaven, and
the Scriptures are the only records in which God has been pleased to
consign his truth to perpetual remembrance, the full authority which
they ought to possess with the faithful is not recognised, unless they
are believed to have come from heaven, as directly as if God had
been heard giving utterance to them.   This subject well deserves to
be treated more at large, and pondered more accurately.   But my
readers will pardon me for having more regard to what my plan
admits than to what the extent of this topic requires.

A most pernicious error has very generally prevailed—viz. that
Scripture is of importance only in so far as conceded to it by the suffrage of the Church ; as if the eternal and inviolable truth of God
could depend on the will of men.   With great insult to the Holy

Spirit, it is asked, Who can assure us that the Scriptures proceeded from God; who guarantee that they have come down safe and unimpaired to our times; who persuade us that *this* book is to be received with reverence, and *that one* expunged from the list, did not the Church regulate all these things with certainty? On the determination of the Church, therefore, it is said, depend both the reverence which is due to Scripture and the books which are to be admitted into the canon. Thus profane men, seeking, under the pretext of the Church, to introduce unbridled tyranny, care not in what absurdities they entangle themselves and others, provided they extort from the simple this one acknowledgment—viz. that there is nothing which the Church cannot do. But what is to become of miserable consciences in quest of some solid assurance of eternal life, if all the promises with regard to it have no better support than man's judgment? On being told so, will they cease to doubt and tremble? On the other hand, to what jeers of the wicked is our faith subjected—into how great suspicion is it brought with all, if believed to have only a precarious authority lent to it by the good-will of men?

2. These ravings are admirably refuted by a single expression of an apostle. Paul testifies that the Church is "built on the foundation of the apostles and prophets" (Eph. ii. 20). If the doctrine of the apostles and prophets is the foundation of the Church, the former must have had its certainty before the latter began to exist. Nor is there any room for the cavil, that though the Church derives her first beginning from thence, it still remains doubtful what writings are to be attributed to the apostles and prophets, until her judgment is interposed. For if the Christian Church was founded at first on the writings of the prophets, and the preaching of the apostles, that doctrine, wheresoever it may be found, was certainly ascertained and sanctioned antecedently to the Church, since, but for this, the Church herself never could have existed.[1] Nothing, therefore, can be more absurd than the fiction, that the power of judging Scripture is in the Church, and that on her nod its certainty depends. When the Church receives it, and gives it the stamp of her authority, she does not make that authentic which was otherwise doubtful or controverted, but, acknowledging it as the truth of God, she, as in duty bound, shows her reverence by an unhesitating assent. As to the question, How shall we be persuaded that it came from God without recurring to a decree of the Church? it is just the same as if it were asked, How shall we learn to distinguish light from darkness, white from black, sweet from bitter? Scripture bears upon the face of it as clear evidence of its truth, as white and black do of their colour, sweet and bitter of their taste.

3. I am aware it is usual to quote a sentence of Augustine, in which

---

[1] The French adds, "Comme le fondement va deuant l'edifice;"—as the foundation goes before the house.

he says that he would not believe the gospel, were he not moved by the authority of the Church (Aug. Cont. Epist. Fundament. c. v.). But it is easy to discover from the context, how inaccurate and unfair it is to give it such a meaning. He was reasoning against the Manichees, who insisted on being implicitly believed, alleging that they had the truth, though they did not show they had. But as they pretended to appeal to the gospel in support of Manes, he asks what they would do if they fell in with a man who did not even believe the gospel—what kind of argument they would use to bring him over to their opinion. He afterwards adds, " But I would not believe the gospel," &c. ; meaning, that were he a stranger to the faith, the only thing which could induce him to embrace the gospel would be the authority of the Church. And is it anything wonderful, that one who does not know Christ should pay respect to men ?

Augustine, therefore, does not here say that the faith of the godly is founded on the authority of the Church ; nor does he mean that the certainty of the gospel depends upon it ; he merely says that unbelievers would have no certainty of the gospel, so as thereby to win Christ, were they not influenced by the consent of the Church. And he clearly shows this to be his meaning, by thus expressing himself a little before : " When I have praised my own creed, and ridiculed yours, who do you suppose is to judge between us ; or what more is to be done than to quit those who, inviting us to certainty, afterwards command us to believe uncertainty, and follow those who invite us, in the first instance, to believe what we are not yet able to comprehend, that waxing stronger through faith itself, we may become able to understand what we believe—no longer men, but God himself internally strengthening and illuminating our minds ?" These unquestionably are the words of Augustine (August. Cont. Epist. Fundament. cap. iv.) ; and the obvious inference from them is, that this holy man had no intention to suspend our faith in Scripture on the nod or decision of the Church,[1] but only to intimate (what we too admit to be true) that those who are not yet enlightened by the Spirit of God, become teachable by reverence for the Church, and thus submit to learn the faith of Christ from the gospel. In this way, though the authority of the Church leads us on, and prepares us to believe in the gospel, it is plain that Augustine would have the certainty of the godly to rest on a very different foundation.[2]

At the same time, I deny not that he often presses the Manichees with the consent of the whole Church, while arguing in support of

---

[1] The French adds, " La destournant du seul fondement qu'elle a en l'Escriture ;"— diverting it from the only foundation which it has in Scripture.

[2] Augustin. De Ordine, lib. ii. c. 9. " Ad discendum dupliciter movemur, auctoritate atque ratione : tempore auctoritas, re autem ratio prior est," &c. " Itaque quamquam bonorum auctoritas imperitæ multitudini videatur esse salubrior, ratio vero aptior eruditis : tamen quia nullus hominum nisi ex imperito peritus fit, &c., evenit ut omnibus bona, magna, occulta discere cupientibus, non aperiat nisi auctoritas januam," &c. He has many other excellent things to the same effect.

the Scriptures, which they rejected. Hence he upbraids Faustus (Lib. xxxii.) for not submitting to evangelical truth—truth so well founded, so firmly established, so gloriously renowned, and handed down by sure succession from the days of the apostles. But he nowhere insinuates that the authority which we give to the Scriptures depends on the definitions or devices of men. He only brings forward the universal judgment of the Church, as a point most pertinent to the cause, and one, moreover, in which he had the advantage of his opponents. Any one who desires to see this more fully proved may read his short treatise, *De Utilitate Credendi* (The Advantages of Believing), where it will be found that the only facility of believing which he recommends is that which affords an introduction, and forms a fit commencement to inquiry; while he declares that we ought not to be satisfied with opinion, but to strive after substantial truth.

4. It is necessary to attend to what I lately said, that our faith in doctrine is not established until we have a perfect conviction that God is its author. Hence, the highest proof of Scripture is uniformly taken from the character of him whose word it is. The prophets and apostles boast not their own acuteness, or any qualities which win credit to speakers, nor do they dwell on reasons; but they appeal to the sacred name of God, in order that the whole world may be compelled to submission. The next thing to be considered is, how it appears not probable merely, but certain, that the name of God is neither rashly nor cunningly pretended. If, then, we would consult most effectually for our consciences, and save them from being driven about in a whirl of uncertainty, from wavering, and even stumbling at the smallest obstacle, our conviction of the truth of Scripture must be derived from a higher source than human conjectures, judgments, or reasons; namely, the secret testimony of the Spirit. It is true, indeed, that if we choose to proceed in the way of argument, it is easy to establish, by evidence of various kinds, that if there is a God in heaven, the Law, the Prophecies, and the Gospel, proceeded from him. Nay, although learned men, and men of the greatest talent, should take the opposite side, summoning and ostentatiously displaying all the powers of their genius in the discussion; if they are not possessed of shameless effrontery, they will be compelled to confess that the Scripture exhibits clear evidence of its being spoken by God, and, consequently, of its containing his heavenly doctrine. We shall see a little farther on, that the volume of sacred Scripture very far surpasses all other writings. Nay, if we look at it with clear eyes and unbiassed judgment, it will forthwith present itself with a divine majesty which will subdue our presumptuous opposition, and force us to do it homage.

Still, however, it is preposterous to attempt, by discussion, to rear up a full faith in Scripture. True, were I called to contend with the craftiest despisers of God, I trust, though I am not possessed of the highest ability or eloquence, I should not find it difficult to stop their obstreperous mouths; I could, without much ado, put down the boastings which they mutter in corners, were anything to be gained by refuting their cavils. But although we may maintain the sacred Word of God against gainsayers, it does not follow that we shall forthwith implant the certainty which faith requires in their hearts. Profane men think that religion rests only on opinion, and, therefore, that they may not believe foolishly, or on slight grounds desire and insist to have it proved by reason that Moses and the prophets were divinely inspired. But I answer, that the testimony of the Spirit is superior to reason. For as God alone can properly bear witness to his own words, so these words will not obtain full credit in the hearts of men, until they are sealed by the inward testimony of the Spirit. The same Spirit, therefore, who spoke by the mouth of the prophets, must penetrate our hearts, in order to convince us that they faithfully delivered the message with which they were divinely intrusted. This connection is most aptly expressed by Isaiah in these words, "My Spirit that is upon thee, and my words which I have put in thy mouth, shall not depart out of thy mouth, nor out of the mouth of thy seed, nor out of the mouth of thy seed's seed, saith the Lord, from henceforth and for ever" (Isa. lix. 21). Some worthy persons feel disconcerted, because, while the wicked murmur with impunity at the word of God, they have not a clear proof at hand to silence them, forgetting that the Spirit is called an earnest and seal to confirm the faith of the godly, for this very reason, that, until he enlightens their minds, they are tossed to and fro in a sea of doubts.

5. Let it therefore be held as fixed, that those who are inwardly taught by the Holy Spirit acquiesce implicitly in Scripture; that Scripture, carrying its own evidence along with it, deigns not to submit to proofs and arguments, but owes the full conviction with which we ought to receive it to the testimony of the Spirit.[1] Enlightened by him, we no longer believe, either on our own judgment or that of others, that the Scriptures are from God; but, in a way superior to human judgment, feel perfectly assured—as much so as if we beheld the divine image visibly impressed on it—that it came to us, by the instrumentality of men, from the very mouth of God. We ask not for proofs or probabilities on which to rest our judgment, but we subject our intellect and judgment to it as too transcendent for us to estimate. This, however, we do, not in the manner in which some are wont to fasten on an unknown object, which, as soon as known, displeases, but because we have a thorough conviction that, in holding it, we hold unassailable truth; not like miserable men, whose minds are enslaved by superstition, but because we feel a divine

---

1 The French adds, " Car jaçoit qu'en sa propre majesté elle ait assez de quoy estre reuerée, neantmoins elle commence lors à nous vrayement toucher, quand elle est scellée en nos cœurs par le Sainct Esprit."—For though in its own majesty it has enough to command reverence, nevertheless, it then begins truly to touch us when it is sealed in our hearts by the Holy Spirit.

energy living and breathing in it—an energy by which we are drawn and animated to obey it, willingly indeed, and knowingly, but more vividly and effectually than could be done by human will or knowledge.   Hence, God most justly exclaims by the mouth of Isaiah, "Ye are my witnesses, saith the Lord, and my servant whom I have chosen, that ye may know and believe me, and understand that I am he" (Isa. xliii. 10).

Such, then, is a conviction which asks not for reasons; such, a knowledge which accords with the highest reason, namely, knowledge in which the mind rests more firmly and securely than in any reasons; such, in fine, the conviction which revelation from heaven alone can produce.   I say nothing more than every believer experiences in himself, though my words fall far short of the reality.   I do not dwell on this subject at present, because we will return to it again: only let us now understand that the only true faith is that which the Spirit of God seals on our hearts.   Nay, the modest and teachable reader will find a sufficient reason in the promise contained in Isaiah, that all the children of the renovated Church "shall be taught of the Lord" (Isaiah liv. 13).   This singular privilege God bestows on his elect only, whom he separates from the rest of mankind.   For what is the beginning of true doctrine but prompt alacrity to hear the word of God?   And God, by the mouth of Moses, thus demands to be heard: "It is not in heaven, that thou shouldst say, Who shall go up for us to heaven, and bring it unto us, that we may hear and do it?   But the word is very nigh unto thee, in thy mouth and in thy heart" (Deut. xxx. 12, 14).   God having been pleased to reserve the treasure of intelligence for his children, no wonder that so much ignorance and stupidity is seen in the generality of mankind.   In the *generality*, I include even those specially chosen, until they are ingrafted into the body of the Church.   Isaiah, moreover, while reminding us that the prophetical doctrine would prove incredible not only to strangers, but also to the Jews, who were desirous to be thought of the household of God, subjoins the reason, when he asks, "To whom hath the arm of the Lord been revealed?" (Isaiah liii. 1.)   If at any time, then, we are troubled at the small number of those who believe, let us, on the other hand, call to mind, that none comprehend the mysteries of God save those to whom it is given.

CHAPTER VIII.

THE CREDIBILITY OF SCRIPTURE SUFFICIENTLY PROVED, IN SO FAR AS NATURAL REASON ADMITS.

This chapter consists of four parts. The first contains certain general proofs which may be easily gathered out of the writings both of the Old and New Testament—viz. the arrangement of the sacred volume, its dignity, truth, simplicity, efficacy, and majesty, sec. 1, 2. The second part contains special proofs taken from the Old Testament—viz the antiquity of the books of Moses, their authority, his miracles and prophecies, sec. 3–7; also, the predictions of the other prophets and their wondrous harmony, sec. 8. There is subjoined a refutation of two objections to the books of Moses and the Prophets, sec. 9, 10. The third part exhibits proof gathered out of the New Testament, *e.g.*, the harmony of the Evangelists in their account of heavenly mysteries, the majesty of the writings of John, Peter, and Paul, the remarkable calling of the Apostles and conversion of Paul, sec. 11. The last part exhibits the proofs drawn from ecclesiastical history, the perpetual consent of the Church in receiving and preserving divine truth, the invincible force of the truth in defending itself, the agreement of the godly (though otherwise differing so much from one another), the pious profession of the same doctrine by many illustrious men ; in fine, the more than human constancy of the martyrs, sec. 12, 13. This is followed by a conclusion of the particular topic discussed.

Sections.

1. Secondary helps to establish the credibility of Scripture. I. The arrangement of the sacred volume. II. Its dignity. III. Its truth. IV. Its simplicity. V. Its efficacy.
2. The majesty conspicuous in the writings of the Prophets.
3. Special proofs from the Old Testament. I. The antiquity of the Books of Moses.
4. This antiquity contrasted with the dreams of the Egyptians. II. The majesty of the Books of Moses.
5. The miracles and prophecies of Moses. A profane objection refuted
6. Another profane objection refuted.
7. The prophecies of Moses as to the sceptre not departing from Judah, and the calling of the Gentiles.
8. The predictions of other prophets. The destruction of Jerusalem ; and the return from the Babylonish captivity. Harmony of the Prophets. The celebrated prophecy of Daniel.
9. Objection against Moses and the Prophets. Answer to it.
10. Another objection and answer. Of the wondrous Providence of God in the preservation of the sacred books. The Greek Translation. The carefulness of the Jews.
11. Special proofs from the New Testament. I. The harmony of the Evangelists, and the sublime simplicity of their writings. II. The majesty of John, Paul, and Peter. III. The calling of the Apostles. IV. The conversion of Paul.
12 Proofs from Church history. I. Perpetual consent of the Church in receiving and preserving the truth. II. The invincible power of the truth itself. III. Agreement among the godly, notwithstanding of their many differences in other respects.
13. The constancy of the martyrs. Conclusion. Proofs of this description only of use after the certainty of Scripture has been established in the heart by the Holy Spirit.

1. In vain were the authority of Scripture fortified by argument, or supported by the consent of the Church, or confirmed by any other

helps, if unaccompanied by an assurance higher and stronger than human judgment can give. Till this better foundation has been laid, the authority of Scripture remains in suspense. On the other hand, when recognising its exemption from the common rule, we receive it reverently, and according to its dignity, those proofs which were not so strong as to produce and rivet a full conviction in our minds, become most appropriate helps. For it is wonderful how much we are confirmed in our belief, when we more attentively consider how admirably the system of divine wisdom contained in it is arranged—how perfectly free the doctrine is from everything that savours of earth—how beautifully it harmonises in all its parts—and how rich it is in all the other qualities which give an air of majesty to composition. Our hearts are still more firmly assured when we reflect that our admiration is excited more by the dignity of the matter than by the graces of style. For it was not without an admirable arrangement of Providence, that the sublime mysteries of the kingdom of heaven have for the greater part been delivered with a contemptible meanness of words. Had they been adorned with a more splendid eloquence, the wicked might have cavilled, and alleged that this constituted all their force. But now, when an unpolished simplicity, almost bordering on rudeness, makes a deeper impression than the loftiest flights of oratory, what does it indicate if not that the Holy Scriptures are too mighty in the power of truth to need the rhetorician's art ?

Hence there was good ground for the Apostle's declaration, that the faith of the Corinthians was founded not on " the wisdom of men," but on " the power of God" (1 Cor. ii. 5),—his speech and preaching among them having been, " not with enticing words of man's wisdom, but in demonstration of the Spirit and of power" (1 Cor. ii. 5). For the truth is vindicated in opposition to every doubt, when, unsupported by foreign aid, it has its sole sufficiency in itself. How peculiarly this property belongs to Scripture appears from this, that no human writings, however skilfully composed, are at all capable of affecting us in a similar way. Read Demosthenes or Cicero, read Plato, Aristotle, or any other of that class : you will, I admit, feel wonderfully allured, pleased, moved, enchanted ; but turn from them to the reading of the sacred volume, and whether you will or not, it will so affect you, so pierce your heart, so work its way into your very marrow, that, in comparison of the impression so produced, that of orators and philosophers will almost disappear ; making it manifest that in the sacred volume there is a truth divine, a something which makes it immeasurably superior to all the gifts and graces attainable by man.

2. I confess, however, that in elegance and beauty, nay, splendour, the style of some of the prophets is not surpassed by the eloquence of heathen writers. By examples of this description, the Holy Spirit was pleased to show that it was not from want of eloquence he in

other instances used a rude and homely style.   But whether you read
David, Isaiah, and others of the same class, whose discourse flows
sweet and pleasant; or Amos the herdsman, Jeremiah and Zechariah,
whose rougher idiom savours of rusticity; that majesty of the Spirit to
which I adverted appears conspicuous in all.   I am not unaware, that
as Satan often apes God, that he may by a fallacious resemblance the
better insinuate himself into the minds of the simple, so he craftily
disseminated the impious errors with which he deceived miserable
men in an uncouth and semi-barbarous style, and frequently employed obsolete forms of expression in order to cloak his impostures.
None possessed of any moderate share of sense need be told how vain
and vile such affectation is.   But in regard to the Holy Scriptures,
however petulant men may attempt to carp at them, they are replete
with sentiments which it is clear that man never could have conceived.   Let each of the prophets be examined, and not one will be
found who does not rise far higher than human reach.   Those who
feel their works insipid must be absolutely devoid of taste.

3. As this subject has been treated at large by others, it will be
sufficient here merely to touch on its leading points.   In addition to
the qualities already mentioned, great weight is due to the antiquity
of Scripture (Euseb. Prepar. Evang. lib. ii. c. i.).   Whatever fables
Greek writers may retail concerning the Egyptian Theology, no
monument of any religion exists which is not long posterior to the
age of Moses.   But Moses does not introduce a new Deity.   He only
sets forth that doctrine concerning the eternal God which the Israelites had received by tradition from their fathers, by whom it had
been transmitted, as it were, from hand to hand, during a long series
of ages.   For what else does he do than lead them back to the covenant which had been made with Abraham?   Had he referred to matters of which they had never heard, he never could have succeeded;
but their deliverance from the bondage in which they were held must
have been a fact of familiar and universal notoriety, the very mention
of which must have immediately aroused the attention of all.   It is,
moreover, probable, that they were intimately acquainted with the
whole period of four hundred years.   Now, if Moses (who is so much
earlier than all other writers) traces the tradition of his doctrine
from so remote a period, it is obvious how far the Holy Scriptures
must, in point of antiquity, surpass all other writings.

4. Some perhaps may choose to credit the Egyptians in carrying
back their antiquity to a period of six thousand years before the
world was created.   But their garrulity, which even some profane
authors have held up to derision, it cannot be necessary for me to refute.   Josephus, however, in his work against Appion, produces important passages from very ancient writers, implying that the doctrine
delivered in the law was celebrated among all nations from the
remotest ages, though it was neither read nor accurately known.
And then, in order that the malignant might have no ground for

suspicion, and the ungodly no handle for cavil, God has provided, in the most effectual manner, against both dangers. When Moses relates the words which Jacob, under Divine inspiration, uttered concerning his posterity almost three hundred years before, how does he ennoble his own tribe? He stigmatises it with eternal infamy in the person of Levi. "Simeon and Levi," says he, "are brethren; instruments of cruelty are in their habitations. O my soul, come not thou into their secret; unto their assembly mine honour be not thou united" (Gen. xlix. 5, 6). This stigma he certainly might have passed in silence, not only that he might spare his own ancestor, but also save both himself and his whole family from a portion of the disgrace. How can any suspicion attach to him, who, by voluntarily proclaiming that the first founder of his family was declared detestable by a Divine oracle, neither consults for his own private interest, nor declines to incur obloquy among his tribe, who must have been offended by his statement of the fact? Again, when he relates the wicked murmuring of his brother Aaron, and his sister Miriam (Numb. xii. 1), shall we say that he spoke his own natural feelings, or that he obeyed the command of the Holy Spirit? Moreover, when invested with supreme authority, why does he not bestow the office of High Priest on his sons, instead of consigning them to the lowest place? I only touch on a few points out of many; but the Law itself contains throughout numerous proofs, which fully vindicate the credibility of Moses, and place it beyond dispute, that he was in truth a messenger sent forth from God.

5. The many striking miracles which Moses relates are so many sanctions of the law delivered, and the doctrine propounded, by him.[1] His being carried up into the mount in a cloud; his remaining there forty days separated from human society; his countenance glistening during the promulgation of the law, as with meridian effulgence; the lightnings which flashed on every side; the voices and thunderings which echoed in the air; the clang of the trumpet blown by no human mouth; his entrance into the tabernacle, while a cloud hid him from the view of the people; the miraculous vindication of his authority, by the fearful destruction of Korah, Dathan, and Abiram, and all their impious faction; the stream instantly gushing forth from the rock when struck with his rod; the manna which rained from heaven at his prayer;—did not God by all these proclaim aloud that he was an undoubted prophet? If any one object that I am taking debatable points for granted, the cavil is easily answered, Moses published all these things in the assembly of the people. How, then, could he possibly impose on the very eyewitnesses of what was done? Is it conceivable that he would have come forward, and, while accusing the people of unbelief, obstinacy, ingratitude, and other crimes, have boasted that his doctrine had been confirmed in their own presence by miracles which they never saw?

1 Exod. xxiv. 18; xxxiv. 29; xix. 16; xl. 34. Numb. xvi. 24; xx. 10; xi. 9.

6. For it is also worthy of remark, that the miracles which he relates are combined with disagreeable circumstances, which must have provoked opposition from the whole body of the people, if there had been the smallest ground for it. Hence it is obvious that they were induced to assent, merely because they had been previously convinced by their own experience. But because the fact was too clear to leave it free for heathen writers to deny that Moses did perform miracles, the father of lies suggested a calumny, and ascribed them to magic (Exod. ix. 11). But with what probability is a charge of magic brought against him, who held it in such abhorrence, that he ordered every one who should consult soothsayers and magicians to be stoned? (Lev. xxx. 6.) Assuredly, no impostor deals in tricks, without studying to raise his reputation by amazing the common people. But what does Moses do? By crying out, that he and Aaron his brother are nothing (Exod. xvi. 7), that they merely execute what God has commanded, he clears himself from every approach to suspicion. Again, if the facts are considered in themselves, what kind of incantation could cause manna to rain from heaven every day, and in sufficient quantity to maintain a people, while any one, who gathered more than the appointed measure, saw his incredulity divinely punished by its turning to worms? To this we may add, that God then suffered his servant to be subjected to so many serious trials, that the ungodly cannot now gain anything by their clamour. When (as often happened) the people proudly and petulantly rose up against him, when individuals conspired, and attempted to overthrow him, how could any impostures have enabled him to elude their rage? The event plainly shows that by these means his doctrine was attested to all succeeding ages.

7. Moreover, it is impossible to deny that he was guided by a prophetic spirit in assigning the first place to the tribe of Judah in the person of Jacob, especially if we take into view the fact itself, as explained by the event. Suppose that Moses was the inventor of the prophecy, still, after he committed it to writing, four hundred years pass away, during which no mention is made of a sceptre in the tribe of Judah. After Saul is anointed, the kingly office seems fixed in the tribe of Benjamin (1 Sam. xi. 15; xvi. 13). When David is anointed by Samuel, what apparent ground is there for the transference? Who could have looked for a king out of the plebeian family of a herdsman? And out of seven brothers, who could have thought that the honour was destined for the youngest? And then by what means did he afterwards come within reach of the throne? Who dare say that his anointing was regulated by human art, or skill, or prudence, and was not rather the fulfilment of a divine prophecy? In like manner, do not the predictions, though obscure, of the admission of the Gentiles into the divine covenant, seeing they were not fulfilled till almost two thousand years after, make it palpable that Moses spoke under divine inspiration? I omit other predictions which so

plainly betoken divine revelation, that all men of sound mind must see they were spoken by God.   In short, his Song itself (Deut. xxxii.) is a bright mirror in which God is manifestly seen.

8. In the case of the other prophets the evidence is even clearer. I will only select a few examples, for it were too tedious to enumerate the whole.   Isaiah, in his own day, when the kingdom of Judah was at peace, and had even some ground to confide in the protection of the Chaldeans, spoke of the destruction of the city and the captivity of the people (Isaiah xlv. 1).   Supposing it not to be sufficient evidence of divine inspiration to foretell, many years before, events which, at the time, seemed fabulous, but which ultimately turned out to be true, whence shall it be said that the prophecies which he uttered concerning their return proceeded, if it was not from God ?   He names Cyrus, by whom the Chaldeans were to be subdued and the people restored to freedom.   After the prophet thus spoke, more than a hundred years elapsed before Cyrus was born, that being nearly the period which elapsed between the death of the one and the birth of the other.   It was impossible at that time to guess that some Cyrus would arise to make war on the Babylonians, and after subduing their powerful monarchy, put an end to the captivity of the children of Israel.   Does not this simple, unadorned narrative plainly demonstrate that what Isaiah spoke was not the conjecture of man, but the undoubted oracle of God?   Again, when Jeremiah, a considerable time before the people were led away, assigned seventy years as the period of captivity, and fixed their liberation and return, must not his tongue have been guided by the Spirit of God ?   What effrontery were it to deny that, by these evidences, the authority of the prophets is established, the very thing being fulfilled to which they appeal in support of their credibility !   " Behold, the former things are come to pass, and new things do I declare ; before they spring forth I tell you of them" (Isaiah xlii. 9).   I say nothing of the agreement between Jeremiah and Ezekiel, who, living so far apart, and yet prophesying at the same time, harmonise as completely in all they say as if they had mutually dictated the words to one another.   What shall I say of Daniel ?   Did not he deliver prophecies embracing a future period of almost six hundred years, as if he had been writing of past events generally known ?   (Dan. ix. &c.)   If the pious will duly meditate on these things, they will be sufficiently instructed to silence the cavils of the ungodly.   The demonstration is too clear to be gainsayed.

9. I am aware of what is muttered in corners by certain miscreants, when they would display their acuteness in assailing divine truth.   They ask, how do we know that Moses and the prophets wrote the books which now bear their names ?   Nay, they even dare to question whether there ever was a Moses.   Were any one to question whether there ever was a Plato, or an Aristotle, or a Cicero, would not the rod or the whip be deemed the fit chastisement of such

folly? The law of Moses has been wonderfully preserved, more by divine providence than by human care; and though, owing to the negligence of the priests, it lay for a short time buried,—from the time when it was found by good King Josiah (2 Kings xxii. 8; 2 Chron. xxxiv. 15),—it has continued in the hands of men, and been transmitted in unbroken succession from generation to generation. Nor, indeed, when Josiah brought it forth, was it as a book unknown or new, but one which had always been matter of notoriety, and was then in full remembrance. The original writing had been deposited in the temple, and a copy taken from it had been deposited in the royal archives (Deut. xvii. 18, 19); the only thing which had occurred was, that the priests had ceased to publish the law itself in due form, and the people also had neglected the wonted reading of it. I may add, that scarcely an age passed during which its authority was not confirmed and renewed. Were the books of Moses unknown to those who had the Psalms of David in their hands? To sum up the whole in one word, it is certain beyond dispute, that these writings passed down, if I may so express it, from hand to hand, being transmitted in an unbroken series from the fathers, who either with their own ears heard them spoken, or learned them from those who had, while the remembrance of them was fresh.

10. An objection taken from the history of the Maccabees (1 Maccab. i. 57, 58) to impugn the credibility of Scripture, is, on the contrary, fitted the best possible to confirm it. First, however, let us clear away the gloss which is put upon it: having done so, we shall turn the engine which they erect against us upon themselves. As Antiochus ordered all the books of Scripture to be burnt, it is asked, where did the copies we now have come from? I, in my turn, ask, In what workshop could they have been so quickly fabricated? It is certain that they were in existence the moment the persecution ceased, and that they were acknowledged without dispute by all the pious who had been educated in their doctrine, and were familiarly acquainted with them. Nay, while all the wicked so wantonly insulted the Jews as if they had leagued together for the purpose, not one ever dared to charge them with having introduced spurious books. Whatever, in their opinion, the Jewish religion might be, they acknowledged that Moses was the founder of it. What, then, do those babblers, but betray their snarling petulance in falsely alleging the spuriousness of books whose sacred antiquity is proved by the consent of all history? But not to spend labour in vain in refuting these vile calumnies, let us rather attend to the care which the Lord took to preserve his Word, when against all hope he rescued it from the truculence of a most cruel tyrant as from the midst of the flames— inspiring pious priests and others with such constancy that they hesitated not, though it should have been purchased at the expense of their lives, to transmit this treasure to posterity, and defeating the keenest search of prefects and their satellites.

Who does not recognise it as a signal and miraculous work of God, that those sacred monuments which the ungodly persuaded themselves had utterly perished, immediately returned to resume their former rights, and, indeed, in greater honour? For the Greek translation appeared to disseminate them over the whole world. Nor does it seem so wonderful that God rescued the tables of his covenant from the sanguinary edicts of Antiochus, as that they remained safe and entire amid the manifold disasters by which the Jewish nation was occasionally crushed, devastated, and almost exterminated. The Hebrew language was in no estimation, and almost unknown; and assuredly, had not God provided for religion, it must have utterly perished. For it is obvious from the prophetical writings of that age, how much the Jews, after their return from the captivity, had lost the genuine use of their native tongue. It is of importance to attend to this, because the comparison more clearly establishes the antiquity of the Law and the Prophets. And whom did God employ to preserve the doctrine of salvation contained in the Law and the Prophets, that Christ might manifest it in its own time? The Jews, the bitterest enemies of Christ; and hence Augustine justly calls them the librarians of the Christian Church, because they supplied us with books of which they themselves had not the use.

11. When we proceed to the New Testament, how solid are the pillars by which its truth is supported! Three evangelists give a narrative in a mean and humble style. The proud often eye this simplicity with disdain, because they attend not to the principal heads of doctrine; for from these they might easily infer that these evangelists treat of heavenly mysteries beyond the capacity of man. Those who have the least particle of candour must be ashamed of their fastidiousness when they read the first chapter of Luke. Even our Saviour's discourses, of which a summary is given by these three evangelists, ought to prevent every one from treating their writings with contempt. John, again, fulminating in majesty, strikes down more powerfully than any thunderbolt the petulance of those who refuse to submit to the obedience of faith. Let all those acute censors, whose highest pleasure it is to banish a reverential regard of Scripture from their own and other men's hearts, come forward; let them read the Gospel of John, and, willing or unwilling, they will find a thousand sentences which will at least arouse them from their sloth; nay, which will burn into their consciences as with a hot iron, and check their derision. The same thing may be said of Peter and Paul, whose writings, though the greater part read them blindfold, exhibit a heavenly majesty, which in a manner binds and rivets every reader. But one circumstance, sufficient of itself to exalt their doctrine above the world, is, that Matthew, who was formerly fixed down to his money-table, Peter and John, who were employed with their little boats, being all rude and illiterate, had never learned in any human school that which they delivered to others. Paul, more-

over, who had not only been an avowed but a cruel and bloody foe, being changed into a new man, shows, by the sudden and unhoped-for change, that a heavenly power had compelled him to preach the doctrine which once he destroyed. Let those dogs deny that the Holy Spirit descended upon the apostles, or, if not, let them refuse credit to the history, still the very circumstances proclaim that the Holy Spirit must have been the teacher of those who, formerly con-temptible among the people, all of a sudden began to discourse so magnificently of heavenly mysteries.

12. Add, moreover, that, for the best of reasons, the consent of the Church is not without its weight. For it is not to be accounted of no consequence, that, from the first publication of Scripture, so many ages have uniformly concurred in yielding obedience to it, and that, notwithstanding of the many extraordinary attempts which Satan and the whole world have made to oppress and overthrow it, or completely efface it from the memory of men, it has flourished like the palm-tree and continued invincible. Though in old times there was scarcely a sophist or orator of any note who did not exert his powers against it, their efforts proved unavailing. The powers of the earth armed themselves for its destruction, but all their attempts vanished into smoke. When thus powerfully assailed on every side, how could it have resisted if it had trusted only to human aid? Nay, its divine origin is more completely established by the fact, that when all human wishes were against it, it advanced by its own energy. Add that it was not a single city or a single nation that concurred in receiving and embracing it. Its authority was recognised as far and as wide as the world extends—various nations who had nothing else in common entering for this purpose into a holy league. Moreover, while we ought to attach the greatest weight to the agreement of minds so diversified, and in all other things so much at variance with each other—an agreement which a Divine Providence alone could have produced—it adds no small weight to the whole when we attend to the piety of those who thus agree; not of all of them indeed, but of those in whom as lights God was pleased that his Church should shine.

13. Again, with what confidence does it become us to sub-scribe to a doctrine attested and confirmed by the blood of so many saints? They, when once they had embraced it, hesitated not boldly and intrepidly, and even with great alacrity, to meet death in its defence. Being transmitted to us with such an earnest, who of us shall not receive it with firm and unshaken conviction? It is there-fore no small proof of the authority of Scripture, that it was sealed with the blood of so many witnesses, especially when it is considered that in bearing testimony to the faith, they met death not with fanatical enthusiasm (as erring spirits are sometimes wont to do), but with a firm and constant, yet sober godly zeal. There are other reasons, neither few nor feeble, by which the dignity and majesty of

the Scriptures may be not only proved to the pious, but also completely vindicated against the cavils of slanderers. These, however, cannot of themselves produce a firm faith in Scripture until our heavenly Father manifest his presence in it, and thereby secure implicit reverence for it. Then only, therefore, does Scripture suffice to give a saving knowledge of God when its certainty is founded on the inward persuasion of the Holy Spirit. Still the human testimonies which go to confirm it will not be without effect, if they are used in subordination to that chief and highest proof, as secondary helps to our weakness. But it is foolish to attempt to prove to infidels that the Scripture is the Word of God. This it cannot be known to be, except by faith. Justly, therefore, does Augustine remind us, that every man who would have any understanding in such high matters must previously possess piety and mental peace.

CHAPTER IX.

ALL THE PRINCIPLES OF PIETY SUBVERTED BY FANATICS, WHO SUBSTITUTE REVELATIONS FOR SCRIPTURE.

Sections.

1. The temper and error of the Libertines, who take to themselves the name of spiritual, briefly described. Their refutation. 1. The Apostles and all true Christians have embraced the written Word. This confirmed by a passage in Isaiah; also by the example and words of Paul. 2. The Spirit of Christ seals the doctrine of the written Word on the minds of the godly.
2. Refutation continued. 3. The impositions of Satan cannot be detected without the aid of the written Word. First objection. The Answer to it.
3. Second Objection from the words of Paul as to the *letter and spirit*. The Answer, with an explanation of Paul's meaning. How the Spirit and the written Word are indissolubly connected:

1. THOSE who, rejecting Scripture, imagine that they have some peculiar way of penetrating to God, are to be deemed not so much under the influence of error as madness. For certain giddy men[r] have lately appeared, who, while they make a great display of the superiority of the Spirit, reject all reading of the Scriptures themselves, and deride the simplicity of those who only delight in what they call the dead and deadly letter. But I wish they would tell me what spirit it is whose inspiration raises them to such a sublime height that they dare despise the doctrine of Scripture as mean and childish. If they answer that it is the Spirit of Christ, their confidence is exceedingly ridiculous; since they will, I presume, admit that the apostles and other believers in the primitive Church were not illuminated by any other Spirit. None of these thereby learned to despise the Word of God, but every one was imbued with greater reverence for it, as their writings most clearly testify. And, indeed, it had been so foretold by the mouth of Isaiah. For when he says, " My Spirit that is upon thee, and my words which I have put in thy mouth, shall not depart out of thy mouth, nor out of the mouth of thy seed, nor out of the mouth of thy seed's seed, saith the Lord, from henceforth and for ever," he does not tie down the ancient Church to external doctrine, as he were a mere teacher of elements;[2] he rather shows that, under the reign of Christ, the true and full felicity of the new Church will consist in their being ruled not less by the Word than by the Spirit of God. Hence we infer that these miscreants are guilty of fearful sacrilege in tearing asunder what the prophet joins in indissoluble union. Add to this, that Paul, though carried up even to the third heaven, ceased not to profit by the doctrine of the law and the prophets, while, in like manner, he exhorts Timothy, a

---

1 Lactantius: Cœlestes literas corruperunt, ut novam sibi doctrinam sine ulla radice ac stabilitate componerent. *Vide* Calvin in Instruct. adv. Libertinos, cap. ix. and x.

2 For the Latin, " ac si elementarius esset," the French has, " comme s'ils eussent étépetis enfans a l'A, B, C ;"—as if they were little children at their A, B, C.

teacher of singular excellence, to give attention to reading (1 Tim. iv. 13). And the eulogium which he pronounces on Scripture well deserves to be remembered—viz., that " it is profitable for doctrine, for reproof, for correction, and for instruction in righteousness, that the man of God may be perfect" (2 Tim. iii. 16). What an infatuation of the devil, therefore, to fancy that Scripture, which conducts the sons of God to the final goal, is of transient and temporary use ? Again, I should like those people to tell me whether they have imbibed any other Spirit than that which Christ promised to his disciples. Though their madness is extreme, it will scarcely carry them the length of making this their boast. But what kind of Spirit did our Saviour promise to send ? One who should not speak of himself (John xvi. 13), but suggest and instil the truths which he himself had delivered through the word. Hence the office of the Spirit promised to us, is not to form new and unheard-of revelations, or to coin a new form of doctrine, by which we may be led away from the received doctrine of the gospel, but to seal on our minds the very doctrine which the gospel recommends.

2. Hence it is easy to understand that we must give diligent heed both to the reading and hearing of Scripture, if we would obtain any benefit from the Spirit of God (just as Peter praises those who attentively study the doctrine of the prophets (2 Pet. i. 19), though it might have been thought to be superseded after the gospel light arose), and, on the contrary, that any spirit which passes by the wisdom of God's Word, and suggests any other doctrine, is deservedly suspected of vanity and falsehood. Since Satan transforms himself into an angel of light, what authority can the Spirit have with us if he be not ascertained by an infallible mark ? And assuredly he is pointed out to us by the Lord with sufficient clearness ; but these miserable men err as if bent on their own destruction, while they seek the Spirit from themselves rather than from Him. But they say that it is insulting to subject the Spirit, to whom all things are to be subject, to the Scripture : as if it were disgraceful to the Holy Spirit to maintain a perfect resemblance throughout, and be in all respects without variation consistent with himself. True, if he were subjected to a human, an angelical, or to any foreign standard, it might be thought that he was rendered subordinate, or, if you will, brought into bondage ; but so long as he is compared with himself, and considered in himself, how can it be said that he is thereby injured ? I admit that he is brought to a test, but the very test by which it has pleased him that his majesty should be confirmed. It ought to be enough for us when once we hear his voice ; but lest Satan should insinuate himself under his name, he wishes us to recognise him by the image which he has stamped on the Scriptures. The author of the Scriptures cannot vary, and change his likeness. Such as he there appeared at first, such he will perpetually remain. There is nothing contumelious to him in this, unless we are to think it would be honourable for him to degenerate, and revolt against himself.

3. Their cavil about our cleaving to the dead letter carries with it the punishment which they deserve for despising Scripture. It is clear that Paul is there arguing against false apostles (2 Cor. iii. 6), who, by recommending the law without Christ, deprived the people of the benefit of the New Covenant, by which the Lord engages that he will write his law on the hearts of believers, and engrave it on their inward parts. The letter therefore is dead, and the law of the Lord kills its readers when it is dissevered from the grace of Christ, and only sounds in the ear without touching the heart. But if it is effectually impressed on the heart by the Spirit; if it exhibits Christ, it is the word of life converting the soul, and making wise the simple. Nay, in the very same passage, the apostle calls his own preaching the ministration of the Spirit (2 Cor. iii. 8), intimating that the Holy Spirit so cleaves to his own truth, as he has expressed it in Scripture, that he then only exerts and puts forth his strength when the word is received with due honour and respect.

There is nothing repugnant here to what was lately said (chap. vii.) that we have no great certainty of the word itself, until it be confirmed by the testimony of the Spirit. For the Lord has so knit together the certainty of his word and his Spirit, that our minds are duly imbued with reverence for the word when the Spirit shining upon it enables us there to behold the face of God; and, on the other hand, we embrace the Spirit with no danger of delusion when we recognise him in his image, that is, in his word. Thus, indeed, it is. God did not produce his word before men for the sake of sudden display, intending to abolish it the moment the Spirit should arrive; but he employed the same Spirit, by whose agency he had administered the word, to complete his work by the efficacious confirmation of the word. In this way Christ explained to the two disciples (Luke xxiv. 27), not that they were to reject the Scriptures and trust to their own wisdom, but that they were to understand the Scriptures. In like manner, when Paul says to the Thessalonians, "Quench not the Spirit," he does not carry them aloft to empty speculation apart from the word; he immediately adds, "Despise not prophesyings" (1 Thess. v. 19, 20). By this, doubtless, he intimates that the light of the Spirit is quenched the moment prophesyings fall into contempt. How is this answered by those swelling enthusiasts, in whose idea the only true illumination consists, in carelessly laying aside, and bidding adieu to the Word of God, while, with no less confidence than folly, they fasten upon any dreaming notion which may have casually sprung up in their minds? Surely a very different sobriety becomes the children of God. As they feel that without the Spirit of God they are utterly devoid of the light of truth, so they are not ignorant that the word is the instrument by which the illumination of the Spirit is dispensed. They know of no other Spirit than the one who dwelt and spake in the apostles—the Spirit by whose oracles they are daily invited to the hearing of the Word.

CHAPTER X.

IN SCRIPTURE, THE TRUE GOD OPPOSED, EXCLUSIVELY, TO ALL THE GODS OF THE HEATHEN.

Sections.

1. Explanation of the knowledge of God resumed. God as manifested in Scripture, the same as delineated in his works.
2. The attributes of God as described by Moses, David, and Jeremiah. Explanation of the attributes. Summary. Uses of this knowledge.
3. Scripture, in directing us to the true God, excludes the gods of the heathen, who, however, in some sense, held the unity of God.

1. WE formerly observed that the knowledge of God, which, in other respects, is not obscurely exhibited in the frame of the world, and in all the creatures, is more clearly and familiarly explained by the word. It may now be proper to show, that in Scripture the Lord represents himself in the same character in which we have already seen that he is delineated in his works. A full discussion of this subject would occupy a large space. But it will here be sufficient to furnish a kind of index, by attending to which the pious reader may be enabled to understand what knowledge of God he ought chiefly to search for in Scripture, and be directed as to the mode of conducting the search. I am not now adverting to the peculiar covenant by which God distinguished the race of Abraham from the rest of the nations. For when by gratuitous adoption he admitted those who were enemies to the rank of sons, he even then acted in the character of a Redeemer. At present, however, we are employed in considering that knowledge which stops short at the creation of the world, without ascending to Christ the Mediator. But though it will soon be necessary to quote certain passages from the New Testament (proofs being there given both of the power of God the Creator, and of his providence in the preservation of what he originally created), I wish the reader to remember what my present purpose is, that he may not wander from the proper subject. Briefly, then, it will be sufficient for him at present to understand how God, the Creator of heaven and earth, governs the world which was made by him. In every part of Scripture we meet with descriptions of his paternal kindness and readiness to do good, and we also meet with examples of severity which show that he is the just punisher of the wicked, especially when they continue obstinate notwithstanding of all his forbearance.

2. There are certain passages which contain more vivid descriptions

of the divine character, setting it before us as if his genuine counte-nance were visibly portrayed. Moses, indeed, seems to have intended briefly to comprehend whatever may be known of God by man, when he said, "The Lord, The Lord God, merciful and gracious, long-suffering, and abundant in goodness and truth, keeping mercy for thousands, forgiving iniquity and transgression and sin, and that will by no means clear the guilty; visiting the iniquity of the fathers upon the children, and upon the children's children, unto the third and to the fourth generation" (Ex. xxxiv. 6, 7). Here we may observe, *first*, that his eternity and self-existence are declared by his magnificent name twice repeated; and, *secondly*, that in the enumera-tion of his perfections, he is described not as he is in himself, but in relation to us, in order that our acknowledgment of him may be more a vivid actual impression than empty visionary speculation. Moreover, the perfections thus enumerated are just those which we saw shining in the heavens, and on the earth—compassion, goodness, mercy, justice, judgment, and truth. For power and energy are comprehended under the name Jehovah. Similar epithets are em-ployed by the prophets when they would fully declare his sacred name. Not to collect a great number of passages, it may suffice at present to refer to one Psalm (cxlv.), in which a summary of the divine per-fections is so carefully given, that not one seems to have been omitted. Still, however, every perfection there set down may be contemplated in creation; and, hence, such as we feel him to be when experience is our guide, such he declares himself to be by his word. In Jeremiah, where God proclaims the character in which he would have us to acknowledge him, though the description is not so full, it is substan-tially the same. "Let him that glorieth," says he, "glory in this, that he understandeth and knoweth me, that I am the Lord which exercise loving-kindness, judgment, and righteousness, in the earth" (Jerem. ix. 24). Assuredly, the attributes which it is most necessary for us to know are these three: Loving-kindness, on which alone our entire safety depends; Judgment, which is daily exercised on the wicked, and awaits them in a severer form, even for eternal destruc-tion; Righteousness, by which the faithful are preserved, and most benignly cherished. The prophet declares, that when you understand these, you are amply furnished with the means of glorying in God. Nor is there here any omission of his truth, or power, or holiness, or goodness. For how could this knowledge of his loving-kindness, judgment, and righteousness, exist, if it were not founded on his in-violable truth? How, again, could it be believed that he governs the earth with judgment and righteousness, without presupposing his mighty power? Whence, too, his loving-kindness, but from his good-ness? In fine, if all his ways are loving-kindness, judgment, and righteousness, his holiness also is thereby conspicuous. Moreover, the knowledge of God, which is set before us in the Scriptures, is designed for the same purpose as that which shines in creation—viz.

that we may thereby learn to worship him with perfect integrity of heart and unfeigned obedience, and also to depend entirely on his goodness.

3. Here it may be proper to give a summary of the general doctrine. First, then, let the reader observe that the Scripture, in order to direct us to the true God, distinctly excludes and rejects all the gods of the heathen, because religion was universally adulterated in almost every age. It is true, indeed, that the name of one God was everywhere known and celebrated. For those who worshipped a multitude of gods, whenever they spoke the genuine language of nature, simply used the name god, as if they had thought one god sufficient. And this is shrewdly noticed by Justin Martyr, who, to the same effect, wrote a treatise, entitled, On the Monarchy of God, in which he shows, by a great variety of evidence, that the unity of God is engraven on the hearts of all. Tertullian also proves the same thing from the common forms of speech.[1] But as all, without exception, have in the vanity of their minds rushed or been dragged into lying fictions, these impressions, as to the unity of God, whatever they may have naturally been, have had no further effect than to render men inexcusable. The wisest plainly discover the vague wanderings of their minds when they express a wish for any kind of Deity, and thus offer up their prayers to unknown gods. And then, in imagining a manifold nature in God, though their ideas concerning Jupiter, Mercury, Venus, Minerva, and others, were not so absurd as those of the rude vulgar, they were by no means free from the delusions of the devil. We have elsewhere observed, that however subtle the evasions devised by philosophers, they cannot do away with the charge of rebellion, in that all of them have corrupted the truth of God. For this reason, Habakkuk (ii. 20), after condemning all idols, orders men to seek God in his temple, that the faithful may acknowledge none but Him, who has manifested himself in his word.

1 In his book, De Idolatria. See also in Augustine, a letter by one Maximus, a grammarian of Medaura, jesting at his gods, and scoffing at the true religion. See, at the same time, Augustine's grave and admirable reply. Ep. xliii. xliv.

CHAPTER XI.

IMPIETY OF ATTRIBUTING A VISIBLE FORM TO GOD.—THE SETTING
UP OF IDOLS A DEFECTION FROM THE TRUE GOD.

There are three leading divisions in this chapter. The first contains a refutation of those who ascribe a visible form to God (s. 1 and 2), with an answer to the objection of those who, because it is said that God manifested his presence by certain symbols, use it as a defence of their error (s. 3 and 4). Various arguments are afterwards adduced, disposing of the trite objection from Gregory's expression, that images are the books of the unlearned (s. 5–7). The second division of the chapter relates to the origin of idols or images, and the adoration of them, as approved by the Papists (s. 8–10). Their evasion refuted (s. 11). The third division treats of the use and abuse of images (s. 12). Whether it is expedient to have them in Christian Churches (s. 13). The concluding part contains a refutation of the second Council of Nice, which very absurdly contends for images in opposition to divine truth, and even to the disparagement of the Christian name.

Sections.

1. God is opposed to idols, that all may know he is the only fit witness to himself. He expressly forbids any attempt to represent him by a bodily shape
2. Reasons fort his prohibition from Moses, Isaiah, and Paul. The complaint of a heathen. It should put the worshippers of idols to shame.
3. Consideration of an objection taken from various passages in Moses. The Cherubim and Seraphim show that images are not fit to represent divine mysteries. The Cherubim belonged to the tutelage of the Law.
4. The materials of which idols are made, abundantly refute the fiction of idolaters. Confirmation from Isaiah and others. Absurd precaution of the Greeks.
5. Objection,—That images are the books of the unlearned. Objection answered, 1. Scripture declares images to be teachers of vanity and lies.
6. Answer continued,—2. Ancient Theologians condemn the formation and worship of idols.
7. Answer continued,—3. The use of images condemned by the luxury and meretricious ornaments given to them in Popish Churches. 4. The Church must be trained in true piety by another method.
8. The second division of the chapter. Origin of idols or images. Its rise shortly after the flood. Its continual progress.
9. Of the worship of images. Its nature. A pretext of idolaters refuted. Pretexts of the heathen. Genius of idolaters.
10. Evasion of the Papists. Their agreement with ancient idolaters.
11. Refutation of another evasion or sophism,—viz. the distinction of *dulia* and *latria*.
12. Third division of the chapter—viz. the use and abuse of images.
13. Whether it is expedient to have images in Christian temples.
14. Absurd defence of the worship of images by the second so-called Council of Nice. Sophisms or perversions of Scripture in defence of images in churches.
15. Passages adduced in support of the worship of images.
16. The blasphemous expressions of some ancient idolaters approved by not a few of the more modern, both in word and deed.

1. As Scripture, in accommodation to the rude and gross intellect of man, usually speaks in popular terms, so whenever its object is to

discriminate between the true God and false deities, it opposes him in particular to idols ; not that it approves of what is taught more elegantly and subtilely by philosophers, but that it may the better expose the folly, nay madness, of the world in its inquiries after God, so long as every one clings to his own speculations.   This exclusive definition, which we uniformly meet with in Scripture, annihilates every deity which men frame for themselves of their own accord— God himself being the only fit witness to himself.   Meanwhile, seeing that this brutish stupidity has overspread the globe, men longing after visible forms of God, and so forming deities of wood and stone, silver and gold, or of any other dead and corruptible matter, we must hold it as a first principle, that as often as any form is assigned to God, his glory is corrupted by an impious lie.   In the Law, accordingly, after God had claimed the glory of divinity for himself alone, when he comes to show what kind of worship he approves and rejects, he immediately adds, "Thou shalt not make unto thee any graven image, or any likeness of anything that is in heaven above, or in the earth beneath, or in the water under the earth" (Exod. xx. 4).   By these words he curbs any licentious attempt we might make to represent him by a visible shape, and briefly enumerates all the forms by which superstition had begun, even long before, to turn his truth into a lie.   For we know that the Sun was worshipped by the Persians.   As many stars as the foolish nations saw in the sky, so many gods they imagined them to be.   Then to the Egyptians, every animal was a figure of God.[1]   The Greeks, again, plumed themselves on their superior wisdom in worshipping God under the human form, (Maximus Tyrius Platonic. Serm. 38).   But God makes no comparison between images, as if one were more, and another less befitting; he rejects, without exception, all shapes and pictures, and other symbols by which the superstitious imagine they can bring him near to them.

2. This may easily be inferred from the reasons which he annexes to his prohibition.   First, it is said in the books of Moses, (Deut. iv. 15), "Take ye therefore good heed unto yourselves; for ye saw no manner of similitude in the day that the Lord spake unto you in Horeb, out of the midst of the fire, lest ye corrupt yourselves, and make you a graven image, the similitude of any figure," &c.   We see how plainly God declares against all figures, to make us aware that all longing after such visible shapes is rebellion against him. Of the prophets, it will be sufficient to mention Isaiah, who is the most copious on this subject (Isaiah xl. 18 ; xli. 7, 29 ; xlv. 9 ; xlvi. 5), in order to show how the majesty of God is defiled by an absurd and indecorous fiction, when he who is incorporeal is assimilated to corporeal matter; he who is invisible to a visible image; he who is a spirit to an inanimate object; and he who fills all space to a bit of

1 The French adds, " voire jusques aux oignons et porreaux ;"—they have gone even to onions and leeks.

paltry wood, or stone, or gold. Paul, too, reasons in the same way, "Forasmuch, then, as we are the offspring of God, we ought not to think that the Godhead is like unto gold, or silver, or stone, graven by art and man's device" (Acts xvii. 29). Hence it is manifest, that whatever statues are set up or pictures painted to represent God, are utterly displeasing to him, as a kind of insults to his majesty. And is it strange that the Holy Spirit thunders such responses from heaven, when he compels even blind and miserable idolaters to make a similar confession on the earth? Seneca's complaint, as given by Augustine, De Civit. Dei, c. 10, is well known. He says, "The sacred, immortal, and invisible gods, they exhibit in the meanest and most ignoble materials, and dress them in the clothing of men and beasts; some confound the sexes, and form a compound out of different bodies, giving the name of deities to objects, which, if they were met alive, would be deemed monsters." Hence, again, it is obvious, that the defenders of images resort to a paltry quibbling evasion, when they pretend that the Jews were forbidden to use them on account of their proneness to superstition; as if a prohibition which the Lord founds on his own eternal essence, and the uniform course of nature, could be restricted to a single nation. Besides, when Paul refuted the error of giving a bodily shape to God, he was addressing not Jews, but Athenians.

3. It is true that the Lord occasionally manifested his presence by certain signs, so that he was said to be seen face to face; but all the signs he ever employed were in apt accordance with the scheme of doctrine, and, at the same time, gave plain intimation of his incomprehensible essence. For the cloud, and smoke, and flame, though they were symbols of heavenly glory (Deut. iv. 11), curbed men's minds as with a bridle, that they might not attempt to penetrate farther. Therefore, even Moses (to whom, of all men, God manifested himself most familiarly) was not permitted, though he prayed for it, to behold that face, but received for answer, that the refulgence was too great for man (Exod. xxxiii. 20). The Holy Spirit appeared under the form of a dove, but as it instantly vanished, who does not see that in this symbol of a moment, the faithful were admonished to regard the Spirit as invisible, to be contented with his power and grace, and not call for any external figure? God sometimes appeared in the form of a man, but this was in anticipation of the future revelation in Christ, and, therefore, did not give the Jews the least pretext for setting up a symbol of Deity under the human form. The mercy-seat, also (Exod. xxv. 17, 18, 21), where, under the Law, God exhibited the presence of his power, was so framed, as to intimate that God is best seen when the mind rises in admiration above itself: the Cherubim with outstretched wings shaded, and the veil covered it, while the remoteness of the place was in itself a sufficient concealment. It is therefore mere infatuation to attempt to defend images of God and the saints by the example of the Cherubim. For

what, pray, did these figures mean, if not that images are unfit to represent the mysteries of God, since they were so formed as to cover the mercy-seat with their wings, thereby concealing the view of God, not only from the eye, but from every human sense, and curbing presumption ?   To this we may add, that the prophets depict the Seraphim, who are exhibited to us in vision, as having their faces veiled ; thus intimating, that the refulgence of the divine glory is so great, that even the angels cannot gaze upon it directly, while the minute beams which sparkle in the face of angels are shrouded from our view.   Moreover, all men of sound judgment acknowledge that the Cherubim in question belonged to the old tutelage of the law.   It is absurd, therefore, to bring them forward as an example for our age. For that period of puerility, if I may so express it, to which such rudiments were adapted, has passed away.   And surely it is disgraceful that heathen writers should be more skilful interpreters of Scripture than the Papists.   Juvenal (Sat. xiv.) holds up the Jews to derision for worshipping the thin clouds and firmament.   This he does perversely and impiously ; still, in denying that any visible shape of deity existed among them, he speaks more accurately than the Papists, who prate about there having been some visible image.   In the fact that the people every now and then rushed forth with boiling haste in pursuit of idols, just like water gushing forth with violence from a copious spring, let us learn how prone our nature is to idolatry, that we may not, by throwing the whole blame of a common vice upon the Jews, be led away by vain and sinful enticements to sleep the sleep of death.

4. To the same effect are the words of the Psalmist (Psalms cxv. 4, cxxxv. 15), "Their idols are silver and gold, the work of men's hands."   From the materials of which they are made, he infers that they are not gods, taking it for granted that every human device concerning God is a dull fiction.   He mentions silver and gold rather than clay or stone, that neither splendour nor cost may procure reverence to idols.   He then draws a general conclusion, that nothing is more unlikely than that gods should be formed of any kind of inanimate matter.   Man is forced to confess that he is but the creature of a day (see Book III. c. ix. s. 2), and yet would have the metal which he has deified to be regarded as God.   Whence had idols their origin, but from the will of man ?   There was ground, therefore, for the sarcasm of the heathen poet (Hor. Sat. I. 8), "I was once the trunk of a fig-tree, a useless log, when the tradesman, uncertain whether he should make me a stool, &c., chose rather that I should be a god."   In other words, an earth-born creature, who breathes out his life almost every moment, is able by his own device to confer the name and honour of deity on a lifeless trunk.   But as that Epicurean poet, in indulging his wit, had no regard for religion, without attending to his jeers or those of his fellows, let the rebuke of the prophet sting, nay, cut us to the heart, when he speaks of the extreme infatuation of

those who take a piece of wood to kindle a fire to warm themselves, bake bread, roast or boil flesh, and out of the residue make a god, before which they prostrate themselves as suppliants (Isaiah xliv. 16). Hence the same prophet, in another place, not only charges idolaters as guilty in the eye of the law, but upbraids them for not learning from the foundations of the earth, nothing being more incongruous than to reduce the immense and incomprehensible Deity to the stature of a few feet. And yet experience shows that this monstrous proceeding, though palpably repugnant to the order of nature, is natural to man. It is, moreover, to be observed, that by the mode of expression which is employed, every form of superstition is denounced. Being works of men, they have no authority from God (Isa. ii. 8, 31; vii. 57; Hos. xiv. 4; Mic. v. 13); and, therefore, it must be regarded as a fixed principle, that all modes of worship devised by man are detestable. The infatuation is placed in a still stronger light by the Psalmist (Psalm cxv. 8), when he shows how aid is implored from dead and senseless objects, by beings who have been endued with intelligence for the very purpose of enabling them to know that the whole universe is governed by Divine energy alone. But as the corruption of nature hurries away all mankind collectively and individually into this madness, the Spirit at length thunders forth a dreadful imprecation, "They that make them are like unto them, so is every one that trusteth in them."[1] And it is to be observed, that the thing forbidden is *likeness*, whether sculptured or otherwise. This disposes of the frivolous precaution taken by the Greek Church. They think they do admirably, because they have no sculptured shape of Deity, while none go greater lengths in the licentious use of pictures. The Lord, however, not only forbids any image of himself to be erected by a statuary, but to be formed by any artist whatever, because every such image is sinful and insulting to his majesty.

5. I am not ignorant, indeed, of the assertion, which is now more than threadbare, "that images are the books of the unlearned." So said Gregory:[2] but the Holy Spirit gives a very different decision; and had Gregory got his lesson in this matter in the Spirit's school, he never would have spoken as he did. For when Jeremiah declares that "the stock is a doctrine of vanities" (Jer. x. 8), and Habakkuk, "that the molten image" is "a teacher of lies," the general doctrine to be inferred certainly is, that everything respecting God which is learned from images is futile and false. If it is objected that the censure of the prophets is directed against those who perverted images to purposes of impious superstition, I admit it to be so; but I add (what must be obvious to all), that the prophets utterly condemn

---

[1] Calvin translates the words of the Psalmist as an imprecation, "Similes illis fiant qui faciunt ea;"—Let those who make them be like unto them.

[2] See Gregory, Ep. ad Serenum Massiliens, Ep. cix. lib. vii.; and Ep. ix. lib. ix.; also Ep. liii. et cxxvi. lib. ii., where Gregory, while wishing to excuse the worship of images, rather accuses it.

what the Papists hold to be an undoubted axiom—viz. that images are substitutes for books. For they contrast images with the true God, as if the two were of an opposite nature, and never could be made to agree. In the passages which I lately quoted, the conclusion drawn is, that seeing there is one true God whom the Jews worshipped, visible shapes made for the purpose of representing him are false and wicked fictions; and all, therefore, who have recourse to them for knowledge are miserably deceived. In short, were it not true that all such knowledge is fallacious and spurious, the prophets would not condemn it in such general terms. This at least I maintain, that when we teach that all human attempts to give a visible shape to God are vanity and lies, we do nothing more than state *verbatim* what the prophets taught.

6. Moreover, let Lactantius and Eusebius [1] be read on this subject. [2] These writers ass me it as an indisputable fact, that all the beings whose images were erected were originally men. In like manner, Augustine distinctly declares, that it is unlawful not only to worship images, but to dedicate them. And in this he says no more than had been long before decreed by the Elibertine Council, the thirty-sixth Canon of which is, "There must be no pictures used in churches: Let nothing which is adored or worshipped be painted on walls." But the most memorable passage of all is that which Augustine quotes in another place from Varro, and in which he expressly concurs:— "Those who first introduced images of the gods both took away fear and brought in error." Were this merely the saying of Varro, it might perhaps be of little weight, though it might well make us ashamed that a heathen, groping as it were in darkness, should have attained to such a degree of light, as to see that corporeal images are unworthy of the majesty of God, and that, because they diminish reverential fear and encourage error. The sentiment itself bears witness that it was uttered with no less truth than shrewdness. But Augustine, while he borrows it from Varro, adduces it as conveying his own opinion. At the outset, indeed, he declares that the first errors into which men fell concerning God did not originate with images, but increased with them, as if new fuel had been added. Afterwards, he explains how the fear of God was thereby extinguished or impaired, his presence being brought into contempt by foolish, and childish, and absurd representations. [3] The truth of this latter remark I wish we did not so thoroughly experience. Whosoever, therefore, is desirous of being instructed in the true knowledge of God must apply to some other teacher than images.

---

1 The French adds, "deux des plus anciens Docteurs de l'Eglise;"—two of the most ancient Doctors of the Church.

2 Lact. Inst. Div. lib. i c. 15; Euseb. Præf. Evang. lib. iii. c. 3, 4; also August. De Civitate Dei, lib. iv. c. 9, 31.

3 The French is, "Pourceque la gloire de sa Divinite est vilipendée en une chose si sotte et lourde comme est un marmouset;"—because the glory of his Divinity is degraded into an object so silly and stupid as a marmoset.

7. Let Papists, then, if they have any sense of shame, henceforth desist from the futile plea, that images are the books of the unlearned —a plea so plainly refuted by innumerable passages of Scripture. And yet were I to admit the plea, it would not be a valid defence of their peculiar idols. It is well known what kind of monsters they obtrude upon us as divine. For what are the pictures or statues to which they append the names of saints, but exhibitions of the most shameless luxury or obscenity? Were any one to dress himself after their model, he would deserve the pillory. Indeed, brothels exhibit their inmates more chastely and modestly dressed than churches do images intended to represent virgins. The dress of the martyrs is is in no respect more becoming. Let Papists then have some little regard to decency in decking their idols, if they would give the least plausibility to the false allegation, that they are books of some kind of sanctity. But even then we shall answer, that this is not the method in which the Christian people should be taught in sacred places. Very different from these follies is the doctrine in which God would have them to be there instructed. His injunction is, that the doctrine common to all should there be set forth by the preaching of the Word, and the administration of the sacraments,—a doctrine to which little heed can be given by those whose eyes are carried to and fro gazing at idols. And who are the unlearned, whose rudeness admits of being taught by images only? Just those whom the Lord acknowledges for his disciples ; those whom he honours with a revelation of his celestial philosophy, and desires to be trained in the saving mysteries of his kingdom. I confess, indeed, as matters now are, there are not a few in the present day who cannot want such books. But, I ask, whence this stupidity, but just because they are defrauded of the only doctrine which was fit to instruct them? The simple reason why those who had the charge of churches resigned the office of teaching to idols was, because they themselves were dumb. Paul declares, that by the true preaching of the gospel Christ is portrayed and in a manner crucified before our eyes (Gal. iii. 1). Of what use, then, were the erection in churches of so many crosses of wood and stone, silver and gold, if this doctrine were faithfully and honestly preached—viz., Christ died that he might bear our curse upon the tree, that he might expiate our sins by the sacrifice of his body, wash them in his blood, and, in short, reconcile us to God the Father? From this one doctrine the people would learn more than from a thousand crosses of wood and stone. As for crosses of gold and silver, it may be true that the avaricious give their eyes and minds to them more eagerly than to any heavenly instructor.

8. In regard to the origin of idols, the statement contained in the Book of Wisdom has been received with almost universal consent— viz., that they originated with those who bestowed this honour on the dead, from a superstitious regard to their memory. I admit that this perverse practice is of very high antiquity, and I deny not that

it was a kind of torch by which the infatuated proneness of mankind to idolatry was kindled into a greater blaze. I do not, however, admit that it was the first origin of the practice. The idols that were in use before the prevalence of that ambitious consecration of the images of the dead, frequently adverted to by profane writers, is evident from the words of Moses (Gen. xxxi. 19). When he relates that Rachel stole her father's images, he speaks of the use of idols as a common vice. Hence we may infer, that the human mind is, so to speak, a perpetual forge of idols. There was a kind of renewal of the world at the deluge, but before many years elapse, men are forging gods at will. There is reason to believe, that in the holy Patriarch's lifetime his grandchildren were given to idolatry: so that he must with his own eyes, not without the deepest grief, have seen the earth polluted with idols—that earth whose iniquities God had lately purged with so fearful a judgment. For Joshua testifies (Josh. xxiv. 2), that Terah and Nachor, even before the birth of Abraham, were the worshippers of false gods. The progeny of Shem having so speedily revolted, what are we to think of the posterity of Ham, who had been cursed long before in their father? Thus, indeed, it is. The human mind, stuffed as it is with presumptuous rashness, dares to imagine a god suited to its own capacity; as it labours under dulness, nay, is sunk in the grossest ignorance, it substitutes vanity and an empty phantom in the place of God. To these evils another is added. The god whom man has thus conceived inwardly he attempts to embody outwardly. The mind, in this way, conceives the idol, and the hand gives it birth. That idolatry has its origin in the idea which men have, that God is not present with them unless his presence is carnally exhibited, appears from the example of the Israelites: "Up," said they, "make us gods, which shall go before us; for as for this Moses, the man that brought us up out of the land of Egypt, we wot not what is become of him" (Exod. xxxii. 1). They knew, indeed, that there was a God whose mighty power they had experienced in so many miracles, but they had no confidence of his being near to them, if they did not with their eyes behold a corporeal symbol of his presence, as an attestation to his actual government. They desired, therefore, to be assured, by the image which went before them, that they were journeying under Divine guidance. And daily experience shows, that the flesh is always restless until it has obtained some figment like itself, with which it may vainly solace itself as a representation of God. In consequence of this blind passion men have, almost in all ages since the world began, set up signs on which they imagined that God was visibly depicted to their eyes.

9. After such a figment is formed, adoration forthwith ensues; for when once men imagined that they beheld God in images, they also worshipped him as being there. At length their eyes and minds becoming wholly engrossed by them, they began to grow more and

more brutish, gazing and wondering as if some divinity were actually before them.   It hence appears that men do not fall away to the worship of images until they have imbibed some idea of a grosser description : not that they actually believe them to be gods, but that the power of divinity somehow or other resides in them.   Therefore, whether it be God or a creature that is imaged, the moment you fall prostrate before it in veneration, you are so far fascinated by superstition.   For this reason, the Lord not only forbad the erection of statues to himself, but also the consecration of titles and stones which might be set up for adoration.   For the same reason, also, the second commandment has an additional part concerning adoration.   For as soon as a visible form is given to God, his power also is supposed to be annexed to it.   So stupid are men, that wherever they figure God, there they fix him, and by necessary consequence proceed to adore him.   It makes no difference whether they worship the idol simply, or God in the idol ; it is always idolatry when divine honours are paid to an idol, be the colour what it may.   And because God wills not to be worshipped superstitiously, whatever is bestowed upon idols is so much robbed from him.

Let those attend to this who set about hunting for miserable pretexts in defence of the execrable indolatry in which for many past ages true religion has been buried and sunk.   It is said that the images are not accounted gods.   Nor were the Jews so utterly thoughtless as not to remember that there was a God whose hand led them out of Egypt before they made the calf.   Indeed, Aaron saying that these were the gods which had brought them out of Egypt, they intimated, in no ambiguous terms, that they wished to retain God, their deliverer, provided they saw him going before them in the calf.   Nor are the heathen to be deemed to have been so stupid as not to understand that God was something else than wood and stone.   For they changed the images at pleasure, but always retained the same gods in their minds ;[1] besides, they daily consecrated new images without thinking they were making new gods.   Read the excuses which Augustine tells us were employed by the idolaters of his time (*August. in Ps.* cxiii.).   The vulgar, when accused, replied that they did not worship the visible object, but the Deity which dwelt in it invisibly.   Those, again, who had what he calls a more refined religion, said, that they neither worshipped the image, nor any inhabiting Deity, but by means of the corporeal image beheld a symbol of that which it was their duty to worship.   What then ?   All idolaters, whether Jewish or Gentile, were actuated in the very way which has been described.   Not contented with spiritual understanding, they thought that images would give them a surer and nearer impression.   When once this preposterous representation of God was adopted, there was

---

[1] The French is, " Neantmoins ils ne disoyent point pour cela qu'un Dieu fut divisé ;" —nevertheless, they did not therefore say that the unity of God was divided.

no limit until, deluded every now and then by new impostures, they came to think that God exerted his power in images.[1] Still the Jews were persuaded, that, under such images, they worshipped the eternal God, the one true Lord of heaven and earth; and the Gentiles, also, in worshipping their own false gods, supposed them to dwell in heaven.

10. It is an impudent falsehood to deny that the thing which was thus anciently done is also done in our day. For why do men prostrate themselves before images? Why, when in the act of praying, do they turn towards them as to the ears of God? It is indeed true, as Augustine says (in Ps. cxiii.), that no person thus prays or worships, looking at an image, without being impressed with the idea that he is heard by it, or without hoping that what he wishes will be performed by it. Why are such distinctions made between different images of the same God, that while one is passed by, or receives only common honour, another is worshipped with the highest solemnities? Why do they fatigue themselves with votive pilgrimages to images, while they have many similar ones at home?[2] Why at the present time do they fight for them to blood and slaughter, as for their altars and hearths, showing more willingness to part with the one God than with their idols? And yet I am not now detailing the gross errors of the vulgar—errors almost infinite in number, and in possession of almost all hearts. I am only referring to what those profess who are most desirous to clear themselves of idolatry. They say, we do not call them our gods. Nor did either the Jews or Gentiles of old so call them; and yet the prophets never ceased to charge them with their adulteries with wood and stone for the very acts which are daily done by those who would be deemed Christians, namely, for worshipping God carnally in wood and stone.

11. I am not ignorant, however, and I have no wish to disguise the fact, that they endeavour to evade the charge by means of a more subtle distinction, which shall afterwards be fully considered (see *infra*, s. 16, and chap. xii. s. 2). The worship which they pay to their images they cloak with the name of εἰδωλοδυλεία (*idolodulia*), and deny to be εἰδωλολατρεία (*idolatria*). So they speak, holding that the worship which they call *dulia* may, without insult to God, be paid to statues and pictures. Hence, they think themselves blameless if they are only the *servants*, and not the *worshippers*, of idols; as if it were not a lighter matter to *worship* than *to serve*. And yet,

---

1 French, " Ne vouloit monstrer sa vertu que sous les images;"—would only show his power under the form of images.

2 The two last sentences in French are, " Car laissans là un crucifix, ou une image de leur nostre-dame, ou n'en tenans point grand comte, ils mettent leur devotion à un autre. Pourquoy est-ce qu'ils trotent si loin en pelerinage pour voir un marmouset, duquel ils ont le semblable à leur porte?"—For there passing by a crucifix, or an image of what they call " Our Lady," or making no great account of them, they pay their devotion to another. Why is it that they trot so far on a pilgrimage to see a marmoset, when they have one like it at their door?

while they take refuge in a Greek term, they very childishly contradict themselves. For the Greek word λατρεύειν having no other meaning than *to worship*, what they say is just the same as if they were to confess that they worship their images without worshipping them. They cannot object that I am quibbling upon words. The fact is, that they only betray their ignorance while they attempt to throw dust in the eyes of the simple. But how eloquent soever they may be, they will never prove by their eloquence that one and the same thing makes two. Let them show how the things differ if they would be thought different from ancient idolaters. For as a murderer or an adulterer will not escape conviction by giving some adventitious name to his crime, so it is absurd for them to expect that the subtle device of a name will exculpate them, if they, in fact, differ in nothing from idolaters whom they themselves are forced to condemn. But so far are they from proving that their case is different, that the source of the whole evil consists in a preposterous rivalship with them, while they with their minds devise, and with their hands execute, symbolical shapes of God.

12. I am not, however, so superstitious as to think that all visible representations of every kind are unlawful. But as sculpture and painting are gifts of God, what I insist for is, that both shall be used purely and lawfully,—that gifts which the Lord has bestowed upon us, for his glory and our good, shall not be preposterously abused, nay, shall not be perverted to our destruction. We think it unlawful to give a visible shape to God, because God himself has forbidden it, and because it cannot be done without, in some degree, tarnishing his glory. And lest any should think that we are singular in this opinion, those acquainted with the productions of sound divines will find that they have always disapproved of it. If it be unlawful to make any corporeal representation of God, still more unlawful must it be to worship such a representation instead of God, or to worship God in it. The only things, therefore, which ought to be painted or sculptured, are things which can be presented to the eye ; the majesty of God, which is far beyond the reach of any eye, must not be dishonoured by unbecoming representations. Visible representations are of two classes—viz. historical, which give a representation of events, and pictorial, which merely exhibit bodily shapes and figures. The former are of some use for instruction or admonition. The latter, so far as I can see, are only fitted for amusement. And yet it is certain, that the latter are almost the only kind which have hitherto been exhibited in churches. Hence we may infer, that the exhibition was not the result of judicious selection, but of a foolish and inconsiderate longing. I say nothing as to the improper and unbecoming form in which they are presented, or the wanton license in which sculptors and painters have here indulged (a point to which I alluded a little ago, *supra*, s. 7). I only say, that though they were otherwise faultless, they could not be of any utility in teaching.

13. But, without reference to the above distinction, let us here consider, whether it is expedient that churches should contain representations of any kind, whether of events or human forms. First, then, if we attach any weight to the authority of the ancient Church, let us remember, that for five hundred years, during which religion was in a more prosperous condition, and a purer doctrine flourished, Christian churches were completely free from visible representations (see Preface, and Book IV., c. ix. s. 9). Hence their first admission as an ornament to churches took place after the purity of the ministry had somewhat degenerated. I will not dispute as to the rationality of the grounds on which the first introduction of them proceeded, but if you compare the two periods, you will find that the latter had greatly declined from the purity of the times when images were unknown. What then? Are we to suppose that those holy fathers, if they had judged the thing to be useful and salutary, would have allowed the Church to be so long without it? Undoubtedly, because they saw very little or no advantage, and the greatest danger in it, they rather rejected it intentionally and on rational grounds, than omitted it through ignorance or carelessness. This is clearly attested by Augustine in these words (Ep. xlix. See also De Civit. Dei, lib. iv. c. 31). "When images are thus placed aloft in seats of honour, to be beheld by those who are praying or sacrificing, though they have neither sense nor life, yet from appearing as if they had both, they affect weak minds just as if they lived and breathed," &c. And again, in another passage (in Ps. cxii.), he says, "The effect produced, and in a manner extorted, by the bodily shape, is, that the mind, being itself in a body, imagines that a body which is so like its own must be similarly affected," &c. A little farther on he says, "Images are more capable of giving a wrong bent to an unhappy soul, from having mouth, eyes, ears, and feet, than of correcting it, as they neither speak, nor see, nor hear, nor walk." This undoubtedly is the reason why John (1 John v. 21) enjoins us to beware, not only of the worship of idols, but also of idols themselves. And from the fearful infatuation under which the world has hitherto laboured, almost to the entire destruction of piety, we know too well from experience that the moment images appear in churches, idolatry has as it were raised its banner; because the folly of manhood cannot moderate itself, but forthwith falls away to superstitious worship. Even were the danger less imminent, still, when I consider the proper end for which churches are erected, it appears to me more unbecoming their sacredness than I well can tell, to admit any other images than those living symbols which the Lord has consecrated by his own word: I mean Baptism and the Lord's Supper, with the other ceremonies. By these our eyes ought to be more steadily fixed, and more vividly impressed, than to require the aid of any images which the wit of man may devise. Such, then, is the incomparable blessing of images—a

blessing, the want of which, if we believe the Papists, cannot possibly be compensated![1]

14. Enough, I believe, would have been said on this subject, were I not in a manner arrested by the Council of Nice; not the celebrated Council which Constantine the Great assembled, but one which was held eight hundred years ago by the orders and under the auspices of the Empress Irene.[2] This Council decreed not only that images were to be used in churches, but also that they were to be worshipped. Everything, therefore, that I have said, is in danger of suffering great prejudice from the authority of this Synod. To confess the truth, however, I am not so much moved by this consideration, as by a wish to make my readers aware of the lengths to which the infatuation has been carried by those who had a greater fondness for images than became Christians. But let us first dispose of this matter. Those who defend the use of images appeal to that Synod for support. But there is a refutation extant which bears the name of Charlemagne, and which is proved by its style to be a production of that period. It gives the opinions delivered by the bishops who were present, and the arguments by which they supported them. John, deputy of the Eastern Churches, said, "God created man in his own image," and thence inferred that images ought to be used. He also thought there was a recommendation of images in the following passage, "Show me thy face, for it is beautiful." Another, in order to prove that images ought to be placed on altars, quoted the passage, "No man, when he hath lighted a candle, putteth it under a bushel." Another, to show the utility of looking at images, quoted a verse of the Psalms, "The light of thy countenance, O Lord, has shone upon us." Another laid hold of this similitude: As the Patriarchs used the sacrifices of the Gentiles, so ought Christians to use the images of saints instead of the idols of the Gentiles. They also twisted to the same effect the words, "Lord, I have loved the beauty of thy house." But the most ingenious interpretation was the following, "As we have heard, so also have we seen;" therefore, God is known not merely by the hearing of the word, but also by the seeing of images. Bishop Theodore was equally acute: "God," says he, "is to be admired in his saints;" and it is elsewhere said, "To the saints who are on earth;" therefore this must refer to images. In short, their absurdities are so extreme that it is painful even to quote them.

15. When they treat of adoration, great stress is laid on the worship of Pharaoh, the staff of Joseph, and the inscription which Jacob set up. In this last case they not only pervert the meaning of Scripture, but quote what is nowhere to be found. Then the passages,

---

[1] The French is, "qu'il n'y ait nulle recompense qui vaille un marmouset guignant à travers et faisant la mine tortue;"—that no compensation can equal the value of a marmoset looking askance and twisting its face.

[2] The French is, "une mechante Proserpine nommée Irene;"—a wicked Proserpine named Irene.

"Worship at his footstool"—"Worship in his holy mountain"—"The rulers of the people will worship before thy face," seem to them very solid and apposite proofs.   Were one, with the view of turning the defenders of images into ridicule, to put words into their mouths, could they be made to utter greater and grosser absurdities?   But to put an end to all doubt on the subject of images, Theodosius Bishop of Mira confirms the propriety of worshipping them by the dreams of his archdeacon, which he adduces with as much gravity as if he were in possession of a response from heaven.   Let the patrons of images now go and urge us with the decree of this Synod, as if the venerable Fathers did not bring themselves into utter discredit by handling Scripture so childishly, or wresting it so shamefully and profanely.

16.   I come now to monstrous impieties, which it is strange they ventured to utter, and twice strange that all men did not protest against with the utmost detestation.[1]   It is right to expose this frantic and flagitious extravagance, and thereby deprive the worship of images of that gloss of antiquity in which Papists seek to deck it.   Theodosius, Bishop of Amora, fires off an anathema at all who object to the worship of images.   Another attributes all the calamities of Greece and the East to the crime of not having worshipped them.   Of what punishment then are the Prophets, Apostles, and Martyrs worthy, in whose day no images existed?   They afterwards add, that if the statue of the Emperor is met with odours and incense, much more are the images of saints entitled to the honour.   Constantius, Bishop of Constantia in Cyprus, professes to embrace images with reverence, and declares that he will pay them the respect which is due to the ever blessed Trinity: every person refusing to do the same thing he anathematises and classes with Marcionites and Manichees.   Lest you should think this the private opinion of an individual, they all assent.   Nay, John the Eastern legate, carried still farther by his zeal, declares it would be better to allow a city to be filled with brothels than be denied the worship of images.   At last it is resolved with one consent that the Samaritans are the worst of all heretics, and that the enemies of images are worse than the Samaritans.   But that the play may not pass off without the accustomed *Plaudite*, the whole thus concludes, " Rejoice and exult, ye who, having the image of Christ, offer sacrifice to it."   Where is now the distinction of *latria* and *dulia* with which they would throw dust in all eyes, human and divine?   The Council unreservedly relies as much on images as on the living God.[2]

1 The French adds, " et qu'il ne se soit trouvé gens qui leur crachassent au visage ;" —and that people were not found to spit in their face.
2 See Calvin, De Vitandis Superstitionibus, where also see Resp. Pastorum, Tigurin. adver. Nicoder. tas.   See also Calvin, De Fugiendis Illicitis Sacris.

CHAPTER XII.

GOD DISTINGUISHED FROM IDOLS, THAT HE MAY BE THE EXCLUSIVE OBJECT OF WORSHIP.

Sections.

1. Scripture, in teaching that there is but one God, does not make a dispute about words, but attributes all honour and religious worship to him alone. This proved, 1st, By the etymology of the term. 2d, By the testimony of God himself, when he declares that he is a jealous God, and will not allow himself to be confounded with any fictitious Deity.
2. The Papists, in opposing this pure doctrine, gain nothing by their distinction of *dulia* and *latria.*
3. Passages of Scripture subversive of the Papistical distinction, and proving that religious worship is due to God alone. Perversions of Divine worship.

1. WE said at the commencement of our work (chap. ii.), that the knowledge of God consists not in frigid speculation, but carries worship along with it ; and we touched by the way (chap. v. s. 6, 9, 10) on what will be more copiously treated in other places (Book II. chap. viii.)—viz. how God is duly worshipped. Now I only briefly repeat, that whenever Scripture asserts the unity of God, it does not contend for a mere name, but also enjoins that nothing which belongs to Divinity be applied to any other ; thus making it obvious in what respect pure religion differs from superstition. The Greek word εὐσέβεια means " right worship ;" for the Greeks, though groping in darkness, were always aware that a certain rule was to be observed, in order that God might not be worshipped absurdly. Cicero truly and shrewdly derives the name *religion* from *relego,* and yet the reason which he assigns is forced and far-fetched—viz. that honest worshippers *read* and *read again,* and ponder what is true.[1] I rather think the name is used in opposition to *vagrant license*—the greater part of mankind rashly taking up whatever first comes in their way, whereas piety, that it may stand with a firm step, confines itself within due bounds. In the same way superstition seems to take its name from its not being contented with the measure which reason prescribes, but accumulating a superfluous mass of vanities. But to say nothing more of words, it has been universally admitted in all ages, that religion is vitiated and perverted whenever false opinions are introduced into it, and hence it is inferred, that whatever is allowed to be done from inconsiderate zeal, cannot be defended by any pretext with which

---

[1] Cic. De Nat. Deor. lib. ii. c. 28. See also Lactant. Inst. Div. lib. iv. c. 28.

the superstitious may choose to cloak it. But although this confession is in every man's mouth, a shameful stupidity is forthwith manifested, inasmuch as men neither cleave to the one God, nor use any selection in their worship, as we have already observed.

But God, in vindicating his own right, first proclaims that he is a jealous God, and will be a stern avenger if he is confounded with any false god; and thereafter defines what due worship is, in order that the human race may be kept in obedience. Both of these he embraces in his Law when he first binds the faithful in allegiance to him as their only Lawgiver, and then prescribes a rule for worshipping him in accordance with his will. The Law, with its manifold uses and objects, I will consider in its own place; at present I only advert to this one, that it is designed as a bridle to curb men, and prevent them from turning aside to spurious worship. But it is necessary to attend to the observation with which I set out—viz. that unless everything peculiar to divinity is confined to God alone, he is robbed of his honour, and his worship is violated.

It may be proper here more particularly to attend to the subtleties which superstition employs. In revolting to strange gods, it avoids the appearance of abandoning the Supreme God, or reducing him to the same rank with others. It gives him the highest place, but at the same time surrounds him with a tribe of minor deities, among whom it portions out his peculiar offices. In this way, though in a dissembling and crafty manner, the glory of the Godhead is dissected, and not allowed to remain entire. In the same way the people of old, both Jews and Gentiles, placed an immense crowd in subordination to the father and ruler of the gods, and gave them, according to their rank, to share with the supreme God in the government of heaven and earth. In the same way, too, for some ages past, departed saints have been exalted to partnership with God, to be worshipped, invoked, and lauded in his stead. And yet we do not even think that the majesty of God is obscured by this abomination, whereas it is in a great measure suppressed and extinguished—all that we retain being a frigid opinion of his supreme power. At the same time, being deluded by these entanglements, we go astray after divers gods.

2. The distinction of what is called *dulia* and *latria* was invented for the very purpose of permitting divine honours to be paid to angels and dead men with apparent impunity. For it is plain that the worship which Papists pay to saints differs in no respect from the worship of God: for this worship is paid without distinction; only when they are pressed they have recourse to the evasion, that what belongs to God is kept unimpaired, because they leave him *latria*. But since the question relates not to the word, but the thing, how can they be allowed to sport at will with a matter of the highest moment? But not to insist on this, the utmost they will obtain by their distinction is, that they give worship to God, and service to the others. For λατρεία in Greek has the same meaning as *worship* in Latin; whereas

δουλεία properly means *service*, though the words are sometimes used in Scripture indiscriminately. But granting that the distinction is invariably preserved, the thing to be inquired into is the meaning of each. Δουλεία unquestionably means service, and λατρεία worship. But no man doubts that to *serve* is something higher than to *worship*. For it were often a hard thing to serve him whom you would not refuse to reverence. It is, therefore, an unjust division to assign the greater to the saints and leave the less to God. But several of the ancient fathers observed this distinction. What if they did, when all men see that it is not only improper, but utterly frivolous?

3. Laying aside subtleties, let us examine the thing. When Paul reminds the Galatians of what they were before they came to the knowledge of God, he says, that they "did service unto them which by nature are no gods" (Gal. iv. 8). Because he does not say *latria*, was their superstition excusable? This superstition, to which he gives the name of *dulia*, he condemns as much as if he had given it the name of *latria*. When Christ repels Satan's insulting proposal with the words, "It is written, Thou shalt worship the Lord thy God, and him only shalt thou serve" (Matth. viii. 10), there was no question of *latria*. For all that Satan asked was προσκύνησις (obeisance). In like manner, when John is rebuked by the angel for falling on his knees before him (Rev. xix. 10; xxii. 8, 9), we ought not to suppose that John had so far forgotten himself as to have intended to transfer the honour due to God alone to an angel. But because it was impossible that a worship connected with religion should not savour somewhat of divine worship, he could not προσκύνειν (do obeisance to) the angel without derogating from the glory of God. True, we often read that men were worshipped; but that was, if I may so speak, civil honour. The case is different with religious honour, which, the moment it is conjoined with worship, carries profanation of the divine honour along with it. The same thing may be seen in the case of Cornelius (Acts x. 25). He had not made so little progress in piety as not to confine supreme worship to God alone. Therefore, when he prostrates himself before Peter, he certainly does it not with the intention of adoring him instead of God. Yet Peter sternly forbids him. And why, but just because men never distinguish so accurately between the worship of God and the creatures as not to transfer promiscuously to the creature that which belongs only to God. Therefore, if we would have one God, let us remember that we can never appropriate the minutest portion of his glory without retaining what is his due. Accordingly, when Zechariah discourses concerning the repairing of the Church, he distinctly says not only that there would be one God, but also that he would have only one name—the reason being, that he might have nothing in common with idols. The nature of the worship which God requires will be seen in its own place (Book II., c. vii. and viii.). He has been pleased to prescribe in his Law what is lawful and right, and thus astrict men to a certain rule,

lest any should allow themselves to devise a worship of their own. But as it is inexpedient to burden the reader by mixing up a variety of topics, I do not now dwell on this one. Let it suffice to remember, that whatever offices of piety are bestowed anywhere else than on God alone, are of the nature of sacrilege. First, superstition attached divine honours to the sun and stars, or to idols : afterwards ambition followed—ambition which, decking man in the spoils of God, dared to profane all that was sacred. And though the principle of worshipping a supreme Deity continued to be held, still the practice was to sacrifice promiscuously to genii and minor gods, or departed heroes : so prone is the descent to this vice of communicating to a crowd that which God strictly claims as his own peculiar right !

CHAPTER XIII.

THE UNITY OF THE DIVINE ESSENCE IN THREE PERSONS TAUGHT, IN
SCRIPTURE, FROM THE FOUNDATION OF THE WORLD.

This chapter consists of two parts. The former delivers the orthodox doctrine concerning the Holy Trinity. This occupies from sec. 1–21, and may be divided into four
heads ; the first, treating of the meaning of Person, including both the term and the
thing meant by it, sec. 2–6 ; the second, proving the deity of the Son, sec. 7–13 ; the
third, the deity of the Holy Spirit, sec, 14 and 15 ; and the fourth, explaining what
to be held concerning the Holy Trinity. The second part of the chapter refutes
certain heresies which have arisen, particularly in our age, in opposition to this orthodox doctrine. This occupies from sec. 21 to the end.

Sections.

1. Scripture, in teaching that the essence of God is immense and spiritual, refutes not
   only idolaters and the foolish wisdom of the world, but also the Manichees and
   Anthropomorphites. These latter briefly refuted.
2. In this one essence are three persons, yet so that neither is there a triple God,
   nor is the simple essence of God divided. Meaning of the word Person in this
   discussion. Three hypostases in God, or the essence of God.
3. Objection of those who, in this discussion, reject the use of the word Person.
   Answer 1. That it is not a foreign term, but is employed for the explanation of
   sacred mysteries.
4. Answer continued, 2. The orthodox compelled to use the terms, Trinity, Subsistence, and Person. Examples from the case of the Arians and Sabellians.
5. Answer continued, 3. The ancient Church, though differing somewhat in the
   explanation of these terms, agree in substance. Proofs from Hilary, Jerome,
   Augustine, in their use of the words Essence, Substance, Hypostasis 4. Provided
   the orthodox meaning is retained, there should be no dispute about mere terms.
   But those who object to the terms usually favour the Arian and Sabellian heresy.
6. After the definition of the term follows a definition and explanation of the thing
   meant by it. The distinction of Persons.
7. Proofs of the eternal Deity of the Son. The Son the λόγος of the Eternal Father,
   and, therefore, the Son Eternal God. Objection. Reply.
8. Objection, that the λόγος began to be when the creating God spoke. Answer confirmed by Scripture and argument.
9. The Son called God and Jehovah. Other names of the Eternal Father applied to
   him in the Old Testament. He is, therefore, the Eternal God. Another objection refuted. Case of the Jews explained.
10. The angel who appeared to the fathers under the Law asserts that he is Jehovah.
    That angel was the λόγος of the Eternal Father. The Son being that λόγος is
    Eternal God. Impiety of Servetus refuted. Why the Son appeared in the form
    of an angel.
11. Passages from the New Testament in which the Son is acknowledged to be the
    Lord of Hosts, the Judge of the world, the God of glory, the Creator of the world,
    the Lord of angels, the King of the Church, the eternal λόγος, God blessed for
    ever, God manifest in the flesh, the equal of God, the true God and eternal life,
    the Lord and God of all believers. Therefore, the Eternal God.
12. Christ the Creator, Preserver, Redeemer, and Searcher of hearts. Therefore, the
    Eternal God.
13. Christ, by his own inherent power, wrought miracles, and bestowed the power of

working them on others. Out of the Eternal God there is no salvation, no right-eousness, no life. All these are in Christ. Christ, consequently, is the Eternal God. He in whom we believe and hope, to whom we pray, whom the Church acknowledges as the Saviour of the faithful, whom to know is life eternal, in whom the pious glory, and through whom eternal blessings are communicated, is the Eternal God. All these Christ is, and, therefore, he is God.

14. The Divinity of the Spirit proved. I. He is the Creator and Preserver of the world. II. He sent the Prophets. III. He quickeneth all things. IV, He is everywhere present. V. He renews the saints, and fits them for eternal life. VI. All the offices of Deity belong to him.

15. The Divinity of the Spirit continued. VII. He is called God. VIII. Blasphemy against him is not forgiven.

16. What view to be taken of the Trinity. The form of Christian baptism proves that there are three persons in one essence. The Arian and Macedonian heresies.

17. Of the distinction of Persons. They are distinct, but not divided. This proved.

18. Analogies taken from human affairs to be cautiously used. Due regard to be paid to those mentioned by Scripture.

19. How the Three Persons not only do not destroy, but constitute the most perfect unity.

20. Conclusion of this part of the chapter, and summary of the true doctrine concern-ing the unity of Essence and the Three Persons.

21. Refutation of Arian, Macedonian, and Antitrinitarian heresies. Caution to be observed.

22. The more modern Antitrinitarians, and especially Servetus, refuted.

23. Other Antitrinitarians refuted. No good objection that Christ is called the Son of God, since he is also called God. Impious absurdities of some heretics.

24. The name of God sometimes given to the Son absolutely as to the Father. Same as to other attributes. Objections refuted.

25. Objections further refuted. Caution to be used.

26. Previous refutations further explained.

27. Reply to certain passages produced from Irenæus. The meaning of Irenæus.

28. Reply to certain passages produced from Tertullian. The meaning of Tertullian.

29. Antitrinitarians refuted by ancient Christian writers ; e g., Justin, Hilary. Ob-jections drawn from writings improperly attributed to Ignatius. Conclusion of the whole discussion concerning the Trinity.

1. THE doctrine of Scripture concerning the immensity and the spirituality of the essence of God, should have the effect not only of dissipating the wild dreams of the vulgar, but also of refuting the subtleties of a profane philosophy. One of the ancients thought he spake shrewdly when he said that everything we see and everything we do not see is God (Senec. Præf. lib. i. Quæst. Nat.). In this way he fancied that the Divinity was transfused into every separate portion of the world. But although God, in order to keep us within the bounds of soberness, treats sparingly of his essence, still, by the two attributes which I have mentioned, he at once suppresses all gross imaginations, and checks the audacity of the human mind. His im-mensity surely ought to deter us from measuring him by our sense, while his spiritual nature forbids us to indulge in carnal or earthly speculation concerning him. With the same view he frequently re-presents heaven as his dwelling-place. It is true, indeed, that as he is incomprehensible, he fills the earth also, but knowing that our minds are heavy and grovel on the earth, he raises us above the world, that he may shake off our sluggishness and inactivity. And here we have a refutation of the error of the Manichees, who, by adopting two first principles, made the devil almost the equal of God.

This, assuredly, was both to destroy his unity and restrict his immensity. Their attempt to pervert certain passages of Scripture proved their shameful ignorance, as the very nature of the error did their monstrous infatuation. The Anthropomorphites also, who dreamed of a corporeal God, because mouth, ears, eyes, hands, and feet are often ascribed to him in Scripture, are easily refuted. For who is so devoid of intellect as not to understand that God, in so speaking, lisps with us as nurses are wont to do with little children? Such modes of expression, therefore, do not so much express what kind of a being God is, as accommodate the knowledge of him to our feebleness. In doing so, he must of course stoop far below his proper height.

2. But there is another special mark by which he designates himself, for the purpose of giving a more intimate knowledge of his nature. While he proclaims his unity, he distinctly sets it before us as existing in three persons. These we must hold, unless the bare and empty name of Deity merely is a flutter in our brain without any genuine knowledge. Moreover, lest any one should dream of a threefold God, or think that the simple essence is divided by the three Persons, we must here seek a brief and easy definition which may effectually guard us from error. But as some strongly inveigh against the term Person as being merely of human invention, let us first consider how far they have any ground for doing so.

When the Apostle calls the Son of God "the express image of his person" (Heb. i. 3), he undoubtedly does assign to the Father some subsistence in which he differs from the Son. For to hold with some interpreters that the term is equivalent to essence (as if Christ represented the substance of the Father like the impression of a seal upon wax), were not only harsh but absurd. For the essence of God being simple and undivided, and contained in himself entire, in full perfection, without partition or diminution, it is improper, nay, ridiculous, to call it his express image (χαρακτηρ). But because the Father, though distinguished by his own peculiar properties, has expressed himself wholly in the Son, he is said with perfect reason to have' rendered his person (hypostasis) manifest in him. And this aptly accords with what is immediately added—viz. that he is "the brightness of his glory." The fair inference from the Apostle's words is, that there is a proper subsistence (hypostasis) of the Father, which shines refulgent in the Son. From this, again, it is easy to infer that there is a subsistence (hypostasis) of the Son which distinguishes him from the Father. The same holds in the case of the Holy Spirit; for we will immediately prove both that he is God, and that he has a separate subsistence from the Father. This, moreover, is not a distinction of essence, which it were impious to multiply. If credit, then, is given to the Apostle's testimony, it follows that there are three persons (hypostases) in God. The Latins having used the word *Persona* to express the same thing as the Greek ὑποστασις, it betrays excessive fastidiousness and even perverseness to quarrel with the term. The most literal translation would be *subsistence*. Many have used *substance* in the same sense. Nor, indeed, was the use of the term Person confined to the Latin Church. For the Greek Church in like manner, perhaps for the purpose of testifying their consent, have taught that there are three προσωπα (*aspects*) in God. All these, however, whether Greeks or Latins, though differing as to the word, are perfectly agreed in substance.

3. Now, then, though heretics may snarl and the excessively fastidious carp at the word Person as inadmissible, in consequence of its human origin, since they cannot displace us from our position that three are named, each of whom is perfect God, and yet that there is no plurality of gods, it is most uncandid to attack the terms which do nothing more than explain what the Scriptures declare and sanction. " It were better," they say, " to confine not only our meanings but our words within the bounds of Scripture, and not scatter about foreign terms to become the future seed-beds of brawls and dissensions. In this way, men grow tired of quarrels about words ; the truth is lost in altercation, and charity melts away amid hateful strife." If they call it a *foreign* term, because it cannot be pointed out in Scripture in so many syllables, they certainly impose an unjust law—a law which would condemn every interpretation of Scripture that is not composed of other words of Scripture. But if by *foreign* they mean that which, after being idly devised, is superstitiously defended,—which tends more to strife than edification,—which is used either out of place, or with no benefit,—which offends pious ears by its harshness, and leads them away from the simplicity of God's Word, I embrace their soberness with all my heart. For I think we are bound to speak of God as reverently as we are bound to think of him. As our own thoughts respecting him are foolish, so our own language respecting him is absurd. Still, however, some medium must be observed. The unerring standard both of thinking and speaking must be derived from the Scriptures : by it all the thoughts of our minds, and the words of our mouths, should be tested. But in regard to those parts of Scripture which, to our capacities, are dark and intricate, what forbids us to explain them in clearer terms —terms, however, kept in reverent and faithful subordination to Scripture truth, used sparingly and modestly, and not without occasion? Of this we are not without many examples. When it has been proved that the Church was impelled, by the strongest necessity, to use the words Trinity and Person, will not he who still inveighs against novelty of terms be deservedly suspected of taking offence at the light of truth, and of having no other ground for his invective, than that the truth is made plain and transparent ?

4. Such novelty (if novelty it should be called) becomes most requisite, when the truth is to be maintained against calumniators who evade it by quibbling. Of this, we of the present day have too much

experience in being constantly called upon to attack the enemies of pure and sound doctrine. These slippery snakes escape by their swift and tortuous windings, if not strenuously pursued, and when caught, firmly held. Thus the early Christians, when harassed with the disputes which heresies produced, were forced to declare their sentiments in terms most scrupulously exact in order that no indirect subterfuges might remain to ungodly men, to whom ambiguity of expression was a kind of hiding-place. Arius confessed that Christ was God, and the Son of God; because the passages of Scripture to this effect were too clear to be resisted, and then, as if he had done well, pretended to concur with others. But, meanwhile, he ceased not to give out that Christ was created, and had a beginning like other creatures. To drag this man of wiles out of his lurking-places, the ancient Church took a further step, and declared that Christ is the eternal Son of the Father, and consubstantial with the Father. The impiety was fully disclosed when the Arians began to declare their hatred and utter detestation of the term ὁμοουσίος. Had their first confession—viz. that Christ was God—been sincere and from the heart, they would not have denied that he was consubstantial with the Father. Who dare charge those ancient writers as men of strife and contention, for having debated so warmly, and disturbed the quiet of the Church for a single word? That little word distinguished between Christians of pure faith and the blasphemous Arians. Next Sabellius arose, who counted the names of Father, Son, and Holy Spirit, as almost nonentities; maintaining that they were not used to mark out some distinction, but that they were different attributes of God, like many others of a similar kind. When the matter was debated, he acknowledged his belief that the Father was God the Son God, the Spirit God; but then he had the evasion ready, that he had said nothing more than if he had called God powerful, and just, and wise. Accordingly, he sang another note—viz. that the Father was the Son, and the Holy Spirit the Father, without order or distinction. The worthy doctors who then had the interests of piety at heart, in order to defeat this man's dishonesty, proclaimed that three subsistences were to be truly acknowledged in the one God. That they might protect themselves against tortuous craftiness by the simple open truth, they affirmed that a Trinity of Persons subsisted in the one God, or (which is the same thing) in the unity of God.

5. Where names have not been invented rashly, we must beware lest we become chargeable with arrogance and rashness in rejecting them. I wish, indeed, that such names were buried, provided all would concur in the belief that the Father, Son, and Spirit, are one God, and yet that the Son is not the Father, nor the Spirit the Son, but that each has his peculiar subsistence. I am not so minutely precise as to fight furiously for mere words. For I observe, that the writers of the ancient Church, while they uniformly spoke with great reverence on these matters, neither agreed with each other, nor were

always consistent with themselves.   How strange the formulæ used by Councils, and defended by Hilary!   How extravagant the view which Augustine sometimes takes!   How unlike the Greeks are to the Latins!   But let one example of variance suffice.   The Latins, in translating ὁμοουσίος, used *consubstantialis* (consubstantial), intimating that there was one substance of the Father and the Son, and thus using the word Substance for Essence.   Hence Jerome, in his Letter to Damascus, says it is profane to affirm that there are three Substances in God.   But in Hilary you will find it said more than a hundred times that there are three substances in God.   Then how greatly is Jerome perplexed with the word Hypostasis!   He suspects some lurking poison, when it is said that there are three Hypostases in God.   And he does not disguise his belief that the expression, though used in a pious sense, is improper ; if, indeed, he was sincere in saying this, and did not rather designedly endeavour, by an unfounded calumny, to throw odium on the Eastern bishops whom he hated.   He certainly shows little candour in asserting, that in all heathen schools οὐσία is equivalent to Hypostasis—an assertion completely refuted by trite and common use.

More courtesy and moderation is shown by Augustine (De Trinit. lib. v. c. 8 and 9), who, although he says that Hypostasis in this sense is new to Latin ears, is still so far from objecting to the ordinary use of the term by the Greeks, that he is even tolerant of the Latins, who had imitated the Greek phraseology.   The purport of what Socrates says of the term, in the Sixth Book of the Tripartite History, is, that it had been improperly applied to this purpose by the unskilful.   Hilary (De Trinitat. lib. ii.) charges it upon the heretics as a great crime, that their misconduct had rendered it necessary to subject to the peril of human utterance, things which ought to have been reverently confined within the mind, not disguising his opinion that those who do so, do what is unlawful, speak what is ineffable, and pry into what is forbidden.   Shortly after, he apologises at great length for presuming to introduce new terms. For, after putting down the natural names of Father, Son, and Spirit, he adds, that all further inquiry transcends the significancy of words, the discernment of sense, and the apprehension of intellect.   And in another place (De Conciliis), he congratulates the Bishops of France in not having framed any other confession, but received, without alteration, the ancient and most simple confession received by all Churches from the days of the Apostles.   Not unlike this is the apology of Augustine, that the term had been wrung from him by necessity, from the poverty of human language in so high a matter: not that the reality could be thereby expressed, but that he might not pass on in silence without attempting to show how the Father, Son, and Spirit are three.

The modesty of these holy men should be an admonition to us not instantly to dip our pen in gall, and sternly denounce those who may be unwilling to swear to the terms which we have devised, provided they do not in this betray pride, or petulance, or unbecoming heat, but are willing to ponder the necessity which compels us so to speak, and may thus become gradually accustomed to a useful form of expression.   Let men also studiously beware, that in opposing the Arians on the one hand, and the Sabellians on the other, and eagerly endeavouring to deprive both of any handle for cavil, they do not bring themselves under some suspicion of being the disciples of either Arius or Sabellius.   Arius says, that *Christ is God*, and then mutters that *he was made, and had a beginning.*   He says, that *he is one with the Father ;* but secretly whispers in the ears of his party, *made one*, like other believers, though with special privilege.   Say, *he is consubstantial*, and you immediately pluck the mask from this chameleon, though you add nothing to Scripture.   Sabellius says, that *the Father, Son, and Spirit, indicate some distinction in God.*   Say, *they are three*, and he will bawl out that you are making three Gods.   Say, that *there is a Trinity of persons in one Divine essence*, you will only express in one word what the Scriptures say, and stop his empty prattle.   Should any be so superstitiously precise as not to tolerate these terms, still do their worst, they will not be able to deny that when *one* is spoken of, a unity of substance must be understood, and when *three* in one essence, the persons in this Trinity are denoted. When this is confessed without equivocation, we dwell not on words. But I was long ago made aware, and indeed, on more than one occasion, that those who contend pertinaciously about words are tainted with some hidden poison ; and, therefore, that it is more expedient to provoke them purposely, than to court their favour by speaking obscurely.

6. But to say nothing more of words, let us now attend to the thing signified.   By *person*, then, I mean a subsistence in the Divine essence,—a subsistence which, while related to the other two, is distinguished from them by incommunicable properties.   By *subsistence* we wish something else to be understood than *essence*.   For if the Word were God simply, and had not some property peculiar to himself, John could not have said correctly that he had always been with God.   When he adds immediately after, that the Word was God, he calls us back to the one essence.   But because he could not be with God without dwelling in the Father, hence arises that subsistence, which, though connected with the essence by an indissoluble tie, being incapable of separation, yet has a special mark by which it is distinguished from it.   Now, I say that each of the three subsistences while related to the others, is distinguished by its own properties.   Here relation is distinctly expressed, because, when God is mentioned simply and indefinitely, the name belongs not less to the Son and Spirit than to the Father.   But whenever the Father is compared with the Son, the peculiar property of each distinguishes the one from the other.   Again, whatever is proper to each I affirm

to be incommunicable, because nothing can apply or be transferred to the Son which is attributed to the Father as a mark of distinction. I have no objections to adopt the definition of Tertullian, provided it is properly understood, "that there is in God a certain arrangement or economy, which makes no change on the unity of essence." —Tertull. Lib. contra Praxeam.

7. Before proceeding farther, it will be necessary to prove the Divinity of the Son and the Holy Spirit. Thereafter, we shall see how they differ from each other. When the Word of God is set before us in the Scriptures, it were certainly most absurd to imagine that it is only a fleeting and evanescent voice, which is sent out into the air, and comes forth beyond God himself, as was the case with the communications made to the patriarchs, and all the prophecies. The reference is rather to the wisdom ever dwelling with God, and by which all oracles and prophecies were inspired. For, as Peter testifies (1 Pet. i. 11), the ancient prophets spake by the Spirit of Christ just as did the apostles, and all who after them were ministers of the heavenly doctrine. But as Christ was not yet manifested, we necessarily understand that the Word was begotten of the Father before all ages. But if that Spirit, whose organs the prophets were, belonged to the Word, the inference is irresistible, that the Word was truly God. And this is clearly enough shown by Moses in his account of the creation, where he places the Word as intermediate. For why does he distinctly narrate that God, in creating each of his works, said, Let there be this—let there be that, unless that the unsearchable glory of God might shine forth in his image? I know prattlers would easily evade this, by saying that *Word* is used for *order* or *command;* but the apostles are better expositors, when they tell us that the worlds were created by the Son, and that he sustains all things by his mighty word (Heb. i. 2). For we here see that *word* is used for the nod or command of the Son, who is himself the eternal and essential Word of the Father. And no man of sane mind can have any doubt as to Solomon's meaning, when he introduces Wisdom as begotten by God, and presiding at the creation of the world, and all other divine operations (Prov. viii. 22). For it were trifling and foolish to imagine any temporary command at a time when God was pleased to execute his fixed and eternal counsel, and something more still mysterious. To this our Saviour's words refer, "My Father worketh hitherto, and I work" (John v. 17). In thus affirming, that from the foundation of the world he constantly worked with the Father, he gives a clearer explanation of what Moses simply touched. The meaning therefore is, that God spoke in such a manner as left the Word his peculiar part in the work, and thus made the operation common to both. But the clearest explanation is given by John, when he states that the Word which was from the beginning, God and with God, was, together with God the Father, the maker of all things. For he both attributes a substantial and permanent

essence to the Word, assigning to it a certain peculiarity, and distinctly showing how God spoke the world into being. Therefore, as all revelations from heaven are duly designated by the title of the Word of God, so the highest place must be assigned to that substantial Word, the source of all inspiration, which, as being liable to no variation, remains for ever one and the same with God, and is God.

8. Here an outcry is made by certain men, who, while they dare not openly deny his divinity, secretly rob him of his eternity. For they contend that the Word only began to be when God opened his sacred mouth in the creation of the world. Thus, with excessive temerity, they imagine some change in the essence of God. For as the names of God, which have respect to external work, began to be ascribed to him from the existence of the work (as when he is called the Creator of heaven and earth), so piety does not recognise or admit any name which might indicate that a change had taken place in God himself. For if anything adventitious took place, the saying of James would cease to be true, that "every good gift, and every perfect gift, is from above, and cometh down from the Father of lights, with whom is no variableness, neither shadow of turning" (James i. 17). Nothing, therefore, is more intolerable than to fancy a beginning to that Word which was always God, and afterwards was the Creator of the world. But they think they argue acutely, in maintaining that Moses, when he says that God then spoke for the first time, must be held to intimate that till then no Word existed in him. This is the merest trifling. It does not surely follow, that because a thing begins to be manifested at a certain time, it never existed previously. I draw a very different conclusion. Since at the very moment when God said, "Let there be light," the energy of the Word was immediately exerted, it must have existed long before. If any inquire how long, he will find it was without beginning. No certain period of time is defined, when he himself says, "Now, O Father, glorify thou me with thine own self, with the glory which I had with thee before the world was" (John xvii. 5). Nor is this omitted by John : for before he descends to the creation of the world, he says, that "in the beginning was the Word, and the Word was with God." We, therefore, again conclude, that the Word was eternally begotten by God, and dwelt with him from everlasting. In this way, his true essence, his eternity, and divinity, are established.

9. But though I am not now treating of the office of the Mediator having deferred it till the subject of redemption is considered, yet because it ought to be clear and incontrovertible to all, that Christ is that Word become incarnate, this seems the most appropriate place to introduce those passages which assert the Divinity of Christ. When it is said in the forty-fifth Psalm, "Thy throne, O God, is for ever and ever," the Jews quibble that the name Elohim is applied to angels and sovereign powers. But no passage is to be found in Scripture, where an eternal throne is set up for a creature. For he

is not called God simply, but also the eternal Ruler. Besides, the title is not conferred on any man, without some addition, as when it is said that Moses would be a God to Pharaoh (Exod. vii. 1). Some read as if it were in the genitive case, but this is too insipid. I admit, that anything possessed of singular excellence is often called divine, but it is clear from the context, that this meaning here were harsh and forced, and totally inapplicable. But if their perverseness still refuses to yield, surely there is no obscurity in Isaiah, where Christ is introduced both as God, and as possessed of supreme power, one of the peculiar attributes of God, "His name shall be called the Mighty God, the Everlasting Father, the Prince of Peace (Isa. xi. 6). Here, too, the Jews object, and invert the passage thus, This is the name by which the mighty God, the Everlasting Father, will call him ; so that all which they leave to the Son is, "Prince of Peace." But why should so many epithets be here accumulated on God the Father, seeing the prophet's design is to present the Messiah with certain distinguished properties which may induce us to put our faith in him ? There can be no doubt, therefore, that he who a little before was called Immanuel, is here called the Mighty God. Moreover, there can be nothing clearer than the words of Jeremiah, "This is the name whereby he shall be called, THE LORD OUR RIGHTEOUSNESS" (Jer. xxiii. 6). For as the Jews themselves teach that the other names of God are mere epithets, whereas this, which they call the ineffable name, is substantive, and expresses his essence, we infer, that the only begotten Son is the eternal God, who elsewhere declares, "My glory will I not give to another" (Isa. xlii. 8). An attempt is made to evade this from the fact, that this name is given by Moses to the altar which he built, and by Ezekiel to the New Jerusalem. But who sees not that the altar was erected as a memorial to show that God was the exalter of Moses, and that the name of God was applied to Jerusalem, merely to testify the Divine presence ? For thus the prophet speaks, "The name of the city from that day shall be, The Lord is there" (Ezek. xlviii. 35). In the same way, "Moses built an altar, and called the name of it JEHOVAH-nissi" (Jehovah my exaltation). But it would seem the point is still more keenly disputed as to another passage in Jeremiah, where the same title is applied to Jerusalem in these words, "In those days shall Judah be saved, and Jerusalem shall dwell safely ; and this is the name wherewith she shall be called, The Lord our Righteousness." But so far is this passage from being adverse to the truth which we defend, that it rather supports it. The prophet having formerly declared that Christ is the true Jehovah from whom righteousness flows, now declares that the Church would be made so sensible of this as to be able to glory in assuming his very name. In the former passage, therefore, the fountain and cause of righteousness is set down ; in the latter, the effect is described.

10. But if this does not satisfy the Jews, I know not what cavils

will enable them to evade the numerous passages in which Jehovah is said to have appeared in the form of an Angel (Judges vi. vii. xiii. 16—23, &c.). This angel claims for himself the name of the Eternal God. Should it be alleged that this is done in respect of the office which he bears, the difficulty is by no means solved. No servant would rob God of his honour, by allowing sacrifice to be offered to himself. But the Angel, by refusing to eat bread, orders the sacrifice due to Jehovah to be offered to him. Thus the fact itself proves that he was truly Jehovah. Accordingly, Manoah and his wife infer from the sign, that they had seen not only an angel, but God. Hence Manoah's exclamation, "We shall die; for we have seen the Lord." When the woman replies, "If Jehovah had wished to slay us, he would not have received the sacrifice at our hand," she acknowledges that he who is previously called an angel was certainly God. We may add, that the angel's own reply removes all doubt, "Why do ye ask my name, which is wonderful?" Hence the impiety of Servetus was the more detestable, when he maintained that God was never manifested to Abraham and the Patriarchs, but that an angel was worshipped in his stead. The orthodox doctors of the Church have correctly and wisely expounded, that the Word of God was the supreme angel, who then began, as it were by anticipation, to perform the office of Mediator. For though he were not clothed with flesh, yet he descended as in an intermediate form, that he might have more familiar access to the faithful. This closer intercourse procured for him the name of the Angel; still, however, he retained the character which justly belonged to him—that of the God of ineffable glory. The same thing is intimated by Hosea, who, after mentioning the wrestling of Jacob with the angel, says, "Even the Lord God of hosts; the Lord is his memorial" (Hosea xii. 5). Servetus again insinuates that God personated an angel; as if the prophet did not confirm what had been said by Moses, "Wherefore is it that thou dost ask after my name?" (Gen. xxxii. 29, 30). And the confession of the holy Patriarch sufficiently declares that he was not a created angel, but one in whom the fulness of the Godhead dwelt, when he says, "I have seen God face to face." Hence also Paul's statement, that Christ led the people in the wilderness (1 Cor. x. 4. See also Calvin on Acts vii. 30, and *infra*, chap. xiv., s. 9). Although the time of humiliation had not yet arrived, the eternal Word exhibited a type of the office which he was to fulfil. Again, if the first chapter of Zechariah (ver. 9, &c.) and the second (ver. 3, &c.) be candidly considered, it will be seen that the angel who sends the other angel is immediately after declared to be the Lord of hosts, and that supreme power is ascribed to him. I omit numberless passages in which our faith rests secure, though they may not have much weight with the Jews. For when it is said in Isaiah, "Lo, this is our God; we have waited for him, and he will save us: this is the Lord; we have waited for him, we will be glad and rejoice in his salvation" (Isa. xxv. 9), even the blind may see that the God referred to is he who again rises up for the deliverance of his people. And the emphatic description, twice repeated, precludes the idea that reference is made to any other than to Christ. Still clearer and stronger is the passage of Malachi, in which a promise is made that the messenger who was then expected would come to his own temple (Mal. iii. 1). The temple certainly was dedicated to Almighty God only, and yet the prophet claims it for Christ. Hence it follows, that he is the God who was always worshipped by the Jews.

11. The New Testament teems with innumerable passages, and our object must therefore be, the selection of a few, rather than an accumulation of the whole. But though the Apostles spoke of him after his appearance in the flesh as Mediator, every passage which I adduce will be sufficient to prove his eternal Godhead. And the first thing deserving of special observation is, that predictions concerning the eternal God are applied to Christ, as either already fulfilled in him, or to be fulfilled at some future period. Isaiah prophesies, that "the Lord of Hosts" shall be "for a stone of stumbling, and for a rock of offence" (Isa. viii. 14). Paul asserts that this prophecy was fulfilled in Christ (Rom. ix. 33), and therefore declares that Christ is that Lord of Hosts. In like manner, he says in another passage, "We shall all stand before the judgment-seat of Christ. For it is written, As I live, saith the Lord, every knee shall bow to me, and every tongue shall confess to God." Since in Isaiah God predicts this of himself (Isa. xlv. 23), and Christ exhibits the reality fulfilled in himself, it follows that he is the very God, whose glory cannot be given to another. It is clear also, that the passage from the Psalms (Ps. lxviii. 19) which he quotes in the Epistle to the Ephesians, is applicable only to God, "When he ascended up on high, he led captivity captive" (Eph. iv. 8). Understanding that such an ascension was shadowed forth when the Lord exerted his power, and gained a glorious victory over heathen nations, he intimates that what was thus shadowed was more fully manifested in Christ. So John testifies that it was the glory of the Son which was revealed to Isaiah in a vision (John xii. 41; Isa. vi. 4), though Isaiah himself expressly says that what he saw was the Majesty of God. Again, there can be no doubt that those qualities which, in the Epistle to the Hebrews, are applied to the Son, are the brightest attributes of God, "Thou, Lord, in the beginning hast laid the foundation of the earth," &c., and, "Let all the angels of God worship him" (Heb. i. 10, 6). And yet he does not pervert the passages in thus applying them to Christ, since Christ alone performed the things which these passages celebrate. It was he who arose and pitied Zion—he who claimed for himself dominion over all nations and islands. And why should John have hesitated to ascribe the Majesty of God to Christ, after saying in his preface that the Word was God? (John i. 14). Why should Paul have feared to place

Christ on the judgment-seat of God (2 Cor. v. 10), after he had so openly proclaimed his divinity, when he said that he was God over all, blessed for ever? And to show how consistent he is in this respect, he elsewhere says that "God was manifest in the flesh" (1 Tim. iii. 16). If he is God blessed for ever, he therefore it is to whom alone, as Paul affirms in another place, all glory and honour is due. Paul does not disguise this, but openly exclaims, that "being in the form of God, (he) thought it not robbery to be equal with God, but made himself of no reputation" (Phil. ii. 6). And lest the wicked should clamour and say that he was a kind of spurious God, John goes farther, and affirms, "This is the true God, and eternal life." Though it ought to be enough for us that he is called God, especially by a witness who distinctly testifies that we have no more gods than one, Paul says, "Though there be that are called gods, whether in heaven or in earth (as there be gods many, and lords many), but to us there is but one God" (1 Cor. viii. 5, 6). When we hear from the same lips that God was manifest in the flesh, that God purchased the Church with his own blood, why do we dream of any second God, to whom he makes not the least allusion? And there is no room to doubt that all the godly entertained the same view. Thomas, by addressing him as his Lord and God, certainly professes that he was the only God whom he had ever adored (John xx. 28).

12. The divinity of Christ, if judged by the works which are ascribed to him in Scripture, becomes still more evident. When he said of himself, "My Father worketh hitherto, and I work," the Jews, though most dull in regard to his other sayings, perceived that he was laying claim to divine power. And, therefore, as John relates (John v. 17), they sought the more to kill him, because he not only broke the Sabbath, but also said that God was his Father, making himself equal with God. What, then, will be our stupidity if we do not perceive from the same passage that his divinity is plainly instructed? To govern the world by his power and providence, and regulate all things by an energy inherent in himself (this an Apostle ascribes to him, Heb. 1. 3), surely belongs to none but the Creator. Nor does he merely share the government of the world with the Father, but also each of the other offices, which cannot be communicated to creatures. The Lord proclaims by his prophet, "I, even I, am he that blotteth out thy transgressions for mine own sake" (Isa. xliii. 25). When, in accordance with this declaration, the Jews thought that injustice was done to God when Christ forgave sins, he not only asserted, in distinct terms, that this power belonged to him, but also proved it by a miracle (Matth. ix. 6). We thus see that he possessed in himself not the ministry of forgiving sins, but the inherent power which the Lord declares he will not give to another. What! Is it not the province of God alone to penetrate and interrogate the secret thoughts of the heart? But Christ also had this power, and therefore we infer that Christ is God.

13. How clearly and transparently does this appear in his miracles? I admit that similar and equal miracles were performed by the prophets and apostles; but there is this very essential difference, that they dispensed the gifts of God as his ministers, whereas he exerted his own inherent might. Sometimes, indeed, he used prayer, that he might ascribe glory to the Father, but we see that for the most part his own proper power is displayed. And how should not he be the true author of miracles, who, of his own authority, commissions others to perform them? For the Evangelist relates that he gave power to the apostles to cast out devils, cure the lepers, raise the dead, &c. And they, by the mode in which they performed this ministry, showed plainly that their whole power was derived from Christ. "In the name of Jesus Christ of Nazareth," says Peter, (Acts iii. 6), "rise up and walk." It is not surprising, then, that Christ appealed to his miracles in order to subdue the unbelief of the Jews, inasmuch as these were performed by his own energy, and therefore bore the most ample testimony to his divinity.

Again, if out of God there is no salvation, no righteousness, no life, Christ, having all these in himself, is certainly God. Let no one object that life or salvation is transfused into him by God. For it is said not that he received, but that he himself is salvation. And if there is none good but God, how could a mere man be pure, how could he be, I say not good and just, but goodness and justice? Then what shall we say to the testimony of the Evangelist, that from the very beginning of the creation "in him was life, and this life was the light of men?" Trusting to such proofs, we can boldly put our hope and faith in him, though we know it is blasphemous impiety to confide in any creature.[1] " Ye believe in God,"[2] says he, " believe also in me" (John xiv. 1). And so Paul (Rom. x. 11, and xv. 12) interprets two passages of Isaiah, " Whoso believeth in him shall not be confounded" (Isa. xxviii. 16); and, " In that day there shall be a root of Jesse, which shall stand for an ensign of the people; to it shall the Gentiles seek" (Isa. xi. 10). But why adduce more passages of Scripture on this head, when we so often meet with the expression, " He that believeth in me hath eternal life"?

Again the prayer of faith is addressed to him—prayer, which specially belongs to the divine majesty, if anything so belongs. For the prophet Joel says, " And it shall come to pass, that whosoever shall call on the name of the Lord (Jehovah) shall be delivered" (Joel ii. 32). And another says, " The name of the Lord (Jehovah) is a strong tower; the righteous runneth into it and is safe" (Prov. xviii. 10). But the name of Christ is invoked for salvation, and therefore it follows that he is Jehovah. Moreover, we have an example of invocation in Stephen, when he said, " Lord Jesus, receive my spirit;"

---

1 The French adds, "Et ne faisons point cela témérairement, mais selon sa parole." —And let us not do this rashly, but in accordance with his Word.
2 Calvin translates interrogatively, " Do ye believe in God?"

and thereafter in the whole Church, when Ananias says in the same
book, " Lord, I have heard by many of this man, how much evil he
hath done to thy saints at Jerusalem ; and here he hath authority
from the chief priests to bind all that call on thy name" (Acts ix.
13, 14). And to make it more clearly understood that in Christ
dwelt the whole fulness of the Godhead bodily, the Apostle declares
that the only doctrine which he professed to the Corinthians, the only
doctrine which he taught, was the knowledge of Christ (1 Cor. ii. 2).
Consider what kind of thing it is, and how great, that the name of
the Son alone is preached to us, though God command us to glory
only in the knowledge of himself (Jer. ix. 24). Who will dare to
maintain that he, whom to know forms our only ground of glorying,
is a mere creature ? To this we may add, that the salutations pre-
fixed to the Epistles of Paul pray for the same blessings from the Son
as from the Father. By this we are taught, not only that the blessings which our heavenly Father bestows come to us through his intercession, but that by a partnership in power, the Son himself is
their author. This practical knowledge is doubtless surer and more
solid than any idle speculation. For the pious soul has the best view
of God, and may almost be said to handle him, when it feels that it
is quickened, enlightened, saved, justified, and sanctified by him.

14. In asserting the divinity of the Spirit, the proof must be derived from the same sources. And it is by no means an obscure testimony which Moses bears in the history of the creation, when he says
that the Spirit of God was expanded over the abyss or shapeless
matter ; for it shows not only that the beauty which the world displays
is maintained by the invigorating power of the Spirit, but that even
before this beauty existed the Spirit was at work cherishing the confused mass.[1] Again, no cavils can explain away the force of what
Isaiah says, " And now the Lord God, and his Spirit, hath sent me"
(Isa. xlviii. 16), thus ascribing a share in the sovereign power of
sending the prophets to the Holy Spirit. (Calvin in Acts xx. 28.)
In this his divine majesty is clear.

But, as I observed, the best proof to us is our familiar experience.
For nothing can be more alien from a creature, than the office which
the Scriptures ascribe to him, and which the pious actually feel him
discharging,—his being diffused over all space, sustaining, invigorating, and quickening all things, both in heaven and on the earth. The
mere fact of his not being circumscribed by any limits raises him
above the rank of creatures, while his transfusing vigour into all
things, breathing into them being, life, and motion, is plainly divine.
Again, if regeneration to incorruptible life is higher, and much more
excellent than any present quickening, what must be thought of him
by whose energy it is produced ? Now, many passages of Scripture
show that he is the author of regeneration, not by a borrowed, but

[1] The French adds, "à ce qu'elle ne fust point aneantie incontinent ;"—so as to prevent its being instantly annihilated.

by an intrinsic energy; and not only so, but that he is also the author of future immortality. In short, all the peculiar attributes of the Godhead are ascribed to him in the same way as to the Son. He searches the deep things of God, and has no counsellor among the creatures; he bestows wisdom and the faculty of speech, though God declares to Moses (Exod. iv. 11) that this is his own peculiar province. In like manner, by means of him we become partakers of the divine nature, so as in a manner to feel his quickening energy within us. Our justification is his work; from him is power, sanctification, truth, grace, and every good thought, since it is from the Spirit alone that all good gifts proceed. Particular attention is due to Paul's expression, that though there are diversities of gifts, "all these worketh that one and the self-same Spirit" (1 Cor. xii. 11), he being not only the beginning or origin, but also the author;[1] as is even more clearly expressed immediately after, in these words, "dividing to every man severally as he will." For were he not something subsisting in God, will and arbitrary disposal would never be ascribed to him. Most clearly, therefore, does Paul ascribe divine power to the Spirit, and demonstrate that he dwells hypostatically in God.

15. Nor does the Scripture, in speaking of him, withhold the name of God. Paul infers that we are the temple of God, from the fact that "the Spirit of God dwelleth in us" (1 Cor. iii. 16; vi. 19; and 2 Cor. vi. 16). Now, it ought not to be slightly overlooked, that all the promises which God makes of choosing us to himself as a temple, receive their only fulfilment by his Spirit dwelling in us. Surely, as it is admirably expressed by Augustine (Ad Maximinum, Ep. 66), "were we ordered to make a temple of wood and stone to the Spirit, inasmuch as such worship is due to God alone, it would be a clear proof of the Spirit's divinity; how much clearer a proof in that we are not to make a temple to him, but to be ourselves that temple." And the Apostle says at one time that we are the temple of God, and at another time, in the same sense, that we are the temple of the Holy Spirit. Peter, when he rebuked Ananias for having lied to the Holy Spirit, said, that he had not lied unto men, but unto God. And when Isaiah had introduced the Lord of Hosts as speaking, Paul says, it was the Holy Spirit that spoke (Acts xxviii. 25, 26). Nay, words uniformly said by the prophets to have been spoken by the Lord of Hosts, are by Christ and his apostles ascribed to the Holy Spirit. Hence it follows that the Spirit is the true Jehovah, who dictated the prophecies. Again, when God complains that he was provoked to anger by the stubbornness of the people, in place of Him, Isaiah says that his Holy Spirit was grieved (Isa. lxiii. 10). Lastly, while blasphemy against the Spirit is not forgiven, either in the present life or that which is to come, whereas he who has blasphemed against the

---

[1] The French adds, "Sainct Paul n'eust jamais ainsi parlé, s'il n'eust cognu la vraie Divinité du Sainct Esprit"—St Paul would never have so spoken, if he had not known the divinity of the Holy Spirit.

Son may obtain pardon, that majesty must certainly be divine which it is an inexpiable crime to offend or impair. I designedly omit several passages which the ancient fathers adduced. They thought it plausible to quote from David, "By the word of the Lord were the heavens made, and all the host of them by the breath (Spirit) of his mouth" (Ps. xxxiii. 6), in order to prove that the world was not less the work of the Holy Spirit than of the Son. But seeing it is usual in the Psalms to repeat the same thing twice, and in Isaiah the *spirit* (breath) of the mouth is equivalent to *word*, that proof was weak; and, accordingly, my wish has been to advert briefly to those proofs on which pious minds may securely rest.

16. But as God has manifested himself more clearly by the advent of Christ, so he has made himself more familiarly known in three persons. Of many proofs let this one suffice. Paul connects together these three, God, Faith, and Baptism, and reasons from the one to the other—viz. because there is one faith, he infers that there is one God; and because there is one baptism, he infers that there is one faith. Therefore, if by baptism we are initiated into the faith and worship of one God, we must of necessity believe that he into whose name we are baptised is the true God. And there cannot be a doubt that our Saviour wished to testify, by a solemn rehearsal, that the perfect light of faith is now exhibited, when he said, "Go and teach all nations, baptising them in the name of the Father, and of the Son, and of the Holy Spirit" (Matth. xxviii. 19), since this is the same thing as to be baptised into the name of the one God, who has been fully manifested in the Father, the Son, and the Spirit. Hence it plainly appears, that the three persons, in whom alone God is known, subsist in the Divine essence. And since faith certainly ought not to look hither and thither, or run up and down after various objects, but to look, refer, and cleave to God alone, it is obvious that were there various kinds of faith, there behoved also to be various gods. Then, as the baptism of faith is a sacrament, its unity assures us of the unity of God. Hence, also, it is proved that it is lawful only to be baptised into one God, because we make a profession of faith in him in whose name we are baptised. What, then, is our Saviour's meaning in commanding baptism to be administered in the name of the Father, and the Son, and the Holy Spirit, if it be not that we are to believe with one faith in the name of the Father, and the Son, and the Holy Spirit?[1] But is this anything else than to declare that the Father, Son, and Spirit, are one God? Wherefore, since it must be held certain that there is one God, not more than one, we conclude that the Word and Spirit are of the very essence of God. Nothing could be more stupid than the trifling of the Arians, who, while acknowledging the divinity of the Son, denied his divine essence. Equally extravagant were the ravings of the Macedonians, who insisted that by the

---

[1] The French entirely omits the three previous sentences, beginning, "Then, as," &c.

Spirit were only meant the gifts of grace poured out upon men. For as wisdom, understanding, prudence, fortitude, and the fear of the Lord, proceed from the Spirit, so he is the one Spirit of wisdom, prudence, fortitude, and piety. He is not divided according to the distribution of his gifts, but, as the Apostle assures us (1 Cor. xii. 11), however they be divided, he remains one and the same.

17. On the other hand, the Scriptures demonstrate that there is some distinction between the Father and the Word, the Word and the Spirit; but the magnitude of the mystery reminds us of the great reverence and soberness which ought to be employed in discussing it. It seems to me, that nothing can be more admirable than the words of Gregory Nanzianzen: "Ού φθάνω το ἓι νοῆσαι, καὶ τοῖς τρισὶ περιλάμπομαι· οὐ φθάνω τὰ τρία διελεῖν καὶ εἰς τὸ ἓν ἀναφέρομαι" (Greg. Nanzian. in Serm. de Sacro Baptis.). "I cannot think of the unity without being irradiated by the Trinity: I cannot distinguish between the Trinity without being carried up to the unity."[1] Therefore, let us beware of imagining such a Trinity of persons as will distract our thoughts, instead of bringing them instantly back to the unity. The words, Father, Son, and Holy Spirit, certainly indicate a real distinction, not allowing us to suppose that they are merely epithets by which God is variously designated from his works. Still they indicate distinction only, not division. The passages we have already quoted show that the Son has a distinct subsistence from the Father, because the Word could not have been with God unless he were distinct from the Father; nor but for this could he have had his glory with the Father. In like manner, Christ distinguishes the Father from himself, when he says that there is another who bears witness of him (John v. 32; viii. 16). To the same effect is it elsewhere said, that the Father made all things by the Word. This could not be, if he were not in some respect distinct from him. Besides, it was not the Father that descended to the earth, but he who came forth from the Father; nor was it the Father that died and rose again, but he whom the Father had sent. This distinction did not take its beginning at the incarnation: for it is clear that the only begotten Son previously existed in the bosom of the Father (John i. 18). For who will dare to affirm that the Son entered his Father's bosom for the first time, when he came down from heaven to assume human nature? Therefore, he was previously in the bosom of the Father, and had his glory with the Father. Christ intimates the distinction between the Holy Spirit and the Father, when he says that the Spirit proceedeth from the Father, and between the Holy Spirit and himself, when he speaks of him as another, as he does when he declares that he will send another

---

[1] Bernard, De Consider. lib. v. "Cum dico unum, non me trinitatis turbat numerus, qui essentiam non multiplicat, non variat, nec partitur. Rursum, quum, dico tria, non me arguit intuitus unitatis, quia illa quæcunque tria, seu illos tres, nec in confusionem cogit, nec in singularitatem redigit."—See also Bernard, Serm. 71, in Cantica.

Comforter; and in many other passages besides (John xiv. 6; xv. 26; xiv. 16).

18. I am not sure whether it is expedient to borrow analogies from human affairs to express the nature of this distinction. The ancient fathers sometimes do so, but they at the same time admit, that what they bring forward as analogous is very widely different. And hence it is that I have a great dread of anything like presumption here, lest some rash saying may furnish an occasion of calumny to the malicious, or of delusion to the unlearned. It were unbecoming, however, to say nothing of a distinction which we observe that the Scriptures have pointed out. This distinction is, that to the Father is attributed the beginning of action, the fountain and source of all things; to the Son, wisdom, counsel, and arrangement in action, while the energy and efficacy of action is assigned to the Spirit. Moreover, though the eternity of the Father is also the eternity of the Son and Spirit, since God never could be without his own wisdom and energy; and though in eternity there can be no room for first or last, still the distinction of order is not unmeaning or superfluous, the Father being considered first, next the Son from him, and then the Spirit from both. For the mind of every man naturally inclines to consider, first, God, secondly, the wisdom emerging from him, and, lastly, the energy by which he executes the purposes of his counsel. For this reason, the Son is said to be of the Father only; the Spirit of both the Father and the Son. This is done in many passages, but in none more clearly than in the eighth chapter to the Romans, where the same Spirit is called indiscriminately the Spirit of Christ, and the Spirit of him who raised up Christ from the dead. And not improperly. For Peter also testifies (1 Pet. i. 21), that it was the Spirit of Christ which inspired the prophets, though the Scriptures so often say that it was the Spirit of God the Father.

19. Moreover, this distinction is so far from interfering with the most perfect unity of God, that the Son may thereby be proved to be one God with the Father, inasmuch as he constitutes one Spirit with him, and that the Spirit is not different from the Father and the Son, inasmuch as he is the Spirit of the Father and the Son. In each hypostasis the whole nature is understood, the only difference being that each has his own peculiar subsistence. The whole Father is in the Son, and the whole Son in the Father, as the Son himself also declares (John xiv. 10), "I am in the Father, and the Father in me;" nor do ecclesiastical writers admit that the one is separated from the other by any difference of essence. "By those names which denote distinction," says Augustine, "is meant the relation which they mutually bear to each other, not the very substance by which they are one." In this way, the sentiments of the Fathers, which might sometimes appear to be at variance with each other, are to be reconciled. At one time they teach that the Father is the beginning of the Son, at another they assert that the Son has both di-

vinity and essence from himself, and therefore is one beginning with the Father. The cause of this discrepancy is well and clearly explained by Augustine, when he says,[1] "Christ, as to himself, is called God, as to the Father he is called Son." And again, "The Father, as to himself, is called God, as to the Son he is called Father. He who, as to the Son, is called Father, is not Son; and he who, as to himself, is called Father, and he who, as to himself, is called Son, is the same God." Therefore, when we speak of the Son simply, without reference to the Father, we truly and properly affirm that he is of himself, and, accordingly, call him the only beginning; but when we denote the relation which he bears to the Father, we correctly make the Father the beginning of the Son. Augustine's fifth book on the Trinity is wholly devoted to the explanation of this subject. But it is far safer to rest contented with the relation as taught by him than get bewildered in vain speculation by subtle prying into a sublime mystery.

20. Let those, then, who love soberness, and are contented with the measure of faith, briefly receive what is useful to be known. It is as follows: When we profess to believe in one God, by the name God is understood the one simple essence, comprehending three persons or hypostases; and, accordingly, whenever the name of God is used indefinitely, the Son and Spirit, not less than the Father, is meant. But when the Son is joined with the Father, relation comes into view, and so we distinguish between the Persons. But as the Personal subsistences carry an order with them, the principle and origin being in the Father, whenever mention is made of the Father and Son, or of the Father and Spirit together, the name of God is specially given to the Father. In this way the unity of essence is retained, and respect is had to the order, which, however, derogates in no respect from the divinity of the Son and Spirit. And surely since we have already seen how the apostles declare the Son of God to have been He whom Moses and the prophets declared to be Jehovah, we must always arrive at an unity of essence. We, therefore hold it detestable blasphemy to call the Son a different God from the Father, because the simple name God admits not of relation, nor can God, considered in himself, be said to be this or that. Then, that the name Jehovah, taken indefinitely, may be applied to Christ, is clear from the words of Paul, "For this thing I besought the Lord thrice." After giving the answer, "My grace is sufficient for thee," he subjoins, "that the power of Christ may rest upon me" (2 Cor. xii. 8, 9). For it is certain that the name of Lord ($Κύριου$) is there put for Jehovah, and, therefore, to restrict it to the person of the Mediator, were puerile and frivolous, the words being used absolutely, and not with the view of comparing the Father and the Son, And

---

[1] August. Homil. De Temp. 38, De Trinitate. See also Ad Pascentium Epist. 174 Cyrill. De Trinit. lib. vii.; Idem, lib. iii. Dialog.; Aug. in Psal. cix.; et Tract. in Joann 89; Idem, in Psal. lxviii.

we know that, in accordance with the received usage of the Greeks, the apostles uniformly substitute the word Κυρίος for Jehovah. Not to go far for an example, Paul besought the Lord in the same sense in which Peter quotes the passage of Joel, "Whosoever shall call upon the name of the Lord shall be saved" (Acts ii. 21 ; Joel ii. 28). Where this name is specially applied to the Son, there is a different ground for it, as will be seen in its own place ; at present it is sufficient to remember that Paul, after praying to God absolutely, immediately subjoins the name of Christ. Thus, too, the Spirit is called God absolutely by Christ himself. For nothing prevents us from holding that he is the entire spiritual essence of God, in which are comprehended Father, Son, and Spirit. This is plain from Scripture. For as God is there called a Spirit, so the Holy Spirit also, in so far as he is a hypostasis of the whole essence, is said to be both of God and from God.

21. But since Satan, in order to pluck up our faith by the roots, has always provoked fierce disputes, partly concerning the divine essence of the Son and Spirit, and partly concerning the distinction of persons ; since in almost every age he has stirred up impious spirits to vex the orthodox doctors on this head, and is attempting in the present day to kindle a new flame out of the old embers, it will be proper here to dispose of some of these perverse dreams. Hitherto our chief object has been to stretch out our hand for the guidance of such as are disposed to learn, not to war with the stubborn and contentious ; but now the truth which was calmly demonstrated must be vindicated from the calumnies of the ungodly. Still, however, it will be our principal study to provide a sure footing for those whose ears are open to the word of God. Here, if anywhere, in considering the hidden mysteries of Scripture, we should speculate soberly and with great moderation, cautiously guarding against allowing either our mind or our tongue to go a step beyond the confines of God's word. For how can the human mind, which has not yet been able to ascertain of what the body of the sun consists, though it is daily presented to the eye, bring down the boundless essence of God to its little measure ? Nay, how can it, under its own guidance, penetrate to a knowledge of the substance of God while unable to understand its own ? Wherefore, let us willingly leave to God the knowledge of himself. In the words of Hilary (De Trinit. lib. i.), " He alone is a fit witness to himself who is known only by himself." This knowledge, then, if we would leave to God, we must conceive of him as he has made himself known, and in our inquiries make application to no other quarter than his word. On this subject we have five homilies of Chrysostom against the Anomœi (De Incomprehensit. Dei Natura), in which he endeavoured, but in vain, to check the presumption of the Sophists, and curb their garrulity. They showed no more modesty here than they are wont to do in everything else. The very unhappy results of their temerity should be a warning to us to bring more docility than acumen to the discussion of this question, never to at-

tempt to search after God anywhere but in his sacred word, and never to speak or think of him farther than we have it for our guide. But if the distinction of Father, Son, and Spirit, subsisting in the one Godhead (certainly a subject of great difficulty), gives more trouble and annoyance to some intellects than is meet, let us remember that the human mind enters a labyrinth whenever it indulges its curiosity, and thus submit to be guided by the divine oracles, how much soever the mystery may be beyond our reach.

22. It were tedious, and to no purpose toilsome, to form a catalogue of the errors by which, in regard to this branch of doctrine, the purity of the faith has been assailed. The greater part of heretics have with their gross deliriums made a general attack on the glory of God, deeming it enough if they could disturb and shake the unwary. ·From a few individuals numerous sects have sprung up, some of them rending the divine essence, and others confounding the distinction of persons. But if we hold, what has already been demonstrated from Scripture, that the essence of the one God, pertaining to the Father, Son, and Spirit, is simple and indivisible, and again, that the Father differs in some special property from the Son, and the Son from the Spirit, the door will be shut against Arius and Sabellius, as well as the other ancient authors of error. But as in our day have arisen certain frantic men, such as Servetus and others, who, by new devices, have thrown everything into confusion, it may be worth while briefly to discuss their fallacies.

The name of Trinity was so much disliked, nay, detested, by Servetus, that he charged all whom he called Trinitarians with being Atheists. I say nothing of the insulting terms in which he thought proper to make his charges. The sum of his speculations was, that a threefold Deity is introduced wherever three Persons are said to exist in his essence, and that this Triad was imaginary, inasmuch as it was inconsistent with the unity of God. At the same time, he would have it that the Persons are certain external ideas which do not truly subsist in the Divine essence, but only figure God to us under this or that form : that at first, indeed, there was no distinction in God, because originally the Word was the same as the Spirit, but ever since Christ came forth God of God, another Spirit, also a God, had proceeded from him. But although he sometimes cloaks his absurdities in allegory, as when he says that the eternal Word of God was the Spirit of Christ with God, and the reflection of the idea, likewise that the Spirit was a shadow of Deity, he at last reduces the divinity of both to nothing ; maintaining that, according to the mode of distribution, there is a part of God as well in the Son as in the Spirit, just as the same spirit substantially is a portion of God in us, and also in wood and stone. His absurd babbling concerning the person of the Mediator will be seen in its own place.[1]

1 See Calvin. Defensio Orthodox. Fid. S. Trinit. Adv. Prod. Error. M. Serveti

The monstrous fiction that a person is nothing else than a visible appearance of the glory of God, needs not a long refutation. For when John declares that before the world was created the Logos was God (John i. 1), he shows that he was something very different from an idea. But if even then, and from the remotest eternity, that Logos, who was God, was with the Father, and had his own distinct and peculiar glory with the Father (John xvii. 5), he certainly could not be an external or figurative splendour, but must necessarily have been a hypostasis which dwelt inherently in God himself. But although there is no mention made of the Spirit antecedent to the account of the creation, he is not there introduced as a shadow, but as the essential power of God, where Moses relates that the shapeless mass was upborne by him (Gen. i. 2). It is obvious that the eternal Spirit always existed in God, seeing he cherished and sustained the confused materials of heaven and earth before they possessed order or beauty. Assuredly he could not then be an image or representation of God, as Servetus dreams. But he is elsewhere forced to make a more open disclosure of his impiety when he says, that God by his eternal reason decreeing a Son to himself, in this way assumed a visible appearance. For if this be true, no other Divinity is left to Christ than is implied in his having been ordained a Son by God's eternal decree. Moreover, those phantoms which Servetus substitutes for the hypostases he so transforms as to make new changes in God. But the most execrable heresy of all is his confounding both the Son and Spirit promiscuously with all the creatures. For he distinctly asserts, that there are parts and partitions in the essence of God, and that every such portion is God. This he does especially when he says, that the spirits of the faithful are co-eternal and consubstantial with God, although he elsewhere assigns a substantial divinity, not only to the soul of man, but to all created things.

23. This pool has bred another monster not unlike the former. For certain restless spirits, unwilling to share the disgrace and obloquy of the impiety of Servetus, have confessed that there were indeed three Persons, but added, as a reason, that the Father, who alone is truly and properly God, transfused his Divinity into the Son and Spirit when he formed them. Nor do they refrain from expressing themselves in such shocking terms as these : that the Father is essentially distinguished from the Son and Spirit by this ; that he is the only *essentiator*. Their first pretext for this is, that Christ is uniformly called the Son of God. From this they infer that there is no proper God but the Father. But they forget that, although the name of God is common also to the Son, yet it is sometimes, by way of excellence, ascribed to the Father, as being the source and principle of Divinity ; and this is done in order to mark the simple unity of essence. They object, that if the Son is truly God, he must be deemed the Son of a person : which is absurd. I answer, that both are true ; namely, that he is the Son of God, because he is the Word, begotten of the Father before

all ages (for we are not now speaking of the Person of the Mediator) ; and yet, that for the purpose of explanation, regard must be had to the Person, so that the name God may not be understood in its absolute sense, but as equivalent to Father. For if we hold that there is no other God than the Father, this rank is clearly denied to the Son.

In every case where the Godhead is mentioned, we are by no means to admit that there is an antithesis between the Father and the Son, as if to the former only the name of God could competently be applied. For assuredly, the God who appeared to Isaiah was the one true God, and yet John declares that he was Christ (Isa. vi. ; John xii. 41). He who declared, by the mouth of Isaiah, that he was to be "for a stone of stumbling" to the Jews, was the one God ; and yet Paul declares that he was Christ (Isa. viii. 14 ; Rom. ix. 33). He who proclaims by Isaiah, " Unto me every knee shall bow," is the one God ; yet Paul again explains that he is Christ (Isa. xlv. 23 ; Rom. xiv. 11). To this we may add the passages quoted by an Apostle, " Thou, Lord, hast laid the foundations of the earth ;" " Let all the angels of God worship him" (Heb. i. 10 ; x. 6 ; Ps. cii. 26 ; xcvii. 7). All these apply to the one God ; and yet the Apostle contends that they are the proper attributes of Christ. There is nothing in the cavil, that what properly applies to God is transferred to Christ, because he is the brightness of his glory. Since the name of Jehovah is everywhere applied to Christ, it follows that, in regard to Deity, he is of himself. For if he is Jehovah, it is impossible to deny that he is the same God who elsewhere proclaims by Isaiah, " I am the first, and I am the last ; and besides me there is no God" (Isa xliv. 6). We would also do well to ponder the words of Jeremiah, " The gods that have not made the heavens and the earth, even they shall perish from the earth, and from under these heavens" (Jer. x. 11) ; whence it follows conversely, that He whose divinity Isaiah repeatedly proves from the creation of the world, is none other than the Son of God. And how is it possible that the Creator, who gives to all, should not be of himself, but should borrow his essence from another ? Whosoever says that the Son was *essentiated* by the Father,[1] denies his self-existence. Against this, however, the Holy Spirit protests, when he calls him Jehovah. On the supposition, then, that the whole essence is in the Father only, the essence becomes divisible, or is denied to the Son, who, being thus robbed of his essence, will be only a titular God. If we are to believe these triflers, divine essence belongs to the Father only, on the ground that he is sole God, and *essentiator* of the Son. In this way, the divinity of the Son will be something abstracted [2] from the essence of God, or the derivation of a part from the whole. On the same principle it must

---

[1] The French adds, "puisque tels abuseurs forgent des noms contre nature ;"— for these perverters forge names against nature.

[2] The French is, " tiré comme par un alambic ;"—extracted as by an alembic.

also be conceded, that the Spirit belongs to the Father only. For if the derivation is from the primary essence which is proper to none but the Father, the Spirit cannot justly be deemed the Spirit of the Son.   This view, however, is refuted by the testimony of Paul, when he makes the Spirit common both to Christ and the Father.   More-over, if the Person of the Father is expunged from the Trinity, in what will he differ from the Son and Spirit, except in being the only God ?   They confess that Christ is God, and that he differs from the Father.   If he differs, there must be some mark of distinction between them.   Those who place it in the essence, manifestly reduce the true divinity of Christ to nothing, since divinity cannot exist without essence, and indeed without entire essence.[1]   The Father certainly cannot differ from the Son, unless he have something peculiar to himself, and not common to him with the Son. What, then, do these men show as the mark of distinction ?   If it is in the essence, let them tell whether or not he communicated essence to the Son. This he could not do in part merely, for it were impious to think of a divided God.   And besides, on this supposition, there would be a rending of the Divine essence.   The whole entire essence must there-fore be common to the Father and the Son ; and if so, in respect of essence there is no distinction between them.   If they reply that the Father, while essentiating, still remains the only God, being the pos-sessor of the essence, then Christ will be a figurative God, one in name or semblance only, and not in reality, because no property can be more peculiar to God than essence, according to the words, "I AM hath sent me unto you" (Ex. iii. 4).

24. The assumption, that whenever God is mentioned absolutely, the Father only is meant, may be proved erroneous by many passages. Even in those which they quote in support of their views they betray a lamentable inconsistency, because the name of Son occurs there by way of contrast, showing that the other name God is used rela-tively, and in that way confined to the person of the Father.   Their objection may be disposed of in a single word. Were not the Father alone the true God, he would, say they, be his own Father.   But there is nothing absurd in the name of God being specially applied, in respect of order and degree, to him who not only of himself begat his own wisdom, but is the God of the Mediator, as I will more fully show in its own place.   For ever since Christ was manifested in the flesh he is called the Son of God, not only because begotten of the Father before all worlds he was the Eternal Word, but because he undertook the person and office of the Mediator that he might unite us to God.   Seeing they are so bold in excluding the Son from the honour of God, I would fain know whether, when he declares that there is "none good but one, that is, God," he deprives himself of

---

[1] See Bernard, Serm. 80, super Cantica., on the heresy of Gilbert, Bishop of Poio-tiers.

goodness. I speak not of his human nature, lest perhaps they should object, that whatever goodness was in it was derived by gratuitous gift: I ask whether the Eternal Word of God is good, yes or no? If they say no, their impiety is manifest; if yes, they refute themselves. Christ's seeming at the first glance to disclaim the name of good (Matth. xix. 17), rather confirms our view. Goodness being the special property of God alone, and yet being at the time applied to him in the ordinary way of salutation, his rejection of false honour intimates that the goodness in which he excels is Divine. Again, I ask whether, when Paul affirms that God alone is "immortal," "wise, and true" (1 Tim. i. 17), he reduces Christ to the rank of beings mortal, foolish, and false. Is not he immortal, who, from the beginning, had life so as to bestow immortality on angels? Is not he wise who is the eternal wisdom of God? Is not he true who is truth itself?

I ask, moreover, whether they think Christ should be worshipped. If he claims justly, that every knee shall bow to him, it follows that he is the God who, in the law, forbade worship to be offered to any but himself. If they insist on applying to the Father only the words of Isaiah, "I am, and besides me there is none else" (Isa. xliv. 6), I turn the passage against themselves, since we see that every property of God is attributed to Christ.[1] There is no room for the cavil that Christ was exalted in the flesh in which he humbled himself, and in respect of which all power is given to him in heaven and on earth. For although the majesty of King and Judge extends to the whole person of the Mediator, yet had he not been God manifested in the flesh, he could not have been exalted to such a height without coming into collision with God. And the dispute is admirably settled by Paul, when he declares that he was equal with God before he humbled himself, and assumed the form of a servant (Phil. ii. 6, 7). Moreover, how could such equality exist, if he were not that God whose name is Jah and Jehovah, who rides upon 'the cherubim, is King of all the earth, and King of ages? Let them clamour as they may, Christ cannot be robbed of the honour described by Isaiah, "Lo, this is our God; we have waited for him" (Isa. xxv. 9); for these words describe the advent of God the Redeemer, who was not only to bring back the people from Babylonish captivity, but restore the Church, and make her completely perfect.

Nor does another cavil avail them, that Christ was God in his Father. For though we admit that, in respect of order and gradation, the beginning of divinity is in the Father, we hold it a detestable fiction to maintain that essence is proper to the Father alone, as if he were the deifier of the Son. On this view either the essence is manifold, or Christ is God only in name and imagination. If they

---

1 The French is expressed somewhat differently, " veu que l'Apostre en l'allegant de Christ, lui attribue tout ce qui est de Dieu ; "—seeing the Apostle, by applying it to Christ, attributes to him everything belonging to God.

grant that the Son is God, but only in subordination to the Father, the essence which in the Father is unformed and unbegotten will in him be formed and begotten. I know that many who would be thought wise deride us for extracting the distinction of persons from the words of Moses when he introduces God as saying, " Let us make man in our own image " (Gen. i. 26). Pious readers, however, see how frigidly and absurdly the colloquy were introduced by Moses, if there were not several persons in the Godhead. It is certain that those whom the Father addresses must have been uncreated. But nothing is uncreated except the one God. Now then, unless they concede that the power of creating was common to the Father, Son, and Spirit, and the power of commanding common, it will follow that God did not speak thus inwardly with himself, but addressed other extraneous architects. In fine, there is a single passage which will at once dispose of these two objections. The declaration of Christ, that " God is a Spirit " (John iv. 24), cannot be confined to the Father only, as if the Word were not of a spiritual nature. But if the name Spirit applies equally to the Son as to the Father, I infer that under the indefinite name of God the Son is included. He adds immediately after, that the only worshippers approved by the Father are those who worship him in spirit and in truth ; and hence I also infer, that because Christ performs the office of teacher under a head, he applies the name God to the Father, not for the purpose of destroying his own Divinity, but for the purpose of raising us up to it as it were step by step.

25. The hallucination consists in dreaming of individuals, each of whom possesses a part of the essence. The Scriptures teach that there is essentially but one God, and therefore that the essence both of the Son and Spirit is unbegotten ; but inasmuch as the Father is first in order, and of himself begat his own Wisdom, he, as we lately observed, is justly regarded as the principle and fountain of all the Godhead. Thus God, taken indefinitely, is unbegotten, and the Father, in respect of his person, is unbegotten. For it is absurd to imagine that our doctrine gives any ground for alleging that we establish a quaternion of gods. They falsely and calumniously ascribe to us the figment of their own brain, as if we virtually held that three persons emanate from one essence,[1] whereas it is plain, from our writings, that we do not disjoin the persons from the essence, but interpose a distinction between the persons residing in it. If the persons were separated from the essence, there might be some plausibility in their argument ; as in this way there would be a trinity of Gods, not of persons comprehended in one God. This affords an answer to their futile question—whether or not the essence concurs in forming the Trinity ; as if we imagined that three Gods were derived from it. Their objection, that there would thus be a Trinity without a God,

1 The French adds, " Comme trois ruisseaux ; "—like three streams.

originates in the same absurdity. Although the essence does not contribute to the distinction, as if it were a part or member, the persons are not without it, or external to it; for the Father, if he were not God, could not be the Father; nor could the Son possibly be Son unless he were God. We say, then, that the Godhead is absolutely of itself. And hence also we hold that the Son, regarded as God, and without reference to person, is also of himself; though we also say that, regarded as Son, he is of the Father. Thus his essence is without beginning, while his person has its beginning in God. And, indeed, the orthodox writers who in former times spoke of the Trinity, used this term only with reference to the Persons. To have included the essence in the distinction, would not only have been an absurd error, but gross impiety. For those who class the three thus— Essence, Son, and Spirit [1]—plainly do away with the essence of the Son and Spirit; otherwise the parts being intermingled would merge into each other—a circumstance which would vitiate any distinction.[2] In short, if God and Father were synonymous terms, the Father would be deifier in a sense which would leave the Son nothing but a shadow; and the Trinity would be nothing more than the union of one God with two creatures.

26. To the objection, that if Christ be properly God, he is improperly called the Son of God, it has been already answered, that when one person is compared with another, the name God is not used indefinitely, but is restricted to the Father, regarded as the beginning of the Godhead, not by *essentiating*, as fanatics absurdly express it, but in respect of order. In this sense are to be understood the words which Christ addressed to the Father, " This is life eternal, that they might know thee the only true God, and Jesus Christ whom thou hast sent" (John xvii. 3). For speaking in the person of the Mediator, he holds a middle place between God and man; yet so that his majesty is not diminished thereby. For though he humbled (emptied) himself, he did not lose the glory which he had with the Father, though it was concealed from the world. So in the Epistle to the Hebrews (Heb. i. 10 ; ii. 9), though the apostle confesses that Christ was made a little lower than the angels, he at the same time hesitates not to assert that he is the eternal God who founded the earth. We must hold, therefore, that as often as Christ, in the character of Mediator, addresses the Father, he, under the term God, includes his own divinity also. Thus, when he says to the apostles, " It is expedient for you that I go away," " My Father is greater than I," he does not attribute to himself a secondary divinity merely, as if in regard

1 The French adds, " Comme si l'essence étoit au lieu de la personne du Pére;"—as if the essence were in place of the person of the Father.
2 The French is somewhat differently expressed: " Car le Fils a quelque l'estre, ou il n'en a point. S'il en a, voila deux essences pour jouster l'un contre autre ; s'il n'en a point, ce ne seroit qu'une ombre." For the Son has some being, or he has none. If some, here are two essences to tilt with each other : if none, he is only a shadow.

to eternal essence he were inferior to the Father; but having obtained celestial glory, he gathers together the faithful to share it with him. He places the Father in the higher degree, inasmuch as the full perfection of brightness conspicuous in heaven, differs from that measure of glory which he himself displayed when clothed in flesh. For the same reason Paul says, that Christ will restore "the kingdom to God, even the Father," "that God may be all in all" (1 Cor. xv. 24, 28). Nothing can be more absurd than to deny the perpetuity of Christ's divinity. But if he will never cease to be the Son of God, but will ever remain the same that he was from the beginning, it follows that under the name of Father the one divine essence common to both is comprehended. And assuredly Christ descended to us for the very purpose of raising us to the Father, and thereby, at the same time, raising us to himself, inasmuch as he is one with the Father. It is therefore erroneous and impious to confine the name of God to the Father, so as to deny it to the Son. Accordingly, John, declaring that he is the true God, has no idea of placing him beneath the Father in a subordinate rank of divinity. I wonder what these fabricators of new gods mean, when they confess that Christ is truly God, and yet exclude him from the godhead of the Father, as if there could be any true God but the one God, or as if transfused divinity were not a mere modern fiction.

27. In the many passages which they collect from Irenæus, in which he maintains that the Father of Christ is the only eternal God of Israel, they betray shameful ignorance, or very great dishonesty. For they ought to have observed, that that holy man was contending against certain frantic persons, who, denying that the Father of Christ was that God who had in old times spoken by Moses and the prophets, held that he was some phantom or other produced from the pollution of the world. His whole object, therefore, is to make it plain, that in the Scriptures no other God is announced but the Father of Christ; that it is wicked to imagine any other. Accordingly, there is nothing strange in his so often concluding that the God of Israel was no other than he who is celebrated by Christ and the apostles. Now, when a different heresy is to be resisted, we also say with truth, that the God who in old times appeared to the fathers, was no other than Christ. Moreover, if it is objected that he was the Father, we have the answer ready, that while we contend for the divinity of the Son, we by no means exclude the Father. When the reader attends to the purpose of Irenæus, the dispute is at an end. Indeed, we have only to look to lib. iii. c. 6, where the pious writer insists on this one point, "that he who in Scripture is called God absolutely and indefinitely, is truly the only God; and that Christ is called God absolutely." Let us remember (as appears from the whole work, and especially from lib. ii. c. 46), that the point under discussion was, that the name of Father is not applied enigmatically and parabolically to one who was not truly God. We may add, that in lib. iii. c. 9, he contends that

the Son as well as the Father united was the God proclaimed by the prophets and apostles. He afterwards explains (lib. iii. c. 12) how Christ, who is Lord of all, and King and Judge, received power from him who is God of all, namely, in respect of the humiliation by which he humbled himself, even to the death of the cross. At the same time he shortly after affirms (lib. iii. c. 16), that the Son is the maker heaven and earth, who delivered the law by the hand of Moses, and appeared to the fathers. Should any babbler now insist that, according to Irenæus, the Father alone is the God of Israel, I will refer him to a passage in which Irenæus distinctly says (lib. iii. c. 18, 23), that Christ is ever one and the same, and also applies to Christ the words of the prophecy of Habakkuk, " God cometh from the south." To the same effect he says (lib. iv. c. 9), " Therefore, Christ himself, with the Father, is the God of the living." And in the 12th chapter of the same book he explains that Abraham believed God, because Christ is the maker of heaven and earth, and very God.

28. With no more truth do they claim Tertullian as a patron. Though his style is sometimes rugged and obscure, he delivers the doctrine which we maintain in no ambiguous manner, namely, that while there is one God, his Word, however, is with dispensation or economy ; that there is only one God, in unity of substance ; but that nevertheless, by the mystery of dispensation, the unity is arranged into Trinity ; that there are three, not in state, but in degree—not in substance, but in form—not in power, but in order.[1] He says, indeed, that he holds the Son to be second to the Father ; but he means that the only difference is by distinction. In one place he says the Son is visible ; but after he has discoursed on both views, he declares that he is invisible regarded as the Word. In fine, by affirming that the Father is characterised by his own Person, he shows that he is very far from countenancing the fiction which we refute. And although he does not acknowledge any other God than the Father, yet explaining himself in the immediate context, he shows that he does not speak exclusively in respect of the Son, because he denies that he is a different God from the Father ; and, accordingly, that the one supremacy is not violated by the distinction of Person. And it is easy to collect his meaning from the whole tenor of his discourse. For he contends against Praxeas, that although God has three distinct Persons, yet there are not several gods, nor is unity divided.

---

[1] Tertullianus, lib. adv. Praxeam :—" Perversitas hæc (Praxeæ scil.) se existimat meram veritatem possidere, dum unicum Deum non alias putat credendum, quam si ipsum eundemque et Patrem et Filium et Spiritum sanctum dicat : quasi non sic quoque unus sit omnia, dum ex uno omnia, per substantiæ scilicet unitatem, et nihilominus custodiatur οἰκονομίας sacramentum, quæ unitatem in trinitatem disponit, tres dirigens, Patrem, Filium, et Spiritum sanctum. Tres autem non statu, sed gradu : nec substantia, sed forma : nec potestate, sed specie : unius autem substantiæ, et unius status, et unius potestatis : quia unus Deus, ex quo et gradus isti, formæ et species, in nomine Patris, et Filii, et Spiritus sancti deputantur. Quomodo numerum sine divisione patiuntur, procedentes tractatus demonstrabunt," &c.

According to the fiction of Praxeas, Christ could not be God without being the Father also ; and this is the reason why Tertullian dwells so much on the distinction. When he calls the Word and Spirit a portion of the whole, the expression, though harsh, may be allowed, since it does not refer to the substance, but only (as Tertullian himself testifies) denotes arrangement and economy which applies to the persons only. Accordingly, he asks, " How many persons, Praxeas, do you think there are, but just as many as there are names for ? " In the same way, he shortly after says, " That they may believe the Father and the Son, each in his own name and person." These things, I think, sufficiently refute the effrontery of those who endeavour to blind the simple by pretending the authority of Tertullian.

29. Assuredly, whosoever will compare the writings of the ancient fathers with each other, will not find anything in Irenæus different from what is taught by those who come after him. Justin is one of the most ancient, and he agrees with us out and out. Let them object that, by him and others, the Father of Christ is called the one God. The same thing is taught by Hilary, who uses the still harsher expression, that Eternity is in the Father. Is it that he may withhold divine essence from the Son ? His whole work is a defence of the doctrine which we maintain ; and yet these men are not ashamed to produce some kind of mutilated excerpts for the purpose of persuading us that Hilary is a patron of their heresy. With regard to what they pretend as to Ignatius, if they would have it to be of the least importance, let them prove that the apostles enacted laws concerning Lent, and other corruptions. Nothing can be more nauseating than the absurdities which have been published under the name of Ignatius ; and, therefore, the conduct of those who provide themselves with such masks for deception is the less entitled to toleration.

Moreover, the consent of the ancient fathers clearly appears from this, that in the Council of Nice, no attempt was made by Arius to cloak his heresy by the authority of any approved author ; and no Greek or Latin writer apologises as dissenting from his predecessors. It cannot be necessary to observe how carefully Augustine, to whom all these miscreants are most violently opposed, examined all ancient writings, and how reverently he embraced the doctrine taught by them (August. lib. de Trinit. &c.). He is most scrupulous in stating the grounds on which he is forced to differ from them, even in the minutest point. On this subject, too, if he finds anything ambiguous or obscure in other writers, he does not disguise it.[1] And he assumes it as an acknowledged fact, that the doctrine opposed by the Arians was received without dispute from the earliest antiquity. At the same time, he was not ignorant of what some others had previously taught. This is obvious from a

---

[1] Athanasius expresses himself thus learnedly and piously :—" On this subject, though you cannot explain yourself, you are not therefore to distrust the Holy Scriptures. It is better, while hesitating through ignorance, to be silent and believe, than not to believe because you hesitate "

single expression. When he says (De Doct. Christ. lib. i.) that "unity is in the Father," will they pretend that he then forgot himself? In another passage, he clears away every such charge, when he calls the Father the beginning of the Godhead, as being from none —thus wisely inferring that the name of God is specially ascribed to the Father, because, unless the beginning were from him, the simple unity of essence could not be maintained. I hope the pious reader will admit that I have now disposed of all the calumnies by which Satan has hitherto attempted to pervert or obscure the pure doctrine of faith. The whole substance of the doctrine has, I trust, been faithfully expounded, if my readers will set bounds to their curiosity, and not long more eagerly than they ought for perplexing disputation. I did not undertake to satisfy those who delight in speculative views, but I have not designedly omitted anything which I thought adverse to me. At the same time, studying the edification of the Church, I have thought it better not to touch on various topics, which could have yielded little profit, while they must have needlessly burdened and fatigued the reader. For instance, what avails it to discuss, as Lombard does at length (lib. i. dist. 9), whether or not the Father always generates? This idea of continual generation becomes an absurd fiction from the moment it is seen, that from eternity there were three persons in one God.

CHAPTER XIV.

IN THE CREATION OF THE WORLD, AND ALL THINGS IN IT, THE TRUE
GOD DISTINGUISHED BY CERTAIN MARKS FROM FICTITIOUS GODS.

In this chapter commences the second part of Book First—viz., the knowledge of
man. Certain things premised. I. The creation of the world generally (s. 1 and 2);
II. The subject of angels considered (s. 3–13); III. Of bad angels or devils (s. 13–20);
and, IV. The practical use to be made of the history of the creation (s. 20–22).

Sections.

1. The mere fact of creation should lead us to acknowledge God, but to prevent our
   falling away to Gentile fictions, God has been pleased to furnish a history of the
   creation. An impious objection, Why the world was not created sooner? Answer
   to it. Shrewd saying of an old man.
2. For the same reason, the world was created, not in an instant, but in six days. The
   order of creation described, showing that Adam was not created until God had,
   with infinite goodness, made ample provision for him.
3. The doctrine concerning angels expounded. 1. That we may learn from them also
   to acknowledge God. 2. That we may be put on our guard against the errors of
   the worshippers of angels and the Manichees. Manicheeism refuted. Rule of
   piety.
4. The angels created by God. At what time and in what order it is inexpedient to
   inquire. The garrulity of the Pseudo-Dionysius.
5. The nature, offices, and various names of angels.
6. Angels the dispensers of the divine beneficence to us.
7. A kind of prefects over kingdoms and provinces, but specially the guardians of the
   elect. Not certain that every believer is under the charge of a single angel.
   Enough, that all angels watch over the safety of the Church.
8. The number and orders of angels not defined. Why angels said to be winged.
9. Angels are ministering spirits and spiritual essences.
10. The heathen error of placing angels on the throne of God refuted. 1. By passages
    of Scripture.
11. Refutation continued. 2. By inferences from other passages. Why God employs
    the ministry of angels.
12. Use of the doctrine of Scripture concerning the holy angels.
13. The doctrine concerning bad angels or devils reduced to four heads. 1. That we
    may guard against their wiles and assaults.
14. That we may be stimulated to exercises of piety. Why one angel in the singular
    number often spoken of.
15. The devil being described as the enemy of man, we should perpetually war against
    him.
16. The wickedness of the devil not by creation but by corruption. Vain and useless
    to inquire into the mode, time, and character of the fall of angels.
17. Though the devil is always opposed in will and endeavour to the will of God, he can
    do nothing without his permission and consent.
18. God so overrules wicked spirits as to permit them to try the faithful, and rule over
    the wicked.
19. The nature of bad angels. They are spiritual essences endued with sense and
    intelligence.
20. The latter part of the chapter briefly embracing the history of creation, and showing
    what it is of importance for us to know concerning God.

21. The special object of this knowledge is to prevent us, through ingratitude or thoughtlessness, from overlooking the perfections of God. Example of this primary knowledge.

22. Another object of this knowledge—viz., that perceiving how these things were created for our use, we may be excited to trust in God, pray to him, and love him.

1. ALTHOUGH Isaiah justly charges the worshippers of false gods with stupidity, in not learning from the foundations of the earth, and the circle of the heavens, who the true God is (Isa. xl. 21) ; yet so sluggish and grovelling is our intellect, that it was necessary he should be more clearly depicted, in order that the faithful might not fall away to Gentile fictions. The idea that God is the soul of the world, though the most tolerable that philosophers have suggested, is absurd ; and, therefore, it was of importance to furnish us with a more intimate knowledge in order that we might not wander to and fro in uncertainty. Hence God was pleased that a history of the creation should exist—a history on which the faith of the Church might lean without seeking any other God than Him whom Moses sets forth as the Creator and Architect of the world. First, in that history, the period of time is marked so as to enable the faithful to ascend by an unbroken succession of years to the first origin of their race and of all things. This knowledge is of the highest use not only as an antidote to the monstrous fables which anciently prevailed both in Egypt and the other regions of the world, but also as a means of giving a clearer manifestation of the eternity of God as contrasted with the birth of creation, and thereby inspiring us with higher admiration. We must not be moved by the profane jeer, that it is strange how it did not sooner occur to the Deity to create the heavens and the earth, instead of idly allowing an infinite period to pass away, during which thousands of generations might have existed, while the present world is drawing to a close before it has completed its six thousandth year. Why God delayed so long it is neither fit nor lawful to inquire. Should the human mind presume to do it, it could only fail in the attempt, nor would it be useful for us to know what God, as a trial of the modesty of our faith, has been pleased purposely to conceal. It was a shrewd saying of a good old man, who when some one pertly asked in derision what God did before the world was created, answered he made a hell for the inquisitive (August. Confess., lib. xi. c. 12). This reproof, not less weighty than severe, should repress the tickling wantonness which urges many to indulge in vicious and hurtful speculation.

In fine, let us remember that that invisible God, whose wisdom, power, and justice, are incomprehensible, is set before us in the history of Moses as in a mirror, in which his living image is reflected. For as an eye, either dimmed by age or weakened by any other cause, sees nothing distinctly without the aid of glasses, so (such is our imbecility) if Scripture does not direct us in our inquiries after God, we immediately turn vain in our imaginations. Those who now indulge their petulance, and refuse to take warning, will learn, when too late, how much better it had been reverently to regard the secret counsels of God, than to belch forth blasphemies which pollute the face of heaven. Justly does Augustine complain that God is insulted whenever any higher reason than his will is demanded (Lib. de Gent.). He also in another place wisely reminds us that it is just as improper to raise questions about infinite periods of time as about infinite space (De Civit. Dei.). However wide the circuit of the heavens may be, it is of some definite extent. But should any one expostulate with God that vacant space remains exceeding creation by a hundredfold, must not every pious mind detest the presumption? Similar is the madness of those who charge God with idleness in not having pleased them by creating the world countless ages sooner than he did create it. In their cupidity they affect to go beyond the world, as if the ample circumference of heaven and earth did not contain objects numerous and resplendent enough to absorb all our senses; as if, in the period of six thousand years, God had not furnished facts enough to exercise our minds in ceaseless meditation. Therefore, let us willingly remain hedged in by those boundaries within which God has been pleased to confine our persons, and, as it were, enclose our minds, so as to prevent them from losing themselves by wandering unrestrained.

2. With the same view Moses relates that the work of creation was accomplished not in one moment, but in six days. By this statement we are drawn away from fiction to the one God who thus divided his work into six days, that we may have no reluctance to devote our whole lives to the contemplation of it. For though our eyes, in what direction soever they turn, are forced to behold the works of God, we see how fleeting our attention is, and how quickly pious thoughts, if any arise, vanish away. Here, too, objection is taken to these progressive steps as inconsistent with the power of God, until human reason is subdued to the obedience of faith, and learns to welcome the calm quiescence to which the sanctification of the seventh day invites us. In the very order of events, we ought diligently to ponder on the paternal goodness of God toward the human race, in not creating Adam until he had liberally enriched the earth with all good things. Had he placed him on an earth barren and unfurnished; had he given life before light, he might have seemed to pay little regard to his interest. But now that he has arranged the motions of the sun and stars for man's use, has replenished the air, earth, and water, with living creatures, and produced all kinds of fruit in abundance for the supply of food, by performing the office of a provident and industrious head of a family, he has shown his wondrous goodness toward us. These subjects, which I only briefly touch, if more attentively pondered, will make it manifest that Moses was a sure witness and herald of the one only Creator. I do not repeat what I have

already explained—viz. that mention is here made not of the bare essence of God, but that his eternal Wisdom and Spirit are also set before us, in order that we may not dream of any other God than Him who desires to be recognised in that express image.

3. But before I begin to treat more fully of the nature of man (chap. xv. and B. II. c. 1), it will be proper to say something of angels. For although Moses, in accommodation to the ignorance of the generality of men, does not in the history of the creation make mention of any other works of God than those which meet our eye, yet, seeing he afterwards introduces angels as the ministers of God, we easily infer that he for whom they do service is their Creator. Hence, though Moses, speaking in popular language, did not at the very commencement enumerate the angels among the creatures of God, nothing prevents us from treating distinctly and explictly of what is delivered by Scripture concerning them in other places. For if we desire to know God by his works, we surely cannot overlook this noble and illustrious specimen. We may add that this branch of doctrine is very necessary for the refutation of numerous errors. The minds of many are so struck with the excellence of angelic natures, that they would think them insulted in being subjected to the authority of God, and so made subordinate. Hence a fancied divinity has been assigned them. Manes, too, has arisen with his sect, fabricating to himself two principles—God and the devil, attributing the origin of good things to God, but assigning all bad natures to the devil as their author. Were this delirium to take possession of our minds, God would be denied his glory in the creation of the world. For, seeing there is nothing more peculiar to God than eternity and αὐτȣσία, *i.e.* self-existence, or existence of himself, if I may so speak, do not those who attribute it to the devil in some degree invest him with the honour of divinity? And where is the omnipotence of God, if the devil has the power of executing whatever he pleases against the will, and notwithstanding of the opposition of God? But the only good ground which the Manichees have—viz. that it were impious to ascribe the creation of anything bad to a good God, militates in no degree against the orthodox faith, since it is not admitted that there is anything naturally bad throughout the universe; the depravity and wickedness, whether of man or of the devil, and the sins thence resulting, being not from nature, but from the corruption of nature; nor, at first, did anything whatever exist that did not exhibit some manifestation of the divine wisdom and justice. To obviate such perverse imaginations, we must raise our minds higher than our eyes can penetrate. It was probably with this view that the Nicene Creed, in calling God the creator of all things, makes express mention of things invisible. My care, however, must be to keep within the bounds which piety prescribes, lest by indulging in speculations beyond my reach, I bewilder the reader, and lead him away from the simplicity of the faith. And since the Holy Spirit

always instructs us in what is useful, but altogether omits, or only touches cursorily on matters which tend little to edification, of all such matters, it certainly is our duty to remain in willing ignorance.

4. Angels being the ministers appointed to execute the commands of God, must of course be admitted to be his creatures; but to stir up questions concerning the time or order in which they were created (see Lombard, lib. ii. dist. 2, sqq.), bespeaks more perverseness than industry. Moses relates that the heavens and the earth were finished, with all their host; what avails it anxiously to inquire at what time other more hidden celestial hosts than the stars and planets also began to be? Not to dwell on this, let us here remember that on the whole subject of religion one rule of modesty and soberness is to be observed, and it is this,—in obscure matters not to speak or think, or even long to know, more than the Word of God has delivered. A second rule is, that in reading the Scriptures we should constantly direct our inquiries and meditations to those things which tend to edification, not indulge in curiosity, or in studying things of no use. And since the Lord has been pleased to instruct us, not in frivolous questions, but in solid piety, in the fear of his name, in true faith, and the duties of holiness, let us rest satisfied with such knowledge. Wherefore, if we would be duly wise, we must renounce those vain babblings of idle men, concerning the nature, ranks, and number of angels, without any authority from the Word of God. I know that many fasten on these topics more eagerly, and take greater pleasure in them than in those relating to daily practice. But if we decline not to be the disciples of Christ, let us not decline to follow the method which he has prescribed. In this way, being contented with him for our master, we will not only refrain from, but even feel averse to, superfluous speculations which he discourages. None can deny that Dionysius (whoever he may have been) has many shrewd and subtle disquisitions in his Celestial Hierarchy; but on looking at them more closely, every one must see that they are merely idle talk. The duty of a Theologian, however, is not to tickle the ear, but confirm the conscience, by teaching what is true, certain, and useful. When you read the work of Dionysius, you would think that the man had come down from heaven, and was relating not what he had learned, but what he had actually seen. Paul, however, though he was carried to the third heaven, so far from delivering anything of the kind, positively declares that it was not lawful for man to speak the secrets which he had seen. Bidding adieu, therefore, to that nugatory wisdom, let us endeavour to ascertain from the simple doctrine of Scripture what it is the Lord's pleasure that we should know concerning angels.

5. In Scripture, then, we uniformly read that angels are heavenly spirits, whose obedience and ministry God employs to execute all the purposes which he has decreed, and hence their name as being a kind of intermediate messengers to manifest his will to men. The names by which several of them are distinguished have reference to the same

office. They are called hosts, because they surround their Prince as his court,—adorn and display his majesty,—like soldiers, have their eyes always turned to their leader's standard, and are so ready and prompt to execute his orders, that the moment he gives the nod, they prepare for, or rather are actually at work. In declaring the magnificence of the divine throne, similar representations are given by the prophets, and especially by Daniel, when he says, that when God stood up to judgment, "thousand thousands ministered unto him, and ten thousand times ten thousand stood before him" (Dan. vii. 10). As by these means the Lord wonderfully exerts and declares the power and might of his hand, they are called Virtues. Again, as his government of the world is exercised and administered by them, they are called at one time Principalities, at another Powers, at another Dominions (Col. i. 16 ; Eph. i. 21). Lastly, as the glory of God in some measure dwells in them, they are also termed Thrones ; though as to this last designation I am unwilling to speak positively, as a different interpretation is equally, if not more congruous. To say nothing, therefore, of the name of Thrones, the former names are often employed by the Holy Spirit in commendation of the dignity of angelic service. Nor is it right to pass by unhonoured those instruments by whom God specially manifests the presence of his power. Nay, they are more than once called Gods, because the Deity is in some measure represented to us in their service, as in a mirror. I am rather inclined, however, to agree with ancient writers, that in those passages[1] wherein it is stated that the angel of the Lord appeared to Abraham, Jacob, and Moses, Christ was that angel. Still it is true, that when mention is made of all the angels, they are frequently so designated. Nor ought this to seem strange. For if princes and rulers have this honour given them, because in their office they are vicegerents of God, the supreme King and Judge, with far greater reason may it be given to angels, in whom the brightness of the divine glory is much more conspicuously displayed.

6. But the point on which the Scriptures specially insist is that which tends most to our comfort, and to the confirmation of our faith, namely, that angels are the ministers and dispensers of the divine bounty towards us. Accordingly, we are told how they watch for our safety, how they undertake our defence, direct our path, and take heed that no evil befall us. There are whole passages which relate, in the first instance, to Christ, the Head of the Church, and after him to all believers. "He shall give his angels charge over thee, to keep thee in all thy ways. They shall bear thee up in their hands, lest thou dash thy foot against a stone." Again, "The angel of the Lord encampeth round about them that fear him, and delivereth them."[2]

[1] Gen. xviii. 2; xxxii. 1, 28; Josh. v. 14; Judges vi. 14; xiii. 10, 22.
[2] Ps. xci. 11; xxxiv. 8; Gen. xvi. 9; xxiv. 7; xlviii. 16; Ex. xiv. 19, 28, 29; Judges ii. 1, 20; vi. 11; xiii. 10; Matth. iv. 11; Luke xxii. 43; Matth. xxviii. 5; Luke xxiv. 5; Acts i. 10; 2 Kings xix. 35; Isa. xxxvii. 36.

By these passages the Lord shows that the protection of those whom he has undertaken to defend he has delegated to his angels. Accordingly, an angel of the Lord consoles Hagar in her flight, and bids her be reconciled to her mistress. Abraham promises to his servant that an angel will be the guide of his journey. Jacob, in blessing Ephraim and Manasseh, prays, "The angel which redeemed me from all evil bless the lads." So an angel was appointed to guard the camp of the Israelites ; and as often as God was pleased to deliver Israel from the hands of his enemies, he stirred up avengers by the ministry of angels. Thus, in fine (not to mention more), angels ministered to Christ, and were present with him in all straits. To the women they announced his resurrection ; to the disciples they foretold his glorious advent. In discharging the office of our protectors, they war against the devil and all our enemies, and execute vengeance upon those who afflict us. Thus we read that an angel of the Lord, to deliver Jerusalem from siege, slew one hundred and eighty-five thousand men in the camp of the king of Assyria in a single night.

7. Whether or not each believer has a single angel assigned to him for his defence, I dare not positively affirm. When Daniel introduces the angel of the Persians and the angel of the Greeks, he undoubtedly intimates that certain angels are appointed as a kind of presidents over kingdoms and provinces.[1] Again, when Christ says that the angels of children always behold the face of his Father, he insinuates that there are certain angels to whom their safety has been intrusted. But I know not if it can be inferred from this, that each believer has his own angel. This, indeed, I hold for certain, that each of us is cared for, not by one angel merely, but that all with one consent watch for our safety. For it is said of all the angels collectively, that they rejoice " over one sinner that repenteth, more than over ninety and nine just persons, which need no repentance." It is also said, that the angels (meaning more than one) carried the soul of Lazarus into Abraham's bosom. Nor was it to no purpose that Elisha showed his servant the many chariots of fire which were specially allotted him.

There is one passage which seems to intimate somewhat more clearly that each individual has a separate angel. When Peter, after his deliverance from prison, knocked at the door of the house where the brethren were assembled, being unable to think it could be himself, they said that it was his angel. This idea seems to have been suggested to them by a common belief that every believer has a single angel assigned to him. Here, however, it may be alleged, that there is nothing to prevent us from understanding it of any one of the angels to whom the Lord might have given the charge of Peter at that particular time, without implying that he was to be his perpetual guardian,

[1] Dan. x. 13, 20 ; xii. 1 ; Matth. xviii. 20 ; Luke xv. 7 ; xvi. 22 ; 2 Kings xvi. 17 ; Acts xii. 15.

according to the vulgar imagination (see Calvin on Mark v. 9), that two angels, a good and a bad, as a kind of genii, are assigned to each individual. After all, it is not worth while anxiously to investigate a point which does not greatly concern us. If any one does not think it enough to know that all the orders of the heavenly host are perpetually watching for his safety, I do not see what he could gain by knowing that he has one angel as a special guardian. Those, again, who limit the care which God takes of each of us to a single angel, do great injury to themselves and to all the members of the Church, as if there were no value in those promises of auxiliary troops, who on every side encircling and defending us, embolden us to fight more manfully.

8. Those who presume to dogmatise on the ranks and numbers of angels, would do well to consider on what foundation they rest. As to their rank, I admit that Michael is described by David as a mighty Prince, and by Jude as an Archangel.[1] Paul also tells us, that an archangel will blow the trumpet which is to summon the world to judgment. But how is it possible from such passages to ascertain the gradations of honour among the angels, to determine the insignia, and assign the place and station of each? Even the two names, Michael and Gabriel, mentioned in Scripture, or a third, if you choose to add it from the history of Tobit, seem to intimate by their meaning that they are given to angels, in accommodation to the weakness of our capacity, though I rather choose not to speak positively on the point. As to the number of angels, we learn from the mouth of our Saviour that there are many legions, and from Daniel that there are many myriads. Elisha's servant saw a multitude of chariots, and their vast number is declared by the fact, that they encamp round about those that fear the Lord. It is certain that spirits have no bodily shape, and yet Scripture, in accommodation to us, describes them under the form of winged Cherubim and Seraphim; not without cause, to assure us that when occasion requires, they will hasten to our aid with incredible swiftness, winging their way to us with the speed of lightning. Farther than this, in regard both to the ranks and numbers of angels, let us class them among those mysterious subjects, the full revelation of which is deferred to the last day, and accordingly refrain from inquiring too curiously, or talking presumptuously.

9. There is one point, however, which, though called into doubt by certain restless individuals, we ought to hold for certain—viz. that angels are ministering spirits (Heb. i. 14); whose service God employs for the protection of his people, and by whose means he distributes his favours among men, and also executes other works. The Sadducees of old maintain, that by angels nothing more was meant

---

[1] Dan. xii. 1; Jude 9; 1 Thess. iv. 16; Dan. x. 13, 21; Luke i. 19, 26; Tobit iii. 17 v. 5; Matth. xxvi. 53; Dan. vii. 10; 2 Kings vi. 17; Ps. xxxiv. 7.

than the movements which God impresses on men, or manifestations which he gives of his own power (Acts xxiii. 8). But this dream is contradicted by so many passages of Scripture, that it seems strange how such gross ignorance could have had any countenance among the Jews. To say nothing of the passages I have already quoted, passages which refer to thousands and legions of angels, speak of them as rejoicing, as bearing up the faithful in their hands, carrying their souls to rest, beholding the face of their Father, and so forth:[1] there are other passages which most clearly prove that they are real beings possessed of spiritual essence. Stephen and Paul say that the Law was enacted in the hands of angels. Our Saviour, moreover, says, that at the resurrection the elect will be like angels ; that the day of judgment is known not even to the angels ; that at that time he himself will come with the holy angels. However much such passages may be twisted, their meaning is plain. In like manner, when Paul beseeches Timothy to keep his precepts as before Christ and his elect angels, it is not qualities or inspirations without substance that he speaks of, but true spirits. And when it is said, in the Epistle to the Hebrews, that Christ was made more excellent than the angels, that the world was not made subject to them, that Christ assumed not their nature, but that of man, it is impossible to give a meaning to the passages without understanding that angels are blessed spirits, as to whom such comparisons may competently be made. The author of that Epistle declares the same thing when he places the souls of believers and the holy angels together in the kingdom of heaven. Moreover, in the passages we have already quoted, the angels of children are said to behold the face of God, to defend us by their protection, to rejoice in our salvation, to admire the manifold grace of God in the Church, to be under Christ their head. To the same effect is their frequent appearance to the holy patriarchs in human form, their speaking, and consenting to be hospitably entertained. Christ, too, in consequence of the supremacy which he obtains as Mediator, is called the Angel (Mal. iii. 1). It was thought proper to touch on this subject in passing, with the view of putting the simple upon their guard against the foolish and absurd imaginations which, suggested by Satan many centuries ago, are ever and anon starting up anew.

10. It remains to give warning against the superstition which usually begins to creep in, when it is said that all blessings are ministered and dispensed to us by angels. For the human mind is apt immediately to think that there is no honour which they ought not to receive, and hence the peculiar offices of Christ and God are bestowed upon them. In this way, the glory of Christ was for several former ages greatly obscured, extravagant eulogiums being pronounced on

---

[1] Luke xv. 10; Ps. xci. 11; Matth. iv. 6; Luke iv. 10, 16, 22; Matth. xviii. 10; Acts vii. 55; Gal. iii. 19; Matth. xxii. 30; xxiv. 36; Eph. iii. 10; 1 Peter i. 12; Heb. i. 6; Ps. xcvii. 7.

angels without any authority from Scripture. Among the corruptions which we now oppose, there is scarcely any one of greater antiquity. Even Paul appears to have had a severe contest with some who so exalted angels as to make them almost the superiors of Christ. Hence he so anxiously urges in his Epistle to the Colossians (Col. i. 16, 20), that Christ is not only superior to all angels, but that all the endowments which they possess are derived from him ; thus warning us against forsaking him, by turning to those who are not sufficient for themselves, but must draw with us at a common fountain. As the refulgence of the Divine glory is manifested in them, there is nothing to which we are more prone than to prostrate ourselves before them in stupid adoration, and then ascribe to them the blessings which we owe to God alone. Even John confesses in the Apocalypse (Rev. xix. 10 ; xxii. 8, 9), that this was his own case, but he immediately adds the answer which was given to him, " See thou do it not : I am thy fellow-servant ; worship God."

11. This danger we will happily avoid, if we consider why it is that God, instead of acting directly without their agency, is wont to employ it in manifesting his power, providing for the safety of his people, and imparting the gifts of his beneficence. This he certainly does not from necessity, as if he were unable to dispense with them. Whenever he pleases, he passes them by, and performs his own work by a single nod : so far are they from relieving him of any difficulty. Therefore, when he employs them, it is as a help to our weakness, that nothing may be wanting to elevate our hopes or strengthen our confidence. It ought, indeed, to be sufficient for us that the Lord declares himself to be our protector. But when we see ourselves beset by so many perils, so many injuries, so many kinds of enemies, such is our frailty and effeminacy, that we might at times be filled with alarm, or driven to despair, did not the Lord proclaim his gracious presence by some means in accordance with our feeble capacities. For this reason, he not only promises to take care of us, but assures us that he has numberless attendants, to whom he has committed the charge of our safety,—that whatever dangers may impend, so long as we are encircled by their protection and guardianship, we are placed beyond all hazard of evil. I admit that after we have a simple assurance of the divine protection, it is improper in us still to look round for help. But since for this our weakness the Lord is pleased, in his infinite goodness and indulgence, to provide, it would ill become us to overlook the favour. Of this we have an example in the servant of Elisha (2 Kings vi. 17), who, seeing the mountain encompassed by the army of the Assyrians, and no means of escape, was completely overcome with terror, and thought it all over with himself and his master. Then Elisha prayed to God to open the eyes of the servant, who forthwith beheld the mountain filled with horses and chariots of fire ; in other words, with a multitude of angels, to whom he and the prophet had been given in charge. Confirmed by the vision he re-

ceived courage, and could boldly defy the enemy, whose appearance previously filled him with dismay.

12. Whatever, therefore, is said as to the ministry of angels, let us employ for the purpose of removing all distrust, and strengthening our confidence in God. Since the Lord has provided us with such protection, let us not be terrified at the multitude of our enemies, as if they could prevail notwithstanding of his aid, but let us adopt the sentiment of Elisha, that more are for us than against us. How preposterous, therefore, is it to allow ourselves to be led away from God by angels who have been appointed for the very purpose of assuring us of his more immediate presence to help us? But we are so led away, if angels do not conduct us directly to him—making us look to him, invoke and celebrate him as our only defender—if they are not regarded merely as hands moving to our assistance just as he directs—if they do not direct us to Christ as the only Mediator on whom we must wholly depend and recline, looking towards him, and resting in him. Our minds ought to give thorough heed to what Jacob saw in his vision (Gen. xxviii. 12),—angels descending to the earth to men, and again mounting up from men to heaven, by means of a ladder, at the head of which the Lord of Hosts was seated, intimating that it is solely by the intercession of Christ that the ministry of angels extends to us, as he himself declares, "Hereafter ye shall see heaven open, and the angels of God ascending and descending upon the Son of man" (John i. 51). Accordingly, the servant of Abraham, though he had been commended to the guardianship of an angel (Gen. xxiv. 7), does not therefore invoke that angel to be present with him, but trusting to the commendation, pours out his prayers before the Lord, and entreats him to show mercy to Abraham. As God does not make angels the ministers of his power and goodness, that he may share his glory with them, so he does not promise his assistance by their instrumentality, that we may divide our confidence between him and them. Away, then, with that Platonic philosophy of seeking access to God by means of angels, and courting them with the view of making God more propitious (*Plat. in Epinomide et Cratylo*),—a philosophy which presumptuous and superstitious men attempted at first to introduce into our religion, and which they persist in even to this day.

13. The tendency of all that Scripture teaches concerning devils is to put us on our guard against their wiles and machinations, that we may provide ourselves with weapons strong enough to drive away the most formidable foes. For when Satan is called the god and ruler of this world, the strong man armed, the prince of the power of the air, the roaring lion,[1] the object of all these descriptions is to make us more cautious and vigilant, and more prepared for the contest. This is sometimes stated in distinct terms. For Peter, after describing the

---

[1] 2 Cor. iv. 4; John xii. 31; Matth. xii. 29; Eph. ii. 2.

devil as a roaring lion, going about seeking whom he may devour, immediately adds the exhortation, "whom resist steadfast in the faith" (1 Pet. v. 8). And Paul, after reminding us that we wrestle not against flesh and blood, but against principalities, against powers, against the rulers of the darkness of this world, against spiritual wickedness in high places, immediately enjoins us to put on armour equal to so great and perilous a contest (Ephes. vi. 12). Wherefore, let this be the use to which we turn all these statements. Being forewarned of the constant presence of an enemy the most daring, the most powerful, the most crafty, the most indefatigable, the most completely equipped with all the engines, and the most expert in the science of war, let us not allow ourselves to be overtaken by sloth or cowardice, but, on the contrary, with minds aroused and ever on the alert, let us stand ready to resist; and, knowing that this warfare is terminated only by death, let us study to persevere. Above all, fully conscious of our weakness and want of skill, let us invoke the help of God, and attempt nothing without trusting in him, since it is his alone to supply counsel, and strength, and courage, and arms.

14. That we may feel the more strongly urged to do so, the Scripture declares that the enemies who war against us are not one or two, or few in number, but a great host. Mary Magdalene is said to have been delivered from seven devils by which she was possessed; and our Saviour assures us that it is an ordinary circumstance, when a devil has been expelled, if access is again given to it, to take seven other spirits, more wicked than itself, and resume the vacant possession. Nay, one man is said to have been possessed by a whole legion.[1] By this, then, we are taught that the number of enemies with whom we have to war is almost infinite, that we may not, from a contemptuous idea of the fewness of their numbers, be more remiss in the contest, or from imagining that an occasional truce is given us, indulge in sloth. In one Satan or devil being often mentioned in the singular number, the thing denoted is that domination of iniquity which is opposed to the reign of righteousness. For, as the Church and the communion of saints has Christ for its head, so the faction of the wicked, and wickedness itself, is portrayed with its prince exercising supremacy. Hence the expression, "Depart, ye cursed, into everlasting fire, prepared for the devil and his angels" (Matth. xxv. 41).

15. One thing which ought to animate us to perpetual contest with the devil is, that he is everywhere called both our adversary and the adversary of God. For, if the glory of God is dear to us, as it ought to be, we ought to struggle with all our might against him who aims at the extinction of that glory. If we are animated with proper zeal to maintain the kingdom of Christ, we must wage irreconcilable war with him who conspires its ruin. Again, if we have any anxiety about our own salvation, we ought to make no peace nor truce with him who

1 Mark xvi. 9; Matth. xii. 43; Luke viii. 30.

is continually laying schemes for its destruction. But such is the character given to Satan in the third chapter of Genesis, where he is seen seducing man from his allegiance to God, that he may both deprive God of his due honour, and plunge man headlong in destruction. Such, too, is the description given of him in the Gospels (Matth. xiii. 28), where he is called the enemy, and is said to sow tares in order to corrupt the seed of eternal life. In one word, in all his actions we experience the truth of our Saviour's description, that he was "a murderer from the beginning, and abode not in the truth" (John viii. 44). Truth he assails with lies, light he obscures with darkness. The minds of men he involves in error; he stirs up hatred, inflames strife and war, and all in order that he may overthrow the kingdom of God, and drown men in eternal perdition with himself. Hence it is evident that his whole nature is depraved, mischievous, and malignant. There must be extreme depravity in a mind bent on assailing the glory of God and the salvation of man. This is intimated by John in his Epistle, when he says that he "sinneth from the beginning" (1 John iii. 8), implying that he is the author, leader, and contriver of all malice and wickedness.

16. But as the devil was created by God, we must remember that this malice which we attribute to his nature is not from creation, but from depravation. Everything damnable in him he brought upon himself, by his revolt and fall. Of this Scripture reminds us, lest, by believing that he was so created at first, we should ascribe to God what is most foreign to his nature. For this reason, Christ declares, (John viii. 44), that Satan, when he lies, "speaketh of his own," and states the reason, "because he abode not in the truth." By saying that he abode not in the truth, he certainly intimates that he once was in the truth, and by calling him the father of lies, he puts it out of his power to charge God with the depravity of which he was himself the cause. But although the expressions are brief and not very explicit, they are amply sufficient to vindicate the majesty of God from every calumny. And what more does it concern us to know of devils? Some murmur because the Scripture does not in various passages give a distinct and regular exposition of Satan's fall, its cause, mode, date, and nature. But as these things are of no consequence to us, it was better, if not entirely to pass them in silence, at least only to touch lightly upon them. The Holy Spirit could not deign to feed curiosity with idle, unprofitable histories. We see it was the Lord's purpose to deliver nothing in his sacred oracles which we might not learn for edification. Therefore, instead of dwelling on superfluous matters, let it be sufficient for us briefly to hold, with regard to the nature of devils, that at their first creation they were the angels of God, but by revolting they both ruined themselves and became the instruments of perdition to others. As it was useful to know this much, it is clearly taught by Peter and Jude: "God," they say, "spared not the angels that sinned, but cast them down to

hell, and delivered them into chains of darkness to be reserved unto judgment" (2 Pet. ii. 4 ; Jude ver. 6). And Paul, by speaking of the elect angels, obviously draws a tacit contrast between them and reprobate angels.

17. With regard to the strife and war which Satan is said to wage with God, it must be understood with this qualification, that Satan cannot possibly do anything against the will and consent of God. For we read in the history of Job, that Satan appears in the presence of God to receive his commands, and dares not proceed to execute any enterprise until he is authorised. In the same way, when Ahab was to be deceived, he undertook to be a lying spirit in the mouth of all the prophets ; and on being commissioned by the Lord, proceeds to do so. For this reason, also, the spirit which tormented Saul is said to be an evil spirit from the Lord, because he was, as it were, the scourge by which the misdeeds of the wicked king were punished. In another place it is said that the plagues of Egypt were inflicted by God through the instrumentality of wicked angels. In conformity with these particular examples, Paul declares generally that unbelievers are blinded by God, though he had previously described it as the doing of Satan.[1] It is evident, therefore, that Satan is under the power of God, and is so ruled by his authority that he must·yield obedience to it. Moreover, though we say that Satan resists God, and does works at variance with His works, we at the same time maintain that this contrariety and opposition depend on the permission of God. I now speak not of Satan's will and endeavour, but only of the result. For the disposition of the devil being wicked, he has no inclination whatever to obey the divine will, but, on the contrary, is wholly bent on contumacy and rebellion. This much, therefore, he has of himself, and his own iniquity, that he eagerly, and of set purpose, opposes God, aiming at those things which he deems most contrary to the will of God. But as God holds him bound and fettered by the curb of his power, he executes those things only for which permission has been given him, and thus, however unwilling, obeys his Creator, being forced, whenever he is required, to do Him service.

18. God thus turning the unclean spirits hither and thither at his pleasure, employs them in exercising believers by warring against them, assailing them with wiles, urging them with solicitations, pressing close upon them, disturbing, alarming, and occasionally wounding, but never conquering or oppressing them ; whereas they hold the wicked in thraldom, exercise dominion over their minds and bodies, and employ them as bond-slaves in all kinds of iniquity. Because believers are disturbed by such enemies, they are addressed in such exhortations as these ; " Neither give place to the devil ;" " Your adversary the devil, as a roaring lion, walketh about seeking

---

[1] Job i. 6 ; ii. 1 ; 1 Kings xxii. 20 ; 1 Sam. xvi. 14 ; xviii. 10 ; 2 Thess. ii. 9, 11.

whom he may devour; whom resist steadfast in the faith" (Eph. iv. 27; 1 Pet. v. 8). Paul acknowledges that he was not exempt from this species of contest when he says, that for the purpose of subduing his pride, a messenger of Satan was sent to buffet him (2 Cor. xii. 7). This trial, therefore, is common to all the children of God. But as the promise of bruising Satan's head (Gen. iii. 15) applies alike to Christ and to all his members, I deny that believers can ever be oppressed or vanquished by him. They are often, indeed, thrown into alarm, but never so thoroughly as not to recover themselves. They fall by the violence of the blows, but they get up again; they are wounded, but not mortally. In fine, they labour on through the whole course of their lives, so as ultimately to gain the victory, though they meet with occasional defeats. We know how David, through the just anger of God, was left for a time to Satan, and by his instigation numbered the people (2 Sam. xxiv. 1); nor without cause does Paul hold out a hope of pardon in case any should have become ensnared by the wiles of the devil (2 Tim. ii. 26). Accordingly, he elsewhere shows that the promise above quoted commences in this life where the struggle is carried on, and that it is completed after the struggle is ended. His words are, "The God of peace shall bruise Satan under your feet shortly" (Rom. xvi. 20). In our Head, indeed, this victory was always perfect, because the prince of the world "had nothing" in him (John xiv. 30); but in us, who are his members, it is now partially obtained, and will be perfected when we shall have put off our mortal flesh, through which we are liable to infirmity, and shall have been filled with the energy of the Holy Spirit. In this way, when the kingdom of Christ is raised up and established, that of Satan falls, as our Lord himself expresses it, "I beheld Satan as lightning fall from heaven" (Luke x. 18). By these words, he confirmed the report which the apostles gave of the efficacy of their preaching. In like manner he says, "When a strong man armed keepeth his palace, his goods are in peace. But when a stronger than he shall come upon him, and overcome him, he taketh from him all his armour wherein he trusted, and divideth his spoils" (Luke xi. 21, 22). And to this end Christ, by dying, overcame Satan, who had the power of death (Heb. ii. 14), and triumphed over all his hosts, that they might not injure the Church, which otherwise would suffer from them every moment. For (such being our weakness, and such his raging fury) how could we withstand his manifold and unintermitted assaults for any period, however short, if we did not trust to the victory of our leader? God, therefore, does not allow Satan to have dominion over the souls of believers, but only gives over to his sway the impious and unbelieving, whom he deigns not to number among his flock. For the devil is said to have undisputed possession of this world until he is dispossessed by Christ. In like manner, he is said to blind all who do not believe the Gospel, and to do his own work in the children of disobedience. And justly; for all the wicked are vessels of wrath, and, accordingly, to whom should they be subjected but to the minister of the divine vengeance? In fine, they are said to be of their father the devil.[1] For as believers are recognised to be the sons of God by bearing his image, so the wicked are properly regarded as the children of Satan, from having degenerated into his image.

19. Having above refuted that nugatory philosophy concerning the holy angels, which teaches that they are nothing but good motions or inspirations which God excites in the minds of men, we must here likewise refute those who foolishly allege that devils are nothing but bad affections or perturbations suggested by our carnal nature. The brief refutation is to be found in passages of Scripture on this subject, passages neither few nor obscure. First, when they are called unclean spirits and apostate angels (Matth. xii. 43; Jude, verse 6), who have degenerated from their original, the very terms sufficiently declare that they are not motions or affections of the mind, but truly, as they are called, minds or spirits endued with sense and intellect. In like manner, when the children of God are contrasted by John, and also by our Saviour, with the children of the devil, would not the contrast be absurd if the term devil meant nothing more than evil inspirations? And John adds still more emphatically, that the devil sinneth from the beginning (1 John iii. 8). In like manner, when Jude introduces the archangel Michael contending with the devil (Jude, verse 9), he certainly contrasts a wicked and rebellious with a good angel. To this corresponds the account given in the Book of Job, that Satan appeared in the presence of God with the holy angels. But the clearest passages of all are those which make mention of the punishment which, from the judgment of God, they already begin to feel, and are to feel more especially at the resurrection, "What have we to do with thee, Jesus, thou Son of God? art thou come hither to torment us before the time?" (Matth. viii. 29); and again, "Depart, ye cursed, into everlasting fire, prepared for the devil and his angels" (Matth. xxv. 41). Again, "If God spared not the angels that sinned, but cast them down to hell, and delivered them into chains of darkness to be reserved unto judgment," &c. (2 Pet. ii. 4). How absurd the expressions, that devils are doomed to eternal punishment, that fire is prepared for them, that they are even now excruciated and tormented by the glory of Christ, if there were truly no devils at all? But as all discussion on this subject is superfluous for those who give credit to the Word of God, while little is gained by quoting Scripture to those empty speculators whom nothing but novelty can please, I believe I have already done enough for my purpose, which was to put the pious on their guard against the delirious dreams with which restless men harass themselves and the simple. The subject, however, deserved to be touched upon, lest any, by embracing that error,

---

[1] 2 Cor. iv. 4; Eph. ii. 2; Rom. ix. 22; John viii. 44; 1 John iii. 8.

should imagine they have no enemy, and thereby be more remiss or less cautious in resisting.

20. Meanwhile, being placed in this most beautiful theatre, let us not decline to take a pious delight in the clear and manifest works of God. For, as we have elsewhere observed, though not the chief, it is, in point of order, the first evidence of faith, to remember to which side soever we turn, that all which meets the eye is the work of God, and at the same time to meditate with pious care on the end which God had in view in creating it. Wherefore, in order that we may apprehend with true faith what it is necessary to know concerning God, it is of importance to attend to the history of the creation, as briefly recorded by Moses, and afterwards more copiously illustrated by pious writers, more especially by Basil and Ambrose. From this history we learn that God, by the power of his Word and his Spirit, created the heavens and the earth out of nothing; that thereafter he produced things inanimate and animate of every kind, arranging an innumerable variety of objects in admirable order, giving each kind its proper nature, office, place, and station; at the same time, as all things were liable to corruption, providing for the perpetuation of each single species, cherishing some by secret methods, and, as it were, from time to time instilling new vigour into them, and bestowing on others a power of continuing their race, so preventing it from perishing at their own death. Heaven and earth being thus most richly adorned, and copiously supplied with all things, like a large and splendid mansion gorgeously constructed and exquisitely furnished, at length man was made—man, by the beauty of his person and his many noble endowments, the most glorious specimen of the works of God. But, as I have no intention to give the history of creation in detail, it is sufficient to have again thus briefly touched on it in passing. I have already reminded my reader, that the best course for him is to derive his knowledge of the subject from Moses and others, who have carefully and faithfully transmitted an account of the creation.

21. It is unnecessary to dwell at length on the end that should be aimed at in considering the works of God. The subject has been in a great measure explained elsewhere, and in so far as required by our present work, may now be disposed of in a few words. Undoubtedly, were one to attempt to speak in due terms of the inestimable wisdom, power, justice, and goodness of God, in the formation of the world, no grace or splendour of diction could equal the greatness of the subject. Still there can be no doubt that the Lord would have us constantly occupied with such holy meditation, in order that, while we contemplate the immense treasures of wisdom and goodness exhibited in the creatures, as in so many mirrors, we may not only run our eye over them with a hasty, and, as it were, evanescent glance, but dwell long upon them, seriously and faithfully turn them in our minds, and every now and then bring them to recollection.

But as the present work is of a didactic nature, we cannot fittingly enter on topics which require lengthened discourse. Therefore, in order to be compendious, let the reader understand that he has a genuine apprehension of the character of God as the Creator of the world; first, if he attends to the general rule, never thoughtlessly or obliviously to overlook the glorious perfections which God displays in his creatures; and, secondly, if he makes a self-application of what he sees, so as to fix it deeply on his heart. The former is exemplified when we consider how great the Architect must be who framed and ordered the multitude of the starry host so admirably, that it is impossible to imagine a more glorious sight, so stationing some, and fixing them to particular spots that they cannot move; giving a fixer course to others, yet setting limits to their wanderings; so tempering the movement of the whole as to measure out day and night, months, years, and seasons, and at the same time so regulating the inequality of days as to prevent everything like confusion. The former course is, moreover, exemplified when we attend to his power in sustaining the vast mass, and guiding the swift revolutions of the heavenly bodies, &c. These few examples sufficiently explain what is meant by recognising the divine perfections in the creation of the world. Were we to attempt to go over the whole subject we should never come to a conclusion, there being as many miracles of divine power, as many striking evidences of wisdom and goodness, as there are classes of objects, nay, as there are individual objects, great or small, throughout the universe.

22. The other course, which has a closer relation to faith, remains to be considered—viz. that while we observe how God has destined all things for our good and salvation, we at the same time feel his power and grace, both in ourselves and in the great blessings which he has bestowed upon us; thence stirring up ourselves to confidence in him, to invocation, praise, and love. Moreover, as I lately observed, the Lord himself, by the very order of creation, has demonstrated that he created all things for the sake of man. Nor is it unimportant to observe, that he divided the formation of the world into six days, though it had been in no respect more difficult to complete the whole work, in all its parts, in one moment than by a gradual progression. But he was pleased to display his providence and paternal care towards us in this, that before he formed man, he provided whatever he foresaw would be useful and salutary to him. How ungrateful, then, were it to doubt whether we are cared for by this most excellent Parent, who we see cared for us even before we were born! How impious were it to tremble in distrust, lest we should one day be abandoned in our necessity by that kindness which, antecedent to our existence, displayed itself in a complete supply of all good things! Moreover, Moses tells us that everything which the world contains is liberally placed at our disposal. This God certainly did not that he might delude us with an empty form of dona-

tion. Nothing, therefore, which concerns our safety will ever be wanting. To conclude, in one word; as often as we call God the Creator of heaven and earth, let us remember that the distribution of all the things which he created are in his hand and power, but that we are his sons, whom he has undertaken to nourish and bring up in allegiance to him, that we may expect the substance of all good from him alone, and have full hope that he will never suffer us to be in want of things necessary to salvation, so as to leave us dependent on some other scource; that in everything we desire we may address our prayers to him, and in every benefit we receive acknowledge his hand and give him thanks; that thus allured by his great goodness and beneficence, we may study with our whole heart to love and serve him.

CHAPTER XV.

STATE IN WHICH MAN WAS CREATED.   THE FACULTIES OF THE SOUL—
THE IMAGE OF GOD—FREE WILL—ORIGINAL RIGHTEOUSNESS.

This chapter is thus divided:—I. The necessary rules to be observed in considering the state of man before the fall being laid down, the point first considered is the creation of the body, and the lesson taught by its being formed out of the earth, and made alive, sec. 1.   II. The immortality of the human soul is proved by various solid arguments, sec. 2.   III. The image of God (the strongest proof of the soul's immortality) is considered, and various absurd fancies are refuted, sec. 3.   IV. Several errors which obscure the light of truth being dissipated, follows a philosophical and theological consideration of the faculties of the soul before the fall.

Sections.

1. A twofold knowledge of God—viz. before the fall and after it.   The former here considered.   Particular rules or precautions to be observed in this discussion. What we are taught by a body formed out of the dust, and tenanted by a spirit.
2. The immortality of the soul proved from, 1. The testimony of conscience.   2. The knowledge of God.   3. The noble faculties with which it is endued.   4. Its activity and wondrous fancies in sleep.   5. Innumerable passages of Scripture.
3. The image of God one of the strongest proofs of the immortality of the soul. What meant by this image.   The dreams of Osiander concerning the image of God refuted.   Whether any difference between " image " and " likeness."   Another objection of Osiander refuted.   The image of God conspicuous in the whole Adam.
4. The image of God is in the soul.   Its nature may be learnt from its renewal by Christ.   What comprehended under this renewal.   What the image of God in man before the fall.   In what things it now appears.   When and where it will be seen in perfection.
5. The dreams of the Manichees and of Servetus, as to the origin of the soul, refuted. Also of Osiander, who denies that there is any image of God in man without essential righteousness.
6. The doctrine of philosophers as to the faculties of the soul generally discordant, doubtful, and obscure.   The excellence of the soul described.   Only one soul in each man.   A brief review of the opinion of philosophers as to the faculties of the soul.   What to be thought of this opinion.
7. The division of the faculties of the soul into intellect and will, more agreeable to Christian doctrine.
8. The power and office of the intellect and will in man before the fall.   Man's free will.   This freedom lost by the fall—a fact unknown to philosophers.   The delusion of Pelagians and Papists.   Objection as to the fall of man when free, refuted.

1. WE have now to speak of the creation of man, not only because of all the works of God it is the noblest, and most admirable specimen of his justice, wisdom, and goodness, but, as we observed at the outset, we cannot clearly and properly know God unless the knowledge of ourselves be added.   This knowledge is twofold,—relating, first, to the condition in which we were at first created; and, secondly, to our condition such as it began to be immediately after Adam's fall. For it would little avail us to know how we were created if we remained

ignorant of the corruption and degradation of our nature in consequence of the fall. At present, however, we confine ourselves to a consideration of our nature in its original integrity. And, certainly, before we descend to the miserable condition into which man has fallen, it is of importance to consider what he was at first. For there is need of caution, lest we attend only to the natural ills of man, and thereby seem to ascribe them to the Author of nature; impiety deeming it a sufficient defence if it can pretend that everything vicious in it proceeded in some sense from God, and not hesitating, when accused, to plead against God, and throw the blame of its guilt upon Him. Those who would be thought to speak more reverently of the Deity catch at an excuse for their depravity from nature, not considering that they also, though more obscurely, bring a charge against God, on whom the dishonour would fall if anything vicious were proved to exist in nature. Seeing, therefore, that the flesh is continually on the alert for subterfuges, by which it imagines it can remove the blame of its own wickedness from itself to some other quarter, we must diligently guard against this depraved procedure, and accordingly treat of the calamity of the human race in such a way as may cut off every evasion, and vindicate the justice of God against all who would impugn it. We shall afterwards see, in its own place (Book II. chap. i. sec. 3), how far mankind now are from the purity originally conferred on Adam. And, first, it is to be observed, that when he was formed out of the dust of the ground a curb was laid on his pride—nothing being more absurd than that those should glory in their excellence who not only dwell in tabernacles of clay, but are themselves in part dust and ashes. But God having not only deigned to animate a vessel of clay, but to make it the habitation of an immortal spirit, Adam might well glory in the great liberality of his Maker.[1]

2. Moreover, there can be no question that man consists of a body and a soul; meaning by soul, an immortal though created essence, which is his nobler part. Sometimes he is called a spirit. But though the two terms, while they are used together, differ in their meaning, still when spirit is used by itself it is equivalent to soul, as when Solomon speaking of death says, that the spirit returns to God who gave it (Eccles. xii. 7). And Christ, in commending his spirit to the Father, and Stephen his to Christ, simply mean, that when the soul is freed from the prison-house of the body, God becomes its perpetual keeper. Those who imagine that the soul is called a spirit because it is a breath or energy divinely infused into bodies, but devoid of essence, err too grossly, as is shown both by the nature of

---

[1] On man's first original, see *Calvin against Pighius;* and on the immortality of the soul, see *Calvin's Psychopannychia* and *Instructio adv. Libertinos,* c. ix. 11, 12. It is curious to see how widely the opinion of Pliny differs from the Christian doctrine: " Omnibus a suprema die eadem quæ ante primam; hic magis a morte sensus ullus aut corpori aut animæ quam ante natales. Eadem enim vanitas in futurum etiam se propagat et in mortis quoque tempora ipsa sibi vitam mentitur."—*Plin. Hist. Nat.* lib. vii. c. 56.

the thing, and the whole tenor of Scripture. It is true, indeed, that men cleaving too much to the earth are dull of apprehension, nay, being alienated from the Father of Lights, are so immersed in darkness as to imagine that they will not survive the grave ; still the light is not so completely quenched in darkness that all sense of immortality is lost. Conscience, which, distinguishing between good and evil, responds to the judgment of God, is an undoubted sign of an immortal spirit. How could motion devoid of essence penetrate to the judgment-seat of God, and under a sense of guilt strike itself with terror ? The body cannot be affected by any fear of spiritual punishment. This is competent only to the soul, which must therefore be endued with essence. Then the mere knowledge of a God sufficiently proves that souls which rise higher than the world must be immortal, it being impossible that any evanescent vigour could reach the very fountain of life. In fine, while the many noble faculties with which the human mind is endued proclaim that something divine is engraven on it, they are so many evidences of an immortal essence. For such sense as the lower animals possess goes not beyond the body, or at least not beyond the objects actually presented to it. But the swiftness with which the human mind glances from heaven to earth, scans the secrets of nature, and, after it has embraced all ages, with intellect and memory digests each in its proper order, and reads the future in the past, clearly demonstrates that there lurks in man a something separated from the body. We have intellect by which we are able to conceive of the invisible God and angels—a thing of which body is altogether incapable. We have ideas of rectitude, justice, and honesty—ideas which the bodily senses cannot reach. The seat of these ideas must therefore be a spirit. Nay, sleep itself, which stupifying the man, seems even to deprive him of life, is no obscure evidence of immortality ; not only suggesting thoughts of things which never existed, but foreboding future events. I briefly touch on topics which even profane writers describe with a more splendid eloquence. For pious readers, a simple reference is sufficient. Were not the soul some kind of essence separated from the body, Scripture would not teach [1] that we dwell in houses of clay, and at death remove from a tabernacle of flesh ; that we put off that which is corruptible, in order that, at the last day, we may finally receive according to the deeds done in the body. These, and similar passages which everywhere occur, not only clearly distinguish the soul from the body, but by giving it the name of man, intimate that it is his principal part. Again, when Paul exhorts believers to cleanse themselves from all filthiness of the flesh and the spirit, he shows that there are two parts in which the taint of sin resides. Peter, also, in calling Christ the

1 Job iv. 19 ; 2 Cor. v 4 ; 2 Pet. i. 13, 14 ; 2 Cor. v. 10 : vii. 1 ; 1 Pet. ii. 25 ; i. 9 ; ii. 11 ; Heb. xiii 17 ; 2 Cor. i. 23 ; Matth. x. 28 ; Luke xii. 5 ; Heb. xii. 9 ; Luke xvi. 22 ; 2 Cor. v. 6, 8 ; Acts xxiii. 8.

Shepherd and Bishop of souls, would have spoken absurdly if there were no souls towards which he might discharge such an office. Nor would there be any ground for what he says concerning the eternal salvation of souls, or for his injunction to purify our souls, or for his assertion that fleshly lusts war against the soul; neither could the author of the Epistle to the Hebrews say, that pastors watch as those who must give an account for our souls, if souls were devoid of essence. To the same effect Paul calls God to witness upon his soul, which could not be brought to trial before God if incapable of suffering punishment. This is still more clearly expressed by our Saviour, when he bids us fear him who, after he hath killed the body, is able also to cast into hell fire. Again, when the author of the Epistle to the Hebrews distinguishes the fathers of our flesh from God, who alone is the Father of our spirits, he could not have asserted the essence of the soul in clearer terms. Moreover, did not the soul, when freed from the fetters of the body, continue to exist, our Saviour would not have represented the soul of Lazarus as enjoying blessedness in Abraham's bosom, while, on the contrary, that of Dives was suffering dreadful torments. Paul assures us of the same thing when he says, that so long as we are present in the body we are absent from the Lord. Not to dwell on a matter as to which there is little obscurity, I will only add, that Luke mentions among the errors of the Sadducees that they believed neither angel nor spirit.

3. A strong proof of this point may be gathered from its being said, that man was created in the image of God. For though the divine glory is displayed in man's outward appearance, it cannot be doubted that the proper seat of the image is in the soul. I deny not, indeed, that external shape, in so far as it distinguishes and separates us from the lower animals, brings us nearer to God; nor will I vehemently oppose any who may choose to include under the image of God that

> " While the mute creation downward bend
> Their sight, and to their earthly mother tend,
> Man looks aloft, and with erected eyes,
> Beholds his own hereditary skies."[1]

Only let it be understood, that the image of God which is beheld or made conspicuous by these external marks, is spiritual. For Osiander (whose writings exhibit a perverse ingenuity in futile devices), extending the image of God indiscriminately as well to the body as to the soul, confounds heaven with earth. He says that the Father, the Son, and the Holy Spirit placed their image in man, because, even though Adam had stood entire, Christ would still have become man. Thus, according to him, the body which was destined for Christ was a model and type of that corporeal figure which was then formed.

---

[1] Ovid, Metam. Lib. I.—*Dryden's Translation.*

But where does he find that Christ is an image of the Spirit? I admit, indeed, that in the person of the Mediator, the glory of the whole Godhead is displayed: but how can the eternal Word, who in order precedes the Spirit, be called his image? In short, the distinction between the Son and the Spirit is destroyed when the former is represented as the image of the latter. Moreover, I should like to know in what respect Christ in the flesh in which he was clothed resembles the Holy Spirit, and by what marks or lineaments the likeness is expressed. And since the expression, " Let us make man in our own image," is used in the person of the Son also, it follows that he is the image of himself—a thing utterly absurd. Add that, according to the figment of Osiander,[1] Adam was formed after the model or type of the man Christ. Hence Christ, inasmuch as he was to be clothed with flesh, was the idea according to which Adam was formed, whereas the Scriptures teach very differently—viz. that he was formed in the image of God. There is more plausibility in the imagination of those who interpret that Adam was created in the image of God, because it was conformable to Christ, who is the only image of God; but not even for this is there any solid foundation. The " image " and " likeness" has given rise to no small discussion ; interpreters searching without cause for a difference between the two terms, since " likeness" is merely added by way of exposition. First, we know that repetitions are common in Hebrew, which often gives two words for one thing ; and, secondly, there is no ambiguity in the thing itself, man being called the image of God because of his likeness to God. Hence there is an obvious absurdity in those who indulge in philosophical speculation as to these names, placing the *Zelem*, that is, the image, in the substance of the soul, and the *Demuth*, that is, the likeness, in its qualities, and so forth. God having determined to create man in his own image, to remove the obscurity which was in this term, adds, by way of explanation, in *his likeness*, as if he had said, that he would make man, in whom he would, as it were, image himself by means of the marks of resemblance impressed upon him. Accordingly, Moses, shortly after repeating the account, puts down the image of God twice, and makes no mention of the likeness. Osiander frivolously objects that it is not a part of the man, or the soul with its faculties, which is called the image of God, but the whole Adam, who received his name from the dust out of which he was taken. I call the objection frivolous, as all sound readers will judge. For though the whole man is called mortal, the soul is not therefore liable to death, nor when he is called a rational animal is reason or intelligence thereby attributed to the body. Hence, although the soul is not the man, there is no absurdity in holding that he is called the

---

1 As to Osiander's absurd fancy, see Book II. cap. 12, sec. 5, sq. In Rom. viii. 3, Christ is said to have been sent by the Father in the likeness of sinful flesh, but nowhere is Adam said to have been formed in the likeness of Christ's future flesh, although Tertullian somewhere says so.

image of God in respect of the soul ; though I retain the principle which I lately laid down, that the image of God extends to everything in which the nature of man surpasses that of all other species of animals. Accordingly, by this term is denoted the integrity with which Adam was endued when his intellect was clear, his affections subordinated to reason, all his senses duly regulated, and when he truly ascribed all his excellence to the admirable gifts of his Maker. And though the primary seat of the divine image was in the mind and the heart, or in the soul and its powers, there was no part even of the body in which some rays of glory did not shine. It is certain that in every part of the world some lineaments of divine glory are beheld ; and hence we may infer, that when his image is placed in man, there is a kind of tacit antithesis, as it were, setting man apart from the crowd, and exalting him above all the other creatures. But it cannot be denied that the angels also were created in the likeness of God, since, as Christ declares (Matth. xxii. 30), our highest perfection will consist in being like them. But it is not without good cause that Moses commends the favour of God towards us by giving us this peculiar title, the more especially that he was only comparing man with the visible creation.

4. But our definition of the image seems not to be complete until it appears more clearly what the faculties are in which man excels, and in which he is to be regarded as a mirror of the divine glory. This, however, cannot be better known than from the remedy provided for the corruption of nature. It cannot be doubted that when Adam lost his first estate he became alienated from God. Wherefore, although we grant that the image of God was not utterly effaced and destroyed in him, it was, however, so corrupted, that any thing which remains is fearful deformity ; and, therefore, our deliverance begins with that renovation which we obtain from Christ, who is, therefore, called the second Adam, because he restores us to true and substantial integrity. For although Paul, contrasting the quickening Spirit which believers receive from Christ, with the living soul which Adam was created (1 Cor. xv. 45), commends the richer measure of grace bestowed in regeneration, he does not, however, contradict the statement, that the end of regeneration is to form us anew in the image of God. Accordingly, he elsewhere shows that the new man is renewed after the image of him that created him (Col. iii. 19). To this corresponds another passage, " Put ye on the new man, who after God is created" (Eph. iv. 24). We must now see what particulars Paul comprehends under this renovation. In the first place, he mentions knowledge ; and, in the second, true righteousness and holiness. Hence we infer, that at the beginning the image of God was manifested by light of intellect, rectitude of heart, and the soundness of every part. For though I admit that the forms of expression are elliptical, this principle cannot be overthrown—viz. that the leading feature in the renovation of the divine image must also have held

the highest place in its creation.   To the same effect Paul elsewhere says that, beholding the glory of Christ with unveiled face, we are transformed into the same image.   We now see how Christ is the most perfect image of God, into which we are so renewed as to bear the image of God in knowledge, purity, righteousness, and true holiness.   This being established, the imagination of Osiander, as to bodily form, vanishes of its own accord.   As to that passage of St Paul (1 Cor. xi. 7), in which the man alone, to the express exclusion of the woman, is called the image and glory of God, it is evident, from the context, that it merely refers to civil order.   I presume it has already been sufficiently proved, that the image comprehends everything which has any relation to the spiritual and eternal life. The same thing, in different terms, is declared by St John when he says, that the light which was from the beginning, in the eternal Word of God, was the light of man (John i. 4).   His object being to extol the singular grace of God in making man excel the other animals, he at the same time shows how he was formed in the image of God, that he may separate him from the common herd, as possessing not ordinary animal existence, but one which combines with it the light of intelligence.   Therefore, as the image of God constitutes the entire excellence of human nature, as it shone in Adam before his fall, but was afterwards vitiated and almost destroyed, nothing remaining but a ruin, confused, mutilated, and tainted with impurity, so it is now partly seen in the elect, in so far as they are regenerated by the Spirit.   Its full lustre, however, will be displayed in heaven. But in order to know the particular properties in which it consists, it will be proper to treat of the faculties of the soul.   For there is no solidity in Augustine's speculation,[1] that the soul is a mirror of the Trinity, inasmuch as it comprehends within itself, intellect, will, and memory.   Nor is there probability in the opinion of those who place likeness to God in the dominion bestowed upon man, as if he only resembled God in this, that he is appointed lord and master of all things.   The likeness must be within, in himself.   It must be something which is not external to him, but is properly the internal good of the soul.

5. But before I proceed farther, it is necessary to advert to the dream of the Manichees, which Servetus has attempted in our day to revive.   Because it is said that God breathed into man's nostrils the breath of life (Gen. ii. 7), they thought that the soul was a transmission of the substance of God; as if some portion of the boundless divinity had passed into man.   It cannot take long time to show how many gross and foul absurdities this devilish error carries in its train.   For if the soul of man is a portion transmitted from the essence of God, the divine nature must not only be liable to passion and change, but also to ignorance, evil desires, infirmity, and all

[1] See Aug. *Lib. de Trin.* 10, et *Lib. de Civit. Dei*, 11. See farther, Calvin, in *Psycho pannychia et Comment. in Genes.*

kinds of vice. There is nothing more inconstant than man, contrary movements agitating and distracting his soul. He is ever and anon deluded by want of skill, and overcome by the slightest temptations; while every one feels that the soul itself is a receptacle for all kinds of pollution. All these things must be attributed to the divine nature, if we hold that the soul is of the essence of God, or a secret influx of divinity. Who does not shudder at a thing so monstrous? Paul, indeed, quoting from Aratus, tells us we are his offspring (Acts xvii. 28); not in substance, however, but in quality, inasmuch as he has adorned us with divine endowments. Meanwhile, to lacerate the essence of the Creator, in order to assign a portion to each individual, is the height of madness. It must, therefore, be held as certain, that souls, notwithstanding of their having the divine image engraven on them, are created just as angels are. Creation, however, is not a transfusion of essence,[1] but a commencement of it out of nothing. Nor, though the spirit is given by God, and when it quits the flesh again returns to him, does it follow that it is a portion withdrawn from his essence.[2] Here, too, Osiander, carried away by his illusions, entangled himself in an impious error, by denying that the image of God could be in man without his essential righteousness; as if God were unable, by the mighty power of his Spirit, to render us conformable to himself, unless Christ were substantially transfused into us. Under whatever colour some attempt to gloss these delusions, they can never so blind the eyes of intelligent readers, as to prevent them from discerning in them a revival of Manicheism. But from the words of Paul, when treating of the removal of the image (2 Cor. iii. 18), the inference is obvious, that man was conformable to God, not by an influx of substance, but by the grace and virtue of the Spirit. He says, that by beholding the glory of Christ, we are transformed into the same image as by the Spirit of the Lord; and certainly the Spirit does not work in us so as to make us of the same substance with God.

6. It were vain to seek a definition of the soul from philosophers, not one of whom, with the exception of Plato, distinctly maintained its immortality. Others of the school of Socrates, indeed, lean the same way, but still without teaching distinctly a doctrine of which they were not fully persuaded. Plato, however, advanced still further, and regarded the soul as an image of God. Others so attach its powers and faculties to the present life, that they leave nothing external to the body. Moreover, having already shown from Scripture that the substance of the soul is incorporeal, we must now add, that though it is not properly enclosed by space, it however occupies the body as a kind of habitation, not only animating all its parts, and

---

[1] The French adds, " comme si on tiroit le vin d'un vaisseau en une bouteille;"—as if one were to draw wine out of a cask into a bottle.

[2] The French is, "qu'il le coupe de sa substance comme une branche d'arbre;"— that he cuts it from his substance like a branch from a tree.

rendering the organs fit and useful for their actions, but also holding the first place in regulating the conduct. This it does not merely in regard to the offices of a terrestrial life, but also in regard to the service of God. This, though not clearly seen in our corrupt state, yet the impress of its remains is seen in our very vices. For whence have men such a thirst for glory but from a sense of shame? And whence this sense of shame, but from a respect for what is honourable? Of this, the first principle and source is a consciousness that they were born to cultivate righteousness,—a consciousness akin to religion. But as man was undoubtedly created to meditate on the heavenly life, so it is certain that the knowledge of it was engraven on the soul. And, indeed, man would want the principal use of his understanding if he were unable to discern his felicity, the perfection of which consists in being united to God. Hence, the principal action of the soul is to aspire thither, and, accordingly, the more a man studies to approach to God, the more he proves himself to be endued with reason.

Though there is some plausibility in the opinion of those who maintain that man has more than one soul, namely, a sentient and a rational, yet as there is no soundness in their arguments, we must reject it, unless we would torment ourselves with things frivolous and useless. They tell us (see chap. v. sec. 4), there is a great repugnance between organic movements and the rational part of the soul. As if reason also were not at variance with herself, and her counsels sometimes conflicting with each other like hostile armies. But since this disorder results from the depravation of nature, it is erroneous to infer that there are two souls, because the faculties do not accord so harmoniously as they ought. But I leave it to philosophers to discourse more subtilely of these faculties. For the edification of the pious, a simple definition will be sufficient. I admit, indeed, that what they ingeniously teach on the subject is true, and not only pleasant, but also useful to be known; nor do I forbid any who are inclined to prosecute the study. First, I admit that there are five senses, which Plato (in Theæteto) prefers calling organs, by which all objects are brought into a common sensorium, as into a kind of receptacle:[1] Next comes the imagination (*phantasia*), which distinguishes between the objects brought into the sensorium: Next, reason, to which the general power of judgment belongs: And, lastly, intellect, which contemplates with fixed and quiet look whatever reason discursively revolves. In like manner,[2] to intellect, fancy, and reason, the three cognitive faculties of the soul, correspond

1 The French is, "Et que par iceux comme par canaux, tous objects qui se presentent à la veuë, au goust, ou au flair, ou a l'attouchement distillent au sens commun, comme en une cisterne qui reçoit d'un coté et d'autre."—"And that by them as by channels, all objects which present themselves to the sight, taste, smell, or touch, drop into the common sensorium, as into a cistern which receives on either side."

2 See Arist. lib. i. Ethic. cap. ult.; item, lib. vi. cap. 2.

three appetive faculties—viz. will—whose office is to choose whatever reason and intellect propound; irascibility, which seizes on what is set before it by reason and fancy; and concupiscence, which lays hold of the objects presented by sense and fancy.

Though these things are true, or at least plausible, still, as I fear they are more fitted to entangle, by their obscurity, than to assist us, I think it best to omit them. If any one chooses to distribute the powers of the mind in a different manner, calling one appetive, which, though devoid of reason, yet obeys reason, if directed from a different quarter, and another intellectual, as being by itself participant of reason, I have no great objection. Nor am I disposed to quarrel with the view, that there are three principles of action—viz. sense, intellect, and appetite. But let us rather adopt a division adapted to all capacities—a thing which certainly is not to be obtained from philosophers. For they,[1] when they would speak most plainly, divide the soul into appetite and intellect, but make both double. To the latter they sometimes give the name of *contemplative*, as being contented with mere knowledge, and having no active power—(which circumstance makes Cicero designate it by the name of intellect, *ingenii*) (De Fin. lib. v.). At other times they give it the name of *practical*, because it variously moves the will by the apprehension of good or evil. Under this class is included the art of living well and justly. The former—viz. appetite—they divide into will and concupiscence, calling it βουλησις, whenever the appetite, which they call ὁρμη, obeys the reason. But when appetite, casting off the yoke of reason, runs to intemperance, they call it παθος. Thus they always presuppose in man a reason by which he 'is able to guide himself aright.

7. From this method of teaching we are forced somewhat to dissent. For philosophers, being unacquainted with the corruption of nature, which is the punishment of revolt, erroneously confound two states of man which are very different from each other. Let us therefore hold, for the purpose of the present work, that the soul consists of two parts, the intellect and the will (Book II. chap. ii. sec. 2, 12)—the office of the intellect being to distinguish between objects, according as they seem deserving of being approved or disapproved; and the office of the will, to choose and follow what the intellect declares to be good, to reject and shun what it declares to be bad (Plato in Phædro). We dwell not on the subtlety of Aristotle, that the mind has no motion of itself; but that the moving power is choice, which he also terms the appetive intellect. Not to lose ourselves in superfluous questions, let it be enough to know that the intellect is to us, as it were, the guide and ruler of the soul; that the will always follows its beck, and waits for its decision, in matters of desire. For which reason Aristotle truly taught, that in the appetite there is a

---

[1] See Themist. lib. iii De Anima, 49, De Dupl. Intellectu.

pursuit and rejection corresponding in some degree to affirmation and negation in the intellect (Aristot. Ethic. lib. vi. c. 2). Moreover, it will be seen in another place (Book II. c. ii. sec. 12—26), how surely the intellect governs the will. Here we only wish to observe, that the soul does not possess any faculty which may not be duly referred to one or other of these members. And in this way we comprehend sense under intellect. Others distinguish thus : They say that sense inclines to pleasure in the same way as the intellect to good ; that hence the appetite of sense becomes concupiscence and lust, while the affection of the intellect becomes will. For the term appetite, which they prefer, I use that of will, as being more common.

8. Therefore, God has provided the soul of man with intellect, by which he might discern good from evil, just from unjust, and might know what to follow or to shun, reason going before with her lamp ; whence philosophers, in reference to her directing power, have called her το ηγεμονικον. To this he has joined will, to which choice belongs. Man excelled in these noble endowments in his primitive condition, when reason, intelligence, prudence, and judgment, not only sufficed for the government of his earthly life, but also enabled him to rise up to God and eternal happiness. Thereafter choice was added to direct the appetites and temper all the organic motions ; the will being thus perfectly submissive to the authority of reason. In this upright state, man possessed freedom of will, by which, if he chose, he was able to obtain eternal life. It were here unseasonable to introduce the question concerning the secret predestination of God, because we are not considering what might or might not happen, but what the nature of man truly was. Adam, therefore, might have stood if he chose, since it was only by his own will that he fell ; but it was because his will was pliable in either direction, and he had not received constancy to persevere, that he so easily fell. Still he had a free choice of good and evil ; and not only so, but in the mind and will there was the highest rectitude, and all the organic parts were duly framed to obedience, until man corrupted its good properties, and destroyed himself. Hence the great darkness of philosophers who have looked for a complete building in a ruin, and fit arrangement in disorder. The principle they set out with was, that man could not be a rational animal unless he had a free choice of good and evil. They also imagined that the distinction between virtue and vice was destroyed, if man did not of his own counsel arrange his life. So far well, had there been no change in man. This being unknown to them, it is not surprising that they throw everything into confusion. But those who, while they profess to be the disciples of Christ, still seek for free-will in man, notwithstanding of his being lost and drowned in spiritual destruction, labour under manifold delusion, making a heterogeneous mixture of inspired doctrine and philosophical opinions, and so erring as to both. But it will be better to leave these things to their own place (see Book II. chap. ii.). At present

it is necessary only to remember, that man at his first creation, was very different from all his posterity; who, deriving their origin from him after he was corrupted, received a hereditary taint. At first every part of the soul was formed to rectitude. There was soundness of mind and freedom of will to choose the good. If any one objects that it was placed, as it were, in a slippery position, because its power was weak, I answer, that the degree conferred was sufficient to take away every excuse. For surely the Deity could not be tied down to this condition,—to make man such, that he either could not or would not sin. Such a nature might have been more excellent;[1] but to expostulate with God as if he had been bound to confer this nature on man, is more than unjust, seeing He had full right to determine how much or how little He would give. Why He did not sustain him by the virtue of perseverance is hidden in his counsel; it is ours to keep within the bounds of soberness. Man had received the power, if he had the will, but he had not the will which would have given the power; for this will would have been followed by perseverance. Still, after he had received so much, there is no excuse for his having spontaneously brought death upon himself. No necessity was laid upon God to give him more than that intermediate and even transient will, that out of man's fall he might extract materials for his own glory.

[1] See August. lib xi., super Gen. cap. vii. viii. ix., and De Corrept. et Gratia ad Valent., cap. xi.

CHAPTER XVI.

THE WORLD, CREATED BY GOD, STILL CHERISHED AND PROTECTED BY
HIM.   EACH AND ALL OF ITS PARTS GOVERNED BY HIS PROVIDENCE.

The divisions of this chapter are, I. The doctrine of the special providence of God over all the creatures, singly and collectively, as opposed to the dreams of the Epicureans about fortune and fortuitous causes.   II. The fiction of the Sophists concerning the omnipotence of God, and the error of philosophers, as to a confused and equivocal government of the world, sec. 1–5. All animals, but especially mankind, from the peculiar superintendence exercised over them, are proofs, evidences, and examples of the providence of God, sec. 6, 7.   III. A consideration of fate, fortune, chance, contingence, and uncertain events (on which the matter here under discussion turns).

Sections.

1. Even the wicked, under the guidance of carnal sense, acknowledge that God is the Creator.   The godly acknowledge not this only, but that he is a most wise and powerful governor and preserver of all created objects.   In so doing, they lean on the Word of God, some passages from which are produced.
2. Refutation of the Epicureans, who oppose fortune and fortuitous causes to Divine Providence, as taught in Scripture.   The sun, a bright manifestation of Divine Providence.
3. Figment of the Sophists as to an indolent Providence refuted.   Consideration of the Omnipotence as combined with the Providence of God.   Double benefit resulting from a proper acknowledgment of the Divine Omnipotence.   Cavils of Infidelity.
4. A definition of Providence refuting the erroneous dogmas of Philosophers.   Dreams of the Epicureans and Peripatetics.
5. Special Providence of God asserted and proved by arguments founded on a consideration of the Divine Justice and Mercy.   Proved also by passages of Scripture, relating to the sky, the earth, and animals.
6. Special Providence proved by passages relating to the human race, and the more especially that for its sake the world was created.
7. Special Providence proved, lastly, from examples taken from the history of the Israelites, of Jonah, Jacob, and from daily experience.
8. Erroneous views as to Providence refuted:—I. The sect of the Stoics.   II. The fortune and chance of the Heathen.
9. How things are said to be fortuitous to us, though done by the determinate counsel of God.   Example.   Error of separating contingency and event from the secret, but just, and most wise counsel of God.   Two examples.

1. IT were cold and lifeless to represent God as a momentary Creator, who completed his work once for all, and then left it. Here, especially, we must dissent from the profane, and maintain that the presence of the divine power is conspicuous, not less in the perpetual condition of the world than in its first creation. For, although even wicked men are forced, by the mere view of the earth and sky, to rise to the Creator, yet faith has a method of its own in assigning the whole praise of creation to God. To this effect is the passage of the Apostle already quoted, that by faith we understand that the worlds

were framed by the Word of God (Heb. xi. 3); because, without proceeding to his Providence, we cannot understand the full force of what is meant by God being the Creator, how much soever we may seem to comprehend it with our mind, and confess it with our tongue. The carnal mind, when once it has perceived the power of God in the creation, stops there, and, at the farthest, thinks and ponders on nothing else than the wisdom, power, and goodness, displayed by the Author of such a work (matters which rise spontaneously, and force themselves on the notice even of the unwilling), or on some general agency on which the power of motion depends, exercised in preserving and governing it. In short, it imagines that all things are sufficiently sustained by the energy divinely infused into them at first. But faith must penetrate deeper. After learning that there is a Creator, it must forthwith infer that he is also a Governor and Preserver, and that, not by producing a kind of general motion in the machine of the globe as well as in each of its parts, but by a special Providence sustaining, cherishing, superintending, all the things which he has made, to the very minutest, even to a sparrow. Thus David, after briefly premising that the world was created by God, immediately descends to the continual course of Providence, "By the word of the Lord were the heavens framed, and all the host of them by the breath of his mouth;" immediately adding, "The Lord looketh from heaven, he beholdeth the children of men" (Ps. xxxiii. 6, 13, &c.). He subjoins other things to the same effect. For although all do not reason so accurately, yet because it would not be credible that human affairs were superintended by God, unless he were the maker of the world, and no one could seriously believe that he is its Creator without feeling convinced that he takes care of his works; David, with good reason, and in admirable order, leads us from the one to the other. In general, indeed, philosophers teach, and the human mind conceives, that all the parts of the world are invigorated by the secret inspiration of God. They do not, however, reach the height to which David rises, taking all the pious along with him, when he says, "These wait all upon thee, that thou mayest give them their meat in due season. That thou givest them they gather: thou openest thine hand, they are filled with good. Thou hidest thy face, they are troubled: thou takest away their breath, they die, and return to their dust. Thou sendest forth thy Spirit, they are created, and thou renewest the face of the earth" (Ps. civ. 27—30). Nay, though they subscribe to the sentiment of Paul, that in God "we live, and move, and have our being" (Acts xvii. 28), yet they are far from having a serious apprehension of the grace which he commends, because they have not the least relish for that special care in which alone the paternal favour of God is discerned.

2. That this distinction may be the more manifest, we must consider that the Providence of God, as taught in Scripture, is opposed

to fortune and fortuitous causes. By an erroneous opinion prevailing in all ages, an opinion almost universally prevailing in our own day— viz. that all things happen fortuitously—the true doctrine of Providence has not only been obscured, but almost buried. If one falls among robbers, or ravenous beasts; if a sudden gust of wind at sea causes shipwreck; if one is struck down by the fall of a house or a tree; if another, when wandering through desert paths, meets with deliverance; or, after being tossed by the waves, arrives in port, and makes some wondrous hairbreadth escape from death — all these occurrences, prosperous as well as adverse, carnal sense will attribute to fortune. But whoso has learned from the mouth of Christ that all the hairs of his head are numbered (Matth. x. 30), will look farther for the cause, and hold that all events whatsoever are governed by the secret counsel of God. With regard to inanimate objects, again, we must hold that though each is possessed of its peculiar properties, yet all of them exert their force only in so far as directed by the immediate hand of God. Hence they are merely instruments, into which God constantly infuses what energy he sees meet, and turns and converts to any purpose at his pleasure. No created object makes a more wonderful or glorious display than the sun. For, besides illuminating the whole world with its brightness, how admirably does it foster and invigorate all animals by its heat, and fertilise the earth by its rays, warming the seeds of grain in its lap, and thereby calling forth the verdant blade! This it supports, increases, and strengthens with additional nurture, till it rises into the stalk; and still feeds it with perpetual moisture, till it comes into flower; and from flower to fruit, which it continues to ripen till it attains maturity. In like manner, by its warmth trees and vines bud, and put forth first their leaves, then their blossom, then their fruit. And the Lord, that he might claim the entire glory of these things as his own, was pleased that light should exist, and that the earth should be replenished with all kinds of herbs and fruits before he made the sun. No pious man, therefore, will make the sun either the necessary or principal cause of those things which existed before the creation of the sun, but only the instrument which God employs, because he so pleases; though he can lay it aside, and act equally well by himself. Again, when we read, that at the prayer of Joshua the sun was stayed in its course (Josh. x. 13); that as a favour to Hezekiah, its shadow receded ten degrees (2 Kings xx. 11); by these miracles God declared that the sun does not daily rise and set by a blind instinct of nature, but is governed by Him in its course, that he may renew the remembrance of his paternal favour toward us. Nothing is more natural than for spring, in its turn, to succeed winter, summer spring, and autumn summer; but in this series the variations are so great and so unequal as to make it very apparent that every single year, month, and day, is regulated by a new and special providence of God.

3. And truly God claims omnipotence to himself, and would have us

to acknowledge it,—not the vain, indolent, slumbering omnipotence which sophists feign, but vigilant, efficacious, energetic, and ever active,—not an omnipotence which may only act as a general principle of confused motion, as in ordering a stream to keep within the channel once prescribed to it, but one which is intent on individual and special movements. God is deemed omnipotent, not because he can act though he may cease or be idle, or because by a general instinct, he continues the order of nature previously appointed; but because, governing heaven and earth by his providence, he so over-rules all things that nothing happens without his counsel. For when it is said in the Psalms, "He hath done whatsoever he hath pleased" (Ps. cxv. 3), the thing meant is his sure and deliberate purpose. It were insipid to interpret the Psalmist's words in philosophic fashion, to mean that God is the primary agent, because the beginning and cause of all motion. This rather is the solace of the faithful, in their adversity, that everything which they endure is by the ordination and command of God, that they are under his hand. But if the government of God thus extends to all his works, it is a childish cavil to confine it to natural influx.[1] Those, moreover, who confine the providence of God within narrow limits, as if he allowed all things to be borne along freely according to a perpetual law of nature, do not more defraud God of his glory than themselves of a most useful doctrine; for nothing were more wretched than man if he were exposed to all possible movements of the sky, the air, the earth, and the water. We may add, that by this view the singular goodness of God towards each individual is unbecomingly impaired. David exclaims (Ps. viii. 3), that infants hanging at their mothers' breasts are eloquent enough to celebrate the glory of God, because, from the very moment of their birth, they find an aliment prepared for them by heavenly care. Indeed, if we do not shut our eyes and senses to the fact, we must see that some mothers have full provision for their infants, and others almost none, according as it is the pleasure of God to nourish one child more liberally, and another more sparingly. Those who attribute due praise to the omnipotence of God, thereby derive a double benefit. He to whom heaven and earth belong, and whose nod all creatures must obey, is fully able to reward the homage which they pay to him, and they can rest secure in the protection of Him to whose control everything that could do them harm is subject, by whose authority, Satan, with all his furies and engines, is curbed as with a bridle, and on whose will everything adverse to our safety depends. In this way, and in no other, can the immoderate and superstitious fears, excited by the dangers to which we are exposed, be calmed or subdued. I say superstitious fears. For such they are, as often as the dangers threatened by any created objects inspire us with such terror, that we tremble as if they had in themselves a

---

[1] See Hyperius in Methodo Theologiæ.

power to hurt us, or could hurt at random or by chance ; or as if we had not in God a sufficient protection against them. For example, Jeremiah forbids the children of God "to be dismayed at the signs of heaven, as the heathen are dismayed at them" (Jer. x. 2). He does not, indeed, condemn every kind of fear. But as unbelievers transfer the government of the world from God to the stars, imagining that happiness or misery depends on their decrees or presages, and not on the Divine will, the consequence is, that their fear, which ought to have reference to him only, is diverted to stars and comets. Let him, therefore, who would beware of such unbelief, always bear in mind, that there is no random power, or agency, or motion in the creatures, who are so governed by the secret counsel of God, that nothing happens but what he has knowingly and willingly decreed.[1]

4. First, then, let the reader remember that the providence we mean is not one by which the Deity, sitting idly in heaven, looks on at what is taking place in the world, but one by which he, as it were, holds the helm, and overrules all events. Hence his providence extends not less to the hand than to the eye.[2] When Abraham said to his son, *God will provide* (Gen. xxii. 8), he meant not merely to assert that the future event was foreknown to God, but to resign the management of an unknown business to the will of Him whose province it is to bring perplexed and dubious matters to a happy result. Hence it appears that providence consists in action. What many talk of bare prescience is the merest trifling. Those do not err quite so grossly who attribute government to God, but still, as I have observed, a confused and promiscuous government which consists in giving an impulse and general movement to the machine of the globe and each of its parts, but does not specially direct the action of every creature. It is impossible, however, to tolerate this error. For, according to its abettors, there is nothing in this providence, which they call universal, to prevent all the creatures from being moved contingently, or to prevent man from turning himself in this direction or in that, according to the mere freedom of his own will. In this way, they make man a partner with God,—God, by his energy, impressing man with the movement by which he can act, agreeably to the nature conferred upon him, while man voluntarily regulates his own actions. In short, their doctrine is, that the world, the affairs of men, and men themselves, are governed by the power, but not by the decree of God. I say nothing of the Epicureans (a pest with which the world has always been plagued), who dream of an inert and idle God,[3] and others, not a whit sounder, who of old feigned that God rules the

---

1 See Calvin adversus Astrolog. Judiciariam. August De Ordine, lib. ii. cap. 15.

2 The French adds, " Cest à dire, que non seulement il voit, mais aussi ordonne ce qu'il veut estre fait;"—" that is to say, he not only sees, but ordains what he wills to be done."

3 Plin. lib. ii. c. 7. " Irridendum vero, agere curam rerum humanarum, illud, quicquid est, summum. Anne tam tristi atque multiplici ministerio non pollui credamus dubitemusve ?"

upper regions of the air, but leaves the inferior to Fortune. Against such evident madness even dumb creatures lift their voice.

My intention now is, to refute an opinion which has very generally obtained—an opinion which, while it concedes to God some blind and equivocal movement, withholds what is of principal moment—viz. the disposing and directing of everything to its proper end by incomprehensible wisdom. By withholding government, it makes God the ruler of the world in name only, not in reality. For what, I ask, is meant by government, if it be not to preside so as to regulate the destiny of that over which you preside? I do not, however, totally repudiate what is said of an universal providence, provided, on the other hand, it is conceded to me that the world is governed by God, not only because he maintains the order of nature appointed by him, but because he takes a special charge of every one of his works. It is true, indeed, that each species of created objects is moved by a secret instinct of nature, as if they obeyed the eternal command of God, and spontaneously followed the course which God at first appointed. And to this we may refer our Saviour's words, that he and his Father have always been at work from the beginning (John v. 17); also the words of Paul, that "in him we live, and move, and have our being" (Acts xvii. 28), also the words of the author of the Epistle to the Hebrews, who, when wishing to prove the divinity of Christ, says, that he upholdeth "all things by the word of his power" (Heb. i. 3). But some, under pretext of the general, hide and obscure the special providence, which is so surely and clearly taught in Scripture, that it is strange how any one can bring himself to doubt of it. And, indeed, those who interpose that disguise are themselves forced to modify their doctrine, by adding that many things are done by the special care of God. This, however, they erroneously confine to particular acts. The thing to be proved, therefore, is that single events are so regulated by God, and all events so proceed from his determinate counsel, that nothing happens fortuitously.

5. Assuming that the beginning of motion belongs to God, but that all things move spontaneously or casually, according to the impulse which nature gives, the vicissitudes of day and night, summer and winter, will be the work of God; inasmuch as he, in assigning the office of each, appointed a certain law, namely, that they should always with uniform tenor observe the same course, day succeeding night, month succeeding month, and year succeeding year. But, as at one time, excessive heat, combined with drought, burns up the fields; at another time excessive rains rot the crops, while sudden devastation is produced by tempests and storms of hail, these will not be the works of God, unless in so far as rainy or fair weather, heat or cold, are produced by the concourse of the stars, and other natural causes. According to this view, there is no place left either for the paternal favour or the judgments of God. If it is said that God fully manifests his beneficence to the human race, by fur-

nishing heaven and earth with the ordinary power of producing food, the explanation is meagre and heathenish: as if the fertility of one year were not a special blessing, the penury and dearth of another a special punishment and curse from God. But as it would occupy too much time to enumerate all the arguments, let the authority of God himself suffice. In the Law and the Prophets he repeatedly declares, that as often as he waters the earth with dew and rain, he manifests his favour, that by his command the heaven becomes hard as iron, the crops are destroyed by mildew and other evils, that storms and hail, in devastating the fields, are signs of sure and special vengeance. This being admitted, it is certain that not a drop of rain falls without the express command of God. David, indeed (Ps. cxlvi. 9), extols the general providence of God in supplying food to the young ravens that cry to him, but when God himself threatens living creatures with famine, does he not plainly declare that they are all nourished by him, at one time with scanty, at another with more ample measure? It is childish, as I have already said, to confine this to particular acts, when Christ says, without reservation, that not a sparrow falls to the ground without the will of his Father (Matth. x. 29). Surely, if the flight of birds is regulated by the counsel of God, we must acknowledge with the prophet, that while he "dwelleth on high," he "humbleth himself to behold the things that are in heaven and in the earth" (Ps. cxiii. 5, 6).

6. But as we know that it was chiefly for the sake of mankind that the world was made, we must look to this as the end which God has in view in the government of it. The prophet Jeremiah exclaims, "O Lord, I know that the way of man is not in himself: it is not in man that walketh to direct his steps" (Jer. x. 23). Solomon again says, "Man's goings are of the Lord: how can a man then understand his own way?" (Prov. xx. 24.) Will it now be said that man is moved by God according to the bent of his nature, but that man himself gives the movement any direction he pleases? Were it truly so, man would have the full disposal of his own ways. To this it will perhaps be answered, that man can do nothing without the power of God. But the answer will not avail, since both Jeremiah and Solomon attribute to God not power only, but also election and decree. And Solomon, in another place, elegantly rebukes the rashness of men in fixing their plans without reference to God, as if they were not led by his hand. "The preparations of the heart in man, and the answer of the tongue, is from the Lord" (Prov. xvi. 1). It is a strange infatuation, surely, for miserable men, who cannot even give utterance except in so far as God pleases, to begin to act without him! Scripture, moreover, the better to show that everything done in the world is according to his decree, declares that the things which seem most fortuitous are subject to him. For what seems more attributable to chance than the branch which falls from a tree, and kills the passing traveller? But the Lord sees very differently, and

declares that He delivered him into the hand of the slayer (Exod. xxi. 13). In like manner, who does not attribute the lot to the blindness of Fortune? Not so the Lord, who claims the decision for himself (Prov. xvi. 33). He says not, that by his power the lot is thrown into the lap, and taken out, bnt declares that the only thing which could be attributed to chance is from him. To the same effect are the words of Solomon, " The poor and the deceitful man meet together ; the Lord lighteneth both their eyes" (Prov. xxix. 13). For although rich and poor are mingled together in the world, in saying that the condition of each is divinely appointed, he reminds us that God, who enlightens all, has his own eye always open, and thus exhorts the poor to patient endurance, seeing that those who are discontented with their lot endeavour to shake off a burden which God has imposed upon them. Thus, too, another prophet upbraids the profane, who ascribe it to human industry, or to fortune, that some grovel in the mire, while others rise to honour. " Promotion cometh neither from the east, nor from the west, nor from the south. But God is the judge : he putteth down one, and setteth up another" (Ps. lxxv. 6, 7). Because God cannot divest himself of the office of judge, he infers that to his secret counsel it is owing that some are elevated, while others remain without honour.

7. Nay, I affirm in general, that particular events are evidences of the special providence of God. In the wilderness, God caused a south wind to blow, and brought the people a plentiful supply of birds (Exod. xix. 13). When he desired that Jonah should be thrown into the sea, he sent forth a whirlwind. Those who deny that God holds the reins of government will say that this was contrary to ordinary practice, whereas I infer from it that no wind ever rises or rages without his special command. In no way could it be true that "he maketh the winds his messengers, and the flames of fire his ministers ;" that " he maketh the clouds his chariot, and walketh upon the wings of the wind" (Ps. civ. 3, 4), did he not at pleasure drive the clouds and winds, and therein manifest the special presence of his power. In like manner, we are èlsewhere taught, that whenever the sea is raised into a storm, its billows attest the special presence of God. " He commandeth and raiseth the stormy wind, which lifteth up the waves." " He maketh the storm a calm, so that the waves thereof are still" (Ps. cvii. 25, 29). He also elsewhere declares, that he had smitten the people with blasting and mildew (Amos iv. 9). Again, while man naturally possesses the power of continuing his species, God describes it as a mark of his special favour, that while some continue childless, others are blessed with offspring : for the fruit of the womb is his gift. Hence the words of Jacob to Rachel, " Am I in God's stead, who hath withheld from thee the fruit of the womb ?" (Gen. xxx. 2.) To conclude in one word. Nothing in nature is more ordi-

nary than that we should be nourished with bread. But the Spirit declares not only that the produce of the earth is God's special gift, but "that man doth not live by bread only" (Deut. viii. 3), because it is not mere fulness that nourishes him, but the secret blessing of God. And hence, on the other hand, he threatens to take away "the stay and the staff, the whole stay of bread, and the whole stay of water" (Is. iii. 1). Indeed, there could be no serious meaning in our prayer for daily bread, if God did not with paternal hand supply us with food. Accordingly, to convince the faithful that God, in feeding them, fulfils the office of the best of parents, the prophet reminds them that he "giveth food to all flesh" (Ps. cxxxvi. 25). In fine, when we hear on the one hand, that "the eyes of the Lord are upon the righteous, and his ears are open unto their cry," and, on the other hand, that "the face of the Lord is against them that do evil, to cut off the remembrance of them from the earth" (Ps. xxxiv. 15, 16), let us be assured that all creatures above and below are ready at his service, that he may employ them in whatever way he pleases. Hence we infer, not only that the general providence of God, continuing the order of nature, extends over the creatures, but that by his wonderful counsel they are adapted to a certain and special purpose.

8. Those who would cast obloquy on this doctrine, calumniate it as the dogma of the Stoics concerning fate. The same charge was formerly brought against Augustine (Lib. ad Bonifac. II., c. vi. et alibi.). We are unwilling to dispute about words; but we do not admit the term Fate, both because it is of the class which Paul teaches us to shun, as profane novelties (1 Tim. vi. 20), and also because it is attempted, by means of an odious term, to fix a stigma on the truth of God. But the dogma itself is falsely and maliciously imputed to us. For we do not with the Stoics imagine a necessity consisting of a perpetual chain of causes, and a kind of involved series contained in nature, but we hold that God is the disposer and ruler of all things,—that from the remotest eternity, according to his own wisdom, he decreed what he was to do, and now by his power executes what he decreed. Hence we maintain that, by his providence, not heaven and earth and inanimate creatures only, but also the counsels and wills of men are so governed as to move exactly in the course which he has destined. What, then, you will say, does nothing happen fortuitously, nothing contingently? I answer, it was a true saying of Basil the Great, that Fortune and Chance are heathen terms; the meaning of which ought not to occupy pious minds. For if all success is blessing from God, and calamity and adversity are his curse, there is no place left in human affairs for Fortune and chance. We ought also to be moved by the words of Augustine (Retract. Lib. i. cap. 1), "In my writings against the Academics," says he, "I regret having so often used the term fortune; although I intended to denote by it not some goddess, but the fortuitous issue of events in external

matters, whether good or evil. Hence, too, those words, Perhaps, Perchance, Fortuitously,[1] which no religion forbids us to use, though everything must be referred to Divine Providence. Nor did I omit to observe this when I said, Although, perhaps, that which is vulgarly called Fortune, is also regulated by a hidden order, and what we call Chance is nothing else than that the reason and cause of which is secret. It is true, I so spoke, but I repent of having mentioned Fortune there as I did, when I see the very bad custom which men have of saying, not as they ought to do, ' So God pleased,' but, ' So Fortune pleased.' " In short, Augustine everywhere teaches, that if anything is left to fortune, the world moves at random. And although he elsewhere declares (Quæstionum, Lib. lxxxiii.), that all things are carried on, partly by the free will of man, and partly by the Providence of God, he shortly after shows clearly enough that his meaning was, that men also are ruled by Providence, when he assumes it as a principle, that there cannot be a greater absurdity than to hold that anything is done without the ordination of God ; because it would happen at random. For which reason, he also excludes the contingency which depends on human will, maintaining a little further on, in clearer terms, that no cause must be sought for but the will of God. When he uses the term permission, the meaning which he attaches to it will best appear from a single passage (De Trinit. Lib. iii. cap. 4), where he proves that the will of God is the supreme and primary cause of all things, because nothing happens without his order or permission. He certainly does not figure God sitting idly in a watch-tower, when he chooses to permit anything. The will which he represents as interposing is, if I may so express it, active (*actualis*), and but for this could not be regarded as a cause.

9. But since our sluggish minds rest far beneath the height of Divine Providence, we must have recourse to a distinction which may assist them in rising. I say then, that though all things are ordered by the counsel and certain arrangement of God, to us, however, they are fortuitous,—not because we imagine that Fortune rules the world and mankind, and turns all things upside down at random (far be such a heartless thought from every Christian breast); but as the order, method, end, and necessity of events, are, for the most part, hidden in the counsel of God, though it is certain that they are produced by the will of God, they have the appearance of being fortuitous, such being the form under which they present themselves to us, whether considered in their own nature, or estimated according to our knowledge and judgment. Let us suppose, for example, that a merchant, after entering a forest in company with trust-worthy individuals, imprudently strays from his companions, and wanders bewildered till he falls into a den of robbers and is murdered. His death was not only foreseen by the eye of God, but had been fixed by his decree. For it is said, not that he foresaw how far the life of each

---

[1] Forte. Forsan. Forsitan. Fortuito.

individual should extend, but that he determined and fixed the bounds, which could not be passed (Job xiv. 5). Still, in relation, to our capacity of discernment, all these things appear fortuitous. How will the Christian feel? Though he will consider that every circumstance which occurred in that person's death was indeed in its nature fortuitous, he will have no doubt that the Providence of God overruled it and guided fortune to his own end. The same thing holds in the case of future contingencies. All future events being uncertain to us, seem in suspense as if ready to take either direction. Still, however, the impression remains seated in our hearts, that nothing will happen which the Lord has not provided. In this sense the term event is repeatedly used in Ecclesiastes, because, at the first glance, men do not penetrate to the primary cause which lies concealed. And yet, what is taught in Scripture of the secret providence of God was never so completely effaced from the human heart, as that some sparks did not always shine in the darkness. Thus the soothsayers of the Philistines, though they waver in uncertainty, attribute the adverse event partly to God and partly to chance. If the ark, say they, "goeth up by the way of his own coast to Bethshemish, then he hath done us this great evil; but if not, then we shall know that it is not his hand that smote us, it was a chance that happened to us" (1 Sam. vi. 9). Foolishly, indeed, when divination fails them they flee to fortune. Still we see them constrained, so as not to venture to regard their disaster as fortuitous. But the mode in which God, by the curb of his Providence, turns events in whatever direction he pleases, will appear from a remarkable example. At the very same moment when David was discovered in the wilderness of Maon, the Philistines make an inroad into the country, and Saul is forced to depart (1 Sam. xxiii. 26, 27). If God, in order to provide for the safety of his servant, threw this obstacle in the way of Saul, we surely cannot say, that though the Philistines took up arms contrary to human expectation, they did it by chance. What seems to us contingence, faith will recognise as the secret impulse of God. The reason is not always equally apparent, but we ought undoubtedly to hold that all the changes which take place in the world are produced by the secret agency of the hand of God. At the same time, that which God has determined, though it must come to pass, is not, however, precisely, or in its own nature, necessary. We have a familiar example in the case of our Saviour's bones. As he assumed a body similar to ours, no sane man will deny that his bones were capable of being broken, and yet it was impossible that they should be broken (John xix. 33, 36). Hence again, we see that there was good ground for the distinction which the Schoolmen made between necessity, *secundum quid*, and necessity absolute, also between the necessity of *consequent* and *of consequence*. God made the bones of his Son frangible, though he exempted them from actual fracture; and thus, in reference to the necessity of his counsel, made that impossible which might have naturally taken place.

CHAPTER XVII.

USE TO BE MADE OF THE DOCTRINE OF PROVIDENCE.

This chapter may be conveniently divided into two parts :—I. A general explanation is given of the doctrine of Divine Providence, in so far as conducive to the solid instruction and consolation of the godly, sect. 1, and specially sect. 2–12. First, however, those are refuted who deny that the world is governed by the secret and incomprehensible counsel of God; those also who throw the blame of all wickedness upon God, and absurdly pretend that exercises of piety are useless, sect. 2–5. Thereafter is added a holy meditation on Divine Providence, which, in the case of prosperity, is painted to the life, sect. 6–11.

II. A solution of two objections from passages of Scripture, which attribute repentance to God, and speak of something like an abrogation of his decrees.

Sections.

1. Summary of the doctrine of Divine Providence. 1. It embraces the future and the past. 2. It works by means, without means, and against means. 3. Mankind, and particularly the Church, the object of special care. 4. The mode of administration usually secret, but always just. This last point more fully considered.
2. The profane denial that the world is governed by the secret counsel of God, refuted by passages of Scripture. Salutary counsel.
3. This doctrine, as to the secret counsel of God in the government of the world, gives no countenance either to the impiety of those who throw the blame of their wickedness upon God, the petulance of those who reject means, or the error of those who neglect the duties of religion.
4. As regards future events, the doctrine of Divine Providence not inconsistent with deliberation on the part of man.
5. In regard to past events, it is absurd to argue that crimes ought not to be punished, because they are in accordance with the divine decrees. 1. The wicked resist the declared will of God. 2. They are condemned by conscience. 3. The essence and guilt of the crime is in themselves, though God uses them as instruments.
6. A holy meditation on Divine Providence. 1. All events happen by the ordination of God. 2. All things contribute to the advantage of the godly. 3. The hearts of men and all their endeavours are in the hand of God. 4. Providence watches for the safety of the righteous. 5. God has a special care of his elect.
7. Meditation on Providence continued. 6. God in various ways curbs and defeats the enemies of the Church. 7. He overrules all creatures, even Satan himself, for the good of his people.
8. Meditation on Providence continued. 8. He trains the godly to patience and moderation. Examples. Joseph, Job, and David. 9. He shakes off their lethargy, and urges them to repentance.
9. Meditation continued. 10. The right use of inferior causes explained. 11. When the godly become negligent or imprudent in the discharge of duty, Providence reminds them of their fault. 12. It condemns the iniquities of the wicked. 13. It produces a right consideration of the future, rendering the servants of God prudent, diligent, and active. 14. It causes them to resign themselves to the wisdom and omnipotence of God, and, at the same time, makes them diligent in their calling.
10. Meditation continued. 15. Though human life is beset with innumerable evils, the righteous, trusting to Divine Providence, feel perfectly secure.
11. The use of the foregoing meditation.
12. The second part of the chapter, disposing of two objections. 1. That Scripture

1. MOREOVER, such is the proneness of the human mind to indulge in vain subtleties, that it becomes almost impossible for those who do not see the sound and proper use of this doctrine, to avoid entangling themselves in perplexing difficulties.   It will, therefore, be proper here to advert to the end which Scripture has in view in teaching that all things are divinely ordained.   And it is to be observed, first, that the Providence of God is to be considered with reference both to the past and the future; and, secondly, that in overruling all things, it works at one time with means, at another without means, and at another against means.   Lastly, the design of God is to show that He takes care of the whole human race, but is especially vigilant in governing the Church, which he favours with a closer inspection.   Moreover, we must add, that although the paternal favour and beneficence, as well as the judicial severity of God, is often conspicuous in the whole course of his Providence, yet occasionally as the causes of events are concealed, the thought is apt to rise, that human affairs are whirled about by the blind impulse of Fortune, or our carnal nature inclines us to speak as if God were amusing himself by tossing men up and down like balls.   It is true, indeed, that if with sedate and quiet minds we were disposed to learn, the issue would at length make it manifest that the counsel of God was in accordance with the highest reason, that his purpose was either to train his people to patience, correct their depraved affections, tame their wantonness, inure them to self-denial, and arouse them from torpor; or, on the other hand, to cast down the proud, defeat the craftiness of the ungodly, and frustrate all their schemes. How much soever causes may escape our notice, we must feel assured that they are deposited with him, and accordingly exclaim with David, "Many, O Lord my God, are thy wonderful works which thou hast done, and thy thoughts which are to us-ward: if I would declare and speak of them, they are more than can be numbered" (Ps. xl. 5). For while our adversities ought always to remind us of our sins, that the punishment may incline us to repentance, we see, moreover, how Christ declares there is something more in the secret counsel of his Father than to chastise every one as he deserves.   For he says of the man who was born blind, "Neither hath this man sinned, nor his parents: but that the works of God should be made manifest in him" (John ix. 3).   Here, where calamity takes precedence even of birth, our carnal sense murmurs as if God were unmerciful in thus afflicting those who have not offended.   But Christ declares that, provided we had eyes clear enough, we should perceive that in this spectacle the

glory of his Father is brightly displayed. We must use modesty, not as it were compelling God to render an account, but so revering his hidden judgments as to account his will the best of all reasons.[1] When the sky is overcast with dense clouds, and a violent tempest arises, the darkness which is presented to our eye, and the thunder which strikes our ears, and stupifies all our senses with terror, make us imagine that everything is thrown into confusion, though in the firmament itself all continues quiet and serene. In the same way, when the tumultuous aspect of human affairs unfits us for judging, we should still hold that God, in the pure light of his justice and wisdom, keeps all these commotions in due subordination, and conducts them to their proper end. And certainly in this matter many display monstrous infatuation, presuming to subject the works of God to their calculation, and discuss his secret counsels, as well as to pass a precipitate judgment on things unknown, and that with greater license than on the doings of mortal men. What can be more preposterous than to show modesty toward our equals, and choose rather to suspend our judgment than incur the blame of rashness, while we petulantly insult the hidden judgments of God, judgments which it becomes us to look up to and to revere.

2. No man, therefore, will duly and usefully ponder on the providence of God save he who recollects that he has to do with his own Maker, and the Maker of the world, and in the exercise of the humility which becomes him, manifests both fear and reverence. Hence it is, that in the present day so many dogs tear this doctrine with envenomed teeth, or, at least, assail it with their bark, refusing to give more license to God than their own reason dictates to themselves. With what petulance, too, are we assailed for not being contented with the precepts of the Law, in which the will of God is comprehended, and for maintaining that the world is governed by his secret counsels? As if our doctrine were the figment of our own brain, and were not distinctly declared by the Spirit, and repeated in innumerable forms of expression! Since some feeling of shame restrains them from daring to belch forth their blasphemies against heaven, that they may give the freer vent to their rage, they pretend to pick a quarrel with us. But if they refuse to admit that every event which happens in the world is governed by the incomprehensible counsel of God, let them explain to what effect Scripture declares, that "his judments are a great deep" (Ps. xxxvi. 7). For when Moses exclaims that the will of God "is not in heaven that thou shouldest say, Who shall go up for us to heaven, and bring it unto us? Neither is it beyond the sea that thou shouldest say, Who shall go over the sea and bring it unto us?" (Deut. xxx. 12, 13) because it was familiarly expounded in the law, it follows that there must be another hidden will which is compared to "a great deep."

1 "Here the words of Cicero admirably apply: Nec si ego quod tu sis sequutus, non perspicio, idcirco minus existimo te nihil sine summa ratione fecisse."

It is of this will Paul exclaims, "O! the depths of the riches of the wisdom and knowledge of God! How unsearchable are his judgments, and his ways past finding out! For who hath known the mind of the Lord, or who hath been his counsellor?" (Rom. xi. 33, 34.) It is true, indeed, that in the law and the gospel are comprehended mysteries which far transcend the measure of our sense; but since God, to enable his people to understand those mysteries which he has deigned to reveal in his word, enlightens their minds with a spirit of understanding, they are now no longer a deep, but a path in which they can walk safely—a lamp to guide their feet—a light of life—a school of clear and certain truth. But the admirable method of governing the world is justly called a deep, because, while it lies hid from us, it is to be reverently adored. Both views Moses has beautifully expressed in a few words. "Secret things," saith he, "belong unto the Lord our God, but those things which are revealed belong unto us and to our children for ever" (Deut. xxix. 29). We see how he enjoins us not only studiously to meditate on the law, but to look up with reverence to the secret Providence of God. The Book of Job also, in order to keep our minds humble, contains a description of this lofty theme. The author of the Book, after taking an ample survey of the universe, and discoursing magnificently on the works of God, at length adds, "Lo, these are parts of his ways: but how little a portion is heard of him?" (Job xxvi. 14.) For which reason he, in another passage, distinguishes between the wisdom which dwells in God, and the measure of wisdom which he has assigned to man (Job xxviii. 21, 28). After discoursing of the secrets of nature, he says that wisdom "is hid from the eyes of all living;" that "God understandeth the way thereof." Shortly after he adds, that it has been divulged that it might be investigated; for "unto man he said, Behold the fear of the Lord, that is wisdom." To this the words of Augustine refer, "As we do not know all the things which God does respecting us in the best order, we ought, with good intention, to act according to the Law, and in some things be acted upon according to the Law, his Providence being a Law immutable" (August. Quæst. Lib. lxxxiii. c. 27). Therefore, since God claims to himself the right of governing the world, a right unknown to us, let it be our law of modesty and soberness to acquiesce in his supreme authority, regarding his will as our only rule of justice, and the most perfect cause of all things,—not that absolute will, indeed, of which sophists prate, when by a profane and impious divorce, they separate his justice from his power, but that universal overruling Providence from which nothing flows that is not right, though the reasons thereof may be concealed.[1]

3. Those who have learned this modesty, will neither murmur against God for adversity in time past, nor charge him with the

---

[1] See Salvian. in Tract. de Vero Judicio et Providentia Dei. Also Bernard. De Interiore Domo, cap. 25. Also Luther in Epist. ad Fratres Antwerpienses.

blame of their own wickedness, as Homer's Agamemnon does.—'Εγω δ' ουχ αἴτιός εἰμι, ἀλλὰ Ζεὺς καὶ μοῖρα. "*Blame not me, but Jupiter and fate.*" On the other hand, they will not, like the youth in Plautus, destroy themselves in despair, as if hurried away by the Fates. "Unstable is the condition of affairs; instead of doing as they list, men only fulfil their fate: I will hie me to a rock, and there end my fortune with my life." Nor will they, after the example of another, use the name of God as a cloak for their crimes. For in another comedy Lyconides thus expresses himself: "God was the impeller: I believe the gods wished it. Did they not wish it, it would not be done, I know." They will rather inquire and learn from Scripture what is pleasing to God, and then, under the guidance of the Spirit, endeavour to attain it. Prepared to follow whithersoever God may call, they will show by their example that nothing is more useful than the knowledge of this doctrine, which perverse men undeservedly assail, because it is sometimes wickedly abused. The profane make such a bluster with their foolish puerilities, that they almost, according to the expression, confound heaven and earth. If the Lord has marked the moment of our death, it cannot be escaped,—it is vain to toil and use precaution. Therefore, when one ventures not to travel on a road which he hears is infested by robbers; when another calls in the physician, and annoys himself with drugs, for the sake of his health; a third abstains from coarser food, that he may not injure a sickly constitution; and a fourth fears to dwell in a ruinous house; when all, in short, devise, and, with great eagerness of mind, strike out paths by which they may attain the objects of their desire; either these are all vain remedies, laid hold of to correct the will of God, or his certain decree does not fix the limits of life and death, health and sickness, peace and war, and other matters which men, according as they desire and hate, study by their own industry to secure or avoid. Nay, these trifles even infer, that the prayers of the faithful must be perverse, not to say superfluous, since they intreat the Lord to make a provision for things which he has decreed from eternity. And then, imputing whatever happens to the providence of God, they connive at the man who is known to have expressly designed it. Has an assassin slain an honest citizen? He has, say they, executed the counsel of God. Has some one committed theft or adultery? The deed having been provided and ordained by the Lord, he is the minister of his providence. Has a son waited with indifference for the death of his parent, without trying any remedy? He could not oppose God, who had so predetermined from eternity. Thus all crimes receive the name of virtues, as being in accordance with divine ordination.

4. As regards future events, Solomon easily reconciles human deliberation with divine providence. For while he derides the stupidity of those who presume to undertake anything without God, as if they were not ruled by his hand, he elsewhere thus expresses himself:

"A man's heart deviseth his way, but the Lord directeth his steps," (Prov. xvi. 9); intimating that the eternal decrees of God by no means prevent us from proceeding, under his will, to provide for ourselves, and arrange all our affairs. And the reason for this is clear. For he who has fixed the boundaries of our life, has at the same time intrusted us with the care of it, provided us with the means of preserving it, forewarned us of the dangers to which we are exposed, and supplied cautions and remedies, that we may not be overwhelmed unawares. Now, our duty is clear, namely, since the Lord has committed to us the defence of our life,—to defend it; since he offers assistance,—to use it; since he forewarns us of danger—not to rush on heedless; since he supplies remedies,—not to neglect them. But it is said, a danger that is not fatal ʼll not hurt us, and one that is fatal cannot be resisted by any precaution. But what if dangers are not fatal, merely because the Lord has furnished you with the means of warding them off, and surmounting them? See how far your reasoning accords with the order of divine procedure: You infer that danger is not to be guarded against, because, if it is not fatal you shall escape without precaution; whereas the Lord enjoins you to guard against it, just because he wills it not to be fatal.[1] These insane cavillers overlook what is plainly before their eyes—viz. that the Lord has furnished men with the arts of deliberation and caution, that they may employ them in subservience to his providence, in the preservation of their life; while, on the contrary, by neglect and sloth, they bring upon themselves the evils which he has annexed to them. How comes it that a provident man, while he consults for his safety, disentangles himself from impending evils; while a foolish man, through unadvised temerity, perishes, unless it be that prudence and folly are, in either case, instruments of divine dispensation? God has been pleased to conceal from us all future events that we may prepare for them as doubtful, and cease not to apply the provided remedies until they have either been overcome, or have proved too much for all our care. Hence, I formerly observed, that the Providence of God does not interpose simply; but, by employing means, assumes, as it were, a visible form.

5. By the same class of persons, past events are referred improperly and inconsiderately to simple providence. As all contingencies whatsoever depend on it, therefore, neither thefts nor adulteries, nor murders, are perpetrated without an interposition of the divine will. Why, then, they ask, should the thief be punished for robbing him whom the Lord chose to chastise with poverty? Why should the murderer be punished for slaying him whose life the Lord had terminated? If all such persons serve the will of God, why should they be punished? I deny that they serve the will of God. For we can-

---

[1] Cic. de Fato. " Recte Chrysippus, tam futile est medicum adhibere, quam convalescere."—See Luther on Genesis xxx. 7, against those who thus abuse the doctrine of Predestination.

not say that he who is carried away by a wicked mind performs service on the order of God, when he is only following his own malignant desires. He obeys God, who, being instructed in his will, hast us in the direction in which God calls him. But how are we so instructed unless by his word? The will declared by his word is, therefore, that which we must keep in view in acting. God requires of us nothing but what he enjoins. If we design anything contrary to his precept, it is not obedience, but contumacy and transgression. But if he did not will it, we could not do it. I admit this. But do we act wickedly for the purpose of yielding obedience to him? This, assuredly, he does not command. Nay, rather we rush on, not thinking of what he wishes, but so inflamed by our own passionate lust, that, with destined purpose, we strive against him. And in this way, while acting wickedly, we serve his righteous ordination, since in his boundless wisdom he well knows how to use bad instruments for good purposes. And see how absurd this mode of arguing is. They will have it that crimes ought not to be punished in their authors, because they are not committed without the dispensation of God. I concede more—that thieves and murderers, and other evil-doers, are instruments of Divine Providence, being employed by the Lord himself to execute the judgments which he has resolved to inflict. But I deny that this forms any excuse for their misdeeds. For how? Will they implicate God in the same iniquity with themselves, or will they cloak their depravity by his righteousness? They cannot exculpate themselves, for their own conscience condemns them: they cannot charge God, since they perceive the whole wickedness in themselves, and nothing in Him save the legitimate use of their wickedness. But it is said he works by their means. And whence, I pray, the foetid odour of a dead body, which has been uncoffined and putrified by the sun's heat? All see that it is excited by the rays of the sun, but no man therefore says that the foetid odour is in them. In the same way, while the matter and guilt of wickedness belongs to the wicked man, why should it be thought that God contracts any impurity in using it at pleasure as his instrument? Have done, then, with that dog-like petulance which may, indeed, bay from a distance at the justice of God, but cannot reach it!

6. These calumnies, or rather frenzied dreams, will easily be dispelled by a pure and holy meditation on Divine Providence, meditation such as piety enjoins, that we may thence derive the best and sweetest fruit. The Christian, then, being most fully persuaded that all things come to pass by the dispensation of God, and that nothing happens fortuitously, will always direct his eye to him as the principal cause of events, at the same time paying due regard to inferior causes in their own place. Next, he will have no doubt that a special providence is awake for his preservation, and will not suffer anything to happen that will not turn to his good and safety. But as its business is first with men and then with the other creatures, he will feel

assured that the providence of God reigns over both. In regard to men, good as well as bad, he will acknowledge that their counsels, wishes, aims, and faculties, are so under his hand, that he has full power to turn them in whatever direction, and constrain them as often as he pleases. The fact that a special providence watches over the safety of believers, is attested by a vast number of the clearest promises.[1] " Cast thy burden upon the Lord, and he shall sustain thee : he shall never suffer the righteous to be moved." " Casting all your care upon him : for he careth for you." " He that dwelleth in the secret place of the Most High, shall abide under the shadow of the Almighty." " He that toucheth you, toucheth the apple of mine eye." " We have a strong city : salvation will God appoint for walls and bulwarks." " Can a woman forget her sucking child, that she should not have compassion on the son of her womb ? yea, they may forget, yet will I not forget thee." Nay, the chief aim of the historical books of Scripture is to show that the ways of his saints are so carefully guarded by the Lord, as to prevent them even from dashing their foot against a stone. Therefore, as we a little ago justly exploded the opinion of those who feign a universal providence, which does not condescend to take special care of every creature, so it is of the highest moment that we should specially recognise this care towards ourselves. Hence, our Saviour, after declaring that even a sparrow falls not to the ground without the will of his Father, immediately makes the application, that being more valuable than many sparrows, we ought to consider that God provides more carefully for us. He even extends this so far, as to assure us that the hairs of our head are all numbered. What more can we wish, if not even a hair of our head can fall, save in accordance with his will ? I speak not merely of the human race in general. God having chosen the Church for his abode, there cannot be a doubt, that in governing it, he gives singular manifestations of his paternal care.

7. The servant of God being confirmed by these promises and examples, will add the passages which teach that all men are under his power, whether to conciliate their minds, or to curb their wickedness, and prevent it from doing harm. For it is the Lord who gives us favour, not only with those who wish us well, but also in the eyes of the Egyptians (Exod. iii. 21), in various ways defeating the malice of our enemies. Sometimes he deprives them of all presence of mind, so that they cannot undertake anything soundly or soberly. In this way, he sends Satan to be a lie in the mouths of all the prophets in order to deceive Ahab (1 Kings xxii. 22) ; by the counsel of the young men he so infatuates Rehoboam, that his folly deprives him of his kingdom (1 Kings xii. 10, 15). Sometimes when he leaves them in possession of intellect, he so fills them with terror and dismay, that they can neither will nor plan the execution of what they had

1 Ps. lv. 23 ; 1 Pet. v. 7 ; Ps. xci. 1 ; Zech. ii. 8 ; Isaiah xxvi. 1 ; xxix. 15.

designed. Sometimes, too, after permitting them to attempt what lust and rage suggested, he opportunely interrupts them in their career, and allows them not to conclude what they had begun. Thus the counsel of Ahithophel, which would have been fatal to David, was defeated before its time (2 Sam. xvii. 7, 14). Thus, for the good and safety of his people, he overrules all the creatures, even the devil himself, who, we see, durst not attempt anything against Job without his permission and command. This knowledge is necessarily followed by gratitude in prosperity, patience in adversity, and incredible security for the time to come. Everything, therefore, which turns out prosperous and according to his wish, the Christian will ascribe entirely to God, whether he has experienced his beneficence through the instrumentality of men, or been aided by inanimate creatures. For he will thus consider with himself: Certainly it was the Lord that disposed the minds of these people in my favour, attaching them to me so as to make them the instruments of his kindness. In an abundant harvest he will think that it is the Lord who listens to the heaven, that the heaven may listen to the earth, and the earth herself to her own offspring ; in other cases, he will have no doubt that he owes all his prosperity to the divine blessing, and, admonished by so many circumstances, will feel it impossible to be ungrateful.

8. If anything adverse befalls him, he will forthwith raise his mind to God, whose hand is most effectual in impressing us with patience and placid moderation of mind. Had Joseph kept his thoughts fixed on the treachery of his brethren, he never could have resumed fraternal affection for them. But turning toward the Lord, he forgot the injury, and was so inclined to mildness and mercy, that he even voluntarily comforts his brethren, telling them, " Be not grieved nor angry with yourselves that ye sold me hither ; for God did send me before you to preserve life." " As for you, ye thought evil against me ; but God meant it unto good" (Gen. xlv. 5 ; l. 20). Had Job turned to the Chaldees, by whom he was plundered, he should instantly have been fired with revenge, but recognising the work of the Lord, he solaces himself with this most beautiful sentiment : " The Lord gave, and the Lord hath taken away ; blessed be the name of the Lord" (Job i. 21). So when David was assailed by Shimei with stones and curses, had he immediately fixed his eyes on the man, he would have urged his people to retaliate the injury ; but perceiving that he acts not without an impulse from the Lord, he rather calms them. " So let him curse," says he, " because the Lord hath said unto him, Curse David." With the same bridle he elsewhere curbs the excess of his grief, " I was dumb, I opened not my mouth, because thou didst it" (Ps. xxxix. 9). If there is no more effectual remedy for anger and impatience, he assuredly has not made little progress who has learned so to meditate on Divine Providence, as to be able always to bring his mind to this, The Lord willed it, it

must therefore be borne ; not only because it is unlawful to strive with him, but because he wills nothing that is not just and befitting. The whole comes to this. When unjustly assailed by men, over-looking their malice (which could only aggravate our grief, and whet our minds for vengeance), let us remember to ascend to God, and learn to hold it for certain that whatever an enemy wickedly com-mitted against us was permitted, and sent by his righteous dispensa-tion. Paul, in order to suppress our desire to retaliate injuries, wisely reminds us that we wrestle not with flesh and blood, but with our spiritual enemy the devil, that we may prepare for the contest (Eph. vi. 12). But to calm all the impulses of passion, the most useful consideration is, that God arms the devil, as well as all the wicked, for conflict, and sits as umpire, that he may exercise our patience. But if the disasters and miseries which press us happen without the agency of men, let us call to mind the doctrine of the Law (Deut. xxviii. 1), that all prosperity has its source in the blessing of God, that all adversity is his curse. And let us tremble at the dreadful denunciation, "And if ye will not be reformed by these things, but will walk contrary unto me ; then will I also walk con-trary unto you" (Lev. xxvi. 23, 24). These words condemn our torpor, when, according to our carnal sense, deeming that whatever happens in any way is fortuitous, we are neither animated by the kindness of God to worship him, nor by his scourge stimulated to repentance. And it is for this reason that Jeremiah (Lament. iii. 38) and Amos (Amos iii. 6) expostulated bitterly with the Jews, for not believing that good as well as evil was produced by the command of God. To the same effect are the words in Isaiah, " I form the light and create darkness : I make peace and create evil. I the Lord do all these things" (Is. xlv. 7).

9. At the same time, the Christian will not overlook inferior causes. For, while he regards those by whom he is benefited as ministers of the divine goodness, he will not, therefore, pass them by, as if their kindness deserved no gratitude, but feeling sincerely obliged to them, will willingly confess the obligation, and endeavour, according to his ability, to return it. In fine, in the blessings which he receives, he will revere and extol God as the principal author, but will also honour men as his ministers, and perceive, as is the truth, that by the will of God he is under obligation to those, by whose hand God has been pleased to show him kindness. If he sustains any loss through negli-gence or imprudence, he will, indeed, believe that it was the Lord's will it should so be, but at the same time, he will impute it to him-self. If one for whom it was his duty to care, but whom he has treated with neglect, is carried off by disease, although aware that the person had reached a limit beyond which it was impossible to pass, he will not, therefore, extenuate his fault, but, as he had neglected to do his duty faithfully towards him, will feel as if he had perished by his guilty negligence. Far less where, in the case of theft or murder,

fraud and preconceived malice have existed, will he palliate it under the pretext of Divine Providence, but in the same crime will distinctly recognise the justice of God, and the iniquity of man, as each is separately manifested. But in future events, especially, will he take account of such inferior causes. If he is not left destitute of human aid, which he can employ for his safety, he will set it down as a divine blessing; but he will not, therefore, be remiss in taking measures, or slow in employing the help of those whom he sees possessed of the means of assisting him. Regarding all the aids which the creatures can lend him, as hands offered him by the Lord, he will avail himself of them as the legitimate instruments of Divine Providence. And as he is uncertain what the result of any business in which he engages is to be (save that he knows, that in all things the Lord will provide for his good), he will zealously aim at what he deems for the best, so far as his abilities enable him. In adopting his measures, he will not be carried away by his own impressions, but will commit and resign himself to the wisdom of God, that under his guidance he may be led into the right path. However, his confidence in external aid will not be such, that the presence of it will make him feel secure, the absence of it fill him with dismay, as if he were destitute. His mind will always be fixed on the Providence of God alone, and no consideration of present circumstances will be allowed to withdraw him from the steady contemplation of it. Thus Joab, while he acknowledges that the issue of the battle is entirely in the hand of God, does not therefore become inactive, but strenuously proceeds with what belongs to his proper calling. "Be of good courage," says he, "and let us play the men for our people, and for the cities of our God; and the Lord do that which seemeth him good" (2 Sam. x. 12). The same conviction keeping us free from rashness and false confidence, will stimulate us to constant prayer, while at the same time filling our minds with good hope, it will enable us to feel secure, and bid defiance to all the dangers by which we are surrounded.

10. Here we are forcibly reminded of the inestimable felicity of a pious mind. Innumerable are the ills which beset human life, and present death in as many different forms. Not to go beyond ourselves, since the body is a receptacle, nay, the nurse, of a thousand diseases, a man cannot move without carrying along with him many forms of destruction. His life is in a manner interwoven with death. For what else can be said where heat and cold bring equal danger? Then, in what direction soever you turn, all surrounding objects not only may do harm, but almost openly threaten and seem to present immediate death. Go on board a ship, you are but a plank's breadth from death. Mount a horse, the stumbling of a foot endangers your life. Walk along the streets, every tile upon the roofs is a source of danger. If a sharp instrument is in your own hand, or that of a friend, the possible harm is manifest. All the savage beasts you see are so many beings armed for your destruction. Even within a high-walled

garden, where everything ministers to delight, a serpent will some-times lurk. Your house, constantly exposed to fire, threatens you with poverty by day, with destruction by night. Your fields, subject to hail, mildew, drought, and other injuries, denounce barrenness, and thereby famine. I say nothing of poison, treachery, robbery, some of which beset us at home, others follow us abroad. Amid these perils, must not man be very miserable, as one who, more dead than alive, with difficulty draws an anxious and feeble breath, just as if a drawn sword were constantly suspended over his neck? It may be said that these things happen seldom, at least not always, or to all, certainly never all at once. I admit it; but since we are reminded by the example of others, that they may also happen to us, and that our life is not an exception any more than theirs, is it impossible not to fear and dread as if they were to befall us? What can you imagine more grievous than such trepidation? Add that there is something like an insult to God when it is said that man, the noblest of the crea-tures, stands exposed to every blind and random stroke of fortune. Here, however, we were only referring to the misery which man should feel, were he placed under the dominion of chance.

11. But when once the light of Divine Providence has illumined the believer's soul, he is relieved and set free, not only from the extreme fear and anxiety which formerly oppressed him, but from all care. For as he justly shudders at the idea of chance, so he can confidently commit himself to God. This, I say, is his comfort, that his heavenly Father so embraces all things under his power —so governs them at will by his nod—so regulates them by his wisdom, that nothing takes place save according to his appointment; that received into his favour, and intrusted to the care of his angels, neither fire, not water, nor sword, can do him harm, except in so far as God their master is pleased to permit. For thus sings the Psalm, "Surely he shall deliver thee from the snare of the fowler, and from the noisome pestilence. He shall cover thee with his feathers, and under his wings shalt thou trust; his truth shall be thy shield and buckler. Thou shalt not be afraid for the terror by night; nor for the arrow that flieth by day; nor for the pestilence that walketh in darkness; nor for the destruction that wasteth at noonday," &c. (Ps. xci. 2–6). Hence the exulting confidence of the saints, " The Lord is on my side; I will not fear: what can man do unto me? The Lord taketh my part with them that help me." "Though an host should encamp against me, my heart shall not fear." "Yea, though I walk through the valley of the shadow of death, I will fear no evil" (Ps. cxviii. 6; xxvii. 3; xxiii. 4).

How comes it, I ask, that their confidence never fails, but just that while the world apparently revolves at random, they know that God is everywhere at work, and feel assured that his work will be their safety? When assailed by the devil and wicked men, were they not confirmed by remembering and meditating on Providence, they should, of necessity, forthwith despond.   But when they call to mind that the devil, and the whole train of the ungodly, are, in all directions, held in by the hand of God as with a bridle, so that they can neither conceive any mischief, nor plan what they have conceived, nor how much-soever they may have planned, move a single finger to perpetrate, unless in so far as he permits, nay, unless in so far as he commands; that they are not only bound by his fetters, but are even forced to do him service,—when the godly think of all these things they have ample sources of consolation.   For, as it belongs to the Lord to arm the fury of such foes, and turn and destine it at pleasure, so it is his also to determine the measure and the end, so as to prevent them from breaking loose and wantoning as they list. Supported by this conviction, Paul, who had said in one place that his journey was hindered by Satan (1 Thess. ii. 18), in another resolves, with the permission of God, to undertake it (1 Cor. xvi. 7). If he had only said that Satan was the obstacle, he might have seemed to give him too much power, as if he were able even to overturn the counsels of God ; but now, when he makes God the disposer, on whose permission all journeys depend, he shows, that however Satan may contrive, he can accomplish nothing except in so far as He pleases to give the word.   For the same reason, David, considering the various turns which human life undergoes as it rolls, and in a manner whirls around, betakes himself to this asylum, "My times are in thy hand" (Ps. xxxi. 15).   He might have said the course of life or *time* in the singular number, but by *times* he meant to express, that how unstable soever the condition of man may be, the vicissitudes which are ever and anon taking place are under divine regulation.   Hence Rezin and the king of Israel, after they had joined their forces for the destruction of Israel, and seemed torches which had been kindled to destroy and consume the land, are termed by the prophet "smoking firebrands."   They could only emit a little smoke (Is. vii. 4).   So Pharaoh, when he was an object of dread to all by his wealth and strength, and the multitude of his troops, is compared to the largest of beasts, while his troops are compared to fishes ; and God declares that he will take both leader and army with his hooks, and drag them whither he pleases (Exod. xxix. 4).   In one word, not to dwell longer on this, give heed, and you will at once perceive that ignorance of Providence is the greatest of all miseries, and the knowledge of it the highest happiness.

12. On the Providence of God, in so far as conducive to the solid instruction and consolation of believers (for, as to satisfying the curiosity of foolish men, it is a thing which cannot be done, and ought not to be attempted), enough would have been said, did not a few passages remain which seem to insinuate, contrary to the view which we have expounded, that the counsel of God is not firm and stable, but varies with the changes of sublunary affairs.   First, in reference to the Providence of God, it is said that he repented of

having made man (Gen. vi. 6), and of having raised Saul to the kingdom (1 Sam. xv. 11), and that he will repent of the evil which he had resolved to inflict on his people as soon as he shall have perceived some amendment in them (Jer. xviii. 8). Secondly, his decrees are sometimes said to be annulled. He had by Jonah proclaimed to the Ninevites, "Yet forty days and Nineveh shall be overthrown," but, immediately on their repentance, he inclined to a more merciful sentence (Jonah iii. 4—10). After he had, by the mouth of Isaiah, given Hezekiah intimation of his death, he was moved by his tears and prayers to defer it (Is. xxxviii. 15; 2 Kings xx. 15). Hence many argue that God has not fixed human affairs by an eternal decree, but according to the merits of each individual, and as he deems right and just, disposes of each single year, and day, and hour. As to repentance, we must hold that it can no more exist in God than ignorance, or error, or impotence. If no man knowingly or willingly reduces himself to the necessity of repentance, we cannot attribute repentance to God without saying either that he knows not what is to happen, or that he cannot evade it, or that he rushes precipitately and inconsiderately into a resolution, and then forthwith regrets it. But so far is this from the meaning of the Holy Spirit, that in the very mention of repentance he declares that God is not influenced by any feeling of regret, that he is not a man that he should repent. And it is to be observed that, in the same chapter, both things are so conjoined, that a comparison of the passages admirably removes the appearance of contradiction. When it is said that God repented of having made Saul king, the term *change* is used figuratively. Shortly after, it is added, "The Strength of Israel will not lie nor repent; for he is not a man, that he should repent" (1 Sam. xv. 29). In these words, his immutability is plainly asserted without figure. Wherefore it is certain that, in administering human affairs, the ordination of God is perpetual, and superior to everything like repentance. That there might be no doubt of his constancy, even his enemies are forced to bear testimony to it. For Balaam, even against his will, behoved to break forth into this exclamation, "God is not a man, that he should lie; neither the son of man, that he should repent: hath he said, and shall he not do it? or hath he spoken, and shall he not make it good?" (Num. xxiii. 19).

13. What then is meant by the term repentance? The very same that is meant by the other forms of expression, by which God is described to us humanly. Because our weakness cannot reach his height, any description which we receive of him must be lowered to our capacity in order to be intelligible. And the mode of lowering is to represent him not as he really is, but as we conceive of him. Though he is incapable of every feeling of perturbation, he declares that he is angry with the wicked. Wherefore, as when we hear that God is angry, we ought not to imagine that there is any emotion in

him, but ought rather to consider the mode of speech accommodated to our sense, God appearing to us like one inflamed and irritated whenever he exercises judgment, so we ought not to imagine anything more under the term repentance than a change of action, men being wont to testify their dissatisfaction by such a change. Hence, because every change whatever among men is intended as a correction of what displeases, and the correction proceeds from repentance, the same term applied to God simply means that his procedure is changed. In the mean time, there is no inversion of his counsel or will, no change of his affection. What from eternity he had foreseen, approved, decreed, he prosecutes with unvarying uniformity, how sudden soever to the eye of man the variation may seem to be.

14. Nor does the Sacred History, while it relates that the destruction which had been proclaimed to the Ninevites was remitted, and the life of Hezekiah, after an intimation of death, prolonged, imply that the decrees of God were annulled. Those who think so labour under delusion as to the meaning of *threatenings*, which, though they affirm simply, nevertheless contain in them a tacit condition dependent on the result. Why did the Lord send Jonah to the Ninevites to predict the overthrow of their city? Why did he by Isaiah give Hezekiah intimation of his death? He might have destroyed both them and him without a message to announce the disaster. He had something else in view than to give them a warning of death, which might let them see it at a distance before it came. It was because he did not wish them destroyed but reformed, and thereby saved from destruction. When Jonah prophesies that in forty days Nineveh will be overthrown, he does it in order to prevent the overthrow. When Hezekiah is forbidden to hope for longer life, it is that he may obtain longer life. Who does not now see that, by threatenings of this kind, God wished to arouse those to repentance whom he terrified, that they might escape the judgment which their sins deserved? If this is so, the very nature of the case obliges us to supply a tacit condition in a simple denunciation. This is even confirmed by analogous cases. The Lord rebuking king Abimelech for having carried off the wife of Abraham, uses these words: " Behold, thou art but a dead man, for the woman which thou hast taken; for she is a man's wife." But, after Abimelech's excuse, he thus speaks: " Restore the man his wife, for he is a prophet, and he shall pray for thee, and thou shalt live; and if thou restore her not, know thou that thou shalt surely die, thou and all that art thine" (Gen. xx. 3, 7). You see that, by the first announcement, he makes a deep impression on his mind, that he may render him eager to give satisfaction, and that by the second he clearly explains his will. Since the other passages may be similarly explained, you must not infer from them that the Lord derogated in any respect from his former counsel, because he recalled what he had promulgated. When, by denouncing punishment, he admonishes to repentance those whom he wishes to spare, he paves

the way for his eternal decree, instead of varying it one whit either in will or in language.   The only difference is, that he does not express, in so many syllables, what is easily understood.   The words of Isaiah must remain true, "The Lord of hosts hath purposed, and who shall disannul it ?   And his hand is stretched out, and who shall turn it back ?" (Isaiah xiv. 27.)

CHAPTER XVIII.

THE INSTRUMENTALITY OF THE WICKED EMPLOYED BY GOD, WHILE HE CONTINUES FREE FROM EVERY TAINT.[1]

This last chapter of the First Book consists of three parts : I. It having been said above that God bends all the reprobate, and even Satan himself, at his will, three objections are started. First, that this happens by the permission, not by the will of God. To this objection there is a twofold reply, the one, that angels and men, good and bad, do nothing but what is appointed by God ; the second, that all movements are secretly directed to their end by the hidden inspiration of God, sec. 1, 2. II. A second objection is, that there are two contrary wills in God, if by a secret counsel he decrees what he openly prohibits by his law. This objection refuted, sec. 3. III. The third objection is, that God is made the author of all wickedness, when he is said not only to use the agency of the wicked, but also to govern their counsels and affections, and that therefore the wicked are unjustly punished. This objection refuted in the last section.

Sections.

1. The carnal mind the source of the objections which are raised against the Providence of God. A primary objection, making a distinction between the *permission* and the *will* of God, refuted. Angels and men, good and bad, do nought but what has been decreed by God. This proved by examples.
2. All hidden movements directed to their end by the unseen but righteous instigation of God. Examples, with answers to objections.
3. These objections originate in a spirit of pride and blasphemy. Objection, that there must be two contrary wills in God, refuted. Why the one simple will of God seems to us as if it were manifold.
4. Objection, that God is the author of sin, refuted by examples. Augustine's answer and admonition.

1. FROM other passages, in which God is said to draw or bend Satan himself, and all the reprobate, to his will, a more difficult question arises. For the carnal mind can scarcely comprehend how, when acting by their means, he contracts no taint from their impurity, nay, how, in a common operation, he is exempt from all guilt, and can justly condemn his own ministers. Hence a distinction has been invented between *doing* and *permitting*, because to many it seemed altogether inexplicable how Satan and all the wicked are so under the hand and authority of God, that he directs their malice to whatever end he pleases, and employs their iniquities to execute his judgments. The modesty of those who are thus alarmed at the appearance of absurdity might perhaps be excused, did they not endeavour to vindicate the justice of God from every semblance of stigma by defending an untruth. It seems absurd that man should be

---

[1] See Calvin, adv. Libertinos, cap. xv. xvi., and Augustin. de Ordine, Lib. i. and ii., where he admirably discusses the question, Whether the order of Divine Providence includes all good and evil ?

blinded by the will and command of God, and yet be forthwith punished for his blindness. Hence recourse is had to the evasion that this is done only by the permission, and not also by the will of God. He himself, however, openly declaring that he *does* this, repudiates the evasion. That men do nothing save at the secret instigation of God, and do not discuss and deliberate on anything but what he has previously decreed with himself, and brings to pass by his secret direction, is proved by numberless clear passages of Scripture. What we formerly quoted from the Psalms, to the effect that he does whatever pleases him, certainly extends to all the actions of men. If God is the arbiter of peace and war, as is there said, and that without any exception, who will venture to say that men are borne along at random with a blind impulse, while He is unconscious or quiescent? But the matter will be made clearer by special examples. From the first chapter of Job we learn that Satan appears in the presence of God to receive his orders, just as do the angels who obey spontaneously. The manner and the end are different, but still the fact is, that he cannot attempt anything without the will of God. But though afterwards his power to afflict the saint seems to be only a bare permission, yet as the sentiment is true, "The Lord gave, and the Lord hath taken away; as it pleased the Lord, so it hath been done," we infer that God was the author of that trial of which Satan and wicked robbers were merely the instruments. Satan's aim is to drive the saint to madness by despair. The Sabeans cruelly and wickedly make a sudden incursion to rob another of his goods. Job acknowledges that he was deprived of all his property, and brought to poverty, because such was the pleasure of God. Therefore, whatever men or Satan himself devise, God holds the helm, and makes all their efforts contribute to the execution of his judgments. God wills that the perfidious Ahab should be deceived; the devil offers his agency for that purpose, and is sent with a definite command to be a lying spirit in the mouth of all the prophets (2 Kings xxii. 20). If the blinding and infatuation of Ahab is a judgment from God, the fiction of bare permission is at an end; for it would be ridiculous for a judge only to permit, and not also to decree, what he wishes to be done at the very time that he commits the execution of it to his ministers. The Jews purposed to destroy Christ. Pilate and the soldiers indulged them in their fury; yet the disciples confess in solemn prayer that all the wicked did nothing but what the hand and counsel of God had decreed (Acts iv. 28), just as Peter had previously said in his discourse, that Christ was delivered to death by the determinate counsel and foreknowledge of God (Acts ii. 23); in other words, that God, to whom all things are known from the beginning, had determined what the Jews had executed. He repeats the same thing elsewhere, "Those things, which God before had showed by the mouth of all his prophets, that Christ should suffer, he hath so fulfilled (Acts iii. 18). Absalom incestuously defiling his father's bed, perpetrates a detestable crime. God, however, declares that it was his work; for the words are, " Thou didst it secretly, but I will do this thing before all Israel, and before the sun." [1] The cruelties of the Chaldeans in Judea are declared by Jeremiah to be the work of God. For which reason, Nebuchadnezzar is called the servant of God. God frequently exclaims, that by his hiss, by the clang of his trumpet, by his authority and command, the wicked are excited to war. He calls the Assyrian the rod of his anger, and the axe which he wields in his hand. The overthrow of the city, and downfall of the temple, he calls his own work. David, not murmuring against God, but acknowledging him to be a just judge, confesses that the curses of Shimei are uttered by his orders. "The Lord," says he, "has bidden him curse." Often in sacred history whatever happens is said to proceed from the Lord, as the revolt of the ten tribes, the death of Eli's sons, and very many others of a similar description. Those who have a tolerable acquaintance with the Scriptures see that, with a view to brevity, I am only producing a few out of many passages, from which it is perfectly clear that it is the merest trifling to substitute a bare permission for the providence of God, as if he sat in a watch-tower waiting for fortuitous events, his judgments meanwhile depending on the will of man.

2. With regard to secret movements, what Solomon says of the heart of a king, that it is turned hither and thither, as God sees meet, certainly applies to the whole human race, and has the same force as if he had said, that whatever we conceive in our minds is directed to its end by the secret inspiration of God. And certainly, did he not work internally in the minds of men, it could not have been properly said, that he takes away the lip from the true, and prudence from the aged—takes away the heart from the princes of the earth, that they wander through devious paths. To the same effect, we often read that men are intimidated when He fills their hearts with terror. Thus David left the camp of Saul while none knew of it, because a sleep from God had fallen upon all. But nothing can be clearer than the many passages which declare, that he blinds the minds of men, and smites them with giddiness, intoxicates them with a spirit of stupor, renders them infatuated, and hardens their hearts. Even these expressions many would confine to permission, as if, by deserting the reprobate, he allowed them to be blinded by Satan. But since the Holy Spirit distinctly says, that the blindness and infatuation are inflicted by the just judgment of God, the solution is altogether inadmissible. He is said to have hardened the heart of Pharaoh, to have hardened it yet more, and confirmed it. Some evade these forms of expression by a silly cavil, because Pharaoh is elsewhere said to have hardened his own heart, thus making his will the cause of hardening it ; as if the two things did not perfectly agree with each other, though

[1] 2 Sam. xii. 12; Jer. l. 25; Is. v. 26; x. 5 : xix. 25; 2 Sam. xvi 10; 1 Kings xi. 31; 1 Sam. ii. 34.

in different senses—viz. that man, though acted upon by God, at the same time also acts. But I retort the objection on those who make it. If to harden means only bare permission, the contumacy will not properly belong to Pharaoh. Now, could anything be more feeble and insipid than to interpret as if Pharaoh had only allowed himself to be hardened? We may add, that Scripture cuts off all handle for such cavils: "I," saith the Lord, "will harden his heart" (Exod. iv. 21). So also, Moses says of the inhabitants of the land of Caanan, that they went forth to battle because the Lord had hardened their hearts (Josh. xi. 20). The same thing is repeated by another prophet, "He turned their hearts to hate his people" (Psalm cv. 25). In like manner, in Isaiah, he says of the Assyrian, "I will send him against a hypocritical nation, and against the people of my wrath will I give him a charge to take the spoil, and to take the prey" (Isaiah x. 6); not that he intends to teach wicked and obstinate man to obey spontaneously, but because he bends them to execute his judgments, just as if they carried their orders engraven on their minds. And hence it appears that they are impelled by the sure appointment of God. I admit, indeed, that God often acts in the reprobate by interposing the agency of Satan; but in such a manner, that Satan himself performs his part, just as he is impelled, and succeeds only in so far as he is permitted. The evil spirit that troubled Saul is said to be from the Lord (1 Sam. xvi. 14), to intimate that Saul's madness was a just punishment from God. Satan is also said to blind the minds of those who believe not (2 Cor. iv. 4). But how so, unless that a spirit of error is sent from God himself, making those who refuse to obey the truth to believe a lie? According to the former view, it is said, "If the prophet be deceived when he hath spoken a thing, I the Lord have deceived that prophet" (Ezek. xiv. 9). According to the latter view, he is said to have given men over to a reprobate mind (Rom. i. 28), because he is the special author of his own just vengeance; whereas Satan is only his minister (see Calv. in Ps. cxli. 4). But as in the Second Book (chap. iv. sec. 3, 4), in discussing the question of man's freedom, this subject will again be considered, the little that has now been said seems to be all that the occasion requires. The sum of the whole is this,—since the will of God is said to be the cause of all things, all the counsels and actions of men must be held to be governed by his providence; so that he not only exerts his power in the elect, who are guided by the Holy Spirit, but also forces the reprobate to do him service.

3. As I have hitherto stated only what is plainly and unambiguously taught in Scripture, those who hesitate not to stigmatise what is thus taught by the sacred oracles, had better beware what kind of censure they employ. If, under a pretence of ignorance, they seek the praise of modesty, what greater arrogance can be imagined than to utter one word in opposition to the authority of God—to say, for instance, "I think otherwise,"—I would not have this subject

touched"? But if they openly blaspheme, what will they gain by assaulting heaven? Such petulance, indeed, is not new. In all ages there have been wicked and profane men, who rabidly assailed this branch of doctrine. But what the Spirit declared of old by the mouth of David (Ps. li. 6), they will feel by experience to be true—God will overcome when he is judged. David indirectly rebukes the infatuation of those whose license is so unbridled, that from their grovelling spot of earth they not only plead against God, but arrogate to themselves the right of censuring him. At the same time, he briefly intimates that the blasphemies which they belch forth against heaven, instead of reaching God, only illustrate his justice, when the mists of their calumnies are dispersed. Even our faith, because founded on the sacred word of God, is superior to the whole world, and is able from its height to look down upon such mists.

Their first objection—that if nothing happens without the will of God, he must have two contrary wills, decreeing by a secret counsel what he has openly forbidden in his law—is easily disposed of. But before I reply to it, I would again remind my readers that this cavil is directed not against me, but against the Holy Spirit, who certainly dictated this confession to that holy man Job, " The Lord gave, and the Lord hath taken away," when, after being plundered by robbers, he acknowledges that their injustice and mischief was a just chastisement from God. And what says the Scripture elsewhere? The sons of Eli " hearkened not unto the voice of their father, because the Lord would slay them " (1 Sam. ii. 25). Another prophet also exclaims, "Our God is in the heavens: he hath done whatsoever he hath pleased" (Ps. cxv. 3). I have already shown clearly enough that God is the author of all those things which, according to these objectors, happen only by his inactive permission. He testifies that he creates light and darkness, forms good and evil (Is. xlv. 7); that no evil happens which he hath not done (Amos iii. 6). Let them tell me whether God exercises his judgments willingly or unwillingly. As Moses teaches that he who is accidentally killed by the blow of an axe, is delivered by God into the hand of him who smites him (Deut. xix. 5), so the Gospel, by the mouth of Luke, declares, that Herod and Pontius Pilate conspired " to do whatsoever thy hand and thy counsel determined before to be done " (Acts iv. 28). And, in truth, if Christ was not crucified by the will of God, where is our redemption? Still, however, the will of God is not at variance with itself. It undergoes no change. He makes no pretence of not willing what he wills, but while in himself the will is one and undivided, to us it appears manifold, because, from the feebleness of our intellect, we cannot comprehend how, though after a different manner, he wills and wills not the very same thing. Paul terms the calling of the Gentiles a hidden mystery, and shortly after adds, that therein was manifested the manifold wisdom of God (Eph. iii. 10). Since, on account of the dulness of our sense, the wisdom of God seems manifold (or, as an old interpreter rendered it, multiform), are we, therefore, to dream of some variation in God, as if he either changed his counsel, or disagreed with himself? Nay, when we cannot comprehend how God can will that to be done which he forbids us to do, let us call to mind our imbecility, and remember that the light in which he dwells is not without cause termed inaccessible (1 Tim. vi. 16), because shrouded in darkness. Hence, all pious and modest men will readily acquiesce in the sentiment of Augustine: "Man sometimes with a good-will wishes something which God does not will, as when a good son wishes his father to live, while God wills him to die. Again, it may happen that man with a bad will wishes what God wills righteously, as when a bad son wishes his father to die, and God also wills it. The former wishes what God wills not, the latter wishes what God also wills. And yet the filial affection of the former is more consonant to the good-will of God, though willing differently, than the unnatural affection of the latter, though willing the same thing; so much does approbation or condemnation depend on what it is befitting in man, and what in God to will, and to what end the will of each has respect. For the things which God rightly wills, he accomplishes by the evil wills of bad men" (*August. Enchirid. ad Laurent.* cap. 101). He had said a little before (cap. 100), that the apostate angels, by their revolt, and all the reprobate, as far as they themselves were concerned, did what God willed not; but, in regard to his omnipotence, it was impossible for them to do so; for, while they act against the will of God, his will is accomplished in them. Hence he exclaims, "Great is the work of God, exquisite in all he wills! so that, in a manner wondrous and ineffable, that is not done without his will which is done contrary to it, because it could not be done if he did not permit; nor does he permit it unwillingly, but willingly; nor would He who is good permit evil to be done, were he not omnipotent to bring good out of evil" (*Augustin. in* Ps. cxi. 2).

4. In the same way is solved, or rather spontaneously vanishes, another objection—viz. If God not only uses the agency of the wicked, but also governs their counsels and affections, he is the author of all their sins; and therefore men, in executing what God has decreed, are unjustly condemned, because they are obeying his will. Here *will* is improperly confounded with *precept*, though it is obvious, from innumerable examples, that there is the greatest difference between them.[1] When Absalom defiled his father's bed, though God was pleased thus to avenge the adultery of David, he did not therefore enjoin an abandoned son to commit incest, unless, perhaps, in respect of David, as David himself says of Shimei's

---

[1] The French is, "Car ils meslent perversement le commandement de Dieu avec son vouloir secret, veu qu'il appert par exemples infinis qu'il y a bien longue distance et diversité de l'un à l'autre;" for they perversely confound the command of God with his secret will, though it appears, by an infinite number of examples, that there is a great distance and diversity between them.

curses. For, while he confesses that Shimei acts by the order of
God, he by no means commends the obedience, as if that petulant
dog had been yielding obedience to a divine command; but, recognising in his tongue the scourge of God, he submits patiently to be
chastised. Thus we must hold, that while by means of the wicked
God performs what he had secretly decreed, they are not excusable
as if they were obeying his precept, which of set purpose they
violate according to their lust.

How these things, which men do perversely, are of God, and are
ruled by his secret providence, is strikingly shown in the election of
king Jeroboam (1 Kings xii. 20), in which the rashness and infatuation of the people are severely condemned for perverting the order
sanctioned by God, and perfidiously revolting from the family of
David. And yet we know it was God's will that Jeroboam should
be anointed. Hence the apparent contradiction in the words of
Hosea (Hosea viii. 4 ; xiii. 11), because, while God complained that
that kingdom was erected without his knowledge, and against his
will, he elsewhere declares, that he had given king Jeroboam in his
anger. How shall we reconcile the two things,—that Jeroboam's
reign was not of God, and yet God appointed him king? In this way:
The people could not revolt from the family of David without shaking off a yoke divinely imposed on them, and yet God himself was
not deprived of the power of thus punishing the ingratitude of Solomon. We therefore see how God, while not willing treachery, with
another view justly wills the revolt ; and hence Jeroboam, by unexpectedly receiving the sacred unction, is urged to aspire to the kingdom. For this reason, the sacred history says, that God stirred up
an enemy to deprive the nos of Solomon of part of the kingdom
(1 Kings xi. 23). Let the reader diligently ponder both points: how,
as it was the will of God that the people should be ruled by the hand
of one king, their being rent into two parties was contrary to his will ;
and yet how this same will originated the revolt. For certainly
when Jeroboam, who had no such thought, is urged by the prophet
verbally, and by the oil of unction, to hope for the kingdom, the
thing was not done without the knowledge or against the will of
God, who had expressly commanded it ; and yet the rebellion of the
people is justly condemned, because it was against the will of God
that they revolted from the posterity of David. For this reason, it is
afterwards added, that when Rehoboam haughtily spurned the prayers
of the people, " the cause was from the Lord, that he might perform
his saying, which the Lord spake by Ahijah " (1 Kings xii. 15). See
how sacred unity was violated against the will of God, while, at the
same time, with his will the ten tribes were alienated from the son
of Solomon. To this might be added another similar example—viz.
the murder of the sons of Ahab, and the extermination of his whole
progeny by the consent, or rather the active agency, of the people.
Jehu says truly, " There shall fall unto the earth nothing of the word

of the Lord, which the Lord spake concerning the house of Ahab : for the Lord hath done that which he spake by his servant Elijah" (2 Kings x. 10). And yet, with good reason, he upbraids the citizens of Samaria for having lent their assistance. " Ye be righteous : behold, I conspired against my master, and slew him, but who slew all these ?"

If I mistake not, I have already shown clearly how the same act at once betrays the guilt of man, and manifests the righteousness of God. Modest minds will always be satisfied with Augustine's answer, " Since the Father delivered up the Son, Christ his own body, and Judas his Master, how in such a case is God just, and man guilty, but just because in the one act which they did, the reasons for which they did it are different ?" (*August. Ep.* 48, *ad Vincentium.*) If any are not perfectly satisfied with this explanation—viz. that there is no concurrence between God and man, when by His righteous impulse man does what he ought not to do—let them give heed to what Augustine elsewhere observes : " Who can refrain from trembling at those judgments when God does according to his pleasure even in the hearts of the wicked, at the same time rendering to them according to their deeds ?" (*De Grat. et Lib. Arbit. ad Valent.* c. 20.) And certainly, in regard to the treachery of Judas, there is just as little ground to throw the blame of the crime upon God, because He was both pleased that his Son should be delivered up to death, and did deliver him, as to ascribe to Judas the praise of our redemption. Hence Augustine, in another place, truly observes, that when God makes his scrutiny, he looks not to what men could do, or to what they did, but to what they wished to do, thus taking account of their will and purpose. Those to whom this seems harsh had better consider how far their captiousness is entitled to any toleration, while, on the ground of its exceeding their capacity, they reject a matter which is clearly taught by Scripture, and complain of the enunciation of truths, which, if they were not useful to be known, God never would have ordered his prophets and apostles to teach. Our true wisdom is to embrace with meek docility, and without reservation, whatever the Holy Scriptures have delivered. Those who indulge their petulance, a petulance manifestly directed against God, are undeserving of a longer refutation.

END OF THE FIRST BOOK.

INSTITUTES

OF

THE CHRISTIAN RELIGION.

BOOK SECOND.

OF THE KNOWLEDGE OF GOD THE REDEEMER,
IN CHRIST, AS FIRST MANIFESTED
TO THE FATHERS, UNDER THE LAW, AND
THEREAFTER TO US UNDER THE GOSPEL.

ARGUMENT.

THE First Part of the Apostles' Creed—viz. the knowledge of God the Creator, being disposed of, we now come to the Second Part, which relates to the knowledge of God as a Redeemer in Christ. The subjects treated of accordingly are, *first*, the Occasion of Redemption—viz. Adam's fall; and, *secondly*, Redemption itself. The first five chapters are devoted to the former subject, and the remainder to the latter.

Under the Occasion of Redemption, the Fall is considered not only in a general way, but also specially in its effects. Hence the first four chapters treat of original sin, free will, the corruption of human nature, and the operation of God in the heart. The fifth chapter contains a refutation of the arguments usually urged in support of free will.

The subject of redemption may be reduced to five particular heads :—

I. The character of him in whom salvation for lost man must be sought, Chap. VI.

II. How he was manifested to the world, namely, in a twofold manner First, under the Law. Here the Decalogue is expounded, and some other points relating to the law discussed, Chap. VII. and VIII. Secondly, under the Gospel. Here the resemblance and difference of the two dispensations are considered, Chap. IX. X. XI.

III. What kind of person Christ was, and behoved to be, in order to perform the office of Mediator—viz. God and man in one person, Chap. XII. XIII. XIV.

IV. For what end he was sent into the world by the Father. Here Christ's prophetical, kingly, and priestly offices are considered, Chap. XV.

V. In what way, or by what successive steps, Christ fulfilled the office of our Redeemer, Chap. XVI. Here are considered his crucifixion, death, burial, descent to hell, resurrection, ascension to heaven, and seat at the right hand of the Father, together with the practical use of the whole doctrine. Chapter XVII. contains an answer to the question, Whether Christ is properly said to have merited the grace of God for us.

INSTITUTES

OF

THE CHRISTIAN RELIGION.

BOOK SECOND.

OF THE KNOWLEDGE OF GOD THE REDEEMER, IN CHRIST, AS FIRST MANIFESTED TO THE FATHERS, UNDER THE LAW, AND THEREAFTER TO US UNDER THE GOSPEL.

CHAPTER I.

THROUGH THE FALL AND REVOLT OF ADAM, THE WHOLE HUMAN RACE MADE ACCURSED AND DEGENERATE. OF ORIGINAL SIN.

I. How necessary the knowledge of ourselves is, its nature, the danger of mistake, its leading parts, sec. 1, 2, 3. II. The causes of Adam's fearful fall, sec. 4. III. The effects of the fall extending to Adam's posterity, and all the creatures, sec. 5, to the end of the Chapter, where the nature, propagation, and effect of original sin are considered.

Sections.

1. The knowledge of ourselves most necessary. To use it properly we must be divested of pride, and clothed with true humility, which will dispose us to consider our fall, and embrace the mercy of God in Christ.
2. Though there is plausibility in the sentiment which stimulates us to self-admiration, the only sound sentiment is that which inclines us to true humbleness of mind. Pretexts for pride. The miserable vanity of sinful man.
3. Different views taken by carnal wisdom and by conscience, which appeals to divine justice as its standard. The knowledge of ourselves, consisting of two parts, the former of which having already been discussed, the latter is here considered.
4. In considering this latter part, two points to be considered: 1. How it happened that Adam involved himself and the whole human race in this dreadful calamity. This the result not of sensual intemperance, but of infidelity (the source of other heinous sins), which led to revolt from God, from whom all true happiness must

1. IT was not without reason that the ancient proverb so strongly recommended to man the knowledge of himself. For if it is deemed disgraceful to be ignorant of things pertaining to the business of life, much more disgraceful is self-ignorance, in consequence of which we miserably deceive ourselves in matters of the highest moment, and so walk blindfold. But the more useful the precept is, the more careful we must be not to use it preposterously, as we see certain philosophers have done. For they, when exhorting man to know himself, state the motive to be, that he may not be ignorant of his own excellence and dignity. They wish him to see nothing in himself but what will fill him with vain confidence, and inflate him with pride. But self-knowledge consists in this, *first*, When reflecting on what God gave us at our creation, and still continues graciously to give, we perceive how great the excellence of our nature would have been had its integrity remained, and, at the same time, remember that we have nothing of our own, but depend entirely on God, from whom we hold at pleasure whatever he has seen it meet to bestow ; *secondly*, When viewing our miserable condition since Adam's fall, all confidence and boasting are overthrown, we blush for shame, and feel truly humble. For as God at first formed us in his own image, that he might elevate our minds to the pursuit of virtue, and the contemplation of eternal life, so to prevent us from heartlessly burying those noble qualities which distinguish us from the lower animals, it is of importance to know that we were endued with reason and intelligence, in order that we might cultivate a holy and honourable life, and regard a blessed immortality as our destined aim. At the same time, it is impossible to think of our primeval dignity without being immediately reminded of the sad spectacle of our ignominy and corruption, ever since we

fell from our original in the person of our first parent. In this way, we feel dissatisfied with ourselves, and become truly humble, while we are inflamed with new desires to seek after God, in whom each may regain those good qualities of which all are found to be utterly destitute.

2. In examining ourselves, the search which divine truth enjoins, and the knowledge which it demands, are such as may indispose us to everything like confidence in our own powers, leave us devoid of all means of boasting, and so incline us to submission. This is the course which we must follow, if we would attain to the true goal, both in speculation and practice. I am not unaware how much more plausible the view is, which invites us rather to ponder on our good qualities than to contemplate what must overwhelm us with shame—our miserable destitution and ignominy. There is nothing more acceptable to the human mind than flattery, and, accordingly, when told that its endowments are of a high order, it is apt to be excessively credulous. Hence it is not strange that the greater part of mankind have erred so egregiously in this matter. Owing to the innate self-love by which all are blinded, we most willingly persuade ourselves that we do not possess a single quality which is deserving of hatred; and hence, independent of any countenance from without, general credit is given to the very foolish idea, that man is perfectly sufficient of himself for all the purposes of a good and happy life. If any are disposed to think more modestly, and concede somewhat to God, that they may not seem to arrogate everything as their own, still, in making the division, they apportion matters so that the chief ground of confidence and boasting always remains with themselves. Then, if a discourse is pronounced which flatters the pride spontaneously springing up in man's inmost heart, nothing seems more delightful. Accordingly, in every age, he who is most forward in extolling the excellence of human nature, is received with the loudest applause. But be this heralding of human excellence what it may, by teaching man to rest in himself, it does nothing more than fascinate by its sweetness, and, at the same time, so delude as to drown in perdition all who assent to it. For what avails it to proceed in vain confidence, to deliberate, resolve, plan, and attempt what we deem pertinent to the purpose, and, at the very outset, prove deficient and destitute both of sound intelligence and true virtue, though we still confidently persist till we rush headlong on destruction? But this is the best that can happen to those who put confidence in their own powers. Whosoever, therefore, gives heed to those teachers who merely employ us in contemplating our good qualities, so far from making progress in self-knowledge, will be plunged into the most pernicious ignorance.

3. While revealed truth concurs with the general consent of mankind in teaching that the second part of wisdom consists in self-knowledge, they differ greatly as to the method by which this

knowledge is to be acquired. In the judgment of the flesh man deems his self-knowledge complete, when, with overweening confidence in his own intelligence and integrity, he takes courage, and spurs himself on to virtuous deeds, and when, declaring war upon vice, he uses his utmost endeavour to attain to the honourable and the fair. But he who tries himself by the standard of divine justice, finds nothing to inspire him with confidence; and hence, the more thorough his self-examination, the greater his despondency. Abandoning all dependence on himself, he feels that he is utterly incapable of duly regulating his conduct. It is not the will of God, however, that we should forget the primeval dignity which he bestowed on our first parents—a dignity which may well stimulate us to the pursuit of goodness and justice. It is impossible for us to think of our first original, or the end for which we were created, without being urged to meditate on immortality, and to seek the kingdom of God. But such meditation, so far from raising our spirits, rather casts them down, and makes us humble. For what is our original? One from which we have fallen. What the end of our creation? One from which we have altogether strayed, so that, weary of our miserable lot, we groan, and groaning sigh for a dignity now lost. When we say that man should see nothing in himself which can raise his spirits, our meaning is, that he possesses nothing on which he can proudly plume himself. Hence, in considering the knowledge which man ought to have of himself, it seems proper to divide it thus, *first*, to consider the end for which he was created, and the qualities—by no means contemptible qualities—with which he was endued, thus urging him to meditate on divine worship and the future life; and, *secondly*, to consider his faculties, or rather want of faculties—a want which, when perceived, will annihilate all his confidence, and cover him with confusion. The tendency of the former view is to teach him what his duty is, of the latter, to make him aware how far he is able to perform it. We shall treat of both in their proper order.

4. As the act which God punished so severely must have been not a trivial fault but a heinous crime, it will be necessary to attend to the peculiar nature of the sin which produced Adam's fall, and provoked God to inflict such fearful vengeance on the whole human race. The common idea of sensual intemperance is childish. The sum and substance of all virtues could not consist in abstinence from a single fruit amid a general abundance of every delicacy that could be desired, the earth, with happy fertility, yielding not only abundance, but also endless variety. We must, therefore, look deeper than sensual intemperance. The prohibition to touch the tree of the knowledge of good and evil was a trial of obedience, that Adam, by observing it, might prove his willing submission to the command of God. For the very term shows the end of the precept to have been to keep him contented with his lot, and not allow him arro-

gantly to aspire beyond it. The promise, which gave him hope of eternal life as long as he should eat of the tree of life, and, on the other hand, the fearful denunciation of death the moment he should taste of the tree of the knowledge of good and evil, were meant to prove and exercise his faith. Hence it is not difficult to infer in what way Adam provoked the wrath of God. Augustine, indeed, is not far from the mark, when he says (in Psal. xix.), that pride was the beginning of all evil, because, had not man's ambition carried him higher than he was permitted, he might have continued in his first estate. A further definition, however, must be derived from the kind of temptation which Moses describes. When, by the subtlety of the devil, the woman faithlessly abandoned the command of God, her fall obviously had its origin in disobedience. This Paul confirms, when he says, that, by the disobedience of one man, all were destroyed. At the same time, it is to be observed, that the first man revolted against the authority of God, not only in allowing himself to be ensnared by the wiles of the devil, but also by despising the truth, and turning aside to lies. Assuredly, when the word of God is despised, all reverence for Him is gone. His majesty cannot be duly honoured among us, nor his worship maintained in its integrity, unless we hang as it were upon his lips. Hence infidelity was at the root of the revolt. From infidelity, again, sprang ambition and pride, together with ingratitude; because Adam, by longing for more than was allotted him, manifested contempt for the great liberality with which God had enriched him. It was surely monstrous impiety that a son of earth should deem it little to have been made in the likeness, unless he were also made the equal of God. If the apostacy by which man withdraws from the authority of his Maker, nay, petulantly shakes off his allegiance to him, is a foul and execrable crime, it is in vain to extenuate the sin of Adam. Nor was it simple apostacy. It was accompanied with foul insult to God, the guilty pair assenting to Satan's calumnies when he charged God with malice, envy, and falsehood. In fine, infidelity opened the door to ambition, and ambition was the parent of rebellion, man casting off the fear of God, and giving free vent to his lust. Hence, Bernard truly says, that, in the present day, a door of salvation is opened to us when we receive the gospel with our ears, just as by the same entrance, when thrown open to Satan, death was admitted. Never would Adam have dared to show any repugnance to the command of God if he had not been incredulous as to his word. The strongest curb to keep all his affections under due restraint, would have been the belief that nothing was better than to cultivate righteousness by obeying the commands of God, and that the highest possible felicity was to be loved by him.[1] Man, therefore, when carried away by the blasphemies of Satan, did his very utmost to annihilate the whole glory of God.

[1] The latter clause of this sentence is omitted in the French.

5. As Adam's spiritual life would have consisted in remaining united and bound to his Maker, so estrangement from him was the death of his soul. Nor is it strange that he who perverted the whole order of nature in heaven and earth deteriorated his race by his revolt. "The whole creation groaneth," saith St Paul, "being made subject to vanity, not willingly" (Rom. viii. 20, 22). If the reason is asked, there cannot be a doubt that creation bears part of the punishment deserved by man, for whose use all other creatures were made. Therefore, since through man's fault a curse has extended above and below, over all the regions of the world, there is nothing unreasonable in its extending to all his offspring. After the heavenly image in man was effaced, he not only was himself punished by a withdrawal of the ornaments in which he had been arrayed—viz. wisdom, virtue, justice, truth, and holiness, and by the substitution in their place of those dire pests, blindness, impotence, vanity, impurity, and unrighteousness, but he involved his posterity also, and plunged them in the same wretchedness. This is the hereditary corruption to which early Christian writers gave the name of Original Sin, meaning by the term the depravation of a nature formerly good and pure. The subject gave rise to much discussion, there being nothing more remote from common apprehension, than that the fault of one should render all guilty, and so become a common sin. This seems to be the reason why the oldest doctors of the church only glance obscurely at the point, or, at least, do not explain it so clearly as it required. This timidity, however, could not prevent the rise of a Pelagius with his profane fiction—that Adam sinned only to his own hurt, but did no hurt to his posterity. Satan, by thus craftily hiding the disease, tried to render it incurable. But when it was clearly proved from Scripture that the sin of the first man passed to all his posterity, recourse was had to the cavil, that it passed by imitation, and not by propagation. The orthodox, therefore, and more especially Augustine, laboured to show, that we are not corrupted by acquired wickedness, but bring an innate corruption from the very womb. It was the greatest impudence to deny this. But no man will wonder at the presumption of the Pelagians and Celestians, who has learned from the writings of that holy man how extreme the effrontery of these heretics was. Surely there is no ambiguity in David's confession, "I was shapen in iniquity; and in sin did my mother conceive me" (Ps. li. 5). His object in the passage is not to throw blame on his parents; but the better to commend the goodness of God towards him, he properly reiterates the confession of impurity from his very birth. As it is clear, that there was no peculiarity in David's case, it follows that it is only an instance of the common lot of the whole human race. All of us, therefore, descending from an impure seed, come into the world tainted with the contagion of sin. Nay, before we behold the light of the sun we are in God's sight defiled and polluted. "Who can bring a clean

thing out of an unclean? Not one," says the Book of Job (Job xiv. 4).

6. We thus see that the impurity of parents is transmitted to their children, so that all, without exception, are originally depraved. The commencement of this depravity will not be found until we ascend to the first parent of all as the fountain head. We must, therefore, hold it for certain that, in regard to human nature, Adam was not merely a progenitor, but, as it were, a root, and that accordingly, by his corruption, the whole human race was deservedly viti ated. This is plain from the contrast which the Apostle draws between Adam and Christ, "Wherefore, as by one man sin entered into the world, and death by sin; and so death passed upon all men, for that all have sinned; even so might grace reign through righteousness unto eternal life by Jesus Christ our Lord" (Rom. v. 19—21). To what quibble will the Pelagians here recur? That the sin of Adam was propagated by imitation? Is the righteousness of Christ then available to us only in so far as it is an example held forth for our imitation? Can any man tolerate such blasphemy? But if, out of all controversy, the righteousness of Christ, and thereby life, is ours by communication, it follows that both of these were lost in Adam that they might be recovered in Christ, whereas sin and death were brought in by Adam, that they might be abolished in Christ. There is no obscurity in the words, "As by one man's disobedience many were made sinners, so by the obedience of one shall many be made righteous." Accordingly, the relation subsisting between the two is this, As Adam, by his ruin, involved and ruined us, so Christ, by his grace, restored us to salvation. In this clear light of truth I cannot see any need of a longer or more laborious proof. Thus, too, in the First Epistle to the Corinthians, when Paul would confirm believers in the confident hope of the resurrection, he shows that the life is recovered in Christ which was lost in Adam (1 Cor. xv. 22). Having already declared that all died in Adam, he now also openly testifies that all are imbued with the taint of sin. Condemnation, indeed, could not reach those who are altogether free from blame. But his meaning cannot be made clearer than from the other member of the sentence, in which he shows that the hope of life is restored in Christ. Every one knows that the only mode in which this is done is, when by a wondrous communication Christ transfuses into us the power of his own righteousness, as it is elsewhere said, "The Spirit is life because of righteousness" (1 Cor. xv. 22). Therefore, the only explanation which can be given of the expression, "in Adam all died," is, that he by sinning not only brought disaster and ruin upon himself, but also plunged our nature into like destruction; and that not only in one fault, in a matter not pertaining to us, but by the corruption into which he himself fell, he infected his whole seed. Paul never could have said that all are "by nature the children of wrath" (Eph. ii. 3), if

they had not been cursed from the womb. And it is obvious, that the nature there referred to is not nature such as God created, but as vitiated in Adam; for it would have been most incongruous to make God the author of death. Adam, therefore, when he corrupted himself, transmitted the contagion to all his posterity. For a heavenly Judge, even our Saviour himself, declares that all are by birth vicious and depraved, when he says that "that which is born of the flesh is flesh" (John iii. 6), and that therefore the gate of life is closed against all until they have been regenerated.

7. To the understanding of this subject, there is no necessity for an anxious discussion (which in no small degree perplexed the ancient doctors) as to whether the soul of the child comes by transmission from the soul of the parent.[1] It should be enough for us to know that Adam was made the depository of the endowments which God was pleased to bestow on human nature, and that, therefore, when he lost what he had received, he lost not only for himself but for us all. Why feel any anxiety about the transmission of the soul, when we know that the qualities which Adam lost he received for us not less than for himself, that they were not gifts to a single man, but attributes of the whole human race? There is nothing absurd, therefore, in the view, that when he was divested, his nature was left naked and destitute, that he having been defiled by sin, the pollution extends to all his seed. Thus, from a corrupt root corrupt branches proceeding, transmit their corruption to the saplings which spring from them. The children being vitiated in their parent, conveyed the taint to the grandchildren; in other words, corruption commencing in Adam, is, by perpetual descent, conveyed from those preceding to those coming after them. The cause of the contagion is neither in the substance of the flesh nor the soul, but God was pleased to ordain that those gifts which he had bestowed on the first man, that man should lose as well for his descendants as for himself. The Pelagian cavil, as to the improbability of children deriving corruption from pious parents, whereas, they ought rather to be sanctified by their purity, is easily refuted. Children come not by spiritual regeneration but carnal descent.[2] Accordingly, as Augustine says, "Both the condemned unbeliever and the acquitted believer beget offspring not acquitted but condemned, because the nature which begets is corrupt."[3] Moreover, though godly parents do in some measure contribute to the holiness of their offspring, this is by the blessing of God; a blessing,

---

[1] The French is, "Assavoir, si l'ame du fils procede de la substance de l'ame paternelle, veu que c'est en l'ame que reside le peché originel." That is, whether the soul of the child is derived from the substance of the soul of the parent, seeing it is in the soul that original sin resides.

[2] The French is, "Les enfans ne descendent point de la generation spirituelle qui les serviteurs de Dieu ont du S. Esprit, mais de la generation charnelle qu'ils ont d'Adam." Children descend not from the spiritual generation which the servants of God have of the Holy Spirit, but the carnal generation which they have of Adam.

[3] Lib. contra Pelag. Cœlest. See also Ep. 157, ad Gregor., Lib. vii. Ep. 53.

however, which does not prevent the primary and universal curse of the whole race from previously taking effect. Guilt is from nature, whereas sanctification is from supernatural grace.

8. But lest the thing itself of which we speak be unknown or doubtful, it will be proper to define original sin (Calvin, in Conc. Trident. I., Dec. Sess. v.). I have no intention, however, to discuss all the definitions which different writers have adopted, but only to adduce the one which seems to me most accordant with truth. Original sin, then, may be defined a hereditary corruption and depravity of our nature, extending to all the parts of the soul, which first makes us obnoxious to the wrath of God, and then produces in us works which in Scripture are termed works of the flesh. This corruption is repeatedly designated by Paul by the term sin[1] (Gal. v. 19); while the works which proceed from it, such as adultery, fornication, theft, hatred, murder, revellings, he terms, in the same way, the fruits of sin, though in various passages of Scripture, and even by Paul himself, they are also termed sins. The two things, therefore, are to be distinctly observed—viz. that being thus perverted and corrupted in all the parts of our nature, we are, merely on account of such corruption, deservedly condemned by God, to whom nothing is acceptable but righteousness, innocence, and purity. This is not liability for another's fault. For when it is said, that the sin of Adam has made us obnoxious to the justice of God, the meaning is not, that we, who are in ourselves innocent and blameless, are bearing his guilt, but that since by his transgression we are all placed under the curse, he is said to have brought us under obligation.[2] Through him, however, not only has punishment been derived, but pollution instilled, for which punishment is justly due. Hence Augustine, though he often terms it another's sin (that he may more clearly show how it comes to us by descent), at the same time asserts that it is each individual's own sin.[3] And the Apostle most distinctly testifies, that "death passed upon all men, for that all have sinned" (Rom. v. 12); that is, are involved in original sin, and polluted by its stain. Hence, even infants bringing their condemnation with them from their mother's womb, suffer not for another's, but for their own defect. For although they have not yet produced the fruits of their own unrighteousness, they have the seed implanted in them. Nay, their whole nature is, as it were, a seed-bed of sin, and therefore cannot

[1] The French adds, " Sans adjouster Originel : "—without adding Original.

[2] The French is, " Car en ce qui est dit, que par Adam nous sommes fait redevables au jugement de Dieu, ce ne'st pas a dire que nous soyons innocens, et que sans avoir merité aucune peine nous portions la folleenchere de son peché ; mais pourceque par sa transgression nous sommes tous enveloppés de confusion, il est dit nous avoir tous obligez." For when it is said, that by Adam we are made liable to the judgment of God, the meaning is, not that we are innocent, and that without having deserved any punishment, we are made to pay dear for his sin, but because by his transgression we are all covered with confusion, he is said to have bound us.

[3] In many passages, and especially in his treatise, De Peccatorum Merit. et Remiss. Lib. iii. cap. 8.

but be odious-and abominable to God. Hence it follows, that it is properly deemed sinful in the sight of God; for there could be no condemnation without guilt. Next comes the other point—viz. that this perversity in us never ceases, but constantly produces new fruits, in other words, those works of the flesh which we formerly described; just as a lighted furnace sends forth sparks and flames, or a fountain without ceasing pours out water. Hence, those who have defined original sin as the want of the original righteousness which we ought to have had, though they substantially comprehend the whole case, do not significantly enough express its power and energy. For our nature is not only utterly devoid of goodness, but so prolific in all kinds of evil, that it can never be idle. Those who term it *concupiscence* use a word not very inappropriate, provided it were added (this, however, many will by no means concede), that everything which is in man, from the intellect to the will, from the soul even to the flesh, is defiled and pervaded with this concupiscence; or, to express it more briefly, that the whole man is in himself nothing else than concupiscence.

9. I have said, therefore, that all the parts of the soul were possessed by sin, ever since Adam revolted from the fountain of righteousness. For not only did the inferior appetites entice him, but abominable impiety seized upon the very citadel of the mind, and pride penetrated to his inmost heart (Rom. vii. 12; Book IV., chap. xv., sec. 10–12), so that it is foolish and unmeaning to confine the corruption thence proceeding to what are called sensual motions, or to call it an excitement, which allures, excites, and drags the single part which they call sensuality into sin. Here Peter Lombard has displayed gross ignorance (Lomb., Lib. ii. Dist. 21). When investigating the seat of corruption, he says it is in the flesh (as Paul declares), not properly, indeed, but as being more apparent in the flesh. As if Paul had meant that only a part of the soul, and not the whole nature, was opposed to supernatural grace. Paul himself leaves no room for doubt, when he says, that corruption does not dwell in one part only, but that no part is free from its deadly taint. For, speaking of corrupt nature, he not only condemns the inordinate nature of the appetites, but, in particular, declares that the understanding is subjected to blindness, and the heart to depravity (Eph. iv. 17, 18). The third chapter of the Epistle to the Romans is nothing but a description of original sin. The same thing appears more clearly from the mode of renovation. For the spirit, which is contrasted with the old man, and the flesh, denotes not only the grace by which the sensual or inferior part of the soul is corrected, but includes a complete reformation of all its parts (Eph. iv. 23). And, accordingly, Paul enjoins not only that gross appetites be suppressed, but that we be renewed in the spirit of our mind (Eph. iv. 23), as he elsewhere tells us to be transformed by the renewing of our mind (Rom. xii. 2). Hence it follows, that that part in which the dignity and excellence of the soul

are most conspicuous, has not only been wounded, but so corrupted, that mere cure is not sufficient. There must be a new nature. How far sin has seized both on the mind and heart, we shall shortly see. Here I only wish briefly to observe, that the whole man, from the crown of the head to the sole of the foot, is so deluged, as it were, that no part remains exempt from sin, and, therefore, everything which proceeds from him is imputed as sin. Thus Paul says, that all carnal thoughts and affections are enmity against God, and consequently death (Rom. viii. 7).

10. Let us have done, then, with those who dare to inscribe the name of God on their vices, because we say that men are born vicious. The divine workmanship, which they ought to look for in the nature of Adam, when still entire and uncorrupted, they absurdly expect to find in their depravity. The blame of our ruin rests with our own carnality, not with God, its only cause being our degeneracy from our original condition. And let no one here clamour that God might have provided better for our safety by preventing Adam's fall. This objection, which, from the daring presumption implied in it, is odious to every pious mind, relates to the mystery of predestination, which will afterwards be considered in its own place (Tertull. de Præscript. Calvin, Lib. de Predest.). Meanwhile, let us remember that our ruin is attributable to our own depravity, that we may not insinuate a charge against God himself, the Author of nature. It is true that nature has received a mortal wound, but there is a great difference between a wound inflicted from without, and one inherent in our first condition. It is plain that this wound was inflicted by sin; and, therefore, we have no ground of complaint except against ourselves. This is carefully taught in Scripture. For the Preacher says, " Lo, this only have I found, that God made man upright; but they have sought out many inventions" (Eccl. vii. 29). Since man, by the kindness of God, was made upright, but by his own infatuation fell away unto vanity, his destruction is obviously attributable only to himself (Athanas. in Orat. Cont. Idola.)

11. We say, then, that man is corrupted by a natural viciousness, but not by one which proceeded from nature. In saying that it proceeded not from nature, we mean that it was rather an adventitious event which befell man, than a substantial property assigned to him from the beginning.[1] We, however, call it *natural* to prevent any one from supposing that each individual contracts it by depraved habit, whereas all receive it by a hereditary law. And we have authority for so calling it. For, on the same ground, the Apostle says, that we are "by nature the children of wrath" (Eph. ii. 3).

---

[1] The French is, "Nous nions qu'elle soit de nature, afin de monstrer que c'est plutot une qualité survenue à l'homme qu'une proprieté de sa substance, laquelle ait eté dés le commencément enracinée en lui;"—we deny that it is of nature, in order to show that it is rather a quality superadded to man than a property of his substance, which has been from the beginning rooted in him.

How could God, who takes pleasure in the meanest of his works, be offended with the noblest of them all ? The offence is not with the work itself, but the corruption of the work. Wherefore, if it is not improper to say that, in consequence of the corruption of human nature, man is naturally hateful to God, it is not improper to say, that he is naturally vicious and depraved. Hence, in the view of our corrupt nature, Augustine hesitates not to call those sins natural which necessarily reign in the flesh wherever the grace of God is wanting. This disposes of the absurd notion of the Manichees, who, imagining that man was essentially wicked, went the length of assigning him a different Creator, that they might thus avoid the appearance of attributing the cause and origin of evil to a righteous God.

CHAPTER II.

MAN NOW DEPRIVED OF FREEDOM OF WILL, AND MISERABLY ENSLAVED.

Having in the first chapter treated of the fall of man, and the corruption of the human race, it becomes necessary to inquire, Whether the sons of Adam are deprived of all liberty ; and if any particle of liberty remains, how far its power extends ?　The four next chapters are devoted to this question.　This second chapter may be reduced to three general heads : I. The foundation of the whole discussion. II. The opinions of others on the subject of human freedom, sec. 2–9. III. The true doctrine on the subject, sec. 10–27.

Sections.

1. Connection of the previous with the four following chapters.　In order to lay a proper foundation for the discussion of free will, two obstacles in the way to be removed—viz. sloth and pride.　The basis and sum of the whole discussion.　The solid structure of this basis, and a clear demonstration of it by the argument à *majori ad minus*.　Also from the inconveniences and absurdities arising from the obstacle of pride.
2. The second part of the chapter containing the opinions of others.　1. The opinions of philosophers.
3. The labyrinths of philosophers.　A summary of the opinion common to all the philosophers.
4. The opinions of others continued—viz. The opinions of the ancient theologians on the subject of free will.　These composed partly of Philosophy and partly of Theology.　Hence their falsehood, extravagance, perplexity, variety, and contradiction.　Too great fondness for philosophy in the Church has obscured the knowledge of God and of ourselves.　The better to explain the opinions of philosophers, a definition of Free Will given.　Wide difference between this definition and these opinions.
5. Certain things annexed to Free Will by the ancient theologians, especially the Schoolmen.　Many kinds of Free Will according to them.
6. Puzzles of scholastic divines in the explanation of this question.
7. The conclusion that so trivial a matter ought not to be so much magnified.　Objection of those who have a fondness for new terms in the Church.　Objection answered.
8. Another answer.　The Fathers, and especially Augustine, while retaining the term Free Will, yet condemned the doctrine of the heretics on the subject, as destroying the grace of God.
9. The language of the ancient writers on the subject of Free Will is, with the exception of that of Augustine, almost unintelligible.　Still they set little or no value on human virtue, and ascribe the praise of all goodness to the Holy Spirit.
10. The last part of the chapter, containing a simple statement of the true doctrine.　The fundamental principle is, that man first begins to profit in the knowledge of himself when he becomes sensible of his ruined condition.　This confirmed, 1. by passages of Scripture.
11. Confirmed, 2. by the testimony of ancient theologians.
12. The foundation being laid, to show how far the power both of the intellect and will now extends, it is maintained in general, and in conformity with the views of Augustine and the Schoolmen, that the natural endowments of man are corrupted, and the supernatural almost entirely lost.　A separate consideration of the powers

of the Intellect and the Will. Some general considerations, 1. The intellect possesses some powers of perception. Still it labours under a twofold defect.
13. Man's intelligence extends both to things terrestrial and celestial. The power of
the intellect in regard to the knowledge of things terrestrial. First, with regard to matters of civil polity.
14. The power of the intellect, secondly, with regard to the arts. Particular gifts in
this respect conferred on individuals, and attesting the grace of God.
15 The use of this knowledge of things terrestrial, first, that we may see how human
nature, notwithstanding of its fall, is still adorned by God with excellent endowments.
16. Use of this knowledge continued. Secondly, that we may see that these endowments bestowed on individuals are intended for the common benefit of mankind.
They are sometimes conferred even on the wicked.
17. Some portion of human nature still left. This, whatever be the amount of it, should
be ascribed entirely to the divine indulgence. Reason of this. Examples.
18. Second part of the discussion, namely, that which relates to the power of the
human intellect in regard to things celestial These reducible to three heads,
namely, divine knowledge, adoption, and will. The blindness of man in regard
to these proved and illustrated by a simile.
19. Proved, moreover, by passages of Scripture, showing, 1. That the sons of Adam
are endued with some light, but not enough to enable them to comprehend God.
Reasons.
20. Adoption not from nature, but from our heavenly Father, being sealed in the elect
by the Spirit of regeneration. Obvious from many passages of Scripture, that,
previous to regeneration, the human intellect is altogether unable to comprehend
the things relating to regeneration. This fully proved. First argument. Second
argument. Third argument.
21. Fourth argument. Scripture ascribes the glory of our adoption and salvation to
God only. The human intellect blind as to heavenly things until it is illuminated. Disposal of a heretical objection.
22. Human intellect ignorant of the true knowledge of the divine law. This proved
by the testimony of an Apostle, by an inference from the same testimony, and
from a consideration of the end and definition of the Law of Nature. Plato obviously mistaken in attributing all sins to ignorance.
23. Themistius nearer the truth in maintaining, that the delusion of the intellect is
manifested not so much in generals as in particulars. Exception to this rule.
24. Themistius, however, mistaken in thinking that the intellect is so very seldom
deceived as to generals. Blindness of the human intellect when tested by the
standard of the Divine Law, in regard both to the first and second tables. Examples.
25. A middle view to be taken—viz. that all sins are not imputable to ignorance, and,
at the same time, that all sins do not imply intentional malice. All the human
mind conceives and plans in this matter is evil in the sight of God. Need of
divine direction every moment.
26. The will examined. The natural desire of good, which is universally felt, no proof
of the freedom of the human will. Two fallacies as to the use of terms, *appetite*
and *good*.
27. The doctrine of the Schoolmen on this subject opposed to and refuted by Scripture.
The whole man being subject to the power of sin, it follows that the will, which
is the chief seat of sin, requires to be most strictly curbed. Nothing ours but
sin.

1. HAVING seen that the dominion of sin, ever since the first man
was brought under it, not only extends to the whole race, but has
complete possession of every soul, it now remains to consider more
closely, whether, from the period of being thus enslaved, we have
been deprived of all liberty; and if any portion still remains, how
far its power extends. In order to facilitate the answer to this question, it may be proper in passing to point out the course which our

inquiry ought to take.   The best method of avoiding error is to consider the dangers which beset us on either side.   Man being devoid
of all uprightness, immediately takes occasion from the fact to indulge in sloth, and having no ability in himself for the study of
righteousness, treats the whole subject as if he had no concern in it.
On the other hand, man cannot arrogate anything, however minute,
to himself, without robbing God of his honour, and through rash
confidence subjecting himself to a fall.   To keep free of both these
rocks,[1] our proper course will be, first, to show that man has no remaining good in himself, and is beset on every side by the most
miserable destitution ; and then teach him to aspire to the goodness
of which he is devoid, and the liberty of which he has been deprived:
thus giving him a stronger stimulus to exertion than he could have
if he imagined himself possessed of the highest virtue.   How necessary the latter point is, everybody sees.   As to the former, several
seem to entertain more doubt than they ought.   For it being admitted as incontrovertible that man is not to be denied anything that
is truly his own, it ought also to be admitted, that he is to be deprived of everything like false boasting.   If man had no title to
glory in himself, when, by the kindness of his Maker, he was distinguished by the noblest ornaments, how much ought he to be
humbled now, when his ingratitude has thrust him down from the
highest glory to extreme ignominy ?   At the time when he was
raised to the highest pinnacle of honour, all which Scripture attributes to him is, that he was created in the image of God, thereby
intimating that the blessings in which his happiness consisted were
not his own, but derived by divine communication.   What remains,
therefore, now that man is stript of all his glory, than to acknowledge the God for whose kindness he failed to be grateful, when he
was loaded with the riches of his grace ?   Not having glorified him
by the acknowledgment of his blessings, now, at least, he ought to
glorify him by the confession of his poverty.   In truth, it is no less
useful for us to renounce all the praise of wisdom and virtue, than
to aim at the glory of God.   Those who invest us with more than
we possess only add sacrilege to our ruin.   For when we are taught
to contend in our own strength, what more is done than to lift us
up, and then leave us to lean on a reed which immediately gives
way ?   Indeed, our strength is exaggerated when it is compared to
a reed.   All that foolish men invent and prattle on this subject is
mere smoke.   Wherefore, it is not without reason that Augustine so
often repeats the well-known saying, that free will is more destroyed
than established by its defenders (August. in Evang. Joann. Tract.
81).   It was necessary to premise this much for the sake of some
who, when they hear that human virtue is totally overthrown, in

---

[1] See *Calvin Adv. Theolog. Parisienses*, Art. 2.   These two rocks are adverted to by
Augustine, *Ep.* 47, *et in Joannem*, cap. 12.

order that the power of God in man may be exalted, conceive an utter dislike to the whole subject, as if it were perilous, not to say superfluous, whereas it is manifestly both most necessary and most useful.[1]

2. Having lately observed that the faculties of the soul are seated in the mind and the heart, let us now consider how far the power of each extends. Philosophers generally maintain that reason dwells in the mind like a lamp, throwing light on all its counsels, and, like a queen, governing the will—that it is so pervaded with divine light as to be able to consult for the best, and so endued with vigour as to be able perfectly to command; that, on the contrary, sense is dull and short-sighted, always creeping on the ground, grovelling among inferior objects, and never rising to true vision; that the appetite, when it obeys reason, and does not allow itself to be subjugated by sense, is borne to the study of virtue, holds a straight course, and becomes transformed into will; but that when enslaved by sense, it is corrupted and depraved so as to degenerate into lust. In a word, since, according to their opinion, the faculties which I have mentioned above—namely, intellect, sense, and appetite, or will (the latter being the term in ordinary use)—are seated in the soul, they maintain that the intellect is endued with reason, the best guide to a virtuous and happy life, provided it duly avails itself of its excellence, and exerts the power with which it is naturally endued; that, at the same time, the inferior movement, which is termed sense, and by which the mind is led away to error and delusion, is of such a nature, that it can be tamed and gradually subdued by the power of reason. To the will, moreover, they give an intermediate place between reason and sense, regarding it as possessed of full power and freedom, whether to obey the former, or yield itself up to be hurried away by the latter.

3. Sometimes, indeed, convinced by their own experience, they do not deny how difficult it is for man to establish the supremacy of reason in himself, inasmuch as he is at one time enticed by the allurements of pleasure; at another, deluded by a false semblance of good; and at another, impelled by unruly passions, and pulled away (to use Plato's expression) as by ropes or sinews (Plato, De Legibus, lib. i.). For this reason, Cicero says, that the sparks given forth by nature are immediately extinguished by false opinions and depraved manners (Cicero, Tusc. Quæst. lib. iii.). They confess that when once diseases of this description have seized upon the mind, their course is too impetuous to be easily checked, and they hesitate not to compare them to fiery steeds, which, having thrown off the charioteer, scamper away without restraint. At the same time, they set it down as beyond

---

1 The French is, " Laquelle toutefois nous cognoistrons etre très-utile et qui plus est, etre un des fondemens de la religion ;"—which, however, we shall know to be very useful, and what is more, to be one of the fundamentals of religion.

dispute, that virtue and vice are in our own power. For (say they), If it is in our choice to do this thing or that, it must also be in our choice not to do it: Again, If it is in our choice nor to act, it must also be in our choice to act: But both in doing and abstaining we seem to act from free choice; and, therefore, if we do good when we please, we can also refrain from doing it; if we commit evil, we can also shun the commission of it (Aristot. Ethic. lib. iii. c. 5). Nay, some have gone the length of boasting (Seneca, *passim*), that it is the gift of the gods that we live, but our own that we live well and purely. Hence Cicero says, in the person of Cotta, that as every one acquires virtue for himself, no wise man ever thanked the gods for it. "We are praised," says he, "for virtue, and glory in virtue, but this could not be, if virtue were the gift of God, and not from ourselves" (Cicero, De Nat. Deorum). A little after, he adds, "The opinion of all mankind is, that fortune must be sought from God, wisdom from ourselves." Thus, in short, all philosophers maintain, that human reason is sufficient for right government; that the will, which is inferior to it, may indeed be solicited to evil by sense, but having a free choice, there is nothing to prevent it from following reason as its guide in all things.

4. Among ecclesiastical writers, although there is none who did not acknowledge that sound reason in man was seriously injured by sin, and the will greatly entangled by vicious desires, yet many of them made too near an approach to the philosophers. Some of the most ancient writers appear to me to have exalted human strength, from a fear that a distinct acknowledgment of its impotence might expose them to the jeers of the philosophers with whom they were disputing, and also furnish the flesh, already too much disinclined to good, with a new pretext for sloth. Therefore, to avoid teaching anything which the majority of mankind might deem absurd, they made it their study, in some measure, to reconcile the doctrine of Scripture with the dogmas of philosophy, at the same time making it their special care not to furnish any occasion to sloth. This is obvious from their words. Chrysostom says, "God having placed good and evil in our power, has given us full freedom of choice; he does not keep back the unwilling, but embraces the willing" (Homil. de Prodit. Judæ.). Again, "He who is wicked is often, when he so chooses, changed into good, and he who is good falls through sluggishness, and becomes wicked. For the Lord has made our nature free. He does not lay us under necessity, but furnishing apposite remedies, allows the whole to depend on the views of the patient" (Homil. 16, in Genesim.). Again, "As we can do nothing rightly until aided by the grace of God, so, until we bring forward what is our own, we cannot obtain favour from above" (Homil. 52). He had previously said, "As the whole is not done by divine assistance, we ourselves must of necessity bring somewhat." Accordingly, one of his common expressions is "Let us bring what is our own, God will supply the rest."

In unison with this, Jerome says, "It is ours to begin, God's to finish: it is ours to offer what we can, his to supply what we cannot" (Dialog. iii. Cont. Pelag.).

From these sentences, you see that they have bestowed on man more than he possesses for the study of virtue, because they thought that they could not skake off our innate sluggishness unless they argued that we sin by ourselves alone. With what skill they have thus argued we shall afterwards see. Assuredly we shall soon be able to show that the sentiments just quoted are most inaccurate.[1] Moreover, although the Greek Fathers, above others, and especially Chrysostom, have exceeded due bounds in extolling the powers of the human will, yet all ancient theologians, with the exception of Augustine, are so confused, vacillating, and contradictory on this subject, that no certainty can be obtained from their writings. It is needless, therefore, to be more particular in enumerating every separate opinion. It will be sufficient to extract from each as much as the exposition of the subject seems to require. Succeeding writers (every one courting applause for his acuteness in the defence of human nature) have uniformly, one after the other, gone more widely astray, until the common dogma came to be, that man was corrupted only in the sensual part of his nature, that reason remained entire, and will was scarcely impaired. Still the expression was often on their lips, that man's natural gifts were corrupted, and his supernatural[2] taken away. Of the thing implied by these words, however, scarcely one in a hundred had any distinct idea. Certainly, were I desirous clearly to express what the corruption of nature is, I would not seek for any other expression. But it is of great importance attentively to consider what the power of man now is when vitiated in all the parts of his nature, and deprived of supernatural gifts. Persons professing to be the disciples of Christ have spoken too much like the philosophers on this subject. As if human nature were still in its integrity, the term free will has always been in use among the Latins, while the Greeks were not ashamed to use a still more presumptuous term—viz. αὐτεξούσιον—as if man had still full power in himself.

But since the principle entertained by all, even the vulgar, is, that man is endued with free will, while some, who would be thought more skilful, know not how far its power extends; it will be necessary, first to consider the meaning of the term, and afterwards ascertain, by a simple appeal to Scripture, what man's natural power for good or evil is. The thing meant by free will, though constantly occurring in all writers, few have defined. Origen,[3] however, seems

---

[1] The French adds, "Pour en dire franchement ce qui en est;"—to speak of them frankly as they deserve.

[2] The French adds the explanation, "Assavoir ceux qui concernoyent la vie celeste;" that is to say, those which concern the heavenly life.

[3] Orig. De Principiis, Lib. iii. It is given by Lombard, Lib. ii. Dist. xxiv. Bernard. de Grat. et Liber Arbit Anselm, Dialog. de Liber. Arbit. cap. xii. xiii. Lombard, Lib. ii. Dist. xxiv. sec. 5.

to have stated the common opinion when he said, It is a power of reason to discern between good and evil; of will, to choose the one or other. Nor does Augustine differ from him when he says, It is a power of reason and will to choose the good, grace assisting,—to choose the bad, grace desisting. Bernard, while aiming at greater acuteness, speaks more obscurely, when he describes it as consent, in regard to the indestructible liberty of the will, and the inalienable judgment of reason. Anselm's definition is not very intelligible to ordinary understandings. He calls it a power of preserving rectitude on its own account. Peter Lombard and the Schoolmen preferred the definition of Augustine, both because it was clearer, and did not exclude divine grace, without which they saw that the will was not sufficient of itself. They, however, add something of their own, because they deemed it either better or necessary for clearer explanation. First, they agree that the term *will* (arbitrium) has reference to reason, whose office it is to distinguish between good and evil, and that the epithet *free* properly belongs to the will, which may incline either way. Wherefore, since liberty properly belongs to the will, Thomas Aquinas says (Part I. Quæst. 83, Art. 3), that the most congruous definition is to call free will an elective power, combining intelligence and appetite, but inclining more to appetite. We now perceive in what it is they suppose the faculty of free will to consist —viz. in reason and will. It remains to see how much they attribute to each.

5. In general, they are wont to place under the free will of man only intermediate things—viz. those which pertain not to the kingdom of God—while they refer true righteousness to the special grace of God and spiritual regeneration. The author of the work, "De Vocatione Gentium" (On the Calling of the Gentiles),[1] wishing to show this, describes the will as threefold—viz. sensitive, animal, and spiritual. The two former, he says, are free to man, but the last is the work of the Holy Spirit. What truth there is in this will be considered in its own place. Our intention at present is only to mention the opinions of others, not to refute them. When writers treat of free will, their inquiry is chiefly directed not to what its power is in relation to civil or external actions, but to the obedience required by the divine law. The latter I admit to be the great question, but I cannot think the former should be altogether neglected; and I hope to be able to give the best reason for so thinking (sec. 12 to 18). The schools, however, have adopted a distinction which enumerates three kinds of freedom (see Lombard, Lib. ii. Dist. 25): the first, a freedom from necessity; the second, a freedom from sin; and the third, a freedom from misery: the first naturally so inherent in man, that he cannot possibly be deprived of it; while through sin the other two have been lost. I willingly admit this

---

[1] The French adds ("qu'en attribue à St Ambroise");—which is attributed to St Ambrose.

distinction, except in so far as it confounds *necessity* with *compulsion*. How widely the things differ, and how important it is to attend to the difference, will appear elsewhere.

6. All this being admitted, it will be beyond dispute, that free will does not enable any man to perform good works, unless he is assisted by grace; indeed, the special grace which the elect alone receive through regeneration. For I stay not to consider the extravagance of those who say that grace is offered equally and promiscuously to all (Lomb. Lib. ii. Dist. 26). But it has not yet been shown whether man is entirely deprived of the power of well-doing, or whether he still possesses it in some, though in a very feeble and limited degree—a degree so feeble and limited, that it can do nothing of itself, but when assisted by grace, is able also to perform its part. The Master of the Sentences (Lombard, ibid.), wishing to explain this, teaches that a twofold grace is necessary to fit for any good work. The one he calls Operating. To it it is owing that we effectually will what is good. The other, which succeeds this good-will, and aids it, he calls Co-operating. My objection to this division (see *infra*, chap. iii. sec. 10, and chap. vii. sec. 9) is, that while it attributes the effectual desire of good to divine grace, it insinuates that man, by his own nature, desires good in some degree, though ineffectually. Thus Bernard, while maintaining that a good-will is the work of God, concedes this much to man—viz. that of his own nature he longs for such a good-will. This differs widely from the view of Augustine, though Lombard pretends to have taken the division from him. Besides, there is an ambiguity in the second division, which has led to an erroneous interpretation. For it has been thought that we co-operate with subsequent grace, inasmuch as it pertains to us either to nullify the first grace, by rejecting it, or to confirm it, by obediently yielding to it. The author of the work De Vocatione Gentium expresses it thus: It is free to those who enjoy the faculty of reason to depart from grace, so that the not departing is a reward, and that which cannot be done without the co-operation of the Spirit is imputed as merit to those whose will might have made it otherwise (Lib ii. cap. iv.). It seemed proper to make these two observations in passing, that the reader may see how far I differ from the sounder of the Schoolmen. Still further do I differ from more modern sophists, who have departed even more widely than the Schoolmen from the ancient doctrine. The division, however, shows in what respect free will is attributed to man. For Lombard ultimately declares (Lib. ii. Dist. 25), that our freedom is not to the extent of leaving us equally inclined to good and evil in act or in thought, but only to the extent of freeing us from compulsion. This liberty is compatible with our being depraved, the servants of sin, able to do nothing but sin.

7. In this way, then, man is said to have free will, not because he has a free choice of good and evil, but because he acts voluntarily,

and not by compulsion. This is perfectly true: but why should so small a matter have been dignified with so proud a title? An admirable freedom! that man is not forced to be the servant of sin, while he is, however, ἐθελοδουλος (a voluntary slave); his will being bound by the fetters of sin. I abominate mere verbal disputes, by which the Church is harassed to no purpose; but I think we ought religiously to eschew terms which imply some absurdity, especially in subjects where error is of pernicious consequence. How few are there who, when they hear free will attributed to man, do not immediately imagine that he is the master of his mind and will in such a sense, that he can of himself incline himself either to good or evil? It may be said that such dangers are removed by carefully expounding the meaning to the people. But such is the proneness of the human mind to go astray, that it will more quickly draw error from one little word, than truth from a lengthened discourse. Of this, the very term in question furnishes too strong a proof. For the explanation given by ancient Christian writers having been lost sight of, almost all who have come after them, by attending only to the etymology of the term, have been led to indulge a fatal confidence.

8. As to the Fathers (if their authority weighs with us), they have the term constantly in their mouths; but they, at the same time, declare what extent of meaning they attach to it. In particular, Augustine hesitates not to call the will *a slave*.[1] In another passage, he is offended with those who deny free will; but his chief reason for this is explained when he says, " Only, lest any one should presume so to deny freedom of will, from a desire to excuse sin." It is certain, he elsewhere admits, that without the Spirit the will of man is not free, inasmuch as it is subject to lusts which chain and master it. And again, that nature began to want liberty the moment the will was vanquished by the revolt into which it fell. Again, that man, by making a bad use of free will, lost both himself and his will. Again, that free will having been made a captive, can do nothing in the way of righteousness. Again, that no will is free which has not been made so by divine grace. Again, that the righteousness of God is not fulfilled when the law orders, and man acts, as it were, by his own strength, but when the Spirit assists, and the will (not the free will of man, but the will freed by God) obeys. He briefly states the ground of all these observations, when he says, that man at his creation received a great degree of free will, but lost it by sinning. In another place, after showing that free will is established by grace, he strongly inveighs against those who arrogate anything to themselves without grace. His words are, " How much soever miserable men presume to plume themselves on free will before they are made free,

[1] August. Lib. i. cont. Julian. For the subsequent quotations, see Homil. 53, in Joannem; Ad Anast. Epist. 144; De Perf. Just; Eucher. ad Laur. c. 30; Idem ad Bonifac. Lib. iii. c. 8; Ibid. c. 7; Idem ad Bonifac. Lib. i. c. 3; Ibid. Lib. iii. cap. 7; Idem, Lib. de Verbis Apost. Serm. 3; Lib. de Spiritu et Litera. cap. 30.

or on their strength after they are made free, they do not consider that, in the very expression *free will*, liberty is implied. 'Where the Spirit of the Lord is, there is liberty' (2 Cor. iii. 17). If, therefore, they are the servants of sin, why do they boast of free will? He who has been vanquished is the servant of him who vanquished him. But if men have been made free, why do they boast of it as of their own work? Are they so free that they are unwilling to be the servants of Him who has said, 'Without me ye can do nothing'?" (John xv. 5). In another passage he even seems to ridicule the word, when he says,[1] "That the will is indeed free, but not freed— free of righteousness, but enslaved to sin." The same idea he elsewhere repeats and explains, when he says, "That man is not free from righteousness save by the choice of his will, and is not made free from sin save by the grace of the Saviour." Declaring that the freedom of man is nothing else than emancipation or manumission from righteousness, he seems to jest at the emptiness of the name. If any one, then, chooses to make use of this term, without attaching any bad meaning to it, he shall not be troubled by me on that account; but as it cannot be retained without very great danger, I think the abolition of it would be of great advantage to the Church. I am unwilling to use it myself; and others, if they will take my advice, will do well to abstain from it.

9. It may, perhaps, seem that I have greatly prejudiced my own view by confessing that all the ecclesiastical writers, with the exception of Augustine, have spoken so ambiguously or inconsistently on this subject, that no certainty is attainable from their writings. Some will interpret this to mean, that I wish to deprive them of their right of suffrage, because they are opposed to me. Truly, however, I have had no other end in view than to consult, simply and in good faith, for the advantage of pious minds, which, if they trust to those writers for their opinion, will always fluctuate in uncertainty. At one time they teach, that man having been deprived of the power of free will must flee to grace alone; at another, they equip or seem to equip him in armour of his own. It is not difficult, however, to show, that notwithstanding of the ambiguous manner in which those writers express themselves, they hold human virtue in little or no account, and ascribe the whole merit of all that is good to the Holy Spirit. To make this more manifest, I may here quote some passages from them. What, then, is meant by Cyprian in the passage so often lauded by Augustine,[2] "Let us glory in nothing, because nothing is ours," unless it be, that man being utterly destitute, considered in himself, should entirely depend on God? What is meant by Augustine and

---

[1] See August. de Corrept. et Grat. cap. 13. Adv. Lib. Arbit. See also August. Epist. 107. Also the first and last parts of Bernard's Treatise De Gratia et Libero Arbitrio.

[2] August. de Prædest. Sanct. Idem ad Bonifacum, Lib. iv. et alibi. Eucher. Lib. in Genesin. Chrysost. Homil. in Adventu.

Eucherius,[1] when they expound that Christ is the tree of life, and that whoso puts forth his hand to it shall live; that the choice of the will is the tree of the knowledge of good and evil, and that he who, forsaking the grace of God, tastes of it shall die? What is meant by Chrysostom, when he says, "That every man is not only naturally a sinner, but is wholly sin"? If there is nothing good in us; if man, from the crown of the head to the sole of the foot, is wholly sin; if it is not even lawful to try how far the power of the will extends,—how can it be lawful to share the merit of a good work between God and man? I might quote many passages to the same effect from others writers; but lest any caviller should say, that I select those only which serve my purpose, and cunningly pass by those which are against me, I desist. This much however, I dare affirm, that though they sometimes go too far in extolling free will, the main object which they had in view was to teach man entirely to renounce all self-confidence, and place his strength in God alone. I now proceed to a simple exposition of the truth in regard to the nature of man.

10. Here, however, I must again repeat what I premised at the outset of this chapter,[2] that he who is most deeply abased and alarmed, by the consciousness of his disgrace, nakedness, want, and misery, has made the greatest progress in the knowledge of himself. Man is in no danger of taking too much from himself, provided he learns that whatever he wants is to be recovered in God. But he cannot arrogate to himself one particle beyond his due, without losing himself in vain confidence, and, by transferring divine honour to himself, becoming guilty of the greatest impiety. And, assuredly, whenever our minds are seized with a longing to possess a somewhat of our own, which may reside in us rather than in God, we may rest assured that the thought is suggested by no other counsellor than he who enticed our first parents to aspire to be like gods, knowing good and evil.[3] It is sweet, indeed, to have so much virtue of our own as to be able to rest in ourselves; but let the many solemn passages by which our pride is sternly humbled, deter us from indulging this vain confidence: "Cursed be the man that trusteth in man, and maketh flesh his arm" (Jer. xvii. 5). "He delighteth not in the strength of the horse; he taketh not pleasure in the legs of a man. The Lord taketh pleasure in those that fear him, in those that hope in his mercy" (Ps. cxlvii. 10, 11). "He giveth power to the faint; and to them that have no might he increaseth strength. Even the youths shall faint and be weary, and the young men shall utterly fall: But they that wait upon the Lord·shall renew their strength"

---

1 The French adds, "Ancien evesque de Lion;" ancient bishop of Lyons.
2 The French has, "Au commencement de ce traité;" at the commencement of this treatise.
3 The French adds, "Si c'est parole diabolique celle qui exalte homme en soy-mesme, il ne nous lui faut donner lieu, sinon que nous veuillions prendre conseil de nostre ennemi;"—if words which exalt man in himself are devilish, we must not give place to them unless we would take counsel of our enemy.

(Is. xl. 29—31). The scope of all these passages is, that we must not entertain any opinion whatever of our own strength, if we would enjoy the favour of God, who "resisteth the proud, but giveth grace unto the humble" (James iv. 6). Then let us call to mind such promises as these, "I will pour water upon him that is thirsty, and floods upon the dry ground" (Is. xliv. 3); "Ho, every one that thirsteth, come ye to the waters" (Is. lv. 1). These passages declare that none are admitted to enjoy the blessings of God save those who are pining under a sense of their own poverty. Nor ought such passages as the following to be omitted: "The sun shall no more be thy light by day; neither for brightness shall the moon give light unto thee: but the Lord shall be unto thee an everlasting light, and thy God thy glory" (Is. lx. 19). The Lord certainly does not deprive his servants of the light of the sun or moon, but as he would alone appear glorious in them, he dissuades them from confidence even in those objects which they deem most excellent.

11. I have always been exceedingly delighted with the words of Chrysostom, "The foundation of our philosophy is humility;"[1] and still more with those of Augustine, "As the orator,[2] when asked, What is the first precept in eloquence? answered, Delivery: What is the second? Delivery: What the third? Delivery: so, if you ask me in regard to the precepts of the Christian Religion, I will answer, first, second, and third, Humility." By humility, he means not when a man, with a consciousness of some virtue, refrains from pride, but when he truly feels that he has no refuge but in humility. This is clear from another passage,[3] "Let no man," says he, "flatter himself: of himself he is a devil: his happiness he owes entirely to God. What have you of your own but sin? Take your sin which is your own: for righteousness is of God." Again, "Why presume so much on the capability of nature? It is wounded, maimed, vexed, lost. The thing wanted is genuine confession, not false defence." "When any one knows that he is nothing in himself, and has no help from himself, the weapons within himself are broken, and the war is ended." All the weapons of impiety must be bruised, and broken, and burnt in the fire; you must remain unarmed, having no help in yourself. The more infirm you are, the more the Lord will sustain you. So, in expounding the seventieth Psalm, he forbids us to remember our own righteousness, in order that we may recognise the righteousness of God, and shows that God bestows his grace upon us, that we may know that we are nothing; that we stand only by the mercy of God, seeing that in ourselves we are altogether wicked. Let us not contend with God for our right, as if anything attributed to him were

---

1 Chrysost. Homil. de Perf. Evang. August. Epist. 56, ad Discur. As to true humility, see *infra*, chap. vii. sec. 4, and lib. iii. c. 12, sec. 6, 7.

2 The French is, "Demosthene orateur Grec;"—the Greek orator Demosthenes.

3 August. Homil. in Joann. 49, lib. de Natura et Gratia, cap. lii.; and in Psalms xlv. set lxx.

lost to our salvation. As our insignificance is his exaltation, so the confession of our insignificance has its remedy provided in his mercy. I do not ask, however, that man should voluntarily yield without being convinced, or that, if he has any powers, he should shut his eyes to them, that he may thus be subdued to true humility; but that getting quit of the disease of self-love and ambition, φιλαυτία καὶ φιλονεικία, under the blinding influences of which he thinks of himself more highly than he ought to think, he may see himself as he really is, by looking into the faithful mirror of Scripture.

12. I feel pleased with the well-known saying which has been borrowed from the writings of Augustine, that man's natural gifts were corrupted by sin, and his supernatural gifts withdrawn; meaning by supernatural gifts the light of faith and righteousness, which would have been sufficient for the attainment of heavenly life and everlasting felicity. Man, when he withdrew his allegiance to God, was deprived of the spiritual gifts by which he had been raised to the hope of eternal salvation. Hence it follows, that he is now an exile from the kingdom of God, so that all things which pertain to the blessed life of the soul are extinguished in him until he recover them by the grace of regeneration. Among these are faith, love to God, charity towards our neighbour, the study of righteousness and holiness. All these, when restored to us by Christ, are to be regarded as adventitious and above nature. If so, we infer that they were previously abolished. On the other hand, soundness of mind and integrity of heart were, at the same time, withdrawn, and it is this which constitutes the corruption of natural gifts. For although there is still some residue of intelligence and judgment as well as will, we cannot call a mind sound and entire which is both weak and immersed in darkness. As to the will, its depravity is but too well known. Therefore, since reason, by which man discerns between good and evil, and by which he understands and judges, is a natural gift, it could not be entirely destroyed; but being partly weakened and partly corrupted, a shapeless ruin is all that remains. In this sense it is said (John i. 5), that "the light shineth in darkness, and the darkness comprehended it not;" these words clearly expressing both points—viz. that in the perverted and degenerate nature of man there are still some sparks which show that he is a rational animal, and differs from the brutes, inasmuch as he is endued with intelligence, and yet, that this light is so smothered by clouds of darkness, that it cannot shine forth to any good effect. In like manner, the will, because inseparable from the nature of man, did not perish, but was so enslaved by depraved lusts as to be incapable of one righteous desire. The definition now given is complete, but there are several points which require to be explained. Therefore, proceeding agreeably to that primary distinction (Book I. c. xv. sec. 7 and 8), by which we divided the soul into intellect and will, we will now inquire into the power of the intellect.

To charge the intellect with perpetual blindness so as to leave it no intelligence of any description whatever, is repugnant not only to the Word of God, but to common experience. We see that there has been implanted in the human mind a certain desire of investigating truth, to which it never would aspire unless some relish for truth antecedently existed. There is, therefore, now, in the human mind, discernment to this extent, that it is naturally influenced by the love of truth, the neglect of which in the lower animals is a proof of their gross and irrational nature. Still it is true that this love of truth fails before it reaches the goal, forthwith falling away into vanity. As the human mind is unable, from dulness, to pursue the right path of investigation, and, after various wanderings, stumbling every now and then like one groping in darkness, at length gets completely bewildered, so its whole procedure proves how unfit it is to search the truth and find it. Then it labours under another grievous defect, in that it frequently fails to discern what the knowledge is which it should study to acquire. Hence, under the influence of a vain curiosity, it torments itself with superfluous and useless discussions, either not adverting at all to the things necessary to be known, or casting only a cursory and contemptuous glance at them. At all events, it scarcely ever studies them in sober earnest. Profane writers are constantly complaining of this perverse procedure, and yet almost all of them are found pursuing it. Hence Solomon, throughout the Book of Ecclesiastes, after enumerating all the studies in which men think they attain the highest wisdom, pronounces them vain and frivolous.

13. Still, however, man's efforts are not always so utterly fruitless as not to lead to some result, especially when his attention is directed to inferior objects. Nay, even with regard to superior objects, though he is more careless in investigating them, he makes some little progress. Here, however, his ability is more limited, and he is never made more sensible of his weakness than when he attempts to soar above the sphere of the present life. It may therefore be proper, in order to make it more manifest how far our ability extends in regard to these two classes of objects, to draw a distinction between them. The distinction is, that we have one kind of intelligence of earthly things, and another of heavenly things. By earthly things, I mean those which relate not to God and his kingdom, to true righteousness and future blessedness, but have some connection with the present life, and are in a manner confined within its boundaries. By heavenly things, I mean the pure knowledge of God, the method of true righteousness, and the mysteries of the heavenly kingdom. To the former belong matters of policy and economy, all mechanical arts and liberal studies. To the latter (as to which, see the eighteenth and following sections) belong the knowledge of God and of his will, and the means of framing the life in accordance with them. As to the former, the view to be taken is this: Since man is by nature a social animal, he is disposed, from natural instinct, to cherish and preserve society;

and accordingly we see that the minds of all men have impressions of civil order and honesty. Hence it is that every individual understands how human societies must be regulated by laws, and also is able to comprehend the principles of those laws. Hence the universal agreement in regard to such subjects, both among nations and individuals, the seeds of them being implanted in the breasts of all without a teacher or lawgiver. The truth of this fact is not affected by the wars and dissensions which immediately arise, while some, such as thieves and robbers, would invert the rules of justice, loosen the bonds of law, and give free scope to their lust; and while others (a vice of most frequent occurrence) deem that to be unjust which is elsewhere regarded as just, and, on the contrary, hold that to be praiseworthy which is elsewhere forbidden. For such persons do not hate the laws from not knowing that they are good and sacred, but, inflamed with headlong passion, quarrel with what is clearly reasonable, and licentiously hate what their mind and understanding approve. Quarrels of this latter kind do not destroy the primary idea of justice. For while men dispute with each other as to particular enactments, their ideas of equity agree in substance. This, no doubt, proves the weakness of the human mind, which, even when it seems on the right path, halts and hesitates. Still, however, it is true, that some principle of civil order is impressed on all. And this is ample proof that, in regard to the constitution of the present life, no man is devoid of the light of reason.

14. Next come manual and liberal arts, in learning which, as all have some degree of aptitude, the full force of human acuteness is displayed. But though all are not equally able to learn all the arts, we have sufficient evidence of a common capacity in the fact, that there is scarcely an individual who does not display intelligence in some particular art. And this capacity extends not merely to the learning of the art, but to the devising of something new, or the improving of what had been previously learned. This led Plato to adopt the erroneous idea, that such knowledge was nothing but recollection.[1] So cogently does it oblige us to acknowledge that its principle is naturally implanted in the human mind. But while these proofs openly attest the fact of an universal reason and intelligence naturally implanted, this universality is of a kind which should lead every individual for himself to recognise it as a special gift of God. To this gratitude we have a sufficient call from the Creator himself, when, in the case of idiots, he shows what the endowments of the soul would be were it not pervaded with his light. Though natural to all, it is so in such a sense that it ought to be regarded as a gratuitous gift of his beneficence to each. Moreover, the invention, the methodical arrangement, and the more thorough and superior knowledge of the arts, being confined to a few individuals, cannot be

---

1 The French adds, " de ce que l'ame savoit avant qu'etre mis dedans le corps;"— of what the soul knew before it was placed within the body.

regarded as a solid proof of common shrewdness. Still, however, as they are bestowed indiscriminately on the good and the bad, they are justly classed among natural endowments.

15. Therefore, in reading profane authors, the admirable light of truth displayed in them should remind us, that the human mind, however much fallen and perverted from its original integrity, is still adorned and invested with admirable gifts from its Creator. If we reflect that the Spirit of God is the only fountain of truth, we will be careful, as we would avoid offering insult to him, not to reject or contemn truth wherever it appears. In despising the gifts, we insult the Giver. How, then, can we deny that truth must have beamed on those ancient lawgivers who arranged civil order and discipline with so much equity? Shall we say that the philosophers, in their exquisite researches and skilful description of nature, were blind? Shall we deny the possession of intellect to those who drew up rules for discourse, and taught us to speak in accordance with reason? Shall we say that those who, by the cultivation of the medical art, expended their industry in our behalf, were only raving? What shall we say of the mathematical sciences? Shall we deem them to be the dreams of madmen? Nay, we cannot read the writings of the ancients on these subjects without the highest admiration; an admiration which their excellence will not allow us to withhold. But shall we deem anything to be noble and praiseworthy, without tracing it to the hand of God? Far from us be such ingratitude; an ingratitude not chargeable even on heathen poets, who acknowledged that philosophy and laws, and all useful arts, were the inventions of the gods. Therefore, since it is manifest that men 'whom the Scriptures term natural, are so acute and clear-sighted in the investigation of inferior things, their example should teach us how many gifts the Lord has left in possession of human nature, notwithstanding of its having been despoiled of the true good.

16. Moreover, let us not forget that there are most excellent blessings which the Divine Spirit dispenses to whom he will for the common benefit of mankind. For if the skill and knowledge required for the construction of the Tabernacle behoved to be imparted to Bezaleel and Aholiab, by the Spirit of God (Exod. xxxi. 2; xxxv. 30), it is not strange that the knowledge of those things which are of the highest excellence in human life is said to be communicated to us by the Spirit. Nor is there any ground for asking what concourse the Spirit can have with the ungodly, who are altogether alienated from God? For what is said as to the Spirit dwelling in believers only, is to be understood of the Spirit of holiness, by which we are consecrated to God as temples. Notwithstanding of this, He fills, moves, and invigorates all things by the virtue of the Spirit, and that according to the peculiar nature which each class of beings has received by the Law of Creation. But if the Lord has been pleased to assist us by the work and ministry of the ungodly in physics, dialectics, mathe-

matics, and other similar sciences, let us avail ourselves of it, lest, by neglecting the gifts of God spontaneously offered to us, we be justly punished for our sloth.   Lest any one, however, should imagine a man to be very happy merely because, with reference to the elements of this world, he has been endued with great talents for the investigation of truth, we ought to add, that the whole power of intellect thus bestowed is, in the sight of God, fleeting and vain whenever it is not based on a solid foundation of truth.   Augustine (*supra*, sec. 4 and 12), to whom, as we have observed. the Master of Sentences (Lib. ii. Dist. 25) and the Schoolmen are forced to subscribe, says most correctly, that as the gratuitous gifts bestowed on man were withdrawn, so the natural gifts which remained were corrupted after the fall.   Not that they can be polluted in themselves in so far as they proceed from God, but that they have ceased to be pure to polluted man, lest he should by their means obtain any praise.

17. The sum of the whole is this : From a general survey of the human race, it appears that one of the essential properties of our nature is reason, which distinguishes us from the lower animals, just as these by means of sense are distinguished from inanimate objects. For although some individuals are born without reason, that defect does not impair the general kindness of God, but rather serves to remind us, that whatever we retain ought justly to be ascribed to the Divine indulgence.   Had God not so spared us, our revolt would have carried along with it the entire destruction of nature.   In that some excel in acuteness, and some in judgment, while others have greater readiness in learning some peculiar art, God, by this variety, commends his favour toward us, lest any one should presume to arrogate to himself that which flows from his mere liberality.   For whence is it that one is more excellent than another, but that in a common nature the grace of God is specially displayed in passing by many, and thus proclaiming that it is under obligation to none.   We may add, that each individual is brought under particular influences according to his calling.   Many examples of this occur in the Book of Judges, in which the Spirit of the Lord is said to have come upon those whom he called to govern his people (Judges vi. 34).   In short, in every distinguished act there is a special inspiration.   Thus it is said of Saul, that " there went with him a band of men whose hearts the Lord had touched" (1 Sam. x. 26).   And when his inauguration to the kingdom is foretold, Samuel thus addresses him, " The Spirit of the Lord will come upon thee, and thou shalt prophesy with them, and shalt be turned into another man" (1 Sam. x. 6).   This extends to the whole course of government, as it is afterwards said of David, " The Spirit of the Lord came upon David from that day forward " (1 Sam. xvi. 13).   The same thing is elsewhere said with reference to particular movements.   Nay, even in Homer, men are said to excel in genius, not only according as Jupiter has distributed to each, but according as he leads them day by day, οἶον ἐπ᾽ ἧμαρ ἄγῃσι.   And

certainly experience shows when those who were most skilful and
ingenious stand stupified, that the minds of men are entirely under
the control of God, who rules them every moment. Hence it is
said, that "He poureth contempt upon princes, and causeth them to
wander in the wilderness where there is no way" (Ps. cvii. 40). Still,
in this diversity we can trace some remains of the divine image distinguishing the whole human race from other creatures.

18. We must now explain what the power of human reason is, in
regard to the kingdom of God, and spiritual discernment, which consists chiefly of three things—the knowledge of God, the knowledge
of his paternal favour towards us, which constitutes our salvation,
and the method of regulating of our conduct in accordance with the
Divine Law. With regard to the former two, but more properly the
second, men otherwise the most ingenious are blinder than moles. I
deny not, indeed, that in the writings of philosophers we meet occasionally with shrewd and apposite remarks on the nature of God,
though they invariably savour somewhat of giddy imagination. As
observed above, the Lord has bestowed on them some slight perception of his Godhead, that they might not plead ignorance as an excuse for their impiety, and has, at times, instigated them to deliver
some truths, the confession of which should be their own condemnation. Still, though seeing, they saw not. Their discernment was
not such as to direct them to the truth, far less to enable them to
attain it, but resembled that of the bewildered traveller, who sees the
flash of lightning glance far and wide for a moment, and then vanish
into the darkness of the night, before he can advance a single step.
So far is such assistance from enabling him to find the right path.
Besides, how many monstrous falsehoods intermingle with those
minute particles of truth scattered up and down in their writings as
if by chance. In short, not one of them even made the least approach
to that assurance of the divine favour, without which the mind of
man must ever remain a mere chaos of confusion. To the great
truths, What God is in himself, and what he is in relation to us,
human reason makes not the least approach. (See Book III. c. ii.
sec. 14, 15, 16.)

19. But since we are intoxicated with a false opinion of our own
discernment, and can scarcely be persuaded that in divine things it
is altogether stupid and blind, I believe the best course will be to
establish the fact, not by argument, but by Scripture. Most admirable to this effect is the passage which I lately quoted from John,
when he says, "In him was life; and the life was the light of men.
And the light shineth in darkness; and the darkness comprehended
it not" (John i. 4, 5). He intimates that the human soul is indeed
irradiated with a beam of divine light, so that it is never left utterly
devoid of some small flame, or rather spark, though not such as to
enable it to comprehend God. And why so? Because its acuteness
is, in reference to the knowledge of God, mere blindness. When the

Spirit describes men under the term *darkness*, he declares them void of all power of spiritual intelligence. For this reason, it is said that believers, in embracing Christ, are "born, not of blood, nor of the will of the flesh, nor of the will of man, but of God" (John i. 13); in other words, that the flesh has no capacity for such sublime wisdom as to apprehend God, and the things of God, unless illumined by his Spirit. In like manner our Saviour, when he was acknowledged by Peter, declared that it was by special revelation from the Father (Matth. xvi. 17).

20. If we were persuaded of a truth which ought to be beyond dispute—viz. that human nature possesses none of the gifts which the elect receive from their heavenly Father through the Spirit of regeneration, there would be no room here for hesitation. For thus speaks the congregation of the faithful, by the mouth of the prophet: "With thee is the fountain of life: in thy light shall we see light" (Ps. xxxvi. 9). To the same effect is the testimony of the apostle Paul, when he declares that "no man can say that Jesus is the Lord, but by the Holy Ghost" (1 Cor. xii. 3). And John the Baptist, on seeing the dulness of his disciples, exclaims, "A man can receive nothing, unless it be given him from heaven" (John iii. 27). That the gift to which he here refers must be understood not of ordinary natural gifts, but of special illumination, appears from this —that he was complaining how little his disciples had profited by all that he had said to them in commendation of Christ. "I see," says he, "that my words are of no effect in imbuing the minds of men with divine things, unless the Lord enlighten their understandings by His Spirit." Nay, Moses also, while upbraiding the people for their forgetfulness, at the same time observes, that they could not become wise in the mysteries of God without his assistance. "Ye have seen all that the Lord did before your eyes in the land of Egypt, unto Pharaoh, and unto all his servants, and unto all his land; the great temptations which thine eyes have seen, the signs, and these great miracles: yet the Lord hath not given you an heart to perceive, and eyes to see, and ears to hear, unto this day" (Deut. xxix. 2, 4). Would the expression have been stronger had he called us mere blocks in regard to the contemplation of divine things? Hence the Lord, by the mouth of the prophet, promises to the Israelites as a singular favour, "I will give them an heart to know me" (Jer. xxiv. 7); intimating, that in spiritual things the human mind is wise only in so far as He enlightens it. This was also clearly confirmed by our Saviour when he said, "No man can come to me, except the Father which hath sent me draw him" (John vi. 44). Nay, is not he himself the living image of his Father, in which the full brightness of his glory is manifested to us? Therefore, how far our faculty of knowing God extends could not be better shown than when it is declared, that though his image is so plainly exhibited, we have not eyes to perceive it. What? Did not Christ descend into the world

that he might make the will of his Father manifest to men, and did he not faithfully perform the office? True! He did; but nothing is accomplished by his preaching unless the inner teacher, the Spirit, open the way into our minds. Only those, therefore, come to him who have heard and learned of the Father. And in what is the method of this hearing and learning? It is when the Spirit, with a wondrous and special energy, forms the ear to hear and the mind to understand. Lest this should seem new, our Saviour refers to the prophecy of Isaiah, which contains a promise of the renovation of the Church. "For a small moment have I forsaken thee; but with great mercies will I gather thee" (Is. liv. 7). If the Lord here predicts some special blessing to his elect, it is plain that the teaching to which he refers is not that which is common to them with the ungodly and profane.

It thus appears that none can enter the kingdom of God save those whose minds have been renewed by the enlightening of the Holy Spirit. On this subject the clearest exposition is given by Paul, who, when expressly handling it, after condemning the whole wisdom of the world as foolishness and vanity, and thereby declaring man's utter destitution, thus concludes, "The natural man receiveth not the things of the Spirit of God: for they are foolishness unto him: neither can he know them, for they are spiritually discerned" (1 Cor. ii. 14). Whom does he mean by the "natural man"? The man who trusts to the light of nature. Such a man has no understanding in the spiritual mysteries of God. Why so? Is it because through sloth he neglects them? Nay, though he exert himself, it is of no avail; they are "spiritually discerned." And what does this mean? That altogether hidden from human discernment, they are made known only by the revelation of the Spirit; so that they are accounted foolishness wherever the Spirit does not give light. The Apostle had previously declared, that "Eye hath not seen, nor ear heard, neither have entered into the heart of man, the things which God hath prepared for them that love him;" nay, that the wisdom of the world is a kind of veil by which the mind is prevented from beholding God (1 Cor. ii. 9). What would we more? The Apostle declares that God hath "made foolish the wisdom of this world" (1 Cor. i. 20); and shall we attribute to it an acuteness capable of penetrating to God, and the hidden mysteries of his kingdom? Far from us be such presumption!

21. What the Apostle here denies to man, he, in another place, ascribes to God alone, when he prays, "that the God of our Lord Jesus Christ, the Father of glory, may give unto you the spirit of wisdom and revelation" (Eph. i. 17). You now hear that all wisdom and revelation is the gift of God. What follows? "The eyes of your understanding being enlightened." Surely, if they require a new enlightening, they must in themselves be blind. The next words are, "that ye may know what is the hope of his calling" (Eph. i. 18). In other words, the minds of men have not capacity enough to know

their calling. Let no prating Pelagian here allege that God obviates this rudeness or stupidity, when, by the doctrine of his word, he directs us to a path which we could not have found without a guide. David had the law, comprehending in it all the wisdom that could be desired, and yet not contented with this, he prays, "Open thou mine eyes, that I may behold wondrous things out of thy law" (Ps. cxix. 18). By this expression, he certainly intimates, that it is like sunrise to the earth when the word of God shines forth; but that men do not derive much benefit from it until he himself, who is for this reason called the Father of lights (James i. 17), either gives eyes or opens them; because, whatever is not illuminated by his Spirit is wholly darkness. The Apostles had been duly and amply instructed by the best of teachers. Still, as they wanted the Spirit of truth to complete their education in the very doctrine which they had previously heard, they were ordered to wait for him (John xiv. 26). If we confess that what we ask of God is lacking to us, and He by the very thing promised intimates our want, no man can hesitate to acknowledge that he is able to understand the mysteries of God, only in so far as illuminated by his grace. He who ascribes to himself more understanding than this, is the blinder for not acknowledging his blindness.

22. It remains to consider the third branch of the knowledge of spiritual things—viz. the method of properly regulating the conduct. This is correctly termed the knowledge of the works of righteousness, a branch in which the human mind seems to have somewhat more discernment than in the former two, since an Apostle declares, "When the Gentiles, which have not the law, do by nature the things contained in the law, these, having not the law, are a law unto themselves: which show the work of the law written in their hearts, their conscience also bearing witness, and their thoughts the meantime accusing or else excusing one another" (Rom. ii. 14, 15). If the Gentiles have the righteousness of the law naturally engraven on their minds, we certainly cannot say that they are altogether blind as to the rule of life. Nothing, indeed, is more common, than for man to be sufficiently instructed in a right course of conduct by natural law, of which the Apostle here speaks. Let us consider, however, for what end this knowledge of the law was given to men. For from this it will forthwith appear how far it can conduct them in the way of reason and truth. This is even plain from the words of Paul, if we attend to their arrangement. He had said a little before, that those who had sinned in the law will be judged by the law; and those who have sinned without the law will perish without the law. As it might seem unaccountable that the Gentiles should perish without any previous judgment, he immediately subjoins, that conscience served them instead of the law, and was therefore sufficient for their righteous condemnation. The end of the natural law, therefore, is to render man inexcusable, and may be not improperly defined—the

judgment of conscience distinguishing sufficiently between just and unjust, and by convicting men on their own testimony, depriving them of all pretext for ignorance. So indulgent is man toward himself, that, while doing evil, he always endeavours as much as he can to suppress the idea of sin. It was this, apparently, which induced Plato (in his Protagoras) to suppose that sins were committed only through ignorance. There might be some ground for this, if hypocrisy were so successful in hiding vice as to keep the conscience clear in the sight of God. But since the sinner, when trying to evade the judgment of good and evil implanted in him, is ever and anon dragged forward, and not permitted to wink so effectually as not to be compelled at times, whether he will or not, to open his eyes, it is false to say that he sins only through ignorance.

23. Themistius is more accurate in teaching (Paraphr. in Lib. iii. de Anima, cap. xlvi.), that the intellect is very seldom mistaken in the general definition or essence of the matter; but that deception begins as it advances farther—namely, when it descends to particulars. That homicide, putting the case in the abstract, is an evil, no man will deny; and yet one who is conspiring the death of his enemy deliberates on it as if the thing was good. The adulterer will condemn adultery in the abstract, and yet flatter himself while privately committing it. The ignorance lies here; that man, when he comes to the particular, forgets the rule which he had laid down in the general case. Augustine treats most admirably on this subject in his exposition of the first verse of the fifty-seventh Psalm. The doctrine of Themistius, however, does not always hold true: for the turpitude of the crime sometimes presses so on the conscience, that the sinner does not impose upon himself by a false semblance of good, but rushes into sin knowingly and willingly. Hence the expression,—I see the better course, and approve it: I follow the worse (Medea of Ovid.). For this reason, Aristotle seems to me to have made a very shrewd distinction between incontinence and intemperance (Ethic. Lib. vii. cap. iii.). Where incontinence (ἀκρασία) reigns, he says, that through the passion (πάθος) particular knowledge is suppressed: so that the individual sees not in his own misdeed the evil which he sees generally in similar cases; but when the passion is over, repentance immediately succeeds. Intemperance (ἀκολασία), again, is not extinguished or diminished by a sense of sin, but, on the contrary, persists in the evil choice which it has once made.

24. Moreover, when you hear of an universal judgment in man distinguishing between good and evil, you must not suppose that this judgment is, in every respect, sound and entire. For if the hearts of men are imbued with a sense of justice and injustice, in order that they may have no pretext to allege ignorance, it is by no means necessary for this purpose that they should discern the truth in particular cases. It is even more than sufficient if they understand so far as to be unable to practise evasion without being convicted by

their own conscience, and beginning even now to tremble at the judgment-seat of God. Indeed, if we would test our reason by the Divine Law, which is a perfect standard of righteousness, we should find how blind it is in many respects. It certainly attains not to the principal heads in the First Table, such as, trust in God, the ascription to him of all praise in virtue and righteousness, the invocation of his name, and the true observance of his day of rest. Did ever any soul, under the guidance of natural sense, imagine that these and the like constitute the legitimate worship of God? When profane men would worship God, how often soever they may be drawn off from their vain trifling, they constantly relapse into it. They admit, indeed, that sacrifices are not pleasing to God, unless accompanied with sincerity of mind; and by this they testify that they have some conception of spiritual worship, though they immediately pervert it by false devices: for it is impossible to persuade them that everything which the law enjoins on the subject is true. Shall I then extol the discernment of a mind which can neither acquire wisdom by itself, nor listen to advice?[1] As to the precepts of the Second Table, there is considerably more knowledge of them, inasmuch as they are more closely connected with the preservation of civil society. Even here, however, there is something defective. Every man of understanding deems it most absurd to submit to unjust and tyrannical domination, provided it can by any means be thrown off, and there is but one opinion among men, that it is the part of an abject and servile mind to bear it patiently, the part of an honourable and high-spirited mind to rise up against it. Indeed, the revenge of injuries is not regarded by philosophers as a vice. But the Lord condemning this too lofty spirit, prescribes to his people that patience which mankind deem infamous. In regard to the general observance of the law, concupiscence altogether escapes our animadversion. For the natural man cannot bear to recognise diseases in his lusts. The light of nature is stifled sooner than take the first step into this profound abyss. For, when philosophers class immoderate movements of the mind among vices, they mean those which break forth and manifest themselves in grosser forms. Depraved desires, in which the mind can quietly indulge, they regard as nothing (see *infra*, chap. viii. sect. 49).

25. As we have above animadverted on Plato's error, in ascribing all sins to ignorance, so we must repudiate the opinion of those who hold that all sins proceed from preconceived pravity and malice. We know too well from experience how often we fall, even when our intention is good. Our reason is exposed to so many forms of delusion, is liable to so many errors, stumbles on so many obstacles, is entangled by so many snares, that it is ever wandering from the right direc-

---

1 The French adds, " Or l'entendement humain a eté tel en cest endroit. Nous appercevons donques qu'il est du tout stupide ; " now, the understanding has proved so in this matter. We see, therefore, that it is quite stupid.

tion. Of how little value it is in the sight of God, in regard to all the parts of life, Paul shows, when he says, that we are not "sufficient of ourselves to think anything as of ourselves" (2 Cor. iii. 5). He is not speaking of the will or affection; he denies us the power of thinking aright how anything can be duly performed. Is it indeed true that all thought, intelligence, discernment, and industry, are so defective, that, in the sight of the Lord, we cannot think or aim at anything that is right? To us, who can scarcely bear to part with acuteness of intellect (in our estimation a most precious endowment), it seems hard to admit this, whereas it is regarded as most just by the Holy Spirit, who "knoweth the thoughts of man, that they are vanity" (Ps. xciv. 11), and distinctly declares, that "every imagination of the thoughts of his heart was only evil continually" (Gen. vi. 5; viii. 21). If everything which our mind conceives, meditates, plans, and resolves, is always evil, how can it ever think of doing what is pleasing to God, to whom righteousness and holiness alone are acceptable? It is thus plain that our mind, in what direction soever it turns, is miserably exposed to vanity. David was conscious of its weakness when he prayed, "Give me understanding, and I shall keep thy law" (Ps. cxix. 34). By desiring to obtain a new understanding, he intimates that his own was by no means sufficient. This he does not once only, but in one Psalm repeats the same prayer almost ten times, the repetition intimating how strong the necessity which urged him to pray. What he thus asked for himself alone, Paul prays for the churches in general. "For this cause," says he, "we also, since the day we heard it, do not cease to pray for you, and to desire that ye might be filled with the knowledge of his will, in all wisdom and spiritual understanding; that you might walk worthy of the Lord," &c. (Col. i. 9, 10). Whenever he represents this as a blessing from God, we should remember that he at the same time testifies that it is not in the power of man. Accordingly, Augustine, in speaking of this inability of human reason to understand the things of God, says, that he deems the grace of illumination not less necessary to the mind than the light of the sun to the eye (*August. de Peccat. Merit. et Remiss.* lib. ii. cap. v.). And, not content with this, he modifies his expression, adding, that we open our eyes to behold the light, whereas the mental eye remains shut, until it is opened by the Lord. Nor does Scripture say that our minds are illuminated in a single day, so as afterwards to see of themselves. The passage, which I lately quoted from the Apostle Paul, refers to continual progress and increase. David, too, expresses this distinctly in these words: "With my whole heart have I sought thee: O let me not wander from thy commandments" (Ps. cxix. 10). Though he had been regenerated, and so had made no ordinary progress in true piety, he confesses that he stood in need of direction every moment, in order that he might not decline from the knowledge with which he had been endued. Hence, he elsewhere prays for a renewal of a right spirit, which he had lost by his sin [1] (Ps. li. 12). For that which God gave at first, while temporarily withdrawn, it is equally his province to restore.

26. We must now examine the will, on which the question of freedom principally turns, the power of choice belonging to it rather than the intellect, as we have already seen (*supra*, sect. 4). And, at the outset, to guard against its being thought that the doctrine taught by philosophers, and generally received—viz. that all things by natural instinct have a desire of good—is any proof of the rectitude of the human will—let us observe, that the power of free will is not to be considered in any of those desires which proceed more from instinct than mental deliberation. Even the Schoolmen admit (*Thomas*, Part I., *Quæst.* 83, art. 3) that there is no act of free will, unless when reason looks at opposites. By this they mean, that the things desired must be such as may be made the object of choice, and that to pave the way for choice, deliberation must precede. And, undoubtedly, if you attend to what this natural desire of good in man is, you will find that it is common to him with the brutes. They, too, desire what is good; and when any semblance of good capable of moving the sense appears, they follow after it. Here, however, man does not, in accordance with the excellence of his immortal nature, rationally choose, and studiously pursue, what is truly for his good. He does not admit reason to his counsel, nor exert his intellect; but without reason, without counsel, follows the bent of his nature like the lower animals. The question of freedom, therefore, has nothing to do with the fact of man's being led by natural instinct to desire good. The question is, Does man, after determining by right reason what is good, choose what he thus knows, and pursue what he thus chooses? Lest any doubt should be entertained as to this, we must attend to the double misnomer. For this *appetite* is not properly a movement of the will, but natural inclination; and this *good* is not one of virtue or righteousness, but of condition —viz. that the individual may feel comfortable. In fine, how much soever man may desire to obtain what is good, he does not follow it. There is no man who would not be pleased with eternal blessedness; and yet, without the impulse of the Spirit, no man aspires to it. Since, then, the natural desire of happiness in man no more proves the freedom of the will, than the tendency in metals and stones to attain the perfection of their nature, let us consider, in other respects, whether the will is so utterly vitiated and corrupted in every part as to produce nothing but evil, or whether it retains some portion uninjured, and productive of good desires.

27. Those who ascribe our willing effectually, to the primary grace of God (*supra*, sect. 6), seem conversely to insinuate that the soul has in itself a power of aspiring to good, though a power too

---

[1] Calvin, in his Commentary on the passage, says, " Lost in part or appearance, or deserved to lose."

feeble to rise to solid affection or active endeavour. There is no doubt that this opinion, adopted from Origen and certain of the ancient Fathers, has been generally embraced by the Schoolmen, who are wont to apply to man in his natural state (*in puris naturalibus*, as they express it) the following description of the apostle:—" For that which I do I allow not: for what I would, that do I not; but what I hate, that do I." " To will is present with me; but how to perform that which is good I find not" (Rom. vii. 15, 18). But, in this way, the whole scope of Paul's discourse is inverted. He is speaking of the Christian struggle (touched on more briefly in the Epistle to the Galatians) which believers constantly experience from the conflict between the flesh and the spirit. But the spirit is not from nature, but from regeneration. That the apostle is speaking of the regenerate is apparent from this, that after saying, " in me dwells no good thing," he immediately adds the explanation, " in my flesh." Accordingly, he declares, " It is no more I that do it, but sin that dwelleth in me." What is the meaning of the correction, " in me (that is, in my flesh?") It is just as if he had spoken in this way, No good thing dwells in me, of myself, for in my flesh nothing good can be found. Hence follows the species of excuse, It is not I myself that do evil, but sin that dwelleth in me. This applies to none but the regenerate, who, with the leading powers of the soul, tend towards what is good. The whole is made plain by the conclusion, " I delight in the law of God after the inward man: but I see another law in my members, warring against the law of my mind" (Rom. vii. 22, 23). Who has this struggle in himself, save those who, regenerated by the Spirit of God, bear about with them the remains of the flesh? Accordingly, Augustine, who had at one time thought that the discourse related to the natural man (August. ad Bonifac. Lib. i. c. 10), afterwards retracted his exposition as unsound and inconsistent. And, indeed, if we admit that men, without grace, have any motions to good, however feeble, what answer shall we give to the apostle, who declares that " we are incapable of thinking a good thought"? (2 Cor. iii. 5.) What answer shall we give to the Lord, who declares, by Moses, that " every imagination of man's heart is only evil continually"? (Gen. viii. 21.) Since the blunder has thus arisen from an erroneous view of a single passage, it seems unnecessary to dwell upon it. Let us rather give due weight to our Saviour's words, " Whosoever committeth sin is the servant of sin" (John viii. 34). We are all sinners by nature, therefore we are held under the yoke of sin. But if the whole man is subject to the dominion of sin, surely the will, which is its principal seat, must be bound with the closest chains. And, indeed, if divine grace were preceded by any will of ours, Paul could not have said that " it is God which worketh in us both to will and to do" (Philip. ii. 13). Away, then, with all the absurd trifling which many have indulged in with regard to preparation. Although believers sometimes ask to have their heart trained to the obedience of the divine law, as David does in several passages (Ps. li. 12), it is to be observed, that even this longing in prayer is from God. This is apparent from the language used. When he prays, " Create in me a clean heart," he certainly does not attribute the beginning of the creation to himself. Let us therefore rather adopt the sentiment of Augustine, " God will prevent you in all things, but do you sometimes prevent his anger. How? Confess that you have all these things from God, that all the good you have is from him, all the evil from yourself" (August. De Verbis Apost. Serm. 10). Shortly after he says, "Of our own we have nothing but sin."

CHAPTER III.

EVERYTHING PROCEEDING FROM THE CORRUPT NATURE OF MAN DAMNABLE.

The principal matters in this chapter are—I. A recapitulation of the former chapter, proving, from passages of Scripture, that the intellect and will of man are so corrupted, that no integrity, no knowledge or fear of God, can now be found in him, sect. 1 and 2. II. Objections to this doctrine, from the virtues which shone in some of the heathen, refuted, sect. 3 and 4. III. What kind of will remains in man, the slave of sin, sect. 5. The remedy and cure, sect. 6. IV. The opinion of Neo-Pelagian sophists concerning the preparation and efficacy of the will, and also concerning perseverance and co-operating grace, refuted, both by reason and Scripture, sect. 7–12. V. Some passages from Augustine confirming the truth of this doctrine, sect. 13 and 14.

Sections.

1. The intellect and will of the whole man corrupt. The term *flesh* applies not only to the sensual, but also to the higher part of the soul. This demonstrated from Scripture.
2. The heart also involved in corruption, and hence in no part of man can integrity or knowledge, or the fear of God, be found.
3. Objection, that some of the heathen were possessed of admirable endowments, and, therefore, that the nature of man is not entirely corrupt. Answer, Corruption is not entirely removed, but only inwardly restrained. Explanation of this answer.
4. Objection still urged, that the virtuous and vicious among the heathen must be put upon the same level, or the virtuous prove that human nature, properly culti- vated, is not devoid of virtue. Answer, That these are not ordinary properties of human nature, but special gifts of God. These gifts defiled by ambition, and hence the actions proceeding from them, however esteemed by man, have no merit with God.
5. Though man has still the faculty of willing, there is no soundness in it. He falls under the bondage of sin necessarily, and yet voluntarily. Necessity must be distinguished from compulsion. The ancient Theologians acquainted with this necessity. Some passages condemning the vacillation of Lombard.
6. Conversion to God constitutes the remedy or soundness of the human will. This not only begun, but continued and completed ; the beginning, continuance, and completion, being ascribed entirely to God. This proved by Ezekiel's description of the stony heart, and from other passages of Scripture.
7. Various Objections.—1. The will is converted by God, but, when once prepared, does its part in the work of conversion. Answer from Augustine. 2. Grace can do nothing without will, nor the will without grace. Answer, Grace itself pro- duces will. God prevents the unwilling, making him willing, and follows up this preventing grace that he may not will in vain. Another answer gathered from various passages of Augustine.
8. Answer to the second Objection continued. No will inclining to good except in the elect. The cause of election out of man. Hence right will, as well as elec- tion, are from the good pleasure of God. The beginning of willing and doing well is of faith ; faith again is the gift of God ; and hence mere grace is the cause of our beginning to will well. This proved by Scripture.
9. Answer to second Objection continued. That good-will is merely of grace proved by the prayers of saints. Three axioms—1. God does not prepare man's heart,

1. THE nature of man, in both parts of his soul—viz. intellect and will—cannot be better ascertained than by attending to the epithets applied to him in Scripture. If he is fully depicted (and it may easily be proved that he is) by the words of our Saviour, "that which is born of the flesh is flesh" (John iii. 6), he must be a very miserable creature. For, as an apostle declares, "to be carnally minded is death" (Rom. viii. 8), "It is enmity against God, and is not subject to the law of God, neither indeed can be." Is it true that the flesh is so perverse, that it is perpetually striving with all its might against God? that it cannot accord with the righteousness of the divine law? that, in short, it can beget nothing but the materials of death? Grant that there is nothing in human nature but flesh, and then extract something good out of it if you can. But it will be said, that the word *flesh* applies only to the sensual, and not to the higher part of the soul. This, however, is completely refuted by the words both of Christ and his apostle. The statement of our Lord is, that a man must be born again, because he is flesh. He requires not to be born again, with reference to the body. But a mind is not born again merely by having some portion of it reformed. It must be totally renewed. This is confirmed by the antithesis used in both passages. In the contrast between the Spirit and the flesh, there is nothing left of an intermediate nature. In this way, everything in man, which is not spiritual, falls under the denomination of carnal. But we have nothing of the Spirit except through regeneration. Everything, therefore, which we have from nature is flesh. Any possible doubt which might exist on the subject is removed by the words of Paul (Eph. iv. 23), where, after a description of the old man, who, he says, "is corrupt according to the deceitful lusts," he bids us "be renewed in the spirit" of our mind. You see that he places unlawful and depraved desires not in the sensual part merely, but in the mind itself, and therefore requires that it should be renewed. Indeed, he had a little before drawn a picture of human nature, which shows that there is no part in which it is not perverted and corrupted. For when he says that the "Gentiles walk in the vanity of their mind, having the understanding darkened, being alienated from the life of

God through the ignorance that is in them, because of the blindness of their heart" (Eph. iv. 17, 18), there can be no doubt that his words apply to all whom the Lord has not yet formed anew both to wisdom and righteousness. This is rendered more clear by the comparison which immediately follows, and by which he reminds believers that they " have not so learned Christ;"—these words implying, that the grace of Christ is the only remedy for that blindness and its evil consequences. Thus, too, had Isaiah prophesied of the kingdom of Christ, when the Lord promised to the Church, that though darkness should " cover the earth, and gross darkness the people," yet that he should " arise" upon it, and " his glory" should be seen upon it (Isaiah lx. 2). When it is thus declared that divine light is to arise on the Church alone, all without the Church is left in blindness and darkness. I will not enumerate all that occurs throughout Scripture, and particularly in the Psalms and Prophetical writings, as to the vanity of man. There is much in what David says, " Surely men of low degree are vanity, and men of high degree are a lie : to be laid in the balance, they are altogether lighter than vanity " (Ps. lxii. 9). The human mind receives a humbling blow when all the thoughts which proceed from it are derided as foolish, frivolous, perverse, and insane.

2. In no degree more lenient is the condemnation of the heart, when it is described as " deceitful above all things, and desperately wicked" (Jer. xvii. 9). But as I study brevity, I will be satisfied with a single passage, one, however, in which, as in a bright mirror, we may behold a complete image of our nature. The Apostle, when he would humble man's pride, uses these words : " There is none righteous, no, not one : there is none that understandeth, there is none that seeketh after God. They are all gone out of the way, they are together become unprofitable ; there is none that doeth good, no, not one. Their throat is an open sepulchre ; with their tongues they have used deceit ; the poison of asps is under their lips : Whose mouth is full of cursing and bitterness : their feet are swift to shed blood : destruction and misery are in their ways : and the way of peace have they not known : there is no fear of God before their eyes " (Rom. iii. 10—18). Thus he thunders not against certain individuals, but against the whole posterity of Adam—not against the depraved manners of any single age, but the perpetual corruption of nature. His object in the passage is not merely to upbraid men in order that they may repent, but to teach that all are overwhelmed with inevitable calamity, and can be delivered from it only by the mercy of God. As this could not be proved without previously proving the overthrow and destruction of nature, he produced those passages to show that its ruin is complete.

Let it be a fixed point, then, that men are such as is here described, not by vicious custom, but by depravity of nature. The reasoning of the Apostle, that there is no salvation for man, save in the mercy of God, because in himself he is desperate and undone, could not otherwise stand. I will not here labour to prove that the passages apply, with the view of removing the doubts of any who might think them quoted out of place. I will take them as if they had been used by Paul for the first time, and not taken from the Prophets. First, then, he strips man of righteousness, that is, integrity and purity; and, secondly, he strips him of sound intelligence. He argues, that defect of intelligence is proved by apostacy from God. To seek Him is the beginning of wisdom, and, therefore, such defect must exist in all who have revolted from Him. He subjoins, that all have gone astray, and become as it were mere corruption; that there is none that doeth good. He then enumerates the crimes by which those who have once given loose to their wickedness pollute every member of their bodies. Lastly, he declares that they have no fear of God, according to whose rule all our steps should be directed. If these are the hereditary properties of the human race, it is vain to look for anything good in our nature. I confess, indeed, that all these iniquities do not break out in every individual. Still it cannot be denied that the hydra lurks in every breast. For as a body, while it contains and fosters the cause and matter of disease, cannot be called healthy, although pain is not actually felt; so a soul, while teeming with such seeds of vice, cannot be called sound. This similitude, however, does not apply throughout. In a body, however morbid, the functions of life are performed; but the soul, when plunged into that deadly abyss, not only labours under vice, but is altogether devoid of good.

3. Here, again, we are met with a question very much the same as that which was previously solved. In every age there have been some who, under the guidance of nature, were all their lives devoted to virtue. It is of no consequence, that many blots may be detected in their conduct; by the mere study of virtue, they evinced that there was somewhat of purity in their nature. The value which virtues of this kind have in the sight of God will be considered more fully when we treat of the merit of works. Meanwhile, however, it will be proper to consider it in this place also, in so far as necessary for the exposition of the subject in hand. Such examples, then, seem to warn us against supposing that the nature of man is utterly vicious, since, under its guidance, some have not only excelled in illustrious deeds, but conducted themselves most honourably through the whole course of their lives. But we ought to consider that, notwithstanding of the corruption of our nature, there is some room for divine grace, such grace as, without purifying it, may lay it under internal restraint. For, did the Lord let every mind loose to wanton in its lusts, doubtless there is not a man who would not show that his nature is capable of all the crimes with which Paul charges it (Rom. iii. compared with Ps. xiv. 3, &c.). What? Can you exempt yourself from the number of those whose feet are swift to shed blood; whose hands are foul

with rapine and murder ; whose throats are like open sepulchres ; whose tongues are deceitful ; whose lips are venomous ; whose actions are useless, unjust, rotten, deadly ; whose soul is without God ; whose inward parts are full of wickedness ; whose eyes are on the watch for deception ; whose minds are prepared for insult ; whose every part, in short, is framed for endless deeds of wickedness ? If every soul is capable of such abominations (and the Apostle declares this boldly), it is surely easy to see what the result would be, if the Lord were to permit human passion to follow its bent. No ravenous beast would rush so furiously, no stream, however rapid and violent, so impetuously burst its banks. In the elect, God cures these diseases in the mode which will shortly be explained ; in others, he only lays them under such restraint as may prevent them from breaking forth to a degree incompatible with the preservation of the established order of things. Hence, how much soever men may disguise their impurity, some are restrained only by shame, others by a fear of the laws, from breaking out into many kinds of wickedness. Some aspire to an honest life, as deeming it most conducive to their interest, while others are raised above the vulgar lot, that, by the dignity of their station, they may keep inferiors to their duty. Thus God, by his providence, curbs the perverseness of nature, preventing it from breaking forth into action, yet without rendering it inwardly pure.

4. The objection, however, is not yet solved. For we must either put Cataline on the same footing with Camillus, or hold Camillus to be an example that nature, when carefully cultivated, is not wholly void of goodness. I admit that the specious qualities which Camillus possessed were divine gifts, and appear entitled to commendation when viewed in themselves. But in what way will they be proofs of a virtuous nature ? Must we not go back to the mind, and from it begin to reason thus ? If a natural man possesses such integrity of manners, nature is not without the faculty of studying virtue. But what if his mind was depraved and perverted, and followed anything rather than rectitude ? Such it undoubtedly was, if you grant that he was only a natural man. How then will you laud the power of human nature for good, if, even where there is the highest semblance of integrity, a corrupt bias is always detected ? Therefore, as you would not commend a man for virtue whose vices impose upon you by a show of virtue, so you will not attribute a power of choosing rectitude to the human will while rooted in depravity (see August. Lib. iv., Cont. Julian). Still, the surest and easiest answer to the objection is, that those are not common endowments of nature, but special gifts of God, which he distributes in divers forms, and in a definite measure, to men otherwise profane. For which reason, we hesitate not, in common language, to say, that one is of a good, another of a vicious nature ; though we cease not to hold that both are placed under the universal condition of human depravity. All we mean is, that God has conferred on the one a special grace which

he has not seen it meet to confer on the other. When he was pleased to set Saul over the kingdom, he made him as it were a new man. This is the thing meant by Plato, when, alluding to a passage in the Iliad, he says, that the children of kings are distinguished at their birth by some special qualities—God, in kindness to the human race, often giving a spirit of heroism to those whom he destines for empire. In this way, the great leaders celebrated in history were formed. The same judgment must be given in the case of private individuals. But as those endued with the greatest talents were always impelled by the greatest ambition (a stain which defiles all virtues, and makes them lose all favour in the sight of God), so we cannot set any value on anything that seems praiseworthy in ungodly men. We may add, that the principal part of rectitude is wanting, when there is no zeal for the glory of God, and there is no such zeal in those whom he has not regenerated by his Spirit. Nor is it without good cause said in Isaiah, that on Christ should rest "the spirit of knowledge, and of the fear of the Lord" (Isa. xi. 2); for by this we are taught that all who are strangers to Christ are destitute of that fear of God which is the beginning of wisdom (Ps. cxi. 10). The virtues which deceive us by an empty show may have their praise in civil society and the common intercourse of life, but before the judgment-seat of God they will be of no value to establish a claim of righteousness.

5. When the will is enchained as the slave of sin, it cannot make a movement towards goodness, far less steadily pursue it. Every such movement is the first step in that conversion to God, which in Scripture is entirely ascribed to divine grace. Thus Jeremiah prays, "Turn thou me, and I shall be turned" (Jer. xxxi. 18). Hence, too, in the same chapter, describing the spiritual redemption of believers, the Prophet says, "The Lord hath redeemed Jacob, and ransomed him from the hand of him that was stronger than he" (Jer. xxxi. 11); intimating how close the fetters are with which the sinner is bound, so long as he is abandoned by the Lord, and acts under the yoke of the devil. Nevertheless, there remains a will which both inclines and hastens on with the strongest affection towards sin ; man, when placed under this bondage, being deprived not of will, but of soundness of will. Bernard says not improperly, that all of us have a will ; but to will well is proficiency, to will ill is defect. Thus simply to will is the part of man, to will ill the part of corrupt nature, to will well the part of grace. Moreover, when I say that the will, deprived of liberty, is led or dragged by necessity to evil, it is strange that any should deem the expression harsh, seeing there is no absurdity in it, and it is not at variance with pious use. It does, however, offend those who know not how to distinguish between necessity and compulsion. Were any one to ask them, Is not God necessarily good, is not the devil necessarily wicked, what answer would they give? The goodness of God is so connected with his Godhead, that it is

not more necessary to be God than to be good; whereas, the devil, by his fall, was so estranged from goodness, that he can do nothing but evil. Should any one give utterance to the profane jeer (see Calvin Adv. Pighium), that little praise is due to God for a goodness to which he is forced, is it not obvious to every man to reply, It is owing not to violent impulse, but to his boundless goodness, that he cannot do evil? Therefore, if the free will of God in doing good is not impeded, because he necessarily must do good; if the devil, who can do nothing but evil, nevertheless sins voluntarily; can it be said that man sins less voluntarily because he is under a necessity of sinning? This necessity is uniformly proclaimed by Augustine, who, even when pressed by the invidious cavil of Celestius, hesitated not to assert it in the following terms: "Man through liberty became a sinner, but corruption, ensuing as the penalty, has converted liberty into necessity" (August. Lib. de Perf. Justit.). Whenever mention is made of the subject, he hesitates not to speak in this way of the necessary bondage of sin (August. de Natura et Gratia, et alibi). Let this, then, be regarded as the sum of the distinction. Man, since he was corrupted by the fall, sins not forced or unwilling, but voluntarily, by a most forward bias of the mind; not by violent compulsion, or external force, but by the movement of his own passion; and yet such is the depravity of his nature, that he cannot move and act except in the direction of evil. If this is true, the thing not obscurely expressed is, that he is under a necessity of sinning. Bernard, assenting to Augustine, thus writes: "Among animals, man alone is free, and yet sin intervening, he suffers a kind of violence, but a violence proceeding from his will, not from nature, so that it does not even deprive him of innate liberty" (Bernard, Sermo. super Cantica, 81). For that which is voluntary is also free. A little after he adds, "Thus, by some means strange and wicked, the will itself, being deteriorated by sin, makes a necessity; but so that the necessity, inasmuch as it is voluntary, cannot excuse the will, and the will, inasmuch as it is enticed, cannot exclude the necessity." For this necessity is in a manner voluntary. He afterwards says that "we are under a yoke, but no other yoke than that of voluntary servitude; therefore, in respect of servitude, we are miserable, and in respect of will, inexcusable; because the will, when it was free, made itself the slave of sin." At length he concludes, "Thus the soul, in some strange and evil way, is held under this kind of voluntary, yet sadly free necessity, both bond and free; bond in respect of necessity, free in respect of will: and what is still more strange, and still more miserable, it is guilty because free, and enslaved because guilty, and therefore enslaved because free." My readers hence perceive that the doctrine which I deliver is not new, but the doctrine which of old Augustine delivered with the consent of all the godly, and which was afterwards shut up in the cloisters of monks for almost a thousand years. Lombard, by not knowing how to distinguish between necessity and compulsion, gave occasion to a pernicious error.[1]

6. On the other hand, it may be proper to consider what the remedy is which divine grace provides for the correction and cure of natural corruption. Since the Lord, in bringing assistance, supplies us with what is lacking, the nature of that assistance will immediately make manifest its converse—viz. our penury. When the Apostle says to the Philippians, "Being confident of this very thing, that he which hath begun a good work in you, will perform it until the day of Jesus Christ" (Phil. i. 6), there cannot be a doubt that, by the good work thus begun, he means the very commencement of conversion in the will. God, therefore, begins the good work in us by exciting in our hearts a desire, a love, and a study of righteousness, or (to speak more correctly) by turning, training, and guiding our hearts unto righteousness; and he completes this good work by confirming us unto perseverance. But lest any one should cavil that the good work thus begun by the Lord consists in aiding the will, which is in itself weak, the Spirit elsewhere declares what the will, when left to itself, is able to do. His words are, "A new heart also will I give you, and a new spirit will I put within you: and I will take away the stony heart out of your flesh, and I will give you an heart of flesh. And I will put my Spirit within you, and cause you to walk in my statutes, and ye shall keep my judgments, and do them" (Ezek. xxxvi. 26, 27). How can it be said that the weakness of the human will is aided so as to enable it to aspire effectually to the choice of good, when the fact is, that it must be wholly transformed and renovated? If there is any softness in a stone; if you can make it tender, and flexible into any shape, then it may be said, that the human heart may be shaped for rectitude, provided that which is imperfect in it is supplemented by divine grace. But if the Spirit, by the above similitude, meant to show that no good can ever be extracted from our heart until it is made altogether new, let us not attempt to share with Him what He claims for himself alone. If it is like turning a stone into flesh when God turns us to the study of rectitude, everything proper to our own will is abolished, and that which succeeds in its place is wholly of God. I say the will is abolished, but not in so far as it is will, for in conversion everything essential to our original nature remains: I also say, that it is created anew, not because the will then begins to exist, but because it is turned from evil to good. This, I maintain, is wholly the work of God, because, as the Apostle testifies, we are not "sufficient of ourselves to think anything as of ourselves" (2 Cor. iii. 5). Accordingly, he elsewhere says, not merely that God assists the weak or corrects the depraved will, but that he worketh in us to will (Philip. ii. 13). From this it is easily inferred,

---

[1] The French adds, "Qui a esté une peste mortelle à l'Eglise, d'estimer que l'homme pouvoit eviter le peché pource qu'il peche franchement;" which has been a deadly pest to the Church—viz. that man could avoid sin, because he sins frankly.

as I have said, that everything good in the will is entirely the result of grace. In the same sense, the Apostle elsewhere says, "It is the same God which worketh all in all" (1 Cor. xii. 6). For he is not there treating of universal government, but declaring that all the good qualities which believers possess are due to God. In using the term "all," he certainly makes God the author of spiritual life from its beginning to its end. This he had previously taught in different terms, when he said that there is "one Lord Jesus Christ, by whom are all things, and we by him" (1 Cor. viii. 6); thus plainly extolling the new creation, by which everything of our common nature is destroyed. There is here a tacit antithesis between Adam and Christ, which he elsewhere explains more clearly when he says, "We are his workmanship, created in Christ Jesus unto good works, which God hath before ordained that we should walk in them" (Eph. ii. 10). His meaning is to show in this way that our salvation is gratuitous, because the beginning of goodness is from the second creation which is obtained in Christ. If any, even the minutest, ability were in ourselves, there would also be some merit. But to show our utter destitution, he argues, that we merit nothing, because we are created in Christ Jesus unto good works, which God hath prepared; again intimating by these words, that all the fruits of good works are originally and immediately from God. Hence the Psalmist, after saying that the Lord "hath made us," to deprive us of all share in the work, immediately adds, "not we ourselves." That he is speaking of regeneration, which is the commencement of the spiritual life, is obvious from the context, in which the next words are, "we are his people, and the sheep of his pasture" (Psalm c. 3). Not contented with simply giving God the praise of our salvation, he distinctly excludes us from all share in it, just as if he had said that not one particle remains to man as a ground of boasting. The whole is of God.

7. But perhaps there will be some who, while they admit that the will is in its own nature averse to righteousness, and is converted solely by the power of God, will yet hold that, when once it is prepared, it performs a part in acting. This they found upon the words of Augustine, that grace precedes every good work; the will accompanying, not leading; a handmaid, and not a guide (August. ad Bonifac. Ep. 106). The words thus not improperly used by this holy writer, Lombard preposterously wrests to the above effect (Lombard, Lib. ii. Dist. 25). But I maintain that, as well in the words of the Psalmist which I have quoted, as in other passages of Scripture, two things are clearly taught—viz. that the Lord both corrects, or rather destroys, our depraved will, and also substitutes a good will from himself. Inasmuch as it is prevented by grace, I have no objection to your calling it a handmaid; but inasmuch as when formed again, it is the work of the Lord, it is erroneous to say, that it accompanies preventing grace as a voluntary attendant. Therefore, Chrysostom is inaccurate in saying, that grace cannot do anything

without will, nor will anything without grace (Serm. de Invent. Sanct. Crucis); as if grace did not, in terms of the passage lately quoted from Paul, produce the very will itself. The intention of Augustine, in calling the human will the handmaid of grace, was not to assign it a kind of second place to grace in the performance of good works. His object merely was to refute the pestilential dogma of Pelagius, who made human merit the first cause of salvation. As was sufficient for his purpose at the time, he contends that grace is prior to all merit, while, in the mean time, he says nothing of the other question as to the perpetual effect of grace, which, however, he handles admirably in other places. For in saying, as he often does, that the Lord prevents the unwilling in order to make him willing, and follows after the willing that he may not will in vain, he makes Him the sole author of good works. Indeed, his sentiments on this subject are too clear to need any lengthened illustration. "Men," says he, "labour to find in our will something that is our own, and not God's; how they can find it, I wot not" (August. de Remiss. Peccat., Lib. ii. c. 18). In his First Book against Pelagius and Celestius, expounding the saying of Christ, "Every man therefore that hath heard, and hath learned of the Father, cometh unto me" (John vi. 45), he says, "The will is aided not only so as to know what is to be done, but also to do what it knows." And thus, when God teaches not by the letter of the Law, but by the grace of the Spirit, he so teaches, that every one who has learned, not only knowing, sees, but also willing, desires, and acting, performs.

8. Since we are now occupied with the chief point on which the controversy turns, let us give the reader the sum of the matter in a few, and those most unambiguous, passages of Scripture; thereafter, lest any one should charge us with distorting Scripture, let us show that the truth, which we maintain to be derived from Scripture, is not unsupported by the testimony of this holy man (I mean Augustine). I deem it unnecessary to bring forward every separate passage of Scripture in confirmation of my doctrine. A selection of the most choice passages will pave the way for the understanding of all which lie scattered up and down in the sacred volume. On the other hand, I thought it not out of place to show my accordance with a man whose authority is justly of so much weight in the Christian world. It is certainly easy to prove that the commencement of good is only with God, and that none but the elect have a will inclined to good. But the cause of election must be sought out of man; and hence it follows that a right will is derived not from man himself, but from the same good pleasure by which we were chosen before the creation of the world. Another argument much akin to this may be added. The beginning of right will and action being of faith, we must see whence faith itself is. But since Scripture proclaims throughout that it is the free gift of God, it follows, that when

men, who are with their whole soul naturally prone to evil, begin to have a good will, it is owing to mere grace. Therefore, when the Lord, in the conversion of his people, sets down these two things as requisite to be done—viz. to take away the heart of stone, and give a heart of flesh—he openly declares that, in order to our conversion to righteousness, what is ours must be taken away, and that what is substituted in its place is of himself. Nor does he declare this in one passage only. For he says in Jeremiah, "I will give them one heart, and one way, that they may fear me for ever;" and a little after he says, "I will put my fear in their hearts, that they shall not depart from me" (Jer. xxxii. 39, 40). Again, in Ezekiel, "I will give them one heart, and I will put a new spirit within you; and I will take the stony heart out of their flesh, and will give them an heart of flesh" (Ezek. xi. 19). He could not more clearly claim to himself, and deny to us, everything good and right in our will, than by declaring, that in our conversion there is the creation of a new spirit and a new heart. It always follows, both that nothing good can proceed from our will until it be formed again, and that after it is formed again, in so far as it is good, it is of God, and not of us.

9. With this view, likewise, the prayers of the saints correspond. Thus Solomon prays that the Lord may "incline our hearts unto him, to walk in his ways, and keep his commandments" (1 Kings viii. 58); intimating that our heart is perverse, and naturally indulges in rebellion against the Divine law, until it be turned. Again it is said in the Psalms, "Incline my heart unto thy testimonies" (Ps. cxix. 36). For we should always note the antithesis between the rebellious movement of the heart, and the correction by which it is subdued to obedience. David, feeling for the time that he was deprived of directing grace, prays, "Create in me a clean heart, O God; and renew a right spirit within me" (Ps. li. 10). Is not this an acknowledgment that all the parts of the heart are full of impurity, and that the soul has received a twist, which has turned it from straight to crooked? And then, in describing the cleansing, which he earnestly demands as a thing to be created by God, does he not ascribe the work entirely to Him? If it is objected, that the prayer itself is a symptom of a pious and holy affection, it is easy to reply, that although David had already in some measure repented, he was here contrasting the sad fall which he had experienced with his former state. Therefore, speaking in the person of a man alienated from God, he properly prays for the blessings which God bestows upon his elect in regeneration. Accordingly, like one dead, he desires to be created anew, so as to become, instead of a slave of Satan, an instrument of the Holy Spirit. Strange and monstrous are the longings of our pride. There is nothing which the Lord enjoins more strictly than the religious observance of his Sabbath, in other words, resting from our works; but in nothing do we show greater reluctance than to renounce our own works, and give due place to

the works of God. Did not arrogance stand in the way, we could not overlook the clear testimony which Christ has borne to the efficacy of his grace. " I," said he, " am the true vine, and my Father is the husbandman." " As the branch cannot bear fruit of itself, except it abide in the vine; no more can ye, except ye abide in me " (John xv. 1, 4). If we can no more bear fruit of ourselves than a vine can bud when rooted up and deprived of moisture, there is no longer any room to ask what the aptitude of our nature is for good. There is no ambiguity in the conclusion, " For without me ye can do nothing." He says not that we are too weak to suffice for ourselves; but, by reducing us to nothing, he excludes the idea of our possessing any, even the least ability. If, when engrafted into Christ, we bear fruit like the vine, which draws its vegetative power from the moisture of the ground, and the dew of heaven, and the fostering warmth of the sun, I see nothing in a good work, which we can call our own, without trenching upon what is due to God. It is vain to have recourse to the frivolous cavil, that the sap and the power of producing are already contained in the vine, and that, therefore, instead of deriving everything from the earth or the original root, it contributes something of its own. Our Saviour's words simply mean, that when separated from him, we are nothing but dry, useless wood, because, when so separated, we have no power to do good, as he elsewhere says, " Every plant which my heavenly Father hath not planted, shall be rooted up " (Matth. xv. 13). Accordingly, in the passage already quoted from the Apostle Paul, he attributes the whole operation to God, " It is God which worketh in you both to will and to do of his good pleasure " (Philip. ii. 13). The first part of a good work is the will, the second is vigorous effort in the doing of it.[1] God is the author of both. It is, therefore, robbery from God to arrogate anything to ourselves, either in the will or the act. Were it said that God gives assistance to a weak will, something might be left us; but when it is said that he makes the will, everything good in it is placed without us. Moreover, since even a good will is still weighed down by the burden of the flesh, and prevented from rising, it is added that, to meet the difficulties of the contest, God supplies the persevering effort until the effect it obtained. Indeed, the Apostle could not otherwise have said, as he elsewhere does, that " it is the same God which worketh all in all " (1 Cor. xii. 6); words comprehending, as we have already observed (sec. 6), the whole course of the spiritual life. For which reason, David, after praying, " Teach me thy way, O Lord, I will walk in thy truth," adds, " unite my heart to fear thy name " (Ps. lxxxvi. 11); by these words intimating, that even those who are well-affected are liable to so many distractions that they easily become vain and fall away, if

---

1 French, " La premiere partie des bonnes œuvres est la volonté; l'autre est de s'efforcer a l'executer et le pouvoir faire."—The first part of good works is the will; the second is the attempt to execute it, and the power to do so.

not strengthened to persevere. And hence, in another passage, after praying, "Order my steps in thy word," he requests that strength also may be given him to carry on the war, "Let not any iniquity have dominion over me" (Ps. cxix. 133). In this way, the Lord both begins and perfects the good work in us, so that it is due to Him, first, that the will conceives a love of rectitude, is inclined to desire, is moved and stimulated to pursue it; secondly, that this choice, desire, and endeavour fail not, but are carried forward to effect; and, lastly, that we go on without interruption, and persevere even to the end.

10. This movement of the will is not of that description which was for many ages taught and believed—viz. a movement which there-after leaves us the choice to obey or resist it—but one which affects us efficaciously. We must, therefore, repudiate the oft-repeated senti-ment of Chrysostom, "Whom he draws, he draws willingly;" insinuat-ing that the Lord only stretches out his hand, and waits to see whether we will be pleased to take his aid. We grant that, as man was originally constituted, he could incline to either side, but since he has taught us by his example how miserable a thing free will is if God works not in us to will and to do, of what use to us were grace imparted in such scanty measure? Nay, by our own ingratitude, we obscure and impair divine grace. The Apostle's doctrine is not, that the grace of a good will is offered to us if we will accept of it, but that God himself is pleased so to work in us as to guide, turn, and govern our heart by his Spirit, and reign in it as his own possession. Ezekiel promises that a new-spirit will be given to the elect, not merely that they may be able to walk in his precepts, but that they may really walk in them (Ezek. xi. 19; xxxvi. 27). And the only meaning which can be given to our Saviour's words, "Every man, therefore, that hath heard and learned of the Father, cometh unto me" (John vi. 45), is, that the grace of God is effectual in itself. This Augustine maintains in his book De Prædestinatione Sancta. This grace is not bestowed on all promiscuously, according to the common brocard (of Occam, if I mistake not), that it is not denied to any one who does what in him lies. Men are indeed to be taught that the favour of God is offered, without exception, to all who ask it; but since those only begin to ask whom heavenly grace inspires, even this minute portion of praise must not be withheld from him. It is the privilege of the elect to be regenerated by the Spirit of God, and then placed under his guidance and government. Wherefore Augustine justly derides some who arrogate to themselves a certain power of willing, as well as censures others who imagine that that which is a special evidence of gratuitous election is given to all (August. de Verbis Apost. Serm. xxi.). He says, "Nature is com-mon to all, but not grace;" and he calls it a showy acuteness "which shines by mere vanity, when that which God bestows on whom he will is attributed generally to all." Elsewhere he says, "How came

you ? By believing. Fear, lest by arrogating to yourself the merit of finding the right way, you perish from the right way. I came, you say, by free choice, came by my own will. Why do you boast ? Would you know that even this was given you ? Hear Christ exclaiming, 'No man cometh unto me, except the Father which hath sent me draw him.'" And from the words of John (vi. 44), he infers it to be an incontrovertible fact, that the hearts of believers are so effectually governed from above, that they follow with undeviating affection. "Whosoever is born of God doth not commit sin ; for his seed remaineth in him" (1 John iii. 9). That intermediate movement which the sophists imagine, a movement which every one is free to obey or to reject, is obviously excluded by the doctrine of effectual perseverance.[1]

11. As to perseverance, it would undoubtedly have been regarded as the gratuitous gift of God, had not the very pernicious error prevailed, that it is bestowed in proportion to human merit, according to the reception which each individual gives to the first grace. This having given rise to the idea that it was entirely in our own power to receive or reject the offered grace of God, that idea is no sooner exploded than the error founded on it must fall. The error, indeed, is twofold. For, besides teaching that our gratitude for the first grace and our legitimate use of it is rewarded by subsequent supplies of grace, its abettors add that, after this, grace does not operate alone, but only co-operates with ourselves. As to the former, we must hold that the Lord, while he daily enriches his servants, and loads them with new gifts of his grace, because he approves of and takes pleasure in the work which he has begun, finds that in them which he may follow up with larger measures of grace. To this effect are the sentences, " To him that hath shall be given." " Well done, good and faithful servant : thou hast been faithful over a few things, I will make thee ruler over many things" (Matth. xxv. 21, 23, 29 ; Luke xix. 17, 26). But here two precautions are necessary. It must not be said that the legitimate use of the first grace is rewarded by subsequent measures of grace, as if man rendered the grace of God effectual by his own industry, nor must it be thought that there is any such remuneration as to make it cease to be the gratuitous grace of God. 1 admit, then, that believers may expect as a blessing from God, that the better the use they make of previous, the larger the supplies they will receive of future grace ; but I say that even

---

1 The French is, " Nous voyons que ce mouvement sans vertu, lequel imaginent les sophistes, est exclus ; J'entend ce qu'ils disent, que Dieu offre seulement sa grace, a telle condition que chacun la refuse ou accepte selon que bon lui semble. Telle reverie di-je, qui n'est ne chair ne poisson, est exclue, quand il est dit que Dieu nous fait tellement perseverer que nous sommes hors de danger de decliver."—We see that this movement without virtue, which the sophists imagine, is excluded, I mean their dogma, that God only offers his grace on such conditions that each may refuse or accept it as seems to him good. Such a reverie, I say, which is neither fish nor flesh, is excluded, when it is said that God makes us so persevere that we are in no danger of declining.

this use is of the Lord, and that this remuneration is bestowed freely of mere good-will.   The trite distinction of operating and co-operating grace is employed no less sinistrously than unhappily.   Augustine, indeed, used it, but softened it by a suitable definition—viz. that God, by co-operating, perfects what he begins by operating,—that both graces are the same, but obtain different names from the different manner in which they produce their effects.   Whence it follows, that he does not make an apportionment between God and man, as if a proper movement on the part of each produced a mutual concurrence.   All he does is to mark a multiplication of grace.   To this effect, accordingly, he elsewhere says, that in man good will precedes many gifts from God ; but among these gifts is this good will itself. (*August. Enchiridion ad Laurent.* cap. 32).   Whence it follows, that nothing is left for the will to arrogate as its own.   This Paul has expressly stated.   For, after saying, " It is God which worketh in you both to will and to do," he immediately adds, " of his good pleasure " (Phil. ii. 13) ; indicating by this expression, that the blessing is gratuitous.   As to the common saying, that after we have given admission to the first grace, our efforts co-operate with subsequent grace, this is my answer :—If it is meant that after we are once subdued by the power of the Lord to the obedience of righteousness, we proceed voluntarily, and are inclined to follow the movement of grace, I have nothing to object.   For it is most certain, that where the grace of God reigns, there is also this readiness to obey.   And whence this readiness, but just that the Spirit of God being everywhere consistent with himself, after first begetting a principle of obedience, cherishes and strengthens it for perseverance ?   If, again, it is meant that man is able of himself to be a fellow-labourer with the grace of God, I hold it to be a most pestilential delusion.

12. In support of this view, some make an ignorant and false application of the Apostle's words : " I laboured more abundantly than they all : yet not I, but the grace of God which was with me" (1 Cor. xv. 10).   The meaning they give them is, that as Paul might have seemed to speak somewhat presumptuously in preferring himself to all the other apostles, he corrects the expression so far by referring the praise to the grace of God, but he, at the same time, calls himself a co-operator with grace.   It is strange that this should have proved a stumbling-block to so many writers, otherwise respectable.   The Apostle says not that the grace of God laboured with him so as to make him a copartner in the labour.   He rather transfers the whole merit of the labour to grace alone, by thus modifying his first expression, " It was not I," says he, " that laboured, but the grace of God that was present with me."   Those who have adopted the erroneous interpretation have been misled by an ambiguity in the expression, or rather by a preposterous translation, in which the force of the Greek article is overlooked.   For to take the words literally, the Apostle does not say that grace was a fellow-worker with him, but

that the grace which was with him was sole worker. And this is taught not obscurely, though briefly, by Augustine when he says, "Good will in man precedes many gifts from God, but not all gifts, seeing that the will which precedes is itself among the number." He adds the reason "for it is written, 'The God of my mercy shall prevent me' (Ps. lix. 10), and 'Surely goodness and mercy shall follow me' (Ps. xxiii. 6) ; it prevents him that is unwilling, and makes him willing ; it follows him that is willing, that he may not will in vain." To this Bernard assents, introducing the Church as praying thus, "Draw me, who am in some measure unwilling, and make me willing ; draw me, who am sluggishly lagging, and make me run" (Serm. II. in Cantic.)

13. Let us now hear Augustine in his own words, lest the Pelagians of our age, I mean the sophists of the Sorbonne, charge us after their wont with being opposed to all antiquity. In this, indeed, they imitate their father Pelagius, by whom of old a similar charge was brought against Augustine. In the second chapter of his Treatise De Correptione et Gratia, addressed to Valentinus, Augustine explains at length what I will state briefly, but in his own words, that to Adam was given the grace of persevering in goodness if he had the will ; to us it is given to will, and by will overcome concupiscence : that Adam, therefore, had the power if he had the will, but did not will to have the power, whereas to us is given both the will and the power ; that the original freedom of man was to be able not to sin, but that we have a much greater freedom—viz. not to be able to sin. And lest it should be supposed, as Lombard erroneously does (Lib. ii. Dist. 25), that he is speaking of the perfection of the future state, he shortly after removes all doubt when he says, "For so much is the will of the saints inflamed by the Holy Spirit that they are able, because they are willing ; and willing, because God worketh in them so to will." For if, in such weakness (in which, however, to suppress pride, "strength" must be made "perfect"), their own will is left to them, in such sense that, by the help of God, they are able, if they will, while at the same time God does not work in them so as to make them will ; among so many temptations and infirmities the will itself would give way, and, consequently, they would not be able to persevere. Therefore, to meet the infirmity of the human will, and prevent it from failing, how weak soever it might be, divine grace was made to act on it inseparably and uninterruptedly. Augustine (ibid. cap. xiv.) next entering fully into the question, how our hearts follow the movement when God affects them, necessarily says, indeed, that the Lord draws men by their own wills ; wills, however, which he himself has produced. We have now an attestation by Augustine to the truth which we are specially desirous to maintain—viz. that the grace offered by the Lord is not merely one which every individual has full liberty of choosing to receive or reject, but a grace which produces in the heart both choice and will :

so that all the good works which follow after are its fruit and effect; the only will which yields obedience being the will which grace itself has made. In another place Augustine uses these words, "Every good work in us is performed only by grace" (August. Ep. 105).

14. In saying elsewhere that the will is not taken away by grace, but out of bad is changed into good, and after it is good is assisted, —he only means, that man is not drawn as if by an extraneous impulse[1] without the movement of the heart, but is inwardly affected so as to obey from the heart. Declaring that grace is given specially and gratuitously to the elect, he writes in this way to Boniface: "We know that Divine grace is not given to all men, and that to those to whom it is given, it is not given either according to the merit of works, or according to the merit of the will, but by free grace : in regard to those to whom it is not given, we know that the not giving of it is a just judgment from God" (August. ad Bonifac. Ep. 106). In the same epistle, he argues strongly against the opinion of those who hold that subsequent grace is given to human merit as a reward for not rejecting the first grace. For he presses Pelagius to confess that gratuitous grace is necessary to us for every action, and that merely from the fact of its being truly grace, it cannot be the recompense of works. But the matter cannot be more briefly summed up than in the eighth chapter of his Treatise De Correptione et Gratia, where he shows, *First*, that human will does not by liberty obtain grace, but by grace obtains liberty. *Secondly*, that by means of the same grace, the heart being impressed with a feeling of delight, is trained to persevere, and strengthened with invincible fortitude. *Thirdly*, that while grace governs the will, it never falls; but when grace abandons it, it falls forthwith. *Fourthly*, that by the free mercy of God, the will is turned to good, and when turned, perseveres. *Fifthly*, that the direction of the will to good, and its constancy after being so directed, depend entirely on the will of God, and not on any human merit. Thus the will (free will, if you choose to call it so), which is left to man, is, as he in another place (Ep. 46) describes it, a will which can neither be turned to God, nor continue in God, unless by grace; a will which, whatever its ability may be, derives all that ability from grace.

---

[1] French, "Comme une pierre;"—like a stone.

CHAPTER IV.

HOW GOD WORKS IN THE HEARTS OF MEN.

The leading points discussed in this chapter are—I. Whether in bad actions any-thing is to be attributed to God; if anything, how much. Also, what is to be attri-buted to the devil and to man, sec. 1—5. II. In indifferent matters, how much is to be attributed to God, and how much is left to man, sec. 6. III. Two objections refuted, sec. 7, 8.

Sections.

1. Connection of this chapter with the preceding. Augustine's similitude of a good and bad rider. Question answered in respect to the devil.
2. Question answered in respect to God and man. Example from the history of Job. The works of God distinguished from the works of Satan and wicked men. 1. By the design or end of acting. How Satan acts in the reprobate. 2. How God acts in them.
3. Old Objection, that the agency of God in such cases is referable to prescience or permission, not actual operation. Answer, showing that God blinds and hardens the reprobate, and this in two ways: 1. By deserting them; 2. By delivering them over to Satan.
4. Striking passages of Scripture, proving that God acts in both ways, and disposing of the objection with regard to prescience. Confirmation from Augustine.
5. A modification of the former answer, proving that God employs Satan to instigate the reprobate, but, at the same time, is free from all taint.
6. How God works in the hearts of men in indifferent matters. Our will in such matters not so free as to be exempt from the overruling providence of God. This confirmed by various examples.
7. Objection, that these examples do not form the rule. An answer, fortified by the testimony of universal experience, by Scripture, and a passage of Augustine.
8. Some, in arguing against the error of free will, draw an argument from the event. How this is to be understood.

1. THAT man is so enslaved by the yoke of sin, that he cannot of his own nature aim at good either in wish or actual pursuit, has, I think, been sufficiently proved. Moreover, a distinction has been drawn between compulsion and necessity, making it clear that man, though he sins necessarily, nevertheless sins voluntarily. But since, from his being brought into bondage to the devil, it would seem that he is actuated more by the devil's will than his own, it is necessary, first, to explain what the agency of each is, and then solve the ques-tion,[1] Whether in bad actions anything is to be attributed to God, Scripture intimating that there is some way in which he interferes? Augustine (in Psalm xxxi. and xxxiii.) compares the human will to

[1] The French adds, "dont on doute communement;" on which doubts are commonly entertained.

a horse preparing to start, and God and the devil the riders. "If God mounts, he, like a temperate and skilful rider, guides it calmly, urges it when too slow, reins it in when too fast, curbs its forwardness and over-action, checks its bad temper, and keeps it on the proper course; but if the devil has seized the saddle, like an ignorant and rash rider, he hurries it over broken ground, drives it into ditches, dashes it over precipices, spurs it into obstinacy or fury." With this simile, since a better does not occur, we shall for the present be contented. When it is said, then, that the will of the natural man is subject to the power of the devil, and is actuated by him, the meaning is, not that the will, while reluctant and resisting, is forced to submit (as masters oblige unwilling slaves to execute their orders), but that, fascinated by the impostures of Satan, it necessarily yields to his guidance, and does him homage. Those whom the Lord favours, not with the direction of his Spirit, he, by a righteous judgment, consigns to the agency of Satan. Wherefore, the Apostle says, that "the god of this world hath blinded the minds of them which believe not, lest the light of the glorious gospel of Christ, who is the image of God, should shine into them." And, in another passage, he describes the devil as "the spirit that now worketh in the children of disobedience" (Eph. ii. 2). The blinding of the wicked, and all the iniquities consequent upon it, are called the works of Satan; works, the cause of which is not to be sought in anything external to the will of man, in which the root of the evil lies, and in which the foundation of Satan's kingdom, in other words, sin, is fixed.

2. The nature of the divine agency in such cases is very different. For the purpose of illustration, let us refer to the calamities brought upon holy Job by the Chaldeans. They having slain his shepherds, carry off his flocks. The wickedness of their deed is manifest,[1] as is also the hand of Satan, who, as the history informs us, was the instigator of the whole. Job, however, recognises it as the work of God, saying, that what the Chaldeans had plundered, "the Lord" had "taken away." How can we attribute the same work to God, to Satan, and to man, without either excusing Satan by the interference of God, or making God the author of the crime? This is easily done if we look first to the end, and then to the mode of acting. The Lord designs to exercise the patience of his servant by adversity; Satan's plan is to drive him to despair; while the Chaldeans are bent on making unlawful gain by plunder. Such diversity of purpose makes a wide distinction in the act. In the mode there is not less difference. The Lord permits Satan to afflict his servant; and the Chaldeans, who had been chosen as the ministers to execute the deed, he hands over to the impulses of Satan, who, pricking on the already depraved

---

[1] The French adds, "Car quand nous voyons des voleurs, qui ont commis quelque meurtre ou larrecin, nous ne doutons point de leur imputer la faute, et de les condamner."—For when we see robbers who have committed some murder or robbery, we hesitate not to impute the blame to them, and condemn them.

Chaldeans with his poisoned darts, instigates them to commit the crime. They rush furiously on to the unrighteous deed, and become its guilty perpetrators. Here Satan is properly said to act in the reprobate, over whom he exercises his sway, which is that of wickedness. God also is said to act in his own way; because even Satan, when he is the instrument of divine wrath, is completely under the command of God, who turns him as he will in the execution of his just judgments. I say nothing here of the universal agency of God, which, as it sustains all the creatures, also gives them all their power of acting. I am now speaking only of that special agency which is apparent in every act. We thus see that there is no inconsistency in attributing the same act to God, to Satan, and to man, while, from the difference in the end and mode of action, the spotless righteousness of God shines forth at the same time that the iniquity of Satan and of man is manifested in all its deformity.

3. Ancient writers sometimes manifest a superstitious dread of making a simple confession of the truth in this matter, from a fear of furnishing impiety with a handle for speaking irreverently of the works of God. While I embrace such soberness with all my heart, I cannot see the least danger in simply holding what Scripture delivers. Even Augustine was not always free from this superstition, as when he says, that blinding and hardening have respect not to the operation of God, but to prescience (Lib. de Predestina. et Gratia). But this subtilty is repudiated by many passages of Scripture, which clearly show that the divine interference amounts to something more than prescience. And Augustine himself, in his book against Julian,[1] contends at length that sins are manifestations not merely of divine permission or patience, but also of divine power, that thus former sins may be punished. In like manner, what is said of permission is too weak to stand. God is very often said to blind and harden the reprobate, to turn their hearts, to incline and impel them, as I have elsewhere fully explained (Book I. c. xviii.). The extent of this agency can never be explained by having recourse to prescience or permission. We, therefore, hold that there are two methods in which God may so act. When his light is taken away, nothing remains but blindness and darkness: when his Spirit is taken away, our hearts become hard as stones: when his guidance is withdrawn, we immediately turn from the right path: and hence he is properly said to incline, harden, and blind those whom he deprives of the faculty of seeing, obeying, and rightly executing. The second method, which comes much nearer to the exact meaning of the words, is when executing his judgments by Satan as the minister of his anger, God both directs men's counsels, and excites their wills, and regulates their efforts as he pleases. Thus when Moses relates that Sihon, king of the Amorites, did not give the Israelites a passage, because the Lord

1 The French adds, "se retractant de l'autre sentence;" retracting the other sentiment.

" had hardened his spirit, and made his heart obstinate," he immediately adds the purpose which God had in view—viz. that he might deliver him into their hand (Deut. ii. 30). As God had resolved to destroy him, the hardening of his heart was the divine preparation for his ruin.

4. In accordance with the former method, it seems to be said,[1] " The law shall perish from the priest, and counsel from the ancients." " He poureth contempt upon princes, and causeth them to wander in the wilderness, where there is no way." Again, " O Lord, why hast thou made us to err from thy ways, and hardened our heart from thy fear ?" These passages rather indicate what men become when God deserts them, than what the nature of his agency is when he works in them. But there are other passages which go farther, such as those concerning tha hardening of Pharaoh : " I will harden his heart, that he shall not let the people go." The same thing is afterwards repeated in stronger terms. Did he harden his heart by not softening it? This is, indeed, true ; but he did something more : he gave it in charge to Satan to confirm him in his obstinacy. Hence he had previously said, " I am sure he will not let you go." The people come out of Egypt, and the inhabitants of a hostile region come forth against them. How were they instigated ? Moses certainly declares of Sihon, that it was the Lord who " had hardened his spirit, and made his heart obstinate" (Deut. ii. 30). The Psalmist, relating the same history, says, " He turned their hearts to hate his people" (Psalm cv. 25). You cannot now say that they stumbled merely because they were deprived of divine counsel. For if they are *hardened* and *turned*, they are purposely bent to the very end in view. Moreover, whenever God saw it meet to punish the people for their transgression, in what way did he accomplish his purpose by the reprobate ? In such a way as shows that the efficacy of the action was in him, and that they were only ministers. At one time he declares, " that he will lift an ensign to the nations from far, and will hiss unto them from the end of the earth ;" at another, that he will take a net to ensnare them ; and at another, that he will be like a hammer to strike them. But he specially declared that he was not inactive among them, when he called Sennacherib an axe, which was formed and destined to be wielded by his own hand.[2] Augustine is not far from the mark when he states the matter thus, That men sin, is attributable to themselves : that in sinning they produce this or that result, is owing to the mighty power of God, who divides the darkness as he pleases (August. de Prædest. Sanct.).

5. Moreover, that the ministry of Satan is employed to instigate the reprobate, whenever the Lord, in the course of his providence, has any purpose to accomplish in them, will sufficiently appear from

[1] Ezek. vii. 26 ; Psalm cvii. 40 ; Job xii. 20, 24 ; Isaiah lxiii. 17 ; Exod. iv. 21 ; vii. 3 ; x. 1 ; iii. 19.
[2] Isa. v. 26 ; vii. 18 ; Ezek. xii. 13 ; xvii. 20 ; Jer. 1. 23 ; Isa. x. 15.

a single passage. It is repeatedly said in the First Book of Samuel, that an evil spirit from the Lord came upon Saul, and troubled him (1 Sam. xvi. 14 ; xviii. 10 ; xix. 9). It were impious to apply this to the Holy Spirit. An impure spirit must therefore be called a spirit from the Lord, because completely subservient to his purpose, being more an instrument in acting than a proper agent. We should also add what Paul says, " God shall send them strong delusion, that they should believe a lie: that they all might be damned who believed not the truth (2 Thess. ii. 11, 12). But in the same trans-action there is always a wide difference between what the Lord does, and what Satan and the ungodly design to do. The wicked instru-ments which he has under his hand, and can turn as he pleases, he makes subservient to his own justice. They, as they are wicked, give effect to the iniquity conceived in their wicked minds. Every-thing necessary to vindicate the majesty of God from calumny, and cut off any subterfuge on the part of the ungodly, has already been expounded in the chapters on Providence (Book I. chapter xvi.—xviii.) Here I only meant to show, in a few words, how Satan reigns in the reprobate, and how God works in both.

6. In those actions which in themselves are neither good nor bad, and concern the corporeal rather than the spiritual life, the liberty which man possesses, although we have above touched upon it (*supra*, Chap. ii. sect. 13—17), has not yet been explained. Some have con-ceded a free choice to man in such actions ; more, I suppose, because they were unwilling to debate a matter of no great moment, than because they wished positively to assert what they were prepared to concede. While I admit that those who hold that man has no abi-lity in himself to do righteousness, hold what is most necessary to be known for salvation, I think it ought not to be overlooked that we owe it to the special grace of God, whenever, on the one hand, we choose what is for our advantage, and whenever our will inclines in that direction ; and on the other, whenever with heart and soul we shun what would otherwise do us harm. And the interference of Divine Providence goes to the extent not only of making events turn out as was foreseen to be expedient, but of giving the wills of men the same direction. If we look at the administration of human affairs with the eye of sense, we will have no doubt that, so far, they are placed at man's disposal ; but if we lend an ear to the many pas-sages of Scripture which proclaim that even in these matters the minds of men are ruled by God, they will compel us to place human choice in subordination to his special influence. Who gave the Israelites such favour in the eyes of the Egyptians, that they lent them all their most valuable commodities ? (Exod. xi. 3.) They never would have been so inclined of their own accord. Their in-clinations, therefore, were more overruled by God than regulated by themselves. And surely, had not Jacob been persuaded that God inspires men with divers affections as seemeth

not have said of his son Joseph (whom he thought to be some heathen Egyptian), "God Almighty give you mercy before the man"
(Gen. xliii. 14). In like manner, the whole Church confesses that
when the Lord was pleased to pity his people, he made them also to
be pitied of all them that carried them captives (Ps. cvi. 46). In
like manner, when his anger was kindled against Saul, so that he
prepared himself for battle, the cause is stated to have been, that a
spirit from God fell upon him (1 Sam. xi. 6). Who dissuaded Ab-
solom from adopting the counsel of Ahithophel, which was wont
to be regarded as an oracle? (2 Sam. xvii. 14.) Who disposed
Rehoboam to adopt the counsel of the young men? (1 Kings xii.
10.) Who caused the approach of the Israelites to strike terror into
nations formerly distinguished for valour? Even the harlot Rahab
recognised the hand of the Lord. Who, on the other hand, filled
the hearts of the Israelites with fear and dread (Lev. xxvi. 36), but
He who threatened in the Law that he would give them a "trembling heart"? (Deut. xxviii. 65.)

7. It may be objected, that these are special examples which cannot be regarded as a general rule. They are sufficient, at all events,
to prove the point for which I contend—viz. that whenever God is
pleased to make way for his providence, he even in external matters
so turns and bends the wills of men, that whatever the freedom of
their choice may be, it is still subject to the disposal of God. That
your mind depends more on the agency of God than the freedom of
your own choice, daily experience teaches. Your judgment often
fails, and in matters of no great difficulty, your courage flags; at
other times, in matters of the greatest obscurity, the mode of expli-
cating them at once suggests itself, while in matters of moment and
danger, your mind rises superior to every difficulty.[1] In this way, I
interpret the words of Solomon, "The hearing ear, and the seeing
eye, the Lord hath made even both of them" (Prov. xx. 12). For
they seem to me to refer not to their creation, but to peculiar grace
in the use of them. When he says, "The king's heart is in the hand
of the Lord as the rivers of water; he turneth it whithersoever he
will" (Prov. xxi. 1), he comprehends the whole race under one particular class. If any will is free from subjection, it must be that of
one possessed of regal power, and in a manner exercising dominion
over other wills. But if it is under the hand of God, ours surely
cannot be exempt from it. On this subject there is an admirable
sentiment of Augustine, "Scripture, if it be carefully examined, will
show not only that the good wills of men are made good by God out
of evil, and when so made, are directed to good acts, even to eternal
life, but those which retain the elements of the world are in the
power of God, to turn them whither he pleases, and when he pleases,
either to perform acts of kindness, or by a hidden, indeed, but, at the

[1] The French adds, "D'où procede cela sinon que Dieu besongne tant d'une part
que d'autre?"—Whence this, but that God interferes thus far in either case?

same time, most just judgment, to inflict punishment" (August. De Gratia et Lib. Arb. ad Valent. cap. xx.).

8. Let the reader here remember, that the power of the human will is not to be estimated by the event, as some unskilful persons are absurdly wont to do. They think it an elegant and ingenious proof of the bondage of the human will, that even the greatest monarchs are sometimes thwarted in their wishes. But the ability of which we speak must be considered as within the man, not measured by outward success. In discussing the subject of free will, the question is not, whether external obstacles will permit a man to execute what he has internally resolved, but whether, in any matter whatever, he has a free power of judging and of willing. If men possess both of these, Attilius Regulus, shut up in a barrel studded with sharp nails, will have a will no less free than Augustus Cæsar ruling with imperial sway over a large portion of the globe.[1]

1 The French is simply, "Car si cela pouvoit etre en l'homme, il ne seroit par moins libre enfermé en un prison que dominant par toute la terre." If that could be in man, he would be no less free shut up in a prison than ruling all the earth.

CHAPTER V.

THE ARGUMENTS USUALLY ALLEGED IN SUPPORT OF FREE WILL REFUTED.

Objections reduced to three principal heads :—I. Four absurdities advanced by the opponents of the orthodox doctrine concerning the slavery of the will, stated and refuted, sec. 1—5. II. The passages of Scripture which they pervert in favour of their error, reduced to five heads, and explained, sec. 6—15. III. Five other passages quoted in defence of free will expounded, sec. 16—19.

Sections.

1. Absurd fictions of opponents first refuted, and then certain passages of Scripture explained. Answer by a negative. Confirmation of the answer.
2. Another absurdity of Aristotle and Pelagius. Answer by a distinction. Answer fortified by passages from Augustine, and supported by the authority of an Apostle.
3. Third absurdity borrowed from the words of Chrysostom. Answer by a negative.
4. Fourth absurdity urged of old by the Pelagians. Answer from the works of Augustine. Illustrated by the testimony of our Saviour. Another answer, which explains the use of exhortations.
5. A third answer, which contains a fuller explanation of the second. Objection to the previous answers. Objection refuted. Summary of the previous answers.
6. First class of arguments which the Neo-Pelagians draw from Scripture in defence of free will. 1. The Law demands perfect obedience; and, therefore, God either mocks us, or requires things which are not in our power. Answer by distinguishing precepts into three sorts. The first of these considered in this and the following section.
7. This general argument from the Law of no avail to the patrons of free will. Promises conjoined with precepts, prove that our salvation is to be found in the grace of God. Objection, that the Law was given to the persons living at the time. Answer, confirmed by passages from Augustine.
8. A special consideration of the three classes of precepts of no avail to the defenders of free will. 1. Precepts enjoining us to turn to God. 2. Precepts which simply speak of the observance of the Law. 3. Precepts which enjoin us to persevere in the grace of God.
9. Objection. Answer. Confirmation of the answer from Jeremiah. Another objection refuted.
10. A second class of arguments in defence of free will drawn from the promises of God—viz. that the promises which God makes to those who seek him are vain if it is not in our power to do, or not do, the thing required. Answer, which explains the use of promises, and removes the supposed inconsistency.
11. Third class of arguments drawn from the divine upbraidings—that it is in vain to upbraid us for evils which it is not in our power to avoid. Answer. Sinners are condemned by their own consciences, and, therefore, the divine upbraidings are just. Moreover, there is a twofold use in these upbraidings. Various passages of Scripture explained by means of the foregoing answers.
12. Objection founded on the words of Moses. Refutation by the words of an Apostle. Confirmation by argument.
13. Fourth class of arguments by the defenders of free will. God waits to see whether or not sinners will repent; therefore they can repent. Answer by a dilemma. Passage in Hosea explained.
14. Fifth class of arguments in defence of free will. Good and bad works described as our own, and therefore we are capable of both. Answer by an exposition,

1. ENOUGH would seem to have been said on the subject of man's will, were there not some who endeavour to urge him to his ruin by a false opinion of liberty, and at the same time, in order to support their own opinion, assail ours. First, they gather together some absurd inferences, by which they endeavour to bring odium upon our doctrine, as if it were abhorrent to common sense, and then they oppose it with certain passages of Scripture (*infra*, sec. 6). Both devices we shall dispose of in their order. If sin, say they, is necessary, it ceases to be sin; if it is voluntary, it may be avoided. Such, too, were the weapons with which Pelagius assailed Augustine. But we are unwilling to crush them by the weight of his name, until we have satisfactorily disposed of the objections themselves. I deny, therefore, that sin ought to be the less imputed because it is necessary; and, on the other hand, I deny the inference, that sin may be avoided because it is voluntary. If any one will dispute with God, and endeavour to evade his judgment, by pretending that he could not have done otherwise, the answer already given is sufficient, that it is owing not to creation, but the corruption of nature, that man has become the slave of sin, and can will nothing but evil. For whence that impotence of which the wicked so readily avail themselves as an excuse, but just because Adam voluntarily subjected himself to the tyranny of the devil? Hence, the corruption by which we are held bound as with chains, originated in the first man's revolt from his Maker. If all men are justly held guilty of this revolt, let them not think themselves excused by a necessity in which they see the clearest cause of their condemnation. But this I have fully explained above; and in the case of the devil himself, have given an example of one who sins not less voluntarily that he sins necessarily. I have also shown, in the case of the elect angels, that though their will cannot decline from good, it does not therefore cease to be will. This Bernard shrewdly explains when he says (Serm. 81, in Cantica), that we are the more miserable in this, that the necessity is voluntary; and yet this necessity so binds us who are subject to it, that we are the slaves of sin, as we have already observed. The second step in the reasoning is vicious, because it leaps from *voluntary* to *free;* whereas we have proved above, that a thing may be done voluntarily, though not subject to free choice.

2. They add, that unless virtue and vice proceed from free choice, it is absurd either to punish man or reward him. Although this argument is taken from Aristotle, I admit that it is also used by Chrysostom and Jerome. Jerome, however, does not disguise that it was familiar to the Pelagians. He even quotes their words, " If grace acts in us, grace, and not we who do the work, will be crowned" (*Hieron. in Ep. ad Ctesiphont. et Dialog. 1.*). With regard to punishment, I answer, that it is properly inflicted on those by whom the guilt is contracted. What matters it whether you sin with a free or an enslaved judgment, so long as you sin voluntarily, especially when man is proved to be a sinner because he is under the bondage of sin ? In regard to the rewards of righteousness, is there any great absurdity in acknowledging that they depend on the kindness of God rather than our own merits ? How often do we meet in Augustine with this expression,—" God crowns not our merits but his own gifts; and the name of reward is given not to what is due to our merits, but to the recompense of grace previously bestowed ?" Some seem to think there is acuteness in the remark, that there is no place at all for the mind, if good works do not spring from free will as their proper source ; but in thinking this so very unreasonable they are widely mistaken. Augustine does not hesitate uniformly to describe as necessary the very thing which they count it impious to acknowledge. Thus he asks, " What is human merit ? He who came to bestow not due recompense but free grace, though himself free from sin, and the giver of freedom, found all men sinners" (Augustin. in Psal. xxxi.). Again, " If you are to receive your due, you must be punished. What then is done ? God has not rendered you due punishment, but bestows upon you unmerited grace. If you wish to be an alien from grace, boast your merits" (in Psal. lxx.). Again, " You are nothing in yourself, sin is yours, merit God's. Punishment is your due ; and when the reward shall come, God shall crown his own gifts, not your merits" (Ep. lii.). To the same effect he elsewhere says (De Verb. Apostol. Serm. xv.), that grace is not of merit, but merit of grace. And shortly after he concludes, that God by his gifts anticipates all our merit, that he may thereby manifest his own merit, and give what is absolutely free, because he sees nothing in us that can be a ground of salvation. But why extend the list of quotations, when similar sentiments are ever and anon recurring in his works ? The abettors of this error would see a still better refutation of it, if they would attend to the source from which the apostle derives the glory of the saints,—" Moreover, whom he did predestinate, them he also called ; and whom he called, them he also justified ; and whom he justified, them he also glorified" (Rom. viii. 30). On what ground, then, the apostle being judge (2 Tim. iv. 8), are believers crowned ? Because by the mercy of God, not their own exertions, they are predestinated, called, and justified. Away, then, with the vain fear, that unless free will stand, there will no longer be

any merit! It is most foolish to take alarm, and recoil from that which Scripture inculcates. "If thou didst receive it, why dost thou glory as if thou hadst not received it?" (1 Cor. iv. 7.) You see how everything is denied to free will, for the very purpose of leaving no room for merit. And yet, as the beneficence and liberality of God are manifold and inexhaustible, the grace which he bestows upon us, inasmuch as he makes it our own, he recompenses as if the virtuous acts were our own.

3. But it is added, in terms which seem to be borrowed from Chrysostom (Homil. 22, in Genes.), that if our will possesses not the power of choosing good or evil, all who are partakers of the same nature must be alike good or alike bad. A sentiment akin to this occurs in the work De Vocatione Gentium (Lib. iv. c. 4), usually attributed to Ambrose, in which it is argued, that no one would ever decline from faith, did not the grace of God leave us in a mutable state. It is strange that such men should have so blundered. How did it fail to occur to Chrysostom, that it is divine election which distinguishes among men? We have not the least hesitation to admit what Paul strenuously maintains, that all, without exception, are depraved and given over to wickedness; but at the same time we add, that through the mercy of God all do not continue in wickedness. Therefore, while we all labour naturally under the same disease, those only recover health to whom the Lord is pleased to put forth his healing hand. The others whom, in just judgment, he passes over, pine and rot away till they are consumed. And this is the only reason why some persevere to the end, and others, after beginning their course, fall away. Perseverance is the gift of God, which he does not lavish promiscuously on all, but imparts to whom he pleases. If it is asked how the difference arises—why some steadily persevere, and others prove deficient in steadfastness—we can give no other reason than that the Lord, by his mighty power, strengthens and sustains the former, so that they perish not, while he does not furnish the same assistance to the latter, but leaves them to be monuments of instability.

4. Still it is insisted, that exhortations are vain, warnings superfluous, and rebukes absurd, if the sinner possesses not the power to obey. When similar objections were urged against Augustine, he was obliged to write his book, De Correptione et Gratia, where he has fully disposed of them. The substance of his answer to his opponents is this: "O, man! learn from the precept what you ought to do; learn from correction, that it is your own fault you have not the power; and learn in prayer, whence it is that you may receive the power." Very similar is the argument of his book, De Spiritu et Litera, in which he shows that God does not measure the precepts of his law by human strength, but, after ordering what is right, freely bestows on his elect the power of fulfilling it. The subject, indeed, does not require a long discussion. For we are not

singular in our doctrine, but have Christ and all his apostles with us. Let our opponents, then, consider how they are to come off victorious in a contest which they wage with such antagonists. Christ declares, "without me ye can do nothing" (John xv. 5). Does he the less censure and chastise those who, without him, did wickedly ? Does he the less exhort every man to be intent on good works ? How severely does Paul inveigh against the Corinthians for want of charity (1 Cor. iii. 3) ; and yet, at the same time, he prays that charity may be given them by the Lord. In the Epistle to the Romans, he declares that "it is not of him that willeth, nor of him that runneth, but of God that showeth mercy" (Rom. ix. 16). Still he ceases not to warn, exhort, and rebuke them. Why then do they not expostulate with God for making sport with men, by demanding of them things which he alone can give, and chastising them for faults committed through want of his grace ? Why do they not admonish Paul to spare those who have it not in their power to will or to run, unless the mercy of God, which has forsaken them, precede ? As if the doctrine were not founded on the strongest reason —reason which no serious inquirer can fail to perceive. The extent to which doctrine, and exhortation, and rebuke, are in themselves able to change the mind, is indicated by Paul when he says, " Neither is he that planteth any thing, neither he that watereth ; but God that giveth the increase" (1 Cor. iii. 7). In like manner, we see that Moses delivers the precepts of the Law under a heavy sanction, and that the prophets strongly urge and threaten transgressors, though they at the same time confess, that men are wise only when an understanding heart is given them ; that it is the proper work of God to circumcise the heart, and to change it from stone into flesh ; to write his law on their inward parts ; in short, to renew souls so as give efficacy to doctrine.

5. What purpose, then, is served by exhortations ? It is this: As the wicked, with obstinate heart, despise them, they will be a testimony against them when they stand at the judgment-seat of God ; nay, they even now strike and lash their consciences. For, however they may petulantly deride, they cannot disapprove them. But what, you will ask, can a miserable mortal do, when softness of heart, which is necessary to obedience, is denied him ? I ask, in reply, Why have recourse to evasion, since hardness of heart cannot be imputed to any but the sinner himself ? The ungodly, though they would gladly evade the divine admonitions, are forced, whether they will or not, to feel their power. But their chief use is to be seen in the case of believers, in whom the Lord, while he always acts by his Spirit, also omits not the instrumentality of his word, but employs it, and not without effect. Let this, then, be a standing truth, that the whole strength of the godly consists in the grace of God, according to the words of the prophet, " I will give them one heart, and I will put a new spirit within you : and I will take the stony heart out

of their flesh, and will give them an heart of flesh, that they may walk in my statutes" (Ezek. xi. 19, 20). But it will be asked, why are they now admonished of their duty, and not rather left to the guidance of the Spirit? Why are they urged with exhortations when they cannot hasten any faster than the Spirit impels them? and why are they chastised, if at any time they go astray, seeing that this is caused by the necessary infirmity of the flesh? "O, man! who art thou that repliest against God?" If, in order to prepare us for the grace which enables us to obey exhortation, God sees meet to employ exhortation, what is there in such an arrangement for you to carp and scoff at? Had exhortations and reprimands no other profit with the godly than to convince them of sin, they could not be deemed altogether useless. Now, when, by the Spirit of God acting within, they have the effect of inflaming their desire of good, of arousing them from lethargy, of destroying the pleasure and honeyed sweetness of sin, making it hateful and loathsome, who will presume to cavil at them as superfluous?

Should any one wish a clearer reply, let him take the following:— God works in his elect in two ways: inwardly, by his Spirit ; outwardly, by his Word. By his Spirit illuminating their minds, and training their hearts to the practice of righteousness, he makes them new creatures, while, by his Word, he stimulates them to long and seek for this renovation. In both, he exerts the might of his hand in proportion to the measure in which he dispenses them. The Word, when addressed to the reprobate, though not effectual for their amendment, has another use. It urges their consciences now, and will render them more inexcusable on the day of judgment. Thus, our Saviour, while declaring that none can come to him but those whom the Father draws, and that the elect come after they have heard and learned of the Father (John vi. 44, 45), does not lay aside the office of teacher, but carefully invites those who must be taught inwardly by the Spirit before they can make any profit. The reprobate, again, are admonished by Paul, that the doctrine is not in vain ; because, while it is in them a savour of death unto death, it is still a sweet savour unto God (2 Cor. ii. 16).

6. The enemies of this doctrine are at great pains in collecting passages of Scripture, as if, unable to accomplish anything by their weight, they were to overwhelm us by their number. But as in battle, when it is come to close quarters, an unwarlike multitude, how great soever the pomp and show they make, give way after a few blows, and take to flight,[1] so we shall have little difficulty here in disposing of our opponents and their host. All the passages which they pervert in opposing us are very similar in their import ; and

1 The French is, "Mais c'est comme si un capitaine assembloit force gens qui ne fussent nullement duits à la guerre pour espouvanter son ennemi. Avant que les mettre en œuvre, il feroient grande monstre ; mais s'il faloit venir en bataille et joindre contre son ennemi on les feroit fuir du premier coup." But it is as if a captain were

hence, when they are arranged under their proper heads, one answer will suffice for several ; it is not necessary to give a separate consideration to each. Precepts seem to be regarded as their stronghold. These they think so accommodated to our abilities, as to make it follow as a matter of course, that whatever they enjoin we are able to perform. Accordingly, they run over all the precepts, and by them fix the measure of our power. For, say they, when God enjoins meekness, submission, love, chastity, piety, and holiness, and when he forbids anger, pride, theft, uncleanness, idolatry, and the like, he either mocks us, or only requires things which are in our power.

All the precepts which they thus heap together may be divided into three classes. Some enjoin a first conversion unto God, others speak simply of the observance of the law, and others inculcate perseverance in the grace which has been received. We shall first treat of precepts in general, and then proceed to consider each separate class. That the abilities of man are equal to the precepts of the divine law, has long been a common idea, and has some show of plausibility. It is founded, however, on the grossest ignorance of the law. Those who deem it a kind of sacrilege to say, that the observance of the law is impossible, insist, as their strongest argument, that, if it is so, the law has been given in vain (*infra*, chap. vii. sec. 5). For they speak just as if Paul had never said anything about the Law. But what, pray, is meant by saying, that the Law " was added because of transgressions ;" " by the law is the knowledge of sin ;" " I had not known sin but by the law ;" " the law entered that the offence might abound "? (Gal. iii. 19 ; Rom. iii. 20 ; vii. 7 ; v. 20.) Is it meant that the Law was to be limited to our strength, lest it should be given in vain ? Is it not rather meant that it was placed far above us, in order to convince us of our utter feebleness ? Paul indeed declares, that charity is the end and fulfilling of the Law (1 Tim. i. 5). But when he prays that the minds of the Thessalonians may be filled with it, he clearly enough acknowledges that the Law sounds in our ears without profit, if God do not implant it thoroughly in our hearts (1 Thess. iii. 12).

7. I admit, indeed, that if the Scripture taught nothing else on the subject than that the Law is a rule of life by which we ought to regulate our pursuits, I should at once assent to their opinion ; but since it carefully and clearly explains that the use of the Law is manifold, the proper course is to learn from that explanation what the power of the Law is in man. In regard to the present question, while it explains what our duty is, it teaches that the power of obeying it is derived from the goodness of God, and it accordingly urges us to pray that this power may be given us. If there were merely a

---

to assemble a large body of people, in no wise trained to war, to astonish the enemy. Before coming into action they would make a great show ; but if they were to go into battle, and come to close quarters with the enemy, the first stroke would make them fly.

command and no promise, it would be necessary to try whether our strength were sufficient to fulfil the command; but since promises are annexed, which proclaim not only that aid, but that our whole power is derived from divine grace, they at the same time abundantly testify that we are not only unequal to the observance of the law, but mere fools in regard to it. Therefore, let us hear no more of a proportion between our ability and the divine precepts, as if the Lord had accommodated the standard of justice which he was to give in the law to our feeble capacities. We should rather gather from the promises how ill provided we are, having in everything so much need of grace. But say they, Who will believe that the Lord designed his Law for blocks and stones? There is no wish to make any one believe this. The ungodly are neither blocks nor stones,when taught by the Law that their lusts are offensive to God; they are proved guilty by their own confession; nor are the godly blocks or stones, when, admonished of their powerlessness, they take refuge in grace. To this effect are the pithy sayings of Augustine, "God orders what we cannot do, that we may know what we ought to ask of him. There is a great utility in precepts, if all that is given to free will is to do greater honour to divine grace. Faith acquires what the law requires; nay, the law requires, in order that faith may acquire what is thus required; nay, more, God demands of us faith itself, and finds not what he thus demands, until by giving he makes it possible to find it." Again, he says, "Let God give what he orders, and order what he wills."[1]

8. This will be more clearly seen by again attending to the three classes of precepts to which we above referred. Both in the Law and in the Prophets, God repeatedly calls upon us to turn to him.[2] But, on the other hand, a prophet exclaims, "Turn thou me, and I shall be turned; for thou art the Lord my God. Surely, after that I was turned, I repented." He orders us to circumcise the foreskins of our hearts; but Moses declares, that that circumcision is made by his own hand. In many passages he demands a new heart, but in others he declares that he gives it. As Augustine says, "What God promises, we ourselves do not through choice or nature, but he himself does by grace." The same observation is made, when, in enumerating the rules of Tichonius, he states the third in effect to be—that we distinguish carefully between the Law and the promises, or between the commands and grace (Augustin. de Doctrina Christiana, Lib. iii.). Let them now go and gather from precepts what man's power of obedience is, when they would destroy the divine grace by which the precepts themselves are accomplished. The precepts of the second class are simply those which enjoin us to worship God, to

---

[1] August. Enchir. ad Laurent. de Gratia et Liber. Arbit. cap. 16. Homil. 29, in Joann. Ep. 24.
[2] Joel ii. 12; Jer. xxxi. 18; Deut. x. 16; xxx. 6; Ezek. xxxvi. 26; Jer. xxxi. 18. Vid. Calvin. adv. Pighium.

obey and adhere to his will, to do his pleasure, and follow his teaching. But innumerable passages testify that every degree of purity,
piety, holiness, and justice, which we possess, is his gift. Of the
third class of precepts is the exhortation of Paul and Barnabas to the
proselytes, as recorded by Luke; they "persuaded them to continue
in the grace of God" (Acts xiii. 43). But the source from which
this power of continuance must be sought is elsewhere explained by
Paul, when he says, "Finally, my brethren, be strong in the Lord"
(Eph. vi. 10). In another passage he says, "Grieve not the Holy
Spirit of God, whereby ye are sealed unto the day of redemption"
(Eph. iv. 30). But as the thing here enjoined could not be performed by man, he prays in behalf of the Thessalonians, that God
would count them "worthy of this calling, and fulfil all the good
pleasure of his goodness, and the work of faith with power" (2 Thess.
i. 11). In the same way, in the Second Epistle to the Corinthians,
when treating of alms, he repeatedly commends their good and pious
inclination. A little farther on, however, he exclaims, "Thanks be
to God, which put the same earnest care into the heart of Titus for
you. For indeed he accepted the exhortation" (2 Cor. viii. 16, 17).
If Titus could not even perform the office of being a mouth to exhort
others, except in so far as God suggested, how could the others have
been voluntary agents in acting, if the Lord Jesus had not directed
their hearts?

9. Some, who would be thought more acute, endeavour to evade
all these passages, by the quibble, that there is nothing to hinder us
from contributing our part, while God, at the same time, supplies
our deficiencies. They, moreover, adduce passages from the Prophets, in which the work of our conversion seems to be shared between God and ourselves; "Turn ye unto me, saith the Lord of
hosts, and I will turn unto you, saith the Lord of hosts" (Zech i. 3).
The kind of assistance which God gives us has been shown above
(sect. 7, 8), and need not now be repeated. One thing only I ask
to be conceded to me, that it is vain to think we have a power of fulfilling the Law, merely because we are enjoined to obey it. Since, in
order to our fulfilling the divine precepts, the grace of the Lawgiver
is both necessary, and has been promised to us, this much at least
is clear, that more is demanded of us than we are able to pay. Nor
can any cavil evade the declaration in Jeremiah, that the covenant
which God made with his ancient people was broken, because it was
only of the letter—that to make it effectual, it was necessary for the
Spirit to interpose and train the heart to obedience (Jer. xxxi. 32).
The opinion we now combat is not aided by the words, "Turn unto
me, and I will turn unto you." The turning there spoken of is not
that by which God renews the heart unto repentance; but that in
which, by bestowing prosperity, he manifests his kindness and favour,
just in the same way as he sometimes expresses his displeasure by
sending adversity. The people complaining under the many calami-

ties which befell them, that they were forsaken by God, he answers, that his kindness would not fail them, if they would return to a right course, and to himself, the standard of righteousness. The passage, therefore, is wrested from its proper meaning when it is made to countenance the idea that the work of conversion is divided between God and man (*supra*, Chap. ii. sec. 27). We have only glanced briefly at this subject, as the proper place for it will occur when we come to treat of the Law (Chap. vii. sec. 2 and 3).

10. The second class of objections is akin to the former. They allege the promises in which the Lord makes a paction with our will. Such are the following: "Seek good, and not evil, that ye may live" (Amos v. 14). "If ye be willing and obedient, ye shall eat the good of the land: but if ye refuse and rebel, ye shall be devoured with the sword: for the mouth of the Lord hath spoken it" (Isaiah i. 19, 20). "If thou wilt put away thine abominations out of my sight, then thou shalt not remove" (Jer. iv. 1). "It shall come to pass, if thou shalt hearken diligently unto the voice of the Lord thy God, to observe and do all the commandments which I command thee this day, that the Lord thy God will set thee on high above all nations of the earth" (Deut. xxviii. 1). There are other similar passages (Lev. xxvi. 3, &c.). They think that the blessings contained in these promises are offered to our will absurdly and in mockery, if it is not in our power to secure or reject them. It is, indeed, an easy matter to indulge in declamatory complaint on this subject,—to say that we are cruelly mocked [1] by the Lord when he declares that his kindness depends on our will, if we are not masters of our will,—that it would be a strange liberality on the part of God to set his blessings before us, while we have no power of enjoying them,—a strange certainty of promises, which, to prevent their ever being fulfilled, are made to depend on an impossibility. Of promises of this description, which have a condition annexed to them, we shall elsewhere speak, and make it plain that there is nothing absurd in the impossible fulfilment of them. In regard to the matter in hand, I deny that God cruelly mocks us when he invites us to merit blessings which he knows we are altogether unable to merit. The promises being offered alike to believers and to the ungodly, have their use in regard to both. As God by his precepts stings the consciences of the ungodly, so as to prevent them from enjoying their sins while they have no remembrance of his judgments, so, in his promises, he in a manner takes them to witness how unworthy they are of his kindness. Who can deny that it is most just and most becoming in God to do good to those who worship him, and to punish with due severity those who despise his majesty? God, therefore, proceeds in due order, when, though the wicked are bound

---

1 The French is, "Et de fait cette raison a grande apparence humainement. Car on peut deduire que ce seroit une cruauté de Dieu," &c.—And, in fact, humanly speaking, there is great plausibility in this argument. For, it may be maintained, that it would be cruelty in God, &c.

by the fetters of sin, he lays down the law in his promises, that he will do them good only if they depart from their wickedness. This would be right, though His only object were to let them understand that they are deservedly excluded from the favour due to his true worshippers. On the other hand, as he desires by all means to stir up believers to supplicate his grace, it surely should not seem strange that he attempts to accomplish by promises the same thing which, as we have shown, he to their great benefit accomplishes by means of precepts. Being taught by precepts what the will of God is, we are reminded of our wretchedness in being so completely at variance with that will, and, at the same time, are stimulated to invoke the aid of the Spirit to guide us into the right path. But as our indolence is not sufficiently aroused by precepts, promises are added, that they may attract us by their sweetness, and produce a feeling of love for the precept. The greater our desire of righteousness, the greater will be our earnestness to obtain the grace of God. And thus it is, that in the protestations, *if ye be willing, if thou shalt hearken*, the Lord neither attributes to us a full power of willing and hearkening, nor yet mocks us for our impotence.[1]

11. The third class of objections is not unlike the other two. For they produce passages in which God upbraids his people for their ingratitude, intimating that it was not his fault that they did not obtain all kinds of favour from his indulgence. Of such passages, the following are examples: "The Amalekites and the Canaanites are before you, and ye shall fall by the sword: because ye are turned away from the Lord, therefore the Lord will not be with you" (Num. xiv. 43). "Because ye have done all these works, saith the Lord, and I spake unto you, rising up early and speaking, but ye heard not; and I called you, but ye answered not; therefore will I do unto this house, which is called by my name, wherein ye trust, and unto the place which I gave to you and to your fathers, as I have done to Shiloh" (Jer. vii. 13, 14). "They obeyed not thy voice, neither walked in thy law: they have done nothing of all that thou commandedst them to do; therefore thou hast caused all this evil to come upon them" (Jer. xxxii. 23). How, they ask, can such upbraiding be directed against those who have it in their power immediately to reply,— Prosperity was dear to us: we feared adversity; that we did not, in order to obtain the one and avoid the other, obey the Lord, and listen to his voice, is owing to its not being free for us to do so in consequence of our subjection to the dominion of sin; in vain, therefore, are we upbraided with evils which it was not in our power to escape. But to say nothing of the pretext of necessity, which is but a feeble and flimsy defence of their conduct, can they, I ask, deny their guilt? If they are held convicted of any fault, the Lord is not unjust in upbraiding them for having, by their own perverseness, deprived them-

---

1 The French adds, " Veu qu'en cela il fait le profit de ses serviteurs et rend les iniques plus damnables ;" seeing that by this he promotes the good of his servants, and rend rs the wicked more deserving of condemnation.

selves of the advantages of his kindness. Let them say, then, whether they can deny that their own will is the depraved cause of their rebellion. If they find within themselves a fountain of wickedness, why do they stand declaiming about extraneous causes, with the view of making it appear that they are not the authors of their own destruction? If it be true that it is not for another's faults that sinners are both deprived of the divine favour, and visited with punishment, there is good reason why they should hear these rebukes from the mouth of God. If they obstinately persist in their vices, let them learn in their calamities to accuse and detest their own wickedness, instead of charging God with cruelty and injustice. If they have not manifested docility, let them, under a feeling of disgust at the sins which they see to be the cause of their misery and ruin, return to the right path, and, with serious contrition, confess the very thing of which the Lord by his rebuke reminds them. Of what use those upbraidings of the prophets above quoted are to believers, appears from the solemn prayer of Daniel, as given in his ninth chapter. Of their use in regard to the ungodly, we see an example in the Jews, to whom Jeremiah was ordered to explain the cause of their miseries, though the event could not be otherwise than the Lord had foretold. "Therefore thou shalt speak these words unto them; but they will not hearken unto thee: thou shalt also call unto them; but they will not answer thee" (Jer. vii. 27). Of what use, then, was it to talk to the deaf? It was, that even against their will they might understand that what they heard was true, and that it was impious blasphemy to transfer the blame of their wickedness to God, when it resided in themselves.

These few explanations will make it very easy for the reader to disentangle himself from the immense heap of passages (containing both precepts and reprimands) which the enemies of divine grace are in the habit of piling up, that they may thereon erect their statue of free will. The Psalmist upbraids the Jews as "a stubborn and rebellious generation; a generation that set not their heart aright" (Psalm lxxviii. 8); and in another passage, he exhorts the men of his time, "Harden not your heart" (Psalm xcv. 8). This implies that the whole blame of the rebellion lies in human depravity. But it is foolish thence to infer, that the heart, the preparation of which is from the Lord, may be equally bent in either direction. The Psalmist says, "I have inclined my heart to perform thy statutes alway" (Psalm cxix. 112); meaning, that with willing and cheerful readiness of mind he had devoted himself to God. He does not boast, however, that he was the author of that disposition, for in the same psalm he acknowledges it to be the gift of God. We must, therefore, attend to the admonition of Paul, when he thus addresses believers, "Work out your own salvation with fear and trembling. For it is God which worketh in you both to will and to do of his good pleasure" (Philip. ii. 12, 13). He ascribes to them a part in acting that they may not indulge in carnal sloth, but by enjoining fear and trembling, he humbles them so as to keep them in remembrance, that the very thing which they are ordered to do is the proper work of God— distinctly intimating, that believers act (if I may so speak) *passively*, inasmuch as the power is given them from heaven, and cannot in any way be arrogated to themselves. Accordingly, when Peter exhorts us to "add to faith virtue" (2 Pet. i. 5), he does not concede to us the possession of a second place, as if we could do anything separately. He only arouses the sluggishness of our flesh, by which faith itself is frequently stifled. To the same effect are the words of Paul. He says, "Quench not the Spirit" (1 Thess. v. 19); because a spirit of sloth, if not guarded against, is ever and anon creeping in upon believers. But should any thence infer that it is entirely in their own power to foster the offered light, his ignorance will easily be refuted by the fact, that the very diligence which Paul enjoins is derived only from God (2 Cor. vii. 1). We are often commanded to purge ourselves of all impurity, though the Spirit claims this as his peculiar office. In fine, that what properly belongs to God is transferred to us only by way of concession, is plain from the words of John, "He that is begotten of God keepeth himself" (1 John v. 18). The advocates of free will fasten upon the expression, as if it implied that we are kept partly by the power of God, partly by our own, whereas the very keeping of which the Apostle speaks is itself from heaven. Hence, Christ prays his Father to keep us from evil (John xvii. 15), and we know that believers, in their warfare against Satan, owe their victory to the armour of God. Accordingly, Peter, after saying, "Ye have purified your souls in obeying the truth," immediately adds by way of correction, "through the Spirit" (1 Pet. i. 22). In fine, the nothingness of human strength in the spiritual contest is briefly shown by John, when he says, that "Whosoever is born of God doth not commit sin; for his seed remaineth in him" (1 John iii. 9). He elsewhere gives the reason, "This is the victory that overcometh the world, even our faith" (1 John v. 4).

12. But a passage is produced from the Law of Moses, which seems very adverse to the view now given. After promulgating the Law, he takes the people to witness in these terms: "This commandment which I command thee this day, it is not hidden from thee, neither is it far off. It is not in heaven, that thou shouldest say, Who shall go up for us to heaven, and bring it unto us, that we may hear it, and do it? But the word is very nigh unto thee, in thy mouth, and in thy heart, that thou mayest do it" (Deut. xxx. 11, 12, 14). Certainly, if this is to be understood of mere precepts, I admit that it is of no little importance to the matter in hand. For, though it were easy to evade the difficulty by saying, that the thing here treated of is not the observance of the law, but the facility and readiness of becoming acquainted with it, some scruple, perhaps, would still remain. The Apostle Paul, however, no mean interpreter, removes all doubt when he affirms, that Moses here spoke of the doctrine of the Gospel (Rom.

x. 8). If any one is so refractory as to contend that Paul violently wrested the words in applying them to the Gospel, though his hardihood is chargeable with impiety, we are still able, independently of the authority of the Apostle, to repel the objection. For, if Moses spoke of precepts merely, he was only inflating the people with vain confidence. Had they attempted the observance of the law in their own strength, as a matter in which they should find no difficulty, what else could have been the result than to throw them headlong? Where, then, was that easy means of observing the law, when the only access to it was over a fatal precipice?[1] Accordingly, nothing, is more certain, than that under these words is comprehended the covenant of mercy, which had been promulgated along with the demands of the law. A few verses before, he had said, "The Lord thy God will circumcise thine heart, and the heart of thy seed, to love the Lord thy God with all thine heart, and with all thy soul, that thou mayest live" (Deut. xxx. 6). Therefore, the readiness of which he immediately after speaks was placed not in the power of man, but in the protection and help of the Holy Spirit, who mightily performs his own work in our weakness. The passage, however, is not to be understood of precepts simply, but rather of the Gospel promises, which, so far from proving any power in us to fulfil righteousness, utterly disprove it. This is confirmed by the testimony of Paul, when he observes that the Gospel holds forth salvation to us, not under the harsh, arduous, and impossible terms on which the law treats with us (namely, that those shall obtain it who fulfil all its demands), but on terms easy, expeditious, and readily obtained. This passage, therefore, tends in no degree to establish the freedom of the human will.

13. They are wont also to adduce certain passages in which God is said occasionally to try men, by withdrawing the assistance of his grace, and to wait until they turn to him, as in Hosea, "I will go and return to my place, till they acknowledge their offence, and seek my face" (Hosea v. 15). It were absurd (say they), that the Lord should wait till Israel should seek his face, if their minds were not flexible, so as to turn in either direction of their own accord. As if anything were more common in the prophetical writings than for God to put on the semblance of rejecting and casting off his people until they reform their lives. But what can our opponents extract from such threats? If they mean to maintain that a people, when abandoned by God, are able of themselves to think of turning unto him, they will do it in the very face of Scripture. On the other hand, if they admit that divine grace is necessary to conversion, why do they dispute with us? But while they admit that grace is so far necessary, they insist on reserving some ability for man. How do they

---

1 The French is, "Où est-ce que sera cette facilité, veu que notre natute succombe en cet endroit, et n'y a celui qui ne trebusche voulant marcher?" Where is this facility, seeing that our nature here gives way, and there is not a man who in wishing to walk does not tumble?

prove it ? Certainly not from this nor any similar passage; for it is one thing to withdraw from man, and look to what he will do when thus abandoned and left to himself, and another thing to assist his powers (whatever they may be), in proportion to their weakness. What, then, it will be asked, is meant by such expressions ? I answer, just the same as if God were to say, Since nothing is gained by admonishing, exhorting, rebuking this stubborn people, I will withdraw for a little, and silently leave them to be afflicted; I shall see whether, after long calamity, any remembrance of me will return, and induce them to seek my face. But by the departure of the Lord to a distance is meant the withdrawal of prophecy. By his waiting to see what men will do is meant that he, while silent, and in a manner hiding himself, tries them for a season with various afflictions. Both he does that he may humble us the more; for we shall sooner be broken than corrected by the strokes of adversity, unless his Spirit train us to docility. Moreover, when the Lord, offended, and, as it were, fatigued with our obstinate perverseness, leaves us for a while (by withdrawing his word, in which he is wont in some degree to manifest his presence), and makes trial of what we will do in his absence, from this it is erroneously inferred, that there is some power of free will, the extent of which is to be considered and tried, whereas the only end which he has in view is to bring us to an acknowledgment of our utter nothingness.

14. Another objection is founded on a mode of speaking which is constantly observed both in Scripture and in common discourse. Good works are said to be ours, and we are said to do what is holy and acceptable to God, just as we are said to commit sin. But if sins are justly imputed to us, as proceeding from ourselves, for the same reason (say they) some share must certainly be attributed to us in works of righteousness. It could not be accordant with reason to say, that we do those things which we are incapable of doing of our own motion, God moving us, as if we were stones. These expressions, therefore, it is said, indicate that while, in the matter of grace, we give the first place to God, a secondary place must be assigned to our agency. If the only thing here insisted on were, that good works are termed *ours*, I, in my turn, would reply, that the bread which we ask God to give us is also termed *ours*. What, then, can be inferred from the title of possession, but simply that, by the kindness and free gift of God, that becomes ours which in other respects is by no means due to us ? Therefore, let them either ridicule the same absurdity in the Lord's Prayer, or let them cease to regard it as absurd, that good works should be called ours, though our only property in them is derived from the liberality of God. But there is something stronger in the fact, that we are often said in Scripture to worship God, do justice, obey the law, and follow good works. These being proper offices of the mind and will, how can they be consistently referred to the Spirit, and, at the same time, attributed to us, unless there be some concur-

rence on our part with the divine agency? This difficulty will be easily disposed of if we attend to the manner in which the Holy Spirit acts in the righteous. The similitude with which they invidiously assail us is foreign to the purpose; for who is so absurd as to imagine that movement in man differs in nothing from the impulse given to a stone? Nor can anything of the kind be inferred from our doctrine. To the natural powers of man we ascribe approving and rejecting, willing and not willing, striving and resisting—viz. approving vanity, rejecting solid good, willing evil and not willing good, striving for wickedness and resisting righteousness. What then does the Lord do? If he sees meet to employ depravity of this description as an instrument of his anger, he gives it whatever aim and direction he pleases, that, by a guilty hand, he may accomplish his own good work. A wicked man thus serving the power of God, while he is bent only on following his own lust, can we compare to a stone, which, driven by an external impulse, is borne along without motion, or sense, or will of its own? We see how wide the difference is. But how stands the case with the godly, as to whom chiefly the question is raised? When God erects his kingdom in them, he, by means of his Spirit, curbs their will, that it may not follow its natural bent, and be carried hither and thither by vagrant lusts; bends, frames, trains, and guides it according to the rule of his justice, so as to incline it to righteousness and holiness, and stablishes it and strengthens it by the energy of his Spirit, that it may not stumble or fall. For which reason Augustine thus expresses himself (De Corrept. et Gratia, cap. ii.), "It will be said we are therefore acted upon, and do not act. Nay, you act and are acted upon, and you then act well when you are acted upon by one that is good. The Spirit of God who actuates you is your helper in acting, and bears the name of helper, because you, too, do something." In the former member of this sentence, he reminds us that the agency of man is not destroyed by the motion of the Holy Spirit, because nature furnishes the will which is guided so as to aspire to good. As to the second member of the sentence, in which he says that the very idea of help implies that we also do something, we must not understand it as if he were attributing to us some independent power of action; but not to foster a feeling of sloth, he reconciles the agency of God with our own agency, by saying, that to wish is from nature, to wish well is from grace. Accordingly, he had said a little before, "Did not God assist us, we should not only not be able to conquer, but not able even to fight."

15. Hence it appears that the grace of God (as this name is used when regeneration is spoken of) is the rule of the Spirit, in directing and governing the human will. Govern he cannot, without correcting, reforming, renovating (hence we say that the beginning of regeneration consists in the abolition of what is ours); in like manner, he cannot govern without moving, impelling, urging, and restraining. Accordingly, all the actions which are afterwards done are truly said

to be wholly his. Meanwhile, we deny not the truth of Augustine's doctrine, that the will is not destroyed, but rather repaired, by grace —the two things being perfectly consistent—viz. that the human will may be said to be renewed when, its vitiosity and perverseness being corrected, it is conformed to the true standard of righteousness, and that, at the same time, the will may be said to be made new, being so vitiated and corrupted that its nature must be entirely changed. There is nothing then to prevent us from saying, that our will does what the Spirit does in us, although the will contributes nothing of itself apart from grace. We must, therefore, remember what we quoted from Augustine, that some men labour in vain to find in the human will some good quality properly belonging to it. Any inter-mixture which men attempt to make by conjoining the effort of their own will with divine grace is corruption, just as when unwholesome and muddy water is used to dilute wine. But though everything good in the will is entirely derived from the influence of the Spirit, yet, because we have naturally an innate power of willing, we are not improperly said to do the things of which God claims for himself all the praise: first, because everything which his kindness produces in us is our own (only we must understand that it is not of ourselves); and, secondly, because it is our mind, our will, our study, which are guided by him to what is good.

16. The other passages which they gather together from different quarters will not give much trouble to any person of tolerable under-standing, who pays due attention to the explanations already given. They adduce the passage of Genesis, "Unto thee shall be his desire, and thou shalt rule over him" (Gen. iv. 7). This they interpret of sin, as if the Lord were promising Cain that the dominion of sin should not prevail over his mind, if he would labour in subduing it. We, however, maintain that it is much more agreeable to the con-text to understand the words as referring to Abel, it being there the purpose of God to point out the injustice of the envy which Cain had conceived against his brother. And this He does in two ways, by showing, first, that it was vain to think he could, by means of wicked-ness, surpass his brother in the favour of God, by whom nothing is esteemed but righteousness; and, secondly, how ungrateful he was for the kindness he had already received, in not being able to bear with a brother who had been subjected to his authority. But lest it should be thought that we embrace this interpretation because the other is contrary to our view, let us grant that God does here speak of sin. If so, his words contain either an order or a promise. If an order, we have already demonstrated that this is no proof of man's ability; if a promise, where is the fulfilment of the promise when Cain yielded to the sin over which he ought to have prevailed? They will allege a tacit condition in the promise, as if it were said that he would gain the victory if he contended. This sul 'erfuge is altogether unavailing. For, if the dominion spoken of refers to sin,

no man can have any doubt that the form of expression is imperative, declaring not what we are able, but what it is our duty to do, even if beyond our ability. Although both the nature of the case, and the rule of grammatical construction, require that it be regarded as a comparison between Cain and Abel, we think the only preference given to the younger brother was, that the elder made himself inferior by his own wickedness.

17. They appeal, moreover, to the testimony of the Apostle Paul, because he says, "It is not of him that willeth, nor of him that runneth, but of God that showeth mercy" (Rom. ix. 15). From this they infer, that there is something in will and endeavour, which, though weak in themselves, still, being mercifully aided by God, are not without some measure of success. But if they would attend in sober earnest to the subject there handled by Paul, they would not so rashly pervert his meaning. I am aware they can quote Origen and Jerome[1] in support of this exposition. To these I might, in my turn, oppose Augustine. But it is of no consequence what they thought, if it is clear what Paul meant. He teaches that salvation is prepared for those only on whom the Lord is pleased to bestow his mercy—that ruin and death await all whom he has not chosen. He had proved the condition of the reprobate by the example of Pharaoh, and confirmed the certainty of gratuitous election by the passage in Moses, "I will have mercy on whom I will have mercy." Thereafter he concludes, that it is not of him that willeth, nor of him that runneth, but of God that showeth mercy. If these words are understood to mean that the will or endeavour are not sufficient, because unequal to such a task, the apostle has not used them very appropriately. We must therefore abandon this absurd mode of arguing, " It is not of him that willeth, nor of him that runneth ;"—therefore, there is some will, some running. Paul's meaning is more simple— there is no will nor running by which we can prepare the way for our salvation—it is wholly of the divine mercy. He indeed says nothing more than he says to Titus, when he writes, "After that the kindness and love of God our Saviour toward man appeared, not by works of righteousness which we have done, but according to his mercy he saved us" (Titus iii. 4, 5). Those who argue that Paul insinuated there was some will and some running when he said, " It is not of him that willeth, nor of him that runneth," would not allow me to argue after the same fashion, that we have done some righteous works, because Paul says that we have attained the divine favour, " not by works of righteousness which we have done." But if they see a flaw in this mode of arguing, let them open their eyes, and they will see that their own mode is not free from a similar fallacy. The argument which Augustine uses is well founded, " If it is said, ' It

---

1 Orig. Lib. vii. in Epist. ad Rom.—Hieron. Dial. i in Pelagium.—For the passage in Augustine, see the extract in Book III. chap. xxiv. sec. i.

is not of him that willeth, nor of him that runneth,' because neither will nor running are sufficient ; it may, on the other hand, be retorted, it is not ' of God that showeth mercy,' because mercy does not act alone" (August. Ep. 170, ad Vital. See also Enchirid. ad Laurent. cap. 32). This second proposition being absurd, Augustine justly concludes the meaning of the words to be, that there is no good will in man until it is prepared by the Lord ; not that we ought not to will and run, but that both are produced in us by God. Some, with equal unskilfulness, wrest the saying of Paul, " We are labourers together with God" (1 Cor. iii. 9). There cannot be a doubt that these words apply to ministers only, who are called " labourers with God," not from bringing anything of their own, but because God makes use of their instrumentality after he has rendered them fit, and provided them with the necessary endowments.

18. They appeal also to Ecclesiasticus, who is well known to be a writer of doubtful authority. But, though we might justly decline his testimony, let us see what he says in support of free will. His words are, " He himself made man from the beginning, and left him in the hand of his counsel ; If thou wilt, to keep the commandments, and perform acceptable faithfulness. He hath set fire and water before thee: stretch forth thy hand unto whether thou wilt. Before man is life and death ; and whether him liketh shall be given him" (Ecclesiasticus xv. 14—17). Grant that man received at his creation a power of acquiring life or death ; what, then, if we, on the other hand, can reply that he has lost it ? Assuredly I have no intention to contradict Solomon, who asserts that " God hath made man upright ;" that " they have sought out many inventions" (Eccl. vii. 29). But since man, by degenerating, has made shipwreck of himself and all his blessings, it certainly does not follow, that everything attributed to his nature, as originally constituted, applies to it now when vitiated and degenerate. Therefore, not only to my opponents, but to the author of Ecclesiasticus himself (whoever he may have been), this is my answer: If you mean to tell man that in himself there is a power of acquiring salvation, your authority with us is not so great as, in the least degree, to prejudice the undoubted word of God ; but if only wishing to curb the malignity of the flesh, which, by transferring the blame of its own wickedness to God, is wont to catch at a vain defence, you say that rectitude was given to man, in order to make it apparent he was the cause of his own destruc- tion, I willingly assent. Only agree with me in this, that it is by his own fault he is stript of the ornaments in which the Lord at first attired him, and then let us unite in acknowledging that what he now wants is a physician, and not a defender.

19. There is nothing more frequent in their mouths than the parable of the traveller who fell among thieves, and was left half dead (Luke x. 32). I am aware that it is a common idea with almost all writers, that under the figure of the traveller is represented

the calamity of the human race. Hence our opponents argue that man was not so mutilated by the robbery of sin and the devil as not to preserve some remains of his former endowments; because it is said he was left half dead. For where is the half living, unless some portion of right will and reason remain? First, were I to deny that there is any room for their allegory, what could they say? There can be no doubt that the Fathers invented it contrary to the genuine sense of the parable. Allegories ought to be carried no further than Scripture expressly sanctions: so far are they from forming a sufficient basis to found doctrines upon. And were I so disposed, I might easily find the means of tearing up this fiction by the roots. The Word of God leaves no half life to man, but teaches that, in regard to life and happiness, he has utterly perished. Paul, when he speaks of our redemption, says not that the half dead are cured (Eph. ii. 5, 30; v. 14), but that those who were dead are raised up. He does not call upon the half dead to receive the illumination of Christ, but upon those who are asleep and buried. In the same way our Lord himself says, "The hour is coming, and now is, when the dead shall hear the voice of the Son of God" (John v. 25). How can they presume to set up a flimsy allegory in opposition to so many clear statements? But be it that this allegory is good evidence, what can they extort out of it? Man is half dead; therefore there is some soundness in him. True! he has a mind capable of understanding, though incapable of attaining to heavenly and spiritual wisdom; he has some discernment of what is honourable; he has some sense of the Divinity, though he cannot reach the true knowledge of God. But to what do these amount? They certainly do not refute the doctrine of Augustine—a doctrine confirmed by the common suffrages even of the Schoolmen, that after the fall, the free gifts on which salvation depends were withdrawn, and natural gifts corrupted and defiled (*supra*, chap. ii. sec. 2). Let it stand, therefore, as an indubitable truth, which no engines can shake, that the mind of man is so entirely alienated from the righteousness of God that he cannot conceive, desire, or design anything but what is wicked, distorted, foul, impure, and iniquitous; that his heart is so thoroughly envenomed by sin, that it can breathe out nothing but corruption and rottenness; that if some men occasionally make a show of goodness, their mind is ever interwoven with hypocrisy and deceit, their soul inwardly bound with the fetters of wickedness.

CHAPTER VI.

REDEMPTION FOR MAN LOST TO BE SOUGHT IN CHRIST.

The parts of this chapter are, I. The excellence of the doctrine of Christ the Redeemer —a doctrine always entertained by the Church, sec. 1. II. Christ, the Mediator in both dispensations, was offered to the faith of the pious Israelites and people of old, as is plain from the institution of sacrifice, the calling of Abraham's family, and the elevation of David and his posterity, sec. 2. III. Hence the consolation, strength, hope, and confidence of the godly under the Law, Christ being offered to them in various ways by their heavenly Father.

Sections.

1. The knowledge of God the Creator of no avail without faith in Christ the Redeemer. First reason. Second reason strengthened by the testimony of an Apostle. Conclusion. This doctrine entertained by the children of God in all ages from the beginning of the world. Error of throwing open heaven to the heathen, who know nothing of Christ. The pretexts for this refuted by passages of Scripture.
2. God never was propitious to the ancient Israelites without Christ the Mediator. First reason founded on the institution of sacrifice. Second reason founded on the calling of Abraham. Third reason founded on the elevation of David's family to regal dignity, and confirmed by striking passages of Scripture.
3. Christ the solace ever promised to the afflicted; the banner of faith and hope always erected. This confirmed by various passages of Scripture.
4. The Jews taught to have respect to Christ. This teaching sanctioned by our Saviour himself. The common saying, that God is the object of faith, requires to be explained and modified. Conclusion of this discussion concerning Christ. No saving knowledge of God in the heathen.

1. THE whole human race having been undone in the person of Adam, the excellence and dignity of our origin, as already described, is so far from availing us, that it rather turns to our greater disgrace, until God, who does not acknowledge man when defiled and corrupted by sin as his own work, appear as a Redeemer in the person of his only begotten Son. Since our fall from life unto death, all that knowledge of God the Creator, of which we have discoursed, would be useless, were it not followed up by faith, holding forth God to us as a Father in Christ. The natural course undoubtedly was, that the fabric of the world should be a school in which we might learn piety, and from it pass to eternal life and perfect felicity. But after looking at the perfection beheld wherever we turn our eye, above and below, we are met by the divine malediction, which, while it involves innocent creatures in our fault, of necessity fills our own souls with despair. For although God is still pleased in many ways to manifest his paternal favour towards us, we cannot, from a mere survey of the world, infer that he is a Father. Conscience urging us within, and showing that sin is a just ground for our being forsaken, will not allow us to think that God accounts or treats us as sons. In addition

to this are our sloth and ingratitude.   Our minds are so blinded that they cannot perceive the truth, and all our senses are so corrupt that we wickedly rob God of his glory.   Wherefore, we must conclude with Paul, "After that in the wisdom of God the world by wisdom knew not God, it pleased God by the foolishness of preaching to save them that believe" (1 Cor. i. 21).   By the "wisdom of God," he designates this magnificent theatre of heaven and earth replenished with numberless wonders, the wise contemplation of which should have enabled us to know God.   But this we do with little profit ; and, therefore, he invites us to faith in Christ,—faith which, by a semblance of foolishness, disgusts the unbeliever.   Therefore, although the preaching of the cross is not in accordance with human wisdom, we must, however, humbly embrace it if we would return to God our Maker, from whom we are estranged, that he may again become our Father.   It is certain that after the fall of our first parent, no knowledge of God without a Mediator was effectual to salvation.   Christ speaks not of his own age merely, but embraces all ages, when he says, " This is life eternal, that they might know thee the only true God, and Jesus Christ, whom thou hast sent" (John xvii. 3).   The more shameful, therefore, is the presumption of those who throw heaven open to the unbelieving and profane, in the absence of that grace which Scripture uniformly describes as the only door by which we enter into life.   Should any confine our Saviour's words to the period subsequent to the promulgation of the Gospel, the refutation is at hand ; since, on a ground common to all ages and nations, it is declared, that those who are estranged from God, and as such, are under the curse, the children of wrath, cannot be pleasing to God until they are reconciled.   To this we may add the answer which our Saviour gave to the Samaritan woman, " Ye worship ye know not what; we know what we worship: for salvation is of the Jews" (John iv. 22).   By these words, he both charges every Gentile religion with falsehood, and assigns the reason—viz., that under the Law the Redeemer was promised to the chosen people only, and that, consequently, no worship was ever pleasing to God in which respect was not had to Christ.   Hence also Paul affirms, that all the Gentiles were "without God," and deprived of the hope of life.   Now, since John teaches that there was life in Christ from the beginning, and that the whole world had lost it (John i. 4), it is necessary to return to that fountain ; and, accordingly, Christ declares that, inasmuch as he is a propitiator, he is life.   And, indeed, the inheritance of heaven belongs to none but the sons of God (John xv. 6).   Now, it were most incongruous to give the place and rank of sons to any who have not been engrafted into the body of the only begotten Son.   And John distinctly testifies that those become the sons of God who believe in his name.   But as it is not my intention at present formally to discuss the subject of faith in Christ, it is enough to have thus touched on it in passing.

2. Hence it is that God never showed himself propitious to his ancient people, nor gave them any hope of grace without a Mediator. I say nothing of the sacrifices of the Law, by which believers were plainly and openly taught that salvation was not to be found anywhere but in the expiation which Christ alone completed. All I maintain is, that the prosperous and happy state of the Church was always founded in the person of Christ. For although God embraced the whole posterity of Abraham in his covenant, yet Paul properly argues (Gal. iii. 16), that Christ was truly the seed in which all the nations of the earth were to be blessed, since we know that all who were born of Abraham, according to the flesh, were not accounted the seed. To omit Ishmael and others, how came it that of the two sons of Isaac, the twin brothers, Esau and Jacob, while yet in the womb, the one was chosen and the other rejected? Nay, how came it that the first-born was rejected, and the younger alone admitted? Moreover, how happens it that the majority are rejected? It is plain, therefore, that the seed of Abraham is considered chiefly in one head, and that the promised salvation is not attained without coming to Christ, whose office it is to gather together those which were scattered abroad. Thus the primary adoption of the chosen people depended on the grace of the Mediator. Although it is not expressed in very distinct terms in Moses, it, however, appears to have been commonly known to all the godly. For before a king was appointed over the Israelites, Hannah, the mother of Samuel, describing the happiness of the righteous, speaks thus in her song, " He shall give strength unto his king, and exalt the horn of his anointed ; " meaning by these words, that God would bless his Church. To this corresponds the prediction, which is afterwards added, " I will raise me up a faithful priest,——and he shall walk before mine anointed for ever" (1 Sam. ii. 10, 35). And there can be no doubt that our heavenly Father intended that a living image of Christ should be seen in David and his posterity. Accordingly, exhorting the righteous to fear Him, he bids them " Kiss the Son" (Psalm ii. 12). Corresponding to this is the passage in the Gospel, " He that honoureth not the Son, honoureth not the Father" (John v. 23). Therefore, though the kingdom was broken up by the revolt of the ten tribes, yet the covenant which God had made in David and his successors behoved to stand, as is also declared by his Prophets, " Howbeit I will not take the whole kingdom out of his hand : but I will make him prince all the days of his life for David my servant's sake" (1 Kings xi. 34). The same thing is repeated a second and third time. It is also expressly said, " I will for this afflict the seed of David, but not for ever" (1 Kings xi. 39). Some time afterwards it was said, " Nevertheless, for David's sake did the Lord his God give him a lamp in Jerusalem, to set up his own after him, and to establish Jerusalem" (1 Kings xv. 4). And when matters were bordering on destruction, it was again said, " Yet the Lord would

not destroy Judah for David his servant's sake, as he had promised to give him alway a light, and to his children" (2 Kings viii.19).

The sum of the whole comes to this—David, all others being excluded, was chosen to be the person in whom the good pleasure of the Lord should dwell; as it is said elsewhere, "He forsook the tabernacle of Shiloh;" "Moreover, he refused the tabernacle of Joseph, and chose not the tribe of Ephraim;" "But chose the tribe of Judah, the mount Zion which he loved;" "He chose David also his servant, and took him from the sheepfolds: from following the ewes great with young he brought him to feed Jacob his people, and Israel his inheritance" (Ps. lxxviii. 60, 67, 70, 71). In fine, God, in thus preserving his Church, intended that its security and salvation should depend on Christ as its head. Accordingly, David exclaims, "The Lord is their strength, and he is the saving strength of his anointed;" and then prays, "Save thy people, and bless thine inheritance;" intimating, that the safety of the Church was indissolubly connected with the government of Christ. In the same sense he elsewhere says, "Save Lord: let the king hear us when we call" (Ps. xx. 9). These words plainly teach that believers, in applying for the help of God, had their sole confidence in this—that they were under the unseen government of the King. This may be inferred from another psalm, "Save now, I beseech thee, O Lord: Blessed be he that cometh in the name of the Lord" (Ps. cxviii. 25, 26). Here it is obvious that believers are invited to Christ, in the assurance that they will be safe when entirely in his hand. To the same effect is another prayer, in which the whole Church implores the divine mercy, "Let thy hand be upon the Man of thy right hand, upon the Son of man, whom thou madest strong (or hast fitted) for thyself" (Ps. lxxx. 17). For though the author of the psalm laments the dispersion of the whole nation, he prays for its revival in him who is sole Head. After the people were led away into captivity, the land laid waste, and matters to appearance desperate, Jeremiah, lamenting the calamity of the Church, especially complains, that by the destruction of the kingdom the hope of believers was cut off; "The breath of our nostrils, the anointed of the Lord, was taken in their pits, of whom we said, Under his shadow we shall live among the heathen" (Lam. iv. 20). From all this it is abundantly plain, that as the Lord cannot be propitious to the human race without a Mediator, Christ was always held forth to the holy Fathers under the Law as the object of their faith.

3. Moreover, when comfort is promised in affliction, especially when the deliverance of the Church is described, the banner of faith and hope in Christ is unfurled. "Thou wentest forth for the salvation of thy people, even for salvation with thine anointed," says Habakkuk (iii. 13). And whenever mention is made in the Prophets of the renovation of the Church, the people are directed to the promise made to David, that his kingdom would be for ever. And

there is nothing strange in this, since otherwise there would have been no stability in the covenant. To this purpose is the remarkable prophecy in Isaiah vii. 14. After seeing that the unbelieving king Ahaz repudiated what he had testified regarding the deliverance of Jerusalem from siege and its immediate safety, he passes as it were abruptly to the Messiah, "Behold, a Virgin shall conceive and bear a son, and shall call his name Immanuel;" intimating indirectly, that though the king and his people wickedly rejected the promise offered to them, as if they were bent on causing the faith of God to fail, the covenant would not be defeated—the Redeemer would come in his own time. In fine, all the prophets, to show that God was placable, were always careful to bring forward that kingdom of David, on which redemption and eternal salvation depended. Thus in Isaiah it is said, "I will make an everlasting covenant with you, even the sure mercies of David. Behold, I have given him for a witness to the people" (Isa. lv. 3, 4); intimating, that believers, in calamitous circumstances, could have no hope, had they not this testimony, that God would be ready to hear them. In the same way, to revive their drooping spirits, Jeremiah says, "Behold, the days come, saith the Lord, that I will raise unto David a righteous Branch, and a King shall reign and prosper, and shall execute judgment and justice in the earth. In his days Judah shall be saved, and Israel shall dwell safely" (Jer. xxiii. 5, 6). In Ezekiel also it is said, "I will set up one Shepherd over them, and he shall feed them, even my servant David; he shall feed them, and he shall be their shepherd. And I the Lord will be their God, and my servant David a prince among them: I the Lord have spoken it. And I will make with them a covenant of peace" (Ezek. xxxiv. 23, 24, 25). And again, after discoursing of this wondrous renovation, he says, "David my servant shall be king over them: and they all shall have one shepherd." "Moreover, I will make a covenant of peace with them; it shall be an everlasting covenant with them" (Ezek. xxxvii. 24—26). I select a few passages our of many, because I merely wish to impress my readers with the fact, that the hope of believers was ever treasured up in Christ alone. All the other prophets concur in this. Thus Hosea, "Then shall the children of Judah and the children of Israel be gathered together, and appoint themselves one head" (Hosea i. 11). This he afterwards explains in clearer terms, "Afterward shall the childen of Israel return, and seek the Lord their God, and David their king" (Hosea iii. 5). Micah, also speaking of the return of the people, says expressly, "Their king shall pass before them, and the Lord on the head of them" (Micah ii. 13). So Amos, in predicting the renovation of the people, says, "In that day will I raise up the tabernacle of David that is fallen, and close up the breaches thereof; and I will raise up the ruins, and I will build it as in the days of old" (Amos ix. 11); in other words, the only banner of salvation was, the exaltation of the family of David to regal splendour, as fulfilled in Christ. Hence, too, Zechariah, as nearer in time to the manifestation of Christ, speaks more plainly, " Rejoice greatly, O daughter of Zion ; shout, O daughter of Jerusalem : behold, thy King cometh unto thee : he is just, and having salvation" (Zech. ix. 9). This corresponds to the passage already quoted from the Psalms, "The Lord is their strength, and he is the saving health of their anointed." Here salvation is extended from the head to the whole body.

4. By familiarising the Jews with these prophecies, God intended to teach them, that in seeking for deliverance, they should turn their eyes directly towards Christ. And though they had sadly degenerated, they never entirely lost the knowledge of this general principle, that God, by the hand of Christ, would be the deliverer of the Church, as he had promised to David ; and that in this way only the free covenant by which God had adopted his chosen people would be fulfilled. Hence it was, that on our Saviour's entry into Jerusalem, shortly before his death, the children shouted, "Hosannah to the son of David" (Matth. xxi. 9). For there seems to have been a hymn known to all, and in general use, in which they sang, that the only remaining pledge which they had of the divine mercy was the promised advent of a Redeemer. For this reason, Christ tells his disciples to believe in him, in order that they might have a distinct and complete belief in God, "Ye believe in God, believe also in me" (John xiv. 1). For although, properly speaking, faith rises from Christ to the Father, he intimates, that even when it leans on God, it gradually vanishes away, unless he himself interpose to give it solid strength. The majesty of God is too high to be scaled up to by mortals, who creep like worms on the earth. Therefore, the common saying that God is the object of faith (Lactantius, Lib. iv. c. 16), requires to be received with some modification. When Christ is called the image of the invisible God (Col. i. 15), the expression is not used without cause, but is designed to remind us that we can have no knowledge of our salvation, until we behold God in Christ. For although the Jewish scribes had by their false glosses darkened what the prophets had taught concerning the Redeemer, yet Christ assumed it to be a fact, received, as it were, with public consent, that there was no other remedy in desperate circumstances, no other mode of delivering the Church, than the manifestation of the Mediator. It is true, that the fact adverted to by Paul was not so generally known as it ought to have been—viz. that Christ is the end of the Law (Rom. x. 4), though this is both true, and clearly appears both from the Law and the Prophets. I am not now, however, treating of faith, as we shall elsewhere have a fitter place (Book III. chap. ii.), but what I wish to impress upon my readers in this way is, that the first step in piety is, to acknowledge that God is a Father, to defend, govern, and cherish us, until he brings us to the eternal inheritance of his kingdom ; that hence it is plain, as we lately observed, there is no

having knowledge of God without Christ, and that, consequently, from the beginning of the world Christ was held forth to all the elect as the object of their faith and confidence. In this sense, Irenæus says, that the Father, who is boundless in himself, is bounded in the Son, because he has accommodated himself to our capacity, lest our minds should be swallowed up by the immensity of his glory (Irenæus, Lib. iv. cap. 8). Fanatics, not attending to this, distort a useful sentiment into an impious dream,[1] as if Christ had only a share of the Godhead, as a part taken from a whole ; whereas the meaning merely is, that God is comprehended in Christ alone. The saying of John was always true, " Whosoever denieth the Son, the same hath not the Father" (1 John ii. 23). For though in old time there were many who boasted that they worshipped the Supreme Deity, the Maker of heaven and earth, yet as they had no Mediator, it was impossible for them truly to enjoy the mercy of God, so as to feel persuaded that he was their Father. Not holding the head, that is, Christ, their knowledge of God was evanescent ; and hence they at length fell away to gross and foul superstitions, betraying their ignorance, just as the Turks in the present day, who, though proclaiming, with full throat, that the Creator of heaven and earth is their God, yet, by their rejection of Christ, substitute an idol in his place.

[1] French, " reverie infernale.

CHAPTER VII.

THE LAW GIVEN, NOT TO RETAIN A PEOPLE FOR ITSELF, BUT TO KEEP ALIVE THE HOPE OF SALVATION IN CHRIST UNTIL HIS ADVENT.

The divisions of this chapter are, I. The Moral and Ceremonial Law a schoolmaster to bring us to Christ, sec. 1, 2. II. This true of the Moral Law, especially its conditional promises. These given for the best reasons. In what respect the observance of the Moral Law is said to be impossible, sec. 3—5. III. Of the threefold office and use of the Moral Law, sec. 6—12. Antinomians refuted, sec. 13. IV. What the abrogation of the Law, Moral and Ceremonial, sec. 14—17.

Sections.

1. The whole system of religion delivered by the hand of Moses, in many ways pointed to Christ. This exemplified in the case of sacrifices, ablutions, and an endless series of ceremonies. This proved, 1. By the declared purpose of God ; 2. By the nature of the ceremonies themselves ; 3. From the nature of God ; 4. From the grace offered to the Jews ; 5. From the consecration of the priests.
2. Proof continued. 6. From a consideration of the kingdom erected in the family of David. 7. From the end of the ceremonies. 8. From the end of the Moral Law.
3. A more ample exposition of the last proof. The Moral Law leads believers to Christ. Showing the perfect righteousness required by God, it convinces us of our inability to fulfil it. It thus denies us life, adjudges us to death, and so urges us to seek deliverance in Christ.
4. The promises of the Law, though conditional, founded on the best reason. This reason explained.
5. No inconsistency in giving a law, the observance of which is impossible. This proved from reason, and confirmed by Scripture. Another confirmation from Augustine.
6. A consideration of the office and use of the Moral Law shows that it leads to Christ. The Law, while it describes the righteousness which is acceptable to God, proves that every man is unrighteous.
7. The Law fitly compared to a mirror, which shows us our wretchedness. This derogates not in any degree from its excellence.
8. When the Law discloses our guilt, we should not despond, but flee to the mercy of God. How this may be done.
9. Confirmation of the first use of the Moral Law from various passages in Augustine.
10. A second use of the Law is to curb sinners. This most necessary for the good of the community at large ; and this in respect not only of the reprobate, but also of the elect, previous to regeneration. This confirmed by the authority of an Apostle.
11. The Law showing our wretchedness, disposes us to admit the remedy. It also tends to keep us in our duty. Confirmation from general experience.
12. The third and most appropriate use of the Law respects the elect. 1. It instructs and teaches them to make daily progress in doing the will of God. 2. Urges them by exhortation to obedience. Testimony of David. How he is to be reconciled with the Apostle.
13. The profane heresy of the Antinomians must be exploded. Argument founded on a passage in David, and another in Moses.
14. Last part of the chapter treating of the abrogation of the Law. In what respect any part of the Moral Law abrogated.

15. The curse of the Law how abrogated.
16. Of the abrogation of the Ceremonial Law in regard to the observance only.
17. The reason assigned by the Apostle applicable not to the Moral Law, but to ceremonial observances only. These abrogated, not only because they separated the Jews from the Gentiles, but still more because they were a kind of formal instruments to attest our guilt and impurity. Christ, by destroying these, is justly said to have taken away the handwriting that was against us, and nailed it to his cross.

1. From the whole course of the observations now made, we may infer that the Law was not superadded about four hundred years after the death of Abraham in order that it might lead the chosen people away from Christ, but, on the contrary, to keep them in suspense until his advent; to inflame their desire, and confirm their expectation, that they might not become dispirited by the long delay. By the Law, I understand not only the Ten Commandments, which contain a complete rule of life, but the whole system of religion delivered by the hand of Moses. Moses was not appointed as a Lawgiver, to do away with the blessing promised to the race of Abraham; nay, we see that he is constantly reminding the Jews of the free covenant which had been made with their fathers, and of which they were heirs; as if he had been sent for the purpose of renewing it. This is most clearly manifested by the ceremonies. For what could be more vain or frivolous than for men to reconcile themselves to God, by offering him the foul odour produced by burning the fat of beasts? or to wipe away their own impurities by besprinkling themselves with water or blood? In short, the whole legal worship (if considered by itself apart from the types and shadows of corresponding truth) is a mere mockery. Wherefore, both in Stephen's address (Acts vii. 44), and in the Epistle to the Hebrews, great weight is justly given to the passage in which God says to Moses, " Look that thou make them after the pattern which was showed thee in the mount" (Exod. xxv. 40). Had there not been some spiritual end to which they were directed, the Jews, in the observance of them, would have deluded themselves as much as the Gentiles in their vanities. Profane men, who have never made religion their serious study, cannot bear without disgust to hear of such a multiplicity of rites. They not merely wonder why God fatigued his ancient people with such a mass of ceremonies, but they despise and ridicule them as childish toys. This they do, because they attend not to the end; from which, if the legal figures are separated, they cannot escape the charge of vanity. But the type shows that God did not enjoin sacrifice, in order that he might occupy his worshippers with earthly exercises, but rather that he might raise their minds to something higher. This is clear even from His own nature. Being a spirit, he is delighted only with spiritual worship. The same thing is testified by the many passages in which the Prophets accuse the Jews of stupidity, for imagining that mere sacrifices have any value in the sight of God. Did they by this mean to derogate in any respect from the Law? By

no means; but as interpreters of its true meaning, they wished in this way to turn the attention of the people to the end which they ought to have had in view, but from which they generally wandered. From the grace offered to the Jews, we may certainly infer, that the law was not a stranger to Christ. Moses declared the end of the adoption of the Israelites to be, that they should be " a kingdom of priests, and an holy nation" (Exod. xix. 6). This they could not attain, without a greater and more excellent atonement than the blood of beasts. For what could be less in accordance with reason, than that the sons of Adam, who, from hereditary taint, are all born the slaves of sin, should be raised to royal dignity, and in this way made partakers of the glory of God, if the noble distinction were not derived from some other source? How, moreover, could the priestly office exist in vigour among those whose vices rendered them abominable in the sight of God, if they were not consecrated in a holy head? Wherefore, Peter elegantly transposes the words of Moses, teaching that the fulness of grace, of which the Jews had a foretaste under the Law, is exhibited in Christ, " Ye are a chosen generation, a royal priesthood" (1 Pet. ii. 9). The transposition of the words intimates that those to whom Christ has appeared in the Gospel, have obtained more than their fathers, inasmuch as they are all endued with priestly and royal honour, and can, therefore, trusting to their Mediator, appear with boldness in the presence of God.

2. And it is to be observed, by the way, that the kingdom, which was at length erected in the family of David, is part of the Law, and is comprehended under the dispensation of Moses; whence it follows, that, as well in the whole tribe of Levi as in the posterity of David, Christ was exhibited to the eyes of the Israelites as in a double mirror. For, as I lately observed (sec. i.), in no other way could those who were the slaves of sin and death, and defiled with corruption, be either kings or priests. Hence appears the perfect truth of Paul's statement, " The law was our schoolmaster to bring us unto Christ," " till the seed should come to whom the promise was made" (Gal. iii. 24, 19). For Christ not yet having been made familiarly known to the Jews, they were like children whose weakness could not bear a full knowledge of heavenly things. How they were led to Christ by the ceremonial law has already been adverted to, and may be made more intelligible by several passages in the Prophets. Although they were required, in order to appease God, to approach him daily with new sacrifices, yet Isaiah promises, that all their sins would be expiated by one single sacrifice, and with this Daniel concurs (Is. liii. 5; Dan. ix. 26, 27). The priests appointed from the tribe of Levi entered the sanctuary, but it was once said of a single priest, " The Lord hath sworn, and will not repent, Thou art a priest for ever, after the order of Melchizedek" (Ps. cx. 4). The unction of oil was then visible, but Daniel in vision declares that there will be another unction. Not to dwell on this, the author of the Epistle to

the Hebrews proves clearly, and at length, from the fourth to the eleventh chapter, that ceremonies were vain, and of no value, unless as bringing us to Christ. In regard to the Ten Commandments, we must, in like manner, attend to the statement of Paul, that "Christ is the end of the law for righteousness to every one that believeth" (Rom. x. 4) ; and, again, that ministers of the New Testament were "not of the letter, but of the spirit : for the letter killeth, but the spirit giveth life" (2 Cor. iii. 6). The former passage intimates, that it is in vain to teach righteousness by precept, until Christ bestow it by free imputation, and the regeneration of the Spirit. Hence he properly calls Christ the end or fulfilling of the Law, because it would avail us nothing to know what God demands, did not Christ come to the succour of those who are labouring, and oppressed under an intolerable yoke and burden. In another place, he says that the Law "was added because of transgressions" (Gal. iii. 19), that it might humble men under a sense of their condemnation. Moreover, inasmuch as this is the only true preparation for Christ, the statements, though made in different words, perfectly agree with each other. But because he had to dispute with perverse teachers, who pretended that men merited justification by the works of the Law, he was sometimes obliged, in refuting their error, to speak of the Law in a more restricted sense, merely as law, though, in other respects, the covenant of free adoption is comprehended under it.

3. But in order that a sense of guilt may urge us to seek for pardon, it is of importance to know how our being instructed in the Moral Law renders us more inexcusable. If it is true, that a perfect righteousness is set before us in the Law, it follows, that the complete observance of it is perfect righteousness in the sight of God ; that is, a righteousness by which a man may be deemed and pronounced righteousness at the divine tribunal. Wherefore Moses, after promulgating the Law, hesitates not to call heaven and earth to witness, that he had set life and death, good and evil before the people. Nor ean it be denied, that the reward of eternal salvation, as promised by the Lord, awaits the perfect obedience of the Law (Deut. xxx. 19). Again, however, it is of importance to understand in what way we perform that obedience for which we justly entertain the hope of that reward. For of what use is it to see that the reward of eternal life depends on the observance of the Law, unless it moreover appears whether it be in our power in that way to attain to eternal life ? Herein, then, the weakness of the Law is manifested ; for, in none of us is that righteousness of the Law manifested, and, therefore, being excluded from the promises of life, we again fall under the curse. I state not only what happens, but what must necessarily happen. The doctrine of the Law transcending our capacity, a man may indeed look from a distance at the promises held forth, but he cannot derive any benefit from them. The only thing, therefore, remaining for him is, from their excellence to form a better estimate of his own

misery, while he considers that the hope of salvation is cut off, and he is threatened with certain death. On the other hand, those fearful denunciations which strike not at a few individuals, but at every individual without exception, rise up; rise up, I say, and, with inexorable severity, pursue us; so that nothing but instant death is presented by the Law.

4. Therefore, if we look merely to the Law, the result must be despondency, confusion, and despair, seeing that by it we are all cursed and condemned, while we are kept far away from the blessedness which it holds forth to its observers. Is the Lord, then, you will ask, only sporting with us? Is it not the next thing to mockery, to hold out the hope of happiness, to invite and exhort us to it, to declare that it is set before us, while all the while the entrance to it is precluded and quite shut up? I answer, Although the promises, in so far as they are conditional, depend on a perfect obedience of the Law, which is nowhere to be found, they have not, however, been given in vain. For when we have learned, that the promises would be fruitless and unavailing, did not God accept us of his free goodness, without any view to our works, and when, having so learned, we, by faith, embrace the goodness thus offered in the gospel, the promises, with all their annexed conditions, are fully accomplished. For God, while bestowing all things upon us freely, crowns his goodness by not disdaining our imperfect obedience; forgiving its deficiencies, accepting it as if it were complete, and so bestowing upon us the full amount of what the Law has promised. But as this point will be more fully discussed in treating of justification by faith, we shall not follow it further at present.

5. What has been said as to the impossible observance of the Law, it will be proper briefly to explain and confirm, the general opinion being, that nothing can be more absurd. Hence Jerome has not hesitated to denounce anathema against it.[1] What Jerome thought, I care not; let us inquire what is the truth. I will not here enter into a long and intricate discussion on the various kinds of possibility. By impossible, I mean, that which never was, and, being prevented by the ordination and decree of God, never will be. I say, that if we go back to the remotest period, we shall not find a single saint who, clothed with a mortal body, ever attained to such perfection as to love the Lord with all his heart, and soul, and mind, and strength; and, on the other hand, not one who has not felt the power of concupiscence. Who can deny this? I am aware, indeed, of a kind of saints whom a foolish superstition imagines, and whose purity the angels of heaven scarcely equal. This, however, is repugnant both to Scripture and experience. But I say further, that no saint ever will attain to perfection, so long as he is in the body. Scripture bears clear testimony to this effect: "There is no man that sinneth

---

1 See among the works of Justin. Quæst. 103; and Hieronymus ad Ctesiphont adv. Pelegianos, where he seems to admit and deny the same proposition.

not," saith Solomon (1 Kings viii. 46). David says, "In thy sight shall no man living be justified" (Psalm cxliii. 2). Job also, in numerous passages, affirms the same thing. But the clearest of all is Paul, who declares that "the flesh lusteth against the Spirit, and the Spirit against the flesh" (Gal. v. 17). And he proves, that "as many as are of the works of the Law are under the curse," for the simple reason, that it is written, "Cursed is every one that continueth not in all things which are written in the book of the law to do them" (Gal. iii. 10; Deut. xxvii. 26); intimating, or rather assuming it as confessed, that none can so continue. But whatever has been declared by Scripture must be regarded as perpetual, and hence necessary. The Pelagians annoyed Augustine with the sophism, that it was insulting to God to hold, that he orders more than believers are able, by his grace, to perform; and he, in order to evade it, acknowledged that the Lord was able, if he chose, to raise a mortal man to angelic purity; but that he had never done, and never would do it, because so the Scripture had declared (Augustine, Lib. de Nat. et Grat.). This I deny not: but I add, that there is no use in absurdly disputing concerning the power of God in opposition to his truth; and therefore there is no ground for cavilling, when it is said that that thing cannot be, which the Scriptures declare will never be. But if it is the word that is objected to, I refer to the answer which our Saviour gave to his disciples when they asked, "Who then can be saved?" "With men," said he, "This is impossible; but with God all things are possible" (Matth. xix. 25). Augustine argues in the most convincing manner, that while in the flesh, we never can give God the love which we owe him. "Love so follows knowledge, that no man can perfectly love God who has not previously a full comprehension of his goodness" (Augustin. de Spiritu et Litera, towards the end and elsewhere). So long as we are pilgrims in the world, we see through a glass darkly, and therefore our love is imperfect. Let it therefore be held incontrovertible, that, in consequence of the feebleness of our nature, it is impossible for us, so long as we are in the flesh, to fulfil the law. This will also be proved elsewhere from the writings of Paul (Rom. viii. 3).[1]

6. That the whole matter may be made clearer, let us take a succinct view of the office and use of the Moral Law. Now, this office and use seems to me to consist of three parts. First, by exhibiting the righteousness of God,—in other words, the righteousness which alone is acceptable to God,—it admonishes every one of his own unrighteousness, certiorates, convicts, and finally condemns him. This is necessary, in order that man, who is blind and intoxicated with self-love, may be brought at once to know and to confess his weakness and impurity. For until his vanity is made perfectly manifest, he is puffed up with infatuated confidence in his own

---

[1] Book II. chap. xii. sec. 4; and Book III. chap. iv. sec. 27; and chap. xi. sec. 23.

powers, and never can be brought to feel their feebleness so long as he measures them by a standard of his own choice. So soon, however, as he begins to compare them with the requirements of the Law, he has something to tame his presumption. How high soever his opinion of his own powers may be, he immediately feels that they pant under the heavy load, then totter and stumble, and finally fall and give way. He, then, who is schooled by the Law, lays aside the arrogance which formerly blinded him. In like manner must he be cured of pride, the other disease under which we have said that he labours. So long as he is permitted to appeal to his own judgment, he substitutes a hypocritical for a real righteousness, and, contented with this, sets up certain factitious observances in opposition to the grace of God. But after he is forced to weigh his conduct in the balance of the Law, renouncing all dependence on this fancied righteousness, he sees that he is at an infinite distance from holiness, and, on the other hand, that he teems with innumerable vices of which he formerly seemed free. The recesses in which concupiscence lies hid are so deep and tortuous that they easily elude our view ; and hence the Apostle had good reason for saying, "I had not known lust, except the law had said, Thou shalt not covet." For, if it be not brought forth from its lurking-places, it miserably destroys in secret before its fatal sting is discerned.

7. Thus the Law is a kind of mirror.. As in a mirror we discover any stains upon our face, so in the Law we behold, first, our impotence ; then, in consequence of it, our iniquity ; and, finally, the curse, as the consequence of both. He who has no power of following righteousness is necessarily plunged in the mire of iniquity, and this iniquity is immediately followed by the curse. Accordingly, the greater the transgression of which the Law convicts us, the severer the judgment to which we are exposed. To this effect is the Apostle's declaration, that "by the law is the knowledge of sin" (Rom. iii. 20). By these words, he only points out the first office of the Law as experienced by sinners not yet regenerated. In conformity to this, it is said, "the law entered that the offence might abound ;" and, accordingly, that it is "the ministration of death ;" that it "worketh wrath" and kills (Rom. v. 20 ; 2 Cor. iii. 7 ; Rom. iv. 15). For there cannot be a doubt that the clearer the consciousness of guilt, the greater the increase of sin ; because then to transgression a rebellious feeling against the Lawgiver is added. All that remains for the Law, is to arm the wrath of God for the destruction of the sinner ; for by itself it can do nothing but accuse, condemn, and destroy him. Thus Augustine says, "If the Spirit of grace be absent, the law is present only to convict and slay us."[1] But to say this neither insults the law, nor derogates in any degree from its excellence. Assuredly, if our whole will were formed and disposed to obedience, the

---

[1] August. de Corrept. et Gratia. Ambros. Lib. i. de Jac. et cap. vi. de Vita Beat.

mere knowledge of the law would be sufficient for salvation ; but since our carnal and corrupt nature is at enmity with the Divine law, and is in no degree amended by its discipline, the consequence is, that the law which, if it had been properly attended to, would have given life, becomes the occasion of sin and death.   When all are convicted of transgression, the more it declares the righteousness of God, the more, on the other hand, it discloses our iniquity ; the more certainly it assures us that life and salvation are treasured up as the reward of righteousness, the more certainly it assures us that the un- righteous will perish.   So far, however, are these qualities from throw- ing disgrace on the Law, that their chief tendency is to give a brighter display of the divine goodness.   For they show that it is only our weakness and depravity that prevents us from enjoying the blessed- ness which the law openly sets before us.   Hence additional sweet- ness is given to divine grace, which comes to our aid without the law, and additional loveliness to the mercy which confers it, because they proclaim that God is never weary in doing good, and in loading us with new gifts.

8. But while the unrighteousness and condemnation of all are attested by the law, it does not follow (if we make the proper use of it) that we are immediately to give up all hope and rush headlong on despair. No doubt, it has some such effect upon the reprobate, but this is owing to their obstinacy.   With the children of God the effect is different.   The Apostle testifies that the law pronounces its sentence of condemnation in order " that every mouth may be stopped, and all the world may become guilty before God " (Rom. iii. 19).   In another place, however, the same Apostle declares that "God hath con- cluded them all in unbelief ;" not that he might destroy all, or allow all to perish, but that " he might have mercy upon all " (Rom. xi. 32) : in other words, that divesting themselves of an absurd opinion of their own virtue, they may perceive how they are wholly depend- ent on the hand of God ; that feeling how naked and destitute they are, they may take refuge in his mercy, rely upon it, and cover them- selves up entirely with it ; renouncing all righteousness and merit, and clinging to mercy alone, as offered in Christ to all who long and look for it in true faith.   In the precepts of the law, God is seen as the rewarder only of perfect righteousness (a righteousness of which all are destitute), and, on the other hand, as the stern avenger of wickedness.   But in Christ his countenance beams forth full of grace and gentleness towards poor unworthy sinners.

9. There are many passages in Augustine, as to the utility of the law in leading us to implore Divine assistance.   Thus he writes to Hilary,[1] " The law orders, that we, after attempting to do what is ordered, and so feeling our weakness under the law, may learn to implore the help of grace."   In like manner, he writes to Assellius,

---

[1] August. Ep. 89, Quæst. 2 ; ad Assell. Ep. 200 ; ad Innocent. Ep. 95 ; Lib. de Cor- rept. et Gratia ad Valent. ; in Ps. lxx. et cxviii. ; Item, Concio. 27.

" The utility of the law is, that it convinces man of his weakness, and compels him to apply for the medicine of grace, which is in Christ." In like manner, he says to Innocentius Romanus, " The law orders ; grace supplies the power of acting." Again, to Valentinus, " God enjoins what we cannot do, in order that we may know what we have to ask of him." Again, " The law was given, that it might make you guilty—being made guilty, might fear ; fearing, might ask indulgence, not presume on your own strength." Again, " The law was given, in order to convert a great into a little man— to show that you have no power of your own for righteousness ; and might thus, poor, needy, and destitute, flee to grace." He afterwards thus addresses the Almighty, " So do, O Lord, so do, O merciful Lord ; command what cannot be fulfilled ; nay, command what cannot be fulfilled, unless by thy own grace : so that when men feel they have no strength in themselves to fulfil it, every mouth may be stopped, and no man seem great in his own eyes. Let all be little ones ; let the whole world become guilty before God." But I am forgetting myself in producing so many passages, since this holy man wrote a distinct treatise, which he entitled *De Spiritu et Litera*. The other branch of this first use he does not describe so distinctly, either because he knew that it depended on the former, or because he was not so well aware of it, or because he wanted words in which he might distinctly and clearly explain its proper meaning. But even in the reprobate themselves, this first office of the law is not altogether wanting. They do not, indeed, proceed so far with the children of God as, after the flesh is cast down, to be renewed in the inner man, and revive again; but stunned by the first terror, give way to despair. Still it tends to manifest the equity of the Divine judgment, when their consciences are thus heaved upon the waves. They would always willingly carp at the judgment of God ; but now, though that judgment is not manifested, still the alarm produced by the testimony of the law and of their conscience bespeaks their deserts.

10. The second office of the Law is, by means of its fearful denunciations and the consequent dread of punishment, to curb those who, unless forced, have no regard for rectitude and justice. Such persons are curbed, not because their mind is inwardly moved and affected, but because, as if a bridle were laid upon them, they refrain their hands from external acts, and internally check the depravity which would otherwise petulantly burst forth. It is true, they are not on this account either better or more righteous in the sight of God. For although restrained by terror or shame, they dare not proceed to what their mind has conceived, nor give full license to their raging lust, their heart is by no means trained to fear and obedience. Nay, the more they restrain themselves, the more they are inflamed, the more they rage and boil, prepared for any act or outbreak whatsoever, were it not for the terror of the law. And not only so, but they thoroughly detest the law itself, and execrate the Lawgiver ; so that

if they could, they would most willingly annihilate him, because they cannot bear either his ordering what is right, or his avenging the despisers of his Majesty. The feeling of all who are not yet regenerate, though in some more, in others less lively, is, that in regard to the observance of the law, they are not led by voluntary submission, but dragged by the force of fear. Nevertheless, this forced and extorted righteousness is necessary for the good of society, its peace being secured by a provision but for which all things would be thrown into tumult and confusion. Nay, this tuition is not without its use, even to the children of God, who, previous to their effectual calling, being destitute of the Spirit of holiness, freely indulge the lusts of the flesh. When, by the fear of Divine vengeance, they are deterred from open outbreakings, though, from not being subdued in mind, they profit little at present, still they are in some measure trained to bear the yoke of righteousness, so that when they are called, they are not like mere novices, studying a discipline of which previously they had no knowledge. This office seems to be especially in the view of the Apostle, when he says, "That the law is not made for a righteous man, but for the lawless and disobedient, for the ungodly and for sinners, for unholy and profane, for murderers of fathers and murderers of mothers, for manslayers, for whoremongers, for them that defile themselves with mankind, for men-stealers, for liars, for perjured persons, and if there be any other thing that is contrary to sound doctrine" (1 Tim. i. 9, 10). He thus indicates that it is a restraint on unruly lusts that would otherwise burst all bonds.

11. To both may be applied the declaration of the Apostle in another place, that "The law was our schoolmaster to bring us unto Christ" (Gal. iii. 24); since there are two classes of persons, whom by its training it leads to Christ. Some (of whom we spoke in the first place), from excessive confidence in their own virtue or righteousness, are unfit to receive the grace of Christ, until they are completely humbled. This the law does by making them sensible of their misery, and so disposing them to long for what they previously imagined they did not want. Others have need of a bridle to restrain them from giving full scope to their passions, and thereby utterly losing all desire after righteousness. For where the Spirit of God rules not, the lusts sometimes so burst forth, as to threaten to drown the soul subjected to them in forgetfulness and contempt of God; and so they would, did not God interpose with this remedy. Those, therefore, whom he has destined to the inheritance of his kingdom, if he does not immediately regenerate, he, through the works of the law, preserves in fear, against the time of his visitation, not, indeed, that pure and chaste fear which his children ought to have, but a fear useful to the extent of instructing them in true piety according to their capacity. Of this we have so many proofs, that there is not the least need of an example. For all who have remained for some

time in ignorance of God will confess, as the result of their own experience, that the law had the effect of keeping them in some degree in the fear and reverence of God, till, being regenerated by his Spirit, they began to love him from the heart.

12. The third use of the Law (being also the principal use, and more closely connected with its proper end) has respect to believers in whose hearts the Spirit of God already flourishes and reigns. For although the Law is written and engraven on their hearts by the finger of God, that is, although they are so influenced and actuated by the Spirit, that they desire to obey God, there are two ways in which they still profit in the Law. For it is the best instrument for enabling them daily to learn with greater truth and certainty what that will of the Lord is which they aspire to follow, and to confirm them in this knowledge; just as a servant who desires with all his soul to approve himself to his master, must still observe, and be careful to ascertain his master's dispositions, that he may comport himself in accommodation to them. Let none of us deem ourselves exempt from this necessity, for none have as yet attained to such a degree of wisdom, as that they may not, by the daily instruction of the Law, advance to a purer knowledge of the Divine will. Then, because we need not doctrine merely, but exhortation also, the servant of God will derive this further advantage from the Law: by frequently meditating upon it, he will be excited to obedience, and confirmed in it, and so drawn away from the slippery paths of sin. In this way must the saints press onward, since, however great the alacrity with which, under the Spirit, they hasten toward righteousness, they are retarded by the sluggishness of the flesh, and make less progress than they ought. The Law acts like a whip to the flesh, urging it on as men do a lazy sluggish ass. Even in the case of a spiritual man, inasmuch as he is still burdened with the weight of the flesh, the Law is a constant stimulus, pricking him forward when he would indulge in sloth. David had this use in view when he pronounced this high eulogium on the Law, "The law of the Lord is perfect, converting the soul: the testimony of the Lord is sure, making wise the simple. The statutes of the Lord are right, rejoicing the heart: the commandment of the Lord is pure, enlightening the eyes" (Ps. xix. 7, 8). Again, "Thy word is a lamp unto my feet, and a light unto my path" (Ps. cxix. 105). The whole Psalm abounds in passages to the same effect. Such passages are not inconsistent with those of Paul, which show not the utility of the law to the regenerate, but what it is able of itself to bestow. The object of the Psalmist is to celebrate the advantages which the Lord, by means of his law, bestows on those whom he inwardly inspires with a love of obedience. And he adverts not to the mere precepts, but also to the promise annexed to them, which alone makes that sweet which in itself is bitter. For what is less attractive than the law, when, by its demands and threatenings, it overawes the soul, and

fills it with terror ?   David specially shows that in the law he saw the Mediator, without whom it gives no pleasure or delight.

13. Some unskilful persons, from not attending to this, boldly discard the whole law of Moses, and do away with both its Tables, imaging it unchristian to adhere to a doctrine which contains the ministration of death.   Far from our thoughts be this profane notion. Moses has admirably shown that the Law, which can produce nothing but death in sinners, ought to have a better and more excellent effect upon the righteous.   When about to die, he thus addressed the people, " Set your hearts unto all the words which I testify among you this day, which ye shall command your children to observe to do, all the words of this law.   For it is not a vain thing for you ; because it is your life" (Deut. xxxii. 46, 47).   If it cannot be denied that it contains a perfect pattern of righteousness, then, unless we ought not to have any proper rule of life, it must be impious to discard it. There are not various rules of life, but one perpetual and inflexible rule ; and, therefore, when David describes the righteous as spending their whole lives in meditating on the Law (Psalm i. 2), we must not confine to a single age, an employment which is most appropriate to all ages, even to the end of the world.   Nor are we to be deterred or to shun its instructions, because the holiness which it prescribes is stricter than we are able to render, so long as we bear about the prison of the body.   It does not now perform toward us the part of a hard taskmaster, who will not be satisfied without full payment ; but, in the perfection to which it exhorts us, points out the goal at which, during the whole course of our lives, it is not less our interest than our duty to aim.   It is well if we thus press onward.   Our whole life is a race, and after we have finished our course, the Lord will enable us to reach that goal to which, at present, we can only aspire in wish.

14. Since, in regard to believers, the law has the force of exhortation, not to bind their consciences with a curse, but by urging them, from time to time, to shake off sluggishness and chastise imperfection, —many, when they would express this exemption from the curse, say, that in regard to believers the Law (I still mean the Moral Law) is abrogated : not that the things which it enjoins are no longer right to be observed, but only that it is not to believers what it formerly was ; in other words, that it does not, by terrifying and confounding their consciences, condemn and destroy.   It is certainly true that Paul shows, in clear terms, that there is such an abrogation of the Law.   And that the same was preached by our Lord appears from this, that he would not have refuted the opinion of his destroying the Law, if it had not been prevalent among the Jews.   Since such an opinion could not have arisen at random without some pretext, there is reason to presume that it originated in a false interpretation of his doctrine, in the same way in which all errors generally arise from a perversion of the truth.   But lest we should stumble against the same

stone, let us distinguish accurately between what has been abrogated
in the Law, and what still remains in force.   When the Lord declares, that he came not to destroy the Law, but to fulfil (Matth. v.
17), that until heaven and earth pass away, not one jot or tittle
shall remain unfulfilled; he shows that his advent was not to derogate, in any degree, from the observance of the Law.   And justly,
since the very end of his coming was to remedy the transgression of
the Law.   Therefore, the doctrine of the Law has not been infringed
by Christ, but remains, that, by teaching, admonishing, rebuking,
and correcting, it may fit and prepare us for every good work.

15. What Paul says, as to the abrogation of the Law, evidently
applies not to the Law itself, but merely to its power of constraining
the conscience.   For the Law not only teaches, but also imperiously
demands.   If obedience is not yielded, nay, if it is omitted in any
degree, it thunders forth its curse.   For this reason, the Apostle says,
that "as many as are of the works of the law are under the curse: for
it is written, Cursed is every one that continueth not in all things
which are written in the book of the law to do them" (Gal. iii. 10;
Deut. xxvii. 26).   Those he describes as under the works of the Law,
who do not place righteousness in that forgiveness of sins by which
we are freed from the rigour of the Law.   He therefore shows, that
we must be freed from the fetters of the Law, if we would not perish
miserably under them.   But what fetters?   Those of rigid and austere
exaction, which remits not one iota of the demand, and leaves no
transgression unpunished.   To redeem us from this curse, Christ was
made a curse for us: for it is written, Cursed is every one that hangeth
on a tree (Deut. xxi. 23, compared with Gal. iii. 13, iv. 4).   In the
following chapter, indeed, he says, that "Christ was made under the
law, in order that he might redeem those who are under the law;"
but the meaning is the same.   For he immediately adds, "That we
might receive the adoption of sons."   What does this mean?   That
we might not be, all our lifetime, subject to bondage, having our
consciences oppressed with the fear of death.   Meanwhile, it must
ever remain an indubitable truth, that the Law has lost none of its
authority, but must always receive from us the same respect and
obedience.

16. The case of ceremonies is different, these having been abrogated
not in effect but in use only.   Though Christ by his advent put an
end to their use, so far is this from derogating from their sacredness,
that it rather commends and illustrates it.   For as these ceremonies
would have given nothing to God's ancient people but empty show,
if the power of Christ's death and resurrection had not been prefigured
by them,—so, if the use of them had not ceased, it would, in the
present day, be impossible to understand for what purpose they were
instituted.   Accordingly, Paul, in order to prove that the observance
of them was not only superfluous, but pernicious also, says that they
"are a shadow of things to come; but the body is of Christ" (Col.

ii. 17). We see, therefore, that the truth is made clearer by their abolition than if Christ, who has been openly manifested, were still figured by them as at a distance, and as under a veil. By the death of Christ, the veil of the temple was rent in twain, the living and express image of heavenly things, which had begun to be dimly shadowed forth, being now brought fully into view, as is described by the author of the Epistle to the Hebrews (Heb. x. 1). To the same effect, our Saviour declares, that "the law and the prophets were until John: since that time the kingdom of God is preached, and every man presseth into it" (Luke xvi. 16); not that the holy fathers were left without the preaching of the hope of salvation and eternal life, but because they only saw at a distance, and under a shadow, what we now behold in full light. Why it behoved the Church to ascend higher than these elements, is explained by John the Baptist, when he says, "The law was given by Moses, but grace and truth came by Jesus Christ" (John i. 17). For though it is true that expiation was promised in the ancient sacrifices, and the ark of the covenant was a sure pledge of the paternal favour of God, the whole would have been elusory had it not been founded on the grace of Christ, wherein true and eternal stability is found. It must be held as a fixed point, that though legal rites ceased to be observed, their end serves to show more clearly how great their utility was before the advent of Christ, who, while he abolished the use, sealed their force and effect by his death.

17. There is a little more difficulty in the following passage of Paul: "You, being dead in your sins and the uncircumcision of your flesh, hath he quickened together with him, having forgiven you all trespasses; blotting out the handwriting of ordinances that was against us, which was contrary to us, and took it out of the way, nailing it to his cross" &c. (Col. ii. 13, 14). He seems to extend the abolition of the Law considerably farther, as if we had nothing to do with its injunctions. Some err in interpreting this simply of the Moral Law, as implying the abolition not of its injunctions, but of its inexorable rigour. Others examining Paul's words more carefully, see that they properly apply to the Ceremonial Law, and show that Paul repeatedly uses the term *ordinance* in this sense. He thus writes to the Ephesians: "He is our peace, who hath made both one, and hath broken down the middle wall of partition between us; having abolished in his flesh the enmity, even the law of commandments contained in ordinances; for to make in himself of twain one new man" (Eph. ii. 14). There can be no doubt that he is there treating of ceremonies, as he speaks of "the middle wall of partition" which separated Jews and Gentiles. I therefore hold that the former view is erroneous; but, at the same time, it does not appear to me that the latter comes fully up to the Apostle's meaning. For I cannot admit that the two passages are perfectly parallel. As his object was to assure the Ephesians that they were admitted to fellowship with

the Jews, he tells them that the obstacle which formerly stood in the way was removed. This obstacle was in the ceremonies. For the rites of ablution and sacrifice, by which the Jews were consecrated to the Lord, separated them from the Gentiles. But who sees not that, in the Epistle to the Colossians, a sublimer mystery is adverted to? No doubt, a question is raised there as to the Mosaic observances, to which false apostles were endeavouring to bind the Christian people. But as in the Epistle to the Galatians he takes a higher view of this controversy, and in a manner traces it to its fountain, so he does in this passage also. For if the only thing considered in rites is the necessity of observing them, of what use was it to call it a handwriting which was contrary to us? Besides, how could the bringing in of it be set down as almost the whole sum of redemption? Wherefore, the very nature of the case clearly shows that reference is here made to something more internal. I cannot doubt that I have ascertained the genuine interpretation, provided I am permitted to assume what Augustine has somewhere most truly affirmed, nay, derived from the very words of the Apostle—viz. that in the Jewish ceremonies there was more a confession than an expiation of sins. For what more was done in sacrifice by those who substituted purifications instead of themselves, than to confess that they were conscious of deserving death? What did these purifications testify but that they themselves were impure? By these means, therefore, the handwriting both of their guilt and impurity was ever and anon renewed. But the attestation of these things was not the removal of them. Wherefore, the Apostle says that Christ is "the mediator of the new testament,—by means of death, for the redemption of the transgressions that were under the first testament" (Heb. ix. 15). Justly, therefore, does the Apostle describe these handwritings as against the worshippers, and contrary to them, since by means of them their impurity and condemnation were openly sealed. There is nothing contrary to this in the fact that they were partakers of the same grace with ourselves. This they obtained through Christ, and not through the ceremonies which the Apostle there contrasts with Christ, showing that by the continued use of them the glory of Christ was obscured. We perceive how ceremonies, considered in themselves, are elegantly and appositely termed handwritings, and contrary to the salvation of man, inasmuch as they were a kind of formal instruments which attested his liability. On the other hand, when false apostles wished to bind them on the Christian Church, Paul, entering more deeply into their signification, with good reason warned the Colossians how seriously they would relapse if they allowed a yoke to be in that way imposed upon them. By so doing, they, at the same time, deprived themselves of all benefit from Christ, who, by his eternal sacrifice once offered, had abolished those daily sacrifices, which were indeed powerful to attest sin, but could do nothing to destroy it.

CHAPTER VIII.

EXPOSITION OF THE MORAL LAW.

This chapter consists of four parts. I. Some general observations necessary for the understanding of the subject are made by way of preface, sec. 1—5. II. Three things always to be attended to in ascertaining and expounding the meaning of the Moral Law, sec. 6—12. III. Exposition of the Moral Law, or the Ten Commandments, sec. 13—15. IV. The end for which the whole Law is intended—viz. to teach not only elementary principles, but perfection—sec. 51, to the end of the chapter.

Sections.

1. The Law was committed to writing, in order that it might teach more fully and perfectly that knowledge, both of God and of ourselves, which the law of nature teaches meagrely and obscurely. Proof of this, from an enumeration of the principal parts of the Moral Law; and also from the dictate of natural law, written on the hearts of all, and, in a manner, effaced by sin.
2. Certain general maxims. 1. From the knowledge of God, furnished by the Law, we learn that God is our Father and Ruler. Righteousness is pleasing, iniquity is an abomination in his sight. Hence, how weak soever we may be, our duty is to cultivate the one, and shun the other.
3. From the knowledge of ourselves, furnished by the Law, we learn to discern our own utter powerlessness, we are ashamed; and seeing it is in vain to seek for righteousness in ourselves, are induced to seek it elsewhere.
4. Hence, God has annexed promises and threatenings to his promises. These not limited to the present life, but embrace things heavenly and eternal. They, moreover, attest the spotless purity of God, his love of righteousness, and also his kindness towards us.
5. The Law shows, moreover, that there is nothing more acceptable to God than obedience. Hence, all superstitious and hypocritical modes of worship are condemned. A remedy against superstitious worship and human presumption.
6. The second part of the chapter, containing three observations or rules. First rule, Our life must be formed by the Law, not only to external honesty, but to inward and spiritual righteousness. In this respect the Law of God differs from civil laws, he being a spiritual Lawgiver, man not. This rule of great extent, and not sufficiently attended to.
7. This first rule confirmed by the authority of Christ, and vindicated from the false dogma of Sophists, who say that Christ is only another Moses.
8. Second observation or rule to be carefully attended to—viz. that the end of the command must be inquired into, until it is ascertained what the Lawgiver approves or disapproves. Example. Where the Law approves, its opposite is condemned, and *vice versa.*
9. Full explanation of this latter point. Example.
10. The Law states what is most impious in each transgression, in order to show how heinous the transgression is. Example.
11. Third observation or rule regards the division of the Law into Two Tables: the former comprehending our duty to God; the latter, our duty to our neighbour. The connection between these necessary and inseparable. Their invariable order. Sum of the Law.
12. Division of the Law into Ten Commandments. Various distinctions made with regard to them, but the best distinction that which divides them into Two Tables. Four commandments belong to the First, and six to the Second Table.

13. The third part of the chapter, containing an exposition of the Decalogue. The preface vindicates the authority of the Law. This it does in three ways. First, by a declaration of its majesty.

14. The preface to the Law vindicates its authority. Secondly, by calling to mind God's paternal kindness.

15. Thirdly, by calling to mind the deliverance out of the land of Egypt. Why God distinguishes himself by certain epithets. Why mention is made of the deliverance from Egypt. In what way, and how far, the remembrance of this deliverance should still affect us.

16. Exposition of the First Commandment. Its end. What it is to have God, and to have strange gods. Adoration due to God, trust, invocation, thanksgiving, and also true religion, required by the Commandment. Superstition, Polytheism, and Atheism, forbidden. What meant by the words, "before me."

17. Exposition of the Second Commandment. The end and sum of it. Two parts. Short enumeration of forbidden shapes.

18. Why a threatening is added. Four titles applied to God, to make a deeper impression. He is called Mighty, Jealous, an Avenger, Merciful. Why said to be jealous. Reason drawn from analogy.

19. Exposition of the threatening which is added. First, as to visiting the iniquity of the fathers upon the children. A misinterpretation on this head refuted, and the genuine meaning of the threatening explained.

20. Whether this visiting of the sins of parents inconsistent with the divine justice. Apparently conflicting passages reconciled.

21. Exposition of the latter part—viz. the showing mercy to thousands. The use of this promise. Consideration of an exception of frequent occurrence. The extent of this blessing.

22. Exposition of the Third Commandment. The end and sum of it. Three parts. These considered. What it is to use the name of God in vain. Swearing. Distinction between this commandment and the Ninth.

23. An oath defined. It is a species of divine worship. This explained.

24. Many modes in which this commandment is violated. 1. By taking God to witness what we know is false. The insult thus offered.

25. Modes of violation continued. 2. Taking God to witness in trivial matters. Contempt thus shown. When and how an oath should be used. 3. Substituting the servants of God instead of himself when taking an oath.

26. The Anabaptists, who condemn all oaths, refuted. 1. By the authority of Christ, who cannot be opposed in anything to the Father. A passage perverted by the Anabaptists explained. The design of our Saviour in the passage. What meant by his there prohibiting oaths.

27. The lawfulness of oaths confirmed by Christ and the apostles. Some approve of public, but not of private oaths. The lawfulness of the latter proved both by reason and example. Instances from Scripture.

28. Exposition of the Fourth Commandment. Its end. Three purposes.

29. Explanation of the first purpose—viz. a shadowing forth of spiritual rest. This the primary object of the precept. God is therein set forth as our sanctifier; and hence we must abstain from work, that the work of God in us may not be hindered.

30. The number seven denoting perfection in Scripture, this commandment may, in that respect, denote the perpetuity of the Sabbath, and its completion at the last day.

31. Taking a simpler view of the commandment, the number is of no consequence, provided we maintain the doctrine of a perpetual rest from all our works, and at the same time, avoid a superstitious observance of days. The ceremonial part of the commandment abolished by the advent of Christ.

32. The second and third purposes of the Commandment explained. These twofold and perpetual. This confirmed. Of religious assemblies.

33. Of the observance of the Lord's day, in answer to those who complain that the Christian people are thus trained to Judaism. Objection.

34. Ground of this institution. There is no kind of superstitious necessity. The sum of the Commandment.

35. The Fifth Commandment (the first of the Second Table) expounded. Its end and substance. How far honour due to parents. To whom the term *father* applies.

36. It makes no difference whether those to whom this honour is required are worthy

1. I BELIEVE it will not be out of place here to introduce the Ten

Commandments of the Law, and give a brief exposition of them. In this way it will be made more clear, that the worship which God originally prescribed is still in force (a point to which I have already adverted) ; and then a second point will be confirmed—viz. that the Jews not only learned from the law wherein true piety consisted, but from feeling their inability to observe it were overawed by the fear of judgment, and so drawn, even against their will, towards the Mediator. In giving a summary of what constitutes the true knowledge of God,[1] we showed that we cannot form any just conception of the character of God, without feeling overawed by his majesty, and bound to do him service. In regard to the knowledge of ourselves, we showed that it principally consists in renouncing all idea of our own strength, and divesting ourselves of all confidence in our own righteousness, while, on the other hand, under a full consciousness of our wants, we learn true humility and self-abasement. Both of these the Lord accomplishes by his Law, first, when, in assertion of the right which he has to our obedience, he calls us to reverence his majesty, and prescribes the conduct by which this reverence is manifested ; and, secondly, when, by promulgating the rule of his justice (a rule, to the rectitude of which our nature, from being depraved and perverted, is continually opposed, and to the perfection of which our ability, from its infirmity and nervelessness for good, is far from being able to attain), he charges us both with impotence and unrighteousness. Moreover, the very things contained in the two tables are, in a manner, dictated to us by that internal law, which, as has been already said, is in a manner written and stamped on every heart. For conscience, instead of allowing us to stifle our perceptions, and sleep on without interruption, acts as an inward witness and monitor, reminds us of what we owe to God, points out the distinction between good and evil, and therbey convicts us of departure from duty. But man, being immured in the darkness of error, is scarcely able, by means of that natural law, to form any tolerable idea of the worship which is acceptable to God. At all events, he is very far from forming any correct knowledge of it. In addition to this, he is so swollen with arrogance and ambition, and so blinded with self-love, that he is unable to survey, and, as it were, descend into himself, that he may so learn to humble and abase himself, and confess his misery. Therefore, as a necessary remedy, both for our dulness and our contumacy, the Lord has given us his written Law, which, by its sure attestations, removes the obscurity of the law of nature, and also, by shaking off our lethargy, makes a more lively and permanent impression on our minds.

2. It is now easy to understand the doctrine of the law—viz. that God, as our Creator, is entitled to be regarded by us as a Father and Master, and should, accordingly, receive from us fear, love, reverence,

[1] This chapter is connected with Book I., chap. i. and ii., and with Book II., chap. i.—vi. See also Book II. chap. ii., sec. 22.

and glory; nay, that we are not our own, to follow whatever course passion dictates, but are bound to obey him implicitly, and to acquiesce entirely in his good pleasure. Again, the Law teaches, that justice and rectitude are a delight, injustice an abomination to him, and, therefore, as we would not with impious ingratitude revolt from our Maker, our whole life must be spent in the cultivation of righteousness. For if we manifest becoming reverence only when we prefer his will to our own, it follows, that the only legitimate service to him is the practice of justice, purity, and holiness. Nor can we plead as an excuse, that we want the power, and, like debtors, whose means are exhausted, are unable to pay. We cannot be permitted to measure the glory of God by our ability; whatever we may be, he ever remains like himself, the friend of righteousness, the enemy of unrighteousness, and whatever his demands from us may be, as he can only require what is right, we are necessarily under a natural obligation to obey. Our inability to do so is our own fault. If lust, in which sin has its dominion, so enthrals us, that we are not free to obey our Father, there is no ground for pleading necessity as a defence, since this evil necessity is within, and must be imputed to ourselves.

3. When, under the guidance of the Law, we have advanced thus far, we must, under the same guidance, proceed to descend into ourselves. In this way, we at length arrive at two results: First, contrasting our conduct with the righteousness of the Law, we see how very far it is from being in accordance with the will of God, and, therefore, how unworthy we are of holding our place among his creatures, far less of being accounted his sons; and, secondly, taking a survey of our powers, we see that they are not only unequal to fulfil the Law, but are altogether null. The necessary consequence must be, to produce distrust of our own ability, and also anxiety and trepidation of mind. Conscience cannot feel the burden of its guilt, without forthwith turning to the judgment of God, while the view of this judgment cannot fail to excite a dread of death. In like manner, the proofs of our utter powerlessness must instantly beget despair of our own strength. Both feelings are productive of humility and abasement, and hence the sinner, terrified at the prospect of eternal death (which he sees justly impending over him for his iniquities), turns to the mercy of God as the only haven of safety. Feeling his utter inability to pay what he owes to the Law, and thus despairing of himself, he bethinks him of applying and looking to some other quarter for help.

4. But the Lord does not count it enough to inspire a reverence for his justice. To imbue our hearts with love to himself, and, at the same time, with hatred to iniquity, he has added promises and threatenings. The eye of our mind being too dim to be attracted by the mere beauty of goodness, our most merciful Father has been pleased, in his great indulgence, to allure us to love and long after it by the hope of

reward. He accordingly declares that rewards for virtue are treasured up with him. That none who yield obedience to his commands will labour in vain. On the other hand, he proclaims not only that iniquity is hateful in his sight, but that it will not escape with impunity, because he will be the avenger of his insulted majesty. That he may encourage us in every way, he promises present blessings, as well as eternal felicity, to the obedience of those who shall have kept his commands, while he threatens transgressors with present suffering, as well as the punishment of eternal death. The promise, " Ye shall therefore keep my statutes, and my judgments ; which if a man do, he shall live in them " (Lev. xviii. 5), and corresponding to this the threatening, " The soul that sinneth, it shall die " (Ezek. xviii. 4, 20) ; doubtless point to a future life and death, both without end. But though in every passage where the favour or anger of God is mentioned, the former comprehends eternity of life and the latter eternal destruction, the Law, at the same time, enumerates a long catalogue of present blessings and curses (Lev. xxvi. 4 ; Deut. xxviii. 1). The threatenings attest the spotless purity of God, which cannot bear iniquity, while the promises attest at once his infinite love of righteousness (which he cannot leave unrewarded), and his wondrous kindness. Being bound to do him homage with all that we have, he is perfectly entitled to demand everything which he requires of us as a debt ; and as a debt, the payment is unworthy of reward. He therefore foregoes his right, when he holds forth reward for services which are not offered spontaneously, as if they were not due. The amount of these services, in themselves, has been partly described, and will appear more clearly in its own place. For the present, it is enough to remember that the promises of the Law are no mean commendation of righteousness, as they show how much God is pleased with the observance of them, while the threatenings denounced are intended to produce a greater abhorrence of unrighteousness, lest the sinner should indulge in the blandishments of vice, and forget the judgment which the divine Lawgiver has prepared for him.

5. The Lord, in delivering a perfect rule of righteousness, has reduced it in all its parts to his mere will, and in this way has shown that there is nothing more acceptable to him than obedience. There is the more necessity for attending to this, because the human mind, in its wantonness, is ever and anon inventing different modes of worship as a means of gaining his favour. This irreligious affectation of religion being innate in the human mind, has betrayed itself in every age, and is still doing so, men always longing to devise some method of procuring righteousness without any sanction from the Word of God.[1] Hence, in those observances which are generally regarded as good works, the precepts of the Law occupy a narrow space, almost

---

[1] See Calvin, De Vera Ecclesiæ Reformandæ Ratione.

the whole being usurped by this endless host of human inventions. But was not this the very license which Moses meant to curb, when, after the promulgation of the Law, he thus addressed the people: "Observe and hear all these words which I command thee, that it may go well with thee, and with thy children after thee for ever, when thou doest that which is good and right in the sight of the Lord thy God." "What thing soever I command you, observe to do it; thou shalt not add thereto, nor diminish from it" (Deut. xii. 28 —32). Previously, after asking "what nation is there so great, that hath statutes and judgments so righteous as all this law, which I set before you this day?" he had added, "Only take heed to thyself, and keep thy soul diligently, lest thou forget the things which thine eyes have seen, and lest they depart from thy heart all the days of thy life" (Deut. iv. 8, 9). God foreseeing that the Israelites would not rest, but after receiving the Law, would, unless sternly prohibited, give birth to new kinds of righteousness, declares that the Law comprehended a perfect righteousness. This ought to have been a most powerful restraint, and yet they desisted not from the presumptuous course so strongly prohibited. How do we act? We are certainly under the same obligation as they were; for there cannot be a doubt that the claim of absolute perfection which God made for his Law is perpetually in force. Not contented with it, however, we labour prodigiously in feigning and coining an endless variety of good works, one after another. The best cure for this vice would be a constant and deeply-seated conviction that the Law was given from heaven to teach us a perfect righteousness; that the only righteousness so taught is that which the divine will expressly enjoins; and that it is, therefore, vain to attempt, by new forms of worship, to gain the favour of God, whose true worship consists in obedience alone; or rather, that to go a-wandering after good works which are not prescribed by the Law of God, is an intolerable violation of true and divine righteousness. Most truly does Augustine say in one place, that the obedience which is rendered to God is the parent and guardian; in another, that it is the source of all the virtues.[1]

6. After we shall have expounded the Divine Law, what has been previously said of its office and use will be understood more easily, and with greater benefit. But before we proceed to the consideration of each separate commandment, it will be proper to take a general survey of the whole. At the outset, it was proved that in the Law human life is instructed not merely in outward decency, but in inward spiritual righteousness. Though none can deny this, yet very few duly attend to it, because they do not consider the Lawgiver, by whose character that of the Law must also be determined. Should a king issue an edict prohibiting murder, adultery, and theft, the

---

[1] See Augustin. De Civitate Dei, Lib. iv. c. 12, and Lib. xiii. c. 20, and Lib. xiv. c. 12. See also Lib. De Bono Conjugali, and Lib. Contra Adversarios Legis et Prophetarum, Lib. i. c. 14.

penalty, I admit, will not be incurred by the man who has only felt a longing in his mind after these vices, but has not actually committed them. The reason is, that a human lawgiver does not extend his care beyond outward order, and, therefore, his injunctions are not violated without outward acts. But God, whose eye nothing escapes, and who regards not the outward appearance so much as purity of heart, under the prohibition of murder, adultery, and theft, includes wrath, hatred, lust, covetousness, and all other things of a similar nature. Being a spiritual Lawgiver, he speaks to the soul not less than the body. The murder which the soul commits is wrath and hatred ; the theft, covetousness, and avarice ; and the adultery, lust. It may be alleged that human laws have respect to intentions and wishes, and not fortuitous events. I admit this, but then these must manifest themselves externally. They consider the *animus* with which the act was done, but do not scrutinise the secret thoughts. Accordingly, their demand is satisfied when the hand merely refrains from transgression. On the contrary, the law of heaven being enacted for our minds, the first thing necessary to a due observance of the Law is to put them under restraint. But the generality of men, even while they are most anxious to conceal their disregard of the Law, only frame their hands and feet and other parts of their body to some kind of observance, but in the meanwhile keep the heart utterly estranged from everything like obedience. They think it enough to have carefully concealed from man what they are doing in the sight of God. Hearing the commandments, " Thou shalt not kill," " Thou shalt not commit adultery," " Thou shalt not steal," they do not unsheathe their sword for slaughter, nor defile their bodies with harlots, nor put forth their hands to other men's goods. So far well ; but with their whole soul they breathe out slaughter, boil with lust, cast a greedy eye at their neighbour's property, and in wish devour it. Here the principal thing which the Law requires is wanting. Whence, then, this gross stupidity, but just because they lose sight of the Lawgiver, and form an idea of righteousness in accordance with their own disposition ? Against this Paul strenuously protests, when he declares that the " *law is spiritual* " (Rom. vii. 14); intimating that it not only demands the homage of the soul, and mind, and will, but requires an angelic purity, which, purified from all filthiness of the flesh, savours only of the Spirit.

7. In saying that this is the meaning of the Law, we are not introducing a new interpretation of our known ; we are following Christ, the best interpreter of the Law (Matth. v. 22, 28, 44). The Pharisees having instilled into the people the erroneous idea that the Law was fulfilled by every one who did not in external act do anything against the Law, he pronounces this a most dangerous delusion, and declares that an immodest look is adultery, and that hatred of a brother is murder. " Whosoever is angry with his brother without a cause, shall be in danger of the judgment ;" whosoever by

whispering or murmuring gives indication of being offended, "shall be in danger of the council;" whosoever by reproaches and evil-speaking gives way to open anger, "shall be in danger of hell-fire." Those who have not perceived this, have pretended that Christ was only a second Moses, the giver of an Evangelical, to supply the deficiency of the Mosaic Law. Hence the common axiom as to the perfection of the Evangelical Law, and its great superiority to that of Moses. This idea is in many ways most pernicious. For it will appear from Moses himself, when we come to give a summary of his precepts, that great indignity is thus done to the Divine Law. It certainly insinuates, that the holiness of the fathers under the Law was little else than hypocrisy, and leads us away from that one unvarying rule of righteousness. It is very easy, however, to confute this error, which proceeds on the supposition that Christ added to the Law, whereas he only restored it to its integrity by maintaining and purifying it when obscured by the falsehood, and defiled by the leaven of the Pharisees.

8. The next observation we would make is, that there is always more in the requirements and prohibitions of the Law than is expressed in words. This, however, must be understood so as not to convert it into a kind of Lesbian code;[1] and thus, by licentiously wresting the Scriptures, make them assume any meaning that we please. By taking this excessive liberty with Scripture, its authority is lowered with some, and all hope of understanding it abandoned by others. We must, therefore, if possible, discover some path which may conduct us with direct and firm step to the will of God. We must consider, I say, how far interpretation can be permitted to go beyond the literal meaning of the words, still making it apparent that no appendix of human glosses is added to the Divine Law, but that the pure and genuine meaning of the Lawgiver is faithfully exhibited. It is true that, in almost all the commandments, there are elliptical expressions, and that, therefore, any man would make himself ridiculous by attempting to restrict the spirit of the Law to the strict letter of the words. It is plain that a sober interpretation of the Law must go beyond these, but how far is doubtful, unless some rule be adopted. The best rule, in my opinion, would be, to be guided by the principle of the commandment—viz. to consider in the case of each what the purpose is for which it was given. For example, every commandment either requires or prohibits; and the nature of each is instantly discerned when we look to the principle of the commandment as its end. Thus, the end of the Fifth Commandment is to render honour to those on whom God bestows it. The sum of the commandment, therefore, is, that it is right in itself, and pleasing to God, to honour those on whom he has conferred some distinction; that to despise and rebel against such persons is offensive to Him. The principle of the First Commandment is, that God only is to be

[1] "Ne sit nobis Lesbiæ regulæ," omitted in the French.

worshipped. The sum of the commandment, therefore, is, that true piety, in other words, the worship of the Deity, is acceptable, and impiety is an abomination to him. So in each of the commandments we must first look to the matter of which it treats, and then consider its end, until we discover what it properly is that the Lawgiver declares to be pleasing or displeasing to him. Only, we must reason from the precept to its contrary in this way: If this pleases God, its opposite displeases; if that displeases, its opposite pleases: if God commands this, he forbids the opposite; if he forbids that, he commands the opposite.

9. What is now touched on somewhat obscurely will become perfectly clear as we proceed and get accustomed to the exposition of the Commandments. It is sufficient thus to have adverted to the subject; but perhaps our concluding statement will require to be briefly confirmed, as it might otherwise not be understood, or, though understood, might, perhaps, at the outset appear unsound. There is no need of proving, that when good is ordered, the evil which is opposed to it is forbidden. This every one admits. It will also be admitted, without much difficulty, that when evil is forbidden, its opposite is enjoined. Indeed, it is a common saying, that censure of vice is commendation of virtue. We, however, demand somewhat more than is commonly understood by these expressions. When the particular virtue opposed to a particular vice is spoken of, all that is usually meant is abstinence from that vice. We maintain that it goes farther, and means opposite duties and positive acts. Hence the commandment, "Thou shalt not kill," the generality of men will merely consider as an injunction to abstain from all injury, and all wish to inflict injury. I hold that it moreover means, that we are to aid our neighbour's life by every means in our power. And not to assert without giving my reason, I prove it thus: God forbids us to injure or hurt a brother, because he would have his life to be dear and precious to us; and, therefore, when he so forbids, he, at the same time, demands all the offices of charity which can contribute to his preservation.

10. But why did God thus deliver his commandments, as it were, by halves, using elliptical expressions with a larger meaning than that actually expressed? Other reasons are given, but the following seems to me the best:—As the flesh is always on the alert to extenuate the heinousness of sin (unless it is made, as it were, perceptible to the touch), and to cover it with specious pretexts, the Lord sets forth, by way of example, whatever is foulest and most iniquitous in each species of transgression, that the delivery of it might produce a shudder in the hearer, and impress his mind with a deeper abhorrence of sin. In forming an estimate of sins, we are often imposed upon by imagining that the more hidden the less heinous they are. This delusion the Lord dispels by accustoming us to refer the whole multitude of sins to particular, heads, which admirably show how great a degree of heinousness there is in each. For example, wrath

and hatred do not seem so very bad when they are designated by their own names; but when they are prohibited under the name of murder, we understand better how abominable they are in the sight of God, who puts them in the same class with that horrid crime. Influenced by his judgment, we accustom ourselves to judge more accurately of the heinousness of offences which previously seemed trivial.

11. It will now be proper to consider what is meant by the division of the divine Law into Two Tables. It will be judged by all men of sense from the formal manner in which these are sometimes mentioned, that it has not been done at random, or without reason. Indeed, the reason is so obvious as not to allow us to remain in doubt with regard to it. God thus divided his Law into two parts, containing a complete rule of righteousness, that he might assign the first place to the duties of religion which relate especially to His worship, and the second to the duties of charity which have respect to man. The first foundation of righteousness undoubtedly is the worship of God. When it is subverted, all the other parts of righteousness, like a building rent asunder, and in ruins, are racked and scattered. What kind of righteousness do you call it, not to commit theft and rapine, if you, in the mean time, with impious sacrilege, rob God of his glory? or not to defile your body with fornication, if you profane his holy name with blasphemy? or not to take away the life of man, if you strive to cut off and destroy the remembrance of God? It is vain, therefore, to talk of righteousness apart from religion. Such righteousness has no more beauty than the trunk of a body deprived of its head.[1] Nor is religion the principal part merely: it is the very soul by which the whole lives and breathes. Without the fear of God, men do not even observe justice and charity among themselves. We say, then, that the worship of God is the beginning and foundation of righteousness; and that wherever it is wanting, any degree of equity, or continence, or temperance, existing among men themselves, is empty and frivolous in the sight of God. We call it the source and soul of righteousness, inasmuch as men learn to live together temperately, and without injury, when they revere God as the judge of right and wrong. In the First Table, accordingly, he teaches us how to cultivate piety, and the proper duties of religion in which his worship consists; in the second, he shows how, in the fear of his name, we are to conduct ourselves towards our fellow-men. Hence, as related by the Evangelists (Matth. xxii. 37; Luke x. 27), our Saviour summed up the whole Law in two heads—viz. to love the Lord with all our heart, with all our soul, and with all our strength, and our neighbour as ourselves. You see how, of the two parts under which he comprehends the whole Law, he devotes the one to God, and assigns the other to mankind.

1 The French is, "Tout ainsi comme si quelcun vouloit faire une belle monstre d'un corps sans teste;" just as if one were to try to make a beautiful monster of a body without a head.

12. But although the whole Law is contained in two heads, yet, in order to remove every pretext for excuse, the Lord has been pleased to deliver more fully and explicitly in Ten Commandments, everything relating to his own honour, fear, and love, as well as everything relating to the charity which, for his sake, he enjoins us to have towards our fellow-men. Nor is it an unprofitable study to consider the division of the commandments, provided we remember that it is one of those matters in which every man should have full freedom of judgment, and on account of which, difference of opinion should not lead to contention. We are, indeed, under the necessity of making this observation, lest the division which we are to adopt should excite the surprise or derision of the reader, as novel or of recent invention.

There is no room for controversy as to the fact, that the Law is divided into ten heads, since this is repeatedly sanctioned by divine authority. The question, therefore, is not as to the number of the parts, but the method of dividing them. Those who adopt a division which gives three commandments to the First Table, and throws the remaining seven into the Second Table, expunge the commandment concerning images from the list, or at least conceal it under the first, though there cannot be a doubt that it was distinctly set down by the Lord as a separate commandment; whereas the tenth, which prohibits the coveting of what belongs to our neighbour, they absurdly break down into two. Moreover, it will soon appear, that this method of dividing was unknown in a purer age. Others count four commandments in the First Table as we do, but for the first set down the introductory promise, without adding the precept. But because I must hold, unless I am convinced by clear evidence to the contrary, that the " ten words " mentioned by Moses are Ten Commandments, and because I see that number arranged in most admirable order, I must, while I leave them to hold their own opinion, follow what appears to me better established—viz. that what they make to be the first commandment is of the nature of a preface to the whole Law, that thereafter follow four commandments in the First Table, and six in the Second, in the order in which they will here be reviewed. This division Origen adopts without discussion, as if it had been everywhere received in his day.[1] It is also adopted by Augustine, in his book addressed to Boniface, where, in enumerating the commandments, he follows this order, Let one God be religiously obeyed, let no idol be worshipped, let the name of God be not used in vain ; while previously he had made separate mention of the typical commandment of the Sabbath. Elsewhere, indeed, he expresses approbation of the first division, but on too slight grounds, because, by the

---

[1] Origen in Exod. cap. xx. Homil. 8; Augustin. contra duas Epist. Pelagii, Lib. iii. cap. 4; Quæst. in Vet. Test. Lib. ii. cap. 74; Epist. cxix. ad Januarium, cap. 11. The opinion of Josephus, and the last-mentioned opinion of Augustine, are briefly refuted by Calvin, in Exod. cap. xx., in expounding the Fifth Commandment.

number three (making the First Table consist of three commandments), the mystery of the Trinity would be better manifested. Even here, however, he does not disguise his opinion, that in other respects, our division is more to his mind. Besides these, we are supported by the author of an unfinished work on Matthew.[1] Josephus, no doubt with the general consent of his age, assigns five commandments to each table. This, while repugnant to reason, inasmuch as it confounds the distinction between piety and charity, is also refuted by the authority of our Saviour, who in Matthew places the command to honour parents in the list of those belonging to the Second Table (Matth. xix. 19). Let us now hear God speaking in his own words.

First Commandment.

I AM THE LORD THY GOD, WHICH BROUGHT THEE OUT OF THE LAND OF
　EGYPT, OUT OF THE HOUSE OF BONDAGE. THOU SHALT HAVE NO
　OTHER GODS BEFORE ME.

13. Whether you take the former sentence as a part of the commandment, or read it separately, is to me a matter of indifference, provided you grant that it is a kind of preface to the whole Law. In enacting laws, the first thing to be guarded against is their being forthwith abrogated by contempt. The Lord, therefore, takes care, in the first place, that this shall not happen to the Law about to be delivered, by introducing it with a triple sanction. He claims to himself power and authority to command, that he may impress the chosen people with the necessity of obedience ; he holds forth a promise of favour, as a means of alluring them to the study of holiness ; and he reminds them of his kindness, that he may convict them of ingratitude, if they fail to make a suitable return. By the name, Lord, are denoted power and lawful dominion. If all things are from him, and by him consist, they ought in justice to bear reference to him, as Paul says (Rom. xi. 36). This name, therefore, is in itself sufficient to bring us under the authority of the divine majesty: for it were monstrous for us to wish to withdraw from the dominion of him, out of whom we cannot even exist.

14. After showing that he has a right to command, and to be obeyed, he next, in order not to seem to drag men by mere necessity, but to allure them, graciously declares, that he is the God of the Church. For the mode of expression implies, that there is a mutual relation included in the promise, " I will be their God, and they shall be my people" (Jer. xxxi. 33). Hence Christ infers the immortality

---

1 The French is, "Nous avous aussi un autre ancien Pere qui accorde a nostre opinion, celui qui a ecrit les Commentaires imparfaits sur Sainct Matthieu." We have also another ancient Father who agrees with us in our opinion, he who wrote the unfinished Commentaries on St Matthew.

of Abraham, Isaac, and Jacob, from the fact that God had declared himself to be their God (Matth. xxii. 52). It is, therefore, the same as if he had said, I have chosen you to myself, as a people to whom I shall not only do good in the present life, but also bestow felicity in the life to come. The end contemplated in this is adverted to in the Law, in various passages. For when the Lord condescends in mercy to honour us so far as to admit us to partnership with his chosen people, he chooses us, as Moses says, "to be a holy people," "a peculiar people unto himself," to "keep all his commandments" (Deut. vii. 6; xiv. 2; xxvi. 18). Hence the exhortation, "Ye shall be holy; for I the Lord your God am holy" (Lev. xix. 2). These two considerations form the ground of the remonstrance, "A son honoureth his father, and a servant his master; if then I be a father, where is mine honour? and if I be a master, where is my fear? saith the Lord of hosts" (Mal. i. 6).

15. Next follows a commemoration of his kindness, which ought to produce upon us an impression strong in proportion to the detestation in which ingratitude is held even among men. It is true, indeed, he was reminding Israel of a deliverance then recent, but one which, on account of its wondrous magnitude, was to be for ever memorable to the remotest posterity. Moreover, it is most appropriate to the matter in hand.[1] For the Lord intimates that they were delivered from miserable bondage, that they might learn to yield prompt submission and obedience to him as the author of their freedom. In like manner, to keep us to his true worship, he often describes himself by certain epithets which distinguish his sacred Deity from all idols and fictitious gods. For, as I formerly observed, such is our proneness to vanity and presumption, that as soon as God is named, our minds, unable to guard against error, immediately fly off to some empty delusion. In applying a remedy to this disease, God distinguishes his divinity by certain titles, and thus confines us, as it were, within distinct boundaries, that we may not wander hither and thither, and feign some new deity for ourselves, abandoning the living God, and setting up an idol. For this reason, whenever the Prophets would bring him properly before us, they invest, and, as it were, surround him with those characters under which he had manifested himself to the people of Israel. When he is called the God of Abraham, or the God of Israel, when he is stationed in the temple of Jerusalem, between the Cherubim, these, and similar modes of expression,[2] do not confine him to one place or one people, but are used merely for the purpose of fixing our thoughts on that God who so manifested himself in the covenant which he made with Israel, as to make it unlawful on any account to deviate from the strict view there given of his character. Let it be understood, then, that mention is made of deliverance, in

---

[1] "Præsenti causæ."—The French is, "du temps que la loi devoit estre publiée;" to the time when the Law was to be published.

[2] Exod. iii. 6; Amos i. 2; Hab. ii. 20; Psalm lxxx. 2; xcix. 1; Isaiah xxxvii. 16.

order to make the Jews submit with greater readiness to that God who justly claims them as his own.   We again, instead of supposing that the matter has no reference to us, should reflect that the bondage of Israel in Egypt was a type of that spiritual bondage, in the fetters of which we are all bound, until the heavenly avenger delivers us by the power of his own arm, and transports us into his free kingdom. Therefore, as in old times, when he would gather together the scattered Israelites to the worship of his name, he rescued them from the intolerable tyranny of Pharaoh, so all who profess him now are delivered from the fatal tyranny of the devil, of which that of Egypt was only a type.   There is no man, therefore, whose mind ought not to be aroused to give heed to the Law, which, as he is told, proceeded from the supreme King, from him who, as he gave all their being, justly destines and directs them to himself as their proper end.   There is no man, I say, who should not hasten to embrace the Lawgiver, whose commands, he knows, he has been specially appointed to obey, from whose kindness he anticipates an abundance of all good, and even a blessed immortality, and to whose wondrous power and mercy he is indebted for deliverance from the jaws of death.[1]

16. The authority of the Law being founded and established, God delivers his First Commandment—

THOU SHALT HAVE NO OTHER GODS BEFORE ME.

The purport of this commandment is, that the Lord will have himself alone to be exalted in his people, and claims the entire possession of them as his own.   That it may be so, he orders us to abstain from ungodliness and superstition of every kind, by which the glory of his divinity is diminished or obscured ; and, for the same reason, he requires us to worship and adore him with truly pious zeal.   The simple terms used obviously amount to this.   For seeing we cannot have God without embracing everything which belongs to him, the prohibition against having strange gods means, that nothing which belongs to him is to be transferred to any other.   The duties which we owe to God are innumerable, but they seem to admit of being not improperly reduced to four heads: Adoration, with its accessory spiritual submission of conscience, Trust, Invocation, Thanksgiving.[2] By Adoration, I mean the veneration and worship which we render to him when we do homage to his majesty ; and hence I make part of it to consist in bringing our consciences into subjection to his Law.[3] Trust, is secure resting in him under a recognition of his perfections, when, ascribing to him all power, wisdom, justice, goodness, and

---

1 " E faucibus mortis."—French, " du gouffre d'enfer ; " from the gulf of hell.

2 Calvin. in Catechismo ; De Necessitate Reformandæ Ecclesiæ ; Vera Reformandæ Ecclesiæ Ratio.

3 The French adds, " Car c'est un hommage spirituel qui se rend a lui comme souverain Roy, et ayant toute superiorité sur nos ames."   For this is a spiritual homage which is rendered to him as sovereign King, having full supremacy over our souls.

truth, we consider ourselves happy in having been brought into intercourse with him. Invocation may be defined the betaking of ourselves to his promised aid as the only resource in every case of need. Thanksgiving is the gratitude which ascribes to him the praise of all our blessings. As the Lord does not allow these to be derived from any other quarter, so he demands that they shall be referred entirely to himself. It is not enough to refrain from other gods. We must, at the same time, devote ourselves wholly to him, not acting like certain impious despisers, who regard it as the shortest method, to hold all religious observance in derision. But here precedence must be given to true religion, which will direct our minds to the living God. When duly imbued with the knowledge of him, the whole aim of our lives will be to revere, fear, and worship his majesty, to enjoy a share in his blessings, to have recourse to him in every difficulty, to acknowledge, laud, and celebrate the magnificence of his works, to make him, as it were, the sole aim of all our actions. Next, we must beware of superstition, by which our minds are turned aside from the true God, and carried to and fro after a multiplicity of gods. Therefore, if we are contented with one God, let us call to mind what was formerly observed, that all fictitious gods are to be driven far away, and that the worship which he claims for himself is not to be mutilated. Not a particle of his glory is to be withheld: everything belonging to him must be reserved to him entire. The words, "before me," go to increase the indignity, God being provoked to jealousy whenever we substitute our fictions in his stead; just as an unfaithful wife stings her husband's heart more deeply when her adultery is committed openly before his eyes. Therefore, God having by his present power and grace declared that he had respect to the people whom he had chosen, now, in order to deter them from the wickedness of revolt, warns them that they cannot adopt strange gods without his being witness and spectator of the sacrilege. To the audacity of so doing is added the very great impiety of supposing that they can mock the eye of God with their evasions. Far from this, the Lord proclaims that everything which we design, plan, or execute, lies open to his sight. Our conscience must, therefore, keep aloof from the most distant thought of revolt, if we would have our worship approved by the Lord. The glory of his godhead must be maintained entire and incorrupt, not merely by external profession, but as under his eye, which penetrates the inmost recesses of his heart.

Second Commandment.

THOU SHALT NOT MAKE UNTO THEE ANY GRAVEN IMAGE, OR ANY
LIKENESS OF ANYTHING THAT IS IN HEAVEN ABOVE, OR THAT IS
IN THE EARTH BENEATH, OR THAT IS IN THE WATER UNDER THE
EARTH: THOU SHALT NOT BOW DOWN THYSELF TO THEM, NOR
SERVE THEM.

17. As in the First Commandment the Lord declares that he is one,
and that besides him no gods must be either worshipped or imagined,
so he here more plainly declares what his nature is, and what the kind
of worship with which he is to be honoured, in order that we may not
presume to form any carnal idea of him. The purport of the commandment, therefore, is, that he will not have his legitimate worship
profaned by superstitious rites. Wherefore, in general, he calls us
entirely away from the carnal frivolous observances which our stupid
minds are wont to devise after forming some gross idea of the divine
nature, while, at the same time, he instructs us in the worship which
is legitimate, namely, spiritual worship of his own appointment. The
grossest vice here prohibited is external idolatry. This commandment consists of two parts. The former curbs the licentious daring
which would subject the incomprehensible God to our senses, or represent him under any visible shape. The latter forbids the worship
of images, on any religious ground. There is, moreover, a brief
enumeration of all the forms by which the Deity was usually represented by heathen and superstitious nations. By "anything which
is in heaven above," is meant the sun, the moon, and the stars, perhaps also birds, as in Deuteronomy, where the meaning is explained,
there is mention of birds as well as stars (Deut. iv. 15). I would
not have made this observation, had I not seen that some absurdly
apply it to the angels. The other particulars I pass, as requiring no
explanation. We have already shown clearly enough (Book I. chap.
xi. xii.) that every visible shape of Deity which man devises is diametrically opposed to the divine nature; and, therefore, that the
moment idols appear, true religion is corrupted and adulterated.

18. The threatening subjoined ought to have no little effect in
shaking off our lethargy. It is in the following terms:—

I THE LORD THY GOD AM A JEALOUS[1] GOD, VISITING THE INIQUITY
OF THE FATHERS UPON THE CHILDREN UNTO THE THIRD AND
FOURTH GENERATION OF THEM THAT HATE ME; AND SHOWING
MERCY UNTO THOUSANDS OF THEM THAT LOVE ME, AND KEEP MY
COMMANDMENTS.

The meaning here is the same as if he had said, that our duty is

---

[1] Or "Strong," this name being derived from a word denoting strength.

to cleave to him alone. To induce us to this, he proclaims his authority, which he will not permit to be impaired or despised with impunity. It is true, the word used is *El*, which means God; but as it is derived from a word meaning *strength*, I have had no hesitation, in order to express the sense more fully, so to render it as inserted on the margin. Secondly, he calls himself *jealous*, because he cannot bear a partner. Thirdly, he declares that he will vindicate his majesty and glory, if any transfer it either to the creatures or to graven images; and that not by a simple punishment of brief duration, but one extending to the third and fourth generation of such as imitate the impiety of their progenitors. In like manner, he declares his constant mercy and kindness to the remote posterity of those who love him, and keep his Law. The Lord very frequently addresses us in the character of a husband;[1] the union by which he connects us with himself, when he receives us into the bosom of the Church, having some resemblance to that of holy wedlock, because founded on mutual faith. As he performs all the offices of a true and faithful husband, so he stipulates for love and conjugal chastity from us; that is, that we do not prostitute our souls to Satan, to be defiled with foul carnal lusts. Hence, when he rebukes the Jews for their apostacy, he complains that they have cast off chastity, and polluted themselves with adultery. Therefore, as the purer and chaster the husband is, the more grievously he is offended when he sees his wife inclining to a rival; so the Lord, who hath betrothed us to himself in truth, declares that he burns with the hottest jealousy whenever, neglecting the purity of his holy marriage, we defile ourselves with abominable lusts, and especially when the worship of his Deity, which ought to have been most carefully kept unimpaired, is transferred to another, or adulterated with some superstition; since, in this way, we not only violate our plighted troth, but defile the nuptial couch, by giving access to adulterers.

19. In the threatening, we must attend to what is meant when God declares that he will visit the iniquity of the fathers upon the children unto the third and fourth generation. It seems inconsistent with the equity of the divine procedure to punish the innocent for another's fault; and the Lord himself declares, that "the son shall not bear the iniquity of the father" (Ezek. xviii. 20). But still we meet more than once with a declaration as to the postponing of the punishment of the sins of fathers to future generations. Thus Moses repeatedly addresses the Lord as "visiting the iniquity of the fathers upon the children unto the third and fourth generation" (Num. xiv. 18). In like manner, Jeremiah, "Thou showest loving-kindness unto thousands, and recompensest the iniquity of the fathers into the bosom of their children after them" (Jer. xxxii. 18). Some feeling sadly perplexed how to solve this difficulty, think it is to be

1 2 Cor. xi. 2; Eph. v. 30; Jer. lxii. 5; Hos. ii. 9; Jer. iii. 1, 2; Hos. ii. 2.

understood of temporal punishments only, which it is said sons may properly bear for the sins of their parents, because they are often inflicted for their own safety.   This is indeed true ; for Isaiah declared to Hezekiah, that his children should be stript of the kingdom, and carried away into captivity, for a sin which he had committed (Isa. xxxix. 7) ; and the households of Pharaoh and Abimelech were made to suffer for an injury done to Abraham (Gen. xii. 17 ; xx. 3—18).   But the attempt to solve the question in this way is an evasion rather than a true interpretation.   For the punishment denounced here and in similar passages is too great to be confined within the limits of the present life.   We must therefore understand it to mean, that a curse from the Lord righteously falls not only on the head of the guilty individual, but also on all his lineage.   When it has fallen, what can be anticipated but that the father, being deprived of the Spirit of God, will live most flagitiously ; that the son, being in like manner forsaken of the Lord, because of his father's iniquity, will follow the same road to destruction ; and be followed in his turn by succeeding generations, forming a seed of evil-doers ?

20. First, let us examine whether such punishment is inconsistent with the divine justice.   If human nature is universally condemned, those on whom the Lord does not bestow the communication of his grace must be doomed to destruction ; nevertheless, they perish by their own iniquity, not by unjust hatred on the part of God.   There is no room to expostulate, and ask why the grace of God does not forward their salvation as it does that of others.   Therefore, when God punishes the wicked and flagitious for their crimes, by depriving their families of his grace for many generations, who will dare to bring a charge against him for this most righteous vengeance ?   But it will be said, the Lord, on the contrary, declares, that the son shall not suffer for the father's sin (Ezek. xviii. 20).   Observe the scope of that passage.   The Israelites, after being subjected to a long period of uninterrupted calamities, had begun to say, as a proverb, that their fathers had eaten the sour grape, and thus set the children's teeth on edge ; meaning that they, though in themselves righteous and innocent, were paying the penalty of sins committed by their parents, and this more from the implacable anger than the duly tempered severity of God.   The prophet declares it was not so : that they were punished for their own wickedness ; that it was not in accordance with the justice of God that a righteous son should suffer for the iniquity of a wicked father ; and that nothing of the kind was exemplified in what they suffered.   For, if the visitation of which we now speak is accomplished when God withdraws from the children of the wicked the light of his truth and the other helps to salvation, the only way in which they are accursed for their fathers' wickedness is in being blinded and abandoned by God, and so left to walk in their parents' steps.   The misery which they suffer in time, and the destruction to which they are finally doomed, are thus punishments

inflicted by divine justice, not for the sins of others, but for their own iniquity.

21. On the other hand, there is a promise of mercy to thousands—a promise which is frequently mentioned in Scripture, and forms an article in the solemn covenant made with the Church—I will be "a God unto thee, and to thy seed after thee" (Gen. xvii. 7). With reference to this, Solomon says, "The just man walketh in his integrity: his children are blessed after him" (Prov. xx. 7); not only in consequence of a religious education (though this certainly is by no means unimportant), but in consequence of the blessing promised in the covenant—viz. that the divine favour will dwell for ever in the families of the righteous. Herein is excellent consolation to believers, and great ground of terror to the wicked; for if, after death, the mere remembrance of righteousness and iniquity have such an influence on the divine procedure, that his blessing rests on the posterity of the righteous, and his curse on the posterity of the wicked, much more must it rest on the heads of the individuals themselves. Notwithstanding of this, however, the offspring of the wicked sometimes amends, while that of believers degenerates; because the Almighty has not here laid down an inflexible rule which might derogate from his free election. For the consolation of the righteous, and the dismay of the sinner, it is enough that the threatening itself is not vain or nugatory, although it does not always take effect. For, as the temporal punishments inflicted on a few of the wicked are proofs of the divine wrath against sin, and of the future judgment that will ultimately overtake all sinners, though many escape with impunity even to the end of their lives, so, when the Lord gives one example of blessing a son for his father's sake, by visiting him in mercy and kindness, it is a proof of constant and unfailing favour to his worshippers. On the other hand, when, in any single instance, he visits the iniquity of the father on the son, he gives intimation of the judgment which awaits all the reprobate for their own iniquities. The certainty of this is the principal thing here taught. Moreover, the Lord, as it were by the way, commends the riches of his mercy by extending it to thousands, while he limits his vengeance to four generations.

Third Commandment.

THOU SHALT NOT TAKE THE NAME OF THE LORD THY GOD IN VAIN.

22. The purport of this Commandment is, that the majesty of the name of God is to be held sacred. In sum, therefore, it means, that we must not profane it by using it irreverently or contemptuously. This prohibition implies a corresponding precept—viz. that it be our

study and care to treat his name with religious veneration. Wherefore it becomes us to regulate our minds and our tongues, so as never to think or speak of God and his mysteries without reverence and great soberness, and never, in estimating his works, to have any feeling towards him but one of deep veneration. We must, I say, steadily observe the three following things :—*First*, Whatever our mind conceives of him, whatever our tongue utters, must bespeak his excellence, and correspond to the sublimity of his sacred name ; in short, must be fitted to extol its greatness. *Secondly*, We must not rashly and preposterously pervert his sacred word and adorable mysteries to purposes of ambition, or avarice, or amusement, but, according as they bear the impress of his dignity, must always maintain them in due honour and esteem. *Lastly*, We must not detract from or throw obloquy upon his works, as miserable men are wont insultingly to do, but must laud every action which we attribute to him as wise, and just, and good. This is to sanctify the name of God. When we act otherwise, his name is profaned with vain and wicked abuse, because it is applied to a purpose foreign to that to which it is consecrated. Were there nothing worse, in being deprived of its dignity it is gradually brought into contempt. But if there is so much evil in the rash and unseasonable employment of the divine name, there is still more evil in its being employed for nefarious purposes, as is done by those who use it in necromancy, cursing, illicit exorcisms, and other impious incantations. But the Commandment refers especially to the case of oaths, in which a perverse employment of the divine name is particularly detestable ; and this it does the more effectually to deter us from every species of profanation. That the thing here commanded relates to the worship of God, and the reverence due to his name, and not to the equity which men are to cultivate towards each other, is apparent from this, that afterwards, in the Second Table, there is a condemnation of the perjury and false testimony by which human society is injured, and that the repetition would be superfluous, if, in this Commandment, the duty of charity were handled. Moreover, this is necessary even for distinction, because, as was observed, God has, for good reason, divided his Law into two tables. The inference then is, that God here vindicates his own right, and defends his sacred name, but does not teach the duties which men owe to men.

23. In the first place, we must consider what an oath is. An oath, then, is calling God to witness that what we say is true. Execrations being manifestly insulting to God, are unworthy of being classed among oaths. That an oath, when duly taken, is a species of divine worship, appears from many passages of Scripture, as when Isaiah prophesies of the admission of the Assyrians and Egyptians to a participation in the covenant, he says, " In that day shall five cities in the land of Egypt speak the language of Canaan, and swear to the Lord of hosts " (Isaiah xix. 18). Swearing by the name of

the Lord here means, that they will make a profession of religion. In like manner, speaking of the extension of the Redeemer's kingdom, it is said, "He who blesseth himself in the earth shall bless himself in the God of truth: and he that sweareth in the earth shall swear by the God of truth" (Isaiah lxv. 16). In Jeremiah it is said, "If they will diligently learn the ways of my people, to swear by my name, The Lord liveth; as they taught my people to swear by Baal; then shall they be built in the midst of my people" (Jer. xii. 16). By appealing to the name of the Lord, and calling him to witness, we are justly said to declare our own religious veneration of him. For we thus acknowledge that he is eternal and unchangeable truth, inasmuch as we not only call upon him, in preference to others, as a fit witness to the truth, but as its only assertor, able to bring hidden things to light, a discerner of the hearts. When human testimony fails, we appeal to God as witness, especially when the matter to be proved lies hid in the conscience. For which reason, the Lord is grievously offended with those who swear by strange gods, and construes such swearing as a proof of open revolt, "Thy children have forsaken me, and sworn by them that are no gods" (Jer. v. 7). The heinousness of the offence is declared by the punishment denounced against it, "I will cut off them that swear by the Lord, and that swear by Malcham" (Zeph. i. 4, 5).

24. Understanding that the Lord would have our oaths to be a species of divine worship, we must be the more careful that they do not, instead of worship, contain insult, or contempt, and vilification. It is no slight insult to swear by him and do it falsely; hence in the Law this is termed profanation (Lev. xix. 12). For if God is robbed of his truth, what is it that remains? Without truth he could not be God. But assuredly he is robbed of his truth, when he is made the approver and attester of what is false. Hence, when Joshua is endeavouring to make Achan confess the truth, he says, "My son, give, I pray thee, glory to the Lord God of Israel" (Joshua vii. 19); intimating, that grievous dishonour is done to God when men swear by him falsely. And no wonder; for, as far as in them lies, his sacred name is in a manner branded with falsehood. That this mode of expression was common among the Jews whenever any one was called upon to take an oath, is evident from a similar obtestation used by the Pharisees, as given in John (John ix. 24). Scripture reminds us of the caution which we ought to use by employing such expressions as the following:—"As the Lord liveth;" "God do so and more also;" "I call God for a record upon my soul."[1] Such expressions intimate, that we cannot call God to witness our statement, without imprecating his vengeance for perjury if it is false.

25. The name of God is vulgarised and vilified when used in oaths, which, though true, are superfluous. This, too, is to take his name

---

[1] 1 Sam. xiv. 44; 2 Kings vi. 31; 2 Cor. i. 23.

in vain. Wherefore, it is not sufficient to abstain from perjury, unless we, at the same time, remember that an oath is not appointed or allowed for passion or pleasure, but for necessity; and that, therefore, a licentious use is made of it by him who uses it on any other than necessary occasions. Moreover, no case of necessity can be pretended, unless where some purpose of religion or charity is to be served. In this matter, great sin is committed in the present day— sin the more intolerable in this, that its frequency has made it cease to be regarded as a fault, though it certainly is not accounted trivial before the judgment-seat of God. The name of God is everywhere profaned by introducing it indiscriminately in frivolous discourse; and the evil is disregarded, because it has been long and audaciously persisted in with impunity. The commandment of the Lord, however, stands; the penalty also stands, and will one day receive effect. Special vengeance will be executed on those who have taken the name of God in vain. Another form of violation is exhibited, when, with manifest impiety, we, in our oaths, substitute the holy servants of God for God himself,[1] thus conferring upon them the glory of his Godhead. It is not without cause the Lord has, by a special commandment, required us to swear by his name, and, by a special prohibition, forbidden us to swear by other gods.[2] The Apostle gives a clear attestation to the same effect, when he says, that "men verily swear by the greater;" but that, "when God made promise to Abraham, because he could swear by no greater, he sware by himself" (Heb. vi. 16, 13).

26. The Anabaptists, not content with this moderate use of oaths, condemn all, without exception, on the ground of our Saviour's general prohibition, "I say unto you, Swear not at all:" "Let your speech be Yea, yea; Nay, nay: for whatsoever is more than these cometh of evil" (Matth. v. 34; James v. 12). In this way, they inconsiderately make a stumbling-stone of Christ, setting him in opposition to the Father, as if he had descended into the world to annul his decrees. In the Law, the Almighty not only permits an oath as a thing that is lawful (this were amply sufficient), but, in a case of necessity, actually commands it (Exod. xxii. 11). Christ again declares, that he and his Father are one; that he only delivers what was commanded of his Father; that his doctrine is not his own, but his that sent him (John x. 18, 30; vii. 16). What then? Will they make God contradict himself, by approving and commanding at one time, what he afterwards prohibits and condemns? But as there is some difficulty in what our Saviour says on the subject of swearing, it may be proper to consider it a little. Here, however, we shall never arrive at the true meaning, unless we attend to the design of Christ, and the subject of which he is treating. His pur-

---

[1] The French adds, "jurans par S. Jaques ou S. Antoine;"—swearing by St James or St Anthony.

[2] Exod. xxiii. 13; Deut. vi. 13; x. 20; Heb. vi. 18.

pose was, neither to relax nor to curtail the Law, but to restore the true and genuine meaning, which had been greatly corrupted by the false glosses of the Scribes and Pharisees. If we attend to this, we shall not suppose that Christ condemned all oaths, but those only which transgressed the rule of the Law. It is evident, from the oaths themselves, that the people were accustomed to think it enough if they avoided perjury, whereas the Law prohibits not perjury merely, but also vain and superfluous oaths. Therefore our Lord, who is the best interpreter of the Law, reminds them that there is a sin not only in perjury, but in swearing. How in swearing? Namely, by swearing vainly. Those oaths, however, which are authorised by the Law, he leaves safe and free. Those who condemn oaths think their argument invincible when they fasten on the expression, *not at all.* The expression applies not to the word *swear*, but to the subjoined forms of oaths. For part of the error consisted in their supposing, that when they swore by the heaven and the earth, they did not touch the name of God. The Lord, therefore, after cutting off the principal source of prevarication, deprives them of all subterfuges, warning them against supposing that they escape guilt by suppressing the name of God, and appealing to heaven and earth. For it ought here to be observed in passing, that although the name of God is not expressed, yet men swear by him in using indirect forms, as when they swear by the light of life, by the bread they eat, by their baptism, or any other pledges of the divine liberality towards them. Some erroneously suppose that our Saviour in that passage, rebukes superstition, by forbidding men to swear by heaven and earth, and Jerusalem. He rather refutes the sophistical subtlety of those who thought it nothing vainly to utter indirect oaths, imagining that they thus spared the holy name of God, whereas that name is inscribed on each of his mercies. The case is different, when any mortal, living or dead, or an angel, is substituted in the place of God, as in the vile form devised by flattery in heathen nations, *By the life or genius of the king;* for, in this case, the false apotheosis obscures and impairs the glory of the one God. But when nothing else is intended than to confirm what is said by an appeal to the holy name of God, although it is done indirectly, yet his majesty is insulted by all frivolous oaths. Christ strips this abuse of every vain pretext when he says, Swear not at all. To the same effect is the passage in which James uses the words of our Saviour above quoted (James v. 12). For this rash swearing has always prevailed in the world, notwithstanding that it is a profanation of the name of God. If you refer the words, *not at all*, to the act itself, as if every oath, without exception, were unlawful, what will be the use of the explanation which immediately follows—Neither by heaven, neither by the earth, &c.? These words make it clear, that the object in view was to meet the cavils by which the Jews thought they could extenuate their fault.

27. Every person of sound judgment must now see that in that passage our Lord merely condemned those oaths which were forbidden by the Law. For he who in his life exhibited a model of the perfection which he taught, did not object to oaths whenever the occasion required them; and the disciples, who doubtless in all things obeyed their Master, followed the same rule. Who will dare to say that Paul would have sworn (Rom. i. 9; 2 Cor. i. 23) if an oath had been altogether forbidden? But when the occasion calls for it, he adjures without any scruple, and sometimes even imprecates. The question, however, is not yet disposed of. For some think that the only oaths exempted from the prohibition are public oaths, such as those which are administered to us by the magistrate, or independent states employ in ratifying treaties, or the people take when they swear allegiance to their sovereign, or the soldier in the case of the military oath, and others of a similar description. To this class they refer (and justly) those protestations in the writings of Paul, which assert the dignity of the Gospel; since the apostles, in discharging their office, were not private individuals, but the public servants of God. I certainly deny not that such oaths are the safest, because they are most strongly supported by passages of Scripture. The magistrate is enjoined, in a doubtful matter, to put the witness upon oath; and he in his turn to answer upon oath; and an apostle says, that in this way there is an end of all strife (Heb. vi. 16). In this commandment, both parties are fully approved. Nay, we may observe, that among the ancient heathens a public and solemn oath was held in great reverence, while those common oaths which were indiscriminately used were in little or no estimation, as if they thought that, in regard to them, the Deity did not interpose. Private oaths used soberly, sacredly, and reverently, on necessary occasions, it were perilous to condemn, supported as they are by reason and example. For if private individuals are permitted, in a grave and serious matter, to appeal to God as a judge, much more may they appeal to him as a witness. Your brother charges you with perfidy. You, as bound by the duties of charity, labour to clear yourself from the charge. He will on no account be satisfied. If, through his obstinate malice, your good name is brought into jeopardy, you can appeal, without offence, to the judgment of God, that he may in time manifest your innocence. If the terms are weighed, it will be found that it is a less matter to call upon him to be witness; and I therefore see not how it can be called unlawful to do so. And there is no want of examples. If it is pretended that the oath which Abraham and Isaac made with Abimelech was of a public nature, that by which Jacob and Laban bound themselves in mutual league was private. Boaz, though a private man, confirmed his promise of marriage to Ruth in the same way. Obadiah, too, a just man, and one that feared God, though a private individual, in seeking to persuade Elijah, asseverates with an oath.[1] I hold, therefore, that there is no better rule than so to regu-

[1] Gen. xxi. 24; xxvi. 31; xxxi. 53; Ruth iii. 13; 1 Kings xviii. 10.

late our oaths that they shall neither be rash, frivolous, promiscuous, nor passionate, but be made to serve a just necessity ; in other words, to vindicate the glory of God, or promote the edification of a brother. This is the end of the Commandment.

Fourth Commandment.

REMEMBER THE SABBATH DAY TO KEEP IT HOLY. SIX DAYS SHALT THOU LABOUR AND DO ALL THY WORK : BUT THE SEVENTH DAY IS THE SABBATH OF THE LORD THY GOD. IN IT THOU SHALT NOT DO ANY WORK, &C.

28. The purport of the commandment is, that being dead to our own affections and works, we meditate on the kingdom of God, and in order to such meditation, have recourse to the means which he has appointed. But as this commandment stands in peculiar circumstances apart from the others, the mode of exposition must be somewhat different. Early Christian writers are wont to call it typical, as containing the external observance of a day which was abolished with the other types on the advent of Christ. This is indeed true ; but it leaves the half of the matter untouched. Wherefore, we must look deeper for our exposition, and attend to three cases in which it appears to me that the observance of this commandment consists. First, under the rest of the seventh day, the divine Lawgiver meant to furnish the people of Israel with a type of the spiritual rest by which believers were to cease from their own works, and allow God to work in them. Secondly, he meant that there should be a stated day on which they should assemble to hear the Law, and perform religious rites, or which, at least, they should specially employ in meditating on his works, and be thereby trained to piety. Thirdly, he meant that servants, and those who lived under the authority of others, should be indulged with a day of rest, and thus have some intermission from labour.

29. We are taught in many passages[1] that this adumbration of spiritual rest held a primary place in the Sabbath. Indeed, there is no commandment the observance of which the Almighty more strictly enforces. When he would intimate by the prophets that religion was entirely subverted, he complains that his sabbaths were polluted, violated, not kept, not hallowed ; as if, after it was neglected, there remained nothing in which he could be honoured. The observance of it he eulogises in the highest terms, and hence, among other divine privileges, the faithful set an extraordinary value on the revelation of the Sabbath. In Nehemiah, the Levites, in the public assembly,

1 Num. xiii. 22; Ezek. xx. 12; xxii. 8; xxiii. 38; Jer. xvii. 21, 22, 27; Isaiah lvi. 2; Neh. ix. 14.

thus speak: "Thou madest known unto them thy holy sabbath, and commandedst them precepts, statutes, and laws, by the hand of Moses thy servant." You see the singular honour which it holds among all the precepts of the Law. All this tends to celebrate the dignity of the mystery, which is most admirably expressed by Moses and Ezekiel. Thus in Exodus: "Verily my sabbaths shall ye keep: for it is a sign between me and you throughout your generations; that ye may know that I am the Lord that doth sanctify you. Ye shall keep my sabbath therefore; for it is holy unto you: every one that defileth it shall surely be put to death: for whosoever doeth any work therein, that soul shall be cut off from among his people. Six days may work be done; but in the seventh is the sabbath of rest, holy to the Lord: whosoever doeth any work in the sabbath day, he shall surely be put to death. Wherefore the children of Israel shall keep the sabbath, to observe the sabbath throughout their generations, for a perpetual covenant. It is a sign between me and the children of Israel for ever" (Exodus xxxi. 13—17). Ezekiel is still more full, but the sum of what he says amounts to this: that the sabbath is a sign by which Israel might know that God is their sanctifier. If our sanctification consists in the mortification of our own will, the analogy between the external sign and the thing signified is most appropriate. We must rest entirely, in order that God may work in us; we must resign our own will, yield up our heart, and abandon all the lusts of the flesh. In short, we must desist from all the acts of our own mind, that God working in us, we may rest in him, as the Apostle also teaches (Heb. iii. 13; iv. 3, 9).

30. This complete cessation was represented to the Jews by the observance of one day in seven, which, that it might be more religiously attended to, the Lord recommended by his own example. For it is no small incitement to the zeal of man to know that he is engaged in imitating his Creator. Should any one expect some secret meaning in the number seven, this being in Scripture the number for perfection, it may have been selected, not without cause, to denote perpetuity. In accordance with this, Moses concludes his description of the succession of day and night on the same day on which he relates that the Lord rested from his works. Another probable reason for the number may be, that the Lord intended that the Sabbath never should be completed before the arrival of the last day. We here begin our blessed rest in him, and daily make new progress in it; but because we must still wage an incessant warfare with the flesh, it shall not be consummated until the fulfilment of the prophecy of Isaiah: "From one new moon to another, and from one sabbath to another, shall all flesh come to worship before me, saith the Lord" (Isaiah lxvi. 23); in other words, when God shall be "all in all" (1 Cor. xv. 28). It may seem, therefore, that by the seventh day the Lord delineated to his people the future perfection of his sabbath

on the last day, that by continual meditation on the Sabbath, they might throughout their whole lives aspire to this perfection.

31. Should these remarks on the number seem to any somewhat far-fetched, I have no objection to their taking it more simply : that the Lord appointied a certain day on which his people might be trained, under the tutelage of the Law, to meditate constantly on the spiritual rest, and fixed upon the seventh, either because he foresaw it would be sufficient, or in order that his own example might operate as a stronger stimulus ; or, at least, to remind men that the Sabbath was appointed for no other purpose than to render them conformable to their Creator. It is of little consequence which of these be adopted, provided we lose not sight of the principal thing delineated—viz. the mystery of perpetual resting from our works. To the contemplation of this, the Jews were every now and then called by the prophets, lest they should think a carnal cessation from labour sufficient. Beside the passages already quoted, there is the following: " If thou turn away thy foot from the Sabbath, from doing thy pleasure on my holy day ; and call the Sabbath a delight, the holy of the Lord, honourable ; and shalt honour him, not doing thine own ways, nor finding thine own pleasure, nor speaking thine own words : then shalt thou delight thyself in the Lord " (Isaiah lviii. 13, 14). Still there can be no doubt, that, on the advent of our Lord Jesus Christ, the ceremonial part of the commandment was abolished. He is the truth, at whose presence all the emblems banish ; the body, at the sight of which the shadows disappear. He, I say, is the true completion of the Sabbath : " We are buried with him by baptism unto death : that like as Christ was raised up from the dead by the glory of the Father, even so we should walk in newness of life " (Rom. vi. 4). Hence, as the Apostle elsewhere says, " Let no man therefore judge you in meat, or in drink, or in respect of an holyday, or of the new moon, or of the Sabbath days ; which are a shadow of things to come ; but the body is of Christ " (Col. ii. 16, 17) ; meaning by body the whole essence of the truth, as is well explained in that passage. This is not contented with one day, but requires the whole course of our lives, until being completely dead to ourselves, we are filled with the life of God. Christians, therefore, should have nothing to do with a superstitious observance of days.

32. The two other cases ought not to be classed with ancient shadows, but are adapted to every age. The Sabbath being abrogated, there is still room among us, first, to assemble on stated days for the hearing of the word, the breaking of the mystical bread, and public prayer : and, secondly, to give our servants and labourers relaxation from labour. It cannot be doubted that the Lord provided for both in the commandment of the Sabbath. The former is abundantly evinced by the mere practice of the Jews. The latter Moses has expressed in Deuteronomy in the following terms : " The seventh day

is the Sabbath of the Lord thy God : in it thou shalt not do any work, thou, nor thy son, nor thy daughter, nor thy man-servant, nor thy maid-servant ;—that thy man-servant and thy maid-servant may rest as well as thou " (Deut. v. 14).   Likewise in Exodus, " That thine ox and thine ass may rest, and the son of thy handmaid, and the stranger, may be refreshed" (Exod. xxiii. 12).   Who can deny that both are equally applicable to us as to the Jews ?   Religious meet-ings are enjoined us by the word of God ; their necessity, experience itself sufficiently demonstrates.   But unless these meetings are stated, and have fixed days allotted to them, how can they be held ?   We must, as the Apostle expresses it, do all things decently and in order (1 Cor. xiv. 40).   So impossible, however, would it be to preserve decency and order without this politic arrangement, that the dissolu-tion of it would instantly lead to the disturbance and ruin of the Church.   But if the reason for which the Lord appointed a Sabbath to the Jews is equally applicable to us, no man can assert that it is a matter with which we have nothing to do.   Our most provident and indulgent Parent has been pleased to provide for our wants not less than for the wants of the Jews.   Why, it may be asked, do we not hold daily meetings, and thus avoid the distinction of days ? Would that we were privileged to do so !   Spiritual wisdom un-doubtedly deserves to have some portion of every day devoted to it. But if, owing to the weakness of many, daily meetings cannot be held, and charity will not allow us to exact more of them, why should we not adopt the rule which the will of God has obviously imposed upon us ?

33. I am obliged to dwell a little longer on this, because some restless spirits are now making an outcry about the observance of the Lord's day.   They complain that Christian people are trained in Judaism, because some observance of days is retained.   My reply is, That those days are observed by us without Judaism, because in this matter we differ widely from the Jews.   We do not celebrate it with most minute formality, as a ceremony by which we imagine that a spiritual mystery is typified, but we adopt it as a necessary remedy for preserving order in the Church.   Paul informs us that Christians are not to be judged in respect of its observance, because it is a shadow of something to come (Col. ii. 16) ; and, accordingly, he expresses a fear lest his labour among the Galatians should prove in vain, because they still observed days (Gal. iv. 10, 11).   And he tells the Romans that it is superstitious to make one day differ from another (Rom. xiv. 5).   But who, except those restless men, does not see what the observance is to which the Apostle refers ?   Those persons had no regard to that politic and ecclesiastical arrangement,[1] but by retaining the days as types of spiritual things, they in so far obscured

---

1 " Finem istum politicum et ecclesiasticum ordinem."—French, "la police et ordre en l'Eglise;" policy and order in the Church.

the glory of Christ, and the light of the Gospel. They did not desist from manual labour on the ground of its interfering with sacred study and meditation, but as a kind of religious observance; because they dreamed that by their cessation from labour, they were cultivating the mysteries which had of old been committed to them. It was, I say, against this preposterous observance of days that the Apostle inveighs, and not against that legitimate selection which is subservient to the peace of Christian society. For in the churches established by him, this was the use for which the Sabbath was retained. He tells the Corinthians to set the first day apart for collecting contributions for the relief of their brethren at Jerusalem (1 Cor. xvi. 2). If superstition is dreaded, there was more danger in keeping the Jewish Sabbath than the Lord's day as Christians now do. It being expedient to overthrow superstition, the Jewish holyday was abolished; and as a thing necessary to retain decency, order, and peace, in the Church, another day was appointed for that purpose.

34. It was not, however, without a reason that the early Christians substituted what we call the Lord's day for the Sabbath. The resurrection of our Lord being the end and accomplishment of that true rest which the ancient Sabbath typified, this day, by which types were abolished, serves to warn Christians against adhering to a shadowy ceremony. I do not cling so to the number seven as to bring the Church under bondage to it, nor do I condemn churches for holding their meetings on other solemn days, provided they guard against superstition. This they will do if they employ those days merely for the observance of discipline and regular order. The whole may be thus summed up: As the truth was delivered typically to the Jews, so it is imparted to us without figure; first, that during our whole lives we may aim at a constant rest from our own works, in order that the Lord may work in us by his Spirit; secondly, that every individual, as he has opportunity, may diligently exercise himself in private, in pious meditation on the works of God, and, at the same time, that all may observe the legitimate order appointed by the Church, for the hearing of the word, the administration of the sacraments, and public prayer: and, thirdly, that we may avoid oppressing those who are subject to us. In this way, we get quit of the trifling of the false prophets, who in later times instilled Jewish ideas into the people, alleging that nothing was abrogated but what was ceremonial in the commandment[1] (this they term in their language the taxation of the seventh day), while the moral part remains—viz. the observance of one day in seven.[2] But this is nothing else than to

---

1 As to this liberty, see Socrates, Hist. Trip. Lib. ix. c. 38.
2 French, "ne discernans entre le Dimanche et le Sabbath autrement, sinon que le septiéme jour estoit abrogé qu'on gardoit pour lors, mais qu'il on faloit neantmoins garder un;"—making no other distinction between the Sunday and the Sabbath, save that the seventh day, which was kept till then, was abrogated, but that it was nevertheless necessary to keep some one day.

insult the Jews, by changing the day, and yet mentally attributing to it the same sanctity; thus retaining the same typical distinction of days as had place among the Jews. And of a truth, we see what profit they have made by such a doctrine. Those who cling to their constitutions go thrice as far as the Jews in the gross and carnal superstition of sabbatism; so that the rebukes which we read in Isaiah (Isa. i. 13; lviii. 13) apply as much to those of the present day,[1] as to those to whom the Prophet addressed them. We must be careful, however, to observe the general doctrine—viz. in order that religion may neither be lost nor languish among us, we must diligently attend on our religious assemblies, and duly avail ourselves of those external aids which tend to promote the worship of God.

Fifth Commandment.

HONOUR THY FATHER AND THY MOTHER, THAT THY DAYS MAY BE LONG UPON THE LAND WHICH THE LORD THY GOD GIVETH THEE.

35. The end of this commandment is, that since the Lord takes pleasure in the preservation of his own ordinance, the degrees of dignity appointed by him must be held inviolable. The sum of the commandment, therefore, will be; that we are to look up to those whom the Lord has set over us, yielding them honour, gratitude, and obedience. Hence it follows, that everything in the way of contempt, ingratitude, or disobedience, is forbidden. For the term *honour* has this extent of meaning in Scripture. Thus when the Apostle says, " Let the elders that rule well be counted worthy of double honour " (1 Tim. v. 17), he refers not only to the reverence which is due to them, but to the recompense to which their services are entitled. But as this command to submit is very repugnant to the perversity of the human mind (which, puffed up with ambitious longings, will scarcely allow itself to be subject), that superiority which is most attractive and least invidious is set forth as an example calculated to soften and bend our minds to habits of submission. From that subjection which is most easily endured, the Lord gradually accustoms us to every kind of legitimate subjection, the same principle regulating all. For to those whom he raises to eminence, he communicates his authority, in so far as necessary to maintain their station. The titles of Father, God, and Lord, all meet in him alone; and hence, whenever any one of them is mentioned, our mind should be impressed with the same feeling of reverence. Those, therefore, to whom he imparts such titles, he distinguishes by some small spark of his refulgence, so as to entitle them to honour, each in his own place. In this way, we must consider that our earthly father possesses something of a divine

---

[1] French, " leur conviendroyent mieux; "—would be more applicable to them.

nature in him, because there is some reason for his bearing a divine title, and that he who is our prince and ruler is admitted to some communion of honour with God.

36. Wherefore, we ought to have no doubt that the Lord here lays down this universal rule—viz. that knowing how every individual is set over us by his appointment, we should pay him reverence, gratitude, obedience, and every duty in our power. And it makes no difference whether those on whom the honour is conferred are deserving or not. Be they what they may, the Almighty, by conferring their station upon them, shows that he would have them honoured. The commandment specifies the reverence due to those to whom we owe our being. This Nature herself should in some measure teach us. For they are monsters, and not men, who petulantly and contumeliously violate the paternal authority. Hence, the Lord orders all who rebel against their parents to be put to death, they being, as it were, unworthy of the light in paying no deference to those to whom they are indebted for beholding it. And it is evident, from the various appendices to the Law, that we were correct in stating, that the honour here referred to consists of three parts, reverence, obedience, and gratitude. The first of these the Lord enforces, when he commands that whoso curseth his father or his mother shall be put to death. In this way he avenges insult and contempt. The second he enforces, when he denounces the punishment of death on disobedient and rebellious children. To the third belongs our Saviour's declaration, that God requires us to do good to our parents (Matth. xv.). And whenever Paul mentions this commandment, he interprets it as enjoining obedience.[1]

37. A promise is added by way of recommendation, the better to remind us how pleasing to God is the submission which is here required. Paul applies that stimulus to rouse us from our lethargy, when he calls this the first commandment with promise ; the promise contained in the First Table not being specially appropriated to any one commandment, but extended to the whole law. Moreover, the sense in which the promise is to be taken is as follows :—The Lord spoke to the Israelites specially of the land which he had promised them for an inheritance. If, then, the possession of the land was an earnest of the divine favour, we cannot wonder if the Lord was pleased to testify his favour, by bestowing long life, as in this way they were able long to enjoy his kindness. The meaning therefore is : Honour thy father and thy mother, that thou mayst be able, during the course of a long life, to enjoy the possession of the land which is to be given thee in testimony of my favour. But, as the whole earth is blessed to believers, we justly class the present life among the number of divine blessings. Whence this promise has, in like manner, refer-

---

1 Exod. xxi. 17; Levit. xx. 9; Prov. xx. 20; Deut. xxi. 18; Matth. xv. 4; Eph. vi. 1; Coloss. iii. 20.

ence to us also, inasmuch as the duration of the present life is a proof of the divine benevolence toward us. It is not promised to us, nor was it promised to the Jews, as if in itself it constituted happiness, but because it is an ordinary symbol of the divine favour to the pious. Wherefore, if any one who is obedient to parents happens to be cut off before mature age (a thing which not unfrequently happens), the Lord nevertheless adheres to his promise as steadily as when he bestows a hundred acres of land where he had promised only one. The whole lies in this: We must consider that long life is promised only in so far as it is a blessing from God, and that it is a blessing only in so far as it is a manifestation of divine favour. This, however, he testifies and truly manifests to his servants more richly and substantially by death.

38. Moreover, while the Lord promises the blessing of present life to children who show proper respect to their parents, he, at the same time, intimates that an inevitable curse is impending over the rebellious and disobedient; and, that it may not fail of execution, he, in his Law, pronounces sentence of death upon them, and orders it to be inflicted. If they escape the judgment, he, in some way or other, will execute vengeance. For we see how great a number of this description of individuals fall either in battle or in brawls; others of them are overtaken by unwonted disasters, and almost all are a proof that the threatening is not used in vain. But if any do escape till extreme old age, yet, because deprived of the blessing of God in this life, they only languish on in wickedness, and are reserved for severer punishment in the world to come; they are far from participating in the blessing promised to obedient children. It ought to be observed, by the way, that we are ordered to obey parents only in the Lord. This is clear from the principle already laid down: for the place which they occupy is one to which the Lord has exalted them, by communicating to them a portion of his own honour. Therefore the submission yielded to them should be a step in our ascent to the Supreme Parent, and hence, if they instigate us to transgress the law, they deserve not to be regarded as parents, but as strangers attempting to seduce us from our obedience to our true Father. The same holds in the case of rulers, masters, and superiors of every description. For it were unbecoming and absurd that the honour of God should be impaired by their exaltation—an exaltation which, being derived from him, ought to lead us up to him.[1]

Sixth Commandment.

THOU SHALT NOT KILL.

39. The purport of this commandment is, that since the Lord has

---

[1] The French adds, "et la doit plustost augmenter, qu'amoindrir confirmer que violer;"—and ought to augment rather than diminish, to confirm rather than violate it.

bound the whole human race by a kind of unity, the safety of all ought to be considered as intrusted to each. In general, therefore, all violence and injustice, and every kind of harm from which our neighbour's body suffers, is prohibited. Accordingly, we are required faithfully to do what in us lies to defend the life of our neighbour, to promote whatever tends to his tranquility, to be vigilant in warding off harm, and, when danger comes, to assist in removing it. Remembering that the Divine Lawgiver thus speaks, consider, moreover, that he requires you to apply the same rule in regulating your mind. It were ridiculous, that he, who sees the thoughts of the heart, and has special regard to them, should train the body only to rectitude. This commandment, therefore, prohibits the murder of the heart, and requires a sincere desire to preserve our brother's life. The hand, indeed, commits the murder, but the mind, under the influence of wrath and hatred, conceives it. How can you be angry with your brother, without passionately longing to do him harm? If you must not be angry with him, neither must you hate him, hatred being nothing but inveterate anger. However you may disguise the fact, or endeavour to escape from it by vain pretexts, where either wrath or hatred is, there is an inclination to do mischief. If you still persist in tergiversation, the mouth of the Spirit has declared, that "whosoever hateth his brother is a murderer" (1 John iii. 15); and the mouth of our Saviour has declared, that "whosoever is angry with his brother without a cause shall be in danger of the judgment: and whosoever shall say to his brother, Raca, shall be in danger of the council: but whosoever shall say, Thou fool, shall be in danger of hell fire" (Matth. v. 22).

40. Scripture notes a twofold equity on which this commandment is founded. Man is both the image of God and our flesh. Wherefore, if we would not violate the image of God, we must hold the person of man sacred—if we would not divest ourselves of humanity, we must cherish our own flesh. The practical inference to be drawn from the redemption and gift of Christ will be elsewhere considered.[1] The Lord has been pleased to direct our attention to these two natural considerations as inducements to watch over our neighbour's preservation—viz. to revere the divine image impressed upon him, and embrace our own flesh. To be clear of the crime of murder, it is not enough to refrain from shedding man's blood. If in act you perpetrate, if in endeavour you plot, if in wish and design you conceive what is adverse to another's safety, you have the guilt of murder. On the other hand, if you do not according to your means and opportunity study to defend his safety, by that inhumanity you violate the law. But if the safety of the body is so carefully provided for, we may hence infer how much care and exertion is due to the safety

---

[1] Book III. Chap. vii. sec 4—7; Chap. xx. sec. 38, 45; Book IV. Chap. i. sec. 13—19; Chap. xviii. sec. 38, 40.

of the soul, which is of immeasurably higher value in the sight of
God.

Seventh Commandment.

THOU SHALT NOT COMMIT ADULTERY.

41. The purport of this commandment is, that as God loves chastity and purity, we ought to guard against all uncleanness. The
substance of the commandment therefore is, that we must not defile
ourselves with any impurity or libidinous excess. To this corresponds
the affirmative, that we must regulate every part of our conduct
chastely and continently. The thing expressly forbidden is adultery,
to which lust naturally tends, that its filthiness (being of a grosser
and more palpable form, inasmuch as it casts a stain even on the
body) may dispose us to abominate every form of lust. As the law
under which man was created was not to lead a life of solitude, but
enjoy a help-meet for him—and ever since he fell under the curse the
necessity for this mode of life is increased—the Lord made the requisite provision for us in this respect by the institution of marriage,
which, entered into under his authority, he has also sanctified with
his blessing. Hence, it is evident, that any mode of cohabitation different from marriage is cursed in his sight, and that the conjugal
relation was ordained as a necessary means of preventing us from
giving way to unbridled lust. Let us beware, therefore, of yielding
to indulgence, seeing we are assured that the curse of God lies on
every man and woman cohabiting without marriage.

42. Now, since natural feeling and the passions inflamed by the
fall make the marriage tie doubly necessary, save in the case of those
whom God has by special grace exempted, let every individual consider how the case stands with himself. Virginity, I admit, is a
virtue not to be despised ; but since it is denied to some, and to
others granted only for a season, those who are assailed by incontinence, and unable successfully to war against it, should betake
themselves to the remedy of marriage, and thus cultivate chastity in
the way of their calling. Those incapable of self-restraint, if they
apply not to the remedy allowed and provided for intemperance, war
with God and resist his ordinance. And let no man tell me (as
many in the present day do) that he can do all things, God helping !
The help of God is present with those only who walk in his ways
(Ps. xci. 14), that is, in his calling, from which all withdraw themselves who, omitting the remedies provided by God, vainly and presumptuously strive to struggle with and surmount their natural
feelings. That continence is a special gift from God, and of the
class of those which are not bestowed indiscriminately on the whole
body of the Church, but only on a few of its members, our Lord

affirms (Matth. xix. 12). He first describes a certain class of individuals who have made themselves eunuchs for the kingdom of heaven's sake; that is, in order that they may be able to devote themselves with more liberty and less restraint to the things of heaven. But lest any one should suppose that such a sacrifice was in every man's power, he had shown a little before that all are not capable, but those only to whom it is specially given from above. Hence he concludes, "He that is able to receive it, let him receive it." Paul asserts the same thing still more plainly when he says, "Every man has his proper gift of God, one after this manner, and another after that" (1 Cor. vii. 7).

43. Since we are reminded by an express declaration, that it is not in every man's power to live chaste in celibacy, although it may be his most strenuous study and aim to do so—that it is a special grace which the Lord bestows only on certain individuals, in order that they may be less encumbered in his service, do we not oppose God, and nature as constituted by him, if we do not accommodate our mode of life to the measure of our ability? The Lord prohibits fornication, therefore he requires purity and chastity. The only method which each has of preserving it is to measure himself by his capacity. Let no man rashly despise matrimony as a thing useless or superfluous to him; let no man long for celibacy unless he is able to dispense with the married state. Nor even here let him consult the tranquility or convenience of the flesh, save only that, freed from this tie, he may be the readier and more prepared for all the offices of piety. And since there are many on whom this blessing is conferred only for a time, let every one, in abstaining from marriage, do it so long as he is fit to endure celibacy. If he has not the power of subduing his passion, let him understand that the Lord has made it obligatory on him to marry. The Apostle shows this when he enjoins: "Nevertheless, to avoid fornication, let every man have his own wife, and let every woman have her own husband." "If they cannot contain, let them marry." He first intimates that the greater part of men are liable to incontinence; and then of those so liable, he orders all, without exception, to have recourse to the only remedy by which unchastity may be obviated. The incontinent, therefore, in neglecting to cure their infirmity by this means, sin by the very circumstance of disobeying the Apostle's command. And let not a man flatter himself, that because he abstains from the outward act he cannot be accused of unchastity. His mind may in the meantime be inwardly inflamed with lust. For Paul's definition of chastity is purity of mind, combined with purity of body. "The unmarried woman careth for the things of the Lord, that she may be holy both in body and spirit" (1 Cor. vii. 34). Therefore, when he gives a reason for the former precept, he not only says that it is better to marry than to live in fornication, but that it is better to marry than to burn.

44. Moreover, when spouses are made aware that their union is blessed by the Lord, they are thereby reminded that they must not give way to intemperate and unrestrained indulgence. For though honourable wedlock veils the turpitude of incontinence, it does not follow that it ought forthwith to become a stimulus to it. Wherefore, let spouses consider that all things are not lawful for them. Let there be sobriety in the behaviour of the husband toward the wife, and of the wife in her turn toward the husband ; each so acting as not to do anything unbecoming the dignity and temperance of married life. Marriage contracted in the Lord ought to exhibit measure and modesty—not run to the extreme of wantonness. This excess Ambrose censured gravely, but not undeservedly, when he described the man who shows no modesty or comeliness in conjugal intercourse, as committing adultery with his wife.[1] Lastly, let us consider who the Lawgiver is that thus condemns fornication : even He who, as he is entitled to possess us entirely, requires integrity of body, soul, and spirit. Therefore, while he forbids fornication, he at the same time forbids us to lay snares for our neighbour's chastity by lascivious attire, obscene gestures, and impure conversation. There was reason in the remark made by Archelaus to a youth clothed effeminately and over-luxuriously, that it mattered not in what part his wantonness appeared. We must have respect to God, who abhors all contamination, whatever be the part of soul or body in which it appears. And that there may be no doubt about it, let us remember, that what the Lord here commends is chastity. If he requires chastity, he condemns everything which is opposed to it. Therefore, if you aspire to obedience, let not your mind burn within with evil concupiscence, your eyes wanton after corrupting objects, nor your body be decked for allurement; let neither your tongue by filthy speeches, nor your appetite by intemperance, entice the mind to corresponding thoughts. All vices of this description are a kind of stains which despoil chastity of its purity.

Eight Commandment.

THOU SHALT NOT STEAL.

The purport is, that injustice being an abomination to God, we must render to every man his due. In substance, then, the commandment forbids us to long after other men's goods, and, accordingly, requires every man to exert himself honestly in preserving his own. For we must consider, that what each individual possesses has not fallen to him by chance, but by the distribution of the sovereign

---

[1] See Ambros. Lib. de Philosoph., quoted by Augustine in his book, Contra Julian, Lib. ii.

Lord of all, that no one can pervert his means to bad purposes without committing a fraud on a divine dispensation. There are very many kinds of theft. One consists in violence, as when a man's goods are forcibly plundered and carried off; another in malicious imposture, as when they are fraudulently intercepted; a third in the more hidden craft which takes possession of them with a semblance of justice; and a fourth in sycophancy, which wiles them away under the pretence of donation. But not to dwell too long in enumerating the different classes, we know that all the arts by which we obtain possession of the goods and money of our neighbours, for sincere affection substituting an eagerness to deceive or injure them in any way, are to be regarded as thefts. Though they may be obtained by an action at law, a different decision is given by God. He sees the long train of deception by which the man of craft begins to lay nets for his more simple neighbour, until he entangles him in its meshes—sees the harsh and cruel laws by which the more powerful oppresses and crushes the feeble—sees the enticements by which the more wily baits the hook for the less wary, though all these escape the judgment of man, and no cognisance is taken of them. Nor is the violation of this commandment confined to money, or merchandise, or lands, but extends to every kind of right; for we defraud our neighbours to their hurt if we decline any of the duties which we are bound to perform towards them. If an agent or an indolent steward wastes the substance of his employer, or does not give due heed to the management of his property; if he unjustly squanders or luxuriously wastes the means intrusted to him; if a servant holds his master in derision, divulges his secrets, or in any way is treacherous to his life or his goods; if, on the other hand, a master cruelly torments his household, he is guilty of theft before God; since every one who, in the exercise of his calling, performs not what he owes to others, keeps back, or makes away with what does not belong to him.

46. This commandment, therefore, we shall duly obey, if, contented with our own lot, we study to acquire nothing but honest and lawful gain; if we long not to grow rich by injustice, nor to plunder our neighbour of his goods, that our own may thereby be increased; if we hasten not to heap up wealth cruelly wrung from the blood of others; if we do not, by means lawful and unlawful, with excessive eagerness, scrape together whatever may glut our avarice or meet our prodigality. On the other hand, let it be our constant aim faithfully to lend our counsel and aid to all so as to assist them in retaining their property; or if we have to do with the perfidious or crafty, let us rather be prepared to yield somewhat of our right than to contend with them. And not only so, but let us contribute to the relief of those whom we see under the pressure of difficulties, assisting their want out of our abundance. Lastly, let each of us consider how far he is bound in duty to others, and in good faith pay what we owe. In the same way, let the people pay all due honour to their rulers,

submit patiently to their authority, obey their laws and orders, and decline nothing which they can bear without sacrificing the favour of God. Let rulers, again, take due charge of their people, preserve the public peace, protect the good, curb the bad, and conduct themselves throughout as those who must render an account of their office to God, the Judge of all. Let the ministers of churches faithfully give heed to the ministry of the word, and not corrupt the doctrine of salvation, but deliver it purely and sincerely to the people of God. Let them teach not merely by doctrine, but by example; in short, let them act the part of good shepherds towards their flocks. Let the people, in their turn, receive them as the messengers and apostles of God, render them the honour which their Supreme Master has bestowed on them, and supply them with such things as are necessary for their livelihood. Let parents be careful to bring up, guide, and teach their children as a trust committed to them by God. Let them not exasperate or alienate them by cruelty, but cherish and embrace them with the lenity and indulgence which becomes their character. The regard due to parents from their children has already been adverted to. Let the young respect those advanced in years, as the Lord has been pleased to make that age honourable. Let the aged also, by their prudence and their experience (in which they are far superior), guide the feebleness of youth, not assailing them with harsh and clamorous invectives, but tempering strictness with ease and affability. Let servants show themselves diligent and respectful in obeying their masters, and this not with eye-service, but from the heart, as the servants of God. Let masters also not be stern and disobliging to their servants, nor harass them with excessive asperity, nor treat them with insult, but rather let them acknowledge them as brethren and fellow-servants of our heavenly Master, whom, therefore, they are bound to treat with mutual love and kindness. Let every one, I say, thus consider what in his own place and order he owes to his neighbours, and pay what he owes. Moreover, we must always have a reference to the Lawgiver, and so remember that the law requiring us to promote and defend the interest and convenience of our fellowmen, applies equally to our minds and our hands.

Ninth Commandment.

THOU SHALT NOT BEAR FALSE WITNESS AGAINST THY NEIGHBOUR.

47. The purport of the commandment is, since God, who is truth, abhors falsehood, we must cultivate unfeigned truth towards each other. The sum, therefore, will be, that we must not by calumnies and false accusations injure our neighbour's name, or by falsehood impair his fortunes; in fine, that we must not injure any one from

petulance, or a love of evil speaking. To this prohibition corresponds the command, that we must faithfully assist every one, as far as in us lies, in asserting the truth, for the maintenance of his good name and his estate. The Lord seems to have intended to explain the commandment in these words: " Thou shalt not raise a false report : put not thine hand with the wicked to be an unrighteous witness." " Keep thee far from a false matter" (Exod. xxiii. 1, 7). In another passage, he not only prohibits that species of falsehood which consists in acting the part of tale-bearers among the people, but says, " Neither shalt thou stand against the blood of thy neighbour" (Lev. xix. 16). Both transgressions are distinctly prohibited. Indeed, there can be no doubt, that as in the previous commandment he prohibited cruelty, unchastity, and avarice, so here he prohibits falsehood, which consists of the two parts to which we have adverted. By malignant or vicious detraction, we sin against our neighbour's good name : by lying, sometimes even by casting a slur upon him, we injure him in his estate. It makes no difference whether you suppose that formal and judicial testimony is here intended, or the ordinary testimony which is given in private conversation. For we must always recur to the consideration, that for each kind of transgression one species is set forth by way of example, that to it the others may be referred, and that the species chiefly selected, is that in which the turpitude of the transgression is most apparent. It seems proper, however, to extend it more generally to calumny and sinister insinuations by which our neighbours are unjustly aggrieved. For falsehood in a court of justice is always accompanied with perjury. But against perjury, in so far as it profanes and violates the name of God, there is a sufficient provision in the third commandment. Hence the legitimate observance of this precept consists in employing the tongue in the maintenance of truth, so as to promote both the good name and the prosperity of our neighbour. The equity of this is perfectly clear. For if a good name is more precious than riches, a man, in being robbed of his good name, is no less injured than if he were robbed of his goods ; while, in the latter case, false testimony is sometimes not less injurious than rapine committed by the hand.

48. And yet it is strange, with what supine security men everywhere sin in this respect. Indeed, very few are found who do not notoriously labour under this disease : such is the envenomed delight we take both in prying into and exposing our neighbour's faults. Let us not imagine it is a sufficient excuse to say that on many occasions our statements are not false. He who forbids us to defame our neighbour's reputation by falsehood, desires us to keep it untarnished in so far as truth will permit. Though the commandment is only directed against falsehood, it intimates that the preservation of our neighbour's good name is recommended. It ought to be a sufficient inducement to us to guard our neighbour's good name, that God takes an interest in it. Wherefore, evil-speaking in general is undoubtedly

condemned. Moreover, by evil-speaking, we understand not the rebuke which is administered with a view of correcting ; not accusation or judicial decision, by which evil is sought to be remedied; not public censure, which tends to strike terror into other offenders ; not the disclosure made to those whose safety depends on being forewarned, lest unawares they should be brought into danger, but the odious crimination which springs from a malicious and petulant love of slander. Nay, the commandment extends so far as to include that scurrilous affected urbanity, instinct with invective, by which the failings of others, under an appearance of sportiveness, are bitterly assailed, as some are wont to do, who court the praise of wit, though it should call forth a blush, or inflict a bitter pang. By petulance of this description, our brethren are sometimes grievously wounded.[1] But if we turn our eye to the Lawgiver, whose just authority extends over the ears and the mind, as well as the tongue, we cannot fail to perceive that eagerness to listen to slander, and an unbecoming proneness to censorious judgment, are heie forbidden. It were absurd to suppose that God hates the disease of evil-speaking in the tongue, and yet disapproves not of its malignity in the mind. Wherefore, if the true fear and love of God dwell in us, we must endeavour, as far as is lawful and expedient, and as far as charity admits, neither to listen nor give utterance to bitter and acrimonious charges, nor rashly entertain sinister suspicions. As just interpreters of the words and actions of other men, let us candidly maintain the honour due to them by our judgment, our ear, and our tongue.

Tenth Commandment.

THOU SHALT NOT COVET THY NEIGHBOUR'S HOUSE, THOU SHALT NOT COVET THY NEIGHBOUR'S WIFE, NOR HIS MAN-SERVANT, NOR HIS MAID-SERVANT, NOR HIS OX, NOR HIS ASS, NOR ANY THING THAT IS. THY NEIGHBOUR'S.

The purport is : Since the Lord would have the whole soul pervaded with love, any feeling of an adverse nature must be banished from our minds. The sum, therefore, will be, that no thought be permitted to insinuate itself into our minds, and inflame them with a noxious concupiscence tending to our neighbour's loss. To this

---

[1] The French is, "D'avantage ce precepte s'estend jusques là, que nous n'affections point une plaisanterie d'honnesteté et une grace de brocarder et mordre en riant les uns et les autres, comme sont aucuns, qui se bagnent quand ils peuvent faire vergogne à quelqu'un : car par telle intemperance souventes fois quelque marque demeure sur l'homme qu'on a ainsi noté."—Moreover, the commandment extends thus far : we must not affect a good-humoured pleasantry and grace in nicknaming, and with a smile say cutting things of others, as some persons do, who are delighted when they can make another blush : by such intemperance a stigma is often fastened on the individual thus attacked.

corresponds the contrary precept, that everything which we conceive, deliberate, will, or design, be conjoined with the good and advantage of our neighbour. But here it seems we are met with a great and perplexing difficulty. For if it was correctly said above, that under the words adultery and theft, lust and an intention to injure and deceive are prohibited, it may seem superfluous afterwards to employ a separate commandment to prohibit a covetous desire of our neighbour's goods. The difficulty will easily be removed by distinguishing between *design* and *covetousness*.[1] Design, such as we have spoken of in the previous commandments, is a deliberate consent of the will, after passion has taken possession of the mind. Covetousness may exist without such deliberation and assent, when the mind is only stimulated and tickled by vain and perverse objects. As, therefore, the Lord previously ordered that charity should regulate our wishes, studies, and actions, so he now orders us to regulate the thoughts of the mind in the same way, that none of them may be depraved and distorted, so as to give the mind a contrary bent. Having forbidden us to turn and incline our mind to wrath, hatred, adultery, theft, and falsehood, he now forbids us to give our thoughts the same direction.

50. Nor is such rectitude demanded without reason. For who can deny the propriety of occupying all the powers of the mind with charity? If it ceases to have charity for its aim, who can question that it is diseased? How comes it that so many desires of a nature hurtful to your brother enter your mind, but just because, disregarding him, you think only of yourself? Were your mind wholly imbued with charity, no portion of it would remain for the entrance of such thoughts. In so far, therefore, as the mind is devoid of charity, it must be under the influence of concupiscence. Some one will object that those fancies which casually rise up in the mind, and forthwith vanish away, cannot properly be condemned as concupiscence, which have their seat in the heart. I answer, That the question here relates to a description of fancies which, while they present themselves to our thoughts, at the same time impress and stimulate the mind with cupidity, since the mind never thinks of making some choice, but the heart is excited and tends towards it. God therefore commands a strong and ardent affection, an affection not to be impeded by any portion, however minute, of concupiscence. He requires a mind so admirably arranged as not to be prompted in the slightest degree contrary to the law of love. Lest you should imagine that this view is not supported by any grave authority, I may mention that it was first suggested to me by Augustine.[2] But although it was the intention of God to prohibit every kind of perverse desire, he, by way of

---

[1] See *supra*, chap. ii., end of sec. 24; and Book III. chap. iii. sec. 11, 12, 13; and Book IV. chap. xv. sec. 11, 12.

[2] See August. Ep. 200, ad Asellicum, et Quæstio, Lib. lxxxiii., sub fin. Quæst. 66; but especially Conscio. 8, in Ps. cxviii. The subject is also touched on in Ps. cxliii. und De Temp. Serm. 45, and Retract. Lib. i. cap. 5, and De Continentia, cap. 8.

example, sets before us those objects which are generally regarded as most attractive : thus leaving no room for cupidity of any kind, by the interdiction of those things in which it especially delights and loves to revel.

Such, then, is the Second Table of the Law, in which we are sufficiently instructed in the duties which we owe to man for the sake of God, on a consideration of whose nature the whole system of love is founded. It were vain, therefore, to inculcate the various duties taught in this table, without placing your instructions on the fear and reverence to God as their proper foundation. I need not tell the considerate reader, that those who make two precepts out of the prohibition of covetousness, perversely split one thing into two. There is nothing in the repetition of the words, " Thou shalt not covet." The " house" being first put down, its different parts are afterwards enumerated, beginning with the " wife ;" and hence it is clear, that the whole ought to be read consecutively, as is properly done by the Jews. The sum of the whole commandment, therefore, is, that whatever each individual possesses remain entire and secure, not only from injury, or the wish to injure, but also from the slightest feeling of covetousness which can spring up in the mind.

51. It will not now be difficult to ascertain the general end contemplated by the whole Law—viz. the fulfilment of righteousness, that man may form his life on the model of the divine purity. For therein God has so delineated his own character, that any one exhibiting in action what is commanded, would in some measure exhibit a living image of God. Wherefore Moses, when he wished to fix a summary of the whole in the memory of the Israelites, thus addressed them, " And now, Israel, what doth the Lord thy God require of thee, but to fear the Lord thy God, to walk in all his ways, and to love him, and to serve the Lord thy God with all thy heart, and with all thy soul, to keep the commandments of the Lord and his statutes which I command thee this day for thy good ?" (Deut. x. 12, 13.) And he ceased not to reiterate the same thing, whenever he had occasion to mention the end of the Law. To this the doctrine of the Law pays so much regard, that it connects man, by holiness of life, with his God ; and, as Moses elsewhere expresses it (Deut. vi. 5 ; xi. 13), and makes him cleave to him. Moreover, this holiness of life is comprehended under the two heads above mentioned. " Thou shalt love the Lord thy God with all thy heart, and with all thy soul, and with all thy mind, and with all thy strength, and thy neighbour as thyself." First, our mind must be completely filled with love to God, and then this love must forthwith flow out toward our neighbour. This the Apostle shows when he says, " The end of the commandment is charity out of a pure heart, and a good conscience, and of faith unfeigned" (1 Tim. i. 5). You see that conscience and faith unfeigned are placed at the head, in other words, true piety ; and that from this charity is derived. It is a mistake then to suppose, that merely

the rudiments and first principles of righteousness are delivered in the Law, to form, as it were, a kind of introduction to good works, and not to guide to the perfect performance of them. For complete perfection, nothing more can be required than is expressed in these passages of Moses and Paul. How far, pray, would he wish to go, who is not satisfied with the instruction which directs man to the fear of God, to spiritual worship, practical obedience ; in fine, purity of conscience, faith unfeigned, and charity ? This confirms that interpretation of the Law which searches out, and finds in its precepts, all the duties of piety and charity. Those who merely search for dry and meagre elements, as if it taught the will of God only by halves, by no means understand its end, the Apostle being witness.

52. As, in giving a summary of the Law, Christ and the Apostles sometimes omit the First Table, very many fall into the mistake of supposing that their words apply to both tables. In Matthew, Christ calls "judgment, mercy, and faith," the "weightier matters of the Law." I think it clear, that by *faith* is here meant veracity towards men. But in order to extend the words to the whole Law, some take it for piety towards God. This is surely to no purpose. For Christ is speaking of those works by which a man ought to approve himself as just. If we attend to this, we will cease to wonder why elsewhere, when asked by the young man, " What good thing shall I do, that I may have eternal life ?" he simply answers, that he must keep the commandments, " Thou shalt do no murder, Thou shalt not commit adultery, Thou shalt not steal, Thou shalt not bear false witness, Honour thy father and thy mother : and, Thou shalt love thy neighbour as thyself" (Matth. xix. 16, 18). For the obedience of the First Table consisted almost entirely either in the internal affection of the heart, or in ceremonies. The affection of the heart was not visible, and hypocrites were diligent in the observance of ceremonies ; but the works of charity were of such a nature as to be a solid attestation of righteousness. The same thing occurs so frequently in the Prophets, that it must be familiar to every one who has any tolerable acquaintance with them.[1] For, almost on every occasion, when they exhort men to repentance, omitting the First Table, they insist on faith, judgment, mercy, and equity. Nor do they, in this way, omit the fear of God. They only require a serious proof of it from its signs. It is well known, indeed, that when they treat of the Law, they generally insist on the Second Table, because therein the cultivation of righteousness and integrity is best manifested. There is no occasion to quote passages. Every one can easily for himself perceive the truth of my observation.

53. Is it then true, you will ask, that it is a more complete summary of righteousness to live innocently with men, than piously towards God ? By no means ; but because no man, as a matter of

---

[1] Is. i. 17 ; lviii. 6 ; Jer. vii. 5, 6 ; Ezek. xviii. 7, 8 ; Hosea vi. 6 ; Zech. vii. 9, 10.

course, observes charity in all respects, unless he seriously fear God, such observance is a proof of piety also. To this we may add, that the Lord, well knowing that none of our good deeds can reach him (as the Psalmist declares, Psalm xvi. 2), does not demand from us duties towards himself, but exercises us in good works towards our neighbour. Hence the Apostle, not without cause, makes the whole perfection of the saints to consist in charity (Eph. iii. 19 ; Col. iii. 14). And in another passage, he not improperly calls it the "ful-filling of the law," adding, that "he that loveth another hath fulfilled the law" (Rom. xiii. 8). And again, "All the law is fulfilled in this: Thou shalt love thy neighbour as thyself" (Gal. v. 14). For this is the very thing which Christ himself teaches when he says, "All things whatsoever ye would that men should do to you, do ye even so to them : fo this is the law and the prophets" (Matth. vii. 12). It is certain that, in the law and the prophets, faith, and whatever pertains to the du worship of God, holds the first place, and that to this charity is made subordinate; but our Lord means, that in the Law the observance of justice and equity towards men is prescribed as the means which we are to employ in testifying a pious fear of God, if we truly possess it.

54. Let us therefore hold, that our life will be framed in best ac-cordance with the will of God, and the requirements of his Law, when it is, in every respect, most advantageous to our brethren. But in the whole Law, there is not one syllable which lays down a rule as to what man is to do or avoid for the advantage of his own carnal nature. And, indeed, since men are naturally prone to excessive self-love, which they always retain, how great soever their departure from the truth may be, there was no need of a law to inflame a love already existing in excess. Hence it is perfectly plain,[1] that the observance of the Commandments consists not in the love of ourselves, but in the love of God and our neighbour ; and that he leads the best and holiest life who as little as may be studies and lives for himself; and that none lives worse and more unrighteously than he who studies and lives only for himself, and seeks and thinks only of his own. Nay, the better to express how strongly we should be inclined to love our neighbour, the Lord has made self-love as it were the standard, there being no feeling in our nature of greater strength and vehemence. The force of the expression ought to be carefully weighed. For he does not (as some sophists have stupidly dreamed) assign the first place to self-love, and the second to charity. He rather transfers to others the love which we naturally feel for ourselves. Hence the Apostle declares, that charity "seeketh not her own" (1 Cor. xiii. 5). Nor is the argument worth a straw, That the thing regulated must always be inferior to the rule. The Lord did not make self-love the rule, as if love towards others was subordinate to it ; but whereas,

---

[1] See Book III. chap. vii. sec. 4. Also August. de Doctrina Christiana, Lib. i. chap. xxiii. et seq.

through natural pravity, the feeling of love usually rests on ourselves, he shows that it ought to diffuse itself in another direction—that we should be prepared to do good to our neighbour with no less alacrity, ardour, and solicitude, than to ourselves.

55. Our Saviour having shown, in the parable of the Samaritan (Luke x. 36), that the term *neighbour* comprehends the most remote stranger, there is no reason for limiting the precept of love to our own connections. I deny not that the closer the relation the more frequent our offices of kindness should be. For the condition of humanity requires that there be more duties in common between those who are more nearly connected by the ties of relationship, or friendship, or neighbourhood. And this is done without any offence to God, by whose providence we are in a manner impelled to do it. But I say that the whole human race, without exception, are to be embraced with one feeling of charity : that here there is no distinction of Greek or Barbarian, worthy or unworthy, friend or foe, since all are to be viewed not in themselves, but in God. If we turn aside from this view, there is no wonder that we entangle ourselves in error. Wherefore, if we would hold the true course in love, our first step must be to turn our eyes not to man, the sight of whom might oftener produce hatred than love, but to God, who requires that the love which we bear to him be diffused among all mankind, so that our fundamental principle must ever be, Let a man be what he may, he is still to be loved, because God is loved.

56. Wherefore, nothing could be more pestilential than the ignorance or wickedness of the Schoolmen in converting the precepts respecting revenge and the love of enemies (precepts which had formerly been delivered to all the Jews, and were then delivered universally to all Christians) into counsels which it was free to obey or disobey, confining the necessary observance of them to the monks, who were made more righteous than ordinary Christians, by the simple circumstance of voluntarily binding themselves to obey counsels. The reason they assign for not receiving them as laws, is that they seem too heavy and burdensome, especially to Christians, who are under the law of grace. Have they, indeed, the hardihood to remodel the eternal law of God concerning the love of our neighbour ? Is there a page of the Law in which any such distinction exists ; or rather, do we not meet in every page with commands which, in the strictest terms, require us to love our enemies ? What is meant by commanding us to feed our enemy if he is hungry, to bring back his ox or his ass if we meet it going astray, or help it up if we see it lying under its burden ? (Prov. xxv. 21 ; Exod. xxiii. 4.) Shall we show kindness to cattle for man's sake, and have no feeling of goodwill to himself ? What ? Is not the word of the Lord eternally true : "Vengeance is mine, I will repay ?" (Deut. xxxii. 35). This is elsewhere more explicitly stated : " Thou shalt not avenge, nor bear any grudge against the children of thy people" (Lev. xix. 18). Let

them either erase these passages from the Law, or let them acknowledge the Lord as a Lawgiver, not falsely feign him to be merely a counsellor.

57. And what, pray, is meant by the following passage, which they have dared to insult with this absurd gloss? " Love your enemies, bless them that curse you, do good to them that hate you, and pray for them which despitefully use you, and persecute you ; that ye may be the children of your Father which is in heaven " (Matth. v. 44, 45). Who does not here concur in the reasoning of Chrysostom (Lib. de Compunctione Cordis, et ad Rom. vii.), that the nature of the motive makes it plain that these are not exhortations, but precepts ? For what is left to us if we are excluded from the number of the children of God? According to the Schoolmen, monks alone will be the children of our Father in heaven—monks alone will dare to invoke God as their Father. And in the mean time, how will it fare with the Church ? By the same rule, she will be confined to heathens and publicans. For our Saviour says, " If ye love them which love you, what reward have ye ? do not even the publicans the same ?" It will truly be well with us if we are left only the name of Christians, while we are deprived of the inheritance of the kingdom of heaven ! Nor is the argument of Augustine less forcible : " When the Lord forbids adultery, he forbids it in regard to the wife of a foe not less than the wife of a friend ; when he forbids theft, he does not allow stealing of any description, whether from a friend or an enemy " (August. Lib. de Doctr. Christ.). Now, these two commandments, " Thou shalt not steal, Thou shalt not commit adultery,". Paul brings under the rule of love ; nay, he says that they are briefly comprehended in this saying, " Thou shalt love thy neighbour as thyself" (Rom. xiii. 9). Therefore, Paul must either be a false interpreter of the Law, or we must necessarily conclude, that under this precept we are bound to love our enemies just as our friends. Those, then, show themselves to be in truth the children of Satan who thus licentiously shake off a yoke common to the children of God. It may be doubted whether, in promulgating this dogma, they have displayed greater stupidity or impudence. There is no ancient writer who does not hold it as certain that these are pure precepts. It was not even doubted in the age of Gregory, as is plain from his decided assertion ; for he holds it to be incontrovertible that they are precepts. And how stupidly they argue ! The burden, say they, were too difficult for Christians to bear ! As if anything could be imagined more difficult than to love the Lord with all the heart, and soul, and strength. Compared with this Law, there is none which may not seem easy, whether it be to love our enemy, or to banish every feeling of revenge from our minds. To our weakness, indeed, everything, even to the minutest tittle of the Law, is arduous and difficult. In the Lord we have strength. It is his to give what he orders, and to order what he wills. That Christians are under the law of grace, means not that

they are to wander unrestrained without law, but that they are engrafted into Christ, by whose grace they are freed from the curse of the Law, and by whose Spirit they have the Law written in their hearts. This grace Paul has termed, but not in the proper sense of the term, a law, alluding to the Law of God, with which he was contrasting it. The Schoolmen, laying hold of the term *Law*, make it the ground-work of their vain speculations.[1]

58. The same must be said of their application of the term, venial sin, both to the hidden impiety which violates the First Table, and the direct transgression of the last commandment of the Second Table [2] They define venial sin to be, desire unaccompanied with deliberate assent, and not remaining long in the heart. But I maintain that it cannot even enter the heart unless through a want of those things which are required in the Law. We are forbidden to have strange gods. When the mind, under the influence of distrust, looks elsewhere, or is seized with some sudden desire to transfer its blessedness to some other quarter, whence are these movements, however evanescent, but just because there is some empty corner in the soul to receive such temptations? And, not to lengthen out the discussion, there is a precept to love God with the whole heart, and mind, and soul; and, therefore, if all the powers of the soul are not directed to the love of God, there is a departure from the obedience of the Law; because those internal enemies which rise up against the dominion of God, and countermand his edicts, prove that his throne is not well established in our consciences. It has been shown that the last commandment goes to this extent. Has some undue longing sprung up in our mind? Then we are chargeable with covetousness, and stand convicted as transgressors of the Law. For the Law forbids us not only to meditate and plan our neighbour's loss, but to be stimulated and inflamed with covetousness. But every transgression of the Law lays us under the curse, and therefore even the slightest desires cannot be exempted from the fatal sentence. "In weighing our sins," says Augustine, "let us not use a deceitful balance, weighing at our own discretion what we will, and how we will, calling this heavy and that light: but let us use the divine balance of the Holy Scriptures, as taken from the treasury of the Lord, and by it weigh every offence, nay, not weigh, but rather recognise what has been already weighed by the Lord" (August. De Bapt. cont. Donatist. Lib. ii. chap. 6). And what saith the Scripture? Certainly when Paul says, that "the wages of sin is death" (Rom. vi. 23), he shows that he knew nothing of this vile distinction. As we are but too prone to hypocrisy, there was very little occasion for this sop to soothe our torpid consciences.

1 The French is, " Ces folastres sans propos prennent un grand mystére en ce mot de Loy;" these foolish fellows absurdly find a great mystery in this term Law.
2 See Book III. chap. iv. sec. 28, where it is also shown that this is not the dogma of the Stoics—that all sins are equal.

59. I wish they would consider what our Saviour meant when he said, " Whosoever shall break one of these least commandments, and shall teach men so, he shall be called the least in the kingdom of heaven" (Matth. v. 19). Are they not of this number when they presume to extenuate the transgression of the Law, as if it were unworthy of death? The proper course had been to consider not simply what is commanded, but who it is that commands, because every least transgression of his Law derogates from his authority. Do they count it a small matter to insult the majesty of God in any one respect? Again, since God has explained his will in the Law, everything contrary to the Law is displeasing to him. Will they feign that the wrath of God is so disarmed that the punishment of death will not forthwith follow upon it? He has declared plainly (if they could be induced to listen to his voice, instead of darkening his clear truth by their insipid subtleties), " The soul that sinneth it shall die" (Ezek. xviii. 20). Again, in the passage lately quoted, " The wages of sin is death." What these men acknowledge to be sin, because they are unable to deny it, they contend is not mortal. Having already indulged this madness too long, let them learn to repent; or, if they persist in their infatuation, taking no further notice of them, let the children of God remember that all sin is mortal, because it is rebellion against the will of God, and necessarily provokes his anger; and because it is a violation of the Law, against every violation of which, without exception, the judgment of God has been pronounced. The faults of the saints are indeed venial, not, however, in their own nature, but because, through the mercy of God, they obtain pardon.

CHAPTER IX.

CHRIST, THOUGH KNOWN TO THE JEWS UNDER THE LAW, YET ONLY MANIFESTED UNDER THE GOSPEL.

There are three principal heads in this chapter. I. Preparatory to a consideration of the knowledge of Christ, and the benefits procured by him; the 1st and 2d sections are occupied with the dispensation of this knowledge, which, after the manifestation of Christ in the flesh, was more clearly revealed than under the Law. II. A refutation of the profane dream of Servetus, that the promises are entirely abrogated, sec. 3. Likewise, a refutation of those who do not properly compare the Law with the Gospel, sec. 4. III. A necessary and brief exposition of the ministry of John Baptist, which occupies an intermediate place between the Law and the Gospel.

Sections.

1. **The holy fathers** under the Law saw the day of Christ, though obscurely. He is more fully revealed to us under the Gospel. A reason for this, confirmed by the testimony of Christ and his Apostles.
2. The term Gospel, used in its most extensive sense, comprehends the attestations of mercy which God gave to the fathers. Properly, however, it means the promulgation of grace exhibited in the God-man Jesus Christ.
3. The notion of Servetus, that the promises are entirely abolished, refuted. Why we must still trust to the promises of God. Another reason. Solution of a difficulty.
4. Refutation of those who do not properly compare the Law and the Gospel. Answer to certain questions here occurring. The Law and the Gospel briefly compared.
5. Third part of the chapter. Of the ministry of John the Baptist.

1. Since God was pleased (and not in vain) to testify in ancient times, by means of expiations and sacrifices, that he was a Father, and to set apart for himself a chosen people, he was doubtless known even then in the same character in which he is now fully revealed to us. Accordingly, Malachi, having enjoined the Jews to attend to the Law of Moses (because after his death there was to be an interruption of the prophetical office), immediately after declares that the Sun of righteousness should arise (Mal. iv. 2); thus intimating, that though the Law had the effect of keeping the pious in expectation of the coming Messiah, there was ground to hope for much greater light on his advent. For this reason, Peter, speaking of the ancient prophets, says, " Unto whom it was revealed, that not unto themselves, but unto us, they did minister the things which are now reported unto you by them that have preached the gospel unto you, with the Holy Ghost sent down from heaven " (1 Pet. i. 12). Not that the prophetical doctrine was useless to the ancient people, or unavailing to the prophets themselves, but that they did not obtain possession of the treasure which God has transmitted to us by their hands. The

grace of which they testified is now set familiarly before our eyes. They had only a slight foretaste; to us is given a fuller fruition. Our Saviour, accordingly, while he declares that Moses testified of him, extols the superior measure of grace bestowed upon us (John v. 46). Addressing his disciples, he says, " Blessed are your eyes, for they see, and your ears, for they hear. For verily I say unto you, That many prophets and righteous men have desired to see those things which ye see, and have not seen them, and to hear those things which ye hear, and have not heard them " (Matth. xiii. 16; Luke x. 23). It is no small commendation of the gospel revelation, that God has preferred us to holy men of old, so much distinguished for piety. There is nothing in this view inconsistent with another passage, in which our Saviour says, " Your father Abraham rejoiced to see my day, and he saw it and was glad " (John viii. 56). For though the event being remote, his view of it was obscure, he had full assurance that it would one day be accomplished; and hence the joy which the holy patriarch experienced even to his death. Nor does John Baptist, when he says, " No man hath seen God at any time; the only begotten Son, which is in the bosom of the Father, he hath declared him " (John i. 18), exclude the pious who had previously died from a participation in the knowledge and light which are manifested in the person of Christ; but comparing their condition with ours, he intimates that the mysteries which they only beheld dimly under shadows are made clear to us; as is well explained by the author of the Epistle to the Hebrews, in these words, " God, who at sundry times and in divers manners spake in time past unto the fathers by the prophets, hath in these last days spoken unto us by his Son " (Heb. i. 1, 2). Hence, although this only begotten Son,·who is now to us the brightness of his Father's glory and the express image of his person, was formerly made known to the Jews, as we have elsewhere shown from Paul, that he was the Deliverer under the old dispensation; it is nevertheless true, as Paul himself elsewhere declares, that " God, who commanded the light to shine out of darkness, hath shined in our hearts, to give the light of the knowledge of the glory of God in the face of Jesus Christ " (2 Cor. iv. 6); because, when he appeared in this his image, he in a manner made himself visible, his previous appearance having been shadowy and obscure. More shameful and more detestable, therefore, is the ingratitude of those who walk blindfold in this meridian light. Accordingly, Paul says that " the god of this world hath blinded their minds, lest the light of the glorious gospel of Christ should shine unto them " (2 Cor. iv. 4).

2. By the Gospel, I understand the clear manifestation of the mystery of Christ. I confess, indeed, that inasmuch as the term Gospel is applied by Paul to the doctrine of faith (2 Tim. iv. 10), it includes all the promises by which God reconciles men to himself, and which occur throughout the Law. For Paul there opposes faith to those terrors which vex and torment the conscience when salvation is sought

by means of works. Hence it follows, that *Gospel*, taken in a large sense, comprehends the evidences of mercy and paternal favour which God bestowed on the Patriarchs. Still, by way of excellence, it is applied to the promulgation of the grace manifested in Christ. This is not only founded on general use, but has the sanction of our Saviour and his Apostles. Hence it is described as one of his peculiar characteristics, that he preached the Gospel of the kingdom (Matth. iv. 23; ix. 35; Mark i. 14). Mark, in his preface to the Gospel, calls it " *The beginning of the Gospel of Jesus Christ.*" There is no use of collecting passages to prove what is already perfectly known. Christ at his advent "brought life and immortality to light through the Gospel" (2 Tim. i. 10). Paul does not mean by these words that the Fathers were plunged in the darkness of death before the Son of God became incarnate; but he claims for the Gospel the honourable distinction of being a new and extraordinary kind of embassy, by which God fulfilled what he had promised, these promises being realised in the person of the Son. For though believers have at all times experienced the truth of Paul's declaration, that "all the promises of God in him are yea and amen," inasmuch as these promises were sealed upon their hearts; yet because he hath in his flesh completed all the parts of our salvation, this vivid manifestation of realities was justly entitled to this new and special distinction. Accordingly, Christ says, "Hereafter ye shall see heaven open, and the angels of God ascending and descending upon the Son of man." For though he seems to allude to the ladder which the Patriarch Jacob saw in vision, he commends the excellence of his advent in this, that it opened the gate of heaven, and gave us familiar access to it.

3. Here we must guard against the diabolical imagination of Servetus, who, from a wish, or at least the pretence of a wish, to extol the greatness of Christ, abolishes the promises entirely, as if they had come to an end at the same time with the Law. He pretends, that by the faith of the Gospel all the promises have been fulfilled; as if there was no distinction between us and Christ. I lately observed that Christ had not left any part of our salvation incomplete; but from this it is erroneously inferred, that we are now put in possession of all the blessings purchased by him; thereby implying, that Paul was incorrect in saying, "We are saved by hope" (Rom. iii. 24). I admit, indeed, that by believing in Christ we pass from death unto life; but we must at the same time remember the words of John, that though we know we are "the sons of God," "it doth not yet appear what we shall be: but we know that, when he shall appear, we shall be like him; for we shall see him as he is" (1 John iii. 2). Therefore, although Christ offers us in the Gospel a present fulness of spiritual blessings, fruition remains in the keeping of hope,[1] until

---

[1] " Sub custodia spei."—French, " sous la garde, et comme sous le cachet d'espoir;" under the guard, and, as it were, under the seal of hope.

we are divested of corruptible flesh, and transformed into the glory of him who has gone before us. Meanwhile, in leaning on the promises, we obey the command of the Holy Spirit, whose authority ought to have weight enough with us to silence all the barkings of that impure dog. We have it on the testimony of Paul, that "Godliness is profitable unto all things, having promise of the life that now is, and of that which is to come" (1 Tim. iv. 8); for which reason, he glories in being "an apostle of Jesus Christ, according to the promise of life which is in Christ Jesus" (2 Tim. i. 1). And he elsewhere reminds us, that we have the same promises which were given to the saints in ancient time (2 Cor. vii. 1). In fine, he makes the sum of our felicity consist in being sealed with the Holy Spirit of promise. Indeed, we have no enjoyment of Christ, unless by embracing him as clothed with his own promises. Hence it is, that he indeed dwells in our hearts, and yet we are as pilgrims in regard to him, because "we walk by faith, not by sight" (2 Cor. v. 6, 7). There is no inconsistency in the two things—viz. that in Christ we possess everything pertaining to the perfection of the heavenly life, and yet that faith is only a vision "of things not seen" (Heb. xi. 1). Only there is this difference to be observed in the nature or quality of the promises, that the Gospel points with the finger to what the Law shadowed under types.

4. Hence, also, we see the error of those who, in comparing the Law with the Gospel, represent it merely as a comparison between the merit of works, and the gratuitous imputation of righteousness. The contrast thus made is by no means to be rejected, because, by the term Law, Paul frequently understands that rule of holy living in which God exacts what is his due, giving no hope of life unless we obey in every respect; and, on the other hand, denouncing a curse for the slightest failure. This Paul does when showing that we are freely accepted of God, and accounted righteous by being pardoned, because that obedience of the Law to which the reward is promised is nowhere to be found. Hence he appropriately represents the righteousness of the Law and the Gospel as opposed to each other. But the Gospel has not succeeded the whole Law in such a sense as to introduce a different method of salvation. It rather confirms the Law, and proves that everything which it promised is fulfilled. What was shadow, it has made substance. When Christ says that the Law and the Prophets were until John, he does not consign the fathers to the curse, which, as the slaves of the Law, they could not escape. He intimates that they were only imbued with the rudiments, and remained far beneath the height of the Gospel doctrine. Accordingly Paul, after calling the Gospel "the power of God unto salvation to every one that believeth," shortly after adds, that it was "witnessed by the Law and the Prophets" (Rom. i. 16; iii. 21). And in the end of the same Epistle, though he describes "the preaching of Jesus Christ" as "the revelation of the mystery which was kept secret since

the world began," he modifies the expression by adding, that it is "now made manifest" "by the scriptures of the prophets" (Rom. xvi. 25, 26). Hence we infer, that when the whole Law is spoken of, the Gospel differs from it only in respect of clearness of manifestation. Still, on account of the inestimable riches of grace set before us in Christ, there is good reason for saying, that by his advent the kingdom of heaven was erected on the earth (Matth. xii. 28).

5. John stands between the Law and the Gospel, holding an intermediate office allied to both. For though he gave a summary of the Gospel when he pronounced Christ to be "the Lamb of God who taketh away the sin of the world," yet, inasmuch as he did not unfold the incomparable power and glory which shone forth in his resurrection, Christ says that he was not equal to the Apostles. For this is the meaning of the words: "Among them that are born of woman, there hath not risen a greater than John the Baptist: notwithstanding, he that is least in the kingdom of heaven is greater than he" (Matth. xi. 11). He is not there commending the persons of men, but after preferring John to all the Prophets, he gives the first place to the preaching of the Gospel, which is elsewhere designated by the kingdom of heaven. When John himself, in answer to the Jews, says that he is only "a voice" (John i. 23), as if he were inferior to the Prophets, it is not in pretended humility, but he means to teach that the proper embassy was not intrusted to him, that he only performed the office of a messenger, as had been foretold by Malachi, "Behold, I will send you Elijah the prophet, before the coming of the great and dreadful day of the Lord" (Mal. iv. 5). And, indeed, during the whole course of his ministry, he did nothing more than prepare disciples for Christ. He even proves from Isaiah that this was the office to which he was divinely appointed. In this sense, he is said by Christ to have been "a burning and a shining light" (John v. 35), because full day had not yet appeared. And yet this does not prevent us from classing him among the preachers of the Gospel, since he used the same baptism which was afterwards committed to the Apostles. Still, however, he only began that which had freer course under the Apostles, after Christ was taken up into the heavenly glory.

CHAPTER X.

THE RESEMBLANCE BETWEEN THE OLD TESTAMENT AND THE NEW.[1]

This chapter consists of four parts. I. The sum, utility, and necessity of this discussion, sec. 1. II. A proof that, generally speaking, the old and new dispensations are in reality one, although differently administered. Three points in which the two dispensations entirely agree, sec. 2—4. III. The Old Testament, as well as the New, had regard to the hope of immortality and a future life, whence two other resemblances or points of agreement follow—viz that both were established by the free mercy of God, and confirmed by the intercession of Christ. This proved by many arguments, passages of Scripture, and examples, sec. 5—23. IV. Conclusion of the whole chapter, where, for fuller confirmation, certain passages of Scripture are produced. Refutation of the cavils of the Sadducees and other Jews.

Sections.

1. Introduction, showing the necessity of proving the similarity of both dispensations in opposition to Servetus and the Anabaptists.
2. This similarity in general. Both covenants truly one, though differently administered. Three things in which they entirely agree.
3. First general similarity, or agreement—viz. that the Old Testament, equally with the New, extended its promises beyond the present life, and held out a sure hope of immortality. Reason for this resemblance. Objection answered.
4. The other two points of resemblance—viz. that both covenants were established in the mercy of God, and confirmed by the mediation of Christ.
5. The first of these points of resemblance being the foundation of the other two, a lengthened proof is given of it. The first argument taken from a passage, in which Paul, showing that the sacraments of both dispensations had the same meaning, proves that the condition of the ancient church was similar to ours.
6. An objection from John vi. 49—viz. that the Israelites ate manna in the wilderness, and are dead, whereas Christians eat the flesh of Christ, and die not. Answer reconciling this passage of the Evangelist with that of the Apostle.
7. Another proof from the Law and the Prophets—viz. the power of the divine word in quickening souls before Christ was manifested. Hence the believing Jews were raised to the hope of eternal life.
8. Third proof from the form of the covenant, which shows that it was in reality one both before and after the manifestation of Christ in the flesh.
9. Confirmation of the former proof from the clear terms in which the form is expressed. Another confirmation derived from the former and from the nature of God.
10. Fourth proof from examples. Adam, Abel, and Noah, when tried with various temptations, neglecting the present, aspired with living faith and invincible hope to a better life. They, therefore, had the same aim as believers under the Gospel.
11. Continuation of the fourth proof from the example of Abraham, whose call and whole course of life shows that he ardently aspired to eternal felicity. Objection disposed of.
12. Continuation of the fourth proof from the examples of Isaac and Jacob.
13. Conclusion of the fourth proof. Adam, Abel, Noah, Abraham, Isaac, Jacob, and others under the Law, looked for the fulfilment of the divine promises not on the earth, but in heaven. Hence they termed this life an earthly pilgrimage, and desired to be buried in the land of Canaan, which was a figure of eternal happiness.

[1] As to the agreement of both dispensations, see August. Lib. de Moribus Eccles. Lat., especially cap. xxviii.

1. FROM what has been said above, it must now be clear, that all whom, from the beginning of the world, God adopted as his peculiar people, were taken into covenant with him on the same conditions, and under the same bond of doctrine, as ourselves; but as it is of no small importance to establish this point, I will here add it by way of appendix, and show, since the Fathers were partakers with us in the same inheritance, and hoped for a common salvation through the grace of the same Mediator, how far their condition in this respect was different from our own. For although the passages which we have collected from the Law and the Prophets for the purpose of proof, make it plain that there never was any other rule of piety and religion among the people of God; yet as many things are written on the subject of the difference between the Old and New Testaments in a manner which may perplex ordinary readers, it will be proper here to devote a special place to the better and more exact discussion of this subject. This discussion, which would have been most useful at any rate, has been rendered necessary by that monstrous miscreant Servetus, and some madmen of the sect of the Anabaptists, who think of the people of Israel just as they would do of some herd of swine, absurdly imagining that the Lord gorged them with temporal blessings here, and gave them no hope of a blessed immortality.[1] Let us guard pious minds against this pestilential error, while we at the same time remove all the difficulties which are wont to start up when mention is made of the difference between the Old and the New Testaments. By the way also, let us consider what resemblance and what difference there is between the covenant which the Lord

1 The French is, " Veu qu'ils pensent que notre Seigneur l'ait voulu seulement engraisser en terre comme en une auge, sans esperance aucune de l'immortalité celeste;"—seeing they think that our Lord only wished to fatten them on the earth as in a sty, without any hope of heavenly immortality.

made with the Israelites before the advent of Christ, and that which he has made with us, now that Christ is manifested.

2. It is possible, indeed, to explain both in one word. The covenant made with all the fathers is so far from differing from ours in reality and substance, that it is altogether one and the same: still the administration differs. But because this brief summary is insufficient to give any one a full understanding of the subject, our explanation to be useful must extend to greater length. It were superfluous, however, in showing the similarity, or rather identity, of the two dispensations, again to treat of the particulars which have already been discussed, as it were unseasonable to introduce those which are still to be considered elsewhere. What we propose to insist upon here may be reduced to three heads:—*First*, That temporal opulence and felicity was not the goal to which the Jews were invited to aspire, but that they were admitted to the hope of immortality, and that assurance of this adoption was given by immediate communications, by the Law and by the Prophets. *Secondly*, That the covenant by which they were reconciled to the Lord was founded on no merits of their own, but solely on the mercy of God, who called them; and, *thirdly*, That they both had and knew Christ the Mediator, by whom they were united to God, and made capable of receiving his promises. The second of these, as it is not yet perhaps sufficiently understood, will be fully considered in its own place (Book III. chap. xv.—xviii). For we will prove by many clear passages in the Prophets, that all which the Lord has ever given or promised to his people is of mere goodness and indulgence. The third also has, in various places, been not obscurely demonstrated. Even the first has not been left unnoticed.

3. As the first is most pertinent to the present subject, and is most controverted, we shall enter more fully into the consideration of it, taking care, at the same time, where any of the others require explanation, to supply it by the way, or afterwards add it in its proper place. The Apostle, indeed, removes all doubt when he says that the Gospel which God gave concerning his Son, Jesus Christ, "he had promised aforetime by his prophets in the holy Scriptures" (Rom. i. 2). And again, that "the righteousness of God without the law is manifested, being witnessed by the law and the prophets" (Rom. iii. 21). For the Gospel does not confine the hearts of men to the enjoyment of the present life, but raises them to the hope of immortality; does not fix them down to earthly delights, but announcing that there is a treasure laid up in heaven, carries the heart thither also. For in another place he thus explains, "After that ye believed [the Gospel], ye were sealed with that Holy Spirit of promise, which is the earnest of our inheritance unto the redemption of the purchased possession" (Eph. i. 13, 14). Again, "Since we heard of your faith in Jesus Christ, and of the love which ye have to all the saints, for the hope which is laid up for you in heaven, whereof ye

heard before in the word of the truth of the Gospel" (Col. i. 4).
Again, "Whereunto he called you by our Gospel to the obtaining of
the glory of our Lord Jesus Christ" (2 Thess. ii. 14). Whence also
it is called the word of salvation and the power of God, with salvation to every one that believes, and the kingdom of heaven.[1] But if
the doctrine of the Gospel is spiritual, and gives access to the possession of incorruptible life, let us not suppose that those to whom it
was promised and declared altogether neglected the care of the soul,
and lived stupidly like cattle in the enjoyment of bodily pleasures.
Let no one here quibble and say, that the promises concerning the
Gospel, which are contained in the Law and the Prophets, were designed for a new people.[2] For Paul, shortly after making that
statement concerning the Gospel promised in the Law, adds, that
"whatsoever things the law saith, it saith to those who are under
the law." I admit, indeed, he is there treating of a different subject,
but when he said that everything contained in the Law was directed
to the Jews, he was not so oblivious as not to remember what he had
said a few verses before of the Gospel promised in the Law. Most
clearly, therefore, does the Apostle demonstrate that the Old Testament had special reference to the future life, when he says that the
promises of the Gospel were comprehended under it.

4. In the same way we infer that the Old Testament was both
established by the free mercy of God and confirmed by the intercession
of Christ. For the preaching of the Gospel declares nothing more
than that sinners, without any merit of their own, are justified by
the paternal indulgence of God. It is wholly summed up in Christ.
Who, then, will presume to represent the Jews as destitute of Christ,
when we know that they were parties to the Gospel covenant, which
has its only foundation in Christ? Who will presume to make them
aliens to the benefit of gratuitous salvation, when we know that they
were instructed in the doctrine of justification by faith? And not
to dwell on a point which is clear, we have the remarkable saying of
our Lord, "Your father Abraham rejoiced to see my day, and he saw
it and was glad" (John viii. 56). What Christ here declares of
Abraham, an apostle shows to be applicable to all believers, when he
says that Jesus Christ is the "same yesterday, to-day, and for ever"
(Heb. xiii. 8). For he is not there speaking merely of the eternal
divinity of Christ, but of his power, of which believers had always
full proof. Hence both the blessed Virgin[3] and Zachariah, in their
hymns, say that the salvation revealed in Christ was a fulfilment of
the mercy promised " to our fathers, to Abraham, and to his seed for
ever" (Luke i. 55, 72). If, by manifesting Christ, the Lord fulfilled

---

[1] Acts xiii. 26; Rom. i. 16; 1 Cor. i. 18; Matth. iii. 2, 4, 17, &c., especially xiii.
[2] "Novo populo." French, "au peuple du Nouveau Testament"—the people of the New Dispensation.
[3] "Beata Virgo." French, "la Vierge Marie;"—the Virgin Mary.

his ancient oath, it cannot be denied that the subject of that oath [1] must ever have been Christ and eternal life.

5. Nay, the Apostle makes the Israelites our equals, not only in the grace of the covenant, but also in the signification of the Sacraments. For employing the example of those punishments, which the Scripture states to have been of old inflicted on the Jews, in order to deter the Corinthians from falling into similar wickedness, he begins with premising that they have no ground to claim for themselves any privilege which can exempt them from the divine vengeance which overtook the Jews, since the Lord not only visited them with the same mercies, but also distinguished his grace among them by the same symbols: as if he had said, If you think you are out of danger, because the Baptism which you received, and the Supper of which you daily partake, have excellent promises, and if, in the mean time, despising the goodness of God, you indulge in licentiousness, know that the Jews, on whom the Lord inflicted his severest judgments, possessed similiar symbols. They were baptised in passing through the sea, and in the cloud which protected them from the burning heat of the sun. It is said, that this passage was a carnal baptism, corresponding in some degree to our spiritual baptism. But if so, there would be a want of conclusiveness in the argument of the Apostle, whose object is to prevent Christians from imagining that they excelled the Jews in the matter of baptism. Besides, the cavil cannot apply to what immediately follows—viz. that they did "all eat the same spiritual meat; and did all drink the same spiritual drink: for they drank of that spiritual Rock that followed them: and that Rock was Christ" (1 Cor. x. 3, 4).

6. To take off the force of this passage of Paul, an objection is founded on the words of our Saviour, "Your fathers did eat manna in the wilderness, and are dead." "If any man eat of this bread, he shall live for ever" (John vi. 49, 51). There is no difficulty in reconciling the two passages. The Lord, as he was addressing hearers who only desired to be filled with earthly food, while they cared not for the true food of the soul, in some degree adapts his speech to their capacity, and, in particular, to meet their carnal view, draws a comparison between manna and his own body. They called upon him to prove his authority by performing some miracle, such as Moses performed in the wilderness when he obtained manna from heaven. In this manna they saw nothing but a relief of the bodily hunger from which the people were then suffering; they did not penetrate to the sublimer mystery to which Paul refers. Christ, therefore, to demonstrate that the blessing which they ought to expect from him was more excellent than the lauded one which Moses had bestowed upon their fathers, draws this comparison: If, in your opinion, it was a great and memorable miracle when the Lord, by

[1] " Ejus finis." French, " la fin du Vieil Testament;"—the end of the Old Testament.

Moses, supplied his people with heavenly food that they might be supported for a season, and not perish in the wilderness from famine; from this infer how much more excellent is the food which bestows immortality. We see why our Lord omitted to mention what was of principal virtue in the manna, and mentioned only its meanest use. Since the Jews had, as it were by way of upbraiding, cast up Moses to him as one who had relieved the necessity of the people by means of manna, he answers, that he was the minister of a much larger grace, one compared with which the bodily nourishment of the people, on which they set so high a value, ought to be held worthless. Paul, again, knowing that the Lord, when he rained manna from heaven, had not merely supplied their bodies with food, but had also dispensed it as containing a spiritual mystery to typify the spiritual quickening which is obtained in Christ, does not overlook that quality which was most deserving of consideration. Wherefore it is surely and clearly proved, that the same promises of celestial and eternal life, which the Lord now gives to us, were not only communicated to the Jews, but also sealed by truly spiritual sacraments. This subject is copiously discussed by Augustine in his work against Faustus the Manichee.

7. But if my readers would rather have passages quoted from the Law and the Prophets, from which they may see, as we have already done from Christ and the Apostles, that the spiritual covenant was common also to the Fathers, I will yield to the wish, and the more willingly, because opponents will thus be more surely convinced, that henceforth there will be no room for evasion. And I will begin with a proof which, though I know it will seem futile and almost ridiculous to supercilious Anabaptists, will have very great weight with the docile and sober-minded. I take it for granted that the word of God has such an inherent efficacy, that it quickens the souls of all whom he is pleased to favour with the communication of it. Peter's statement has ever been true, that it is an incorruptible seed, "which liveth and abideth for ever" (1 Peter i. 23), as he infers from the words of Isaiah (Is. xl. 6). Now when God, in ancient times, bound the Jews to him by this sacred bond, there cannot be a doubt that he separated them unto the hope of eternal life. When I say that they embraced the word which brought them nearer to God, I refer not to that general method of communication which is diffused through heaven and earth, and all the creatures of the world, and which, though it quickens all things, each according to its nature, rescues none from the bondage of corruption. I refer to that special mode of communication by which the minds of the pious are both enlightened in the knowledge of God, and, in a manner, linked to him. Adam, Abel, Noah, Abraham, and the other patriarchs, having been united to God by this illumination of the word, I say there cannot be the least doubt that entrance was given them into the immortal kingdom of God. They had that solid participation in God which cannot exist without the blessing of everlasting life.

8. If the point still seems somewhat involved, let us pass to the form of the covenant, which will not only satisfy calm thinkers, but sufficiently establish the ignorance of gainsayers. The covenant which God always made with his servants was this, "I will walk among you, and will be your God, and ye shall be my people" (Lev. xxvi. 12). These words, even as the prophets are wont to expound them, comprehend life and salvation, and the whole sum of blessedness. For David repeatedly declares, and with good reason, "Happy is that people whose God is the Lord." "Blessed is the nation whose God is the Lord; and the people whom he hath chosen for his own inheritance" (Psalm cxliv. 15; xxxiii. 12); and this not merely in respect of earthly happiness, but because he rescues from death, constantly preserves, and, with eternal mercy, visits those whom he has adopted for his people. As is said in other prophets, "Art not thou from everlasting, O Lord my God, mine Holy One? we shall not die." "The Lord is our judge, the Lord is our lawgiver, the Lord is our king; he will save us." "Happy art thou, O Israel: who is like unto thee, O people saved by the Lord?" (Hab. 1, 12; Isaiah xxxiii. 22; Deut. xxxiii. 29.) But not to labour superfluously, the prophets are constantly reminding us that no good thing, and, consequently, no assurance of salvation, is wanting, provided the Lord is our God. And justly. For if his face, the moment it hath shone upon us, is a perfect pledge of salvation, how can he manifest himself to any one as his God, without opening to him the treasures of salvation? The terms on which God makes himself ours is to dwell in the midst of us, as he declared by Moses (Lev. xxvi. 11). But such presence cannot be enjoyed without life being, at the same time, possessed along with it. And though nothing more had been expressed, they had a sufficiently clear promise of spiritual life in these words, "I am your God" (Exod. vi. 7). For he declared that he would be a God not to their bodies only, but specially to their souls. Souls, however, if not united to God by righteousness, remain estranged from him in death. On the other hand, that union, wherever it exists, will bring perpetual salvation with it.

9. To this we may add, that he not only declared he was, but also promised that he would be, their God. By this their hope was extended beyond present good, and stretched forward into eternity. Moreover, that this observance of the future had the effect, appears from the many passages in which the faithful console themselves not only in their present evils, but also for the future, by calling to mind that God was never to desert them. Moreover, in regard to the second part of the promise—viz. the blessing of God, its extending beyond the limits of the present life was still more clearly confirmed by the words, I will be the God of your seed after you (Gen. xvii. 7). If he was to manifest his favour to the dead by doing good to their posterity, much less would he deny his favour to themselves. God is not like men, who transfer their love to the children of their

friends, because the opportunity of bestowing kind offices as they wished upon themselves is interrupted by death. But God, whose kindness is not impeded by death, does not deprive the dead of the benefit of his mercy, which, on their account, he continues to a thousand generations. God, therefore, was pleased to give a striking proof of the abundance and greatness of his goodness which they were to enjoy after death, when he described it as overflowing to all their posterity (Exod. xx. 6). The truth of this promise was sealed, and in a manner completed, when, long after the death of Abraham, Isaac, and Jacob, he called himself their God (Exod. xx. 6). And why? Was not the name absurd if they had perished? It would have been just the same as if he had said, I am the God of men who exist not. Accordingly, the Evangelists relate that, by this very argument, our Saviour refuted the Sadducees (Matth. xxii. 23; Luke xx. 32), who were, therefore, unable to deny that the resurrection of the dead was attested by Moses, inasmuch as he had taught them that all the saints are in his hand (Deut. xxxiii. 3). Whence it is easy to infer that death is not the extinction of those who are taken under the tutelage, guardianship, and protection of him who is the disposer of life and death.

10. Let us now see (and on this the controversy principally turns) whether or not believers themselves were so instructed by the Lord, as to feel that they had elsewhere a better life, and to aspire to it while disregarding the present. First, the mode of life which heaven had imposed upon them made it a constant exercise, by which they were reminded, that if in this world only they had hope, they were of all men the most miserable. Adam, most unhappy even in the mere remembrance of his lost felicity, with difficulty supplies his wants by anxious labours; and that the divine curse might not be restricted to bodily labour, his only remaining solace becomes a source of the deepest grief. Of two sons, the one is torn from him by the parricidal hand of his brother; while the other, who survives, causes detestation and horror by his very look. Abel, cruelly murdered in the very flower of his days, is an example of the calamity which had come upon man. While the whole world are securely living in luxury, Noah, with much fatigue, spends a great part of his life in building an ark. He escapes death, but by greater troubles than a hundred deaths could have given. Besides his ten months' residence in the ark, as in a kind of sepulchre, nothing could have been more unpleasant than to have remained so long pent up among the filth of beasts. After escaping these difficulties he falls into a new cause of sorrow. He sees himself mocked by his own son, and is forced, with his own mouth, to curse one whom, by the great kindness of God, he had received safe from the deluge.

11. Abraham alone ought to be to us equal to tens of thousands if we consider his faith, which is set before us as the best model of believing, to whose race also we must be held to belong in order that

we may be the children of God.[1] What could be more absurd than that Abraham should be the father of all the faithful, and not even occupy the meanest corner among them? He cannot be denied a place in the list; nay, he cannot be denied one of the most honourable places in it, without the destruction of the whole Church. Now, as regards his experience in life, the moment he is called by the command of God, he is torn away from friends, parents, and country, objects in which the chief happiness of life is deemed to consist, as if it had been the fixed purpose of the Lord to deprive him of all the sources of enjoyment. No sooner does he enter the land in which he was ordered to dwell, than he is driven from it by famine. In the country to which he retires to obtain relief, he is obliged, for his personal safety, to expose his wife to prostitution. This must have been more bitter than many deaths. After returning to the land of his habitation, he is again expelled by famine. What is the happiness of inhabiting a land where you must so often suffer from hunger, nay, perish from famine, unless you flee from it? Then, again, with Abimelech, he is reduced to the same necessity of saving his head by the loss of his wife (Gen. xii. 12). While he wanders up and down uncertain for many years, he is compelled, by the constant quarrelling of servants, to part with his nephew, who was to him as a son. This departure must doubtless have cost him a pang something like the cutting off of a limb. Shortly after, he learns that his nephew is carried off captive by the enemy. Wherever he goes, he meets with savage-hearted neighbours, who will not even allow him to drink of the wells which he has dug with great labour. For he would not have purchased the use from the king of Gerar if he had not been previously prohibited. After he had reached the verge of life, he sees himself childless (the bitterest and most unpleasant feeling to old age), until, beyond expectation, Ishmael is born; and yet he pays dearly for his birth in the reproaches of Sarah, as if he was the cause of domestic disturbance by encouraging the contumacy of a female slave. At length Isaac is born, but in return, the first-born Ishmael is displaced, and almost hostilely driven forth and abandoned. Isaac remains alone, and the good man, now worn out with age, has his heart upon him, when shortly after he is ordered to offer him up in sacrifice. What can the human mind conceive more dreadful than for the father to be the murderer of his son? Had he been carried off by disease, who would not have thought the old man much to be pitied in having a son given to him in mockery, and in having his grief for being childless doubled to him? Had he been slain by some stranger, this would, indeed, have been much worse than natural death. But all these calamities are little compared with the murder of him by his father's hand. Thus, in fine, during the whole course of his life, he was harassed and tossed in such a way, that any one

[1] Calv. in Genes. cap. xii. 11—15.

desirous to give a picture of a calamitous life could not find one more appropriate. Let it not be said that he was not so very distressed, because he at length escaped from all these tempests. He is not said to lead a happy life who, after infinite difficulties during a long period, at last laboriously works out his escape, but he who calmly enjoys present blessings without any alloy of suffering.

12. Isaac is less afflicted, but he enjoys very few of the sweets of life. He also meets with those vexations which do not permit a man to be happy on the earth. Famine drives him from the land of Canaan ; his wife is torn from his bosom ; his neighbours are ever and anon annoying and vexing him in all kinds of ways, so that he is even obliged to fight for water. At home, he suffers great annoyance from his daughters-in-law ; he is stung by the dissension of his sons, and has no other cure for this great evil than to send the son whom he had blessed into exile (Gen. xxvi. xxvii.). Jacob, again, is nothing but a striking example of the greatest wretchedness. His boyhood is passed most uncomfortably at home amidst the threats and alarms of his elder brother, and to these he is at length forced to give way (Gen. xxvii. xxviii.). A fugitive from his parents and his native soil, in addition to the hardships of exile, the treatment he receives from his uncle Laban is in no respect milder and more humane (Gen. xxix.). As if it had been little to spend seven years of hard and rigorous servitude, he is cheated in the matter of a wife. For the sake of another wife, he must undergo a new servitude, during which, as he himself complains, the heat of the sun scorches him by day, while in frost and cold he spends the sleepless night (Gen. xxxi. 40, 41). For twenty years he spends this bitter life, and daily suffers new injuries from his father-in-law. Nor is he quiet at home, which he sees disturbed and almost broken up by the hatreds, quarrels, and jealousies of his wives. When he is ordered to return to his native land, he is obliged to take his departure in a manner resembling an ignominious flight. Even then he is unable to escape the injustice of his father-in-law, but in the midst of his journey is assailed by him with contumely and reproach (Gen. xxxi. 20.[1]) By-and-by a much greater difficulty befalls him (Gen. xxxii. xxxiii.). For as he approaches his brother, he has as many forms of death in prospect as a cruel foe could invent. Hence, while waiting for his arrival, he is distracted and excruciated by direful terrors ; and when he comes into his sight, he falls at his feet like one half dead, until he perceives him to be more placable than he had ventured to hope. Moreover, when he first enters the land, he is bereaved of Rachel his only beloved

---

[1] The French is, " Et encore ne peut il pas ainsi eviter l'iniquité de son beau père, qu'il ne soit de lui persecuté, et atteint au milieu du chemin ; et pourceque Dieu ne permettoit point qu'il lui advint pis, il est vexé de beaucoup d'opprobres et contumelies, par celui du quel il avoit bonne matiere de se plaindre."—Even thus he cannot escape the injustice of his father-in-law, but is persecuted by him, and attacked in the midst of his journey ; and because God did not allow worse to happen, he is assailed with much contumely and reproach by one of whom he had good cause to complain.

wife. Afterwards he hears that the son whom she had borne him,
and whom he loved more than all his other children, is devoured by
a wild beast (Gen. xxxvii. 33). How deep the sorrow caused by his
death he himself evinces, when, after long tears, he obstinately refuses
to be comforted, declaring that he will go down to the grave to his
son mourning. In the mean time, what vexation, anxiety, and grief,
must he have received from the carrying off and dishonour of his
daughter, and the cruel revenge of his sons, which not only brought
him into bad odour with all the inhabitants of the country, but exposed him to the greatest danger of extermination? (Gen. xxxiv.)
Then follows the horrid wickedness of Reuben his first-born, wickedness than which none could be committed more grievous (Gen. xxxvi.
22). The dishonour of a wife being one of the greatest of calamities,
what must be said when the atrocity is perpetrated by a son? Some
time after, the family is again polluted with incest (Gen. xxxviii. 18).
All these disgraces might have crushed a mind otherwise the most
firm and unbroken by misfortune. Towards the end of his life, when
he seeks relief for himself and his family from famine, he is struck
by the announcement of a new misfortune, that one of his sons is
detained in prison, and that to recover him he must intrust to others
his dearly beloved Benjamin (Gen. xlii. xliii.). Who can think that
in such a series of misfortunes, one moment was given him in which
he could breathe secure? Accordingly, his own best witness, he declares
to Pharaoh, " Few and evil have the days of the years of my life been"
(Gen. xlvii. 9). In declaring that he had spent his life in constant
wretchedness, he denies that he had experienced the prosperity which
had been promised him by the Lord. Jacob, therefore, either formed
a malignant and ungrateful estimate of the Lord's favour, or he truly
declared that he had lived miserable on the earth. If so, it follows
that his hope could not have been fixed on earthly objects.

13. If these holy Patriarchs expected a happy life from the hand
of God (and it is indubitable that they did), they viewed and contemplated a different happiness from that of a terrestrial life. This is
admirably shown by an Apostle, " By faith, he [Abraham] sojourned
in the land of promise, as in a strange country, dwelling in tabernacles with Isaac and Jacob, the heirs with him of the same promise :
for he looked for a city which hath foundations, whose builder and
maker is God." "These all died in faith, not having received the
promises, but having seen them afar off, and were persuaded of them,
and embraced them, and confessed that they were strangers and pilgrims on the earth. For they that say such things declare plainly
that they seek a country. And truly, if they had been mindful of
that country from whence they came out, they might have had opportunity to have returned. But now they desire a better country, that
is, an heavenly : wherefore God is not ashamed to be called their God :
for he hath prepared for them a city" (Heb. xi. 9, 10, 13–16). They
had been duller than blocks in so pertinaciously pursuing promises,

no hope of which appeared upon the earth, if they had not expected their completion elsewhere. The thing which the Apostle specially urges, and not without reason, is, that they called this world a pilgrimage, as Moses also relates (Gen. xlvii. 9). If they were pilgrims and strangers in the land of Canaan, where is the promise of the Lord which appointed them heirs of it? It is clear, therefore, that the promise of possession which they had received looked farther. Hence, they did not acquire a footbreadth in the land of Canaan, except for sepulture; thus testifying that they hoped not to receive the benefit of the promise till after death. And this is the reason why Jacob set so much value on being buried there, that he took Joseph bound by oath to see it done; and why Joseph wished that his bones should some ages later, long after they had mouldered into dust, be carried thither (Gen. xlvii. 29, 30; l. 25).

14. In short, it is manifest, that in the whole course of their lives, they had an eye to future blessedness. Why should Jacob have aspired so earnestly to primogeniture, and intrigued for it at so much risk, if it was to bring him only exile and destitution, and no good at all, unless he looked to some higher blessing? And that this was his feeling, he declared in one of the last sentences he uttered, "I have waited for thy salvation, O God" (Gen. xlix. 18). What salvation could he have waited for, when he felt himself breathing his last, if he did not see in death the beginning of a new life? And why talk of saints and the children of God, when even one, who otherwise strove to resist the truth, was not devoid of some similar impression? For what did Balaam mean when he said, "Let me die the death of the righteous, and let my last end be like his" (Num. xxiii. 10), unless he felt convinced of what David afterward declares, "Precious in the sight of the Lord is the death of his saints" (Ps. cxvi. 15; xxxiv. 12). If death were the goal and ultimate limit, no distinction could be observed between the righteous and the wicked. The true distinction is the different lot which awaits them after death.

15. We have not yet come farther down than the books of Moses whose only office, according to our opponents, was to induce the people to worship God, by setting before them the fertility of the land, and its general abundance; and yet to every one who does not voluntarily shun the light, there is clear evidence of a spiritual covenant. But if we come down to the Prophets, the kingdom of Christ and eternal life are there exhibited in the fullest splendour. First, David, as earlier in time, in accordance with the order of the Divine procedure, spoke of heavenly mysteries more obscurely than they, and yet with what clearness and certainty does he point to it in all he says. The value he put upon his earthly habitation is attested by these words, "I am a stranger with thee, and a sojourner, as all my fathers were. Verily every man at his best estate is altogether vanity. Surely every man walketh in a vain show. And now, Lord, what

wait I for? my hope is in thee" (Ps. xxxix. 12, 5, 6, 7). He who confesses that there is nothing solid or stable on the earth, and yet firmly retains his hope in God, undoubtedly contemplates a happiness reserved for him elsewhere. To this contemplation he is wont to invite believers whenever he would have them to be truly comforted. For, in another passage, after speaking of human life as a fleeting and evanescent show, he adds, "The mercy of the Lord is from everlasting to everlasting upon them that fear him" (Ps. ciii. 17). To this there is a corresponding passage in another psalm, "Of old thou hast laid the foundation of the earth; and the heavens are the work of thy hands. They shall perish, but thou shalt endure; yea, all of them shall wax old like a garment; as a vesture shalt thou change them, and they shall be changed; but thou art the same, and thy years shall have no end. The children of thy servants shall continue, and their seed shall be established before thee" (Ps. cii. 25–28). If, notwithstanding of the destruction of the heavens and the earth, the godly cease not to be established before God, it follows, that their salvation is connected with his eternity. But this hope could have no existence, if it did not lean upon the promise as expounded by Isaiah, "The heavens shall vanish away like smoke, and the earth shall wax old like a garment, and they that dwell therein shall die in like manner; but my salvation shall be for ever, and my righteousness shall not be abolished" (Isa. li. 6). Perpetuity is here attributed to righteousness and salvation, not as they reside in God, but as they are experienced by men.

16. Nor can those things which are everywhere said as to the prosperous success of believers be understood in any other sense than as referring to the manifestation of celestial glory. Of this nature are the following passages: "He preserveth the souls of his saints; he delivereth them out of the hand of the wicked. Light is sown for the righteous, and gladness for the upright in heart." "His righteousness endureth for ever; his horn shall be exalted with honour— the desire of the wicked shall perish." "Surely the righteous shall give thanks unto thy name; the upright shall dwell in thy presence." "The righteous shall be in everlasting remembrance." "The Lord redeemeth the soul of his servants." [1] But the Lord often leaves his servants, not only to be annoyed by the violence of the wicked, but to be lacerated and destroyed; allows the good to languish in obscurity and squalid poverty, while the ungodly shine forth, as it were, among the stars; and even by withdrawing the light of his countenance does not leave them lasting joy. Wherefore, David by no means disguises the fact, that if believers fix their eyes on the present condition of the world, they will be grievously tempted to believe that with God integrity has neither favour nor reward; so much does impiety prosper and flourish, while the godly are oppressed with ignominy,

---

[1] Ps. xcvii. 10, 11; cxii. 9, 10; cxl. 18; cxii. 6; xxxiv. 22.

poverty, contempt, and every kind of cross. The Psalmist says, "But as for me, my feet were almost gone; my steps had well nigh slipped. For I was envious of the foolish, when I saw the prosperity of the wicked." At length, after a statement of the case, he concludes, "When I thought to know this, it was too painful for me: until I went into the sanctuary of God; then understood I their end" (Ps. lxxiii. 2, 3, 16, 17).

17. Therefore, even from this confession of David, let us learn that the holy fathers under the Old Testament were not ignorant that in this world God seldom or never gives his servants the fulfilment of what is promised them, and therefore has directed their minds to his sanctuary, where the blessings not exhibited in the present shadowy life are treasured up for them. This sanctuary was the final judgment of God, which, as they could not at all discern it by the eye, they were contented to apprehend by faith. Inspired with this confidence, they doubted not that whatever might happen in the world, a time would at length arrive when the divine promises would be fulfilled. This is attested by such expressions as these: "As for me, I will behold thy face in righteousness: I shall be satisfied, when I awake, with thy likeness" (Psalm xvii. 15). "I am like a green olive tree in the house of God" (Psalm lii. 8). Again, "The righteous shall flourish like the palm tree: he shall grow like a cedar in Lebanon. Those that be planted in the house of the Lord shall flourish in the courts of our God. They shall still bring forth fruit in old age; they shall be fat and flourishing" (Psalm xcii. 12—14). He had exclaimed a little before, "O Lord, how great are thy works! and thy thoughts are very deep." "When the wicked spring as the grass, and when all the workers of iniquity do flourish: it is that they shall be destroyed for ever." Where was this splendour and beauty of the righteous, unless when the appearance of this world was changed by the manifestation of the heavenly kingdom? Lifting their eyes to the eternal world, they despised the momentary hardships and calamities of the present life, and confidently broke out into these exclamations: "He shall never suffer the righteous to be moved. But thou, O God, shalt bring them down into the pit of destruction: bloody and deceitful men shall not live out half their days" (Psalm. lv. 22, 23). Where in this world is there a pit of eternal destruction to swallow up the wicked, of whose happiness it is elsewhere said, "They spend their days in wealth, and in a moment go down to the grave"? (Job xxi. 13). Where, on the other hand, is the great stability of the saints, who, as David complains, are not only disturbed, but everywhere utterly bruised and oppressed? It is here. He set before his eyes not merely the unstable vicissitudes of the world, tossed like a troubled sea, but what the Lord is to do when he shall one day sit to fix the eternal constitution of heaven and earth, as he in another place elegantly describes: "They that trust in their wealth, and boast themselves in the multitude of their

riches; none of them can by any means redeem his brother, nor give to God a ransom for him." "For he seeth that wise men die, likewise the fool and the brutish person perish, and leave their wealth to others. Their inward thought is, that their houses shall continue for ever, and their dwelling-places to all generations; they call their lands after their own names. Nevertheless, man being in honour abideth not: he is like the beasts that perish. This their way is their folly: yet their posterity approve their sayings. Like sheep they are laid in the grave; death shall feed on them; and the upright shall have dominion over them in the morning; and their beauty shall consume in the grave from their dwelling" (Psalm xlix. 6, 7, 10—14). By this derision of the foolish for resting satisfied with the slippery and fickle pleasures of the world, he shows that the wise must seek for a very different felicity. But he more clearly unfolds the hidden doctrine of the resurrection when he sets up a kingdom to the righteous after the wicked are cast down and destroyed. For what, pray, are we to understand by the "morning," unless it be the revelation of a new life, commencing when the present comes to an end?

18. Hence the consideration which believers employed as a solace for their sufferings, and a remedy for their patience: "His anger endureth but a moment: in his favour is life" (Psalm xxx. 5). How did their afflictions, which continued almost throughout the whole course of life, terminate in a moment? Where did they see the long duration of the divine benignity, of which they had only the slightest taste? Had they clung to earth, they could have found nothing of the kind; but looking to heaven, they saw that the period during which the Lord afflicted his saints was but a moment, and that the mercies with which he gathers them are everlasting: on the other hand, they foresaw that for the wicked, who only dreamed of happiness for a day, there was reserved an eternal and never-ending destruction. Hence those expressions: "The memory of the just is blessed, but the name of the wicked shall rot" (Prov. x. 7). "Precious in the sight of the Lord is the death of his saints (Psalm cxvi. 15). Again in Samuel: "The Lord will keep the feet of his saints, and the wicked shall be silent in darkness" (1 Sam. ii. 9); showing they knew well, that however much the righteous might be tossed about, their latter end was life and peace; that how pleasant soever the delights of the wicked, they gradually lead down to the chambers of death. They accordingly designated the death of such persons as the death "of the uncircumcised," that is, persons cut off from the hope of resurrection (Ezek. xxviii. 10; xxxi. 18). Hence David could not imagine a greater curse than this: "Let them be blotted out of the book of the living, and not be written with the righteous" (Psalm lxix. 28).

19. The most remarkable passage of all is that of Job: "I know that my Redeemer liveth, and that he shall stand at the latter day

upon the earth: and though after my skin worms destroy this body, yet in my flesh shall I see God: whom I shall see for myself, and mine eyes shall behold, and not another" (Job xix. 25—27). Those who would make a display of their acuteness, pretend that these words are to be understood not of the last resurrection, but of the day when Job expected that God would deal more gently with him. Granting that this is partly meant, we shall, however, compel them, whether they will or not, to admit that Job never could have attained to such fulness of hope if his thoughts had risen no higher than the earth. It must, therefore, be confessed, that he who saw that the Redeemer would be present with him when lying in the grave, must have raised his eyes to a future immortality. To those who think only of the present life, death is the extremity of despair; but it could not destroy the hope of Job. "Though he slay me," said he, "yet will I trust in him" (Job xiii. 15). Let no trifler here burst in with the objection that these are the sayings of a few, and do not by any means prove that there was such a doctrine among the Jews. To this my instant answer is, that these few did not in such passages give utterance to some hidden wisdom, to which only distinguished individuals were admitted privately and apart from others, but that having been appointed by the Holy Spirit to be the teachers of the people, they openly promulgated the mysteries of God, which all in common behoved to learn as the principles of public religion. When, therefore, we hear that those passages in which the Holy Spirit spoke so distinctly and clearly of the spiritual life were public oracles in the Jewish Church, it were intolerably perverse to confine them entirely to a carnal covenant relating merely to the earth and earthly riches.

20. When we descend to the later prophets, we have it in our power to expatiate freely as in our own field. If, when David, Job, and Samuel were in question, the victory was not difficult, much easier is it here; for the method and economy which God observed in administering the covenant of his mercy was, that the nearer the period of its full exhibition approached, the greater the additions which were daily made to the light of revelation. Accordingly, at the beginning, when the first promise of salvation was given to Adam (Gen. iii. 15), only a few slender sparks beamed forth: additions being afterwards made, a greater degree of light began to be displayed, and continued gradually to increase and shine with greater brightness, until at length, all the clouds being dispersed, Christ the Sun of righteousness arose, and with full refulgence illumined all the earth (Mal. iv). In appealing to the Prophets, therefore, we can have no fear of any deficiency of proof; but as I see an immense mass of materials, which would occupy us much longer than is compatible with the nature of our present work (the subject, indeed, would require a large volume), and as I trust that, by what has already been said, I have paved the way, so that every reader of the very least discernment may proceed without stumbling, I will avoid a

prolixity, for which at present there is little necessity; only reminding my readers to facilitate the entrance by means of the key which was formerly put into their hands (*supra*, Chap. IV. sec. 3, 4)— namely, that whenever the Prophets make mention of the happiness of believers (a happiness of which scarcely any vestiges are discernible in the present life), they must have recourse to this distinction: that the better to commend the Divine goodness to the people, they used temporal blessings as a kind of lineaments to shadow it forth, and yet gave such a portrait as might lift their minds above the earth, the elements of this world, and all that will perish, and compel them to think of the blessedness of a future and spiritual life.

21. One example will suffice. When the Israelites were carried away to Babylon, their dispersion seemed to be the next thing to death, and they could scarcely be dissuaded from thinking that Ezekiel's prophecy of their restoration (Ezek. xxxvii. 4) was a mere fable, because it seemed to them the same thing as if he had prophesied that putrid carcases would be raised to life. The Lord, in order to show that, even in that case, there was nothing to prevent him from making room for his kindness, set before the prophet in vision a field covered with dry bones, to which, by the mere power of his word, he in one moment restored life and strength. The vision served, indeed, to correct the unbelief of the Jews at the time, but it also reminded them how much farther the power of the Lord extended than to the bringing back of the people, since by a single nod it could so easily give life to dry scattered bones. Wherefore, the passage may be fitly compared with one in Isaiah, " Thy dead men shall live, together with my dead body shall they arise. Awake and sing, ye that dwell in dust: for thy dew is as the dew of herbs, and the earth shall cast out the dead. Come, my people, enter thou into thy chambers, and shut thy doors about thee: hide thyself as it were for a little moment, until the indignation be overpast. For, behold, the Lord cometh out of his place to punish the inhabitants of the earth for their iniquity: the earth also shall disclose her blood, and shall no more cover her slain" (Isa. xxvi. 19—21).

22. It were absurd, however, to interpret all the passages on a similar principle; for there are several which point without any veil to the future immortality which awaits believers in the kingdom of heaven. Some of them we have already quoted, and there are many others, but especially the following two. The one is in Isaiah, "As the new heavens and the new earth, which I will make, shall remain beforeme, saith the Lord, so shall your seed and your name remain. And it shall come to pass, that from one new moon to another, and from one sabbath to another, shall all flesh come to worship before me, saith the Lord. And they shall go forth, and look upon the carcases of the men that have transgressed against me: for their worm shall not die, neither shall their fire be quenched; and they shall be an abhorring unto all flesh" (Isa. lxvi. 22—24). The other passage

is in Daniel. " At that shall Michael stand up, the great prince which standeth for the children of thy people : and there shall be a time of trouble, such as there never was since there was a nation even to that same time : and at that time thy people shall be delivered, every one shall be found written in the book. And many of them that sleep in the dust of the earth shall awake, some to everlasting life, and some to shame and everlasting contempt" (Dan. xii. 1, 2).

23. In proving the two remaining points—viz. that the Patriarchs had Christ as the pledge of their covenant, and placed all their hope of blessing in him—as they are clearer, and not so much controverted, I will be less particular. Let us then lay it down confidently as a truth which no engines of the devil can destroy—that the Old Testament, or covenant which the Lord made with the people of Israel, was not confined to earthly objects, but contained a promise of spiritual and eternal life, the expectation of which behoved to be impressed on the minds of all who truly consented to the covenant. Let us put far from us the senseless and pernicious notion, that the Lord proposed nothing to the Jews, or that they sought nothing but full supplies of food, carnal delights, abundance of wealth, external influence. a numerous offspring, and all those things which our animal nature deems valuable. For, even now, the only kingdom of heaven which our Lord Jesus Christ promises to his followers, is one in which they may sit down with Abraham, and Isaac, and Jacob (Matth. viii. 11) ; and Peter declared of the Jews of his day, that they were heirs of gospel grace because they were the sons of the prophets, and comprehended in the covenant which the Lord of old made with his people (Acts iii. 25). And that this might not be attested by words merely, our Lord also approved it by act (Matth. xxvii. 52). At the moment when he rose again, he deigned to make many of the saints partakers of his resurrection, and allowed them to be seen in the city ; thus giving a sure earnest, that everything which he did and suffered in the purchase of eternal salvation, belonged to believers under the Old Testament just as much as to us. Indeed, as Peter testifies, they were endued with the same spirit of faith by which we are regenerated to life (Acts xv. 8). When we hear that that spirit, which is, as it were, a kind of spark of immortality in us (whence it is called the " earnest" of our inheritance, Eph. i. 14), dwelt in like manner in them, how can we presume to deny them the inheritance ? Hence, it is the more wonderful how the Sadducees of old fell into such a degree of sottishness as to deny both the resurrection and the substantive existence[1] of spirits, both of which were attested to them by so many striking passages of Scripture. Nor would the stupidity of the whole nation in the present day, in expecting an earthly reign of the Messiah, be less wonderful, had not the Scriptures foretold this long before as the punishment which they were to suffer for rejecting the

---

1 " Animarum substantiam." French, "immortalité des ames ;"—immortality of souls.

Gospel, God, by a just judgment, blinding minds which voluntarily invite darkness, by rejecting the offered light of heaven. They read, and are constantly turning over the pages of Moses, but a veil prevents them from seeing the light which beams forth in his countenance (2 Cor. iii. 14) ; and thus to them he will remain covered and veiled until they are converted to Christ, between whom and Moses they now study, as much as in them lies, to maintain a separation.

CHAPTER XI.

THE DIFFERENCE BETWEEN THE TWO TESTAMENTS.

This chapter consists principally of three parts. I. Five points of difference between the Old and the New Testaments, sec. 1–11. II. The last of these points being, that the Old Testament belonged to the Jews only, whereas the New Testament belongs to all; the calling of the Gentiles is shortly considered, sec. 12. III. A reply to two objections usually taken to what is here taught concerning the difference between the Old and the New Testaments, sec. 13, 14.

Sections.

1. Five points of difference between the Old and the New Testaments. These belong to the mode of administration rather than the substance. First difference. In the Old Testament the heavenly inheritance is exhibited under temporal blessings; in the New, aids of this description are not employed.
2. Proof of this first difference from the simile of an heir in pupillarity, as in Gal. iv. 1.
3. This the reason why the Patriarchs, under the Law, set a higher value on this life, and the blessings of it, and dreaded the punishments, these being even more striking. Why severe and sudden punishments existed under the Law.
4. A second difference. The Old Testament typified Christ under ceremonies. The New exhibits the immediate truth and the whole body. The scope of the Epistle to the Hebrews in explaining this difference. Definition of the Old Testament.
5. Hence the Law our Schoolmaster to bring us unto Christ.
6. Notwithstanding, among those under the Law, some of the strongest examples of faith are exhibited, their equals being scarcely to be found in the Christian Church. The ordinary method of the divine dispensation to be here attended to. These excellent individuals placed under the Law, and aided by ceremonies, that they might behold and hail Christ afar off.
7. Third difference. The Old Testament is literal, the New spiritual. This difference considered first generally.
8. Next treated specially, on a careful examination of the Apostle's text. A threefold antithesis. The Old Testament is literal, deadly, temporary. The New is spiritual, quickening, eternal. Difference between the letter and the spirit.
9. Fourth difference. The Old Testament belongs to bondage, the New to liberty. This confirmed by three passages of Scripture. Two objections answered.
10. Distinction between the three last differences and the first. Confirmation of the above from Augustine. Condition of the patriarchs under the Old Testament.
11. Fifth difference. The Old Testament belonged to one people only, the New to all.
12. The second part of the chapter depending on the preceding section. Of the calling of the Gentiles. Why the calling of the Gentiles seemed to the Apostles so strange and new.
13. The last part of the chapter. Two objections considered. 1. God being immutable cannot consistently disapprove what he once ordered. Answer confirmed by a passage of Scripture.
14. Objections. 2. God could at first have transacted with the Jews as he now does with Christians. Answer, showing the absurdity of this objection. Another answer founded on a just consideration of the divine will and the dispensation of grace.

1. WHAT, then? you will say, Is there no difference between the Old and the New Testaments? What is to become of the many

passages of Scripture in which they are contrasted as things differing most widely from each other? I readily admit the differences which are pointed out in Scripture, but still hold that they derogate in no respect from their established unity, as will be seen after we have considered them in their order. These differences (so far as I have been able to observe them and can remember) seem to be chiefly four, or if you choose to add a fifth, I have no objections. I hold, and think I will be able to show, that they all belong to the mode of administration rather than to the substance. In this way, there is nothing in them to prevent the promises of the Old and New Testament from remaining the same, Christ being the foundation of both. The first difference then is, that though, in old time, the Lord was pleased to direct the thoughts of his people, and raise their minds to the heavenly inheritance, yet, that their hope of it might be the better maintained, he held it forth, and, in a manner, gave a foretaste of it under earthly blessings, whereas the gift of future life, now more clearly and lucidly revealed by the gospel, leads our minds directly to meditate upon it, the inferior mode of exercise formerly employed in regard to the Jews being now laid aside. Those who attend not to the divine purpose in this respect, suppose that God's ancient people ascended no higher than the blessings which were promised to the body. They hear the land of Canaan so often named as the special, and as it were the only, reward of the Divine Law to its worshippers; they hear that the severest punishment which the Lord denounces against the transgressors of the Law is expulsion from the possession of that land and dispersion into other countries; they see that this forms almost the sum of the blessings and curses declared by Moses; and from these things they confidently conclude that the Jews were separated from other nations not on their own account, but for another reason—viz. that the Christian Church might have an emblem in whose outward shape might be seen an evidence of spiritual things. But since the Scripture sometimes demonstrates that the earthly blessings thus bestowed were intended by God himself to guide them to a heavenly hope, it shows great unskilfulness, not to say dulness, not to attend to this mode of dispensation. The ground of controversy is this: our opponents hold that the land of Canaan was considered by the Israelites as supreme and final happiness, and now, since Christ was manifested, typifies to us the heavenly inheritance; whereas we maintain that, in the earthly possession which the Israelites enjoyed, they beheld, as in a mirror, the future inheritance which they believed to be reserved for them in heaven.

2. This will better appear from the similitude which Paul uses in Galatians (Gal. iv. 1). He compares the Jewish nation to an heir in pupillarity, who, as yet unfit to govern himself, follows the direction of a tutor or guide to whose charge he has been committed. Though this simile refers especially to ceremonies, there is nothing to prevent us from applying it most appropriately here also. The

same inheritance was destined to them as to us, but from nonage they were incapable of entering to it, and managing it. They had the same Church, though it was still in puerility. The Lord, therefore, kept them under this tutelage, giving them spiritual promises, not clear and simple, but typified by earthly objects. Hence, when he chose Abraham, Isaac, and Jacob, and their posterity, to the hope of immortality, he promised them the land of Canaan for an inheritance, not that it might be the limit of their hopes, but that the view of it might train and confirm them in the hope of that true inheritance, which, as yet, appeared not. And, to guard against delusion, they received a better promise, which attested that this earth was not the highest measure of the divine kindness. Thus, Abraham is not allowed to keep down his thoughts to the promised land : by a greater promise his views are carried upward to the Lord. He is thus addressed, "Fear not, Abram : I am thy shield, and thy exceeding great reward" (Gen. xv. 1). Here we see that the Lord is the final reward promised to Abraham, that he might not seek a fleeting and evanescent reward in the elements of this world, but look to one which was incorruptible. A promise of the land is afterwards added for no other reason than that it might be a symbol of the divine benevolence, and a type of the heavenly inheritance, as the saints declare their understanding to have been. Thus David rises from temporal blessings to the last and highest of all, "My flesh and my heart faileth : but God is the strength of my heart, and my portion for ever." "My heart and my flesh crieth out for the living God" (Ps. lxxiii. 26 ; lxxxiv. 2). Again, "The Lord is the portion of mine inheritance and of my cup : thou maintainest my lot" (Ps. xvi. 5). Again, "I cried unto thee, O Lord : I said, Thou art my refuge and my portion in the land of the living" (Ps. cxlii. 5). Those who can venture to speak thus, assuredly declare that their hope rises beyond the world and worldly blessings. This future blessedness, however, the prophets often describe under a type which the Lord had taught them. In this way are to be understood the many passages in Job (Job xviii. 17) and Isaiah, to the effect, That the righteous shall inherit the earth, that the wicked shall be driven out of it, that Jerusalem will abound in all kinds of riches, and Sion overflow with every species of abundance. In strict propriety, all these things obviously apply not to the land of our pilgrimage, nor to the earthly Jerusalem, but to the true country, the heavenly city of believers, in which the Lord hath commanded blessing and life for evermore (Ps. cxxxiii. 3).

3. Hence the reason why the saints under the Old Testament set a higher value on this mortal life and its blessings than would now be meet. For, though they well knew that in their race they were not to halt at it as the goal, yet, perceiving that the Lord, in accommodation to their feebleness, had there imprinted the lineaments of his favour, it gave them greater delight than it could have done if considered only in itself. For as the Lord, in testifying his good-will

towards believers by means of present blessings, then exhibited spiritual felicity under types and emblems, so, on the other hand, by temporal punishments he gave proofs of his judgment against the reprobate. Hence, by earthly objects, the favour of the Lord was displayed, as well as his punishment inflicted. The unskilful, not considering this analogy and correspondence (if I may so speak) between rewards and punishments, wonder that there is so much variance in God, that those who, in old time, were suddenly visited for their faults with severe and dreadful punishments, he now punishes much more rarely and less severely, as if he had laid aside his former anger ; and, for this reason, they can scarcely help imagining, like the Manichees, that the God of the Old Testament was different from that of the New. But we shall easily disencumber ourselves of such doubts if we attend to that mode of divine administration to which I have adverted—that God was pleased to indicate and typify both the gift of future and eternal felicity by terrestrial blessings, as well as the dreadful nature of spiritual death by bodily punishments, at that time when he delivered his covenant to the Israelites as under a kind of veil.

4. Another distinction between the Old and New Testaments is in the types, the former exhibiting only the image of truth, while the reality was absent, the shadow instead of the substance, the latter exhibiting both the full truth and the entire body. Mention is usually made of this, whenever the New Testament is contrasted with the Old,[1] but it is nowhere so fully treated as in the Epistle to the Hebrews (chap. vii.—x.). The Apostle is there arguing against those who thought that the observances of the Mosaic Law could not be abolished without producing the total ruin of religion. In order to refute this error, he adverts to what the Psalmist had foretold concerning the priesthood of Christ (Ps cx. 4). Seeing that an eternal priesthood is assigned to him, it is clear that the priesthood in which there was a daily succession of priests is abolished. And he proves that the institution of this new Priest must prevail, because confirmed by an oath. He afterwards adds, that a change of the priest necessarily led to a change of the covenant. And the necessity of this he confirms by the reason, that the weakness of the law was such, that it could make nothing perfect. He then goes on to show in what this weakness consists—namely, that it had external carnal observances which could not render the worshippers perfect in respect of conscience, because its sacrifices of beasts could neither take away sins nor procure true holiness. He therefore concludes that it was a shadow of good things to come, and not the very image of the things,

---

.[1] The French is, " et à icelle se doivent reduire quasi tous les passages, auxquels le vieil Testament est opposé au Nouveau par comparaison."—And to this ought in a manner to be referred all the passages in which the Old Testament is, by way of comparison, opposed to the New.

and accordingly had no other office than to be an introduction to the better hope which is exhibited in the Gospel.

Here we may see in what respect the legal is compared with the evangelical covenant, the ministry of Christ with that of Moses. If the comparison referred to the substance of the promises, there would be a great repugnance between the two covenants ; but since the nature of the case leads to a different view, we must follow it in order to discover the truth. Let us, therefore, bring forward the covenant which God once ratified as eternal and unending. Its completion, whereby it is fixed and ratified, is Christ. Till such completion takes place, the Lord, by Moses, prescribes ceremonies which are, as it were, formal symbols of confirmation. The point brought under discussion was, Whether or not the ceremonies ordained in the Law behoved to give way to Christ. Although these were merely accidents of the covenant, or at least additions and appendages, and, as they are commonly called, accessories, yet because they were the means of administering it, the name of covenant is applied to them, just as is done in the case of other sacraments.[1] Hence, in general, the Old Testament is the name given to the solemn method of confirming the covenant comprehended under ceremonies and sacrifices. Since there is nothing substantial in it, until we look beyond it, the Apostle contends that it behoved to be annulled and become antiquated (Heb. vii. 22), to make room for Christ, the surety and mediator of a better covenant, by whom the eternal sanctification of the elect was once purchased, and the transgressions which remained under the Law wiped away. But if you prefer it, take it thus : the covenant of the Lord was old, because veiled by the shadowy and ineffectual observance of ceremonies ; and it was therefore temporary, being, as it were, in suspense until it received a firm and substantial confirmation. Then only did it become new and eternal when it was consecrated and established in the blood of Christ. Hence the Saviour, in giving the cup to his disciples in the last supper, calls it the cup of the new testament in his blood ; intimating, that the covenant of God was truly realised, made new, and eternal, when it was sealed with his blood.

5. It is now clear in what sense the Apostle said (Gal. iii. 24 ; iv. 1), that by the tutelage of the Law the Jews were conducted to Christ, before he was exhibited in the flesh. He confesses that they were sons and heirs of God, though, on account of nonage, they were placed under the guardianship of a tutor. It was fit, the Sun of Righteousness not yet having risen, that there should neither be so much light of revelation nor such clear understanding. The Lord dispensed the light of his word, so that they could behold it at a distance, and

---

[1] " Qualiter et aliis Sacramentis dari solet." French, " comme l'Escriture a coustume d'attribuer aux sacremens le nom des choses qu'ils representent ;"—just as Scripture is wont to give sacraments the names of the things which they represent.

obscurely. Accordingly, this slender measure of intelligence is designated by Paul by the term *childhood*, which the Lord was pleased to train by the elements of this world, and external observances, until Christ should appear. Through him the knowledge of believers was to be matured. This distinction was noted by our Saviour himself when he said that the Law and the Prophets were until John, that from that time the gospel of the kingdom was preached (Matth. xi. 13). What did the Law and the Prophets deliver to the men of their time ? They gave a foretaste of that wisdom which was one day to be clearly manifested, and showed it afar off. But where Christ can be pointed to with the finger, there the kingdom of God is manifested. In him are contained all the treasures of wisdom and understanding, and by these we penetrate almost to the very shrine of heaven.

6. There is nothing contrary to this in the fact, that in the Christian Church scarcely one is to be found who, in excellence of faith, can be compared to Abraham, and that the Prophets were so distinguished by the power of the Spirit, that even in the present day they give light to the whole world. For the question here is, not what grace the Lord conferred upon a few, but what was the ordinary method which he followed in teaching the people, and which even was employed in the case of those very prophets who were endued with special knowledge above others. For their preaching was both obscure as relating to distant objects, and was included in types. Moreover, however wonderful the knowledge displayed in them, as they were under the necessity of submitting to the tutelage common to all the people, they must also be ranked among children. Lastly, none of them ever had such a degree of discernment as not to savour somewhat of the obscurity of the age. Whence the words of our Saviour, " Many kings and prophets have desired to see the things which you see, and have not seen them ; and to hear the things which ye hear, and have not heard them. Blessed are your eyes, for they see ; and your ears, for they hear " (Matth. xiii. 17). And it was right that the presence of Christ should have this distinguishing feature, that by means of it the revelation of heavenly mysteries should be made more transparent. To the same effect is the passage which we formerly quoted from the First Epistle of Peter, that to them it was revealed that their labour should be useful not so much to themselves as to our age.

7. I proceed to the third distinction, which is thus expressed by Jeremiah : " Behold, the days come, saith the Lord, that I will make a new covenant with the house of Israel, and with the house of Judah : not according to the covenant that I made with their fathers in the day that I took them by the hand to bring them out of the land of Egypt ; which my covenant they brake, although I was an husband unto them, saith the Lord : but this shall be the covenant that I will make with the house of Israel ; After those days, saith the Lord, I

will put my law in their inward parts, and write it in their hearts ; and will be their God, and they shall be my people. And they shall teach no more every man his neighbour, and every man his brother, saying, Know the Lord: for they shall all know me, from the least of them unto the greatest of them " (Jer. xxxi. 31—34). From these words, the Apostle took occasion to institute a comparison between the Law and the Gospel, calling the one a doctrine of the letter, the other a doctrine of the spirit ; describing the one as formed on tables of stone, the other on tables of the heart ; the one the preaching of death, the other of life ; the one of condemnation, the other of justification ; the one made void, the other permanent (2 Cor. iii. 5, 6). The object of the Apostle being to explain the meaning of the Prophet, the words of the one furnish us with the means of ascertaining what was understood by both. And yet there is some difference between them. For the Apostle speaks of the Law more disparagingly than the Prophet. This he does not simply in respect of the Law itself, but because there were some false zealots of the Law who, by a perverse zeal for ceremonies, obscured the clearness of the Gospel, he treats of the nature of the Law with reference to their error and foolish affection. It will, therefore, be proper to attend to this peculiarity in Paul. Both, however, as they are contrasting the Old and New Testament, consider nothing in the Law but what is peculiar to it. For example, the Law everywhere [1] contains promises of mercy; but as these are adventitious to it, they do not enter into the account of the Law as considered only in its own nature. All which is attributed to it is, that it commands what is right, prohibits crimes, holds forth rewards to the cultivators of righteousness, and threatens transgressors with punishment, while at the same time it neither changes nor amends that depravity of heart which is naturally inherent in all.

8. Let us now explain the Apostle's contrast step by step. The Old Testament is literal, because promulgated without the efficacy of the Spirit: the New spiritual, because the Lord has engraven it on the heart. The second antithesis is a kind of exposition of the first. The Old is deadly, because it can do nothing but involve the whole human race in a curse; the New is the instrument of life, because those who are freed from the curse it restores to favour with God. The former is the ministry of condemnation, because it charges the whole sons of Adam with transgression; the latter the ministry of righteousness, because it unfolds the mercy of God, by which we are justified. The last antithesis must be referred to the Ceremonial Law. Being a shadow of things to come, it behoved in time to perish and vanish away; whereas the Gospel, inasmuch as it exhibits the very body, is firmly established for ever. Jeremiah, indeed, calls the Moral Law also a weak and fragile covenant; but for another

---

[1] "Passim." French, "çá et lá ;"—here and there.

reason—namely, because it was immediately broken by the sudden
defection of an ungrateful people; but as the blame of such violation
is in the people themselves, it is not properly alleged against the
covenant.   The ceremonies, again, inasmuch as through their very
weakness they were dissolved by the advent of Christ, had the cause
of weakness from within.   Moreover, the difference between the spirit
and the letter must not be understood as if the Lord had delivered
his Law to the Jews without any good result ; *i.e.* as if none had been
converted to him.   It is used comparatively to commend the riches
of the grace with which the same Lawgiver, assuming, as it were, a
new character, honoured the preaching of the Gospel.   When we
consider the multitude of those whom, by the preaching of the Gospel,
he has regenerated by his Spirit, and gathered out of all nations into
the communion of his Church, we may say that those of ancient Israel
who, with sincere and heartfelt affection, embraced the covenant of
the Lord, were few or none, though the number is great when they
are considered in themselves without comparison.

9. Out of the third distinction a fourth arises.   In Scripture, the
term bondage is applied to the Old Testament, because it begets fear,
and the term freedom to the New, because productive of confidence
and security.   Thus Paul says to the Romans, " Ye have not received
the spirit of bondage again to fear ; but ye have received the Spirit
of adoption, whereby we cry, Abba, Father" (Rom. viii. 15).   To the
same effect is the passage in the Hebrews, " For ye are not come unto
the mount that might be touched, and that burned with fire, nor unto
blackness, and darkness, and tempest, and the sound of a trumpet,
and the voice of words ; which voice they that heard entreated that
the word should not be spoken to them any more (for they could not
endure that which was commanded, And if so much as a beast touch
the mountain, it shall be stoned, or thrust through with a dart : and
so terrible was the sight, that Moses said, I exceedingly fear and
quake): but ye are come unto Mount Sion, and unto the city of
the living God, the heavenly Jerusalem," &c. (Heb. xii. 18—22).
What Paul briefly touches on in the passage which we have quoted
from the Romans, he explains more fully in the Epistle to the Galatians, where he makes an allegory of the two sons of Abraham in this
way : " Agar is mount Sinai in Arabia, and answereth to Jerusalem
which now is, and is in bondage with her children.   But Jerusalem
which is above is free, which is the mother of us all" (Gal. iv. 25,
26).   As the offspring of Agar was born in slavery, and could never
attain to the inheritance, while that of Sara was free and entitled to
the inheritance, so by the Law we are subjected to slavery, and by the
Gospel alone regenerated into liberty.   The sum of the matter comes
to this : The Old Testament filled the conscience with fear and
trembling, the New inspires it with gladness.   By the former the
conscience is held in bondage, by the latter it is manumitted and
made free.   If it be objected, that the holy fathers among the Israel-

ites, as they were endued with the same spirit of faith, must also have been partakers of the same liberty and joy, we answer, that neither was derived from the Law; but feeling that by the Law they were oppressed like slaves, and vexed with a disquieted conscience, they fled for refuge to the Gospel; and, accordingly, the peculiar advantage of the Gospel was, that, contrary to the common rule of the Old Testament, it exempted those who were under it from those evils. Then, again, we deny that they did possess the spirit of liberty and security in such a degree as not to experience some measure of fear and bondage. For however they might enjoy the privilege which they had obtained through the grace of the Gospel, they were under the same bonds and burdens of observances as the rest of their nation. Therefore, seeing they were obliged to the anxious observance of ceremonies (which were the symbols of a tutelage bordering on slavery, and handwritings by which they acknowledged their guilt, but did not escape from it), they are justly said to have been, comparatively, under a covenant of fear and bondage, in respect of that common dispensation under which the Jewish people were then placed.

10. The three last contrasts to which we have adverted (sec. 4, 7, 9), are between the Law and the Gospel, and hence in these the Law is designated by the name of the Old, and the Gospel by that of the New Testament. The first is of wider extent (sec. 1), comprehending under it the promises which were given even before the Law. When Augustine maintained that these were not to be included under the name of the Old Testament (August. ad Bonifac. Lib. iii. c. 14), he took a most correct view, and meant nothing different from what we have now taught; for he had in view those passages of Jeremiah and Paul in which the Old Testament is distinguished from the word of grace and mercy. In the same passage, Augustine, with great shrewdness, remarks, that from the beginning of the world the sons of promise, the divinely regenerated, who, through faith working by love, obeyed the commandments, belonged to the New Testament; entertaining the hope not of carnal, earthly, temporal, but spiritual, heavenly, and eternal blessings, believing especially in a Mediator, by whom they doubted not both that the Spirit was administered to them, enabling them to do good, and pardon imparted as often as they sinned. The thing which he thus intended to assert was, that all the saints mentioned in Scripture, from the beginning of the world, as having been specially selected by God, were equally with us partakers of the blessing of eternal salvation. The only difference between our division and that of Augustine is, that ours (in accordance with the words of our Saviour, "All the prophets and the law prophesied until John," Matth. xi. 13) distinguishes between the gospel light and that more obscure dispensation of the word which preceded it, while the other division simply distinguishes between the weakness of the Law and the strength of the Gospel. And here also, with regard to the holy

fathers, it is to be observed, that though they lived under the Old Testament, they did not stop there, but always aspired to the New, and so entered into sure fellowship with it. Those who, contented with existing shadows, did not carry their thoughts to Christ, the Apostle charges with blindness and malediction. To say nothing of other matters, what greater blindness can be imagined, than to hope for the expiation of sin from the sacrifice of a beast, or to seek mental purification in external washing with water, or to attempt to appease God with cold ceremonies, as if he were greatly delighted with them? Such are the absurdities into which those fall who cling to legal observances, without respect to Christ.

11. The fifth distinction which we have to add consists in this, that until the advent of Christ, the Lord set apart one nation, to which he confined the covenant of his grace. Moses says, "When the Most High divided to the nations their inheritance, when he separated the sons of Adam, he set the bounds of the people according to the number of the children of Israel. For the Lord's portion is his people; Jacob is the lot of his inheritance" (Deut. xxxii. 8, 9). In another passage he thus addresses the people: "Behold, the heaven and the heaven of heavens is the Lord's thy God, the earth also, with all that therein is. Only the Lord had a delight in thy fathers to love them, and he chose their seed, after them, even you, above all people, as it is this day" (Deut. x. 14, 15). That people, therefore, as if they had been the only part of mankind belonging to him, he favoured exclusively with the knowledge of his name, depositing his covenant, as it were, in their bosom, manifesting to them the presence of his divinity, and honouring them with all privileges. But to say nothing of other favours, the only one here considered is his binding them to him by the communion of his word, so that he was called and regarded as their God. Meanwhile other nations, as if they had had no kind of intercourse with him, he allowed to wander in vanity, not even supplying them with the only means of preventing their destruction—viz. the preaching of his word. Israel was thus the Lord's favourite child, the others were aliens. Israel was known and admitted to trust and guardianship, the others left in darkness; Israel was made holy, the others were profane; Israel was honoured with the presence of God, the others kept far aloof from him. But on the fulness of the time destined to renew all things, when the Mediator between God and man was manifested, the middle wall of partition, which had long kept the divine mercy within the confines of Israel, was broken down, peace was preached to them who were afar off, as well as to those who were nigh, that being together reconciled to God, they might unite as one people. Wherefore, there is now no respect of Jew or Greek, of circumcision or uncircumcision, but Christ is all and in all. To him the heathen have been given for his inheritance, and the uttermost parts of the earth for his possession (Ps. ii. 8), that he may rule

without distinction "from sea to sea, and from the river unto the ends of the earth" (Ps. lxxii. 8).

12. The calling of the Gentiles, therefore, is a distinguishing feature illustrative of the superiority of the New over the Old Testament. This, it is true, had been previously declared by the prophets, in passages both numerous and clear, but still the fulfilment of it was deferred to the reign of the Messiah. Even Christ did not acknowledge it at the very outset of his ministry, but delayed it until having completed the whole work of redemption in all its parts, and finished the period of his humiliation, he received from the Father "a name which is above every name, that at the name of Jesus every knee should bow" (Philip. ii. 9, 10). Hence the period being not yet completed, he declared to the woman of Canaan, "I am not sent but unto the lost sheep of the house of Israel" (Matth. xv. 24). Nor in his first commission to the Apostles does he permit them to pass the same limits, "Go not into the way of the Gentiles, and into any city of the Samaritans enter ye not: but go rather to the lost sheep of the house of Israel" (Matth. x. 5, 6). However plainly the thing may have been declared in numerous passages, when it was announced to the Apostles, it seemed to them so new and extraordinary, that they were horrified at is as something monstrous. At length, when they did act upon it, it was timorously, and not without reluctance. Nor is this strange; for it seemed by no means in accordance with reason, that the Lord, who for so many ages had selected Israel from the rest of the nations, should suddenly, as it were, change his purpose, and abandon his choice. Prophecy, indeed, had foretold it, but they could not be so attentive to prophecies, as not to be somewhat startled by the novel spectacle thus presented to their eye. It was not enough that God had in old times given specimens of the future calling of the Gentiles. Those whom he had so called were very few in number, and, moreover, he in a manner adopted them into the family of Abraham, before allowing them to approach his people. But by this public call, the Gentiles were not only made equal to the Jews, but seemed to be substituted into their place, as if the Jews had been dead.[1] We may add, that any strangers whom God had formerly admitted into the body of the Church, had never been put on the same footing with the Jews. Wherefore, it is not without cause that Paul describes it as "the mystery which hath been hid from ages and from generations, but now is made manifest to his saints" (Col. i. 26).

13. The whole difference between the Old and New Testaments has, I think, been fully and faithfully explained, under these four or five heads, in so far as requisite for ordinary instruction. But since this variety in governing the Church, this diversity in the mode

---

[1] "In demortuorum locum." The French is simply, "en leur lieu;"—into their place.

of teaching, this great change in rites and ceremonies, is regarded by some as an absurdity, we must reply to them before passing to other matters. And this can be done briefly, because the objections are not so strong[1] as to require a very careful refutation. It is unreasonable, they say, to suppose that God, who is always consistent with himself, permitted such a change as afterwards to disapprove what he had once ordered and commended. I answer, that God ought not to be deemed mutable, because he adapts different forms to different ages, as he knows to be expedient for each. If the husbandman prescribes one set of duties to his household in winter, and another in summer, we do not therefore charge him with fickleness, or think he deviates from the rules of good husbandry, which depends on the regular course of nature. In like manner, if a father of a family, in educating, governing, and managing his children, pursues one course in boyhood, another in adolescence, and another in manhood, we do not therefore say that he is fickle, or abandons his opinions. Why, then, do we charge God with inconstancy, when he makes fit and congruous arrangements for diversities of times? The latter similitude ought to be completely satisfactory. Paul likens the Jews to children, and Christians to grown men (Gal. iv. 1). What irregularity is there in the Divine arrangement, which confined them to the rudiments which were suitable to their age, and trains us by a firmer and more manly discipline? The constancy of God is conspicuous in this, that he delivered the same doctrine to all ages, and persists in requiring that worship of his name which he commanded at the beginning. His changing the external form and manner does not show that he is liable to change. In so far he has only accommodated himself to the mutable and diversified capacities of man.

14. But it is said, Whence this diversity, save that God chose to make it? Would it not have been as easy for him from the first, as after the advent of Christ, to reveal eternal life in clear terms without any figures, to instruct his people by a few clear sacraments, to bestow his Holy Spirit, and diffuse his grace over the whole globe? This is very much the same as to bring a charge against God, because he created the world at so late a period, when he could have done it at the first, or because he appointed the alternative changes of summer and winter, of day and night. With the feeling common to every pious mind, let us not doubt that everything which God has done has been done wisely and justly, although we may be ignorant of the cause which required that it should be so done. We should arrogate too much to ourselves were we not to concede to God that he may have reasons for his counsel, which we are unable to discern. It is strange, they say, that he now repudiates and abominates the sacrifices of beasts, and the whole apparatus of

---

[1] "Firmæ," French, "Ne si fortes, ne si urgentes;"—neither so strong, nor so pressing.

that Levitical priesthood in which he formerly delighted. As if those external and transient matters could delight God, or affect him in any way![1] It has already been observed, that he appointed none of these things on his own account, but instituted them all for the salvation of men. If a physician, adopting the best method, effects a cure upon a youth, and afterwards, when the same individual has grown old, and is again subject to the same disease, employs a different method of cure, can it be said that he repudiates the method which he formerly approved? Nay, continuing to approve of it, he only adapts himself to the different periods of life. In like manner, it was necessary in representing Christ in his absence, and predicting his future advent, to employ a different set of signs from those which are employed, now that his actual manifestation is exhibited. It is true, that since the advent of Christ, the calling of God is more widely addressed to all nations, and the graces of the Spirit more liberally bestowed than they had previously been. But who, I ask, can deny the right of God to have the free and uncontrolled disposal of his gifts, to select the nations which he may be pleased to illuminate, the places which he may be pleased to illustrate by the preaching of his word, and the mode and measure of progress and success which he may be pleased to give to his doctrine,—to punish the world for its ingratitude, by withdrawing the knowledge of his name for certain ages, and again, when he so pleases, to restore it in mercy? We see, then, that in the calumnies which the ungodly employ in this matter, to perplex the minds of the simple, there is nothing that ought to throw doubt either on the justice of God or the veracity of Scripture.

1 " Aut ullo modo afficiant." French, " ou comme si jamais il s'y fust arreté ; "—or as if he could ever have stopped at them.

CHAPTER XII.

CHRIST, TO PERFORM THE OFFICE OF MEDIATOR, BEHOVED TO BECOME
MAN.

The two divisions of this chapter are, I. The reasons why our Mediator behoved to be
very God, and to become man, sec. 1—3. II. Disposal of various objections by some
fanatics, and especially by Osiander, to the orthodox doctrine concerning the Mediator,
sec. 4—7.

Sections.

1. Necessary, not absolutely, but by divine decree, that the Mediator should be God,
   and become man. Neither man nor angel, though pure, could have sufficed. The
   Son of God behoved to come down. Man in innocence could not penetrate to God
   without a Mediator, much less could he after the fall.
2. A second reason why the Mediator behoved to be God and man—viz. that he had to
   convert those who were heirs of hell into children of God.
3. Third reason, that in our flesh he might yield a perfect obedience, satisfy the divine
   justice, and pay the penalty of sin. Fourth reason, regarding the consolation and
   confirmation of the whole Church.
4. First objection against the orthodox doctrine: Answer to it. Confirmation from the
   sacrifices of the Law, the testimony of the Prophets, Apostles, Evangelists, and
   even Christ himself.
5. Second objection: Answer: Answer confirmed. Third objection: Answer. Fourth
   objection by Osiander: Answer.
6. Fifth objection, forming the basis of Osiander's errors on this subject: Answer.
   Nature of the divine image in Adam. Christ the head of angels and men.
7. Sixth objection: Answer. Seventh objection: Answer. Eighth objection: Answer.
   Ninth objection: Answer. Tenth objection: Answer. Eleventh objection: Answer.
   Twelfth objection: Answer. The sum of the doctrine.

1. It deeply concerned us, that he who was to be our Mediator
should be very God and very man. If the necessity be inquired into,
it was not what is commonly termed simple or absolute, but flowed
from the divine decree on which the salvation of man depended.
What was best for us, our most merciful Father determined. Our
iniquities, like a cloud intervening between Him and us, having utterly
alienated us from the kingdom of heaven, none but a person reaching
to him could be the medium of restoring peace. But who could
thus reach to him? Could any of the sons of Adam? All of them,
with their parent, shuddered at the sight of God. Could any of the
angels? They had need of a head, by connection with which they
might adhere to their God entirely and inseparably. What then?
The case was certainly desperate, if the Godhead itself did not descend
to us, it being impossible for us to ascend. Thus the Son of God
behoved to become our Emmanuel, *i.e.* God with us; and in such a
way, that by mutual union his divinity and our nature might be com-

bined; otherwise, neither was the proximity near enough, nor the affinity strong enough, to give us hope that God would dwell with us; so great was the repugnance between our pollution and the spotless purity of God. Had man remained free from all taint, he was of too humble a condition to penetrate to God without a Mediator. What, then, must it have been, when by fatal ruin he was plunged into death and hell, defiled by so many stains, made loathsome by corruption; in fine, overwhelmed with every curse? It is not without cause, therefore, that Paul, when he would set forth Christ as the Mediator, distinctly declares him to be man. There is, says he, " one Mediator between God and man, the man Christ Jesus" (1 Tim. ii. 5). He might have called him God, or at least, omitting to call him God, he might also have omitted to call him man: but because the Spirit, speaking by his mouth, knew our infirmity, he opportunely provides for it by the most appropriate remedy, setting the Son of God familiarly before us as one of ourselves. That no one, therefore, may feel perplexed where to seek the Mediator, or by what means to reach him, the Spirit, by calling him man, reminds us that he is near, nay, contiguous to us, inasmuch as he is our flesh. And, indeed, he intimates the same thing in another place, where he explains at greater length that he is not a high priest who "cannot be touched with the feeling of our infirmities; but was in all points tempted like as we are, yet without sin" (Heb. iv. 15).

2. This will become still clearer if we reflect, that the work to be performed by the Mediator was of no common description: being to restore us to the divine favour, so as to make us, instead of sons of men, sons of God; instead of heirs of hell, heirs of a heavenly kingdom. Who could do this unless the Son of God should also become the Son of man, and so receive what is ours as to transfer to us what is his, making that which is his by nature to become ours by grace? Relying on this earnest, we trust that we are the sons of God, because the natural Son of God assumed to himself a body of our body, flesh of our flesh, bones of our bones, that he might be one with us; he declined not to take what was peculiar to us, that he might in his turn extend to us what was peculiarly his own, and thus might be in common with us both Son of God and Son of man. Hence that holy brotherhood which he commends with his own lips, when he says, " I ascend to my Father, and your Father, to my God, and your God" (John xx. 17). In this way, we have a sure inheritance in the heavenly kingdom, because the only Son of God, to whom it entirely belonged, has adopted us as his brethren; and if brethren, then partners with him in the inheritance (Rom. viii. 17). Moreover, it was especially necessary for this cause also that he who was to be our Redeemer should be truly God and man. It was his to swallow up death: who but Life could do so? It was his to conquer sin: who could do so save Righteousness itself? It was his to put to flight the powers of the air and the world: who could do so but the mighty power superior

to both ? But who possesses life and righteousness, and the dominion and government of heaven, but God alone? Therefore God, in his infinite mercy, having determined to redeem us, became himself our Redeemer in the person of his only-begotten Son.

3. Another principal part of our reconciliation with God was, that man, who had lost himself by his disobedience, should by way of remedy, oppose to it obedience, satisfy the justice of God, and pay the penalty of sin. Therefore, our Lord came forth very man, adopted the person of Adam, and assumed his name, that he might in his stead obey the Father ; that he might present our flesh as the price of satisfaction to the just judgment of God, and in the same flesh pay the penalty which we had incurred. Finally, since as God only he could not suffer, and as man only could not overcome death, he united the human nature with the divine, that he might subject the weakness of the one to death as an expiation of sin, and by the power of the other, maintaining a struggle with death, might gain us the victory. Those, therefore, who rob Christ of divinity or humanity, either detract from his majesty and glory, or obscure his goodness. On the other hand, they are no less injurious to men, undermining and subverting their faith, which, unless it rest on this foundation, cannot stand. Moreover, the expected Redeemer was that son of Abraham and David whom God had promised in the Law and in the Prophets. Here believers have another advantage. Tracing up his origin in regular series to David and Abraham, they more distinctly recognise him as the Messiah celebrated by so many oracles. But special attention must be paid to what I lately explained, namely, that a common nature is the pledge of our union with the Son of God ; that, clothed with our flesh, he warred to death with sin that he might be our triumphant conqueror ; that the flesh which he received of us he offered in sacrifice, in order that by making expiation he might wipe away our guilt, and appease the just anger of his Father.

4. He who considers these things with due attention, will easily disregard vague speculations, which attract giddy minds and lovers of novelty. One speculation of this class is, that Christ, even though there had been no need of his interposition to redeem the human race, would still have become man. I admit that in the first ordering of creation, while the state of nature was entire, he was appointed head of angels and men ; for which reason Paul designates him " the first-born of every creature" (Col. i. 15). But since the whole Scripture proclaims that he was clothed with flesh in order to become a Redeemer, it is presumptuous to imagine any other cause or end. We know well why Christ was at first promised—viz. that he might renew a fallen world, and succour lost man. Hence under the Law he was typified by sacrifices, to inspire believers with the hope that God would be propitious to them after he was reconciled by the expiation of their sins. Since from the earliest age, even before the Law was promulgated, there was never any promise of a Mediator without

blood, we justly infer that he was destined in the eternal counsel of God to purge the pollution of man, the shedding of blood being the symbol of expiation. Thus, too, the prophets, in discoursing of him, foretold that he would be the Mediator between God and man. It is sufficient to refer to the very remarkable prophecy of Isaiah (Is. liii. 4, 5), in which he foretells that he was " smitten for our iniquities;" that " the chastisement of our peace was upon him ; " that as a priest " he was made an offering for sin : " " that by his stripes we are healed ; " that as all " like lost sheep have gone astray," " it pleased the Lord to bruise him, and put him to grief," that he might " bear our iniquities." After hearing that Christ was divinely appointed to bring relief to miserable sinners, whoso overleaps these limits gives too much indulgence to a foolish curiosity.

Then when he actually appeared, he declared the cause of his advent to be, that by appeasing God he might bring us from death unto life. To the same effect was the testimony of the Apostles concerning him (John i. 9 ; x. 14). Thus John, before teaching that the Word was made flesh, narrates the fall of man. But above all, let us listen to our Saviour himself when discoursing of his office: " God so loved the world, that he gave his only-begotten Son, that whosoever believeth in him should not perish, but have everlasting life." Again, " The hour is coming, and now is, when the dead shall hear the voice of the Son of God: and they that hear shall live." " I am the resurrection and the life: he that believeth in me, though he were dead, yet shall he live." " The Son of man is come to save that which was lost." Again, " They that be whole need not a physician."[1] I should never have done were I to quote all the passages. Indeed, the Apostles, with one consent, lead us back to this fountain ; and assuredly, if he had not come to reconcile God, the honour of his priesthood would fall, seeing it was his office as priest to stand between God and men, and " offer both gifts and sacrifices for sins " (Heb. v. 1); nor could he be our righteousness, as having been made a propitiation for us in order that God might not impute to us our sins (2 Cor. v. 19). In short, he would be stript of all the titles with which Scripture invests him. Nor could Paul's doctrine stand. " What the law could not do, in that it was weak through the flesh, God sending his own Son in the likeness of sinful flesh, and for sin, condemned sin in the flesh " (Rom. viii. 3). Nor what he states in another passage: " The grace of God that bringeth salvation hath appeared to all men "(Tit. ii. 11). In fine, the only end which the Scripture uniformly assigns for the Son of God voluntarily assuming our nature, and even receiving it as a command from the Father, is, that he might propitiate the Father to us by becoming a victim. " Thus it is written, and thus it behoved Christ to suffer ;"—" and that repentance and remission of sins should be preached in his name."

1 John iii. 16 ; v. 25 ; xi. 25 ; Matth. xviii. 11 ; ix. 12.

" Therefore doth my Father love me, because I lay down my life, that I might take it again." " This commandment have I received of my Father." " As Moses lifted up the serpent in the wilderness, even so must the Son of man be lifted up." " Father, save me from this hour: but for this cause came I unto this hour. Father, glorify thy name."[1] Here he distinctly assigns as the reason for assuming our nature, that he might become a propitiatory victim to take away sin. For the same reason Zacharias declares (Luke i. 79), that he came " to perform the mercy promised to our fathers," " to give light to them that sit in darkness, and in the shadow of death." Let us remember that all these things are affirmed of the Son of God, in whom, as Paul elsewhere declares, were " hid all the treasures of wisdom and knowledge," and save whom it was his determination " not to know anything" (Col. ii. 3: 1 Cor. ii. 2).

5. Should any one object, that in this there is nothing to prevent the same Christ who redeemed us when condemned from also testifying his love to us when safe by assuming our nature, we have the brief answer, that when the Spirit declares that by the eternal decree of God the two things were connected together—viz. that Christ should be our Redeemer, and, at the same time, a partaker of our nature, it is unlawful to inquire further. He who is tickled with a desire of knowing something more, not contented with the immutable ordination of God, shows also that he is not even contented with that Christ who has been given us as the price of redemption. And, indeed, Paul not only declares for what end he was sent, but rising to the sublime mystery of predestination, seasonably represses all the wantonness and pruriency of the human mind. " He hath chosen us in him before the foundation of the world, that we should be holy and without blame before him in love: having predestinated us unto the adoption of children by Jesus Christ to himself, according to the good pleasure of his will, to the praise of the glory of his grace, wherein he hath made us accepted in the Beloved: In whom we have redemption through his blood" (Eph. i. 4–7). Here certainly the fall of Adam is not presupposed as anterior in point of time, but our attention is directed to what God predetermined before all ages, when he was pleased to provide a cure for the misery of the human race. If, again, it is objected that this counsel of God depended on the fall of man, which he foresaw, to me it is sufficient and more to reply, that those who propose to inquire, or desire to know more of Christ than God predestinated by his secret decree, are presuming with impious audacity to invent a new Christ. Paul, when discoursing of the proper office of Christ, justly prays for the Ephesians that God would strengthen them " by his Spirit in the inner man," that they might " be able to comprehend with all saints what is the breadth and length, and depth and height; and to know the love of Christ

---

[1] Luke xxiv. 46; John x. 17; iii. 14; xii. 27, 28.

which passeth knowledge" (Eph. iii. 16, 18); as if he intended of set purpose to set barriers around our minds, and prevent them from declining one iota from the gift of reconciliation whenever mention is made of Christ. Wherefore, seeing it is as Paul declares it to be, "a faithful saying, and worthy of all acceptation, that Christ Jesus came into the world to save sinners" (1 Tim. i. 15), in it I willingly acquiesce. And since the same Apostle elsewhere declares that the grace which is now manifested by the Gospel "was given us in Christ Jesus before the world began" (2 Tim. i. 9), I am resolved to adhere to it firmly even to the end. This moderation is unjustly vituperated by Osiander, who has unhappily, in the present day, again agitated this question, which a few had formerly raised. He brings a charge of overweening confidence against those who deny that the Son of God would have appeared in the flesh if Adam had not fallen, because this notion is not repudiated by any passage of Scripture. As if Paul did not lay a curb on perverse curiosity when, after speaking of the redemption obtained by Christ, he bids us "avoid foolish questions" (Tit. iii. 9). To such insanity have some proceeded in their preposterous eagerness to seem acute, that they have made it a question whether the Son of God might not have assumed the nature of an ass. This blasphemy, at which all pious minds justly shudder with detestation, Osiander excuses by the pretext that it is nowhere distinctly refuted in Scripture; as if Paul, when he counted nothing valuable or worth knowing "save Jesus Christ and him crucified" (1 Cor. ii. 2), were admitting that the author of salvation is an ass. He who elsewhere declares that Christ was by the eternal counsel of the Father appointed "head over all things to the church," would never have acknowledged another to whom no office of redemption had been assigned.

6. The principle on which Osiander founds is altogether frivolous. He will have it that man was created in the image of God, inasmuch as he was formed on the model of the future Messiah, in order to resemble him whom the Father had already determined to clothe with flesh. Hence he infers, that though Adam had never fallen from his first and pure original, Christ would still have been man. How silly and distorted this view is, all men of sound judgment will at once discern; still he thinks he was the first to see what the image of God was—namely, that not only did the divine glory shine forth in the excellent endowments with which he was adorned, but God dwelt in him essentially. But while I grant that Adam bore the image of God, inasmuch as he was united to God (this being the truest and highest perfection of dignity), yet I maintain, that the likeness of God is to be sought for only in those marks of superiority with which God has distinguished Adam above the other animals. All, likewise, with one consent, acknowledge that Christ was even then the image of God, and, accordingly, whatever excellence was engraven on Adam had its origin in this, that by means of the only begotten Son he ap-

proximated to the glory of his Maker. Man, therefore, was created in the image of God (Gen. i. 27), and in him the Creator was pleased to behold, as in a mirror, his own glory. To this degree of honour he was exalted by the kindness of the only-begotten Son. But I add, that, as the Son was the common head both of men and angels, so the dignity which was conferred on man belonged to the angels also. For when we hear them called the sons of God (Ps. lxxxii. 6), it would be incongruous to deny that they were endued with some quality in which they resembled the Father. But if he was pleased that his glory should be represented in men and angels, and made manifest in both natures, it is ignorant trifling in Osiander to say, that angels were postponed to men, because they did not bear the image of Christ. They could not constantly enjoy the immediate presence of God if they were not like to him ; nor does Paul teach (Col. iii. 10) that men are renewed in the image of God in any other way than by being associated with angels, that they may be united together under one head. In fine, if we believe Christ, our felicity will be perfected when we shall have been received into the heavens, and made like the angels. But if Osiander is entitled to infer that the primary type of the image of God was in the man Christ, on the same ground may any one maintain that Christ behoved to partake of the angelic nature, seeing that angels also possess the image of God.

7. Osiander has no reason to fear that God would be found a liar, if the decree to incarnate the Son was not previously immutably fixed in his mind. Even had Adam not lost his integrity, he would, with the angels, have been like to God ; and yet it would not therefore have been necessary that the Son of God should become either a man or an angel. In vain does he entertain the absurd fear, that unless it had been determined by the immutable counsel of God, before man was created, that Christ should be born, not as the Redeemer, but as the first man, he might lose his precedence, since he would not have been born, except for an accidental circumstance—namely, that he might restore the lost race of man ; and in this way would have been created in the image of Adam. For why should he be alarmed at what the Scripture plainly teaches, that " he was in all points tempted like as we are, yet without sin ?" (Heb. iv. 15.) Hence Luke, also, hesitates not to reckon him in his genealogy as a son of Adam (Luke iii. 38). I should like to know why Christ is termed by Paul the second Adam (1 Cor. xv. 47), unless it be that a human condition was decreed him, for the purpose of raising up the ruined posterity of Adam. For if in point of order, that condition was antecedent to creation, he ought to have been called the first Adam. Osiander confidently affirms, that because Christ was in the purpose of God foreknown as man, men were formed after him as their model. But Paul, by calling him the second Adam, gives that revolt which made it necessary to restore nature to its primitive condition an intermediate place between its original formation and the restitution which we

obtain by Christ : hence it follows, that it was this restitution which made the Son of God be born, and thereby become man. Moreover, Osiander argues ill and absurdly, that as long as Adam maintained his integrity, he would have been the image of himself, and not of Christ. I maintain, on the contrary, that although the Son of God had never become incarnate, nevertheless the image of God was conspicuous in Adam, both in his body and his soul ; in the rays of this image it always appeared that Christ was truly head, and had in all things the pre-eminence. In this way we dispose of the futile sophism put forth by Osiander, that the angels would have been without this head, had not God purposed to clothe his Son with flesh, even independent of the sin of Adam. He inconsiderately assumes what no rational person will grant, that Christ could have had no supremacy over the angels, so that they might enjoy him as their prince, unless in so far as he was man. But it is easy to infer from the words of Paul (Col. i. 15), that inasmuch as he is the eternal Word of God, he is the first-born of every creature, not because he is created, or is to be reckoned among the creatures, but because the entire structure of the world, such as it was from the beginning, when adorned with exquisite beauty, had no other beginning ; then, inasmuch as he was made man, he is the first-born from the dead. For in one short passage (Col. i. 16—18), the Apostle calls our attention to both views : that by the Son all things were created, so that he has dominion over angels ; and that he became man, in order that he might begin to be a Redeemer. Owing to the same ignorance, Osiander says that men would not have had Christ for their king unless he had been a man ; as if the kingdom of God could not have been established by his eternal Son, though not clothed with human flesh, holding the supremacy, while angels and men were gathered together to participate in his celestial life and glory. But he is always deluded, or imposes upon himself by this false principle, that the church would have been ἀκέφαλον—without a head—had not Christ appeared in the flesh. In the same way as angels enjoyed him for their head, could he not by his divine energy preside over men, and by the secret virtue of his Spirit quicken and cherish them as his body, until they were gathered into heaven to enjoy the same life with the angels ? The absurdities which I have been refuting, Osiander regards as infallible oracles. Taking an intoxicating delight in his own speculations, his wont is to extract ridiculous pæans out of nothing. He afterwards says that he has a much stronger passage to produce—namely, the prophecy of Adam, who, when the woman was brought to him, said, " This is now bone of my bone, and flesh of my flesh " (Gen. ii. 23). But how does he prove it to be a prophecy ? Because in Matthew Christ attributes the same expression to God ! as if everything which God has spoken by man contained a prophecy. On the same principle, as the law proceeded from God, let Osiander in each precept find a prophecy. Add, that our Saviour's exposition would have been harsh and grovelling, had he confined himself to the literal meaning. He was not referring to the mystical union with which he has honoured the Church, but only to conjugal fidelity, and states, that the reason why God declared man and wife to be one flesh, was to prevent any one from violating that indissoluble tie by divorce. If this simple meaning is too low for Osiander, let him censure Christ for not leading his disciples to the hidden sense, by interpreting his Father's words with more subtlety. Paul gives no countenance to Osiander's dream, when, after saying that "we are members of his body, of his flesh, and of his bones," he immediately adds, "This is a great mystery" (Eph. v. 30—32). For he meant not to refer to the sense in which Adam used the words, but sets forth, under the figure and similitude of marriage, the sacred union which makes us one with Christ. His words have this meaning; for reminding us that he is speaking of Christ and the Church, he, by way of correction, distinguishes between the marriage tie and the spiritual union of Christ with his Church. Wherefore, this subtlety vanishes at once. I deem it unnecessary to discuss similar absurdities: for from this very brief refutation, the vanity of them all will be discovered. Abundantly sufficient for the solid nurture of the children of God is this sober truth, that "when the fulness of the time was come, God sent forth his Son, made of a woman, made under the law, to redeem them who were under the law" (Gal. iv. 4, 5).

CHAPTER XIII.

CHRIST CLOTHED WITH THE TRUE SUBSTANCE OF HUMAN NATURE.

The heads of this chapter are, I. The orthodox doctrine as to the true humanity of our Saviour, proved from many passages of Scripture, sec. 1. II. Refutation of the impious objections of the Marcionites, Manichees, and similar heretics, sec. 2–4.

Sections.

1. Proof of the true humanity of Christ, against the Manichees and Marcionites.
2. Impious objections of heretics farther discussed. Six objections answered.
8. Other eight objections answered.

1. OF the divinity of Christ, which has elsewhere been established by clear and solid proofs, I presume it were superfluous again to treat. It remains, therefore, to see how, when clothed with our flesh, he fulfilled the office of Mediator. In ancient times, the reality of his human nature was impugned by the Manichees and Marcionites, the latter figuring to themselves a phantom instead of the body of Christ, and the former dreaming of his having been invested with celestial flesh. The passages of Scripture contradictory to both are numerous and strong. The blessing is not promised in a heavenly seed, or the mask of a man, but the seed of Abraham and Jacob; nor is the everlasting throne promised to an aërial man but to the Son of David, and the fruit of his loins. Hence, when manifested in the flesh, he is called the Son of David and Abraham, not because he was born of a virgin, and yet created in the air, but because, as Paul explains, he was "made of the seed of David, according to the flesh" (Rom. i. 3), as the same apostle elsewhere says, that he came of the Jews (Rom. ix. 5). Wherefore, our Lord himself, not contented with the name of man, frequently calls himself the Son of man. wishing to express more clearly that he was a man by true human descent. The Holy Spirit having so often, by so many organs, with so much care and plainness, declared a matter which in itself is not abstruse, who could have thought that mortals would have had the effrontery to darken it with their glosses? Many other passages are at hand, were it wished to produce more: for instance, that one of Paul, that "God sent forth his Son, made of a woman" (Gal. iv. 4), and innumerable others, which show that he was subject to hunger, thirst, cold, and the other infirmities of our nature. But from the many we must chiefly select those which may conduce to build up our minds in true faith, as when it is said, "Verily, he took not on

him the nature of angels, but he took on him the seed of Abraham," "that through death he might destroy him that had the power of death" (Heb. ii. 16, 14). Again, " Both he that sanctifieth and they who are sanctified are all of one : for which cause he is not ashamed to call them brethren." "Wherefore in all things it behoved him to be made like unto his brethren, that he might be a merciful and faithful high priest" (Heb. ii. 11, 17). Again, "We have not an high priest which cannot be touched with the feeling of our infirmities" (Heb. iv. 15), and the like. To the same effect is the passage to which we lately referred, in which Paul distinctly declares, that the sins of the world behoved to be expiated in our flesh (Rom. viii. 3). And certainly everything which the Father conferred on Christ pertains to us for this reason, that "he is the head," that from him the whole body is "fitly joined together, and compacted by that which every joint supplieth" (Eph. iv. 16). Nay, in no other way could it hold true as is said, that the Spirit was given to him without measure (John i. 16), and that out of his fulness have all we received ; since nothing could be more absurd than that God, in his own essence, should be enriched by an adventitious gift. For this reason also, Christ himself elsewhere says, "For their sakes I sanctify myself" (John xvii. 19).

2. The passages which they produce in confirmation of their error are absurdly wrested, nor do they gain anything by their frivolous subtleties when they attempt to do away with what I have now adduced in opposition to them. Marcion imagines that Christ, instead of a body, assumed a phantom, because it is elsewhere said, that he was made in the likeness of man, and found in fashion as a man. Thus he altogether overlooks what Paul is then discussing (Philip. ii. 7). His object is not to show what kind of body Christ assumed, but that, when he might have justly asserted his divinity, he was pleased to exhibit nothing but the attributes of a mean and despised man. For, in order to exhort us to submission by his example, he shows, that when as God he might have displayed to the world the brightness of his glory, he gave up his right, and voluntarily emptied himself; that he assumed the form of a servant, and, contented with that humble condition, suffered his divinity to be concealed under a veil of flesh. Here, unquestionably, he explains not what Christ was, but in what way he acted. Nay, from the whole context, it is easily gathered, that it was in the true nature of man that Christ humbled himself. For what is meant by the words, he was "found in fashion as a man," but that for a time, instead of being resplendent with divine glory, the human form only appeared in a mean and abject condition? Nor would the words of Peter, that he was "put to death in the flesh, but quickened by the Spirit" (1 Pet. iii. 18), hold true, unless the Son of God had become weak in the nature of man. This is explained more clearly by Paul, when he declares that "he was crucified through weakness" (2 Cor. xiii. 4). And

hence his exaltation; for it is distinctly said, that Christ acquired new glory after he humbled himself. This could fitly apply only to a man endued with a body and a soul. "Manes" dreams of an aërial body, because, Christ is called the second Adam, the Lord from heaven. But the apostle does not there speak of the essence of his body as heavenly, but of the spiritual life which, derived from Christ, quickens us (1 Cor. xv. 47). This life Paul and Peter, as we have seen, separate from his flesh. Nay, that passage admirably confirms the doctrine of the orthodox, as to the human nature of Christ. If his body were not of the same nature with ours, there would be no soundness in the argument which Paul pursues with so much earnestness,—If Christ is risen, we shall rise also; if we rise not, neither hath Christ risen. Whatever be the cavils by which the ancient Manichees, or their modern disciples, endeavour to evade this, they cannot succeed. It is a frivolous and despicable evasion to say, that Christ is called the Son of man, because he was promised to men; it being obvious that, in the Hebrew idiom, the Son of man means a true man: and Christ, doubtless, retained the idiom of his own tongue.[1] Moreover, there cannot be a doubt as to what is to be understood by the sons of Adam. Not to go farther, a passage in the eighth psalm, which the apostles apply to Christ, will abundantly suffice: "What is man, that thou art mindful of him? and the son of man, that thou visitest him?" (Ps. viii. 4). Under this figure is expressed the true humanity of Christ. For although he was not immediately descended of an earthly father, yet he originally sprang from Adam. Nor could it otherwise be said in terms of the passage which we have already quoted, "Forasmuch, then, as the children are partakers of flesh and blood, he also himself likewise took part of the same;" these words plainly proving that he was an associate and partner in the same nature with ourselves. In this sense also it is said, that "both he that sanctifieth and they who are sanctified are all of one." The context proves that this refers to a community of nature; for it is immediately added, "For which cause he is not ashamed to call them brethren" (Heb. ii. 11). Had he said at first that believers are of God, where could there have been any ground for being ashamed of persons possessing such dignity? But when Christ of his boundless grace associates himself with the mean and ignoble, we see why it was said that "he is not ashamed." It is vain to object, that in this way the wicked will be the brethren of Christ; for we know that the children of God are not born of flesh and blood, but of the Spirit through faith. Therefore, flesh alone does not constitute the union of brotherhood. But although the apostle assigns to believers only the honour of being one with Christ, it does not, however, follow, that unbelievers have not the same origin accordingly to the flesh; just as when we say that Christ became

---

[1] The last clause of the sentence is omited in the French.

man, that he might make us sons of God, the expression does not extend to all classes of persons; the intervention of faith being necessary to our being spiritually ingrafted into the body of Christ. A dispute is also ignorantly raised as to the term *first-born*. It is alleged that Christ ought to have been the first son of Adam, in order that he might be the first-born among the brethren (Rom. viii. 29). But primogeniture refers not to age, but to degree of honour and pre-eminence of virtue. There is just as little colour for the frivolous assertion that Christ assumed the nature of man, and not that of angels (Heb. ii. 16), because it was the human race that he restored to favour. The apostle, to magnify the honour which Christ has conferred upon us, contrasts us with the angels, to whom we are in this respect preferred. And if due weight is given to the testimony of Moses (Gen. iii. 15), when he says that the seed of the woman would bruise the head of the serpent, the dispute is at an end. For the words there used refer not to Christ alone, but to the whole human race. Since the victory was to be obtained for us by Christ. God declares generally, that the posterity of the woman would overcome the devil. From this it follows, that Christ is a descendant of the human race, the purpose of God in thus addressing Eve being to raise her hopes, and prevent her from giving way to despair.

3. The passages in which Christ is called the seed of Abraham, and the fruit of the loins of David, those persons, with no less folly than wickedness, wrap up in allegory. Had the term *seed* been used allegorically, Paul surely would not have omitted to notice it, when he affirms clearly, and without figure, that the promise was not given "to seeds, as of many; but as of one, And to thy seed, which is Christ" (Gal. iii. 16). With similar absurdity they pretend that he was called the Son of David, for no other reason but because he had been promised, and was at length in due time manifested. For Paul, after he had called him the Son of David, by immediately subjoining *according to the flesh*, certainly designates his nature. So also (Rom. ix. 5), while declaring him to be "God blessed for ever," he mentions separately, that, "as concerning the flesh, he was descended from the Jews." Again, if he had not been truly begotten of the seed of David, what is the meaning of the expression, that he is the "fruit of his loins;" or what the meaning of the promise, "Of the fruit of thy body will I set upon thy throne?" (Ps. cxxxii. 11). Moreover, their mode of dealing with the genealogy of Christ, as given by Matthew, is mere sophistry; for though he reckons up the progenitors not of Mary, but of Joseph, yet as he was speaking of a matter then generally understood, he deems it enough to show that Joseph was descended from the seed of David, since it is certain that Mary was of the same family. Luke goes still farther, showing that the salvation brought by Christ is common to the whole human race, inasmuch as Christ, the author of salvation, is descended from Adam, the common father of us all. I confess, indeed, that the genealogy proves Christ

to be the Son of David, only as being descended of the Virgin ; but the new Marcionites, for the purpose of giving a gloss to their heresy— namely, to prove that the body which Christ assumed was unsubstantial, too confidently maintain that the expression as to seed is applicable only to males, thus subverting the elementary principles of nature. But as this discussion belongs not to theology, and the arguments which they adduce are too futile to require any laboured refutation, I will not touch on matters pertaining to philosophy and the medical art. It will be sufficient to dispose of the objection drawn from the statement of Scripture, that Aaron and Jehoiadah married wives out of the tribe of Judah, and that thus the distinction of tribes was confounded, if proper descent could come through the female. It is well known, that in regard to civil order, descent is reckoned through the male ; and yet the superiority on his part does not prevent the female from having her proper share in the descent. This solution applies to all the genealogies. When Scripture gives a list of individuals, it often mentions males only. Must we therefore say that females go for nothing ? Nay, the very children know that they are classified with men. For this reason, wives are said to give children to their husbands, the name of the family always remaining with the males. Then, as the male sex has this privilege, that sons are deemed of noble or ignoble birth, according to the condition of their fathers, so, on the other hand, in slavery, the condition of the child is determined by that of the mother, as lawyers say, *partus sequitur ventrem*. Whence we may infer, that offspring is partly procreated by the seed of the mother. According to the common custom of nations, mothers are deemed progenitors, and with this the divine law agrees, which could have had no ground to forbid the marriage of the uncle with the niece, if there was no consanguinity between them. It would also be lawful for a brother and sister uterine to intermarry, when their fathers are different. But while I admit that the power assigned to the woman is passive, I hold that the same thing is affirmed indiscriminately of her and of the male. Christ is not said to have been made by a woman, but of a woman (Gal. iv. 4). But some of this herd, laying aside all shame, publicly ask whether we mean to maintain that Christ was procreated of the proper seed of a Virgin.[1] I, in my turn, ask, whether they are not forced to admit that he was nourished to maturity in the Virgin's womb. Justly, therefore, we infer from the words of Matthew, that Christ, inasmuch as he was begotten of Mary, was procreated of her seed ; as a similar generation is denoted when Boaz is said to have been begotten of Rachab (Matth. i. 5, 16). Matthew does not here describe the Virgin as the channel through which Christ flowed, but distinguishes his miraculous from an ordinary birth, in that Christ was begotten by her of the seed of David. For the same reason for

---

[1] Latin, "An dicere velimus ex semine menstruali virginis procreatur esse Christum."

which Isaac is said to be begotten of Abraham, Joseph of Jacob, Solomon of David, is Christ said to have been begotten of his mother. The Evangelist has arranged his discourse in this way. Wishing to prove that Christ derives his descent from David, he deems it enough to state, that he was begotten of Mary. Hence it follows, that he assumed it as an acknowledged fact, that Mary was of the same lineage as Joseph.

4. The absurdities which they wish to fasten upon us are mere puerile calumnies. They reckon it base and dishonouring to Christ to have derived his descent from men; because, in that case, he could not be exempted from the common law which includes the whole offspring of Adam, without exception, under sin. But this difficulty is easily solved by Paul's antithesis, "As by one man sin entered into the world, and death by sin"—"even so by the righteousness of one the free gift came upon all men unto justification of life" (Rom. v. 12, 18). Corresponding to this is another passage, "The first man is of the earth, earthy: the second man is the Lord from heaven" (1 Cor. xv. 47). Accordingly, the same apostle, in another passage, teaching that Christ was sent "in the likeness of sinful flesh, that the righteousness of the law might be fulfilled in us," distinctly separates him from the common lot, as being true man, and yet without fault and corruption (Rom. viii. 3). It is childish, trifling to maintain, that if Christ is free from all taint, and was begotten of the seed of Mary, by the secret operation of the Spirit, it is not therefore the seed of the woman that is impure, but only that of the man. We do not hold Christ to be free from all taint, merely because he was born of a woman unconnected with a man, but because he was sanctified by the Spirit, so that the generation was pure and spotless, such as it would have been before Adam's fall. Let us always bear in mind, that wherever Scripture adverts to the purity of Christ, it refers to his true human nature, since it were superfluous to say that God is pure. Moreover, the sanctification of which John speaks in his seventeenth chapter is inapplicable to the divine nature. This does not suggest the idea of a twofold seed in Adam, although no contamination extended to Christ, the generation of man not being in itself vicious or impure, but an accidental circumstance of the fall. Hence, it is not strange that Christ, by whom our integrity was to be restored, was exempted from the common corruption. Another absurdity which they obtrude upon us—viz. that if the Word of God became incarnate, it must have been enclosed in the narrow tenement of an earthly body, is sheer petulance. For although the boundless essence of the Word was united with human nature into one person, we have no idea of any enclosing. The Son of God descended miraculously from heaven, yet without abandoning heaven; was pleased to be conceived miraculously in the Virgin's womb, to live on the earth, and hang upon the cross, and yet always filled the world as from the beginning.

CHAPTER XIV.

HOW TWO NATURES CONSTITUTE THE PERSON OF THE MEDIATOR.

This chapter contains two principal heads: I. A brief exposition of the doctrine of Christ's two natures in one person, sec. 1—4. II. A refutation of the heresies of Servetus, which destroy the distinction of natures in Christ, and the eternity of the divine nature of the Son.

Sections.

1. Proof of two natures in Christ—a human and a divine. Illustrated by analogy, from the union of body and soul. Illustration applied.
2. Proof from passages of Scripture which distinguish between the two natures. Proof from the communication of properties.
3. Proof from passages showing the union of both natures. A rule to be observed in this discussion.
4. Utility and use of the doctrine concerning the two natures. The Nestorians. The Eutychians. Both justly condemned by the Church.
5. The heresies of Servetus refuted. General answer or sum of the orthodox doctrine concerning Christ. What meant by the hypostatic union. Objections of Servetus to the deity of Christ. Answer.
6. Another objection and answer. A twofold filiation of Christ.
7. Other objections answered.
8. Conclusion of the former objections. Other pestilential heresies of Servetus.

1. WHEN it is said that the Word was made flesh, we must not understand it as if he were either changed into flesh, or confusedly intermingled with flesh, but that he made choice of the Virgin's womb as a temple in which he might dwell. He who was the Son of God became the Son of man, not by confusion of substance, but by unity of person. For we maintain, that the divinity was so conjoined and united with the humanity, that the entire properties of each nature remain entire, and yet the two natures constitute only one Christ. If, in human affairs, anything analogous to this great mystery can be found, the most apposite similitude[1] seems to be that of man, who obviously consists of two substances, neither of which, however, is so intermingled with the other as that both do not retain their own properties. For neither is soul body, nor is body soul. Wherefore that is said separately of the soul which cannot in any way apply to the body; and that, on the other hand, of the body which is altogether inapplicable to the soul; and that, again, of the whole man, which cannot be affirmed without absurdity either of the body or of the soul separately. Lastly, the properties of the soul are

---

[1] Augustine employs the same similitude, Epist. cii.

transferred to the body, and the properties of the body to the soul, and yet these form only one man, not more than one. Such modes of expression intimate both that there is in man one person formed of two compounds, and that these two different natures constitute one person. Thus the Scriptures speak of Christ. They sometimes attribute to him qualities which should be referred specially to his humanity, and sometimes qualities applicable peculiarly to his divinity, and sometimes qualities which embrace both natures, and do not apply specially to either. This combination of a twofold nature in Christ they express so carefully, that they sometimes communicate them with each other, a figure of speech which the ancients termed ἰδιωμάτων κοινωνια (a communication of properties).

2. Little dependence could be placed on these statements, were it not proved by numerous passages throughout the sacred volume that none of them is of man's devising. What Christ said of himself, " Before Abraham was I am" (John viii. 58), was very foreign to his humanity. I am not unaware of the cavil by which erroneous spirits distort this passage—viz. that he was before all ages, inasmuch as he was foreknown as the Redeemer, as well in the counsel of the Father as in the minds of believers. But seeing he plainly distinguishes the period of his manifestation from his eternal existence, and professedly founds on his ancient government, to prove his precedence to Abraham, he undoubtedly claims for himself the peculiar attributes of divinity. Paul's assertion that he is " the first-born of every creature," that " he is before all things, and by him all things consist" (Col. i. 15, 17) ; his own declaration, that he had glory with the Father before the world was, and that he worketh together with the Father, are equally inapplicable to man. These and similar properties must be specially assigned to his divinity. Again, his being called the servant of the Father, his being said to grow in stature, and wisdom, and favour with God and man, not to seek his own glory, not to know the last day, not to speak of himself, not to do his own will, his being seen and handled,[1] apply entirely to his humanity; since, as God, he cannot be in any respect said to grow, works always for himself, knows everything, does all things after the counsel of his own will, and is incapable of being seen or handled. And yet he not merely ascribes these things separately to his human nature, but applies them to himself as suitable to his office of Mediator. There is a communication of ἰδιωμάτα, or properties, when Paul says, that God purchased the Church " with his own blood" (Acts xx. 28), and that the Jews crucified the Lord of glory (1 Cor. ii. 8). In like manner, John says, that the Word of God was " handled." God certainly has no blood, suffers not, cannot be touched with hands ; but since that Christ, who was true God and true man, shed

---

[1] Isaiah xli. 1, &c.; John v. 17; Luke ii. 52; John viii. 50; Mark xiii. 32; John xiv. 10; vi. 38; Luke xxiv. 39.

his blood on the cross for us, the acts which were performed in his human nature are transferred improperly, but not causelessly, to his divinity. We have a similar example in the passage where John says that God laid down his life for us (1 John iii. 16). Here a property of his humanity is communicated with his other nature. On the other hand, when Christ, still living on the earth, said, " No man hath ascended up to heaven, but he that came down from heaven, even the Son of man, which is in heaven" (John iii. 13), certainly regarded as man in the flesh which he had put on, he was not then in heaven, but inasmuch as he was both God and man, he, on account of the union of a twofold nature, attributed to the one what properly belonged to the other.

3. But, above all, the true substance of Christ is most clearly declared in those passages which comprehend both natures at once. Numbers of these exist in the Gospel of John. What we there read as to his having received power from the Father to forgive sins; as to his quickening whom he will; as to his bestowing righteousness, holiness, and salvation; as to his being appointed judge both of the quick and the dead; as to his being honoured even as the Father,[1] are not peculiar either to his Godhead or his humanity, but applicable to both. In the same way he is called the Light of the world, the good Shepherd, the Door, the true Vine. With such prerogatives the Son of God was invested on his manifestation in the flesh, and though he possessed the same with the Father before the world was created, still it was not in the same manner or respect; neither could they be attributed to one who was a man and nothing more. In the same sense we ought to understand the saying of Paul, that at the end Christ shall deliver up " the kingdom to God, even the Father" (1 Cor. xv. 24). The kingdom of God assuredly had no beginning, and will have no end: but because he was hid under a humble clothing of flesh, and took upon himself the form of a servant, and humbled himself (Phil. ii. 8), and laying aside the insignia of majesty, became obedient to the Father; and after undergoing this subjection was at length crowned with glory and honour (Heb. ii. 7), and exalted to supreme authority, that at his name every knee should bow (Phil. ii. 10); so at the end he will subject to the Father both the name and the crown of glory, and whatever he received of the Father, that God may be all in all (1 Cor. xv. 28). For what end were that power and authority given to him, save that the Father might govern us by his hand? In the same sense, also, he is said to sit at the right hand of the Father. But this is only for a time, until we enjoy the immediate presence of his Godhead. And here we cannot excuse the error of some ancient writers, who, by not attending to the office of Mediator, darken the genuine meaning of almost the whole doctrine which we read in the Gospel of John, and entangle themselves in many snares.

---

[1] John i. 29; v. 21—23; ix. 5; x. 9—11; xv. 1.

Let us, therefore, regard it as the key of true interpretation, that those things which refer to the office of Mediator are not spoken of the divine or human nature simply.[1]   Christ, therefore, shall reign until he appear to judge the world, inasmuch as, according to the measure of our feeble capacity, he now connects us with the Father.   But when, as partakers of the heavenly glory, we shall see God as he is, then Christ, having accomplished the office of Mediator, shall cease to be the vicegerent of the Father, and will be content with the glory which he possessed before the world was.   Nor is the name of Lord specially applicable to the person of Christ in any other respect than in so far as he holds a middle place between God and us.   To this effect are the words of Paul, "To us there is but one God, the Father, of whom are all things, and we in him; and one Lord Jesus Christ, by whom are all things, and we by him" (1 Cor. viii. 6); that is, to the letter a temporary authority has been committed by the Father until his divine majesty shall be beheld face to face.   His giving up of the kingdom to the Father, so far from impairing his majesty, will give a brighter manifestation of it.   God will then cease to be the head of Christ, and Christ's own Godhead will then shine forth of itself, whereas it is now in a manner veiled.

4. This observation, if the readers apply it properly, will be of no small use in solving a vast number of difficulties.   For it is strange how the ignorant, nay, some who are not altogether without learning, are perplexed by these modes of expression which they see applied to Christ, without being properly adapted either to his divinity or his humanity, not considering their accordance with the character in which he was manifested as God and man, and with his office of Mediator. It is very easy to see how beautifully they accord with each other, provided they have a sober interpreter, one who examines these great mysteries with the reverence which is meet.   But there is nothing which furious and frantic spirits cannot throw into confusion.[2]   They fasten on the attributes of humanity to destroy his divinity; and, on the other hand, on those of his divinity to destroy his humanity: while those which, spoken conjointly of the two natures, apply to neither, they employ to destroy both.   But what else is this than to contend that Christ is not man because he is God, not God because he is man, and neither God nor man because he is both at once. Christ, therefore, as God and man, possessing natures which are united but not confused, we conclude that he is our Lord and the true Son of God, even according to his humanity, though not by means of his humanity.   For we must put far from us the heresy of Nestorius, who, presuming to dissect rather than distinguish between the two natures, devised a double Christ.   But we see the Scripture loudly protesting against this, when the name of the Son of God is given to him who is born of a Virgin, and the Virgin herself is called the

1 *Vide* Calv. Epist. ad Polonos adversus Stancarum.
2 See August. in Enchir. ad Laurent. c. 36.

mother of our Lord (Luke i. 32, 43). We must beware also of the insane fancy of Eutyches, lest, when we would demonstrate the unity of person, we destroy the two natures. The many passages we have already quoted, in which the divinity is distinguished from the humanity, and the many other passages existing throughout Scripture, may well stop the mouth of the most contentious. I will shortly add a few observations, which will still better dispose of this fiction. For the present, one passage will suffice—Christ would not have called his body a temple (John ii. 19), had not the Godhead distinctly dwelt in it. Wherefore, as Nestorius had been justly condemned in the Council of Ephesus, so afterwards was Eutyches in those of Constantinople and Chalcedon, it being not more lawful to confound the two natures of Christ than to divide them.

5. But in our age, also, has arisen a not less fatal monster, Michael Servetus, who for the Son of God has substituted a figment composed of the essence of God, spirit, flesh, and three uncreated elements. First, indeed, he denies that Christ is the Son of God, for any other reason than because he was begotten in the womb of the Virgin by the Holy Spirit. The tendency of this crafty device is to make out, by destroying the distinction of the two natures, that Christ is somewhat composed of God and man, and yet is not to be deemed God and man. His aim throughout is to establish, that before Christ was manifested in the flesh there were only shadowy figures in God, the truth or effect of which existed for the first time, when the Word who had been destined to that honour truly began to be the Son of God. We indeed acknowledge that the Mediator who was born of the Virgin is properly the Son of God. And how could the man Christ be a mirror of the inestimable grace of God, had not the dignity been conferred upon him both of being and of being called the only-begotten Son of God? Meanwhile, however, the definition of the Church stands unmoved, that he is accounted the Son of God, because the Word begotten by the Father before all ages assumed human nature by hypostatic union,—a term used by ancient writers to denote the union which of two natures constitutes one person, and invented to refute the dream of Nestorius, who pretended that the Son of God dwelt in the flesh in such a manner as not to be at the same time man. Servetus calumniously charges us with making the Son of God double, when we say that the eternal Word before he was clothed with flesh was already the Son of God: as if we said anything more than that he was manifested in the flesh. Although he was God before he became man, he did not therefore begin to be a new God. Nor is there any greater absurdity in holding that the Son of God, who by eternal generation ever had the property of being a Son, appeared in the flesh. This is intimated by the angel's words to Mary: "That holy thing which shall be born of thee shall be called the Son of God" (Luke i. 35); as if he had said said that the name of Son, which was more obscure under the law, would become

celebrated and universally known.   Corresponding to this is the passage of Paul, that being now the sons of God by Christ, we "have received the Spirit of adoption, whereby we cry, Abba, Father" (Rom. viii. 15).   Were not also the holy patriarchs of old reckoned among the sons of God ?   Yea, trusting to this privilege, they invoked God as their Father.   But because ever since the only-begotten Son of God came forth into the world, his celestial paternity has been more clearly manifested, Paul assigns this to the kingdom of Christ as its distinguishing feature.   We must, however, constantly hold, that God never was a Father to angels and men save in respect of his only-begotten Son : that men, especially, who by their iniquity were rendered hateful to God, are sons by gratuitous adoption, because he is a Son by nature.   Nor is there anything in the assertion of Servetus, that this depends on the filiation which God had decreed with himself.   Here we deal not with figures, as expiation by the blood of beasts was shown to be ; but since they could not be the sons of God in reality, unless their adoption was founded in the head, it is against all reason to deprive the head of that which is common to the members.   I go farther : since the Scripture gives the name of sons of God to the angels, whose great dignity in this respect depended not on the future redemption, Christ must in order take precedence of them that he may reconcile the Father to them. I will again briefly repeat and add the same thing concerning the human race.   Since angels as well as men were at first created on the condition that God should be the common Father of both ; if it is true, as Paul says, that Christ always was the head, " the first-born of every creature—that in all things he might have the pre-eminence" (Col. i. 15, 18), I think I may legitimately infer, that he existed as the Son of God before the creation of the world.

6. But if his filiation (if I may so express it) had a beginning at the time when he was manifested in the flesh, it follows that he was a Son in respect of human nature also.   Servetus, and others similarly frenzied, hold that Christ who appeared in the flesh is the Son of God, inasmuch as but for his incarnation he could not have possessed this name.   Let them now answer me, whether, according to both natures, and in respect of both, he is a Son ?   So indeed they prate ; but Paul's doctrine is very different.   We acknowledge, indeed, that Christ in human nature is called a Son, not like believers by gratuitous adoption merely, but the true, natural, and, therefore, only Son, this being the mark which distinguishes him from all others. Those of us who are regenerated to a new life God honours with the name of sons ; the name of true and only-begotten Son he bestows on Christ alone.   But how is he an only Son in so great a multitude of brethren, except that he possesses by nature what we acquire by gift ?   This honour we extend to his whole character of Mediator, so that He who was born of a Virgin, and on the cross offered himself in sacrifice to the Father, is truly and properly the Son of God ; but

still in respect of his Godhead : as Paul teaches when he says, that he "was separated unto the gospel of God (which he had promised afore by his prophets in the Holy Scriptures), concerning his Son Jesus Christ our Lord, which was made of the seed of David according to the flesh ; and declared to be the Son of God with power" (Rom. i. 1—4). When distinctly calling him the Son of David according to the flesh, why should he also say that he was "declared to be the Son of God," if he meant not to intimate, that this depended on something else than his incarnation ? For in the same sense in which he elsewhere says, that "though he was crucified through weakness, yet he liveth by the power of God" (2 Cor. xiii. 4), so he now draws a distinction between the two natures. They must certainly admit, that as on account of his mother he is called the Son of David, so, on account of his Father, he is the Son of God, and that in some respect differing from his human nature. The Scripture gives him both names, calling him at one time the Son of God, at another the Son of Man. As to the latter, there can be no question that he is called a Son in accordance with the phraseology of the Hebrew language, because he is of the offspring of Adam On the other hand, I maintain that he is called a Son on account of his Godhead and eternal essence, because it is no less congruous to refer to his divine nature his being called the Son of God, than to refer to his human nature his being called the Son of Man. In fine, in the passage which I have quoted, Paul does not mean that he who, according to the flesh, was begotten of the seed of David, was declared to be the Son of God in any other sense than he elsewhere teaches that Christ, who, descended of the Jews according to the flesh, is "over all, God blessed for ever" (Rom. ix. 5). But if in both passages the distinction of two natures is pointed out, how can it be denied, that he who according to the flesh is the Son of Man, is also in respect of his divine nature the Son of God ?

7. They indeed find a blustering defence of their heresy in its being said, that "God spared not his own Son," and in the communication of the angel, that He who was to be born of the Virgin should be called the "Son of the Highest" (Rom. viii. 32 ; Luke i. 32). But before pluming themselves on this futile objection, let them for a little consider with us what weight there is in their argument. If it is legitimately concluded, that at conception he began to be the Son of God, because he who has been conceived is called a Son, it will follow, that he began to be the Word after his manifestation in the flesh, because John declares, that the Word of life of which he spoke was that which "our hands have handled" (1 John i. 1). In like manner we read in the prophet, "Thou, Bethlehem Ephratah, though thou be little among the thousands of Israel, yet out of thee shall he come forth that is to be a ruler in Israel ; whose goings forth have been from of old, from everlasting" (Mic. v. 2). How will they be forced to interpret if they will follow such a method of arguing?

I have declared that we by no means assent to Nestorius, who imagined a twofold Christ, when we maintain that Christ, by means of brotherly union, made us sons of God with himself, because in the flesh, which he took from us, he is the only-begotten Son of God. And Augustine wisely reminds us,[1] that he is a bright mirror of the wonderful and singular grace of God, because as man he obtained honour which he could not merit. With this distinction, therefore, according to the flesh, was Christ honoured even from the womb —viz. to be the Son of God. Still, in the unity of person we are not to imagine any intermixture which takes away from the Godhead what is peculiar to it. Nor is it more absurd that the eternal Word of God and Christ, uniting the two natures in one person, should in different ways be called the Son of God, than that he should in various respects be called at one time the Son of God, at another the Son of Man. Nor are we more embarrased by another cavil of Servetus—viz. that Christ, before he appeared in the flesh, is nowhere called the Son of God, except under a figure. For though the description of him was then more obscure, yet it has already been clearly proved, that he was not otherwise the eternal God, than as he was the Word begotten of the eternal Father. Nor is the name applicable to the office of Mediator which he undertook, except in that he was God manifest in the flesh. Nor would God have thus from the beginning been called a Father, had there not been even then a mutual relation to the Son, "of whom the whole family in heaven and earth is named" (Eph. iii. 15). Hence it is easy to infer, that under the Law and the Prophets he was the Son of God before this name was celebrated in the Church. But if we are to dispute about the word merely, Solomon, speaking of the incomprehensibility of God, affirms that his Son is like himself, incomprehensible: "What is his name, and what is his Son's name, if thou canst tell"? (Prov. xxx. 4). I am well aware that with the contentious this passage will not have sufficient weight; nor do I found much upon it, except as showing the malignant cavils of those who affirm that Christ is the Son of God only in so far as he became man. We may add, that all the most ancient writers, with one mouth and consent, testified the same thing so plainly, that the effrontery is no less ridiculous than detestable, which dares to oppose us with Irenæus and Tertullian, both of whom acknowledge that He who was afterwards visibly manifested was the invisible Son of God.[2]

8. But though Servetus heaped together a number of horrid dogmas, to which, perhaps, others would not subscribe, you will find, that all who refuse to acknowledge the Son of God except in the flesh, are obliged, when urged more closely, to admit that he was a Son,

---

[1] See August. De Corruptione et Gratia. cap. xi., et De Civitate Dei, lib. x. cap 29, et alibi   See also cap. xvii. s. 1.

[2] See Irenæus, lib. iv. cap 14 et 37 ; Tertullian adversus Praxeam. The above passages from The Proverbs is quoted by Augustine, Ep 49, Quæs. 5.

for no other reason than because he was conceived in the womb of the Virgin by the Holy Spirit; just like the absurdity of the ancient Manichees, that the soul of man was derived by transfusion from God, from its being said, that he breathed into Adam's nostrils the breath of life (Gen. ii. 7). For they lay such stress on the name of Son that they leave no distinction between the natures, but babblingly maintain that the man Christ is the Son of God, because, according to his human nature, he was begotten of God. Thus, the eternal generation of Wisdom, celebrated by Solomon (Prov. viii. 22, seq.), is destroyed, and no kind of Godhead exists in the Mediator: or a phantom is substituted instead of man. The grosser delusions of Servetus, by which he imposed upon himself and some others, it were useful to refute, that pious readers might be warned by the example, to confine themselves within the bounds of soberness and modesty: however, I deem it superfluous here, as I have already done it in a special treatise.[1] The whole comes to this, that the Son of God was from the beginning an idea, and was even then a preordained man, who was to be the essential image of God. Nor does he acknowledge any other word of God except in external splendour. The generation he interprets to mean, that from the beginning a purpose of generating the Son was begotten in God, and that this purpose extended itself by act to creation. Meanwhile, he confounds the Spirit with the Word, saying that God arranged the invisible Word and Spirit into flesh and soul. In short, in his view the typifying of Christ occupies the place of generation; but he says, that he who was then in appearance a shadowy Son, was at length begotten by the Word, to which he attributes a generating power. From this it will follow, that dogs and swine are not less sons of God, because created of the original seed of the Divine Word. But although he compounds Christ of three uncreated elements, that he may be begotten of the essence of God, he pretends that he is the first-born among the creatures, in such a sense that, according to their degree, stones have the same essential divinity. But lest he should seem to strip Christ of his Deity, he admits that his flesh is $\delta\mu oo\acute{u}\sigma\iota o\nu$, of the same substance with God, and that the Word was made man, by the conversion of flesh into Deity. Thus, while he cannot comprehend that Christ was the Son of God, until his flesh came forth from the essence of God and was converted into Deity, he reduces the eternal personality (*hypostasis*) of the Word to nothing, and robs us of the Son of David, who was the promised Redeemer. It is true, he repeatedly declares that the Son was begotten of God by knowledge and predestination, but that he was at length made man out of that matter which, from the beginning, shone with God in the three elements, and afterwards appeared in the first light of the world, in

---

[1] Vide Calv. Defensio Orthodoxæ Fidei Sacræ Trinitatis adversus Prodigiosos Errores Michaelis Serveti Hispani.

the cloud and pillar of fire.   How shamefully inconsistent with himself he ever and anon becomes, it were too tedious to relate.   From this brief account sound readers will gather, that by the subtle ambiguities of this infatuated man, the hope of salvation was utterly extinguished.   For if the flesh were the Godhead itself, it would cease to be its temple.   Now, the only Redeemer we can have is He who being begotten of the seed of Abraham and David according to the flesh, truly became man.   But he erroneously insists on the expression of John, " The Word was made flesh."   As these words refute the heresy of Nestorius, so they give no countenance to the impious fiction of which Eutyches was the inventor, since all that the Evangelist intended was to assert a unity of person in two natures.

CHAPTER XV.

THREE THINGS CHIEFLY TO BE REGARDED IN CHRIST—VIZ. HIS OFFICES OF PROPHET, KING, AND PRIEST.

The principal parts of this chapter are—I. Of the Prophetical Office of Christ, its dignity and use, sec. 1, 2. II. The nature of the Kingly power of Christ, and the advantage we derive from it, sec. 3—5. III. Of the Priesthood of Christ, and the efficacy of it, sec. 6.

Sections.

1. Among heretics and false Christians, Christ is found in name only; but by those who are truly and effectually called of God, he is acknowledged as a Prophet, King, and Priest. In regard to the Prophetical Office, the Redeemer of the Church is the same from whom believers under the Law hoped for the full light of understanding.
2. The unction of Christ, though it has respect chiefly to the Kingly Office, refers also to the Prophetical and Priestly Offices. The dignity, necessity, and use of this unction.
3. From the spirituality of Christ's kingdom its eternity is inferred. This twofold, referring both to the whole body of the Church, and to its individual members.
4. Benefits from the spiritual kingdom of Christ. 1. It raises us to eternal life. 2. It enriches us with all things necessary to salvation. 3. It makes us invincible by spiritual foes. 4. It animates us to patient endurance. 5. It inspires confidence and triumph. 6. It supplies fortitude and love.
5. The unction of our Redeemer heavenly. Symbol of this unction. A passage in the apostle reconciled with others previously quoted, to prove the eternal kingdom of Christ.
6. What necessary to obtain the benefit of Christ's Priesthood. We must set out with the death of Christ. From it follows, 1. His intercession for us. 2. Confidence in prayer. 3. Peace of conscience. 4. Through Christ, Christians themselves become priests. Grievous sin of the Papists in pretending to sacrifice Christ.

1. THOUGH heretics pretend the name of Christ, truly does Augustine affirm (Enchir. ad Laurent. cap. v.), that the foundation is not common to them with the godly, but belongs exclusively to the Church: for if those things which pertain to Christ be diligently considered, it will be found that Christ is with them in name only, not in reality. Thus, in the present day, though the Papists have the words, Son of God, Redeemer of the world, sounding in their mouths, yet, because contented with an empty name, they deprive him of his virtue and dignity; what Paul says of "not holding the head," is truly applicable to them (Col. ii. 19). Therefore, that faith may find in Christ a solid ground of salvation, and so rest in him, we must set out with this principle, that the office which he received from the Father consists of three parts. For he was ap-

pointed both Prophet, King, and Priest; though little were gained by holding the names unaccompanied by a knowledge of the end and use. These, too, are spoken of in the Papacy, but frigidly, and with no great benefit, the full meaning comprehended under each title not being understood. We formerly observed, that though God, by supplying an uninterrupted succession of prophets, never left his people destitute of useful doctrine, such as might suffice for salvation; yet the minds of believers were always impressed with the conviction that the full light of understanding was to be expected only on the advent of the Messiah. This expectation, accordingly, had reached even the Samaritans, to whom the true religion had never been made known. This is plain from the expression of the woman, "I know that Messias cometh, which is called Christ: when he is come, he will tell us all things" (John iv. 25). Nor was this a mere random presumption which had entered the minds of the Jews. They believed what sure oracles had taught them. One of the most remarkable passages is that of Isaiah, "Behold, I have given him for a witness to the people, a leader and commander to the people" (Is. lv. 4); that is, in the same way in which he had previously in another place styled him "Wonderful, Counsellor" (Is. ix. 6).[1] For this reason the apostle, commending the perfection of gospel doctrine, first says that "God, at sundry times and in divers manners spake in times past unto the prophets," and then adds, that he "hath in these last days spoken unto us by his Son" (Heb. i. 1, 2). But as the common office of the prophets was to hold the Church in suspense, and at the same time support it until the advent of the Mediator; we read, that the faithful, during the dispersion, complained that they were deprived of that ordinary privilege. "We see not our signs: there is no more any prophet, neither is there among us any that knoweth how long" (Ps. lxxiv. 9). But when Christ was now not far distant, a period was assigned to Daniel "to seal up the vision and prophecy" (Daniel ix. 24), not only that the authority of the prediction there spoken of might be established, but that believers might, for a time, patiently submit to the want of the prophets, the fulfilment and completion of all the prophecies being at hand.

2. Moreover, it is to be observed, that the name *Christ* refers to those three offices: for we know that under the Law, prophets as well as priests and kings were anointed with holy oil. Whence, also, the celebrated name of Messiah was given to the promised Mediator. But although I admit (as, indeed, I have elsewhere shown) that he was so called from a view to the nature of a kingly office, still the prophetical and sacerdotal unctions have their proper place, and must not be overlooked. The former is expressly mentioned by Isaiah in these words; "The Spirit of the Lord God is upon me: because the

---

[1] Calvin translates, "Angelum vel Interpretem magni consilii;"—"the Angel or interpreter of the great counsel."

Lord hath anointed me to preach good tidings unto the meek; he hath sent me to bind up the broken-hearted, to proclaim liberty to the captive, and the opening of the prison to them that are bound; to proclaim the acceptable year of the Lord" (Is. lx. 1, 2). We see that he was anointed by the Spirit to be a herald and witness of his Father's grace, and not in the usual way; for he is distinguished from other teachers who had a similar office. And here, again, it is to be observed, that the unction which he received, in order to perform the office of teacher, was not for himself, but for his whole body, that a corresponding efficacy of the Spirit might always accompany the preaching of the Gospel. This, however, remains certain, that by the perfection of doctrine which he brought, an end was put to all the prophecies, so that those who, not contented with the Gospel, annex somewhat extraneous to it, derogate from its authority. The voice which thundered from heaven, "This is my beloved Son, hear him," gave him a special privilege above all other teachers. Then from him, as head, this unction is diffused through the members, as Joel has foretold, "Your sons and your daughters shall prophesy, your old men shall dream dreams, and your young men shall see visions" (Joel ii. 28). Paul's expressions, that he was "made unto us wisdom" (1 Cor. i. 30), and elsewhere that in him "are hid all the treasures of wisdom and knowledge" (Col. ii. 3), have a somewhat different meaning—namely, that out of him there is nothing worth knowing, and that those who, by faith, apprehend his true character, possess the boundless immensity of heavenly blessings. For which reason, he elsewhere says, "I determined not to know anything among you, save Jesus Christ and him crucified" (1 Cor. ii. 2). And most justly: for it is unlawful to go beyond the simplicity of the Gospel. The purpose of this prophetical dignity in Christ is to teach us, that in the doctrine which he delivered is substantially included a wisdom which is perfect in all its parts.

3. I come to the Kingly office, of which it were in vain to speak, without previously reminding the reader that its nature is spiritual; because it is from thence we learn its efficacy, the benefits it confers, its whole power and eternity. Eternity, moreover, which in Daniel an angel attributes to the office of Christ (Dan. ii. 44), in Luke an angel justly applies to the salvation of his people (Luke i. 33). But this is also twofold, and must be viewed in two ways; the one pertains to the whole body of the Church, the other is proper to each member. To the former is to be referred what is said in the Psalms, "Once have I sworn by my holiness, that I will not lie unto David. His seed shall endure for ever, and his throne as the sun before me. It shall be established for ever, as the moon, and as a faithful witness in heaven" (Ps. lxxxix. 35, 37). There can be no doubt that God here promises that he will be, by the hand of his Son, the eternal governor and defender of the Church. In none but Christ will the fulfilment of this prophecy be found; since immediately after Solo-

mon's death the kingdom in a great measure lost its dignity, and, with ignominy to the family of David, was transferred to a private individual.   Afterwards decaying by degrees, it at length came to a sad and dishonourable end.   In the same sense are we to understand the exclamation of Isaiah, "Who shall declare his generation?" (Isaiah liii. 8).   For he asserts that Christ will so survive death as to be connected with his members.   Therefore, as often as we hear that Christ is armed with eternal power, let us learn that the perpetuity of the Church is thus effectually secured; that amid the turbulent agitations by which it is constantly harassed, and the grievous and fearful commotions which threaten innumerable disasters, it still remains safe.   Thus, when David derides the audacity of the enemy who attempt to throw off the yoke of God and his anointed, and says, that kings and nations rage "in vain" (Ps. ii. 2—4), because he who sitteth in the heaven is strong enough to repel their assaults, assuring believers of the perpetual preservation of the Church, he animates them to have good hope whenever it isoccasionally oppressed.   So, in another place, when speaking in the person of God, he says, "The Lord said unto my Lord, Sit thou at my right hand, until I make thine enemies thy footstool" (Ps. cx. 1), he reminds us, that however numerous and powerful the enemies who conspire to assault the Church, they are not possessed of strength sufficient to prevail against the immortal decree by which he appointed his Son eternal King. Whence it follows that the devil, with the whole power of the world, can never possibly destroy the Church, which is founded on the eternal throne of Christ.   Then in regard to the special use to be made by each believer, this same eternity ought to elevate us to the hope of a blessed immortality.   For we see that everything which is earthly, and of the world, is temporary, and soon fades away.   Christ, therefore, to raise our hope to the heavens, declares that his kingdom is not of this world (John xviii. 36).   In fine, let each of us, when he hears that the kingdom of Christ is spiritual, be roused by the thought to entertain the hope of a better life, and to expect that as it is now protected by the hand of Christ, so it will be fully realised in a future life.

4. That the strength and utility of the kingdom of Christ cannot, as we have said, be fully perceived, without recognising it as spiritual, is sufficiently apparent, even from this, that having during the whole course of our lives to war under the cross, our condition here is bitter and wretched.   What then would it avail us to be ranged under the government of a heavenly King, if its benefits were not realised beyond the present earthly life?   We must, therefore, know that the happiness which is promised to us in Christ does not consist in external advantages—such as leading a joyful and tranquil life, abounding in wealth, being secure against all injury, and having an affluence of delights, such as the flesh is wont to long for—but properly belongs to the heavenly life.   As in the world the prosperous and desirable

condition of a people consists partly in the abundance of temporal good and domestic peace, and partly in the strong protection which gives security against external violence; so Christ also enriches his people with all things necessary to the eternal salvation of their souls, and fortifies them with courage to stand unassailable by all the attacks of spiritual foes. Whence we infer, that he reigns more for us than for himself, and that both within us and without us; that being replenished, in so far as God knows to be expedient, with the gifts of the Spirit, of which we are naturally destitute, we may feel from their first fruits, that we are truly united to God for perfect blessedness; and then trusting to the power of the same Spirit, may not doubt that we shall always be victorious against the devil, the world, and everything that can do us harm. To this effect was our Saviour's reply to the Pharisees, "The kingdom of God is within you." "The kingdom of God cometh not with observation" (Luke xvii. 21, 22). It is probable that on his declaring himself to be that King under whom the highest blessing of God was to be expected, they had in derision asked him to produce his insignia. But to prevent those who were already more than enough inclined to the earth from dwelling on its pomp, he bids them enter into their consciences, for "the kingdom of God" is "righteousness, and peace, and joy in the Holy Ghost" (Rom. xiv. 17). These words briefly teach what the kingdom of Christ bestows upon us. Not being earthly or carnal, and so subject to corruption, but spiritual, it raises us even to eternal life, so that we can patiently live at present under toil, hunger, cold, contempt, disgrace, and other annoyances; contented with this, that our King will never abandon us, but will supply our necessities until our warfare is ended, and we are called to triumph: such being the nature of his kingdom, that he communicates to us whatever he received of his Father. Since then he arms and equips us by his power, adorns us with splendour and magnificence, enriches us with wealth, we here find most abundant cause of glorying, and also are inspired with boldness, so that we can contend intrepidly with the devil, sin, and death. In fine, clothed with his righteousness, we can bravely surmount all the insults of the world: and as he replenishes us liberally with his gifts, so we can in our turn bring forth fruit unto his glory.

5. Accordingly, his royal unction is not set before us as composed of oil or aromatic perfumes; but he is called the Christ of God, because "the Spirit of the Lord" rested upon him; "the Spirit of wisdom and understanding, the Spirit of counsel and might, the Spirit of knowledge and of the fear of the Lord" (Isaiah xi. 2). This is the oil of joy with which the Psalmist declares that he was anointed above his fellows (Ps. xlv. 7). For, as has been said, he was not enriched privately for himself, but that he might refresh the parched and hungry with his abundance. For as the Father is said to have given the Spirit to the Son without measure (John iii. 34), so the reason is

expressed, that we might all receive of his fulness, and grace for grace (John i. 16). From this fountain flows the copious supply (of which Paul makes mention, Eph. iv. 7) by which grace is variously distributed to believers according to the measure of the gift of Christ. Here we have ample confirmation of what I said, that the kingdom of Christ consists in the Spirit, and not in earthly delights or pomp, and that hence, in order to be partakers with him, we must renounce the world. A visible symbol of this grace was exhibited at the baptism of Christ, when the Spirit rested upon him in the form of a dove. To designate the Spirit and his gifts by the term *unction*, is not new, and ought not to seem absurd (see 1 John ii. 20, 27), because this is the only quarter from which we derive life; but especially in what regards the heavenly life, there is not a drop of vigour in us save what the Holy Spirit instils, who has chosen his seat in Christ, that thence the heavenly riches, of which we are destitute, might flow to us in copious abundance. But because believers stand invincible in the strength of their King, and his spiritual riches abound towards them, they are not improperly called Christians. Moreover, from this eternity of which we have spoken, there is nothing derogatory in the expression of Paul, "Then cometh the end, when he shall have delivered up the kingdom to God, even the Father" (1 Cor. xv. 24); and also, "Then shall the Son also himself be subject unto him that put all things under him, that God may be all in all" (1 Cor. xv. 28); for the meaning merely is, that, in that perfect glory, the administration of the kingdom will not be such as it now is. For the Father hath given all power to the Son, that by his hand he may govern, cherish, sustain us, keep us under his guardianship, and give assistance to us. Thus, while we wander far as pilgrims from God, Christ interposes, that he may gradually bring us to full communion with God. And, indeed, his sitting at the right hand of the Father has the same meaning as if he was called the vicegerent of the Father, intrusted with the whole power of government. For God is pleased, mediately (so to speak) in his person to rule and defend the Church. Thus also his being seated at the right hand of the Father is explained by Paul, in the Epistle to the Ephesians, to mean that "he is the head over all things to the Church, which is his body" (Eph. i. 20, 22). Nor is this different in purport from what he elsewhere teaches, that God hath "given him a name which is above every name; that at the name of Jesus every knee shall bow, of things in heaven, and things in earth, and things under the earth, and that every tongue should confess that Jesus Christ is Lord, to the glory of God the Father" (Phil. ii. 9—11). For in these words, also, he commends an arrangement in the kingdom of Christ, which is necessary for our present infirmity. Thus Paul rightly infers that God will then be the only Head of the Church, because the office of Christ, in defending the Church, shall then have been completed. For the same reason, Scripture throughout calls him *Lord*, the Father having appointed him over us for the express purpose of exercising his government through him. For though many lordships are celebrated in the world, yet Paul says, " To us there is but one God, the Father, of whom are all things, and we in him ; and one Lord Jesus Christ, by whom are all things, and we by him " (1 Cor. viii. 6). Whence it is justly inferred that he is the same God who, by the mouth of Isaiah, declared, " The Lord is our Judge, the Lord is our Lawgiver, the Lord is our King : he will save us " (Isaiah xxxiii. 22). For though he everywhere describes all the power which he possesses as the benefit and gift of the Father, the meaning simply is, that he reigns by divine authority, because his reason for assuming the office of Mediator was, that descending from the bosom and incomprehensible glory of the Father, he might draw near to us. Wherefore there is the greater reason that we all should with one consent prepare to obey, and with the greatest alacrity yield implicit obedience to, his will. For as he unites the offices of King and Pastor towards believers, who voluntarily submit to him, so, on the other hand, we are told that he wields an iron sceptre to break and bruise all the rebellious like a potter's vessel (Ps. ii. 9). We are also told that he will be the Judge of the Gentiles, that he will cover the earth with dead bodies, and level down every opposing height (Ps. cx. 6). Of this examples are seen at present, but full proof will be given at the final judgment, which may be properly regarded as the last act of his reign.

6. With regard to his Priesthood, we must briefly hold its end and use to be, that as a Mediator, free from all taint he may by his own holiness procure the favour of God for us. But because a deserved curse obstructs the entrance, and God in his character of Judge is hostile to us, expiation must necessarily intervene, that as a priest employed to appease the wrath of God, he may reinstate us in his favour. Wherefore, in order that Christ might fulfil this office, it behoved him to appear with a sacrifice. For even under the law of the priesthood it was forbidden to enter the sanctuary without blood, to teach the worshipper that however the priest might interpose to deprecate, God could not be propitiated without the expiation of sin. On this subject the Apostle discourses at length in the Epistle to the Hebrews, from the seventh almost to the end of the tenth chapter. The sum comes to this, that the honour of the priesthood was competent to none but Christ, because, by the sacrifice of his death, he wiped away our guilt, and made satisfaction for sin. Of the great importance of this matter, we are reminded by that solemn oath which God uttered, and of which he declared he would not repent, " Thou art a priest for ever, after the order of Melchizedek " (Ps. cx. 4). For, doubtless, his purpose was to ratify that point on which he knew that our salvation chiefly hinged. For, as has been said, there is no access to God for us or for our prayers until the priest, purging away our defilements, sanctify us, and obtain for

us that favour of which the impurity of our lives and hearts deprives us.   Thus we see, that if the benefit and efficacy of Christ's priesthood is to reach us, the commencement must be with his death. Whence it follows, that he by whose aid we obtain favour, must be a perpetual intercessor.   From this again arises not only confidence in prayer, but also the tranquillity of pious minds, while they recline in safety on the paternal indulgence of God, and feel assured, that whatever has been consecrated by the Mediator is pleasing to him. But since God under the Law ordered sacrifices of beasts to be offered to him, there was a different and new arrangement in regard to Christ —viz. that he should be at once victim and priest, because no other fit satisfaction for sin could be found, nor was any one worthy of the honour of offering an only-begotten son to God.   Christ now bears the office of priest, not only that by the eternal law of reconciliation he may render the Father favourable and propitious to us, but also admit us into this most honourable alliance.   For we, though in ourselves polluted, in him being priests (Rev. i. 6), offer ourselves and our all to God, and freely enter the heavenly sanctuary, so that the sacrifices of prayer and praise which we present are grateful and of sweet odour before him.   To this effect are the words of Christ, " For their sakes I sanctify myself " (John xvii. 19) ; for being clothed with his holiness, inasmuch as he has devoted us to the Father with himself (otherwise we were an abomination before him), we please him as if we were pure and clean, nay, even sacred.   Hence that unction of the sanctuary of which mention is made in Daniel (Dan. ix. 24).   For we must attend to the contrast between this unction and the shadowy one which was then in use ; as if the angel had said, that when the shadows were dispersed, there would be a clear priesthood in the person of Christ.   The more detestable, therefore, is the fiction of those who, not content with the priesthood of Christ, have dared to take it upon themselves to sacrifice him, a thing daily attempted in the Papacy, where the mass is represented as an immolation of Christ.

CHAPTER XVI.

HOW CHRIST PERFORMED THE OFFICE OF REDEEMER IN PROCURING OUR SALVATION. THE DEATH, RESURRECTION, AND ASCENSION OF CHRIST.

This chapter contains four leading heads—I. A general consideration of the whole subject, including a discussion of a necessary question concerning the justice of God and his mercy in Christ, sec. 1—4. II. How Christ fulfilled the office of Redeemer in each of its parts, sec. 5—17. His death, burial, descent to hell, resurrection, ascension, to heaven, seat at the right hand of the Father, and return to judgment. III. A great part of the Creed being here expounded, a statement is given of the view which ought to be taken of the Creed commonly ascribed to the Apostles, sec. 18. IV. Conclusion, setting forth the doctrine of Christ the Redeemer, and the use of the doctrine, sec. 19.

1. ALL that we have hitherto said of Christ leads to this one result, that condemned, dead, and lost in ourselves, we must in him seek righteousness, deliverance, life, and salvation, as we are taught by the celebrated words of Peter, "Neither is there salvation in any other: for there is none other name under heaven given among men whereby we must be saved" (Acts iv. 12). The name of Jesus was not given him at random, or fortuitously, or by the will of man, but was brought from heaven by an angel, as the herald of the supreme decree;[1] the reason also being added, "for he shall save his people from their sins" (Matt. i. 21). In these words attention should be paid to what we have elsewhere observed, that the office of Redeemer was assigned him in order that he might be our Saviour. Still, however, redemption would be defective if it did not conduct us by an uninterrupted progression to the final goal of safety. Therefore, the moment we turn aside from him in the minutest degree, salvation, which resides entirely in him, gradually disappears; so that all who do not rest in him voluntarily deprive themselves of all grace. The observation of Bernard well deserves to be remembered: The name of Jesus is not only light but food also, yea, oil, without which all the food of the soul is dry; salt, without which as a condiment whatever is set before us is insipid; in fine, honey in the mouth, melody in the ear, joy in the heart, and, at the same time, medicine; every discourse where this name is not heard is absurd (Bernard in Cantica., Serm. 15). But here it is necessary diligently to consider in what way we obtain salvation from him, that we may not only be persuaded that he is the author of it, but having embraced whatever is sufficient as a sure foundation of our faith, may eschew all that might make us waver. For seeing no man can descend into himself, and seriously consider what he is, without feeling that God is angry and at enmity with him, and therefore anxiously longing for the means of regaining his favour (this cannot be without satisfaction), the certainty here required is of no ordinary description,—sinners, until freed from guilt, being always liable to the wrath and curse of God, who, as he is a just judge, cannot permit his law to be violated with impunity, but is armed for vengeance.

2. But before we proceed farther, we must see in passing, how can

---

[1] Latin, "Supremi decreti." French, "Decret eternel et inviolable;"—Eternal and inviolable decree.

it be said that God, who prevents us with his mercy, was our enemy until he was reconciled to us by Christ. For how could he have given us in his only-begotten Son a singular pledge of his love, if he had not previously embraced us with free favour? As there thus arises some appearance of contradiction, I will explain the difficulty. The mode in which the Spirit usually speaks in Scripture is, that God was the enemy of men until they were restored to favour by the death of Christ (Rom. v. 10); that they were cursed until their iniquity was expiated by the sacrifice of Christ (Gal. iii. 10, 13); that they were separated from God, until by means of Christ's body they were received into union (Col. i. 21, 22). Such modes of expression are accommodated to our capacity, that we may the better understand how miserable and calamitous our condition is without Christ. For were it not said in clear terms, that Divine wrath, and vengeance, and eternal death, lay upon us, we should be less sensible of our wretchedness without the mercy of God, and less disposed to value the blessing of deliverance. For example, let a person be told, Had God at the time you were a sinner hated you, and cast you off as you deserved, horrible destruction must have been your doom; but spontaneously and of free indulgence he retained you in his favour, not suffering you to be estranged from him, and in this way rescued you from danger,—the person will indeed be affected, and made sensible in some degree how much he owes to the mercy of God. But again, let him be told, as Scripture teaches, that he was estranged from God by sin, an heir of wrath, exposed to the curse of eternal death, excluded from all hope of salvation, a complete alien from the blessing of God, the slave of Satan, captive under the yoke of sin; in fine, doomed to horrible destruction, and already involved in it; that then Christ interposed, took the punishment upon himself, and bore what by the just judgment of God was impending over sinners; with his own blood expiated the sins which rendered them hateful to God, by this expiation satisfied and duly propitiated God the Father, by this intercession appeased his anger, on this basis founded peace between God and men, and by this tie secured the Divine benevolence toward them; will not these considerations move him the more deeply, the more strikingly they represent the greatness of the calamity from which he was delivered? In short, since our mind cannot lay hold of life through the mercy of God with sufficient eagerness, or receive it with becoming gratitude, unless previously impressed with fear of the Divine anger, and dismayed at the thought of eternal death, we are so instructed by divine truth, as to perceive that without Christ God is in a manner hostile to us, and has his arm raised for our destruction. Thus taught, we look to Christ alone for divine favour and paternal love.

3. Though this is said in accommodation to the weakness of our capacity, it is not said falsely. For God, who is perfect righteousness, cannot love the iniquity which he sees in all. All of us, there-

fore, have that within which deserves the hatred of God. Hence, in respect, first, of our corrupt nature; and, secondly, of the depraved conduct following upon it, we are all offensive to God, guilty in his sight, and by nature the children of hell. But as the Lord wills not to destroy in us that which is his own, he still finds something in us which in kindness he can love. For though it is by our own fault that we are sinners, we are still his creatures; though we have brought death upon ourselves, he had created us for life. Thus, mere gratuitous love prompts him to receive us into favour. But if there is a perpetual and irreconcilable repugnance between righteousness and iniquity, so long as we remain sinners we cannot be completely received. Therefore, in order that all ground of offence may be removed, and he may completely reconcile us to himself, he, by means of the expiation set forth in the death of Christ, abolishes all the evil that is in us, so that we, formerly impure and unclean, now appear in his sight just and holy. Accordingly, God the Father, by his love, prevents and anticipates our reconciliation in Christ. Nay, it is because he first loves us, that he afterwards reconciles us to himself. But because the iniquity, which deserves the indignation of God, remains in us until the death of Christ comes to our aid, and that iniquity is in his sight accursed and condemned, we are not admitted to full and sure communion with God, unless in so far as Christ unites us. And, therefore, if we would indulge the hope of having God placable and propitious to us, we must fix our eyes and minds on Christ alone, as it is to him alone it is owing that our sins, which necessarily provoked the wrath of God, are not imputed to us.

4. For this reason Paul says, that God "hath blessed us with all spiritual blessings in heavenly places in Christ: according as he hath chosen us in him before the foundation of the world" (Eph. i. 3, 4). These things are clear and conformable to Scripture, and admirably reconcile the passages in which it is said, that "God so loved the world, that he gave his only-begotten Son" (John iii. 16); and yet that it was "when we were enemies we were reconciled to God by the death of his Son" (Rom. v. 10). But to give additional assurance to those who require the authority of the ancient Church, I will quote a passage of Augustine to the same effect: "Incomprehensible and immutable is the love of God. For it was not after we were reconciled to him by the blood of his Son that he began to love us, but he loved us before the foundation of the world, that with his only-begotten Son we too might be sons of God before we were anything at all. Our being reconciled by the death of Christ must not be understood as if the Son reconciled us, in order that the Father, then hating, might begin to love us, but that we were reconciled to him already, loving, though at enmity with us because of sin. To the truth of both propositions we have the attestation of the Apostle, 'God commendeth his love toward us, in that while we were yet sinners, Christ died for us' (Rom. v. 8). Therefore he had this love

towards us even when, exercising enmity towards him, we were the workers of iniquity. Accordingly, in a manner wondrous and divine, he loved even when he hated us. For he hated us when we were such as he had not made us, and yet because our iniquity had not destroyed his work in every respect, he knew in regard to each one of us, both to hate what we had made, and love what he had made." Such are the words of Augustine (Tract in Jo. 110).

5. When it is asked then how Christ, by abolishing sin, removed the enmity between God and us, and purchased a righteousness which made him favourable and kind to us, it may be answered generally, that he accomplished this by the whole course of his obedience. This is proved by the testimony of Paul, " As by one man's disobedience many were made sinners, so by the obedience of one shall many be made righteous" (Rom. v. 19). And indeed he elsewhere extends the ground of pardon which exempts from the curse of the law to the whole life of Christ, " When the fulness of the time was come, God sent forth his Son, made of a woman, made under the law, to redeem them that were under the law" (Gal. iv. 4, 5). Thus even at his baptism he declared that a part of righteousness was fulfilled by his yielding obedience to the command of the Father. In short, from the moment when he assumed the form of a servant, he began, in order to redeem us, to pay the price of deliverance. Scripture, however, the more certainly to define the mode of salvation, ascribes it peculiarly and specially to the death of Christ. He himself declares that he gave his life a ransom for many (Matth. xx. 28). Paul teaches that he died for our sins (Rom. iv. 25). John Baptist exclaimed, " Behold the Lamb of God, which taketh away the sin of the world" (John i. 29). Paul in another passage declares, " that we are justified freely by his grace, through the redemption that is in Christ Jesus: whom God hath set forth to be a propitiation through faith in his blood" (Rom. iii. 25). Again, being "justified by his blood, we shall be saved from wrath through him" (Rom. v. 9). Again, " He hath made him to be sin for us, who knew no sin ; that we might be made the righteousness of God in him" (2 Cor. v. 21). I will not search out all the passages, for the list would be endless, and many are afterwards to be quoted in their order. In the Confession of Faith, called the Apostles' Creed, the transition is admirably made from the birth of Christ to his death and resurrection, in which the completion of a perfect salvation consists. Still there is no exclusion of the other part of obedience which he performed in life. Thus Paul comprehends, from the beginning even to the end, his having assumed the form of a servant, humbled himself, and become obedient to death, even the death of the cross (Phil. ii. 7). And, indeed, the first step in obedience was his voluntary subjection ; for the sacrifice would have been unavailing to justification if not offered spontaneously. Hence our Lord, after testifying, " I lay down my life for the sheep," distinctly adds, " No man taketh it from me"

(John x. 15, 18). In the same sense Isaiah says, "Like a sheep before her shearers is dumb, so he opened not his mouth" (Is. liii. 7). The Gospel History relates that he came forth to meet the soldiers; and in presence of Pilate, instead of defending himself, stood to receive judgment. This, indeed, he did not without a struggle, for he had assumed our infirmities also, and in this way it behoved him to prove that he was yielding obedience to his Father. It was no ordinary example of incomparable love towards us to struggle with dire terrors, and amid fearful tortures to cast away all care of himself that he might provide for us. We must bear in mind, that Christ could not duly propitiate God without renouncing his own feelings, and subjecting himself entirely to his Father's will. To this effect the Apostle appositely quotes a passage from the Psalms, "Lo, I come (in the volume of the book it is written of me) to do thy will, O God" (Heb. x. 5.; Ps. xl. 7, 8). Thus, as trembling consciences find no rest without sacrifice and ablution by which sins are expiated, we are properly directed thither, the source of our life being placed in the death of Christ. Moreover, as the curse consequent upon guilt remained for the final judgment of God, one principal point in the narrative is his condemnation before Pontius Pilate, the governor of Judea, to teach us, that the punishment to which we were liable was inflicted on that Just One. We could not escape the fearful judgment of God; and Christ, that he might rescue us from it, submitted to be condemned by a mortal, nay, by a wicked and profane man. For the name of Governor is mentioned not only to support the credibility of the narrative, but to remind us of what Isaiah says, that "the chastisement of our peace was upon him;" and that "with his stripes we are healed" (Is. liii. 5). For, in order to remove our condemnation, it was not sufficient to endure any kind of death. To satisfy our ransom, it was necessary to select a mode of death in which he might deliver us, both by giving himself up to condemnation, and undertaking our expiation. Had he been cut off by assassins, or slain in a seditious tumult, there could have been no kind of satisfaction in such a death. But when he is placed as a criminal at the bar, where witnesses are brought to give evidence against him, and the mouth of the judge condemns him to die, we see him sustaining the character of an offender and evil-doer. Here we must attend to two points which had both been foretold by the prophets, and tend admirably to comfort and confirm our faith. When we read that Christ was led away from the judgment-seat to execution, and was crucified between thieves, we have a fulfilment of the prophecy which is quoted by the Evangelist, "He was numbered with the transgressors" (Is. liii. 12; Mark xv. 28). Why was it so? That he might bear the character of a sinner, not of a just or innocent person, inasmuch as he met death on account not of innocence, but of sin. On the other hand, when we read that he was acquitted by the same lips that condemned him (for Pilate was forced once and again to bear public testimony to his innocence), let us call to mind what is said by another prophet, "I restored that which I took not away" (Ps. lxix. 4). Thus we perceive Christ representing the character of a sinner and a criminal, while, at the same time, his innocence shines forth, and it becomes manifest that he suffers for another's and not for his own crime. He therefore suffered under Pontius Pilate, being thus, by the formal sentence of the judge, ranked among criminals, and yet he is declared innocent by the same judge, when he affirms that he finds no cause of death in him. Our acquittal is in this—that the guilt which made us liable to punishment was transferred to the head of the Son of God (Is. liii. 12). We must specially remember this substitution in order that we may not be all our lives in trepidation and anxiety, as if the just vengeance, which the Son of God transferred to himself, were still impending over us.

6. The very form of the death embodies a striking truth. The cross was cursed not only in the opinion of men, but by the enactment of the Divine Law. Hence Christ, while suspended on it, subjects himself to the curse. And thus it behoved to be done, in order that the whole curse, which on account of our iniquities awaited us, or rather lay upon us, might be taken from us by being transferred to him. This was also shadowed in the Law, since אשמות, the word by which sin itself is properly designated, was applied to the sacrifices and expiations offered for sin. By this application of the term, the Spirit intended to intimate, that they were a kind of καθαρ-μάτων (purifications), bearing, by substitution, the curse due to sin. But that which was represented figuratively in the Mosaic sacrifices is exhibited in Christ the archetype. Wherefore, in order to accomplish a full expiation, he made his soul אשם, i.e., a propitiatory victim for sin (as the prophet says, Is. liii. 5, 10), on which the guilt and penalty being in a manner laid, ceases to be imputed to us. The Apostle declares this more plainly when he says, that "he made him to be sin for us, who knew no sin ; that we might be made the righteousness of God in him" (2 Cor. v. 21). For the Son of God, though spotlessly pure, took upon him the disgrace and ignominy of our iniquities, and in return clothed us with his purity. To the same thing he seems to refer, when he says, that he "condemned sin in the flesh" (Rom. viii. 3), the Father having destroyed the power of sin when it was transferred to the flesh of Christ. This term, therefore, indicates that Christ, in his death, was offered to the Father as a propitiatory victim ; that, expiation being made by his sacrifice, we might cease to tremble at the divine wrath. It is now clear what the prophet means when he says that "the Lord hath laid upon him the iniquity of us all" (Is. liii. 6) ; namely, that as he was to wash away the pollution of sins, they were transferred to him by imputation. Of this the cross to which he was nailed was a symbol, as the Apostle declares, "Christ hath redeemed us from the curse of the law, being made a curse for us : for it is written, Cursed is every one that hangeth

on a tree: that the blessing of Abraham might come on the Gentiles through Jesus Christ" (Gal. iii. 13, 14). In the same way Peter says, that he "bare our sins in his own body on the tree" (1 Peter ii. 24), inasmuch as from the very symbol of the curse, we perceive more clearly that the burden with which we were oppressed was laid upon him. Nor are we to understand that by the curse which he endured he was himself overwhelmed, but rather that by enduring it he repressed, broke, annihilated all its force. Accordingly, faith apprehends acquittal in the condemnation of Christ, and blessing in his curse. Hence it is not without cause that Paul magnificently celebrates the triumph which Christ obtained upon the cross, as if the cross, the symbol of ignominy, had been converted into a triumphal chariot. For he says, that he blotted out the handwriting of ordinances that was against us, which was contrary to us, and took it out of the way, nailing it to his cross: that, "having spoiled principalities and powers, he made a show of them openly, triumphing over them in it" (Col. ii. 14, 15). Nor is this to be wondered at; for, as another Apostle declares, Christ, " through the eternal Spirit, offered himself without spot to God" (Heb. ix. 14), and hence that transformation of the cross which were otherwise against its nature. But that these things may take deep root and have their seat in our inmost hearts, we must never lose sight of sacrifice and ablution. For, were not Christ a victim, we could have no sure conviction of his being ἀπολύτρωσις, ἀντίλυτρον, καὶ ἱλαστηριον, *our substitute-ransom and propitiation.* And hence mention is always made of blood whenever Scripture explains the mode of redemption: although the shedding of Christ's blood was available not only for propitiation, but also acted as a laver to purge our defilements.

7. The Creed next mentions, that he " was dead and buried." Here again it is necessary to consider how he substituted himself in order to pay the price of our redemption. Death held us under its yoke, but he in our place delivered himself into its power, that he might exempt us from it. This the Apostle means when he says, " that he tasted death for every man" (Heb. ii. 9). By dying he prevented us from dying; or (which is the same thing) he by his death purchased life for us (see Calvin in Psychopann). But in this he differed from us, that in permitting himself to be overcome of death, it was not so as to be ingulfed in its abyss, but rather to annihilate it, as it must otherwise have annihilated us; he did not allow himself to be so subdued by it as to be crushed by its power; he rather laid it prostrate, when it was impending over us, and exulting over us as already overcome. In fine, his object was, " that through death he might destroy him that had the power of death, that is, the devil, and deliver them who through fear of death were all their lifetime subject to bondage" (Heb. ii. 14, 15). This is the first fruit which his death produced to us. Another is, that by fellowship with him he mortifies our earthly members, that they may

not afterwards exert themselves in action, and kills the old man, that he may not hereafter be in vigour and bring forth fruit. An effect of his burial, moreover, is, that we as his fellows are buried to sin. For when the Apostle says, that we are ingrafted into the likeness of Christ's death, and that we are buried with him unto sin, that by his cross the world is crucified unto us and we unto the world, and that we are dead with him, he not only exhorts us to manifest an example of his death, but declares that there is an efficacy in it which should appear in all Christians, if they would not render his death unfruitful and useless. Accordingly, in the death and burial of Christ a twofold blessing is set before us—viz. deliverance from death, to which we were enslaved, and the mortification of our flesh (Rom. vi. 5 ; Gal. ii. 19, vi. 14 ; Col. iii. 3).

8. Here we must not omit the descent to hell, which was of no little importance to the accomplishment of redemption. For although it is apparent from the writings of the ancient Fathers, that the clause which now stands in the Creed was not formerly so much used in the churches, still, in giving a summary of doctrine, a place must be assigned to it, as containing a matter of great importance which ought not by any means to be disregarded. Indeed, some of the ancient Fathers do not omit it,[1] and hence we may conjecture, that having been inserted in the Creed after a considerable lapse of time, it came into use in the Church not immediately but by degrees.[2] This much is uncontroverted, that it was in accordance with the general sentiment of all believers, since there is none of the Fathers who does not mention Christ's descent into hell, though they have various modes of explaining it. But it is of little consequence by whom and at what time it was introduced. The chief thing to be attended to in the Creed is, that it furnishes us with a full and every way complete summary of faith, containing nothing but what has been derived from the infallible word of God. But should any still scruple to give it admission into the Creed, it will shortly be made plain, that the place which it holds in a summary of our redemption is so important, that the omission of it greatly detracts from the benefit of Christ's death. There are some again who think that the article contains nothing new, but is merely a repetition in different words of what was previously said respecting burial, the word Hell (Infernis) being often used in Scripture for sepulchre. I admit the truth of what they allege with regard to the not unfrequent use of the term *infernis* for *sepulchre ;* but I cannot adopt their opinion, for two obvious reasons. First, What folly would it have been, after explaining a matter attended with no difficulty in clear and unambiguous terms, afterwards

---

1 It is not adverted to by Augustine, Lib. i. De Symbolo de Catechumenos.

2 The French of this sentence is, "Dont on peut conjecturer qu'il a esté tantost aprés le tems des Apostres adjousté ; mais que peu a peu il est venu en usage."—Whence we may conjecture that it was added some time after the days of the Apostles, but gradually came into use.

to involve rather than illustrate it by clothing it in obscure phraseology? When two expressions having the same meaning are placed together, the latter ought to be explanatory of the former. But what kind of explanation would it be to say, the expression, *Christ was buried*, means, that *he descended into hell?* My second reason is, the improbability that a superfluous tautology of this description should have crept into this compendium, in which the principal articles of faith are set down summarily in the fewest possible number of words. I have no doubt that all who weigh the matter with some degree of care will here agree with me.

9. Others interpret differently—viz. That Christ descended to the souls of the Patriarchs who died under the law, to announce his accomplished redemption, and bring them out of the prison in which they were confined. To this effect they wrest the passage[1] in the Psalms, "He hath broken the gates of brass, and cut the bars of iron in sunder" (Ps. cvii. 16); and also the passage in Zechariah, "I have sent forth thy prisoners out of the pit wherein is no water" (Zech. ix. 11). But since the psalm foretells the deliverance of those who were held captive in distant lands, and Zechariah comparing the Babylonish disaster into which the people had been plunged to a deep dry well or abyss, at the same time declares, that the salvation of the whole Church was an escape from a profound pit, I know not how it comes to pass, that posterity imagined it to be a subterraneous cavern, to which they gave the name of *Limbus*. Though this fable has the countenance of great authors, and is now also seriously defended by many as truth,[2] it is nothing but a fable. To conclude from it that the souls of the dead are in prison is childish. And what occasion was there that the soul of Christ should go down thither to set them at liberty? I readily admit that Christ illumined them by the power of his Spirit, enabling them to perceive that the grace of which they had only had a foretaste was then manifested to the world. And to this not improbably the passage of Peter may be applied, wherein he says, that Christ "went and preached to the spirits that were in prison" (or rather "a watch-tower") (1 Pet. iii. 19). The purport of the context is, that believers who had died before that time were partakers of the same grace with ourselves: for he celebrates the power of Christ's death, in that he penetrated even to the dead, pious souls obtaining an immediate view of that visitation for which they had anxiously waited; while, on the other hand, the reprobate were more clearly convinced that they were completely excluded from salvation. Although the passage in Peter is not perfectly definite, we

[1] The French is, "Pour colorer leur fantasie, ils tirent par les cheveux quelques temoignages."—To colour their fancy, they pull by the hair (violently wrest) certain passages.
[2] See Justin, Ambrose, Jerome. The opinions of the Fathers and Rabbis on Hell and Limbus are collected by Peter Martyr, Loci Communes, Lib. iii. Loc. xvi. sect. 8: see Augustine, Ep. 99.

must not interpret as if he made no distinction between the righteous and the wicked: he only means to intimate, that the death of Christ was made known to both.

10. But, apart from the Creed, we must seek for a surer exposition of Christ's descent to hell: and the word of God furnishes us with one not only pious and holy, but replete with excellent consolation. Nothing had been done if Christ had only endured corporeal death. In order to interpose between us and God's anger, and satisfy his righteous judgment, it was necessary that he should feel the weight of divine vengeance. Whence also it was necessary that he should engage, as it were, at close quarters with the powers of hell and the horrors of eternal death. We lately quoted from the Prophet that the "chastisement of our peace was laid upon him," that he "was bruised for our iniquities," that he "bore our infirmities;" expressions which intimate, that, like a sponsor and surety for the guilty, and, as it were, subjected to condemnation, he undertook and paid all the penalties which must have been exacted from them, the only exception being, that the pains of death could not hold him. Hence there is nothing strange in its being said that he descended to hell, seeing he endured the death which is inflicted on the wicked by an angry God. It is frivolous and ridiculous to object that in this way the order is perverted, it being absurd that an event which preceded burial should be placed after it. But after explaining what Christ endured in the sight of man, the Creed appropriately adds the invisible and incomprehensible judgment which he endured before God, to teach us that not only was the body of Christ given up as the price of redemption, but that there was a greater and more excellent price—that he bore in his soul the tortures of condemned and ruined man.

11. In this sense, Peter says that God raised up Christ, "having loosed the pains of death: because it was not possible he should be holden of it" (Acts ii. 24). He does not mention death simply, but says that the Son of God endured the pains produced by the curse and wrath of God, the source of death. How small a matter had it been to come forth securely, and as it were in sport to undergo death. Herein was a true proof of boundless mercy, that he shunned not the death he so greatly dreaded. And there can be no doubt that, in the Epistle to the Hebrews, the Apostle means to teach the same thing when he says that he "was heard in that he feared" (Heb. v. 7). Some, instead of "feared," use a term meaning reverence or piety, but how inappropriately, is apparent both from the nature of the thing and the form of expression.[1] Christ then praying in a loud voice, and with tears, is heard in that he feared, not so as to be ex-

---

[1] French, "Les autres translatent Reverence ou Pieté; mais la Grammaire et la matiere qui est la tracté monstrent que c'est mal à propos."—Others translate Reverence or Piety; but Grammar and the subject-matter show that they do it very unseasonably

empted from death, but so as not to be swallowed up of it like a sinner, though standing as our representative. And certainly no abyss can be imagined more dreadful than to feel that you are abandoned and forsaken of God, and not heard when you invoke him, just as if he had conspired your destruction. To such a degree was Christ dejected, that in the depth of his agony he was forced to exclaim, "My God, my God, why hast thou forsaken me?" The view taken by some, that he here expressed the opinion of others rather than his own conviction, is most improbable; for it is evident that the expression was wrung from the anguish of his inmost soul. We do not, however, insinuate that God was ever hostile to him or angry with him.[1] How could he be angry with the beloved Son, with whom his soul was well pleased? or how could he have appeased the Father by his intercession for others if He were hostile to himself? But this we say, that he bore the weight of the divine anger, that, smitten and afflicted, he experienced all the signs of an angry and avenging God. Hence Hilary argues, that to this descent we owe our exemption from death. Nor does he dissent from this view in other passages, as when he says, "The cross, death, hell, are our life." And again, "The Son of God is in hell, but man is brought back to heaven." And why do I quote the testimony of a private writer, when an Apostle asserts the same thing, stating it as one fruit of his victory that he delivered "them who through fear of death were all their lifetime subject to bondage?" (Heb. ii. 15). He behoved, therefore, to conquer the fear which incessantly vexes and agitates the breasts of all mortals; and this he could not do without a contest. Moreover, it will shortly appear with greater clearness that his was no common sorrow, was not the result of a trivial cause. Thus by engaging with the power of the devil, the fear of death, and the pains of hell, he gained the victory, and achieved a triumph, so that we now fear not in death those things which our Prince has destroyed.[2]

12. Here some miserable creatures, who, though unlearned, are however impelled more by malice than ignorance, cry out that I am offering an atrocious insult to Christ, because it were most incongruous to hold that he feared for the safety of his soul. And then in harsher terms they urge the calumnious charge that I attribute despair to the Son of God, a feeling the very opposite of faith. First, they wickedly raise a controversy as to the fear and dread which Christ felt, though these are openly affirmed by the Evangelists. For before the hour of his death arrived, he was troubled in spirit, and affected with grief; and at the very onset began to be exceedingly amazed. To speak of these feelings as merely assumed, is a shameful evasion. It becomes us, therefore (as Ambrose truly teaches), boldly

---

[1] See Cyril. Lib. ii. De Recta Fide ad Reginas; Item, Hilarius de Trinitate, Lib. iv c. 2 and 3.

[2] Vide Luther, tom. i. in Concione de Morte, fol. 87.

to profess the agony of Christ, if we are not ashamed of the cross. And certainly had not his soul shared in the punishment, he would have been a Redeemer of bodies only. The object of his struggle was to raise up those who were lying prostrate; and so far is this from detracting from his heavenly glory, that his goodness, which can never be sufficiently extolled, becomes more conspicuous in this, that he declined not to bear our infirmities. Hence also that solace to our anxieties and griefs which the Apostle sets before us: "We have not an high priest who cannot be touched with the feeling of our infirmities; but was in all respects tempted like as we are, yet without sin" (Heb. iv. 15). These men pretend that a thing in its nature vitious is improperly ascribed to Christ; as if they were wiser than the Spirit of God, who in the same passage reconciles the two things —viz. that he was tempted in all respects like as we are, and yet was without sin. There is no reason, therefore, to take alarm at infirmity in Christ, infirmity to which he submitted not under the constraint of violence and necessity, but merely because he loved and pitied us. Whatever he spontaneously suffered, detracts in no degree from his majesty. One thing which misleads these detractors is, that they do not recognise in Christ an infirmity which was pure and free from every species of taint, inasmuch as it was kept within the limits of obedience. As no moderation can be seen in the depravity of our nature, in which all affections with turbulent impetuosity exceed their due bounds, they improperly apply the same standard to the Son of God. But as he was upright, all his affections were under such restraint as prevented everything like excess. Hence he could resemble us in grief, fear, and dread, but still with this mark of distinction. Thus refuted. they fly off to another cavil, that although Christ feared death, yet he feared not the curse and wrath of God, from which he knew that he was safe. But let the pious reader consider how far it is honourable to Christ to make him more effeminate and timid than the generality of men. Robbers and other malefactors contumaciously hasten to death, many men magnanimously despise it, others meet it calmly. If the Son of God was amazed and terror-struck at the prospect of it, where was his firmness or magnanimity? We are even told, what in a common death would have been deemed most extraordinary, that in the depth of his agony his sweat was like great drops of blood falling to the ground. Nor was this a spectacle exhibited to the eyes of others, since it was from a secluded spot that he uttered his groans to his Father. And that no doubt may remain, it was necessary that angels should come down from heaven to strengthen him with miraculous consolation. How shamefully effeminate would it have been (as I have observed) to be so excruciated by the fear of an ordinary death as to sweat drops of blood, and not even be revived by the presence of angels? What? Does not that prayer, thrice repeated, "Father, if it be possible, let this cup pass from me" (Matth. xxvi. 39), a prayer dictated by incredible bitterness of soul, show that Christ had a fiercer and more arduous struggle than with ordinary death?

Hence it appears that these triflers, with whom I am disputing, presume to talk of what they know not, never having seriously considered what is meant and implied by ransoming us from the justice of God. It is of consequence to understand aright how much our salvation cost the Son of God. If any one now ask, Did Christ descend to hell at the time when he deprecated death? I answer, that this was the commencement, and that from it we may infer how dire and dreadful were the tortures which he endured when he felt himself standing at the bar of God as a criminal in our stead. And although the divine power of the Spirit veiled itself for a moment, that it might give place to the infirmity of the flesh, we must understand that the trial arising from feelings of grief and fear was such as not to be at variance with faith. And in this was fulfilled what is said in Peter's sermon as to having been loosed from the pains of death, because "it was not possible he could be holden of it" (Acts ii. 24). Though feeling, as it were, forsaken of God, he did not cease in the slightest degree to confide in his goodness. This appears from the celebrated prayer in which, in the depth of his agony, he exclaimed, "My God, my God, why hast thou forsaken me?" (Matth. xxvii. 46). Amid all his agony he ceases not to call upon his God, while exclaiming that he is forsaken by him. This refutes the Apollinarian heresy, as well as that of those who are called Monothelites. Apollinaris pretended, that in Christ the eternal Spirit supplied the place of a soul, so that he was only half a man; as if he could have expiated our sins in any other way than by obeying the Father. But where does the feeling or desire of obedience reside but in the soul? and we know that his soul was troubled in order that ours, being free from trepidation, might obtain peace and quiet. Moreover, in opposition to the Monothelites, we see that in his human he felt a repugnance to what he willed in his divine nature. I say nothing of his subduing the fear of which we have spoken by a contrary affection. This appearance of repugnance is obvious in the words, "Father, save me from this hour: but for this cause came I unto this hour. Father, glorify thy name" (John xii. 27, 28). Still, in this perplexity, there was no violent emotion, such as we exhibit while making the strongest endeavours to subdue our own feelings.

13. Next follows the resurrection from the dead, without which all that has hitherto been said would be defective. For seeing that in the cross, death and burial of Christ, nothing but weakness appears, faith must go beyond all these, in order that it may be provided with full strength. Hence, although in his death we have an effectual completion of salvation, because by it we are reconciled to God, satisfaction is given to his justice, the curse is removed, and the penalty paid; still it is not by his death, but by his resurrection, that we are said to be begotten again to a living hope (1 Pet. i. 3); because, as

he, by rising again, became victorious over death, so the victory of our faith consists only in his resurrection. The nature of it is better expressed in the words of Paul, "Who (Christ) was delivered for our offences, and was raised again for our justification" (Rom. iv. 25); as if he had said, By his death sin was taken away, by his resurrection righteousness was renewed and restored. For how could he by dying have freed us from death, if he had yielded to its power? how could he have obtained the victory for us, if he had fallen in the contest?

Our salvation may be thus divided between the death and the resurrection of Christ: by the former, sin was abolished and death annihilated; by the latter, righteousness was restored and life revived, the power and efficacy of the former being still bestowed upon us by means of the latter. Paul accordingly affirms, that he was declared to be the Son of God by his resurrection (Rom. i. 4), because he then fully displayed that heavenly power which is both a bright mirror of his divinity, and a sure support of our faith; as he also elsewhere teaches, that "though he was crucified through weakness, yet he liveth by the power of God" (2 Cor. xiii. 4). In the same sense, in another passage, treating of perfection, he says, "That I may know him and the power of his resurrection" (Phil. iii. 10). Immediately after he adds, "being made conformable unto his death." In perfect accordance with this is the passage in Peter, that God "raised him up from the dead, and gave him glory, that your faith and hope might be in God" (1 Pet. i. 21). Not that faith founded merely on his death is vacillating, but that the divine power by which he maintains our faith is most conspicuous in his resurrection. Let us remember, therefore, that when death only is mentioned, everything peculiar to the resurrection is at the same time included, and that there is a like synecdoche in the term *resurrection*, as often as it is used apart from death, everything peculiar to death being included. But as, by rising again, he obtained the victory, and became the resurrection and the life, Paul justly argues, "If Christ be not raised, your faith is vain; ye are yet in your sins" (1 Cor. xv. 17). Accordingly, in another passage, after exulting in the death of Christ in opposition to the terrors of condemnation, he thus enlarges, "Christ that died, yea rather, that is risen again, who is even at the right hand of God, who also maketh intercession for us" (Rom. viii. 34). Then, as we have already explained that the mortification of our flesh depends on communion with the cross, so we must also understand, that a corresponding benefit is derived from his resurrection. For as the Apostle says, "Like as Christ was raised up from the dead by the glory of the Father, even so we also should walk in newness of life" (Rom. vi. 4). Accordingly, as in another passage, from our being dead with Christ, he inculcates, "Mortify therefore your members which are upon the earth" (Col. iii. 5); so from our being risen with Christ he infers, "seek those things which are above, where Christ sitteth at the right hand of God" (Col. iii. 1). In these words we are not only urged by the example of a risen Saviour to follow newness of life, but are taught that by his power we are renewed unto righteousness. A third benefit derived from it is, that, like an earnest, it assures us of our own resurrection, of which it is certain that his is the surest representation. This subject is discussed at length (1 Cor. xv). But it is to be observed, in passing, that when he is said to have "risen from the dead," these terms express the reality both of his death and resurrection, as if it had been said, that he died the same death as other men naturally die, and received immortality in the same mortal flesh which he had assumed.

14. The resurrection is naturally followed by the ascension into heaven. For although Christ, by rising again, began fully to display his glory and virtue, having laid aside the abject and ignoble condition of a mortal life, and the ignominy of the cross, yet it was only by his ascension to heaven that his reign truly commenced. This the Apostle shows, when he says he ascended "that he might fill all things" (Eph. iv. 10); thus reminding us that, under the appearance of contradiction, there is a beautiful harmony, inasmuch as though he departed from us, it was that his departure might be more useful to us than that presence which was confined in a humble tabernacle of flesh during his abode on the earth. Hence John, after repeating the celebrated invitation, "If any man thirst, let him come unto me and drink," immediately adds, "the Holy Ghost was not yet given; because that Jesus was not yet glorified" (John vii. 37, 39). This our Lord himself also declared to his disciples, "It is expedient for you that I go away; for if I go not away, the Comforter will not come unto you" (John xvi. 7). To console them for his bodily absence, he tells them that he will not leave them comfortless, but will come again to them in a manner invisible indeed, but more to be desired, because they were then taught by a surer experience that the government which he had obtained, and the power which he exercises, would enable his faithful followers not only to live well, but also to die happily. And, indeed, we see how much more abundantly his Spirit was poured out, how much more gloriously his kingdom was advanced, how much greater power was employed in aiding his followers and discomfiting his enemies. Being raised to heaven, he withdrew his bodily presence from our sight, not that he might cease to be with his followers, who are still pilgrims on the earth, but that he might rule both heaven and earth more immediately by his power; or rather, the promise which he made to be with us even to the end of the world, he fulfilled by this ascension, by which, as his body has been raised above all heavens, so his power and efficacy have been propagated and diffused beyond all the bounds of heaven and earth. This I prefer to explain in the words of Augustine rather than my own: "Through death Christ was to go to the right hand of the Father, whence he is to come to judge the quick and the dead, and

that in corporal presence, according to the sound doctrine and rule of faith. For, in spiritual presence, he was to be with them after his ascension" (August. Tract. in Joann. 109). In another passage he is more full and explicit: "In regard to ineffable and invisible grace, is fulfilled what he said, Lo, I am with you alway, even to the end of the world (Matth. xxviii. 20); but in regard to the flesh which the Word assumed, in regard to his being born of a Virgin, in regard to his being apprehended by the Jews, nailed to the tree, taken down from the cross, wrapt in linen clothes, laid in the sepulchre, and manifested on his resurrection, it may be said, Me ye have not always with you. Why? because, in bodily presence, he conversed with his disciples forty days, and leading them out where they saw, but followed not, he ascended into heaven, and is not here: for there he sits at the right hand of the Father: and yet he is here, for the presence of his Godhead was not withdrawn. Therefore, as regards his divine presence, we have Christ always: as regards his bodily presence, it was truly said to the disciples, Me ye have not always. For a few days the Church had him bodily present. Now, she apprehends him by faith, but sees him not by the eye" (August. Tract. 51).

15. Hence it is immediately added, that he "sitteth at the right hand of God the Father;" a similitude borrowed from princes, who have their assessors to whom they commit the office of ruling and issuing commands. Thus Christ, in whom the Father is pleased to be exalted, and by whose hand he is pleased to reign, is said to have been received up, and seated on his right hand (Mark xvi. 19); as if it had been said, that he was installed in the government of heaven and earth, and formally admitted to possession of the administration committed to him, and not only admitted for once, but to continue until he descend to judgment. For so the Apostle interprets, when he says, that the Father "set him at his own right hand in the heavenly places, far above all principality, and power, and might, and dominion, and every name that is named not only in this world, but also in that which is to come; and hath put all things under his feet, and given him to be the head over all things to the Church."[1] You see to what end he is so seated—namely, that all creatures both in heaven and earth should reverence his majesty, be ruled by his hand, do him implicit homage, and submit to his power. All that the Apostles intend, when they so often mention his seat at the Father's hand, is to teach that everything is placed at his disposal. Those therefore are in error, who suppose that his blessedness merely is indicated. We may observe, that there is nothing contrary to this doctrine in the testimony of Stephen, that he saw him standing (Acts vii. 56), the subject here considered being not the position of his body, but the majesty of his empire, *sitting* meaning nothing more than presiding on the judgment-seat of heaven.

[1] Ephes. i. 20; Phil. ii. 9; 1 Cor. xv. 27; Ephes. iv. 15; Acts ii. 33; iii. 21; Heb. i. 4.

16. From this doctrine faith derives manifold advantages.[1] First, it perceives that the Lord, by his ascension to heaven, has opened up the access to the heavenly kingdom, which Adam had shut. For having entered it in our flesh, as it were in our name, it follows, as the Apostle says, that we are in a manner now seated in heavenly places, not entertaining a mere hope of heaven, but possessing it in our head. Secondly, faith perceives that his seat beside the Father is not without great advantage to us. Having entered the temple not made with hands, he constantly appears as our advocate and intercessor in the presence of the Father; directs attention to his own righteousness, so as to turn it away from our sins; so reconciles him to us, as by his intercession to pave for us a way of access to his throne, presenting it to miserable sinners, to whom it would otherwise be an object of dread, as replete with grace and mercy. Thirdly, it discerns his power, on which depend our strength, might, resources, and triumph over hell, " When he ascended up on high, he led captivity captive" (Eph. iv. 8). Spoiling his foes, he gave gifts to his people, and daily loads them with spiritual riches. He thus occupies his exalted seat, that, thence transferring his virtue unto us, he may quicken us to spiritual life, sanctify us by his Spirit, and adorn his Church with various graces, by his protection preserve it safe from all harm, and by the strength of his hand curb the enemies raging against his cross and our salvation; in fine, that he may possess all power in heaven and earth, until he have utterly routed all his foes, who are also ours, and completed the structure of his Church. Such is the true nature of the kingdom, such the power which the Father has conferred upon him, until he arrive to complete the last act by judging the quick and the dead.

17. Christ, indeed, gives his followers no dubious proofs of present power, but as his kingdom in the world is in a manner veiled by the humiliation of a carnal condition, faith is most properly invited to meditate on the visible presence which he will exhibit on the last day. For he will descend from heaven in visible form, in like manner as he was seen to ascend,[2] and appear to all, with the ineffable majesty of his kingdom, the splendour of immortality, the boundless power of divinity, and an attending company of angels. Hence we are told to wait for the Redeemer against that day on which he will separate the sheep from the goats, and the elect from the reprobate, and when not one individual either of the living or the dead shall escape his judgment. From the extremities of the universe shall be heard the clang of the trumpet summoning all to his tribunal; both those whom that day shall find alive, and those whom death shall previously have removed from the society of the living. There are some who take the words, *quick* and *dead*, in a different sense;[3] and, indeed, some an-

---

[1] August. de Fide et Symbolo, cap. 8; Eph. ii. 6; Heb. vii. 25; ix. 11.
[2] Acts i. 11; Matth. xxiv. 30; xxv. 31; 1 Thess. iv. 16, 17.
[3] The French is, " Il y en a aucuns qui exposent par les vivans et les morts, les bons

cient writers appear to have hesitated as to the exposition of them ; but our meaning being plain and clear, is much more accordant with the Creed, which was certainly written for popular use.   There is nothing contrary to it in the Apostle's declaration, that it is appointed unto all men once to die.   For though those who are surviving at the last day shall not die after a natural manner, yet the change which they are to undergo, as it shall resemble, is not improperly. called, death (Heb. ix. 27).   " We shall not all sleep, but we shall all be changed" (1 Cor. xv. 51).   What does this mean?   Their mortal life shall perish and be swallowed up in one moment, and be transformed into an entirely new nature.   Though no one can deny that that destruction of the flesh will be death, it still remains true that the quick and the dead shall be summoned to judgment (1 Thess. iv. 16) : for " the dead in Christ shall rise first ; then we which are alive and remain shall be caught up together with them in the clouds to meet the Lord in the air."   Indeed, it is probable, that these words in the Creed were taken from Peter's sermon as related by Luke (Acts x. 42), and from the solemn charge of Paul to Timothy (2 Tim. iv. 1).

18. It is most consolatory to think, that judgment is vested in him who has already destined us to share with him in the honour of judgment (Matth. xix. 28) ; so far is it from being true, that he will ascend the judgment-seat for our condemnation.   How could a most merciful prince destroy his own people ? how could the head disperse its own members ? how could the advocate condemn his clients ? For if the Apostle, when contemplating the interposition of Christ, is bold to exclaim, " Who is he that condemneth?" (Rom. viii. 33), much more certain is it that Christ, the intercessor, will not condemn those whom he has admitted to his protection.   It certainly gives no small security, that we shall be sisted at no other tribunal than that of our Redeemer, from whom salvation is to be expected; and that he who in the Gospel now promises eternal blessedness, will then as judge ratify his promise.[1] The end for which the Father has honoured the Son by committing all judgment to him (John v. 22), was to pacify the consciences of his people when alarmed at the thought of judgment. Hitherto I have followed the order of the Apostles' Creed, because it states the leading articles of redemption in a few words, and may thus serve as a tablet in which the points of Christian doctrine, most deserving of attention, are brought separately and distinctly before us.[2] I call it the Apostles' Creed, though I am by no

et les mauvais."—There are some who, by the quick and the dead, understand the good and the bad.

[1] Vide Ambros. de Jac. et Vita Beata, Lib. i. c. 6.

[2] The French is, " Jusques ici j'ay suivi l'ordre du Symbole qu'on appelle des Apostres, pource que la nous pouvons voir comme en un tableau, par les articles qui y sont contenus, en quoy gist nostre salut : et par ce moyen aussi entendons a quelles choses il nous faut arrester pour obtenir salut en Jesus Christ."—Hitherto I have followed the order of what is called the Apostles' Creed, because there we may see, as in a tablet,

means solicitous as to its authorship. The general consent of ancient writers certainly does ascribe it to the Apostles, either because they imagined it was written and published by them for common use, or because they thought it right to give the sanction of such authority to a compendium faithfully drawn up from the doctrine delivered by their hands. I have no doubt that, from the very commencement of the Church, and, therefore, in the very days of the Apostles, it held the place of a public and universally received confession, whatever be the quarter from which it originally proceeded. It is not probable that it was written by some private individual, since it is certain that, from time immemorial, it was deemed of sacred authority by all Christians. The only point of consequence we hold to be incontrovertible—viz. that it gives, in clear and succinct order, a full statement of our faith, and in everything which it contains is sanctioned by the sure testimony of Scripture. This being understood, it were to no purpose to labour anxiously, or quarrel with any one as to the authorship, unless, indeed, we think it not enough to possess the sure truth of the Holy Spirit, without, at the same time, knowing by whose mouth it was pronounced, or by whose hand it was written.

19. When we see that the whole sum of our salvation, and every single part of it, are comprehended in Christ, we must beware of deriving even the minutest portion of it from any other quarter. If we seek salvation, we are taught by the very name of Jesus that he possesses it;[1] if we seek any other gifts of the Spirit, we shall find them in his unction; strength in his government; purity in his conception; indulgence in his nativity, in which he was made like us in all respects, in order that he might learn to sympathise with us: if we seek redemption, we shall find it in his passion; acquittal in his condemnation; remission of the curse in his cross; satisfaction in his sacrifice; purification in his blood; reconciliation in his descent to hell; mortification of the flesh in his sepulchre; newness of life in his resurrection; immortality also in his resurrection; the inheritance of a celestial kingdom in his entrance into heaven; protection, security, and the abundant supply of all blessings, in his kingdom; secure anticipation of judgment in the power of judging committed to him. In fine, since in him all kinds of blessings are treasured up; let us draw a full supply from him, and none from any other quarter. Those who, not satisfied with him alone, entertain various hopes from others, though they may continue to look to him chiefly, deviate from the right path by the simple fact, that some portion of their thought takes a different direction. No distrust of this description can arise when once the abundance of his blessings is properly known:

by the articles which are contained in it, wherein consists our salvation, and by this means also understand on what things we ought to dwell in order to obtain salvation in Jesus Christ.

[1] Acts iv. 12; 1 Cor. i. 30; Heb. ii. 17; Gal. iii. 8.

CHAPTER XVII.

CHRIST RIGHTLY AND PROPERLY SAID TO HAVE MERITED GRACE AND
SALVATION FOR US.

The three leading divisions of this chapter are,—I. A proof from reason and from
Scripture that the grace of God and the merit of Christ (the prince and author of our
salvation) are perfectly compatible, sec. 1 and 2. II. Christ, by his obedience, even
to the death of the cross (which was the price of our redemption), merited divine favour
for us, sec. 3—5. III. The presumptuous rashness of the Schoolmen in treating this
branch of doctrine.

Sections.

1. Christ not only the minister, but also the author and prince of salvation. Divine
   grace not obscured by this mode of expression. The merit of Christ not opposed
   to the mercy of God, but depends upon it.
2. The compatibility of the two proved by various passages of Scripture.
3. Christ by his obedience truly merited divine grace for us.
4. This grace obtained by the shedding of Christ's blood and his obedience even unto
   death.
5. In this way he paid our ransom.
6. The presumptuous manner in which the Schoolmen handle this subject.

1. A QUESTION must here be considered by way of supplement.
Some men too much given to subtilty, while they admit that we
obtain salvation through Christ, will not hear of the name of merit,
by which they imagine that the grace of God is obscured ; and therefore insist that Christ was only the instrument or minister, not the
author or leader, or prince of life, as he is designated by Peter (Acts
iii. 15).   I admit that were Christ opposed simply, and by himself,
to the justice of God, there could be no room for merit, because there
cannot be found in man a worth which could make God a debtor ;
nay, as Augustine says most truly,[1] "The Saviour, the man Christ
Jesus, is himself the brightest illustration of predestination and
grace : his character as such was not procured by any antecedent
merit of works or faith in his human nature.   Tell me, I pray, how
that man, when assumed into unity of person by the Word, co-eternal
with the Father, as the only begotten Son of God, could merit this."
—"Let the very fountain of grace, therefoie, appear in our head,
whence, according to the measure of each, it is diffused through all
his members.   Every man, from the commencement of his faith,
becomes a Christian, by the same grace by which that man from his

---

[1] August. de Prædest. Sanct. Lib. i. c. xv. ; De Bono Perseverantia, cap. ult. See
supra, chapter xiv. sec. 7.

formation became Christ." Again, in another passage, "There is not a more striking example of predestination than the Mediator himself. He who made him (without any antecedent merit in his will) of the seed of David a righteous man never to be unrighteous, also converts those who are members of his head from unrighteous into righteous," and so forth. Therefore, when we treat of the merit of Christ, we do not place the beginning in him, but we ascend to the ordination of God as the primary cause, because of his mere good pleasure he appointed a Mediator to purchase salvation for us. Hence the merit of Christ is inconsiderately opposed to the mercy of God. It is a well-known rule, that principal and accessory are not incompatible, and therefore there is nothing to prevent the justification of man from being the gratuitous result of the mere mercy of God, and, at the same time, to prevent the merit of Christ from intervening in subordination to this mercy. The free favour of God is as fitly opposed to our works as is the obedience of Christ, both in their order: for Christ could not merit anything save by the good pleasure of God, but only inasmuch as he was destined to appease the wrath of God by his sacrifice, and wipe away our transgressions by his obedience: in one word, since the merit of Christ depends entirely on the grace of God (which provided this mode of salvation for us), the latter is no less appropriately opposed to all righteousness of men than is the former.

2. This distinction is found in numerous passages of Scripture: "God so loved the world, that he gave his only begotten Son, that whosoever believeth in him might not perish (John iii. 16). We see that the first place is assigned to the love of God as the chief cause or origin, and that faith in Christ follows as the second and more proximate cause. Should any one object that Christ is only the formal cause,[1] he lessens his energy more than the words justify. For if we obtain justification by a faith which leans on him, the groundwork of our salvation must be sought in him. This is clearly proved by several passages: "Herein is love, not that we loved God, but that he loved us, and sent his Son to be the propitiation for our sins" (1 John iv. 10). These words clearly demonstrate that God, in order to remove any obstacle to his love towards us, appointed the method of reconciliation in Christ. There is great force in this word *propitiation;* for in a manner which cannot be expressed, God, at the very time when he loved us, was hostile to us until reconciled in Christ. To this effect are all the following passages: "He is the propitiation for our sins;" "It pleased the Father that in him should all fulness dwell, and having made peace by the blood of his cross, by him to reconcile all things unto himself;" "God was in Christ reconciling the world unto himself, not imputing their trespasses

---

[1] The French adds, "C'est a dire, qui n'emporte en soy vrai effect;"—that is to say, which in itself produces no true effect.

unto them;" "He hath made us accepted in the Beloved," "That he might reconcile both into one body by the cross."[1] The nature of this mystery is to be learned from the first chapter to the Ephesians, where Paul, teaching that we were chosen in Christ, at the same time adds, that we obtained grace in him. How did God begin to embrace with his favour those whom he had loved before the foundation of the world, unless in displaying his love when he was reconciled by the blood of Christ? As God is the fountain of all righteousness, he must necessarily be the enemy and judge of man so long as he is a sinner. Wherefore, the commencement of love is the bestowing of righteousness, as described by Paul: "He hath made him to be sin for us who knew no sin; that we might be made the righteousness of God in him" (2 Cor. v. 21). He intimates, that by the sacrifice of Christ we obtain free justification, and become pleasing to God, though we are by nature the children of wrath, and by sin estranged from him. This distinction is also noted whenever the grace of Christ is connected with the love of God (2 Cor. xiii. 13); whence it follows, that he bestows upon us of his own which he acquired by purchase. For otherwise there would be no ground for the praise ascribed to him by the Father, that grace is his, and proceeds from him.

3. That Christ, by his obedience, truly purchased and merited grace for us with the Father, is accurately inferred from several passages of Scripture. I take it for granted, that if Christ satisfied for our sins, if he paid the penalty due by us, if he appeased God by his obedience; in fine, if he suffered the just for the unjust, salvation was obtained for us by his righteousness; which is just equivalent to meriting. Now, Paul's testimony is, that we were reconciled, and received reconciliation through his death (Rom. v. 11). But there is no room for reconciliation unless where offence[2] has preceded. The meaning therefore is, that God, to whom we were hateful through sin, was appeased by the death of his Son, and made propitious to us. And the antithesis which immediately follows is carefully to be observed, "As by one man's disobedience many were made sinners, so by the obedience of one shall many be made righteous" (Rom. v. 19). For the meaning is—As by the sin of Adam we were alienated from God and doomed to destruction, so by the obedience of Christ we are restored to his favour as if we were righteous. The future tense of the verb does not exclude present righteousness, as is apparent from the context. For he had previously said, "the free gift *is* of many offences unto justification."

4. When we say, that grace was obtained for us by the merit of Christ, our meaning is, that we were cleansed by his blood, that his death was an expiation for sin, "His blood cleanses us from all sin."

---

[1] 1 John ii. 2; Col. i. 19, 20; 2 Cor. v. 19; Eph. i. 6; ii. 16.
[2] French, "Offense, haine, divorce;"—offence, hatred, divorce.

"This is my blood, which is shed for the remission of sins" (1 John i. 7; Luke xxii. 20). If the effect of his shed blood is, that our sins are not imputed to us, it follows, that by that price the justice of God was satisfied. To the same effect are the Baptist's words, "Behold the Lamb of God, which taketh away the sin of the world" (John i. 29). For he contrasts Christ with all the sacrifices of the Law, showing that in him alone was fulfilled what these figures typified. But we know the common expression in Moses—Iniquity shall be expiated, sin shall be wiped away and forgiven. In short, we are admirably taught by the ancient figures what power and efficacy there is in Christ's death. And the Apostle, skilfully proceeding from this principle, explains the whole matter in the Epistle to the Hebrews, showing that without shedding of blood there is no remission (Heb. ix. 22). From this he infers, that Christ appeared once for all to take away sin by the sacrifice of himself. Again, that he was offered to bear the sins of many (Heb. ix. 28). He had previously said, that not by the blood of goats or of heifers, but by his own blood, he had once entered into the holy of holies, having obtained eternal redemption for us. Now, when he reasons thus, "If the blood of bulls and of goats, and the ashes of an heifer sprinkling the unclean, sanctifieth to the purifying of the flesh: how much more shall the blood of Christ, who through the eternal Spirit offered himself to God, purge your consciences from dead works to serve the living God?" (Heb. ix. 13, 14), it is obvious that too little effect is given to the grace of Christ, unless we concede to his sacrifice the power of expiating, appeasing, and satisfying: as he shortly after adds, "For this cause he is the mediator of the new testament, that by means of his death, for the redemption of the transgressions that were under the first testament, they which are called might receive the promise of eternal inheritance" (Heb. ix. 15). But it is especially necessary to attend to the analogy which is drawn by Paul as to his having been made a curse for us (Gal. iii. 13). It had been superfluous and therefore absurd, that Christ should have been burdened with a curse, had it not been in order that, by paying what others owed, he might acquire righteousness for them. There is no ambiguity in Isaiah's testimony, "He was wounded for our transgressions, he was bruised for our iniquities: the chastisement of our peace was laid upon him; and with his stripes we are healed" (Is. liii. 5). For had not Christ satisfied for our sins, he could not be said to have appeased God by taking upon himself the penalty which we had incurred. To this corresponds what follows in the same place, "for the transgression of my people was he stricken" (Is. liii. 8). We may add the interpretation of Peter, who unequivocally declares, that he "bare our sins in his own body on the tree" (1 Pet. ii. 24), that the whole burden of condemnation, of which we were relieved, was laid upon him.

5. The Apostles also plainly declare that he paid a price to ransom us from death: "Being justified freely by his grace, through the re-

demption that is in Christ Jesus: whom God hath set forth to be a propitiation through faith in his blood" (Rom. iii. 24, 25). Paul commends the grace of God, in that he gave the price of redemption in the death of Christ; and he exhorts us to flee to his blood, that having obtained righteousness, we may appear boldly before the judgment-seat of God. To the same effect are the words of Peter: "Forasmuch as ye know that ye were not redeemed with corruptible things, as silver and gold,"——" but with the precious blood of Christ, as of a lamb without blemish and without spot" (1 Pet. i. 18, 19). The antithesis would be incongruous if he had not by this price made satisfaction for sins. For which reason, Paul says, " Ye are bought with a price." Nor could it be elsewhere said, there is " one mediator between God and men, the man Christ Jesus; who gave himself a ransom for all" (1 Tim. ii. 5, 6), had not the punishment which we deserved been laid upon him. Accordingly, the same Apostle declares, that "we have redemption through his blood, even the forgiveness of sins" (Col. i. 14); as if he had said, that we are justified or acquitted before God, because that blood serves the purpose of satisfaction. With this another passage agrees—viz. that he blotted out "the handwriting of ordinances which was against us, which was contrary to us" (Col. ii. 14). These words denote the payment or compensation which acquits us from guilt. There is great weight also in these words of Paul: " If righteousness come by the law, then Christ is dead in vain" (Gal. ii. 21). For we hence infer, that it is from Christ we must seek what the Law would confer on any one who fulfilled it; or, which is the same thing, that by the grace of Christ we obtain what God promised in the Law to our works: " If a man do, he shall live in them" (Lev. xviii. 5). This is no less clearly taught in the discourse at Antioch, when Paul declares, "That through this man is preached unto you the forgiveness of sins; and by him all that believe are justified from all things, from which ye could not be justified by the law of Moses" (Acts xiii. 38, 39). For if the observance of the Law is righteousness, who can deny that Christ, by taking this burden upon himself, and reconciling us to God, as if we were the observers of the Law, merited favour for us? Of the same nature is what he afterwards says to the Galatians: " God sent forth his Son, made of a woman, made under the law, to redeem them that were under the law" (Gal. iv. 4, 5). For to what end that subjection, unless that he obtained justification for us by undertaking to perform what we were unable to pay? Hence that imputation of righteousness without works, of which Paul treats (Rom. iv. 5), the righteousness found in Christ alone being accepted as if it were ours. And certainly the only reason why Christ is called our " meat" (John vi. 55), is because we find in him the substance of life. And the source of this efficacy is just that the Son of God was crucified as the price of our justification; as Paul says, Christ " hath given himself for us an offering and a sacrifice to God for a sweet-smelling savour" (Eph. v. 2); and elsewhere, he "was delivered for our offences, and was raised again for our justification" (Rom. iv. 25). Hence it is proved not only that salvation was given us by Christ, but that on account of him the Father is now propitious to us. For it cannot be doubted that in him is completely fulfilled what God declares by Isaiah under a figure, "I will defend this city to save it for mine own sake, and for my servant David's sake" (Isaiah xxxvii. 35). Of this the Apostle is the best witness, when he says, "Your sins are forgiven you for his name's sake" (1 John. ii. 12). For although the name of Christ is not expressed, John, in his usual manner, designates him by the pronoun "He" (αὐτὸς). In the same sence also our Lord declares, "As the living Father hath sent me, and I live by the Father: so he that eateth me, even he shall live by me" (John vi. 57). To this corresponds the passage of Paul, "Unto you it is given in the behalf of Christ, not only to believe in him, but also to suffer for his sake" (Phil i. 29).

6. To inquire, as Lombard and the Schoolmen do (Sent. Lib. III. Dist. 18), whether he merited for himself, is foolish curiosity. Equally rash is their decision when they answer in the affirmative. How could it be necessary for the only Son of God to come down in order to acquire some new quality for himself? The exposition which God gives of his own purpose removes all doubt. The Father is not said to have consulted the advantage of his Son in his services, but to have given him up to death, and not spared him, because he loved the world (Rom. viii). The prophetical expressions should be observed: "To us a Son is born;" "Rejoice greatly, O daughter of Zion: shout, O daughter of Jerusalem: behold, thy King cometh unto thee" (Isaiah ix. 6; Zech. ix. 9). It would otherwise be a cold commendation of love which Paul describes, when he says, "God commendeth his love toward us, in that, while we were yet sinners, Christ died for us" (Rom. v. 8). Hence, again, we infer that Christ had no regard to himself; and this he distinctly affirms, when he says, "For their sakes I sanctify myself" (John xvii. 19). He who transfers the benefit of his holiness to others, testifies that he acquires nothing for himself. And surely it is most worthy of remark, that Christ, in devoting himself entirely to our salvation, in a manner forgot himself. It is absurd to wrest the testimony of Paul to a different effect: "Wherefore God hath highly exalted him, and given him a name which is above every name" (Phil. ii. 9).[1] By what services could a man merit to become the judge of the world, the head of angels, to obtain the supreme government of God, and become the residence of that majesty of which all the virtues of men and angels

---

[1] The sentence stands thus in the French :—"Les Sorbonnistes pervertissent le passage de S. Paul, l'appliquans a ce propos c'est que pource que Jesus Christ s'est humilié, le Pere l'a exalté et lui donné un nom souverain :"—The Sorbonnists pervert the passage of St Paul, and apply it in this way—that because **Christ humbled himself, the Father exalted him, and gave him a sovereign name.**

cannot attain one thousandth part? The solution is easy and complete. Paul is not speaking of the cause of Christ's exaltation, but only pointing out a consequence of it by way of example to us. The meaning is not much different from that of another passage: "Ought not Christ to have suffered these things, and to enter into his glory?" (Luke xxiv. 26.)

END OF THE SECOND BOOK.

INSTITUTES

OF

THE CHRISTIAN RELIGION.

BOOK THIRD

THE MODE OF OBTAINING THE GRACE OF CHRIST.
THE BENEFITS IT CONFERS, AND THE
EFFECTS RESULTING FROM IT.

ARGUMENT.

The two former Books treated of God the Creator and Redeemer. This Book, which contains a full exposition of the Third Part of the Apostles' Creed, treats of the mode of procuring the grace of Christ, the benefits which we derive and the effects which follow from it, or of the operations of the Holy Spirit in regard to our salvation.

The subject is comprehended under seven principal heads, which almost all point to the same end—namely, the doctrine of faith.

I. As it is by the secret and special operation of the Holy Spirit that we enjoy Christ and all his benefits, the First Chapter treats of this operation, which is the foundation of faith, new life, and all holy exercises.

II. Faith being, as it were, the hand by which we embrace Christ the Redeemer, offered to us by the Holy Spirit, Faith is fully considered in the Second Chapter.

III. In further explanation of Saving Faith, and the benefits derived from it, it is mentioned that true repentance always flows from true faith. The doctrine of Repentance is considered generally in the Third Chapter, Popish repentance in the Fourth Chapter, Indulgences and Purgatory in the Fifth Chapter. Chapters Sixth to Tenth are devoted to a special consideration of the different parts of true Repentance—viz., mortification of the flesh, and quickening of the Spirit.

IV. More clearly to show the utility of this Faith, and the effects resulting from it, the doctrine of Justification by Faith is explained in the Eleventh Chapter, and certain questions connected with it explained from the Twelfth to the Eighteenth Chapter. Christian liberty a kind of accessory to Justification, is considered in the Nineteenth Chapter.

V. The Twentieth Chapter is devoted to Prayer, the principal exercise of faith, and, as it were, the medium or instrument through which we daily procure blessings from God.

VI. As all do not indiscriminately embrace the fellowship of Christ offered in the Gospel, but those only whom the Lord favours with the effectual and special grace of his Spirit, lest any should impugn this arrangement, Chapters Twenty-First to Twenty-Fourth are occupied with a necessary and apposite discussion of the subject of Election.

VII. Lastly, As the hard warfare which the Christian is obliged constantly to wage may have the effect of disheartening him, it is shown how it may be alleviated by meditating on the final resurrection. Hence the subject of the Resurrection is considered in the Twenty-Fifth Chapter.

INSTITUTES

OF

THE CHRISTIAN RELIGION.

BOOK THIRD.

THE MODE OF OBTAINING THE GRACE OF CHRIST. THE BENEFITS IT CONFERS, AND THE EFFECTS RESULTING FROM IT.

CHAPTER I.

THE BENEFITS OF CHRIST MADE AVAILABLE TO US BY THE SECRET OPERATION OF THE SPIRIT.

The three divisions of this chapter are,—I. The secret operation of the Holy Spirit, which seals our salvation, should be considered first in Christ the Mediator as our Head, sec. 1 and 2. II. The titles given to the Holy Spirit show that we become members of Christ by his grace and energy, sec. 3. III. As the special influence of the Holy Spirit is manifested in the gift of faith, the former is a proper introduction to the latter, and thus prepares for the second chapter, sec. 4.

Sections.

1. The Holy Spirit the bond which unites us with Christ. This the result of faith produced by the secret operation of the Holy Spirit. This obvious from Scripture.
2. In Christ the Mediator the gifts of the Holy Spirit are to be seen in all their fulness. To what end. Why the Holy Spirit is called the Spirit of the Father and the Son.
3. Titles of the Spirit,—1. The Spirit of adoption. 2. An earnest and seal. 3. Water. 4. Life. 5 Oil and unction. 6. Fire. 7. A fountain. 8. The word of God. Use of these titles.
4. Faith being the special work of the Holy Spirit, the power and efficacy of the Holy Spirit usually ascribed to it.

1. WE must now see in what way we become possessed of the blessings which God has bestowed on his only begotten Son, not for

private use, but to enrich the poor and needy. And the first thing to be attended to is, that so long as we are without Christ and separated from him, nothing which he suffered and did for the salvation of the human race is of the least benefit to us. To communicate to us the blessings which he received from the Father, he must become ours and dwell in us. Accordingly, he is called our Head, and the first-born among many brethren, while, on the other hand, we are said to be ingrafted into him and clothed with him,[1] all which he possesses being, as I have said, nothing to us until we become one with him. And although it is true that we obtain this by faith, yet since we see that all do not indiscriminately embrace the offer of Christ which is made by the gospel, the very nature of the case teaches us to ascend higher, and inquire into the secret efficacy of the Spirit, to which it is owing that we enjoy Christ and all his blessings. I have already treated of the eternal essence and divinity of the Spirit (Book I. chap. xiii. sect. 14, 15); let us at present attend to the special point, that Christ came by water and blood, as the Spirit testifies concerning him, that we might not lose the benefits of the salvation which he has purchased. For as there are said to be three witnesses in heaven, the Father, the Word, and the Spirit, so there are also three on the earth—namely, water, blood, and Spirit. It is not without cause that the testimony of the Spirit is twice mentioned, a testimony which is engraven on our hearts by way of seal, and thus seals the cleansing and sacrifice of Christ. For which reason, also, Peter says, that believers are "elect" "through sanctification of the Spirit, unto obedience and sprinkling of the blood of Jesus Christ" (1 Pet. i. 2). By these words he reminds us, that if the shedding of his sacred blood is not to be in vain, our souls must be washed in it by the secret cleansing of the Holy Spirit. For which reason, also, Paul, speaking of cleansing and purification, says, "But ye are washed, but ye are sanctified, but ye are justified in the name of the Lord Jesus, and by the Spirit of our God" (1 Cor. vi. 11). The whole comes to this; that the Holy Spirit is the bond by which Christ effectually binds us to himself. Here we may refer to what was said in the last Book concerning his anointing.

2. But in order to have a clearer view of this most important subject, we must remember that Christ came provided with the Holy Spirit after a peculiar manner—namely, that he might separate us from the world, and unite us in the hope of an eternal inheritance. Hence the Spirit is called the Spirit of sanctification, because he quickens and cherishes us, not merely by the general energy which is seen in the human race, as well as other animals, but because he is the seed and root of heavenly life in us. Accordingly, one of the highest commendations which the prophets give to the kingdom of Christ is, that under it the Spirit would be poured out in richer abundance. One

---

1 Eph. iv. 15; Rom. vi. 5; xi. 17; viii. 29; Gal. iii. 27.

of the most remarkable passages is that of Joel, "It shall come to pass afterward, that I will pour out my Spirit upon all flesh" (Joel ii. 28). For although the prophet seems to confine the gifts of the Spirit to the office of prophesying, he yet intimates, under a figure, that God will, by the illumination of his Spirit, provide himself with disciples who had previously been altogether ignorant of heavenly doctrine. Moreover, as it is for the sake of his Son that God bestows the Holy Spirit upon us, and yet has deposited him in all his fulness with the Son, to be the minister and dispenser of his liberality, he is called at one time the Spirit of the Father, at another the Spirit of the Son: " Ye are not in the flesh but in the Spirit, if so be that the Spirit of God dwell in you. Now, if any man have not the Spirit of Christ, he is none of his" (Rom. viii. 9) ; and hence he encourages us to hope for complete renovation : " If the Spirit of him that raised up Jesus from the dead dwell in you, he that raised up Christ from the dead shall also quicken your mortal bodies by his Spirit that dwelleth in you " (Rom. viii. 11). There is no inconsistency in ascribing the glory of those gifts to the Father, inasmuch as he is the author of them, and, at the same time, ascribing them to Christ, with whom they have been deposited, that he may bestow them on his people. Hence he invites all the thirsty to come unto him and drink (John vii. 37). And Paul teaches, that " unto every one of us is given grace, according to the measure of the gift of Christ" (Eph. iv. 7). And we must remember that the Spirit is called the Spirit of Christ, not only inasmuch as the eternal Word of God is with the Father united with the Spirit, but also in respect of his office of Mediator ; because, had he not been endued with the energy of the Spirit, he had come to us in vain. In this sense he is called the " last Adam," and said to have been sent from heaven " a quickening Spirit" (1 Cor. xv. 45), where Paul contrasts the special life which Christ breathes into his people, that they may be one with him, with the animal life which is common even to the reprobate. In like manner, when he prays that believers may have " the grace of our Lord Jesus Christ, and the love of God," he at the same time adds, " the communion of the Holy Ghost," without which no man shall ever taste the paternal favour of God, or the benefits of Christ. Thus, also, in another passage he says, " The love of God is shed abroad in our hearts by the Holy Ghost, which is given unto us" (Rom. v. 5).

3. Here it will be proper to point out the titles which the Scripture bestows on the Spirit, when it treats of the commencement and entire renewal of our salvation. First, he is called the " Spirit of adoption," because he is witness to us of the free favour with which God the Father embraced us in his well-beloved and only-begotten Son, so as to become our Father, and give us boldness of access to him ; nay, he dictates the very words, so that we can boldly cry, " Abba, Father." For the same reason, he is said to have " sealed us, and given the earnest of the Spirit in our hearts," because, as

pilgrims in the world, and persons in a manner dead, he so quickens us from above as to assure us that our salvation is safe in the keeping of a faithful God. Hence, also, the Spirit is said to be "life because of righteousness." But since it is his secret irrigation that makes us bud forth and produce the fruits of righteousness, he is repeatedly described as *water*. Thus in Isaiah, "Ho, every one that thirsteth, come ye to the waters." Again, "I will pour water upon him that is thirsty, and floods upon the dry ground." Corresponding to this are the words of our Saviour, to which I lately referred, "If any man thirst, let him come unto me and drink." Sometimes, indeed, he receives this name from his energy in cleansing and purifying, as in Ezekiel, where the Lord promises, "Then will I sprinkle you with clean water, and ye shall be clean." As those sprinkled with the Spirit are restored to the full vigour of life, he hence obtains the names of *"Oil"* and *"Unction."* On the other hand, as he is constantly employed in subduing and destroying the vices of our concupiscence, and inflaming our hearts with the love of God and piety, he hence receives the name of *Fire*. In fine, he is described to us as a *Fountain*, whence all heavenly riches flow to us; or as the *Hand* by which God exerts his power, because by his divine inspiration he so breathes divine life into us, that we are no longer acted upon by ourselves, but ruled by his motion and agency, so that everything good in us is the fruit of his grace, while our own endowments without him are mere darkness of mind and perverseness of heart. Already, indeed, it has been clearly shown, that until our minds are intent on the Spirit, Christ is in a manner unemployed, because we view him coldly without us, and so at a distance from us. Now we know that he is of no avail save only to those to whom he is a head and the first-born among the brethren, to those, in fine, who are clothed with him.[1] To this union alone it is owing that, in regard to us, the Saviour has not come in vain. To this is to be referred that sacred marriage, by which we become bone of his bone, and flesh of his flesh, and so one with him (Eph. v. 30), for it is by the Spirit alone that he unites himself to us. By the same grace and energy of the Spirit we become his members, so that he keeps us under him, and we in our turn possess him.

4. But as faith is his principal work, all those passages which express his power and operations are, in a great measure, referred to it, as it is only by faith that he brings us to the light of the Gospel, as John teaches, that to those who believe in Christ is given the privilege "to become the Sons of God, even to them that believe in his name, which were born not of blood, nor of the will of the flesh, nor of the will of man, but of God" (John i. 12). Opposing *God* to *flesh and blood*, he declares it to be a supernatural gift, that those

1 Rom. viii. 15; Gal. iv. 6; 2 Cor. i. 22; Eph. i. 13, 14; Rom. viii. 10; Isa. lv. 1; xliv. 3; John viii. 37; Ezek. xxxvi. 25; John ii. 14; 1 John ii. 20, 27; Luke iii. 16.; Acts xi. 21.

who would otherwise remain in unbelief receive Christ by faith. Similar to this is our Saviour's reply to Peter, " Flesh and blood hath not revealed it unto thee, but my Father which is in heaven " (Matt. xvi. 17). These things I now briefly advert to, as I have fully considered them elsewhere. To the same effect Paul says to the Ephesians, " Ye were sealed with that Holy Spirit of promise" (Eph. i. 13) ; thus showing that he is the internal teacher, by whose agency the promise of salvation, which would otherwise only strike the air or our ears, penetrates into our minds. In like manner, he says to the Thessalonians, " God hath from the beginning chosen you to salvation, through sanctification of the Spirit and belief of the truth" (2 Thess. ii. 13) ; by this passage briefly reminding us, that faith itself is produced only by the Spirit. This John explains more distinctly, " We know that he abideth in us, by the Spirit which he hath given us ;" again, " Hereby know we that we dwell in him and he in us, because he hath given us of his Spirit" (1 John iii. 24 ; iv. 13). Accordingly, to make his disciples capable of heavenly wisdom, Christ promised them " the Spirit of truth, whom the world cannot receive" (John xiv. 17). And he assigns it to him, as his proper office, to bring to remembrance the things which he had verbally taught ; for in vain were light offered to the blind, did not that Spirit of understanding open the intellectual eye ; so that he himself may be properly termed the key by which the treasures of the heavenly kingdom are unlocked, and his illumination, the eye of the mind by which we are enabled to see : hence Paul so highly commends the ministry of the Spirit[1] (2 Cor. iii. 6), since teachers would cry aloud to no purpose, did not Christ, the internal teacher, by means of his Spirit, draw to himself those who are given him of the Father. Therefore, as we have said that salvation is perfected in the person of Christ, so, in order to make us partakers of it, he baptises us " with the Holy Spirit and with fire" (Luke iii. 16), enlightening us into the faith of his Gospel, and so regenerating us to be new creatures. Thus cleansed from all pollution, he dedicates us as holy temples to the Lord.

---

[1] The French adds, " qui vaut autant a dire comme la predication ayant avec soy vivacité spirituelle ;"—that is to say, preaching carrying spiritual quickening along with it.

CHAPTER II.

OF FAITH.   THE DEFINITION OF IT.   ITS PECULIAR PROPERTIES.

This chapter consists of three principal parts.—I. A brief explanation of certain matters pertaining to the doctrine of Faith, sec. 1—14. First, of the object of faith, sec. 1. Second, of Implicit Faith, sec. 2—6. Third, Definition of Faith, sec. 7. Fourth, the various meanings of the term Faith, sec. 8—13. II. A full exposition of the definition given in the seventh section, sec. 14—40. III. A brief confirmation of the definition by the authority of an Apostle. The mutual relation between faith, hope, and charity, sec. 41—43.

Sections.

15. Why this knowledge must be sure and firm. Reason drawn from the consideration of our weakness. Another reason from the certainty of the promises of God.

16. The leading point in this certainty. Its fruits. A description of the true believer.

17. An objection to this certainty. Answer. Confirmation of the answer from the example of David. This enlarged upon from the opposite example of Ahaz. Also from the uniform experience and the prayers of believers.

18. For this reason the conflict between the flesh and the Spirit in the soul of the believer described. The issue of this conflict, the victory of faith.

19. On the whole, the faith of the elect certain and indubitable. Confirmation from analogy.

20. Another confirmation from the testimony of an Apostle, making it apparent that, though the faith of the elect is as yet imperfect, it is nevertheless firm and sure.

21. A fuller explanation of the nature of faith. 1. When the believer is shaken with fear, he betakes himself to the bosom of a merciful God. 2. He does not even shun God when angry, but hopes in him. 3. He does not suffer unbelief to reign in his heart. 4. He opposes unbelief, and is never finally lost. 5. Faith, however often assailed, at length comes off victorious.

22. Another species of fear, arising from a consideration of the judgment of God against the wicked. This also faith overcomes. Examples of this description, placed before the eyes of believers, repress presumption, and fix their faith in God.

23. Nothing contrary to this in the exhortation of the Apostle to work out our salvation with fear and trembling. Fear and faith mutually connected. Confirmation from the words of a Prophet.

24. This doctrine gives no countenance to the error of those who dream of a confidence mingled with incredulity. Refutation of this error, from a consideration of the dignity of Christ dwelling in us. The argument retorted. Refutation confirmed by the authority of an Apostle. What we ought to hold on this question.

25. Confirmation of the preceding conclusion by a passage from Bernard.

26. True fear caused in two ways—viz. when we are required to reverence God as a Father, and also to fear him as Lord.

27. Objection from a passage in the Apostle John. Answer founded on the distinction between filial and servile fear.

28. How faith is said to have respect to the divine benevolence. What comprehended under this benevolence. Confirmation from David and Paul.

29. Of the Free Promise which is the foundation of Faith. Reason. Confirmation.

30. Faith not divided in thus seeking a Free Promise in the Gospel. Reason. Conclusion confirmed by another reason.

31. The word of God the prop and root of faith. The word attests the divine goodness and mercy. In what sense faith has respect to the power of God. Various passages of Isaiah, inviting the godly to behold the power of God, explained. Other passages from David. We must beware of going beyond the limits prescribed by the word, lest false zeal lead us astray, as it did Sarah, Rebekah, and Isaac. In this way faith is obscured, though not extinguished. We must not depart one iota from the word of God.

32. All the promises included in Christ. Two objections answered. A third objection drawn from example. Answer explaining the faith of Naaman, Cornelius, and the Eunuch.

33. Faith revealed to our minds, and sealed on our hearts, by the Holy Spirit. 1. The mind is purified so as to have a relish for divine truth. 2. The mind is thus established in the truth by the agency of the Holy Spirit.

34. Proof of the former. 1. By reason. 2. By Scripture. 3. By example. 4. By analogy.

35. 5. By the excellent qualities of faith. 6. By a celebrated passage from Augustine.

36. Proof of the latter by the argument *a minore ad majus*. Why the Spirit is called a seal, an earnest, and the Spirit of promise.

37. Believers sometimes shaken, but not so as to perish finally. They ultimately overcome their trials, and remain stedfast. Proofs from Scripture.

38. Objection of the Schoolmen. Answer. Attempt to support the objection by a passage in Ecclesiastes. Answer, explaining the meaning of the passage.

39. Another objection, charging the elect in Christ with rashness and presumption. Answer. Answer confirmed by various passages from the Apostle Paul. Also from John and Isaiah.

1. ALL these things will be easily understood after we have given a clearer definition of faith, so as to enable the readers to apprehend its nature and power. Here it is of importance to call to mind what was formerly taught, first, That since God by his Law prescribes what we ought to do, failure in any one respect subjects us to the dreadful judgment of eternal death, which it denounces. Secondly, Because it is not only difficult, but altogether beyond our strength and ability, to fulfil the demands of the Law, if we look only to ourselves and consider what is due to our merits, no ground of hope remains, but we lie forsaken of God under eternal death. Thirdly, That there is only one method of deliverance which can rescue us from this miserable calamity—viz. when Christ the Redeemer appears, by whose hand our heavenly Father, out of his infinitè goodness and mercy, has been pleased to succour us, if we with true faith embrace this mercy, and with firm hope rest in it. It is now proper to consider the nature of this faith, by means of which, those who are adopted into the family of God obtain possession of the heavenly kingdom. For the accomplishment of so great an end, it is obvious that no mere opinion or persuasion is adequate. And the greater care and diligence is necessary in discussing the true nature of faith, from the pernicious delusions which many, in the present day, labour under with regard to it. Great numbers, on hearing the term, think that nothing more is meant than a certain common assent to the Gospel History; nay, when the subject of faith is discussed in the Schools, by simply representing God as its object, they by empty speculation, as we have elsewhere said (Book II. chap. vi. sec. 4), hurry wretched souls away from the right mark instead of directing them to it. For seeing that God dwells in light that is inaccessible, Christ must intervene. Hence he calls himself "the light of the world;" and in another passage, "the way, the truth, and the life." None cometh to the Father (who is the fountain of life), except by him; for "no man knoweth who the Father is but the Son, and he to whom the Son will reveal him." For this reason, Paul declares, "I count all things as loss for the excellency of the knowledge of Christ Jesus my Lord." In the twentieth chapter of the Acts, he states that he preached "faith towards our Lord Jesus Christ;" and in another passage, he introduces Christ as thus addressing him: "I have appeared unto thee for this purpose, to make thee a minister and a witness;"—— "delivering

thee from the people, and from the Gentiles, unto whom now I send thee,"——" that they may receive forgiveness of sins, and inheritance among them which are sanctified through faith which is in me." Paul further declares, that in the person of Christ the glory of God is visibly manifested to us, or, which is the same thing, we have "the light of the knowledge of the glory of God in the face of Jesus Christ."[1] It is true, indeed, that faith has respect to God only; but to this we should add, that it acknowledges Jesus Christ whom he hath sent. God would remain far off, concealed from us, were we not irradiated by the brightness of Christ. All that the Father had, he deposited with his only begotten Son, in order that he might manifest himself in him, and thus by the communication of blessings express the true image of his glory. Since, as has been said, we must be led by the Spirit, and thus stimulated to seek Christ, so must we also remember that the invisible Father is to be sought nowhere but in this image. For which reason Augustine, treating of the object of faith (De Civitate Dei, Lib. xi. c. 2), elegantly says, " The thing to be known is, whither we are to go, and by what way;" and immediately after infers, that " the surest way to avoid all errors is to know him who is both God and man. It is to God we tend, and it is by man we go, and both of these are found only in Christ."[2] Paul, when he preaches faith towards God, surely does not intend to overthrow what he so often inculcates—viz. that faith has all its stability in Christ. Peter most appropriately connects both, saying, that by him "we believe in God" (1 Pet. i. 21).

2. This evil, therefore, must, like innumerable others, be attributed to the Schoolmen,[3] who have in a manner drawn a veil over Christ, to whom, if our eye is not directly turned, we must always wander through many labyrinths. But besides impairing, and almost anni-hilating, faith by their obscure definition, they have invented the fiction of implicit faith, with which name decking the grossest ignor-ance, they delude the wretched populace to their great destruction.[4] Nay, to state the fact more truly and plainly, this fiction not only buries true faith, but entirely destroys it. Is it faith to understand nothing, and merely submit your convictions implicitly to the Church? Faith consists not in ignorance, but in knowledge—knowledge not of God merely, but of the divine will. We do not obtain salvation either because we are prepared to embrace every dictate of the Church as true, or leave to the Church the province of inquiring and deter-mining; but when we recognise God as a propitious Father through the reconciliation made by Christ, and Christ as given to us for

[1] 1 Tim. vi. 16; John viii. 12; xiv. 6; Luke x. 22; 1 Cor. ii. 2; Acts xx. 21; xxvi. 17, 18; 2 Cor. iv. 6.
[2] The French is, " Car nous tendons a Dieu, et par l'humanité de Jesus Christ, nous y sommes conduits; "—For we tend to God, and by the humanity of Christ are conducted to him.
[3] French, " Theologiens Sorboniques; "—Theologians of Sorbonne.
[4] In opposition to this ignorance, see Chrysostom in Joann. Homil. xvi.

righteousness, sanctification, and life. By this knowledge, I say, not by the submission of our understanding, we obtain an entrance into the kingdom of heaven. For when the Apostle says, " With the heart man believeth unto righteousness; and with the mouth confession is made unto salvation" (Rom. x. 10), he intimates, that it is not enough to believe implicitly without understanding, or even inquiring. The thing requisite is an explicit recognition of the divine goodness, in which our righteousness consists.

3. I indeed deny not (so enveloped are we in ignorance), that to us very many things now are and will continue to be completely involved until we lay aside this weight of flesh, and approach nearer to the presence of God. In such cases the fittest course is to suspend our judgment, and resolve to maintain unity with the Church. But under this pretext, to honour ignorance, tempered with humility, with the name of faith, is most absurd. Faith consists in the knowledge of God and Christ (John xvii. 3), not in reverence for the Church. And we see what a labyrinth they have formed out of this implicit faith—everything, sometimes even the most monstrous errors, being received by the ignorant as oracles without any discrimination, provided they are prescribed to them under the name of the Church. This inconsiderate facility, though the surest precipice to destruction, is, however, excused on the ground that it believes nothing definitely, but only with the appended condition, If such is the faith of the Church. Thus they pretend to find truth in error, light in darkness, true knowledge in ignorance. Not to dwell longer in refuting these views, we simply advise the reader to compare them with ours. The clearness of truth will itself furnish a sufficient refutation. For the question they raise is not, whether there may be an implicit faith with many remains of ignorance, but they maintain, that persons living and even indulging in a stupid ignorance duly believe, provided, in regard to things unknown, they assent to the authority and judgment of the Church : as if Scripture did not uniformly teach, that with faith understanding is conjoined.

4. We grant, indeed, that so long as we are pilgrims in the world faith is implicit, not only because as yet many things are hidden from us, but because, involved in the mists of error, we attain not to all. The highest wisdom, even of him who has attained the greatest perfection, is to go forward, and endeavour in a calm and teachable spirit to make further progress. Hence Paul exhorts believers to wait for further illumination in any matter in which they differ from each other (Phil. iii. 15).[1] And certainly experience teaches, that so long as we are in the flesh, our attainments are less than is to be desired. In our daily reading we fall in with many obscure passages which

[1] See Augustin. Ep. 102, " Si propter eos solos Christus mortuus est, qui certa intelligentia possunt ista discernera, pæne frustra in ecclesia laboramus," &c. ;—If Christ died for those only who are able to discern these things with true understanding, our labour in the Church is almost in vain.

convict us of ignorance. With this curb God keeps us modest, assigning to each a measure of faith, that every teacher, however excellent, may still be disposed to learn. Striking examples of this implicit faith may be observed in the disciples of Christ before they were fully illuminated. We see with what difficulty they take in the first rudiments, how they hesitate in the minutest matters, how, though hanging on the lips of their Master, they make no great progress; nay, even after running to the sepulchre on the report of the women, the resurrection of their Master appears to them a dream. As Christ previously bore testimony to their faith, we cannot say that they were altogether devoid of it; nay, had they not been persuaded that Christ would rise again, all their zeal would have been extinguished. Nor was it superstition that led the women to prepare spices to embalm a dead body of whose revival they had no expectation; but, although they gave credit to the words of one whom they knew to be true, yet the ignorance which still possessed their minds involved their faith in darkness, and left them in amazement. Hence they are said to have believed only when, by the reality, they perceive the truth of what Christ had spoken; not that they then began to believe, but the seed of a hidden faith, which lay as it were dead in their hearts, then burst forth in vigour. They had, therefore, a true but implicit faith, having reverently embraced Christ as the only teacher. Then, being taught by him, they felt assured that he was the author of salvation: in fine, believed that he had come from heaven to gather disciples, and take them thither through the grace of the Father. There cannot be a more familiar proof of this, than that in all men faith is always mingled with incredulity.

5. We may also call their faith implicit, as being properly nothing else than a preparation for faith. The Evangelists describe many as having believed, although they were only roused to admiration by the miracles, and went no farther than to believe that Christ was the promised Messiah, without being at all imbued with Evangelical doctrine. The reverence which subdued them, and made them willingly submit to Christ, is honoured with the name of faith, though it was nothing but the commencement of it. Thus the nobleman who believed in the promised cure of his son, on returning home, is said by the Evangelist (John iv. 53) to have again believed; that is, he had first received the words which fell from the lips of Christ as an oracular response, and thereafter submitted to his authority and received his doctrine. Although it is to be observed that he was docile and disposed to learn, yet the word " *believed* " in the former passage denotes a particular faith, and in the latter gives him a place among those disciples who had devoted themselves to Christ. Not unlike this is the example which John gives of the Samaritans, who believed the woman, and eagerly hastened to Christ; but, after they had heard him, thus express themselves, " Now we believe, not because of thy saying, for we have heard him ourselves, and know

that this is indeed the Christ, the Saviour of the world" (John iv. 42). From these passages it is obvious, that even those who are not yet imbued with the first principles, provided they are disposed to obey, are called *believers*, not properly indeed, but inasmuch as God is pleased in kindness so highly to honour their pious feeling. But this docility, with a desire of further progress, is widely different from the gross ignorance in which those sluggishly indulge who are contented with the implicit faith of the Papists. If Paul severely condemns those who are "ever learning, and never able to come to the knowledge of the truth," how much more sharply ought those to be rebuked who avowedly affect to know nothing?

6. The true knowledge of Christ consists in receiving him as he is offered by the Father—namely, as invested with his Gospel. For, as he is appointed as the end of our faith, so we cannot directly tend towards him except under the guidance of the Gospel. Therein are certainly unfolded to us treasures of grace. Did these continue shut, Christ would profit us little. Hence Paul makes faith the inseparable attendant of doctrine in these words, "Ye have not so learned Christ; if so be that ye have heard him, and have been taught by him, as the truth is in Jesus" (Eph. iv. 20, 21). Still I do not confine faith to the Gospel in such a sense as not to admit that enough was delivered to Moses and the Prophets to form a foundation of faith; but as the Gospel exhibits a fuller manifestation of Christ, Paul justly terms it the doctrine of faith (1 Tim. iv. 6). For which reason, also, he elsewhere says, that, by the coming of faith, the Law was abolished (Rom. x. 4), including under the expression a new and unwonted mode of teaching, by which Christ, from the period of his appearance as the great Master, gave a fuller illustration of the Father's mercy, and testified more surely of our salvation. But an easier and more appropriate method will be to descend from the general to the particular. First, we must remember, that there is an inseparable relation between faith and the word, and that these can no more be disconnected from each other than rays of light from the sun. Hence in Isaiah the Lord explains, "Hear, and your soul shall live" (Is. lv. 3). And John points to this same fountain of faith, in the following words, "These are written that ye might believe" (John xx. 31). The Psalmist also, exhorting the people to faith, says, "To-day, if ye will hear his voice" (Ps. xcv. 7), to *hear* being uniformly taken for to *believe*. In fine, in Isaiah the Lord distinguishes the members of the Church from strangers by this mark, "All thy children shall be taught of the Lord" (Is liv. 13); for if the benefit was indiscriminate, why should he address his words only to a few? Corresponding with this, the Evangelists uniformly employ the terms *believers* and *disciples* as synonymous. This is done especially by Luke in several passages of the Acts. He even applies the term *disciple* to a woman (Acts ix. 36). Wherefore, if faith declines in the least degree from the mark at which it ought to

aim, it does not retain its nature, but becomes uncertain credulity and vague wandering of mind. The same word is the basis on which it rests and is sustained. Declining from it, it falls. Take away the word, therefore, and no faith will remain. We are not here discussing whether, in order to propagate the word of God by which faith is engendered, the ministry of man is necessary (this will be considered elsewhere); but we say that the word itself, whatever be the way in which it is conveyed to us, is a kind of mirror in which faith beholds God. In this, therefore, whether God uses the agency of man, or works immediately by his own power, it is always by his word that he manifests himself to those whom he designs to draw to himself. Hence Paul designates faith as the obedience which is given to the Gospel (Rom. i. 5); and writing to the Philippians, he commends them for the obedience of faith (Phil. ii. 17). For faith includes not merely the knowledge that God is, but also, nay chiefly, a perception of his will towards us. It concerns us to know not only what he is in himself, but also in what character he is pleased to manifest himself to us. We now see, therefore, that faith is the knowledge of the divine will in regard to us, as ascertained from his word. And the foundation of it is a previous persuasion of the truth of God. So long as your mind entertains any misgivings as to the certainty of the word, its authority will be weak and dubious, or rather it will have no authority at all. Nor is it sufficient to believe that God is true, and cannot lie or deceive, unless you feel firmly persuaded that every word which proceeds from him is sacred, inviolable truth.

7. But since the heart of man is not brought to faith by every word of God, we must still consider what it is that faith properly has respect to in the word. The declaration of God to Adam was, "Thou shalt surely die" (Gen. ii. 17); and to Cain, "The voice of thy brother's blood crieth unto me from the ground" (Gen. iv. 10); but these, so far from being fitted to establish faith, tend only to shake it. At the same time, we deny not that it is the office of faith to assent to the truth of God whenever, whatever, and in whatever way he speaks: we are only inquiring what faith can find in the word of God to lean and rest upon. When conscience sees only wrath and indignation, how can it but tremble and be afraid? and how can it avoid shunning the God whom it thus dreads? But faith ought to seek God, not shun him. It is evident, therefore, that we have not yet obtained a full definition of faith, it being impossible to give the name to every kind of knowledge of the divine will. Shall we, then, for *will*, which is often the messenger of bad news and the herald of terror, substitute the benevolence or mercy of God? In this way, doubtless, we make a nearer approach to the nature of faith. For we are allured to seek God when told that our safety is treasured up in him; and we are confirmed in this when he declares that he studies and takes an interest in our welfare. Hence there is

need of the gracious promise, in which he testifies that he is a propitious Father; since there is no other way in which we can approach to him, the promise being the only thing on which the heart of man can recline.   For this reason, the two things, mercy and truth, are uniformly conjoined in the Psalms as having a mutual connection with each other.   For it were of no avail to us to know that God is true, did He not in mercy allure us to himself; nor could we of ourselves embrace his mercy did not He expressly offer it.   "I have declared thy faithfulness and thy salvation: I have not concealed thy loving-kindness and thy truth.   Withhold not thy tender mercies from me, O Lord: let thy loving-kindness and thy truth continually preserve me" (Ps. xl. 10, 11).   "Thy mercy, O Lord, is in the heavens; and thy faithfulness reacheth unto the clouds" (Ps. xxxvi. 5).   "All the paths of the Lord are mercy and truth unto such as keep his covenant and his testimonies" (Ps. xxv. 10).   "His merciful kindness is great towards us: and the truth of the Lord endureth for ever" (Ps. cxvii. 2).   "I will praise thy name for thy loving-kindness and thy truth" (Ps. cxxxviii. 2).   I need not quote what is said in the Prophets, to the effect that God is merciful and faithful in his promises.   It were presumptuous in us to hold that God is propitious to us, had we not his own testimony, and did he not prevent us by his invitation, which leaves no doubt or uncertainty as to his will.   It has already been seen that Christ is the only pledge of love, for without him all things, both above and below, speak of hatred and wrath.   We have also seen, that since the knowledge of the divine goodness cannot be of much importance unless it leads us to confide in it, we must exclude a knowledge mingled with doubt, —a knowledge which, so far from being firm, is continually wavering.   But the human mind, when blinded and darkened, is very far from being able to rise to a proper knowledge of the divine will; nor can the heart, fluctuating with perpetual doubt, rest secure in such knowledge.   Hence, in order that the word of God may gain full credit, the mind must be enlightened, and the heart confirmed, from some other quarter.   We shall now have a full definition of faith [1] if we say that it is a firm and sure knowledge of the divine favour toward us, founded on the truth of a free promise in Christ, and revealed to our minds, and sealed on our hearts, by the Holy Spirit.

8. But before I proceed farther, it will be necessary to make some preliminary observations for the purpose of removing difficulties which might otherwise obstruct the reader.   And first, I must refute the nugatory distinction of the Schoolmen as to formed and unformed faith. [2]   For they imagine that persons who have no fear of God, and no sense of piety, may believe all that is necessary to be known for salvation; as if the Holy Spirit were not the witness of our adoption

1 This definition is explained, sections 14, 15, 28, 29, 32, 33, 31, of this chapter.
2 See Lombard, Lib. iii. Dist. 23.   See the refutation in the middle of sections 41 42, 43, where it is shown that faith produces, and is inseparable from, hope and love.

by enlightening our hearts unto faith. Still, however, though the whole Scripture is against them, they dogmatically give the name of faith to a persuasion devoid of the fear of God. It is unnecessary to go farther in refuting their definition, than simply to state the nature of faith as declared in the word of God. From this it will clearly appear how unskilfully and absurdly they babble, rather than discourse, on this subject. I have already done this in part, and will afterwards add the remainder in its proper place. At present, I say that nothing can be imagined more absurd than their fiction. They insist that faith is an assent with which any despiser of God may receive what is delivered by Scripture. But we must first see whether any one can by his own strength acquire faith, or whether the Holy Spirit, by means of it, becomes the witness of adoption. Hence it is childish trifling in them to inquire whether the faith formed by the supervening quality of love be the same, or a different and new faith. By talking in this style, they show plainly that they have never thought of the special gift of the Spirit; since one of the first elements of faith is reconciliation implied in man's drawing near to God. Did they duly ponder the saying of Paul, "With the heart man believeth unto righteousness" (Rom. x. 10), they would cease to dream of that frigid quality. There is one consideration which ought at once to put an end to the debate—viz. that assent itself (as I have already observed, and will afterwards more fully illustrate) is more a matter of the heart than the head, of the affection than the intellect. For this reason, it is termed "the obedience of faith" (Rom. i. 5), which the Lord prefers to all other service, and justly, since nothing is more precious to him than his truth, which, as John Baptist declares, is in a manner signed and sealed by believers (John iii. 33). As there can be no doubt on the matter, we in one word conclude, that they talk absurdly when they maintain that faith is formed by the addition of pious affection as an accessory to assent, since assent itself, such at least as the Scripture describes, consists in pious affection. But we are furnished with a still clearer argument. Since faith embraces Christ as he is offered by the Father, and he is offered not only for justification, for forgiveness of sins and peace, but also for sanctification, as the fountain of living waters, it is certain that no man will ever know him aright without at the same time receiving the sanctification of the Spirit; or, to express the matter more plainly, faith consists in the knowledge of Christ; Christ cannot be known without the sanctification of his Spirit: therefore faith cannot possibly be disjoined from pious affection.

9. In their attempt to mar faith by divesting it of love, they are wont to insist on the words of Paul, "Though I have all faith, so that I could remove mountains, and have not charity, I am nothing" (1 Cor. xiii. 2). But they do not consider what the faith is of which the Apostle there speaks. Having, in the previous chapter, discoursed of the various gifts of the Spirit (1 Cor. xii. 10), including

diversity of tongues, miracles, and prophecy, and exhorted the Corinthians to follow the better gifts, in other words, those from which the whole body of the Church would derive greater benefit, he adds, "Yet show I unto you a more excellent way" (1 Cor. xii. 30). All other gifts, how excellent soever they may be in themselves, are of no value unless they are subservient to charity. They were given for the edification of the Church, and fail of their purpose if not so applied. To prove this he adopts a division, repeating the same gifts which he had mentioned before, but under different names. Miracles and faith are used to denote the same thing—viz. the power of working miracles. Seeing, then, that this miraculous power or faith is the particular gift of God, which a wicked man may possess and abuse, as the gift of tongues, prophecy, or other gifts, it is not strange that he separates it from charity. Their whole error lies in this, that while the term faith has a variety of meanings, overlooking this variety, they argue as if its meaning were invariably one and the same. The passage of James, by which they endeavour to defend their error, will be elsewhere discussed (*infra*, chap. xvii. sec. 11). Although, in discoursing of faith, we admit that it has a variety of forms; yet, when our object is to show what knowledge of God the wicked possess, we hold and maintain, in accordance with Scripture, that the pious only have faith. Multitudes undoubtedly believe that God is, and admit the truth of the Gospel History, and the other parts of Scripture, in the same way in which they believe the records of past events, or events which they have actually witnessed. There are some who go even farther: they regard the Word of God as an infallible oracle; they do not altogether disregard its precepts, but are moved to some degree by its threatenings and promises. To such the testimony of faith is attributed, but by *catachresis;* because they do not with open impiety impugn, reject, or contemn, the Word of God, but rather exhibit some semblance of obedience.

10. But as this shadow or image of faith is of no moment, so it is unworthy of the name. How far it differs from true faith will shortly be explained at length. Here, however, we may just indicate it in passing. Simon Magus is said to have believed, though he soon after gave proof of his unbelief (Acts viii. 13–18). In regard to the faith attributed to him, we do not understand with some, that he merely pretended a belief which had no existence in his heart: we rather think that, overcome by the majesty of the Gospel, he yielded some kind of assent, and so far acknowledged Christ to be the author of life and salvation, as willingly to assume his name. In like manner, in the Gospel of Luke, those in whom the seed of the word is choked before it brings forth fruit, or in whom, from having no depth of earth, it soon withereth away, are said to believe for a time. Such, we doubt not, eagerly receive the word with a kind of relish, and have some feeling of its divine power, so as not only to impose upon men by a false semblance of faith, but even to impose upon them-

selves. They imagine that the reverence which they give to the
word is genuine piety, because they have no idea of any impiety but
that which consists in open and avowed contempt. But whatever
that assent may be, it by no means penetrates to the heart, so as to
have a fixed seat there. Although it sometimes seems to have
planted its roots, these have no life in them. The human heart has
so many recesses for vanity, so many lurking places for falsehood, is
so shrouded by fraud and hypocrisy, that it often deceives itself. Let
those who glory in such semblances of faith know that, in this respect, they are not a whit superior to devils. The one class, indeed,
is inferior to them, inasmuch as they are able without emotion to
hear and understand things, the knowledge of which makes devils
tremble (James ii. 19). The other class equals them in this, that
whatever be the impression made upon them, its only result is terror and consternation.

11. I am aware it seems unaccountable to some how faith is attributed to the reprobate, seeing that it is declared by Paul to be one
of the fruits of election ;[1] and yet the difficulty is easily solved : for
though none are enlightened into faith, and truly feel the efficacy of
the Gospel, with the exception of those who are fore-ordained to salvation, yet experience shows that the reprobate are sometimes affected
in a way so similar to the elect, that even in their own judgment
there is no difference between them. Hence it is not strange, that
by the Apostle a taste of heavenly gifts, and by Christ himself a
temporary faith, is ascribed to them. Not that they truly perceive
the power of spiritual grace and the sure light of faith ; but the Lord,
the better to convict them, and leave them without excuse, instils
into their minds such a sense of his goodness as can be felt without
the Spirit of adoption. Should it be objected, that believers have no
stronger testimony to assure them of their adoption, I answer, that
though there is a great resemblance and affinity between the elect of
God and those who are impressed for a time with a fading faith, yet
the elect alone have that full assurance which is extolled by Paul, and
by which they are enabled to cry, Abba, Father. Therefore, as God
regenerates the elect only for ever by incorruptible seed, as the seed
of life once sown in their hearts never perishes, so he effectually seals
in them the grace of his adoption, that it may be sure and stedfast.
But in this there is nothing to prevent an inferior operation of the
Spirit from taking its course in the reprobate. Meanwhile, believers
are taught to examine themselves carefully and humbly, lest carnal
security creep in and take the place of assurance of faith. We may
add, that the reprobate never have any other than a confused sense
of grace, laying hold of the shadow rather than the substance, because
the Spirit properly seals the forgiveness of sins in the elect only, applying it by special faith to their use. Still it is correctly said, that

---

[1] 1 Thess. i. 3, 4; 2 Thess. ii. 13; Tit. i.

the reprobate believe God to be propitious to them, inasmuch as they accept the gift of reconciliation, though confusedly and without due discernment; not that they are partakers of the same faith or regeneration with the children of God; but because, under a covering of hypocrisy, they seem to have a principle of faith in common with them. Nor do I even deny that God illumines their minds to this extent, that they recognise his grace; but that conviction he distinguishes from the peculiar testimony which he gives to his elect in this respect, that the reprobate never obtain to the full result or to fruition. When he shows himself propitious to them, it is not as if he had truly rescued them from death, and taken them under his protection. He only gives them a manifestation of his present mercy.[1] In the elect alone he implants the living root of faith, so that they persevere even to the end. Thus we dispose of the objection, that if God truly displays his grace, it must endure for ever. There is nothing inconsistent in this with the fact of his enlightening some with a present sense of grace, which afterwards proves evanescent.

12. Although faith is a knowledge of the divine favour towards us, and a full persuasion of its truth, it is not strange that the sense of the divine love, which though akin to faith differs much from it, vanishes in those who are temporarily impressed. The will of God is, I confess, immutable, and his truth is always consistent with itself; but I deny that the reprobate ever advance so far as to penetrate to that secret revelation which Scripture reserves for the elect only. I therefore deny that they either understand his will considered as immutable, or steadily embrace his truth, inasmuch as they rest satisfied with an evanescent impression; just as a tree not planted deep enough may take root, but will in process of time wither away, though it may for several years not only put forth leaves and flowers, but produce fruit. In short, as by the revolt of the first man, the image of God could be effaced from his mind and soul, so there is nothing strange in His shedding some rays of grace on the reprobate, and afterwards allowing these to be extinguished. There is nothing to prevent His giving some a' slight knowledge of his Gospel, and imbuing others thoroughly. Meanwhile, we must remember that however feeble and slender the faith of the elect may be, yet as the Spirit of God is to them a sure earnest and seal of their adoption, the impression once engraven can never be effaced from their hearts, whereas the light which glimmers in the reprobate is afterwards quenched.[2] Nor can it be said that the Spirit therefore deceives, because he does not quicken the seed which lies in their hearts, so as to make it ever remain incorruptible as in the elect. I go farther: seeing it is evident, from the doctrine of Scripture and from daily experience, that

---

1 The French adds, "Comme par une bouffée,"—as by fits and starts.
2 See section 13, where it is said that this impression, sometimes existing in the reprobate, is called faith, but improperly.

the reprobate are occasionally impressed with a sense of divine grace, some desire of mutual love must necessarily be excited in their hearts. Thus for a time a pious affection prevailed in Saul, disposing him to love God. Knowing that he was treated with paternal kindness, he was in some degree attracted by it. But as the reprobate have no rooted conviction of the paternal love of God, so they do not in return yield the love of sons, but are led by a kind of mercenary affection. The Spirit of love was given to Christ alone, for the express purpose of conferring this Spirit upon his members; and there can be no doubt that the following words of Paul apply to the elect only: "The love of God is shed abroad in our hearts, by the Holy Ghost which is given unto us" (Rom. v. 5); namely, the love which begets that confidence in prayer to which I have above adverted. On the other hand, we see that God is mysteriously offended with his children, though he ceases not to love them. He certainly hates them not, but he alarms them with a sense of his anger, that he may humble the pride of the flesh, arouse them from lethargy, and urge them to repentance. Hence they, at the same instant, feel that he is angry with them for their sins, and also propitious to their persons. It is not from fictitious dread that they deprecate his anger, and yet they betake themselves to him with tranquil confidence. It hence appears that the faith of some, though not true faith, is not mere pretence. They are borne along by some sudden impulse of zeal, and erroneously impose upon themselves, sloth undoubtedly preventing them from examining their hearts with due care. Such probably was the case of those whom John describes as believing on Christ; but of whom he says, "Jesus did not commit himself unto them, because he knew all men, and needed not that any should testify of man: for he knew what was in man" (John ii. 24, 25). Were it not true that many fall away from the common faith (I call it common, because there is a great resemblance between temporary and living, ever-during faith), Christ would not have said to his disciples, "If ye continue in my word, then are ye my disciples indeed; and ye shall know the truth, and the truth shall make you free" (John viii. 31, 32). He is addressing those who had embraced his doctrine, and urging them to progress in the faith, lest by their sluggishness they extinguish the light which they have received. Accordingly, Paul claims faith as the peculiar privilege of the elect, intimating that many, from not being properly rooted, fall away (Tit. i. 1). In the same way, in Matthew, our Saviour says, "Every plant which my heavenly Father hath not planted shall be rooted up" (Matth. xvi. 13). Some who are not ashamed to insult God and man are more grossly false. Against this class of men, who profane the faith by impious and lying pretence, James inveighs (James ii. 14). Nor would Paul require the faith of believers to be unfeigned (1 Tim. i. 5), were there not many who presumptuously arrogate to themselves what they have not, deceiving others and sometimes even themselves, with empty show. Hence he compares a good conscience to the ark in which faith is preserved, because many, by falling away, have in regard to it made shipwreck.

13. It is necessary to attend to the ambiguous meaning of the term: for *faith* is often equivalent in meaning to *sound doctrine*, as in the passage which we lately quoted, and in the same Epistle where Paul enjoins the deacons to hold "the mystery of the faith in a pure conscience;" in like manner, when he denounces the defection of certain from the faith. The meaning again is the same, when he says that Timothy had been brought up in the faith; and in like manner, when he says that profane babblings and oppositions of science, falsely so called, lead many away from the faith. Such persons he elsewhere calls reprobate as to the faith. On the other hand, when he enjoins Titus, " Rebuke them sharply, that they may be sound in the faith;"[1] by soundness he means purity of doctrine, which is easily corrupted, and degenerates through the fickleness of men. And indeed, since in Christ, as possessed by faith, are "hid all the treasures of wisdom and knowledge" (Col. i. 2, 3), the term *faith* is justly extended to the whole sum of heavenly doctrine, from which it cannot be separated. On the other hand, it is sometimes confined to a particular object, as when Matthew says of those who let down the paralytic through the roof. that Jesus saw their faith (Matth. ix. 2); and Jesus himself exclaims in regard to the centurion, "I have not found so great faith, no, not in Israel" (Matth. viii. 10). Now, it is probable that the centurion was thinking only of the cure of his son, by whom his whole soul was engrossed;[2] but because he is satisfied with the simple answer and assurance of Christ, and does not request his bodily presence, this circumstance calls forth the eulogium on his faith. And we have lately shown how Paul uses the term faith for the gift of miracles—a gift possessed by persons who were neither regenerated by the Spirit of God, nor sincerely reverenced him. In another passage, he uses faith for the doctrine by which we are instructed in the faith. For when he says, that "that which is in part shall be done away" (1 Cor. xiii. 10), there can be no doubt that reference is made to the ministry of the Church, which is necessary in our present imperfect state; in these forms of expression the analogy is obvious. But when the name of faith is improperly transferred to a false profession or lying assumption, the *catachresis* ought not to seem harsher than when the fear of God is used for vitious and perverse worship; as when it is repeatedly said in sacred history, that the foreign nations which had been transported to Samaria and the neighbouring districts, feared false gods and the God of Israel: in other words, confounded heaven with earth. But we have now been inquiring what the faith is which distinguishes the children of God from unbelievers, the faith

[1] 1 Tim. iii. 9; iv. 1, 6; 2 Tim. ii. 15; iii. 18; Tit. i. 13; ii. 2.
[2] The French adds, "Comme il montre par ses propos quel souci il en avoit;"—as ʒe shows by his urgency what anxiety he felt.

by which we invoke God the Father, by which we pass from death unto life, and by which Christ, our eternal salvation and life, dwells in us. Its power and nature have, I trust, been briefly and clearly explained.

14. Let us now again go over the parts of the definition separately: I should think that, after a careful examination of them, no doubt will remain. By knowledge we do not mean comprehension, such as that which we have of things falling under human sense. For that knowledge is so much superior, that the human mind must far surpass and go beyond itself in order to reach it. Nor even when it has reached it does it comprehend what it feels, but persuaded of what it comprehends not, it understands more from mere certainty of persuasion than it could discern of any human matter by its own capacity. Hence it is elegantly described by Paul as ability " to comprehend with all saints what is the breadth, and length, and depth, and height; and to know the love of Christ, which passeth knowledge" (Eph. iii. 18, 19). His object was to intimate, that what our mind embraces by faith is every way infinite, that this kind of knowledge far surpasses all understanding. But because the "mystery which hath been hid from ages and from generations" is now "made manifest to the saints" (Col. i. 26), *faith* is, for good reason, occasionally termed in Scripture *understanding* (Col. ii. 2); and *knowledge*, as by John (1 John iii. 2), when he declares that believers know themselves to be the sons of God. And certainly they do know, but rather as confirmed by a belief of the divine veracity than taught by any demonstration of reason. This is also indicated by Paul when he says, that "whilst we are at home in the body, we are absent from the Lord: (for we walk by faith, not by sight)" (2 Cor. v. 6, 7): thus showing that what we understand by faith is yet distant from us and escapes our view. Hence we conclude that the knowledge of faith consists more of certainty than discernment.

15. We add, that it is *sure and firm*, the better to express strength and constancy of persuasion. For as faith is not contented with a dubious and fickle opinion, so neither is it contented with an obscure and ill-defined conception. The certainty which it requires must be full and decisive, as is usual in regard to matters ascertained and proved. So deeply rooted in our hearts is unbelief, so prone are we to it, that while all confess with the lips that God is faithful, no man ever believes it without an arduous struggle. Especially when brought to the test,[1] we by our wavering betray the vice which lurked within. Nor is it without cause that the Holy Spirit bears such distinguished testimony to the authority of God, in order that it may cure the disease of which I have spoken, and induce us to give full credit to the divine promises: "The words of the Lord"

---

[1] Latin, "Præsentim ubi ad rem ventum est."—French, "Principalement quand les tentations nous pressent;"—especially when temptations press us.

(says David, Ps. xii. 6) " are pure words, as silver tried in a furnace of earth, purified seven times:" " The word of the Lord is tried: he is a buckler to all those that trust in him" (Ps. xviii. 30). And Solomon declares the same thing almost in the same words, " Every word of God is pure" (Prov. xxx. 5). But further quotation is superfluous, as the cxix. Psalm is almost wholly occupied with this subject. Certainly, whenever God thus recommends his word, he indirectly rebukes our unbelief, the purport of all that is said being to eradicate perverse doubt from our hearts. There are very many also who form such an idea of the divine mercy as yields them very little comfort. For they are harassed by miserable anxiety while they doubt whether God will be merciful to them. They think, indeed, that they are most fully persuaded of the divine mercy, but they confine it within too narrow limits. The idea they entertain is, that this mercy is great and abundant, is shed upon many, is offered and ready to be bestowed upon all; but that it is uncertain whether it will reach to them individually, or rather whether they can reach to it. Thus their knowledge stopping short leaves them only midway; not so much confirming and tranquillising the mind as harassing it with doubt and disquietude. Very different is that feeling of full assurance ($\pi\lambda\eta\rho o\phi o\rho\iota a$) which the Scriptures uniformly attribute to faith—an assurance which leaves no doubt that the goodness of God is clearly offered to us. This assurance we cannot have without truly perceiving its sweetness, and experiencing it in ourselves. Hence from faith the Apostle deduces confidence, and from confidence boldness. His words are, " In whom (Christ) we have boldness and access with confidence by the faith of him" (Eph. iii. 12): thus undoubtedly showing that our faith is not true unless it enables us to appear calmly in the presence of God. Such boldness springs only from confidence in the divine favour and salvation. So true is this, that the term *faith* is often used as equivalent to *confidence*.

16. The principal hinge on which faith turns is this: We must' not suppose that any promises of mercy which the Lord offers are only true out of us, and not at all in us: we should rather make them ours by inwardly embracing them. In this way only is engendered that confidence which he elsewhere terms peace (Rom. v. 1); though perhaps he rather means to make peace follow from it. This is the security which quiets and calms the conscience in the view of the judgment of God, and without which it is necessarily vexed and almost torn with tumultuous dread, unless when it happens to slumber for a moment, forgetful both of God and of itself. And verily it is but for a moment. It never long enjoys that miserable obliviousness, for the memory of the divine judgment, ever and anon recurring, stings it to the quick. In one word, he only is a true believer who, firmly persuaded that God is reconciled, and is a kind Father to him, hopes everything from his kindness, who, trusting to the promises of the divine favour, with undoubting confidence anti-

cipates salvation; as the Apostle shows in these words, "We are made partakers of Christ, if we hold the beginning of our confidence stedfast unto the end" (Heb. iii. 14). He thus holds, that none hope well in the Lord save those who confidently glory in being the heirs of the heavenly kingdom. No man, I say, is a believer but he who, trusting to the security of his salvation, confidently triumphs over the devil and death, as we are taught by the noble exclamation of Paul, "I am persuaded, that neither death, nor life, nor angels, nor principalities, nor powers, nor things present, nor things to come, nor height, nor depth, nor any other creature, shall be able to separate us from the love of God, which is in Christ Jesus our Lord" (Rom. viii. 38). In like manner, the same Apostle does not consider that the eyes of our understanding are enlightened unless we know what is the hope of the eternal inheritance to which we are called (Eph. i. 18). Thus he uniformly intimates throughout his writings, that the goodness of God is not properly comprehended when security does not follow as its fruit.

17. But it will be said that this differs widely from the experience of believers, who, in recognising the grace of God toward them, not only feel disquietude (this often happens), but sometimes tremble, overcome with terror,[1] so violent are the temptations which assail their minds. This scarcely seems consistent with certainty of faith. It is necessary to solve this difficulty, in order to maintain the doctrine above laid down. When we say that faith must be certain and secure, we certainly speak not of an assurance which is never affected by doubt, nor a security which anxiety never assails, we rather maintain that believers have a perpetual struggle with their own distrust, and are thus far from thinking that their consciences possess a placid quiet, uninterrupted by perturbation. On the other hand, whatever be the mode in which they are assailed, we deny that they fall off and abandon that sure confidence which they have formed in the mercy of God. Scripture does not set before us a brighter or more memorable example of faith than in David, especially if regard be had to the constant tenor of his life. And yet how far his mind was from being always at peace is declared by innumerable complaints, of which it will be sufficient to select a few. When he rebukes the turbulent movements of his soul, what else is it but a censure of his unbelief? "Why art thou cast down, my soul? and why art thou disquieted in me? hope thou in God" (Psalm xlii. 6). His alarm was undoubtedly a manifest sign of distrust, as if he thought that the Lord had forsaken him. In another passage we have a fuller confession: "I said in my haste, I am cut off from before thine eyes" (Psalm xxxi. 22). In another passage, in anxious and wretched perplexity, he debates with himself, nay, raises a question as to the

---

[1] As to the imperfection, strengthening, and increase of faith, see Book **IV.** chap. xiv. sec. 7, 8.

nature of God: "Hath God forgotten to be gracious? hath he in anger shut up his tender mercies?" (Psalm lxxvii. 9.) What follows is still harsher: "I said this is my infirmity; but I will remember the years of the right hand of the Most High."[1] As if desperate, he adjudges himself to destruction.[2] He not only confesses that he is agitated by doubt, but, as if he had fallen in the contest, leaves himself nothing in reserve,—God having deserted him, and made the hand which was wont to help him the instrument of his destruction. Wherefore, after having been tossed among tumultuous waves, it is not without reason he exhorts his soul to return to her quiet rest (Psalm cxvi. 7). And yet (what is strange) amid those commotions, faith sustains the believer's heart, and truly acts the part of the palm-tree, which supports any weights laid upon it, and rises above them; thus David, when he seemed to be overwhelmed, ceased not by urging himself forward to ascend to God. But he who, anxiously contending with his own infirmity, has recourse to faith, is already in a great measure victorious. This we may infer from the following passage, and others similar to it: "Wait on the Lord: be of good courage, and he shall strengthen thine heart: wait, I say, on the Lord" (Psalm xxvii. 14). He accuses himself of timidity, and repeating the same thing twice, confesses that he is ever and anon exposed to agitation. Still he is not only dissatisfied with himself for so feeling, but earnestly labours to correct it. Were we to take a nearer view of his case, and compare it with that of Ahaz, we should find a great difference between them. Isaiah is sent to relieve the anxiety of an impious and hypocritical king, and addresses him in these terms: "Take heed, and be quiet; fear not," &c. (Isaiah vii. 4). How did Ahaz act? As has already been said, his heart was shaken as a tree is shaken by the wind: though he heard the promise, he ceased not to tremble. This, therefore, is the proper hire and punishment of unbelief, so to tremble as in the day of trial to turn away from God, who gives access to himself only by faith. On the other hand, believers, though weighed down and almost overwhelmed with the burden of temptation, constantly rise up, though not without toil and difficulty; hence, feeling conscious of their own weakness, they pray with the Prophet, "Take not the word of truth utterly out of my mouth" (Psalm cxix. 43). By these words, we are taught that they at times become dumb, as if their faith were overthrown, and yet that they do not withdraw or turn their backs, but persevere in the contest, and by prayer stimulate their sluggishness, so as not to fall into stupor by giving way to it. (See Calv. in Psalm lxxxviii. 16.)

18. To make this intelligible, we must return to the distinction

---

[1] Calvin's Latin translation of the passage is, "Atque dixi, occidere meum est; mutationes dexteræ excelsi."—The French is, "J'ay dit, Il-me faut mourir. Voicy un changement de la main de Dieu;"—I said I must die. Behold a change in the hand of God.

[2] See Calv adv. Pighium, near the commencement.

between flesh and spirit, to which we have already adverted, and which here becomes most apparent. The believer finds within himself two principles : the one filling him with delight in recognising the divine goodness, the other filling him with bitterness under a sense of his fallen state ; the one leading him to recline on the promise of the Gospel, the other alarming him by the conviction of his iniquity; the one making him exult with the anticipation of life, the other making him tremble with the fear of death. This diversity is owing to imperfection of faith, since we are never so well in the course of the present life as to be entirely cured of the disease of distrust, and completely replenished and engrossed by faith. Hence those conflicts : the distrust cleaving to the remains of the flesh rising up to assail the faith existing in our hearts. But if in the believer's mind certainty is mingled with doubt, must we not always be carried back to the conclusion that faith consists not of a sure and clear, but only of an obscure and confused, understanding of the divine will in regard to us? By no means. Though we are distracted by various thoughts, it does not follow that we are immediately divested of faith. Though we are agitated and carried to and fro by distrust, we are not immediately plunged into the abyss ; though we are shaken, we are not therefore driven from our place. The invariable issue of the contest is, that faith in the long-run surmounts the difficulties by which it was beset and seemed to be endangered.

19. The whole, then, comes to this : As soon as the minutest particle of faith is instilled into our minds, we begin to behold the face of God placid, serene, and propitious; far off, indeed, but still so distinctly as to assure us that there is no delusion in it. In proportion to the progress we afterwards make (and the progress ought to be uninterrupted), we obtain a nearer and surer view, the very continuance making it more familiar to us. Thus we see that a mind illumined with the knowledge of God is at first involved in much ignorance,—ignorance, however, which is gradually removed. Still this partial ignorance or obscure discernment does not prevent that clear knowledge of the divine favour which holds the first and principal part in faith. For as one shut up in a prison, where from a narrow opening he receives the rays of the sun indirectly and in a manner divided, though deprived of a full view of the sun, has no doubt of the source from which the light comes, and is benefited by it ; so believers, while bound with the fetters of an earthly body, though surrounded on all sides with much obscurity, are so far illumined by any slender light which beams upon them and displays the divine mercy as to feel secure.

20 The Apostle elegantly adverts to both in different passages. When he says, " We know in part, and we prophecy in part ;" and " Now we see through a glass darkly " (1 Cor. xiii. 9, 12), he intimates how very minute a portion of divine wisdom is given to us in the present life. For although those expressions do not simply indicate that **faith is imperfect so long as we groan under a weight of flesh, but**

that the necessity of being constantly engaged in learning is owing to our imperfection, he at the same time reminds us, that a subject which is of boundless extent cannot be comprehended by our feeble and narrow capacities. This Paul affirms of the whole Church, each individual being retarded and impeded by his own ignorance from making so near an approach as were to be wished. But that the foretaste which we obtain from any minute portion of faith is certain, and by no means fallacious, he elsewhere shows, when he affirms that " We all, with open face beholding as in a glass the glory of the Lord, are changed into the same image, from glory to glory, even as by the Spirit of the Lord" (2 Cor. iii. 18). In such degrees of ignorance much doubt and trembling is necessarily implied, especially seeing that our heart is by its own natural bias prone to unbelief. To this we must add the temptations which, various in kind and infinite in number, are ever and anon violently assailing us. In particular, conscience itself, burdened with an incumbent load of sins, at one time complains and groans, at another accuses itself; at one time murmurs in secret, at another openly rebels. Therefore, whether adverse circumstances betoken the wrath of God, or conscience finds the subject and matter within itself, unbelief thence draws weapons and engines to put faith to flight, the aim of all its efforts being to make us think that God is adverse and hostile to us, and thus, instead of hoping for any assistance from him, to make us dread him as a deadly foe.

21. To withstand these assaults, faith arms and fortifies itself with the word of God. When the temptation suggested is, that God is an enemy because he afflicts, faith replies, that while he afflicts he is merciful, his chastening proceeding more from love than anger. To the thought that God is the avenger of wickedness, it opposes the pardon ready to be bestowed on all offences whenever the sinner betakes himself to the divine mercy. Thus the pious mind, how much soever it may be agitated and torn, at length rises superior to all difficulties, and allows not its confidence in the divine mercy to be destroyed. Nay, rather, the disputes which exercise and disturb it tend to establish this confidence. A proof of this is, that the saints, when the hand of God lies heaviest upon them, still lodge their complaints with him, and continue to invoke him, when to all appearance he is least disposed to hear. But of what use were it to lament before him if they had no hope of solace? They never would invoke him did they not believe that he is ready to assist them. Thus the disciples, while reprimanded by their Master for the weakness of their faith in crying out that they were perishing, still implored his aid (Matth. viii. 25). And he, in rebuking them for their want of faith, does not disown them or class them with unbelievers, but urges them to shake off the vice. Therefore, as we have already said, we again maintain, that faith remaining fixed in the believer's breast never can be eradicated from it. However it may seem shaken and bent in this direction or in that, its flame is never so completely quenched as not at least to lurk under the embers.

In this way, it appears that the word, which is an incorruptible seed, produces fruit similar to itself. Its germ never withers away utterly and perishes. The saints cannot have a stronger ground for despair than to feel that, according to present appearances, the hand of God is armed for their destruction; and yet Job thus declares the strength of his confidence: "Though he slay me, yet will I trust in him." The truth is, that unbelief reigns not in the hearts of believers, but only assails them from without; does not wound them mortally with its darts, but annoys them, or, at the utmost, gives them a wound which can be healed. Faith, as Paul declares (Eph. vi. 16), is our shield, which receiving these darts, either wards them off entirely, or at least breaks their force, and prevents them from reaching the vitals. Hence when faith is shaken, it is just as when, by the violent blow of a javelin, a soldier standing firm is forced to step back and yield a little; and again, when faith is wounded, it is as if the shield were pierced, but not perforated by the blow. The pious mind will always rise, and be able to say with David, "Yea, though I walk through the valley of the shadow of death, I will fear no evil: for thou art with me" (Psalm. xxiii. 4). Doubtless it is a terrific thing to walk in the darkness of death, and it is impossible for believers, however great their strength may be, not to shudder at it; but since the prevailing thought is that God is present and providing for their safety, the feeling of security overcomes that of fear. As Augustine says,—whatever be the engines which the devil erects against us, as he cannot gain the heart where faith dwells, he is cast out. Thus, if we may judge by the event, not only do believers come off safe from every contest, so as to be ready, after a short repose, to descend again into the arena, but the saying of John, in his Epistle, is fulfilled, "This is the victory that overcometh the world, even our faith" (1 John v. 4). It is not said that it will be victorious in a single fight, or a few, or some one assault, but that it will be victorious over the whole world, though it should be a thousand times assailed.

22. There is another species of fear and trembling, which, so far from impairing the security of faith, tends rather to establish it— namely, when believers, reflecting that the examples of the divine vengeance on the ungodly are a kind of beacons warning them not to provoke the wrath of God by similar wickedness, keep anxious watch, or, taking a view of their own inherent wretchedness, learn their entire dependence on God, without whom they feel themselves to be fleeting and evanescent as the wind. For when the Apostle sets before the Corinthians the scourges which the Lord in ancient times inflicted on the people of Israel, that they might be afraid of subjecting themselves to similar calamities, he does not in any degree destroy the ground of their confidence; he only shakes off their carnal torpor which suppresses faith, but does not strengthen it. Nor when he takes occasion from the case of the Israelites to exhort, "Let him that thinketh he standeth take heed lest he fall" (1 Cor.

x. 12), he does not bid us waver, as if we had no security for our stedfastness : he only removes arrogance and rash confidence in our strength, telling the Gentiles not to presume because the Jews had been cast off, and they had been admitted to their place (Rom. xi. 20). In that passage, indeed, he is not addressing believers only, but also comprehends hypocrites, who gloried merely in external appearance; nor is he addressing individuals, but contrasting the Jews and Gentiles, he first shows that the rejection of the former was a just punishment of their ingratitude and unbelief, and then exhorts the latter to beware lest pride and presumption deprive them of the grace of adoption which had lately been transferred to them. For as in that rejection of the Jews there still remained some who were not excluded from the covenant of adoption, so there might be some among the Gentiles who, possessing no true 'faith were only puffed up with vain carnal confidence, and so abused the goodness of God to their own destruction. But though you should hold that the words were addressed to elect believers, no inconsistency will follow. It is one thing, in order to prevent believers from indulging vain confidence, to repress the temerity which, from the remains of the flesh, sometimes gains upon them, and it is another thing to strike terror into their consciences, and prevent them from feeling secure in the mercy of God.

23. Then, when he bids us work out our salvation with fear and trembling, all he requires is, that we accustom ourselves to think very meanly of our own strength, and confide in the strength of the Lord. For nothing stimulates us so strongly to place all our confidence and assurance on the Lord as self-diffidence, and the anxiety produced by a consciousness of our calamitous condition. In this sense are we to understand the words of the Psalmist : " I will come into thy house in the multitude of thy mercy : and in thy fear will I worship toward thy holy temple" (Ps. v. 7). Here he appropriately unites confident faith leaning on the divine mercy with religious fear, which of necessity we must feel whenever coming into the presence of the divine majesty, we are made aware by its splendour of the extent of our own impurity. Truly also does Solomon declare : " Happy is the man that feareth alway ; but he that hardeneth his heart falleth into mischief" (Prov. xxviii. 14). The fear he speaks of is that which renders us more cautious, not that which produces despondency ; the fear which is felt when the mind confounded in itself resumes its equanimity in God, downcast in itself, takes courage in God, distrusting itself, breathes confidence in God. Hence there is nothing inconsistent in believers being afraid, and at the same time possessing secure consolation as they alternately behold their own vanity, and direct their thoughts to the truth of God. How, it will be asked, can fear and faith dwell in the same mind ? Just in the same way as sluggishness and anxiety can so dwell. The ungodly court a state of lethargy that the fear of God may not annoy them ; and yet the

judgment of God so urges that they cannot gain their desire.   In the same way God can train his people to humility, and curb them by the bridle of modesty, while yet fighting bravely.   And it is plain, from the context, that this was the Apostle's meaning, since he states, as the ground of fear and trembling, that it is God who worketh in us to will and to do of his good pleasure.   In the same sense must we understand the words of the Prophet, " The children of Israel" " shall fear the Lord and his goodness in the latter days" (Hos. iii. 5). For not only does piety beget reverence to God, but the sweet attractiveness of grace inspires a man, though desponding of himself, at once with fear and admiration, making him feel his dependence on God, and submit humbly to his power.

24. Here, however, we give no countenance to that most pestilential philosophy which some semi-papists are at present beginning to broach in corners.   Unable to defend the gross doubt inculcated by the Schoolmen, they have recourse to another fiction, that they may compound a mixture of faith and unbelief.   They admit, that whenever we look to Christ we are furnished with full ground for hope ; but as we are ever unworthy of all the blessings which are offered us in Christ, they will have us to fluctuate and hesitate in the view of our unworthiness.   In short, they give conscience a position between hope and fear, making it alternate, by successive turns, to the one and the other.   Hope and fear, again, they place in complete contrast,—the one falling as the other rises, and rising as the other falls. Thus Satan, finding the devices by which he was wont to destroy the certainty of faith too manifest to be now of any avail, is endeavouring, by indirect methods, to undermine it.[1]   But what kind of confidence is that which is ever and anon supplanted by despair ?   They tell you, if you look to Christ salvation is certain ; if you return to yourself damnation is certain.   Therefore, your mind must be alternately ruled by diffidence and hope ; as if we were to imagine Christ standing at a distance, and not rather dwelling in us.   We expect salvation from him—not because he stands aloof from us, but because ingrafting us into his body he not only makes us partakers of all his benefits, but also of himself.   Therefore, I thus retort the argument, If you look to yourself damnation is certain : but since Christ has been communicated to you with all his benefits, so that all which is his is made yours, you become a member of him, and hence one with him.   His righteousness covers your sins—his salvation extinguishes your condemnation ; he interposes with ·his worthiness, and so prevents your unworthiness from coming into the view of God.   Thus it truly is.   It will never do to separate Christ from us, nor us from

---

[1] The French is, " Voila comme Satan, quand il voit que par mensonge clair et ouvert il ne peust plus destruire la certitude de la foy, s'efforce en cachette et comme par dessous terre la ruiner."—Behold how Satan, when he sees that by clear and open falsehood he can no longer destroy the certainty of faith, is striving in secret, and as it were below ground, to ruin it.

him; but we must, with both hands, keep firm hold of that alliance by which he has riveted us to himself. This the Apostle teaches us: "The body is dead because of sin; but the spirit is life because of righteousness" (Rom. viii. 10). According to the frivolous trifling of these objectors he ought to have said, Christ indeed has life in himself, but you, as you are sinners, remain liable to death and condemnation. Very different is his language. He tells us that the condemnation which we of ourselves deserve is annihilated by the salvation of Christ; and to confirm this he employs the argument to which I have referred—viz. that Christ is not external to us, but dwells in us; and not only unites us to himself by an undivided bond of fellowship, but by a wondrous communion brings us daily into closer connection, until he becomes altogether one with us. And yet I deny not, as I lately said, that faith occasionally suffers certain interruptions when, by violent assault, its weakness is made to bend in this direction or in that; and its light is buried in the thick darkness of temptation. Still happen what may, faith ceases not to long after God.

25. The same doctrine is taught by Bernard when he treats professedly on this subject in his Fifth Homily on the Dedication of the Temple: "By the blessing of God, sometimes meditating on the soul, methinks I find in it as it were two contraries. When I look at it as it is in itself and of itself, the truest thing I can say of it is, that it has been reduced to nothing. What need is there to enumerate each of its miseries? how burdened with sin, obscured with darkness, ensnared by allurements, teeming with lusts, ruled by passion, filled with delusions, ever prone to evil, inclined to every vice; lastly, full of ignominy and confusion. If all its righteousnesses, when examined by the light of truth, are but as filthy rags (Is. lxiv. 6), what must we suppose its unrighteousness to be? 'If, therefore, the light that is in thee be darkness, how great is that darkness?' (Matth. vi. 23.) What then? man doubtless has been made subject to vanity—man has been reduced to nothing—man is nothing. And yet how is he whom God exalts utterly nothing? How is he nothing to whom a divine heart has been given? Let us breathe again, brethren. Although we are nothing in our hearts, perhaps something of us may lurk in the heart of God. O Father of mercies! O Father of the miserable! how plantest thou thy heart in us? Where thy heart is, there is thy treasure also. But how are we thy treasure if we are nothing? All nations before thee are as nothing. Observe, *before* thee; not *within* thee. Such are they in the judgment of thy truth, but not such in regard to thy affection. Thou callest the things which be not as though they were; and they are not, because thou callest them 'things that be not:' and yet they are because thou callest them. For though they are not as to themselves, yet they are with thee according to the declaration of Paul: 'Not of works, but of him that calleth'" (Rom. ix. 11). He then goes on to

say that the connection is wonderful in both points of view. Certainly things which are connected together do not mutually destroy each other. This he explains more clearly in his conclusion in the following terms: " If, in both views, we diligently consider what we are,—in the one view our nothingness, in the other our greatness,—I presume our glorying will seem restrained; but perhaps it is rather increased and confirmed, because we glory not in ourselves, but in the Lord. Our thought is, if he determined to save us we shall be delivered; and here we begin again to breathe. But, ascending to a loftier height, let us seek the city of God, let us seek the temple, let us seek our home, let us seek our spouse. I have not forgotten myself when, with fear and reverence, I say, We are,—are in the heart of God. We are, by his dignifying, not by our own dignity."

26. Moreover, the fear of the Lord, which is uniformly attributed to all the saints, and which, in one passage, is called " the beginning of wisdom," in another *wisdom* itself, although it is one, proceeds from a twofold cause. God is entitled to the reverence of a Father and a Lord. Hence he who desires duly to worship him, will study to act the part both of an obedient son and a faithful servant. The obedience paid to God as a Father he by his prophet terms *honour;* the service performed to him as a master he terms *fear.* "A son honoureth his father, and a servant his master. If then I be a father, where is mine honour? and if I be a master, where is my fear?"[1] But while he thus distinguishes between the two, it is obvious that he at the same time confounds them. The fear of the Lord, therefore, may be defined reverence mingled with honour and fear. It is not strange that the same mind can entertain both feelings; for he who considers with himself what kind of a father God is to us, will see sufficient reason, even were there no hell, why the thought of offending him should seem more dreadful than any death. But so prone is our carnal nature to indulgence in sin, that, in order to curb it in every way, we must also give place to the thought that all iniquity is abomination to the Master under whom we live; that those who, by wicked lives, provoke his anger, will not escape his vengeance.

27. There is nothing repugnant to this in the observation of John: " There is no fear in love; but perfect love casteth out fear: because fear hath torment" (1 John iv. 18). For he is speaking of the fear of unbelief, between which and the fear of believers there is a wide difference. The wicked do not fear God from any unwillingness to offend him, provided they could do so with impunity; but knowing that he is armed with power for vengeance, they tremble in dismay on hearing of his anger. And they thus dread his anger, because they think it is impending over them, and they every moment expect it to fall upon their heads. But believers, as has been said, dread the offence even more than the punishment. They are not alarmed

---

[1] Ps. cxi. 10; Prov. i. 7, ix. 10, xv. 24; Job xxviii. 28; Mal. i. 6.

by the fear of punishment, as if it were impending over them,[1] but are rendered the more cautious of doing anything to provoke it. Thus the Apostle addressing believers says, "Let no man deceive you with vain words; for because of these things, the wrath of God cometh upon the children of disobedience" (Eph. v. 6; Col. iii. 6). He does not threaten that wrath will descend upon them; but he admonishes them, while they think how the wrath of God is prepared for the wicked, on account of the crimes which he had enumerated, not to run the risk of provoking it. It seldom happens that mere threatenings have the effect of arousing the reprobate; nay, becoming more callous and hardened when God thunders verbally from heaven, they obstinately persist in their rebellion. It is only when actually smitten by his hand that they are forced, whether they will or not, to fear. This fear the sacred writers term *servile*, and oppose to the free and voluntary fear which becomes sons. Some, by a subtle distinction, have introduced an intermediate species, holding that that forced and servile fear sometimes subdues the mind, and leads spontaneously to proper fear.

28. The divine favour to which faith is said to have respect, we understand to include in it the possession of salvation and eternal life. For if, when God is propitious, no good thing can be wanting to us, we have ample security for our salvation when assured of his love. "Turn us again, O God, and cause thy face to shine," says the Prophet, "and we shall be saved" (Ps. lxxx. 3). Hence the Scriptures make the sum of our salvation to consist in the removal of all enmity, and our admission into favour; thus intimating, that when God is reconciled all danger is past, and everything good will befall us. Wherefore, faith apprehending the love of God has the promise both of the present and the future life, and ample security for all blessings (Eph. ii. 14). The nature of this must be ascertained from the word. Faith does not promise us length of days, riches, and honours (the Lord not having been pleased that any of these should be appointed us); but is contented with the assurance, that however poor we may be in regard to present comforts, God will never fail us. The chief security lies in the expectation of future life, which is placed beyond doubt by the word of God. Whatever be the miseries and calamities which await the children of God in this world, they cannot make his favour cease to be complete happiness. Hence, when we were desirous to express the sum of blessedness, we designated it by the favour of God, from which, as their source, all kinds of blessings flow. And we may observe throughout the Scriptures, that they refer us to the love of God, not only when they treat of our eternal salvation, but of any blessing whatever. For which reason David sings, that the loving-kindness of God experienced by the pious heart is sweeter and more to be desired than life itself (Ps. lxiii. 3). In short, if we have

1 Latin, "acsi cervicibus suis impenderet."—French, "comme si l'enfer leur etoit desia present pour les englouter;"—as if hell were already present to engulf them.

every earthly comfort to a wish, but are uncertain whether we have the love or the hatred of God, our felicity will be cursed, and therefore miserable. But if God lift on us the light of his fatherly countenance, our very miseries will be blessed, inasmuch as they will become helps to our salvation. Thus Paul, after bringing together all kinds of adversity, boasts that they cannot separate us from the love of God: and in his prayers he uniformly begins with the grace of God as the source of all prosperity. In like manner, to all the terrors which assail us David opposes merely the favour of God,— " Yea, though I walk through the valley of the shadow of death, I will fear no evil : for thou art with me" (Ps. xxiii. 4). And we feel that our minds always waver until, contented with the grace of God, we in it seek peace, and feel thoroughly persuaded of what is said in the psalm, " Blessed is the nation whose God is the Lord, and the people whom he hath chosen for his own inheritance" (Ps. xxxiii. 12).

29. Free promise we make the foundation of faith, because in it faith properly consists. For though it holds that God is always true, whether in ordering or forbidding, promising or threatening ; though it obediently receive his commands, observe his prohibitions, and give heed to his threatenings ; yet it properly begins with promise, continues with it, and ends with it. It seeks life in God, life which is not found in commands or the denunciations of punishment, but in the promise of mercy. And this promise must be gratuitous ; for a conditional promise, which throws us back upon our works, promises life only in so far as we find it existing in ourselves. Therefore, if we would not have faith to waver and tremble, we must support it with the promise of salvation, which is offered by the Lord spontaneously and freely, from a regard to our misery, rather than our worth. Hence the Apostle bears this testimony to the Gospel, that it is the word of faith (Rom. x. 8). This he concedes not either to the precepts or the promises of the Law, since there is nothing which can establish our faith, but that free embassy by which God reconciles the world to himself. Hence he often uses faith and the Gospel as correlative terms, as when he says, that the ministry of the Gospel was committed to him for " obedience to the faith ;" that " it is the power of God unto salvation to every one that believeth ;" that "therein is the righteousness of God revealed from faith to faith " (Rom. i. 5, 16, 17). No wonder : for seeing that the Gospel is " the ministry of reconciliation" (2 Cor. v. 18), there is no other sufficient evidence of the divine favour, such as faith requires to know. Therefore, when we say, that faith must rest on a free promise, we deny not that believers accept and embrace the word of God in all its parts, but we point to the promise of mercy as its special object. Believers, indeed, ought to recognise God as the judge and avenger of wickedness ; and yet mercy is the object to which they properly look, since he is exhibited to their contemplation as " good and ready to forgive," " plenteous in mercy," " slow to anger," " good to all," and

shedding "his tender mercies over all his works" (Ps. lxxxvi. 5; ciii. 8; cxlv. 8, 9).

30. I stay not to consider the rabid objections of Pighius, and others like-minded, who inveigh against this restriction, as rending faith, and laying hold of one of its fragments. I admit, as I have already said, that the general object of faith (as they express it) is the truth of God, whether he threatens or gives hope of his favour. Accordingly, the Apostle attributes it to faith in Noah, that he feared the destruction of the world, when as yet it was not seen (Heb. xi. 17). If fear of impending punishment was a work of faith, threatenings ought not to be excluded in defining it. This is indeed true; but we are unjustly and calumniously charged with denying that faith has respect to the whole word of God. We only mean to maintain these two points,—that faith is never decided until it attain to a free promise; and that the only way in which faith reconciles us to God is by uniting us with Christ. Both are deserving of notice. We are inquiring after a faith which separates the children of God from the reprobate, believers from unbelievers. Shall every man, then, who believes that God is just in what he commands, and true in what he threatens, be on that account classed with believers? Very far from it. Faith, then, has no firm footing until it stand in the mercy of God. Then what end have we in view in discoursing of faith? Is it not that we may understand the way of salvation? But how can faith be saving, unless in so far as it engrafts us into the body of Christ? There is no absurdity, therefore, when, in defining it, we thus press its special object, and, by way of distinction, add to the generic character the particular mark which distinguishes the believer from the unbeliever. In short, the malicious have nothing to carp at in this doctrine, unless they are to bring the same censure against the Apostle Paul, who specially designates the Gospel as "the word of faith" (Rom. x. 8).

31. Hence again we infer, as has already been explained, that faith has no less need of the word than the fruit of a tree has of a living root; because, as David testifies, none can hope in God but those who know his name (Ps. ix. 10). This knowledge, however, is not left to every man's imagination, but depends on the testimony which God himself gives to his goodness. This the same Psalmist confirms in another passage, "Thy salvation according to thy word" (Ps. cxix. 41). Again, "Save me," "I hoped in thy word" (Ps. cxix. 146, 147). Here we must attend to the relation of faith to the word, and to salvation as its consequence. Still, however, we exclude not the power of God. If faith cannot support itself in the view of this power, it never will give Him the honour which is due. Paul seems to relate a trivial or very ordinary circumstance with regard to Abraham, when he says, that he believed that God, who had given him the promise of a blessed seed, was able also to perform it (Rom. iv. 21). And in like manner, in another passage, he says of himself, "I

know whom I have believed, and am persuaded that he is able to keep that which I have committed unto him against that day" (2 Tim. i. 12). But let any one consider with himself, how he is ever and anon assailed with doubts in regard to the power of God, and he will readily perceive, that those who duly magnify it have made no small progress in faith. We all acknowledge that God can do whatsoever he pleases; but while every temptation, even the most trivial, fills us with fear and dread, it is plain that we derogate from the power of God, by attaching less importance to his promises than to Satan's threatenings against them.[1]

This is the reason why Isaiah, when he would impress on the hearts of the people the certainty of faith, discourses so magnificently of the boundless power of God. He often seems, after beginning to speak of the hope of pardon and reconciliation, to digress, and unnecessarily take a long circuitous course, describing how wonderfully God rules the fabric of heaven and earth, with the whole course of nature; and yet he introduces nothing which is not appropriate to the occasion; because, unless the power of God, to which all things are possible, is presented to our eye, our ears malignantly refuse admission to the word, or set no just value upon it. We may add, that an effectual power is here meant; for piety, as it has elsewhere been seen, always makes a practical application of the power of God; in particular, keeps those works in view in which he has declared himself to be a Father. Hence the frequent mention in Scripture of redemption; from which the Israelites might learn, that he who had once been the author of salvation would be its perpetual guardian. By his own example, also, David reminds us, that the benefits which God has bestowed privately on any individual, tend to confirm his faith for the time to come; nay, that when God seems to have forsaken us, we ought to extend our view farther, and take courage from his former favours, as is said in another Psalm, " I remember the days of old: I meditate on all thy works" (Ps. cxliii. 5). Again, "I will remember the works of the Lord; surely I will remember thy wonders of old" (Ps. lxxvii. 11). But because all our conceptions of the power and works of God are evanescent without the word, we are not rash in maintaining, that there is no faith until God present us with clear evidence of his grace.

Here, however, a question might be raised as to the view to be taken of Sarah and Rebekah, both of whom, impelled as it would seem by zeal for the faith, went beyond the limits of the word. Sarah, in her eager desire for the promised seed, gave her maid to her husband. That she sinned in many respects is not to be denied; but the only fault to which I now refer is her being carried away by zeal, and not confining herself within the limits prescribed by the

---

[1] The French adds, "Combien que nous ayons les promesses de Dieu pour nous munir à l'encontre;"—although we have the promise of God to strengthen us for the encounter.

word. It is certain, however, that her desire proceeded from faith. Rebekah, again, divinely informed of the election of her son Jacob, procures the blessing for him by a wicked stratagem ; deceives her husband, who was a witness and minister of divine grace ; forces her son to lie ; by various frauds and impostures corrupts divine truth ; in fine, by exposing his promise to scorn, does what in her lies to make it of no effect. And yet this conduct, however vicious and reprehensible, was not devoid of faith. She must have overcome many obstacles before she obtained so strong a desire of that which, without any hope of earthly advantage, was full of difficulty and danger. In the same way, we cannot say that the holy patriarch Isaac was altogether void of faith, in that, after he had been similarly informed of the honour transferred to the younger son, he still continues his predilection in favour of his first-born, Esau. These examples certainly show that error is often mingled with faith ; and yet that when faith is real, it always obtains the pre-eminence. For as the particular error of Rebekah did not render the blessing of no effect, neither did it nullify the faith which generally ruled in her mind, and was the principle and cause of that action. In this, nevertheless, Rebekah showed how prone the human mind is to turn aside whenever it gives itself the least indulgence. But though defect and infirmity obscure faith, they do not extinguish it. Still they admonish us how carefully we ought to cling to the word of God, and at the same time confirm what we have taught—viz. that faith gives way when not supported by the word, just as the minds of Sarah, Isaac, and Rebekah, would have lost themselves in devious paths, had not the secret restraint of Providence kept them obedient to the word.

32. On the other hand, we have good ground for comprehending all the promises in Christ, since the Apostle comprehends the whole Gospel under the knowledge of Christ, and declares that all the promises of God are in him, yea, and amen.[1] The reason for this is obvious. Every promise which God makes is evidence of his good will. This is invariably true, and is not inconsistent with the fact, that the large benefits which the divine liberality is constantly bestowing on the wicked are preparing them for heavier judgment. As they neither think that these proceed from the hand of the Lord, nor acknowledge them as his, or if they do so acknowledge them, never regard them as proofs of his favour, they are in no respect more instructed thereby in his mercy than brute beasts, which, according to their condition, enjoy the same liberality, and yet never look beyond it. Still it is true, that by rejecting the promises generally offered to them, they subject themselves to severer punishment. For though it is only when the promises are received in faith that their efficacy is manifested, still their reality and power are never extinguished by our infidelity or ingratitude. Therefore, when the Lord by his pro-

---

[1] Rom. i. 3; 1 Cor. ii. 2; 2 Cor. i. 20.

mises invites us not only to enjoy the fruits of his kindness, but also to meditate upon them, he at the same time declares his love. Thus we are brought back to our statement, that every promise is a manifestation of the divine favour toward us. Now, without controversy, God loves no man out of Christ. He is the beloved Son, in whom the love of the Father dwells, and from whom it afterwards extends to us. Thus Paul says, "In whom he hath made us accepted in the Beloved" (Eph. i. 6). It is by his intervention, therefore, that love is diffused so as to reach us. Accordingly, in another passage, the Apostle calls Christ "our peace" (Eph. ii. 14), and also represents him as the bond by which the Father is united to us in paternal affection (Rom. viii. 3). It follows, that whenever any promise is made to us, we must turn our eyes toward Christ. Hence, with good reason, Paul declares that in him all the promises of God are confirmed and completed (Rom. xv. 8). Some examples are brought forward as repugnant to this view. When Naaman the Syrian made inquiry at the prophet as to the true mode of worshipping God, we cannot (it is said) suppose that he was informed of the Mediator, and yet he is commended for his piety (2 Kings v. 17—19). Nor could Cornelius, a Roman heathen, be acquainted with what was not known to all the Jews, and at best known obscurely. And yet his alms and prayers were acceptable to God (Acts x. 31), while the prophet by his answer approved of the sacrifices of Naaman. In both, this must have been the result of faith. In like manner, the eunuch to whom Philip was sent, had he not been endued with some degree of faith, never would have incurred the fatigue and expense of a long and difficult journey to obtain an opportunity of worship (Acts viii. 27, 31); and yet we see how, when interrogated by Philip, he betrays his ignorance of the Mediator. I admit that, in some respect, their faith was not explicit either as to the person of Christ, or the power and office assigned him by the Father. Still it is certain that they were imbued with principles which might give some, though a slender, foretaste of Christ. This should not be thought strange; for the eunuch would not have hastened from a distant country to Jerusalem to an unknown God; nor could Cornelius, after having once embraced the Jewish religion, have lived so long in Judea without becoming acquainted with the rudiments of sound doctrine. In regard to Naaman, it is absurd to suppose that Elisha, while he gave him many minute precepts, said nothing of the principal matter. Therefore, although their knowledge of Christ may have been obscure, we cannot suppose that they had no such knowledge at all. They used the sacrifices of the Law, and must have distinguished them from the spurious sacrifices of the Gentiles, by the end to which they referred—viz. Christ.

33. A simple external manifestation of the word ought to be amply sufficient to produce faith, did not our blindness and perverseness prevent. But such is the proneness of our mind to vanity, that it

can never adhere to the truth of God, and such its dulness, that it is always blind even in his light. Hence without the illumination of the Spirit the word has no effect; and hence also it is obvious that faith is something higher than human understanding. Nor were it sufficient for the mind to be illumined by the Spirit of God unless the heart also were strengthened and supported by his power. Here the Schoolmen go completely astray, dwelling entirely in their consideration of faith, on the bare simple assent of the understanding, and altogether overlooking confidence and security of heart. Faith is the special gift of God in both ways,—in purifying the mind so as to give it a relish for divine truth, and afterwards in establishing it therein. For the Spirit does not merely originate faith, but gradually increases it, until by its means he conducts us into the heavenly kingdom. "That good thing which was committed unto thee," says Paul, "keep by the Holy Ghost which dwelleth in us" (2 Tim. i. 14). In what sense Paul says (Gal. iii. 2), that the Spirit is given by the hearing of faith, may be easily explained. If there were only a single gift of the Spirit, he who is the author and cause of faith could not without absurdity be said to be its effect; but after celebrating the gifts with which God adorns his church, and by successive additions of faith leads it to perfection, there is nothing strange in his ascribing to faith the very gifts which faith prepares us for receiving. It seems to some paradoxical, when it is said that none can believe Christ save those to whom it is given; but this is partly because they do not observe how recondite and sublime heavenly wisdom is, or how dull the mind of man in discerning divine mysteries, and partly because they pay no regard to that firm and stable constancy of heart which is the chief part of faith.

34.[1] But as Paul argues, "What man knoweth the things of a man, save the spirit of man which is in him? even so the things of God knoweth no man but the Spirit of God" (1 Cor. ii. 11). If in regard to divine truth we hesitate even as to those things which we see with the bodily eye, how can we be firm and stedfast in regard to those divine promises which neither the eye sees nor the mind comprehends? Here human discernment is so defective and lost, that the first step of advancement in the school of Christ is to renounce it (Matth. xi. 25; Luke x. 21). Like a veil interposed, it prevents us from beholding divine mysteries, which are revealed only to babes. "Flesh and blood" doth not reveal them (Matth. xvi. 17). "The natural man receiveth not the things of the Spirit of God: for they are foolishness unto him; neither can he know them, for they are spiritually discerned" (1 Cor. ii. 14). The supplies of the Holy Spirit are therefore necessary, or rather his agency is here the only strength. "For who hath known the mind of the Lord? or who hath been his counsellor?" (Rom. xi. 34;) but "The Spirit searcheth

---

[1] The French thus begins the section: "Lequel erreur est facile a convaincre;"— This error is easily refuted

all things, yea, the deep things of God" (1 Cor. ii. 10). Thus it is that we attain to the mind of Christ: " No man can come to me, except the Father which hath sent me draw him: and I will raise him up at the last day." " Every man therefore that hath heard, and learned of the Father, cometh unto me. Not that any man hath seen the Father, save he which is of God, he hath seen the Father" (John vi. 44, 45, 46). Therefore, as we cannot possibly come to Christ unless drawn by the Spirit, so when we are drawn we are both in mind and spirit exalted far above our own understanding. For the soul, when illumined by him, receives as it were a new eye, enabling it to contemplate heavenly mysteries, by the splendour of which it was previously dazzled. And thus, indeed, it is only when the human intellect is irradiated by the light of the Holy Spirit that it begins to have a taste of those things which pertain to the kingdom of God; previously it was too stupid and senseless to have any relish for them. Hence our Saviour, when clearly declaring the mysteries of the kingdom to the two disciples, makes no impression till he opens their minds to understand the Scriptures (Luke xxiv. 27, 45). Hence also, though he had taught the Apostles with his own divine lips, it was still necessary to send the Spirit of truth to instil into their minds the same doctrine which they had heard with their ears. The word is, in regard to those to whom it is preached, like the sun which shines upon all, but is of no use to the blind. In this matter we are all naturally blind; and hence the word cannot penetrate our mind unless the Spirit, that internal teacher, by his enlightening power make an entrance for it.

35. Having elsewhere shown more fully, when treating of the corruption of our nature, how little able men are to believe (Book II. c. ii. iii.), I will not fatigue the reader by again repeating it. Let it suffice to observe, that the spirit of faith is used by Paul as synonymous with the very faith which we receive from the Spirit, but which we have not naturally (2 Cor. iv. 13). Accordingly, he prays for the Thessalonians, "that our God would count you worthy of this calling, and fulfil all the good pleasure of his goodness, and the work of faith with power" (2 Thess. i. 2). Here, by designating faith the *work* of God, and distinguishing it by way of epithet, appropriately calling it his *good pleasure*, he declares that it is not of man's own nature; and not contented with this, he adds, that it is an illustration of divine power. In addressing the Corinthians, when he tells them that faith stands not " in the wisdom of man, but in the power of God" (1 Cor. ii. 4), he is no doubt speaking of external miracles; but as the reprobate are blinded when they behold them, he also includes that internal seal of which he elsewhere makes mention. And the better to display his liberality in this most excellent gift, God does not bestow it upon all promiscuously, but, by special privilege, imparts it to whom he will. To this effect we have already quoted passages of Scripture, as to which Augustine, their faithful expositor,

exclaims (De Verbo Apost. Serm. ii.), "Our Saviour, to teach that faith in him is a gift, not a merit, says, 'No man can come to me, except the Father, which hath sent me, draw him' (John vi. 44). It is strange when two persons hear, the one despises, the other ascends. Let him who despises impute it to himself; let him who ascends not arrogate it to himself." In another passage, he asks, "Wherefore is it given to the one, and not to the other? I am not ashamed to say, This is one of the deep things of the cross. From some unknown depth of the judgments of God, which we cannot scrutinise, all our ability proceeds. I see that I am able; but how I am able I see not:—this far only I see, that it is of God. But why the one, and not the other? This is too great for me: it is an abyss, a depth of the cross. I can cry out with wonder; not discuss and demonstrate." The whole comes to this, that Christ, when he produces faith in us by the agency of his Spirit, at the same time ingrafts us into his body, that we may become partakers of all blessings.

36. The next thing necessary is, that what the mind has imbibed be transferred into the heart. The word is not received in faith when it merely flutters in the brain, but when it has taken deep root in the heart, and become an invincible bulwark to withstand and repel all the assaults of temptation. But if the illumination of the Spirit is the true source of understanding in the intellect, much more manifest is his agency in the confirmation of the heart; inasmuch as there is more distrust in the heart than blindness in the mind; and it is more difficult to inspire the soul with security than to imbue it with knowledge. Hence the Spirit performs the part of a seal, sealing upon our hearts the very promises, the certainty of which was previously impressed upon our minds. It also serves as an earnest in establishing and confirming these promises. Thus the Apostle says, "In whom also, after that ye believed, ye were sealed with that holy Spirit of promise, which is the earnest of our inheritance" (Eph. i. 13, 14). You see how he teaches that the hearts of believers are stamped with the Spirit as with a seal, and calls it the Spirit of promise, because it ratifies the gospel to us. In like manner he says to the Corinthians, "God hath also sealed us, and given the earnest of the Spirit in our hearts" (2 Cor. i. 22). And again, when speaking of a full and confident hope, he founds it on the "earnest of the Spirit" (2 Cor. v. 5).

37. I am not forgetting what I formerly said, and experience brings daily to remembrance—viz. that faith is subject to various doubts,[1] so that the minds of believers are seldom at rest, or at least are not always tranquil. Still, whatever be the engines by which they are shaken, they either escape from the whirlpool of temptation, or remain stedfast in their place. Faith finds security and protection in the words of the psalm, "God is our refuge and strength, a very present help in trouble; therefore will not we fear, though the earth be

---

[1] French, "Doutes, solicitudes, et detresses;"—doubts, anxieties, and distresses.

removed, and the mountains be carried into the midst of the sea" (Ps. xlvi. 1, 2). This delightful tranquillity is elsewhere described: "I laid me down and slept; I awaked, for the Lord sustained me" (Ps. iii. 5). Not that David was uniformly in this joyful frame; but in so far as the measure of his faith made him sensible of the divine favour, he glories in intrepidly despising everything that could disturb his peace of mind. Hence the Scripture, when it exhorts us to faith, bids us be at peace. In Isaiah it is said, "In quietness and in confidence shall be your strength" (Is. xxx. 15); and in the psalm, "Rest in the Lord, and wait patiently for him." Corresponding to this is the passage in the Hebrews, "Ye have need of patience," &c. (Heb. x. 36).

38. Hence we may judge how pernicious is the scholastic dogma,[1] that we can have no stronger evidence of the divine favour toward us than moral conjecture, according as each individual deems himself not unworthy of it. Doubtless, if we are to determine by our works in what way the Lord stands affected towards us, I admit that we cannot even get the length of a feeble conjecture: but since faith should accord with the free and simple promise, there is no room left for ambiguity. With what kind of confidence, pray, shall we be armed if we reason in this way—God is propitious to us, provided we deserve it by the purity of our lives? But since we have reserved this subject for discussion in its proper place, we shall not prosecute it farther at present, especially seeing it is already plain that nothing is more adverse to faith than conjecture, or any other feeling akin to doubt. Nothing can be worse than their perversion of the passage of Ecclesiastes, which is ever in their mouths: "No man knoweth either love or hatred by all that is before them" (Eccl. ix. 1).[2] For without insisting that the passage is erroneously rendered in the common version—even a child cannot fail to perceive what Solomon's meaning is—viz. that any one who would ascertain, from the present state of things, who are in the favour or under the displeasure of God, labours in vain, and torments himself to no useful purpose, since "all things come alike to all;" "to him that sacrificeth, and to him that sacrificeth not:" and hence God does not always declare his love to those on whom he bestows uninterrupted prosperity, nor his hatred against those whom he afflicts. And it tends to prove the vanity of the human intellect, that it is so completely in the dark as to matters which it is of the highest importance to know. Thus Solomon had said a little before, "That which befalleth the sons of men befalleth beasts; even one thing befalleth them: as the one dieth, so dieth the other" (Eccl. iii. 19). Were any one thence to infer that we hold the immortality of the soul by conjecture merely, would he not justly be deemed insane? Are those then sane who

---

[1] French, "La doctrine des theologiens sophistes;"—the doctrine of sophistical theologians.

[2] See Bernard, Serm. ii. in Die Ascensionis, and Serm. ii. in Octava Paschæ.

cannot obtain any certainty of the divine favour, because the carnal eye is now unable to discern it from the present appearance of the world?

39. But, they say, it is rash and presumptuous to pretend to an undoubted knowledge of the divine will. I would grant this, did we hold that we were able to subject the incomprehensible counsel of God to our feeble intellect. But when we simply say with Paul, " We have received not the spirit of the world, but the Spirit which is of God ; that we might know the things that are freely given to us of God" (1 Cor. ii. 12), what can they oppose to this, without offering insult to the Spirit of God ? But if it is sacrilege to charge the revelation which he has given us with falsehood, or uncertainty, or ambiguity, how can we be wrong in maintaining its certainty? But they still exclaim, that there is great temerity in our presuming to glory in possessing the Spirit of God.[1] Who could believe that these men, who desire to be thought the masters of the world, could be so stupid as to err thus grossly in the very first principles of religion? To me, indeed, it would be incredible, did not their own writings make it manifest. Paul declares that those only are the sons of God who are led by his Spirit (Rom. viii. 14); these men would have those who are the sons of God to be led by their own, and void of the divine Spirit. He tells us that we call God our Father in terms dictated by the Spirit, who alone bears witness with our spirit that we are the sons of God (Rom. viii. 16); they, though they forbid us not to invoke God, withdraw the Spirit, by whose guidance he is duly invoked. He declares that those only are the servants of Christ who are led by the Spirit of Christ (Rom. viii. 9); they imagine a Christianity which has no need of the Spirit of Christ. He holds out the hope of a blessed resurrection to those only who feel His Spirit dwelling in them (Rom. viii. 11); they imagine hope when there is no such feeling. But perhaps they will say, that they deny not the necessity of being endued with the Spirit, but only hold it to be the part of modesty and humility not to recognise it. What, then, does Paul mean, when he says to the Corinthians, " Examine yourselves whether ye be in the faith: prove your ownselves. Know ye not your ownselves, that Jesus Christ is in you, except ye be reprobates?" (2 Cor. xiii. 5.) John, moreover, says, " Hereby we know that he abideth in us by the Spirit which he hath given us" (1 John iii. 24). And what else is it than to bring the promises of Christ into doubt, when we would be deemed servants of Christ without having his Spirit, whom he declared that he would pour out on all his people ? (Isa. xliv. 3.) What! do we not insult the Holy Spirit, when we separate faith, which is his peculiar work, from himself? These being the first rudiments of religion, it is the most wretched blindness to charge Christians with arrogance, for presum-

1 The French adds, " En quoy ils demonstrent grandement leur betise ;"—In this they give a great demonstration of their stupidity.

ing to glory in the presence of the Holy Spirit ; a glorying without which Christianity itself does not exist.   The example of these men illustrates the truth of our Saviour's declaration, that his Spirit " the world cannot receive, because it seeth him not, neither knoweth him ; but ye know him, for he dwelleth with you, and shall be in you" (John xiv. 17).

40. That they may not attempt to undermine the certainty of faith in one direction only, they attack it in another—viz. that though it be lawful for the believer, from his actual state of righteousness, to form a judgment as to the favour of God, the knowledge of final perseverance still remains in suspense.   An admirable security, indeed, is left us, if, for the present moment only, we can judge from moral conjecture that we are in grace, but know not how we are to be to-morrow !   Very different is the language of the Apostle, " I am persuaded that neither death, nor life, nor angels, nor principalities, nor powers, nor things present nor things to come, nor height, nor depth, nor any other creature, shall be able to separate us from the love of God, which is in Christ Jesus our Lord" (Rom. viii. 38). They endeavour to evade the force of this by frivolously pretending that the Apostle had this assurance by special revelation.   They are too well caught thus to escape ; for in that passage he is treating not of his individual experience, but of the blessings which all believers in common derive from faith.   But then Paul in another passage alarms us by the mention of our weakness and inconstancy, " Let him that thinketh he standeth take heed lest he fall" (1 Cor. x. 12). True ; but this he says not to inspire us with terror, but that we may learn to humble ourselves under the mighty hand of God, as Peter explains (1 Pet. v. 6).   Then how preposterous is it to limit the certainty of faith to a point of time ; seeing it is the property of faith to pass beyond the whole course of this life, and stretch forward to a future immortality ?   Therefore, since believers owe it to the favour of God, that, enlightened by his Spirit, they, through faith, enjoy the prospect of heavenly life ; there is so far from an approach to arrogance in such glorying, that any one ashamed to confess it, instead of testifying modesty or submission, rather betrays extreme ingratitude, by maliciously suppressing the divine goodness.

41. Since the nature of faith could not be better or more clearly evinced than by the substance of the promise on which it leans as its proper foundation, and without which it immediately falls or rather vanishes away, we have derived our definition from it—a definition, however, not at all at variance with that definition, or rather description, which the Apostle accommodates to his discourse, when he says that faith is "the substance of things hoped for, the evidence of things not seen" (Heb. xi. 1).   For by the term substance ($\upsilon\pi\acute{o}\sigma\tau\alpha\sigma\iota\varsigma$), he means a kind of prop on which the pious mind rests and leans.   As if he had said, that faith is a kind of certain and secure possession of those things which are promised to us by God ; unless we prefer

taking ὑπόστασις for *confidence.* I have no objection to this, though I am more inclined to adopt the other interpretation, which is more generally received. Again, to intimate that until the last day, when the books will be opened (Dan. vii. 10; Rev. xx. 12), the things pertaining to our salvation are too lofty to be perceived by our sense, seen by our eyes, or handled by our hands, and that in the meantime there is no possible way in which these can be possessed by us, unless we can transcend the reach of our own intellect, and raise our eye above all worldly objects; in short, surpass ourselves, he adds that this certainty of possession relates to things which are only hoped for, and therefore not seen. For as Paul says (Rom. viii. 24), "hope that is seen is not hope," that we "hope for that we see not." When he calls it the evidence or proof, or, as Augustine repeatedly renders it (see *Hom. in Joann.* 79 and 95), the convictions of things not present, the Greek term being ἔλεγχος, it is the same as if he had called it the appearance of things not apparent, the sight of things not seen, the clearness of things obscure, the presence of things absent, the manifestation of things hid. For the mysteries of God (and to this class belong the things which pertain to our salvation) cannot be discerned in themselves, or, as it is expressed, in their own nature; but we behold them only in his word, of the truth of which we ought to be as firmly persuaded as if we held that everything which it says were done and completed. But how can the mind rise to such a perception and foretaste of the divine goodness, without being at the same time wholly inflamed with love to God? The abundance of joy which God has treasured up for those who fear him cannot be truly known without making a most powerful impression. He who is thus once affected is raised and carried entirely towards him. Hence it is not strange that no sinister perverse heart ever experiences this feeling, by which, transported to heaven itself, we are admitted to the most hidden treasures of God, and the holiest recesses of his kingdom, which must not be profaned by the entrance of a heart that is impure. For what the Schoolmen say as to the priority of love to faith and hope is a mere dream (see Sent. Lib. iii. Dist. 25, &c.), since it is faith alone that first engenders love. How much better is Bernard, "The testimony of conscience, which Paul calls 'the rejoicing' of believers, I believe to consist in three things. It is necessary, first of all, to believe that you cannot have remission of sins except by the indulgence of God; secondly, that you cannot have any good work at all unless he also give it; lastly, that you cannot by any works merit eternal life unless it also be freely given," (Bernard, Serm. i. in Annuntiatione). Shortly after he adds, "These things are not sufficient, but are a kind of commencement of faith; for while believing that your sins can only be forgiven by God, you must also hold that they are not forgiven until persuaded by the testimony of the Holy Spirit that salvation is treasured up for us; that as God pardons sins, and gives merits, and after merits rewards, you cannot halt at that beginning." But these and other topics will be considered in their own place; let it suffice at present to understand what faith is.

42. Wherever this living faith exists, it must have the hope of eternal life as its inseparable companion, or rather must of itself beget and manifest it; where it is wanting, however clearly and elegantly we may discourse of faith, it is certain we have it not. For if faith is (as has been said) a firm persuasion of the truth of God—a persuasion that it can never be false, never deceive, never be in vain, those who have received this assurance must at the same time expect that God will perform his promises, which in their conviction are absolutely true; so that in one word hope is nothing more than the expectation of those things which faith previously believes to have been truly promised by God. Thus, faith believes that God is true; hope expects that in due season he will manifest his truth. Faith believes that he is our Father; hope expects that he will always act the part of a Father towards us. Faith believes that eternal life has been given to us; hope expects that it will one day be revealed. Faith is the foundation on which hope rests; hope nourishes and sustains faith. For as no man can expect anything from God without previously believing his promises, so, on the other hand, the weakness of our faith, which might grow weary and fall away, must be supported and cherished by patient hope and expectation. For this reason Paul justly says, "We are saved by hope" (Rom. viii. 24). For while hope silently waits for the Lord, it restrains faith from hastening on with too much precipitation, confirms it when it might waver in regard to the promises of God or begin to doubt of their truth, refreshes it when it might be fatigued, extends its view to the final goal, so as not to allow it to give up in the middle of the course, or at the very outset. In short, by constantly renovating and reviving, it is ever and anon furnishing more vigour for perseverance. On the whole, how necessary the reinforcements of hope are to establish faith will better appear if we reflect on the numerous forms of temptation by which those who have embraced the word of God are assailed and shaken. First, the Lord often keeps us in suspense, by delaying the fulfilment of his promises much longer than we could wish. Here the office of hope is to perform what the prophet enjoins, "Though it tarry, wait for it" (Hab. ii. 3). Sometimes he not only permits faith to grow languid, but even openly manifests his displeasure. Here there is still greater necessity for the aid of hope, that we may be able to say with another prophet, "I will wait upon thet Lord that hideth his face from the house of Jacob, and I will look for him" (Isaiah viii. 17). Scoffers also rise up, as Peter tells us, and ask, "Where is the promise of his coming? for since the fathers fell asleep, all things continue as they were from the beginning of the creation" (2 Pet. iii. 4). Nay, the world and the flesh insinuate the same thing. Here faith must be supported by the patience of hope,

and fixed on the contemplation of eternity, consider that "one day is with the Lord as a thousand years, and a thousand years as one day" (2 Pet. iii. 8; Ps. xc. 4).

43. On account of this connection and affinity Scripture sometimes confounds the two terms, faith and hope. For when Peter says that we are "kept by the power of God through faith until salvation, ready to be revealed in the last time" (1 Pet. i. 5), he attributes to faith what more properly belongs to hope. And not without cause, since we have already shown that hope is nothing else than the food and strength of faith. Sometimes the two are joined together, as in the same Epistle, "That your faith and hope might be in God" (1 Pet. i. 21). Paul, again, in the Epistle to the Philippians, from hope deduces expectation (Phil. i. 20), because in hoping patiently we suspend our wishes until God manifest his own time. The whole of this subject may be better understood from the tenth chapter of the Epistle to the Hebrews, to which I have already adverted. Paul, in another passage, though not in strict propriety of speech, expresses the same thing in these words, " For we through the Spirit wait for the hope of righteousness by faith" (Gal. v. 5) ; that is, after embracing the testimony of the Gospel as to free love, we wait till God openly manifest what is now only an object of hope. It is now obvious how absurdly Peter Lombard lays down a double foundation of hope—viz. the grace of God and the merit of works (Sent. Lib. iii. Dist. 26). Hope cannot have any other object than faith has. But we have already shown clearly that the only object of faith is the mercy of God, to which, to use the common expression, it must look with both eyes. But it is worth while to listen to the strange reason which he adduces. If you presume, says he, to hope for anything without merit, it should be called not hope, but presumption. Who, dear reader, does not execrate the gross stupidity[1] which calls it rashness and presumption to confide in the truth of God ? The Lord desires us to expect everything from his goodness, and yet these men tell us it is presumption to rest in it. O teacher, worthy of the pupils whom you found in these insane raving schools ! Seeing that, by the oracles of God, sinners are enjoined to entertain the hope of salvation, let us willingly presume so far on his truth as to cast away all confidence in our works, and trusting in his mercy, venture to hope. He who hath said, " According to your faith be it unto you" (Matth. ix. 29), will never deceive.

---

1 Latin, " Quis non merito, amice lector, tales bestias execretur ?" French, " Je vous prie, mes amis, qui se tiendra de maudire telles bestes ?"—I pray you, my friends, who can refrain from execrating such beasts ?

CHAPTER III.

REGENERATION BY FAITH.   OF REPENTANCE.

This chapter is divided into five parts. I. The title of the chapter seems to promise a treatise on Faith, but the only subject here considered is Repentance, the inseparable attendant of faith. And, first, various opinions on the subject of repentance are stated, sec. 1—4. II. An exposition of the orthodox doctrine of Repentance, sec. 5—9. III. Reasons why repentance must be prolonged to the last moment of life, sec. 10—14. IV. Of the fruits of repentance, or its object and tendency, sec. 15—20. V. The source whence repentance proceeds, sec. 21—24. Of the sin against the Holy Spirit, and the impenitence of the reprobate, sec. 25.

Sections.

1. Connection of this chapter with the previous one and the subsequent chapters. Repentance follows faith, and is produced by it. Reason. Error of those who take a contrary view.
2. Their First Objection. Answer. In what sense the origin of Repentance ascribed to Faith. Cause of the erroneous idea that faith is produced by repentance. Refutation of it. The hypocrisy of Monks and Anabaptists in assigning limits to repentance exposed.
3. A second opinion concerning repentance considered.
4. A third opinion, assigning two forms to repentance, a legal and an Evangelical. Examples of each.
5. The orthodox doctrine of Repentance. 1. Faith and Repentance to be distinguished, not confounded or separated. 2. A consideration of the name. 3. A definition of the thing, or what repentance is. Doctrine of the Prophets and Apostles.
6. Explanation of the definition. This consists of three parts. 1. Repentance is a turning of our life unto God. This described and enlarged upon.
7. 2. Repentance produced by fear of God. Hence the mention of divine judgment by the Prophets and Apostles. Example. Exposition of the second branch of the definition from a passage in Paul. Why the fear of God is the first part of Repentance.
8. 3. Repentance consists in the mortification of the flesh and the quickening of the Spirit. These required by the Prophets. They are explained separately.
9. How this mortification and quickening are produced. Repentance just a renewal of the divine image in us. Not completed in a moment, but extends to the last moment of life.
10. Reasons why repentance must so extend. Augustine's opinion as to concupiscence in the regenerate examined. A passage of Paul which seems to confirm that opinion.
11. Answer. Confirmation of the answer by the Apostle himself. Another confirmation from a precept of the law. Conclusion.
12. Exception, that those desires only are condemned which are repugnant to the order of God. Desires not condemned in so far as natural, but in so far as inordinate. This held by Augustine.
13. Passages from Augustine to show that this was his opinion. Objection from a passage in James.
14. Another objection of the Anabaptists and Libertines to the continuance of repentance throughout the present life. An answer disclosing its impiety. Another answer, founded on the absurdities to which it leads. A third answer, contrasting sincere Christian repentance with the erroneous view of the objectors. Confirmation from the example and declaration of an Apostle.

1. ALTHOUGH we have already in some measure shown how faith possesses Christ, and gives us the enjoyment of his benefits, the subject would still be obscure were we not to add an exposition of the effects resulting from it. The sum of the Gospel is, not without good reason, made to consist in repentance and forgiveness of sins; and, therefore, where these two heads are omitted, any discussion concerning faith will be meagre and defective, and indeed almost useless. Now, since Christ confers upon us, and we obtain by faith, both free reconciliation and newness of life, reason and order require that I should here begin to treat of both. The shortest transition, however, will be from faith to repentance; for repentance being properly understood, it will better appear how a man is justified freely by faith alone, and yet that holiness of life, *real* holiness, as it is called, is inseparable from the free imputation of righteousness.[1] That repentance not only always follows faith, but is produced by it, ought to be without controversy (see Calvin in Joann. i. 13). For since pardon and forgiveness are offered by the preaching of the Gospel, in order that the sinner, delivered from the tyranny of Satan, the yoke of sin, and the miserable bondage of iniquity, may pass into

---

[1] The French adds in explanation, " C'est à dire, que cela s'accorde bien, que nous ne soyons pas sans bonnes œuvres, et toutesfois que nous soyons reputés justes sans bonnes œuvres;"—That is to say, that the two propositions are quite consistent—viz. that we are not without good works, and yet that we are accounted righteous without works.

the kingdom of God, it is certain that no man can embrace the grace of the Gospel without betaking himself from the errors of his former life into the right path and making it his whole study to practise repentance. Those who think that repentance precedes faith instead of flowing from, or being produced by it, as the fruit by the tree, have never understood its nature, and are moved to adopt that view on very insufficient grounds.

2. Christ and John. it is said, in their discourses, first exhort the people to repentance, and then add, that the kingdom of heaven is at hand (Matth. iii. 2; iv. 17). Such, too, is the message which the Apostles received, and such the course which Paul followed, as is narrated by Luke (Acts xx. 21). But clinging superstitiously to the juxta-position of the syllables, they attend not to the coherence of meaning in the words. For when our Lord and John begin their preaching thus, "Repent, for the kingdom of heaven is at hand" (Matth. iii. 2), do they not deduce repentance as a consequence of the offer of grace and promise of salvation? The force of the words, therefore, is the same as if it were said, As the kingdom of heaven is at hand, for that reason repent. For Matthew, after relating that John so preached, says that therein was fulfilled the prophecy concerning the voice of one crying in the desert, "Prepare ye the way of the Lord, make straight in the desert a highway for our God" (Isaiah xl. 3). But in the Prophet that voice is ordered to commence with consolation and glad tidings. Still, when we attribute the origin of repentance to faith, we do not dream of some period of time in which faith is to give birth to it: we only wish to show that a man cannot seriously engage in repentance unless he know that he is of God. But no man is truly persuaded that he is of God until he have embraced his offered favour. These things will be more clearly explained as we proceed. Some are perhaps misled by this, that not a few are subdued by terror of conscience, or disposed to obedience before they have been imbued with a knowledge, nay, before they have had any taste of the divine favour (see Calvin in Acts xx. 21). This is that initial fear[1] which some writers class among the virtues, because they think it approximates to true and genuine obedience. But we are not here considering the various modes in which Christ draws us to himself, or prepares us for the study of piety: All I say is, that no righteousness can be found where the Spirit, whom Christ received in order to communicate it to his members, reigns not. Then, according to the passage in the Psalms, "There is forgiveness with thee, that thou mayest be feared" (Psalm cxxx. 4), no man will ever reverence God who does not trust that God is propitious to him, no man will ever willingly set himself to observe the Law who is not persuaded that his services are pleas-

---

[1] Latin, "Initialis timor," which is thus paraphrased by the French: "Et c'est une crainte comme on la voit aux petits enfans, qui ne sont point gouvernés par raison;"— And it is a fear such as we see in little children, who are not governed by reason.

ing to God. The indulgence of God in tolerating and pardoning our iniquities is a sign of paternal favour. This is also clear from the exhortation in Hosea, " Come, and let us return unto the Lord : for he hath torn, and he will heal us ; he hath smitten, and he will bind us up" (Hos. vi. 1); the hope of pardon is employed as a stimulus to prevent us from becoming reckless in sin. But there is no semblance of reason in the absurd procedure of those who, that they may begin with repentance, prescribe to their neophytes certain days during which they are to exercise themselves in repentance, and after these are elapsed, admit them to communion in Gospel grace. I allude to great numbers of Anabaptists, those of them especially who plume themselves on being spiritual, and their associates the Jesuits, and others of the same stamp. Such are the fruits which their giddy spirit produces, that repentance, which in every Christian man lasts as long as life, is with them completed in a few short days.

3. Certain learned men, who lived long before the present day, and were desirous to speak simply and sincerely, according to the rule of Scripture, held that repentance consists of two parts, mortification and quickening. By mortification they mean, grief of soul and terror, produced by a conviction of sin and a sense of the divine judgment. For when a man is brought to a true knowledge of sin, he begins truly to hate and abominate sin. He also is sincerely dissatisfied with himself, confesses that he is lost and undone, and wishes he were different from what he is. Moreover, when he is touched with some sense of the divine justice (for the one conviction immediately follows the other), he lies terror-struck and amazed, humbled and dejected, desponds and despairs. This, which they regarded as the first part of repentance, they usually termed *contrition*. By quickening they mean, the comfort which is produced by faith, as when a man prostrated by a consciousness of sin, and smitten with the fear of God, afterwards beholding his goodness, and the mercy, grace, and salvation obtained through Christ, looks up, begins to breathe, takes courage, and passes, as it were, from death unto life. I admit that these terms, when rightly interpreted, aptly enough express the power of repentance ; only I cannot assent to their using the term *quickening*, for the joy which the soul feels after being calmed from perturbation and fear. It more properly means, that desire of pious and holy living which springs from the new birth ; as if it were said, that the man dies to himself that he may begin to live unto God.

4. Others seeing that the term is used in Scripture in different senses, have set down two forms of repentance, and, in order to distinguish them, have called the one Legal repentance ; or that by which the sinner, stung with a sense of his sin, and overwhelmed with fear of the divine anger, remains in that state of perturbation, unable to escape from it. The other they term Evangelical repent-

ance ; or that by which the sinner, though grievously downcast in himself, yet looks up and sees in Christ the cure of his wound, the solace of his terror, the haven of rest from his misery. They give Cain, Saul, and Judas,[1] as examples of legal repentance. Scripture, in describing what is called their repentance, means that they perceived the heinousness of their sins, and dreaded the divine anger ; but, thinking only of God as a judge and avenger, were overwhelmed by the thought. Their repentance, therefore, was nothing better than a kind of threshold to hell, into which having entered even in the present life, they began to endure the punishment inflicted by the presence of an offended God. Examples of evangelical repentance we see in all those who, first stung with a sense of sin, but afterwards raised and revived by confidence in the divine mercy, turned unto the Lord.[2] Hezekiah was frightened on receiving the message of his death, but praying with tears, and beholding the divine goodness, regained his confidence. The Ninevites were terrified at the fearful announcement of their destruction ; but clothing themselves in sackcloth and ashes, they prayed, hoping that the Lord might relent and avert his anger from them. David confessed that he had sinned greatly in numbering the people, but added, " Now, I beseech thee, O Lord, take away the iniquity of thy servant." When rebuked by Nathan, he acknowledged the crime of adultery, and humbled himself before the Lord ; but he, at the same time, looked for pardon. Similar was the repentance of those who, stung to the heart by the preaching of Peter, yet trusted in the divine goodness, and added, " Men and brethren, what shall we do ? " Similar was the case of Peter himself, who indeed wept bitterly, but ceased not to hope.

5. Though all this is true, yet the term *repentance* (in so far as I can ascertain from Scripture) must be differently taken. For in comprehending faith under repentance, they are at variance with what Paul says in the Acts, as to his " testifying both to the Jews and also to the Greeks, repentance toward God, and faith toward our Lord Jesus Christ" (Acts xx. 21). Here he mentions faith and repentance as two different things. What then ? Can true repentance exist without faith ? By no means. But although they cannot be separated, they ought to be distinguished. As there is no faith without hope, and yet faith and hope are different, so repentance and faith, though constantly linked together, are only to be united, not confounded. I am not unaware that under the term *repentance* is comprehended the whole work of turning to God, of which not the least important part is faith ; but in what sense this is done will be perfectly obvious, when its nature and power shall have been explained. The term repentance is derived in the Hebrew from con-

---

[1] Gen. iv. 13; 1 Sam. xv. 30; Matt. xxvii. 3, 4.
[2] 2 Kings xx. 2; Isa. xxxviii. 2; Jonah iii. 5; 2 Sam. xxiv. 10; xii. 13, 16; Acts ii. 37; Matth. xxvi 75; Luke xxii. 62.

version, or turning again; and in the Greek from a change of mind and purpose; nor is the thing meant inappropriate to both derivations, for it is substantially this, that withdrawing from ourselves we turn to God, and laying aside the old, put on a new mind. Wherefore, it seems to me, that repentance may be not inappropriately defined thus: A real conversion of our life unto God, proceeding from sincere and serious fear of God; and consisting in the mortification of our flesh and the old man, and the quickening of the Spirit. In this sense are to be understood all those addresses in which the prophets first, and the apostles afterwards, exhorted the people of their time to repentance. The great object for which they laboured was, to fill them with confusion for their sins and dread of the divine judgment, that they might fall down and humble themselves before him whom they had offended, and, with true repentance, betake themselves to the right path. Accordingly, they use indiscriminately in the same sense, the expressions, turning, or returning to the Lord; repenting, doing repentance.[1] Whence, also, the sacred history describes it as repentance towards God, when men who disregarded him and wantoned in their lusts begin to obey his word, and are prepared to go whithersoever he may call them. And John Baptist and Paul, under the expression, bringing forth fruits meet for repentance, described a course of life exhibiting and bearing testimony, in all its actions, to such a repentance.

6. But before proceeding farther, it will be proper to give a clearer exposition of the definition which we have adopted. There are three things, then, principally to be considered in it. First, in the conversion of the life to God, we require a transformation not only in external works, but in the soul itself, which is able only after it has put off its old habits to bring forth fruits conformable to its renovation. The prophet, intending to express this, enjoins those whom he calls to repentance to make them "a new heart and a new spirit" (Ezek. xviii. 31). Hence Moses, on several occasions, when he would show how the Israelites were to repent and turn to the Lord, tells them that it must be done with the whole heart, and the whole soul (a mode of expression of frequent recurrence in the prophets), and by terming it the circumcision of the heart, points to the internal affections. But there is no passage better fitted to teach us the genuine nature of repentance than the following: "If thou wilt return, O Israel, saith the Lord, return unto me." "Break up your fallow ground, and sow not among thorns. Circumcise yourselves to the Lord, and take away the foreskins of your heart" (Jer. iv. 1—4). See how he declares to them that it will be of no avail to commence the study of righteousness unless impiety shall first have been eradicated from their inmost heart. And to make the deeper impression, he reminds them that they have to do with God, and can gain nothing by deceit,

---

[1] Matth iii. 2; 1 Sam. vii. 8; Luke iii. 8; Rom. vi. 4; Acts xxvi. 20.

because he hates a double heart. For this reason Isaiah derides the preposterous attempts of hypocrites, who zealously aimed at an external repentance by the observance of ceremonies, but in the meanwhile cared not " to loose the bands of wickedness, to undo the heavy burdens, and to let the oppressed go free " (Isaiah lviii. 6). In these words he admirably shows wherein the acts of unfeigned repentance consist.

7 The second part of our definition is, that repentance proceeds from a sincere fear of God. Before the mind of the sinner can be inclined to repentance, he must be aroused by the thought of divine judgment ; but when once the thought that God will one day ascend his tribunal to take an account of all words and actions has taken possession of his mind, it will not allow him to rest, or have one moment's peace, but will perpetually urge him to adopt a different plan of life, that he may be able to stand securely at that judgment-seat. Hence the Scripture, when exhorting to repentance, often introduces the subject of judgment as in Jeremiah, " Lest my fury come forth like fire, and burn that none can quench it, because of the evil of your doings" (Jer. iv. 4). Paul, in his discourse to the Athenians, says, " The times of this ignorance God winked at ; but now commandeth all men everywhere to repent : because he hath appointed a day, in the which he will judge the world in righteousness " (Acts xvii. 30, 31). The same thing is repeated in several other passages. Sometimes God is declared to be a judge, from the punishments already inflicted, thus leading sinners to reflect that worse awaits them if they do not quickly repent. There is an example of this in the xxixth chapter of Deuteronomy. As repentance begins with dread and hatred of sin, the Apostle sets down godly sorrow as one of its causes (2 Cor vii. 10). By godly sorrow he means when we not only tremble at the punishment, but hate and abhor the sin, because we know it is displeasing to God. It is not strange that this should be, for unless we are stung to the quick, the sluggishness of our carnal nature cannot be corrected ; nay, no degree of pungency would suffice for our stupor and sloth, did not God lift the rod and strike deeper. There is, moreover, a rebellious spirit which must be broken as with hammers. The stern threatenings which God employs are extorted from him by our depraved dispositions. For while we are asleep it were in vain to allure us by soothing measures. Passages to this effect are everywhere to be met with, and I need not quote them. But there is another reason why the fear of God lies at the root of repentance—viz. that though the life of man were possessed of all kinds of virtue, still if they do not bear reference to God, how much soever they may be lauded in the world, they are mere abomination in heaven, inasmuch as it is the principal part of righteousness to render to God that service and honour of which he is impiously defrauded, whenever it is not our express purpose to submit to his authority.

8. We must now explain the third part of the definition, and show

what is meant when we say that repentance consists of two parts—viz. the mortification of the flesh, and the quickening of the Spirit. The prophets, in accommodation to a carnal people, express this in simple and homely terms, but clearly, when they say, " Depart from evil, and do good " (Ps. xxxiv. 14). " Wash you, make you clean, put away the evil of your doings from before mine eyes ; cease to do evil ; learn to do well ; seek judgment ; relieve the oppressed," &c. (Isaiah i. 16, 17). In dissuading us from wickedness they demand the entire destruction of the flesh, which is full of perverseness and malice. It is a most difficult and arduous achievement to renounce ourselves, and lay aside our natural disposition. For the flesh must not be thought to be destroyed unless everything that we have of our own is abolished. But seeing that all the desires of the flesh are enmity against God (Rom. viii. 7), the first step to the obedience of his law is the renouncement of our own nature. Renovation is afterwards manifested by the fruits produced by it—viz. justice, judgment, and mercy. Since it were not sufficient duly to perform such acts, were not the mind and heart previously endued with sentiments of justice, judgment, and mercy, this is done when the Holy Spirit, instilling his holiness into our souls, so inspires them with new thoughts and affections, that they may justly be regarded as new. And, indeed, as we are naturally averse to God, unless self-denial precede, we shall never tend to that which is right. Hence we are so often enjoined to put off the old man, to renounce the world and the flesh, to forsake our lusts, and be renewed in the spirit of our mind. Moreover, the very name *mortification* reminds us how difficult it is to forget our former nature, because we hence infer that we cannot be trained to the fear of God, and learn the first principles of piety, unless we are violently smitten with the sword of the Spirit and annihilated, as if God were declaring, that to be ranked among his sons there must be a destruction of our ordinary nature.

9. Both of these we obtain by union with Christ. For if we have true fellowship in his death, our old man is crucified by his power, and the body of sin becomes dead, so that the corruption of our original nature is never again in full vigour (Rom. vi. 5, 6). If we are partakers in his resurrection, we are raised up by means of it to newness of life which conforms us to the righteousness of God. In one word, then, by repentance I understand regeneration,[1] the only aim of which is to form in us anew the image of God, which was sullied, and all but effaced by the transgression of Adam. So the Apostle teaches when he says, " We all with open face beholding as in a glass the glory of the Lord, are changed into the same image from glory to glory, as by the Spirit of the Lord." Again, " Be renewed in the spirit of your mind," and " put ye on the new man, which after God is created in righteousness and true holiness." Again, " Put ye on

---

[1] French, " une regeneration spirituelle ;"—a spiritual regeneration.

the new man, which is renewed in knowledge after the image of him that created him."[1]   Accordingly through the blessing of Christ we are renewed by that regeneration into the righteousness of God from which we had fallen through Adam, the Lord being pleased in this manner to restore the integrity of all whom he appoints to the inheritance of life. This renewal, indeed, is not accomplished in a moment, a day, or a year, but by uninterrupted, sometimes even by slow, progress God abolishes the remains of carnal corruption in his elect, cleanses them from pollution, and consecrates them as his temples, restoring all their inclinations to real purity, so that during their whole lives they may practise repentance, and know that death is the only termination to this warfare. The greater is the effrontery of an impure raver and apostate, named Staphylus, who pretends that I confound the condition of the present life with the celestial glory, when, after Paul, I make the image of God to consist in righteousness and true holiness ; as if in every definition it were not necessary to take the thing defined in its integrity and perfection. It is not denied that there is room for improvement; but what I maintain is that the nearer any one approaches in resemblance to God, the more does the image of God appear in him. That believers may attain to it, God assigns repentance as the goal towards which they must keep running during the whole course of their lives.

10. By regeneration the children of God are delivered from the bondage of sin, but not as if they had already obtained full possession of freedom, and no longer felt any annoyance from the flesh. Materials for an unremitting contest remain, that they may be exercised, and not only exercised, but may better understand their weakness. All writers of sound judgment agree in this, that, in the regenerate man, there is still a spring of evil which is perpetually sending forth desires that allure and stimulate him to sin. They also acknowledge that the saints are still so liable to the disease of concupiscence, that, though opposing it, they cannot avoid being ever and anon prompted and incited to lust, avarice, ambition, or other vices. It is unnecessary to spend much time in investigating the sentiments of ancient writers. Augustine alone may suffice, as he has collected all their opinions with great care and fidelity.[2] Any reader who is desirous to know the sense of antiquity may obtain it from him. There is this difference apparently between him and us, that while he admits that believers, so long as they are in the body, are so liable to concupiscence that they cannot but feel it, he does not venture to give this disease the name of sin. He is contented with giving it the name of infirmity, and says, that it only becomes sin when either external act or consent is added to conception or apprehension; that is, when the will yields to the first desire. We

---

[1] 2 Cor. iii. 18; Eph. iv. 23, 24; Col. iii. 10; 2 Cor. iv. 16.
[2] See August. ad Bonif. Lib. iv. et cont. Julianum, Lib. i. and ii. See also Serm. 6, de Verbis Apost. See also Calv. cont. Pighium, and Calv. ad Conc. Trident.

again regard it as sin whenever man is influenced in any degree by any desire contrary to the law of God; nay, we maintain that the very pravity which begets in us such desires is sin. Accordingly, we hold that there is always sin in the saints, until they are freed from their mortal frame, because depraved concupiscence resides in their flesh, and is at variance with rectitude. Augustine himself does not always refrain from using the name of sin, as when he says, "Paul gives the name of sin to that carnal concupiscence from which all sins arise. This in regard to the saints loses its dominion in this world, and is destroyed in heaven." In these words he admits that believers, in so far as they are liable to carnal concupiscence, are chargeable with sin.

11. When it is said that God purifies his Church, so as to be "holy and without blemish" (Eph. v. 26, 27), that he promises this cleansing by means of baptism, and performs it in his elect, I understand that reference is made to the guilt rather than to the matter of sin. In regenerating his people God indeed accomplishes this much for them; he destroys the dominion of sin,[1] by supplying the agency of the Spirit, which enables them to come off victorious from the contest. Sin, however, though it ceases to reign, ceases not to dwell in them. Accordingly, though we say that the old man is crucified, and the law of sin is abolished in the children of God (Rom. vi. 6), the remains of sin survive, not to have dominion, but to humble them under a consciousness of their infirmity. We admit that these remains, just as if they had no existence, are not imputed, but we, at the same time, contend that it is owing to the mercy of God that the saints are not charged with the guilt which would otherwise make them sinners before God. It will not be difficult for us to confirm this view, seeing we can support it by clear passages of Scripture. How can we express our view more plainly than Paul does in Rom. vii. 6? We have elsewhere shown, and Augustine by solid reasons proves, that Paul is there speaking in the person of a regenerated man. I say nothing as to his use of the words evil and sin. However those who object to our view may quibble on these words, can any man deny that aversion to the law of God is an evil, and that hinderance to righteousness is sin? In short, who will not admit that there is guilt where there is spiritual misery? But all these things Paul affirms of this disease. Again, the law furnishes us with a clear demonstration by which the whole question may be quickly disposed of. We are enjoined to love God with all our heart, with all our soul, with all our strength. Since all the faculties of our soul ought thus to be engrossed with the love of God, it is certain that the commandment is not fulfilled by those who receive the smallest desire into their heart, or admit into their minds any thought whatever which may lead them away from the love of God to vanity. What

---

[1] Latin, "Reatus."—French, "l'imputation du peché;"—the imputation of sin.

then ?   Is it not through the faculties of mind that we are assailed with sudden motions, that we perceive sensual, or form conceptions of mental objects ?   Since these faculties give admission to vain and wicked thoughts, do they not show that to that extent they are devoid of the love of God ?   He, then, who admits not that all the desires of the flesh are sins, and that that disease of concupiscence, which they call a stimulus, is a fountain of sin, must of necessity deny that the transgression of the law is sin.

12. If any one thinks it absurd thus to condemn all the desires by which man is naturally affected, seeing they have been implanted by God the author of nature, we answer, that we by no means condemn those appetites which God so implanted in the mind of man at his first creation, that they cannot be eradicated without destroying human nature itself, but only the violent lawless movements which war with the order of God. But as, in consequence of the corruption of nature, all our faculties are so vitiated and corrupted, that a perpetual disorder and excess is apparent in all our actions, and as the appetites cannot be separated from this excess, we maintain that therefore they are vicious ; or, to give the substance in fewer words, we hold that all human desires are evil, and we charge them with sin not in as far as they are natural, but because they are inordinate, and inordinate because nothing pure and upright can proceed from a corrupt and polluted nature. Nor does Augustine depart from this doctrine in reality so much as in appearance. From an excessive dread of the invidious charge with which the Pelagians assailed him, he sometimes refrains from using the term sin in this sense ; but when he says (ad Bonif.) that *the law of sin remaining in the saints, the guilt only is taken away,* he shows clearly enough that his view is not very different from ours.

13. We will produce some other passages to make it more apparent what his sentiments were. In his second book against Julian, he says, " This law of sin is both remitted in spiritual regeneration and remains in the mortal flesh ; remitted, because the guilt is forgiven in the sacrament by which believers are regenerated, and yet remains, inasmuch as it produces desires against which believers fight." Again, " Therefore the law of sin (which was in the members of this great Apostle also) is forgiven in baptism, not ended." Again, " The law of sin, the guilt of which, though remaining, is forgiven in baptism, Ambrose called iniquity, for it is iniquitous for the flesh to lust against the Spirit." Again, " Sin is dead in the guilt by which it bound us ; and until it is cured by the perfection of burial, though dead it rebels." In the fifth book he says still more plainly, " As blindness of heart is the sin by which God is not believed ; and the punishment of sin, by which a proud heart is justly punished ; and the cause of sin, when through the error of a blinded heart any evil is committed : so the lust of the flesh, against which the good Spirit wars, is also sin, because disobedient to the authority of the mind ; and the punish-

ment of sin, because the recompense rendered for disobedience; and the cause of sin, consenting by revolt or springing up through contamination." He here without ambiguity calls it sin, because the Pelagian heresy being now refuted, and the sound doctrine confirmed, he was less afraid of calumny. Thus, also, in his forty-first Homily on John, where he speaks his own sentiments without controversy, he says, " If with the flesh you serve the law of sin, do what the Apostle himself says, ' Let not sin, therefore, reign in your mortal body, that ye should obey it in the lusts thereof' (Rom. vi. 12). He does not say, *Let it not be*, but *Let it not reign*. As long as you live there must be sin in your members; but at least let its dominion be destroyed; do not what it orders." Those who maintain that concupiscence is not sin, are wont to found on the passage of James, "Then, when lust hath conceived, it bringeth forth sin" (James i. 15). But this is easily refuted: for unless we understand him as speaking only of wicked works or actual sins, even a wicked inclination will not be accounted sin. But from his calling crimes and wicked deeds the fruits of lust, and also giving them the name of sins, it does not follow that the lust itself is not an evil, and in the sight of God deserving of condemnation.

14. Some Anabaptists in the present age mistake some indescribable sort of frenzied excess for the regeneration of the Spirit, holding that the children of God are restored to a state of innocence, and, therefore, need give themselves no anxiety about curbing the lust of the flesh; that they have the Spirit for their guide, and under his agency never err.[1] It would be incredible that the human mind could proceed to such insanity, did they not openly and exultingly give utterance to their dogma. It is indeed monstrous, and yet it is just, that those who have resolved to turn the word of God into a lie, should thus be punished for their blasphemous audacity. Is it indeed true, that all distinction between base and honourable, just and unjust, good and evil, virtue and vice, is abolished? The distinction, they say, is from the curse of the old Adam, and from this we are exempted by Christ. There will be no difference, then, between whoredom and chastity, sincerity and craft, truth and falsehood, justice and robbery. Away with vain fear! (they say), the Spirit will not bid you do anything that is wrong, provided you sincerely and boldly leave yourself to his agency. Who is not amazed at such monstrous doctrines? And yet this philosophy is popular with those who, blinded by insane lusts, have thrown off common sense. But what kind of Christ, pray, do they fabricate? what kind of Spirit do they belch forth? We acknowledge one Christ, and his one Spirit, whom the prophets foretold and the Gospel proclaims as actually manifested, but we hear nothing of this kind respecting him. That Spirit is not the patron of murder, adultery, drunkenness, pride, contention, avarice, and fraud,

---

[1] See Calvin, adv. Libertinos, cap. xviii.

but the author of love, chastity, sobriety, modesty, peace, moderation, and truth.   He is not a Spirit of giddiness, rushing rashly and pre-cipitately, without regard to right and wrong, but full of wisdom and understanding, by which he can duly distinguish between justice and injustice.   He instigates not to lawless and unrestrained licentious-ness, but, discriminating between lawful and unlawful, teaches tem-perance and moderation.   But why dwell longer in refuting that brutish frenzy?   To Christians the Spirit of the Lord is not a turbulent phantom, which they themselves have produced by dreaming, or received ready-made by others; but they religiously seek the know-ledge of him from Scripture, where two things are taught concerning him : *first*, that he is given to us for sanctification, that he may purge us from all iniquity and defilement, and bring us to the obedience of divine rigteousness, an obedience which cannot exist unless the lusts to which these men would give loose reins are tamed and subdued; *secondly*, that though purged by his sanctification, we are still beset by many vices and much weakness, so long as we are enclosed in the prison of the body.   Thus it is, that placed at a great distance from perfection, we must always be endeavouring to make some progress, and daily struggling with the evil by which we are entangled. Whence, too, it follows that, shaking off sloth and security, we must be intently vigilant, so as not to be taken unawares in the snares of our flesh; unless, indeed, we presume to think that we have made greater progress than the Apostle, who was buffeted by a messenger of Satan, in order that his strength might be perfected in weakness, and who gives in his own person a true, not a fictitious representation, of the strife between the Spirit and the flesh (2 Cor. xii. 7, 9 ; Rom. vii. 6).

15. The Apostle, in his description of repentance (2 Cor. vii. 2), enumerates seven causes, effects, or parts belonging to it, and that on the best grounds.   These are carefulness, excuse, indignation, fear, desire, zeal, revenge.   It should not excite surprise that I venture not to determine whether they ought to be regarded as causes or effects : both views may be maintained.   They may also be called affections conjoined with repentance ; but as Paul's meaning may be ascertained without entering into any of these questions, we shall be contented with a simple exposition.   He says then that godly sorrow produces *carefulness*.   He who is really dissatisfied with himself for sinning against his God, is, at the same time, stimulated to care and attention, that he may completely disentangle himself from the chains of the devil, and keep a better guard against his snares, so as not afterwards to lose the guidance of the Holy Spirit, or be overcome by security.   Next comes *excuse*, which in this place means not de-fence, in which the sinner to escape the judgment of God either denies his fault or extenuates it, but apologising, which trusts more to intercession than to the goodness of the cause ; just as children not altogether abandoned, while they acknowledge and confess their

errors, yet employ deprecation; and to make room for it, testify, by every means in their power, that they have by no means cast off the reverence which they owe to their parents; in short, endeavour by excuse not to prove themselves righteous and innocent, but only to obtain pardon. Next follows *indignation*, under which the sinner inwardly murmurs, expostulates, and is offended with himself on recognising his perverseness and ingratitude to God. By the term *fear* is meant that trepidation which takes possession of our minds whenever we consider both what we have deserved, and the fearful severity of the divine anger against sinners. Accordingly, the exceeding disquietude which we must necessarily feel, both trains us to humility and makes us more cautious for the future. But if the carefulness or anxiety which he first mentioned is the result of fear, the connection between the two becomes obvious. *Desire* seems to me to be used as equivalent to diligence in duty, and alacrity in doing service, to which the sense of our misdeeds ought to be a powerful stimulus. To this also pertains *zeal*, which immediately follows; for it signifies the ardour with which we are inflamed when such goads as these are applied to us. "What have I done? Into what abyss had I fallen had not the mercy of God prevented?" The last of all is *revenge*, for the stricter we are with ourselves, and the severer the censure we pass upon our sins, the more ground we have to hope for the divine favour and mercy. And certainly when the soul is overwhelmed with a dread of divine judgment, it cannot but act the part of an avenger in inflicting punishment upon itself. Pious men, doubtless, feel that there is punishment in the shame, confusion, groans, self-displeasure, and other feelings produced by a serious review of their sins. Let us remember, however, that moderation must be used, so that we may not be overwhelmed with sadness, there being nothing to which trembling consciences are more prone than to rush into despair. This, too, is one of Satan's artifices. Those whom he sees thus overwhelmed with fear he plunges deeper and deeper into the abyss of sorrow, that they may never again rise. It is true that the fear which ends in humility without relinquishing the hope of pardon cannot be in excess. And yet we must always beware, according to the apostolic injunction, of giving way to extreme dread, as this tends to make us shun God while he is calling us to himself by repentance. Wherefore, the advice of Bernard is good, "Grief for sins is necessary, but must not be perpetual. My advice is to turn back at times from sorrow and the anxious remembrance of your ways, and escape to the plain, to a calm review of the divine mercies. Let us mingle honey with wormwood, that the salubrious bitter may give health when we drink it tempered with a mixture of sweetness: while you think humbly of yourselves, think also of the goodness of the Lord" (Bernard in Cant. Serm. xi.).

16. We can now understand what are the fruits of repentance—viz. offices of piety towards God, and love towards men, general holi-

ness and purity of life. In short, the more a man studies to conform his life to the standard of the divine law, the surer signs he gives of his repentance. Accordingly, the Spirit, in exhorting us to repentance, brings before us at one time each separate precept of the law ; at another the duties of the second table ; although there are also passages in which, after condemning impurity in its fountain in the heart, he afterwards descends to external marks, by which repentance is proved to be sincere. A portraiture of this I will shortly set before the eye of the reader when I come to describe the Christian life (*infra*, chapter vi.). I will not here collect the passages from the prophets in which they deride the frivolous observances of those who labour to appease God with ceremonies, and show that they are mere mockery ; or those in which they show that outward integrity of conduct is not the chief part of repentance, seeing that God looks at the heart. Any one moderately versant in Scripture will understand by himself, without being reminded by others, that when he has to do with God, nothing is gained without beginning with the internal affections of the heart. There is a passage of Joel which will avail not a little for the understanding of others : " Rend your heart, and not your garments " (Joel ii. 13). Both are also briefly expressed by James in these words : "Cleanse your hands, ye sinners ; and purify your hearts, ye double-minded" (James iv. 8). Here, indeed, the accessory is set down first ; but the source and principle is afterwards pointed out—viz. that hidden defilements must be wiped away, and an altar erected to God in the very heart. There are, moreover, certain external exercises which we employ in private as remedies to humble us and tame our flesh, and in public, to testify our repentance. These have their origin in that revenge of which Paul speaks (2 Cor. vii. 2), for when the mind is distressed it naturally expresses itself in sackcloth, groans, and tears, shuns ornament and every kind of show, and abandons all delights. Then he who feels how great an evil the rebellion of the flesh is, tries every means of curbing it. Besides, he who considers aright how grievous a thing it is to have offended the justice of God, cannot rest until, in his humility, he have given glory to God. Such exercises are often mentioned by ancient writers when they speak of the fruits of repentance. But although they by no means place the power of repentance in them, yet my readers must pardon me for saying what I think— they certainly seem to insist on them more than is right. Any one who judiciously considers the matter will, I trust, agree with me that they have exceeded in two ways ; first, by so strongly urging and extravagantly commending that corporal discipline, they indeed succeeded in making the people embrace it with greater zeal ; but they in a manner obscured what they should have regarded as of much more serious moment. Secondly, the inflictions which they enjoined were considerably more rigorous than ecclesiastical mildness demands, as will be elsewhere shown.

17. But as there are some who, from the frequent mention of sackcloth, fasting, and tears, especially in (Joel ii. 12), think that these constitute the principal part of repentance, we must dispel their delusion. In that passage the proper part of repentance is described by the words, "turn ye even to me with your whole heart;" "rend your heart, and not your garments." The "fasting," "weeping," and "mourning," are introduced not as invariable or necessary effects, but as special circumstances.[1] Having foretold that most grievous disasters were impending over the Jews, he exhorts them to turn away the divine anger, not only by repenting, but by giving public signs of sorrow. For as a criminal, to excite the commiseration of the judge, appears in a supplicating posture, with a long beard, uncombed hair, and coarse clothing, so should those who are charged at the judgment-seat of God deprecate his severity in a garb of wretchedness. But although sackcloth and ashes were perhaps more conformable to the customs of these times,[2] yet it is plain that weeping and fasting are very appropriate in our case whenever the Lord threatens us with any defeat or calamity. In presenting the appearance of danger, he declares that he is preparing, and, in a manner, arming himself for vengeance. Rightly, therefore, does the Prophet exhort those, on whose crimes he had said a little before that vengeance was to be executed, to weeping and fasting,—that is, to the mourning habit of criminals. Nor in the present day do ecclesiastical teachers act improperly when, seeing ruin hanging over the necks of their people,[3] they call aloud on them to hasten with weeping and fasting: only they must always urge, with greater care and earnestness, "rend your hearts, and not your garments." It is beyond doubt that fasting is not always a concomitant of repentance, but is specially destined for seasons of calamity.[4] Hence our Saviour connects it with mourning (Matth. ix. 15), and relieves the Apostles of the necessity of it until, by being deprived of his presence, they were filled with sorrow. I speak of formal fasting. For the life of Christians ought ever to be tempered with frugality and sobriety, so that the whole course of it should present some appearance of fasting. As this subject will be fully discussed when the discipline of the Church comes to be considered, I now dwell less upon it.

18. This much, however, I will add: when the name *repentance* is applied to the external profession, it is used improperly, and not

1 French, "Circonstances qui convenoyent specialement alors;"—circumstances which were then specially suitable.

2 French, "Fust la coustume de ce temps-la, et ne nous appartienne aujourdhui de rien;"—was the custom of that time, and we have nowadays nothing to do with it.

3 The French adds, "Soit de guerre, de famine, ou de pestilence;"—whether of war, famine, or pestilence.

4 Latin, "Calamitosis temporibus peculiariter destinari."—French, "Convient particulierement a ceux qui veulent testifier quils se recognoissant avoir merité l'ire de Dieu, et neantmoins requierent pardon de sa clemence;"—is particularly suitable to those who acknowledge they have deserved the wrath of God, and yet seek pardon of his mercy.

in the genuine meaning as I have explained it. For that is not so much a turning unto God as the confession of a fault accompanied with deprecation of the sentence and punishment. Thus to repent in sackcloth and ashes (Matth. xi. 21 ; Luke x. 13), is just to testify self-dissatisfaction when God is angry with us for having grievously offended him. It is, indeed, a kind of public confession by which, condemning ourselves before angels and the world, we prevent the judgment of God. For Paul, rebuking the sluggishness of those who indulge in their sins, says, "If we would judge ourselves, we should not be judged" (1 Cor xi. 31). It is not always necessary, however, openly to inform others, and make them the witnesses of our repentance ; but to confess privately to God is a part of true repentance which cannot be omitted. Nothing were more incongruous than that God should pardon the sins in which we are flattering ourselves, and hypocritically cloaking that he may not bring them to light. We must not only confess the sins which we daily commit, but more grievous lapses ought to carry us farther, and bring to our remembrance things which seemed to have been long ago buried. Of this David sets an example before us in his own person (Ps. li). Filled with shame for a recent crime he examines himself, going back to the womb, and acknowledging that even then he was corrupted and defiled. This he does not to extenuate his fault, as many hide themselves in the crowd, and catch at impunity by involving others along with them. Very differently does David, who ingenuously makes it an aggravation of his sin, that being corrupted from his earliest infancy he ceased not to add iniquity to iniquity. In another passage, also, he takes a survey of his past life, and implores God to pardon the errors of his youth (Ps. xxv. 7). And, indeed, we shall not prove that we have thoroughly shaken off our stupor until, groaning under the burden, and lamenting our sad condition, we seek relief from God. It is, moreover, to be observed, that the repentance which we are enjoined assiduously to cultivate, differs from that which raises, as it were, from death those who had fallen more shamefully, or given themselves up to sin without restraint, or by some kind of open revolt, had thrown off the authority of God. For Scripture, in exhorting to repentance, often speaks of it as a passage from death unto life, and when relating that a people had repented, means that they had abandoned idolatry, and other forms of gross wickedness. For which reason Paul denounces woe to sinners, "who have not repented of the uncleanness, and fornication, and lasciviousness which they have committed" (2 Cor. xii. 21). This distinction ought to be carefully observed, lest when we hear of a few individuals having been summoned to repent we indulge in supine security, as if we had nothing to do with the mortification of the flesh ; whereas, in consequence of the depraved desires which are always enticing us, and the iniquities which are ever and anon springing from them, it must engage our unremitting care. The special repentance enjoined upon those whom the devil has entangled in deadly snares, and withdrawn from the fear of God, does not abolish that ordinary repentance which the corruption of nature obliges us to cultivate during the whole course of our lives.

19. Moreover, if it is true, and nothing can be more certain, than that a complete summary of the Gospel is included under these two heads—viz. repentance and the remission of sins—do we not see that the Lord justifies his people freely, and at the same time renews them to true holiness by the sanctification of his Spirit? John, the messenger sent before the face of Christ to prepare his ways, proclaimed, "Repent, for the kingdom of heaven is at hand" (Matth. xi. 10; iii. 2). By inviting them to repentance, he urged them to acknowledge that they were sinners, and in all respects condemned before God, that thus they might be induced earnestly to seek the mortification of the flesh, and a new birth in the Spirit. By announcing the kingdom of God, he called for faith, since by the kingdom of God which he declared to be at hand, he meant forgiveness of sins, salvation, life, and every other blessing which we obtain in Christ; wherefore we read in the other Evangelists, "John did baptise in the wilderness, and preach the baptism of repentance for the remission of sins" (Mark i. 4; Luke iii. 3). What does this mean, but that, weary and oppressed with the burden of sin, they should turn to the Lord, and entertain hopes of forgiveness and salvation?[1] Thus, too, Christ began his preaching, "The kingdom of God is at hand: repent ye, and believe the Gospel" (Mark i. 15). First, he declares that the treasures of the divine mercy were opened in him; next, he enjoins repentance; and, lastly, he encourages confidence in the promises of God. Accordingly, when intending to give a brief summary of the whole Gospel, he said that he behoved "to suffer, and to rise from the dead the third day, and that repentance and remission of sins should be preached in his name among all nations" (Luke xxiv. 26, 46). In like manner, after his resurrection the Apostles preached, "Him hath God exalted with his right hand, to be a Prince and a Saviour, for to give repentance to Israel and forgiveness of sins" (Acts v. 31). Repentance is preached in the name of Christ, when men learn, through the doctrines of the Gospel, that all their thoughts, affections, and pursuits, are corrupt and vicious; and that, therefore, if they would enter the kingdom of God they must be born again. Forgiveness of sins is preached when men are taught that Christ "is made unto us wisdom, and righteousness, and sanctification, and redemption" (1 Cor. i. 30), that on his account they are freely deemed righteous and innocent in the sight of God. Though both graces are obtained by faith (as has been shown elsewhere), yet as the goodness of God, by which sins are forgiven, is the proper object of faith, it was proper carefully to distinguish it from repentance.

1 The French adds, "pource qu'il lui est propre, et comme naturel, de sauver ce que est perdu;"—because it is proper, and, as it were, natural to him to save that which is lost

20. Moreover, as hatred of sin, which is the beginning of repentance, first gives us access to the knowledge of Christ, who manifests himself to none but miserable and afflicted sinners, groaning, labouring, burdened, hungry, and thirsty, pining away with grief and wretchedness, so if we would stand in Christ, we must aim at repentance, cultivate it during our whole lives, and continue it to the last. Christ came to call sinners, but to call them to repentance. He was sent to bless the unworthy, but by " turning away every one " " from his iniquities." The Scripture is full of similar passages. Hence, when God offers forgiveness of 'sins, he in return usually stipulates for repentance, intimating that his mercy should induce men to repent. " Keep ye judgment," saith he, " and do justice : for my salvation is near to come." Again, " The Redeemer shall come to Zion, and unto them that turn from transgression in Jacob." Again, " Seek ye the Lord while he may be found, call ye upon him while he is near. Let the wicked forsake his way, and the unrighteous man his thoughts, and let him return unto the Lord, and he will have mercy upon him." " Repent ye, therefore, and be converted, that your sins may be blotted out."[1] Here, however, it is to be observed, that repentance is not made a condition in such a sense as to be a foundation for meriting pardon ; nay, it rather indicates the end at which they must aim if they would obtain favour, God having resolved to take pity on men for the express purpose of leading them to repent. Therefore, so long as we dwell in the prison of the body, we must constantly struggle with the vices of our corrupt nature, and so with our natural disposition. Plato sometimes says,[2] that the life of the philosopher is to meditate on death. More truly may we say, that the life of a Christian man is constant study and exercise in mortifying the flesh, until it is certainly slain, and the Spirit of God obtains dominion in us. Wherefore, he seems to me to have made most progress who has learned to be most dissatisfied with himself. He does not, however, remain in the miry clay without going forward ; but rather hastens and sighs after God, that, ingrafted both into the death and the life of Christ, he may constantly meditate on repentance. Unquestionably those who have a genuine hatred of sin cannot do otherwise : for no man ever hated sin without being previously enamoured of righteousness. This view, as it is the simplest of all, seemed to me also to accord best with Scripture truth.

21. Moreover, that repentance is a special gift of God, I trust is too well understood from the above doctrine to require any lengthened discourse. Hence the Church[3] extols the goodness of God, and looks on in wonder, saying, " Then hath God also to the Gentiles granted repentance unto life"(Acts xi. 18); and Paul, enjoining Timothy to

---

[1] Isaiah lvi. 1 ; lix. 20 ; lv. 6, 7 ; Acts ii. 38 ; iii. 19.
[2] This is to be found in different passages of his work, and often in the Phaido.
[3] French, " L'Eglise primitive du temps des Apostres;"—the primitive Church of the Apostles' time.

deal meekly and patiently with unbelievers, says, "If God peradventure will give them repentance to the acknowledging of the truth, and that they may recover themselves out of the snare of the devil"(2 Tim. ii. 25, 26). God indeed declares, that he would have all men to repent, and addresses exhortations in common to all; their efficacy, however, depends on the Spirit of regeneration. It were easier to create us at first, than for us by our own strength to acquire a more excellent nature. Wherefore, in regard to the whole process of regeneration, it is not without cause we are called God's " workmanship, created in Christ Jesus unto good works, which God hath before ordained that we should walk in them" (Eph. ii. 10).[1] Those whom God is pleased to rescue from death, he quickens by the Spirit of regeneration; not that repentance is properly the cause of salvation, but because, as already seen, it is inseparable from the faith and mercy of God; for, as Isaiah declares, " The Redeemer shall come to Zion, and unto them that turn from trangression in Jacob." This, indeed, is a standing truth, that wherever the fear of God is in vigour, the Spirit has been carrying on his saving work. Hence, in Isaiah, while believers complain and lament that they have been forsaken of God, they set down the supernatural hardening of the heart as a sign of reprobation. The Apostle also, intending to exclude apostates from the hope of salvation, states, as the reason, that it is impossible to renew them to repentance (Heb. vi. 6); that is, God by renewing those whom he wills not to perish, gives them a sign of paternal favour, and in a manner attracts them to himself, by the beams of a calm and reconciled countenance; on the other hand, by hardening the reprobate whose impiety is not to be forgiven, he thunders against them. This kind of vengeance the Apostle denounces against voluntary apostates, (Heb. x. 29), who, in falling away from the faith of the gospel, mock God, insultingly reject his favour, profane and trample under foot the blood of Christ, nay, as far as in them lies, crucify him afresh. Still, he does not, as some austere persons preposterously insist, leave no hope of pardon to voluntary sins, but shows that apostacy being altogether without excuse, it is not strange that God is inexorably rigorous in punishing sacrilegious contempt thus shown to himself. For, in the same Epistle, he says, that " it is impossible for those who were once enlightened, and have tasted of the heavenly gift, and were made partakers of the Holy Ghost, and have tasted the word of God, and the powers of the world to come, if they shall fall away to renew them again to repentance, seeing they crucify the Son of God afresh, and put him to an open shame" (Heb. vi. 4—6). And in another passage, " If we sin willingly, after that we have received the knowledge of the truth, there remaineth no more sacrifice for sins, but a certain fearful looking for of judgment," &c. (Heb. xi.

---

1 The French adds, " Et ce non seulement au regard d'un jour. mais de tout le cours de notre vocation;"—and this in regard not only to a single day, but to the whole course of our vocation.

25, 26). There are other passages, from a misinterpretation of which the Novatians of old extracted materials for their heresy; so much so, that some good men taking offence at their harshness, have deemed the Epistle altogether spurious, though it truly savours in every part of it of the apostolic spirit. But as our dispute is only with those who receive the Epistle, it is easy to show that those passages give no support to their error. First, the Apostle must of necessity agree with his Master, who declares, that " all manner of sin and blasphemy shall be forgiven unto men, but the blasphemy against the Holy Ghost shall not be forgiven unto men," " neither in this world, neither in the world to come"(Matth. xii. 31; Luke xii. 10). We must hold that this was the only exception which the Apostle recognised, unless we would set him in opposition to the grace of God. Hence it follows, that to no sin is pardon denied save to one, which proceeding from desperate fury cannot be ascribed to infirmity, and plainly shows that the man guilty of it is possessed by the devil.

22. Here, however, it is proper to consider what the dreadful iniquity is which is not to be pardoned. The definition which Augustine somewhere gives [1]—viz. that it is obstinate perverseness, with distrust of pardon, continued till death—scarcely agrees with the words of Christ, that it shall not be forgiven in this world. For either this is said in vain, or it may be committed in this world. But if Augustine's definition is correct, the sin is not committed unless persisted in till death. Others say, that the sin against the Holy Spirit consists in envying the grace conferred upon a brother; but I know not on what it is founded. Here, however, let us give the true definition, which, when once it is established by sound evidence, will easily of itself overturn all the others. I say, therefore, that he sins against the Holy Spirit who, while so constrained by the power of divine truth that he cannot plead ignorance, yet deliberately resists, and that merely for the sake of resisting. For Christ, in explanation of what he had said, immediately adds, " Whosoever speaketh a word against the Son of man, it shall be forgiven him; but whosoever speaketh against the Holy Ghost, it shall not be forgiven him" (Matth. xii. 31). And Matthew uses the term spirit of blasphemy [2] for blasphemy against the Spirit. How can any one insult the Son, without at the same time attacking the Spirit? In this way. Those who in ignorance assail the unknown truth of God, and yet are so disposed that they would be unwilling to extinguish the truth of God when manifested to them, or utter one word against-him whom they knew to be the Lord's Anointed, sin against the Father and the Son. Thus there are many in the present day who have the greatest abhorrence to the doctrine of the Gospel, and yet, if they knew it to be the doctrine of the Gospel, would be prepared to venerate it with their

1 August. Lib. de Correp. et Gratia, cap. xii.
2 The Greek is, " τοῦ πνεύματος βλασφημία." This Calvin translates in Latin, " Spiritum blasphemiæ," and in French, " Esprit de blaspheme."

whole heart. But those who are convinced in conscience that what they repudiate and impugn is the word of God, and yet cease not to impugn it, are said to blaspheme against the Spirit, inasmuch as they struggle against the illumination which is the work of the Spirit. Such were some of the Jews, who, when they could not resist the Spirit speaking by Stephen, yet were bent on resisting (Acts vi. 10). There can be no doubt that many of them were carried away by zeal for the law; but it appears that there were others who maliciously and impiously raged against God himself, that is, against the doctrine which they knew to be of God. Such, too, were the Pharisees, on whom our Lord denounced woe. To depreciate the power of the Holy Spirit, they defamed him by the name of Beelzebub (Matth. ix. 3, 4; xii. 24). The spirit of blasphemy, therefore, is, when a man audaciously, and of set purpose, rushes forth to insult his divine name. This Paul intimates when he says, "but I obtained mercy, because I did it ignorantly in unbelief;" otherwise he had deservedly been held unworthy of the grace of God.[1] If ignorance joined with unbelief made him obtain pardon, it follows that there is no room for pardon when knowledge is added to unbelief.

23. If you attend properly, you will perceive that the Apostle speaks not of one particular lapse or two, but of the universal revolt by which the reprobate renounce salvation. It is not strange that God should be implacable to those whom John, in his Epistle, declares not to have been of the elect, from whom they went out (1 John ii. 19). For he is directing his discourse against those who imagined that they could return to the Christian religion though they had once revolted from it. To divest them of this false and pernicious opinion, he says, as is most true, that those who had once knowingly and willingly cast off fellowship with Christ, had no means of returning to it. It is not, however, so cast off by those who merely, by the dissoluteness of their lives, transgress the word of the Lord, but by those who avowedly reject his whole doctrine. There is a paralogism in the expression *casting off* and *sinning. Casting off*, as interpreted by the Novatians, is when any one, notwithstanding of being taught by the Law of the Lord not to steal or commit adultery, refrains not from theft or adultery. On the contrary, I hold that there is a tacit antithesis, in which all the things, contrary to those which had been said, must be held to be repeated, so that the thing expressed is not some particular vice, but universal aversion to God, and (so to speak) the apostasy of the whole man. Therefore, when he speaks of those falling away "who were once enlightened, and have tasted of the heavenly gift, and were made partakers of the Holy Ghost, and have tasted of the good word of God, and the powers of the world to come," we must understand him as referring to those who, with deliberate impiety, have quenched the light of the Spirit, tasted of the heavenly

---

[1] The omission of this last clause in the French seems to be an improvement.

word and spurned it, alienated themselves from the sanctification of the Spirit, and trampled under foot the word of God and the powers of a world to come. The better to show that this was the species of impiety intended, he afterwards expressly adds the term *wilfully*. For when he says, "If we sin wilfully, after that we have received the knowledge of the truth, there remaineth no more sacrifice for sins," he denies not that Christ is a perpetual victim to expiate the transgressions of saints (this the whole Epistle, in explaining the priesthood of Christ, distinctly proclaims), but he says that there remains no other sacrifice after this one is abandoned. And it is abandoned when the truth of the Gospel is professedly abjured.

24. To some it seems harsh, and at variance with the divine mercy, utterly to deny forgiveness to any who betake themselves to it. This is easily disposed of. It is not said that pardon will be refused if they turn to the Lord, but it is altogether denied that they can turn to repentance, inasmuch as for their ingratitude they are struck by the just judgment of God with eternal blindness. There is nothing contrary to this in the application which is afterwards made of the example of Esau, who tried in vain, by crying and tears, to recover his lost birthright; nor in the denunciation of the Prophet, "They cried, and I would not hear." Such modes of expression do not denote true conversion or calling upon God, but that anxiety with which the wicked, when in calamity, are compelled to see what they before securely disregarded—viz. that nothing can avail but the assistance of the Lord. This, however, they do not so much implore as lament the loss of. Hence all that the Prophet means by crying, and the Apostle by tears, is the dreadful torment which stings and excruciates the wicked in despair. It is of consequence carefully to observe this: for otherwise God would be inconsistent with himself when he proclaims through the Prophet, that "If the wicked will turn from all his sins that he hath committed," —"he shall surely live, he shall not die" (Ezek. xviii. 21, 22). And (as I have already said) it is certain that the mind of man cannot be changed for the better unless by his preventing grace. The promise as to those who call upon him will never fail; but the names of conversion and prayer are improperly given to that blind torment by which the reprobate are distracted when they see that they must seek God if they would find a remedy for their calamities, and yet shun to approach him.

25. But as the Apostle declares that God is not appeased by feigned repentance, it is asked how Ahab obtained pardon, and averted the punishment denounced against him (1 Kings xxi. 28, 29), seeing, it appears, he was only amazed on the sudden, and afterwards continued his former course of life. He, indeed, clothed himself in sackcloth, covered himself with ashes, lay on the ground, and (as the testimony given to him bears) humbled himself before God. It was a small matter to rend his garments while his heart

continued obstinate and swollen with wickedness, and yet we see that God was inclined to mercy. I answer, that though hypocrites are thus occasionally spared for a time, the wrath of God still lies upon them, and that they are thus spared not so much on their own account as for a public example. For what did Ahab gain by the mitigation of his punishment except that he did not suffer it alive on the earth? The curse of God, though concealed, was fixed on his house, and he himself went to eternal destruction. We may see the same thing in Esau (Gen. xxvii. 38, 39). For though he met with a refusal, a temporal blessing was granted to his tears. But as, according to the declaration of God, the spiritual inheritance could be possessed only by one of the brothers, when Jacob was selected instead of Esau, that event excluded him from the divine mercy; but still there was given to him, as a man of a grovelling nature, this consolation, that he should be filled with the fatness of the earth and the dew of heaven. And this, as I lately said, should be regarded as done for the example of others, that we may learn to apply our minds, and exert ourselves with greater alacrity, in the way of sincere repentance, as there cannot be the least doubt that God will be ready to pardon those who turn to him truly and with the heart, seeing his mercy extends even to the unworthy, though they bear marks of his displeasure. In this way also, we are taught how dreadful the judgment is which awaits all the rebellious who with audacious brow and iron heart make it their sport to despise and disregard the divine threatenings. God in this way often stretched forth his hand to deliver the Israelites from their calamities, though their cries were pretended, and their minds double and perfidious, as he himself complains in the Psalms, that they immediately returned to their former course (Psalm lxxviii. 36, 37). But he designed thus by kindness and forbearance to bring them to true repentance, or leave them without excuse. And yet by remitting the punishment for a time, he does not lay himself under any perpetual obligation. He rather at times rises with greater severity against hypocrites, and doubles their punishment, that it may thereby appear how much hypocrisy displeases him. But, as I have observed, he gives some examples of his inclination to pardon, that the pious may thereby be stimulated to amend their lives, and the pride of those who petulantly kick against the pricks be more severely condemned.

CHAPTER IV.

PENITENCE, AS EXPLAINED IN THE SOPHISTICAL JARGON OF THE
SCHOOLMEN, WIDELY DIFFERENT FROM THE PURITY REQUIRED
BY THE GOSPEL.   OF CONFESSION AND SATISFACTION.

The divisions of this chapter are,—I. The orthodox doctrine of repentance being
already expounded, the false doctrine is refuted in the present chapter; a general
summary survey being at the same time taken of the doctrine of the Schoolmen, sec. 1,
2.   II. Its separate parts are afterwards examined.   Contrition, sec. 2 and 3.   Confession, sec. 4–20   Sanctification, from sec. 20 to the end of the chapter.

Sections.

18. Another refutation of the first error from analogy. Sum of the whole refutation. Third refutation, laying down the surest rule of confession. Explanation of the rule. Three objections answered.
19. Fourth objection—viz. that auricular confession does no harm, and is even useful. Answer, unfolding the hypocrisy, falsehood, impiety, and monstrous abominations of the patrons of this error.
20. Refutation of the second error. 1. Priests not successors of the Apostles. 2. They have not the Holy Spirit, who alone is arbiter of the keys.
21. Refutation of the third error. 1. They are ignorant of the command and promise of Christ. By abandoning the word of God they run into innumerable absurdities.
22. Objection to the refutation of the third error. Answers, reducing the Papists to various absurdities.
23. Refutation of the fourth error. 1. Petitio principii. 2. Inversion of ecclesiastical discipline. Three objections answered.
24. Conclusion of the whole discussion against this fictitious confession.
25. Of satisfaction, to which the Sophists assign the third place in repentance. Errors and falsehoods. These views opposed by the terms,—1. Forgiveness. 2. Free forgiveness. 3. God destroying iniquities. 4. By and on account of Christ. No need of our satisfaction.
26. Objection, confining the grace and efficacy of Christ within narrow limits. Answers by both John the Evangelist and John the Baptist. Consequence of these answers.
27. Two points violated by the fiction of satisfaction. First, the honour of Christ impaired. Secondly, the conscience cannot find peace. Objection, confining the forgiveness of sins to Catechumens, refuted.
28. Objection, founded on the arbitrary distinction between venial and mortal sins. This distinction insulting to God and repugnant to Scripture. Answer, showing the true distinction in regard to venial sin.
29. Objection, founded on a distinction between guilt and the punishment of it. Answer, illustrated by various passages of Scripture. Admirable saying of Augustine.
30. Answer, founded on a consideration of the efficacy of Christ's death, and the sacrifices under the law. Our true satisfaction.
31. An objection, perverting six passages of Scripture. Preliminary observations concerning a twofold judgment on the part of God. 1. For punishment. 2. For correction.
32. Two distinctions hence arising. Objection, that God is often angry with his elect. Answer, God in afflicting his people does not take his mercy from them. This confirmed by his promise, by Scripture, and the uniform experience of the Church. Distinction between the reprobate and the elect in regard to punishment.
33. Second distinction. The punishment of the reprobate a commencement of the eternal punishment awaiting them ; that of the elect designed to bring them to repentance. This confirmed by passages of Scripture and of the Fathers.
34. Two uses of this doctrine to the believer. In affliction he can believe that God, though angry, is still favourable to him. In the punishment of the reprobate, he sees a prelude to their final doom.
35. Objection, as to the punishment of David, answered. Why all men here subjected to chastisement.
36. Objections, founded on five other passages, answered.
37. Answer continued.
38. Objection, founded on passages in the Fathers. Answer, with passages from Chrysostom and Augustine.
39. These satisfactions had reference to the peace of the Church, and not to the throne of God. The Schoolmen have perverted the meaning of some absurd statements by obscure monks.

1. I COME now to an examination of what the scholastic sophists teach concerning repentance. This I will do as briefly as possible ; for I have no intention to take up every point, lest this work, which I am desirous to frame as a compendium of doctrine, should exceed

all bounds. They have managed to envelop a matter, otherwise not
much involved, in so many perplexities, that it will be difficult to
find an outlet if once you get plunged but a little way into their mire.
And, first, in giving a definition, they plainly show they never understood what repentance means. For they fasten on some expressions
in the writings of the Fathers which are very far from expressing the
nature of repentance. For instance, that to *repent* is to deplore past
sins and not commit what is to be deplored. Again, that it is to
bewail past evils, and not again to do what is to be bewailed. Again,
that it is a kind of grieving revenge, punishing in itself what it
grieves to have committed. Again, that it is sorrow of heart
and bitterness of soul for the evils which the individual has committed, or to which he has consented.[1] Supposing we grant
that these things were well said by Fathers (though, if one were
inclined to dispute, it were not difficult to deny it), they were
not, however, said with the view of describing repentance, but
only of exhorting penitents not again to fall into the same faults
from which they had been delivered. But if all descriptions of this
kind are to be converted into definitions, there are others which have
as good a title to be added. For instance, the following sentence of
Chrysostom: " Repentance is a medicine for the cure of sin, a gift
bestowed from above, an admirable virtue, a grace surpassing the
power of laws." Moreover, the doctrine which they[2] afterwards
deliver is somewhat worse than their definition. For they are so
keenly bent on external exercises, that all you can gather from immense volumes[3] is, that repentance is a discipline, and austerity,
which serves partly to subdue the flesh, partly to chasten and punish
sins: of internal renovation of mind, bringing with it true amendment of life, there is a strange silence.[4] No doubt, they talk much
of contrition and attrition, torment the soul with many scruples, and
involve it in great trouble and anxiety; but when they seem to have
deeply wounded the heart, they cure all its bitterness by a slight
sprinkling of ceremonies. Repentance thus shrewdly defined, they
divide into contrition of the heart, confession of the mouth, and satisfaction of works.[5] This is not more logical than the definition,
though they would be thought to have spent their whole lives in
framing syllogisms.[6] But if any one argues from the definition (a

1 The first definition is that of Gregory, and is contained Sentent. Lib. iv. Dist. 14,
c. 1.   The second, which is that of Ambrose, is given same place, and also Decret. Dist.
3, de Pœnitentia C. Pœnit. Prior. The third is Augustine's, as stated in the same
place, and C. Pœnit. Poster. The fourth is from Ambrose, and is given Dist. 1, de
Pœnit. C. Vera Pœnitentia.
2 French, " Ces bons glosateurs;"—these worthy glossers.
3 Latin, " Immensis voluminibus."—French, " Leur gros bobulaire de livres;"—
their large lumbering books.
4 Latin, " Mirum silentium."—French, " Il n'en est nulles nouuelles en leur quar-
tier;"—there are no news in their quarter.
5 Sent. Lib. iv. Dist. 16, cap. 1; De Pœnit. Dist. 1; C. Perfecta Pœnit.
6 French, " Combien qu'ils n'estudient autre chose en toute leur vie que la Dialecti-
que, que est l'art de definir et partir;"—although they study nought else during their
whole life but Dialectics, which is the art of defining and dividing.

mode of argument prevalent with dialecticians) that a man may
weep over his past sins, and not commit things that cause weeping;
may bewail past evils, and not commit things that are to be bewailed;
may punish what he is grieved for having committed, though he
does not confess it with the mouth,—how will they defend their
division? For if he may be a true penitent and not confess, repentance can exist without confession. If they answer, that this division
refers to repentance regarded as a sacrament, or is to be understood
of repentance in its most perfect form, which they do not comprehend
in their definitions, the mistake does not rest with me: let them
blame themselves for not defining more purely and clearly. When
any matter is discussed, I certainly am dull enough to refer everything to the definition as the hinge and foundation of the whole discussion. But granting that this is a licence which masters have, let
us now survey the different parts in their order. In omitting as
frivolous several things which they vend with solemn brow as
mysteries, I do it not from ignorance. It were not very difficult to
dispose of all those points which they plume themselves on their
acuteness and subtilty in discussing: but I consider it a sacred duty
not to trouble the reader to no purpose with such absurdities. It is
certainly easy to see from the questions which they move and agitate,
and in which they miserably entangle themselves, that they are prating of things they know not. Of this nature are the following:
Whether repentance of one sin is pleasing to God, while there is an
obstinate adherence to other sins. Again, whether punishments
divinely inflicted are available for satisfaction. Again, whether repentance can be several times repeated for mortal sins, whereas they
grossly and wickedly define that daily repentance has to do with none
but venial sins. In like manner, with gross error, they greatly
torment themselves with a saying of Jerome, that repentance is a
second plank after shipwreck.[1] Herein they show that they have
never awoke from brutish stupor, so as to obtain a distant view of
the thousandth part of their sins.

2. I would have my readers to observe, that the dispute here
relates not to a matter of no consequence;[2] but to one of the most
important of all—viz. the forgiveness of sins. For while they require three things in repentance—viz. compunction of heart, confession of the mouth, and satisfaction of work[3]—they at the same time
teach that these are necessary to obtain the pardon of sins. If there
is anything in the whole compass of religion which it is of importance

---

1 Latin, "Secundam tabulam post naufragium."—French, "Une seconde planche,
sur laquelle celui que estoit pour perir en la mer, nage pour venir au port;"—a second
plank on which he who was on the point of perishing in the sea swims to gain the
harbour.
2 Latin, "De asini umbra rixam."—French, "En un combat frivole;"—engaged in
a frivolous combat.
3 Luther (adv. Bullam Antichristi, Art. vi.) shows that those who set down these
three parts of repentance, speak neither according to Scripture nor the ancient Fathers.

to us to know, this certainly is one of the most important—viz. to perceive and rightly hold by what means, what rule, what terms, with what facility or difficulty, forgiveness of sins may be obtained. Unless our knowledge here is clear and certain, our conscience can have no rest at all, no peace with God, no confidence or security, but is continually trembling, fluctuating, boiling, and distracted; dreads, hates, and shuns the presence of God. But if forgiveness of sins depends on the conditions to which they bind it, nothing can be more wretched and deplorable than our situation. *Contrition* they represent as the first step in obtaining pardon; and they exact it as due, that is, full and complete: meanwhile, they decide not when one may feel secure of having performed this contrition in due measure. I admit that we are bound strongly and incessantly to urge every man bitterly to lament his sins, and thereby stimulate himself more and more to dislike and hate them. For this is the "repentance to salvation not to be repented of" (2 Cor. vii. 10). But when such bitterness of sorrow is demanded as may correspond to the magnitude of the offence, and be weighed in the balance with confidence of pardon, miserable consciences are sadly perplexed and tormented when they see that the contrition due for sin is laid upon them, and yet that they have no measure of what is due, so as to enable them to determine that they have made full payment. If they say we are to do what in us lies, we are always brought back to the same point;[1] for when will any man venture to promise himself that he has done his utmost in bewailing sin? Therefore, when consciences, after a lengthened struggle and long contests with themselves, find no haven in which they may rest, as a means of alleviating their condition in some degree, they extort sorrow and wring out tears, in order to perfect their contrition.

3. If they say that this is calumny on my part, let them come forward and point out a single individual who, by this doctrine of contrition, has not either been driven to despair, or has not, instead of true, opposed pretended fear to the justice of God. We have elsewhere observed, that forgiveness of sins never can be obtained without repentance, because none but the afflicted, and those wounded by a consciousness of sins, can sincerely implore the mercy of God; but we, at the same time, added, that repentance cannot be the cause of the forgiveness of sins: and we also did away with that torment of souls—the dogma that it must be performed as due. Our doctrine was, that the soul looked not to its own compunction or its own tears, but fixed both eyes on the mercy of God alone. Only we observed, that those who labour and are heavy laden are called by Christ, seeing he was sent " to preach good tidings to the meek;" " to bind up the broken-hearted; to proclaim liberty to the captives, and the opening of the prison to them that are bound;" "to comfort all that

---

[1] French, "Nous tournerons toujours en un même circuit";—we shall always revolve in the same circle.

mourn."[1] Hence the Pharisees were excluded, because, full of their own righteousness, they acknowledged not their own poverty; and despisers, because, regardless of the divine anger, they sought no remedy for their wickedness. Such persons neither labour nor are heavy laden, are not broken-hearted, bound, nor in prison. But there is a great difference between teaching that forgiveness of sins is merited by a full and complete contrition (which the sinner never can give), and instructing him to hunger and thirst after the mercy of God, that recognising his wretchedness, his .turmoil, weariness, and captivity, you may show him where he should seek refreshment, rest, and liberty; in fine, teach him in his humility to give glory to God.

4. *Confession* has ever been a subject of keen contest between the Canonists and the Scholastic Theologians; the former contending that confession is of divine authority—the latter insisting, on the contrary, that it is merely enjoined by ecclesiastical constitution. In this contest great effrontery has been displayed by the Theologians, who have corrupted and violently wrested every passage of Scripture they have quoted in their favour.[2] And when they saw that even thus they could not gain their object, those who wished to be thought particularly acute had recourse to the evasion that confession is of divine authority in regard to the substance, but that it afterwards received its form from positive enactment. Thus the silliest of these quibblers refer the citation to divine authority, from its being said, " Adam, where art thou ?" (Gen. iii. 9, 12) ; and also the exception from Adam having replied as if excepting, " The woman whom thou gavest to be with me," &c. ; but say that the form of both was appointed by civil law. Let us see by what arguments they prove that this confession, formed or unformed, is a divine commandment. The Lord, they say, sent the lepers to the priests (Matth. viii. 4). What? did he send them to confession ? Who ever heard tell that the Levitical priests were appointed to hear confession ? Here they resort to allegory. The priests were appointed by the Mosaic law to discern between leper and leper : sin is spiritual leprosy ; therefore it belongs to the priests to decide upon it. Before I answer, I would ask, in passing, why, if this passage makes them judges of spiritual leprosy, they claim the cognisance of natural and carnal leprosy ? This, forsooth, is not to play upon Scripture ![3] The law gives the cognisance of leprosy to the Levitical priests : let us usurp this to ourselves. Sin is spiritual leprosy : let us also have cognisance of sin. I now give my answer : There being a change of the priesthood, there must of necessity be a change of the law. All the sacer-

[1] Matth. xi. 28 ; Is. lxi. 1 ; Luke iv. 18.

[2] Erasmus, in a letter to the Augustine Steuchus in 1531, while flattering, at the same time laughs at him, for thinking that the fifth chapter of Numbers sufficiently proves, in opposition to Luther, that auricular confession is of God.

[3] French, " N'est ce pas bien se jouer des Escritures, de les tourner en ceste façon ?" —is it not indeed to make game of Scripture, to turn it in this fashion ?

dotal functions were transferred to Christ, and in him fulfilled and ended (Heb. vii. 12). To him alone, therefore, all the rights and honours of the priesthood have been transferred: If they are so fond then of hunting out allegories, let them set Christ before them as the only priest, and place full and universal jurisdiction on his tribunal: this we will readily admit. Besides, there is an incongruity in their allegory: it classes a merely civil enactment among ceremonies. Why, then, does Christ send the lepers to the priests? Lest the priests should be charged with violating the law, which ordained that the person cured of leprosy should present himself before the priest, and be purified by the offering of a sacrifice, he orders the lepers who had been cleansed to do what the law required. " Go and show thyself to the priest, and offer for thy cleansing according as Moses commanded for a testimony unto them " (Luke v. 14). And assuredly this miracle would be a testimony to them: they had pronounced them lepers; they now pronounce them cured. Whether they would or not, they are forced to become witnesses to the miracles of Christ. Christ allows them to examine the miracle, and they cannot deny it: yet, as they still quibble, they have need of a testimony. So it is elsewhere said, " This gospel of the kingdom shall be preached in all the world, for a witness unto all nations" (Matth. xxiv. 14). Again, " Ye shall be brought before governors and kings for my sake, for a testimony against them and the Gentiles " (Matth. x. 18); that is, in order that, in the judgment of God, they might be more fully convicted. But if they prefer taking the view of Chrysostom (Hom. xii. de Muliere Cananæa), he shows that this was done by Christ for the sake of the Jews also, that he might not be regarded as a violator of the law. But we are ashamed to appeal to the authority of any man in a matter so clear, when Christ declares that he left the legal right of the priests entire, as professed enemies of the Gospel, who were always intent on making a clamour if their mouths were not stopped. Wherefore, let the Popish priests, in order to retain this privilege, openly make common cause with those whom it was necessary to restrain, by forcible means, from speaking evil of Christ.[1] For there is here no reference to his true ministers.

5. They draw their second argument from the same fountain,—I mean allegory; as if allegories were of much avail in confirming any doctrine. But, indeed, let them avail, if those which I am able to produce are not more specious than theirs. They say, then, that the Lord, after raising Lazarus, commanded his disciples to " loose him and let him go " (John xi. 44). Their first statement is untrue: we no where read that the Lord said this to the disciples; and it is much more probable that he spoke to the Jews who were standing by, that from there being no suspicion of fraud the miracle might be more

---

1 The French is, " Car ce que Jesus Christ laisse aux Prestres de la loy, n'appartient en rien à ses vrais ministres;"—for that which Jesus Christ leaves to the Priests, belongs not in any respect to his true ministers.

manifest, and his power might be the more conspicuous from his raising the dead without touching him, by a mere word. In the same way, I understand that our Lord, to leave no ground of suspicion to the Jews, wished them to roll back the stone, feel the stench, perceive the sure signs of death, see him rise by the mere power of a word, and first handle him when alive. And this is the view of Chrysostom (Serm. C. Jud. Gent. et Hæret.). But granting that it was said to the disciples, what can they gain by it? That the Lord gave the apostles the power of loosing? How much more aptly and dexterously might we allegorise and say, that by this symbol the Lord designed to teach his followers to loose those whom he raises up; that is, not to bring to remembrance the sins which he himself had forgotten not to condemn as sinners those whom he had acquitted, not still to upbraid those whom he had pardoned, not to be stern and severe in punishing, while he himself was merciful and ready to forgive. Certainly nothing should more incline us to pardon than the example of the Judge who threatens that he will be inexorable to the rigid and inhumane. Let them go now and vend their allegories.[1]

6. They now come to closer quarters, while they support their view by passages of Scripture which they think clearly in their favour.[2] Those who came to John's baptism confessed their sins, and James bids us confess our sins one to another (James v. 16). It is not strange that those who wished to be baptised confessed their sins. It has already been mentioned, that John preached the baptism of repentance, baptised with water unto repentance. Whom then could he baptise, but those who confessed that they were sinners? Baptism is a symbol of the forgiveness of sins; and who could be admitted to receive the symbol but sinners acknowledging themselves as such? They therefore confessed their sins that they might be baptised. Nor without good reason does James enjoin us to confess our sins one to another. But if they would attend to what immediately follows, they would perceive that this gives them little support. The words are, "Confess your sins one to another, and pray one for another." He joins together mutual confession and mutual prayer. If, then, we are to confess to priests only, we are also to pray for them only. What? It would even follow from the words of James, that priests alone can confess. In saying that we are to confess mutually, he must be addressing those only who can hear the confession of others. He says, ἀλλήολυς, *mutually*, *by turns*, or, if they prefer it, *reciprocally*. But those only can confess reciprocally who are fit to hear confession. This being a privilege which they bestow upon priests only, we also leave them the office of confessing to each other. Have done then with such frivolous absurdities, and let us receive the true meaning of the

---

1 French, "Qu'ils voisent maintenant, et facent un bouclier de leur allegories;"— let them go now and make a buckler of their allegories,
2 Augustin. Epist. 54.

apostle, which is plain and simple; *first*, That we are to deposit our infirmities in the breasts of each other, with the view of receiving mutual counsel, sympathy, and comfort; and, *secondly*, That mutually conscious of the infirmities of our brethren, we are to pray to the Lord for them. Why then quote James against us who so earnestly insist on acknowledgment of the divine mercy? No man can acknowledge the mercy of God without previously confessing his own misery. Nay, we pronounce every man to be anathema who does not confess himself a sinner before God, before his angels, before the Church; in short, before all men. " The Scripture hath concluded all under sin," "that every mouth may be stopped, and all the world may become guilty before God," that God alone may be justified and exalted (Gal. iii. 22; Rom. iii. 9, 19).

7. I wonder at their effrontery in venturing to maintain that the confession of which they speak is of divine authority. We admit that the use of it is very ancient; but we can easily prove that at one time it was free. It certainly appears, from their own records, that no law or constitution respecting it was enacted before the days of Innocent III. Surely if there had been a more ancient law they would have fastened on it, instead of being satisfied with the decree of the Council of Lateran, and so making themselves ridiculous even to children. In other matters, they hesitate not to coin fictitious decrees, which they ascribe to the most ancient Councils, that they may blind the eyes of the simple by veneration for antiquity. In this instance it has not occurred to them to practise this deception, and hence, themselves being witnesses, three centuries have not yet elapsed since the bridle was put, and the necessity of confession imposed by Innocent III. And to say nothing of the time, the mere barbarism of the terms used destroys the authority of the law. For when these worthy fathers enjoin that every person of *both sexes* (utriusque sexus) must once a-year confess his sins to his own priest, men of wit humorously object that the precept binds hermaphrodites only, and has no application to any one who is either a male or a female. A still grosser absurdity has been displayed by their disciples, who are unable to explain what is meant by one's own priest (proprius sacerdos). Let all the hired ravers of the Pope babble as they may,[1] we hold that Christ is not the author of this law, which compels men to enumerate their sins; nay, that twelve hundred years elapsed after the resurrection of Christ before any such law was made, and that, consequently, this tyranny was not introduced until piety and doctrine were extinct, and pretended pastors had usurped to themselves unbridled licence. There is clear evidence in historians, and other ancient writers, to show that this was a politic discipline introduced by bishops, not a law enacted by Christ or the

---

[1] French, " Quoy que tous les advocats et procureurs du Pape, et tous les caphars qu'il a à louage gazouillent;"—whatever all the advocates and procurators of the Pope, and all the caphars whom he has in his pay may gabble.

Apostles. Out of many I will produce only one passage, which will be no obscure proof. Sozomen[1] relates,[2] that this constitution of the bishops was carefully observed in the Western churches, but especially at Rome; thus intimating that it was not the universal custom of all churches. He also says, that one of the presbyters was specially appointed to take charge of this duty. This abundantly confutes their falsehood as to the keys being given to the whole priesthood indiscriminately for this purpose, since the function was not common to all the priests, but specially belonged to the one priest whom the bishop had appointed to it. He it was (the same who at present in each of the cathedral churches has the name of pœnitentiary) who had cognisance of offences which were more heinous, and required to be rebuked for the sake of example. He afterwards adds, that the same custom extited at Constantinpole, until a certain matron, while prentending to confess, was discovered to have used it as a cloak to cover her intercourse with a deacon. In consequence of that crime, Nectarious, the bishop of that church—a man famous for learning and sanctity—abolished the custom of confessing. Here, then, let these asses prick up their ears. If auricular confession was a divine law, how could Nectarius have dared to abolish or remodel it? Nectarius, a holy man of God, approved by the suffrage of all antiquity, will they charge with heresy and schism? With the same vote they will condemn the church of Constantinople, in which Sozomen affirms that the custom of confessing was not only disguised for a time, but even in his own memory abolished. Nay, let them charge with defection, not only Constantinople, but all the Eastern churches, which (if they say true) disregarded an inviolable law enjoined on all Christians.

8. This abrogation is clearly attested in so many passages by Chrysostom, who lived at Constantinople, and was himself prelate of the church, that it is strange they can venture to maintain the contrary: "Tell your sins," says he, that you may efface them: if you blush to tell another what sins you have committed, tell them daily in your soul. I say not, tell them to your fellow-servant who may upbraid you, but tell them to God who cures them. Confess your sins upon your bed, that your conscience may there daily recognise its iniquities." Again, "Now, however, it is not necessary to confess before witnesses; let the examination of your faults be made in your own thought: let the judgment be without a witness: let God alone see you confessing." Again, "I do not lead you publicly into the view of your fellow-servants; I do not force you to disclose your sins to men; review and lay open your conscience before God. Show your wounds to the Lord, the best of physicians, and seek medicine from him. Show to him who upbraids not, but cures most kindly." Again, "Certainly tell it not to man lest he upbraid you. Nor must you

---

1 The French adds, "l'un des auteurs de l'Histoire Ecclesiastique;"—one of the authors of the Ecclesiastical History.
2 Eccles Hist. Lib. viii. cap. 17, et Trepont. Hist. Lib. ix.

confess to your fellow-servant, who may make it public; but show your wounds to the Lord, who takes care of you, who is kind and can cure." He afterwards introduces God speaking thus: "I oblige you not to come into the midst of a theatre, and have many witnesses; tell your sins to me alone in private, that I may cure the ulcer."[1] Shall we say that Chrysostom, in writing these and similar passages, carried his presumption so far as to free the consciences of men from those chains with which they are bound by the divine law? By no means; but knowing that it was not at all prescribed by the word of God, he dares not exact it as necessary.

9. But that the whole matter may be more plainly unfolded, we shall first honestly state the nature of confession as delivered in the word of God, and thereafter subjoin their inventions—not all of them indeed (who could drink up that boundless sea?), but those only which contain a summary of their secret confession. Here I am grieved to mention how frequently the old interpreter [2] has rendered the word *confess* instead of *praise*, a fact notorious to the most illiterate, were it not fitting to expose their effrontery in transferring to their tyrannical edict what was written concerning the praises of God. To prove that confession has the effect of exhilarating the mind, they obtrude the passage in the psalm, "with the voice of joy and praise" (Vulgate, *confessionis*) (Ps. xlii. 4). But if such a metamorphosis is valid, anything may be made of anything. But, as they have lost all shame, let pious readers reflect how, by the just vengeance of God, they have been given over to a reprobate mind, that their audacity may be the more detestable. If we are disposed to acquiesce in the simple doctrine of Scripture, there will be no danger of our being misled by such glosses. There one method of confessing is prescribed; since it is the Lord who forgives, forgets, and wipes away sins, to him let us confess them, that we may obtain pardon. He is the physician, therefore, let us show our wounds to him. He is hurt and offended, let us ask peace of him. He is the discerner of the heart, and knows all our thoughts; let us hasten to pour out our hearts before him. He it is, in fine, who invites sinners; let us delay not to draw near to him. " I acknowledge my sin unto thee," says David; "and mine iniquity have I not hid. I said, I will confess my transgressions unto the Lord; and thou forgavest the iniquity of my sin" (Ps. xxxii. 5). Another specimen of David's confession is as follows: "Have mercy upon me, O God, according to thy loving kindness" (Ps. li. 1). The following is Daniel's confession: "We have sinned, and have committed iniquity, and have done wickedly, and have rebelled, even by departing from thy precepts and thy judgments" (Dan. ix. 5). Other examples everywhere occur in Scripture:

---

[1] Chrysost. Hom. ii. in Psal. 1. Serm. de Pœnit. et Confess. Hom. v. De Incomprehensibili Dei. Nat. cont. Anomeos. Item, Hom. iv. de Lazaro.

[2] Latin, "Vetus interpres."—French, "Le translateur tant Grec qui Latin;"—the Greek as well as Latin translator.

the quotation of them would almost fill a volume. "If we confess our sins," says John, "he is faithful and just to forgive us our sins" (1 John i. 9). To whom are we to confess? to him surely;—that is, we are to fall down before him with a grieved and humbled heart, and, sincerely accusing and condemning ourselves, seek forgiveness of his goodness and mercy.

10. He who has adopted this confession from the heart and as in the presence of God, will doubtless have a tongue ready to confess whenever there is occasion among men to publish the mercy of God. He will not be satisfied to whisper the secret of his heart for once into the ear of one individual, but will often, and openly, and in the hearing of the whole world, ingenuously make mention both of his own ignominy, and of the greatness and glory of the Lord. In this way David, after he was accused by Nathan, being stung in his conscience, confesses his sin before God and men. "I have sinned unto the Lord," says he (2 Sam. xii. 13); that is, I have now no excuse, no evasion; all must judge me a sinner; and that which I wished to be secret with the Lord must also be made manifest to men. Hence the secret confession which is made to God is followed by voluntary confession to men, whenever that is conducive to the divine glory or our humiliation. For this reason the Lord anciently enjoined the people of Israel that they should repeat the words after the priest, and make public confession of their iniquities in the temple; because he foresaw that this was a necessary help to enable each one to form a just idea of himself. And it is proper that, by confession of our misery, we should manifest the mercy of our God both among ourselves and before the whole world.

11. It is proper that this mode of confession should both be ordinary in the Church, and also be specially employed on extraordinary occasions, when the people in common happen to have fallen into any fault. Of this latter description we have an example in the solemn confession which the whole people made under the authority and guidance of Ezra and Nehemiah (Neh. i. 6, 7). For their long captivity, the destruction of the temple, and suppression of their religion, having been the common punishment of their defection, they could not make meet acknowledgment of the blessing of deliverance without previous confession of their guilt. And it matters not though in one assembly it may sometimes happen that a few are innocent, seeing that the members of a languid and sickly body cannot boast of soundness. Nay, it is scarcely possible that these few have not contracted some taint, and so bear part of the blame. Therefore, as often as we are afflicted with pestilence, or war, or famine, or any other calamity whatsoever, if it is our duty to betake ourselves to mourning, fasting, and other signs of guiltiness, confession also, on which all the others depend, is not to be neglected. That ordinary confession which the Lord has moreover expressly commended, no sober man, who has reflected on its usefulness, will venture to disap-

prove. Seeing that in every sacred assembly we stand in the view of God and angels, in what way should our service begin but in acknowledging our own unworthiness? But this you will say is done in every prayer; for as often as we pray for pardon, we confess our sins. I admit it. But if you consider how great is our carelessness, or drowsiness, or sloth, you will grant me that it would be a salutary ordinance if the Christian people were exercised in humiliation by some formal method of confession. For though the ceremony which the Lord enjoined on the Israelites belonged to the tutelage of the Law, yet the thing itself belongs in some respect to us also. And, indeed, in all well-ordered churches, in observance of an useful custom, the minister, each Lord's day, frames a formula of confession in his own name and that of the people, in which he makes a common confession of iniquity, and supplicates pardon from the Lord. In short, by this key a door of prayer is opened privately for each, and publicly for all.

12. Two other forms of private confession are approved by Scripture. The one is made on our own account, and to it reference is made in the passage in James, "Confess your sins one to another" (James v. 16); for the meaning is, that by disclosing our infirmities to each other, we are to obtain the aid of mutual counsel and consolation. The other is to be made for the sake of our neighbour, to appease and reconcile him if by our fault he has been in any respect injured. In the former, although James, by not specifying any particular individual into whose bosom we are to disburden our feelings, leaves us the free choice of confessing to any member of the church who may seem fittest; yet as for the most part pastors are to be supposed better qualified than others, our choice ought chiefly to fall upon them. And the ground of preference is, that the Lord, by calling them to the ministry, points them out as the persons by whose lips we are to be taught to subdue and correct our sins, and derive consolation from the hope of pardon. For as the duty of mutual admonition and correction is committed to all Christians, but is specially enjoined on ministers, so while we ought all to console each other mutually, and confirm each other in confidence in the divine mercy, we see that ministers, to assure our consciences of the forgiveness of sins, are appointed to be the witnesses and sponsors of it, so that they are themselves said to forgive sins and loose souls (Matth. xvi. 19; xviii. 18). When you hear this attributed to them, reflect that it is for your use. Let every believer, therefore, remember, that if in private he is so agonised and afflicted by a sense of his sins that he cannot obtain relief without the aid of others, it is his duty not to neglect the remedy which God provides for him—viz. to have recourse for relief to a private confession to his own pastor, and for consolation privately implore the assistance of him whose business it is, both in public and private, to solace the people of God with Gospel doctrine. But we are always to use moderation, lest in a matter as to

which God prescribes no certain rule, our consciences be burdened with a certain yoke. Hence it follows, first, that confession of this nature ought to be free so as not to be exacted of all, but only recommended to those who feel that they have need of it; and, secondly, even those who use it according to their necessity must neither be compelled by any precept, nor artfully induced to enumerate all their sins, but only in so far as they shall deem it for their interest, that they may obtain the full benefit of consolation. Faithful pastors, as they would both eschew tyranny in their ministry, and superstition in the people, must not only leave this liberty to churches, but defend and strenuously vindicate it.

13. Of the second form of confession, our Saviour speaks in Matthew. "If thou bring thy gift to the altar, and there remember that thy brother hath ought against thee; leave there thy gift before the altar; first be reconciled to thy brother, and then come and offer thy gift" (Matth. v. 23, 24). Thus love, which has been interrupted by our fault, must be restored by acknowledging and asking pardon for the fault. Under this head is included the confession of those who by their sin have given offence to the whole Church (*supra*, sec. 10). For if Christ attaches so much importance to the offence of one individual, that he forbids the sacrifice of all who have sinned in any respect against their brethren, until by due satisfaction they have regained their favour, how much greater reason is there that he, who by some evil example has offended the Church, should be reconciled to it by the acknowledgment of his fault? Thus the member of the Church of Corinth was restored to communion after he had humbly submitted to correction (2 Cor. ii. 6). This form of confession existed in the ancient Christian Church, as Cyprian relates: "They practise repentance," says he, "for a proper time, then they come to confession, and by the laying on of the hands of the bishop and clergy, are admitted to communion. Scripture knows nothing of any other form or method of confessing, and it belongs not to us to bind new chains upon consciences which Christ most strictly prohibits from being brought into bondage. Meanwhile, that the flock present themselves before the pastor whenever they would partake of the Holy Supper, I am so far from disapproving, that I am most desirous it should be everywhere observed. For both those whose conscience is hindered may thence obtain singular benefit, and those who require admonition thus afford an opportunity for it; provided always no countenance is given to tyranny and superstition."

14. The *power of the keys* has place in the three following modes of confession,—either when the whole Church, in a formal acknowledgment of its defects,[1] supplicates pardon; or when a private individual, who has given public offence by some notable delinquency, testifies his repentance; or when he who from disquiet of conscience

[1] As to the form of repentance enjoined by the primitive Church for more flagrant offences, see Book IV. chap i. sec. 29.

needs the aid of his minister, acquaints him with his infirmity. With regard to the reparation of offence, the case is different. For though in this also provision is made for peace of conscience, yet the principal object is to suppress hatred, and reunite brethren in the bond of peace. But the benefit of which I have spoken is by no means to be despised, that we may the more willingly confess our sins. For when the whole Church stands as it were at the bar of God, confesses her guilt, and finds her only refuge in the divine mercy, it is no common or light solace to have an ambassador of Christ present, invested with the mandate of reconciliation, by whom she may hear her absolution pronounced. Here the utility of the keys is justly commended when that embassy is duly discharged with becoming order and reverence. In like manner, when he who has as it were become an alien from the Church receives pardon, and is thus restored to brotherly unity, how great is the benefit of understanding that he is pardoned by those to whom Christ said, " Whose soever sins ye remit, they are remitted unto them" (John xx. 23). Nor is private absolution of less benefit or efficacy when asked by those who stand in need of a special remedy for their infirmity. It not seldom happens, that he who hears general promises which are intended for the whole congregation of the faithful, nevertheless remains somewhat in doubt, and is still disquieted in mind, as if his own remission were not yet obtained. Should this individual lay open the secret wound of his soul to his pastor, and hear these words of the Gospel specially addressed to him, "Son, be of good cheer ; thy sins be forgiven thee" (Matth. ix. 2),[1] his mind will feel secure, and escape from the trepidation with which it was previously agitated. But when we treat of the keys, we must always beware of dreaming of any power apart from the preaching of the Gospel. This subject will be more fully explained, when we come to treat of the government of the Church (Book IV. chap. xi. xii.). There we shall see, that whatever privilege of binding and loosing Christ has bestowed on his Church is annexed to the word. This is especially true with regard to the ministry of the keys, the whole power of which consists in this, that the grace of the Gospel is publicly and privately sealed on the minds of believers by means of those whom the Lord has appointed ; and the only method in which this can be done is by preaching.

15. What say the Roman theologians ? That all persons of both sexes,[2] so soon as they shall have reached the years of discretion, must, once a-year at least, confess all their sins to their own priest ; that the sin is not discharged unless the resolution to confess has been firmly conceived ; that if this resolution is not carried into effect when

[1] The French is, " Et que le Pasteur addressant sa parole à lui, l'asseure comme lui appliquant en particulier la doctrine generale ;"—and when the Pastor, addressing his discourse to him, assures him as applying the general doctrine to him in particular.

[2] " C Omnis utriusque sexus ;"—every one of both sexes. Innocent's decree is in the Lateran Council, De Summa Trinitate et Fide Cathol. It is also given Sent. Lib. iv. Dist. 14, cap. 2, et Dist. 18. cap. 2.

an opportunity offers, there is no entrance into Paradise; that the priest, moreover, has the power of the keys, by which he can loose and bind the sinner; because the declaration of Christ is not in vain: "Whatsoever ye shall bind on earth shall be bound in heaven" (Matth. xviii. 18). Concerning this power, however, they wage a fierce war among themselves. Some say there is only one key essentially—viz. the power of binding and loosing; that knowledge, indeed, is requisite for the proper use of it, but only as an accessory, not as essentially inherent in it. Others, seeing that this gave too unrestrained licence, have imagined two keys—viz. discernment and power. Others, again, seeing that the licence of priests was curbed by such restraint, have forged other keys (*infra*, sec. 21), the authority of discerning to be used in defining, and the power to carry their sentences into execution; and to these they add knowledge as a counsellor. This binding and loosing, however, they do not venture to interpret simply, to forgive and wipe away sins, because they hear the Lord proclaiming by the prophet, "I, even I, am the Lord; and beside me there is no saviour." "I, even I, am he that blotteth out thy transgressions" (Isaiah xliii. 11, 25). But they say it belongs to the priest to declare who are bound or loosed, and whose sins are remitted or retained; to declare, moreover, either by confession, when he absolves and retains sins, or by sentence, when he excommunicates or admits to communion in the Sacraments. Lastly, perceiving that the knot is not yet untied, because it may always be objected that persons are often undeservedly bound and loosed, and therefore not bound or loosed in heaven; as their ultimate resource, they answer, that the conferring of the keys must be taken with limitation, because Christ has promised that the sentence of the priest, properly pronounced, will be approved at his judgment-seat according as the bound or loosed asked what they merited. They say, moreover, that those keys which are conferred by bishops at ordination were given by Christ to all priests, but that the free use of them is with those only who discharge ecclesiastical functions; that with priests excommunicated or suspended the keys themselves indeed remain, but tied and rusty. Those who speak thus may justly be deemed modest and sober compared with others, who on a new anvil have forged new keys, by which they say that the treasury of heaven is locked up: these we shall afterwards consider in their own place (chap. v. sec. 2).

16. To each of these views I will briefly reply. As to their binding the souls of believers by their laws, whether justly or unjustly, I say nothing at present, as it will be seen at the proper place; but their enacting it as a law, that all sins are to be enumerated; their denying that sin is discharged except under the condition that the resolution to confess has been firmly conceived; their pretence that there is no admission into Paradise if the opportunity of confession has been neglected, are things which it is impossible to bear. Are all sins to be enumerated? But David, who, I presume, had honestly pondered

with himself as to the confession of his sins, exclaimed, "Who can understand his errors? cleanse thou me from secret faults" (Ps. xix. 12); and in another passage, "Mine iniquities are gone over my head: as a heavy burden they are too heavy for me" (Ps. xxxviii. 4). He knew how deep was the abyss of our sins, how numerous the forms of wickedness, how many heads the hydra carried, how long a tail it drew. Therefore, he did not sit down to make a catalogue, but from the depth of his distress cried unto the Lord, "I am overwhelmed, and buried, and sore vexed; the gates of hell have encircled me: let thy right hand deliver me from the abyss into which I am plunged, and from the death which I am ready to die." Who can now think of a computation of his sins when he sees David's inability to number his?

17. By this ruinous procedure, the souls of those who were affected with some sense of God have been most cruelly racked. First, they betook themselves to calculation, proceeding according to the formula given by the Schoolmen, and dividing their sins into boughs, branches, twigs, and leaves; then they weighed the qualities, quantities, and circumstances; and in this way, for some time, matters proceeded. But after they had advanced farther, when they looked around, nought was seen but sea and sky; no road, no harbour. The longer the space they ran over, a longer still met the eye; nay, lofty mountains began to rise, and there seemed no hope of escape; none at least till after long wanderings. They were thus brought to a dead halt, till at length the only issue was found in despair. Here these cruel murderers, to ease the wounds which they had made, applied certain fomentations. Every one was to do his best. But new cares again disturbed, nay, new torments excruciated their souls. "I have not spent enough of time; I have not exerted myself sufficiently: many things I have omitted through negligence: forgetfulness proceeding from want of care is not excusable." Then new drugs were supplied to alleviate their pains. "Repent of your negligence; and provided it is not done supinely, it will be pardoned." All these things, however, could not heal the wound, being not so much alleviations of the sore as poison besmeared with honey, that its bitterness might not at once offend the taste, but penetrate to the vitals before it could be detected. The dreadful voice, therefore, was always heard pealing in their ears, "Confess all your sins," and the dread thus occasioned could not be pacified without sure consolation. Here let my readers consider whether it be possible to take an account of the actions of a whole year, or even to collect the sins committed in a single day, seeing every man's experience convinces him that at evening, in examining the faults of that single day, memory gets confused, so great is the number and variety presented. I am not speaking of dull and heartless hypocrites, who, after animadverting on three or four of their grosser offences, think the work finished; but of the true worshippers of God, who, after they have performed their examination,

feeling themselves overwhelmed, still add the words of John : " If our heart condemn us, God is greater than our heart, and knoweth all things" (1 John iii. 20) ; and, therefore, tremble at the thought of that Judge whose knowledge far surpasses our comprehension.

18. Though a good part of the world rested in these soothing suggestions, by which this fatal poison was somewhat tempered, it was not because they thought that God was satisfied, or they had quite satisfied themselves ; it was rather like an anchor cast out in the middle of the deep, which for a little interrupts the navigation, or a weary, worn-out traveller, who lies down by the way.[1] I give myself no trouble in proving the truth of this fact. Every one can be his own witness. I will mention generally what the nature of this law is. First, The observance of it is simply impossible ; and hence its only result is to destroy, condemn, confound, to plunge into ruin and despair. Secondly, By withdrawing sinners from a true sense of their sins, it makes them hypocritical, and ignorant both of God and themselves. For, while they are wholly occupied with the enumeration of their sins, they lose sight of that lurking hydra, their secret iniquities and internal defilements, the knowledge of which would have made them sensible of their misery. But the surest rule of confession is, to acknowledge and confess our sins to be an abyss so great as to exceed our comprehension. On this rule we see the confession of the publican was formed, " God be merciful to me, a sinner" (Luke xviii. 13); as if he had said, How great, how very great a sinner, how utterly sinful I am ! the extent of my sins I can neither conceive nor express. Let the depth of thy mercy ingulf the depth of sin ! What ! you will say, are we not to confess every single sin ? Is no confession acceptable to God but that which is contained in the words, " I am a sinner" ? Nay, our endeavour must rather be, as much as in us lies, to pour out our whole heart before the Lord. Nor are we only in one word to confess ourselves sinners, but truly and sincerely acknowledge ourselves as such ; to feel with our whole soul how great and various the pollutions of our sins are ; confessing not only that we are impure, but what the nature of our impurity is, its magnitude and its extent ; not only that we are debtors, but what the debts are which burden us, and how they were incurred ; not only that we are wounded, but how numerous and deadly are the wounds. When thus recognising himself, the sinner shall have poured out his whole heart before God, let him seriously and sincerely reflect that a greater number of sins still remains, and that their recesses are too deep for him thoroughly to penetrate. Accordingly, let him exclaim with

---

[1] The French is, " Mais comme les nautonniers fichans l'anchre au milieu de la mer, se reposent du trauail de leur navigation ; ou comme un pelerin lassé ou defaillant se sied au milieu de la voye pour reposer : en telle maniere ils prenoyent ce repos, combien qu'il ne leur fust suffisant;"—but as mariners casting anchor in the midst of the sea, repose from the toil of navigation ; or as a pilgrim, weary or faint, sits down in the middle of the way to rest himself : in this way they took this rest, though it was not sufficient for them.

David, "Who can understand his errors? cleanse thou me from
secret faults" (Ps. xix. 12). But when the Schoolmen affirm that
sins are not forgiven, unless the resolution to confess has been firmly
conceived, and that the gate of Paradise is closed on him who has
neglected the opportunity of confessing when offered, far be it from
us to concede this to them. The remission of sins is not different
now from what it has ever been. In all the passages in which we
read that sinners obtained forgiveness from God, we read not that
they whispered into the ear of some priest.[1] Indeed, they could not
then confess, as priests were not then confessionaries, nor did the con-
fessional itself exist. And for many ages afterwards, this mode of
confession, by which sins were forgiven on this condition, was unheard
of. But not to enter into a long discussion, as if the matter were
doubtful, the word of God, which abideth for ever, is plain, "When
the wicked shall turn away from all his sins that he hath committed,
and keep all my statutes, and do that which is lawful and right, he
shall surely live, he shall not die" (Ezek. xviii. 21). He who presumes to add to this declaration binds not sins, but the mercy of God.
When they contend that judgment cannot be given unless the case
is known, the answer is easy, that they usurp the right of judging,
being only self-created judges. And it is strange, how confidently
they lay down principles, which no man of sound mind will admit.
They give out, that the office of binding and loosing has been committed to them, as a kind of jurisdiction annexed to the right of
inquiry. That the jurisdiction was unknown to the Apostles their
whole doctrine proclaims. Nor does it belong to the priest to know
for certainty whether or not a sinner is loosed, but to Him from whom
acquittal is asked; since he who only hears can ever know whether
or not the enumeration is full and complete. Thus there would be
no absolution, without restricting it to the words of him who is to be
judged. We may add, that the whole system of loosing depends on
faith and repentance, two things which no man can know of another,
so as to pronounce sentence. It follows, therefore, that the certainty
of binding and loosing is not subjected to the will of an earthly judge,
because the minister of the word, when he duly executes his office,
can only acquit conditionally, when, for the sake of the sinner, he
repeats the words, "Whose soever sins ye remit;" lest he should
doubt of the pardon, which, by the command and voice of God, is
promised to be ratified in heaven.

19. It is not strange, therefore, that we condemn that auricular
confession, as a thing pestilent in its nature, and in many ways injurious to the Church, and desire to see it abolished. But if the
thing were in itself indifferent, yet, seeing it is of no use or benefit,

---

[1] "Tous ceux que nous lisons avoir obtenu de Christ la remission de leurs pechez,
ne sont pas dits s'etre confessés à l'aureille de quelque Messire Jean;"—None of whom
we read as having obtained the forgiveness of their sins from Christ, are said to have
confessed in the ear of some Mess John.

and has given occasion to so much impiety, blasphemy, and error, who does not think that it ought to be immediately abolished? They enumerate some of its uses, and boast of them as very beneficial, but they are either fictitious or of no importance. One thing they specially commend, that the blush of shame in the penitent is a severe punishment, which makes him more cautious for the future, and anticipates divine punishment, by his punishing himself. As if a man was not sufficiently humbled with shame when brought under the cognisance of God at his supreme tribunal. Admirable proficiency—if we cease to sin because we are ashamed to make one man acquainted with it, and blush not at having God as the witness of our evil conscience! The assertion, however, as to the effect of shame, is most unfounded, for we may everywhere see, that there is nothing which gives men greater confidence and licence in sinning than the idea, that after making confession to priests, they can *wipe their lips and say, I have not done it.* And not only do they during the whole year become bolder in sin, but, secure against confession for the remainder of it, they never sigh after God, never examine themselves, but continue heaping sins upon sins, until, as they suppose, they get rid of them all at once. And when they have got rid of them, they think they are disburdened of their load, and imagine they have deprived God of the right of judging, by giving it to the priest; have made God forgetful, by making the priest conscious. Moreover, who is glad when he sees the day of confession approaching? Who goes with a cheerful mind to confess, and does not rather, as if he were dragged to prison with a rope about his neck, go unwillingly, and, as it were, struggling against it? with the exception, perhaps, of the priests themselves, who take a fond delight in the mutual narrative of their own misdeeds, as a kind of merry tales. I will not pollute my page by retailing the monstrous abominations with which auricular confession teems; I only say, that if that holy man (Nectarius, of whom *supra*, sec. 7) did not act unadvisedly, when for one rumour of whoredom he banished confession from his church, or rather from the memory of his people, the innumerable acts of prostitution, adultery, and incest, which it produces in the present day, warns us of the necessity of abolishing it.

20. As to the pretence of the confessionaries respecting the power of the keys, and their placing in it, so to speak, the sum and substance of their kingdom, we must see what force it ought to have. Were the keys, then (they ask), given without a cause? Was it said without a cause, "Whatsoever ye shall bind on earth shall be bound in heaven, and whatsoever ye shall loose on earth shall be loosed in heaven"? (Matth. xviii. 18.) Do we make void the word of Christ? I answer, that there was a weighty reason for giving the keys, as I lately explained, and will again show at greater length when I come to treat of Excommunication (Book IV. cap. 12). But what if I should cut off the handle for all such questions with one sword—

viz. that priests are neither vicars nor successors of the Apostles? But that also will be elsewhere considered (Book IV. 6). Now, at the very place where they are most desirous to fortify themselves, they erect a battering-ram, by which all their own machinations are overthrown. Christ did not give his Apostles the power of binding and loosing before he endued them with the Holy Spirit. I deny, therefore, that any man, who has not previously received the Holy Spirit, is competent to possess the power of the keys. I deny that any one can use the keys, unless the Holy Spirit precede, teaching and dictating what is to be done. They pretend, indeed, that they have the Holy Spirit, but by their works deny him; unless, indeed, we are to suppose that the Holy Spirit is some vain thing of no value, as they certainly do feign, but we will not believe them. With this engine they are completely overthrown; whatever be the door of which they boast of having the key, we must always ask, whether they have the Holy Spirit, who is arbiter and ruler of the keys? If they reply, that they have, we must again ask, whether the Holy Spirit can err? This they will not venture to say distinctly, although by their doctrine they indirectly insinuate it. Therefore, we must infer, that no priestlings have the power of the keys, because they everywhere and indiscriminately loose what the Lord was pleased should be bound, and bind what he has ordered to be loosed.

21. When they see themselves convicted on the clearest evidence, of loosing and binding worthy and unworthy without distinction, they lay claim to power without knowledge. And although they dare not deny that knowledge is requisite for the proper use, they still affirm that the power itself has been given to bad administrators. This, however, is the power, " Whatsoever ye shall bind on earth shall be bound in heaven, and whatsoever ye shall loose on earth shall be loosed in heaven." Either the promise of Christ must be false, or those who are endued with this power bind and loose properly. There is no room for the evasion, that the words of Christ are limited, according to the merits of him who is loosed or bound. We admit, that none can be bound or loosed but those who are worthy of being bound or loosed. But the preachers of the Gospel and the Church have the word by which they can measure this worthiness. By this word preachers of the Gospel can promise forgiveness of sins to all who are in Christ by faith, and can declare a sentence of condemnation against all, and upon all, who do not embrace Christ. In this word the Church declares, that " neither fornicators, nor idolators, nor adulterers," "nor thieves, nor covetous, nor drunkards, nor revilers, nor extortioners, shall inherit the kingdom of God" (1 Cor. vi. 9, 10). Such it binds in sure fetters. By the same word it looses and consoles the penitent. But what kind of power is it which knows not what is to be bound or loosed? You cannot bind or loose without knowledge. Why, then, do they say, that they absolve by authority given to them, when absolution is uncertain? As regards us, this

power is merely imaginary, if it cannot be used. Now, I hold, either that there is no use, or one so uncertain as to be virtually no use at all. For when they confess that a good part of the priests do not use the keys duly, and that power without the legitimate use is ineffectual, who is to assure me, that the one by whom I am loosed is a good dispenser of the keys? But if he is a bad one, what better has he given me than this nugatory dispensation,—What is to be bound or loosed in you I know not, since I have not the proper use of the keys; but if you deserve it, I absolve you? As much might be done, I say not by a laic, (since they would scarcely listen to such a statement), but by the Turk or the devil. For it is just to say, I have not the word of God, the sure rule for loosing, but authority has been given me to absolve you, if you deserve it. We see, therefore, what their object was, when they defined (see sec. 16) the keys as authority to discern and power to execute; and said, that knowledge is added as a counsellor, and counsels the proper use; their object was to reign libidinously and licentiously, without God and his word.

22. Should any one object, first, that the lawful ministers of Christ will be no less perplexed in the discharge of their duty, because the absolution, which depends on faith, will always be equivocal; and, secondly, that sinners will receive no comfort at all, or cold comfort, because the minister, who is not a fit judge of their faith, is not certain of their absolution, we are prepared with an answer. They say that no sins are remitted by the priest, but such sins as he is cognisant of; thus, according to them, remission depends on the judgment of the priest, and unless he accurately discriminate as to who are worthy of pardon, the whole procedure is null and void. In short, the power of which they speak is a jurisdiction annexed to examination, to which pardon and absolution are restricted. Here no firm footing can be found, nay, there is a profound abyss; because, where confession is not complete, the hope of pardon also is defective; next, the priest himself must necessarily remain in suspense, while he knows not whether the sinner gives a faithful enumeration of his sins; lastly, such is the rudeness and ignorance of priests, that the greater part of them are in no respect fitter to perform this office than a cobbler to cultivate the fields, while almost all the others have good reason to suspect their own fitness. Hence the perplexity and doubt as to the Popish absolution, from their choosing to found it on the person of the priest, and not on his person only, but on his knowledge, so that he can only judge of what is laid before him, investigated, and ascertained. Now, if any should ask at these good doctors, Whether the sinner is reconciled to God when some sins are remitted? I know not what answer they could give, unless that they should be forced to confess, that whatever the priest pronounces with regard to the remission of sins which have been enumerated to him will be unavailing, so long as others are not exempted from condemnation. On the

part of the penitent, again, it is hence obvious in what a state of pernicious anxiety his conscience will be held; because, while he leans on what they call the discernment of the priest, he cannot come to any decision from the word of God. From all these absurdities the doctrine which we deliver is completely free. For absolution is conditional, allowing the sinner to trust that God is propitious to him, provided he sincerely seek expiation in the sacrifice of Christ, and accept of the grace offered to him. Thus, he cannot err who, in the capacity of a herald, promulgates what has been dictated to him from the word of God. The sinner, again, can receive a clear and sure absolution when, in regard to embracing the grace of Christ, the simple condition annexed is in terms of the general rule of our Master himself,—a rule impiously spurned by the Papacy,—"According to your faith be it unto you" (Matth. ix. 29).

23. The absurd jargon which they make of the doctrine of Scripture concerning the power of the keys, I have promised to expose elsewhere; the proper place will be in treating of the Goverment of the Church (Book IV. c. 12). Meanwhile let the reader remember how absurdly they wrest to auricular and secret confession what was said by Christ partly of the preaching of the Gospel, and partly of excommunication. Wherefore, when they object that the power of loosing was given to the Apostles, and that this power priests exercise by remitting sins acknowledged to them, it is plain that the principle which they assume is false and frivolous: for the absolution which is subordinate to faith is nothing else than an evidence of pardon, derived from the free promise of the Gospel, while the other absolution, which depends on the discipline of the Church, has nothing to do with secret sins; but is more a matter of example for the purpose of removing the public offence given to the Church. As to their diligence in searching up and down for passages by which they may prove that it is not sufficient to confess sins to God alone, or to laymen, unless the priest take cognisance, it is vile and disgraceful. For when the ancient fathers advise sinners to disburden themselves to their pastor, we cannot understand them to refer to a recital which was not then in use. Then, so unfair are Lombard and others likeminded, that they seem intentionally to have devoted themselves to spurious books, that they might use them as a cloak to deceive the simple. They, indeed, acknowledge truly, that as forgiveness always accompanies repentance, no obstacle properly remains after the individual is truly penitent, though he may not have actually confessed; and, therefore, that the priest does not so much remit sins, as pronounce and declare that they are remitted; though in the term *declaring*, they insinuate a gross error, surrogating ceremony[1] in place of doctrine. But in pretending that he who has already obtained pardon before God is acquitted in the face of the Church, they

1 Latin simply, "ceremoniam." French, "la ceremonie de faire une croix sur le dos;"—the ceremony of making a cross upon the back

unseasonably apply to the special use of every individual, that which we have already said was designed for common discipline when the offence of a more heinous and notorious trangression was to be removed. Shortly after they pervert and destroy their previous moderation, by adding that there is another mode of remission—namely, by the infliction of penalty and satisfaction, in which they arrogate to their priests the right of dividing what God has everywhere promised to us entire. While He simply requires repentance and faith, their division or exception is altogether blasphemous. For it is just as if the priest, assuming the office of tribune, were to interfere with God,[1] and try to prevent him from admitting to his favour by his mere liberality any one who had not previously lain prostrate at the tribunicial bench, and there been punished.

24. The whole comes to this,[2] when they wish to make God the author of this fictitious confession their vanity is proved, as I have shown their falsehood in expounding the few passages which they cite. But while it is plain, that the law was imposed by men, I say that it is both tyrannical and insulting to God, who, in binding consciences to his word, would have them free from human rule. Then when confession is prescribed as necessary to obtain pardon, which God wished to be free, I say that the sacrilege is altogether intolerable, because nothing belongs more peculiarly to God than the forgiveness of sins, in which our salvation consists. I have, moreover, shown that this tyranny was introduced when the world was sunk in shameful barbarism.[3] Besides, I have proved that the law is pestiferous, inasmuch as when the fear of God exists, it plunges men into despair, and when there is security soothing itself with vain flattery, it blunts it the more. Lastly, I have explained that all the mitigations which they employ have no other tendency than to entangle, obscure, and corrupt the pure doctrine, and cloak their iniquities with deceitful colours.

25. In repentance they assign the third place to satisfaction, all their absurd talk as to which can be refuted in one word. They say,[4] that it is not sufficient for the penitent to abstain from past sins, and change his conduct for the better, unless he satisfy God for what he has done; and that there are many helps by which we may redeem sins, such as tears, fastings, oblations,[5] and offices of charity; that by them the Lord is to be propitiated; by them the

---

1 French, " Car cela vaut autant comme si les prestres se faisoyent contrerolleurs de Dieu;"—for that is as much as if the priests made themselves controllers of God.

2 See on the subject of this section, Calv. ad Concil. Trident. Also Vera Ecclesiæ Reformandæ Ratio, Epist. ad Sadoletum· Epist. adversus Theologos Parisienses. De Scandalis. De Necessitate Reformandæ Ecclesiæ, Lib. iv.

3 French, " une barbarie si vileine que rien plus;"—a barbarism so vile that nothing could be more so.

4 See Lombard, Sent. Lib. iv. Dist. 10, c. 4. C. Non sufficit. de Pœnit. C. (middle of same Dist.) C. Nullus (same Dist.). See also on the subject of satisfaction, *infra*, s. 29, and chap. xvi. 4.

5 The French adds, " aumosnes;"--alms.

debts due to divine justice are to be paid; by them our faults are to be compensated; by them pardon is to be deserved: for though in the riches of his mercy he has forgiven the guilt, he yet, as a just discipline, retains the penalty, and that this penalty must be bought off by satisfaction. The sum of the whole comes to this: that we indeed obtain pardon of our sins from the mercy of God, but still by the intervention of the merit of works, by which the evil of our sins is compensated, and due satisfaction made to divine justice. To such false views I oppose the free forgiveness of sins, one of the doctrines most clearly taught in Scripture.[1] First, what is forgiveness but a gift of mere liberality? A creditor is not said to forgive when he declares, by granting a discharge, that the money has been paid to him; but when, without any payment, through voluntary kindness he expunges the debt. And why is the term *gratis* (free) afterwards added, but to take away all idea of satisfaction? With what confidence, then, do they still set up their satisfactions, which are thus struck down as with a thunderbolt? What? When the Lord proclaims by Isaiah, "I, even I, am he that blotteth out thy transgressions for mine own sake, and will not remember thy sins," does he not plainly declare, that the cause and foundation of forgiveness is to be sought from his goodness alone? Besides, when the whole of Scripture bears this testimony to Christ, that through his name the forgiveness of sins is to be obtained (Acts x. 43), does it not plainly exclude all other names? How then do they teach that it is obtained by the name of satisfaction? Let them not deny that they attribute this to satisfactions, though they bring them in as subsidiary aids.[2] For when Scripture says, *by the name of Christ*, it means, that we are to bring nothing, pretend nothing of our own, but lean entirely on the recommendation of Christ. Thus Paul, after declaring that "God was in Christ reconciling the world unto himself, not imputing their trespasses unto them," immediately adds the reason and the method, "For he hath made him to be sin for us who knew no sin" (2 Cor. v. 19, 20).

26. But with their usual perverseness, they maintain that both the forgiveness of sins and reconciliation take place at once when we are received into the favour of God through Christ in baptism; that in lapses after baptism we must rise again by means of satisfactions; that the blood of Christ is of no avail unless in so far as it is dispensed by the keys of the Church. I speak not of a matter as to which there can be any doubt; for this impious dogma is declared in the plainest terms, in the writings not of one or two, but of the whole Schoolmen. Their master (Sent. Lib. iii. Dist. 9), after acknow-

---

[1] Isa. lii. 3; Rom. v. 8; Col. ii. 14; Tit. iii. 5.
[2] The French is, "Et ne faut pas qu'ils disent, que combien que les satisfactions en soyent moyens, neantmoins ce n'est pas en leur nom, mais au nom de Jesus Christ;" —and they must not say that though satisfactions are the means, nevertheless it is not in their name, but in the name of Jesus Christ.

ledging, according to the doctrine of Peter, that Christ "bare our sins in his own body on the tree" (1 Pet. ii. 24), immediately modifies the doctrine by introducing the exception, that in baptism all the temporal penalties of sin are relaxed; but that after baptism they are lessened by means of repentance, the cross of Christ and our repentance thus co-operating together. St John speaks very differently, "If any man sin, we have an advocate with the Father, Jesus Christ the righteous; and he is the propitiation for our sins." "I write unto you, little children, because your sins are forgiven you for his name's sake" (1 John ii. 1, 2, 12). He certainly is addressing believers, and while setting forth Christ as the propitiation for sins, shows them that there is no other satisfaction by which an offended God can be propitiated or appeased. He says not: God was once reconciled to you by Christ; now, seek other methods; but he makes him a perpetual advocate, who always, by his intercession, reinstates us in his Father's favour—a perpetual propitiation by which sins are expiated. For what was said by another John will ever hold true, "Behold the Lamb of God, which taketh away the sins of the world" (John i. 29). He, I say, takes them away, and no other; that is, since he alone is the Lamb of God, he alone is the offering for our sins; he alone is expiation; he alone is satisfaction. For though the right and power of pardoning properly belongs to the Father, when he is distinguished from the Son, as has already been seen, Christ is here exhibited in another view, as transferring to himself the punishment due to us, and wiping away our guilt in the sight of God. Whence it follows, that we could not be partakers of the expiation accomplished by Christ, were he not possessed of that honour of which those who try to appease God by their compensations seek to rob him.

27. Here it is necessary to keep two things in view: that the honour of Christ be preserved entire and unimpaired, and that the conscience, assured of the pardon of sin, may have peace with God. Isaiah says that the Father "hath laid on him the iniquity of us all;" that "with his stripes we are healed" (Isa. liii. 5, 6). Peter repeating the same thing, in other words says, that he "bare our sins in his own body on the tree" (1 Pet. ii. 24). Paul's words are, "God sending his own Son in the likeness of sinful flesh, and for sin condemned sin in the flesh," "being made a curse for us" (Rom. viii. 3; Gal. iii. 13); in other words, the power and curse of sin was destroyed in his flesh when he was offered as a sacrifice, on which the whole weight of our sins was laid, with their curse and execration, with the fearful judgment of God, and condemnation to death. Here there is no mention of the vain dogma, that after the initial cleansing no man experiences the efficacy of Christ's passion in any other way than by means of satisfying penance: we are directed to the satisfaction of Christ alone for every fall. Now call to mind their pestilential dogma: that the grace of God is effective only in the first

forgiveness of sins; but if we afterwards fall, our works co-operate in obtaining the second pardon. If these things are so, do the properties above attributed to Christ remain entire? How immense the difference between the two propositions—that our iniquities were laid upon Christ, that in his own person he might expiate them, and that they are expiated by our works; that Christ is the propitiation for our sins, and that God is to be propitiated by works. Then, in regard to pacifying the conscience, what pacification will it be to be told that sins are redeemed by satisfactions? How will it be able to ascertain the measure of satisfaction? It will always doubt whether God is propitious; will always fluctuate, always tremble. Those who rest satisfied with petty satisfactions form too contemptible an estimate of the justice of God, and little consider the grievous heinousness of sin, as shall afterwards be shown. Even were we to grant that they can buy off some sins by due satisfaction, still what will they do while they are overwhelmed with so many sins, that not even a hundred lives, though wholly devoted to the purpose, could suffice to satisfy for them? We may add, that all the passages in which the forgiveness of sins is declared refer not only to catechumens,[1] but to the regenerate children of God; to those who have long been nursed in the bosom of the Church. That embassy which Paul so highly extols, " we pray you in Christ's stead, be ye reconciled to God" (2 Cor. v. 20), is not directed to strangers, but to those who had been regenerated long before. Setting satisfactions altogether aside, he directs us to the cross of Christ. Thus when he writes to the Colossians that Christ had "made peace through the blood of his cross," "to reconcile all things unto himself," he does not restrict it to the moment at which we are received into the Church, but extends it to our whole course. This is plain from the context, where he says that in him " we have redemption by his blood, even the forgiveness of sins" (Col. i. 14). It is needless to collect more passages, as they are ever occurring.

28. Here they take refuge in the absurd distinction that some sins are *venial*, and others *mortal;* that for the latter a weighty satisfaction is due, but that the former are purged by easier remedies; by the Lord's Prayer, the sprinkling of holy water, and the absolution of the Mass. Thus they insult and trifle with God.[2] And yet, though they have the terms venial and mortal sin continually in their mouth, they have not yet been able to distinguish the one from the other, except by making impiety and impurity of heart[3] to be venial sin. We, on the contrary, taught by the Scripture standard of righteousness and unrighteousness, declare that " the wages of sin

1 Latin, " Catechumenos."—French, " Ceux qui ne sont point encore baptisez;"—those who are not yet baptised.

2 See on this Section, Book II. chap. viii. s. 58, 59.

3 The French adds, " Qui est le plus horrible peché devant Dieu;"—which is the most heinous sin in the sight of God.

is death;" and that "the soul that sinneth, it shall die" (Rom. vi. 23; Ezek. xviii. 20). The sins of believers are venial, not because they do not merit death, but because by the mercy of God there is "now no condemnation to those which are in Christ Jesus," their sin being not imputed, but effaced by pardon. I know how unjustly they calumniate this our doctrine; for they say it is the paradox of of the Stoics concerning the equality of sins: but we shall easily convict them out of their own mouths. I ask them whether, among those sins which they hold to be mortal, they acknowledge a greater and a less? If so, it cannot follow, as a matter of course, that all sins which are mortal are equal. Since Scripture declares that the wages of sin is death,—that obedience to the law is the way to life, —the transgression of it the way to death,—they cannot evade this conclusion. In such a mass of sins, therefore, how will they find an end to their satisfactions? If the satisfaction for one sin requires one day, while preparing it they involve themselves in more sins; since no man, however righteous, passes one day without falling repeatedly. While they prepare themselves for their satisfactions, number, or rather numbers without number, will be added.[1] Confidence in satisfaction being thus destroyed, what more would they have? how do they still dare to think of satisfying?

29. They endeavour, indeed, to disentangle themselves, but it is impossible. They pretend a distinction between penalty and guilt, holding that the guilt is forgiven by the mercy of God; but that though the guilt is remitted, the punishment which divine justice requires to be paid remains. Satisfactions then properly relate to the remission of the penalty. How ridiculous this levity! They now confess that the remission of guilt is gratuitous; and yet they are ever and anon telling us to merit it by prayers and tears, and other preparations of every kind. Still the whole doctrine of Scripture regarding the remission of sins is diametrically opposed to that distinction. But although I think I have already done more than enough to establish this, I will subjoin some other passages, by which these slippery snakes will be so caught as to be afterwards unable to writhe even the tip of their tail: "Behold, the days come, saith the Lord, that I will make a new covenant with the house of Israel, and with the house of Judah." "I will forgive their iniquity, and I will remember their sin no more" (Jer. xxxi. 31, 34). What this means we learn from another Prophet, when the Lord says, "When the righteous turneth away from his righteousness," "all his righteousness that he hath done shall not be mentioned." "Again, when the wicked man turneth away from his wickedness that he hath committed, and doth that which is lawful and right, he shall save his soul alive"

---

[1] French, "Et quand ils voudront satisfaire pour plusieurs, ils en commettront encore davantage jusques à venir à un abysme sans fin. Je traite encore des plus justes;"—And when they would satisfy for several sins, they will commit still more, until they come at last to a bottomless abyss. I am still speaking of the best.

(Ezek. xviii. 24, 27). When he declares that he will not remember righteousness, the meaning is, that he will take no account of it to reward it. In the same way, not to remember sins is not to bring them to punishment. The same thing is denoted in other passages,[1] by casting them behind his back, blotting them out as a cloud, casting them into the depths of the sea, not imputing them, hiding them. by such forms of expression the Holy Spirit has explained his meaning not obscurely, if we would lend a willing ear. Certainly if God punishes sins, he imputes them; if he avenges, he remembers; if he Brings them to judgment, he has not hid them; if he examines, he has not cast them behind his back; if he investigates, he has not blotted them out like a cloud; if he exposes them, he has not thrown them into the depths of the sea. In this way Augustine clearly interprets: " If God has covered sins, he willed not to advert to them; if he willed not to advert, he willed not to animadvert; if he willed not to animadvert, he willed not to punish: he willed not to take knowledge of them, he rather willed to pardon them. Why then did he say that sins were hid? Just that they might not be seen. What is meant by God seeing sins but punishing them?" (August. in Ps. xxxii. 1.) But let us hear from another prophetical passage on what terms the Lord forgives sins : " Though your sins be as scarlet, they shall be white as snow; though they be red like crimson, they shall be as wool" (Isa. i. 18). In Jeremiah again we read: " In those days, and in that time, saith the Lord, the iniquity of Israel shall be sought for, and there shall be none; and the sins of Judah, they shall not be found: for I will pardon them whom I reserve" (Jer. l. 20). Would you briefly comprehend the meaning of these words? Consider what, on the contrary, is meant by these expressions, "that transgression is sealed up in a bag;" "that the iniquity of Ephraim is bound up ; his sin is hid;" that "the sin of Judah is written with a pen of iron, and with the point of a diamond."[2] If they mean, as they certainly do, that vengeance will be recompensed, there can be no doubt that, by the contrary passages, the Lord declares that he renounces all thought of vengeance. Here I must entreat the reader not to listen to any glosses of mine, but only to give some deference to the word of God.

30. What, pray, did Christ perform for us if the punishment of sin is still exacted ? For when we say that he " bare our sins in his own body on the tree" (1 Pet. ii. 24), all we mean is, that he endured the penalty and punishment which was due to our sins. This is more significantly declared by Isaiah, when he says that the " chastisement (or correction) of our peace was upon him" (Isaiah liii. 5). But what is the correction of our peace, unless it be the punishment due to our sins, and to be paid by us before we could be reconciled to God, had he not become our substitute ? Thus you clearly see that

---

[1] Isa. xxxviii. 17; xliv. 22; Micah vii. 19; Ps. xxxii. 1.
[2] Job xiv. 17; Hos. xiii. 12; Jer. xxii. 1.

Christ bore the punishment of sin that he might thereby exempt his people from it. And whenever Paul makes mention of the redemption procured by him,[1] he calls it ἀπολύτρωσις, by which he does not simply mean *redemption*, as it is commonly understood, but the very *price* and satisfaction of redemption.[2] For which reason, he also says, that Christ gave himself an ἀντίλυτρον (ransom) for us. " What is propitiation with the Lord (says Augustine) but sacrifice ? And what is sacrifice but that which was offered for us in the death of Christ?" But we have our strongest argument in the injunctions of the Mosaic Law as to expiating the guilt of sin. The Lord does not there appoint this or that method of satisfying, but requires the whole compensation to be made by sacrifice, though he at the same time enumerates all the rites of expiation with the greatest care and exactness. How comes it that he does not at all enjoin works as the means of procuring pardon, but only requires sacrifices for expiation, unless it were his purpose thus to testify that this is the only kind of satisfaction by which his justice is appeased ? For the sacrifices which the Israelites then offered were not regarded as human works, but were estimated by their antitype, that is, the sole sacrifice of Christ. The kind of compensation which the Lord receives from us is elegantly and briefly expressed by Hosea : " Take with you words, and turn to the Lord : say unto him, Take away all iniquity, and receive us graciously," here is remission : " so will we render the calves of our lips," here is satisfaction (Hos. xiv. 2). I know that they have still a more subtle evasion,[3] by making a distinction between eternal and temporal punishment ; but as they define temporal punishment to be any kind of infliction with which God visits either the body or the soul, eternal death only excepted, this restriction avails them little. The passages which we have quoted above say expressly that the terms on which God receives us into favour are these—viz. he remits all the punishment which we deserved by pardoning our guilt. And whenever David or the other prophets ask pardon for their sins, they deprecate punishment. Nay, a sense of the divine justice impels them to this. On the other hand, when they promise mercy from the Lord, they almost always discourse of punishments and the forgiveness of them. Assuredly, when the Lord declares in Ezekiel, that he will put an end to the Babylonish captivity, not "for your sakes, O house of Israel, but for mine holy name's sake" (Ezek. xxxvi. 22), he sufficiently demonstrates that both are gratuitous. In short, if we are freed from guilt by Christ, the punishment consequent upon guilt must cease with it.

31. But since they also arm themselves with passages of Scripture, let us see what the arguments are which they employ. David, they

---

1 Rom. iii. 24 ; 1 Cor. i. 30 ; Eph. i. 7 ; Col. i. 14 ; 1 Tim ii. 6.
2 The French adds, " Que nous appellons Rançon en François ;"—which we call Ransom in French.
3 See Calvin, ad Concil. Tridentini, Sess. cap. i. ad xv.

say, when upbraided by Nathan the Prophet for adultery and murder, receives pardon of the sin, and yet by the death of the son born of adultery is afterwards punished (2 Sam. xii. 13, 14). Such punishments, which were to be inflicted after the remission of the guilt, we are taught to ransom by satisfactions. For Daniel exhorted Nebuchadnezzar : " Break off thy sins by righteousness, and thine iniquities by showing mercy to the poor" (Dan. iv. 27). And Solomon says, " By mercy and truth iniquity is purged" (Prov. xvi. 6); and again, " love covereth all sins" (Prov. x. 12). This sentiment is confirmed by Peter (1 Pet. iv. 8). Also in Luke, our Lord says of the woman that was a sinner, " Her sins, which are many, are forgiven ; for she loved much" (Luke vii. 47). How perverse and preposterous the judgment they ever form of the doings of God !¹ Had they observed, what certainly they ought not to have overlooked, that there are two kinds of divine judgment, they would have seen in the correction of David a very different form of punishment from that which must be thought designed for vengeance. But since it in no slight degree concerns us to understand the purpose of God in the chastisements by which he animadverts upon our sins, and how much they differ from the exemplary punishments which he indignantly inflicts on the wicked and reprobate, I think it will not be improper briefly to glance at it. For the sake of distinction, we may call the one kind of judgment *punishment*, the other *chastisement*. In judicial punishment, God is to be understood as taking vengeance on his enemies, by displaying his anger against them, confounding, scattering, and annihilating them. By divine punishment, properly so called, let us then understand punishment accompanied with indignation. In judicial chastisement, he is offended, but not in wrath ; he does not punish by destroying or striking down as with a thunderbolt. Hence it is not properly punishment or vengeance, but correction and admonition. The one is the act of a judge, the other of a father. When the judge punishes a criminal, he animadverts upon the crime, and demands the penalty. When a father corrects his son sharply, it is not to mulct or avenge, but rather to teach him, and make him more cautious for the future. Chrysostom in his writings employs a simile which is somewhat different, but the same in purport. He says, " A son is whipt, and a slave is whipt, but the latter is punished as a slave for his offence : the former is chastised as a free-born son, standing in need of correction." The correction of the latter is designed to prove and amend him ; that of the former is scourging and punishment.

32. To have a short and clear view of the whole matter, we must make two distinctions. First, whenever the infliction is designed to avenge, then the curse and wrath of God displays itself. This is never the case with believers. On the contrary, the chastening of

¹ For a full exposition of these passages, see *infra*, sec. 35–37.

God carries his blessing with it, and is an evidence of love, as Scripture teaches.[1] This distinction is plainly marked throughout the word of God. All the calamities which the wicked suffer in the present life are depicted to us as a kind of anticipation of the punishment of hell. In these they already see, as from a distance, their eternal condemnation: and so far are they from being thereby reformed, or deriving any benefit, that by such preludes they are rather prepared for the fearful doom which finally awaits them. The Lord chastens his servants sore, but does not give them over unto death (Ps. cxviii. 18). When afflicted, they acknowledge it is good for them, that they may learn his statutes (Ps. cxix. 71). But as we everywhere read that the saints received their chastisements with placid mind, so inflictions of the latter kind they always most earnestly deprecated. "O Lord, correct me," says Jeremiah, "but with judgment; not in thine anger, lest thou bring me to nothing. Pour out thy fury upon the heathen that know thee not, and upon the families that call not on thy name" (Jer. x. 24, 25). David says, "O Lord, rebuke me not in thine anger, neither chasten me in thy hot displeasure" (Ps. vi. 1). There is nothing inconsistent with this in its being repeatedly said, that the Lord is angry with his saints when he chastens them for their sins (Ps. xxxviii. 7). In like manner, in Isaiah, "And in that day thou shalt say, O Lord, I will praise thee: though thou wast angry with me, thine anger is turned away, and thou comfortedst me" (Isa. xii. 1). Likewise in Habakkuk, "In wrath remember mercy" (Hab. iii. 2); and in Micah, "I will bear the indignation of the Lord, because I have sinned against him" (Mic. vii. 9). Here we are reminded not only that those who are justly punished gain nothing by murmuring, but that believers obtain a mitigation of their pain by reflecting on the divine intention. For the same reason, he is said to profane his inheritance; and yet we know that he will never profane it. The expression refers not to the counsel or purpose of God in punishing, but to the keen sense of pain, endured by those who are visited with any measure of divine severity. For the Lord not only chastens his people with a slight degree of austerity, but sometimes so wounds them, that they seem to themselves on the very eve of perdition. He thus declares that they have deserved his anger, and it is fitting so to do, that they may be dissatisfied with themselves for their sins, may be more careful in their desires to appease God, and anxiously hasten to seek his pardon; still, at this very time, he gives clearer evidence of his mercy than of his anger. For He who cannot deceive has declared, that the covenant made with us in our true Solomon[2] stands fast and will never be broken, "If his children forsake my law, and walk not in my judgments; if they break my statutes, and keep not my commandments;

---

[1] Job. v. 17; Prov. iii. 11; Heb. xii. 5.
[2] French, "Car l'alliance qu'il a une fois faite avec Jesus Christ et ses membres;"—
For the covenant which he once made with Jesus Christ and his members.

then will I visit their transgressions with the rod, and their iniquity with stripes. Nevertheless, my loving-kindness will I not utterly take from him, nor suffer my faithfulness to fail" (Ps. lxxxix. 31–34). To assure us of this mercy, he says, that the *rod* with which he will chastise the posterity of Solomon will be the "rod of men," and "the stripes of the children of men" (2 Sam. vii. 14). While by these terms he denotes moderation and lenity, he, at the same time, intimates, that those who feel the hand of God opposed to them cannot but tremble and be confounded. How much regard he has to this lenity in chastening his Israel he shows by the Prophet, "Behold, I have refined thee, but not with silver; I have chosen thee in the furnace of affliction" (Isa. xlviii. 10). Although he tells them that they are chastisements with a view to purification, he adds, that even these are so tempered, that they are not to be too much crushed by them. And this is very necessary, for the more a man reveres God, and devotes himself to the cultivation of piety, the more tender he is in bearing his anger (Ps. xc. 11; and ibid. Calv.). The reprobate, though they groan under the lash,[1] yet, because they weigh not the true cause, but rather turn their back, as well upon their sins as upon the divine judgment, become hardened in their stupor; or, because they murmur and kick, and so rebel against their judge, their infatuated violence fills them with frenzy and madness. Believers, again, admonished by the rod of God, immediately begin to reflect on their sins, and, struck with fear and dread, betake themselves as suppliants to implore mercy. Did not God mitigate the pains by which wretched souls are excruciated, they would give way a hundred times, even at slight signs of his anger.

33. The second distinction is, that when the reprobate are brought under the lash of God, they begin in a manner to pay the punishment due to his justice; and though their refusal to listen to these proofs of the divine anger will not escape with impunity, still they are not punished with the view of bringing them to a better mind, but only to teach them by dire experience that God is a judge and avenger. The sons of God are beaten with rods, not that they may pay the punishment due to their faults, but that they may thereby be led to repent. Accordingly, we perceive that they have more respect to the future than to the past. I prefer giving this in the words of Chrysostom rather than my own: "His object in imposing a penalty upon us, is not to inflict punishment on our sins, but to correct us for the future" (Chrysost. Serm. de Pœnit. et Confess.). So also Augustine, "The suffering at which you cry, is medicine, not punishment; chastisement, not condemnation. Do not drive away the rod, if you would not be driven away from the inheritance. Know, brethren, that the whole of that misery of the human race, under which the world groans, is a medicinal pain, not a penal sentence"

[1] French, "Car combien les reprouvés souspirent ou grincent les dents sous les coups;"—For though the reprobate sigh or gnash their teeth under the strokes.

(August. in Psal. cii. circa finem). It seemed proper to quote these passages, lest any one should think the mode of expression which I have used to be novel or uncommon. To the same effect are the indignant terms in which the Lord expostulates with his people, for their ingratitude in obstinately despising all his inflictions. In Isaiah he says, " Why should ye be stricken any more ? ye will revolt more and more. The whole head is sick, and the whole heart faint" (Isa. i. 5, 6). But as such passages abound in the Prophets, it is sufficient briefly to have shown, that the only purpose of God in punishing his Church is to subdue her to repentance. Thus, when he rejected Saul from the kingdom, he punished in vengeance (1 Sam. xv. 23); when he deprived David of his child, he chastised for amendment (2 Sam. xii. 18). In this sense Paul is to be understood when he says, " When we are judged, we are chastened of the Lord, that we should not be condemned with the world" (1 Cor. xi. 32); that is, while we as sons of God are afflicted by our heavenly Father's hand, it is not punishment to confound, but only chastisement to train us. On this subject Augustine is plainly with us (De Peccator. Meritis ac Remiss. Lib. ii. cap. 33, 34). For he shows that the punishments with which men are equally chastened by God are to be variously considered ; because the saints after the forgiveness of their sins have struggles and exercises, the reprobate without forgiveness are punished for their iniquity. Enumerating the punishments inflicted on David and other saints, he says, it was designed, by thus humbling them, to prove and exercise their piety. The passage in Isaiah, in which it is said, " Speak ye comfortably to Jerusalem, and cry unto her, that her warfare is accomplished, that her iniquity is pardoned ; for she has received of the Lord's hands double for all her sins " (Isa. xl. 2), proves not that the pardon of sin depends on freedom from punishment. It is just as if he had said, sufficient punishment has now been exacted ; as for their number and heinousness, you have long been oppressed with sorrow and mourning, it is time to send you a message of complete mercy, that your minds may be filled with joy on feeling me to be a Father. For God there assumes the character of a father who repents even of the just severity which he has been compelled to use towards his son.

34. These are the thoughts with which the believer ought to be provided in the bitterness of affliction, " The time is come that judgment must begin at the house of God," " the city which is called by my name" (1 Pet. iv. 17; Jer. xxv. 29). What could the sons of God do, if they thought that the severity which they feel was vengeance ? He who, smitten by the hand of God, thinks that God is a judge inflicting punishment, cannot conceive of him except as angry and at enmity with him ; cannot but detest the rod of God as curse and condemnation ; in short, can never persuade himself that he is loved by God, while he feels that he is still disposed to inflict punishment upon him. He only profits under the divine chastening

who considers that God, though offended with his sins, is still propitious and favourable to him. Otherwise, the feeling must necessarily be what the Psalmist complains that he had experienced, "Thy wrath lieth hard upon me, and thou hast afflicted me with all thy waves." Also what Moses says, "For we are consumed by thine anger, and by thy wrath we are troubled. Thou hast set our iniquities before thee, our secret sins in the light of thy countenance. For all our days are passed away in thy wrath; we spend our years as a tale that is told" (Ps. xc. 7–9). On the other hand, David, speaking of fatherly chastisements, to show how believers are more assisted than oppressed by them, thus sings, "Blessed is the man whom thou chastenest, O Lord, and teachest him out of thy law; that thou mayest give him rest from the days of adversity, until the pit be digged for the wicked" (Ps. xciv. 12, 13). It is certainly a sore temptation, when God, sparing unbelievers and overlooking their crimes, appears more rigid towards his own people. Hence, to solace them, he adds the admonition of the law which teaches them, that their salvation is consulted when they are brought back to the right path, whereas the wicked are borne headlong in their errors, which ultimately lead to the pit. It matters not whether the punishment is eternal or temporary. For disease, pestilence, famine, and war are curses from God, as much as even the sentence of eternal death, whenever their tendency is to operate as instruments of divine wrath and vengeance against the reprobate.

35. All, if I mistake not, now see what view the Lord had in chastening David—namely, to prove that murder and adultery are most offensive to God, and to manifest this offensiveness in a beloved and faithful servant, that David himself might be taught never again to dare to commit such wickedness; still, however, it was not a punishment designed in payment of a kind of compensation to God. In the same way are we to judge of that other correction, in which the Lord subjects his people to a grievous pestilence, for the disobedience of David in forgetting himself so far as to number the people. He indeed freely forgave David the guilt of his sin; but because it was necessary, both as a public example to all ages and also to humble David himself, not to allow such an offence to go unpunished, he chastened him most sharply with his whip. We ought also to keep this in view in the universal curse of the human race. For since after obtaining grace we still continue to endure the miseries denounced to our first parent as the penalty of transgression, we ought thereby to be reminded, how offensive to God is the transgression of his law, that thus humbled and dejected by a consciousness of our wretched condition, we may aspire more ardently to true happiness. But it were most foolish in any one to imagine, that we are subjected to the calamities of the present life for the guilt of sin. This seems to me to have been Chrysostom's meaning when he said, "If the purpose of God in inflicting punishment is to bring those persisting in evil to

repentance, when repentance is manifested punishment would be superfluous" (Chrysos. Homil. iii. de Provid.). Wherefore, as he knows what the disposition of each requires, he treats one with greater harshness, and another with more indulgence. Accordingly, when he wishes to show that he is not excessive in exacting punishment, he upbraids a hard-hearted and obstinate people, because, after being smitten, they still continued in sin (Jer. v. 3). In the same sense he complains, that "Ephraim is a cake not turned" (Hos. vii. 8), because chastisement did not make a due impression on their minds, and, correcting their vices, make them fit to receive pardon. Surely he who thus speaks shows, that as soon as any one repents he will be ready to receive him, and that the rigour which he exercises in chastising faults is wrung from him by our perverseness, since we should prevent him by a voluntary correction. Such, however, being the hardness and rudeness of all hearts, that they stand universally in need of castigation, our infinitely wise Parent hath seen it meet to exercise all without exception, during their whole lives, with chastisement. It is strange how they fix their eyes so intently on the one example of David, and are not moved by the many examples in which they might have beheld the free forgiveness of sins. The publican is said to have gone down from the temple justified (Luke xviii. 14) ; no punishment follows. Peter obtained the pardon of his sin (Luke xxii. 61). "We read of his tears," says Ambrose, (Serm. 46, De Pœnit. Petri), "we read not of satisfaction." To the paralytic it is said, "Son, be of good cheer; thy sins be forgiven thee," (Matth. ix. 2) ; no penance is enjoined. All the acts of forgiveness mentioned in Scripture are gratuitous. The rule ought to be drawn from these numerous examples, rather than from one example which contains a kind of specialty.

36. Daniel, in exhorting Nebuchadnezzar to break off his sins by righteousness, and his iniquities by showing mercy to the poor (Dan. iv. 27), meant not to intimate, that righteousness and mercy are able to propitiate God and redeem from punishment (far be it from us to suppose that there ever was any other ἀπολύτρωσις (ransom) than the blood of Christ) ; but the breaking off referred to in that passage has reference to man rather than to God: as if he had said, O king, you have exercised an unjust and violent domination, you have oppressed the humble, spoiled the poor, treated your people harshly and unjustly ; instead of unjust exaction, instead of violence and oppression, now practise mercy and justice. In like manner, Solomon says, that love covers a multitude of sins ; not, however, with God, but among men. For the whole verse stands thus, "Hatred stirreth up strifes ; out love covereth all sins" (Prov. x. 12). Here, after his manner, he contrasts the evils produced by hatred with the fruits of charity, in this sense, Those who hate are incessantly biting, carping at, upbraiding, lacerating each other, making everything a fault ; but those who love mutually conceal each other's faults, wink at many,

forgive many: not that the one approves the vices of the other, but tolerates and cures by admonishing, rather than exasperates by assailing. That the passage is quoted by Peter (1 Pet. iv. 8) in the same sense we cannot doubt, unless we would charge him with corrupting or craftily wresting Scripture. When it is said that "by mercy and truth iniquity is purged" (Prov. xvi. 6), the meaning is, not that by them compensation is made to the Lord, so that he being thus satisfied remits the punishment which he would otherwise have exacted; but intimation is made after the familiar manner of Scripture, that those who, forsaking their vices and iniquities, turn to the Lord in truth and piety, will find him propitious: as if he had said, that the wrath of God is calmed, and his judgment is at rest, whenever we rest from our wickedness. But, indeed, it is not the cause of pardon that is described, but rather the mode of true conversion; just as the Prophets frequently declare, that it is in vain for hypocrites to offer God fictitious rites instead of repentance, seeing his delight is in integrity and the duties of charity.[1] In like manner, also, the author of the Epistle to the Hebrews, commending kindness and humanity, reminds us, that "with such sacrifices God is well pleased" (Heb. xiii. 16). And indeed when Christ, rebuking the Pharisees because, intent merely on the outside of the cup and platter, they neglected purity of heart, enjoins them, in order that they may be clean in all respects, to give alms, does he exhort them to give satisfaction thereby? He only tells them what the kind of purity is which God requires. Of this mode of expression we have treated elsewhere (Matth. xxiii. 25; Luke xi. 39-41; see Calv. in Harm. Evang.).

37. In regard to the passage in Luke (Luke vii. 36, sq.) no man of sober judgment who reads the parable there employed by our Lord, will raise any controversy with us. The Pharisee thought that the Lord did not know the character of the woman whom he had so easily admitted to his presence. For he presumed that he would not have admitted her if he had known what kind of a sinner she was; and from this he inferred, that one who could be deceived in this way was not a prophet. Our Lord, to show that she was not a sinner, inasmuch as she had already been forgiven, spake this parable: "There was a certain creditor which had two debtors; the one owed five hundred pence, and the other fifty. And when they had nothing to pay he frankly forgave them both. Tell me, therefore, which of them will love him most? The Pharisee answers: "I suppose that he to whom he forgave most." Then our Saviour rejoins: "Her sins, which are many, are forgiven; for she loved much." By these words it is plain he does not make love the cause of forgiveness, but the proof of it. The similitude is borrowed from the case of a debtor, to whom a debt of five hundred pence had been forgiven. It is not said that the debt is forgiven because he loved much, but that he loved

---

1 French, "Integrité, pitié, droiture, et choses semblables;"—integrity, pity, uprightness, and the like.

much because it was forgiven. The similitude ought to be applied in this way: You think this woman is a sinner; but you ought to have acknowledged her as not a sinner, in respect that her sins have been forgiven her. Her love ought to have been to you a proof of her having obtained forgiveness, that love being an expression of gratitude for the benefit received. It is an argument *a posteriori*, by which something is demonstrated by the results produced by it Our Lord plainly attests the ground on which she had obtained forgiveness, when he says, "Thy faith hath saved thee." By faith, therefore, we obtain forgiveness: by love we give thanks, and bear testimony to the loving-kindness of the Lord.

38. I am little moved by the numerous passages in the writings of the Fathers relating to satisfaction. I see indeed that some (I will frankly say almost all whose books are extant) have either erred in this matter, or spoken too roughly and harshly; but I cannot admit that they were so rude and unskilful as to write these passages in the sense in which they are read by our new satisfactionaries. Chrysostom somewhere says, "When mercy is implored, interrogation ceases; when mercy is asked, judgment rages not; when mercy is sought, there is no room for punishment; where there is mercy, no question is asked; where there is mercy, the answer gives pardon" (Chrysos. Hom. ii. in Psal. 1). How much soever these words may be twisted, they can never be reconciled with the dogmas of the Schoolmen. In the book *De Dogmatibus Ecclesiasticis*, which is attributed to Augustine, you read (cap. 54), "The satisfaction of repentance is to cut off the causes of sins, and not to indulge an entrance to their suggestions." From this it appears that the doctrine of satisfaction, said to be paid for sins committed, was everywhere derided in those ages; for here the only satisfaction referred to is caution, abstinence from sin for the future. I am unwilling to quote what Chrysostom says (Hom. x. in Genes.), that God requires nothing more of us than to confess our faults before him with tears, as similar sentiments abound both in his writings and those of others. Augustine indeed calls works of mercy remedies for obtaining forgiveness of sins (Enchir. ad Laur.); but lest any one should stumble at the expression, he himself, in another passage, obviates the difficulty. "The flesh of Christ," says he, "is the true and only sacrifice for sins—not only for those which are all effaced in baptism, but those into which we are afterwards betrayed through infirmity, and because of which the whole Church daily cries, 'Forgive us our debts' (Matth. vi. 12). And they are forgiven by that special sacrifice."

39. By satisfaction, however, they. for the most part, meant not compensation to be paid to God, but the public testimony, by which those who had been punished with excommunication, and wished again to be received into communion, assured the Church of their repentance. For those penitents were enjoined certain fasts and other things, by which they might prove that they were truly, and from

the heart, weary of their former life, or rather might obliterate the remembrance of their past deeds: in this way they were said to give satisfaction, not to God, but to the Church. The same thing is expressed by Augustine in a passage in his Enchiridion ad Laurentium, cap. 65.[1] From that ancient custom the satisfactions and confessions now in use took their rise. It is indeed a viperish progeny, not even a vestige of the better form now remaining. I know that ancient writers sometimes speak harshly; nor do I deny, as I lately said, that they have perhaps erred; but dogmas, which were tainted with a few blemishes, now that they have fallen into the unwashed hands of those men, are altogether defiled. And if we were to decide the contest by authority of the Fathers, what kind of Fathers are those whom they obtrude upon us? A great part of those, from whom Lombard their Coryphæus framed his centos, are extracted from the absurd dreams of certain monks passing under the names of Ambrose, Jerome, Augustine, and Chrysostom. On the present subject almost all his extracts are from the book of Augustine *De Pœnitentia*, a book absurdly compiled by some rhapsodist, alike from good and bad authors—a book which indeed bears the name of Augustine, but which no person of the least learning would deign to acknowledge as his. Wishing to save my readers trouble, they will pardon me for not searching minutely into all their absurdities. For myself it were not very laborious, and might gain some applause, to give a complete exposure of dogmas which have hitherto been vaunted as mysteries; but as my object is to give useful instruction, I desist.

1 It is quoted in the Decret. c. in Art. de Pœnit. Dist. i.

CHAPTER V.

OF THE MODES OF SUPPLEMENTING SATISFACTION—VIZ., INDULGENCES AND PURGATORY.

Divisions of the chapter,—I. A summary description and refutation of Popish indulgences, sec. 1, 2. II. Confutation by Leo and Augustine. Answer to two objections urged in support of them, sec. 3, 4. A profane love of filthy lucre on the part of the Pope. The origin of indulgences unfolded, sec. 5. III. An examination of Popish purgatory. Its horrible impiety, sec. 6. An explanation of five passages of Scripture by which Sophists endeavour to support that dream, sec. 7, 8. Sentiments of the ancient Theologians concerning purgatory, sec. 10.

Sections.

1. The dogma of satisfaction the parent of indulgences. Vanity of both. The reason of it. Evidence of the avarice of the Pope and the Romish clergy: also of the blindness with which the Christian world was smitten.
2. View of indulgences given by the Sophists. Their true nature. Refutation of them. Refutation confirmed by seven passages of Scripture.
3. Confirmed also by the testimony of Leo, a Roman Bishop, and by Augustine. Attempts of the Popish doctors to establish the monstrous doctrine of indulgences, and even support it by Apostolical authority. First answer.
4. Second answer to the passage of an Apostle adduced to support the dogma of indulgences. Answer confirmed by a comparison with other passages, and from a passage in Augustine, explaining the Apostle's meaning. Another passage from the same Apostle confirming this view.
5. The Pope's profane thirst for filthy lucre exposed. The origin of indulgences.
6. Examination of the fictitious purgatory of the Papists. 1. From the nature of the thing itself. 2. From the authority of God. 3. From the consideration of the merit of Christ, which is destroyed by this fiction. Purgatory, what it is. 4. From the impiety teeming from this fountain.
7. Exposition of the passages of Scripture quoted in support of purgatory. 1. Of the unpardonable sin, from which it is inferred that there are some sins afterwards to be forgiven. 2. Of the passage as to paying the last farthing.
8. 3. The passage concerning the bending of the knee to Christ by things under the earth. 4. The example of Judas Maccabæus in sending an oblation for the dead to Jerusalem.
9. 5. Of the fire which shall try every man's work. The sentiment of the ancient theologians. Answer, containing a *reductio ad absurdum*. Confirmation by a passage of Augustine. The meaning of the Apostle. What to be understood by fire. A clear exposition of the metaphor. The day of the Lord. How those who suffer loss are saved by fire.
10. The doctrine of purgatory ancient, but refuted by a more ancient Apostle. Not supported by ancient writers, by Scripture, or solid argument. Introduced by custom and a zeal not duly regulated by the word of God. Ancient writers, as Augustine, speak doubtfully in commending prayer for the dead. At all events, we must hold by the word of God, which rejects this fiction. A vast difference between the more ancient and the more modern builders of purgatory. This shown by comparing them.

1. FROM this dogma of satisfaction that of indulgences takes its rise. For the pretence is, that what is wanting to our own ability is

hereby supplied; and they go the insane length of defining them to be a dispensation of the merits of Christ, and the martyrs which the Pope makes by his bulls. Though they are fitter for hellebore than for argument,—and it is scarcely worth while to refute these frivolous errors, which, already battered down, begin of their own accord to grow antiquated, and totter to their fall;—yet, as a brief refutation may be useful to some of the unlearned, I will not omit it. Indeed, the fact that indulgences have so long stood safe and with impunity, and wantoned with so much fury and tyranny, may be regarded as a proof into how deep a night of ignorance mankind were for some ages plunged. They saw themselves insulted openly, and without disguise, by the Pope and his bull-bearers; they saw the salvation of the soul made the subject of a lucrative traffic, salvation taxed at a few pieces of money, nothing given gratuitously; they saw what was squeezed from them in the form of oblations basely consumed on strumpets, pimps, and gluttony, the loudest trumpeters of indulgences being the greatest despisers; they saw the monsters stalking abroad, and every day luxurating with greater licence, and that without end, new bulls being constantly issued, and new sums extracted. Still indulgences were received with the greatest reverence, worshipped, and bought. Even those who saw more clearly than others deemed them pious frauds, by which, even in deceiving, some good was gained. Now, at length, that a considerable portion of the world have begun to bethink themselves, indulgences grow cool, and gradually even begin to freeze, preparatory to their final extinction.

2. But since very many who see the vile imposture, theft, and rapine (with which the dealers in indulgences have hitherto deluded and sported with us), are not aware of the true source of the impiety, it may be proper to show not only what indulgences truly are, but also that they are polluted in every part.[1] They give the name of *treasury of the Church* to the merits of Christ, the holy Apostles and Martyrs. They pretend as I have said, that the radical custody of the granary has been delivered to the Roman bishop, to whom the dispensation of these great blessings belongs in such a sense, that he can both exercise it by himself, and delegate the power of exercising it to others. Hence we have from the Pope at one time plenary indulgences, at another for certain years; from the cardinals for a hundred days, and from the bishops for forty. These, to describe them truly, are a profanation of the blood of Christ, and a delusion of Satan, by which the Christian people are led away from the grace of God and the life which is in Christ, and turned aside from the true way of salvation. For how could the blood of Christ be more shamefully profaned than

1 French, "Il est expedient de monstrer ici non seulement quelles sont les indul gences, comme ils en usent; mais du tout que c'est, à les prendre en leur propre et meilleure nature, sans quelque qualité ou vice accidental;"—it is expedient here to show not only what indulgences are as in use, but in themselves, taking them in their proper and best form, without any qualification or accidental vice.

by denying its sufficiency for the remission of sins, for reconciliation and satisfaction, unless its defects, as if it were dried up and exhausted, are supplemented from some other quarter ? Peter's words are : " To him give all the prophets witness, that through his name whosoever believeth in him shall receive remission of sins" (Acts x. 43) ; but indulgences bestow the remission of sins through Peter, Paul, and the Martyrs. " The blood of Jesus Christ his Son cleanseth us from all sin," says John (1 John i. 7). Indulgences make the blood of the martyrs an ablution of sins. " He hath made him to be sin (*i.e.* a satisfaction for sin) for us who knew no sin," says Paul (2 Cor. v. 21), " that we might be made the righteousness of God in him." Indulgences make the satisfaction of sin to depend on the blood of the martyrs. Paul exclaimed and testified to the Corinthians, that Christ alone was crucified, and died for them (1 Cor. i. 13). Indulgences declare that Paul and others died for us. Paul elsewhere says that Christ purchased the Church with his own blood (Acts xx. 28). Indulgences assign another purchase to the blood of martyrs. " By one offering he hath perfected for ever them that are sanctified," says the Apostle (Heb. x. 14). Indulgences, on the other hand, insist that sanctification, which would otherwise be insufficient, is perfected by martyrs. John says that all the saints " have washed their robes, and made them white in the blood of the Lamb " (Rev. vii. 14). Indulgences tell us to wash our robes in the blood of saints.

3. There is an admirable passage in opposition to their blasphemies in Leo, a Roman Bishop (ad Palæstinos, Ep. 81). " Although the death of many saints was precious in the sight of the Lord (Ps. cxvi. 15), yet no innocent man's slaughter was the propitiation of the world. The just received crowns, did not give them ; and the fortitude of believers produced examples of patience, not gifts of righteousness ; for their deaths were for themselves ; and none by his final end paid the debt of another, except Christ our Lord, in whom alone all are crucified—all dead, buried, and raised up." This sentiment, as it was of a memorable nature, he has elsewhere repeated (Epist. 95). Certainly one could desire a clearer confutation of this impious dogma. Augustine introduces the same sentiment not less appositely : " Although brethren die for brethren, yet no martyr's blood is shed for the remission of sins : this Christ did for us, and in this conferred upon us not what we should imitate, but what should make us grateful," (August. Tract. in Joann. 84). Again, in another passage : " As he alone became the Son of God and the Son of man, that he might make us to be with himself sons of God, so he alone, without any ill desert, undertook the penalty for us, that through him we might, without good desert, obtain undeserved favour " (ad Bonif. Lib. iv. cap. 4). Indeed, as their whole doctrine is a patchwork of sacrilege and blasphemy, this is the most blasphemous of the whole. Let them acknowledge whether or not they hold the following dogmas : That the martyrs, by their death, performed more to God, and merited

more than was necessary for themselves, and they have a large surplus of merits which may be applied to others; that in order that this great good may not prove superfluous, their blood is mingled with the blood of Christ, and out of both is formed the treasury of the Church, for the forgiveness and satisfaction of sins; and that in this sense we must understand the words of Paul: "Who now rejoice in my sufferings, and fill up that which is behind of the afflictions of Christ in my flesh for his body's sake, which is the Church" (Col. i. 24). What is this but merely to leave the name of Christ, and at the same time make him a vulgar saintling, who can scarcely be distinguished in the crowd? He alone ought to be preached, alone held forth, alone named, alone looked to, whenever the subject considered is the obtaining of the forgiveness of sins, expiation, and sanctification. But let us hear their propositions. That the blood of martyrs may not be shed without fruit, it must be employed for the common good of the Church. Is it so? Was there no fruit in glorifying God by death? in sealing his truth with their blood? in testifying, by contempt of the present life, that they looked for a better? in confirming the faith of the Church, and at the same time disabling the pertinacity of the enemy by their constancy? But thus it is. They acknowledge no fruit if Christ is the only propitiation, if he alone died for our sins, if he alone was offered for our redemption. Nevertheless, they say, Peter and Paul would have gained the crown of victory though they had died in their beds a natural death. But as they contended to blood, it would not accord with the justice of God to leave their doing so barren and unfruitful. As if God were unable to augment the glory of his servants in proportion to the measure of his gifts. The advantage derived in common by the Church is great enough, when, by their triumphs, she is inflamed with zeal to fight.

4. How maliciously they wrest the passage in which Paul says, that he supplies in his body that which was lacking in the sufferings of Christ! (Col. i. 24). That defect or supplement refers not to the work of redemption, satisfaction, or expiation, but to those afflictions with which the members of Christ, in other words, all believers, behove to be exercised, so long as they are in the flesh. He says, therefore, that part of the sufferings of Christ still remains—viz. that what he suffered in himself he daily suffers in his members. Christ so honours us as to regard and count our afflictions as his own. By the additional words—for *the Church*, Paul means not for the redemption or reconciliation, or satisfaction of the Church, but for edification and progress. As he elsewhere says, " I endure all things for the elect's sakes, that they may also obtain the salvation which is in Christ Jesus with eternal glory" (2 Tim. ii. 10). He also writes to the Corinthians: " Whether we be afflicted, it is for your consolation and salvation, which is effectual in the enduring of the same sufferings which we also suffer" (2 Cor. i. 6). In the same place he immediately explains his meaning by adding, that he was made a minister

of the Church, not for redemption, but according to the dispensation which he received to preach the Gospel of Christ. But if they still desire another interpreter, let them hear Augustine: "The sufferings of Christ are in Christ alone, as in the head; in Christ and the Church as in the whole body. Hence Paul, being one member, says, 'I fill up in my body that which is behind of the sufferings of Christ.' Therefore, O hearer, whoever you be, if you are among the members of Christ, whatever you suffer from those who are not members of Christ, was lacking to the sufferings of Christ" (August. in Ps. xvi.). He elsewhere explains the end of the sufferings of the Apostles undertaken for Christ: "Christ is my door to you, because ye are the sheep of Christ purchased by his blood: acknowledge your price, which is not paid by me, but preached by me" (August. Tract. in Joann. 47). He afterwards adds, "As he laid down his life, so ought we to lay down our lives for the brethren, to build up peace and maintain faith." Thus far Augustine. Far be it from us to imagine that Paul thought anything was wanting to the sufferings of Christ in regard to the complete fulness of righteousness, salvation, and life, or that he wished to make any addition to it, after showing so clearly and eloquently that the grace of Christ was poured out in such rich abundance as far to exceed all the power of sin (Rom. v. 15). All saints have been saved by it alone, not by the merit of their own life or death, as Peter distinctly testifies (Acts xv. 11); so that it is an insult to God and his Anointed to place the worthiness of any saint in anything save the mercy of God alone. But why dwell longer on this, as if the matter were obscure, when to mention these monstrous dogmas is to refute them?

5. Moreover, to say nothing of these abominations, who taught the Pope to enclose the grace of Jesus Christ in lead and parchment, grace which the Lord is pleased to dispense by the word of the Gospel? Undoubtedly either the Gospel of God or indulgences must be false. That Christ is offered to us in the Gospel with all the abundance of heavenly blessings, with all his merits, all his righteousness, wisdom, and grace, without exception, Paul bears witness when he says, "Now then we are ambassadors for Christ, as though God did beseech you by us: we pray you in Christ's stead, be ye reconciled to God. For he hath made him to be sin for us, who knew no sin; that we might be made the righteousness of God in him" (2 Cor. v. 20, 21). And what is meant by the fellowship (κοινωνία) of Christ, which, according to the same Apostle (1 Cor. i. 9), is offered to us in the Gospel, all believers know. On the contrary, indulgences, bringing forth some portion of the grace of God from the armoury of the Pope, fix it to lead, parchment, and a particular place, but dissever it from the word of God. When we inquire into the origin of this abuse, it appears to have arisen from this, that when in old times the satisfactions imposed on penitents were too severe to be borne, those who felt themselves burdened beyond measure by the penance imposed,

petitioned the Church for relaxation. The remission so given was called indulgence. But as they transferred satisfactions to God, and called them compensations by which men redeem themselves from the justice of God, they in the same way transferred indulgences, representing them as expiatory remedies which free us from merited punishment. The blasphemies to which we have referred have been feigned with so much effrontery that there is not the least pretext for them.

6. Their purgatory cannot now give us much trouble, since with this axe we have struck it, thrown it down, and overturned it from its very foundations. I cannot agree with some who think that we ought to dissemble in this matter, and make no mention of purgatory, from which (as they say) fierce contests arise, and very little edification can be obtained. I myself would think it right to disregard their follies did they not tend to serious consequences. But since purgatory has been reared on many, and is daily propped up by new blasphemies; since it produces many grievous offences, assuredly it is not to be connived at, however it might have been disguised for a time, that without any authority from the word of God, it was devised by prying audacious rashness, that credit was procured for it by fictitious revelations, the wiles of Satan, and that certain passages of Scripture were ignorantly wrested to its support. Although the Lord bears not that human presumption should thus force its way to the hidden recesses of his judgments; although he has issued a strict prohibition against neglecting his voice, and making inquiry at the dead (Deut. xviii. 11), and permits not his word to be so erroneously contaminated. Let us grant, however, that all this might have been tolerated for a time as a thing of no great moment; yet when the expiation of sins is sought elsewhere than in the blood of Christ, and satisfaction is transferred to others, silence were most perilous. We are bound, therefore, to raise our voice to its highest pitch, and cry aloud that purgatory is a deadly device of Satan; that it makes void the cross of Christ; that it offers intolerable insult to the divine mercy; that it undermines and overthrows our faith. For what is this purgatory but the satisfaction for sin paid after death by the souls of the dead? Hence when this idea of satisfaction is refuted, purgatory itself is forthwith completely overturned.[1] But if it is perfectly clear, from what was lately said, that the blood of Christ is the only satisfaction, expiation, and cleansing for the sins of believers, what remains but to hold that purgatory is mere blasphemy, horrid blasphemy against Christ? I say nothing of the sacrilege by which it is daily defended, the offences which it begets in religion, and the other innumerable evils which we see teeming forth from that fountain of impiety.

7. Those passages of Scripture on which it is their wont falsely and iniquitously to fasten, it may be worth while to wrench out of

---

1 French, "Tellement que si on ote la fantasie de satisfaire, leur purgatorie s'en va bas;"—so that if the fancy of satisfying is taken away, down goes their purgatory.

their hands.[1] When the Lord declares that the sin against the Holy Ghost will not be forgiven either in this world or the world to come, he thereby intimates (they say) that there is a remission of certain sins hereafter. But who sees not that the Lord there speaks of the guilt of sin? But if this is so, what has it to do with their purgatory, seeing they deny not that the guilt of those sins, the punishment of which is there expiated, is forgiven in the present life? Lest, however, they should still object, we shall give a plainer solution. Since it was the Lord's intention to cut off all hope of pardon from this flagitious wickedness, he did not consider it enough to say, that it would never be forgiven, but in the way of amplification, employed a division by which he included both the judgment which every man's conscience pronounces in the present life, and the final judgment which will be publicly pronounced at the resurrection; as if he had said, Beware of this malignant rebellion, as you would of instant destruction; for he who of set purpose endeavours to extinguish the offered light of the Spirit, shall not obtain pardon either in this life, which has been given to sinners for conversion, or on the last day when the angels of God shall separate the sheep from the goats, and the heavenly kingdom shall be purged of all that offends. The next passage they produce is the parable in Matthew: " Agree with thine adversary quickly, whiles thou art in the way with him; lest at any time the adversary deliver thee to the judge, and the judge deliver thee to the officer, and thou be cast into prison. Verily, I say unto thee, Thou shalt by no means come out thence, till thou hast paid the uttermost farthing" (Matth. v. 25, 26). If in this passage the judge means God, the adversary the devil, the officer an angel, and the prison purgatory, I give in at once. But if every man sees that Christ there intended to show to how many perils and evils those expose themselves who obstinately insist on their utmost right, instead of being satisfied with what is fair and equitable, that he might thereby the more strongly exhort his followers to concord, where, I ask, are we to find their purgatory?[2]

8. They seek an argument in the passage in which Paul declares, that all things shall bow the knee to Christ, " things in heaven, and things in earth, and things under the earth" (Phil. ii. 10). They take it for granted, that by " things under the earth" cannot be meant those who are doomed to eternal damnation, and that the only remaining conclusion is, that they must be souls suffering in purgatory. They would not reason very ill if, by the bending of the knee, the Apostle designated true worship; but since he simply says that Christ has received a dominion to which all creatures are subject, what pre-

---

1 Matth. xii. 32; Mark iii. 28; Luke xii. 10; Matth. v. 25.
2 The French adds the following sentence: " Brief, que le passage soit regardé et prins en sa simple intelligence, et il n'y sera rien trouvé de ce qu'ils pretendent;"— In short, let the passage be looked at and taken in its simple meaning, and there will be nothing found in it of what they pretend.

vents us from understanding those "under the earth" to mean the devils, who shall certainly be sisted before the judgment-seat of God, there to recognise their Judge with fear and trembling ? In this way Paul himself elsewhere interprets the same prophecy : " We shall all stand before the judgment-seat of Christ. For it is written, As I live, saith the Lord, every knee shall bow to me, and every tongue shall confess to God" (Rom. xiv. 10, 11). But we cannot in this way interpret what is said in the Apocalypse : " Every creature which is in heaven, and on the earth, and under the earth, and such as are in the sea, heard I saying, Blessing, and honour, and glory, and power, be unto him that sitteth upon the throne, and unto the Lamb, for ever and ever" (Rev. v. 13). This I readily admit ; but what kinds of creatures do they suppose are here enumerated ? It is absolutely certain, that both irrational and inanimate creatures are comprehended. All, then, which is affirmed is, that every part of the universe, from the highest pinnacle of heaven to the very centre of the earth, each in its own way proclaims the glory of the Creator.

To the passage which they produce from the history of the Maccabees (1 Maccab. xii. 43), I will not deign to reply, lest I should seem to include that work among the canonical books. But Augustine[1] holds it to be canonical. First, with what degree of confidence ? " The Jews," says he, " do not hold the book of the Maccabees as they do the Law, the Prophets, and the Psalms, to which the Lord bears testimony as to his own witnesses, saying, Ought not all things which are written in the Law, and the Psalms, and the Prophets, concerning me be fulfilled ? (Luke xxiv. 44.) But it has been received by the Church not uselessly, if it be read or heard with soberness." Jerome, however, unhesitatingly affirms, that it is of no authority in establishing doctrine ; and from the ancient little book, *De Expositione Symboli*, which bears the name of Cyprian, it is plain that it was in no estimation in the ancient Church. And why do I here contend in vain ? As if the author himself did not sufficiently show what degree of deference is to be paid him, when in the end he asks pardon for anything less properly expressed (2 Maccab. xv. 38). He who confesses that his writings stand in need of pardon, certainly proclaims that they are not oracles of the Holy Spirit. We may add, that the piety of Judas is commended for no other reason than for having a firm hope of the final resurrection, in sending his oblation for the dead to Jerusalem. For the writer of the history does not represent what he did as furnishing the price of redemption, but merely that they might be partakers of eternal life, with the other saints who had fallen for their country and religion. The act, indeed, was not free from superstition and misguided zeal ; but it is mere fatuity to extend the legal sacrifice to us, seeing we are assured that the sacrifices then in use ceased on the advent of Christ.

---

[1] See August. contra Secundum Gaudentii Epistolam, cap. 23.

9. But, it seems, they find in Paul an invincible support, which cannot be so easily overthrown. His words are, "Now if any man build upon this foundation gold, silver, precious stones, wood, hay, stubble ; every man's work shall be made manifest : for the day shall declare it, because it shall be revealed by fire ; and the fire shall try every man's work of what sort it is. If any man's work shall be burnt, he shall suffer loss : but he himself shall be saved ; yet so as by fire " (1 Cor. iii. 12—15). What fire (they ask) can that be but the fire of purgatory, by which the defilements of sin are wiped away, in order that we may enter pure into the kingdom of God ? But most of the Fathers [1] give it a different meaning—viz. the tribulation or cross by which the Lord tries his people, that they may not rest satisfied with the defilements of the flesh. This is much more probable than the fiction of a purgatory. I do not, however, agree with them, for I think I see a much surer and clearer meaning to the passage. But, before I produce it, I wish they would answer me, whether they think the Apostle and all the saints have to pass through this purgatorial fire ? I am aware they will say, no ; for it were too absurd to hold that purification is required by those whose superfluous merits they dream of as applicable to all the members of the Church. But this the Apostle affirms ; for he says, not that the works of certain persons, but the works of all will be tried.[2] And this is not my argument, but that of Augustine, who thus impugns that interpretation.[3] And (what makes the thing more absurd) he says, not that they will pass through fire for certain works, but that even if they should have edified the Church with the greatest fidelity, they will receive their reward after their works shall have been tried by fire. First, we see that the Apostle used a metaphor when he gave the names of wood, hay, and stubble, to doctrines of man's device. The ground of the metaphor is obvious—viz. that as wood when it is put into the fire is consumed and destroyed, so neither will those doctrines be able to endure when they come to be tried. Moreover, every one sees that the trial is made by the Spirit of God. Therefore, in following out the thread of the metaphor, and adapting its parts properly to each other, he gave the name of fire to the examination of the Holy Spirit. For just as silver and gold, the nearer they are brought to the fire, give stronger proof of their genuineness and purity, so the Lord's truth, the more thoroughly it is submitted to spiritual examination, has its authority the better confirmed. As hay, wood, and stubble, when the fire is applied to them, are suddenly consumed, so the inventions of man, not founded on the word of God, cannot stand the trial of the Holy Spirit, but forthwith give way and perish. In fine, if spurious doc-

---

1 Chrysostom, Augustine, and others ; see August. Enchirid. ad Laurent. cap. 68.

2 The French adds, " auquel nombre universel sont enclos les Apostres ;"—in which universal number the Apostles are included.

3 French, " l'exposition que font aujourdhui nos adversaires ;"—the exposition which our opponents give in the present day.

trines are compared to wood, hay, and stubble, because, like wood, hay, and stubble, they are burned by fire and fitted for destruction, though the actual destruction is only completed by the Spirit of the Lord, it follows that the Spirit is that fire by which they will be proved. This proof Paul calls the *day of the Lord;* using a term common in Scripture. For the day of the Lord is said to take place whenever he in some way manifests his presence to men, his face being specially said to shine when his truth is manifested. It has now been proved, that Paul has no idea of any other fire than the trial of the Holy Spirit. But how are those who suffer the loss of their works saved by fire? This it will not be difficult to understand, if we consider of what kind of persons he speaks. For he designates them builders of the Church, who, retaining the proper foundation, build different materials upon it; that is, who, not abandoning the principal and necessary articles of faith, err in minor and less perilous matters, mingling their own fictions with the word of God. Such, I say, must suffer the loss of their work by the destruction of their fictions. They themselves, however, are saved, yet so as by fire; that is, not that their ignorance and delusions are approved by the Lord, but they are purified from them by the grace and power of the Holy Spirit. All those, accordingly, who have tainted the golden purity of the divine word with the pollution of purgatory, must necessarily suffer the loss of their work.

10. But the observance of it in the Church is of the highest antiquity. This objection is disposed of by Paul, when, including even his own age in the sentence, he declares, that all who in building the Church have laid up something not conformable to the foundation, must suffer the loss of their work. When, therefore, my opponents object, that it has been the practice for thirteen hundred years to offer prayers for the dead, I, in return, ask them, by what word of God, by what revelation, by what example it was done? For here not only are passages of Scripture wanting, but in the examples of all the saints of whom we read, nothing of the kind is seen. We have numerous, and sometimes long narratives, of their mourning and sepulchral rites, but not one word is said of prayers.[1] But the more important the matter was, the more they ought to have dwelt upon it. Even those who in ancient times offered prayers for the dead, saw that they were not supported by the command of God and legitimate example. Why then did they presume to do it? I hold that herein they suffered the common lot of man, and therefore maintain, that what they did is not to be imitated. Believers ought not to engage in any work without a firm conviction of its propriety, as Paul enjoins,

---

[1] French, "L'Escriture raconte souventesfois et bien au long, comment les fideles ont pleuré la mort de leurs parens, et comment ils les ont ensevelis; mais qu'ils ayent prié pour eux, il n'en est nouvelles;"—Scripture relates oftentimes and at great length, how the faithful lamented the death of their relations, and how they buried them: but that they prayed for them is never hinted at.

(Rom. xiv. 23) ; and this conviction is expressly requisite in prayer. It is to be presumed, however, that they were influenced by some reason ; they sought a solace for their sorrow, and it seemed cruel not to give some attestation of their love to the dead, when in the presence of God. All know by experience how natural it is for the human mind thus to feel.

Received custom too was a kind of torch, by which the minds of many were inflamed. We know that among all the Gentiles, and in all ages, certain rites were paid to the dead, and that every year lustrations were performed for their manes. Although Satan deluded foolish mortals by these impostures, yet the means of deceiving were borrowed from a sound principle—viz. that death is not destruction, but a passage from this life to another. And there can be no doubt that superstition itself always left the Gentiles without excuse before the judgment-seat of God, because they neglected to prepare for that future life which they professed to believe. Thus, that Christians might not seem worse than heathens, they felt ashamed of paying no office to the dead, as if they had been utterly annihilated. Hence their ill-advised assiduity; because they thought they would expose themselves to great disgrace, if they were slow in providing funeral feasts and oblations. What was thus introduced by perverse rivalship, ever and anon received new additions, until the highest holiness of the Papacy consisted in giving assistance to the suffering dead. But far better and more solid comfort is furnished by Scripture when it declares, " Blessed are the dead that die in the Lord ;" and adds the reason, " for they rest from their labours " (Rev. xiv. 13). We ought not to indulge our love so far as to set up a perverse mode of prayer in the Church. Surely every person possessed of the least prudence easily perceives, that whatever we meet with on this subject in ancient writers, was in deference to public custom, and the ignorance of the vulgar. I admit they were themselves also carried away into error, the usual effect of rash credulity being to destroy the judgment. Meanwhile the passages themselves show, that when they recommended prayer for the dead, it was with hesitation. Augustine relates in his Confessions, that his mother Monica earnestly entreated to be remembered when the solemn rites at the altar were performed; doubtless an old woman's wish, which her son did not bring to the test of Scripture, but from natural affection wished others to approve. His book, *De Cura pro Mortuis Agenda, On showing Care for the Dead*, is so full of doubt, that its coldness may well extinguish the heat of a foolish zeal. Should any one, in pretending to be a patron of the dead, deal merely in probabilities, the only effect will be to make those indifferent who were formerly solicitous.[1]

[1] French, "Le liure qu'il à composé tout expres de cest argument, et qu'il a intitule. Du soin pour les morts, est enveloppée en tant de doutes, qu'il doit suffire pour refroidir ceux qui y auroyent devotion; pour le moins en voyant qu'il ne s'aide que de conjectures bien legeres et foibles, on verra qu'on ne se doit point fort empescher d'une chose

The only support of this dogma is, that as a custom of praying for the dead prevailed, the duty ought not to be despised. But granting that ancient ecclesiastical writers deemed it a pious thing to assist the dead, the rule which can never deceive is always to be observed —viz. that we must not introduce anything of our own into our prayers, but must keep all our wishes in subordination to the word of God, because it belongs to Him to prescribe what he wishes us to ask. Now, since the whole Law and Gospel do not contain one syllable which countenances the right of praying for the dead, it is a profanation of prayer to go one step farther than God enjoins. But, lest our opponents boast of sharing their error with the ancient Church, I say, that there is a wide difference between the two. The latter made a commemoration of the dead, that they might not seem to have cast off all concern for them; but they, at the same time, acknowledged that they were doubtful as to their state; assuredly they made no such assertion concerning purgatory as implied that they did not hold it to be uncertain. The former insist, that their dream of purgatory shall be received without question as an article of faith. The latter sparingly and in a perfunctory manner only commended their dead to the Lord, in the communion of the holy supper. The former are constantly urging the care of the dead, and by their importunate preaching of it, make out that it is to be preferred to all the offices of charity. But it would not be difficult for us to produce some passages from ancient writers,[1] which clearly overturn all those prayers for the dead which were then in use. Such is the passage of Augustine, in which he shows that the resurrection of the flesh and eternal glory is expected by all, but that rest which follows death is received by every one who is worthy of it when he dies. Accordingly, he declares that all the righteous, not less than the Apostles, Prophets, and Martyrs, immediately after death enjoy blessed rest. If such is their condition, what, I ask, will our prayers contribute to them?[2] I say nothing of those grosser superstitions by which they have fascinated the minds of the simple; and yet they are innumerable, and most of them so monstrous, that they cannot cover them with any cloak of decency. I say nothing, moreover, of those most shameful traffickings, which they plied as they listed while the world was stupified. For I would never come to an end; and, without enumerating them, the pious reader will here find enough to establish his conscience.

où il n'y a nulle importance;"—The book which he has composed expressly on this subject, and which he has entitled, Of Care for the Dead, is enveloped in so many doubts, that it should be sufficient to cool those who are devoted to it; at least, as he supports his view only by very slight and feeble conjectures, it will be seen, that we ought not to trouble ourselves much with a matter in which there is no importance.

[1] See August. Homil. in Joann. 49. De Civitate Dei, Lib. xxi. cap. xiii.-xxiv.

[2] The French of the latter clause of this sentence is, " et toutesfois il y aura matiere assez ample de les pourmener en cette campagne, veu qu'ils n'ont nulle couleur pour s'excuser, qu'ils ne soyent conveincus d'etre les plus vilains trompeurs qui furent jamais;"—and yet there is ample space to travel them over this field, seeing they have no colour of excuse, but must be convicted of being the most villanous deceivers that ever were.

INSTITUTES

OF

THE CHRISTIAN RELIGION.

BOOK THIRD

CONTINUED.

CHAPTER VI.

THE LIFE OF A CHRISTIAN MAN. SCRIPTURAL ARGUMENTS EXHORTING TO IT.

This and the four following chapters treat of the Life of the Christian, and are so arranged as to admit of being classed under two principal heads.

First, it must be held to be a universally acknowledged point, that no man is a Christian who does not feel some special love for righteousness, chap. vi. Secondly, in regard to the standard by which every man ought to regulate his life, although it seems to be considered in chap. vii. only, yet the three following chapters also refer to it. For it shows that the Christian has two duties to perform. First, the observance being so arduous, he needs the greatest patience. Hence chap. viii. treats professedly of the utility of the cross, and chap. ix. invites to meditation on the future life. Lastly, chap. x. clearly shows, as in no small degree conducive to this end, how we are to use this life and its comforts without abusing them.

This sixth chapter consists of two parts,—I. Connection between this treatise on the Christian Life and the doctrine of Regeneration and Repentance. Arrangement of the treatise, sec. 1–3. II. Extremes to be avoided; 1. False Christians denying Christ, by their works condemned, sec. 4. 2, Christians should not despair, though they have not attained perfection, provided they make daily progress in piety and righteousness.

Sections.

1. Connection between this chapter and the doctrine of Regeneration. Necessity of the doctrine concerning the Christian Life. The brevity of this treatise: The method of it. Plainness and unadorned simplicity of the Scripture system of morals.

2. Two divisions. First, Personal holiness. 1. Because God is holy. 2. Because of our communion with his saints.

3. Second division, relating to our Redemption. Admirable moral system of Scripture. Five special inducements or exhortations to a Christian Life.

4. False Christians who are opposed to this life censured. 1. They have not truly learned Christ. 2. The Gospel not the guide of their words or actions. 3. They do not imitate Christ the Master. 4. They would separate the Spirit from his word.

5. Christians ought not to despond: Provided, 1. They take the word of God for their guide. 2. Sincerely cultivate righteousness. 3. Walk, according to their capacity, in the ways of the Lord. 4. Make some progress. 5. Persevere.

1. WE have said that the object of regeneration is to bring the life of believers into concord and harmony with the righteousness of God, and so confirm the adoption by which they have been received as sons. But although the law comprehends within it that new life by which the image of God is restored in us, yet, as our sluggishness stands greatly in need both of helps and incentives, it will be useful to collect out of Scripture a true account of this reformation, lest any who have a heartfelt desire of repentance should in their zeal go astray. Moreover, I am not unaware that, in undertaking to describe the life of the Christian, I am entering on a large and extensive subject, one which, when fully considered in all its parts, is sufficient to fill a large volume. We see the length to which the Fathers, in treating of individual virtues, extend their exhortations. This they do, not from mere loquaciousness; for whatever be the virtue which you undertake to recommend, your pen is spontaneously led by the copiousness of the matter so to amplify, that you seem not to have discussed it properly if you have not done it at length. My intention, however, in the plan of life which I now propose to give, is not to extend it so far as to treat of each virtue specially, and expatiate in exhortation. This must be sought in the writings of others, and particularly in the Homilies of the Fathers.[1] For me it will be sufficient to point out the method by which a pious man may be taught how to frame his life aright, and briefly lay down some universal rule by which he may not improperly regulate his conduct. I shall one day possibly find time for more ample discourse [or leave others to perform an office for which I am not so fit. I have a natural love of brevity, and, perhaps, any attempt of mine at copiousness would not succeed. Even if I could gain the highest applause by being more prolix, I would scarcely be disposed to attempt it],[2] while the nature of my present work requires me to glance at simple doctrine with as much brevity as possible. As philosophers have certain definitions of rectitude and honesty, from which they derive particular duties and the whole train of virtues; so in this respect Scripture is not without order, but presents a most beautiful arrangement, one too which is every way much more certain than that of philosophers. The only difference is, that they, under the influence of ambition, constantly affect an exquisite perspicuity of arrangement, which may serve to display their genius, whereas the Spirit of God, teaching without affectation, is not so perpetually observant of exact method, and yet by observing it at times sufficiently intimates that it is not to be neglected.

2. The Scripture system of which we speak aims chiefly at two objects. The former is, that the love of righteousness, to which we are by no means naturally inclined, may be instilled and implanted into our minds. The latter is (see chap. vii.), to prescribe a rule

---

[1] The French adds, "C'est a dire, sermons populaires;"—that is to say, popular sermons.

[2] The passage in brackets is omitted in the French.

which will prevent us while in the pursuit of righteousness from going astray. It has numerous admirable methods of recommending righteousness.[1] Many have been already pointed out in different parts of this work; but we shall here also briefly advert to some of them. With what better foundation can it begin than by reminding us that we must be holy, because "God is holy"? (Lev. xix. 1; 1 Pet. i. 16.) For when we were scattered abroad like lost sheep, wandering through the labyrinth of this world, he brought us back again to his own fold. When mention is made of our union with God, let us remember that holiness must be the bond; not that by the merit of holiness we come into communion with him (we ought rather first to cleave to him, in order that, pervaded with his holiness, we may follow whither he calls), but because it greatly concerns his glory not to have any fellowship with wickedness and impurity. Wherefore he tells us that this is the end of our calling, the end to which we ought ever to have respect, if we would answer the call of God. For to what end were we rescued from the iniquity and pollution of the world into which we were plunged, if we allow ourselves, during our whole lives, to wallow in them? Besides, we are at the same time admonished, that if we would be regarded as the Lord's people, we must inhabit the holy city Jerusalem (Isaiah xxxv. 8, *et alibi*), which, as he hath consecrated it to himself, it were impious for its inhabitants to profane by impurity. Hence the expressions, "Who shall abide in thy tabernacle? who shall dwell in thy holy hill? He that walketh uprightly, and worketh righteousness" (Ps. xv. 1, 2; xxiv. 3, 4); for the sanctuary in which he dwells certainly ought not to be like an unclean stall.

3. The better to arouse us, it exhibits God the Father, who, as he hath reconciled us to himself in his Anointed, has impressed his image upon us, to which he would have us to be conformed (Rom. v. 4). Come, then, and let them show me a more excellent system among philosophers, who think that they only have a moral philosophy duly and orderly arranged. They, when they would give excellent exhortations to virtue, can only tell us to live agreeably to nature. Scripture derives its exhortations from the true source,[2] when it not only enjoins us to regulate our lives with a view to God its author to whom it belongs; but after showing us that we have degenerated from our true origin—viz. the law of our Creator, adds, that Christ, through whom we have returned to favour with God, is set before us as a model, the image of which our lives should express. What do you require more effectual than this? Nay, what do you require beyond this? If the Lord adopts us for his sons on the condition that our life be a representation of Christ, the bond of our

---

1 The French begins the sentence thus, "Quant est du premier poinct;"—As to the former point.

2 Mal. i. 6; Eph. v. 1; 1 John iii. 1, 3; Eph. v. 26; Rom. vi. 1–4; 1 Cor. vi. 11; 1 Pet. i. 15, 19; 1 Cor. vi. 15; John xv. 3; Eph. v. 2, 3; Col. iii. 1, 2; 1 Cor. iii. 16; vi. 17; 2 Cor. vi. 16; 1 Thess. v. 23.

adoption,—then, unless we dedicate and devote ourselves to right-eousness, we not only, with the utmost perfidy, revolt from our Creator, but also abjure the Saviour himself. Then, from an enu-meration of all the blessings of God, and each part of our salvation, it finds materials for exhortation. Ever since God exhibited himself to us as a Father, we must be convicted of extreme ingratitude if we do not in turn exhibit ourselves as his sons. Ever since Christ puri-fied us by the laver of his blood, and communicated this purification by baptism, it would ill become us to be defiled with new pollution. Ever since he ingrafted us into his body, we, who are his members, should anxiously beware of contracting any stain or taint. Ever since he who is our head ascended to heaven, it is befitting in us to withdraw our affections from the earth, and with our whole soul aspire to heaven. Ever since the Holy Spirit dedicated us as temples to the Lord, we should make it our endeavour to show forth the glory of God, and guard against being profaned by the defilement of sin. Ever since our soul and body were destined to heavenly incorrupti-bility and an unfading crown, we should earnestly strive to keep them pure and uncorrupted against the day of the Lord. These, I say, are the surest foundations of a well-regulated life, and you will search in vain for anything resembling them among philosophers, who, in their commendation of virtue, never rise higher than the natural dig-nity of man.

4. This is the place to address those who, having nothing of Christ but the name and sign, would yet be called Christians. How dare they boast of this sacred name? None have intercourse with Christ but those who have acquired the true knowledge of him from the Gospel. The Apostle denies that any man truly has learned Christ who has not learned to put off "the old man, which is corrupt ac-cording to the deceitful lusts, and put on Christ" (Eph. iv. 22). They are convicted, therefore, of falsely and unjustly pretending a know-ledge of Christ, whatever be the volubility and eloquence with which they can talk of the Gospel. Doctrine is not an affair of the tongue, but of the life; is not apprehended by the intellect and memory merely, like other branches of learning; but is received only when it possesses the whole soul, and finds its seat and habitation in the inmost recesses of the heart. Let them, therefore, either cease to insult God, by boasting that they are what they are not, or let them show themselves not unworthy disciples of their divine Master. To doctrine in which our religion is contained we have given the first place, since by it our salvation commences; but it must be transfused into the breast, and pass into the conduct, and so transform us into itself, as not to prove unfruitful. If philosophers are justly offended, and banish from their company with disgrace those who, while professing an art which ought to be the mistress of their conduct, convert it into mere loquacious sophistry, with how much better reason shall we detest those flimsy sophists who are contented to let the Gospel play upon their lips, when, from its efficacy, it ought to penetrate the inmost affections

of the heart, fix its seat in the soul, and pervade the whole man a hundred times more than the frigid discourses of philosophers?

5. I insist not that the life of the Christian shall breathe nothing but the perfect Gospel, though this is to be desired, and ought to be attempted. I insist not so strictly on evangelical perfection, as to refuse to acknowledge as a Christian any man who has not attained it. In this way all would be excluded from the Church, since there is no man who is not far removed from this perfection, while many, who have made but little progress, would be undeservedly rejected. What then? Let us set this before our eye as the end at which we ought constantly to aim. Let it be regarded as the goal towards which we are to run. For you cannot divide the matter with God, undertaking part of what his word enjoins, and omitting part at pleasure. For, in the first place, God uniformly recommends integrity as the principal part of his worship, meaning by integrity real singleness of mind, devoid of gloss and fiction, and to this is opposed a double mind; as if it had been said that the spiritual commencement of a good life is when the internal affections are sincerely devoted to God, in the cultivation of holiness and justice. But seeing that, in this earthly prison of the body, no man is supplied with strength sufficient to hasten in his course with due alacrity, while the greater number are so oppressed with weakness, that hesitating, and halting, and even crawling on the ground, they make little progress, let every one of us go as far as his humble ability enables him, and prosecute the journey once begun. No one will travel so badly as not daily to make some degree of progress. This, therefore, let us never cease to do, that we may daily advance in the way of the Lord; and let us not despair because of the slender measure of success. How little soever the success may correspond with our wish, our labour is not lost when to-day is better than yesterday, provided with true singleness of mind we keep our aim, and aspire to the goal, not speaking flattering things to ourselves, nor indulging our vices, but making it our constant endeavour to become better, until we attain to goodness itself. If during the whole course of our life we seek and follow, we shall at length attain it, when relieved from the infirmity of flesh we are admitted to full fellowship with God.

CHAPTER VII.

A SUMMARY OF THE CHRISTIAN LIFE. OF SELF-DENIAL.[1]

The divisions of the chapter are,—I. The rule which permits us not to go astray in the study of righteousness, requires two things—viz. that man, abandoning his own will, devote himself entirely to the service of God; whence it follows, that we must seek not our own things, but the things of God, sec. 1, 2. II. A description of this renovation or Christian life taken from the Epistle to Titus, and accurately explained under certain special heads, sec. 3 to end.

Sections.

1. Consideration of the second general division in regard to the Christian life. Its beginning and sum. A twofold respect. 1. We are not our own. Respect to both the fruit and the use. Unknown to philosophers, who have placed reason on the throne of the Holy Spirit.
2. Since we are not our own, we must seek the glory of God, and obey his will. Self-denial recommended to the disciples of Christ. He who neglects it, deceived either by pride or hypocrisy, rushes on destruction.
3. Three things to be followed, and two to be shunned in life. Impiety and worldly lusts to be shunned. Sobriety, justice, and piety, to be followed. An inducement to right conduct.
4. Self-denial the sum of Paul's doctrine. Its difficulty. Qualities in us which make it difficult. Cures for these qualities. 1. Ambition to be suppressed. 2. Humility to be embraced. 3. Candour to be esteemed. 4. Mutual charity to be preserved. 5. Modesty to be sincerely cultivated.
5. The advantage of our neighbour to be promoted. Here self-denial most necessary, and yet most difficult. Here a double remedy. 1. The benefits bestowed upon us are for the common benefit of the Church. 2. We ought to do all we can for our neighbour. This illustrated by analogy from the members of the human body. This duty of charity founded on the divine command.
6. Charity ought to have for its attendants patience and kindness. We should consider the image of God in our neighbours, and especially in those who are of the household of faith. Hence a fourfold consideration which refutes all objections. A common objection refuted.
7. Christian life cannot exist without charity. Remedies for the vices opposed to charity. 1. Mercy. 2. Humility. 3. Modesty. 4. Diligence. 5. Perseverance.
8. Self-denial, in respect of God, should lead to equanimity and tolerance. 1. We are always subject to God. 2. We should shun avarice and ambition. 3. We should expect all prosperity from the blessing of God, and entirely depend on him.
9. We ought not to desire wealth or honours without the divine blessing, nor follow the arts of the wicked. We ought to cast all our care upon God, and never envy the prosperity of others.
10. We ought to commit ourselves entirely to God. The necessity of this doctrine. Various uses of affliction. Heathen abuse and corruption.

[1] On this and the three following chapters, which contain the second part of the Treatise on the Christian Life, see Augustin. De Moribus Ecclesiæ Catholicæ, and Calvin de Scandalis.

1. ALTHOUGH the Law of God contains a perfect rule of conduct admirably arranged, it has seemed proper to our divine Master to train his people by a more accurate method, to the rule which is enjoined in the Law ; and the leading principle in the method is, that it is the duty of believers to present their "bodies a living sacrifice, holy and acceptable unto God, which is their reasonable service" (Rom. xii. 1). Hence he draws the exhortation : "Be not conformed to this world : but be ye transformed by the renewing of your mind, that ye may prove what is that good, and acceptable, and perfect will of God." The great point, then, is, that we are consecrated and dedicated to God, and therefore should not henceforth think, speak, design, or act, without a view to his glory. What he hath made sacred cannot, without signal insult to him, be applied to profane use. But if we are not our own, but the Lord's, it is plain both what error is to be shunned, and to what end the actions of our lives ought to be directed. We are not our own ; therefore, neither is our own reason or will to rule our acts and counsels. We are not our own ; therefore, let us not make it our end to seek what may be agreeable to our carnal nature. We are not our own ; therefore, as far as possible, let us forget ourselves and the things that are ours. On the other hand, we are God's ; let us, therefore, live and die to him (Rom. xiv. 8). We are God's ; therefore, let his wisdom and will preside over all our actions. We are God's ; to him, then, as the only legitimate end, let every part of our life be directed. O how great the proficiency of him who, taught that he is not his own, has withdrawn the dominion and government of himself from his own reason that he may give them to God ! For as the surest source of destruction to men is to obey themselves, so the only haven of safety is to have no other will, no other wisdom, than to follow the Lord wherever he leads. Let this, then, be the first step, to abandon ourselves, and devote the whole energy of our minds to the service of God. By service, I mean not only that which consists in verbal obedience, but that by which the mind, divested of its own carnal feelings, implicitly obeys the call of the Spirit of God. This transformation (which Paul calls *the renewing of the mind*, Rom. xii. 2 ; Eph. iv. 23), though it is the first entrance to life, was unknown to all the philosophers. They give the government of man to reason alone, thinking that she alone is to be listened to ; in short, they assign to her the sole direction of the conduct. But Christian philosophy bids her give place, and yield complete submission to the Holy Spirit, so that the man himself no longer lives, but Christ lives and reigns in him (Gal. ii. 20).

2. Hence follows the other principle, that we are not to seek our own, but the Lord's will, and act with a view to promote his glory. Great is our proficiency, when, almost forgetting ourselves, certainly postponing our own reason, we faithfully make it our study to obey God and his commandments. For when Scripture enjoins us to lay aside private regard to ourselves, it not only divests our minds of an excessive longing for wealth, or power, or human favour, but eradi-

cates all ambition and thirst for worldly glory, and other more secret
pests. The Christian ought, indeed, to be so trained and disposed
as to consider, that during his whole life he has to do with God.
For this reason, as he will bring all things to the disposal and estimate of God, so he will religiously direct his whole mind to him. For
he who has learned to look to God in everything he does, is at the
same time diverted from all vain thoughts. This is that self-denial
which Christ so strongly enforces on his disciples from the very outset (Matth. xvi. 24), which, as soon as it takes hold of the mind,
leaves no place either, first, for pride, show, and ostentation; or,
secondly, for avarice, lust, luxury, effeminacy, or other vices which
are engendered by self-love. On the contrary, wherever it reigns not,
the foulest vices are indulged in without shame; or, if there is some
appearance of virtue, it is vitiated by a depraved longing for applause.
Show me, if you can, an individual who, unless he has renounced
himself in obedience to the Lord's command, is disposed to do good
for its own sake. Those who have not so renounced themselves have
followed virtue at least for the sake of praise. The philosophers who
have contended most strongly that virtue is to be desired on her own
account, were so inflated with arrogance as to make it apparent that
they sought virtue for no other reason than as a ground for indulging
in pride. So far, therefore, is God from being delighted with these
hunters after popular applause with their swollen breasts, that he
declares they have received their reward in this world (Matth. vi. 2),
and that harlots and publicans are nearer the kingdom of heaven
than they (Matth. xxi. 31). We have not yet sufficiently explained
how great and numerous are the obstacles by which a man is impeded
in the pursuit of rectitude, so long as he has not renounced himself.
The old saying is true, There is a world of iniquity treasured up in
the human soul. Nor can you find any other remedy for this than to
deny yourself, renounce your own reason, and direct your whole mind
to the pursuit of those things which the Lord requires of you,
and which you are to seek only because they are pleasing to Him.

3. In another passage, Paul gives a brief, indeed, but more distinct
account of each of the parts of a well-ordered life: "The grace of
God that bringeth salvation hath appeared to all men, teaching us
that, denying ungodliness and worldly lusts, we should live soberly,
righteously, and godly, in this present world; looking for that blessed
hope, and the glorious appearance of the great God and our Saviour
Jesus Christ; who gave himself for us, that he might redeem us from
all iniquity, and purify to himself a peculiar people, zealous of good
works" (Tit. ii. 11—14). After holding forth the grace of God to
animate us, and pave the way for His true worship, he removes the
two greatest obstacles which stand in the way—viz. ungodliness, to
which we are by nature too prone, and worldly lusts, which are of
still greater extent. Under *ungodliness,* he includes not merely
superstition, but everything at variance with the true fear of God.
Worldly lusts are equivalent to the lusts of the flesh. Thus he en-

joins us, in regard to both tables of the Law, to lay aside our own mind, and renounce whatever our own reason and will dictate. Then he reduces all the actions of our lives to three branches, sobriety, righteousness, and godliness. *Sobriety* undoubtedly denotes as well chastity and temperance as the pure and frugal use of temporal goods, and patient endurance of want. *Righteousness* comprehends all the duties of equity, in rendering to every one his due. Next follows *godliness*, which separates us from the pollutions of the world, and connects us with God in true holiness. These, when connected together by an indissoluble chain, constitute complete perfection. But as nothing is more difficult than to bid adieu to the will of the flesh, subdue, nay, abjure our lusts, devote ourselves to God and our brethren, and lead an angelic life amid the pollutions of the world, Paul, to set our minds free from all entanglements, recalls us to the hope of a blessed immortality, justly urging us to contend, because as Christ has once appeared as our Redeemer, so on his final advent he will give full effect to the salvation obtained by him. And in this way he dispels all the allurements which becloud our path, and prevent us from aspiring as we ought to heavenly glory; nay, he tells us that we must be pilgrims in the world, that we may not fail of obtaining the heavenly inheritance.

4. Moreover, we see by these words that self-denial has respect partly to men and partly (more especially) to God (sec. 8–10). For when Scripture enjoins us, in regard to our fellow-men, to prefer them in honour to ourselves, and sincerely labour to promote their advantage (Rom. xii. 10; Phil. ii. 3), he gives us commands which our mind is utterly incapable of obeying until its natural feelings are suppressed. For so blindly do we all rush in the direction of self-love, that every one thinks he has a good reason for exalting himself and despising all others in comparison. If God has bestowed on us something not to be repented of, trusting to it, we immediately become elated, and not only swell, but almost burst with pride. The vices with which we abound we both carefully conceal from others, and flatteringly represent to ourselves as minute and trivial, nay, sometimes hug them as virtues. When the same qualities which we admire in ourselves are seen in others, even though they should be superior, we, in order that we may not be forced to yield to them, maliciously lower and carp at them; in like manner, in the case of vices, not contented with severe and keen animadversion, we studiously exaggerate them. Hence the insolence with which each, as if exempted from the common lot, seeks to exalt himself above his neighbour, confidently and proudly despising others, or at least looking down upon them as his inferiors. The poor man yields to the rich, the plebeian to the noble, the servant to the master, the unlearned to the learned, and yet every one inwardly cherishes some idea of his own superiority. Thus each flattering himself, sets up a kind of kingdom in his breast; the arrogant, to satisfy themselves, pass censure on the minds and manners of other men, and when conten-

tion arises, the full venom is displayed. Many bear about with them some measure of mildness so long as all things go smoothly and lovingly with them, but how few are there who, when stung and irritated, preserve the same tenor of moderation? For this there is no other remedy than to pluck up by the roots those most noxious pests, self-love and love of victory (φιλονεικία και φιλαυτία). This the doctrine of Scripture does. For it teaches us to remember, that the endowments which God has bestowed upon us are not our own, but His free gifts, and that those who plume themselves upon them betray their ingratitude. "Who maketh thee to differ," saith Paul, "and what hast thou that thou didst not receive? now if thou didst receive it, why dost thou glory, as if thou hadst not received it?" (1 Cor. iv. 7.) Then by a diligent examination of our faults, let us keep ourselves humble. Thus while nothing will remain to swell our pride, there will be much to subdue it. Again, we are enjoined, whenever we behold the gifts of God in others, so to reverence and respect the gifts, as also to honour those in whom they reside. God having been pleased to bestow honour upon them, it would ill become us to deprive them of it. Then we are told to overlook their faults, not, indeed, to encourage by flattering them, but not because of them to insult those whom we ought to regard with honour and good-will.[1] In this way, with regard to all with whom we have intercourse, our behaviour will be not only moderate and modest, but courteous and friendly. The only way by which you can ever attain to true meekness, is to have your heart imbued with a humble opinion of yourself and respect for others.

5. How difficult it is to perform the duty of seeking the good of our neighbour! Unless you leave off all thought of yourself, and in a manner cease to be yourself, you will never accomplish it. How can you exhibit those works of charity which Paul describes unless you renounce yourself, and become wholly devoted to others? "Charity (says he, 1 Cor. xiii. 4) suffereth long, and is kind; charity envieth not; charity vaunteth not itself, is not puffed up, doth not behave itself unseemly, seeketh not her own, is not easily provoked," &c. Were it the only thing required of us to seek not our own, nature would not have the least power to comply: she so inclines us to love ourselves only, that she will not easily allow us carelessly to pass by ourselves and our own interests that we may watch over the interests of others, nay, spontaneously to yield our own right, and resign it to another. But Scripture, to conduct us to this, reminds us, that whatever we obtain from the Lord is granted on the condition of our employing it for the common good of the Church, and that, therefore, the legitimate use of all our gifts is a kind and liberal communication of them with others. There cannot be a surer rule, nor a stronger exhortation to the observance of it, than when we are tauhgt that all the endowments which we possess are divine deposits

---

[1] Calvin. de Sacerdotiis Eccles. Papal. in fine.

intrusted to us for the very purpose of being distributed for the good of our neighbour. But Scripture proceeds still farther when it likens these endowments to the different members of the body (1 Cor. xii. 12). No member has its function for itself, or applies it for its own private use, but transfers it to its fellow-members; nor does it derive any other advantage from it than that which it receives in common with the whole body. Thus, whatever the pious man can do, he is bound to do for his brethren, not consulting his own interest in any other way than by striving earnestly for the common edification of the Church. Let this, then, be our method of showing good-will and kindness, considering that, in regard to everything which God has bestowed upon us, and by which we can aid our neighbour, we are his stewards, and are bound to give account of our stewardship; moreover, that the only right mode of administration is that which is regulated by love. In this way, we shall not only unite the study of our neighbour's advantage with a regard to our own, but make the latter subordinate to the former. And lest we should have omitted to perceive that this is the law for duly administering every gift which we receive from God, he of old applied that law to the minutest expressions of his own kindness. He commanded the first-fruits to be offered to him as an attestation by the people that it was impious to reap any advantage from goods not previously consecrated to him (Exod. xxii. 29; xxiii. 19). But if the gifts of God are not sanctified to us until we have with our own hand dedicated them to the Giver, it must be a gross abuse that does not give signs of such dedication. It is in vain to contend that you cannot enrich the Lord by your offerings. Though, as the Psalmist says, "Thou art my Lord: my goodness extendeth not unto thee," yet you can extend it "to the saints that are in the earth" (Ps. xvi. 2, 3); and therefore a comparison is drawn between sacred oblations and alms as now corresponding to the offerings under the Law.[1]

6. Moreover, that we may not weary in well-doing (as would otherwise forthwith and infallibly be the case), we must add the other quality in the Apostle's enumeration, "Charity suffereth long, and is kind, is not easily provoked" (1 Cor. xiii. 4). The Lord enjoins us to do good to all without exception, though the greater part, if estimated by their own merit, are most unworthy of it. But Scripture subjoins a most excellent reason, when it tells us that we are not to look to what men in themselves deserve, but to attend to the image of God, which exists in all, and to which we owe all honour and love. But in those who are of the household of faith, the same rule is to be more carefully observed, inasmuch as that image is renewed and restored in them by the Spirit of Christ. Therefore, whoever be the man that is presented to you as needing your assistance, you have no ground for declining to give it to him. Say he is a stranger. The Lord has given him a mark which ought

to be familiar to you: for which reason he forbids you to despise your own flesh (Gal. vi. 10). Say he is mean and of no consideration. The Lord points him out as one whom he has distinguished by the lustre of his own image (Isaiah lviii. 7). Say that you are bound to him by no ties of duty. The Lord has substituted him as it were into his own place, that in him you may recognise the many great obligations under which the Lord has laid you to himself. Say that he is unworthy of your least exertion on his account; but the image of God, by which he is recommended to you, is worthy of yourself and all your exertions. But if he not only merits no good, but has provoked you by injury and mischief, still this is no good reason why you should not embrace him in love, and visit him with offices of love. He has deserved very differently from me, you will say. But what has the Lord deserved?[2] Whatever injury he has done you, when he enjoins you to forgive him, he certainly means that it should be imputed to himself. In this way only we attain to what is not to say difficult, but altogether against nature,[1] to love those that hate us, render good for evil, and blessing for cursing, remembering that we are not to reflect on the wickedness of men, but look to the image of God in them, an image which, covering and obliterating their faults, should by its beauty and dignity allure us to love and embrace them.

7. We shall thus succeed in mortifying ourselves if we fulfil all the duties of charity. Those duties, however, are not fulfilled by the mere discharge of them, though none be omitted, unless it is done from a pure feeling of love. For it may happen that one may perform every one of these offices, in so far as the external act is concerned, and be far from performing them aright. For you see some who would be thought very liberal, and yet accompany every thing they give with insult, by the haughtiness of their looks, or the violence of their words. And to such a calamitous condition have we come in this unhappy age, that the greater part of men never almost give alms without contumely. Such conduct ought not to have been tolerated even among the heathen; but from Christians something more is required than to carry cheerfulness in their looks, and give attractiveness to the discharge of their duties by courteous language. First, they should put themselves in the place of him whom they see in need of their assistance, and pity his misfortune as if they felt and bore it, so that a feeling of pity and humanity should incline them to assist him just as they would themselves. He who is thus minded will go and give assistance to his brethren, and not only not taint his acts with arrogance or upbraiding, but will neither look down upon the brother to whom he does a kindness, as one who

---

1 French, " Car si nous disons qu'il n'a merité que mal de nous; Dieu nous pourra demander quel mal il nous a fait, lui dont nous tenons tout notre bien;"—For if we say that he has deserved nothing of us but evil, God may ask us what evil he has done us, he of whom we hold our every blessing.

2 Matth. v. 44; vi. 14; xviii. 35; Luke xvii. 3.

needed his help, or keep him in subjection as under obligation to him, just as we do not insult a diseased member when the rest of the body labours for its recovery, nor think it under special obligation to the other members, because it has required more exertion than it has returned. A communication of offices between members is not regarded as at all gratuitous, but rather as the payment of that which being due by the law of nature it were monstrous to deny. For this reason, he who has performed one kind of duty will not think himself thereby discharged, as is usually the case when a rich man, after contributing somewhat of his substance, delegates remaining burdens to others as if he had nothing to do with them. Every one should rather consider, that however great he is, he owes himself to his neighbours, and that the only limit to his beneficence is the failure of his means. The extent of these should regulate that of his charity.

8. The principal part of self-denial, that which as we have said has reference to God, let us again consider more fully. Many things have already been said with regard to it which it were superfluous to repeat; and, therefore, it will be sufficient to view it as forming us to equanimity and endurance. First, then, in seeking the convenience or tranquillity of the present life, Scripture calls us to resign ourselves, and all we have, to the disposal of the Lord, to give him up the affections of the heart, that he may tame and subdue them. We have a frenzied desire, an infinite eagerness, to pursue wealth and honour, intrigue for power, accumulate riches, and collect all those frivolities which seem conducive to luxury and splendour. On the other hand, we have a remarkable dread, a remarkable hatred of poverty, mean birth, and a humble condition, and feel the strongest desire to guard against them. Hence, in regard to those who frame their life after their own counsel, we see how restless they are in mind, how many plans they try, to what fatigues they submit, in order that they may gain what avarice or ambition desires, or, on the other hand, escape poverty and meanness. To avoid similiar entanglements, the course which Christian men must follow is this: first, they must not long for, or hope for, or think of any kind of prosperity apart from the blessing of God; on it they must cast themselves, and there safely and confidently recline. For, however much the carnal mind may seem sufficient for itself when in the pursuit of honour or wealth, it depends on its own industry and zeal, or is aided by the favour of men, it is certain that all this is nothing, and that neither intellect nor labour will be of the least avail, except in so far as the Lord prospers both. On the contrary, his blessing alone makes a way through all obstacles, and brings everything to a joyful and favourable issue. Secondly, though without this blessing we may be able to acquire some degree of fame and opulence (as we daily see wicked men loaded with honours and riches), yet since those on whom the curse of God lies do not enjoy the least particle of true happiness, whatever we obtain without his blessing must turn

out ill. But surely men ought not to desire what adds to their misery.

9. Therefore, if we believe that all prosperous and desirable success depends entirely on the blessing of God, and that when it is wanting all kinds of misery and calamity await us, it follows that we should not eagerly contend for riches and honours, trusting to our own dexterity and assiduity, or leaning on the favour of men, or confiding in any empty imagination of fortune; but should always have respect to the Lord, that under his auspices we may be conducted to whatever lot he has provided for us. Firs;, the result will be, that instead of rushing on regardless of right and wrong, by wiles and wicked arts, and with injury to our neighbours, to catch at wealth and seize upon honours, we will only follow such fortune as we may enjoy with innocence. Who can hope for the aid of the divine blessing amid fraud, rapine, and other iniquitous arts? As this blessing attends him only who thinks purely and acts uprightly, so it calls off all who long for it from sinister designs and evil actions. Secondly, a curb will be laid upon us, restraining a too eager desire of becoming rich, or an ambitious striving after honour. How can any one have the effrontery to expect that God will aid him in accomplishing desires at variance with his word? What God with his own lips pronounces cursed, never can be prosecuted with his blessing. Lastly, if our success is not equal to our wish and hope, we shall, however, be kept from impatience and detestation of our condition, whatever it be, knowing that so to feel were to murmur against God, at whose pleasure riches and poverty, contempt and honours, are dispensed. In short, he who leans on the divine blessing in the way which has been described, will not, in the pursuit of those things which men are wont most eagerly to desire, employ wicked arts which he knows would avail him nothing; nor when any thing prosperous befalls him will he impute it to himself and his own diligence, or industry, or fortune, instead of ascribing it to God as its author. If, while the affairs of others flourish, his make little progress, or even retrograde, he will bear his humble lot with greater equanimity and moderation than any irreligious man does the moderate success which only falls short of what he wished; for he has a solace in which he can rest more tranquilly than at the very summit of wealth or power, because he considers that his affairs are ordered by the Lord in the manner most conducive to his salvation. This, we see, is the way in which David was affected, who, while he follows God and gives up himself to his guidance, declares, "Neither do I exercise myself in great matters, or in things too high for me. Surely I have behaved and quieted myself as a child that is weaned of his mother" (Ps. cxxxi. 1, 2).

10. Nor is it in this respect only that pious minds ought to manifest this tranquillity and endurance; it must be extended to all the accidents to which this present life is liable. He alone, therefore, has properly denied himself, who has resigned himself entirely to the Lord, placing all the course of his life entirely at his disposal. Happen

what may, he whose mind is thus composed will neither deem himself wretched or murmur against God because of his lot.   How necessary this disposition is will appear, if you consider the many accidents to which we are liable.   Various diseases ever and anon attack us: at one time pestilence rages ; at another we are involved in all the calamities of war.   Frost and hail, destroying the promise of the year, cause sterility, which reduces us to penury ; wife, parents, children, relatives, are carried off by death ; our house is destroyed by fire. These are the events which make men curse their life, detest the day of their birth, execrate the light of heaven, even censure God, and (as they are eloquent in blasphemy) charge him with cruelty and injustice.   The believer must in these things also contemplate the mercy and truly paternal indulgence of God.   Accordingly, should he see his house by the removal of kindred reduced to solitude, even then he will not cease to bless the Lord ; his thought will be, Still the grace of the Lord, which dwells within my house, will not leave it desolate.   If his crops are blasted, mildewed, or cut off by frost, or struck down by hail,[1] and he sees famine before him, he will not however despond or murmur against God, but maintain his confidence in him ; "We thy people, and sheep of thy pasture, will give thee thanks for ever" (Ps. lxxix. 13); he will supply me with food, even in the extreme of sterility.   If he is afflicted with disease, the sharpness of the pain will not so overcome him, as to make him break out with impatience, and expostulate with God ; but recognising justice and lenity in the rod, will patiently endure.   In short, whatever happens, knowing that it is ordered by the Lord, he will receive it with a placid and grateful mind, and will not contumaciously resist the government of him, at whose disposal he has placed himself and all that he has.   Especially let the Christian breast eschew that foolish and most miserable consolation of the heathen, who, to strengthen their mind against adversity, imputed it to fortune, at which they deemed it absurd to feel indignant, as she was ἄσκοπος (aimless) and rash, and blindly wounded the good equally with the bad.   On the contrary, the rule of piety is, that the hand of God is the ruler and arbiter of the fortunes of all, and, instead of rushing on with thoughtless violence, dispenses good and evil with perfect regularity.

1 The French is, " Soit que ses bleds et vignes soyent gastées et destruites par gelée, gresle, ou autre tempeste ;"—whether his corn and vines are hurt and destroyed by frost, hail, or other tempest.

CHAPTER VIII.

OF BEARING THE CROSS—ONE BRANCH OF SELF-DENIAL.

The four divisions of this chapter are,—I. The nature of the cross, its necessity and dignity, sec. 1, 2. II. The manifold advantages of the cross described, sec. 3–6. III. The form of the cross the most excellent of all, and yet it by no means removes all sense of pain, sec 7, 8. IV. A description of warfare under the cross, and of true patience (not that of philosophers), after the example of Christ, sec. 9–11.

Sections.

1. What the cross is By whom, and on whom, and for what cause imposed. *Its necessity and dignity.
2. The cross necessary : 1. To humble our pride. 2. To make us apply to God for aid. Example of David. 3. To give us experience of God's presence.
3. Manifold uses of the cross 1. Produces patience, hope, and firm confidence in God, gives us victory and perseverance. Faith invincible.
4. 2. Frames us to obedience. Example of Abraham. This training how useful.
5. The cross necessary to subdue the wantonness of the flesh. This portrayed by an apposite simile. Various forms of the cross.
6. 3. God permits our infirmities, and corrects past faults, that he may keep us in obedience. This confirmed by a passage from Solomon and an Apostle.
7. Singular consolation under the cross, when we suffer persecution for righteousness. Some parts of this consolation
8. This form of the cross most appropriate to believers, and should be borne willingly and cheerfully. This cheerfulness is not unfeeling hilarity, but, while groaning under the burden, waits patiently for the Lord.
9. A description of this conflict. Opposed to the vanity of the Stoics. Illustrated by the authority and example of Christ.
10. Proved by the testimony and uniform experience of the elect. Also by the special example of the Apostle Peter. The nature of the patience required of us.
11. Distinction between the patience of Christians and philosophers. The latter pretend a necessity which cannot be resisted. The former hold forth the justice of God and his care of our safety A full exposition of this difference.

1. THE pious mind must ascend still higher—namely, whither Christ calls his disciples when he says, that every one of them must "take up his cross" (Matth. xvi. 24). Those whom the Lord has chosen and honoured with his intercourse must prepare for a hard, laborious, troubled life, a life full of many and various kinds of evils: it being the will of our heavenly Father to exercise his people in this way while putting them to the proof. Having begun this course with Christ the first-born, he continues it towards all his children. For though that Son was dear to him above others, the Son in whom he was "well pleased," yet we see, that far from being treated gently and indulgently, we may say, that not only was he subjected to a perpetual cross while he dwelt on earth, but his whole life was nothing else than a kind of perpetual cross. The Apostle assigns the reason, "Though he was a Son, yet learned he obedience by the things which he suffered" (Heb. v. 8). Why then should we exempt ourselves

from that condition to which Christ our Head behoved to submit; especially since he submitted on our account, that he might in his own person exhibit a model of patience? Wherefore, the Apostle declares, that all the children of God are destined to be conformed to him. Hence it affords us great consolation in hard and difficult circumstances, which men deem evil and adverse, to think that we are holding fellowship with the sufferings of Christ; that as he passed to celestial glory through a labyrinth of many woes, so we too are conducted thither through various tribulations. For, in another passage, Paul himself thus speaks, "we must through much tribulation enter the kingdom of God" (Acts xiv. 22); and again, "that I may know him, and the power of his resurrection, and the fellowship of his sufferings, being made conformable unto his death" (Rom. viii. 29). How powerfully should it soften the bitterness of the cross, to think that the more we are afflicted with adversity, the surer we are made of our fellowship with Christ; by communion with whom our sufferings are not only blessed to us, but tend greatly to the furtherance of our salvation.

2. We may add, that the only thing which made it necessary for our Lord to undertake to bear the cross, was to testify and prove his obedience to the Father; whereas there are many reasons which make it necessary for us to live constantly under the cross. Feeble as we are by nature, and prone to ascribe all perfection to our flesh, unless we receive as it were ocular demonstration of our weakness, we readily estimate our virtue above its proper worth, and doubt not that, whatever happens, it will stand unimpared and invincible against all difficulties. Hence we indulge a stupid and empty confidence in the flesh, and then trusting to it wax proud against the Lord himself; as if our own faculties were sufficient without his grace. This arrogance cannot be better repressed than when He proves to us by experience, not only how great our weakness, but also our frailty is. Therefore, he visits us with disgrace, or poverty, or bereavement, or disease, or other afflictions. Feeling altogether unable to support them, we forthwith, in so far as regards ourselves, give way, and thus humbled learn to invoke his strength, which alone can enable us to bear up under a weight of affliction. Nay, even the holiest of men, however well aware that they stand not in their own strength, but by the grace of God, would feel too secure in their own fortitude and constancy, were they not brought to a more thorough knowledge of themselves by the trial of the cross. This feeling gained even upon David, "In my prosperity I said, I shall never be moved. Lord, by thy favour thou hast made my mountain to stand strong: thou didst hide thy face, and I was troubled" (Ps. xxx. 6, 7). He confesses that in prosperity his feelings were dulled and blunted, so that, neglecting the grace of God, on which alone he ought to have depended, he leant to himself, and promised himself perpetuity. If it so happened to this great prophet, who of us should not fear and study caution?

Though in tranquillity they flatter themselves with the idea of greater constancy and patience, yet, humbled by adversity, they learn the deception.   Believers, I say, warned by such proofs of their diseases, make progress in humility, and, divesting themselves of a depraved confidence in the flesh, betake themselves to the grace of God, and, when they have so betaken themselves, experience the presence of the divine power, in which is ample protection.

3. This Paul teaches, when he says that tribulation worketh patience, and patience experience.   God having promised that he will be with believers in tribulation, they feel the truth of the promise ; while supported by his hand, they endure patiently.   This they could never do by their own strength.   Patience, therefore, gives the saints an experimental proof that God in reality furnishes the aid which he has promised whenever there is need.   Hence also their faith is confirmed, for it were very ungrateful not to expect that in future the truth of God will be, as they have already found it, firm and constant.   We now see how many advantages are at once produced by the cross.   Overturning the overweening opinion we form of our own virtue, and detecting the hypocrisy in which we delight, it removes our pernicious carnal confidence, teaching us, when thus humbled, to recline on God alone, so that we neither are oppressed nor despond.   Then victory is followed by hope, inasmuch as the Lord, by performing what he has promised, establishes his truth in regard to the future.   Were these the only reasons, it is surely plain how necessary it is for us to bear the cross.   It is of no little importance to be rid of your self-love and made fully conscious of your weakness ; so impressed with a sense of your weakness as to learn to distrust yourself—to distrust yourself so as to transfer your confidence to God, reclining on him with such heartfelt confidence as to trust in his aid, and continue invincible to the end, standing by his grace so as to perceive that he is true to his promises, and so assured of the certainty of his promises as to be strong in hope.

4. Another end which the Lord has in afflicting his people is to try their patience, and train them to obedience—not that they can yield obedience to him except in so far as he enables them ; but he is pleased thus to attest and display striking proofs of the graces which he has conferred upon his saints, lest they should remain within unseen and unemployed.   Accordingly, by bringing forward openly the strength and constancy of endurance with which he has provided his servants, he is said to try their patience.   Hence the expressions that God tempted Abraham (Gen. xxi. 1, 12), and made proof of his piety by not declining to sacrifice his only son.   Hence, too, Peter tells us that our faith is proved by tribulation, just as gold is tried in a furnace of fire.   But who will say it is not expedient that the most excellent gift of patience which the believer has received from his God should be applied to use, by being made sure and manifest ?   Otherwise men would never value it according to its worth.   But if God himself, to prevent the virtues which he has conferred upon believers from

lurking in obscurity, nay, lying useless and perishing, does aright in supplying materials for calling them forth, there is the best reason for the afflictions of the saints, since without them their patience could not exist. I say, that by the cross they are also trained to obedience, because they are thus taught to live not according to their own wish, but at the disposal of God. Indeed, did all things proceed as they wish, they would not know what it is to follow God. Seneca mentions (De Vit. Beata, cap. xv.) that there was an old proverb when any one was exhorted to endure adversity, "*Follow God;*" thereby intimating, that men truly submitted to the yoke of God only when they gave their back and hand to his rod. But if it is most right that we should in all things prove our obedience to our heavenly Father, certainly we ought not to decline any method by which he trains us to obedience.

5. Still, however, we see not how necessary that obedience is, unless we at the same time consider how prone our carnal nature is to shake off the yoke of God whenever it has been treated with some degree of gentleness and indulgence. It just happens to it as with refractory horses, which, if kept idle for a few days at hack and manger, become ungovernable, and no longer recognise the rider, whose command before they implicitly obeyed. And we invariably become what God complains of in the people of Israel—waxing gross and fat, we kick against him who reared and nursed us (Deut. xxxii. 15). The kindness of God should allure us to ponder and love his goodness; but since such is our malignity, that we are invariably corrupted by his indulgence, it is more than necessary for us to be restrained by discipline from breaking forth into such petulance. Thus, lest we become emboldened by an over-abundance of wealth; lest elated with honour, we grow proud; lest inflated with other advantages of body, or mind, or fortune, we grow insolent, the Lord himself interferes as he sees to be expedient by means of the cross, subduing and curbing the arrogance of our flesh, and that in various ways, as the advantage of each requires. For as we do not all equally labour under the same disease, so we do not all need the same difficult cure. Hence we see that all are not exercised with the same kind of cross. While the heavenly Physician treats some more gently, in the case of others he employs harsher remedies, his purpose being to provide a cure for all. Still none is left free and untouched, because he knows that all, without a single exception, are diseased.

6. We may add, that our most merciful Father requires not only to prevent our weakness, but often to correct our past faults, that he may keep us in due obedience. Therefore, whenever we are afflicted we ought immediately to call to mind our past life. In this way we will find that the faults which we have committed are deserving of such castigation. And yet the exhortation to patience is not to be founded chiefly on the acknowledgment of sin. For Scripture supplies a far better consideration when it says, that in adversity " we are chastened of the Lord, that we should not be condemned with the

world" (1 Cor. xi. 32). Therefore, in the very bitterness of tribulation we ought to recognise the kindness and mercy of our Father, since even then he ceases not to further our salvation. For he afflicts, not that he may ruin or destroy, but rather that he may deliver us from the condemnation of the world. Let this thought lead us to what Scripture elsewhere teaches: " My son, despise not the chastening of the Lord; neither be weary of his correction: For whom the Lord loveth he correcteth; even as a father the son in whom he delighteth" (Prov. iii. 11, 12). When we perceive our Father's rod, is it not our part to behave as obedient docile sons, rather than rebelliously imitate desperate men, who are hardened in wickedness? God dooms us to destruction, if he does not, by correction, call us back when we have fallen off from him, so that it is truly said, " If ye be without chastisement," " then are ye bastards, and not sons" (Heb. xii. 8). We are most perverse then if we cannot bear him while he is manifesting his good-will to us, and the care which he takes of our salvation. Scripture states the difference between believers and unbelievers to be, that the latter, as the slaves of inveterate and deep-seated iniquity, only become worse and more obstinate under the lash; whereas the former, like free-born sons, turn to repentance. Now, therefore, choose your class. But as I have already spoken of this subject, it is sufficient to have here briefly adverted to it.

7. There is singular consolation, moreover, when we are persecuted for righteousness' sake. For our thought should then be, How high the honour which God bestows upon us in distinguishing us by the special badge of his soldiers. By suffering persecution for righteousness' sake, I mean not only striving for the defence of the Gospel, but for the defence of righteousness in any way. Whether, therefore, in maintaining the truth of God against the lies of Satan, or defending the good and innocent against the injuries of the bad, we are obliged to incur the offence and hatred of the world, so as to endanger life, fortune, or honour, let us not grieve or decline so far to spend ourselves for God; let us not think ourselves wretched in those things in which he with his own lips has pronounced us blessed (Matth. v. 10). Poverty, indeed, considered in itself, is misery; so are exile, contempt, imprisonment, ignominy: in fine, death itself is the last of all calamities. But when the favour of God breathes upon us, there is none of these things which may not turn out to our happiness. Let us then be contented with the testimony of Christ rather than with the false estimate of the flesh, and then, after the example of the Apostles, we will rejoice in being " counted worthy to suffer shame for his name" (Acts v. 41). For why? If, while conscious of our innocence, we are deprived of our substance by the wickedness of man, we are, no doubt, humanly speaking, reduced to poverty; but in truth our riches in heaven are increased: if driven from our homes, we have a more welcome reception into the family of God; if vexed and despised, we are more firmly rooted in Christ; if stigmatised by disgrace and ignominy, we have a higher place in the kingdom of God;

and if we are slain, entrance is thereby given us to eternal life. The Lord having set such a price upon us, let us be ashamed to estimate ourselves at less than the shadowy and evanescent allurements of the present life.

8. Since by these, and similar considerations, Scripture abundantly solaces us for the ignominy or calamities which we endure in defence of righteousness, we are very ungrateful if we do not willingly and cheerfully receive them at the hand of the Lord, especially since this form of the cross is the most appropriate to believers, being that by which Christ desires to be glorified in us, as Peter also declares (1 Pet. iv. 11, 14). But as to ingenuous natures, it is more bitter to suffer disgrace than a hundred deaths, Paul expressly reminds us that not only persecution, but also disgrace awaits us, " because we trust in the living God" (1 Tim. iv. 10). So in another passage he bids us, after his example, walk " by evil report and good report" (2 Cor. vi. 8). The cheerfulness required, however, does not imply a total insensibility to pain. The saints could show no patience under the cross if they were not both tortured with pain and grievously molested. Were there no hardship in poverty, no pain in disease, no sting in ignominy, no fear in death, where would be the fortitude and moderation in enduring them ? But while every one of these, by its inherent bitterness, naturally vexes the mind, the believer in this displays his fortitude, that though fully sensible of the bitterness, and labouring grievously, he still withstands and struggles boldly ; in this displays his patience, that though sharply stung, he is however curbed by the fear of God from breaking forth into any excess ; in this displays his alacrity, that though pressed with sorrow and sadness, he rests satisfied with spiritual consolation from God.

9. This conflict which believers maintain against the natural feeling of pain, while they study moderation and patience, Paul elegantly describes in these words : " We are troubled on every side, yet not distressed ; we are perplexed, but not in despair ; persecuted, but not forsaken ; cast down, but not destroyed" (2 Cor. iv. 8, 9). You see that to bear the cross patiently is not to have your feelings altogether blunted, and to be absolutely insensible to pain, according to the absurd description which the Stoics of old gave of their hero as one who, divested of humanity, was affected in the same way by adversity and prosperity, grief and joy ; or rather, like a stone, was not affected by anything. And what did they gain by that sublime wisdom ? they exhibited a shadow of patience, which never did, and never can, exist among men. Nay, rather by aiming at a too exact and rigid patience, they banished it altogether from human life. Now also we have among Christians a new kind of Stoics, who hold it vicious not only to groan and weep, but even to be sad and anxious. These paradoxes are usually started by indolent men who, employing themselves more in speculation than in action, can do nothing else for us than beget such paraxoxes. But we have nothing to do with

that iron philosophy which our Lord and Master condemned—not only in word, but also by his own example. For he both grieved and shed tears for his own and others' woes. Nor did he teach his disciples differently: "Ye shall weep and lament, but the world shall rejoice" (John xvi. 20). And lest any one should regard this as vicious, he expressly declares, "Blessed are they that mourn" (Matth. v. 4). And no wonder. If all tears are condemned, what shall we think of our Lord himself, whose "sweat was as it were great drops of blood falling down to the ground"? Luke xxii. 44; Matth. xxvi. 38.) If every kind of fear is a mark of unbelief, what place shall we assign to the dread which, it is said, in no slight degree amazed him; if all sadness is condemned, how shall we justify him when he confesses, "My soul is exceeding sorrowful, even unto death"?

10. I wished to make these observations to keep pious minds from despair, lest, from feeling it impossible to divest themselves of the natural feeling of grief, they might altogether abandon the study of patience. This must necessarily be the result with those who convert patience into stupor, and a brave and firm man into a block. Scripture gives saints the praise of endurance when, though afflicted by the hardships they endure, they are not crushed; though they feel bitterly, they are at the same time filled with spiritual joy; though pressed with anxiety, breathe exhilarated by the consolation of God. Still there is a certain degree of repugnance in their hearts, because natural sense shuns and dreads what is adverse to it, while pious affection, even through these difficulties, tries to obey the divine will. This repugnance the Lord expressed when he thus addressed Peter: "Verily, verily, I say unto thee, When thou wast young, thou girdedst thyself and walkedst whither thou wouldest: but when thou shalt be old, thou shalt stretch forth thy hands, and another shall gird thee, and carry thee whither thou wouldest not" (John xxi. 18). It is not probable, indeed, that when it became necessary to glorify God by death, he was driven to it unwilling and resisting; had it been so, little praise would have been due to his martyrdom. But though he obeyed the divine ordination with the greatest alacrity of heart, yet, as he had not divested himself of humanity, he was distracted by a double will. When he thought of the bloody death which he was to die, struck with horror, he would willingly have avoided it: on the other hand, when he considered that it was God who called him to it, his fear was vanquished and suppressed, and he met death cheerfully. It must therefore be our study, if we would be disciples of Christ, to imbue our minds with such reverence and obedience to God as may tame and subjugate all affections contrary to his appointment. In this way, whatever be the kind of cross to which we are subjected, we shall in the greatest straits firmly maintain our patience. Adversity will have its bitterness, and sting us. When afflicted with disease, we shall groan and be disquieted, and long for health; pressed with

poverty, we shall feel the stings of anxiety and sadness, feel the pain of ignominy, contempt, and injury, and pay the tears due to nature at the death of our friends ; but our conclusion will always be, The Lord so willed it, therefore let us follow his will. Nay, amid the pungency of grief, among groans and tears, this thought will necessarily suggest itself, and incline us cheerfully to endure the things for which we are so afflicted.

11. But since the chief reason for enduring the cross has been derived from a consideration of the divine will, we must in few words explain wherein lies the difference between philosophical and Christian patience. Indeed, very few of the philosophers advanced so far as to perceive that the hand of God tries us by means of affliction, and that we ought in this matter to obey God. The only reason which they adduce is, that *so it must be*. But is not this just to say, that we must yield to God, because it is in vain to contend against him ? For if we obey God only because it is necessary, provided we can escape, we shall cease to obey him. But what Scripture calls us to consider in the will of God is very different—namely, first justice and equity, and then a regard to our own salvation. Hence Christian exhortations to patience are of this nature, Whether poverty, or exile, or imprisonment, or contumely, or disease, or bereavement, or any such evil affects us, we must think that none of them happens except by the will and providence of God ; moreover, that everything he does is in the most perfect order. What ! do not our numberless daily faults deserve to be chastised, more severely, and with a heavier rod than his mercy lays upon us ? Is it not most right that our flesh should be subdued, and be, as it were, accustomed to the yoke, so as not to rage and wanton as it lists ? Are not the justice and the truth of God worthy of our suffering on their account ?[1] But if the equity of God is undoubtedly displayed in affliction, we cannot murmur or struggle against them without iniquity. We no longer hear the frigid cant, Yield, because it is necessary; but a living and energetic precept, Obey, because it is unlawful to resist; bear patiently, because impatience is rebellion against the justice of God. Then as that only seems to us attractive which we perceive to be for our own safety and advantage, here also our heavenly Father consoles us, by the assurance, that in the very cross with which he afflicts us he provides for our salvation. But if it is clear that tribulations are salutary to us, why should we not receive them with calm and grateful minds ? In bearing them patiently we are not submitting to necessity, but resting satisfied with our own good. The effect of these thoughts is, that to whatever extent our minds are contracted by the bitterness which we naturally feel under the cross, to the same extent will they be expanded with spiritual joy. Hence arises thanksgiving, which cannot exist unless joy be felt. But if the praise of the Lord

---

[1] See end of sec. 4, and sec. 5, 7, 8.

and thanksgiving can emanate only from a cheerful and gladdened breast, and there is nothing which ought to interrupt these feelings in us, it is clear how necessary it is to temper the bitterness of the cross with spiritual joy.

CHAPTER IX.

OF MEDITATING ON THE FUTURE LIFE.

The three divisions of this chapter,—I. The principal use of the cross is, that it in various ways accustoms us to despise the present, and excites us to aspire to the future life, sec. 1, 2. II. In withdrawing from the present life we must neither shun it nor feel hatred for it; but desiring the future life, gladly quit the present at the command of our sovereign Master, sec. 3, 4. III. Our infirmity in dreading death described. The correction and safe remedy, sec. 6.

Sections.

1. The design of God in afflicting his people. 1. To accustom us to despise the present life. Our infatuated love of it. Afflictions employed as the cure. 2. To lead us to aspire to heaven.
2. Excessive love of the present life prevents us from duly aspiring to the other. Hence the disadvantages of prosperity. Blindness of the human judgment. Our philosophising on the vanity of life only of momentary influence. The necessity of the cross.
3. The present life an evidence of the divine favour to his people; and, therefore, not to be detested. On the contrary, should call forth thanksgiving. The crown of victory in heaven after the contest on earth.
4. Weariness of the present life how to be tempered. The believer's estimate of life. Comparison of the present and the future life. How far the present life should be hated.
5. Christians should not tremble at the fear of death. Two reasons. Objection. Answer. Other reasons.
6. Reasons continued. Conclusion.

1. WHATEVER be the kind of tribulation with which we are afflicted, we should always consider the end of it to be, that we may be trained to despise the present, and thereby stimulated to aspire to the future life. For since God well knows how strongly we are inclined by nature to a slavish love of this world, in order to prevent us from clinging too strongly to it, he employs the fittest reason for calling us back, and shaking off our lethargy. Every one of us, indeed, would be thought to aspire and aim at heavenly immortality during the whole course of his life. For we would be ashamed in no respect to excel the lower animals; whose condition would not be at all inferior to ours, had we not a hope of immortality beyond the grave. But when you attend to the plans, wishes, and actions of each, you see nothing in them but the earth. Hence our stupidity; our minds being so dazzled with the glare of wealth, power, and honours, that they can see no farther. The heart also, engrossed with avarice, ambition, and lust, is weighed down and cannot rise above them. In short, the whole soul, ensnared by the allurements of the flesh, seeks its happiness on the earth. To meet this disease, the Lord makes his people sensible of the vanity of the present life,

by a constant proof of its miseries. Thus, that they may not promise themselves deep and lasting peace in it, he often allows them to be assailed by war, tumult, or rapine, or to be disturbed by other injuries. That they may not long with too much eagerness after fleeting and fading riches, or rest in those which they already possess, he reduces them to want, or, at least, restricts them to a moderate allowance, at one time by exile, at another by sterility, at another by fire, or by other means. That they may not indulge too complacently in the advantages of married life, he either vexes them by the misconduct of their partners, or humbles them by the wickedness of their children, or afflicts them by bereavement. But if in all these he is indulgent to them, lest they should either swell with vain-glory, or be elated with confidence, by diseases and dangers he sets palpably before them how unstable and evanescent are all the advantages competent to mortals. We duly profit by the discipline of the cross, when we learn that this life, estimated in itself, is restless, troubled, in numberless ways wretched, and plainly in no respect happy ; that what are estimated its blessings are uncertain, fleeting, vain, and vitiated by a great admixture of evil. From this we conclude, that all we have to seek or hope for here is contest ; that when we think of the crown we must raise our eyes to heaven. For we must hold, that our mind never rises seriously to desire and aspire after the future, until it has learned to despise the present life.

2. For there is no medium between the two things : the earth must either be worthless in our estimation, or keep us enslaved by an intemperate love of it. Therefore, if we have any regard to eternity, we must carefully strive to disencumber ourselves of these fetters. Moreover, since the present life has many enticements to allure us, and great semblance of delight, grace, and sweetness to soothe us, it is of great consequence to us to be now and then called off from its fascinations.[1] For what, pray, would happen, if we here enjoyed an uninterrupted course of honour and felicity, when even the constant stimulus of affliction cannot arouse us to a due sense of our misery ? That human life is like smoke or a shadow, is not only known to the learned ; there is not a more trite proverb among the vulgar. Considering it a fact most useful to be known, they have recommended it in many well-known expressions. Still there is no fact which we ponder less carefully, or less frequently remember. For we form all our plans just as if we had fixed our immortality on the earth. If we see a funeral, or walk among graves, as the image of death is then present to the eye, I admit we philosophise

---

1 French, " Or pource que la vie presente a tousiours force de delices pour nous attraire, et a grande apparence d'amenité, de grace et de douceur pour nous amieller, il nous est bien mestier d'estre retiré d'heure en d'heure, à ce que nous ne soyons point abusez, et comme ensorcelez de telles flatteries ;"—Now because the present life has always a host of delights to attract us, and has great appearance of amenity, grace, and sweetness to entice us, it is of great importance to us to be hourly withdrawn, in order that we may not be deceived, and, as it were, bewitched with such flattery.

admirably on the vanity of life. We do not indeed always do so, for those things often have no effect upon us at all. But, at the best, our philosophy is momentary. It vanishes as soon as we turn our back, and leaves not the vestige of remembrance behind; in short, it passes away, just like the applause of a theatre at some pleasant spectacle. Forgetful not only of death, but also of mortality itself, as if no rumour of it had ever reached us, we indulge in supine security as expecting a terrestrial immortality. Meanwhile, if any one breaks in with the proverb, that man is the creature of a day,[1] we indeed acknowledge its truth, but, so far from giving heed to it, the thought of perpetuity still keeps hold of our minds. Who then can deny that it is of the highest importance to us all, I say not, to be admonished by words, but convinced by all possible experience of the miserable condition of our earthly life; since even when convinced we scarcely cease to gaze upon it with vicious, stupid admiration, as if it contained within itself the sum of all that is good? But if God finds it necessary so to train us, it must be our duty to listen to him when he calls, and shakes us from our torpor, that we may hasten to despise the world, and aspire with our whole heart to the future life.

3. Still the contempt which believers should train themselves to feel for the present life, must not be of a kind to beget hatred of it or ingratitude to God. This life, though abounding in all kinds of wretchedness, is justly classed among divine blessings which are not to be despised. Wherefore, if we do not recognise the kindness of God in it, we are chargeable with no little ingratitude towards him. To believers, especially, it ought to be a proof of divine benevolence, since it is wholly destined to promote their salvation. Before openly exhibiting the inheritance of eternal glory, God is pleased to manifest himself to us as a Father by minor proofs—viz. the blessings which he daily bestows upon us. Therefore, while this life serves to acquaint us with the goodness of God, shall we disdain it as if it did not contain one particle of good? We ought, therefore, to feel and be affected towards it in such a manner as to place it among those gifts of the divine benignity which are by no means to be despised. Were there no proofs in Scripture (they are most numerous and clear), yet nature herself exhorts us to return thanks to God for having brought us forth into light, granted us the use of it, and bestowed upon us all the means necessary for its preservation. And there is a much higher reason when we reflect that here we are in a manner prepared for the glory of the heavenly kingdom. For the Lord hath ordained, that those who are ultimately to be crowned in heaven must maintain a previous warfare on the earth, that they may not triumph before they have overcome the difficulties of war, and obtained the victory. Another reason is, that we here begin to experience in various ways a foretaste of the divine benignity, in

---

[1] Latin, " Animal esse ἐφήμερον;"—is an ephemeral animal.

order that our hope and desire may be whetted for its full manifestation. When once we have concluded that our earthly life is a gift
of the divine mercy, of which, agreeably to our obligation, it behoves
us to have a grateful remembrance, we shall then properly descend
to consider its most wretched condition, and thus escape from that
excessive fondness for it, to which, as I have said, we are naturally
prone.

4. In proportion as this improper love diminishes, our desire of a
better life should increase. I confess, indeed, that a most accurate
opinion was formed by those who thought, that the best thing was
not to be born, the next best to die early. For, being destitute of
the light of God and of true religion, what could they see in it that
was not of dire and evil omen? Nor was it unreasonable for those [1]
who felt sorrow and shed tears at the birth of their kindred, to keep
holiday at their deaths. But this they did without profit; because,
devoid of the true doctrine of faith, they saw not how that which in
itself is neither happy nor desirable turns to the advantage of the
righteous: and hence their opinion issued in despair. Let believers,
then, in forming an estimate of this mortal life, and perceiving that
in itself it is nothing but misery, make it their aim to exert themselves with greater alacrity, and less hinderance, in aspiring to the
future and eternal life. When we contrast the two, the former may
not only be securely neglected, but, in comparison of the latter, be
disdained and contemned. If heaven is our country, what can the
earth be but a place of exile? If departure from the world is entrance into life, what is the world but a sepulchre, and what is residence in it but immersion in death? If to be freed from the body
is to gain full possession of freedom, what is the body but a prison?
If it is the very summit of happiness to enjoy the presence of God, is
it not miserable to want it? But "whilst we are at home in the
body, we are absent from the Lord" (2 Cor. v. 6). Thus when the
earthly is compared with the heavenly life, it may undoubtedly be
despised and trampled under foot. We ought never, indeed, to
regard it with hatred, except in so far as it keeps us subject to sin;
and even this hatred ought not to be directed against life itself. At
all events, we must stand so affected towards it in regard to weariness or hatred as, while longing for its termination, to be ready at
the Lord's will to continue in it, keeping far from everything like
murmuring and impatience. For it is as if the Lord had assigned us
a post, which we must maintain till he recalls us. Paul, indeed,
laments his condition, in being still bound with the fetters of the
body, and sighs earnestly for redemption (Rom. vii. 24); nevertheless, he declared that, in obedience to the command of God, he was
prepared for both courses, because he acknowledges it as his duty to
God to glorify his name whether by life or by death, while it belongs
to God to determine what is most conducive to His glory (Phil. i.

---

1 French, "Le peuple des Scythes;"—the Scythians.

20–24). Wherefore, if it becomes us to live and die to the Lord, let us leave the period of our life and death at his disposal. Still let us ardently long for death, and constantly meditate upon it, and in comparison with future immortality, let us despise life, and, on account of the bondage of sin, long to renounce it whenever it shall so please the Lord.

5. But, most strange to say, many who boast of being Christians, instead of thus longing for death, are so afraid of it that they tremble at the very mention of it as a thing ominous and dreadful. We cannot wonder, indeed, that our natural feelings should be somewhat shocked at the mention of our dissolution. But it is altogether intolerable that the light of piety should not be so powerful in a Christian breast as with greater consolation to overcome and suppress that fear. For if we reflect that this our tabernacle, unstable, defective, corruptible, fading, pining, and putrid, is dissolved, in order that it may forthwith be renewed in sure, perfect, incorruptible, in fine, in heavenly glory, will not faith compel us eagerly to desire what nature dreads? If we reflect that by death we are recalled from exile to inhabit our native country, a heavenly country, shall this give us no comfort? But everything longs for permanent existence. I admit this, and therefore contend that we ought to look to future immortality, where we may obtain that fixed condition which nowhere appears on the earth. For Paul admirably enjoins believers to hasten cheerfully to death, not because they "would be unclothed, but clothed upon" (2 Cor. v. 2). Shall the lower animals, and inanimate creatures themselves, even wood and stone, as conscious of their present vanity, long for the final resurrection, that they may with the sons of God be delivered from vanity (Rom. viii. 19); and shall we, endued with the light of intellect, and more than intellect, enlightened by the Spirit of God, when our essence is in question, rise no higher than the corruption of this earth? But it is not my purpose, nor is this the place, to plead against this great perverseness. At the outset, I declared that I had no wish to engage in a diffuse discussion of common-places. My advice to those whose minds are thus timid is to read the short treatise of Cyprian De Mortalitate, unless it be more accordant with their deserts to send them to the philosophers, that by inspecting what they say on the contempt of death, they may begin to blush. This, however, let us hold as fixed, that no man has made much progress in the school of Christ who does not look forward with joy to the day of death and final resurrection (2 Tim. iv. 18; Tit. ii. 13); for Paul distinguishes all believers by this mark; and the usual course of Scripture is to direct us thither whenever it would furnish us with an argument for substantial joy. "Look up," says our Lord, "and lift up your heads: for your redemption draweth nigh" (Luke xxi. 28). Is it reasonable, I ask, that what he intended to have a powerful effect in stirring us up to alacrity and exultation should produce nothing but sadness and consternation? If it is so, why do we still glory in him as our Master?

Therefore, let us come to a sounder mind, and how repugnant so ever the blind and stupid longing of the flesh may be, let us doubt not to desire the advent of the Lord not in wish only, but with earnest sighs, as the most propitious of all events.   He will come as a Redeemer to deliver us from an immense abyss of evil and misery, and lead us to the blessed inheritance of his life and glory.

6. Thus, indeed, it is; the whole body of the faithful, so long as they live on the earth, must be like sheep for the slaughter, in order that they may be conformed to Christ their head (Rom. viii. 36). Most deplorable, therefore, would their situation be did they not, by raising their mind to heaven, become superior to all that is in the world, and rise above the present aspect of affairs (1 Cor. xv. 19). On the other hand, when once they have raised their head above all earthly objects, though they see the wicked flourishing in wealth and honour, and enjoying profound peace, indulging in luxury and splendour, and revelling in all kinds of delights, though they should moreover be wickedly assailed by them, suffer insult from their pride, be robbed by their avarice, or assailed by any other passion, they will have no difficulty in bearing up under these evils.   They will turn their eye to that day (Isaiah xxv. 8; Rev. vii. 17) on which the Lord will receive his faithful servants, wipe away all tears from their eyes, clothe them in a robe of glory and joy, feed them with the ineffable sweetness of his pleasures, exalt them to share with him in his greatness; in fine, admit them to a participation in his happiness. But the wicked who may have flourished on the earth, he will cast forth in extreme ignominy, will change their delights into torments, their laughter and joy into wailing and gnashing of teeth, their peace into the gnawing of conscience, and punish their luxury with unquenchable fire.   He will also place their necks under the feet of the godly, whose patience they abused.   For, as Paul declares, "it is a righteous thing with God to recompense tribulation to them that trouble you; and to you who are troubled rest with us, when the Lord Jesus shall be revealed from heaven" (2 Thess. i. 6, 7).   This, indeed, is our only consolation; deprived of it, we must either give way to despondency, or resort to our destruction to the vain solace of the world.   The Psalmist confesses, "My feet were almost gone, my steps had well nigh slipt: for I was envious at the foolish when I saw the prosperity of the wicked" (Psalm lxxiii. 3, 4); and he found no resting-place until he entered the sanctuary, and considered the latter end of the righteous and the wicked.   To conclude in one word, the cross of Christ then only triumphs in the breasts of believers over the devil and the flesh, sin and sinners, when their eyes are directed to the power of his resurrection.

CHAPTER X.

HOW TO USE THE PRESENT LIFE, AND THE COMFORTS OF IT.

The divisions of this chapter are,—I. The necessity and usefulness of this doctrine. Extremes to be avoided, if we would rightly use the present life and its comforts, sec. 1, 2. II. One of these extremes—viz. the intemperance of the flesh—to be carefully avoided. Four methods of doing so described in order, sec. 3–6.

Sections.

1. Necessity of this doctrine. Use of the goods of the present life. Extremes to be avoided. 1. Excessive austerity. 2. Carnal intemperance and lasciviousness.
2. God, by creating so many mercies, consulted not only for our necessities, but also for our comfort and delight. Confirmation from a passage in the Psalms, and from experience.
3. Excessive austerity, therefore, to be avoided. So also must the wantonness of the flesh. 1. The creatures invite us to know, love, and honour the Creator. 2. This not done by the wicked, who only abuse these temporal mercies.
4. All earthly blessings to be despised in comparison of the heavenly life. Aspiration after this life destroyed by an excessive love of created objects. First, Intemperance.
5. Second, Impatience and immoderate desire. Remedy of these evils. The creatures assigned to our use. Man still accountable for the use he makes of them.
6. God requires us in all our actions to look to his calling. Use of this doctrine. It is full of comfort.

1. By such rudiments we are at the same time well instructed by Scripture in the proper use of earthly blessings, a subject which, in forming a scheme of life, is by no means to be neglected. For if we are to live, we must use the necessary supports of life; nor can we even shun those things which seem more subservient to delight than to necessity. We must therefore observe a mean, that we may use them with a pure conscience, whether for necessity or for pleasure. This the Lord prescribes by his word, when he tells us that to his people the present life is a kind of pilgrimage by which they hasten to the heavenly kingdom. If we are only to pass through the earth, there can be no doubt that we are to use its blessings only in so far as they assist our progress, rather than retard it. Accordingly, Paul, not without cause, admonishes us to use this world without abusing it, and to buy possessions as if we were selling them (1 Cor. vii. 30, 31). But as this is a slippery place, and there is great danger of falling on either side, let us fix our feet where we can stand safely. There have been some good and holy men who, when they saw intemperance and luxury perpetually carried to excess, if not strictly curbed, and were desirous to correct so pernicious an evil, imagined that there was no other method than to allow man to use corporeal goods

only in so far as they were necessaries: a counsel pious indeed, but unnecessarily austere; for it does the very dangerous thing of binding consciences in closer fetters than those in which they are bound by the word of God. Moreover, necessity, according to them,[1] was abstinence from everything which could be wanted, so that they held it scarcely lawful to make any addition to bread and water. Others were still more austere, as is related of Cratetes the Theban, who threw his riches into the sea, because he thought that unless he destroyed them they would destroy him. Many also in the present day, while they seek a pretext for carnal intemperance in the use of external things, and at the same time would pave the way for licentiousness, assume for granted, what I by no means concede, that this liberty is not to be restrained by any modification, but that it is to be left to every man's conscience to use them as far as he thinks lawful. I indeed confess that here consciences neither can nor ought to be bound by fixed and definite laws; but that Scripture having laid down general rules for the legitimate use, we should keep within the limits which they prescribe.

2. Let this be our principle, that we err not in the use of the gifts of Providence when we refer them to the end for which their author made and destined them, since he created them for our good, and not for our destruction. No man will keep the true path better than he who shall have this end carefully in view. Now then, if we consider for what end he created food, we shall find that he consulted not only for our necessity, but also for our enjoyment and delight. Thus, in clothing, the end was, in addition to necessity, comeliness and honour; and in herbs, fruits, and trees, besides their various uses, gracefulness of appearance and sweetness of smell. Were it not so, the Prophet would not enumerate among the mercies of God " wine that maketh glad the heart of man, and oil to make his face to shine " (Ps. civ. 15). The Scriptures would not everywhere mention, in commendation of his benignity, that he had given such things to men. The natural qualities of things themselves demonstrate to what end, and how far, they may be lawfully enjoyed. Has the Lord adorned flowers with all the beauty which spontaneously presents itself to the eye, and the sweet odour which delights the sense of smell, and shall it be unlawful for us to enjoy that beauty and this odour? What? Has he not so distinguished colours as to make some more agreeable than others? Has he not given qualities to gold and silver, ivory and marble, thereby rendering them precious above other metals or stones? In short, has he not given many things a value without having any necessary use?

3. Have done, then, with that inhuman philosophy which, in allowing no use of the creatures but for neccessity, not only maliciously deprives us of the lawful fruit of the divine beneficence, but cannot be realised without depriving man of all his senses, and reducing him

[1] See Chrysost. ad Heb. xi. As to Cratetes the Theban, see Plutarch, Lib. de Vitand. ære alien. and Philostratus in Vita Apollonii.

to a block. But, on the other hand, let us with no less care guard against the lusts of the flesh, which, if not kept in order, break through all bounds, and are, as I have said, advocated by those who, under pretence of liberty, allow themselves every sort of licence. First, one restraint is imposed when we hold that the object of creating all things was to teach us to know their author, and feel grateful for his indulgence. Where is the gratitude, if you so gorge or stupify yourself with feasting and wine as to be unfit for offices of piety, or the duties of your calling? Where the recognition of God, if the flesh, boiling forth in lust through excessive indulgence, infects the mind with its impurity, so as to lose the discernment of honour and rectitude? Where thankfulness to God for clothing, if on account of sumptuous raiment we both admire ourselves and disdain others? if, from a love of show and splendour, we pave the way for immodesty? Where our recognition of God, if the glare of these things captivates our minds? For many are so devoted to luxury in all their senses, that their mind lies buried: many are so delighted with marble, gold, and pictures, that they become marble-hearted—are changed as it were into metal, and made like painted figures. The kitchen, with its savoury smells, so engrosses them that they have no spiritual savour. The same thing may be seen in other matters. Wherefore it is plain that there is here great necessity for curbing licentious abuse, and conforming to the rule of Paul, "make not provision for the flesh to fulfil the lusts thereof" (Rom. xiii. 14). Where too much liberty is given to them, they break forth without measure or restraint.

4. There is no surer or quicker way of accomplishing this than by despising the present life and aspiring to celestial immortality. For hence two rules arise: First, "it remaineth, that both they that have wives be as though they had none;" "and they that use this world, as not abusing it" (1 Cor. vii. 29, 31). Secondly, we must learn to be no less placid and patient in enduring penury, than moderate in enjoying abundance. He who makes it his rule to use this world as if he used it not, not only cuts off all gluttony in regard to meat and drink, and all effeminacy, ambition, pride, excessive show, and austerity, in regard to his table, his house, and his clothes, but removes every care and affection which might withdraw or hinder him from aspiring to the heavenly life, and cultivating the interest of his soul.[1] It was well said by Cato: Luxury causes great care, and produces great carelessness as to virtue; and it is an old proverb,—Those who are much occupied with the care of the body, usually give little care to the soul. Therefore, while the liberty of the Christian in external matters is not to be tied down to a strict rule, it is, however, subject to this law—he must indulge as little as possible; on the other hand,

---

[1] French, "Parer notre ame de ses vrais ornemens;"—deck our soul with its true ornaments.

it must be his constant aim, not only to curb luxury, but to cut off all show of superfluous abundance, and carefully beware of converting a help into a hinderance.

5. Another rule is, that those in narrow and slender circumstances should learn to bear their wants patiently, that they may not become immoderately desirous of things, the moderate use of which implies no small progress in the school of Christ. For in addition to the many other vices which accompany a longing for earthly good, he who is impatient under poverty almost always betrays the contrary disease in abundance. By this I mean, that he who is ashamed of a sordid garment will be vain-glorious of a splendid one ; he who not contented with a slender, feels annoyed at the want of a more luxurious supper, will intemperately abuse his luxury if he obtains it ; he who has a difficulty, and is dissatisfied in submitting to a private and humble condition, will be unable to refrain from pride if he attain to honour. Let it be the aim of all who have any unfeigned desire for piety to learn, after the example of the Apostle, " both to be full and to be hungry, both to abound and to suffer need " (Philip. iv. 12). Scripture, moreover, has a third rule for modifying the use of earthly blessings. We have already adverted to it when considering the offices of charity. For it declares that they have all been given us by the kindness of God, and appointed for our use under the condition of being regarded as trusts, of which we must one day give account. We must, therefore, administer them as if we constantly heard the words sounding in our ears, " Give an account of your stewardship." At the same time, let us remember by whom the account is to be taken—viz. by him who, while he so highly commends abstinence, sobriety, frugality, and moderation, abominates luxury, pride, ostentation, and vanity ; who approves of no administration but that which is combined with charity, who with his own lips has already condemned all those pleasures which withdraw the heart from chastity and purity, or darken the intellect.

6. The last thing to be observed is, that the Lord enjoins every one of us, in all the actions of life, to have respect to our own calling. He knows the boiling restlessness of the human mind, the fickleness with which it is borne hither and thither, its eagerness to hold opposites at one time in its grasp, its ambition. Therefore, lest all things should be thrown into confusion by our folly and rashness, he has assigned distinct duties to each in the different modes of life. And that no one may presume to overstep his proper limits, he has distinguished the different modes of life by the name of callings. Every man's mode of life, therefore, is a kind of station assigned him by the Lord, that he may not be always driven about at random. So necessary is this distinction, that all our actions are thereby estimated in his sight, and often in a very different way from that in which human reason or philosophy would estimate them. There is no more illustrious deed even among philosophers than to free one's country from tyranny, and yet the private individual who stabs the tyrant is

openly condemned by the voice of the heavenly Judge. But I am unwilling to dwell on particular examples; it is enough to know that in everything the call of the Lord is the foundation and beginning of right action.   He who does not act with reference to it will never, in the discharge of duty, keep the right path.   He will sometimes be able, perhaps, to give the semblance of something laudable, but whatever it may be in the sight of man, it will be rejected before the throne of God; and besides, there will be no harmony in the different parts of his life.   Hence, he only who directs his life to this end will have it properly framed; because, free from the impulse of rashness, he will not attempt more than his calling justifies, knowing that it is unlawful to overleap the prescribed bounds.   He who is obscure will not decline to cultivate a private life, that he may not desert the post at which God has placed him.   Again, in all our cares, toils, annoyances, and other burdens, it will be no small alleviation to know that all these are under the superintendence of God. The magistrate will more willingly perform his office, and the father of a family confine himself to his proper sphere.   Every one in his particular mode of life will, without repining, suffer its inconveniences, cares, uneasiness, and anxiety, persuaded that God has laid on the burden.   This, too, will afford admirable consolation, that in following your proper calling, no work will be so mean and sordid as not to have a splendour and value in the eye of God.

CHAPTER XI.

OF JUSTIFICATION BY FAITH. BOTH THE NAME AND THE REALITY DEFINED.

In this chapter and the seven which follow, the doctrine of Justification by Faith is expounded, and opposite errors refuted. The following may be regarded as the arrangement of these chapters:—Chapter XI. states the doctrine, and the four subsequent chapters, by destroying the righteousness of works, confirm the righteousness of faith, each in the order which appears in the respective titles of these chapters. In Chapter XII. the doctrine of Justification is confirmed by a description of perfect righteousness; in Chapter XIII. by calling attention to two precautions; in Chapter XIV. by a consideration of the commencement and progress of regeneration in the regenerate; and in Chapter XV. by two very pernicious effects which constantly accompany the righteousness of works. The three other chapters are devoted to refutation; Chapter XVI. disposes of the objections of opponents; Chapter XVII. replies to the arguments drawn from the promises of the Law or the Gospel; Chapter XVIII. refutes what is said in support of the righteousness of faith from the promise of reward.

There are three principal divisions in the Eleventh Chapter. I. The terms used in this discussion are explained, sec. 1–4. II. Osiander's dream as to essential righteousness impugned, sec. 5–13. III. The righteousness of faith established in opposition to the righteousness of works.

Sections.

1. Connection between the doctrine of Justification and that of Regeneration. The knowledge of this doctrine very necessary for two reasons.
2. For the purpose of facilitating the exposition of it, the terms are explained. 1. What it is to be justified in the sight of God. 2. To be justified by works. 3. To be justified by faith. Definition.
3. Various meanings of the term Justification. 1. To give praise to God and truth. 2. To make a vain display of righteousness. 3. To impute righteousness by faith, by and on account of Christ. Confirmation from an expression of Paul, and another of our Lord.
4. Another confirmation from a comparison with other expressions, in which justification means free righteousness before God through faith in Jesus Christ. 1. Acceptance. 2. Imputation of righteousness. 3. Remission of sins. 4 Blessedness. 5. Reconciliation with God. 6. Righteousness by the obedience of Christ.
5. The second part of the chapter. Osiander's dream as to essential righteousness refuted. 1. Osiander's argument: Answer. 2. Osiander's second argument: Answer. Third argument: Answer.
6. Necessity of this refutation. Fourth argument: Answer. Confirmation: Another answer. Fifth and sixth arguments and answers.
7. Seventh and eighth arguments: Answers.
8. Ninth argument: Answer.
9. Tenth argument: Answer.
10. In what sense Christ is said to be our righteousness. Eleventh and twelfth arguments and answers.
11. Thirteenth and fourteenth arguments: Answers. An exception by Osiander. Imputed and begun righteousness to be distinguished. Osiander confounds them. Fifteenth argument: Answer.
12. Sixteenth argument, a dream of Osiander: Answer. Other four arguments and answers. Conclusion of the refutation of Osiander's errors.
13. Last part of the chapter. Refutation of the Sophists pretending a righteousness compounded partly of faith and partly of works.

1. I TRUST I have now sufficiently shown[1] how man's only resource
for escaping from the curse of the law, and recovering salvation, lies
in faith; and also what the nature of faith is, what the benefits which
it confers, and the fruits which it produces. The whole may be thus
summed up: Christ given to us by the kindness of God is apprehended and possessed by faith, by means of which we obtain in particular a twofold benefit: first, being reconciled by the righteousness
of Christ, God becomes, instead of a judge, an indulgent Father;
and, secondly, being sanctified by his Spirit, we aspire to integrity
and purity of life. This second benefit—viz. regeneration—appears
to have been already sufficiently discussed. On the other hand, the
subject of justification was discussed more cursorily, because it seemed
of more consequence first to explain that the faith by which alone,
through the mercy of God, we obtain free justification, is not destitute
of good works; and also to show the true nature of these good works
on which this question partly turns. The doctrine of Justification
is now to be fully discussed, and discussed under the conviction, that
as it is the principal ground on which religion must be supported, so
it requires greater care and attention. For unless you understand
first of all what your position is before God, and what the judgment
which he passes upon you, you have no foundation on which your
salvation can be laid, or on which piety towards God can be reared.
The necessity of thoroughly understanding this subject will become
more apparent as we proceed with it.

2. Lest we should stumble at the very threshold (this we should
do were we to begin the discussion without knowing what the subject
is), let us first explain the meaning of the expressions, *To be justified
in the sight of God, To be justified by faith or by works.* A man is
said to be justified in the sight of God when in the judgment of God
he is deemed righteous, and is accepted on account of his righteous-

---

[1] See Institutes, Book II. chap. vi. and vii., and Book III. from the commencement
to the present chapter.

ness; for as iniquity is abominable to God, so neither can the sinner find grace in his sight, so far as he is and so long as he is regarded as a sinner. Hence, wherever sin is, there also are the wrath and vengeance of God. He, on the other hand, is justified who is regarded not as a sinner, but as righteous, and as such stands acquitted at the judgment-seat of God, where all sinners are condemned. As an innocent man, when charged before an impartial judge, who decides according to his innocence, is said to be justified by the judge, so a man is said to be justified by God when, removed from the catalogue of sinners, he has God as the witness and assertor of his righteousness. In the same manner, a man will be said to be *justified by works*, if in his life there can be found a purity and holiness which merits an attestation of righteousness at the throne of God, or if by the perfection of his works he can answer and satisfy the divine justice. On the contrary, a man will be *justified by faith* when, excluded from the righteousness of works, he by faith lays hold of the righteousness of Christ, and clothed in it appears in the sight of God not as a sinner, but as righteous. Thus we simply interpret justification, as the acceptance with which God receives us into his favour as if we were righteous; and we say that this justification consists in the forgiveness of sins and the imputation of the righteousness of Christ (see sec. 21 and 23).

3. In confirmation of this there are many clear passages of Scripture. First, it cannot be denied that this is the proper and most usual signification of the term. But as it were too tedious to collect all the passages, and compare them with each other, let it suffice to have called the reader's attention to the fact: he will easily convince himself of its truth. I will only mention a few passages in which the justification of which we speak is expressly handled. First, when Luke relates that all the people that heard Christ "justified God" (Luke vii. 29), and when Christ declares, that "Wisdom is justified of all her children" (Luke vii. 35), Luke means not that they conferred righteousness, which always dwells in perfection with God, although the whole world should attempt to wrest it from him, nor does Christ mean that the doctrine of salvation is made just: this it is in its own nature; but both modes of expression are equivalent to attributing due praise to God and his doctrine. On the other hand, when Christ upbraids the Pharisees for justifying themselves (Luke xvi. 15), he means not that they acquired righteousness by acting properly, but that they ambitiously courted a reputation for righteousness of which they were destitute. Those acquainted with Hebrew understand the meaning better; for in that language the name of wicked is given not only to those who are conscious of wickedness, but to those who receive sentence of condemnation. Thus, when Bathsheba says, "I and my son Solomon shall be counted offenders," she does not acknowledge a crime, but complains that she and her son will be exposed to the disgrace of being numbered among reprobates and criminals (1 Kings i. 21). It is, indeed, plain from the

context that the term even in Latin[1] must be thus understood—viz. *relatively*—and does not denote any quality. In regard to the use of the term with reference to the present subject, when Paul speaks of the Scripture, "foreseeing that God would justify the heathen through faith" (Gal. iii. 8), what other meaning can you give it than that God imputes righteousness by faith? Again, when he says "that he (God) might be just, and the justifier of him who believeth in Jesus" (Rom. iii. 26), what can the meaning be, if not that God, in consideration of their faith, frees them from the condemnation which their wickedness deserves? This appears still more plainly at the conclusion, when he exclaims, "Who shall lay anything to the charge of God's elect? It is God that justifieth. Who is he that condemneth? It is Christ that died, yea rather, that is risen again, who is even at the right hand of God, who also maketh intercession for us" (Rom. viii. 33, 34). For it is just as if he had said, Who shall accuse those whom God has acquitted? Who shall condemn those for whom Christ pleads? *To justify*, therefore, is nothing else than to acquit from the charge of guilt, as if innocence were proved. Hence, when God justifies us through the intercession of Christ, he does not acquit us on a proof of our own innocence, but by an imputation of righteousness, so that though not righteous in ourselves, we are deemed righteous in Christ. Thus it is said in Paul's discourse, in the Acts, "Through this man is preached unto you the forgiveness of sins; and by him all that believe are justified from all things from which ye could not be justified by the law of Moses" (Acts xiii. 38, 39). You see that after remission of sins justification is set down by way of explanation; you see plainly that it is used for acquittal; you see how it cannot be obtained by the works of the law; you see that it is entirely through the interposition of Christ; you see that it is obtained by faith; you see, in fine, that satisfaction intervenes, since it is said that we are justified from our sins by Christ. Thus when the publican is said to have gone down to his house "justified" (Luke xviii. 14), it cannot be held that he obtained this justification by any merit of works. All that is said is, that after obtaining the pardon of sins he was regarded in the sight of God as righteous. He was justified, therefore, not by any approval of works, but by gratuitous acquittal on the part of God. Hence Ambrose elegantly terms confession of sins "legal justification" (Ambrose on Psalm cxviii. Serm. x.).

4. Without saying more about the term, we shall have no doubt as to the thing meant if we attend to the description which is given of it. For Paul certainly designates justification by the term *acceptance*, when he says to the Ephesians, "Having predestinated us unto the adoption of children by Jesus Christ to himself, according to the good pleasure of his will, to the praise of the glory of his grace, wherein he

---

[1] Latin, "etiam dum Latine legitur."—French, "mesme en Grec et en Latin;" even in Greek and Latin.

hath made us accepted in the Beloved" (Eph. i. 5, 6). His meaning
is the very same as where he elsewhere says, "being justified freely by
his grace" (Rom. iii. 24). In the fourth chapter of the Epistle to the
Romans, he first terms it the *imputation* of righteousness, and hesitates not to place it in forgiveness of sins: "Even as David also
describeth the blessedness of the man unto whom God imputeth
righteousness without works, saying, Blessed are they whose iniquities are forgiven" &c. (Rom. iv. 6–8). There, indeed, he is not
speaking of a part of justification, but of the whole. He declares,
moreover, that a definition of it was given by David, when he pronounced him *blessed* who has obtained the *free* pardon of his sins.
Whence it appears that this righteousness of which he speaks is
simply opposed to judicial guilt.[1] But the most satisfactory passage
on this subject is that in which he declares the sum of the Gospel
message to be reconciliation to God, who is pleased, through Christ,
to receive us into favour by not imputing our sins (2 Cor v. 18–21).
Let my readers carefully weigh the whole context. For Paul shortly
after adding, by way of explanation, in order to designate the mode
of reconciliation, that Christ who knew no sin was made sin for us,
undoubtedly understands by reconciliation nothing else than justification. Nor, indeed, could it be said, as he elsewhere does, that we
are made righteous "by the obedience" of Christ (Rom. v. 19), were
it not that we are deemed righteous in the sight of God in him and
not in ourselves.

5. But as Osiander has introduced a kind of monstrosity termed
essential righteousness, by which, although he designed not to abolish
free righteousness, he involves it in darkness, and by that darkness
deprives pious minds of a serious sense of divine grace;[2] before I
pass to other matters, it may be proper to refute this delirious dream.
And, first, the whole speculation is mere empty curiosity. He, indeed, heaps together many passages of Scripture showing that Christ
is one with us, and we likewise one with him, a point which needs no
proof; but he entangles himself by not attending to the bond of this
unity. The explanation of all difficulties is easy to us, who hold
that we are united to Christ by the secret agency of his Spirit, but
he had formed some idea akin to that of the Manichees, desiring to
transfuse the divine essence into men.[3] Hence his other notion, that
Adam was formed in the image of God, because even before the fall
Christ was destined to be the model of human nature. But as I
study brevity, I will confine myself to the matter in hand. He says,
that we are one with Christ. This we admit, but still we deny that

---

1 French, "Dont il appert qu'il note ces deux choses comme opposites, Estre justifies
et Estre tenu coulpable; à ce que le proces soit fait à l'homme qui aura failli;"—
whence it appears that he sets down as opposites the two things, To be justified, and
To be held guilty, in that the process is brought against man who has failed.

2 French, "Que les poures ames ne sauroyent comprendre en telle obscurité la grace
de Christ;"—that poor souls cannot in such obscurity comprehend the grace of Christ.

3 French, "C'est, que l'ame est de l'essence de Dieu;"—that is, that the soul is of
the essence of God.

the essence of Christ is confounded with ours. Then we say that he absurdly endeavours to support his delusions by means of this principle: that Christ is our righteousness, because he is the eternal God, the fountain of righteousness, the very righteousness of God. My readers will pardon me for now only touching on matters which method requires me to defer to another place. But although he pretends that, by the term essential righteousness, he merely means to oppose the sentiment that we are reputed righteous on account of Christ, he however clearly shows, that not contented with that righteousness, which was procured for us by the obedience and sacrificial death of Christ, he maintains that we are substantially righteous in God by an infused essence as well as quality. For this is the reason why he so vehemently contends, that not only Christ but the Father and the Spirit dwell in us. The fact I admit to be true, but still I maintain it is wrested by him. He ought to have attended to the mode of dwelling—viz. that the Father and the Spirit are in Christ; and as in him the fulness of the Godhead dwells, so in him we possess God entire. Hence, whatever he says separately concerning the Father and the Spirit, has no other tendency than to lead away the simple from Christ. Then he introduces a substantial mixture, by which God, transfusing himself into us, makes us as it were a part of himself. Our being made one with Christ by the agency of the Spirit, he being the head and we the members, he regards as almost nothing unless his essence is mingled with us. But, as I have said, in the case of the Father and the Spirit he more clearly betrays his views—namely, that we are not justified by the mere grace of the Mediator, and that righteousness is not simply or entirely offered to us in his person, but that we are made partakers of divine righteousness when God is essentially united to us.

6. Had he only said, that Christ by justifying us becomes ours by an essential union, and that he is our head not only in so far as he is man, but that as the essence of the divine nature is diffused into us, he might indulge his dreams with less harm, and perhaps, it were less necessary to contest the matter with him; but since this principle is like a cuttle-fish, which, by the ejection of dark and inky blood, conceals its many tails,[1] if we would not knowingly and willingly allow ourselves to be robbed of that righteousness which alone gives us full assurance of our salvation, we must strenuously resist. For, in the whole of this discussion, the noun *righteousness*, and the verb *to justify*, are extended by Osiander to two parts; to be justified being not only to be reconciled to God by a free pardon, but also to be made just; and righteousness being not a free impu-

---

1 French, "Mais comme le principe qu'il prend est comme une seche, laquelle en jettant son sang qui est noir comme encre, trouble l'eau d'alentour pour cacher une grande multitude de queues;"—But as the principle which he adopts is like a cuttle-fish, which, casting out its blood, which is black as ink, troubles the water all around, to hide a great multitude of tails.

tation, but the holiness and integrity which the divine essence dwelling in us inspires. And he vehemently asserts (see sec. 8) that Christ is himself our righteousness, not in so far as he, by expiating sins, appeased the Father, but because he is the eternal God and life. To prove the first point—viz. that God justifies not only by pardoning but by regenerating—he asks, whether he leaves those whom he justifies as they were by nature, making no change upon their vices? The answer is very easy : as Christ cannot be divided into parts, so the two things, justification and sanctification, which we perceive to be united together in him, are inseparable. Whomsoever, therefore, God receives into his favour, he presents with the Spirit of adoption, whose agency forms them anew into his image. But if the brightness of the sun cannot be separated from its heat, are we therefore to say, that the earth is warmed by light and illumined by heat? Nothing can be more apposite to the matter in hand than this simile. The sun by its heat quickens and fertilises the earth ; by its rays enlightens and illumines it. Here is a mutual and undivided connection, and yet reason itself prohibits us from transferring the peculiar properties of the one to the other. In the confusion of a twofold grace, which Osiander obtrudes upon us, there is a similar absurdity. Because those whom God freely regards as righteous, he in fact renews to the cultivation of righteousness, Osiander confounds that free acceptance with this gift of regeneration, and contends that they are one and the same. But Scripture, while combining both, classes them separately, that it may the better display the manifold grace of God. Nor is Paul's statement superfluous, that Christ is made unto us " righteousness and sanctification" (1 Cor. i. 30). And whenever he argues from the salvation procured for us, from the paternal love of God and the grace of Christ, that we are called to purity and holiness, he plainly intimates, that to be justified is something else than to be made new creatures. Osiander on coming to Scripture corrupts every passage which he quotes. Thus when Paul says, " to him that worketh not, but believeth on him that justifieth the ungodly, his faith is counted for righteousness," he expounds *justifying* as *making just*. With the same rashness he perverts the whole of the fourth chapter to the Romans. He hesitates not to give a similar gloss to the passage which I lately quoted, " Who shall lay any thing to the charge of God's elect? It is God that justifieth." Here it is plain that guilt and acquittal simply are considered, and that the Apostle's meaning depends on the antithesis. Therefore his futility is detected both in his argument and his quotations for support from Scripture. He is not a whit sounder in discussing the term righteousness, when it is said, that faith was imputed to Abraham for righteousness after he had embraced Christ (who is the righteousness of God and God himself), and was distinguished by excellent virtues. Hence it appears, that two things which are perfect are viciously converted by him into one which is corrupt. For the righteousness which is there mentioned pertains not to the whole course of life; or rather, the Spirit testifies, that though Abraham greatly excelled in virtue, and by long perseverance in it had made so much progress, the only way in which he pleased God was by receiving the grace which was offered by the promise, in faith. From this it follows, that, as Paul justly maintains, there is no room for works in justification.

7. When he objects that the power of justifying exists not in faith, considered in itself, but only as receiving Christ, I willingly admit it. For did faith justify of itself, or (as it is expressed) by its own intrinsic virtue, as it is always weak and imperfect, its efficacy would be partial, and thus our righteousness being maimed, would give us only a portion of salvation. We indeed imagine nothing of the kind, but say, that, properly speaking, God alone justifies. The same thing we likewise transfer to Christ, because he was given to us for righteousness; while we compare faith to a kind of vessel, because we are incapable of receiving Christ, unless we are emptied and come with open mouth to receive his grace. Hence it follows, that we do not withdraw the power of justifying from Christ, when we hold that, previous to his righteousness, he himself is received by faith. Still, however, I admit not the tortuous figure of the sophist, that faith is Christ; as if a vessel of clay were a treasure, because gold is deposited in it.[1] And yet this is no reason why faith, though in itself of no dignity or value, should not justify us by giving Christ; just as such a vessel filled with coin may give wealth. I say, therefore, that faith, which is only the instrument for receiving justification, is ignorantly confounded with Christ, who is the material cause, as well as the author and minister of this great blessing. This disposes of the difficulty—viz. how the term *faith* is to be understood when treating of justification.

8. Osiander goes still farther in regard to the mode of receiving Christ, holding, that by the ministry of the external word the internal word is received; that he may thus lead us away from the priesthood of Christ, and his office of Mediator, to his eternal divinity.[2] We, indeed, do not divide Christ, but hold that he who, reconciling us to God in his flesh, bestowed righteousness upon us, is the eternal Word of God; and that he could not perform the office of Mediator, nor acquire righteousness for us, if he were not the eternal God. Osiander will have it, that as Christ is God and man, he was made our righteousness in respect not of his human but of his divine nature. But if this is a peculiar property of the Godhead, it will not be peculiar to Christ, but common to him with the Father and the Spirit, since

1 French, "Quant à d'autres folies extravagantes d'Osiander, tout homme de sain jugement les rejettera; comme quand il dit que la foy est Jesus Christ, autant que s'il disoit, qu'un pot de terre est le thresor qui est caché dedans;"—As to the other extravagant follies of Osiander, every man of sound judgment will reject them; for instance, when he says that faith is Jesus Christ, as much as if he said, that an earthen pot is the treasure which is hidden in it.

2 French, "Faisant semblant de les rauir à la divinité d'icelui;"—under pretence of leading them to his divinity.

their righteousness is one and the same. Thus it would be incongruous to say, that that which existed naturally from eternity was made ours. But granting that God was made unto us righteousness, what are we to make of Paul's interposed statement, that he was so made by God? This certainly is peculiar to the office of Mediator, for although he contains in himself the divine nature, yet he receives his own proper title, that he may be distinguished from the Father and the Spirit. But he makes a ridiculous boast of a single passage of Jeremiah, in which it is said, that Jehovah will be our righteousness (Jer. xxiii. 6; xxxiii. 16). But all he can extract from this is, that Christ, who is our righteousness, was God manifest in the flesh. We have elsewhere quoted from Paul's discourse, that God purchased the Church with his own blood (Acts xx. 28). Were any one to infer from this that the blood by which sins were expiated was divine, and of a divine nature, who could endure so foul a heresy? But Osiander, thinking that he has gained the whole cause by this childish cavil, swells, exults, and stuffs whole pages with his bombast, whereas the solution is simple and obvious—viz. that Jehovah, when made of the seed of David, was indeed to be the righteousness of believers, but in what sense Isaiah declares, "By his knowledge shall my righteous servant justify many" (Isa. liii. 11). Let us observe that it is the Father who speaks. He attributes the office of justifying to the Son, and adds the reason—because he is "righteous." He places the method, or *medium* (as it is called), in the doctrine by which Christ is known. For the word דעת is more properly to be understood in a passive sense. Hence I infer, first, that Christ was made righteousness when he assumed the form of a servant; secondly, that he justified us by his obedience to the Father; and, accordingly, that he does not perform this for us in respect of his divine nature, but according to the nature of the dispensation laid upon him. For though God alone is the fountain of righteousness, and the only way in which we are righteous is by participation with him, yet as by our unhappy revolt we are alienated from his righteousness, it is necessary to descend to this lower remedy, that Christ may justify us by the power of his death and resurrection.

9. If he objects, that this work by its excellence transcends human, and therefore can only be ascribed to the divine nature; I concede the former point, but maintain, that on the latter he is ignorantly deluded. For although Christ could neither purify our souls by his own blood, nor appease the Father by his sacrifice, nor acquit us from the charge of guilt, nor, in short, perform the office of priest, unless he had been very God, because no human ability was equal to such a burden, it is however certain that he performed all these things in his human nature. If it is asked, in what way we are justified? Paul answers, *by the obedience of Christ.* Did he obey in any other way than by assuming the form of a servant? We infer, therefore, that righteousness was manifested to us in his flesh. In like manner, in another passage (which I greatly wonder that Osiander does not

blush repeatedly to quote), he places the fountain of righteousness entirely in the incarnation of Christ, "He hath made him to be sin for us who knew no sin, that we might be made the righteousness of God in him" (2 Cor. v. 21). Osiander in turgid sentences lays hold of the expression, *righteousness of God*, and shouts victory! as if he had proved it to be his own phantom of essential righteousness,[1] though the words have a very different meaning—viz. that we are justified through the expiation made by Christ. That the righteousness of God is used for the righteousness which is approved by God, should be known to mere tyros, as in John, the praise of God is contrasted with the praise of men [2] (John xii. 43). I know that by the righteousness of God is sometimes meant that of which God is the author, and which he bestows upon us; but that here the only thing meant is, that being supported by the expiation of Christ, we are able to stand at the tribunal of God, sound readers perceive without any observation of mine. The word is not of so much importance, provided Osiander agrees with us in this, that we are justified by Christ in respect he was made an expiatory victim for us. This he could not be in his divine nature. For which reason also, when Christ would seal the righteousness and salvation which he brought to us, he holds forth the sure pledge of it in his flesh. He indeed calls himself "living bread," but, in explanation of the mode, adds, "my flesh is meat indeed, and my blood is drink indeed" (John vi. 55). The same doctrine is clearly seen in the sacraments; which, though they direct our faith to the whole, not to a part of Christ, yet, at the same time, declare that the materials of righteousness and salvation reside in his flesh; not that the mere man of himself justifies or quickens, but that God was pleased, by means of a Mediator, to manifest his own hidden and incomprehensible nature. Hence I often repeat, that Christ has been in a manner set before us as a fountain, whence we may draw what would otherwise lie without use in that deep and hidden abyss which streams forth to us in the person of the Mediator.[3] In this way, and in this meaning, I deny not that Christ, as he is God and man, justifies us; that this work is common also to

1 French, "Il magnifie la justice de Dieu tant et plus; mais c'est pour triompher comme s'il auoit gagné ce poinct, que la justice de Dieu nous est essencielle;"—He magnifies the righteousness of God above measure; but it is to triumph, as if he had gained this point, that the righteousness of God is essential to us.

2 The French adds, "signifiant, que ceux desquels il parle ont nagé entre deux eaux; pource qu'ils aimoyent mieux garder leur bonne reputation au monde, que d'etre priser devant Dieu;"—meaning, that those of whom he speaks were swimming between two streams; that they preferred keeping their good reputation in the world, to being prized in the sight of God.

3 French, "Pour ceste cause j'ay accoustume de dire que Christ nous est comme une fontaine, dont chacun peut puiser et boire à son aise et à souhait; et que par son moyen les biens celestes sourdent et decoulent à nous, lesquels ne nous profiteroyent rien demeurans en la majesté de Dieu, qui est comme une source profonde;"—For this cause I am accustomed to say, that Christ is to us like a fountain, of which every man may draw and drink at his ease, and to the fill; and that by his means heavenly blessings rise and flow to us, which blessings would profit us nothing, remaining in the majesty of God, which is, as it were, a profound abyss.

the Father and the Holy Spirit; in fine, that the righteousness of which God makes us partakers is the eternal righteousness of the eternal God, provided effect is given to the clear and valid reasons to which I have adverted.

10. Moreover, lest by his cavils he deceive the unwary, I acknowledge that we are devoid of this incomparable gift until Christ become ours. Therefore, to that union of the head and members, the residence of Christ in our hearts, in fine, the mystical union, we assign the highest rank, Christ when he becomes ours making us partners with him in the gifts with which he was endued. Hence we do not view him as at a distance and without us, but as we have put him on, and been ingrafted into his body, he deigns to make us one with himself, and, therefore, we glory in having a fellowship of righteousness with him. This disposes of Osiander's calumny, that we regard faith as righteousness; as if we were robbing Christ of his rights when we say, that, destitute in ourselves, we draw near to him by Faith, to make way for his grace, that he alone may fill us. But Osiander, spurning this spiritual union, insists on a gross mixture of Christ with believers; and, accordingly, to excite prejudice, gives the name of Zuinglians[1] to all who subscribe not to his fanatical heresy of essential righteousness, because they do not hold that, in the supper, Christ is eaten substantially. For my part, I count it the highest honour to be thus assailed by a haughty man, devoted to his own impostures; though he assails not me only, but writers of known reputation throughout the world, and whom it became him modestly to venerate. This, however, does not concern me, as I plead not my own cause, and plead the more sincerely that I am free from every sinister feeling. In insisting so vehemently on essential righteousness, and an essential inhabitation of Christ within us, his meaning is, first, that God by a gross mixture[2] transfuses himself into us, as he pretends that there is a carnal eating in the supper; and, secondly, that by instilling his own righteousness into us, he makes us really righteous with himself, since, according to him, this righteousness is as well God himself as the probity, or holiness, or integrity of God. I will not spend much time in disposing of the passages of Scripture which he adduces, and which, though used in reference to the heavenly life, he wrests to our present state. Peter says, that through the knowledge of Christ "are given unto us exceeding great and precious promises, that by them ye might be partakers of the divine nature" (2 Pet. i. 4);[3] as if we now were what the gospel promises we shall be at the final advent of Christ; nay, John reminds us, that "when he shall appear we shall be like him,

---

1 The Latin, "ideo Zuinglianos odiose nominat;" is in the French simply, "condamne furieusement;"—furiously condemns.

2 Latin, "crassa mixtura;"—French, "mixtion telle que les viandes que nous mangeons;"—mixture such as the victuals we eat.

3 The French adds, "Osiander tire de la que Dieu a meslée son essence avec la nostre;"—Osiander implies from this that God has mingled his essence with ours.

for we shall see him as he is" (1 John iii. 2). I only wished to give my readers a slender specimen of Osiander, it being my intention to decline the discussion of his frivolities, not because there is any difficulty in disposing of them, but because I am unwilling to annoy the reader with superfluous labour.

11. But more poison lurks in the second branch, when he says that we are righteous together with God. I think I have already sufficiently proved, that although the dogma were not so pestiferous, yet because it is frigid and jejune, and falls by its own vanity, it must justly be disrelished by all sound and pious readers. But it is impossible to tolerate the impiety which, under the pretence of a twofold righteousness, undermines our assurance of salvation, and, hurrying us into the clouds, tries to prevent us from embracing the gift of expiation in faith, and invoking God with quiet minds. Osiander derides us for teaching, that *to be justified* is a forensic term, because it behoves us to be in reality just: there is nothing also to which he is more opposed than the idea of our being justified by a free imputation. Say, then, if God does not justify us by acquitting and pardoning, what does Paul mean when he says, "God was in Christ reconciling the world unto himself, not imputing their trespasses unto them"? "He made him to be sin for us who knew no sin; that we might be made the righteousness of God in him" (2 Cor. v. 19, 21). Here I learn, first, that those who are reconciled to God are regarded as righteous: then the method is stated, God justifies by pardoning; and hence, in another place, justification is opposed to accusation (Rom. viii. 33); this antithesis clearly demonstrating that the mode of expression is derived from forensic use. And, indeed, no man, moderately versant in the Hebrew tongue (provided he is also of sedate brain), is ignorant that this phrase thus took its rise, and thereafter derived its tendency and force. Now, then, when Paul says that David "describeth the blessedness of the man unto whom God imputeth righteousness without works, saying, Blessed are they whose iniquities are forgiven" (Rom. iv. 6, 7; Ps. xxxii. 1), let Osiander say whether this is a complete or only a partial definition. He certainly does not adduce the Psalmist as a witness that pardon of sins is a part of righteousness, or concurs with something else in justifying, but he includes the whole of righteousness in gratuitous forgiveness, declaring those to be blessed "whose iniquities are forgiven, and whose sins are covered," and "to whom the Lord will not impute sin." He estimates and judges of his happiness from this, that in this way he is righteous not in reality, but by imputation.

Osiander objects that it would be insulting to God, and contrary to his nature, to justify those who still remain wicked. But it ought to be remembered, as I already observed, that the gift of justification is not separated from regeneration, though the two things are distinct. But as it is too well known by experience, that the remains of sin always exist in the righteous, it is necessary that justification should be something very different from reformation to newness of life. This latter God begins in his elect, and carries on during the whole course of life, gradually and sometimes slowly, so that if placed at his judgment-seat they would always deserve sentence of death. He justifies not partially, but freely, so that they can appear in the heavens as if clothed with the purity of Christ. No portion of righteousness could pacify the conscience. It must be decided that we are pleasing to God, as being without exception righteous in his sight. Hence it follows that the doctrine of justification is perverted and completely overthrown whenever doubt is instilled into the mind, confidence in salvation is shaken, and free and intrepid prayer is retarded ; yea, whenever rest and tranquillity with spiritual joy are not established. Hence Paul argues against objectors, that " if the inheritance be of the law, it is no more of promise " (Gal. iii. 18), that in this way faith would be made vain ; for if respect be had to works it fails, the holiest of men in that case finding nothing in which they can confide. This distinction between justification and regeneration (Osiander confounding the two, calls them a twofold righteousness) is admirably expressed by Paul. Speaking of his real righteousness, or the integrity bestowed upon him (which Osiander terms his essential righteousness), he mournfully exclaims, " O wretched man that I am ! who shall deliver me from the body of this death ?" (Rom. vii. 24); but betaking himself to the righteousness which is founded solely on the mercy of God, he breaks forth thus magnificently into the language of triumph: " Who shall lay any thing to the charge of God's elect ? It is God that justifieth." " Who shall separate us from the love of Christ ? shall tribulation, or distress, or persecution, or famine, or nakedness, or peril, or sword ?" (Rom. viii. 33, 35.) He clearly declares that the only righteousness for him is that which alone suffices for complete salvation in the presence of God, so that that miserable bondage, the consciousness of which made him a little before lament his lot, derogates not from his confidence, and is no obstacle in his way. This diversity is well known, and indeed is familiar to all the saints who groan under the burden of sin, and yet with victorious assurance rise above all fears. Osiander's objection as to its being inconsistent with the nature of God, falls back upon himself; for though he clothes the saints with a twofold righteousness as with a coat of skins, he is, however, forced to admit, that without forgiveness no man is pleasing to God. If this be so, let him at least admit, that with reference to what is called the proportion of imputation, those are regarded as righteous who are not so in reality. But how far shall the sinner extend this gratuitous acceptance, which is substituted in the room of righteousness ? Will it amount to the whole pound, or will it be only an ounce ? He will remain in doubt, vibrating to this side and to that, because he will be unable to assume to himself as much righteousness as will be necessary to give confidence. It is well that he who would prescribe a law to God is not the judge in this cause. But this saying will ever stand true, " That thou mightest be justified when thou speakest, and be clear when thou judgest " (Ps. li. 4).

What arrogance to condemn the Supreme Judge when he acquits freely, and try to prevent the response from taking effect: " I will have mercy on whom I will have mercy." And yet the intercession of Moses, which God calmed by this answer, was not for pardon to some individual, but to all alike, by wiping away the guilt to which all were liable. And we, indeed, say, that the lost are justified before God by the burial of their sins; for (as he hates sin) he can only love those whom he justifies. But herein is the wondrous method of justification, that, clothed with the righteousness of Christ, they dread not the judgment of which they are worthy; and while they justly condemn themselves, are yet deemed righteous out of themselves.

12. I must admonish the reader carefully to attend to the mystery which he boasts he is unwilling to conceal from them. For after contending with great prolixity that we do not obtain favour with God through the mere imputation of the righteousness of Christ, because (to use his own words) it were impossible for God to hold those as righteous who are not so, he at length concludes that Christ was given to us for righteousness, in respect not of his human, but of his divine nature; and though this can only be found in the person of the Mediator, it is, however, the righteousness not of man, but of God. He does not now twist his rope of two righteousnesses, but plainly deprives the human nature of Christ of the office of justifying. It is worth while to understand what the nature of his argument is. It is said in the same passage that Christ is made unto us *wisdom* (1 Cor. i. 30); but this is true only of the eternal Word, and, therefore, it is not the man Christ that is made *righteousness*. I answer, that the only-begotten Son of God was indeed his eternal wisdom, but that this title is applied to him by Paul in a different way—viz. because " in him are hid all the treasures of wisdom and righteousness" (Col. ii. 3). That, therefore, which he had with the Father he manifested to us; and thus Paul's expression refers not to the essence of the Son of God, but to our use, and is fitly applied to the human nature of Christ; for although the light shone in darkness before he was clothed with flesh, yet he was a hidden light until he appeared in human nature as the *Sun of Righteousness*, and hence he calls himself the *light of the world*. It is also foolishly objected by Osiander, that justifying far transcends the power both of men and angels, since it depends not on the dignity of any creature, but on the ordination of God. Were angels to attempt to give satisfaction to God, they could have no success, because they are not appointed for this purpose, it being the peculiar office of Christ, who " hath redeemed us from the curse of the law, being made a curse for us" (Gal. iii. 13). Those who deny that Christ is our righteousness, in respect of his divine nature, are wickedly charged by Osiander with leaving only a part of Christ, and (what is worse) with making two Gods; because, while admitting that God dwells in us, they still insist that we are not justified by the righteousness of God. For

though we call Christ the author of life, inasmuch as he endured death that he might destroy him who had the power of death (Heb. ii. 14), we do not thereby rob him of this honour, in his whole character as God manifested in the flesh. We only make a distinction as to the manner in which the righteousness of God comes to us, and is enjoyed by us,—a matter as to which Osiander shamefully erred. We deny not that that which was openly exhibited to us in Christ flowed from the secret grace and power of God; nor do we dispute that the righteousness which Christ confers upon us is the righteousness of God, and proceeds from him. What we constantly maintain is, that our righteousness and life are in the death and resurrection of Christ. I say nothing of that absurd accumulation of passages with which, without selection or common understanding, he has loaded his readers, in endeavouring to show, that whenever mention is made of righteousness, this essential righteousness of his should be understood; as when David implores help from the righteousness of God. This David does more than a hundred times, and as often Osiander hesitates not to pervert his meaning. Not a whit more solid is his objection, that the name of righteousness is rightly and properly applied to that by which we are moved to act aright, but that it is God only that worketh in us both to will and to do (Phil. ii. 13). For we deny not that God by his Spirit forms us anew to holiness and righteousness of life; but we must first see whether he does this of himself, immediately, or by the hand of his Son, with whom he hath deposited all the fulness of the Holy Spirit, that out of his own abundance he may supply the wants of his members. Then, although righteousness comes to us from the secret fountain of the Godhead, it does not follow that Christ, who sanctified himself in the flesh on our account, is our righteousness in respect of his divine nature (John xvii. 19). Not less frivolous is his observation, that the righteousness with which Christ himself was righteous was divine; for had not the will of the Father impelled him, he could not have fulfilled the office assigned him. For although it has been elsewhere said that all the merits of Christ flow from the mere good pleasure of God, this gives no countenance to the phantom by which Osiander fascinates both his own eyes and those of the simple. For who will allow him to infer, that because God is the source and commencement of our righteousness, we are essentially righteous, and the essence of the divine righteousness dwells in us? In redeeming us, says Isaiah, "he (God) put on righteousness as a breastplate, and an helmet of salvation upon his head" (Isaiah lix. 17), was this to deprive Christ of the armour which he had given him, and prevent him from being a perfect Redeemer? All that the Prophet meant was, that God borrowed nothing from an external quarter, that in redeeming us he received no external aid. The same thing is briefly expressed by Paul in different terms, when he says that God set him forth "to declare his righteousness for the remission of sins." This is not the least repugnant to his doctrine: in another place, that " by the obedience of one shall many be made righteous" (Rom. v. 19).   In short, every one who, by the entanglement of a twofold righteousness, prevents miserable souls from resting entirely on the mere mercy of God, mocks Christ by putting on him a crown of plaited thorns.

13. But since a great part of mankind imagine a righteousness compounded of faith and works, let us here show that there is so wide a difference between justification by faith and by works, that the establishment of the one necessarily overthrows the other.   The Apostle says, " Yea doubtless, and I count all things but loss for the excellency of the knowledge of Christ Jesus my Lord: for whom I have suffered the loss of all things, and do count them but dung, that I may win Christ, and be found in him, not having mine own righteousness, which is of the law, but that which is through the faith of Christ, the righteousness which is of God by faith" (Phil. iii. 8, 9). You here see a comparison of contraries, and an intimation that every one who would obtain the righteousness of Christ must renounce his own.   Hence he elsewhere declares the cause of the rejection of the Jews to have been, that " they being ignorant of God's righteousness, and going about to establish their own righteousness, have not submitted themselves unto the righteousness of God" (Rom. x. 3).   If we destroy the righteousness of God by establishing our own righteousness, then, in order to obtain his righteousness, our own must be entirely abandoned.   This also he shows, when he declares that boasting is not excluded by the Law, but by faith (Rom. iii. 27). Hence it follows, that so long as the minutest portion of our own righteousness remains, we have still some ground for boasting.   Now if faith utterly excludes boasting, the righteousness of works cannot in any way be associated with the righteousness of faith.   This meaning is so clearly expressed in the fourth chapter to the Romans as to leave no room for cavil or evasion.   " If Abraham were justified by works, he hath whereof to glory;" and then it is added, " but not before God" (Rom. iv. 2).   The conclusion therefore is, that he was not justified by works.   He then employs another argument from contraries—viz. when *reward* is paid to works, it is done *of debt*, not *of grace;* but the righteousness of faith is of grace: therefore it is not of the merit of works.   Away, then, with the dream of those who invent a righteousness compounded of faith and works, (see Calvin. ad Concilium Tridentinum).

14. The Sophists, who delight in sporting with Scripture and in empty cavils, think they have a subtle evasion when they expound *works* to mean, such as unregenerated men do literally, and by the effect of free will, without the grace of Christ, and deny that these have any reference to spiritual works.[1]   Thus, according to them, man is justified by faith as well as by works, provided these are not

1 French, " Ainsi ils disent que cela n'appartient de rien aux bonnes œuvres des fideles qui se font par la vertu du Sainct Esprit; "—Thus they say that that has no reference at all to the good works of believers, which are done by the power of the Holy Spirit.

his own works, but gifts of Christ and fruits of regeneration ; Paul's only object in so expressing himself being to convince the Jews, that in trusting to their own strength they foolishly arrogated righteousness to themselves, whereas it is bestowed upon us by the Spirit of Christ alone, and not by studied efforts of our own nature.   But they observe not that in the antithesis between Legal and Gospel righteousness, which Paul elsewhere introduces, all kinds of works, with whatever name adorned, are excluded (Gal. iii. 11, 12).   For he says that the righteousness of the Law consists in obtaining salvation by doing what the Law requires, but that the righteousness of faith consists in believing that Christ died and rose again (Rom. x. 5–9).   Moreover, we shall afterwards see, at the proper place, that the blessings of sanctification and justification, which we derive from Christ, are different.   Hence it follows, that not even spiritual works are taken into account when the power of justifying is ascribed to faith.   And, indeed, the passage above quoted, in which Paul declares that Abraham had no ground of glorying before God, because he was not justified by works, ought not to be confined to a literal and external form of virtue, or to the effort of free will.   The meaning is, that though the life of the Patriarch had been spiritual and almost angelic, yet he could not by the merit of works have procured justification before God.

15. The Schoolmen treat the matter somewhat more grossly by mingling their preparations with it ; and yet the others instil into the simple and unwary a no less pernicious dogma, when, under cover of the Spirit and grace, they hide the divine mercy, which alone can give peace to the trembling soul.   We, indeed, hold with Paul, that those who fulfil the Law are justified by God; but because we are all far from observing the Law, we infer that the works which should be most effectual to justification are of no avail to us, because we are destitute of them.   In regard to vulgar Papists or Schoolmen, they are here doubly wrong, both in calling faith assurance of conscience while waiting to receive from God the reward of merits, and in interpreting divine grace to mean not the imputation of gratuitous righteousness, but the assistance of the Spirit in the study of holiness. They quote from an Apostle : " He that cometh to God must believe that he is, and that he is the rewarder of them that diligently seek him " (Heb. xi. 6).   But they observe not what the method of seeking is.   Then in regard to the term *grace*, it is plain from their writings that they labour under a delusion.   For Lombard holds that justification is given to us by Christ in two ways.   " First," says he (Lombard, Sent. Lib. iii. Dist. 16, c. 11), " the death of Christ justifies us when by means of it the love by which we are made righteous is excited in our hearts ; and, secondly, when by means of it sin is extinguished, sin by which the devil held us captive, but by which he cannot now procure our condemnation."   You see here that the chief office of divine grace in our justification he considers to be its directing us to good works by the agency of the Holy Spirit.   He intended, no doubt, to follow the opinion of Augustine, but he follows it at a distance,

and even wanders far from a true imitation of him, both obscuring what was clearly stated by Augustine, and making what in him was less pure more corrupt. The Schools have always gone from worse to worse, until at length, in their downward path, they have degenerated into a kind of Pelagianism. Even the sentiment of Augustine, or at least his mode of expressing it, cannot be entirely approved of. For although he is admirable in stripping man of all merit of righteousness, and transferring the whole praise of it to God, yet he classes the grace by which we are regenerated to newness of life under the head of sanctification.

16. Scripture, when it treats of justification by faith, leads us in a very different direction. Turning away our view from our own works, it bids us look only to the mercy of God and the perfection of Christ. The order of justification which it sets before us in this: first, God of his mere gratuitous goodness is pleased to embrace the sinner, in whom he sees nothing that can move him to mercy but wretchedness, because he sees him altogether naked and destitute of good works. He, therefore, seeks the cause of kindness in himself, that thus he may affect the sinner by a sense of his goodness, and induce him, in distrust of his own works, to cast himself entirely upon his mercy for salvation. This is the meaning of faith by which the sinner comes into the possession of salvation, when, according to the doctrine of the Gospel, he perceives that he is reconciled by God; when, by the intercession of Christ, he obtains the pardon of his sins, and is justified; and, though renewed by the Spirit of God, considers that, instead of leaning on his own works, he must look solely to the righteousness which is treasured up for him in Christ. When these things are weighed separately, they will clearly explain our view, though they may be arranged in a better order than that in which they are here presented. But it is of little consequence, provided they are so connected with each other as to give us a full exposition and solid confirmation of the whole subject.

17. Here it is proper to remember the relation which we previously established between faith and the Gospel; faith being said to justify because it receives and embraces the righteousness offered in the Gospel. By the very fact of its being said to be offered by the Gospel, all consideration of works is excluded. This Paul repeatedly declares, and in two passages, in particular, most clearly demonstrates. In the Epistle to the Romans, comparing the Law and the Gospel, he says, " Moses describeth the righteousness which is of the law, That the man which doeth those things shall live by them. But the righteousness which is of faith speaketh on this wise,—If thou shalt confess with thy mouth the Lord Jesus, and shalt believe in thine heart that God hath raised him from the dead, thou shalt be saved" (Rom. x. 5, 6, 9). Do you see how he makes the distinction between the Law and the Gospel to be, that the former gives justification to works, whereas the latter bestows it freely without any help from works? This is a notable passage, and may free us from many difficulties if

we understand that the justification which is given us by the Gospel is free from any terms of Law. It is for this reason he more than once places the promise in diametrical opposition to the Law. "If the inheritance be of the law, it is no more of promise" (Gal. iii. 18). Expressions of similar import occur in the same chapter. Undoubtedly the Law also has its promises; and, therefore, between them and the Gospel promises there must be some distinction and difference, unless we are to hold that the comparison is inept. And in what can the difference consist unless in this, that the promises of the Gospel are gratuitous, and founded on the mere mercy of God, whereas the promises of the Law depend on the condition of works? But let no prater here allege that only the righteousness which men would obtrude upon God of their own strength and free will is repudiated; since Paul declares, without exception, that the Law gained nothing by its commands, being such as none, not only of mankind in general, but none even of the most perfect, are able to fulfil. Love assuredly is the chief commandment in the Law; and since the Spirit of God trains us to love, it cannot but be a cause of righteousness in us, though that righteousness even in the saints is defective, and therefore of no value as a ground of merit.

18. The second passage is, "That no man is justified by the law in the sight of God, it is evident: for, The just shall live by faith. And the law is not of faith: but, The man that doeth them shall live in them" (Gal. iii. 11, 12; Hab. ii. 4). How could the argument hold unless it be true that works are not to be taken into account, but are to be altogether separated? The Law, he says, is different from faith. Why? Because to obtain justification by it, works are required; and hence it follows, that to obtain justification by the Gospel they are not required. From this statement, it appears that those who are justified by faith are justified independent of, nay, in the absence of, the merit of works, because faith receives that righteousness which the Gospel bestows. But the Gospel differs from the Law in this, that it does not confine justification to works, but places it entirely in the mercy of God. In like manner, Paul contends, in the Epistle to the Romans, that Abraham had no ground of glorying, because faith was imputed to him for righteousness (Rom. iv. 2); and he adds in confirmation, that the proper place for justification by faith is where there are no works to which reward is due. "To him that worketh is the reward not reckoned of grace, but of debt." What is given to faith is gratuitous, this being the force of the meaning of the words which he there employs. Shortly after he adds, "Therefore it is of faith, that it might be by grace" (Rom. iv. 16); and hence infers that the inheritance is gratuitous because it is procured by faith. How so but just because faith, without the aid of works, leans entirely on the mercy of God? And in the same sense, doubtless, he elsewhere teaches, that the righteousness of God without the Law was manifested, being witnessed by the Law and the Prophets (Rom. iii. 21); for excluding the Law, he

declares that it is not aided by works, that we do not obtain it by working, but are destitute when we draw near to receive it.

19. The reader now perceives with what fairness the Sophists of the present day cavil at our doctrine, when we say that a man is justified by faith alone (Rom. iv. 2). They dare not deny that *he is justified by faith*, seeing Scripture so often declares it ; but as the word *alone* is nowhere expressly used, they will not tolerate its being added.[1] Is it so ? What answer, then, will they give to the words of Paul, when he contends that righteousness is not of faith unless it be gratuitous ? How can it be gratuitous, and yet by works ? By what cavils, moreover, will they evade his declaration in another place, that in the Gospel the righteousness of God is manifested ? (Rom. i. 17.) If righteousness is manifested in the Gospel, it is certainly not a partial or mutilated, but a full and perfect righteousness. The Law, therefore, has no part in it, and their objection to the exclusive word *alone* is not only unfounded, but is obviously absurd. Does he not plainly enough attribute everything to faith alone when he disconnects it with works ? What, I would ask, is meant by the expressions, " The righteousness of God without the law is manifest ;" " Being justified freely by his grace ;" " Justified by faith without the deeds of the law"? (Rom. iii. 21, 24, 28). Here they have an ingenious subterfuge, one which, though not of their own devising, but taken from Origen and some ancient writers, is most childish. They pretend that the works excluded are ceremonial, not moral works. Such profit do they make by their constant wrangling, that they possess not even the first elements of logic. Do they think the Apostle was raving when he produced, in proof of his doctrine, these passages ? " The man that doeth them shall live in them" (Gal. iii. 12). " Cursed is every one that continueth not in all things that are written in the book of the law to do them" (Gal. iii. 10). Unless they are themselves raving, they will not say that life was promised to the observers of ceremonies, and the curse denounced only against the transgressors of them. If these passages are to be understood of the Moral Law, there cannot be a doubt that moral works also are excluded from the power of justifying. To the same effect are the arguments which he employs. " By the deeds of the law there shall no flesh be justified in his sight : for by the law is the knowledge of sin" (Rom. iii. 20). " The law worketh wrath" (Rom. iv. 15), and therefore not righteousness. " The law cannot pacify the conscience," and therefore cannot confer righteousness. " Faith is imputed for righteousness," and therefore righteousness is not the reward of works, but is given without being due. Because "we are justified by faith," boasting is excluded. " Had there been a law given which could have given life, verily righteousness should

---

1 French. " Mais pource que ce mot Seule, n'y est point exprimé, ils nous reprochent qu'il est adjousté du notre ;" —but because this word Alone is not expressed, they upbraid us with having it added of our own accord.

have been by the law.   But the Scripture hath concluded all under
sin, that the promise by faith of Jesus Christ might be given to
them that believe" (Gal. iii. 21, 22).   Let them maintain, if they
dare, that these things apply to ceremonies, and not to morals, and
the very children will laugh at their effrontery.   The true conclusion therefore is, that the whole Law is spoken of when the power
of justifying is denied to it.

20. Should any one wonder why the Apostle, not contented with
having named works, employs this addition, the explanation is easy.
However highly works may be estimated, they have their whole
value more from the approbation of God than from their own dignity.
For who will presume to plume himself before God on the righteousness of works, unless in so far as He approves of them?   Who will
presume to demand of Him a reward except in so far as He has promised it?   It is owing entirely to the goodness of God that works
are deemed worthy of the honour and reward of righteousness; and,
therefore, their whole value consists in this, that by means of them
we endeavour to manifest obedience to God.   Wherefore, in another
passage, the Apostle, to prove that Abraham could not be justified
by works, declares, "that the covenant, that was confirmed before of
God in Christ, the law, which was four hundred and thirty years
after, cannot disannul, that it should make the promise of none
effect" (Gal. iii. 17).   The unskilful would ridicule the argument
that there could be righteous works before the promulgation of the
Law, but the Apostle, knowing that works could derive this value
solely from the testimony and honour conferred on them by God,
takes it for granted that, previous to the Law, they had no power of
justifying.   We see why he expressly terms them works of Law
when he would deny the power of justifying to them—viz. because
it was only with regard to such works that a question could be
raised; although he sometimes, without addition, excepts all kinds
of works whatever, as when on the testimony of David he speaks of
the man to whom the Lord imputeth righteousness without works
(Rom. iv. 5, 6).   No cavils, therefore, can enable them to prove
that the exclusion of works is not general.   In vain do they lay hold
of the frivolous subtilty, that the *faith alone*, by which we are justified, "*worketh by love*," and that love, therefore, is the foundation of
justification.   We, indeed, acknowledge with Paul, that the only
faith which justifies is that which works by love (Gal. v. 6); but
love does not give it its justifying power.   Nay, its only means of
justifying consists in its bringing us into communication with the
righteousness of Christ.   Otherwise the whole argument, on which
the Apostle insists with so much earnestness, would fall.   " To him
that worketh is the reward not reckoned of grace, but of debt.   But
to him that worketh not, but believeth on him that justifieth the
ungodly, his faith is counted for righteousness."   Could he express
more clearly than in this way, that there is justification in faith
only where there are no works to which reward is due, and that

faith is imputed for righteousness only when righteousness is conferred freely without merit?

21. Let us now consider the truth of what was said in the definition—viz. that justification by faith is reconciliation with God, and that this consists solely in the remission of sins. We must always return to the axiom, that the wrath of God lies upon all men so long as they continue sinners. This is elegantly expressed by Isaiah in these words: "Behold, the Lord's hand is not shortened, that it cannot save; neither his ear heavy, that it cannot hear: but your iniquities have separated between you and your God, and your sins have hid his face from you, that he will not hear" (Isaiah lix. 1, 2). We are here told that sin is a separation between God and man; that His countenance is turned away from the sinner; and that it cannot be otherwise, since to have any intercourse with sin is repugnant to his righteousness. Hence the Apostle shows that man is at enmity with God until he is restored to favour by Christ (Rom. v. 8–10). When the Lord, therefore, admits him to union, he is said to justify him, because he can neither receive him into favour, nor unite him to himself, without changing his condition from that of a sinner into that of a righteous man. We add, that this is done by remission of sins. For if those whom the Lord hath reconciled to himself are estimated by works, they will still prove to be in reality sinners, while they ought to be pure and free from sin. It is evident, therefore, that the only way in which those whom God embraces are made righteous, is by having their pollutions wiped away by the remission of sins, so that this justification may be termed in one word the remission of sins.

22. Both of these become perfectly clear from the words of Paul: "God was in Christ reconciling the world unto himself, not imputing their trespasses unto them; and hath committed unto us the word of reconciliation." He then subjoins the sum of his embassy: "He hath made him to be sin for us who knew no sin; that we might be made the righteousness of God in him" (2 Cor. v. 19–21). He here uses righteousness and reconciliation indiscriminately, to make us understand that the one includes the other. The mode of obtaining this righteousness he explains to be, that our sins are not imputed to us. Wherefore, you cannot henceforth doubt how God justifies us when you hear that he reconciles us to himself by not imputing our faults. In the same manner, in the Epistle to the Romans, he proves, by the testimony of David, that righteousness is imputed without works, because he declares the man to be blessed "whose transgression is forgiven, whose sin is covered," and "unto whom the Lord imputeth not iniquity" (Rom. iv. 6; Ps. xxxii. 1, 2). There he undoubtedly uses blessedness for righteousness; and as he declares that it consists in forgiveness of sins, there is no reason why we should define it otherwise. Accordingly, Zacharias, the father of John the Baptist, sings that the knowledge of salvation consists in the forgiveness of sins (Luke i. 77). The same course

was followed by Paul when, in addressing the people of Antioch, he gave them a summary of salvation. Luke states that he concluded in this way: "Through this man is preached unto you the forgiveness of sins, and by him all that believe are justified from all things from which ye could not be justified by the law of Moses" (Acts xii. 38, 39). Thus the Apostle connects forgiveness of sins with justification in such a way as to show that they are altogether the same; and hence he properly argues that justification, which we owe to the indulgence of God, is gratuitous. Now should it seem an unusual mode of expression to say that believers are justified before God not by works, but by gratuitous acceptance, seeing it is frequently used in Scripture, and sometimes also by ancient writers. Thus Augustine says: "The righteousness of the saints in this world consists more in the forgiveness of sins than the perfection of virtue" (August. de Civitate Dei, Lib. xix. cap. 27). To this corresponds the well-known sentiment of Bernard: "Not to sin is the righteousness of God, but the righteousness of man is the indulgence of God" (Bernard, Serm. xxii. xxiii. in Cant.). He previously asserts that Christ is our righteousness in absolution, and, therefore, that those only are just who have obtained pardon through mercy.

23. Hence also it is proved, that it is entirely by the intervention of Christ's righteousness that we obtain justification before God. This is equivalent to saying that man is not just in himself, but that the righteousness of Christ is communicated to him by imputation, while he is strictly deserving of punishment. Thus vanishes the absurd dogma, that man is justified by faith, inasmuch as it brings him under the influence of the Spirit of God by whom he is rendered righteous. This is so repugnant to the above doctrine that it never can be reconciled with it. There can be no doubt that he who is taught to seek righteousness out of himself does not previously possess it in himself.[1] This is most clearly declared by the Apostle, when he says, that he who knew no sin was made an expiatory victim for sin, that we might be made the righteousness of God in him (2 Cor. v. 21). You see that our righteousness is not in ourselves, but in Christ; that the only way in which we become possessed of it is by being made partakers with Christ, since with him we possess all riches. There is nothing repugnant to this in what he elsewhere says: "God sending his own Son in the likeness of sinful flesh, and for sin condemned sin in the flesh: that the righteousness of the law might be fulfilled in us" (Rom. viii. 3, 4). Here the only fulfilment to which he refers is that which we obtain by imputation. Our Lord Jesus Christ communicates his righteousness to us, and so by some wondrous way, in so far as pertains to the

---

[1] French, "Ceci est fort contraire a la doctrine ci dessus mise: car il n'y a nulle doute que celui qui doit cercher justice hors de soy-mesme, ne soit desnué de la sienne propre;"—This is quite contrary to the doctrine above laid down; for there is no doubt, that he who is to seek righteousness out of himself, is devoid of righteousness in himself.

justice of God, transfuses its power into us. That this was the Apostle's view is abundantly clear from another sentiment which he had expressed a little before: "As by one man's disobedience many were made sinners, so by the obedience of one shall many be made righteous" (Rom. v. 19). To declare that we are deemed righteous, solely because the obedience of Christ is imputed to us as if it were our own, is just to place our righteousness in the obedience of Christ. Wherefore, Ambrose appears to me to have most elegantly adverted to the blessing of Jacob as an illustration of this righteousness, when he says that as he who did not merit the birthright in himself personated his brother, put on his garments, which gave forth a most pleasant odour, and thus introduced himself to his father that he might receive a blessing to his own advantage, though under the person of another, so we conceal ourselves under the precious purity[1] of Christ, our first-born brother, that we may obtain an attestation of righteousness from the presence of God. The words of Ambrose are, —"Isaac's smelling the odour of his garments, perhaps means that we are justified not by works, but by faith, since carnal infirmity is an impediment to works, but errors of conduct are covered by the brightness of faith, which merits the pardon of faults" (Ambrose de Jacobo et Vita Beata, Lib. ii. c. 2). And so indeed it is; for in order to appear in the presence of God for salvation, we must send forth that fragrant odour, having our vices covered and buried by his perfection.

1 French, "Sous la robbe;"—under the robe.

CHAPTER XII.

NECESSITY OF CONTEMPLATING THE JUDGMENT-SEAT OF GOD, IN ORDER TO BE SERIOUSLY CONVINCED OF THE DOCTRINE OF GRA-TUITOUS JUSTIFICATION.

The divisions of this chapter are,—I. A consideration of the righteousness of God overturns the righteousness of works, as is plain from passages of Scripture, and the confession and example of the saints, sec. 1–3. II. The same effect produced by a serious examination of the conscience, and a constant citation to the divine tribunal, sec. 4 and 5. III. Hence arises, in the hearts of the godly, not hypocrisy, or a vain opinion of merit, but true humility. This illustrated by the authority of Scripture and the example of the Publican, sec. 6, 7. IV. Conclusion—arrogance and security must be discarded, every man throwing an impediment in the way of the divine goodness in proportion as he trusts to himself.

Sections.

1. Source of error on the subject of Justification. Sophists speak as if the question were to be discussed before some human tribunal. It relates to the majesty and justice of God. Hence nothing accepted without absolute perfection. Passages confirming this doctrine. If we descend to the righteousness of the Law, the curse immediately appears.
2. Source of hypocritical confidence. Illustrated by a simile. Exhortation. Testimony of Job, David, and Paul.
3. Confession of Augustine and Bernard.
4. Another engine overthrowing the righteousness of works—viz. a serious examination of the conscience, and a comparison between the perfection of God and the imperfection of man.
5. How it is that we so indulge this imaginary opinion of our own works. The proper remedy to be found in a consideration of the majesty of God and our own misery. A description of this misery.
6. Christian humility consists in laying aside the imaginary idea of our own righteousness, and trusting entirely to the mercy of God, apprehended by faith in Christ. This humility described. Proved by passages of Scripture.
7. The parable of the Publican explained.
8. Arrogance, security, and self-confidence, must be renounced. General rule, or summary of the above doctrine.

1. ALTHOUGH the perfect truth of the above doctrine is proved by clear passages of Scripture, yet we cannot clearly see how necessary it is, before we bring distinctly into view the foundations on which the whole discussion ought to rest. First, then, let us remember that the righteousness which we are considering is not that of a human, but of a heavenly tribunal; and so beware of employing our own little standard to measure the perfection which is to satisfy the justice of God. It is strange with what rashness and presumption this is commonly defined. Nay, we see that none talk more confidently, or, so to speak, more blusteringly, of the righteousness of works, than those whose diseases are most palpable, and blemishes most apparent. This

they do because they reflect not on the righteousness of Christ, which, if they had the slightest perception of it, they would never treat with so much insult. It is certainly undervalued, if not recognised to be so perfect that nothing can be accepted that is not in every respect entire and absolute, and tainted by no impurity; such indeed as never has been, and never will be, found in man. It is easy for any man, within the precincts of the schools, to talk of the sufficiency of works for justification; but when we come into the presence of God there must be a truce to such talk. The matter is there discussed in earnest, and is no longer a theatrical logomachy. Hither must we turn our minds if we would inquire to any purpose concerning true righteousness; the question must be, How shall we answer the heavenly Judge when he calls us to account? Let us contemplate that Judge, not as our own unaided intellect conceives of him, but as he is pourtrayed to us in Scripture (see especially the Book of Job), with a brightness which obscures the stars, a strength which melts the mountains, an anger which shakes the earth, a wisdom which takes the wise in their own craftiness, a purity before which all things become impure, a righteousness to which not even angels are equal (so far is it from making the guilty innocent), a vengeance which once kindled burns to the lowest hell (Exod. xxxiv. 7; Nahum i. 3; Deut. xxxii. 22). Let him, I say, sit in judgment on the actions of men, and who will feel secure in sisting himself before his throne? "Who among us," says the prophet, "shall dwell with the devouring fire? who among us shall dwell with everlasting burnings? He that walketh righteously, and speaketh uprightly," &c. (Isaiah xxxiii. 14, 15). Let whoso will come forth. Nay, the answer shows that no man can. For, on the other hand, we hear the dreadful voice: "If thou, Lord, shouldst mark our iniquities, O Lord, who shall stand?" (Ps. cxxx. 3.) All must immediately perish, as Job declares, "Shall mortal man be more just than God? shall a man be more pure than his Maker? Behold, he put no trust his servants; and his angels he charged with folly: How much less in in them that dwell in houses of clay, whose foundation is in the dust, which are crushed before the moth? They are destroyed from morning to evening" (Job iv. 17–20). Again, "Behold, he putteth no trust in his saints; yea, the heavens are not clean in his sight. How much more abominable and filthy is man, which drinketh iniquity like water?" (Job xv. 15, 16.) I confess, indeed, that in the Book of Job reference is made to a righteousness of a more exalted description than the observance of the Law. It is of importance to attend to this distinction; for even could a man satisfy the Law, he could not stand the scrutiny of that righteousness which transcends all our thoughts. Hence, although Job was not conscious of offending, he is still dumb with astonishment, because he sees that God could not be appeased even by the sanctity of angels, were their works weighed in that supreme balance. But to advert no farther to this righteousness, which is incomprehensible,

I only say, that if our life is brought to the standard of the written law, we are lethargic indeed if we are not filled with dread at the many maledictions which God has employed for the purpose of arousing us, and among others, the following general one: "Cursed be he that confirmeth not all the words of this law to do them" (Deut. xxvii. 26). In short, the whole discussion of this subject will be insipid and frivolous, unless we sist ourselves before the heavenly Judge, and, anxious for our acquittal, voluntarily humble ourselves, confessing our nothingness.

2. Thus, then, must we raise our eyes that we may learn to tremble instead of vainly exulting. It is easy, indeed, when the comparison is made among men, for every one to plume himself on some quality which others ought not to despise; but when we rise to God that confidence instantly falls and dies away. The case of the soul with regard to God is very analogous to that of the body in regard to the visible firmament. The bodily eye, while employed in surveying adjacent objects, is pleased with its own perspicacity; but when directed to the sun, being dazzled and overwhelmed by the refulgence, it becomes no less convinced of its weakness than it formerly was of its power in viewing inferior objects. Therefore, lest we deceive ourselves by vain confidence, let us recollect that even though we deem ourselves equal or superior to other men, this is nothing to God, by whose judgment the decision must be given. But if our presumption cannot be tamed by these considerations, he will answer us as he did the Pharisees, "Ye are they which justify yourselves before men; but God knoweth your hearts: for that which is highly esteemed among men is abomination in the sight of God" (Luke xvi. 15). Go now and make a proud boast of your righteousness among men, while God in heaven abhors it. But what are the feelings of the servants of God, of those who are truly taught by his Spirit? "Enter not into judgment with thy servant; for in thy sight shall no man living be justified" (Ps. cxliii. 2). Another, though in a sense somewhat different, says, "How should man be just with God? If he will contend with him he cannot answer him one of a thousand" (Job ix. 2, 3). Here we are plainly told what the righteousness of God is—namely, a righteousness which no human works can satisfy, which charges us with a thousand sins, while not one sin can be excused. Of this righteousness Paul, that chosen vessel of God, had formed a just idea, when he declared, "I know nothing by myself, yet am I not hereby justified" (1 Cor. iv. 4).

3. Such examples exist not in the sacred volume only; all pious writers show that their sentiment was the same. Thus, Augustine says, "Of all pious men groaning under this burden of corruptible flesh, and the infirmities of this life, the only hope is, that we have one Mediator Jesus Christ the righteous, and that he intercedes for our sins" (August. ad Bonif. Lib. iii. c. 5). What do we hear? If this is their only hope, where is their confidence in works? When

he says *only*, he leaves no other. Bernard says, "And, indeed, where have the infirm firm security and safe rest, but in the wounds of the Saviour? Hold it then the more securely, the more powerful he is to save. The world frowns, the body presses, the devil lays snares: I fall not, because I am founded on a firm rock. I have sinned a grievous sin: conscience is troubled, but it shall not be overwhelmed, for I will remember the wounds of the Lord." He afterwards concludes, "My merit, therefore, is the compassion of the Lord; plainly I am not devoid of merit so long as he is not devoid of commiseration. But if the mercies of the Lord are many, equally many are my merits. Shall I sing of my own righteousness? O Lord, I will make mention of thy righteousness alone. That righteousness is mine also, being made mine by God" (Bernard, Serm. 61, in Cantic). Again, in another passage, "Man's whole merit is to place his whole hope in him who makes the whole man safe" (in Psal. Qui Habitat. Serm. 15). In like manner, reserving peace to himself, he leaves the glory to God: "Let thy glory remain unimpaired: it is well with me if I have peace; I altogether abjure boasting, lest if I should usurp what is not mine, I lose also what is offered" (Serm. 13, in Cantic). He says still more plainly in another place: "Why is the Church solicitous about merits? God purposely supplies her with a firmer and more secure ground of boasting. There is no reason for asking by what merits may we hope for blessings, especially when you hear in the prophet, 'Thus saith the Lord God, I do not this for your sakes, O house of Israel, but for mine holy name's sake' (Ezek. xxxvi. 22, 32). It is sufficient for merit to know that merits suffice not; but as it is sufficient for merit not to presume on merit, so to be without merits is sufficient for condemnation" (Bernard, Serm. 68). The free use of the term merits for good works must be pardoned to custom. Bernard's purpose was to alarm hypocrites, who turned the grace of God into licentiousness, as he shortly after explains: "Happy the church which neither wants merit without presumption, nor presumption without merit. It has ground to presume, but not merit. It has merit, merit to deserve, not presume. Is not the absence of presumption itself a merit? He, therefore, to whom the many mercies of the Lord furnish ample grounds of boasting, presumes the more securely that he presumes not" (Bernard, Serm. 68).

4. Thus, indeed, it is. Aroused consciences, when they have to do with God, feel this to be the only asylum in which they can breathe safely. For if the stars which shine most brightly by night lose their brightness on the appearance of the sun, what think we will be the case with the highest purity of man when contrasted with the purity of God? For the scrutiny will be most strict, penetrating to the most hidden thoughts of the heart. As Paul says, it "will bring to light the hidden things of darkness, and will make manifest the counsels of the heart" (1 Cor. iv. 5); will compel the reluctant and dissembling conscience to bring forward everything,

even things which have now escaped our memory. The devil, aware of all the iniquities which he has induced us to perpetrate, will appear as accuser; the external show of good works, the only thing now considered, will then be of no avail; the only thing demanded will be the true intent of the will. Hence hypocrisy, not only that by which a man, though consciously guilty before God, affects to make an ostentatious display before man, but that by which each imposes upon himself before God (so prone are we to soothe and flatter ourselves), will fall confounded, how much soever it may now swell with pride and presumption. Those who do not turn their thoughts to this scene, may be able for the moment calmly and complacently to rear up a righteousness for themselves; but this the judgment of God will immediately overthrow, just as great wealth amassed in a dream vanishes the moment we awake. Those who, as in the presence of God, inquire seriously into the true standard of righteousness, will certainly find that all the works of men, if estimated by their own worth, are nothing but vileness and pollution, that what is commonly deemed justice is with God mere iniquity; what is deemed integrity is pollution; what deemed glory is ignominy.

5. Let us not decline to descend from this contemplation of the divine perfection, to look into ourselves without flattery or blind self-love. It is not strange that we are so deluded in this matter, seeing none of us can avoid that pestilential self-indulgence, which, as Scripture proclaims, is naturally inherent in all: "Every way of a man is right in his own eyes," says Solomon (Prov. xxi. 2). And again, "All the ways of a man are clean in his own eyes" (Prov. xvi. 2). What then? does this hallucination excuse him? No, indeed, as Solomon immediately adds, "The Lord weigheth the spirits;" that is, while man flatters himself by wearing an external mask of righteousness, the Lord weighs the hidden impurity of the heart in his balance. Seeing, therefore, that nothing is gained by such flattery, let us not votuntarily delude ourselves to our own destruction. To examine ourselves properly, our conscience must be called to the judgment-seat of God. His light is necessary to disclose the secret recesses of wickedness, which otherwise lie too deeply hid. Then only shall we clearly perceive what the value of our works is; that man, so far from being just before God, is but rottenness and a worm, abominable and vain, drinking in "iniquity like water." For "who can bring a clean thing out of an unclean? not one" (Job xiv. 5). Then we shall experience the truth of what Job said of himself: "If I justify myself, mine own mouth shall condemn me: if I say I am perfect, it shall prove me perverse" (Job. ix. 20). Nor does the complaint which the prophet made concerning Israel apply to one age only. It is true of every age, that "all we like sheep have gone astray; we have turned every one to his own way" (Isaiah liii. 6). Indeed, he there comprehends all to whom the gift of redemption was to come. And the strictness of the examination ought to be

continued until it have completely alarmed us, and in that way prepared us for receiving the grace of Christ. For he is deceived who
thinks himself capable of enjoying it, until he have laid aside all
loftiness of mind. There is a well-known declaration, "God resist-
eth the proud, but giveth grace to the humble" (1 Pet. v. 5).

6. But what means is there of humbling us if we do not make way
for the mercy of God, by our utter indigence and destitution? For
I call it not humility, so long as we think there is any good remaining in us. Those who have joined together the two things, to think
humbly as ourselves before God and yet hold our own righteousness
in some estimation, have hitherto taught a pernicious hypocrisy.
For if we confess to God contrary to what we feel, we wickedly lie to
him; but we cannot feel as we ought without seeing that everything
like a ground of boasting is completely crushed. Therefore, when
you hear from the prophet, "thou wilt save the afflicted people; but
wilt bring down high looks" (Ps. xviii. 27), consider, first, that
there is no access to salvation unless all pride is laid aside and true
humility embraced; secondly, that that humility is not a kind of
moderation by which you yield to God some article of your right
(thus men are called humble in regard to each other when they
neither conduct themselves haughtily nor insult over other, though
they may still entertain some consciousness of their own excellence),
but that it is the unfeigned submission of a mind overwhelmed by a
serious conviction of its want and misery. Such is the description
everywhere given by the word of God. When in Zephaniah the
Lord speaks thus, "I will take away out of the midst of thee them
that rejoice in thy pride, and thou shalt no more be haughty because
of my holy mountain. I will also leave in the midst of thee an
afflicted and poor people, and they shall trust in the name of the
Lord" (Zeph. iii. 11, 12), does he not plainly show who are the
humble—viz. those who lie afflicted by a knowledge of their poverty?
On the contrary, he describes the proud as rejoicing (*exultantes*),
such being the mode in which men usually express their delight in
prosperity. To the humble, whom he designs to save, he leaves
nothing but hope in the Lord. Thus, also, in Isaiah, "To this man
will I look, even to him that is poor and of a contrite spirit, and
trembleth at my word" (Isaiah lxvi. 2). Again, "Thus saith the
high and lofty One that inhabiteth eternity, whose name is Holy; I
dwell in the high and holy place, with him also that is of a contrite
and humble spirit, to revive the spirit of the humble, and to revive
the heart of the contrite ones" (Isaiah lvii. 15). By the term *contrition*, which you so often hear, understand a wounded heart, which,
humbling the individual to the earth, allows him not to rise. With
such contrition must your heart be wounded, if you would, according
to the declaration of God, be exalted with the humble. If this is
not your case, you shall be humbled by the mighty hand of God
to your shame and disgrace.

7. Our divine Master, not confining himself to words, has by a parable set before us, as in a picture, a representation of true humility. He brings forward a publican, who standing afar off, and not daring to lift up his eyes to heaven, smites upon his breast, laments aloud, and exclaims, " God be merciful to me a sinner" (Luke xviii. 13). Let us not suppose that he gives the signs of a fictitious modesty when he dares not come near or lift up his eyes to heaven, but, smiting upon his breast, confesses himself a sinner; let us know that these are the evidences of his internal feeling. With him our Lord contrasts the Pharisee, who thanks God " I am not as other men are, extortioners, unjust, adulterers, or even as this publican. I fast twice in the week. I give tithes of all that I possess." In this public confession he admits that the righteousness which he possesses is the gift of God; but because of his confidence that he is righteous, he departs from the presence of God unaccepted and abominated. The publican acknowledging his iniquity is justified. Hence we may see how highly our humility is valued by the Lord: our breast cannot receive his mercy until deprived completely of all opinion of its own worth. When such an opinion is entertained, the door of mercy is shut. That there might be no doubt on this matter, the mission on which Christ was sent into the world by his Father was "to preach good tidings to the meek," " to bind up the broken-hearted, to proclaim liberty to the captives, and the opening of the prison to them that are bound; to proclaim the acceptable year of the Lord, and the day of vengeance of our God; to comfort all that mourn; to appoint unto them that mourn in Zion, to give unto them beauty for ashes, the oil of joy for mourning, the garment of praise for the spirit of heaviness" (Isa. lxi. 1–3). In fulfilment of that mission, the only persons whom he invites to share in his beneficence are the " weary and heavy laden." In another passage he says, " I am not come to call the righteous, but sinners to repentance" (Matth. xi. 28; ix. 13).

8. Therefore, if we would make way for the call of Christ, we must put far from us all arrogance and confidence. The former is produced by a foolish persuasion of self-righteousness, when a man thinks that he has something in himself which deservedly recommends him to God; the latter may exist without any confidence in works.[1] For many sinners, intoxicated with the pleasures of vice, think not of the judgment of God. Lying stupified, as it were, by a kind of lethargy, they aspire not to the offered mercy. It is not less necessary to shake off torpor of this description than every kind of confidence in ourselves, in order that we may haste to Christ unencumbered, and while hungry and empty be filled with his blessings. Never shall we have suffici-

---

1 French, " Par arrogance j'enten l'orgueil qui s'engendre d'une fole persuasion de justice, quand l'homme pense avoir quelque chose, dont il merite d'estre agreable à Dieu; par presomption j'enten une nonchalance charnelle, qui peut estre sans aucune fiance des œuvres;"—by arrogance I mean the pride which is engendered by a foolish persuasion of righteousness, when man thinks he has something for which he deserves to be agreeable to God. By presumption I understand a carnal indifference, which may exist without any confidence in works.

ent confidence in him unless utterly distrustful of ourselves; never shall we take courage in him until we first despond of ourselves; never shall we have full consolation in him until we cease to have any in ourselves. When we have entirely discarded all self-confidence, and trust solely in the certainty of his goodness, we are fit to apprehend and obtain the grace of God. "When" (as Augustine says) "forgetting our own merits, we embrace the gifts of Christ, because if he should seek for merits in us we should not obtain his gifts" (August. de Verb. Apost. 8). With this Bernard admirably accords, comparing the proud, who presume in the least on their merits, to unfaithful servants, who wickedly take the merit of a favour merely passing through them, just as if a wall were to boast of producing the ray which it receives through the window (Bernard, Serm. 13, in Cant.). Not to dwell longer here, let us lay down this short but sure and general rule, That he is prepared to reap the fruits of the divine mercy who has thoroughly emptied himself, I say not of righteousness (he has none), but of a vain and blustering show of righteousness; for to whatever extent any man rests in himself, to the same extent he impedes the beneficence of God.

CHAPTER XIII.

TWO THINGS TO BE OBSERVED IN GRATUITOUS JUSTIFICATION.

The divisions of this chapter are,—I. The glory of God, and peace of conscience, both secured by gratuitous justification. An insult to the glory of God to glory in ourselves and seek justification out of Christ, whose righteousness, apprehended by faith, is imputed to all the elect for reconciliation and eternal salvation, sec. 1, 2. II. Peace of conscience cannot be obtained in any other way than by gratuitous justification. This fully proved, sec. 3–5.

Sections.

1. The glory of God remains untarnished, when he alone is acknowledged to be just. This proved from Scripture.
2. Those who glory in themselves glory against God. Objection. Answer, confirmed by the authority of Paul and Peter.
3. Peace of conscience obtained by free justification only. Testimony of Solomon, of conscience itself, and the Apostle Paul, who contends that faith is made vain if righteousness come by the law.
4. The promise confirmed by faith in the mercy of Christ. This is confirmed by Augustine and Bernard, is in accordance with what has been above stated, and is illustrated by clear predictions of the prophets.
5. Farther demonstration by an Apostle. Refutation of a sophism.

1. HERE two ends must be kept specially in view—namely, that the glory of God be maintained unimpaired, and that our consciences, in the view of his tribunal, be secured in peaceful rest and calm tranquillity. When the question relates to righteousness, we see how often and how anxiously Scripture exhorts us to give the whole praise of it to God. Accordingly, the Apostle testifies that the purpose of the Lord in conferring righteousness upon us in Christ, was to demonstrate his own righteousness. The nature of this demonstration he immediately subjoins—viz. "that he might be just, and the justifier of him which believeth in Jesus" (Rom. iii. 25). Observe, that the righteousness of God is not sufficiently displayed, unless He alone is held to be righteous, and freely communicates righteousness to the undeserving. For this reason it is his will, that "every mouth may be stopped, and all the world may become guilty before God" (Rom. iii. 19). For so long as a man has anything, however small, to say in his own defence, so long he deducts somewhat from the glory of God. Thus, we are taught in Ezekiel how much we glorify his name by acknowledging our iniquity: "Then shall ye remember your ways and all your doings, wherein ye have been defiled; and ye shall loathe yourselves in your own sight, for all your evils that ye have committed. And ye shall know that I am the Lord, when I have wrought with you for my name's sake, not according to your

wicked ways, nor according to your corrupt doings" (Ezek. xx. 43, 44). If part of the true knowledge of God consists in being oppressed by a consciousness of our own iniquity, and in recognising him as doing good to those who are unworthy of it, why do we attempt, to our great injury, to steal from the Lord even one particle of the praise of unmerited kindness? In like manner, when Jeremiah exclaims, " Let not the wise man glory in his wisdom, neither let the mighty man glory in his might, let not the rich man glory in his riches : but let him that glorieth glory" in the Lord (Jer. ix. 23, 24), does he not intimate, that the glory of the Lord is infringed when man glories in himself? To this purpose, indeed, Paul accommodates the words when he says, that all the parts of our salvation are treasured up with Christ, that we may glory only in the Lord (1 Cor. i. 29). For he intimates, that whosoever imagines he has anything of his own, rebels against God, and obscures his glory.

2. Thus, indeed, it is : we never truly glory in him until we have utterly discarded our own glory. It must, therefore, be regarded as an universal proposition, that whoso glories in himself glories against God. Paul indeed considers, that the whole world is not made subject to God until every ground of glorying has been withdrawn from men (Rom. iii. 19). Accordingly, Isaiah, when he declares that " in the Lord shall all the seed of Israel be justified", adds, "and shall glory" (Isa. xlv. 25); as if he had said, that the elect are justified by the Lord, in order that they may glory in him, and in none else. The way in which we are to glory in the Lord he had explained in the preceding verse, " Unto me every knee shall bow, every tongue shall swear ;" " Surely, shall one say, in the Lord have I righteousness and strength, even to him shall men come." Observe, that the thing required is not simple confession, but confession confirmed by an oath, that it might not be imagined that any kind of fictitious humility might suffice. And let no man here allege that he does not glory, when without arrogance he recognises his own righteousness ; such a recognition cannot take place without generating confidence, nor such confidence without begetting boasting. Let us remember, therefore, that in the whole discussion concerning justification the great thing to be attended to is, that God's glory be maintained entire and unimpaired ; since, as the Apostle declares, it was in demonstration of his own righteousness that he shed his favour upon us ; it was " that he might be just, and the justifier of him which believeth in Jesus" (Rom. iii. 26). Hence, in another passage, having said that the Lord conferred salvation upon us, in order that he might show forth the glory of his name (Eph. i. 6), he afterwards, as if repeating the same thing, adds, " By grace are ye saved through faith ; and that not of yourselves : it is the gift of God : not of works, lest any man should boast" (Eph. ii. 8). And Peter, when he reminds us that we are called to the hope of salvation, " that ye should show forth the praises of him who hath called you out of darkness into his marvellous light" (1 Pet. ii. 9), doubtless intends thus to proclaim

in the ears of believers only the praises of God, that they may bury in profound silence all arrogance of the flesh. The sum is, that man cannot claim a single particle of righteousness to himself, without at the same time detracting from the glory of the divine righteousness.

3. If we now inquire in what way the conscience can be quieted as in the view of God, we shall find that the only way is by having righteousness bestowed upon us freely by the gift of God. Let us always remember the words of Solomon, "Who can say I have made my heart clean, I am free from my sin?" (Prov. xx. 9). Undoubtedly, there is not one man who is not covered with infinite pollutions. Let the most perfect man descend into his own conscience, and bring his actions to account, and what will the result be? Will he feel calm and quiescent, as if all matters were well arranged between himself and God; or will he not rather be stung with dire torment, when he sees that the ground of condemnation is within him if he be estimated by his works? Conscience, when it beholds God, must either have sure peace with his justice, or be beset by the terrors of hell. We gain nothing, therefore, by discoursing of righteousness, unless we hold it to be a righteousness stable enough to support our souls before the tribunal of God. When the soul is able to appear intrepidly in the presence of God, and receive his sentence without dismay, then only let us know that we have found a righteousness that is not fictitious. It is not, therefore, without cause, that the Apostle insists on this matter. I prefer giving it in his words rather than my own: "If they which are of the law be heirs, faith is made void, and the promise made of no effect" (Rom. iv. 14). He first infers that faith is made void if the promise of righteousness has respect to the merit of our works, or depends on the observance of the law. Never could any one rest securely in it, for never could he feel fully assured that he had fully satisfied the law; and it is certain that no man ever fully satisfies it by works. Not to go far for proof of this, every one who will use his eyes aright may be his own witness. Hence it appears how deep and dark the abyss is into which hypocrisy plunges the minds of men, when they indulge so securely as, without hesitation, to oppose their flattery to the judgment of God, as if they were relieving him from his office as judge. Very different is the anxiety which fills the breasts of believers, who sincerely examine themselves.[1] Every mind, therefore, would first begin to hesitate, and at length to despair, while each determined for itself with how great a load of debt it was still oppressed, and how far it was from coming up to the enjoined condition. Thus, then, faith would be oppressed and extinguished. To have faith is not to fluctuate, to vary, to be carried up and down, to hesitate, remain in suspense, vacillate, in fine, to despair; it is to possess sure certainty and complete security of mind, to have whereon to rest and fix your foot.

---

[1] The two previous sentences are omitted in the French.

4. Paul, moreover, adds, that the promise itself would be rendered null and void. For if its fulfilment depends on our merit, when, pray, will we be able to come the length of meriting the favour of God? Nay, the second clause is a consequence of the former, since the promise will not be fulfilled unless to those who put faith in it. Faith therefore failing, no power will remain in the promise. "Therefore it is of faith, that it might be by grace, to the end the promise might be sure to all the seed" (Rom. iv. 16). It was abundantly confirmed when made to rest on the mercy of God alone, for mercy and truth are united by an indissoluble tie; that is, whatever God has mercifully promised he faithfully performs. Thus David, before he asks salvation according to the word of God, first places the source of it in his mercy. "Let, I pray thee, thy merciful kindness be for my comfort, according to thy word unto thy servant" (Ps. cxix. 76). And justly, for nothing but mere mercy induces God to promise. Here, then, we must place, and, as it were, firmly fix our whole hope, paying no respect to our works, and asking no assistance from them. And lest you should suppose that there is anything novel in what I say, Augustine also enjoins us so to act. "Christ," says he, "will reign for ever among his servants. This God has promised, God has spoken; if this is not enough, God has sworn. Therefore, as the promise stands firm, not in respect of our merits, but in respect of his mercy, no one ought to tremble in announcing that of which he cannot doubt" (August. in Ps. lxxxviii. Tract. 1). Thus Bernard also, "Who can be saved? ask the disciples of Christ. He replies, With men it is impossible, but not with God. This is our whole confidence; this our only consolation; this the whole ground of our hope: but being assured of the possibility, what are we to say as to his willingness? Who knows whether he is deserving of love or hatred? (Eccles. ix. 1.) 'Who hath known the mind of the Lord that he may instruct him?' (1 Cor. ii. 16.) Here it is plain, faith must come to our aid: here we must have the assistance of truth, in order that the secret purpose of the Father respecting us may be revealed by the Spirit, and the Spirit testifying may persuade our hearts that we are the sons of God. But let him persuade by calling and justifying freely by faith: in these there is a kind of transition from eternal predestination to future glory" (Berd. in Dedica. Templi. Serm. 5). Let us thus briefly conclude: Scripture indicates that the promises of God are not sure, unless they are apprehended with full assurance of conscience; it declares that wherever there is doubt or uncertainty, the promises are made void; on the other hand, that they can only waver and fluctuate if they depend on our works. Therefore, either our righteousness must perish, or without any consideration of our works, place must be given to faith alone, whose nature it is to prick up the ear, and shut the eye; that is, to be intent on the promise only, to give up all idea of any dignity or merit in man. Thus is fulfilled the celebrated prophecy of Zechariah: "I will remove the iniquity of that land in one day. In that

day, saith the Lord of hosts, shall ye call every man his neighbour
under the vine, and under the fig-tree" (Zech. iii. 9, 10). Here
the prophet intimates that the only way in which believers can enjoy
true peace, is by obtaining the remission of their sins. For we must
attend to this peculiarity in the prophets, that when they discourse
of the kingdom of Christ, they set forth the external mercies of God
as types of spiritual blessings. Hence Christ is called *the Prince of
Peace, and our peace* (Isaiah ix. 6; Eph. ii. 14), because he calms
all the agitations of conscience. If the method is asked, we must
come to the sacrifice by which God was appeased, for no man will
ever cease to tremble, until he hold that God is propitiated solely by
that expiation in which Christ endured his anger. In short, peace
must be sought no where but in the agonies of Christ our Redeemer.

5. But why employ a more obscure testimony? Paul uniformly
declares that the conscience can have no peace or quiet joy until it is
held for certain that we are justified by faith. And he at the same
time declares whence this certainty is derived—viz. when " the love
of God is shed abroad in our hearts by the Holy Ghost" (Rom. v.
5); as if he had said, that our souls cannot have peace until we are
fully assured that we are pleasing to God. Hence he elsewhere exclaims in the person of believers in general, " Who shall separate us
from the love of Christ?" (Rom. viii. 35). Until we have reached
that haven, the slightest breeze will make us tremble, but so long as
the Lord is our Shepherd, we shall walk without fear in the valley
of the shadow of death (Ps. xxiii.). Thus those who pretend that
justification by faith consists in being regenerated and made just, by
living spiritually, have never tasted the sweetness of grace in trusting that God will be propitious. Hence also, they know no more of
praying aright than do the Turks or any other heathen people. For,
as Paul declares, faith is not true, unless it suggest and dictate the
delightful name of Father; nay, unless it open our mouths and
enable us freely to cry, Abba, Father. This he expresses more
clearly in another passage, " In whom we have boldness and access
with confidence by the faith of him " (Eph. iii. 12). This, certainly,
is not obtained by the gift of regeneration, which, as it is always defective in the present state, contains within it many grounds of
doubt. Wherefore, we must have recourse to this remedy; we must
hold that the only hope which believers have of the heavenly inheritance is, that being ingrafted into the body of Christ, they are justified freely. For, in regard to justification, faith is merely passive,
bringing nothing of our own to procure the favour of God, but receiving from Christ everything that we want.

CHAPTER XIV.

THE BEGINNING OF JUSTIFICATION.   IN WHAT SENSE PROGRESSIVE.

To illustrate what has been already said, and show what kind of righteousness man can have during the whole course of his life, mankind are divided into four classes. I. First class considered, sec. 1–6. II. Second and third classes considered together, sec. 7, 8. III. Fourth class considered, sec. 9 to end.

Sections.

1. Men either idolatrous, profane, hypocritical, or regenerate. 1. Idolaters void of righteousness, full of unrighteousness, and hence in the sight of God altogether wretched and undone.
2. Still a great difference in the characters of men. This difference manifested. 1. In the gifts of God. 2. In the distinction between honourable and base. 3. In the blessings of the present life.
3. All human virtue, how praiseworthy soever it may appear, is corrupted. 1. By impurity of heart. 2. By the absence of a proper nature.
4. By the want of Christ, without whom there is no life.
5. Natural condition of man as described by Scripture. All men dead in sins before regeneration.
6. Passages of Scripture to this effect. Vulgar error confounding the righteousness of works with the redemption purchased by Christ.
7. The second and third classes of men, comprehending hypocrites and Christians in name only. Every action of theirs deserves condemnation. Passage from Haggai. Objection. Answer.
8. Other passages. Quotations from Augustine and Gregory.
9. The fourth class—viz. the regenerate. Though guided by the Spirit, corruption adheres to all they do, especially when brought to the bar of God.
10. One fault sufficient to efface all former righteousness. Hence they cannot possibly be justified by works.
11. In addition to the two former arguments, a third adduced against the Sophists, to show that whatever be the works of the regenerate, they are justified solely by faith and the free imputation of Christ's righteousness.
12. Sophism of the Schoolmen in opposition to the above doctrine. Answer.
13. Answer explained. Refutation of the fiction of partial righteousness, and compensation by works of supererogation. This fiction necessarily falls with that of satisfaction.
14. Statement of our Saviour—viz. that after we have done all, we are still unprofitable servants.
15. Objection founded on Paul's boasting. Answer, showing the Apostle's meaning. Other answers, stating the general doctrine out of Chrysostom. Third answer, showing that supererogation is the merest vanity.
16. Fourth answer, showing how Scripture dissuades us from all confidence in works. Fifth answer, showing that we have no ground of boasting.
17. Sixth answer, showing in regard to four different causes, that works have no part in procuring our salvation. 1. The efficient cause is the free love of the Father, 2. The material cause is Christ acquiring righteousness for us. 3. The instrumental cause is faith. 4. The final cause the display of the divine justice and praise of the divine goodness.
18. A second objection, founded on the glorying of saints. An answer, explaining these modes of expression. How the saints feel in regard to the certainty of salvation. The opinion they have of their own works as in the sight of God.
19. Another answer—viz. that the elect, by this kind of glorying, refer only to their adoption by the Father as proved by the fruits of their calling. The order of this glorying. Its foundation, structure, and parts.
20. Conclusion. The saints neither attribute anything to the merits of works, nor

derogate in any degree from the righteousness which they obtain in Christ. Confirmation from a passage of Augustine, in which he gives two reasons why no believer will presume to boast before God of his works.
21. A third objection—viz. that the good works of believers are the causes of divine blessings. Answer. There are inferior causes, but these depend on free justification, which is the only true cause why God blesses us. These modes of expression designate the order of sequence rather than the cause.

1. In farther illustration of the subject, let us consider what kind of righteousness man can have, during the whole course of his life, and for this purpose let us make a fourfold division. Mankind, either endued with no knowledge of God, are sunk in idolatry; or, initiated in the sacraments, but by the impurity of their lives denying him whom they confess with their mouths, are Christians in name only; or they are hypocrites, who with empty glosses hide the iniquity of the heart; or they are regenerated by the Spirit of God, and aspire to true holiness. In the first place, when men are judged by their natural endowments, not an iota of good will be found from the crown of the head to the sole of the foot, unless we are to charge Scripture with falsehood, when it describes all the sons of Adam by such terms as these: "The heart is deceitful above all things, and desperately wicked." "The imagination of man's heart is evil from his youth." "The Lord knoweth the thoughts of man that they are vanity." "They are all gone aside: they are altogether become filthy; there is none that doeth good, no, not one." In short, that they are *flesh*, under which name are comprehended all those works which are enumerated by Paul; adultery, fornication, uncleanness, lasciviousness, idolatry, witchcraft, hatred, variance, emulation, wrath, strife, seditions, heresies, envyings, murders, drunkenness, revellings, and all kinds of pollution and abomination which it is possible to imagine.[1] Such, then, is the worth on which men are to plume themselves. But if any among them possess an integrity of manners which presents some semblance of sanctity among men, yet because we know that God regards not the outward appearance, we must penetrate to the very source of action, if we would see how far works avail for righteousness. We must, I say, look within, and see from what affection of the heart these works proceed. This is a very wide field of discussion, but as the matter may be explained in few words, I will use as much brevity as I can.

2. First, then, I deny not, that whatever excellent endowments appear in unbelievers[2] are divine gifts. Nor do I set myself so much in opposition to common sense, as to contend that there was no difference between the justice, moderation, and equity of Titus and Trajan, and the rage, intemperance, and cruelty of Caligula, Nero, and Domitian; between the continence of Vespasian, and the obscene lusts of Tiberius; and (not to dwell on single virtues and vices) be-

[1] Jer. xvii. 9; Gen. viii. 21; Ps. xciv. 11; xxxvi. 2; xiv. 2, 3; Gen. vi. 3; Gal. v. 19.
[2] Latin, "in incredulis." French, "en la vie des infideles et idolatres;"—in the life of infidels and idolaters.

tween the observance of law and justice, and the contempt of them. So great is the difference between justice and injustice, that it may be seen even where the former is only a lifeless image. For what order would remain in the world if we were to confound them? Hence this distinction between honourable and base actions God has not only engraven on the minds of each, but also often confirms in the administration of his providence. For we see how he visits those who cultivate virtue with many temporal blessings. Not that that external image of virtue in the least degree merits his favour, but he is pleased thus to show how much he delights in true righteousness, since he does not leave even the outward semblance of it to go unrewarded. Hence it follows, as we lately observed, that those virtues, or rather images of virtues, of whatever kind, are divine gifts, since there is nothing in any degree praiseworthy which proceeds not from him.

3. Still the observation of Augustine is true, that all who are strangers to the true God, however excellent they may be deemed on account of their virtues, are more deserving of punishment than of reward, because, by the pollution of their heart, they contaminate the pure gifts of God (August. contra Julian. Lib. iv.). For though they are instruments of God to preserve human society by justice, continence, friendship, temperance, fortitude, and prudence, yet they execute these good works of God in the worst manner, because they are kept from acting ill, not by a sincere love of goodness, but merely by ambition or self-love, or some other sinister affection. Seeing then that these actions are polluted as in their very source, by impurity of heart, they have no better title to be classed among virtues than vices, which impose upon us by their affinity or resemblance to virtue. In short, when we remember that the object at which righteousness always aims is the service of God, whatever is of a different tendency deservedly forfeits the name. Hence, as they have no regard to the end which the divine wisdom prescribes, although from the performance the act seems good, yet from the perverse motive it is sin. Augustine, therefore, concludes that all the Fabriciuses, the Scipios, and Catos,[1] in their illustrious deeds, sinned in this, that, wanting the light of faith, they did not refer them to the proper end, and that, therefore, there was no true righteousness in them, because duties are estimated not by acts but by motives.

4. Besides, if it is true, as John says, that there is no life without the Son of God (1 John v. 12), those who have no part in Christ, whoever they be, whatever they do or devise, are hastening on, during their whole career, to destruction and the judgment of eternal death. For this reason, Augustine says, " Our religion distinguishes the righteous from the wicked, by the law, not of works but of faith, without which works which seem good are converted into sins" (August. ad Bonif. Lib. iii. c. v.). He finely expresses the same

1 Latin, " omnes Fabricios, Scipiones, Catones." French, "tous ceux qui ont esté prisez entre les Pagans ;"—all those who have been prized among the Heathen.

idea in another passage, when he compares the zeal of such men to those who in a race mistake the course (August. Præf. in Ps. xxxi.). He who is off the course, the more swiftly he runs is the more distant from the goal; and, therefore, the more unhappy. It is better to limp in the way than run out of the way. Lastly, as there is no sanctification without union with Christ, it is evident that they are bad trees which are beautiful and fair to look upon, and may even produce fruit, sweet to the taste, but are still very far from good. Hence we easily perceive that everything which man thinks, designs, and performs, before he is reconciled to God by faith, is cursed, and not only of no avail for justification, but merits certain damnation. And why do we talk of this as if it were doubtful, when it has already been proved by the testimony of an apostle, that "without faith it is impossible to please God"? (Heb. xi. 6.)

5. But the proof will be still clearer if divine grace is set in opposition to the natural condition of man. For Scripture everywhere proclaims that God finds nothing in man to induce him to show kindness, but that he prevents him by free liberality. What can a dead man do to obtain life? But when he enlightens us with the knowledge of himself, he is said to raise us from the dead, and make us new creatures (John v. 25). On this ground we see that the kindness of God toward us is often commended, especially by the apostle: "God," says he, "who is rich in mercy, for his great love wherewith he loved us, even when we were dead in sins, hath quickened us together with Christ" (Eph. ii. 4). In another passage, when treating of the general call of believers under the type of Abraham, he says, "God quickeneth the dead, and calleth those things which be not as though they were" (Rom. iv. 17). If we are nothing, what, pray, can we do? Wherefore, in the Book of Job the Lord sternly represses all arrogance in these words, "Who hath prevented me, that I should repay him? whatsoever is under the whole heaven is mine" (Job xli. 11). Paul explaining this sentence applies it in this way,—Let us not imagine that we bring to the Lord anything but the mere disgrace of want and destitution (Rom. xi. 35). Wherefore, in the passage above quoted, to prove that we attain to the hope of salvation, not by works but only by grace, he affirms that "we are his workmanship, created in Christ Jesus unto good works, which God hath before ordained that we should walk in them" (Eph. ii. 10); as if he had said, Who of us can boast of having challenged God by his righteousness, seeing our first power to act aright is derived from regeneration? For, as we are formed by nature, sooner shall oil be extracted from stone than good works from us. It is truly strange how man, convicted of such ignominy, dares still to claim anything as his own. Let us acknowledge, therefore, with that chosen vessel, that God "hath called us with an holy calling, not according to our works, but according to his own purpose and grace;" and "that the kindness and love of God our Saviour toward men appeared not by works of righteousness which we have done,

but according to his mercy he saved us;" that being justified by his grace, we might become the heirs of everlasting life (2 Tim. i. 9; Tit. iii. 4, 5). By this confession we strip man of every particle of righteousness, until by mere mercy he is regenerated unto the hope of eternal life, since it is not true to say we are justified by grace, if works contribute in any degree to our justification. The apostle undoubtedly had not forgotten himself in declaring that justification is gratuitous, seeing he argues in another place, that if works are of any avail, " grace is no more grace" (Rom xi. 6). And what else does our Lord mean, when he declares, " I am not come to call the righteous, but sinners to repentance"? (Matth. ix. 13). If sinners alone are admitted, why do we seek admission by means of fictitious righteousness?

6. The thought is ever and anon recurring to me, that I am in danger of insulting the mercy of God by labouring with so much anxiety to maintain it, as if it were doubtful or obscure. Such, however, is our malignity in refusing to concede to God what belongs to him until most strongly urged, that I am obliged to insist at greater length. But as Scripture is clear enough on this subject, I shall contend in its words rather than my own. Isaiah, after describing the universal destruction of the human race, finely subjoins the method of restitution. " The Lord saw it, and it displeased him that there was no judgment. And he saw that there was no man, and wondered that there was no intercessor: therefore his arm brought salvation unto him; and his righteousness, it sustained him" (Isaiah lix. 15, 16). Where is our righteousness, if the prophet says truly, that no man in recovering salvation gives any assistance to the Lord? Thus another prophet, introducing the Lord as treating concerning the reconciliation of sinners, says, " I will betroth thee unto me for ever; yea, I will betroth thee unto me in righteousness, and in judgment, and in loving-kindness, and in mercies." " I will have mercy upon her that had not obtained mercy" (Hosea ii. 19, 23). If a covenant of this kind, evidently forming our first union with God, depends on mercy, there is no foundation left for our righteousness. And, indeed, I would fain know, from those who pretend that man meets God with some righteousness of works, whether they imagine there is any kind of righteousness save that which is acceptable to Him. If it were insane to think so, can anything agreeable to God proceed from his enemies, whom he abominates with all their deeds? Truth declares that we are all the avowed and inveterate enemies of God until we are justified and admitted to his friendship (Rom. v. 6; Col. i. 21). If justification is the beginning of love, how can the righteousness of works precede it? Hence John, to put down the arrogant idea, carefully reminds us that God first loved us (1 John iv. 10). The Lord had formerly taught the same thing by his prophet: " I will love them freely: for mine anger is turned away from him" (Hosea xiv. 4). Assuredly he is not influenced by works if his love turns to us spontaneously. But the rude and vulgar idea

entertained is, that we did not merit the interposition of Christ for our redemption, but that we are aided by our works in obtaining possession of it. On the contrary, though we may be redeemed by Christ, still, until we are ingrafted into union with him by the calling of the Father, we are darkness, the heirs of death, and the enemies of God. For Paul declares that we are not purged and washed from our impurities by the blood of Christ until the Spirit accomplishes that cleansing in us (1 Cor. vi. 11). Peter, intending to say the same thing, declares that the sanctification of the Spirit avails "unto obedience and sprinkling of the blood of Jesus Christ" (1 Pet. i. 2). If the sprinkling of the blood of Christ by the Spirit gives us purification, let us not think that, previous to this sprinkling, we are anything but sinners without Christ. Let us, therefore, hold it as certain, that the beginning of our salvation is as it were a resurrection from death unto life, because, when it is given us on behalf of Christ to believe on him (Phil. i. 29), then only do we begin to pass from death unto life.

7. Under this head the second and third class of men noted in the above division is comprehended. Impurity of conscience proves that as yet neither of these classes is regenerated by the Spirit of God. And, again, their not being regenerated proves their want of faith. Whence it is clear that they are not yet reconciled, not yet justified, since it is only by faith that these blessings are obtained. What can sinners, alienated from God, produce save that which is abominable in his sight? Such, however, is the stupid confidence entertained by all the wicked, and especially by hypocrites, that however conscious that their whole heart teems with impurity, they yet deem any spurious works which they may perform as worthy of the approbation of God. Hence the pernicious consequence, that though convicted of a wicked and impious mind, they cannot be induced to confess that they are devoid of righteousness. Even acknowledging themselves to be unrighteous, because they cannot deny it, they yet arrogate to themselves some degree of righteousness. This vanity the Lord admirably refutes by the prophet: "Ask now the priests concerning the law, saying, If one bear holy flesh in the skirt of his garment, and with his skirt do touch bread, or pottage, or wine, or oil, or any meat, shall it be holy? And the priests answered and said, No. Then said Haggai, If one that is unclean by a dead body touch any of these, shall it be unclean? And the priests answered and said, It shall be unclean. Then answered Haggai, and said, So is this people, and so is this nation before me, saith the Lord; and so is every work of their hands; and that which they offer there is unclean" (Haggai ii. 11–14). I wish these sentiments could obtain full credit with us, and be deeply fixed on our memories. For there is no man, however flagitious the whole tenor of his life may be, who will allow himself to be convinced of what the Lord here so clearly declares. As soon as any person, even the most wicked, has performed some one duty of the law, he hesitates not to impute it to

himself for righteousness; but the Lord declares that no degree of holiness is thereby acquired, unless the heart has previously been made pure. And not contented with this, he declares that all the works performed by sinners are contaminated by impurity of heart. Let us cease then to give the name of righteousness to works which the mouth of the Lord condemns as polluted. How well is this shown by that elegant similitude? It might be objected, that what the Lord has commanded is inviolably holy. But he, on the contrary, replies, that it is not strange that those things which are sanctified in the law are contaminated by the impurity of the wicked, the unclean hand profaning that which is sacred by handling it.

8. The same argument is admirably followed out by Isaiah: "Bring no more vain oblations; incense is an abomination unto me; the new moons and sabbaths, the calling of assemblies, I cannot away with; it is iniquity, even the solemn meeting. Your new moons and your appointed feasts my soul hateth: they are a trouble unto me; I am weary to bear them. And when ye spread forth your hands, I will hide mine eyes from you; yea, when ye make many prayers, I will not hear: your hands are full of blood. Wash you, make you clean; put away the evil of your doings from before mine eyes" (Isaiah i. 13–16, compared with lviii.). What is meant by the Lord thus nauseating the observance of his law? Nay, indeed, he does not repudiate anything relating to the genuine observance of the law, the beginning of which is, as he uniformly declares, the sincere fear of his name. When this is wanting, all the services which are offered to him are not only nugatory, but vile and abominable. Let hypocrites now go, and while keeping depravity wrapt up in their heart, study to lay God under obligation by their works. In this way they will only offend him more and more. "The sacrifice of the wicked is an abomination to the Lord; but the prayer of the upright is his delight" (Prov. xv. 8). We hold it, therefore, as indubitable, indeed it should be notorious to all tolerably versant with Scripture, that the most splendid works performed by men, who are not yet truly sanctified, are so far from being righteousness in the sight of the Lord, that he regards them as sins. And, therefore, it is taught with perfect truth, that no man procures favour with God by means of works, but that, on the contrary, works are not pleasing to God unless the person has previously found favour in his sight.[1] Here we should carefully observe the order which Scripture sets before us. Moses says, that "the Lord had respect unto Abel and to his offering" (Gen. iv. 4). Observe how he says that the Lord was propitious (had respect) to Abel, before he had respect to his works. Wherefore, purification of heart ought to precede, in order that the works performed by us may be graciously accepted by God: for the saying of Jeremiah is always true, "O Lord, are not thine eyes upon the truth?" (Jer. v. 3). Moreover, the Holy Spirit declared by the mouth of

1 See August. Lib. de Poenit., and Gregory, whose words are quoted, Sent. Lib. iii. Quæst. 7.

Peter, that it is by faith alone the heart is purified (Acts xv. 9). Hence it is evident, that the primary foundation is in true and living faith.

9. Let us now see what kind of righteousness belongs to those persons whom we have placed in the fourth class. We admit, that when God reconciles us to himself by the intervention of the righteousness of Christ, and bestowing upon us the free pardon of sins regards us as righteous, his goodness is at the same time conjoined with mercy, so that he dwells in us by means of his Holy Spirit, by whose agency the lusts of our flesh are every day more and more mortified, while that we ourselves are sanctified; that is, consecrated to the Lord for true purity of life, our hearts being trained to the obedience of the law. It thus becomes our leading desire to obey his will, and in all things advance his glory only. Still, however, while we walk in the ways of the Lord, under the guidance of the Holy Spirit, lest we should become unduly elated, and forget ourselves, we have still remains of imperfection which serve to keep us humble: " There is no man that sinneth not," saith Scripture (1 Kings viii. 46). What righteousness then can men obtain by their works? First, I say, that the best thing which can be produced by them is always tainted and corrupted by the impurity of the flesh, and has, as it were, some mixture of dross in it. Let the holy servant of God, I say, select from the whole course of his life the action which he deems most excellent, and let him ponder it in all its parts; he will doubtless find in it something that savours of the rottenness of the flesh, since our alacrity in well-doing is never what it ought to be, but our course is always retarded by much weakness. Although we see that the stains by which the works of the righteous are blemished are by no means unapparent, still, granting that they are the minutest possible, will they give no offence to the eye of God, before which even the stars are not clean? We thus see, that even saints cannot perform one work which, if judged on its own merits, is not deserving of condemnation.

10. Even were it possible for us to perform works absolutely pure, yet one sin is sufficient to efface and extinguish all remembrance of former righteousness, as the prophet says (Ezek. xviii. 24). With this James agrees, " Whosoever shall keep the whole law, and yet offend in one point, is guilty of all" (James ii. 10). And since this mortal life is never entirely free from the taint of sin, whatever righteousness we could acquire would ever and anon be corrupted, overwhelmed, and destroyed, by subsequent sins, so that it could not stand the scrutiny of God, or be imputed to us for righteousness. In short, whenever we treat of the righteousness of works, we must look not to the legal work but to the command. Therefore, when righteousness is sought by the Law, it is in vain to produce one or two single works; we must show an uninterrupted obedience. God does not (as many foolishly imagine) impute that forgiveness of sins, once for all, as righteousness; so that having obtained the pardon of our past

life we may afterwards seek righteousness in the Law. This were only to mock and delude us by the entertainment of false hopes. For since perfection is altogether unattainable by us, so long as we are clothed with flesh, and the Law denounces death and judgment against all who have not yielded a perfect righteousness, there will always be ground to accuse and convict us unless the mercy of God interpose, and ever and anon absolve us by the constant remission of sins. Wherefore the statement with which we set out is always true, If we are estimated by our own worthiness, in everything that we think or devise, with all our studies and endeavours we deserve death and destruction.

11. We must strongly insist on these two things: That no believer ever performed one work which, if tested by the strict judgment of God, could escape condemnation; and, moreover, that were this granted to be possible (though it is not), yet the act being vitiated and polluted by the sins of which it is certain that the author of it is guilty, it is deprived of its merit. This is the cardinal point of the present discussion. There is no controversy between us and the sounder Schoolmen as to the beginning of justification.[1] They admit that the sinner, freely delivered from condemnation, obtains justification, and that by forgiveness of sins; but under the term justification they comprehend the renovation by which the Spirit forms us anew to the obedience of the Law; and in describing the righteousness of the regenerate man, maintain that being once reconciled to God by means of Christ, he is afterwards deemed righteous by his good works, and is accepted in consideration of them. The Lord, on the contrary, declares, that he imputed Abraham's faith for righteousness (Rom. iv. 3), not at the time when he was still a worshipper of idols, but after he had been many years distinguished for holiness. Abraham had long served God with a pure heart, and performed that obedience of the Law which a mortal man is able to perform: yet his righteousness still consisted in faith. Hence we infer, according to the reasoning of Paul, that it was *not of works*. In like manner, when the prophet says, "The just shall live by his faith" (Hab. ii. 4), he is not speaking of the wicked and profane, whom the Lord justifies by converting them to the faith: his discourse is directed to believers, and life is promised to them by faith. Paul also removes every doubt, when in confirmation of this sentiment he quotes the words of David, "Blessed is he whose transgression is forgiven, whose sin is covered"

1 The following sentence is added in the French:—"Il est bien vray que le poure monde a esté seduit jusques la, de penser que l'homme se preparast de soy-mesme pour estre justifié de Dieu : et que ce blaspheme a regné communement tant en predications qu'aux escoles ; comme encore aujourdhui il est soustenue de ceux qui veulent maintenir toutes les abominations de la Papauté."—It is very true that the poor world has been seduced hitherto, to think that man could of himself prepare to be justified by God, and that this blasphemy has commonly reigned both in sermons and schools, as it is still in the present day asserted by those who would maintain all the abominations of the Papacy.

(Ps. xxxii. 1). It is certain that David is not speaking of the ungodly, but of believers such as he himself was, because he was giving utterance to the feelings of his own mind. Therefore we must have this blessedness not once only, but must hold it fast during our whole lives. Moreover, the message of free reconciliation with God is not promulgated for one or two days, but is declared to be perpetual in the Church (2 Cor. v. 18, 19). Hence believers have not even to the end of life any other righteousness than that which is there described. Christ ever remains a Mediator to reconcile the Father to us, and there is a perpetual efficacy in his death—viz. ablution, satisfaction, expiation; in short, perfect obedience, by which all our iniquities are covered. In the Epistle to the Ephesians, Paul says not that the beginning of salvation is of grace, but "by grace are ye saved," "not of works, lest any man should boast" (Eph. ii. 8, 9).

12. The subterfuges by which the Schoolmen here endeavour to escape will not disentangle them. They say that good works are not of such intrinsic worth as to be sufficient to procure justification, but it is owing to accepting grace that they have this effect. Then because they are forced to confess that here the righteousness of works is always imperfect, they grant that so long as we are in this life we stand in need of the forgiveness of sin in order to supply the deficiency of works, but that the faults which are committed are compensated by works of supererogation. I answer, that the grace which they call accepting, is nothing else than the free goodness with which the Father embraces us in Christ when he clothes us with the innocence of Christ, and accepts it as ours, so that in consideration of it he regards us as holy, pure, and innocent. For the righteousness of Christ (as it alone is perfect, so it alone can stand the scrutiny of God) must be sisted for us, and as a surety represent us judicially. Provided with this righteousness, we constantly obtain the remission of sins through faith. Our imperfection and impurity, covered with this purity, are not imputed, but are as it were buried, so as not to come under judgment until the hour arrive when the old man being destroyed, and plainly extinguished in us, the divine goodness shall receive us into beatific peace with the new Adam, there to await the day of the Lord, on which, being clothed with incorruptible bodies, we shall be translated to the glory of the heavenly kingdom.

13. If these things are so, it is certain that our works cannot in themselves make us agreeable and acceptable to God, and even cannot please God, except in so far as being covered with the righteousness of Christ we thereby please him, and obtain forgiveness of sins. God has not promised life as the reward of certain works, but only declares, "which if a man do, he shall live in them" (Lev. xviii. 5), denouncing the well-known curse against all who do not continue in all things that are written in the book of the Law to do them. In this way is completely refuted the fiction of a partial righteousness, the only righteousness acknowledged in heaven being the perfect observance of the law. There is nothing more solid in their dogma

of compensation by means of works of supererogation. For must they not always return to the proposition which has already been disproved—viz. that he who observes the Law in part is so far justified by works? This, which no man of sound judgment will concede to them, they are not ashamed to take for granted. The Lord having so often declared that he recognises no justification by works unless they be works by which the Law is perfectly fulfilled,—how perverse is it, while we are devoid of such works, to endeavour to secure some ground of glorying to ourselves; that is, not to yield it entirely to God, by boasting of some kind of fragments of works, and trying to supply the deficiency by other satisfactions? Satisfactions have already been so completely disposed of, that we ought never again even to dream of them. Here all I say is, that those who thus trifle with sin do not at all consider how execrable it is in the sight of God; if they did, they would assuredly understand, that all the righteousness of men collected into one heap would be inadequate to compensate for a single sin. For we see that by one sin man was so cast off and forsaken by God, that he at the same time lost all power of recovering salvation. He was, therefore, deprived of the power of giving satisfaction. Those who flatter themselves with this idea will never satisfy God, who cannot possibly accept or be pleased with any thing that proceeds from his enemies. But all to whom he imputes sin are enemies, and, therefore, our sins must be covered and forgiven before the Lord has respect to any of our works. From this it follows, that the forgiveness of sins is gratuitous, and this forgiveness is wickedly insulted by those who introduce the idea of satisfaction. Let us, therefore, after the example of the Apostle, "forgetting those things which are behind, and reaching forth unto those things which are before," "press toward the mark for the prize of the high calling of God in Jesus Christ" (Philip. iii. 13, 14).

14. How can boasting in works of supererogation agree with the command given to us: "When ye shall have done all those things which are commanded you, say, We are unprofitable servants: we have done that which was our duty to do"? (Luke xvii. 10.) To *say* or speak in the presence of God is not to feign or lie, but to declare what we hold as certain. Our Lord, therefore, enjoins us sincerely to feel and consider with ourselves that we do not perform gratuitous duties, but pay him service which is due. And truly. For the obligations of service under which we lie are so numerous, that we cannot discharge them though all our thoughts and members were devoted to the observance of the Law; and, therefore, when he says, "When ye shall have done all those things which are commanded you," it is just as if he had said, that all the righteousness of men would not amount to one of these things. Seeing, then, that every one is very far distant from that goal, how can we presume to boast of having accumulated more than is due? It cannot be objected that a person, though failing in some measure in what is necessary, may yet in intention go beyond what is necessary. For it must

ever be held, that in whatever pertains to the worship of God, or to charity, nothing can ever be thought of that is not comprehended under the Law. But if it is part of the Law, let us not boast of voluntary liberality in matters of necessary obligation.

15. On this subject, they causelessly allege the boast of Paul, that among the Corinthians he spontaneously renounced a right which, if he had otherwise chosen, he might have exercised (1 Cor. ix. 15); thus not only paying what he owed them in duty, but gratuitously bestowing upon them more than duty required. They ought to have attended to the reason there expressed, that his object was to avoid giving offence to the weak. For wicked and deceitful workmen employed this pretence of kindness that they might procure favour to their pernicious dogmas, and excite hatred against the Gospel, so that it was necessary for Paul either to peril the doctrine of Christ, or to thwart their schemes. Now, if it is a matter of indifference to a Christian man whether or not he cause a scandal when it is in his power to avoid it, then I admit that the Apostle performed a work of supererogation to his Master; but if the thing which he did was justly required in a prudent minister of the Gospel, then I say he did what he was bound to do. In short, even when no such reason appears, yet the saying of Chrysostom is always true, that everything which we have is held on the same condition as the private property of slaves; it is always due to our Master. Christ does not disguise this in the parable; for he asks in regard to the master who, on return from his labour, requires his servant to gird himself and serve him, "Does he thank that servant because he did the things that were commanded him? I trow not" (Luke xvii. 9). But possibly the servant was more industrious than the master would have ventured to exact. Be it so: still he did nothing to which his condition as a servant did not bind him, because his utmost ability is his master's. I say nothing as to the kind of supererogations on which these men would plume themselves before God. They are frivolities which he never commanded, which he approves not, and will not accept when they come to give in their account. The only sense in which we admit works of supererogation is that expressed by the prophet, when he says, "Who hath required this at your hand?" (Isaiah i. 12). But let them remember what is elsewhere said of them: "Wherefore do ye spend money for that which is not bread? and your labour for that which satisfieth not?" (Isaiah lv. 2). It is, indeed, an easy matter for these indolent Rabbins to carry on such discussions sitting in their soft chairs under the shade; but when the Supreme Judge shall sit on his tribunal, all these blustering dogmas will behove to disappear.[1] This, this I say, was the true question: not what we can fable and talk in schools and corners, but what ground of defence we can produce at his judgment-seat.

---

[1] French, "Tout ce qu'ils auront determiné ne profitera gueres, ains s'evanouisra comme fumee;"—All their decisions will scarcely avail them, but will vanish like smoke.

16. In this matter the minds of men must be specially guarded against two pestiferous dogmas—viz. against putting any confidence in the righteousness of works, or ascribing any glory to them. From all such confidence the Scriptures uniformly dissuade us when they declare that our righteousness is offensive in the sight of God unless it derives a sweet odour from the purity of Christ: that it can have no other effect than to excite the divine vengeance unless sustained by his indulgent mercy. Accordingly, the only thing they leave to us is to deprecate our Judge with that confession of David: "Enter not into judgment with thy servant: for in thy sight shall no living be justified" (Psalm cxliii. 2). And when Job says, "If I be wicked, woe unto me: and if I be righteous, yet will I not lift up my head" (Job x. 15). Although he refers to that spotless righteousness of God, before which even angels are not clean, he however shows, that when brought to the bar of God, all that mortals can do is to stand dumb. He does not merely mean that he chooses rather to give way spontaneously than to risk a contest with the divine severity, but that he was not conscious of possessing any righteousness that would not fall the very first moment it was brought into the presence of God. Confidence being banished, all glorying must necessarily cease. For who can attribute any merit of righteousness to works, which instead of giving confidence, only make us tremble in the presence of God? We must, therefore, come to what Isaiah invites us: "In the Lord shall all the seed of Israel be justified, and shall glory" (Isaiah xlv. 25); for it is most true, as he elsewhere says, that we are "the planting of the Lord, that he might be glorified" (Isaiah lxi. 3). Our soul, therefore, will not be duly purified until it ceases to have any confidence, or feel any exultation in works. Foolish men are puffed up to this false and lying confidence by the erroneous idea that the cause of their salvation is in works.

17. But if we attend to the four kinds of causes which philosophers bring under our view in regard to effects, we shall find that not one of them is applicable to works as a cause of salvation. The efficient cause of our eternal salvation the Scripture uniformly proclaims to be the mercy and free love of the heavenly Father towards us; the material cause to be Christ, with the obedience by which he purchased righteousness for us; and what can the formal or instrumental cause be but faith? John includes the three in one sentence when he says, "God so loved the world, that he gave his only begotten Son, that whosoever believeth in him should not perish, but have everlasting life" (John iii. 16). The Apostle, moreover, declares that the final cause is the demonstration of the divine righteousness and the praise of his goodness. There also he distinctly mentions the other three causes; for he thus speaks to the Romans: "All have sinned, and come short of the glory of God; being justified freely by his grace" (Rom. iii. 23, 24). You have here the head and primary source— God has embraced us with free mercy. The next words are, "through the redemption that is in Christ Jesus;" this is as it were the material

cause by which righteousness is procured for us. " Whom God hath set forth to be a propitiation through faith." Faith is thus the instrumental cause by which righteousness is applied to us. He lastly subjoins the final cause when he says, " To declare at this time his righteousness; that he might be just, and the justifier of him that believeth in Jesus." And to show by the way that this righteousness consists in reconciliation, he says that Christ was " set forth to be a propitiation." Thus also, in the Epistle to the Ephesians, he tells us that we are received into the favour of God by mere mercy; that this is done by the intervention of Christ; that it is apprehended by faith; the end of all being that the glory of the divine goodness may be fully displayed. When we see that all the parts of our salvation thus exist without us, what ground can we have for glorying or confiding in our works? Neither as to the efficient nor the final cause can the most sworn enemies of divine grace raise any controversy with us unless they would abjure the whole of Scripture. In regard to the material or formal cause they make a gloss, as if they held that our works divide the merit with faith and the righteousness of Christ. But here also Scripture reclaims, simply affirming that Christ is both righteousness and life, and that the blessing of justification is possessed by faith alone.

18. When the saints repeatedly confirm and console themselves with the remembrance of their innocence and integrity, and sometimes even abstain not from proclaiming them, it is done in two ways: either because by comparing their good cause with the bad cause of the ungodly, they thence feel secure of victory, not so much from commendation of their own righteousness, as from the just and merited condemnation of their adversaries; or because, reviewing themselves before God, even without any comparison with others, the purity of their conscience gives them some comfort and security. The former reason will afterwards be considered (chap. xvii. sec. 14, and chap. xx. sec. 10); let us now briefly show, in regard to the latter, how it accords with what we have above said, that we can have no confidence in works before the bar of God, that we cannot glory in any opinion of their worth. The accordance lies here, that when the point considered is the constitution and foundation of salvation, believers, without paying any respect to works, direct their eyes to the goodness of God alone. Nor do they turn to it only in the first instance, as to the commencement of blessedness, but rest in it as the completion. Conscience being thus founded, built up, and established, is farther established by the consideration of works, inasmuch as they are proofs of God dwelling and reigning in us. Since, then, this confidence in works has no place unless you have previously fixed your whole confidence on the mercy of God, it should not seem contrary to that on which it depends. Wherefore, when we exclude confidence in works, we merely mean, that the Christian mind must not turn back to the merit of works as an aid to salvation, but must dwell entirely on the free promise of justification. But we forbid no

believer to confirm and support this faith by the signs of the divine favour towards him. For if when we call to mind the gifts which God has bestowed upon us, they are like rays of the divine countenance, by which we are enabled to behold the highest light of his goodness; much more is this the case with the gift of good works, which shows that we have received the Spirit of adoption.

19. When believers, therefore, feel their faith strengthened by a consciousness of integrity, and entertain sentiments of exultation, it is just because the fruits of their calling convince them that the Lord has admitted them to a place among his children. Accordingly, when Solomon says, " In the fear of the Lord is strong confidence" (Prov. xiv. 26), and when the saints sometimes beseech the Lord to hear them, because they walked before his face in simplicity and integrity (Gen. xxiv. 10; 2 Kings xx. 3), these expressions apply not to laying the foundation of a firm conscience, but are of force only when taken *a posteriori*.[1] For there is nowhere such a fear of God as can give full security, and the saints are always conscious that any integrity which they may possess is mingled with many remains of the flesh. But as the fruits of regeneration furnish them with a proof of the Holy Spirit dwelling in them, experiencing God to be a Father in a matter of so much moment, they are strengthened in no slight degree to wait for his assistance in all their necessities. Even this they could not do, had they not previously perceived that the goodness of God is sealed to them by nothing but the certainty of the promise. Should they begin to estimate it by their good works, nothing will be weaker or more uncertain; works, when estimated by themselves, no less proving the divine displeasure by their imperfection, than his good-will by their incipient purity. In short, while proclaiming the mercies of the Lord, they never lose sight of his free favour, with all its "breadth and length, and depth and height," testified by Paul (Eph. iii. 18); as if he had said, Whithersoever the believer turns, however loftily he climbs, however far and wide his thoughts extend, he must not go farther than the love of Christ, but must be wholly occupied in meditating upon it, as including in itself all dimensions. Accordingly, he declares that it "passeth knowledge," that "to know the love of Christ" is to "be filled with all the fulness of God" (Eph. iii. 19). In another passage, where he glories that believers are victorious in every contest, he adds the reason, "through him that loved us" (Rom. viii. 37).

20. We now see that believers have no such confidence in works as to attribute any merit to them (since they regard them only as divine gifts, in which they recognise his goodness and signs of calling, in which they discern their election); nor such confidence as to derogate in any respect from the free righteousness of Christ; since on this it depends, and without this cannot subsist. The same thing is briefly but elegantly expressed by Augustine when he says, "I do

---

[1] Latin, "a posteriori;" French, "comme enseigne de la vocation de Dieu;"—as a sign of the calling of God.

not say to the Lord, Despise not the works of my hands; I have sought the Lord with my hands, and have not been deceived. But I commend not the works of my hands, for I fear that when thou examinest them thou wilt find more faults than merits. This only I say, this ask, this desire, Despise not the works of thy hands. See in me thy work, not mine. If thou seest mine, thou condemnest; if thou seest thine own, thou crownest. Whatever good works I have are of thee" (August. in Ps. cxxxvii.). He gives two reasons for not venturing to boast of his works before God: first, that if he has any good works, he does not see in them anything of his own; and, secondly, that these works are overwhelmed by a multitude of sins. Whence it is, that the conscience derives from them more fear and alarm than security. Therefore, the only way in which he desires God to look at any work which he may have done aright is, that he may therein see the grace of his calling, and perfect the work which he has begun.

21. Moreover, when Scripture intimates that the good works of believers are causes why the Lord does them good, we must still understand the meaning so as to hold unshaken what has previously been said—viz. that the efficient cause of our salvation is placed in the love of God the Father; the material cause in the obedience of the Son; the instrumental cause in the illumination of the Spirit, that is, in faith; and the final cause in the praise of the divine goodness. In this, however, there is nothing to prevent the Lord from embracing works as inferior causes. But how so? In this way: Those whom in mercy he has destined for the inheritance of eternal life, he, in his ordinary adminstration, introduces to the possession of it by means of good works. What precedes in the order of administration is called the cause of what follows. For this reason, he sometimes makes eternal life a consequent of works; not because it is to be ascribed to them, but because those whom he has elected he justifies, that he may at length glorify (Rom. viii. 30); he makes the prior grace to be a kind of cause, because it is a kind of step to that which follows. But whenever the true cause is to be assigned, he enjoins us not to take refuge in works, but to keep our thoughts entirely fixed on the mercy of God; " The wages of sin is death; but the gift of God is eternal life" (Rom. vi. 23). Why, as he contrasts life with death, does he not also contrast righteousness with sin? Why, when setting down sin as the cause of death, does he not also set down righteousness as the cause of life? The antithesis which would otherwise be complete is somewhat marred by this variation; but the Apostle employed the comparison to express the fact, that death is due to the deserts of men, but that life was treasured up solely in the mercy of God. In short, by these expressions, the order rather than the cause is noted.[1] The Lord adding grace to

---

[1] French, " Brief, en toutes ces façons de parler, ou il est fait mention de bonnes œuvres, il n'est pas question de la cause pourquoy Dieu fait bien aux siens, mais seule-

grace, takes occasion from a former to add a subsequent, so that he may omit no means of enriching his servants. Still, in following out his liberality, he would have us always look to free election as its source and beginning. For although he loves the gifts which he daily bestows upon us, inasmuch as they proceed from that fountain, still our duty is to hold fast by that gratuitous acceptance, which alone can support our souls; and so to connect the gifts of the Spirit which he afterwards bestows, with their primary cause, as in no degree to detract from it.

ment de l'ordre qu'il y tient;"—In short, in all those forms of expression in which mention is made of good works, there is no question as to the cause why God does good to his people, but only to the order which he observes in it.

CHAPTER XV.

THE BOASTED MERIT OF WORKS SUBVERSIVE BOTH OF THE GLORY OF
GOD, IN BESTOWING RIGHTEOUSNESS, AND OF THE CERTAINTY OF
SALVATION.

The divisions of this chapter are,—I. To the doctrine of free justification is opposed
the question, Whether or not works merit favour with God, sec. 1. This question
answered, sec. 2 and 3. II. An exposition of certain passages of Scripture produced
in support of the erroneous doctrine of merit, sec. 4 and 5. III. Sophisms of Semi-
pelagian Schoolmen refuted, sec. 6 and 7. IV. Conclusion, proving the sufficiency of
the orthodox doctrine, sec. 8.

Sections.

1. After a brief recapitulation, the question, Whether or not good works merit favour
   with God, considered.
2. First answer, fixing the meaning of the term Merit. This term improperly applied to works, but used in a good sense, as by Augustine, Chrysostom, Bernard.
3. A second answer to the question. First by a negative, then by a concession. In
   the rewarding of works what to be attributed to God, and what to man. Why
   good works please God, and are advantageous to those who do them. The ingratitude of seeking righteousness by works. This shown by a double similitude.
4. First objection taken from Ecclesiasticus. Second objection from the Epistle to the
   Hebrews. Two answers to both objections. A weak distinction refuted.
5. A third and most complete answer, calling us back to Christ as the only foundation
   of salvation. How Christ is our righteousness. Whence it is manifest that we
   have all things in Christ and he nothing in us.
6. We must abhor the sophistry which destroys the merit of Christ, in order to establish that of man. This impiety refuted by clear passages of Scripture.
7. Errors of the younger Sophists extracted from Lombard. Refuted by Augustine.
   Also by Scripture.
8. Conclusion, showing that the foundation which has been laid is sufficient for doctrine, exhortation, and comfort. Summary of the orthodox doctrine of Justification.

1. THE principal point in this subject has been now explained: as
justification, if dependant upon works, cannot possibly stand in the
sight of God, it must depend solely on the mercy of God and communion with Christ, and therefore on faith alone. But let us carefully attend to the point on which the whole subject hinges, lest we
get entangled in the common delusion, not only of the vulgar, but
of the learned. For the moment the question is raised as to the
justification by faith or works, they run off to those passages which
seem to ascribe some merit to works in the sight of God, just as if
justification by works were proved whenever it is proved that works
have any value with God. Above we have clearly shown that justification by works consists only in a perfect and absolute fulfilment of
the law ; and that, therefore, no man is justified by works unless he

has reached the summit of perfection, and cannot be convicted of even the smallest transgression.   But there is another and a separate question, Though works by no means suffice to justify, do they not merit favour with God?

2. First, I must premise with regard to the term Merit, that he, whoever he was, that first applied it to human works, viewed in reference to the divine tribunal, consulted very ill for the purity of the faith.   I willingly abstain from disputes about words, but I could wish that Christian writers had always observed this soberness—that when there was no occasion for it, they had never thought of using terms foreign to the Scriptures—terms which might produce much offence, but very little fruit.   I ask, what need was there to introduce the word Merit, when the value of works might have been fully expressed by another term, and without offence?   The quantity of offence contained in it the world shows to its great loss.   It is certain that, being a high sounding term, it can only obscure the grace of God, and inspire men with pernicious pride.   I admit it was used by ancient ecclesiastical writers, and I wish they had not by the abuse of one term furnished posterity with matter of heresy, although in some passages they themselves show that they had no wish to injure the truth.   For Augustine says, " Let human merits, which perished by Adam, here be silent, and let the grace of God reign by Jesus Christ" (August. de. Prædest. Sanct.).   Again, "The saints ascribe nothing to their merits; every thing will they ascribe solely to thy mercy, O God" (August. in Psal. cxxxix.).   Again, "And when a man sees that whatever good he has he has not of himself, but of his God, he sees that every thing in him which is praised is not of his own merits, but of the divine mercy" (August. in Psal. lxxxviii.). You see how he denies man the power of acting aright, and thus lays merit prostrate.   Chrysostom says, " If any works of ours follow the free calling of God, they are return and debt; but the gifts of God are grace, and beneficence, and great liberality."   But to say nothing more of the name, let us attend to the thing.   I formerly quoted a passage from Bernard: " As it is sufficient for merit not to presume on merit, so to be without merit is sufficient for condemnation" (Bernard in Cantic. Serm. 98).   He immediately adds an explanation which softens the harshness of the expression, when he says, " Hence be careful to have merits; when you have them, know that they were given; hope for fruit from the divine mercy, and you have escaped all the perils of poverty, ingratitude, and presumption. Happy the Church which neither wants merit without presumption, nor presumption without merit."   A little before he had abundantly shown that he used the words in a sound sense, saying, " Why is the Church anxious about merits?   God has furnished her with a firmer and surer ground of boasting.   God cannot deny himself; he will do what he has promised.   Thus there is no reason for asking by what merits may we hope for blessings; especially when you hear, ' Thus saith the Lord God; I do not this for your sakes, O house of Israel,

but for mine holy name's sake' (Ezek. xxxvi. 22). It suffices for merit to know that merits suffice not."

3. What all our works can merit Scripture shows when it declares that they cannot stand the view of God, because they are full of impurity ; it next shows what the perfect observance of the law (if it can anywhere be found) will merit when it enjoins, "So likewise ye, when ye shall have done all those things which are commanded you, say, We are unprofitable servants, we have done that which was our duty to do" (Luke xvii. 10); because we make no free-offering to God, but only perform due service by which no favour is deserved. And yet those good works which the Lord has bestowed upon us he counts ours also, and declares, that they are not only acceptable to him, but that he will recompense them. It is ours in return to be animated by this great promise, and to keep up our courage, that we may not weary in well-doing, but feel duly grateful for the great kindness of God. There cannot be a doubt, that everything in our works which deserves praise is owing to divine grace, and that there is not a particle of it which we can properly ascribe to ourselves. If we truly and seriously acknowledge this, not only confidence, but every idea of merit vanishes. I say we do not, like the Sophists, share the praise of works between God and man, but we keep it entire and unimpaired for the Lord. All we assign to man is, that, by his impurity, he pollutes and contaminates the very works which were good. The most perfect thing which proceeds from man is always polluted by some stain. Should the Lord, therefore, bring to judgment the best of human works, he would indeed behold his own righteousness in them ; but he would also behold man's dishonour and disgrace. Thus good works please God, and are not without fruit to their authors, since, by way of recompense, they obtain more ample blessings from God, not because they so deserve, but because the divine benignity is pleased of itself to set this value upon them. Such, however, is our malignity, that, not contented with this liberality on the part of God, which bestows rewards on works that do not at all deserve them, we with profane ambition maintain that that which is entirely due to the divine munificence is paid to the merit of works. Here I appeal to every man's common sense. If one who by another's liberality possesses the usufruct of a field, rear up a claim to the property of it, does he not by his ingratitude deserve to lose the possession formerly granted? In like manner, if a slave, who has been manumitted, conceals his humble condition of freedman, and gives out that he was free-born, does he not deserve to be reduced to his original slavery? A benefit can only be legitimately enjoyed when we neither arrogate more to ourselves than has been given, nor defraud the author of it of his due praise ; nay, rather when we so conduct ourselves as to make it appear that the benefit conferred still in a manner resides with him who conferred it. But if this is the moderation to be observed towards men, let every one reflect and consider for himself what is due to God.

4. I know that the Sophists abuse some passages in order to prove that the Scriptures use the term *merit* with reference to God. They quote a passage from Ecclesiasticus: "Mercy will give place to every man according to the merit of his works" (Ecclesiasticus xvi. 14); and from the Epistle to the Hebrews: "To do good and communicate forget not; for with such sacrifices God is well pleased" (Heb. xiii. 16). I now renounce my right to repudiate the authority of Ecclesiasticus; but I deny that the words of Ecclesiasticus, whoever the writer may have been, are faithfully quoted. The Greek is as follows: Πάσῃ ἐλεημοσύνῃ ποιήσει τόπον· ἕκαστος γάρ κατὰ τὰ ἔργα αὐτοῦ εὑρήσει. "He will make room for all mercy: for each shall find according to his works." That this is the genuine reading, and has been corrupted in the Latin version, is plain, both from the very structure of the sentence, and from the previous context. In the Epistle to the Hebrews there is no room for their quibbling on one little word, for in the Greek the Apostle simply says, that *such sacrifices are pleasing* and acceptable to God. This alone should amply suffice to quell and beat down the insolence of our pride, and prevent us from attaching value to works beyond the rule of Scripture. It is the doctrine of Scripture, moreover, that our good works are constantly covered with numerous stains by which God is justly offended and made angry against us, so far are they from being able to conciliate him, and call forth his favour towards us; and yet because of his indulgence, he does not examine them with the utmost strictness, he accepts them just as if they were most pure; and therefore rewards them, though undeserving, with innumerable blessings, both present and future. For I admit not the distinction laid down by otherwise learned and pious men, that good works merit the favours which are conferred upon us in this life, whereas eternal life is the reward of faith only. The recompense of our toils, and crown of our contest, our Lord almost uniformly places in heaven. On the other hand, to attribute to the merit of works, so as to deny it to grace, that we are loaded with other gifts from the Lord, is contrary to the doctrine of Scripture. For though Christ says, "Unto every one that hath shall be given;" "thou hast been faithful over a few things, I will make thee ruler over many things" (Matth. xxv. 29, 21), he, at the same time, shows that all additional gifts to believers are of his free benignity: "Ho, every one that thirsteth, come ye to the waters, and he that hath no money, come ye, buy, and eat: yea, come, buy wine and milk, without money and without price" (Isaiah lv. 1). Therefore, every help to salvation bestowed upon believers, and blessedness itself, are entirely the gift of God, and yet in both the Lord testifies that he takes account of works, since to manifest the greatness of his love toward us, he thus highly honours not ourselves only, but the gifts which he has bestowed upon us.

5. Had these points been duly handled and digested in past ages, never could so many tumults and dissensions have arisen. Paul says, that in the architecture of Christian doctrine, it is necessary to

retain the foundation which he had laid with the Corinthians, "Other foundation can no man lay than that which is laid, which is Jesus Christ" (1 Cor. iii. 11). What then is our foundation in Christ? Is it that he begins salvation and leaves us to complete it? Is it that he only opened up the way, and left us to follow it in our own strength? By no means, but as Paul had a little before declared, it is to acknowledge that he has been given us for righteousness. No man, therefore, is well founded in Christ who has not entire righteousness in him, since the Apostle says not that he was sent to assist us in procuring, but was himself to be our righteousness. Thus it is said that God "hath chosen us in him before the foundation of the world" not according to our merit, but "according to the good pleasure of his will;" that in him " we have redemption through his blood, even the forgiveness of sins;" that peace has been made "through the blood of his cross;" that we are reconciled by his blood; that, placed under his protection, we are delivered from the danger of finally perishing; that thus ingrafted into him we are made partakers of eternal life, and hope for admission into the kingdom of God.[1] Nor is this all. Being admitted to participation in him, though we are still foolish, he is our wisdom ; though we are still sinners, he is our righteousness; though we are unclean, he is our purity; though we are weak, unarmed, and exposed to Satan, yet ours is the power which has been given him in heaven and in earth, to bruise Satan under our feet, and burst the gates of hell (Matth. xxviii. 18); though we still bear about with us a body of death, he is our life; in short, all things of his are ours, we have all things in him, he nothing in us. On this foundation, I say, we must be built, if we would grow up into a holy temple in the Lord.

6. For a long time the world has been taught very differently. A kind of good works called *moral* has been found out, by which men are rendered agreeable to God before they are ingrafted into Christ; as if Scripture spoke falsely when it says, "He that hath the Son hath life, and he that hath not the Son of God hath not life" (1 John v. 12). How can they produce the materials of life if they are dead? Is there no meaning in its being said, that "whatsoever is not of faith is sin"? (Rom. xiv. 23); or can good fruit be produced from a bad tree? What have these most pestilential Sophists left to Christ on which to exert his virtue? They say that he merited for us the first grace, that is, the occasion of meriting, and that it is our part not to let slip the occasion thus offered. O the daring effrontery of impiety! Who would have thought that men professing the name of Christ would thus strip him of his power, and all but trample him under foot? The testimony uniformly borne to him in Scripture is, that whoso believeth in him is justified ; the doctrine of these men is, that the only benefit which proceeds from him is to open up a way for each to justify himself. I wish they could get a taste of what is

---

[1] 1 Cor. i. 30; Eph. i. 3-5; Col. i. 14, 20; John i. 12; x. 28.

meant by these passages : " He that hath the Son hath life.'   " He
that heareth my word, and believeth on him that sent me," " is passed
from death unto life." Whoso believeth in him " is passed from death
unto life."   " Being justified freely by his grace, through the redemption that is in Christ Jesus."   " He that keepeth his commandments
dwelleth in him, and he in him."   God " hath raised us up together,
and made us sit together in heavenly places in Christ."   " Who hath
delivered us from the power of darkness, and hath translated us into
the kingdom of his dear Son."[1]   There are similar passages without
number. Their meaning is not, that by faith in Christ an opportunity is given us of procuring justification, or acquiring salvation, but
that both are given us.   Hence, so soon as you are ingrafted into
Christ by faith, you are made a son of God, an heir of heaven, a partaker of righteousness, a possessor of life, and (the better to manifest
the false tenets of these men) you have not obtained an opportunity
of meriting), but all the merits of Christ, since they are communicated to you.

7. In this way the schools of Sorbonne, the parents of all heresies,
have deprived us of justification by faith, which lies at the root of all
godliness.   They confess, indeed, in word, that men are justified by
a formed faith, but they afterwards explain this to mean that of faith
they have good works, which avail to justification, so that they almost
seem to use the term faith in mockery, because they were unable,
without incurring great obloquy, to pass it in silence, seeing it is so
often repeated by Scripture.   And yet not contented with this, they
by the praise of good works transfer to man what they steal from
God.   And seeing that good works give little ground for exultation,
and are not even properly called merits, if they are regarded as the
fruits of divine grace, they derive them from the power of free-will ;
in other words, extract oil out of stone.   They deny not that the
principal cause is in grace ; but they contend that there is no exclusion of free-will through which all merit comes. This is the doctrine,
not only of the later Sophists, but of Lombard their Pythagoras
(Sent. Lib. ii. Dist. 28), who, in comparison of them, may be called
sound and sober. It was surely strange blindness, while he had
Augustine so often in his mouth, not to see how cautiously he guarded
against ascribing a single particle of praise to man because of good
works.   Above, when treating of free-will, we quoted some passages
from him to this effect, and similar passages frequently occur in his
writings (see in Psal. civ. ; Ep. cv.), as when he forbids us ever to
boast of our merits, because they themselves also are the gifts of God,
and when he says that all our merits are only of grace, are not provided by our sufficiency, but are entirely the production of grace, &c.
It is less strange that Lombard was blind to the light of Scripture, in
which it is obvious that he had not been a very successful student.[2]

[1] 1 John v. 12; John v. 24; Rom. iii. 24; 1 John iii. 24; Eph. ii. 6; Col. i. 13.
[2] French, " d'autant qu'il n'y estoit gueres exercité ;"—inasmuch as he was little
versant in it.

Still there cannot be a stronger declaration against him and his disciples than the words of the Apostle, who, after interdicting all Christians from glorying, subjoins the reason why glorying is unlawful: "For we are his workmanship, created in Christ Jesus unto good works, which God hath before ordained that we should walk in them" (Eph. ii. 10). Seeing, then, that no good proceeds from us unless in so far as we are regenerated—and our regeneration is without exception wholly of God—there is no ground for claiming to ourselves one iota in good works. Lastly, while these men constantly inculcate good works, they, at the same time, train the conscience in such a way as to prevent it from venturing to confide that works will render God favourable and propitious. We, on the contrary, without any mention of merit, give singular comfort to believers when we teach them that in their works they please, and doubtless are accepted of God. Nay, here we even insist that no man shall attempt or enter upon any work without faith, that is, unless he previously have a firm conviction that it will please God.

8. Wherefore, let us never on any account allow ourselves to be drawn away one nail's breadth[1] from that only foundation. After it is laid, wise architects build upon it rightly and in order. For whether there is need of doctrine or exhortation, they remind us that "for this purpose the Son of God was manifested, that he might destroy the works of the devil;" that "whosoever is born of God doth not commit sin;" that "the time past of our life may suffice us to have wrought the will of the Gentiles;" that the elect of God are vessels of mercy, appointed "to honour," purged, "sanctified, and meet for the Master's use, and prepared unto every good work." The whole is expressed at once, when Christ thus describes his disciples, "If any man will come after me, let him deny himself, and take up his cross daily, and follow me."[2] He who has denied himself has cut off the root of all evil, so as no longer to seek his own; he who has taken up his cross has prepared himself for all meekness and endurance. The example of Christ includes this and all offices of piety and holiness. He obeyed his Father even unto death; his whole life was spent in doing the works of God; his whole soul was intent on the glory of his Father; he laid down his life for the brethren; he did good to his enemies, and prayed for them. And when there is need of comfort, it is admirably afforded in these words: "We are troubled on every side, yet not distressed; we are perplexed, but not in despair; persecuted, but not forsaken; cast down, but not destroyed; always bearing about in the body the dying of the Lord Jesus, that the life also of Jesus might be made manifest in our body." "For if we be dead with him, we shall also live with him; if we suffer, we shall also reign with him;" by means of "the fellowship of his sufferings, being made conformable unto his death;" the Father having predestinated us "to be conformed to the image

1 French, "ne fust ce que de la pointe d'une espingle;"—were it only a pin's point.
2 1 John iii. 8; 1 Pet. iv. 3; 2 Tim. ii. 20, 21; Luke ix. 23.

of his Son, that he might be the first-born among many brethren." Hence it is, that "neither death, nor life, nor angels, nor principalities, nor powers, nor things present, nor things to come, nor height, nor depth, nor any other creature, shall be able to separate us from the love of God which is in Christ Jesus our Lord;"[1] nay, rather all things will work together for our good. See how it is that we do not justify men before God by works, but say, that all who are of God are regenerated and made new creatures, so that they pass from the kingdom of sin into the kingdom of righteousness. In this way they make their calling sure, and, like trees, are judged by their fruits.

[1] 2 Cor. iv. 8; 2 Tim. ii. 11; Phil. iii. 10; Rom. viii. 29, 39.

CHAPTER XVI.

REFUTATION OF THE CALUMNIES BY WHICH IT IS ATTEMPTED TO THROW ODIUM ON THIS DOCTRINE.

The divisions of this chapter are,—I. The calumnies of the Papists against the ortho-dox doctrine of Justification by Faith are reduced to two classes. The first class, with its consequences, refuted, sec. 1–3. II. The second class, which is dependant on the first, refuted in the last section.

Sections.

1. Calumnies of the Papists. 1. That we destroy good works, and give encouragement to sin. Refutation of the first calumny. 1. Character of those who censure us. 2. Justification by faith establishes the necessity of good works.
2. Refutation of a consequent of the former calumny—viz. that men are dissuaded from well-doing when we destroy merit. Two modes of refutation. First mode con-firmed by many invincible arguments.
3. The Apostles make no mention of merit, when they exhort us to good works. On the contrary, excluding merit, they refer us entirely to the mercy of God. Another mode of refutation.
4. Refutation of the second calumny and of an inference from it—viz. that the obtain-ing righteousness is made too easy, when it is made to consist in the free remission of sins.

1. OUR last sentence may refute the impudent calumny of certain ungodly men, who charge us, first, with destroying good works, and leading men away from the study of them, when we say, that men are not justified, and do not merit salvation by works; and, secondly, with making the means of justification too easy, when we say that it consists in the free remission of sins, and thus alluring men to sin to which they are already too much inclined. These calumnies, I say, are sufficiently refuted by that one sentence; however, I will briefly reply to both. The allegation is, that justification by faith destroys good works. I will not describe what kind of zealots for good works the persons are who thus charge us. We leave them as much liberty to bring the charge, as they take licence to taint the whole world with the pollution of their lives.[1] They pretend to lament[2] that when faith is so highly extolled, works are deprived of their proper place. But what if they are rather ennobled and established? We dream not of a faith which is devoid of good works, nor of a justification which can exist without them: the only difference is, that while we acknowledge that faith and works are necessarily connected, we, how-ever, place justification in faith, not in works. How this is done is easily explained, if we turn to Christ only, to whom our faith is directed, and from whom it derives all its power. Why, then, are

---

1 This sentence is wholly omitted in the French.
2 Latin, " Dolere sibi simulant."—French, " Ils alleguent ; "—they allege.

we justified by faith? Because by faith we apprehend the righteousness of Christ, which alone reconciles us to God. This faith, however, you cannot apprehend without at the same time apprehending sanctification; for Christ "is made unto us wisdom, and righteousness, and sanctification, and redemption" (1 Cor. i. 30). Christ, therefore, justifies no man without also sanctifying him. These blessings are conjoined by a perpetual and inseparable tie. Those whom he enlightens by his wisdom he redeems; whom he redeems he justifies; whom he justifies he sanctifies. But as the question relates only to justification and sanctification, to them let us confine ourselves. Though we distinguish between them, they are both inseparably comprehended in Christ. Would ye then obtain justification in Christ? You must previously possess Christ. But you cannot possess him without being made a partaker of his sanctification: for Christ cannot be divided. Since the Lord, therefore, does not grant us the enjoyment of these blessings without bestowing himself, he bestows both at once, but never the one without the other. Thus it appears how true it is that we are justified not without, and yet not by works, since in the participation of Christ, by which we are justified, is contained not less sanctification than justification.

2. It is also most untrue that men's minds are withdrawn from the desire of well-doing when we deprive them of the idea of merit. Here, by the way, the reader must be told that those men absurdly infer merit from reward, as I will afterwards more clearly explain. They thus infer, because ignorant of the principle that God gives no less a display of his liberality when he assigns reward to works, than when he bestows the faculty of well-doing. This topic it will be better to defer to its own place. At present, let it be sufficient merely to advert to the weakness of their objection. This may be done in two ways.[1] For, *first*, they are altogether in error when they say that, unless a hope of reward is held forth, no regard will be had to the right conduct of life. For if all that men do when they serve God is to look to the reward, and hire out or sell their labour to him, little is gained: he desires to be freely worshipped, freely loved: I say he approves the worshipper who, even if all hope of reward were cut off, would cease not to worship him. Moreover, when men are to be urged, there cannot be a stronger stimulus than that derived from the end of our redemption and calling, such as the word of God employs when it says, that it were the height of impiety and ingratitude not to "love him who first loved us;" that by "the blood of Christ" our conscience is purged "from dead works to serve the living God;" that it were impious sacrilege in any one to count "the blood of the covenant, wherewith he was sanctified, an unholy thing;" that we have been "delivered out of the hands of our enemies," that we "might serve him without fear, in holiness and righteousness before him, all the days of our life;" that being "made free from sin," we

---

[1] All the previous sentences of this section, except the first, are omitted in the French.

" become the servants of righteousness;" " that our old man is crucified with him," in order that we might rise to newness of life.   Again,
" if ye then be risen with Christ (as becomes his members), seek those
things which are above," living as pilgrims in the world, and aspiring
to heaven, where our treasure is.   " The grace of God hath appeared
to all men, bringing salvation, teaching us that, denying ungodliness
and worldly lusts, we should live soberly, righteously, and godly, in
this present world ; looking for that blessed hope, and the glorious appearing of the great God and our Saviour Jesus Christ."   " For God
hath not appointed us to wrath, but to obtain salvation through our
Lord Jesus Christ."   " Know ye not that ye are the temples of the Holy
Spirit," which it were impious to profane ?   " Ye were sometimes
darkness, but now are ye light in the Lord: walk as the children of
light."   "God hath not called us unto uncleanness, but unto holiness."
" For this is the will of God, even your sanctification, that ye should
abstain" from all illicit desires: ours is a " holy calling," and we
respond not to it except by purity of life.   " Being then made free
from sin, ye became the servants of righteousness."   Can there be a
stronger argument in exciting us to charity than that of John ?   " If
God so loved us, we ought also to love one another."   " In this the
children of God are manifest, and the children of the devil: whosoever doeth not righteousness is not of God, neither he that loveth not
his brother."   Similar is the argument of Paul, " Know ye not that
your bodies are the members of Christ ?"   " For as the body is one,
and hath many members, and all the members of that one body being
many, are one body, so also is Christ."   Can there be a stronger in-
centive to holiness than when we are told by John, " Every man that
hath this hope in him purifieth himself, even as he is pure" ? and by
Paul, " Having, therefore, these promises, dearly beloved, cleanse
yourselves from all filthiness of the flesh and spirit;" or when we
hear our Saviour hold forth himself as an example to us that we should
follow his steps ?[1]

3. I have given these few passages merely as a specimen ; for were
I to go over them all, I should form a large volume. All the Apostles
abound in exhortations, admonitions, and rebukes, for the purpose of
training the man of God to every good work, and that without any
mention of merit. Nay, rather their chief exhortations are founded
on the fact, that without any merit of ours, our salvation depends
entirely on thme ercy of God. Thus Paul, who during a whole Epistle
had maintained that there was no hope of life for us save in the righteousness of Christ, when he comes to exhortation, beseeches us by
the mercy which God has bestowed upon us (Rom. xii. 1). And,
indeed, this one reason ought to have been sufficient, that God may
be glorified in us. But if any are not so ardently desirous to promote

1 1 John iv. 10, 19 ; Heb. ix. 14 ; x. 29 ; Luke i. 74, 75 ; Rom. vi. 18 ; Col. iii. 1 ; Tit.
ii. 11 ; 1 Thess. v. 9 ; 1 Cor. iii. 16 ; Eph. ii. 21 ; v. 8 ; 2 Cor. vi. 16 ; 1 Thess. iv. 3, 7 ;
2 Tim. i. 9 ; Rom. vi. 18 ; 1 John iv. 10 ; iii. 11 ; 1 Cor. vi. 15, 17 ; xii. 12 ; 1 John iii.
3 ; 2 Cor. vii. 1 ; John xv. 10.

the glory of God, still the remembrance of his kindness is most sufficient to incite them to do good (see Chrysost. Homil. in Genes.). But
those men,[1] because, by introducing the idea of merit, they perhaps
extract some forced and servile obedience of the Law, falsely allege,
that as we do not adopt the same course, we have no means of exhorting to good works. As if God were well pleased with such services
when he declares that he loves a cheerful giver, and forbids anything
to be given him grudgingly or of necessity (2 Cor. ix. 7). I say not
that I would reject that or omit any kind of exhortation which Scripture employs, its object being not to leave any method of animating
us untried. For it states, that the recompense which God will render
to every one is *according to his deeds;* but, first, I deny that that is
the only, or, in many instances, the principal motive; and, secondly,
I admit not that it is the motive with which we are to begin. Moreover, I maintain that it gives not the least countenance to those
merits which these men are always preaching. This will afterwards
be seen. Lastly, there is no use in this recompense, unless we have
previously embraced the doctrine that we are justified solely by the
merits of Christ as apprehended by faith, and not by any merit of
works; because the study of piety can be fitly prosecuted only by
those by whom this doctrine has been previously imbibed. This is
beautifully intimated by the Psalmist when he thus addresses God.
"There is forgiveness with thee, that thou mayest be feared" (Ps.
cxxx. 4). For he shows that the worship of God cannot exist without acknowledging his mercy, on which it is founded and established.
This is specially deserving of notice, as showing us not only that the
beginning of the due worship of God is confidence in his mercy; but
that the fear of God (which Papists will have to be meritorious) cannot be entitled to the name of merit, for this reason, that it is founded
on the pardon and remission of sins.

4. But the most futile calumny of all is, that men are invited to
sin when we affirm that the pardon in which we hold that justification
consists is gratuitous. Our doctrine is, that justification is a thing
of such value, that it cannot be put into the balance with any good
quality of ours; and, therefore, could never be obtained unless it were
gratuitous: moreover, that it is gratuitous to us, but not also to Christ,
who paid so dearly for it—namely, his own most sacred blood, out
of which there was no price of sufficient value to pay what was due
to the justice of God. When men are thus taught, they are reminded
that it is owing to no merit of theirs that the shedding of that most
sacred blood is not repeated every time they sin. Moreover, we say
that our pollution is so great, that it can never be washed away save
in the fountain of his pure blood. Must not those who are thus addressed conceive a greater horror of sin than if it were said to be
wiped off by a sprinkling of good works? If they have any reverence
for God, how can they, after being once purified, avoid shuddering

----

1 French, "ces Pharisiens;"—those Pharisees.

at the thought of again wallowing in the mire, and as much as in them lies troubling and polluting the purity of this fountain? "I have washed my feet" (says the believing soul in the Song of Solomon, v. 3), "how shall I defile them?" It is now plain which of the two makes the forgiveness of sins of less value, and derogates from the dignity of justification. They pretend that God is appeased by their frivolous satisfactions; in other words, by mere dross. We maintain that the guilt of sin is too heinous to be so frivolously expiated; that the offence is too grave to be forgiven to such valueless satisfactions; and, therefore, that forgiveness is the prerogative of Christ's blood alone. They say that righteousness, wherever it is defective, is renewed and repaired by works of satisfaction. We think it too precious to be balanced by any compensation of works, and, therefore, in order to restore it, recourse must be had solely to the mercy of God. For the other points relating to the forgiveness of sins, see the following chapter.

CHAPTER XVII.

THE PROMISES OF THE LAW AND THE GOSPEL RECONCILED.

In the following chapter, the arguments of Sophists, who would destroy or impair the doctrine of Justification by Faith, are reduced to two classes. The former is general, the latter special, and contains some arguments peculiar to itself. I. The first class, which is general, and in a manner contains the foundation of all the arguments, draws an argument from the promises of the law. This is considered from sec. 1–3. II. The second class following from the former, and containing special proofs. An argument drawn from the history of Cornelius explained, sec. 4, 5. III. A full exposition of those passages of Scripture which represent God as showing mercy and favour to the cultivators of righteousness, sec. 6. IV. A third argument from the passages which distinguish good works by the name of righteousness, and declare that men are justified by them, sec. 7, 8. V. The adversaries of justification by faith placed in a dilemma. Their partial righteousness refuted, sec. 9, 10. VI. A fourth argument, setting the Apostle James in opposition to Paul, considered, sec. 11, 12. VII. Answer to a fifth argument, that, according to Paul, not the hearers but the doers of the law are justified, sec. 13. VIII. Consideration of a sixth argument, drawn from those passages in which believers boldly submit their righteousness to the judgment of God, and ask him to decide according to it, sec. 14. IX. Examination of the last argument, drawn from passages which ascribe righteousness and life to the ways of believers, sec. 15.

A double paralogism in the term Faith. In James the faith said not to justify is a mere empty opinion; in Paul it is the instrument by which we apprehend Christ our righteousness.

12. Another paralogism on the word *justify*. Paul speaks of the cause, James of the effects, of justification. Sum of the discussion.

13. Argument founded on Rom. ii. 13. Answer, explaining the Apostle's meaning. Another argument, containing a *reductio ad impossibili*. Why Paul used the argument.

14. An argument founded on the passages in which believers confidently appeal to their righteousness. Answer, founded on a consideration of two circumstances. 1. They refer only to a special cause. 2. They claim righteousness in comparison with the wicked.

15. Last argument from those passages which ascribe righteousness and life to the ways of believers. Answer. This proceeds from the paternal kindness of God. What meant by the perfection of saints.

1. LET us now consider the other arguments which Satan by his satellites invents to destroy or impair the doctrine of Justification by Faith. I think we have already put it out of the power of our calumniators to treat us as if we were the enemies of good works—justification being denied to works, not in order that no good works may be done, or that those which are done may be denied to be good; but only that we may not trust or glory in them, or ascribe salvation to them. Our only confidence and boasting, our only anchor of salvation is, that Christ the Son of God is ours, and that we are in him sons of God and heirs of the heavenly kingdom, being called, not by our worth, but the kindness of God, to the hope of eternal blessedness. But since, as has been said, they assail us with other engines, let us now proceed to demolish them also. First, they recur to the legal promises which the Lord proclaimed to the observers of the law, and they ask us whether we hold them to be null or effectual. Since it were absurd and ridiculous to say they are null, they take it for granted that they have some efficacy. Hence they infer that we are not justified by faith only. For the Lord thus speaks: "Wherefore it shall come to pass, if ye hearken to these judgments, and keep and do them, that the Lord thy God 'shall keep unto thee the covenant and the mercy which he sware unto thy fathers; and he will love thee, and bless thee, and multiply thee" (Deut. vii. 12, 13). Again, "If ye thoroughly amend your ways and your doings: if ye thoroughly execute judgment between a man and his neighbour; if ye oppress not the stranger, the fatherless, and the widow, and shed not innocent blood in this place, neither walk after other gods to your hurt: then will I cause you to dwell in this place, in the land that I gave to your fathers, for ever and ever" (Jer. vii. 5–7). It were to no purpose to quote a thousand similar passages, which, as they are not different in meaning, are to be explained on the same principle. In substance, Moses declares that in the law is set down "a blessing and a curse," life and death (Deut. xi. 26); and hence they argue, either that that blessing is become inactive and unfruitful, or that justification is not by faith only. We have already shown,[1] that if

---

[1] See Book II. chap. vii: sec. 2–8, 15; chap. viii. sec. 3; chap. xi. sec. 8; Book III. chap. xix. sec. 2.

we cleave to the law we are devoid of every blessing, and have nothing but the curse denounced on all transgressors. The Lord does not promise anything except to the perfect observers of the law ; and none such are anywhere to be found. The result, therefore, is, that the whole human race is convicted by the law, and exposed to the wrath and curse of God : to be saved from this they must escape from the power of the law, and be as it were brought out of bondage into freedom,—not that carnal freedom which indisposes us for the obser- vance of the law, tends to licentiousness, and allows our passions to wanton unrestrained with loosened reins ; but that spiritual freedom which consoles and raises up the alarmed and smitten conscience, proclaiming its freedom from the curse and condemnation under which it was formerly held bound. This freedom from subjection to the law, this manumission, if I may so express it, we obtain when by faith we apprehend the mercy of God in Christ, and are thereby assured of the pardon of sins, with a consciousness of which the law stung and tortured us.

2. For this reason, the promises offered in the law would all be null and ineffectual, did not God in his goodness send the Gospel to our aid, since the condition on which they depend, and under which only they are to be performed—viz. the fulfilment of the law—will never be accomplished. Still, however, the aid which the Lord gives consists not in leaving part of justification to be obtained by works, and in supplying part out of his indulgence, but in giving us Christ as in himself alone the fulfilment of righteousness. For the Apostle, after premising that he and the other Jews, aware that " a man is not jus- tified by the works of the law," had " believed in Jesus Christ," adds as the reason, not that they might be assisted to make up the sum of righteousness, by faith in Christ, but that they " might be justified by the faith of Christ, and not by the works of the law " (Gal. ii. 16). If believers withdraw from the law to faith, that in the latter they may find the justification which they see is not in the former, they certainly disclaim justification by the law. Therefore, whoso will, let him amplify the rewards which are said to await the observer of the law, provided he at the same time understand that, owing to our depravity, we derive no benefit from them until we have obtained another righteousness by faith. Thus David, after making mention of the reward which the Lord has prepared for his servants (Ps. xxv. almost throughout), immediately descends to an acknowledgment of sins, by which the reward is made void. In Psalm xix., also, he loudly extols the benefits of the law ; but immediately exclaims, " Who can understand his errors ? cleanse thou me from secret faults " (Ps. xix. 12). This passage perfectly accords with the former, when, after saying, " All the paths of the Lord are mercy and truth unto such as keep his covenant and his testimonies," he adds, " For thy name's sake, O Lord, pardon mine iniquity : for it is great " (Ps. xxv. 10, 11). Thus, too, we ought not to acknowledge that the favour of God is offered to us in the law, provided by our works we can

deserve it; but that it never actually reaches us through any such desert.

3. What then? Were the promises given that they might vanish away without fruit? I lately declared that this is not my opinion. I say, indeed, that their efficacy does not extend to us so long as they have respect to the merit of works, and therefore that, considered in themselves, they are in some sense abolished. Hence the Apostle shows, that the celebrated promise, " Ye shall therefore keep my statutes and my judgments: which if a man do, he shall live in them" (Levit. xviii. 5; Ezek. xx. 10), will, if we stop at it, be of no avail, and will profit us not a whit more than if it were not given, being inaccessible even to the holiest servants of God, who are all far from fulfilling the law, being encompassed with many infirmities. But when the Gospel promises are substituted, promises which announce the free pardon of sins, the result is not only that our persons are accepted of God, but his favour also is shown to our works, and that not only in respect that the Lord is pleased with them, but also because he visits them with the blessings which were due by agreement to the observance of his law. I admit, therefore, that the works of the faithful are rewarded with the promises which God gave in his law to the cultivators of righteousness and holiness; but in this reward we should always attend to the cause which procures favour to works. This cause, then, appears to be threefold. First, God turning his eye away from the works of his servants which merit reproach more than praise, embraces them in Christ, and by the intervention of faith alone reconciles them to himself without the aid of works. Secondly, the works not being estimated by their own worth, he, by his fatherly kindness and indulgence, honours so far as to give them some degree of value. Thirdly, he extends his pardon to them, not imputing the imperfection by which they are all polluted, and would deserve to be regarded as vices rather than virtues. Hence it appears how much Sophists[1] were deluded in thinking they admirably escaped all absurdities when they said, that works are able to merit salvation, not from their intrinsic worth, but according to agreement, the Lord having, in his liberality, set this high value upon them. But, meanwhile, they observed not how far the works which they insisted on regarding as meritorious must be from fulfilling the condition of the promises, were they not preceded by a justification founded on faith alone, and on forgiveness of sins—a forgiveness necessary to cleanse even good works from their stains. Accordingly, of the three causes of divine liberality to which it is owing that good works are accepted, they attended only to one; the other two, though the principal causes, they suppressed.

4. They quote the saying of Peter as given by Luke in the Acts. " Of a truth I perceive that God is no respecter of persons: but in every nation he that feareth him, and worketh righteousness, is ac-

---

1 French, " Les Sophistes de Sorbonne;"—the Sophists of Sorbonne.

cepted with him" (Acts x. 34, 35). And hence they infer, as a thing which seems to them beyond a doubt, that if man by right conduct procures the favour of God, his obtaining salvation is not entirely the gift of God. Nay, that when God in his mercy assists the sinner, he is inclined to mercy by works. There is no way of reconciling the passages of Scripture unless you observe that man's acceptance with God is twofold. As man is by nature, God finds nothing in him which can incline him to mercy, except merely his wretchedness. If it is clear then that man, when God first interposes for him, is naked and destitute of all good, and, on the other hand, loaded and filled with all kinds of evil,—for what quality, pray, shall we say that he is worthy of the heavenly kingdom? Where God thus clearly displays free mercy, have done with that empty imagination of merit. Another passage in the same book—viz. where Cornelius hears fron the lips of an angel, " Thy prayer and thine alms are come up for a memorial before God" (Acts x. 4), is miserably wrested to prove that man is prepared by the study of good works to receive the favour of God. Cornelius being endued with true wisdom, in other words, with the fear of God, must have been enlightened by the Spirit of wisdom, and, being an observer of righteousness, must have been sanctified by the same Spirit; righteousness being, as the Apostle testifies, one of the most certain fruits of the Spirit (Gal. v. 5). Therefore all those qualities by which he is said to have pleased God he owed to divine grace: so far was he from preparing himself by his own strengh to receive it. Indeed not a syllable of Scripture can be produced which does not accord with the doctrine, that the only reason why God receives man into his favour is, because he sees that he is in every respect lost when left to himself; lost, if he does not display his mercy in delivering him. We now see that in thus accepting, God looks not to the righteousness of the individual, but merely manifests the divine goodness towards miserable sinners, who are altogether undeserving of this great mercy.

5. But after the Lord has withdrawn the sinner from the abyss of perdition, and set him apart for himself by means of adoption, having begotten him again and formed him to newness of life, he embraces him as a new creature, and bestows the gifts of his Spirit. This is the acceptance to which Peter refers, and by which believers after their calling are approved by God even in respect of works; for the Lord cannot but love and delight in the good qualities which he produces in them by means of his Spirit. But we must always bear in mind, that the only way in which men are accepted of God in respect of works is, that whatever good works he has conferred upon those whom he admits to favour, he by an increase of liberality honours with his acceptance. For whence their good works, but just that the Lord having chosen them as vessels of honour, is pleased to adorn them with true purity? And how are their actions deemed good as if there was no deficiency in them, but just that their merciful Father indulgently pardons the spots and blemishes which adhere to them?

In one word, the only meaning of acceptance in this passage is, that God accepts and takes pleasure in his children, in whom he sees the traces and lineaments of his own countenance. We have elsewhere said, that regeneration is a renewal of the divine image in us. Since God therefore, whenever he beholds his own face, justly loves it and holds it in honour, the life of believers, when formed to holiness and justice, is said, not without cause, to be pleasing to him. But because believers, while encompassed with mortal flesh, are still sinners, and their good works only begun savour of the corruption of the flesh, God cannot be propitious either to their persons or their works, unless he embraces them more in Christ than in themselves. In this way are we to understand the passages in which God declares that he is clement and merciful to the cultivators of righteousness. Moses said to the Israelites, " Know, therefore, that the Lord thy God, he is God, the faithful God, which keepeth covenant and mercy with them that love him and keep his commandments, to a thousand generations." These words afterwards became a common form of expression among the people. Thus Solomon in his prayer at the dedication says, " Lord God of Israel, there is no God like thee, in heaven above, or on earth beneath, who keepest covenant and mercy with thy servants that walk before thee with all their heart" (1 Kings viii. 23). The same words are repeated by Nehemiah (Neh. i. 5). As the Lord in all covenants of mercy stipulates on his part for integrity and holiness of life in his servants (Deut. xxix. 18), lest his goodness might be held in derision, or any one, puffed up with exultation in it, might speak flatteringly to his soul while walking in the depravity of his heart, so he is pleased that in this way those whom he admits to communion in the covenant should be kept to their duty. Still, however, the covenant was gratuitous at first, and such it ever remains. Accordingly, while David declares, "according to the cleanness of my hands hath he recompensed me," yet does he not omit the fountain to which I have referred ; "he delivered me, because he delighted in me" (2 Sam. xxii. 20, 21). In commending the goodness of his cause, he derogates in no respect from the free mercy which takes precedence of all the gifts of which it is the origin.

6. Here, by the way, it is of importance to observe how those forms of expression differ from legal promises. By legal promises, I mean not those which lie scattered in the books of Moses (for there many Evangelical promises occur), but those which properly belong to the legal dispensation. All such promises, by whatever name they may be called, are made under the condition that the reward is to be paid on the things commanded being done. But when it is said that the Lord keeps a covenant of mercy with those who love him, the words rather demonstrate what kind of servants those are who have sincerely entered into the covenant, than express the reason why the Lord blesses them. The nature of the demonstration is this : As the end for which God bestows upon us the gift of eternal life is, that he may be loved, feared, and worshipped by us, so the end of all the promises

of mercy contained in Scripture justly is, that we may reverence and serve their author. Therefore, whenever we hear that he does good to those that observe his law, let us remember that the sons of God are designated by the duty which they ought perpetually to observe, that his reason for adopting us is, that we may reverence him as a father. Hence, if we would not deprive ourselves of the privilege of adoption, we must always strive in the direction of our calling. On the other hand, however, let us remember, that the completion of the Divine mercy depends not on the works of believers, but that God himself fulfils the promise of salvation to those who by right conduct correspond to their calling, because he recognises the true badges of sons in those only who are directed to good by his Spirit. To this we may refer what is said of the members of the Church, " Lord, who shall abide in thy tabernacle? who shall dwell in thy holy hill? He that walketh uprightly, and worketh righteousness, and speaketh the truth in his heart," &c. (Ps. xv. 1, 2). Again, in Isaiah, " Who among us shall dwell with the devouring fire? who among us shall dwell with everlasting burnings? He that walketh righteously," &c. (Isa. xxxiii. 14, 15). For the thing described is not the strength with which believers can stand before the Lord, but the manner in which our most merciful Father introduces them into his fellowship, and defends and confirms them therein. For as he detests sin and loves righteousness, so those whom he unites to himself he purifies by his Spirit, that he may render them conformable to himself and to his kingdom. Therefore, if it be asked, What is the first cause which gives the saints free access to the kingdom of God, and a firm and permanent footing in it? the answer is easy. The Lord in his mercy once adopted and ever defends them. But if the question relates to the manner, we must descend to regeneration, and the fruits of it, as enumerated in the fifteenth Psalm.

7. There seems much more difficulty in those passages which distinguish good works by the name of righteousness, and declare that man is justified by them. The passages of the former class are very numerous, as when the observance of the commandments is termed justification or righteousness. Of the other classes we have a description in the words of Moses, " It shall be our righteousness, if we observe to do all these commandments" (Deut. vi. 25). But if you object, that it is a legal promise, which, having an impossible condition annexed to it, proves nothing, there are other passages to which the same answer cannot be made; for instance, " If the man be poor," " thou shalt deliver him the pledge again when the sun goeth down:" " and it shall be righteousness unto thee before the Lord thy God" (Deut. xxiv. 13). Likewise the words of the prophet, " Then stood up Phinehas, and executed judgment: and so the plague was stayed. And that was counted unto him for righteousness unto all generations for evermore" (Psal. cvi. 30, 31). Accordingly, the Pharisees of our day think they have here full scope for exultation.[1] For, as

---

1 French, " de crier contre nous en cest endroit;"—here to raise an outcry against us.

we say, that when justification by faith is established, justification by works falls; they argue on the same principle, If there is a justification by works, it is false to say that we are justified by faith only. When I grant that the precepts of the law are termed righteousness, I do nothing strange: for they are so in reality. I must, however, inform the reader, that the Hebrew word חקים has been rendered by the Septuagint, not very appropriately, δικαιώματα, *justifications*, instead of *edicts*.[1] But I readily give up any dispute as to the word. Nor do I deny that the Law of God contains a perfect righteousness. For although we are debtors to do all the things which it enjoins, and therefore, even after a full obedience, are unprofitable servants; yet, as the Lord has deigned to give it the name of righteousness, it is not ours to take from it what he has given. We readily admit, therefore, that the perfect obedience of the law is righteousness, and the observance of any precept a part of righteousness, the whole substance of righteousness being contained in the remaining parts. But we deny that any such righteousness ever exists. Hence we discard the righteousness of the law, not as being in itself maimed and defective, but because of the weakness of our flesh it nowhere appears. But then Scripture does not merely call the precepts of the law righteousness, it also gives this name to the works of the saints: as when it states that Zacharias and his wife " were both righteous before God, walking in all the commandments and ordinances of the Lord blameless" (Luke i. 6). Surely when it thus speaks, it estimates works more according to the nature of the law than their own proper character. And here, again, I must repeat the observation which I lately made, that the law is not to be ascertained from a careless translation of the Greek interpreter. Still, as Luke chose not to make any change on the received version, I will not contend for this. The things contained in the law God enjoined upon man for righteousness, but that righteousness we attain not unless by observing the whole law: every transgression whatever destroys it. While, therefore, the law commands nothing but righteousness, if we look to itself, every one of its precepts is righteousness: if we look to the men by whom they are performed, being transgressors in many things, they by no means merit the praise of righteousness for one work, and that a work which, through the imperfection adhering to it, is always in some respect vicious.[2]

8. I come to the second class (sec. 1, 7, ad init.), in which the

---

1 French, " Edits ou Statuts;"—Edicts or Statutes.

2 The French here adds the two following sentences:—" Nostre response donc est, que quand les œuvres des saincts sont nommées justice, cela ne vient point de leurs merites: mais entant qu'elles tendent à la justice que Dieu nous a commandee, laquelle est nulle, si elle n'est parfaite. Or elle ne se trouve parfaite en nul homme de monde; pourtant faut conclure, q'une bonne œuvre de soy ne merite pas le nom de justice."—Our reply then is, that when the works of the saints are called righteousness, it is not owing to their merits, but is in so far as they tend to the righteousness which God has commanded, and which is null if it be not perfect. Now it is not found perfect in any man in the world. Hence we must conclude, that no good work merits in itself the name of righteousness.

chief difficulty lies. Paul finds nothing stronger to prove justification by faith than that which is written of Abraham, he "believed God, and it was counted unto him for righteousness" (Rom. iv. 3; Gal. iii. 6). Therefore, when it is said that the achievement of Phinehas "was counted unto him for righteousness" (Psal. cvi. 30, 31), we may argue that what Paul contends for respecting faith applies also to works. Our opponents, accordingly, as if the point were proved, set it down that though we are not justified without faith, it is not by faith only; that our justification is completed by works. Here I beseech believers, as they know that the true standard of righteousness must be derived from Scripture alone, to consider with me seriously and religiously, how Scripture can be fairly reconciled with that view. Paul, knowing that justification by faith was the refuge of those who wanted righteousness of their own, confidently infers, that all who are justified by faith are excluded from the righteousness of works. But as it is clear that this justification is common to all believers, he with equal confidence infers that no man is justified by works; nay, more, that justification is without any help from works. But it is one thing to determine what power works have in themselves, and another to determine what place they are to hold after justification by faith has been established. If a price is to be put upon works according to their own worth, we hold that they are unfit to appear in the presence of God: that man, accordingly, has no works in which he can glory before God, and that hence, deprived of all aid from works, he is justified by faith alone. Justification, moreover, we thus define: The sinner being admitted into communion with Christ is, for his sake, reconciled to God; when purged by his blood he obtains the remission of sins, and clothed with righteousness, just as if it were his own, stands secure before the judgment-seat of heaven. Forgiveness of sins being previously given, the good works which follow have a value different from their merit, because whatever is imperfect in them is covered by the perfection of Christ, and all their blemishes and pollutions are wiped away by his purity, so as never to come under the cognisance of the divine tribunal. The guilt of all transgressions, by which men are prevented from offering God an acceptable service, being thus effaced, and the imperfection which is wont to sully even good works being buried, the good works which are done by believers are deemed righteous, or, which is the same thing, are imputed for righteousness.

9. Now, should any one state this to me as an objection to justification by faith, I would first ask him, Whether a man is deemed righteous for one holy work or two, while in all the other acts of his life he is a transgressor of the law? This were, indeed, more than absurd. I would next ask, Whether he is deemed righteous on account of many good works if he is guilty of transgression in some one part? Even this he will not venture to maintain in opposition to the authority of the law, which pronounces, "Cursed be he that

confirmeth not all the words of this law to do them" (Deut xxvii. 26). I would go still farther and ask, Whether there be any work which may not justly be convicted of impurity or imperfection? How, then, will it appear to that eye before which even the heavens are not clean, and angels are chargeable with folly? (Job. iv. 18.) Thus he will be forced to confess that no good work exists that is not defiled, both by contrary transgression and also by its own corruption, so that it cannot be honoured as righteousness. But if it is certainly owing to justification by faith that works, otherwise impure, unclean, defective, unworthy of the sight, not to say of the love of God, are imputed for righteousness, why do they by boasting of this imputation aim at the destruction of that justification, but for which the boast were vain? Are they desirous of having a viper's birth?[1] To this their ungodly language tends. They cannot deny that justification by faith is the beginning, the foundation, the cause, the subject, the substance, of works of righteousness, and yet they conclude that justification is not by faith, because good works are counted for righteousness. Let us have done then with this frivolity, and confess the fact as it stands; if any righteousness which works are supposed to possess depends on justification by faith, this doctrine is not only not impaired, but on the contrary confirmed, its power being thereby more brightly displayed. Nor let us suppose, that after free justification works are commended, as if they afterwards succeeded to the office of justifying, or shared the office with faith. For did not justification by faith always remain entire, the impurity of works would be disclosed. There is nothing absurd in the doctrine, that though man is justified by faith, he is himself not only not righteous, but the righteousness attributed to his works is beyond their own deserts.

10. In this way we can admit not only that there is a partial righteousness in works (as our adversaries maintain), but that they are approved by God as if they were absolutely perfect. If we remember on what foundation this is rested, every difficulty will be solved. The first time when a work begins to be acceptable is when it is received with pardon. And whence pardon, but just because God looks upon us and all that belongs to us as in Christ? Therefore, as we ourselves when ingrafted into Christ appear righteous before God, because our iniquities are covered with his innocence; so our works are, and are deemed righteous, because everything otherwise defective in them being buried by the purity of Christ is not imputed. Thus we may justly say, that not only ourselves, but our works also, are justified by faith alone. Now, if that righteousness of works, whatever it be, depends on faith and free justification, and is produced by it, it ought to be included under it, and, so to speak, made subordinate to it, as the effect to its cause; so far is it from

---

[1] French. "Voudrions nous faire une lignee serpentine, que les enfans meurtrissent leur mere?"—Would we have a viperish progeny, where the children murder the parent?

being entitled to be set up to impair or destroy the doctrine of justification.[1] Thus Paul, to prove that our blessedness depends not on
our works, but on the mercy of God, makes special use of the words
of David, " Blessed is he whose transgression is forgiven, whose sin is
covered ;" " Blessed is the man unto whom the Lord imputeth not
iniquity." Should any one here obtrude the numberless passages in
which blessedness seems to be attributed to works, as " Blessed is the
man that feareth the Lord ;" " He that hath mercy on the poor,
happy is he ;" " Blessed is the man that walketh not in the counsel
of the ungodly," and " that endureth temptation ;" " Blessed are they
that keep judgment," that are " pure in heart," " meek," " merciful,"
&c.,[2] they cannot make out that Paul's doctrine is not true. For
seeing that the qualities thus extolled never all so exist in man as to
obtain for him the approbation of God, it follows, that man is always
miserable until he is exempted from misery by the pardon of his sins.
Since, then, all the kinds of blessedness extolled in the Scripture are
vain, so that man derives no benefit from them until he obtains blessedness by the forgiveness of sins, a forgiveness which makes way for
them, it follows that this is not only the chief and highest, but the
only blessedness, unless you are prepared to maintain that it is impaired by things which owe their entire existence to it. There is
much less to trouble us in the name of *righteous* which is usually
given to believers. I admit that they are so called from the holiness
of their lives, but as they rather exert themselves in the study of
righteousness than fulfil righteousness itself, any degree of it which
they possess must yield to justification by faith, to which it is owing
that it is what it is.

11. But they say that we have a still more serious business with
James, who in express terms opposes us. For he asks, " Was not
Abraham our father justified by works ?" and adds, " You see then
how that by works a man is justified, and not by faith only " (James
ii. 21, 24). What then ? Will they engage Paul in a quarrel with
James ? If they hold James to be a servant of Christ, his sentiments
must be understood as not dissenting from Christ speaking by the
mouth of Paul. By the mouth of Paul the Spirit declares that Abraham obtained justification by faith, not by works ; we also teach that
all are justified by faith without the works of the law. By James the
same Spirit declares that both Abraham's justification and ours consists of works, and not of faith only. It is certain that the Spirit
cannot be at variance with himself. Where, then, will be the agree-

---

1 The whole sentence in French stands thus :—" Or si cette justice des œuvres telle
quelle procede de la foy et de la justification gratuite, il ne faut pas qu'on la prenne
pour destruire ou obscurcir la grace dont elle depend ; mais plustost doit estre enclose
en icelle, comme le fruict à l'arbre."—Now, if this righteousness of works, such as it is,
proceeds from faith and free justification, it must not be employed to destroy or obscure
the grace on which it depends, but should rather be included in it, like the fruit in the tree.
2 Rom. iv. 7 ; Ps xxxii. 1, 2 ; cxii. 1 ; Prov. xiv. 21 ; Ps. i. 1 ; cvi. 3 ; cxix. 11 ; Matth.
v. 3.

ment? It is enough for our opponents, provided they can tear up that justification by faith which we regard as fixed by the deepest roots:[1] to restore peace to the conscience is to them a matter of no great concern. Hence you may see, that though they indeed carp at the doctrine of justification by faith, they meanwhile point out no goal of righteousness at which the conscience may rest. Let them triumph then as they will, so long as the only victory they can boast of is, that they have deprived righteousness of all its certainty. This miserable victory they will indeed obtain when the light of truth is extinguished, and the Lord permits them to darken it with their lies. But wherever the truth of God stands they cannot prevail. I deny, then, that the passage of James which they are constantly holding up before us as if it were the shield of Achilles, gives them the slightest countenance. To make this plain, let us first attend to the scope of the Apostle, and then show wherein their hallucination consists. As at that time (and the evil has existed in the Church ever since) there were many who, while they gave manifest proof of their infidelity, by neglecting and omitting all the works peculiar to believers, ceased not falsely to glory in the name of faith. James here dissipates their vain confidence. His intention therefore is, not to derogate in any degree from the power of true faith, but to show how absurdly these triflers laid claim only to the empty name, and resting satisfied with it, felt secure in unrestrained indulgence in vice. This state of matters being understood, it will be easy to see where the error of our opponents lies. They fall into a double paralogism, the one in the term *faith*, the other in the term *justifying*. The Apostle, in giving the name of *faith* to an empty opinion altogether differing from true faith, makes a concession which derogates in no respect from his case. This he demonstrates at the outset by the words, " What doth it profit, my brethren, though a man say he hath faith, and have not works?" (James ii. 14). He says not, " If a man *have* faith without works," but " if he say that he has." This becomes still clearer when a little after he derides this faith as worse than that of devils, and at last when he calls it " dead." You may easily ascertain his meaning by the explanation, " Thou believest that there is one God." Surely if all which is contained in that faith is a belief in the existence of God, there is no wonder that it does not justify. The denial of such a power to it cannot be supposed to derogate in any degree from Christian faith, which is of a very different description. For how does true faith justify unless by uniting us to Christ, so that being made one with him, we may be admitted to a participation in his righteousness? It does not justify because it forms an idea of the divine existence, but because it reclines with confidence on the divine mercy.

---

1 French, " Il suffit à nos adversaires s'ils peuvent deraciner la justice de foy, laquelle nous voulons estre plantee au profond du cœur."—It is enough for our opponents if they can root up justification by faith, which we desire to be planted at the bottom of the heart.

12. We have not made good our point until we dispose of the other paralogism: since James places a part of justification in works. If you would make James consistent with the other Scriptures and with himself, you must give the word *justify*, as used by him, a different meaning from what it has with Paul. In the sense of Paul we are said to be justified when the remembrance of our unrighteousness is obliterated, and we are counted righteous. Had James had the same meaning it would have been absurd for him to quote the words of Moses, " Abraham believed God," &c. The context runs thus: " Was not Abraham our father justified by works when he had offered Isaac his son upon the altar? Seest thou how faith wrought with his works, and by works was faith made perfect? And the Scripture was fulfilled which saith, Abraham believed God, and it was imputed unto him for righteousness." If it is absurd to say that the effect was prior to its cause, either Moses falsely declares in that passage that Abraham's faith was imputed for righteousness, or Abraham, by his obedience in offering up Isaac, did not merit righteousness. Before the existence of Ishmael, who was a grown youth at the birth of Isaac. Abraham was justified by his faith. How then can we say that he obtained justification by an obedience which followed long after? Wherefore, either James erroneously inverts the proper order (this it were impious to suppose), or he meant not to say that he was justified, as if he deserved to be deemed just. What then? It appears certain that he is speaking of the manifestation, not of the imputation of righteousness, as if he had said, Those who are justified by true faith prove their justification by obedience and good works, not by a bare and imaginary semblance of faith. In one word, he is not discussing the mode of justification, but requiring that the justification of believers shall be operative. And as Paul contends that men are justified without the aid of works, so James will not allow any to be regarded as justified who are destitute of good works. Due attention to the scope will thus disentangle every doubt; for the error of our opponents lies chiefly in this, that they think James is defining the mode of justification, whereas his only object is to destroy the depraved security of those who vainly pretended faith as an excuse for their contempt of good works. Therefore, let them twist the words of James as they may, they will never extract out of them more than the two propositions: That an empty phantom of faith does not justify, and that the believer, not contented with such an imagination, manifests his justification by good works.

13. They gain nothing by quoting from Paul to the same effect, that " not the hearers of the law are just before God, but the doers of the law shall be justified " (Rom. ii. 13). I am unwilling to evade the difficulty by the solution of Ambrose, that Paul spoke thus because faith in Christ is the fulfilment of the law. This I regard as a mere subterfuge, and one too for which there is no occasion, as the explanation is perfectly obvious. The Apostle's object is to suppress the absurd confidence of the Jews, who gave out that they alone had

a knowledge of the law, though at the very time they were its greatest despisers.   That they might not plume themselves so much on a bare acquaintance with the law, he reminds them that when justification is sought by the law, the thing required is not the knowledge but the observance of it.   We certainly mean not to dispute that the righteousness of the law consists in works, and not only so, but that justification consists in the dignity and merits of works.   But this proves not that we are justified by works unless they can produce some one who has fulfilled the law.   That Paul had no other meaning is abundantly obvious from the context.   After charging Jews and Gentiles in common with unrighteousness, he descends to particulars, and says, that "as many as have sinned without law shall also perish without law," referring to the Gentiles ; and that "as many as have sinned in the law shall be judged by the law," referring to the Jews. Moreover, as they, winking at their transgressions, boasted merely of the law, he adds most appropriately, that the law was passed with the view of justifying not those who only heard it, but those only who obeyed it ; as if he had said, Do you seek righteousness in the law ? do not bring forward the mere hearing of it, which is in itself of little weight, but bring works by which you may show that the law has not been given to you in vain.   Since in these they were all deficient, it followed that they had no ground of boasting in the law.   Paul's meaning, therefore, rather leads to an opposite argument.   The righteousness of the law consists in the perfection of works ; but no man can boast of fulfilling the law by works, and therefore there is no righteousness by the law.

14.   They now betake themselves to those passages in which believers boldly submit their righteousness to the judgment of God, and wish to be judged accordingly ; as in the following passages : "Judge me, O Lord, according to my righteousness, and according to mine integrity that is in me."   Again, "Hear the right, O Lord ;" "Thou hast proved mine heart ; thou hast visited me in the night ; thou hast tried me, and shalt find nothing."   Again, "The Lord rewarded me according to my righteousness ; according to the cleanness of my hands hath he recompensed me.   For I have kept the ways of the Lord, and have not wickedly departed from my God."   "I was also upright before him, and I kept myself from mine iniquity."   Again, "Judge me, O Lord ; for I have walked in mine integrity ;"   "I have not sat with vain persons ; neither will I go in with dissemblers ;" "Gather not my soul with sinners, nor my life with bloody men ; in whose hands is mischief, and their right hand is full of bribes.   But as for me, I will walk in mine integrity."[1]   I have already spoken of the confidence which the saints seem to derive simply from works. The passages now quoted will not occasion much difficulty, if we attend to their περίστασις, their connection, or (as it is commonly called) special circumstances.   These are of two kinds ; for those who use

[1] Ps. vii. 9 ; xvii. 1 ; xviii. 20 ; xxvi. 1, 9, 10.   Farther on, see Chap. xiv. s. 18 ; Chap. xx. s. 10.

them have no wish that their whole life should be brought to trial, so that they may be acquitted or condemned according to its tenor; all they wish is, that a decision, should be given on the particular case; and even here the righteousness which they claim is not with reference to the divine perfection, but only by comparison with the wicked and profane. When the question relates to justification, the thing required is not that the individual have a good ground of acquittal in regard to some particular matter, but that his whole life be in accordance with righteousness. But when the saints implore the divine justice in vindication of their innocence, they do not present themselves as free from fault, and in every respect blameless, but while placing their confidence of salvation in the divine goodness only, and trusting that he will vindicate his poor when they are afflicted contrary to justice and equity, they truly commit to him the cause in which the innocent are oppressed. And when they sist themselves with their adversaries at the tribunal of God, they pretend not to an innocence corresponding to the divine purity were inquiry strictly made, but knowing that in comparison of the malice, dishonesty, craft, and iniquity of their enemies, their sincerity, justice, simplicity, and purity, are ascertained and approved by God, they dread not to call upon him to judge between them. Thus when David said to Saul, "The Lord render to every man his righteousness and his faithfulness" (1 Sam. xxvi. 23), he meant not that the Lord should examine and reward every one according to his deserts, but he took the Lord to witness how great his innocence was in comparison of Saul's injustice. Paul, too, when he indulges in the boast, "Our rejoicing is this, the testimony of our conscience, that in simplicity and godly sincerity, not with fleshly wisdom, but by the grace of God, we have had our conversation in the world, and more abundantly to you-ward" (2 Cor. i. 12), means not to call for the scrutiny of God, but compelled by the calumnies of the wicked he appeals, in contradiction of all their slanders, to his faith and probity, which he knew that God had indulgently accepted. For we see how he elsewhere says, "I know nothing by myself; yet am I not hereby justified" (1 Cor. iv. 4); in other words, he was aware that the divine judgment far transcended the blind estimate of man. Therefore, however believers may, in defending their integrity against the hypocrisy of the ungodly, appeal to God as their witness and judge, still when the question is with God alone, they all with one mouth exclaim, "If thou, Lord, should mark iniquities, O Lord, who shall stand?" Again, "Enter not into judgment with thy servant; for in thy sight shall no man living be justified." Distrusting their own works, they gladly exclaim, "Thy loving-kindness is better than life" (Ps. cxxx. 3; cxliii. 2; lxiii. 3).

15. There are other passages not unlike those quoted above, at which some may still demur. Solomon says, "The just man walketh in his integrity" (Prov. xx. 7). Again, "In the way of righteousness is life; and in the pathway thereof there is no death" (Prov.

xii. 28). For this reason Ezekiel says, He that " hath walked in my statutes, and hath kept my judgments to deal truly; he is just, he shall surely live" (Ezek. xviii. 9, 21; xxxiii. 15). None of these declarations do we deny or obscure. But let one of the sons of Adam come forward with such integrity. If there is none, they must perish from the presence of God, or betake themselves to the asylum of mercy. Still we deny not that the integrity of believers, though partial and imperfect, is a step to immortality. How so, but just that the works of those whom the Lord has assumed into the covenant of grace, he tries not by their merit, but embraces with paternal indulgence. By this we understand not with the Schoolmen, that works derive their value from accepting grace. For their meaning is, that works otherwise unfit to obtain salvation in terms of law, are made fit for such a purpose by the divine acceptance. On the other hand, I maintain that these works being sullied both by other transgressions and by their own deficiencies, have no other value than this, that the Lord indulgently pardons them; in other words, that the righteousness which he bestows on man is gratuitous. Here they unseasonably obtrude those passages in which the Apostle prays for all perfection to believers, " To the end he may establish your hearts unblameable in holiness before God, even our Father" (1 Thess. iii. 13, and elsewhere). These words were strongly urged by the Celestines of old, in maintaining the perfection of holiness in the present life. To this we deem it sufficient briefly to reply with Augustine, that the goal to which all the pious ought to aspire is, to appear in the presence of God without spot and blemish; but as the course of the present life is at best nothing more than progress, we shall never reach the goal until we have laid aside the body of sin, and been completely united to the Lord. If any one choose to give the name of perfection to the saints, I shall not obstinately quarrel with him, provided he defines this perfection in the words of Augustine, " When we speak of the perfect virtue of the saints, part of this perfection consists in the recognition of our imperfection both in truth and in humility" (August. ad Bonif. Lib. iii. c. 7).

CHAPTER XVIII.

THE RIGHTEOUSNESS OF WORKS IMPROPERLY INFERRED FROM REWARDS.

There are three divisions in this chapter,—I. A solution of two general objections which are urged in support of justification by works. First, That God will render to every one according to his works, sec. 1. Second that the reward of works is called eternal, sec. 2-6. II. Answer to other special objections derived from the former, and a perversion of passages of Scripture, sec. 6-9. III. Refutation of the sophism that faith itself is called a work, and therefore justification by it is by works, sec. 10.

Sections.

1. Two general objections. The former solved and explained. What meant by the term *working*.
2. Solution of the second general objection. 1. Works not the cause of salvation. This shown from the name and nature of inheritance. 2. A striking example that the Lord rewards the works of believers with blessings which he had promised before the works were thought of.
3. First reason why eternal life said to be the reward of works. This confirmed by passages of Scripture. The concurrence of Ambrose. A rule to be observed. Declarations of Christ and an Apostle.
4. Other four reasons. Holiness the way to the kingdom, not the cause of obtaining it. Proposition of the Sophists.
5. Objection that God crowns the works of his people. Three answers from Augustine. A fourth from Scripture.
6. First special objection—viz. that we are ordered to lay up treasure in heaven. Answer, showing in what way this can be done.
7. Second objection—viz. that the righteous enduring affliction are said to be worthy of the kingdom of heaven. Answer. What meant by righteousness.
8. A third objection founded on three passages of Paul. Answer.
9. Fourth objection founded on our Saviour's words, " If ye would enter into life, keep the commandments." Answer, giving an exposition of the passage.
10. Last objection—viz. that faith itself is called a work. Answer—it is not as a work that faith justifies.

1. LET us now proceed to those passages which affirm that God will render to every one according to his deeds. Of this description are the following: " We must all appear before the judgment-seat of Christ; that every one may receive the things done in his body, according to that he hath done, whether it be good or bad;" " Who will render to every man according to his deeds: to them who by patient continuance in well-doing seek for glory, and honour, and immortality, eternal life;" but " tribulation and anguish upon every soul of man that doeth evil;" " They that have done good, unto the resurrection of life; and they that have done evil, unto the resurrection of damnation;" " Come, ye blessed of my Father;" " For I was an hungered, and ye gave me meat; I was thirsty, and ye gave me drink," &c. To these we may add the passages which describe eter-

nal life as the reward of works, such as the following: "The recompense of a man's hands shall be rendered unto him;" "He that feareth the commandment shall be rewarded;" "Rejoice and be exceeding glad, for great is your reward in heaven;" "Every man shall receive his own reward, according to his own labour."[1] The passages in which it is said that God will reward every man according to his works are easily disposed of. For that mode of expression indicates not the cause but the order of sequence. Now, it is beyond a doubt that the steps by which the Lord in his mercy consummates our salvation are these, "Whom he did predestinate, them he also called; and whom he called, them he also justified; and whom he justified, them he also glorified" (Rom. viii. 30). But though it is by mercy alone that God admits his people to life, yet as he leads them into possession of it by the course of good works, that he may complete his work in them in the order which he has destined, it is not strange that they are said to be crowned according to their works, since by these doubtless they are prepared for receiving the crown of immortality. Nay, for this reason they are aptly said to work out their own salvation (Phil. ii. 12), while by exerting themselves in good works they aspire to eternal life, just as they are elsewhere told to labour for the meat which perisheth not (John vi. 27), while they acquire life for themselves by believing in Christ; and yet it is immediately added, that this meat "the Son of man shall give unto you." Hence it appears, that *working* is not at all opposed to *grace*, but refers to pursuit,[2] and therefore it follows not that believers are the authors of their own salvation, or that it is the result of their works. What then? The moment they are admitted to fellowship with Christ, by the knowledge of the gospel, and the illumination of the Holy Spirit, their eternal life is begun, and then He which hath begun a good work in them "will perform it until the day of Jesus Christ" (Phil. i. 6). And it is performed when in righteousness and holiness they bear a resemblance to their heavenly Father, and prove that they are not degenerate sons.

2. There is nothing in the term *reward* to justify the inference that our works are the cause of salvation. First, let it be a fixed principle in our hearts, that the kingdom of heaven is not the hire of servants, but the inheritance of sons (Eph. i. 18); an inheritance obtained by those only whom the Lord has adopted as sons, and obtained for no other cause than this adoption, "The son of the bond-woman shall not be heir with the son of the free-woman" (Gal. iv. 30). And hence in those very passages in which the Holy Spirit promises eternal glory as the reward of works, by expressly calling it an inheritance, he demonstrates that it comes to us from some other quarter. Thus Christ enumerates the works for which he bestows

---

[1] Matth. xvi. 27; 2 Cor. v. 10; Rom. ii. 6; John v. 29: Matth. xxv. 34; Prov. xii. 14; xiii. 13; Matth. v. 12; Luke vi. 23; 1 Cor. iii. 8.

[2] French, "mais seulement emporte zele et estude;"—but only imports zeal and study.

heaven as a recompense, while he is calling his elect to the possession of it, but he at the same time adds, that it is to be possessed by right of inheritance (Matth. xxv. 34). Paul, too, encourages servants, while faithfully doing their duty, to hope for reward from the Lord, but adds, "of the inheritance" (Col. iii. 24). You see how, as it were, in formal terms they carefully caution us to attribute eternal blessedness not to works, but to the adoption of God. Why then do they at the same time make mention of works? This question will be elucidated by an example from Scripture (Gen. xv. 5; xvii. 1). Before the birth of Isaac, Abraham had received promise of a seed in whom all the families of the earth should be blessed; the propagation of a seed that for number should equal the stars of heaven, and the sand of the sea, &c. Many years after he prepares, in obedience to a divine message, to sacrifice his son. Having done this act of obedience, he receives the promise, "By myself have I sworn, saith the Lord, for because thou hast done this thing, and hast not withheld thy son, thine only son; that in blessing I will bless thee, and in multiplying I will multiply thy seed as the stars of the heaven, and as the sand which is upon the sea-shore, and thy seed shall possess the gate of his enemies; and in thy seed shall all the nations of the earth be blessed, because thou hast obeyed my voice" (Gen. xxii. 16–18). What is it we hear? Did Abraham by his obedience merit the blessing which had been promised him before the precept was given? Here assuredly we see without ambiguity that God rewards the works of believers with blessings which he had given them before the works were thought of, there still being no cause for the blessings which he bestows but his own mercy.

3. And yet the Lord does not act in vain, or delude us when he says, that he renders to works what he had freely given previous to works. As he would have us to be exercised in good works, while aspiring to the manifestation, or, if I may so speak, the fruition of the things which he has promised, and by means of them to hasten on to the blessed hope set before us in heaven, the fruit of the promises is justly ascribed to those things by which it is brought to maturity. Both things were elegantly expressed by the Apostle, when he told the Colossians to study the offices of charity, "for the hope which is laid up for you in heaven, whereof ye heard before in the word of the truth of the gospel" (Col. i. 5). For when he says that the gospel informed them of the hope which was treasured up for them in heaven, he declares that it depends on Christ alone, and not at all upon works. With this accords the saying of Peter, that believers "are kept by the power of God through faith unto salvation, ready to be revealed in the last time" (1 Pet. i. 5). When he says that they strive on account of it, he intimates that believers must continue running during the whole course of their lives, in order that they may attain it. But to prevent us from supposing that the reward which is promised becomes a kind of merit, our Lord introduced a parable, in which he represented himself as a householder,

who sent all the labourers whom he met to work in his vineyard, some at the first hour of the day, others at the second, others at the third, some even at the eleventh; at evening he paid them all alike. The interpretation of this parable is briefly and truly given by that ancient writer (whoever he was) who wrote the book *De Vocatione Gentium*, which goes under the name of Ambrose. I will give it in his words rather than my own:[1] "By means of this comparison, our Lord represented the many various modes of calling as pertaining to grace alone, where those who were introduced into the vineyard at the eleventh hour, and made equal to those who had toiled the whole day, doubtless represent the case of those whom the indulgence of God, to commend the excellence of grace, has rewarded in the decline of the day and the conclusion of life; not paying the price of labour, but shedding the riches of his goodness on those whom he chose without works; in order that even those who bore the heat of the day, and yet received no more than those who came last, may understand that they received a gift of grace, not the hire of works" (Lib. i. cap. 5). Lastly, it is also worthy of remark, that in those passages in which eternal life is called the reward of works, it is not taken simply for that communion which we have with God preparatory to a blessed immortality, when with paternal benevolence he embraces us in Christ, but for the possession, or, as it is called, the fruition of blessedness, as the very words of Christ express it, "in the world to come eternal life" (Mark x. 30); and elsewhere, "Come, ye blessed of my Father, inherit the kingdom," &c. (Matth. xxv. 34). For this reason also, Paul gives the name of *adoption* to that revelation of adoption which shall be made at the resurrection; and which adoption he afterwards interprets to mean, the redemption of our body (Rom. viii. 23). But, otherwise, as alienation from God is eternal death,—so when man is received into favour by God that he may enjoy communion with him and become one with him, he passes from death unto life. This is owing to adoption alone. Although after their manner they pertinaciously urge the term *reward*, we can always carry them back to the declaration of Peter, that eternal life is the reward of faith (1 Pet. i. 9).

4. Let us not suppose, then, that the Holy Spirit, by this promise, commends the dignity of our works, as if they were deserving of such a reward. For Scripture leaves us nothing of which we may glory in the sight of God. Nay, rather its whole object is to repress, humble, cast down, and completely crush our pride. But in this way help is given to our weakness, which would immediately give way were it not sustained by this expectation, and soothed by this comfort. First, let every man reflect for himself how hard it is not only to leave all things, but to leave and abjure one's self. And yet

---

[1] French, "Pource que c'est un Docteur ancien, j'aime mieux user de ses paroles que des miennes;"—Because he is an ancient Doctor, I prefer making use of his words rather than my own.

this is the training by which Christ initiates his disciples, that is, all the godly. Secondly, he thus keeps them all their lifetime under the discipline of the cross, lest they should allow their heart to long for or confide in present good. In short, his treatment is usually such, that wherever they turn their eyes, as far as this world extends, they see nothing before them but despair; and hence Paul says, "If in this life only we have hope in Christ, we are of all men most miserable" (1 Cor. xv. 19). That they may not fail in these great straits, the Lord is present reminding them to lift their head higher and extend their view farther, that in him they may find a happiness which they see not in the world: to this happiness he gives the name of reward, hire, recompense, not as estimating the merit of works, but intimating that it is a compensation for their straits, sufferings, and affronts, &c. Wherefore, there is nothing to prevent us from calling eternal life a recompense after the example of Scripture, because in it the Lord brings his people from labour to quiet, from affliction to a prosperous and desirable condition, from sorrow to joy, from poverty to affluence, from ignominy to glory; in short, exchanges all the evils which they endured for blessings. Thus there will be no impropriety in considering holiness of life as the way, not indeed the way which gives access to the glory of the heavenly kingdom; but a way by which God conducts his elect to the manifestation of that kingdom, since his good pleasure is to glorify those whom he has sanctified (Rom. viii. 30). Only let us not imagine that merit and hire are correlative terms, a point on which the Sophists absurdly insist, from not attending to the end to which we have adverted. How preposterous is it when the Lord calls us to one end to look to another? Nothing is clearer than that a reward is promised to good works, in order to support the weakness of our flesh by some degree of comfort; but not to inflate our minds with vain glory. He, therefore, who from merit infers reward, or weighs works and reward in the same balance, errs very widely from the end which God has in view.

5. Accordingly, when the Scripture speaks of "a crown of righteousness which God the righteous Judge shall give" "at that day" (2 Tim. iv. 8), I not only say with Augustine, "To whom could the righteous Judge give the crown if the merciful Father had not given grace, and how could there have been righteousness but for the precedence of grace which justifies the ungodly? how could these be paid as things due were not things not due previously given?" (August. ad Valent. de Grat. et Lib. Art.); but I also add, how could he impute righteousness to our works, did not his indulgence hide the unrighteousness that is in them? How could he deem them worthy of reward, did he not with boundless goodness destroy what is unworthy in them? Augustine is wont to give the name of grace to eternal life, because, while it is the recompense of works, it is bestowed by the gratuitous gifts of God. But Scripture humbles us more, and at the same time elevates us. For besides forbidding us to glory in works, because they are the gratuitous gifts of God, it tells us that they are

always defiled by some degrees of impurity, so that they cannot satisfy
God when they are tested by the standard of his justice; but that,
lest our activity should be destroyed, they please merely by pardon.
But though Augustine speaks somewhat differently from us, it is
plain from his words that the difference is more apparent than real.
After drawing a contrast between two individuals, the one with a life
holy and perfect almost to a miracle; the other honest indeed, and
of pure morals, yet not so perfect as not to leave much room for
desiring better, he at length infers, "He who seems inferior in conduct, yet on account of the true faith in God by which he lives (Hab.
ii. 4), and in conformity to which he accuses himself in all his faults,
praises God in all his good works, takes shame to himself, and ascribes
glory to God, from whom he receives both forgiveness for his sins,
and the love of well-doing, the moment he is set free from this life
is translated into the society of Christ. Why, but just on account
of his faith? For though it saves no man without works (such faith
being reprobate and not working by love), yet by means of it sins are
forgiven; for the just lives by faith: without it works which seem
good are converted into sins" (August. ad Bonifac., Lib. iii. c. 5).
Here he not obscurely acknowledges what we so strongly maintain,
that the righteousness of good works depends on their being approved
by God in the way of pardon.[1]

6. In a sense similar to the above passages our opponents quote
the following: "Make to yourselves friends of the mammon of unrighteousness; that when ye fail, they may receive you into everlasting habitations" (Luke xvi. 9). "Charge them that are rich in this
world, that they be not high-minded, nor trust in uncertain riches,
but in the living God, who giveth us richly all things to enjoy: that
they do good, that they be rich in good works, ready to distribute,
willing to communicate; laying up in store for themselves a good
foundation against the time to come, that they may lay hold on eternal
life" (1 Tim. vi. 17-19). For the good works which we enjoy in
eternal blessedness are compared to riches. I answer, that we shall
never attain to the true knowledge of these passages unless we attend
to the scope of the Spirit in uttering them. If it is true, as Christ
says, "Where your treasure is, there will your heart be also" (Matth.
vi. 21), then, as the children of the world are intent on providing
those things which form the delight of the present life, so it is the
duty of believers, after they have learned that this life will shortly
pass away like a dream, to take care that those things which they
would truly enjoy be transmitted thither where their entire life is to
be spent. We must, therefore, do like those who begin to remove to
any place where they mean to fix their abode. As they send forward
their effects, and grudge not to want them for a season, because they
think the more they have in their future residence the happier they
are; so, if we think that heaven is our country, we should send our

---

[1] The French adds, "C'est à dire, en misericorde, et non pas en jugement;"—that is
to say, in mercy, and not in judgment.

wealth thither rather than retain it here, where on our sudden departure it will be lost to us. But how shall we transmit it? By contributing to the necessities of the poor, the Lord imputing to himself
whatever is given to them. Hence that excellent promise, "He that
hath pity on the poor lendeth to the Lord" (Prov. xix. 17; Matth.
xxv. 40); and again, "He which soweth bountifully shall reap also
bountifully" (2 Cor. ix. 6). What we give to our brethren in the
exercise of charity is a deposit with the Lord, who, as a faithful de-
positary, will ultimately restore it with abundant interest. Are our
duties, then, of such value with God that they are as a kind of treasure
placed in his hand? Who can hesitate to say so when Scripture so
often and so plainly attests it? But if any one would leap from the
mere kindness of God to the merit of works,[1] his error will receive
no support from these passages. For all you can properly infer from
them is the inclination on the part of God to treat us with indulgence.
For, in order to animate us in well-doing, he allows no act of obedience, however unworthy of his eye, to pass unrewarded.

7. But they insist more strongly on the words of the apostle when,
in consoling the Thessalonians under their tribulations, he tells them
that these were sent, "that ye may be counted worthy of the kingdom
of God, for which ye also suffer; seeing it is a righteous thing with
God to recompense tribulation to them that trouble you; and to you
who are troubled, rest with us, when the Lord Jesus shall be revealed
from heaven with his mighty angels" (2 Thess. i. 5–7). The author
of the Epistle to the Hebrews says, "God is not unrighteous to forget your work and labour of love, which ye have showed towards his
name, in that ye have ministered to the saints, and do minister"
(Heb. vi. 10). To the former passage I answer, that the worthiness
spoken of is not that of merit, but as God the Father would have
those whom he has chosen for sons to be conformed to Christ the first
born, and as it behoved him first to suffer, and then to enter into his
glory, so we also, through much tribulation, enter the kingdom of
heaven. Therefore, while we suffer tribulation for the name of Christ,
we in a manner receive the marks with which God is wont to stamp
the sheep of his flock (Gal. vi. 17). Hence we are counted worthy
of the kingdom of God, because we bear in our body the· marks of
our Lord and Master, these being the insignia of the children of God.
In this sense are we to understand the passages: "Always bearing
about in the body the dying of the Lord Jesus, that the life also of
Jesus might be made manifest in our body" (2 Cor. iv. 10). "That
I may know him and the power of his resurrection, and the fellowship
of his sufferings, being made conformable unto his death" (Phil. iii.
10). The reason which is subjoined is intended not to prove any
merit, but to confirm our hope of the kingdom of God; as if he had
said, As it is befitting the just judgment of God to take vengeance

1 French, "Mais si quelcun pour obscurcir la benignité de Dieu veut establir la
dignité des œuvres;"—but if any one to obscure the benignity of God would establish
the dignity of works.

on your enemies for the tribulation which they have brought upon you, so it is also befitting to give you release and rest from these tribulations. The other passage, which speaks as if it were becoming the justice of God not to overlook the services of his people, and almost insinuates that it were unjust to forget them, is to be thus explained: God, to arouse us from sloth, assures us that every labour which we undertake for the glory of his name shall not be in vain. Let us always remember that this promise, like all other promises, will be of no avail unless it is preceded by the free covenant of mercy, on which the whole certainty of our salvation depends. Trusting to it, however, we ought to feel secure that, however unworthy our services, the liberality of God will not allow them to pass unrewarded. To confirm us in this expectation, the Apostle declares that God is not unrighteous; but will act consistently with the promise once given. Righteousness, therefore, refers rather to the truth of the divine promise than to the equity of paying what is due. In this sense there is a celebrated saying of Augustine, which, as containing a memorable sentiment, that holy man declined not repeatedly to employ, and which I think not unworthy of being constantly remembered: "Faithful is the Lord, who hath made himself our debtor, not by receiving anything from us, but by promising us all things" (August. in Ps. xxxii., cix., *et alibi*).

8. Our opponents also adduce the following passages from Paul: "Though I have all faith so that I could remove mountains, and have not charity, I am nothing" (1 Cor. xiii. 2). Again, "Now abideth faith, hope, charity, these three; but the greatest of these is charity" (1 Cor. 13). "Above all these things put on charity, which is the bond of perfectness" (Col. iii. 14). From the two first passages our Pharisees[1] contend that we are justified by charity rather than by faith, charity being, as they say, the better virtue. This mode of arguing is easily disposed of. I have elsewhere shown that what is said in the first passage refers not to true faith. In the second passage we admit that charity is said to be greater than true faith, but not because charity is more meritorious, but because it is more fruitful, because it is of wider extent, of more general service, and always flourishes, whereas the use of faith is only for a time. If we look to excellence, the love of God undoubtedly holds the first place. Of it, however, Paul does not here speak; for the only thing he insists on is, that we should by mutual charity edify one another in the Lord. But let us suppose that charity is in every respect superior to faith, what man of sound judgment, nay, what man with any soundness in his brain, would argue that it therefore does more to justify? The power of justifying which belongs to faith consists not in its worth as a work. Our justification depends entirely on the mercy of God and the merits of Christ: when faith apprehends these,

---

[1] See Calvin's Answer to Sadolet, who had said that charity is the first and principal cause of our salvation.

it is said to justify. Now, if you ask our opponents in what sense they ascribe justification to charity, they will answer, Being a duty acceptable to God, righteousness is in respect of its merit imputed to us by the acceptance of the divine goodness. Here you see how beautifully the argument proceeds. We say that faith justifies not because it merits justification for us by it own worth, but because it is an instrument by which we freely obtain the righteousness of Christ. They, overlooking the mercy of God, and passing by Christ, the sum of righteousness, maintain that we are justified by charity as being superior to faith; just as if one were to maintain that a king is fitter to make a shoe than a shoemaker, because the king is infinitely the superior of the two. This one syllogism is ample proof that all the schools of Sorbonne have never had the slightest apprehension of what is meant by justification by faith. Should any disputant here interpose, and ask why we give different meanings to the term faith as used by Paul in passages so near each other, I can easily show that I have not slight grounds for so doing. For while those gifts which Paul enumerates are in some degree subordinate to faith and hope, because they relate to the knowledge of God, he by way of summary comprehends them all under the name of faith and hope; as if he had said, Prophecy and tongues, and the gift of interpreting, and knowledge, are all designed to lead us to the knowledge of God. But in this life it is only by faith and hope that we acknowledge God. Therefore, when I name faith and hope, I at the same time comprehend the whole. "Now abideth faith, hope, charity, these three;" that is, how great soever the number of the gifts, they are all to be referred to them; but "the greatest of these is charity." From the third passage they infer, If charity is the bond of perfection, it must be the bond of righteousness, which is nothing else than perfection. First, without objecting that the name of perfection is here given by Paul to proper union among the members of a rightly constituted church, and admitting that by charity we are perfected before God, what new result do they gain by it? I will always object in reply, that we never attain to that perfection unless we fulfil all the parts of charity; and will thence infer, that as all are most remote from such fulfilment, the hope of perfection is excluded.

9. I am unwilling to discuss all the things which the foolish Sorbonnists have rashly laid hold of in Scripture as it chanced to come in their way, and throw out against us. Some of them are so ridiculous, that I cannot mention them without laying myself open to a charge of trifling. I will, therefore, conclude with an exposition of one of our Saviour's expressions with which they are wondrously pleased. When the lawyer asked him, "Good Master, what good thing shall I do, that I may have eternal life?" he answers, "If thou wilt enter into life, keep the commandments" (Matth. xix. 16, 17). What more (they ask) would we have, when the very author of grace bids us acquire the kingdom of heaven by the observance of the commandments? As if it were not plain that Christ adapted his answers

to the characters of those whom he addressed. Here he is questioned by a Doctor of the Law as to the means of obtaining eternal life ; and the question is not put simply, but is, What can men do to attain it ? Both the character of the speaker and his question induced our Lord to give this answer. Imbued with a persuasion of legal righteousness, the lawyer had a blind confidence in works. Then all he asked was, what are the works of righteousness by which salvation is obtained ? Justly, therefore, is he referred to the law, in which there is a perfect mirror of righteousness. We also distinctly declare, that if life is sought in works, the commandments are to be observed. And the knowledge of this doctrine is necessary to Christians ; for how should they betake themselves to Christ, unless they perceived that they had fallen from the path of life over the precipice of death ? Or how could they understand how far they have wandered from the way of life unles sthey previously understand what that way is ? Then only do they feel that the asylum of safety is in Christ when they see how much their conduct is at variance with the divine righteousness, which consists in the observance of the law. The sum of the whole is this, If salvation is sought in works, we must keep the commandments, by which we are instructed in perfect righteousness. But we cannot remain here unless we would stop short in the middle of our course ; for none of us is able to keep the commandments. Being thus excluded from the righteousness of the law, we must betake ourselves to another remedy—viz. to the faith of Christ. Wherefore, as a teacher of the law, whom our Lord knew to be puffed up with a vain confidence in works, was here directed by him to the law, that he might learn he was a sinner exposed to the fearful sentence of eternal death ; so others, who were already humbled with this knowledge, he elsewhere solaces with the promise of grace, without making any mention of the law. "Come unto me, all ye that labour and are heavy laden, and I will give you rest." "Take my yoke upon you, and learn of me; for I am meek and lowly in heart: and ye shall find rest unto your souls" (Matth. xi. 28, 29).

10. At length, after they have wearied themselves with perverting Scripture, they have recourse to subtleties and sophisms. One cavil is, that faith is somewhere called a work (John vi. 29) ; hence they infer that we are in error in opposing faith to works ; as if faith, regarded as obedience to the divine will, could by its own merit procure our justification, and did not rather, by embracing the mercy of God, thereby seal upon our hearts the righteousness of Christ, which is offered to us in the preaching of the Gospel. My readers will pardon me if I stay not to dispose of such absurdities ; their own weakness, without external assault, is sufficient to destroy them. One objection, however, which has some semblance of reason, it will be proper to dispose of in passing, lest it give any trouble to those less experienced. As common sense dictates that contraries must be tried by the same rule, and as each sin is charged against us as unright-

eousness, so it is right (say our opponents) that each good work should receive the praise of righteousness. The answer which some give, that the condemnation of men proceeds on unbelief alone, and not on particular sins, does not satisfy me. I agree with them, indeed, that infidelity is the fountain and root of all evil; for it is the first act of revolt from God, and is afterwards followed by particular transgressions of the law. But as they seem to hold, that in estimating righteousness and unrighteousness, the same rule is to be applied to good and bad works, in this I dissent from them.[1] The righteousness of works consists in perfect obedience to the law. Hence you cannot be jusitfied by works unless you follow this straight line (if I may so call it) during the whole course of your life. The moment you decline from it you have fallen into unrighteousness. Hence it appears, that righteousness is not obtained by few works, but by an indefatigable and inflexible observance of the divine will. But the rule with regard to unrighteousness is very different. The adulterer or the thief is by one act guilty of death, because he offends against the majesty of God. The blunder of these arguers of ours lies here: they attend not to the words of James, "Whosoever shall keep the whole law, and yet offend in one point, he is guilty of all. For he that said, Do not commit adultery, said also, Do not kill," &c. (James ii. 10, 11). Therefore, it should not seem absurd when we say that death is the just recompense of every sin, because each sin merits the just indignation and vengeance of God. But you reason absurdly if you infer the converse, that one good work will reconcile a man to God notwithstanding of his meriting wrath by many sins.

---

[1] French, "Mais touchant ce qu'ils semblent advis contrepoiser en une mesme balance les bonnes œuvres et les mauvaises, pour estimer la justice ou l'injustice de l'homme, en cela je suis contreint de leur repugner."—But as they seem disposed to put good and bad works into the opposite scales of the same balance, in order to estimate the righteousness or unrighteousness of man, in this I am forced to dissent from them.

CHAPTER XIX.

OF CHRISTIAN LIBERTY.

The three divisions of this chapter are,—1. Necessity of the doctrine of Christian Liberty, sec. 1. The principal parts of this liberty explained, sec. 2–8. II. The nature and efficacy of this liberty against the Epicureans and others who take no account whatever of the weak, sec. 9 and 10. III. Of offence given and received. A lengthened and not unnecessary discussion of this subject, sec. 11–16.

Sections.

1. Connection of this chapter with the previous ones on Justification. A true knowledge of Christian liberty useful and necessary. 1. It purifies the conscience. 2. It checks licentiousness. 3. It maintains the merits of Christ, the truth of the Gospel, and the peace of the soul.
2. This liberty consists of three parts. First, Believers renouncing the righteousness of the law, look only to Christ. Objection. Answer, distinguishing between Legal and Evangelical righteousness.
3. This first part clearly established by the whole Epistle to the Galatians.
4. The second part of Christian liberty—viz. that the conscience, freed from the yoke of the law, voluntarily obeys the will of God. This cannot be done so long as we are under the law. Reason.
5. When freed from the rigorous exactions of the law, we can cheerfully and with much alacrity answer the call of God.
6. Proof of this second part from an Apostle. The end of this liberty.
7. Third part of liberty—viz. the free use of things indifferent. The knowledge of this part necessary to remove despair and superstition. Superstition described.
8. Proof of this third part from the Epistle to the Romans. Those who observe it not only use evasion. 1. Despisers of God. 2. The desperate. 3. The ungrateful. The end and scope of this third part.
9. Second part of the chapter, showing the nature and efficacy of Christian liberty, in opposition to the Epicureans. Their character described. Pretext and allegation. Use of things indifferent. Abuse detected. Mode of correcting it.
10. This liberty maintained in opposition to those who pay no regard to the weak. Error of this class of men refuted. A most pernicious error. Objection. Reply.
11. Application of the doctrine of Christian liberty to the subject of offences. These of two kinds. Offence given. Offence received. Of offence given, a subject comprehended by few. Of Pharisaical offence, or offence received.
12. Who are to be regarded as weak and Pharisaical. Proved by examples and the doctrine of Paul. The just moderation of Christian liberty. Necessity of vindicating it. No regard to be paid to hypocrites. Duty of edifying our weak neighbours.
13. Application of the doctrine to things indifferent. Things necessary not to be omitted from any fear of offence.
14. Refutation of errors in regard to Christian liberty. The consciences of the godly not to be fettered by human traditions in matters of indifference.
15. Distinction to be made between Spiritual and Civil government. These must not be confounded. How far conscience can be bound by human constitutions. Definition of conscience. Definition explained by passages from the Apostolic writings.
16. The relation which conscience bears to external obedience : first, in things good and evil ; secondly, in things indifferent.

1. WE are now to treat of Christian Liberty, the explanation of which certainly ought not to be omitted by any one proposing to give

a compendious summary of Gospel doctrine. For it is a matter of primary necessity, one without the knowledge of which the conscience can scarcely attempt anything without hesitation, in many must demur and fluctuate, and in all proceed with fickleness and trepidation. In particular, it forms a proper appendix to Justification, and is of no little service in understanding its force. Nay, those who seriously fear God will hence perceive the incomparable advantages of a doctrine which wicked scoffers are constantly assailing with their jibes ; the intoxication of mind under which they labour leaving their petulance without restraint. This, therefore, seems the proper place for considering the subject. Moreover, though it has already been occasionally adverted to, there was an advantage in deferring the fuller consideration of it till now, for the moment any mention is made of Christian liberty lust begins to boil, or insane commotions arise, if a speedy restraint is not laid on those licentious spirits by whom the best things are perverted into the worst. For they either, under pretext of this liberty, shake off all obedience to God, and break out into unbridled licentiousness, or they feel indignant, thinking that all choice, order, and restraint, are abolished. What can we do when thus encompassed with straits ? Are we to bid adieu to Christian liberty, in order that we may cut off all opportunity for such perilous consequences ? But, as we have said, if the subject be not understood, neither Christ, nor the truth of the Gospel, nor the inward peace of the soul, is properly known. Our endeavour must rather be, while not suppressing this very necessary part of doctrine, to obviate the absurd objections to which it usually gives rise.

2. Christian liberty seems to me to consist of three parts. First, the consciences of believers, while seeking the assurance of their justification before God, must rise above the law, and think no more of obtaining justification by it. For while the law, as has already been demonstrated (*supra,* chap. xvii. sec. 1), leaves not one man righteous, we are either excluded from all hope of justification, or we must be loosed from the law, and so loosed as that no account at all shall be taken of works. For he who imagines that in order to obtain justification he must bring any degree of works whatever, cannot fix any mode or limit, but makes himself debtor to the whole law. Therefore, laying aside all mention of the law, and all idea of works, we must in the matter of justification have recourse to the mercy of God only ; turning away our regard from ourselves, we must look only to Christ. For the question is, not how we may be righteous, but how, though unworthy and unrighteous, we may be regarded as righteous. If consciences would obtain any assurance of this, they must give no place to the law. Still it cannot be rightly inferred from this that believers have no need of the law. It ceases not to teach, exhort, and urge them to good, although it is not recognised by their consciences before the judgment-seat of God. The two things are very different, and should be well and carefully distinguished. The whole lives of Christians ought to be a kind of aspiration after piety, seeing they

are called unto holiness (Eph. i. 4; 1 Thess. iv. 5). The office of the law is to excite them to the study of purity and holiness, by reminding them of their duty. For when the conscience feels anxious as to how it may have the favour of God, as to the answer it could give, and the confidence it would feel, if brought to his judgment-seat, in such a case the requirements of the law are not to be brought forward, but Christ, who surpasses all the perfection of the law, is alone to be held forth for righteousness.

3. On this almost the whole subject of the Epistle to the Galatians hinges; for it can be proved from express passages that those are absurd interpreters who teach that Paul there contends only for freedom from ceremonies. Of such passages are the following: "Christ hath redeemed us from the curse of the law, being made a curse for us." "Stand fast, therefore, in the liberty wherewith Christ has made us free, and be not entangled again with the yoke of bondage. Behold, I Paul say unto you, that if ye be circumcised, Christ shall profit you nothing. For I testify again to every man that is circumcised, that he is a debtor to do the whole law. Christ is become of no effect unto you, whosoever of you are justified by the law; ye are fallen from grace" (Gal. iii. 13; v. 1–4). These words certainly refer to something of a higher order than freedom from ceremonies. I confess, indeed, that Paul there treats of ceremonies, because he was contending with false apostles, who were plotting to bring back into the Christian Church those ancient shadows of the law which were abolished by the advent of Christ. But, in discussing this question, it was necessary to introduce higher matters, on which the whole controversy turns. First, because the brightness of the Gospel was obscured by those Jewish shadows, he shows that in Christ we have a full manifestation of all those things which were typified by Mosaic ceremonies. Secondly, as those impostors instilled into the people the most pernicious opinion, that this obedience was sufficient to merit the grace of God, he insists very strongly that believers shall not imagine that they can obtain justification before God by any works, far less by those paltry observances. At the same time, he shows that by the cross of Christ they are free from the condemnation of the law, to which otherwise all men are exposed, so that in Christ alone they can rest in full security. This argument is pertinent to the present subject (Gal. iv. 5, 21, &c.). Lastly, he asserts the right of believers to liberty of conscience, a liberty which may not be restrained without necessity.

4. Another point which depends on the former is, that consciences obey the law, not as if compelled by legal necessity; but being free from the yoke of the law itself, voluntarily obey the will of God. Being constantly in terror so long as they are under the dominion of the law, they are never disposed promptly to obey God, unless they have previously obtained this liberty. Our meaning shall be explained more briefly and clearly by an example. The command of the law is, " Thou shalt love the Lord thy God with all thine heart,

and with all thy soul, and with all thy might" (Deut. vi. 5). To accomplish this, the soul must previously be divested of every other thought and feeling, the heart purified from all its desires, all its powers collected and united on this one object. Those who, in comparison of others, have made much progress in the way of the Lord, are still very far from this goal. For although they love God in their mind, and with a sincere affection of heart, yet both are still in a great measure occupied with the lusts of the flesh, by which they are retarded and prevented from proceeding with quickened pace towards God. They indeed make many efforts, but the flesh partly enfeebles their strength, and partly binds them to itself. What can they do while they thus feel that there is nothing of which they are less capable than to fulfil the law? They wish, aspire, endeavour; but do nothing with the requisite perfection. If they look to the law, they see that every work which they attempt or design is accursed. Nor can any one deceive himself by inferring that the work is not altogether bad, merely because it is imperfect, and, therefore, that any good which is in it is still accepted of God. For the law demanding perfect love condemns all imperfection, unless its rigour is mitigated. Let any man therefore consider his work which he wishes to be thought partly good, and he will find that it is a transgression of the law by the very circumstance of its being imperfect.

5. See how our works lie under the curse of the law if they are tested by the standard of the law. But how can unhappy souls set themselves with alacrity to a work from which they cannot hope to gain anything in return but cursing? On the other hand, if freed from this severe exaction, or rather from the whole rigour of the law, they hear themselves invited by God with paternal lenity, they will cheerfully and alertly obey the call, and follow his guidance. In one word, those who are bound by the yoke of the law are like servants who have certain tasks daily assigned them by their masters. Such servants think that nought has been done; and they dare not come into the presence of their masters until the exact amount of labour has been performed. But sons who are treated in a more candid and liberal manner by their parents, hesitate not to offer them works that are only begun or half finished, or even with something faulty in them, trusting that their obedience and readiness of mind will be accepted, although the performance be less exact than was wished. Such should be our feelings, as we certainly trust that our most indulgent Parent will approve our services, however small they may be, and however rude and imperfect. Thus He declares to us by the prophet, "I will spare them as a man spareth his own son that serveth him" (Mal. iii. 17); where the word *spare* evidently means indulgence, or connivance at faults, while at the same time service is remembered. This confidence is necessary in no slight degree, since without it everything should be attempted in vain; for

God does not regard any work of ours as done to himself, unless truly done from a desire to serve him. But how can this be amidst these terrors, while we doubt whether God is offended or served by our work?

6. This is the reason why the author of the Epistle to the Hebrews ascribes to faith all the good works which the holy patriarchs are said to have performed, and estimates them merely by faith (Heb. xi. 2). In regard to this liberty there is a remarkable passage in the Epistle to the Romans, where Paul argues, "Sin shall not have dominion over you; for ye are not under the law, but under grace" (Rom. vi. 14). For after he had exhorted believers, "Let not sin therefore reign in your mortal body, that ye should obey it in the lusts thereof: Neither yield ye your members as instruments of un-righteousness unto sin; but yield yourselves unto God, as those that are alive from the dead, and your members as instruments of right-eousness unto God;" they might have objected that they still bore about with them a body full of lust, that sin still dwelt in them. He therefore comforts them by adding, that they are freed from the law; as if he had said, Although you feel that sin is not yet extin-guished, and that righteousness does not plainly live in you, you have no cause for fear and dejection, as if God were always offended because of the remains of sin, since by grace you are freed from the law, and your works are not tried by its standard. Let those, how-ever, who infer that they may sin because they are not under the law, understand that they have no right to this liberty, the en d of which is to encourage us in well-doing.

7. The third part of this liberty is, that we are not bound before God to any observance of external things which are in themselves indifferent (ἀδιάφορα), but that we are now at full liberty either to use or omit them. The knowledge of this liberty is very necessary to us; where it is wanting our consciences will have no rest, there will be no end .of superstition. In the present day many think us absurd in raising a question as to the free eating of flesh, the free use of dress and holidays, and similar frivolous trifles, as they think them; but they are of more importance than is commonly supposed. For when once the conscience is entangled in the net, it enters a long and inextricable labyrinth, from which it is afterwards most difficult to escape. When a man begins to doubt whether it is law-ful for him to use linen for sheets, shirts, napkins, and handkerchiefs, he will not long be secure as to hemp, and will at last have doubts as to tow; for he will revolve in his mind whether he cannot sup without napkins, or dispense with handkerchiefs, Should he deem a daintier food unlawful, he will afterwards feel uneasy for using loaf-bread and common eatables, because he will think that his body might possibly be supported on a still meaner food. If he hesitates as to a more genial wine, he will scarcely drink the worst with a good conscience; at last he will not dare to touch water if more than

usually sweet and pure. In fine, he will come to this, that he will deem it criminal to trample on a straw lying in his way. For it is no trivial dispute that is here commenced, the point in debate being, whether the use of this thing or that is in accordance with the divine will, which ought to take precedence of all our acts and counsels. Here some must by despair be hurried into an abyss, while others, despising God and casting off his fear, will not be able to make a way for themselves without ruin. When men are involved in such doubts, whatever be the direction in which they turn, everything they see must offend their conscience.

8. "I know," says Paul, "that there is nothing unclean of itself" (by unclean meaning unholy); "but to him that esteemeth anything to be unclean, to him it is unclean" (Rom. xiv. 14). By these words he makes all external things subject to our liberty, provided the nature of that liberty approves itself to our minds as before God. But if any superstitious idea suggests scruples, those things which in their own nature were pure are to us contaminated. Wherefore the apostle adds, "Happy is he that condemneth not himself in that which he alloweth. And he that doubteth is damned if he eat, because he eateth not of faith: for whatsoever is not of faith is sin" (Rom. xiv. 22, 23). When men, amid such difficulties, proceed with greater confidence, securely doing whatever pleases them, do they not in so far revolt from God? Those who are thoroughly impressed with some fear of God, if forced to do many things repugnant to their conscience, are discouraged and filled with dread. All such persons receive none of the gifts of God with thanksgiving, by which alone Paul declares that all things are sanctified for our use (1 Tim. iv. 5). By thanksgiving I understand that which proceeds from a mind recognising the kindness and goodness of God in his gifts. For many, indeed, understand that the blessings which they enjoy are the gifts of God, and praise God in their works; but not being persuaded that these have been given to them, how can they give thanks to God as the giver? In one word, we see whither this liberty tends—viz. that we are to use the gifts of God without any scruple of conscience, without any perturbation of mind, for the purpose for which he gave them: in this way our souls may both have peace with him, and recognise his liberality towards us. For here are comprehended all ceremonies of free observance, so that while our consciences are not to be laid under the necessity of observing them, we are also to remember that, by the kindness of God, the use of them is made subservient to edification.

9. It is, however, to be carefully observed, that Christian liberty is in all its parts a spiritual matter, the whole force of which consists in giving peace to trembling consciences, whether they are anxious and disquieted as to the forgiveness of sins, or as to whether their imperfect works, polluted by the infirmities of the flesh, are pleasing to God, or are perplexed as to the use of things indifferent. It is, therefore, perversely interpreted by those who use it as a cloak for

their lusts, and they may licentiously abuse the good gifts of God, or who think there is no liberty unless it is used in the presence of men, and, accordingly, in using it pay no regard to their weak brethren. Under this head, the sins of the present age are more numerous. For there is scarcely any one whose means allow him to live sumptuously, who does not delight in feasting, and dress, and the luxurious grandeur of his house, who wishes not to surpass his neighbour in every kind of delicacy, and does not plume himself amazingly on his splendour. And all these things are defended under the pretext of Christian liberty. They say they are things indifferent: I admit it, provided they are used indifferently. But when they are too eagerly longed for, when they are proudly boasted of, when they are indulged in luxurious profusion, things which otherwise were in themselves lawful are certainly defiled by these vices. Paul makes an admirable distinction in regard to things indifferent: "Unto the pure all things are pure: but unto them that are defiled and unbelieving is nothing pure; but even their mind and conscience is defiled" (Tit. i. 15). For why is a woe pronounced upon the rich who have received their consolation? (Luke vi. 24), who are full, who laugh now, who "lie upon beds of ivory, and stretch themselves upon their couches;" "join house to house," and "lay field to field;" "and the harp and the viol, the tabret and pipe, and wine, are in their feasts?" (Amos. vi. 6; Is. v. 8, 10). Certainly ivory and gold, and riches, are the good creatures of God, permitted, nay, destined, by divine providence for the use of man; nor was it ever forbidden to laugh, or to be full, or to add new to old and hereditary possessions, or to be delighted with music, or to drink wine. This is true, but when the means are supplied, to roll and wallow in luxury, to intoxicate the mind and soul with present, and be always hunting after new pleasures, is very far from a legitimate use of the gifts of God. Let them, therefore, suppress immoderate desire, immoderate profusion, vanity, and arrogance, that they may use the gifts of God purely with a pure conscience. When their mind is brought to this state of soberness, they will be able to regulate the legitimate use. On the other hand, when this moderation is wanting, even plebeian and ordinary delicacies are excessive. For it is a true saying, that a haughty mind often dwells in a coarse and homely garb, while true humility lurks under fine linen and purple. Let every one then live in his own station, poorly or moderately, or in splendour; but let all remember that the nourishment which God gives is for life, not luxury, and let them regard it as the law of Christian liberty, to learn with Paul in whatever state they are, "therewith to be content," to know "both how to be abased," and "how to abound," "to be full and to be hungry, both to abound and to suffer need" (Phil. iv. 11).

10. Very many also err in this: as if their liberty were not safe and entire, without having men to witness it, they use it indiscriminately and imprudently, and in this way often give offence to weak brethren. You may see some in the present day who cannot think

they possess their liberty unless they come into possession of it by eating flesh on Friday. Their eating I blame not, but this false notion must be driven from their minds : for they ought to think that their liberty gains nothing new by the sight of men, but is to be enjoyed before God, and consists as much in abstaining as in using. If they understand that it is of no consequence in the sight of God whether they eat flesh or eggs, whether they are clothed in red or in black, this is amply sufficient. The conscience to which the benefit of this liberty was due is loosed. Therefore, though they should afterwards, during their whole life, abstain from flesh, and constantly wear one colour, they are not less free. Nay, just because they are free, they abstain with a free conscience. But they err most egregiously in paying no regard to the infirmity of their brethren, with which it becomes us to bear, so as not rashly to give them offence. But[1] it is sometimes also of consequence that we should assert our liberty before men. This I admit : yet must we use great caution in the mode, lest we should cast off the care of the weak whom God has specially committed to us.

11. I will here make some observations on offences, what distinctions are to be made between them, what kind are to be avoided and what disregarded. This will afterwards enable us to determine what scope there is for our liberty among men. We are pleased with the common division into *offence given* and *offence taken*, since it has the plain sanction of Scripture, and not improperly expresses what is meant. If from unseasonable levity or wantonness, or rashness, you do anything out of order or not in its own place, by which the weak or unskilful are offended, it may be said that offence has been *given* by you, since the ground of offence is owing to your fault. And in general, offence is said to be *given* in any matter where the person from whom it has proceeded is in fault. Offence is said to be *taken* when a thing otherwise done, not wickedly or unseasonably, is made an occasion of offence from malevolence or some sinister feeling. For here offence was not given, but sinister interpreters causelessly take offence. By the former kind, the weak only, by the latter, the ill-tempered and Pharisaical are offended. Wherefore, we shall call the one the offence of the weak, the other the offence of Pharisees, and we will so temper the use of our liberty as to make it yield to the ignorance of weak brethren, but not to the austerity of Pharisees. What is due to infirmity is fully shown by Paul in many passages. "Him that is weak in the faith receive ye." Again, "Let us not judge one another any more : but judge this rather, that no man put a stumbling-block, or an occasion to fall, in his brother's way ;" and many others to the same effect in the same place, to which, instead of quoting them here, we refer the reader. The sum is, "We then that are strong ought to bear the infirmities of the weak, and not to please ourselves. Let every one of us please his neighbour for his

---

1 French, "Mais quelcun dira;"—But some one will say.

good to edification." Elsewhere he says, "Take heed lest by any means this liberty of yours become a stumbling-block to them that are weak." Again, "Whatsoever is sold in the shambles, that eat, asking no question for conscience sake." "Conscience, I say, not thine own, but of the other." Finally, "Give none offence, neither to the Jews, nor to the Gentiles, nor to the Church of God." Also in another passage, "Brethren, ye have been called into liberty, only use not liberty for an occasion to the flesh, but by love serve one another."[1] Thus, indeed, it is: our liberty was not given us against our weak neighbours, whom charity enjoins us to serve in all things, but rather that, having peace with God in our minds, we should live peaceably among men. What value is to be set upon the offence of the Pharisees we learn from the words of our Lord, in which he says, "Let them alone: they be blind leaders of the blind" (Matth. xv. 14). The disciples had intimated that the Pharisees were offended at his words. He answers, that they are to be let alone, that their offence is not to be regarded.

12. The matter still remains uncertain, unless we understand who are the weak and who the Pharisees; for if this distinction is destroyed, I see not how, in regard to offences, any liberty at all would remain without being constantly in the greatest danger. But Paul seems to me to have marked out most clearly, as well by example as by doctrine, how far our liberty, in the case of offence, is to be modified or maintained. When he adopts Timothy as his companion, he circumcises him: nothing can induce him to circumcise Titus (Acts xvi. 3; Gal. ii. 3). The acts are different, but there is no difference in the purpose or intention; in circumcising Timothy, as he was free from all men, he made himself the servant of all: "Unto the Jews I became as a Jew, that I might gain the Jews; to them that are under the law, as under the law, that I might gain them that are under the law; to them that are without law, as without law (being not without law to God, but under the law to Christ), that I might gain them that are without law. To the weak became I as weak, that I might gain the weak: I am made all things to all men, that I might by all means save some" (1 Cor. ix. 20-22). We have here the proper modification of liberty, when in things indifferent it can be restrained with some advantage. What he had in view in firmly resisting the circumcision of Titus, he himself testifies when he thus writes: "But neither Titus, who was with me, being a Greek, was compelled to be circumcised: and that because of false brethren unawares brought in, who came in privily to spy out our liberty which we have in Christ Jesus, that they might bring us into bondage: to whom we gave place by subjection, no, not for an hour, that the truth of the gospel might continue with you" (Gal. ii. 3-5). We here see the necessity of vindicating our liberty when, by the unjust exactions of false apostles, it is

[1] Rom. xiv. 1, 13; xv. 1; 1 Cor. viii. 9; x. 25, 29, 32; Gal. v. 13.

brought into danger with weak consciences. In all cases we must study charity, and look to the edification of our neighbour. " All things are lawful for me," says he, " but all things are not expedient ; all things are lawful for me, but all things edify not. Let no man seek his own, but every man another's wealth" (1 Cor. x. 23, 24). There is nothing plainer than this rule, that we are to use our liberty if it tends to the edification of our neighbour, but if inexpedient for our neighbour, we are to abstain from it. There are some who pretend to imitate this prudence of Paul by abstinence from liberty, while there is nothing for which they less employ it than for purposes of charity. Consulting their own ease, they would have all mention of liberty buried though it is not less for the interest of our neighbour to use liberty for their good and edification, than to modify it occasionally for their advantage. It is the part of a pious man to think, that the free power conceded to him in external things is to make him the readier in all offices of charity.

13. Whatever I have said about avoiding offences, I wish to be referred to things indifferent.[1] Things which are necessary to be done cannot be omitted from any fear of offence. For as our liberty is to be made subservient to charity, so charity must in its turn be subordinate to purity of faith. Here, too, regard must be had to charity, but it must go as far as the altar ; that is, we must not offend God for the sake of our neighbour. We approve not of the intemperance of those who do everything tumultuously, and would rather burst through every restraint at once than proceed step by step. But neither are those to be listened to who, while they take the lead in a thousand forms of impiety, pretend that they act thus to avoid giving offence to their neighbour, as if in the meantime they did not train the consciences of their neighbours to evil, especially when they always stick in the same mire without any hope of escape. When a neighbour is to be instructed, whether by doctrine or by example, then smooth-tongued men say that he is to be fed with milk, while they are instilling into him the worst and most pernicious opinions. Paul says to the Corinthians, "I have fed you with milk, and not with meat" (1 Cor. iii. 2); but had there then been a Popish mass among them, would he have sacrificed as one of the modes of giving them milk ? By no means : milk is not poison. It is false then to say they nourish those whom, under a semblance of soothing, they cruelly murder. But granting that such dissimulation may be used for a time, how long are they to make their pupils drink that kind of milk ? If they never grow up so as to be able to bear at least some gentle food, it is certain that they have never been reared on milk.[2] Two reasons prevent me from now entering farther into contest with these people : first, their follies are scarcely worthy of refutation, seeing all men of sense must nauseate them ; and,

1 The French adds, "Lesquelles ne sont de soy ne bonnes ne mauvais ;"—which in themselves are neither good nor bad.
2 French, " de bon laict ;"—good milk.

secondly, having already amply refuted them in special treatises, I am unwilling to do it over again.[1] Let my readers only bear in mind, first, that whatever be the offences by which Satan and the world attempt to lead us away from the law of God, we must nevertheless strenuously proceed in the course which he prescribes; and, secondly, that whatever dangers impend, we are not at liberty to deviate one nail's breadth from the command of God, that on no pretext is it lawful to attempt anything but what he permits.

14. Since by means of this privilege of liberty which we have described, believers have derived authority from Christ not to entangle themselves by the observance of things in which he wished them to be free, we conclude that their consciences are exempted from all human authority. For it were unbecoming that the gratitude due to Christ for his liberal gift should perish, or that the consciences of believers should derive no benefit from it. We must not regard it as a trivial matter when we see how much it cost our Saviour, being purchased not with silver or gold, but with his own blood (1 Pet. i. 18, 19); so that Paul hesitates not to say that Christ has died in vain, if we place our souls under subjection to men (Gal. v. 1, 4; 1 Cor. vii. 23). Several chapters of the Epistle to the Galatians are wholly occupied with showing that Christ is obscured, or rather extinguished to us, unless our consciences maintain their liberty; from which they have certainly fallen, if they can be bound with the chains of laws and constitutions at the pleasure of men. But as the knowledge of this subject is of the greatest importance, so it demands a longer and clearer exposition. For the moment the abolition of human constitutions is mentioned, the greatest disturbances are excited, partly by the seditious, and partly by calumniators, as if obedience of every kind were at the same time abolished and overthrown.

15. Therefore, lest this prove a stumbling-block to any, let us observe that in man government is twofold: the one spiritual, by which the conscience is trained to piety and divine worship; the other civil, by which the individual is instructed in those duties which, as men and citizens, we are bound to perform (see Book IV. chap. x. sec. 3–6). To these two forms are commonly given the not inappropriate names of spiritual and temporal jurisdiction, intimating that the former species has reference to the life of the soul, while the latter relates to matters of the present life, not only to food and clothing, but to the enacting of laws which require a man to live among his fellows purely, honourably, and modestly. The former has its seat within the soul, the latter only regulates the external conduct. We may call the one the spiritual, the other the civil kingdom. Now, these two, as we have divided them, are always to be viewed apart from each other. When the one is considered, we should call off our minds, and not allow them to think of the other.

---

[1] See Epist. de Fugiendis Impiorum Illicitis Sacris. Also Epist. de Abjiciendis vel Administrandis Sacerdotiis Also the short treatise, De Vitandis Superstitionibus.

For there exists in man a kind of two worlds, over which different kings and different laws can preside. By attending to this distinction, we will not erroneously transfer the doctrine of the gospel concerning spiritual liberty to civil order, as if in regard to external government Christians were less subject to human laws, because their consciences are unbound before God, as if they were exempted from all carnal service, because in regard to the Spirit they are free. Again, because even in those constitutions which seem to relate to the spiritual kingdom, there may be some delusion, it is necessary to distinguish between those which are to be held legitimate as being agreeable to the word of God, and those, on the other hand, which ought to have no place among the pious. We shall elsewhere have an opportunity of speaking of civil government (see Book IV. chap. xx.). For the present, also, I defer speaking of ecclesiastical laws, because that subject will be more fully discussed in the Fourth Book when we come to treat of the Power of the Church. We would thus conclude the present discussion. The question, as I have said, though not very obscure, or perplexing in itself, occasions difficulty to many, because they do not distinguish with sufficient accuracy between what is called the external *forum*, and the *forum* of conscience. What increases the difficulty is, that Paul commands us to obey the magistrate, "not only for wrath, but also for conscience sake" (Rom. xiii. 1, 5). Whence it follows that civil laws also bind the conscience. Were this so, then what we said a little ago, and are still to say of spiritual government, would fall. To solve this difficulty, the first thing of importance is to understand what is meant by *conscience*. The definition must be sought in the etymology of the word. For as men, when they apprehend the knowledge of things by the mind and intellect, are said to know, and hence arises the term knowledge or *science*, so when they have a sense of the divine justice added as a witness which allows them not to conceal their sins, but drags them forward as culprits to the bar of God, that sense is called *conscience*. For it stands as it were between God and man, not suffering man to suppress what he knows in himself; but following him on even to conviction. It is this that Paul means when he says, "Their conscience also bearing witness, and their thoughts the meanwhile accusing, or else excusing one another" (Rom. ii. 15). Simple knowledge may exist in man, as it were shut up; therefore this sense, which sists man before the bar of God, is set over him as a kind of sentinel to observe and spy out all his secrets, that nothing may remain buried in darkness. Hence the ancient proverb, Conscience is a thousand witnesses. For the same reason Peter also employs the expression, "the answer of a good conscience" (1 Pet. iii. 21), for tranquillity of mind; when persuaded of the grace of Christ, we boldly present ourselves before God. And the author of the Epistle to the Hebrews says, that we have "no more conscience of sins" (Heb. x. 2), that we are held as freed or acquitted, so that sin no longer accuses us.

16. Wherefore, as works have respect to men, so conscience bears reference to God, a good conscience being nothing else than inward integrity of heart. In this sense Paul says, that "the end of the commandment is charity, out of a pure heart, and of a good conscience, and of faith unfeigned" (1 Tim. i. 5). He afterwards, in the same chapter, shows how much it differs from intellect when he speaks of "holding faith, and a good conscience; which some having put away, have made shipwreck" (1 Tim. i. 19). For by these words he intimates, that it is a lively inclination to serve God, a sincere desire to live in piety and holiness. Sometimes, indeed, it is even extended to men, as when Paul testifies, "Herein do I exercise myself, to have always a conscience void of offence toward God, and toward men" (Acts xxiv. 16). He speaks thus, because the fruits of a good conscience go forth and reach even to men. But, as I have said, properly speaking, it refers to God only. Hence a law is said to bind the conscience, because it simply binds the individual, without looking at men, or taking any account of them. For example, God not only commands us to keep our mind chaste and pure from lust, but prohibits all external lasciviousness or obscenity of language. My conscience is subjected to the observance of this law, though there were not another man in the world, and he who violates it sins not only by setting a bad example to his brethren, but stands convicted in his conscience before God. The same rule does not hold in things indifferent. We ought to abstain from everything that produces offence, but with a free conscience. Thus Paul, speaking of meat consecrated to idols, says, "If any man say unto you, This is offered in sacrifice unto idols, eat not for his sake that showed it, and for conscience sake:" "Conscience, I say, not thine own, but of the other" (1 Cor. x. 28, 29). A believer, after being previously admonished, would sin were he still to eat meat so offered. But though abstinence, on his part, is necessary, in respect of a brother, as it is prescribed by God, still he ceases not to retain liberty of conscience. We see how the law, while binding the external act, leaves the conscience unbound.

CHAPTER XX.

OF PRAYER—A PERPETUAL EXERCISE OF FAITH. THE DAILY
BENEFITS DERIVED FROM IT.

The principal divisions of this chapter are,—I. Connection of the subject of prayer
with the previous chapters. The nature of prayer, and its necessity as a Christian
exercise, sec. 1, 2. II. To whom prayer is to be offered. Refutation of an objection
which is too apt to present itself to the mind, sec. 3. III. Rules to be observed in
prayer, sec. 4–16. IV. Through whom prayer is to be made, sec. 17–19. V. Refutation of an error as to the doctrine of our Mediator and Intercessor, with answers to the
leading arguments urged in support of the intercession of saints, sec. 20–27. VI. The
nature of prayer, and some of its accidents, sec. 28–33. VII. A perfect form of invocation, or an exposition of the Lord's Prayer, sec. 34–50. VIII. Some rules to be observed
with regard to prayer, as time, perseverance, the feeling of the mind, and the assurance
of faith, sec. 50–52.

Sections.

1. A general summary of what is contained in the previous part of the work. A transition to the doctrine of prayer. Its connection with the subject of faith.
2. Prayer defined. Its necessity and use.
3. Objection, that prayer seems useless, because God already knows our wants.
   Answer, from the institution and end of prayer. Confirmation by example. Its
   necessity and propriety. Perpetually reminds us of our duty, and leads to
   meditation on divine providence. Conclusion. Prayer a most useful exercise.
   This proved by three passages of Scripture.
4. Rules to be observed in prayer. First, reverence to God. How the mind ought to
   be composed.
5. All giddiness of mind must be excluded, and all our feelings seriously engaged.
   This confirmed by the form of lifting the hand in prayer. We must ask only in
   so far as God permits. To help our weakness, God gives the Spirit to be our
   guide in prayer. What the office of the Spirit in this respect. We must still
   pray both with the heart and the lips.
6. Second rule of prayer, a sense of our want. This rule violated, 1. By perfunctory
   and formal prayer. 2. By hypocrites, who have no sense of their sins. 3. By
   giddiness in prayer. Remedies.
7. Objection, that we are not always under the same necessity of praying. Answer,
   we must pray always. This answer confirmed by an examination of the dangers
   by which both our life and our salvation are every moment threatened. Confirmed farther by the command and permission of God, by the nature of true repentance, and a consideration of impenitence. Conclusion.
8. Third rule, the suppression of all pride. Examples. Daniel, David, Isaiah, Jeremiah, Baruch.
9. Advantage of thus suppressing pride. It leads to earnest entreaty for pardon,
   accompanied with humble confession and sure confidence in the Divine mercy.
   This may not always be expressed in words. It is peculiar to pious penitents.
   A general introduction to procure favour to our prayers never to be omitted.
10. Objection to the third rule of prayer. Of the glorying of the saints. Answer.
    Confirmation of the answer.
11. Fourth rule of prayer,—a sure confidence of being heard animating us to prayer.
    The kind of confidence required—viz. a serious conviction of our misery, joined
    with sure hope. From these true prayer springs. How diffidence impairs prayer.
    In general, faith is required.
12 This faith and sure hope regarded by our opponents as most absurd. Their error

described and refuted by various passages of Scripture, which show that acceptable prayer is accompanied with these qualities. No repugnance between this certainty and an acknowledgment of our destitution.

13. To our unworthiness we oppose, 1. The command of God. 2. The promise. Rebels and hypocrites completely condemned. Passages of Scripture confirming the command to pray.

14. Other passages respecting the promises which belong to the pious when they invoke God. These realised though we are not possessed of the same holiness as other distinguished servants of God, provided we indulge no vain confidence, and sincerely betake ourselves to the mercy of God. Those who do not invoke God under urgent necessity are no better than idolaters. This concurrence of fear and confidence reconciles the different passages of Scripture, as to humbling ourselves in prayer, and causing our prayers to ascend.

15. Objection founded on some examples—viz. that prayers have proved effectual, though not according to the form prescribed. Answer. Such examples, though not given for our imitation, are of the greatest use. 2. Objection, the prayers of the faithful sometimes not effectual. Answer confirmed by a noble passage of Augustine. Rule for right prayer.

16. The above four rules of prayer not so rigidly exacted, as that every prayer deficient in them in any respect is rejected by God. This shown by examples. Conclusion, or summary of this section.

17. Through whom God is to be invoked—viz. Jesus Christ. This founded on a consideration of the divine majesty, and the precept and promise of God himself. God therefore to be invoked only in the name of Christ.

18. From the first all believers were heard through him only: yet this specially restricted to the period subsequent to his ascension. The ground of this restriction.

19. The wrath of God lies on those who reject Christ as a Mediator. This excludes not the mutual intercession of saints on the earth.

20. Refutation of errors interfering with the intercession of Christ. 1. Christ the Mediator of redemption; the saints mediators of intercession. Answer confirmed by the clear testimony of Scripture, and by a passage from Augustine. The nature of Christ's intercession.

21. Of the intercession of saints living with Christ in heaven. Fiction of the Papists in regard to it. Refuted. 1. Its absurdity. 2. It is nowhere mentioned by Scripture. 3. Appeal to the conscience of the superstitious. 4. Its blasphemy. Exception. Answers.

22. Monstrous errors resulting from this fiction. Refutation. Exception by the advocates of this fiction. Answer.

23. Arguments of the Papists for the intercession of saints. 1. From the duty and office of angels. Answer. 2. From an expression of Jeremiah respecting Moses and Samuel. Answer, retorting the argument. 3. The meaning of the prophet confirmed by a similar passage in Ezekiel, and the testimony of an apostle.

24. 4. Fourth papistical argument from the nature of charity, which is more perfect in the saints in glory. Answer.

25. Argument founded on a passage in Moses. Answer.

26. Argument from its being said that the prayers of saints are heard. Answer, confirmed by Scripture, and illustrated by examples.

27. Conclusion, that the saints cannot be invoked without impiety. 1. It robs God of his glory. 2. Destroys the intercession of Christ. 3. Is repugnant to the word of God. 4. Is opposed to the due method of prayer. 5. Is without approved example. 6. Springs from distrust. Last objection. Answer.

28. Kinds of prayer. Vows. Supplications. Petitions. Thanksgiving. Connection of these, their constant use and necessity. Particular explanation confirmed by reason, Scripture, and example. Rule as to supplication and thanksgiving.

29. The accidents of prayer—viz. private and public, constant, at stated seasons, &c. Exception in time of necessity. Prayer without ceasing. Its nature. Garrulity of Papists and hypocrites refuted. The scope and parts of prayer. Secret prayer. Prayer at all places. Private and public prayer.

30. Of public places or churches in which common prayers are offered up. Right use of churches. Abuse.

31. Of utterance and singing. These of no avail if not from the heart. The use of the voice refers more to public than private prayer.

32. Singing of the greatest antiquity, but not universal. How to be performed.

33. Public prayers should be in the vulgar, not in a foreign tongue. Reason, 1. The

1. FROM the previous part of the work we clearly see how com-

pletely destitute man is of all good, how devoid of every means of procuring his own salvation. Hence, if he would obtain succour in his necessity, he must go beyond himself, and procure it in some other quarter. It has farther been shown that the Lord kindly and spontaneously manifests himself in Christ, in whom he offers all happiness for our misery, all abundance for our want, opening up the treasures of heaven to us, so that we may turn with full faith to his beloved Son, depend upon him with full expectation, rest in him, and cleave to him with full hope. This, indeed, is that secret and hidden philosophy which cannot be learned by syllogisms, a philosophy thoroughly understood by those whose eyes God has so opened as to see light in his light. But after we have learned by faith to know that whatever is necessary for us or defective in us is supplied in God and in our Lord Jesus Christ, in whom it hath pleased the Father that all fulness should dwell, that we may thence draw as from an inexhaustible fountain, it remains for us to seek and in prayer implore of him what we have learned to be in him. To know God as the sovereign disposer of all good, inviting us to present our requests, and yet not to approach or ask of him, were so far from availing us, that it were just as if one told of a treasure were to allow it to remain buried in the ground. Hence the Apostle, to show that a faith unaccompanied with prayer to God cannot be genuine, states this to be the order: As faith springs from the Gospel, so by faith our hearts are framed to call upon the name of God (Rom. x. 14). And this is the very thing which he had expressed some time before—viz. that the *Spirit of adoption*, which seals the testimony of the Gospel on our hearts, gives us courage to make our requests known unto God, calls forth groanings which cannot be uttered, and enables us to cry, Abba, Father (Rom. viii. 26). This last point, as we have hitherto only touched upon it slightly in passing, must now be treated more fully.

2. To *prayer*, then, are we indebted for penetrating to those riches which are treasured up for us with our heavenly Father. For there is a kind of intercourse between God and men, by which, having entered the upper sanctuary, they appear before Him and appeal to his promises, that when necessity requires, they may learn by experience, that what they believed merely on the authority of his word was not in vain. Accordingly, we see that nothing is set before us as an object of expectation from the Lord which we are not enjoined to ask of Him in prayer, so true it is that prayer digs up those treasures which the Gospel of our Lord discovers to the eye of faith. The necessity and utility of this exercise of prayer no words can sufficiently express. Assuredly it is not without cause our heavenly Father declares that our only safety is in calling upon his name, since by it we invoke the presence of his providence to watch over our interests, of his power to sustain us when weak and almost fainting, of his goodness to receive us into favour, though miserably loaded with sin; in fine, call upon him to manifest himself to us in all his

perfections. Hence, admirable peace and tranquillity are given to our consciences; for the straits by which we were pressed being laid before the Lord, we rest fully satisfied with the assurance that none of our evils are unknown to him, and that he is both able and willing to make the best provision for us.

3. But some one will say, Does he not know without a monitor both what our difficulties are, and what is meet for our interest, so that it seems in some measure superfluous to solicit him by our prayers, as if he were winking, or even sleeping, until aroused by the sound of our voice?[1] Those who argue thus attend not to the end for which the Lord taught us to pray. It was not so much for his sake as for ours. He wills indeed, as is just, that due honour be paid him by acknowledging that all which men desire or feel to be useful, and pray to obtain, is derived from him. But even the benefit of the homage which we thus pay him redounds to ourselves. Hence the holy patriarchs, the more confidently they proclaimed the mercies of God to themselves and others, felt the stronger incitement to prayer. It will be sufficient to refer to the example of Elijah, who being assured of the purpose of God, had good ground for the promise of rain which he gives to Ahab, and yet prays anxiously upon his knees, and sends his servant seven times to inquire (1 Kings xviii. 42); not that he discredits the oracle, but because he knows it to be his duty to lay his desires before God, lest his faith should become drowsy or torpid. Wherefore, although it is true that while we are listless or insensible to our wretchedness, he wakes and watches for us, and sometimes even assists us unasked; it is very much for our interest to be constantly supplicating him: first, that our heart may always be inflamed with a serious and ardent desire of seeking, loving, and serving him, while we accustom ourselves to have recourse to him as a sacred anchor in every necessity; secondly, that no desire, no longing whatever, of which we are ashamed to make him the witness, may enter our minds, while we learn to place all our wishes in his sight, and thus pour out our heart before him; and, lastly, that we may be prepared to receive all his benefits with true gratitude and thanksgiving, while our prayers remind us that they proceed from his hand. Moreover, having obtained what we asked, being persuaded that he has answered our prayers, we are led to long more earnestly for his favour, and at the same time have greater pleasure in welcoming the blessings which we perceive to have been obtained by our prayers. Lastly, use and experience confirm the thought of his providence in our minds in a manner adapted to our weakness, when we understand that he not only promises that he will never fail us, and spontaneously gives us access to approach him in every time of need,

---

1 French, "Dont il sembleroit que ce fust chose superflue de le soliciter par prieres; veu que nous avons accoustumé de soliciter ceux qui ne pensent à nostre affaire, et qui sont endormis."—Whence it would seem that it was a superfluous matter to solicit him by prayer; seeing we are accustomed to solicit those who think not of our business, and who are slumbering.

but has his hand always stretched out to assist his people, not amusing them with words, but proving himself to be a present aid. For these reasons, though our most merciful Father never slumbers nor sleeps he very often seems to do so, that thus he may exercise us, when we might otherwise be listless and slothful, in asking, entreating, and earnestly beseeching him to our great good. It is very absurd, therefore, to dissuade men from prayer, by pretending that Divine Providence, which is always watching over the government of the universe, is in vain importuned by our supplications, when, on the contrary, the Lord himself declares, that he is "nigh unto all that call upon him, to all that call upon him in truth" (Ps. cxlv. 18). No better is the frivolous allegation of others, that it is superfluous to pray for things which the Lord is ready of his own accord to bestow; since it is his pleasure that those very things which flow from his spontaneous liberality should be acknowledged as conceded to our prayers. This is testified by that memorable sentence in the psalm, to which many others correspond, "The eyes of the Lord are upon the righteous, and his ears are open unto their cry" (Ps. xxxiv. 15), This passage, while extolling the care which Divine Providence spontaneously exercises over the safety of believers, omits not the exercise of faith by which the mind is aroused from sloth. The eyes of God are awake to assist the blind in their necessity, but he is likewise pleased to listen to our groans, that he may give us the better proof of his love. And thus both things are true, "He that keepeth Israel shall neither slumber nor sleep" (Ps. cxxi. 4); and yet whenever he sees us dumb and torpid, he withdraws as if he had forgotten us.

4. Let the first rule of right prayer then be, to have our heart and mind framed as becomes those who are entering into converse with God. This we shall accomplish in regard to the mind, if, laying aside carnal thoughts and cares which might interfere with the direct and pure contemplation of God, it not only be wholly intent on prayer, but also, as far as possible, be borne and raised above itself. I do not here insist on a mind so disengaged as to feel none of the gnawings of anxiety; on the contrary, it is by much anxiety that the fervour of prayer is inflamed. Thus we see that the holy servants of God betray great anguish, not to say solicitude, when they cause the voice of complaint to ascend to the Lord from the deep abyss and the jaws of death. What I say is, that all foreign and extraneous cares must be dispelled by which the mind might be driven to and fro in vague suspense, be drawn down from heaven, and kept grovelling on the earth. When I say it must be raised above itself, I mean that it must not bring into the presence of God any of those things which our blind and stupid reason is wont to devise, nor keep itself confined within the little measure of its own vanity, but rise to a purity worthy of God.

5. Both things are specially worthy of notice. First, let every one in professing to pray turn thither all his thoughts and feelings, and be not (as is usual) distracted by wandering thoughts; because

nothing is more contrary to the reverence due to God than that levity which bespeaks a mind too much given to license and devoid of fear. In this matter we ought to labour the more earnestly the more difficult we experience it to be; for no man is so intent on prayer as not to feel many thoughts creeping in, and either breaking off the tenor of his prayer, or retarding it by some turning or digression. Here let us consider how unbecoming it is when God admits us to familiar intercourse, to abuse his great condescension by mingling things sacred and profane, reverence for him not keeping our minds under restraint; but just as if in prayer we were conversing with one like ourselves, forgetting him, and allowing our thoughts to run to and fro. Let us know, then, that none duly prepare themselves for prayer but those who are so impressed with the majesty of God that they engage in it free from all earthly cares and affections. The ceremony of lifting up our hands in prayer is designed to remind us that we are far removed from God, unless our thoughts rise upward: as it is said in the psalm, "Unto thee, O Lord, do I lift up my soul" (Psalm xxv. 1). And Scripture repeatedly uses the expression to *raise our prayer*, meaning, that those who would be heard by God must not grovel in the mire. The sum is, that the more liberally God deals with us, condescendingly inviting us to disburden our cares into his bosom, the less excusable we are if this admirable and incomparable blessing does not in our estimation outweigh all other things, and win our affection, that prayer may seriously engage our every thought and feeling. This cannot be unless our mind, strenuously exerting itself against all impediments, rise upward.

Our second proposition was, that we are to ask only in so far as God permits. For though he bids us pour out our hearts (Ps. lxii. 8), he does not indiscriminately give loose reins to foolish and depraved affections; and when he promises that he will grant believers their wish, his indulgence does not proceed so far as to submit to their caprice. In both matters grievous delinquencies are everywhere committed. For not only do many without modesty, without reverence, presume to invoke God concerning their frivolities, but impudently bring forward their dreams, whatever they may be, before the tribunal of God. Such is the folly or stupidity under which they labour, that they have the hardihood to obtrude upon God desires so vile, that they would blush exceedingly to impart them to their fellow-men. Profane writers have derided and even expressed their detestation of this presumption, and yet the vice has always prevailed. Hence, as the ambitious adopted Jupiter as their patron; the avaricious, Mercury; the literary aspirants, Apollo and Minerva; the warlike, Mars; the licentious, Venus: so in the present day, as I lately observed, men in prayer give greater license to their unlawful desires than if they were telling jocular tales among their equals. God does not suffer his condescension to be thus mocked, but vindicating his own right, places our wishes under the restraint of his authority. We must, therefore, attend to the observation of John,

" This is the confidence that we have in him, that if we ask anything according to his will, he heareth us" (1 John v. 14).

But as our faculties are far from being able to attain to such high perfection, we must seek for some means to assist them. As the eye of our mind should be intent upon God, so the affection of our heart ought to follow in the same course. But both fall far beneath this, or rather, they faint and fail, and are carried in a contrary direction. To assist this weakness, God gives us the guidance of the Spirit in our prayers to dictate what is right, and regulate our affections. For seeing " we know not what we should pray for as we ought," " the Spirit itself maketh intercession for us with groanings which cannot be uttered" (Rom. viii. 26) ; not that he actually prays or groans, but he excites in us sighs, and wishes, and confidence, which our natural powers are not at all able to conceive. Nor is it without cause Paul gives the name of *groanings which cannot be uttered* to the prayers which believers send forth under the guidance of the Spirit. For those who are truly exercised in prayer are not unaware that blind anxieties so restrain and perplex them, that they can scarcely find what it becomes them to utter ; nay, in attempting to lisp they halt and hesitate. Hence it appears that to pray aright is a special gift. We do not speak thus in indulgence to our sloth, as if we were to leave the office of prayer to the Holy Spirit, and give way to that carelessness to which we are too prone. Thus we sometimes hear the impious expression, that we are to wait in suspense until he take possession of our minds while otherwise occupied. Our meaning is that, weary of our own heartlessness and sloth, we are to long for the aid of the Spirit. Nor indeed does Paul, when he enjoins us to pray *in the Spirit* (1 Cor. xiv. 15), cease to exhort us to vigilance, intimating, that while the inspiration of the Spirit is effectual to the formation of prayer, it by no means impedes or retards our own endeavours ; since in this matter God is pleased to try how efficiently faith influences our hearts.

6. Another rule of prayer is, that in asking we must always truly feel our wants, and seriously considering that we need all the things which we ask, accompany the prayer with a sincere, nay, ardent desire of obtaining them. Many repeat prayers in a perfunctory manner from a set form, as if they were performing a task to God ; and though they confess that this is a necessary remedy for the evils of their condition, because it were fatal to be left without the divine aid which they implore, it still appears that they perform the duty from custom, because their minds are meanwhile cold, and they ponder not what they ask. A general and confused feeling of their necessity leads them to pray, but it does not make them solicitous as in a matter of present consequence, that they may obtain the supply of their need. Moreover, can we suppose anything more hateful or even more execrable to God than this fiction of asking the pardon of sins, while he who asks at the very time either thinks that he is not a sinner or at least is not thinking that he is a sinner ; in other words, a fiction by

which God is plainly held in derision? But mankind, as I have
lately said, are full of depravity, so that in the way of perfunctory
service they often ask many things of God which they think come to
them without his beneficence, or from some other quarter, or are
already certainly in their possession. There is another fault which
seems less heinous, but is not to be tolerated. Some murmur out
prayers without meditation, their only principle being that God is to
be propitiated by prayer. Believers ought to be specially on their
guard never to appear in the presence of God with the intention of
presenting a request unless they are under some serious impression,
and are, at the same time, desirous to obtain it. Nay, although in
these things which we ask only for the glory of God, we seem not at
first sight to consult for our necessity, yet we ought not to ask with
less fervour and vehemency of desire. For instance, when we pray
that his name be hallowed, that hallowing must, so to speak, be
earnestly hungered and thirsted after.

7. If it is objected, that the necessity which urges us to pray is not
always equal, I admit it, and this distinction is profitably taught us
by James: "Is any among you afflicted? let him pray. Is any
merry? let him sing psalms" (James v. 13). Therefore, common
sense itself dictates, that as we are too sluggish, we must be stimulated by God to pray earnestly whenever the occasion requires. This
David calls a time when God " may be found" (a seasonable time);
because, as he declares in several other passages, that the more hardly
grievances, annoyances, fears, and other kinds of trial press us, the
freer is our access to God, as if he were inviting us to himself. Still
not less true is the injunction of Paul to pray "always" (Eph. vi. 18);
because, however prosperously, according to our view, things proceed,
and however we may be surrounded on all sides with grounds of joy,
there is not an instant of time during which our want does not exhort
us to prayer. A man abounds in wheat and wine; but as he cannot
enjoy a morsel of bread, unless by the continual bounty of God, his
granaries or cellars will not prevent him from asking for daily bread.
Then, if we consider how many dangers impend every moment, fear
itself will teach us that no time ought to be without prayer. This,
however, may be better known in spiritual matters. For when will
the many sins of which we are conscious allow us to sit secure without suppliantly entreating freedom from guilt and punishment?
When will temptation give us a truce, making it unnecessary to
hasten for help? Moreover, zeal for the kingdom and glory of God
ought not to seize us by starts, but urge us without intermission, so that
every time should appear seasonable. It is not without cause, therefore,
that assiduity in prayer is so often enjoined.. I am not now speaking
of perseverance, which shall afterwards be considered; but Scripture,
by reminding us of the necessity of constant prayer, charges us with
sloth, because we feel not how much we stand in need of this care
and assiduity. By this rule hypocrisy and the device of lying to God
are restrained, nay, altogether banished from prayer. God promises

that he will be near to those who call upon him in truth, and declares that those who seek him with their whole heart will find him : those, therefore, who delight in their own pollution cannot surely aspire to him.

One of the requisites of legitimate prayer is repentance. Hence the common declaration of Scripture, that God does not listen to the wicked ; that their prayers, as well as their sacrifices, are an abomination to him. For it is right that those who seal up their hearts should find the ears of God closed against them, that those who, by their hard-heartedness, provoke his severity should find him inflexible. In Isaiah he thus threatens : " When ye make many prayers, I will not hear : your hands are full of blood" (Isaiah i. 15). In like manner, in Jeremiah, "Though they shall cry unto me, I will not hearken unto them" (Jer. xi. 7, 8, 11) ; because he regards it as the highest insult for the wicked to boast of his covenant while profaning his sacred name by their whole lives. Hence he complains in Isaiah : " This people draw near to me with their mouth, and with their lips do honour me; but have removed their heart far from me" (Isaiah xxix. 13). Indeed, he does not confine this to prayers alone, but declares that he abominates pretence in every part of his service. Hence the words of James, " Ye ask and receive not, because ye ask amiss, that ye may consume it upon your lusts" (James iv. 3). It is true indeed (as we shall again see in a little) that the pious, in the prayers which they utter, trust not to their own worth ; still the admonition of John is not superfluous : " Whatsoever we ask, we receive of him, because we keep his commandments" (1 John iii. 22) ; an evil conscience shuts the door against us. Hence it follows, that none but the sincere worshippers of God pray aright, or are listened to. Let every one, therefore, who prepares to pray feel dissatisfied with what is wrong in his condition, and assume, which he cannot do without repentance, the character and feelings of a poor suppliant.

8. The third rule to be added is, that he who comes into the presence of God to pray must divest himself of all vain-glorious thoughts, lay aside all idea of worth ; in short, discard all self-confidence, humbly giving God the whole glory, lest by arrogating anything, however little, to himself, vain pride cause him to turn away his face. Of this submission, which casts down all haughtiness, we have numerous examples in the servants of God. The holier they are, the more humbly they prostrate themselves when they come into the presence of the Lord. Thus Daniel, on whom the Lord himself bestowed such high commendation, says, " We do not present our supplications before thee for our righteousness, but for thy great mercies. O Lord, hear ; O Lord, forgive ; O Lord, hearken and do ; defer not, for thine own sake, O my God : for thy city and thy people are called by thy name." This he does not indirectly in the usual manner, as if he were one of the individuals in a crowd : he rather confesses his guilt apart, and as a suppliant betaking himself to the asylum of pardon, he distinctly declares that he was confessing his own sin, and

the sin of his people Israel (Dan. ix. 18-20).   David also sets us an example of this humility : " Enter not into judgment with thy servant : for in thy sight shall no man living be justified" (Psalm cxliii. 2).   In like manner, Isaiah prays, " Behold, thou art wroth ; for we have sinned : in those is continuance, and we shall be saved. But we are all as an unclean thing, and all our righteousness are as filthy rags ; and we all do fade as a leaf ; and our iniquities, like the wind, have taken us away.   And there is none that calleth upon thy name that stirreth up himself to take hold of thee : for thou hast hid thy face from us, and hast consumed us, because of our iniquities. But now, O Lord, thou art our Father ; we are the clay, and thou our potter ; and we all are the work of thy hand.   Be not wroth very sore, O Lord, neither remember iniquity for ever : Behold, see, we beseech thee, we are all thy people" (Isa. lxiv. 5-9).   You see how they put no confidence in anything but this : considering that they are the Lord's, they despair not of being the objects of his care.   In the same way, Jeremiah says, " O Lord, though our iniquities testify against us, do thou it for thy name's sake" (Jer. xiv. 7).   For it was most truly and piously written by the uncertain author (whoever he may have been) that wrote the book which is attributed to the prophet Baruch,[1] " but the soul that is greatly vexed, which goeth stooping and feeble, and the eyes that fail, and the hungry soul, will give thee praise and righteousness, O Lord.   Therefore, we do not make our humble supplication before thee, O Lord our God, for the righteousness of our fathers, and of our kings." " Hear, O Lord, and have mercy ; for thou art merciful : and have pity upon us, because we have sinned before thee" (Baruch ii. 18, 19 ; iii. 2).

9. In fine, supplication for pardon, with humble and ingenuous confession of guilt, forms both the preparation and commencement of right prayer.   For the holiest of men cannot hope to obtain anything from God until he has been freely reconciled to him.   God cannot be propitious to any but those whom he pardons.   Hence it is not strange that this is the key by which believers open the door of prayer, as we learn from several passages in The Psalms.   David, when presenting a request on a different subject, says, "Remember not the sins of my youth, nor my transgressions ; according to thy mercy remember me, for thy goodness sake, O Lord" (Psalm xxv. 7).   Again, " Look upon my affliction and my pain, and forgive my sins" (Psalm xxv. 18).   Here also we see that it is not sufficient to call ourselves to account for the sins of each passing day ; we must also call to mind those which might seem to have been long before buried in oblivion.   For in another passage the same prophet, confessing one grievous crime, takes occasion to go back to his very birth, " I was shapen in iniquity, and in sin did my mother conceive me" (Psalm

---

[1] French, "Pourtant ce qui est escrit en la prophetie qu'on attribue à Baruch, combien que l'autheur soit incertain, est tres sainctement dit ;"—However, what is written in the prophecy which is attributed to Baruch, though the author is uncertain, is very holily said.

li. 5) ; not to extenuate the fault by the corruption of his nature, but as it were to accumulate the sins of his whole life, that the stricter he was in condemning himself, the more placable God might be. But although the saints do not always in express terms ask forgiveness of sins, yet if we carefully ponder those prayers as given in Scripture, the truth of what I say will readily appear—namely, that their courage to pray was derived solely from the mercy of God, and that they always began with appeasing him. For when a man interrogates his conscience, so far is he from presuming to lay his cares familiarly before God, that if he did not trust to mercy and pardon, he would tremble at the very thought of approaching him. There is, indeed, another special confession. When believers long for deliverance from punishment, they at the same time pray that their sins may be pardoned ;[1] for it were absurd to wish that the effect should be taken away while the cause remains. For we must beware of imitating foolish patients, who, anxious only about curing accidental symptoms, neglect the root of the disease.[2] Nay, our endeavour must be to have God propitious even before he attests his favour by external signs, both because this is the order which he himself chooses, and it were of little avail to experience his kindness, did not conscience feel that he is appeased, and thus enable us to regard him as altogether lovely. Of this we are even reminded by our Saviour's reply. Having determined to cure the paralytic, he says, " Thy sins are forgiven thee ;" in other words, he raises our thoughts to the object which is especially to be desired—viz. admission into the favour of God—and then gives the fruit of reconciliation by bringing assistance to us. But besides that special confession of present guilt which believers employ, in supplicating for pardon of every fault and punishment, that general introduction which procures favour for our prayers must never be omitted, because prayers will never reach God unless they are founded on free mercy. To this we may refer the words of John, " If we confess our sins, he is faithful and just to forgive us our sins, and to cleanse us from all unrighteousness" (1 John i. 9). Hence under the law it was necessary to consecrate prayers by the expiation of blood, both that they might be accepted, and that the people might be warned that they were unworthy of the high privilege, until being purged from their defilements, they founded their confidence in prayer entirely on the mercy of God.

10. Sometimes, however, the saints, in supplicating God, seem to appeal to their own righteousness, as when David says, " Preserve my soul ; for I am holy" (Ps. lxxxvi. 2). Also Hezekiah, " Remember now, O Lord, I beseech thee, how I have walked before thee in truth, and with a perfect heart, and have done that which is good in

---

1 French, " il recognoissent le chastiement qu'ils ont merité ;"—they acknowledge the punishment which they have deserved.
2 The French adds, " Ile voudront qu'on leur oste le mal de teste et des reins, et seront contens qu'on ne touche point a la fievre ;"—They would wish to get quit of the pain in the head and the loins, and would be contented to leave the fever untouched.

thy sight" (Is. xxxviii. 3). All they mean by such expressions is, that regeneration declares them to be among the servants and children to whom God engages that he will show favour. We have already seen how he declares by the Psalmist that his eyes "are upon the righteous, and his ears are open unto their cry" (Ps. xxxiv. 16): and again by the apostle, that "whatsoever we ask of him we obtain, because we keep his commandments" (John iii. 22). In these passages he does not fix a value on prayer as a meritorious work, but designs to establish the confidence of those who are conscious of an unfeigned integrity and innocence, such as all believers should possess. For the saying of the blind man who had received his sight is in perfect accordance with divine truth—"God heareth not sinners" (John ix. 31)—provided we take the term sinners in the sense commonly used by Scripture to mean those who, without any desire for righteousness, are sleeping secure in their sins; since no heart will ever rise to genuine prayer that does not at the same time long for holiness. Those supplications in which the saints allude to their purity and integrity correspond to such promises, that they may thus have, in their own experience, a manifestation of that which all the servants of God are made to expect. Thus they almost always use this mode of prayer when before God they compare themselves with their enemies, from whose injustice they long to be delivered by his hand. When making such comparisons, there is no wonder that they bring forward their integrity and simplicity of heart, that thus, by the justice of their cause, the Lord may be the more disposed to give them succour. We rob not the pious breast of the privilege of enjoying a consciousness of purity before the Lord, and thus feeling assured of the promises with which he comforts and supports his true worshippers, but we would have them to lay aside all thought of their own merit, and found their confidence of success in prayer solely on the divine mercy.

11. The fourth rule of prayer is, that notwithstanding of our being thus abased and truly humbled, we should be animated to pray with the sure hope of succeeding. There is, indeed, an appearance of contradiction between the two things, between a sense of the just vengeance of God and firm confidence in his favour, and yet they are perfectly accordant, if it is the mere goodness of God that raises up those who are overwhelmed by their own sins. For, as we have formerly shown (chap. iii. sec. 1, 2) that repentance and faith go hand in hand, being united by an indissoluble tie, the one causing terror, the other joy, so in prayer they must both be present. This concurrence David expresses in a few words: "But as for me, I will come into thy house in the multitude of thy mercy; and in thy fear will I worship toward thy holy temple" (Ps. v. 7). Under the goodness of God he comprehends faith, at the same time not excluding fear; for not only does his majesty compel our reverence, but our own unworthiness also divests us of all pride and confidence, and keeps us in fear. The confidence of which I speak is not one which

frees the mind from all anxiety, and soothes it with sweet and perfect rest, such rest is peculiar to those who, while all their affairs are flowing to a wish, are annoyed by no care, stung with no regret, agitated by no fear. But the best stimulus which the saints have to prayer is when, in consequence of their own necessities, they feel the greatest disquietude, and are all but driven to despair, until faith seasonably comes to their aid; because in such straits the goodness of God so shines upon them, that while they groan, burdened by the weight of present calamities, and tormented with the fear of greater, they yet trust to this goodness, and in this way both lighten the difficulty of endurance, and take comfort in the hope of final deliverance. It is necessary, therefore, that the prayer of the believer should be the result of both feelings, and exhibit the influence of both—namely, that while he groans under present and anxiously dreads new evils, he should, at the same time, have recourse to God, not at all doubting that God is ready to stretch out a helping hand to him. For it is not easy to say how much God is irritated by our distrust, when we ask what we expect not of his goodness. Hence nothing is more accordant to the nature of prayer than to lay it down as a fixed rule, that it is not to come forth at random, but is to follow in the footsteps of faith. To this principle Christ directs all of us in these words, "Therefore, I say unto you, What things soever ye desire, when ye pray, believe that ye receive them, and ye shall have them" (Mark xi. 24). The same thing he declares in another passage, "All things, whatsoever ye shall ask in prayer, believing, ye shall receive" (Matth. xxi. 22). In accordance with this are the words of James, "If any of you lack wisdom, let him ask of God, that giveth to all men liberally, and upbraideth not, and it shall be given him. But let him ask in faith, nothing wavering" (James i. 5). He most aptly expresses the power of faith by opposing it to wavering. No less worthy of notice is his additional statement, that those who approach God with a doubting, hesitating mind, without feeling assured whether they are to be heard or not, gain nothing by their prayers. Such persons he compares to a wave of the sea, driven with the wind and tossed. Hence in another passage he terms genuine prayer "the prayer of faith" (James v. 15). Again, since God so often declares that he will give to every man according to his faith, he intimates that we cannot obtain anything without faith. In short, it is faith which obtains everything that is granted to prayer. This is the meaning of Paul in the well-known passage to which dull men give too little heed, "How then shall they call upon him in whom they have not believed? and how shall they believe in him of whom they have not heard?" "So then faith cometh by hearing, and hearing by the word of God" (Rom. x. 14, 17). Gradually deducing the origin of prayer from faith, he distinctly maintains that God cannot be invoked sincerely except by those to whom, by the preaching of the Gospel, his mercy and willingness have been made known, nay, familiarly explained.

12. This necessity our opponents do not at all consider. Therefore, when we say that believers ought to feel firmly assured, they think we are saying the absurdest thing in the world. But if they had any experience in true prayer, they would assuredly understand that God cannot be duly invoked without this firm sense of the Divine benevolence. But as no man can well perceive the power of faith, without at the same time feeling it in his heart, what profit is there in disputing with men of this character, who plainly show that they have never had more than a vain imagination? The value and necessity of that assurance for which we contend is learned chiefly from prayer. Every one who does not see this gives proof of a very stupid conscience. Therefore, leaving those who are thus blinded, let us fix our thoughts on the words of Paul, that God can only be invoked by such as have obtained a knowledge of his mercy from the Gospel, and feel firmly assured that that mercy is ready to be bestowed upon them. What kind of prayer would this be? "O Lord, I am indeed doubtful whether or not thou art inclined to hear me; but being oppressed with anxiety, I fly to thee, that if I am worthy, thou mayest assist me." None of the saints whose prayers are given in Scripture thus supplicated. Nor are we thus taught by the Holy Spirit, who tells us to "come boldly unto the throne of grace, that we may obtain mercy, and find grace to help in time of need" (Heb. iv. 16); and elsewhere teaches us to "have boldness and access with confidence by the faith of Christ" (Eph. iii. 12). This confidence of obtaining what we ask, a confidence which the Lord commands, and all the saints teach by their example, we must therefore hold fast with both hands, if we would pray to any advantage. The only prayer acceptable to God is that which springs (if I may so express it) from this presumption of faith, and is founded on the full assurance of hope. He might have been contented to use the simple name of faith, but he adds not only confidence, but liberty or boldness, that by this mark he might distinguish us from unbelievers, who indeed like us pray to God, but pray at random. Hence the whole Church thus prays, "Let thy mercy, O Lord, be upon us, according as we hope in thee" (Ps. xxxiii. 22). The same condition is set down by the Psalmist in another passage, "When I cry unto thee, then shall mine enemies turn back: this I know, for God is for me" (Ps. lvi. 9). Again, "In the morning will I direct my prayer unto thee, and will look up" (Ps. v. 3). From these words we gather, that prayers are vainly poured out into the air unless accompanied with faith, in which, as from a watch-tower, we may quietly wait for God. With this agrees the order of Paul's exhortation. For before urging believers to pray in the Spirit always, with vigilance and assiduity, he enjoins them to take "the shield of faith," the helmet of salvation, and the sword of the Spirit, which is the word of God" (Eph. vi. 16–18).

Let the reader here call to mind what I formerly observed, that faith by no means fails, though accompanied with a recognition of our wretchedness, poverty, and pollution. How much soever believers may feel that they are oppressed by a heavy load of iniquity, and are not only devoid of everything which can procure the favour of God for them, but justly burdened with many sins which make him an object of dread, yet they cease not to present themselves, this feeling not deterring them from appearing in his presence, because there is no other access to him. Genuine prayer is not that by which we arrogantly extol ourselves before God, or set a great value on any thing of our own, but that by which, while confessing our guilt, we utter our sorrows before God, just as children familiarly lay their complaints before their parents. Nay, the immense accumulation of our sins should rather spur us on and incite us to prayer. Of this the Psalmist gives us an example, " Heal my soul : for I have sinned against thee" (Ps. xli. 4). I confess, indeed, that these stings would prove mortal darts, did not God give succour ; but our heavenly Father has, in ineffable kindness, added a remedy, by which, calming all perturbation, soothing our cares, and dispelling our fears, he condescendingly allures us to himself ; nay, removing all doubts, not to say obstacles, makes the way smooth before us.

13. And first, indeed, in enjoining us to pray, he by the very injunction convicts us of impious contumacy if we obey not. He could not give a more precise command than that which is contained in the psalm, " Call upon me in the day of trouble" (Ps. l. 15). But as there is no office of piety more frequently enjoined by Scripture, there is no occasion for here dwelling longer upon it. " Ask," says our Divine Master, " and it shall be given you ; seek, and ye shall find ; knock, and it shall be opened unto you" (Matth. vii. 7). Here, indeed, a promise is added to the precept, and this is necessary. For though all confess that we must obey the precept, yet the greater part would shun the invitation of God, did he not promise that he would listen and be ready to answer. These two positions being laid down, it is certain that all who cavillingly allege that they are not to come to God directly, are not only rebellious and disobedient, but are also convicted of unbelief, inasmuch as they distrust the promises. There is the more occasion to attend to this, because hypocrites, under a pretence of humility and modesty, proudly contemn the precept, as well as deny all credit to the gracious invitation of God ; nay, rob him of a principal part of his worship. For when he rejected sacrifices, in which all holiness seemed then to consist, he declared that the chief thing, that which above all others is precious in his sight, is to be invoked in the day of necessity. Therefore, when he demands that which is his own, and urges us to alacrity in obeying, no pretexts for doubt, how specious soever they may be, can excuse us. Hence all the passages throughout Scripture in which we are commanded to pray, are set up before our eyes as so many banners, to inspire us with confidence. It were presumption to go forward into the presence of God, did he not anticipate us by his invitation. Accordingly, he opens up the way for us by his own voice,

"I will say, It is my people: and they shall say, The Lord is my God" (Zech. xiii. 9). We see how he anticipates his worshippers, and desires them to follow, and therefore we cannot fear that the melody which he himself dictates will prove unpleasing. Especially let us call to mind that noble description of the divine character, by trusting to which we shall easily overcome every obstacle: "O thou that hearest prayer, unto thee shall all flesh come" (Ps. lxv. 2). What can be more lovely or soothing than to see God invested with a title which assures us that nothing is more proper to his nature than to listen to the prayers of suppliants? Hence the Psalmist infers, that free access is given not to a few individuals, but to all men, since God addresses all in these terms, "Call upon me in the day of trouble: I will deliver thee, and thou shalt glorify me" (Ps. l. 15). David, accordingly, appeals to the promise thus given, in order to obtain what he asks: "Thou, O Lord of hosts, God of Israel, hast revealed to thy servant, saying, I will build thee an house: therefore hath thy servant found in his heart to pray this prayer unto thee" (2 Sam. vii. 27). Here we infer, that he would have been afraid but for the promise which emboldened him. So in another passage he fortifies himself with the general doctrine, "He will fulfil the desire of them that fear him" (Ps. cxlv. 19). Nay, we may observe in The Psalms, how the continuity of prayer is broken, and a transition is made at one time to the power of God, at another to his goodness, at another to the faithfulness of his promises. It might seem that David, by introducing these sentiments, unseasonably mutilates his prayers; but believers well know by experience, that their ardour grows languid unless new fuel be added, and, therefore, that meditation as well on the nature as the word of God during prayer, is by no means superfluous. Let us not decline to imitate the example of David, and introduce thoughts which may reanimate our languid minds with new vigour.

14. It is strange that these delightful promises affect us coldly, or scarcely at all, so that the generality of men prefer to wander up and down, forsaking the fountain of living waters, and hewing out to themselves broken cisterns, rather than embrace the divine liberality voluntarily offered to them. "The name of the Lord," says Solomon, "is a strong tower; the righteous runneth into it, and is safe." Joel, after predicting the fearful disaster which was at hand, subjoins the following memorable sentence: "And it shall come to pass, that whosoever shall call on the name of the Lord shall be delivered." This we know properly refers to the course of the Gospel. Scarcely one in a hundred is moved to come into the presence of God, though he himself exclaims by Isaiah, "And it shall come to pass, that before they call, I will answer; and while they are yet speaking, I will hear." This honour he elsewhere bestows upon the whole Church in general, as belonging to all the members of Christ: "He shall call upon me, and I will answer him: I will be with him in trouble;

I will deliver him, and honour him."[1]   My intention, however, as I already observed, is not to enumerate all, but only select some admirable passages as a specimen how kindly God allures us to himself, and how extreme our ingratitude must be when with such powerful motives our sluggishness still retards us. Wherefore, let these words always resound in our ears: "The Lord is nigh unto all them that call upon him, to all that call upon him in truth" (Ps. cxlv. 18). Likewise those passages which we have quoted from Isaiah and Joel, in which God declares that his ear is open to our prayers, and that he is delighted as with a sacrifice of sweet savour when we cast our cares upon him. The special benefit of these promises we receive when we frame our prayer, not timorously or doubtingly, but when trusting to his word whose majesty might otherwise deter us, we are bold to call him Father, he himself deigning to suggest this most delightful name.   Fortified by such invitations, it remains for us to know that we have therein sufficient materials for prayer, since our prayers depend on no merit of our own, but all their worth and hope of success are founded and depend on the promises of God, so that they need no other support, and require not to look up and down on this hand and on that. It must therefore be fixed in our minds, that though we equal not the lauded sanctity of patriarchs, prophets, and apostles, yet as the command to pray is common to us as well as them, and faith is common, so if we lean on the word of God, we are in respect of this privilege their associates.   For God declaring, as has already been seen, that he will listen and be favourable to all, encourages the most wretched to hope that they shall obtain what they ask; and, accordingly, we should attend to the general forms of expression, which, as it is commonly expressed, exclude none from first to last; only let there be sincerity of heart, self-dissatisfaction, humility, and faith, that we may not, by the hypocrisy of a deceitful prayer, profane the name of God. Our most merciful Father will not reject those whom he not only encourages to come, but urges in every possible way.   Hence David's method of prayer to which I lately referred: "And now, O Lord God, thou art that God, and thy words be true, and thou hast promised this goodness unto thy servant, that it may continue for ever before thee" (2 Sam. vii. 28). So also, in another passage, "Let, I pray thee, thy merciful kindness be for my comfort, according to thy word unto thy servant" (Psalm cxix. 76).   And the whole body of the Israelites, whenever they fortify themselves with the remembrance of the covenant, plainly declare, that since God thus prescribes they are not to pray timorously (Gen. xxxii. 10).   In this they imitated the example of the patriarchs, particularly Jacob, who, after confessing that he was unworthy of the many mercies which he had received of the Lord's hand, says, that he is encouraged to make still larger requests, because God had promised that he would grant them. But whatever be the pretexts

---

1 Jer. ii. 13; Prov. xviii. 10; Joel ii. 32; Is. lxv. 24; Ps. xci. 15; cxlv. 18.

which unbelievers employ, when they do not flee to God as often as necessity urges, nor seek after him, nor implore his aid, they defraud him of his due honour just as much as if they were fabricating to themselves new gods and idols, since in this way they deny that God is the author of all their blessings.   On the contrary, nothing more effectually frees pious minds from every doubt, than to be armed with the thought that no obstacle should impede them while they are obeying the command of God, who declares that nothing is more grateful to him than obedience.   Hence, again, what I have previously said becomes still more clear—namely, that a bold spirit in prayer well accords with fear, reverence, and anxiety, and that there is no inconsistency when God raises up those who had fallen prostrate.   In this way forms of expression apparently inconsistent admirably harmonise.   Jeremiah and David speak of humbly laying their supplications [1] before God.   In another passage Jeremiah says, " Let, we beseech thee, our supplication be accepted before thee, and pray for us unto the Lord thy God, even for all this remnant."   On the other hand, believers are often said to *lift up prayer.*   Thus Hezekiah speaks, when asking the prophet to undertake the office of interceding.   And David says, " Let my prayer be set forth before thee as incense ; and the lifting up of my hands as the evening sacrifice." [2]   The explanation is, that though believers, persuaded of the paternal love of God, cheerfully rely on his faithfulness, and have no hesitation in imploring the aid which he voluntarily offers, they are not elated with supine or presumptuous security ; but climbing up by the ladder of the promises, still remain humble and abased suppliants.

15. Here, by way of objection, several questions are raised. Scripture relates that God sometimes complied with certain prayers which had been dictated by minds not duly calmed or regulated.   It is true, that the cause for which Jotham imprecated on the inhabitants of Shechem the disaster which afterwards befell them was well founded ; but still he was inflamed with anger and revenge (Judges ix. 20); and hence God, by complying with the execration, seems to approve of passionate impulses.   Similar fervour also seized Samson when he prayed, "Strengthen me, I pray thee, only this once, O God, that I may be at once avenged of the Philistines for my two eyes" (Judges xvi. 28).   For although there was some mixture of good zeal, yet his ruling feeling was a fervid, and therefore vicious longing for vengeance.   God assents, and hence apparently it might be inferred that prayers are effectual, though not framed in conformity to the rule of the word.   But I answer, *first,* that a perpetual law is not abrogated by singular examples ; and, *secondly,* that special suggestions have sometimes been made to a few individuals,

---

[1] Latin, "prosternere preces."   French, "mettent bas leurs prieres ;"—lay low their prayers.
[2] Jer. xlii. 9 ; Dan. ix. 18 ; Jer. xlii. 2 ; 2 Kings xix. 4 ; Ps. cxliv. 2.

whose case thus becomes different from that of the generality of men. For we should attend to the answer which our Saviour gave to his disciples when they inconsiderately wished to imitate the example of Elias, " Ye know not what manner of spirit ye are of" (Luke ix. 55). We must, however, go farther and say, that the wishes to which God assents are not always pleasing to him ; but he assents, because it is necessary, by way of example, to give clear evidence of the doctrine of Scripture—viz. that he assists the miserable, and hears the groans of those who unjustly afflicted implore his aid : and, accordingly, he executes his judgments when the complaints of the needy, though in themselves unworthy of attention, ascend to him. For how often, in inflicting punishment on the ungodly for cruelty, rapine, violence, lust, and other crimes, in curbing audacity and fury, and also in overthrowing tyrannical power, has he declared that he gives assistance to those who are unworthily oppressed, though they by addressing an unknown deity only beat the air ? There is one psalm which clearly teaches that prayers are not without effect, though they do not penetrate to heaven by faith (Ps. cvii.). For it enumerates the prayers which, by natural instinct, necessity extorts from unbelievers not less than from believers, and to which it shows by the event, that God is, notwithstanding, propitious. Is it to testify by such readiness to hear that their prayers are agreeable to him ? Nay ; it is, first, to magnify or display his mercy by the circumstance, that even the wishes of unbelievers are not denied ; and, secondly, to stimulate his true worshippers to more urgent prayer, when they see that sometimes even the wailings of the ungodly are not without avail. This, however, is no reason why believers should deviate from the law divinely imposed upon them, or envy unbelievers, as if they gained much in obtaining what they wished. We have observed (chap. iii. sec. 25), that in this way God yielded to the feigned repentance of Ahab, that he might show how ready he is to listen to his elect when, with true contrition, they seek his favour. Accordingly he upbraids the Jews, that shortly after experiencing his readiness to listen to their prayers, they returned to their own perverse inclinations. It is also plain from the Book of Judges that, whenever they wept, though their tears were deceitful, they were delivered from the hands of their enemies. Therefore, as God sends his sun indiscrimately on the evil and on the good, so he despises not the tears of those who have a good cause, and whose sorrows are deserving of relief. Meanwhile, though he hears them, it has no more to do with salvation than the supply of food which he gives to other despisers of his goodness.

There seems to be a more difficult question concerning Abraham and Samuel, the one of whom, without any instructions from the word of God, prayed in behalf of the people of Sodom, and the other, contrary to an express prohibition, prayed in behalf of Saul (Gen. xviii. 23 ; 1 Sam. xv. 11). Similar is the case of Jeremiah, who prayed that the city might not be destroyed (Jer. xxxii. 16). It is true their prayers were refused, but it seems harsh to affirm that they prayed without faith. Modest readers will, I hope, be satisfied with this solution— viz. that leaning to the general principle on which God enjoins us to be merciful even to the unworthy, they were not altogether devoid of faith, though in this particular instance their wish was disappointed. Augustine shrewdly remarks, " How do the saints pray in faith when they ask from God contrary to what he has decreed ? Namely, because they pray according to his will, not his hidden and immutable will, but that which he suggests to them, that he may hear them in another manner ; as he wisely distinguishes" (August. de Civit. Dei, Lib. xxii. c. 2). This is truly said : for, in his incomprehensible counsel, he so regulates events, that the prayers of the saints, though involving a mixture of faith and error, are not in vain. And yet this no more sanctions imitation than it excuses the saints themselves, who I deny not exceeded due bounds. Wherefore, whenever no certain promise exists, our request to God must have a condition annexed to it. Here we may refer to the prayer of David, "Awake for me to the judgment that thou hast commanded" (Ps. vii. 6) ; for he reminds us that he had received special instruction to pray for a temporal blessing.[1]

16. It is also of importance to observe, that the four laws of prayer of which I have treated are not so rigorously enforced, as that God rejects the prayers in which he does not find perfect faith or repentance, accompanied with fervent zeal and wishes duly framed. We have said (sec. 4), that though prayer is the familiar intercourse of believers with God, yet reverence and modesty must be observed : we must not give loose reins to our wishes, nor long for anything farther than God permits ; and, moreover, lest the majesty of God should be despised, our minds must be elevated to pure and chaste veneration. This no man ever performed with due perfection. For, not to speak of the generality of men, how often do David's complaints savour of intemperance ? Not that he actually means to expostulate with God, or murmur at his judgments, but failing, through infirmity, he finds no better solace than to pour his griefs into the bosom of his heavenly Father. Nay, even our stammering is tolerated by God, and pardon is granted to our ignorance as often as anything rashly escapes us : indeed, without this indulgence, we should have no freedom to pray. But although it was David's intention to submit himself entirely to the will of God, and he prayed with no less patience than fervour, yet irregular emotions appear, nay, sometimes burst forth,— emotions not a little at variance with the first law which we laid down. In particular, we may see in a clause of the thirty-ninth Psalm, how this saint was carried away by the vehemence of his grief, and unable to keep within bounds. " O spare me,[2] that I may recover strength, before I go hence, and be no more" (Ps. xxxix. 13).

---

1 The French adds, "duquel il n'eust pas autrement esté asseuré;"—of which he would not otherwise have felt assured

2 Latin, " Desine a me." French, " Retire-toy ;"—Withdraw from me.

You would call this the language of a desperate man, who had no other desire than that God should withdraw and leave him to perish in his distresses. Not that his devout mind rushes into such intemperance, or that, as the reprobate are wont, he wishes to have done with God; he only complains that the divine anger is more than he can bear. During those trials, wishes often escape which are not in accordance with the rule of the word, and in which the saints do not duly consider what is lawful and expedient. Prayers contaminated by such faults, indeed, deserve to be rejected; yet provided the saints lament, administer self-correction, and return to themselves, God pardons.

Similar faults are committed in regard to the second law (as to which, see sec. 6), for the saints have often to struggle with their own coldness, their want and misery not urging them sufficiently to serious prayer. It often happens, also, that their minds wander, and are almost lost; hence in this matter also there is need of pardon, lest their prayers, from being languid or mutilated, or interrupted and wandering, should meet with a refusal. One of the natural feelings which God has imprinted on our mind is, that prayer is not genuine unless the thoughts are turned upward. Hence the ceremony of raising the hands, to which we have adverted, a ceremony known to all ages and nations, and still in common use. But who, in lifting up his hands, is not conscious of sluggishness, the heart cleaving to the earth? In regard to the petition for remission of sins (sec. 8), though no believer omits it, yet all who are truly exercised in prayer feel that they bring scarcely a tenth of the sacrifice of which David speaks, "The sacrifices of God are a broken spirit: a broken and a contrite heart, O God, thou wilt not despise" (Ps. li. 17). Thus a twofold pardon is always to be asked. first, because they are conscious of many faults, the sense of which, however, does not touch them so as to make them feel dissatisfied with themselves as they ought; and, secondly, in so far as they have been enabled to profit in repentance and the fear of God, they are humbled with just sorrow for their offences, and pray for the remission of punishment by the judge. The thing which most of all vitiates prayer, did not God indulgently interpose, is weakness or imperfection of faith; but it is not wonderful that this defect is pardoned by God, who often exercises his people with severe trials, as if he actually wished to extinguish their faith. The hardest of such trials is when believers are forced to exclaim, "O Lord God of hosts, how long wilt thou be angry against the prayer of thy people?" (Ps. lxxx. 4), as if their very prayers offended him. In like manner, when Jeremiah says, "Also when I cry and shout, he shutteth out my prayer" (Lam. iii. 8), there cannot be a doubt that he was in the greatest perturbation. Innumerable examples of the same kind occur in the Scriptures, from which it is manifest that the faith of the saints was often mingled with doubts and fears, so that while believing and hoping, they however betrayed some degree of unbelief.

But because they do not come so far as were to be wished, that is only an additional reason for their exerting themselves to correct their faults, that they may daily approach nearer to the perfect law of prayer, and at the same time feel into what an abyss of evils those are plunged, who, in the very cures they use, bring new diseases upon themselves: since there is no prayer which God would not deservedly disdain, did he not overlook the blemishes with which all of them are polluted. I do not mention these things that believers may securely pardon themselves in any faults which they commit, but that they may call themselves to strict account, and thereby endeavour to surmount these obstacles; and though Satan endeavours to block up all the paths in order to prevent them from praying, they may, nevertheless, break through, being firmly persuaded that though not disencumbered of all hinderances, their attempts are pleasing to God, and their wishes are approved, provided they hasten on and keep their aim, though without immediately reaching it.

17. But since no man is worthy to come forward in his own name, and appear in the presence of God, our heavenly Father, to relieve us at once from fear and shame, with which all must feel oppressed,[1] has given us his Son, Jesus Christ our Lord, to be our Advocate and Mediator, that under his guidance we may approach securely, confiding that with him for our Intercessor nothing which we ask in his name will be denied to us, as there is nothing which the Father can deny to him (1 Tim. ii. 5; 1 John ii. 1; see sec. 36, 37). To this it is necessary to refer all that we have previously taught concerning faith; because, as the promise gives us Christ as our Mediator, so, unless our hope of obtaining what we ask is founded on him, it deprives us of the privilege of prayer. For it is impossible to think of the dread majesty of God without being filled with alarm; and hence the sense of our own unworthiness must keep us far away, until Christ interpose, and convert a throne of dreadful glory into a throne of grace; as the Apostle teaches that thus we can "come boldly unto the throne of grace, that we may obtain mercy, and find grace to help in time of need" (Heb. iv. 16). And as a rule has been laid down as to prayer, as a promise has been given that those who pray will be heard, so we are specially enjoined to pray in the name of Christ, the promise being that we shall obtain what we ask in his name. "Whatsoever ye shall ask in my name," says our Saviour, "that will I do; that the Father may be glorified in the Son;" "Hitherto ye have asked nothing in my name; ask, and ye shall receive, that your joy may be full" (John xiv. 13; xvi. 24). Hence it is incontrovertibly clear that those who pray to God in any other name than that of Christ contumaciously falsify his orders, and regard his will as nothing, while they have no promise that they shall obtain. For, as Paul says, "All the promises of God in him

---

1 French, "Confusion que nous avons, ou devons avoir en nousmesmes;"—confusion which we have, or ought to have, in ourselves.

are yea, and in him amen;" that is, are confirmed and fulfilled in him.

18. And we must carefully attend to the circumstance of time. Christ enjoins his disciples to have recourse to his intercession after he shall have ascended to heaven: "At that day ye shall ask in my name" (John xvi. 26). It is certain, indeed, that from the very first all who ever prayed were heard only for the sake of the Mediator. For this reason God had commanded in the Law, that the priest alone should enter the sanctuary, bearing the names of the twelve tribes of Israel on his shoulders, and as many precious stones on his breast, while the people were to stand at a distance in the outer court, and thereafter unite their prayers with the priest. Nay, the sacrifice had even the effect of ratifying and confirming their prayers. That shadowy ceremony of the Law therefore taught, first, that we are all excluded from the face of God, and, therefore, that there is need of a Mediator to appear in our name, and carry us on his shoulders, and keep us bound upon his breast, that we may be heard in his person; and, secondly, that our prayers, which, as has been said, would otherwise never be free from impurity, are cleansed by the sprinkling of his blood. And we see that the saints, when they desired to obtain anything, founded their hopes on sacrifices, because they knew that by sacrifice all prayers were ratified: "Remember all thy offerings," says David, "and accept thy burnt sacrifice" (Ps. xx. 3). Hence we infer, that in receiving the prayers of his people, God was from the very first appeased by the intercession of Christ. Why then does Christ speak of a new period ("at that day") when the disciples were to begin to pray in his name, unless it be that this grace, being now more brightly displayed, ought also to be in higher estimation with us? In this sense he had said a little before, "Hitherto ye have asked nothing in my name; ask." Not that they were altogether ignorant of the office of Mediator (all the Jews were instructed in these first rudiments), but they did not clearly understand that Christ by his ascent to heaven would be more the advocate of the Church than before. Therefore, to solace their grief for his absence by some more than ordinary result, he asserts his office of advocate, and says, that hitherto they had been without the special benefit which it would be their privilege to enjoy, when aided by his intercession they should invoke God with greater freedom. In this sense the Apostle says, that we have "boldness to enter into the holiest by the blood of Jesus, by a new and living way, which he hath consecrated for us" (Heb. x. 19, 20). Therefore, the more inexcusable we are, if we do not with both hands (as it is said) embrace the inestimable gift which is properly destined for us.

19. Moreover, since he himself is the only way and the only access by which we can draw near to God, those who deviate from this way, and decline this access, have no other remaining; his throne presents nothing but wrath, judgment, and terror. In short, as the Father has consecrated him our guide and head, those who abandon or turn

aside from him in any way endeavour, as much as in them lies, to sully and efface the stamp which God has impressed. Christ, therefore, is the only Mediator by whose intercession the Father is rendered propitious and exorable (1 Tim. ii. 5). For though the saints are still permitted to use intercessions, by which they mutually beseech God in behalf of each other's salvation, and of which the Apostle makes mention (Eph. vi. 18, 19; 1 Tim. ii. 1); still these depend on that one intercession, so far are they from derogating from it. For as the intercessions which as members of one body we offer up for each other, spring from the feeling of love, so they have reference to this one head. Being thus also made in the name of Christ, what more do they than declare that no man can derive the least benefit from any prayers without the intercession of Christ? As there is nothing in the intercession of Christ to prevent the different members of the Church from offering up prayers for each other, so let it be held as a fixed principle, that all the intercessions thus used in the Church must have reference to that one intercession. Nay, we must be specially careful to show our gratitude on this very account, that God pardoning our unworthiness, not only allows each individual to pray for himself, but allows all to intercede mutually for each other. God having given a place in his Church to intercessors who would deserve to be rejected when praying privately on their own account, how presumptuous were it to abuse this kindness by employing it to obscure the honour of Christ.

20. Moreover, the Sophists are guilty of the merest trifling when they allege that Christ is the Mediator of *redemption*, but that believers are mediators of *intercession ;* as if Christ had only performed a temporary mediation, and left an eternal and imperishable mediation to his servants. Such, forsooth, is the treatment which he receives from those who pretend only to take from him a minute portion of honour. Very different is the language of Scripture, with whose simplicity every pious man will be satisfied, without paying any regard to those impostors. For when John says, "If any man sin, we have an advocate with the Father, Jesus Christ the righteous" (1 John ii. 1), does he mean merely that we once had an advocate; does he not rather ascribe to him a perpetual intercession? What does Paul mean when he declares that he " is even at the right hand of God, who also maketh intercession for us"? (Rom. viii. 32.) But when in another passage he declares that he is the only Mediator between God and man (1 Tim. ii. 5), is he not referring to the supplications which he had mentioned a little before? Having previously said that prayers were to be offered up for all men, he immediately adds, in confirmation of that statement, that there is one God, and one Mediator between God and man. Nor does Augustine give a different interpretation when he says, "Christian men mutually recommend each other in their prayers. But he for whom none intercedes, while he himself intercedes for all, is the only true Mediator. Though the Apostle Paul was under the head a principal

member, yet because he was a member of the body of Christ, and knew that the most true and High Priest of the Church had entered not by figure into the inner veil to the holy of holies, but by firm and express truth into the inner sanctuary of heaven to holiness, holiness not imaginary, but eternal, he also commends himself to the prayers of the faithful. He does not make himself a mediator between God and the people, but asks that all the members of the body of Christ should pray mutually for each other, since the members are mutually sympathetic: if one member suffers, the others suffer with it. And thus the mutual prayers of all the members still labouring on the earth ascend to the Head, who has gone before into heaven, and in whom there is propitiation for our sins. For if Paul were a mediator, so would also the other apostles, and thus there would be many mediators, and Paul's statement could not stand, 'There is one God, and one Mediator between God and men, the man Christ Jesus;' in whom we also are one if we keep the unity of the faith in the bond of peace"[1] (August. Contra Parmenian, Lib. ii. cap. 8). Likewise in another passage Augustine says, "If thou requirest a priest, he is above the heavens, where he intercedes for those who on earth died for thee" (August. in Ps. xciv.). We imagine not that he throws himself before his Father's knees, and suppliantly intercedes for us; but we understand with the Apostle, that he appears in the presence of God, and that the power of his death has the effect of a perpetual intercession for us; that having entered into the upper sanctuary, he alone continues to the end of the world to present the prayers of his people, who are standing far off in the outer court.

21. In regard to the saints who having died in the body live in Christ, if we attribute prayer to them, let us not imagine that they have any other way of supplicating God than through Christ who alone is the way, or that their prayers are accepted by God in any other name. Wherefore, since the Scripture calls us away from all others to Christ alone, since our heavenly Father is pleased to gather together all things in him, it were the extreme of stupidity, not to say madness, to attempt to obtain access by means of others, so as to be drawn away from him without whom access cannot be obtained. But who can deny that this was the practice for several ages, and is still the practice, wherever Popery prevails? To procure the favour of God, human merits are ever and anon obtruded, and very frequently while Christ is passed by, God is supplicated in their name. I ask if this is not to transfer to them that office of sole intercession which we have above claimed for Christ? Then what angel or devil ever announced one syllable to any human being concerning that fancied intercession of theirs? There is not a word on the subject in Scripture. What ground then was there for the fiction? Certainly, while the human mind thus seeks help for itself in which it is not sanctioned by the word of God, it plainly manifests its distrust

[1] Heb. ix. 11, 24; Rom. xv. 30; Eph. vi. 19; Col. iv. 3; 1 Cor. xii. 25; 1 Tim. ii. 5; Eph. iv. 3.

(see s. 27). But if we appeal to the consciences of all who take pleasure in the intercession of saints, we shall find that their only reason for it is, that they are filled with anxiety, as if they supposed that Christ were insufficient or too rigorous. By this anxiety they dishonour Christ, and rob him of his title of sole Mediator, a title which being given him by the Father as his special privilege, ought not to be transferred to any other. By so doing they obscure the glory of his nativity and make void his cross; in short, divest and defraud of due praise everything which he did or suffered, since all which he did and suffered goes to show that he is and ought to be deemed sole Mediator. At the same time, they reject the kindness of God in manifesting himself to them as a Father, for he is not their Father if they do not recognise Christ as their brother. This they plainly refuse to do if they think not that he feels for them a brother's affection; affection than which none can be more gentle or tender. Wherefore Scripture offers him alone, sends us to him, and establishes us in him. "He," says Ambrose, "is our mouth by which we speak to the Father; our eye by which we see the Father; our right hand by which we offer ourselves to the Father. Save by his intercession neither we nor any saints have any intercourse with God" (Ambros. Lib. de Isaac et Anima). If they object that the public prayers which are offered up in churches conclude with the words, *through Jesus Christ our Lord*, it is a frivolous evasion; because no less insult is offered to the intercession of Christ by confounding it with the prayers and merits of the dead, than by omitting it altogether, and making mention only of the dead. Then, in all their litanies, hymns, and proses, where every kind of honour is paid to dead saints, there is no mention of Christ.

22. But here stupidity has proceeded to such a length as to give a manifestation of the genius of superstition, which, when once it has shaken off the rein, is wont to wanton without limit. After men began to look to the intercession of saints, a peculiar administration was gradually assigned to each, so that, according to diversity of business, now one, now another, intercessor was invoked. Then individuals adopted particular saints, and put their faith in them, just as if they had been tutelar deities. And thus not only were gods set up according to the number of the cities (the charge which the prophet brought against Israel of old, Jer. ii. 28; xi. 13), but according to the number of individuals. But while the saints in all their desires refer to the will of God alone, look to it, and acquiesce in it, yet to assign to them any other prayer than that of longing for the arrival of the kingdom of God, is to think of them stupidly, carnally, and even insultingly. Nothing can be farther from such a view than to imagine that each, under the influence of private feeling, is disposed to be most favourable to his own worshippers. At length vast numbers have fallen into the horrid blasphemy of invoking them not merely as helping but presiding over their salvation. See the depth to which miserable men fall when they forsake their proper station,

that is, the word of God. I say nothing of the more monstrous specimens of impiety in which, though detestable to God, angels, and men, they themselves feel no pain or shame. Prostrated at a statue or picture of Barbara or Catherine, and the like, they mutter a *Pater Noster*;[1] and so far are their pastors[2] from curing or curbing this frantic course, that, allured by the scent of gain, they approve and applaud it. But while seeking to relieve themselves of the odium of this vile and criminal procedure, with what pretext can they defend the practice of calling upon Eloy or Medard to look upon their servants, and send them help from heaven? or the Holy Virgin to order her Son to do what they ask?[3] The Council of Carthage forbade direct prayer to be made at the altar to saints. It is probable that these holy men, unable entirely to suppress the force of depraved custom, had recourse to this check, that public prayers might not be vitiated with such forms of expression as *Sancti Petre, ora pro nobis —St Peter, pray for us.* But how much farther has this devilish extravagance proceeded when men hesitate not to transfer to the dead the peculiar attributes of Christ and God?

23. In endeavouring to prove that such intercession derives some support from Scripture they labour in vain. We frequently read (they say) of the prayers of angels; and not only so, but the prayers of believers are said to be carried into the presence of God by their hands. But if they would compare saints who have departed this life with angels, it will be necessary to prove that saints are ministering spirits, to whom has been delegated the office of superintending our salvation, to whom has been assigned the province of guiding us in all our ways, of encompassing, admonishing, and comforting us, of keeping watch over us. All these are assigned to angels, but none of them to saints. How preposterously they confound departed saints with angels is sufficiently apparent from the many different offices

---

1 Erasmus, though stumbling and walking blindfold in clear light, ventures to write thus in a letter to Sadolet, 1530: " Primum, constat nullum esse locum in divinis voluminibus, qui permittat invocare divos, nisi fortasse detorquere huc placet, quod dives in Evangelica parabola implorat opem Abrahæ. Quanquam autem in re tanta novare quicquam præter auctoritatem Scripturæ, merito periculosum videri possit, tamen invocationem divorum nusquam improbo," &c.—First, it is clear that there is no passage in the Sacred Volume which permits the invocation of saints, unless we are pleased to wrest to this purpose what is said in the parable as to the rich man imploring the help of Abraham. But though in so weighty a matter it may justly seem dangerous to introduce anything without the authority of Scripture, I by no means condemn the invocation of saints, &c.

2 Latin, " Pastores;"—French, " ceux qui se disent prelats, curés, ou precheurs;"— those who call themselves prelates, curates, or preachers.

3 French, " Mais encore qu'ils taschent de laver leur mains d'un si vilain sacrilege, d'autant qu'il ne se commet point en leurs messes ni en leurs vespres; sous quelle couleur defendront ils ces blasphemes qu'il lisent a pleine gorge, où ils prient St Eloy ou St Medard, de regarder du ciel leurs serviteurs pour les aider? mesmes où ils supplient la vierge Maire de commander a son fils qu'il leur ottroye leur requestes?—But although they endeavour to wash their hands of the vile sacrilege, inasmuch as it is not committed in their masses or vespers, under what pretext will they defend those blasphemies which they repeat with full throat, in which they pray St Eloy or St Medard to look from heaven upon their servants and assist them; even supplicate the Virgin Mary to command her Son to grant their requests?

by which Scripture distinguishes the one from the other. No one unless admitted will presume to perform the office of pleader before an earthly judge; whence then have worms such licence as to obtrude themselves on God as intercessors, while no such office has been assigned them? God has been pleased to give angels the charge of our safety. Hence they attend our sacred meetings, and the Church is to them a theatre in which they behold the manifold wisdom of God (Eph. iii. 10). Those who transfer to others this office which is peculiar to them, certainly pervert and confound the order which has been established by God and ought to be inviolable. With similar dexterity they proceed to quote other passages. God said to Jeremiah, "Though Moses and Samuel stood before me, yet my mind could not be toward this people" (Jer. xv. 1). How (they ask) could he have spoken thus of the dead but because he knew that they interceded for the living? My inference, on the contrary, is this: since it thus appears that neither Moses nor Samuel interceded for the people of Israel, there was then no intercession for the dead. For who of the saints can be supposed to labour for the salvation of the people, while Moses who, when in life, far surpassed all others in this matter, does nothing? Therefore, if they persist in the paltry quibble, that the dead intercede for the living, because the Lord said, "*If they stood before me*" (*intercesserint*), I will argue far more speciously in this way: Moses, of whom it is said, *if he interceded*, did not intercede for the people in their extreme necessity: it is probable, therefore, that no other saint intercedes, all being far behind Moses in humanity, goodness, and paternal solicitude. Thus all they gain by their cavilling is to be wounded by the very arms with which they deem themselves admirably protected. But it is very ridiculous to wrest this simple sentence in this manner; for the Lord only declares that he would not spare the iniquities of the people, though some Moses or Samuel, to whose prayers he had shown himself so indulgent, should intercede for them. This meaning is most clearly elicited from a similar passage in Ezekiel: "Though these three men, Noah, Daniel, and Job, were in it, they should deliver but their own souls by their righteousness, saith the Lord God" (Ezek. xiv. 14). Here there can be no doubt that we are to understand the words as if it had been said, If two of the persons named were again to come alive; for the third was still living—namely, Daniel, who it is well known had then in the bloom of youth given an incomparable display of piety. Let us therefore leave out those whom Scripture declares to have completed their course. Accordingly, when Paul speaks of David, he says not that by his prayers he assisted posterity, but only that he "served his own generation" (Acts xiii. 36).

24. They again object, Are those, then, to be deprived of every pious wish, who, during the whole course of their lives, breathed nothing but piety and mercy? I have no wish curiously to pry into what they do or meditate; but the probability is, that instead of

being subject to the impulse of various and particular desires, they, with one fixed and immoveable will, long for the kingdom of God, which consists not less in the destruction of the ungodly, than in the salvation of believers. If this be so, there cannot be a doubt that their charity is confined to the communion of Christ's body, and extends no farther than is compatible with the nature of that communion. But though I grant that in this way they pray for us, they do not, however, lose their quiescence so as to be distracted with earthly cares : far less are they, therefore, to be invoked by us. Nor does it follow that such invocation is to be used, because, while men are alive upon the earth, they can mutually commend themselves to each other's prayers. It serves to keep alive a feeling of charity when they, as it were, share each other's wants, and bear each other's burdens. This they do by the command of the Lord, and not without a promise, the two things of primary importance in prayer. But all such reasons are inapplicable to the dead, with whom the Lord, in withdrawing them from our society, has left us no means of intercourse (Eccles. ix. 5, 6), and to whom, so far as we can conjecture, he has left no means of intercourse with us. But if any one allege that they certainly must retain the same charity for us, as they are united with us in one faith, who has revealed to us that they have ears capable of listening to the sounds of our voice, or eyes clear enough to discern our necessities. Our opponents, indeed, talk in the shade of their schools of some kind of light which beams upon departed saints from the divine countenance, and in which, as in a mirror, they, from their lofty abode, behold the affairs of men ; but to affirm this with the confidence which these men presume to use, is just to desire, by means of the extravagant dreams of our own brain, and without any authority, to pry and penetrate into the hidden judgments of God, and trample upon Scripture, which so often declares that the wisdom of our flesh is at enmity with the wisdom of God, utterly condemns the vanity of our mind, and humbling our reason, bids us look only to the will of God.

25. The other passages of Scripture which they employ to defend their error are miserably wrested. Jacob (they say) asks for the sons of Joseph, " Let my name be named on them, and the name of my fathers, Abraham and Isaac" (Gen. xlviii. 16). First, let us see what the nature of this invocation was among the Israelites. They do not implore their fathers to bring succour to them, but they beseech God to remember his servants, Abraham, Isaac, and Jacob. Their example, therefore, gives no countenance to those who use addresses to the saints themselves. But such being the dulness of these blocks, that they comprehend not what it is to invoke the name of Jacob, nor why it is to be invoked, it is not strange that they blunder thus childishly as to the mode of doing it. The expression repeatedly occurs in Scripture. Isaiah speaks of women being called by the name of men, when they have them for husbands and live under their protection (Isa. iv. 1). The calling of the name of Abraham

over the Israelites consists in referring the origin of their race to him, and holding him in distinguished remembrance as their author and parent. Jacob does not do so from any anxiety to extend the celebrity of his name, but because he knows that all the happiness of his posterity consisted in the inheritance of the covenant which God had made with them. Seeing that this would give them the sum of all blessings, he prays that they may be regarded as of his race, this being nothing else than to transmit the succession of the covenant to them. They again, when they make mention of this subject in their prayers, do not betake themselves to the intercession of the dead, but call to remembrance that covenant in which their most merciful Father undertakes to be kind and propitious to them for the sake of Abraham, Isaac, and Jacob. How little, in other respects, the saints trusted to the merits of their fathers, the public voice of the Church declares in the prophet, " Doubtless thou art our Father, though Abraham be ignorant of us, and Israel acknowledge us not; thou, O Lord, art our Father, our Redeemer" (Isa. lxiii. 16). And while the Church thus speaks, she at the same time adds, " Return for thy servants' sake," not thinking of anything like intercession, but adverting only to the benefit of the covenant. Now, indeed, when we have the Lord Jesus, in whose hand the eternal covenant of mercy was not only made but confirmed, what better name can we bear before us in our prayers ? And since those good Doctors would make out by these words that the Patriarchs are intercessors, I should like them to tell me why, in so great a multitude,[1] no place whatever is given to Abraham, the father of the Church ? We know well from what a crew they select their intercessors.[2] Let them then tell me what consistency there is in neglecting and rejecting Abraham, whom God preferred to all others, and raised to the highest degree of honour. The only reason is, that as it was plain there was no such practice in the ancient Church, they thought proper to conceal the novelty of the practice by saying nothing of the Patriarchs: as if by a mere diversity of names they could excuse a practice at once novel and impure. They sometimes, also, object that God is entreated to have mercy on his people "for David's sake" (Ps. cxxxii. 1, 10; see Calv. Com.). This is so far from supporting their error, that it is the strongest refutation of it. We must consider the character which David bore. He is set apart from the whole body of the faithful to establish the covenant which God made in his hand. Thus regard is had to the covenant rather than to the individual. Under him as a type the sole intercession of Christ is asserted. But what was peculiar to David as a type of Christ is certainly inapplicable to others.

26. But some seem to be moved by the fact, that the prayers of

---

1 The French adds, "et quasi en une fourmiliere de saincts;"—and as it were a swarm of saints.

2 " C'est chose trop notoire de quel bourbieu ou de quelle racaille ils tirent leur saincts."—It is too notorious out of what mire or rubbish they draw their saints.

saints are often said to have been heard. Why? Because they prayed. "They cried unto thee" (says the Psalmist), "and were delivered: they trusted in thee, and were not confounded" (Ps. xxii. 5). Let us also pray after their example, that like them we too may be heard. Those men, on the contrary, absurdly argue that none will be heard but those who have been heard already. How much better does James argue, "Elias was a man subject to like passions as we are, and he prayed earnestly that it might not rain: and it rained not on the earth by the space of three years and six months. And he prayed again, and the heaven gave rain, and the earth brought forth her fruit" (James v. 17, 18). What? Does he infer that Elias possessed some peculiar privilege, and that we must have recourse to him for the use of it? By no means. He shows the perpetual efficacy of a pure and pious prayer, that we may be induced in like manner to pray. For the kindness and readiness of God to hear others is malignantly interpreted, if their example does not inspire us with stronger confidence in his promise, since his declaration is not that he will incline his ear to one or two, or a few individuals, but to all who call upon his name. In this ignorance they are the less excusable, because they seem as it were avowedly to contemn the many admonitions of Scripture. David was repeatedly delivered by the power of God. Was this to give that power to him that we might be delivered on his application? Very different is his affirmation: "The righteous shall compass me about; for thou shalt deal bountifully with me" (Ps. cxlii. 7). Again, "The righteous also shall see, and fear, and shall laugh at him" (Ps. lii. 6). "This poor man cried, and the Lord heard him, and saved him out of all his troubles" (Ps. xxxiv. 6). In The Psalms are many similar prayers, in which David calls upon God to give him what he asks, for this reason—viz. that the righteous may not be put to shame, but by his example encouraged to hope. Here let one passage suffice, "For this shall every one that is godly pray unto thee in a time when thou mayest be found" (Ps. xxxii. 6, Calv. Com.). This passage I have quoted the more readily, because those ravers who employ their hireling tongues in defence of the Papacy, are not ashamed to adduce it in proof of the intercession of the dead. As if David intended anything more than to show the benefit which he shall obtain from the divine clemency and condescension when he shall have been heard. In general, we must hold that the experience of the grace of God, as well towards ourselves as towards others, tends in no slight degree to confirm our faith in his promises. I do not quote the many passages in which David sets forth the lovingkindness of God to him as a ground of confidence, as they will readily occur to every reader of The Psalms. Jacob had previously taught the same thing by his own example, "I am not worthy of the least of all thy mercies, and of all the truth which thou hast showed unto thy servant: for with my staff I passed over this Jordan; and now I am become two bands" (Gen. xxxii. 10). He, indeed, alleges the promise, but not the promise only; for he at the same time adds the effect, to animate him with greater confidence in the future kindness of God. God is not like men who grow weary of their liberality, or whose means of exercising it become exhausted; but he is to be estimated by his own nature, as David properly does when he says, "Thou hast redeemed me, O Lord God of truth" (Ps. xxxi. 5). After ascribing the praise of his salvation to God, he adds that he is true: for were he not ever like himself, his past favour would not be an infallible ground for confidence and prayer. But when we know that as often as he assists us, he gives us a specimen and proof of his goodness and faithfulness, there is no reason to fear that our hope will be ashamed or frustrated.

27. On the whole, since Scripture places the principal part of worship in the invocation of God (this being the office of piety which he requires of us in preference to all sacrifices), it is manifest sacrilege to offer prayer to others. Hence it is said in the psalm: "If we have forgotten the name of our God, or stretched out our hands to a strange God, shall not God search this out?" (Ps. xliv. 20, 21.) Again, since it is only in faith that God desires to be invoked, and he distinctly enjoins us to frame our prayers according to the rule of his word: in fine, since faith is founded on the word, and is the parent of right prayer, the moment we decline from the word, our prayers are impure. But we have already shown, that if we consult the whole volume of Scripture, we shall find that God claims this honour to himself alone. In regard to the office of intercession, we have also seen that it is peculiar to Christ, and that no prayer is agreeable to God which he as Mediator does not sanctify. And though believers mutually offer up prayers to God in behalf of their brethren, we have shown that this derogates in no respect from the sole intercession of Christ, because all trust to that intercession in commending themselves as well as others to God. Moreover, we have shown that this is ignorantly transferred to the dead, of whom we nowhere read that they were commanded to pray for us. The Scripture often exhorts us to offer up mutual prayers; but says not one syllable concerning the dead; nay, James tacitly excludes the dead, when he combines the two things, to "confess our sins one to another, and to pray one for another" (James v. 16). Hence it is sufficient to condemn this error, that the beginning of right prayer springs from faith, and that faith comes by the hearing of the word of God, in which there is no mention of fictitious intercession, superstition having rashly adopted intercessors who have not been divinely appointed. While the Scripture abounds in various forms of prayer, we find no example of this intercession, without which Papists think there is no prayer. Moreover, it is evident that this superstition is the result of distrust, because they are either not contented with Christ as an intercessor, or have altogether robbed him of this honour. This last is easily proved by their effrontery in maintaining, as the strongest of all their arguments for the intercession of the saints, that we are

unworthy of familiar access to God.   This, indeed, we acknowledge
to be most true, but we thence infer that they leave nothing to
Christ, because they consider his intercession as nothing, unless it is
supplemented by that of George and Hypolyte, and similar phantoms.

28. But though prayer is properly confined to vows and supplications, yet so strong is the affinity between petition and thanksgiving,
that both may be conveniently comprehended under one name.   For
the forms which Paul enumerates (1 Tim. ii. 1) fall under the first
member of this division.   By prayer and supplication we pour out
our desires before God, asking as well those things which tend to
promote his glory and display his name, as the benefits which contribute to our advantage.   By thanksgiving we duly celebrate his kind-
nesses toward us, ascribing to his liberality every blessing which
enters into our lot.   David accordingly includes both in one sentence,
" Call upon me in the day of trouble : I will deliver thee, and thou
shalt glorify me " (Ps. l. 15).   Scripture, not without reason, commands us to use both continually.   We have already described the
greatness of our want, while experience itself proclaims the straits
which press us on every side to be so numerous and so great, that all
have sufficient ground to send forth sighs and groans to God without
intermission, and suppliantly implore him.   For even should they be
exempt from adversity, still the holiest ought to be stimulated first
by their sins, and, secondly, by the innumerable assaults of temptation, to long for a remedy.   The sacrifice of praise and thanksgiving
can never be interrupted without guilt, since God never ceases to
load us with favour upon favour, so as to force us to gratitude, however slow and sluggish we may be.   In short, so great and widely
diffused are the riches of his liberality towards us, so marvellous and
wondrous the miracles which we behold on every side, that we never
can want a subject and materials for praise and thanksgiving.

To make this somewhat clearer : since all our hopes and resources
are placed in God (this has already been fully proved), so that neither
our persons nor our interests can prosper without his blessing, we
must constantly submit ourselves and our all to him.   Then whatever we deliberate, speak, or do, should be deliberated, spoken, and
done under his hand and will ; in fine, under the hope of his assistance.   God has pronounced a curse upon all who, confiding in themselves or others, form plans and resolutions, who, without regarding
his will, or invoking his aid, either plan or attempt to execute (James
iv. 14 ; Isaiah xxx. 1 ; xxxi. 1).   And since, as has already been
observed, he receives the honour which is due when he is acknowledged to be the author of all good, it follows that, in deriving all
good from his hand, we ought continually to express our thankfulness, and that we have no right to use the benefits which proceed
from his liberality, if we do not assiduously proclaim his praise, and
give him thanks, these being the ends for which they are given.
When Paul declares that every creature of God " is sanctified by the
word of God and prayer " (1 Tim. iv. 5), he intimates that without

the word and prayer, none of them are holy and pure, *word* being used metonymically for *faith*. Hence David, on experiencing the loving-kindness of the Lord, elegantly declares, "He hath put a new song in my mouth" (Ps. xl. 3); intimating, that our silence is malignant when we leave his blessings unpraised, seeing every blessing he bestows is a new ground of thanksgiving. Thus Isaiah, proclaiming the singular mercies of God, says, "Sing unto the Lord a new song." In the same sense David says in another passage, "O Lord, open thou my lips; and my mouth shall show forth thy praise" (Ps. li. 15). In like manner, Hezekiah and Jonah declare that they will regard it as the end of their deliverance "to celebrate the goodness of God with songs in his temple" (Is. xxxviii. 20; Jonah ii. 10). David lays down a general rule for all believers in these words, "What shall I render unto the Lord for all his benefits toward me? I will take the cup of salvation, and call upon the name of the Lord" (Ps. cxvi. 12, 13). This rule the Church follows in another psalm, "Save us, O Lord our God, and gather us from among the heathen, to give thanks unto thy holy name, and to triumph in thy praise" (Ps. cvi. 47). Again, "He will regard the prayer of the destitute, and not despise their prayer. This shall be written for the generation to come: and the people which shall be created shall praise the Lord." "To declare the name of the Lord in Zion, and his praise in Jerusalem" (Ps. cii. 18, 21). Nay, whenever believers beseech the Lord to do anything *for his own name's sake*, as they declare themselves unworthy of obtaining it in their own name, so they oblige themselves to give thanks, and promise to make the right use of his loving-kindness by being the heralds of it. Thus Hosea, speaking of the future redemption of the Church, says, "Take away all iniquity, and receive us graciously; so will we render the calves of our lips" (Hos. xiv. 2). Not only do our tongues proclaim the kindness of God, but they naturally inspire us with love to him. "I love the Lord, because he hath heard my voice and my supplications" (Ps. cxvi. 1). In another passage, speaking of the help which he had experienced, he says, "I will love thee, O Lord, my strength" (Ps. xviii. 1). No praise will ever please God that does not flow from this feeling of love. Nay, we must attend to the declaration of Paul, that all wishes are vicious and perverse which are not accompanied with thanksgiving. His words are, "In everything by prayer and supplication with thanksgiving let your requests be made known unto God" (Phil. iv. 6). Because many, under the influence of moroseness, weariness, impatience, bitter grief and fear, use murmuring in their prayers, he enjoins us so to regulate our feelings as cheerfully to bless God even before obtaining what we ask. But if this connection ought always to subsist in full vigour between things that are almost contrary, the more sacred is the tie which binds us to celebrate the praises of God whenever he grants our requests. And as we have already shown that our prayers, which otherwise would be polluted, are sanctified by the intercession of Christ, so the Apostle, by enjoining us "to offer the sacrifice of praise to God continually" by Christ (Heb. xiii. 15), reminds us, that without the intervention of his priesthood our lips are not pure enough to celebrate the name of God. Hence we infer that a monstrous delusion prevails among Papists, the great majority of whom wonder when Christ is called an intercessor. The reason why Paul enjoins, "Pray without ceasing; in everything give thanks" (1 Thess. v. 17, 18), is, because he would have us with the utmost assiduity, at all times, in every place, in all things, and under all circumstances, direct our prayers to God, to expect all the things which we desire from him, and when obtained ascribe them to him; thus furnishing perpetual grounds for prayer and praise.

29. This assiduity in prayer, though it specially refers to the peculiar private prayers of individuals, extends also in some measure to the public prayers of the Church. These, it may be said, cannot be continual, and ought not to be made, except in the manner which, for the sake of order, has been established by public consent. This I admit, and hence certain hours are fixed beforehand, hours which, though indifferent in regard to God, are necessary for the use of man, that the general convenience may be consulted, and all things be done in the Church, as Paul enjoins, "decently and in order" (1 Cor. xiv. 40). But there is nothing in this to prevent each church from being now and then stirred up to a more frequent use of prayer, and being more zealously affected under the impulse of some greater necessity. Of perseverance in prayer, which is much akin to assiduity, we shall speak towards the close of the chapter (sec. 51, 52). This assiduity, moreover, is very different from the Βαττολογία, *vain speaking*, which our Saviour has prohibited (Matth. vi. 7). For he does not there forbid us to pray long or frequently, or with great fervour, but warns as against supposing that we can extort anything from God by importuning him with garrulous loquacity, as if he were to be persuaded after the manner of men. We know that hypocrites, because they consider not that they have to do with God, offer up their prayers as pompously as if it were part of a triumphal show. The pharisee, who thanked God that he was not as other men, no doubt proclaimed his praises before men, as if he had wished to gain a reputation for sanctity by his prayers. Hence that *vain speaking*, which for a similar reason prevails so much in the Papacy in the present day, some vainly spinning out the time by a reiteration of the same frivolous prayers, and others employing a long series of verbiage for vulgar display.[1] This childish garrulity being a mockery of God, it is not

1 French, "Cette longueur de priere a aujourd'hui sa vogue en la Papauté, et procede de cette mesme source; c'est que les uns barbotant force Ave Maria, et reiterant cent fois un chapelet, perdent une partie du temps; les autres, comme les chanoines et caphars, en abayant le parchemin jour et nuict, et barbotant leur breviaire vendent leur coquilles au peuple."—This long prayer is at present in vogue among the Papists, and proceeds from the same cause: some muttering a host of Ave Marias, and going over their beads a hundred times, lose part of their time; others, as the canons and monks, grumbling over their parchment night and day, and muttering their breviary, sell their cockleshells to the people.

strange that it is prohibited in the Church, in order that every feeling there expressed may be sincere, proceeding from the inmost heart. Akin to this abuse is another which our Saviour also condemns— namely, when hypocrites for the sake of ostentation court the presence of many witnesses, and would sooner pray in the market place than pray without applause. The true object of prayer being, as we have already said (sec. 4, 5), to carry our thoughts directly to God, whether to celebrate his praise or implore his aid, we can easily see that its primary seat is in the mind and heart, or rather that prayer itself is properly an effusion and manifestation of internal feeling before Him who is the searcher of hearts. Hence (as has been said), when our divine Master was pleased to lay down the best rule for prayer, his injunction was, " Enter into thy closet, and when thou hast shut thy door, pray to thy Father which is in secret, and thy Father which seeth in secret shall reward thee openly" (Matth. vi. 6). Dissuading us from the example of hypocrites, who sought the applause of men by an ambitious ostentation in prayer, he adds the better course— enter thy chamber, shut thy door, and there pray. By these words (as I understand them) he taught us to seek a place of retirement which might enable us to turn all our thoughts inwards, and enter deeply into our hearts, promising that God would hold converse with the feelings of our mind, of which the body ought to be the temple. He meant not to deny that it may be expedient to pray in other places also, but he shows that prayer is somewhat of a secret nature, having its chief seat in the mind, and requiring a tranquillity far removed from the turmoil of ordinary cares. And hence it was not without cause that our Lord himself, when he would engage more earnestly in prayer, withdrew into a retired spot beyond the bustle of the world, thus reminding us by his example that we are not to neglect those helps which enable the mind, in itself too much dis- posed to wander, to become sincerely intent on prayer. Meanwhile, as he abstained not from prayer when the occasion required it, though he were in the midst of a crowd, so must we, whenever there is need, lift up "pure hands" (1 Tim. ii. 8) at all places. And hence we must hold that he who declines to pray in the public meeting of the saints, knows not what it is to pray apart, in retirement, or at home. On the other hand, he who neglects to pray alone and in private, however sedulously he frequents public meetings, there gives his prayers to the wind, because he defers more to the opinion of man than to the secret judgment of God. Still, lest the public prayers of the Church should be held in contempt, the Lord anciently bestowed upon them the most honourable appellation, especially when he called the temple the " *house of prayer* " (Isa. lvi. 7). For by this expres- sion he both showed that the duty of prayer is a principal part of his worship, and that to enable believers to engage in it with one consent his temple is set up before them as a kind of banner. A noble promise was also added, " Praise waiteth for thee, O God, in Sion:

and unto thee shall the vow be performed"[1] (Ps. lxv. 1). By these
words the Psalmist reminds us that the prayers of the Church are
never in vain; because God always furnishes his people with materials for a song of joy. But although the shadows of the law have
ceased, yet because God was pleased by this ordinance to foster the
unity of the faith among us also, there can be no doubt that the
same promise belongs to us—a promise which Christ sanctioned
with his own lips, and which Paul declares to be perpetually in
force.

30. As God in his word enjoins common prayer, so public temples
are the places destined for the performance of them, and hence those
who refuse to join with the people of God in this observance have no
ground for the pretext, that they enter their chamber in order that
they may obey the command of the Lord. For he who promises to
grant whatsoever two or three assembled in his name shall ask (Matth.
xviii. 20), declares, that he by no means despises the prayers which
are publicly offered up, provided there be no ostentation, or catching
at human applause, and provided there be a true and sincere affection in the secret recesses of the heart.[2] If this is the legitimate use
of churches (and it certainly is), we must, on the other hand, beware
of imitating the practice which commenced some centuries ago, of
imagining that churches are the proper dwellings of God, where he
is more ready to listen to us, or of attaching to them some kind
of secret sanctity, which makes prayer there more holy. For seeing
we are the true temples of God, we must pray in ourselves if we would
invoke God in his holy temple. Let us leave such gross ideas to the
Jews or the heathen, knowing that we have a command to pray,
without distinction of place, "in spirit and in truth" (John iv. 23).
It is true that by the order of God the temple was anciently dedicated for the offerings of prayers and sacrifices, but this was at
a time when the truth (which being now fully manifested, we are not
permitted to confine to any material temple) lay hid under the figure
of shadows. Even the temple was not represented to the Jews as
confining the presence of God within its walls, but was meant to
train them to contemplate the image of the true temple. Accordingly,
a severe rebuke is administered both by Isaiah and Stephen, to those
who thought that God could in any way dwell in temples made with
hands (Isa. lxvi. 2; Acts vii. 48).

31. Hence it is perfectly clear that neither words nor singing (if
used in prayer) are of the least consequence, or avail one iota with
God, unless they proceed from deep feeling in the heart. Nay, rather
they provoke his anger against us, if they come from the lips and
throat only, since this is to abuse his sacred name, and hold his
majesty in derision. This we infer from the words of Isaiah, which,

---

[1] Calvin translates, " Te expectat Deus, laus in Sion;"—God, the praise in Sion
waiteth for thee.
[2] See Book I. chap. xi. sec. 7, 13, on the subject of images in churches. Also Book
IV. chap. iv. sec. 8, and chap. v. sec. 18, as to the ornaments of churches.

though their meaning is of wider extent, go to rebuke this vice also : " Forasmuch as this people draw near me with their mouth, and with their lips do honour me, but have removed their heart far from me, and their fear toward me is taught by the precept of men : therefore, behold, I will proceed to do a marvellous work among this people, even a marvellous work and a wonder : for the wisdom of their wise men shall perish, and the understanding of their prudent men shall be hid" (Isa. xxix. 13).   Still we do not condemn words or singing, but rather greatly commend them, provided the feeling of the mind goes along with them.   For in this way the thought of God is kept alive on our minds, which, from their fickle and versatile nature, soon relax, and are distracted by various objects, unless various means are used to support them.   Besides, since the glory of God ought in a manner to be displayed in each part of our body, the special service to which the tongue should be devoted is that of singing and speaking, inasmuch as it has been expressly created to declare and proclaim the praise of God.   This employment of the tongue is chiefly in the public services which are performed in the meeting of the saints.   In this way the God whom we serve in one spirit and one faith, we glorify together as it were with one voice and one mouth ; and that openly, so that each may in turn receive the confession of his brother's faith, and be invited and incited to imitate it.

32. It is certain that the use of singing in churches (which I may mention in passing) is not only very ancient, but was also used by the Apostles, as we may gather from the words of Paul, " I will sing with the spirit, and I will sing with the understanding also" (1 Cor. xiv. 15).   In like manner he says to the Colossians, " Teaching and admonishing one another in psalms, and hymns, and spiritual songs, singing with grace in your hearts to the Lord" (Col. iii. 16).   In the former passage, he enjoins us to sing with the voice and the heart ; in the latter, he commends spiritual songs, by which the pious mutually edify each other.   That it was not a universal practice, however, is attested by Augustine (Confess. lib. ix. cap. 7), who states that the church of Milan first began to use singing in the time of Ambrose, when the orthodox faith being persecuted by Justina, the mother of Valentinian, the vigils of the people were more frequent than usual ;[1] and that the practice was afterwards followed by the other Western churches. He had said a little before that the custom came from the East.[2] He also intimates (Retract. Lib. ii.) that it was received in Africa in his own time.   His words are, " Hilarius, a man of tribunitial rank, assailed with the bitterest invectives he could use the custom which then began to exist at Carthage, of singing hymns from the book of Psalms at the altar, either before the oblation, or when it was distributed to the people ; I answered him, at the request of my brethren."[3]   And certainly if singing is

---

1 This clause of the sentence is omitted in the French.
2 The French adds, " où on en avoit tousjours usé ; "—where it had always been used.
3 The whole of this quotation is omitted in the French.

tempered to a gravity befitting the presence of God and angels, it both gives dignity and grace to sacred actions, and has a very powerful tendency to stir up the mind to true zeal and ardour in prayer. We must, however, carefully beware, lest our ears be more intent on the music than our minds on the spiritual meaning of the words. Augustine confesses (Confess. Lib. x. cap. 33) that the fear of this danger sometimes made him wish for the introduction of a practice observed by Athanasius, who ordered the reader to use only a gentle inflection of the voice, more akin to recitation than singing. But on again considering how many advantages were derived from singing, he inclined to the other side.[1] If this moderation is used, there cannot be a doubt that the practice is most sacred and salutary. On the other hand, songs composed merely to tickle and delight the ear are unbecoming the majesty of the Church, and cannot but be most displeasing to God.

33. It is also plain that the public prayers are not to be couched in Greek among the Latins, nor in Latin among the French or English (as hitherto has been everywhere practised), but in the vulgar tongue, so that all present may understand them, since they ought to be used for the edification of the whole Church, which cannot be in the least degree benefited by a sound not understood. Those who are not moved by any reason of humanity or charity, ought at least to be somewhat moved by the authority of Paul, whose words are by no means ambiguous: "When thou shalt bless with the spirit, how shall he that occupieth the room of the unlearned say, Amen, at thy giving of thanks, seeing he understandeth not what thou sayest? For thou verily givest thanks, but the other is not edified" (1 Cor. xiv. 16, 17). How then can one sufficiently admire the unbridled licence of the Papists, who, while the Apostle publicly protests against it, hesitate not to brawl out the most verbose prayers in a foreign tongue, prayers of which they themselves sometimes do not understand one syllable, and which they have no wish that others should understand?[2] Different is the course which Paul prescribes, "What is it then? I will pray with the spirit, and I will pray with the understanding also ; I will sing with the spirit, and I will sing with the understanding also :" meaning by the *spirit* the special gift of tongues, which some who had received it abused when they dissevered

---

[1] French, " Mais il adjouste d'autre part, que quand il se souvenoit du fruict et de l'edification qu'il avoit recue en oyant chanter à l'Église il enclinoit plus à l'autre partie, c'est, approuver le chant ;"—but he adds on the other hand, that when he called to mind the fruit and edification which he had received from hearing singing in the church, he inclined more to the other side ; that is, to approve singing.

[2] French, " Qui est-ce donc qui se pourra assez esmerveiller d'une audace tant effrenee qu'ont eu les Papistes et ont encore, qui contre la defense de l'Apostre, chantent et brayent de langue estrange et inconnue, en laquelle le plus souvent ils n'entendent pas eux mesmes une syllabe, et ne veulent que les autres y entendent ?"—Who then can sufficiently admire the unbridled audacity which the Papists have had, and still have, who, contrary to the prohibition of the Apostle, chant and bray in a foreign and unknown tongue, in which, for the most part, they do not understand one syllable, and which they have no wish that others understand ?

it from the mind, that is, the understanding. The principle we must always hold is, that in all prayer, public and private, the tongue without the mind must be displeasing to God. Moreover, the mind must be so incited, as in ardour of thought far to surpass what the tongue is able to express. Lastly, the tongue is not even necessary to private prayer, unless in so far as the internal feeling is insufficient for incitement, or the vehemence of the incitement carries the utterance of the tongue along with it. For although the best prayers are sometimes without utterance, yet when the feeling of the mind is overpowering, the tongue spontaneously breaks forth into utterance, and our other members into gesture. Hence that dubious muttering of Hannah (1 Sam. i. 13), something similar to which is experienced by all the saints when concise and abrupt expressions escape from them. The bodily gestures usually observed in prayer, such as kneeling and uncovering of the head (Calv. in Acts xx. 36), are exercises by which we attempt to rise to higher veneration of God.

34. We must now attend not only to a surer method, but also form of prayer, that—namely, which our heavenly Father has delivered to us by his beloved Son, and in which we may recognise his boundless goodness and condescension (Matth. vi. 9 ; Luke xi. 2). Besides admonishing us and exhorting us to seek him in our every necessity (as children are wont to betake themselves to the protection of their parents when oppressed with any anxiety), seeing that we are not fully aware how great our poverty was, or what was right or for our interest to ask, he has provided for this ignorance ; that wherein our capacity failed he has sufficiently supplied. For he has given us a form in which is set before us as in a picture everything which it is lawful to wish, everything which is conducive to our interest, everything which it is necessary to demand. From his goodness in this respect we derive the great comfort of knowing, that as we ask almost in his words, we ask nothing that is absurd, or foreign, or unseasonable ; nothing, in short, that is not agreeable to him. Plato, seeing the ignorance of men in presenting their desires to God, desires which if granted would often be most injurious to them, declares the best form of prayer to be that which an ancient poet has furnished : " O king Jupiter, give what is best, whether we wish it or wish it not ; but avert from us what is evil even though we ask it" (Plato, Alcibid. i.). This heathen shows his wisdom in discerning how dangerous it is to ask of God what our own passion dictates ; while, at the same time, he reminds us of our unhappy condition in not being able to open our lips before God without danger, unless his Spirit instruct us how to pray aright (Rom. viii. 26). The higher value, therefore, ought we to set on the privilege, when the only begotten Son of God puts words into our lips, and thus relieves our minds of all hesitation.

35. This form or rule of prayer is composed of *six petitions*. For I am prevented from agreeing with those who divide it into *seven* by the adversative mode of diction used by the Evangelist, who appears

to have intended to unite the two members together: as if he had said, Do not allow us to be overcome by temptation, but rather bring assistance to our frailty, and deliver us that we may not fall. Ancient writers[1] also agree with us, that what is added by Matthew as a seventh head is to be considered as explanatory of the sixth petition.[2] But though in every part of the prayer the first place is assigned to the glory of God, still this is more especially the object of the three first petitions, in which we are to look to the glory of God alone, without any reference to what is called our own advantage. The three remaining petitions are devoted to our interest, and properly relate to things which it is useful for us to ask. When we ask that the name of God may be hallowed, as God wishes to prove whether we love and serve him freely, or from the hope of reward, we are not to think at all of our own interest; we must set his glory before our eyes, and keep them intent upon it alone. In the other similar petitions, this is the only manner in which we ought to be affected. It is true, that in this way our own interest is greatly promoted, because, when the name of God is hallowed in the way we ask, our own sanctification is also thereby promoted. But in regard to this advantage, we must, as I have said, shut our eyes, and be in a manner blind, so as not even to see it; and hence were all hope of our private advantage cut off, we still should never cease to wish and pray for this hallowing, and everything else which pertains to the glory of God. We have examples in Moses and Paul, who did not count it grievous to turn away their eyes and minds from themselves, and with intense and fervent zeal long for death, if by their loss the kingdom and glory of God might be promoted (Exod. xxxii. 32; Rom. ix. 3). On the other hand, when we ask for daily bread, although we desire what is advantageous for ourselves we ought also especially to seek the glory of God, so much so that we would not ask at all unless it were to turn to his glory. Let us now proceed to an exposition of the Prayer.

OUR FATHER WHICH ART IN HEAVEN.

36. The first thing suggested at the very outset is, as we have already said (sec. 17–19), that all our prayers to God ought only to be presented in the name of Christ, as there is no other name which can recommend them. In calling God our Father, we certainly plead the name of Christ. For with what confidence could any man call God his Father? Who would have the presumption to arrogate

---

[1] August. in Enchirid. ad Laurent. cap. 116. Chrysost. in an imperfect work. See end of sec. 53.

[2] " Dont il est facile de juger que cè qui est adjousté en S. Matthieu, et qu'aucuns ont pris pour une septieme requeste, n'est qu'un explication de la sixieme, et se doit a icelle rapporter;"—Whence it is easy to perceive that what is added in St Matthew, and which some have taken for a seventh petition, is only an explanation of the sixth, and ought to be referred to it.

to himself the honour of a son of God were we not gratuitously adopted as his sons in Christ? He being the true Son, has been given to us as a brother, so that that which he possesses as his own by nature becomes ours by adoption, if we embrace this great mercy with firm faith. As John says, "As many as receive him, to them gave he power to become the sons of God, even to them that believe in his name" (John i. 12). Hence he both calls himself our Father, and is pleased to be so called by us, by this delightful name relieving us of all distrust, since nowhere can a stronger affection be found than in a father. Hence, too, he could not have given us a stronger testimony of his boundless love than in calling us his sons. But his love towards us is so much the greater and more excellent than that of earthly parents, the farther he surpasses all men in goodness and mercy (Isaiah lxiii. 18). Earthly parents, laying aside all paternal affection, might abandon their offspring; he will never abandon us (Ps. xxvii. 10), seeing he cannot deny himself. For we have his promise, "If ye then, being evil, know how to give good gifts unto your children, how much more shall your Father which is in heaven give good things to them that ask him?" (Matth. vii. 11.) In like manner in the prophet, "Can a woman forget her sucking child, that she should not have compassion on the son of her womb? Yea, they may forget, yet will not I forget thee" (Isaiah xlix. 15). But if we are his sons, then as a son cannot betake himself to the protection of a stranger and a foreigner without at the same time complaining of his father's cruelty or poverty, so we cannot ask assistance from any other quarter than from him, unless we would upbraid him with poverty, or want of means, or cruelty and excessive austerity.

37. Nor let us allege that we are justly rendered timid by a consciousness of sin, by which our Father, though mild and merciful, is daily offended. For if among men a son cannot have a better advocate to plead his cause with his father, and cannot employ a better intercessor to regain his lost favour, than if he come himself suppliant and downcast, acknowledging his fault, to implore the mercy of his father, whose paternal feelings cannot but be moved by such entreaties, what will that "Father of all mercies, and God of all comfort," do? (2 Cor. i. 3.) Will he not rather listen to the tears and groans of his children, when supplicating for themselves (especially seeing he invites and exhorts us to do so), than to any advocacy of others to whom the timid have recourse, not without some semblance of despair, because they are distrustful of their father's mildness and clemency? The exuberance of his paternal kindness he sets before us in the parable (Luke xv. 20; see Calv. Comm.), when the father with open arms receives the son who had gone away from him, wasted his substance in riotous living, and in all ways grievously sinned against him. He waits not till pardon is asked in words, but, anticipating the request, recognises him afar off, runs to meet him, consoles him, and restores him to favour. By setting before us this admirable example of mildness in a man, he de-

signed to show in how much greater abundance we may expect it from him who is not only a Father, but the best and most merciful of all fathers, however ungrateful, rebellious, and wicked sons we may be, provided only we throw ourselves upon his mercy. And the better to assure us that he is such a Father if we are Christians, he has been pleased to be called not only a Father, but OUR Father, as if we were pleading with him after this manner, O Father, who art possessed of so much affection for thy children, and art so ready to forgive, we thy children approach thee and present our requests, fully persuaded that thou hast no other feelings towards us than those of a father, though we are unworthy of such a parent.[1] But as our narrow hearts are incapable of comprehending such boundless favour, Christ is not only the earnest and pledge of our adoption, but also gives us the Spirit as a witness of this adoption, that through him we may freely cry aloud, Abba, Father. Whenever, therefore, we are restrained by any feeling of hesitation, let us remember to ask of him that he may correct our timidity, and placing us under the magnanimous guidance of the Spirit, enable us to pray boldly.

38. The instruction given us, however, is not that every individual in particular is to call him Father, but rather that we are all in common to call him Our Father. By this we are reminded how strong the feeling of brotherly love between us ought to be, since we are all alike, by the same mercy and free kindness, the children of such a Father. For if He from whom we all obtain whatever is good is our common Father (Matth. xxiii. 9), everything which has been distributed to us we should be prepared to communicate to each other, as far as occasion demands. But if we are thus desirous, as we ought, to stretch out our hand, and give assistance to each other, there is nothing by which we can more benefit our brethren than by committing them to the care and protection of the best of parents, since if He is propitious and favourable nothing more can be desired. And, indeed, we owe this also to our Father. For as he who truly and from the heart loves the father of a family, extends the same love and good-will to all his household, so the zeal and affection which we feel for our heavenly Parent it becomes us to extend towards his people, his family, and, in fine, his heritage, which he has honoured so highly as to give them the appellation of the "fulness" of his only begotten Son (Eph. i. 23). Let the Christian, then, so regulate his prayers as to make them common, and embrace all who are his brethren in Christ; not only those whom at present he sees and knows to be such, but all men who are alive upon the earth. What God has determined with regard to them is beyond our knowledge, but to wish and hope the best concerning them is both pious and humane. Still it becomes us to regard with special affection those who are of the household of faith, and whom the

---

1 French, "Quelque mauvaistié qu'ayons euë, ou quelque imperfection ou poureté qui soit en nous;"—whatever wickedness we may have done, or whatever imperfection or poverty there may be in us.

Apostle has in express terms recommended to our care in everything (Gal. vi. 10). In short, all our prayers ought to bear reference to that community which our Lord has established in his kingdom and family.

39. This, however, does not prevent us from praying specially for ourselves, and certain others, provided our mind is not withdrawn from the view of this community, does not deviate from it, but constantly refers to it. For prayers, though couched in special terms, keeping that object still in view, cease not to be common. All this may easily be understood by analogy. There is a general command from God to relieve the necessities of all the poor, and yet this command is obeyed by those who with that view give succour to all whom they see or know to be in distress, although they pass by many whose wants are not less urgent, either because they cannot know or are unable to give supply to all. In this way there is nothing repugnant to the will of God in those who, giving heed to this common society of the Church, yet offer up particular prayers, in which, with a public mind, though in special terms, they commend to God themselves or others, with whose necessity he has been pleased to make them more familiarly acquainted. It is true that prayer and the giving of our substance are not in all respects alike. We can only bestow the kindness of our liberality on those of whose wants we are aware, whereas in prayer we can assist the greatest strangers, how wide soever the space which may separate them from us. This is done by that general form of prayer which, including all the sons of God, includes them also. To this we may refer the exhortation which Paul gave to the believers of his age, to lift up "holy hands, without wrath and doubting" (1 Tim. ii. 8). By reminding them that dissension is a bar to prayer, he shows it to be his wish that they should with one accord present their prayers in common.

40. The next words are, WHICH ART IN HEAVEN. From this we are not to infer that he is enclosed and confined within the circumference of heaven, as by a kind of boundaries. Hence Solomon confesses, "The heaven of heavens cannot contain thee" (1 Kings viii. 27); and he himself says by the Prophet, "The heaven is my throne, and the earth is my footstool" (Isa. lxvi. 1); thereby intimating, that his presence, not confined to any region, is diffused over all space. But as our gross minds are unable to conceive of his ineffable glory, it is designated to us by *heaven*, nothing which our eyes can behold being so full of splendour and majesty. While, then, we are accustomed to regard every object as confined to the place where our senses discern it, no place can be assigned to God; and hence, if we would seek him, we must rise higher than all corporeal or mental discernment. Again, this form of expression reminds us that he is far beyond the reach of change or corruption, that he holds the whole universe in his grasp, and rules it by his power. The effect of the expression, therefore, is the same as if it had been said, that he is of infinite majesty, incomprehensible essence,

boundless power, and eternal duration. When we thus speak of God, our thoughts must be raised to their highest pitch; we must not ascribe to him anything of a terrestrial or carnal nature, must not measure him by our little standards, or suppose his will to be like ours. At the same time, we must put our confidence in him, understanding that heaven and earth are governed by his providence and power. In short, under the name of Father is set before us that God, who hath appeared to us in his own image, that we may invoke him with sure faith; the familiar name of Father being given not only to inspire confidence, but also to curb our minds, and prevent them from going astray after doubtful or fictitious gods. We thus ascend from the only begotten Son to the supreme Father of angels and of the Church. Then when his throne is fixed in heaven, we are reminded that he governs the world, and, therefore, that it is not in vain to approach him whose present care we actually experience. "He that cometh to God," says the Apostle, "must believe that he is, and that he is a rewarder of them that diligently seek him" (Heb. xi. 6). Here Christ makes both claims for his Father, *first*, that we place our faith in him; and, *secondly*, that we feel assured that our salvation is not neglected by him, inasmuch as he condescends to extend his providence to us. By these elementary principles Paul prepares us to pray aright; for before enjoining us to make our requests known unto God, he premises in this way, "The Lord is at hand. Be careful for nothing" (Phil. iv. 5, 6). Whence it appears that doubt and perplexity hang over the prayers of those in whose minds the belief is not firmly seated, that "the eyes of the Lord are upon the righteous" (Ps. xxxiv. 15).

41. The first petition is, HALLOWED BE THY NAME. The necessity of presenting it bespeaks our great disgrace. For what can be more unbecoming than that our ingratitude and malice should impair, our audacity and petulance should as much as in them lies destroy, the glory of God? But though all the ungodly should burst with sacrilegious rage, the holiness of God's name still shines forth. Justly does the Psalmist exclaim, "According to thy name, O God, so is thy praise unto the ends of the earth" (Ps. xlviii. 10). For wherever God hath made himself known, his perfections must be displayed, his power, goodness, wisdom, justice, mercy, and truth, which fill us with admiration, and incite us to show forth his praise. Therefore, as the name of God is not duly hallowed on the earth, and we are otherwise unable to assert it, it is at least our duty to make it the subject of our prayers. The sum of the whole is, It must be our desire that God may receive the honour which is his due: that men may never think or speak of him without the greatest reverence. The opposite of this reverence is profanity, which has always been too common in the world, and is very prevalent in the present day. Hence the necessity of the petition, which, if piety had any proper existence among us, would be superfluous. But if the name of God is duly hallowed only when separated from all other names it alone is glori-

fied, we are in the petition enjoined to ask not only that God would vindicate his sacred name from all contempt and insult, but also that he would compel the whole human race to reverence it. Then since God manifests himself to us partly by his word, and partly by his works, he is not sanctified unless in regard to both of these we ascribe to him what is due, and thus embrace whatever has proceeded from him, giving no less praise to his justice than to his mercy. On the manifold diversity of his works he has inscribed the marks of his glory, and these ought to call forth from every tongue an ascription of praise. Thus Scripture will obtain its due authority with us, and no event will hinder us from celebrating the praises of God, in regard to every part of his government. On the other hand, the petition implies a wish that all impiety which pollutes this sacred name may perish and be extinguished, that everything which obscures or impairs his glory, all detraction and insult, may cease ; that all blasphemy being suppressed, the divine majesty may be more and more signally displayed.

42. The second petition is, THY KINGDOM COME. This contains nothing new, and yet there is good reason for distinguishing it from the first. For if we consider our lethargy in the greatest of all matters, we shall see how necessary it is that what ought to be in itself perfectly known should be inculcated at greater length. Therefore, after the injunction to pray that God would reduce to order, and at length completely efface every stain which is thrown on his sacred name, another petition, containing almost the same wish, is added—viz. Thy kingdom come. Although a definition of this kingdom has already been given, I now briefly repeat that God reigns when men, in denial of themselves, and contempt of the world and this earthly life, devote themselves to righteousness and aspire to heaven (see Calvin, Harm. Matth. vi.). Thus this kingdom consists of two parts : the first is, when God by the agency of his Spirit corrects all the depraved lusts of the flesh, which in bands war against Him ; and the second, when he brings all our thoughts into obedience to his authority. This petition, therefore, is duly presented only by those who begin with themselves ; in other words, who pray that they may be purified from all the corruptions which disturb the tranquillity and impair the purity of God's kingdom. Then as the word of God is like his royal sceptre, we are here enjoined to pray that he would subdue all minds and hearts to voluntary obedience. This is done when by the secret inspiration of his Spirit he displays the efficacy of his word, and raises it to the place of honour which it deserves. We must next descend to the wicked, who perversely and with desperate madness resist his authority. God, therefore, sets up his kingdom, by humbling the whole world, though in different ways, taming the wantonness of some, and breaking the ungovernable pride of others. We should desire this to be done every day, in order that God may gather churches to himself from all quarters of the world, may extend and increase their numbers, enrich them with his gifts,

establish due order among them; on the other hand, beat down all the enemies of pure doctrine and religion, dissipate their counsels, defeat their attempts. Hence it appears that there is good ground for the precept which enjoins daily progress, for human affairs are never so prosperous as when the impurities of vice are purged away, and integrity flourishes in full vigour. The completion, however, is deferred to the final advent of Christ, when, as Paul declares, "God will be all in all" (1 Cor. xv. 28). This prayer, therefore, ought to withdraw us from the corruptions of the world which separate us from God, and prevent his kingdom from flourishing within us; secondly, it ought to inflame us with an ardent desire for the mortification of the flesh; and, lastly, it ought to train us to the endurance of the cross; since this is the way in which God would have his kingdom to be advanced. It ought not to grieve us that the outward man decays, provided the inner man is renewed. For such is the nature of the kingdom of God, that while we submit to his righteousness he makes us partakers of his glory. This is the case when continually adding to his light and truth, by which the lies and the darkness of Satan and his kingdom are dissipated, extinguished, and destroyed, he protects his people, guides them aright by the agency of his Spirit, and confirms them in perseverance; while, on the other hand, he frustrates the impious conspiracies of his enemies, dissipates their wiles and frauds, prevents their malice, and curbs their petulance, until at length he consume Antichrist " with the spirit of his mouth," and destroy all impiety " with the brightness of his coming" (2 Thess. ii. 8, Calv. Com.).

43. The third petition is, THY WILL BE DONE ON EARTH AS IT IS IN HEAVEN. Though this depends on his kingdom, and cannot be disjoined from it, yet a separate place is not improperly given to it on account of our ignorance, which does not at once or easily apprehend what is meant by God reigning in the world. This, therefore, may not improperly be taken as the explanation, that God will be King in the world when all shall subject themselves to his will. We are not here treating of that secret will by which he governs all things, and destines them to their end (see chap. xxiv. s. 17). For although devils and men rise in tumult against him, he is able by his incomprehensible counsel not only to turn aside their violence, but make it subservient to the execution of his decrees. What we here speak of is another will of God—namely, that of which voluntary obedience is the counterpart; and, therefore, heaven is expressly contrasted with earth, because, as is said in The Psalms, the angels "do his commandments, hearkening unto the voice of his word" (Ps ciii. 20). We are, therefore, enjoined to pray that as everything done in heaven is at the command of God, and the angels are calmly disposed to do all that is right, so the earth may be brought under his authority, all rebellion and depravity having been extinguished. In presenting this request we renounce the desires of the flesh, because he who does not entirely resign his affections to God, does as much as in him lies

to oppose the divine will, since everything which proceeds from us is vicious.   Again, by this prayer we are taught to deny ourselves, that God may rule us according to his pleasure ; and not only so, but also having annihilated our own may create new thoughts and new minds, so that we shall have no desire save that of entire agreement with his will ; in short, wish nothing of ourselves, but have our hearts governed by his Spirit, under whose inward teaching we my learn to love those things which please and hate those things which displease him. Hence also we must desire that he would nullify and suppress all affections which are repugnant to his will.

Such are the three first heads of the prayer, in presenting which we should have the glory of God only in view, taking no account of ourselves, and paying no respect to our own advantage, which, though it is thereby greatly promoted, is not here to be the subject of request.   And though all the events prayed for must happen in their own time, without being either thought of, wished, or asked by us, it is still our duty to wish and ask for them.   And it is of no slight importance to do so, that we may testify and profess that we are the servants and children of God, desirous by every means in our power to promote the honour due to him as our Lord and Father, and truly and thoroughly devoted to his service.   Hence if men, in praying that the name of God may be hallowed, that his kingdom may come, and his will be done, are not influenced by this zeal for the promotion of his glory, they are not to be accounted among the servants and children of God ; and as all these things will take place against their will, so they will turn out to their confusion and destruction.

44. Now comes the second part of the prayer, in which we descend to our own interests, not, indeed, that we are to lose sight of the glory of God (to which, as Paul declares, we must have respect even in meat and drink, 1 Cor. x. 31), and ask only what is expedient for ourselves ; but the distinction, as we have already observed, is this : God claiming the three first petitions as specially his own, carries us entirely to himself, that in this way he may prove our piety.   Next he permits us to look to our own advantage, but still on the condition, that when we ask anything for ourselves it must be in order that all the benefits which he confers may show forth his glory, there being nothing more incumbent on us than to live and die to him.

By the first petition of the second part, GIVE US THIS DAY OUR DAILY BREAD, we pray in general that God would give us all things which the body requires in this sublunary state, not only food and clothing, but everything which he knows will assist us to eat our bread in peace.   In this way we briefly cast our care upon him, and commit ourselves to his providence, that he may feed, foster, and preserve us.   For our heavenly Father disdains not to take our body under his charge and protection, that he may exercise our faith in those minute matters, while we look to him for everything, even to a morsel of bread and a drop of water.   For since, owing to some strange inequality, we feel more concern for the body than for the soul, many who can trust the latter to God still continue anxious about the former, still hesitate as to what they are to eat, as to how they are to be clothed, and are in trepidation whenever their hands are not filled with corn, and wine, and oil (Ps. iv. 8): so much more value do we set on this shadowy, fleeting life, than on a blessed immortality. But those who, trusting to God, have once cast away that anxiety about the flesh, immediately look to him for greater gifts, even salvation and eternal life. It is no slight exercise of faith, therefore, to hope in God for things which would otherwise give us so much concern; nor have we made little progress when we get quit of this unbelief, which cleaves, as it were, to our very bones.

The speculations of some concerning supersubstantial bread seem to be very little accordant with our Saviour's meaning; for our prayer would be defective were we not to ascribe to God the nourishment even of this fading life. The reason which they give is heathenish —viz. that it is inconsistent with the character of sons of God, who ought to be spiritual, not only to occupy their mind with earthly cares, but to suppose God also occupied with them. As if his blessing and paternal favour were not eminently displayed in giving us food, or as if there were nothing in the declaration that godliness hath "the promise of the life that now is, and of that which is to come" (1 Tim. iv. 8). But although the forgiveness of sins is of far more importance than the nourishment of the body, yet Christ has set down the inferior in the prior place, in order that he might gradually raise us to the other two petitions, which properly belong to the heavenly life,—in this providing for our sluggishness. We are enjoined to ask *our bread*, that we may be contented with the measure which our heavenly Father is pleased to dispense, and not strive to make gain by illicit arts. Meanwhile, we must hold that the title by which it is ours is donation, because, as Moses says (Levit. xxvi. 20; Deut. viii. 17), neither our industry, nor labour, nor hands, acquire anything for us, unless the blessing of God be present; nay, not even would abundance of bread be of the least avail were it not divinely converted into nourishment. And hence this liberality of God is not less necessary to the rich than the poor, because, though their cellars and barns were full, they would be parched and pine with want did they not enjoy his favour along with their bread. The terms *this day*, or, as it is in another Evangelist, *daily*, and also the epithet *daily*, lay a restraint on our immoderate desire of fleeting good—a desire which we are extremely apt to indulge to excess, and from which other evils ensue: for when our supply is in richer abundance we ambitiously squander it in pleasure, luxury, ostentation, or other kinds of extravagance. Wherefore, we are only enjoined to ask as much as our necessity requires, and as it were for each day, confiding that our heavenly Father, who gives us the supply of to-day, will not fail us on the morrow. How great soever our abundance may be, however well filled our cellars and granaries, we must still always ask for daily bread, for we must feel assured that all substance is nothing, unless in so far as the Lord, by pouring out his blessing, make it fruitful during its whole progress; for even that which is in our hand is not ours except in so far as he every hour portions it out, and permits us to use it. As nothing is more difficult to human pride than the admission of this truth, the Lord declares that he gave a special proof for all ages, when he fed his people with manna in the desert (Deut. viii. 3), that he might remind us that "man shall not live by bread alone, but by every word that proceedeth out of the mouth of God" (Matth. iv. 4). It is thus intimated, that by his power alone our life and strength are sustained, though he ministers supply to us by bodily instruments. In like manner, whenever it so pleases, he gives us a proof of an opposite description, by breaking the strength, or, as he himself calls it, the *staff* of bread (Levit. xxvi. 26), and leaving us even while eating to pine with hunger, and while drinking to be parched with thirst. Those who, not contented with daily bread, indulge an unrestrained insatiable cupidity, or those who are full of their own abundance, and trust in their own riches, only mock God by offering up this prayer. For the former ask what they would be unwilling to obtain, nay, what they most of all abominate—namely, daily bread only—and as much as in them lies disguise their avarice from God, whereas true prayer should pour out the whole soul and every inward feeling before him. The latter, again, ask what they do not at all expect to obtain—namely, what they imagine that they in themselves already possess. In its being called *ours*, God, as we have already said, gives a striking display of his kindness, making that to be ours to which we have no just claim. Nor must we reject the view to which I have already adverted—viz. that this name is given to what is obtained by just and honest labour, as contrasted with what is obtained by fraud and rapine, nothing being our own which we obtain with injury to others. When we ask God to *give us*, the meaning is, that the thing asked is simply and freely the gift of God, whatever be the quarter from which it comes to us, even when it seems to have been specially prepared by our own art and industry, and procured by our hands, since it is to his blessing alone that all our labours owe their success.

45. The next petition is, FORGIVE US OUR DEBTS. In this and the following petition our Saviour has briefly comprehended whatever is conducive to the heavenly life, as these two members contain the spiritual covenant which God made for the salvation of his Church, " I will put my law in their inward parts, and write it on their hearts." " I will pardon all their iniquities" (Jer. xxxi. 33; xxxiii. 8). Here our Saviour begins with the forgiveness of sins, and then adds the subsequent blessing—viz. that God would protect us by the power, and support us by the aid of his Spirit, so that we may stand invincible against all temptations. To sins he gives the name of *debts*, because

we owe the punishment due to them, a debt which we could not possibly pay were we not discharged by this remission, the result of his free mercy, when he freely expunges the debt, accepting nothing in return; but of his own mercy receiving satisfaction in Christ, who gave himself a ransom for us (Rom. iii. 24). Hence, those who expect to satisfy God by merits of their own or of others, or to compensate and purchase forgiveness by means of satisfactions, have no share in this free pardon, and while they address God in this petition, do nothing more than subscribe their own accusation, and seal their condemnation by their own testimony. For they confess that they are debtors, unless they are discharged by means of forgiveness. This forgiveness, however, they do not receive, but rather reject, when they obtrude their merits and satisfactions upon God, since by so doing they do not implore his mercy, but appeal to his justice. Let those, again, who dream of a perfection which makes it unnecessary to seek pardon, find their disciples among those whose itching ears incline them to imposture[1] (see Calv. on Dan. ix. 20); only let them understand that those whom they thus acquire have been carried away from Christ, since he, by instructing all to confess their guilt, receives none but sinners, not that he may soothe, and so encourage them in their sins, but because he knows that believers are never so divested of the sins of the flesh as not to remain obnoxious to the justice of God. It is, indeed, to be wished, it ought even to be our strenuous endeavour, to perform all the parts of our duty, so as truly to congratulate ourselves before God as being pure from every stain; but as God is pleased to renew his image in us by degrees, so that to some extent there is always a residue of corruption in our flesh, we ought by no means to neglect the remedy. But if Christ, according to the authority given him by his Father, enjoins us, during the whole course of our lives, to implore pardon, who can tolerate those new teachers who, by the phantom of perfect innocence, endeavour to dazzle the simple, and make them believe that they can render themselves completely free from guilt? This, as John declares, is nothing else than to make God a liar (1 John i. 10). In like manner, those foolish men mutilate the covenant in which we have seen that our salvation is contained by concealing one head of it, and so destroying it entirely; being guilty not only of profanity in that they separate things which ought to be indissolubly connected; but also of wickedness and cruelty in overwhelming wretched souls with despair —of treachery also to themselves and their followers, in that they encourage themselves in a carelessness diametrically opposed to the mercy of God. It is excessively childish to object that when they long for the advent of the kingdom of God, they at the same time pray for the abolition of sin. In the former division of the prayer absolute perfection is set before us; but in the latter our own weakness. Thus the two fitly correspond to each other—we strive for the

---

[1] French, "Telles disciples qu'ils voudront;"—such disciples as they will.

goal, and at the same time neglect not the remedies which our necessities require.

In the next part of the petition we pray to be forgiven, *"as we forgive our debtors;"* that is, as we spare and pardon all by whom we are in any way offended, either in deed by unjust, or in word by contumelious treatment. Not that we can forgive the guilt of a fault or offence: this belongs to God only; but we can forgive to this extent; we can voluntarily divest our minds of wrath, hatred, and revenge, and efface the remembrance of injuries by a voluntary oblivion. Wherefore, we are not to ask the forgiveness of our sins from God, unless we forgive the offences of all who are or have been injurious to us. If we retain any hatred in our minds, if we meditate revenge, and devise the means of hurting; nay, if we do not return to a good understanding with our enemies, perform every kind of friendly office, and endeavour to effect a reconciliation with them, we by this petition beseech God not to grant us forgiveness. For we ask him to do to us as we do to others. This is the same as asking him not to do unless we do also. What, then, do such persons obtain by this petition but a heavier judgment? Lastly, it is to be observed that the condition of being forgiven as we forgive our debtors, is not added because by forgiving others we deserve forgiveness, as if the cause of forgiveness were expressed; but by the use of this expression the Lord has been pleased partly to solace the weakness of our faith, using it as a sign to assure us that our sins are as certainly forgiven as we are certainly conscious of having forgiven others, when our mind is completely purged from all envy, hatred, and malice; and partly using as a badge by which he excludes from the number of his children all who, prone to revenge and reluctant to forgive, obstinately keep up their enmity, cherishing against others that indignation which they deprecate from themselves; so that they should not venture to invoke him as a Father. In the Gospel of Luke we have this distinctly stated in the words of Christ.

46. The sixth petition corresponds (as we have observed) to the promise[1] of *writing the law upon our hearts;* but because we do not obey God without a continual warfare, without sharp and arduous contests, we here pray that he would furnish us with armour, and defend us by his protection, that we may be able to obtain the victory. By this we are reminded that we not only have need of the gift of the Spirit inwardly to soften our hearts, and turn and direct them to the obedience of God, but also of his assistance, to render us invincible by all the wiles and violent assaults of Satan. The forms of temptation are many and various. The depraved conceptions of our minds provoking us to transgress the law—conceptions which our concupiscence suggests or the devil excites, are temptations; and things which in their own nature are not evil, become temptations by the wiles of the devil, when they are presented to our eyes in such

[1] The French adds, "que Dieu nous a donnee et faite;"—which God has given and performed to us.

a way that the view of them makes us withdraw or decline from God.[1] These temptations are both on the right hand and on the left. On the right, when riches, power, and honours, which by their glare, and the semblance of good which they present, generally dazzle the eyes of men, and so entice by their blandishments, that, caught by their snares, and intoxicated by their sweetness, they forget their God: on the left, when offended by the hardship and bitterness of poverty, disgrace, contempt, afflictions, and other things of that description, they despond, cast away their confidence and hope, and are at length totally estranged from God. In regard to both kinds of temptation, which either enkindled in us by concupiscence, or presented by the craft of Satan, war against us, we pray God the Father not to allow us to be overcome, but rather to raise and support us by his hand, that strengthened by his mighty power we may stand firm against all the assaults of our malignant enemy, whatever be the thoughts which he sends into our minds; next we pray that whatever of either description is allotted us, we may turn to good, that is, may neither be inflated with prosperity, nor cast down by adversity. Here, however, we do not ask to be altogether exempted from temptation, which is very necessary to excite, stimulate, and urge us on, that we may not become too lethargic. It was not without reason that David wished to be tried, nor is it without cause that the Lord daily tries his elect, chastising them by disgrace, poverty, tribulation, and other kinds of cross.[2] But the temptations of God and Satan are very different: Satan tempts, that he may destroy, condemn, confound, throw headlong; God, that by proving his people he may make trial of their sincerity, and by exercising their strength confirm it; may mortify, tame, and cauterise their flesh, which, if not curbed in this manner, would wanton and exult above measure. Besides, Satan attacks those who are unarmed and unprepared, that he may destroy them unawares; whereas, whatever God sends, he " will with the temptation also make a way to escape, that ye may be able to bear it." Whether by the term *evil* we understand the devil or sin, is not of the least consequence. Satan is indeed the very enemy who lays snares for our life, but it is by sin that he is armed for our destruction.

Our petition, therefore, is, that we may not be overcome or overwhelmed with temptation, but in the strength of the Lord may stand firm against all the powers by which we are assailed; in other words, may not fall under temptation: that being thus taken under his charge and protection, we may remain invincible by sin, death, the gates of hell, and the whole power of the devil; in other words, be delivered from evil. Here it is carefully to be observed, that we have no strength to contend with such a combatant as the devil, or to

[1] James i. 2, 14; Matth. iv. 1, 3; 1 Thess. iii. 5; 2 Cor. vi. 7, 8.
[2] Ps. xxvi. 2; Gen. xxii. 1; Deut. viii. 2; xiii. 3; 1 Cor. x. 13; 2 Pet. ii. 9; 1 Pet. v. 8. For the sense in which God is said to lead us into temptation, see the end of this section.

sustain the violence of his assault.   Were it otherwise, it would be
mockery of God to ask of him what we already possess in ourselves.
Assuredly those who in self-confidence prepare for such a fight, do
not understand how bold and well-equipped the enemy is with whom
they have to do.   Now we ask to be delivered from his power, as
from the mouth of some furious raging lion, who would instantly
tear us with his teeth and claws, and swallow us up, did not the Lord
rescue us from the midst of death ; at the same time knowing that if
the Lord is present and will fight for us while we stand by, through
him " we shall do valiantly" (Ps. lx. 12).   Let others if they will
confide in the powers and resources of their free will which they think
they possess ; enough for us that we stand and are strong in the
power of God alone.   But the prayer comprehends more than at first
sight it seems to do.   For if the Spirit of God is our strength in
waging the contest with Satan, we cannot gain the victory unless we
are filled with him, and thereby freed from all infirmity of the flesh.
Therefore, when we pray to be delivered from sin and Satan, we at
the same time desire to be enriched with new supplies of divine grace,
until completely replenished with them, we triumph over every evil.
To some it seems rude and harsh to ask God not to lead us into
temptation, since, as James declares (James i. 13), it is contrary to
his nature to do so.   This difficulty has already been partly solved
by the fact that our concupiscence is the cause, and therefore properly
bears the blame of all the temptations by which we are overcome.
All that James means is, that it is vain and unjust to ascribe to God
vices which our own consciousness compels us to impute to ourselves.
But this is no reason why God may not when he sees it meet bring
us into bondage to Satan, give us up to a reprobate mind and shameful lusts, and so by a just, indeed, but often hidden judgment, lead
us into temptation.   Though the cause is often concealed from men,
it is well known to him.   ·Hence we may see that the expression is
not improper, if we are persuaded that it is not without cause he so
often threatens to give sure signs of his vengeance, by blinding the
reprobate, and hardening their hearts.

47. These three petitions, in which we specially commend ourselves
and all that we have to God, clearly show what we formerly observed
(sec. 38, 39), that the prayers of Christians should be public, and
have respect to the public edification of the Church and the advancement of believers in spiritual communion.   For no one requests that
anything should be given to him as an individual, but we all ask in
common for daily bread and the forgiveness of sins, not to be led
into temptation, but delivered from evil.   Moreover, there is subjoined
the reason for our great boldness in asking and confidence of obtaining (sec. 11, 36).   Although this does not exist in the Latin copies,
yet as it accords so well with the whole, we cannot think of omitting
it.

The words are, THINE IS THE KINGDOM, AND THE POWER, AND THE
GLORY, FOR EVER.   Here is the calm and firm assurance of our faith.

For were our prayers to be commended to God by our own worth, who would venture even to whisper before him? Now, however wretched we may be, however unworthy, however devoid of commendation, we shall never want a reason for prayer, nor a ground of confidence, since the kingdom, power, and glory, can never be wrested from our Father. The last word is AMEN, by which is expressed the eagerness of our desire to obtain the things which we ask, while our hope is confirmed, that all things have already been obtained, and will assuredly be granted to us, seeing they have been promised by God, who cannot deceive. This accords with the form of expression to which we have already adverted: "Grant, O Lord, for thy name's sake, not on account of us or of our righteousness." By this the saints not only express the end of their prayers, but confess that they are unworthy of obtaining did not God find the cause in himself, and were not their confidence founded entirely on His nature.

48. All things that we ought, indeed all that we are able, to ask of God, are contained in this formula, and as it were rule, of prayer delivered by Christ, our divine Master, whom the Father has appointed to be our teacher, and to whom alone he would have us to listen (Matth. xvii. 5). For he ever was the eternal wisdom of the Father, and being made man, was manifested as the Wonderful, the Counsellor (Isa. xi. 2). Accordingly, this prayer is complete in all its parts, so complete, that whatever is extraneous and foreign to it, whatever cannot be referred to it, is impious and unworthy of the approbation of God. For he has here summarily prescribed what is worthy of him, what is acceptable to him, and what is necessary for us; in short, whatever he is pleased to grant. Those, therefore, who presume to go further and ask something more from God, first seek to add of their own to the wisdom of God (this it is insane blasphemy to do); secondly, refusing to confine themselves within the will of God, and despising it, they wander as their cupidity directs; lastly, they will never obtain anything, seeing they pray without faith. For there cannot be a doubt that all such prayers are made without faith, because at variance with the word of God, on which if faith do not always lean it cannot possibly stand. Those who, disregarding the Master's rule, indulge their own wishes, not only have not the word of God, but as much as in them lies oppose it. Hence Tertullian (De Fuga in Persequutione) has not less truly than elegantly termed it *Lawful Prayer*, tacitly intimating that all other prayers are lawless and illicit.

49. By this, however, we would not have it understood that we are so astricted to this form of prayer as to make it unlawful to change a word or syllable of it. For in Scripture we meet with many prayers differing greatly from it in word, yet written by the same Spirit, and capable of being used by us with the greatest advantage. Many prayers also are continually suggested to believers by the same Spirit, though in expression they bear no great resemblance to it. All we mean to say is, that no man should wish, expect, or ask anything

which is not summarily comprehended in this prayer. Though the words may be very different, there must be no difference in the sense. In this way, all prayers, both those which are contained in the Scripture, and those which come forth from pious breasts, must be referred to it, certainly none can ever equal it, far less surpass it in perfection. It omits nothing which we can conceive in praise of God, nothing which we can imagine advantageous to man, and the whole is so exact that all hope of improving it may well be renounced. In short, let us remember that we have here the doctrine of heavenly wisdom. God has taught what he willed; he willed what was necessary.

50. But although it has been said above (sec. 7, 27, &c.) that we ought always to raise our minds upwards towards God, and pray without ceasing, yet such is our weakness, which requires to be supported, such our torpor, which requires to be stimulated, that it is requisite for us to appoint special hours for this exercise, hours which are not to pass away without prayer, and during which the whole affections of our minds are to be completely occupied—namely, when we rise in the morning, before we commence our daily work, when we sit down to food, when by the blessing of God we have taken it, and when we retire to rest. This, however, must not be a superstitious observance of hours, by which, as it were, performing a task to God, we think we are discharged as to other hours; it should rather be considered as a discipline by which our weakness is exercised, and ever and anon stimulated. In particular, it must be our anxious care, whenever we are ourselves pressed, or see others pressed by any strait, instantly to have recourse to him not only with quickened pace, but with quickened minds; and again, we must not in any prosperity of ourselves or others omit to testify our recognition of his hand by praise and thanksgiving. Lastly, we must in all our prayers carefully avoid wishing to confine God to certain circumstances, or prescribe to him the time, place, or mode of action. In like manner, we are taught by this prayer not to fix any law or impose any condition upon him, but leave it entirely to him to adopt whatever course of procedure seems to him best, in respect of method, time, and place. For before we offer up any petition for ourselves, we ask that his will may be done, and by so doing place our will in subordination to his, just as if we had laid a curb upon it, that, instead of presuming to give law to God, it may regard him as the ruler and disposer of all its wishes.

51. If, with minds thus framed to obedience, we allow ourselves to be governed by the laws of Divine Providence, we shall easily learn to persevere in prayer, and suspending our own desires wait patiently for the Lord, certain, however little the appearance of it may be, that he is always present with us, and will in his own time show how very far he was from turning a deaf ear to prayers, though to the eyes of men they may seem to be disregarded. This will be a very present consolation, if at any time God does not grant an immediate answer to our prayers, preventing us from fainting or giving way to despond

ency, as those are wont to do who, in invoking God, are so borne away by their own fervour, that unless he yield on their first importunity and give present help, they immediately imagine that he is angry and offended with them, and abandoning all hope of success cease from prayer. On the contrary, deferring our hope with well tempered equanimity, let us insist with that perseverance which is so strongly recommended to us in Scripture. We may often see in The Psalms how David and other believers, after they are almost weary of praying, and seem to have been beating the air by addressing a God who would not hear, yet cease not to pray, because due authority is not given to the word of God, unless the faith placed in it is superior to all events. Again, let us not tempt God, and by wearying him with our importunity, provoke his anger against us. Many have a practice of formally bargaining with God on certain conditions, and, as if he were the servant of their lusts, binding him to certain stipulations; with which if he do not immediately comply, they are indignant and fretful, murmur, complain, and make a noise. Thus offended, he often in his anger grants to such persons what in mercy he kindly denies to others. Of this we have a proof in the children of Israel, for whom it had been better not to have been heard by the Lord, than to swallow his indignation with their flesh (Num. xi. 18, 33).

52. But if our sense is not able till after long expectation to perceive what the result of prayer is, or experience any benefit from it, still our faith will assure us of that which cannot be perceived by sense—viz. that we have obtained what was fit for us, the Lord having so often and so surely engaged to take an interest in all our troubles from the moment they have been deposited in his bosom. In this way we shall possess abundance in poverty, and comfort in affliction. For though all things fail, God will never abandon us, and he cannot frustrate the expectation and patience of his people. He alone will suffice for all, since in himself he comprehends all good, and will at last reveal it to us on the day of judgment, when his kingdom shall be plainly manifested. We may add, that although God complies with our request, he does not always give an answer in the very terms of our prayer, but while apparently holding us in suspense, yet in an unknown way, shows that our prayers have not been in vain. This is the meaning of the words of John, "If we know that he hear us, whatsoever we ask, we know that we have the petitions that we desired of him" (1 John v. 15). It might seem that there is here a great superfluity of words, but the declaration is most useful—namely, that God, even when he does not comply with our requests, yet listens and is favourable to our prayers, so that our hope founded on his word is never disappointed. But believers have always need of being supported by this patience, as they could not stand long if they did not lean upon it. For the trials by which the Lord proves and exercises us are severe, nay, he often drives us to extremes, and when driven allows us long to stick fast in the mire

before he gives us any taste of his sweetness. As Hannah says, " The Lord killeth, and maketh alive; he bringeth down to the grave, and bringeth up" (1 Sam. ii. 6). What could they here do but become dispirited and rush on despair, were they not, when afflicted, desolate, and half dead, comforted with the thought that they are regarded by God, and that there will be an end to their present evils. But however secure their hopes may stand, they in the meantime cease not to pray, since prayer unaccompanied by perseverance leads to no result.

CHAPTER XXI.

OF THE ETERNAL ELECTION, BY WHICH GOD HAS PREDESTINATED SOME TO SALVATION, AND OTHERS TO DESTRUCTION.

The divisions of this chapter are,—I. The necessity and utility of the doctrine of eternal Election explained. Excessive curiosity restrained, sec. 1, 2. II. Explanation to those who through false modesty shun the doctrine of Predestination, sec. 3, 4. III. The orthodox doctrine expounded.

Sections.

1. The doctrine of Election and Predestination. It is useful, necessary, and most sweet. Ignorance of it impairs the glory of God, plucks up humility by the roots, begets and fosters pride. The doctrine establishes the certainty of salvation, peace of conscience, and the true origin of the Church. Answer to two classes of men : 1. The curious.
2. A sentiment of Augustine confirmed by an admonition of our Saviour and a passage of Solomon.
3. An answer to a second class—viz. those who are unwilling that the doctrine should be adverted to. An objection founded on a passage of Solomon, solved by the words of Moses.
4. A second objection—viz. That this doctrine is a stumbling-block to the profane. Answer 1. The same may be said of many other heads of doctrine. 2. The truth of God will always defend itself. Third objection—viz. That this doctrine is dangerous even to believers. Answer 1. The same objection made to Augustine. 2. We must not despise anything that God has revealed. Arrogance and blasphemy of such objections.
5. Certain cavils against the doctrine. 1. Prescience regarded as the cause of predestination. Prescience and predestination explained. Not prescience, but the good pleasure of God the cause of predestination. This apparent from the gratuitous election of the posterity of Abraham and the rejection of all others.
6. Even of the posterity of Abraham some elected and others rejected by special grace.
7. The Apostle shows that the same thing has been done in regard to individuals under the Christian dispensation.

1. THE covenant of life is not preached equally to all, and among those to whom it is preached, does not always meet with the same reception. This diversity displays the unsearchable depth of the divine judgment, and is without doubt subordinate to God's purpose of eternal election. But if it is plainly owing to the mere pleasure of God that salvation is spontaneously offered to some, while others have no access to it, great and difficult questions immediately arise, questions which are inexplicable, when just views are not entertained concerning election and predestination. To many this seems a perplexing subject, because they deem it most incongruous that of the great body of mankind some should be predestinated to salvation, and others to destruction. How causelessly they entangle themselves will appear as we proceed. We may add, that in the very obscurity

which deters them, we may see not only the utility of this doctrine, but also its most pleasant fruits. We shall never feel persuaded as we ought that our salvation flows from the free mercy of God as its fountain, until we are made acquainted with his eternal election, the grace of God being illustrated by the contrast—viz. that he does not adopt promiscuously to the hope of salvation, but gives to some what he denies to others. It is plain how greatly ignorance of this principle detracts from the glory of God, and impairs true humility. But though thus necessary to be known, Paul declares that it cannot be known unless God, throwing works entirely out of view, elect those whom he has predestined. His words are, "Even so then at this present time also, there is a remnant according to the election of grace. And if by grace, then it is no more of works: otherwise grace is no more grace. But if it be of works, then it is no more grace: otherwise work is no more work" (Rom. xi. 6). If to make it appear that our salvation flows entirely from the good mercy of God, we must be carried back to the origin of election, then those who would extinguish it, wickedly do as much as in them lies to obscure what they ought most loudly to extol, and pluck up humility by the very roots. Paul clearly declares that it is only when the salvation of a remnant is ascribed to gratuitous election, we arrive at the knowledge that God saves whom he wills of his mere good pleasure, and does not pay a debt, a debt which never can be due. Those who preclude access, and would not have any one to obtain a taste of this doctrine, are equally unjust to God and men, there being no other means of humbling us as we ought, or making us feel how much we are bound to him. Nor, indeed, have we elsewhere any sure ground of confidence. This we say on the authority of Christ, who, to deliver us from all fear, and render us invincible amid our many dangers, snares, and mortal conflicts, promises safety to all that the Father hath taken under his protection (John x. 26). From this we infer, that all who know not that they are the peculiar people of God, must be wretched from perpetual trepidation, and that those, therefore, who, by overlooking the three advantages which we have noted, would destroy the very foundation of our safety, consult ill for themselves and for all the faithful. What? Do we not here find the very origin of the Church, which, as Bernard rightly teaches (Serm. in Cantic.), could not be found or recognised among the creatures, because it lies hid (in both cases wondrously) within the lap of blessed predestination, and the mass of wretched condemnation?

But before I enter on the subject, I have some remarks to address to two classes of men. The subject of predestination, which in itself is attended with considerable difficulty, is rendered very perplexed, and hence perilous by human curiosity, which cannot be restrained from wandering into forbidden paths, and climbing to the clouds, determined if it can that none of the secret things of God shall remain unexplored. When we see many, some of them in other respects not bad men, everywhere rushing into this audacity and wickedness, it is necessary to remind them of the course of duty in this matter. First, then, when they inquire into predestination, let them remember that they are penetrating into the recesses of the divine wisdom, where he who rushes forward securely and confidently instead of satisfying his curiosity will enter an inextricable labyrinth.[1] For it is not right that man should with impunity pry into things which the Lord has been pleased to conceal within himself, and scan that sublime eternal wisdom which it is his pleasure that we should not apprehend but adore, that therein also his perfections may appear. Those secrets of his will, which he has seen it meet to manifest, are revealed in his word—revealed in so far as he knew to be conducive to our interest and welfare.

2. "We have come into the way of faith," says Augustine: "let us constantly adhere to it. It leads to the chambers of the king, in which are hidden all the treasures of wisdom and knowledge. For our Lord Jesus Christ did not speak invidiously to his great and most select disciples when he said, 'I have yet many things to say unto you, but ye cannot bear them now' (John xvi. 12). We must walk, advance, increase, that our hearts may be able to comprehend those things which they cannot now comprehend. But if the last day shall find us making progress, we shall there learn what here we could not" (August. Hom. in Joann.). If we give due weight to the consideration, that the word of the Lord is the only way which can conduct us to the investigation of whatever it is lawful for us to hold with regard to him—is the only light which can enable us to discern what we ought to see with regard to him, it will curb and restrain all presumption. For it will show us that the moment we go beyond the bounds of the word we are out of the course, in darkness, and must every now and then stumble, go astray, and fall. Let it, therefore, be our first principle that to desire any other knowledge of predestination than that which is expounded by the word of God, is no less infatuated than to walk where there is no path, or to seek light in darkness. Let us not be ashamed to be ignorant in a matter in which ignorance is learning. Rather let us willingly abstain from the search after knowledge, to which it is both foolish as well as perilous, and even fatal to aspire. If an unrestrained imagination urges us, our proper course is to oppose it with these words, "It is not good to eat much honey: so for men to search their own glory is not glory" (Prov. xxv. 27). There is good reason to dread a presumption which can only plunge us headlong into ruin.

3. There are others who, when they would cure this disease, recommend that the subject of predestination should scarcely if ever be mentioned, and tell us to shun every question concerning it as we would a rock. Although their moderation is justly commendable in thinking that such mysteries should be treated with moderation, yet

---

[1] Thus Eck boasts that he had written of predestination to exercise his youthful spirits.

because they keep too far within the proper measure, they have little influence over the human mind, which does not readily allow itself to be curbed. Therefore, in order to keep the legitimate course in this matter, we must return to the word of God, in which we are furnished with the right rule of understanding. For Scripture is the school of the Holy Spirit, in which as nothing useful and necessary to be known has been omitted, so nothing is taught but what it is of importance to know. Everything, therefore, delivered in Scripture on the subject of predestination, we must beware of keeping from the faithful lest we seem either maliciously to deprive them of the blessing of God, or to accuse and scoff at the Spirit, as having divulged what ought on any account to be suppressed. Let us, I say, allow the Christian to unlock his mind and ears to all the words of God which are addressed to him, provided he do it with this moderation—viz. that whenever the Lord shuts his sacred mouth, he also desists from inquiry. The best rule of sobriety is, not only in learning to follow wherever God leads, but also when he makes an end of teaching, to cease also from wishing to be wise. The danger which they dread is not so great that we ought on account of it to turn away our minds from the oracles of God. There is a celebrated saying of Solomon, "It is the glory of God to conceal a thing" (Prov. xxv. 2). But since both piety and common sense dictate that this is not to be understood of everything, we must look for a distinction, lest under the pretence of modesty and sobriety we be satisfied with a brutish ignorance. This is clearly expressed by Moses in a few words, "The secret things belong unto the Lord our God: but those things which are revealed belong unto us, and to our children for ever" (Deut. xxix. 29). We see how he exhorts the people to study the doctrine of the law in accordance with a heavenly decree, because God has been pleased to promulgate it, while he at the same time confines them within these boundaries, for the simple reason that it is not lawful for men to pry into the secret things of God.

4. I admit that profane men lay hold of the subject of predestination to carp, or cavil, or snarl, or scoff. But if their petulance frightens us, it will be necessary to conceal all the principal articles of faith, because they and their fellows leave scarcely one of them unassailed with blasphemy. A rebellious spirit will display itself no less insolently when it hears that there are three persons in the divine essence, than when it hears that God when he created man foresaw everything that was to happen to him. Nor will they abstain from their jeers when told that little more than five thousand years have elapsed since the creation of the world. For they will ask, Why did the power of God slumber so long in idleness? In short, nothing can be stated that they will not assail with derision. To quell their blasphemies, must we say nothing concerning the divinity of the Son and Spirit? Must the creation of the world be passed over in silence? No! The truth of God is too powerful, both here and everywhere, to dread the slanders of the ungodly, as Augustine powerfully maintains

in his treatise, De Bono Perseverantiæ (cap. xiv.–xx.). For we see that the false apostles were unable, by defaming and accusing the true doctrine of Paul, to make him ashamed of it. There is nothing in the allegation that the whole subject is fraught with danger to pious minds, as tending to destroy exhortation, shake faith, disturb and dispirit the heart. Augustine disguises not that on these grounds he was often charged with preaching the doctrine of predestination too freely, but, as it was easy for him to do, he abundantly refutes the charge. As a great variety of absurd objections are here stated, we have thought it best to dispose of each of them in its proper place (see chap. xxiii.). Only I wish it to be received as a general rule, that the secret things of God are not to be scrutinised, and that those which he has revealed are not to be overlooked, lest we may, on the one hand, be chargeable with curiosity, and, on the other, with ingratitude. For it has been shrewdly observed by Augustine (de Genesi ad Literam, Lib. v.), that we can safely follow Scripture, which walks softly, as with a mother's step, in accommodation to our weakness. Those, however, who are so cautious and timid, that they would bury all mention of predestination in order that it may not trouble weak minds, with what colour, pray, will they cloak their arrogance, when they indirectly charge God with a want of due consideration, in not having foreseen a danger for which they imagine that they prudently provide? Whoever, therefore, throws obloquy on the doctrine of predestination, openly brings a charge against God, as having inconsiderately allowed something to escape from him which is injurious to the Church.

5. The predestination by which God adopts some to the hope of life, and adjudges others to eternal death, no man who would be thought pious ventures simply to deny ; but it is greatly cavilled at, especially by those who make prescience its cause. We, indeed, ascribe both prescience and predestination to God ; but we say that it is absurd to make the latter subordinate to the former (see chap. xxii. sec. 1). When we attribute prescience to God, we mean that all things always were, and ever continue, under his eye ; that to his knowledge there is no past or future, but all things are present, and indeed so present, that it is not merely the idea of them that is before him (as those objects are which we retain in our memory), but that he truly sees and contemplates them as actually under his immediate inspection. This prescience extends to the whole circuit of the world, and to all creatures. By predestination we mean the eternal decree of God, by which he determined with himself whatever he wished to happen with regard to every man. All are not created on equal terms, but some are preordained to eternal life, others to eternal damnation ; and, accordingly, as each has been created for one or other of these ends, we say that he has been predestinated to life or to death. This God has testified, not only in the case of single individuals ; he has also given a specimen of it in the whole posterity of Abraham, to make it plain

that the future condition of each nation was entirely at his disposal : " When the Most High divided to the nations their inheritance, when he separated the sons of Adam, he set the bounds of the people according to the number of the children of Israel. For the Lord's portion is his people ; Jacob is the lot of his inheritance" (Deut. xxxii. 8, 9). The separation is before the eyes of all ; in the person of Abraham, as in a withered stock, one people is specially chosen, while the others are rejected ; but the cause does not appear, except that Moses, to deprive posterity of any handle for glorying, tells them that their superiority was owing entirely to the free love of God. The cause which he assigns for their deliverance is, "Because he loved thy fathers, therefore he chose their seed after them" (Deut. iv. 37) ; or more explicitly in another chapter, "The Lord did not set his love upon you, nor choose you, because you were more in number than any people : for ye were the fewest of all people : but because the Lord loved you" (Deut. vii. 7, 8). He repeatedly makes the same intimation, "Behold, the heaven, and the heaven of heavens, is the Lord's thy God, the earth also, with all that therein is. Only the Lord had a delight in thy fathers to love them, and he chose their seed after them" (Deut. x. 14, 15). Again, in another passage, holiness is enjoined upon them, because they have been chosen to be a peculiar people ; while in another, love is declared to be the cause of their protection (Deut. xxiii. 5). This, too, believers with one voice proclaim, "He shall choose our inheritance for us, the excellency of Jacob, whom he loved" (Ps. xlvii. 4). The endowments with which God had adorned them, they all ascribe to gratuitous love, not only because they knew that they had not obtained them by any merit, but that not even was the holy patriarch endued with a virtue that could procure such distinguished honour for himself and his posterity. And the more completely to crush all pride, he upbraids them with having merited nothing of the kind, seeing they were a rebellious and stiff-necked people (Deut. ix. 6). Often, also, do the prophets remind the Jews of this election by way of disparagement and opprobrium, because they had shamefully revolted from it. Be this as it may, let those who would ascribe the election of God to human worth or merit come forward. When they see that one nation is preferred to all others, when they hear that it was no feeling of respect that induced God to show more favour to a small and ignoble body, nay, even to the wicked and rebellious, will they plead against him for having chosen to give such a manifestation of mercy ? But neither will their obstreperous words hinder his work, nor will their invectives, like stones thrown against heaven, strike or hurt his righteousness ; nay, rather they will fall back on their own heads. To this principle of a free covenant, moreover, the Israelites are recalled whenever thanks are to be returned to God, or their hopes of the future to be animated. " The Lord he is God," says the Psalmist ; " it is he that hath made us, and not we ourselves : we are his people, and the sheep of his pasture" (Ps. c. 3 ; xcv. 7). The negation which is added, "not we ourselves," is not superfluous, to teach us that God is not only the author of all the good qualities in which men excel, but that they originate in himself, there being nothing in them worthy of so much honour. In the following words also they are enjoined to rest satisfied with the mere good pleasure of God: "O ye seed of Abraham, his servant; ye children of Jacob, his chosen" (Ps. cv. 6). And after an enumeration of the continual mercies of God as fruits of election, the conclusion is, that he acted thus kindly because he remembered his covenant. With this doctrine accords the song of the whole Church, "They got not the land in possession by their own sword, neither did their own arm save them; but thy right hand, and thine arm, and the light of thy countenance, because thou hadst a favour unto them" (Ps. xliv. 3). It is to be observed, that when the land is mentioned, it is a visible symbol of the secret election in which adoption is comprehended. To like gratitude David elsewhere exhorts the people, "Blessed is the nation whose God is the Lord, and the people whom he hath chosen for his own inheritance" (Ps. xxxiii. 12). Samuel thus animates their hopes, "The Lord will not forsake his people for his great name's sake: because it hath pleased the Lord to make you his people" (1 Sam. xii. 22). And when David's faith is assailed, how does he arm himself for the battle? "Blessed is the man whom thou choosest, and causest to approach unto thee, that he may dwell in thy courts" (Ps. lxv. 4). But as the hidden election of God was confirmed both by a first and second election, and by other intermediate mercies, Isaiah thus applies the term, "The Lord will have mercy on Jacob, and will yet choose Israel" (Isa. xiv. 1). Referring to a future period, the gathering together of the dispersion, who seemed to have been abandoned, he says, that it will be a sign of a firm and stable election, notwithstanding of the apparent abandonment. When it is elsewhere said, "I have chosen thee, and not cast thee away" (Isa. xli. 9), the continual course of his great liberality is ascribed to paternal kindness. This is stated more explicitly in Zechariah by the angel, the Lord "shall choose Jerusalem again," as if the severity of his chastisements had amounted to reprobation, or the captivity had been an interruption of election, which, however, remains inviolable, though the signs of it do not always appear.

6. We must add a second step of a more limited nature, or one in which the grace of God was displayed in a more special form, when of the same family of Abraham God rejected some, and by keeping others within his Church showed that he retained them among his sons. At first Ishmael had obtained the same rank with his brother Isaac, because the spiritual covenant was equally sealed in him by the symbol of circumcision. He is first cut off, then Esau, at last an innumerable multitude, almost the whole of Israel. In Isaac was the seed called. The same calling held good in the case of Jacob. God gave a similar example in the rejection of Saul. This is also celebrated in the psalm, "Moreover, he refused the tabernacle of

Joseph, and chose not the tribe of Ephraim : but chose the tribe of Judah" (Ps. lxxviii. 67, 68). This the sacred history sometimes repeats, that the secret grace of God may be more admirably displayed in that change. I admit that it was by their own fault Ishmael, Esau, and others, fell from their adoption ; for the condition annexed was, that they should faithfully keep the covenant of God, whereas they perfidiously violated it. The singular kindness of God consisted in this, that he had been pleased to prefer them to other nations ; as it is said in the psalm, " He hath not dealt so with any nation : and as for his judgments, they have not known them" (Ps. cxlvii. 20). But I had good reason for saying that two steps are here to be observed ; for in the election of the whole nation, God had already shown that in the exercise of his mere liberality he was under no law, but was free, so that he was by no means to be restricted to an equal division of grace, its very inequality proving it to be gratuitous. Accordingly, Malachi enlarges on the ingratitude of Israel, in that being not only selected from the whole human race, but set peculiarly apart from a sacred household, they perfidiously and impiously spurn God their beneficent parent. " Was not Esau Jacob's brother ? saith the Lord : yet I loved Jacob, and I hated Esau" (Mal. i. 2, 3). For God takes it for granted, that as both were the sons of a holy father, and successors of the covenant, in short, branches from a sacred root, the sons of Jacob were under no ordinary obligation for having been admitted to that dignity ; but when by the rejection of Esau the first-born, their progenitor though inferior in birth was made heir, he charges them with double ingratitude, in not being restrained by a double tie.

7. Although it is now sufficiently plain that God by his secret counsel chooses whom he will while he rejects others, his gratuitous election has only been partially explained until we come to the case of single individuals, to whom God not only offers salvation, but so assigns it, that the certainty of the result remains not dubious or suspended.[1] These are considered as belonging to that one seed of which Paul makes mention (Rom. ix. 8 ; Gal. iii. 16, &c.). For although adoption was deposited in the hand of Abraham, yet as many of his posterity were cut off as rotten members, in order that election may stand and be effectual, it is necessary to ascend to the head in whom the heavenly Father hath connected his elect with each other, and bound them to himself by an indissoluble tie. Thus in the adoption of the family of Abraham, God gave them a liberal display of favour which he has denied to others ; but in the members of Christ there is a far more excellent display of grace, because those ingrafted into him as their head never fail to obtain salvation.

---

[1] On predestination, see the pious and very learned observations of Luther, tom. i. p. 86, fin., and p. 87, fin. Tom. iii. ad Psal. xxii. 8. Tom. v. in Joann. cxvii. Also his Prefatio in Epist. ad Rom. and Adv. Erasmum de Servo Arbitrio, p. 429, sqq. 452, 463. Also in Psal. cxxxix.

Hence Paul skilfully argues from the passage of Malachi which I quoted (Rom. ix. 13; Mal. i. 2), that when God, after making a covenant of eternal life, invites any people to himself, a special mode of election is in part understood, so that he does not with promiscuous grace effectually elect all of them. The words, "Jacob have I loved," refer to the whole progeny of the patriarch, which the prophet there opposes to the posterity of Esau. But there is nothing in this repugnant to the fact, that in the person of one man is set before us a specimen of election, which cannot fail of accomplishing its object. It is not without cause Paul observes, that these are called *a remnant* (Rom. ix. 27; xi. 5); because experience shows that of the general body many fall away and are lost, so that often a small portion only remains. The reason why the general election of the people is not always firmly ratified, readily presents itself—viz. that on those with whom God makes the covenant, he does not immediately bestow the Spirit of regeneration, by whose power they persevere in the covenant even to the end. The external invitation, without the internal efficacy of grace which would have the effect of retaining them, holds a kind of middle place between the rejection of the human race and the election of a small number of believers. The whole people of Israel are called the Lord's inheritance, and yet there were many foreigners among them. Still, because the covenant which God had made to be their Father and Redeemer was not altogether null, he has respect to that free favour rather than to the perfidious defection of many; even by them his truth was not abolished, since by preserving some residue to himself, it appeared that his calling was without repentance. When God ever and anon gathered his Church from among the sons of Abraham rather than from profane nations, he had respect to his covenant, which, when violated by the great body, he restricted to a few, that it might not entirely fail. In short, that common adoption of the seed of Abraham was a kind of visible image of a greater benefit which God deigned to bestow on some out of many. This is the reason why Paul so carefully distinguishes between the sons of Abraham according to the flesh and the spiritual sons, who are called after the example of Isaac. Not that simply to be a son of Abraham was a vain or useless privilege (this could not be said without insult to the covenant), but that the immutable counsel of God, by which he predestinated to himself whomsoever he would, was alone effectual for their salvation. But until the proper view is made clear by the production of passages of Scripture, I advise my readers not to prejudge the question. We say, then, that Scripture clearly proves this much, that God by his eternal and immutable counsel determined once for all those whom it was his pleasure one day to admit to salvation, and those whom, on the other hand, it was his pleasure to doom to destruction. We maintain that this counsel, as regards the elect, is founded on his free mercy, without any respect to human worth, while those whom he dooms to destruction are excluded from access to life by a just and blameless, but at the same time incomprehensible judgment. In regard to the elect, we regard calling as the evidence of election, and justification as another symbol of its manifestation, until it is fully accomplished by the attainment of glory. But as the Lord seals his elect by calling and justification, so by excluding the reprobate either from the knowledge of his name or the sanctification of his Spirit, he by these marks in a manner discloses the judgment which awaits them. I will here omit many of the fictions which foolish men have devised to overthrow predestination. There is no need of refuting objections which the moment they are produced abundantly betray their hollowness. I will dwell only on those points which either form the subject of dispute among the learned, or may occasion any difficulty to the simple, or may be employed by impiety as specious pretexts for assailing the justice of God.

CHAPTER XXII.

THIS DOCTRINE CONFIRMED BY PROOFS FROM SCRIPTURE.

The divisions of this chapter are,—I. A confirmation of the orthodox doctrine in opposition to two classes of individuals. This confirmation founded on a careful exposition of our Saviour's words, and passages in the writings of Paul, sec. 1–7. II. A refutation of some objections taken from ancient writers, Thomas Aquinas, and more modern writers, sec. 8–10. III. Of reprobation, which is founded entirely on the righteous will of God, sec. 11.

Sections.

1. Some imagine that God elects or reprobates according to a foreknowledge of merit. Others make it a charge against God that he elects some and passes by others. Both refuted, 1. By invincible arguments; 2. By the testimony of Augustine.
2. Who are elected, when, in whom, to what, for what reason.
3. The reason is the good pleasure of God, which so reigns in election that no works, either past or future, are taken into consideration. This proved by notable declarations of our Saviour and passages of Paul.
4. Proved by a striking discussion in the Epistle to the Romans. Its scope and method explained. The advocates of foreknowledge refuted by the Apostle, when he maintains that election is special and wholly of grace.
5. Evasion refuted. A summary and analysis of the Apostle's discussion.
6. An exception, with three answers to it. The efficacy of gratuitous election extends only to believers, who are said to be elected according to foreknowledge. This foreknowledge or prescience is not speculative but active.
7. This proved from the words of Christ. Conclusion of the answer, and solution of the objection with regard to Judas.
8. An objection taken from the ancient fathers. Answer from Augustine, from Ambrose, as quoted by Augustine, and an invincible argument by an Apostle. Summary of this argument.
9. Objection from Thomas Aquinas. Answer.
10. Objection of more modern writers. Answers. Passages in which there is a semblance of contradiction reconciled. Why many called and few chosen. An objection founded on mutual consent between the word and faith. Solution confirmed by the words of Paul, Augustine, and Bernard. A clear declaration by our Saviour.
11. The view to be taken of reprobation. It is founded on the righteous will of God.

1. MANY controvert all the positions which we have laid down, especially the gratuitous election of believers, which however cannot be overthrown. For they commonly imagine that God distinguishes between men according to the merits which he foresees that each individual is to have, giving the adoption of sons to those whom he foreknows will not be unworthy of his grace, and dooming those to destruction whose dispositions he perceives will be prone to mischief and wickedness. Thus by interposing foreknowledge as a veil, they not only obscure election, but pretend to give it a different origin. Nor is this the commonly received opinion of the vulgar merely, for

it has in all ages had great supporters (see sec. 8).   This I candidly confess, lest any one should expect greatly to prejudice our cause by opposing it with their names.   The truth of God is here too certain to be shaken, too clear to be overborne by human authority. Others, who are neither versed in Scripture, nor entitled to any weight, assail sound doctrine with a petulance and improbity which it is impossible to tolerate.[1]   Because God of his mere good pleasure electing some passes by others, they raise a plea against him.   But if the fact is certain, what can they gain by quarrelling with God ? We teach nothing but what experience proves to be true—viz. that God has always been at liberty to bestow his grace on whom he would.   Not to ask in what respect the posterity of Abraham excelled others, if it be not in a worth, the cause of which has no existence out of God, let them tell why men are better than oxen or asses. God might have made them dogs when he formed them in his own image.   Will they allow the lower animals to expostulate with God, as if the inferiority of their condition were unjust ?   It is certainly not more equitable that men should enjoy the privilege which they have not acquired by any merit, than that he should variously distribute favours as seems to him meet.   If they pass to the case of individuals where inequality is more offensive to them, they ought at least, in regard to the example of our Saviour, to be restrained by feelings of awe from talking so confidently of this sublime mystery. He is conceived a mortal man of the seed of David ; what, I would ask them, are the virtues by which he deserved to become in the very womb, the head of angels, the only begotten Son of God, the image and glory of the Father, the light, righteousness, and salvation of the world ?   It is wisely observed by Augustine,[2] that in the very head of the Church we have a bright mirror of free election, lest it should give any trouble to us the members—viz. that he did not become the Son of God by living righteously, but was freely presented with this great honour, that he might afterwards make others partakers of his gifts.   Should any one here ask, why others are not what he was, or why we are all at so great a distance from him, why we are all corrupt while he is purity, he would not only betray his madness, but his effrontery also.   But if they are bent on depriving God of the free right of electing and reprobating, let them at the same time take away what has been given to Christ.   It will now be proper to attend to what Scripture declares concerning each.   When Paul declares that we were chosen in Christ before the foundation of the world (Eph. i. 4), he certainly shows that no regard is had to our

---

1 French, " Il y en a d'aucuns, lesquels n'estans exercés en l'Ecriture ne sont dignes d'aucun credit ne reputation ; et toutes fois sont plus hardis et temeraires à diffamer la doctrine qui leur est incognue ; et ainsi ce n'est pas raison que leur arrogance soit supportée."—There are some who, not being exercised in Scripture, are not worthy of any credit or reputation, and yet are more bold and presumptuous in defaming the doctrine which is unknown to them, and hence their arrogance is insupportable.

2 August. de Corrept. et Gratia ad Valent. c. 15.   Hom. de Bono Perseveran. c. 8. Item, de Verbis Apost. Serm. viii.

own worth; for it is just as if he had said, Since in the whole seed of Adam our heavenly Father found nothing worthy of his election, he turned his eye upon his own Anointed, that he might select as members of his body those whom he was to assume into the fellowship of life.   Let believers, then, give full effect to this reason—viz. that we were in Christ adopted unto the heavenly inheritance, because in ourselves we were incapable of such excellence.   This he elsewhere observes in another passage, in which he exhorts the Colossians to give thanks that they had been made meet to be partakers of the inheritance of the saints (Col. i. 12).   If election precedes that divine grace by which we are made fit to obtain immortal life, what can God find in us to induce him to elect us?   What I mean is still more clearly explained in another passage: God, says he, "hath chosen us in him before the foundation of the world, that we might be holy and without blame before him in love: having predestinated us unto the adoption of children by Jesus Christ to himself, according to the good pleasure of his will" (Eph. i. 4, 5).   Here he opposes the good pleasure of God to our merits of every description.

2. That the proof may be more complete, it is of importance to attend to the separate clauses of that passage.   When they are connected together they leave no doubt.   From giving them the name of elect, it is clear that he is addressing believers, as indeed he shortly after declares.   It is, therefore, a complete perversion of the name to confine it to the age in which the gospel was published.   By saying they were elected before the foundation of the world, he takes away all reference to worth.   For what ground of distinction was there between persons who as yet existed not, and persons who were afterwards like them to exist in Adam?   But if they were elected in Christ, it follows not only that each was elected on some extrinsic ground, but that some were placed on a different footing from others, since we see that all are not members of Christ.   In the additional statement that they were elected that they might be holy, the apostle openly refutes the error of those who deduce election from prescience, since he declares that whatever virtue appears in men is the result of election.   Then, if a higher cause is asked, Paul answers that God so predestined, and predestined according to the good pleasure of his will.   By these words, he overturns all the grounds of election which men imagine to exist in themselves.   For he shows that whatever favours God bestows in reference to the spiritual life flow from this one fountain, because God chose whom he would, and before they were born had the grace which he designed to bestow upon them set apart for their use.

3. Wherever this good pleasure of God reigns, no good works are taken into account.   The Apostle, indeed, does not follow out the antithesis, but it is to be understood, as he himself explains it in another passage, "Who hath called us with a holy calling, not according to our works, but according to his own purpose and grace, which was given us in Christ Jesus before the world began" (1 Tim.

ii. 9).　We have already shown that the additional words, "that we might be holy," remove every doubt.　If you say that he foresaw they would be holy, and therefore elected them, you invert the order of Paul.　You may, therefore, safely infer, If he elected us that we might be holy, he did not elect us because he foresaw that we would be holy.　The two things are evidently inconsistent—viz. that the pious owe it to election that they are holy, and yet attain to election by means of works.　There is no force in the cavil to which they are ever recurring, that the Lord does not bestow election in recompense of preceding, but bestows it in consideration of future merits.　For when it is said that believers were elected that they might be holy, it is at the same time intimated that the holiness which was to be in them has its origin in election.　And how can it be consistently said, that things derived from election are the cause of election?　The very thing which the Apostle had said, he seems afterwards to confirm by adding, "According to his good pleasure which he hath purposed in himself" (Eph. i. 9); for the expression that God "purposed in himself," is the same as if it had been said, that in forming his decree he considered nothing external to himself; and, accordingly, it is immediately subjoined, that the whole object contemplated in our election is, that "we should be to the praise of his glory."　Assuredly divine grace would not deserve all the praise of election, were not election gratuitous; and it would not be gratuitous, did God in electing any individual pay regard to his future works.　Hence, what Christ said to his disciples is found to be universally applicable to all believers, "Ye have not chosen me, but I have chosen you" (John xv. 16).　Here he not only excludes past merits, but declares that they had nothing in themselves for which they could be chosen, except in so far as his mercy anticipated.　And how are we to understand the words of Paul, "Who hath first given to him, and it shall be recompensed unto him again?" (Rom. xi. 35).　His meaning obviously is, that men are altogether indebted to the preventing goodness of God, there being nothing in them, either past or future, to conciliate his favour.

4. In the Epistle to the Romans (Rom. ix. 6), in which he again treats this subject more reconditely and at greater length, he declares that "they are not all Israel which are of Israel;" for though all were blessed in respect of hereditary right, yet all did not equally obtain the succession.　The whole discussion was occasioned by the pride and vain-glorying of the Jews, who, by claiming the name of the Church for themselves, would have made the faith of the Gospel dependent on their pleasure; just as in the present day the Papists would fain under this pretext substitute themselves in place of God.　Paul, while he concedes that in respect of the covenant they were the holy offspring of Abraham, yet contends that the greater part of them were strangers to it, and that not only because they were degenerate, and so had become bastards instead of sons, but because the principal point to be considered was the special election of God, by which alone his adop-

tion was ratified. If the piety of some established them in the hope of salvation, and the revolt of others was the sole cause of their being rejected, it would have been foolish and absurd in Paul to carry his readers back to a secret election. But if the will of God (no cause of which external to him either appears or is to be looked for) distinguishes some from others, so that all the sons of Israel are not true Israelites, it is vain for any one to seek the origin of his condition in himself. He afterwards prosecutes the subject at greater length, by contrasting the cases of Jacob and Esau. Both being sons of Abraham, both having been at the same time in the womb of their mother, there was something very strange in the change by which the honour of the birthright was transferred to Jacob, and yet Paul declares that the change was an attestation to the election of the one and the reprobation of the other.

The question considered is the origin and cause of election. The advocates of foreknowledge insist that it is to be found in the virtues and vices of men. For they take the short and easy method of asserting, that God showed in the person of Jacob, that he elects those who are worthy of his grace; and in the person of Esau, that he rejects those whom he foresees to be unworthy. Such is their confident assertion; but what does Paul say? "For the children being not yet born, neither having done any good or evil, that the purpose of God according to election might stand, not of works, but of him that calleth; it was said unto her [Rebecca], The elder shall serve the younger. As it is written, Jacob have I loved, but Esau have I hated" (Rom. ix. 11—13). If foreknowledge had anything to do with this distinction of the brothers, the mention of time would have been out of place. Granting that Jacob was elected for a worth to be obtained by future virtues, to what end did Paul say that he was not yet born? Nor would there have been any occasion for adding, that as yet he had done no good, because the answer was always ready, that nothing is hid from God, and that therefore the piety of Jacob was present before him. If works procure favour, a value ought to have been put upon them before Jacob was born, just as if he had been of full age. But in explaining the difficulty, the Apostle goes on to show, that the adoption of Jacob proceeded not on works but on the calling of God. In works he makes no mention of past or future, but distinctly opposes them to the calling of God, intimating, that when place is given to the one the other is overthrown; as if he had said, The only thing to be considered is what pleased God, not what men furnished of themselves. Lastly, it is certain that all the causes which men are wont to devise as external to the secret counsel of God, are excluded by the use of the terms *purpose* and *election*.

5. Why should men attempt to darken these statements by assigning some place in election to past or future works? This is altogether to evade what the Apostle contends for—viz. that the distinction between the brothers is not founded on any ground of works, but on

the mere calling of God, inasmuch as it was fixed before the children were born. Had there been any solidity in this subtlety, it would not have escaped the notice of the Apostle, but being perfectly aware that God foresaw no good in man, save that which he had already previously determined to bestow by means of his election, he does not employ a preposterous arrangement which would make good works antecedent to their cause. We learn from the Apostle's words, that the salvation of believers is founded entirely on the decree of divine election, that the privilege is procured not by works but free calling. We have also a specimen of the thing itself set before us. Esau and Jacob are brothers, begotten of the same parents, within the same womb, not yet born. In them all things are equal, and yet the judgment of God with regard to them is different. He adopts the one and rejects the other. The only right of precedence was that of primogeniture; but that is disregarded, and the younger is preferred to the elder. Nay, in the case of others, God seems to have disregarded primogeniture for the express purpose of excluding the flesh from all ground of boasting. Rejecting Ishmael he gives his favour to Isaac, postponing Manasseh he honours Ephraim.

6. Should any one object that these minute and inferior favours do not enable us to decide with regard to the future life, that it is not to be supposed that he who received the honour of primogeniture was thereby adopted to the inheritance of heaven (many objectors do not even spare Paul, but accuse him of having in the quotation of these passages wrested Scripture from its proper meaning); I answer as before, that the Apostle has not erred through inconsideration, or spontaneously misapplied the passages of Scripture; but he saw (what these men cannot be brought to consider) that God purposed under an earthly sign to declare the spiritual election of Jacob, which otherwise lay hidden at his inaccessible tribunal. For unless we refer the primogeniture bestowed upon him to the future world, the form of blessing would be altogether vain and ridiculous, inasmuch as he gained nothing by it but a multitude of toils and annoyances, exile, sharp sorrows, and bitter cares. Therefore, when Paul knew beyond a doubt that by the external, God manifested the spiritual and unfading blessings, which he had prepared for his servant in his kingdom, he hesitated not in proving the latter to draw an argument from the former. For we must remember that the land of Canaan was given in pledge of the heavenly inheritance; and that therefore there cannot be a doubt that Jacob was like the angels ingrafted into the body of Christ, that he might be a partaker of the same life. Jacob therefore is chosen, while Esau is rejected; the predestination of God makes a distinction where none existed in respect of merit. If you ask the reason the Apostle gives it, "For he saith to Moses, I will have mercy on whom I will have mercy, and I will have compassion on whom I will have compassion" (Rom. ix. 15). And what, pray, does this mean? It is just a clear declaration by the Lord that he finds nothing in men themselves to induce him to show kind-

ness, that it is owing entirely to his own mercy, and accordingly that their salvation is his own work. Since God places your salvation in himself alone, why should you descend to yourself? Since he assigns you his own mercy alone, why will you recur to your own merits? Since he confines your thoughts to his own mercy, why do you turn partly to the view of your own works?

We must therefore come to that smaller number whom Paul elsewhere describes as foreknown of God (Rom. xi. 2); not foreknown, as these men imagine, by idle, inactive comtemplation, but in the sense which it often bears. For surely when Peter says that Christ was "delivered by the determinate counsel and foreknowledge of God" (Acts ii. 23), he does not represent God as contemplating merely, but as actually accomplishing our salvation. Thus also Peter, in saying that the believers to whom he writes are elect "according to the foreknowledge of God" (1 Pet. i. 2), properly expresses that secret predestination by which God has sealed those whom he has been pleased to adopt as sons. In using the term *purpose* as synonymous with a term which uniformly denotes what is called a fixed determination, he undoubtedly shows that God, in being the author of our salvation, does not go beyond himself. In this sense he says in the same chapter, that Christ as "a lamb" "was foreordained before the creation of the world" (1 Pet. i. 19, 20). What could have been more frigid or absurd than to have represented God as looking from the height of heaven to see whence the salvation of the human race was to come? By a people foreknown, Peter means the same thing as Paul does by a remnant selected from a multitude falsely assuming the name of God. In another passage, to suppress the vain boasting of those who, while only covered with a mask, claim for themselves in the view of the world a first place among the godly, Paul says, "The Lord knoweth them that are his" (2 Tim. ii. 19). In short, by that term he designates two classes of people, the one consisting of the whole race of Abraham, the other a people separated from that race, and though hidden from human view, yet open to the eye of God. And there is no doubt that he took the passage from Moses, who declares that God would be merciful to whomsoever he pleased (although he was speaking of an elect people whose condition was apparently equal); just as if he had said, that in a common adoption was included a special grace which he bestows on some as a holier treasure, and that there is nothing in the common covenant to prevent this number from being exempted from the common order. God being pleased in this matter to act as a free dispenser and disposer, distinctly declares, that the only ground on which he will show mercy to one rather than to another is his sovereign pleasure; for when mercy is bestowed on him who asks it, though he indeed does not suffer a refusal, he however either anticipates or partly acquires a favour, the whole merit of which God claims for himself.

7. Now, let the supreme Judge and Master decide on the whole case. Seeing such obduracy in his hearers, that his words fell upon

the multitude almost without fruit, he, to remove this stumbling-block, exclaims, "All that the Father giveth me shall come to me." "And this is the Father's will which hath sent me, that of all which he hath given me I should lose nothing" (John vi. 37, 39). Observe that the donation of the Father is the first step in our delivery into the charge and protection of Christ. Some one, perhaps, will here turn round and object, that those only peculiarly belong to the Father who make a voluntary surrender by faith. But the only thing which Christ maintains is, that though the defections of vast multitudes should shake the world, yet the counsel of God would stand firm, more stable than heaven itself, that his election would never fail. The elect are said to have belonged to the Father before he bestowed them on his only begotten Son. It is asked if they were his by nature? Nay, they were aliens, but he makes them his by delivering them. The words of Christ are too clear to be rendered obscure by any of the mists of caviling. "No man can come to me except the Father which hath sent me draw him." "Every man, therefore, that hath heard and learned of the Father cometh unto me" (John vi. 44, 45). Did all promiscuously bend the knee to Christ, election would be common; whereas now in the small number of believers a manifest diversity appears. Accordingly our Saviour, shortly after declaring that the disciples who were given to him were the common property of the Father, adds, "I pray not for the world, but for them which thou hast given me; for they are thine" (John xvii. 9). Hence it is that the whole world no longer belongs to its Creator, except in so far as grace rescues from malediction, divine wrath, and eternal death, some, not many, who would otherwise perish, while he leaves the world to the destruction to which it is doomed. Meanwhile, though Christ interpose as a Mediator, yet he claims the right of electing in common with the Father, "I speak not of you all: I know whom I have chosen" (John xiii. 18). If it is asked whence he hath chosen them, he answers in another passage, "Out of the world;" which he excludes from his prayers when he commits his disciples to the Father (John xv. 19). We must indeed hold, when he affirms that he knows whom he has chosen, first, that some individuals of the human race are denoted; and, secondly, that they are not distinguished by the quality of their virtues, but by a heavenly decree. Hence it follows, that since Christ makes himself the author of election, none excel by their own strength or industry. In elsewhere numbering Judas among the elect, though he was a devil (John vi. 70), he refers only to the apostolical office, which, though a bright manifestation of divine favour (as Paul so often acknowledges it to be in his own person), does not however contain within itself the hope of eternal salvation. Judas, therefore, when he discharged the office of Apostle perfidiously, might have been worse than a devil; but not one of those whom Christ has once ingrafted into his body will he ever permit to perish, for in securing their salvation, he will perform what he has promised; that is, exert a divine power greater than all (John x. 28). For when he says, "Those that thou gavest me I have kept, and none of them is lost but the son of perdition" (John xvii. 12), the expression, though there is a catachresis in it, is not at all ambiguous. The sum is, that God by gratuitous adoption forms those whom he wishes to have for sons; but that the intrinsic cause is in himself, because he is contented with his secret pleasure.

8. But Ambrose, Origen, and Jerome, were of opinion, that God dispenses his grace among men according to the use which he foresees that each will make of it. It may be added, that Augustine also was for some time of this opinion; but after he had made greater progress in the knowledge of Scripture, he not only retracted it as evidently false, but powerfully confuted it (August. Retract. Lib. i. c. 13). Nay, even after the retractation, glancing at the Pelagians who still persisted in that error, he says, "Who does not wonder that the Apostle failed to make this most acute observation? For after stating a most startling proposition concerning those who were not yet born, and afterwards putting the question to himself by way of objection, 'What then? Is there unrighteousness with God?' he had an opportunity of answering, that God foresaw the merits of both, he does not say so, but has recourse to the justice and mercy of God" (August. Epist. 106, ad Sixtum). And in another passage, after excluding all merit before election, he says, "Here, certainly, there is no place for the vain argument of those who defend the foreknowledge of God against the grace of God, and accordingly maintain that we were elected before the foundation of the world, because God foreknew that we would be good, not that he himself would make us good. This is not the language of him who says, 'Ye have not chosen me, but I have chosen you' (John xv. 16). For had he chosen us because he foreknew that we would be good, he would at the same time also have foreknown that we were to choose him" (August. in Joann. viii.; see also what follows to the same effect). Let the testimony of Augustine prevail with those who willingly acquiesce in the authority of the Fathers; although Augustine allows not that he differs from the others,[1] but shows by clear evidence that the difference which the Pelagians invidiously objected to him is unfounded. For he quotes from Ambrose (Lib. de Prædest. Sanct. cap. 19), "Christ calls whom he pities." Again, "Had he pleased, he could have made them devout instead of undevout; but God calls whom he deigns to call, and makes religious whom he will." Were we disposed to frame an entire volume out of Augustine, it were easy to show the reader that I have no occasion to use any other words than his: but I am unwilling to burden him with a prolix statement. But assuming that the fathers did not speak thus, let us attend to the thing itself. A difficult question had been raised—viz. Did God do justly in bestowing his grace on certain individuals? Paul might

---

[1] Latin, "a reliquis;" French, "les autre Docteurs anciens;"—the other ancient Doctors.

have disencumbered himself of this question at once by saying, that God had respect to works. Why does he not do so? Why does he rather continue to use a language which leaves him exposed to the same difficulty? Why, but just because it would not have been right to say it. There was no obliviousness on the part of the Holy Spirit, who was speaking by his mouth. He therefore answers without ambiguity, that God favours his elect, because he is pleased to do so, and shows mercy because he is pleased to do so. For the words, "I will be gracious to whom I will be gracious, and show mercy on whom I will show mercy" (Exod. xxxiii. 19), are the same in effect as if it had been said, God is moved to mercy by no other reason than that he is pleased to show mercy. Augustine's declaration, therefore, remains true. The grace of God does not find, but makes persons fit to be chosen.

9. Nor let us be detained by the subtlety of Thomas, that the foreknowledge of merit is the cause of predestination, not indeed in respect of the predestinating act, but that on our part it may in some sense be so called—namely, in respect of a particular estimate of predestination; as when it is said, that God predestinates man to glory according to his merit, inasmuch as he decreed to bestow upon him the grace by which he merits glory. For while the Lord would have us to see nothing more in election than his mere goodness, for any one to desire to see more is preposterous affectation. But were we to make a trial of subtlety, it would not be difficult to refute the sophistry of Thomas. He maintains that the elect are in a manner predestinated to glory on account of their merits, because God predestines to give them the grace by which they merit glory What if I should, on the contrary, object that predestination to grace is subservient to election unto life, and follows as its handmaid; that grace is predestined to those to whom the possession of glory was previously assigned, the Lord being pleased to bring his sons by election to justification? For it will hence follow that the predestination to glory is the cause of the predestination to grace, and not the converse. But let us have done with these disputes as superfluous among those who think that there is enough of wisdom for them in the word of God. For it has been truly said by an old ecclesiastical writer, Those who ascribe the election of God to merits, are wise above what they ought to be (Ambros. de Vocat. Gentium, Lib. i. c. 2).

10. Some object that God would be inconsistent with himself, in inviting all without distinction while he elects only a few. Thus, according to them, the universality of the promise destroys the distinction of special grace. Some moderate men speak in this way, not so much for the purpose of suppressing the truth, as to get quit of puzzling questions, and curb excessive curiosity. The intention is laudable, but the design is by no means to be approved, dissimulation being at no time excusable. In those again who display their petulance, we see only a vile cavil or a disgraceful error. The mode in which Scripture reconciles the two things—viz. that by external

preaching all are called to faith and repentance, and that yet the Spirit of faith and repentance is not given to all—I have already explained, and will again shortly repeat. But the point which they assume I deny as false in two respects: for he who threatens that when it shall rain on one city there will be drought in another (Amos iv. 7); and declares in another passage, that there will be a famine of the word (Amos viii. 11), does not lay himself under a fixed obligation to call all equally. And he who, forbidding Paul to preach in Asia, and leading him away from Bithynia, carries him over to Macedonia (Acts xvi. 6), shows that it belongs to him to distribute the treasure in what way he pleases. But it, is by Isaiah he more clearly demonstrates how he destines the promises of salvation specially to the elect (Isa. viii. 16); for he declares that his disciples would consist of them only, and not indiscriminately of the whole human race. Whence it is evident that the doctrine of salvation, which is said to be set apart for the sons of the Church only, is abused when it is represented as effectually available to all. For the present let it suffice to observe, that though the word of the gospel is addressed generally to all, yet the gift of faith is rare. Isaiah assigns the cause when he says, that the arm of the Lord is not revealed to all (Isa. liii. 1). Had he said, that the gospel is malignantly and perversely contemned, because many obstinately refuse to hear, there might perhaps be some colour for this universal call. It is not the purpose of the Prophet, however, to extenuate the guilt of men, when he states the source of their blindness to be, that God deigns not to reveal his arm to them; he only reminds us that since faith is a special gift, it is in vain that external doctrine sounds in the ear. But I would fain know from those doctors whether it is mere preaching or faith that makes men sons of God. Certainly when it is said, "As many as received him, to them gave he power to become the sons of God, even to them that believe on his name" (John i. 12), a confused mass is not set before us, but a special order is assigned to believers, who are "born not of blood, nor of the will of the flesh, nor of the will of man, but of God."

But it is said, there is a mutual agreement between faith and the word. That must be wherever there is faith. But it is no new thing for the seed to fall among thorns or in stony places; not only because the majority appear in fact to be rebellious against God, but because all are not gifted with eyes and ears. How, then, can it consistently be said, that God calls while he knows that the called will not come? Let Augustine answer for me: "Would you dispute with me? Wonder with me, and exclaim, O the depth! Let us both agree in dread, lest we perish in error" (August. de Verb. Apost. Serm. xi.). Moreover, if election is, as Paul declares, the parent of faith, I retort the argument, and maintain that faith is not general, since election is special. For it is easily inferred from the series of causes and effects, when Paul says, that the Father "hath blessed us with all spiritual blessings in heavenly places in Christ, according

as he hath chosen us in him before the foundation of the world"
(Eph. i. 3, 4), that these riches are not common to all, because God
has chosen only whom he would.   And the reason why in another
passage he commends the faith of the elect is, to prevent any one
from supposing that he acquires faith of his own nature; since to
God alone belongs the glory of freely illuminating those whom he
had previously chosen (Tit. i. 1).   For it is well said by Bernard,
"His friends hear apart when he says to them, Fear not, little
flock: to you it is given to know the mysteries of the kingdom. Who
are these?   Those whom he foreknew and predestinated to be conformed to the image of his Son.   He has made known his great and
secret counsel.   The Lord knoweth them that are his, but that which
was known to God was manifested to men; nor, indeed, does he
deign to give a participation in this great mystery to any but those
whom he foreknew and predestinated to be his own" (Bernard. ad
Thomam Præpos. Benerlae. Epist. 107).   Shortly after he concludes,
"The mercy of the Lord is from everlasting to everlasting upon them
that fear him; from everlasting through predestination, to everlasting through glorification: the one knows no beginning, the other no
end."   But why cite Bernard as a witness, when we hear from the
lips of our Master, "Not that any man hath seen the Father, save he
which is of God"? (John vi. 46).   By these words he intimates that
all who are not regenerated by God are amazed at the brightness of
his countenance.   And, indeed, faith is aptly conjoined with election,
provided it hold the second place.   This order is clearly expressed
by our Saviour in these words, "This is the Father's will which hath
sent me, that of all which he hath given me I should lose nothing;"
"And this is the will of him that sent me, that every one which
seeth the Son, and believeth on him, may have everlasting life"
(John vi. 39, 40).   If he would have all to be saved, he would appoint his Son their guardian, and would ingraft them all into his
body by the sacred bond of faith.   It is now clear that faith is a
singular pledge of paternal love, treasured up for the sons whom he
has adopted.   Hence Christ elsewhere says, that the sheep follow
the shepherd because they know his voice, but that they will not
follow a stranger, because they know not the voice of strangers
(John x. 4).   But whence that distinction, unless that their ears
have been divinely bored?   For no man makes himself a sheep, but
is formed by heavenly grace.   And why does the Lord declare that
our salvation will always be sure and certain, but just because it is
guarded by the invincible power of God? (John x. 29.)   Accordingly, he concludes that unbelievers are not of his sheep (John x.
16).   The reason is, because they are not of the number of those
who, as the Lord promised by Isaiah, were to be his disciples. Moreover, as the passages which I have quoted imply perseverance, they
are also attestations to the inflexible constancy of election.

11. We come now to the reprobate, to whom the Apostle at the
same time refers (Rom. ix. 13).   For as Jacob, who as yet had

merited nothing by good works, is assumed into favour; so Esau, while as yet unpolluted by any crime, is hated. If we turn our view to works, we do injustice to the Apostle, as if he had failed to see the very thing which is clear to us. Moreover, there is complete proof of his not having seen it, since he expressly insists that when as yet they had done neither good nor evil, the one was elected, the other rejected, in order to prove that the foundation of divine predestination is not in works. Then after starting the objection, Is God unjust? instead of employing what would have been the surest and plainest defence of his justice—viz. that God had recompensed Esau according to his wickedness—he is contented with a different solution —viz. that the reprobate are expressly raised up, in order that the glory of God may thereby be displayed. At last, he concludes that God hath mercy on whom he will have mercy, and whom he will he hardeneth (Rom. ix. 18). You see how he refers both to the mere pleasure of God. Therefore, if we cannot assign any reason for his bestowing mercy on his people, but just that it so pleases him, neither can we have any reason for his reprobating others but his will. When God is said to visit in mercy or harden whom he will, men are reminded that they are not to seek for any cause beyond his will.

CHAPTER XXIII.

REFUTATION OF THE CALUMNIES BY WHICH THIS DOCTRINE IS ALWAYS UNJUSTLY ASSAILED.

This chapter consists of four parts, which refute the principal objections to this doctrine, and the various pleas and exceptions founded on these objections. These are preceded by a refutation of those who hold election but deny reprobation, sec. 1. Then follows, I. A refutation of the first objection to the doctrine of reprobation and election, sec. 2–5. II. An answer to the second objection, sec. 6–9. III A refutation of the third objection. IV. A refutation of the fourth objection; to which is added a useful and necessary caution, sec. 12–14.

Sections.

1. THE human mind, when it hears this doctrine, cannot restrain its petulance, but boils and rages as if aroused by the sound of a trumpet. Many professing a desire to defend the Deity from an invidious charge admit the doctrine of election, but deny that any one

is reprobated (Bernard, in Die Ascensionis, Serm. 2). This they do ignorantly and childishly, since there could be no election without its opposite reprobation. God is said to set apart those whom he adopts for salvation. It were most absurd to say, that he admits others fortuitously, or that they by their industry acquire what election alone confers on a few. Those, therefore, whom God passes by he reprobates, and that for no other cause but because he is pleased to exclude them from the inheritance which he predestines to his children. Nor is it possible to tolerate the petulance of men, in refusing to be restrained by the word of God, in regard to his incomprehensible counsel, which even angels adore. We have already been told that hardening is not less under the immediate hand of God than mercy. Paul does not, after the example of those whom I have mentioned, labour anxiously to defend God, by calling in the aid of falsehood; he only reminds us that it is unlawful for the creature to quarrel with its Creator. Then how will those who refuse to admit that any are reprobated by God explain the following words of Christ? "Every plant which my heavenly Father hath not plantèd shall be rooted up" (Matth. xv. 13). They are plainly told that all whom the heavenly Father has not been pleased to plant as sacred trees in his garden, are doomed and devoted to destruction. If they deny that this is a sign of reprobation, there is nothing, however clear, that can be proved to them. But if they will still murmur, let us in the soberness of faith rest contented with the admonition of Paul, that it can be no ground of complaint that God, "willing to show his wrath, and to make his power known, endured with much long-suffering the vessels of wrath fitted for destruction: and that he might make known the riches of his glory on the vessels of mercy, which he had afore prepared unto glory" (Rom. ix. 22, 23). Let my readers observe that Paul, to cut off all handle for murmuring and detraction, attributes supreme sovereignty to the wrath and power of God; for it were unjust that those profound judgments, which transcend all our powers of discernment, should be subjected to our calculation. It is frivolous in our opponents to reply, that God does not altogether reject those whom in lenity he tolerates, but remains in suspense with regard to them, if peradventure they may repent; as if Paul were representing God as patiently waiting for the conversion of those whom he describes as fitted for destruction. For Augustine, rightly expounding this passage, says, that where power is united to endurance, God does not permit, but rules (August. Cont. Julian., Lib. v. c. 5). They add also, that it is not without cause the vessels of wrath are said to be fitted for destruction, and that God is said to have prepared the vessels of mercy, because in this way the praise of salvation is claimed for God, whereas the blame of perdition is thrown upon those who of their own accord bring it upon themselves. But were I to concede that by the different forms of expression Paul softens the harshness of the former clause, it by no means follows, that he transfers the preparation for destruction to any other cause than the secret counsel of God.   This, indeed, is asserted in the preceding context, where God is said to have raised up Pharaoh, and to harden whom he will.   Hence it follows, that the hidden counsel of God is the cause of hardening.   I at least hold with Augustine, that when God makes sheep out of wolves, he forms them again by the powerful influence of grace, that their hardness may thus be subdued, and that he does not convert the obstinate, because he does not exert that more powerful grace, a grace which he has at command, if he were disposed to use it (August. de Prædest. Sanct., Lib. i. c. 2).

2. These observations would be amply sufficient for the pious and modest, and such as remember that they are men.   But because many are the species of blasphemy which these virulent dogs utter against God, we shall, as far as the case admits, give an answer to each.   Foolish men raise many grounds of quarrel with God, as if they held him subject to their accusations.   First, they ask why God is offended with his creatures, who have not provoked him by any previous offence; for to devote to destruction whomsoever he pleases, more resembles the caprice of a tyrant than the legal sentence of a judge; and, therefore, there is reason to expostulate with God, if at his mere pleasure men are, without any desert of their own, predestinated to eternal death.   If at any time thoughts of this kind come into the minds of the pious, they will be sufficiently armed to repress them, by considering how sinful it is to insist on knowing the causes of the divine will, since it is itself, and justly ought to be, the cause of all that exists.   For if his will has any cause, there must be something antecedent to it, and to which it is annexed; this it were impious to imagine.   The will of God is the supreme rule of righteousness,[1] so that everything which he wills must be held to be righteous by the mere fact of his willing it.   Therefore, when it is asked why the Lord did so, we must answer, Because he pleased.   But if you proceed farther to ask why he pleased, you ask for something greater and more sublime than the will of God, and nothing such can be found.   Let human temerity then be quiet, and cease to inquire after what exists not, lest perhaps it fails to find what does exist.   This, I say, will be sufficient to restrain any one who would reverently contemplate the secret things of God.   Against the audacity of the wicked, who hesitate not openly to blaspheme, God will sufficiently defend himself by his own righteousness, without our assistance, when depriving their consciences of all means of evasion, he shall hold them under conviction, and make them feel their guilt.   We, however, give no countenance to the fiction of absolute power,[2] which, as it is heathenish, so it ought justly to be held in detestation by us.   We do not imagine God to be lawless.   He is a law to himself; because, as Plato says, men labouring under the influence of concupiscence

1 This is taken from Auguste Dein Gen. cont. Manich., Lib. i. c. 3.

2 French, "Toutesfois en parlant ainsi, nous n'approuvons pas la reverie des theologiens Papistes touchant la puissance absolue de Dieu;"—still in speaking thus, we approve not of the reverie of the Popish theologians touching the absolute power of God.

need law; but the will of God is not only free from all vice, but is the supreme standard of perfection, the law of all laws. But we deny that he is bound to give an account of his procedure; and we moreover deny that we are fit of our own ability to give judgment in such a case. Wherefore, when we are tempted to go farther than we ought, let this consideration deter us, Thou shalt be "justified when thou speakest, and be clear when thou judgest" (Ps. li. 4).

3. God may thus quell his enemies by silence. But lest we should allow them with impunity to hold his sacred name in derision, he supplies us with weapons against them from his word. Accordingly, when we are accosted in such terms as these, Why did God from the first predestine some to death, when, as they were not yet in existence, they could not have merited sentence of death? let us by way of reply ask in our turn, What do you imagine that God owes to man, if he is pleased to estimate him by his own nature? As we are all vitiated by sin, we cannot but be hateful to God, and that not from tyrannical cruelty, but the strictest justice. But if all whom the Lord predestines to death are naturally liable to sentence of death, of what injustice, pray, do they complain? Should all the sons of Adam come to dispute and contend with their Creator, because by his eternal providence they were before their birth doomed to perpetual destruction, when God comes to reckon with them, what will they be able to mutter against this defence? If all are taken from a corrupt mass, it is not strange that all are subject to condemnation. Let them not, therefore, charge God with injustice, if by his eternal judgment they are doomed to a death to which they themselves feel that whether they will or not they are drawn spontaneously by their own nature. Hence it appears how perverse is this affectation of murmuring, when of set purpose they suppress the cause of condemnation which they are compelled to recognise in themselves, that they may lay the blame upon God. But though I should confess a hundred times that God is the author (and it is most certain that he is), they do not, however, thereby efface their own guilt, which, engraven on their own consciences, is ever and anon presenting itself to their view.

4. They again object, Were not men predestinated by the ordination of God to that corruption which is now held forth as the cause of condemnation? If so, when they perish in their corruption, they do nothing else than suffer punishment for that calamity, into which, by the predestination of God, Adam fell, and dragged all his posterity headlong with him. Is not he, therefore, unjust in thus cruelly mocking his creatures? I admit that by the will of God all the sons of Adam fell into that state of wretchedness in which they are now involved; and this is just what I said at the first, that we must always return to the mere pleasure of the divine will, the cause of which is hidden in himself. But it does not forthwith follow that God lies open to this charge. For we will answer with Paul in these words, "Nay but, O man, who art thou that repliest against God? Shall the thing formed say to him that formed it, Why hast thou made me

thus? Hath not the potter power over the clay, of the same lump to make one vessel unto honour, and another unto dishonour?" (Rom. ix. 20, 21). They will deny that the justice of God is thus truly defended, and will allege that we seek an evasion, such as those are wont to employ who have no good excuse. For what more seems to be said here than just that the power of God is such as cannot be hindered, so that he can do whatsoever he pleases? But it is far otherwise. For what stronger reason can be given than when we are ordered to reflect who God is? How could he who is the Judge of the world commit any unrighteousness? If it properly belongs to the nature of God to do judgment, he must naturally love justice and abhor injustice. Wherefore, the Apostle did not, as if he had been caught in a difficulty, have recourse to evasion; he only intimated that the procedure of divine justice is too high to be scanned by human measure, or comprehended by the feebleness of human intellect. The Apostle, indeed, confesses that in the divine judgments there is a depth in which all the minds of men must be engulfed if they attempt to penetrate into it. But he also shows how unbecoming it is to reduce the works of God to such a law as that we can presume to condemn them the moment they accord not with our reason. There is a well-known saying of Solomon (which, however, few properly understand), "The great God that formed all things both rewardeth the fool and rewardeth transgressors" (Prov. xxvi. 10). For he is speaking of the greatness of God, whose pleasure it is to inflict punishment on fools and transgressors, though he is not pleased to bestow his Spirit upon them. It is a monstrous infatuation in men to seek to subject that which has no bounds to the little measure of their reason. Paul gives the name of *elect* to the angels who maintained their integrity. If their steadfastness was owing to the good pleasure of God, the revolt of the others proves that they were abandoned.[1] Of this no other cause can be adduced than reprobation, which is hidden in the secret counsel of God.

5. Now, should some Manes or Cœlestinus[2] come forward to arraign Divine Providence (see sec. 8), I say with Paul, that no account of it can be given, because by its magnitude it far surpasses our understanding. Is there anything strange or absurd in this? Would we have the power of God so limited as to be unable to do more than our mind can comprehend? I say with Augustine, that the Lord has created those who, as he certainly foreknew, were to go to destruction, and he did so because he so willed. Why he willed it is not ours to ask, as we cannot comprehend, nor can it become us even to raise a controversy as to the justice of the divine will. Whenever we speak of it, we are speaking of the supreme standard of justice. (See August. Ep. 106). But when justice clearly appears, why

---

1 French, "Si leur constance et fermeté a été fondée au bon plaisir de Dieu, la revolte des diables monstre qu'ils n'ont pas été retenus, mais plustost delaissez;"—if their constancy and firmness was founded on the good pleasure of God, the revolt of the devils shows that they were not restrained, but rather abandoned.

2 The French adds, "ou autre heretique;"—or other heretic.

should we raise any question of injustice? Let us not, therefore, be ashamed to stop their mouths after the example of Paul. Whenever they presume to carp, let us begin to repeat: Who are ye, miserable men, that bring an accusation against God, and bring it because he does not adapt the greatness of his works to your meagre capacity? As if everything must be perverse that is hidden from the flesh. The immensity of the divine judgments is known to you by clear experience. You know that they are called "a great deep" (Ps. xxxvi. 6). Now, look at the narrowness of your own mind, and say whether it can comprehend the decrees of God. Why then should you, by infatuated inquisitiveness, plunge yourselves into an abyss which reason itself tells you will prove your destruction? Why are you not deterred, in some degree at least, by what the Book of Job, as well as the Prophetical books, declare concerning the incomprehensible wisdom and dreadful power of God? If your mind is troubled, decline not to embrace the counsel of Augustine, "You a man expect an answer from me: I also am a man. Wherefore, let us both listen to him who says, 'O man, who art thou?' Believing ignorance is better than presumptuous knowledge. Seek merits; you will find nought but punishment. O the height! Peter denies, a thief believes. O the height! Do you ask the reason? I will tremble at the height. Reason you, I will wonder; dispute you, I will believe. I see the height; I cannot sound the depth. Paul found rest, because he found wonder. He calls the judgments of God 'unsearchable;' and have you come to search them? He says that his ways are 'past finding out,' and do you seek to find them out?" (August. de Verb. Apost. Serm. 20). We shall gain nothing by proceeding farther. For neither will the Lord satisfy the petulance of these men, nor does he need any other defence than that which he used by his Spirit, who spoke by the mouth of Paul. We unlearn the art of speaking well when we cease to speak with God.

6. Impiety starts another objection, which however seeks not so much to criminate God as to excuse the sinner; though he who is condemned by God as a sinner cannot ultimately be acquitted without impugning the judge. This, then, is the scoffing language which profane tongues employ. Why should God blame men for things the necessity of which he has imposed by his own predestination? What could they do? Could they struggle with his decrees? It were in vain for them to do it, since they could not possibly succeed. It is not just, therefore, to punish them for things the principal cause of which is in the predestination of God. Here I will abstain from a defence to which ecclesiastical writers usually recur, that there is nothing in the prescience of God to prevent him from regarding man as a sinner, since the evils which he foresees are man's, not his. This would not stop the caviller, who would still insist that God might, if he had pleased, have prevented the evils which he foresaw, and not having done so, must with determinate counsel have created man for the very purpose of so acting on the earth. But if by the providence

of God man was created, on the condition of afterwards doing whatever he does, then that which he cannot escape, and which he is constrained by the will of God to do, cannot be charged upon him as a crime. Let us, therefore, see what is the proper method of solving the difficulty. First, all must admit what Solomon says, " The Lord hath made all things for himself; yea, even the wicked for the day of evil" (Prov. xvi. 4). Now, since the arrangement of all things is in the hand of God, since to him belongs the disposal of life and death, he arranges all things by his sovereign counsel, in such a way that individuals are born, who are doomed from the womb to certain death, and are to glorify him by their destruction. If any one alleges that no necessity is laid upon them by the providence of God, but rather that they are created by him in that condition, because he foresaw their future depravity, he says something, but does not say enough. Ancient writers, indeed, occasionally employ this solution, though with some degree of hesitation. The Schoolmen, again, rest in it as if it could not be gainsayed. I, for my part, am willing to admit, that mere prescience lays no necessity on the creatures; though some do not assent to this, but hold that it is itself the cause of things. But Valla, though otherwise not greatly skilled in sacred matters, seems to me to have taken a shrewder and more acute view, when he shows that the dispute is superfluous, since life and death are acts of the divine will rather than of prescience. If God merely foresaw human events, and did not also arrange and dispose of them at his pleasure, there might be room for agitating the question, how far his foreknowledge amounts to necessity; but since he foresees the things which are to happen, simply because he has decreed that they are so to happen, it is vain to debate about prescience, while it is clear that all events take place by his sovereign appointment.

7. They deny that it is ever said in distinct terms, God decreed that Adam should perish by his revolt.[1] As if the same God, who is declared in Scripture to do whatsoever he pleases, could have made the noblest of his creatures without any special purpose. They say that, in accordance with free-will, he was to be the architect of his own fortune, that God had decreed nothing but to treat him according to his desert. If this frigid fiction is received, where will be the omnipotence of God, by which, according to his secret counsel on which everything depends, he rules over all? But whether they will allow it or not, predestination is manifest in Adam's posterity. It was not owing to nature that they all lost salvation by the fault of one parent. Why should they refuse to admit with regard to one man that which against their will they admit with regard to the whole human race? Why should they in cavilling lose their labour? Scripture proclaims that all were, in the person of one, made liable to eternal death. As this cannot be ascribed to nature, it is plain that it is owing to the wonderful counsel of God. It is very absurd

---

[1] See Calvin, De Prædestinatione.

in these worthy defenders of the justice of God to strain at a gnat and swallow a camel. I again ask how it is that the fall of Adam involves so many nations with their infant children in eternal death without remedy, unless that it so seemed meet to God? Here the most loquacious tongues must be dumb. The decree, I admit, is dreadful; and yet it is impossible to deny that God foreknew what the end of man was to be before he made him, and foreknew, because he had so ordained by his decree. Should any one here inveigh against the prescience of God, he does it rashly and unadvisedly. For why, pray, should it be made a charge against the heavenly Judge, that he was not ignorant of what was to happen? Thus, if there is any just or plausible complaint, it must be directed against predestination. Nor ought it to seem absurd when I say, that God not only foresaw the fall of the first man, and in him the ruin of his posterity; but also at his own pleasure arranged it. For as it belongs to his wisdom to foreknow all future events, so it belongs to his power to rule and govern them by his hand. This question, like others, is skilfully explained by Augustine: "Let us confess with the greatest benefit, what we believe with the greatest truth, that the God and Lord of all things, who made all things very good, both foreknew that evil was to arise out of good, and knew that it belonged to his most omnipotent goodness to bring good out of evil, rather than not permit evil to be, and so ordained the life of angels and men as to show in it, first, what free-will could do; and, secondly, what the benefit of his grace and his righteous judgment could do" (August. Enchir. ad Laurent.).

8. Here they recur to the distinction between will and permission, the object being to prove that the wicked perish only by the permission, but not by the will of God. But why do we say that he permits, but just because he wills? Nor, indeed, is there any probability in the thing itself—viz. that man brought death upon himself, merely by the permission, and not by the ordination of God; as if God had not determined what he wished the condition of the chief of his creatures to be. I will not hesitate, therefore, simply to confess with Augustine that the will of God is necessity, and that everything is necessary which he has willed; just as those things will certainly happen which he has foreseen (August. de Gen. ad Lit., Lib. vi. cap. 15). Now, if in excuse of themselves and the ungodly, either the Pelagians, or Manichees, or Anabaptists, or Epicureans (for it is with these four sects we have to discuss this matter), should object the necessity by which they are constrained, in consequence of the divine predestination, they do nothing that is relevant to the cause. For if predestination is nothing else than a dispensation of divine justice, secret indeed, but unblameable, because it is certain that those predestinated to that condition were not unworthy of it, it is equally certain, that the destruction consequent upon predestination is also most just. Moreover, though their perdition depends on the predestination of God, the cause and matter of it is in themselves. The

first man fell because the Lord deemed it meet that he should : why he deemed it meet, we know not. It is certain, however, that it was just, because he saw that his own glory would thereby be displayed. When you hear the glory of God mentioned, understand that his justice is included. For that which deserves praise must be just. Man therefore falls, divine providence so ordaining, but he falls by his own fault. The Lord had a little before declared that all the things which he had made were very good (Gen. i. 31). Whence then the depravity of man, which made him revolt from God? Lest it should be supposed that it was from his creation, God had expressly approved what proceeded from himself. Therefore, man's own wickedness corrupted the pure nature which he had received from God, and his ruin brought with it the destruction of all his posterity. Wherefore, let us in the corruption of human nature contemplate the evident cause of condemnation (a cause which comes more closely home to us), rather than inquire into a cause hidden and almost incomprehensible in the predestination of God. Nor let us decline to submit our judgment to the boundless wisdom of God, so far as to confess its insufficiency to comprehend many of his secrets. Ignorance of things which we are not able, or which it is not lawful to know, is learning, while the desire to know them is a species of madness.

9. Some one, perhaps, will say, that I have not yet stated enough to refute this blasphemous excuse. I confess that it is impossible to prevent impiety from murmuring and objecting ; but I think I have said enough, not only to remove the ground, but also the pretext for throwing blame upon God. The reprobate would excuse their sins by alleging that they are unable to escape the necessity of sinning, especially because a necessity of this nature is laid upon them by the ordination of God. We deny that they can thus be validly excused, since the ordination of God, by which they complain that they are doomed to destruction, is consistent with equity,—an equity, indeed, unknown to us, but most certain. Hence we conclude, that every evil which they bear is inflicted by the most just judgment of God. Next we have shown that they act preposterously when, in seeking the origin of their condemnation, they turn their view to the hidden recesses of the divine counsel, and wink at the corruption of nature, which is the true source. They cannot impute this corruption to God, because he bears testimony to the goodness of his creation. For though, by the eternal providence of God, man was formed for the calamity under which he lies, he took the matter of it from himself, not from God, since the only cause of his destruction was his degenerating from the purity of his creation into a state of vice and impurity.

10. There is a third absurdity by which the adversaries of predestination defame it. As we ascribe it entirely to the counsel of the divine will, that those whom God adopts as the heirs of his kingdom are exempted from universal destruction, they infer that he is an accepter of persons ; but this Scripture uniformly denies : and, therefore, Scripture is either at variance with itself, or respect is had to

merit in election. First, the sense in which Scripture declares that God is not an acceptor of persons, is different from that which they suppose: since the term *person* means not *man*, but those things which, when conspicuous in a man, either procure favour, grace, and dignity, or, on the contrary, produce hatred, contempt, and disgrace. Among these are, on the one hand, riches, wealth, power, rank, office, country, beauty, &c. ; and, on the other hand, poverty, want, mean birth, sordidness, contempt, and the like. Thus Peter and Paul say, that the Lord is no accepter of persons, because he makes no distinction between the Jew and the Greek ; does not make the mere circumstance of country the ground for rejecting one or embracing the other (Acts x. 34 ; Rom. ii. 10 ; Gal. iii. 28). Thus James also uses the same words, when he would declare that God has no respect to riches in his judgment (James ii. 5). Paul also says in another passage, that in judging God has no respect to slavery or freedom (Eph. vi. 9 ; Col. iii. 25). There is nothing inconsistent with this when we say, that God, according to the good pleasure of his will, without any regard to merit, elects those whom he chooses for sons, while he rejects and reprobates others. For fuller satisfaction the matter may be thus explained (see August. Epist. 115, et ad Bonif., Lib. ii. cap. 7). It is asked, how it happens that of two, between whom there is no difference of merit, God in his election adopts the one, and passes by the other ? I, in my turn, ask, Is there anything in him who is adopted to incline to God towards him ? If it must be confessed that there is nothing, it will follow, that God looks not to the man, but is influenced entirely by his own goodness to do him good. Therefore, when God elects one and rejects another, it is owing not to any respect to the individual, but entirely to his own mercy, which is free to display and exert itself when and where he pleases. For we have elsewhere seen, that in order to humble the pride of the flesh, " not many wise men after the flesh, not many mighty, not many noble, are called" (1 Cor. i. 26) ; so far is God in the exercise of his favour from showing any respect to persons.

11. Wherefore, it is false and most wicked to charge God with dispensing justice unequally, because in this predestination he does not observe the same course towards all. If (say they) he finds all guilty, let him punish all alike : if he finds them innocent, let him relieve all from the severity of judgment. But they plead with God as if he were either interdicted from showing mercy, or were obliged, if he show mercy, entirely to renounce judgment. What is it that they demand ? That if all are guilty, all shall receive the same punishment. We admit that the guilt is common, but we say, that God in mercy succours some. Let him (they say) succour all. We object, that it is right for him to show by punishing that he is a just judge. When they cannot tolerate this, what else are they attempting than to deprive God of the power of showing mercy ; or, at least, to allow it to him only on the condition of altogether renouncing judgment ? Here the words of Augustine most admirably apply :

" Since in the first man the whole human race fell under condemnation, those vessels which are made of it unto honour, are not vessels of self-righteousness, but of divine mercy.   When other vessels are made unto dishonour, it must be imputed not to injustice, but to judgment" (August. Epist. 106, De Prædest. et Gratia ; De Bono Persever., cap. 12).   Since God inflicts due punishment on those whom he reprobates, and bestows unmerited favour on those whom he calls, he is free from every accusation ; just as it belongs to the creditor to forgive the debt to one, and exact it of another.   The Lord therefore may show favour to whom he will, because he is merciful ; not show it to all, because he is a just judge.   In giving to some what they do not merit, he shows his free favour ; in not giving to all, he declares what all deserve.   For when Paul says, " God hath concluded them all in unbelief, that he might have mercy upon all " it ought also to be added, that he is debtor to none ; for " who hath first given to him, and it shall be recompensed unto him again ?" (Rom. xi. 32, 35.)

12. Another argument which they employ to overthrow predestination is, that if it stand, all care and study of well-doing must cease. For what man can hear (say they) that life and death are fixed by an eternal and immutable decree of God, without immediately concluding that it is of no consequence how he acts, since no work of his can either hinder or further the predestination of God ?   Thus all will rush on, and like desperate men plunge headlong wherever lust inclines.   And it is true that this is not altogether a fiction ; for there are multitudes of a swinish nature who defile the doctrine of predestination by their profane blasphemies, and employ them as a cloak to evade all admonition and censure.   " God knows what he has determined to do with regard to us : if he has decreed our salvation, he will bring us to it in his own time ; if he has doomed us to death, it is vain for us to fight against it."   But Scripture, while it enjoins us to think of this high mystery with much greater reverence and religion, gives very different instruction to the pious, and justly condemns the accursed licence of the ungodly.   For it does not remind us of predestination to increase our audacity, and tempt us to pry with impious presumption into the inscrutable counsels of God, but rather to humble and abase us, that we may tremble at his judgment, and learn to look up to his mercy.   This is the mark at which believers will aim.   The grunt of these filthy swine is duly silenced by Paul. They say that they feel secure in vice, because, if they are of the number of the elect, their vices will be no obstacle to the ultimate attainment of life.   But Paul reminds us that the end for which we are elected is, " that we should be holy, and without blame before him" (Eph. i. 4).   If the end of election is holiness of life, it ought to arouse and stimulate us strenuously to aspire to it, instead of serving as a pretext for sloth.   How wide the difference between the two things, between ceasing from well-doing because election is sufficient for salvation, and its being the very end of election, that we

should devote ourselves to the study of good works. Have done, then, with blasphemies which wickedly invert the whole order of election. When they extend their blasphemies farther, and say that he who is reprobated by God will lose his pains if he studies to approve himself to him by innocence and probity of life, they are convicted of the most impudent falsehood. For whence can any such study arise but from election? As all who are of the number of the reprobate are vessels formed unto dishonour, so they cease not by their perpetual crimes to provoke the anger of God against them, and give evident signs of the judgment which God has already passed upon them; so far is it from being true that they vainly contend against it.

13. Another impudent and malicious calumny against this doctrine is, that it destroys all exhortations to a pious life. The great odium to which Augustine was at one time subjected on this head he wiped away in his treatise De Correptione et Gratia, to Valentinus, a perusal of which will easily satisfy the pious and docile. Here, however, I may touch on a few points, which will, I hope, be sufficient for those who are honest and not contentious. We have already seen how plainly and audibly Paul preaches the doctrine of free election: is he, therefore, cold in admonishing and exhorting? Let those good zealots compare his vehemence with theirs, and they will find that they are ice, while he is all fervour. And surely every doubt on this subject should be removed by the principles which he lays down, that God hath not called us to uncleanness; that every one should possess his vessel in honour; that we are the workmanship of God, "created in Christ Jesus unto good works, which God hath before ordained that we should walk in them" (1 Thess iv. 4, 7; Eph. ii. 10). In one word, those who have any tolerable acquaintance with the writings of Paul will understand, without a long demonstration, how well he reconciles the two things which those men pretend to be contradictory to each other. Christ commands us to believe in him, and yet there is nothing false or contrary to this command in the statement which he afterwards makes: "No man can come unto me, except it were given him of my Father" (John vi. 65). Let preaching then have its free course, that it may lead men to faith, and dispose them to persevere with uninterrupted progress. Nor, at the same time, let there be any obstacle to the knowledge of predestination, so that those who obey may not plume themselves on anything of their own, but glory only in the Lord. It is not without cause our Saviour says, "Who hath ears to hear, let him hear" (Matth. xiii. 9). Therefore, while we exhort and preach, those who have ears willingly obey: in those, again, who have no ears is fulfilled what is written: "Hear ye indeed, but understand not" (Isaiah vi. 9). "But why (says Augustine) have some ears, and others not? Who hath known the mind of the Lord? Are we, therefore, to deny what is plain because we cannot comprehend what is hid?" This is a faithful quotation from Augustine; but because his words will perhaps have more

authority than mine, let us adduce the following passage from his treatise, De Bono Persever., cap. 15.

" Should some on hearing this turn to indolence and sloth, and, leaving off all exertion, rush headlong into lust, are we therefore to suppose that what has been said of the foreknowledge of God is not true ?   If God foreknew that they would be good, will they not be good, however great their present wickedness ? and if God foreknew that they would be wicked, will they not be wicked, how great soever the goodness now seen in them ?   For reasons of this description, must the truth which has been stated on the subject of divine fore-knowledge be denied or not mentioned ? and more especially when, if it is not stated, other errors will arise ?"   In the sixteenth chapter he says, " The reason for not mentioning the truth is one thing, the necessity for telling the truth is another.   It were tedious to inquire into all the reasons for silence.   One however is, lest those who understand not become worse, while we are desirous to make those who understand better informed.   Now, such persons, when we say anything of this kind, do not indeed become better informed, but neither do they become worse.   But when the truth is of such a nature, that he who cannot comprehend it becomes worse by our tell-ing it, and he who can comprehend it becomes worse by our not telling it, what think ye ought we to do?   Are we not to tell the truth, that he who can comprehend may comprehend, rather than not tell it, and thereby not only prevent both from comprehending, but also make the more intelligent of the two to become worse, whereas if he heard and comprehended others might learn through him ? And we are unwilling to say what, on the testimony of Scripture, it is lawful to say.   For we fear lest, when we speak, he who cannot comprehend may be offended ; but we have no fear lest, while we are silent, he who can comprehend the truth be involved in falsehood." In chapter twentieth, glancing again at the same view, he more clearly confirms it.   " Wherefore, if the apostles and teachers of the Church who came after them did both ; if they discoursed piously of the eternal election of God, and at the same time kept believers under the discipline of a pious life, how can those men of our day, when shut up by the invincible force of truth, think they are right in say-ing, that what is said of predestination, though it is true, must not be preached to the people ?   Nay, it ought indeed to be preached, that whoso hath ears to hear may hear.   And who hath ears if he hath not received them from him who has promised to give them ? Certainly, let him who receives not, reject.   Let him who receives, take and drink, drink and live.   For as piety is to be preached, that God may be duly worshipped ; so predestination also is to be preached, that he who hath ears to hear may, in regard to divine grace, glory not in himself, but in God."

14. And yet as that holy man had a singular desire to edify, he so regulates his method of teaching as carefully, and as far as in him lay, to avoid giving offence.   For he reminds us, that those things

which are truly should also be fitly spoken. Were any one to address the people thus: If you do not believe, the reason is, because God has already doomed you to destruction: he would not only encourage sloth, but also give countenance to wickedness. Were any one to give utterance to the sentiment in the future tense, and say, that those who hear will not believe because they are reprobates, it were imprecation rather than doctrine. Wherefore, Augustine not undeservedly orders such, as senseless teachers or sinister and ill-omened prophets, to retire from the Church. He, indeed, elsewhere truly contends that " a man profits by correction only when He who causes those whom He pleases to profit without correction, pities and assists. But why is it thus with some, and differently with others? Far be it from us to say that it belongs to the clay and not to the potter to decide." He afterwards says, " When men by correction either come or return to the way of righteousness, who is it that works salvation in their hearts but he who gives the increase, whoever it be that plants and waters? When he is pleased to save, there is no free-will in man to resist. Wherefore, it cannot be doubted that the will of God (who hath done whatever he hath pleased in heaven and in earth, and who has even done things which are to be) cannot be resisted by the human will, or prevented from doing what he pleases, since with the very wills of men he does so." Again, " When he would bring men to himself, does he bind them with corporeal fetters? He acts inwardly, inwardly holds, inwardly moves their hearts, and draws them by the wills which he has wrought in them." What he immediately adds must not be omitted: " Because we know not who belongs to the number of the predestinated, or does not belong, our desire ought to be that all may be saved; and hence every person we meet, we will desire to be with us a partaker of peace. But our peace will rest upon the sons of peace. Wherefore, on our part, let correction be used as a harsh yet salutary medicine for all, that they may neither perish, nor destroy others. To God it will belong to make it available to those whom he has foreknown and predestinated."

CHAPTER XXIV.

ELECTION CONFIRMED BY THE CALLING OF GOD. THE REPROBATE
BRING UPON THEMSELVES THE RIGHTEOUS DESTRUCTION TO WHICH
THEY ARE DOOMED.

The title of this chapter shows that it consists of two parts,—I. The case of the Elect,
from sec. 1–11. II. The case of the Reprobate, from sec. 12–17.

Sections.

1. The election of God is secret, but is manifested by effectual calling. The nature
   of this effectual calling. How election and effectual calling are founded on the
   free mercy of God. A cavil of certain expositors refuted by the words of Augustine. An exception disposed of.
2. Calling proved to be free, 1. By its nature and the mode in which it is dispensed.
   2. By the word of God. 3. By the calling of Abraham, the father of the faithful.
   4. By the testimony of John. 5. By the example of those who have been called.
3. The pure doctrine of the calling of the elect misunderstood, 1. By those who attribute too much to the human will. 2. By those who make election dependent on
   faith. This error amply refuted.
4. In this and the five following sections the certainty of election vindicated from the
   assaults of Satan. The leading arguments are : 1. Effectual calling. 2. Christ
   apprehended by faith. 3. The protection of Christ, the guardian of the elect.
   We must not attempt to penetrate to the hidden recesses of the divine wisdom,
   in order to learn what is decreed with regard to us at the judgment-seat. We
   must begin and end with the call of God. This confirmed by an apposite saying
   of Bernard.
5. Christ the foundation of this calling and election. He who does not lean on him
   alone cannot be certain of his election. He is the faithful interpreter of the
   eternal counsel in regard to our salvation.
6. Another security of our election is the protection of Christ our Shepherd. How it
   is manifested to us. Objection 1. As to the future state. 2. As to perseverance.
   Both objections refuted.
7. Objection, that those who seem elected sometimes fall away. Answer. A passage
   of Paul dissuading us from security explained. The kind of fear required in
   the elect.
8. Explanation of the saying, that many are called, but few chosen. A twofold call.
9. Explanation of the passage, that none is lost but the son of perdition. Refutation
   of an objection to the certainty of election.
10. Explanation of the passages urged against the certainty of election. Examples by
    which some attempt to prove that the seed of election is sown in the hearts of the
    elect from their very birth. Answer 1. One or two examples do not make the
    rule. 2. This view opposed to Scripture. 3. Is expressly opposed by an
    apostle.
11. An explanation and confirmation of the third answer.
12. Second part of the chapter, which treats of the reprobate. Some of them God de-
    prives of the opportunity of hearing his word. Others he blinds and stupifies
    the more by the preaching of it.
13. Of this no other account can be given than that the reprobate are vessels fitted for
    destruction. This confirmed by the case of the elect; of Pharaoh and of the
    Jewish people both before and after the manifestation of Christ.
14. Question, Why does God blind the reprobate ? Two answers. These confirmed by
    different passages of Scripture. Objection of the reprobate. Answer.
15. Objection to this doctrine of the righteous rejection of the reprobate. The first
    founded on a passage in Ezekiel. The passage explained.
16. A second objection founded on a passage in Paul. The apostle's meaning explained.
    A third objection and fourth objection answered.

17. A fifth objection—viz. that there seems to be a twofold will in God. Answer. Other objections and answers. Conclusion.

1. But that the subject may be more fully illustrated, we must treat both of the calling of the elect, and of the blinding and hardening of the ungodly.   The former I have already in some measure discussed (chap. xxii. sec. 10, 11), when refuting the error of those who think that the general terms in which the promises are made place the whole human race on a level.   The special election which otherwise would remain hidden in God, he at length manifests by his calling.   " For whom he did foreknow, he also did predestinate to be conformed to the image of his Son."   Moreover, " whom he did predestinate, them he also called ; and whom he called, them he also justified," that he may one day glorify (Rom. viii. 29, 30).   Though the Lord, by electing his people, adopted them as his sons, we however see that they do not come into possession of this great good until they are called ; but when called, the enjoyment of their election is in some measure communicated to them.   For which reason the Spirit which they receive is termed by Paul both the " Spirit of adoption," and the " seal " and " earnest " of the future inheritance ; because by his testimony he confirms and seals the certainty of future adoption on their hearts.   For although the preaching of the gospel springs from the fountain of election, yet being common to them with the reprobate, it would not be in itself a solid proof.   God, however, teaches his elect effectually when he brings them to faith, as we formerly quoted from the words of our Saviour, " Not that any man hath seen the Father, save he which is of God, he hath seen the Father " (John vi. 46).   Again, " I have manifested thy name unto the men which thou gavest me out of the world " (John xvii. 6). He says in another passage, " No man can come to me except the Father which hath sent me draw him " (John vi. 44).   This passage Augustine ably expounds in these words : "If (as Truth says) every one who has learned cometh, then every one who does not come has not learned.   It does not therefore follow, that he who can come does come, unless he have willed and done it ; but every one who hath learned of the Father, not only can come, but also comes ; the antecedence of possibility,[1] the affection of will, and the effect of action being now present " (August. de Grat. Chr. Cont. Pelag., Lib. i. c. 14, 31).   In another passage, he says still more clearly, " What means, Every one that hath heard and learned of the Father cometh unto me, but just that there is no one who hears and learns of the Father that does not come to me ?   For if every one who has heard and learned, comes ; assuredly every one who does not come, has neither heard nor learned of the Father ; for if he had heard and learned, he would come.   Far removed from carnal sense is this school in which the Father is heard and teaches us to come to the Son " (August. de Prædes. Sanct. c. 8).   Shortly after, he says, " This grace, which is secretly imparted to the hearts of men, is not

---

[1] Latin, " possibilitatis profectus."—French, " l'avancement de possibilité.

received by any hard heart; for the reason for which it is given is, that the hardness of the heart may first be taken away. Hence, when the Father is heard within, he takes away the stony heart, and gives a heart of flesh. Thus he makes them sons of promise and vessels of mercy, which he has prepared for glory. Why then does he not teach all to come to Christ, but just because all whom he teaches he teaches in mercy, while those whom he teaches not he teaches not in judgment? for he pities whom he will, and hardens whom he will." Those, therefore, whom God has chosen he adopts as sons, while he becomes to them a Father. By calling, moreover, he admits them to his family, and unites them to himself, that they may be one with him. When calling is thus added to election, the Scripture plainly intimates that nothing is to be looked for in it but the free mercy of God. For if we ask whom it is he calls, and for what reason, he answers, it is those whom he had chosen. When we come to election, mercy alone everywhere appears; and, accordingly, in this the saying of Paul is truly realised, "So then, it is not of him that willeth, nor of him that runneth, but of God that showeth mercy" (Rom. ix. 16); and that not as is commonly understood by those who share the result between the grace of God and the will and agency of man. For their exposition is, that the desire and endeavour of sinners are of no avail by themselves, unless accompanied by the grace of God, but that when aided by his blessing, they also do their part in procuring salvation. This cavil I prefer refuting in the words of Augustine rather than my own: "If all that the apostle meant is, that it is not alone of him that willeth, or of him that runneth, unless the Lord be present in mercy, we may retort and hold the converse, that it is not of mercy alone, unless willing and running be present" (August. Enchir. ad Laurent. c. 31). But if this is manifestly impious, let us have no doubt that the apostle attributes all to the mercy of the Lord, and leaves nothing to our wills or exertions. Such were the sentiments of that holy man. I set not the value of a straw on the subtlety to which they have recourse—viz. that Paul would not have spoken thus had there not been some will and effort on our part. For he considered not what might be in man; but seeing that certain persons ascribed a part of salvation to the industry of man, he simply condemned their error in the former clause, and then claimed the whole substance of salvation for the divine mercy. And what else do the prophets than perpetually proclaim the free calling of God?

2. Moreover, this is clearly demonstrated by the nature and dispensation of calling, which consists not merely of the preaching of the word, but also of the illumination of the Spirit. Who those are to whom God offers his word is explained by the prophet, "I am sought of them that asked not for me: I am found of them that sought me not: I said, Behold me, behold me, unto a nation that was not called by my name" (Isaiah lxv. 1). And lest the Jews

should think that that mercy applied only to the Gentiles, he calls to their remembrance whence it was he took their father Abraham when he condescended to be his friend (Isaiah xxiv. 3)—namely, from the midst of idolatry, in which he was plunged with all his people. When he first shines with the light of his word on the undeserving, he gives a sufficiently clear proof of his free goodness. Here, therefore, boundless goodness is displayed, but not so as to bring all to salvation, since a heavier judgment awaits the reprobate for rejecting the evidence of his love. God also, to display his own glory, withholds from them the effectual agency of his Spirit. Therefore, this inward calling is an infallible pledge of salvation. Hence the words of John, "Hereby we know that he abideth in us by the Spirit which he hath given us" (1 John iii. 24). And lest the flesh should glory, in at least responding to him, when he calls and spontaneously offers himself, he affirms that there would be no ears to hear, no eyes to see, did not he give them. And he acts not according to the gratitude of each, but according to his election. Of this you have a striking example in Luke, when the Jews and Gentiles in common heard the discourse of Paul and Barnabas. Though they were all instructed in the same word, it is said, that "as many as were ordained to eternal life believed" (Acts xiii. 48). How can we deny that calling is gratuitous, when election alone reigns in it even to its conclusion?

3. Two errors are here to be avoided. Some make man a fellow-worker with God in such a sense, that man's suffrage ratifies election, so that, according to them, the will of man is superior to the counsel of God. As if Scripture taught that only the power of being able to believe is given us, and not rather faith itself. Others, although they do not so much impair the grace of the Holy Spirit, yet, induced by what means I know not, make election dependent on faith, as if it were doubtful and ineffectual till confirmed by faith. There can be no doubt, indeed, that in regard to us it is so confirmed. Moreover, we have already seen, that the secret counsel of God, which lay concealed, is thus brought to light, by this nothing more being understood than that that which was unknown is proved, and as it were sealed. But it is false to say that election is then only effectual after we have embraced the gospel, and that it thence derives its vigour. It is true that we must there look for its certainty, because, if we attempt to penetrate to the secret ordination of God, we shall be engulfed in that profound abyss. But when the Lord hath manifested it to us, we must ascend higher in order that the effect may not bury the cause. For what can be more absurd and unbecoming, than while Scripture teaches that we are illuminated as God has chosen us, our eyes should be so dazzled with the brightness of this light, as to refuse to attend to election? Meanwhile, I deny not that, in order to be assured of our salvation, we must begin with the word, and that our confidence ought to go no farther than the word when we invoke God the Father. For some, to obtain more certainty of the counsel of God (which is nigh us in our mouth, and in our hearts, Deut. xxx.

14), absurdly desire to fly above the clouds. We must, therefore, curb that temerity by the soberness of faith, and be satisfied to have God as the witness of his hidden grace in the external word; provided always that the channel in which the water flows, and out of which we may freely drink, does not prevent us from paying due honour to the fountain.

4. Therefore, as those are in error who make the power of election dependent on the faith by which we perceive that we are elected, so we shall follow the best order, if, in seeking the certainty of our election, we cleave to those posterior signs which are sure attestations to it. Among the temptations with which Satan assaults believers, none is greater or more perilous, than when disquieting them with doubts as to their election, he at the same time stimulates them with a depraved desire of inquiring after it out of the proper way. (See Luther in Genes. cap. xxvi.) By inquiring out of the proper way, I mean when puny man endeavours to penetrate to the hidden recesses of the divine wisdom, and goes back even to the remotest eternity, in order that he may understand what final determination God has made with regard to him. In this way he plunges headlong into an immense abyss, involves himself in numberless inextricable snares, and buries himself in the thickest darkness. For it is right that the stupidity of the human mind should be punished with fearful destruction, whenever it attempts to rise in its own strength to the height of divine wisdom. And this temptation is the more fatal, that it is the temptation to which of all others almost all of us are most prone. For there is scarcely a mind in which the thought does not sometimes rise, Whence your salvation but from the election of God? But what proof have you of your election? When once this thought has taken possession of any individual, it keeps him perpetually miserable, subjects him to dire torment, or throws him into a state of complete stupor. I cannot wish a stronger proof of the depraved ideas, which men of this description form of predestination, than experience itself furnishes, since the mind cannot be infected by a more pestilential error than that which disturbs the conscience, and deprives it of peace and tranquillity in regard to God. Therefore, as we dread shipwreck, we must avoid this rock, which is fatal to every one who strikes upon it. And though the discussion of predestination is regarded as a perilous sea, yet in sailing over it the navigation is calm and safe, nay, pleasant, provided we do not voluntarily court danger. For as a fatal abyss engulfs those who, to be assured of their election, pry into the eternal counsel of God without the word, yet those who investigate it rightly, and in the order in which it is exhibited in the word, reap from it rich fruits of consolation.

Let our method of inquiry then be, to begin with the calling of God and to end with it. Although there is nothing in this to prevent believers from feeling that the blessings which they daily receive from the hand of God originate in that secret adoption, as they themselves express it in Isaiah, " Thou hast done wonderful things; thy counsels of old are faithfulness and truth" (Isa. xxv. 1). For with this as a pledge, God is pleased to assure us of as much of his counsel as can be lawfully known. But lest any should think that testimony weak, let us consider what clearness and certainty it gives us. On this subject there is an apposite passage in Bernard. After speaking of the reprobate, he says, " The purpose of God stands, the sentence of peace on those that fear him also stands, a sentence concealing their bad and recompensing their good qualities; so that, in a wondrous manner, not only their good but their bad qualities work together for good. Who will lay anything to the charge of God's elect? It is completely sufficient for my justification to have him propitious against whom only I have sinned. Everything which he has decreed not to impute to me, is as if it had never been." A little after he says, "O the place of true rest, a place which I consider not unworthy of the name of inner-chamber, where God is seen, not as if disturbed with anger, or distracted by care, but where his will is proved to be good, and acceptable, and perfect. That vision does not terrify but soothe, does not excite restless curiosity but calms it, does not fatigue but tranquillises the senses. Here is true rest. A tranquil God traquillises all things; and to see him at rest, is to be at rest" (Bernard, super Cantic. Serm. xiv.).

5. First, if we seek for the paternal mercy and favour of God, we must turn our eyes to Christ, in whom alone the Father is well pleased (Matth. iii. 17). When we seek for salvation, life, and a blessed immortality, to him also must we betake ourselves, since he alone is the fountain of life, and the anchor of salvation, and the heir of the kingdom of heaven. Then what is the end of election, but just that, being adopted as sons by the heavenly Father, we may by his favour obtain salvation and immortality? How much soever you may speculate and discuss, you will perceive that in its ultimate object it goes no farther. Hence, those whom God has adopted as sons, he is said to have elected, not in themselves, but in Christ Jesus (Eph. i. 4); because he could love them only in him, and only as being previously made partakers with him, honour them with the inheritance of his kingdom. But if we are elected in him, we cannot find the certainty of our election in ourselves; and not even in God the Father, if we look at him apart from the Son. Christ, then, is the mirror in which we ought, and in which, without deception, we may contemplate our election. For since it is into his body that the Father has decreed to ingraft those whom from eternity he wished to be his, that he may regard as sons all whom he acknowledges to be his members, if we are in communion with Christ, we have proof sufficiently clear and strong that we are written in the Book of Life. Moreover, he admitted us to sure communion with himself, when, by the preaching of the gospel, he declared that he was given us by the Father, to be ours with all his blessings (Rom. viii. 32). We are said to be clothed with him, to be one with him, that we may live, because he himself lives. The doctrine is often repeated, " God so

loved the world, that he gave his only begotten Son, that whosoever believeth in him should not perish, but have everlasting life" (John iii. 16). He who believes in him is said to have passed from death unto life (John v. 24). In this sense he calls himself the *bread of life*, of which if a man eat, he shall never die (John vi. 35). He, I say, was our witness, that all by whom he is received in faith will be regarded by our heavenly Father as sons. If we long for more than to be regarded as sons of God and heirs, we must ascend above Christ. But if this is our final goal, how infatuated is it to seek out of him what we have already obtained in him, and can only find in him? Besides, as he is the Eternal Wisdom, the Immutable Truth, the Determinate Counsel of the Father, there is no room for fear that anything which he tells us will vary in the minutest degree from that will of the Father after which we inquire. Nay, rather he faithfully discloses it to us as it was from the beginning, and always will be. The practical influence of this doctrine ought also to be exhibited in our prayers. For though a belief of our election animates us to invoke God, yet when we frame our prayers, it were preposterous to obtrude it upon God, or to stipulate in this way, "O Lord, if I am elected, hear me." He would have us to rest satisfied with his promises, and not to inquire elsewhere whether or not he is disposed to hear us. We shall thus be disentangled from many snares, if we know how to make a right use of what is rightly written; but let us not inconsiderately wrest it to purposes different from that to which it ought to be confined.

6. Another confirmation tending to establish our confidence is, that our election is connected with our calling. For those whom Christ enlightens with the knowledge of his name, and admits into the bosom of his Church, he is said to take under his guardianship and protection. All whom he thus receives are said to be committed and intrusted to him by the Father, that they may be kept unto life eternal. What would we have? Christ proclaims aloud that all whom the Father is pleased to save he hath delivered into his protection (John vi. 37–39; xvii. 6, 12). Therefore, if we would know whether God cares for our salvation, let us ask whether he has committed us to Christ, whom he has appointed to be the only Saviour of all his people. Then, if we doubt whether we are received into the protection of Christ, he obviates the doubt when he spontaneously offers himself as our Shepherd, and declares that we are of the number of his sheep if we hear his voice (John x. 3, 16). Let us, therefore, embrace Christ, who is kindly offered to us, and comes forth to meet us : he will number us among his flock, and keep us within his fold. But anxiety arises as to our future state.[1] For as Paul teaches, that those are called who were previously elected, so our

---

1 French, "Mas quelcun dira qu'il nous faut soucier de ce qui peut nous advenir : et quand nous pensons au temps futur que nostre imbecilité nous admoneste d'etre en solicitude :"—But some one will say, that we must feel anxious as to what may happen to us ; and that when we think on the future, our weakness warns us to be solicitous.

Saviour shows that many are called, but few chosen (Matth. xxii. 14). Nay, even Paul himself dissuades us from security, when he says, "Let him that thinketh he standeth take heed lest he fall" (1 Cor. x. 12). And again, "Well, because of unbelief they were broken off, and thou standest by faith. Be not high-minded, but fear: for if God spared not the natural branches, take heed lest he also spare not thee" (Rom. xi. 20, 21). In fine, we are sufficiently taught by experience itself, that calling and faith are of little value without perseverance, which, however, is not the gift of all. But Christ has freed us from anxiety on this head; for the following promises undoubtedly have respect to the future: "All that the Father giveth me shall come to me, and him that cometh to me I will in no wise cast out." Again, "This is the will of him that sent me, that of all which he hath given me I should lose nothing; but should raise it up at the last day" (John vi. 37, 39). Again, "My sheep hear my voice, and I know them, and they follow me: and I give unto them eternal life, and they shall never perish, neither shall any man pluck them out of my hand. My Father which gave them me is greater than all: and no man is able to pluck them out of my Father's hand" (John x. 27, 28). Again, when he declares, "Every plant which my heavenly Father hath not planted shall be rooted up" (Matth. xv. 13), he intimates conversely that those who have their root in God can never be deprived of their salvation. Agreeable to this are the words of John, "If they had been of us, they would no doubt have continued with us" (1 John ii. 19). Hence, also, the magnificent triumph of Paul over life and death, things present, and things to come (Rom. viii. 38). This must be founded on the gift of perseverance. There is no doubt that he employs the sentiment as applicable to all the elect. Paul elsewhere says, "Being confident of this very thing, that he who hath begun a good work in you will perform it until the day of Jesus Christ" (Phil. i. 6). David, also, when his faith threatened to fail, leant on this support, "Forsake not the works of thy hands." Moreover, it cannot be doubted, that since Christ prays for all the elect, he asks the same thing for them as he asked for Peter—viz. that their faith fail not (Luke xxii. 32). Hence we infer, that there is no danger of their falling away, since the Son of God, who asks that their piety may prove constant, never meets with a refusal. What then did our Saviour intend to teach us by this prayer, but just to confide, that whenever we are his our eternal salvation is secure?

7. But it daily happens that those who seemed to belong to Christ revolt from him and fall away: Nay, in the very passage where he declares that none of those whom the Father hath given to him have perished, he excepts the son of perdition. This, indeed, is true; but it is equally true that such persons never adhered to Christ with that heartfelt confidence by which I say that the certainty of our election is established: "They went out from us," says John, "but they were not of us; for if they had been of us, they would, no doubt, have con-

tinued with us" (1 John ii. 19). I deny not that they have signs of calling similar to those given to the elect; but I do not at all admit that they have that sure confirmation of election which I desire believers to seek from the word of the gospel. Wherefore, let not examples of this kind move us away from tranquil confidence in the promise of the Lord, when he declares that all by whom he is received in true faith have been given him by the Father, and that none of them, while he is their Guardian and Shepherd, will perish (John iii. 16; vi. 39). Of Judas we shall shortly speak (sec. 9). Paul does not dissuade Christians from security simply, but from careless, carnal security, which is accompanied with pride, arrogance, and contempt of others, which extinguishes humility and reverence for God, and produces a forgetfulness of grace received (Rom. xi. 20). For he is addressing the Gentiles, and showing them that they ought not to exult proudly and cruelly over the Jews, in consequence of whose rejection they had been substituted in their stead. He also enjoins fear, not a fear under which they may waver in alarm, but a fear which, teaching us to receive the grace of God in humility, does not impair our confidence in it, as has elsewhere been said. We may add, that he is not speaking to individuals, but to sects in general (see 1 Cor. x. 12). The Church having been divided into two parties, and rivalship producing dissension, Paul reminds the Gentiles that their having been substituted in the place of a peculiar and holy people was a reason for modesty and fear. For there were many vain-glorious persons among them, whose empty boasting it was expedient to repress. But we have elsewhere seen, that our hope extends into the future, even beyond death, and that nothing is more contrary to its nature than to be in doubt as to our future destiny.

8. The expression of our Saviour, " Many are called, but few are chosen" (Matth. xxii. 14), is also very improperly interpreted (see Book III. chap. ii. sec. 11, 12). There will be no ambiguity in it if we attend to what our former remarks ought to have made clear—viz. that there are two species of calling;—for there is a universal call, by which God, through the external preaching of the word, invites all men alike, even those for whom he designs the call to be a savour of death, and the ground of a severer condemnation. Besides this there is a special call which, for the most part, God bestows on believers only, when by the internal illumination of the Spirit he causes the word preached to take deep root in their hearts. Sometimes, however, he communicates it also to those whom he enlightens only for a time, and whom afterwards, in just punishment for their ingratitude, he abandons and smites with greater blindness. Now, our Lord seeing that the Gospel was published far and wide, was despised by multitudes, and justly valued by few, describes God under the character of a King, who, preparing a great feast, sends his servants all around to invite a great multitude, but can only obtain the presence of a very few, because almost all allege causes of excuse; at length, in consequence of their refusal, he is obliged to send his

servants out into the highways to invite every one they meet. It is perfectly clear, that thus far the parable is to be understood of external calling. He afterwards adds, that God acts the part of a kind entertainer, who goes round his table and affably receives his guests; but still if he finds any one not adorned with the nuptial garment, he will by no means allow him to insult the festivity by his sordid dress. I admit that this branch of the parable is to be understood of those who, by a profession of faith, enter the Church, but are not at all invested with the sanctification of Christ. Such disgraces to his Church, such cankers God will not always tolerate, but will cast them forth as their turpitude deserves. Few, then, out of the great number of called are chosen; the calling, however, not being of that kind which enables believers to judge of their election. The former call is common to the wicked, the latter brings with it the spirit of regeneration, which is the earnest and seal of the future inheritance by which our hearts are sealed unto the day of the Lord (Eph. i. 13, 14). In one word, while hypocrites pretend to piety, just as if they were true worshippers of God, Christ declares that they will ultimately be ejected from the place which they improperly occupy, as it is said in the psalm, " Lord, who shall abide in thy tabernacle? who shall dwell in thy holy hill? He that walketh uprightly, and worketh righteousness, and speaketh the truth in his heart" (Psalm xv. 1. 2). Again, in another passage, " This is the generation of them that seek him, that seek thy face, O Jacob" (Psalm xxiv. 6). And thus the Spirit exhorts believers to patience, and not to murmur because Ishmaelites are mingled with them in the Church, since the mask will at length be torn off, and they will be ejected with disgrace.

9. The same account is to be given of the passage lately quoted, in which Christ says, that none is lost but the son of perdition (John xvii. 12). The expression is not strictly proper; but it is by no means obscure: for Judas was not numbered among the sheep of Christ, because he was one truly, but because he held a place among them. Then, in another passage, where the Lord says, that he was elected with the apostles, reference is made only to the office, " Have I not chosen you twelve," says he, " and one of you is a devil?" (John vi. 70). That is, he had chosen him to the office of apostle. But when he speaks of election to salvation, he altogether excludes him from the number of the elect, " I speak not of you all: I know whom I have chosen" (John xiii. 18). Should any one confound the term *election* in the two passages, he will miserably entangle himself; whereas if he distinguish between them, nothing can be plainer. Gregory, therefore, is most grievously and perniciously in error, when he says that we are conscious only of our calling, but are uncertain of our election; and hence he exhorts all to fear and trembling, giving this as the reason, that though we know what we are to-day, yet we know not what we are to be (Gregor. Hom. 38). But in that passage he clearly shows how he stumbled on that stone. By suspending election on the merit of works, he had too good a

reason for dispiriting the minds of his readers, while, at the same time, as he did not lead them away from themselves to confidence in the divine goodness, he was unable to confirm them.   Hence believers may in some measure perceive the truth of what we said at the out-set—viz. predestination duly considered does not shake faith, but rather affords the best confirmation of it.   I deny not, however, that the Spirit sometimes accommodates his language to our feeble capac-ity; as when he says, "They shall not be in the assembly of my people, neither shall they be written in the writing of the house of Israel" (Ezek. xiii. 9).   As if God were beginning to write the names of those whom he counts among his people in the Book of Life; whereas we know, even on the testimony of Christ, that the names of the children of God were written in the Book of Life from the beginning (Luke x. 20).   The words simply indicate the abandon-ment of those who seemed to have a chief place among the elect, as is said in the psalm, "Let them be blotted out of the Book of the Living, and not be written with the righteous" (Psalm lxix. 28).

10. For the elect are brought by calling into the fold of Christ, not from the very womb, nor all at the same time, but according as God sees it meet to dispense his grace.   Before they are gathered to the supreme Shepherd they wander dispersed in a common desert, and in no respect differ from others, except that by the special mercy of God they are kept from rushing to final destruction.   Therefore, if you look to themselves, you will see the offspring of Adam giving token of the common corruption of the mass.   That they proceed not to extreme and desperate impiety is not owing to any innate goodness in them, but because the eye of God watches for their safety, and his hand is stretched over them.   Those who dream of some seed of election implanted in their hearts from their birth, by the agency of which they are ever inclined to piety and the fear of God, are not supported by the authority of Scripture, but refuted by experience. They, indeed, produce a few examples to prove that the elect before they were enlightened were not aliens from religion; for instance, that Paul led an unblemished life during his Pharisaism, that Cor-nelius was accepted for his prayers and alms, and so forth (Phil. iii. 5; Acts x. 2).   The case of Paul we admit, but we hold that they are in error as to Cornelius; for it appears that he was already en-lightened and regenerated, so that all which he wanted was a clear revelation of the Gospel.   But what are they to extract from these few examples?   Is it that all the elect were always endued with the spirit of piety?   Just as well might any one, after pointing to the integrity of Aristides, Socrates, Xenocrates, Scipio, Curius, Camillus, and others (see Book II. c. iv. sec. 4), infer that all who are left in the blindness of idolatry are studious of virtue and holiness.   Nay, even Scripture is plainly opposed to them in more passages than one. The description which Paul gives of the state of the Ephesians before regeneration shows not one grain of this seed.   His words are, "You hath he quickened, who were dead in trespasses and sins; wherein

in time past ye walked according to the course of this world, according to the prince of the power of the air, the spirit that now worketh in the children of disobedience: among whom also we all had our conversation in times past in the lusts of our flesh, fulfilling the desires of the flesh and of the mind ; and were by nature the children of wrath, even as others" (Eph. ii. 1—3). And again, "At that time ye were without Christ," "having no hope, and without God in the world" (Eph. ii. 12). Again, "Ye were sometimes darkness, but now are ye light in the Lord: walk as children of light" (Eph. v. 8). But perhaps they will insist that in this last passage reference is made to that ignorance of the true God, in which they deny not that the elect lived before they were called. Though this is grossly inconsistent with the Apostle's inference, that they were no longer to lie or steal (Eph. iv. 28). What answer will they give to other passages; such as that in which, after declaring to the Corinthians that "neither fornicators, nor idolaters, nor adulterers, nor effeminate, nor abusers of themselves with mankind, nor thieves, nor covetous, nor drunkards, nor revilers, nor extortioners, shall inherit the kingdom of God," he immediately adds, " Such were some of you : but ye are washed, but be are sanctified, but ye are justified in the name of the Lord Jesus, and by the Spirit of our God"? (1 Cor. vi. 9—11.) Again, he says to the Romans, "As ye have yielded your members servants to uncleanness and to iniquity unto iniquity ; even so now yield your members servants to righteousness unto holiness. For when ye were the servants of sin, ye were free from righteousness. What fruit had ye then in those things whereof ye are now ashamed?" (Rom. vi.19—21.)

11. Say, then, what seed of election germinated in those who, contaminated in various ways during their whole lives, indulged as with desperate wickedness in every kind of abomination? Had Paul meant to express this view, he ought to have shown how much they then owed to the kindness of God, by which they had been preserved from falling into such pollution. Thus, too, Peter ought to have exhorted his countrymen to gratitude for a perpetual seed of election. On the contrary, his admonition is, " The time past of our life may suffice us to have wrought the will of the Gentiles" (1 Pet. iv. 3). What if we come to examples? Was there any germ of righteousness in Rahab the harlot before she believed? (Josh. ii. 4); in Manasseh when Jerusalem was dyed and almost deluged with the blood of the prophets? (2 Kings xxiii. 16) ; in the thief who only with his last breath thought of repentance ? (Luke xxiii. 42.) Have done, then, with those arguments which curious men of themselves rashly devise without any authority from Scripture. But let us hold fast what Scripture states—viz. that " All we like sheep have gone astray, we have turned every one to his own way" (Isa. liii. 6); that is, to perdition. In this gulf of perdition God leaves those whom he has determined one day to deliver until his own time arrive ; he only preserves them from plunging into irremediable blasphemy.

12. As the Lord by the efficacy of his calling accomplishes towards his elect the salvation to which he had by his eternal counsel destined them, so he has judgments against the reprobate, by which he executes his counsel concerning them. Those, therefore, whom he has created for dishonour during life and destruction at death, that they may be vessels of wrath and examples of severity, in bringing to their doom, he at one time deprives of the means of hearing his word, at another by the preaching of it blinds and stupifies them the more. The examples of the former case are innumerable, but let us select one of the most remarkable of all. Before the advent of Christ, about four thousand years passed away, during which he hid the light of saving doctrine from all nations. If any one answer, that he did not put them in possession of the great blessing, because he judged them unworthy, then their posterity will be in no respect more worthy. Of this in addition to experience, Malachi is a sufficient witness; for while charging them with mixed unbelief and blasphemy, he yet declares that the Redeemer will come. Why then is he given to the latter rather than to the former? They will in vain torment themselves in seeking for a deeper cause than the secret and inscrutable counsel of God. And there is no occasion to fear lest some disciple of Porphyry with impunity arraign the justice of God, while we say nothing in its defence. For while we maintain that none perish without deserving it, and that it is owing to the free goodness of God that some are delivered, enough has been said for the display of his glory; there is not the least occasion for our cavilling. The Supreme Disposer then makes way for his own predestination, when depriving those whom he has reprobated of the communication of his light, he leaves them in blindness. Every day furnishes instances of the latter case, and many of them are set before us in Scripture. Among a hundred to whom the same discourse is delivered, twenty, perhaps, receive it with the prompt obedience of faith; the others set no value upon it, or deride, or spurn, or abominate it. If it is said that this diversity is owing to the malice and perversity of the latter, the answer is not satisfactory: for the same wickedness would possess the minds of the former, did not God in his goodness correct it. And hence we will always be entangled until we call in the aid of Paul's question, "Who maketh thee to differ?" (1 Cor. iv. 7), intimating that some excel others, not by their own virtue, but by the mere favour of God.

13. Why, then, while bestowing grace on the one, does he pass by the other? In regard to the former, Luke gives the reason, Because they "were ordained to eternal life" (Acts xiii. 48). What, then, shall we think of the latter, but that they are vessels of wrath unto dishonour? Wherefore, let us not decline to say with Augustine, "God could change the will of the wicked into good, because he is omnipotent. Clearly he could. Why, then, does he not do it? Because he is unwilling. Why he is unwilling remains with himself" (August. de Genes. ad Lit. Lib. ii.). We should not attempt to be

wise above what is meet, and it is much better to take Augustine's explanation, than to quibble with Chrysostom, "that he draws him who is willing, and stretching forth his hand" (Chrysost. Hom. de Convers. Pauli), lest the difference should seem to lie in the judgment of God, and not in the mere will of man. So far is it, indeed, from being placed in the mere will of man, that we may add, that even the pious, and those who fear God, need this special inspiration of the Spirit. Lydia, a seller of purple, feared God, and yet it was necessary that her heart should be opened, that she might attend to the doctrine of Paul, and profit in it (Acts xvi. 14). This was not said of one woman only, but to teach us that all progress in piety is the secret work of the Spirit. Nor can it be questioned, that God sends his word to many whose blindness he is pleased to aggravate. For why does he order so many messages to be taken to Pharaoh ? Was it because he hoped that he might be softened by the repetition ? Nay, before he began he both knew and had foretold the result : " The Lord said unto Moses, When thou goest to return into Egypt, see that thou do all those wonders before Pharaoh, which I have put in thine hand : but I will harden his heart, that he will not let the people go" (Exod iv. 21). So when he raises up Ezekiel, he fore-warns him, " I send thee to the children of Israel, to a rebellious nation that hath rebelled against me." " Be not afraid of their words." " Thou dwellest in the midst of a rebellious house, which hath eyes to see, and see not ; they have ears to hear, and hear not" (Ezek. ii. 3, 6 ; xii. 2). Thus he foretells to Jeremiah that the effect of his doctrine would be, " to root out, and pull down, and to destroy" (Jer. i. 10). But the prophecy of Isaiah presses still more closely ; for he is thus commissioned by the Lord, " Go and tell this people, Hear ye indeed, but understand not, and see ye indeed, but perceive not. Make the heart of this people fat, and make their ears heavy, and shut their eyes ; lest they see with their eyes, and hear with their ears, and understand with their heart, and convert and be healed" (Isa. vi. 9, 10). Here he directs his voice to them, but it is that they may turn a deafer ear ; he kindles a light, but it is that they may become more blind ; he produces a doctrine, but it is that they may be more stupid ; he employs a remedy, but it is that they may not be cured. And John, referring to this prophecy, declares that the Jews could not believe the doctrine of Christ, because this curse from God lay upon them. It is also incontrovertible, that to those whom God is not pleased to illumine, he delivers his doctrine wrapt up in enigmas, so that they may not profit by it, but be given over to greater blindness. Hence our Saviour declares that the parables in which he had spoken to the multitude he expounded to the Apostles only, " because it is given unto you to know the mysteries of the kingdom of heaven, but to them it is not given" (Matth. xiii. 11). What, you will ask, does our Lord mean, by teaching those by whom he is careful not to be understood ? Consider where the fault lies, and then cease to ask. How obscure soever the word may be, there is always sufficient light in it to convince the consciences of the ungodly.

14. It now remains to see why the Lord acts in the manner in which it is plain that he does. If the answer be given, that it is because men deserve this by their impiety, wickedness, and ingratitude, it is indeed well and truly said; but still, because it does not yet appear what the cause of the difference is, why some are turned to obedience, and others remain obdurate, we must, in discussing it, pass to the passage from Moses, on which Paul has commented—namely, " Even for this same purpose have I raised thee up, that I might show my power in thee, and that my name might be declared throughout all the earth " (Rom. ix. 17). The refusal of the reprobate to obey the word of God when manifested to them, will be properly ascribed to the malice and depravity of their hearts, provided it be at the same time added, that they were adjudged to this depravity, because they were raised up by the just but inscrutable judgment of God, to show forth his glory by their condemnation. In like manner, when it is said of the sons of Eli, that they would not listen to salutary admonitions, " because the Lord would slay them " (1 Sam. ii. 25), it is not denied that their stubbornness was the result of their own iniquity; but it is at the same time stated why they were left to their stubbornness, when the Lord might have softened their hearts— namely, because his immutable decree had once for all doomed them to destruction. Hence the words of John, " Though he had done so many miracles before them, yet they believed not on him; that the saying of Esaias the prophet might be fulfilled which he spake, Lord, who hath believed our report?" (John xii. 37, 38); for though he does not exculpate their perverseness, he is satisfied with the reason that the grace of God is insipid to men, until the Holy Spirit gives it its savour. And Christ, in quoting the prophecy of Isaiah, " They shall be all taught of God " (John vi. 45), designs only to show that the Jews were reprobates and aliens from the Church, because they would not be taught: and gives no other reason than that the promise of God does not belong to them. Confirmatory of this are the words of Paul, " Christ crucified " was " unto the Jews a stumbling-block, and unto the Greeks foolishness; but unto them which are called, both Jews and Greeks, Christ the power of God, and the wisdom of God " (1 Cor. i. 23). For after mentioning the usual result wherever the Gospel is preached, that it exasperates some, and is despised by others, he says, that it is precious to them only who are called. A little before he had given them the name of believers, but he was unwilling to refuse the proper rank to divine grace, which precedes faith; or rather, he added the second term by way of correction, that those who had embraced the Gospel might ascribe the merit of their faith to the calling of God. Thus, also, he shortly after shows that they were elected by God. When the wicked hear these things, they complain that God abuses his inordinate power, to make cruel sport with the miseries of his creatures. But let us, who

know that all men are liable on so many grounds to the judgment of God, that they cannot answer for one in a thousand of their transgressions (Job ix. 3), confess that the reprobate suffer nothing which is not accordant with the most perfect justice. When unable clearly to ascertain the reason, let us not decline to be somewhat in ignorance in regard to the depths of the divine wisdom.

15. But since an objection is often founded on a few passages of Scripture, in which God seems to deny that the wicked perish through his ordination, except in so far as they spontaneously bring death upon themselves in opposition to his warning, let us briefly explain these passages, and demonstrate that they are not adverse to the above view. One of the passages adduced is, "Have I any pleasure at all that the wicked should die? saith the Lord God; and not that he should return from his ways and live?" (Ezek. xviii. 23.) If we are to extend this to the whole human race, why are not the very many whose minds might be more easily bent to obey urged to repentance, rather than those who by his invitations become daily more and more hardened? Our Lord declares that the preaching of the gospel and miracles would have produced more fruit among the people of Nineveh and Sodom than in Judea (Matth. xiii. 23). How comes it, then, that if God would have all to be saved, he does not open a door of repentance for the wretched, who would more readily have received grace? Hence we may see that the passage is violently wrested, if the will of God, which the prophet mentions, is opposed to his eternal counsel, by which he separated the elect from the reprobate.[1] Now, if the genuine meaning of the prophet is inquired into, it will be found that he only means to give the hope of pardon to them who repent. The sum is, that God is undoubtedly ready to pardon whenever the sinner turns. Therefore, he does not will his death, in so far as he wills repentance. But experience shows that this will, for the repentance of those whom he invites to himself, is not such as to make him touch all their hearts. Still, it cannot be said that he acts deceitfully; for though the external word only renders those who hear it, and do not obey it, inexcusable, it is still truly regarded as an evidence of the grace by which he reconciles men to himself. Let us therefore hold the doctrine of the prophet, that God has no pleasure in the death of the sinner: that the godly may feel confident that whenever they repent God is ready to pardon them; and that the wicked may feel that their guilt is doubled, when they respond not to the great mercy and condescension of God. The mercy of God, therefore, will ever be ready to meet the penitent; but all the prophets, and apostles, and Ezekiel himself, clearly tell us who they are to whom repentance is given.

16. The second passage adduced is that in which Paul says that "God will have all men to be saved" (1 Tim. ii. 4). Though the reason here differs from the former, they have somewhat in common.

[1] Bernard, in his Sermon on the Nativity, on 2 Cor. i. 3, quoting the two passages, Rom. ix. 18, and Ezek. xviii. 32, admirably reconciles them.

I answer, first, That the mode in which God thus wills is plain from the context; for Paul connects two things, a will to be saved, and to come to the knowledge of the truth. If by this they will have it to be fixed by the eternal counsel of God that they are to receive the doctrine of salvation, what is meant by Moses in these words, "What nation is there so great, who hath God so nigh unto them?" (Deut. iv. 7.) How comes it that many nations are deprived of that light of the Gospel which others enjoy? How comes it that the pure knowledge of the doctrine of godliness has never reached some, and others have scarcely tasted some obscure rudiments of it? It will now be easy to extract the purport of Paul's statement. He had commanded Timothy that prayers should be regularly offered up in the church for kings and princes; but as it seemed somewhat absurd that prayer should be offered up for a class of men who were almost hopeless (all of them being not only aliens from the body of Christ, but doing their utmost to overthrow his kingdom), he adds, that it was acceptable to God, who will have all men to be saved. By this he assuredly means nothing more than that the way of salvation was not shut against any order of men; that, on the contrary, he had manifested his mercy in such a way, that he would have none debarred from it. Other passages do not declare what God has, in his secret judgment, determined with regard to all, but declare that pardon is prepared for all sinners who only turn to seek after it. For if they persist in urging the words, "God hath concluded all in unbelief, that he might have mercy upon all" (Rom. xi. 32), I will, on the contrary, urge what is elsewhere written, "Our God is in the heavens: he hath done whatsoever he hath pleased" (Ps. cxv. 3). We must, therefore, expound the passage so as to reconcile it with another, I "will be gracious to whom I will be gracious, and will show mercy on whom I will show mercy" (Exod. xxxiii. 19). He who selects those whom he is to visit in mercy does not impart it to all. But since it clearly appears that he is there speaking not of individuals, but of orders of men, let us have done with a longer discussion. At the same time, we ought to observe, that Paul does not assert what God does always, everywhere, and in all circumstances, but leaves it free to him to make kings and magistrates partakers of heavenly doctrine, though in their blindness they rage against it. A stronger objection seems to be founded on the passage in Peter; the Lord is "not willing that any should perish, but that all should come to repentance" (2 Pet. iii. 9). But the solution of the difficulty is to be found in the second branch of the sentence, for his will that they should come to repentance cannot be used in any other sense than that which is uniformly employed. Conversion is undoubtedly in the hand of God, whether he designs to convert all can be learned from himself, when he promises that he will give some a heart of flesh, and leave to others a heart of stone (Ezek. xxxvi. 26). It is true, that if he were not disposed to receive those who implore his mercy, it could not have been said, "Turn ye unto me, saith the Lord of Hosts, and I will turn unto you, saith the

Lord of Hosts" (Zech. i. 3); but I hold that no man approaches God unless previously influenced from above. And if repentance were placed at the will of man, Paul would not say, "If God peradventure will give them repentance" (2 Tim. ii. 25). Nay, did not God at the very time when he is verbally exhorting all to repentance, influence the elect by the secret movement of his Spirit, Jeremiah would not say, "Turn thou me, and I shall be turned; for thou art the Lord my God. Surely after that I was turned, I repented" (Jer. xxxi. 18).

17. But if it is so (you will say), little faith can be put in the Gospel promises, which, in testifying concerning the will of God, declare that he wills what is contrary to his inviolable decree. Not at all; for however universal the promises of salvation may be, there is no discrepancy between them and the predestination of the reprobate, provided we attend to their effect. We know that the promises are effectual only when we receive them in faith, but, on the contrary, when faith is made void, the promise is of no effect. If this is the nature of the promises, let us now see whether there be any inconsistency between the two things—viz. that God, by an eternal decree, fixed the number of those whom he is pleased to embrace in love, and on whom he is pleased to display his wrath, and that he offers salvation indiscriminately to all. I hold that they are perfectly consistent, for all that is meant by the promise is, just that his mercy is offered to all who desire and implore it, and this none do, save those whom he has enlightened. Moreover, he enlightens those whom he has predestinated to salvation. Thus the truth of the promises remains firm and unshaken, so that it cannot be said there is any disagreement between the eternal election of God and the testimony of his grace which he offers to believers. But why does he mention all men? Namely, that the consciences of the righteous may rest the more secure when they understand that there is no difference between sinners, provided they have faith, and that the ungodly may not be able to allege that they have not an asylum to which they may betake themselves from the bondage of sin, while they ungratefully reject the offer which is made to them. Therefore, since by the Gospel the mercy of God is offered to both, it is faith, in other words, the illumination of God, which distinguishes between the righteous and the wicked; the former feeling the efficacy of the Gospel, the latter obtaining no benefit from it. Illumination itself has eternal election for its rule.

Another passage quoted is the lamentation of our Saviour, "O Jerusalem, Jerusalem, how often would I have gathered thy children together, even as a hen gathereth her chickens under her wings, and ye would not!" (Matth. xxiii. 37); but it gives them no support. I admit that here Christ speaks not only in the character of man, but upbraids them with having, in every age, rejected his grace. But this will of God, of which we speak, must be defined. For it is well known what exertions the Lord made to retain that people, and how perversely, from the highest to the lowest, they followed their own wayward desires, and refused to be gathered together. But it does not follow that by the wickedness of men the counsel of God was frustrated. They object that nothing is less accordant with the nature of God than that he should have a double will. This I concede, provided they are sound interpreters. But why do they not attend to the many passages in which God clothes himself with human affections, and descends beneath his proper majesty?[1] He says, " I have spread out my hands all the day unto a rebellious people" (Isa. lxv. 1), exerting himself early and late to bring them back. Were they to apply these qualities without regarding the figure, many unnecessary disputes would arise which are quashed by the simple solution, that what is human is here transferred to God. Indeed, the solution which we have given elsewhere (see Book I. c. xviii. sec. 3 ; and Book III. c. xx. sec. 43) is amply sufficient—viz. that though to our apprehension the will of God is manifold, yet he does not in himself will opposites, but, according to his manifold wisdom (so Paul styles it, Eph. iii. 10), transcends our senses, until such time as it shall be given us to know how he mysteriously wills what now seems to be adverse to his will. They also amuse themselves with the cavil, that since God is the Father of all, it is unjust to discard any one before he has by his misconduct merited such a punishment. As if the kindness of God did not extend even to dogs and swine. But if we confine our view to the human race, let them tell why God selected one people for himself and became their father, and why, from that one people, he plucked only a small number as if they were the flower. But those who thus charge God are so blinded by their love of evil speaking, that they consider not that as God "maketh his sun to rise on the evil and on the good" (Matth. v. 45), so the inheritance is treasured up for a few to whom it shall one day be said, "Come, ye blessed of my Father, inherit the kingdom," &c. (Matth. xxv. 34). They object, moreover, that God does not hate any of the things which he has made. This I concede, but it does not affect the doctrine which I maintain, that the reprobate are hateful to God, and that with perfect justice, since those destitute of his Spirit cannot produce anything that does not deserve cursing. They add, that there is no distinction of Jew and Gentile, and that, therefore, the grace of God is held forth to all indiscriminately ; true, provided they admit (as Paul declares) that God calls as well Jews as Gentiles, according to his good pleasure, without being astricted to any. This disposes of their gloss upon another passage, "God hath concluded all in unbelief, that he might have mercy upon all" (Rom. xi. 32); in other words, he wills that all who are saved should ascribe their salvation to his mercy, although the blessing of salvation is not common to all. Finally, after all that has been adduced

---

[1] The French adds, "pour se conformer à notre rudesse ;"—in accommodation to our weakness.

on this side and on that, let it be our conclusion to feel overawed with
Paul at the great depth, and if petulant tongues will still murmur,
let us not be ashamed to join in his exclamation, " Nay but, O man,
who art thou that repliest against God ?" (Rom. ix. 20.)   Truly does
Augustine maintain that it is perverse to measure divine by the
standard of human justice (De Prædest. et Gra. c. ii.).

CHAPTER XXV.

OF THE LAST RESURRECTION.

There are four principal heads in this chapter,—I. The utility, necessity, truth, and irrefragable evidence of the orthodox doctrine of a final resurrection—a doctrine unknown to philosophers, sec. 1–4. II. Refutation of the objections to this doctrine by Atheists, Sadducees, Chiliasts, and other fanatics, sec. 5–7. III. The nature of the final resurrection explained, sec. 8, 9. IV. Of the eternal felicity of the elect, and the everlasting misery of the reprobate.

Sections.

1. For invincible perseverance in our calling, it is necessary to be animated with the blessed hope of our Saviour's final advent.
2. The perfect happiness reserved for the elect at the final resurrection unknown to philosophers.
3. The truth and necessity of this doctrine of a final resurrection. To confirm our belief in it we have, 1. The example of Christ; and, 2. The omnipotence of God. There is an inseparable connection between us and our risen Saviour. The bodies of the elect must be conformed to the body of their Head. It is now in heaven. Therefore our bodies also must rise, and, reanimated by their souls, reign with Christ in heaven. The resurrection of Christ a pledge of ours.
4. As God is omnipotent, he can raise the dead. Resurrection explained by a natural process. The vision of dry bones.
5. Second part of the chapter, refuting objections to the doctrine of resurrection. 1. Atheists. 2. Sadducees. 3. Chiliasts. Their evasion. Various answers. 4. Universalists. Answer.
6. Objections continued. 5. Some speculators who imagine that death destroys the whole man. Refutation. The condition and abode of souls from death till the last day. What meant by the bosom of Abraham.
7. Refutation of some weak men and Manichees, pretending that new bodies are to be given. Refutation confirmed by various arguments and passages of Scripture.
8. Refutation of the fiction of new bodies continued.
9. Shall the wicked rise again? Answer in the affirmative. Why the wicked shall rise again. Why resurrection promised to the elect only.
10. The last part of the chapter, treating of eternal felicity; 1. Its excellence transcends our capacity. Rules to be observed. The glory of all the saints will not be equal.
11. Without regarding questions which merely puzzle, an answer given to some which are not without use.
12. As the happiness of the elect, so the misery of the reprobate, will be without measure, and without end.

1. ALTHOUGH Christ, the Sun of righteousness, shining upon us through the gospel, hath, as Paul declares, after conquering death, given us the light of life; and hence on believing we are said to have passed from "death unto life," being no longer strangers and pilgrims, but fellow-citizens with the saints, and of the household of God, who has made us sit with his only begotten Son in heavenly places, so that nothing is wanting to our complete felicity; yet, lest we should feel it grievous to be exercised under a hard warfare, as if the victory obtained by Christ had produced no fruit, we must attend to what is elsewhere taught concerning the nature of hope. For since we hope

for what we see not, and faith, as is said in another passage, is " the evidence of things not seen," so long as we are imprisoned in the body we are absent from the Lord. For which reason Paul says, " Ye are dead, and your life is hid with Christ in God. When Christ, who is our life, shall appear, then shall ye also appear with him in glory." Our present condition, therefore, requires us to " live soberly, right-eously, and godly ;" " looking for that blessed hope, and the glorious appearing of the great God and our Saviour Jesus Christ." Here there is need of no ordinary patience, lest, worn out with fatigue, we either turn backwards or abandon our post. Wherefore, all that has hitherto been said of our salvation calls upon us to raise our minds towards heaven, that, as Peter exhorts, though we now see not Christ, " yet believing," we may " rejoice with joy unspeakable and full of glory," receiving the end of our faith, even the salvation of our souls.[1] For this reason Paul says, that the faith and charity of the saints have respect to the faith and hope which is laid up for them in heaven (Col. i. 5). When we thus keep our eyes fixed upon Christ in heaven, and nothing on earth prevents us from directing them to the promised blessedness, there is a true fulfilment of the saying, " where your treasure is, there will your heart be also" (Matth. vi. 21). Hence the reason why faith is so rare in the world ; nothing being more difficult for our sluggishness than to surmount innumer-able obstacles in striving for the prize of our high calling. To the immense load of miseries which almost overwhelm us, are added the jeers of profane men, who assail us for our simplicity, when spontan-eously renouncing the allurements of the present life we seem, in seeking a happiness which lies hid from us, to catch at a fleeting shadow. In short, we are beset above and below, behind and before, with violent temptations, which our minds would be altogether un-able to withstand, were they not set free from earthly objects, and devoted to the heavenly life, though apparently remote from us. Wherefore, he alone has made solid progress in the gospel who has acquired the habit of meditating continually on a blessed resurrection.

2. In ancient times philosophers discoursed, and even debated with each other, concerning the chief good : none however, except Plato, acknowledged that it consisted in union with God. He could not, however, form even an imperfect idea of its true nature ; nor is this strange, as he had learned nothing of the sacred bond of that union. We even in this our earthly pilgrimage know wherein our perfect and only felicity consists,—a felicity which, while we long for it, daily inflames our hearts more and more, until we attain to full fruition. Therefore I said, that none participate in the benefits of Christ save those who raise their minds to the resurrection. This, accordingly, is the mark which Paul sets before believers, and at which he says they are to aim, forgetting everything until they reach it (Phil. iii. 8). The more strenuously, therefore, must we contend for it, lest if

[1] 2 Tim. i. 10; John v. 24; Eph. ii. 6, 19; Rom. viii. 16–18; Heb. xi. 1 ; 2 Cor. v. 6; Col. iii. 3 ; Titus ii. 12.

the world engross us we be severely punished for our sloth.[1] Accordingly, he in another passage distinguishes believers by this mark, that their conversation is in heaven, from whence they look for the Saviour (Phil. iii. 20). And that they may not faint in their course, he associates all the other creatures with them. As shapeless ruins are everywhere seen, he says, that all things in heaven and earth struggle for renovation. For since Adam by his fall destroyed the proper order of nature, the creatures groan under the servitude to which they have been subjected through his sin ; not that they are at all endued with sense, but that they naturally long for the state of perfection from which they have fallen. Paul therefore describes them as groaning and travailing in pain (Rom. viii. 19) ; so that we who have received the first-fruits of the Spirit may be ashamed to grovel in our corruption, instead of at least imitating the inanimate elements which are bearing the punishment of another's sin. And in order that he may stimulate us the more powerfully, he terms the final advent of Christ *our redemption*. It is true, indeed, that all the parts of our redemption are already accomplished ; but as Christ was once offered for sins (Heb. ix. 28), so he shall again appear without sin unto salvation. Whatever, then, be the afflictions by which we are pressed, let this redemption sustain us until its final accomplishment.

3. The very importance of the subject ought to increase our ardour. Paul justly contends, that if Christ rise not the whole gospel is delusive and vain (1 Cor. xv. 13–17) ; for our condition would be more miserable than that of other mortals, because we are exposed to much hatred and insult, and incur danger every hour ; nay, are like sheep destined for slaughter ; and hence the authority of the gospel would fail, not in one part merely, but in its very essence, including both our adoption and the accomplishment of our salvation. Let us, therefore, give heed to a matter of all others the most serious, so that no length of time may produce weariness. I have deferred the brief consideration to be given of it to this place, that my readers may learn, when they have received Christ, the author of perfect salvation, to rise higher, and know that he is clothed with heavenly immortality and glory, in order that the whole body may be rendered conformable to the Head. For thus the Holy Spirit is ever setting before us in his person an example of the resurrection. It is difficult to believe that after our bodies have been consumed with rottenness, they will rise again at their appointed time. And hence, while many of the philosophers maintained the immortality of the soul, few of them assented to the resurrection of the body. Although in this they were inexcusable, we are thereby reminded that the subject is too difficult for human apprehension to reach it. To enable faith to surmount the great difficulty, Scripture furnishes two auxiliary proofs, the one the likeness of Christ's resurrection, and the other the omnipotence of God. Therefore, whenever the subject of the resurrection is con-

---

1 French, " nous recevions un povre salaire de nostre lascheté et paresse ; "—we receive a poor salary for our carelessness and sloth.

sidered, let us think of the case of our Saviour, who, having completed his mortal course in our nature which he had assumed, obtained immortality, and is now the pledge of our future resurrection. For in the miseries by which we are beset, we always bear "about in the body the dying of the Lord Jesus, that the life also of Jesus might be made manifest in our mortal flesh" (2 Cor. iv. 10). It is not lawful, it is not even possible, to separate him from us, without dividing him. Hence Paul's argument, "If there be no resurrection of the dead, then is Christ not risen" (1 Cor. xv. 13) ; for he assumes it as an acknowledged principle, that when Christ was subjected to death, and by rising gained a victory over death, it was not on his own account, but in the Head was begun what must necessarily be fulfilled in all the members, according to the degree and order of each. For it would not be proper to be made equal to him in all respects. It is said in the psalm, "Neither wilt thou suffer thine Holy One to see corruption" (Ps. xvi. 10). Although a portion of this confidence appertain to us according to the measure bestowed on us, yet the full effect appeared only in Christ, who, free from all corruption, resumed a spotless body. Then, that there may be no doubt as to our fellowship with Christ in a blessed resurrection, and that we may be contented with this pledge, Paul distinctly affirms that he sits in the heavens, and will come as a judge on the last day for the express purpose of changing our vile body, "that it may be fashioned like unto his glorious body" (Phil. iii. 21). For he elsewhere says that God did not raise up his Son from death to give an isolated specimen of his mighty power, but that the Spirit exerts the same efficacy in regard to them that believe ; and accordingly he says, that the Spirit when he dwells in us is life, because the end for which he was given is to quicken our mortal body (Rom. viii. 10, 11 ; Col. iii. 4). I briefly glance at subjects which might be treated more copiously, and deserve to be adorned more splendidly, and yet in the little I have said I trust pious readers will find sufficient materials for building up their faith. Christ rose again, that he might have us as partakers with him of future life. He was raised up by the Father, inasmuch as he was the Head of the Church, from which he cannot possibly be dissevered. He was raised up by the power of the Spirit, who also in in us performs the office of quickening. In fine, he was raised up to be the resurrection and the life. But as we have said, that in this mirror we behold a living image of the resurrection, so it furnishes a sure evidence to support our minds, provided we faint not, nor grow weary at the long delay, because it is not ours to measure the periods of time at our own pleasure ; but to rest patiently till God in his own time renew his kingdom. To this Paul refers when he says, "But every man in his own order : Christ the first-fruits ; afterward they that are Christ's at his coming" (1 Cor. xv. 23).

But lest any question should be raised as to the resurrection of Christ on which ours is founded, we see how often and in what various ways he has borne testimony to it. Scoffing men will deride the narrative which is given by the Evangelist as a childish fable. For what importance will they attach to a message which timid women bring, and the disciples, almost dead with fear, afterwards confirm? Why does not Christ rather place the illustrious trophies of his victory in the midst of the temple and the forum? Why does he not come forth, and in the presence of Pilate strike terror? Why does he not show himself alive again to the priests and all Jerusalem? Profane men will scarcely admit that the witnesses whom he selects are well qualified. I answer, that though at the commencement their infirmity was contemptible, yet the whole was directed by the admirable providence of God, so that partly from love to Christ and religious zeal, partly from incredulity, those who were lately overcome with fear now hurry to the sepulchre, not only that they might be eyewitnesses of the fact, but that they might hear angels announce what they actually saw. How can we question the veracity of those who regarded what the women told them as a fable, until they saw the reality? It is not strange that the whole people and also the governor, after they were furnished with sufficient evidence for conviction, were not allowed to see Christ or the other signs (Matth. xxvii. 66; xxviii. 11). The sepulchre is sealed, sentinels keep watch, on the third day the body is not found. The soldiers are bribed to spread the report that his disciples had stolen the body. As if they had had the means of deforcing a band of soldiers, or been supplied with weapons, or been trained so as to make such a daring attempt. But if the soldiers had not courage enough to repel them, why did they not follow and apprehend some of them by the aid of the populace? Pilate, therefore, in fact, put his signet to the resurrection of Christ, and the guards who were placed at the sepulchre by their silence or falsehood also became heralds of his resurrection. Meanwhile, the voice of angels was heard, "He is not here, but is risen" (Luke xxiv. 6). The celestial splendour plainly shows that they were not men but angels. Afterwards, if any doubt still remained, Christ himself removed it. The disciples saw him frequently; they even touched his hands and his feet, and their unbelief is of no little avail in confirming our faith. He discoursed to them of the mysteries of the kingdom of God, and at length, while they beheld, ascended to heaven. This spectacle was exhibited not to eleven apostles only, but was seen by more than five hundred brethren at once (1 Cor. xv. 6). Then by sending the Holy Spirit he gave a proof not only of life but also of supreme power, as he had foretold, "It is expedient for you that I go away: for if I go not away, the Comforter will not come unto you" (John xvi. 7). Paul was not thrown down on the way by the power of a dead man, but felt that he whom he was opposing was possessed of sovereign authority. To Stephen he appeared for another purpose—viz. that he might overcome the fear of death by the certainty of life. To refuse assent to these numerous and authentic proofs is not diffidence, but depraved and therefore infatuated obstinacy.

4. We have said that in proving the resurrection our thoughts must be directed to the immense power of God. This Paul briefly teaches, when he says that the Lord Jesus Christ "shall change our vile body, that it may be fashioned like unto his glorious body, according to the working of that mighty power whereby he is able even to subdue all things unto himself" (Phil. iii. 21). Wherefore, nothing can be more incongruous than to look here at what can be done naturally when the subject presented to us is an inestimable miracle, which by its magnitude absorbs our senses. Paul, however, by producing a proof from nature, confutes the senselessness of those who deny the resurrection. "Thou fool, that which thou sowest is not quickened except it die" &c. (1 Cor. xv. 36). He says that in seed there is a species of resurrection, because the crop is produced from corruption. Nor would the thing be so difficult of belief were we as attentive as we ought to be to the wonders which meet our eye in every quarter of the world. But let us remember that none is truly persuaded of the future resurrection save he who, carried away with admiration, gives God the glory.

Elated with this conviction, Isaiah exclaims, "Thy dead men shall live, together with my dead body shall they arise. Awake and sing, ye that dwell in dust" (Isaiah xxvi. 19). In desperate circumstances he rises to God, the author of life, in whose hand are "the issues from death" (Psalm lxviii. 20). Job also, when liker a dead body than a living being, trusting to the power of God, hesitates not as if in full vigour to rise to that day: "I know that my Redeemer liveth, and that he will stand at the latter day upon the earth" (that is, that he will there exert his power): "and though after my skin worms destroy this body, yet in my flesh shall I see God; whom I shall see for myself, and mine eyes shall behold, and not another" (Job xix· 25–27). For though some have recourse to a more subtle interpretation, by which they wrest these passages, as if they were not to be understood of the resurrection, they only confirm what they are desirous to overthrow; for holy men, in seeking consolation in their misfortunes, have recourse for alleviation merely to the similitude of a resurrection. This is better learned from a passage in Ezekiel. When the Jews scouted the promise of return, and objected that the probability of it was not greater than that of the dead coming forth from the tomb, there is presented to the prophet in vision a field covered with dry bones, which at the command of God recover sinews and flesh. Though under that figure he encourages the people to hope for return, yet the ground of hope is taken from the resurrection, as it is the special type of all the deliverances which believers experience in this world. Thus Christ declares that the voice of the Gospel gives life; but because the Jews did not receive it, he immediately adds, "Marvel not at this; for the hour is coming in which all that are in the grave shall hear his voice, and shall come forth" (John v. 28, 29). Wherefore, amid all our conflicts let us exult after the example of Paul, that he who has promised us future

life " is able to keep that " which " is committed unto him " and thus
glory that there is laid up for us " a crown of righteousness, which
the Lord, the righteous judge, shall give " (2 Tim. i. 12; iv. 8).
Thus all the hardships which we may endure will be a demonstration
of our future life, " seeing it is a righteous thing with God to recompense tribulation to them that trouble you; and to you who are
troubled rest with us, when the Lord Jesus shall be revealed from
heaven with his mighty angels, in flaming fire " (2 Thess. i. 6–8).
But we must attend to what he shortly after adds—viz. that he
" shall come to be glorified in his saints, and to be admired in all
them that believe "—by receiving the Gospel.

5. Although the minds of men ought to be perpetually occupied
with this pursuit, yet, as if they actually resolved to banish all remembrance of the resurrection, they have called death the end of all
things, the extinction of man. For Solomon certainly expresses the
commonly received opinion when he says, " A living dog is better
than a dead lion " (Eccl. ix. 4). And again, " Who knoweth the
spirit of man that goeth upward, and the spirit of the beast that
goeth downward to the earth ?"[1] In all ages a brutish stupor has
prevailed, and accordingly it has made its way into the very Church;
for the Sadducees had the hardihood openly to profess that there was
no resurrection, nay, that the soul was mortal (Mark xii. 18; Luke
xx. 27). But that this gross ignorance might be no excuse, unbelievers have always by natural instinct had an image of the resurrection before their eyes. For why the sacred and inviolable custom
of burying, but that it might be the earnest of a new life ? Nor can
it be said that it had its origin in error, for the solemnity of sepulture
always prevailed among the holy patriarchs, and God was pleased
that the same custom should continue among the Gentiles, in order
that the image of the resurrection thus presented might shake off
their torpor. But although that ceremony was without profit, yet it
is useful to us if we prudently consider its end; because it is no
feeble refutation of infidelity that all men agreed in professing what
none of them believed. But not only did Satan stupify the senses of
mankind, so that with their bodies they buried the remembrance of
the resurrection; but he also managed by various fictions so to corrupt this branch of doctrine that it at length was lost. Not to mention that even in the days of Paul he began to assail it (1 Cor. xv.).
shortly after the Chiliasts arose, who limited the reign of Christ to a
thousand years. This fiction is too puerile to need or to deserve refutation. Nor do they receive any countenance from the Apocalypse,
from which it is known that they extracted a gloss for their error
(Rev. xx. 4), since the thousand years there mentioned refer not to
the eternal blessedness of the Church, but only to the various troubles
which await the Church militant in this world. The whole Scripture
proclaims that there will be no end either to the happiness of the

---

[1] Calvin translates, " Quis scit an hominis anima ascendit sursum?" &c.—Who
knows whether the soul of man goes upward? &c.

elect, or the punishment of the reprobate. Moreover, in regard to all things which lie beyond our sight, and far transcend the reach of our intellect, belief must either be founded on the sure oracles of God, or altogether renounced. Those who assign only a thousand years to the children of God to enjoy the inheritance of future life, observe not how great an insult they offer to Christ and his kingdom. If they are not to be clothed with immortality, then Christ himself, into whose glory they shall be transformed, has not been received into immortal glory; if their blessedness is to have an end, the kingdom of Christ, on whose solid structure it rests, is temporary. In short, they are either most ignorant of all divine things, or they maliciously aim at subverting the whole grace of God and power of Christ, which cannot have their full effect, unless sin is obliterated, death swallowed up, and eternal life fully renewed. How stupid and frivolous their fear that too much severity will be ascribed to God, if the reprobate are doomed to eternal punishment, even the blind may see. The Lord, forsooth, will be unjust if he exclude from his kingdom those who, by their ingratitude, shall have rendered themselves unworthy of it. But their sins are temporary (see Bernard, Epist. 254). I admit it; but then the majesty of God, and also the justice which they have violated by their sins, are eternal. Justly, therefore, the memory of their iniquity does not perish. But in this way the punishment will exceed the measure of the fault. It is intolerable blasphemy to hold the majesty of God in so little estimation, as not to regard the contempt of it as of greater consequence than the destruction of a single soul. But let us have done with these triflers, that we may not seem (contrary to what we first observed) to think their dreams deserving of refutation.

6. Besides these, other two dreams have been invented by men who indulge a wicked curiosity. Some, under the idea that the whole man perishes, have thought that the soul will rise again with the body; while others, admitting that spirits are immortal, hold that they will be clothed with new bodies, and thus deny the resurrection of the flesh. Having already adverted to the former point when speaking of the creation of man, it will be sufficient again to remind the reader how grovelling an error it is to convert a spirit, formed after the image of God, into an evanescent breath, which animates the body only during this fading life, and to reduce the temple of the Holy Spirit to nothing; in short, to rob of the badge of immortality that part of ourselves in which the divinity is most refulgent, and the marks of immortality conspicuous, so as to make the condition of the body better and more excellent than that of the soul. Very different is the course taken by Scripture, which compares the body to a tabernacle, from which it describes us as migrating when we die, because it estimates us by that part which distinguishes us from the lower animals. Thus Peter, in reference to his approaching death, says, " Knowing that shortly I must put off this my tabernacle " (2 Pet. i. 14). Paul, again, speaking of believers, after saying,

" If our earthly house of this tabernacle were dissolved, we have a building of God," adds, " Whilst we are at home in the body, we are absent from the Lord " (2 Cor. v. 1, 6). Did not the soul survive the body, how could it be present with the Lord on being separated from the body ? But an Apostle removes all doubt when he says that we go " to the spirits of just men made perfect " (Heb. xii. 23) ; by these words meaning, that we are associated with the holy patriarchs, who, even when dead, cultivate the same piety, so that we cannot be the members of Christ unless we unite with them. And did not the soul, when unclothed from the body, retain its essence, and be capable of beatific glory, our Saviour would not have said to the thief, " To-day shalt thou be with me in paradise " (Luke xxiii. 43). Trusting to these clear proofs, let us doubt not, after the example of our Saviour, to commend our spirits to God when we come to die, or, after the example of Stephen, to commit ourselves to the protection of Christ, who, with good reason, is called " The Shepherd and Bishop " of our souls (Acts vii. 59 ; 1 Pet. ii. 25). Moreover, to pry curiously into their intermediate state is neither lawful nor expedient (see Calv. Psychopannychia). Many greatly torment themselves with discussing what place they occupy, and whether or not they already enjoy celestial glory. It is foolish and rash to inquire into hidden things, farther than God permits us to know. Scripture, after telling that Christ is present with them, and receives them into paradise (John xii. 32), and that they are comforted, while the souls of the reprobate suffer the torments which they have merited, goes no farther. What teacher or doctor will reveal to us what God has concealed ? As to the place of abode, the question is not less futile and inept, since we know that the dimension of the soul is not the same as that of the body.[1] When the abode of blessed spirits is designated as the *bosom* of *Abraham*, it is plain that, on quitting this pilgrimage, they are received by the common father of the faithful, who imparts to them the fruit of his faith. Still, since Scripture uniformly enjoins us to look with expectation to the advent of Christ, and delays the crown of glory till that period, let us be contented with the limits divinely prescribed to us—viz. that the souls of the righteous, after their warfare is ended, obtain blessed rest where in joy they wait for the fruition of promised glory, and that thus the final result is suspended till Christ the Redeemer appear. There can be no doubt that the reprobate have the same doom as that which Jude assigns to the devils, they are " reserved in everlasting chains under darkness, unto the judgment of the great day " (Jude, ver. 6).

7. Equally monstrous is the error of those who imagine that the soul, instead of resuming the body with which it is now clothed, will obtain a new and different body. Nothing can be more futile than

---

1 French, " La question quant au lieu est bien frivole et sotte : veu que nous savons que l'ame n'a pas ses mesures de long et de large, comme le corps ;"—the question as to place is very frivolous and foolish, seeing we know that the soul has no measures of length and breadth like the body.

the reason given by the Manichees—viz. that it were incongruous for impure flesh to rise again : as if there were no impurity in the soul ; and yet this does not exclude it from the hope of heavenly life. It is just as if they were to say, that what is infected by the taint of sin cannot be divinely purified ; for I now say nothing to the delirious dream that flesh is naturally impure as having been created by the devil. I only maintain, that nothing in us at present, which is unworthy of heaven, is any obstacle to the resurrection. But, first, Paul enjoins believers to purify themselves from " all filthiness of the flesh and spirit" (2 Cor. vii. 1) ; and then denounces the judgment which is to follow, that every one shall " receive the things done in his body, according to that he hath done, whether it be good or bad" (2 Cor. v. 10). With this accords what he says to the Corinthians, " That the life also of Jesus might be made manifest in our body" (2 Cor. iv. 10). For which reason he elsewhere says, " I pray God your whole spirit and soul and body be preserved blameless unto the coming of our Lord Jesus Christ" (1 Thess. v. 23). He says "body" as well as " spirit and soul," and no wonder ; for it were most absurd that bodies which God has dedicated to himself as temples should fall into corruption without hope of resurrection. What ? are they not also the members of Christ ? Does he not pray that God would sanctify every part of them, and enjoin them to celebrate his name with their tongues, lift up pure hands, and offer sacrifices ? That part of man, therefore, which the heavenly Judge so highly honours, what madness is it for any mortal man to reduce to dust without hope of revival ? In like manner, when Paul exhorts, " Glorify God in your body, and in your spirit, which are God's," he certainly does not allow that that which he claims for God as sacred is to be adjudged to eternal corruption. Nor, indeed, on any subject does Scripture furnish clearer explanation than on the resurrection of our flesh. " This corruptible (says Paul) must put on incorruption, and this mortal must put on immortality" (1 Cor. xv. '53). If God formed new bodies, where would be this change of quality ? If it were said that we must be renewed, the ambiguity of the expression might, perhaps, afford room for cavil ; but here pointing with the finger to the bodies with which we are clothed, and promising that they shall be incorruptible, he very plainly affirms that no new bodies are to be fabricated. " Nay," as Tertullian says, " he could not have spoken more expressly, if he had held his skin in his hands" (Tertull. de Resurrect. Carnis.). Nor can any cavil enable them to evade the force of another passage, in which saying that Christ will be the Judge of the world, he quotes from Isaiah, " As I live, saith the Lord, every knee shall bow to me " (Rom. xiv. 11 ; Isa. xix. 18); since he openly declares that those whom he was addressing will have to give an account of their lives. This could not be true if new bodies were to be sisted to the tribunal. Moreover, there is no ambiguity in the words of Daniel, " Many of them that sleep in the dust of the earth shall awake, some to everlasting life, and some to shame and everlasting contempt" (Dan. xii. 2); since he does not bring new matter from the four elements to compose men, but calls forth the dead from their graves. And the reason which dictates this is plain. For if death, which originated in the fall of man, is adventitious, the renewal produced by Christ must be in the same body which began to be mortal. And, certainly, since the Athenians mocked Paul for asserting the resurrection (Acts xvii. 32), we may infer what his preaching was: their derision is of no small force to confirm our faith. The saying of our Saviour also is worthy of observation, "Fear not them which kill the body, but are not able to kill the soul: but rather fear him which is able to destroy both soul and body in hell" (Matth. x. 28). Here there would be no ground for fear, were not the body which we now have liable to punishment. Nor is another saying of our Saviour less obscure, "The hour is coming, in the which all that are in the graves shall hear his voice, and shall come forth; they that have done good, unto the resurrection of life; and they that have done evil, unto the resurrection of damnation" (John v. 28, 29). Shall we say that the soul rests in the grave, that it may there hear the voice of Christ, and not rather that the body shall at his command resume the vigour which it had lost? Moreover, if we are to receive new bodies, where will be the conformity of the Head and the members? Christ rose again. Was it by forming for himself a new body? Nay, he had foretold, "Destroy this temple, and in three days I will raise it up" (John ii. 19). The mortal body which he had formerly carried he again received; for it would not have availed us much if a new body had been substituted, and that which had been offered in expiatory sacrifice been destroyed. We must, therefore, attend to that connection which the Apostle celebrates, that we rise because Christ rose (1 Cor. xv. 12); nothing being less probable than that the flesh in which we bear about the dying of Christ, shall have no share in the resurrection of Christ. This was even manifested by a striking example, when, at the resurrection of Christ, many bodies of the saints came forth from their graves. For it cannot be denied that this was a prelude, or rather earnest, of the final resurrection for which we hope, such as already existed in Enoch and Elijah, whom Tertullian calls *candidates for resurrection*, because, exempted from corruption, both in body and soul, they were received into the custody of God.

8. I am ashamed to waste so many words on so clear a matter; but my readers will kindly submit to the annoyance, in order that perverse and presumptuous minds may not be able to avail themselves of any flaw to deceive the simple. The volatile spirits with whom I now dispute adduce the fiction of their own brain, that in the resurrection there will be a creation of new bodies. Their only reason for thinking so is, that it seems to them incredible that a dead body, long wasted by corruption, should return to its former state. Therefore, mere unbelief is the parent of their opinion. The Spirit of God, on the contrary, uniformly exhorts us in Scripture to hope for the resurrection of our flesh. For this reason Baptism is, according to Paul,

a seal of our future resurrection; and in like manner the holy Supper invites us confidently to expect it, when with our mouths we receive the symbols of spiritual grace. And certainly the whole exhortation of Paul, "Yield ye your members as instruments of righteousness unto God" (Rom. vi. 13), would be frigid, did he not add, as he does in another passage, "He that raised up Christ from the dead shall also quicken your mortal bodies" (Rom. viii. 11). For what would it avail to apply feet, hands, eyes, and tongues, to the service of God, did not these afterwards participate in the benefit and reward? This Paul expressly confirms when he says, "The body is not for fornication, but for the Lord; and the Lord for the body. And God hath both raised up the Lord, and will also raise up us by his own power" (1 Cor. vi. 13, 14). The words which follow are still clearer, "Know ye not that your bodies are the members of Christ?" "Know ye not that your body is the temple of the Holy Ghost?" (1 Cor. vi. 15, 19.) Meanwhile, we see how he connects the resurrection with chastity and holiness, as he shortly after includes our bodies in the purchase of redemption. It would be inconsistent with reason, that the body, in which Paul bore the marks of his Saviour, and in which he magnificently extolled him (Gal. vi. 17), should lose the reward of the crown. Hence he glories thus, "Our conversation is in heaven; from whence also we look for the Saviour, the Lord Jesus Christ: Who shall change our vile body, that it may be fashioned like unto his glorious body" (Phil. iii. 20, 21). As it is true, "That we must through much tribulation enter into the kingdom of God" (Acts xiv. 22); so it were unreasonable that this entrance should be denied to the bodies which God exercises under the banner of the cross, and adorns with the palm of victory.

Accordingly, the saints never entertained any doubt that they would one day be the companions of Christ, who transfers to his own person all the afflictions by which we are tried, that he may show their quickening power.[1] Nay, under the law, God trained the holy patriarch in this belief, by means of an external ceremony. For to what end was the rite of burial, as we have already seen, unless to teach that new life was prepared for the bodies thus deposited? Hence, also, the spices and other symbols of immortality, by which under the law the obscurity of the doctrine was illustrated in the same way as by sacrifices. That custom was not the offspring of superstition, since we see that the Spirit is not less careful in narrating burials than in stating the principal mysteries of the faith. Christ commends these last offices as of no trivial importance (Matth. xvi. 10), and that, certainly, for no other reason than just that they raise our eyes from the view of the tomb, which corrupts and destroys all things, to the prospect of renovation. Besides, that careful observance of the ceremony for which the patriarchs are praised, sufficiently proves that they found in it a special and valuable help to their faith. Nor

---

[1] Latin, "ut vivificas esse doceat"—French, "pour monstrer quelles nous meinent à vie;"— to show that they conduct us to life.

would Abraham have been so anxious about the burial of his wife (Gen. xxiii. 4, 19), had not the religious view, and something superior to any worldly advantage, been present to his mind; in other words, by adorning her dead body with the insignia of the resurrection, he confirmed his own faith, and that of his family. A clearer proof of this appears in the example of Jacob, who, to testify to his posterity that even death did not destroy the hope of the promised land, orders his bones to be carried thither. Had he been to be clothed with a new body, would it not have been ridiculous in him to give commands concerning a dust which was to be reduced to nothing? Wherefore, if Scripture has any authority with us, we cannot desire a clearer or stronger proof of any doctrine. Even tyros understand this to be the meaning of the words, *resurrection*, and *raising up*. A thing which is created for the first time cannot be said to rise again; nor could our Saviour have said, "This is the father's will which hath sent me, that of all which he hath given me I should lose nothing, but should raise it up again at the last day" (John vi. 39). The same is implied in the word *sleeping*, which is applicable only to the body. Hence, too, the name of cemetery, applied to burying-grounds.

It remains to make a passing remark on the mode of resurrection. I speak thus because Paul, by styling it a mystery, exhorts us to soberness, in order that he may curb a licentious indulgence in free and subtle speculation. First, we must hold, as has already been observed, that the body in which we shall rise will be the same as at present in respect of substance, but that the quality will be different; just as the body of Christ which was raised up was the same as that which had been offered in sacrifice, and yet excelled in other qualities, as if it had been altogether different. This Paul declares by familiar examples (1 Cor. xv. 39). For as the flesh of man and of beasts is the same in substance, but not in quality: as all the stars are made of the same matter, but have different degrees of brightness: so he shows, that though we shall retain the substance of the body, there will be a change, by which its condition will become much more excellent. The corruptible body therefore, in order that we may be raised, will not perish or vanish away, but, divested of corruption, will be clothed with incorruption. Since God has all the elements at his disposal, no difficulty can prevent him from commanding the earth, the fire, and the water, to give up what they seem to have destroyed. This, also, though not without figure, Isaiah testifies, "Behold the Lord cometh out of his place to punish the inhabitants of the earth for their iniquity: the earth also shall disclose her blood, and shall no more cover her slain" (Isa. xxvi. 21). But a distinction must be made between those who died long ago, and those who on that day shall be found alive. For as Paul declares, "We shall not all sleep, but we shall all be changed" (1 Cor. xv. 51); that is, it will not be necessary that a period should elapse between death and the beginning of the second life, for in a moment of time, in the twinkling of an eye, the trumpet shall sound, raising up the dead incorruptible, and, by a sudden change, fitting those who are alive for the same glory. So, in another passage, he comforts believers who were to undergo death, telling them that those who are then alive shall not take precedence of the dead, because those who have fallen asleep in Christ shall rise first (1 Thess. iv. 15). Should any one urge the Apostle's declaration, "It is appointed unto all men once to die" (Heb. ix. 27), the solution is easy, that when the natural state is changed there is an appearance of death, which is fitly so denominated, and therefore there is no inconsistency in the two things—viz. that all when divested of their mortal body shall be renewed by death; and yet that where the change is sudden, there will be no necessary separation between the soul and the body.

9. But a more difficult question here arises, How can the resurrection, which is a special benefit of Christ, be common to the ungodly, who are lying under the curse of God? We know that in Adam all died. Christ has come to be the resurrection and the life (John xi. 25). Is it to revive the whole human race indiscriminately? But what more incongruous than that the ungodly in their obstinate blindness should obtain what the pious worshippers of God receive by faith only? It is certain, therefore, that there will be one resurrection to judgment, and another to life, and that Christ will come to separate the kids from the goats (Matth. xxv. 32). I observe, that this ought not to seem very strange, seeing something resembling it occurs every day. We know that in Adam we were deprived of the inheritance of the whole world, and that the same reason which excludes us from eating of the tree of life, excludes us also from common food. How comes it, then, that God not only makes his sun to rise on the evil and on the good, but that, in regard to the uses of the present life, his inestimable liberality is constantly flowing forth in rich abundance? Hence we certainly perceive, that things which are proper to Christ and his members, abound to the wicked also: not that their possession is legitimate, but that they may thus be rendered more inexcusable. Thus the wicked often experience the beneficence of God, not in ordinary measures, but such as sometimes throw all the blessings of the godly into the shade, though they eventually lead to greater damnation. Should it be objected, that the resurrection is not properly compared to fading and earthly blessings, I again answer, that when the devils were first alienated from God, the fountain of life, they deserved to be utterly destroyed; yet, by the admirable counsel of God, an intermediate state was prepared, where without life they might live in death. It ought not to seem in any respect more absurd that there is to be an adventitious resurrection of the ungodly which will drag them against their will before the tribunal of Christ, whom they now refuse to receive as their master and teacher. To be consumed by death would be a light punishment were they not, in order to the punishment of their rebellion, to be sisted before the Judge whom they have provoked to a vengeance without measure and without

end. But although we are to hold, as already observed, and as is contained in the celebrated confession of Paul to Felix, "That there shall be a resurrection of the dead, both of the just and unjust" (Acts xxiv. 15); yet Scripture more frequently sets forth the resurrection as intended, along with celestial glory, for the children of God only: because, properly speaking, Christ comes not for the destruction, but for the salvation of the world; and, therefore, in the Creed the life of blessedness only is mentioned.

10. But since the prophecy, that death shall be swallowed up in victory (Hosea xiii. 14), will then only be completed, let us always remember that the end of the resurrection is eternal happiness, of whose excellence scarcely the minutest part can be described by all that human tongues can say. For though we are truly told that the kingdom of God will be full of light, and gladness, and felicity, and glory, yet the things meant by these words remain most remote from sense, and as it were involved in enigma, until the day arrive on which he will manifest his glory to us face to face (1 Cor. xv. 54). "Now," says John, "are we the sons of God; and it doth not yet appear what we shall be: but we know that, when he shall appear, we shall be like him; for we shall see him as he is" (1 John iii. 2). Hence, as the prophets were unable to give a verbal description of that spiritual blessedness, they usually delineated it by corporeal objects. On the other hand, because the fervour of desire must be kindled in us by some taste of its sweetness, let us specially dwell upon this thought, If God contains in himself as an inexhaustible fountain all fulness of blessing, those who aspire to the supreme good and perfect happiness must not long for anything beyond him. This we are taught in several passages, "Fear not, Abraham; I am thy shield, and thy exceeding great reward" (Gen. xv. 1). With this accords David's sentiment, "The Lord is the portion of mine inheritance, and of my cup: thou maintainest my lot. The lines are fallen unto me in pleasant places" (Ps. xvi. 5, 6). Again, "I shall be satisfied when I awake with thy likeness" (Ps. xvii. 15). Peter declares that the purpose for which believers are called is, that they may be "partakers of the divine nature" (2 Pet. i. 4). How so? Because "he shall come to be glorified in his saints, and to be admired in all them that believe" (2 Thess. i. 10). If our Lord will share his glory, power, and righteousness with the elect, nay, will give himself to be enjoyed by them; and what is better still, will, in a manner, become one with them, let us remember that every kind of happiness is herein included. But when we have made great progress in thus meditating, let us understand that if the conceptions of our minds be contrasted with the sublimity of the mystery, we are still halting at the very entrance.[1] The more necessary is it for us

---

[1] French, Et encore quand nous aurons bien profité en cette meditation, si nous faut il entendre que nous sommes encore tout au bas et à la premiere entree, et que jamais nous n'approcherons durant cette vie à la hautesse de çe mystere."—And still, when

to cultivate sobriety in this matter, lest, unmindful of our feeble capacity, we presume to take too lofty a flight, and be overwhelmed by the brightness of the celestial glory. We feel how much we are stimulated by an excessive desire of knowing more than is given us to know, and hence frivolous and noxious questions are ever and anon springing forth: by frivolous, I mean questions from which no advantage can be extracted. But there is a second class which is worse than frivolous; because those who indulge in them involve themselves in hurtful speculations. Hence I call them noxious. The doctrine of Scripture on the subject ought not to be made the ground of any controversy, and it is that as God, in the varied distribution of gifts to his saints in this world, gives them unequal degrees of light, so when he shall crown his gifts, their degrees of glory in heaven will also be unequal. When Paul says, "Ye are our glory and our joy" (2 Thess. ii. 19), his words do not apply indiscriminately to all; nor do those of our Saviour to his apostles, "Ye also shall sit on twelve thrones judging the twelve tribes of Israel" (Matth. xix. 28). But Paul, who knew that as God enriches the saints with spiritual gifts in this world, he will in like manner adorn them with glory in heaven, hesitates not to say, that a special crown is laid up for him in proportion to his labours. Our Saviour, also, to commend the dignity of the office which he had conferred on the apostles, reminds them that the fruit of it is laid up in heaven. This, too, Daniel says, "They that be wise shall shine as the brightness of the firmament; and they that turn many to righteousness as the stars for ever and ever" (Dan. xii. 3). Any one who attentively considers the Scriptures will see not only that they promise eternal life to believers, but a special reward to each. Hence the expression of Paul, "The Lord grant unto him that he may find mercy of the Lord in that day" (2 Tim. i. 18; iv. 14). This is confirmed by our Saviour's promise, that they "shall receive an hundredfold, and shall inherit everlasting life" (Matth. xix. 29). In short, as Christ, by the manifold variety of his gifts, begins the glory of his body in this world, and gradually increases it, so he will complete it in heaven.

11. While all the godly with one consent will admit this, because it is sufficiently attested by the word of God, they will, on the other hand, avoid perplexing questions which they feel to be a hinderance in their way, and thus keep within the prescribed limits. In regard to myself, I not only individually refrain from a superfluous investigation of useless matters, but also think myself bound to take care that I do not encourage the levity of others by answering them. Men puffed up with vain science are often inquiring how great the difference will be between prophets and apostles, and again, between apostles and martyrs; by how many degrees virgins will surpass those who are married; in short, they leave not a corner of heaven un-

we shall have profited much by thus meditating, we must understand that we are still far beneath it, and at the very threshold, and that never during this life shall we approach the height of this mystery.

touched by their speculations. Next it occurs to them to inquire to what end the world is to be repaired, since the children of God will not be in want of any part of this great and incomparable abundance, but will be like the angels, whose abstinence from food is a symbol of eternal blessedness. I answer, that independent of use, there will be so much pleasantness in the very sight, so much delight in the very knowledge, that this happiness will far surpass all the means of enjoyment which are now afforded. Let us suppose ourselves placed in the richest quarter of the globe, where no kind of pleasure is wanting, who is there that is not ever and anon hindered and excluded by disease from enjoying the gifts of God? who does not oftentimes interrupt the course of enjoyment by intemperance? Hence it follows, that fruition, pure and free from all defect, though it be of no use to a corruptible life, is the summit of happiness. Others go further, and ask whether dross and other impurities in metals will have no existence at the restitution, and are inconsistent with it. Though I should go so far as concede this to them, yet I expect with Paul a reparation of those defects which first began with sin, and on account of which the whole creation groaneth and travaileth with pain (Rom. viii. 22). Others go a step further, and ask, What better condition can await the human race, since the blessing of offspring shall then have an end? The solution of this difficulty also is easy. When Scripture so highly extols the blessing of offspring, it refers to the progress by which God is constantly urging nature forward to its goal; in perfection itself we know that the case is different. But as such alluring speculations instantly captivate the unwary, who are afterwards led farther into the labyrinth, until at length, every one becoming pleased with his own view, there is no limit to disputation, the best and shortest course for us will be to rest contented with seeing through a glass darkly until we shall see face to face. Few out of the vast multitude of mankind feel concerned how they are to get to heaven; all would fain know before the time what is done in heaven. Almost all, while slow and sluggish in entering upon the contest, are already depicting to themselves imaginary triumphs.

12. Moreover, as language cannot describe the severity of the divine vengeance on the reprobate, their pains and torments are figured to us by corporeal things, such as darkness, wailing and gnashing of teeth, unextinguishable fire, the ever-gnawing worm (Matth. viii. 12; xxii. 13; Mark ix. 43; Isa. lxvi. 24). It is certain that by such modes of expression the Holy Spirit designed to impress all our senses with dread, as when it is said, " Tophet is ordained of old; yea, for the king it is prepared: he hath made it deep and large; the pile thereof is fire and much wood; the breath of the Lord, like a stream of brimstone, doth kindle it (Isa. xxx. 33). As we thus require to be assisted to conceive the miserable doom of the reprobate, so the consideration on which we ought chiefly to dwell is the fearful consequence of being estranged from all fellowship with God, and not only so, but of feeling that his majesty is

adverse to us, while we cannot possibly escape from it. For, first, his indignation is like a raging fire, by whose touch all things are devoured and annihilated. Next, all the creatures are the instruments of his judgment, so that those to whom the Lord will thus publicly manifest his anger will feel that heaven, and earth, and sea, all beings, animate and inanimate, are, as it were, inflamed with dire indignation against them, and armed for their destruction. Wherefore, the Apostle made no trivial declaration, when he said that unbelievers shall be "punished with everlasting destruction from the presence of the Lord, and from the glory of his power" (2 Thess. i. 9). And whenever the prophets strike terror by means of corporeal figures, although in respect of our dull understanding there is no extravagance in their language, yet they give preludes of the future judgment in the sun and the moon, and the whole fabric of the world. Hence unhappy consciences find no rest, but are vexed and driven about by a dire whirlwind, feeling as if torn by an angry God, pierced through with deadly darts, terrified by his thunderbolt, and crushed by the weight of his hand; so that it were easier to plunge into abysses and whirlpools than endure these terrors for a moment. How fearful, then, must it be to be thus beset throughout eternity! On this subject there is a memorable passage in the ninetieth Psalm: Although God by a mere look scatters all mortals, and brings them to nought, yet as his worshippers are more timid in this world, he urges them the more, that he may stimulate them, while burdened with the cross, to press onward until he himself shall be all in all.

END OF THE THIRD BOOK.

INSTITUTES

OF

THE CHRISTIAN RELIGION.

BOOK FOURTH.

OF THE HOLY CATHOLIC CHURCH.

ARGUMENT.

In the former Books an exposition has been given of the three parts of the Apostles' Creed concerning God the Creator, the Redeemer, and the Sanctifier. It now remains to treat, in this last Book, of the Church and the Communion of Saints, or of the external means or helps by which God invites us to fellowship with Christ, and keeps us in it.

The twenty Chapters of which it consists may be conveniently reduced to three particular heads—viz. I. Of the Church. II. Of the Sacraments. III. Of Civil Government.

The first head occupies the first thirteen chapters; but these may all be reduced to four—viz. I. Of the marks of the Church, or the means by which the Church may be discerned, since it is necessary to cultivate unity with the Church. This is considered in Chapters I. and II. —II. Of the rule or government of the Church. The order of government, Chap. III. The form in use in the primitive Church, Chap. IV. The form at present existing in the Papacy, Chap. V. The primacy of the Pope, Chap. VI. The gradual rise of his usurpation, Chap. VII.—III. Of the power of the Church. The power in relation to doctrine as possessed either by individuals, Chap. VIII.; or universally as in Councils, Chap. IX. The power of enacting laws, Chap. X. The extent of ecclesiastical jurisdiction, Chap. XI.—IV. Of the discipline of the Church. The chief use of discipline, Chap. XII. The abuse of it, Chap. XIII.

The second general head, Of the Sacraments, comprehends three particulars,—I. Of the Sacraments in general, Chap. XIV.—II. Of the two Sacraments in particular. Of Baptism, Chap. XV. Of Pædobaptism, Chap. XVI. Of the Lord's Supper, Chap. XVII. Of profaning the Lord's Supper, Chap. XVIII. Of the five Sacraments falsely so called, Chap. XIX.

The third general head, Of Civil Government. This considered first generally, and then under the separate heads of Magistrates, Laws, and People.

INSTITUTES

OF

THE CHRISTIAN RELIGION.

BOOK FOURTH.

OF THE HOLY CATHOLIC CHURCH.

CHAPTER I.

OF THE TRUE CHURCH. DUTY OF CULTIVATING UNITY WITH HER, AS THE MOTHER OF ALL THE GODLY.

The three divisions of this chapter are,—I. The article of the Creed concerning the Holy Catholic Church and the Communion of Saints briefly expounded. The grounds on which the Church claims our reverence, sec. 1–6. II. Of the marks of the Church, sec. 7–9. III. The necessity of cleaving to the Holy Catholic Church and the Communion of Saints. Refutation of the errors of the Novatians, Anabaptists, and other schismatics, in regard to this matter, sec. 10–29.

Sections.

1. The church now to be considered. With her God has deposited whatever is necessary to faith and good order. A summary of what is contained in this Book. Why it begins with the Church.
2. In what sense the article of the Creed concerning the Church is to be understood. Why we should say, "I believe the Church," not "I believe in the Church." The purport of this article. Why the Church is called Catholic or Universal.
3. What meant by the Communion of Saints. Whether it is inconsistent with various gifts in the saints, or with civil order. Uses of this article concerning the Church and the Communion of Saints. Must the Church be visible in order to our maintaining unity with her?
4. The name of Mother given to the Church shows how necessary it is to know her. No salvation out of the Church.
5. The Church is our mother, inasmuch as God has committed to her the kind office of bringing us up in the faith until we attain full age. This method of education not to be despised. Useful to us in two ways. This utility destroyed by those who despise the pastors and teachers of the Church. The petulance of such despisers repressed by reason and Scripture. For this education of the Church her children enjoined to meet in the sanctuary. The abuse of churches both before and since the advent of Christ. Their proper use.

6. Her ministry effectual, but not without the Spirit of God. Passages in proof of this.
7. Second part of the Chapter. Concerning the marks of the Church. In what respect the Church is invisible. In what respect she is visible.
8. God alone knoweth them that are his. Still he has given marks to discern his children.
9. These marks are the ministry of the word, and administration of the sacraments instituted by Christ. The same rule not to be followed in judging of individuals and of churches.
10. We must on no account forsake the Church distinguished by such marks. Those who act otherwise are apostates, deserters of the truth and of the household of God, deniers of God and Christ, violators of the mystical marriage.
11. These marks to be the more carefully observed, because Satan strives to efface them, or to make us revolt from the Church. The twofold error of despising the true, and submitting to a false Church.
12. Though the common profession should contain some corruption, this is not a sufficient reason for forsaking the visible Church. Some of these corruptions specified. Caution necessary. The duty of the members.
13. The immoral lives of certain professors no ground for abandoning the Church. Error on this head of the ancient and modern Cathari. Their first objection. Answer to it from three of our Saviour's parables.
14. Second objection. Answer from a consideration of the state of the Corinthian Church, and the Churches of Galatia.
15. Third objection and answer.
16. The origin of these objections. A description of Schismatics. Their portraiture by Augustine. A pious counsel respecting these scandals, and a safe remedy against them.
17. Fourth objection and answer. Answer confirmed by the divine promises.
18. Another confirmation from the example of Christ and of the faithful servants of God. The appearance of the Church in the days of the prophets.
19. Appearance of the Church in the days of Christ and the apostles, and their immediate followers.
20. Fifth objection. Answer to the ancient and modern Cathari, and to the Novatians, concerning the forgiveness of sins.
21. Answer to the fifth objection continued. By the forgiveness of sins believers are enabled to remain perpetually in the Church.
22. The keys of the Church given for the express purpose of securing this benefit. A summary of the answer to the fifth objection.
23. Sixth objection, formerly advanced by the Novatians, and renewed by the Anabaptists. This error confuted by the Lord's Prayer.
24. A second answer, founded on some examples under the Old Testament.
25. A third answer, confirmed by passages from Jeremiah, Ezekiel, and Solomon. A fourth answer, derived from sacrifices.
26. A fifth answer, from the New Testament. Some special examples.
27. General examples. A celebrated passage. The arrangement of the Creed.
28. Objection, that voluntary transgression excludes from the Church.
29. Last objection of the Novatians, founded on the solemn renewal of repentance required by the Church for more heinous offences. Answer.

1. In the last Book, it has been shown, that by the faith of the gospel Christ becomes ours, and we are made partakers of the salvation and eternal blessedness procured by him. But as our ignorance and sloth (I may add, the vanity of our mind) stand in need of external helps, by which faith may be begotten in us, and may increase and make progress until its consummation, God, in accommodation to our infirmity, has added such helps, and secured the effectual preaching of the gospel, by depositing this treasure with the Church. He has appointed pastors and teachers, by whose lips he might edify his people (Eph. iv. 11); he has invested them with authority, and, in short, omitted nothing that might conduce to holy consent in the

faith, and to right order. In particular, he has instituted sacraments, which we feel by experience to be most useful helps in fostering and confirming our faith. For seeing we are shut up in the prison of the body, and have not yet attained to the rank of angels, God, in accommodation to our capacity, has in his admirable providence provided a method by which, though widely separated, we might still draw near to him. Wherefore, due order requires that we first treat of the Church, of its Government, Orders, and Power; next, of the Sacraments; and, lastly, of Civil Government;—at the same time guarding pious readers against the corruptions of the Papacy, by which Satan has adulterated all that God had appointed for our salvation. I will begin with the Church, into whose bosom God is pleased to collect his children, not only that by her aid and ministry they may be nourished so long as they are babes and children, but may also be guided by her maternal care until they grow up to manhood, and, finally, attain to the perfection of faith. What God has thus joined, let not man put asunder (Mark x. 9): to those to whom he is a Father, the Church must also be a mother. This was true not merely under the Law, but even now after the advent of Christ; since Paul declares that we are the children of a new, even a heavenly Jerusalem (Gal. iv. 26).

2. When in the Creed we profess to believe the Church, reference is made not only to the visible Church of which we are now treating, but also to all the elect of God, including in the number even those who have departed this life. And, accordingly, the word used is " believe," because oftentimes no difference can be observed between the children of God and the profane, between his proper flock and the untamed herd. The particle *in* is often interpolated, but without any probable ground. I confess, indeed, that it is the more usual form, and is not unsupported by antiquity, since the Nicene Creed, as quoted in Ecclesiastical History, adds the preposition. At the same time, we may perceive from early writers, that the expression received without controversy in ancient times was to believe "the Church," and not "in the Church." This is not only the expression used by Augustine, and that ancient writer, whoever he may have been, whose treatise, *De Symboli Expositione*, is extant under the name of Cyprian, but they distinctly remark that the addition of the preposition would make the expression improper, and they give good grounds for so thinking. We declare that we believe in God, both because our mind reclines upon him as true, and our confidence is fully satisfied in him. This cannot be said of the Church, just as it cannot be said of the forgiveness of sins, or the resurrection of the body. Wherefore, although I am unwilling to dispute about words, yet I would rather keep to the proper form, as better fitted to express the thing that is meant, than affect terms by which the meaning is causelessly obscured. The object of the expression is to teach us, that though the devil leaves no stone unturned in order to destroy the grace of Christ, and the enemies of God rush with insane violence in the same

direction, it cannot be extinguished,—the blood of Christ cannot be rendered barren, and prevented from producing fruit. Hence, regard must be had both to the secret election and to the internal calling of God, because he alone "knoweth them that are his" (2 Tim. ii. 19); and as Paul expresses it, holds them as it were enclosed under his seal, although, at the same time, they wear his insignia, and are thus distinguished from the reprobate. But as they are a small and despised number, concealed in an immense crowd, like a few grains of wheat buried among a heap of chaff, to God alone must be left the knowledge of his Church, of which his secret election forms the foundation. Nor is it enough to embrace the number of the elect in thought and intention merely. By the unity of the Church we must understand a unity into which we feel persuaded that we are truly ingrafted. For unless we are united with all the other members under Christ our head, no hope of the future inheritance awaits us. Hence the Church is called Catholic or Universal (August. Ep. 48), for two or three cannot be invented without dividing Christ; and this is impossible. All the elect of God are so joined together in Christ, that as they depend on one head, so they are as it were compacted into one body, being knit together like its different members; made truly one by living together under the same Spirit of God in one faith, hope, and charity, called not only to the same inheritance of eternal life, but to participation in one God and Christ. For although the sad devastation which everywhere meets our view may proclaim that no Church remains, let us know that the death of Christ produces fruit, and that God wondrously preserves his Church, while placing it as it were in concealment. Thus it was said to Elijah, "Yet I have left me seven thousand in Israel" (1 Kings xix. 18).

3. Moreover, this article of the Creed relates in some measure to the external Church, that every one of us must maintain brotherly concord with all the children of God, give due authority to the Church, and, in short, conduct ourselves as sheep of the flock. And hence the additional expression, the "communion of saints;" for this clause, though usually omitted by ancient writers, must not be overlooked, as it admirably expresses the quality of the Church; just as if it had been said, that saints are united in the fellowship of Christ on this condition, that all the blessings which God bestows upon them are mutually communicated to each other. This, however, is not incompatible with a diversity of graces, for we know that the gifts of the Spirit are variously distributed; nor is it incompatible with civil order, by which each is permitted privately to possess his own means, it being necessary for the preservation of peace among men that distinct rights of property should exist among them. Still a community is asserted, such as Luke describes when he says, "The multitude of them that believed were of one heart and of one soul" (Acts iv. 32); and Paul, when he reminds the Ephesians, "There is one body, and one Spirit, even as ye are called in one hope of your call-

ing" (Eph. iv. 4). For if they are truly persuaded that God is the common Father of them all, and Christ their common head, they cannot but be united together in brotherly love, and mutually impart their blessings to each other. Then it is of the highest importance for us to know what benefit thence redounds to us. For when we believe the Church, it is in order that we may be firmly persuaded that we are its members. In this way our salvation rests on a foundation so firm and sure, that though the whole fabric of the world were to give way, it could not be destroyed. First, it stands with the election of God, and cannot change or fail, any more than his eternal providence. Next, it is in a manner united with the stability of Christ, who will no more allow his faithful followers to be dissevered from him, than he would allow his own members to be torn to pieces. We may add, that so long as we continue in the bosom of the Church, we are sure that the truth will remain with us. Lastly, we feel that we have an interest in such promises as these, "In Mount Zion and in Jerusalem shall be deliverance" (Joel ii. 32; Obad. 17); "God is in the midst of her, she shall not be moved" (Ps. xlvi. 5). So available is communion with the Church to keep us in the fellowship of God. In the very term communion there is great consolation; because, while we are assured that everything which God bestows on his members belongs to us, all the blessings conferred upon them confirm our hope. But in order to embrace the unity of the Church in this manner, it is not necessary, as I have observed, to see it with our eyes, or feel it with our hands. Nay, rather from its being placed in faith, we are reminded that our thoughts are to dwell upon it, as much when it escapes our perception as when it openly appears. Nor is our faith the worse for apprehending what is unknown, since we are not enjoined here to distinguish between the elect and the reprobate (this belongs not to us, but to God only), but to feel firmly assured in our minds, that all those who, by the mercy of God the Father, through the efficacy of the Holy Spirit, have become partakers with Christ, are set apart as the proper and peculiar possession of God, and that as we are of the number, we are also partakers of this great grace.

4. But as it is now our purpose to discourse of the visible Church, let us learn, from her single title of Mother, how useful, nay, how necessary the knowledge of her is, since there is no other means of entering into life unless she conceive us in the womb and give us birth, unless she nourish us at her breasts, and, in short, keep us under her charge and government, until, divested of mortal flesh, we become like the angels (Matth. xxii. 30). For our weakness does not permit us to leave the school until we have spent our whole lives as scholars. Moreover, beyond the pale of the Church no forgiveness of sins, no salvation, can be hoped for, as Isaiah and Joel testify (Isa. xxxvii. 32; Joel ii. 32). To their testimony Ezekiel subscribes, when he declares, "They shall not be in the assembly of my people, neither shall they be written in the writing of the house of Israel"

(Ezek. xiii. 9); as, on the other hand, those who turn to the cultivation of true piety are said to inscribe their names among the citizens of Jerusalem. For which reason it is said in the psalm, "Remember me, O Lord, with the favour that thou bearest unto thy people: O visit me with thy salvation; that I may see the good of thy chosen, that I may rejoice in the gladness of thy nation, that I may glory with thine inheritance" (Ps. cvi. 4, 5). By these words the paternal favour of God and the special evidence of spiritual life are confined to his peculiar people, and hence the abandonment of the Church is always fatal.

5. But let us proceed to a full exposition of this view. Paul says that our Saviour "ascended far above all heavens, that he might fill all things. And he gave some, apostles; and some, prophets; and some, evangelists; and some, pastors and teachers; for the perfecting of the saints, for the work of the ministry, for the edifying of the body of Christ: till we all come in the unity of the faith, and of the knowledge of the Son of God, unto a perfect man, unto the measure of the stature of the fulness of Christ" (Eph. iv. 10–13). We see that God, who might perfect his people in a moment, chooses not to bring them to manhood in any other way than by the education of the Church. We see the mode of doing it expressed; the preaching of celestial doctrine is committed to pastors. We see that all without exception are brought into the same order, that they may with meek and docile spirit allow themselves to be governed by teachers appointed for this purpose. Isaiah had long before given this as the characteristic of the kingdom of Christ, "My Spirit that is upon thee, and my words which I have put in thy mouth, shall not depart out of thy mouth, nor out of the mouth of thy seed, nor out of the mouth of thy seed's seed, saith the Lord, from henceforth and for ever" (Isa. lix. 21). Hence it follows, that all who reject the spiritual food of the soul divinely offered to them by the hands of the Church, deserve to perish of hunger and famine. God inspires us with faith, but it is by the instrumentality of his gospel, as Paul reminds us, "Faith cometh by hearing" (Rom. x. 17). God reserves to himself the power of maintaining it, but it is by the preaching of the gospel, as Paul also declares, that he brings it forth and unfolds it. With this view, it pleased him in ancient times that sacred meetings should be held in the sanctuary, that consent in faith might be nourished by doctrine proceeding from the lips of the priest. Those magnificent titles, as when the temple is called God's rest, his sanctuary, his habitation, and when he is said to dwell between the cherubims (Ps. cxxxii. 13, 14; lxxx. 1), are used for no other purpose than to procure respect, love, reverence, and dignity to the ministry of heavenly doctrine, to which otherwise the appearance of an insignificant human being might be in no slight degree derogatory. Therefore, to teach us that the treasure offered to us in earthen vessels is of inestimable value (2 Cor. iv. 7), God himself appears and, as the author of this ordinance, requires his presence to be recognised in his own institu-

tion. Accordingly, after forbidding his people to give heed to familiar spirits, wizards, and other superstitions (Lev. xix. 30, 31), he adds, that he will give what ought to be sufficient for all—namely, that he will never leave them without prophets. For, as he did not commit his ancient people to angels, but raised up teachers on the earth to perform a truly angelical office, so he is pleased to instruct us in the present day by human means. But as anciently he did not confine himself to the law merely, but added priests as interpreters, from whose lips the people might inquire after his true meaning, so in the present day he would not only have us to be attentive to reading, but has appointed masters to give us their assistance. In this there is a twofold advantage. For, on the one hand, he by an admirable test proves our obedience when we listen to his ministers just as we would to himself; while, on the other hand, he consults our weakness in being pleased to address us after the manner of men by means of interpreters, that he may thus allure us to himself, instead of driving us away by his thunder. How well this familiar mode of teaching is suited to us all the godly are aware, from the dread with which the divine majesty justly inspires them.

Those who think that the authority of the doctrine is impaired by the insignificance of the men who are called to teach, betray their ingratitude; for among the many noble endowments with which God has adorned the human race, one of the most remarkable is, that he deigns to consecrate the mouths and tongues of men to his service, making his own voice to be heard in them. Wherefore, let us not on our part decline obediently to embrace the doctrine of salvation, delivered by his command and mouth; because, although the power of God is not confined to external means, he has, however, confined us to his ordinary method of teaching, which method, when fanatics refuse to observe, they entangle themselves in many fatal snares. Pride, or fastidiousness, or emulation, induces many to persuade themselves that they can profit sufficiently by reading and meditating in private, and thus to despise public meetings, and deem preaching superfluous. But since as much as in them lies they loose or burst the sacred bond of unity, none of them escapes the just punishment of this impious divorce, but become fascinated with pestiferous errors, and the foulest delusions. Wherefore, in order that the pure simplicity of the faith may flourish among us, let us not decline to use this exercise of piety, which God by his institution of it has shown to be necessary, and which he so highly recommends. None, even among the most petulant of men, would venture to say, that we are to shut our ears against God, but in all ages prophets and pious teachers have had a difficult contest to maintain with the ungodly, whose perverseness cannot submit to the yoke of being taught by the lips and ministry of men. This is just the same as if they were to destroy the impress of God as exhibited to us in doctrine. For no other reason were believers anciently enjoined to seek the face of God in the sanctuary (Ps. cv. 4) (an injunction so often repeated in the Law), than because the doctrine of the Law, and the exhortations of the prophets, were to them a living image of God. Thus Paul declares, that in his preaching the glory of God shone in the face of Jesus Christ (2 Cor. iv. 6). The more detestable are the apostates who delight in producing schisms in churches, just as if they wished to drive the sheep from the fold, and throw them into the jaws of wolves. Let us hold, agreeably to the passage we quoted from Paul, that the Church can only be edified by external preaching, and that there is no other bond by which the saints can be kept together than by uniting with one consent to observe the order which God has appointed in his Church for learning and making progress. For this end, especially, as I have observed, believers were anciently enjoined under the Law to flock together to the sanctuary; for when Moses speaks of the habitation of God, he at the same time calls it the place of the name of God, the place where he will record his name (Exod. xx. 24); thus plainly teaching that no use could be made of it without the doctrine of godliness. And there can be no doubt that, for the same reason, David complains with great bitterness of soul, that by the tyrannical cruelty of his enemies he was prevented from entering the tabernacle (Ps. lxxxiv.). To many the complaint seems childish, as if no great loss were sustained, not much pleasure lost, by exclusion from the temple, provided other amusements were enjoyed. David, however, laments this one deprivation, as filling him with anxiety and sadness, tormenting, and almost destroying him. This he does because there is nothing on which believers set a higher value than on this aid, by which God gradually raises his people to heaven. For it is to be observed, that he always exhibited himself to the holy patriarchs in the mirror of his doctrine in such a way as to make their knowledge spiritual. Whence the temple is not only styled his face, but also, for the purpose of removing all superstition, is termed his footstool (Ps. cxxxii. 7; xcix. 5). Herein is the unity of the faith happily realised, when all, from the highest to the lowest, aspire to the head. All the temples which the Gentiles built to God with a different intention were a mere profanation of his worship,—a profanation into which the Jews also fell, though not with equal grossness. With this Stephen upbraids them in the words of Isaiah when he says, "Howbeit the Most High dwelleth not in temples made with hands; as saith the Prophet, Heaven is my throne," &c. (Acts vii. 48). For God only consecrates temples to their legitimate use by his word. And when we rashly attempt anything without his order, immediately setting out from a bad principle, we introduce adventitious fictions, by which evil is propagated without measure. It was inconsiderate in Xerxes when, by the advice of the magians, he burnt or pulled down all the temples of Greece, because he thought it absurd that God, to whom all things ought to be free and open, should be enclosed by walls and roofs, as if it were not in the power of God in a manner to descend to us, that he may be near to us, and yet neither change his place nor affect us by earthly means, but rather, by a kind of vehicles, raise us aloft to his own heavenly glory, which, with its immensity, fills all things, and in height is above the heavens.

6. Moreover, as at this time there is a great dispute as to the efficacy of the ministry, some extravagantly overrating its dignity, and others erroneously maintaining, that what is peculiar to the Spirit of God is transferred to mortal man, when we suppose that ministers and teachers penetrate to the mind and heart, so as to correct the blindness of the one, and the hardness of the other ; it is necessary to place this controversy on its proper footing. The arguments on both sides will be disposed of without trouble, by distinctly attending to the passages in which God, the author of preaching, connects his Spirit with it, and then promises a beneficial result ; or, on the other hand, to the passages in which God, separating himself from external means, claims for himself alone both the commencement and the whole course of faith. The office of the second Elias was, as Malachi declares, to "turn the heart of the fathers to the children, and the heart of the children to their fathers" (Mal. iv. 6). Christ declares that he sent the Apostles to produce fruit from his labours (John xv. 16). What this fruit is Peter briefly defines, when he says that we are begotten again of incorruptible seed (1 Pet. i. 23). Hence Paul glories, that by means of the Gospel he had begotten the Corinthians, who were the seals of his apostleship (1 Cor. iv. 15); moreover, that his was not a ministry of the letter, which only sounded in the ear, but that the effectual agency of the Spirit was given to him, in order that his doctrine might not be in vain (1 Cor. ix. 2 ; 2 Cor. iii. 6). In this sense he elsewhere declares that his Gospel was not in word, but in power (1 Thess. i. 5). He also affirms that the Galatians received the Spirit by the hearing of faith (Gal. iii. 2). In short, in several passages he not only makes himself a fellow-worker with God, but attributes to himself the province of bestowing salvation (1 Cor. iii. 9). All these things he certainly never uttered with the view of attributing to himself one iota apart from God, as he elsewhere briefly explains. "For this cause also thank we God without ceasing, because, when ye received the word of God which ye heard of us, ye received it not as the word of men, but (as it is in truth) the word of God, which effectually worketh also in you that believe" (1 Thess. ii. 13). Again, in another place, " He that wrought effectually in Peter to the apostleship of the circumcision, the same was mighty in me toward the Gentiles" (Gal. ii. 8). And that he allows no more to ministers is obvious from other passages. " So then neither is he that planteth anything, neither he that watereth ; but God that giveth the increase" (1 Cor. iii. 7). Again, " I laboured more abundantly than they all : yet not I, but the grace of God which was with me" (1 Cor. xv. 10). And it is indeed necessary to keep these sentences in view, since God, in ascribing to himself the illumination of the mind and renewal of the heart, reminds us that it is sacrilege for man to claim any part of either to himself. Still every one who listens with docility to the ministers whom God appoints, will know by the beneficial result, that for good reason God is pleased with this method of teaching, and for good reason has laid believers under this modest yoke.

7. The judgment which ought to be formed concerning the visible Church which comes under our observation, must, I think, be sufficiently clear from what has been said. I have observed that the Scriptures speak of the Church in two ways. Sometimes when they speak of the Church they mean the Church as it really is before God—the Church into which none are admitted but those who by the gift of adoption are sons of God, and by the sanctification of the Spirit true members of Christ. In this case it not only comprehends the saints who dwell on the earth, but all the elect who have existed from the beginning of the world. Often, too, by the name of Church is designated the whole body of mankind scattered throughout the world, who profess to worship one God and Christ, who by baptism are initiated into the faith; by partaking of the Lord's Supper profess unity in true doctrine and charity, agree in holding the word of the Lord, and observe the ministry which Christ has appointed for the preaching of it. In this Church there is a very large mixture of hypocrites, who have nothing of Christ but the name and outward appearance: of ambitious, avaricious, envious, evil-speaking men, some also of impurer lives, who are tolerated for a time, either because their guilt cannot be legally established, or because due strictness of discipline is not always observed. Hence, as it is necessary to believe the invisible Church, which is manifest to the eye of God only, so we are also enjoined to regard this Church which is so called with reference to man, and to cultivate its communion.

8. Accordingly, inasmuch as it was of importance to us to recognise it, the Lord has distinguished it by certain marks, and as it were symbols. It is, indeed, the special prerogative of God to know those who are his, as Paul declares in the passage already quoted (2 Tim. ii. 19). And doubtless it has been so provided as a check on human rashness, the experience of every day reminding us how far his secret judgments surpass our apprehension. For even those who seemed most abandoned, and who had been completely despaired of, are by his goodness recalled to life, while those who seemed most stable often fall. Hence, as Augustine says, " In regard to the secret predestination of God, there are very many sheep without, and very many wolves within" (August. Hom. in Joan. 45). For he knows, and has his mark on those who know neither him nor themselves. Of those again who openly bear his badge, his eyes alone see who of them are unfeignedly holy, and will persevere even to the end, which alone is the completion of salvation. On the other hand, foreseeing that it was in some degree expedient for us to know who are to be regarded by us as his sons, he has in this matter accommodated himself to our capacity. But as here full certainty was not necessary, he has in its place substituted the judgment of charity, by which we acknowledge all as members of the Church who by confession of faith,

regularity of conduct, and participation in the sacraments, unite with us in acknowledging the same God and Christ. The knowledge of his body, inasmuch as he knew it to be more necessary for our salvation, he has made known to us by surer marks.

9. Hence the form of the Church appears and stands forth conspicuous to our view. Wherever we see the word of God sincerely preached and heard, wherever we see the sacraments administered according to the institution of Christ, there we cannot have any doubt that the Church of God has some existence, since his promise cannot fail, "Where two or three are gathered together in my name, there am I in the midst of them" (Matth. xviii. 20). But that we may have a clear summary of this subject, we must proceed by the following steps:—The Church universal is the multitude collected out of all nations, who, though dispersed and far distant from each other, agree in one truth of divine doctrine, and are bound together by the tie of a common religion. In this way it comprehends single churches, which exist in different towns and villages, according to the wants of human society, so that each of them justly obtains the name and authority of the Church; and also comprehends single individuals, who by a religious profession are accounted to belong to such churches, although they are in fact aliens from the Church, but have not been cut off by a public decision. There is, however, a slight difference in the mode of judging of individuals and of churches. For it may happen in practice that those whom we deem not altogether worthy of the fellowship of believers, we yet ought to treat as brethren, and regard as believers, on account of the common consent of the Church in tolerating and bearing with them in the body of Christ. Such persons we do not approve by our suffrage as members of the Church, but we leave them the place which they hold among the people of God, until they are legitimately deprived of it. With regard to the general body we must feel differently; if they have the ministry of the word, and honour the administration of the sacraments, they are undoubtedly entitled to be ranked with the Church, because it is certain that these things are not without a beneficial result. Thus we both maintain the Church universal in its unity, which malignant minds .have always been eager to dissever, and deny not due authority to lawful assemblies distributed as circumstances require.

10. We have said that the symbols by which the Church is discerned are the preaching of the word and the observance of the sacraments, for these cannot anywhere exist without producing fruit and prospering by the blessing of God. I say not that wherever the word is preached fruit immediately appears; but that in every place where it is received, and has a fixed abode, it uniformly displays its efficacy. Be this as it may, when the preaching of the gospel is reverently heard, and the sacraments are not neglected, there for the time the face of the Church appears without deception or ambiguity

and no man may with impunity spurn her authority, or reject her admonitions, or resist her counsels, or make sport of her censures, far less revolt from her, and violate her unity (see Chap. II. sec. 1, 10, and Chap. VIII. sec. 12). For such is the value which the Lord sets on the communion of his Church, that all who contumaciously alienate themselves from any Christian society, in which the true ministry of his word and sacraments is maintained, he regards as deserters of religion. So highly does he recommend her authority, that when it is violated he considers that his own authority is impaired. For there is no small weight in the designation given to her, "the house of God," "the pillar and ground of the truth" (1 Tim. iii. 15). By these words Paul intimates, that to prevent the truth from perishing in the world, the Church is its faithful guardian, because God has been pleased to preserve the pure preaching of his word by her instrumentality, and to exhibit himself to us as a parent while he feeds us with spiritual nourishment, and provides whatever is conducive to our salvation. Moreover, no mean praise is conferred on the Church when she is said to have been chosen and set apart by Christ as his spouse, "not having spot or wrinkle, or any such thing" (Eph. v. 27), as "his body, the fulness of him that filleth all in all" (Eph. i. 23). Whence it follows, that revolt from the Church is denial of God and Christ. Wherefore there is the more necessity to beware of a dissent so iniquitous; for seeing by it we aim as far as in us lies at the destruction of God's truth, we deserve to be crushed by the full thunder of his anger. No crime can be imagined more atrocious than that of sacrilegiously and perfidiously violating the sacred marriage which the only begotten Son of God has condescended to contract with us.

11. Wherefore let these marks be carefully impressed upon our minds, and let us estimate them as in the sight of the Lord. There is nothing on which Satan is more intent than to destroy and efface one or both of them—at one time to delete and abolish these marks, and thereby destroy the true and genuine distinction of the Church; at another, to bring them into contempt, and so hurry us into open revolt from the Church. To his wiles it was owing that for several ages the pure preaching of the word disappeared, and now, with the same dishonest aim, he labours to overthrow the ministry, which, however, Christ has so ordered in his Church, that if it is removed the whole edifice must fall. How perilous, then, nay, how fatal the temptation, when we even entertain a thought of separating ourselves from that assembly in which are beheld the signs and badges which the Lord has deemed sufficient to characterise his Church! We see how great caution should be employed in both respects. That we may not be imposed upon by the name of Church, every congregation which claims the name must be brought to that test as to a Lydian stone. If it holds the order instituted by the Lord in word and sacraments there will be no deception; we may safely pay it the honour due to a church: on the other hand, if it exhibit itself with-

out word and sacraments, we must in this case be no less careful to avoid the imposture than we were to shun pride and presumption in the other.

12. When we say that the pure ministry of the word and pure celebration of the sacraments is a fit pledge and earnest, so that we may safely recognise a church in every society in which both exist, our meaning is, that we are never to discard it so long as these remain, though it may otherwise teem with numerous· faults. Nay, even in the administration of word and sacraments defects may creep in which ought not to alienate us from its communion. For all the heads of true doctrine are not in the same position. Some are so necessary to be known, that all must hold them to be fixed and undoubted as the proper essentials of religion : for instance, that God is one, that Christ is God, and the Son of God, that our salvation depends on the mercy of God, and the like. Others, again, which are the subject of controversy among the churches, do not destroy the unity of the faith ; for why should it be regarded as a ground of dissension between churches, if one, without any spirit of contention or perverseness in dogmatising, hold that the soul on quitting the body flies to heaven, and another, without venturing to speak positively as to the abode, holds it for certain that it lives with the Lord ?[1] The words of the Apostle are, " Let us therefore, as many as be perfect, be thus minded: and if in anything ye be otherwise minded, God shall reveal even this unto you" (Phil. iii. 15). Does he not sufficiently intimate that a difference of opinion as to these matters which are not absolutely necessary, ought not to be a ground of dissension among Christians ? The best thing, indeed, is to be perfectly agreed, but seeing there is no man who is not involved in some mist of ignorance, we must either have no church at all, or pardon delusion in those things of which one may be ignorant, without violating the substance of religion and forfeiting salvation. Here, however, I have no wish to patronise even the minutest errors, as if I thought it right to foster them by flattery or connivance ; what I say is, that we are not on account of every minute difference to abandon a church, provided it retain sound and unimpaired that doctrine in which the safety of piety consists,[2] and keep the use of the sacraments instituted by the Lord. Meanwhile, if we strive to reform what is offensive, we act in the discharge of duty. To this effect are the words of Paul, " If anything be revealed to another that sitteth by, let the first hold his peace" (1 Cor.

French, " Pour donner exemple, s'il advenoit qu'une Eglise tint que les ames etant separées des corps fussent transferés au ciel incontinent : une autre, sans oser determiner du lieu pensât semplement qu'elles vivent en Dieu; et que telle diversité fut sans contention et sans opiniatreté pourquoy se diviseroient elles d'ensemble?"—To give an example, should one church happen to hold that the soul when separated from the body is forthwith transported to heaven, and should another, without venturing to determine the place, simply think that it lives in God, and should such diversity be without contention and obstinacy, why should they be divided?

2 French, " La doctrine principale de nostre salut;"—the fundamental doctrine of our salvation.

xiv. 30).   From this it is evident that to each member of the Church, according to his measure of grace, the study of public edification has been assigned, provided it be done decently and in order.   In other words, we must neither renounce the communion of the Church, nor, continuing in it, disturb peace and discipline when duly arranged.[1]

13. Our indulgence ought to extend much farther in tolerating imperfection of conduct.   Here there is great danger of falling, and Satan employs all his machinations to ensnare us.   For there always have been persons who, imbued with a false persuasion of absolute holiness, as if they had already become a kind of aërial spirits,[2] spurn the society of all in whom they see that something human still remains.   Such of old were the Cathari and the Donatists, who were similarly infatuated.   Such in the present day are some of the Anabaptists, who would be thought to have made superior progress.   Others, again, sin in this respect, not so much from that insane pride as from inconsiderate zeal.   Seeing that among those to whom the gospel is preached, the fruit produced is not in accordance with the doctrine, they forthwith conclude that there no church exists.   The offence is indeed well founded, and it is one to which in this most unhappy age we give far too much occasion.   It is impossible to excuse our accursed sluggishness, which the Lord will not leave unpunished, as he is already beginning sharply to chastise us.   Woe then to us who, by our dissolute licence of wickedness, cause weak consciences to be wounded !   Still those of whom we have spoken sin intheir turn, by not knowing how to set bounds to their offence.   For where the Lord requires mercy they omit it, and give themselves up to immoderate severity.   Thinking there is no church where there is not complete purity and integrity of conduct, they, through hatred of wickedness, withdraw from a genuine church, while they think they are shunning the company of the ungodly.   They allege that the Church of God is holy.   But that they may at the same time understand that it contains a mixture of good and bad, let them hear from the lips of our Saviour that parable in which he compares the Church to a net in which all kinds of fishes are taken, but not separated until they are brought ashore.   Let them hear it compared to a field which, planted with good seed, is by the fraud of an enemy mingled with tares, and is not freed of them until the harvest is brought into the barn.   Let them hear, in fine, that it is a thrashing-floor in which the collected wheat lies concealed under the chaff, until, cleansed by the fanners and the sieve, it is at length laid up in the granary.   If the Lord declares that the Church will labour under the defect of being burdened with a multitude of wicked until the day of judgment, it is in vain to look for a church altogether free from blemish (Matth. xiii.).

1 French, " Et aussi que demeurant en icelle nous ne troublions point la police ni la discipline ; "—and also that, remaining in it, we disturb not its order and discipline.
2 French, " Comme s'ils eussent ete quelques anges de Paradis ; "—as if they had bean some angels of Paradise.

14. They exclaim that it is impossible to tolerate the vice which everywhere stalks abroad like a pestilence. What if the apostle's sentiment applies here also? Among the Corinthians it was not a few that erred, but almost the whole body had become tainted; there was not one species of sin merely, but a multitude, and those not trivial errors, but some of them execrable crimes. There was not only corruption in manners, but also in doctrine. What course was taken by the holy apostle, in other words, by the organ of the heavenly Spirit, by whose testimony the Church stands and falls? Does he seek separation from them? Does he discard them from the kingdom of Christ? Does he strike them with the thunder of a final anathema? He not only does none of these things, but he acknowledges and heralds them as a Church of Christ, and a society of saints. If the Church remains among the Corinthians, where envyings, divisions, and contentions rage; where quarrels, lawsuits, and avarice prevail; where a crime, which even the Gentiles would execrate, is openly approved; where the name of Paul, whom they ought to have honoured as a father, is petulantly assailed; where some hold the resurrection of the dead in derision, though with it the whole gospel must fall; where the gifts of God are made subservient to ambition, not to charity; where many things are done neither decently nor in order:[1] If there the Church still remains, simply because the ministration of word and sacrament is not rejected, who will presume to deny the title of church to those to whom a tenth part of these crimes cannot be imputed? How, I ask, would those who act so morosely against present churches have acted to the Galatians, who had done all but abandon the gospel (Gal. i. 6), and yet among them the same apostle found churches?[2]

15. They also object, that Paul sharply rebukes the Corinthians for permitting an heinous offender in their communion, and then lays down a general sentence, by which he declares it unlawful even to eat bread with a man of impure life (1 Cor. v. 11, 12). Here they exclaim, If it is not lawful to eat ordinary bread, how can it be lawful to eat the Lord's bread? I admit, that it is a great disgrace if dogs and swine are admitted among the children of God; much more, if the sacred body of Christ is prostituted to them. And, indeed, when churches are well regulated, they will not bear the wicked in their bosom, nor will they admit the worthy and unworthy indiscriminately to that sacred feast. But because pastors are not always sedulously vigilant, are sometimes also more indulgent than they ought, or are prevented from acting so strictly as they could wish; the consequence is, that even the openly wicked are not always excluded from the fellowship of the saints. This I admit to be a vice, and I have no wish to extenuate it, seeing that Paul sharply rebukes it in the Corinthians. But although the Church fail in her

1 1 Cor. i. 11; iii. 3; v. 1; vi. 7; ix. 1; xv. 12.
2 French, " Toutesfois Sainct Paul recognoissoit entre eux quelque Eglise;"—yet St Paul recognised some church among them.

duty, it does not therefore follow that every private individual is to decide the question of separation for himself. I deny not that it is the duty of a pious man to withdraw from all private intercourse with the wicked, and not entangle himself with them by any voluntary tie ; but it is one thing to shun the society of the wicked, and another to renounce the communion of the Church through hatred of them. Those who think it sacrilege to partake the Lord's bread with the wicked, are in this more rigid than Paul.[1] For when he exhorts us to pure and holy communion, he does not require that we should examine others, or that every one should examine the whole church, but that each should examine himself (1 Cor. xi. 28, 29). If it were unlawful to communicate with the unworthy, Paul would certainly have ordered us to take heed that there were no individual in the whole body by whose impurity we might be defiled, but now that he only requires each to examine himself, he shows that it does no harm to us though some who are unworthy present themselves along with us. To the same effect he afterwards adds, " He that eateth and drinketh unworthily, eateth and drinketh damnation to himself." He says not *to others*, but *to himself*. And justly ; for the right of admitting or excluding ought not to be left to the decision of individuals. Cognisance of this point, which cannot be exercised without due order, as shall afterwards be more fully shown, belongs to the whole church. It would therefore be unjust to hold any private individual as polluted by the unworthiness of another, whom he neither can nor ought to keep back from communion.

16. Still, however, even the good are sometimes affected by this inconsiderate zeal for righteousness, though we shall find that this excessive moroseness is more the result of pride and a false idea of sanctity, than genuine sanctity itself, and true zeal for it. Accordingly, those who are the most forward, and, as it were, leaders in producing revolt from the Church, have, for the most part, no other motive than to display their own superiority by despising all other men. Well and wisely, therefore, does Augustine say, " Seeing that pious reason and the mode of ecclesiastical discipline ought specially to regard the unity of the Spirit in the bond of peace, which the Apostle enjoins us to keep, by bearing with one another (for if we keep it not, the application of medicine is not only superfluous, but pernicious, and therefore proves to be no medicine); those bad sons who, not from hatred of other men's iniquities, but zeal for their own contentions, attempt altogether to draw away, or at least to divide, weak brethren ensnared by the glare of their name, while swollen with pride, stuffed with petulance, insidiously calumnious, and turbulently seditious, use the cloak of a rigorous severity, that they may not seem devoid of the light of truth, and pervert to sacrilegious schism, and purposes of excision, those things which are enjoined in the Holy Scriptures (due regard being had to sincere love, and the

1 See Calvin, Lib. de Cœna Domini ; item, Instructio adv. Anabapt.

unity of peace), to correct a brother's faults by the appliance of a moderate cure" (August. Cont. Parmen. cap. i.). To the pious and placid his advice is, mercifully to correct what they can, and to bear patiently with what they cannot correct, in love lamenting and mourning until God either reform or correct, or at the harvest root up the tares, and scatter the chaff (Ibid. cap. ii.). Let all the godly study to provide themselves with these weapons, lest, while they deem themselves strenuous and ardent defenders of righteousness, they revolt from the kingdom of heaven, which is the only kingdom of righteousness. For as God has been pleased that the communion of his Church shall be maintained in this external society, any one who, from hatred of the ungodly, violates the bond of this society, enters on a downward course, in which he incurs great danger of cutting himself off from the communion of saints. Let them reflect, that in a numerous body there are several who may escape their notice, and yet are truly righteous and innocent in the eyes of the Lord. Let them reflect, that of those who seem diseased, there are many who are far from taking pleasure or flattering themselves in their faults, and who, ever and anon aroused by a serious fear of the Lord, aspire to greater integrity. Let them reflect, that they have no right to pass judgment on a man for one act, since the holiest sometimes make the most grievous fall. Let them reflect, that in the ministry of the word and participation of the sacraments, the power to collect the Church is too great to be deprived of all its efficacy, by the fault of some ungodly men. Lastly, let them reflect, that in estimating the Church, divine is of more force than human judgment.

17. Since they also argue that there is good reason for the Church being called holy, it is necessary to consider what the holiness is in which it excels, lest by refusing to acknowledge any church, save one that is completely perfect, we leave no church at all. It is true, indeed, as Paul says, that Christ "loved the church, and gave himself for it, that he might sanctify and cleanse it with the washing of water by the word, that he might present it to himself a glorious church, not having spot, or wrinkle, or any such thing; but that it should be holy and without blemish" (Eph. v. 25–27). Nevertheless, it is true, that the Lord is daily smoothing its wrinkles, and wiping away its spots. Hence it follows, that its holiness is not yet perfect. Such, then, is the holiness of the Church: it makes daily progress, but is not yet perfect; it daily advances, but as yet has not reached the goal, as will elsewhere be more fully explained. Therefore, when the Prophets foretel, "Then shall Jerusalem be holy, and there shall no strangers pass through her any more;"—"It shall be called, The way of holiness; the unclean shall not pass over it" (Joel iii. 17; Isa. xxxv. 8), let us not understand it as if no blemish remained in the members of the Church: but only that with there whole heart they aspire after holiness and perfect purity: and hence, that purity which they have not yet fully attained is, by the kindness of God, attributed to them. And though the indications of such a kind of holiness existing among men

are too rare, we must understand, that at no period since the world began has the Lord been without his Church, nor ever shall be till the final consummation of all things. For although, at the very outset, the whole human race was vitiated and corrupted by the sin of Adam, yet of this kind of polluted mass he always sanctifies some vessels to honour, that no age may be left without experience of his mercy. This he has declared by sure promises, such as the following: "I have made a covenant with my chosen, I have sworn unto David my servant, Thy seed will I establish for ever, and build up thy throne to all generations" (Ps. lxxxix. 3, 4). "The Lord hath chosen Zion; he hath desired it for his habitation. This is my rest for ever; here will I dwell" (Ps. cxxxii. 13, 14). Thus saith the Lord, which giveth the sun for a light by day, and the ordinances of the moon and of the stars for a light by night, which divideth the sea when the waves thereof roar; The Lord of hosts is his name: If those ordinances depart from before me, saith the Lord, then the seed of Israel also shall cease from being a nation before me for ever" (Jer. xxxi. 35, 36).

18. On this head, Christ himself, his apostles, and almost all the prophets, have furnished us with examples. Fearful are the descriptions in which Isaiah, Jeremiah, Joel, Habakkuk, and others, deplore the diseases of the Church of Jerusalem. In the people, the rulers, and the priests, corruption prevailed to such a degree, that Isaiah hesitates not to liken Jerusalem to Sodom and Gomorrah (Isa. i. 10). Religion was partly despised, partly adulterated, while in regard to morals, we everywhere meet with accounts of theft, robbery, perfidy, murder, and similar crimes. The prophets, however, did not therefore either form new churches for themselves, or erect new altars on which they might have separate sacrifices, but whatever their countrymen might be, reflecting that the Lord had deposited his word with them, and instituted the ceremonies by which he was then worshipped, they stretched out pure hands to him, though amid the company of the ungodly. Certainly, had they thought that they thereby contracted any pollution, they would have died a hundred deaths sooner than suffered themselves to be dragged thither. Nothing, therefore, prevented them from separating themselves, but a desire of preserving unity. But if the holy prophets felt no obligation to withdraw from the Church on account of the very numerous and heinous crimes, not of one or two individuals, but almost of the whole people, we arrogate too much to ourselves, if we presume forthwith to withdraw from the communion of the Church, because the lives of all accord not with our judgment, or even with the Christian profession.

19. Then what kind of age was that of Christ and the apostles? Yet neither could the desperate impiety of the Pharisees, nor the dissolute licentiousness of manners which everywhere prevailed, prevent them from using the same sacred rites with the people, and meeting in one common temple for the public exercises of religion. And why so, but just because they knew that those who joined in

these sacred rites with a pure conscience were not at all polluted by the society of the wicked? If any one is little moved by prophets and apostles, let him at least defer to the authority of Christ. Well, therefore, does Cyprian say, "Although tares or unclean vessels are seen in the Church, that is no reason why we ourselves should withdraw from the Church; we must only labour that we may be able to be wheat; we must give our endeavour, and strive as far as we can, to be vessels of gold or silver. But to break the earthen vessels belongs to the Lord alone, to whom a rod of iron has been given: let no one arrogate to himself what is peculiar to the Son alone, and think himself sufficient to winnow the floor and cleanse the chaff, and separate all the tares by human judgment. What depraved zeal thus assumes to itself is proud obstinacy and sacrilegious presumption" (Cyprian, Lib. iii. Ep. v). Let both points, therefore, be regarded as fixed; *first*, that there is no excuse for him who spontaneously abandons the external communion of a church in which the word of God is preached and the sacraments are administered; *secondly*, that notwithstanding of the faults of a few or of many, there is nothing to prevent us from there duly professing our faith in the ordinances instituted by God, because a pious conscience is not injured by the unworthiness of another, whether he be a pastor or a private individual; and sacred rites are not less pure and salutary to a man who is holy and upright, from being at the same time handled by the impure.

20. Their moroseness and pride proceed even to greater lengths. Refusing to acknowledge any church that is not pure from the minutest blemish, they take offence at sound teachers for exhorting believers to make progress, and so teaching them to groan during their whole lives under the burden of sin, and flee for pardon. For they pretend[1] that in this way believers are led away from perfection. I admit that we are not to labour feebly or coldly in urging perfection, far less to desist from urging it; but I hold that it is a device of the devil to fill our minds with a confident belief of it while we are still in our course. Accordingly, in the Creed forgiveness of sins is appropriately subjoined to belief as to the Church, because none obtain forgiveness but those who are citizens, and of the household of the Church, as we read in the Prophet (Is. xxxiii. 24). The first place, therefore, should be given to the building of the heavenly Jerusalem, in which God afterwards is pleased to wipe away the iniquity of all who betake themselves to it. I say, however, that the Church must first be built; not that there can be any church without forgiveness of sins, but because the Lord has not promised his mercy save in the communion of saints. Therefore, our first entrance into the Church and the kingdom of God is by forgiveness of sins, without which we have no covenant nor union with God. For thus he speaks by the Prophet, "In that day will I make a covenant for them

---

1 Latin, "Jactant."—French, "Ces grands correcteurs leur reprochent;"—those great reformers upbraid them.

with the beasts of the field, and with the fowls of heaven, and with the creeping things of the ground: and I will break the bow, and the sword, and the battle, out of the earth, and will make them to lie down safely. And I will betroth thee unto me for ever; yea, I will betroth thee unto me in righteousness, and in judgment, and in loving-kindness, and in mercies" (Hos. ii. 18, 19). We see in what way the Lord reconciles us to himself by his mercy. So in another passage, where he foretells that the people whom he had scattered in anger will again be gathered together, " I will cleanse them from all their iniquity, whereby they have sinned against me" (Jer. xxxiii. 8). Wherefore, our initiation into the fellowship of the Church is, by the symbol of ablution, to teach us that we have no admission into the family of God, unless by his goodness our impurities are previously washed away.

21. Nor by remission of sins does the Lord only once for all elect and admit us into the Church, but by the same means he preserves and defends us in it. For what would it avail us to receive a pardon of which we were afterwards to have no use? That the mercy of the Lord would be vain and delusive if only granted once, all the godly can bear witness; for there is none who is not conscious, during his whole life, of many infirmities which stand in need of divine mercy. And truly it is not without cause that the Lord promises this gift specially to his own household, nor in vain that he orders the same message of reconciliation to be daily delivered to them. Wherefore, as during our whole lives we carry about with us the remains of sin, we could not continue in the Church one single moment were we not sustained by the uninterrupted grace of God in forgiving our sins. On the other hand, the Lord has called his people to eternal salvation, and therefore they ought to consider that pardon for their sins is always ready. Hence let us surely hold that if we are admitted and ingrafted into the body of the Church, the forgiveness of sins has been bestowed, and is daily bestowed on us, in divine liberality, through the intervention of Christ's merits, and the sanctification of the Spirit.

22. To impart this blessing to us, the keys have been given to the Church (Matth. xvi. 19; xviii. 18). For when Christ gave the command to the apostles, and conferred the power of forgiving sins, he not merely intended that they should loose the sins of those who should be converted from impiety to the faith of Christ;[1] but, moreover, that they should perpetually perform this office among believers. This Paul teaches, when he says that the embassy of reconciliation has been committed to the ministers of the Church, that they may ever and anon in the name of Christ exhort the people to be reconciled to God (2 Cor. v. 20). Therefore, in the communion of saints

---

[1] French, " Ce n'a pas été seulement afin qu'ils deliassent ceux qui si convertiroient alla foy Christienne, et qu'ils fissent cela pour une fois."—It was not only that they might loose those who should be converted to the Christian faith, and that they should do so once for all.

our sins are constantly forgiven by the ministry of the Church, when presbyters or bishops, to whom the office has been committed, confirm pious consciences, in the hope of pardon and forgiveness by the promises of the gospel, and that as well in public as in private, as the case requires. For there are many who, from their infirmity, stand in need of special pacification, and Paul declares that he testified of the grace of Christ not only in the public assembly, but from house to house, reminding each individually of the doctrine of salvation (Acts xx. 20, 21). Three things are here to be observed. First, Whatever be the holiness which the children of God possess, it is always under the condition, that so long as they dwell in a mortal body, they cannot stand before God without forgiveness of sins. Secondly, This benefit is so peculiar to the Church, that we cannot enjoy it unless we continue in the communion of the Church. Thirdly, It is dispensed to us by the ministers and pastors of the Church, either in the preaching of the Gospel or the administration of the Sacraments, and herein is especially manifested the power of the keys, which the Lord has bestowed on the company of the faithful. Accordingly, let each of us consider it to be his duty to seek forgiveness of sins only where the Lord has placed it. Of the public reconciliation which relates to discipline, we shall speak at the proper place.

23. But since those frantic spirits of whom I have spoken attempt to rob the Church of this the only anchor of salvation, consciences must be more firmly strengthened against this pestilential opinion. The Novatians, in ancient times, agitated the Churches with this dogma, but in our day, not unlike the Novatians are some of the Anabaptists, who have fallen into the same delirious dreams. For they pretend that in baptism, the people of God are regenerated to a pure and angelical life, which is not polluted by any carnal defilements. But if a man sin after baptism, they leave him nothing except the inexorable judgment of God. In short, to the sinner who has lapsed after receiving grace they give no hope of pardon, because they admit no other forgiveness of sins save that by which we are first regenerated. But although no falsehood is more clearly refuted by Scripture, yet as these men find means of imposition (as Novatus also of old had very many followers), let us briefly show how much they rave, to the destruction both of themselves and others. In the first place, since by the command of our Lord the saints daily repeat this prayer, " Forgive us our debts" (Matth. vi. 12), they confess that they are debtors. Nor do they ask in vain ; for the Lord has only enjoined them to ask what he will give. Nay, while he has declared that the whole prayer will be heard by his Father, he has sealed this absolution with a peculiar promise. What more do we wish ? The Lord requires of his saints confession of sins during their whole lives, and that without ceasing, and promises pardon. How presumptuous, then, to exempt them from sin, or when they have stumbled, to exclude them altogether from grace ? Then whom does he enjoin us to pardon seventy and seven times ? Is it not our brethren ? (Matth.

xviii. 22.)   And why has he so enjoined but that we may imitate his clemency ?   He therefore pardons not once or twice only, but as often as, under a sense of our faults, we feel alarmed, and sighing call upon him.

24. And to begin almost with the very first commencement of the Church : the Patriarchs had been circumcised, admitted to a participation in the covenant, and doubtless instructed by their father's care in righteousness and integrity, when they conspired to commit fratricide.   The crime was one which the most abandoned robbers would have abominated.[1]   At length, softened by the remonstrances of Judah, they sold him ; this also was intolerable cruelty.   Simeon and Levi took a nefarious revenge on the sons of Sychem, one, too, condemned by the judgment of their father.   Reuben, with execrable lust, defiled his father's bed.   Judah, when seeking to commit whoredom, sinned against the law of nature with his daughter-in-law.   But so far are they from being expunged from the chosen people, that they are rather raised to be its heads.   What, moreover, of David ? when on the throne of righteousness, with what iniquity did he make way for blind lust, by the shedding of innocent blood ?   He had already been regenerated, and, as one of the regenerated, received distinguished approbation from the Lord.   But he perpetrated a crime at which even the Gentiles would have been horrified, and yet obtained pardon.   And not to dwell on special examples, all the promises of divine mercy extant in the Law and the Prophets are so many proofs that the Lord is ready to forgive the offences of his people.   For why does Moses promise a future period, when the people who had fallen into rebellion should return to the Lord ? " Then the Lord thy God will turn thy captivity, and have compassion upon thee, and will return and gather thee from all the nations whither the Lord thy God hath scattered thee" (Deut. xxx. 3).

25. But I am unwilling to begin an enumeration which never could be finished.   The prophetical books are filled with similar promises, offering mercy to a people covered with innumerable transgressions.   What crime is more heinous than rebellion ?   It is styled divorce between God and the Church, and yet, by his goodness, it is surmounted.   They say, " If a man put away his wife, and she go from him, and become another man's, shall he return unto her again ? shall not that land be greatly polluted ?   But thou hast played the harlot with many lovers ; yet return again unto me, saith the Lord." " Return, thou backsliding Israel, saith the Lord ; and I will not cause mine anger to fall upon you ; for I am merciful, saith the Lord, and I will not keep anger for ever" (Jer. iii. 1, 12).   And surely he could not have a different feeling who declares, " I have no pleasure in the death of him that dieth ;" " Wherefore turn yourselves, and live ye" (Ezek. xviii. 23, 32).   Accordingly, when Solomon dedicated the temple, one of the uses for which it was destined was, that prayers

---

[1] Gen. xxxvii. 18, 28 ; xxxiv. 25 ; xxxv. 22 ; xxxviii. 16 ; 2 Sam xi. 4, 15 ; xii 13.

offered up for the pardon of sins might there be heard. " If they sin against thee (for there is no man that sinneth not), and thou be angry with them, and deliver them to the enemy, so that they carry them away captive unto the land of the enemy, far or near ; yet if they shall bethink themselves in the land whither they were carried captives, and repent, and make supplication unto thee in the land of them that carried them captives, saying, We have sinned, and have done perversely, we have committed wickedness ; and so return unto thee with all their heart, and with all their soul, in the land of their enemies which led them away captive, and pray unto thee towards their land, which thou gavest unto their fathers, the city which thou hast chosen, and the house which I have built for thy name : then hear thou their prayer and their supplication in heaven thy dwelling-place, and maintain their cause, and forgive thy people that have sinned against thee, and all their transgressions wherein they have transgressed against thee " (1 Kings viii. 46-50). Nor in vain in the Law did God ordain a daily sacrifice for sins. Had he not foreseen that his people were constantly to labour under the disease of sin, he never would have appointed these remedies.

26. Did the advent of Christ, by which the fulness of grace was displayed, deprive believers of this privilege of supplicating for the pardon of their sins ? If they offended against the Lord, were they not to obtain any mercy ? What were it but to say that Christ came not for the salvation, but for the destruction of his people, if the divine indulgence in pardoning sin, which was constantly provided for the saints under the Old Testament, is now declared to have been taken away ? But if we give credit to the Scriptures, when distinctly proclaiming that in Christ alone the grace and loving-kindness of the Lord have fully appeared, the riches of his mercy been poured out, reconciliation between God and man accomplished (Tit. ii. 11 ; iii. 4 ; 2 Tim. i. 9, 10), let us not doubt that the clemency of our heavenly Father, instead of being cut off or curtailed, is in much greater exuberance. Nor are proofs of this wanting. Peter, who had heard our Saviour declare that he who did not confess his name before men would be denied before the angels of God, denied him thrice in one night, and not without execration ; yet he is not denied pardon (Mark viii. 38). Those who lived disorderly among the Thessalonians, though chastised, are still invited to repentance (2 Thess. iii. 6). Not even is Simon Magus thrown into despair. He is rather told to hope, since Peter invites him to have recourse to prayer (Acts viii. 22).

27. What shall we say to the fact, that occasionally whole churches have been implicated in the grossest sins, and yet Paul, instead of giving them over to destruction, rather mercifully extricated them ? The defection of the Galatians was no trivial fault ; the Corinthians were still less excusable, the iniquities prevailing among them being more numerous and not less heinous, yet neither are excluded from

the mercy of the Lord. Nay, the very persons who had sinned above others in uncleanness and fornication are expressly invited to repentance. The covenant of the Lord remains, and ever will remain, inviolable, that covenant which he solemnly ratified with Christ the true Solomon, and his members, in these words: "If his children forsake my law, and walk not in my judgments; if they break my statutes, and keep not my commandments; then will I visit their transgression with the rod, and their iniquity with stripes. Nevertheless, my loving-kindness will I not utterly take from him" (Ps. lxxxix. 30–33). In short, by the very arrangement of the Creed, we are reminded that forgiveness of sins always resides in the Church of Christ, for after the Church is as it were constituted, forgiveness of sins is subjoined.

28. Some persons who have somewhat more discernment, seeing that the dogma of Novatus is so clearly refuted in Scripture, do not make every fault unpardonable, but that voluntary transgression of the Law into which a man falls knowingly and willingly. Those who speak thus allow pardon to those sins only that have been committed through ignorance. But since the Lord has in the Law ordered some sacrifices to be offered in expiation of the voluntary sins of believers, and others to redeem sins of ignorance (Lev. iv.), how perverse is it to concede no expiation to a voluntary sin? I hold nothing to be more plain, than that the one sacrifice of Christ avails to remit the voluntary sins of believers, the Lord having attested this by carnal sacrifices as emblems. Then how is David, who was so well instructed in the Law, to be excused by ignorance? Did David, who was daily punishing it in others, not know how heinous a crime murder and adultery was? Did the patriarchs deem fratricide a lawful act? Had the Corinthians made so little proficiency as to imagine that God was pleased with lasciviousness, impurity, whoredom, hatred, and strife? Was Peter, after being so carefully warned, ignorant how heinous it was to forswear his Master? Therefore, let us not by our malice shut the door against the divine mercy, when so benignly manifested.

29. I am not unaware, that by the sins which are daily forgiven to believers, ancient writers have understood the lighter errors which creep in through the infirmity of the flesh, while they thought that the formal repentance which was then exacted for more heinous crimes was no more to be repeated than Baptism. This opinion is not to be viewed as if they wished to plunge those into despair who had fallen from their first repentance, or to extenuate those errors as if they were of no account before God. For they knew that the saints often stumble through unbelief, that superfluous oaths occasionally escape them, that they sometimes boil with anger, nay, break out into open invectives, and labour, besides, under other evils, which are in no slight degree offensive to the Lord; but they so called them to distinguish them from public crimes, which came under the cogni-

sance of the Church, and produced much scandal.[1] The great difficulty they had in pardoning those who had done something that
called for ecclesiastical animadversion, was not because they thought
it difficult to obtain pardon from the Lord, but by this severity they
wished to deter others from rushing precipitately into crimes, which,
by their demerit, would alienate them from the communion of the
Church. Still the word of the Lord, which here ought to be our
only rule, certainly prescribes greater moderation, since it teaches
that the rigour of discipline must not be stretched so far as to overwhelm with grief the individual for whose benefit it should specially
be designed (2 Cor. ii. 7), as we have above discoursed at greater
length.

1 French, " Ils usoient de cette maniere de parler afin de mettre difference autre les
fautes privees, et les crimes publiques qui emportoient grands scandales en l'Eglise."—
They used this manner of speech, in order to make a difference between private faults
and the public crimes which brought great scandals into the Church.

CHAPTER II.

COMPARISON BETWEEN THE FALSE CHURCH AND THE TRUE.

The divisions of the chapter are,—I. Description of a spurious Church, resembling the Papacy vaunting of personal succession, of which a refutation is subjoined, sec. 1–4. II. An answer, in name of the orthodox Churches, to the Popish accusations of heresy and schism. A description of the Churches existing at present under the Papacy.

Sections.

1. Recapitulation of the matters treated in the previous chapter. Substance of the present chapter—viz. Where lying and falsehood prevail, no Church exists. There is falsehood wherever the pure doctrine of Christ is not in vigour.
2. This falsehood prevails under the Papacy. Hence the Papacy is not a Church. Still the Papists extol their own Church, and charge those who dissent from it with heresy and schism. They attempt to defend their vaunting by the name of personal succession. A succession which abandons the truth of Christ proved to be of no importance.
3. This proof confirmed, 1. By examples and passages of Scripture; 2. By reason and the authority of Augustine.
4. Whatever the Papists may pretend, there is no Church where the word of God appears not.
5. The objection of personal succession, and the charge of heresy and schism, refuted, both from Scripture and Augustine.
6. The same thing confirmed by the authority of Cyprian. The anathemas of the Papists of no consequence.
7. The churches of the Papists in the same situation as those of the Israelites, which revolted to superstition and idolatry under Jeroboam.
8. The character of those Israelitish churches.
9. Hence the Papists act unjustly when they would compel us to communion with their Church. Their two demands. Answer to the first. Sum of the question. Why we cannot take part in the external worship of the Papists.
10. Second demand of the Papists answered.
11. Although the Papacy cannot properly be called a Church, still against the will of Antichrist himself, there is some vestige of a Church in the Papacy, as Baptism and some other remnants.
12. The name of Church not conceded to the Papacy, though under its domination there have been some kind of churches. Herein is a fulfilment of Paul's prophecy, that Antichrist would sit in the temple of God. Deplorable condition of such churches. Summary of the chapter.

1. How much the ministry of the word and sacraments should weigh with us, and how far reverence for it should extend, so as to be a perpetual badge for distinguishing the Church, has been explained; for we have shown, first, that wherever it exists entire and unimpaired, no errors of conduct, no defects should prevent us from giving the name of Church;[1] and, secondly, that trivial errors in this ministry

---

[1] French, "Secondement, qu'encore il y ait quelques petites fautes, ou en la doctrine ou aux sacremens qu'icelui ne laisse point d'avoir sa vigueur."—Secondly, that though there may be some little faults either in doctrine or in the sacraments, the Church ceases not to be in vigour.

ought not to make us regard it as illegitimate. Moreover, we have shown that the errors to which such pardon is due, are those by which the fundamental doctrine of religion is not injured, and by which those articles of religion, in which all believers should agree, are not suppressed, while, in regard to the sacraments, the defects are such as neither destroy nor impair the legitimate institution of their Author. But as soon as falsehood has forced its way into the citadel of religion, as soon as the sum of necessary doctrine is inverted, and the use of the sacraments is destroyed, the death of the Church undoubtedly ensues, just as the life of man is destroyed when his throat is pierced, or his vitals mortally wounded. This is clearly evinced by the words of Paul when he says, that the Church is " built upon the foundation of the apostles and prophets, Jesus Christ himself being the chief corner-stone" (Eph. ii. 20). If the Church is founded on the doctrine of the apostles and prophets, by which believers are enjoined to place their salvation in Christ alone, then if that doctrine is destroyed, how can the Church continue to stand? The Church must necessarily fall whenever that sum of religion which alone can sustain it has given way. Again, if the true Church is "the pillar and ground of the truth" (1 Tim. iii. 15), it is certain that there is no Church where lying and falsehood have usurped the ascendancy.

2. Since this is the state of matters under the Papacy, we can understand how much of the Church there survives.[1] There, instead of the ministry of the word, prevails a perverted government, compounded of lies, a government which partly extinguishes, partly suppresses, the pure light. In place of the Lord's Supper, the foulest sacrilege has entered, the worship of God is deformed by a varied mass of intolerable superstitions; doctrine (without which Christianity exists not) is wholly buried and exploded, the public assemblies are schools of idolatry and impiety. Wherefore, in declining fatal participation in such wickedness, we run no risk of being dissevered from the Church of Christ. The communion of the Church was not instituted to be a chain to bind us in idolatry, impiety, ignorance of God, and other kinds of evil, but rather to retain us in the fear of God and obedience of the truth. They, indeed, vaunt loudly of their Church,[2] as if there was not another in the world; and then, as if the matter were ended, they make out that all are schismatics who withdraw from obedience to that Church which they thus depict, that all are heretics who presume to whisper against its doctrine (see sec. 5). But by what arguments do they prove their possession of the true Church? They appeal to ancient records which formerly existed in Italy, France, and Spain, pretending to derive their origin from those holy men who, by sound doctrine, founded and raised up churches, confirmed the doctrine, and reared the edifice of the Church

---

1 See chap. i. sec. 10; ii. sec. 10; viii. sec. 12.
2 French, " Je say bien que les flatteurs du Pape magnifient grandement leur Eglise."—I know that the flatterers of the Pope greatly extol their Church.

with their blood; they pretend that the Church thus consecrated by spiritual gifts and the blood of martyrs was preserved from destruction by a perpetual succession of bishops. They dwell on the importance which Irenæus, Tertullian, Origen, Augustine, and others, attached to this succession (see sec. 3). How frivolous and plainly ludicrous these allegations are, I will enable any, who will for a little consider the matter with me, to understand without any difficulty. I would also exhort our opponents to give their serious attention, if I had any hope of being able to benefit them by instruction; but since they have laid aside all regard to truth, and make it their only aim to prosecute their own ends in whatever way they can, I will only make a few observations by which good men and lovers of truth may disentangle themselves from their quibbles. First, I ask them why they do not quote Africa, and Egypt, and all Asia, just because in all those regions there was a cessation of that sacred succession, by the aid of which they vaunt of having continued churches. They therefore fall back on the assertion, that they have the true Church, because ever since it began to exist it was never destitute of bishops, because they succeeded each other in an unbroken series. But what if I bring Greece before them? Therefore, I again ask them, Why they say that the Church perished among the Greeks, among whom there never was any interruption in the succession of bishops—a succession, in their opinion, the only guardian and preserver of the Church? They make the Greeks schismatics. Why? because, by revolting from the Apostolic See, they lost their privilege. What? Do not those who revolt from Christ much more deserve to lose it? It follows, therefore, that the pretence of succession is vain, if posterity do not retain the truth of Christ, which was handed down to them by their fathers, safe and uncorrupted, and continue in it.

3. In the present day, therefore, the pretence of the Romanists is just the same as that which appears to have been formerly used by the Jews, when the Prophets of the Lord charged them with blindness, impiety, and idolatry. For as the Jews proudly vaunted of their temple, ceremonies, and priesthood, by which, with strong reason, as they supposed, they measured the Church, so, instead of the Church, we are presented by the Romanists with certain external masks, which often are far from being connected with the Church, and without which the Church can perfectly exist. Wherefore, we need no other argument to refute them than that with which Jeremiah opposed the foolish confidence of the Jews—namely, "Trust ye not in lying words, saying, The temple of the Lord, The temple of the Lord, The temple of the Lord are these" (Jer. vii. 4). The Lord recognises nothing as his own, save when his word is heard and religiously observed. Thus, though the glory of God sat in the sanctuary between the cherubim (Ezek. x. 4), and he had promised that he would there have his stated abode, still when the priests corrupted his worship by depraved superstitions, he transferred it elsewhere, and left the place without any sanctity. If that temple which

seemed consecrated for the perpetual habitation of God, could be abandoned by God and become profane, the Romanists have no ground to pretend that God is so bound to persons or places, and fixed to external observances, that he must remain with those who have only the name and semblance of a Church. This is the question which Paul discusses in the Epistle to the Romans, from the ninth to the twelfth chapter. Weak consciences were greatly disturbed, when those who seemed to be the people of God not only rejected, but even persecuted the doctrine of the Gospel. Therefore, after expounding doctrine, he removes this difficulty, denying that those Jews, the enemies of the truth, were the Church, though they wanted nothing which might otherwise have been desired to the external form of the Church. The ground of his denial is, that they did not embrace Christ. In the Epistle to the Galatians, when comparing Ishmael with Isaac, he says still more expressly, that many hold a place in the Church to whom the inheritance does not belong, because they were not the offspring of a free parent. From this he proceeds to draw a contrast between two Jerusalems, because, as the Law was given on Mount Sinai, but the Gospel proceeded from Jerusalem, so many who were born and brought up in servitude confidently boast that they are the sons of God and of the Church; nay, while they are themselves degenerate, proudly despise the genuine sons of God. Let us also, in like manner, when we hear that it was once declared from heaven, " Cast out the bondmaid and her son," trust to this inviolable decree, and boldly despise their unmeaning boasts. For if they plume themselves on external profession, Ishmael also was circumcised: if they found on antiquity, he was the first-born: and yet we see that he was rejected. If the reason is asked, Paul assigns it (Rom. ix. 6), that those only are accounted sons who are born of the pure and legitimate seed of doctrine. On this ground God declares that he was not astricted to impious priests, though he had made a covenant with their father Levi, to be their angel, or interpreter (Mal. ii. 4); nay, he retorts the false boast by which they were wont to rise against the Prophets—namely, that the dignity of the priesthood was to be held in singular estimation. This he himself willingly admits: and he disputes with them, on the ground that he is ready to fulfil the covenant, while they, by not fulfilling it on their part, deserve to be rejected. Here, then, is the value of succession when not conjoined with imitation and corresponding conduct: posterity, as soon as they are convicted of having revolted from their origin, are deprived of all honour; unless, indeed, we are prepared to say, that because Caiaphas succeeded many pious priests (nay, the series from Aaron to him was continuous), that accursed assembly deserved the name of Church. Even in earthly governments, no one would bear to see the tyranny of Caligula, Nero, Heliogabalus, and the like, described as the true condition of a republic, because they succeeded such men as Brutus,

Scipio, and Camillus.[1]   That in the government of the Church
especially, nothing is more absurd than to disregard doctrine, and
place succession in persons.   Nor, indeed, was anything farther from
the intention of the holy teachers, whom they falsely obtrude upon
us, than to maintain distinctly that churches exist, as by hereditary
right, wherever bishops have been uniformly succeeded by bishops.
But while it was without controversy that no change had been made
in doctrine from the beginning down to their day, they assumed it
to be a sufficient refutation of all their errors, that they were opposed
to the doctrine maintained constantly, and with unanimous consent,
even by the apostles themselves.   They have, therefore, no longer
any ground for proceeding to make a gloss of the name of the
Church, which we regard with due reverence; but when we come to
definition, not only (to use the common expression) does the water
adhere to them, but they stick in their own mire, because they substitute a vile prostitute for the sacred spouse of Christ.   That the
substitution may not deceive us, let us, among other admonitions,
attend to the following from Augustine. ˌSpeaking of the Church,
he says, "She herself is sometimes obscured, and, as it were, be-
clouded by a multitude of scandals; sometimes, in a time of tranquillity, she appears quiet and free; sometimes she is covered and
tossed by the billows of tribulation and trial."—(August. ad Vincent.
Epist. 48).   As instances, he mentions that the strongest pillars of
the Church often bravely endured exile for the faith, or lay hid
throughout the world.

4. In this way the Romanists assail us in the present day, and
terrify the unskilful with the name of Church, while they are the
deadly adversaries of Christ.   Therefore, although they exhibit a
temple, a priesthood, and other similar masks, the empty glare by
which they dazzle the eyes of the simple should not move us in the
least to admit that there is a Church where the word of God appears
not.   The Lord furnished us with an unfailing test when he said,
"Every one that is of the truth heareth my voice" (John xviii. 37).
Again, "I am the good shepherd, and know my sheep, and am
known of mine."   "My sheep hear my voice, and I know them, and
they follow me."   A little before he had said, when the shepherd
"putteth forth his own sheep, he goeth before them, and the sheep
follow him; for they know his voice.   And a stranger will they not
follow, but will flee from him: for they know not the voice of
strangers" (John x. 14, 4, 5).   Why then do we. of our own accord,
form so infatuated an estimate of the Church, since Christ has des-

---

[1] French, "Or tant s'en faut que cela ait lieu, que mesmes aux gouvernemens ter-
restres il ne seroit point supportable.   Comme il n'y a nul propos de dire que la
tyrannie de Caligula, Neron, Heliogabale, et leurs semblables soit le vrai etat de la
cité de Rome, pourcequ'ils ont succedé aux bons governeurs qui etoient establis par la
peuple."—Now, so far is this from being the case, that even in earthly governments
it would not be supportable.   As there is no ground for saying that the tyranny of Caligula, Nero, Heliogabalus, and the like, is the true state of the city of Rome, because
they succeeded the good governors who were established by the people.

ignated it by a sign in which is nothing in the least degree equivocal, a sign which is everywhere seen, the existence of which infallibly proves the existence of the Church, while its absence proves the absence of everything that properly bears the name of Church? Paul declares that the Church is not founded either upon the judgments of men or the priesthood, but upon the doctrine of the Apostles and Prophets (Eph. ii. 20). Nay, Jerusalem is to be distinguished from Babylon, the Church of Christ from a conspiracy of Satan, by the discriminating test which our Saviour has applied to them, "He that is of God, heareth God's words: ye therefore hear them not, because ye are not of God" (John viii. 47). In short, since the Church is the kingdom of Christ, and he reigns only by his word, can there be any doubt as to the falsehood of those statements by which the kingdom of Christ is represented without his sceptre, in other words, without his sacred word?

5. As to their charge of heresy and schism, because we preach a different doctrine, and submit not to their laws, and meet apart from them for Prayer, Baptism, the administration of the Supper, and other sacred rites, it is indeed a very serious accusation, but one which needs not a long and laboured defence. The name of heretics and schismatics is applied to those who, by dissenting from the Church, destroy its communion. This communion is held together by two chains—viz. consent in sound doctrine and brotherly charity. Hence the distinction which Augustine makes between heretics and schismatics is, that the former corrupt the purity of the faith by false dogmas, whereas the latter sometimes, even while holding the same faith, break the bond of union (August. Lib. Quæst. in Evang. Matth.). But the thing to be observed is, that this union of charity so depends on unity of faith, as to have in it its beginning, its end, in fine, its only rule. Let us therefore remember, that whenever ecclesiastical unity is commended to us, the thing required is, that while our minds consent in Christ, our wills also be united together by mutual good-will in Christ. Accordingly Paul, when he exhorts us to it, takes for his fundamental principle that there is "one God, one faith, one baptism" (Eph. iv. 5). Nay, when he tells us to be "of one accord, of one mind," he immediately adds, "Let this mind be in you which was also in Christ Jesus" (Phil. ii. 2, 5); intimating, that where the word of the Lord is not, it is not a union of believers, but a faction of the ungodly.

6. Cyprian, also, following Paul, derives the fountain of ecclesiastical concord from the one bishopric of Christ, and afterwards adds, "There is one Church, which by increase from fecundity is more widely extended to a multitude, just as there are many rays of the sun, but one light, and many branches of a tree, but one trunk upheld by the tenacious root. When many streams flow from one fountain, though there seems wide spreading numerosity from the overflowing copiousness of the supply, yet unity remains in the origin. Pluck a ray from the body of the sun, and the unity sustains no di-

vision. Break a branch from a tree, and the branch will not germinate. Cut off a stream from a fountain, that which is thus cut
off dries up. So the Church, pervaded by the light of the Lord,
extends over the whole globe, and yet the light which is everywhere
diffused is one" (Cyprian, de Simplicit. Prælat.). Words could not
more elegantly express the inseparable connection which all the
members of Christ have with each other. We see how he constantly
calls us back to the head. Accordingly, he declares that when
heresies and schisms arise, it is because men return not to the origin
of the truth, because they seek not the head, because they keep not
the doctrine of the heavenly Master. Let them now go and clamour
against us as heretics for having withdrawn from their Church, since
the only cause of our estrangement is, that they cannot tolerate a
pure profession of the truth. I say nothing of their having expelled
us by anathemas and curses. The fact is more than sufficient to
excuse us, unless they would also make schismatics of the apostles,
with whom we have a common cause. Christ, I say, forewarned his
apostles, " they shall put you out of the synagogues" (John xvi. 2).
The synagogues of which he speaks were then held to be lawful
churches. Seeing then it is certain that we were cast out, and we
are prepared to show that this was done for the name of Christ, the
cause should first be ascertained before any decision is given either
for or against us. This, however, if they choose, I am willing to
leave to them; to me it is enough that we behoved to withdraw from
them in order to draw near to Christ.

7. The place which we ought to assign to all the churches on
which the tyranny of the Romish idol has seized will better appear if
we compare them with the ancient Israelitish Church, as delineated
by the prophets. So long as the Jews and Israelites persisted in the
laws of the covenant, a true Church existed among them; in other
words, they by the kindness of God obtained the benefits of a Church.
True doctrine was contained in the law, and the ministry of it was
committed to the prophets and priests. They were initiated in
religion by the sign of circumcision, and by the other sacraments
trained and confirmed in the faith. There can be no doubt that the
titles with which the Lord honoured his Church were applicable to
their society. After they forsook the law of the Lord, and degenerated into idolatry and superstition, they partly lost the privilege. For
who can presume to deny the title of the Church to those with whom
the Lord deposited the preaching of his word and the observance of
his mysteries? On the other hand, who may presume to give the
name of Church, without reservation, to that assembly by which the
word of God is openly and with impunity trampled under foot—
where his ministry, its chief support, and the very soul of the Church,
is destroyed?

8. What then? (some one will say); was there not a particle of
the Church left to the Jews from the date of their revolt to idolatry?
The answer is easy. First, I say that in the defection itself there

were several gradations; for we cannot hold that the lapses by which both Judah and Israel turned aside from the pure worship of God were the same. Jeroboam, when he fabricated the calves against the express prohibition of God, and dedicated an unlawful place for worship, corrupted religion entirely. The Jews became degenerate in manners and superstitious opinions before they made any improper change in the external form of religion. For although they had adopted many perverse ceremonies under Rehoboam, yet, as the doctrine of the law and the priesthood, and the rites which God had instituted, continued at Jerusalem, the pious still had the Church in a tolerable state. In regard to the Israelites, matters which, up to the time of Ahab, had certainly not been reformed, then became worse. Those who succeeded him, until the overthrow of the kingdom, were partly like him, and partly (when they wished to be somewhat better) followed the example of Jeroboam, while all, without exception, were wicked and idolatrous. In Judea different changes now and then took place, some kings corrupting the worship of God by false and superstitious inventions, and others attempting to reform it, until, at length, the priests themselves polluted the temple of God by profane and abominable rites.

9. Now then let the Papists, in order to extenuate their vices as much as possible, deny, if they can, that the state of religion is as much vitiated and corrupted with them as it was in the kingdom of Israel under Jeroboam. They have a grosser idolatry, and in doctrine are not one whit more pure; rather, perhaps, they are even still more impure. God, nay, even those possessed of a moderate degree of judgment, will bear me witness, and the thing itself is too manifest to require me to enlarge upon it. When they would force us to the communion of their Church, they make two demands upon us—first, that we join in their prayers, their sacrifices, and all their ceremonies; and, secondly, that whatever honour, power, and jurisdiction, Christ has given to his Church, the same we must attribute to theirs. In regard to the first, I admit that all the prophets who were at Jerusalem, when matters there were very corrupt, neither sacrificed apart nor held separate meetings for prayer. For they had the command of God, which enjoined them to meet in the temple of Solomon, and they knew that the Levitical priests, whom the Lord had appointed over sacred matters, and who were not yet discarded, how unworthy soever they might be of that honour, were still entitled to hold it [1] (Exod. xxix. 9). But the principal point in the whole question is, that they were no tcompelled to any superstitious worship, nay, they undertook nothing but what had been instituted by God. But in these men, I mean the Papists, where is the resemblance?

[1] French, "Ils savoient que les pretres Levitiques, combien qu'ils fussent indignes d'un tel office, neantmoins pourcequ'ils avoient eté ordonnez de Dieu, et n'etoient point encore deposés, devoient etre recognus pour ministres legitimes, ayant le degré de pretrise."—They knew that the Levitical priests, although they were unworthy of such an office, nevertheless, because they had been ordained of God, and were not yet deposed, were to be recognised as lawful ministers, having the rank of priesthood.

Scarcely can we hold any meeting with them without polluting ourselves with open idolatry. Their principal bond of communion is
undoubtedly in the Mass, which we abominate as the greatest sacrilege. Whether this is justly or rashly done will be elsewhere seen
(see chap. xviii.; see also Book II., chap. xv., sec. 6). It is now
sufficient to show that our case is different from that of the prophets,
who, when they were present at the sacred rites of the ungodly, were
not obliged to witness or use any ceremonies but those which were
instituted by God. But if we would have an example in all respects
similar, let us take one from the kingdom of Israel. Under the
ordinance of Jeroboam, circumcision remained, sacrifices were offered,
the law was deemed holy, and the God whom they had received from
their fathers was worshipped; but in consequence of invented and
forbidden modes of worship, everything which was done there God
disapproved and condemned. Show me one prophet or pious man
who once worshipped or offered sacrifice in Bethel. They knew that
they could not do it without defiling themselves with some kind of
sacrilege. We hold, therefore, that the communion of the Church
ought not to be carried so far by the godly as to lay them under a
necessity of following it when it has degenerated to profane and
polluted rites.

10. With regard to the second point, our objections are still
stronger. For when the Church is considered in that particular point
of view as the Church, whose judgment we are bound to revere, whose
authority acknowledge, whose admonitions obey, whose censures
dread, whose communion religiously cultivate in every respect, we
cannot concede that they have a Church, without obliging ourselves
to subjection and obedience. Still we are willing to concede what
the Prophets conceded to the Jews and Israelites of their day, when
with them matters were in a similar, or even in a better condition.
For we see how they uniformly exclaim against their meetings as
profane conventicles, to which it is not more lawful for them to assent
than to abjure God (Isa. i. 14). And certainly if those were churches,
it follows, that Elijah, Micaiah, and others in Israel, Isaiah, Jeremiah, Hosea, and those of like character in Judah, whom the prophets, priests, and people of their day, hated and execrated more
than the uncircumcised, were aliens from the Church of God. If
those were churches, then the Church was no longer the pillar of the
truth, but the stay of falsehood, not the tabernacle of the living God,
but a receptacle of idols. They were, therefore, under the necessity
of refusing consent to their meetings, since consent was nothing else
than impious conspiracy against God. For this same reason, should
any one acknowledge those meetings of the present day, which are
contaminated by idolatry, superstition, and impious doctrine, as
churches, full communion with which a Christian must maintain so
far as to agree with them even in doctrine, he will greatly err. For
if they **are** churches, the power of the keys belongs to them, whereas
the keys are inseparably connected with the word which they have

put to flight.   Again, if they are churches, they can claim the promise of Christ, " Whatsoever ye bind," &c. ; whereas, on the contrary, they discard from their communion all who sincerely profess themselves the servants of Christ.   Therefore, either the promise of Christ is vain, or in this respect, at least, they are not churches.   In fine, instead of the ministry of the word, they have schools of impiety, and sinks of all kinds of error.   Therefore, in this point of view, they either are not churches, or no badge will remain by which the lawful meetings of the faithful can be distinguished from the meetings of Turks.

11. Still, as in ancient times, there remained among the Jews certain special privileges of a Church, so in the present day we deny not to the Papists those vestiges of a Church which the Lord has allowed to remain among them amid the dissipation.   When the Lord had once made his covenant with the Jews, it was preserved not so much by them as by its own strength, supported by which it withstood their impiety.   Such, then, is the certainty and constancy of the divine goodness, that the covenant of the Lord continued there, and his faith could not be obliterated by their perfidy ; nor could circumcision be so profaned by their impure hands as not still to be a true sign and sacrament of his covenant.   Hence the children who were born to them the Lord called his own (Ezek. xvi. 20), though, unless by special blessing, they in no respect belonged to him.   So having deposited his covenant in Gaul, Italy, Germany, Spain, and England, when these countries were oppressed by the tyranny of Antichrist, He, in order that his covenant might remain inviolable, first preserved baptism there as an evidence of the covenant ;—baptism, which, consecrated by his lips, retains its power in spite of human depravity ; secondly, He provided by his providence that there should be other remains also to prevent the Church from utterly perishing.   But as in pulling down buildings the foundations and ruins are often permitted to remain, so he did not suffer Antichrist either to subvert his Church from its foundation, or to level it with the ground (though, to punish the ingratitude of men who had despised his word, he allowed a fearful shaking and dismembering to take place), but was pleased that amid the devastation the edifice should remain, though half in ruins.

12. Therefore, while we are unwilling simply to concede the name of Church to the Papists, we do not deny that there are churches among them.   The question we raise only relates to the true and legitimate constitution of the Church, implying communion in sacred rites, which are the signs of profession, and especially in doctrine.[1]   Daniel and Paul foretold that Antichrist would sit in the temple of God (Dan. ix. 27 ; 2 Thess. ii. 4); we regard the Roman Pontiff as

---

[1] French, "Mais nous contendons seulement du vrai etat de l'Eglise, qui emporte communion, tant en doctrine, qu'en tout qui appartient à la profession de notre Chretienté ; "—but we contend only for the true state of the Church, implying communion, as well as everything which pertains to the profession of our Christianity.

the leader and standard-bearer of that wicked and abominable king-dom.[1] By placing his seat in the temple of God, it is intimated that his kingdom would not be such as to destroy the name either of Christ or of his Church.   Hence, then, it is obvious that we do not at all deny that churches remain under his tyranny ; churches, how-ever, which by sacrilegious impiety he has profaned, by cruel domina-tion has oppressed, by evil and deadly doctrines like poisoned potions has corrupted and almost slain ; churches where Christ lies half-buried, the gospel is suppressed, piety is put to flight, and the wor-ship of God almost abolished ; where, in short, all things are in such disorder as to present the appearance of Babylon rather than the holy city of God.   In one word, I call them churches, inasmuch as the Lord there wondrously preserves some remains of his people, though miserably torn and scattered, and inasmuch as some symbols of the Church still remain—symbols especially whose efficacy neither the craft of the devil nor human depravity can destroy.   But as, on the other hand, those marks to which we ought especially to have respect in this discussion are effaced, I say that the whole body, as well as every single assembly, want the form of a legitimate Church.

[1] The French adds, "pour le moins en l'Eglise Occidentale ; "—at least in the West-ern Church.

CHAPTER III.

OF THE TEACHERS AND MINISTERS OF THE CHURCH. THEIR ELECTION AND OFFICE.

The three heads of this chapter are,—I. A few preliminary remarks on Church order, on the end, utility, necessity, and dignity of the Christian ministry, sec. 1–3. II. A separate consideration of the persons performing Ecclesiastical functions, sec. 4–10. III. Of the Ordination or calling of the ministers of the Church, sec. 10–16.

Sections.

1. Summary of the chapter. Reasons why God, in governing the Church, uses the ministry of men. 1. To declare his condescension. 2. To train us to humility and obedience. 3. To bind us to each other in mutual charity. These reasons confirmed by Scripture.
2. This ministry of men most useful to the whole Church. Its advantages enumerated.
3. The honourable terms in which the ministry is spoken of. Its necessity established by numerous examples.
4. Second part of the chapter, treating of Ecclesiastical office-bearers in particular. Some of them, as Apostles, Prophets, and Evangelists, temporary. Others, as Pastors and Teachers, perpetual and indispensable.
5. Considering the office of Evangelist and Apostle as one, we have Pastors corresponding with Apostles, and Teachers with Prophets. Why the name of Apostles specially conferred on the twelve.
6. As to the Apostles so also to Pastors the preaching of the Word and the administration of the sacraments has been committed. How the Word should be preached.
7. Regularly every Pastor should have a separate church assigned to him. This, however, admits of modification, when duly and regularly made by public authority.
8. Bishops, Presbyters, Pastors, and Ministers, are used by the Apostles as one and the same. Some functions, as being temporary, are omitted. Two—namely, those of Elders and Deacons—as pertaining to the ministry of the Word, are retained.
9. Distinction between Deacons. Some employed in distributing alms, others in taking care of the poor.
10. Third part of the chapter, treating of the Ordination or calling of the ministers of the Church.
11. A twofold calling—viz. an external and an internal. Mode in which both are to be viewed.
12. 1. Who are to be appointed ministers? 2. Mode of appointment.
13. 3. By whom the appointment is to be made. Why the Apostles were elected by Christ alone. Of the calling and election of St Paul.
14. Ordinary Pastors are designated by other Pastors. Why certain of the Apostles also were designated by men.
15. The election of Pastors does not belong to one individual. Other Pastors should preside, and the people consent and approve.
16. Form in which the ministers of the Church are to be ordained. No express precept but one. Laying on of hands.

1. WE are now to speak of the order in which the Lord has been pleased that his Church should be governed. For though it is right

that he alone should rule and reign in the Church, that he should preside and be conspicuous in it, and that its government should be exercised and administered solely by his word; yet as he does not dwell among us in visible presence, so as to declare his will to us by his own lips, he in this (as we have said) uses the ministry of men, by making them, as it were, his substitutes,[1] not by transferring his right and honour to them, but only doing his own work by their lips, just as an artificer uses a tool for any purpose. What I have previously expounded (chap. i. sec. 5) I am again forced to repeat. God might have acted, in this respect, by himself, without any aid or instrument, or might even have done it by angels; but there are several reasons why he rather chooses to employ men.[2] First, in this way he declares his condescension towards us, employing men to perform the function of his ambassadors in the world, to be the interpreters of his secret will; in short, to represent his own person. Thus he shows by experience that it is not to no purpose he calls us his temples, since by man's mouth he gives responses to men as from a sanctuary. Secondly, it forms a most excellent and useful training to humility, when he accustoms us to obey his word though preached by men like ourselves, or, it may be, our inferiors in worth. Did he himself speak from heaven, it were no wonder if his sacred oracles were received by all ears and minds reverently and without delay. For who would not dread his present power? who would not fall prostrate at the first view of his great majesty? who would not be overpowered by that immeasurable splendour? But when a feeble man, sprung from the dust, speaks in the name of God, we give the best proof of our piety and obedience, by listening with docility to his servant, though not in any respect our superior. Accordingly, he hides the treasure of his heavenly wisdom in frail earthen vessels (2 Cor. iv. 7), that he may have a more certain proof of the estimation in which it is held by us. Moreover, nothing was fitter to cherish mutual charity than to bind men together by this tie, appointing one of them as a pastor to teach the others who are enjoined to be disciples, and receive the common doctrine from a single mouth. For did every man suffice for himself, and stand in no need of another's aid (such is the pride of the human intellect), each would despise all others, and be in his turn despised. The Lord, therefore, has astricted his Church to what he foresaw would be the strongest bond of unity when he deposited the doctrine of eternal life and salvation with men, that by their hands he might communicate it to others. To this Paul had respect when he wrote to the Ephesians, "There is one body, and one Spirit, even as ye are called in one hope of your calling; one Lord, one faith, one baptism, one God and Father of all, who is above all, and through all, and in you all. But unto every one of us is given grace according to the measure of the

---

1 Latin, " quasi vicariam operam."—French, " les faisans comme ses lieutenans;"— making them as it were his substitutes.

2 See on this subject August. de Doctrina Christiana, Lib. i.

gift of Christ. Wherefore he saith, When he ascended up on high, he led captivity captive, and gave gifts unto men. (Now that he ascended, what is it but that he also descended first into the lower parts of the earth? He that descended is the same also that ascended up far above all heavens, that he might fill all things.) And he gave some, apostles; and some, prophets; and some, evangelists; and some, pastors and teachers; for the perfecting of the saints, for the work of the ministry, for the edifying of the body of Christ: till we all come in the unity of the faith, and of the knowledge of the Son of God, unto a perfect man, unto the measure of the stature of the fulness of Christ: that we henceforth be no more children, tossed to and fro, and carried about with every wind of doctrine, by the sleight of men, and cunning craftiness, whereby they lie in wait to deceive; but speaking the truth in love, may grow up into him in all things, which is the head, even Christ: from whom the whole body fitly joined together and compacted by that which every joint supplieth, according to the effectual working in the measure of every part, maketh increase of the body unto the edifying of itself in love" (Eph. iv. 4–16).

2. By these words he shows that the ministry of men, which God employs in governing the Church, is a principal bond by which believers are kept together in one body. He also intimates, that the Church cannot be kept safe, unless supported by those guards to which the Lord has been pleased to commit its safety. Christ "ascended up far above all heavens, that he might fill all things" (Eph. iv. 10). The mode of filling is this: By the ministers to whom he has committed this office, and given grace to discharge it, he dispenses and distributes his gifts to the Church, and thus exhibits himself as in a manner actually present by exerting the energy of his Spirit in this his institution, so as to prevent it from being vain or fruitless. In this way, the renewal of the saints is accomplished, and the body of Christ is edified; in this way we grow up in all things unto Him who is the Head, and unite with one another; in this way we are all brought into the unity of Christ, provided prophecy flourishes among us, provided we receive his apostles, and despise not the doctrine which is administered to us. Whoever, therefore, studies to abolish this order and kind of government of which we speak, or disparages it as of minor importance, plots the devastation, or rather the ruin and destruction, of the Church. For neither are the light and heat of the sun, nor meat and drink, so necessary to sustain and cherish the present life, as is the apostolical and pastoral office to preserve a Church in the earth.

3. Accordingly, I have observed above, that God has repeatedly commended its dignity by the titles which he has bestowed upon it, in order that we might hold it in the highest estimation, as among the most excellent of our blessings. He declares, that in raising up teachers, he confers a special benefit on men, when he bids his prophet exclaim, "How beautiful upon the mountains are the feet of him that bringeth good tidings, that publisheth peace" (Isa. lii. 7); when

he calls the apostles the light of the world and the salt of the earth (Matth. v. 13, 14). Nor could the office be more highly eulogised than when he said, "He that heareth you heareth me; and he that despiseth you despiseth me" (Luke x. 16). But the most striking passage of all is that in the Second Epistle to the Corinthians, where Paul treats as it were professedly of this question. He contends, that there is nothing in the Church more noble and glorious than the ministry of the Gospel, seeing it is the administration of the Spirit of righteousness and eternal life. These and similar passages should have the effect of preventing that method of governing and maintaining the Church by ministers, a method which the Lord has ratified for ever, from seeming worthless in our eyes, and at length becoming obsolete by contempt. How very necessary it is, he has declared not only by words but also by examples. When he was pleased to shed the light of his truth in greater effulgence on Cornelius, he sent an angel from heaven to despatch Peter to him (Acts x. 3). When he was pleased to call Paul to the knowledge of himself, and ingraft him into the Church, he does not address him with his own voice, but sends him to a man from whom he may both obtain the doctrine of salvation and the sanctification of baptism (Acts ix. 6–20). If it was not by mere accident that the angel, who is the interpreter of God, abstains from declaring the will of God, and orders a man to be called to declare it; that Christ, the only Master of believers, commits Paul to the teaching of a man, that Paul whom he had determined to carry into the third heaven, and honour with a wondrous revelation of things that could not be spoken (2 Cor. xii. 2), who will presume to despise or disregard as superfluous that ministry, whose utility God has been pleased to attest by such evidence?

4. Those who preside over the government of the Church, according to the institution of Christ, are named by Paul, first, *Apostles;* secondly, *Prophets;* thirdly, *Evangelists;* fourthly, *Pastors;* and, lastly, *Teachers* (Eph. iv. 11). Of these, only the two last have an ordinary office in the Church. The Lord raised up the other three at the beginning of his kingdom, and still occasionally raises them up when the necessity of the times requires. The nature of the apostolic function is clear from the command, "Go ye into all the world, and preach the Gospel to every creature" (Mark xvi. 15). No fixed limits are given them, but the whole world is assigned to be reduced under the obedience of Christ, that by spreading the Gospel as widely as they could, they might everywhere erect his kingdom. Accordingly, Paul, when he would approve his apostleship, does not say that he had acquired some one city for Christ, but had propagated the Gospel far and wide—had not built on another man's foundation, but planted churches where the name of his Lord was unheard. The apostles, therefore, were sent forth to bring back the world from its revolt to the true obedience of God, and everywhere establish his kingdom by the preaching of the Gospel; or, if you choose, they were like the first architects of the Church, to lay its foundations

throughout the world. By *Prophets*, he means not all interpreters of the divine will, but those who excelled by special revelation ; none such now exist, or they are less manifest. By *Evangelists*, I mean those who, while inferior in rank to the apostles, were next them in office, and even acted as their substitutes. Such were Luke, Timothy, Titus, and the like ; perhaps, also, the seventy disciples whom our Saviour appointed in the second place to the apostles (Luke x. 1). According to this interpretation, which appears to me consonant both to the words and the meaning of Paul, those three functions were not instituted in the Church to be perpetual, but only to endure so long as churches were to be formed where none previously existed, or at least where churches were to be transferred from Moses to Christ ; although I deny not, that afterward God occasionally raised up Apostles, or at least Evangelists, in their stead, as has been done in our time. For such were needed to bring back the Church from the revolt of Antichrist. The office I nevertheless call extraordinary, because it has no place in churches duly constituted. Next come *Pastors* and *Teachers*, with whom the Church never can dispense, and between whom, I think, there is this difference, that teachers preside not over discipline, or the administration of the sacraments, or admonitions, or exhortations, but the interpretation of Scripture only, in order that pure and sound doctrine may be maintained among believers. But all these are embraced in the pastoral office.

5. We now understand what offices in the government of the Church were temporary, and what offices were instituted to be of perpetual duration. But if we class evangelists with apostles, we shall have two like offices in a manner corresponding to each other. For the same resemblance which our teachers have to the ancient prophets pastors have to the apostles. The prophetical office was more excellent in respect of the special gift of revelation which accompanied it, but the office of teachers was almost of the same nature, and had altogether the same end. In like manner, the twelve, whom the Lord chose to publish the new preaching of the Gospel to the world (Luke vi. 13), excelled others in rank and dignity. For although, from the nature of the case, and etymology of the word, all ecclesiastical officers may be properly called apostles, because they are all sent by the Lord and are his messengers, yet as it was of great importance that a sure attestation should be given to the mission of those who delivered a new and extraordinary message, it was right that the twelve (to the number of whom Paul was afterwards added) should be distinguished from others by a peculiar title. The same name, indeed, is given by Paul to Andronicus and Junia, who, he says, were " of note among the apostles" (Rom. xvi. 7); but when he would speak properly, he confines the term to that primary order. And this is the common use of Scripture. Still pastors (except that each has the government of a particular church assigned to him) have the same function as apostles. The nature of this function let us now see still more clearly.

6. When our Lord sent forth the apostles, he gave them a commission (as has been lately said) to preach the Gospel, and baptise those who believed for the remission of sins. He had previously commanded that they should distribute the sacred symbols of his body and blood after his example (Matth. xxviii. 19; Luke xxii. 19). Such is the sacred, inviolable, and perpetual law, enjoined on those who succeed to the place of the apostles,—they receive a commission to preach the Gospel and administer the sacraments. Whence we infer that those who neglect both of these falsely pretend to the office of apostles. But what shall we say of pastors? Paul speaks not of himself only but of all pastors, when he says, " Let a man so account of us, as of the ministers of Christ, and stewards of the mysteries of God" (1 Cor. iv. 1). Again, in another passage, he describes a bishop as one " holding fast the faithful word as he hath been taught, that he may be able by sound doctrine both to exhort and convince the gainsayers " (Tit. i. 9). From these and similar passages which everywhere occur, we may infer that the two principal parts of the office of pastors are to preach the Gospel and administer the sacraments. But the method of teaching consists not merely in public addresses, it extends also to private admonitions. Thus Paul takes the Ephesians to witness, " I kept back nothing that was profitable to you, but have showed you, and have taught you publicly, and from house to house, testifying both to the Jews, and also to the Greeks, repentance toward God, and faith toward our Lord Jesus Christ." A little after he says, " Remember, that, for the space of three years, I ceased not to warn every one night and day with tears" (Acts xx. 20, 31). Our present purpose, however, is not to enumerate the separate qualities of a good pastor, but only to indicate what those profess who call themselves pastors—viz. that in presiding over the Church they have not an indolent dignity, but must train the people to true piety by the doctrine of Christ, administer the sacred mysteries, preserve and exercise right discipline. To those who are set as watchmen in the Church the Lord declares, " When I say unto the wicked, Thou shalt surely die; and thou givest him not warning, nor speakest to warn the wicked from his wicked way, to save his life; the same wicked man shall die in his iniquity; but his blood will I require at thine hand" (Ezek. iii. 18). What Paul says of himself is applicable to all pastors: " For though I preach the Gospel, I have nothing to glory of: for necessity is laid upon me; yea, woe is unto me if I preach not the Gospel" (1 Cor. ix. 16). In short, what the apostles did to the whole world, every pastor should do to the flock over which he is appointed.

7. While we assign a church to each pastor, we deny not that he who is fixed to one church may assist other churches, whether any disturbance has occurred which requires his presence, or his advice is asked on some doubtful matter. But because that policy is necessary to maintain the peace of the Church, each has his proper duty assigned, lest all should become disorderly, run up and down with-

out any certain vocation, flock together promiscuously to one spot, and capriciously leave the churches vacant, being more solicitous for their own convenience than for the edification of the Church. This arrangement ought, as far as possible, to be commonly observed, that every one, content with his own limits, may not encroach on another's province. Nor is this a human invention. It is an ordinance of God. For we read that Paul and Barnabas appointed presbyters over each of the churches of Lystra, Antioch, and Iconium (Acts xiv. 23); and Paul himself enjoins Titus to ordain presbyters in every town (Tit. i. 5). In like manner, he mentions the bishops of the Philippians, and Archippus, the bishop of the Colossians (Phil. i. 1 ; Col. iv. 17). And in the Acts we have his celebrated address to the presbyters of the Church of Ephesus (Acts xx. 28). Let every one, then, who undertakes the government and care of one church, know that he is bound by this law of divine vocation, not that he is astricted to the soil (as lawyers speak), that is, enslaved, and, as it were, fixed, as to be unable to move a foot if public utility so require, and the thing is done duly and in order ; but he who has been called to one place ought not to think of removing, nor seek to be set free when he deems it for his own advantage. Again, if it is expedient for any one to be transferred to another place, he ought not to attempt it of his own private motive, but to wait for public authority.

8. In giving the name of bishops, presbyters, and pastors, indiscriminately to those who govern churches, I have done it on the authority of Scripture, which uses the words as synonymous. To all who discharge the ministry of the word it gives the name of bishops. Thus Paul, after enjoining Titus to ordain elders in every city, immediately adds, " A bishop must be blameless," &c. (Tit. i. 5, 7). So in another place he salutes several bishops in one church (Phil. i. 1). And in the Acts, the elders of Ephesus, whom he is said to have called together, he, in the course of his address, designates as bishops (Acts xx. 17). Here it is to be observed, that we have hitherto enumerated those offices only which consist in the ministry of the word ; nor does Paul make mention of any others in the passage which we have quoted from the fourth chapter of the Epistle to the Ephesians. But in the Epistle to the Romans, and the First Epistle to the Corinthians, he enumerates other offices, as powers, gifts of healing, interpretation, government, care of the poor (Rom. xii. 7 : 1 Cor. xii. 28). As to those which were temporary, I say nothing, for it is not worth while to dwell upon them. But there are two of perpetual duration—viz. government and care of the poor. By these governors I understand seniors selected from the people to unite with the bishops in pronouncing censures and exercising discipline. For this is the only meaning which can be given to the passage, "He that ruleth with diligence" (Rom. xii. 8). From the beginning, therefore, each church had its senate,[1] composed of pious, grave, and

---

[1] Latin, " senatum."—French, " conseil ou consistoire ;"—council or consistory.

venerable men, in whom was lodged the power of correcting faults. Of this power we shall afterwards speak. Moreover, experience shows that this arrangement was not confined to one age, and therefore we are to regard the office of government as necessary for all ages.

9. The care of the poor was committed to deacons, of whom two classes are mentioned by Paul in the Epistle to the Romans, "He that giveth, let him do it with simplicity;" "he that showeth mercy, with cheerfulness" (Rom. xii. 8). As it is certain that he is here speaking of public offices of the Church, there must have been two distinct classes. If I mistake not, he in the former clause designates deacons, who administered alms; in the latter, those who had devoted themselves to the care of the poor and the sick. Such were the widows of whom he makes mention in the Epistle to Timothy (1 Tim. v. 10). For there was no public office which women could discharge save that of devoting themselves to the service of the poor. If we admit this (and it certainly ought to be admitted), there will be two classes of deacons, the one serving the Church by administering the affairs of the poor; the other, by taking care of the poor themselves. For although the term διακονία has a more extensive meaning, Scripture specially gives the name of deacons to those whom the Church appoints to dispense alms, and take care of the poor, constituting them as it were stewards of the public treasury of the poor. Their origin, institution, and office, is described by Luke (Acts vi. 3). When a murmuring arose among the Greeks, because in the administration of the poor their widows were neglected, the apostles, excusing themselves that they were unable to discharge both offices, to preach the word and serve tables, requested the multitude to elect seven men of good report, to whom the office might be committed. Such deacons as the Apostolic Church had, it becomes us to have after her example.

10. Now seeing that in the sacred assembly all things ought to be done decently and in order (1 Cor. xiv. 40), there is nothing in which this ought to be more carefully observed than in settling government, irregularity in any respect being nowhere more perilous. Wherefore, lest restless and turbulent men should presumptuously push themselves forward to teach or rule (an event which actually was to happen), it was expressly provided that no one should assume a public office in the Church without a call (Heb. v. 4; Jer. xvii. 16). Therefore, if any one would be deemed a true minister of the Church, he must *first* be duly called; and, *secondly*, he must answer to his calling; that is, undertake and execute the office assigned to him. This may often be observed in Paul, who, when he would approve his apostleship, almost always alleges a call, together with his fidelity in discharging the office. If so great a minister of Christ dares not arrogate to himself authority to be heard in the Church, unless as having been appointed to it by the command of his Lord, and faithfully performing what has been intrusted to him, how great the effrontery for any man, devoid of one or both of them, to demand

for himself such honour. But as we have already touched on the necessity of executing the office, let us now treat only of the call.

11. The subject is comprehended under four heads—viz. *who* are to be appointed ministers, *in what way, by whom,* and *with what rite or initiatory ceremony.* I am speaking of the external and formal call which relates to the public order of the Church, while I say nothing of that secret call of which every minister is conscious before God, but has not the Church as a witness of it ; I mean, the good testimony of our heart, that we undertake the offered office neither from ambition nor avarice, nor any other selfish feeling, but a sincere fear of God and desire to edify the Church. This, as I have said, is indeed necessary for every one of us, if we would approve our ministry to God. Still, however, a man may have been duly called by the Church, though he may have accepted with a bad conscience, provided his wickedness is not manifest. It is usual also to say, that private men are called to the ministry when they seem fit and apt to discharge it ; that is, because learning, conjoined with piety and the other endowments of a good pastor, is a kind of preparation for the office. For those whom the Lord has destined for this great office he previously provides with the armour which is requisite for the discharge of it, that they may not come empty and unprepared. Hence Paul, in the First Epistle to the Corinthians, when treating of the offices, first enumerates the gifts in which those who performed the offices ought to excel. But as this is the first of the four heads which I mentioned, let us now proceed to it.

12. What persons should be elected bishops is treated at length by Paul in two passages (Tit. i. 7 ; 1 Tim. iii. 1). The substance is, that none are to be chosen save those who are of sound doctrine and holy lives, and not notorious for any defect which might destroy their authority and bring disgrace on the ministry. The description of deacons and elders is entirely similar (see chapter iv. sec. 10–13). We must always take care that they are not unfit for or unequal to the burden imposed upon them ; in other words, that they are provided with the means which will be necessary to fulfil their office. Thus our Saviour, when about to send his apostles, provided them with the arms and instruments which were indispensably requisite.[1] And Paul, after portraying the character of a good and genuine bishop, admonishes Timothy not to contaminate himself by choosing an improper person for the office. The expression, *in what way,* I use not in reference to the rite of choosing, but only to the religious fear which is to be observed in election. Hence the fastings and prayers which Luke narrates that the faithful employed when they elected presbyters (Acts xiv. 23). For, understanding that the business was the most serious in which they could engage, they did not venture to act without the greatest reverence and solicitude. But above all, they were earnest in prayer, imploring from God the spirit of wisdom and discernment.

[1] Luke xxi. 15 ; xxiv. 49 ; Mark vi. 15 ; Acts i. 8 ; 1 Tim. v. 22.

13. The third division which we have adopted is, *by whom* ministers are to be chosen. A certain rule on this head cannot be obtained from the appointment of the apostles, which was somewhat different from the common call of others. As theirs was an extraordinary ministry, in order to render it conspicuous by some more distinguished mark, those who were to discharge it behoved to be called and appointed by the mouth of the Lord himself. It was not, therefore, by any human election, but at the sole command of God and Christ, that they prepared themselves for the work. Hence, when the apostles were desirous to substitute another in the place of Judas, they did not venture to nominate any one certainly, but brought forward two, that the Lord might declare by lot which of them he wished to succeed (Acts i. 23). In this way we ought to understand Paul's declaration, that he was made an apostle, "not of men, neither by man, but by Jesus Christ, and God the Father" (Gal. i. 1). The former —viz. *not of men*—he had in common with all the pious ministers of the word, for no one could duly perform the office unless called by God. The other was proper and peculiar to him. And while he glories in it, he boasts that he had not only what pertains to a true and lawful pastor, but he also brings forward the insignia of his apostleship. For when there were some among the Galatians who, seeking to disparage his authority, represented him as some ordinary disciple, substituted in place of the primary apostles, he, in order to maintain unimpaired the dignity of his ministry, against which he knew that these attempts were made, felt it necessary to show that he was in no respect inferior to the other apostles. Accordingly, he affirms that he was not chosen by the judgment of men, like some ordinary bishop, but by the mouth and manifest oracle of the Lord himself.

14. But no sober person will deny that the regular mode of lawful calling is; that bishops should be designated by men, since there are numerous passages of Scripture to this effect. Nor, as has been said, is there anything contrary to this in Paul's protestation, that he was not sent either of man, or by man, seeing he is not there speaking of the ordinary election of ministers, but claiming for himself what was peculiar to the apostles: although the Lord in thus selecting Paul by special privilege, subjected him in the meantime to the discipline of an ecclesiastical call: for Luke relates, "As they ministered to the Lord, and fasted, the Holy Ghost said, Separate me Barnabas and Saul for the work whereunto I have called them" (Acts xiii. 2). Why this separation and laying on of hands after the Holy Spirit had attested their election, unless that ecclesiastical discipline might be preserved in appointing ministers by men? God could not give a more illustrious proof of his approbation of this order, than by causing Paul to be set apart by the Church after he had previously declared that he had appointed him to be the Apostle of the Gentiles. The same thing we may see in the election of Matthias. As the apostolic office was of such importance that they did not venture to appoint any one to it of their own judgment, they

bring forward two, on one of whom the lot might fall, that thus the election might have a sure testimony from heaven, and, at the same time, the policy of the Church might not be disregarded.

15. The next question is, Whether a minister should be chosen *by the whole Church*, or only by *colleagues* and *elders*, who have the charge of discipline; or whether they may be appointed by the authority of one individual ?[1] Those who attribute this right to one individual quote the words of Paul to Titus " For this cause left I thee in Crete, that thou shouldest set in order the things that are wanting, and ordain elders in every city" (Tit. i. 5); and also to Timothy, " Lay hands suddenly on no man" (1 Tim. v. 22). But they are mistaken if they suppose that Timothy so reigned at Ephesus, and Titus in Crete, as to dispose of all things at their own pleasure. They only presided by previously giving good and salutary counsels to the people, not by doing alone whatever pleased them, while all others were excluded. Lest this should seem to be a fiction of mine, I will make it plain by a similar example. Luke relates that Barnabas and Paul ordained elders throughout the churches, but he at the same time marks the plan or mode when he says that it was done by suffrage. The words are, Χειροτονήσαντες πρεσβυτέρους κατ' ἐκκλησίαν (Acts xiv. 23). They therefore selected (*creabant*) two ; but the whole body, as was the custom of the Greeks in elections, declared by a show of hands which of the two they wished to have. Thus it is not uncommon for Roman historians to say, that the consul who held the comitia elected the new magistrates, for no other reason but because he received the suffrages, and presided over the people at the election. Certainly it is not credible that Paul conceded more to Timothy and Titus than he assumed to himself. Now we see that his custom was to appoint bishops by the suffrages of the people. We must therefore interpret the above passages, so as not to infringe on the common right and liberty of the Church. Rightly, therefore, does Cyprian contend for it as of divine authority, that the priest be chosen in presence of the people, before the eyes of all, and be approved as worthy and fit by public judgment and testimony, (Cyprian, Lib. i. Ep. 3). Indeed, we see that by the command of the Lord, the practice in electing the Levitical priests was to bring them forward in view of the people before consecration. Nor is Matthias enrolled among the number of the apostles, nor are the seven deacons elected in any other way, than at the sight and approval of the people (Acts vi. 2). " Those examples," says Cyprian, " show that the ordination of a priest behoved not to take place, unless under the consciousness of the people assisting, so that that ordination was just and legitimate which was vouched by the testimony of all." We see, then, that ministers are legitimately called according to the word of God, when those who may have seemed fit are elected on the consent and approbation of the people. Other

1 See chap. iv. sec. 10, 11; chap. v. sec. 2, 3.   Also Calv. in Acts vi. 3, and Luther, tom. ii. p. 374.

pastors, however, ought to preside over the election, lest any error should be committed by the general body either through levity, or bad passion, or tumult.

16. It remains to consider the form of ordination, to which we have assigned the last place in the call (see chap. iv., sec. 14, 15). It is certain, that when the apostles appointed any one to the ministry, they used no other ceremony than the laying on of hands. This form was derived, I think, from the custom of the Jews, who, by the laying on of hands, in a manner presented to God whatever they wished to be blessed and consecrated. Thus Jacob, when about to bless Ephraim and Manasseh, placed his hands upon their heads (Gen. xlviii. 14). The same thing was done by our Lord, when he prayed over the little children (Matth. xix. 15). With the same intent (as I imagine), the Jews, according to the injunction of the law, laid hands upon their sacrifices. Wherefore, the apostles, by the laying on of hands, intimated that they made an offering to God of him whom they admitted to the ministry; though they also did the same thing over those on whom they conferred the visible gifts of the Spirit (Acts viii. 17; xix. 6). However this be, it was the regular form, whenever they called any one to the sacred ministry. In this way they consecrated pastors and teachers; in this way they consecrated deacons. But though there is no fixed precept concerning the laying on of hands, yet as we see that it was uniformly observed by the apostles, this careful observance ought to be regarded by us in the light of a precept (see chap. xiv., sec. 29; chap. xix., sec. 31). And it is certainly useful, that by such a symbol the dignity of the ministry should be commended to the people, and he who is ordained, reminded that he is no longer his own, but is bound in service to God and the Church. Besides, it will not prove an empty sign, if it be restored to its genuine origin. For if the Spirit of God has not instituted anything in the Church in vain, this ceremony of his appointment we shall feel not to be useless, provided it be not superstitiously abused. Lastly, it is to observed, that it was not the whole people, but only pastors, who laid hands on ministers, though it is uncertain whether or not several always laid their hands: it is certain, that in the case of the deacons, it was done by Paul and Barnabas, and some few others (Acts vi. 6; xiii. 3). But in another place, Paul mentions that he himself, without any others, laid hands on Timothy. "Wherefore, I put thee in remembrance, that thou stir up the gift of God which is in thee, by the putting on of my hands" (2 Tim. i. 6). For what is said in the First Epistle, of the *laying on of the hands of the presbytery*, I do not understand as if Paul were speaking of the college of Elders. By the expression, I understand the ordination itself; as if he had said, Act so, that the gift which you received by the laying on of hands, when I made you a presbyter, may not be in vain.

CHAPTER IV.

OF THE STATE OF THE PRIMITIVE CHURCH, AND THE MODE OF GOVERNMENT IN USE BEFORE THE PAPACY.

The divisions of this chapter are,—I. The mode of government in the primitive Church, sec 1–10. II. The formal ordination of Bishops and Ministers in the primitive Church, sec. 10–15.

Sections.

1. The method of government in the primitive Church. Not in every respect con formable to the rule of the word of God. Three distinct orders of Ministers.
2. First, the Bishop, for the sake of preserving order, presided over the Presbyters or Pastors. The office of Bishop. Presbyter and Bishop the same. The institution of this order ancient.
3. The office of Bishop and Presbyters. Strictly preserved in the primitive Church.
4. Of Archbishops and Patriarchs. Very seldom used. For what end instituted. Hierarchy an improper name, and not used in Scripture.
5. Deacons, the second order of Ministers in the primitive Church. Their proper office. The Bishop their inspector. Subdeacons, their assistants. Archdeacons, their presidents. The reading of the Gospel, an adventitious office conferred in honour on the Deacons.
6. Mode in which the goods of the Church were anciently dispensed. 1. The support of the poor. 2. Due provision for the ministers of the Church.
7. The administration at first free and voluntary. The revenues of the Church afterwards classed under four heads.
8. A third part of the revenues devoted to the fabric of churches. To this, however, when necessary, the claim of the poor was preferred. Sayings, testimonies, and examples to this effect, from Cyril, Acatius, Jerome, Exuperius, Ambrose.
9. The Clerici, among whom were the Doorkeepers and Acolytes, were the names given to exercises used as a kind of training for tyros.
10. Second part of the chapter, treating of the calling of Ministers. Some error introduced in course of time in respect to celibacy from excessive strictness. In regard to the ordination of Ministers, full regard not always paid to the consent of the people. Why the people less anxious to maintain their right. Ordinations took place at stated times.
11. In the ordination of Bishops the liberty of the people maintained.
12. Certain limits afterwards introduced to restrain the inconsiderate licence of the multitude.
13 This mode of election long prevailed. Testimony of Gregory. Nothing repugnant to this in the decretals of Gratian.
14. The form of ordination in the ancient Church.
15. This form gradually changed.

1. HITHERTO we have discoursed of the order of church government as delivered to us in the pure word of God, and of ministerial offices as instituted by Christ (chap. i. sec. 5, 6 ; chap. iii.). Now that the whole subject may be more clearly and familiarly explained, and also better fixed in our minds, it will be useful to attend to the form of the early church, as this will give us a kind of visible representation of the divine institution. For although the bishops of those

times published many canons, in which they seemed to express more than is expressed by the sacred volume, yet they were so cautious in framing all their economy on the word of God, the only standard, that it is easy to see that they scarcely in any respect departed from it. Even if something may be wanting in these enactments, still, as they were sincerely desirous to preserve the divine institution, and have not strayed far from it, it will be of great benefit here briefly to explain what their observance was. As we have stated that three classes of ministers are set before us in Scripture, so the early Church distributed all its ministers into three orders. For from the order of presbyters, part were selected as pastors and teachers, while to the remainder was committed the censure of manners and discipline. To the deacons belonged the care of the poor and the dispensing of alms. Readers and Acolytes were not the names of certain offices; but those whom they called clergy, they accustomed from their youth to serve the Church by certain exercises, that they might the better understand for what they were destined, and afterwards come better prepared for their duty, as I will shortly show at greater length. Accordingly, Jerome, in setting forth five orders in the Church, enumerates Bishops, Presbyters, Deacons, Believers, Catechumens: to the other Clergy and Monks he gives no proper place [1] (Hieron. in Jes. c. ix.).

2. All, therefore, to whom the office of teaching was committed, they called presbyters, and in each city these presbyters selected one of their number to whom they gave the special title of bishop, lest, as usually happens, from equality dissension should arise. The bishop, however, was not so superior in honour and dignity as to have dominion over his colleagues, but as it belongs to a president in an assembly to bring matters before them, collect their opinions, take precedence of others in consulting, advising, exhorting, guide the whole procedure by his authority, and execute what is decreed by common consent, a bishop held the same office in a meeting of presbyters. And the ancients themselves confess that this practice was introduced by human arrangement, according to the exigency of the times. Thus Jerome, on the Epistle to Titus, cap. i., says, " A bishop is the same as a presbyter. And before dissensions were introduced into religion by the instigation of the devil, and it was said among the people, I am of Paul, and I of Cephas, churches were governed by a common council of presbyters. Afterwards, that the seeds of dissension might be plucked up, the whole charge was devolved upon

---

[1] " Pourtant Sainct Hierome apres avoir divisé l'Eglise en cinq ordres, nomme les Eveques, secondement, les Pretres, tiercement, les Diacres, puis les fideles en commun, finalement, ceux qui n'etoient pas baptisés encore, mais qui s'etoient presentés pour etre instruits en la foy Chretienne; et puis recevoient le baptéme. Ainsi il n'attribue point de certain lieu au reste du Clergé ni aux Moines."—However, St Jerome, after dividing the Church into five orders, names the Bishops, secondly, the Priests, thirdly, the Deacons, then the faithful in common, lastly, those who were not yet baptised, but had presented themselves to be instructed in the Christian faith, and thereafter received baptism. Thus he attributes no certain place to the remainder of the Clergy or to the Monks.

mendatory rescripts, preventions, and the like. But they all conduct one. Therefore, as presbyters know that by the custom of the Church they are subject to him who presides, so let bishops know that they are greater than presbyters more by custom than in consequence of our Lord's appointment, and ought to rule the Church for the common good." In another place he shows how ancient the custom was (Hieron. Epist. ad Evang.). For he says that at Alexandria, from Mark the Evangelist, as far down as Heraclas and Dionysius, presbyters always placed one, selected from themselves, in a higher rank, and gave him the name of bishop. Each city, therefore, had a college of presbyters, consisting of pastors and teachers. For they all performed to the people that office of teaching, exhorting, and correcting, which Paul enjoins on bishops (Tit. i. 9); and that they might leave a seed behind them, they made it their business to train the younger men who had devoted themselves to the sacred warfare. To each city was assigned a certain district which took presbyters from it, and was considered as it were incorporated into that church. Each presbyter, as I have said, merely to preserve order and peace, was under one bishop, who, though he excelled others in dignity, was subject to the meeting of the brethren. But if the district which was under his bishopric was too large for him to be able to discharge all the duties of bishop, presbyters were distributed over it in certain places to act as his substitutes in minor matters. These were called *Chorepiscopi* (rural bishops), because they represented the bishops throughout the province.

3. But, in regard to the office of which we now treat, the bishop as well as the presbyters behoved to employ themselves in the administration of word and sacraments. For, at Alexandria only (as Arius had there troubled the Church), it was enacted, that no presbyter should deliver an address to the people, as Socrates says, Tripartit. Hist. Lib. ix. Jerome does not conceal his dissatisfaction with the enactment (Hieron. Epist. ad Evagr.). It certainly would have been deemed monstrous for one to give himself out as a bishop, and yet not show himself a true bishop by his conduct. Such, then, was the strictness of those times, that all ministers were obliged to fulfil the office as the Lord requires of them. Nor do I refer to the practice of one age only, since not even in the time of Gregory, when the Church had almost fallen (certainly had greatly degenerated from ancient purity), would any bishop have been tolerated who abstained from preaching. In some part of his twenty-fourth Epistle he says, " The priest dies when no sound is heard from him : for he calls forth the wrath of the unseen Judge against him if he walks without the sound of preaching." Elsewhere he says, " When Paul testifies that he is pure from the blood of all men (Acts xx. 26), by his words, we, who are called priests, are charged, are arraigned, are shown to be guilty, since to those sins which we have of our own we add the deaths of other men, for we commit murder as often as lukewarm and silent we see them daily going to destruction " (Gregor. Hom. in

Ezek. xi. 26). He calls himself and others silent when less assiduous in their work than they ought to be. Since he does not spare even those who did their duty partially, what think you would he do in the case of those who entirely neglected it? For a long time, therefore, it was regarded in the Church as the first duty of a bishop to feed the people by the word of God, or to edify the Church, in public and private, with sound doctrine.

4. As to the fact, that each province had an archbishop among the bishops (see chap. vii. sec. 15), and, moreover, that, in the Council of Nice, patriarchs were appointed to be superior to archbishops, in order and dignity, this was designed for the preservation of discipline, although, in treating of the subject here, it ought not to be omitted, that the practice was very rare. The chief reason for which these orders were instituted was, that if anything occurred in any church which could not well be explicated by a few, it might be referred to a provincial synod. If the magnitude or difficulty of the case demanded a larger discussion, patriarchs were employed along with synods,[1] and from them there was no appeal except to a General Council. To the government thus constituted some gave the name of Hierarchy—a name, in my opinion, improper, certainly one not used by Scripture. For the Holy Spirit designed to provide that no one should dream of primacy or domination in regard to the government of the Church. But if, disregarding the term, we look to the thing, we shall find that the ancient bishops had no wish to frame a form of church government different from that which God has prescribed in his word.

5. Nor was the case of deacons then different from what it had been under the apostles (chap. iii. sec. 6). For they received the daily offerings of the faithful, and the annual revenues of the Church, that they might apply them to their true uses; in other words, partly in maintaining ministers, and partly in supporting the poor; at the sight of the bishop, however, to whom they every year gave an account of their stewardship. For, although the canons uniformly make the bishop the dispenser of all the goods of the Church, this is not to be understood as if he by himself undertook that charge, but because it belonged to him to prescribe to the deacon who were to be admitted to the public alimony of the Church, and point out to what persons, and in what portions, the residue was to be distributed, and because he was entitled to see whether the deacon faithfully performed his office. Thus, in the canons which they ascribe to the apostles, it is said, "We command that the bishop have the affairs of the Church under his control. For if the souls of men, which are more precious, have been intrusted to him, much more is he entitled to have the charge of money matters, so that under his control all may be dispensed to the poor by the presbyters and deacons, that the ministra-

1 French, "La cognoissance venoit aux patriarches, qui assemblerent le concile de tous les eveques respondant a leur primauté;"—the cognisance fell to the patriarchs, who assembled a council of all the bishops corresponding to their precedence.

tion may be made reverently and with due care." And in the Council of Antioch, it was decreed (cap. xxxv.), that bishops, who intermeddled with the effects of the Church, without the knowledge of the presbyters and deacons, should be restrained. But there is no occasion to discuss this point farther, since it is evident, from many of the letters of Gregory, that even at that time, when the ecclesiastical ordinances were otherwise much vitiated, it was still the practice for the deacons to be, under the bishops, the stewards of the poor. It is probable that at the first subdeacons were attached to the deacons, to assist them in the management of the poor; but the distinction was gradually lost. Archdeacons began to be appointed when the extent of the revenues demanded a new and more exact method of administration, though Jerome mentions that it already existed in his day.[1] To them belonged the amount of revenues, possessions, and furniture, and the charge of the daily offerings. Hence Gregory declares to the Archdeacon Solitanus, that the blame rested with him, if any of the goods of the Church perished through his fraud or negligence. The reading of the word to the people, and exhortation to prayer, was assigned to them, and they were permitted, moreover, to give the cup in the sacred Supper; but this was done for the purpose of honouring their office, that they might perform it with greater reverence, when they were reminded by such symbols that what they discharged was not some profane stewardship, but a spiritual function dedicated to God.

6. Hence, also, we may judge what was the use, and of what nature was the distribution of ecclesiastical goods. You may everywhere find, both from the decrees of synods, and from ancient writers, that whatever the Church possessed, either in lands or in money, was the patrimony of the poor. Accordingly, the saying is ever and anon sounded in the ears of bishops and deacons, Remember that you are not handling your own property, but that destined for the necessities of the poor; if you dishonestly conceal or dilapidate it, you will be guilty of blood. Hence they are admonished to distribute them to those to whom they are due, with the greatest fear and reverence, as in the sight of God, without respect of persons. Hence, also, in Chrysostom, Ambrose, Augustine, and other like bishops, those grave obtestations in which they assert their integrity before the people. But since it is just in itself, and was sanctioned by a divine law, that those who devote their labour to the Church shall be supported at the public expense of the Church, and some presbyters in that age having consecrated their patrimony to God, had become voluntarily poor, the distribution was so made that aliment was afforded to ministers, and the poor were not neglected. Meanwhile, it was provided that the ministers themselves, who ought to be an example of frugality to others, should not have so much as might be abused for luxury or delicacy; but only what might be needful to support their wants:

[1] Hieronymus, Epist. ad Nepotianum. It is mentioned also by Chrysostom, Epist. ad Innocent.

"For those clergy, who can be supported by their own patrimony," says Jerome, "commit sacrilege if they accept what belongs to the poor, and by such abuse eat and drink judgment to themselves."

7. At first the administration was free and voluntary, when bishops and deacons were faithful of their own accord, and when integrity of conscience and purity of life supplied the place of laws. Afterwards, when, from the cupidity and depraved desires of some, bad examples arose, canons were framed, to correct these evils, and divided the revenues of the Church into four parts, assigning one to the clergy, another to the poor, another to the repair of churches and other edifices, a fourth to the poor, whether[1] strangers or natives. For though other canons attribute this last part to the bishop, it differs in no respect from the division which I have mentioned. For they do not mean that it is his property, which he may devour alone or squander in any way he pleases, but that it may enable him to use the hospitality which Paul requires in that order (1 Tim. iii. 2). This is the interpretation of Gelasius and Gregory. For the only reason which Gelasius gives why the bishop should claim anything to himself is, that he may be able to bestow it on captives and strangers. Gregory speaks still more clearly: "It is the custom of the Apostolic See," says he, "to give command to the bishop who has been ordained, to divide all the revenues into four portions— namely, one to the bishop and his household for hospitality and main- tenance, another to the clergy, a third to the poor, a fourth to the repair of churches." The bishop, therefore, could not lawfully take for his own use more than was sufficient for moderate and frugal food and clothing. When any one began to wanton either in luxury or ostentation and show, he was immediately reprimanded by his col- leagues, and if he obeyed not, was deprived of his honours.

8. Moreover, the sum expended on the adorning of churches was at first very trifling, and even afterwards, when the Church had become somewhat more wealthy, they in that matter observed medi- ocrity. Still, whatever money was then collected was reserved for the poor, when any greater necessity occurred. Thus Cyril, when a famine prevailed in the province of Jerusalem, and the want could not otherwise be supplied, took the vessels and robes and sold them for the support of the poor. In like manner, Acatius, Bishop of Amida, when a great multitude of the Persians were almost destroyed by famine, having assembled the clergy, and delivered this noble address, "Our God has no need either of chalices or salvers, for he neither eats nor drinks" (Tripart. Hist. Lib. v. and Lib. xi. c. 16), melted down the plate, that he might be able to furnish food and obtain the means of ransoming the miserable. Jerome also, while inveighing against the excessive splendour of churches, relates that Exuperius, Bishop of Tholouse, in his day, though he carried the

---

[1] In the Amsterdam edition the words are only "quartam vero advenis pauperibus." The Geneva edition of 1559, the last published under Calvin's own eye, has "quartam vero tam advenis quam indigenis pauperibus." With this Tholuck agrees.

body of the Lord in a wicker basket, and his blood in a glass, nevertheless suffered no poor man to be hungry (Hieron. ad Nepotian). What I lately said of Acatius, Ambrose relates of himself. For when the Arians assailed him for having broken down the sacred vessels for the ransom of captives, he made this most admirable excuse : " He who sent the apostles without gold has also gathered churches without gold. The Church has gold not to keep but to distribute, and give support in necessity. What need is there of keeping what is of no benefit ? Are we ignorant how much gold and silver the Assyrians carried off from the temple of the Lord ? Is it not better for a priest to melt them for the support of the poor, if other means are wanting, than for a sacrilegious enemy to carry them away ? Would not the Lord say, Why have you suffered so many poor to die of hunger, and you certainly had gold wherewith to minister to their support ? Why have so many captives been carried away and not redeemed ? Why have so many been slain by the enemy ? It had been better to preserve living than metallic vessels. These charges you will not be able to answer : for what could you say ? I feared lest the temple of God should want ornament. He would answer, Sacraments require not gold, and things which are not bought with gold please not by gold. The ornament of the Sacraments is the ransom of captives" (Ambros. de Offic. Lib. ii. c. 28). In a word, we see the exact truth of what he elsewhere says—viz. that whatever the Church then possessed was the revenue of the needy. Again, A bishop has nothing but what belongs to the poor (Ambros. Lib. v. Ep. 31, 33).

9. We have now reviewed the ministerial offices of the ancient Church. For others, of which ecclesiastical writers make mention, were rather exercises and preparations than distinct offices. These holy men, that they might leave a nursery of the Church behind them, received young men, who, with the consent and authority of their parents, devoted themselves to the spiritual warfare under their guardianship and training, and so formed them from their tender years, that they might not enter on the discharge of the office as ignorant novices. All who received this training were designated by the general name of *Clerks*. I could wish that some more appropriate name had been given them, for this appellation had its origin in error, or at least improper feeling, since the whole church is by Peter denominated κληρος (*clerus*), that is, the inheritance of the Lord (1 Pet. v. 3). It was in itself, however, a most sacred and salutary institution, that those who wished to devote themselves and their labour to the Church should be brought up under the charge of the bishop ; so that no one should minister in the Church unless he had been previously well trained, unless he had in early life imbibed sound doctrine, unless by stricter discipline he had formed habits of gravity and severer morals, been withdrawn from ordinary business, and accustomed to spiritual cares and studies. For as tyros in the military art are trained by mock fights for true and serious warfare, so there was a rudimental training by which they were exercised in

clerical duty before they were actually appointed to office. First, then, they intrusted them with the opening and shutting of the church, and called them Ostiarii. Next, they gave the name of Acolytes to those who assisted the bishop in domestic services, and constantly attended him, first, as a mark of respect; and, secondly, that no suspicion might arise.[1] Moreover, that they might gradually become known to the people, and recommend themselves to them, and at the same time might learn to stand the gaze of all, and speak before all, that they might not, when appointed presbyters, be overcome with shame when they came forward to teach, the office of reading in the desk was given them.[2] In this way they were gradually advanced, that they might prove their carefulness in separate exercises, until they were appointed subdeacons. All I mean by this is, that these were rather the rudimentary exercises of tyros than functions which were accounted among the true ministries of the Church.

10. In regard to what we have set down as the first and second heads in the calling of ministers—viz. the persons to be elected and the religious care to be therein exercised—the ancient Church followed the injunction of Paul, and the examples of the apostles. For they were accustomed to meet for the election of pastors with the greatest reverence, and with earnest prayer to God. Moreover, they had a form of examination by which they tested the life and doctrine of those who were to be elected by the standard of Paul (1 Tim. iii. 2); only here they sometimes erred from excessive strictness, by exacting more of a bishop than Paul requires, and especially, in process of time, by exacting celibacy: but in other respects their practice corresponded with Paul's description. In regard to our third head, however—viz. Who were entitled to appoint ministers?—they did not always observe the same rule. Anciently none were admitted to the number of the clergy without the consent of the whole people: and hence Cyprian makes a laboured apology for having appointed Aurelius a reader without consulting the Church, because, although done contrary to custom, it was not done without reason. He thus premises: " In ordaining clergy, dearest brethren, we are wont previously to consult you, and weigh the manners and merits of each by the common advice" (Cyprian. Lib. ii. Ep. 5). But as in these minor exercises[3] there was no great danger, inasmuch as they were appointed to a long probation and unimportant function, the consent of the people ceased to be asked. Afterwards, in other orders also, with the exception of the bishopric, the people usually left the choice and decision to the bishop and presbyters, who thus determined who were fit and worthy, unless, perhaps, when new presbyters were appointed to parishes, for then the express consent of the inhabitants of the place behoved to be given. Nor is it strange that in this matter the people

---

[1] The French adds, " Afin qu'il n'allâ nulle part sans compagnie et sans temoin; "—in order that he might not go anywhere without company and without witness

[2] French, " On leur ordonnoit de faire la lecture des Pseaumes au pulpitre;"—they ordered them to read the Psalms in the desk.

[3] The French adds, " Comme de Lecteurs et Acolytes;"—as Readers and Acolytes.

were not very anxious to maintain their right, for no subdeacon was appointed who had not given a long proof of his conduct in the clerical office, agreeably to the strictness of discipline then in use. After he had approved himself in that degree, he was appointed deacon, and thereafter, if he conducted himself faithfully, he attained to the honour of a presbyter. Thus none were promoted whose conduct had not, in truth, been tested for many years under the eye of the people. There were also many canons for punishing their faults, so that the Church, if she did not neglect the remedies, was not burdened with bad presbyters or deacons. In the case of presbyters, indeed, the consent of the citizens was always required, as is attested by the canon (Primus Distinct. 67), which is attributed to Anacletus. In fine, all ordinations took place at stated periods of the year, that none might creep in stealthily without the consent of the faithful, or be promoted with too much facility without witnesses.

11. In electing bishops, the people long retained their right of preventing any one from being intruded who was not acceptable to all. Accordingly, it was forbidden by the Council of Antioch to induct any one on the unwilling. This also Leo I. carefully confirms. Hence these passages: "Let him be elected whom the clergy and people or the majority demand." Again. "Let him who is to preside over all be elected by all" (Leo, Ep. 90, cap. 2). He, therefore, who is appointed while unknown and unexamined, must of necessity be violently intruded. Again, "Let him be elected who is chosen by the clergy, and called by the people, and let him be consecrated by the provincials with the judgment of the metropolitan." So careful were the holy fathers that this liberty of the people should on no account be diminished, that when a general council, assembled at Constantinople, were ordaining Nectarius, they declined to do it without the approbation of the whole clergy and people, as their letter to the Roman synod testified. Accordingly, when any bishop nominated his successor, the act was not ratified without consulting the whole people. Of this you have not only an example, but the form, in Augustine, in the nomination of Eradius (August. Ep. 110). And Theodoret, after relating that Peter was the successor nominated by Athanasius, immediately adds, that the sacerdotal order ratified it, that the magistracy, chief men, and whole people, by their acclamation approved.[1]

12. It was, indeed, decreed (and I admit on the best grounds) by the Council of Laodicea (Can. xviii.) that the election should not be left to crowds. For it scarcely ever happens that so many heads, with one consent, settle any affair well. It generally holds true, "Incertum scindi studia in contraria vulgus;"—"Opposing wishes rend the fickle crowd." For, first, the clergy alone selected, and presented him whom they had selected to the magistrate, or senate, and chief men. These, after deliberation, put their signature to the

---

1 The whole narrative in Theodoret is most deserving of notice. Theodoret. Lib. iv. cap. xx.

election, if it seemed proper, if not, they chose another whom they more highly approved. The matter was then laid before the multitude, who, although not bound by those previous proceedings, were less able to act tumultuously. Or, if the matter began with the multitude, it was only that it might be known whom they were most desirous to have; the wishes of the people being heard, the clergy at length elected. Thus, it was neither lawful for the clergy to appoint whom they chose, nor were they, however, under the necessity of yielding to the foolish desires of the people. Leo sets down this order, when he says, " The wishes of the citizens, the testimonies of the people, the choice of the honourable, the election of the clergy, are to be waited for" (Leo, Ep. 87). Again, " Let the testimony of the honourable, the subscription of the clergy, the consent of the magistracy and people, be obtained; otherwise (says he) it must on no account be done." Nor is anything more intended by the decree of the Council of Laodicea, than that the clergy and rulers were not to allow themselves to be carried away by the rash multitude, but rather by their prudence and gravity to repress their foolish desires whenever there was occasion.

13. This mode of election was still in force in the time of Gregory, and probably continued to a much later period. Many of his letters which are extant clearly prove this, for whenever a new bishop is to be elected, his custom is to write to the clergy, magistrates, and people; sometimes also to the governor, according to the nature of the government. But if, on account of the unsettled state of the Church, he gives the oversight of the election to a neighbouring bishop, he always requires a formal decision confirmed by the subscriptions of all. Nay, when one Constantius was elected Bishop of Milan, and in consequence of the incursions of the Barbarians many of the Milanese had fled to Genoa, he thought that the election would not be lawful unless they too were called together and gave their assent (Gregor. Lib. ii. Ep. 69). Nay, five hundred years have not elapsed since Pope Nicholas fixed the election of the Roman Pontiff in this way, first, that the cardinals should precede; next, that they should join to themselves the other clergy; and, lastly, that the election should be ratified by the consent of the people. And in the end he recites the decree of Leo, which I lately quoted, and orders it to be enforced in future. But should the malice of the wicked so prevail that the clergy are obliged to quit the city, in order to make a pure election, he, however, orders that some of the people shall, at the same time, be present. The suffrage of the Emperor, as far as we can understand, was required only in two churches, those of Rome and Constantinople, these being the two seats of empire. For when Ambrose was sent by Valentinianus to Milan with authority to superintend the election of a new bishop, it was an extraordinary proceeding, in consequence of the violent factions which raged among the citizens. But at Rome the authority of the Emperor in the election of the bishop was so great, that Gregory says he was appointed to the government

of the Church by his order (Gregor. Lib. i. Ep. 5), though he had been called by the people in regular form. The custom, however, was, that when the magistrates, clergy, and people, nominated any one, he was forthwith presented to the Emperor, who either by approving ratified, or by disapproving annulled the election. There is nothing contrary to this practice in the decretals which are collected by Gratian, where all that is said is, that it was on no account to be tolerated, that canonical election should be abolished, and a king should at pleasure appoint a bishop, and that one thus promoted by violent authority was not to be consecrated by the metropolitans. For it is one thing to deprive the Church of her right, and transfer it entirely to the caprice of a single individual ; it is another thing to assign to a king or emperor the honour of confirming a legitimate election by his authority.

14. It now remains to treat of the form by which the ministers of the ancient Church were initiated to their office after election. This was termed by the Latins, Ordination or consecration, and by the Greeks χειροτονία, sometimes also χειροθεσία, though χειροτονία properly denotes that mode of election by which suffrages are declared by a show of hands. There is extant a decree of the Council of Nice, to the effect that the metropolitans, with all the bishops of the province, were to meet to ordain him who was chosen. But if, from distance, or sickness, or any other necessary cause, part were prevented, three at least should meet, and those who were absent signify their consent by letter. And this canon, after it had fallen into desuetude, was afterwards renewed by several councils. All, or at least all who had not an excuse, were enjoined to be present, in order that a stricter examination might be had of the life and doctrine of him who was to be ordained ; for the thing was not done without examination. And it appears, from the words of Cyprian, that, in old time, they were not wont to be called after the election, but to be present at the election, and with the view of their acting as moderators, that no disorder might be committed by the crowd. For after saying that the people had the power either of choosing worthy or refusing unworthy priests, he immediately adds, " For which reason, we must carefully observe and hold by the divine and apostolic tradition (which is observed by us also, and almost by all the provinces), that for the due performance of ordinations all the nearest bishops of the province should meet with the people over whom the person is proposed to be ordained, and the bishop should be elected in presence of the people. But as they were sometimes too slowly assembled, and there was a risk that some might abuse the delay for purposes of intrigue, it was thought that it would be sufficient if they came after the designation was made, and on due investigation consecrated him who had been approved.

15. While this was done everywhere without exception, a different custom gradually gained ground—namely, that those who were elected

should go to the metropolitan to obtain ordination.   This was owing
more to ambition, and the corruption of the ancient custom, than to
any good reason.   And not long after, the authority of the Romish
See being now increased, another still worse custom was introduced,
of applying to it for the consecration of the bishops of almost all
Italy.   This we may observe from the letters of Gregory (Lib. ii.
Ep. 69, 76).   The ancient right was preserved by a few cities only
which had not yielded so easily; for instance, Milan.   Perhaps metropolitan sees only retained their privilege.   For, in order to consecrate an archbishop, it was the practice for all the provincial bishops
to meet in the metropolitan city.   The form used was the laying on
of hands (chap. xix. sec. 28, 31).   I do not read that any other ceremonies were used, except that, in the public meeting, the bishops
had some dress to distinguish them from the other presbyters.   Presbyters, also, and deacons, were ordained by the laying on of hands ;
but each bishop, with the college of presbyters, ordained his own
presbyters.   But though they all did the same act, yet because the
bishop presided, and the ordination was performed as it were under
his auspices, it was said to be his.   Hence ancient writers often say
that a presbyter does not differ in any respect from a bishop except
in not having the power of ordaining.

CHAPTER V.

THE ANCIENT FORM OF GOVERNMENT UTTERLY CORRUPTED BY THE TYRANNY OF THE PAPACY.

This chapter consists of two parts,—I. Who are called to the ministry under the Papacy, their character, and the ground of their appointment, sec. 1–7. II. How far they fulfil their office, sec. 8–19.

Sections.

1. It may now be proper to bring under the eye of the reader the order of church government observed by the Roman See and all its satellites, and the whole of that hierarchy, which they have perpetually in their mouths, and compare it with the description we have given of the primitive and early Church, that the contrast may make it manifest what kind of church those have who plume themselves on the very title, as sufficient to outweigh, or rather overwhelm us. It will be best to begin with the call, that we may see who are called to the ministry, with what character, and on what grounds. Thereafter we will consider how far they faithfully fulfil their office. We shall give the first place to the bishops; would that they could claim the honour of holding the first rank in this disscussion! But the subject does not allow me even to touch it lightly, without exposing their disgrace. Still, let me remember in what kind of writing I am engaged, and not allow my discourse, which ought to be framed for simple teaching, to wander beyond its proper limits. But let any of them, who have not laid aside all modesty, tell me what kind of bishops are uniformly elected in the present day. Any examination of doctrine is too old fashioned, but if any respect is had to doctrine, they make choice of some lawyer who knows better how to plead in the forum than to preach in the church. This much is certain, that for a hundred years, scarcely one in a hundred has been elected who had any acquaintance with sacred doctrine. I do not spare former ages because they were much better, but because the question now relates only to the present Church. If morals be inquired into, we shall find few or almost none whom the ancient canons would not have judged unworthy. If one was not a drunkard, he was a fornicator; if one was free from this vice, he was either a gambler or sportsman, or a loose liver in some respect. For there are lighter faults which, according to the ancient canons, exclude from the episcopal office. But the most absurd thing of all is, that even boys scarcely ten years of age are, by the permission of the Pope, made bishops. Such is the effrontery and stupidity to which they have arrived, that they have no dread even of that last and monstrous iniquity, which is altogether abhorrent even from natural feeling. Hence it appears what kind of elections these must have been, when such supine negligence existed.

2. Then in election, the whole right has been taken from the people. Vows, assents, subscriptions, and all things of this sort, have disappeared; the whole power has been given to the canons alone. First, they confer the episcopal office on whomsoever they please; by-and-by they bring him forth into the view of the people, but it is to be adored, not examined. But Leo protests that no reason permits this, and declares it to be a violent imposition (Leo, Ep. 90, cap. 2). Cyprian, after declaring it to be of divine authority, that election should not take place without the consent of the people, shows that a different procedure is at variance with the word of God. Numerous decrees of councils most strictly forbid it to be

otherwise done, and if done, order it to be null. If this is true, there is not throughout the whole Papacy in the present day any canonical election in accordance either with divine or ecclesiastical law. Now, were there no other evil in this, what excuse can they give for having robbed the Church of her right? But the corruption of the times required (they say), that since hatred and party-spirit prevailed with the people and magistrates in the election of bishops more than right and sound judgment, the determination should be confined to a few. Allow that this was the last remedy in desperate circumstances. When the cure was seen to be more hurtful than the disease, why was not a remedy provided for this new evil? But it is said that the course which the Canons must follow is strictly prescribed. But can we doubt, that even in old times the people, on meeting to elect a bishop, were aware that they were bound by the most sacred laws, when they saw a rule prescribed by the word of God? That one sentence in which God describes the true character of a bishop ought justly to be of more weight than ten thousand canons. Nevertheless, carried away by the worst of feelings, they had no regard to law or equity. So in the present day, though most excellent laws have been made, they remain buried in writing. Meanwhile, the general and approved practice is (and it is carried on as it were systematically), that drunkards, fornicators, gamblers, are everywhere promoted to this honour; nay, this is little: bishoprics are the rewards of adulterers and panders: for when they are given to hunters and hawkers, things may be considered at the best. To excuse such unworthy procedure in any way, were to be wicked over much. The people had a most excellent canon prescribed to them by the word of God—viz. that a bishop must be blameless, apt to teach, not a brawler, &c. (1 Tim. iii. 2). Why, then, was the province of electing transferred from the people to these men? Just because among the tumults and factions of the people the word of God was not heard. And, on the other hand, why is it not in the present day transferred from these men, who not only violate all laws, but having cast off shame, libidinously, avariciously, and ambitiously, mix and confound things human and divine?

3. But it is not true to say that the thing was devised as a remedy. We read, that in old times tumults often arose in cities at the election of bishops; yet no one ever ventured to think of depriving the citizens of their right: for they had other methods by which they could either prevent the fault, or correct it when committed. I will state the matter as it truly is. When the people began to be negligent in making their choice, and left the business, as less suited to them, to the presbyters, these abused the opportunity to usurp a domination, which they afterwards established by putting forth new canons. Ordination is now nothing else than a mere mockery. For the kind of examination of which they make a display is so empty and trifling, that it even entirely wants the semblance. Therefore. when sovereigns, by paction with the Roman Pontiffs, obtained for

themselves the right of nominating bishops, the Church sustained no new injury, because the canons were merely deprived of an election which they had seized without any right, or acquired by stealth. Nothing, indeed, can be more disgraceful, than that bishops should be sent from courts to take possession of churches, and pious princes would do well to desist from such corruption. For there is an impious spoliation of the Church whenever any people have a bishop intruded whom they have not asked, or at least freely approved. But that disorderly practice, which long existed in churches, gave occasion to sovereigns to assume to themselves the presentation of bishops. They wished the benefice to belong to themselves, rather than to those who had no better right to it, and who equally abused it.

4. Such is the famous call, on account of which bishops boast that they are the successors of the apostles. They say, moreover, that they alone can competently appoint presbyters. But herein they most shamefully corrupt the ancient institution, that they by their ordination appoint not presbyters to guide and feed the people, but priests to sacrifice. In like manner, when they consecrate deacons, they pay no regard to their true and proper office, but only ordain to certain ceremonies concerning the cup and paten. But in the Council of Chalcedon it was, on the contrary, decreed that there should be no absolute ordinations, that is, ordinations without assigning to the ordained a place where they were to exercise their office. This decree is most useful for two reasons—first, That churches may not be burdened with superfluous expense, nor idle men receive what ought to be distributed to the poor ; and, secondly, That those who are ordained may consider that they are not promoted merely to an honorary office, but intrusted with a duty which they are solemnly bound to discharge. But the Roman authorities (who think that nothing is to be cared for in religion but their belly) consider the first title to be a revenue adequate to their support, whether it be from their own patrimony or from the priesthood. Accordingly, when they ordain presbyters or deacons, without any anxiety as to where they ought to minister, they confer the order, provided those ordained are sufficiently rich to support themselves. But what man can admit that the title which the decree of the council requires is an annual revenue for sustenance ? Again, when more recent canons made bishops liable in the support of those whom they had ordained without a fit title, that they might thus repress too great facility, a method was devised of eluding the penalty. For he who is ordained promises that whatever be the title named he will be contented with it. In this way he is precluded from an action for aliment. I say nothing of the thousand frauds which are here committed, as when some falsely claim the empty titles of benefices, from which t! ey cannot obtain a sixpence of revenue, and others by secret stipulation obtain a temporary appointment, which they promise that they will immediately restore, but sometimes do not. There are still more mysteries of the same kind.

5. But although these grosser abuses were removed, is it not at all times absurd to appoint a presbyter without assigning him a locality? For when they ordain it is only to sacrifice.   But the legitimate ordination of a presbyter is to the government of the Church, while deacons are called to the charge of alms.   It is true, many pompous ceremonies are used to disguise the act, that mere show may excite veneration in the simple ; but what effect can these semblances have upon men of sound minds, when beneath them there is nothing solid or true ?   They used ceremonies either borrowed from Judaism or devised by themselves ; from these it were better if they would abstain. Of the trial (for it is unnecessary to say anything of the shadow which they retain), of the consent of the people, of other necessary things, there is no mention.   By shadow, I mean those ridiculous gesticulations framed in inept and frigid imitation of antiquity.   The bishops have their vicars, who, previous to ordination, inquire into doctrine. But what is the inquiry ?   Is it whether they are able to read their Missals, or whether they can decline some common noun which occurs in the lesson, or conjugate a verb, or give the meaning of some one word ?   For it is not necessary to give the sense of a single sentence. And yet even those who are deficient in these puerile elements are not repelled, provided they bring the recommendation of money or influence.   Of the same nature is the question which is thrice put in an unintelligible voice, when the persons who are to be ordained are brought to the altar—viz. Are they worthy of the honour ?   One (who never saw them, but has his part in the play, that no form may be wanting) answers, They are worthy.[1]   What can you accuse in these venerable fathers save that, by indulging in such sacrilegious sport, they shamelessly laugh at God and man ?   But as they have long been in possession of the thing, they think they have now a legal title to it.   For any one who ventures to open his lips against these palpable and flagrant iniquities is hurried off to a capital trial, like one who had in old time divulged the mysteries of Ceres.   Would they act thus if they had any belief in a God ?

6. Then in the collation of benefices (which was formerly conjoined with ordination, but is now altogether separate), how much better do they conduct themselves ?   But they have many reasons to give, for it is not bishops alone who confer the office of priests (and even in their case, where they are called Collators, they have not always the full right), but others have the presentation, while they only retain the honorary title of collations.   To these are added nominations from schools, resignations, either simple or by way of exchange, com-

---

1 " C'est un acte semblable, que quand ceux qu'on doit promouvoir se presentent à l'autel, on demande par trois fois en Latin, s'il ést digne ; et quelcun qui ne l'a jamais vue, ou quelque valet de chambre que n'entend point Latin, repond en Latin qu'il est digne : tout ainsi qu'un personnage joueroit son rolle en une farce."—In like manner, when those whom they are to promote present themselves at the altar, they ask, three times in Latin, if he is worthy ; and some one who has never seen him, or some valet who does not understand Latin, replies, in Latin, that he is worthy : just as a person would play his part in a farce.

mendatory rescripts, preventions, and the like. But they all conduct themselves in such a way that one cannot upbraid another. I maintain that, in the Papacy in the present day, scarcely one benefice in a hundred is conferred without simony, as the ancients have defined it (Calv. in Art. viii. 21). I say not that all purchase for a certain sum; but show me one in twenty who does not attain to the priesthood by some sinister method. Some owe their promotion to kindred or affinity, others to the influence of their parents, while others procure favour by obsequiousness. In short, the end for which the offices are conferred is, that provision may be made not for churches, but for those who receive them. Accordingly, they call them benefices, by which name they sufficiently declare, that they look on them in no other light than as the largesses by which princes either court the favour or reward the services of their soldiers. I say nothing of the fact, that these rewards are conferred on barbers, cooks, grooms, and dross of that sort. At present, indeed, there are no cases in law courts which make a greater noise than those concerning sacerdotal offices, so that you may regard them as nothing else than game set before dogs to be hunted. Is it tolerable even to hear the name of pastors given to those who have forced their way into the possession of a church as into an enemy's country? who have evicted it by forensic brawls? who have bought it for a price? who have laboured for it by sordid sycophancy? who, while scarcely lisping boys, have obtained it like heritage from uncles and relatives? Sometimes even bastards obtain it from their fathers.

7. Was the licentiousness of the people, however corrupt and lawless, ever carried to such a height? But a more monstrous thing still is, that one man (I say not what kind of man, but certainly one who cannot govern himself) is appointed to the charge of five or six churches. In the courts of princes in the present day, you may see youths who are thrice abbots, twice bishops, once archbishops. Everywhere are Canons loaded with five, six, or seven cures, of not one of which they take the least charge, except to draw the income. I will not object that the word of God cries aloud against this: it has long ceased to have the least weight with them. I will not object that many councils denounce the severest punishment against this dishonest practice; these, too, when it suits them, they boldly contemn. But I say that it is monstrous wickedness, altogether opposed to God, to nature, and to ecclesiastical government, that one thief should lie brooding over several churches, that the name of pastor should be given to one who, even if he were willing, could not be present among his flock, and yet (such is their impudence) they cloak these abominations with the name of church, that they may exempt them from all blame. Nay, if you please, in these iniquities is contained that sacred succession to which, as they boast, it is owing that the Church does not perish.

8. Let us now see, as the second mark for estimating a legitimate pastor, how faithfully they discharge their office. Of the priests

who are there elected, some are called monks, others seculars. The former herd was unknown to the early Church; even to hold such a place in the Church is so repugnant to the monastic profession, that in old times, when persons were elected out of monasteries to clerical offices, they ceased to be monks. And, accordingly, Gregory, though in his time there were many abuses, did not suffer the offices to be thus confounded (Gregor. Lib. iii. Ep. 11). For he insists that those who have been appointed abbots shall resign the clerical office, because no one can be properly at the same time a monk and a clerk, the one being an obstacle to the other. Now, were I to ask how he can well fulfil his office who is declared by the canons to be unfit, what answer, pray, will they give? They will quote those abortive decrees of Innocent and Boniface, by which monks are admitted to the honour and power of the priesthood, though they remain in their monasteries. But is it at all reasonable that any unlearned ass, as soon as he has seized upon the Roman See, may by one little word overturn all antiquity? But of this matter afterwards. Let it now suffice, that in the purer times of the Church it was regarded as a great absurdity for a monk to hold the office of priest. For Jerome declares that he does not the office of priest while he is living among monks, and ranks himself as one of the people to be governed by the priests. But to concede this to them, what duty do they perform? Some of the mendicants preach, while all the other monks chant or mutter masses in their cells; as if either our Saviour had wished, or the nature of the office permits, presbyters to be made for such a purpose. When Scripture plainly testifies that it is the duty of a presbyter to rule his own church (Acts xx. 28), is it not impious profanation to transfer it to another purpose, nay, altogether to change the sacred institution of God? For when they are ordained, they are expressly forbidden to do what God enjoins on all presbyters. For this is their cant, Let a monk, contented with his cell, neither presume to administer the sacraments, nor hold any other public office. Let them deny, if they can, that it is open mockery of God when any one is appointed a presbyter in order to abstain from his proper and genuine office, and when he who has the name is not able to have the thing.

9. I come to the seculars, some of whom are (as they speak) beneficiaries; that is, have offices by which they are maintained, while others let out their services, day by day, to chant or say masses, and live in a manner on a stipend thus collected. Benefices either have a cure of souls, as bishoprics and parochial charges, or they are the stipends of delicate men, who gain a livelihood by chanting; as prebends, canonries, parsonships, deaneries, chaplainships, and the like; although, things being now turned upside down, the offices of abbot and prior are not only conferred on secular presbyters, but on boys also by privilege, that is, by common and usual custom. In regard to the mercenaries who seek their food from day to day, what else could they do than they actually do, in other words, prostitute

themselves in an illiberal and disgraceful manner for gain, especially from the vast multitude of them with which the world now teems? Hence, as they dare not beg openly, or think that in this way they would gain little, they go about like hungry dogs, and by a kind of barking importunity extort from the unwilling what they may deposit in their hungry stomachs. Were I here to attempt to describe how disgraceful it is to the Church, that the honour and office of a presbyter should come to this, I should never have done. My readers, therefore, must not expect from me a discourse which can fully represent this flagitious indignity. I briefly say, that if it is the office of a presbyter (and this both the word of God prescribes (1 Cor. iv. 1) and the ancient canons enjoin) to feed the Church, and administer the spiritual kingdom of Christ, all those priests who have no work or stipend, save in the traffic of masses, not only fail in their office, but have no lawful office to discharge. No place is given them to teach, they have no people to govern. In short, nothing is left them but an altar on which to sacrifice Christ; this is to sacrifice not to God but to demons, as we shall afterwards show (see chap. xviii. sec. 3, 9, 14).

10. I am not here touching on extraneous faults,[1] but only on the intestine evil which lies at the root of the very institution. I will add a sentence which will sound strange in their ears, but which, as it is true, it is right to express, that canons, deans, chaplains, provosts, and all who are maintained in idle offices of priesthood, are to be viewed in the same light. For what service can they perform to the Church? The preaching of the word, the care of discipline, and the administration of the sacraments, they have shaken off as burdens too grievous to be borne. What then remains on which they can plume themselves as being true presbyters? Merely chanting and pompous ceremonies. But what is this to the point? If they allege custom, use, or the long prescription, I, on the contrary, appeal to the definition by which our Saviour has described true presbyters, and shown the qualities of those who are to be regarded as presbyters. But if they cannot endure the hard law of submitting to the rule of Christ, let them at least allow the cause to be decided by the authority of the primitive Church. Their condition will not be one whit improved when decided according to the ancient canons. Those who have degenerated into Canons ought to be presbyters, as they formerly were, to rule the Church in common with the bishop, and be, as it were, his colleagues in the pastoral office. What they call deaneries of the chapter have no concern with the true government of the Church, much less chaplainships and other similar worthless names. In what light then are they all to be regarded? Assuredly, both the word of Christ and the practice of the primitive Church exclude them from the honour of presbyters. They maintain, however, that they are presbyters; but we must unmask them, and we shall find that their whole profession is most alien from the office of presbyters, as that office is described to us by the apostles, and was

---

[1] French, "les vices des personnes;"—the faults of individuals.

discharged in the primitive Church. All such offices, therefore, by whatever titles they are distinguished, as they are novelties, and certainly not supported either by the institution of God or the ancient practice of the Church, ought to have no place in a description of that spiritual government which the Church received, and was consecrated by the mouth of the Lord himself. Or (if they would have me express it in ruder and coarser terms), since chaplains, canons, deans, provosts, and such like lazy-bellies, do not even, with one finger, touch a particle of the office, which is necessarily required in presbyters, they must not be permitted falsely to usurp the honour, and thereby violate the holy institution of Christ.

11. There still remain bishops and rectors of parishes; and I wish that they would contend for the maintenance of their office. I would willingly grant that they have a pious and excellent office if they would discharge it; but when they desert the churches committed to them, and throwing the care upon others, would still be considered pastors, they just act as if the office of pastor were to do nothing. If any usurer, who never stirs from the city, were to give himself out as a ploughman or vine-dresser; or a soldier, who has constantly been in the field or the camp, and has never seen books or the forum, to pass for a lawyer, who could tolerate the absurdity? Much more absurdly do those act who would be called and deemed lawful pastors of the Church, and are unwilling so to be. How few are those who in appearance even take the superintendence of their church? Many spend their lives in devouring the revenues of churches which they never visit even for the purpose of inspection. Some once a-year go themselves or send a steward, that nothing may be lost in the letting of them. When the corruption first crept in, those who wished to enjoy this kind of vacation pleaded privilege, but it is now a rare case for any one to reside in his church. They look upon them merely in the light of farms, over which they appoint their vicars as grieves or husbandmen. But it is repugnant to common sense to regard him as a shepherd who has never seen a sheep of his flock.

12. It appears that in the time of Gregory some of the seeds of this corruption existed, the rulers of churches having begun to be more negligent in teaching; for he thus bitterly complains: "The world is full of priests, and yet labourers in the harvest are rare, for we indeed undertake the office of the priesthood, but we perform not the work of the office" (Gregor. Hom. 17). Again, "As they have no bowels of love, they would be thought lords, but do not at all acknowledge themselves to be fathers. They change a post of humility into the elevation of ascendancy." Again, "But we, O pastors! what are we doing, we who obtain the hire but are not labourers? We have fallen off to extraneous business; we undertake one thing, we perform another; we leave the ministry of the word, and, to our punishment, as I see, are called bishops, holding the honour of the name, not the power." Since he uses such bitterness of expression against those who were only less diligent or sedulous in their office,

what, pray, would he have said if he had seen that very few bishops, if any at all, and scarcely one in a hundred of the other clergy, mounted the pulpit once in their whole lifetime? For to such a degree of infatuation have men come, that it is thought beneath the episcopal dignity to preach a sermon to the people. In the time of Bernard things had become still worse. Accordingly, we see how bitterly he inveighs against the whole order, and yet there is reason to believe that matters were then in a much better state than now.

13. Whoever will duly examine and weigh the whole form of ecclesiastical government as now existing in the Papacy, will find that there is no kind of spoliation in which robbers act more licentiously, without law or measure. Certainly all things are so unlike, nay, so opposed to the institution of Christ, have so degenerated from the ancient customs and practices of the Church, are so repugnant to nature and reason, that a greater injury cannot be done to Christ than to use his name in defending this disorderly rule. We (say they) are the pillars of the Church, the priests of religion, the vicegerents of Christ, the heads of the faithful, because the apostolic authority has come to us by succession. As if they were speaking to stocks, they perpetually plume themselves on these absurdities. Whenever they make such boasts, I, in my turn, will ask, What have they in common with the apostles? We are not now treating of some hereditary honour which can come to men while they are asleep, but of the office of preaching, which they so greatly shun. In like manner, when we maintain that their kingdom is the tyranny of Antichrist, they immediately object that their venerable hierarchy has often been extolled by great and holy men, as if the holy fathers, when they commended the ecclesiastical hierarchy or spiritual government handed down to them by the apostles, ever dreamed of that shapeless and dreary chaos where bishoprics are held for the most part by ignorant asses, who do not even know the first and ordinary rudiments of the faith, or occasionally by boys who have just left their nurse; or if any are more learned (this, however, is a rare case), they regard the episcopal office as nothing else than a title of magnificence and splendour; where the rectors of churches no more think of feeding the flock than a cobbler does of ploughing, where all things are so confounded by a confusion worse than that of Babel, that no genuine trace of paternal government is any longer to be seen.

14. But if we descend to conduct, where is that light of the world which Christ requires, where the salt of the earth, where that sanctity which might operate as a perpetual censorship? In the present day, there is no order of men more notorious for luxury, effeminacy, delicacy, and all kinds of licentiousness; in no order are more apt or skilful teachers of imposture, fraud, treachery, and perfidy; nowhere is there more skill or audacity in mischief, to say nothing of ostentation, pride, rapacity, and cruelty. In bearing these the world is so disgusted, that there is no fear lest I seem to exaggerate. One thing I say, which even they themselves will not be able to deny: Among

bishops there is scarcely an individual, and among the parochial clergy not one in a hundred, who, if sentence were passed on his conduct according to the ancient canons, would not deserve to be excommunicated, or at least deposed from his office. I seem to say what is almost incredible, so completely has that ancient discipline which enjoined strict censure of the morals of the clergy become obsolete ; but such the fact really is. Let those who serve under the banner and auspices of the Romish See now go and boast of their sacerdotal order. It is certain that that which they have is neither from Christ, nor his apostles, nor the fathers, nor the early Church.

15. Let the deacons now come forward and show their most sacred distribution of ecclesiastical goods (see chap. xix. sec. 32). Although their deacons are not at all elected for that purpose, for the only injunction which they lay upon them is to minister at the altar, to read the Gospel, or chant and perform I know not what frivolous acts. Nothing is said of alms, nothing of the care of the poor, nothing at all of the function which they formerly performed. I am speaking of the institution itself; for if we look to what they do, theirs, in fact, is no office, but only a step to the priesthood. In one thing, those who hold the place of deacons in the mass exhibit an empty image of antiquity, for they receive the offerings previous to consecration. Now, the ancient practice was, that before the communion of the Supper the faithful mutually kissed each other, and offered alms at the altar ; thus declaring their love, first by symbol, and afterwards by an act of beneficence. The deacon, who was steward of the poor, received what was given that he might distribute it. Now, of these alms no more comes to the poor than if they were cast into the sea. They, therefore, delude the Church by that lying deaconship. Assuredly in this they have nothing resembling the apostolical institution or the ancient practice. The very distribution of goods they have transferred elsewhere, and have so settled it that nothing can be imagined more disorderly. For as robbers, after murdering their victims, divide the plunder, so these men, after extinguishing the light of God's word, as if they had murdered the Church, have imagined that whatever had been dedicated to pious uses was set down for prey and plunder. Accordingly, they have made a division, each seizing for himself as much as he could.

16. All those ancient methods which we have explained are not only disturbed but altogether disguised and expunged. The chief part of the plunder has gone to bishops and city presbyters, who, having thus enriched themselves, have been converted into canons. That the partition was a mere scramble is apparent from this, that even to this day they are litigating as to the proportions. Be this as it may, the decision has provided that out of all the goods of the Church not one penny shall go to the poor, to whom at least the half belonged. The canons expressly assign a fourth part to them, while the other fourth they destine to the bishops, that they may expend it in hospitality and other offices of kindness. I say nothing as to what

the clergy ought to do with their portion, or the use to which they ought to apply it, for it has been clearly shown that what is set apart for churches, buildings, and other expenditure, ought in necessity to be given to the poor. If they had one spark of the fear of God in their heart, could they, I ask, bear the consciousness that all their food and clothing is the produce of theft, nay, of sacrilege? But as they are little moved by the judgment of God, they should at least reflect that those whom they would persuade that the orders of their Church are so beautiful and well arranged as they are wont to boast, are men endued with sense and reason. Let them briefly answer whether the diaconate is a licence to rob and steal. If they deny this, they will be forced to confess that no diaconate remains among them, since the whole administration of their ecclesiastical resources has been openly converted into sacrilegious depredation.

17. But here they use a very fair gloss, for they say that the dignity of the Church is not unbecomingly maintained by this magnificence. And certain of their sect are so impudent as to dare openly to boast that thus only are fulfilled the prophecies, in which the ancient prophets describe the splendour of Christ's kingdom, where the sacerdotal order is exhibited in royal attire, that it was not without cause that God made the following promises to his Church: "All kings shall fall down before him: all nations shall serve him" (Ps. lxxii. 11). "Awake, awake; put on thy strength, O Sion; put on thy beautiful garments, O Jerusalem, the holy city" (Isa. lii. 1). "All they from Sheba shall come; they shall bring gold and incense, and they shall show forth the praises of the Lord. All the flocks of Kedar shall be gathered together unto thee" (Isa. lx. 6, 7). I fear I should seem childish were I to dwell long in refuting this dishonesty. I am unwilling, therefore, to use words unnecessarily; I ask, however, were any Jew to misapply these passages, what answer would they give? They would rebuke his stupidity in making a carnal and worldly application of things spiritually said of Christ's spiritual kingdom. For we know that under the image of earthly objects the prophets have delineated to us the heavenly glory which ought to shine in the Church. For in those blessings with these words literally express, the Church never less abounded than under the apostles; and yet all admit that the power of Christ's kingdom was then most flourishing. What, then, is the meaning of the above passages? That everything which is precious, sublime, and illustrious, ought to be made subject to the Lord. As to its being said expressly of kings, that they will submit to Christ, that they will throw their diadems at his feet, that they will dedicate their resources to the Church, when was this more truly and fully manifested than when Theodosius, having thrown aside the purple and left the insignia of empire, like one of the people humbled himself before God and the Church in solemn repentance? than when he and other like pious princes made it their study and their care to preserve pure doctrine in the Church, to cherish and protect sound teachers? But that priests did not

then luxuriate in superfluous wealth is sufficiently declared by this one sentence of the Council of Aquileia, over which Ambrose presided, " *Poverty in the priests of the Lord is glorious.*" It is certain that the bishops then had some means by which they might have rendered the glory of the Church conspicuous, if they had deemed them the true ornaments of the Church. But knowing that nothing was more adverse to the duty of pastors than to plume themselves on the delicacies of the table, on splendid clothes, numerous attendants, and magnificent places, they cultivated and followed the humility and modesty, nay, the very poverty, which Christ has consecrated among his servants.

18. But not to be tedious, let us again briefly sum up and show how far that distribution, or rather squandering, of ecclesiastical goods which now exists differs from the true diaconate, which both the word of God recommends and the ancient Church observed (Book I. chap. xi. sec. 7, 13 ; Book III. chap. xx. sec. 30 ; *supra*, chap. iv. sec. 8). I say, that what is employed on the adorning of churches is improperly laid out, if not accompanied with that moderation which the very nature of sacred things prescribes, and which the apostles and other holy fathers prescribed, both by precept and example. But is anything like this seen in churches in the present day ? Whatever accords, I do not say with that ancient frugality, but with decent mediocrity, is rejected. Nought pleases but what savours of luxury and the corruption of the times. Meanwhile, so far are they from taking due care of living temples, that they would allow thousands of the poor to perish sooner than break down the smallest cup or platter to relieve their necessity. That I may not decide too severely at my own hand, I would only ask the pious reader to consider what Exuperius, the Bishop of Thoulouse, whom we have mentioned, what Acatius, or Ambrose, or any one like minded, if they were to rise from the dead, would say ? Certainly, while the necessities of the poor are so great, they would not approve of their funds being carried away from them as superfluous ; not to mention that, even were there no poor, the uses to which they are applied are noxious in many respects and useful in none. But I appeal not to men. These goods have been dedicated to Christ, and ought to be distributed at his pleasure. In vain, however, will they make that to be expenditure for Christ which they have squandered contrary to his commands, though, to confess the truth, the ordinary revenue of the Church is not much curtailed by these expenses. No bishoprics are so opulent, no abbacies so productive, in short, no benefices so numerous and ample, as to suffice for the gluttony of priests. But while they would spare themselves, they induce the people by superstition to employ what ought to have been distributed to the poor in building temples, erecting statues, buying plate, and providing costly garments. Thus the daily alms are swallowed up in this abyss.

19. Of the revenue which they derive from lands and property, what else can I say than what I have already said, and is manifest

before the eyes of all ? We see with what kind of fidelity the greatest portion is administered by those who are called bishops and abbots. What madness is it to seek ecclesiastical order here ? Is it becoming in those whose life ought to have been a singular example of frugality, modesty, continence, and humility, to rival princes in the number of their attendants, the splendour of their dwellings, the delicacies of dressing and feasting ? Can anything be more contrary to the duty of those whom the eternal and inviolable edict of God forbids to long for filthy lucre, and orders to be contented with simple food, not only to lay hands on villages and castles, but also invade the largest provinces, and even seize on empire itself ? If they despise the word of God, what answer will they give to the ancient canons of councils, which decree that the bishop shall have a little dwelling not far from the church, a frugal table and furniture ? (Conc. Carth. cap. 14, 15). What answer will they give to the declaration of the Council of Aquileia, in which poverty in the priests of the Lord is pronounced glorious ? For, the injunction which Jerome gives to Nepotian, to make the poor and strangers acquainted with his table, and have Christ with them as a guest, they would, perhaps, repudiate as too austere. What he immediately adds it would shame them to acknowledge—viz. that the glory of a bishop is to provide for the sustenance of the poor, that the disgrace of all priests is to study their own riches. This they cannot admit without covering themselves with disgrace. But it is unnecessary here to press them so hard, since all we wished was to demonstrate that the legitimate order of deacons has long ago been abolished, and that they can no longer plume themselves on this order in commendation of their Church. This, I think, has been completely established.

CHAPTER VI.

OF THE PRIMACY OF THE ROMISH SEE.

The divisions of this chapter are,—I. Question stated, and an argument for the primacy of the Roman Pontiff drawn from the Old Testament refuted, sec. 1, 2. II. Reply to various arguments in support of the Papacy founded on the words, " Thou art Peter," &c., sec. 3–17.

Sections.

1. HITHERTO we have reviewed those ecclesiastical orders which existed in the government of the primitive Church; but afterwards corrupted by time, and thereafter more and more vitiated, now only retain the name in the Papal Church, and are, in fact, nothing but mere masks, so that the contrast will enable the pious reader to judge what kind of Church that is, for revolting from which we are charged with schism. But, on the head and crown of the whole matter, I mean the primacy of the Roman See, from which they undertake to prove that the Catholic Church is to be found only with them,[1] we

---

[1] See Calv. Adversus Concilium Tridentinum. Also Adversus Theologos Parisienses.

have not yet touched, because it did not take its origin either in the
institution of Christ, or the practice of the early Church, as did those
other parts, in regard to which we have shown, that though they
were ancient in their origin, they in process of time altogether degenerated, nay, assumed an entirely new form.　And yet they
endeavour to persuade the world that the chief and only bond of
ecclesiastical unity is to adhere to the Roman See, and continue in
subjection to it.　I say, the prop on which they chiefly lean, when
they would deprive us of the Church, and arrogate it to themselves,
is, that they retain the head on which the unity of the Church depends, and without which it must necessarily be rent and go to pieces.
For they regard the Church as a kind of mutilated trunk if it be not
subject to the Romish See as its head.　Accordingly, when they debate about their hierarchy they always set out with the axiom : The
Roman Pontiff (as the vicar of Christ, who is the Head of the Church)
presides in his stead over the universal Church, and the Church is
not rightly constituted unless that See hold the primacy over all
others.　The nature of this claim must, therefore, be considered, that
we may not omit anything which pertains to the proper government
of the Church.

2. The question, then, may be thus stated, Is it necessary for the
true order of the hierarchy (as they term it), or of ecclesiastical order,
that one See should surpass the others in dignity and power, so as to
be the head of the whole body ?　We subject the Church to unjust
laws if we lay this necessity upon her without sanction from the word
of God.　Therefore, if our opponents would prove what they maintain, it behoves them first of all to show that this economy was instituted by Christ.　For this purpose, they refer to the office of high
priest under the law, and the supreme jurisdiction which God appointed at Jerusalem.[1]　But the solution is easy, and it is manifold
if one does not satisfy them.　First, no reason obliges us to extend
what was useful in one nation to the whole world ; nay, the cases of
one nation and of the whole world are widely different.　Because the
Jews were hemmed in on every side by idolaters, God fixed the seat
of his worship in the central region of the earth, that they might not
be distracted by a variety of religions ; there he appointed one priest
to whom they might all look up, that they might be the better kept
in unity.　But now when the true religion has been diffused over the
whole globe, who sees not that it is altogether absurd to give the
government of East and West to one individual ?　It is just as if one
were to contend that the whole world ought to be governed by one
prefect, because one district has not several prefects.[2]　But there is

[1] French, " Pour ce faire, ils alleguent la pretrise souveraine qui etoit en la loy, et
la jurisdiction souveraine du grand sacrificateur, que Dieu avoit establie en Jerusalem."—For this purpose, they allege the sovereign priesthood which was under the
law, and the sovereign jurisdiction of the high priest which God had established at
Jerusalem.
[2] " Car c'est tout ainsi comme si quelcun debattoit que le monde doit etre gouverné
par un baillie ou seneschal parce que chacune province a le sien."—For it is just as if

still another reason why that institution ought not to be drawn into a precedent. Every one knows that the high priest was a type of Christ; now, the priesthood being transferred, that right must also be transferred. To whom, then, was it transferred? certainly not to the Pope, as he dares impudently to boast when he arrogates this title to himself, but to Christ, who, as he alone holds the office without vicar or successor, does not resign the honour to any other. For this priesthood consists not in doctrine only, but in the propitiation which Christ made by his death, and the intercession which he now makes with the Father (Heb. vii. 11).

3. That example, therefore, which is seen to have been temporary, they have no right to bind upon us as by a perpetual law. In the New Testament there is nothing which they can produce in confirmation of their opinion, but its having been said to one, "Thou art Peter, and upon this rock I will build my Church" (Matth. xvi. 18). Again, "Simon, son of Jonas, lovest thou me?" "Feed my lambs" (John xxi. 15). But to give strength to these proofs, they must, in the first place, show, that to him who is ordered to feed the flock of Christ power is given over all churches, and that to bind and loose is nothing else than to preside over the whole world. But as Peter had received a command from the Lord, so he exhorts all other presbyters to feed the Church (1 Pet. v. 2). Hence we are entitled to infer, that, by that expression of Christ, nothing more was given to Peter than to the others, or that the right which Peter had received he communicated equally to others. But not to argue to no purpose, we elsewhere have, from the lips of Christ himself, a clear exposition of what it is to bind and loose. It is just to retain and remit sins (John x. 23). The mode of loosing and binding is explained throughout Scripture: but especially in that passage in which Paul declares that the ministers of the Gospel are commissioned to reconcile men to God, and at the same time to exercise discipline over those who reject the benefit (2 Cor. v. 18; x. 16).

4. How unbecomingly they wrest the passages of binding and loosing I have elsewhere glanced at, and will in a short time more fully explain. It may now be worth while merely to see what they can extract from our Saviour's celebrated answer to Peter. He promised him the keys of the kingdom of heaven, and said, that whatever things he bound on earth should be bound in heaven (Matth. xvi. 19). The moment we are agreed as to the meaning of the keys, and the mode of binding, all dispute will cease. For the Pope will willingly omit that office assigned to the apostles, which, full of labour and toil, would interfere with his luxuries without giving any gain. Since heaven is opened to us by the doctrine of the Gospel, it is by an elegant metaphor distinguished by the name of *keys*. Again, the only mode in which men are bound and loosed is, in the latter case, when they are reconciled to God by faith, and in the former, more

one were to maintain that the whole world ought to be governed by a bailie or seneschal, because each province has its own.

strictly bound by unbelief. Were this all that the Pope arrogated to himself, I believe there would be none to envy him or stir the question. But because this laborious and very far from lucrative succession is by no means pleasing to the Pope, the dispute immediately arises as to what it was that Christ promised to Peter. From the very nature of the case, I infer that nothing more is denoted than the dignity which cannot be separated from the burden of the apostolic office. For, admitting the definition which I have given (and it cannot without effrontery be rejected), nothing is here given to Peter that was not common to him with his colleagues. On any other view, not only would injustice be done to their persons, but the very majesty of the doctrine would be impaired. They object; but what, pray, is gained by striking against this stone? The utmost they can make out is, that as the preaching of the same gospel was enjoined on all the apostles, so the power of binding and loosing was bestowed upon them in common. Christ (they say) constituted Peter prince of the whole Church when he promised to give him the keys. But what he then promised to one he elsewhere delivers, and as it were hands over, to all the rest. If the same right, which was promised to one, is bestowed upon all, in what respect is that one superior to his colleagues? He excels (they say) in this, that he receives both in common, and by himself, what is given to the others in common only. What if I should answer with Cyprian, and Augustine, that Christ did not do this to prefer one to the other, but in order to commend the unity of his Church? For Cyprian thus speaks: "In the person of one man he gave the keys to all, that he might denote the unity of all; the rest, therefore, were the same that Peter was, being admitted to an equal participation of honour and power, but a beginning is made from unity that the Church of Christ may be shown to be one" (Cyprian, de Simplic. Prælat.). Augustine's words are, " Had not the mystery of the Church been in Peter, our Lord would not have said to him, I will give thee the keys. For if this was said to Peter, the Church has them not; but if the Church has them, then when Peter received the keys he represented the whole Church" (August. Hom. in Joann. 50). Again, " All were asked, but Peter alone answers, Thou art the Christ; and it is said to him, I will give thee the keys; as if he alone had received the power of loosing and binding; whereas he both spoke for all, and received in common with all, being, as it were, the representative of unity. One received for all, because there is unity in all" (Hom. 124).

5. But we nowhere read of its being said to any other, " Thou art Peter, and upon this rock I will build my Church"! (Matth. xvi. 18); as if Christ then affirmed anything else of Peter, than Paul and Peter himself affirm of all Christians (Eph. ii. 20; 1 Peter ii. 5). The former describes Christ as the chief corner-stone, on whom are built all who grow up into a holy temple in the Lord; the latter describes us as living stones who are founded on that elect and precious stone, and being so joined and compacted, are united to our God, and

to each other. Peter (they say) is above others, because the name was specially given to him. I willingly concede to Peter the honour of being placed among the first in the building of the Church, or (if they prefer it) of being the first among the faithful; but I will not allow them to infer from this that he has a primacy over others. For what kind of inference is this? Peter surpasses others in fervid zeal, in doctrine, in magnanimity; therefore, he has power over them: as if we might not with greater plausibility infer, that Andrew is prior to Peter in order, because he preceded him in time, and brought him to Christ (John i. 40, 42); but this I omit. Let Peter have the pre-eminence, still there is a great difference between the honour of rank and the possession of power. We see that the Apostles usually left it to Peter to address the meeting, and in some measure take precedence in relating, exhorting, admonishing, but we nowhere read anything at all of power.

6. Though we are not yet come to that part of the discussion, I would merely observe at present, how futilely those argue who, out of the mere name of Peter, would rear up a governing power over the whole Church. For the ancient quibble which they at first used to give a colour—viz. The Church is founded upon Peter, because it is said, "On this rock," &c.—is undeserving of notice, not to say of refutation. Some of the Fathers so expounded![1] But when the whole of Scripture is repugnant to the exposition, why is their authority brought forward in opposition to God? nay, why do we contend about the meaning of these words, as if it were obscure or ambiguous, when nothing can be more clear and certain? Peter had confessed in his own name, and that of his brethren, that Christ was the Son of God (Matth. xvi. 16). On this rock Christ builds his Church, because it is the only foundation; as Paul says, "Other foundation than this can no man lay" (1 Cor. iii. 11). Therefore, I do not here repudiate the authority of the Fathers, because I am destitute of passages from them to prove what I say, were I disposed to quote them; but as I have observed, I am unwilling to annoy my readers by debating so clear a matter, especially since the subject has long ago been fully handled and expounded by our writers.

7. And yet, in truth, none can solve this question better than Scripture, if we compare all the passages in which it shows what office and power Peter held among the apostles, how he acted among them, how he was received by them (Acts xv. 7). Run over all these passages, and the utmost you will find is, that Peter was one of twelve, their equal and colleague, not their master. He indeed brings the matter before the council when anything is to be done, and advises as to what is necessary, but he, at the same time, listens to the others, not only conceding to them an opportunity of expressing their sentiments, but allowing them to decide; and when they have decided, he follows and obeys. When he writes to pastors, he

---

[1] French, "Ils ont pour leur bouclier, qu'aucuns des Peres les ont ainsi exposees."—They regard it as their buckler, that some of the Fathers have so expounded them.

does not command authoritatively as a superior, but makes them his colleagues, and courteously advises as equals are wont to do (1 Pet. v. 1). When he is accused of having gone in to the Gentiles, though the accusation is unfounded, he replies to it, and clears himself (Acts xi. 3). Being ordered by his colleagues to go with John into Samaria, he declines not (Acts viii. 14). The apostles, by sending him, declare that they by no means regard him as a superior, while he, by obeying and undertaking the embassy committed to him, confesses that he is associated with them, and has no authority over them. But if none of these facts existed, the one Epistle to the Galatians would easily remove all doubt, there being almost two chapters in which the whole for which Paul contends is, that in regard to the honour of the apostleship, he is the equal of Peter (Gal. i. 18; ii. 8). Hence he states, that he went to Peter, not to acknowledge subjection, but only to make their agreement in doctrine manifest to all; that Peter himself asked no acknowledgment of the kind, but gave him the right hand of fellowship, that they might be common labourers in the vineyard; that not less grace was bestowed on him among the Gentiles than on Peter among the Jews: in fine, that Peter, when he was not acting with strict fidelity, was rebuked by him, and submitted to the rebuke (Gal. ii. 11). All these things make it manifest, either that there was an equality between Paul and Peter, or, at least, that Peter had no more authority over the rest than they had over him. This point, as I have said, Paul handles professedly, in order that no one might give a preference over him, in respect of apostleship, to Peter or John, who were colleagues, not masters.

8. But were I to concede to them what they ask with regard to Peter—viz. that he was the chief of the apostles, and surpassed the others in dignity—there is no ground for making a universal rule out of a special example, or wresting a single fact into a perpetual enactment, seeing that the two things are widely different. One was chief among the apostles, just because they were few in number. If one man presided over twelve, will it follow that one ought to preside over a hundred thousand? That twelve had one among them to direct all is nothing strange. Nature admits, the human mind requires, that in every meeting, though all are equal in power, there should be one as a kind of moderator to whom the others should look up. There is no senate without a consul, no bench of judges without a president or chancellor, no college without a provost, no company without a master. Thus there would be no absurdity were we to confess that the apostles had conferred such a primacy on Peter. But an arrangement which is effectual among a few must not be forthwith transferred to the whole world, which no one man is able to govern. But (say they) it is observed that not less in nature as a whole, than in each of its parts, there is one supreme head. Proof of this it pleases them to derive from cranes and bees, which always place themselves under the guidance of one, not of several. I admit

the examples which they produce ; but do bees flock together from all parts of the world to choose one queen ? Each queen is contented with her own hive. So among cranes, each flock has its own king. What can they prove from this, except that each church ought to have its bishop ? They refer us to the examples of states, quoting from Homer, Οὐκ ἀγαθὸν πολυκοιρανίη, " a many-headed rule is not good ;" and other passages to the same effect from heathen writers in commendation of monarchy. The answer is easy. Monarchy is not lauded by Homer's Ulysses, or by others, as if one individual ought to govern the whole world ; but they mean to intimate that one kingdom does not admit of two kings, and that empire, as one expresses it (Lucan. Lib. i.), cannot bear a partner.

9. Be it, however, as they will have it (though the thing is most absurd ; be it), that it were good and useful for the whole world to be under one monarchy, I will not, therefore, admit that the same thing should take effect in the government of the Church. Her only Head is Christ, under whose government we are all united to each other, according to that order and form of policy which he himself has prescribed. Wherefore they offer an egregious insult to Christ, when under this pretext they would have one man to preside over the whole Church, seeing the Church can never be without a head, " even Christ, from whom the whole body fitly joined together, and compacted by that which every joint supplieth, according to the effectual working in the measure of every part, maketh increase of the body" (Eph. iv. 15, 16). See how all men, without exception, are placed in the body, while the honour and name of Head is left to Christ alone. See how to each member is assigned a certain measure, a finite and limited function, while both the perfection of grace and the supreme power of government reside only in Christ. I am not unaware of the cavilling objection which they are wont to urge—viz. that Christ is properly called the only Head, because he alone reigns by his own authority and in his own name ; but that there is nothing in this to prevent what they call another *ministerial* head from being under him, and acting as his substitute. But this cavil cannot avail them, until they previously show that this office was ordained by Christ. For the apostle teaches, that the whole subministration is diffused through the members, while the power flows from one celestial Head;[1] or, if they will have it more plainly, since Scripture testifies that Christ is Head, and claims this honour for himself alone, it ought not to be transferred to any other than him whom Christ himself has made his vicegerent. But not only is there no passage to this effect, but it can be amply refuted by many passages.

10. Paul sometimes depicts a living image of the Church, but makes no mention of a single head. On the contrary, we may infer from his description, that it is foreign to the institution of Christ. Christ, by his ascension, took away his visible presence from us, and

---

1 Eph. i. 22 ; iv. 15 ; v. 23 ; Col. i. 18 ; ii. 10.

yet he ascended that he might fill all things: now, therefore, he is present in the Church, and always will be. When Paul would show the mode in which he exhibits himself, he calls our attention to the ministerial offices which he employs: " Unto every one of us is given grace according to the measure of the gift of Christ;" " And he gave some, apostles; and some, prophets; and some, evangelists; and some, pastors and teachers."[1] Why does he not say, that one presided over all to act as his substitute? The passage particularly required this, and it ought not on any account to have been omitted if it had been true. Christ, he says, is present with us. How? By the ministry of men whom he appointed over the government of the Church. Why not rather by a ministerial head whom he appointed his substitute? He speaks of unity, but it is in God and in the faith of Christ. He attributes nothing to men but a common ministry, and a special mode to each. Why, when thus commending unity, does he not, after saying, " one body, one Spirit, even as ye are called in one hope of your calling, one Lord, one faith, one baptism" (Eph. iv. 4), immediately add, one Supreme Pontiff to keep the Church in unity? Nothing could have been said more aptly if the case had really been so. Let that passage be diligently pondered, and there will be no doubt that Paul there meant to give a complete representation of that sacred and ecclesiastical government to which posterity have given the name of hierarchy. Not only does he not place a monarchy among ministers, but even intimates that there is none. There can also be no doubt, that he meant to express the mode of connection by which believers unite with Christ the Head. There he not only makes no mention of a ministerial head, but attributes a particular operation to each of the members, according to the measure of grace distributed to each. Nor is there any ground for subtle philosophical comparisons between the celestial and the earthly hierarchy. For it is not safe to be wise above measure with regard to the former, and in constituting the latter, the only type which it behoves us to follow is that which our Lord himself has delineated in his own word.

11. I will now make them another concession, which they will never obtain from men of sound mind—viz. that the primacy of the Church was fixed in Peter, with the view of remaining for ever by perpetual succession. Still how will they prove that his See was so fixed at Rome, that whosoever becomes Bishop of that city is to preside over the whole world? By what authority do they annex this dignity to a particular place, when it was given without any mention of place? Peter, they say, lived and died at Rome. What did Christ himself do? Did he not discharge his episcopate while he lived, and complete the office of the priesthood by dying at Jerusalem? The Prince of pastors, the chief Shepherd, the Head of the Church, could not procure honour for a place, and Peter, so far his inferior, could! Is

2 Eph. iv. 10, 7, 11.

not this worse than childish trifling? Christ conferred the honour of primacy on Peter. Peter had his See at Rome, therefore he fixed the seat of the primacy there. In this way the Israelites of old must have placed the seat of the primacy in the wilderness, where Moses, the chief teacher and prince of prophets, discharged his ministry and died.

12. Let us see, however, how admirably they reason. Peter, they say, had the first place among the apostles; therefore, the church in which he sat ought to have the privilege. But where did he first sit? At Antioch, they say. Therefore, the church of Antioch justly claims the primacy. They acknowledge that she was once the first, but that Peter, by removing from it, transferred the honour which he had brought with him to Rome. For there is extant, under the name of Pope Marcellus, a letter to the presbyters of Antioch, in which he says, "The See of Peter, at the outset, was with you, and was afterwards, by the order of the Lord, translated hither." Thus the church of Antioch, which was once the first, yielded to the See of Rome. But by what oracle did that good man learn that the Lord had so ordered? For if the question is to be determined in regular form, they must say whether they hold the privilege to be personal, or real, or mixed. One of the three it must be. If they say personal, then it has nothing to do with place; if real, then when once given to a place it is not lost by the death or departure of the person. It remains that they must hold it to be mixed; then the mere consideration of place is not sufficient unless the person also correspond. Let them choose which they will, I will forthwith infer, and easily prove, that Rome has no ground to arrogate the primacy.

13. However, be it so. Let the primacy have been (as they vainly allege) transferred from Antioch to Rome. Why did not Antioch retain the second place? For if Rome has the first, simply because Peter had his See there at the end of his life, to which place should the second be given sooner than to that where he first had his See? How comes it, then, that Alexandria takes precedence of Antioch? How can the church of a disciple be superior to the See of Peter? If honour is due to a church according to the dignity of its founder, what shall we say of other churches? Paul names three individuals who seemed to be pillars—viz. James, Peter, and John (Gal. ii. 9). If, in honour of Peter, the first place is given to the Roman See, do not the churches of Ephesus and Jerusalem, where John and James were fixed, deserve the second and third places? But in ancient times Jerusalem held the last place among the Patriarchates, and Ephesus was not able to secure even the lowest corner. Other churches too have passed away, churches which Paul founded, and over which the apostles presided. The See of Mark, who was only one of the disciples, has obtained honour. Let them either confess that that arrangement was preposterous, or let them concede that it is not always true that each church is entitled to the degree of honour which its founder possessed.

14. But I do not see that any credit is due to their allegation of Peter's occupation of the Roman See. Certainly it is, that the statement of Eusebius, that he presided over it for twenty-five years, is easily refuted. For it appears from the first and second chapters of Galatians, that he was at Jerusalem about twenty years after the death of Christ, and afterwards came to Antioch. How long he remained here is uncertain; Gregory counts seven, and Eusebius twenty-five years. But from our Saviour's death to the end of Nero's reign (under which they state that he was put to death), will be found only thirty-seven years. For our Lord suffered in the eighteenth year of the reign of Tiberius. If you cut off the twenty years, during which, as Paul testifies, Peter dwelt at Jerusalem, there will remain at most seventeen years; and these must be divided between his two episcopates. If he dwelt long at Antioch, his See at Rome must have been of short duration. This we may demonstrate still more clearly. Paul wrote to the Romans while he was on his journey to Jerusalem, where he was apprehended and conveyed to Rome (Rom. xv. 15, 16). It is therefore probable that this letter was written four years before his arrival at Rome. Still there is no mention of Peter, as there certainly would have been if he had been ruling that church. Nay, in the end of the Epistle, where he enumerates a long list of individuals whom he orders to be saluted, and in which it may be supposed he includes all who were known to him, he says nothing at all of Peter. To men of sound judgment, there is no need here of a long and subtle demonstration; the nature of the case itself, and the whole subject of the Epistle, proclaim that he ought not to have passed over Peter if he had been at Rome.

15. Paul is afterwards conveyed as a prisoner to Rome. Luke relates that he was received by the brethren, but says nothing of Peter. From Rome he writes to many churches. He even sends salutations from certain individuals, but does not by a single word intimate that Peter was then there. Who, pray, will believe that he would have said nothing of him if he had been present? Nay, in the Epistle to the Philippians, after saying that he had no one who cared for the work of the Lord so faithfully as Timothy, he complains, that "all seek their own" (Phil. ii. 20). And to Timothy he makes the more grievous complaint, that no man was present at his first defence, that all men forsook him (2 Tim. iv. 16). Where then was Peter? If they say that he was at Rome, how disgraceful the charge which Paul brings against him of being a deserter of the Gospel! For he is speaking of believers, since he adds, "The Lord lay it not to their charge." At what time, therefore, and how long, did Peter hold that See? The uniform opinion of authors is, that he governed that church until his death. But these authors are not agreed as to who was his successor. Some say Linus, others Clement. And they relate many absurd fables concerning a discussion between him and Simon Magus. Nor does Augustine, when treating of superstition, disguise the fact, that owing to an opinion rashly entertained, it had

become customary at Rome to fast on the day on which Peter carried away the palm from Simon Magus (August. ad Januar. Ep. 2). In short, the affairs of that period are so involved from the variety of opinions, that credit is not to be given rashly to anything we read concerning it. And yet, from this agreement of authors, I do not dispute that he died there, but that he was bishop, particularly for a long period, I cannot believe. I do not, however, attach much importance to the point, since Paul testifies, that the apostleship of Peter pertained especially to the Jews, but his own specially to us. Therefore, in order that that compact which they made between themselves, nay, that the arrangement of the Holy Spirit may be firmly established among us, we ought to pay more regard to the apostleship of Paul than to that of Peter, since the Holy Spirit, in allotting them different provinces, destined Peter for the Jews and Paul for us. Let the Romanists, therefore, seek their primacy somewhere else than in the word of God, which gives not the least foundation for it.

16. Let us now come to the Primitive Church, that it may also appear that our opponents plume themselves on its support, not less falsely and unadvisedly than on the testimony of the word of God. When they lay it down as an axiom, that the unity of the Church cannot be maintained unless there be one supreme head on earth whom all the members should obey; and that, accordingly, our Lord gave the primacy to Peter, and thereafter, by right of succession, to the See of Rome, there to remain even to the end, they assert that this has always been observed from the beginning. But since they improperly wrest many passages, I would first premise, that I deny not that the early Christians uniformly give high honour to the Roman Church, and speak of it with reverence. This, I think, is owing chiefly to three causes. The opinion which had prevailed (I know not how), that that Church was founded and constituted by the ministry of Peter, had great effect in procuring influence and authority. Hence, in the East, it was, as a mark of honour, designated the Apostolic See. Secondly, as the seat of empire was there, and it was for this reason to be presumed, that the most distinguished for learning, prudence, skill, and experience, were there more than elsewhere, account was justly taken of the circumstance, lest the celebrity of the city, and the much more excellent gifts of God also, might seem to be despised. To these was added a third cause, that when the churches of the East, of Greece and of Africa, were kept in a constant turmoil by differences of opinion, the Church of Rome was calmer and less troubled. To this it was owing, that pious and holy bishops, when driven from their sees, often betook themselves to Rome as an asylum or haven. For as the people of the West are of a less acute and versatile turn of mind than those of Asia or Africa, so they are less desirous of innovations. It therefore added very great authority to the Roman Church, that in those dubious times it was not so much unsettled as others, and adhered more firmly to the

doctrine once delivered, as shall immediately be better explained. For these three causes, I say, she was held in no ordinary estimation, and received many distinguished testimonies from ancient writers.

17. But since on this our opponents would rear up a primacy and supreme authority over other churches, they, as I have said, greatly err. That this may better appear, I will first briefly show what the views of early writers are as to this unity which they so strongly urge. Jerome, in writing to Nepotian, after enumerating many examples of unity, descends at length to the ecclesiastical hierarchy. He says, " Every bishop of a church, every archpresbyter, every archdeacon, and the whole ecclesiastical order, depends on its own rulers." Here a Roman presbyter speaks and commends unity in ecclesiastical order. Why does he not mention that all the churches are bound together by one Head as a common bond? There was nothing more appropriate to the point in hand, and it cannot be said that he omitted it through forgetfulness; there was nothing he would more willingly have mentioned had the fact permitted. He therefore undoubtedly owns, that the true method of unity is that which Cyprian admirably describes in these words: " The episcopate is one, part of which is held entire by each bishop, and the Church is one, which, by the increase of fecundity, extends more widely in numbers. As there are many rays of the sun and one light, many branches of a tree and one trunk, upheld by its tenacious root, and as very many streams flow from one fountain, and though numbers seem diffused by the largeness of the overflowing supply, yet unity is preserved entire in the source, so the Church, pervaded with the light of the Lord, sends her rays over the whole globe, and yet is one light, which is everywhere diffused without separating the unity of the body, extends her branches over the whole globe, and sends forth flowing streams ; still the head is one, and the source one" (Cyprian, de Simplic. Prælat.). Afterwards he says, " The spouse of Christ cannot be an adulteress : she knows one house, and with chaste modesty keeps the sanctity of one bed." See how he makes the bishopric of Christ alone universal, as comprehending under it the whole Church : See how he says that part of it is held entire by all who discharge the episcopal office under this head. Where is the primacy of the Roman See, if the entire bishopric resides in Christ alone, and a part of it is held entire by each? My object in these remarks is, to show the reader, in passing, that that axiom of the unity of an earthly kind in the hierarchy, which the Romanists assume as confessed and indubitable, was altogether unknown to the ancient Church.

CHAPTER VII.

OF THE BEGINNING AND RISE OF THE ROMISH PAPACY, TILL IT AT-
TAINED A HEIGHT BY WHICH THE LIBERTY OF THE CHURCH WAS
DESTROYED, AND ALL TRUE RULE OVERTHROWN.

There are five heads in this chapter. I. The Patriarchate given and confirmed to
the Bishop of Rome, first by the Council of Nice, and afterwards by that of Chalcedon,
though by no means approved of by other bishops, was the commencement of the Papacy, sec. 1–4. II. The Church at Rome, by taking pious exiles under its protection,
and also thereby protecting wicked men who fled to her, helped forward the mystery
of iniquity, although at that time neither the ordination of bishops, nor admonitions
and censures, nor the right of convening Councils, nor the right of receiving appeals,
belonged to the Roman Bishop, whose profane meddling with these things was condemned by Gregory, sec. 5–13. III. After the Council of Turin, disputes arose as to
the authority of Metropolitans. Disgraceful strife between the Patriarchs of Rome and
Constantinople. The vile assassin Phocas put an end to these brawls at the instigation
of Boniface, sec. 14–18. IV. To the dishonest arts of Boniface succeeded fouler frauds
devised in more modern times, and expressly condemned by Gregory and Bernard. sec.
19–21. V. The Papacy at length appeared complete in all its parts, the seat of Antichrist. Its impiety, execrable tyranny, and wickedness, portrayed, sec. 23–30.

Sections.

1. In regard to the antiquity of the primacy of the Roman See, there is nothing in favour of its establishment more ancient than the decree of the Council of Nice, by which the first place among the Patriarchs is assigned to the Bishop of Rome, and he is enjoined to take care of the suburban churches.   While the council, in dividing between him and the other Patriarchs, assigns the proper limits of each, it certainly does not appoint him head of all, but only one of the chief.   Vitus and Vincentius attended on the part of Julius, who then governed the Roman Church, and to them the fourth place was given.   I ask, if Julius was acknowledged the head of the Church, would his legates have been consigned to the fourth place?   Would Athanasius have presided in the council where a representative of the hierarchal order should have been most conspicuous?   In the Council of Ephesus, it appears that Celestinus (who was then Roman Pontiff) used a cunning device to secure the dignity of his See.   For when he sent his deputies, he made Cyril of Alexandria, who otherwise would have presided, his substitute.   Why that commission, but just that his name might stand connected with the first See?   His legates sit in an inferior place, are asked their opinion along with others, and subscribe in their order, while, at the same time, his name is coupled with that of the Patriarch of Alexandria.   What shall I say of the second Council of Ephesus, where, while the deputies of Leo

were present, the Alexandrian Patriarch Dioscorus presided as in his own right? They will object that this was not an orthodox council, since by it the venerable Flavianus was condemned, Eutyches acquitted, and his heresy approved. Yet when the council was met, and the bishops distributed the places among themselves, the deputies of the Roman Church sat among the others just as in a sacred and lawful Council. Still they contend not for the first place, but yield it to another: this they never would have done if they had thought it their own by right. For the Roman bishops were never ashamed to stir up the greatest strife in contending for honours, and for this cause alone, to trouble and harass the Church with many pernicious contests; but because Leo saw that it would be too extravagant to ask the first place for his legates, he omitted to do it.

2. Next came the Council of Chalcedon, in which, by concession of the Emperor, the legates of the Roman Church occupied the first place. But Leo himself confesses that this was an extraordinary privilege; for when he asks it of the Emperor Marcian and Pulcheria Augusta, he does not maintain that it is due to him, but only pretends that the Eastern bishops who presided in the Council of Ephesus had thrown all into confusion, and made a bad use of their power. Therefore, seeing there was need of a grave moderator, and it was not probable that those who had once been so fickle and tumultuous would be fit for this purpose, he requests that, because of the fault and unfitness of others, the office of governing should be transferred to him. That which is asked as a special privilege, and out of the usual order, certainly is not due by a common law. When it is only pretended that there is need of a new president, because the former ones had behaved themselves improperly, it is plain that the thing asked was not previously done, and ought not to be made perpetual, being done only in respect of a present danger. The Roman Pontiff, therefore, holds the first place in the Council of Chalcedon, not because it is due to his See, but because the council is in want of a grave and fit moderator, while those who ought to have presided exclude themselves by their intemperance and passion. This statement the successor of Leo approved by his procedure. For when he sent his legates to the fifth Council, that of Constantinople, which was held long after, he did not quarrel for the first seat, but readily allowed Mennas, the patriarch of Constantinople, to preside. In like manner, in the Council of Carthage, at which Augustine was present, we perceive that not the legates of the Roman See, but Aurelius, the archbishop of the place, presided, although there was then a question as to the authority of the Roman Pontiff. Nay, even in Italy itself, a universal council was held (that of Aquileia), at which the Roman Bishop was not present. Ambrose, who was then in high favour with the Emperor, presided, and no mention is made of the Roman Pontiff. Therefore, owing to the dignity of Ambrose, the See of Milan was then more illustrious than that of Rome.

3. In regard to the mere title of primate and other titles of pride,

of which that pontiff now makes a wondrous boast, it is not difficult to understand how and in what way they crept in. Cyprian often makes mention of Cornelius (Cyprian. Lib. ii. Ep. 2; Lib. iv. Ep. 6), nor does he distinguish him by any other name than that of brother, or fellow bishop, or colleague. When he writes to Stephen, the successor of Cornelius, he not only makes him the equal of himself and others, but addresses him in harsh terms, charging him at one time with presumption, at another with ignorance. After Cyprian, we have the judgment of the whole African Church on the subject. For the Council of Carthage enjoined that none should be called chief of the priests, or first bishop, but only bishop of the first See. But any one who will examine the more ancient records will find that the Roman Pontiff was then contented with the common appellation of brother. Certainly, as long as the true and pure form of the Church continued, all these names of pride on which the Roman See afterwards began to plume itself, were altogether unheard of; none knew what was meant by the supreme Pontiff, and the only head of the Church on earth. Had the Roman Bishop presumed to assume any such title, there were right-hearted men who would immediately have repressed his folly. Jerome, seeing he was a Roman presbyter, was not slow to proclaim the dignity of his church, in as far as fact and the circumstances of the times permitted, and yet we see how he brings it under due subordination. "If authority is asked, the world is greater than a city. Why produce to me the custom of one city? Why vindicate a small number with whom superciliousness has originated against the laws of the Church? Wherever the bishop be, whether at Rome, or Eugubium, or Constantinople, or Rhegium, the merit is the same, and the priesthood the same. The power of riches, or the humbleness of poverty, do not make a bishop superior or inferior" (Hieron. Ep. ad Evagr.).

4. The controversy concerning the title of universal bishop arose at length in the time of Gregory, and was occasioned by the ambition of John of Constantinople. For he wished to make himself universal, a thing which no other had ever attempted. In that controversy, Gregory does not allege that he is deprived of a right which belonged to him, but he strongly insists that the appellation is profane, nay, blasphemous, nay the forerunner of Antichrist. "The whole Church falls from its state, if he who is called universal falls" (Greg. Lib. iv. Ep. 76). Again, "It is very difficult to bear patiently that one who is our brother and fellow bishop should alone be called bishop, while all others are despised. But in this pride of his, what else is intimated but that the days of Antichrist are already near? For he is imitating him, who, despising the company of angels, attempted to ascend the pinnacle of greatness" (Lib. iv. Ep. 76). He elsewhere says to Eulogius of Alexandria and Anastasius of Antioch: "None of my predecessors ever desired to use this profane term: for if one patriarch is called universal, it is derogatory to the name of patriarch in others. But far be it from any Christian mind to wish to arrogate

to itself that which would in any degree, however slight, impair the honour of his brethren" (Lib. iv. Ep. 80). " To consent to that impious term is nothing else than to lose the faith" (Lib. iv. Ep. 83). " What we owe to the preservation of the unity of the faith is one thing, what we owe to the suppression of pride is another. I speak with confidence, for every one that calls himself, or desires to be called, universal priest, is by his pride a forerunner of Antichrist, because he acts proudly in preferring himself to others" (Lib. vii. Ep. 154). Thus, again, in a letter to Anastasius of Antioch, " I said, that he could not have peace with us unless he corrected the presumption of a superstitious and haughty term which the first apostate invented; and (to say nothing of the injury to your honour) if one bishop is called universal, the whole Church goes to ruin when that universal bishop falls" (Lib. vi. Ep. 188). But when he writes, that this honour was offered to Leo in the Council of Chalcedon (Lib. iv. Ep. 76, 80; Lib. vii. Ep. 76), he says what has no semblance of truth; nothing of the kind is found among the acts of that council. And Leo himself, who, in many letters, impugns the decree which was then made in honour of the See of Constantinople, undoubtedly would not have omitted this argument, which was the most plausible of all, if it was true that he himself repudiated what was given to him. One who, in other respects, was rather too desirous of honour, would not have omitted what would have been to his praise. Gregory, therefore, is incorrect in saying, that that title was conferred on the Roman See by the Council of Chalcedon; not to mention how ridiculous it is for him to say, that it proceeded from that sacred council, and yet to term it wicked, profane, nefarious, proud, and blasphemous, nay, devised by the devil, and promulgated by the herald of Antichrist. And yet he adds, that his predecessor refused it, lest by that which was given to one individually, all priests should be deprived of their due honour. In another place, he says, " None ever wished to be called by such a name; none arrogated this rash name to himself, lest, by seizing on the honour of supremacy in the office of the Pontificate, he might seem to deny it to all his brethren" (Gregor. Lib. iv. Ep. 82).

5. I come now to jurisdiction, which the Roman Pontiff asserts as an incontrovertible proposition that he possesses over all churches. I am aware of the great disputes which anciently existed on this subject: for there never was a time when the Roman See did not aim at authority over other churches. And here it will not be out of place to investigate the means by which she gradually attained to some influence. I am not now referring to that unlimited power which she seized at a comparatively recent period. The consideration of that we shall defer to its own place. But it is worth while here briefly to show in what way, and by what means, she formerly raised herself, so as to arrogate some authority over other churches. When the churches of the East were troubled and rent by the fac-

tions of the Arians, under the Emperors Constantius and Constans, sons of Constantine the Great; and Athanasius, the principal defender of the orthodox faith, had been driven from his see, the calamity obliged him to come to Rome, in order that by the authority of this see he might both repress the rage of his enemies, and confirm the orthodox under their distress. He was honourably received by Julius, who was then bishop, and engaged those of the West to undertake the defence of his cause. Therefore, when the orthodox stood greatly in need of external aid, and perceived that their chief protection lay in the Roman See, they willingly bestowed upon it all the authority they could. But the utmost extent of this was, that its communion was held in high estimation, and it was deemed ignominious to be excommunicated by it. Dishonest bad men afterwards added much to its authority, for when they wished to escape lawful tribunals, they betook themselves to Rome as an asylum. Accordingly, if any presbyter was condemned by his bishop, or if any bishop was condemned by the synod of his province, he appealed to Rome. These appeals the Roman bishops received more eagerly than they ought, because it seemed a species of extraordinary power to interpose in matters with which their connection was so very remote. Thus, when Eutyches was condemned by Flavianus, Bishop of Constantinople, he complained to Leo that the sentence was unjust. He, nothing loth, no less presumptuously than abruptly, undertook the patronage of a bad cause, and inveighed bitterly against Flavianus, as having condemned an innocent man without due investigation: and thus the effect of Leo's ambition was, that for some time the impiety of Eutyches was confirmed. It is certain that in Africa the same thing repeatedly occurred, for whenever any miscreant had been condemned by his ordinary judge, he fled to Rome, and brought many calumnious charges against his own people. The Roman See was always ready to interpose. This dishonesty obliged the African bishops to decree that no one should carry an appeal beyond sea under pain of excommunication.

6. Be this as it may, let us consider what right or authority the Roman See then possessed. Ecclesiastical power may be reduced to four heads—viz. ordination of bishops, calling of councils, hearing of appeals (or jurisdiction), inflicting monitory chastisements or censures. All ancient councils enjoin that bishops shall be ordained by their own Metropolitans; they nowhere enjoin an application to the Roman Bishop, except in his own patriarchate. Gradually, however, it became customary for all Italian bishops to go to Rome for consecration, with the exception of the Metropolitans, who did not allow themselves to be thus brought into subjection; but when any Metropolitan was to be ordained, the Roman Bishop sent one of his presbyters merely to be present, but not to preside. An example of this kind is extant in Gregory (Lib. ii. Ep. 68, 70), in the consecration of Constantius of Milan, after the death of Laurence. I do not, however, think that this was a very ancient custom. At first, as a mark

of respect and good-will, they sent deputies to one another to witness the ordination, and attest their communion. What was thus voluntary afterwards began to be regarded as necessary. However this be, it is certain that anciently the Roman Bishop had no power of ordaining except within the bounds of his own patriarchate, that is, as a canon of the Council of Nice expresses it, in suburban churches. To ordination was added the sending of a *synodical epistle*, but this implied no authority. The patriarchs were accustomed, immediately after consecration, to attest their faith by a formal writing, in which they declared that they assented to sacred and orthodox councils. Thus, by rendering an account of their faith, they mutually approved of each other. If the Roman Bishop had received this confession from others, and not given it, he would therein have been acknowledged superior ; but when it behoved to give as well as to receive, and to be subject to the common law, this was a sign of equality, not of lordship. Of this we have an example in a letter of Gregory to Anastasius and Cyriac of Constantinople, and in another letter to all the patriarchs together (Gregor. Lib. i. Ep. 24, 25 ; Lib. vi. Ep. 169).

7. Next come *admonitions* or *censures*. These the Roman Bishops anciently employed towards others, and in their turn received. Irenæus sharply rebuked Victor for rashly troubling the Church with a pernicious schism, for a matter of no moment. He submitted without objecting. Holy bishops were then wont to use the freedom as brethren, of admonishing and rebuking the Roman Prelate when he happened to err. He in his turn, when the case required, reminded others of their duty, and reprimanded them for their faults. For Cyprian, when he exhorts Stephen to admonish the bishops of France, does not found on his larger power, but on the common right which priests have in regard to each other (Cyprian. Lib. iii. Ep. 13). I ask if Stephen had then presided over France, would not Cyprian have said, " Check them, for they are yours" ? but his language is very different. " The brotherly fellowship which binds us together requires that we should mutually admonish each other " (Cyprian. ad Pomp. Cont. Epist. Steph.). And we see also with what severity of expression, a man otherwise of a mild temper, inveighs against Stephen himself, when he thinks him chargeable with insolence. Therefore, it does not yet appear in this respect that the Roman Bishop possessed any jurisdiction over those who did not belong to his province.

8. In regard to calling of councils, it was the duty of every Metropolitan to assemble a provincial synod at stated times. Here the Roman Bishop had no jurisdiction, while the Emperor alone could summon a general council. Had any of the bishops attempted this, not only would those out of the province not have obeyed the call, but a tumult would instantly have arisen. Therefore the Emperor gave intimation to all alike to attend. Socrates, indeed, relates that Julius expostulated with the Eastern bishops for not having called

him to the Council of Antioch, seeing it was forbidden by the canons that anything should be decided without the knowledge of the Roman Bishop (Tripart. Hist. Lib. iv.). But who does not perceive that this is to be understood of those decrees which bind the whole Church? At the same time, it is not strange if, in deference both to the antiquity and largeness of the city, and the dignity of the see, no universal decree concerning religion should be made in the absence of the Bishop of Rome, provided he did not refuse to be present. But what has this to do with the dominion of the whole Church? For we deny not that he was one of the principal bishops, though we are unwilling to admit what the Romanists now contend for—viz. that he had power over all.

9. The fourth remaining species of power is that of hearing *appeals*. It is evident that the supreme power belongs to him to whose tribunal appeals are made. Many had repeatedly appealed to the Roman Pontiff. He also had endeavoured to bring causes under his cognisance, but he had always been derided whenever he went beyond his own boundaries. I say nothing of the East and of Greece, but it is certain, that the bishops of France stoutly resisted when he seemed to assume authority over them. In Africa, the subject was long disputed, for in the Council of Milevita, at which Augustine was present, when those who carried appeals beyond seas were excommunicated, the Roman Pontiff attempted to obtain an alteration of the decree, and sent legates to show that the privilege of hearing appeals was given him by the Council of Nice. The legates produced acts of the council drawn from the armoury of their church. The African bishops resisted, and maintained, that credit was not to be given to the Bishop of Rome in his own cause; accordingly, they said that they would send to Constantinople, and other cities of Greece, where less suspicious copies might be had. It was found that nothing like what the Romanists had pretended was contained in the acts, and thus the decree which abrogated the supreme jurisdiction of the Roman Pontiff was confirmed. In this matter was manifested the egregious effrontery of the Roman Pontiff. For when he had fraudulently substituted the Council of Sardis for that of Nice, he was disgracefully detected in a palpable falsehood; but still greater and more impudent was the iniquity of those who added a fictitious letter to the Council, in which some Bishop of Carthage condemns the arrogance of Aurelius his predecessor, in promising to withdraw himself from obedience to the Apostolic See, and making a surrender of himself and his church, suppliantly prays for pardon. These are the noble records of antiquity on which the majesty of the Roman See is founded, while, under the pretext of antiquity, they deal in falsehoods so puerile, that even a blind man might feel them. "Aurelius (says he), elated by diabolical audacity and contumacy, was rebellious against Christ and St Peter, and, accordingly, deserved to be anathematised." What does Augustine say? and what the many Fathers who were present at the Council of Milevita? But what need is

there to give a lengthened refutation of that absurd writing, which not even Romanists, if they have any modesty left them, can look at without a deep feeling of shame ?   Thus Gratian, whether through malice or ignorance, I know not, after quoting the decree, That those are to be deprived of communion who carry appeals beyond seas, subjoins the exception, Unless, perhaps, they have appealed to the Roman See (Grat. 2, Quæst. 4, cap. Placuit.).   What can you make of creatures like these, who are so devoid of common sense that they set down as an exception from the law the very thing on account of which, as everybody sees, the law was made ?   For the Council, in condemning transmarine appeals, simply prohibits an appeal to Rome.   Yet this worthy expounder excepts Rome from the common law.

10. But (to end the question at once) the kind of jurisdiction which belonged to the Roman Bishop one narrative will make manifest. Donatus of Casa Nigra had accused Cecilianus the Bishop of Carthage. Cecilianus was condemned without a hearing : for, having ascertained that the bishops had entered into a conspiracy against him, he refused to appear.   The case was brought before the Emperor Constantine, who, wishing the matter to be ended by an ecclesiastical decision, gave the cognisance of it to Melciades, the Roman Bishop, appointing as his colleagues some bishops from Italy, France, and Spain. If it formed part of the ordinary jurisdiction of the Roman See to hear appeals in ecclesiastical causes, why did he allow others to be conjoined with him at the Emperor's discretion ? nay, why does he undertake to decide more from the command of the Emperor than his own office ?   But let us hear what afterwards happened (see August. Ep. 162, *et alibi*).   Cecilianus prevails.   Donatus of Casa Nigra is thrown in his calumnious action and appeals.   Constantine devolves the decision of the appeal on the Bishop of Arles, who sits as judge, to give sentence after the Roman Pontiff.[1]   If the Roman See has supreme power not subject to appeal, why does Melciades allow himself to be so greatly insulted as to have the Bishop of Arles preferred to him ?   And who is the Emperor that does this ?   Constantine, who they boast not only made it his constant study, but employed all the resources of the empire to enlarge the dignity of that see.   We see, therefore, how far in every way the Roman Pontiff was from that supreme dominion, which he asserts to have been given him by Christ over all churches, and which he falsely alleges that he possessed in all ages, with the consent of the whole world.

11. I know how many epistles there are, how many rescripts and edicts in which there is nothing which the pontiffs do not ascribe and confidently arrogate to themselves.   But all men of the least intellect and learning know, that the greater part of them are in themselves

---

1 French. " Voila l'Archeveque d'Arles assis pour retracter; si bon lui semble la sentence de l'Eveque Romain. au moins pour juger par dessus lui."—Here is the Archbishop of Arles seated to recall, if he thinks fit, the sentence of the Bishop of Rome, or at least to judge as his superior.

so absurd, that it is easy at the first sight to detect the forge from which they have come.   Does any man of sense and soberness think that Anacletus is the author of that famous interpretation which is given in Gratian, under the name of Anacletus—viz. that Cephas is head? (Dist. 22, cap. Sacrosancta.)   Numerous follies of the same kind which Gratian has heaped together without judgment, the Romanists of the present day employ against us in defence of their see. The smoke, by which, in the former days of ignorance, they imposed upon the ignorant, they would still vend in the present light.   I am unwilling to take much trouble in refuting things which, by their extreme absurdity, plainly refute themselves.   I admit the existence of genuine epistles by ancient Pontiffs, in which they pronounce magnificent eulogiums on the extent of their see.   Such are some of the epistles of Leo.   For as he possessed learning and eloquence, so he was excessively desirous of glory and dominion; but the true question is, whether or not, when he thus extolled himself, the churches gave credit to his testimony?   It appears that many were offended with his ambition, and also resisted his cupidity.   He in one place appoints the Bishop of Thessalonica his vicar throughout Greece and other neighbouring regions (Leo, Ep. 85), and elsewhere gives the same office to the Bishop of Arles or some other throughout France (Ep. 83).   In like manner, he appointed Hormisdas, Bishop of Hispala, his vicar throughout Spain, but he uniformly makes this reservation, that in giving such commissions, the ancient privileges of the Metropolitans were to remain safe and entire.   These appointments, therefore, were made on the condition, that no bishop should be impeded in his ordinary jurisdiction, no Metropolitan in taking cognisance of appeals, no provincial council in constituting churches. But what else was this than to decline all jurisdiction, and to interpose for the purpose of settling discord only, in so far as the law and nature of ecclesiastical communion admit?

12. In the time of Gregory, that ancient rule was greatly changed. For when the empire was convulsed and torn, when France and Spain were suffering from the many disasters which they ever and anon received, when Illyricum was laid waste, Italy harassed, and Africa almost destroyed by uninterrupted calamities, in order that, during these civil convulsions, the integrity of the faith might remain, or at least not entirely perish, the bishops in all quarters attached themselves more to the Roman Pontiff.   In this way, not only the dignity, but also the power of the see, exceedingly increased, although I attach no great importance to the means by which this was accomplished.   It is certain, that it was then greater than in former ages. And yet it was very different from the unbridled dominion of one ruling others as he pleased.   Still the reverence paid to the Roman See was such, that by its authority it could guide and repress those whom their own colleagues were unable to keep to their duty; for Gregory is careful ever and anon to testify that he was not less faithful in preserving the rights of others, that in insisting that his

own should be preserved. "I do not," says he, "under the stimulus of ambition, derogate from any man's right, but desire to honour my brethren in all things" (Gregor. Lib. ii. Ep. 68). There is no sentence in his writings in which he boasts more proudly of the extent of his primacy than the following: "I know not what bishop is not subject to the Roman See, when he is discovered in a fault" (Leo. Lib. ii., Epist. 68). However, he immediately adds, "Where faults do not call for interference, all are equal according to the rule of humility." He claims for himself the right of correcting those who have sinned; if all do their duty, he puts himself on a footing of equality. He, indeed, claimed this right, and those who chose assented to it, while those who were not pleased with it were at liberty to object with impunity; and it is known that the greater part did so. We may add, that he is then speaking of the primate of Byzantium, who, when condemned by a provincial synod, repudiated the whole judgment. His colleagues had informed the Emperor of his contumacy, and the Emperor had given the cognisance of the matter to Gregory. We see, therefore, that he does not interfere in any way with the ordinary jurisdiction, and that, in acting as a subsidiary to others, he acts entirely by the Emperor's command.

13. At this time, therefore, the whole power of the Roman Bishop consisted in opposing stubborn and ungovernable spirits, where some extraordinary remedy was required, and this in order to assist other bishops, not to interfere with them. Therefore, he assumes no more power over others than he elsewhere gives others over himself, when he confesses that he is ready to be corrected by all, amended by all (Lib. ii. Ep. 37). So, in another place, though he orders the Bishop of Aquileia to come to Rome to plead his cause in a controversy as to doctrine which had arisen between himself and others, he thus orders not of his own authority, but in obedience to the Emperor's command. Nor does he declare that he himself will be sole judge, but promises to call a synod, by which the whole business may be determined. But although the moderation was still such, that the power of the Roman See had certain limits which it was not permitted to overstep, and the Roman Bishop himself was not more above than under others, it appears how much Gregory was dissatisfied with this state of matters. For he ever and anon complains, that he, under the colour of the episcopate, was brought back to the world, and was more involved in earthly cares than when living as a laic; that he, in that honourable office, was oppressed by the tumult of secular affairs. Elsewhere he says, "So many burdensome occupations depress me, that my mind cannot at all rise to things above. I am shaken by the many billows of causes, and after they are quieted, am afflicted by the tempests of a tumultuous life, so that I may truly say I am come into the depths of the sea, and the flood has overwhelmed me." From this I infer what he would have said if he had fallen on the present times. If he did not fulfil, he at least did the duty of a pastor. He declined the administration of civil power, and

acknowledged himself subject, like others, to the Emperor. He did not interfere with the management of other churches, unless forced by necessity. And yet he thinks himself in a labyrinth, because he cannot devote himself entirely to the duty of a bishop.

14. At that time, as has already been said, the Bishop of Constantinople was disputing with the Bishop of Rome for the primacy. For after the seat of empire was fixed at Constantinople, the majesty of the empire seemed to demand that that church should have the next place of honour to that of Rome. And certainly, at the outset, nothing had tended more to give the primacy to Rome, than that it was then the capital of the empire. In Gratian (Dist. 80), there is a rescript under the name of Pope Lucinus, to the effect that the only way in which the cities where Metropolitans and Primates ought to preside were distinguished, was by means of the civil government which had previously existed. There is a similar rescript under the name of Pope Clement, in which he says, that patriarchs were appointed in those cities which had previously had the first flamens. Although this is absurd, it was borrowed from what was true. For it is certain, that in order to make as little change as possible, provinces were distributed according to the state of matters then existing, and Primates and Metropolitans were placed in those cities which surpassed others in honours and power. Accordingly, it was decreed in the Council of Turin, that the cities of every province which were first in the civil government should be the first sees of bishops. But if it should happen that the honour of civil government was transferred from one city to another, then the right of the metropolis should be at the same time transferred thither. But Innocent, the Roman Pontiff, seeing that the ancient dignity of the city had been decaying ever since the seat of empire had been transferred to Constantinople, and fearing for his see, enacted a contrary law, in which he denies the necessity of changing metropolitan churches as imperial metropolitan cities were changed. But the authority of a synod is justly to be preferred to the opinion of one individual, and Innocent himself should be suspected in his own cause. However this be, he by his caveat shows the original rule to have been, that Metropolitans should be distributed according to the order of the empire.

15. Agreeably to this ancient custom, the first Council of Constantinople decreed that the bishop of that city should take precedence after the Roman Pontiff, because it was a new Rome. But long after, when a similar decree was made at Chalcedon, Leo keenly protested (Socrat. Hist. Trop. Lib. ix. cap. 13). And not only did he permit himself to set at nought what six hundred bishops or more had decreed, but he even assailed them with bitter reproaches, because they had derogated from other sees in the honour which they had presumed to confer on the Church of Constantinople (in Decr. 22, Distinct. cap. Constantinop.). What, pray, could have incited the man to trouble the world for so small an affair but mere ambition? He says, that what the Council of Nice had once sanctioned

ought to have been inviolable; as if the Christian faith was in any danger if one church was preferred to another; or as if separate Patriarchates had been established on any other grounds than that of policy. But we know that policy varies with times, nay, demands various changes. It is therefore futile in Leo to pretend that the See of Constantinople ought not to receive the honour which was given to that of Alexandria, by the authority of the Council of Nice. For it is the dictate of common sense, that the decree was one of those which might be abrogated, in respect of a change of times. What shall we say to the fact, that none of the Eastern churches, though chiefly interested, objected? Proterius, who had been appointed at Alexandria instead of Dioscorus, was certainly present; other patriarchs whose honour was impaired were present. It belonged to them to interfere, not to Leo, whose station remained entire. While all of them are silent, many assent, and the Roman Bishop alone resists, it is easy to judge what it is that moves him; just because he foresaw what happened not long after, that when the glory of ancient Rome declined, Constantinople, not contented with the second place, would dispute the primacy with her. And yet his clamour was not so successful as to prevent the decree of the council from being ratified. Accordingly, his successors seeing themselves defeated, quietly desisted from that petulance, and allowed the Bishop of Constantinople to be regarded as the second Patriarch.

16. But shortly after, John, who, in the time of Gregory, presided over the church of Constantinople, went so far as to say that he was universal Patriarch. Here Gregory, that he might not be wanting to his See in a most excellent cause, constantly opposed. And certainly it was impossible to tolerate the pride and madness of John, who wished to make the limits of his bishopric equal to the limits of the empire. This, which Gregory denies to another, he claims not for himself, but abominates the title by whomsoever used, as wicked, impious, and nefarious. Nay, he is offended with Eulogius, Bishop of Alexandria, who had honoured him with this title, "See (says he, Lib. vii. Ep. 30) in the address of the letter which you have directed to me, though I prohibited you, you have taken care to write a word of proud signification by calling me universal Pope. What I ask is, that your holiness do not go farther, because, whatever is given to another more than reason demands is withdrawn from you. I do not regard that as honour by which I see that the honour of my brethren is diminished. For my honour is the universal honour of the Church, and entire prerogative of my brethren. If your holiness calls me universal Pope, it denies itself to be this whole which it acknowledges me to be." The cause of Gregory was indeed good and honourable; but John, aided by the favour of the Emperor Maurice, could not be dissuaded from his purpose. Cyriac also, his successor, never allowed himself to be spoken to on the subject.

17. At length Phocas, who had slain Maurice, and usurped his place (more friendly to the Romans, for what reason I know not, or

rather because he had been crowned king there without opposition), conceded to Boniface III. what Gregory by no means demanded— viz. that Rome should be the head of all the churches. In this way the controversy was ended. And yet this kindness of the Emperor to the Romans would not have been of very much avail had not other circumstances occurred. For shortly after Greece and all Asia were cut off from his communion, while all the reverence which he received from France was obedience only in so far as she pleased. She was brought into subjection for the first time when Pepin got possession of the throne. For Zachary, the Roman Pontiff, having aided him in his perfidy and robbery when he expelled the lawful sovereign, and seized upon the kingdom, which lay exposed as a kind of prey, was rewarded by having the jurisdiction of the Roman See established over the churches of France. In the same way as robbers are wont to divide and share the common spoil, those two worthies arranged that Pepin should have the worldly and civil power by spoiling the true prince, while Zachary should become the head of all the bishops, and have the spiritual power. This, though weak at the first (as usually happens with new power), was afterwards confirmed by the authority of Charlemagne for a very similar cause. For he too was under obligation to the Roman Pontiff, to whose zeal he was indebted for the honour of empire. Though there is reason to believe that the churches had previously been greatly altered, it is certain that the ancient form of the Church was then only completely effaced in Gaul and Germany. There are still extant among the archives of the Parliament of Paris short commentaries on those times, which, in treating of ecclesiastical affairs, make mention of the compacts both of Pepin and Charlemagne with the Roman Pontiff. Hence we may infer that the ancient state of matters was then changed.

18. From that time, while everywhere matters were becoming daily worse, the tyranny of the Roman Bishop was established, and ever and anon increased, and this partly by the ignorance, partly by the sluggishness, of the bishops. For while he was arrogating everything to himself, and proceeding more and more to exalt himself without measure, contrary to law and right, the bishops did not exert themselves so zealously as they ought in curbing his pretensions. And though they had not been deficient in spirit, they were devoid of true doctrine and experience, so that they were by no means fit for so important an effort. Accordingly, we see how great and monstrous was the profanation of all sacred things, and the dissipation of the whole ecclesiastical order at Rome, in the age of Bernard. He complains (Lib. i. de Consider. ad Eugen.) that the ambitious, avaricious, demoniacal, sacrilegious, fornicators, incestuous, and similar miscreants, flocked from all quarters of the world to Rome, that by apostolic authority they might acquire or retain ecclesiastical honours: that fraud, circumvention, and violence, prevailed. The mode of judging causes then in use he describes as

execrable, as disgraceful, not only to the Church, but the bar. He exclaims that the Church is filled with the ambitious: that not one is more afraid to perpetrate crimes than robbers in their den when they share the spoils of the traveller. "Few (say he) look to the mouth of the legislator, but all to his hands. Not without cause, however: for their hands do the whole business of the Pope. What kind of thing is it when those are bought by the spoils of the Church, who say to you, Well done, well done? The life of the poor is sown in the highways of the rich: silver glitters in the mire: they run together from all sides: it is not the poorer that takes it up, but the stronger, or, perhaps, he who runs fastest. That custom, however, or rather that death, comes not of you: I wish it would end in you. While these things are going on, you, a pastor, come forth robed in much costly clothing. If I might presume to say it, this is more the pasture of demons than of sheep. Peter, forsooth, acted thus; Paul sported thus. Your court has been more accustomed to receive good men than to make them. The bad do not gain much there, but the good degenerate." Then when he describes the abuses of appeals, no pious man can read them without being horrified. At length, speaking of the unbridled cupidity of the Roman See in usurping jurisdiction, he thus concludes (Lib. iii. de Concil.), " I express the murmur and common complaint of the churches. Their cry is, that they are maimed and dismembered. There are none, or very few, who do not lament or fear that plague. Do you ask what plague? Abbots are encroached upon by bishops, bishops by archbishops, &c. It is strange if this can be excused. By thus acting, you prove that you have the fulness of power, but not the fulness of righteousness. You do this because you are able; but whether you also ought to do it is the question. You are appointed to preserve, not to envy, the honour and rank of each." I have thought it proper to quote these few passages out of many, partly that my readers may see how grievously the Church had then fallen, partly, too, that they may see with what grief and lamentation all pious men beheld this calamity.

19. But though we were to concede to the Roman Pontiff of the present day the eminence and extent of jurisdiction which his see had in the middle ages, as in the time of Leo and Gregory, what would this be to the existing Papacy? I am not now speaking of worldly dominion, or of civil power, which will afterwards be explained in their own place (chap. xi. sec. 8–14); but what resemblance is there between the spiritual government of which they boast and the state of those times? The only definition which they give of the Pope is, that he is the supreme head of the Church on earth, and the universal bishop of the whole globe. The Pontiffs themselves, when they speak of their authority, declare with great superciliousness, that the power of commanding belongs to them,—that the necessity of obedience remains with others,—that all their decrees are to be regarded as confirmed by the divine voice of Peter,—that

provincial synods, from not having the presence of the Pope, are
deficient in authority,—that they can ordain the clergy of any church,
—and can summon to their See any who have been ordained elsewhere.   Innumerable things of this kind are contained in the farrago
of Gratian, which I do not mention, that I may not be tedious to my
readers.   The whole comes to this, that to the Roman Pontiff belongs the supreme cognisance of all ecclesiastical causes, whether in
determining and defining doctrines, or in enacting laws, or in appointing discipline, or in giving sentences.   It were also tedious and
superfluous to review the privileges which they assume to themselves
in what they call reservations.   But the most intolerable of all things
is their leaving no judicial authority in the world to restrain and
curb them when they licentiously abuse their immense power.   " No
man (say they[1]) is entitled to alter the judgment of this See, on
account of the primacy of the Roman Church."   Again, " The judge
shall not be judged either by the emperor, or by kings, or by the
clergy, or by the people."   It is surely imperious enough for one man
to appoint himself the judge of all, while he will not submit to the
judgment of any.   But what if he tyrannises over the people of God?
if he dissipates and lays waste the kingdom of Christ ? if he troubles
the whole Church ? if he convert the pastoral office into robbery ?
Nay, though he should be the most abandoned of all, he insists that
none can call him to account.   The language of Pontiffs is, " God
has been pleased to terminate the causes of other men by men, but
the Prelate of this See he has reserved unquestioned for his own
judgment."   Again, " The deeds of subjects are judged by us ; ours
by God only."

20. And in order that edicts of this kind might have more weight,
they falsely substituted the names of ancient Pontiffs, as if matters
had been so constituted from the beginning, while it is absolutely
certain that whatever attributes more to the Pontiff than we have
stated to have been given to him by ancient councils, is new and of
recent fabrication.   Nay, they have carried their effrontery so far as
to publish a rescript under the name of Anastasius, the Patriarch of
Constantinople, in which he testifies that it was appointed by ancient
regulations, that nothing should be done in the remotest provinces
without being previously referred to the Roman See.   Besides its
extreme folly, who can believe it credible that such an eulogium on
the Roman See proceeded from an opponent and rival of its honour
and dignity ?   But doubtless it was necessary that those Antichrists
should proceed to such a degree of madness and blindness, that their
iniquity might be manifest to all men of sound mind who will only
open their eyes.   The decretal epistles collected by Gregory IX.,
also the Clementines and Extravagants of Martin, breathe still more
plainly, and in more bombastic terms bespeak this boundless ferocity

1 Nicolas, whose view is given in Decretis 17, Quæst. 3, cap. Nemini; Innocent IX.
Quæst. 3. cap. Nemo. Symmachi 9. Quæst. 3, cap. Aliorum. Antherius, ibidem, cap.
Facta.

and tyranny, as it were, of barbarian kings. But these are the
oracles out of which the Romanists would have their Papacy to be
judged.   Hence have sprung those famous axioms which have the
force of oracles throughout the Papacy in the present day—viz. that
the Pope cannot err ; that the Pope is superior to councils ; that the
Pope is the universal bishop of all churches, and the chief Head of
the Church on earth.   I say nothing of the still greater absurdities
which are babbled by the foolish canonists in their schools, absurdities, however, which Roman theologians not only assent to, but
even applaud in flattery of their idol.

21. I will not treat with them on the strictest terms.   In opposition
to their great insolence, some would quote the language which Cyprian
used to the bishops in the council over which he presided : " None of
us styles himself bishop of bishops, or forces his colleagues to the
necessity of obeying by the tyranny of terror."   Some might object
what was long after decreed at Carthage, " Let no one be called the
prince of priests or first bishop ; " and might gather many proofs from
history, and canons from councils, and many passages from ancient
writers, which bring the Roman Pontiff into due order.   But these I
omit, that I may not seem to press too hard upon them.   However,
let these worthy defenders of the Roman See tell me with what face
they can defend the title of universal bishop, while they see it so often
anathematised by Gregory.   If effect is to be given to his testimony,
then they, by making their Pontiff universal, declare him to be Antichrist.   The name of *head* was not more approved.   For Gregory
thus speaks: "Peter was the chief member in the body, John, Andrew,
and James, the heads of particular communities.   All, however, are
under one head members of the Church : nay, the saints before the
law, the saints under the law, the saints under grace, all perfecting
the body of the Lord, are constituted members: none of them ever
wished to be styled universal" (Gregor. Lib. iv. Ep. 83).   When the
Pontiff arrogates to himself the power of ordering, he little accords
with what Gregory elsewhere says.   For Eulogius, Bishop of Alexandria, having said that he had received an order from him, he replies
in this manner : " This word *order* I beg you to take out of my hearing, for I know who I am, and who you are: in station you are my
brethren, in character my fathers.   I therefore did not order, but
took care to suggest what seemed useful" (Gregor. Lib. vii. Ep. 80).
When the Pope extends his jurisdiction without limit, he does great
and atrocious injustice not only to other bishops, but to each single
church, tearing and dismembering them, that he may build his see
upon their ruins.   When he exempts himself from all tribunals, and
wishes to reign in the manner of a tyrant, holding his own caprice
to be his only law, the thing is too insulting, and too foreign to ecclesiastical rule, to be on any account submitted to.   It is altogether
abhorrent, not only from pious feeling, but also from common sense.

22. But that I may not be forced to discuss and follow out each
point singly, I again appeal to those who, in the present day, would

be thought the best and most faithful defenders of the Roman See, whether they are not ashamed to defend the existing state of the Papacy, which is clearly a hundred times more corrupt than in the days of Gregory and Bernard, though even then these holy men were so much displeased with it.   Gregory everywhere complains (Lib. i. Ep. 5 ; *item,* Ep. 7, 25, &c.) that he was distracted above measure by foreign occupations : that under colour of the episcopate he was taken back to the world, being subject to more worldly cares than he remembered to have ever had when a laic ; that he was so oppressed by the trouble of secular affairs, as to be unable to raise his mind to things above ; that he was so tossed by the many billows of causes, and afflicted by the tempests of a tumultuous life, that he might well say, " I am come into the depths of the sea."   It is certain, that amid these worldly occupations, he could teach the people in sermons, admonish in private, and correct those who required it ; order the Church, give counsel to his colleagues, and exhort them to their duty. Moreover, some time was left for writing, and yet he deplores it as his calamity, that he was plunged into the very deepest sea.   If the administration at that time was a sea, what shall we say of the present Papacy ?   For what resemblance is there between the periods ? Now there are no sermons, no care for discipline, no zeal for churches, no spiritual function ; nothing, in short, but the world.   And yet this labyrinth is lauded as if nothing could be found better ordered and arranged.   What complaints also does Bernard pour forth, what groans does he utter, when he beholds the vices of his own age ? What then would he have done on beholding this iron, or, if possible, worse than iron, age of ours ?   How dishonest, therefore, not only obstinately to defend as sacred and divine what all the saints have always with one mouth disapproved, but to abuse their testimony in favour of the Papacy, which, it is evident, was altogether unknown to them ?   Although I admit, in respect to the time of Bernard, that all things were so corrupt as to make it not unlike our own.   But it betrays a want of all sense of shame to seek any excuse from that middle period—namely, from that of Leo, Gregory, and the like—for it is just as if one were to vindicate the monarchy of the Cæsars by lauding the ancient state of the Roman empire ; in other words, were to borrow the praises of liberty in order to eulogise tyranny.

23. Lastly, Although all these things were granted, an entirely new question arises, when we deny that there is at Rome a Church in which privileges of this nature can reside ; when we deny that there is a bishop to sustain the dignity of these privileges.   Assume, therefore, that all these things are true (though we have already extorted the contrary from them), that Peter was by the words of Christ constituted head of the universal Church, and that the honour thus conferred upon him he deposited in the Roman See, that this was sanctioned by the authority of the ancient Church, and confirmed by long use ; that supreme power was always with one consent devolved by all on the Roman Pontiff, that while he was the judge of all causes

and all men, he was subject to the judgment of none. Let even more be conceded to them if they will, I answer, in one word, that none of these things avail if there be not a Church and a Bishop at Rome. They must of necessity concede to me that she is not a mother of churches who is not herself a church, that he cannot be the chief of bishops who is not himself a bishop. Would they then have the Apostolic See at Rome? Let them give me a true and lawful apostleship. Would they have a supreme pontiff, let them give me a bishop. But how? Where will they show me any semblance of a church? They, no doubt, talk of one, and have it ever in their mouths. But surely the Church is recognised by certain marks, and bishopric is the name of an office. I am not now speaking of the people but of the government, which ought perpetually to be conspicuous in the Church. Where, then, is a ministry such as the institution of Christ requires? Let us remember what was formerly said of the duty of presbyters and bishops. If we bring the office of cardinals to that test, we will acknowledge that they are nothing less than presbyters. But I should like to know what one quality of a bishop the Pope himself has? The first point in the office of a bishop is to instruct the people in the word of God; the second and next to it is to administer the sacraments; the third is to admonish and exhort, to correct those who are in fault, and restrain the people by holy discipline. Which of these things does he do? Nay, which of these things does he pretend to do? Let them say, then, on what ground they will have him to be regarded as a bishop, who does not even in semblance touch any part of the duty with his little finger.

24. It is not with a bishop as with a king; the latter, though he does not execute the proper duty of a king, nevertheless retains the title and the honour; but in deciding on a bishop respect is had to the command of Christ, to which effect ought always to be given in the Church. Let the Romanists then untie this knot. I deny that their pontiff is the prince of bishops, seeing he is no bishop. This allegation of mine they must prove to be false if they would succeed in theirs. What then do I maintain? That he has nothing proper to a bishop, but is in all things the opposite of a bishop. But with what shall I here begin? With doctrine or with morals? What shall I say, or what shall I pass in silence, or where shall I end? This I maintain: while in the present day the world is so inundated with perverse and impious doctrines, so full of all kinds of superstition, so blinded by error and sunk in idolatry, there is not one of them which has not emanated from the Papacy, or at least been confirmed by it. Nor is there any other reason why the pontiffs are so enraged against the reviving doctrine of the Gospel, why they stretch every nerve to oppress it, and urge all kings and princes to cruelty, than just that they see their whole dominion tottering and falling to pieces the moment the Gospel of Christ prevails. Leo was cruel and Clement sanguinary, Paul is truculent. But in assailing the truth, it is not so much natural temper that impels them as the conviction

that they have no other method of maintaining their power.   Therefore, seeing they cannot be safe unless they put Christ to flight, they
labour in this cause as if they were fighting for their altars and
hearths, for their own lives and those of their adherents.   What
then ? Shall we recognise the Apostolic See where we see nothing
but horrible apostacy ? Shall he be the vicar of Christ who, by his
furious efforts in persecuting the Gospel, plainly declares himself to
be Antichrist ? Shall he be the successor of Peter who goes about with
fire and sword demolishing everything that Peter built ? Shall he
be the Head of the Church who, after dissevering the Church from
Christ, her only true Head, tears and lacerates her members ? Rome,
indeed, was once the mother of all the churches, but since she began
to be the seat of Antichrist she ceased to be what she was.

25. To some we seem slanderous and petulant, when we call the
Roman Pontiff Antichrist. But those who think so perceive not that
they are bringing a charge of intemperance against Paul, after whom
we speak, nay, in whose very words we speak.   But lest any one
object that Paul's words have a different meaning, and are wrested by
us against the Roman Pontiff, I will briefly show that they can only
be understood of the Papacy.   Paul says that Antichrist would sit in
the temple of God (2 Thess. ii. 4).   In another passage, the Spirit,
portraying him in the person of Antiochus, says that his reign would
be with great swelling words of vanity (Dan. vii. 25).   Hence we
infer that his tyranny is more over souls than bodies, a tyranny set
up in opposition to the spiritual kingdom of Christ.   Then his nature
is such, that he abolishes not the name either of Christ or the Church,
but rather uses the name of Christ as a pretext, and lurks under the
name of Church as under a mask.   But though all the heresies and
schisms which have existed from the beginning belong to the kingdom of Antichrist, yet when Paul foretells that defection will come,
he by the description intimates that that seat of abomination will be
erected, when a kind of universal defection comes upon the Church,
though many members of the Church scattered up and down should
continue in the true unity of the faith.   But when he adds, that in
his own time, the mystery of iniquity, which was afterwards to be
openly manifested, had begun to work in secret, we thereby understand that this calamity was neither to be introduced by one man,
nor to terminate in one man (see Calv. in 2 Thess. ii. 3 ; Dan. vii.
9).   Moreover, when the mark by which he distinguishes Antichrist
is, that he would rob God of his honour and take it to himself, he
gives the leading feature which we ought to follow in searching out
Antichrist ; especially when pride of this description proceeds to the
open devastation of the Church.   Seeing then it is certain that the
Roman Pontiff has impudently transferred to himself the most
peculiar properties of God and Christ, there cannot be a doubt that
he is the leader and standard-bearer of an impious and abominable
kingdom.

26. Let the Romanists now go and oppose us with antiquity ; as

if, amid such a complete change in every respect, the honour of the See can continue where there is no See. Eusebius says that God, to make way for his vengeance, transferred the Church which was at Jerusalem to Pella (Euseb. Lib. iii. cap. 5). What we are told was once done may have been done repeatedly. Hence it is too absurd and ridiculous so to fix the honour of the primacy to a particular spot, as that he who is in fact the most inveterate enemy of Christ, the chief adversary of the Gospel, the greatest devastator and waster of the Church, the most cruel slayer and murderer of the saints, should be, nevertheless, regarded as the vicegerent of Christ, the successor of Peter, the first priest of the Church, merely because he occupies what was formerly the first of all sees. I do not say how great the difference is between the chancery of the Pope and well-regulated order in the Church; although this one fact might well set the question at rest. For no man of sound mind will include the episcopate in lead and bulls, much less in that administration of captions and circumscriptions, in which the spiritual government of the Pope is supposed to consist. It has therefore been elegantly said, that that vaunted Roman Church was long ago converted into a temporal court, the only thing which is now seen at Rome. I am not here speaking of the vices of individuals, but demonstrating that the Papacy itself is diametrically opposed to the ecclesiastical system.

27. But if we come to individuals, it is well known what kind of vicars of Christ we shall find. No doubt, Julius and Leo, and Clement and Paul, will be pillars of the Christian faith, the first interpreters of religion, though they knew nothing more of Christ than they had learned in the school of Lucian. But why give the names of three or four pontiffs? as if there were any doubt as to the kind of religion professed by pontiffs, with their College of Cardinals, and professors, in the present day. The first head of the secret theology which is in vogue among them is, that there is no God. Another, that whatever things have been written and are taught concerning Christ are lies and imposture.[1] A third, that the doctrine of a future life and final resurrection is a mere fable. All do not think, few speak thus; I confess it. Yet it is long since this began to be the ordinary religion of pontiffs; and though the thing is notorious to all who know Rome, Roman theologians cease not to boast that by special privilege our Saviour has provided that the Pope cannot err, because it was said to Peter, "I have prayed for thee that thy faith fail not" (Luke xxii. 32). What, pray, do they gain by their effrontery, but to let the whole world understand that they have reached the extreme of wickedness, so as neither to fear God nor regard man?

---

[1] Erasmus, in a letter to Steuchus, says, "It may be that in Germany there are persons who do not refrain from blasphemy against God, but the severest punishment is inflicted on them. But at Rome, I have with my own ears heard men belching out

28. But let us suppose that the iniquity of these pontiffs whom I have mentioned is not known, as they have not published it either in sermons or writings, but betrayed it only at table or in their chamber, or at least within the walls of their court. But if they would have the privilege which they claim to be confirmed, they must expunge from their list of pontiffs John XXII.,[1] who publicly maintained that the soul is mortal, and perishes with the body till the day of resurrection. And to show you that the whole See with its chief props then utterly fell, none of the Cardinals opposed his madness, only the Faculty of Paris urged the king to insist on a recantation. The king interdicted his subjects from communion with him, unless he would immediately recant, and published his interdict in the usual way by a herald. Thus necessitated, he abjured his error. This example relieves me from the necessity of disputing further with my opponents, when they say that the Roman See and its pontiffs cannot err in the faith, from its being said to Peter, " I have prayed for thee that thy faith fail not." Certainly by this shameful lapse he fell from the faith, and became a noted proof to posterity, that all are not Peters who succeed Peter in the episcopate; although the thing is too childish in itself to need an answer: for if they insist on applying everything that was said to Peter to the successors of Peter, it will follow, that they are all Satans, because our Lord once said to Peter, " Get thee behind me, Satan, thou art an offence unto me." It is as easy for us to retort the latter saying as for them to adduce the former.

29. But I have no pleasure in this absurd mode of disputation, and therefore return to the point from which I digressed. To fix down Christ and the Holy Spirit and the Church to a particular spot, so that every one who presides in it, should he be a devil, must still be deemed vicegerent of Christ, and the head of the Church, because that spot was formerly the See of Peter, is not only impious and insulting to Christ, but absurd and contrary to common sense. For a long period, the Roman Pontiffs have either been altogether devoid of religion, or been its greatest enemies. The see which they occupy, therefore, no more makes them the vicars of Christ, than it makes an idol to become God, when it is placed in the temple of God (2 Thess. ii. 4). Then, if manners be inquired into, let the Popes answer for themselves, what there is in them that can make them be recognised for bishops. First, the mode of life at Rome, while they not only connive and are silent, but also tacitly approve, is altogether unworthy of bishops, whose duty it is to curb the licence of the people by the strictness of discipline. But I will not be so rigid with them as to charge them with the faults of others. But when they with their household, with almost the whole College of Cardinals, and the whole body of their clergy, are so devoted to wickedness, obscenity, unclean-

horrid blasphemies against Christ and his apostles, in the presence of many besides myself, and doing it with impunity! "

1 John Gerson, who lived at the time, attests that John XXII. openly denied the immortality of the soul.

ness, iniquity, and crime of every description, that they resemble monsters more than men, they herein betray that they are nothing less than bishops. They need not fear that I will make a farther disclosure of their turpitude. For it is painful to wade through such filthy mire, and I must spare modest ears. But I think I have amply demonstrated what I proposed—viz. that though Rome was formerly the first of churches, she deserves not in the present day to be regarded as one of her minutest members.

30. In regard to those whom they call Cardinals, I know not how it happened that they rose so suddenly to such a height. In the age of Gregory, the name was applied to bishops only (Gregor. Lib. ii. Ep. 15, 77, 79 ; Ep. 6, 25). For whenever he makes mention of cardinals, he assigns them not only to the Roman Church, but to every other church, so that, in short, *a Cardinal priest* is nothing else than a bishop. I do not find the name among the writers of a former age. I see, however, that they were inferior to bishops, whom they now far surpass. There is a well-known passage in Augustine : " Although, in regard to terms of honour which custom has fixed in the Church, the office of bishop is greater than that of presbyter, yet in many things, Augustine is inferior to Jerome " (August. ad Hieron. Ep. 19). Here, certainly, he is not distinguishing a presbyter of the Roman Church from other presbyters, but placing all of them alike after bishops. And so strictly was this observed, that at the Council of Carthage, when two legates of the Roman See were present, one a bishop, and the other a presbyter, the latter was put in the lowest place. But not to dwell too much on ancient times, we have account of a Council held at Rome, under Gregory, at which the presbyters sit in the lowest place, and subscribe by themselves, while deacons do not subscribe at all. And, indeed, they had no office at that time, unless to be present under the bishop, and assist him in the administration of word and sacraments. So much is their lot now changed, that they have become associates of kings and Cesars. And there can be no doubt that they have grown gradually with their head, until they reached their present pinnacle of dignity. This much it seemed proper to say in passing, that my readers may understand how very widely the Roman See, as it now exists, differs from the ancient See, under which it endeavours to cloak and defend itself. But whatever they were formerly, as they have no true and legitimate office in the Church, they only retain a colour and empty mask ; nay, as they are in all respects the opposite of true ministers, the thing which Gregory so often writes must, of necessity, have befallen them. His words are, " Weeping, I say, groaning, I declare it ; when the sacerdotal order has fallen within, it cannot long stand without " (Gregor. Lib. iv. Ep. 55, 56 ; Lib. v. Ep. 7). Nay, rather what Malachi says of such persons must be fulfilled in them : " Ye are departed out of the way ; ye have caused many to stumble at the law ; ye have corrupted the covenant of Levi, saith the Lord of hosts. Therefore have I also made you contemptible and base before all the people " (Mal. ii. 8,

9).   I now leave all the pious to judge what the supreme pinnacle of the Roman hierarchy must be, to which the Papists, with nefarious effrontery, hesitate not to subject the word of God itself, that word which should be venerable and holy in earth and heaven, to men and angels.

CHAPTER VIII.

OF THE POWER OF THE CHURCH IN ARTICLES OF FAITH.   THE UN-
BRIDLED LICENCE OF THE PAPAL CHURCH IN DESTROYING PURITY
OF DOCTRINE.

This chapter is divided into two parts,—I. The limits within which the Church ought to confine herself in matters of this kind, sec. 1–9. II. The Roman Church convicted of having transgressed these limits, sec. 10–16.

Sections.

1. The marks and government of the Church having been considered in the seven previous chapters, the power of the Church is now considered under three heads —viz. Doctrine, Legislation, Jurisdiction.
2. The authority and power given to Church-officers not given to themselves, but their office. This shown in the case of Moses and the Levitical priesthood.
3. The same thing shown in the case of the Prophets.
4. Same thing shown in the case of the Apostles, and of Christ himself.
5. The Church astricted to the written Word of God. Christ the only teacher of the Church. From his lips ministers must derive whatever they teach for the salvation of others. Various modes of divine teaching. 1. Personal revelations.
6. Second mode of teaching—viz. by the Law and the Prophets. The Prophets were, in regard to doctrine, the expounders of the Law. To these were added Historical Narratives and the Psalms.
7. Last mode of teaching by our Saviour himself manifested in the flesh. Different names given to this dispensation, to show that we are not to dream of anything more perfect than the written word.
8. Nothing can be lawfully taught in the Church, that is not contained in the writings of the Prophets and Apostles, as dictated by the Spirit of Christ.
9. Neither the Apostles, nor apostolic men, nor the whole Church, allowed to overstep these limits. This confirmed by passages of Peter and Paul. Argument *a fortiori*.
10. The Roman tyrants have taught a different doctrine—viz. that Councils cannot err, and, therefore, may coin new dogmas.
11. Answer to the Papistical arguments for the authority of the Church. Argument, that the Church is to be led into all truth. Answer. This promise made not only to the whole Church, but to every individual believer.
12. Answers continued.
13. Answers continued.
14. Argument, that the Church should supply the deficiency of the written word by traditions. Answer.
15. Argument founded on Matth. xviii. 17. Answer.
16. Objections founded on Infant Baptism, and the Canon of the Council of Nice, as to the consubstantiality of the Son. Answer.

1. WE come now to the third division—viz. the *Power of the Church,* as existing either in individual bishops, or in councils, whether provincial or general. I speak only of the spiritual power which is proper to the Church, and which consists either in doctrine, or jurisdiction, or in enacting laws. In regard to doctrine, there are two divisions—viz. the authority of delivering dogmas, and the interpretation of them. Before we begin to treat of each in particular, I wish to remind the pious reader, that whatever is taught respecting

the power of the Church, ought to have reference to the end for which Paul declares (2 Cor. x. 8; xiii. 10) that it was given—namely, for edification, and not for destruction, those who use it lawfully deeming themselves to be nothing more than servants of Christ, and, at the same time, servants of the people in Christ. Moreover, the only mode by which ministers can edify the Church is, by studying to maintain the authority of Christ, which cannot be unimpaired, unless that which he received of the Father is left to him—viz. to be the only Master of the Church. For it was not said of any other but of himself alone, "Hear him" (Matth. xvii. 5). Ecclesiastical power, therefore, is not to be mischievously adorned, but it is to be confined within certain limits, so as not to be drawn hither and thither at the caprice of men. For this purpose, it will be of great use to observe how it is described by Prophets and Apostles. For if we concede unreservedly to men all the power which they think proper to assume, it is easy to see how soon it will degenerate into a tyranny which is altogether alien from the Church of Christ.

2. Therefore, it is here necessary to remember, that whatever authority and dignity the Holy Spirit in Scripture confers on priests, or prophets, or apostles, or successors of Apostles, is wholly given not to men themselves, but to the ministry to which they are appointed; or, to speak more plainly, to the word, to the ministry of which they are appointed. For were we to go over the whole in order, we should find that they were not invested with authority to teach or give responses, save in the name and word of the Lord. For whenever they are called to office, they are enjoined not to bring anything of their own, but to speak by the mouth of the Lord. Nor does he bring them forward to be heard by the people, before he has instructed them what they are to speak, lest they should speak anything but his own word. Moses, the prince of all the prophets, was to be heard in preference to others (Exod. iii. 4; Deut. xvii. 9); but he is previously furnished with his orders, that he may not be able to speak at all except from the Lord. Accordingly, when the people embraced his doctrine, they are said to have believed the Lord, and his servant Moses (Exod. xiv. 31). It was also provided under the severest sanctions, that the authority of the priests should not be despised (Exod. xvii. 9). But the Lord, at the same time, shows in what terms they were to be heard, when he says that he made his covenant with Levi, that the law of truth might be in his mouth (Mal. ii. 4–6). A little after he adds, "The priest's lips should keep knowledge, and they should seek the law at his mouth; for he is the messenger of the Lord of hosts." Therefore, if the priest would be heard, let him show himself to be the messenger of God; that is, let him faithfully deliver the commands which he has received from his Maker. When the mode of hearing, then, is treated of, it is expressly said, "According to the sentence of the law which they shall teach thee" (Deut. xvii. 11).

3. The nature of the power conferred upon the prophets in general

is elegantly described by Ezekiel: " Son of man, I have made thee a watchman unto the house of Israel: therefore hear the word at my mouth, and give them warning from me" (Ezek. iii. 17). Is not he who is ordered to hear at the mouth of the Lord prohibited from devising anything of himself? And what is meant by giving a warning from the Lord, but just to speak so as to be able confidently to declare that the word which he delivers is not his own but the Lord's? The same thing is expressed by Jeremiah in different terms, " The prophet that hath a dream, let him tell a dream; and he that hath my word, let him speak my word faithfully" (Jer. xxiii. 28). Surely God here declares the law to all, and it is a law which does not allow any one to teach more than he has been ordered. He afterwards gives the name of chaff to whatever has not proceeded from himself alone. Accordingly, none of the prophets opened his mouth unless preceded by the word of the Lord. Hence we so often meet with the expressions, " The word of the Lord, The burden of the Lord, Thus saith the Lord, The mouth of the Lord hath spoken it."[1] And justly, for Isaiah exclaims that his lips are unclean (Isa. vi. 5); and Jeremiah confesses that he knows not how to speak because he is a child (Jer. i. 6). Could anything proceed from the unclean lips of the one, and the childish lips of the other, if they spoke their own language, but what was unclean or childish? But their lips were holy and pure when they began to be organs of the Holy Spirit. The prophets, after being thus strictly bound not to deliver anything but what they received, are invested with great power and illustrious titles. For when the Lord declares. " See, I have this day set thee over the nations, and over the kingdoms, to root out, and to pull down, and to destroy, and to throw down, to build, and to plant," he at the same time gives the reason, " Behold, I have put my words in thy mouth" (Jer. i. 9, 10).

4. Now, if you look to the apostles, they are commended by many distinguished titles, as the Light of the world, and the Salt of the earth, to be heard in Christ's stead, whatever they bound or loosed on earth being bound or loosed in heaven (Matth. v. 13, 14; Luke x. 16; John xx. 23). But they declare in their own name what the authority was which their office conferred on them—viz. if they are apostles they must not speak their own pleasure, but faithfully deliver the commands of him by whom they are sent. The words in which Christ defined their embassy are sufficiently clear, " Go ye, therefore, and teach all nations, teaching them to observe all things whatsoever I have commanded you" (Matth. xxviii. 19, 20). Nay, that none might be permitted to decline this law, he received it and imposed it on himself. " My doctrine is not mine, but his that sent me" (John vii. 16). He who always was the only and eternal counsellor of the Father, who by the Father was constituted Lord and Master of all, yet because he per-

---

[1] The French adds, " Vision receue du Seigneur; Le Seigneur des armees l'a dit;" —A vision received from the Lord; The Lord of hosts hath spoken it.

formed the ministry of teaching, prescribed to all ministers by his example the rule which they ought to follow in teaching. The power of the Church, therefore, is not infinite, but is subject to the word of the Lord, and, as it were, included in it.

5. But though the rule which always existed in the Church from the beginning, and ought to exist in the present day, is, that the servants of God are only to teach what they have learned from himself, yet, according to the variety of times, they have had different methods of learning. The mode which now exists differs very much from that of former times. First, if it is true, as Christ says, " Neither knoweth any man the Father save the Son, and he to whomsoever the Son will reveal him " (Matth. xi. 27), then those who wish to attain to the knowledge of God behoved always to be directed by that eternal wisdom. For how could they have comprehended the mysteries of God in their mind, or declared them to others, unless by the teaching of him, to whom alone the secrets of the Father are known ? The only way, therefore, by which in ancient times holy men knew God, was by beholding him in the Son as in a mirror. When I say this, I mean that God never manifested himself to men by any other means than by his Son, that is, his own only wisdom, light, and truth. From this fountain Adam, Noah, Abraham, Isaac, Jacob, and others, drew all the heavenly doctrine which they possessed. From the same fountain all the prophets also drew all the heavenly oracles which they published. For this wisdom did not always display itself in one manner. With the patriarchs he employed secret revelations, but, at the same time, in order to confirm these, had recourse to signs so as to make it impossible for them to doubt that it was God that spake to them. What the patriarchs received they handed down to posterity, for God had, in depositing it with them, bound them thus to propagate it, while their children and descendants knew by the inward teaching of God, that what they heard was of heaven and not of earth.

6. But when God determined to give a more illustrious form to the Church, he was pleased to commit and consign his word to writing, that the priests might there seek what they were to teach the people, and every doctrine delivered be brought to it as a test (Mal. ii. 7). Accordingly, after the promulgation of the Law, when the priests are enjoined to teach from the mouth of the Lord, the meaning is, that they are not to teach anything extraneous or alien to that kind of doctrine which God had summed up in the Law, while it was unlawful for them to add to it or take from it. Next followed the prophets, by whom God published the new oracles which were added to the Law, not so new, however, but that they flowed from the Law, and had respect to it. For in so far as regards doctrine, they were only interpreters of the Law, adding nothing to it but predictions of future events. With this exception, all that they delivered was pure exposition of the Law. But as the Lord was pleased that doctrine should exist in a clearer and more ample form, the better to satisfy weak

consciences, he commanded the prophecies also to be committed to writing, and to be held part of his word. To these at the same time were added historical details, which are also the composition of prophets, but dictated by the Holy Spirit; I include the Psalms among the Prophecies, the quality which we attribute to the latter belonging also to the former. The whole body, therefore, composed of the Law, the Prophets, the Psalms, and Histories, formed the word of the Lord to his ancient people, and by it as a standard, priests and teachers, before the advent of Christ, were bound to test their doctrine, nor was it lawful for them to turn aside either to the right hand or the left, because their whole office was confined to this—to give responses to the people from the mouth of God. This is gathered from a celebrated passage of Malachi, in which it is enjoined to remember the Law, and give heed to it until the preaching of the Gospel (Mal. iv. 4). For he thus restrains men from all adventitious doctrines, and does not allow them to deviate in the least from the path which Moses had faithfully pointed out. And the reason why David so magnificently extols the Law, and pronounces so many encomiums on it (Ps. xix., cxix.), was, that the Jews might not long after any 'extraneous aid, all perfection being included in it.

7. But when at length the Wisdom of God was manifested in the flesh, he fully unfolded to us all that the human mind can comprehend, or ought to think of the heavenly Father. Now, therefore, since Christ, the Sun of Righteousness, has arisen, we have the perfect refulgence of divine truth, like the brightness of noon-day, whereas the light was previously dim. It was no ordinary blessing which the apostle intended to publish when he wrote: "God, who at sundry times and in divers manners, spake in time past unto the fathers by the prophets, hath in these last days spoken unto us by his Son" (Heb. i. 1, 2); for he intimates, nay, openly declares, that God will not henceforth, as formerly, speak by this one and by that one, that he will not add prophecy to prophecy, or revelation to revelation, but has so completed all the parts of teaching in the Son, that it is to be regarded as his last and eternal testimony. For which reason, the whole period of the new dispensation, from the time when Christ appeared to us with the preaching of his Gospel, until the day of judgment, is designated by the *last hour, the last times, the last days*, that, contented with the perfection of Christ's doctrine, we may learn to frame no new doctrine for ourselves, or admit any one devised by others. With good cause, therefore, the Father appointed the Son our teacher, with special prerogative, commanding that he and no human being should be heard. When he said, " Hear him" (Matth. xvii. 5), he commended his office to us, in few words, indeed, but words of more weight and energy than is commonly supposed, for it is just as if he had withdrawn us from all doctrines of man, and confined us to him alone, ordering us to seek the whole doctrine of salvation from him alone, to depend on him alone, and cleave to him alone; in short (as the words express), to listen only to his voice.

And, indeed, what can now be expected or desired from man, when the very Word of life has appeared before us, and familiarly explained himself? Nay, every mouth should be stopped when once he has spoken, in whom, according to the pleasure of our heavenly Father, "are hid all the treasures of wisdom and knowledge" (Col. ii. 3), and spoken as became the Wisdom of God (which is in no part defective) and the Messiah (from whom the revelation of all things was expected) (John iv. 25); in other words, has so spoken as to leave nothing to be spoken by others after him.

8. Let this then be a sure axiom—that there is no word of God to which place should be given in the Church save that which is contained, first, in the Law and the Prophets; and, secondly, in the writings of the Apostles, and that the only due method of teaching in the Church is according to the prescription and rule of his word. Hence also we infer that nothing else was permitted to the apostles than was formerly permitted to the prophets—namely, to expound the ancient Scriptures, and show that the things there delivered are fulfilled in Christ: this, however, they could not do unless from the Lord; that is, unless the Spirit of Christ went before, and in a manner dictated words to them. For Christ thus defined the terms of their embassy, when he commanded them to go and teach, not what they themselves had at random fabricated, but whatsoever he had commanded (Matth. xxviii. 20). And nothing can be plainer than his words in another passage, "Be not ye called Rabbi: for one is your Master, even Christ" (Matth. xxiii. 8–10). To impress this more deeply in their minds, he in the same place repeats it twice. And because from ignorance they were unable to comprehend the things which they had heard and learned from the lips of their Master, the Spirit of truth is promised to guide them unto all truth (John xiv. 26; xvi. 13). The restriction should be carefully attended to. The office which he assigns to the Holy Spirit is to bring to remembrance what his own lips had previously taught.

9. Accordingly, Peter, who was perfectly instructed by his Master as to the extent of what was permitted to him, leaves nothing more to himself or others than to dispense the doctrine delivered by God. "If any man speak, let him speak as the oracles of God" (1 Peter iv. 11); that is, not hesitatingly, as those are wont whose convictions are imperfect, but with the full confidence which becomes a servant of God, provided with a sure message. What else is this than to banish all the inventions of the human mind (whatever be the head which may have devised them), that the pure word of God may be taught and learned in the Church of the faithful,—than to discard the decrees, or rather fictions of men (whatever be their rank), that the decrees of God alone may remain steadfast? These are "the weapons of our warfare," which "are not carnal, but mighty through God to the pulling down of strongholds; casting down imaginations, and every high thing that exalteth itself against the knowledge of God, and bringing into captivity every thought to the obedience of Christ"

(2 Cor. x. 4, 5). Here is the supreme power with which pastors of the Church, by whatever name they are called, should be invested— namely, to dare all boldly for the word of God, compelling all the virtue, glory, wisdom, and rank of the world to yield and obey its majesty; to command all from the highest to the lowest, trusting to its power to build up the house of Christ and overthrow the house of Satan; to feed the sheep and chase away the wolves; to instruct and exhort the docile, to accuse, rebuke, and subdue the rebellious and petulant, to bind and loose; in fine, if need be, to fire and fulminate, but all in the word of God. Although, as I have observed, there is this difference between the apostles and their successors, they were sure and authentic amanuenses of the Holy Spirit; and, therefore, their writings are to be regarded as the oracles of God, whereas others have no other office than to teach what is delivered and sealed in the holy Scriptures. We conclude, therefore, that it does not now belong to faithful ministers to coin some new doctrine, but simply to adhere to the doctrine to which all, without exception, are made subject. When I say this, I mean to show not only what each individual, but what the whole Church, is bound to do. In regard to individuals, Paul certainly had been appointed an apostle to the Corinthians, and yet he declares that he has no dominion over their faith (2 Cor. i. 24). Who will now presume to arrogate a dominion to which the apostle declares that he himself was not competent? But if he had acknow- ledged such licence in teaching, that every pastor could justly demand implicit faith in whatever he delivered, he never would have laid it down as a rule to the Corinthians, that while two or three prophets spoke, the others should judge, and that, if anything was revealed to one sitting by, the first should be silent (1 Cor. xiv. 29, 30). Thus he spared none, but subjected the authority of all to the censure of the word of God. But it will be said, that with regard to the whole Church the case is different. I answer, that in another place Paul meets the objection also when he says, that faith cometh by hearing, and hearing by the word of God (Rom. x. 17). In other words, if faith depends upon the word of God alone, if it regards and reclines on it alone, what place is left for any word of man? He who knows what faith is can never hesitate here, for it must possess a strength sufficient to stand intrepid and invincible against Satan, the machina- tions of hell, and the whole world. This strength can be found only in the word of God. Then the reason to which we ought here to have regard is universal: God deprives man of the power of produc- ing any new doctrine, in order that he alone may be our master in spiritual teaching, as he alone is true, and can neither lie nor deceive. This reason applies not less to the whole Church than to every individual believer.

10. But if this power of the church which is here described be contrasted with that which spiritual tyrants, falsely styling them- selves bishops and religious prelates, have now for several ages exer- cised among the people of God, there will be no more agreement

than that of Christ with Belial. It is not my intention here to unfold the manner, the unworthy manner, in which they have used their tyranny; I will only state the doctrine which they maintain in the present day, first, in writing, and then, by fire and sword. Taking it for granted, that a universal council is a true representation of the Church, they set out with this principle, and, at the same time, lay it down as incontrovertible, that such councils are under the immediate guidance of the Holy Spirit, and therefore cannot err. But as they rule councils, nay, constitute them, they in fact claim for themselves whatever they maintain to be due to councils. Therefore, they will have our faith to stand and fall at their pleasure, so that whatever they have determined on either side must be firmly seated in our minds; what they approve must be approved by us without any doubt; what they condemn we also must hold to be justly condemned. Meanwhile, at their own caprice, and in contempt of the word of God, they coin doctrines to which they in this way demand our assent, declaring that no man can be a Christian unless he assent to all their dogmas, affirmative as well as negative, if not with explicit, yet with implicit faith, because it belongs to the Church to frame new articles of faith.

11. First, let us hear by what arguments they prove that this authority was given to the Church, and then we shall see how far their allegations concerning the Church avail them. The Church, they say, has the noble promise that she will never be deserted by Christ her spouse, but be guided by his Spirit into all truth. But of the promises which they are wont to allege, many were given not less to private believers than to the whole Church. For although the Lord spake to the twelve apostles, when he said, "Lo! I am with you alway, even unto the end of the world" (Matth. xxviii. 20); and again, "I will pray the Father, and he shall give you another Comforter, that he may abide with you for ever: even the Spirit of truth" (John xiv. 16, 17), he made these promises not only to the twelve, but to each of them separately, nay, in like manner, to other disciples whom he already had received, or was afterwards to receive. When they interpret these promises, which are replete with consolation, in such a way as if they were not given to any particular Christian but to the whole Church together, what else is it but to deprive Christians of the confidence which they ought thence to have derived, to animate them in their course? I deny not that the whole body of the faithful is furnished with a manifold variety of gifts, and endued with a far larger and richer treasure of heavenly wisdom than each Christian apart; nor do I mean that this was said of believers in general, as implying that all possess the spirit of wisdom and knowledge in an equal degree: but we are not to give permission to the adversaries of Christ to defend a bad cause, by wresting Scripture from its proper meaning. Omitting this, however, I simply hold what is true—viz. that the Lord is always present with his people, and guides them by his Spirit. He is the Spirit,

not of error, ignorance, falsehood, or darkness, but of sure revelation, wisdom, truth, and light, from whom they can, without deception, learn the things which have been given to them (1 Cor. ii. 12); in other words, "what is the hope of their calling, and what the riches of the glory of their inheritance in the saints" (Eph. i. 18). But while believers, even those of them who are endued with more excellent graces, obtain in the present life only the first-fruits, and, as it were, a foretaste of the Spirit, nothing better remains to them than, under a consciousness of their weakness, to confine themselves anxiously within the limits of the word of God, lest, in following their own sense too far, they forthwith stray from the right path, being left without that Spirit, by whose teaching alone truth is discerned from falsehood. For all confess with Paul, that "they have not yet reached the goal" (Phil. iii. 12). Accordingly, they rather aim at daily progress than glory in perfection.

12. But it will be objected, that whatever is attributed in part to any of the saints, belongs in complete fulness to the Church. Although there is some semblance of truth in this, I deny that it is true. God, indeed, measures out the gifts of his Spirit to each of the members, so that nothing necessary to the whole body is wanting, since the gifts are bestowed for the common advantage. The riches of the Church, however, are always of such a nature, that much is wanting to that supreme perfection of which our opponents boast. Still the Church is not left destitute in any part, but always has as much as is sufficient, for the Lord knows what her necessities require. But to keep her in humility and pious modesty, he bestows no more on her than he knows to be expedient. I am aware, it is usual here to object, that Christ hath cleansed the Church "with the washing of water by the word: that he might present it to himself a glorious Church, not having spot or wrinkle" (Eph. v. 26, 27), and that it is therefore called the "pillar and ground of the truth" (1 Tim. iii. 15). But the former passage rather shows what Christ daily performs in it, than what he has already perfected. For if he daily sanctifies all his people, purifies, refines them, and wipes away their stains, it is certain that they have still some spots and wrinkles, and that their sanctification is in some measure defective. How vain and fabulous is it to suppose that the Church, all whose members are somewhat spotted and impure, is completely holy and spotless in every part? It is true, therefore, that the Church is sanctified by Christ, but here the commencement of her sanctification only is seen; the end and entire completion will be effected when Christ, the Holy of holies, shall truly and completely fill her with his holiness. It is true also, that her stains and wrinkles have been effaced, but so that the process is continued every day, until Christ at his advent will entirely remove every remaining defect. For unless we admit this, we shall be constrained to hold with the Pelagians, that the righteousness of believers is perfected in this life: like the Cathari and Donatists we shall tolerate no infirmity in

the Church.[1]   The other passage, as we have elsewhere seen (chap.
i. sec. 10), has a very different meaning from what they put upon it.
For when Paul instructed Timothy, and trained him to the office of
a true bishop, he says, he did it in order that he might learn how to
behave himself in the Church of God.   And to make him devote
himself to the work with greater seriousness and zeal, he adds, that
the Church is the pillar and ground of the truth.   And what else do
these words mean, than just that the truth of God is preserved in
the Church, and preserved by the instrumentality of preaching; as
he elsewhere says, that Christ "gave some, apostles; and some,
prophets; and some, evangelists; and some, pastors and teachers;"
"that we henceforth be no more children, tossed to and fro, and
carried about with every wind of doctrine, by the sleight of men,
and cunning craftiness, whereby they lie in wait to deceive; but,
speaking the truth in love, may grow up into him in all things, who
is the head, even Christ"? (Eph. iv. 11, 14, 15.)   The reason,
therefore, why the truth, instead of being extinguished in the world,
remains unimpaired, is, because he has the Church as a faithful
guardian, by whose aid and ministry it is maintained.   But if this
guardianship consists in the ministry of the Prophets and Apostles,
it follows, that the whole depends upon this—viz. that the word of
the Lord is faithfully preserved and maintained in purity.

13. And that my readers may the better understand the hinge on
which the question chiefly turns, I will briefly explain what our
opponents demand, and what we resist.   When they deny that the
Church can err, their end and meaning are to this effect: Since the
Church is governed by the Spirit of God, she can walk safely without
the word; in whatever direction she moves, she cannot think or
speak anything but the truth, and hence, if she determines anything
without or beside the word of God, it must be regarded in no other
light than if it were a divine oracle.   If we grant the first point—
viz. that the Church cannot err in things necessary to salvation—our
meaning is, that she cannot err, because she has altogether discarded
her own wisdom, and submits to the teaching of the Holy Spirit
through the word of God.   Here then is the difference.   They place
the authority of the Church without the word of God; we annex it
to the word, and allow it not to be separated from it.   And is it
strange if the spouse and pupil of Christ is so subject to her lord and
master as to hang carefully and constantly on his lips?   In every
well-ordered house the wife obeys the command of her husband, in
every well-regulated school the doctrine of the master only is listened
to.   Wherefore, let not the Church be wise in herself, nor think any
thing of herself, but let her consider her wisdom terminated when he
ceases to speak.   In this way she will distrust all the inventions of
her own reason; and when she leans on the word of God, will not
waver in diffidence or hesitation, but rest in full assurance and un-

1 The French adds, "Or, nos adversaires mesmes tiennent tous ceux-la pour here-
tiques."—Now, our opponents themselves regard all those as heretics.

wavering constancy. Trusting to the liberal promises which she has received, she will have the means of nobly maintaining her faith, never doubting that the Holy Spirit is always present with her to be the perfect guide of her path. At the same time, she will remember the use which God wishes to be derived from his Spirit. "When he, the Spirit of truth, is come, he will guide you into all truth" (John xvi. 13). How? "He shall bring to your remembrance all things whatsoever I have said unto you." He declares, therefore, that nothing more is to be expected of his Spirit than to enlighten our minds to perceive the truth of his doctrine. Hence Chrysostom most shrewdly observes, "Many boast of the Holy Spirit, but with those who speak their own it is a false pretence. As Christ declared that he spoke not of himself (John xii. 50; xiv. 10), because he spoke according to the Law and the Prophets; so, if anything contrary to the Gospel is obtruded under the name of the Holy Spirit, let us not believe it. For as Christ is the fulfilment of the Law and the Prophets, so is the Spirit the fulfilment of the Gospel" (Chrysost. Serm. de Sancto et Adorando Spiritu.) Thus far Chrysostom. We may now easily infer how erroneously our opponents act in vaunting of the Holy Spirit, for no other end than to give the credit of his name to strange doctrines, extraneous to the word of God, whereas he himself desires to be inseparably connected with the word of God; and Christ declares the same thing of him, when he promises him to the Church. And so indeed it is. The soberness which our Lord once prescribed to his Church, he wishes to be perpetually observed. He forbade that anything should be added to his word, and that anything should be taken from it. This is the inviolable decree of God and the Holy Spirit, a decree which our opponents endeavour to annul when they pretend that the Church is guided by the Spirit without the word.

14. Here again they mutter that the Church behoved to add something to the writings of the apostles, or that the apostles themselves behoved orally to supply what they had less clearly taught, since Christ said to them, " I have yet many things to say unto you, but ye cannot bear them now" (John xvi. 12), and that these are the points which have been received, without writing, merely by use and custom. But what effrontery is this? The disciples, I admit, were ignorant and almost indocile when our Lord thus addressed them, but were they still in this condition when they committed his doctrine to writing, so as afterwards to be under the necessity of supplying orally that which, through ignorance, they had omitted to write? If they were guided by the Spirit of truth unto all truth when they published their writings, what prevented them from embracing a full knowledge of the Gospel, and consigning it therein? But let us grant them what they ask, provided they point out the things which behoved to be revealed without writing. Should they presume to attempt this, I will address them in the words of Augustine, "When the Lord is silent, who of us may say, this is, or that is? or if we

should presume to say it, how do we prove it?," (August. in Joann. 96.) But why do I contend superfluously? Every child knows that in the writings of the apostles, which these men represent as mutilated and incomplete, is contained the result of that revelation which the Lord then promised to them.

15. What, say they, did not Christ declare that nothing which the Church teaches and decrees can be gainsayed, when he enjoined that every one who presumes to contradict should be regarded as a heathen man and a publican? (Matth. xviii. 17.) First, there is here no mention of doctrine, but her authority to censure, for correction is asserted, in order that none who had been admonished or reprimanded might oppose her judgment. But to say nothing of this, it is very strange that those men are so lost to all sense of shame, that they hesitate not to plume themselves on this declaration. For what, pray, will they make of it, but just that the consent of the Church, a consent never given but to the word of God, is not to be despised? The Church is to be heard, say they. Who denies this? since she decides nothing but according to the word of God. If they demand more than this, let them know that the words of Christ give them no countenance. I ought not to seem contentious when I so vehemently insist that we cannot concede to the Church any new doctrine; in other words, allow her to teach and oracularly deliver more than the Lord has revealed in his word. Men of sense see how great the danger is if so much authority is once conceded to men. They see also how wide a door is opened for the jeers and cavils of the ungodly, if we admit that Christians are to receive the opinions of men as if they were oracles. We may add, that our Saviour, speaking according to the circumstances of his times, gave the name of Church to the Sanhedrim, that the disciples might learn afterwards to revere the sacred meetings of the Church. Hence it would follow, that single cities and districts would have equal liberty in coining dogmas.

16. The examples which they bring do not avail them. They say that pædobaptism proceeds not so much on a plain command of Scripture, as on a decree of the Church. It would be a miserable asylum if, in defence of pædobaptism, we were obliged to betake ourselves to the bare authority of the Church; but it will be made plain enough elsewhere (chap. xvi.) that it is far otherwise. In like manner, when they object that we nowhere find in the Scriptures what was declared in the Council of Nice—viz. that the Son is consubstantial with the Father (see August. Ep. 178)—they do a grievous injustice to the Fathers, as if they had rashly condemned Arius for not swearing to their words, though professing the whole of that doctrine which is contained in the writings of the Apostles and Prophets. I admit that the expression does not exist in Scripture, but seeing it is there so often declared that there is one God, and Christ is so often called true and eternal God, one with the Father, what do the Nicene Fathers do when they affirm that he is of one essence, than simply

declare the genuine meaning of Scripture? Theodoret relates that Constantine, in opening their meeting, spoke as follows: "In the discussion of divine matters, the doctrine of the Holy Spirit stands recorded. The Gospels and apostolical writings, with the oracles of the prophets, fully show us the meaning of the Deity. Therefore, laying aside discord, let us take the exposition of questions from the words of the Spirit" (Theodoret. Hist. Eccles. Lib. i. c. 5). There was none who opposed this sound advice; none who objected that the Church could add something of her own, that the Spirit did not reveal all things to the apostles, or at least that they did not deliver them to posterity, and so forth. If the point on which our opponents insist is true, Constantine, first, was in error in robbing the Church of her power; and, secondly, when none of the bishops rose to vindicate it, their silence was a kind of perfidy, and made them traitors to Ecclesiastical law. But since Theodoret relates that they readily embraced what the Emperor said, it is evident that this new dogma was then wholly unknown.

CHAPTER IX.

OF COUNCILS AND THEIR AUTHORITY.[1]

Since Papists regard their Councils as expressing the sentiment and consent of the Church, particularly as regards the authority of declaring dogmas and the exposition of them, it was necessary to treat of Councils before proceeding to consider that part of ecclesiastical power which relates to doctrine. I. First, the authority of Councils in delivering dogmas is discussed, and it is shown that the Spirit of God is not so bound to the Pastors of the Church as opponents suppose. Their objections refuted, sec. 1–7. II. The errors, contradictions, and weaknesses, of certain Councils exposed. A refutation of the subterfuge, that those set over us are to be obeyed without distinction, sec. 8–12. III. Of the authority of Councils as regards the interpretation of Scripture, sec. 13. 14.

Sections.

1. WERE I now to concede all that they ask concerning the Church, it would not greatly aid them in their object. For everything that

[1] See Calvin's Antidote to the Articles of Sorbonne; Letter to Sadolet; Necessity of Reforming the Church; Antidote to the Council of Trent; Remarks on the Paternal Admonition of the Pope.

is said of the Church they immediately transfer to councils, which, in their opinion, represent the Church. Nay, when they contend so doggedly for the power of the Church, their only object is to devolve the whole which they extort on the Roman Pontiff and his conclave. Before I begin to discuss this question, two points must be briefly premised. First, though I mean to be more rigid in discussing this subject, it is not because I set less value than I ought on ancient councils. I venerate them from my heart, and would have all to hold them in due honour.[1] But there must be some limitation, there must be nothing derogatory to Christ. Moreover, it is the right of Christ to preside over all councils, and not share the honour with any man. Now, I hold that he presides only when he governs the whole assembly by his word and Spirit. Secondly, in attributing less to councils than my opponents demand, it is not because I have any fear that councils are favourable to their cause and adverse to ours. For as we are amply provided by the word of the Lord with the means of proving our doctrine and overthrowing the whole Papacy, and thus have no great need of other aid, so, if the case required it, ancient councils furnish us in a great measure with what might be sufficient for both purposes.

2. Let us now proceed to the subject itself. If we consult Scripture on the authority of councils, there is no promise more remarkable than that which is contained in these words of our Saviour, "Where two or three are gathered together in my name, there am I in the midst of them." But this is just as applicable to any particular meeting as to a universal council. And yet the important part of the question does not lie here, but in the condition which is added—viz. that Christ will be in the midst of a council, provided it be assembled in his name. Wherefore, though our opponents should name councils of thousands of bishops it will little avail them; nor will they induce us to believe that they are, as they maintain, guided by the Holy Spirit, until they make it credible that they assemble in the name of Christ: since it is as possible for wicked and dishonest to conspire against Christ, as for good and honest bishops to meet together in his name. Of this we have a clear proof in very many of the decrees which have proceeded from councils. But this will be afterwards seen. At present I only reply in one word, that our Saviour's promise is made to those only who assemble in his name. How, then, is such an assembly to be defined? I deny that those assemble in the name of Christ who, disregarding his command by which he forbids anything to be added to the word of God or taken from it, determine everything at their own pleasure, who, not contented with the oracles of Scripture, that is, with the only rule of perfect wisdom, devise

---

1 French, "Si je tien ici la bride roide pour ne lascher rien facilement à nos adversaires, ce n'est pas a dire pourtant que je prise les conciles anciens moins que je ne doy. Car je les honore de bonne affection, et desire que chacun les estime, et les ait en reverence."—If I here keep the reins tight, and do not easily yield anything to our opponents, it is not because I prize ancient councils less than I ought. For I honour them sincerely and desire that every man esteem them, and hold them in reverence.

some novelty out of their own head (Deut. iv. 2; Rev. xxii. 18). Certainly, since our Saviour has not promised to be present with all councils of whatever description, but has given a peculiar mark for distinguishing true and lawful councils from others, we ought not by any means to lose sight of the distinction. The covenant which God anciently made with the Levitical priests was to teach at his mouth (Mal. ii. 7). This he always required of the prophets, and we see also that it was the law given to the apostles. On those who violate this covenant God bestows neither the honour of the priesthood nor any authority. Let my opponents solve this difficulty if they would subject my faith to the decrees of man, without authority from the word of God.

3. Their idea that the truth cannot remain in the Church unless it exist among pastors, and that the Church herself cannot exist unless displayed in general councils, is very far from holding true if the prophets have left us a correct description of their own times. In the time of Isaiah there was a Church at Jerusalem which the Lord had not yet abandoned. But of pastors he thus speaks: "His watchmen are blind; they are all ignorant, they are all dumb dogs, they cannot bark; sleeping, lying down, loving to slumber. Yea, they are greedy dogs which never have enough, and they are shepherds that cannot understand: they all look to their own way" (Isa. lvi. 10, 11). In the same way Hosea says, "The watchman of Ephraim was with my God: but the prophet is a snare of a fowler in all his ways, and hatred in the house of his God" (Hosea ix. 8). Here, by ironically connecting them with God, he shows that the pretext of the priesthood was vain. There was also a Church in the time of Jeremiah. Let us hear what he says of pastors: "From the prophet even unto the priest, every one dealeth falsely." Again, "The prophets prophesy lies in my name: I sent them not, neither have I commanded them, neither spake unto them" (Jer. vi. 13; xiv. 14). And not to be prolix with quotations, read the whole of his thirty-third and fortieth chapters. Then, on the other hand, Ezekiel inveighs against them in no milder terms. "There is a conspiracy of her prophets in the midst thereof, like a roaring lion ravening the prey; they have devoured souls." "Her priests have violated my law, and profaned mine holy things" (Ezek. xxii. 25, 26). There is more to the same purpose. Similar complaints abound throughout the prophets; nothing is of more frequent recurrence.

4. But perhaps, though this great evil prevailed among the Jews, our age is exempt from it. Would that it were so; but the Holy Spirit declared that it would be otherwise. For Peter's words are clear, "But there were false prophets among the people, even as there shall be false teachers among you, who privily will bring in damnable heresies" (2 Peter ii. 1). See how he predicts impending danger, not from ordinary believers, but from those who should plume themselves on the name of pastors and teachers. Besides, how often did Christ and his apostles foretell that the greatest dangers with

which the Church was threatened would come from pastors ? (Matth. xxiv. 11, 24). Nay, Paul openly declares, that Antichrist would have his seat in the temple of God (2 Thess. ii. 4); thereby intimating, that the fearful calamity of which he was speaking would come only from those who should have their seat in the Church as pastors. And in another passage he shows that the introduction of this great evil was almost at hand. For in addressing the Elders of Ephesus, he says, " I know this, that after my departing shall grievous wolves enter in among you, not sparing the flock. Also of your own selves shall men arise, speaking perverse things, to draw away disciples after them" (Acts xx. 29, 30). How great corruption might a long series of years introduce among pastors, when they could degenerate so much within so short a time ? And not to fill my pages with details, we are reminded by the examples of almost every age, that the truth is not always cherished in the bosoms of pastors, and that the safety of the Church depends not on their state. It was becoming that those appointed to preserve the peace and safety of the Church should be its presidents and guardians; but it is one thing to perform what you owe, and another to owe what you do not perform.

5. Let no man, however, understand me as if I were desirous in everything rashly and unreservedly to overthrow the authority of pastors.[1] All I advise is, to exercise discrimination, and not suppose, as a matter of course, that all who call themselves pastors are so in reality. But the Pope, with the whole crew of his bishops, for no other reason but because they are called pastors, shake off obedience to the word of God, invert all things, and turn them hither and thither at their pleasure; meanwhile, they insist that they cannot be destitute of the light of truth, that the Spirit of God perpetually resides in them, that the Church subsists in them, and dies with them, as if the Lord did not still inflict his judgments, and in the present day punish the world for its wickedness, in the same way in which he punished the ingratitude of the ancient people—namely, by smiting pastors with astonishment and blindness (Zech. xii. 4). These stupid men understand not that they are just chiming in with those of ancient times who warred with the word of God. For the enemies of Jeremiah thus set themselves against the truth, " Come, and let us devise devices against Jeremiah ; for the law shall not perish from the priest, nor counsel from the wise, nor the word from the prophet" (Jer. xviii. 18).

6. Hence it is easy to reply to their allegation concerning general councils. It cannot be denied, that the Jews had a true Church under the prophets. But had a general council then been composed of the priests, what kind of appearance would the Church have had? We hear the Lord denouncing not against one or two of them, but

---

1 French, " Toutesfois je ne veux point que ces propos soyent entendus comme si je vouloye amoindrir l'authorité des pasteurs, et induire le peuple à la mepriser legerement."—However, I would not have these statements to be understood as if I wished to lessen the authority of pastors, and induce the people lightly to despise it.

the whole order: "The priests shall be astonished, and the prophets shall wonder" (Jer. iv. 9). Again, "The law shall perish from the priest, and counsel from the ancients" (Ezek. vii. 26). Again, "Therefore night shall be unto you, that ye shall not have a vision; and it shall be dark unto you, that ye shall not divine; and the sun shall go down over the prophets, and the day shall be dark over them," &c. (Micah iii. 6). Now, had all men of this description been collected together, what spirit would have presided over their meeting? Of this we have a notable instance in the council which Ahab convened (1 Kings xxii. 6, 22). Four hundred prophets were present. But because they had met with no other intention than to flatter the impious king, Satan is sent by the Lord to be a lying spirit in all their mouths. The truth is there unanimously condemned. Micaiah is judged a heretic, is smitten, and cast into prison. So was it done to Jeremiah, and so to the other prophets.

7. But there is one memorable example which may suffice for all. In the council which the priests and Pharisees assembled at Jerusalem against Christ (John xi. 47), what is wanting, in so far as external appearance is concerned? Had there been no Church then at Jerusalem, Christ would never have joined in the sacrifices and other ceremonies. A solemn meeting is held; the high priest presides; the whole sacerdotal order take their seats, and yet Christ is condemned, and his doctrine is put to flight. This atrocity proves that the Church was not at all included in that council. But there is no danger that anything of the kind will happen with us. Who has told us so? Too much security in a matter of so great importance lies open to the charge of sluggishness. Nay, when the Spirit, by the mouth of Paul, foretells, in distinct terms, that a defection will take place, a defection which cannot come until pastors first forsake God (2 Thess. ii. 3), why do we spontaneously walk blindfold to our own destruction? Wherefore, we cannot on any account admit that the Church consists in a meeting of pastors, as to whom the Lord has nowhere promised that they would always be good, but has sometimes foretold that they would be wicked. When he warns us of danger, it is to make us use greater caution.

8. What, then, you will say, is there no authority in the definitions of councils? Yes, indeed; for I do not contend that all councils are to be condemned, and all their acts rescinded, or, as it is said, made one complete erasure. But you are bringing them all (it will be said) under subordination, and so leaving every one at liberty to receive or reject the decrees of councils as he pleases. By no means; but whenever the decree of a council is produced, the first thing I would wish to be done is, to examine at what time it was held, on what occasion, with what intention, and who were present at it; next I would bring the subject discussed to the standard of Scripture. And this I would do in such a way that the decision of the council should have its weight, and be regarded in the light of a prior judgment, yet not so as to prevent the application of

the test which I have mentioned. I wish all had observed the method which Augustine prescribes in his Third Book against Maximinus, when he wished to silence the cavils of this heretic against the decrees of councils, " I ought not to oppose the Council of Nice to you, nor ought you to oppose that of Ariminum to me, as prejudging the question. I am not bound by the authority of the latter, nor you by that of the former. Let thing contend with thing, cause with cause, reason with reason, on the authority of Scripture, an authority not peculiar to either, but common to all." In this way, councils would be duly respected, and yet the highest place would be given to Scripture, everything being brought to it as a test. Thus those ancient Councils of Nice, Constantinople, the first of Ephesus, Chalcedon, and the like, which were held for refuting errors, we willingly embrace, and reverence as sacred, in so far as relates to doctrines of faith, for they contain nothing but the pure and genuine interpretation of Scripture, which the holy Fathers with spiritual prudence adopted to crush the enemies of religion who had then arisen. In some later councils, also, we see displayed a true zeal for religion, and moreover unequivocal marks of genius, learning, and prudence. But as matters usually become worse and worse, it is easy to see in more modern councils how much the Church gradually degenerated from the purity of that golden age.. I doubt not, however, that even in those more corrupt ages, councils had their bishops of better character. But it happened with them as the Roman senators of old complained in regard to their decrees. Opinions being numbered, not weighed, the better were obliged to give way to the greater number. They certainly put forth many impious sentiments. There is no need here to collect instances, both because it would be tedious, and because it has been done by others so carefully, as not to leave much to be added.

9. Moreover, why should I review the contests of council with council ? Nor is there any ground for whispering to me, that when councils are at variance, one or other of them is not a lawful council. For how shall we ascertain this ? Just, if I mistake not, by judging from Scripture that the decrees are not orthodox. For this alone is the sure law of discrimination. It is now about nine hundred years since the Council of Constantinople, convened under the Emperor Leo, determined that the images set up in temples were to be thrown down and broken to pieces. Shortly after, the Council of Nice, which was assembled by Irene, through dislike of the former, decreed that images were to be restored. Which of the two councils shall we acknowledge to be lawful ? The latter has usually prevailed, and secured a place for images in churches. But Augustine maintains that this could not be done without the greatest danger of idolatry. Epiphanius, at a later period, speaks much more harshly (Epist. ad Joann. Hierosolym. et Lib. iii. contra Hæres.). For he says, it is an unspeakable abomination to see images in a Christian temple. Could those who speak thus approve of that council if they were alive in

the present day ?   But if historians speak true, and we believe their acts, not only images themselves, but the worship of them, were there sanctioned.   Now it is plain that this decree emanated from Satan: Do they not show, by corrupting and wresting Scripture, that they held it in derision ?   This I have made sufficiently clear in a former part of the work (see Book I. chap. xi. sec. 14).   Be this as it may, we shall never be able to distinguish between contradictory and dissenting councils, which have been many, unless we weigh them all in that balance for men and angels, I mean, the word of God.   Thus we embrace the Council of Chalcedon, and repudiate the second of Ephesus, because the latter sanctioned the impiety of Eutyches, and the former condemned it.   The judgment of these holy men was founded on the Scriptures, and while we follow it, we desire that the word of God, which illuminated them, may now also illuminate us. Let the Romanists now go and boast after their manner, that the Holy Spirit is fixed and tied to their councils.

10.   Even in their ancient and purer councils there is something to be desiderated, either because the otherwise learned and prudent men who attended, being distracted by the business in hand, did not attend to many things beside ; or because, occupied with grave and more serious measures, they winked at some of lesser moment ; or simply because, as men, they were deceived through ignorance, or were sometimes carried headlong by some feeling in excess.   Of this last case (which seems the most difficult of all to avoid) we have a striking example in the Council of Nice, which has been unanimously received, as it deserves, with the utmost veneration.   For when the primary article of our faith was there in peril, and Arius, its enemy, was present, ready to engage any one in combat, and it was of the utmost moment that those who had come to attack Arius should be agreed, they nevertheless, feeling secure amid all these dangers, nay, as it were, forgetting their gravity, modesty, and politeness, laying aside the discussion which was before them (as if they had met for the express purpose of gratifying Arius), began to give way to intestine dissensions, and turn the pen, which should have been employed against Arius, against each other.   Foul accusations were heard, libels flew up and down, and they never would have ceased from their contention until they had stabbed each other with mutual wounds, had not the Emperor Constantine interfered, and declaring that the investigation of their lives was a matter above his cognisance, repressed their intemperance by flattery rather than censure.   In how many respects is it probable that councils, held subsequently to this, have erred ?   Nor does the fact stand in need of a long demonstration ; any one who reads their acts will observe many infirmities, not to use a stronger term.

11.   Even Leo, the Roman Pontiff, hesitates not to charge the Council of Chalcedon, which he admits to be orthodox in its doctrines, with ambition and inconsiderate rashness.   He denies not that it was lawful, but openly maintains that it might have erred.   Some

may think me foolish in labouring to point out errors of this description, since my opponents admit that councils may err in things not necessary to salvation. My labour, however, is not superfluous. For although compelled, they admit this in word, yet by obtruding upon us the determination of all councils, in all matters without distinction, as the oracles of the Holy Spirit, they exact more than they had at the outset assumed. By thus acting what do they maintain but just that councils cannot err, of if they err, it is unlawful for us to perceive the truth, or refuse assent to their errors? At the same time, all I mean to infer from what I have said is, that though councils, otherwise pious and holy, were governed by the Holy Spirit, he yet allowed them to share the lot of humanity, lest we should confide too much in men. This is a much better view than that of Gregory Nanzianzen, who says (Ep. 55), that he never saw any council end well. In asserting that all, without exception, ended ill, he leaves them little authority. There is no necessity for making separate mention of provincial councils, since it is easy to estimate, from the case of general councils, how much authority they ought to have in framing articles of faith, and deciding what kind of doctrine is to be received.

12. But our Romanists, when, in defending their cause, they see all rational grounds slip from beneath them, betake themselves to a last miserable subterfuge. Although they should be dull in intellect and counsel, and most depraved in heart and will, still the word of the Lord remains, which commands us to obey those who have the rule over us (Heb. xiii. 17). Is it indeed so? What if I should deny that those who act thus have the rule over us? They ought not to claim for themselves more than Joshua had, who was both a prophet of the Lord and an excellent pastor. Let us then hear in what terms the Lord introduced him to his office. "This book of the law shall not depart out of thy mouth; but thou shalt meditate therein day and night, that thou mayest observe to do according to all that is written therein: for then shalt thou make thy way prosperous, and thou shalt have good success" (Josh. i. 7, 8). Our spiritual rulers, therefore, will be those who turn not from the law of the Lord to the right hand or the left. But if the doctrine of all pastors is to be received without hesitation, why are we so often and so anxiously admonished by the Lord not to give heed to false prophets? "Thus saith the Lord of Hosts, Hearken not unto the words of the prophets that prophesy unto you; they make you vain: they speak a vision of their own heart, and not out of the mouth of the Lord" (Jer. xxiii. 16). Again, "Beware of false prophets, which come to you in sheep's clothing but inwardly they are ravening wolves" (Matth. vii. 15). In vain also would John exhort us to try the spirits whether they be of God (1 John iv. 1). From this judgment not even angels are exempted (Gal. i. 8); far less Satan with his lies. And what is meant by the expression, "If the blind lead the blind, both shall fall into the ditch"? (Matth. xv. 14.) Does it

not sufficiently declare that there is a great difference among the pastors who are to be heard, that all are not to be heard indiscriminately? Wherefore they have no ground for deterring us by their name, in order to draw us into a participation of their blindness, since we see, on the contrary, that the Lord has used special care to guard us from allowing ourselves to be led away by the errors of others, whatever be the mask under which they may lurk. For if the answer of our Saviour is true, blind guides, whether high priests, prelates, or pontiffs, can do nothing more than hurry us over the same precipice with themselves. Wherefore, let no names of councils, pastors, and bishops (which may be used on false pretences as well as truly), hinder us from giving heed to the evidence both of words and facts, and bringing all spirits to the test of the divine word, that we may prove whether they are of God.

13. Having proved that no power was given to the Church to set up any new doctrine, let us now treat of the power attributed to them in the interpretation of Scripture. We readily admit, that when any doctrine is brought under discussion, there is not a better or surer remedy than for a council of true bishops to meet and discuss the controverted point. There will be much more weight in a decision of this kind, to which the pastors of churches have agreed in common after invoking the Spirit of Christ, than if each, adopting it for himself, should deliver it to his people, or a few individuals should meet in private and decide. Secondly, When bishops have assembled in one place, they deliberate more conveniently in common, fixing both the doctrine and the form of teaching it, lest diversity give offence. Thirdly, Paul prescribes this method of determining doctrine. For when he gives the power of deciding to a single church, he shows what the course of procedure should be in more important cases—namely, that the churches together are to take common cognisance. And the very feeling of piety tells us, that if any one trouble the Church with some novelty in doctrine, and the matter be carried so far that there is danger of a greater dissension, the churches should first meet, examine the question, and at length, after due discussion, decide according to Scripture, which may both put an end to doubt in the people, and stop the mouths of wicked and restless men, so as to prevent the matter from proceeding farther. Thus when Arius arose, the Council of Nice was convened, and by its authority both crushed the wicked attempts of this impious man, and restored peace to the churches which he had vexed, and asserted the eternal divinity of Christ in opposition to his sacrilegious dogma. Thereafter, when Eunomius and Macedonius raised new disturbances, their madness was met with a similar remedy by the Council of Constantinople; the impiety of Nestorius was defeated by the Council of Ephesus. In short, this was from the first the usual method of preserving unity in the Church whenever Satan commenced his machinations. But let us remember, that all ages and places are not favoured with an Athanasius, a Basil, a Cyril, and like vindica-

tors of sound doctrine, whom the Lord then raised up. Nay, let us consider what happened in the 'second Council of Ephesus when the Eutychian heresy prevailed. Flavianus, of holy memory, with some pious men, was driven into exile, and many similar crimes were committed, because, instead of the Spirit of the Lord, Dioscorus, a factious man, of a very bad disposition, presided. But the Church was not there. I admit it; for I always hold that the truth does not perish in the Church though it be oppressed by one council, but is wondrously preserved by the Lord to rise again, and prove victorious in his own time. I deny, however, that every interpretation of Scripture is true and certain which has received the votes of a council.

14. But the Romanists have another end in view when they say that the power of interpreting Scripture belongs to councils, and that without challenge. For they employ it as a pretext for giving the name of an interpretation of Scripture to everything which is determined in councils. Of purgatory, the intercession of saints, and auricular confession, and the like, not one syllable can be found in Scripture. But as all these have been sanctioned by the authority of the Church, or, to speak more correctly, have been received by opinion and practice, every one of them is to be held as an interpretation of Scripture. And not only so, but whatever a council has determined against Scripture is to have the name of an interpretation. Christ bids all drink of the cup which he holds forth in the Supper. The Council of Constance prohibited the giving of it to the people, and determined that the priest alone should drink. Though this is diametrically opposed to the institution of Christ (Matth. xxvi. 26), they will have it to be regarded as his interpretation. Paul terms the prohibition of marriage a doctrine of devils (1 Tim. iv. 1, 3); and the Spirit elsewhere declares that "marriage is honourable in all" (Heb. xiii. 4). Having afterwards interdicted their priests from marriage, they insist on this as a true and genuine interpretation of Scripture, though nothing can be imagined more alien to it. Should any one venture to open his lips in opposition, he will be judged a heretic, since the determination of the Church is without challenge, and it is unlawful to have any doubt as to the accuracy of her interpretation. Why should I assail such effrontery? to point to it is to condemn it. Their dogma with regard to the power of approving Scripture I intentionally omit. For to subject the oracles of God in this way to the censure of men, and hold that they are sanctioned because they please men, is a blasphemy which deserves not to be mentioned. Besides, I have already touched upon it (Book I. chap. vii. viii. sec. 9). I will ask them one question, however. If the authority of Scripture is founded on the approbation of the Church, will they quote the decree of a council to that effect? I believe they cannot. Why, then, did Arius allow himself to be vanquished at the Council of Nice by passages adduced from the Gospel of John? According to these, he was at liberty to re-

pudiate them, as they had not previously been approved by any general council. They allege an old catalogue, which they call the Canon, and say that it originated in a decision of the Church. But I again ask, In what council was that Canon published? Here they must be dumb. Besides, I wish to know what they believe that Canon to be. For I see that the ancients are little agreed with regard to it. If effect is to be given to what Jerome says (Præf. in Lib. Solom.), the Maccabees, Tobit, Ecclesiasticus, and the like, must take their place in the Apocrypha: but this they will not tolerate on any account.

CHAPTER X.

OF THE POWER OF MAKING LAWS. THE CRUELTY OF THE POPE AND
HIS ADHERENTS, IN THIS RESPECT, IN TYRANNICALLY OPPRESSING
AND DESTROYING SOULS.

This chapter treats,—I. Of human constitutions in general. Of the distinction between Civil and Ecclesiastical Laws. Of conscience, why and in what sense ministers cannot impose laws on the conscience, sec. 1–8. II. Of traditions or Popish
constitutions relating to ceremonies and discipline. The many vices inherent in them,
sec. 9–17. Arguments in favour of those traditions refuted, sec. 17-26. III. Of Ecclesiastical constitutions that are good and lawful, sec. 27–32.

Sections.

1. The power of the Church in enacting laws. This made a source of human traditions. Impiety of these traditions.
2. Many of the Papistical traditions not only difficult, but impossible to be observed.
3. That the question may be more conveniently explained, nature of conscience must
   be defined.
4. Definition of conscience explained. Examples in illustration of the definition.
5. Paul's doctrine of submission to magistrates for conscience sake, gives no countenance to the Popish doctrine of the obligation of traditions.
6. The question stated. A brief mode of deciding it.
7. A perfect rule of life in the Law. God our only Lawgiver.
8. The traditions of the Papacy contradictory to the Word of God.
9. Ceremonial traditions of the Papists. Their impiety. Substituted for the true
   worship of God.
10. Through these ceremonies the commandment of God made void.
11. Some of these ceremonies useless and childish. Their endless variety. Introduce
    Judaism.
12. Absurdity of these ceremonies borrowed from Judaism and Paganism.
13. Their intolerable number condemned by Augustine.
14. Injury thus done to the Church. They cannot be excused.
15. Mislead the superstitious. Used as a kind of show and for incantation. Prosti-
    tuted to gain.
16. All such traditions liable to similar objections.
17. Arguments in favour of traditions answered.
18. Answer continued.
19. Illustration taken from the simple administration of the Lord's Supper, under the
    Apostles, and the complicated ceremonies of the Papists.
20. Another illustration from the use of Holy Water.
21. An argument in favour of traditions founded on the decision of the Apostles and
    elders at Jerusalem. This decision explained.
22. Some things in the Papacy may be admitted for a time for the sake of weak
    brethren.
23. Observance of the Popish traditions inconsistent with Christian liberty, torturing
    to the conscience, and insulting to God.
24. All human inventions in religion displeasing to God. Reason. Confirmed by an
    example.
25. An argument founded on the examples of Samuel and Manoah. Answer.
26. Argument that Christ wished such burdens to be borne. Answer.
27. Third part of the chapter, treating of lawful Ecclesiastical arrangements. Their
    foundation in the general axiom, that all things be done decently and in order.
    Two extremes to be avoided.

1. WE come now to the second part of power, which, according to them, consists in the enacting of laws, from which source innumerable traditions have arisen, to be as many deadly snares to miserable souls. For they have not been more scrupulous than the Scribes and Pharisees in laying burdens on the shoulders of others, which they would not touch with their finger (Matth xxiii. 4; Luke xi. 16). I have elsewhere shown (Book III. chap. iv. sec. 4–7) how cruel murder they commit by their doctrine of auricular confession. The same violence is not apparent in other laws, but those which seem most tolerable press tyrannically on the conscience. I say nothing as to the mode in which they adulterate the worship of God, and rob God himself, who is the only Lawgiver, of his right. The power we have now to consider is, whether it be lawful for the Church to bind laws upon the conscience? In this discussion, civil order is not touched; but the only point considered is, how God may be duly worshipped according to the rule which he has prescribed, and how our spiritual liberty, with reference to God, may remain unimpaired. In ordinary language, the name of human traditions is given to all decrees concerning the worship of God, which men have issued without the authority of his word. We contend against these, not against the sacred and useful constitutions of the Church, which tend to preserve discipline, or decency, or peace. Our aim is to curb the unlimited and barbarous empire usurped over souls by those who would be thought pastors of the Church, but who are in fact its most cruel murderers. They say that the laws which they enact are spiritual, pertaining to the soul, and they affirm that they are necessary to eternal life. But thus the kingdom of Christ, as I lately observed, is invaded; thus the liberty, which he has given to the consciences of believers, is completely oppressed and overthrown. I say nothing as to the great impiety with which, to sanction the observance of their laws, they declare that from it they seek forgiveness of sins, righteousness and salvation, while they make the whole sum of religion and piety to consist in it. What I contend for is, that necessity ought not to be laid on consciences in matters in which Christ has made them free; and unless freed, cannot, as we have previously shown (Book III. chap. xix.), have peace with God. They must acknowledge Christ their deliverer, as their only king, and be ruled by the only law of liberty—namely, the sacred word of the Gospel—if they would retain the grace which they have once received in Christ: they must be subject to no bondage, be bound by no chains.

2. These Solons, indeed, imagine that their constitutions are laws of liberty, a pleasant yoke, a light burden ; but who sees not that this is mere falsehood. They themselves, indeed, feel not the burden of their laws. Having cast off the fear of God, they securely and assiduously disregard their own laws as well as those which are divine. Those, however, who feel any interest in their salvation, are far from thinking themselves free so long as they are entangled in these snares. We see how great caution Paul employed in this matter, not venturing to impose a fetter in any one thing, and with good reason : he certainly foresaw how great a wound would be inflicted on the conscience if these things should be made necessary which the Lord had left free. On the contrary, it is scarcely possible to count the constitutions which these men have most grievously enforced, under the penalty of eternal death, and which they exact with the greatest rigour, as necessary to salvation. And while very many of them are most difficult of observance, the whole taken together are impossible ; so great is the mass. How, then, possibly can those, on whom this mountain of difficulty lies, avoid being perplexed with extreme anxiety, and filled with terror ? My intention here then is, to impugn constitutions of this description ; constitutions enacted for the purpose of binding the conscience inwardly before God, and imposing religious duties, as if they enjoined things necessary to salvation.

3. Many are greatly puzzled with this question, from not distinguishing, with sufficient care, between what is called the external forum and the forum of conscience [1] (Book III. chap. xix. sec 15). Moreover, the difficulty is increased by the terms in which Paul enjoins obedience to magistrates, "not only for wrath, but also for conscience sake" (Rom. xiii. 5); and from which it would follow, that civil laws also bind the conscience. But if this were so, nothing that we have said of spiritual government, in the last chapter, and are to say in this, would stand. To solve this difficulty, we must first understand what is meant by conscience. The definition must be derived from the etymology of the term. As when men, with the mind and intellect, apprehend the knowledge of things, they are thereby said to know, and hence the name of science or knowledge is used ; so, when they have, in addition to this, a sense of the divine judgment, as a witness not permitting them to hide their sins, but bringing them as criminals before the tribunal of the judge, that sense is called conscience. For it occupies a kind of middle place between God and man, not suffering man to suppress what he knows in himself, but following him out until it bring him to conviction. This is what Paul means, when he says that conscience bears witness, "our thoughts the meanwhile accusing or else excusing each other" (Rom. ii. 15). Simple knowledge, therefore, might exist in a man, as it were, shut up, and therefore the sense which sists men before the judgment-seat of God has been placed over him as a sentinel, to

---

[1] French, "entre le siege judicial de Dieu, qui est spirituel, et la justice terrestre des hommes;"—between the judgment-seat of God and the terrestrial justice of men.

observe and spy out all his secrets, that nothing may remain buried in darkness. Hence the old proverb, Conscience is a thousand witnesses. For this reason, Peter also uses the "answer of a good conscience towards God" (1 Pet. iii. 21); for tranquillity of mind, when, persuaded of the grace of Christ, we with boldness present ourselves before God. And the author of the Epistle to the Hebrews says, that we have "no more conscience of sins," that we are freed or acquitted, so that sin no longer accuses us (Heb. x. 2).

4. Wherefore, as works have respect to men, so conscience bears reference to God ; and hence a good conscience is nothing but inward integrity of heart. In this sense, Paul says, that "the end of the commandment is charity out of a pure heart, and of a good conscience, and of faith unfeigned" (1 Tim. i. 5). He afterwards, in the same chapter, shows how widely it differs from intellect, saying, that "some having put away" a good conscience, "concerning faith have made shipwreck." For by these words he intimates, that it is a living inclination to worship God, a sincere desire to live piously and holily. Sometimes, indeed, it is extended to men also, as when Paul declares, "Herein do I exercise myself, to have always a conscience void of offence toward God, and toward men" (Acts xxiv. 16). But this is said, because the benefits of a good conscience flow forth and reach even to men. Properly speaking, however, it respects God alone, as I have already said. Hence a law may be said to bind the conscience when it simply binds a man without referring to men, or taking them into account. For example, God enjoins us not only to keep our mind chaste and pure from all lust, but prohibits every kind of obscenity in word, and all external lasciviousness. This law my conscience is bound to observe, though there were not another man in the world. Thus he who behaves intemperately not only sins by setting a bad example to his brethren, but stands convicted in his conscience before God. Another rule holds in the case of things which are in themselves indifferent. For we ought to abstain when they give offence, but conscience is free. Thus Paul says of meat consecrated to idols, "If any man say unto you, This is offered in sacrifice unto idols, eat not for his sake that showed it, and for conscience sake;" "conscience, I say, not thine own, but of the other" (1 Cor. x. 28, 29). A believer would sin, if, after being warned, he should still eat such kind of meat. But however necessary abstinence may be in respect of a brother, as prescribed by the Lord, conscience ceases not to retain its liberty. We see how the law, while binding the external work, leaves the conscience free.

5. Let us now return to human laws. If they are imposed for the purpose of forming a religious obligation, as if the observance of them was in itself necessary, we say that the restraint thus laid on the conscience is unlawful. Our consciences have not to do with men but with God only. Hence the common distinction between the

earthly forum and the forum of conscience.[1] When the whole world was enveloped in the thickest darkness of ignorance, it was still held (like a small ray of light which remained unextinguished) that conscience was superior to all human judgments. Although this, which was acknowledged in word, was afterwards violated in fact, yet God was pleased that there should even then exist an attestation to liberty, exempting the conscience from the tyranny of man. But we have not yet explained the difficulty which arises from the words of Paul. For if we must obey princes not only from fear of punishment but for conscience sake, it seems to follow, that the laws of princes have dominion over the conscience. If this is true, the same thing must be affirmed of ecclesiastical laws. I answer, that the first thing to be done here is to distinguish between the genus and the species. For though individual laws do not reach the conscience, yet we are bound by the general command of God, which enjoins us to submit to magistrates. And this is the point on which Paul's discussion turns—viz. that magistrates are to be honoured, because they are ordained of God (Rom. xiii. 1). Meanwhile, he does not at all teach that the laws enacted by them reach to the internal government of the soul, since he everywhere proclaims that the worship of God, and the spiritual rule of living righteously, are superior to all the decrees of men. Another thing also worthy of observation, and depending on what has been already said, is, that human laws, whether enacted by magistrates or by the Church, are necessary to be observed (I speak of such as are just and good), but do not therefore in themselves bind the conscience, because the whole necessity of observing them respects the general end, and consists not in the things commanded. Very different, however, is the case of those which prescribe a new form of worshipping God, and introduce necessity into things that are free.

6. Such, however, are what in the present day are called ecclesiastical constitutions by the Papacy, and are brought forward as part of the true and necessary worship of God. But as they are without number, so they form innumerable fetters to bind and ensnare the soul. Though, in expounding the law, we have adverted to this subject (Book III. chap. iv. 5), yet as this is more properly the place for a full discussion of it, I will now study to give a summary of it as carefully as I can. I shall, however, omit the branch relating to the tyranny with which false bishops arrogate to themselves the right of teaching whatever they please, having already considered it as far as seemed necessary, but shall treat at length of the power which they claim of enacting laws. The pretext, then, on which our

---

[1] French, "Et de fait, tel a eté le sens de cette distinction vulgaire qu'on a tenue par toutes les ecoles ; que c'est autre choses des jurisdictions humaines et politiques, que de celles qui touchent à la conscience ;"—And in fact, such is the import of the common distinction which has been held by all the schools, that human and civil jurisdictions are quite different from those which touch the conscience.

false bishops burden the conscience with new laws is, that the Lord has constituted them spiritual legislators, and given them the government of the Church. Hence they maintain that everything which they order and prescribe must, of necessity, be observed by the Christian people, that he who violates their commands is guilty of a twofold disobedience, being a rebel both against God and the Church. Assuredly, if they were true bishops, I would give them some authority in this matter, not so much as they demand, but so much as is requisite for duly arranging the polity of the Church; but since they are anything but what they would be thought, they cannot possibly assume anything to themselves, however little, without being in excess. But as this also has been elsewhere shown, let us grant for the present, that whatever power true bishops possess justly belongs to them, still I deny that they have been set over believers as legislators to prescribe a rule of life at their own hands, or bind the people committed to them to their decrees. When I say this, I mean that they are not at all entitled to insist that whatever they devise without authority from the word of God shall be observed by the Church as matter of necessity. Since such power was unknown to the apostles, and was so often denied to the ministers of the Church by our Lord himself, I wonder how any have dared to usurp, and dare in the present day to defend it, without any precedent from the apostles, and against the manifest prohibition of God.

7. Everything relating to a perfect rule of life the Lord has so comprehended in his law, that he has left nothing for men to add to the summary there given. His object in doing this was, first, that since all rectitude of conduct consists in regulating all our actions by his will as a standard, he alone should be regarded as the master and guide of our life; and, secondly, that he might show that there is nothing which he more requires of us than obedience. For this reason James says, " He that speaketh evil of his brother, and judgeth his brother, speaketh evil of the law, and judgeth the law: " " There is one lawgiver, who is able to save and to destroy" (James iv. 11, 12). We hear how God claims it as his own peculiar privilege to rule us by his laws. This had been said before by Isaiah, though somewhat obscurely, " The Lord is our judge, the Lord is our lawgiver, the Lord is our king; he will save us" (Isa. xxxiii. 22). Both passages show that the power of life and death belongs to him who has power over the soul. Nay, James clearly expresses this. This power no man may assume to himself. God, therefore, to whom the power of saving and destroying belongs, must be acknowledged as the only King of souls, or, as the words of Isaiah express it, he is our king and judge, and lawgiver and saviour. So Peter, when he reminds pastors of their duty, exhorts them to feed the flock without lording it over the heritage (1 Pet. v. 2); meaning by heritage the body of believers. If we duly consider that it is unlawful to transfer to man what God declares to belong only to himself,

we shall see that this completely cuts off all the power claimed by those who would take it upon them to order anything in the Church without authority from the word of God.

8. Moreover, since the whole question depends on this, that God being the only lawgiver, it is unlawful for men to assume that honour to themselves, it will be proper to keep in mind the two reasons for which God claims this solely for himself. The one reason is, that his will is to us the perfect rule of all righteousness and holiness, and that thus in the knowledge of it we have a perfect rule of life. The other reason is, that when the right and proper method of worshipping him is in question, he whom we ought to obey, and on whose will we ought to depend, alone has authority over our souls. When these two reasons are attended to, it will be easy to decide what human constitutions are contrary to the word of the Lord. Of this description are all those which are devised as part of the true worship of God, and the observance of which is bound upon the conscience, as of necessary obligation. Let us remember then to weigh all human laws in this balance, if we would have a sure test which will not allow us to go astray. The former reason is urged by Paul in the Epistle to the Colossians against the false apostles who attempted to lay new burdens on the churches. The second reason he more frequently employs in the Epistle to the Galatians in a similar case. In the Epistle to the Colossians, then, he maintains that the doctrine of the true worship of God is not to be sought from men, because the Lord has faithfully and fully taught us in what way he is to be worshipped. To demonstrate this, he says in the first chapter, that in the gospel is contained all wisdom, that the man of God may be made perfect in Christ. In the beginning of the second chapter, he says that all the treasures of wisdom and knowledge are hidden in Christ, and from this he concludes that believers should beware of being led away from the flock of Christ by vain philosophy, according to the constitutions of men (Col. ii. 10). In the end of the chapter, he still more decisively condemns all ἐθελοθρησκείας that is, fictitious modes of worship which men themselves devise or receive from others, and all precepts whatsoever which they presume to deliver at their own hand concerning the worship of God. We hold, therefore, that all constitutions are impious in the observance of which the worship of God is pretended to be placed. The passages in the Galatians in which he insists that fetters are not to be bound on the conscience (which ought to be ruled by God alone), are sufficiently plain, especially chapter v. Let it, therefore, suffice to refer to them.

9. But that the whole matter may be made plainer by examples, it will be proper, before we proceed, to apply the doctrine to our own times. The constitutions which they call ecclesiastical, and by which the Pope, with his adherents, burdens the Church, we hold to be pernicious and impious, while our opponents defend them as sacred and salutary. Now there are two kinds of them, some relating to ceremonies and rites, and others more especially to discipline. Have

we, then, any just cause for impugning both? Assuredly a juster cause than we could wish. First, do not their authors themselves distinctly declare that the very essence of the worship of God (so to speak) is contained in them? For what end do they bring forward their ceremonies but just that God may be worshipped by them? Nor is this done merely by error in the ignorant multitude, but with the approbation of those who hold the place of teachers. I am not now adverting to the gross abominations by which they have plotted the adulteration of all godliness, but they would not deem it to be so atrocious a crime to err in any minute tradition, did they not make the worship of God subordinate to their fictions. Since Paul then declares it to be intolerable that the legitimate worship of God should be subjected to the will of men, wherein do we err when we are unable to tolerate this in the present day? especially when we are enjoined to worship God according to the elements of this world—a thing which Paul declares to be adverse to Christ (Col. ii. 20). On the other hand, the mode in which they lay consciences under the strict necessity of observing whatever they enjoin, is not unknown. When we protest against this, we make common cause with Paul, who will on no account allow the consciences of believers to be brought under human bondage.

10. Moreover, the worst of all is, that when once religion begins to be composed of such vain fictions, the perversion is immediately succeeded by the abominable depravity with which our Lord upbraids the Pharisees of making the commandment of God void through their traditions (Matth. xv. 3). I am unwilling to dispute with our present legislators in my own words;—let them gain the victory if they can clear themselves from this accusation of Christ. But how can they do so, seeing they regard it as immeasurably more wicked to allow the year to pass without auricular confession, than to have spent it in the greatest iniquity: to have infected their tongue with a slight tasting of flesh on Friday, than to have daily polluted the whole body with whoredom: to have put their hand to honest labour on a day consecrated to some one or other of their saintlings, than to have constantly employed all their members in the greatest crimes: for a priest to be united to one in lawful wedlock, than to be engaged in a thousand adulteries: to have failed in performing a votive pilgrimage, than to have broken faith in every promise: not to have expended profusely on the monstrous, superfluous, and useless luxury of churches, than to have denied the poor in their greatest necessities: to have passed an idol without honour, than to have treated the whole human race with contumely: not to have muttered long unmeaning sentences at certain times, than never to have framed one proper prayer? What is meant by making the word of God void by tradition, if this is not done when recommending the ordinances of God only frigidly and perfunctorily, they nevertheless studiously and anxiously urge strict obedience to their own ordinances, as if the whole power of piety was contained in them;—when

vindicating the transgression of the divine Law with trivial satisfactions, they visit the minutest violation of one of their decrees with no lighter punishment than imprisonment, exile, fire, or sword ?—When neither severe nor inexorable against the despisers of God, they persecute to extremity, with implacable hatred, those who despise themselves, and so train all those whose simplicity they hold in thraldom, that they would sooner see the whole law of God subverted than one iota of what they call the precepts of the Church infringed. First, there is a grievous delinquency in this, that one contemns, judges, and casts off his neighbour for trivial matters,—matters which, if the judgment of God is to decide, are free. But now, as if this were a small evil, those frivolous elements of this world (as Paul terms them in his Epistle to the Galatians, Gal. iv. 9) are deemed of more value than the heavenly oracles of God. He who is all but acquitted for adultery is judged in meat; and he to whom whoredom is permitted is forbidden to marry. This, forsooth, is all that is gained by that prevaricating obedience, which only turns away from God to the same extent that it inclines to men.

11. There are other two grave vices which we disapprove in these constitutions. First, They prescribe observances which are in a great measure useless, and are sometimes absurd ; secondly, by the vast multitude of them, pious consciences are oppressed, and being carried back to a kind of Judaism, so cling to shadows that they cannot come to Christ. My allegation that they are useless and absurd will, I know, scarcely be credited by carnal wisdom, to which they are so pleasing, that the Church seems to be altogether defaced when they are taken away. But this is just what Paul says, that they " have indeed a show of wisdom in will-worship, and humility, and neglecting of the body" (Col. ii. 23) ; a most salutary admonition, of which we ought never to lose sight. Human traditions, he says, deceive by an appearance of wisdom. Whence this show ? Just that being framed by men, the human mind recognises in them that which is its own, and embraces it when recognised more willingly than anything, however good, which is less suitable to its vanity. Secondly, That they seem to be a fit training to humility, while they keep the minds of men grovelling on the ground under their yoke ; hence they have another recommendation. Lastly, Because they seem to have a tendency to curb the will of the flesh, and to subdue it by the rigour of abstinence, they seem to be wisely devised. But what does Paul say to all this ? Does he pluck off those masks lest the simple should be deluded by a false pretext ? Deeming it sufficient for their refutation to say that they were devices of men, he passes all these things without refutation, as things of no value. Nay, because he knew that all fictitious worship is condemned in the Church, and is the more suspected by believers, the more pleasing it is to the human mind—because he knew that this false show of outward humility differs so widely from true humility that it can be easily discerned ; —finally, because he knew that this tutelage is valued at no more

than bodily exercise, he wished the very things which commended human traditions to the ignorant to be regarded by believers as the refutation of them.

12. Thus, in the present day, not only the unlearned vulgar, but every one in proportion as he is inflated by worldly wisdom, is won-derfully captivated by the glare of ceremonies, while hypocrites and silly women think that nothing can be imagined better or more beautiful. But those who thoroughly examine them, and weigh them more truly according to the rule of godliness, in regard to the value of all such ceremonies, know, first, that they are trifles of no utility; secondly, that they are impostures which delude the eyes of the spec-tators with empty show. I am speaking of those ceremonies which the Roman masters will have to be great mysteries, while we know by experience that they are mere mockery. Nor is it strange that their authors have gone the length of deluding themselves and others by mere frivolities, because they have taken their model partly from the dreams of the Gentiles, partly, like apes, have rashly imitated the ancient rites of the Mosaic Law, with which we have nothing more to do than with the sacrifices of animals and other similar things. Assuredly, were there no other proof, no sane man would expect any good from such an ill-assorted farrago. And the case itself plainly demonstrates that very many ceremonies have no other use than to stupify the people rather than teach them. In like manner, to those new canons which pervert discipline rather than preserve it, hypo-crites attach much importance; but a closer examination will show that they are nothing but the shadowy and evanescent phantom of discipline.

13. To come to the second fault, who sees not that ceremonies, by being heaped one upon another, have grown to such a multitude, that it is impossible to tolerate them in the Christian Church? Hence it is, that in ceremonies a strange mixture of Judaism is apparent, while other observances prove a deadly snare to pious minds. Augus-tine complained that in his time, while the precepts of God were neglected, prejudice everywhere prevailed to such an extent, that he who touched the ground barefoot during his octave was censured more severely than he who buried his wits in wine. He complained that the Church, which God in mercy wished to be free, was so op-pressed that the condition of the Jews was more tolerable (August. Ep. 119). Had that holy man fallen on our day, in what terms would he have deplored the bondage now existing? For the number is tenfold greater, and each iota is exacted a hundred times more rigidly than then. This is the usual course; when once those per-verse legislators have usurped authority, they make no end of their commands and prohibitions until they reach the extreme of harsh-ness. This Paul elegantly intimated by these words,—"If ye be dead with Christ from the rudiments of the world, why, as though living in the world, are ye subject to ordinances? Touch not, taste not, handle not" (Col. ii. 20, 21). For while the word ἅπτεσθαι sig-

nifies both to eat and to touch, it is doubtless taken in the former sense, that there may not be a superfluous repetition. Here, therefore, he most admirably describes the progress of false apostles. The way in which superstition begins is this : they forbid not only to eat, but even to chew gently ; after they have obtained this, they forbid even to taste. This also being yielded to them, they deem it unlawful to touch even with the finger.

14. We justly condemn this tyranny in human constitutions, in consequence of which miserable consciences are strangely tormented by innumerable edicts, and the excessive exaction of them. Of the canons relating to discipline, we have spoken elsewhere (*supra*, sec. 12 ; also chapter xii.). What shall I say of ceremonies, the effect of which has been, that we have almost buried Christ, and returned to Jewish figures ? " Our Lord Christ (says Augustine, Ep. 118) bound together the society of his new people by sacraments, very few in number, most excellent in signification, most easy of observance." How widely different this simplicity is from the multitude and variety of rites in which we see the Church entangled in the present day, cannot well be told. I am aware of the artifice by which some acute men excuse this perverseness. They say that there are numbers among us equally rude as any among the Israelitish people, and that for their sakes has been introduced this tutelage, which though the stronger may do without, they, however, ought not to neglect, seeing that it is useful to weak brethren. I answer, that we are not unaware of what is due to the weakness of brethren, but, on the other hand, we object that the method of consulting for the weak is not to bury them under a great mass of ceremonies. It was not without cause that God distinguished between us and his ancient people, by training them like children by means of signs and figures, and training us more simply, without so much external show. Paul's words are, " The heir, as long as he is a child,"—" is under tutors and governors" (Gal. iv. 1, 2). This was the state of the Jews under the law. But we are like adults who, being freed from tutory and curatory, have no need of puerile rudiments. God certainly foresaw what kind of people he was to have in his Church, and in what way they were to be governed. Now, he distinguished between us and the Jews in the way which has been described. Therefore, it is a foolish method of consulting for the ignorant to set up the Judaism which Christ has abrogated. This dissimilitude between the ancient and his new people Christ expressed when he said to the woman of Samaria, " The hour cometh, and now is, when the true worshippers shall worship the Father in spirit and in truth" (John iv. 23). This, no doubt, had always been done ; but the new worshippers differ from the old in this, that while under Moses the spiritual worship of God was shadowed, and, as it were, entangled by many ceremonies, these have been abolished, and worship is now more simple. Those, accordingly, who confound this distinction, subvert the order instituted and sanctioned by Christ. Therefore you will ask, Are no ceremonies to

be given to the more ignorant, as a help to their ignorance? I do not say so; for I think that help of this description is very useful to them. All I contend for is the employment of such a measure as may illustrate, not obscure Christ. Hence a few ceremonies have been divinely appointed, and these by no means laborious, in order that they may evince a present Christ. To the Jews a greater number were given, that they might be images of an absent Christ. In saying he was absent, I mean not in power, but in the mode of expression. Therefore, to secure due moderation, it is necessary to retain that fewness in number, facility in observance, and significancy of meaning which consists in clearness. Of what use is it to say that this is not done? The fact is obvious to every eye.

15. I here say nothing of the pernicious opinions with which the minds of men are imbued, as that these are sacrifices by which propitiation is made to God, by which sins are expiated, by which righteousness and salvation are procured. It will be maintained that things good in themselves are not vitiated by errors of this description, since in acts expressly enjoined by God similar errors may be committed. There is nothing, however, more unbecoming than the fact, that works devised by the will of man are held in such estimation as to be thought worthy of eternal life. The works commanded by God receive a reward, because the Lawgiver himself accepts of them as marks of obedience. They do not, therefore, take their value from their own dignity or their own merit, but because God sets this high value on our obedience toward him. I am here speaking of that perfection of works which is commanded by God, but is not performed by men. The works of the law are accepted merely by the free kindness of God, because the obedience is infirm and defective. But as we are not here considering how far works avail without Christ, let us omit that question. I again repeat, as properly belonging to the present subject, that whatever commendation works have, they have it in respect of obedience, which alone God regards, as he testifies by the prophet, "I spake not unto your fathers, nor commanded them in the day that I brought them out of the land of Egypt, concerning burnt-offerings or sacrifices: but this thing commanded I them, saying, Obey my voice" (Jer. vii. 22). Of fictitious works he elsewhere speaks, "Wherefore do you spend your money for that which is not bread"? (Isa. lv. 2; xxix. 13). Again, "In vain do they worship me, teaching for doctrines the commandments of men" (Matth. xv. 9). They cannot, therefore, excuse themselves from the charge of allowing wretched people to seek in these external frivolities a righteousness which they may present to God, and by which they may stand before the celestial tribunal. Besides, it is not a fault deservedly stigmatised, that they exhibit unmeaning ceremonies as a kind of stage-play or magical incantation? For it is certain that all ceremonies are corrupt and noxious which do not direct men to Christ. But the ceremonies in use in the Papacy are separated from doctrine, so that they confine men to signs altogether

devoid of meaning. Lastly (as the belly is an ingenious contriver), it is clear, that many of their ceremonies have been invented by greedy priests as lures for catching money. But whatever be their origin, they are all so prostituted to filthy lucre, that a great part of them must be rescinded if we would prevent a profane and sacrilegious traffic from being carried on in the Church.

16. Although I seem not to be delivering the general doctrine concerning human constitutions, but adapting my discourse wholly to our own age, yet nothing has been said which may not be useful to all ages. For whenever men begin the superstitious practice of worshipping God with their own fictions, all the laws enacted for this purpose forthwith degenerate into those gross abuses. For the curse which God denounces—viz. to strike those who worship him with the doctrines of men with stupor and blindness—is not confined to any one age, but applies to all ages. The uniform result of this blindness is, that there is no kind of absurdity escaped by those who, despising the many admonitions of God, spontaneously entangle themselves in these deadly fetters. But if, without any regard to circumstances, you would simply know the character belonging at all times to those human traditions which ought to be repudiated by the Church, and condemned by all the godly,[1] the definition which we formerly gave is clear and certain—viz. That they include all the laws enacted by men, without authority from the word of God, for the purpose either of prescribing the mode of divine worship, or laying a religious obligation on the conscience, as enjoining things necessary to salvation. If to one or both of these are added the other evils of obscuring the clearness of the Gospel by their multitude, of giving no edification, of being useless and frivolous occupations rather than true exercises of piety, of being set up for sordid ends and filthy lucre, of being difficult of observance, and contaminated by pernicious superstitions, we shall have the means of detecting the quantity of mischief which they occasion.

17. I understand what their answer will be—viz. that these traditions are not from themselves, but from God. For to prevent the Church from erring, it is guided by the Holy Spirit, whose authority resides in them. This being conceded, it at the same time follows, that their traditions are revelations by the Holy Spirit, and cannot be disregarded without impiety and contempt of God. And that they may not seem to have attempted anything without high authority, they will have it to be believed that a great part of their observances is derived from the apostles. For they contend, that in one instance they have a sufficient proof of what the apostles did in other cases. The instance is, when the apostles assembled in council, announced to all the Gentiles as the opinion of the council, that they should "abstain from pollution of idols, and from fornication, and from things strangled, and from blood" (Acts xv. 20, 29). We have

---

[1] Calvin on the Necessity of Reforming the Church.

already explained, how, in order to extol themselves, they falsely assume the name of Church (Chap. viii. sec. 10–13). If, in regard to the present cause, we remove all masks and glosses (a thing, indeed, which ought to be our first care, and also is our highest interest), and consider what kind of Church Christ wishes to have, that we may form and adapt ourselves to it as a standard, it will readily appear that it is not a property of the Church to disregard the limits of the word of God, and wanton and luxuriate in enacting new laws. Does not the law which was once given to the Church endure for ever? "What things soever I command you, observe to do it: thou shalt not add thereto, nor diminish from it" (Deut. xii. 32). And in another place, "Add thou not unto his words, lest he reprove thee, and thou be found a liar" (Prov. xxx. 6). Since they cannot deny that this was said to the Church, what else do they proclaim but their contumacy, when, notwithstanding of such prohibitions, they profess to add to the doctrine of God, and dare to intermingle their own with it? Far be it from us to assent to the falsehood by which they offer such insult to the Church. Let us understand that the name of Church is falsely pretended wherever men contend for that rash human licence which cannot confine itself within the boundaries prescribed by the word of God, but petulantly breaks out, and has recourse to its own inventions. In the above passage there is nothing involved, nothing obscure, nothing ambiguous; the whole Church is forbidden to add to, or take from the word of God, in relation to his worship and salutary precepts. But that was said merely of the Law, which was succeeded by the Prophets and the whole Gospel dispensation! This I admit, but I at the same time add, that these are fulfilments of the Law, rather than additions or diminutions. Now, if the Lord does not permit anything to be added to, or taken from the ministry of Moses, though wrapt up, if I may so speak, in many folds of obscurity, until he furnish a clearer doctrine by his servants the Prophets, and at last by his beloved Son, why should we not suppose that we are much more strictly prohibited from making any addition to the Law, the Prophets, the Psalms, and the Gospel? The Lord cannot forget himself, and it is long since he declared that nothing is so offensive to him as to be worshipped by human inventions. Hence those celebrated declarations of the Prophets, which ought continually to ring in our ears, "I spake not unto your fathers, nor commanded them in the day that I brought them out of the land of Egypt, concerning burnt-offerings or sacrifices; but this thing commanded I them, saying, Obey my voice, and I will be your God, and ye shall be my people: and walk ye in all the ways that I have commanded you" (Jer. vii. 22, 23). "I earnestly protested unto your fathers, in the day that I brought them out of the land of Egypt, even unto this day, rising early and protesting, saying, Obey my voice" (Jer. xi. 7). There are other passages of the same kind, but the most noted of all is, "Hath the Lord as great delight in burnt-offerings and sacrifices, as in obeying the voice of the Lord? Behold, to obey is better than sacrifice, and to hearken than the fat of rams. For rebellion is as the sin of witchcraft, and stubbornness is as iniquity and idolatry" (1 Sam. xv. 22, 23). It is easy, therefore, to prove, that whenever human inventions in this respect are defended by the authority of the Church, they cannot be vindicated from the charge of impiety, and that the name of Church is falsely assumed.

18. For this reason we freely inveigh against that tyranny of human traditions which is haughtily obtruded upon us in the name of the Church. Nor do we hold the Church in derision (as our adversaries, for the purpose of producing obloquy, unjustly accuse us), but we attribute to her the praise of obedience, than which there is none which she acknowledges to be greater. They themselves rather are emphatically injurious to the Church, in representing her as contumacious to her Lord, when they pretend that she goes farther than the word of God allows, to say nothing of their combined impudence and malice, in continually vociferating about the power of the Church, while they meanwhile disguise both the command which the Lord has given her, and the obedience which she owes to the command. But if our wish is as it ought to be, to agree with the Church, it is of more consequence to consider and remember the injunction which the Lord has given both to us and to the Church, to obey him with one consent. For there can be no doubt that we shall best agree with the Church when we show ourselves obedient to the Lord in all things. But to ascribe the origin of the traditions by which the Church has hitherto been oppressed to the apostles is mere imposition, since the whole substance of the doctrine of the apostles is, that conscience must not be burdened with new observances, nor the worship of God contaminated by our inventions. Then, if any credit is to be given to ancient histories and records, what they attribute to the apostles was not only unknown to them, but was never heard by them. Nor let them pretend that most of their decrees, though not delivered in writing, were received by use and practice, being things which they could not understand while Christ was in the world, but which they learned after his ascension, by the revelation of the Holy Spirit. The meaning of that passage has been explained elsewhere (Chap. viii. sec. 14). In regard to the present question, they make themselves truly ridiculous, seeing it is manifest that all those mysteries which so long were undiscovered by the apostles, are partly Jewish or Gentile observances, the former of which had anciently been promulgated among the Jews, and the latter among all the Gentiles, partly absurd gesticulations and empty ceremonies, which stupid priests, who have neither sense nor letters, can duly perform; nay, which children and mountebanks perform so appropriately, that it seems impossible to have fitter priests for such sacrifices. If there were no records, men of sense would judge from the very nature of the case, that such a mass of rites and observances did not rush into the Church all at once, but crept in gradually. For though the venerable bishops, who were nearest in time to the apostles, introduced some things

pertaining to order and discipline, those who came after them, and those after them again, had not enough of consideration, while they had too much curiosity and cupidity, he who came last always vying in foolish emulation with his predecessors, so as not to be surpassed in the invention of novelties. And because there was a danger that these inventions, from which they anticipated praise from posterity, might soon become obsolete, they were much more rigorous in insisting on the observance of them. This false zeal has produced a great part of the rites which these men represent as apostolical. This history attests.

19. And not to become prolix, by giving a catalogue of all, we shall be contented with one example. Under the apostles there was great simplicity in administering the Lord's Supper. Their immediate successors made some additions to the dignity of the ordinance, which are not to be disapproved. Afterwards came foolish imitators, who, by ever and anon patching various fragments together, have left us those sacerdotal vestments which we see in the mass, those altar ornaments, those gesticulations, and whole farrago of useless observances.[1] But they object, that in old time the persuasion was, that those things which were done with the consent of the whole Church proceeded from the apostles. Of this they quote Augustine as a witness. I will give the explanation in the very words of Augustine. " Those things which are observed over the whole world we may understand to have been appointed either by the apostles themselves, or by general councils, whose authority in the Church is most beneficial, as the annual solemn celebration of our Lord's passion, resurrection, and ascension to heaven, and of the descent of the Holy Spirit, and any other occurrence observed by the whole Church wherever it exists" (August. Ep. 118). In giving so few examples, who sees not that he meant to refer the observances then in use to authors deserving of faith and reverence ;—observances few and sober, by which it was expedient that the order of the Church should be maintained ? How widely does this differ from the view of our Roman masters, who insist that there is no paltry ceremony among them which is not apostolical ?

20. Not to be tedious, I will give only one example. Should any one ask them where they get their holy water, they will at once answer, —from the apostles. As if I did not know who the Roman bishop is, to whom history ascribes the invention, and who, if he had admitted the apostles to his council, assuredly never would have adulterated baptism by a foreign and unseasonable symbol; although it does not seem probable to me that the origin of that consecration is

---

[1] French, " Mais depuis sont survenus d'autres singes, qui ont eu une folle affectation de coudre piece sur piece, et ainsi ont composé tant les accoustremens du prestre, que les paremens de l'autel, et le badinage et jeu de farce que nous voyons à present à la Messe, avec tout le reste du borgage."—But other apes have since appeared, who have had a foolish affectation of sewing piece to piece, and thus have formed all the furnishings of the priests, as well as altar ornaments, the trifling and farce play which we now see in the Mass, with all the other garniture.

so ancient as is there recorded. For when Augustine says (Ep. 118) that certain churches in his day rejected the formal imitation of Christ in the washing of feet, lest that rite should seem to pertain to baptism, he intimates that there was then no kind of washing which had any resemblance to baptism. Be this as it may, I will never admit that the apostolic spirit gave rise to that daily sign by which baptism, while brought back to remembrance, is in a manner repeated. I attach no importance to the fact, that Augustine elsewhere ascribes other things to the apostles. For as he has nothing better than conjecture, it is not sufficient for forming a judgment concerning a matter of so much moment. Lastly, though we should grant that the things which he mentions are derived from the apostolic age, there is a great difference between instituting some exercise of piety, which believers may use with a free conscience, or may abstain from if they think the observance not to be useful, and enacting a law which brings the conscience into bondage. Now, indeed, whoever is the author from whom they are derived, since we see the great abuses to which they have led, there is nothing to prevent us from abrogating them without any imputation on him, since he never recommended them in such a way as to lay us under a fixed and immovable obligation to observe them.

21. It gives them no great help, in defending their tyranny, to pretend the example of the apostles. The apostles and elders of the primitive Church, according to them, sanctioned a decree without any authority from Christ, by which they commanded all the Gentiles to abstain from meat offered to idols, from things strangled, and from blood (Acts xv. 20). If this was lawful for them, why should not their successors be allowed to imitate the example as often as occasion requires ? Would that they would always imitate them both in this and in other matters ! For I am ready to prove, on valid grounds, that here nothing new has been instituted or decreed by the apostles. For when Peter declares in that council, that God is tempted if a yoke is laid on the necks of the disciples, he overthrows his own argument if he afterwards allows a yoke to be imposed on them. But it is imposed if the apostles, on their own authority, prohibit the Gentiles from touching meat offered to idols, things strangled, and blood. The difficulty still remains, that they seem nevertheless to prohibit them. But this will easily be removed by attending more closely to the meaning of their decree. The first thing in order, and the chief thing in importance, is, that the Gentiles were to retain their liberty, which was not to be disturbed, and that they were not to be annoyed with the observances of the Law. As yet, the decree is all in our favour. The reservation which immediately follows is not a new law enacted by the apostles, but a divine and eternal command of God against the violation of charity, which does not detract one iota from that liberty. It only reminds the Gentiles how they are to accommodate themselves to their brother, and to not abuse their liberty for an occasion of offence. Let the second head, therefore, be,

that the Gentiles are to use an innoxious liberty, giving no offence to the brethren. Still, however, they prescribe some certain thing— viz. they show and point out, as was expedient at the time, what those things are by which they may give offence to their brethren, that they may avoid them; but they add no novelty of their own to the eternal law of God, which forbids the offence of brethren.

22. As in the case where faithful pastors, presiding over churches not yet well constituted, should intimate to their flocks not to eat flesh on Friday until the weak among whom they live become strong, or to work on a holiday, or any other similar things, although, when superstition is laid aside, these matters are in themselves indifferent, still, where offence is given to the brethren, they cannot be done without sin; so there are times when believers cannot set this example before weak brethren without most grievously wounding their consciences. Who but a slanderer would say that a new law is enacted by those who, it is evident, only guard against scandals which their Master has distinctly forbidden? But nothing more than this can be said of the apostles, who had no other end in view, in removing grounds of offence, than to enforce the divine Law, which prohibits offence; as if they had said, The Lord hath commanded you not to hurt a weak brother; but meats offered to idols, things strangled, and blood, ye cannot eat, without offending weak brethren; we, therefore, require you, in the word of the Lord, not to eat with offence. And to prove that the apostles had respect to this, the best witness is Paul, who writes as follows, undoubtedly according to the sentiments of the council: "As concerning, therefore, the eating of those things which are offered in sacrifice unto idols, we know that an idol is nothing in the world, and that there is none other God but one."— "Howbeit, there is not in every man that knowledge: for some with conscience of the idol unto this hour eat it as a thing offered unto an idol; and their conscience being weak is defiled."—"But take heed lest by any means this liberty of yours become a stumbling-block to them that are weak" (1 Cor. viii. 4-9). Any one who duly considers these things will not be imposed upon by the gloss which these men employ when, as a cloak to their tyranny, they pretend that the apostles had begun by their decree to infringe the liberty of the Church. But that they may be unable to escape without confessing the accuracy of this explanation, let them tell me by what authority they have dared to abrogate this very decree. It was, it seems, because there was no longer any danger of those offences and dissensions which the apostles wished to obviate, and they knew that the law was to be judged by its end. Seeing, therefore, the law was passed with a view to charity, there is nothing prescribed in it except in so far as required by charity. In confessing that the transgression of this law is nothing but a violation of charity, do they not at the same time acknowledge that it was not some adventitious supplement to the law of God, but a genuine and simple adaptation of it to the times and manners for which it was destined?

23. But though such laws are hundreds of times unjust and injurious to us, still they contend that they are to be heard without exception ; for the thing asked of us is not to consent to errors, but only to submit to the strict commands of those set over us,—commands which we are not at liberty to decline (1 Pet. ii. 18). But here also the Lord comes to the succour of his word, and frees us from this bondage by asserting the liberty which he has purchased for us by his sacred blood, and the benefit of which he has more than once attested by his word. For the thing required of us is not (as they maliciously pretend) to endure some grievous oppression in our body, but to be tortured in our consciences, and brought into bondage : in other words, robbed of the benefits of Christ's blood. Let us omit this, however, as if it were irrelevant to the point. Do we think it a small matter that the Lord is deprived of his kingdom which he so strictly claims for himself ? Now, he is deprived of it as often as he is worshipped with laws of human invention, since his will is to be sole legislator of his worship. And lest any one should consider this as of small moment, let us hear how the Lord himself estimates it. " Forasmuch as this people draw near me with their mouth, and with their lips do honour me, but have removed their heart far from me, and their fear toward me is taught by the precept of men : therefore, behold, I will proceed to do a marvellous work among the people, even a marvellous work and a wonder ; for the wisdom of their wise men shall perish, and the understanding of their prudent men shall be hid" (Isaiah xxix. 13-14). And in another place, " But in vain do they worship me, teaching for doctrines the commandments of men" (Matth. xv. 9). And, indeed, when the children of Israel polluted themselves with manifold idolatries, the cause of the whole evil is ascribed to that impure mixture caused by their disregarding the commandments of God, and framing new modes of worship. Accordingly, sacred history relates that the new inhabitants who had been brought by the king of Assyria from Babylon to inhabit Samaria were torn and destroyed by wild beasts, because they knew not the judgment or statutes of the God of that land (2 Kings xvii. 24-34). Though they had done nothing wrong in ceremonies, still their empty show could not have been approved by God. Meanwhile he ceased not to punish them for the violation of his worship by the introduction of fictions alien from his word. Hence it is afterwards said that, terrified by the punishment, they adopted the rites prescribed in the Law ; but as they did not yet worship God purely, it is twice repeated that, they feared him and feared not. Hence we infer that part of the reverence due to him consists in worshipping him simply in the way which he commands, without mingling any inventions of our own. And, accordingly, pious princes are repeatedly praised (2 Kings xxii. 1, &c.) for acting according to all his precepts, and not declining either to the right hand or the left. I go further : although there be no open manifestation of impiety in fictitious worship, it is strictly condemned by the Spirit,

inasmuch as it is a departure from the command of God. The altar of Ahaz, a model of which had been brought from Damascus (2 Kings xvi. 10), might have seemed to give additional ornament to the temple, seeing it was his intention there to offer sacrifices to God only, and to do it more splendidly than at the first ancient altar : yet we see how the Spirit detests the audacious attempt, for no other reasons but because human inventions are in the worship of God impure corruptions. And the more clearly the will of God has been manifested to us, the less excusable is our petulance in attempting anything. Accordingly, the guilt of Manasses is aggravated by the circumstance of having erected a new altar at Jerusalem, of which the Lord said, " In Jerusalem will I put my name" (2 Kings xxii. 3, 4), because the authority of God was thereby professedly rejected.

24. Many wonder why God threatens so sternly that he will bring astonishment on the people who worship him with the commandments of men, and declares that it is in vain to worship him with the commandments of men. But if they would consider what it is in the matter of religion, that is, of heavenly wisdom, to depend on God alone, they would, at the same time, see that it is not on slight grounds the Lord abominates perverse service of this description, which is offered him at the caprice of the human will. For although there is some show of humility in the obedience of those who obey such laws in worshipping God, yet they are by no means humble, since they prescribe to him the very laws which they observe. This is the reason why Paul would have us so carefully to beware of being deceived by the traditions of men, and what is called ἐθελοθρησκεία, that is, voluntary worship, worship devised by men without sanction from God. Thus it is, indeed : we must be fools in regard to our own wisdom and all the wisdom of men, in order that we may allow him alone to be wise. This course is by no means observed by those who seek to approve themselves to him by paltry observances of man's devising, and, as it were, against his will obtrude upon him a prevaricating obedience which is yielded to men. This is the course which has been pursued for several ages, and within our own recollection, and is still pursued in the present day in those places in which the power of the creature is more than that of the Creator, where religion (if religion it deserves to be called) is polluted with more numerous, and more absurd superstitions, than ever Paganism was. For what could human sense produce but things carnal and fatuous, and savouring of their authors ?

25. When the patrons of superstition cloak them, by pretending that Samuel sacrificed in Ramath, and though he did so contrary to the Law, yet pleased God (1 Sam vii. 17), it is easy to answer, that he did not set up any second altar in opposition to the only true one; but, as the place for the Ark of the Covenant had not been fixed, he sacrificed in the town where he dwelt, as being the most convenient. It certainly never was the intention of the holy prophet to make any innovation in sacred things, in regard to which the Lord had so

strictly forbidden addition or diminution. The case of Manoah I consider to have been extraordinary and special. He, though a private man, offered sacrifice to God, and did it not without approbation, because he did it not from a rash movement of his own mind, but by divine inspiration (Judges xiii. 19). How much God abominates all the devices of men in his worship, we have a striking proof in the case of one not inferior to Manoah—viz. Gideon, whose ephod brought ruin not only on himself and his family, but on the whole people (Judges viii. 27). In short, every adventitious invention, by which men desire to worship God, is nothing else than a pollution of true holiness.

26. Why then, they ask, did Christ say that the intolerable burdens, imposed by Scribes and Pharisees, were to be borne? (Matth. xxiii. 3.) Nay, rather, why did he say in another place that we were to beware of the leaven of the Pharisees? (Matth. xvi. 6,) meaning by leaven, as the Evangelist Matthew explains it, whatever of human doctrine is mingled with the pure word of God. What can be plainer than that we are enjoined to shun and beware of their whole doctrine? From this it is most certain, that in the other passage our Lord never meant that the consciences of his people were to be harassed by the mere traditions of the Pharisees. And the words themselves, unless when wrested, have no such meaning. Our Lord, indeed, beginning to inveigh against the manners of the Pharisees, first instructs his hearers simply, that though they saw nothing to follow in the lives of the Pharisees, they should not, however, cease to do what they verbally taught when they sat in the seat of Moses, that is, to expound the Law. All he meant, therefore, was to guard the common people against being led by the bad example of their teachers to despise doctrine. But as some are not at all moved by reason, and always require authority, I will quote a passage from Augustine, in which the very same thing is expressed. " The Lord's sheepfold has persons set over it, of whom some are faithful, others hirelings. Those who are faithful are true shepherds ; learn, however, that hirelings also are necessary. For many in the Church, pursuing temporal advantages, preach Christ, and the voice of Christ is heard by them, and the sheep follow not a hireling, but the shepherd by means of a hireling. Learn that hirelings were pointed out by the Lord himself. The Scribes and Pharisees, says he, sit in Moses' seat ; what they tell you, do, but what they do, do ye not. What is this but to say, Hear the voice of the shepherd by means of hirelings ? Sitting in the chair, they teach the Law of God, and therefore God teaches by them ; but if they choose to teach their own, hear not, do not." Thus far Augustine. (August. in Joann. Tract. 46.)

27. But as very many ignorant persons, on hearing that it is impious to bind the conscience, and vain to worship God with human traditions, apply one blot to all the laws by which the order of the

Church is established, it will be proper to obviate their error. Here, indeed, the danger of mistake is great: for it is not easy to see at first sight how widely the two things differ. But I will, in a few words, make the matter so clear, that no one will be imposed upon by the resemblance. First, then, let us understand that if in every human society some kind of government is necessary to insure the common peace and maintain concord, if in transacting business some form must always be observed, which public decency, and hence humanity itself, require us not to disregard, this ought especially to be observed in churches, which are best sustained by a constitution in all respects well ordered, and without which concord can have no existence. Wherefore, if we would provide for the safety of the Church, we must always carefully attend to Paul's injunction, that all things be done decently and in order (1 Cor. xiv. 40). But seeing there is such diversity in the manners of men, such variety in their minds, such repugnance in their judgments and dispositions, no policy is sufficiently firm unless fortified by certain laws, nor can any rite be observed without a fixed form. So far, therefore, are we from condemning the laws which conduce to this, that we hold that the removal of them would unnerve the Church, deface and dissipate it entirely. For Paul's injunction, that all things be done decently and in order, cannot be observed unless order and decency be secured by the addition of ordinances, as a kind of bonds. In these ordinances, however, we must always attend to the exception, that they must not be thought necessary to salvation, nor lay the conscience under a religious obligation ; they must not be compared to the worship of God, nor substituted for piety.

28. We have, therefore, a most excellent and sure mark to distinguish between those impious constitutions (by which, as we have said, true religion is overthrown, and conscience subverted) and the legitimate observances of the Church, if we remember that one of two things, or both together, are always intended—viz. that in the sacred assembly of the faithful, all things may be done decently, and with becoming dignity, and that human society may be maintained in order by certain bonds, as it were, of moderation and humanity. For when a law is understood to have been made for the sake of public decency, there is no room for the superstition into which those fall who measure the worship of God by human inventions. On the the other hand, when a law is known to be intended for common use, that false idea of its obligation and necessity, which gives great alarm to the conscience, when traditions are deemed necessary to salvation, is overthrown ; since nothing here is sought but the maintenance of charity by a common office. But it may be proper to explain more clearly what is meant by the decency which Paul commends, and also what is comprehended under order. And the object of decency is, partly that by the use of rites, which produce reverence in sacred matters, we may be excited to piety, and partly that the modesty and gravity which ought to be seen in all honourable actions may here

especially be conspicuous.　In order, the first thing is, that those who preside know the law and rule of right government, while those who are governed be accustomed to obedience and right discipline.　The second thing is, that by duly arranging the state of the Church, provision be made for peace and tranquillity.

29. We shall not, therefore, give the name of decency to that which only ministers an empty pleasure: such, for example, as is seen in that theatrical display which the Papists exhibit in their public service, where nothing appears but a mask of useless splendour, and luxury without any fruit.　But we give the name of decency to that which, suited to the reverence of sacred mysteries, forms a fit exercise for piety, or at least gives an ornament adapted to the action, and is not without fruit, but reminds believers of the great modesty, seriousness, and reverence, with which sacred things ought to be treated. Moreover, ceremonies, in order to be exercises of piety, must lead us directly to Christ.　In like manner, we shall not make order consist in that nugatory pomp which gives nothing but evanescent splendour, but in that arrangement which removes all confusion, barbarism, contumacy, all turbulence and dissension.　Of the former class we have examples (1 Cor. xi. 5, 21), where Paul says, that profane entertainments must not be intermingled with the sacred Supper of the Lord; that women must not appear in public uncovered.　And there are many other things which we have in daily practice, such as praying on our knees, and with our head uncovered, administering the sacraments of the Lord, not sordidly, but with some degree of dignity; employing some degree of solemnity in the burial of our dead, and so forth.　In the other class are the hours set apart for public prayer, sermon, and solemn services; during sermon, quiet and silence, fixed places, singing of hymns, days set apart for the celebration of the Lord's Supper, the prohibition of Paul against women teaching in the Church, and such like.　To the same list especially may be referred those things which preserve discipline, as catechising, ecclesiastical censures, excommunication, fastings, &c.　Thus all ecclesiastical constitutions, which we admit to be sacred and salutary, may be reduced to two heads, the one relating to rites and ceremonies, the other to discipline and peace.

30. But as there is here a danger, on the one hand, lest false bishops should thence derive a pretext for their impious and tyrannical laws, and, on the other, lest some, too apt to take alarm, should, from fear of the above evils, leave no place for laws, however holy, it may here be proper to declare, that I approve of those human constitutions only which are founded on the authority of God, and derived from Scripture, and are therefore altogether divine.　Let us take, for example, the bending of the knee which is made in public prayer.　It is asked, whether this is a human tradition, which any one is at liberty to repudiate or neglect?　I say, that it is human, and that at the same time it is divine.　It is of God, inasmuch as it is a part of that decency, the care and observance of which is re-

commended by the apostle; and it is of men, inasmuch as it specially determines what was indicated in general, rather than expounded. From this one example, we may judge what is to be thought of the whole class—viz. that the whole sum of righteousness, and all the parts of divine worship, and everything necessary to salvation, the Lord has faithfully comprehended, and clearly unfolded, in his sacred oracles, so that in them he alone is the only Master to be heard. But as in external discipline and ceremonies, he has not been pleased to prescribe every particular that we ought to observe (he foresaw that this depended on the nature of the times, and that one form would not suit all ages), in them we must have recourse to the general rules which he has given, employing them to test whatever the necessity of the Church may require to be enjoined for order and decency. Lastly, as he has not delivered any express command, because things of this nature are not necessary to salvation, and, for the edification of the Church, should be accommodated to the varying circumstances of each age and nation, it will be proper, as the interest of the Church may require, to change and abrogate the old, as well as to introduce new forms. I confess, indeed, that we are not to innovate rashly or incessantly, or for trivial causes. Charity is the best judge of what tends to hurt or to edify : if we allow her to be guide, all things will be safe.

31. Things which have been appointed according to this rule, it is the duty of the Christian people to observe with a free conscience indeed, and without superstition, but also with a pious and ready inclination to obey. They are not to hold them in contempt, nor pass them by with careless indifference, far less openly to violate them in pride and contumacy. You will ask, What liberty of conscience will there be in such cautious observances? Nay, this liberty will admirably appear when we shall hold that these are not fixed and perpetual obligations to which we are astricted, but external rudiments for human infirmity, which, though we do not all need, we, however, all use, because we are bound to cherish mutual charity towards each other. This we may recognise in the examples given above. What? Is religion placed in a woman's bonnet, so that it is unlawful for her to go out with her head uncovered? Is her silence fixed by a decree which cannot be violated without the greatest wickedness? Is there any mystery in bending the knee, or in burying a dead body, which cannot be omitted without a crime? By no means. For should a woman require to make such haste in assisting a neighbour that she has not time to cover her head, she sins not in running out with her head uncovered. And there are some occasions on which it is not less seasonable for her to speak than on others to be silent. Nothing, moreover, forbids him who, from disease, cannot bend his knees, to pray standing. In fine, it is better to bury a dead man quickly, than from want of grave-clothes, or the absence of those who should attend the funeral, to wait till it rot away unburied. Nevertheless, in those matters the custom and in-

stitutions of the country, in short, humanity and the rules of modesty itself, declare what is to be done or avoided. Here, if any error is committed through imprudence or forgetfulness, no crime is perpetrated; but if this is done from contempt, such contumacy must be disapproved. In like manner, it is of no consequence what the days and hours are, what the nature of the edifices, and what psalms are sung on each day. But it is proper that there should be certain days and stated hours, and a place fit for receiving all, if any regard is had to the preservation of peace. For what a seed-bed of quarrels will confusion in such matters be, if every one is allowed at pleasure to alter what pertains to common order? All will not be satisfied with the same course if matters, placed as it were on debateable ground, are left to the determination of individuals. But if any one here becomes clamorous, and would be wiser than he ought, let him consider how he will approve his moroseness to the Lord. Paul's answer ought to satisfy us, " If any man seem to be contentious, we have no such custom, neither the churches of God."

32. Moreover, we must use the utmost diligence to prevent any error from creeping in which may either taint or sully this pure use. In this we shall succeed, if whatever observances we use are manifestly useful, and very few in number; especially if to this is added the teaching of a faithful pastor, which may prevent access to erroneous opinions. The effect of this procedure is, that in all these matters each retains his freedom, and yet at the same time voluntarily subjects it to a kind of necessity, in so far as the *decency* of which we have spoken or charity demands. Next, that in the observance of these things we may not fall into any superstition, nor rigidly require too much from others, let us not imagine that the worship of God is improved by a multitude of ceremonies: let not church despise church because of a difference in external discipline. Lastly, instead of here laying down any perpetual law for ourselves, let us refer the whole end and use of observances to the edification of the Church, at whose request let us without offence allow not only something to be changed, but even observances which were formerly in use to be inverted. For the present age is a proof that the nature of times allows that certain rites, not otherwise impious or unbecoming, may be abrogated according to circumstances. Such was the ignorance and blindness of former times; with such erroneous ideas and pertinacious zeal did churches formerly cling to ceremonies, that they can scarcely be purified from monstrous superstitions without the removal of many ceremonies which were formerly established, not without cause, and which in themselves are not chargeable with any impiety.

CHAPTER XI.

OF THE JURISDICTION OF THE CHURCH, AND THE ABUSES OF IT, AS EXEMPLIFIED IN THE PAPACY.

This chapter may be conveniently comprehended under two heads,—I. Ecclesiastical jurisdiction, its necessity, origin, description, and essential parts—viz. the sacred ministry of the word, and discipline of excommunication, of which the aim, use, and abuse are explained, sec. 1–8. II. Refutation of the arguments advanced by Papists in defence of the tyranny of Pontiffs, the right of both swords, imperial pomp and dignity, foreign jurisdiction, and immunity from civil jurisdiction, sec. 9–16.

Sections.

1. IT remains to consider the third, and, indeed, when matters are well arranged, the principal part of ecclesiastical power, which, as we have said, consists in jurisdiction. Now, the whole jurisdiction of the Church relates to discipline, of which we are shortly to treat. For as no city or village can exist without a magistrate and government, so the Church of God, as I have already taught, but am again obliged to repeat, needs a kind of spiritual government. This is altogether

distinct from civil government, and is so far from impeding or impairing it, that it rather does much to aid and promote it.   Therefore, this power of jurisdiction is, in one word, nothing but the order provided for the preservation of spiritual polity.   To this end, there were established in the Church from the first, tribunals which might take cognisance of morals, animadvert on vices, and exercise the office of the keys.   This order is mentioned by Paul in the First Epistle to the Corinthians under the name of governments (1 Cor. xii. 28): in like manner, in the Epistle to the Romans, when he says, " He that ruleth with diligence" (Rom. xii. 8).   For he is not addressing magistrates, none of whom were then Christians, but those who were joined with pastors in the spiritual government of the Church.   In the Epistle to Timothy, also, he mentions two kinds of presbyters, some who labour in the word, and others who do not perform the office of preaching, but rule well (1 Tim. v. 17).   By this latter class there is no doubt he means those who were appointed to the inspection of manners, and the whole use of the keys.   For the power of which we speak wholly depends on the keys which Christ bestowed on the Church in the eighteenth chapter of Matthew, where he orders, that those who depise private admonition should be sharply rebuked in public, and if they persist in their contumacy, be expelled from the society of believers.   Moreover, those admonitions and corrections cannot be made without investigation, and hence the necessity of some judicial procedure and order.   Wherefore, if we would not make void the promise of the keys, and abolish altogether excommunication, solemn admonitions, and everything of that description, we must, of necessity, give some jurisdiction to the Church.   Let the reader observe that we are not here treating of the general authority of doctrine, as in Matth. xxi. and John xx., but maintaining that the right of the Sanhedrim is transferred to the fold of Christ.   Till that time, the power of government had belonged to the Jews.   This Christ establishes in his Church, in as far as it was a pure institution, and with a heavy sanction.   Thus it behoved to be, since the judgment of a poor and despised Church might otherwise be spurned by rash and haughty men.   And lest it occasion any difficulty to the reader, that Christ in the same words makes a considerable difference between the two things, it will here be proper to explain.   There are two passages which speak of binding and loosing.   The one is Matth. xvi., where Christ, after promising that he will give the keys of the kingdom of heaven to Peter, immediately adds, " Whatsoever thou shalt bind on earth shall be bound in heaven ; and whatsoever thou shalt loose on earth shall be loosed in heaven" (Matth. xvi. 19). These words have the very same meaning as those in the Gospel of John, where, being about to send forth the disciples to preach, after breathing on them, he says, " Whose soever sins ye remit, they are remitted unto them ; and whose soever sins ye retain, they are retained" (John xx. 23).   I will give an interpretation, not subtle, not forced, not wrested, but genuine, natural, and obvious.   This command concerning remitting and retaining sins, and that promise made to Peter concerning binding and loosing, ought to be referred to nothing but the ministry of the word. When the Lord committed it to the apostles, he, at the same time, provided them with this power of binding and loosing. For what is the sum of the gospel, but just that all being the slaves of sin and death, are loosed and set free by the redemption which is in Christ Jesus, while those who do not receive and acknowledge Christ as a deliverer and redeemer are condemned and doomed to eternal chains? When the Lord delivered this message to his apostles, to be carried by them into all nations, in order to prove that it was his own message, and proceeded from him, he honoured it with this distinguished testimony, and that as an admirable confirmation both to the apostles themselves, and to all those to whom it was to come. It was of importance that the apostles should have a constant and complete assurance of their preaching, which they were not only to exercise with infinite labour, anxiety, molestation, and peril, but ultimately to seal with their blood. That they might know that it was not vain or void, but full of power and efficacy, it was of importance, I say, that amidst all their anxieties, dangers, and difficulties, they might feel persuaded that they were doing the work of God; that though the whole world withstood and opposed them, they might know that God was for them; that not having Christ the author of their doctrine bodily present on the earth, they might understand that he was in heaven to confirm the truth of the doctrine which he had delivered to them. On the other hand, it was necessary that their hearers should be most certainly assured that the doctrine of the gospel was not the word of the apostles, but of God himself; not a voice rising from the earth, but descending from heaven. For such things as the forgiveness of sins, the promise of eternal life, and message of salvation, cannot be in the power of man. Christ therefore testified, that in the preaching of the gospel the apostles only acted ministerially; that it was he who, by their mouths as organs, spoke and promised all; that, therefore, the forgiveness of sins which they announced was the true promise of God; the condemnation which they pronounced, the certain judgment of God. This attestation was given to all ages, and remains firm, rendering all certain and secure, that the word of the gospel, by whomsoever it may be preached, is the very word of God, promulgated at the supreme tribunal, written in the book of life, ratified firm and fixed in heaven. We now understand that the power of the keys is simply the preaching of the gospel in those places, and in so far as men are concerned, it is not so much power as ministry. Properly speaking, Christ did not give this power to men but to his word, of which he made men the ministers.

2. The other passage, in which binding and loosing are mentioned, is in the eighteenth chapter of Matthew, where Christ says, " If he shall neglect to hear them, tell it unto the Church: but if he neglect to hear the Church, let him be unto thee as an heathen man and

a publican. Verily I say unto you, Whatsoever ye shall bind on earth shall be bound in heaven; and whatsoever ye shall loose on earth shall be loosed in heaven" (Matth. xviii. 17, 18). This passage is not altogether similar to the former, but is to be understood somewhat differently. But in saying that they are different, I do not mean that there is not much affinity between them. First, they are similar in this, that they are both general statements, that there is always the same power of binding and loosing (namely, by the word of God), the same command, the same promise. They differ in this, that the former passage relates specially to the preaching which the ministers of the word perform, the latter relates to the discipline of excommunication which has been committed to the Church. Now, the Church binds him whom she excommunicates, not by plunging him into eternal ruin and despair, but condemning his life and manners, and admonishing him, that, unless he repent, he is condemned. She looses him whom she receives into communion, because she makes him, as it were, a partaker of the unity which she has in Christ Jesus. Let no one, therefore, contumaciously despise the judgment of the Church, or account it a small matter that he is condemned by the suffrages of the faithful. The Lord testifies that such judgment of the faithful is nothing else than the promulgation of his own sentence, and that what they do on earth is ratified in heaven. For they have the word of God by which they condemn the perverse: they have the word by which they take back the penitent into favour. Now, they cannot err nor disagree with the judgment of God, because they judge only according to the law of God, which is not an uncertain or worldly opinion, but the holy will of God, an oracle of heaven. On these two passages, which I think I have briefly, as well as familiarly and truly expounded, these madmen, without any discrimination, as they are borne along by their spirit of giddiness, attempt to found at one time confession, at another excommunication, at another jurisdiction, at another the right of making laws, at another indulgences. The former passage they adduce for the purpose of rearing up the primacy of the Roman See. So well known are the keys to those who have thought proper to fit them with locks and doors, that you would say their whole life had been spent in the mechanic art.

3. Some, in imagining that all these things were temporary, as magistrates were still strangers to our profession of religion, are led astray, by not observing the distinction and dissimilarity between ecclesiastical and civil power. For the Church has not the right of the sword to punish or restrain, has no power to coerce, no prison nor other punishments which the magistrate is wont to inflict. Then the object in view is not to punish the sinner against his will, but to obtain a profession of penitence by voluntary chastisement. The two things, therefore, are widely different, because neither does the Church assume anything to herself which is proper to the magistrate, nor is the magistrate competent to what is done by the Church. This will

be made clearer by an example. Does any one get intoxicated. In a well-ordered city his punishment will be imprisonment. Has he committed whoredom? The punishment will be similar, or rather more severe. Thus satisfaction will be given to the laws, the magistrates, and the external tribunal. But the consequence will be, that the offender will give no signs of repentance, but will rather fret and murmur. Will the Church not here interfere? Such persons cannot be admitted to the Lord's Supper without doing injury to Christ and his sacred institution. Reason demands that he who, by a bad example, gives offence to the Church, shall remove the offence which he has caused by a formal declaration of repentance. The reason adduced by those who take a contrary view is frigid. Christ, they say, gave this office to the Church when there were no magistrates to execute it. But it often happens that the magistrate is negligent, nay, sometimes himself requires to be chastised; as was the case with the Emperor Theodosius. Moreover, the same thing may be said regarding the whole ministry of the word. Now, therefore, according to that view, let pastors cease to censure manifest iniquities, let them cease to chide, accuse, and rebuke. For there are Christian magistrates who ought to correct these things by the laws and the sword. But as the magistrate ought to purge the Church of offences by corporal punishment and coercion, so the minister ought, in his turn, to assist the magistrate in diminishing the number of offenders. Thus they ought to combine their efforts, the one being not an impediment but a help to the other.

4. And, indeed, on attending more closely to the words of Christ, it will readily appear that the state and order of the Church there described is perpetual, not temporary. For it were incongruous that those who refuse to obey our admonitions should be transferred to the magistrate—a course, however, which would be necessary if he were to succeed to the place of the Church. Why should the promise, "Verily I say unto you, What thing soever ye shall bind on earth," be limited to one, or to a few years? Moreover, Christ has here made no new enactment, but followed the custom always observed in the Church of his ancient people, thereby intimating, that the Church cannot dispense with the spiritual jurisdiction which existed from the beginning. This has been confirmed by the consent of all times. For when emperors and magistrates began to assume the Christian name, spiritual jurisdiction was not forthwith abolished, but was only so arranged as not in any respect to impair civil jurisdiction, or be confounded with it. And justly. For the magistrate, if he is pious, will have no wish to exempt himself from the common subjection of the children of God, not the least part of which is to subject himself to the Church, judging according to the word of God; so far is it from being his duty to abolish that judgment. For, as Ambrose says, "What more honourable title can an emperor have than to be called a son of the Church? A good emperor is within the Church, not above the Church" (Ambros. ad Valent. Ep. 32).

Those, therefore, who to adorn the magistrate strip the Church of this power, not only corrupt the sentiment of Christ by a false interpretation, but pass no light condemnation on the many holy bishops who have existed since the days of the apostles, for having on a false pretext usurped the honour and office of the civil magistrate.

5. But, on the other hand, it will be proper to see what was anciently the true use of ecclesiastical discipline, and how great the abuses which crept in, that we may know what of ancient practice is to be abolished, and what restored, if we would, after overthrowing the kingdom of Antichrist, again set up the true kingdom of Christ. First, the object in view is to prevent the occurrence of scandals, and when they arise, to remove them. In the use two things are to be considered: first, that this spiritual power be altogether distinct from the power of the sword; secondly, that it be not administered at the will of one individual, but by a lawful consistory (1 Cor. v. 4). Both were observed in the purer times of the Church. For holy bishops did not exercise their power by fine, imprisonment, or other civil penalties, but as became them, employed the word of God only. For the severest punishment of the Church, and, as it were, her last thunderbolt, is excommunication, which is not used unless in necessity.[1] This, moreover, requires neither violence nor physical force, but is contented with the might of the word of God. In short, the jurisdiction of the ancient Church was nothing else than (if I may so speak) a practical declaration of what Paul teaches concerning the spiritual power of pastors. " The weapons of our warfare are not carnal, but mighty through God to the pulling down of strongholds; casting down imaginations, and every high thing that exalteth itself against the knowledge of God, and bringing into captivity every thought to the obedience of Christ; and having in a readiness to revenge all disobedience" (2 Cor. x. 4–6). As this is done by the preaching of doctrine, so in order that doctrine may not be held in derision, those who profess to be of the household of faith ought to be judged according to the doctrine which is taught. Now this cannot be done without connecting with the office of the ministry a right of summoning those who are to be privately admonished or sharply rebuked, a right, moreover, of keeping back from the communion of the Lord's Supper, those who cannot be admitted without profaning this high ordinance. Hence, when Paul elsewhere asks, "What have I to do to judge them also that are without?" (1. Cor. v. 12), he makes the members of the Church subject to censures for the correction of their vices, and intimates the existence of tribunals from which no believer is exempted.

6. This power, as we have already stated, did not belong to an individual who could exercise it as he pleased, but belonged to the consistory of elders, which was in the Church what a council is in a

---

[1] There is nothing repugnant to this in the statement of Augustine (Ep. 119), that as the teachers of liberal arts and pursuits, so bishops also were often accustomed, in their judicial proceedings, to chastise with the rod.

city.   Cyprian, when mentioning those by whom it was exercised in
his time, usually associates the whole clergy with the bishop (Cyprian,
Lib. iii. Ep. 14, 19).   In another place, he shows that though the
clergy presided, the people, at the same time, were not excluded from
cognisance : for he thus writes :—" From the commencement of my
bishopric, I determined to do nothing without the advice of the clergy,
nothing without the consent of the people."   But the common and
usual method of exercising this jurisdiction was by the council of
presbyters, of whom, as I have said, there were two classes.   Some
were for teaching, others were only censors of manners.   This institution gradually degenerated from its primitive form, so that, in the
time of Ambrose, the clergy alone had cognisance of ecclesiastical
causes.   Of this he complains in the following terms :—"The ancient
synagogue, and afterwards the Church, had elders, without whose
advice nothing was done : this has grown obsolete, by whose fault I
know not, unless it be by the sloth, or rather the pride, of teachers,
who would have it seem that they only are somewhat" (Ambros. in
1 Tim. v.).   We see how indignant this holy man was because the
better state was in some degree impaired, and yet the order which
then existed was at least tolerable.   What, then, had he seen those
shapeless ruins which exhibit no trace of the ancient edifice ?   How
would he have lamented ?   First, contrary to what was right and
lawful, the bishop appropriated to himself what was given to the
whole Church.   For this is just as if the consul had expelled the
senate, and usurped the whole empire.   For as he is superior in rank
to the others, so the authority of the consistory is greater than that
of one individual.   It was, therefore, a gross iniquity, when one man,
transferring the common power to himself, paved the way for tyrannical licence, robbed the Church of what was its own, suppressed and
discarded the consistory ordained by the Spirit of Christ.

7. But as evil always produces evil, the bishops, disdaining this
jurisdiction as a thing unworthy of their care, devolved it on others.
Hence the appointment of officials to supply their place.   I am not
now speaking of the character of this class of persons; all I say is,
that they differ in no respect from civil judges.   And yet they call it
spiritual jurisdiction, though all the litigation relates to worldly affairs.
Were there no other evil in this, how can they presume to call a
litigious forum a church court ?   But there are admonitions ; there is
excommunication.   This is the way in which God is mocked.   Does
some poor man owe a sum of money ?   He is summoned: if he
appears, he is found liable ; when found liable, if he pays not, he is
admonished.   After the second admonition, the next step is excommunication.   If he appears not, he is admonished to appear ; if he
delays, he is admonished, and by-and-by excommunicated.   I ask,
is there any resemblance whatever between this and the institution
of Christ, or ancient custom or ecclesiastical procedure ?   But there,
too, vices are censured.   Whoredom, lasciviousness, drunkenness, and
similar iniquities, they not only tolerate, but by a kind of tacit ap-

probation encourage and confirm, and that not among the people only, but also among the clergy. Out of many they summon a few, either that they may not seem to wink too strongly, or that they may mulct them in money. I say nothing of the plunder, rapine, peculation, and sacrilege, which are there committed. I say nothing of the kind of persons who are for the most part appointed to the office. It is enough, and more than enough, that when the Romanists boast of their spiritual jurisdiction, we are ready to show that nothing is more contrary to the procedure instituted by Christ, that it has no more resemblance to ancient practice than darkness has to light.

8. Although we have not said all that might here be adduced, and even what has been said is only briefly glanced at, enough, I trust, has been said to leave no man in doubt that the spiritual power on which the Pope plumes himself, with all his adherents, is impious contradiction of the word of God, and unjust tyranny against his people. Under the name of spiritual power, I include both their audacity in framing new doctrines, by which they led the miserable people away from the genuine purity of the word of God, the iniquitous traditions by which they ensnared them, and the pseudo-ecclesiastical jurisdiction which they exercise by suffragans and officials. For if we allow Christ to reign amongst us, the whole of that domination cannot but immediately tumble and fall. The right of the sword which they also claim for themselves, not being exercised against consciences, does not fall to be considered in this place. Here, however, it is worth while to observe, that they are always like themselves, there being nothing which they less resemble than that which they would be thought to be—viz. pastors of the Church. I speak not of the vices of particular men, but of the common wickedness, and, consequently, the pestiferous nature of the whole order, which is thought to be mutilated if not distinguished by wealth and haughty titles. If in this matter we seek the authority of Christ, there can be no doubt that he intended to debar the ministers of his word from civil domination and worldly power when he said, "The princes of the Gentiles exercise dominion over them, and they that are great exercise authority upon them. But it shall not be so among you" (Matth. xx. 25, 26). For he intimates not only that the office of pastor is distinct from the office of prince, but that the things differ so widely that they cannot be united in the same individual. Moses indeed held both (Exod. xviii. 16); but, first, this was the effect of a rare miracle; and, secondly, it was temporary, until matters should be better arranged. For when a certain form is prescribed by the Lord, the civil government is left to Moses, and he is ordered to resign the priesthood to his brother. And justly; for it is more than nature can do, for one man to bear both burdens. This has in all ages been carefully observed in the Church. Never did any bishop, so long as any true appearance of a church remained, think of usurping the right of the sword: so that, in the age of Am-

brose, it was a common proverb, that emperors longed more for the priesthood than priests for imperial power.[1] For the expression which he afterwards adds was fixed in all minds, Palaces belong to the emperor, churches to the priest.

9. But after a method was devised by which bishops might hold the title, honour, and wealth of their office without burden and solicitude, that they might be left altogether idle, the right of the sword was given them, or rather, they themselves usurped it. With what pretext will they defend this effrontery? Was it the part of bishops to entangle themselves with the cognisance of causes, and the administration of states and provinces, and embrace occupations so very alien to them—of bishops, who require so much time and labour in their own office, that though they devote themselves to it diligently and entirely, without distraction from other avocations, they are scarcely sufficient? But such is their perverseness, that they hesitate not to boast that in this way the dignity of Christ's kingdom is duly maintained, and they, at the same time, are not withdrawn from their own vocation. In regard to the former allegation, if it is a comely ornament of the sacred office, that those holding it be so elevated as to become formidable to the greatest monarchs, they have ground to expostulate with Christ, who in this respect has grievously curtailed their honour. For what, according to their view, can be more insulting than these words, "The kings of the Gentiles exercise authority over them"? "But ye shall not be so" (Luke xxii. 25, 26). And yet he imposes no harder law on his servants than he had previously laid on himself. "Who," says he, "made me a judge or divider over you?" (Luke xii. 14.) We see that he unreservedly refuses the office of judging; and this he would not have done if the thing had been in accordance with his office. To the subordination to which the Lord thus reduced himself, will his servants not submit? The other point I wish they would prove by experience as easily as they allege it. But as it seemed to the apostles not good to leave the word of God and serve tables, so these men are thereby forced to admit, though they are unwilling to be taught, that it is not possible for the same person to be a good bishop and a good prince. For if those who, in respect of the largeness of the gifts with which they were endued, were able for much more numerous and weighty cares than any who have come after them, confessed that they could not serve the ministry of the word and of tables, without giving way under the burden, how are these, who are no men at all when compared with the apostles, possibly to surpass them a hundred times in diligence? The very attempt is most impudent and audacious presumption. Still we see the thing done; with what success is plain. The result could not but be that they have deserted their own functions, and removed to another camp.

10. There can be no doubt that this great progress has been made

[1] This is stated by Ambrose, Hom. de Basilic. Tradend. See also August. De Fide et Operibus, cap. 4.

from slender beginnings. They could not reach so far at one step, but at one time by craft and wily art, secretly raised themselves before any one foresaw what was to happen; at another time, when occasion offered, by means of threats and terror, extorted some increase of power from princes; at another time, when they saw princes disposed to give liberally, they abused their foolish and inconsiderate facility. The godly in ancient times, when any dispute arose, in order to escape the necessity of a lawsuit, left the decision to the bishop, because they had no doubt of his integrity. The ancient bishops were often greatly dissatisfied at being entangled in such matters, as Augustine somewhere declares; but lest the parties should rush to some contentious tribunal, unwillingly submitted to the annoyance. These voluntary decisions, which altogether differed from forensic strife, these men have converted into ordinary jurisdiction. As cities and districts, when for some time pressed with various difficulties, betook themselves to the patronage of the bishops, and threw themselves on their protection, these men have, by a strange artifice, out of patrons made themselves masters. That they have seized a good part by the violence of faction cannot be denied. The princes, again, who spontaneously conferred jurisdiction on bishops, were induced to it by various causes. Though their indulgence had some appearance of piety, they did not by this preposterous liberality consult in the best manner for the interests of the Church, whose ancient and true discipline they thus corrupted, nay, to tell the truth, completely abolished. Those bishops who abuse the goodness of princes to their own advantage, gave more than sufficient proof by this one specimen of their conduct, that they were not at all true bishops. Had they had one spark of the apostolic spirit, they would doubtless have answered in the words of Paul, "The weapons of our warfare are not carnal," but spiritual (2 Cor. x. 4). But hurried away by blind cupidity, they lost themselves, and posterity, and the Church.

11. At length the Roman Pontiff, not content with moderate districts, laid hands first on kingdoms, and thereafter on empire. And that he may on some pretext or other retain possession, secured by mere robbery, he boasts at one time that he holds it by divine right, at another, he pretends a donation from Constantine, at another, some different title. First, I answer with Bernard, "Be it that on some ground or other he can claim it, it is not by apostolic right. For Peter could not give what he had not, but what he had he gave to his successors—viz. care of the churches. But when our Lord and Master says that he was not appointed a judge between two, the servant and disciple ought not to think it unbecoming not to be judge of all" (Bernard. de Considerat. Lib. ii.). Bernard is speaking of civil judgments, for he adds, "Your power then is in sins, not in rights of property, since for the former and not the latter you received the keys of the kingdom of heaven. Which of the two seems to you the higher dignity, the forgiving of sins or the dividing of lands? There is no comparison. These low earthly things have for

their judges the kings and princes of the earth. Why do you invade the territories of others?" &c. Again, "You are made superior" (he is addressing Pope Eugenius), "for what? not to domineer, I presume. Let us therefore remember, however highly we think of ourselves, that a ministry is laid upon us, not a dominion given to us. Learn that you have need of a slender rod, not of a sceptre, to do the work of a prophet." Again, "It is plain that the apostles are prohibited to exercise dominion. Go you, therefore, and dare to usurp for yourself, either apostleship with dominion, or dominion with apostleship." Immediately after he says, "The apostolic form is this; dominion is interdicted, ministry is enjoined." Though Bernard speaks thus, and so speaks as to make it manifest to all that he speaks truth, nay, though without a word the thing itself is manifest, the Roman Pontiff was not ashamed at the Council of Arles to decree that the supreme right of both swords belonged to him of divine right.

12. As far as pertains to the donation of Constantine, those who are moderately versant in the history of the time have no need of being told, that the claim is not only fabulous but also absurd. But to say nothing of history, Gregory alone is a fit and most complete witness to this effect. For wherever he speaks of the emperor he calls him His Most Serene Lord, and himself his unworthy servant.[1] Again, in another passage he says, " Let not our Lord in respect of worldly power be too soon offended with priests, but with excellent consideration, on account of him whose servants they are, let him while ruling them also pay them due reverence." We see how in a common subjection he desires to be accounted one of the people. For he there pleads not another's but his own cause. Again, "I trust in Almighty God that he will give long life to pious rulers, and place us under your hand according to his mercy." I have not adduced these things here from any intention thoroughly to discuss the question of Constantine's donation, but only to show my readers by the way, how childishly the Romanists tell lies when they attempt to claim an earthly empire for their Pontiff. The more vile the impudence of Augustine Steuchus, who, in so desperate a cause, presumed to lend his labour and his tongue to the Roman Pontiff. Valla, as was easy for a man of learning and acuteness to do, had completely refuted this fable. And yet, as he was little versant in ecclesiastical affairs, he had not said all that was relevant to the subject. Steuchus breaks in, and scatters his worthless quibbles, trying to bury the clear light. And certainly he pleads the cause of his master not less frigidly than some wit might, under pretence of defending the same view, support that of Valla. But the cause is a worthy one, which the Pope may well hire such patrons to defend; equally worthy are the hired ravers whom the hope of gain may deceive, as was the case with Eugubinus.

13. Should any one ask at what period this fictitious empire began to emerge, five hundred years have not yet elasped since the Roman

1 Gregor. Lib. ii. Ep. 5; Lib. iii. Ep. 20; Lib. ii. Ep. 61; Lib. iv. Ep. 31, 34.

Pontiffs were under subjection to the emperors, and no pontiff was elected without the emperor's authority. An occasion of innovating on this order was given to Gregory VII. by Henry IV., a giddy and rash man, of no prudence, great audacity, and a dissolute life. When he had the whole bishoprics of Germany in his court partly for sale, and partly exposed to plunder, Hildebrand, who had been provoked by him, seized the plausible pretext for asserting his claim. As his cause seemed good and pious, it was viewed with great favour, while Henry, on account of the insolence of his government, was generally hated by the princes. At length Hildebrand, who took the name of Gregory VII., an impure and wicked man, betrayed his sinister intentions. On this he was deserted by many who had joined him in his conspiracy. He gained this much, however, that his successors were not only able to shake off the yoke with impunity, but also to bring the emperors into subjection to them. Moreover, many of the subsequent emperors were liker Henry than Julius Cæsar. These it was not difficult to overcome while they sat at home sluggish and secure, instead of vigorously exerting themselves, as was most necessary, by all legitimate means to repress the cupidity of the pontiffs. We see what colour there is for the grand donation of Constantine, by which the Pope pretends that the western empire was given to him.

14. Meanwhile the pontiff ceased not, either by fraud, or by perfidy, or by arms, to invade the dominions of others. Rome itself, which was then free, they, about a hundred and thirty years ago, reduced under their power. At length they obtained the dominion which they now possess, and to retain or increase which, now for two hundred years (they had begun before they usurped the dominion of the city) they have so troubled the Christian world that they have almost destroyed it. Formerly, when in the time of Gregory, the guardians of ecclesiastical property seized upon lands which they considered to belong to the Church, and, after the manner of the exchequer, affixed their seals in attestation of their claim, Gregory having assembled a council of bishops, and bitterly inveighed against that profane custom, asked whether they would not anathematise the churchman who, of his own accord, attempted to seize some possession by the inscription of a title, and in like manner, the bishop who should order it to be done, or not punish it when done without his order. All pronounced the anathema. If it is a crime deserving of anathema for a churchman to claim a property by the inscription of a title— then, now that for two hundred years, the pontiffs meditate nothing but war and bloodshed, the destruction of armies, the plunder of cities, the destruction or overthrow of nations, and the devastation of kingdoms, only that they may obtain possession of the property of others — what anathemas can sufficiently punish such conduct? Surely it is perfectly obvious that the very last thing they aim at is the glory of Christ. For were they spontaneously to resign every

portion of secular power which they possess, no peril to the glory of
God, no peril to sound doctrine, no peril to the safety of the Church
ensues ; but they are borne blind and headlong by a lust for power,
thinking that nothing can be safe unless they rule, as the prophet
says, " with force and with cruelty " (Ezek. xxxiv. 4).

15. To jurisdiction is annexed the immunity claimed by the
Romish clergy. They deem it unworthy of them to answer before a
civil judge in personal causes ; and consider both the liberty and
dignity of the Church to consist in exemption from ordinary tribunals and laws. But the ancient bishops, who otherwise were most
resolute in asserting the rights of the Church, did not think it any
injury to themselves and their order to act as subjects. Pious emperors also, as often as there was occasion, summoned clergy to their
tribunals, and met with no opposition. For Constantine, in a letter
to the Nicomedians, thus speaks :—" Should any of the bishops unadvisedly excite tumult, his audacity shall be restrained by the minister
of God, that is, by my executive " (Theodoret. Lib. i. c. 20). Valentinian says, " Good bishops throw no obloquy on the power of the
emperor, but sincerely keep the commandments of God, the great
King, and obey our laws " (Theodoret. Lib. iv. c. 8). This was unquestionably the view then entertained by all. Ecclesiastical causes,
indeed, were brought before the episcopal court; as when a clergyman had offended, but not against the laws, he was only charged by
the Canons ; and instead of being cited before the civil court, had
the bishop for his judge in that particular case. In like manner,
when a question of faith was agitated, or one which properly pertained to the Church, cognisance was left to the Church. In this
sense the words of Ambrose are to be understood : " Your father, of
august memory, not only replied verbally, but enacted by law, that,
in a question of faith, the judge should be one who was neither unequal from office, nor incompetent from the nature of his jurisdiction "
(Ambros. Ep. 32). Again, " If we attend to the Scriptures, or to
ancient examples, who can deny that in a question of faith, a question
of faith, I say, bishops are wont to judge Christian emperors, not
emperors to judge bishops?" Again, " I would have come before
your consistory, O emperor, would either the bishops or the people
have allowed me to come : they say that a question of faith should
be discussed in the Church before the people." He maintains, indeed, that a spiritual cause, that is, one pertaining to religion, is
not to be brought before the civil court, where worldly disputes are
agitated. His firmness in this respect is justly praised by all. And
yet, though he has a good cause, he goes so far as to say, that if it
comes to force and violence, he will yield. " I will not desert the
post committed to me, but, if forced, I will not resist: prayers and
tears are our weapons" (Ambros. Hom. de Basilic. Traden.). Let us
observe the singular moderation of this holy man, his combination of
prudence, magnanimity, and boldness. Justina, the mother of the
emperor, unable to bring him over to the Arian party, sought to

drive him from the government of the Church.   And this would have been the result had he, when summoned, gone to the palace to plead his cause.   He maintains, therefore, that the emperor is not fit to decide such a controversy.   This both the necessity of the times, and the very nature of the thing, demanded.   He thought it were better for him to die than consent to transmit such an example to posterity ; and yet if violence is offered, he thinks not of resisting. For he says, it is not the part of a bishop to defend the faith and rights of the Church by arms.   But in all other causes he declares himself ready to do whatever the emperor commands.   " If he asks tribute, we deny it not: the lands of the Church pay tribute.   If he asks lands, he has the power of evicting them; none of us interposes." Gregory speaks in the same manner.   " I am not ignorant of the mind of my most serene lord: he is not wont to interfere in sacerdotal causes, lest he may in some degree burden himself with our sins."   He does not exclude the emperor generally from judging priests, but says that there are certain causes which he ought to leave to the ecclesiastical tribunal.

16. And hence all that these holy men sought by this exception was, to prevent irreligious princes from impeding the Church in the discharge of her duty, by their tyrannical caprice and violence.   They did not disapprove when princes interposed their authority in ecclesiastical affairs, provided this was done to preserve, not to disturb, the order of the Church, to establish, not to destroy discipline.   For, seeing the Church has not, and ought not to wish to have, the power of compulsion (I speak of civil coercion), it is the part of pious kings and princes to maintain religion by laws, edicts, and sentences.   In this way, when the emperor Maurice had commanded certain bishops to receive their neighbouring colleagues, who had been expelled by the Barbarians, Gregory confirms the order, and exhorts them to obey.[1] He himself, when admonished by the same emperor to return to a good understanding with John, Bishop of Constantinople, endeavours to show that he is not to be blamed ; but so far from boasting of immunity from the secular forum, rather promises to comply as far as conscience would permit: he at the same time says, that Maurice had acted as became a religious prince, in giving these commands to priests.

[1] Lib. i. Ep. 43; Lib. iv. Ep. 32, 34; Lib. vii. Ep. 39.

CHAPTER XII.

OF THE DISCIPLINE OF THE CHURCH, AND ITS PRINCIPAL USE IN CENSURES AND EXCOMMUNICATION.

This chapter consists of two parts :—I. The first part of ecclesiastical discipline, which respects the people, and is called common, consists of two parts, the former depending on the power of the keys, which is considered, sec. 1-14; the latter consisting in the appointment of times for fasting and prayer, sec. 14-21. II. The second part of ecclesiastical discipline relating to the clergy, sec. 22-28.

Sections.

1. Of the power of the keys, or the common discipline of the Church. Necessity and very great utility of this discipline.
2. Its various degrees. 1. Private admonition. 2. Rebukes before witnesses. 3. Excommunication.
3. Different degrees of delinquency. Modes of procedure in both kinds of chastisement.
4. Delicts to be distinguished from flagitious wickedness. The last to be more severely punished.
5. Ends of this discipline. 1. That the wicked may not, by being admitted to the Lord's Table, put insult on Christ. 2. That they may not corrupt others. 3. That they themselves may repent.
6. In what way sins public as well as secret are to be corrected. Trivial and grave offences.
7. No person, not even the sovereign, exempted from this discipline. By whom and in what way it ought to be exercised.
8. In what spirit discipline is to be exercised. In what respect some of the ancient Christians exercised it too rigorously. This done more from custom than in accordance with their own sentiments. This shown from Cyprian, Chrysostom, and Augustine.
9. Moderation to be used, not only by the whole Church, but by each individual member.
10. Our Saviour's words concerning binding and loosing wrested if otherwise understood. Difference between anathema and excommunication. Anathema rarely if ever to be used.
11. Excessive rigour to be avoided, as well by private individuals as by pastors.
12. In this respect the Donatists erred most grievously, as do also the Anabaptists in the present day. Portraiture by Augustine.
13. Moderation especially to be used when not a few individuals, but the great body of the people, have gone astray.
14. A second part of common discipline relating to fastings, prayer, and other holy exercises. These used by believers under both dispensations. To what purposes applied. Of Fasting.
15. Three ends of fasting. The first refers more especially to private fasting. Second and third ends.
16. Public fasting and prayer appointed by pastors on any great emergency.
17. Examples of this under the Law.
18. Fasting consists chiefly in three things—viz. time, the quality, and sparing use of food.
19. To prevent superstition, three things to be inculcated. 1. The heart to be rent, not the garments. 2. Fasting not to be regarded as a meritorious work or kind of divine worship. 3. Abstinence must not be immoderately extolled.
20. Owing to an excess of this kind the observance of Lent was established. This superstitious observance refuted by three arguments. It was indeed used by the ancients, but on different grounds.

1. THE discipline of the Church, the consideration of which has been deferred till now, must be briefly explained, that we may be able to pass to other matters. Now discipline depends in a very great measure on the power of the keys and on spiritual jurisdiction. That this may be more easily understood, let us divide the Church into two principal classes—viz. clergy and people. The term clergy I use in the common acceptation for those who perform a public ministry in the Church.[1] We shall speak first of the common discipline to which all ought to be subject, and then proceed to the clergy, who have besides that common discipline one peculiar to themselves. But as some, from hatred of discipline, are averse to the very name, for their sake we observe,—If no society, nay, no house with even a moderate family, can be kept in a right state without discipline, much more necessary is it in the Church, whose state ought to be the best ordered possible. Hence as the saving doctrine of Christ is the life of the Church, so discipline is, as it were, its sinews; for to it it is owing that the members of the body adhere together, each in its own place. Wherefore, all who either wish that discipline were abolished, or who impede the restoration of it, whether they do this of design or through thoughtlessness, certainly aim at the complete devastation of the Church. For what will be the result if every one is allowed to do as he pleases? But this must happen if to the preaching of the gospel are not added private admonition, correction, and similar methods of maintaining doctrine, and not allowing it to become lethargic. Discipline, therefore, is a kind of curb to restrain and tame those who war against the doctrine of Christ, or it is a kind of stimulus by which the indifferent are aroused; sometimes, also, it is a kind of fatherly rod, by which those who have made some more grievous lapse are chastised in mercy with the meekness of the spirit of Christ. Since, then, we already see some beginnings of a fearful devastation in the Church from the total want of care and method in managing the people, necessity itself cries

---

1 French, " J'use de ce mot de Clercs pource qu'il est commun, combien qu'il soit impropre; par lequel j'entens ceux qui ont office et ministere en l'Eglise."—I use this word Clergy because it is common, though it is improper; by it I mean those who have an office and ministry in the Church.

aloud that there is need of a remedy. Now the only remedy is this which Christ enjoins, and the pious have always had in use.

2. The first foundation of discipline is to provide for private admonition; that is, if any one does not do his duty spontaneously, or behaves insolently, or lives not quite honestly, or commits something worthy of blame, he must allow himself to be admonished; and every one must study to admonish his brother when the case requires. Here especially is there occasion for the vigilance of pastors and presbyters, whose duty is not only to preach to the people, but to exhort and admonish from house to house, whenever their hearers have not profited sufficiently by general teaching; as Paul shows, when he relates that he taught "publicly, and from house to house," and testifies that he is "pure from the blood of all men," because he had not shunned to declare "all the counsel of God" (Acts xx. 20, 26, 27.) Then does doctrine obtain force and authority, not only when the minister publicly expounds to all what they owe to Christ, but has the right and means of exacting this from those whom he may observe to be sluggish or disobedient to his doctrine. Should any one either perversely reject such admonitions, or by persisting in his faults, show that he contemns them, the injunction of Christ is, that after he has been a second time admonished before witnesses, he is to be summoned to the bar of the Church, which is the consistory of elders, and there admonished more sharply, as by public authority, that if he reverence the Church he may submit and obey (Matth. xviii. 15, 17). If even in this way he is not subdued, but persists in his iniquity, he is then, as a despiser of the Church, to be debarred from the society of believers.

3. But as our Saviour is not there speaking of secret faults merely, we must attend to the distinction that some sins are private, others public or openly manifest. Of the former, Christ says to every private individual, "go and tell him his fault between thee and him alone" (Matth. xviii. 15). Of open sins Paul says to Timothy, "Those that sin rebuke before all, that others also may fear" (1 Tim. v. 20). Our Saviour had previously used the words, "If thy brother shall trespass against thee." This clause, unless you would be captious, you cannot understand otherwise than, If this happens *in a manner known to yourself*, others not being privy to it. The injunction which Paul gave to Timothy to rebuke those openly who sin openly, he himself followed with Peter (Gal. ii. 14). For when Peter sinned so as to give public offence, he did not admonish him apart, but brought him forward in face of the Church. The legitimate course, therefore, will be to proceed in correcting secret faults by the steps mentioned by Christ, and in open sins, accompanied with public scandal, to proceed at once to solemn correction by the Church.

4. Another distinction to be attended to is, that some sins are mere delinquencies, others crimes and flagrant iniquities. In correcting the latter, it is necessary to employ not only admonition or

rebuke, but a sharper remedy, as Paul shows when he not only verbally rebukes the incestuous Corinthian, but punishes him with excommunication, as soon as he was informed of his crime (1 Cor. v. 4). Now then we begin better to perceive how the spiritual jurisdiction of the Church, which animadverts on sins according to the word of the Lord, is at once the best help to sound doctrine, the best foundation of order, and the best bond of unity. Therefore, when the Church banishes from its fellowship open adulterers, fornicators, thieves, robbers, the seditious, the perjured, false witnesses, and others of that description; likewise the contumacious, who, when duly admonished for lighter faults, hold God and his tribunal in derision, instead of arrogating to itself anything that is unreasonable, it exercises a jurisdiction which it has received from the Lord. Moreover, lest any one should despise the judgment of the Church, or count it a small matter to be condemned by the suffrages of the faithful, the Lord has declared that it is nothing else than the promulgation of his own sentence, and that that which they do on earth is ratified in heaven. For they act by the word of the Lord in condemning the perverse, and by the word of the Lord in taking the penitent back into favour (John xx. 23). Those, I say, who trust that churches can long stand without this bond of discipline are mistaken, unless, indeed, we can with impunity dispense with a help which the Lord foresaw would be necessary. And, indeed, the greatness of the necessity will be better perceived by its manifold uses.

5. There are three ends to which the Church has respect in thus correcting and excommunicating. The first is, that God may not be insulted by the name of Christians being given to those who lead shameful and flagitious lives, as if his holy Church were a combination of the wicked and abandoned. For seeing that the Church is the body of Christ, she cannot be defiled by such fetid and putrid members, without bringing some disgrace on her Head. Therefore, that there may be nothing in the Church to bring disgrace on his sacred name, those whose turpitude might throw infamy on the name must be expelled from his family. And here, also, regard must be had to the Lord's Supper, which might be profaned by a promiscuous admission.[1] For it is most true, that he who is intrusted with the dispensation of it, if he knowingly and willingly admits any unworthy person whom he ought and is able to repel, is as guilty of sacrilege as if he had cast the Lord's body to dogs. Wherefore, Chrysostom bitterly inveighs against priests, who, from fear of the great, dare not keep any one back. " Blood (says he, Hom. 83, in Matth.) will be required at your hands. If you fear man, he will mock you, but if you fear God, you will be respected also by men. Let us not tremble at fasces, purple, or diadems; our power here is greater. Assuredly I will sooner give up my body to death, and allow my blood to be shed, than be a partaker of that pollution." Therefore, lest this most sacred mystery should be exposed to ignominy, great selection is

1 Vide Cyril in Joann. cap. 50, et Luther, de Commun. Populi, tom. ii.

required in dispensing it, and this cannot be except by the jurisdiction of the Church. A second end of discipline is, that the good may not, as usually happens, be corrupted by constant communication with the wicked. For such is our proneness to go astray, that nothing is easier than to seduce us from the right course by bad example. To this use of discipline the apostle referred when he commanded the Corinthians to discard the incestuous man from their society. "A little leaven leaveneth the whole lump" (1 Cor. v. 6.) And so much danger did he foresee here, that he prohibited them from keeping company with such persons. "If any man that is called a brother be a fornicator, or covetous, or an idolater, or a railer, or a drunkard, or an extortioner; with such an one, no not to eat" (1 Cor. v. 11). A third end of discipline is, that the sinner may be ashamed, and begin to repent of his turpitude. Hence it is for their interest also that their iniquity should be chastised, that whereas they would have become more obstinate by indulgence, they may be aroused by the rod. This the apostle intimates when he thus writes —"If any man obey not our word by this epistle, note that man, and have no company with him, that he may be ashamed" (2 Thess. iii. 14). Again, when he says that he had delivered the Corinthian to Satan, "that the spirit may be saved in the day of the Lord Jesus" (1 Cor. v. 5); that is, as I interpret it, he gave him over to temporal condemnation, that he might be made safe for eternity. And he says that he gave him over to Satan because the devil is without the Church, as Christ is in the Church. Some interpret this of a certain infliction on the flesh, but this interpretation seems to me most improbable. (August. de Verb. Apostol. Serm. 68.)

6. These being the ends proposed, it remains to see in what way the Church is to execute this part of discipline, which consists in jurisdiction. And, first, let us remember the division above laid down, that some sins are public, others private or secret. Public are those which are done not before one or two witnesses, but openly, and to the offence of the whole Church. By secret, I mean not such as are altogether concealed from men, such as those of hypocrites (for these fall not under the judgment of the Church), but those of an intermediate description, which are not without witnesses, and yet are not public. The former class requires not the different steps which Christ enumerates; but whenever anything of the kind occurs, the Church ought to do her duty by summoning the offender, and correcting him according to his fault. In the second class, the matter comes not before the Church, unless there is contumacy, according to the rule of Christ. In taking cognisance of offences, it is necessary to attend to the distinction between delinquencies and flagrant iniquities. In lighter offences there is not so much occasion for severity, but verbal chastisement is sufficient, and that gentle and fatherly, so as not to exasperate or confound the offender, but to bring him back to himself, so that he may rather rejoice than be grieved at the correction. Flagrant iniquities require a sharper

remedy.   It is not sufficient verbally to rebuke him who, by some open act of evil example, has grievously offended the Church; but he ought for a time to be denied the communion of the Supper, until he gives proof of repentance.   Paul does not merely administer a verbal rebuke to the Corinthian, but discards him from the Church, and reprimands the Corinthians for having borne with him so long (1 Cor. v. 5).   This was the method observed by the ancient and purer Church, when legitimate government was in vigour.   When any one was guilty of some flagrant iniquity, and thereby caused scandal, he was first ordered to abstain from participation in the sacred Supper, and thereafter to humble himself before God, and testify his penitence before the Church.   There were, moreover, solemn rites, which, as indications of repentance, were wont to be prescribed to those who had lapsed.   When the penitent had thus made satisfaction to the Church, he was received into favour by the laying on of hands.   This admission often receives the name of *peace* from Cyprian, who briefly describes the form.[1]   " They act as penitents for a certain time, next they come to confession, and receive the right of communion by the laying on of hands of the bishop and clergy."   Although the bishop with the clergy thus superintended the restoration of the penitent, the consent of the people was at the same time required, as he elsewhere explains.

7. So far was any one from being exempted from this discipline, that even princes submitted to it in common with their subjects; and justly, since it is the discipline of Christ, to whom all sceptres and diadems should be subject.   Thus Theodosius,[2] when excommunicated by Ambrose, because of the slaughter perpetrated at Thessalonica, laid aside all the royal insignia with which he was surrounded, and publicly in the Church bewailed the sin into which he had been betrayed by the fraud of others, with groans and tears imploring pardon.   Great kings should not think it a disgrace to them to prostrate themselves suppliantly before Christ, the King of kings; nor ought they to be displeased at being judged by the Church.   For seeing they seldom hear anything in their courts but mere flattery, the more necessary is it that the Lord should correct them by the mouth of his priests.   Nay, they ought rather to wish the priests not to spare them, in order that the Lord may spare.   I here say nothing as to those by whom the jurisdiction ought to be exercised, because it has been said elsewhere (Chap. xi. sec. 5, 6).   I only add, that the legitimate course to be taken in excommunication, as shown by Paul, is not for the elders alone to act apart from others, but with the knowledge and approbation of the Church, so that the body of the people, without regulating the procedure, may, as witnesses and guardians, observe it, and prevent the few from doing anything capriciously.   Throughout the whole procedure, in addition to invocation of the name of God, there should be a gravity bespeaking the pre-

---

1 Cyprian, Lib. i. Ep. 2; Lib. iii. Ep. 14, 26.
2 Ambros. Lib. i. Ep. 3; et Oratio habita in Funere Theodosii.

sence of Christ, and leaving no room to doubt that he is presiding over his own tribunal.

8. It ought not, however, to be omitted, that the Church, in exercising severity, ought to accompany it with the spirit of meekness. For, as Paul enjoins, we must always take care that he on whom discipline is exercised be not "swallowed up with overmuch sorrow" (2 Cor. ii. 7): for in this way, instead of cure there would be destruction. The rule of moderation will be best obtained from the end contemplated. For the object of excommunication being to bring the sinner to repentance and remove bad examples, in order that the name of Christ may not be evil spoken of, nor others tempted to the same evil courses: if we consider this, we shall easily understand how far severity should be carried, and at what point it ought to cease. Therefore, when the sinner gives the Church evidence of his repentance, and by this evidence does what in him lies to obliterate the offence, he ought not on any account to be urged farther. If he is urged, the rigour now exceeds due measure. In this respect it is impossible to excuse the excessive austerity of the ancients, which was altogether at variance with the injunction of our Lord, and strangely perilous. For when they enjoined a formal repentance, and excluded from communion for three, or four, or seven years, or for life, what could the result be, but either great hypocrisy or very great despair? In like manner, when any one who had again lapsed was not admitted to a second repentance, but ejected from the Church, to the end of his life (August. Ep. 54), this was neither useful nor agreeable to reason. Whosoever, therefore, looks at the matter with sound judgment, will here regret a want of prudence. Here, however, I rather disapprove of the public custom, than blame those who complied with it. Some of them certainly disapproved of it, but submitted to what they were unable to correct. Cyprian, indeed, declares that it was not with his own will he was thus rigorous. "Our patience, facility, and humanity (he says, Lib. i. Ep. 3), are ready to all who come. I wish all to be brought back into the Church: I wish all our fellow-soldiers to be contained within the camp of Christ and the mansions of God the Father. I forgive all; I disguise much; from an earnest desire of collecting the brotherhood, I do not minutely scrutinise all the faults which have been committed against God. I myself often err, by forgiving offences more than I ought. Those returning in repentance, and those confessing their sins with simple and humble satisfaction, I embrace with prompt and full delight." Chrysostom, who is somewhat more severe, still speaks thus: "If God is so kind, why should his priest wish to appear austere?" We know, moreover, how indulgently Augustine treated the Donatists; not hesitating to admit any who returned from schism to their bishopric, as soon as they declared their repentance. But, as a contrary method had prevailed, they were compelled to follow it, and give up their own judgment.

9. But as the whole body of the Church are required to act thus

mildly, and not to carry their rigour against those who have lapsed to an extreme, but rather to act charitably towards them, according to the precept of Paul, so every private individual ought proportionately to accommodate himself to this clemency and humanity. Such as have, therefore, been expelled from the Church, it belongs not to us to expunge from the number of the elect, or to despair of, as if they were already lost. We may lawfully judge them aliens from the Church, and so aliens from Christ, but only during the time of their excommunication. If then, also, they give greater evidence of petulance than of humility, still let us commit them to the judgment of the Lord, hoping better of them in future than we see at present, and not ceasing to pray to God for them. And (to sum up in one word) let us not consign to destruction their person, which is in the hand, and subject to the decision, of the Lord alone; but let us merely estimate the character of each man's acts according to the law of the Lord. In following this rule, we abide by the divine judgment rather than give any judgment of our own. Let us not arrogate to ourselves greater liberty in judging, if we would not limit the power of God, and give the law to his mercy. Whenever it seems good to Him, the worst are changed into the best; aliens are ingrafted, and strangers are adopted into the Church. This the Lord does, that he may disappoint the thoughts of men, and confound their rashness; a rashness which, if not curbed, would usurp a power of judging to which it has no title.

10. For when our Saviour promises that what his servants bound on earth should be bound in heaven (Matth. xviii. 18), he confines the power of binding to the censure of the Church, which does not consign those who are excommunicated to perpetual ruin and damnation, but assures them, when they hear their life and manners condemned, that perpetual damnation will follow if they do not repent. Excommunication differs from anathema in this, that the latter completely excluding pardon, dooms and devotes the individual to eternal destruction, whereas the former rather rebukes and animadverts upon his manners; and although it also punishes, it is to bring him to salvation, by forewarning him of his future doom. If it succeeds, reconciliation and restoration to communion are ready to be given. Moreover, anathema is rarely if ever to be used. Hence, though ecclesiastical discipline does not allow us to be on familiar and intimate terms with excommunicated persons, still we ought to strive by all possible means to bring them to a better mind, and recover them to the fellowship and unity of the Church: as the apostle also says, "Yet count him not as an enemy, but admonish him as a brother" (2 Thess. iii. 15). If this humanity be not observed in private as well as public, the danger is, that our discipline shall degenerate into destruction.[1]

---

[1] French, "Il y a danger, que de discipline nous ne tombions en une maniere de gehene, et que de correcteurs nous ne devenions bourreaux."—There is a danger, lest instead of discipline we fall into a kind of gehenna, and instead of correctors become executioners.

11. Another special requisite to moderation of discipline is, as Augustine discourses against the Donatists, that private individuals must not, when they see vices less carefully corrected by the Council of Elders, immediately separate themselves from the Church; nor must pastors themselves, when unable to reform all things which need correction to the extent which they could wish, cast up their ministry, or by unwonted severity throw the whole Church into confusion. What Augustine says is perfectly true: "Whoever corrects what he can, by rebuking it, or without violating the bond of peace, excludes what he cannot correct, or unjustly condemns while he patiently tolerates what he is unable to exclude without violating the bond of peace, is free and exempted from the curse" (August. contra Parmen. Lib. ii. c. 4). He elsewhere gives the reason. "Every pious reason and mode of ecclesiastical discipline ought always to have regard to the unity of the Spirit in the bond of peace. This the apostle commands us to keep by bearing mutually with each other. If it is not kept, the medicine of discipline begins to be not only superfluous, but even pernicious, and therefore ceases to be medicine" (Ibid. Lib. iii. c. 1). "He who diligently considers these things, neither in the preservation of unity neglects strictness of discipline, nor by intemperate correction bursts the bond of society" (Ibid. cap. 2). He confesses, indeed, that pastors ought not only to exert themselves in removing every defect from the Church, but that every individual ought to his utmost to do so; nor does he disguise the fact, that he who neglects to admonish, accuse, and correct the bad, although he neither favours them, nor sins with them, is guilty before the Lord; and if he conducts himself so that though he can exclude them from partaking of the Supper, he does it not, then the sin is no longer that of other men, but his own. Only he would have that prudence used which our Lord also requires, "lest while ye gather up the tares, ye root up also the wheat with them" (Matth. xiii. 29). Hence he infers from Cyprian, "Let a man then mercifully correct what he can; what he cannot correct, let him bear patiently, and in love bewail and lament."

12. This he says on account of the moroseness of the Donatists, who, when they saw faults in the Church which the bishops indeed rebuked verbally, but did not punish with excommunication (because they did not think that anything would be gained in this way), bitterly inveighed against the bishops as traitors to discipline, and by an impious schism separated themselves from the flock of Christ. Similar, in the present day, is the conduct of the Anabaptists, who, acknowledging no assembly of Christ unless conspicuous in all respects for angelic perfection, under pretence of zeal overthrow everything which tends to edification.[1] "Such (says Augustin. contra Parmen. Lib. iii. c. 4), not from hatred of other men's iniquity, but zeal for their own disputes, ensnaring the weak by the credit of their name, attempt to draw them entirely away, or at least to separate them;

1 See a lengthened refutation in Calv. Instructio adv. Anabap. Art. 2. See also Calv. de Cœna Domini.

swollen with pride, raving with petulance, insidious in calumny, turbulent in sedition. That it may not be seen how void they are of the light of truth, they cover themselves with the shadow of a stern severity: the correction of a brother's fault, which in Scripture is enjoined to be done with moderation, without impairing the sincerity of love or breaking the bond of peace, they pervert to sacrilegious schism and purposes of excision. Thus Satan transforms himself into an angel of light (2 Cor. xi. 14) when, under pretext of a just severity, he persuades to savage cruelty, desiring nothing more than to violate and burst the bond of unity and peace; because, when it is maintained, all his power of mischief is feeble. his wily traps are broken, and his schemes of subversion vanish."

13. One thing Augustine specially commends—viz. that if the contagion of sin has seized the multitude, mercy must accompany living discipline. "For counsels of separation are vain, sacrilegious, and pernicious, because impious and proud, and do more to disturb the weak good than to correct the wicked proud" (August. Ep. 64). This which he enjoins on others he himself faithfully practised. For, writing to Aurelius, Bishop of Carthage, he complains that drunkenness, which is so severely condemned in Scripture, prevails in Africa with impunity, and advises a council of bishops to be called for the purpose of providing a remedy. He immediately adds, "In my opinion, such things are not removed by rough, harsh, and imperious measures, but more by teaching than commanding, more by admonishing than threatening. For thus ought we to act with a multitude of offenders. Severity is to be exercised against the sins of a few" (August. Ep. 64). He does not mean, however, that the bishops were to wink or be silent because they are unable to punish public offences severely, as he himself afterwards explains. But he wishes to temper the mode of correction, so as to give soundness to the body rather than cause destruction. And, accordingly, he thus concludes: "Wherefore, we must on no account neglect the injunction of the apostle, to separate from the wicked, when it can be done without the risk of violating peace, because he did not wish it to be done otherwise (1 Cor. v. 13); we must also endeavour, by bearing with each other, to keep the unity of the Spirit in the bond of peace" (Eph. iv. 2).

14. The remaining part of discipline, which is not, strictly speaking, included in the power of the keys, is when pastors, according to the necessity of the times, exhort the people either to fasting and solemn prayer, or to other exercises of humiliation, repentance, and faith, the time, mode, and form of these not being prescribed by the Word of God, but left to the judgment of the Church. As the observance of this part of discipline is useful, so it was always used in the Church, even from the days of the apostles. Indeed, the apostles themselves were not its first authors, but borrowed the example from the Law and Prophets. For we there see,[1] that as often as any

---

[1] See a striking instance in Ezra viii. 21, on the appointment of a fast at the river Ahava, on the return of the people from the Babylonish captivity.

weighty matter occurred the people were assembled, and supplication and fasting appointed. In this, therefore, the apostles followed a course which was not new to the people of God, and which they foresaw would be useful. A similar account is to be given of the other exercises by which the people may either be aroused to duty, or kept in duty and obedience. We everywhere meet with examples in Sacred History, and it is unnecessary to collect them. In general, we must hold that whenever any religious controversy arises, which either a council or ecclesiastical tribunal behoves to decide;[1] whenever a minister is to be chosen; whenever, in short, any matter of difficulty and great importance is under consideration : on the other hand, when manifestations of the divine anger appear, as pestilence, war, and famine, the sacred and salutary custom of all ages has been for pastors to exhort the people to public fasting and extraordinary prayer. Should any one refuse to admit the passages which are adduced from the Old Testament, as being less applicable to the Christian Church, it is clear that the apostles also acted thus; although, in regard to prayer, I scarcely think any one will be found to stir the question. Let us, therefore, make some observations on fasting, since very many, not understanding what utility there can be in it, judge it not to be very necessary, while others reject it altogether as superfluous. Where its use is not well known it is easy to fall into superstition.

15. A holy and lawful fast has three ends in view. We use it either to mortify and subdue the flesh, that it may not wanton, or to prepare the better for prayer and holy meditation; or to give evidence of humbling ourselves before God, when we would confess our guilt before him. The first end is not very often regarded in public fasting, because all have not the same bodily constitution, nor the same state of health, and hence it is more applicable to private fasting. The second end is common to both, for this preparation for prayer is requisite for the whole Church, as well as for each individual member. The same thing may be said of the third. For it sometimes happens that God smites a nation with war or pestilence, or some kind of calamity. In this common chastisement it behoves the whole people to plead guilty, and confess their guilt. Should the hand of the Lord strike any one in private, then the same thing is to be done by himself alone, or by his family. The thing, indeed, is properly a feeling of the mind. But when the mind is effected as it ought, it cannot but give vent to itself in external manifestation, especially when it tends to the common edification, that all, by openly confessing their sin, may render praise to the divine justice, and by their example mutually encourage each other.

16. Hence fasting, as it is a sign of humiliation, has a more frequent use in public than among private individuals, although as we

1 French, "Quand il advient quelque different en Chretienté, qui tire grande conséquence."—When some difference on a matter of great consequence takes place ir Christendom.

have said, it is common to both. In regard, then, to the discipline of which we now treat, whenever supplication is to be made to God on any important occasion, it is befitting to appoint a period for fasting and prayer. Thus when the Christians of Antioch laid hands on Barnabas and Paul, that they might the better recommend their ministry, which was of so great importance, they joined fasting and prayer (Acts xiii. 3). Thus these two apostles afterwards, when they appointed ministers to churches, were wont to use prayer and fasting (Acts xiv. 23). In general, the only object which they had in fasting was to render themselves more alert and disencumbered for prayer. We certainly experience that after a full meal the mind does not so rise toward God as to be borne along by an earnest and fervent longing for prayer, and perseverance in prayer. In this sense is to be understood the saying of Luke concerning Anna, that she " served God with fastings and prayers, night and day " (Luke ii. 37). For he does not place the worship of God in fasting, but intimates that in this way the holy woman trained herself to assiduity in prayer. Such was the fast of Nehemiah, when with more intense zeal he prayed to God for the deliverance of his people (Neh. i. 4). For this reason Paul says, that married believers do well to abstain for a season (1 Cor. vii. 5), that they may have greater freedom for prayer and fasting, when by joining prayer to fasting, by way of help, he reminds us it is of no importance in itself, save in so far as it refers to this end. Again, when in the same place he enjoins spouses to render due benevolence to each other, it is clear that he is not referring to daily prayer, but prayers which require more than ordinary attention.

17. On the other hand, when pestilence begins to stalk abroad, or famine or war, or when any other disaster seems to impend over a province and people (Esther iv. 16), then also it is the duty of pastors to exhort the Church to fasting, that she may suppliantly deprecate the Lord's anger. For when he makes danger appear, he declares that he is prepared and in a manner armed for vengeance. In like manner, therefore, as persons accused were anciently wont, in order to excite the commiseration of the judge, to humble themselves suppliantly with long beard, dishevelled hair, and coarse garments, so when we are charged before the divine tribunal, to deprecate his severity in humble raiment is equally for his glory and the public edification, and useful and salutary to ourselves. And that this was common among the Israelites we may infer from the words of Joel. For when he says, " Blow the trumpet in Zion, sanctify a fast, call a solemn assembly," &c. (Joel ii. 15), he speaks as of things received by common custom. A little before he had said that the people were to be tried for their wickedness, and that the day of judgment was at hand, and he had summoned them as criminals to plead their cause: then he exclaims that they should hasten to sackcloth and ashes, to weeping and fasting; that is, humble themselves before God with external manifestations. The sackcloth and ashes, indeed, were per-

haps more suitable for those times, but the assembly, and weeping and fasting, and the like, undoubtedly belong, in an equal degree, to our age, whenever the condition of our affairs so requires. For seeing it is a holy exercise both for men to humble themselves, and confess their humility, why should we in similar necessity use this less than did those of old ? We read not only that the Israelitish Church, formed and constituted by the word of God, fasted in token of sadness, but the Ninevites also, whose only teaching had been the preaching of Jonah.[1] Why, therefore, should not we do the same ? But it is an external ceremony, which, like other ceremonies, terminated in Christ. Nay, in the present day it is an admirable help to believers, as it always was, and a useful admonition to arouse them, lest by too great security and sloth they provoke the Lord more and more when they are chastened by his rod. Accordingly, when our Saviour excuses his apostles for not fasting, he does not say that fasting was abrogated, but reserves it for calamitous times, and conjoins it with mourning. " The days will come when the bridegroom shall be taken from them" (Matth. ix. 35; Luke v. 34).

18. But that there may be no error in the name, let us define what fasting is; for we do not understand by it simply a restrained and sparing use of food, but something else. The life of the pious should be tempered with frugality and sobriety, so as to exhibit, as much as may be, a kind of fasting during the whole course of life. But there is another temporary fast, when we retrench somewhat from our accustomed mode of living, either for one day or a certain period, and prescribe to ourselves a stricter and severer restraint in the use of that ordinary food. This consists in three things—viz. the time, the quality of food, and the sparing use of it. By the time I mean, that while fasting we are to perform those actions for the sake of which the fast is instituted. For example, when a man fasts because of solemn prayer, he should engage in it without having taken food. The quality consists in putting all luxury aside, and, being contented with common and meaner food, so as not to excite our palate by dainties. In regard to quantity, we must eat more lightly and sparingly, only for necessity and not for pleasure.

19. But the first thing always to be avoided is, the encroachment of superstition, as formerly happened, to the great injury of the Church. It would have been much better to have had no fasting at all, than have it carefully observed, but at the same time corrupted by false and pernicious opinions, into which the world is ever and anon falling, unless pastors obviate them by the greatest fidelity and prudence. The first thing is constantly to urge the injunction of Joel, " Rend your heart, and not your garments" (Joel ii. 13); that is, to remind the people that fasting in itself is not of great value in the sight of God, unless accompanied with internal affection of the heart, true dissatisfaction with sin and with one's self, true humiliation, and true grief, from the fear of God; nay, that fasting is use-

[1] 1 Sam. vii. 6; xxxi. 13; 2 Kings i. 12; Jonah iii. 5.

ful for no other reason than because it is added to these as an inferior help. There is nothing which God more abominates than when men endeavour to cloak themselves by substituting signs and external appearance for integrity of heart. Accordingly, Isaiah inveighs most bitterly against the hypocrisy of the Jews, in thinking that they had satisfied God when they had merely fasted, whatever might be the impiety and impure thoughts which they cherished in their hearts. " Is it such a fast that I have chosen ?" (Isa. lviii. 5.) See also what follows. The fast of hypocrites is, therefore, not only useless and superfluous fatigue, but the greatest abomination. Another evil akin to this, and greatly to be avoided, is, to regard fasting as a meritorious work and species of divine worship. For seeing it is a thing which is in itself indifferent, and has no importance except on account of those ends to which it ought to have respect, it is a most pernicious superstition to confound it with the works enjoined by God, and which are necessary in themselves without reference to anything else. Such was anciently the dream of the Manichees, in refuting whom Augustine clearly shows,[1] that fasting is to be estimated entirely by those ends which I have mentioned, and cannot be approved by God, unless in so far as it refers to them. Another error, not indeed so impious, but perilous, is to exact it with greater strictness and severity as one of the principal duties, and extol it with such extravagant encomiums as to make men imagine that they have done something admirable when they have fasted. In this respect I dare not entirely excuse ancient writers[2] from having sown some seeds of superstition, and given occasion to the tyranny which afterwards arose. We sometimes meet with sound and prudent sentiments on fasting, but we also ever and anon meet with extravagant praises, lauding it as one of the cardinal virtues.

20. Then the superstitious observance of Lent had everywhere prevailed : for both the vulgar imagined that they thereby perform some excellent service to God, and pastors commended it as a holy imitation of Christ ; though it is plain that Christ did not fast to set an example to others, but, by thus commencing the preaching of the gospel, meant to prove that his doctrine was not of men, but had come from heaven. And it is strange how men of acute judgment could fall into this gross delusion, which so many clear reasons refute : for Christ did not fast repeatedly (which he must have done had he meant to lay down a law for an anniversary fast), but once only, when preparing for the promulgation of the gospel. Nor does he fast after the manner of men, as he would have done had he meant to invite men to imitation ; he rather gives an example, by which he may raise all to admire rather than study to imitate him. In short, the nature of his fast is not different from that which Moses observed

[1] August. de Morib. Manich. Lib. ii. c. 13 ; et cont. Faustum, Lib. xxx.
[2] See Chrysostom. Homil. sub. initium Quadragesimæ, where he terms fasting a cure of souls and ablution for sins.

when he received the law at the hand of the Lord (Exod. xxiv. 18 ; xxxiv. 28). For, seeing that that miracle was performed in Moses to establish the law, it behoved not to be omitted in Christ, lest the gospel should seem inferior to the law. But from that day, it never occurred to any one, under pretence of imitating Moses, to set up a similar form of fast among the Israelites. Nor did any of the holy prophets and fathers follow it, though they had inclination and zeal enough for all pious exercises ; for though it is said of Elijah that he passed forty days without meat and drink (1 Kings xix. 8), this was merely in order that the people might recognise that he was raised up to maintain the law, from which almost the whole of Israel had revolted. It was therefore merely false zeal, replete with superstition, which set up a fast under the title and pretext of imitating Christ ; although there was then a strange diversity in the mode of the fast, as is related by Cassiodorus in the ninth book of the History of Socrates : "The Romans," says he, " had only three weeks, but their fast was continuous, except on the Lord's day and the Sabbath. The Greeks and Illyrians had, some six, others seven, but the fast was at intervals. Nor did they differ less in the kind of food : some used only bread and water, others added vegetables ; others had no objecttion to fish and fowls ; others made no difference in their food." Augustine also makes mention of this difference in his latter epistle to Januarius.

21. Worse times followed. To the absurd zeal of the vulgar were added rudeness and ignorance in the bishops, lust of power, and tyrannical rigour. Impious laws were passed, binding the conscience in deadly chains. The eating of flesh was forbidden, as if a man were contaminated by it. Sacrilegious opinions were added, one after another, until all became an abyss of error. And that no kind of depravity might be omitted, they began, under a most absurd pretence of abstinence, to make a mock of God ;[1] for in the most exquisite delicacies they seek the praise of fasting : no dainties now suffice ; never was there greater abundance or variety or savouriness of food. In this splendid display they think that they serve God. I do not mention that at no time do those who would be thought the holiest of them wallow more fully. In short, the highest worship of God is to abstain from flesh, and, with this reservation, to indulge in delicacies of every kind. On the other hand, it is the greatest impiety, impiety scarcely to be expiated by death, for any one to taste the smallest portion of bacon or rancid flesh with his bread. Jerome, writing to Nepotian, relates, that even in his day there were some who mocked God with such follies : those who would not even put oil in their food caused the greatest delicacies to be procured from every quarter ; nay, that they might do violence to nature, abstained from drinking water, and caused sweet and costly

---

[1] Bernard, in Serm. I. in die Paschæ, censures, among others, princes also, for longing, during the season of Lent, for the approaching festival of our Lord's resurrection, that they might indulge more freely.

potions to be made for them, which they drank, not out of a cup, but a shell. What was then the fault of a few is now common among all the rich: they do not fast for any other purpose than to feast more richly and luxuriously. But I am unwilling to waste many words on a subject as to which there can be no doubt. All I say is, that, as well in fasts as in all other parts of discipline, the Papists are so far from having anything right, anything sincere, anything duly framed and ordered, that they have no occasion to plume themselves as if anything was left them that is worthy of praise.

22. We come now to the second part of discipline, which relates specially to the clergy. It is contained in the canons, which the ancient bishops framed for themselves and their order: for instance, let no clergyman spend his time in hunting, in gaming, or in feasting; let none engage in usury or in trade; let none be present at lascivious dances, and the like. Penalties also were added to give a sanction to the authority of the canons, that none might violate them with impunity. With this view, each bishop was intrusted with the superintendence of his own clergy, that he might govern them according to the canons, and keep them to their duty. For this purpose, certain annual visitations and synods were appointed, that if any one was negligent in his office he might be admonished; if any one sinned, he might be punished according to his fault. The bishops also had their provincial synods once, anciently twice, a-year, by which they were tried, if they had done anything contrary to their duty. For if any bishop had been too harsh or violent with his clergy, there was an appeal to the synod, though only one individual complained. The severest punishment was deposition from office, and exclusion, for a time, from communion. But as this was the uniform arrangement, no synod rose without fixing the time and place of the next meeting. To call a universal council belonged to the emperor alone, as all the ancient summonings testify. As long as this strictness was in force, the clergy demanded no more in word from the people than they performed in act and by example; nay, they were more strict against themselves than the vulgar; and, indeed, it is becoming that the people should be ruled by a kindlier, and, if I may so speak, laxer discipline; that the clergy should be stricter in their censures, and less indulgent to themselves than to others. How this whole procedure became obsolete it is needless to relate, since, in the present day, nothing can be imagined more lawless and dissolute than this order, whose licentiousness is so extreme that the whole world is crying out. I admit that, in order not to seem to have lost all sight of antiquity, they, by certain shadows, deceive the eyes of the simple; but these no more resemble ancient customs than the mimicry of an ape resembles what men do by reason and counsel. There is a memorable passage in Xenophon, in which he mentions, that when the Persians had shamefully degenerated from the customs of their ancestors, and had fallen away from an austere mode of life to luxury and effeminacy, they still, to hide the disgrace,

were sedulously observant of ancient rites (Cyrop. Lib. viii.). For while, in the time of Cyrus, sobriety and temperance so flourished that no Persian required to wipe his nose, and it was even deemed disgraceful to do so, it remained with their posterity, as a point of religion, not to remove the mucus from the nostril, though they were allowed to nourish within, even to putridity, those fetid humours which they had contracted by gluttony. In like manner, according to the ancient custom, it was unlawful to use cups at table; but it was quite tolerable to swallow wine so as to make it necessary to be carried off drunk. It was enjoined to use only one meal a-day: this these good successors did not abrograte, but they continued their surfeit from mid-day to midnight. To finish the day's march, fasting, as the law enjoined it, was the uniform custom; but in order to avoid lassitude, the allowed and usual custom was to limit the march to two hours. As often as the degenerate Papists obtrude their rules that they may show their resemblance to the holy fathers, this example will serve to expose their ridiculous imitation. Indeed, no painter could paint them more to the life.

23. In one thing they are more than rigid and inexorable—in not permitting priests to marry. It is of no consequence to mention with what impunity whoredom prevails among them, and how, trusting to their vile celibacy, they have become callous to all kinds of iniquity. The prohibition, however, clearly shows how pestiferous all traditions are, since this one has not only deprived the Church of fit and honest pastors, but has introduced a fearful sink of iniquity, and plunged many souls into the gulf of despair. Certainly, when marriage was interdicted to priests, it was done with impious tyranny, not only contrary to the word of God, but contrary to all justice. First, men had no title whatever to forbid what God had left free; secondly, it is too clear to make it necessary to give any lengthened proof that God has expressly provided in his Word that this liberty shall not be infringed. I omit Paul's injunction, in numerous passages, that a bishop be the husband of one wife; but what could be stronger than his declaration, that in the latter days there would be impious men " forbidding to marry"? (1 Tim. iv. 3.) Such persons he calls not only impostors, but devils. We have therefore a prophecy, a sacred oracle of the Holy Spirit, intended to warn the Church from the outset against perils, and declaring that the prohibition of marriage is a doctrine of devils. They think that they get finely off when they wrest this passage, and apply it to Montanus, the Tatians, the Encratites, and other ancient heretics. These (they say) alone condemned marriage; we by no means condemn it, but only deny it to the ecclesiastical order, in whom we think it not befitting. As if, even granting that this prophecy was primarily fulfilled in those heretics, it is not applicable also to themselves; or, as if one could listen to the childish quibble that they do not forbid marriage, because they do not forbid it to all. This is just as if a tyrant were to

contend that a law is not unjust because its injustice presses only on a part of the state.

24. They object that there ought to be some distinguishing mark between the clergy and the people; as if the Lord had not provided the ornaments in which priests ought to excel. Thus they charge the apostle with having disturbed the ecclesiastical order, and destroyed its ornament, when, in drawing the picture of a perfect bishop, he presumed to set down marriage among the other endowments which he required of them. I am aware of the mode in which they expound this—viz. that no one was to be appointed a bishop who had a second wife. This interpretation, I admit, is not new; but its unsoundness is plain from the immediate context, which prescribes the kind of wives whom bishops and deacons ought to have. Paul enumerates marriage among the qualities of a bishop; those men declare that, in the ecclesiastical order, marriage is an intolerable vice; and, indeed, not content with this general vituperation, they term it, in their canons, the uncleanness and pollution of the flesh (Siric. ad Episc. Hispaniar.). Let every one consider with himself from what forge these things have come. Christ deigns so to honour marriage as to make it an image of his sacred union with the Church. What greater eulogy could be pronounced on the dignity of marriage? How, then, dare they have the effrontery to give the name of unclean and polluted to that which furnishes a bright representation of the spiritual grace of Christ?

25. Though their prohibition is thus clearly repugnant to the word of God, they, however, find something in the Scriptures to defend it. The Levitical priests, as often as their ministerial course returned, behoved to keep apart from their wives, that they might be pure and immaculate in handling sacred things; and it were therefore very indecorous that our sacred things, which are more noble, and are ministered every day, should be handled by those who are married: as if the evangelical ministry were of the same character as the Levitical priesthood. These, as types, represented Christ, who, as Mediator between God and men, was, by his own spotless purity, to reconcile us to the Father. But as sinners could not in every respect exhibit a type of his holiness, that they might, however, shadow it forth by certain lineaments, they were enjoined to purify themselves beyond the manner of men when they approached the sanctuary, inasmuch as they then properly prefigured Christ appearing in the tabernacle, an image of the heavenly tribunal, as pacificators, to reconcile men to God. As ecclesiastical pastors do not sustain this character in the present day, the comparison is made in vain. Wherefore the apostle declares distinctly, without reservation, " Marriage is honourable in all, and the bed undefiled; but whoremongers and adulterers God will judge" (Heb. xiii. 4). And the apostles showed, by their own example, that marriage is not unbefitting the holiness of any function, however excellent; for Paul de-

clares, that they not only retained their wives, but led them about with them (1 Cor. ix. 5).

26. Then how great the effrontery when, in holding forth this ornament of chastity as a matter of necessity, they throw the greatest obloquy on the primitive Church, which, while it abounded in admirable divine erudition, excelled more in holiness. For if they pay no regard to the apostles (they are sometimes wont strenuously to contemn them), what, I ask, will they make of all the ancient fathers, who, it is certain, not only tolerated marriage in the episcopal order, but also approved it? They, forsooth, encouraged a foul profanation of sacred things when the mysteries of the Lord were thus irregularly performed by them. In the Council of Nice, indeed, there was some question of proclaiming celibacy : as there are never wanting little men of superstitious minds, who are always devising some novelty as a means of gaining admiration for themselves. What was resolved? The opinion of Paphnutius was adopted, who pronounced legitimate conjugal intercourse to be chastity (Hist. Trip. Lib. ii. c. 14). The marriage of priests, therefore, continued sacred, and was neither regarded as a disgrace, nor thought to cast any stain on their ministry.

27. In the times which succeeded, a too superstitious admiration of celibacy prevailed. Hence, ever and anon, unmeasured encomiums were pronounced on virginity, so that it became the vulgar belief that scarcely any virtue was to be compared to it. And although marriage was not condemned as impurity, yet its dignity was lessened, and its sanctity obscured ; so that he who did not refrain from it was deemed not to have a mind strong enough to aspire to perfection. Hence those canons which enacted, first, that those who had attained the priesthood should not contract marriage ; and, secondly, that none should be admitted to that order but the unmarried, or those who, with the consent of their wives, renounced the marriage-bed. These enactments, as they seemed to procure reverence for the priesthood, were, I admit, received even in ancient times with great applause. But if my opponents plead antiquity, my first answer is, that both under the apostles, and for several ages after, bishops were at liberty to have wives : that the apostles themselves, and other pastors of primitive authority who succeeded them, had no difficulty in using this liberty, and that the example of the primitive Church ought justly to have more weight than allow us to think that what was then received and used with commendation is either illicit or unbecoming. My second answer is, that the age, which, from an immoderate affection for virginity, began to be less favourable to marriage, did not bind a law of celibacy on the priests, as if the thing were necessary in itself, but gave a preference to the unmarried over the married. My last answer is, that they did not exact this so rigidly as to make continence necessary and compulsory on those who were unfit for it. For while the strictest laws were made against

fornication, it was only enacted with regard to those who contracted marriage that they should be superseded in their office.

28. Therefore, as often as the defenders of this new tyranny appeal to antiquity in defence of their celibacy, so often should we call upon them to restore the ancient chastity of their priests, to put away adulterers and whoremongers, not to allow those whom they deny an honourable and chaste use of marriage, to rush with impunity into every kind of lust, to bring back that obsolete discipline by which all licentiousness is restrained, and free the Church from the flagitious turpitude by which it has long been deformed. When they have conceded this, they will next require to be reminded not to represent as necessary that which, being in itself free, depends on the utility of the Church. I do not, however, speak thus as if I thought that on any condition whatever effect should be given to those canons which lay a bond of celibacy on the ecclesiastical order, but that the better-hearted may understand the effrontery of our enemies in employing the name of antiquity to defame the holy marriage of priests. In regard to the Fathers, whose writings are extant, none of them, when they spoke their own mind, with the exception of Jerome, thus malignantly detracted from the honour of marriage. We will be contented with a single passage from Chrysostom, because he being a special admirer of virginity, cannot be thought to be more lavish than others in praise of matrimony. Chrysostom thus speaks: " The first degree of chastity is pure virginity ; the second, faithful marriage. Therefore, a chaste love of matrimony is the second species of virginity" (Chrysost. Hom. de Invent. Crucis.).

CHAPTER XIII.

OF VOWS.   THE MISERABLE ENTANGLEMENTS CAUSED BY VOWING
RASHLY.

This chapter consists of two parts,—I. Of vows in general, sec. 1-8.   II. Of monastic vows, and specially of the vow of celibacy, sec. 8-21.

Sections.

1. It is indeed deplorable that the Church, whose freedom was
purchased by the inestimable price of Christ's blood, should have
been thus oppressed by a cruel tyranny, and almost buried under a
huge mass of traditions; but, at the same time, the private infatuation of each individual shows, that not without just cause has so
much power been given from above to Satan and his ministers.   It
was not enough to neglect the command of Christ, and bear any
burdens which false teachers might please to impose, but each individual behoved to have his own peculiar burdens, and thus sink
deeper by digging his own cavern.   This has been the result when
men set about devising vows, by which a stronger and closer obliga-

tion might be added to common ties. Having already shown that the worship of God was vitiated by the audacity of those who, under the name of pastors, domineered in the Church, when they ensnared miserable souls by their iniquitous laws, it will not be out of place here to advert to a kindred evil, to make it appear that the world, in accordance with its depraved disposition, has always thrown every possible obstacle in the way of the helps by which it ought to have been brought to God. Moreover, that the very grievous mischief introduced by such vows may be more apparent, let the reader attend to the principles formerly laid down. First, we showed (Book II. chap. viii. sec. 5) that everything requisite for the ordering of a pious and holy life is comprehended in the law. Secondly, we showed that the Lord, the better to dissuade us from devising new works, included the whole of righteousness in simple obedience to his will. If these positions are true, it is easy to see that all fictitious worship, which we ourselves devise for the purpose of serving God, is not in the least degree acceptable to him, how pleasing soever it may be to us. And, unquestionably, in many passages the Lord not only openly rejects, but grievously abhors such worship. Hence arises a doubt with regard to vows which are made without any express authority from the word of God; in what light are they to be viewed? can they be duly made by Christian men, and to what extent are they binding? What is called a promise among men is a vow when made to God. Now, we promise to men either things which we think will be acceptable to them, or things which we in duty owe them. Much more careful, therefore, ought we to be in vows which are directed to God, with whom we ought to act with the greatest seriousness. Here superstition has in all ages strangely prevailed; men at once, without judgment and without choice, vowing to God whatever came into their minds, or even rose to their lips. Hence the foolish vows, nay, monstrous absurdities, by which the heathen insolently sported with their gods. Would that Christians had not imitated them in this their audacity! Nothing, indeed, could be less becoming; but it is obvious that for some ages nothing has been more usual than this misconduct—the whole body of the people everywhere despising the Law of God,[1] and burning with an insane zeal of vowing according to any dreaming notion which they had formed. I have no wish to exaggerate invidiously, or particularise the many grievous sins which have here been committed; but it seemed right to advert to it in passing, that it may the better appear, that when we treat of vows we are not by any means discussing a superfluous question.

2. If we would avoid error in deciding what vows are legitimate, and what preposterous, three things must be attended to—viz. who

---

[1] See Ps. cxix. 106. "I have sworn, and I will perform it, that I will keep thy righteous judgments." Calvin observes on these words, that the vow and oath to keep the law cannot be charged with rashness, because it trusted to the promises of God concerning the forgiveness of sins, and to the spirit of regeneration.

he is to whom the vow is made; who we are that make it; and, lastly, with what intention we make it. In regard in the first, we should consider that we have to do with God, whom our obedience so delights, that he abominates all will-worship, how specious and splendid soever it be in the eyes of men (Col. ii. 23). If all will-worship, which we devise without authority, is abomination to God, it follows that no worship can be acceptable to him save that which is approved by his word. Therefore, we must not arrogate such licence to ourselves as to presume to vow anything to God without evidence of the estimation in which he holds it. For the doctrine of Paul, that whatsoever is not of faith is sin (Rom. xiv. 23), while it extends to all actions of every kind, certainly applies with peculiar force in the case where the thought is immediately turned towards God. Nay, if in the minutest matters (Paul was then speaking of the distinction of meats) we err or fall, where the sure light of faith shines not before us, how much more modesty ought we to use when we attempt a matter of the greatest weight? For in nothing ought we to be more serious than in the duties of religion. In vows, then, our first precaution must be, never to proceed to make any vow without having previously determined in our conscience to attempt nothing rashly. And we shall be safe from the danger of rashness when we have God going before, and, as it were, dictating from his word what is good, and what is useless.

3. In the second point which we have mentioned as requiring consideration is implied, that we measure our strength, that we attend to our vocation so as not to neglect the blessing of liberty which God has conferred upon us. For he who vows what is not within his means, or is at variance with his calling, is rash, while he who contemns the beneficence of God in making him lord of all things, is ungrateful. When I speak thus, I mean not that anything is so placed in our hand, that, leaning on our own strength, we may promise it to God. For in the Council of Arausica (cap. 11) it was most truly decreed, that nothing is duly vowed to God save what we have received from his hand, since all things which are offered to him are merely his gifts. But seeing that some things are given to us by the goodness of God, and others withheld by his justice, every man should have respect to the measure of grace bestowed on him, as Paul enjoins (Rom. xii. 3; 1 Cor. xii. 11). All then I mean here is, that your vows should be adapted to the measure which God by his gifts prescribes to you, lest by attempting more than he permits, you arrogate too much to yourself, and fall headlong. For example, when the assassins, of whom mention is made in the Acts, vowed "that they would neither eat nor drink till they had killed Paul" (Acts xxiii. 12), though it had not been an impious conspiracy, it would still have been intolerably presumptuous, as subjecting the life and death of a man to their own power. Thus Jephthah suffered for his folly, when with precipitate fervour he made a rash vow (Judges xi. 30). Of this class, the first place of

insane audacity belongs to celibacy. Priests, monks, and nuns, forgetful of their infirmity, are confident of their fitness for celibacy.[1] But by what oracle have they been instructed, that the chastity which they vow to the end of life, they will be able through life to maintain? They hear the voice of God concerning the universal condition of mankind, " It is not good that the man should be alone" (Gen. ii. 18). They understand, and I wish they did not feel that the sin remaining in us is armed with the sharpest stings. How can they presume to shake off the common feelings of their nature for a whole lifetime, seeing the gift of continence is often granted for a certain time as occasion requires? In such perverse conduct they must not expect God to be their helper; let them rather remember the words, " Ye shall not tempt the Lord your God" (Deut. vi. 16). But it is to tempt the Lord to strive against the nature implanted by him, and to spurn his present gifts as if they did not appertain to us. This they not only do, but marriage, which God did not think it unbecoming his majesty to institute, which he pronounced honourable in all, which Christ our Lord sanctified by his presence, and which he deigned to honour with his first miracle, they presume to stigmatise as pollution, so extravagant are the terms in which they eulogise every kind of celibacy; as if in their own life they did not furnish a clear proof that celibacy is one thing and chastity another. This life, however, they most impudently style angelical, thereby offering no slight insult to the angels of God, to whom they compare whoremongers and adulterers, and something much worse and fouler still.[2] And, indeed, there is here very little occasion for argument, since they are abundantly refuted by fact. For we plainly see the fearful punishments with which the Lord avenges this arrogance and contempt of his gifts from overweening confidence. More hidden crimes I spare through shame; what is known of them is too much. Beyond all controversy, we ought not to vow anything which will hinder us in fulfilling our vocation; as if the father of a family were to vow to leave his wife and children, and undertake other burdens; or one who is fit for a public office should, when elected to it, vow to live private. But the meaning of what we have said as to not despising our liberty may occasion some difficulty if not explained. Wherefore, understand it briefly thus: Since God has given us dominion over all things, and so subjected them to us that we may use them for our convenience, we cannot hope that our service will be acceptable to God if we bring ourselves into bondage to external things, which ought to be subservient to us. I say this, because

1 On the vow of celibacy, see Calv. de Fugiend. Micit. sacris, Adv. Theolog. Paris. De Necessit. Reform. Eccl.; Præfat. Antidoti ad Concil. Trident.; Vera Eccles. Reform. Ratio; De Scandalis.

2 Bernard, de Convers. ad Clericos, cap. 29, inveighing against the crimes of the clergy, says, "Would that those who cannot contain would fear to take the vow of celibacy! For it is a weighty saying, that all cannot receive it. Many are either unable to conceal from the multitude, or seek not to do it. They abstain from the remedy of marriage, and thereafter give themselves up to all wickedness.

some aspire to the praise of humility, for entangling themselves in a variety of observances from which God for good reason wished us to be entirely free. Hence, if we would escape this danger, let us always remember that we are by no means to withdraw from the economy which God has appointed in the Christian Church.

4. I come now to my third position—viz. that if you would approve your vow to God, the mind in which you undertake it is of great moment. For seeing that God looks not to the outward appearance but to the heart, the consequence is, that according to the purpose which the mind has in view, the same thing may at one time please and be acceptable to him, and at another be most displeasing. If you vow abstinence from wine, as if there were any holiness in so doing, you are superstitious; but if you have some end in view which is not perverse, no one can disapprove. Now, as far as I can see, there are four ends to which our vows may be properly directed; two of these, for the sake of order, I refer to the past, and two to the future. To the past belong vows by which we either testify our gratitude toward God for favours received, or in order to deprecate his wrath, inflict punishment on ourselves for faults committed. The former, let us if you please call acts of thanksgiving; the latter, acts of repentance. Of the former class, we have an example in the tithes which Jacob vowed (Gen. xxviii. 20), if the Lord would conduct him safely home from exile; and also in the ancient peace-offerings which pious kings and commanders, when about to engage in a just war, vowed that they would give if they were victorious, or, at least, if the Lord would deliver them when pressed by some greater difficulty. Thus are to be understood all the passages in the Psalms which speak of vows (Ps. xxii. 26; lvi. 13; cxvi. 14, 18). Similar vows may also be used by us in the present day, whenever the Lord has rescued us from some disaster or dangerous disease, or other peril. For it is not abhorrent from the office of a pious man thus to consecrate a votive offering to God as a formal symbol of acknowledgment that he may not seem ungrateful for his kindness. The nature of the second class it will be sufficient to illustrate merely by one familiar example. Should any one, from gluttonous indulgence, have fallen into some iniquity, there is nothing to prevent him, with the view of chastising his intemperance, from renouncing all luxuries for a certain time, and in doing so, from employing a vow for the purpose of binding himself more firmly. And yet I do not lay down this as an invariable law to all who have similarly offended; I merely show what may be lawfully done by those who think that such a vow will be useful to them. Thus while I hold it lawful so to vow, I at the same time leave it free.

5. The vows which have reference to the future tend partly, as we have said, to render us more cautious, and partly to act as a kind of stimulus to the discharge of duty. A man sees that he is so prone to a certain vice, that in a thing which is otherwise not bad he cannot restrain himself from forthwith falling into evil: he will

not act absurdly in cutting off the use of that thing for some time by a vow. If, for instance, one should perceive that this or that bodily ornament brings him into peril, and yet allured by cupidity he eagerly longs for it, what can he do better than by throwing a curb upon himself, that is, imposing the necessity of abstinence, free himself from all doubt? In like manner, should one be oblivious or sluggish in the necessary duties of piety, why should he not, by forming a vow, both awaken his memory and shake off his sloth? In both, I confess, there is a kind of tutelage, but inasmuch as they are helps to infirmity, they are used not without advantage by the ignorant and imperfect. Hence we hold that vows which have respect to one of these ends, especially in external things, are lawful, provided they are supported by the approbation of God, are suitable to our calling, and are limited to the measure of grace bestowed upon us.

6. It is not now difficult to infer what view on the whole ought to be taken of vows. There is one vow common to all believers, which taken in baptism we confirm, and as it were sanction, by our Catechism,[1] and partaking of the Lord's Supper. For the sacraments are a kind of mutual contracts by which the Lord conveys his mercy to us, and by it eternal life, while we in our turn promise him obedience. The formula, or at least substance, of the vow is, That renouncing Satan we bind ourselves to the service of God, to obey his holy commands, and no longer follow the depraved desires of our flesh. It cannot be doubted that this vow, which is sanctioned by Scripture, nay, is exacted from all the children of God, is holy and salutary. There is nothing against this in the fact, that no man in this life yields that perfect obedience to the law which God requires of us. This stipulation being included in the covenant of grace, comprehending forgiveness of sins and the spirit of holiness, the promise which we there make is combined both with entreaty for pardon and petition for assistance. It is necessary, in judging of particular vows, to keep the three former rules in remembrance: from them any one will easily estimate the character of each single vow. Do not suppose, however, that I so commend the vows which I maintain to be holy that I would have them made every day. For though I dare not give any precept as to time or number, yet if any one will take my advice, he will not undertake any but what are sober and temporary. If you are ever and anon launching out into numerous vows, the whole solemnity will be lost by the frequency, and you will readily fall into superstition. If you bind yourself by a perpetual vow, you will have great trouble and annoyance in getting free, or, worn out by length of time, you will at length make bold to break it.

7. It is now easy to see under how much superstition the world has laboured in this respect for several ages. One vowed that he would be abstemious, as if abstinence from wine were in itself an acceptable service to God. Another bound himself to fast, another to

---

1 Latin, "Catechism."—French, "En faisant protestation de notre foy;"—in making profession of our faith.

abstain from flesh on certain days, which he had vainly imagined to be more holy than other days. Things much more boyish were vowed though not by boys. For it was accounted great wisdom to undertake votive pilgrimages to holy places, and sometimes to perform the journey on foot, or with the body half naked, that the greater merit might be acquired by the greater fatigue. These and similar things, for which the world has long bustled with incredible zeal, if tried by the rules which we formerly laid down, will be discovered to be not only empty and nugatory, but full of manifest impiety. Be the judgment of the flesh what it may, there is nothing which God more abhors than fictitious worship. To these are added pernicious and damnable notions, hypocrites, after performing such frivolities, thinking that they have acquired no ordinary righteousness, placing the substance of piety in external observances, and despising all others who appear less careful in regard to them.

8. It is of no use to enumerate all the separate forms. But as monastic vows **are** held in great veneration, because they seem to be approved by the public judgment of the Church, I will say a few words concerning them. And, first, lest any one defend the monachism of the present day on the ground of the long prescription, it is to be observed, that the ancient mode of living in monasteries was very different. The persons who retired to them were those who wished to train themselves to the greatest austerity and patience. The discipline practised by the monks then resembled that which the Lacedemonians are said to have used under the laws of Lycurgus, and was even much more rigorous. They slept on the ground, their drink was water, their food bread, herbs, and roots, their chief luxuries oil and pulse. From more delicate food and care of the body they abstained. These things might seem hyperbolical were they not vouched by experienced eye witnesses, as Gregory Nazianzen, Basil, and Chrysostom. By such rudimentary training they prepared themselves for greater offices. For of the fact that monastic colleges were then a kind of seminaries of the ecclesiastical order, both those whom we lately named are very competent witnesses (they were all brought up in monasteries, and thence called to the episcopal office), as well as several other great and excellent men of their age. Augustine also shows that in his time the monasteries were wont to furnish the Church with clergy. For he thus addresses the monks of the island of Caprae: " We exhort you, brethren in the Lord, to keep your purpose, and persevere to the end; and if at any time our mother Church requires your labour, you will neither undertake it with eager elation, nor reject it from the blandishment of sloth, but with meek hearts obey God. You will not prefer your own ease to the necessities of the Church. Had no good men been willing to minister to her when in travail, it would have been impossible for you to be born "[1] (August. Ep. 82). He is speak-

---

1 At the same place, he admirably says, "Dearly beloved, love ease, but with the

ing of the ministry by which believers are spiritually born again. In like manner, he says to Aurelius (Ep. 76), "It is both an occasion of lapse to them, and a most unbecoming injury to the clerical order, if the deserters of monasteries are elected to the clerical warfare, since from those who remain in the monastery our custom is to appoint to the clerical office only the better and more approved. Unless, perhaps, as the vulgar say, A bad chorister is a good symphonist, so, in like manner, it will be jestingly said of us, A bad monk is a good clergyman. There will be too much cause for grief if we stir up monks to such ruinous pride, and deem the clergy deserving of so grave an affront, seeing that sometimes a good monk scarcely makes a good clerk; he may have sufficient continence, but be deficient in necessary learning." From these passages, it appears that pious men were wont to prepare for the government of the Church by monastic discipline, that thus they might be more apt and better trained to undertake the important office: not that all attained to this object, or even aimed at it, since the great majority of monks were illiterate men. Those who were fit were selected.

9. Augustine, in two passages in particular, gives a portraiture of the form of ancient monasticism. The one is in his book, *De Moribus Ecclesiæ Catholicæ* (*On the Manners of the Catholic Church*), where he maintains the holiness of that profession against the calumnies of the Manichees; the other in a treatise, entitled, *De Opere Monachorum* (*On the Work of Monks*), where he inveighs against certain degenerate monks who had begun to corrupt that institution. I will here give a summary of what he there delivers, and, as far as I can, in his own words: "Despising the allurements of this world, and congregated in common for a most chaste and most holy life, they pass their lives together, spending their time in prayer, reading, and discourse, not swollen with pride, not turbulent through petulance, not livid with envy. No one possesses anything of his own: no one is burdensome to any man. They labour with their hands in things by which the body may be fed, and the mind not withdrawn from God. The fruit of their labour they hand over to those whom they call deans. Those deans, disposing of the whole with great care, render an account to one whom they call father. These fathers, who are not only of the purest morals, but most distinguished for divine learning, and noble in all things, without any pride, consult those whom they call their sons, though the former have full authority to command, and the latter a great inclination to obey. At the close of the day they assemble each from his cell, and without having broken their fast, to hear their father, and to the number of three thousand at least (he is speaking of Egypt and the East) they assemble under each father. Then the body is refreshed, so far as suffices for safety and health, every one curbing his concupiscence so as not to be profuse in the scanty and very mean diet which is pro-

view of restraining from all worldly delight, and remember that there is no place where he who dreads our return to God is not able to lay his snares."

vided. Thus they not only abstain from flesh and wine for the purpose of subduing lust, but from those things which provoke the appetite of the stomach and gullet more readily, from seeming to some, as it were, more refined. In this way the desire of exquisite dainties, in which there is no flesh, is wont to be absurdly and shamefully defended. Any surplus, after necessary food (and the surplus is very great from the labour of their hands and the frugality of their meals), is carefully distributed to the needy, the more carefully that it was not procured by those who distribute. For they never act with the view of having abundance for themselves, but always act with the view of allowing no superfluity to remain with them" (August. De Mor. Eccl. Cath. c. 31). Afterwards describing their austerity, of which he had himself seen instances both at Milan and elsewhere, he says, " Meanwhile, no one is urged to austerities which he is unable to bear: no one is obliged to do what he declines, nor condemned by the others, whom he acknowledges himself too weak to imitate. For they remember how greatly charity is commended: they remember that to the pure all things are pure (Tit. i. 15). Wherefore, all their vigilance is employed, not in rejecting kinds of food as polluted, but in subduing concupiscence, and maintaining brotherly love. They remember, ' Meats for the belly, and the belly for meats,' &c. (1 Cor. vi. 13). Many, however strong, abstain because of the weak. In many this is not the cause of action ; they take pleasure in sustaining themselves on the meanest and least expensive food. Hence the very persons who in health restrain themselves, decline not in sickness to use what their health requires. Many do not drink wine, and yet do not think themselves polluted by it, for they most humanely cause it to be given to the more sickly, and to those whose health requires it; and some who foolishly refuse, they fraternally admonish, lest by vain superstition they sooner become more weak than more holy. Thus they sedulously practise piety, while they know that bodily exercise is only for a short time. Charity especially is observed : their food is adapted to charity, their speech to charity, their dress to charity, their looks to charity. They go together, and breathe only charity : they deem it as unlawful to offend charity as to offend God ; if any one opposes it, he is cast out and shunned ; if any one offends it, he is not permitted to remain one day" (August. De Moribus Eccl. Cath. c. 33). Since this holy man appears in these words to have exhibited the monastic life of ancient times as in a picture, I have thought it right to insert them here, though somewhat long, because I perceive that I would be considerably longer if I collected them from different writers, however compendious I might study to be.

10. Here, however, I had no intention to discuss the whole subject. I only wished to show, by the way, what kind of monks the early Church had, and what the monastic profession then was, that from the contrast sound readers might judge how great the effrontery is of those who allege antiquity in support of present monkism. Augus-

tine, while tracing out a holy and legitimate monasticism, would keep away all rigorous exaction of those things which the word of the Lord has left free.   But in the present day nothing is more rigorously exacted.   For they deem it an inexpiable crime if any one deviates in the least degree from the prescribed form in colour or species of dress, in the kind of food, or in other frivolous and frigid ceremonies.   Augustine strenuously contends that it is not lawful for monks to live in idleness on other men's means.   (August. De Oper. Monach.)   He denies that any such example was to be found in his day in a well-regulated monastery.   Our monks place the principal part of their holiness in idleness.   For if you take away their idleness, where will that contemplative life by which they glory that they excel all others, and make a near approach to the angels?   Augustine, in fine, requires a monasticism which may be nothing else than a training and assistant to the offices of piety which are recommended to all Christians.   What? When he makes charity its chief and almost its only rule, do we think he praises that combination by which a few men, bound to each other, are separated from the whole body of the Church?   Nay, he wishes them to set an example to others of preserving the unity of the Church.   So different is the nature of present monachism in both respects, that it would be difficult to find anything so dissimilar, not to say contrary.   For our monks, not satisfied with that piety, on the study of which alone Christ enjoins his followers to be intent, imagine some new kind of piety, by aspiring to which they are more perfect than all other men.

11. If they deny this, I should like to know why they honour their own order only with the title of perfection, and deny it to all other divine callings.[1]   I am not unaware of the sophistical solution that their order is not so called because it contains perfection in itself, but because it is the best of all for acquiring perfection.   When they would extol themselves to the people; when they would lay a snare for rash and ignorant youth; when they would assert their privileges and exalt their own dignity to the disparagement of others, they boast that they are in a state of perfection.   When they are too closely pressed to be able to defend this vain arrogance, they betake themselves to the subterfuge that they have not yet obtained perfection, but that they are in a state in which they aspire to it more than others; meanwhile, the people continue to admire as if the monastic life alone were angelic, perfect, and purified from every vice.   Under this pretence they ply a most gainful traffic, while their moderation lies buried in a few volumes.[2]   Who sees not that this

1 Laurentius, defending his written assertion, that the monks falsely imagined that by means of their profession they merited more than others, admirably concludes. "There is no safer, no better way than that taught by Christ, and in it no profession is enjoined."

2 French, "Par ce moyen ils attirent farine au moulin et vendent leur sainteté tres cherement; cependant cette glose est cachee et comme ensevelie en peu de livres;"— by this means they bring grist to their mill, and sell their holiness very dear; meanwhile, the gloss is concealed, and is, as it were, buried in a few books.

is intolerable trifling? But let us treat with them as if they ascribed nothing more to their profession than to call it a state for acquiring perfection. Surely by giving it this name, they distinguish it by a special mark from other modes of life. And who will allow such honour to be transferred to an institution of which not one syllable is said in approbation, while all the other callings of God are deemed unworthy of the same, though not only commanded by his sacred lips, but adorned with distinguished titles? And how great the insult offered to God, when some device of man is preferred to all the modes of life which he has ordered, and by his testimony approved?

12. But let them say I calumniated them when I declared that they were not contented with the rule prescribed by God. Still, though I were silent, they more than sufficiently accuse themselves; for they plainly declare that they undertake a greater burden than Christ has imposed on his followers, since they promise that they will keep evangelical counsels regarding the love of enemies, the suppression of vindictive feelings, and abstinence from swearing, counsels to which Christians are not commonly astricted. In this what antiquity can they pretend? None of the ancients ever thought of such a thing: all with one voice proclaim that not one syllable proceeded from Christ which it is not necessary to obey. And the very things which these worthy expounders pretend that Christ only counselled they uniformly declare, without any doubt, that he expressly enjoined. But as we have shown above, that this is a most pestilential error, let it suffice here to have briefly observed that monasticism, as it now exists, founded on an idea which all pious men ought to execrate— namely, the pretence that there is some more perfect rule of life than that common rule which God has delivered to the whole Church. Whatever is built on this foundation cannot but be abominable.

13. But they produce another argument for their perfection, and deem it invincible. Our Lord said to the young man who put a question to him concerning the perfection of righteousness, " If thou wilt be perfect, go and sell that thou hast, and give to the poor" (Matth. xix. 21). Whether they do so, I do not now dispute. Let us grant for the present that they do. They boast, then, that they have become perfect by abandoning their all. If the sum of perfection consists in this, what is the meaning of Paul's doctrne, that though a man should give all his goods to feed the poor, and have not charity, he is nothing? (1 Cor. xiii. 3). What kind of perfection is that which, if charity be wanting, is with the individual himself reduced to nothing? Here they must of necessity answer that it is indeed the highest, but is not the only work of perfection. But here again Paul interposes; and hesitates not to declare that charity, without any renunciation of that sort, is the " bond of perfectness " (Col. iii. 14). If it is certain that there is no disagreement between the scholar and the master, and the latter clearly denies that the perfection of a man consists in renouncing all his goods, and on the other hand asserts that perfection may exist without it, we must see

in what sense we should understand the words of Christ, " If thou wilt be perfect, go and sell that thou hast." Now, there will not be the least obscurity in the meaning if we consider (this ought to be attended to in all our Saviour's discourses) to whom the words are addressed (Luke x. 25). A young man asks by what works he shall enter into eternal life. Christ, as he was asked concerning works, refers him to the law. And justly ; for, considered in itself, it is the way of eternal life, and its inefficacy to give eternal life is owing to our depravity. By this answer Christ declared that he did not deliver any other rule of life than that which had formerly been delivered in the law of the Lord. Thus he both bore testimony to the divine law, that it was a doctrine of perfect righteousness, and at the same time met the calumnious charge of seeming, by some new rule of life, to incite the people to revolt from the law. The young man, who was not ill-disposed, but was puffed up with vain confidence, answers that he had observed all the precepts of the law from his youth. It is absolutely certain that he was immeasurably distant from the goal which he boasted of having reached. Had his boast been true, he would have wanted nothing of absolute perfection. For it has been demonstrated above, that the law contains in it a perfect righteousness. This is even obvious from the fact, that the observance of it is called the way to eternal life. To show him how little progress he had made in that righteousness which he too boldly answered that he had fulfilled, it was right to bring before him his besetting sin. Now, while he abounded in riches, he had his heart set upon them. Therefore, because he did not feel this secret wound, it is probed by Christ—" Go," says he, " and sell that thou hast." Had he been as good a keeper of the law as he supposed, he would not have gone away sorrowful on hearing these words. For he who loves God with his whole heart, not only regards everything which wars with his love as dross, but hates it as destruction (Phil. iii. 8). Therefore, when Christ orders a rich miser to leave all that he has, it is the same as if he had ordered the ambitious to renounce all his honours, the voluptuous all his luxuries, the unchaste all the instruments of his lust. Thus consciences, which are not reached by any general admonition, are to be recalled to a particular feeling of their particular sin. In vain, therefore, do they wrest that special case to a general interpretation, as if Christ had decided that the perfection of man consists in the abandonment of his goods, since he intended nothing more by the expression than to bring a youth who was out of measure satisfied with himself to feel his sore, and so understand that he was still at a great distance from that perfect obedience of the law which he falsely ascribed to himself. I admit that this passage was ill understood by some of the Fathers ; [1] and hence arose an affectation of voluntary poverty, those only being thought

---

[1] Chrysostom, in his Homily on the words of Paul, " Salute Prisca," &c., says, " All who retire to monasteries separate themselves from the Church, seeing they plainly assert that their monasticism is the form of a second baptism."

blest who abandoned all earthly goods, and in a state of destitution devoted themselves to Christ. But I am confident that, after my exposition, no good and reasonable man will have any dubiety here as to the mind of Christ.

14. Still there was nothing with the Fathers less intended than to establish that kind of perfection which was afterwards fabricated by cowled monks, in order to rear up a speices of double Christianity. For as yet the sacrilegious dogma was not broached which compares the profession of monasticism to baptism, nay, plainly asserts that it is the form of a second baptism. Who can doubt that the Fathers with their whole hearts abhorred such blasphemy? Then what need is there to demonstrate, by words, that the last quality which Augustine mentions as belonging to the ancient monks—viz. that they in all things accommodated themselves to charity—is most alien from this new profession? The thing itself declares that all who retire into monasteries withdraw from the Church. For how? Do they not separate themselves from the legitimate society of the faithful, by acquiring for themselves a special ministry and private administration of the sacraments? What is meant by destroying the communion of the Church if this is not? And to follow out the comparison with which I began, and at once close the point, what resemblance have they in this respect to the ancient monks? These, though they dwelt separately from others, had not a separate Church; they partook of the sacraments with others, they attended public meetings, and were then a part of the people. But what have those men done in erecting a private altar for themselves but broken the bond of unity? For they have excommunicated themselves from the whole body of the Church, and contemned the ordinary ministry by which the Lord has been pleased that peace and charity should be preserved among his followers. Wherefore I hold that as many monasteries as there are in the present day, so many conventicles are there of schismatics, who have disturbed ecclesiastical order, and been cut off from the legitimate society of the faithful. And that there might be no doubt as to their separation, they have given themselves the various names of factions. They have not been ashamed to glory in that which Paul so execrates, that he is unable to express his detestation too strongly. Unless, indeed, we suppose that Christ was not divided by the Corinthians, when one teacher set himself above another (1 Cor. i. 12, 13; iii. 4); and that now no injury is done to Christ when, instead of Christians, we hear some called Benedictines, others Franciscans, others Dominicans, and so called, that while they affect to be distinguished from the common body of Christians, they proudly substitute these names for a religious profession.

15. The differences which I have hitherto pointed out between the ancient monks and those of our age are not in manners, but in profession. Hence let my readers remember that I have spoken of monachism rather than of monks; and marked, not the vices which cleave to a few, but vices which are inseparable from the very mode of life. In regard to

manners, of what use is it to particularise and show how great the difference? This much is certain,[1] that there is no order of men more polluted by all kinds of vicious turpitude; nowhere do faction, hatred, party-spirit, and intrigue, more prevail. In a few monasteries, indeed, they live chastely, if we are to call it chastity, where lust is so far repressed as not to be openly infamous; still you will scarcely find one in ten which is not rather a brothel than a sacred abode of chastity. But how frugally they live? Just like swine wallowing in their sties. But lest they complain that I deal too unmercifully with them, I go no farther; although any one who knows the case will admit, that in the few things which I have said, I have not spoken in the spirit of an accuser. Augustine though he testifies, that the monks excelled so much in chastity, yet complains that there were many vagabonds, who, by wicked arts and impostures, extracted money from the more simple, plying a shameful traffic, by carrying about the relics of martyrs, and vending any dead man's bones for relics, bringing ignominy on their order by many similar iniquities. As he declares that he had seen none better than those who had profited in monasteries; so he laments that he had seen none worse than those who had backslidden in monasteries. What would he say were he, in the present day, to see now almost all monasteries overflowing, and in a manner bursting, with numerous deplorable vices? I say nothing but what is notorious to all; and yet this charge does not apply to all without a single exception; for, as the rule and discipline of holy living was never so well framed in monasteries as that there were not always some drones very unlike the others; so I hold that, in the present day, monks have not so completely degenerated from that holy antiquity as not to have some good men among them; but these few lie scattered up and down among a huge multitude of wicked and dishonest men, and are not only despised, but even petulantly assailed, sometimes even treated cruelly by the others, who, according to the Milesian proverb, think they ought to have no good man among them.

16. By this contrast between ancient and modern monasticism, I trust I have gained my object, which was to show that our cowled monks falsely pretend the example of the primitive Church in defence of their profession; since they differ no less from the monks of that period than apes do from men. Meanwhile I disguise not that even in that ancient form which Augustine commends, there was something which little pleases me. I admit that they were not superstitious in the external exercises of a more rigorous discipline, but I say that they were not without a degree of affectation and false zeal. It was a fine thing to cast away their substance, and free themselves from all worldly cares; but God sets more value on the pious management of a household, when the head of it, discarding all avarice,

---

[1] See Bernard. ad Guliel. Abbat. "I wonder why there is so much intemperance among monks. O vanity of vanities! but not more vain than insane." See also August. de Opere Monach. in fin

ambition, and other lusts of the flesh, makes it his purpose to serve God in some particular vocation. It is fine to philosophise in seclusion, far away from the intercourse of society; but it ill accords with Christian meekness for any one, as if in hatred of the human race, to fly to the wilderness and to solitude, and at the same time desert the duties which the Lord has especially commanded. Were we to grant that there was nothing worse in that profession, there is certainly no small evil in its having introduced a useless and perilous example into the Church.

17. Now, then, let us see the nature of the vows by which the monks of the present day are initiated into this famous order. First, as their intention is to institute a new and fictitious worship with a view to gain favour with God, I conclude from what has been said above, that everything which they vow is abomination to God. Secondly, I hold that as they frame their own mode of life at pleasure, without any regard to the calling of God, or to his approbation, the attempt is rash and unlawful; because their conscience has no ground on which it can support itself before God; and "whatsoever is not of faith is sin" (Rom. xiv. 23). Moreover, I maintain that in astricting themselves to many perverse and impious modes of worship, such as are exhibited in modern monasticism, they consecrate themselves not to God but to the devil. For why should the prophets have been permitted to say that the Israelites sacrificed their sons to devils and not to God (Deut. xxxii. 17; Ps. cvi. 37), merely because they had corrupted the true worship of God by profane ceremonies; and we not be permitted to say the same thing of monks who, along with the cowl, cover themselves with the net of a thousand impious superstitions? Then what is their species of vows? They offer God a promise of perpetual virginity, as if they had previously made a compact with him to free them from the necessity of marriage. They cannot allege that they make this vow trusting entirely to the grace of God; for, seeing he declares this to be a special gift not given to all (Matth. xix. 11), no man has a right to assume that the gift will be his. Let those who have it use it; and if at any time they feel the infirmity of the flesh, let them have recourse to the aid of him by whose power alone they can resist. If this avails not, let them not despise the remedy which is offered to them. If the faculty of continence is denied, the voice of God distinctly calls upon them to marry. By continence I mean not merely that by which the body is kept pure from fornication, but that by which the mind keeps its chastity untainted. For Paul enjoins caution not only against external lasciviousness, but also burning of mind (1 Cor. vii. 9). It has been the practice (they say) from the remotest period, for those who wished to devote themselves entirely to God, to bind themselves by a vow of continence. I confess that the custom is ancient, but I do not admit that the age when it commenced was so free from every defect that all that was then done is to be regarded as a rule. Moreover, the inexorable rigour of holding that after the vow is conceived there is

no room for repentance, crept in gradually. This is clear from Cyprian. "If virgins have dedicated themselves to Christian faith, let them live modestly and chastely, without pretence. Thus strong and stable, let them wait for the reward of virginity. But if they will not, or cannot persevere, it is better to marry, than by their faults to fall into the fire." In the present day, with what invectives would they not lacerate any one who should seek to temper the vow of continence by such an equitable course? Those, therefore, have wandered far from the ancient custom who not only use no moderation, and grant no pardon when any one proves unequal to the performance of his vow, but shamelessly declare that it is a more heinous sin to cure the intemperance of the flesh by marriage, than to defile body and soul by whoredom.

18. But they still insist and attempt to show that this vow was used in the days of the apostles, because Paul says that widows who marry after having once undertaken a public office, "cast off their first faith" (1 Tim. v. 12). I by no means deny that widows who dedicated themselves and their labours to the Church, at the same time came under an obligation of perpetual celibacy, not because they regarded it in the light of a religious duty, as afterwards began to be the case, but because they could not perform their functions unless they had their time at their own command, and were free from the nuptial tie. But if, after giving their pledge, they began to look to a new marriage, what else was this but to shake off the calling of God? It is not strange, therefore, when Paul says that by such desires they grow wanton against Christ. In further explanation he afterwards adds, that by not performing their promises to the Church, they violate and nullify their first faith given in baptism; one of the things contained in this first faith being, that every one should correspond to his calling. Unless you choose rather to interpret that, having lost their modesty, they afterwards cast off all care of decency, prostituting themselves to all kinds of lasciviousness and pertness, leading licentious and dissolute lives, than which nothing can less become Christian women. I am much pleased with this exposition. Our answer then is, that those widows who were admitted to a public ministry came under an obligation of perpetual celibacy, and hence we easily understand how, when they married, they threw off all modesty, and became more insolent than became Christian women that in this way they not only sinned by violating the faith given to the Church, but revolted from the common rule of pious women. But, first, I deny that they had any other reason for professing celibacy than just because marriage was altogether inconsistent with the function which they undertook. Hence they bound themselves to celibacy only in so far as the nature of their function required. Secondly, I do not admit that they were bound to celibacy in such a sense that it was not better for them to marry than to suffer by the incitements of the flesh, and fall into uncleanness. Thirdly, I hold that what Paul enjoined was in the common case free from danger,

because he orders the selection to be made from those who, contented with one marriage, had already given proof of continence. Our only reason for disapproving of the vow of celibacy is, because it is improperly regarded as an act of worship, and is rashly undertaken by persons who have not the power of keeping it.

19. But what ground can there be for applying this passage to nuns? For deaconesses were appointed, not to soothe God by chantings or unintelligible murmurs, and spend the rest of their time in idleness; but to perform a public ministry of the Church toward the poor, and to labour with all zeal, assiduity, and diligence, in offices of charity. They did not vow celibacy, that they might thereafter exhibit abstinence from marriage as a kind of worship rendered to God, but only that they might be freer from encumbrance in executing their office. In fine, they did not vow on attaining adolescence, or in the bloom of life, and so afterwards learn, by too late experience, over what a precipice they had plunged themselves, but after they were thought to have surmounted all danger, they took a vow not less safe than holy. But not to press the two former points, I say that it was unlawful to allow women to take a vow of continence before their sixtieth year, since the apostle admits such only, and enjoins the younger to marry and beget children. Therefore, it is impossible, on any ground, to excuse the deduction, first of twelve, then of twenty, and, lastly, of thirty years. Still less possible is it to tolerate the case of miserable girls, who, before they have reached an age at which they can know themselves, or have any experience of their character, are not only induced by fraud, but compelled by force and threats, to entangle themselves in these accursed snares. I will not enter at length into a refutation of the other two vows. This only I say, that besides involving (as matters stand in the present day) not a few superstitions, they seem to be purposely framed in such a manner, as to make those who take them mock God and men. But lest we should seem, with too malignant feeling, to attack every particular point, we will be contented with the general refutation which has been given above.

20. The nature of the vows which are legitimate and acceptable to God, I think I have sufficiently explained. Yet, because some ill-informed and timid consciences, even when a vow displeases, and is condemned, nevertheless hesitate as to the obligation, and are grievously tormented, shuddering at the thought of violating a pledge given to God, and, on the other hand, fearing to sin more by keeping it,—we must here come to their aid, and enable them to escape from this difficulty. And to take away all scruple at once, I say that all vows not legitimate, and not duly conceived, as they are of no account with God, should be regarded by us as null. (See Calv. ad Concil. Trident.) For if, in human contracts, those promises only are binding in which he with whom we contract wishes to have us bound, it is absurd to say that we are bound to perform things which God does not at all require of us, especially since our works can only

be right when they please God, and have the testimony of our consciences that they do please him. For it always remains fixed, that "whatsoever is not of faith is sin" (Rom. xiv. 23). By this Paul means, that any work undertaken in doubt is vicious, because at the root of all good works lies faith, which assures us that they are acceptable to God. Therefore, if Christian men may not attempt anything without this assurance, why, if they have undertaken anything rashly through ignorance, may they not afterwards be freed, and desist from their error? Since vows rashly undertaken are of this description, they not only oblige not, but must necessarily be rescinded. What, then, when they are not only of no estimation in the sight of God, but are even an abomination, as has already been demonstrated? It is needless farther to discuss a point which does not require it. To appease pious consciences, and free them from all doubt, this one argument seems to me sufficient—viz. that all works whatsoever which flow not from a pure fountain, and are not directed to a proper end, are repudiated by God, and so repudiated, that he no less forbids us to continue than to begin them. Hence it follows, that vows dictated by error and superstition are of no weight with God, and ought to be abandoned by us.

21. He who understands this solution is furnished with the means of repelling the calumnies of the wicked against those who withdraw from monasticism to some honest kind of livelihood. They are grievously charged with having perjured themselves, and broken their faith, because they have broken the bond (vulgarly supposed to be indissoluble) by which they had bound themselves to God and the Church. But I say, first, there is no bond when that which man confirms God abrogates; and, secondly, even granting that they were bound when they remained entangled in ignorance and error, now, since they have been enlightened by the knowledge of the truth, I hold that they are, at the same time, free by the grace of Christ. For if such is the efficacy of the cross of Christ, that it frees us from the curse of the divine law by which we were held bound, how much more must it rescue us from extraneous chains, which are nothing but the wily nets of Satan? There can be no doubt, therefore, that all on whom Christ shines with the light of his Gospel, he frees from all the snares in which they had entangled themselves through superstition. At the same time, they have another defence if they were unfit for celibacy. For if an impossible vow is certain destruction to the soul, which God wills to be saved and not destroyed, it follows that it ought by no means to be adhered to. Now, how impossible the vow of continence is to those who have not received it by special gift, we have shown, and experience, even were I silent, declares: while the great obscenity with which almost all monasteries teem is a thing not unknown. If any seem more decent and modest than others, they are not, however, chaste. The sin of unchastity urges, and lurks within. Thus it is that God, by fearful examples, punishes the audacity of men, when, unmindful of their

infirmity, they, against nature, affect that which has been denied to them, and despising the remedies which the Lord has placed in their hands, are confident in their ability to overcome the disease of incontinence by contumacious obstinacy. For what other name can we give it, when a man, admonished of his need of marriage, and of the remedy with which the Lord has thereby furnished, not only despises it, but binds himself by an oath to despise it?

CHAPTER XIV.

OF THE SACRAMENTS.

This chapter consists of two principal parts,—I. Of sacraments in general. The sum of the doctrine stated, sec. 1–6. Two classes of opponents to be guarded against—viz. those who undervalue the power of the sacraments, sec. 7–13; and those who attribute too much to the sacraments, sec. 14–17. II. Of the sacraments in particular, both of the Old and the New Testament. Their scope and meaning. Refutation of those who have either too high or too low ideas of the sacraments.

Sections.

1. Of the sacraments in general. A sacrament defined.
2. Meaning of the word sacrament.
3. Definition explained. Why God seals his promises to us by sacraments.
4. The word which ought to accompany the element, that the sacrament may be complete.
5. Error of those who attempt to separate the word, or promise of God, from the element.
6. Why sacraments are called Signs of the Covenant.
7. They are such signs, though the wicked should receive them, but are signs of grace only to believers.
8. Objections to this view answered.
9. No secret virtue in the sacraments. Their whole efficacy depends on the inward operation of the Spirit.
10. Objections answered. Illustrated by a simile.
11. Of the increase of faith by the preaching of the word.
12. In what way, and how far, the sacraments are confirmations of our faith.
13. Some regard the sacraments as mere signs. This view refuted.
14. Some again attribute too much to the sacraments. Refutation.
15. Refutation confirmed by a passage from Augustine.
16. Previous views more fully explained.
17. The matter of the sacrament always present when the sacrament is duly administered.
18. Extensive meaning of the term sacrament.
19. The ordinary sacraments in the Church. How necessary they are.
20. The sacraments of the Old and of the New Testament. The end of both the same —viz. to lead us to Christ.
21. This apparent in the sacraments of the Old Testament.
22. Apparent also in the sacraments of the New Testament.
23. Impious doctrine of the Schoolmen as to the difference between the Old and the New Testaments.
24. Scholastic objection answered.
25. Another objection answered.
26. Sacraments of the New Testament sometimes excessively extolled by early Theologians. Their meaning explained.

1. AKIN to the preaching of the gospel, we have another help to our faith in the sacraments, in regard to which, it greatly concerns us that some sure doctrine should be delivered, informing us both of the end for which they were instituted, and of their present use. First, we must attend to what a sacrament is. It seems to me, then, a simple and appropriate definition to say, that it is an external sign,

by which the Lord seals on our consciences his promises of good-will toward us, in order to sustain the weakness of our faith, and we in our turn testify our piety towards him, both before himself, and before angels as well as men. We may also define more briefly by calling it a testimony of the divine favour toward us, confirmed by an external sign, with a corresponding attestation of our faith towards Him. You may make your choice of these definitions, which in meaning differ not from that of Augustine, which defines a sacrament to be a visible sign of a sacred thing, or a visible form of an invisible grace, but does not contain a better or surer explanation. As its brevity makes it somewhat obscure, and thereby misleads the more illiterate, I wished to remove all doubt, and make the definition fuller by stating it at greater length.

2. The reason why the ancients used the term in this sense is not obscure. The old interpreter, whenever he wished to render the Greek term μυστήριον into Latin, especially when it was used with reference to divine things, used the word *sacramentum*. Thus, in Ephesians, "Having made known unto us the mystery (*sacramentum*) of his will;" and again, "If ye have heard of the dispensation of the grace of God, which is given me to you-wards, how that by revelation he made known unto me the mystery" (*sacramentum*) (Eph. i. 9; iii. 2). In the Colossians, "Even the mystery which hath been hid from ages and from generations, but is now made manifest to his saints, to whom God would make known what is the riches of the glory of this mystery" (*sacramentum*) (Col. i. 26). Also in the First Epistle to Timothy, "Without controversy, great is the mystery (*sacramentum*) of godliness: God was manifest in the flesh" (1 Tim. iii. 16). He was unwilling to use the word *arcanum* (secret), lest the word should seem beneath the magnitude of the thing meant. When the thing, therefore, was sacred and secret, he used the term *sacramentum*. In this sense it frequently occurs in ecclesiastical writers. And it is well known, that what the Latins call *sacramenta*, the Greeks call μυστήρια (mysteries). The sameness of meaning removes all dispute. Hence it is that the term was applied to those signs which gave an august representation of things spiritual and sublime. This is also observed by Augustine, "It were tedious to discourse of the variety of signs; those which relate to divine things are called sacraments" (August. Ep. 5. ad Marcell.).

3. From the definition which we have given, we perceive that there never is a sacrament without an antecedent promise, the sacrament being added as a kind of appendix, with the view of confirming and sealing the promise, and giving a better attestation, or rather, in a manner, confirming it. In this way God provides first for our ignorance and sluggishness, and, secondly, for our infirmity; and yet, properly speaking, it does not so much confirm his word as establish us in the faith of it. For the truth of God is in itself sufficiently stable and certain, and cannot receive a better confirmation from any

other quarter than from itself.   But as our faith is slender and weak, so if it be not propped up on every side, and supported by all kinds of means, it is forthwith shaken and tossed to and fro, wavers, and even falls.   And here, indeed, our merciful Lord, with boundless condescension, so accommodates himself to our capacity, that seeing how from our animal nature we are always creeping on the ground, and cleaving to the flesh, having no thought of what is spiritual, and not even forming an idea of it, he declines not by means of these earthly elements to lead us to himself, and even in the flesh to exhibit a mirror of spiritual blessings.   For, as Chrysostom says (Hom. 60, ad Popul.).   " Were we incorporeal, he would give us these things in a naked and incorporeal form.   Now because our souls are implanted in bodies, he delivers spiritual things under things visible.   Not that the qualities which are set before us in the sacraments are inherent in the nature of the things, but God gives them this signification."

4. This is commonly expressed by saying that a sacrament consists of the word and the external sign.   By the word we ought to understand not one which, muttered without meaning and without faith, by its sound merely, as by a magical incantation, has the effect of consecrating the element, but one which, preached, makes us understand what the visible sign means.   The thing, therefore, which was frequently done, under the tyranny of the Pope, was not free from great profanation of the mystery, for they deemed it sufficient if the priest muttered the formula of consecration, while the people, without understanding, looked stupidly on.   Nay, this was done for the express purpose of preventing any instruction from thereby reaching the people: for all was said in Latin to illiterate hearers.   Superstition afterwards was carried to such a height, that the consecration was thought not to be duly performed except in a low grumble, which few could hear.   Very different is the doctrine of Augustine concerning the sacramental word.   " Let the word be added to the element, and it will become a sacrament.   For whence can there be so much virtue in water as to touch the body and cleanse the heart, unless by the agency of the word, and this not because it is said, but because it is believed?   For even in the word the transient sound is one thing, the permanent power another.   This is the word of faith which we preach says the Apostle (Rom. x. 8).   Hence, in the Acts of the Apostles, we have the expression, " Purify their hearts by faith" (Acts xv. 9).   And the Apostle Peter says, " The like figure whereunto even baptism doth now save us (not the putting away of the filth of the flesh, but the answer of a good conscience) " (1 Pet. iii. 21).   " This is the word of faith which we preach : by which word doubtless baptism also, in order that it may be able to cleanse, is consecrated " (August. Hom. in Joann. 13).   You see how he requires preaching to the production of faith.   And we need not labour to prove this, since there is not the least room for doubt as to what Christ did, and commanded us to do, as to what the apostles followed, and a purer Church observed.   Nay, it is known that, from the very

beginning of the world, whenever God offered any sign to the holy Patriarchs, it was inseparably attached to doctrine, without which our senses would gaze bewildered on an unmeaning object. Therefore, when we hear mention made of the sacramental word, let us understand the promise which, proclaimed aloud by the minister, leads the people by the hand to that to which the sign tends and directs us.

5. Nor are those to be listened to who oppose this view with a more subtle than solid dilemma. They argue thus: We either know that the word of God which precedes the sacrament is the true will of God, or we do not know it. If we know it, we learn nothing new from the sacrament which succeeds. If we do not know it, we cannot learn it from the sacrament, whose whole efficacy depends on the word. Our brief reply is: The seals which are affixed to diplomas, and other public deeds, are nothing considered in themselves, and would be affixed to no purpose if nothing was written on the parchment, and yet this does not prevent them from sealing and confirming when they are appended to writings. It cannot be alleged that this comparison is a recent fiction of our own, since Paul himself used it, terming *circumcision a seal* (Rom. iv. 11), where he expressly maintains that the circumcision of Abraham was not for justification, but was an attestation to the covenant, by the faith of which he had been previously justified. And how, pray, can any one be greatly offended when we teach that the promise is sealed by the sacrament, since it is plain, from the promises themselves, that one promise confirms another? The clearer any evidence is, the fitter is it to support our faith. But sacraments bring with them the clearest promises, and, when compared with the word, have this peculiarity, that they represent promises to the life, as if painted in a picture. Nor ought we to be moved by an objection founded on the distinction between sacraments and the seals of documents—viz. that since both consist of the carnal elements of this world, the former cannot be sufficient or adequate to seal the promises of God, which are spiritual and eternal, though the latter may be employed to seal the edicts of princes concerning fleeting and fading things. But the believer, when the sacraments are presented to his eye, does not stop short at the carnal spectacle, but by the steps of analogy which I have indicated, rises with pious consideration to the sublime mysteries which lie hidden in the sacraments.

6. As the Lord calls his promises covenants (Gen. vi. 18 ; ix. 9 ; xvii. 2), and sacraments signs of the covenants, so something similar may be inferred from human covenants. What could the slaughter of a hog effect, unless words were interposed or rather preceded? Swine are often killed without any interior or occult mystery. What could be gained by pledging the right hand, since hands are not unfrequently joined in giving battle? But when words have preceded, then by such symbols of covenant sanction is given to laws, though previously conceived, digested, and enacted by words. Sacra-

ments, therefore, are exercises which confirm our faith in the word of God; and because we are carnal, they are exhibited under carnal objects, that thus they may train us in accommodation to our sluggish capacity, just as nurses lead children by the hand. And hence Augustine calls a sacrament a *visible word* (August. in Joann. Hom. 89), because it represents the promises of God as in a picture, and places them in our view in a graphic bodily form (August. cont. Faust. Lib. xix.). We might refer to other similitudes, by which sacraments are more plainly designated, as when they are called the pillars of our faith. For just as a building stands and leans on its foundation, and yet is rendered more stable when supported by pillars, so faith leans on the word of God as its proper foundation, and yet when sacraments are added leans more firmly, as if resting on pillars. Or we may call them mirrors, in which we may contemplate the riches of the grace which God bestows upon us. For then, as has been said, he manifests himself to us in as far as our dulness can enable us to recognise him, and testifies his love and kindness to us more expressly than by word.

7. It is irrational to contend that sacraments are not manifestations of divine grace toward us, because they are held forth to the ungodly also, who, however, so far from experiencing God to be more propitious to them, only incur greater condemnation. By the same reasoning, the gospel will be no manifestation of the grace of God, because it is spurned by many who hear it; nor will Christ himself be a manifestation of grace, because of the many by whom he was seen and known, very few received him. Something similar may be seen in public enactments. A great part of the body of the people deride and evade the authenticating seal, though they know it was employed by their sovereign to confirm his will; others trample it under foot, as a matter by no means appertaining to them; while others even execrate it: so that, seeing the condition of the two things to be alike, the appropriateness of the comparison which I made above ought to be more readily allowed. It is certain, therefore, that the Lord offers us his mercy, and a pledge of his grace, both in his sacred word and in the sacraments; but it is not apprehended save by those who receive the word and sacraments with firm faith: in like manner as Christ, though offered and held forth for salvation to all, is not, however, acknowledged and received by all. Augustine, when intending to intimate this, said that the efficacy of the word is produced in the sacrament, *not because it is spoken, but because it is believed.* Hence Paul, addressing believers, includes communion with Christ, in the sacraments, as when he says, " As many of you as have been baptized into Christ have put on Christ" (Gal. iii. 27). Again, " For by one Spirit we are all baptized into one body" (1 Cor. xii. 13). But when he speaks of a preposterous use of the sacraments, he attributes nothing more to them than to frigid, empty figures; thereby intimating, that however the ungodly and hypocrites may, by their perverseness, either suppress, or obscure, or impede

the effect of divine grace in the sacraments, that does not prevent them, where and whenever God is so pleased, from giving a true evidence of communion with Christ, or prevent them from exhibiting, and the Spirit of God from performing, the very thing which they promise. We conclude, therefore, that the sacraments are truly termed evidences of divine grace, and, as it were, seals of the good-will which he entertains toward us. They, by sealing it to us, sustain, nourish, confirm, and increase our faith. The objections usually urged against this view are frivolous and weak. They say that our faith, if it is good, cannot be made better; for there is no faith save that which leans unshakingly, firmly, and undividedly, on the mercy of God. It had been better for the objectors to pray, with the apostles, " Lord, increase our faith" (Luke xvii. 5), than confidently to maintain a perfection of faith which none of the sons of men ever attained, none ever shall attain, in this life. Let them explain what kind of faith his was who said, "Lord, I believe; help thou mine unbelief" (Mark ix. 24). That faith, though only commenced, was good, and might, by the removal of the unbelief, be made better. But there is no better argument to refute them than their own consciousness. For if they confess themselves sinners (this, whether they will or not, they cannot deny), then they must of necessity impute this very quality to the imperfection of their faith.

8. But Philip, they say, replied to the eunuch who asked to be baptized, "If thou believest with all thine heart thou mayest" (Acts viii. 37). What room is there for a confirmation of baptism when faith fills the whole heart? I, in my turn, ask them, Do they not feel that a good part of their heart is void of faith—do they not perceive new additions to it every day? There was one who boasted that he grew old while learning. Thrice miserable, then, are we Christians if we grow old without making progress, we whose faith ought to advance through every period of life until it grow up into a perfect man (Eph. iv. 13). In this passage, therefore, to believe *with the whole heart*, is not to believe Christ perfectly, but only to embrace him sincerely with heart and soul; not to be filled with him, but with ardent affection to hunger and thirst, and sigh after him. It is usual in Scripture to say that a thing is done with the whole heart, when it is done sincerely and cordially. Of this description are the following passages:—" With my whole heart have I sought thee" (Ps. cxix. 10) ; " I will confess unto thee with my whole heart," &c. In like manner, when the fraudulent and deceitful are rebuked, it is said " with flattering lips, and with a double heart, do they speak " (Ps. xii. 2). The objectors next add—" If faith is increased by means of the sacraments, the Holy Spirit is given in vain, seeing it is his office to begin, sustain, and consummate our faith." I admit, indeed, that faith is the proper and entire work of the Holy Spirit, enlightened by whom we recognise God and the treasures of his grace, and without whose illumination our mind is so blind that it can see nothing, so stupid that it has no relish for spiritual things. But

for the one Divine blessing which they proclaim we count three. For, first, the Lord teaches and trains us by his word; next, he confirms us by his sacraments; lastly, he illumines our mind by the light of his Holy Spirit, and opens up an entrance into our hearts for his word and sacraments, which would otherwise only strike our ears, and fall upon our sight, but by no means affect us inwardly.

9. Wherefore, with regard to the increase and confirmation of faith, I would remind the reader (though I think I have already expressed it in unambiguous terms), that in assigning this office to the sacraments, it is not as if I thought that there is a kind of secret efficacy perpetually inherent in them, by which they can of themselves promote or strengthen faith, but because our Lord has instituted them for the express purpose of helping to establish and increase our faith. The sacraments duly perform their office only when accompanied by the Spirit, the internal Master, whose energy alone penetrates the heart, stirs up the affections, and procures access for the sacraments into our souls. If he is wanting, the sacraments can avail us no more than the sun shining on the eyeballs of the blind, or sounds uttered in the ears of the deaf. Wherefore, in distributing between the Spirit and the sacraments, I ascribe the whole energy to him, and leave only a ministry to them; this ministry, without the agency of the Spirit, is empty and frivolous, but when he acts within, and exerts his power, it is replete with energy. It is now clear in what way, according to this view, a pious mind is confirmed in faith by means of the sacraments—viz. in the same way in which the light of the sun is seen by the eye, and the sound of the voice heard by the ear; the former of which would not be at all affected by the light unless it had a pupil on which the light might fall; nor the latter reached by any sound, however loud, were it not naturally adapted for hearing. But if it is true, as has been explained, that in the eye it is the power of vision which enables it to see the light, and in the ear the power of hearing which enables it to perceive the voice, and that in our hearts it is the work of the Holy Spirit to commence, maintain, cherish, and establish faith, then it follows, both that the sacraments do not avail one iota without the energy of the Holy Spirit; and that yet in hearts previously taught by that preceptor, there is nothing to prevent the sacraments from strengthening and increasing faith. There is only this difference, that the faculty of seeing and hearing is naturally implanted in the eye and ear; whereas, Christ acts in our minds above the measure of nature by special grace.

10. In this way, also, we dispose of certain objections by which some anxious minds are annoyed. If we ascribe either an increase or confirmation of faith to creatures, injustice is done to the Spirit of God, who alone ought to be regarded as its author. But we do not rob him of the merit of confirming and increasing faith; nay, rather, we maintain that that which confirms and increases faith, is nothing else than the preparing of our minds by his internal illumination to re-

ceive that confirmation which is set forth by the sacraments. But if the subject is still obscure, it will be made plain by the following similitude: Were you to begin to persuade a person by word to do something, you would think of all the arguments by which he may be brought over to your view, and in a manner compelled to serve your purpose. But nothing is gained if the individual himself possess not a clear and acute judgment, by which he may be able to weigh the value of your arguments; if, moreover, he is not of a docile disposition, and ready to listen to doctrine ; if, in fine, he has no such idea of your faith and prudence as in a manner to prejudice him in your favour, and secure his assent. For there are many obstinate spirits who are not to be bent by any arguments ; and where faith is suspected, or authority contemned, little progress is made even with the docile. On the other hand, when opposite feelings exist, the result will be, that the person whose interests you are consulting will acquiesce in the very counsels which he would otherwise have derided. The same work is performed in us by the Spirit. That the word may not fall upon our ear, or the sacraments be presented to our eye in vain, he shows that it is God who there speaks to us, softens our obdurate hearts, and frames them to the obedience which is due to his word ; in short, transmits those external words and sacraments from the ear to the soul. Both word and sacraments, therefore, confirm our faith, bringing under view the kind intentions of our heavenly Father, in the knowledge of which the whole assurance of our faith depends, and by which its strength is increased ; and the Spirit also confirms our faith when, by engraving that assurance on our minds, he renders it effectual. Meanwhile, it is easy for the Father of lights, in like manner as he illumines the bodily eye by the rays of the sun, to illumine our minds by the sacraments, as by a kind of intermediate brightness.

11. This property our Lord showed to belong to the external word, when, in the parable, he compared it to seed (Matth. xiii. 4 ; Luke viii. 15). For as the seed, when it falls on a deserted and neglected part of the field, can do nothing but die, but when thrown into ground properly laboured and cultivated, will yield a hundred-fold ; so the word of God, when addressed to any stubborn spirit, will remain without fruit, as if thrown upon the barren waste, but when it meets with a soul which the hand of the heavenly Spirit has subdued, will be most fruitful. But if the case of the seed and of the word is the same, and from the seed corn can grow and increase, and attain to maturity, why may not faith also take its beginning, increase, and completion from the word ? Both things are admirably explained by Paul in different passages. For when he would remind the Corinthians how God had given effect to his labours, he boasts that he possessed the ministry of the Spirit (1 Cor. ii. 4); just as if his preaching were inseparably connected with the power of the Holy Spirit, in inwardly enlightening the mind, and stimulating it. But in another passage, when he would remind them what the power of the word is

in itself, when preached by man, he compares ministers to husbandmen, who, after'they have expended labour and industry in cultivating the ground, have nothing more that they can do.   For what would ploughing, and sowing, and watering avail, unless that which was sown should, by the kindness of Heaven, vegetate?   Wherefore he concludes, that he that planteth, and he that watereth is nothing, but that the whole is to be ascribed to God, who alone gives the increase.   The apostles, therefore, exert the power of the Spirit in their preaching, inasmuch as God uses them as instruments which he has ordained for the unfolding of his spiritual grace.   Still, however, we must not lose sight of the distinction, but remember what man is able of himself to do, and what is peculiar to God.

12. The sacraments are confirmations of our faith in such a sense, that the Lord, sometimes, when he sees meet to withdraw our assurance of the things which he had promised in the sacraments, takes away the sacraments themselves.   When he deprives Adam of the gift of immortality, and expels him from the garden, " lest he put forth his hand and take also of the tree of life, and live for ever " (Gen. iii. 22)ı   What is this we hear?   Could that fruit have restored Adam to the immortality from which he had already fallen ?   By no means.   It is just as if he had said, Lest he indulge in vain confidence, if allowed to retain the symbol of my promise, let that be withdrawn which might give him some hope of immortality.   On this ground, when the apostle urges the Ephesians to remember, that they " were without Christ, being aliens from the commonwealth of Israel, and strangers from the covenants of promise, having no hope, and without God in the world" (Eph. ii. 12), he says that they were not partakers of circumcision.   He thus intimates metonymically, that all were excluded from the promise who had not received the badge of the promise.   To the other objection—viz. that when so much power is attributed to creatures, the glory of God is bestowed upon them, and thereby impaired—it is obvious to reply, that we attribute no power to the creatures.   All we say is, that God uses the means and instruments which he sees to be expedient, in order that all things may be subservient to his glory, he being the Lord and disposer of all.   Therefore, as by bread and other aliment he feeds our bodies, as by the sun he illumines, and by fire gives warmth to the world, and yet bread, sun, and fire are nothing, save inasmuch as they are instruments under which he dispenses his blessings to us; so in like manner he spiritually nourishes our faith by means of the sacraments, whose only office is to make his promises visible to our eye, or rather, to be pledges of his promises.   And as it is our duty in regard to the other creatures which the divine liberality and kindness has destined for our use, and by whose instrumentality he bestows the gifts of his goodness upon us, to put no confidence in them, nor to admire and extol them as the causes of our mercies; so neither ought our confidence to be fixed on the sacraments, nor ought the glory of God to be transferred to them, but passing beyond them all, our faith and

confession should rise to Him who is the Author of the sacraments and of all things.

13. There is nothing in the argument which some found on the very term *sacrament*. This term, they say, while it has many significations in approved authors, has only one which is applicable to signs—namely, when it is used for the formal oath which the soldier gives to his commander on entering the service. For as by that military oath recruits bind themselves to be faithful to their commander, and make a profession of military service; so by our signs we acknowledge Chirst to be our commander, and declare that we serve under his standard. They add similitudes, in order to make the matter more clear. As the toga distinguished the Romans from the Greeks, who wore the pallium; and as the different orders of Romans were distinguished from each other by their peculiar insignia; *e. g.*, the senatorial from the equestrian by purple, and crescent shoes, and the equestrian from the plebeian by a ring, so we wear our symbols to distinguish us from the profane. But it is sufficiently clear from what has been said above, that the ancients, in giving the name of sacraments to signs, had not at all attended to the use of the term by Latin writers, but had, for the sake of convenience, given it this new signification, as a means of simply expressing sacred signs. But were we to argue more subtilely, we might say that they seem to have given the term this signification in a manner analogous to that in which they employ the term faith in the sense in which it is now used. For while faith is truth in performing promises, they have used it for the certainty or firm persuasion which is had of the truth. In this way, while a sacrament is the act of the soldier when he vows obedience to his commander, they made it the act by which the commander admits soldiers to the ranks. For in the sacraments the Lord promises that he will be our God, and we that we will be his people. But we omit such subtleties, since I think I have shown by arguments abundantly plain, that all which ancient writers intended was to intimate, that sacraments are the signs of sacred and spiritual things. The similitudes which are drawn from external objects (chap. xv. sec. 1), we indeed admit; but we approve not, that that which is a secondary thing in sacraments is by them made the first, and indeed the only thing. The first thing is, that they may contribute to our faith in God; the secondary, that they may attest our confession before men. These similitudes are applicable to the secondary reason. Let it therefore remain a fixed point, that mysteries would be frigid (as has been seen) were they not helps to our faith, and adjuncts annexed to doctrine for the same end and purpose.

14. On the other hand, it is to be observed, that as these objectors impair the force, and altogether overthrow the use of the sacraments, so there are others who ascribe to the sacraments a kind of secret virtue, which is nowhere said to have been implanted in them by God. By this error the more simple and unwary are perilously deceived,

while they are taught to seek the gifts of God where they cannot possibly be found, and are insensibly withdrawn from God, so as to embrace instead of his truth mere vanity. For the schools of the Sophists have taught with general consent that the sacraments of the new law, in other words, those now in use in the Christian Church, justify, and confer grace, provided only that we do not interpose the obstacle of mortal sin. It is impossible to describe how fatal and pestilential this sentiment is, and the more so, that for many ages it has, to the great loss of the Church, prevailed over a considerable part of the world. It is plainly of the devil : for, first, in promising a righteousness without faith, it drives souls headlong on destruction ; secondly, in deriving a cause of righteousness from the sacraments, it entangles miserable minds, already of their own accord too much inclined to the earth, in a superstitious idea, which, makes them acquiesce in the spectacle of a corporeal object rather than in God himself. I wish we had not such experience of both evils as to make it altogether unnecessary to give a lengthened proof of them. For what is a sacrament received without faith, but most certain destruction to the Church ? For, seeing that nothing is to be expected beyond the promise, and the promise no less denounces wrath to the unbeliever than offers grace to the believer, it is an error to suppose that anything more is conferred by the sacraments than is offered by the word of God, and obtained by true faith. From this another thing follows—viz. that assurance of salvation does not depend on participation in the sacraments, as if justification consisted in it. This, which is treasured up in Christ alone, we know to be communicated, not less by the preaching of the Gospel than by the seal of the sacrament, and may be completely enjoyed without this seal. So true is it, as Augustine declares, that there may be invisible sanctification without a visible sign, and, on the other hand, a visible sign without true sanctification (August. de Quæst. Vet. Test. Lib. iii.). For, as he elsewhere says, " Men put on Christ, sometimes to the extent of partaking in the sacrament, and sometimes to the extent of holiness of life " (August. de Bapt. Cont. Donat. cap. xxiv.). The former may be common to the good and the bad, the latter is peculiar to the good.

15. Hence the distinction, if properly understood, repeatedly made by Augustine between the *sacrament* and the *matter of the sacrament*. For he does not mean merely that the figure and truth are therein contained, but that they do not so cohere as not to be separable, and that in this connection it is always necessary to distinguish the thing from the sign, so as not to transfer to the one what belongs to the other. Augustine speaks of the separation when he says that in the elect alone the sacraments accomplish what they represent (Augustin. de Bapt. Parvul.). Again, when speaking of the Jews, he says, " Though the sacraments were common to all, the grace was not common : yet grace is the virtue of the sacraments. Thus, too, the laver of regeneration is now common to all, but the grace by which

the members of Christ are regenerated with their head is not common to all" (August. in Ps. 78). Again, in another place, speaking of the Lord's Supper, he says, " We also this day receive visible food; but the sacrament is one thing, the virtue of the sacrament another. Why is it that many partake of the altar and die, and die by partaking ? For even the cup of the Lord was poison to Judas, not because he received what was evil, but being wicked he wickedly received what was good" (August. in Joann. Hom. 26). A little after, he says, " The sacrament of this thing, that is, of the unity of the body and blood of Christ, is in some places prepared every day, in others at certain intervals at the Lord's table, which is partaken by some unto life, by others unto destruction. But the thing itself, of which there is a sacrament, is life to all, and destruction to none who partake of it." Some time before he had said, " He who may have eaten shall not die, but he must be one who attains to the virtue of the sacrament, not to the visible sacrament; who eats inwardly, not outwardly ; who eats with the heart, and not with the teeth." Here you are uniformly told that a sacrament is so separated from the reality by the unworthiness of the partaker, that nothing remains but an empty and useless figure. Now, in order that you may have not a sign devoid of truth, but the thing with the sign, the Word which is included in it must be apprehended by faith. Thus, in so far as by means of the sacraments you will profit in the communion of Christ, will you derive advantage from them.

16. If this is obscure from brevity, I will explain it more at length. I say that Christ is the matter, or, if you rather choose it, the substance of all the sacraments, since in him they have their whole solidity, and out of him promise nothing. Hence the less toleration is due to the error of Peter Lombard, who distinctly makes them causes of the righteousness and salvation of which they are parts (Sent. Lib. iv. Dist. 1). Bidding adieu to all other causes of righteousness which the wit of man devises, our duty is to hold by this only. In so far, therefore, as we are assisted by their instrumentality in cherishing, confirming, and increasing the true knowledge of Christ, so as both to possess him more fully, and enjoy him in all his richness, so far are they effectual in regard to us. This is the case when that which is there offered is received by us in true faith. Therefore, you will ask, Do the wicked, by their ingratitude, make the ordinance of God fruitless and void ? I answer, that what I have said is not to be understood as if the power and truth of the sacrament depended on the condition or pleasure of him who receives it. That which God instituted continues firm, and retains its nature, however men may vary; but since it is one thing to offer, and another to receive, there is nothing to prevent a symbol, consecrated by the word of the Lord, from being truly what it is said to be, and preserving its power, though it may at the same time confer no benefit on the wicked and ungodly. This question is well solved by Augustine in a few words : " If you receive carnally, it ceases not to

be spiritual, but it is not spiritual to you" (August. Hom. in Joann. 26). But as Augustine shows in the above passages that a sacrament is a thing of no value if separated from its truth; so also, when the two are conjoined, he reminds us that it is necessary to distinguish, in order that we may not cleave too much to the external sign. "As it is servile weakness to follow the latter, and take the signs for the thing signified, so to interpret the signs as of no use is an extravagant error" (August. de Doct. Christ. Lib. iii. c. 9). He mentions two faults which are here to be avoided; the one when we receive the signs as if they had been given in vain, and by malignantly destroying or impairing their secret meanings, prevent them from yielding any fruit—the other, when by not raising our minds beyond the visible sign, we attribute to it blessings which are conferred upon us by Christ alone, and that by means of the Holy Spirit, who makes us to be partakers of Christ, external signs assisting if they invite us to Christ; whereas, when wrested to any other purpose, their whole utility is overthrown.

17. Wherefore, let it be a fixed point, that the office of the sacraments differs not from the word of God; and this is to hold forth and offer Christ to us, and, in him, the treasures of heavenly grace. They confer nothing, and avail nothing, if not received in faith, just as wine and oil, or any other liquor, however large the quantity which you pour out, will run away and perish unless there be an open vessel to receive it. When the vessel is not open, though it may be sprinkled all over, it will nevertheless remain entirely empty. We must be aware of being led into a kindred error by the terms, somewhat too extravagant, which ancient Christian writers have employed in extolling the dignity of the sacraments. We must not suppose that there is some latent virtue inherent in the sacraments by which they, in themselves, confer the gifts of the Holy Spirit upon us, in the same way in which wine is drunk out of a cup, since the only office divinely assigned them is to attest and ratify the benevolence of the Lord towards us; and they avail no farther than accompanied by the Holy Spirit to open our minds and hearts, and make us capable of receiving this testimony, in which various distinguished graces are clearly manifested. For the sacraments, as we lately observed (chap. xiii. sec. 6; and xiv. sec. 6, 7), are to us what messengers of good news are to men, or earnests in ratifying pactions. They do not of themselves bestow any grace, but they announce and manifest it, and, like earnests and badges, give a ratification of the gifts which the divine liberality has bestowed upon us. The Holy Spirit, whom the sacraments do not bring promiscuously to all, but whom the Lord specially confers on his people, brings the gifts of God along with him, makes way for the sacraments, and causes them to bear fruit. But though we deny not that God, by the immediate agency of his Spirit, countenances his own ordinance, preventing the administration of the sacraments which he has instituted from being fruitless and vain, still we maintain that the internal grace of the Spirit, as

it is distinct from the external ministration, ought to be viewed and considered separately. God, therefore, truly performs whatever he promises and figures by signs ; nor are the signs without effect, for they prove that he is their true and faithful author. The only question here is, whether the Lord works by proper and intrinsic virtue (as it is called), or resigns his office to external symbols? We maintain, that whatever organs he employs detract nothing from his primary operation. In this doctrine of the sacraments, their dignity is highly extolled, their use plainly shown, their utility sufficiently proclaimed, and moderation in all things duly maintained ; so that nothing is attributed to them which ought not to be attributed, and nothing denied them which they ought to possess. Meanwhile, we get rid of that fiction by which the cause of justification and the power of the Holy Spirit are included in elements as vessels and vehicles, and the special power which was overlooked is distinctly explained. Here, also, we ought to observe, that what the minister figures and attests by outward action, God performs inwardly, lest that which God claims for himself alone should be ascribed to mortal man. This Augustine is careful to observe : " How does both God and Moses sanctify? Not Moses for God, but Moses by visible sacraments through his ministry, God by invisible grace through the Holy Spirit. Herein is the whole fruit of visible sacraments ; for what do these visible sacraments avail without that sanctification of invisible grace ? "

18. The term sacrament, in the view we have hitherto taken of it, includes, generally, all the signs which God ever commanded men to use, that he might make them sure and confident of the truth of his promises. These he was pleased sometimes to place in natural objects—sometimes to exhibit in miracles. Of the former class we have an example, in his giving the tree of life to Adam and Eve, as an earnest of immortality, that they might feel confident of the promise as often as they ate of the fruit. Another example was, when he gave the bow in the cloud to Noah and his posterity, as a memorial that he would not again destroy the earth by a flood. These were to Adam and Noah as sacraments : not that the tree could give Adam and Eve the immortality which it could not give to itself ; or the bow (which is only a reflection of the solar rays on the opposite clouds) could have the effect of confining the waters ; but they had a mark engraven on them by the word of God, to be proofs and seals of his covenant. The tree was previously a tree, and the bow a bow ; but when they were inscribed with the word of God, a new form was given to them : they began to be what they previously were not. Lest any one suppose that these things were said in vain, the bow is even in the present day a witness to us of the covenant which God made with Noah (Calv. in Gen. ix. 6). As often as we look upon it, we read this promise from God, that the earth will never be destroyed by a flood. Wherefore, if any philosophaster, to deride the simplicity of our faith, shall contend that the variety of

colours arises naturally from the rays reflected by the opposite cloud, let us admit the fact; but, at the same time, deride his stupidity in not recognising God as the Lord and governor of nature, who, at his pleasure, makes all the elements subservient to his glory. If he had impressed memorials of this description on the sun, the stars, the earth, and stones, they would all have been to us as sacraments. For why is the shapeless and the coined silver not of the same value, seeing they are the same metal? Just because the former has nothing but its own nature, whereas the latter, impressed with the public stamp, becomes money, and receives a new value. And shall the Lord not be able to stamp his creatures with his word, that things which were formerly bare elements may become sacraments? Examples of the second class were given when he showed light to Abraham in the smoking furnace (Gen. xv. 17), when he covered the fleece with dew while the ground was dry; and, on the other hand, when the dew covered the ground while the fleece was untouched, to assure Gideon of victory (Judges vi. 37); also, when he made the shadow go back ten degrees on the dial, to assure Hezekiah of his recovery (2 Kings xx. 9 ; Isa. xxxviii. 7). These things, which were done to assist and establish their faith, were also sacraments.

19. But my present purpose is to discourse especially of those sacraments which the Lord has been pleased to institute as ordinary sacraments in his Church, to bring up his worshippers and servants in one faith, and the confession of one faith. For, to use the words of Augustine, "In no name of religion, true or false, can men be assembled, unless united by some common use of visible signs or sacraments" (August. cont. Faustum, Lib. ix. c. 11). Our most merciful Father, foreseeing this necessity, from the very first appointed certain exercises of piety to his servants; these, Satan, by afterwards transferring to impious and superstitious worship, in many ways corrupted and depraved. Hence those initiations of the Gentiles into their mysteries, and other degenerate rites. Yet, although they were full of error and superstition, they were, at the same time, an indication that men could not be without such external signs of religion. But, as they were neither founded on the word of God, nor bore reference to that truth which ought to be held forth by all signs, they are unworthy of being named when mention is made of the sacred symbols which were instituted by God, and have not been perverted from their end—viz. to be helps to true piety. And they consist not of simple signs, like the rainbow and the tree of life, but of ceremonies, or (if you prefer it) the signs here employed are ceremonies. But since, as has been said above, they are testimonies of grace and salvation from the Lord, so, in regard to us, they are marks of profession by which we openly swear by the name of God, binding ourselves to be faithful to him. Hence Chrysostom somewhere shrewdly gives them the name of pactions, by which God enters into covenant with us, and we become bound to holiness and purity of life, because a mutual stipulation is here interposed be-

tween God and us. For as God there promises to cover and efface any guilt and penalty which we may have incurred by transgression, and reconciles us to himself in his only begotten Son, so we, in our turn, oblige ourselves by this profession to the study of piety and righteousness. And hence it may be justly said, that such sacraments are ceremonies, by which God is pleased to train his people, first, to excite, cherish, and strengthen faith within; and, secondly, to testify our religion to men.

20. Now these have been different at different times, according to the dispensation which the Lord has seen meet to employ in manifesting himself to men. Circumcision was enjoined on Abraham and his posterity, and to it were afterwards added purifications and sacrifices, and other rites of the Mosaic Law. These were the sacraments of the Jews even until the advent of Christ. After these were abrogated, the two sacraments of Baptism and the Lord's Supper, which the Christian Church now employs, were instituted. I speak of those which were instituted for the use of the whole Church. For the laying on of hands, by which the ministers of the Church are initiated into their office, though I have no objection to its being called a sacrament, I do not number among ordinary sacraments. The place to be assigned to the other commonly reputed sacraments we shall see by-and-by. Still the ancient sacraments had the same end in view as our own—viz. to direct and almost lead us by the hand to Christ, or rather, were like images to represent him and hold him forth to our knowledge. But as we have already shown that sacraments are a kind of seals of the promises of God, so let us hold it as a most certain truth, that no divine promise has ever been offered to man except in Christ, and that hence when they remind us of any divine promise, they must of necessity exhibit Christ. Hence that heavenly pattern of the tabernacle and legal worship which was shown to Moses in the mount. There is only this difference, that while the former shadowed forth a promised Christ while he was still expected, the latter bear testimony to him as already come and manifested.

21. When these things are explained singly and separately, they will be much clearer. Circumcision was a sign by which the Jews were reminded that whatever comes of the seed of man—in other words, the whole nature of man—is corrupt, and requires to be cut off; moreover, it was a proof and memorial to confirm them in the promise made to Abraham, of a seed in whom all the nations of the earth should be blessed, and from whom they themselves were to look for a blessing. That saving seed, as we are taught by Paul (Gal. v. 16), was Christ, in whom alone they trusted to recover what they had lost in Adam. Wherefore circumcision was to them what Paul says it was to Abraham—viz. a sign of the righteousness of faith (Rom. iv. 11):—viz. a seal by which they were more certainly assured that their faith in waiting for the Lord would be accepted by God for righteousness. But we shall have a better opportunity elsewhere (chap. xvi. sec. 3, 4) of following out the comparison between circum-

cision and baptism.[1] Their washings and purifications placed under their eye the uncleanness, defilement, and pollution with which they were naturally contaminated, and promised another laver in which all their impurities might be wiped and washed away. This laver was Christ, washed by whose blood we bring his purity into the sight of God, that he may cover all our defilements. The sacrifices convicted them of their unrighteousness, and at the same time taught that there was a necessity for paying some satisfaction to the justice of God; and that, therefore, there must be some high priest, some mediator between God and man, to satisfy God by the shedding of blood, and the immolation of a victim which might suffice for the remission of sins. The high priest was Christ: he shed his own blood, he was himself the victim: for in obedience to the Father, he offered himself to death, and by this obedience abolished the disobedience by which man had provoked the indignation of God (Phil. ii. 8; Rom. v. 19).

22. In regard to our sacraments, they present Christ the more clearly to us, the more familiarly he has been manifested to man, ever since he was exhibited by the Father, truly as he had been promised. For Baptism testifies that we are washed and purified; the Supper of the Eucharist that we are redeemed. Ablution is figured by water, satisfaction by blood. Both are found in Christ, who, as John says, " came by water and blood;" that is, to purify and redeem. Of this the Spirit of God also is a witness. Nay, there are three witnesses in one, water, Spirit, and blood. In the water and blood we have an evidence of purification and redemption, but the Spirit is the primary witness who gives us a full assurance of this testimony. This sublime mystery was illustriously displayed on the cross of Christ, when water and blood flowed from his sacred side (John xix. 34); which, for this reason, Augustine justly termed the fountain of our sacraments (August. Hom. in Joann. 26). Of these we shall shortly treat at greater length. There is no doubt that, if you compare time with time, the grace of the Spirit is now more abundantly displayed. For this forms part of the glory of the kingdom of Christ, as we gather from several passages, and especially from the seventh chapter of John. In this sense are we to understand the words of Paul, that the law was "a shadow of good things to come, but the body is of Christ" (Col. ii. 17). His purpose is not to declare the inefficacy of those manifestations of grace in which God was pleased to prove his truth to the patriarchs, just as he proves it to us in the present day in Baptism and the Lord's Supper, but to contrast the two, and show the great value of what is given to us, that no one may think it strange that by the advent of Christ the ceremonies of the law have been abolished.

23. The Scholastic dogma (to glance at it in passing), by which the difference between the sacraments of the old and the new dispensa-

---

[1] Heb. ix. 1-14; 1 John i. 7; Rev. i. 5; Heb. iv. 14; v, 5; ix. 11.

tion is made so great, that the former did nothing but shadow forth the grace of God, while the latter actually confer that it, must be altogether exploded. Since the apostle speaks in no higher terms of the one than of the other, when he says that the fathers ate of the same spiritual food, and explains that that food was Christ (1 Cor. x. 3), who will presume to regard as an empty sign that which gave a manifestation to the Jews of true communion with Christ? And the state of the case which the apostle is there treating militates strongly for our view. For to guard against confiding in a frigid knowledge of Christ, an empty title of Christianity and external observances, and thereby daring to contemn the judgment of God, he exhibits signal examples of divine severity in the Jews, to make us aware that if we indulge in the same vices, the same punishments which they suffered are impending over us. Now, to make the comparison appropriate, it was necessary to show that there is no inequality between us and them in those blessings in which he forbade us to glory. Therefore, he first makes them equal to us in the sacraments, and leaves us not one iota of privilege which could give us hopes of impunity. Nor can we justly attribute more to our baptism than he elsewhere attributes to circumcision, when he terms it a seal of the righteousness of faith (Rom. iv. 11). Whatever, therefore, is now exhibited to us in the sacraments, the Jews formerly received in theirs—viz. Christ, with his spiritual riches. The same efficacy which ours possess they experienced in theirs—viz. that they were seals of the divine favour toward them in regard to the hope of eternal salvation. Had the objectors been sound expounders of the Epistle to the Hebrews, they would not have been so deluded, but reading therein that sins were not expiated by legal ceremonies, nay, that the ancient shadows were of no importance to justification, they overlooked the contrast which is there drawn, and fastening on the single point, that the law in itself was of no avail to the worshipper, thought that they were mere figures, devoid of truth. The purpose of the apostle is to show that there is nothing in the ceremonial law until we arrive at Christ, on whom alone the whole efficacy depends.

24. But they will found on what Paul says of the circumcision of the letter,[1] and object that it is in no esteem with God; that it confers nothing, is empty; that passages such as these seem to set it far beneath our baptism. But by no means. For the very same thing might justly be said of baptism. Indeed, it is said; first by Paul himself, when he shows that God regards not the external ablution by which we are initiated into religion, unless the mind is purified inwardly, and maintains its purity to the end; and, secondly, by Peter, when he declares that the reality of baptism consists not in external ablution, but in the testimony of a good conscience. But it seems that in another passage he speaks with the greatest contempt of circumcision made with hands, when he contrasts it with the cir-

---

1 Rom. ii. 25–29; 1 Cor. vii. 19; Gal. vi. 15; 1 Cor. x. 5; 1 Pet. iii. 21; Col. ii. 11.

cumcision made by Christ. I answer, that not even in that passage is there anything derogatory to its dignity. Paul is there disputing against those who insisted upon it as necessary, after it had been abrogated. He therefore admonishes believers to lay aside ancient shadows, and cleave to truth. These teachers, he says, insist that your bodies shall be circumcised. But you have been spiritually circumcised both in soul and body. You have, therefore, a manifestation of the reality, and this is far better than the shadow. Still any one might have answered, that the figure was not to be despised because they had the reality, since among the fathers also was exemplified that putting off of the old man of which he was speaking, and yet to them external circumcision was not superfluous. This objection he anticipates, when he immediately adds, that the Colossians were buried together with Christ by baptism, thereby intimating that baptism is now to Christians what circumcision was to those of ancient times; and that the latter, therefore, could not be imposed on Christians without injury to the former.

25. But there is more difficulty in explaining the passage which follows, and which I lately quoted[1]—viz. that all the Jewish ceremonies were shadows of things to come, but the body is of Christ (Col. ii. 17). The most difficult point of all, however, is that which is discussed in several chapters of the Epistle to the Hebrews—namely, that the blood of beasts did not reach to the conscience; that the law was a shadow of good things to come, but not the very image of the things (Heb. x. 1); that worshippers under the Mosaic ceremonies obtained no degree of perfection, and so forth. I repeat what I have already hinted, that Paul does not represent the ceremonies as shadowy because they had nothing solid in them, but because their completion was in a manner suspended until the manifestation of Christ. Again, I hold that the words are to be understood not of their efficiency, but rather of the mode of significancy. For until Christ was manifested in the flesh, all signs shadowed him as absent, however he might inwardly exert the presence of his power, and consequently of his person on believers. But the most important observation is, that in all these passages Paul does not speak simply but by way of reply. He was contending with false apostles, who maintained that piety consisted in mere ceremonies, without any respect to Christ; for their refutation it was sufficient merely to consider what effect ceremonies have in themselves. This, too, was the scope of the author of the Epistle to the Hebrews. Let us remember, therefore, that he is here treating of ceremonies not taken in their true and native signification, but when wrested to a false and vicious interpretation, not of the legitimate use, but of the superstitious abuse of them. What wonder, then, if ceremonies, when separated from Christ, are devoid of all virtue? All signs become null when the thing signified is taken away. Thus Christ, when addressing those who thought that manna

1 French, "Mais on fera encore un autre argument."—But there is still another argument which they will employ.

was nothing more than food for the body, accommodates his language to their gross opinion, and says, that he furnished a better food, one which fed souls for immortality. But if you require a clearer solution, the substance comes to this: First, the whole apparatus of ceremonies under the Mosaic law, unless directed to Christ, is evanescent and null. Secondly, these ceremonies had such respect to Christ, that they had their fulfilment only when Christ was manifested in the flesh. Lastly, at his advent they behoved to disappear, just as the shadow vanishes in the clear light of the sun. But I now touch more briefly on the point, because I defer the future consideration of it till I come to the place where I intend to compare baptism with circumcision.

26. Those wretched sophists are perhaps deceived by the extravagant eulogiums on our signs which occur in ancient writers: for instance, the following passage of Augustine: "The sacraments of the old law only promised a Saviour, whereas ours give salvation" (August. Proem. in Ps. 73). Not perceiving that these and similar figures of speech are hyperbolical, they too have promulgated their hyperbolical dogmas, but in a sense altogether alien from that of ancient writers. For Augustine means nothing more than in another place where he says, "The sacraments of the Mosaic law foretold Christ, ours announce him" (Quæst. sup. Numer. c. 33). And again, "Those were promises of things to be fulfilled, these indications of the fulfilment" (Contra Faustum, Lib. xix. c. 14); as if he had said, Those figured him when he was still expected, ours, now that he has arrived, exhibit him as present. Moreover, with regard to the mode of signifying, he says, as he also elsewhere indicates, "The Law and the Prophets had sacraments foretelling a thing future, the sacraments of our time attest that what they foretold as to come has come" (Cont. Liter. Petil. Lib. ii. c. 37). His sentiments concerning the reality and efficacy, he explains in several passages, as when he says, "The sacraments of the Jews were different in the signs, alike in the things signified; different in the visible appearance, alike in spiritual power" (Hom. in Joann. 26). Again, "In different signs there was the same faith: it was thus in different signs as in different words, because the words change the sound according to times, and yet words are nothing else than signs. The fathers drank of the same spiritual drink, but not of the same corporeal drink. See then, how, while faith remains, signs vary. There the rock was Christ; to us that is Christ which is placed on the altar. They as a great sacrament drank of the water flowing from the rock: believers know what we drink. If you look at the visible appearance there was a difference; if at the intelligible signification, they drank of the same spiritual drink." Again, "In this mystery their food and drink are the same as ours; the same in meaning, not in form, for the same Christ was figured to them in the rock; to us he has been manifested in the flesh" (in Ps. 77). Though we grant that in this respect also there is some difference. Both testify that

the paternal kindness of God, and the graces of the Spirit, are offered us in Christ, but ours more clearly and splendidly. In both there is an exhibition of Christ, but in ours it is more full and complete, in accordance with that distinction between the Old and New Testaments of which we have discoursed above. And this is the meaning of Augustine (whom we quote more frequently, as being the best and most faithful witness of all antiquity), where he says that after Christ was revealed, sacraments were instituted, fewer in number, but of more august significancy and more excellent power (De Doct. Christ. Lib. iii. ; et Ep. ad Janur.). It is here proper to remind the reader, that all the trifling talk of the sophists concerning the *opus operatum*,[1] is not only false, but repugnant to the very nature of sacraments, which God appointed in order that believers, who are void and in want of all good, might bring nothing of their own, but simply beg. Hence it follows, that in receiving them they do nothing which deserves praise, and that in this action (which in respect of them is merely passive [2]) no work can be ascribed to them.

[1] The French adds, "Qu'ils appellent en leur gergon."—So called in their jargon.

[2] The French adds, "J'appel le acte passif, pourceque Dieu fait le tout, et seulement nous recevons."—I call the act passive, because God does the whole, and we only receive.

CHAPTER XV.

OF BAPTISM.

There are two parts of this chapter,—I. Dissertation on the two ends of Baptism, sec, 1–13. II. The second part may be reduced to four heads. Of the use of Baptism, sec. 14, 15. Of the worthiness or unworthiness of the minister, sec. 16–18. Of the corruptions by which this sacrament was polluted, sec. 19. To whom reference is had in the dispensation, sec. 20–22.

Sections.

1. Baptism defined. Its primary object. This consists of three things. 1. To attest the forgiveness of sins.
2. Passages of Scripture proving the forgiveness of sins.
3. Forgiveness not only of past but also of future sins. This no encouragement to license in sin.
4. Refutation of those who share forgiveness between Baptism and Repentance.
5. Second thing in Baptism—viz. to teach that we are ingrafted into Christ for mortification and newness of life.
6. Third thing in Baptism—viz. to teach us that we are united to Christ so as to be partakers of all his blessings. Second and third things conspicuous in the baptism both of John and the apostles.
7. Identity of the baptism of John and the apostles.
8. An objection to this refuted.
9. The benefits of baptism typified to the Israelites by the passage of the Red Sea and the pillar of cloud.
10. Objection of those who imagine that there is some kind of perfect renovation after baptism. Original depravity remains after baptism. Its existence in infants. The elect after baptism are righteous in this life only by imputation.
11. Original corruption trying to the pious during the whole course of their lives. They do not, on this account, seek a licence for sin. They rather walk more cautiously and safely in the ways of the Lord.
12. The trouble occasioned by corruption, shown by the example and testimony of the Apostle Paul.
13. Another end of baptism is to serve as our confession to men.
14. Second part of the chapter. Of baptism as a confirmation of our faith.
15. This illustrated by the examples of Cornelius and Paul. Of the use of baptism as a confession of faith.
16. Baptism not affected by the worthiness or unworthiness of the minister. Hence no necessity to rebaptise those who were baptised under the Papacy.
17. Nothing in the argument that those so baptised remained some years blind and unbelieving. The promise of God remains firm. God, in inviting the Jews to repentance, does not enjoin them to be again circumcised.
18. No ground to allege that Paul rebaptised certain of John's disciples. The baptism of John. What it is to be baptised in the name of Christ.
19. The corruptions introduced into baptism. The form of pure Christian baptism. Immersion or sprinkling should be left free.
20. To whom the dispensation of baptism belongs. Not to private individuals or women, but to the ministers of the Church. Origin of the baptism of private individuals and women. An argument in favour of it refuted.
21. Exploded also by Tertullian and Epiphanius.
22. Objection founded on the case of Zipporah. Answer. Children dying before baptism not excluded from heaven, provided the want of it was not caused by negligence or contempt.

1. BAPTISM is the initiatory sign by which we are admitted to the fellowship of the Church, that being ingrafted into Christ we may be accounted children of God. Moreover, the end for which God has given it (this I have shown to be common to all mysteries) is, first, that it may be conducive to our faith in him; and, secondly, that it may serve the purpose of a confession among men. The nature of both institutions we shall explain in order. Baptism contributes to our faith three things, which require to be treated separately. The first object, therefore, for which it is appointed by the Lord, is to be a sign and evidence of our purification, or (better to explain my meaning) it is a kind of sealed instrument by which he assures us that all our sins are so deleted, covered, and effaced, that they will never come into his sight, never be mentioned, never imputed. For it is his will that all who have believed, be baptised for the remission of sins. Hence those who have thought that baptism is nothing else than the badge and mark by which we profess our religion before men, in the same way as soldiers attest their profession by bearing the insignia of their commander, having not attended to what was the principal thing in baptism; and this is, that we are to receive it in connection with the promise, " He that believeth and is baptised shall be saved " (Mark xvi. 16).

2. In this sense is to be understood the statement of Paul, that " Christ loved the Church, and gave himself for it, that he might sanctify and cleanse it with the washing of water by the word " (Eph. v. 25, 26) ; and again, " not by works of righteousness which we have done, but according to his mercy he saved us, by the washing of regeneration and renewing of the Holy Ghost " (Titus iii. v.). Peter also says that " baptism also doth now save us " (1 Peter iii. 21). For he did not mean to intimate that our ablution and salvation are perfected by water, or that water possesses in itself the virtue of purifying, regenerating, and renewing; nor does he mean that it is the cause of salvation, but only that the knowledge and certainty of such gifts are perceived in this sacrament. This the words themselves evidently show. For Paul connects together the word of life and baptism of water, as if he had said, by the gospel the message of our ablution and sanctification is announced; by baptism this message is sealed. And Peter immediately subjoins, that that baptism is " not the putting away of the filth of the flesh, but the answer of a good conscience toward God, which is of faith." Nay, the only purification which baptism promises is by means of the sprinkling of the blood of Christ, who is figured by water from the resemblance to cleansing and washing. Who, then, can say that we are cleansed by that water which certainly attests that the blood of Christ is our true and only laver? So that we cannot have a better argument to refute the hallucination of those who ascribe the whole to the virtue of water than we derive from the very meaning of baptism, which leads us away as well from the visible element which is

presented to our eye, as from all other means, that it may fix our minds on Christ alone.

3. Nor is it to be supposed that baptism is bestowed only with reference to the past, so that, in regard to new lapses into which we fall after baptism, we must seek new remedies of expiation in other so-called sacraments, just as if the power of baptism had become obsolete. To this error, in ancient times, it was owing that some refused to be initiated by baptism until their life was in extreme danger, and they were drawing their last breath, that they might thus obtain pardon for all the past. Against this preposterous precaution ancient bishops frequently inveigh in their writings. We ought to consider that at whatever time we are baptised, we are washed and purified once for the whole of life. Wherefore, as often as we fall, we must recall the remembrance of our baptism, and thus fortify our minds, so as to feel certain and secure of the remission of sins. For though, when once administered, it seems to have passed, it is not abolished by subsequent sins. For the purity of Christ was therein offered to us, always is in force, and is not destroyed by any stain: it wipes and washes away all our defilements. Nor must we hence assume a licence of sinning for the future (there is certainly nothing in it to countenance such audacity), but this doctrine is intended only for those who, when they have sinned, groan under their sins burdened and oppressed, that they may have wherewith to support and console themselves, and not rush headlong into despair. Thus Paul says that Christ was made a propitiation for us for the remission of sins that are past (Rom. iii. 25). By this he denies not that constant and perpetual forgiveness of sins is thereby obtained even till death: he only intimates that it is designed by the Father for those poor sinners who, wounded by remorse of conscience, sigh for the physician. To these the mercy of God is offered. Those who, from hopes of impunity, seek a licence for sin, only provoke the wrath and justice of God.

4. I know it is a common belief that forgiveness, which at our first regeneration we receive by baptism alone, is after baptism procured by means of penitence and the keys (see chap. xix. sec. 17). But those who entertain this fiction err from not considering that the power of the keys, of which they speak, so depends on baptism, that it ought not on any account to be separated from it. The sinner receives forgiveness by the ministry of the Church; in other words, not without the preaching of the gospel. And of what nature is this preaching? That we are washed from our sins by the blood of Christ. And what is the sign and evidence of that washing if it be not baptism? We see, then, that that forgiveness has reference to baptism. This error had its origin in the fictitious sacrament of penance, on which I have already touched. What remains will be said at the proper place. There is no wonder if men who, from the grossness of their minds, are excessively attached to external things, have here also betrayed the defect,—if not contented with the pure

institution of God, they have introduced new helps devised by themselves, as if baptism were not itself a sacrament of penance.   But if repentance is recommended during the whole of life, the power of baptism ought to have the same extent.   Wherefore, there can be no doubt that all the godly may, during the whole course of their lives, whenever they are vexed by a consciousness of their sins, recall the remembrance of their baptism, that they may thereby assure themselves of that sole and perpetual ablution which we have in the blood of Christ.

5. Another benefit of baptism is, that it shows us our mortification in Christ and new life in him.   "Know ye not," says the apostle, "that as many of us as were baptised into Jesus Christ, were baptised into his death?   Therefore we are buried with him by baptism into death," that we "should walk in newness of life" (Rom. vi. 3, 4).   By these words, he not only exhorts us to imitation of Christ, as if he had said, that we are admonished by baptism, in like manner as Christ died, to die to our lusts, and as he rose, to rise to righteousness; but he traces the matter much higher, that Christ by baptism has made us partakers of his death, ingrafting us into it. And as the twig derives substance and nourishment from the root to which it is attached, so those who receive baptism with true faith truly feel the efficacy of Christ's death in the mortification of their flesh, and the efficacy of his resurrection in the quickening of the Spirit.   On this he founds his exhortation, that if we are Christians we should be dead unto sin, and alive unto righteousness.   He elsewhere uses the same argument—viz. that we are circumcised, and put off the old man, after we are buried in Christ by baptism (Col. ii. 12).   And in this sense, in the passage which we formerly quoted, he calls it "the washing of regeneration, and renewing of the Holy Ghost" (Tit. iii. 5).   We are promised, first, the free pardon of sins and imputation of righteousness; and, secondly, the grace of the Holy Spirit, to form us again to newness of life.

6. The last advantage which our faith receives from baptism is its assuring us not only that we are ingrafted into the death and life of Christ, but so united to Christ himself as to be partakers of all his blessings.   For he consecrated and sanctified baptism in his own body, that he might have it in common with us as the firmest bond of union and fellowship which he deigned to form with us; and hence Paul proves us to be the sons of God, from the fact that we put on Christ in baptism (Gal. iii. 27).   Thus we see the fulfilment of our baptism in Christ, whom for this reason we call the proper object of baptism.   Hence it is not strange that the apostles are said to have baptised in the name of Christ, though they were enjoined to baptise in the name of the Father and Spirit also (Acts viii. 16; xix. 5; Matth. xxviii. 19).   For all the divine gifts held forth in baptism are found in Christ alone.   And yet he who baptises into Christ cannot but at the same time invoke the name of the Father and the Spirit.   For we are cleansed by his blood, just because our

gracious Father, of his incomparable mercy, willing to receive us into favour, appointed him Mediator to effect our reconciliation with himself. Regeneration we obtain from his death and resurrection only, when sanctified by his Spirit we are imbued with a new and spiritual nature. Wherefore we obtain, and in a manner distinctly perceive, in the Father the cause, in the Son the matter, and in the Spirit the effect of our purification and regeneration. Thus first John baptised, and thus afterwards the apostles by the baptism of repentance for the remission of sins, understanding by the term *repentance*, regeneration, and by the *remission* of sins, ablution.

7. This makes it perfectly certain that the ministry of John was the very same as that which was afterwards delegated to the apostles. For the different hands by which baptism is administered do not make it a different baptism, but sameness of doctrine proves it to be the same. John and the apostles agreed in one doctrine. Both baptised unto repentance, both for remission of sins, both in the name of Christ, from whom repentance and remission of sins proceed. John pointed to him as the Lamb of God who taketh away the sins of the world (John i. 29), thus describing him as the victim accepted of the Father, the propitiation of righteousness, and the author of salvation. What could the apostles add to this confession? Wherefore, let no one be perplexed because ancient writers labour to distinguish the one from the other. Their views ought not to be in such esteem with us as to shake the certainty of Scripture. For who would listen to Chrysostom denying that remission of sins was included in the baptism of John (Hom. in Matth. i. 14), rather than to Luke asserting, on the contrary, that John preached "the baptism of repentance for the remission of sins"? (Luke iii. 3). Nor can we admit Augustine's subtlety, that by the baptism of John sins were forgiven in hope, but by the baptism of Christ are forgiven in reality. For seeing the Evangelist clearly declares that John in his baptism promised the remission of sins, why detract from this eulogium when no necessity compels it? Should any one ask what difference the word of God makes, he will find it to be nothing more than that John baptised in the name of him who was to come, the apostles in the name of him who was already manifested (Luke iii. 16 ; Acts xix. 4).

8. This fact, that the gifts of the Spirit were more liberally poured out after the resurrection of Christ, does not go to establish a diversity of baptisms. For baptism, administered by the apostles while he was still on the earth, was called his baptism, and yet the Spirit was not poured out in larger abundance on it than on the baptism of John. Nay, not even after the ascension did the Samaritans receive the Spirit above the ordinary measure of former believers, till Peter and John were sent to lay hands on them (Acts viii. 14–17). I imagine that the thing which imposed on ancient writers, and made them say that the one baptism was only a preparative to the other, was, because they read that those who had received the baptism of

John were again baptised by Paul (Acts xix. 3–5 ; Matth. iii. 11).
How greatly they are mistaken in this will be most clearly explained
in its own place. Why, then, did John say that he baptised with
water, but there was one coming who would baptise with the Holy
Ghost and with fire ? This may be explained in a few words. He
did not mean to distinguish the one baptism from the other, but he
contrasted his own person with the person of Christ, saying, that
while he was a minister of water, Christ was the giver of the Holy
Spirit, and would declare this virtue by a visible miracle on the day on
which he would send the Holy Spirit on the apostles, under the form of
tongues of fire. What greater boast could the apostles make, and
what greater those who baptise in the present day ? For they are
only ministers of the external sign, whereas Christ is the Author of
internal grace, as those same ancient writers uniformly teach, and,
in particular, Augustine, who, in his refutation of the Donatists,
founds chiefly on this axiom, Whoever it is that baptises, Christ
alone presides.

9. The things which we have said, both of mortification and
ablution, were adumbrated among the people of Israel, who, for that
reason, are described by the apostle as having been baptised in the
cloud and in the sea (1 Cor. x. 2). Mortification was figured when
the Lord, vindicating them from the hand of Pharaoh and from cruel
bondage, paved a way for them through the Red Sea, and drowned
Pharaoh himself and their Egyptian foes, who were pressing close
behind, and threatening them with destruction. For in this way
also he promises us in baptism, and shows by a given sign that we
are led by his might, and delivered from the captivity of Egypt, that
is, from the bondage of sin, that our Pharaoh is drowned ; in other
words, the devil, although he ceases not to try and harass us. But as
that Egyptian was not plunged into the depth of the sea, but cast out
upon the shore, still alarmed the Israelites by the terror of his look,
though he could not hurt them, so our enemy still threatens, shows his
arms and is felt, but cannot conquer. The cloud was a symbol of purification (Num. ix. 18). For as the Lord then covered them by an opposite cloud, and kept them cool, that they might not faint or pine
away under the burning rays of the sun ; so in baptism we perceive
that we are covered and protected by the blood of Christ, lest the
wrath of God, which is truly an intolerable flame, should lie upon
us. Although the mystery was then obscure, and known to few, yet
as there is no other method of obtaining salvation than in those two
graces, God was pleased that the ancient fathers, whom he had
adopted as heirs, should be furnished with both badges.

10. It is now clear how false the doctrine is which some long ago
taught, and others still persist in, that by baptism we are exempted
and set free from original sin, and from the corruption which was
propagated by Adam to all his posterity, and that we are restored to
the same righteousness and purity of nature which Adam would have
had if he had maintained the integrity in which he was created. This

class of teachers never understand what is meant by original sin, original righteousness, or the grace of baptism. Now, it has been previously shown (Book II. chap. i. sec. 8), that original sin is the depravity and corruption of our nature, which first makes us liable to the wrath of God, and then produces in us works which Scripture terms *the works of the flesh* (Gal. v. 19). The two things, therefore, must be distinctly observed—viz. that we are vitiated and perverted in all parts of our nature, and then, on account of this corruption, are justly held to be condemned and convicted before God, to whom nothing is acceptable but purity, innocence, and righteousness. And hence, even infants bring their condemnation with them from their mother's womb ; for although they have not yet brought forth the fruits of their unrighteousness, they have its seed included in them. Nay, their whole nature is, as it were, a seed of sin, and, therefore, cannot but be odious and abominable to God. Believers become assured by baptism, that this condemnation is entirely withdrawn from them, since (as has been said) the Lord by this sign promises that a full and entire remission has been made, both of the guilt which was imputed to us, and the penalty incurred by the guilt. They also apprehend righteousness, but such righteousness as the people of God can obtain in this life—viz. by imputation only, God, in his mercy, regarding them as righteous and innocent.

11. Another point is, that this corruption never ceases in us, but constantly produces new fruits—viz. those works of the flesh which we previously described, just as a burning furnace perpetually sends forth flame and sparks, or a fountain is ever pouring out water. For concupiscence never wholly dies or is extinguished in men, until, freed by death from the body of death, they have altogether laid aside their own nature (Book III. chap. iii. sec. 10-13). Baptism, indeed, tells us that our Pharaoh is drowned and sin mortified ; not so, however, as no longer to exist, or give no trouble, but only so as not to have dominion. For as long as we live shut up in this prison of the body, the remains of sin dwell in us, but if we faithfully hold the promise which God has given us in baptism, they will neither rule nor reign. But let no man deceive himself, let no man look complacently on his disease, when he hears that sin always dwells in us. When we say so, it is not in order that those who are otherwise too prone to sin may sleep securely in their sins, but only that those who are tried and stung by the flesh may not faint and despond. Let them rather reflect that they are still on the way, and think that they have made great progress when they feel that their concupiscence is somewhat diminished from day to day, until they shall have reached the point at which they aim—viz. the final death of the flesh ; a death which shall be completed at the termination of this mortal life. Meanwhile, let them cease not to contend strenuously, and animate themselves to further progress, and press on to complete victory. Their efforts should be stimulated by the consideration, that after a lengthened struggle much still remains to be done. We ought to

hold that we are baptised for the mortification of our flesh, which is begun in baptism, is prosecuted every day, and will be finished when we depart from this life to go to the Lord.

12. Here we say nothing more than the apostle Paul expounds most clearly in the sixth and seventh chapters of the Epistle to the Romans. He had discoursed of free justification, but as some wicked men thence inferred that they were to live as they listed, because their acceptance with God was not procured by the merit of works, he adds, that all who are clothed with the righteousness of Christ are at the same time regenerated by the Spirit, and that we have an earnest of this regeneration in baptism. Hence he exhorts believers not to allow sin to reign in their members. And because he knew that there is always some infirmity in believers, lest they should be cast down on this account, he adds, for their consolation, that they are not under the law. Again, as there may seem a danger that Christians might grow presumptuous because they were not under the yoke of the law, he shows what the nature of the abrogation is, and at the same time what the use of the law is. This question he had already postponed a second time. The substance is, that we are freed from the rigour of the law in order that we may adhere to Christ, and that the office of the law is to convince us of our depravity, and make us confess our impotence and wretchedness. Moreover, as this malignity of nature is not so easily apparent in a profane man who, without fear of God, indulges his passions, he gives an example in the regenerate man, in other words, in himself. He therefore says that he had a constant struggle with the remains of his flesh, and was kept in miserable bondage, so as to be unable to devote himself entirely to the obedience of the divine law. Hence he is forced to groan and exclaim, " O wretched man that I am ! who shall deliver me from the body of this death?"(Rom. vii. 24). But if the children of God are kept captive in prison as long as they live, they must necessarily feel very anxious at the thought of their danger, unless their fears are allayed. For this single purpose, then, he subjoins the consolation, that there is " now no condemnation to them which are in Christ Jesus" (Rom. viii. 1). Hence he teaches that those whom the Lord has once admitted into favour, and ingrafted into communion with Christ, and received into the fellowship of the Church by baptism, are freed from guilt and condemnation while they persevere in the faith of Christ, though they may be beset by sin and thus bear sin about with them. If this is the simple and genuine interpretation of Paul's meaning, we cannot think that there is anything strange in the doctrine which he here delivers.[1]

1 French, " Nous suivons donc de mot à mot la doctrine de Sainct Paul, en ce que nous disons que le peché est remis au Baptesme, quant à la coulpe, mais qu'il demeure toujours quant à la matière, en tous Chretiens jusques à la mort."—We therefore follow the doctrine of St Paul, word for word, when we say that in Baptism, sin is forgiven as to the guilt, but that it always remains as to the matter in all Christians until death.

13. Baptism serves as our confession before men, inasmuch as it is a mark by which we openly declare that we wish to be ranked among the people of God, by which we testify that we concur with all Christians in the worship of one God, and in one religion; by which, in short, we publicly assert our faith, so that not only do our hearts breathe, but our tongues also, and all the members of our body, in every way they can, proclaim the praise of God. In this way, as is meet, everything we have is made subservient to the glory of God, which ought everywhere to be displayed, and others are stimulated by our example to the same course. To this Paul referred when he asked the Corinthians whether or not they had been baptised in the name of Christ (1 Cor. i. 13); intimating, that by the very circumstance of having been baptised in his name, they had devoted themselves to him, had sworn and bound themselves in allegiance to him before men, so that they could no longer confess any other than Christ alone, unless they would abjure the confession which they had made in baptism.

14. Now that the end to which the Lord had regard in the institution of baptism has been explained, it is easy to judge in what way we ought to use and receive it. For inasmuch as it is appointed to elevate, nourish, and confirm our faith, we are to receive it as from the hand of its author, being firmly persuaded that it is himself who speaks to us by means of the sign; that it is himself who washes and purifies us, and effaces the remembrance of our faults; that it is himself who makes us the partakers of his death, destroys the kingdom of Satan, subdues the power of concupiscence, nay, makes us one with himself, that being clothed with him we may be accounted the children of God. These things, I say, we ought to feel as truly and certainly in our mind as we see our body washed, immersed, and surrounded with water. For this analogy or similitude furnishes the surest rule in the sacraments—viz. that in corporeal things we are to see spiritual, just as if they were actually exhibited to our eye, since the Lord has been pleased to represent them by such figures; not that such graces are included and bound in the sacrament, so as to be conferred by its efficacy, but only that by this badge the Lord declares to us that he is pleased to bestow all these things upon us. Nor does he merely feed our eyes with bare show; he leads us to the actual object, and effectually performs what he figures.

15. We have a proof of this in Cornelius the centurion, who, after he had been previously endued with the graces of the Holy Spirit, was baptised for the remission of sins, not seeking a fuller forgiveness from baptism, but a surer exercise of faith; nay, an argument for assurance from a pledge. It will, perhaps, be objected, Why did Ananias say to Paul that he washed away his sins by baptism (Acts xxii. 16), if sins are not washed away by the power of baptism? I answer, we are said to receive, procure, and obtain, whatever according to the perception of our faith is exhibited to us by the Lord, whether he then attests it for the first time, or gives additional con-

firmation to what he had previously attested. All then that Ananias meant to say was, Be baptised, Paul, that you may be assured that your sins are forgiven you. In baptism, the Lord promises forgiveness of sins : receive it, and be secure. I have no intention, however, to detract from the power of baptism. I would only add to the sign the substance and reality, inasmuch as God works by external means. But from this sacrament, as from all others, we gain nothing, unless in so far as we receive in faith. If faith is wanting, it will be an evidence of our ingratitude, by which we are proved guilty before God, for not believing the promise there given. In so far as it is a sign of our confession, we ought thereby to testify that we confide in the mercy of God, and are pure, through the forgiveness of sins which Christ Jesus has procured for us ; that we have entered into the Church of God, that with one consent of faith and love we may live in concord with all believers. This last was Paul's meaning, when he said that " by one Spirit are we all baptised into one body" (1 Cor. xii. 13).

16. Moreover, if we have rightly determined that a sacrament is not to be estimated by the hand of him by whom it is administered, but is to be received as from the hand of God himself, from whom it undoubtedly proceeded, we may hence infer that its dignity neither gains nor loses by the administrator. And, just as among men, when a letter has been sent, if the hand and seal is recognised, it is not of the least consequence who or what the messenger was ; so it ought to be sufficient for us to recognise the hand and seal of our Lord in his sacraments, let the administrator be who he may. This confutes the error of the Donatists, who measured the efficacy and worth of the sacrament by the dignity of the minister. Such in the present day are our Catabaptists, who deny that we are duly baptised, because we were baptised in the Papacy by wicked men and idolaters; hence they furiously insist on anabaptism. Against these absurdities we shall be sufficiently fortified if we reflect that by baptism we were initiated not into the name of any man, but into the name of the Father, and the Son, and the Holy Spirit ; and, therefore, that baptism is not of man, but of God, by whomsoever it may have been administered. Be it that those who baptised us were most ignorant of God and all piety, or were despisers, still they did not baptise us into a fellowship with their ignorance or sacrilege, but into the faith of Jesus-Christ, because the name which they invoked was not their own but God's, nor did they baptise into any other name. But if baptism was of God, it certainly included in it the promise of forgiveness of sin, mortification of the flesh, quickening of the Spirit, and communion with Christ. Thus it did not harm the Jews that they were circumcised by impure and apostate priests. It did not nullify the symbol so as to make it necessary to repeat it. It was enough to return to its genuine origin. The objection that baptism ought to be celebrated in the assembly of the godly, does not prove that it loses its whole efficacy because it is partly defective. When we show what

ought to be done to keep baptism pure and free from every taint, we do not abolish the institution of God though idolaters may corrupt it. Circumcision was anciently vitiated by many superstitions, and yet ceased not to be regarded as a symbol of grace ; nor did Josiah and Hezekiah, when they assembled out of all Israel those who had revolted from God, call them to be circumcised anew.

17. Then, again, when they ask us what faith for several years followed our baptism, that they may thereby prove that our baptism was in vain, since it is not sanctified unless the word of the promise is received with faith, our answer is, that being blind and unbelieving, we for a long time did not hold the promise which was given us in baptism, but that still the promise, as it was of God, always remained fixed, and firm, and true. Although all men should be false and perfidious, yet God ceases not to be true (Rom. iii. 3, 4); though all were lost, Christ remains safe. We acknowledge, therefore, that at that time baptism profited us nothing, since in us the offered promise, without which baptism is nothing, lay neglected. Now, when by the grace of God we begin to repent, we accuse our blindness and hardness of heart in having been so long ungrateful for his great goodness. But we do not believe that the promise itself has vanished, we rather reflect thus : God in baptism promises the remission of sins, and will undoubtedly perform what he has promised to all believers. That promise was offered to us in baptism, let us therefore embrace it in faith. In regard to us, indeed, it was long buried on account of unbelief; now, therefore, let us with faith receive it. Wherefore, when the Lord invites the Jewish people to repentance, he gives no injunction concerning another circumcision, though (as we have said) they were circumcised by a wicked and sacrilegious hand, and had long lived in the same impiety. All he urges is conversion of heart. For how much soever the covenant might have been violated by them, the symbol of the covenant always remained, according to the appointment of the Lord, firm and inviolable. Solely, therefore, on the condition of repentance, were they restored to the covenant which God had once made with them in circumcision, though this which they had received at the hand of a covenant-breaking priest, they had themselves as much as in them lay polluted and extinguished.

18. But they seem to think the weapon which they brandish irresistible, when they allege that Paul rebaptised those who had been baptised with the baptism of John (Acts xix. 3, 5). For if, by our confession, the baptism of John was the same as ours, then, in like manner as those who had been improperly trained, when they learned the true faith, were rebaptised into it, ought that baptism which was without true doctrine to be accounted as nothing, and hence we ought to be baptised anew into the true religion with which we are now, for the first time, imbued? It seems to some that it was a foolish imitator of John, who, by a former baptism, had initiated them into vain superstition. This, it is thought, may be conjectured

from the fact, that they acknowledge their entire ignorance of the
Holy Spirit, an ignorance in which John never would have left his
disciples.   But it is not probable that the Jews, even though they
had not been baptised at all, would have been destitute of all knowledge of the Spirit, who is celebrated in so many passages of Scripture.   Their answer, therefore, that they knew not whether there
was a Spirit, must be understood as if they had said, that they had
not yet heard whether or not the gifts of the Spirit, as to which Paul
questioned them, were given to the disciples of Christ.   I grant that
John's was a true baptism, and one and the same with the baptism
of Christ.   But I deny that they were rebaptised (see Calv. Instruct.
adv. Anabapt.).   What then is meant by the words, "They were
baptised in the name of the Lord Jesus"?   Some interpret that they
were only instructed in sound doctrine by Paul; but I would rather
interpret more simply, that the baptism of the Holy Spirit, in other
words, the visible gifts of the Holy Spirit, were given by the laying
on of hands.   These are sometimes designated under the name of
baptism.   Thus, on the day of Pentecost, the apostles are said to
have remembered the words of the Lord concerning the baptism of
the Spirit and of fire.   And Peter relates that the same words occurred to him when he saw these gifts poured out on Cornelius and
his family and kindred.   There is nothing repugnant to this interpretation in its being afterwards added, "When Paul had laid his
hands upon them, the Holy Ghost came on them" (Acts xix. 6).
For Luke does not narrate two different things, but follows the form
of narrative common to the Hebrews, who first give the substance,
and then explain more fully.   This any one may perceive from the
mere context.   For he says, "When they heard this they were
baptised in the name of the Lord Jesus.   And when Paul laid his
hands upon them, the Holy Ghost came on them."   In this last
sentence is described what the nature of the baptism was.   But if
ignorance vitiates a former, and requires to be corrected by a second
baptism, the apostles should first of all have been rebaptised, since
for more than three full years after their baptism they had scarcely
received any slender portion of purer doctrine.   Then so numerous
being the acts of ignorance which by the mercy of God are daily
corrected in us, what rivers would suffice for so many repeated
baptisms?

19. The force, dignity, utility, and end of the sacrament must
now, if I mistake not, be sufficiently clear.   In regard to the external symbol, I wish the genuine institution of Christ had been
maintained as fit to repress the audacity of men.   As if to be baptised with water, according to the precept of Christ, had been a contemptible thing, a benediction, or rather incantation, was devised to pollute the true consecration of water.   There was afterwards added the
taper and chrism, while exorcism[1] was thought to open the door for
baptism.   Though I am not unaware how ancient the origin of this

1 Latin, "Exsufflatio."—French, "Le souffle pour conjurer le diable."

adventitious farrago is, still it is lawful for me and all the godly to reject whatever men have presumed to add to the institution of Christ. When Satan saw that by the foolish credulity of the world his impostures were received almost without objection at the commencement of the gospel, he proceeded to grosser mockery: hence spittle and other follies, to the open disgrace of baptism, were introduced with unbridled licence.[1] From our experience of them, let us learn that there is nothing holier, or better, or safer, than to be contented with the authority of Christ alone. How much better, therefore, is it to lay aside all theatrical pomp, which dazzles the eyes of the simple, and dulls their minds, and when any one is to be baptised to bring him forward and present him to God, the whole Church looking on as witnesses, and praying over him; to recite the Confession of Faith, in which the catechumen has been instructed, explain the promises which are given in baptism, then baptise in the name of the Father, and the Son, and the Holy Spirit, and conclude with prayer and thanksgiving. In this way, nothing which is appropriate would be omitted, and the one ceremony, which proceeded from its divine Author, would shine forth most brightly, not being buried or polluted by extraneous observances. Whether the person baptised is to be wholly immersed, and that whether once or thrice, or whether he is only to be sprinkled with water, is not of the least consequence: churches should be at liberty to adopt either, according to the diversity of climates, although it is evident that the term *baptise* means to immerse, and that this was the form used by the primitive Church.[2]

20. It is here also pertinent to observe, that it is improper for private individuals to take upon themselves the administration of baptism; for it, as well as the dispensation of the Supper, is part of the ministerial office. For Christ did not give command to any men or women whatever to baptise, but to those whom he had appointed apostles. And when, in the administration of the Supper, he ordered his disciples to do what they had seen him do (he having done the part of a legitimate dispenser), he doubtless meant that in this they should imitate his example. The practice which has been in use for many ages, and even almost from the very commencement of the Church, for laics to baptise, in danger of death, when a minister

---

[1] Vid. Calv. in Epist. de Fugiendis illicitis sacris. Item, Vera Ecclesia Reformandæ Ratio. See also infra, chap. xvii. sec. 43. As to the form of baptism, see Cyprian, Lib. iv. Ep. 7.

[2] French, " Au reste, c'est une chose de nulle importance, si on baptise en plongeant du tout dans l'eau celui qui est baptisé, ou en repandant seulement de l'eau sur lui : mais selon la diversité des regions cela doit demeura en la liberté des Eglises. Car le signe est representé en l'un et en l'autre. Combien que le mot mesme de Baptiser signifie du tout plonger et qu'il soit certain que la coustume d'ainsi totalement plonger, ait eté anciennement observée en l'Eglise."—Moreover, it is a matter of no importance whether we baptise by entirely immersing the person baptised in the water, or only by sprinkling water upon him, but, according to the diversity of countries, this should remain free to the churches. For the sign is represented in either. Although the mere term Baptise means to immerse entirely, and it is certain that the custom of thus entirely immersing was anciently observed in the Church.

could not be present in time, cannot, it appears to me, be defended on sufficient grounds. Even the early Christians who observed or tolerated this practice were not clear whether it were rightly done. This doubt is expressed by Augustine when he says, "Although a laic have given baptism when compelled by necessity, I know not whether any one can piously say that it ought to be repeated. For if it is done without any necessity compelling it, it is usurpation of another's office; but if necessity urges, it is either no fault, or a venial one" (August. Cont. Epist. Parmen. Lib. ii. c. 13). With regard to women, it was decreed, without exception, in the Council of Carthage (cap. 100), that they were not to presume to baptise at all. But there is a danger that he who is sick may be deprived of the gift of regeneration if he decease without baptism! By no means. Our children, before they are born, God declares that he adopts for his own when he promises that he will be a God to us, and to our seed after us. In this promise their salvation is included. None will dare to offer such an insult to God as to deny that he is able to give effect to his promise. How much evil has been caused by the dogma, ill expounded, that baptism is necessary to salvation, few perceive, and therefore think caution the less necessary. For when the opinion prevails that all are lost who happen not to be dipped in water, our condition becomes worse than that of God's ancient people, as if his grace were more restrained than under the Law. In that case, Christ will be thought to have come not to fufil, but to abolish the promises, since the promise, which was then effectual in itself to confer salvation before the eighth day, would not now be effectual without the help of a sign.

21. What the custom was before Augustine's day is gathered, first, from Tertullian, who says, that a woman is not permitted to speak in the Church, nor yet to teach, or baptise, or offer, that she may not claim to herself any office of the man, not to say of the priest (Tertull. Cont. Hæres. Lib. i.). Of the same thing we have a sufficient witness in Epiphanius, when he upbraids Marcian with giving permission to women to baptise. I am not unaware of the answer given by those who take an opposite view—viz. that common use is very different from an extraordinary remedy used under the pressure of extreme necessity—but since he declares it mockery to allow women to baptise, and makes no exception, it is sufficiently plain that the corruption is condemned as inexcusable on any pretext. In his Third Book, also, when he says that it was not even permitted to the holy mother of Christ, he makes no reservation.

22. The example of Zipporah (Exod. iv. 25) is irrelevantly quoted. Because the angel of God was appeased after she took a stone and circumcised her son, it is erroneously inferred that her act was approved by God. Were it so, we must say that God was pleased with a worship which Gentiles brought from Assyria, and set up in Samaria.[1] But other valid reasons prove, that what a foolish woman

1 French, "Car par une mesme raison il faudroit dire, le service meslé que dres-

did is ignorantly drawn into a precedent. Were I to say that there was something special in the case, making it unfit for a precedent—and especially as we nowhere read that the command to circumcise was specially given to priests, the cases of baptism and circumcision are different—I should give a sufficient refutation. For the words of Christ are plain: " Go ye, therefore, and teach all nations, baptising them" (Matth. xxviii. 19). Since he appointed the same persons to be preachers of the Gospel, and dispensers of baptism—and in the Church, " no man taketh this honour unto himself," as the apostle declares (Heb. v. 4), " but he that is called of God, as was Aaron "—any one who baptises without a lawful call usurps another's office. Paul declares, that whatever we attempt with a dubious conscience, even in the minutest matters, as in meat and drink, is sin (Rom. xiv. 23). Therefore, in baptism by women, the sin is the greater, when it is plain that the rule delivered by Christ is violated, seeing we know it to be unlawful to put asunder what God has joined. But all this I pass; only I would have my readers to observe, that the last thing intended by Zipporah was to perform a service to God. Seeing her son in danger, she frets and murmurs, and, not without indignation, throws down the foreskin on the ground; thus upbraiding her husband, and taking offence at God. In short, it is plain that her whole procedure is dictated by passion: she complains both against her husband and against God, because she is forced to spill the blood of her son. We may add, that however well she might have conducted herself in all other respects, yet her presumption is inexcusable in this, in circumcising her son while her husband is present, and that husband not a mere private individual, but Moses, the chief prophet of God, than whom no greater ever arose in Israel. This was no more allowable in her, than it would be for women in the present day under the eye of a bishop. But this controversy will at once be disposed of when we maintain, that children who happen to depart this life before an opportunity of immersing them in water, are not excluded from the kingdom of heaven. Now, it has been seen, that unless we admit this position, great injury is done to the covenant of God, as if in itself it were weak, whereas its effect depends not either on baptism, or on any accessaries. The sacrament is afterwards added as a kind of seal, not to give efficacy to the promise, as if in itself invalid, but merely to confirm it to us. Hence it follows, that the children of believers are not baptised, in order that though formerly aliens from the Church, they may then, for the first time, become children of God, but rather are received into the Church by a formal sign, because, in virtue of 'the promise, they previously belonged to the body of Christ. Hence if, in omitting the sign, their is neither sloth, nor

serent en Samarie ceux qui etoient la envoyés d'Orient, eut eté agreable a Dieu, veu que depuis ils ne furent plus molestes des betes sauvages."—For the same reason it would be necessary to say, that the mongrel worship set up in Samaria by those who came from the East was agreeable to God, seeing that thereafter they were not molested by wild beasts.

contempt, nor negligence, we are safe from all danger. By far the better course, therefore, is to pay such respect to the ordinance of God as not to seek the sacraments in any other quarter than where the Lord has deposited them. When we cannot receive them from the Church, the grace of God is not so inseparably annexed to them that we cannot obtain it by faith, according to his word.

CHAPTER XVI.

PÆDOBAPTISM. ITS ACCORDANCE WITH THE INSTITUTION OF CHRIST,
AND THE NATURE OF THE SIGN.

Divisions of this chapter,—I. Confirmation of the orthodox doctrine of Pædobaptism,
sec. 1–9. II. Refutation of the arguments which the Anabaptists urge against Pædobaptism, sec. 10–30. III. Special objections of Servetus refuted, sec. 31, 32.

Sections.

1. Pædobaptism. The consideration of the question necessary and useful. Pædobaptism of divine origin.
2. This demonstrated from a consideration of the promises. These explain the nature
and validity of Pædobaptism.
3. Promises annexed to the symbol of water cannot be better seen than in the institution of circumcision.
4. The promise and thing figured in circumcision and baptism one and the same.
The only difference in the external ceremony.
5. Hence the baptism of the children of Christian parents as competent as the circumcision of Jewish children. An objection founded on a stated day for circumcision refuted.
6. An argument for Pædobaptism founded on the covenant which God made with
Abraham. An objection disposed of. The grace of God not diminished by the
advent of Christ.
7. Argument founded on Christ's invitation to children. Objection answered.
8. Objection, that no infants were baptised by the apostles. Answer. Objection,
that pædobaptism is a novelty. Answer.
9. Twofold use and benefit of pædobaptism. In respect, 1. Of parents. 2. Of
children baptised.
10. Second part of the chapter, stating the arguments of Anabaptists. Alleged dissimilitude between baptism and circumcision. First answer.
11. Second answer. The covenant in baptism and circumcision not different.
12. Third answer.
13. Infants, both Jewish and Christian, comprehended in the covenant.
14. Objection considered.
15. The Jews being comprehended in the covenant, no substantial difference between
baptism and circumcision.
16. Another argument of the Anabaptists considered.
17. Argument that children are not fit to understand baptism, and therefore should
not be baptised.
18. Answer continued.
19. Answer continued.
20. Answer continued.
21. Answer continued.
22. Argument, that baptism being appointed for the remission of sins, infants, not
having sinned, ought not to be baptised. Answer.
23. Argument against pædobaptism, founded on the practice of the apostles. Answer.
24. Answer continued.
25. Argument founded on a saying of our Lord to Nicodemus. Answer.
26. Error of those who adjudge all who die unbaptised to eternal destruction.
27. Argument against pædobaptism, founded on the precept and example of our
Saviour, in requiring instruction to precede baptism. Answer.
28. Answer continued.
29. Answer continued.

1. BUT since, in this age, certain frenzied spirits have raised, and even now continue to raise, great disturbance in the Church on account of pædobaptism, I cannot avoid here, by way of appendix, adding something to restrain their fury. Should any one think me more prolix than the subject is worth, let him reflect that, in a matter of the greatest moment, so much is due to the peace and purity of the Church, that we should not fastidiously object to whatever may be conducive to both. I may add, that I will study so to arrange this discussion, that it will tend, in no small degree, still farther to illustrate the subject of baptism.[1] The argument by which pædobaptism is assailed is, no doubt, specious—viz. that it is not founded on the institution of God, but was introduced merely by human presumption and depraved curiosity, and afterwards, by a foolish facility, rashly received in practice ; whereas a sacrament has not a thread to hang upon, if it rest not on the sure foundation of the word of God. But what if, when the matter is properly attended to, it should be found that a calumny is falsely and unjustly brought against the holy ordinance of the Lord ? First, then, let us inquire into its origin. Should it appear to have been devised merely by human rashness, let us abandon it, and regulate the true observance of baptism entirely by the will of the Lord ; but should it be proved to be by no means destitute of his sure authority, let us beware of discarding the sacred institutions of God, and thereby insulting their Author.

2. In the first place, then, it is a well-known doctrine, and one as to which all the pious are agreed,—that the right consideration of signs does not lie merely in the outward ceremonies, but depends chiefly on the promise and the spiritual mysteries, to typify which the ceremonies themselves are appointed. He, therefore, who would thoroughly understand the effect of baptism—its object and true character—must not stop short at the element and corporeal object.

---

1 The French from the beginning of the chapter is as follows :—" Or d'autant que nous voyons l'observation que nous tenons de baptiser les petits enfans etre impugnée et debatue par aucuns esprits malins, comme si elle n'avoit point eté instituée de Dieu mais inventée nouvellement des hommes, ou pour le moins quelques années apres le tems des Apostres; j'estime qu'il viendra bien à propos, de confermer en cest endroit les consciences imbecilles, et refuter les objections mensonges qui pourroient faire teis seducteurs, pour renverser le verité de Dieu aux cœur des simples, qui ne seraient pas exercités pour repondre a leur cauteles et cavillations."—Now, inasmuch as we see that the practice which we have of baptising little children is impugned and assailed by some malignant spirits, as if it had not been appointed by God, but newly invented by men, or at least some years after the days of the Apostles, I think it will be very seasonable to confirm weak consciences in this matter, and refute the lying objections which such seducers might make, in order to overthrow the truth of God in the hearts of the simple, who might not be skilled in answering their cavils and objections.

but look forward to the divine promises which are therein offered to us, and rise to the internal secrets which are therein represented. He who understands these has reached the solid truth, and, so to speak, the whole substance of baptism, and will thence perceive the nature and use of outward sprinkling. On the other hand, he who passes them by in contempt, and keeps his thoughts entirely fixed on the visible ceremony, will neither understand the force, nor the proper nature of baptism, nor comprehend what is meant, or what end is gained by the use of water. This is confirmed by passages of Scripture too numerous and too clear to make it necessary here to discuss them more at length. It remains, therefore, to inquire into the nature and efficacy of baptism, as evinced by the promises therein given. Scripture shows, *first*, that it points to that cleansing from sin which we obtain by the blood of Christ; and, *secondly*, to the mortification of the flesh, which consists in participation in his death, by which believers are regenerated to newness of life, and thereby to the fellowship of Christ. To these general heads may be referred all that the Scriptures teach concerning baptism, with this addition, that it is also a symbol to testify our religion to men.

3. Now, since prior to the institution of baptism, the people of God had circumcision in its stead, let us see how far these two signs differ, and how far they resemble each other. In this way it will appear what analogy there is between them. When the Lord enjoins Abraham to observe circumcision (Gen. xvii. 10), he premises that he would be a God unto him and to his seed, adding, that in himself was a perfect sufficiency of all things, and that Abraham might reckon on his hand as a fountain of every blessing. These words include the promise of eternal life, as our Saviour interprets when he employs it to prove the immortality and resurrection of believers: " God," says he, "is not the God of the dead, but of the living" (Matth. xxii. 32). Hence, too, Paul, when showing to the Ephesians how great the destruction was from which the Lord had delivered them, seeing that they had not been admitted to the covenant of circumcision, infers that at that time they were aliens from the covenant of promise, without God, and without hope (Eph. ii. 12), all these being comprehended in the covenant. Now, the first access to God, the first entrance to immortal life, is the remission of sins. Hence it follows, that this corresponds to the promise of our cleansing in baptism. The Lord afterwards covenants with Abraham, that he is to walk before him in sincerity and innocence of heart: this applies to mortification or regeneration. And lest any should doubt whether circumcision were the sign of mortification, Moses explains more clearly elsewhere when he exhorts the people of Israel to circumcise the foreskin of their heart, because the Lord had chosen them for his own people, out of all the nations of the earth. As the Lord, in choosing the posterity of Abraham for his people, commands them to be circumcised, so Moses declares that they are to be circumcised in heart, thus explaining what is typified by that carnal

circumcision. Then, lest any one should attempt this in his own strength, he shows that it is the work of divine grace. All this is so often inculcated by the prophets, that there is no occasion here to collect the passages which everywhere occur. We have, therefore, a spiritual promise given to the fathers in circumcision, similar to that which is given to us in baptism, since it figured to them both the forgiveness of sins and the mortification of the flesh. Besides, as we have shown that Christ, in whom both of these reside, is the foundation of baptism, so must he also be the foundation of circumcision. For he is promised to Abraham, and in him all nations are blessed. To seal this grace, the sign of circumcision is added.

4. There is now no difficulty in seeing wherein the two signs agree, and wherein they differ. The promise, in which we have shown that the power of the signs consists, is one in both—viz. the promise of the paternal favour of God, of forgiveness of sins, and eternal life. And the thing figured is one and the same—viz. regeneration. The foundation on which the completion of these things depends is one in both. Wherefore, there is no difference in the internal meaning, from which the whole power and peculiar nature of the sacrament is to be estimated. The only difference which remains is in the external ceremony, which is the least part of it, the chief part consisting in the promise and the thing signified. Hence we may conclude, that everything applicable to circumcision applies also to baptism, excepting always the difference in the visible ceremony. To this analogy and comparison we are led by that rule of the apostle, in which he enjoins us to bring every interpretation of Scripture to the analogy of faith (Rom. xii. 3, 6). And certainly in this matter the truth may almost be felt. For just as circumcision, which was a kind of badge to the Jews, assuring them that they were adopted as the people and family of God, was their first entrance into the Church, while they, in their turn, professed their allegiance to God, so now we are initiated by baptism, so as to be enrolled among his people, and at the same time swear unto his name. Hence it is incontrovertible, that baptism has been substituted for circumcision, and performs the same office.

5. Now, if we are to investigate whether or not baptism is justly given to infants, will we not say that the man trifles, or rather is delirious, who would stop short at the element of water, and the external observance, and not allow his mind to rise to the spiritual mystery? If reason is listened to, it will undoubtedly appear that baptism is properly administered to infants as a thing due to them. The Lord did not anciently bestow circumcision upon them without making them partakers of all the things signified by circumcision. He would have deluded his pepole with mere imposture, had he quieted them with fallacious symbols: the very idea is shocking. He distinctly declares, that the circumcision of the infant will be instead of a seal of the promise of the covenant. But if the covenant remains firm and fixed, it is no less applicable to the children of Christians

in the present day, than to the children of the Jews under the Old Testament. Now, if they are partakers of the thing signified, how can they be denied the sign? If they obtain the reality, how can they be refused the figure? The external sign is so united in the sacrament with the word, that it cannot be separated from it: but if they can be separated, to which of the two shall we attach the greater value? Surely, when we see that the sign is subservient to the word, we shall say that it is subordinate, and assign it the inferior place. Since, then, the word of baptism is destined for infants, why should we deny them the sign, which is an appendage of the word? This one reason, could no other be furnished, would be amply sufficient to refute all gainsayers. The objection, that there was a fixed day for circumcision, is a mere quibble. We admit that we are not now, like the Jews, tied down to certain days; but when the Lord declares, that though he prescribes no day, yet he is pleased that infants shall be formally admitted to his covenant, what more do we ask?

6. Scripture gives us a still clearer knowledge of the truth. For it is most evident that the covenant, which the Lord once made with Abraham, is not less applicable to Christians now than it was anciently to the Jewish people, and therefore that word has no less reference to Christians than to Jews. Unless, indeed, we imagine that Christ, by his advent, diminished, or curtailed the grace of the Father—an idea not free from execrable blasphemy. Wherefore, both the children of the Jews, because, when made heirs of that covenant, they were separated from the heathen, were called a holy seed, and for the same reason the children of Christians, or those who have only one believing parent, are called holy, and, by the testimony of the apostle, differ from the impure seed of idolaters. Then, since the Lord, immediately after the covenant was made with Abraham, ordered it to be sealed in infants by an outward sacrament, how can it be said that Christains are not to attest it in the present day, and seal it in their children? Let it not be objected, that the only symbol by which the Lord ordered his covenant to be confirmed was that of circumcision, which was long ago abrogated. It is easy to answer, that, in accordance with the form of the old dispensation, he appointed circumcision to confirm his covenant, but that it being abrogated, the same reason for confirmation still continues, a reason which we have in common with the Jews. Hence it is always necessary carefully to consider what is common to both, and wherein they differed from us. The covenant is common, and the reason for confirming it is common. The mode of confirming it is so far different, that they had circumcision, instead of which we now have baptism. Otherwise, if the testimony by which the Jews were assured of the salvation of their seed is taken from us, the consequence will be, that, by the advent of Christ, the grace of God. which was formerly given to the Jews, is more obscure and less perfectly attested to us. If this cannot be said without extreme insult to Christ, by whom the infinite goodness of the Father has

been more brightly and benignly than ever shed upon the earth, and declared to men, it must be confessed that it cannot be more confined, and less clearly manifested, than under the obscure shadows of the law.

7. Hence our Lord Jesus Christ, to give an example from which the world might learn that he had come to enlarge rather than to limit the grace of the Father, kindly takes the little children in his arms, and rebukes his disciples for attempting to prevent them from coming (Matth. xix. 13), because they were keeping those to whom the kingdom of heaven belonged away from him, through whom alone there is access to heaven. But it will be asked, What resemblance is there between baptism and our Saviour embracing little children? He is not said to have baptised, but to have received, embraced, and blessed them; and, therefore, if we would imitate his example, we must give infants the benefit of our prayers, not baptise them. But let us attend to the act of our Saviour a little more carefully than these men do. For we must not lightly overlook the fact, that our Saviour, in ordering little children to be brought to him, adds the reason, " of such is the kingdom of heaven." And he afterwards testifies his good-will by act, when he embraces them, and with prayer and benediction commends them to his Father. If it is right that children should be brought to Christ, why should they not be admitted to baptism, the symbol of our communion and fellowship with Christ? If the kingdom of heaven is theirs, why should they be denied the sign by which access, as it were, is opened to the Church, that being admitted into it they may be enrolled among the heirs of the heavenly kingdom? How unjust were we to drive away those whom Christ invites to himself, to spoil those whom he adorns with his gifts, to exclude those whom he spontaneously admits. But if we insist on discussing the difference between our Saviour's act and baptism, in how much higher esteem shall we hold baptism (by which we testify that infants are included in the divine covenant), than the taking up, embracing, laying hands on children, and praying over them, acts by which Christ, when present, declares both that they are his, and are sanctified by him. By the other cavils by which the objectors endeavour to evade this passage, they only betray their ignorance: they quibble that, because our Saviour says, " Suffer little children to come," they must have been several years old, and fit to come. But they are called by the Evangelists βρέφη καὶ παιδία, terms which denote infants still at their mothers' breasts. The term "come" is used simply for "approach." See the quibbles to which men are obliged to have recourse when they have hardened themselves against the truth! There is nothing more solid in their allegation, that the kingdom of heaven is not assigned to children, but to those like children, since the expression is, " of such," not "of themselves." If this is admitted, what will be the reason which our Saviour employs to show that they are not strangers to him from nonage? When he orders that little children shall be allowed to

come to him, nothing is plainer than that mere infancy is meant. Lest this should seem absurd, he adds, " Of such is the kingdom of heaven." But if infants must necessarily be comprehended, the expression, " of such," clearly shows that infants themselves, and those like them, are intended.

8. Every one must now see that pædobaptism, which receives such strong support from Scripture, is by no means of human invention. Nor is there anything plausible in the objection, that we nowhere read of even one infant having been baptised by the hands of the apostles. For although this is not expressly narrated by the Evangelists, yet as they are not expressly excluded when mention is made of any baptised family (Acts xvi. 15, 32), what man of sense will argue from this that they were not baptised? If such kinds of argument were good, it would be necessary, in like manner, to interdict women from the Lord's Supper, since we do not read that they were ever admitted to it in the days of the apostles. But here we are contented with the rule of faith. For when we reflect on the nature of the ordinance of the Lord's Supper, we easily judge who the persons are to whom the use of it is to be communicated. The same we observe in the case of baptism. For, attending to the end for which it was instituted, we clearly perceive that it is not less applicable to children than to those of more advanced years, and that, therefore, they cannot be deprived of it without manifest fraud to the will of its divine Author. The assertion which they disseminate among the common people, that a long series of years elapsed after the resurrection of Christ, during which pædobaptism was unknown, is a shameful falsehood, since there is no writer, however ancient, who does not trace its origin to the days of the apostles.

9. It remains briefly to indicate what benefit redounds from the observance, both to believers who bring their children to the church to be baptised, and to the infants themselves, to whom the sacred water is applied, that no one may despise the ordinance as useless or superfluous : though any one who would think of ridiculing baptism under this pretence, would also ridicule the divine ordinance of circumcision : for what can they adduce to impugn the one, that may not be retorted against the other ? Thus the Lord punishes the arrogance of those who forthwith condemn whatever their carnal sense cannot comprehend. But God furnishes us with other weapons to repress their stupidity. His holy institution, from which we feel that our faith derives admirable consolation, deserves not to be called superfluous. For the divine symbol communicated to the child, as with the impress of a seal, confirms the promise given to the godly parent, and declares that the Lord will be a God not to him only, but to his seed ; not merely visiting him with his grace and goodness, but his posterity also to the thousandth generation. When the infinite goodness of God is thus displayed, it, in the first place, furnishes most ample materials for proclaiming his glory, and fills pious

breasts with no ordinary joy, urging them more strongly to love their affectionate Parent, when they see that, on their account, he extends his care to their posterity. I am not moved by the objection, that the promise ought to be sufficient to confirm the salvation of our children. It has seemed otherwise to God, who, seeing our weakness, has herein been pleased to condescend to it. Let those, then, who embrace the promise of mercy to their children, consider it as their duty to offer them to the Church, to be sealed with the symbol of mercy, and animate themselves to surer confidence, on seeing with the bodily eye the covenant of the Lord engraven on the bodies of their children. On the other hand, children derive some benefit from their baptism, when, being ingrafted into the body of the Church, they are made an object of greater interest to the other members. Then when they have grown up, they are thereby strongly urged to an earnest desire of serving God, who has received them as sons by the formal symbol of adoption, before, from nonage, they were able to recognise him as their Father. In fine, we ought to stand greatly in awe of the denunciation, that God will take vengeance on every one who despises to impress the symbol of the covenant on his child (Gen. xvii. 15), such contempt being a rejection, and, as it were, abjuration of the offered grace.

10. Let us now discuss the arguments by which some furious madmen cease not to assail this holy ordinance of God. And, first, feeling themselves pressed beyond measure by the resemblance between baptism and circumcision, they contend that there is a wide difference between the two signs, that the one has nothing in common with the other. They maintain that the things meant are different, that the covenant is altogether different, and that the persons included under the name of children are different. When they first proceed to the proof, they pretend that circumcision was a figure of mortification, not of baptism. This we willingly concede to them, for it admirably supports our view, in support of which the only proof we use is, that baptism and circumcision are signs of mortification. Hence we conclude that the one was substituted for the other, baptism representing to us the very thing which circumcision signified to the Jews. In asserting a difference of covenant, with what barbarian audacity do they corrupt and destroy Scripture ? and that not in one passage only, but so as not to leave any passage safe and entire. The Jews they depict as so carnal as to resemble brutes more than men, representing the covenant which was made with them as reaching no farther than a temporary life, and the promises which were given to them as dwindling down into present and corporeal blessings. If this dogma is received, what remains but that the Jewish nation was overloaded for a time with divine kindness (just as swine are gorged in their sty), that they might at last perish eternally ? Whenever we quote circumcision and the promises annexed to it, they answer, that circumcision was a literal sign, and that its promises were carnal.

11. Certainly, if circumcision was a literal sign, the same view must be taken of baptism, since, in the second chapter to the Colossians, the apostle makes the one to be not a whit more spiritual than the other. For he says that in Christ we " are circumcised with the circumcision made without hands, in putting off the body of the sins of the flesh, by the circumcision of Christ." In explanation of his sentiment he immediately adds, that we are " buried with him in baptism." What do these words mean, but just that the truth and completion of baptism is the truth and completion of circumcision, since they represent one thing? For his object is to show that baptism is the same thing to Christians that circumcision formerly was to the Jews. Now, since we have already clearly shown that the promises of both signs, and the mysteries which are represented by them, agree, we shall not dwell on the point longer at present. I would only remind believers to reflect, without anything being said by me, whether that is to be regarded as an earthly and literal sign, which has nothing heavenly or spiritual under it. But lest they should blind the simple with their smoke, we shall, in passing, dispose of one objection by which they cloak this most impudent falsehood. It is absolutely certain that the original promises comprehending the covenant which God made with the Israelites under the old dispensation were spiritual, and had reference to eternal life, and were, of course, in like manner spiritually received by the fathers, that they might thence entertain a sure hope of immortality, and aspire to it with their whole soul. Meanwhile, we are far from denying that he testified his kindness to them by carnal and earthly blessings; though we hold that by these the hope of spiritual promises was confirmed. In this manner, when he promised eternal blessedness to his servant Abraham, he, in order to place a manifest indication of favour before his eye, added the promise of possession of the land of Canaan. In the same way we should understand all the terrestrial promises which were given to the Jewish nation, the spiritual promise, as the head to which the others bore reference, always holding the first place. Having handled this subject fully when treating of the difference between the old and the new dispensations, I now only glance at it.

12. Under the appellation of *children* the difference they observe is this, that the children of Abraham, under the old dispensation, were those who derived their origin from his seed, but that the appellation is now given to those who imitate his faith, and therefore that carnal infancy, which was ingrafted into the fellowship of the covenant by circumcision, typified the spiritual children of the new covenant, who are regenerated by the word of God to immortal life. In these words we indeed discover a small spark of truth, but these giddy spirits err grievously in this, that laying hold of whatever comes first to their hand, when they ought to proceed farther, and compare many things together, they obstinately fasten upon one single word. Hence it cannot but happen that they are every now

and then deluded, because they do not exert themselves to obtain a full knowledge of any subject. We certainly admit that the carnal seed of Abraham for a time held the place of the spiritual seed, which is ingrafted into him by faith (Gal. iv. 28; Rom. iv. 12). For we are called his sons, though we have no natural relationship with him. But if they mean, as they not obscurely show, that the spiritual promise was never made to the carnal seed of Abraham, they are greatly mistaken. We must, therefore, take a better aim, one to which we are directed by the infallible guidance of Scripture. The Lord therefore promises to Abraham that he shall have a seed in whom all the nations of the earth will be blessed, and at the same time assures him that he will be a God both to him and his seed. All who in faith receive Christ as the author of the blessing are the heirs of this promise, and accordingly are called the children of Abraham.

13. Although, after the resurrection of Christ, the boundaries of the kingdom began to be extended far and wide into all nations indiscriminately, so that, according to the declaration of Christ, believers were collected from all quarters to sit down with Abraham, Isaac, and Jacob, in the kingdom of heaven (Matth. viii. 11), still, for many ages before, the Jews had enjoyed this great mercy. And as he had selected them (while passing by all other nations) to be for a time the depositaries of his favour, he designated them as his peculiar purchased people (Exod. xix. 5). In attestation of this kindness, he appointed circumcision, by which symbol the Jews were taught that God watched over their safety, and they were thereby raised to the hope of eternal life. For what can ever be wanting to him whom God has once taken under his protection? Wherefore the apostle, to prove that the Gentiles, as well as the Jews, were the children of Abraham, speaks in this way: " Faith was reckoned to Abraham for righteousness. How was it then reckoned? when he was in circumcision, or in uncircumcision? Not in circumcision, but in uncircumcision. And he received the sign of circumcision, a seal of the righteousness of the faith which he had yet being uncircumcised; that he might be the father of all them that believe, though they be not circumcised: that righteousness might be imputed to them also: and the father of circumcision to them who are not of the circumcision only, but who also walk in the steps of that faith of our father Abraham, which he had yet being uncircumcised" (Rom. iv. 9-12). Do we not see that both are made equal in dignity? For, to the time appointed by the divine decree, he was the father of circumcision. But when, as the apostle elsewhere writes (Eph. ii. 14), the wall of partition which separated the Gentiles from the Jews was broken down, to them, also, access was given to the kingdom of God, and he became their father, and that without the sign of circumcision, its place being supplied by baptism. In saying expressly that Abraham was not the father of those who were of the circumcision only, his object was to repress the superciliousness of some who, laying aside all regard to godliness, plumed themselves

on mere ceremonies. In like manner, we may, in the present day, refute the vanity of those who, in baptism, seek nothing but water.

14. But in opposition to this is produced a passage from the Epistle to the Romans, in which the apostle says, that those who are of the flesh are not the children of Abraham, but that those only who are the children of promise are considered as the seed (Rom. ix. 7). For he seems to insinuate, that carnal relationship to Abraham, which we think of some consequence, is nothing. But we must attend carefully to the subject which the apostle is there treating. His object being to show to the Jews that the goodness of God was not restricted to the seed of Abraham, nay, that of itself it contributes nothing, produces, in proof of the fact, the cases of Ishmael and Esau. These being rejected, just as if they had been strangers, although, according to the flesh, they were the genuine offspring of Abraham, the blessing resides in Isaac and Jacob. This proves what he afterwards affirms—viz. that salvation depends on the mercy which God bestows on whomsoever he pleases, but that the Jews have no ground to glory or plume themselves on the name of the covenant, unless they keep the law of the covenant, that is, obey the word. On the other hand, after casting down their vain confidence in their origin, because he was aware that the covenant which had been made with the posterity of Abraham could not properly prove fruitless, he declares, that due honour should still be paid to carnal relationship to Abraham, in consequence of which, the Jews were the primary and native heirs of the gospel, unless in so far as they were, for their ingratitude, rejected as unworthy, and yet rejected so as not to leave their nation utterly destitute of the heavenly blessing. For this reason, though they were contumacious breakers of the covenant, he styles them holy (such respect does he pay to the holy generation which God had honoured with his sacred covenant), while we, in comparison of them, are termed posthumous, or abortive children of Abraham, and that not by nature, but by adoption, just as if a twig were broken from its own tree, and ingrafted on another stock. Therefore, that they might not be defrauded of their privilege, it was necessary that the gospel should first be preached to them. For they are, as it were, the first-born in the family of God. The honour due, on this account, must therefore be paid them, until they have rejected the offer, and, by their ingratitude, caused it to be transferred to the Gentiles. Nor, however great the contumacy with which they persist in warring against the gospel, are we therefore to despise them. We must consider, that in respect of the promise, the blessing of God still resides among them ; and, as the apostle testifies, will never entirely depart from them, seeing that " the gifts and calling of God are without repentance " (Rom. xi. 29).

15. Such is the value of the promise given to the posterity of Abraham,—such the balance in which it is to be weighed. Hence, though we have no doubt that in distinguishing the children of God from bastards and foreigners, that the election of God reigns freely,

we, at the same time, perceive that he was pleased specially to embrace the seed of Abraham with his mercy, and, for the better attestation of it, to seal it by circumcision. The case of the Christian Church is entirely of the same description; for as Paul there declares that the Jews are sanctified by their parents, so he elsewhere says that the children of Christians derive sanctification from their parents. Hence it is inferred, that those who are chargeable with impurity are justly separated from others. Now, who can have any doubt as to the falsehood of their subsequent averment—viz. that the infants who were formerly circumcised only typified the spiritual infancy which is produced by the regeneration of the word of God? When the apostle says, that "Jesus Christ was a minister of the circumcision for the truth of God, to confirm the promises made unto the fathers" (Rom. xv. 8), he does not philosophise subtilely, as if he had said, Since the covenant made with Abraham has respect unto his seed, Christ, in order to perform and discharge the promise made by the Father, came for the salvation of the Jewish nation. Do you see how he considers that, after the resurrection of Christ, the promise is to be fulfilled to the seed of Abraham, not allegorically, but literally, as the words express? To the same effect is the declaration of Peter to the Jews: "The promise is unto you and to your children" (Acts ii. 39); and in the next chapter, he calls them *the children of the covenant*, that is, heirs. Not widely different from this is the other passage of the apostle, above quoted, in which he regards and describes circumcision performed on infants as an attestation to the communion which they have with Christ. And, indeed, if we listen to the absurdities of those men, what will become of the promise by which the Lord, in the second commandment of his law, engages to be gracious to the seed of his servants for a thousand generations? Shall we here have recourse to allegory? This were the merest quibble. Shall we say that it has been abrogated? In this way, we should do away with the law which Christ came not to destroy, but to fulfil, inasmuch as it turns to our everlasting good. Therefore, let it be without controversy, that God is so good and liberal to his people, that he is pleased, as a mark of his favour, to extend their privileges to the children born to them.

16. The distinctions which these men attempt to draw between baptism and circumcision are not only ridiculous, and void of all semblance of reason, but at variance with each other. For, when they affirm that baptism refers to the first day of spiritual contest, and circumcison to the eighth day, mortification being already accomplished, they immediately forget the distinction, and change their song, representing circumcision as typifying the mortification of the flesh, and baptism as a burial, which is given to none but those who are already dead. What are these giddy contradictions but frenzied dreams? According to the former view, baptism ought to precede circumcision; according to the latter, it should come after it. It is not the first time we have seen the minds of men wander

to and fro when they substitute their dreams for the infallible word of God. We hold, therefore, that their former distinction is a mere imagination. Were we disposed to make an allegory of the eighth day, theirs would not be the proper mode of it. It were much better with the early Christians to refer the number eight to the resurrection, which took place on the eighth day, and on which we know that newness of life depends, or to the whole course of the present life, during which, mortification ought to be in progress, only terminating when life itself terminates; although it would seem that God intended to provide for the tenderness of infancy by deferring circumcision to the eighth day, as the wound would have been more dangerous if inflicted immediately after birth. How much more rational is the declaration of Scripture, that we, when already dead, are buried by baptism (Rom. vi. 4); since it distinctly states, that we are buried into death that we may thoroughly die, and thenceforth aim at that mortification? Equally ingenious is their cavil, that women should not be baptised if baptism is to be made conformable to circumcision. For if it is most certain that the sanctification of the seed of Israel was attested by the sign of circumcision, it cannot be doubted that it was appointed alike for the sanctification of males and females. But though the right could only be performed on males, yet the females were, through them, partners and associates in circumcision. Wherefore, disregarding all such quibbling distinctions, let us fix on the very complete resemblance between baptism and circumcision, as seen in the internal office, the promise, the use, and the effect.

17. They seem to think they produce their strongest reason for denying baptism to children, when they allege, that they are as yet unfit, from nonage, to understand the mystery which is there sealed— viz. spiritual regeneration, which is not applicable to earliest infancy. Hence they infer, that children are only to be regarded as sons of Adam until they have attained an age fit for the reception of the second birth. But all this is directly opposed to the truth of God. For if they are to be accounted sons of Adam, they are left in death, since, in Adam, we can do nothing but die. On the contrary, Christ bids them be brought to him. Why so? Because he is life. Therefore, that he may quicken them, he makes them partners with himself; whereas these men would drive them away from Christ, and adjudge them to death. For if they pretend that infants do not perish when they are accounted the sons of Adam, the error is more than sufficiently confuted by the testimony of Scripture (1 Cor. xv. 22). For seeing it declares that in Adam all die, it follows, that no hope of life remains unless in Christ. Therefore, that we may become heirs of life, we must communicate with him. Again, seeing it is elsewhere written that we are all by nature the children of wrath (Eph. ii. 3), and conceived in sin (Ps. li. 5), of which condemnation is the inseparable attendant, we must part with our own nature before we have any access to the kingdom of God. And what can be clearer than the expression, " Flesh and blood cannot inherit the kingdom of God"? (1 Cor. xv. 50.) Therefore, let

everything that is our own be abolished (this cannot be without regeneration), and then we shall perceive this possession of the kingdom. In fine, if Christ speaks truly when he declares that he is life, we must necessarily be ingrafted into him by whom we are delivered from the bondage of death. But how, they ask, are infants regenerated, when not possessing a knowledge of either good or evil? We answer, that the work of God, though beyond the reach of our capacity, is not therefore null. Moreover, infants who are to be saved (and that some are saved at this age is certain) must, without question, be previously regenerated by the Lord. For if they bring innate corruption with them from their mother's womb, they must be purified before they can be admitted into the kingdom of God, into which shall not enter anything that defileth (Rev. xxi. 27). If they are born sinners, as David and Paul affirm, they must either remain unaccepted and hated by God, or be justified. And why do we ask more, when the Judge himself publicly declares, that "except a man be born again, he cannot see the kingdom of God"? (John iii. 3.) But to silence this class of objectors, God gave, in the case of John the Baptist, whom he sanctified from his mother's womb (Luke i. 15), a proof of what he might do in others. They gain nothing by the quibble to which they here resort—viz. that this was only once done, and therefore it does not forthwith follow that the Lord always acts thus with infants. That is not the mode in which we reason. Our only object is to show, that they unjustly and malignantly confine the power of God within limits, within which it cannot be confined. As little weight is due to another subterfuge. They allege that, by the usual phraseology of Scripture, "from the womb," has the same meaning as "from childhood." But it is easy to see that the angel had a different meaning when he announced to Zacharias that the child not yet born would be filled with the Holy Spirit. Instead of attempting to give a law to God, let us hold that he sanctifies whom he pleases, in the way in which he sanctified John, seeing that his power is not impaired.

18. And, indeed, Christ was sanctified from earliest infancy, that he might sanctify his elect in himself at any age, without distinction. For as he, in order to wipe away the guilt of disobedience which had been committed in our flesh, assumed that very flesh, that in it he might, on our account, and in our stead, perform a perfect obedience, so he was conceived by the Holy Spirit, that, completely pervaded with his holiness in the flesh which he had assumed, he might transfuse it into us. If in Christ we have a perfect pattern of all the graces which God bestows on all his children, in this instance we have a proof that the age of infancy is not incapable of receiving sanctification. This, at least, we set down as incontrovertible, that none of the elect is called away from the present life without being previously sanctified and regenerated by the Spirit of God. As to their objection that, in Scripture, the Spirit acknowledges no sanctification save that from incorruptible seed, that is, the word of God, they erron-

eously interpret Peter's words, in which he comprehends only believers who had been taught by the preaching of the gospel (1 Pet. i. 23). We confess, indeed, that the word of the Lord is the only seed of spiritual regeneration ; but we deny the inference that, therefore, the power of God cannot regenerate infants. This is as possible and easy for him, as it is wondrous and incomprehensible to us. It were dangerous to deny that the Lord is able to furnish them with the knowledge of himself in any way he pleases.

19. But *faith*, they say, *cometh by hearing*, the use of which infants have not yet obtained, nor can they be fit to know God, being, as Moses declares, without the knowledge of good and evil (Deut. i. 39). But they observe not that where the apostle makes hearing the beginning of faith, he is only describing the usual economy and dispensation which the Lord is wont to employ in calling his people, and not laying down an invariable rule, for which no other method can be substituted. Many he certainly has called and endued with the true knowledge of himself, by internal means, by the illumination of the Spirit, without the intervention of preaching. But since they deem it very absurd to attribute any knowledge of God to infants, whom Moses makes void of the knowledge of good and evil, let them tell me where the danger lies if they are said now to receive some part of that grace, of which they are to have the full measure shortly after. For if fulness of life consists in the perfect knowledge of God, since some of those whom death hurries away in the first moments of infancy pass into life eternal, they are certainly admitted to behold the immediate presence of God. Those, therefore, whom the Lord is to illumine with the full brightness of his light, why may he not, if he so pleases, irradiate at present with some small beam, especially if he does not remove their ignorance, before he delivers them from the prison of the flesh ? I would not rashly affirm that they are endued with the same faith which we experience in ourselves, or have any knowledge at all resembling faith (this I would rather leave undecided) ; but I would somewhat curb the stolid arrogance of those men who, as with inflated cheeks, affirm or deny whatever suits them.

20. In order to gain a stronger footing here, they add, that baptism is a sacrament of penitence and faith, and as neither of these is applicable to tender infancy, we must beware of rendering its meaning empty and vain, by admitting infants to the communion of baptism. But these darts are directed more against God then against us ; since the fact that circumcision was a sign of repentance is completely established by many passages of Scripture (Jer. iv. 4). Thus Paul terms it a seal of the righteousness of faith (Rom. iv. 11). Let God, then, be demanded why he ordered circumcision to be performed on the bodies of infants ? For baptism and circumcision being here in the same case, they cannot give anything to the latter without conceding it to the former. If they recur to their usual evasion, that, by the age of infancy, spiritual infants were then figured, we have already

closed this means of escape against them. We say, then, that since God imparted circumcision, the sign of repentance and faith, to infants, it should not seem absurd that they are now made partakers of baptism, unless men choose to clamour against an institution of God. But as in all his acts, so here also, enough of wisdom and righteousness shines forth to repress the slanders of the ungodly. For although infants, at the moment when they were circumcised, did not comprehend what the sign meant, still they were truly circumcised for the mortification of their corrupt and polluted nature—a mortification at which they afterwards aspired when adults. In fine, the objection is easily disposed of by the fact, that children are baptised for future repentance and faith. Though these are not yet formed in them, yet the seed of both lies hid in them by the secret operation of the Spirit. This answer at once overthrows all the objections which are twisted against us out of the meaning of baptism; for instance, the title by which Paul distinguishes it when he terms it the "washing of regeneration and renewing" (Tit. iii. 5). Hence they argue, that it is not to be given to any but to those who are capable of such feelings. But we, on the other hand, may object, that neither ought circumcision, which is designated regeneration, to be conferred on any but the regenerate. In this way, we shall condemn a divine institution. Thus, as we have already hinted, all the arguments which tend to shake circumcision are of no force in assailing baptism. Nor can they escape by saying, that everything which rests on the authority of God is absolutely fixed, though there should be no reason for it, but that this reverence is not due to pædobaptism, nor other similar things which are not recommended to us by the express word of God. They always remain caught in this dilemma. The command of God to circumcise infants was either legitimate and exempt from cavil, or deserved reprehension. If there was nothing incompetent or absurd in it, no absurdity can be shown in the observance of pædobaptism.

21. The charge of absurdity with which they attempt to stigmatise it, we thus dispose of. If those on whom the Lord has bestowed his election, after receiving the sign of regeneration, depart this life before they become adults, he, by the incomprehensible energy of his Spirit, renews them in the way which he alone sees to be expedient. Should they reach an age when they can be instructed in the meaning of baptism, they will thereby be animated to greater zeal for renovation, the badge of which they will learn that they received in earliest infancy, in order that they might aspire to it during their whole lives. To the same effect are the two passages in which Paul teaches, that we are buried with Christ by baptism (Rom. vi. 4; Col. ii. 12). For by this he means not that he who is to be initiated by baptism must have previously been buried with Christ; he simply declares the doctrine which is taught by baptism, and that to those already baptised: so that the most senseless cannot maintain from this passage that it ought to precede baptism. In this way, Moses

and the prophets reminded the people of the thing meant by circumcision, which however infants received. To the same effect, Paul says to the Galatians, "As many of you as have been baptised into Christ have put on Christ" (Gal. iii. 27). Why so? That they might thereafter live to Christ, to whom previously they had not lived. And though, in adults, the receiving of the sign ought to follow the understanding of its meaning, yet, as will shortly be explained, a different rule must be followed with children. No other conclusion can be drawn from a passage in Peter, on which they strongly found. He says, that baptism is "not the putting away of the filth of the flesh, but the answer of a good conscience toward God by the resurrection of Jesus Christ" (1 Pet. iii. 21). From this they contend that nothing is left for pædobaptism, which becomes mere empty smoke, as being altogether at variance with the meaning of baptism. But the delusion which misleads them is, that they would always have the thing to precede the sign in the order of time. For the truth of circumcision consisted in the same answer of a good conscience; but if the truth must necessarily have preceded, infants would never have been circumcised by the command of God. But he himself, showing that the answer of a good conscience forms the truth of circumcision, and, at the same time, commanding infants to be circumcised, plainly intimates that, in their case, circumcision had reference to the future. Wherefore, nothing more of present effect is to be required in pædobaptism, than to confirm and sanction the covenant which the Lord has made with them. The other part of the meaning of the sacrament will follow at the time which God himself has provided.

22. Every one must, I think, clearly perceive, that all arguments of this stamp are mere perversions of Scripture. The other remaining arguments akin to these we shall cursorily examine. They object, that baptism is given for the remission of sins. When this is conceded, it strongly supports our view; for, seeing we are born sinners, we stand in need of forgiveness and pardon from the very womb. Moreover, since God does not preclude this age from the hope of mercy, but rather gives assurance of it, why should we deprive it of the sign, which is much inferior to the reality? The arrow, therefore, which they aim at us, we throw back upon themselves. Infants receive forgiveness of sins; therefore, they are not to be deprived of the sign. They adduce the passage from the Ephesians, that Christ gave himself for the Church, "that he might sanctify and cleanse it with the washing of water by the word" (Eph. v. 26). Nothing could be quoted more appropriate than this to overthrow their error: it furnishes us with an easy proof. If, by baptism, Christ intends to attest the ablution by which he cleanses his Church, it would seem not equitable to deny this attestation to infants, who are justly deemed part of the Church, seeing they are called heirs of the heavenly kingdom. For Paul comprehends the whole Church when he says that it was cleansed by the washing of water. In like

manner, from his expression in another place, that by baptism we are ingrafted into the body of Christ (1 Cor. xii. 13), we infer, that infants, whom he enumerates among his members, are to be baptised, in order that they may not be dissevered from his body. See the violent onset which they make with all their engines on the bulwarks of our faith.

23. They now come down to the custom and practice of the apostolic age, alleging that there is no instance of any one having been admitted to baptism without a previous profession of faith and repentance. For when Peter is asked by his hearers, who were pricked in their heart, " What shall we do ?" his advise is, " Repent and be baptised, every one of you, in the name of Jesus Christ, for the remission of sins" (Acts ii. 37, 38). In like manner, when Philip was asked by the eunuch to baptise him, he answered, " If thou believest with all thine heart, thou mayest." Hence they think they can make out that baptism cannot be lawfully given to any one without previous faith and repentance. If we yield to this argument, the former passage, in which there is no mention of faith, will prove that repentance alone is sufficient, and the latter, which makes no requirement of repentance, that there is need only of faith. They will object, I presume, that the one passage helps the other, and that both, therefore, are to be connected. I, in my turn, maintain that these two must be compared with other passages which contribute somewhat to the solution of this difficulty. There are many passages of Scripture whose meaning depends on their peculiar position. Of this we have an example in the present instance. Those to whom these things are said by Peter and Philip are of an age fit to aim at repentance, and receive faith. We strenuously insist that such men are not to be baptised unless their conversion and faith are discerned, at least in as far as human judgment can ascertain it. But it is perfectly clear that infants must be placed in a different class. For when any one formerly joined the religious communion of Israel, he behoved to be taught the covenant, and instructed in the law of the Lord, before he received circumcision, because he was of a different nation ; in other words, an alien from the people of Israel, with whom the covenant, which circumcision sanctioned, had been made.

24. Thus the Lord, when he chose Abraham for himself, did not commence with circumcision, in the meanwhile concealing what he meant by that sign, but first announced that he intended to make a covenant with him, and, after his faith in the promise, made him partaker of the sacrament. Why does the sacrament come after faith in Abraham, and precede all intelligence in his son Isaac ? It is right that he who, in adult age, is admitted to the fellowship of a covenant by one from whom he had hitherto been alienated, should previously learn its conditions ; but it is not so with the infant born to him. He, according to the terms of the promise, is included in the promise by hereditary right from his mother's womb. Or, to

state the matter more briefly and more clearly, If the children of
believers, without the help of understanding, are partakers of the
covenant, there is no reason why they should be denied the sign,
because they are unable to swear to its stipulations. This undoubtedly is the reason why the Lord sometimes declares that the children
born to the Israelites are begotten and born to him (Ezek. xvi. 20;
xxiii. 37). For he undoubtedly gives the place of sons to the
children of those to whose seed he has promised that he will be a
Father. But the child descended from unbelieving parents is deemed
an alien to the covenant until he is united to God by faith. Hence,
it is not strange that the sign is withheld when the thing signified
would be vain and fallacious. In that view, Paul says that the
Gentiles, so long as they were plunged in idolatry, were strangers to
the covenant (Eph. ii. 11). The whole matter may, if I mistake
not, be thus briefly and clearly expounded: Those who, in adult age,
embrace the faith of Christ, having hitherto been aliens from the
covenant, are not to receive the sign of baptism without previous
faith and repentance. These alone can give them access' to the
fellowship of the covenant, whereas children, deriving their origin
from Christians, as they are immediately on their birth received by
God as heirs of the covenant, are also to be admitted to baptism.
To this we must refer the narrative of the Evangelist, that those who
were baptised by John confessed their sins (Matth. iii. 6). This
example, we hold, ought to be observed in the present day. Were
a Turk to offer himself for baptism, we would not at once perform the
rite without receiving a confession which was satisfactory to the
Church.

25. Another passage which they adduce is from the third chapter
of John, where our Saviour's words seem to them to imply that a
present regeneration is required in baptism, " Except a man be born
of water, and of the Spirit, he cannot enter into the kingdom of God"
(John iii. 5). See, they say, how baptism is termed regeneration by
the lips of our Lord himself, and on what pretext, therefore, with
what consistency is baptism given to those who, it is perfectly
obvious, are not at all capable of regeneration? First, they are in
error in imagining that there is any mention of baptism in this
passage, merely because the word water is used. Nicodemus, after
our Saviour had explained to him the corruption of nature, and the
necessity of being born again, kept dreaming of a corporeal birth,
and hence our Saviour intimates the mode in which God regenerates
us—viz. by water and the Spirit; in other words, by the Spirit,
who, in irrigating and cleansing the souls of believers, operates in the
manner of water. By " water and the Spirit," therefore, I simply
understand the Spirit, which is water. Nor is the expression new.
It perfectly accords with that which is used in the third chapter of
Matthew, " He that cometh after me is mightier than I;" " he shall
baptise you with the Holy Ghost, and with fire" (Matth. iii. 11).
Therefore, as to baptise with the Holy Spirit, and with fire, is to

confer the Holy Spirit, who, in regeneration, has the office and nature of fire, so to be born again of water, and of the Spirit, is nothing else than to receive that power of the Spirit, which has the same effect on the soul that water has on the body. I know that a different interpretation is given, but I have no doubt that this is the genuine meaning, because our Saviour's only purpose was to teach, that all who aspire to the kingdom of heaven must lay aside their own disposition. And yet were we disposed to imitate these men in their mode of cavilling, we might easily, after conceding what they wish, reply to them, that baptism is prior to faith and repentance, since, in this passage, our Saviour mentions it before the Spirit. This certainly must be understood of spiritual gifts, and if they follow baptism, I have gained all I contend for. But, cavilling aside, the simple interpretation to be adopted is that which I have given—viz. that no man, until renewed by living water, that is, by the Spirit, can enter the kingdom of God.

26. This, moreover, plainly explodes the fiction of those who consign all the unbaptised to eternal death.[1] Let us suppose, then, that, as they insist, baptism is administered to adults only. What will they make of a youth who, after being embued duly and properly with the rudiments of piety, while waiting for the day of baptism, is unexpectedly carried off by sudden death? The promise of our Lord is clear, " He that heareth my word, and believeth on him that sent me, hath everlasting life, and shall not come into condemnation, but is passed from death unto life" (John v. 24). We nowhere read of his having condemned him who was not yet baptised. I would not be understood as insinuating that baptism may be contemned with impunity. So far from excusing this contempt, I hold that it violates the covenant of the Lord. The passage only serves to show, that we must not deem baptism so necessary as to suppose that every one who has lost the opportunity of obtaining it has forthwith perished. By assenting to their fiction, we should condemn all, without exception, whom any accident may have prevented from procuring baptism, how much soever they may have been endued with the faith by which Christ himself is possessed. Moreover, baptism being, as they hold, necessary to salvation, they, in denying it to infants, consign them all to eternal death. Let them now consider what kind of agreement they have with the words of Christ, who says, that " of such is the kingdom of heaven" (Matth. xix. 14). And though we were to concede everything to them, in regard to the meaning of this passage, they will extract nothing from it, until they have previously overthrown the doctrine which we have already established concerning the regeneration of infants.

27. But they boast of having their strongest bulwark in the very

---

[1] See Calv. Cont. Articulos Theologorum Paris. Art 4. Item, Ad. Concil. Trident. Item, Vera Eccles. Reformand. Ratio, et in Append. Nævus in August. Lib. i. ad Bonifac. et Epist. 28. Ambros. de Vocat. Gentium, Lib. ii. cap. 8, de Abraham. Lib. ii. cap. 11.

institution of baptism, which they find in the last chapter of Matthew, where Christ, sending his disciples into all the world, commands them to teach and then baptise. Then, in the last chapter of Mark, it is added, " He that believeth, and is baptised, shall be saved" (Mark xvi. 16). What more (say they) do we ask, since the words of Christ distinctly declare, that teaching must precede baptism, and assign to baptism the place next to faith? Of this arrangement our Lord himself gave an example, in choosing not to be baptised till his thirtieth year. In how many ways do they here entangle themselves, and betray their ignorance! They err more than childishly in this, that they derive the first institution of baptism from this passage, whereas Christ had, from the commencement of his ministry, ordered it to be administered by the apostles. There is no ground, therefore, for contending that the law and rule of baptism is to be sought from these two passages, as containing the first institution. But to indulge them in their error, how nerveless is this mode of arguing? Were I disposed to evasion, I have not only a place of escape, but a wide field to expatiate in. For when they cling so desperately to the order of the words, insisting that because it is said, " Go, preach and baptise," and again, " Whosoever believes and is baptised," they must preach before baptising, and believe before being baptised, why may not we in our turn object, that they must baptise before teaching the observance of those things which Christ commanded, because it is said, " Baptise, teaching whatsoever I have commanded you"? The same thing we observed in the other passage in which Christ speaks of the regeneration of water and of the Spirit. For if we interpret as they insist, then baptism must take precedence of spiritual regeneration, because it is first mentioned. Christ teaches that we are to be born again, not of the Spirit and of water, but of water and of the Spirit.

28. This unassailable argument, in which they confide so much, seems already to be considerably shaken ; but as we have sufficient protection in the simplicity of truth, I am unwilling to evade the point by paltry subtleties. Let them, therefore, have a solid answer. The command here given by Christ relates principally to the preaching of the gospel : to it baptism is added as a kind of appendage. Then he merely speaks of baptism in so far as the dispensation of it is subordinate to the function of teaching. For Christ sends his disciples to publish the gospel to all nations of the world, that by the doctrine of salvation they may gather men, who were previously lost, into his kingdom. But who or what are those men ? It is certain that mention is made only of those who are fit to receive his doctrine. He subjoins, that such, after being taught, were to be baptised, adding the promise, Whosoever believeth and is baptised, shall be saved. Is there one syllable about infants in the whole discourse ? What, then, is the form of argument with which they assail us ? Those who are of adult age are to be instructed and brought to the faith before being baptised, and therefore it is unlawful to make

baptism common to infants. They cannot, at the very utmost, prove any other thing out of this passage, than that the gospel must be preached to those who are capable of hearing it before they are baptised ; for of such only the passage speaks. From this let them, if they can, throw an obstacle in the way of baptising infants.

29. But I will make their fallacies palpable even to the blind, by a very plain similitude. Should any one insist that infants are to be deprived of food, on the pretence that the apostle permits none to eat but those who labour (2 Thess. iii. 10), would he not deserve to be scouted by all ? Why so ? Because that which was said of a certain class of men, and a certain age, he wrests and applies to all indifferently. The dexterity of these men in the present instance is not greater. That which every one sees to be intended for adult age merely, they apply to infants, subjecting them to a rule which was laid down only for those of riper years. With regard to the example of our Saviour, it gives no countenance to their case. He was not baptised before his thirtieth year. This is indeed true, but the reason is obvious ; because he then determined to lay the solid foundation of baptism by his preaching, or rather to confirm the foundation which John had previously laid. Therefore, when he was pleased with his doctrine to institute baptism, that he might give the greater authority to his institution, he sanctified it in his own person, and that at the most befitting time, namely, the commencement of his ministry. In fine, they can prove nothing more than that baptism received its origin and commencement with the preaching of the gospel. But if they are pleased to fix upon the thirtieth year, why do they not observe it, but admit any one to baptism according to the view which they may have formed of his proficiency ? Nay, even Servetus, one of their masters, although he pertinaciously insisted on this period, had begun to act the prophet in his twenty-first year ; as if any man could be tolerated in arrogating to himself the office of a teacher in the Church before he was a member of the Church.

30. At length they object, that there is not greater reason for admitting infants to baptism than to the Lord's Supper, to which, however, they are never admitted : as if Scripture did not in every way draw a wide distinction between them. In the early Church, indeed, the Lord's Supper was frequently given to infants, as appears from Cyprian and Augustine (August. ad Bonif. Lib. i.) ; but the practice justly became obsolete. For if we attend to the peculiar nature of baptism, it is a kind of entrance, and as it were initiation into the Church, by which we are ranked among the people of God, a sign of our spiritual regeneration, by which we are again born to be children of God ; whereas, on the contrary, the Supper is intended for those of riper years, who, having passed the tender period of infancy, are fit to bear solid food. This distinction is very clearly pointed out in Scripture. For there, as far as regards baptism, the Lord makes no selection of age, whereas he does not admit all to

partake of the Supper, but confines it to those who are fit to discern the body and blood of the Lord, to examine their own conscience, to show forth the Lord's death, and understand its power. Can we wish anything clearer than what the apostle says, when he thus exhorts, " Let a man examine himself, and so let him eat of that bread, and drink of that cup " ? (1 Cor. xi. 28.) Examination, therefore, must precede, and this it were vain to expect from infants. Again, " He that eateth and drinketh unworthily, eateth and drinketh damnation to himself, not discerning the Lord's body." If they cannot partake worthily without being able duly to discern the sanctity of the Lord's body, why should we stretch out poison to our young children instead of vivifying food ? Then what is our Lord's injunction ? " Do this in remembrance of me." And what the inference which the apostle draws from this ? " As often as ye eat this bread, and drink this cup, ye do show the Lord's death till he come." How, pray, can we require infants to commemorate any event of which they have no understanding ; how require them " to show forth the Lord's death," of the nature and benefit of which they have no idea ? Nothing of the kind is prescribed by baptism. Wherefore, there is the greatest difference between the two signs. This also we observe in similar signs under the old dispensation. Circumcision, which, as is well known, corresponds to our baptism, was intended for infants, but the passover, for which the Supper is substituted, did not admit all kinds of guests promiscuously, but was duly eaten only by those who were of an age sufficient to ask the meaning of it (Exod. xii. 26). Had these men the least particle of soundness in their brain, would they be thus blind as to a matter so very clear and obvious ?

31. Though I am unwilling to annoy the reader with the series of conceits which Servetus, not the least among the Anabaptists, nay, the great honour of this crew, when girding himself for battle, deemed, when he adduced them, to be specious arguments, it will be worth while briefly to dispose of them.[1] He pretends that as the symbols of Christ are perfect, they require persons who are perfect, or at least capable of perfection. But the answer is plain. The perfection of baptism, which extends even to death, is improperly restricted to one moment of time ; moreover, perfection, in which baptism invites us to make continual progress during life, is foolishly exacted by him all at once. He objects, that the symbols of Christ were appointed for remembrance, that every one may remember that he was buried together with Christ. I answer, that what he coined out of his own brain does not need refutation, nay, that which he transfers to baptism properly belongs to the Supper, as appears from Paul's words, " Let a man examine

---

1 French, " Combien qu'il me fasche d'amasser tant de reveries frivoles que pourront ennuyer les lecteurs, toutesfcis pource que Servet, se meslant aussi de mesdire du baptesme des petis enfans, a cuide amener de fort belles raisons, il sera raison de les rabattre brievement."—Although I am sorry to amass so many frivolous reveries which may annoy the reader, yet as Servetus, taking it upon him to calumniate baptism also, has seemed to adduce very fine arguments, it will be right briefly to dispose of them.

himself," words similar to which are nowhere used with reference to baptism. Whence we infer, that those who from nonage are incapable of examination are duly baptised. His third point is, That all who believe not in the Son remain in death, the wrath of God abideth on them (John iii. 36) ; and, therefore, infants who are unable to believe lie under condemnation. I answer, that Christ does not there speak of the general guilt in which all the posterity of Adam are involved, but only threatens the despisers of the gospel, who proudly and contumaciously spurn the grace which is offered to them. But this has nothing to do with infants. At the same time, I meet him with the opposite argument. Every one whom Christ blesses is exempted from the curse of Adam, and the wrath of God. Therefore, seeing it is certain that infants are blessed by him, it follows that they are freed from death. He nexts falsely quotes a passage which is nowhere found, Whosoever is born of the Spirit, hears the voice of the Spirit. Though we should grant that such a passage occurs in Scripture, all he can extract from it is, that believers, according as the Spirit works in them, are framed to obedience. But that which is said of a certain number, it is illogical to apply to all alike. His fourth objection is, As that which precedes is animal (1 Cor. xv. 46), we must wait the full time for baptism, which is spiritual. But while I admit that all the posterity of Adam, born of the flesh, bear their condemnation with them from the womb, I hold that this is no obstacle to the immediate application of the divine remedy. Servetus cannot show that by divine appointment, several years must elapse before the new spiritual life begins. Paul's testimony is, that though lost by nature, the children of believers are holy by supernatural grace. He afterwards brings forward the allegory that David, when going up into mount Zion, took with him neither the blind nor the lame, but vigorous soldiers (2 Sam. v. 8). But what if I meet this with the parable in which God invites to the heavenly feast the lame and the blind ? In what way will Servetus disentangle this knot ? I ask, moreover, whether the lame and the maimed had not previously served with David ? But it is superfluous to dwell longer on this argument, which, as the reader will learn from the sacred history, is founded on mere misquotation. He adds another allegory— viz. that the apostles were fishers of men, not of children. I ask, then, What does our Saviour mean when he says that in the net are caught all kinds of fishes ? (Matth. iv. 19 ; xiii. 47.) But as I have no pleasure in sporting with allegory, I answer, that when the office of teaching was committed to the apostles, they were not prohibited from baptising infants. Moreover, I should like to know why, when the Evangelist uses the term ἀνθρώπους (which comprehends the whole human race without exception), he denies that infants are included. His seventh argument is, Since spiritual things accord with spiritual (1 Cor ii. 13), infants, not being spiritual, are unfit for baptism. It is plain how perversely he wrests this passage of Paul. It relates to doctrine. The Corinthians, pluming themselves excessively on a vain acuteness, Paul rebukes their folly, because they still require to be imbued with the first rudiments of heavenly doctrine. Who can infer from this that baptism is to be denied to infants, whom, when begotten of the flesh, the Lord consecrates to himself by gratuitous adoption? His objection, that if they are new men, they must be fed with spiritual food, is easily obviated. By baptism they are admitted into the fold of Christ, and the symbol of adoption is sufficient for them, until they grow up and become fit to bear solid food. We must, therefore, wait for the time of examination, which God distinctly demands in the sacred Supper. His next objection is, that Christ invites all his people to the sacred Supper. But as it is plain that he admits those only who are prepared to celebrate the commemoration of his death, it follows that infants, whom he honoured with his embrace, remain in a distinct and peculiar position until they grow up, and yet are not aliens. When he objects, that it is strange why the infant does not partake of the Supper, I answer, that souls are fed by other food than the external eating of the Supper, and that accordingly Christ is the food of infants, though they partake not of the symbol. The case is different with baptism, by which the door of the Church is thrown open to them. He again objects, that a good householder distributes meat to his household in due season (Matth. xxiv. 45). This I willingly admit; but how will he define the time of baptism, so as to prove that it is not seasonably given to infants? He, moreover, adduces Christ's command to the apostles to make haste, because the fields are already white to the harvest (John iv. 35). Our Saviour only means that the apostles, seeing the present fruit of their labour, should bestir themselves with more alacrity to teach. Who will infer from this, that harvest only is the fit time for baptism? His eleventh argument is, That in the primitive Church, Christians and disciples were the same; but we have already seen that he argues unskilfully from the part to the whole. The name of disciples is given to men of full age, who had already been taught, and had assumed the name of Christ, just as the Jews behoved to be disciples under the law of Moses. Still none could rightly infer from this that infants, whom the Lord declared to be of his household, were strangers. Moreover, he alleges that all Christians are brethren, and that infants cannot belong to this class, so long as we exclude them from the Supper. But I return to my position, first, that none are heirs of the kingdom of heaven but those who are the members of Christ; and, secondly, that the embracing of Christ was the true badge of adoption, in which infants are joined in common with adults, and that temporary abstinence from the Supper does not prevent them from belonging to the body of the Church. The thief on the cross, when converted, became the brother of believers, though he never partook of the Lord's Supper. Servetus afterwards adds, that no man becomes our brother unless by the Spirit of adoption, who is only conferred by the hearing of faith. I answer, that he always falls back into the same paralogism, because he preposterously applies to infants what is said only of adults.

Paul there teaches that the ordinary way in which God calls his elect, and brings them to the faith, is by raising up faithful teachers, and thus stretching out his hand to them by their ministry and labours. Who will presume from this to give the law to God, and say that he may not ingraft infants into Christ by some other secret method? He objects, that Cornelius was baptised after receiving the Holy Spirit; but how absurdly he would convert a single example into a general rule, is apparent from the case of the Eunuch and the Samaritans, in regard to whom the Lord observed a different order, baptism preceding the gifts of the Holy Spirit. The fifteenth argument is more than absurd. He says that we become gods by regeneration, but that they are gods to whom the word of God is sent (John x. 35; 2 Pet. i. 4), a thing not possible to infant children. The attributing of deity to believers is one of his ravings, which this is not the proper place to discuss; but it betrays the utmost effrontery to wrest the passage in the psalm (Ps. lxxxii. 6) to a meaning so alien to it. Christ says, that kings and magistrates are called gods by the prophet, because they perform an office divinely appointed them. This dexterous interpreter transfers what is addressed by special command to certain individuals to the doctrine of the Gospel, so as to exterminate infants from the Church. Again, he objects, that infants cannot be regarded as new men, because they are not begotten by the word. But what I have said again and again I now repeat, that, for regenerating us, doctrine is an incorruptible seed, if indeed we are fit to perceive it; but when, from nonage, we are incapable of being taught, God takes his own methods of regenerating. He afterwards returns to his allegories, and says, that under the law, the sheep and the goat were not offered in sacrifice the moment they were dropt (Exod. xii. 5). Were I disposed to deal in figures, I might obviously reply, first, that all the first-born, on opening the matrix, were sacred to the Lord (Exod. xiii. 12); and, secondly, that a lamb of a year old was to be sacrificed: whence it follows, that it was not necessary to wait for mature age, the young and tender offspring having been selected by God for sacrifice. He contends, moreover, that none could come to Christ but those who were previously prepared by John; as if John's ministry had not been temporary. But, to omit this, assuredly there was no such preparation in the children whom Christ took up in his arms and blessed. Wherefore, let us have done with his false principle. He at length calls in the assistance of Trismegistus and the Sybils, to prove that sacred ablutions are fit only for adults. See how honourably he thinks of Christian baptism, when he tests it by the profane rites of the Gentiles, and will not have it administered except in the way pleasing to Trismegistus. We defer more to the authority of God, who has seen it meet to consecrate infants to himself, and initiate them by a sacred symbol, the significancy of which they are unable from nonage to understand. We do not think it lawful to borrow from the expiations of the Gentiles, in order to change, in our baptism, that eternal and inviolable law which God enacted in circumcision. His last argument is, If infants, without understanding, may be baptised, baptism may be mimicked and jestingly administered by boys in sport. Here let him plead the matter with God, by whose command circumcision was common to infants before they received understanding. Was it, then, a fit matter for ridicule or boyish sport, to overthrow the sacred institution of God? But no wonder that these reprobate spirits, as if they were under the influence of frenzy, introduce the grossest absurdities in defence of their errors, because God, by this spirit of giddiness, justly avenges their pride and obstinacy. I trust I have made it apparent how feebly Servetus has supported his friends the Anabaptists.

32. No sound man, I presume, can now doubt how rashly the Church is disturbed by those who excite quarrels and disturbances because of pædobaptism. For it is of importance to observe what Satan means by all this craft—viz. to rob us of the singular blessing of confidence and spiritual joy, which is hence to be derived, and in so far to detract from the glory of the divine goodness. For how sweet is it to pious minds to be assured not only by word, but even by ocular demonstration, that they are so much in favour with their heavenly Father, that he interests himself in their prosperity! Here we may see how he acts towards us as a most provident parent, not ceasing to care for us even after our death, but consulting and providing for our children. Ought not our whole heart to be stirred up within us, as David's was (Ps. xlviii. 11), to bless his name for such a manifestation of goodness? Doubtless the design of Satan in assaulting pædobaptism with all his forces is to keep out of view, and gradually efface, that attestation of divine grace which the promise itself presents to our eyes. In this way, not only would men be impiously ungrateful for the mercy of God, but be less careful in training their children to piety. For it is no slight stimulus to us to bring them u₊ in the fear of God, and the observance of his law, when we reflect, that from their birth they have been considered and acknowledged by him as his children. Wherefore, if we would not maliciously obscure the kindness of God, let us present to him our infants, to whom he has assigned a place among his friends and family, that is, the members of the Church.

CHAPTER XVII.

OF THE LORD'S SUPPER, AND THE BENEFITS CONFERRED BY IT.

This chapter is divided into two principal heads. —I. The first part shows what it is that God exhibits in the Holy Supper, sec. 1–4; and then in what way and how far it becomes ours, sec. 5–11. II. The second part is chiefly occupied with a refutation of the errors which superstition has introduced in regard to the Lord's Supper. And, first, Transubstantiation is refuted, see. 12–15. Next, Consubstantiation and Ubiquity, sec. 16–19. Thirdly, It is shown that the institution itself is opposed to those hyperbolical doctors, sec. 20–25. Fourth, The orthodox view is confirmed by other arguments derived from Scripture, sec. 26–27. Fifth, The authority of the Fathers is shown to support the same view. Sixth, The presence for which opponents contend is overthrown, and another presence established, sec. 29–32. Seventh, What the nature of our communion ought to be, sec. 33, 34. Eighth, The adoration introduced by opponents refuted. For what end the Lord's Supper was instituted, sec. 35–39. Lastly, The examination of communicants is considered, sec. 40–42. Of the external rites to be observed. Of frequent communion in both kinds. Objections refuted, sec. 43–50.

Sections.

1. Why the Holy Supper was instituted by Christ. The knowledge of the sacrament, how necessary. The signs used. Why there are no others appointed.
2. The manifold uses and advantages of this sacrament to the pious.
3. The Lord's Supper exhibits the great blessings of redemption, and even Christ himself. This even evident from the words of the institution. The thing specially to be considered in them. Congruity of the signs and the things signified.
4. The chief parts of this sacrament.
5. How Christ, the Bread of Life, is to be received by us. Two faults to be avoided. The receiving of it must bear reference both to faith and the effect of faith. What meant by eating Christ. In what sense Christ the bread of life.
6. This mode of eating confirmed by the authority of Augustine and Chrysostom.
7. It is not sufficient, while omitting all mention of flesh and blood, to recognise this communion merely as spiritual. It is impossible fully to comprehend it in the present life.
8. In explanation of it, it may be observed,—I. There is no life at all save in Christ. II. Christ has life in a twofold sense; first, in himself, as he is God; and, secondly, by transfusing it into the flesh which he assumed, that he might thereby communicate life to us.
9. This confirmed from Cyril, and by a familiar example. How the flesh of Christ gives life, and what the nature of our communion with Christ.
10. No distance of place can impede it. In the Supper it is not presented as an empty symbol, but, as the apostle testifies, we receive the reality. Objection, that the expression is figurative. Answer. A sure rule with regard to the sacraments.
11. Conclusion of the first part of the chapter. The sacrament of the Supper consists of two parts—viz. corporeal signs, and spiritual truth. These comprehend the meaning, matter, and effect. Christ truly exhibited to us by symbols.
12. Second part of the chapter, reduced to nine heads. The transubstantiation of the Papists considered and refuted. Its origin and absurdity. Why it should be exploded. .
13. Transubstantiation as feigned by the Schoolmen. Refutation. The many superstitions introduced by their error.

1. AFTER God has once received us into his family, it is not that he may regard us in the light of servants, but of sons, performing the part of a kind and anxious parent, and providing for our maintenance during the whole course of our lives. And, not contented with this, he has been pleased by a pledge to assure us of his continued liberality. To this end, he has given another sacrament to his Church by the hand of his only-begotten Son—viz. a spiritual feast, at which Christ testifies that he himself is living bread (John vi. 51), on which our souls feed, for a true and blessed immortality. Now, as the knowledge of this great mystery is most necessary, and, in proportion to its importance, demands an accurate exposition, and Satan, in order to deprive the Church of this inestimable treasure, long ago introduced, first, mists, and then darkness, to obscure its light, and stirred up strife and contention to alienate the minds of the simple from a relish for this sacred food, and in our age, also, has tried the same artifice, I will proceed, after giving a simple summary adapted to the capacity of the ignorant, to explain those difficulties by which Satan has tried to ensnare the world. First, then, the signs are bread and wine, which represent the invisible food which we receive from the body and blood of Christ. For as God, regenerating us in baptism, ingrafts us into the fellowship of his Church, and makes us his by adoption, so we have said that he performs the office of a provident parent, in continually supplying the food by which he may sustain and preserve us in the life to which he has begotten us by his word. Moreover, Christ is the only food of our soul, and, therefore, our heavenly Father invites us to him, that, refreshed by communion with him, we may ever and anon gather new vigour until we reach the heavenly immortality. But as this mystery of the secret union of Christ with believers is incomprehensible by nature, he exhibts its figure and image in visible signs adapted to our capacity, nay, by giving, as it were, earnests and badges, he makes it as certain to us as if it were seen by the eye; the familiarity of the similitude giving it access to minds however dull, and showing that souls are fed by Christ just as the corporeal life is sustained by bread and wine. We now, therefore, understand the end which this mystical benediction has in view—viz. to assure us that the body of Christ was once sacrificed for us, so that we may now eat it, and, eating, feel within ourselves the efficacy of that one sacrifice,—that his blood was once shed for us so as to be our perpetual drink. This is the force of the promise which is added, " Take, eat; this is my body, which is broken for you" (Matth. xxvi. 26, &c.). The body which was once offered for our salvation we are enjoined to take and eat, that, while we see ourselves made partakers of it, we may safely conclude that the virtue of that death will be efficacious in us. Hence he terms the cup the covenant in his blood. For the covenant which he once sanctioned by his blood he in a manner renews, or rather continues, in so far as

regards the confirmation of our faith, as often as he stretches forth his sacred blood as drink to us.

2. Pious souls can derive great confidence and delight from this sacrament, as being a testimony that they form one body with Christ, so that everything which is his they may call their own. Hence it follows, that we can confidently assure ourselves, that eternal life, of which he himself is the heir, is ours, and that the kingdom of heaven, into which he has entered, can no more be taken from us than from him; on the other hand, that we cannot be condemned for our sins, from the guilt of which he absolves us, seeing he has been pleased that these should be imputed to himself as if they were his own. This is the wondrous exchange made by his boundless goodness. Having become with us the Son of Man, he has made us with himself sons of God. By his own descent to the earth he has prepared our ascent to heaven. Having received our mortality, he has bestowed on us his immortality. Having undertaken our weakness, he has made us strong in his strength. Having submitted to our poverty, he has transferred to us his riches. Having taken upon himself the burden of unrighteousness with which we were oppressed, he has clothed us with his righteousness.

3. To all these things we have a complete attestation in this sacrament, enabling us certainly to conclude that they are as truly exhibited to us as if Christ were placed in bodily presence before our view, or handled by our hands. For these are words which can never lie nor deceive—Take, eat, drink. This is my body, which is broken for you: this is my blood, which is shed for the remission of sins. In bidding us take, he intimates that it is ours: in bidding us eat, he intimates that it becomes one substance with us: in affirming of his body that it was broken, and of his blood that it was shed for us, he shows that both were not so much his own as ours, because he took and laid down both, not for his own advantage, but for our salvation. And we ought carefully to observe, that the chief, and almost the whole energy of the sacrament, consists in these words, It is broken for you: it is shed for you. It would not be of much importance to us that the body and blood of the Lord are now distributed, had they not once been set forth for our redemption and salvation. Wherefore they are represented under bread and wine, that we may learn that they are not only ours, but intended to nourish our spiritual life; that is, as we formerly observed, by the corporeal things which are produced in the sacrament, we are by a kind of analogy conducted to spiritual things. Thus when bread is given as a symbol of the body of Christ, we must immediately think of this similitude. As bread nourishes, sustains, and protects our bodily life, so the body of Christ is the only food to invigorate and keep alive the soul. When we behold wine set forth as a symbol of blood, we must think that such use as wine serves to the body, the same is spiritually bestowed by the blood of Christ; and the use is to foster, refresh, strengthen, and exhilarate. For if we duly consider

what profit we have gained by the breaking of his sacred body, and the shedding of his blood, we shall clearly perceive that these properties of bread and wine, agreeably to this analogy, most appropriately represent it when they are communicated to us.

4. Therefore, it is not the principal part of a sacrament simply to hold forth the body of Christ to us without any higher consideration, but rather to seal and confirm that promise by which he testifies that his flesh is meat indeed, and his blood drink indeed, nourishing us unto life eternal, and by which he affirms that he is the bread of life, of which, whosoever shall eat, shall live for ever—I say, to seal and confirm that promise, and in order to do so, it sends us to the cross of Christ, where that promise was performed and fulfilled in all its parts. For we do not eat Christ duly and savingly unless as crucified, while with lively apprehension we perceive the efficacy of his death. When he called himself the bread of life, he did not take that appellation from the sacrament, as some perversely interpret ; but such as he was given to us by the Father, such he exhibited himself when becoming partaker of our human mortality, he made us partakers of his divine immortality ; when offering himself in sacrifice, he took our curse upon himself, that he might cover us with his blessing, when by his death he devoured and swallowed up death, when in his resurrection he raised our corruptible flesh, which he had put on, to glory and incorruption.

5. It only remains that the whole become ours by application. This is done by means of the gospel, and more clearly by the sacred Supper, where Christ offers himself to us with all his blessings, and we receive him in faith. The sacrament, therefore, does not make Christ become for the first time the bread of life ; but, while it calls to remembrance that Christ was made the bread of life that we may constantly eat him, it gives us a taste and relish for that bread, and makes us feel its efficacy. For it assures us, first, that whatever Christ did or suffered was done to give us life ; and, secondly, that this quickening is eternal ; by it we are ceaselessly nourished, sustained, and preserved in life. For as Christ would not have not been the bread of life to us if he had not been born, if he had not died and risen again ; so he could not now be the bread of life, were not the efficacy and fruit of his nativity, death, and resurrection, eternal. All this Christ has elegantly expressed in these words, " The bread that I will give is my flesh, which I will give for the life of the world" (John vi. 51) ; doubtless intimating, that his body will be as bread in regard to the spiritual life of the soul, because it was to be delivered to death for our salvation, and that he extends it to us for food when he makes us partakers of it by faith. Wherefore he once gave himself that he might become bread, when he gave himself to be crucified for the redemption of the world ; and he gives himself daily, when in the word of the gospel he offers himself to be partaken by us, inasmuch as he was crucified, when he seals that offer by the sacred mystery of the Supper, and when he accomplishes inwardly

what he externally designates. Moreover, two faults are here to be avoided. We must neither, by setting too little value on the signs, dissever them from their meanings to which they are in some degree annexed, nor by immoderately extolling them, seem somewhat to obscure the mysteries themselves. That Christ is the bread of life by which believers are nourished unto eternal life, no man is so utterly devoid of religion as not to acknowledge. But all are not agreed as to the mode of partaking of him. For there are some who define the eating of the flesh of Christ, and the drinking of his blood, to be, in one word, nothing more than believing in Christ himself. But Christ seems to me to have intended to teach something more express and more sublime in that noble discourse, in which he recommends the eating of his flesh—viz. that we are quickened by the true partaking of him, which he designated by the terms eating and drinking, lest any one should suppose that the life which we obtain from him is obtained by simple knowledge. For as it is not the sight but the eating of bread that gives nourishment to the body, so the soul must partake of Christ truly and thoroughly, that by his energy it may grow up into spiritual life. Meanwhile, we admit that this is nothing else than the eating of faith, and that no other eating can be imagined. But there is this difference between their mode of speaking and mine. According to them, to eat is merely to believe ; while I maintain that the flesh of Christ is eaten by believing, because it is made ours by faith, and that that eating is the effect and fruit of faith ; or, if you will have it more clearly, according to them, eating is faith, whereas it rather seems to me to be a consequence of faith. The difference is little in words, but not little in reality. For, although the apostle teaches that Christ dwells in our hearts by faith (Eph. iii. 17), no one will interpret that dwelling to be faith. All see that it explains the admirable effect of faith, because to it it is owing that believers have Christ dwelling in them. In this way, the Lord was pleased, by calling himself the bread of life, not only to teach that our salvation is treasured up in the faith of his death and resurrection, but also, by virtue of true communication with him, his life passes into us and becomes ours, just as bread when taken for food gives vigour to the body.

6. When Augustine, whom they claim as their patron, wrote, that we eat by believing, all he meant was to indicate that that eating is of faith, and not of the mouth. This I deny not ; but I at the same time add, that by faith we embrace Christ, not as appearing at a distance, but as uniting himself to us, he being our head, and we his members. I do not absolutely disapprove of that mode of speaking ; I only deny that it is a full interpretation, if they mean to define what it is to eat the flesh of Christ. I see that Augustine repeatedly used this form of expression, as when he said (De Doct. Christ. Lib. iii.), " Unless ye eat the flesh of the Son of Man" is a figurative expression enjoining us to have communion with our Lord's passion, and sweetly and usefully to treasure in our memory

that his flesh was crucified and wounded for us.   Also when he says, " These three thousand men who were converted at the preaching of Peter (Acts ii. 41), by believing, drank the blood which they had cruelly shed."[1]   But in very many other passages he admirably commends faith for this, that by means of it our souls are not less refreshed by the communion of the blood of Christ, than our bodies with the bread which they eat.   The very same thing is said by Chrysostom, "Christ makes us his body, not by faith only, but in reality."   He does not mean that we obtain this blessing from any other quarter than from faith : he only intends to prevent any one from thinking of mere imagination when he hears the name of faith. I say nothing of those who hold that the Supper is merely a mark of external profession, because I think I sufficiently refuted their error when I treated of the sacraments in general (Chap. xiv. sec. 13). Only let my readers observe, that when the cup is called the covenant in blood (Luke xxii. 20), the promise which tends to confirm faith is expressed.   Hence it follows, that unless we have respect to God, and embrace what he offers, we do not make a right use of the sacred Supper.

7. I am not satisfied with the view of those who, while acknowledging that we have some kind of communion with Christ, only make us partakers of the Spirit, omitting all mention of flesh and blood.   As if it were said to no purpose at all, that his flesh is meat indeed, and his blood is drink indeed ; that we have no life unless we eat that flesh and drink that blood ; and so forth.   Therefore, if it is evident that full communion with Christ goes beyond their description, which is too confined, I will attempt briefly to show how far it extends, before proceeding to speak of the contrary vice of excess. For I shall have a longer discussion with these hyperbolical doctors, who, according to their gross ideas, fabricate an absurd mode of eating and drinking, and transfigure Christ, after divesting him of his flesh, into a phantom : if, indeed, it be lawful to put this great mystery into words, a mystery which I feel, and therefore freely confess that I am unable to comprehend with my mind, so far am I from wishing any one to measure its sublimity by my feeble capacity.   Nay, I rather exhort my readers not to confine their apprehension within those too narrow limits, but to attempt to rise much higher than I can guide them.   For whenever this subject is considered, after I have done my utmost, I feel that I have spoken far beneath its dignity.   And though the mind is more powerful in thought than the tongue in expression, it too is overcome and overwhelmed by the magnitude of the subject.   All then that remains is to break forth in admiration of the mystery, which it is plain that the mind is inadequate to comprehend, or the tongue to express.   I will, however, give a summary of my view as I best can,

[1] See August. Hom. in Joann. 31 et 40, &c. ; Chrysost. Hom. ad Popul. Antioch., 60, 61 ; et Hom. in Marc. 89.

not doubting its truth, and therefore trusting that it will not be disapproved by pious breasts.

8. First of all, we are taught by the Scriptures that Christ was from the beginning the living Word of the Father, the fountain and origin of life, from which all things should always receive life. Hence John at one time calls him the Word of life, and at another says, that in him was life; intimating, that he, even then pervading all creatures, instilled into them the power of breathing and living. He afterwards adds, that the life was at length manifested, when the Son of God, assuming our nature, exhibited himself in bodily form to be seen and handled. For although he previously diffused his virtue into the creatures, yet as man, because alienated from God by sin, had lost the communication of life, and saw death on every side impending over him, he behoved, in order to regain the hope of immortality, to be restored to the communion of that Word. How little confidence can it give you, to know that the Word of God, from which you are at the greatest distance, contains within himself the fulness of life, whereas in yourself, in whatever direction you turn, you see nothing but death? But ever since that fountain of life began to dwell in our nature, he no longer lies hid at a distance from us, but exhibits himself openly for our participation. Nay, the very flesh in which he resides he makes vivifying to us, that by partaking of it we may feed for immortality. · "I," says he, "am that bread of life;" "I am the living bread which came down from heaven;" "And the bread that I will give is my flesh, which I will give for the life of the world" (John vi. 48, 51). By these words he declares, not only that he is life, inasmuch as he is the eternal Word of God who came down to us from heaven, but, by coming down, gave vigour to the flesh which he assumed, that a communication of life to us might thence emanate. Hence, too, he adds, that his flesh is meat indeed, and that his blood is drink indeed: by this food believers are reared to eternal life. The pious, therefore, have admirable comfort in this, that they now find life in their own flesh. For they not only reach it by easy access, but have it spontaneously set forth before them. Let them only throw open the door of their hearts that they may take it into their embrace, and they will obtain it.

9. The flesh of Christ, however, has not such power in itself as to make us live, seeing that by its own first condition it was subject to mortality, and even now, when endued with immortality, lives not by itself. Still it is properly said to be life-giving, as it is pervaded with the fulness of life for the purpose of transmitting it to us. In this sense I understand our Saviour's words as Cyril interprets them, "As the Father hath life in himself, so hath he given to the Son to have life in himself" (John v. 26). For there properly he is speaking not of the properties which he possessed with the Father from the beginning, but of those with which he was invested in the flesh in which he appeared. Accordingly, he shows that in his humanity also

fulness of life resides, so that every one who communicates in his flesh and blood, at the same time enjoys the participation of life. The nature of this may be explained by a familiar example. As water is at one time drunk out of the fountain, at another drawn, at another led away by conduits to irrigate the fields, and yet does not flow forth of itself for all these uses, but is taken from its source, which, with perennial flow, ever and anon sends forth a new and sufficient supply; so the flesh of Christ is like a rich and inexhaustible fountain, which transfuses into us the life flowing forth from the Godhead into itself. Now, who sees not that the communion of the flesh and blood of Christ is necessary to all who aspire to the heavenly life? Hence those passages of the apostle: The Church is the "body" of Christ; his "fulness." He is "the head," "from whence the whole body fitly joined together, and compacted by that which every joint supplieth," "maketh increase of the body" (Eph. i. 23; iv. 15, 16). Our bodies are the "members of Christ" (1 Cor. vi. 15). We perceive that all these things cannot possibly take place unless he adheres to us wholly in body and spirit. But the very close connection which unites us to his flesh, he illustrated with still more splendid epithets, when he said that we "are members of his body, of his flesh, and of his bones" (Eph. v. 30). At length, to testify that the matter is too high for utterance, he concludes with exclaiming, "This is a great mystery" (Eph. v. 32). It were, therefore, extreme infatuation not to acknowledge the communion of believers with the body and blood of the Lord, a communion which the apostle declares to be so great, that he chooses rather to marvel at it than to explain it.

10. The sum is, that the flesh and blood of Christ feed our souls just as bread and wine maintain and suport our corporeal life. For there would be no aptitude in the sign, did not our souls find their nourishment in Christ. This could not be, did not Christ truly form one with us, and refresh us by the eating of his flesh, and the drinking of his blood. But though it seems an incredible thing that the flesh of Christ, while at such a distance from us in respect of place, should be food to us, let us remember how far the secret virtue of the Holy Spirit surpasses all our conceptions, and how foolish it is to wish to measure its immensity by our feeble capacity. Therefore, what our mind does not comprehend let faith conceive—viz. that the Spirit truly unites things separated by space. That sacred communion of flesh and blood by which Christ transfuses his life into us, just as if it penetrated our bones and marrow, he testifies and seals in the Supper, and that not by presenting a vain or empty sign, but by there exerting an efficacy of the Spirit by which he fulfils what he promises. And truly the thing there signified he exhibits and offers to all who sit down at that spiritual feast, although it is beneficially received by believers only who receive this great benefit with true faith and heartfelt gratitude. For this reason the apostle said, "The cup of blessing which we bless, is it not the communion of the blood of Christ? The bread which we break, is it not the communion of

the body of Christ "?   (1 Cor. x. 16.)   There is no ground to object that the expression is figurative, and gives the sign the name of the thing signified.   I admit, indeed, that the breaking of bread is a symbol, not the reality.   But this being admitted, we duly infer from the exhibition of the symbol that the thing itself is exhibited.   For unless we would charge God with deceit, we will never presume to say that he holds forth an empty symbol.   Therefore, if by the break- ing of bread the Lord truly represents the partaking of his body, there ought to be no doubt whatever that he truly exhibits and per- forms it.   The rule which the pious ought always to observe is, whenever they see the symbols instituted by the Lord, to think and feel surely persuaded that the truth of the thing signified is also pre- sent.   For why does the Lord put the symbol of his body into your hands, but just to assure you that you truly partake of him ?   If this is true let us feel as much assured that the visible sign is given us in seal of an invisible gift as that his body itself is given to us.

11. I hold then (as has always been received in the Church, and is still taught by those who feel aright), that the sacred mystery of the Supper consists of two things—the corporeal signs, which, presented to the eye, represent invisible things in a manner adapted to our weak capacity, and the spiritual truth, which is at once figured and exhibited by the signs.   When attempting familiarly to explain its nature, I am accustomed to set down three things—the thing meant, the matter which depends on it, and the virtue or efficacy consequent upon both.   The thing meant consists in the promises which are in a manner included in the sign.   By the matter, or substance, I mean Christ, with his death and resurrection.   By the effect, I understand redemption, justification, sanctification, eternal life, and all other benefits which Christ bestows upon us.   Moreover, though all these things have respect to faith, I leave no room for the cavil, that when I say Christ is conceived by faith, I mean that he is only conceived by the intellect and imagination.   He is offered by the promises, not that we may stop short at the sight or mere knowledge of him, but that we may enjoy true communion with him.   And, indeed, I see not how any one can expect to have redemption and righteousness in the cross of Christ, and life in his death, without trusting first of all to true communion with Christ himself.   Those blessings could not reach us, did not Christ previously make himself ours.   I say then, that in the mystery of the Supper, by the symbols of bread and wine, Christ, his body and his blood, are truly exhibited to us, that in them he fulfilled all obedience, in order to procure righteousness for us— first that we might become one body with him ; and, secondly, that being made partakers of his substance, we might feel the result of this fact in the participation of all his blessings.

12. I now come to the hyperbolical mixtures which superstition has introduced.   Here Satan has employed all his wiles, withdrawing the minds of men from heaven, and imbuing them with the perverse error that Christ is annexed to the element of bread.   And, first, we are not to

dream of such a presence of Christ in the sacrament as the artificers of the Romish court have imagined, as if the body of Christ, locally present, were to be taken into the hand, and chewed by the teeth, and swallowed by the throat.   This was the form of Palinode, which Pope Nicholas dictated to Berengarius, in token of his repentance, a form expressed in terms so monstrous, that the author of the Gloss exclaims, that there is danger, if the reader is not particularly cautious, that he will be led by it into a worse heresy than was that of Berengarius (Distinct. ii. c. Ego Berengarius).   Peter Lombard, though he labours much to excuse the absurdity, rathers inclines to a different opinion.   As we cannot at all doubt that it is bounded according to the invariable rule in the human body, and is contained in heaven, where it was once received, and will remain till it return to judgment, so we deem it altogether unlawful to bring it back under these corruptible elements, or to imagine it everywhere present.   And, indeed, there is no need of this, in order to our partaking of it, since the Lord by his Spirit bestows upon us the blessing of being one with him in soul, body, and spirit.   The bond of that connection, therefore, is the Spirit of Christ, who unites us to him, and is a kind of channel by which everything that Christ has and is, is derived to us.   For if we see that the sun, in sending forth its rays upon the earth, to generate, cherish, and invigorate its offspring, in a manner transfuses its substance into it, why should the radiance of the Spirit be less in conveying to us the communion of his flesh and blood?   Wherefore the Scripture, when it speaks of our participation with Christ, refers its whole efficacy to the Spirit.   Instead of many, one passage will suffice.   Paul, in the Epistle to the Romans (Rom. viii. 9–11), shows that the only way in which Christ dwells in us is by his Spirit.   By this, however, he does not take away that communion of flesh and blood of which we now speak, but shows that it is owing to the Spirit alone that we possess Christ wholly, and have him abiding in us.

13. The Schoolmen, horrified at this barbarous impiety, speak more modestly, though they do nothing more than amuse themselves with more subtle delusions.   They admit that Christ is not contained in the sacrament circumscriptively, or in a bodily manner, but they afterwards devise a method which they themselves do not understand, and cannot explain to others.   It, however, comes to this, that Christ may be sought in what they call the species of bread.   What ?   When they say that the substance of bread is converted into Christ, do they not attach him to the white colour, which is all they leave of it ?   But they say, that though contained in the sacrament, he still remains in heaven, and has no other presence there than that of abode.   But, whatever be the terms in which they attempt to make a gloss, the sum of all is, that that which was formerly bread, by consecration becomes Christ : so that Christ thereafter lies hid under the colour of bread.   This they are not ashamed distinctly to express. For Lombard's words are, " The body of Christ, which is visible in itself, lurks and lies covered after the

act of consecration under the species of bread" (Lombard. Sent. Lib. iv. Dist. 12). Thus the figure of the bread is nothing but a mask which conceals the view of the flesh from our eye. But there is no need of many conjectures to detect the snare which they intended to lay by these words, since the thing itself speaks clearly. It is easy to see how great is the superstition under which not only the vulgar but the leaders also, have laboured for many ages, and still labour, in Popish Churches. Little solicitous as to true faith (by which alone we attain to the fellowship of Christ, and become one with him), provided they have his carnal presence, which they have fabricated without authority from the word, they think he is sufficiently present. Hence we see, that all which they have gained by their ingenious subtlety is to make bread to be regarded as God.

14. Hence proceeded that fictitious transubstantiation for which they fight more fiercely in the present day than for all the other articles of their faith. For the first architects of local presence could not explain, how the body of Christ could be mixed with the substance of bread, without forthwith meeting with many absurdities. Hence it was necessary to have recourse to the fiction, that there is a conversion of the bread into body, not that properly instead of bread it becomes body, but that Christ, in order to conceal himself under the figure, reduces the substance to nothing. It is strange that they have fallen into such a degree of ignorance, nay, of stupor, as to produce this monstrous fiction not only against Scripture, but also against the consent of the ancient Church. I admit, indeed, that some of the ancients occasionally used the term *conversion*, not that they meant to do away with the substance in the external signs, but to teach that the bread devoted to the sacrament was widely different from ordinary bread, and was now something else. All clearly and uniformly teach that the sacred Supper consists of two parts, an earthly and a heavenly. The earthly they without dispute interpret to be bread and wine. Certainly, whatever they may pretend, it is plain that antiquity, which they often dare to oppose to the clear word of God, gives no countenance to that dogma. It is not so long since it was devised; indeed, it was unknown not only to the better ages, in which a purer doctrine still flourished, but after that purity was considerably impaired. There is no early Christian writer who does not admit in distinct terms that the sacred symbols of the Supper are bread and wine, although, as has been said, they sometimes distinguish them by various epithets, in order to recommend the dignity of the mystery. For when they say that a secret conversion takes place at consecration, so that it is now something else than bread and wine, their meaning, as I already observed, is, not that these are annihilated, but that they are to be considered in a different light from common food, which is only intended to feed the body, whereas in the former the spiritual food and drink of the mind are exhibited. This we deny not. But, say our opponents, if there is conversion, one thing must become another. If

they mean that something becomes different from what it was before, I assent. If they will wrest it in support of their fiction, let them tell me of what kind of change they are sensible in baptism. For here, also, the Fathers make out a wonderful conversion, when they say that out of the corruptible element is made the spiritual laver of the soul, and yet no one denies that it still remains water. But say they, there is no such expression in Baptism as that in the Supper, *This is my body;* as if we were treating of these words, which have a meaning sufficiently clear, and not rather of that term *conversion,* which ought not to mean more in the Supper than in Baptism. Have done, then, with those quibbles upon words, which betray nothing but their silliness. The meaning would have no congruity, unless the truth which is there figured had a living image in the external sign. Christ wished to testify by an external symbol that his flesh was food. If he exhibited merely an empty show of bread, and not true bread, where is the analogy or similitude to conduct us from the visible thing to the invisible ? For, in order to make all things consistent, the meaning cannot extend to more than this, that we are fed by the species of Christ's flesh ; just as, in the case of baptism, if the figure of water deceived the eye, it would not be to us a sure pledge of our ablution ; nay, the fallacious spectacle would rather throw us into doubt. The nature of the sacrament is therefore overthrown, if in the mode of signifying the earthly sign corresponds not to the heavenly reality ; and, accordingly, the truth of the mystery is lost if true bread does not represent the true body of Christ. I again repeat, since the Supper is nothing but a conspicuous attestation to the promise which is contained in the sixth chapter of John—viz. that Christ is the bread of life, who came down from heaven, that visible bread must intervene, in order that that spiritual bread may be figured, unless we would destroy all the benefits with which God here favours us for the purpose of sustaining our infirmity. Then on what ground could Paul infer that we are all one bread, and one body in partaking together of that one bread, if only the semblance of bread, and not the natural reality, remained ?

15. They could not have been so shamefully deluded by the impostures of Satan had they not been fascinated by the erroneous idea, that the body of Christ included under the bread is transmitted by the bodily mouth into the belly. The cause of this brutish imagination was, that consecration had the same effect with them as magical incantation. They overlooked the principle, that bread is a sacrament to none but those to whom the word is addressed, just as the water of baptism is not changed in itself, but begins to be to us what it formerly was not, as soon as the promise is annexed. This will better appear from the example of a similar sacrament. The water gushing from the rock in the desert was to the Israelites a badge and sign of the same thing that is figured to us in the Supper by wine. For Paul declares that they drank the same spiritual drink (1 Cor. x. 4.) But the water was common to the herds and

flocks of the people. Hence it is easy to infer, that in the earthly elements, when employed for a spiritual use, no other conversion takes place than in respect of men, inasmuch as they are to them seals of promises. Moreover, since it is the purpose of God, as I have repeatedly inculcated, to raise us up to himself by fit vehicles, those who indeed call us to Christ, but to Christ lurking invisibly under bread, impiously, by their perverseness, defeat this object. For it is impossible for the mind of man to disentangle itself from the immensity of space, and ascend to Christ even above the heavens. What nature denied them, they attempted to gain by a noxious remedy. Remaining on the earth, they felt no need of a celestial proximity to Christ. Such was the necessity which impelled them to transfigure the body of Christ. In the age of Bernard, though a harsher mode of speech had prevailed, transubstantiation was not yet recognised. And in all previous ages, the similitude in the mouths of all was, that a spiritual reality was conjoined with bread and wine in this sacrament. As to the terms, they think they answer acutely, though they adduce nothing relevant to the case in hand. The rod of Moses (they say), when turned into a serpent, though it acquires the name of a serpent, still retains its former name, and is called a rod; and thus, according to them, it is equally probable that though the bread passes into a new substance, it is still called by catachresis, and not inaptly, what it still appears to the eye to be. But what resemblance, real or apparent, do they find between an illustrious miracle and their fictitious illusion, of which no eye on the earth is witness? The magi by their impostures had persuaded the Egyptians, that they had a divine power above the ordinary course of nature to change created beings. Moses comes forth, and after exposing their fallacies, shows that the invincible power of God is on his side, since his rod swallows up all the other rods. But as that conversion was visible to the eye, we have already observed, that it has no reference to the case in hand. Shortly after the rod visibly resumed its form. It may be added, that we know not whether this was an extemporary conversion of substance.[1] For we must attend to the illusion to the rods of the magicians, which the prophet did not choose to term serpents, lest he might seem to insinuate a conversion which had no existence, because those impostors had done nothing more than blind the eyes of the spectators. But what resemblance is there between that expression and the following? "The bread which we break;"—"As often as ye eat this bread;"—"They communicated in the breaking of bread;" and so forth. It is certain that the eye only was deceived by the incantation of the magicians. The matter is more doubtful with regard to Moses, by whose hand it was not more difficult for God to make a serpent out of a rod, and again to make a rod out of a serpent, than to clothe angels with corporeal

---

[1] Compare together Ambrose on those who are initiated in the sacraments (cap. 9), and Augustine, De Trinitate, Lib. iii. cap. 10, and it will be seen that both are opposed to transubstantiation.

bodies, and a little after unclothe them. If the case of the sacrament were at all akin to this, there might be some colour for their explanation. Let it, therefore, remain fixed that there is no true and fit promise in the Supper, that the flesh of Christ is truly meat, unless there is a correspondence in the true substance of the external symbol. But as one error gives rise to another, a passage in Jeremiah has been so absurdly wrested, to prove transubstantiation, that it is painful to refer to it. The prophet complains that wood was placed in his bread, intimating that by the cruelty of his enemies his bread was infected with bitterness, as David by a similar figure complains, " They gave me also gall for my meat : and in my thirst they gave me vinegar to drink" (Psalm lxix. 21). These men would allegorise the expression to mean, that the body of Christ was nailed to the wood of the cross. But some of the Fathers thought so ! As if we ought not rather to pardon their ignorance and bury the disgrace, than to add impudence, and bring them into hostile conflict with the genuine meaning of the prophet.

16. Some, who see that the analogy between the sign and the thing signified cannot be destroyed without destroying the truth of the sacrament, admit that the bread of the Supper is truly the substance of an earthly and corruptible element, and cannot suffer any change in itself, but must have the body of Christ included under it. If they would explain this to mean, that when the bread is held forth in the sacrament, an exhibition of the body is annexed, because the truth is inseparable from its sign, I would not greatly object. But because fixing the body itself in the bread, they attach to it an ubiquity contrary to its nature, and by adding *under* the bread, will have it that it lies hid under it, I must employ a short time in exposing their craft, and dragging them forth from their concealments. Here, however, it is not my intention· professedly to discuss the whole case ; I mean only to lay the foundations of a discussion which will afterwards follow in its own place. They insist, then, that the body of Christ is invisible and immense, so that it may be hid under bread, because they think that there is no other way by which they can communicate with him than by his descending into the bread, though they do not comprehend the mode of descent by which he raises us up to himself. They employ all the colours they possibly can, but after they have said all, it is sufficiently apparent that they insist on the local presence of Christ. How so ? Because they cannot conceive any other participation of flesh and blood than that which consists either· in local conjunction and contact, or in some gross method of enclosing.

17. Some, in order obstinately to maintain the error which they have once rashly adopted, hesitate not to assert that the dimensions of Christ's flesh are not more circumscribed than those of heaven and earth. His birth as an infant, his growth, his extension on the cross, his confinement in the sepulchre, were effected, they say, by a kind of dispensation, that he might perform the offices of being

born, of dying, and of other human acts: his being seen with his wonted bodily appearance after the resurrection, his ascension into heaven, his appearance, after his ascension, to Stephen and Paul, were the effect of the same dispensation, that it might be made apparent to the eye of man that he was constituted King in heaven. What is this but to call forth Marcion from his grave? For there cannot be a doubt that the body of Christ, if so constituted, was a phantasm, or was phantastical. Some employ a rather more subtle evasion, That the body which is given in the sacrament is glorious and immortal, and that, therefore, there is no absurdity in its being contained under the sacrament in various places, or in no place, and in no form. But, I ask, what did Christ give to his disciples the day before he suffered? Do not the words say that he gave the mortal body, which was to be delivered shortly after? But, say they, he had previously manifested his glory to the three disciples on the mount (Matth. xvii. 2). This is true; but his purpose was to give them for the time a taste of immortality. Still they cannot find there a twofold body, but only the one which he had assumed, arrayed in new glory. When he distributed his body in the first Supper, the hour was at hand in which he was "stricken, smitten of God, and afflicted" (Isa. liii. 4). So far was he from intending at that time to exhibit the glory of his resurrection. And here what a door is opened to Marcion, if the body of Christ was seen humble and mortal in one place, glorious and immortal in another! And yet, if their opinion is well-founded, the same thing happens every day, because they are forced to admit that the body of Christ, which is in itself visible, lurks invisibly under the symbol of bread. And yet those who send forth such monstrous dogmas, so far from being ashamed at the disgrace, assail us with virulent invectives for not subscribing to them.

18. But assuming that the body and blood of Christ are attached to the bread and wine, then the one must necessarily be dissevered from the other. For as the bread is given separately from the cup, so the body, united to the bread, must be separated from the blood, included in the cup. For since they affirm that the body is in the bread, and the blood is in the cup, while the bread and wine are, in regard to space, at some distance from each other, they cannot, by any quibble, evade the conclusion that the body must be separated from the blood. Their usual pretence—viz. that the blood is in the body, and the body again in the blood, by what they call concomitance, is more than frivolous, since the symbols in which they are included are thus distinguished. But if we are carried to heaven with our eyes and minds, that we may there behold Christ in the glory of his kingdom, as the symbols invite us to him in his integrity, so, under the symbol of bread, we must feed on his body, and, under the symbol of wine, drink separately of his blood, and thereby have the full enjoyment of him. For though he withdrew his flesh from us, and with his body ascended to heaven, he, however, sits at the right hand of the

Father ; that is, he reigns in power and majesty, and the glory of the Father. This kingdom is not limited by any intervals of space, nor circumscribed by any dimensions. Christ can exert his energy wherever he pleases, in earth and heaven, can manifest his presence by the exercise of his power, can always be present with his people, breathing into them his own life, can live in them, sustain, confirm, and invigorate them, and preserve them safe, just as if he were with them in the body ; in fine, can feed them with his own body, communion with which he transfuses into them. After this manner, the body and blood of Christ are exhibited to us in the sacrament.

19. The presence of Christ in the Supper we must hold to be such as neither affixes him to the element of bread, nor encloses him in bread, nor circumscribes him in any way (this would obviously detract from his celestial glory); and it must, moreover, be such as neither divests him of his just dimensions, nor dissevers him by differences of place, nor assigns to him a body of boundless dimensions, diffused through heaven and earth. All these things are clearly repugnant to his true human nature. Let us never allow ourselves to lose sight of the two restrictions. First, Let there be nothing derogatory to the heavenly glory of Christ. This happens whenever he is brought under the corruptible elements of this world, or is affixed to any earthly creatures. Secondly, Let no property be assigned to his body inconsistent with his human nature. This is done when it is either said to be infinite, or made to occupy a variety of places at the same time. But when these absurdities are discarded, I willingly admit anything which helps to express the true and substantial communication of the body and blood of the Lord, as exhibited to believers under the sacred symbols of the Supper, understanding that they are received not by the imagination or intellect merely, but are enjoyed in reality as the food of eternal life. For the odium with which this view is regarded by the world, and the unjust prejudice incurred by its defence, there is no cause, unless it be in the fearful fascinations of Satan. What we teach on the subject is in perfect accordance with Scripture, contains nothing absurd, obscure, or ambiguous, is not unfavourable to true piety and solid edification ; in short, has nothing in it to offend, save that, for some ages, while the ignorance and barbarism of sophists reigned in the Church, the clear light and open truth were unbecomingly suppressed. And yet as Satan, by means of turbulent spirits, is still, in the present day, exerting himself to the utmost to bring dishonour on this doctrine by all kinds of calumny and reproach, it is right to assert and defend it with the greatest care.

20. Before we proceed farther, we must consider the ordinance itself, as instituted by Christ, because the most plausible objection of our opponents is, that we abandon his words. To free ourselves from the obloquy with which they thus load us, the fittest course will be to begin with an interpretation of the words. Three Evangelists and Paul relate that our Saviour took bread, and after giving

thanks, brake it, and gave it to his disciples, saying, Take, eat: this is my body which is given or broken for you. Of the cup, Matthew and Mark say, "This is my blood of the new testament, which is shed for many for the remission of sins" (Matth. xxvi. 26; Mark xiv. 22). Luke and Paul say, "This cup is the new testament in my blood" (Luke xxii. 20; 1 Cor. xi. 25). The advocates of transubstantiation insist, that by the pronoun, *this*, is denoted the appearance of bread, because the whole complexion of our Saviour's address is an act of consecration, and there is no substance which can be demonstrated. But if they adhere so religiously to the words, inasmuch as that which our Saviour gave to his disciples he declared to be his body, there is nothing more alien from the strict meaning of the words than the fiction, that what was bread is now body. What Christ takes into his hands, and gives to the apostles, he declares to be his body; but he had taken bread, and, therefore, who sees not that what is given is still bread? Hence, nothing can be more absurd than to transfer what is affirmed of bread to the species of bread. Others, in interpreting the particle *is*, as equivalent to being transubstantiated, have recourse to a gloss which is forced and violently wrested. They have no ground, therefore, for pretending that they are moved by a reverence for the words. The use of the term *is*, for being converted into something else, is unknown to every tongue and nation. With regard to those who leave the bread in the Supper, and affirm that it is the body of Christ, there is great diversity among them. Those who speak more modestly, though they insist upon the letter, This is my body, afterwards abandon this strictness, and observe that it is equivalent to saying that the body of Christ is with the bread, in the bread, and under the bread. To the reality which they affirm, we have already adverted, and will by-and-by, at greater length. I am not only considering the words by which they say they are prevented from admitting that the bread is called body, because it is a sign of the body. But if they shun everything like metaphor, why do they leap from the simple demonstration of Christ to modes of expression which are widely different? For there is a great difference between saying that the bread is the body, and that the body is with the bread. But seeing it impossible to maintain the simple proposition that the bread is the body, they endeavoured to evade the difficulty by concealing themselves under those forms of expression. Others, who are bolder, hesitate not to assert that, strictly speaking, the bread is body, and in this way prove that they are truly of the letter. If it is objected that the bread, therefore, is Christ, and, being Christ, is God,—they will deny it, because the words of Christ do not expressly say so. But they gain nothing by their denial, since all agree that the whole Christ is offered to us in the Supper. It is intolerable blasphemy to affirm, without figure, of a fading and corruptible element, that it is Christ. I now ask them, if they hold the two propositions to be identical, Christ is the Son of God, and Bread is the body of

Christ? If they concede that they are different (and this, whether they will or not, they will be forced to do), let them tell wherein is the difference. All which they can adduce is, I presume, that the bread is called body in a sacramental manner. Hence it follows, that the words of Christ are not subject to the common rule, and ought not to be tested grammatically. I ask all these rigid and obstinate exactors of the letter, whether, when Luke and Paul call the cup *the testament in blood,* they do not express the same thing as in the previous clause, when they call bread the body? There certainly was the same solemnity in the one part of the mystery as in the other, and, as brevity is obscure, the longer sentence better elucidates the meaning. As often, therefore, as they contend, from the one expression, that the bread is body, I will adduce an apt interpretation from the longer expression, That it is a testament in the body. What? Can we seek for surer or more faithful expounders than Luke and Paul? I have no intention, however, to detract, in any respect, from the communication of the body of Christ, which I have acknowledged. I only meant to expose the foolish perverseness with which they carry on a war of words. The bread I understand, on the authority of Luke and Paul, to be the body of Christ, because it is a covenant in the body. If they impugn this, their quarrel is not with me, but with the Spirit of God. However often they may repeat, that reverence for the words of Christ will not allow them to give a figurative interpretation to what is spoken plainly, the pretext cannot justify them in thus rejecting all the contrary arguments which we adduce. Meanwhile, as I have already observed, it is proper to attend to the force of what is meant by a testament in the body and blood of Christ. The covenant, ratified by the sacrifice of death, would not avail us without the addition of that secret communication, by which we are made one with Christ.

21. It remains, therefore, to hold, that on account of the affinity which the things signified have with their signs, the name of the thing itself is given to the sign figuratively, indeed, but very appropriately. I say nothing of allegories and parables, lest it should be alleged that I am seeking subterfuges, and slipping out of the present question. I say that the expression which is uniformly used in Scripture, when the sacred mysteries are treated of, is metonymical. For you cannot otherwise understand the expressions, that circumcision is a "covenant"—that the lamb is the Lord's "passover"—that the sacrifices of the law are expiations—that the rock from which the water flowed in the desert was Christ,—unless you interpret them metonymically."[1] Nor is the name merely transferred from the superior to the inferior, but, on the contrary, the name of the visible sign is given to the thing signified, as when God is said to have appeared to Moses in the bush; the ark of the covenant is called God, and the face of God, and the dove is called the Holy Spirit.[2]

---

[1] Gen. xvii. 10; Exod. xii. 11; xvii. 6; 1 Cor. x. 4.
[2] Exod. iii. 2; Psalm lxxxiv. 8; xlii. 3; Matth. iii. 16.

For although the sign differs essentially from the thing signified, the latter being spiritual and heavenly, the former corporeal and visible, —yet, as it not only figures the thing which it is employed to represent as a naked and empty badge, but also truly exhibits it, why should not its name be justly applied to the thing? But if symbols humanly devised, which are rather the images of absent than the marks of present things, and of which they are very often most fallacious types, are sometimes honoured with their names,—with much greater reason do the institutions of God borrow the names of things, of which they always bear a sure, and by no means fallacious signification, and have the reality annexed to them. So great, then, is the similarity, and so close the connection between the two, that it is easy to pass from the one to the other. Let our opponents, therefore, cease to indulge their mirth in calling us Tropists, when we explain the sacramental mode of expression according to the common use of Scripture. For, while the sacraments agree in many things, there is also, in this metonymy, a certain community in all respects between them. As, therefore, the apostle says that the rock from which spiritual water flowed forth to the Israelites was Christ (1 Cor. x. 4), and was thus a visible symbol under which, that spiritual drink was truly perceived, though not by the eye, so the body of Christ is now called bread, inasmuch as it is a symbol under which our Lord offers us the true eating of his body. Lest any one should despise this as a novel invention, the view which Augustine took and expressed was the same: "Had not the sacraments a certain resemblance to the things of which they are sacraments, they would not be sacraments at all. And from this resemblance, they generally have the names of the things themselves. This, as the sacrament of the body of Christ, is, after a certain manner, the body of Christ, and the sacrament of Christ is the blood of Christ; so the sacrament of faith is faith" (August. Ep. 23, ad Bonifac.). He has many similar passages, which it would be superfluous to collect, as that one may suffice. I need only remind my readers, that the same doctrine is taught by that holy man in his Epistle to Evodius. Where Augustine teaches that nothing is more common than metonymy in mysteries, it is a frivolous quibble to object that there is no mention of the Supper. Were this objection sustained, it would follow, that we are not entitled to argue from the genus to the species; e. g., Every animal is endued with motion; and, therefore, the horse and the ox are endued with motion.[1] Indeed, longer discussion is rendered unnecessary by the words of the Saint himself, where he says, that when Christ gave the symbol of his body, he did not hesitate to call it his body (August. Cont. Adimantum, cap. 12). He elsewhere says, "Wonderful was the patience of Christ in admitting Judas to the

---

[1] French, "Certes si on ne veut abolir toute raison, on ne peut dire que ce qui est commun à tous sacremens n'appartienne aussi à la Cene."—Certainly if we would not abolish reason altogether, we cannot say that that which is common to all the sacraments belongs not also to the Supper.

feast, in which he committed and delivered to the disciples the symbol of his body and blood" (August. in. Ps. iii).

22. Should any morose person, shutting his eyes to everything else, insist upon the expression, *This is*, as distinguishing this mystery from all others, the answer is easy. They say that the substantive verb is so emphatic, as to leave no room for interpretation. Though I should admit this, I answer, that the substantive verb occurs in the words of Paul (1 Cor. x. 16), where he calls the bread the *communion* of the body of Christ. But communion is something different from the body itself. Nay, when the sacraments are treated of, the same word occurs: " My covenant shall be in your flesh for an everlasting covenant" (Gen. xvii. 13). " This is the ordinance of the passover" (Exod. xii. 43). To say no more, when Paul declares that the rock was Christ (1 Cor. x. 4), why should the substantive verb, in that passage, be deemed less emphatic than in the discourse of Christ? When John says, " The Holy Ghost was not yet given, because that Jesus was not yet glorified" (John vii. 39), I should like to know what is the force of the substantive verb? If the rule of our opponents is rigidly observed, the eternal essence of the Spirit will be destroyed, as if he had only begun to be after the ascension of Christ. Let them tell me, in fine, what is meant by the declaration of Paul, that baptism is " the washing of regeneration, and renewing of the Holy Ghost" (Tit. iii. 5); though it is certain that to many it was of no use. But they cannot be more effectually refuted than by the expression of Paul, that the Church is Christ. For, after introducing the similitude of the human body, he adds, " So also is Christ" (1 Cor. xii. 12), when he means not the only-begotten Son of God in himself, but in his members. I think I have now gained this much, that all men of sense and integrity will be disgusted with the calumnies of our enemies, when they give out that we discredit the words of Christ; though we embrace them not less obediently than they do, and ponder them with greater reverence. Nay, their supine security proves that they do not greatly care what Christ meant, provided it furnishes them with a shield to defend their obstinacy, while our careful investigation should be an evidence of the authority which we yield to Christ. They invidiously pretend that human reason will not allow us to believe what Christ uttered with his sacred mouth ; but how naughtily they endeavour to fix this odium upon us, I have already, in a great measure, shown, and will still show more clearly. Nothing, therefore, prevents us from believing Christ speaking, and from acquiescing in everything to which he intimates his assent. The only question here is, whether it be unlawful to inquire into the genuine meaning ?

23. Those worthy masters, to show that they are of the letter, forbid us to deviate, in the least, from the letter. On the contrary, when Scripture calls God a man of war, as I see that the expression would be too harsh if not interpreted, I have no doubt that the similitude is taken from man. And, indeed, the only pretext which enabled

the Anthropomorphites to annoy the orthodox Fathers was by fastening on the expressions, "The eyes of God see;" "It ascended to his ears;" "His hand is stretched out;" "The earth is his footstool;" and exclaimed, that God was deprived of the body which Scripture assigns to him. Were this rule admitted, complete barbarism would bury the whole light of faith. What monstrous absurdities shall fanatical men not be able to extract, if they are allowed to urge every knotty point in support of their dogmas? Their objection, that it is not probable that when Christ was providing special comfort for the apostles in adversity, he spoke enigmatically or obscurely, —supports our view. For, had it not occurred to the apostles that the bread was called the body figuratively, as being a symbol of the body, the extraordinary nature of the thing would doubtless have filled them with perplexity. For, at this very period, John relates, that the slightest difficulties perplexed them (John xiv. 5, 8; xvi. 17). They debate, among themselves, how Christ is to go to the Father, and not understanding that the things which were said referred to the heavenly Father, raise a question as to how he is to go out of the world until they shall see him? How, then, could they have been so ready to believe what is repugnant to all reason—viz. that Christ was seated at table under their eye, and yet was contained invisible under the bread? As they attest their consent by eating this bread without hesitation, it is plain that they understood the words of Christ in the same sense as we do, considering what ought not to seem unusual when mysteries are spoken of, that the name of the thing signified was transferred to the sign. There was therefore to the disciples, as there is to us, clear and sure consolation, not involved in any enigma; and the only reason why certain persons reject our interpretation is, because they are blinded by a delusion of the devil to introduce the darkness of enigma, instead of the obvious interpretation of an appropriate figure. Besides, if we insist strictly on the words, our Saviour will be made to affirm erroneously something of the bread different from the cup. He calls the bread body, and the wine blood. There must either be a confusion in terms, or there must be a division separating the body from the blood. Nay, "This is my body," may be as truly affirmed of the cup as of the bread; and it may in turn be affirmed that the bread is the blood.[1] If they answer, that we must look to the end or use for which symbols were instituted, I admit it: but still they will not disencumber themselves of the absurdity which their error drags along with it—viz. that the bread is blood, and the wine is body. Then I know not what they mean when they concede that bread and body are different things, and yet maintain that the one is predicated of the other, properly and without figure, as if one were to say that a garment is different from a man, and yet is properly called a man. Still, as if the victory depended on obstinacy and invective, they say that Christ

---

[1] The French adds, "Je di si Jesus Christ est enclos sous chacun des deux signes." —I mean, if Jesus Christ is included under each of the two signs.

is charged with falsehood, when it is attempted to interpret his words. It will now be easy for the reader to understand the injustice which is done to us by those carpers at syllables, when they possess the simple with the idea that we bring discredit on the words of Christ; words which, as we have shown, are madly perverted and confounded by them, but are faithfully and accurately expounded by us.

24. This infamous falsehood cannot be completely wiped away without disposing of another charge. They give out that we are so wedded to human reason, that we attribute nothing more to the power of God than the order of nature admits, and common sense dictates.[1] From these wicked calumnies, I appeal to the doctrine which I have delivered,—a doctrine which makes it sufficiently clear that I by no means measure this mystery by the capacity of human reason, or subject it to the laws of nature. I ask, whether it is from physics we have learned that Christ feeds our souls from heaven with his flesh, just as our bodies are nourished by bread and wine? How has flesh this virtue of giving life to our souls? All will say, that it is not done naturally. Not more agreeable is it to human reason to hold that the flesh of Christ penetrates to us, so as to be our food. In short, every one who may have tasted our doctrine, will be carried away with admiration of the secret power of God. But these worthy zealots fabricate for themselves a miracle, and think that without it God himself and his power vanish away. I would again admonish the reader carefully to consider the nature of our doctrine, whether it depends on common apprehension, or whether, after having surmounted the world on the wings of faith, it rises to heaven. We say that Christ descends to us, as well by the external symbol as by his Spirit, that he may truly quicken our souls by the substance of his flesh and blood. He who feels not that in these few words are many miracles, is more than stupid ; since nothing is more contrary to nature than to derive the spiritual and heavenly life of the soul from flesh, which received its origin from the earth, and was subjected to death, nothing more incredible than that things separated by the whole space between heaven and earth should, notwithstanding of the long distance, not only be connected, but united, so that souls receive aliment from the flesh of Christ. Let preposterous men, then, cease to assail us with the vile calumny, that we malignantly restrict the boundless power of God. They either foolishly err, or wickedly lie. The question here is not, What could God do? but, What has he been pleased to do? We affirm that he has done what pleased him, and it pleased him that Christ should be in all respects like his brethren, " yet without sin" (Heb. iv. 15). What is our flesh? Is it not that which consists of certain dimensions? is confined within a certain place? is touched and seen? And why,

---

1 The French adds, " En lisant nos ecrits, on verra incontinent combien ces calomnies sont vilaines et puantes."—In reading our writings, it will at once be seen how vile and foul these calumnies are.

say they, may not God make the same flesh occupy several different places, so as not to be confined to any particular place, and so as to have neither measure nor species? Fool! why do you require the power of God to make a thing to be at the same time flesh and not flesh? It is just as if you were to insist on his making light to be at the same time light and darkness. He wills light to be light, darkness to be darkness, flesh to be flesh. True, when he so chooses, he will convert darkness into light, and light into darkness: but when you insist that there shall be no difference between light and darkness, what do you but pervert the order of the divine wisdom? Flesh must therefore be flesh, and spirit spirit; each under the law and condition on which God has created them. Now, the condition of flesh is, that it should have one certain place, its own dimensions, its own form. On that condition, Christ assumed the flesh, to which, as Augustine declares (Ep. ad Dardan.), he gave incorruption and glory, but without destroying its nature and reality.

25. They object that they have the word by which the will of God has been openly manifested; that is if we permit them to banish from the Church the gift of interpretation, which should throw light upon the word. I admit that they have the word, but just as the Anthropomorphites of old had it, when they made God corporeal; just as Marcion and the Manichees had it when they made the body of Christ celestial or phantastical. They quoted the passages, "The first man is of the earth, earthy; the second man is the Lord from heaven" (1 Cor. xv. 47): Christ "made himself of no reputation, and took upon him the form of a servant, and was made in the likeness of men" (Phil. ii. 7). But these vain boasters think that there is no power of God unless they fabricate a monster in their own brains, by which the whole order of nature is subverted. This rather is to circumscribe the power of God, to attempt to try, by our fictions, what he can do. From this word, they have assumed that the body of Christ is visible in heaven, and yet lurks invisible on the earth under innumerable bits of bread. They will say that this is rendered necessary, in order that the body of Christ may be given in the Supper. In other words, because they have been pleased to extract a carnal eating from the words of Christ, carried away by their own prejudice, they have found it necessary to coin this subtlety, which is wholly repugnant to Scripture. That we detract, in any respect, from the power of God, is so far from being true, that our doctrine is the loudest in extolling it. But as they continue to charge us with robbing God of his honour, in rejecting what, according to common apprehension, it is difficult to believe, though it had been promised by the mouth of Christ; I answer, as I lately did, that in the mysteries of faith we do not consult common apprehension, but, with the placid docility and spirit of meekness which James recommends (James i. 21), receive the doctrine which has come from heaven. Wherein they perniciously err, I am confident that we follow a proper moderation. On hearing the words of Christ, this

is my body, they imagine a miracle most remote from his intention ; and when, from this fiction, the grossest absurdities arise, having already, by their precipitate haste, entangled themselves with snares, they plunge themselves into the abyss of the divine omnipotence, that, in this way, they may extinguish the light of truth.[1] Hence the supercilious moroseness. We have no wish to know how Christ is hid under the bread : we are satisfied with his own words, " This is my body." We again study, with no less obedience than care, to obtain a sound understanding of this passage, as of the whole of Scripture. We do not, with preposterous fervour, rashly, and without choice, lay hold on whatever first presents itself to our minds ; but, after careful meditation, embrace the meaning which the Spirit of God suggests. Trusting to him, we look down, as from a height, on whatever opposition may be offered by earthly wisdom. Nay, we hold our minds captive, not allowing one word of murmur, and humble them, that they may not presume to gainsay. In this way, we have arrived at that exposition of the words of Christ, which all who are moderately versant in Scripture know to be perpetually used with regard to the sacraments. Still, in a matter of difficulty, we deem it not unlawful to inquire, after the example of the blessed Virgin, " How shall this be ?" (Luke i. 34).

26. But as nothing will be more effectual to confirm the faith of the pious than to show them that the doctrine which we have laid down is taken from the pure word of God, and rests on its authority, I will make this plain with as much brevity as I can. The body with which Christ rose is declared, not by Aristotle, but by the Holy Spirit, to be finite, and to be contained in heaven until the last day. I am not unaware how confidently our opponents evade the passages which are quoted to this effect. Whenever Christ says that he will leave the world and go away (John xiv. 2, 28), they reply, that that departure was nothing more than a change of mortal state. Were this so, Christ would not substitute the Holy Spirit, to supply, as they express it, the defect of his absence, since he does not succeed in place of him, nor, on the other hand, does Christ himself descend from the heavenly glory to assume the condition of a mortal life. Certainly the advent of the Spirit and the ascension of Christ are set against each other, and hence it necessarily follows that Christ dwells with us according to the flesh, in the same way as that in which he sends his Spirit. Moreover, he distinctly says that he would not always be in the world with his disciples (Matth. xxvi. 11). This saying, also, they think they admirably dispose of, as if it were a denial by Christ that he would always be poor and mean, or liable to the necessities of a fading life. But this is plainly repugnant to the context, since reference is made not to poverty and want, or the wretched condition of an earthly life, but to worship and honour.

---

[1] Thus Augustine, speaking of certain persons, says : " It is strange, when they are confined in their straits, over what precipices they plunge themselves, fearing the nets of truth " (Aug. Ep. 105).

The disciples were displeased with the anointing by Mary, because they thought it a superfluous and useless expenditure, akin to luxury, and would therefore have preferred that the price which they thought wasted should have been expended on the poor. Christ answers, that he will not be always with them to receive such honour. No different exposition is given by Augustine, whose words are by no means ambiguous. When Christ says, " Me ye have not always," he spoke of his bodily presence. In regard to his majesty, in regard to his providence, in regard to his ineffable and invisible grace, is fulfilled what he said : " Lo, I am with you alway, even unto the end of the world " (Matth. xxviii. 20); but in regard to the flesh which the Word assumed—in regard to that which was born of the Virgin —in regard to that which was apprehended by the Jews, nailed to the tree, suspended on the cross, wrapt in linen clothes, laid in the tomb, and manifested in the resurrection,—"Me ye have not always." Why? Since he conversed with his disciples in bodily presence for forty days, and, going out with them, ascended, while they saw but followed not. He is not here, for he sits there, at the right hand of the Father. And yet he is here : for the presence of his majesty is not withdrawn. Otherwise, as regards the presence of his majesty, we have Christ always ; while, in regard to his bodily presence, it was rightly said, " Me ye have not always." In respect of bodily presence, the Church had him for a few days: now she holds him by faith, but sees him not with the eye (August. Tract. in Joann. 50). Here (that I may briefly note this) he makes him present with us in three ways—in majesty, providence, and ineffable grace ; under which I comprehend that wondrous communion of his body and blood, provided we understand that it is effected by the power of the Holy Spirit, and not by that fictitious enclosing of his body under the element, since our Lord declared that he had flesh and bones which could be handled and seen. *Going away*, and *ascending*, intimate, not that he had the appearance of one going away and ascending, but that he truly did what the words express. Some one will ask, Are we then to assign a certain region of heaven to Christ? I answer with Augustine, that this is a curious and superfluous question, provided we believe that he is in heaven.

27. What? Does not the very name of ascension, so often repeated, intimate removal from one place to another? This they deny, because by height, according to them, the majesty of empire only is denoted. But what was the very mode of ascending? Was he not carried up while the disciples looked on ? Do not the Evangelists clearly relate that he was carried into heaven ? These acute Sophists reply, that a cloud intervened, and took him out of their sight, to teach the disciples that he would not afterwards be visible in the world. As if he ought not rather to have vanished in a moment, to make them believe in his invisible presence, or the cloud to have gathered around him before he moved a step. When he is carried aloft into the air, and the interposing cloud shows that he is no more

to be sought on earth, we safely infer that his dwelling now is in the heavens, as Paul also asserts, bidding us look for him from thence (Phil. iii. 20).   For this reason, the angels remind the disciples that it is vain to keep gazing up into heaven, because Jesus, who was taken up, would come in like manner as they had seen him ascend.   Here the adversaries of sound doctrine escape, as they think, by the ingenious quibble, that he will come in visible form, though he never departed from the earth, but remained invisible among his people. As if the angels had insinuated a two-fold presence, and not simply made the disciples eye-witnesses of the ascent, that no doubt might remain.   It was just as if they had said, By ascending to heaven, while you looked on, he has asserted his heavenly power: it remains for you to wait patiently until he again arrive to judge the world. He has not entered into heaven to occupy it alone, but to gather you and all the pious along with him.

28. Since the advocates of this spurious dogma are not ashamed to honour it with the suffrages of the ancients, and especially of Augustine, how perverse they are in the attempt I will briefly explain. Pious and learned men have collected the passages, and therefore I am unwilling to plead a concluded cause: any one who wishes may consult their writings.   I will not even collect from Augustine what might be pertinent to the matter,[1] but will be contented to show briefly, that without all controversy he is wholly ours.   The pretence of our opponents, when they would wrest him from us, that throughout his works the flesh and blood of Christ are said to be dispensed in the Supper—namely, the victim once offered on the cross, is frivolous, seeing he, at the same time, calls it either the eucharist or sacrament of the body.   But it is unnecessary to go far to find the sense in which he uses the terms *flesh* and *blood*, since he himself explains, saying (Ep. 23, ad Bonif.) that the sacraments receive names from their similarity to the things which they designate; and that, therefore, the sacrament of the body is after a certain manner the body. With this agrees another well-know passage, " The Lord hesitated not to say, This is my body, when he gave the sign " (Cont. Adimant. Manich. cap. 12).   They again object that Augustine says distinctly that the body of Christ falls upon the earth, and enters the mouth. But this is in the same sense in which he affirms that it is consumed, for he conjoins both at the same time.   There is nothing repugnant to this in his saying that the bread is consumed after the mystery is performed: for he had said a little before, " As these things are known to men, when they are done by men they may receive honour as being religious, but not as being wonderful " (De Trinit. Lib. iii. c. 10).   His meaning is not different in the passage which our opponents too rashly appropriate to themselves—viz. that

---

[1] That the dogma of those who place the body of Christ in the bread is not aided by passages from Augustine, or the authority of Scripture, is proved here and sec. 29–31. There is no ambiguity in what he says, De Civit. Dei, 16, cap. 27.   In Psal. 26 et 46. In Joann. Tract. 13, 102, 106, 107, &c.

Christ in a manner carried himself in his own hands, when he held out the mystical bread to his disciples. For by interposing the expression, *in a manner*, he declares that he was not really or truly included under the bread. Nor is it strange, since he elsewhere plainly contends, that bodies could not be without particular localities, and being nowhere, would have no existence. It is a paltry cavil that he is not there treating of the Supper, in which God exerts a special power. The question had been raised as to the flesh of Christ, and the holy man professedly replying, says, " Christ gave immortality to his flesh, but did not destroy its nature. In regard to this form, we are not to suppose that it is everywhere diffused: for we must beware not to rear up the divinity of the man, so as to take away the reality of the body. It does not follow that that which is in God is everywhere as God" (Ep. ad Dardan.). He immediately subjoins the reason, " One person is God and man, and both one Christ, everywhere, inasmuch as he is God, and in heaven, inasmuch as he is man." How careless would it have been not to except the mystery of the Supper, a matter so grave and serious, if it was in any respect adverse to the doctrine which he was handling ? And yet, if any one will attentively read what follows shortly after, he will find that under that general doctrine the Supper also is comprehended, that Christ, the only-begotten Son of God, and also Son of man, is everywhere wholly present as God, in the temple of God, that is, in the Church, as an inhabiting God, and in some place in heaven, because of the dimensions of his real body. We see how, in order to unite Christ with the Church, he does not bring his body out of heaven. This he certainly would have done had the body of Christ not been truly our food, unless when included under the bread. Elsewhere, explaining how believers now possess Christ, he says, " You have him by the sign of the cross, by the sacrament of baptism, by the meat and drink of the altar " (Tract. in Joann. 50). How rightly he enumerates a superstitious rite, among the symbols of Christ's presence, I dispute not ; but in comparing the presence of the flesh to the sign of the cross, he sufficiently shows that he has no idea of a twofold body of Christ, one lurking concealed under the bread, and another sitting visible in heaven. If there is any need of explanation, it is immediately added, " In respect of the presence of his majesty, we have Christ always: in respect of the presence of his flesh, it is rightly said, ' Me ye have not always.' " They object that he also adds, " In respect of ineffable and invisible grace is fulfilled what was said by him, ' I am with you always, even to the end of the world.' " But this is nothing in their favour. For it is at length restricted to his majesty, which is always opposed to body, while the flesh is expressly distinguished from grace and virtue. The same antithesis elsewhere occurs, when he says that "Christ left the disciples in bodily presence, that he might be with them in spiritual presence." Here it is clear that the essence of the flesh is distinguished from the virtue of the Spirit, which conjoins us with Christ, when, in respect of space, we are at a great distance from him. He repeatedly uses the same mode of expression, as when he says, " He is to come to the quick and the dead in bodily presence, according to the rule of faith and sound doctrine: for in spiritual presence he was to come to them, and to be with the whole Church in the world until its consummation. There-fore, this discourse is directed to believers, whom he had begun al-ready to save by corporeal presence, and whom he was to leave in coporeal absence, that by spiritual presence he might preserve them with the Father." By corporeal to understand visible is mere trifling, since he both opposes his body to his divine power, and by adding, that he might " preserve them with the Father," clearly expresses that he sends his grace to us from heaven by means of the Spirit.

29. Since they put so much confidence in his hiding-place of in-visible presence, let us see how well they conceal themselves in it. First, they cannot produce a syllable from Scripture to prove that Christ is invisible ; but they take for granted what no sound man will admit, that the body of Christ cannot be given in the Supper, unless covered with the mask of bread.   This is the very point in dispute ; so far is it from occupying the place of the first principle. And while they thus prate, they are forced to give Christ a twofold body, because, according to them, it is visible in itself in heaven, but in the Supper is invisible, by a special mode of dispensation.   The beautiful consistency of this may easily be judged, both from other passages of Scripture, and from the testimony of Peter.   Peter says that the heavens must receive, or contain Christ, till he come again (Acts iii. 21).   These men teach that he is in every place, but with-out form.   They say that it is unfair to subject a glorious body to the ordinary laws of nature.   But this answer draws along with it the delirious dream of Servetus, which all pious minds justly abhor, that his body was absorbed by his divinity.   I do not say that this is their opinion ; but if it is considered one of the properties of a glori-fied body to fill all things in an invisible manner, it is plain that the corporeal substance is abolished, and no distinction is left between his Godhead and his human nature.   Again, if the body of Christ is so multiform and diversified, that it appears in one place, and in another is invisible, where is there anything of the nature of body with its proper dimensions, and where is its unity?   Far more correct is Tertullian, who contends that the body of Christ was natural and real, because its figure is set before us in the mystery of the Supper, as a pledge and assurance of spiritual life (Tertull. Cont. Marc. Lib. iv.).[1]   And certainly Christ said of his glorified body, " Handle me, and see ; for a spirit hath not flesh and bones, as ye see me have " (Luke xxiv. 39).   Here, by the lips of Christ himself, the reality of his flesh is proved, by its admitting of being seen and handled.   Take these away, and it will cease to be flesh.   They always betake them-selves to their lurking-place of dispensation, which they have fabri-

1 The French adds, "Car la figure seroit fausse, si ce qu'elle represente n'estoit vray." —For the figure would be false, if the thing which it represents were not real.

cated. But it is our duty so to embrace what Christ absolutely declares, as to give it an unreserved assent. He proves that he is not a phantom, because he is visible in his flesh. Take away what he claims as proper to the nature of his body, and must not a new definition of body be devised? Then, however they may turn themselves about, they will not find any place for their fictitious dispensation in that passage, in which Paul says, that "our conversation is in heaven; from whence we look for the Saviour, the Lord Jesus Christ: who shall change our vile body, that it may be fashioned like unto his glorious body" (Phil. iii. 20, 21). We are not to hope for conformity to Christ in these qualities which they ascribe to him as a body, without bounds, and invisible. They will not find any one so stupid as to be persuaded of this great absurdity. Let them not, therefore, set it down as one of the properties of Christ's glorious body, that it is, at the same time, in many places, and in no place. In short, let them either openly deny the resurrection of his flesh, or admit that Christ, when invested with celestial glory, did not lay aside his flesh, but is to make us, in our flesh, his associates, and partakers of the same glory, since we are to have a common resurrection with him. For what does Scripture throughout deliver more clearly than that, as Christ assumed our flesh when he was born of the Virgin, and suffered in our true flesh when he made satisfaction for us, so on rising again he resumed the same true flesh, and carried it with him to heaven? The hope of our resurrection, and ascension to heaven, is, that Christ rose again and ascended, and, as Tertullian says (De Resurrect. Carnis), " Carried an earnest of our resurrection along with him into heaven." Morever, how weak and fragile would this hope be, had not this very flesh of ours in Christ been truly raised up, and entered into the kingdom of heaven. But the essential properties of a body are to be confined by space, to have dimension and form. Have done, then, with that foolish fiction, which affixes the minds of men, as well as Christ, to bread. For to what end this occult presence under the bread, save that those who wish to have Christ conjoined with them may stop short at the symbol? But our Lord himself wished us to withdraw not only our eyes, but all our senses, from the earth, forbidding the woman to touch him until he had ascended to the Father (John xx. 17). When he sees Mary, with pious reverential zeal, hastening to kiss his feet, there could be no reason for his disapproving and forbidding her to touch him before he had ascended to heaven, unless he wished to be sought nowhere else. The objection, that he afterwards appeared to Stephen, is easily answered. It was not necessary for our Saviour to change his place, as he could give the eyes of his servant a power of vision which could penetrate to heaven. The same account is to be given of the case of Paul. The objection, that Christ came forth from the closed sepulchre, and came in to his disciples while the doors were shut (Matth. xxviii. 6 ; John xx. 19), gives no better support to their error. For as the water, just as if it had been a solid pavement, furnished a path to our Saviour when he walked on it (Matth. xiv.), so it is not strange that the hard stone yielded to his step; although it is more probable that the stone was removed at his command, and forthwith, after giving him a passage, returned to its place.   To enter while the doors were shut, was not so much to penetrate through solid matter, as to make a passage for himself by divine power, and stand in the midst of his disciples in a most miraculous manner.   They gain nothing by quoting the passage from Luke, in which it is said, that Christ suddenly vanished from the eyes of the disciples, with whom he had journed to Emmaus (Luke xxiv. 31).   In withdrawing from their sight, he did not become invisible : he only disappeared.   Thus Luke declares that, on the journeying with them, he did not assume a new form, but that "their eyes were holden."   But these men not only transform Christ that he may live on the earth, but pretend that there is another elsewhere of a different description.   In short, by thus trifling, they, not in direct terms indeed, but by a circumlocution, make a spirit of the flesh of Christ; and, not contented with this, give him properties altogether opposite.   Hence it necessarily follows that he must be twofold.

30. Granting what they absurdly talk of the invisible presence, it will still be necessary to prove the immensity, without which it is vain to attempt to include Christ under the bread.   Unless the body of Christ can be everywhere without any boundaries of space, it is impossible to believe that he is hid in the Supper under the bread. Hence, they have been under the necessity of introducing the monstrous dogma of ubiquity.   But it has been demonstrated by strong and clear passages of Scripture, first, that it is bounded by the dimensions of the human body ; and, secondly, that its ascension into heaven made it plain that it is not in all places, but on passing to a new one, leaves the one formerly occupied.   The promise to which they appeal, "I am with you always, even to the end of the world," is not to be applied to the body.   First, then, a perpetual connection with Christ could not exist, unless he dwells in us corporeally, independently of the use of the Supper; and, therefore, they have no good ground for disputing so bitterly concerning the words of Christ, in order to include him under the bread in the Supper.[1]   Secondly, the context proves that Christ is not speaking at all of his flesh, but promising the disciples his invincible aid to guard and sustain them against all the assaults of Satan and the world.   For, in appointing them to a difficult office, he confirms them by the assurance of his presence, that they might neither hesitate to undertake it, nor be timorous in the discharge of it ; as if he had said, that his invincible protection would not fail them.   Unless we would throw everything into confusion, must it not be necessary to distinguish the mode of presence?   And, indeed, some, to their great disgrace, choose rather to betray their ignorance than give up one iota of their error.   I

[1] The French adds, "veu qu'ils confessent que nous l'avons aussi bien sans la Cene;" —seeing they acknowledge that we have him as well without the Supper.

speak not of Papists, whose doctrine is more tolerable, or at least more modest; but some are so hurried away by contention as to say, that on account of the union of natures in Christ, wherever his divinity is, there his flesh, which cannot be separated from it, is also; as if that union formed a kind of medium of the two natures, making him to be neither God nor man. So held Eutyches, and after him Servetus. But it is clearly gathered from Scripture that the one person of Christ is composed of two natures, but so that each has its peculiar properties unimpaired. That Eutyches was justly condemned, they will not have the hardihood to deny. It is strange that they attend not to the cause of condemnation—viz. that destroying the distinction between the natures, and insisting only on the unity of person, he converted God into man and man into God.[1] What madness, then, is it to confound heaven with earth, sooner than not withdraw the body of Christ from its heavenly sanctuary? In regard to the passages which they adduce, "No man has ascended up to heaven, but he that came down from heaven, even the Son of man which is in heaven" (John iii. 13); "The only-begotten Son, who is in the bosom of the Father, he hath declared him" (John i. 18), they betray the same stupidity, scouting the communion of properties (*idiomatum*, κοινωνιαν), which not without reason was formerly invented by holy Fathers. Certainly when Paul says of the princes of this world that they "crucified the Lord of glory" (1 Cor. ii. 8), he means not that he suffered anything in his divinity, but that Christ, who was rejected and despised, and suffered in the flesh, was likewise God and the Lord of glory. In this way, both the Son of man was in heaven because he was also Christ; and he who, according to the flesh, dwelt as the Son of man on earth, was also God in heaven. For this reason, he is said to have descended from heaven in respect of his divinity, not that his divinity quitted heaven to conceal itself in the prison of the body, but because, although he filled all things, it yet resided in the humanity of Christ coporeally, that is, naturally, and in an ineffable manner. There is a trite distinction in the schools which I hesitate not to quote. Although the whole Christ is everywhere, yet everything which is in him is not eveywhere. I wish the Schoolmen had duly weighed the force of this sentence, as it would have obviated their absurd fiction of the corporeal presence of Christ. Therefore, while our whole Mediator is everywhere, he is always present with his people, and in the Supper exhibits his presence in a special manner; yet so, that while he is wholly present, not everything which is in him is present, because, as has been said, in his flesh he will remain in heaven till he come to judgment.

31. They are greatly mistaken in imagining that there is no presence of the flesh of Christ in the Supper, unless it be placed in the bread. They thus leave nothing for the secret operation of the Spirit, which

---

French, "Il faisoit Jesus Christ homme en tant qu'il est Dieu, et Dieu en tant qu'il est homme."—He made Jesus Christ man, in so far as he is God, and God in so far as he is man.

unites Christ himself to us. Christ does not seem to them to be present unless he descends to us, as if we did not equally gain his presence when he raises us to himself. The only question, therefore, is as to the mode, they placing Christ in the bread, while we deem it unlawful to draw him down from heaven. Which of the two is more correct, let the reader judge. Only have done with the calumny that Christ is withdrawn from his Supper if he lurk not under the covering of bread. For seeing this mystery is heavenly, there is no necessity to bring Christ on the earth that he may be connected with us.

32. Now, should any one ask me as to the mode, I will not be ashamed to confess that it is too high a mystery either for my mind to comprehend or my words to express; and to speak more plainly, I rather feel than understand it. The truth of God, therefore, in which I can safely rest, I here embrace without controversy. He declares that his flesh is the meat, his blood the drink, of my soul; I give my soul to him to be fed with such food. In his sacred Supper he bids me take, eat, and drink his body and blood under the symbols of bread and wine. I have no doubt that he will truly give and I receive. Only, I reject the absurdities which appear to be unworthy of the heavenly majesty of Christ, and are inconsistent with the reality of his human nature. Since they must also be repugnant to the word of God, which teaches both that Christ was received into the glory of the heavenly kingdom, so as to be exalted above all the circumstances of the world (Luke xxiv. 26), and no less carefully ascribes to him the properties belonging to a true human nature. This ought not to seem incredible or contradictory to reason (Iren. Lib. iv. cap. 34); because, as the whole kindgom of Christ is spiritual, so whatever he does in his Church is not to be tested by the wisdom of this world; or, to use the words of Augustine, "this mystery is performed by man like the others, but in a divine manner, and on earth, but in a heavenly manner." Such, I say, is the corporeal presence which the nature of the sacrament requires, and which we say is here displayed in such power and efficacy, that it not only gives our minds undoubted assurance of eternal life, but also secures the immortality of our flesh, since it is now quickened by his immortal flesh, and in a manner shines in his immortality. Those who are carried beyond this with their hyperboles, do nothing more by their extravagancies than obscure the plain and simple truth. If any one is not yet satisfied, I would have him here to consider with himself that we are speaking of the sacrament, every part of which ought to have reference to faith. Now by participation of the body, as we have explained, we nourish faith not less richly and abundantly than do those who drag Christ himself from heaven. Still I am free to confess that that mixture or transfusion of the flesh of Christ with our soul, which they teach, I repudiate, because it is enough for us that Christ, out of the substance of his flesh, breathes life into our souls, nay, diffuses his own life into us, though

the real flesh of Christ does not enter us.[1] I may add, that there can be no doubt that the analogy of faith by which Paul enjoins us to test every interpretation of Scripture, is clearly with us in this matter. Let those who oppose a truth so clear, consider to what standard of faith they conform themselves: "Ever spirit that confesseth not that Jesus Christ is come in the flesh is not of God" (1 John iv. 23 ; 2 John ver. 7). These men, though they disguise the fact, or perceive it not, rob him of his flesh.

33. The same view must be taken of communion, which, according to them, has no existence unless they swallow the flesh of Christ under the bread. But no slight insult is offered to the Spirit if we refuse to believe that it is by his incomprehensible agency that we communicate in the body and blood of Christ. Nay, if the nature of the mystery, as delivered to us, and known to the ancient Church for four hundred years, had been considered as it deserves, there was more than enough to satisfy us; the door would have been shut against many disgraceful errors. These have kindled up fearful dissensions, by which the Church, both anciently and in our own times, has been miserably vexed ; curious men insisting on an extravagant mode of presence to which Scripture gives no countenance. And for a matter thus foolishly and rashly devised they keep up a turmoil, as if the including of Christ under the bread were, so to speak, the beginning and end of piety. It was of primary importance to know how the body of Christ once delivered to us becomes ours, and how we become partakers of his shed blood, because this is to possess the whole of Christ crucified, so as to enjoy all his blessings. But overlooking these points, in which there was so much importance, nay, neglecting and almost suppressing them, they occupy themselves only with this one perplexing question, How is the body of Christ hidden under the bread, or under the appearance of bread ? They falsely pretend that all which we teach concerning spiritual eating is opposed to true and what they call real eating, since we have respect only to the mode of eating. This, according to them, is carnal, since they include Christ under the bread, but according to us is spiritual, inasmuch as the sacred agency of the Spirit is the bond of our union with Christ. Not better founded is the other objection, that we attend only to the fruit or effect which believers receive from eating the flesh of Christ. We formerly said, that Christ himself is the matter of the Supper, and that the effect follows from this, that by the sacrifice of his death our sins are expiated, by his blood we are washed, and by his resurrection we are raised to the hope of life in heaven. But a foolish imagination, of which Lombard was the author, perverts their minds, while they think that the sacrament is the eating of the flesh of Christ. His words are, " The sacrament and not the thing are the forms of bread and wine ; the sacrament and the thing are the flesh and blood of Christ ; the thing and not the sacrament is his mystical flesh" (Lombard,

---

[1] See Bernard in Cant. Serm. 74, 75 ; et Trad. de Gratia et Liber. Arbit.

Lib. iv. Dist. 8). Again a little after, "The thing signified and contained is the proper flesh of Christ; the thing signified and not contained is his mystical body." To his distinction between the flesh of Christ and the power of nourishing which it possesses, I assent; but his maintaining it to be a sacrament, and a sacrament contained under the bread, is an error not to be tolerated. Hence has arisen that false interpretation of sacramental eating, because it was imagined that even the wicked and profane, however much alienated from Christ, eat his body. But the very flesh of Christ in the mystery of the Supper is no less a spiritual matter than eternal salvation. Whence we infer, that all who are devoid of the Spirit of Christ can no more eat the flesh of Christ than drink wine that has no savour. Certainly Christ is shamefully lacerated, when his body, as lifeless and without any vigour, is prostituted to unbelievers. This is clearly repugnant to his words, " He that eateth my flesh, and drinketh my blood, dwelleth in me, and I in him" (John vi. 56). They object that he is not there speaking of sacramental eating; this I admit, provided they will not ever and anon stumble on this stone, that his flesh itself is eaten without any benefit. I should like to know how they confine it after they have eaten. Here, in my opinion, they will find no outlet. But they object, that the ingratitude of man cannot in any respect detract from, or interfere with, faith in the promises of God. I admit and hold that the power of the sacrament remains entire, however the wicked may labour with all their might to annihilate it. Still, it is one thing to be offered, another to be received. Christ gives this spiritual food and holds forth this spiritual drink to all. Some eat eagerly, others superciliously reject it. Will their rejection cause the meat and drink to lose their nature? They will say that this similitude supports their opinion—viz. that the flesh of Christ, though it be without taste, is still flesh. But I deny that it can be eaten without the taste of faith, or (if it is more agreeable to speak with Augustine), I deny that men carry away more from the sacrament than they collect in the vessel of faith. Thus nothing is detracted from the sacrament, nay, its reality and efficacy remain unimpaired, although the wicked, after externally partaking of it, go away empty. If, again, they object, that it derogates from the expression, " This is my body," if the wicked receive corruptible bread and nothing besides, it is easy to answer, that God wills not that his truth should be recognised in the mere reception, but in the constancy of his goodness, while he is prepared to perform, nay, liberally offers to the unworthy what they reject. The integrity of the sacrament, an integrity which the whole world cannot violate, lies here, that the flesh and blood of Christ are not less truly given to the unworthy than to the elect believers of God; and yet it is true, that just as the rain falling on the hard rock runs away because it cannot penetrate, so the wicked by their hardness repel the grace of God, and prevent it from reaching them. We may add, that it is no more possible to receive Christ without faith, than it is for seed to germinate in the fire. They ask how Christ can have come for the condemnation of some, unless they unworthily receive him; but this is absurd, since we nowhere read that they bring death upon themselves by receiving Christ unworthily, but by rejecting him. They are not aided by the parable in which Christ says, that the seed which fell among thorns sprung up, but was afterwards choked (Matth. xiii. 7), because he is there speaking of the effect of a temporary faith, a faith which those who place Judas in this respect on a footing with Peter, do not think necessary to the eating of the flesh and the drinking of the blood of Christ. Nay, their error is refuted by the same parable, when Christ says that some seed fell upon the wayside, and some on stony ground, and yet neither took root. Hence it follows that the hardness of believers is an obstacle which prevents Christ from reaching them. All who would have our salvation to be promoted by this sacrament, will find nothing more appropriate than to conduct believers to the fountain, that they may draw life from the Son of God. The dignity is amply enough commended when we hold, that it is a help by which we may be ingrafted into the body of Christ, or, already ingrafted, may be more and more united to him, until the union is completed in heaven. They object, that Paul could not have made them guilty of the body and blood of the Lord if they had not partaken of them (1 Cor. xi. 27); I answer, that they were not condemned for having eaten. but only for having profaned the ordinance by trampling under foot the pledge, which they ought to have reverently received, the pledge of sacred union with God.

34. Moreover, as among ancient writers, Augustine especially maintained [1] this head of doctrine, that the grace figured by the sacraments is not impaired or made void by the infidelity or malice of men, it will be useful to prove clearly from his words, how ignorantly and erroneously those who cast forth the body of Christ to be eaten by dogs, wrest them to their present purpose. Sacramental eating, according to them, is that by which the wicked receive the body and blood of Christ without the agency of the Spirit, or any gracious effect. Augustine, on the contrary, prudently pondering the expression, "Whoso eateth my flesh, and drinketh my blood, hath eternal life" (John vi. 54), says: "That is the virtue of the sacrament, and not merely the visible sacrament: the sacrament of him who eats inwardly, not of him who eats outwardly, or merely with the teeth" (Hom. in Joann. 26). Hence he at length concludes, that the sacrament of this thing, that is, of the unity of the body and blood of Christ in the Lord's Supper, is set before some for life, before others for destruction: while the matter itself, of which it is the sacrament, is to all for life, to none for destruction, whoever may have been the partaker. Lest any one should here cavil that by *thing* is not meant body, but the grace of the Spirit, which may be separated from it, he dissipates these mists by the antithetical epithets, Visible and Invisible. For the body of Christ cannot be

[1] See August. Cont. Liter. Petiliani, Lib. ii. c. 47, et Tract. in Joann.

included under the former. Hence it follows, that unbelievers communicate only in the visible symbol; and the better to remove all doubt, after saying that this bread requires an appetite in the inner man, he adds (Hom. in Joann. 59), "Moses, and Aaron, and Phinehas, and many others who ate manna, pleased God. Why? Because the visible food they understood spiritually, hungered for spiritually, tasted spiritually, and feasted on spiritually. We, too, in the present day, have received visible food: but the sacrament is one thing, the virtue of the sacrament is another." A little after, he says: "And hence, he who remains not in Christ, and in whom Christ remains not, without doubt neither spiritually eats his flesh, nor drinks his blood, though with his teeth he may carnally and visibly press the symbol of his body and blood." Again, we are told that the visible sign is opposed to spiritual eating. This refutes the error that the invisible body of Christ is sacramentally eaten in reality, although not spiritually. We are told, also, that nothing is given to the impure and profane beyond the visible taking of the sign. Hence his celebrated saying, that the other disciples ate *bread which was the Lord*, whereas Judas ate *the bread of the Lord* (Hom. in Joann. 62). By this, he clearly excludes unbelievers from participation in his body and blood. He has no other meaning when he says, "Why do you wonder that the bread of Christ was given to Judas, though he consigned him to the devil, when you see, on the contrary, that a messenger of the devil was given to Paul to perfect him in Christ?" (August. de Bapt. Cont. Donat. Lib. v.). He indeed says elsewhere, that the bread of the Supper was the body of Christ to those to whom Paul said, "He that eateth and drinketh unworthily, eateth and drinketh damnation to himself; and that it does not follow that they received nothing because they received unworthily." But in what sense he says this, he explains more fully in another passage (De Civit. Dei, Lib. xxi. c. 25). For undertaking professedly to explain how the wicked and profane, who, with the mouth, profess the faith of Christ, but in act deny him, eat the body of Christ; and, indeed, refuting the opinion of some who thought that they ate not only sacramentally, but really, he says: "Neither can they be said to eat the body of Christ, because they are not to be accounted among the members of Christ. For, not to mention other reasons, they cannot be at the same time the members of Christ and the members of a harlot. In fine, when Christ himself says, 'He that eateth my flesh, and drinketh my blood, dwelleth in me, and I in him' (John vi. 56), he shows what it is to eat the body of Christ, not sacramentally, but in reality. It is to abide in Christ, that Christ may abide in him. For it is just as if he had said, Let not him who abides not in me, and in whom I abide not, say or think that he eats my body or drinks my blood." Let the reader attend to the antithesis between eating sacramentally and eating really, and there will be no doubt. The same thing he confirms not less clearly in these words: "Prepare not the jaws, but the heart; for which alone the Supper is appointed. We believe in Christ when we receive him in faith: in receiving, we know what we think: we receive a small portion, but our heart is filled: it is not therefore that which is seen, but that which is believed, that feeds (August. Cont. Faust. Lib. xiii. c. 16). Here, also, he restricts what the wicked take to be the visible sign, and shows that the only way of receiving Christ is by faith. So, also, in another passage, declaring distinctly that the good and the bad communicate by signs, he excludes the latter from the true eating of the flesh of Christ. For had they received the reality, he would not have been altogether silent as to a matter which was pertinent to the case. In another passage, speaking of eating, and the fruit of it, he thus concludes: "Then will the body and blood of Christ be life to each, if that which is visibly taken in the sacrament is in reality spiritually eaten, spiritually drunk" (De Verb. Apost. Serm. ii.) Let those, therefore, who make unbelievers partakers of the flesh and blood of Christ, if they would agree with Augustine, set before us the visible body of Christ, since, according to him, the whole truth is spiritual. And certainly his words imply that sacramental eating, when unbelief excludes the entrance of the reality, is only equivalent to visible or external eating. But if the body of Christ may be truly and yet not spiritually eaten, what could he mean when he elsewhere says: "Ye are not to eat this body which you see, nor to drink the blood which will be shed by those who are to crucify me? I have committed a certain sacrament to you: it is the spiritual meaning which will give you life" (August. in Ps. xcviii.). He certainly meant not to deny that the body offered in the Supper is the same as that which Christ offered in sacrifice; but he adverted to the mode of eating—viz. that the body, though received into the celestial glory, breathes life into us by the secret energy of the Spirit. I admit, indeed, that he often uses the expression, "that the body of Christ is eaten by unbelievers;" but he explains himself by adding, "in the sacrament." And he elsewhere speaks of a spiritual eating, in which our teeth do not chew grace (Hom. in Joann. 27). And, lest my opponents should say that I am trying to overwhelm them with the mass of my quotations, I would ask how they get over this one sentence: "In the elect alone, the sacraments effect what they figure." Certainly they will not venture to deny, that by the bread in the Supper, the body of Christ is figured. Hence it follows, that the reprobate are not allowed to partake of it. That Cyril did not think differently is clear from these words: "As one in pouring melted wax on melted wax mixes the whole together, so it is necessary, when one receives the body and blood of the Lord, to be conjoined with him, that Christ may be found in him, and he in Christ." From these words, I think it plain that there is no true and real eating by those who only eat the body of Christ sacramentally, seeing the body cannot be separated from its virtue, and that the promises of God do not fail, though, while he ceases not to rain from heaven, rocks and stones are not penetrated by the moisture.

35. This consideration will easily dissuade us from that carnal adoration which some men, have, with perverse temerity, introduced into the sacrament, reasoning thus with themselves : If it is body, then it is also soul and divinity which go along with the body, and cannot be separated from it ; and, therefore, Christ must there be adored. First, if we deny their pretended concomitance, what will they do ? For, as they chiefly insist on the absurdity of separating the body of Christ from his soul and divinity, what sane and sober man can persuade himself that the body of Christ is Christ ? They think that they completely establish this by their syllogisms. But since Christ speaks separately of his body and blood, without describing the mode of his presence, how can they in a doubtful matter arrive at the certainty which they wish ? What then ? Should their consciences be at any time exercised with some more grievous apprehension, will they forthwith set them free, and dissolve the apprehensions by their syllogisms ? In other words, when they see that no certainty is to be obtained from the word of God, in which alone our minds can rest, and without which they go astray the very first moment when they begin to reason, when they see themselves opposed by the doctrine and practice of the apostles, and that they are supported by no authority but their own, how will they feel ? To such feelings other sharp stings will be added. What ? Was it a matter of little moment to worship God under this form without any express injunction ? In a matter relating to the true worship of God, were we thus lightly to act without one word of Scripture ? Had all their thoughts been kept in due subjection to the word of God, they certainly would have listened to what he himself has said, " Take, eat, and drink," and obeyed the command by which he enjoins us to receive the sacrament, not worship it. Those who receive, without adoration, as commanded by God, are secure that they deviate not from the command. In commencing any work, nothing is better than this security. They have the example of the apostles, of whom we read not that they prostrated themselves and worshipped, but that they sat down, took and ate. They have the practice of the apostolic Church, where, as Luke relates, believers communicated not in adoration, but in the breaking of bread (Acts ii. 42). They have the doctrine of the apostles as taught to the Corinthian Church by Paul, who declares that what he delivered he had received of the Lord (1 Cor. xi. 23).

36. The object of these remarks is to lead pious readers to reflect how dangerous it is in matters of such difficulty to wander from the simple word of God to the dreams of our own brain. What has been said above should free us from all scruple in this matter. That the pious soul may duly apprehend Christ in the sacrament, it must rise to heaven. But if the office of the sacrament is to aid the infirmity of the human mind, assisting it in rising upwards, so as to perceive the height of spiritual mysteries, those who stop short at the

external sign stray from the right path of seeking Christ. What then? Can we deny that the worship is superstitious when men prostrate themselves before bread that they may therein worship Christ? The Council of Nice undoubtedly intended to meet this evil when it forbade us to give humble heed to the visible signs. And for no other reason was it formerly the custom, previous to consecration, to call aloud upon the people to raise their hearts, *sursum corda.* Scripture itself, also, besides carefully narrating the ascension of Christ, by which he withdrew his bodily presence from our eye and company, that it might make us abandon all carnal thoughts of him, whenever it makes mention of him, enjoins us to raise our minds upwards and seek him in heaven, seated at the right hand of the Father (Col. iii. 2). According to this rule, we should rather have adored him spiritually in the heavenly glory, than devised that perilous species of adoration replete with gross and carnal ideas of God. Those, therefore, who devised the adoration of the sacrament, not only dreamed it of themselves, without any authority from Scripture, where no mention of it can be shown (it would not have been omitted, had it been agreeable to God); but, disregarding Scripture, forsook the living God, and fabricated a god for themselves, after the lust of their own hearts. For what is idolatry if it is not to worship the gifts instead of the giver? Here the sin is twofold. The honour robbed from God is transferred to the creature, and God, moreover, is dishonoured by the pollution and profanation of his own goodness, while his holy sacrament is converted into an execrable idol. Let us, on the contrary, that we may not fall into the same pit, wholly confine our eyes, ears, hearts, minds, and tongues, to the sacred doctrine of God. For this is the school of the Holy Spirit, that best of masters, in which such progress is made, that while nothing is to be acquired anywhere else, we must willingly be ignorant of whatever is not there taught.

37. Then, as superstition, when once it has passed the proper bounds, has no end to its errors, men went much farther; for they devised rites altogether alien from the institution of the Supper, and to such a degree that they paid divine honours to the sign. They say that their veneration is paid to Christ. First, if this were done in the Supper, I would say that that adoration only is legitimate which stops not at the sign, but rises to Christ sitting in heaven. Now, under what pretext do they say that they honour Christ in that bread, when they have no promise of this nature? They consecrate the host, as they call it, and carry it about in solemn show, and formally exhibit it to be admired, reverenced, and invoked. I ask by what virtue they think it duly consecrated? They will quote the words, "This is my body." I, on the contrary, will object, that it was at the same time said, "Take, eat." Nor will I count the other passage as nothing; for I hold that since the promise is annexed to the command, the former is so included under the latter, that it cannot possibly be separated from it. This will be made clearer by

an example. God gave a command when he said, "Call upon me," and added a promise, "I will deliver thee" (Psal. l. 15). Should any one invoke Peter or Paul, and found on this promise, will not all exclaim that he does it in error? And what else, pray, do those do who, disregarding the command to eat, fasten on the mutilated promise, "This is my body," that they may pervert it to rites alien from the institution of Christ? Let us remember, therefore, that this promise has been given to those who observe the command connected with it, and that those who transfer the sacrament to another end, have no countenance from the word of God. We formerly showed how the mystery of the sacred Supper contributes to our faith in God. But since the Lord not only reminds us of this great gift of his goodness, as we formerly explained, but passes it, as it were, from hand to hand, and urges us to recognise it, he, at the same time, admonishes us not to be ungrateful for the kindness thus bestowed, but rather to proclaim it with such praise as is meet, and celebrate it with thanksgiving. Accordingly, when he delivered the institution of the sacrament to the apostles, he taught them to do it in remembrance of him, which Paul interprets, "to show forth his death" (1 Cor. xi. 26). And this is, that all should publicly and with one mouth confess that all our confidence of life and salvation is placed in our Lord's death, that we ourselves may glorify him by our confession, and by our example excite others also to give him glory. Here, again, we see what the aim of the sacrament is—namely, to keep us in remembrance of Christ's death. When we are ordered to show forth the Lord's death till he come again, all that is meant is, that we should, with confession of the mouth, proclaim what our faith has recognised in the sacrament—viz. that the death of Christ is our life. This is the second use of the sacrament, and relates to outward confession.

38. Thirdly, The Lord intended it to be a kind of exhortation, than which no other could urge or animate us more strongly, both to purity and holiness of life, and also to charity, peace, and concord. For the Lord there communicates his body so that he may become altogether one with us, and we with him. Moreover, since he has only one body of which he makes us all to be partakers, we must necessarily, by this participation, all become one body. This unity is represented by the bread which is exhibited in the sacrament. As it is composed of many grains, so mingled together, that one cannot be distinguished from another; so ought our minds to be so cordially united, as not to allow of any dissension or division. This I prefer giving in the words of Paul: "The cup of blessing which we bless, is it not the communion of the blood of Christ? The bread which we break, is it not the communion of the body of Christ? For we being many, are one bread and one body, for we are all partakers of that one bread" (1 Cor. x. 15, 16). We shall have profited admirably in the sacrament, if the thought shall have been impressed and engraven on our minds, that none of our brethren is hurt, despised,

rejected, injured, or in any way offended, without our, at the same time, hurting, despising, and injuring Christ; that we cannot have dissension with our brethren, without at the same time dissenting from Christ; that we cannot love Christ without loving our brethren; that the same care we take of our own body we ought to take of that of our brethren, who are members of our body; that as no part of our body suffers pain without extending to the other parts, so every evil which our brother suffers ought to excite our compassion. Wherefore Augustine not inappropriately often terms this sacrament *the bond of charity*. What stronger stimulus could be employed to excite mutual charity, than when Christ, presenting himself to us, not only invites us by his example to give and devote ourselves mutually to each other, but inasmuch as he makes himself common to all, also makes us all to be one in him.

39. This most admirably confirms what I elsewhere said—viz. that there cannot be a right administration of the Supper without the word. Any utility which we derive from the Supper requires the word. Whether we are to be confirmed in faith, or exercised in confession, or aroused to duty, there is need of preaching. Nothing, therefore, can be more preposterous than to convert the Supper into a dumb action. This is done under the tyranny of the Pope, the whole effect of consecration being made to depend on the intention of the priest, as if it in no way concerned the people, to whom especially the mystery ought to have been explained. This error has originated from not observing that those promises by which consecration is effected are intended, not for the elements themselves, but for those who receive them. Christ does not address the bread and tell it to become his body, but bids his disciples eat, and promises them the communion of his body and blood. And, according to the arrangement which Paul makes, the promises are to be offered to believers along with the bread and the cup. Thus, indeed, it is. We are not to imagine some magical incantation, and think it sufficient to mutter the words, as if they were heard by the elements; but we are to regard those words as a living sermon, which is to edify the hearers, penetrate their minds, being impressed and seated in their hearts, and exert its efficacy in the fulfilment of that which it promises. For these reasons, it is clear that the setting apart of the sacrament, as some insist, that an extraordinary distribution of it may be made to the sick, is useless. They will either receive it without hearing the words of the institution read, or the minister will conjoin the true explanation of the mystery with the sign. In the silent dispensation, there is abuse and defect. If the promises are narrated, and the mystery is expounded, that those who are to receive may receive with advantage, it cannot be doubted that this is the true consecration. What then becomes of that other consecration, the effect of which reaches even to the sick? But those who do so have the example of the early Church. I confess it; but in so important

a matter, where error is so dangerous, nothing is safer than to follow the truth.

40. Moreover, as we see that this sacred bread of the Lord's Supper is spiritual food, is sweet and savoury, not less than salutary, to the pious worshippers of God, on tasting which they feel that Christ is their life, are disposed to give thanks, and exhorted to mutual love; so, on the other hand, it is converted into the most noxious poison to all whom it does not nourish and confirm in the faith, nor urge to thanksgiving and charity. For, just as corporeal food, when received into a stomach subject to morbid humours, becomes itself vitiated and corrupted, and rather hurts than nourishes, so this spiritual food also, if given to a soul polluted with malice and wickedness, plunges it into greater ruin, not indeed by any defect in the food, but because to the "defiled and unbelieving is nothing pure" (Titus i. 15), however much it may be sanctified by the blessing of the Lord. For, as Paul says, "Whosoever shall eat this bread, and drink this cup of the Lord, unworthily, shall be guilty of the body and blood of the Lord;" "eateth and drinketh damnation to himself, not discerning the Lord's body" (1 Cor. xi. 27, 29). For men of this description, who without any spark of faith, without any zeal for charity, rush forward like swine to seize the Lord's Supper, do not at all discern the Lord's body. For, inasmuch as they do not believe that body to be their life, they put every possible affront upon it, stripping it of all its dignity, and profane and contaminate it by so receiving; inasmuch as while alienated and estranged from their brethren, they dare to mingle the sacred symbol of Christ's body with their dissensions. No thanks to them if the body of Christ is not rent and torn to pieces. Wherefore they are justly held guilty of the body and blood of the Lord, which, with sacrilegious impiety, they so vilely pollute. By this unworthy eating, they bring judgment on themselves. For while they have no faith in Christ, yet, by receiving the sacrament, they profess to place their salvation only in him, and abjure all other confidence. Wherefore they themselves are their own accusers; they bear witness against themselves; they seal their own condemnation. Next being divided and separated by hatred and ill-will from their brethren, that is, from the members of Christ, they have no part in Christ, and yet they declare that the only safety is to communicate with Christ, and be united to him. For this reason Paul commands a man to examine himself before he eats of that bread, and drinks of that cup (1 Cor. xi. 28). By this, as I understand, he means that each individual should descend into himself, and consider, first, whether, with inward confidence of heart, he leans on the salvation obtained by Christ, and with confession of the mouth, acknowledges it; and, secondly, whether with zeal for purity and holiness he aspires to imitate Christ; whether, after his example, he is prepared to give himself to his brethren, and to hold himself in common with those with whom he has Christ in common; whether, as he himself is

regarded by Christ, he in his turn regards all his brethren as members of his body, or, like his members, desires to cherish, defend, and assist them, not that the duties of faith and charity can now be perfected in us, but because it behoves us to contend and seek, with all our heart, daily to increase our faith.

41. In seeking to prepare for eating worthily, men have often dreadfully harassed and tortured miserable consciences, and yet have in no degree attained the end. They have said that those *eat worthily* who are in a state of grace. *Being in a state of grace*, they have interpreted to be pure and free from all sin. By this definition, all the men that ever have been, and are upon the earth, were debarred from the use of this sacrament. For if we are to seek our worthiness from ourselves, it is all over with us ; only despair and fatal ruin await us. Though we struggle to the utmost, we will not only make no progress, but then be most unworthy after we have laboured most to make ourselves worthy. To cure this ulcer, they have devised a mode of procuring worthiness—viz. after having, as far as we can, made an examination, and taken an account of all our actions, to expiate our unworthiness by contrition, confession, and satisfaction. Of the nature of this expiation we have spoken at the proper place (Book III. chap. iv. sec. 2, 17, 27). As far as regards our present object, I say that such things give poor and evanescent comfort to alarmed and downcast consciences, struck with terror at their sins. For if the Lord, by his prohibition, admits none to partake of his Supper but the righteous and innocent, every man would require to be cautious before feeling secure of that righteousness of his own which he is told that God requires. But how are we to be assured that those who have done what in them lay have discharged their duty to God ? Even were we assured of this, who would venture to assure himself that he had done what in him lay ? Thus there being no certain security for our worthiness, access to the Supper would always be excluded by the fearful interdict, " He that eateth and drinketh unworthily, eateth and drinketh damnation to himself."

42. It is now easy to judge what is the nature, and who is the author, of that doctrine which prevails in the Papacy, and which, by its inhuman austerity, deprives and robs wretched sinners, oppressed with sorrow and trembling, of the consolation of this sacrament, a sacrament in which all that is delightful in the gospel was set before them. Certainly the devil could have no shorter method of destroying men than by thus infatuating them, and so excluding them from the taste and savour of this food with which their most merciful Father in heaven had been pleased to feed them. Therefore, lest we should rush over such a precipice, let us remember that this sacred feast is medicine to the sick, comfort to the sinner, and bounty to the poor ; while to the healthy, the righteous, and the rich, if any such could be found, it would be of no value. For while Christ is therein given us for food, we perceive that without him we fail, pine,

and waste away, just as hunger destroys the vigour of the body. Next, as he is given for life, we perceive that without him we are certainly dead. Wherefore, the best and only worthiness which we can bring to God, is to offer him our own vileness, and, if I may so speak, unworthiness, that his mercy may make us worthy ; to despond in ourselves, that we may be consoled in him ; to humble ourselves, that we may be elevated by him ; to accuse ourselves, that we may be justified by him ; to aspire, moreover, to the unity which he recommends in the Supper ; and, as he makes us all one in himself, to desire to have all one soul, one heart, one tongue. If we ponder and meditate on these things, we may be shaken, but will never be overwhelmed by such considerations as these, how shall we, who are devoid of all good, polluted by the defilements of sin, and half dead, worthily eat the body of the Lord ? We shall rather consider that we, who are poor, are coming to a benevolent giver, sick to a physician, sinful to the author of righteousness, in fine, dead to him who gives life ; that worthiness which is commanded by God, consists especially in faith, which places all things in Christ, nothing in ourselves, and in charity, charity which, though imperfect, it may be sufficient to offer to God, that he may increase it, since it cannot be fully rendered. Some, concurring with us in holding that worthiness consists in faith and charity, have widely erred in regard to the measure of worthiness, demanding a perfection of faith to which nothing can be added, and a charity equivalent to that which Christ manifested towards us. And in this way, just as the other class, they debar all men from access to this sacred feast. For, were their view well founded, every one who receives must receive unworthily, since all, without exception, are guilty, and chargeable with imperfection. And certainly it were too stupid, not to say idiotical, to require to the receiving of the sacrament a perfection which would render the sacrament vain and superfluous, because it was not instituted for the perfect, but for the infirm and weak, to stir up, excite, stimulate, exercise the feeling of faith and charity, and at the same time correct the deficiency of both.

43. In regard to the external form of the ordinance, whether or not believers are to take into their hands and divide among themselves, or each is to eat what is given to him : whether they are to return the cup to the deacon or hand it to their neighbour ; whether the bread is to be leavened or unleavened, and the wine to be red or white, is of no consequence. These things are indifferent, and left free to the Church, though it is certain that it was the custom of the ancient Church for all to receive into their hand. And Christ said, " Take this, and divide it among yourselves" (Luke xxii. 17). History relates that leavened and ordinary bread was used before the time of Alexander the Bishop of Rome, who was the first that was delighted with unleavened bread : for what reason I see not, unless it was to draw the wondering eyes of the populace by the novelty of the spectacle, more than to train them in sound religion.

I appeal to all who have the least zeal for piety, whether they do not evidently perceive both how much more brightly the glory of God is here displayed, and how much more abundant spiritual consolation is felt by believers than in these rigid and histrionic follies, which have no other use than to impose on the gazing populace. They call it restraining the people by religion, when, stupid and infatuated, they are drawn hither and thither by superstition. Should any one choose to defend such inventions by antiquity, I am not unaware how ancient is the use of chrism and exorcism in baptism, and how, not long after the age of the apostles, the Supper was tainted with adulteration; such, indeed, is the forwardness of human confidence, which cannot restrain itself, but is always sporting and wantoning in the mysteries of God. But let us remember that God sets so much value on obedience to his word, that, by it, he would have us to judge his angels and the whole world. All this mass of ceremonies being abandoned, the sacrament might be celebrated in the most becoming manner, if it were dispensed to the Church very frequently, at least once a-week. The commencement should be with public prayer; next, a sermon should be delivered : then the minister, having placed bread and wine on the table, should read the institution of the Supper. He should next explain the promises which are therein given ; and, at the same time, keep back from communion all those who are debarred by the prohibition of the Lord. He should afterwards pray that the Lord, with the kindness with which he has bestowed this sacred food upon us, would also form and instruct us to receive it with faith and gratitude ; and, as we are of ourselves unworthy, would make us worthy of the feast by his mercy. Here, either a psalm should be sung, or something read, while the faithful, in order, communicate at the sacred feast, the minister breaking the bread, and giving it to the people. The Supper being ended, an exhortation should be given to sincere faith, and confession of faith, to charity, and lives becoming Christians. Lastly, thanks should be offered, and the praises of God should be sung. This being done, the Church should be dismissed in peace.

44. What we have hitherto said of the sacrament, abundantly shows that it was not instituted to be received once a-year and that perfunctorily (as is now commonly the custom) ; but that all Christians might have it in frequent use, and frequently call to mind the sufferings of Christ, thereby sustaining and confirming their faith : stirring themselves up to sing the praises of God, and proclaim his goodness ; cherishing and testifying towards each other that mutual charity, the bond of which they see in the unity of the body of Christ. As often as we communicate in the symbol of our Saviour's body, as if a pledge were given and received, we mutually bind ourselves to all the offices of love, that none of us may do anything to offend his brother, or omit anything by which he can assist him when necessity demands, and opportunity occurs. That such was the practice of the Apostolic Church, we are informed by Luke in the Acts, when he says, that

"they continued stedfastly in the apostles' doctrine and fellowship, and in breaking of bread, and in prayers" (Acts ii. 42). Thus we ought always to provide that no meeting of the Church is held without the word, prayer, the dispensation of the Supper, and alms. We may gather from Paul that this was the order observed by the Corinthians, and it is certain that this was the practice many ages after. Hence, by the ancient canons, which are attributed to Anacletus and Calixtus, after the consecration was made, all were to communicate who did not wish to be without the pale of the Church. And in those ancient canons, which bear the name of Apostolical, it is said that those who continue not to the end, and partake not of the sacred communion, are to be corrected, as causing disquiet to the Church. In the Council of Antioch it was decreed, that those who enter the Church, hear the Scriptures, and abstain from communion, are to be removed from the Church until they amend their fault. And although, in the first Council of Tholouse, this was mitigated, or at least stated in milder terms, yet there also it was decreed, that those who, after hearing the sermon, never communicated, were to be admonished, and if they still abstained after admonition, were to be excluded.

45. By these enactments, holy men wished to retain and ensure the use of frequent communion, as handed down by the apostles themselves; and which, while it was most salutary to believers, they saw gradually falling into desuetude by the negligence of the people. Of his own age, Augustine testifies: "The sacrament of the unity of our Lord's body is, in some places, provided daily, and in others at certain intervals, at the Lord's table; and at that table some partake to life, and others to destruction" (August. Tract. 26, in Joann. 6). And in the first Epistle to Januarius he says: "Some communicate daily in the body and blood of the Lord; others receive it on certain days: in some places, not a day intervenes on which it is not offered: in others, it is offered only on the Sabbath and the Lord's day: in others, on the Lord's day only." But since, as we have said, the people were sometimes remiss, holy men urged them with severe rebukes, that they might not seem to connive at their sluggishness. Of this we have an example in Chrysostom, on the Epistle to the Ephesians (Hom. 26). "It was not said to him who dishonoured the feast, Why have you not taken your seat? 'But how camest thou in?' (Matth. xxii. 12). Whoever partakes not of the sacred rites is wicked and impudent in being present: should any one who was invited to a feast come in, wash his hands, take his seat, and seem to prepare to eat, and thereafter taste nothing, would he not, I ask, insult both the feast and the entertainer? So you, standing among those who prepare themselves by prayer to take the sacred food, profess to be one of the number by the mere fact of your not going away, and yet you do not partake,—would it not have been better not to have made your appearance? I am unworthy, you say. Then neither were you worthy of the communion of prayer, which is the preparation for taking the sacred mystery."

46. Most assuredly, the custom which prescribes communion once a-year is an invention of the devil, by what instrumentality soever it may have been introduced. They say that Zephyrinus was the author of the decree, though it is not possible to believe that it was the same as we now have it. It may be, that as times then were, he did not, by his ordinance, consult ill for the Church. For there cannot be a doubt that at that time the sacred Supper was dispensed to the faithful at every meeting; nor can it be doubted that a great part of them communicated. But as it scarcely ever happened that all could communicate at the same time, and it was necessary that those who were mingled with the profane and idolaters, should testify their faith by some external symbol, this holy man, with a view to order and government, had appointed that day, that on it the whole of Christendom might give a confession of their faith by partaking of the Lord's Supper. The ordinance of Zephyrinus, which was otherwise good, posterity perverted, when they made a fixed law of one communion in the year. The consequence is, that almost all, when they have once communicated, as if they were discharged as to all the rest of the year, sleep on secure. It ought to have been far otherwise. Each week, at least, the table of the Lord ought to have been spread for the company of Christians, and the promises declared on which we might then spiritually feed. No one, indeed, ought to be forced, but all ought to be exhorted and stimulated; the torpor of the sluggish, also, ought to be rebuked, that all, like persons famishing, should come to the feast. It was not without cause, therefore, I complained, at the outset, that this practice had been introduced by the wile of the devil; a practice which, in prescribing one day in the year, makes the whole year one of sloth. We see, indeed, that this perverse abuse had already crept in in the time of Chrysostom; but we, also, at the same time, see how much it displeased him. For he complains in bitter terms, in the passage which I lately quoted, that there is so great an inequality in this matter, that they did not approach often, at other times of the year, even when prepared, but only at Easter, though unprepared. Then he exclaims: "O custom! O presumption! In vain, then, is the daily oblation made: in vain do we stand at the altar. There is none who partakes along with us." So far is he from having approved the practice by interposing his authority to it.

47. From the same forge proceeded another constitution, which snatched or robbed a half of the Supper from the greater part of the people of God—namely, the symbol of blood, which, interdicted to laics and profane (such are the titles which they give to God's heritage), became the peculiar possession of a few shaven and anointed individuals. The edict of the eternal God is, that all are to drink. This an upstart dares to antiquate and abrogate by a new and contrary law, proclaiming that all are not to drink. And that such legislators may not seem to fight against their God without any ground, they make a pretext of the dangers which might happen if

the sacred cup were given indiscriminately to all : as if these had not been observed and provided for by the eternal wisdom of God. Then they reason acutely, forsooth, that the one is sufficient for the two.   For if the body is, as they say, the whole Christ, who cannot be separated from his body, then the blood includes the body by concomitance.   Here we see how far our sense accords with God, when to any extent whatever it begins to rage and wanton with loosened reins.   The Lord, pointing to the bread, says, " This is my body." Then pointing to the cup, he calls it his blood.   The audacity of human reason objects and says, The bread is .the blood, the wine is the body, as if the Lord had without reason distinguished his body from his blood, both by words and signs ; and it had ever been heard that the body of Christ or the blood is called God and man. Certainly, if he had meant to designate himself wholly, he might have said, It is I, according to the Scriptural mode of expression, and not, " This is my body," " This is my blood."   But wishing to succour the weakness of our faith, he placed the cup apart from the bread, to show that he suffices not less for drink than for food.   Now, if one part be taken away, we can only find the half of the elements in what remains.   Therefore, though it were true, as they pretend, that the blood is in the bread, and, on the other hand, the body in the cup, by concomitance, yet they deprive the pious of that confirmation of faith which Christ delivered as necessary.   Bidding adieu, therefore, to their subtleties, let us retain the advantage which, by the ordinance of Christ, is obtained by a double pledge.

48. I am aware, indeed, how the ministers of Satan, whose usual practice is to hold the Scriptures in derision, here cavil.[1]   First, they allege that from a simple fact we are not to draw a rule which is to be perpetually obligatory on the Church.   But they state an untruth when they call it a simple fact.   For Christ not only gave the cup, but appointed that the apostles should do so in future.   For his words contain the command, " Drink ye all of it."   And Paul relates, that it was so done, and recommends it as a fixed institution.   Another subterfuge is, that the apostles alone were admitted by Christ to partake of this sacred Supper, because he had already selected and chosen them to the priesthood.   I wish they would answer the five following questions, which they cannot evade, and which easily refute them and their lies.   First, By what oracle was this solution so much at variance with the word of God revealed to them ?   Scripture mentions twelve who sat down with Jesus, but it does not so derogate from the dignity of Christ as to call them priests.   Of this appellation we shall afterwards speak in its own place.   Although he then gave to twelve, he commanded them to " do this ;" in other words, to distribute thus among themselves.   Secondly, Why during that purer age, from the days of the apostles downward for· a thousand years, did all, without exception, partake of both symbols ?

1 See Calvin de Cœna Domini.   Item, Adv. Theol. Paris.   Item, Vera Eccles. Reform. Ratio.

Did the primitive Church not know who the guests were whom Christ would have admitted to his Supper? It were the most shameless impudence to carp and quibble here. We have extant ecclesiastical histories, we have the writings of the Fathers, which furnish clear proofs of this fact. "The flesh," says Tertullian, "feeds on the body and blood of Christ, that the soul may be satiated by God" (Tertull. de Resurr. Carnis.). "How," says Ambrose to Theodosius, "will you receive the sacred body of the Lord with such hands? how will you have the boldness to put the cup of precious blood to your lips?" Jerome speaks of "the priests who perform the Eucharist and distribute the Lord's blood to the people" (Hieron. in Malach. cap. 2). Chrysostom says, "Not as under the ancient law the priest ate a part and the people a part, but one body and one cup is set before all. All the things which belong to the Eucharist are common to the priest and the people" (Chrysost. in Cor. cap. 8, Hom. 18). The same thing is attested by Augustine in numerous passages.

49. But why dispute about a fact which is perfectly notorious? Look at all Greek and Latin writers. Passages of the same kind everywhere occur. Nor did this practice fall into desuetude so long as there was one particle of integrity in the Church. Gregory, whom you may with justice call the last Bishop of Rome, says that it was observed in his age. "What the blood of the Lamb is you have learned, not by hearing, but by drinking it. His blood is poured into the mouths of the faithful." Nay, four hundred years after his death, when all things had degenerated, the practice still remained. Nor was it regarded as the custom merely, but as an inviolable law. Reverence for the divine institution was then maintained, and they had no doubt of its being sacrilege to separate what the Lord had joined. For Gelasius thus speaks : "We find that some taking only a portion of the sacred body, abstain from the cup. Undoubtedly let those persons, as they seem entangled by some strange superstition, either receive the whole sacrament, or be debarred from the whole. For the division of this mystery is not made without great sacrilege" (De Consec. Dist. 2). Reasons were given by Cyprian, which surely ought to weigh with Christian minds. "How," says he, "do we teach or incite them to shed their blood in confessing Christ, if we deny his blood to those who are to serve ; or how do we make them fit for the cup of martyrdom, if we do not previously admit them by right of communion in the Church, to drink the cup of the Lord?" (Cyprian, Serm. 5, de Lapsis). The attempt of the Canonists to restrict the decree of Gelasius to priests is a cavil too puerile to deserve refutation.

50. Thirdly, Why did our Saviour say of the bread simply, "Take, eat," and of the cup, "drink ye all of it ;" as if he had purposely intended to provide against the wile of Satan? Fourthly, If, as they will have it, the Lord honoured priests only with his Supper, what man would ever have dared to call strangers, whom the Lord had ex-

cluded, to partake of it, and to partake of a gift which he had not in his power, without any command from him who alone could give it? Nay, what presumption do they show in the present day in distributing the symbol of Christ's body to the common people, if they have no command or example from the Lord? Fifthly, Did Paul lie when he said to the Corinthians, "I have received of the Lord that which also I delivered unto you?" (1 Cor. xi. 23). The thing delivered, he afterwards declares to be, that all should communicate promiscuously in both symbols. But if Paul received of the Lord that all were to be admitted without distinction, let those who drive away almost the whole people of God see from whom they have received, since they cannot now pretend to have their authority from God, with whom there is not "yea and nay" (2 Cor. i. 19, 20). And yet these abominations they dare to cloak with the name of the Church, and defend under this pretence, as if those Antichrists were the Church who so licentiously trample under foot, waste, and abrogate the doctrine and institutions of Christ, or as if the Apostolic Church, in which religion flourished in full vigour, were not the Church.

CHAPTER XVIII.[1]

OF THE POPISH MASS. HOW IT NOT ONLY PROFANES, BUT
ANNIHILATES THE LORD'S SUPPER.

The principal heads of this chapter are,—I. The abomination of the Mass, sec. 1.
Its manifold impiety included under five heads, sec. 2–7. Its origin described, sec.
8, 9. II. Of the name of sacrifice which the ancients gave to the holy Supper, sec.
10–12. An apposite discussion on sacrifice, refuting the arguments of the Papists for
the sacrifice of the Mass, sec. 13–18. III. A summary of the doctrine of the Christian
Church respecting sacraments, paving the way for the subsequent discussion of the
five sacraments, falsely so called, sec. 19, 20.

Sections.

[1] Vid. Calv. Ep. de Fugiend. Illic. Sacris. Item, De Sacerdotiis Eccles. Papal.
Item, De Necessitate Reform. Eccles. Item, Epist. ad Sadoletum.

1. By these and similar inventions, Satan has attempted to adulterate and envelop the sacred Supper of Christ as with thick darkness, that its purity might not be preserved in the Church. But the head of this horrid abomination was, when he raised a sign by which it was not only obscured and perverted, but altogether obliterated and abolished, vanished away and disappeared from the memory of man—namely, when, with most pestilential error, he blinded almost the whole world into the belief that the Mass was a sacrifice and oblation for obtaining the remission of sins. I say nothing as to the way in which the sounder Schoolmen at first received this dogma.[1] I leave them with their puzzling subtleties, which, however they may be defended by cavilling, are to be repudiated by all good men, because, all they do is to envelop the brightness of the Supper in great darkness. Bidding adieu to them, therefore, let my readers understand that I am here combating that opinion with which the Roman Antichrist and his prophets have imbued the whole world— viz. that the mass is a work by which the priest who offers Christ, and the others who in the oblation receive him, gain merit with God, or that it is an expiatory victim by which they regain the favour of God. And this is not merely the common opinion of the vulgar, but the very act has been so arranged as to be a kind of propitiation, by which satisfaction is made to God for the living and the dead. This is also expressed by the words employed, and the same thing may be inferred from daily practice. I am aware how deeply this plague has struck its roots; under what a semblance of good it conceals its true character, bearing the name of Christ before it, and making many believe that under the single name of Mass is comprehended the whole sum of faith. But when it shall have been most clearly proved by the word of God, that this mass, however glossed and splendid, offers the greatest insult to Christ, suppresses and buries his cross, consigns his death to oblivion, takes away the benefit which it was designed to convey, enervates and dissipates the sacrament, by which the remembrance of his death was retained, will its roots be so deep that this most powerful axe, the word of God, will not cut it down and destroy it? Will any semblance be so specious that this light will not expose the lurking evil?

2. Let us show, therefore, as was proposed in the first place, that in the mass intolerable blasphemy and insult are offered to Christ. For he was not appointed Priest and Pontiff by the Father[2] for a time merely, as priests were appointed under the Old Testament. Since their life was mortal, their priesthood could not be immortal, and hence there was need of successors, who might ever and anon be substituted in the room of the dead. But Christ being immortal, had not the least occasion to have a vicar substituted for him.

---

[1] The French adds, "qui ont parlé un petit plus passablement que leur successeurs qui sont venus depuis;"—who have spoken somewhat more tolerably than their successors who have come since.

[2] Heb. v. 5-10; vii. 17, 21; ix. 11; x. 21; Ps. cx, 4; Gen. xiv. 18.

Wherefore he was appointed by his Father a priest for ever, after the order of Melchizedek, that he might eternally exercise a permanent priesthood. This mystery had been typified long before in Melchizedek, whom Scripture, after once introducing as the priest of the living God, never afterwards mentions, as if he had had no end of life. In this way Christ is said to be a priest after his order. But those who sacrifice daily must necessarily give the charge of their oblations to priests, whom they surrogate as the vicars and successors of Christ. By this surrogation they not only rob Christ of his honour, and take from him the prerogative of an eternal priesthood, but attempt to remove him from the right hand of his Father, where he cannot sit immortal without being an eternal priest. Nor let them allege that their priestlings are not substituted for Christ, as if he were dead, but are only substitutes in that eternal priesthood, which therefore ceases not to exist. The words of the apostle are too stringent to leave them any means of evasion—viz. " They truly were many priests, because they were not suffered to continue by reason of death : but this man, because he continueth ever, hath an unchangeable priesthood" (Heb. vii. 23, 24). Yet such is their dishonesty, that to defend their impiety they arm themselves with the example of Melchizedek. As he is said to have "brought forth (*obtulisse*) bread and wine" (Gen. xiv. 18), they infer that it was a prelude to their mass, as if there was any resemblance between him and Christ in the offering of bread and wine. This is too silly and frivolous to need refutation. Melchizedek gave bread and wine to Abraham and his companions, that he might refresh them when worn out with the march and the battle. What has this to do with sacrifice? The humanity of the holy king is praised by Moses : these men absurdly coin a mystery of which there is no mention. They, however, put another gloss upon their error, because it is immediately added, he was " priest of the most high God." I answer, that they erroneously wrest to bread and wine what the apostle refers to blessing. " This Melchizedek, king of Salem, priest of the most high God, who met Abraham," "and blessed him." Hence the same apostle (and a better interpreter cannot be desired) infers his excellence. " Without all contradiction, the less is blessed of the better." But if the oblation of Melchizedek was a figure of the sacrifice of the mass, I ask, would the apostle, who goes into the minutest details, have forgotten a matter so grave and serious? Now, however they quibble, it is in vain for them to attempt to destroy the argument which is adduced by the apostle himself—viz. that the right and honour of the priesthood has ceased among mortal men, because Christ, who is immortal, is the one perpetual priest.

3. Another iniquity chargeable on the mass is, that it sinks and buries the cross and passion of Christ. This much, indeed, is most certain,—the cross of Christ is overthrown the moment an altar is erected. For if, on the cross, he offered himself in sacrifice that he

might sanctify us for ever, and purchase eternal redemption for us,[1] undoubtedly the power and efficacy of his sacrifice continues without end. Otherwise, we should not think more honourably of Christ than of the oxen and calves which were sacrificed under the law, the offering of which is proved to have been weak and inefficacious because often repeated. Wherefore, it must be admitted, either that the sacrifice which Christ offered on the cross wanted the power of eternal cleansing, or that he performed this once for ever by his one sacrifice. Accordingly, the apostle says, "Now once in the end of the world hath he appeared to put away sin by the sacrifice of himself." Again: "By the which act we are sanctified through the offering of the body of Jesus Christ once for all." Again: "For by one offering he hath perfected for ever them that are sanctified." To this he subjoins the celebrated passage: "Now, where remission of these is, there is no more offering for sin." The same thing Christ intimated by his latest voice, when, on giving up the ghost, he exclaimed, "It is finished." We are accustomed to observe the last words of the dying as oracular. Christ, when dying, declares, that by his one sacrifice is perfected and fulfilled whatever was necessary to our salvation. To such a sacrifice, whose perfection he so clearly declared, shall we, as if it were imperfect, presume daily to append innumerable sacrifices? Since the sacred word of God not only affirms, but proclaims and protests, that this sacrifice was once accomplished, and remains eternally in force, do not those who demand another, charge it with imperfection and weakness? But to what tends the mass which has been established, that a hundred thousand sacrifices may be performed every day, but just to bury and suppress the passion of our Lord, in which he offered himself to his Father as the only victim? Who but a blind man does not see that it was Satanic audacity to oppose a truth so clear and transparent? I am not unaware of the impostures by which the father of lies is wont to cloak his fraud—viz. that the sacrifices are not different or various, but that the one sacrifice is repeated. Such smoke is easily dispersed. The apostle, during his whole discourse, contends not only that there are no other sacrifices, but that that one was once offered, and is no more to be repeated. The more subtle try to make their escape by a still narrower loophole—viz. that it is not repetition, but application. But there is no more difficulty in confuting this sophism also. For Christ did not offer himself once, in the view that his sacrifice should be daily ratified by new oblations, but that by the preaching of the gospel and the dispensation of the sacred Supper, the benefit of it should be communicated to us. Thus Paul says, that "Christ, our passover, is sacrificed for us," and bids us "keep the feast" (1 Cor. v. 7, 8). The method, I say, in which the cross of Christ is duly applied to us is when the enjoyment is communicated to us, and we receive it with true faith.

[1] Heb. ix. 11, 12, 26; x. 10. 14, 16.

4. But it is worth while to hear on what other foundation besides they rear up their sacrifice of the mass. To this end they drag in the prophecy of Malachi, in which the Lord promises that "in every place incense shall be offered unto my name, and a pure offering" (Mal. i. 11). As if it were new or unusual for the prophets, when they speak of the calling of the Gentiles, to designate the spiritual worship of God to which they call them, by the external rites of the law, more familiarly to intimate to the men of their age that they were to be called into the true fellowship of religion, just as in general they are wont to describe the truth which has been exhibited by the gospel by the types of their own age. Thus they use going up to Jerusalem for conversion to the Lord, the bringing of all kinds of gifts for the adoration of God—dreams and visions for the more ample knowledge with which believers were to be endued in the kingdom of Christ. The passage they quote from Malachi resembles one in Isaiah, in which the prophet speaks of three altars to be erected in Assyria, Egypt, and Judea. First, I ask, whether or not they grant that this prophecy is fulfilled in the kingdom of Christ? Secondly, Where are those altars, or when were they ever erected? Thirdly, Do they suppose that a single temple is destined for a single kingdom, as was that of Jerusalem? If they ponder these things, they will confess, I think, that the prophet, under types adapted to his age, prophesied concerning the propagation of the spiritual worship of God over the whole world. This is the answer which we give them; but, as obvious examples everywhere occur in the Scripture, I am not anxious to give a longer enumeration; although they are miserably deluded in this also, that they acknowledge no sacrifice but that of the mass, whereas in truth believers now sacrifice to God and offer him a pure offering, of which we shall speak by-and-by.

5. I now come to the third part of the mass, in regard to which, we are to explain how it obliterates the true and only death of Christ, and drives it from the memory of men. For as among men, the confirmation of a testament depends upon the death of the testator, so also the testament by which he has bequeathed to us remission of sins and eternal righteousness, our Lord has confirmed by his death. Those who dare to make any change or innovation on this testament deny his death, and hold it as of no moment. Now, what is the mass but a new and altogether different testament? What? Does not each mass promise a new forgiveness of sins, a new purchase of righteousness, so that now there are as many testaments as there are masses? Therefore, let Christ come again, and, by another death, make this new testament; or rather, by innumerable deaths, ratify the innumerable testaments of the mass. Said I not true, then, at the outset, that the only true death of Christ is obliterated by the mass? For what is the direct aim of the mass but just to put Christ again to death, if that were possible? For, as the apostle says, "Where a testament is, there must also of necessity be the death of the testator" (Heb. ix. 16). The novelty of the mass bears,

on the face of it, to be a testament of Christ, and therefore demands his death. Besides, it is necessary that the victim which is offered be slain and immolated. If Christ is sacrificed at each mass, he must be cruelly slain every moment in a thousand places. This is not my argument, but the apostle's: "Nor yet that he should offer himself often;" "for then must he often have suffered since the foundation of the world" (Heb. ix. 25, 26). I admit that they are ready with an answer, by which they even charge us with calumny; for they say that we object to them what they never thought, and could not even think. We know that the life and death of Christ are not at all in their hand. Whether they mean to slay him, we regard not: our intention is only to show the absurdity consequent on their impious and accursed dogma. This I demonstrate from the mouth of the apostle. Though they insist a hundred times that this sacrifice is bloodless (ἀναίμακτον), I will reply, that it depends not on the will of man to change the nature of sacrifice, for in this way the sacred and inviolable institution of God would fall. Hence it follows, that the principle of the apostle stands firm, "without shedding of blood is no remission" (Heb. ix. 22).

6. The fourth property of the mass which we are to consider is, that it robs us of the benefit which redounded to us from the death of Christ, while it prevents us from recognising it and thinking of it. For who can think that he has been redeemed by the death of Christ when he sees a new redemption in the mass? Who can feel confident that his sins have been remitted when he sees a new remission? It will not do to say that the only ground on which we obtain forgiveness of sins in the mass is, because it has been already purchased by the death of Christ. For this is just equivalent to saying that we are redeemed by Christ on the condition that we redeem ourselves. For the doctrine which is disseminated by the ministers of Satan, and which, in the present day, they defend by clamour, fire, and sword, is, that when we offer Christ to the Father in the mass, we, by this work of oblation, obtain remission of sins, and become partakers of the sufferings of Christ. What is now left for the sufferings of Christ, but to be an example of redemption, that we may thereby learn to be our own redeemers? Christ himself, when he seals our assurance of pardon in the Supper, does not bid his disciples stop short at that act, but sends them to the sacrifice of his death; intimating, that the Supper is the memento, or, as it is commonly expressed, the memorial from which they may learn that the expiatory victim by which God was to be appeased was to be offered only once. For it is not sufficient to hold that Christ is the only victim, without adding that his is the only immolation, in order that our faith may be fixed to his cross.

7. I come now to the crowning point—viz. that the sacred Supper, on which the Lord left the memorial of his passion formed and engraved, was taken away, hidden, and destroyed, when the mass was erected. While the supper itself is a gift of God, which was to be

received with thanksgiving, the sacrifice of the mass pretends to give a price to God to be received as satisfaction. As widely as giving differs from receiving, does sacrifice differ from the sacrament of the Supper. But herein does the wretched ingratitude of man appear,— that when the liberality of the divine goodness ought to have been recognised, and thanks returned, he makes God to be his debtor. The sacrament promised, that by the death of Christ we were not only restored to life once, but constantly quickened, because all the parts of our salvation were then completed. The sacrifice of the mass uses a very different language—viz. that Christ must be sacrificed daily, in order that he may lend something to us. The Supper was to be dispensed at the public meeting of the Church, to remind us of the communion by which we are all united in Christ Jesus. This communion the sacrifice of the mass dissolves, and tears asunder. For after the heresy prevailed, that there behoved to be priests to sacrifice for the people, as if the Supper had been handed over to them, it ceased to be communicated to the assembly of the faithful according to the command of the Lord. Entrance has been given to private masses, which more resemble a kind of excommunication than that communion ordained by the Lord, when the priestling, about to devour his victim apart, separates himself from the whole body of the faithful. That there may be no mistake, I call it a private mass whenever there is no partaking of the Lord's Supper among believers, though, at the same time, a great multitude of persons may be present.

8. The origin of the name of Mass I have never been able certainly to ascertain. It seems probable that it was derived from the offerings which were collected. Hence the ancients usually speak of it in the plural number. But without raising any controversy as to the name, I hold that private masses are diametrically opposed to the institution of Christ, and are, therefore, an impious profanation of the sacred Supper. For what did the Lord enjoin? Was it not to take and divide amongst ourselves? What does Paul teach as to the observance of this command? Is it not that the breaking of bread is the communion of body and blood? (1 Cor. x. 16). Therefore, when one person takes without distributing, where is the resemblance? But that one acts in the name of the whole Church. By what command? Is it not openly to mock God when one privately seizes for himself what ought to have been distributed among a number? But as the words, both of our Saviour and of Paul, are sufficiently clear, we must briefly conclude, that wherever there is no breaking of bread for the communion of the faithful, there is no Supper of the Lord, but a false and preposterous imitation of the Supper. But false imitation is adulteration. Moreover, the adulteration of this high ordinance is not without impiety. In private masses, therefore, there is an impious abuse: and as in religion, one fault ever and anon begets another, after that custom of offering without communion once crept in, they began gradually to make innumerable masses

in all the separate corners of the churches, and to draw the people hither and thither, when they ought to have formed one meeting, and thus recognised the mystery of their unity. Let them now go and deny their idolatry when they exhibit the bread in their masses, that it may be adored for Christ. In vain do they talk of those promises of the presence of Christ, which, however they may be understood, were certainly not given that impure and profane men might form the body of Christ as often as they please, and for whatever abuse they please ; but that believers, while, with religious observance, they follow the command of Christ in celebrating the Supper, might enjoy the true participation of it.

9. We may add, that this perverse course was unknown to the purer Church. For however the more impudent among our opponents may attempt to gloss the matter, it is absolutely certain that all antiquity is opposed to them, as has been above demonstrated in other instances, and may be more surely known by the diligent reading of the Fathers.[1] But before I conclude, I ask our missal doctors, seeing they know that obedience is better than sacrifice, and God commands us to listen to his voice rather than to offer sacrifice (1 Sam. xv. 22),—how they can believe this method of sacrificing to be pleasing to God, since it is certain that he does not command it, and they cannot support it by one syllable of Scripture ? Besides, when they hear the apostle declaring that " no man taketh this honour to himself, but he that is called of God, as was Aaron," so also Christ glorified not himself to be made an high priest, but he that said unto him, " Thou art my Son : this day have I begotten thee " (Heb. v. 4, 5). They must either prove God to be the author and founder of their priesthood, or confess that there is no honour from God in an office, into which, without being called, they have rushed with wicked temerity. They cannot produce one iota of Scripture in support of their priesthood. And must not the sacrifices be vain, since they cannot be offered without a priest ?

10. Should any one here obtrude concise sentences of the ancients, and contend, or their authority, that the sacrifice which is performed in the Supper is to be understood differently from what we have explained it, let this be our brief reply,—that if the question relates to the approval of the fiction of sacrifice, as imagined by Papists in the mass, there is nothing in the Fathers to countenance the sacrilege. They indeed use the term sacrifice, but they, at the same time, explain that they mean nothing more than the commemoration of that one true sacrifice which Christ, our only sacrifice (as they themselves

1 The French of this sentence is, " Car combien que ceux qui sont les plus effrontés entre les Papistes fassent un bouclier des anciens docteurs, abusant faussement de leurs tesmoignages, toutesfois c'est une chose claire comme le soleil en plein midi, que ce qu'ils font est tout contraire a l'usage ancien : et que c'est un abus qui est venu en avant du temps que tout etoit depravé et corrompu en l'Eglise."—For although those who have the most effrontery among the Papists make a shield of the ancient doctors, falsely abusing their testimony, it is clear as the sun at noon-day, that what they do is quite contrary to ancient practice, and that is an abuse which immediately preceded the time when everything was depraved and corrupted in the Church.

everywhere proclaim), performed on the cross. " The Hebrews," says Augustine (Cont. Faust. Lib. xx. c. 18), "in the victims of beasts which they offered to God, celebrated the prediction of the future victim which Christ offered: Christians now celebrate the commemoration of a finished sacrifice by the sacred oblation and participation of the body of Christ." Here he certainly teaches the same doctrine which is delivered at greater length in the Treatise on Faith, addressed to Peter the deacon, whoever may have been the author. The words are, "Hold most firmly, and have no doubt at all, that the Only-Begotten became incarnate for us, that he offered himself for us, an offering and sacrifice to God for a sweet-smelling savour ; to whom, with the Father and the Holy Spirit, in the time of the Old Testament, animals were sacrificed, and to whom now, with the Father and the Holy Spirit (with whom there is one Godhead), the holy Church, throughout the whole world, ceases not to offer the sacrifice of bread and wine. For, in those carnal victims, there was a typifying of the flesh of Christ, which he himself was to offer for our sins, and of the blood which he was to shed for the forgiveness of sins. But in that sacrifice there is thanksgiving and commemoration of the flesh of Christ which he offered for us, and of the blood which he shed for us." Hence Augustine himself, in several passages (Ep. 120, ad Honorat. Cont. Advers. Legis.), explains, that it is nothing else than a sacrifice of praise. In short, you will find in his writings, *passim*, that the only reason for which the Lord's Supper is called a sacrifice is, because it is a commemoration, an image, a testimonial of that singular, true, and only sacrifice by which Christ expiated our guilt. For there is a memorable passage (De Trinitate, Lib. iv. c. 24), where, after discoursing of the only sacrifice, he thus concludes: "Since, in a sacrifice, four things are considered—viz. to whom it is offered, by whom, what and for whom, the same one true Mediator, reconciling us to God by the sacrifice of peace, remains one with him to whom he offered, made himself one with those for whom he offered, is himself the one who offered, and the one thing which he offered." Chrysostom speaks to the same effect. They so strongly claim the honour of the priesthood for Christ alone, that Augustine declares it would be equivalent to Antichrist for any one to make a bishop to be an intercessor between God and man (August. Cont. Parmen. Lib. ii c. 8).[1]

11. And yet we deny not that in the Supper the sacrifice of Christ is so vividly exhibited as almost to set the spectacle of the cross before our eyes, just as the apostle says to the Galatians, that Jesus Christ had been evidently set forth before their eyes, when the preaching of the cross was delivered to them (Gal. iii. 1). But because I see that those ancient writers have wrested this commemoration to a different purpose than was accordant to the divine institution (the Supper somehow seemed to them to present the appearance of a re-

---

[1] This last sentence forms, in the French, the first of sec. 11.

peated, or at least renewed, immolation), nothing can be safer for the pious than to rest satisfied with the pure and simple ordinance of God, whose Supper it is said to be, just because his authority alone ought to appear in it. Seeing that they retained a pious and orthodox view of the whole ordinance—and I cannot discover that they wished to derogate in the least from the one sacrifice of the Lord—I cannot charge them with any impiety, and yet I think they cannot be excused from having erred somewhat in the mode of action. They imitated the Jewish mode of sacrificing more closely than either Christ had ordained, or the nature of the gospel allowed. The only thing, therefore, for which they may be justly censured is, that preposterous analogy, that not contented with the simple and genuine institution of Christ, they declined too much to the shadows of the law.

12. Any who will diligently consider, will perceive that the word of the Lord makes this distinction between the Mosaic sacrifices and our eucharist—that while the former represented to the Jewish people the same efficacy of the death of Christ which is now exhibited to us in the Supper, yet the form of representation was different. There the Levitical priests were ordered to typify the sacrifice which Christ was to accomplish; a victim was placed to act as a substitute for Christ himself; an altar was erected on which it was to be sacrificed; the whole, in short, was so conducted as to bring under the eye an image of the sacrifice which was to be offered to God in expiation. But now that the sacrifice has been performed, the Lord has prescribed a different method to us—viz. to transmit the benefit of the sacrifice offered to him by his Son to his believing people. The Lord, therefore, has given us a table at which we may feast, not an altar on which a victim may be offered; he has not consecrated priests to sacrifice, but ministers to distribute a sacred feast. The more sublime and holy this mystery is, the more religiously and reverently ought it to be treated. Nothing, therefore, is safer than to banish all the boldness of human sense, and adhere solely to what Scripture delivers. And certainly, if we reflect that it is the Supper of the Lord and not of men, why do we allow ourselves to be turned aside one nail's-breadth from Scripture, by any authority of man or length of prescription? [1] Accordingly, the apostle, in desiring completely to remove the vices which had crept into the Church of Corinth, as the most expeditious method, recalls them to the institution itself, showing that thence a perpetual rule ought to be derived.

13. Lest any quarrelsome person should raise a dispute with us as to the terms *sacrifice* and *priest*, I will briefly explain what in the whole of this discussion we mean by sacrifice, and what by priest. Some, on what rational ground I see not, extend the term *sacrifice* to all sacred ceremonies and religious acts. We know that by the uniform

1 French, " n'aucun authorite humaine, ne longeur de temps, ne toutes autres apparences;"—no human authority, no length of time, nor any other appearnces.

use of Scripture, the name of sacrifice is given to what the Greeks call at one time θυσια, at another προσφορὰ, at another τελετὴ. This, in its general acceptation, includes everything whatever that is offered to God. Wherefore, we ought to distinguish, but so that the distinction may derive its analogy from the sacrifices of the Mosaic Law, under whose shadows the Lord was pleased to represent to his people the whole reality of sacrifices. Though these were various in form, they may all be referred to two classes. For either an oblation for sin was made by a certain species of satisfaction, by which the penalty was redeemed before God, or it was a symbol and attestation of religion and divine worship, at one time in the way of supplication to demand the favour of God; at another, by way of thanksgiving, to testify gratitude to God for benefits received; at another, as a simple exercise of piety, to renew the sanction of the covenant, to which latter branch, burnt-offerings, and libations, oblations, first-fruits, and peace offerings, referred. Hence let us also distribute them into two classes. The other class, with the view of explaining, let us call λατρευτικὸν, and σεβαστικὸν, as consisting of the veneration and worship which believers both owe and render to God; or, if you prefer it, let us call it ευχαριστικὸν, since it is exhibited to God by none but those who, enriched with his boundless benefits, offer themselves and all their actions to him in return. The other class let us call *propitiatory* or *expiatory*. A sacrifice of expiation is one whose object is to appease the wrath of God, to satisfy his justice, and thereby wipe and wash away the sins, by which the sinner being cleansed and restored to purity, may return to favour with God. Hence the name which was given in the Law to the victims which were offered in expiation of sin (Exod. xxix. 36); not that they were adequate to regain the favour of God, and wipe away guilt, but because they typified the true sacrifice of this nature, which was at length performed in reality by Christ alone; by him alone, because no other could, and once, because the efficacy and power of the one sacrifice performed by Christ is eternal, as he declared by his voice, when he said, " It is finished ;" that is, that everything necessary to regain the favour of the Father, to procure forgiveness of sins, righteousness, and salvation, that all this was performed and consummated by his one oblation, and that hence nothing was wanting. No place was left for another sacrifice.

14. Wherefore, I conclude, that it is an abominable insult and intolerable blasphemy, as well against Christ as the sacrifice, which, by his death, he performed for us on the cross, for any one to think of repeating the oblation, of purchasing the forgiveness of sins, of propitiating God, and obtaining justification. But what else is done in the mass than to make us partakers of the sufferings of Christ by means of a new oblation? And that there might be no limit to their extravagance, they have deemed it little to say, that it properly becomes a common sacrifice for the whole Church, without adding, that it is at their pleasure to apply it specially to this one or

that, as they choose ; or rather, to any one who is willing to purchase their merchandise from them for a price paid. Moreover, as
they could not come up to the estimate of Judas, still, that they
might in some way refer to their author, they make the resemblance
to consist in the number. He sold for thirty pieces of silver : they,
according to the French method of computation, sell for thirty pieces
of brass. He did it once : they as often as a purchaser is met with.
We deny that they are priests in this sense—namely, that by such
oblations they intercede with God for the people, that by propitiating
God they make expiation for sins. Christ is the only Pontiff and
Priest of the New Testament: to him all priestly offices were transferred, and in him they closed and terminated. Even had Scripture
made no mention of the eternal priesthood of Christ, yet, as God,
after abolishing those ancient sacrifices, appointed no new priest, the
argument of the apostle remains invincible, " No man taketh this
honour unto himself, but he that is called of God, as was Aaron"
(Heb. v. 4). How, then, can those sacrilegious men, who by their
own account are murderers of Christ, dare to call themselves the
priests of the living God ?

15. There is a most elegant passage in the second book of Plato's
Republic. Speaking of ancient expiations, and deriding the foolish
confidence of wicked and iniquitous men, who thought that by them,
as a kind of veils, they concealed their crimes from the gods ; and,
as if they had made a paction with the gods, indulged themselves
more securely, he seems accurately to describe the use of the expiation of the mass, as it exists in the world in the present day. All
know that it is unlawful to defraud and circumvent another. To do
injustice to widows, to pillage pupils, to molest the poor, to seize
the goods of others by wicked arts, to get possession of any man's
succession by fraud and perjury, to oppress by violence and tyrannical terror, all admit to be impious. How then do so many, as if
assured of impunity, dare to do all those things ? Undoubtedly, if
we duly consider, we will find that the only thing which gives them
so much courage is, that by the sacrifice of the mass as a price paid,
they trust that they will satisfy God, or at least will easily find a
means of transacting with him. Plato next proceeds to deride the
gross stupidity of those who think by such expiations to redeem the
punishments which they must otherwise suffer after death. And
what is meant by anniversaries and the greater part of masses in the
present day, but just that those who through life have been the
most cruel tyrants, or most rapacious plunderers, or adepts in all
kinds of wickedness, may, as if redeemed at this price, escape the fire
of purgatory ?

16. Under the other kind of sacrifice, which we have called
eucharistic, are included all the offices of charity, by which, while
we embrace our brethren, we honour the Lord himself in his members ; in fine, all our prayers, praises, thanksgivings, and every act of
worship which we perform to God. All these depend on the greater

sacrifice with which we dedicate ourselves, soul and body, to be a holy temple to the Lord.   For it is not enough that our external acts be framed to obedience, but we must dedicate and consecrate first ourselves, and, secondly, all that we have, so that all which is in us may be subservient to his glory, and be stirred up to magnify it. This kind of sacrifice has nothing to do with appeasing God, with obtaining remission of sins, with procuring justification, but is wholly employed in magnifying and extolling God, since it cannot be grateful and acceptable to God unless at the hand of those who, having received forgiveness of sins, have already been reconciled and freed from guilt.   This is so necessary to the Church, that it cannot be dispensed with.   Therefore, it will endure for ever, so long as the people of God shall endure, as we have already seen above from the prophet.   For in this sense we may understand the prophecy, "From the rising of the sun, even unto the going down of the same, my name shall be great among the Gentiles ; and in every place incense shall be offered unto my name, and a pure offering : for my name shall be great among the heathen, said the Lord of hosts " (Malachi i. 11) ; so far are we from doing away with this sacrifice.   Thus Paul beseeches us by the mercies of God, to present our bodies " a living sacrifice, holy, acceptable unto God," our " reasonable service " (Rom. xii. 1).   Here he speaks very significantly when he adds, that this service is reasonable, for he refers to the spiritual mode of worshipping God, and tacitly opposes it to the carnal sacrifices of the Mosaic Law.   Thus to do good and communicate are called sacrifices with which God is well pleased (Heb. xiii. 16).   Thus the kindness of the Philippians in relieving Paul's want is called " an odour of a sweet smell, a sacrifice acceptable, well pleasing to God" (Phil. iv. 18) ; and thus all the good works of believers are called spiritual sacrifices.

17. And why do I enumerate ?   This form of expression is constantly occurring in Scripture.   Nay, even while the people of God were kept under the external tutelage of the law, the prophets clearly expressed that under these carnal sacrifices there was a reality which is common both to the Jewish people and the Christian Church. For this reason David prayed, " Let my prayer ascend forth before thee as incense" (Ps. cxli. 2).   And Hosea gives the name of " calves of the lips" (Hos. xiv. 3) to thanksgivings, which David elsewhere calls " sacrifices of praise ;" the apostle, imitating him, speaks of offering " the sacrifice of praise," which he explains to mean, " the fruit of our lips, giving thanks to his name" (Heb. xiii. 15).   This kind of sacrifice is indispensable in the Lord's Supper, in which, while we show forth his death, and give him thanks, we offer nothing but the sacrifice of praise.   From this office of sacrificing, all Christians are called " a royal priesthood," because by Christ we offer that sacrifice of praise of which the apostle speaks, the fruit of our lips, giving thanks to his name (1 Pet. ii. 9 ; Heb. xiii. 15).   We do not appear with our gifts in the presence of God without an intercessor.

Christ is our Mediator, by whose intervention we offer ourselves and our all to the Father; he is our High Priest, who, having entered into the upper sanctuary, opens up an access for us; he is the altar on which we lay our gifts, that whatever we do attempt, we may attempt in him; he it is, I say, who "hath made us kings and priests unto God and his Father" (Rev. i. 6).

18. What remains but for the blind to see, the deaf to hear, children even to perceive this abomination of the mass, which, held forth in a golden cup,[1] has so intoxicated all the kings and nations of the earth, from the highest to the lowest; so struck them with stupor and giddiness, that, duller than the lower animals, they have placed the vessel of their salvation in this fatal vortex. Certainly Satan never employed a more powerful engine to assail and storm the kingdom of Christ. This is the Helen for whom the enemies of the truth in the present day fight with so much rage, fury, and atrocity; and truly the Helen with whom they commit spiritual whoredom, the most execrable of all. I am not here laying my little finger on those gross abuses by which they might pretend that the purity of their sacred mass is profaned; on the base traffic which they ply; the sordid gain which they make; the rapacity with which they satiate their avarice. I only indicate, and that in few and simple terms, how very sacred the sanctity of the mass is, how well it has for several ages deserved to be admired and held in veneration! It were a greater work to illustrate these great mysteries as they deserve, and I am unwilling to meddle with their obscene impurities, which are daily before the eyes and faces of all, that it may be understood that the mass, taken in the most choice form in which it can be exhibited, without any appendages, teems from head to foot with all kinds of impiety, blasphemy, idolatry, and sacrilege.

19. My readers have here a compendious view of all that I have thought it of importance to know concerning these two sacraments, which have been delivered to the Christian Church, to be used from the beginning of the new dispensation to the end of the world, Baptism being a kind of entrance into the Church, an initiation into the faith, and the Lord's Supper the constant aliment by which Christ spiritually feeds his family of believers. Wherefore, as there is but one God, one faith, one Christ, one Church, which is his body, so Baptism is one, and is not repeated. But the Supper is ever and anon dispensed, to intimate, that those who are once allured into the Church are constantly fed by Christ. Besides these two, no other has been instituted by God, and no other ought to be recognised by the assembly of the faithful. That sacraments are not to be instituted and set up by the will of men, is easily understood by him who remembers what has been above with sufficient plainness expounded —viz. that the sacraments have been appointed by God to instruct

1 The French explains, "c'est à dire, sous le nom de la parole de Dieu;"—that is to say, under the name of the word of God.

us in his promise, and testify his goodwill towards us; and who, moreover, considers, that the Lord has no counsellor (Isa. xl. 13; Rom. xi. 34); who can give us any certainty as to his will, or assure us how he is disposed towards us, what he is disposed to give, and what to deny? From this it follows, that no one can set forth a sign which is to be a testimonial of his will, and of some promise. He alone can give the sign, and bear witness to himself. I will express it more briefly, perhaps in homelier, but also in clearer terms,— There never can be a sacrament without a promise of salvation. All men collected into one cannot, of themselves, give us any promise of salvation, and, therefore, they cannot, of themselves, give out and set up a sacrament.

20. With these two, therefore, let the Christian Church be contented, and not only not admit or acknowledge any third at present, but not even desire or expect it even until the end of the world. For though to the Jews were given, besides his ordinary sacraments, others differing somewhat according to the nature of the times (as the manna, the water gushing from the rock, the brazen serpent, and the like),[1] by this variety they were reminded not to stop short at such figures, the state of which could not be durable, but to expect from God something better, to endure without decay and without end. Our case is very different. To us Christ has been revealed. In him are hidden all the treasures of wisdom and knowledge (Col. ii. 3), in such richness and abundance, that to ask or hope for any new addition to these treasures is truly to offend God and provoke him against us. It behoves us to hunger after Christ only, to seek him, look to him, learn of him, and learn again, until the arrival of the great day on which the Lord will fully manifest the glory of his kingdom, and exhibit himself as he is to our admiring eye (1 John iii. 2). And, for this reason, this age of ours is designated in Scripture[2] by the last hour, the last days, the last times, that no one may deceive himself with the vain expectation of some new doctrine or revelation. Our heavenly Father, who "at sundry times, and in divers manners, spake in time past unto the fathers by the prophets, hath in these last days spoken unto us" by his beloved Son, who alone can manifest, and, in fact, has fully manifested, the Father, in so far as is of importance to us, while we now see him through a mirror. Now, since men have been denied the power of making new sacraments in the Church of God, it were to be wished, that in those which are of God, there should be the least possible admixture of human invention. For just as when water is infused, the wine is diluted, and when leaven is put in, the whole mass is leavened, so the purity of the ordinances of God is impaired, whenever man makes any addition of his own. And yet we see how far the sacraments as at present used have degenerated from their genuine purity. There is everywhere more than enough of pomp,

---

1 Exod. xvi. 13–15; xvii. 6; Num. xx. 8; xxi. 9; 1 Cor. x. 4; John iii. 14.
2 1 John ii. 18; 1 Pet. i. 20; Luke x. 22; Heb. i. 1; 1 Cor. xiii. 12.

ceremony, and gesticulation, while no account is taken, or mention made, of the word of God, without which, even the sacraments themselves are not sacraments.   Nay, in such a crowd, the very ceremonies ordained by God cannot raise their head, but lie as it were oppressed.   In Baptism, as we have elsewhere justly complained, how little is seen of that which alone ought to shine and be conspicuous there, I mean Baptism itself?   The Supper was altogether buried when it was turned into the Mass.   The utmost is, that it is seen once a year, but in a garbled, mutilated, and lacerated form.[1]

1 French, " deschiree, decouppee, departie, brisee, divisee, et toute difformee.

CHAPTER XIX.

OF THE FIVE SACRAMENTS, FALSELY SO CALLED. THEIR SPURIOUSNESS PROVED, AND THEIR TRUE CHARACTER EXPLAINED.

There are two divisions of this chapter,—I. A general discussion of these five sacraments, sec. 1–3. II. A special consideration of each. 1. Of Confirmation, sec. 4–13. 2. Of Penance, sec. 14–17. 3. Of Extreme Unction, sec. 18–21. 4 Of Order, in which the seven so-called sacraments have originated, sec. 22–23. 5. Of Marriage, sec. 34-37.

Sections.

1. THE above discourse concerning the sacraments might have the effect, among the docile and sober-minded, of preventing them from indulging their curiosity, or from embracing, without authority from the word, any other sacraments than those two, which they know to have been instituted by the Lord.   But since the idea of seven sacraments, almost common in the mouths of all, and circulated in all schools and sermons, by mere antiquity, has struck its roots, and is even now seated in the minds of men, I thought it might be worth while to give a separate and closer consideration of the other five, which are vulgarly classed with the true and genuine sacraments of the Lord, and, after wiping away every gloss, to hold them up to the view of the simple, that they may see what their true nature is, and how falsely they have hitherto been regarded as sacraments.   Here, at the outset, I would declare to all the pious, that I engage not in this dispute about a word for love of wrangling, but am induced, by weighty causes, to impugn the abuse of it.   I am not unaware that Christians are the masters of words, as they are of all things, and that, therefore, they may at pleasure adapt words to things, provided a pious meaning is retained, though there should be some impropriety in the mode of expression.   All this I concede, though it were better to make words subordinate to things than things to words.   But in the name of sacrament, the case is different.   For those who set down seven sacraments, at the same time give this definition to all—viz. that they are visible forms of invisible grace; and at the same time, make them all vehicles of the Holy Spirit, instruments for conferring righteousness, causes of procuring grace.   Accordingly, the Master of Sentences himself denies that the sacraments of the Mosaic Law are properly called by this name, because they exhibited not what they figured.   Is it tolerable, I ask, that the symbols which the Lord has consecrated with his own lips, which he has distinguished by excellent promises, should be regarded as no sacraments, and that, meanwhile, this honour should be transferred to those rites which men have either devised of themselves, or at least observe without any express command from God?   Therefore, let them either change the definition, or refrain from this use of the word, which may after-

wards give rise to false and absurd opinions.   Extreme unction, they say, is a figure and cause of invisible grace, because it is a sacrament. If we cannot possibly admit the inference, we must certainly meet them on the subject of the name, that we may not receive it on terms which may furnish occasion for such an error.   On the other hand, when they prove it to be a sacrament, they add the reason, because it consists of the external sign and the word.   If we find neither command nor promise, what else can we do than protest against it?

2. It now appears that we are not quarrelling about a word, but raising a not unnecessary discussion as to the reality.   Accordingly, we most strenuously maintain what we formerly confirmed by invincible argument, that the power of instituting a sacrament belongs to God alone, since a sacrament ought, by the sure promise of God, to raise up and comfort the consciences of believers, which could never receive this assurance from men.   A sacrament ought to be a testimony of the good-will of God toward us.   Of this no man or angel can be witness, since God has no counsellor (Isa. xl. 13 ; Rom. xi. 34).   He himself alone, with legitimate authority, testifies of himself to us by his word.   A sacrament is a seal of attestation or promise of God.   Now, it could not be sealed by corporeal things, or the elements of this world, unless they were confirmed and set apart for this purpose by the will of God.   Man, therefore, cannot institute a sacrament, because it is not in the power of man to make such divine mysteries lurk under things so abject.   The word of God must precede to make a sacrament to be a sacrament, as Augustine most admirably shows (Hom. in Joann. 80).   Moreover, it is useful to keep up some distinction between sacraments and other ceremonies, if we would not fall into many absurdities.   The apostles prayed on their bended knees ; therefore our knees may not be bent without a sacrament (Acts ix. 20 ; xx. 36).   The disciples are said to have prayed toward the east ; thus looking at the east is a sacrament. Paul would have men in every place to lift up pure hands (1 Tim. ii. 8) ; and it is repeatedly stated that the saints prayed with uplifted hands, let the outstretching, therefore, of hands also become a sacrament ; in short, let all the gestures of saints pass into sacraments, though I should not greatly object to this, provided it was not connected with those greater inconveniences.

3. If they would press us with the authority of the ancient Church, I say that they are using a gloss.   This number seven is nowhere found in the ecclesiastical writers, nor is it well ascertained at what time it crept in.   I confess, indeed, that they sometimes use freedom with the term *sacrament*, but what do they mean by it ? all ceremonies, external writs, and exercises of piety.   But when they speak of those signs which ought to be testimonies of the divine favour toward us, they are contented with those two, Baptism and the Eucharist.   Lest any one suppose that this is falsely alleged by me, I will here give a few passages from Augustine.   " First, I wish you to hold that the principle point in this discussion is, that our Lord Jesus

Christ (as he himself says in the gospel) has placed us under a yoke which is easy, and a burden which is light. Hence he has knit together the society of his new people by sacraments, very few in number, most easy of observance, and most excellent in meaning; such is baptism consecrated by the name of the Trinity : such is the communion of the body and blood of the Lord, and any other, if recommended in the canonical Scriptures" (August. ad. Januar. Ep. 118). Again, "After the resurrection of our Lord, our Lord himself, and apostolic discipline, appointed, instead of many, a few signs, and these most easy of performance, most august in meaning, most chaste in practice; such is baptism and the celebration of the body and blood of the Lord" (August. De. Doct. Christ. Lib. iii. cap. 9). Why does he here make no mention of the sacred number, I mean seven ? Is it probable that he would have omitted it if it had then been established in the Church, especially seeing he is otherwise more curious in observing numbers than might be necessary ? Nay, when he makes mention of Baptism and the Supper, and is silent as to others,[1] does he not sufficiently intimate that these two ordinances excel in special dignity, and that other ceremonies sink down to an inferior place ? Wherefore, I say, that those sacramentary doctors are not only unsupported by the word of God, but also by the consent of the early Church, however much they may plume themselves on the pretence that they have this consent. But let us now come to particulars.

OF CONFIRMATION.[2]

4. It was anciently customary for the children of Christians, after they had grown up, to appear before the bishop to fulfil that duty which was required of such adults as presented themselves for baptism. These sat among the catechumens until they were duly instructed in the mysteries of the faith, and could make a confession of it before bishop and people. The infants, therefore, who had been initiated by baptism, not having then given a confession of faith to the Church, were again, toward the end of their boyhood, or on adolescence, brought forward by their parents, and were examined by the bishop in terms of the Catechism which was then in common use. In order that this act, which otherwise justly required to be grave and holy, might have more reverence and dignity, the ceremony of laying on of hands was also used. Thus the boy, on his faith being approved, was dismissed with a solemn blessing. Ancient writers often make mention of this custom. Pope Leo says (Ep. 39), "If any one returns from heretics, let him not be baptised

---

[1] Ambros. de iis qui init. Mysteriis et de Sacrament.
[2] Calv. adv. Concil. Trident. Præfat. in Catechis. Latinum. Viret. de Adulter. Sacrament. cap. 2–5.

again, but let that which was there wanting to him—viz. the virtue of the Spirit, be conferred by the laying on of the hands of the bishop." Our opponents will here exclaim, that the name of sacrament is justly given to that by which the Holy Spirit is conferred. But Leo elsewhere explains what he means by these words (Ep. 77) ; "Let not him who was baptised by heretics be rebaptised, but be confirmed by the laying on of hands with the invocation of the Holy Spirit, because he received only the form of baptism without sanctification." Jerome also mentions it (Contra Luciferian). Now though I deny not that Jerome is somewhat under delusion when he says that the observance is apostolical, he is, however, very far from the follies of these men. And he softens the expression when he adds, that this benediction is given to bishops only, more in honour of the priesthood than from any necessity of law. This laying on of hands, which is done simply by way of benediction, I commend, and would like to see restored to its pure use in the present day.

5. A later age having almost obliterated the reality, introduced a kind of fictitious confirmation as a divine sacrament. They feigned that the virtue of confirmation consisted in conferring the Holy Spirit, for increase of grace, on him who had been prepared in baptism for righteousness, and in confirming for contest those who in baptism were regenerated to life. This confirmation is performed by unction, and the following form of words : " I sign thee with the sign of the holy cross, and confirm thee with the chrism of salvation, in the name of the Father, and of the Son, and of the Holy Spirit." All fair and venerable. But where is the word of God which promises the presence of the Holy Spirit here ? Not one iota can they allege. How will they assure us that their chrism is a vehicle of the Holy Spirit? We see oil, that is, a thick and greasy liquid, but nothing more. " Let the word be added to the element," says Augustine, " and it will become a sacrament." Let them, I say, produce this word if they would have us to see anything more in the oil than oil. But if they would show themselves to be ministers of the sacraments as they ought, there would be no room for further dispute. The first duty of a minister is not to do anything without a command. Come, then, and let them produce some command for this ministry, and I will not add a word. If they have no command, they cannot excuse their sacrilegious audacity. For this reason our Saviour interogated the Pharisees as to the baptism of John, " Was it from heaven, or of men ?" (Matth. xxi. 25). If they had answered, Of men, he held them confessed that it was frivolous and vain ; if Of heaven, they were forced to acknowledge the doctrine of John. Accordingly, not to be too contumelious to John, they did not venture to say that it was of men. Therefore, if confirmation is of men, it is proved to be frivolous and vain ; if they would persuade us that it is of heaven, let them prove it.

6. They indeed defend themselves by the example of the apostles,

who, they presume, did nothing rashly.   In this they are right, nor
would they be blamed by us if they showed tnemselves to be imi
tators of the apostles.   But what did the apostles do ?   Luke narrates
(Acts viii. 15, 17), that the apostles who were at Jerusalem, when
they heard that Samaria had received the word of God, sent thither
Peter and John, that Peter and John prayed for the Samaritans,
that they might receive the Holy Spirit, who had not yet come upon
any of them, they having only been baptised in the name of Jesus ;
that after prayer they laid their hands upon them, and that by this
laying on of hands the Samaritans received the Holy Spirit.   Luke
repeatedly mentions this laying on of hands.   I hear what the
apostles did, that is, they faithfully executed their ministry.   It
pleased the Lord that those visible and admirable gifts of the Holy
Spirit, which he then poured out upon his people, should be administered and distributed by his apostles by the laying on of hands.   I
think that there was no deeper mystery under this laying on of hands,
but I interpret that this kind of ceremony was used by them to intimate, by the outward act, that they commended to God, and, as it
were, offered him on whom they laid hands.   Did this ministry,
which the apostles then performed, still remain in the Church, it
would also behove us to observe the laying on of hands ; but since
that gift has ceased to be conferred, to what end is the laying on of
hands ?   Assuredly the Holy Spirit is still present with the people of
God ; without his guidance and direction the Church of God cannot
subsist.   For we have a promise of perpetual duration, by which
Christ invites the thirsty to come to him, that they may drink living
water (John vii. 37).   But those miraculous powers and manifest
operations, which were distributed by the laying on of hands, have
ceased.   They were only for a time.   For it was right that the new
preaching of the gospel, the new kingdom of Christ, should be
signalised and magnified by unwonted and unheard-of miracles.
When the Lord ceased from these, he did not forthwith abandon his
Church, but intimated that the magnificence of his kingdom, and the
dignity of his word, had been sufficiently manifested.   In what
respect then can these stage-players say that they imitate the
apostles ?   The object of the laying on of hands was, that the evident
power of the Holy Spirit might be immediately exerted.   This they
effect not.   Why then do they claim to themselves the laying on of
hands, which is indeed said to have been used by the apostles, but
altogether to a different end ?

7. The same account is to be given were any one to insist that the
breathing of our Lord upon his disciples (John xx. 22) is a sacrament by which the Holy Spirit is conferred.   But the Lord did this
once for all, and did not also wish us to do it.   In the same way,
also, the apostles laid their hands, agreeably to that time at which it
pleased the Lord that the visible gifts of the Spirit should be dispensed in answer to their prayers ; not that posterity might, as those
apes do, mimic the empty and useless sign without the reality.   But

if they prove that they imitate the apostles in the laying on of hands (though in this they have no resemblance to the apostles, except it be in manifesting some absurd false zeal),[1] where did they get their oil which they call the oil of salvation ? Who taught them to seek salvation in oil ? Who taught them to attribute to it the power of strengthening ? Was it Paul, who draws us far away from the elements of this world, and condemns nothing more than clinging to such observances.? This I boldly declare, not of myself, but from the Lord: Those who call oil the oil of salvation abjure the salvation which is in Christ, deny Christ, and have no part in the kingdom of God. Oil for the belly, and the belly for oil, but the Lord will destroy both. For all these weak elements, which perish even in the using, have nothing to do with the kingdom of God, which is spiritual, and will never perish. What, then, some one will say, do you apply the same rule to the water by which we are baptised, and the bread and wine under which the Lord's Supper is exhibited ? I answer, that in the sacraments of divine appointment, two things are to be considered : the substance of the corporeal thing which is set before us, and the form which has been impressed upon it by the word of God, and in which its whole force lies. In as far, then, as the bread, wine, and water, which are presented to our view in the sacraments, retain their substance, Paul's declaration applies, "meats for the belly, and the belly for meats : but God shall destroy both it and them" (1 Cor. vi. 13). For they pass and vanish away with the fashion of this world. But in as far as they are sanctified by the word of God to be sacraments, they do not confine us to the flesh, but teach truly and spiritually.

8. But let us make a still closer inspection, and see how many monsters this greasy oil fosters and nourishes. Those anointers say that the Holy Spirit is given in baptism for righteousness, and in confirmation, for increase of grace, that in baptism we are regenerated for life, and in confirmation, equipped for contest. And, accordingly, they are not ashamed to deny that baptism can be duly completed without confirmation. How nefarious ! Are we not, then, buried with Christ by baptism, and made partakers of his death, that we may also be partners of his resurrection ? This fellowship with the life and death of Christ, Paul interprets to mean the mortification of our flesh, and the quickening of the Spirit, our old man being crucified in order that we may walk in newness of life (Rom vi. 6). What is it to be equipped for contest, if this is not ? But if they deemed it as nothing to trample on the word of God, why did they not at least reverence the Church, to which they would be thought to be in everything so obedient ? What heavier charge can be brought against their doctrine than the decree of the Council of

---

1 French, " en laquelle toutesfois ils n'ont rien semblable a eux, sinon une folle et perverse singerie ;—in which, however, they have nothing like them but a foolish and perverse aping.

Melita?[1] "Let him who says that baptism is given for the remission of sins only, and not in aid of future grace, be anathema." When Luke, in the passage which we have quoted, says, that the Samaritans were only "baptised in the name of the Lord Jesus" (Acts viii. 16), but had not received the Holy Spirit, he does not say absolutely that those who believed in Christ with the heart, and confessed him with the mouth, were not endued with any gift of the Spirit. He means that receiving of the Spirit by which miraculous power and visible graces were received. Thus the apostles are said to have received the Spirit on the day of Pentecost (Acts ii. 4), whereas Christ had long before said to them, " It is not ye that speak, but the Spirit of your Father which speaketh in you" (Matth. x. 20). Ye who are of God see the malignant and pestiferous wile of Satan. What was truly given in baptism, is falsely said to be given in the confirmation of it, that he may stealthily lead away the unwary from baptism. Who can now doubt that this doctrine, which dissevers the proper promises of baptism from baptism, and transfers them elsewhere, is a doctrine of Satan? We have discovered on what foundation this famous unction rests. The word of God says, that as many as have been baptised into Christ, have put on Christ with his gifts (Gal. iii. 27). The word of the anointers says that they received no promise in baptism to equip them for contest (De Consecr. Dist. 5, cap. Spir. Sanct). The former is the word of truth, the latter must be the word of falsehood. I can define this baptism more truly than they themselves have hitherto defined it— viz. that it is a noted insult to baptism, the use of which it obscures— nay, abolishes : that it is a false suggestion of the devil, which draws us away from the truth of God ; or, if you prefer it, that it is oil polluted with a lie of the devil, deceiving the minds of the simple by shrouding them, as it were, in darkness.

9. They add, moreover, that all believers ought, after baptism, to receive the Holy Spirit by the laying on of hands, that they may become complete Christians, inasmuch as there never can be a Christian who has not been *chrismed* by episcopal confirmation. These are their exact words.[2] I thought that everything pertaining to Christianity was prescribed and contained in Scripture. Now I see that the true form of religion must be sought and learned elsewhere than in Scripture. Divine wisdom, heavenly truth, the whole doctrine of Christ, only begins the Christian ; it is the oil that perfects him. By this sentence are condemned all the apostles and the many martyrs who, it is absolutely certain, were never chrismed, the oil not yet being made, besmeared with which, they might fufil all the parts of Christianity, or rather become Christians, which, as yet, they were not. Though I were silent, they abundantly refute themselves. How small the proportion of the people whom they anoint after baptism! Why, then, do they allow among their flock so many

---

[1] The French adds, " du temps de Sainct Augustin ;"—of the time of St Augustine.
[2] De Consecr. Dist. 5, Concil. Aurel. cap. Ut Jejuni de Consecr. Dist. 5.

half Christians, whose imperfection they might easily remedy? Why, with such supine negligence, do they allow them to omit what cannot be omitted without grave offence? Why do they not more rigidly insist on a matter so necessary, that, without it, salvation cannot be obtained unless, perhaps, when the act has been anticipated by sudden death? When they allow it to be thus licentiously despised, they tacitly confess that it is not of the importance which they pretend.

10. Lastly, they conclude that this sacred unction is to be held in greater veneration than baptism, because the former is specially administered by the higher order of priests, whereas the latter is dispensed in common by all priests whatever (Distinct. 5, De his vero). What can you here say, but that they are plainly mad in thus pluming themselves on their own inventions, while, in comparison with these, they carelessly contemn the sacred ordinances of God? Sacrilegious mouth! dare you oppose oil merely polluted with your fœtid breath, and charmed by your muttered words, to the sacrament of Christ, and compare it with water sanctified by the word of God? But even this was not enough for your improbity: you must also prefer it. Such are the responses of the holy see, such the oracles of the apostolic tripod. But some of them have begun to moderate this madness, which, even in their own opinion, was carried too far (Lombard. Sent. Lib. iv. Dist. 7, c. 2). It is to be held in greater veneration, they say, not perhaps because of the greater virtue and utility which it confers, but because it is given by more dignified persons, and in a more dignified part of the body, the forehead; or because it gives a greater increase of virtue, though baptism is more effectual for forgiveness. But do they not, by their first reason, prove themselves to be Donatists, who estimate the value of the sacrament by the dignity of the minister? Grant, however, that confirmation may be called more dignified from the dignity of the bishop's hand, still should any one ask how this great perrogative was conferred on the bishops, what reason can they give but their own caprice? The right was used only by the apostles, who alone dispensed the Holy Spirit. Are bishops alone apostles? Are they apostles at all? However, let us grant this also; why do they not, on the same grounds, maintain that the sacrament of blood in the Lord's Supper is to be touched only by bishops? Their reason for refusing it to laics is, that it was given by our Lord to the apostles only. If to the apostles only, why not infer then to bishops only? But in that place, they make the apostles simple Presbyters, whereas here another vertigo seizes them, and they suddenly elect them bishops. Lastly, Ananias was not an apostle, and yet Paul was sent to him to receive his sight, to be baptised and filled with the Holy Spirit (Acts ix. 17). I will add, though cumulatively, if, by divine right, this office was peculiar to bishops, why have they dared to transfer it to plebeian Presbyters, as we read in one of the Epistles of Gregory? (Dist. 95, cap. Pervenis).

11. How frivolous, inept, and stolid the other reason, that their confirmation is worthier than the baptism of God, because in confirmation it is the forehead that is besmeared with oil, and in baptism the cranium. As if baptism were performed with oil, and not with water! I take all the pious to witness, whether it be not the one aim of these miscreants to adulterate the purity of the sacraments by their leaven. I have said elsewhere, that what is of God in the sacraments, can scarcely be got a glimpse of among the crowd of human inventions. If any did not then give me credit for the fact, let them now give it to their own teachers. Here, passing over water, and making it of no estimation, they set a great value on oil alone in baptism. We maintain, against them, that in baptism also the forehead is sprinkled with water, in comparison with which, we do not value your oil one straw, whether in baptism or in confirmation. But if any one alleges that oil is sold for more, I answer, that by this accession of value any good which might otherwise be in it is vitiated, so far is it from being lawful fraudulently to vend this most vile imposture. They betray their impiety by the third reason, when they pretend that a greater increase of virtue is conferred in confirmation than in baptism. By the laying on of hands the apostles dispensed the visible gifts of the Spirit. In what respect does the oil of these men prove its fecundity? But have done with these guides, who cover one sacrilege with many acts of sacrilege. It is a Gordian knot, which it is better to cut than to lose so much labour in untying.

12. When they see that the word of God, and everything like plausible argument, fail them, they pretend, as usual, that the observance is of the highest antiquity, and is confirmed by the consent of many ages. Even were this true, they gain nothing by it. A sacrament is not of earth, but of heaven; not of men, but of God only. They must prove God to be the author of their confirmation, if they would have it to be regarded as a sacrament. But why obtrude antiquity, seeing that ancient writers, whenever they would speak precisely, nowhere mention more than two sacraments? Were the bulwark of our faith to be sought from men, we have an impregnable citadel in this, that the fictitious sacraments of these men were never recognised as sacraments by ancient writers. They speak of the laying on of hands, but do they call it a sacrament? Augustine distinctly affirms that it is nothing but prayer (De Bapt. cont. Donat. Lib. iii. cap. 16). Let them not here yelp out one of their vile distinctions, that the laying on of hands to which Augustine referred was not the confirmatory, but the curative or reconciliatory. His book is extant and in men's hands; if I wrest it to any meaning different from that which Augustine himself wrote it, they are welcome not only to load me with reproaches after their wonted manner, but to spit upon me. He is speaking of those who returned from schism to the unity of the Church. He says that they have no need of a repetition of baptism, for the laying on of hands is sufficient, that the Lord may bestow the Holy Spirit upon them by the bond of

peace. But as it might seem absurd to repeat laying on of hands more than baptism, he shows the difference: "What," he asks, "is the laying on of hands but prayer over the man?" That this is his meaning is apparent from another passage, where he says, "Because of the bond of charity, which is the greatest gift of the Holy Spirit, without which all the other holy qualities which a man may possess are ineffectual for salvation, the hand is laid on reformed heretics" (Lib. v. cap. 23).

13. I wish we could retain the custom, which, as I have observed, existed in the early Church, before this abortive mask of a sacrament appeared. It would not be such a confirmation as they pretend, one which cannot even be named without injury to baptism, but catechising by which those in boyhood, or immediately beyond it, would give an account of their faith in the face of the Church. And the best method of catechising would be, if a form were drawn up for this purpose, containing, and briefly explaining, the substance of almost all the heads of our religion, in which the whole body of the faithful ought to concur without controversy. A boy of ten years of age would present himself to the Church, to make a profession of faith, would be questioned on each head, and give answers to each. If he was ignorant of any point, or did not well understand it, he would be taught. Thus, while the whole Church looked on and witnessed, he would profess the one true sincere faith with which the body of the faithful, with one accord, worship one God. Were this discipline in force in the present day, it would undoubtedly whet the sluggishness of certain parents, who carelessly neglect the instruction of their children, as if it did not at all belong to them, but who could not then omit it without public disgrace; there would be greater agreement in faith among the Christian people, and not so much ignorance and rudeness; some persons would not be so readily carried away by new and strange dogmas; in fine, it would furnish all with a methodical arrangement of Christian doctrine.

OF PENITENCE.

14. The next place they give to Penitence, of which they discourse so confusedly and unmethodically, that consciences cannot derive anything certain or solid from their doctrine. In another place (Book III. chap. iii. and iv.), we have explained at length, first, what the Scriptures teach concerning repentance, and, secondly, what these men teach concerning it. All we have now to advert to is the grounds of that opinion of it as a sacrament which has long prevailed in schools and churches. First, however, I will speak briefly of the rite of the early Church, which those men have used as a pretext for establishing their fiction. By the order observed in public repentance, those who had performed the satisfactions imposed upon them were reconciled by the formal laying on of hands. This was

the symbol of absolution by which the sinner himself regained his confidence of pardon before God, and the Church was admonished to lay aside the remembrance of the offence, and kindly receive him into favour. This Cyprian often terms *to give peace*. In order that the act might have more weight and estimation with the people, it was appointed that the authority of the bishop should always be interposed. Hence the decree of the second Council of Carthage, "No presbyter may publicly at mass reconcile a penitent;" and another, of the Council of Arausica, "Let those who are departing this life, at the time of penitence, be admitted to communion without the reconciliatory laying on of hands; if they recover from the disease, let them stand in the order of penitents, and after they have fulfilled their time, receive the reconciliatory laying on of hands from the bishop." Again, in the third Council of Carthage, "A presbyter may not reconcile a penitent without the authority of the bishop." The object of all these enactments was to prevent the strictness, which they wished to be observed in that matter, from being lost by excessive laxity. Accordingly, they wished cognisance to be taken by the bishop, who, it was probable, would be more circumspect in examining. Although Cyprian somewhere says that not the bishop only laid hands, but also the whole clergy. For he thus speaks, "They do penitence for a proper time; next they come to communion, and receive the right of communion by the laying on of the hands of the bishop and clergy" (Lib. iii. Ep 14). Afterwards, in process of time, the matter came to this, that they used the ceremony in private absolutions also without public penitence. Hence the distinction in Gratian (Decret. 26, Quæst. 6) between public and private reconciliation. I consider that ancient observance of which Cyprian speaks to have been holy and salutary to the Church, and I could wish it restored in the present day. The more modern form, though I dare not disapprove, or at least strongly condemn, I deem to be less necessary. Be this as it may, we see that the laying on of hands in penitence was a ceremony ordained by men, not by God, and is to be ranked among indifferent things, and external exercises, which indeed are not to be despised, but occupy an inferior place to those which have been recommended to us by the word of the Lord.

15. The Romanists and Schoolmen, whose wont it is to corrupt all things by erroneous interpretation, anxiously labour to find a sacrament here, and it cannot seem wonderful, for they seek a thing where it is not. At best, they leave the matter involved, undecided, uncertain, confused, and confounded by the variety of opinions. Accordingly, they say (Sent. Lib. iv. Dist. 22, cap. 3), either that external penitence is a sacrament, and, if so, ought to be regarded as a sign of internal penitence; *i. e.*, contrition of heart, which will be the matter of the sacrament, or that both together make a sacrament, not two, but one complete; but that the external is the sacrament merely, the internal, the matter, and the sacrament, whereas the

forgiveness of sins is the matter only, and not the sacrament. Let those who remember the definition of a sacrament, which we have given •above, test by it that which they say is a sacrament, and it will be found that it is not an external ceremony appointed by God for the confirmation of our faith. But if they allege that my definition is not a law which they are necessarily bound to obey, let them hear Augustine, whom they pretend to regard as a saint.[1] "Visible sacraments were instituted for the sake of carnal men, that by the ladder of sacraments they may be conveyed from those things which are seen by the eye, to those which are perceived by the understanding" (August. Quæst. Vet. Test. Lib. iii). Do they themselves see, or can they show to others, anything like this in that which they call the sacrament of penance? In another passage, he says, "It is called a sacrament, because in it one thing is seen, another thing is understood. What is seen has bodily appearance, what is understood has spiritual fruit" (Serm. de Bapt. Infant). These things in no way apply to the sacrament of penance, as they feign it; there, there is no bodily form to represent spiritual fruit.

16. And (to despatch these beasts in their own arena) if any sacrament is sought here, would it not have been much more plausible to maintain that the absolution of the priest is a sacrament, than penitence either external or internal? For it might obviously have been said that it is a ceremony'to confirm our faith in the forgiveness of sins, and that it has the promise of the keys, as they describe them: "Whatsoever ye shall bind or loose on earth, shall be bound or loosed in heaven." But some one will object that to most of those who are absolved by priests nothing of the kind is given by the absolution, whereas, according to their dogma, the sacraments of the new dispensation ought to effect what they figure. This is ridiculous. As in the eucharist, they make out a twofold eating—a sacramental, which is common to the good and bad alike, and a spiritual, which is proper only to the good; why should they not also pretend that absolution is given in *wo ways? And yet I have never been able to understand what they meant by their dogma. How much it is at variance with the truth of God, we showed when we formally discussed that subject. Here I only wish to show that no scruple should prevent them from giving the name of a sacrament to the absolution of the priest. For they might have answered by the mouth of Augustine,[2] that there is a sanctification without a visible sacrament, and a visible sacrament without internal sanctification. Again, that in the elect alone sacraments effect what they figure. Again, that some put on Christ so far as the receiving of the sacrament, and others so far as sanctification; that the former is done equally by the good and the bad, the latter by the good only. Surely they were more deluded than children, and blind in the full light of the sun when

---

1 French, "Auquel ils font semblant de porter une reverence inviolable;"—for whom they pretend to have an inviolable respect.
2 August. Quæst. Vet. Test. Lib. iii. De Bapt. Parvul. De Bapt. Cont. Donat. Lib. v

they toiled with so much difficulty, and perceived not a matter so plain and obvious to every man.

17. Lest they become elated, however, whatever be the part in which they place the sacrament, I deny that it can justly be regarded as a sacrament ; first, because there exists not to this effect any special promise of God, which is the only ground of a sacrament ;[1] and, secondly, because whatever ceremony is here used is a mere invention of man ; whereas, as has already been shown, the ceremonies of sacraments can only be appointed by God. Their fiction of the sacrament of penance, therefore, was falsehood and imposture. This fictitious sacrament they adorned with the befitting eulogium, that it was the second plank in the case of shipwreck, because if any one had, by sin, injured the garment of innocence received in baptism, he might repair it by penitence.[2] This was a saying of Jerome. Let it be whose it may, as it is plainly impious, it cannot be excused if understood in this sense ; as if baptism were effaced by sin, and were not rather to be recalled to the mind of the sinner whenever he thinks of the forgiveness of sins, that he may thereby recollect himself, regain courage, and be confirmed in the belief that he shall obtain the forgiveness of sins which was promised him in baptism. What Jerome said harshly and improperly—viz. that baptism, which is fallen from by those who deserve to be excommunicated from the Church, is repaired by penitence, these worthy expositors wrest to their own impiety. You will speak most correctly, therefore, if you call baptism the sacrament of penitence, seeing it is given to those who aim at repentance to confirm their faith and seal their confidence. But lest you should think this our invention, it appears, that besides being conformable to the words of Scripture, it was generally regarded in the early Church as an indubitable axiom. For in the short Treatise on Faith addressed to Peter, and bearing the name of Augustine, it is called, *The sacrament of faith and repentance.* But why have recourse to doubtful writings, as if anything can be required more distinct than the statement of the Evangelist, that John preached " the baptism of repentance for the remission of sins"? (Mark i. 4 ; Luke iii. 3).

---

[1] The French adds, " Car, comme nous avons assez declairé ci dessus, la promesse des clefs n'appartient nullement a faire quelque estat particulier d'absolution, mais seulement à la predication de l'Evangile soit qu'elle soit faite ou a plusieurs, ou a un seul, sans y mettre difference ; c'est a dire, que par icelle promesse notre Seigneur ne fonde point une absolution speciale qui soit faite distinctement à un chacun mais celle qui se fait indifferement a tous pecheurs, sans addresse particuliere."—For, as we have sufficiently shown above, the promise of the keys pertains not to the making of any particular state of absolution, but only to the preaching of the Gospel, whether it is made to several or to one only, without making any difference ; that is to say, that by this promise our Lord does not found a special absolution which is given separately to each, but one which is given indifferently to all sinners, without particular application.

[2] Sent. Lib. iv. Dist. 14, cap. 1. De Pœnit. Dist. 1, cap. 2. August. Dictum in Decret. 15. Quæst. 1, Cap. Fermissime.

OF EXTREME UNCTION, SO CALLED.

18. The third fictitious sacrament is Extreme Unction, which is performed only by a priest, and, as they express it, *in extremis*, with oil consecrated by the bishop, and with this form of words, " By this holy unction, and his most tender mercy, may God forgive you whatever sin you have committed, by the eye, the ear, the smell, the touch, the taste" (see Calv. Epist. de Fugiend. Illicit. Sac.). They pretend that there are two virtues in it—the forgiveness of sins, and relief of bodily disease, if so expedient; if not expedient, the salvation of the soul. For they say, that the institution was set down by James, whose words are, " Is any sick among you ? let him send for the elders of the Church ; and let them pray over him, anointing him with oil in the name of the Lord ; and the prayer of faith shall save the sick, and the Lord shall raise him up : and if he have committed sins, they shall be forgiven him" (James v. 14). The same account is here to be given of this unction as we lately gave of the laying on of hands ; in other words, it is mere hypocritical stage-play, by which, without reason or result, they would resemble the apostles. Mark relates that the apostles, on their first mission, agreeably to the command which they had received of the Lord, raised the dead, cast out devils, cleansed lepers, healed the sick, and, in healing, used oil. He says, they "anointed with oil many that were sick, and healed them" (Mark vi. 13). To this James referred when he ordered the presbyters of the Church to be called to anoint the sick. That no deeper mystery lay under this ceremony will easily be perceived by those who consider how great liberty both our Lord and his apostles used in those external things.[1] Our Lord, when about to give sight to the blind man, spat on the ground, and made clay of the spittle ; some he cured by a touch, others by a word. In like manner the apostles cured some diseases by word only, others by touch, others by anointing. But it is probable that neither this anointing nor any of the other things were used at random. I admit this ; not, however, that they were instruments of the cure, but only symbols to remind the ignorant whence this great virtue proceeded, and prevent them from ascribing the praise to the apostles. To designate the Holy Spirit and his gifts by oil is trite and common (Ps. xlv. 8). But the gift of hearing disappeared with the other miraculous powers which the Lord was pleased to give for a time, that it might render the new preaching of the gospel for ever wonderful. Therefore, even were we to grant that anointing was a sacrament of those powers which were then administered by the hands of the apostles, it pertains not to us, to whom no such powers have been committed.

19. And what better reason have they for making a sacrament of

---

[1] John ix. 6; Matth. ix. 29; Luke xviii. 42: Acts iii. 6 ; v. 16 ; xix. 12.

this unction, than of any of the other symbols which are mentioned in Scripture ?   Why do they not dedicate some pool of Siloam, into which, at certain seasons the sick may plunge themselves ?   That, they say, were done in vain.   Certainly not more in vain than unction.   Why do they not lay themselves on the dead, seeing that Paul, in raising up the dead youth, lay upon him ?   Why is not clay made of dust and spittle a sacrament ?   The other cases were special, but this is commanded by James.   In other words, James spake agreeably to the time when the Church still enjoyed this blessing from God.   They affirm, indeed, that there is still the same virtue in their unction, but we experience differently.   Let no man now wonder that they have with so much confidence deluded souls, which they knew to be stupid and blind, because deprived of the word of God, that is, of his light and life, seeing they blush not to attempt to deceive the bodily perceptions of those who are alive, and have all their senses about them.   They make themselves ridiculous, therefore, by pretending that they are endued with the gift of healing. The Lord, doubtless, is present with his people in all ages, and cures their sicknesses as often as there is need, not less than formerly ; and yet he does not exert those manifest powers, nor dispense miracles by the hands of apostles, because that gift was temporary, and owing, in some measure, to the ingratitude of men, immediately ceased.

20. Wherefore, as the apostles, not without cause, openly declared, by the symbol of oil, that the gift of healing committed to them was not their own, but the power of the Holy Spirit ; so, on the other hand, these men insult the Holy Spirit by making his power consist in a filthy oil of no efficacy.   It is just as if one were to say that all oil is the power of the Holy Spirit, because it is called by that name in Scripture, and that every dove is the Holy Spirit, because he appeared in that form.   Let them see to this : it is sufficient for us that we perceive, with absolute certainty, that their unction is no sacrament, as it is neither a ceremony appointed by God, nor has any promise.   For when we require, in a sacrament, these two things, that it be a ceremony appointed by God, and have a promise from God, we at the same time demand that that ceremony be delivered to us, and that that promise have reference to us.   No man contends that circumcision is now a sacrament of the Christian Church, although it was both an ordinance of God, and had his promise annexed to it, because it was neither commanded to us, nor was the promise annexed to it given us on the same condition.   The promise of which they vaunt so much in unction, as we have clearly demonstrated, and they themselves show by experience, has not been given to us.   The ceremony behoved to be used only by those who had been endued with the gift of healing, not by those murderers, who do more by slaying and butchering than by curing.

21. Even were it granted that this precept of unction, which has nothing to do with the present age, were perfectly adapted to it, they

will not even thus have advanced much in support of their unction, with which they have hitherto besmeared us. James would have all the sick to be anointed: these men besmear, with their oil, not the sick, but half-dead carcasses, when life is quivering on the lips, or, as they say, *in extremis.* If they have a present cure in their sacrament, with which they can either alleviate the bitterness of disease, or at least give some solace to the soul, they are cruel in never curing in time. James would have the sick man to be anointed by the elders of the Church. They admit no anointer but a priestling. When they interpret the elders of James to be priests, and allege that the plural number is used for honour, the thing is absurd; as if the Church had at that time abounded with swarms of priests, so that they could set out in long procession, bearing a dish of sacred oil. James, in ordering simply that the sick be anointed, seems to me to mean no other anointing than that of common oil, nor is any other mentioned in the narrative of Mark. These men deign not to use any oil but that which has been consecrated by a bishop, that is warmed with much breath, charmed by much muttering, and saluted nine times on bended knee, Thrice Hail, holy oil! thrice Hail, holy chrism! thrice Hail, holy balsam! From whom did they derive these exorcisms? James says, that when the sick man shall have been anointed with oil, and prayer shall have been made over him, if he have committed sins, they shall be forgiven him—viz. that his guilt being forgiven, he shall obtain a mitigation of the punishment, not meaning that sins are effaced by oil, but that the prayers by which believers commended their afflicted brother to God would not be in vain. These men are impiously false in saying that sins are forgiven by their sacred, that is, abominable unction. See how little they gain, even when they are allowed to abuse the passage of James as they list. And to save us the trouble of a laborious proof, their own annals relieve us from all difficulty; for they relate that Pope Innocent, who presided over the church of Rome in the age of Augustine, ordained, that not elders only, but all Christians, should use oil in anointing, in their own necessity, or in that of their friends.[1] Our authority for this is Sigebert, in his Chronicles.

OF ECCLESIASTICAL ORDERS.

22. The fourth place in their catalogue is held by the sacrament of Orders, one so prolific, as to beget of itself seven lesser sacraments. It is very ridiculous that, after affirming that there are seven sacraments, when they begin to count, they make out thirteen. It cannot be alleged that they are one sacrament, because they all tend to one priesthood, and are a kind of steps to the same thing. For while it is certain that the ceremonies in each are different, and they them-

1 The French adds, "Comment accorderont ils cela avec ce qu'ils veulent faire accroire"?—How will they reconcile this with what they wish to be believed?

selves say that the graces are different, no man can doubt that if their dogmas are admitted, they ought to be called seven sacraments. And why debate it as a doubtful matter, when they themselves plainly and distinctly declare that they are seven? First, then, we shall glance at them in passing, and show to how many absurdities they introduce us when they would recommend their orders to us as sacraments; and, secondly, we shall see whether the ceremony which churches use in ordaining ministers ought at all to be called a sacrament. They make seven ecclesiastical orders, or degrees, which they distinguish by the title of a sacrament. These are Doorkeepers, Readers, Exorcists, Acolytes, Subdeacons, Deacons, and Priests. And they say that they are seven, because of the seven kinds of graces of the Holy Spirit with which those who are promoted to them ought to be endued. This grace is increased and more liberally accumulated on promotion. The mere number has been consecrated by a perversion of Scripture, because they think they read in Isaiah that there are seven gifts of the Holy Spirit, whereas truly not more than six are mentioned by Isaiah, who, however, meant not to include all in that passage. For, in other passages are mentioned the spirit of life, of sanctification, of the adoption of sons, as well as there, the spirit of wisdom and understanding, the spirit of counsel and might, the spirit of knowledge, and of the fear of the Lord.[1] Although others who are more acute make not seven orders, but nine, in imitation, as they say, of the Church triumphant. But among these, also, there is a contest; because some insist that the clerical tonsure is the first order of all, and the episcopate the last; while others, excluding the tonsure, class the office of archbishop among the orders. Isiodorus distinguishes differently, for he makes Psalmists and Readers different.[2] To the former, he gives the charge of chanting; to the latter, that of reading the Scriptures for the instruction of the common people. And this distinction is observed by the canons. In this great variety, what would they have us to follow or to avoid? Shall we say that there are seven orders? So the master of the school teaches, but the most illuminated doctors determine otherwise. On the other hand, they are at variance among themselves. Besides, the most sacred canons call us in a different direction. Such, indeed, is the concord of men when they discuss divine things apart from the word of God.

23. But the crowning folly of all is, that in each of these they make Christ their colleague. First, they say[3] he performed the office of Doorkeeper when, with a whip of small cords, he drove the buyers and sellers from the temple. He intimates that he is a Doorkeeper when he says, " I am the door." He assumed the office of Reader,

---

[1] Isa. xi. 2; Ezek. i. 20; Rom. i. 4; viii. 15.
[2] Isidor. Lib. vii., Etymolog. allegatim, cap. Cleros. Dist. 21, 33, cap. Lector, et cap. Ostier.
[3] John ii. 15; x. 7; Luke iv. 17; Matth. vii. 33; John viii. 12; xiii. 5; Matth. xxvi. 26; xxvii. 50.

when he read Isaiah in the synagogue. He performed the office of Exorcist when, touching the tongue and ears of the deaf and dumb man with spittle, he restored his hearing. He declared that he was an Acolyte by the words, " He that followeth me shall not walk in darkness." He performed the office of Subdeacon, when, girding himself with a towel, he washed the feet of his disciples. He acted the part of a Deacon, when he distributed his body and blood in the Supper. He performed the part of a Priest, when, on the cross, he offered himself in sacrifice to the Father. As these things cannot be heard without laughter, I wonder how they could have been written without laughter, if, indeed, they were men who wrote them. But their most noteable subtlety is that in which they speculate on the name of Acolyte, calling him Ceroferarius—a magical term, I presume, one certainly unknown to all nations and tongues ; ἀκόλουθος, in Greek, meaning simply *attendant*. Were I to stop and seriously refute these things, I might myself justly be laughed at, so frivolous are they and ludicrous.

24. Still, lest they should be able to impose on silly women, their vanity must be exposed in passing. With great pomp and solemnity they elect their readers, psalmists, doorkeepers, acolytes, to perform those services which they give in charge, either to boys, or at least to those whom they call laics. Who, for the most part, lights the tapers, who pours wine and water from the pitcher, but a boy or some mean person among laics, who gains his bread by so doing ? Do not the same persons chant ? Do they not open and shut the doors of Churches ? Who ever saw, in their churches, either an acolyte or doorkeeper performing his office ? Nay, when he who as a boy performed the office of acolyte, is admitted to the order of acolyte, he ceases to be the very thing he begins to be called, so that they seem professedly to wish to cast away the office when they assume the title. See why they hold it necessary to be consecrated by sacraments, and to receive the Holy Spirit! It is just to do nothing. If they pretend that this is the defect of the times, because they neglect and abandon their offices, let them, at the same time, confess that there is not in the Church, in the present day, any use or benefit of these sacred orders which they wondrously extol, and that their whole Church is full of anathema, since the tapers and flagons, which none are worthy to touch but those who have been consecrated acolytes, she allows to be handled by boys and profane persons ; since her chants, which ought to be heard only from consecrated lips, she delegates to children. And to what end, pray, do they consecrate exorcists ? I hear that the Jews had their exorcists, but I see they were so called from the exorcisms which they practised (Acts xix. 13). Who ever heard of those fictitious exorcists having given one specimen of their profession ? It is pretended that power has been given them to lay their hands on energumens, catechumens, and demoniacs, but they cannot persuade demons that they are endued with such power, not only because demons do not

submit to their orders, but even command themselves. Scarcely will you find one in ten who is not possessed by a wicked spirit. All, then, which they babble about their paltry orders is a compound of ignorant and stupid falsehoods. Of the ancient acolytes, door-keepers, and readers, we have spoken when explaining the government of the Church. All that we here proposed was to combat that novel invention of a sevenfold sacrament in ecclesiastical orders of which we nowhere read except among silly raving Sorbonnists and Canonists.

25. Let us now attend to the ceremonies which they employ. And first, all whom they enrol among their militia they initiate into the clerical status by a common symbol. They shave them on the top of the head, that the crown may denote regal honour, because clergy ought to be kings in governing themselves and others. Peter thus speaks of them: " Ye are a chosen generation, a royal priesthood, a holy nation, a peculiar people" (1 Pet. ii. 9). But it was sacrilege in them to arrogate to themselves alone what is given to the whole Church, and proudly to glory in a title of which they had robbed the faithful. Peter addresses the whole Church : these men wrest it to a few shaven crowns, as if it had been said to them alone, Be ye holy : as if they alone had been purchased by the blood of Christ : as if they alone had been made by Christ kings and priests unto God. Then they assign other reasons (Sent. Lib. iv. Dist. 24). The top of the head is bared, that their mind may be shown to be free, with unveiled face, to behold the glory of God ; or that they may be taught to cut off the vices of the eye and the lip. Or the shaving of the head is the laying aside of temporal things, while the circumference of the crown is the remnants of good which are retained for support. Everything is in figure, because forsooth, the veil of the temple is not yet rent. Accordingly, persuaded that they have excellently performed their part because they have figured such things by their crown, they perform none of them in reality. How long will they delude us with such masks and impostures ? The clergy, by shaving off some hair, intimate (Sent. loco cit.) that they have cast away abundance of temporal good— that they contemplate the glory of God—that they have mortified concupiscence of the ear and the eye : but no class of men is more rapacious, more stupid, more libidinous. Why do they not rather exhibit true sanctity, than give a hypocritical semblance of it in false and lying signs?

26. Moreover, when they say that the clerical crown has its origin and nature from the Nazarenes, what else do they say than that their mysteries are derived from Jewish ceremonies, or rather are mere Judaism? When they add that Priscilla, Aquila, and Paul himself, after they had taken a vow, shaved their head that they might be purified, they betray their gross ignorance. For we nowhere read this of Priscilla, while, with regard to Aquila, it is uncertain, since that tonsure may refer equally well to Paul as to Aquila (Acts xviii.

18). But not to leave them in possession of what they ask—viz. that they have an example in Paul, it is to be observed, to the more simple, that Paul never shaved his head for any sanctification, but only in subservience to the weakness of brethren. Vows of this kind I am accustomed to call vows of charity, not of piety; in other words, vows not undertaken for divine worship, but only in deference to the infirmity of the weak, as he himself says, that to the Jews he became a Jew (1 Cor. ix. 20). This, therefore, he did, and that once and for a short time, that he might accommodate himself for a little to the Jews. When these men would, for no end, imitate the purifications of the Nazarenes (Num. vi. 18), what else do they than set up a new, while they improperly affect to rival the ancient Judaism? In the same spirit the Decretal Epistle was composed, which enjoins the clergy, after the apostle, not to nourish their hair, but to shave it all round (Cap. Prohibitur, Dist. 24); as if the apostle, in showing what is comely for all men, had been solicitous for the spherical tonsure of the clergy. Hence, let my readers consider what kind of force or dignity there can be in the subsequent mysteries, to which this is the introduction.

27. Whence the clerical tonsure had its origin, is abundantly clear from Augustine alone (De Opera. Monach. et Retract). While in that age none wore long hair but the effeminate, and those who affected an unmanly beauty and elegance, it was thought to be of bad example to allow the clergy to do so. They were therefore enjoined either to cut or shave their hair, that they might not have the appearance of effeminate indulgence. And so common was the practice, that some monks, to appear more sanctimonious than others by a notable difference in dress, let their locks hang loose.[1] But when hair returned to use, and some nations, which had always worn long hair, as France, Germany, and England, embraced Christianity, it is probable that the clergy everywhere shaved the head, that they might not seem to affect ornament. At length, in a more corrupt age, when all ancient customs were either changed, or had degenerated into superstition, seeing no reason for the clerical tonsure (they had retained nothing but a foolish imitation), they betook themselves to mystery, and now superstitiously obtrude it upon us in support of their sacrament. The Doorkeepers, on consecration, receive the keys of the Church, by which it is understood that the custody of it is committed to them; the Readers receive the Holy Bible; the Exorcists, forms of exorcism which they use over the possessed and catechumens; the Acolytes, tapers and the flagon. Such are the ceremonies which, it would seem, possess so much secret virtue, that they cannot only be signs and badges, but even causes of invisible grace. For this, according to their definition, they demand, when they would have them to be classed among sacraments. But to despatch the

---

[1] The French adds, "Voila comment la tonsure n'estoit point une chose speciale aux clercs, mais estoit en usance quasi à tous."—See how the tonsure was not a thing peculiar to the clergy, but was used, as it were, by all.

matter in a few words, I say that it is absurd for schools and canons to make sacraments of those minor orders, since, even by the confession of those who do so, they were unknown to the primitive Church, and were devised many ages after. But sacraments as containing a divine promise ought not to be appointed, either by angels or men, but by God only, to whom alone it belongs to give the promise.

28. There remain the three orders which they call major. Of these, what they call the subdeaconate was transferred to this class, after the crowd of minor began to be prolific. But as they think they have authority for these from the word of God, they honour them specially with the name of Holy Orders. Let us see how they wrest the ordinances of God to their own ends. We begin with the order of presbyter or priest. To these two names they give one meaning, understanding by them, those to whom, as they say, it pertains to offer the sacrifice of Christ's body and blood on the altar, to frame prayers, and bless the gifts of God. Hence, at ordination, they receive the patena with the host, as symbols of the power conferred upon them of offering sacrifices to appease God, and their hands are anointed, this symbol being intended to teach that they have received the power of consecrating. But of the ceremonies afterwards. Of the thing itself, I say that it is so far from having, as they pretend, one particle of support from the word of God, that they could not more wickedly corrupt the order which he has appointed. And first, it ought to be held as confessed (this we maintained when treating of the Papal Mass), that all are injurious to Christ who call themselves priests in the sense of offering expiatory victims. He was constituted and consecrated Priest by the Father, with an oath, after the order of Melchisedek, without end and without successor (Psalm cx. 4; Heb. v. 6; vii. 3). He once offered a victim of eternal expiation and reconciliation, and now also having entered the sanctuary of heaven, he intercedes for us. In him we all are priests, but to offer praise and thanksgiving, in fine, ourselves, and all that is ours, to God. It was peculiar to him alone to appease God and expiate sins by his oblation. When these men usurp it to themselves, what follows, but that they have an impious and sacrilegious priesthood? It is certainly wicked over much to dare to distinguish it with the title of sacrament. In regard to the true office of presbyter, which was recommended to us by the lips of Christ, I willingly give it that place. For in it there is a ceremony which, first, is taken from the Scriptures; and, secondly, is declared by Paul to be not empty or superfluous, but to be a faithful symbol of spiritual grace (1 Tim. iv. 14). My reason for not giving a place to the third is, because it is not ordinary or common to all believers, but is a special rite for a certain function. But while this honour is attributed to the Christian ministry, Popish priests may not plume themselves upon it. Christ ordered dispensers of his gospel and his sacred mysteries to be ordained, not sacrificers to be inaugurated, and his command was to preach the gospel and feed the flock, not to immolate victims. He

promised the gift of the Holy Spirit, not to make expiation for sins, but duly to undertake and maintain the government of the Church (Matt. xxviii. 19 ; Mark xvi. 15 ; John xxi. 15).

29. With the reality the ceremonies perfectly agree. When our Lord commissioned the apostles to preach the gospel, he breathed upon them (John xx. 22). By this symbol he represented the gift of the Holy Spirit which he bestowed upon them. This breathing these worthy men have retained ; and, as they were bringing the Holy Spirit from their throat, mutter over their priestlings, " Receive the Holy Spirit." Accordingly, they omit nothing which they do not preposterously mimic. I say not in the manner of players (who have art and meaning in their gestures), but like apes who imitate at random without selection. We observe, say they, the example of the Lord. But the Lord did many things which he did not intend to be examples to us. Our Lord said to his disciples, " Receive the Holy Spirit" (John xx. 22). He said also to Lazarus, " Lazarus, come forth" (John xi. 43). He said to the paralytic, " Rise, take up thy bed, and walk" (John v. 8). Why do they not say the same to all the dead and paralytic ? He gave a specimen of his divine power when, in breathing on the apostles, he filled them with the gift of the Holy Spirit. If they attempt to do the same, they rival God, and do all but challenge him to the contest. But they are very far from producing the effect, and only mock Christ by that absurd gesture. Such, indeed, is the effrontery of some, that they dare to assert that the Holy Spirit is conferred by them ; but what truth there is in this, we learn from experience, which cries aloud that all who are consecrated priests, of horses become asses, and of fools, madmen. And yet it is not here that I am contending against them ; I am only condemning the ceremony itself, which ought not to be drawn into a precedent, since it was used as the special symbol of a miracle, so far. is it from furnishing them with an example for imitation.

30. But from whom, pray, did they receive their unction ? They answer, that they received it from the sons of Aaron, from whom also their order derived its origin (Sent. Lib. iv. Dist. 14, cap. 8, et in Canon. Dist. 21, cap. 1). Thus they constantly choose to defend themselves by perverse examples, rather than confess that any of their rash practices is of their own devising. Meanwhile, they observe not that in professing to be the successors of the sons of Aaron, they are injurious to the priesthood of Christ, which alone was adumbrated and typified by all ancient priesthoods. In him, therefore, they were all concluded and completed, in him they ceased, as we have repeatedly said, and as the Epistle to the Hebrews, unaided by any gloss, declares. But if they are so much delighted with Mosaic ceremonies, why do they not hurry oxen, calves, and lambs, to their sacrifices ? They have, indeed, a great part of the ancient tabernacle, and of the whole Jewish worship. The only thing wanted to their religion is, that they do not sacrifice oxen and calves. Who sees not that this

practice of unction is much more pernicious than circumcision, especially when to it is added superstition and a Pharisaical opinion of the merit of the work ? The Jews placed their confidence of justification in circumcision, these men look for spiritual gifts in unction. Therefore, in desiring to be rivals of the Levites, they become apostates from Christ, and discard themselves from the pastoral office.

31. It is, if you please, the sacred oil which impresses an indelible character. As if oil could not be washed away by sand and salt, or if it sticks the closer, with soap. But that character is spiritual. What has oil to do with the soul ? Have they forgotten what they quote from Augustine, that if the word be withdrawn from the water, there will be nothing but water, but that it is owing to the word that it is a sacrament ? What word can they show in their oil ? Is it because Moses was commanded to anoint the sons of Aaron ? (Exod. xxx. 30). But he there receives command concerning the tunic, the ephod, the breastplate, the mitre, the crown of holiness with which Aaron was to be adorned ; and concerning the tunics, belts, and mitres which his sons were to wear. He receives command about sacrificing the calf, burning its fat, about cutting and burning rams, about sanctifying ear-rings and vestments with the blood of one of the rams, and innumerable other observances. Having passed over all these, I wonder why the unction of oil alone pleases them. If they delight in being sprinkled, why are they sprinkled with oil rather than with blood? They are attempting, forsooth, an ingenious device ; they are trying, by a kind of patchwork, to make one religion out of Christianity, Judaism, and Paganism. Their unction, therefore, is without savour ; it wants salt, that is, the word of God. There remains the laying on of hands, which, though I admit it to be a sacrament in true and legitimate ordination, I do deny to have any such place in this fable, where they neither obey the command of Christ, nor look to the end to which the promise ought to lead us. If they would not have the sign denied them, they must adapt it to the reality to which it is dedicated.

32. As to the order of the diaconate, I would raise no dispute, if the office which existed under the apostles, and a purer Church, were restored to its integrity. But what resemblance to it do we see in their fictitious deacons? I speak not of the men, lest they should complain that I am unjustly judging their doctrine by the vices of those who profess it ; but I contend that those whom their doctrine declares to us, derive no countenance from those deacons whom the apostolic Church appointed. They say that it belongs to their deacons to assist the priests, and minister at all the things which are done in the sacraments, as in baptism, in chrism, the patena, and chalice, to bring the offerings and lay them on the altar, to prepare and dress the table of the Lord, to carry the cross, announce and read out the gospel and epistle to the people (Sent. Lib. iv. Dist. 24, cap. 8 ; Item, Cap. Perlectis, Dist. 25). Is there here one word about

the true office of deacon ?   Let us now attend to the appointment.
The bishop alone lays hands on the deacon who is ordained ; he
places the prayer-book and stole upon his left shoulder, that he may
understand that he has received the easy yoke of the Lord, in order
that he may subject to the fear of the Lord every thing pertaining to
the left side : he gives him a text of the gospel, to remind him that
he is its herald.   What have these things to do with deacons ?   But
they act just as if one were to say he was ordaining apostles, when
he was only appointing persons to kindle the incense, clean the
images, sweep the churches, set traps for mice, and put out dogs.
Who can allow this class of men to be called apostles, and to be
compared with the very apostles of Christ ?   After this, let them not
pretend that those whom they appoint to mere stage-play are deacons.
Nay, they even declare, by the very name, what the nature of the
office is.   For they call them Levites, and wish to trace their nature
and origin to the sons of Levi.   As far as I am concerned, they are
welcome, provided they do not afterwards deck themselves in borrowed
feathers.

33. What use is there in speaking of subdeacons ?   For, whereas
in fact they anciently had the charge of the poor, they attribute to
them some kind of nugatory function, as carrying the chalice and
patena, the pitcher with water, and the napkin to the altar, pouring
out water for the hands, &c.   Then, by the offerings which they are
said to receive and bring in, they mean those which they swallow up,
as if they had been destined to anathema.   There is an admirable
correspondence between the office and the mode of inducting to it—
viz. receiving from the bishop the patena and chalice, and from the
archdeacon the pitcher with water, the manual and trumpery of this
kind.   They call upon us to admit that the Holy Spirit is included
in these frivolities.   What pious man can be induced to grant this ?
But to have done at once, we may conclude the same of this as of the
others, and there is no need to repeat at length what has been explained above.   To the modest and docile (it is such I have undertaken to instruct), it will be enough that there is no sacrament of
God, unless where a ceremony is shown annexed to a promise, or
rather where a promise is seen in a ceremony.   Here there is not one
syllable of a certain promise, and it is vain, therefore, to seek for a
ceremony to confirm the promise.   On the other hand, we read of no
ceremony appointed by God in regard to those usages which they
employ, and, therefore, there can be no sacrament.

OF MARRIAGE.

The last of all is marriage, which, while all admit it to be an
institution of God, no man ever saw to be a sacrament, until the time
of Gregory.   And would it ever have occurred to the mind of any
sober man ?   It is a good and holy ordinance of God   And agri-

culture, architecture, shoemaking, and shaving, are lawful ordinances of God; but they are not sacraments. For in a sacrament, the thing required is not only that it be a work of God, but that it be an external ceremony appointed by God to confirm a promise. That there is nothing of the kind in marriage, even children can judge. But it is a sign, they say, of a sacred thing, that is, of the spiritual union of Christ with the Church. If by the term sign they understand a symbol set before us by God to assure us of our faith, they wander widely from the mark. If they mean merely a sign because it has been employed as a similitude, I will show how acutely they reason. Paul says, "One star differeth from another star in glory. So also is the resurrection of the dead" (1 Cor. xv. 41, 42). Here is one sacrament. Christ says, "The kingdom of heaven is like to a grain of mustard-seed" (Matth. xiii. 31). Here is another sacrament. Again, "The kingdom of heaven is like unto leaven" (Matth. xiii. 33). Here is a third sacrament. Isaiah says, "He shall feed his flock like a shepherd" (Isaiah xl. 11). Here is a fourth sacrament. In another passage he says, "The Lord shall go forth as a mighty man" (Isaiah xlii. 13). Here is a fifth sacrament. And where will be the end or limit? Everything in this way will be a sacrament. All the parables and similitudes in Scripture will be so many sacraments. Nay, even theft will be a sacrament, seeing it is written, "The day of the Lord so cometh as a thief in the night" (1 Thess. v. 2). Who can tolerate the ignorant garrulity of these sophists? I admit, indeed, that whenever we see a vine, the best thing is to call to mind what our Saviour says, "I am the true vine, and my father is the husbandman." "I am the vine, ye are the branches" (John xv. 1, 5). And whenever we meet a shepherd with his flock, it is good also to remember, "I am the good shepherd, and know my sheep, and am known of mine" (John x. 14). But any man who would class such similitudes with sacraments should be sent to bedlam.

35. They adduce the words of Paul, by which they say that the name of a sacrament is given to marriage, "He that loveth his wife loveth himself. For no man ever yet hated his own flesh; but nourisheth and cherisheth it, even as the Lord the Church: for we are members of his body, of his flesh, and of his bones. For this cause shall a man leave his father and mother, and shall be joined unto his wife, and they two shall be one flesh. This is a great mystery: but I speak concerning Christ and the Church" (Eph. v. 28, 32). To treat Scripture thus is to confound heaven and earth. Paul, in order to show husbands how they ought to love their wives, sets Christ before them as an example. As he shed his bowels of affection for the Church, which he has espoused to himself, so he would have every one to feel affected toward his wife. Then he adds, "He that loveth his wife loveth himself," "even as the Lord the Church." Moreover, to show how Christ loved the Church as himself, nay, how he made himself one with his spouse the Church, he

applies to her what Moses relates that Adam said of himself. For after Eve was brought into his presence, knowing that she had been formed out of his side, he exclaimed, " This is now bone of my bones, and flesh of my flesh" (Gen. ii. 23). That all this was spiritually fulfilled in Christ, and in us, Paul declares, when he says, that we are members of his body, of his flesh, and of his bones, and so one flesh with him. At length he breaks out into the exclamation," This is a great mystery ;" and lest any one should be misled by the ambiguity, he says, that he is not speaking of the connection between husband and wife, but of the spiritual marriage of Christ and the Church. And truly it is a great mystery that Christ allowed a rib to be taken from himself, of which we might be formed; that is, that when he was strong, he was pleased to become weak, that we might be strengthened by his strength, and should no longer live ourselves, but he live in us (Gal. ii. 20).

36. The thing which misled them was the term *sacrament*.[1] But, was it right that the whole Church should be punished for the ignorance of these men ? Paul called it a mystery. When the Latin interpreter might have abandoned this mode of expression as uncommon to Latin ears, or converted it into " secret," he preferred calling it *sacramentum*, but in no other sense than the Greek term μυστηριον was used by Paul. Let them go now and clamour against skill in languages, their ignorance of which leads them most shamefully astray in a matter easy and obvious to every one. But why do they so strongly urge the term sacrament in this one passage, and in others pass it by with neglect ? For both in the First Epistle to Timothy (1 Tim. iii. 9, 16), and also in the Epistle to the Ephesians, it is used by the Vulgate interpreter, and in every instance, for mystery. Let us, however, pardon them this lapsus, though liars ought to have good memories. Marriage being thus recommended by the title of a sacrament,[2] can it be anything but vertiginous levity afterwards to call it uncleanness, and pollution, and carnal defilement ? How absurd is it to debar priests from a sacrament ! If they say that they debar not from a sacrament but from carnal connection, they will not thus escape me. They say that this connection is part of the sacrament, and thereby figures the union which we have with Christ in conformity of nature, inasmuch as it is by this connection that husband and wife become one flesh; although some have here found two sacraments, the one of God and the soul, in bridegroom and bride, another of Christ and the Church, in husband and wife. Be this as it may, this connection is a sacrament from which no Christian can lawfully be debarred, unless, indeed, the sacraments of Christians accord so ill that they cannot stand together. There is

1 French, " Ils ont eto trompé du mot de Sacrement qui est en la translation commune."—They have been misled by the word Sacrament, which is in the common translation.

2 Lat. Lib. iv. Dist. 26, cap. 6, et in Decret 27, Quæst. 2, cap. Quæ Societas, etc. Gloss. eod. c. Lex Divina. Ibid. Lib. iv. Dist. 33, cap. 2. et in Decret. 32, Quæst. 2. cap. Quicquid, &c.

also another absurdity in these dogmas. They affirm that in a sacrament the gift of the Holy Spirit is conferred ; this connection they hold to be a sacrament, and yet they deny that in it the Holy Spirit is ever present.

37. And, that they might not delude the Church in this matter merely, what a long series of errors, lies, frauds, and iniquities have they appended to one error ?   So that you may say they sought nothing but a hiding-place for abominations when they converted marriage into a sacrament.   When once they obtained this, they appropriated to themselves the cognisance of conjugal causes : as the thing was spiritual, it was not to be intermeddled with by profane judges.   Then they enacted laws by which they confirmed their tyranny,—laws partly impious toward God, partly fraught with injustice toward men ; such as, that marriages contracted between minors, without the consent of their parents, should be valid ; that no lawful marriages can be contracted between relations within the seventh degree, and that such marriages, if contracted, should be dissolved.   Moreover, they frame degrees of kindred contrary to the laws of all nations, and even the polity of Moses, and enact that a husband who has repudiated an adulteress may not marry again—that spiritual kindred cannot be joined in marriage—that marriage cannot be celebrated from Septuagesimo to the Octaves of Easter, three weeks before the nativity of John, nor from Advent to Epiphany, and innumerable others, which it were too tedious to mention.   We must now get out of their mire, in which our discourse has stuck longer than our inclination.   Methinks, however, that much has been gained if I have, in some measure, deprived these asses of their lion's skin.

CHAPTER XX.

OF CIVIL GOVERNMENT.

This chapter consists of two principal heads,—I. General discourse on the necessity, dignity, and use of Civil Government, in opposition to the frantic proceedings of the Anabaptists, sec. 1–3. II. A special exposition of the three leading parts of which Civil Government consists, sec. 4–32.

The first part treats of the function of Magistrates, whose authority and calling is proved, sec. 4–7. Next, the three forms of civil government are added, sec. 8. Thirdly, Consideration of the office of the civil magistrate in respect of piety and righteousness. Here, of rewards and punishments—viz. punishing the guilty, protecting the innocent, repressing the seditious, managing the affairs of peace and war, sec. 9–13. The second part treats of Laws, their utility, necessity, form, authority, constitution, and scope; sec. 14–16.   The last part relates to the People, and explains the use of laws, courts, and magistrates, to the common society of Christians, sec. 17–21. Deference which private individuals owe to magistrates, and how far obedience ought to be carried, sec. 22–32.

Sections.

1. HAVING shown above that there is a twofold government in man, and having fully considered the one which, placed in the soul or inward man, relates to eternal life, we are here called to say something of the other, which pertains only to civil institutions and the external regulation of manners. For although this subject seems from its nature to be unconnected with the spiritual doctrine of faith, which I have undertaken to treat, it will appear as we proceed, that I have properly connected them, nay, that I am under the necessity of doing so, especially while, on the one hand, frantic and barbarous men are furiously endeavouring to overturn the order established by God, and, on the other, the flatterers of princes, extolling their power without measure, hesitate not to oppose it to the government of God. Unless we meet both extremes, the purity of the faith will perish. We may add, that it in no small degree concerns us to know how kindly God has here consulted for the human race, that pious zeal may the more strongly urge us to testify our gratitude. And first, before entering on the subject itself, it is necessary to attend to the distinction which we formerly laid down (Book III. Chap. xix. sec. 16, et supra, Chap. x.), lest, as often happens to many, we imprudently confound these two things, the nature of which is altogether different. For some, on hearing that liberty is promised in the gospel, a liberty which acknowledges no king and no magistrate among men, but looks to Christ alone, think that they can receive no benefit from their liberty so long as they see any power placed over them. Accordingly, they think that nothing will be safe until the whole world is changed into a new form, when there will be neither courts, nor laws, nor magistrates, nor anything of the kind to interfere, as they suppose, with their liberty. But he who knows to distinguish between the body and the soul, between the present fleeting life and that which is future and eternal, will have no difficulty in understanding that the spiritual kingdom of Christ and civil government are things very widely separated. Seeing, therefore, it is a Jewish vanity to seek and include the kingdom of Christ under the elements of this world, let us, considering, as Scripture clearly teaches, that the blessings which we derive from Christ are spiritual, remember to confine the liberty which is promised and offered to us in him within its proper limits. For why is it that the very same apostle who bids us " stand fast in the liberty wherewith Christ hath made us free, and be not again entangled with the yoke of bondage " (Gal. v. 1), in another

passage forbids slaves to be solicitous about their state (1 Cor. vii, 21), unless it be that spiritual liberty is perfectly compatible with civil servitude? In this sense the following passages are to be understood: "There is neither Jew nor Greek, there is neither bond nor free, there is neither male nor female" (Gal. iii. 28). Again, "There is neither Greek nor Jew, circumcision nor uncircumcision, barbarian, Scythian, bond nor free: but Christ is all and in all" (Col. iii. 11). It is thus intimated, that it matters not what your condition is among men, nor under what laws you live, since in them the kingdom of Christ does not at all consist.

2. Still the distinction does not go so far as to justify us in supposing that the whole scheme of civil government is matter of pollution, with which Christian men have nothing to do. Fanatics, indeed, delighting in unbridled license, insist and vociferate that, after we are dead by Christ to the elements of this world, and being translated into the kingdom of God sit among the celestials, it is unworthy of us, and far beneath our dignity, to be occupied with those profane and impure cares which relate to matters alien from a Christian man. To what end, they say, are laws without courts and tribunals? But what has a Christian man to do with courts? Nay, if it is unlawful to kill, what have we to do with laws and courts? But as we lately taught that that kind of government is distinct from the spiritual and internal kingdom of Christ, so we ought to know that they are not adverse to each other. The former, in some measure, begins the heavenly kingdom in us, even now upon earth, and in this mortal and evanescent life commences immortal and incorruptible blessedness, while to the latter it is assigned, so long as we live among men, to foster and maintain the external worship of God, to defend sound doctrine and the condition of the Church, to adapt our conduct to human society, to form our manners to civil justice, to conciliate us to each other, to cherish common peace and tranquillity. All these I confess to be superfluous, if the kingdom of God, as it now exists within us, extinguishes the present life. But if it is the will of God that while we aspire to true piety we are pilgrims upon the earth, and if such pilgrimage stands in need of such aids, those who take them away from man rob him of his humanity. As to their allegation that there ought to be such perfection in the Church of God that her guidance should suffice for law, they stupidly imagine her to be such as she never can be found in the community of men. For while the insolence of the wicked is so great, and their iniquity so stubborn, that it can scarcely be curbed by any severity of laws, what do we expect would be done by those whom force can scarcely repress from doing ill, were they to see perfect impunity for their wickedness?

3. But we shall have a fitter opportunity of speaking of the use of civil government. All we wish to be understood at present is, that it is perfect barbarism to think of exterminating it, its use among men being not less than that of bread and water, light and air, while its dignity is much more excellent. Its object is not merely, like

those things, to enable men to breathe, eat, drink, and be warmed (though it certainly includes all these, while it enables them to live together); this, I say, is not its only object, but it is, that no idolatry, no blasphemy against the name of God, no calumnies against his truth, nor other offences to religion, break out and be disseminated among the people ; that the public quiet be not disturbed, that every man's property be kept secure, that men may carry on innocent commerce with each other, that honesty and modesty be cultivated ; in short, that a public form of religion may exist among Christians, and humanity among men.   Let no one be surprised that I now attribute the task of constituting religion aright to human polity, though I seem above to have placed it beyond the will of man, since I no more than formerly allow men at pleasure to enact laws concerning religion and the worship of God, when I approve of civil order which is directed to this end—viz. to prevent the true religion, which is contained in the law of God, from being with impunity openly violated and polluted by public blasphemy.   But the reader, by the help of a perspicuous arrangement, will better understand what view is to be taken of the whole order of civil government, if we treat of each of its parts separately.   Now these are three: The Magistrate, who is president and guardian of the laws ; the Laws, according to which he governs ; and the People, who are governed by the laws, and obey the magistrate.   Let us consider, then, first, What is the function of the magistrate ?   Is it a lawful calling approved by God ?   What is the nature of his duty ?   What the extent of his power ?   Secondly, What are the laws by which Christian polity is to be regulated ? And, lastly, What is the use of laws as regards the people ?   And, What obedience is due to the magistrate ?

4. With regard to the function of magistrates, the Lord has not only declared that he approves and is pleased with it, but, moreover, has strongly recommended it to us by the very honourable titles which he has conferred upon it.   To mention a few.[1]   When those who bear the office of magistrate are called gods, let no one suppose that there is little weight in that appellation.   It is thereby intimated that they have a commission from God, that they are invested with divine authority, and, in fact, represent the person of God, as whose substitutes they in a manner act.   This is not a quibble of mine, but is the interpretation of Christ.   " If Scripture," says he, " called them Gods, to whom the word of God came."   What is this but that the business was committed to them by God, to serve him in their office, and (as Moses and Jehoshaphat said to the judges whom they were appointing over each of the cities of Judah) to exercise judgment, not for man, but for God ?   To the same effect Wisdom affirms, by the mouth of Solomon, " By me kings reign, and princes decree justice.   By me princes rule, and nobles, even all the judges of the earth" (Prov. viii. 15, 16).   For it is just as if it had

---

[1] Exod. xxii. 8, 9 ; Ps. lxxxii. 1, 6 ; John x. 34, 35 ; Deut. i. 16, 17 ; 2 Chron. xix. 6, 7 ; Prov. viii. 15.

been said, that it is not owing to human perverseness that supreme power on earth is lodged in kings and other governors, but by Divine Providence, and the holy decree of Him to whom it has seemed good so to govern the affairs of men, since he is present, and also presides in enacting laws and exercising judicial equity. This Paul also plainly teaches when he enumerates offices of rule among the gifts of God, which, distributed variously, according to the measure of grace, ought to be employed by the servants of Christ for the edification of the Church (Rom. xii. 8). In that place, however, he is properly speaking of the senate of grave men who were appointed in the primitive Church to take charge of public discipline. This office, in the Epistle to the Corinthians, he calls κυβερνήσεις, *governments* (1 Cor. xii. 28). Still, as we see that civil power has the same end in view, there can be no doubt that he is recommending every kind of just government. He speaks much more clearly when he comes to a proper discussion of the subject. For he says that " there is no power but of God : the powers that be are ordained of God ;" that rulers are the ministers of God, "not a terror to good works, but to the evil" (Rom. xiii. 1, 3). To this we may add the examples of saints, some of whom held the offices of kings, as David, Josiah, and Hezekiah ; others of governors, as Joseph and Daniel ; others of civil magistrates among a free people, as Moses, Joshua, and the Judges. Their functions were expressly approved by the Lord. Wherefore no man can doubt that civil authority is, in the sight of God, not only sacred and lawful, but the most sacred, and by far the most honourable, of all stations in mortal life.

5. Those who are desirous to introduce anarchy[1] object that, though anciently kings and judges presided over a rude people, yet that, in the present day, that servile mode of governing does not at all accord with the perfection which Christ brought with his gospel. Herein they betray not only their ignorance, but their devilish pride, arrogating to themselves a perfection of which not even a hundredth part is seen in them. But be they what they may, the refutation is easy. For when David says, " Be wise now therefore, O ye kings : be instructed, ye judges of the earth ;" " Kiss the Son, lest he be angry" (Psalm ii. 10, 12), he does not order them to lay aside their authority and return to private life, but to make the power with which they are invested subject to Christ, that he may rule over all. In like manner, when Isaiah predicts of the Church, " Kings shall be thy nursing-fathers, and their queens thy nursing-mothers" (Isaiah xlix. 23), he does not bid them abdicate their authority ; he rather gives them the honourable appellation of patrons of the pious worshippers of God ; for the prophecy refers to the advent of Christ. I intentionally omit very many passages which occur throughout Scripture, and especially in the Psalms, in which the due authority of all rulers is asserted. The most celebrated passage of all is that in which Paul,

---

[1] French, " Ceux qui voudroyent que les hommes vesquissent pesle mesle comme rats en paille ;"—Those who would have men to live pell-mell like rats among straw.

admonishing Timothy, that prayers are to be offered up in the public assembly for kings, subjoins the reason, "that we may lead a quiet and peaceable life in all godliness and honesty" (1 Tim. ii. 2). In these words, he recommends the condition of the Church to their protection and guardianship.

6. This consideration ought to be constantly present to the minds of magistrates, since it is fitted to furnish a strong stimulus to the discharge of duty, and also afford singular consolation, smoothing the difficulties of their office, which are certainly numerous and weighty. What zeal for integrity, prudence, meekness, continence, and innocence, ought to sway those who know that they have been appointed ministers of the divine justice! How will they dare to admit iniquity to their tribunal, when they are told that it is the throne of the living God? How will they venture to pronounce an unjust sentence with that mouth which they understand to be an ordained organ of divine truth? With what conscience will they subscribe impious decrees with that hand which they know has been appointed to write the acts of God? In a word, if they remember that they are the vicegerents of God, it behoves them to watch with all care, diligence, and industry, that they may in themselves exhibit a kind of image of the Divine Providence, guardianship, goodness, benevolence, and justice. And let them constantly keep the additional thought in view, that if a curse is pronounced on him that "doeth the work of the Lord deceitfully," a much heavier curse must lie on him who deals deceitfully in a righteous calling. Therefore, when Moses and Jehoshaphat would urge their judges to the discharge of duty, they had nothing by which they could more powerfully stimulate their minds than the consideration to which we have already referred,—"Take heed what ye do: for ye judge not for man, but for the Lord, who is with you in the judgment. Wherefore now let the fear of the Lord be upon you; take heed and do it: for there is no iniquity with the Lord our God, nor respect of persons, nor taking of gifts" (2 Chron. xix. 6, 7, compared with Deut. i. 16, &c.). And in another passage it is said, "God standeth in the congregation of the mighty; he judgeth among the gods" (Psalm lxxxii. 1; Isaiah iii. 14), that they may be animated to duty when they hear that they are the ambassadors of God, to whom they must one day render an account of the province committed to them. This admonition ought justly to have the greatest effect upon them; for if they sin in any respect, not only is injury done to the men whom they wickedly torment, but they also insult God himself, whose sacred tribunals they pollute. On the other hand, they have an admirable source of comfort when they reflect that they are not engaged in profane occupations, unbefitting a servant of God, but in a most sacred office, inasmuch as they are the ambassadors of God.

7. In regard to those who are not debarred by all these passages of Scripture from presuming to inveigh against this sacred ministry, as if it were a thing abhorrent from religion and Christian piety, what

else do they than assail God himself, who cannot but be insulted when his servants are disgraced? These men not only speak evil of dignities, but would not even have God to reign over them (1 Sam. vii. 7). For if this was truly said of the people of Israel, when they declined the authority of Samuel, how can it be less truly said in the present day of those who allow themselves to break loose against all the authority established by God? But it seems that when our Lord said to his disciples, " The kings of the gentiles exercise lordship over them ; and they that exercise authority upon them are called benefactors. But ye shall not be so: but he that is greatest among you, let him be as the younger ; and he that is chief, as he that doth serve" (Luke xxii. 25, 26) ; he by these words prohibited all Christians from becoming kings or governors. Dexterous expounders ! A dispute had arisen among the disciples as to which of them should be greatest. To suppress this vain ambition, our Lord taught them that their ministry was not like the power of earthly sovereigns, among whom one greatly surpasses another. What, I ask, is there in this comparison disparaging to royal dignity? nay, what does it prove at all unless that the royal office is not the apostolic ministry? Besides, though among magisterial offices themselves there are different forms, there is no difference in this respect, that they are all to be received by us as ordinances of God. For Paul includes all together when he says that " there is no power but of God," and that which was by no means the most pleasing of all, was honoured with the highest testimonial—I mean the power of one. This, as carrying with it the public servitude of all (except the one to whose despotic will all is subject), was anciently disrelished by heroic and more excellent natures. But Scripture, to obviate these unjust judgments, affirms expressly that it is by divine wisdom that " kings reign," and gives special command " to honour the king" (1 Peter ii. 17).

8. And certainly it were a very idle occupation for private men to discuss what would be the best form of polity in the place where they live, seeing these deliberations cannot have any influence in determining any public matter. Then the thing itself could not be defined absolutely without rashness, since the nature of the discussion depends on circumstances. And if you compare the different states with each other, without regard to circumstances, it is not easy to determine which of these has the advantage in point of utility, so equal are the terms on which they meet. Monarchy is prone to tyranny. In an aristocracy, again, the tendency is not less to the faction of a few, while in popular ascendancy there is the strongest tendency to sedition.[1] When these three forms of government, of

French, " On conte trois especes de regime civil : c'est assavoir Monarchie, qui est la domination d'un seul, soit qu'on le nomme Roy ou Duc, ou autrement : Aristocratie, qui est une domination gouvernee par les principaux et gens d'apparence : et Democratie, qui est une domination populaire, en laquelle chacun du peuple a puissance."— There are three kinds of civil government; namely, Monarchy, which is the domination which philosophers treat, are considered in themselves, I, for my part, am far from denying that the form which greatly surpasses the others is aristocracy, either pure or modified by popular government, not indeed in itself, but because it very rarely happens that kings so rule themselves as never to dissent from what is just and right, or are possessed of so much acuteness and prudence as always to see correctly.   Owing, therefore, to the vices or defects of men, it is safer and more tolerable when several bear rule, that they may thus mutually assist, instruct, and admonish each other, and should any one be disposed to go too far, the others are censors and masters to curb his excess.   This has already been proved by experience, and confirmed also by the authority of the Lord himself, when he established an aristocracy bordering on popular government among the Israelites, keeping them under that as the best form, until he exhibited an image of the Messiah in David.   And as I willingly admit that there is no kind of government happier than where liberty is framed with becoming moderation, and duly constituted so as to be durable, so I deem those very happy who are permitted to enjoy that form, and I admit that they do nothing at variance with their duty when they strenuously and constantly labour to preserve and maintain it.   Nay, even magistrates ought to do their utmost to prevent the liberty, of which they have been appointed guardians, from being impaired, far less violated.   If in this they are sluggish or little careful, they are perfidious traitors to their office and their country. But should those to whom the Lord has assigned one form of government, take it upon them anxiously to long for a change, the wish would not only be foolish and superfluous, but very pernicious.   If you fix your eyes not on one state merely, but look around the world, or at least direct your view to regions widely separated from each other, you will perceive that Divine Providence has not, without good cause, arranged that different countries should be governed by different forms of polity.   For as only elements of unequal temperature adhere together, so in different regions a similar inequality in the form of government is best.   All this, however, is said unnecessarily to those to whom the will of God is a sufficient reason.   For if it has pleased him to appoint kings over kingdoms, and senates or burgomasters over free states, whatever be the form which he has appointed in the places in which we live, our duty is to obey and submit.

9. The duty of magistrates, its nature, as described by the word of God, and the things in which it consists, I will here indicate in passing.   That it extends to both tables of the law, did Scripture not teach, we might learn from profane writers; for no man has discoursed of the duty of magistrates, the enacting of laws, and the common weal, without beginning with religion and divine worship.

of one only, whether he be called King or Duke, or otherwise; Aristocracy, which is a government composed of the chiefs and people of note; and Democracy, which is a popular government, in which each of the people has power.

Thus all have confessed that no polity can be successfully established unless piety be its first care, and that those laws are absurd which disregard the rights of God, and consult only for men. Seeing then that among philosophers religion holds the first place, and that the same thing has always been observed with the universal consent of nations, Christian princes and magistrates may be ashamed of their heartlessness if they make it not their care. We have already shown that this office is specially assigned them by God, and indeed it is right that they exert themselves in asserting and defending the honour of him whose vicegerents they are, and by whose favour they rule. Hence in Scripture holy kings are especially praised for restoring the worship of God when corrupted or overthrown, or for taking care that religion flourished under them in purity and safety. On the other hand, the sacred history sets down anarchy among the vices, when it states that there was no king in Israel, and, therefore, every one did as he pleased (Judges xxi. 25). This rebukes the folly of those who would neglect the care of divine things, and devote themselves merely to the administration of justice among men; as if God had appointed rulers in his own name to decide earthly controversies, and omitted what was of far greater moment, his own pure worship as prescribed by his law. Such views are adopted by turbulent men, who, in their eagerness to make all kinds of innovations with impunity, would fain get rid of all the vindicators of violated piety. In regard to the second table of the law, Jeremiah addresses rulers, "Thus saith the Lord, Execute ye judgment and righteousness, and deliver the spoiled out of the hand of the oppressor: and do no wrong, do no violence to the stranger, the fatherless, nor the widow, neither shed innocent blood" (Jer. xxii. 3). To the same effect is the exhortation in the Psalm, "Defend the poor and fatherless; do justice to the afflicted and needy. Deliver the poor and needy; rid them out of the hand of the wicked" (Psalm lxxxii. 3, 4). Moses also declared to the princes whom he had substituted for himself, "Hear the causes between your brethren, and judge righteously between every man and his brother, and the stranger that is with him. Ye shall not respect persons in judgment; but ye shall hear the small as well as the great: ye shall not be afraid of the face of man, for the judgment is God's" (Deut. i. 16). I say nothing as to such passages as these, "He shall not multiply horses to himself, nor cause the people to return to Egypt;" "neither shall he multiply wives to himself; neither shall he greatly multiply to himself silver and gold;" "he shall write him a copy of this law in a book;" "and it shall be with him, and he shall read therein all the days of his life, that he may learn to fear the Lord his God;" "that his heart be not lifted up above his brethren" (Deut. xvii. 16–20). In here explaining the duties of magistrates, my exposition is intended not so much for the instruction of magistrates themselves, as to teach others why there are magistrates, and to what end they have been appointed by God. We say, therefore, that they are the ordained guardians and vindicators of public innocence, modesty, honour, and tranquillity, so that it should be their only study to provide for the common peace and safety. Of these things David declares that he will set an example when he shall have ascended the throne. "A froward heart shall depart from me: I will not know a wicked person. Whoso privily slandereth his neighbour, him will I cut off: him that hath an high look and a proud heart will not I suffer. Mine eyes shall be upon the faithful of the land, that they may dwell with me: he that walketh in a perfect way, he shall serve me" (Psalm ci. 4–6). But as rulers cannot do this unless they protect the good against the injuries of the bad, and give aid and protection to the oppressed, they are armed with power to curb manifest evil-doers and criminals, by whose misconduct the public tranquillity is disturbed or harassed. For we have full experience of the truth of Solon's saying, that all public matters depend on reward and punishment; that where these are wanting, the whole discipline of states totters and falls to pieces. For in the minds of many the love of equity and justice grows cold, if due honour be not paid to virtue, and the licentiousness of the wicked cannot be restrained, without strict discipline and the infliction of punishment. The two things are comprehended by the prophet when he enjoins kings and other rulers to execute "judgment and righteousness" (Jer. xxi. 12; xxii. 3). It is righteousness (justice) to take charge of the innocent, to defend and avenge them, and set them free: it is judgment to withstand the audacity of the wicked, to repress their violence, and punish their faults.

10. But here a difficult, and, as it seems, a perplexing question arises. If all Christians are forbidden to kill, and the prophet predicts concerning the holy mountain of the Lord, that is, the Church,[1] "They shall not hurt or destroy," how can magistrates be at once pious and yet shedders of blood? But if we understand that the magistrate, in inflicting punishment, acts not of himself, but executes the very judgments of God, we shall be disencumbered of every doubt. The law of the Lord forbids to kill; but, that murder may not go unpunished, the Lawgiver himself puts the sword into the hands of his ministers, that they may employ it against all murderers. It belongs not to the pious to afflict and hurt; but to avenge the afflictions of the pious, at the command of God, is neither to afflict nor hurt.[2] I wish it could always be present to our mind, that nothing is done here by the rashness of man, but all in obedience to the authority of

---

[1] Exod. xx. 13; Deut. v. 17; Matth. v. 21; Isa. xi. 9; lxv. 25.

[2] The French adds, "Pourtant il est facile de conclure, qu'en cette partie il ne sont sujets a la loy commune; par laquelle combien que le Seigneur lie les mains de tous les hommes, toutes fois il ne lie pas sa justice laquelle il exerce par les mains des magistrats. Tout ainsi que quand un prince defend à tou sses sujets de porter baston, ou blesser aucun, il n'empeche pas neantmoins ses officiers d'executer la justice, laquelle il leur a specialement commise."—Therefore, it is easy to conclude, that in this respect they are not subject to the common law, by which, although the Lord ties the hands of all men, still he ties not his justice which he exercises by the hands of magistrates. Just as when a prince forbids all his subjects to beat or hurt any oue, he nevertheless prohibits not his officers from executing the justice which he has specially committed to them.

God. When it is the guide, we never stray from the right path, unless, indeed, divine justice is to be placed under restraint, and not allowed to take punishment on crimes. But if we dare not give the law to it, why should we bring a charge against its ministers? " He beareth not the sword in vain," says Paul, "for he is the minister of God, a revenger to execute wrath on him that doeth evil" (Rom. xiii. 4). Wherefore, if princes and other rulers know that nothing will be more acceptable to God than their obedience, let them give themselves to this service if they are desirous to improve their piety, justice, and integrity to God. This was the feeling of Moses[1] when, recognising himself as destined to deliver his people by the power of the Lord, he laid violent hands on the Egyptian, and afterwards took vengeance on the people for sacrilege, by slaying three thousand of them in one day. This was the feeling of David also, when, towards the end of his life, he ordered his son Solomon to put Joab and Shimei to death. Hence, also, in an enumeration of the virtues of a king, one is to cut off the wicked from the earth, and banish all workers of iniquity from the city of God. To the same effect is the praise which is bestowed on Solomon, " Thou lovest righteousness, and hatest wickedness." How is it that the meek and gentle temper of Moses becomes so exasperated, that, besmeared and reeking with the blood of his brethren, he runs through the camp making new slaughter ? How is it that David, who, during his whole life, showed so much mildness, almost at his last breath, leaves with his son the bloody testament, not to allow the grey hairs of Joab and Shimei to go to the grave in peace ? Both, by their sternness, sanctified the hands which they would have polluted by showing mercy, inasmuch as they executed the vengeance committed to them by God. Solomon says,[2] " It is an abomination to kings to commit wickedness; for the throne is established by righteousness." Again, "A king that sitteth in the throne of judgment, scattereth away all evil with his eyes." Again, " A wise king scattereth the wicked, and bringeth the wheel over them." Again, " Take away the dross from the silver, and there shall come forth a vessel for the finer. Take away the wicked men from before the king, and his throne shall be established in righteousness." Again, " He that justifieth the wicked, and he that condemneth the just, even they both are an abomination to the Lord." Again, " An evil man seeketh only rebellion, therefore an evil messenger shall be sent against him." Again, " He that saith unto the wicked, Thou art righteous ; him shall the people curse, nations shall abhor him." Now, if it is true justice in them to pursue the guilty and impious with drawn sword, to sheath the sword, and keep their hands pure from blood, while nefarious men wade through murder and slaughter, so far from redounding to the praise of their goodness and justice, would be to incur the guilt of the greatest impiety ; provided always they eschew reckless and cruel

1 Exod. ii. 12; Acts vii. 21; Exod. xxxii. 26; 1 Kings ii. 5; Ps. ci. 8; xlv. 8.
2 Prov. xvi. 12; xx. 26; xxv. 4, 5; xvii. 15; xvii. 14; xxiv. 24.

ssperity, and that tribunal which may be justly termed a rock on which the accused must founder. For I am not one of those who would either favour an unseasonable severity, or think that any tribunal could be accounted just that is not presided over by mercy, that best and surest counsellor of kings, and, as Solomon declares, "upholder of the throne" (Prov. xx. 28). This, as was truly said by one of old, should be the primary endowment of princes. The magistrate must guard against both extremes; he must neither, by excessive severity, rather wound than cure, nor by a superstitious affectation of clemency, fall into the most cruel inhumanity, by giving way to soft and dissolute indulgence to the destruction of many. It was well said by one under the empire of Nerva, It is indeed a bad thing to live under a prince with whom nothing is lawful, but a much worse to live under one with whom all things are lawful.

11. As it is sometimes necessary for kings and states to take up arms in order to execute public vengeance, the reason assigned furnishes us with the means of estimating how far the wars which are thus undertaken are lawful. For if power has been given them to maintain the tranquillity of their subjects, repress the seditious movements of the turbulent, assist those who are violently oppressed, and animadvert on crimes, can they use it more opportunely than in repressing the fury of him who disturbs both the ease of individuals and the common tranquillity of all; who excites seditious tumult, and perpetrates acts of violent oppression and gross wrongs? If it becomes them to be the guardians and maintainers of the laws, they must repress the attempts of all alike by whose criminal conduct the discipline of the laws is impaired. Nay, if they justly punish those robbers whose injuries have been afflicted only on a few, will they allow the whole country to be robbed and devastated with impunity? Since it makes no difference whether it is by a king or by the lowest of the people that a hostile and devastating inroad is made into a district over which they have no authority, all alike are to be regarded and punished as robbers. Natural equity and duty, therefore, demand that princes be armed not only to repress private crimes by judicial inflictions, but to defend the subjects committed to their guardianship whenever they are hostilely assailed. Such even the Holy Spirit, in many passages of Scripture, declares to be lawful.

12. But if it is objected, that in the New Testament there is no passage or example teaching that war is lawful for Christians, I answer, first, that the reason for carrying on war, which anciently existed, still exists in the present day, and that, on the other hand, there is no ground for debarring magistrates from the defence of those under them; and, secondly, that in the Apostolical writings we are not to look for a distinct exposition of those matters, their object being not to form a civil polity, but to establish the spiritual kingdom of Christ; lastly, that there also it is indicated, in passing, that our Saviour, by his advent, made no change in this respect. For (to use the words of Augustine) "if Christian discipline con-

demned all wars, when the soldiers ask counsel as to the way of salvation, they would have been told to cast away their arms, and withdraw altogether from military service.   Whereas it was said (Luke
iii. 14), Concuss no one, do injury to no one, be contented with your
pay.   Those whom he orders to be contented with their pay he certainly does not forbid to serve" (August. Ep. v. ad Marcell.)   But
all magistrates must here be particularly cautious not to give way,
in the slightest degree, to their passions.   Or rather, whether punishments are to be inflicted, they must not be borne headlong by anger,
nor hurried away by hatred, nor burn with implacable severity;
they must, as Augustine says (De Civit. Dei. Lib. v. cap. 24), "even
pity a common nature in him in whom they punish an individual
fault;" or whether they have to take up arms against an enemy,
that is, an armed robber, they must not readily catch at the opportunity, nay, they must not take it when offered, unless compelled by
the strongest necessity.   For if we are to do far more than that
heathen demanded, who wished war to appear as desired peace, assuredly all other means must be tried before having recourse to arms.
In fine, in both cases, they must not allow themselves to be carried
away by any private feeling, but be guided solely by regard for the
public.   Acting otherwise, they wickedly abuse their power which
was given them, not for their own advantage, but for the good and
service of others.   On this right of war depends the right of garrisons, leagues, and other civil munitions.   By garrisons, I mean those
which are stationed in states for defence of the frontiers; by leagues,
the alliances which are made by neighbouring princes, on the ground
that if any disturbance arise within their territories, they will mutually assist each other, and combine their forces to repel the common
enemies of the human race; under civil munitions, I include everything pertaining to the military art.

13. Lastly, we think it proper to add, that taxes and imposts are
the legitimate revenues of princes, which they are chiefly to employ
in sustaining the public burdens of their office.   These, however,
they may use for the maintenance of their domestic state, which is
in a manner combined with the dignity of the authority which they
exercise.   Thus we see that David, Hezekiah, Josiah, Jehoshaphat,
and other holy kings, Joseph also, and Daniel, in proportion to the
office which they sustained, without offending piety, expended liberally of the public funds; and we read in Ezekiel, that a very large
extent of territory was assigned to kings (Ezek. xlviii. 21).   In that
passage, indeed, he is depicting the spiritual kingdom of Christ, but
still he borrows his representation from lawful dominion among men.
Princes, however, must remember, in their turn, that their revenues
are not so much private chests as treasuries of the whole people (this
Paul testifies, Rom. xiii. 6), which they cannot, without manifest
injustice, squander or dilapidate; or rather, that they are almost the
blood of the people, which it were the harshest inhumanity not to
spare.   They should also consider that their levies and contributions,

and other kinds of taxes, are merely subsidies of the public necessity, and that it is tyrannical rapacity to harass the poor people with them without cause. These things do not stimulate princes to profusion and luxurious expenditure (there is certainly no need to inflame the passions, when they are already, of their own accord, inflamed more than enough), but seeing it is of the greatest consequence that, whatever they venture to do, they should do with a pure conscience, it is necessary to teach them how far they can lawfully go, lest, by impious confidence, they incur the divine displeasure. Nor is this doctrine superfluous to private individuals, that they may not rashly and petulantly stigmatise the expenditure of princes, though it should exceed the ordinary limits.

14. In states, the thing next in importance to the magistrates is laws, the strongest sinews of government, or, as Cicero calls them after Plato, the soul, without which, the office of the magistrate cannot exist; just as, on the other hand, laws have no vigour without the magistrate. Hence nothing could be said more truly than that the law is a dumb magistrate, the magistrate a living law. As I have undertaken to describe the laws by which Christian polity is to be governed, there is no reason to expect from me a long discussion on the best kind of laws. The subject is of vast extent, and belongs not to this place. I will only briefly observe, in passing, what the laws are which may be piously used with reference to God, and duly administered among men. This I would rather have passed in silence, were I not aware that many dangerous errors are here committed. For there are some who deny that any commonwealth is rightly framed which neglects the law of Moses, and is ruled by the common law of nations. How perilous and seditious these views are, let others see: for me it is enough to demonstrate that they are stupid and false. We must attend to the well known division which distributes the whole law of God, as promulgated by Moses, into the moral, the ceremonial, and the judicial law, and we must attend to each of these parts, in order to understand how far they do, or do not, pertain to us. Meanwhile, let no one be moved by the thought that the judicial and ceremonial laws relate to morals. For the ancients who adopted this division, though they were not unaware that the two latter classes had to do with morals, did not give them the name of moral, because they might be changed and abrogated without affecting morals. They give this name specially to the first class, without which, true holiness of life and an immutable rule of conduct cannot exist.

15. The moral law, then (to begin with it), being contained under two heads, the one of which simply enjoins us to worship God with pure faith and piety, the other to embrace men with sincere affection, is the true and eternal rule of righteousness prescribed to the men of all nations and of all times, who would frame their life agreeably to the will of God. For his eternal and immutable will is, that we are all to worship him and mutually love one another. The ceremonial

law of the Jews was a tutelage by which the Lord was pleased to exercise, as it were, the childhood of that people, until the fulness of the time should come when he was fully to manifest his wisdom to the world, and exhibit the reality of those things which were then adumbrated by figures (Gal. iii. 24 ; iv. 4). The judicial law, given them as a kind of polity, delivered certain forms of equity and justice, by which they might live together innocently and quietly. And as that exercise in ceremonies properly pertained to the doctrine of piety, inasmuch as it kept the Jewish Church in the worship and religion of God, yet was still distinguishable from piety itself, so the judicial form, though it looked only to the best method of preserving that charity which is enjoined by the eternal law of God, was still something distinct from the precept of love itself. Therefore, as ceremonies might be abrogated without at all interfering with piety, so, also, when these judicial arrangements are removed, the duties and precepts of charity can still remain perpetual. But if it is true that each nation has been left at liberty to enact the laws which it judges to be beneficial, still these are always to be tested by the rule of charity, so that while they vary in form, they must proceed on the same principle. Those barbarous and savage laws, for instance, which conferred honour on thieves, allowed the promiscuous intercourse of the sexes, and other things even fouler and more absurd, I do not think entitled to be considered as laws, since they are not only altogether abhorrent to justice, but to humanity and civilised life.

16. What I have said will become plain if we attend, as we ought, to two things connected with all laws—viz. the enactment of the law, and the equity on which the enactment is founded and rests. Equity, as it is natural, cannot be the same in all, and therefore ought to be proposed by all laws, according to the nature of the thing enacted. As constitutions have some circumstances on which they partly depend, there is nothing to prevent their diversity, provided they all alike aim at equity as their end. Now, as it is evident that the law of God which we call moral, is nothing else than the testimony of natural law, and of that conscience which God has engraven on the minds of men, the whole of this equity of which we now speak is prescribed in it. Hence it alone ought to be the aim, the rule, and the end of all laws. Wherever laws are formed after this rule, directed to this aim, and restricted to this end, there is no reason why they should be disapproved by us, however much they may differ from the Jewish law, or from each other (August. de Civit. Dei, Lib. xix. c. 17). The law of God forbids to steal. The punishment appointed for theft in the civil polity of the Jews may be seen in Exodus xxii. Very ancient laws of other nations punished theft by exacting the double of what was stolen, while subsequent laws made a distinction between theft manifest and not manifest. Other laws went the length of punishing with exile, or with branding, while others made the punishment capital. Among the Jews, the punishment of the false witness was to " do unto him as he had thought to have done

with his brother" (Deut. xix. 19). In some countries, the punishment is infamy, in others hanging, in others crucifixion. All laws alike avenge murder with blood, but the kinds of death are different. In some countries, adultery was punished more severely, in others more leniently. Yet we see that amidst this diversity they all tend to the same end. For they all with one mouth declare against those crimes which are condemned by the eternal law of God—viz. murder, theft, adultery, and false witness; though they agree not as to the mode of punishment. This is not necessary, nor even expedient. There may be a country which, if murder were not visited with fearful punishments, would instantly become a prey to robbery and slaughter. There may be an age requiring that the severity of punishments should be increased. If the state is in troubled condition, those things from which disturbances usually arise must be corrected by new edicts. In time of war, civilisation would disappear amid the noise of arms, were not men overawed by an unwonted severity of punishment. In sterility, in pestilence, were not stricter discipline employed, all things would grow worse. One nation might be more prone to a particular vice, were it not most severely repressed. How malignant were it, and invidious of the public good, to be offended at this diversity, which is admirably adapted to retain the observance of the divine law. The allegation, that insult is offered to the law of God enacted by Moses, where it is abrogated, and other new laws are preferred to it, is most absurd. Others are not preferred when they are more approved, not absolutely, but from regard to time and place, and the condition of the people, or when those things are abrogated which were never enacted for us. The Lord did not deliver it by the hand of Moses to be promulgated in all countries, and to be everywhere enforced; but having taken the Jewish nation under his special care, patronage, and guardianship, he was pleased to be specially its legislator, and as became a wise legislator, he had special regard to it in enacting laws.

17. It now remains to see, as was proposed in the last place, what use the common society of Christians derive from laws, judicial proceedings, and magistrates. With this is connected another question —viz. What difference ought private individuals to pay to magistrates, and how far ought obedience to proceed? To very many it seems that among Christians the office of magistrate is superfluous, because they cannot piously implore his aid, inasmuch as they are forbidden to take revenge, cite before a judge, or go to law. But when Paul, on the contrary, clearly declares that he is the minister of God to us for good (Rom. xiii. 4), we thereby understand that he was so ordained of God, that, being defended by his hand and aid against the dishonesty and injustice of wicked men, we may live quiet and secure. But if he would have been appointed over us in vain, unless we were to use his aid, it is plain that it cannot be wrong to appeal to it and implore it. Here, indeed, I have to do with two classes of men. For there are very many who boil with

such a rage for litigation, that they never can be quiet with themselves unless they are fighting with others. Law-suits they prosecute with the bitterness of deadly hatred, and with an insane eagerness to hurt and revenge, and they persist in them with implacable obstinacy, even to the ruin of their adversary. Meanwhile, that they may be thought to do nothing but what is legal, they use this pretext of judicial proceedings as a defence of their perverse conduct. But if it is lawful for brother to litigate with brother, it does not follow that it is lawful to hate him, and obstinately pursue him with a furious desire to do him harm.

18. Let such persons then understand that judicial proceedings are lawful to him who makes a right use of them; and the right use, both for the pursuer and for the defender, is for the latter to sist himself on the day appointed, and, without bitterness, urge what he can in his defence, but only with the desire of justly maintaining his right; and for the pursuer, when undeservedly attacked in his life or fortunes, to throw himself upon the protection of the magistrate, state his complaint, and demand what is just and good; while, far from any wish to hurt or take vengeance—far from bitterness or hatred —far from the ardour of strife, he is rather disposed to yield and suffer somewhat than to cherish hostile feelings towards his opponent. On the contrary, when minds are filled with malevolence, corrupted by envy, burning with anger, breathing revenge, or, in fine, so inflamed by the heat of the contest, that they, in some measure, lay aside charity, the whole pleading, even of the justest cause, cannot but be impious. For it ought to be an axiom among all Christians, that no plea, however equitable, can be rightly conducted by any one who does not feel as kindly towards his opponent as if the matter in dispute were amicably transacted and arranged. Some one, perhaps, may here break in and say, that such moderation in judicial proceedings is so far from being seen, that an instance of it would be a kind of prodigy. I confess that in these times it is rare to meet with an example of an honest litigant; but the thing itself, untainted by the accession of evil, ceases not to be good and pure. When we hear that the assistance of the magistrate is a sacred gift from God, we ought the more carefully to beware of polluting it by our fault.

19. Let those who distinctly condemn all judicial distinction know, that they repudiate the holy ordinance of God, and one of those gifts which to the pure are pure, unless, indeed, they would charge Paul with a crime,[1] because he repelled the calumnies of his accusers, exposing their craft and wickedness, and, at the tribunal, claimed for himself the privilege of a Roman citizen, appealing, when necessary, from the governor to Cæsar's judgment-seat. There is nothing contrary to this in the prohibition, which binds all Christians to refrain from revenge, a feeling which we drive far away from all Christian tribunals. For whether the action be of a civil nature, he only takes

---

[1] Acts xxii. xxiv. 12; xvi. 37; xxii. 25; xxv. 10; Lev. xix. 18; Matth. v. 39; Deut. xxxii. 35; Rom. xii. 19.

the right course who, with innocuous simplicity, commits his cause to the judge as the public protector, without any thought of returning evil for evil (which is the feeling of revenge); or whether the action is of a graver nature, directed against a capital offence, the accuser required is not one who comes into court, carried away by some feeling of revenge or resentment from some private injury, but one whose only object is to prevent the attempts of some bad men to injure the commonweal. But if you take away the vindictive mind, you offend in no respect against that command which forbids Christians to indulge revenge. But they are not only forbidden to thirst for revenge, they are also enjoined to wait for the hand of the Lord, who promises that he will be the avenger of the oppressed and afflicted. But those who call upon the magistrate to give assistance to themselves or others, anticipate the vengeance of the heavenly Judge. By no means, for we are to consider that the vengeance of the magistrate is the vengeance not of man, but of God, which, as Paul says, he exercises by the ministry of man for our good (Rom. xiii. 8).

20. No more are we at variance with the words of Christ, who forbids us to resist evil, and adds, " Whosoever shall smite thee on thy right cheek, turn to him the other also. And if any man will sue thee at the law, and take away thy coat, let him have thy cloak also" (Matth. v. 39, 40). He would have the minds of his followers to be so abhorrent to everything like retaliation, that they would sooner allow the injury to be doubled than desire to repay it. From this patience we do not dissuade them. For verily Christians were to be a class of men born to endure affronts and injuries, and be exposed to the iniquity, imposture, and derision of abandoned men, and not only so, but were to be tolerant of all these evils; that is, so composed in the whole frame of their minds, that, on receiving one offence, they were to prepare themselves for another, promising themselves nothing during the whole of life but the endurance of a perpetual cross. Meanwhile, they must do good to those who injure them, and pray for those who curse them, and (this is their only victory) strive to overcome evil with good (Rom. xii. 20, 21). Thus affected, they will not seek eye for eye, and tooth for tooth (as the Pharisees taught their disciples to long for vengeance), but (as we are instructed by Christ), they will allow their body to be mutilated, and their goods to be maliciously taken from them, prepared to remit and spontaneously pardon those injuries the moment they have been inflicted. This equity and moderation, however, will not prevent them, with entire friendship for their enemies, from using the aid of the magistrate for the preservation of their goods, or, from zeal for the public interest, to call for the punishment of the wicked and pestilential man, whom they know nothing will reform but death. All these precepts are truly expounded by Augustine, as tending to prepare the just and pious man patiently to sustain the malice of those whom he desires to become good, that he may thus increase the number of the good, not add himself to the number of the bad

by imitating their wickedness. Moreover, it pertains more to the preparation of the heart which is within, than to the work which is done openly, that patience and good-will may be retained within the secret of the heart, and that may be done openly which we see may do good to those to whom we ought to wish well (August. Ep. v. ad. Marcell.).

21. The usual objection, that law-suits are universally condemned by Paul (1 Cor. vi. 6), is false. It may easily be understood from his words, that a rage for litigation prevailed in the Church of Corinth to such a degree, that they exposed the gospel of Christ, and the whole religion which they professed, to the calumnies and cavils of the ungodly. Paul rebukes them, first for traducing the gospel to un-believers by the intemperance of their dissensions ; and, secondly, for so striving with each other while they were brethren. For so far were they from bearing injury from another, that they greedily coveted each other's effects, and voluntarily provoked and injured them. He inveighs, therefore, against that madness for litigation, and not absolutely against all kinds of disputes. He declares it to be alto-gether a vice or infirmity, that they do not submit to the loss of their effects, rather than strive, even to contention, in preserving them ; in other words, seeing they were so easily moved by every kind of loss, and on every occasion, however slight, ran off to the forum and to law-suits, he says, that in this way they showed that they were of too irritable a temper, and not prepared for patience. Christians should always feel disposed rather to give up part of their right than to go into court, out of which they can scarcely come without a troubled mind, a mind inflamed with hatred of their brother. But when one sees that his property, the want of which he would griev-ously feel, he is able, without any loss of charity, to defend, if he should do so, he offends in no respect against that passage of Paul. In short, as we said at first, every man's best adviser is charity. Everything in which we engage without charity, and all the dis-putes which carry us beyond it, are unquestionably unjust and impious.

22. The first duty of subjects towards their rulers, is to entertain the most honourable views of their office, recognising it as a delegated jurisdiction from God, and on that account receiving and reverencing them as the ministers and ambassadors of God. For you will find some who show themselves very obedient to magistrates, and would be unwilling that there should be no magistrates to obey, because they know this is expedient for the public good, and yet the opinion which those persons have of magistrates is, that they are a kind of necessary evils. But Peter requires something more of us when he says, " Honour the king" (1 Pet. ii. 17); and Solomon, when he says, " My son, fear thou the Lord and the king" (Prov. xxiv. 21). For, under the term honour, the former includes a sincere and candid esteem, and the latter, by joining the king with God, shows that he is invested with a kind of sacred veneration and dignity. We have

also the remarkable injunction of Paul, " Be subject not only for wrath, but also for conscience sake" (Rom. xiii. 5). By this he means, that subjects, in submitting to princes and governors, are not to be influenced merely by fear (just as those submit to an armed enemy who see vengeance ready to be executed if they resist), but because the obedience which they yield is rendered to God himself, inasmuch as their power is from God. I speak not of the men as if the mask of dignity could cloak folly, or cowardice, or cruelty, or wicked or flagitious manners, and thus acquire for vice the praise of virtue ; but I say that the station itself is deserving of honour and reverence, and that those who rule should, in respect of their office, be held by us in esteem and veneration.

23. From this, a second consequence is, that we must with ready minds prove our obedience to them, whether in complying with edicts, or in paying tribute, or in undertaking public offices and burdens, which relate to the common defence, or in executing any other orders. " Let every soul," says Paul, " be subject unto the higher powers." " Whosoever, therefore, resisteth the power, resist-eth the ordinance of God" (Rom. xiii. 1, 2). Writing to Titus, he says, " Put them in mind to be subject to principalities and powers, to obey magistrates, to be ready to every good work" (Tit. iii. 1). Peter also says, " Submit yourselves to every human creature" (or rather, as I understand it, " ordinance of man"), " for the Lord's sake : whether it be to the king, as supreme ; or unto governors, as unto them that are sent by him for the punishment of evil-doers, and for the praise of them that do well" (1 Pet. ii. 13). Moreover, to testify that they do not feign subjection, but are sincerely and cordially subject, Paul adds, that they are to commend the safety and prosperity of those under whom they live to God. " I exhort, therefore," says he, " that, first of all, supplications, prayers, inter-cessions, and giving of thanks, be made for all men ; for kings, and for all that are in authority : that we may lead a quiet and peaceable life in all godliness and honesty" (1 Tim. ii. 1, 2). Let no man here deceive himself, since we cannot resist the magistrate without resisting God. For, although an unarmed magistrate may seem to be despised with impunity, yet God is armed, and will signally avenge this contempt. Under this obedience, I comprehend the restraint which private men ought to impose on themselves in public, not interfering with public business, or rashly encroaching on the province of the magistrate, or attempting anything at all of a public nature. If it is proper that anything in a public ordinance should be corrected, let them not act tumultuously, or put their hands to a work where they ought to feel that their hands are tied, but let them leave it to the cognisance of the magistrate, whose hand alone here is free. My meaning is, let them not dare to do it without being ordered. For when the command of the magistrate is given, they too are invested with public authority. For as, according to the common saying, the eyes and ears of the prince are his counsellors,

so one may not improperly say that those who, by his command, have the charge of managing affairs, are his hands.

24. But as we have hitherto described the magistrate who truly is what he is called—viz. the father of his country, and (as the Poet speaks) the pastor of the people, the guardian of peace, the president of justice, the vindicator of innocence, he is justly to be deemed a madman who disapproves of such authority. And since in almost all ages we see that some princes, careless about all their duties on which they ought to have been intent, live, without solicitude, in luxurious sloth; others, bent on their own interest, venally prostitute all rights, privileges, judgments, and enactments; others pillage poor people of their money, and afterwards squander it in insane largesses; others act as mere robbers, pillaging houses, violating matrons, and slaying the innocent; many cannot be persuaded to recognise such persons for princes, whose command, as far as lawful, they are bound to obey. For while in this unworthy conduct, and among atrocities so alien, not only from the duty of the magistrate, but also of the man, they behold no appearance of the image of God, which ought to be conspicuous in the magistrate, while they see not a vestige of that minister of God, who was appointed to be a praise to the good and a terror to the bad, they cannot recognise the ruler whose dignity and authority Scripture recommends to us. And, undoubtedly, the natural feeling of the human mind has always been not less to assail tyrants with hatred and execration, than to look up to just kings with love and veneration.

25. But if we have respect to the word of God, it will lead us farther, and make us subject not only to the authority of those princes who honestly and faithfully perform their duty toward us, but all princes, by whatever means they have so become, although there is nothing they less perform than the duty of princes. For though the Lord declares that a ruler to maintain our safety is the highest gift of his beneficence, and prescribes to rulers themselves their proper sphere, he at the same time declares, that of whatever description they may be, they derive their power from none but him. Those, indeed, who rule for the public good, are true examples and specimens of his beneficence, while those who domineer unjustly and tyrannically are raised up by him to punish the people for their iniquity. Still all alike possess that sacred majesty with which he has invested lawful power. I will not proceed further without subjoining some distinct passages to this effect.[1] We need not labour to prove that an impious king is a mark of the Lord's anger, since I presume no one will deny it, and that this is not less true of a king than of a robber who plunders your goods, an adulterer who defiles your bed, and an assassin who aims at your life, since all such calamities are classed by Scripture among the curses of God. But let us insist at greater length in proving what does not so easily fall in with

---

[1] Job xxxiv. 30; Hos. xiii. 11; Isa. iii 4; x. 5; Deut. xxviii. 29.

the views of men, that even an individual of the worst character, one most unworthy of all honour, if invested with public authority, receives that illustrious divine power which the Lord has by his word devolved on the ministers of his justice and judgment, and that, accordingly, in so far as public obedience is concerned, he is to be held in the same honour and reverence as the best of kings.

26. And, first, I would have the reader carefully to attend to that Divine Providence which, not without cause, is so often set before us in Scripture, and that special act of distributing kingdoms, and setting up as kings whomsoever he pleases. In Daniel it is said, "He changeth the times and the seasons: he removeth kings, and setteth up kings" (Dan. ii. 21, 37). Again, "That the living may know that the Most High ruleth in the kingdom of men, and giveth it to whomsoever he will" (Dan. iv. 17, 25). Similar sentiments occur throughout Scripture, but they abound particularly in the prophetical books. What kind of king Nebuchadnezzar, he who stormed Jerusalem, was, is well known. He was an active invader and devastator of other countries. Yet the Lord declares in Ezekiel that he had given him the land of Egypt as his hire for the devastation which he had committed. Daniel also said to him, "Thou, O king, art a king of kings: for the God of heaven hath given thee a kingdom, power, and strength, and glory. And wheresoever the children of men dwell, the beasts of the field and the fowls of the heaven hath he given into thine hand, and hath made thee ruler over them all" (Dan. ii. 37, 38). Again, he says to his son Belshazzar, "The most high God gave Nebuchadnezzar thy father a kingdom, and majesty, and glory, and honour: and for the majesty that he gave him, all people, nations, and languages, trembled and feared before him" (Dan. v. 18, 19). When we hear that the king was appointed by God, let us, at the same time, call to mind those heavenly edicts as to honouring and fearing the king, and we shall have no doubt that we are to view the most iniquitous tyrant as occupying the place with which the Lord has honoured him. When Samuel declared to the people of Israel what they would suffer from their kings, he said, "This will be the manner of the king that shall reign over you: He will take your sons, and appoint them for himself, for his chariots, and to be his horsemen; and some shall run before his chariots. And he will appoint him captains over thousands, and captains over fifties; and will set them to ear his ground, and to reap his harvest, and to make his instruments of war, and instruments of his chariots. And he will take your daughters to be confectionaries, and to be cooks, and to be bakers. And he will take your fields, and your vineyards, and your oliveyards, even the best of them, and give them to his servants. And he will take the tenth of your seed, and of your vineyards, and give to his officers, and to his servants. And he will take your men-servants, and your maid-servants, and your goodliest young men, and your asses, and put them to his work. He will take the tenth of your sheep: and ye shall be his servants" (1

Sam. viii. 11–17). Certainly these things could not be done legally by kings, whom the law trained most admirably to all kinds of restraint ; but it was called justice in regard to the people, because they were bound to obey, and could not lawfully resist: as if Samuel had said, To such a degree will kings indulge in tyranny, which it will not be for you to restrain. The only thing remaining for you will be to receive their commands, and be obedient to their words.

27. But the most remarkable and memorable passage is in Jeremiah. Though it is rather long, I am not indisposed to quote it, because it most clearly settles this whole question. " I have made the earth, the man and the beast that are upon the ground, by my great power, and by my outstretched arm, and have given it unto whom it seemed meet unto me. And now have I given all these lands into the hand of Nebuchadnezzar the king of Babylon, my servant: and the beasts of the field have I given him also to serve him. And all nations shall serve him, and his son, and his son's son, until the very time of his land come : and then many nations and great kings shall serve themselves of him. And it shall come to pass, that the nation and kingdom which will not serve the same Nebuchadnezzer the king of Babylon, and that will not put their neck under the yoke of the king of Babylon, that nation will I punish, saith the Lord, with the sword, and with famine, and with pestilence, until I have consumed them by his hand " (Jer. xxvii. 5–8). Therefore " bring your necks under the yoke of the king of Babylon, and serve him and his people, and live " (v. 12). We see how great obedience the Lord was pleased to demand for this dire and ferocious tyrant, for no other reason than just that he held the kingdom. In other words, the divine decree had placed him on the throne of the kingdom, and admitted him to regal majesty, which could not be lawfully violated. If we constantly keep before our eyes and minds the fact, that even the most iniquitous kings are appointed by the same decree which establishes all regal authority, we will never entertain the seditious thought, that a king is to be treated according to his deserts, and that we are not bound to act the part of good subjects to him who does not in his turn act the part of a king to us.

28. It is vain to object, that that command was specially given to the Israelites. For we must attend to the ground on which the Lord places it—" I have given the kingdom to Nebuchadnezzar ; therefore serve him and live." Let us doubt not that on whomsoever the kingdom has been conferred, him we are bound to serve. Whenever God raises any one to royal honour, he declares it to be his pleasure that he should reign. To this effect we have general declarations in Scripture. Solomon says—" For the transgression of a land, many are the princes thereof" (Prov. xxviii. 2). Job says—" He looseth the bond of kings, amd girdeth their loins with a girdle " (Job. xii. 18). This being confessed, nothing remains for us but to serve and live. There is in Jeremiah another command in which the Lord thus orders his people—" Seek the peace of the city whither I

have caused you to be carried away captives, and pray unto the Lord for it : for in the peace thereof shall ye have peace " (Jer. xxix. 7). Here the Israelites, plundered of all their property, torn from their homes, driven into exile, thrown into miserable bondage, are ordered to pray for the prosperity of the victor, not as we are elsewhere ordered to pray for our persecutors, but that his kingdom may be preserved in safety and tranquillity, that they too may live prosperously under him. Thus David, when already king elect by the ordination of God, and anointed with his holy oil, though causelessly and unjustly assailed by Saul, holds the life of one who was seeking his life to be sacred, because the Lord had invested him with royal honour. "The Lord forbid that I should do this thing unto my master, the Lord's anointed, to stretch forth mine hand against him, seeing he is the anointed of the Lord." " Mine eyes spare thee ; and I said, I will not put forth mine hand against my lord ; for he is the Lord's anointed " (1 Sam. xxiv. 6, 11). Again,—" Who can stretch forth his hand against the Lord's anointed, and be guiltless"? " As the Lord liveth the Lord shall smite him, or his day shall come to die, or he shall descend into battle, and perish. The Lord forbid that I should stretch forth mine hand against the Lord's anointed " (1 Sam. xxiv. 9–11).

29. This feeling of reverence, and even of piety, we owe to the utmost to all our rulers, be their characters what they may. This I repeat the oftener, that we may learn not to consider the individuals themselves, but hold it to be enough that by the will of the Lord they sustain a character on which he has impressed and engraven inviolable majesty. But rulers, you will say, owe mutual duties to those under them. This I have already confessed. But if from this you conclude that obedience is to be returned to none but just governors, you reason absurdly. Husbands are bound by mutual duties to their wives, and parents to their children. Should husbands and parents neglect their duty ; should the latter be harsh and severe to the children whom they are enjoined not to provoke to anger, and by their severity harass them beyond measure ; should the former treat with the greatest contumely the wives whom they are enjoined to love and to spare as the weaker vessels; would children be less bound in duty to their parents, and wives to their husbands? They are made subject to the froward and undutiful. Nay, since the duty of all is not to look behind them, that is, not to inquire into the duties of one another, but to submit each to his own duty, this ought especially to be exemplified in the case of those who are placed under the power of others. Wherefore, if we are cruelly tormented by a savage, if we are rapaciously pillaged by an avaricious or luxurious, if we are neglected by a sluggish, if, in short, we are persecuted for righteousness' sake by an impious and sacrilegious prince, let us first call up the remembrance of our faults, which doubtless the Lord is chastising by such scourges. In this way humility will

curb our impatience. And let us reflect that it belongs not to us to cure these evils, that all that remains for us is to implore the help of the Lord, in whose hands are the hearts of kings, and inclinations of kingdoms.[1] " God standeth in the congregation of the mighty ; he judgeth among the gods." Before his face shall fall and be crushed all kings and judges of the earth, who have not kissed his anointed, who have enacted unjust laws to oppress the poor in judgment, and do violence to the cause of the humble, to make widows a prey, and plunder the fatherless.

30. Herein is the goodness, power, and providence of God wondrously displayed. At one time he raises up manifest avengers from among his own servants, and gives them his command to punish accursed tyranny, and deliver his people from calamity when they are unjustly oppressed; at another time he employs, for this purpose, the fury of men who have other thoughts and other aims. Thus he rescued his people Israel from the tyranny of Pharaoh by Moses; from the violence of Chusa, king of Syria, by Othniel; and from other bondage by other kings or judges. Thus he tamed the pride of Tyre by the Egyptians ; the insolence of the Egyptians by the Assyrians ; the ferocity of the Assyrians by the Chaldeans; the confidence of Babylon by the Medes and Persians,—Cyrus having previously subdued the Medes, while the ingratitude of the kings of Judah and Israel, and their impious contumacy after all his kindness, he subdued and punished,—at one time by the Assyrians, at another by the Babylonians. All these things, however, were not done in the same way. The former class of deliverers being brought forward by the lawful call of God to perform such deeds, when they took up arms against kings, did not at all violate that majesty with which kings are invested by divine appointment, but armed from heaven, they, by a greater power, curbed a less, just as kings may lawfully punish their own satraps. The latter class, though they were directed by the hand of God, as seemed to him good, and did his work without knowing it, had nought but evil in their thoughts.

31. But whatever may be thought of the acts of the men themselves,[2] the Lord by their means equally executed his own work, when he broke the bloody sceptres of insolent kings, and overthrew their intolerable dominations. Let princes hear and be afraid ; but let us at the same time guard most carefully against spurning or violating the venerable and majestic authority of rulers, an authority which God has sanctioned by the surest edicts, although those invested with it should be most unworthy of it, and, as far as in them lies, pollute it by their iniquity. Although the Lord takes vengeance on unbridled domination, let us not therefore suppose that that vengeance is committed to us, to whom no command has been given but

1 Dan. ix. 7 ; Prov. xxi. 1 ; Psalm lxxxii. 1 ; ii. 10 ; Isaiah x. 1.
2 The French adds, " Car les uns les faisoyent estans asseurez qu'ils faisoyent bien, et les autres par autre zele (comme nous avons dit)."—For the former acted under the full conviction, that they were doing right, and the latter, from a different feeling, as we have said.

to obey and suffer. I speak only of private men. For when popular magistrates have been appointed to curb the tyranny of kings (as the Ephori, who were opposed to kings among the Spartans, or Tribunes of the people to consuls among the Romans, or Demarchs to the senate among the Athenians; and perhaps there is something similar to this in the power exercised in each kingdom by the three orders, when they hold their primary diets). So far am I from forbidding these officially to check the undue license of kings, that if they connive at kings when they tyrannise and insult over the humbler of the people, I affirm that their dissimulation is not free from nefarious perfidy, because they fradulently betray the liberty of the people, while knowing that, by the ordinance of God, they are its appointed guardians.

32. But in that obedience which we hold to be due to the commands of rulers, we must always make the exception, nay, must be particularly careful that it is not incompatible with obedience to Him to whose will the wishes of all kings should be subject, to whose decrees their commands must yield, to whose majesty their sceptres must bow. And, indeed, how preposterous were it, in pleasing men, to incur the offence of Him for whose sake you obey men! The Lord, therefore, is King of kings. When he opens his sacred mouth, he alone is to be heard, instead of all and above all. We are subject to the men who rule over us, but subject only in the Lord. If they command anything against Him let us not pay the least regard to it, nor be moved by all the dignity which they possess as magistrates— a dignity to which no injury is done when it is subordinated to the special and truly supreme power of God. On this ground Daniel denies that he had sinned in any respect against the king when he refused to obey his impious decree (Dan. vi. 22), because the king had exceeded his limits, and not only been injurious to men, but, by raising his horn against God, had virtually abrogated his own power. On the other hand, the Israelites are condemned for having too readily obeyed the impious edict of the king. For, when Jeroboam made the golden calf, they forsook the temple of God, and, in submissiveness to him, revolted to new superstitions (1 Kings xii. 28). With the same facility posterity had bowed before the decrees of their kings. For this they are severely upbraided by the Prophet (Hosea. v. 11). So far is the praise of modesty from being due to that pretence by which flattering courtiers cloak themselves, and deceive the simple, when they deny the lawfulness of declining anything imposed by their kings, as if the Lord had resigned his own rights to mortals by appointing them to rule over their fellows, or as if earthly power were diminished when it is subjected to its author, before whom even the principalities of heaven tremble as suppliants. I know the imminent peril to which subjects expose themselves by this firmness, kings being most indignant when they are contemned. As Solomon says, " The wrath of a king is as messengers of death " (Prov. xvi. 14). But since Peter, one of heaven's heralds, has pub-

lished the edict, "We ought to obey God rather than men" (Acts v. 29), let us console ourselves with the thought, that we are rendering the obedience which the Lord requires, when we endure anything rather than turn aside from piety. And that our courage may not fail, Paul stimulates us by the additional consideration (1 Cor. vii. 23), that we were redeemed by Christ at the great price which our redemption cost him, in order that we might not yield a slavish obedience to the depraved wishes of men, far less do homage to their impiety.

END OF THE INSTITUTES.

ONE HUNDRED APHORISMS,*

CONTAINING,

WITHIN A NARROW COMPASS, THE SUBSTANCE AND ORDER OF
THE FOUR BOOKS OF THE

INSTITUTES OF THE CHRISTIAN RELIGION.

BOOK I.

1. THE true wisdom of man consists in the knowledge of God the Creator and Redeemer.

2. This knowledge is naturally implanted in us, and the end of it ought to be the worship of God rightly performed, or reverence for the Deity accompanied by fear and love.

3. But this seed is corrupted by ignorance, whence arises superstitious worship ; and by wickedness, whence arise slavish dread and hatred of the Deity.

4. It is also from another source that it is derived—namely, from the structure of the whole world, and from the Holy Scriptures.

5. This structure teaches us what is the goodness, power, justice, and wisdom of God in creating all things in heaven and earth, and in preserving them by ordinary and extraordinary government, by which his Providence is more clearly made known.   It teaches also what are our wants, that we may learn to place our confidence in the goodness, power, and wisdom of God,—to obey his commandments, —to flee to him in adversity,—and to offer thanksgiving to him for the gifts which we enjoy.

6. By the Holy Scriptures, also, God the Creator is known.   We ought to consider what these Scriptures are ; that they are true, and have proceeded from the Spirit of God ; which is proved by the testimony of the Holy Spirit, by the efficacy and antiquity of the Scriptures, by the certainty of the Prophecies, by the miraculous preservation of the Law, by the calling and writings of the Apostles, by the consent of the Church, and by the steadfastness of the martyrs,

---

* THE ONE HUNDRED APHORISMS, with the various TABLES and INDICES, which must greatly facilitate reference, and enhance the utility ·and value of the present translation of THE INSTITUTES OF THE CHRISTIAN RELIGION, have been kindly furnished by the Rev. WILLIAM PRINGLE of Auchterarder.

whence it is evident that all the principles of piety are overthrown by those fanatics who, laying aside the Scripture, fly to revelations.

7. Next, what they teach; or, what is the nature of God in himself, and in the creation and government of all things.

8. The nature of God in himself is infinite, invisible, eternal, almighty; whence it follows that they are mistaken who ascribe to God a visible form. In his one essence there are three persons, the Father, the Son, and the Holy Spirit.

9. In the creation of all things there are chiefly considered, 1. Heavenly and spiritual substances, that is, angels, of which some are good and the protectors of the godly, while others are bad, not by creation, but by corruption; 2. Earthly substances, and particularly man, whose perfection is displayed in soul and in body.

10. In the government of all things the nature of God is manifested. Now his government is, in one respect, universal, by which he directs all the creatures according to the properties which he bestowed on each when he created them.

11. In another respect, it is special; which appears in regard to contingent events, so that if any person is visited either by adversity or by any prosperous result, he ought to ascribe it wholly to God; and with respect to those things which act according to a fixed law of nature, though their peculiar properties were naturally bestowed on them, still they exert their power only so far as they are directed by the immediate hand of God.

12. It is viewed also with respect to time past and future. *Past*, that we may learn that all things happen by the appointment of God, who acts either by means, or without means, or contrary to means; so that everything which happens yields good to the godly and evil to the wicked. *Future*, to which belong human deliberations, and which shows that we ought to employ lawful means; since that Providence on which we rely furnishes its own means.

13. Lastly, by attending to the advantage which the godly derive from it. For we know certainly, 1. That God takes care of the whole human race, but especially of his Church. 2. That God governs all things by his will, and regulates them by his wisdom. 3. That he has most abundant power of doing good; for in his hand are heaven and earth, all creatures are subject to his sway, the godly rest on his protection, and the power of hell is restrained by his authority. That nothing happens by chance, though the causes may be concealed, but by the will of God; by his secret will which we are unable to explore, but adore with reverence, and by his will which is conveyed to us in the Law and in the Gospel.

BOOK II.

14. The knowledge of God the Redeemer is obtained from the fall of man, and from the material cause of redemption.

15. In the fall of man, we must consider what he ought to be, and what he may be.

16. For he was created after the image of God ; that is, he was made a partaker of the divine Wisdom, Righteousness, and Holiness, and, being thus perfect in soul and in body, was bound to render to God a perfect obedience to his commandments.

17. The immediate causes of the fall were—Satan, the Serpent, Eve, the forbidden fruit ; the remote causes were—unbelief, ambition, ingratitude, obstinacy. Hence followed the obliteration of the image of God in man, who became unbelieving, unrighteous, liable to death.

18. We must now see what he may be, in respect both of soul and of body. The understanding of the soul in divine things, that is, in the knowledge and true worship of God, is blinder than a mole ; good works it can neither contrive nor perform. In human affairs, as in the liberal and mechanical arts, it is exceedingly blind and variable. Now the will, so far as regards divine things, chooses only what is evil. So far as regards lower and human affairs, it is uncertain, wandering, and not wholly at its own disposal.

19. The body follows the depraved appetites of the soul, is liable to many infirmities, and at length to death.

20. Hence it follows that redemption for ruined man must be sought through Christ the Mediator ; because the first adoption of a chosen people, the preservation of the Church, her deliverance from dangers, her recovery after dispersions, and the hope of the godly, always depended on the grace of the Mediator. Accordingly, the law was given, that it might keep their minds in suspense till the coming of Christ ; which is evident from the history of a gracious covenant frequently repeated, from ceremonies, sacrifices, and washings, from the end of adoption, and from the law of the priesthood.

21. The material cause of redemption is Christ, in whom we must consider three things ; 1. How he is exhibited to men ; 2. How he is received ; 3. How men are retained in his fellowship.

22. Christ is exhibited to men by the Law and by the Gospel.

23. The Law is threefold : Ceremonial, Judicial, Moral. The use of the Ceremonial Law is repealed, its effect is perpetual. The Judicial or Political Law was peculiar to the Jews, and has been set aside, while that universal justice which is described in the Moral Law remains. The latter, or Moral Law, the object of which is to cherish and maintain godliness and righteousness, is perpetual, and is incumbent on all.

24. The use of the Moral Law is threefold. The first use shows our weakness, unrighteousness, and condemnation ; not that we may despair, but that we may flee to Christ. The second is, that those who are not moved by promises, may be urged by the terror of threatenings. The third is, that we may know what is the will of God ; that we may consider it in order to obedience ; that our minds

may be strengthened for that purpose; and that we may be kept from falling.

25. The sum of the Law is contained in the Preface, and in the two Tables. In the Preface we observe, 1. The power of God, to constrain the people by the necessity of obedience; 2. A promise of grace, by which he declares himself to be the God of the Church; 3. A kind act, on the ground of which he charges the Jews with ingratitude, if they do not requite his goodness.

26. The first Table, which relates to the worship of God, consists of four commandments.

27. The design of the First Commandment is, that God alone may be exalted in his people. To God alone, therefore, we owe adoration, trust, invocation, thanksgiving.

28. The design of the Second Commandment is, that God will not have his worship profaned by superstitious rites. It consists of two parts. The former restrains our licentious daring, that we may not subject God to our senses, or represent him under any visible shape. The latter forbids us to worship any images on religious grounds, and, therefore, proclaims his power, which he cannot suffer to be despised,—his jealousy, for he cannot bear a partner,—his vengeance on children's children,—his mercy to those who adore his majesty.

29. The Third Commandment enjoins three things: 1. That whatever our mind conceives, or our tongue utters, may have a regard to the majesty of God; 2. That we may not rashly abuse his holy word and adorable mysteries for the purposes of ambition or avarice; 3. That we may not throw obloquy on his works, but may speak of them with commendatians of his Wisdom, Long-suffering, Power, Goodness, Justice. With these is contrasted a threefold profanation of the name of God, by perjury, unnecessary oaths, and idolatrous rites; that is, when we substitute in the place of God saints, or creatures animate or inanimate.

30. The design of the Fourth Commandment is, that, being dead to our own affections and works, we may meditate on the kingdom of God. Now there are three things here to be considered: 1. A spiritual rest, when believers abstain from their own works, that-God may work in them; 2. That there may be a stated day for calling on the name of God, for hearing his word, and for performing religious rites; 3. That servants may have some remission from labour.

31. The Second Table, which relates to the duties of charity towards our neighbour, contains the last Six Commandments. The design of the Fifth Commandment is, that, since God takes pleasure in the observance of his own ordinance, the degrees of dignity appointed by him must be held inviolable. We are therefore forbidden to take anything from the dignity of those who are above us, by contempt, obstinacy, or ingratitude; and we are commanded to pay them reverence, obedience, and gratitude.

32. The design of the Sixth Commandment is, that, since God has bound mankind by a kind of unity, the safety of all ought to be

considered by each person; whence it follows that we are forbidden to do violence to private individuals, and are commanded to exercise benevolence.

33. The design of the Seventh Commandment is, that, because God loves purity, we ought to put away from us all uncleanness. He therefore forbids adultery in mind, word, and deed.

34. The design of the Eighth Commandment is, that, since injustice is an abomination to God, he requires us to render to every man what is his own. Now men steal, either by violence, or by malicious imposture, or by craft, or by sycophancy, &c.

35. The design of the Ninth Commandment is, that, since God, who is truth, abhors falsehood, he forbids calumnies and false accusations, by which the name of our neighbour is injured,—and lies, by which any one suffers loss in his fortunes. On the other hand, he requires every one of us to defend the name and property of our neighbour by asserting the truth.

36. The design of the Tenth Commandment is, that, since God would have the whole soul pervaded by love, every desire averse to charity must be banished from our minds; and therefore every feeling which tends to the injury of another is forbidden.

37. We have said that Christ is revealed to us by the Gospel. And, first, the agreement between the Gospel, or the New Testament, and the Old Testament is demonstrated: 1. Because the godly, under both dispensations, have had the same hope of immortality; 2. They have had the same covenant, founded not on the works of men, but on the mercy of God; 3. They have had the same Mediator between God and men—Christ.

38. Next, five points of difference between the two dispensations are pointed out. 1. Under the Law the heavenly inheritance was held out to them under earthly blessings; but under the Gospel our minds are led directly to meditate upon it. 2. The Old Testament, by means of figures, presented the image only, while the reality was absent; but the New Testament exhibits the present truth. 3. The former, in respect of the Law, was the ministry of condemnation and death; the latter, of righteousness and life. 4. The former is connected with bondage, which begets fear in the mind; the latter is connected with freedom, which produces confidence. 5. The word had been confined to the single nation of the Jews; but now it is preached to all nations.

39. The sum of evangelical doctrine is, to teach, 1. What Christ is; 2. Why he was sent; 3. In what manner he accomplished the work of redemption.

40. Christ is God and man: *God*, that he may bestow on his people righteousness, sanctification, and redemption; *Man*, because he had to pay the debt of man.

41. He was sent to perform the office, 1. Of a Prophet, by preaching the truth, by fulfilling the prophecies, by teaching and doing the will of his Father; 2. Of a King, by governing the whole Church

and every member of it, and by defending his people from every kind of adversaries; 3. Of a Priest, by offering his body as a sacrifice for sins, by reconciling God to us though his obedience, and by perpetual intercession for his people to the Father.

42. He performed the office of a Redeemer by dying for our sins, by rising again for our justification, by opening heaven to us through his ascension, by sitting at the right hand of the Father whence he will come to judge the quick and the dead; and, therefore, he procured for us the grace of God and salvation.

BOOK III.

43. We receive Christ the Redeemer by the power of the Holy Spirit, who unites us to Christ; and, therefore, he is called the Spirit of sanctification and adoption, the earnest and seal of our salvation, water, oil, a fountain, fire, the hand of God.

44. Faith is the hand of the soul, which receives, through the same efficacy of the Holy Spirit, Christ offered to us in the Gospel.

45. The general office of faith is, to assent to the truth of God, whenever, whatever, and in what manner soever he speaks; but its peculiar office is, to behold the will of God in Christ, his mercy, the promises of grace, for the full conviction of which the Holy Spirit enlightens our minds and strengthens our hearts.

46. Faith, therefore, is a steady and certain knowledge of the divine kindness towards us, which is founded on a gracious promise through Christ, and is revealed to our minds and sealed on our hearts by the Holy Spirit.

47. The effects of faith are four: 1. Repentance; 2. A Christian life; 3. Justification; 4. Prayer.

48. True repentance consists of two parts: 1. Mortification, which proceeds from the acknowledgment of sin, and a real perception of the divine displeasure; 2. Quickening, the fruits of which are— piety towards God, charity towards our neighbour, the hope of eternal life, holiness of life. With this true repentance is contrasted false repentance, the parts of which are, Contrition, Confession, and Satisfaction. The two former may be referred to true repentance, provided that there be contrition of heart on account of the acknowledgment of sin, and that it be not separated from the hope of forgiveness through Christ; and provided that the confession be either *private* to God alone, or made to the pastors of the Church willingly and for the purpose of consolation, not for the enumeration of offences, and for introducing a torture of the conscience; or *public*, which is made to the whole Church, or to one or many persons in presence of the whole Church. What was formerly called Ecclesiastical Satisfaction, that is, what was made for the edification of the Church on account of repentance and public confession of sins, was introduced as due to God by the Sophists; whence sprung the supplements of

Indulgences in this world, and the fire of Purgatory after death. But that Contrition of the Sophists, and auricular Confession (as they call it), and the Satisfaction of actual performance, are opposed to the free forgiveness of sins.

49. The two parts of a Christian life are laid down: 1. The love of righteousness; that we may be holy, because God is holy, and because we are united to him, and are reckoned among his people; 2. That a rule may be prescribed to us, which does not permit us to wander in the course of righteousness, and that we may be conformed to Christ. A model of this is laid down to us, which we ought to copy in our whole life. Next are mentioned the blessings of God, which it will argue extreme ingratitude if we do not requite.

50. The sum of the Christian life is denial of ourselves.

51. The ends of this self-denial are four. 1. That we may devote ourselves to God as a living sacrifice. 2. That we may not seek our own things, but those which belong to God and to our neighbour. 3. That we may patiently bear the cross, the fruits of which are—acknowledgment of our weakness, the trial of our patience, correction of faults, more earnest prayer, more cheerful meditation on eternal life. 4. That we may know in what manner we ought to use the present life and its aids, for necessity and delight. Necessity demands that we possess all things as though we possessed them not; that we bear poverty with mildness, and abundance with moderation; that we know how to endure patiently fulness, and hunger, and want; that we pay regard to our neighbour, because we must give account of our stewardship; and that all things correspond to our calling. The delight of praising the kindness of God ought to be with us a stronger argument.

52. In considering Justification, which is the third effect of faith, the first thing that occurs is an explanation of the word. He is said to be justified who, in the judgment of God, is deemed righteous. He is justified by works, whose life is pure and blameless before God; and no such person ever existed except Christ. They are justified by faith who, shut out from the righteousness of works, receive the righteousness of Christ. Such are the elect of God.

53. Hence follows the strongest consolation; for instead of a severe Judge, we have a most merciful Father. Justified in Christ, and having peace, trusting to his power, we aim at holiness.

54. Next follows Christian liberty, consisting of three parts. 1. That the consciences of believers may rise above the Law, and may forget the whole righteousness of the Law. 2. That the conscience, free from the yoke of the Law, may cheerfully obey the will of God. 3. That they may not be bound by any religious scruples before God about things indifferent. But here we must avoid two precipices. 1. That we do not abuse the gifts of God. 2. That we avoid giving and taking offence.

55. The fourth effect of faith is Prayer; in which are considered its fruits, laws, faults, and petitions.

56. The fruit of prayer is fivefold. 1. When we are accustomed to flee to God, our heart is inflamed with a stronger desire to seek, love, and adore him. 2. Our heart is not a prey to any wicked desire, of which we would be ashamed to make God our witness. 3. We receive his benefits with thanksgiving. 4. Having obtained a gift, we more earnestly meditate on the goodness of God. 5. Experience confirms to us the Goodness, Providence, and Truth of God.

57. The laws are Four. 1. That we should have our heart framed as becomes those who enter into converse with God ; and therefore the lifting up of the hands, the raising of the heart, and perseverance, are recommended. 2. That we should feel our wants. 3. That we should divest ourselves of every thought of our own glory, giving the whole glory to God. 4. That while we are prostrated amidst overwhelming evils, we should be animated by the sure hope of succeeding, since we rely on the command and promise of God.

58. They err who call on the Saints that are placed beyond this life. 1. Because Scripture teaches that prayer ought to be offered to God alone, who alone knows what is necessary for us. He chooses to be present, because he has promised. He can do so, for he is Almighty. 2. Because he requires that he be addressed in faith, which rests on his word and promise. 3. Because faith is corrupted as soon as it departs from this rule. But in calling on the saints there is no word, no promise ; and therefore there is no faith ; nor can the saints themselves either hear or assist.

59. The summary of prayer, which has been delivered to us by Christ the Lord, is contained in a Preface and two Tables.

.60. In the Preface, the Goodness of God is conspicuous, for he is called *our Father*. It follows that we are his children, and that to seek supplies from any other quarter would be to charge God either with poverty or with cruelty ; that sins ought not to hinder us from humbly imploring mercy ; and that a feeling of brotherly love ought to exist amongst us. The power of God is likewise conspicuous in this Preface, for he is *in Heaven*. Hence we infer that God is present everywhere, and that when we seek him, we ought to rise above perceptions of the body and the soul ; that he is far beyond all risk of change or corruption ; that he holds the whole universe in his grasp, and governs it by his power.

61. The First Table is entirely devoted to the glory of God, and contains Three petitions. 1. That the *name* of God, that is, his power, goodness, wisdom, justice, and truth, *may be hallowed;* that is, that men may neither speak nor think of God but with the deepest veneration. 2. That God may correct, by the agency of his Spirit, all the depraved lusts of the flesh ; may bring all our thoughts into obedience to his authority ; may protect his children ; and may defeat the attempts of the wicked. The use of this petition is threefold. (1). It withdraws us from the corruptions of the world. (2). It inflames us with the desire of mortifying the flesh. (3). It ani-

mates us to endure the cross. 3. The Third petition relates not to the secret will of God, but to that which is made known by the Scriptures, and to which voluntary obedience is the counterpart.

62. The Second Table contains the Three remaining petitions, which relate to ourselves and our neighbours. 1. It asks everything which the body needs in this sublunary state; for we commit ourselves to the care and providence of God, that he may feed, foster, and preserve us. 2. We ask those things which contribute to the spiritual life, namely, *the forgiveness of sins*, which implies satisfaction, and to which is added a condition, that when we have been offended by deed or by word, we nevertheless forgive them their offences against us. 3. We ask *deliverance from temptations*, or, that we may be furnished with armour and defended by the Divine protection, that we may be able to obtain the victory. *Temptations* differ in their *cause*, for God, Satan, the world, and the flesh *tempt;* in their.*matter*, for we are tempted, on the right hand, in respect of riches, honours, beauty, &c., and on the left hand, in respect of poverty, contempt, and afflictions: and in their *end*, for God tempts the godly for good, but Satan, the flesh, and the world, tempt them for evil.

63. Those Four effects of faith bring us to the certainty of election, and of the final resurrection.

64. The causes of election are these. The *efficient* cause is—the free mercy of God, which we ought to acknowledge with humility and thanksgiving. The *material* cause is—Christ, the well-beloved Son. The *final* cause is—that, being assured of our salvation, because we are God's people, we may glorify him both in this life and in the life which is to come, to all eternity. The effects are, in respect either of many persons, or of a single individual; and that by electing some, and justly reprobating others. The elect are called by the preaching of the word and the illumination of the Holy Spirit, are justified, and sanctified, that they may at length be glorified.

65. The final resurrection will take place. 1. Because on any other supposition we cannot be perfectly glorified. 2. Because Christ rose in our flesh. 3. Because God is Almighty.

BOOK IV.

66. God keeps us united in the fellowship of Christ by means of Ecclesiastical and Civil government.

57. In Ecclesiastical government Three things are considered. 1. What is the Church? 2. How is it governed? 3. What is its power?

68. The Church is regarded in two points of view; as Invisible and Universal, which is the communion of saints; and as Visible and Particular. The Church is discerned by the pure preaching of the word, and by the lawful administration of the sacraments.

69. As to the government of the Church, there are Five points of inquiry. 1. Who rule? 2. What are they? 3. What is their calling? 4. What is their office? 5. What was the condition of the ancient Church?

70. They that rule are not Angels, but Men. In this respect, God declares his condescension towards us: we have a most excellent training to humility and obedience, and it is singularly fitted to bind us to mutual charity.

71. These are Prophets, Apostles, Evangelists, whose office was temporary; Pastors and Teachers, whose office is of perpetual duration.

72. Their calling is twofold; *internal* and *external*. The *internal* is from the Spirit of God. In the *external* there are Four things to be considered. 1. What sort of persons ought to be chosen? Men of sound doctrine and holy lives. 2. In what manner? With fasting and prayer. 3. By whom? Immediately, by God, as Prophets and Apostles. Mediately, with the direction of the word, by Bishops, by Elders, and by the people. 4. With what rite of ordination? By the laying on of hands, the use of which is threefold. 1. That the dignity of the ministry may be commended. 2. That he who is called may know that he is devoted to God. 3. That he may believe that the Holy Spirit will not desert this holy ministry.

73. The duty of Pastors in the Church is, to preach the Word, to administer the Sacraments, to exercise Discipline.

74. The condition of the ancient Church was distributed into Presbyters, Elders, Deacons, who dispensed the funds of the Church to the Bishops, the Clergy, the poor, and for repairing churches.

75. The power of the Church is viewed in relation to Doctrine, Legislation, and Jurisdiction.

76. Doctrine respects the articles of faith, none of which must be laid down without the authority of the word of God, but all must be directed to the glory of God and the edification of the Church. It respects also the application of the articles, which must agree with the analogy of faith.

77. Ecclesiastical laws, in precepts necessary to be observed, must be in accordance with the written word of God. In things indifferent, regard must be had to places, persons, times, with a due attention to order and decorum. Those constitutions ought to be avoided which have been laid down by pretended pastors instead of the pure worship of God, which bind the consciences by rigid necessity, which make void a commandment of God, which are useless and trifling, which oppress the consciences by their number, which lead to theatrical display, which are considered to be propitiatory sacrifices, and which are turned to the purposes of gain.

78. Jurisdiction is twofold. 1. That which belongs to the Clergy, which was treated of under the head of Provincial and General Synods. 2. That which is common to the Clergy and the people, the design of which is twofold, that scandals may be prevented, and

that scandal which has arisen may be removed. The exercise of it consists in private and public admonitions, and likewise in excommunication, the object of which is threefold. 1. That the Church may not be blamed; 2. That the good may not be corrupted by intercourse with the bad; 3. That they who are excommunicated may be ashamed, and may begin to repent.

79. With regard to Times, Fasts are appointed, and Vows are made. The design of Fasts is, that the flesh may be mortified, that we may be better prepared for prayer, and that they may be evidences of humility and obedience. They consist of Three things, the time, the quality, and the quantity of food. But here we must beware lest we rend our garments only, and not our hearts, as hypocrites do, lest those actions be regarded as a meritorious performance, and lest they be too rigorously demanded as necessary to salvation.

80. In Vows we must consider; 1. To whom the vow is made—namely, to God. Hence it follows that nothing must be attempted but what is approved by his word, which teaches us what is pleasing and what is displeasing to God. 2. Who it is that vows—namely, a man. We must, therefore, beware lest we disregard our liberty, or promise what is beyond our strength or inconsistent with our calling. 3. What is vowed. Here regard must be had to time; to the *past*, such as a vow of thanksgiving and repentance; to the *future*, that we may afterwards be more cautious, and may be stimulated by them to the performance of duty. Hence it is evident what opinion we ought to form respecting Popish vows.

81. In explaining the Sacraments, there are Three things to be considered. 1. What a sacrament is;—namely, an external sign, by which God seals on our consciences the promises of his good-will towards us, in order to sustain the weakness of our faith. We in our turn testify our piety towards him. 2. What things are necessary;—namely, the Sign, the Thing signified, the Promise, and the general Participation. 3. What is the number of them;—namely, Baptism and the Lord's Supper.

82. The Sign in Baptism is water; the Thing Signified is the blood of Christ; the Promise is eternal life; the Communicants or Partakers are, adults, after making a confession of their faith, and likewise infants; for Baptism came in the place of Circumcision, and in both the mystery, promise, use, and efficacy, are the same. Forgiveness of sins also belongs to infants, and therefore it is likewise a sign of this forgiveness.

83. The end of Baptism is twofold. 1. To promote our faith towards God. For it is a sign of our washing by the blood of Christ, and of the mortification of our flesh, and the renewal of our souls in Christ. Besides, being united to Christ, we believe that we shall be partakers of all his blessings, and that we shall never fall under condemnation. 2. To serve as our confession before our neighbour; for it is a mark that we choose to be regarded as the people of God,

and we testify that we profess the Christian religion, and that our desire is, that all the members of our body may proclaim the praise of God.

84. The Lord's Supper is a spiritual feast, by which we are preserved in that life into which God hath begotten us by his word.

85. The design of the Lord's Supper is threefold. 1. To aid in confirming our faith towards God. 2. To serve as a confession before men. 3. To be an exhortation to charity.

86. We must beware lest, by undervaluing the signs, we separate them too much from their mysteries, with which they are in some measure connected; and lest, on the other hand, by immoderately extolling them, we appear to obscure the mysteries themselves.

87. The parts are two. 1. The *spiritual truth* in which the meaning is beheld, consists in the promises; the *matter*, or substance, is Christ dead and risen; and the *effect* is our redemption and justification. 2. The visible signs are, bread and wine.

88. With the Lord's Supper is contrasted the Popish Mass. 1. It offers insult and blasphemy to Christ. 2. It buries the cross of Christ. 3. It obliterates his death. 4. It robs us of the benefits which we obtain in Christ. 5. It destroys the Sacraments in which the memorial of his death was left.

89. The Sacraments, falsely so called, are enumerated, which are, Confirmation, Penitence, Extreme Unction, Orders [which gave rise to the (seven) less and the (three) greater], and Marriage.

90. Next comes Civil government, which belongs to the external regulation of manners.

91. Under this head are considered Magistrates, Laws, and the People.

92. The Magistrate is God's vicegerent, the father of his country, the guardian of the laws, the administrator of justice, the defender of the Church.

93. By these names he is excited to the performance of duty. 1. That he may walk in holiness before God, and before men may maintain uprightness, prudence, temperance, harmlessness, and righteousness. 2. That by wonderful consolation it may smooth the difficulties of his office.

94. The kinds of Magistracy or Civil Government are, Monarchy, Aristocracy, Democracy.

95. As to Laws, we must see what is their constitution in regard to God and to men: and what is their equity in regard to times, places, and nations.

96. The People owe to the Magistrate, 1. Reverence heartily rendered to him as God's ambassador. 2. Obedience, or compliance with edicts, or paying taxes, or undertaking public offices and burdens. 3. That love which will lead us to pray to God for his prosperity.

97. We are enjoined to obey not only good magistrates, but all who possess authority, though they may exercise tyranny; for it

was not without the authority of God that they were appointed to be princes.

98. When tyrants reign, let us first remember our faults, which are chastised by such scourges; and, therefore, humility will restrain our impatience. Besides, it is not in our power to remedy these evils, and all that remains for us is to implore the assistance of the Lord, in whose hand are the hearts of men and the revolutions of kingdoms.

99. In Two ways God restrains the fury of tyrants; either by raising up from among their own subjects open avengers, who rid the people of their tyranny, or by employing for that purpose the rage of men whose thoughts and contrivances are totally different, thus overturning one tyranny by means of another.

100. The obedience enjoined on subjects does not prevent the interference of any popular Magistrates whose office it is to restrain tyrants and to protect the liberty of the people. Our obedience to Magistrates ought to be such, that the obedience which we owe to the King of kings shall remain entire and unimpaired.

GENERAL INDEX.

THE REFERENCES ARE TO THE VOLUMES AND PAGES.

teaching in the Church is according to the prescription of the written word, 394.

Circumcision, how far it agrees with baptism, ii. 530; and differs from it, 531; is a sign of mortification, 535; was never repeated, 521.

Clement, Pope, cruelty of, ii. 383.

Clergy, or Clerks, who they were, ii. 333, 453; impropriety of the name, 333; claim of, to immunity from civil jurisdiction, 450.

Collation of benefices, how simonical it became among the Papists, ii. 343.

Commandments of God, the, must not be estimated by the ability of man, i. 278; in expounding them, the end or object must always be considered, 322; division of the Law into Ten Commandments, 325. See Ten Commandments.

Communication of properties explained, i. 415.

Communion of saints, what is meant by, ii. 282; ought never to be broken up, 484.

Confession must be directed to God alone, i. 542; Popish errors concerning, 546; secret, blessed effects of, 543; private, of two kinds, 544; public, both ordinary and extraordinary, 542; auricular, is altogether a tyrannical imposition, 536; has been a subject of keen contest between the Canonists and the Scholastic Theologians, 537; refutation of arguments in support of it drawn from allegory, 538; from John's Baptism, and the words of the Apostle James, 539; effrontery in venturing to maintain that it is of Divine authority, 540.

Confirmation, what it was in the ancient Church, ii. 625; Augustine's view of, 631; the fictitious, taught by the Papists, 626; is impiously extolled above baptism, 628; is falsely called a Sacrament, 626; derives no countenance from the example of the apostles, 627; the oil used in it is blasphemously called the oil of salvation, 628; the ancient custom of confirmation was praiseworthy, and ought to be restored, 632.

Conformity to Christ in the afflictions of believers, ii. 17; in their resurrection, 262.

Conscience, what is meant by, ii. 141, 415; distinction between the earthly forum and the forum of, 417; bears reference to God alone, 142, 416; duty of obeying princes for the sake of, 352; this does not imply that the laws of princes have dominion over the, ib.

Consecration, or ordination, of ministers, the form and order of, ii. 337.

Constantine, the Emperor, greatly enlarged the dignity of the Roman See, ii. 373; inquiry into the foolish story of his donation, i. 575.

Consubstantial with the Father, Christ is said to be, i. 112: this expression, used by the Council of Nice, does not exist in Scripture, but declares the genuine meaning of Scripture, ii. 400.

Consubstantiation led to the foolish idea of the ubiquity of the body of Christ, ii. 569; confounds the two natures of Christ, 570; involves many absurdities, 571.

Continence defined, ii. 486; is a special gift from God, i. 349.

Contrition, when it is true or false, i. 535,

Conversion is the work of God alone, i. 255; is the remedy which divine grace provides for the cure of natural corruption, 254; is not only begun but completed by divine grace, 255; reply to the objection, that the will does its part in the work of conversion, 256; reply to the objection, that grace can do nothing without the will, ib.

Cornelius the Centurion, faith of, i. 498; why he was baptised, ii. 522; was not accepted by God on the ground of his own merit, i. 107.

Corruption of man, the, proceeds from a natural viciousness, but not from nature, i. 249; extends both to the intellect, and to the will, 219; exists in the heart, 250; does not arise from vicious custom, but from depravity of nature, ib.; objection that there have been some who, under the guidance of nature, were all their lives devoted to

virtue, 251; answer, that these are not common endowments, but special gifts of God, 252; the remedy which divine grace provides for the corruption of man is conversion, 255.

Councils of the Church, the true nature of, ii. 403; whence their authority is derived, ib.; by whom they are to be assembled, 371; in what manner they have often erred, 405; have authority only so far as they accord with Scripture, 406; are believed by Papists to be under the immediate guidance of the Holy Spirit, and therefore to be incapable of erring, 396; the most celebrated among them are the Council of Aquileia, 351; of Nice, i. 102; of Chalcedon, ii. 367; of Laodicea, 335; of Milevita, 372; the Elibertine, i. 95; everything determined by them is pronounced by the Romanists to be an authoritative interpretation of Scripture, ii. 411.

Cratetes, the Theban, excessive austerity of, ii. 32.

Creation of the world, advantages derived from the history of the, i. 141; was completed in six days, 142; answer to the impious question, why it was not created sooner, 141; in the order of it, the goodness of God to the human race was displayed, 142; is fitted to prevent us from overlooking the glorious perfections of God, 157; and to lead us to trust in God, and pray to him, ib.

Cross, the duty of Christians to bear the, ii. 16; is necessary on many accounts, 17; by whom, and on whom, and for what cause, it is imposed, 16; is a correction for past faults, 19; is attended by singular consolations when they are persecuted for righteousness' sake, 20; produces patience, hope, and firm confidence in God, 18; ought to be willingly and cheerfully received at the hand of God, 21; but this cheerfulness does not imply a total insensibility to pain, ib.; accords with the uniform experience of the saints, 22; the wide difference between philosophical and Christian patience, 23.

Cross of Christ, the, was accursed, i. 439; and yet, though a symbol of ignominy, it was converted into a triumphal chariot, 440.

David was a type of Christ, i. 301: under him, as a type, the sole intercession of Christ is asserted, ii. 173.

Deacons in the Church are of two classes, ii. 322; what sort of persons they were under the Papacy, 349; in the ancient Church, there were Subdeacons and Archdeacons, 330; in what manner they distributed the ecclesiastical goods, 331; devoted a fourth part to the repairs of churches, 332; vast difference between Popish deacons and those of the ancient Church, 646.

Deaconesses of the ancient Church, what resemblance do they bear to modern nuns? ii. 488.

Death was met by the martyrs boldly and intrepidly, i. 82; ought not to excite in Christians trembling at the mention of it, ii. 29; the unreasonableness of such fears demonstrated by nine arguments, ib.

Death of Christ, the great efficacy of the, i. 436; salvation is peculiarly and specially ascribed to, 437; by it Christ obtained grace for us, 455; and paid a price to ransom us from death, 456; presumptuous manner in which this subject is handled by the Schoolmen, 458; why it was the death of the cross, 439.

Debts, or the duties which we owe to God, i. 317, 328; why our sins are so called, ii. 429.

Devils are almost infinite in number, i. 151; the tendency of what Scripture teaches us concerning them, 150; are employed by God in exercising believers, but can never oppress or vanquish them, 153; can do nothing without the will and consent of God, ib.; are said to blind all who do not believe the gospel, 154; reasons why one Devil, or Satan, is often mentioned in the singular number, 151; the wickedness of his nature is not from creation, but from depravation, 152; is everywhere called our adversary, and the adver-

ii. 8 ; superiority of the inspired writers over, 2 ; hesitation of, about the immortality of the soul, i. 166 ; extraordinary attainments of, in legislation, eloquence, and the mathematical sciences, ii. 49 ; endless variety and confusion of, about the existence and perfections of God, i. 60.

Phocas the robber, having slain Maurice, conceded to Boniface III., that Rome should be the head of all the other Churches, ii. 377.

Pighius, the rabid objections of, answered, i. 495.

Plato regarded the soul as an image of God, i. 166.

Poor, the care of the, committed to Deacons, ii. 322 ; how faithfully the ancient Bishops attended to, 332.

Pope, the, proclaims himself vicar of Christ, ii. 354 ; but, on the contrary, he is Antichrist, 313 ; on what pretences he proceeded in the person of Leo in the Council of Chalcedon, 367 ; was not acknowledged as primate by the ancient Fathers, *ib.*; gradually attained to influence and jurisdiction, 369 ; the ecclesiastical power of, was long confined to his own Patriarchate, 370 ; was gradually extended in the time of Gregory, 374 ; great progress of, from slender beginnings, 446 ; obtained the concession of the primacy, in the person of Boniface III., from Phocas the robber, 377 ; tyranny of, was increased partly by the ignorance, and partly by the sluggishness, of the bishops, 378 ; is not a bishop in the house of God, 383 ; is proved from Daniel and Paul to be Antichrist, 384 ; laid hands, first, on kingdoms, and thereafter on empire, 447 ; cannot plead the donation of Constantine, which is fabulous, 448 ; by what means he attained to imperial dignity, of which Hildebrand was the founder, 449 ; by what fraud, perfidy, and arms, he invaded the dominion of others, *ib.*; indulgences sprung from the avarice of, i. 574.

Popes, personal characters of, Julius, Leo, Clement, and Paul, ii. 385 ; John XXII., heretical opinion of, that the soul is mortal, 386.

Power of God, the, is displayed in the whole universe, i. 158 ; is not idle, but incessantly active, 174.

Prayer always accompanies true faith, ii. 146 ; is absolutely necessary, though God needs not a monitor, 147 ; four rules of : first, to have our hearts formed as becomes those who are entering into converse with God, 148 ; second, in asking we must always truly feel our wants, 150 ; third, we must divest ourselves of all vain-glorious thoughts, 152 ; fourth, we must be animated to prayer by the sure hope of succeeding, 155 ; yet those laws are not so rigorously enforced as that God rejects the prayers in which he does not find perfect faith or repentance, 163 ; must be offered in the name of Christ alone, many traces of which are to be found in the ceremonies of the Law, 166 ; public, ought to be at stated seasons, except in cases of necessity, 178 ; ostentation forbidden in, 179 ; ought to be in the vulgar tongue, 182 ; secret, 179 ; perseverance in, recommended, 199 ; connection between supplication and thanksgiving in, 176 ; uncovering of the head in, is a token of humility, 183 ; the Lord's. *See* Lord's Prayer.

Preaching of the Gospel to the reprobate, what purpose is served by, ii. 241.

Predestination, the doctrine of, is highly useful and necessary, ii. 202 ; admonition respecting, to two classes of men ; *first*, the curious, 204 ; *second*, those who recommend that the doctrine should scarcely, if ever, be mentioned, 205 ; is wickedly abused by profane men, *ib.*; in the whole history of Abraham was given a specimen of, 206 ; as also in a second step, by which some of Abraham's family were rejected, and others were kept within the Church of God, 208 ; is altogether gratuitous, 212 ; the good pleasure of God is the only reason of, 214 ; is falsely ascribed by some to human merit, 213 ; no good works, either past or future, are taken into consideration in, 214 ; is proved by

a striking discussion in the Epistle to the Romans, 215 ; reply to objections taken from the ancient Fathers, 220 ; from Thomas Aquinas, and more modern authors, 221 ; view to be taken of reprobation, 223.

Presbyters, Bishops, Pastors, and Ministers, are used as synonymous terms, ii. 321 ; were divided by Papists into seculars and beneficiaries, 345.

Pride is natural to man, i. 38 ; pretexts for, 211.

Priesthood of Christ, the, must be viewed in connection with his other offices, i. 426 ; was prefigured by the shadows of the law, 431 ; was of such a nature that it was competent to none but Christ, *ib.*

Primacy of the Roman See, the, is represented by Papists as the bond of ecclesiastical unity, ii. 353 ; question as to the necessity of, 354 ; arguments drawn from the office of High Priest under the law in support of, 355 ; Peter's superiority, though admitted, would afford no proof of, 285 ; on the hypothesis of the Papists, belongs justly to the See of Antioch, 288 ; was first assigned to the Bishop of Rome by the second Nicene Council, 366 ; was not attributed to him by the Council of Chalcedon, or by the ancient Fathers, 367 ; was disputed between the Bishop of Constantinople and the Bishop of Rome, 376 ; for a long period was not acknowledged to have any jurisdiction over other Churches, 373.

Promises of God, the, were all founded on Christ, i. 497 ; are the foundation of faith, 494 ; Naaman the Syrian and Cornelius were brought to the knowledge of God by, 498 ; were added by God to the commandments, in order to imbue our hearts with love to himself, 318 ; though conditional, were not given in vain, 303 ; how the promises of the Law and of the Gospel are reconciled, i. 104.

Prophetical office of Christ, i. 426.

Prophets, who they were, ii. 319 ; harmony of all the, i. 79 ; were interpreters of the law, 66.

Proverb, false, i. 358 ; Milesian, ii. 485.

Providence of God, the, the duty of believing, i. 172 ; definition of, 175 ; is distinctly taught by David and other inspired writers, 172 ; the sun is a bright manifestation of, 183 ; the almighty power of God ought to be viewed in connection with, 174 ; advantages arising from the acknowledgment of, *ib.*; no place is left either for the favour or the judgments of God, without the doctrine of, 176 ; special, proved from passages relating to the human race, 177 ; from the history of the Israelites, and from Jonah, 178 ; from the history of Jacob, and from daily experience, *ib.*; reply to various assailants of, 184 ; gives no countenance to those who use the name of God as a cloak for their crimes, 185 ; is no apology for the neglect of means or of the duties of religion, 186 ; differs widely from the heathen doctrine of fate, 179 ; is not inconsistent with human deliberation, 186 ; simple, past events are often referred inconsiderately to, 187 ; fruits of holy meditation on, 188 ; employs men as instruments, but this forms no excuse for their misdeeds, 188 ; the great happiness arising from trust in, 192 ; the greatest of all miseries is ignorance of, 194 ; makes all things contribute to the advantage of the good, 188 ; in various ways curbs the wickedness of men, 189 ; overrules all for the good and safety of the people of God, 190 ; does not encourage the Christian to overlook inferior causes, 191 ; produces confidence in God, and stimulates to prayer and activity, 192 ; trains the godly to patience and moderation, as in the cases of Joseph, Job, and David, 190 ; shakes off their lethargy, and urges them to repentance, *ib.*; all the objections to, proceed from the carnal mind, 198.

Prudence, which ought to be exercised in the use of means, i. 187.

Publican, parable of the, illustrates the nature of humility, ii. 66.

Punishment, the, of the wicked differs from the

from labour, 341 ; reply to those who complain of the observance of the Lord's Day as Judaism, 342.

Sabellius, the erroneous views of, respecting the Holy Trinity, i. 112.

Sackcloth and ashes were signs of repentance, i. 523 ; ii. 463.

Sacraments what they are, ii. 491 ; extensive meaning of the term, 504 ; cannot exist without an antecedent promise, of which they are the seal, 492 ; consist of the word and the external sign, 493 ; in what sense the word was used by the ancients, 492 ; must be accompanied by the word, that they may be complete, 493 ; why they are called Signs of the Covenants, 494 ; are signs, though held forth to the ungodly, but are signs of grace to none but believers, 495 ; the whole efficacy of, depends on the inward operation of the Holy Spirit, 497 ; are called by Augustine *a visible word*, 495 ; how far they are confirmations of our faith, 499 ; are unjustly regarded by many as mere signs, 500 ; are unduly exalted by others, who ascribe to them a kind of secret virtue, *ib.* ; of the Old Testament, 506 ; of the New Testament, 507 ; are sometimes unduly extolled by the early theologians, 510 ; distinction made by Augustine between the sacrament and the matter of, 501 ; inquiry into the Five Sacraments falsely so called, 622.

Sacrifices were intended to prefigure Christ, i. 300 ; what they strictly are, ii. 615 ; some were eucharistic, and others were propitiatory, 616 ; of Samuel, Manoah, and Gideon, what they were, 432 ; the Mosaic, difference between and our Eucharist, 615 ; of believers are thanksgiving, i. 432 ; and in this respect are priests to God, but this does not interfere with the priesthood of Christ, ii. 618.

Sadducees, erroneous opinions of, concerning angels, i. 147 ; concerning the soul, 163 ; concerning the resurrection, ii. 265.

Saints, unspeakable glory of the, in heaven, ii. 273 ; all, even the most blameless, are struck and overwhelmed whenever they behold the presence of God, i. 39 ; in the presence of God sometimes plead their own innocence, and why, ii. 86, 116, 154 ; departed, do they intercede for us ? 168.

Salvation, four causes of, ii. 85 ; the gospel includes the whole doctrine of, 371

Samson, the prayers of, when he was about to slay the Philistines, were they free from all blame ? ii. 161.

Samuel, what was the sacrifice of, at Ramah, ii. 432 ; not he, but the Lord, was rejected by the Israelites, when his authority was declined, 656.

Satan, various names of, i. 150 ; why he is sometimes said to be *from the Lord*, 201, 269 ; with what dexterity he has laboured to deprive the Church of the ordinance of the Lord's Supper, ii. 557 ; often apes God, i. 76 ; the whole nature of is depraved, mischievous, and malignant, 152 ; cannot possibly do anything against the consent and will of God, 153 ; has been vanquished by Christ, and will be vanquished by all his people 154 ; what it is to deliver to, ii. 456 ; is said to blind those who do not believe the gospel, i. 154 ; the wickedness of the nature of, is not from creation, but from depravation, 152 ; is employed by God in exercising believers, 153.

Schism and heresy, difference between, ii. 309.

Scribes, the intolerable burdens imposed by, ii. 433.

Scripture was necessary in order to a perfect knowledge of God, i. 64 ; why it was committed to writing, 65 ; describes accurately, and to the life, the character of God, 66 ; is the proper school for training the children of God, 67 ; very far surpasses all other writings, 71 ; credibility of, proved by the admirable arrangement of the sacred volume, 74 ; by the majestic style of the Prophets, 75 ; by the harmony of the Evangelists, 81 ; by the heavenly majesty of John, Paul, and Peter, *ib.* ; by the calling of the apostles and the

conversion of Paul, 82 ; by the amazing power of the truth itself, and by the steadfastness of the martyrs, 82 ; never receives full credit, till it is sealed by the testimony of the Holy Spirit, 72 ; without it, the brightness of the divine countenance is an inextricable labyrinth, 67 ; signal work of God in preserving, 81 ; subverted by fanatics, who substitute pretended revelations for, 84 ; objection that it is insulting to subject the Spirit to, answered, 85 ; the tendency of, what it teaches concerning devils, 150 ; in what manner it exhorts to holiness of life, ii. 2 ; the authority of, does not depend on the judgment of the Church, i. 68 ; cavil about cleaving to the dead letter of, answered, 86 ; carefulness of the preservation of, by the Jews, whom Augustine calls the librarians of the Christian Church, 81 ; simplicity of. *See* Simplicity of the Holy Scriptures.

Sculpture and painting are gifts of God, and may be used purely and lawfully, but with what limitations, i. 100.

Self-denial, the beginning and sum of, ii. 7 ; leads us to shun ungodliness and worldly lusts, and to follow sobriety, righteousness, and godliness, 8 ; is most necessary, and yet most difficult, 10 ; how it ought to be cultivated, 9 ; has respect partly to men, and partly to God, *ib.* ; will lead us to equanimity and endurance, 13 ; will prevent us from eagerly contending for riches and honours, 14 ; will keep us from envying the prosperity of others, *ib.* ; will lead us to resign ourselves entirely to the Lord, *ib.* ; necessity of the doctrine of, 15.

Seraphim placed in the temple lent no countenance to the use of images, i. 93.

Simon Magus, fabulous account of the dispute of, with the Apostle Peter, ii. 362.

Simonides, the celebrated answer of, to King Hiero, i. 60.

Simplicity of the Holy Scriptures, the, is a proof of their divine original, i. 75, 81 ; is often beheld by the proud with disdain, 81.

Sin is erroneously supposed by Plato to be always committed through ignorance, i. 242 ; does not always proceed from preconceived depravity or malice, 243 ; of parents, in what respect God punishes on the children, 331 ; good intention does not hinder us from falling into, 243 ; against the Holy Spirit, what it is, 528 ; venial and mortal, absurd distinction of the Schoolmen between, 361, 558.

Singing in the worship is very ancient, ii. 181 ; was not universal, *ib.* ; ought to proceed from deep feeling of the heart, 180.

Sinner, the woman who was a, on what ground she obtained the forgiveness of sins, i. 568.

Sinners are justly punished, though they fulfil the appointment of Providence, i. 187.

Sins are called Debts, and why, ii. 194.

Sitting at the right hand of God the Father, what is meant by, i. 449 ; reasons why Christ is so seated, 420.

Slander is forbidden by the Ninth Commandment, i. 352.

Sobriety ought to be displayed in the whole life of the Christian, i. 523 ; ought to be constantly maintained by us in inquiring into the meaning of the Holy Scriptures, i. 144.

Solon, saying of, ii. 659.

Son of God, in what sense Christ is called, i. 420 ; the twofold filiation of, explained, 421 ; that he is so does not weaken the proof of his supreme Divinity, i. 130. *See* Christ.

Soul, the excellencies of the, described, i. 167 ; dreams of the Manichees, of Servetus, and of Osiander, as to the origin of, refuted, 165 ; faculties of, opinions of philosophers concerning, reviewed, 168 ; division of, into the intellect and the will, 169 ; immortality of, 160 ; proved by various arguments, *ib.* ; a strong proof of, taken from man having been created in the image of God, 162 ; not distinctly maintained by any of the ancient philosophers, 166.

Modern
Residential
Wiring

Harvey N. Holzman

Master Electrician
Member, International Association
of Electrical Inspectors

Based
on the
2005 NEC®

Publisher
The Goodheart-Willcox Company, Inc.
Tinley Park, Illinois
www.g-w.com

The Goodheart-Willcox Company, Inc. Brand Disclaimer: Brand names, company names, and illustrations for products and services included in this text are provided for educational purposes only and do not represent or imply endorsement or recommendation by the author or the publisher.

The Goodheart-Willcox Company, Inc. Safety Notice: The reader is expressly advised to carefully read, understand, and apply all safety precautions and warnings described in this book or that might also be indicated in undertaking the activities and exercises described herein to minimize risk of personal injury or injury to others. Common sense and good judgment should also be exercised and applied to help avoid all potential hazards. The reader should always refer to the appropriate manufacturer's technical information, directions, and recommendations; then proceed with care to follow specific equipment operating instructions. The reader should understand these notices and cautions are not exhaustive.
  The publisher makes no warranty or representation whatsoever, either expressed or implied, including but not limited to equipment, procedures, and applications described or referred to herein, their quality, performance, merchantability, or fitness for a particular purpose. The publisher assumes no responsibility for any changes, errors, or omissions in this book. The publisher specifically disclaims any liability whatsoever, including any direct, indirect, incidental, consequential, special, or exemplary damages resulting, in whole or in part, from the reader's use or reliance upon the information, instructions, procedures, warnings, cautions, applications, or other matter contained in this book.
  The publisher assumes no responsibility for the activities of the reader.

Library of Congress Cataloging-in-Publication Data

Holzman, Harvey N.
  Modern residential wiring / by Harvey N. Holzman.
    p. cm.
  ISBN-13: 978-1-59070-443-1
  ISBN-10: 1-59070-443-6
  1. Electric wiring, Interior. 2. Dwellings—Electric equipment. I. Title.

TK3285.H65   2006
621.319'24—dc22

                                    2005055035

Introduction

Modern Residential Wiring provides you with a solid background of electrical principles and practices, as well as a thorough understanding of **National Electrical Code®** requirements. Once having mastered the information given here, you will be well equipped to design and install modern and safe residential wiring systems that meet the electrical power demands of the new millennium.

Modern Residential Wiring covers not only the "how" but the "why" of safe electrical wiring practice. Although the content is concerned primarily with residential installations, many of the same concepts and principles may be applied to commercial and industrial electrical construction.

The chapters are arranged in a logical sequence. The order of instruction follows the normal order in which the installation would be made. However, each chapter is designed to stand alone and may be studied independently to suit a specific need.

Modern Residential Wiring makes the study of electrical wiring easy. Even the most complicated procedures are simply explained and easy to understand. Procedures are explained step-by-step while the many illustrations are fully integrated into the easy-to-read text. The illustrations should be carefully examined as they will often clarify and explain the more difficult principles of electricity and the requirements of the **National Electrical Code®**.

This new edition of **Modern Residential Wiring** is revised to be consistent with changes in the trade practices, materials, and the requirements of the **2005 National Electrical Code**. It has been expanded to cover new areas and methods of residential wiring.

The principles of electricity remain fixed. The methods, materials, and tools of the trade are continuously evolving. **Modern Residential Wiring** presents both the fundamentals of electrical wiring and the latest practices used in the trade.

The author wishes to express his sincere appreciation to each of the individuals, organizations, and associations that provided input, assistance and illustrative materials for the new edition. A special thanks to my wife, Linda, for her active assistance in the creation of this edition.

Harvey N. Holzman

Modern Residential Wiring Chapter Components

Objectives. Provide an overview of the chapter content and explain what should be understood on completion of the chapter.

Technical Terms. List of important technical terms introduced in the chapter. The terms in this list appear in **_bold-italic type_** when they first appear in the chapter.

Safety Note. Identify procedures that can result in personal injury or damage if the proper safety measures are not followed.

Procedures. Present installation or repair techniques in an easy-to-follow, step-by-step format. Procedures help promote a logical approach to common residential wiring tasks.

Web Site. Highlight Web sites that provide supplemental information related to the procedures, products, or associations discussed in the text.

Pro Tip. Supplemental information and hints related to the components or procedures discussed in the text.

3

Tools for the Electrician

Objectives

Information in this chapter will enable you to:

- Select essential tools for residential wiring.
- Know the specialty tools available for infrequent applications.
- Discuss basic principles of tool use and care.

Technical Terms

Blanket heater	Hickey
Box heater	Hydraulic bender
Cable ripper	Level
Circuit tester	Lineman's hammer
Conduit bender	Lineman's pliers
Continuity tester	Locking pliers
Diagonal cutter	Long tape rule
Digital voltage tester	Multimeter
Electric drill	Needle-nose pliers
Electrical voltage tester	Pipe cutter
Electrician's hammer	Pliers
Electrician's knife	Reamer
Fish tape	Receptacle tester
Flux	Reciprocating saw
Folding rule	Rotary-hammer drill
Grooved joint pliers	
Hacksaw	
Hammer-drill	

Sharpening stone	Steel tape
Solder	Torpedo level
Soldering gun	Whetstone
Soldering paste (flux)	Wire stripper
Solenoid voltage tester	

An electrician must have proper tools for the job. Tools must be kept in good repair as well. If tools are not available or are in poor condition, time is wasted and good work is impossible. Invest in good-quality tools and take the time to inspect and care for them, and you will be able to rely on them for many years.

Safety Note
Homemade Insulated Tools

Insulated tools have been tested to prevent conductivity at the voltage for which the tool is rated. Do not think that you can insulate a tool by dipping its handles in a polymer or wrapping them with tape. These methods create a weak and inconsistent thickness of insulation. If you must work on energized equipment, the cost of insulated tools is a small price to pay to prevent injury or death.

51

...gs, elbows, and ...allation of rigid

...be bent using ...g elements to ...be easily bent ...ig. Preformed ...o connect the RNC and fittings, a special glue and primer are used. See **Figure 4-29.**

Attaching Fittings to RNC

1. Clean the inside of the fitting and the end of the conduit with a rag.
2. Dry-fit the fitting on the conduit to check the final position.
3. Remove the fitting.
4. Apply primer to the inside of the fitting and the outside of the conduit.
5. Apply cement to the primed areas.
6. Push the conduit into the fitting while turning the fitting a quarter turn.
7. Look at the seam for a bead of glue to indicate a proper amount of cement.

Intermediate Metal Conduit

Intermediate metal conduit (IMC) is permitted for use in all atmospheric conditions and in all types of occupancies. Like its counterpart rigid metal conduit, IMC is available in 10' lengths. Each length or part of a length must be properly connected and joined to other lengths or enclosures using the correct fittings. IMC is available with or without threads. Installation is the same as rigid metal conduit.

Step 1
Apply primer to the inside of the fitting.

Step 2
Apply primer to the outside of the conduit.

Step 3
Apply glue to the inside of the fitting.

Step 4
Apply glue to the outside of the conduit.

Step 5
Push the conduit into the fitting. Turn the conduit 1/4 turn to spread the glue evenly.

Step 6
This is a cutaway view of the completed assembly.

Figure 4-29. Follow these steps to make the RNC attachments watertight.

...ble type is ...en remod-

...nch. These ...conductor

...o work in

...use most ...waste time

...is able to ...bolts.

...wood step-...needed at

...n of screws ...tarter hole ...e tools.

...eeded for

...uickly cut ...er hole

- **Wood chisel.** This tool will trim away small amounts of wood in framing members to make room for conduit, cable, or boxes.
- **Aviation or tin snips.** These sheet metal cutting tools are useful for some cabling covers. To create the leverage to cut metal, aviation snips use compound action and the tin snips have long handles.

Pro Tip
Mark Your Screwdrivers

Mark the top of your screwdriver handles with a + or a − symbol so you know the tip style before pulling the screwdriver out of your pouch.

Care and Repair of Tools

Knives, drill bits, chisels, saws, and other tools meant for cutting should be kept sharp. A dull tool does poor work and is also more likely to cause injury to a worker or damage nearby materials. Gripping tools or turning tools such as pliers and screwdrivers should be inspected frequently. Pliers with rounded teeth will slip and may cause damage or scraped knuckles. Inspect screwdriver blades for rounding and other signs of damage and wear. If reconditioning the tool is impossible or costs more than a new one, replace the tool.

Handles of striking tools should be inspected frequently for looseness and weakness. Wooden handles can crack and splinter from misuse or misdirected blows. Loose wooden handles can be repaired with new wedges. Broken handles should be replaced. Proper use and care of tools should be a part of every electrician's training.

Web Site
www.hti.org

For additional information concerning the proper use of hand tools, visit the Hand Tool Institute Web site.

Review Questions

Write your answers on a separate sheet of paper. Do not write in this book.

1. List the three types of rules needed for measuring distance or length.
2. *True or False?* A cable ripper is used on a single conductor wire.
3. How is an electrician's hammer different from a standard claw hammer?
4. Which of the following statements is true when using cutting tools such as cable cutters and side cutters?
   A. Never use more than reasonable hand pressure.
   B. Use a handle extender if the material does not cut easily.
   C. It is acceptable to use a hammer to make the cutters cut the material.
5. _____ are used for holding, shaping, and cutting wire.

Review Questions. Designed to reinforce the material covered in the chapter.

Know the Code. A few *National Electrical Code* questions at the end of each chapter. These questions require a copy of the *NEC* and help the student become familiar with its overall layout.

Code Alert. Call attention to the *National Electrical Code* and possible local codes. Where possible, these notes relate directly to the content of the chapter. Specific codes may be cited, when applicable. It is essential that you refer to your local code to determine the requirements in your area.

Caution. Warn readers of situations that may have an increased potential of injury.

History Brief. Provide background information and help build an appreciation for the development of residential wiring and the electrical trade. This feature will help you gain greater perspective and understand the importance of safe and reliable wiring.

Running Glossary. Provides definitions of the important technical terms introduced on the page. It reinforces the terminology electricians will encounter on the job.

Rigid Metal Conduit: Type RMC — *Article 344*		
Locations Allowed	**Sizes**	**Maximum Mounting Distance**
Dry	1/2"	
Wet	through	
Corrosive	6"	

Rigid Metal Conduit

Rigid metal conduit (RMC) is galvanized and somewhat similar to water pipe. It is used for both indoor and outdoor applications. Inside and out, the conduit is smooth and can be cut, threaded, reamed, and bent as necessary for proper installation. To cut RMC with a pipe cutter, follow the cutting procedure demostrated in the previous EMT section. RMC must be firmly connected to items such as electrical outlet boxes, and panels with a threaded locknut and bushing. This solid connection is necessary because the conduit itself serves as the grounding conductor. Thus, a separate grounding conductor is not required when using RMC. Fittings should maintain a continuous ground throughout the system. See **Figure 4-26.**

Code Alert
Section 344.46

Where a conduit enters a box, fitting, or other enclosure, a bushing shall be provided to protect the wire from abrasion unless the design of the box, fitting, or enclosure is such as to afford equivalent protection.

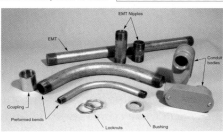

Figure 4-26. Rigid metallic conduit is threaded so that it can be attached to fittings and couplings.

rigid metal conduit (RMC): This is the original conduit, used before thin-wall and IMC. RMC, also called *heavy-wall conduit,* has thick walls and provides the greatest protection for the wires inside. Small sizes can be bent by hand with difficulty; larger sizes must be machine-bent.

Figure 8-4. A dual-element fuse. A—Normal condition. B—Fuse opens from overload after a brief time delay. C—After an overload. D—Short melts fusible element. E—After a short circuit. (Bussmann Division of Cooper Industries)

Figure 8-5. Type S plug fuses (left) have a thinner stem than Edison-base type fuses (right).

Plug fuses
Plug fuses are available in two varieties: Edison-base and Type S, **Figure 8-5.** Plug fuses have a maximum rating of 30 amps. Fuses rated as 15 amps or less have a hexagonal window, while higher-rated fuses have a circular window, **Figure 8-6.**

Figure 8-6. Fuses rated for 15 amps or less have a hexagonal window.

Plug fuses are limited by the following

of lesser capacities. This potentially dangerous oversizing problem is eliminated by using a Type S fuse, which uses a screwshell adapter. Type S fuses must be used on all new installations and for replacement installations. There are three classifications of Type S fuses with specific adapters based on their ampere ratings: 0–15 amps, 16–20 amps, and 21–30 amps.

Caution
Edison-Base Plug Fuses

Edison-base plug fuses have no inherent limit to the use of higher ampacities. For example, nothing prevents a 30-amp fuse from being installed in a 15-amp circuit. Using a fuse with an ampere rating higher than that of the circuit is a fire hazard.

Cartridge fuses
Cartridge fuses are used in fused systems over 120 volts or 30 amps. There are two types of cartridge fuse connections: ferrule type and knife-blade type. See **Figure 8-7.**

Figure 4-11. A—The setscrew connector cannot be used on aluminum AC. B—The clamping connector can be used on steel or aluminum AC. Always read the cable manufacturer's installation instructions for any restrictions.

Nonmetallic Sheathed Cable

Nonmetallic sheathed cable (NM) has two or more insulated conductors wrapped in a strong plastic or braided outer sheath. Often included is a bare copper ground wire, **Figure 4-12.** NM is the easiest and, in many areas, the most popular system to install. NM is easily cut to length with cable cutters. A cable ripper is used to split the outer jacket from the point where the wires will be exposed to the end of the cable. Place the cutting tooth in the center of the cable about 8" from the end. Squeeze the ripper closed to pierce the jacket and pull it to the end of the cable. Use a knife to carefully cut the jacket completely off the cable. See **Figure 4-13.**

History Brief
Romex®

Type NM cable is referred to almost universally as *Romex,* regardless of which company makes the cable. Originally developed by General Cable in Rome, New York, in 1922, NM cable is now made by many different companies.

Nonmetallic Sheathed Cable: Types NM, NMC, and NMS — *Article 334*		
Locations Allowed	**Sizes**	**Maximum Mounting Distance**
Type NM: Normally Dry	14 AWG	
Type NMC: Moist, damp, or corrosive	through	
Type NMS: Normally Dry	2 AWG	

nonmetallic sheathed cable (NM): A cable with 2 or more conductors and a ground all within an outer jacket, suitable for use in most residential installations except where conduit is required. NM is called Romex in the trade.

About the Author

Harvey Holzman is a master electrician licensed in the state of Texas. He has over thirty years of experience installing, repairing, and upgrading electrical systems for residential and commercial customers. He is a long-time member of the International Association of Electrical Inspectors.

The National Electrical Code®

The most informative and authoritative body of information concerning electrical wiring installation in the United States, and perhaps the world, is the *National Electrical Code® (NEC)*. It establishes a set of rules, regulations, and criteria for the installation of electrical equipment. Compliance with these methods will result in a safe installation.

The *NEC* is drafted by a team of experts assembled for this purpose by the National Fire Protection Association (NFPA). This team is formally called the *National Electrical Code* committee. They revise and update the *NEC* every three years. It is imperative that anyone installing electrical wiring obtains and studies the *NEC*. Articles and sections of the *NEC* are referred to throughout this text. Although certain portions, tables, and examples are directly quoted from its text, there is enough useful information in the *NEC* that not having it available would be a tremendous hindrance. The latest edition of the *National Electrical Code* can be purchased from the National Fire Protection Association by visiting their Web site, www.nfpa.org, or writing to:

NFPA
1 Batterymarch Park
Quincy, MA 02169-7471

Brief Contents

Contents

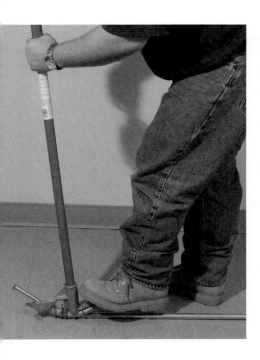

Section 2
Installation

Section 3
Planning

Section 4
Specialized Installations

Section 1
Fundamentals

Safety

Objectives

Information in this chapter will enable you to:

- Understand the effects of electrical shock.

- Describe conditions likely to affect severity of electrical shock.

- Maintain safety during installation.

- List basic workplace safety rules.

- Explain a lockout/tagout/blockout program.

- Describe steps for helping a shock victim.

Technical Terms

Arc flash
Blockout device
Electrical burn
Insulated tools
Lockout device
Personal protective equipment (PPE)
Tagout

Workplace Injuries

The information in this chapter is designed to instill the knowledge that is required to work safely in a residential wiring environment. This knowledge will boost your confidence so that you may do your job well without any fear or apprehension. However, be very careful about letting this confidence turn into complacency. Shortcuts around safe practices quickly become shortcuts to disaster.

There are many types of injuries that may occur on the work site, the obvious one being electrical shock. The others include burns, eye wounds, punctures, cuts, and back injuries.

The effects of these injuries range from stopping an installation because a cut needed to be bandaged to inflicting grief onto family and friends because carelessness caused a death. These are situations that you can avoid if you learn about safe methods, practice those methods, and repeat the practice until safety becomes a habit.

Electrical Shock

Electricity passing through the human body causes an electrical shock. The severity of a shock does not have as much to do with the voltage as with the amount of current. A shock of 10,000 V is no more deadly than that of 120 V. On the other hand, a shock approaching 10 milliamperes (0.01 A) is painful and could cause severe injury. See **Figure 1-1**. The values and the bodily effects listed in the table are only an average. Conditions of body size, skin

| Average Effects of Electric Current on the Body ||
Amount of Current	Effects on the Body
0.001 A (1 mA)	Felt slightly as a tingle
0.001 A to 0.01 A (1 mA to 10 mA)	Would probably cause muscles to contract and prevent victim from releasing the object
0.01 A to 0.1 A (10 mA to 100 mA)	Fatal after several seconds duration
0.1 A or more (100 mA or more)	Almost always fatal

Figure 1-1. Even very small amounts of current passing through the body can be lethal.

moisture, amount of food and liquids in the body, surrounding humidity, and clothing change the severity of the shock. You will learn more about volts and amperes later in the text. For now, know that the electricity in most homes is far more than required to electrocute a person.

Burn

There are two types of electricity-related burns that can occur. Both are life threatening. The first is called an *electrical burn*, which occurs when electricity passes through the body. Just as wires heat up when too much electricity passes through, so will the human body. Often, the victim has extensive internal damage and very little external indication of any injury.

The second type of electricity-related burn is a result of arc flash. *Arc flash* is an explosion that takes place when electricity short-circuits through the air or across inadequate insulation. The temperatures during an arc flash are high enough to melt metal. An arc flash projects melted metal outward, injuring any unprotected workers in the area. The best way to prevent an arc flash is to de-energize the equipment before working on it. If this is not possible, be sure to wear the appropriate clothing and eye protection.

---

electrical burn: A burn that occurs when electricity passes through the body.

arc flash: An explosion that takes place when electricity short-circuits through the air or across inadequate insulation.

A first step in protecting yourself is to wear clothing that is made of flame-resistant fabrics.

Treating a burn involves removing the source of the heat and calling for medical help. Burns caused by electrical shock or arc flash are usually too severe to be treated by anyone other than a doctor or paramedic. While waiting for help to arrive, cool the burn with sterile gauze soaked in cool (not cold) water. Do not apply ice to a burn, and never put butter, grease, or medical ointments on the burn. Be prepared to treat the person for shock.

> **Caution**
> **Calling for Emergency Help**
>
> It is important to know where you are working and be able to describe the location of the work site if you have to call for emergency help. Some work sites may not have a street address yet. Most will not have a telephone. If you call 911 from a cellular phone, the address will not appear at the dispatch center. Not all locations can receive cellular 911 calls. Be sure you know the number to call.

Eye Injury

An eye injury can be one of the most devastating wounds a person can receive and one of the easiest to prevent. Always wear your safety glasses whenever there is the slightest chance of an object being projected. You should also wear safety glasses when working in a position that causes you to look overhead. Dust and debris often fall from upper areas during construction. If any of this material falls into your eye, you may suffer an injury ranging from eye irritation to a scratched eye. There are many styles of safety glasses available to suit your needs and preferences. See **Figure 1-2**.

Puncture Wound

Puncture wounds will typically result from carelessness or sloppy housekeeping. Using a file without a handle, pushing a chisel toward your body, or working around wood scraps with nails are all habits that can lead to a puncture wound. If you or a coworker

Figure 1-2. There are many types and styles of safety glasses available. (Mine Safety Appliances Company)

experience a puncture wound, the first step is to call for help. If the object is still embedded in the victim, do not try to remove it. Instead, lay the victim down and stabilize the object. Removing it may cause further harm. If the victim remains standing or sitting, there is a chance of falling or fainting, which may cause additional injury.

Cuts

Most cuts occur on the hands and arms. Sharp edges of electrical components and carelessness with cutting tools are two of the many causes of cuts. When a cut occurs, you will need to clean and dress the wound quickly to prevent any infection. Wash the cut by running cool water over it. If the cut appears deep, you should see a doctor in case stitches are needed. Use an adhesive bandage to keep the cut clean and closed.

Working Safely

Being aware of the types of injuries that can occur on the work site is important. More important, however, is practicing safe work habits to prevent these injuries from occurring. In order to work safely, you must dress appropriately, use ladders and scaffolds correctly, operate tools safely, and practice safe work habits.

Personal Protective Equipment (PPE)

Personal protective equipment (PPE) is the clothing and equipment you must wear in order to be protected from known hazards. This equipment may be the only barrier between you and 240 volts. There are basic pieces of PPE that you should always have available. These include gloves, safety glasses, flame-resistant clothing, and a hard hat. There may be situations that require earplugs and a face shield. See **Figure 1-3**. When shopping for PPE, purchase items that are certified by a nationally recognized testing laboratory (NRTL).

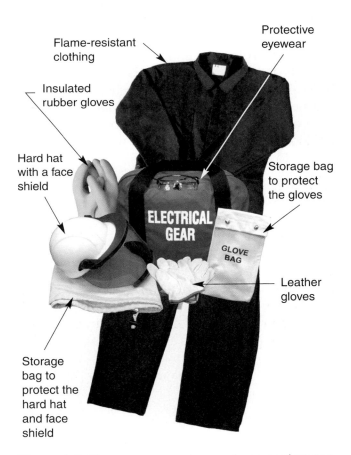

Flame-resistant clothing

Protective eyewear

Insulated rubber gloves

Hard hat with a face shield

Storage bag to protect the gloves

ELECTRICAL GEAR

GLOVE BAG

Leather gloves

Storage bag to protect the hard hat and face shield

Figure 1-3. There are many types of personal protective equipment (PPE). This is often the only barrier between you and dangerous current or arc flash. (National Safety Apparel, Inc.)

personal protective equipment (PPE): The clothing and equipment worn to provide protection from hazards.

Ladders and Scaffolding

There are many instances where you must use a ladder to get to a work area. Sometimes, the work area will require an elevated platform, such as a scaffold. Never use a ladder or scaffold without proper supervision and training. Also, review the manufacturer's instructions before using a ladder or scaffold. Both scaffolding and ladders should be handled carefully to prevent injury or property damage. Be particularly careful not to contact overhead wires or exposed wires. Falls from ladders and scaffolds account for a high percentage of work-related deaths.

Ladders

Ladders used by electricians should be made of wood or fiberglass. See **Figure 1-4**. They should be set at a safe angle and tied off to prevent a slip or fall. As a rule of thumb, the horizontal distance from the base of the ladder to the structure should be one-quarter of the height where the ladder touches the structure, **Figure 1-5**. Make certain the base of the ladder has firm support. The ground or floor should be level. If it is not, use a ladder leveler to position the ladder safely. See **Figure 1-6**.

Figure 1-4. Use only nonmetallic ladders when working around electricity. (Werner Co.)

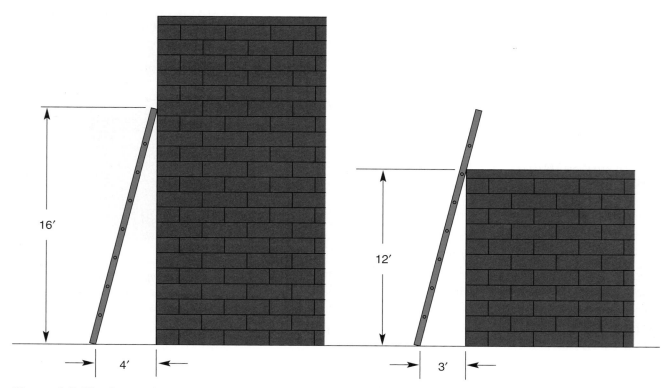

Figure 1-5. The base of an extension ladder should be away from the structure one-quarter of the height where the ladder rests on the structure.

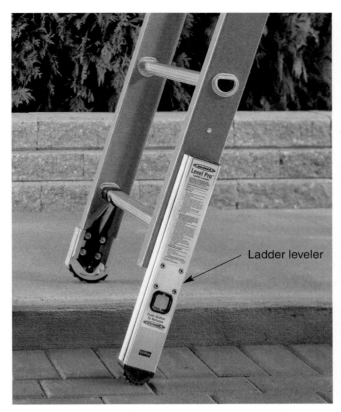

Figure 1-6. Use a ladder leveler when positioning a ladder on an uneven surface. (Werner Co.)

Figure 1-7. Always face the ladder and never stand on the top rung. (Werner Co.)

Use extreme care if the surface is wet or icy. Special blocking may be needed to prevent slipping.

Stepladders should be set level. They must be fully opened so the hinges will lock. Never use a stepladder while it is leaning against a structure. Always open the ladder. Keep the joints tight so the ladder does not wobble or lean.

When working on the ladder, always face it. See **Figure 1-7**. Never use the top rung or step of any ladder for support. Check ladders often for step rot or other structural damage. Discard ladders in poor condition.

Scaffolds

Wooden scaffolds are preferred to metal scaffolds for electrical work. If a metal scaffold must be used, it should be grounded. Handrails and toe boards should be secured to the top level. Lock all wheels, if equipped, to prevent unwanted movement. See **Figure 1-8**. Tie the scaffold off as well, especially if it is several platforms high. Always use a ladder to get onto a scaffold. NEVER climb the braces.

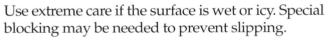

Locking wheels

Figure 1-8. This scaffold is equipped with locking wheels to prevent it from moving during use. (Werner Co.)

Proper Tool Use

There are many tools available for you to use during your electrical training and career. You will see many of these in Chapter 3, **Tools**. When operated correctly, these hand and power tools can be very safe. As always, these are general guidelines to follow—refer to the manufacturer's instructions for full safe operating procedures.

Power tools

Power tools have made many jobs easier, but they have also introduced additional safety risks. Power cords and moving parts are two potential hazards. Be sure that the tool is switched to the "off" position before plugging it in. Inspect the cords for damage regularly. If the insulation becomes damaged or the cord cut, do not splice it or wrap it with electrical tape. This is not a proper repair. Install a new cord to maintain the original safety of the tool.

Hand tools

Injuries commonly caused by hand tools include cuts and puncture wounds. Improper use, especially of cutting tools, is a certain path to injury. Always remember to use hand tools in such a manner that if the tool slips, it will not injure you or a coworker.

Insulated tools

You should always turn the power off before working on electrical equipment. This is the simplest preventive measure you can take to guard against electrical shock. There may be times when you will need to work on equipment with the power on. In these rare instances, you should use insulated tools and the proper PPE. *Insulated tools* have a nonconductive covering that prevents the transfer of electricity from the tool to the user. Just because a tool has a nonmetallic coating or plastic handles does not mean that the tool will protect you from electrical shock. The tool

must be identified as an insulated tool that is capable of resisting a specific amount of electricity. See **Figure 1-9**.

Safe Work Methods

There are many tasks that you will do repeatedly throughout your electrical training and career. Choosing to apply safe work methods when performing these tasks will greatly reduce the chance of injury. This will allow you to continue to be a productive worker and enjoy life outside of work as well.

Lifting and carrying

Improper lifting is a major cause of back injuries in the workplace. Bending over to pick something up and twisting your back while lifting are sure ways to invite back pain. This pain can quickly escalate to the point where you may not be able to get out of bed, and that means a day of lost wages. To reduce the risk of back injury, always follow the basic rules of lifting shown in **Figure 1-10**.

Good housekeeping

Cleaning a work site may seem like the task that is reserved for the end of the day or even the end of the week. After all, it is during this cleanup time that many workers think about

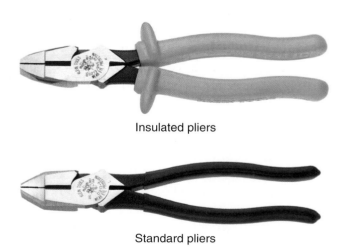

Insulated pliers

Standard pliers

Figure 1-9. A tool is considered insulated only if the manufacturer has certified it at a specific level of electricity. (Klein Tools, Inc.)

---

insulated tools: Tools, with a nonconductive covering, that are designed to prevent the transfer of electricity from the tool to the user.

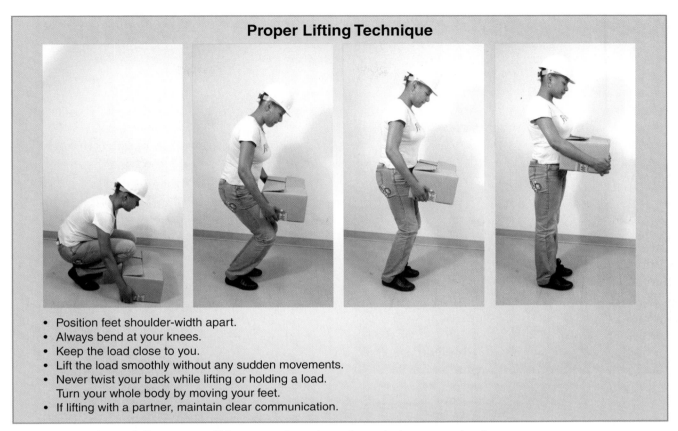

Proper Lifting Technique

- Position feet shoulder-width apart.
- Always bend at your knees.
- Keep the load close to you.
- Lift the load smoothly without any sudden movements.
- Never twist your back while lifting or holding a load.
  Turn your whole body by moving your feet.
- If lifting with a partner, maintain clear communication.

Figure 1-10. Always follow proper lifting procedures to reduce strain on your back.

everything they have accomplished that day and all of the tasks they need to do tomorrow. However, it is during the workday that you should also be maintaining a clean work area. Tripping hazards, lost tools and materials, and general disorganization are all time-wasting consequences of working in an untidy area.

Excavating

There are times when you will have to work around another crew that is excavating or you will have to dig into the earth yourself. Either situation will present a set of hazards. The first hazard is contacting an underground conductor. Always notify the local utility before digging. They will mark the ground where any electric cables, gas lines, water pipe, or television cable are buried. Do not use any powered excavating equipment within 24″ of the utility markings. See **Figure 1-11**.

The second hazard when excavating is the possibility of a wall collapse. Any trench over 5′ deep must be reinforced to prevent the sides

from collapsing. There are various types of shoring designed to eliminate this hazard. Also, make sure to install barricades and warning signs around the trench. Without these warnings, other workers or passersby may fall into the trench.

Lockout/Tagout/Blockout

One of the most important procedures designed to protect the electrician is the lockout/tagout/blockout procedure. This is a combination of rules and devices that prevent the energizing of a circuit that could injure a worker. If an electrician flips a breaker to open a circuit and starts to work on that circuit, what prevents another worker from resetting the breaker? Placing a strip of tape across the breaker or attaching a tag to it does not prevent the closing of the circuit. Tape falls off, tags are ignored, and as a result workers get hurt or killed. Always follow proper lockout/tagout/blockout procedures whether working on residential, commercial, or industrial projects. See **Figure 1-12**.

Lockout

Figure 1-11. The local utilities mark the position of underground equipment. You may use powered equipment to excavate no closer than 24″ to the markings. Any digging within the 24″ zone must be done with a hand shovel.

A *lockout device* prevents the release of energy by attaching one or more locks to switches, breakers, valves (gas and liquid), and enclosures. The person working on the circuit is the only one with a key for that lock. If more than one person is working on the circuit, each is able to attach a lock to the device.

Tagout is the identification procedure that is used to let other workers know who applied the lockout. Your name should be on the tag so other workers know that you are working on the circuit. You may also include the date and time of lockout, your phone number, when you expect to be done, and your company's name. All of this information is intended to improve communication between workers. Write your name on a handful of tags and keep them in your toolbox. A tagout should never be used without a lockout or blockout.

Tagout

Figure 1-12. Lockout, tagout, and blockout are three procedures that help to prevent other workers from energizing a circuit that is being worked on. (Brady Corporation)

A *blockout device* is used to stop dangerous machinery if energy is accidentally applied. Opening a circuit does not mean all energy has been controlled. The power to a fan may be turned off and locked out, but if the fan blades have not been blocked, there is still the possibility of injury. Air movement from another fan can cause the blades to move with enough force to cause injury. Also, switches have been known to fail and close a circuit. In this situation, a lockout device will not prevent the machinery on this circuit from running, but a blockout device will. There are devices that are designed as blockouts for specific equipment, but a board or pipe can be used if it is properly secured.

Turn the power off!

These four words will be repeated to you throughout this book and probably during your apprenticeship. Turn the power off! Never work on energized equipment unless it is absolutely necessary AND you have the proper training, equipment, and PPE. "Turning the power off will take more time than the actual work" is not a reason to work on energized equipment. Replacing damaged equipment or making a trip to the hospital usually takes more time than turning the power off. "I have insulated tools" is also not a reason to work on energized equipment. Turn the power off and use lockout/tagout/blockout methods to ensure that nobody else turns it back on.

Responding to an Accident

Since you may be the first person to respond to an accident, there are some basic procedures to know. This book is not intended to give you all of the information for aiding a victim. Instead, this is a brief overview of the techniques that could be applied. You are encouraged to enlist in a certified cardiopulmonary resuscitation (CPR) and first aid training program. The skills you learn in these programs may help you save the life of a coworker or a family member.

Helping a Shock Victim

If a coworker is a victim of electric shock, tell someone to call for help while you start to assist the victim. Immediate action must be taken to help a shock victim. This is particularly true if the victim is still in contact with the source of electrical current. If you cannot shut off the power immediately, remove the source of electric shock without touching the conductor or the victim. Use great care that you do not receive a shock yourself. After all, you will not be able to help the victim if you become one yourself. Use a stick or insulated material to separate the conductor from the victim.

After the electricity has been removed and safely controlled, begin talking to the victim in a loud and clear voice. You want to see if the victim is conscious. If there is no response, try to keep the victim still while checking for signs of breathing. If the victim is not breathing, get someone who is trained to initiate CPR. Try to stay with the victim throughout the entire rescue. Let the medical team take over when they arrive.

Hazardous Environments

All construction sites are, to some degree, hazardous environments. It is very easy to look around these sites and see dangerous situations and be aware of them. As an electrical worker, you must also be aware of the invisible—the electricity within wires and electrical panels. When you step into this environment, you must be able to focus on the job at hand and be aware of the activity around you.

---

lockout device: A safety device that prevents the energizing of a circuit by locking switches, breakers, valves (gas and liquid), or enclosures.

tagout: The identification procedure that is used to let other workers know who applied a lockout.

blockout device: A safety device used to stop machinery from moving.

Recognize the Hazard

You cannot avoid or control a hazard if you do not know that it exists. Through training and experience you will be able to recognize a hazard and take action. If you see a situation that you believe may be a hazard, but are not sure, let your supervisor or instructor know.

Overhead

Overhead power lines can create one of the most hazardous situations. These lines are high-voltage conductors that are often uninsulated and low to the ground. Carrying a metal ladder or conduit near these conductors should be done with extreme caution. If the equipment contacts the power lines, the electricity will flow through the equipment, through your body, and into the ground. Even if the equipment does not touch the power lines, it can come close enough to draw an arc. To reduce this risk, carry the equipment horizontally or avoid walking under the power lines.

Improper installation

Whether working in new or existing construction, you may come across an installation that is not safe or is not acceptable under local codes. The worst reaction to this situation is to ignore it. Doing so would put you, your coworkers, and future homeowners at risk. Warn those in the area of the danger and immediately notify your supervisor or teacher. If the worker made the improper installation without knowing, a lesson was learned and the person is a better worker. If the improper installation was made because of carelessness or laziness, the supervisor or teacher knows to pay close attention to that person's work.

Worn components

When working in older construction, you may come across outlets, light fixtures, switches, or wires that are worn to the point of being unsafe. Broken plastic, stripped screws, and brittle wire insulation are indications that these items need to be replaced. Do not try to reuse any components that are not in good mechanical or electrical condition. The cost of a new part is very small when compared to the possible costs of not replacing it. See **Figure 1-13**.

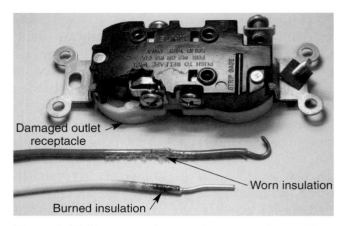

Damaged outlet receptacle
Worn insulation
Burned insulation

Figure 1-13. Never use damaged components or wiring.

Wet conditions

Often, utility workers must repair power lines in the rain. Water is an excellent conductor of electricity, so special equipment and training are necessary to prepare them for these high-risk situations. Although you may not find yourself in a rainstorm, the rules of working in any wet conditions are the same. The first rule is to avoid it. If you are working on an entire house, work on the interior wiring on rainy days and install the service on a dry day. If you must work in wet conditions, make sure that you have the proper equipment and training to complete the job safely and TURN THE POWER OFF. The proper equipment includes ground-fault circuit interrupters for power tools, insulated tools, and PPE that is designed for these situations. See **Figure 1-14**.

Figure 1-14. This power supply contains ground-fault circuit interrupters to protect workers in wet working conditions. (Coleman Cable, Inc.)

Fumes

This may not seem to be a concern of electrical workers, but flammable fumes affect everybody on the work site. Always avoid allowing flammable fumes near any electrical equipment. A simple light switch can create a spark large enough to ignite the fumes.

Nonflammable fumes, although not a fire hazard, can be just as dangerous. Gasoline-powered tools emit carbon monoxide, a colorless and odorless gas that can be deadly. Especially in an unventilated area, fumes from these tools can cause dizziness, headache, and illness. If you feel any of these symptoms, exit the building immediately and tell someone about your condition.

Report the Hazard

As stated earlier, you must report any hazardous situations. There are different methods of reporting the hazard, depending on the severity and risk involved. You already know what to do if you come across an improper installation: notify your supervisor or teacher. Other situations may only require that you notify your coworkers through tagout procedures. Barricades and warning tape are effective tools to alert others of hazardous areas. The main purpose of all of these methods is to let others know about the environment they are working in. Another technique is holding morning meetings to alert all crews of an unusual hazard, such as an overhead crane lift, that is scheduled for that day. Communication among all involved is the most effective tool against accidents. See **Figure 1-15**.

Repair the Hazard

Correcting hazardous situations may be as simple as practicing good housekeeping or as involved as reworking an improper installation. Some hazards may not be able to be removed at all, such as overhead power lines. Removing this hazard involves notifying others in the area by speaking to them or erecting barricades.

Review the Hazard

Once a hazardous situation has been recognized, reported, and repaired, you should take time to review the preceding events, on your own or with your instructor or supervisor. The following are the questions to ask:

- Why did this happen?
- What are the chances that it will happen again?
- How can this be prevented from happening again?
- Was the appropriate action taken?
- Is this situation covered in the *National Electrical Code?*

Reference

There are organizations that research, develop, and maintain rules, codes, and laws that are designed to promote safety. Some organizations are intended to make the workplace safe. Others are intended to make the final installation safe for the building's occupants. More information regarding each organization will be presented in the chapter that relates to the organization's purpose. You should be aware of these organizations and you may want to review their findings or become a member.

Figure 1-15. Communication between crews working on the same job site is essential for worker's safety.

OSHA

Occupational Safety and Health
Administration
200 Constitution Avenue, NW
Washington, DC 20210
800-321-OSHA (6742)
www.osha.gov

NFPA

National Fire Protection Association
(Publisher of the *National Electrical Code®*)
1 Batterymarch Park
Quincy, Massachusetts 02169-7471
617-770-3000
www.nfpa.org

NIOSH

The National Institute for Occupational
Safety and Health
200 Independence Ave., SW
Room 715H
Washington, DC 20201
800-35-NIOSH (1-800-356-4674)
www.cdc.gov/niosh

ICC

International Code Council
5203 Leesburg Pike, Suite 600
Falls Church, VA 22041
888-ICC-SAFE (422-7233)
www.iccsafe.org

IBEW

International Brotherhood of
Electrical Workers®
900 Seventh Street, N.W.
Washington, DC 20001
202-833-7000
www.ibew.org

NECA

National Electrical Contractors Association
3 Bethesda Metro Center, Suite 1100
Bethesda, MD 20814
301-657-3110
www.necanet.org

Review Questions

Write your answers on a separate sheet of paper.
Do not write in this book.

1. List eight safety rules an electrician ought to observe when working with electrical equipment and tools.

2. *True or False?* An aluminum ladder should *not* be used when working around electrical wiring.

3. *True or False?* Lockout procedures apply to only industrial and commercial work.

4. The amount of current passing through the body is an important factor to remember in electrical shock. A current approaching _____ is painful and possibly severe effects will be experienced.

5. To aid a victim of electrical shock, list all of the following you would NOT do and explain why:

   A. Quickly grasp the victim and drag him/her away from the current-carrying material.

   B. Shut off the power.

   C. Give artificial respiration until medical help arrives.

   D. If the shutoff switch is too far away, use a wooden stick to remove victim from current-carrying equipment.

   E. When there is no danger of shock, check to see if the patient is breathing. If not, give CPR until medical help arrives.

   F. Have someone call a doctor or paramedics.

6. Wearing personal protective equipment during an _____ will help prevent burns to the skin and eyes.

Know the Code

A copy of the NEC 2005 is required to answer these questions.

1. What is an Authority Having Jurisdiction (AHJ)?

2. What is meant by FPN? What is it?

3. What does the term *listed* mean?

Electrical Energy Fundamentals

Objectives

Information in this chapter will enable you to:

- Explain the electron theory for current.

- Explain conductors and insulating materials.

- Define and explain the difference between direct current and alternating current.

- Define basic electrical terms.

- Describe the makeup of an electrical circuit.

- Differentiate between series and parallel circuits.

- Apply Ohm's law to resistance, voltage, and current.

- Explain Ohm's law and give its formula.

- Apply Watt's law to power, voltage, and current.

- Explain Watt's law and give its formula.

- Explain electromagnetic induction.

- Discuss the operation of electric motors.

- Discuss electric power transmission.

- Explain the operation of transformers.

Technical Terms

Alternating current (ac)
Amperage (A)
Ampere
Anode
Atom
Battery
Branch
Cathode
Circuit
Complex circuit
Conductor
Current
Cycles
Direct current (dc)
Dry cell
Electrical potential
Electrolyte
Electromagnetic induction
Electromotive force
Electrons
Energy
Equilibrium
Fleming's rule
Free electrons
Generator
Hertz
Insulator
Joules

Joule's law
Kilowatt-hours (kWh)
Left-hand rule
Load
Neutrons
Ohms
Ohm's law
Parallel circuit
Power (P)
Primary winding
Protons
Resistance (R)
Secondary winding
Series circuit
Step-down
    transformer
Step-up
    transformer
Substation
Transformer
Voltage
Volt-amperes (VA)
Volts (V)
Wattage
Watts (W)
Watt's law
Wet cell
Windings
Work

Electron Theory

According to the electron theory, all matter is made up of atoms. An *atom* is the smallest particle of an element. If you take an atom apart, it will not be recognizable as its original element. You can look at each atom and say "This is the building block of copper" or "This atom is hydrogen."

Each atom has a nucleus or center made up of *protons* (positively charged particles) and *neutrons* (particles with no charge). Negatively charged particles called *electrons* orbit the nucleus. See **Figure 2-1**. Electrons are attracted to the protons in the atom. This attraction keeps the electrons in orbit. There can be one or more electrons traveling around in any one atom and they can be at different distances from the nucleus in their orbital paths.

Electrons have the ability to travel from one atom to another. In some types of matter, electrons are tightly bound to the nucleus and travel only with great difficulty. In other types of matter, the bond is so relaxed that moving is easy. These easy-moving electrons are called *free electrons*.

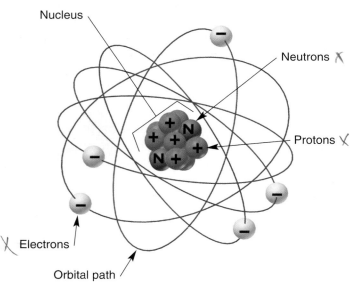

Figure 2-1. The basis of electricity is the atom, which is the foundation of all matter. In some elements, such as metals, orbiting electrons can easily be made to leave the atom and travel.

Electron Travel

A material in which electrons move easily is called a *conductor*. A material in which movement is difficult is called an *insulator*.

Pure metals, carbon, and most liquids are excellent conductors. Among good insulators are dry gases, glass, rubber, mica, silk, and cork. According to the commonly held electron theory, metals conduct electricity well because they have a great number of free electrons. In insulators, there are few, if any, free electrons; thus, little or no electricity is conducted.

Equilibrium

If a conductor, such as a wire, connects a negatively charged body to a positively charged body, the electrons will be attracted to the positive particles. Nature prefers everything to be neutral—equal numbers of positive and negative charges. As a result, electrons will flow from the negatively charged body to the positively charged body. See **Figure 2-2**. This flow is called *current*. Even if two negatively charged bodies are connected in this manner, free electrons will flow from the body with more electrons to the one with fewer electrons. Flow will continue until both bodies have an equal number of electrons. This balance is called *equilibrium*.

---

atom: The smallest particle of an element.

protons: The positively charged particles of an atom.

neutrons: The particles with no charge in the nucleus of an atom.

electrons: Negatively charged particles that orbit the nucleus of an atom.

free electrons: Electrons that are loosely bound to the nucleus of an atom and can easily leave to join other atoms.

conductor: A substance that allows electrons to flow freely through it; an object having good conductivity.

insulators: Substances that prevent electrons from flowing freely.

current: The flow of electrons.

equilibrium: When two connected bodies have the same number of electrons; a balanced condition.

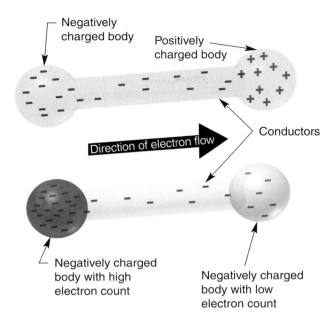

Figure 2-2. Electrons will move from a body with an excess of electrons to a body with fewer or no electrons, provided there is a path (conductor).

Electrical potential is the ability to provide free electrons. Bodies with different concentrations of free electrons are said to be at different potentials. In electricity, differences in potential are measured in units called *volts (V)*.

Types of Electric Current

There are two types of electric current, depending on the direction of the current flow. The first type is called ***direct current (dc)***. In this type, current flows in one direction only. Direct current is used in battery-operated devices, such as radios, flashlights, and automobiles.

The second type of current, ***alternating current (ac)***, continually reverses the direction of flow. This constant change in direction is represented by a sine wave, **Figure 2-3**. In the United States, the standard current is 60 ***cycles***, also known as 60 ***hertz*** (60 Hz). Hertz is a term for frequency meaning "cycles per second." The cycles occur at a frequency of 60 hertz. Thus, there are 60 complete cycles in every second. Notice that the direction changes twice in each cycle. This means that the current reverses its direction 120 times each second. This happens so rapidly that the changes generally cannot be

electrical potential: The ability to provide free electrons.

direct current (dc): A current that always flows in one direction.

alternating current (ac): A periodic current that continuously reverses direction.

cycles: A cycle is one complete repetition of a waveform or signal. The rate at which the signal repeats itself is expressed in cycles per second, or hertz.

Hertz (Hz): A unit of frequency that equals one cycle per second. Named after Heinrich Hertz.

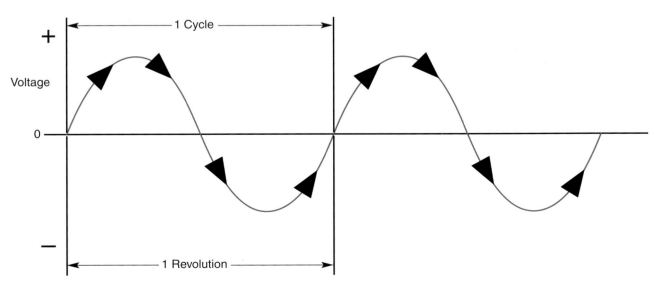

Figure 2-3. A cycle of alternating current is created by one complete revolution of the alternator.

North American electric systems did not use 120 volts ac (VAC) and 60 Hz in their early days. Thomas Edison was using and promoting dc power in his early electric distribution systems. There were problems with dc, however. It was not very easy to change the voltage, so transmitting more power meant higher current in the wires. The current became so high that wires were actually melting from being overloaded. Due to the high current, there were large losses due to voltage drop over short distances. It was also very inconvenient to use devices that required different voltages.

Nikola Tesla championed the use of ac systems. It was easy to change the voltage, so large amounts of power could be delivered by increasing the voltage and decreasing the current in the wires. With lower currents, the wires would not overheat and melt. Losses due to voltage drop were greatly reduced, meaning that electricity could be transmitted over much longer distances. Tesla had the backing of George Westinghouse, who also had the financial backing of John Jacob Astor and J. P. Morgan.

Edison tried to prove how unsafe the ac system was by holding public electrocutions of animals, including Topsy the Elephant. He went so far as to have two of his employees invent the electric chair to demonstrate how effective ac was at killing people. Ultimately, the Westinghouse ac system won the battle based on its technical superiority, and Edison's General Electric Company changed from dc to ac.

It is less clear how the frequency of 60 Hz was adopted, but it seems that it was a high enough frequency that the human eye could not see lightbulbs flickering at 60 Hz. Tesla had calculated that 60 Hz was the most effective frequency, but his early systems were originally 240 V. Other countries adopted 50 Hz because it was still too fast to see the flicker and it matched the 1 2 5 10 standard popular with the "metric countries."

Sources of Electrical Energy

To maintain a flow of electrons or electricity, it is necessary to have a source that is always at a greater electrical potential. That is, it always has an excess of free electrons that are ready to move along a conductor to where the electrical potential is less. The energy may be produced chemically, as with a battery, or mechanically, as with a generator.

Battery

A basic chemical device for providing electrical power is the voltaic cell. **Figure 2-4** shows a simplified cell made up of two metal plates suspended in a mild acid solution. The plates react chemically with the acid. Electrons on the surface of the copper plate are stripped away and travel to the zinc plate. Then the copper plate has fewer electrons and is positively charged. The copper plate becomes the positive pole, or *anode*. The zinc plate has excess electrons and becomes the negative pole, or *cathode*.

It is common practice to group a number of cells in a single container. See **Figure 2-5**. A group of cells is called a *battery*. A *wet cell* battery uses a liquid chemical. A *dry cell* battery uses a somewhat dry chemical paste. The liquid or paste is called an *electrolyte*. When the battery is connected to a circuit, current will flow through the circuit from the cathode to the anode.

Generator

A battery is just one of the ways to generate and drive an electrical current. A second method is with a generator. Driven by some mechanical

---

anode: The positive terminal of a battery.

cathode: The negative terminal of a battery.

battery: A group of voltaic cells that are connected in series or parallel, usually contained in one case.

wet cell: A battery that uses a liquid electrolyte.

dry cell: A battery that uses a chemical paste electrolyte.

electrolyte: The chemical that is a liquid or paste that allows the flow of electrons in a battery.

---

detected, not even as flicker in an electric light. Various cycles and voltages have become the standard in different areas of the world.

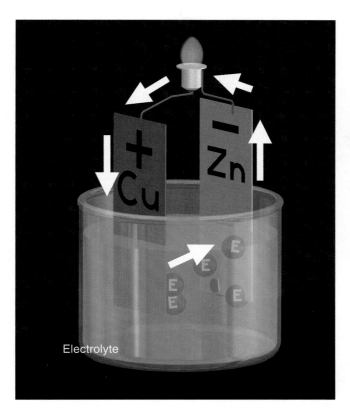

Figure 2-4. A simple wet cell can store electricity as a chemical solution. One electrode is made from copper and the other from zinc. Conductors and a lightbulb complete this simple circuit.

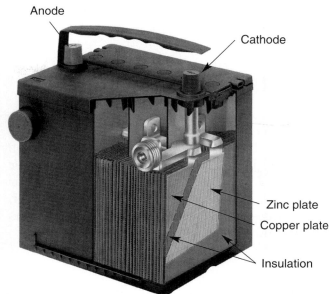

Figure 2-5. A group of wet cells connected electrically and suspended in electrolyte is called a battery. Batteries can supply a steady current of electricity. (East Penn Manufacturing Co., Inc., manufacturer of Deka Batteries, Lyon Station, PA)

force, a *generator* is a device that creates differences in electrical potential between two electrical poles. It moves electrons from one terminal and deposits them on the other terminal. This is accomplished through electromagnetic induction. This process will be explained later as we discuss generators and alternators.

Measuring Electricity

Measuring electricity is essentially finding out how much, how fast, and with what force the electricity flows through a conductor. The terms or units used to measure electricity are amperage, voltage, resistance, and wattage. The full definition of these terms is vital not only to measuring electricity but to understanding its very nature.

Current

The flow of electricity, as you have learned, is called current. The rate of this flow is known as *amperage* (represented in equations by the letter *I*). The *ampere (A)*, or amp, is the unit used when measuring current. The equipment where electricity enters a house is usually rated at 100 A or 200 A.

Voltage

The pressure (electrical potential) that moves electrons through a conductor is called voltage or *electromotive force (E or emf)*. Its

---

generator: A device that uses electromagnetic induction to convert mechanical energy to electrical energy.

amperage: The measurement of the rate of flow of electrons.

ampere (A): The unit used in measuring amperage or current. Abbreviated as amp (plural amps). Named after André-Marie Ampère.

electromotive force (E or emf): The force that causes current to flow between two objects with different electrical potential.

unit of measure is the *volt (V)*. Most residential wiring is rated at 120 volts and 240 volts.

Resistance

The opposition to the flow of electrons through a conductor is called *resistance (R)* and is similar to friction. This electrical resistance is measured in units called *ohms (Ω)*. Like other forms of friction, resistance is responsible for creating heat and consequent loss of power. All devices that use electric power are forms of resistance.

Power

Power (P) is the rate of doing work and, in electricity, is measured in *watts (W)* or *volt-amperes (VA)*. Power determines how fast a certain amount of work can be done, or determines how fast a certain amount of *energy* is consumed by a load. Watts are relatively small units, and we often speak in terms of kilowatts (1,000 watts) and megawatts (1,000,000 watts).

Work

Work is a measure of how much power is applied (or consumed) over a period of time. Work is measured in *joules*. One joule is one watt-second. Electrical energy in particular is measured in power-time units called watt-hours or *kilowatt-hours (kWh)*. One kilowatt-hour is equivalent to 1,000 watts (power) being used for one hour (time). **Figure 2-6** is a summary of these electrical terms.

---

volt (V): The units of measurement of electromotive force caused by the difference in potential between two bodies. Named after Alessandro Volta.

resistance (R): The opposition to the flow of electrons through a conductor.

ohms (Ω): The units of measurement used to express resistance. Named after Georg Simon Ohm.

power (P): The rate of doing work. Electric power is measured in watts or volt-amperes.

watts (W): The units of measurement used in expressing power delivered to or consumed by an electrical device. Named after James Watt.

volt-amperes (VA): Very simply, volts multiplied by amps. The amount of power an electric system can provide or the amount of power an electrical device requires. Equivalent to watts in simple systems. Abbreviated as volt-amps.

energy: The ability to do work.

work: The process of changing energy from one form to another, or causing an object too gain or lose energy.

joules: A unit of electrical power. One joule equals one watt-second. Named after James Prescott Joule.

kilowatt-hours (kWh): A unit of electrical power. One kilowatt-hour is the equivalent of 1,000 watts being used for a 1-hour period.

Electrical Units and Measurements				
Electrical Property	**Property Abbreviation**	**Measurement Units**	**Units Abbreviation**	**Named After**
Electromotive Force or Potential or Voltage	EMF or E (do not confuse with energy)	Volts	V	Alessandro Volta
Current or Amperage	I	Amperes (Amps)	A	André-Marie Ampère
Resistance	R	Ohms	Ω	Georg Simon Ohm
Power or Wattage	P	Watts	W	James Watt
Energy or Work	E or W	Joules or Kilowatt-hour	J or kWh	James Prescott Joule

Figure 2-6. Nearly all units used to measure electrical properties are named after persons who made significant contributions in electrical research and discovery. There are many more electrical properties than those shown here. These are just the basic building blocks that are discussed in this chapter.

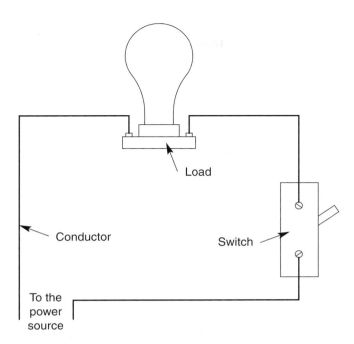

Figure 2-7. A simple electrical circuit includes a pathway (conductors), power source, load (light), and a switch.

Circuits

No electron flow will occur unless there is a pathway in which the electrons can move. In a water system, the pathway is the piping, which moves the water from storage to where it is used. In electrical devices, wires form the pathway, which is called a *circuit*, **Figure 2-7**. The circuit allows the electrons to flow through its conductors as long as the power source supplies electricity. A simple circuit consists of the following elements:

- **Power source.** For a residence, the power source could be considered the electrical generating stations. However, primary sources include small generators and batteries.

- **Conductors.** Wires provide a path for the current to travel.

---

circuit: The pathway over which electrons can move.

series circuit: A circuit having a single path for current flow.

- **Loads.** These are devices through which the electricity produces work.

- **Devices for controlling current.** These devices include switches, fuses, and circuit breakers.

Types of Circuits

The two basic types of electrical circuits are called series and parallel. A third, called a complex circuit, is a combination of these two.

Series circuit

In a *series circuit*, only one path is provided for the current to flow. The electricity flows through every device in the circuit. If one device is burned out, the circuit will not function. **Figure 2-8** is a simple diagram of a series circuit.

Apart from switches and fuses or circuit breakers that are used to control the flow of electricity, series circuitry is not practical for residential wiring. A simple example will explain why. Older Christmas tree lights were often wired in series. Current had to pass through every lightbulb for the string of lights to work. If one bulb burned out, all the lights went out. Finding the defective bulb was a trial-and-error

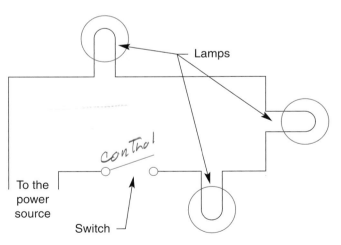

Figure 2-8. Simple diagram of a series circuit. The three lights are wired into the circuit so that if one were not working, the circuit would be open and all lights would go out.

operation. Each bulb had to be removed and tested. Residential circuits are set up so that a nonfunctioning load will not stop electrical current in the remainder of the circuit.

Parallel circuit

The *parallel circuit* has more than one path available for the current to flow, **Figure 2-9**. Like the series circuit, the parallel circuit has a complete path for the current to follow. Each path goes to a load that can operate independently of the other branches and loads in the circuit. If one load, such as a lamp, burns out, the other branches would continue to operate since a path still exists from one supply terminal through the circuit to the other supply terminal.

Under normal conditions, another advantage of parallel circuits is that the current draw of each branch affects only that branch. In a series circuit, current draw in one load affects the rest of the loads on the circuit. Loads such as lamps, heaters, or motors might not operate properly in a series circuit. Except for switches, fuses, and circuit breakers, all residential wiring is done in parallel.

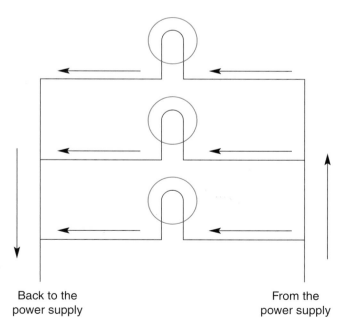

Back to the power supply

From the power supply

Figure 2-9. Parallel circuit diagram. Note that each lamp is on its own electrical path. Should one burn out when the circuit is closed, the others would remain lit.

Loads

In electrical systems, a *load* is any device that uses an electric current and converts the energy to another form. Loads include:

- Lamps and lightbulbs (convert electrical energy to light)
- Electric furnaces and space heaters (convert electrical energy to heat)
- Power tools and motor-driven appliances (convert electrical energy to mechanical energy)
- Radios, televisions, and other electronic devices (convert electrical energy to sound)

Each load is designed to operate at a specific voltage. A voltage rating is given with every device. It is important that the device be operated at its rating. Otherwise, the device can be damaged or destroyed. In some cases the entire circuit can be damaged. This is an important reason series circuits are not used in residential wiring.

Circuit Fundamentals

Electrical circuits consist of a source of electromotive force and one or more complete pathways of electron flow. Both dc and ac circuits require a definite pathway to be useful. A circuit normally consists of a power source, protective devices (fuses or circuit breakers), one or more loads, a switching device, and conductors.

Electrical Resistance— Ohm's Law

To understand circuit theory you must understand electrical resistance. Without it, electrical current could create neither heat nor light.

parallel circuit: A circuit with multiple paths available for current flow.

load: Device that converts electricity into another form of energy.

Georg Simon Ohm first explored resistance in 1827. He expressed the relationship between current, voltage, and resistance: *Current in a circuit is directly proportional to the voltage applied to the circuit and is inversely proportional to the resistance of the circuit.* This statement is called **Ohm's law**. This law can be applied to the entire circuit or to any part of the circuit.

Mathematically, the law takes the following form:

$$I = \frac{E}{R}$$

I is the current measured in amperes. *E* is the voltage or emf (electromotive force) measured in volts. *R* is the resistance measured in ohms.

Electrical Power— Watt's law

A load in an electrical circuit consumes energy. The rate at which it consumes energy is called *power.* The relationship between power, voltage, and current was established by James Watt and is called **Watt's law**. It states that:

$$P = I \times E$$

where *P* is power measured in watts, *I* is current measured in amps, and *E* is emf measured in volts.

Series Circuits

A series circuit has only one loop or path. When devices such as resistors are in series, they are placed one after another so that the current flows through all of them in succession. The three resistors illustrated in **Figure 2-10** are in series arrangement.

Ohm's law: The law that states the relationship between voltage, resistance, and current.

Watt's law: The law that states the relationship between power, voltage, and current.

Series circuit rules

Series circuits follow certain rules that may be summarized as follows:

- Total resistance (R_T) is the sum of the individual resistances. Therefore, the total resistance of the series circuit in Figure 2-10 is:

$$R_T = R_A + R_B + R_C$$
$$= 1\,\Omega + 2\,\Omega + 3\,\Omega$$
$$= 6\,\Omega$$

- The current (amperage) of a series circuit is the same throughout. Thus, the total current (I_T) of the circuit is the same as the current running through each load. By applying Ohm's law, we can find the current in Figure 2-10:

$$I_T = I_A = I_B = I_C$$
$$I_T = \frac{E}{R_T}$$
$$= \frac{6\,V}{6\,\Omega}$$
$$= 1\,A$$

Therefore, 1 A is not only the total amperage, but also the amperage flowing through each of the resistors.

- The total voltage at the source (V_T) is equal to the sum of the voltages at each of the resistances. The voltage at each load is calculated

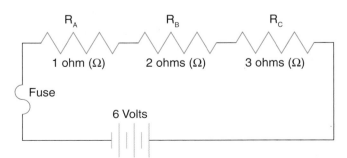

Figure 2-10. A simple series circuit. It has three resistors connected to form a single loop.

using Ohm's law:

Voltage of Resistor A   =
Amperage A × Resistance A

$$V_A = I_A \times R_A$$

$$= 1\,A \times 1\,\Omega$$

$$= 1\,V$$

Voltage of Resistor B   =
Amperage B × Resistance B

$$V_B = I_B \times R_B$$

$$= 1\,A \times 2\,\Omega$$

$$= 2\,V$$

Voltage of Resistor C   =
Amperage C × Resistance C

$$V_C = I_C \times R_C$$

$$= 1\,A \times 3\,\Omega$$

$$= 3\,V$$

The total voltage (V_T) can then be calculated by adding the voltages for all loads:

$$V_T = V_A + V_B + V_C$$

$$= 1\,V + 2\,V + 3\,V$$

$$= 6\,V$$

- A break anywhere in the circuit stops the electron flow in the entire circuit. This is the main disadvantage of series circuits.
- Ohm's law applies to any part of the entire series circuit.

Example: Using the circuit shown in **Figure 2-11**, find:
A. The total resistance, R_T.
B. The total current at the source, I_T.
C. The voltages of resistors 1 and 3, V_1 and V_3.
Solution:
A. Add the individual resistances to find the total resistance, R_T:

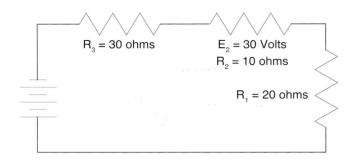

Figure 2-11. In this series circuit, find total resistance, total amperage, and voltage at two resistors.

$$R_T = R_1 + R_2 + R_3$$

$$= 20\,\Omega + 10\,\Omega + 30\,\Omega$$

$$= 60\,\Omega$$

B. The current in a series circuit is constant. Therefore, the total current (I_T) equals the current at resister 2 (I_T). The current at resister 2 can be found using Ohm's law:

$$I_T = I_2 = \frac{E_2}{R_2}$$

$$= 30\,V/10\,\Omega$$

$$= 3\,A$$

C. The current through each resister is equal to the total current (3A). Use Ohm's law to calculate the voltage at resisters 1 and 3:

$$V_1 = I_1 \times R_1$$

$$= 3\,A \times 20\,\Omega$$

$$= 60\,V$$

$$V_3 = I_3 \times R_3$$

$$= 3\,A \times 30\,\Omega$$

$$= 90\,V$$

You can also check to see if the total voltage is equal to the sum of the individual voltages:

$$V_T = I_T \times R_T$$
$$= 3\,A \times 60\,\Omega$$
$$= 180\,V$$

$$V_T = V_1 + V_2 + V_3$$
$$= 60\,V + 30\,V + 90\,V$$
$$= 180\,V$$

Parallel Circuits

As you learned earlier, a parallel circuit is an electrical circuit having two or more different conducting pathways. The term parallel, in electricity, does not necessarily mean physically or geometrically parallel, but simply alternate routes. Each of these alternate routes is called a **branch**. Parallel circuits are more commonly used in electrical circuitry for reasons that will become clear as we go on. **Figure 2-12** shows a simple parallel circuit containing three resistors. Arrows indicate the electron flow.

Parallel circuit rules

Like series circuits, parallel circuits follow certain rules:

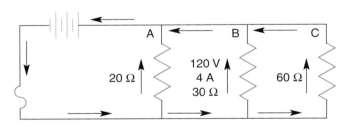

Figure 2-12. Parallel circuits provide numerous alternate routes for the electrons to follow. These routes are called branches.

---

branch: One of the pathways in a parallel circuit

- A break or opening in any branch of a parallel circuit does not stop the flow of electrons to the remaining branches.
- The voltages across all branches of a parallel circuit are the same, and are equal to the voltage at the source. In Figure 2-12, the voltage in branch B is 120 V. Therefore, the total voltage and the voltage in branches A and C are also 120 V. Mathematically:

  Source voltage = branch A voltage = branch B voltage = branch C voltage

$$E_T = V_A = V_B = V_C$$
$$= 120\,V$$

- Ohm's law applies equally well to the total circuit or any of the loops or branches:

$$I_A = \frac{E_A}{R_A}$$
$$= \frac{120V}{20\,\Omega}$$
$$= 6\,A$$

$$I_C = \frac{E_C}{R_C}$$
$$= \frac{120V}{60\,\Omega}$$
$$= 2\,A$$

- The total current (I_T) is equal to the sum of the currents flowing through each of the branches. For Figure 2-12:

$$I_T = I_A + I_B + I_C$$
$$= 6\,A + 4\,A + 2A$$
$$= 12\,A$$

- The total resistance in a parallel circuit is the reciprocal of the sum of the reciprocals of the separate resistances in parallel. Now, before throwing up our hands, let us look at this mathematically:

$$\frac{1}{R}\ total = \frac{1}{R}\ branch\ A + \frac{1}{R}\ branch\ B + \frac{1}{R}\ branch\ C$$

$$\frac{1}{R_T} = \frac{1}{R_A} + \frac{1}{R_B} + \frac{1}{R_C}\ \text{which can be written as:}$$

$$R_T = \frac{1}{\left(\dfrac{1}{R_A} + \dfrac{1}{R_B} + \dfrac{1}{R_C}\right)}$$

Now use the resistance information from the circuit in Figure 2-12:

$$\frac{1}{R_T} = \frac{1}{20}\ \Omega + \frac{1}{30}\ \Omega + \frac{1}{60}\ \Omega$$

Find a common denominator:

$$\frac{1}{R_T} = \frac{3}{60}\ \Omega + \frac{2}{60}\ \Omega + \frac{1}{60}\ \Omega$$

$$\frac{1}{R_T} = \frac{6}{60}\ \Omega$$

$$\frac{R_T}{1} = \frac{60\Omega}{6}$$

$$R_T = 10\ \Omega$$

Series-Parallel Combination Circuits

Practical circuits, for the most part, are far more difficult than those just outlined. Quite often, loads in a particular circuit are designed in both series and parallel configurations. When loads are arranged both ways in a single circuit, the circuit is called a *complex circuit*. An example of this type is shown in **Figure 2-13**. We will use this circuit to show the steps taken to simplify a complex circuit.

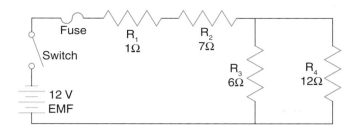

Figure 2-13. A complex circuit uses the advantages of both series and parallel circuits.

In the circuit shown, the source voltage is 12 V. The resistance of each component resistor is also given. First, we need to find the total resistance. To do this we must reduce the parallel resistances into an equivalent single resistance (R_{eq}) and add this resistance to the resistances arranged in series.

Equivalent resistance from parallel portion:

$$\frac{1}{R_{eq}} = \frac{1}{R_3} + \frac{1}{R_4}$$

$$= \frac{1}{6}\ \Omega + \frac{1}{12}\ \Omega$$

$$= \frac{2}{12}\ \Omega + \frac{1}{12}\ \Omega$$

$$= \frac{3}{12}\ \Omega$$

$$\frac{R_{eq}}{1} = 12\ \frac{\Omega}{3}$$

$$R_{eq} = 4\ \Omega$$

We may draw a simpler equivalent circuit showing the equivalent resistance in series with R_1 and R_2. See **Figure 2-14**. Now add this resistance to resistors 1 and 2 to find the total resistance:

$$R_T = R_{eq} + R_1 + R_2$$

$$= 4\ \Omega + 1\ \Omega + 7\ \Omega$$

$$= 12\ \Omega$$

complex circuit: A combination of series and parallel circuits.

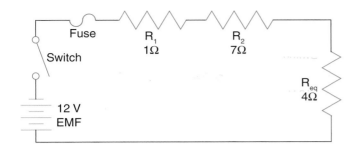

Figure 2-14. An equivalent circuit of Figure 2-13. R_3 and R_4 have been reduced to one resistance, R_{eq}.

Having found the total resistance, and given the total voltage, we can find the total current through the circuit using Ohm's law:

$$I_T = \frac{E_T}{R_T}$$

$$= \frac{12V}{12\,\Omega}$$

$$= 1\,A$$

Next, find the voltages across each of the resistors. Since resistor 1, resistor 2, and the "equivalent resistor" are in series, the current at each resister is the same as the total current (1 A). Using Ohm's law to calculate the voltage at resistors 1 and 2 and the voltage across the "equivalent resistance."

$$V_1 = I_1 \times R_1$$

$$= 1\,A \times 1\,\Omega$$

$$= 1\,V$$

$$V_2 = I_2 \times R_2$$

$$= 1\,A \times 7\,\Omega$$

$$= 7\,V$$

$$V_{eq} = I_T \times R_{eq}$$

$$= 1\,A \times 4\,\Omega$$

$$= 4\,V$$

This is verified by the fact that the total voltage is equal to the sum of the various voltages in a series circuit.

All that remains is to find the portion of the total current (1 ampere) that goes through each of the parallel resistors. (Remember, $V_{eq} = V_3 = V_4 = 4$ V.)

$$I_3 = \frac{V_3}{R_3}$$

$$= \frac{4\,V}{6\,\Omega}$$

$$= 0.67\,A$$

$$I_4 = \frac{V_3}{R_4}$$

$$= \frac{4\,V}{12\,\Omega}$$

$$= 0.33\,A$$

Again, verification comes from the fact that the total current (1 ampere) is equal to the sum of the current through each branch of the parallel resistors. Thus:

$$1\,A = 0.67\,A + 0.33\,A$$

Considered as a whole, electrical circuits are mostly of the complex type. The source voltage is carried by means of wires across every device, appliance, and branch circuit. These are connected in parallel.

Circuits Summary

Figure 2-15 is a summary of the various circuits discussed in this chapter. **Figure 2-16** is a simple aid to remembering Ohm's law. Simply cover the part you wish to find and you discover what to multiply or divide by. Thus, to find E, multiply R by I. To find R, divide E by I. To find I divide E by R.

Series Circuit—Parallel Circuit Network			
Electrical Property	**Series Circuits**	**Parallel Circuits**	**Complex Circuits**
Resistance (R) Unit: Ohm Symbol: Ω	$R_t = R_1 + R_2 + R_3$ Sum of individual resistances	$\dfrac{1}{R_t} = \dfrac{1}{R_1} + \dfrac{1}{R_2} + \dfrac{1}{R_3}$	Total resistance equals resistance of parallel portion and sum of series resistors.
Current (I) Unit: Ampere Symbol: A	$I_t = I_1 = I_2 = I_3$ The same throughout entire circuit	$I_t = I_1 + I_2 + I_3$ Sum of individual currents	Series rules apply to the series portion of the circuit. Parallel rules apply to the parallel portion of the circuit.
Voltage (E) Unit: Volt Symbol: V, E	$E_t = E_1 + E_2 + E_3$ Sum of individual voltages	$E_t = E_1 = E_2 = E_3$ Total voltage and branch voltage are the same	The total voltage is the sum of the voltage drops across each series resistor and each of the branches of parallel portion of the circuit.

Figure 2-15. Characteristics of electrical circuits can be summarized as shown.

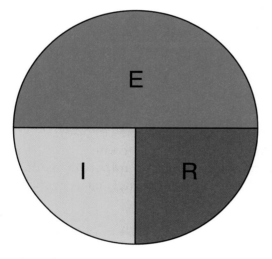

Figure 2-16. This drawing is an easy way to remember the mathematical relationships of Ohm's law. It will tell you when to multiply or divide.

Power and Work

Electrical power is a combination of current and voltage. It is actually current times voltage:

$$P = E \times I$$

Power expresses the rate at which electricity is being consumed regardless of the voltage or the current. For example, a 120 V air conditioner drawing 10 A of current is using the same amount of power as a 240 V air conditioner that is only drawing 5 A of current. The power in both cases is 1200 W. Power indicates how fast a certain amount of work can be done.

Energy and work are almost the same thing. The work done equals the change in energy. Work (W) is a certain amount of power (P) applied (or consumed) for a certain period of time (t):

$$W = P \times t$$

Substituting $E \times I$ for P:

$$W = E \times I \times t$$

You have a 100 W lightbulb and you leave it turned on for 5 hours. The total power consumed is:

$$\begin{aligned} W &= P \times t \\ &= 100 \text{ W} \times 5 \text{ hrs} \\ &= 500 \text{ watt-hours} \end{aligned}$$

Now you change it to a 250 W lightbulb and you leave it turned on for 2 hours. The total power consumed is:

$$\begin{aligned} W &= P \times t \\ &= 250 \text{ W} \times 2 \text{ hrs} \\ &= 500 \text{ watt-hours} \end{aligned}$$

Both lightbulbs use the same amount of total energy. Because the second lightbulb is more powerful, it is brighter and it uses energy faster.

Electromagnetic Induction

In a battery, chemical action displaces the electrons and produces the current through a conductor. Current can also be produced by using magnetic fields.

Two men working independently discovered they could produce a flow of electrons in a wire by passing the wire through a magnetic field, **Figure 2-17**. Michael Faraday and Joseph Henry discovered *electromagnetic induction*, the process of producing an electromotive force

by varying the magnetic field surrounding a conductor. If you were to fashion the conductor into many loops (a coil), and rotate it between two magnetic poles, you would have a crude generator. See **Figure 2-18**.

The strength of the electron flow in a generator is increased by four factors:

- A greater number of turns (loops) of wire in the coil

- A faster speed of the conducting loop rotation

- An increased strength of the magnets

- Positioning the moving coil at right angles to the magnetic field lines of force (**Figure 2-19**)

---

electromagnetic induction: The process of producing an electromotive force by varying the magnetic field surrounding a conductor.

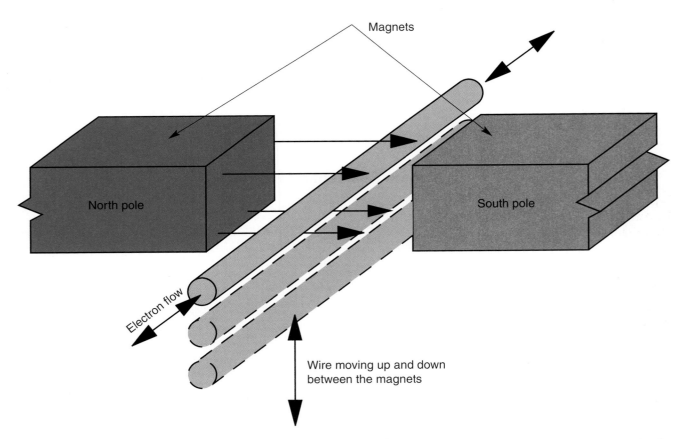

Figure 2-17. Moving a conductor up and down between the poles of a magnet displaces electrons in the conducting wire and causes the electrons to move through the conductor. This event is called electromagnetic induction.

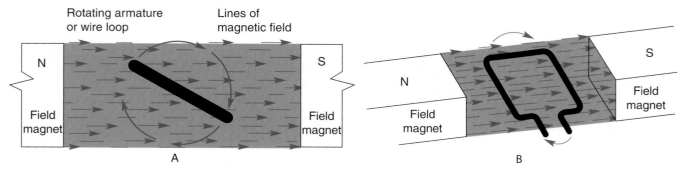

Figure 2-18. A simple generator. The rotating coil of wire has current induced in it as the loop cuts through a magnetic field created between the poles of the magnet. A—Straight-on view of a generator. Voltage would be low with the loop in this position. Wire would be cutting through the field at a sloping angle. B—Perspective view showing loop cutting the magnetic field at a right angle. Voltage is at its highest level at this point.

Generators and Alternators

Alternators, like generators, are rotating machines driven by some mechanical force. They use the electromagnetic induction principle to convert the mechanical force to electrical energy. There are ac generators and dc generators. The ac generator is usually called an alternator.

Direction of induced current

Current from a spinning generator will always move in a specified direction. You can determine this direction by knowing the *left-hand rule* for generators, **Figure 2-20**. Point your thumb, forefinger, and middle finger of the left hand at right angles to each other. According to the rule, the thumb is pointing in the direction the wire is moving, the forefinger is pointing

left-hand rule: A rule for determining the direction of flow in a conductor caused by electromagnetic induction. Also known as *Fleming's rule*.

Modern Residential Wiring

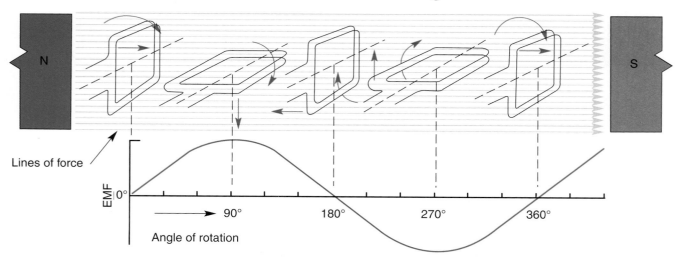

Figure 2-19. Voltage produced by the generator varies. Compare the position of the coil above with the sine wave below. Peaks in wave represent points of highest voltage during one complete rotation cycle.

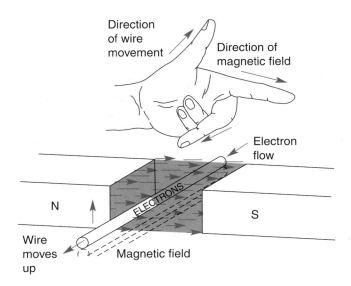

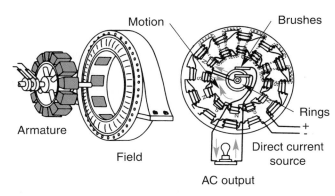

Figure 2-21. A commercial ac generator (alternator) looks much different from the simple sketches you have seen. This unit uses some of the current it produces to magnetize the field.

Figure 2-20. Left-hand rule for generators. If a wire is moving in the direction of the thumb and the magnetic field is moving in the direction of the forefinger (north pole to south pole), electric current is flowing in the direction of the middle finger.

in the direction of the magnetic field (north to south), and the middle finger is pointing in the direction of the induced electron flow. This statement is also known as *Fleming's rule*.

Alternating current generator

The ac generator, or alternator, consists of several distinct parts, **Figure 2-21**. Each has a specific function:

- **Coil or armature.** This part rotates. It has the conducting wire that cuts across a magnetic field. The electron flow begins in the coil.
- **Nonmoving magnetic poles.** These poles create the magnetic field. In some generators, the poles are magnetized by a portion of the generated electrical current.
- **Slip rings.** These metal rings are connected to the ends of the coil wires. The slip rings rotate with the coil and transfer the current to the brushes.

- **Brushes.** Two brushes are in contact with the slip rings and transfer current from the slip rings to the external circuit. One brush is in contact with each slip ring.

As the armature is turned, it cuts through the magnetic field created by the field magnets. Electrons flow through the wires of the armature. The electrons move into one of the slip rings, then to one of the brushes and, finally, into the external circuit. See **Figure 2-22**.

With every half-turn of the armature, the electron flow reverses, following the left-hand rule. Then the electrons flow out to the external circuit through the opposite slip ring and brush.

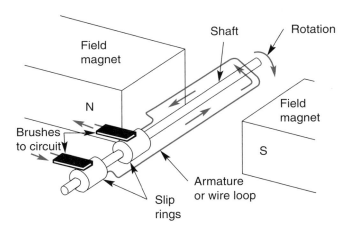

Figure 2-22. Basic elements of an alternator. The wire loop carries induced current. Electrons flow out through one brush, through the circuit, and back in through the other brush.

This creates the reversal of electron flow, which accounts for alternating current. The speed at which the generator is turned determines the frequency of the current. One complete turn is a cycle, and 60 turns each second creates 60 Hz electric current.

Direct current generator

The dc generator is similar in construction to the alternator except that the two slip rings are replaced by a single slip ring with two halves, commonly called a commutator. The two segments of the commutator are connected to the two ends of the armature, **Figure 2-23**, and rotate with it.

As the armature rotates, an alternating current is set up in the coil exactly as in the alternator. However, because the segments of the commutator change brushes every half-turn, the ac of the coil is changed into a pulsating dc in the external circuit, **Figure 2-24**.

Single-Phase and Three-Phase Electricity

An ac generator may produce either single-phase or three-phase electric power. A generator with a single armature coil produces single-phase power. To produce three-phase power, the generator must have three armature coils.

The coils of a three-phase generator are located exactly 120° apart. During each turn of the rotor, voltage is created at three different intervals. The separate voltages or phases are said to be 120° electrically apart in time, or 120° out of phase.

Power plants generate three-phase power because it is more efficient. The electric power is converted to single-phase for residential use. Three-phase power is supplied to commercial and industrial customers for either of the following reasons. Three-phase power is necessary for high-demand applications and cost-effective where there are many motors. Three-phase motors are simpler, less expensive, and more powerful than single-phase motors.

Electric Motors

Electric motors, **Figure 2-25**, are like generators. They transform one kind of energy to another. While generators convert mechanical energy to electrical energy, electric motors change electrical energy to rotating mechanical energy.

A dc motor is constructed exactly like a dc generator. Rotation takes place when the

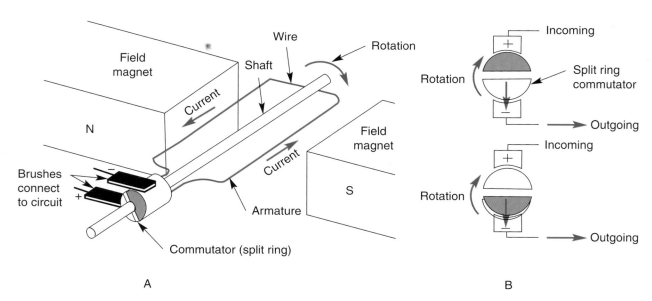

A

B

Figure 2-23. If you look at a simple dc generator, you can see why current always flows in the same direction. A—Each end of an armature coil connects to a different half of the commutator. B—As current reverses in the armature, opposite sides of the commutator contact the brushes so current always flows through the brushes in the same direction.

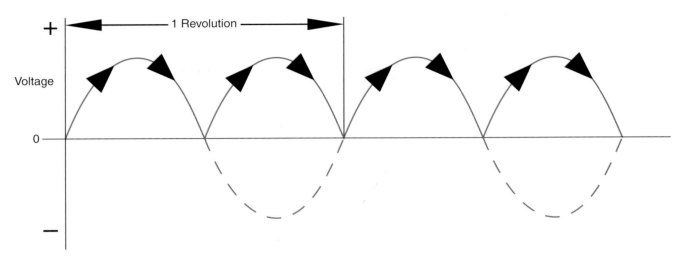

Figure 2-24. Typical dc current pulsates as shown in the wave pattern. The dotted line shows where the sine wave would go if it were alternating current.

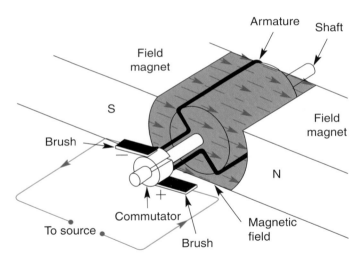

Figure 2-25. A dc motor is constructed in the same way as a dc generator.

Transformers

A *transformer* is a device that uses electromagnetic induction to change the voltage as it transfers electrical energy from one circuit to another. Basically, a transformer is made up of two coils of wire wrapped around an iron core, **Figure 2-26**. There is no connection between the two coils of wire. Each is linked to a different circuit. These coils are commonly known as *windings*.

The coil that is connected to the power source side of a transformer is called the *primary winding*. The coil connected to the load side is

polarity of the armature is in opposition to the poles of the field magnet. In other words, like magnetic poles in the motor repel each other to start the rotation. Constant shifting of the magnetic polarity keeps the motor spinning.

AC motors are somewhat different in construction, but their operation is similar. These motors will be discussed in a later chapter.

---

transformer: A device that transfers electrical energy from one circuit to another, usually at a different voltage, through electromagnetic induction.

windings: The coils of wire in an electrical device. Windings are used in generators, motors, and transformers.

primary winding: The winding of a transformer that creates a magnetic field and is connected to the power source side.

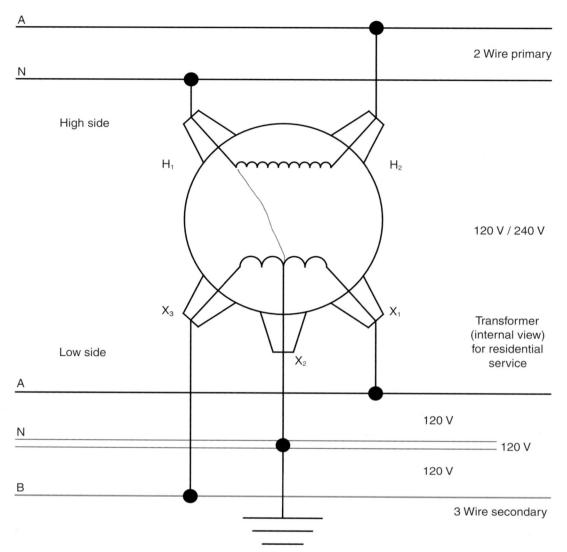

Figure 2-26. Simple diagram of a transformer. The coil of wire on the primary side creates a magnetic field. A current is induced in the secondary coil at a different voltage.

called the *secondary winding*. The current in the primary winding creates a magnetic field that induces current in the secondary winding.

Voltage out of a transformer is directly related to the number of turns of wire in the windings. If there are more turns in the secondary winding than in the primary, the voltage out will be greater than the voltage in. Such a transformer is called a *step-up transformer* because the voltage steps up, or increases, from the primary to the secondary. In fact, the change in voltage from primary to secondary is directly proportional to the change in number of wire turns.

$$V_{out} = \frac{V_{in} \times N_{sec}}{N_{pri}}$$

Suppose that the incoming electrical power is at 110 volts on a transformer that has 100

secondary winding: The transformer winding connected to the load.

step-up transformer: A transformer that steps up, or increases, the voltage exiting the transformer.

turns on the primary coil and 600 turns on the secondary coil. The secondary has six times as many turns as the primary. Therefore, the output voltage will be six times greater.

$$V_{out} = 110 \text{ V} \times \frac{600}{100}$$

$$V_{out} = 660 \text{ V}$$

In a ***step-down transformer***, the secondary coil has fewer turns than the primary coil. Therefore, the output voltage is less than the input voltage.

Electrical System Overview

Electricity is generated at large power stations. These stations have huge generators that are spun by a turbine. High-pressure steam causes the turbine to spin by blowing past the turbine blades. A turbine looks like dozens of fans all connected to the same shaft. If you think of the wind causing a windmill to turn, then you have the right idea. The steam is produced by boiling water in a boiler. The heat for the boiler can come from many sources. Natural gas, coal, oil, and uranium (nuclear fuel) are the most common sources.

Most electrical power is generated at 24,000 V and is stepped up to 132,000 V, 238,000 V, or 345,000 V at the power station. The electricity is sent out to substations over high-voltage cable. See **Figure 2-27**. A *substation* is a collection of transformers, located away from the power station, that lowers the voltage of the electrical power and redistributes it along another set of conductors (distribution lines). Before being brought into homes, the voltage is further reduced to 120 V and 240 V, **Figure 2-28**.

---

step-down transformer: A transformer that steps down, or decreases, the voltage exiting the transformer.

substation: A collection of transformers that changes the voltage of the electrical power and redistributes it along another set of conductors.

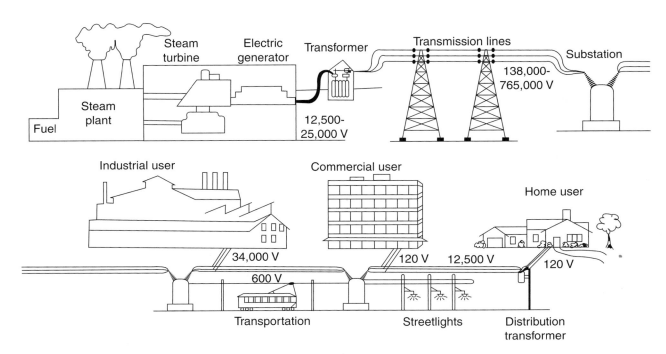

Figure 2-27. Electric power used in residences is generated in power stations and transmitted over long distances through high-voltage lines. Before it is brought into a house, voltage is reduced to 240 or 120 volts.

Figure 2-28. A 240/120 V step-down transformer. This type of transformer is used to reduce voltage to levels that can be used in houses. This transformer is rated at 37.5 kVA or 37.5 kW.

From the point of generation up to the service transformer, the power is all three-phase power. Your service transformer is connected to one of the three phases, while your neighbors' transformers are connected to other phases. The houses are split up among the different phases in order to keep the load on each phase balanced.

The power enters your house through the *service entrance*, which is where the electric meter is located. The electric meter records the amount of power you use each month. The electric company reads the meter every month, and charges you for the amount of energy used.

After passing through the electric meter, the power passes through the main disconnect switch or panel. This is where the power is divided up into branch circuits for the different parts of your house. The panel contains circuit breakers, which will shut off the power if a circuit becomes overloaded. Individual conductors are connected to each circuit breaker and are further connected to the light switches, devices, equipment, and receptacles in your house. The electricity thus reaches your lights, stereo, computer, toaster, and other devices that convert it into forms of useful energy.

Review Questions

Write your answers on a separate sheet of paper.
Do not write in this book.

1. Electricity is a form of _____ .
2. Substances that allow electricity to pass through them easily are called _____, whereas those that block the electron flow are called _____ .

3. The two types of electric current we use are called _____ current and _____ current.

4. A _____ is a pathway for electric current.

5. In a _____ circuit, current must go through every device in the circuit or it will not work.

6. The loads in the circuit shown are connected in (series, parallel).

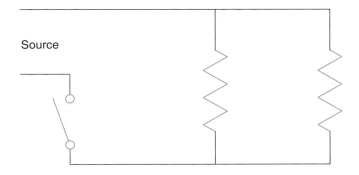

Source

7. What did Faraday and Henry discover?

8. In what important way do ac and dc generators differ?

9. Explain Fleming's Rule.

10. A transformer uses _____ principles to increase or decrease voltage between an electrical power source and its load.

11. Ohm's law relates resistance, _____ , and _____ in an electrical circuit.

12. _____ law relates power, voltage, and current in an electrical circuit.

13. A series circuit has a current of 2 amperes. What is the source voltage, if the total resistance is 6 ohms?

14. Which of the following graphs would best express the correct relationship of resistance to other conductor characteristics:

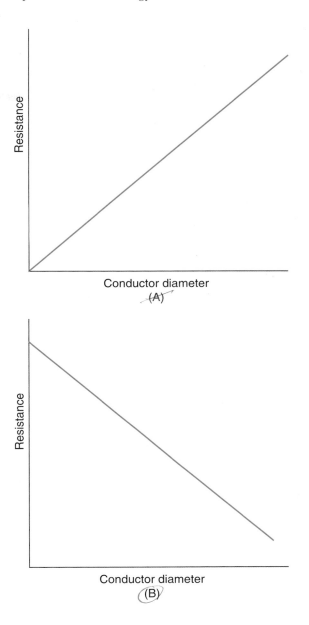

Conductor diameter
(A)

Conductor diameter
(B)

15. What is the total amperage of a parallel circuit having a total resistance of 12 ohms and a source voltage of 24 volts?

16. *True or False?* Ohm's law applies to series, parallel, and complex circuits.

17. *True or False?* Power is the rate of doing work.

18. Electrical energy is measured in units called _____.

A. joules
B. watts
C. horsepower
D. kilowatt-hours

Know the Code

A copy of the NEC 2005 is required to answer these questions.

1. The first issue of the *National Electrical Code* was published in what year?

2. The *National Electrical Code* is published by what organization?

3. What is the primary purpose of the *National Electrical Code*?

3

Tools for the Electrician

Objectives

Information in this chapter will enable you to:

- Select essential tools for residential wiring.

- Know the specialty tools available for infrequent applications.

- Discuss basic principles of tool use and care.

Technical Terms

Blanket heater
Box heater
Cable ripper
Circuit tester
Conduit bender
Continuity tester
Diagonal cutter
Digital voltage tester
Electric drill
Electrical voltage tester
Electrician's hammer
Electrician's knife
Fish tape
Flux
Folding rule
Grooved joint pliers
Hacksaw
Hammer-drill

Hickey
Hydraulic bender
Level
Lineman's hammer
Lineman's pliers
Locking pliers
Long tape rule
Multimeter
Needle-nose pliers
Pipe cutter
Pliers
Reamer
Receptacle tester
Reciprocating saw
Rotary-hammer
   drill

Sharpening stone
Solder
Soldering gun
Soldering paste (flux)
Solenoid voltage
   tester

Steel tape
Torpedo level
Whetstone
Wire stripper

An electrician must have proper tools for the job. Tools must be kept in good repair, as well. If tools are not available or are in poor condition, time is wasted and good work is impossible. Invest in good-quality tools and take the time to inspect and care for them, and you will be able to rely on them for many years.

Safety Note

Homemade Insulated Tools

Insulated tools have been tested to prevent conductivity at the voltage for which the tool is rated. Do not think that you can insulate a tool by dipping its handles in a polymer or wrapping them with tape. These methods create a weak and inconsistent thickness of insulation. If you must work on energized equipment, the cost of insulated tools is a small price to pay to prevent injury or death.

Measuring Tools

One of the most important tasks for an electrician is measuring. Whether you need to measure distances, electrical properties, or wire diameter, proper measuring techniques and tools will make the installation quicker, more accurate, and safer. All measuring tools must be handled with care to ensure accuracy is maintained.

Tools for Measuring Distances

The most-frequently used measuring tool is the power return steel tape rule, also known as the steel tape. See **Figure 3-1**. The *steel tape* is a coiled strip of thin steel that is marked with fractions of an inch. The bent-metal hook on the end of the tape butts up against surfaces for inside

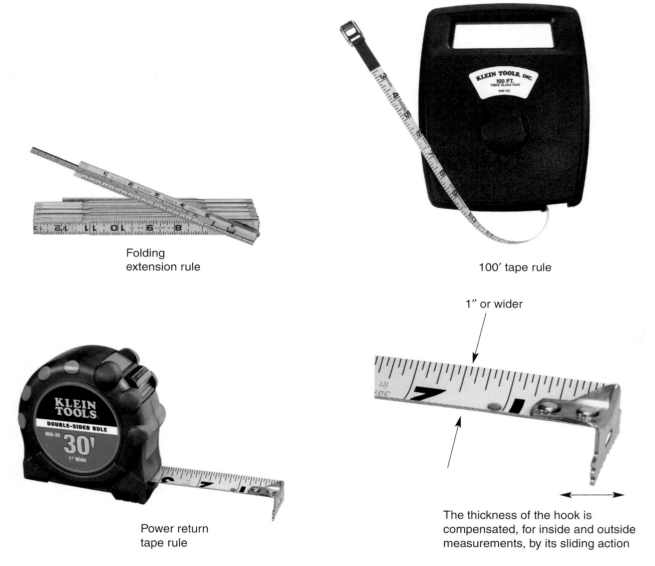

Folding
extension rule

100′ tape rule

1″ or wider

Power return
tape rule

The thickness of the hook is compensated, for inside and outside measurements, by its sliding action

Figure 3-1. These basic measuring tools have specific functions. The steel tape is used for most measurements under 30′. The long tape rule can quickly measure beyond 30′. The folding rule is used near live circuits because it is nonconductive. (Klein Tools, Inc.)

---

steel tape: A measuring tape with U.S. customary or metric markings (or both) made of flexible steel that rolls up into a case when not in use.

measurements or hooks over objects for outside measurements. The hook is designed to slide a distance equal to its thickness. This ensures an accurate measurement whether placing the hook up against an object (an inside measurement) or hooking it over the end of an object (an outside measurement). Always slow the end of the tape just prior to it entering the case to prevent the hook from breaking off the tape.

Typical steel tape lengths are 20′ to 35′, with 25′ being the most common. The width of the tape should be at least 1″ so that the tape remains stiff enough for a single person to make most measurements. Be careful when using a steel tape near powered equipment and conductors. If the steel tape contacts an energized conductor or component, you could receive a shock. A safer measuring tool near live equipment is a folding rule.

Distances that are beyond the steel tape's reach should be measured with a 50′, 100′, or 150′ *long tape rule*. These rules are made of steel or woven fiberglass and are retrieved with a manual crank.

Folding rules are distance-measuring tools that are available in wood or fiberglass, which makes them safer near live equipment. Typical folding rules are 6′, 8′, and 10′ long with hinges for folding at 6″ intervals. A well-built folding rule will last for many years, requiring only a drop of oil at the hinges once a year. Both the steel tape and the folding rule can be found with U.S. customary, metric, or both scales.

Tools for Testing and Measuring Electrical Properties

One of the most important tools for preventing electrical shock is the *electrical voltage tester*. This simple electronic device will indicate if a voltage is present on a circuit. Some testers will also show the amount of voltage, usually 120 V or 240 V. A *digital voltage tester* is a tool that uses indicator lights or a digital readout to indicate the amount of

voltage present. This tester draws very little current from the circuit. A *solenoid voltage tester (Wiggy®)* uses a higher amount of current to activate the tester's solenoid, which indicates the presence of voltage. This meter has been called a *Wiggy®* since the Wigginton Company developed early solenoid meters over one hundred years ago. See **Figure 3-2**.

An inexpensive tool called a *circuit tester* is simply a neon lightbulb attached to two conductive leads. When one lead contacts a powered terminal or wire while the other lead touches a grounded conductor, the neon bulb will light. A version of this tool called a *receptacle tester* plugs into a receptacle and will test correct wiring, open ground, reverse polarity, open hot, open neutral, and hot on neutral in ac circuits. Some units will even test GFCI receptacles for proper operation. See **Figure 3-3**.

Safety Note

Test the Test Light

Use the test light on a circuit known to be live to make sure the light itself is working. Then use it on the circuit you are about to work on.

---

long tape rule: A steel or cloth tape that may be as long as 100′ or 150′.

folding rule: A ruler made of wood, fiberglass, or plastic, that folds into 6″ sections. Usually 6′ total length.

electrical voltage tester: An electronic device that indicates if a voltage is present on a circuit.

digital voltage tester: A tool that uses indicator lights or a digital readout to indicate the amount of voltage present.

solenoid voltage tester (Wiggy®): A tester that uses a solenoid to indicate the presence of voltage.

circuit tester: A simple light with conductive leads used to determine if a circuit is energized or deenergized.

receptacle tester: A tester that plugs into an outlet receptacle and indicates the status of the polarity, ground, and sometimes the ground fault capability.

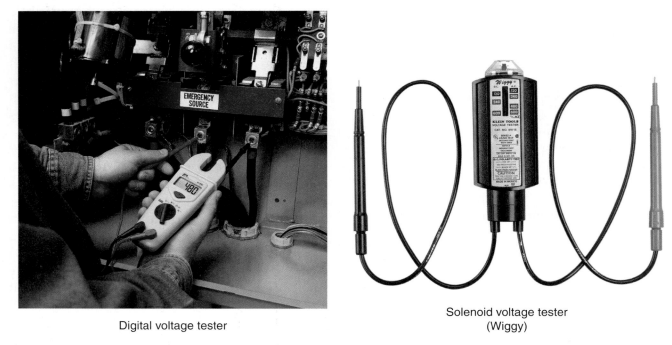

Digital voltage tester

Solenoid voltage tester
(Wiggy)

Figure 3-2. A tester will let you know if there is any voltage in a circuit. (Ideal Industries, Inc. and Klein Tools, Inc.)

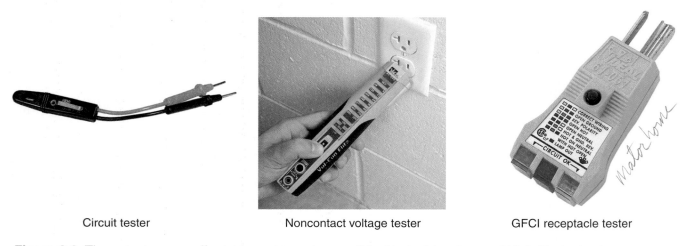

Circuit tester

Noncontact voltage tester

GFCI receptacle tester

Figure 3-3. These testers are affordable and easy to use. (Ideal Industries, Inc. and Klein Tools, Inc.)

To measure electrical properties, such as electromotive force, current, and resistance, you will need a *multimeter*. See **Figure 3-4**. A multimeter, also known as a VOM (volt-ohm-milliammeter), comes in a variety of configurations and prices. Some models only test for the basics: voltage, resistance, and current. Others include settings to test for capacitance, temperature, and frequency. A digital multimeter will display the measurement on a digital readout.

An analog multimeter is recognizable by its multi-scaled display with a needle that rotates from left to right. Before using a multimeter you must know the type of current (ac or dc),

multimeter: A digital or analog meter that measures multiple electrical properties: voltage, resistance, and current. Some will also measure capacitance, temperature, and frequency.

Analog multimeter

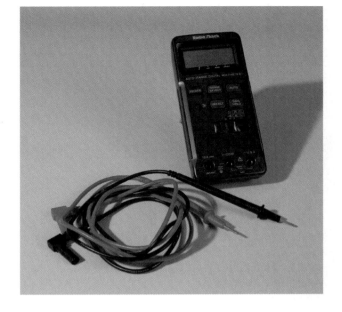

Digital multimeter

Figure 3-4. A multimeter is a versatile tool that can measure current, voltage, and resistance. (Ideal Industries, Inc.)

the approximate voltage, and the approximate current. A multimeter is quickly destroyed if it is connected to a circuit that has more amperage or voltage than the capability of the meter.

Safety Note

Know What You Are Measuring

Always know how much voltage is present in the circuit. Using a handheld meter in a high voltage circuit may damage the meter and possibly cause an injury.

Finally, there may be times when you do not have a meter handy but need to test a wire or device for continuity. A *continuity tester* is an inexpensive tool that lights up when a circuit is continuous. These testers are small enough to carry in your tool pouch or shirt pocket. See **Figure 3-5**.

Tools for Measuring Level

A *level* has clear tubes that contain fluid and an air bubble. When the bubble is centered between the marks on the tube, the tool is level.

A *torpedo level* is a level that is small enough to be carried in a pouch. Some models are magnetic, which is a handy feature when mounting steel

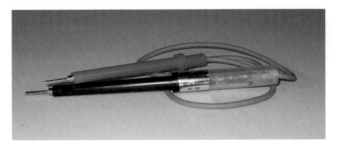

Continuity tester

Figure 3-5. A continuity tester is used to detect a break in a circuit.

---

continuity tester: Checks for electrical continuity between two objects or devices.

level: An essential tool used to make sure conduit and devices are installed plumb (vertical) and level (horizontal).

torpedo level: A special level that is only several inches long, usually not more than a foot. It is handier than an ordinary level since it fits in a toolbox or tool pouch.

boxes. A groove that runs along the length of the level is used when leveling conduit or pipe. All levels have bubbles for horizontal and vertical alignment. Some also can align objects at a 45° angle. See **Figure 3-6**.

> ### Pro Tip
> **Levels**
>
> Your wiring job will not appear professional if the switches and outlet receptacles are not plumb (straight up and down). These are the devices that the homeowners will see every day. When installing boxes, always use a level to ensure the box is plumb instead of relying on your sight alone.

Wire Tools

Having the proper tools to cut, strip, grip, and pull electrical wiring is critical to being an efficient electrician. There are many different types of wire and cabling that you will need to work with. Having the right tools and skills to use them will make the job easier.

Cutting

Most wire in a residential installation will be small enough to cut with a pair of side-cutting *lineman's pliers*. A tool that is designed to only cut wire, such as a *diagonal cutter*, is handy when you have to reach into a crowded space to cut a wire. However, a dual-purpose tool, such as a pair of lineman's pliers, will be used for most wire holding, shaping, and cutting. See **Figure 3-7**.

Larger cable is cut with long-handled cable cutters, ratcheting cable cutters, or hydraulic cutting tools. If there are only a few large cables to cut, a hacksaw is slower but certainly adequate for the job. Never use more than reasonable hand pressure, handle extenders, or a hammer to squeeze the handles of a cable cutter closed. Get a larger cutter or a hacksaw instead.

> ### Safety Note
> **Insulated Tools**
>
> If you must work on powered circuits, always use insulated tools. The insulated tools should be rated for the voltage of the circuit.

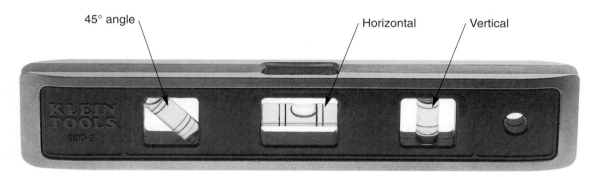

Torpedo level

Figure 3-6. All levels align objects horizontally and vertically, and some can align objects at 45°. A torpedo level is small enough to store in your tool pouch. (Klein Tools, Inc.)

lineman's pliers: Pliers with a square nose for pulling wire. Most also have a cutting blade.

diagonal cutter: Pliers with two sharpened jaws for cutting wires.

Lineman's pliers

Diagonal cutters

Long-handled cable cutter

Ratcheting cutter

Figure 3-7. Use the proper tool for cutting wire or cable. Lineman's pliers will cut the most frequently installed wire. Diagonal cutters can reach into boxes to cut wire. Long-handled cable cutters provide the leverage to cut medium cable. A ratcheting cutter will cut larger cable and it fits in a toolbox. (Klein Tools, Inc.)

Stripping

Stripping insulation off of the end of a wire without damaging the conductor is a skill that takes practice and the proper tool. If the tool cuts too deep, the conductor could be nicked and be unusable. If the tool does not cut deep enough, the insulation will be very difficult to remove. A simple *wire stripper* has circular notches that are sized for standard wire sizes, **Figure 3-8**. Place the wire into the correct notch,

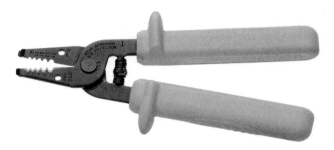

Insulated wire strippers

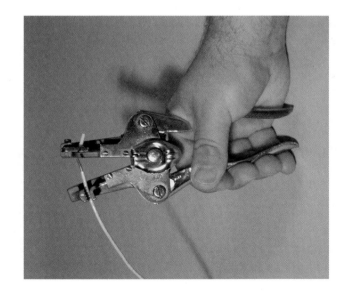

Automatic wire strippers

Figure 3-8. Stripping the insulation off wire must be done without damaging the conductor. A simple wire stripper has notches for standard wire sizes. This one is insulated. An automatic wire stripper will hold the wire, then cut and remove the insulation in one motion. (Klein Tools, Inc.)

wire stripper: A form of pliers with various cutting surfaces for standard wire gages.

squeeze the handles, and slide the insulation off the conductor. Some automatic wire strippers will grip the wire and strip the insulation in one squeeze of the handles. Wire strippers are specifically designed for solid and stranded wire. Be sure to use the tool that is made for the wire you are stripping. See Chapter 5, **Conductors** for more information on solid and stranded wire.

A multipurpose tool has features that will cut and strip wire, crimp terminals, and cut small bolts without damaging the threads. See **Figure 3-9**.

A *cable ripper* is a tool that cuts the outer jacket lengthwise on multi-conductor cables. See **Figure 3-10**. To use a cable ripper, place tool on the cable so the blade makes contact with the cable's jacket. Squeeze the ripper together until

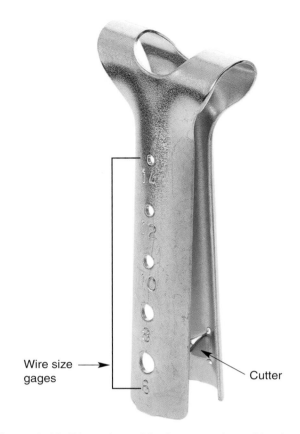

Wire size gages →   Cutter

Figure 3-10. Place the cable ripper on the cable. Apply pressure until the cutter pierces the jacket. Pull the ripper toward the end of the cable. Finish by cutting off the jacket with a knife. (Klein Tools, Inc.)

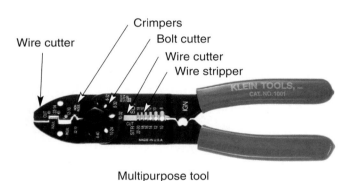

Wire cutter   Crimpers   Bolt cutter   Wire cutter   Wire stripper

Multipurpose tool

Figure 3-9. A multipurpose tool has features for cutting, stripping, and terminating wire. This tool will also cut small bolts. (Klein Tools, Inc.)

cable ripper: A tool used to cut the outer jacket of a cable for removal.

electrician's knife: A single-bladed knife with a curved blade that locks open. Usually used to remove insulation or cable jacket from wire.

sharpening stone: A small stone used to sharpen knife blades.

whetstone: A hard, fine-grained stone for sharpening tools.

the blade pierces the jacket. Now slide the ripper to the end of the cable to rip the jacket. Finally, a knife is used to cut the jacket completely off the cable.

An *electrician's knife* has many uses. It can also be used to strip insulation and cut electrical tape. See **Figure 3-11**. A good-quality electrician's knife will remain sharp for many uses, but eventually all knives will need to be sharpened. A small *sharpening stone* or *whetstone* is used to sharpen the knife. See **Figure 3-12**. To sharpen a knife, push it away from your body at a consistent angle on the sharpening stone. Make sure to sharpen each side of the blade an equal number of times.

Figure 3-11. With practice, an electrician's knife can be used to strip insulation cleanly and safely. The blade locks open to avoid closing on fingers during use. (Klein Tools, Inc.)

Figure 3-12. Sharpen the blade of a knife with a sharpening stone. (Klein Tools, Inc.)

Gripping

Pliers are used to shape the end of a wire so it can be attached to a switch or receptacle properly. *Needle-nose pliers* provide the perfect form to wrap a wire around for this purpose. You have learned about the cutting feature of lineman's pliers. The gripping feature is just as important.

Electrical boxes have partially punched features called *knockouts* that are easily removed with the gripping power and leverage of pliers. There are many different styles of pliers offering unique advantages. These styles include *locking pliers*, for a strong grip, and *grooved joint pliers*, for a larger range of sizes. See **Figure 3-13**.

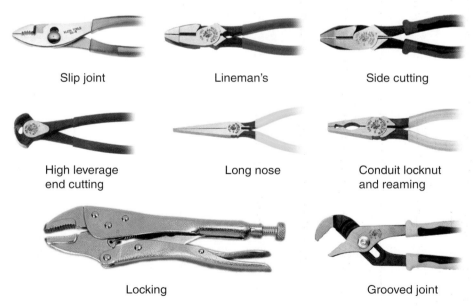

Slip joint

Lineman's

Side cutting

High leverage end cutting

Long nose

Conduit locknut and reaming

Locking

Grooved joint

Figure 3-13. There are many types of pliers used in the electrical trade. (Klein Tools, Inc.)

---

pliers: A tool used for gripping or cutting.

needle-nose pliers: Pliers with a long, skinny nose for reaching into crowded spaces.

locking pliers: Pliers that, when squeezed, will remain locked on an object until a release lever engaged.

grooved joint pliers: Pliers that allow the jaws to be adjusted to several different spacings.

As you can see, pliers are quite versatile. These tools can grip, clamp, tighten, turn, pull, and cut objects. Certain rules should be followed to prolong their usefulness and make them safe:

- Never use pliers to strike another object.
- Do not use pliers for cutting, unless the pliers are designed to do so.
- Keep pliers properly oiled.
- For electrical work, use pliers that have insulated handles. This will help protect against electrical shock.

Pulling

Pull wire through conduit with a tool called a fish tape. See **Figure 3-14**. A *fish tape* is a spool of steel or fiberglass that is stiff enough to be pushed into conduit yet flexible enough to follow the conduit bends. After the tape is pushed into the conduit and the tape's end emerges, the wire or wires are attached to the end. The fish tape is then retrieved, pulling the wires into the conduit.

Conduit

Conduit is a flexible or rigid protective tubing used to contain wires. There are specific methods and tools that make cutting and bending conduit effortless and precise. Some tools may be used on all conduit, but most are designed for conduit that is made of a particular material. Learn how to use all of these tools and practice cutting and bending conduit with them. These are important skills to have as an electrician.

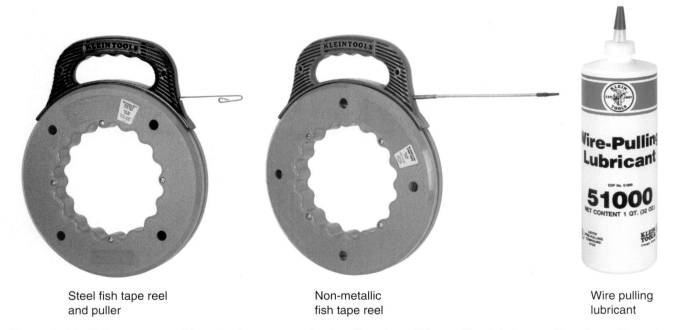

Steel fish tape reel
and puller

Non-metallic
fish tape reel

Wire pulling
lubricant

Figure 3-14. Fish tapes are either steel or nonconductive fiberglass. Wire-pulling lubricant will make pulling wire easier, and it will reduce the chance of damaging the wire's insulation. (Klein Tools, Inc.)

---

fish tape: A long tape, either metal or fiberglass, used to pull wires through walls or conduit.

Cutting

Steel conduit is typically cut with either a powered or manual saw. A good power tool for cutting conduit is a *reciprocating saw*. This saw comes in a corded or battery-powered model and can be outfitted with different blade types and lengths, depending on the material being cut. See **Figure 3-15**.

For manual sawing, a *hacksaw* is a popular metal-cutting tool. See **Figure 3-16**. The blades for a hacksaw are selected based on the number of teeth per inch. A blade with 18 to 24 teeth per inch is a good choice for cutting most types of conduit. To ensure straight cuts, the conduit should be held in a pipe vise. This vise is also required when cutting threads onto rigid conduit. See **Figure 3-17**.

A tool called a *pipe cutter* is sometimes used to cut various types of conduit. See **Figure 3-18**. This tool works by forcing a hardened cutting wheel into the conduit as the tool is rotated around it. The wheel is pushed deeper into the conduit by turning the handle after every rotation. The drawback to this tool is that it creates a large burr on the inside edge of the conduit. All cutting tools will create some type of burr, but a pipe cutter creates the largest.

The burr on the inside edge of the conduit can damage the wiring. After the conduit is cut, this burr must be removed. This is done with a *reamer*, a tool that scrapes the burrs off the conduit edge. There are a few types of tools that will quickly ream the edge of the conduit. A cone-shaped reamer works by scraping a bevel on the inside edge of the conduit as the tool is

Corded reciprocating saw

Cordless reciprocating saw

Figure 3-15. A reciprocating saw and a variety of blade types and lengths will handle most cutting tasks. (Makita Corp.)

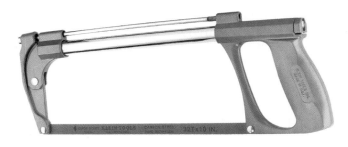

Figure 3-16. A hacksaw outfitted with a blade that has 18 to 24 teeth per inch is useful for cutting conduit. (Klein Tools, Inc.)

reciprocating saw: A power tool with a cutting blade that moves back and forth to provide the cutting action.

hacksaw: A hand or power saw used to cut metal and PVC pipe. Can create a crooked cut.

pipe cutter: A tool that provides a very straight cut, but leaves a large burr.

reamer: Removes the burrs left behind after cutting metal conduit.

Tri-stand yoke vise

Bench-mounted yoke vise

Chain vise with a tubing bender

Stand chain vise

Figure 3-17. There are many vises that will hold conduit for cutting or threading. (Ridge Tool Co.)

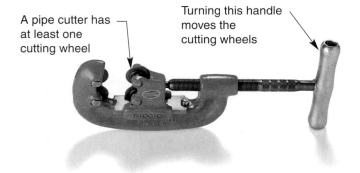

A pipe cutter has at least one cutting wheel

Turning this handle moves the cutting wheels

Figure 3-18. A pipe cutter produces a square cut, but it also creates a large burr. (Ridge Tool Co.)

rotated. Another type of reamer is attached to the shank of a screwdriver and contains a cutting edge for 1/2″, 3/4″, and 1″ conduit. The tool is inserted into the conduit and rotated to remove the burrs on the inside and outside edges at the same time. Finally, a metal file may be used to accomplish the same task as the previous specialty tools, while having many other uses as well. See **Figure 3-19.**

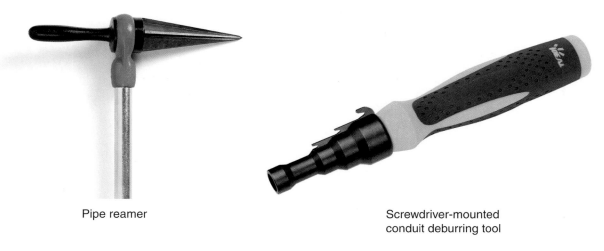

Pipe reamer

Screwdriver-mounted
conduit deburring tool

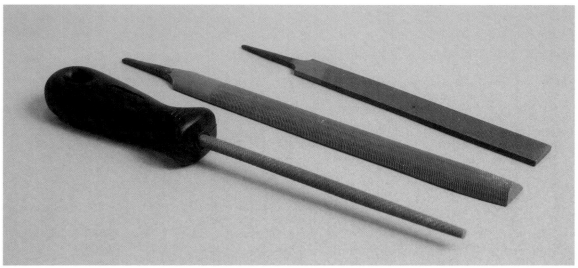

Round and flat files

Figure 3-19. Always remove burrs immediately from conduit ends using one of these tools.
(Ridge Tool Co., Ideal Industries, Inc.)

Bending

Smaller conduit can be bent with an appropriately named *conduit bender*. There are markings on these tools that, with practice, make conduit bending a reliable and consistent process. Conduit that is too rigid or large for a bender can be bent with a *hickey*, a tool that bends the conduit with multiple movements per bend. See **Figure 3-20.** If the conduit is too large for either of these tools, a power-assisted *hydraulic bender* is needed.

Nonmetallic conduit must be heated before it can be bent. A *blanket heater* or a *box heater* will bring the nonmetallic conduit to the proper temperature for bending. Do not use a blowtorch, automobile exhaust, or any other method

conduit bender: A special tool for bending conduit to the proper bend radius. Contains special markings for making consistent bends at the proper angles.

hickey: A tool for bending conduit. It does not have the special markings of a conduit bender.

hydraulic bender: A conduit bender that uses a hydraulic pump for bending.

blanket heater: A heater to bring nonmetallic electrical conduit up to the proper temperature for bending.

box heater: A device for heating nonmetallic electrical conduit to the proper bending temperature.

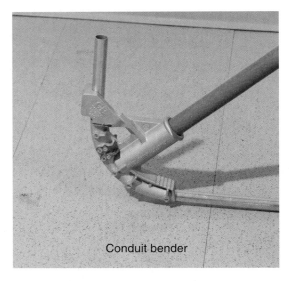

Conduit bender

Conduit hickey

Figure 3-20. Bending conduit is done with a tool that is specific for the size and type of conduit. A hickey is used to bend large or rigid conduit in multiple steps. (Appleton Electric Co.)

that may be suggested as an "electrician's tip." These shortcuts are not only dangerous, they are not allowed by the *National Electrical Code*.

Striking

A hammer is used for driving nails and staples, attaching hangers and electrical boxes, striking chisels, and driving ground rods. Many electricians prefer the *electrician's hammer* to a standard claw hammer because the electrician's hammer has an extra long neck for driving nails through the bottom of an electrical box. The claw, which is straight rather than curved, is used to remove nails or loosen structural materials such as plaster during electrical remodeling. See **Figure 3-21**. A *lineman's hammer* is heavy enough to drive a ground rod.

General rules regarding the proper use of striking tools follow:

- Always choose the right size and weight hammer for the intended use.
- Never strike tools together unless they are designed for that purpose.
- Striking tools should strike a surface squarely, never at an angle.
- Always wear safety glasses when using striking tools.

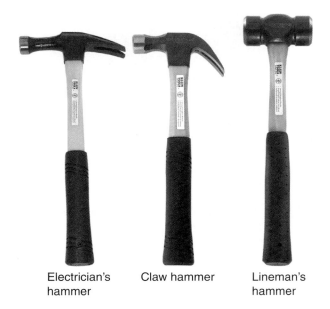

Electrician's   Claw hammer   Lineman's
hammer   hammer

Figure 3-21. Choose the correct hammer to make each task safer and easier. An electrician's hammer has a long neck for mounting boxes. A lineman's hammer is used for heavier work, such as driving a ground rod. (Klein Tools, Inc.)

electrician's hammer: A specialized hammer with a long neck and a straight claw.

lineman's hammer: A heavy hammer, like a mallet, used to drive ground rods into the ground.

Drilling

Whether using a corded or cordless *electric drill*, the common function is to make a round hole. In order to accomplish this, the tool must be in good working condition. The bit must be sharp, the proper type, and the correct size for the hole and material you are drilling. **Figure 3-22** illustrates a typical cordless drill kit, a variety of drill bits, accessories, and hole saws.

Cordless drill set

Twist drill bit

Masonary drill bit

Auger drill bit

Step drill bit

Drill bit set

Hole saw set

Figure 3-22. An electric drill and a variety of drill bits and hole saws will handle most drilling tasks. (Makita Corp., Klein Tools, Inc.)

electric drill: An electric-motor-powered tool for making a round hole.

A *hammer drill* is a drill that delivers an impact to the drill bit while it is turning. This is useful when drilling in cinder block or concrete. A *rotary hammer drill* is a tool that delivers a significant impact to the drill bit while it is turning. The impact is so strong that special bits must be used. Rotary hammer drills are used when drilling large diameter holes in hard materials. See **Figure 3-23**.

Hammer drill   Rotary hammer drill

Figure 3-23. A rotary hammer drill and masonry drill bits are needed to drill into concrete. (Milwaukee Electric Tool Corp.)

Soldering

The development of various types of wire connectors has all but eliminated the once common technique of joining wires by soldering. Still, soldering may occasionally be necessary. Upon such rare occasions, a *soldering gun*, a spool of *solder*, and *soldering paste*, also known as *flux*, will handle the task. See **Figure 3-24**.

Soldering tools require almost no maintenance, except for occasional tinning or cleaning of the soldering tip. Complete instructions provided by the manufacturer are adequate for the care and use of these tools.

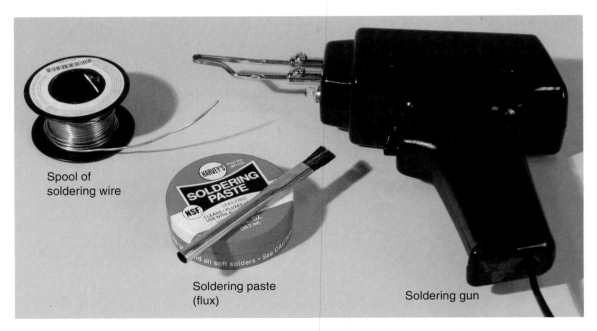

Spool of soldering wire

Soldering paste (flux)

Soldering gun

Figure 3-24. These are the basic items needed to solder wires. Soldering paste or flux is used to clean the area to be soldered.

hammer drill: An electric hand drill that delivers an impact to the drill bit while drilling. Used for materials such as cinder block and for small diameter holes in concrete.

rotary hammer drill: A hammer drill that delivers significant impact to the drill bit while turning it. The impact is so strong that special bits must be used.

soldering gun: An electric tool used to heat solder to its melting point.

solder: A metal alloy that melts easily to join wires together. Also used for joining copper water pipe.

soldering paste: A special paste applied to wires prior to soldering.

Miscellaneous

In addition to those previously described, the following basic hand tools should be included in your toolbox. See **Figure 3-25**.

- **Screwdrivers.** Assorted sizes and types including both Phillips and standard tips.
- **Allen wrench set.** This is necessary to tighten main lugs on certain load centers and panels.

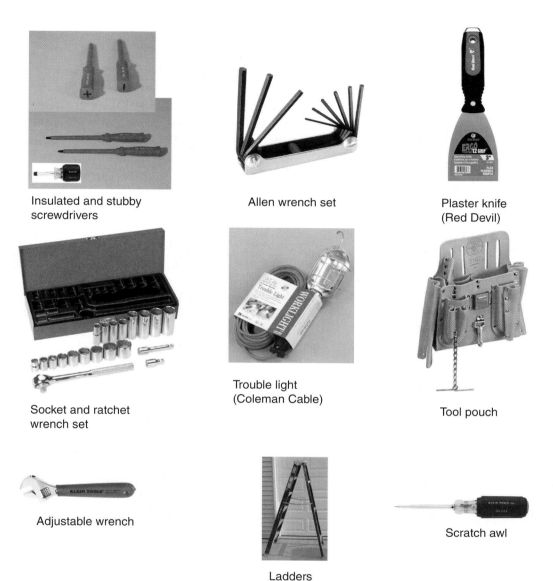

Insulated and stubby screwdrivers

Allen wrench set

Plaster knife (Red Devil)

Socket and ratchet wrench set

Trouble light (Coleman Cable)

Tool pouch

Adjustable wrench

Ladders

Scratch awl

Crosscut saw

Keyhole saw

Wood chisel

Aviation snips

Figure 3-25. These basic hand tools are useful for residential wiring. (Klein Tools, Inc., Red Devil, Inc., Ace Hardware Corp., Coleman Cable, Inc.)

- **Plaster knife.** A wide and flexible type is used to repair damaged plaster when remodeling old work.
- **Set of sockets and a ratchet wrench.** These tools are used when attaching a conductor to a grounding rod.
- **Trouble light.** You may have to work in unlit attics and crawlspaces.
- **Tool pouch.** Carry the tools you use most often in a pouch so you do not waste time going back to your toolbox.
- **Adjustable wrench.** This wrench is able to tighten and loosen most nuts and bolts.
- **Ladders.** A good fiberglass or wood stepladder and extension ladder are needed at most jobs.
- **Gimlet or scratch awl.** Installation of screws is much easier and faster when a starter hole has been created with one of these tools.
- **Crosscut saw.** This saw is needed for notching or cutting studs.
- **Keyhole saw.** Use this tool to quickly cut drywall without requiring a starter hole.
- **Wood chisel.** This tool will trim away small amounts of wood in framing members to make room for conduit, cable, or boxes.
- **Aviation or tin snips.** These sheet metal cutting tools are useful for some cabling covers. To create the leverage to cut metal, aviation snips use compound action and the tin snips have long handles.

Pro Tip

Mark Your Screwdrivers

Mark the top of your screwdriver handles with a + or a – symbol so you know the tip style before pulling the screwdriver out of your pouch.

Care and Repair of Tools

Knives, drill bits, chisels, saws, and other tools meant for cutting should be kept sharp. A dull tool does poor work and is also more likely to cause injury to a worker or damage nearby materials. Gripping tools or turning tools such as pliers and screwdrivers should be inspected frequently. Pliers with rounded teeth will slip and may cause damage or scraped knuckles. Inspect screwdriver blades for rounding and other signs of damage and wear. If reconditioning the tool is impossible or costs more than a new one, replace the tool.

Handles of striking tools should be inspected frequently for looseness and weakness. Wooden handles can crack and splinter from misuse or misdirected blows. Loose wooden handles can be repaired with new wedges. Broken handles should be replaced. Proper use and care of tools should be a part of every electrician's training.

Web Site

www.hti.org

For additional information concerning the proper use of hand tools, visit the Hand Tool Institute Web site.

Review Questions

Write your answers on a separate sheet of paper. Do not write in this book.

1. List the three types of rules needed for measuring distance or length.
2. *True or False?* A cable ripper is used on a single conductor wire.
3. How is an electrician's hammer different from a standard claw hammer?
4. Which of the following statements is true when using cutting tools such as cable cutters and side cutters?
   A. Never use more than reasonable hand pressure.
   B. Use a handle extender if the material does not cut easily.
   C. It is acceptable to use a hammer to make the cutters cut the material.
5. _____ are used for holding, shaping, and cutting wire.

6. Carry your most frequently-used tools in a _____ to prevent multiple trips to your toolbox.

7. Why are insulated tools important?

Know the Code

A copy of the NEC 2005 is required to answer these questions.

1. Is the NFPA responsible for enforcing the requirements of the *NEC*? If not, who is?

2. Are all requirements of the *NEC* mandatory? Explain.

3. What units of measurement (measurement system) are used in the *NEC*?

Section 2 Installation

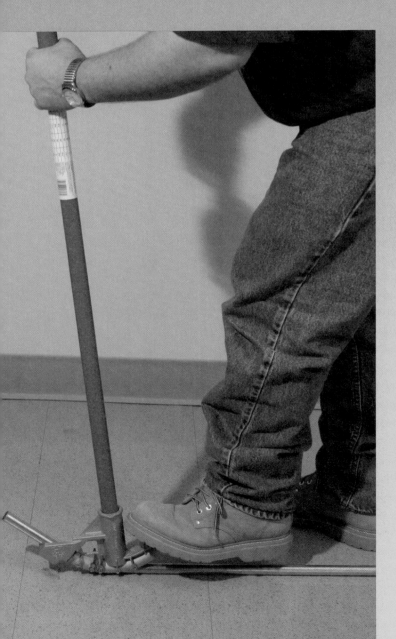

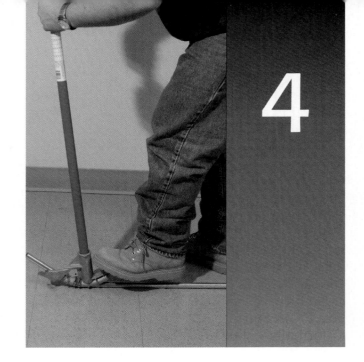

Wiring Systems

Objectives

Information in this chapter will enable you to:

- Know where to find codes and authorities for an installation.
- Recognize the marks of the most popular testing agencies.
- List the different conductor systems used in residential and light commercial wiring.
- Explain the basics of conduit bending.
- Become familiar with the many different types of raceway systems.

Technical Terms

Anti-short bushing
Armor
Armored cable (AC)
Authority having jurisdiction (AHJ)
Back-to-back bend
Bonding strip
Box offset
BX
Cable
Conduit
Electrical metallic tubing (EMT)
Electrical nonmetallic tubing (ENT)
Field bend
Flexible metal conduit (FMC)
Greenfield
Intermediate metal conduit (IMC)
Liquidtight flexible metal conduit (LFMC)
Nonmetallic sheathed cable (NM)
National Electrical Code® (NEC)
Nationally recognized testing laboratory (NRTL)
Offset bend
Occupational Safety and Health Administration (OSHA)
Raceways
Rigid metal conduit (RMC)
Rigid nonmetallic conduit (RNC)
Romex
Saddle bend
Service-entrance cable (SE)
Shrink
Stub bend
Underground feeder and branch-circuit cable (UF)
Underground service-entrance cable (USE)
Wiring
Wiring system

Electrical Codes and Safety Agencies

There are many different methods of providing electricity to the occupants of a modern residence. You will learn about the various types of conductors, devices, and procedures available to use and those that cannot be used. Before selecting any of these systems, you should be aware of the agencies and codes that ensure the materials and procedures you use are safe and reliable.

The National Electrical Code

The most informative and authoritative body of information concerning electrical wiring installation in the United States, and perhaps the world, is the **National Electrical Code® (NEC)**. See **Figure 4-1**. It establishes a set of rules, regulations, and criteria for the installation of electrical equipment. Compliance with these methods will result in a safe installation.

The *NEC* is drafted by a team of experts assembled for this purpose by the National Fire Protection Association (NFPA). This team is formally called the *National Electrical Code* committee. They revise and update the *NEC* every three years. It is imperative that anyone installing electrical wiring obtains and studies the *NEC*. Articles and sections of the *NEC* are referred to throughout this text. Although certain portions, tables, and examples are directly quoted from its text, there is so much useful information in the *NEC* that not having it available would be a tremendous hindrance.

Figure 4-1. *The National Electrical Code* is the set of rules that most installations must follow.

used instead of a specific title, such as *electrical inspector* or *county building commission*, because the approving systems vary.

Code enforcement

Almost every state, region, or locality has some sort of electrical code. Many use the *NEC* in whole or in part. *Article 90.4* of the *NEC* grants full power to the local inspection authority to interpret and modify meanings and intentions of the *NEC*. Further, some communities add regulations beyond those outlined in the *NEC*. For these reasons, the local inspector should be consulted for a copy of the local codes. Failure to do so will probably result in violations and an inspection failure.

Inspection, permits, and licensing

In many areas, permits and licensing are required to do electrical work. In such areas, the utility company requires that permits be obtained and the work be done by or under a licensed electrician *before* they will furnish power. Contact the electrical inspector or power company supervisor for information pertaining to permits and licensing.

Web Site

www.nfpa.org

For a copy of the National Electrical Code, visit the Web site of the National Fire Protection Association or write to:

NFPA

Batterymarch Park

Quincy, MA 02169

State and Local Codes

Although the *NEC*, itself, has no legal basis, it is often made mandatory under local or state rulings. In such cases it becomes a legal document. The **authority having jurisdiction (AHJ)** is the person or group of people responsible for approving the equipment, materials, an installation, or a procedure. The *NEC* is not an AHJ, but the building commission of your municipality may be the AHJ and will probably use the *NEC* for most electrical installations. The phrase "authority having jurisdiction" is

---

National Electrical Code (NEC): The most informative and authoritative body of information concerning electrical wiring installation in the United States.

authority having jurisdiction (AHJ): The person or group of people responsible for approving the equipment, materials, an installation, or a procedure.

Equipment Testing Agencies

There are many recognized testing agencies throughout the U.S. and Canada. Each of these agencies, known as a ***nationally recognized testing laboratory (NRTL)*** tests materials and equipment submitted to them by electrical material manufacturers. If the materials and equipment submitted measure up to the testing agencies' expectations, the items are listed as suitable for electrical installation. In addition, the product will be labeled with a recognized mark to identify the testing agency that approved the product. See **Figure 4-2**.

Almost all reputable manufacturers of electrical materials and equipment submit their products for testing. Products that are not listed should be avoided. In fact, it violates the *NEC* to use an unlisted product when there are listed ones available.

The most widely known testing agencies are Underwriters Laboratories (UL), Canadian Standards Association (CSA), and Intertek Testing Services NA (formerly ETL). Products listed by these and other testing agencies are sure to be well-constructed and safe. See **Figure 4-3**.

Occupational Safety and Health Administration (OSHA)

The ***Occupational Safety and Health Administration (OSHA)*** is the agency with the responsibility of creating and enforcing health and safety standards to protect persons in all occupations within the U.S. OSHA is an agency within the United States Department of Labor.

Underwriters Laboratory

Intertek Testing Services NA (Formerly ETL)

Canadian Standards Association

Figure 4-2. These are a few of the marks that indicate approval by an NRTL.

The regulations can be obtained by contacting the Office of Information Services, OSHA, U.S. Department of Labor, Washington, D.C. These safety regulations are often more detailed than those of the *NEC* and, in some instances, supercede the *NEC* rulings. When in doubt, consult the AHJ.

---

nationally recognized testing laboratory (NRTL): A recognized testing agency that tests materials and equipment submitted to them by electrical material manufacturers to verify that the item is suitable for electrical installation.

Occupational Safety and Health Administration (OSHA): An agency within the United States Department of Labor that is responsible for creating and enforcing health and safety standards to protect persons in all occupations within the U.S.

Web Site

www.osha.gov/SLTC/electrical/index.html

This Web site contains electrical-related OSHA standards, hazards information, and news.

Figure 4-3. Engineers test electrical appliances and equipment to ensure that the products are safe. (Underwriters Laboratories, Inc.)

All persons involved in the electrical trade should become familiar with the OSHA electrical standards, which specifically address the following areas:

- Hazardous locations
- Wiring methods, components and equipment
- Special systems
- Specific purpose equipment
- Wiring design and protection
- Electric utilization systems
- Definitions
- General requirements

Wiring Systems

Conductors for carrying electricity are commonly called *wiring*. A *wiring system* includes the wire, its insulating cover, a protective cover, and connectors that fasten it to an electrical box. See **Figure 4-4**. In some systems, the protective covering and the wire are purchased separately and the electrician assembles them on the job. In other cases, the protective covering is installed during manufacture.

Depending on the structure being wired, several different systems may be used. Regardless of the wiring system, it is important to have a continuous ground throughout every part of the system and every circuit. Refer to Chapter 9, **Grounding** of this text for grounding requirements. All of these systems are adequate for most installations. Some cannot be used where there are unusual hazards such as extreme moisture, explosive gases, or corrosive chemicals.

The wiring system selected depends on:
- Type of dwelling (style)
- Materials and type of construction used (such as log, concrete, post and beam, or platform)

wiring: The wires installed in a building that provide the electrical power throughout.

wiring system: In residential construction, the materials and components used to deliver electricity from the service panel to electrical devices. The wiring system includes the wire, its insulating cover, a protective cover, and the connectors that fasten it to an electrical box.

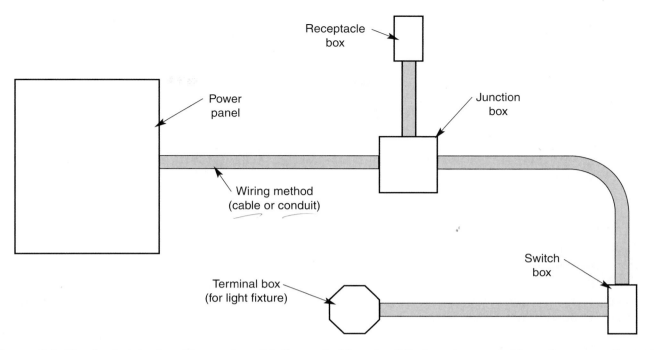

Figure 4-4. Simple sketch of a wiring system. It is the part of the circuit that carries current from the source through the boxes to a load.

- Surroundings of dwelling (hot, cold, wet, or dry)
- Cost of the electrical materials
- Contractor's preference
- Building code requirements
- Preference of owner (client)

Cables

A *cable* is an arrangement of two or more conductors in a protective covering and is assembled by the manufacturer. The protective covering may be plastic, rubber, steel, or aluminum.

Armored Cable: Type AC — *Article 320*		
Locations Allowed	**Sizes**	**Maximum Mounting Distance**
Dry	14 AWG through 1 AWG	12″ / 4 1/2′

cable: An arrangement of two or more conductors in a protective covering assembled by the manufacturer.

Armored Cable

Armored cable (AC) is a manufactured assembly of conductors and ribbed flexible metal tubing, **Figure 4-5**. AC is frequently called *BX*, a trade name for armored cable produced at the Sprague Electric division of General Electric.

The conductors in AC may be copper, aluminum, or copper clad aluminum. The outer covering is called *armor* and is made of steel or aluminum. As always, see the manufacturer's instructions before installing. One of the conductors in the cable is an uninsulated conductor that is in continuous contact with the armor. This wire is called a *bonding strip*.

The use of AC is generally limited to dry locations where it is not subject to physical damage. Thus, it may be used in masonry block, tile walls, attics, and wall spaces, as well as along studs, rafters, and joists. Also, care must be taken to maintain a bend radius of the AC that is five times its diameter.

Armored cable is expressly forbidden for use in:

- Commercial garages.
- Hoistways, elevators, or cranes.
- Theaters or motion picture studios.

AC is quite flexible and can be pulled through bored holes with ease. The holes should be slightly larger than the cable to avoid strain during installation. AC can be measured and cut before it is pulled through the holes in the framing members. Measure the distance along the route the cable will run and transfer this measurement to the cable. Allow 6″ to 8″ extra at each end for making connections. Cut the length of cable needed using a hacksaw, or reciprocating saw, **Figure 4-6**.

Stripping armored cable

There are several methods for cutting through the metal armor and stripping the cable end. Regardless of the method used, always be careful to not damage the wires inside the armor.

- **Hacksaw.** The most common tool for cutting the armor is the hacksaw. The hacksaw blade is placed on the armor so that it makes a diagonal cut across one of the high ridges. See **Figure 4-7**. Once the armor is cut through, it can be twisted off the inside wires.

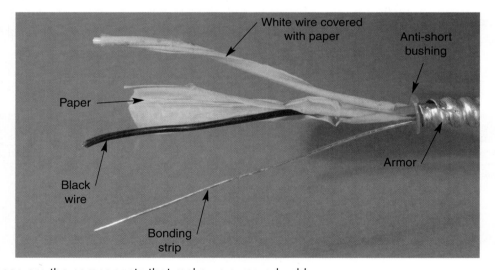

Figure 4-5. These are the components that make up armored cable.

armored cable (AC): An assembly of wires contained within a flexible metallic armor for protection.

BX: Another name for armored cable (AC). BX is a trade name attributed to the Sprague Electric division of General Electric.

armor: The metallic spiral tubing that protects the conductors in armored cable.

bonding strip: A piece of wire manufactured into AC that runs the length of the armor and is in constant contact with it. It provides the continuous ground necessary in a bonded system.

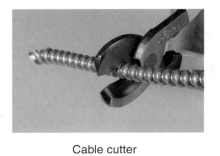

Cable cutter

Hacksaw

Reciprocating saw

Figure 4-6. A hacksaw, reciprocating saw, or special cable cutter will cut AC.

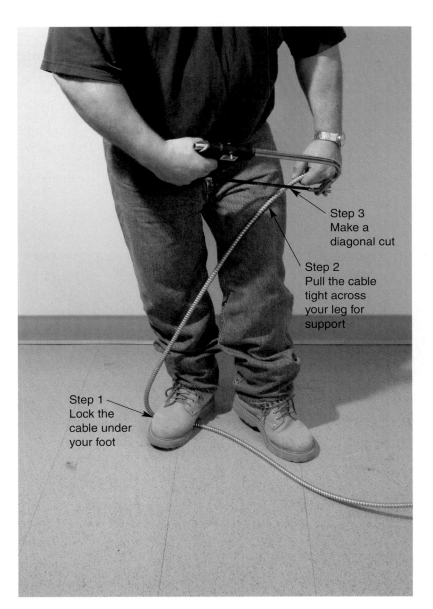

Step 3
Make a
diagonal cut

Step 2
Pull the cable
tight across
your leg for
support

Step 1
Lock the
cable under
your foot

**The armor cable can be supported by
your leg or a wood block**

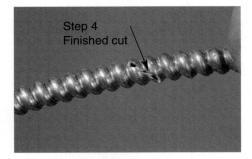

Step 4
Finished cut

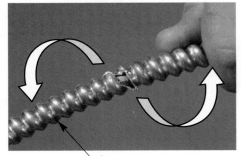

Step 5
Twist the armor in
opposing directions to
break it free

Figure 4-7. A hacksaw can be used to notch AC for stripping the armor.

- **Aviation or tin snips.** The first step is to bend the cable sharply where the armor will be cut. This will cause the interlocked armor to disengage. Twist the armor to force it to expand and expose one twist in the armor. Place one jaw of the snips under this exposed section and cut the armor. Remove the armor and trim any sharp corners. See **Figure 4-8**.

- **Roto-Split®.** The specific directions will come with the tool when you purchase it, but here are the basic steps. First, place the cable into the channel of the tool. Squeeze the handle to hold the cable in place. Turn the crank until the pressure decreases. Remove the cable from the tool and rotate the armor until it breaks free. See **Figure 4-9**.

After you have stripped the armor from the cable, you must install an *anti-short bushing*. This red, split, plastic sleeve is placed between the wires and the rough edge of the armor. Make sure to place the split of the bushing opposite the armor end for maximum protection. See **Figure 4-10**. This bushing keeps the insulation from rubbing against the sharp edge of the armor. The bushing must be in place to pass an electrical inspection. Purchase plenty of bushings when buying armored cable.

When the anti-short bushing is in place, bend the bonding strip back over the bushing and wrap the cable as shown. Add the connector and tighten the setscrew or the clamp. The setscrew type of connector cannot be used on aluminum AC. See **Figure 4-11**.

Code Alert

Section 320.100

  Construction. Type AC cable shall have an armor of flexible metal tape and shall have an internal bonding strip of copper or aluminum in intimate contact with the armor for its entire length.

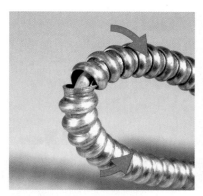

Bend the cable
sharply to buckle it.

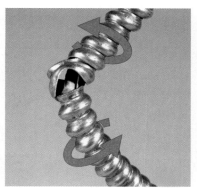

Twist against
the direction
of the spiral.

Cut the armor and
trim off sharp edges.

Figure 4-8. Snips may be used to strip the armor from AC.

---

anti-short bushing: A red, split, plastic sleeve placed between the wires and the rough edge of the armor in AC.

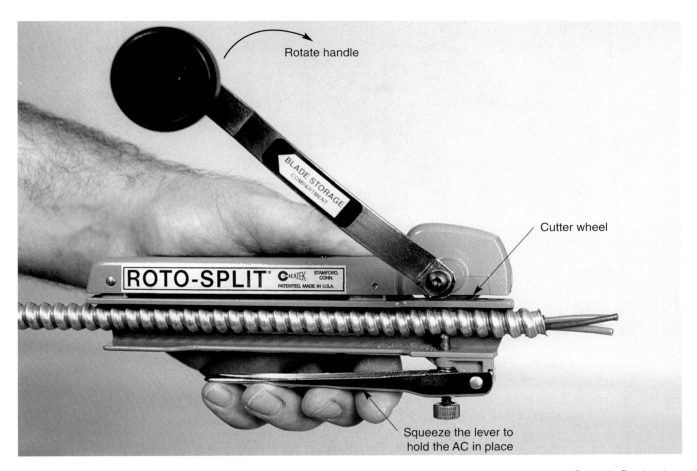

Rotate handle

Cutter wheel

BLADE STORAGE COMPARTMENT

ROTO-SPLIT® SEATEK STAMFORD, CONN. PATENTED. MADE IN U.S.A.

Squeeze the lever to
hold the AC in place

Figure 4-9. A Roto-Split® is a tool that slices the armor so that it can be twisted off the cable. (Seatek Co. Inc.)

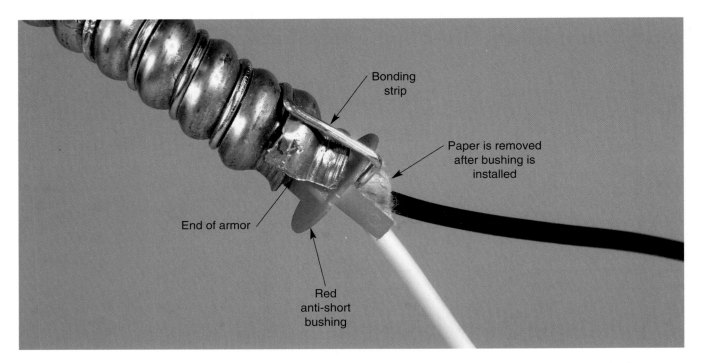

Bonding
strip

Paper is removed
after bushing is
installed

End of armor

Red
anti-short
bushing

Figure 4-10. Always install an anti-short bushing to protect the wires. The tab on the bushing helps the inspector see that it is installed.

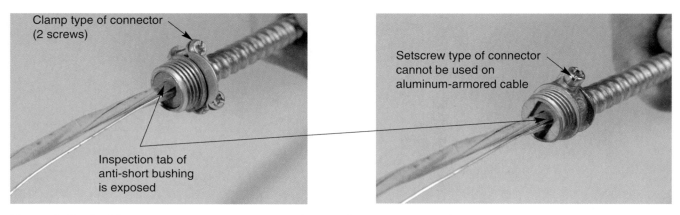

Figure 4-11. A—The setscrew connector cannot be used on aluminum AC. B—The clamping connector can be used on steel or aluminum AC. Always read the cable manufacturer's installation instructions for any restrictions.

Nonmetallic Sheathed Cable

Nonmetallic sheathed cable (NM) has two or more insulated conductors wrapped in a strong plastic or braided outer sheath. Often included is a bare copper ground wire, **Figure 4-12**. NM is the easiest and, in many areas, the most popular system to install. NM is easily cut to length with cable cutters. A cable ripper is used to split the outer jacket from the point where the wires will be exposed to the end of the cable. Place the cutting tooth in the center of the cable about 8″ from the end. Squeeze the ripper closed to pierce

the jacket and pull it to the end of the cable. Use a knife to carefully cut the jacket completely off the cable. See **Figure 4-13**.

History Brief

Romex®

Type NM cable is referred to almost universally as **Romex,** regardless of which company makes the cable. Originally developed by General Cable in Rome, New York, in 1922, NM cable is now made by many different companies.

Nonmetallic Sheathed Cable: Types NM, NMC, and NMS — *Article 334*		
Locations Allowed	**Sizes**	**Maximum Mounting Distance**
Type NM: Normally Dry **Type NMC:** Moist, damp, or corrosive **Type NMS:** Normally Dry	14 AWG through 2 AWG	⟶ ⟵12″ ——— 4 1/2′ ⟶

nonmetallic sheathed cable (NM): A cable with 2 or more conductors and a ground all within an outer jacket, suitable for use in most residential installations except where conduit is required. NM is called Romex in the trade.

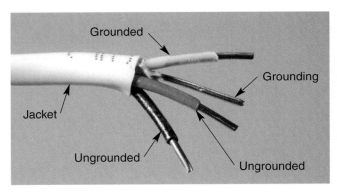

Figure 4-12. This is typical nonmetallic sheathed cable with two current-carrying conductors, a grounded conductor, and a grounding conductor.

Code Alert

Section 300.14

At least 6″ of free conductor, measured from the point in the box where it emerges from its raceway or cable sheath, shall be left at each outlet, junction, and switch point for splices or the connection of luminaires (fixtures) or devices. Where the opening to an outlet, junction, or switch point is less than 8″ in any dimension, each conductor shall be long enough to extend at least 3″ outside the opening.

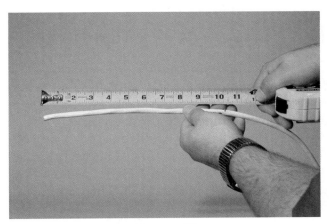

Measure 8″.

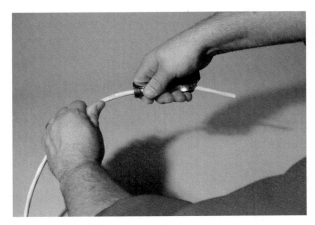

Place the cable ripper over the cable and press the cutter into the jacket.

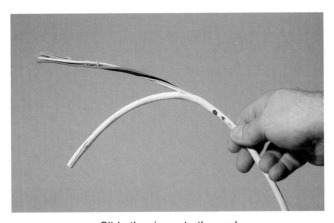

Slide the ripper to the end of the cable. You should be able to peel the jacket off as shown.

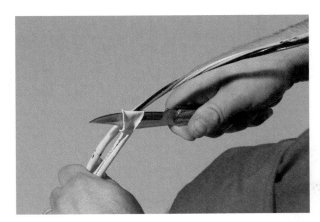

Use a knife to cut the jacket off the cable. Always cut away from your body.

Figure 4-13. Strip off about 8″ of outer covering from NM cable with a special knife or a cable ripper as shown.

Romex: The trade name for NM cable invented by General Cable. It has come into popular use when referring to any brand of NM cable.

Service-Entrance Cable: Types SE and USE — *Article 338*		
Locations Allowed	**Sizes**	**Maximum Mounting Distance**
Dry Wet **USE only:** Underground	14 AWG through 2000 kcmil	

Service-Entrance Cable

Service-entrance cable (SE) may be a single conductor or a multiconductor assembly with or without an overall covering. It is used to bring electricity into a customer's building from an overhead utility pole. *Underground service-entrance cable (USE)* is used to supply electricity underground.

Stripping the insulation off the conductor is done with an electrician's knife. Cut into the insulation around the circumference of the cable, without nicking the conductor. Cut the insulation lengthwise from the first cut to the end of the cable. Now, peel off the insulation.

Since the conductors in these cables must be large enough to handle the power requirements of an entire building, they may be stiff and difficult to work into position. A cable bender is handy to create small-radius bends in the heavy cable.

Underground Feeder and Branch-Circuit Cable

Underground feeder and branch-circuit cable (UF) is a nonmetallic sheathed cable that is run underground between the service equipment and the final branch circuit overcurrent device. A typical installation would be a branch from the main service panel to a detached garage. Although the materials in UF are designed for underground use, the cutting and stripping procedure is exactly the same as standard NM cable. As with all underground cables and conduit, review the local codes for proper burial depth.

Underground Feeder and Branch-Circuit Cable: Type UF — *Article 340*		
Locations Allowed	**Sizes**	**Maximum Mounting Distance**
Dry Wet Corrosive Underground Direct Burial	14 AWG through 4/0 AWG	N/A

service-entrance cable (SE): The cable used to bring power from the utility pole to the customer's building.

underground service-entrance cable (USE): Service-entrance cable that is approved for direct burial in the ground.

underground feeder and branch-circuit cable (UF): Similar to NM, this cable is suitable for direct burial in the ground. It is used for providing power to detached garages, yard lamps, and outbuildings.

Raceways

Raceways are protective coverings installed on site and used to contain wires. Raceway materials are selected depending on the intended application. Wire size and ampacity, environment, installation conditions (new or remodel), building codes, and cost are all factors that will determine the selection of a raceway. Raceways consist of conduit, boxes, and fittings. *Conduit* is the tubing connecting the boxes together. The wires are pulled from box to box through the conduit. Boxes can be used for either junctions to connect the wires or mounting devices such as lamp fixtures, switches, and outlet receptacles. Fittings are used to connect pieces of conduit together, and connectors are used to connect the conduit to the boxes.

Electrical Metallic Tubing

Electrical metallic tubing (EMT) is called thin-wall conduit. EMT is not designed to be threaded; therefore, it is connected length-to-length or to electrical boxes with suitable compression or setscrew fittings. When installed correctly, EMT is used as an effective grounding conductor. See **Figure 4-14.**

Electrical Metallic Tubing: Type EMT — *Article 358*		
Locations Allowed	**Sizes**	**Maximum Mounting Distance**
Dry	1/2″ through 4″	

Setscrew fitting
(coupling)

Compression fitting
(coupling)

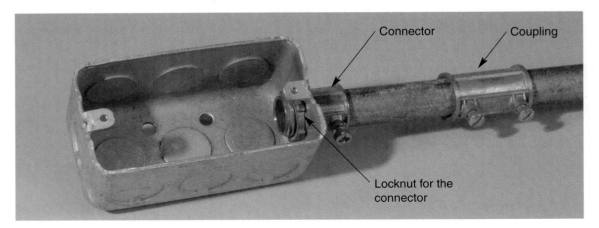

Figure 4-14. These are various types of EMT fittings.

Cutting conduit

The first step when cutting conduit is to secure it in a vise. This will help you make straighter cuts and avoid broken blades. If a vise is not available, brace the conduit against a secure surface such as a wall stud or a sawhorse. A hacksaw is normally used to cut all types of conduit. A reciprocating saw outfitted with a metal-cutting blade is also used to cut conduit. Either saw should be fitted with a blade having 18 to 24 teeth per inch for a clean cut. See **Figure 4-15**.

A square cut can be made with a pipe cutter, although it creates a large burr. Apply a small amount of cutting oil where the cut will be made. Slip the cutter mouth over the conduit and adjust the cutter wheel until the tool is snug. Rotate the cutter around the conduit. If the tool is too difficult to rotate, the wheel is too tight. Adjust the cutter wheel until the tool is firm but not difficult to rotate. Continue to rotate the tool and tighten the cutter slightly after each turn until the conduit is completely cut. See **Figure 4-16**.

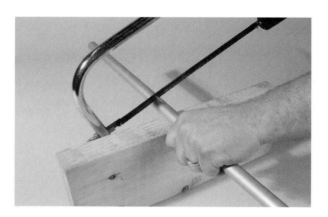

Hacksaw

Reciprocating saw

Figure 4-15. To cut EMT, secure it in a vise or hold it firmly and use a hacksaw, reciprocating saw, or a pipe cutter.

Tighten the pipe cutter
until it is snug.

Rotate the pipe cutter
around the conduit.

Repeat the first two steps
until the conduit breaks.

Figure 4-16. A pipe cutter can be used to cut conduit.

raceways: A system of conduit, boxes, and fittings through which wires are pulled.

conduit: Round hollow tubing that is metal or plastic, rigid or flexible, that is used to protect wires from physical damage.

electrical metallic tubing (EMT): Conduit made of aluminum with relatively thin walls, also called thin-wall conduit. The smaller sizes can be easily bent with a hand tool.

Reaming conduit

The ends of a length of conduit must be smooth to prevent any damage to the wire's insulation. After cutting the conduit, use a reamer, round file, or a deburring tool to remove the burrs. See **Figure 4-17**.

Bending metallic conduit

The purpose of bending conduit is to route it around corners and over obstructions. There are numerous special manufactured fittings available that could be used to achieve similar routing, but field bends are preferred. A *field bend* is a bend that is made on the construction site. This generally saves time and is far more economical than installing fittings.

Most bends in EMT are made with a conduit bender. Always use the correct size bender for the conduit you are bending. This tool is designed to create a bend with the proper bend radius. The *NEC* lists the minimum radius of conduit bends in *Chapter 9, Table 2*.

Typical bends include stub (also known as stub-up), back-to-back, offset, and saddle. The following sections will help you make these fundamental bends. Bending conduit is an important skill you can master with practice.

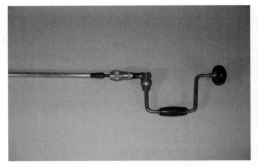
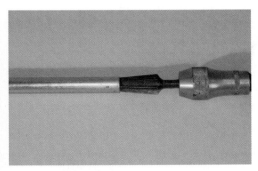

A pipe reamer mounted in a brace will quickly remove any burrs. Insert the reamer into the conduit end and rotate the reamer.

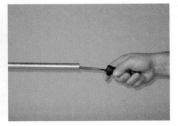

Burrs may be removed with metal files. Use a flat file to remove any burrs on the outside of the conduit. Slide a round file in and out at a slight angle while rotating the conduit.

A deburring tool designed for EMT is available. Insert the tool into the end of the conduit and rotate the tool. The deburring tool will work on 1/2″, 3/4″, and 1″ trade size EMT.

Figure 4-17. The burr created by cutting must be removed, or it may damage the insulation when pulling wires through the conduit.

Stub Bend

A ***stub bend*** is a 90° bend that usually brings a horizontal run of conduit up or down to an outlet box. Practicing this basic bend will help you become familiar with the conduit bender.

1. Measure the height of the total bend. This is typically from the bottom of the horizontal conduit to the bottom of an electrical box.
2. Take this distance and subtract the radius of the conduit bender. The resulting number is the distance to mark from the end of the conduit.
3. Place the conduit in the bender with this mark aligned to the bender's arrow.
4. Press down on the foot pedal of the bender (while guiding the handle to keep the bend perpendicular to the floor) until the stub is 90°.
5. Use a torpedo level to confirm that the stub is vertical. See **Figure 4-18**.

Back-to-Back Bend

A ***back-to-back bend*** produces two 90° bends on a single length of conduit. After the bends are made, both ends of the conduit are pointing in the same direction.

1. Create the first bend by following the stub bend procedure.
2. Mark the distance from the outside of the first bend to the position where the outside of the second bend should be.
3. Place the conduit into the bender so that the star point is aligned with this mark.
4. Create the second bend.
5. Mark the conduit where the height of the second bend should be.
6. Cut the second bend at the mark. This is much more accurate than trying to control the height prior to bending, as you would while making a stub bend. See **Figure 4-19**.

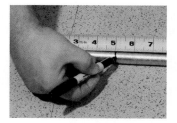

Step 1
Subtract 5″ from the total height of the stub bend. This will be a 10″ stub.

Step 2
Align the arrow of the bender with the mark on the conduit.

Step 3
Apply pressure on the bender with your foot. Your hand should only guide the direction of the bend.

Step 4
Stop bending the conduit when it reaches 90°.

Figure 4-18. Make a stub bend with a conduit bender and check it with a torpedo level.

field bend: A conduit bend that is made in the field (on the work site).

stub bend: A 90° bend used to bring a usually horizontal run of conduit up into a device box. Also called a stub-up bend.

back-to-back bend: Describes two 90° bends in the same piece of conduit, regardless of the distance between bends.

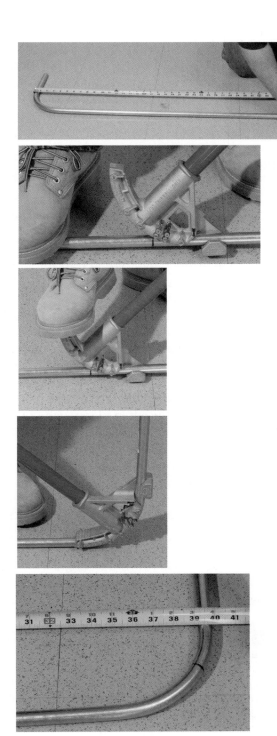

Step 1
The distance between the outside of both bends when completed will be 40″. Measure this distance from the outside of the first bend and mark.

Step 2
Align the star of the bender with the mark on the conduit.

Step 3
Apply pressure on the bender with your foot. Your hand should only guide the direction of the bend.

Step 4
Stop bending the conduit when it reaches 90°.

Step 5
Verify the distance from the outside of both bends.

Figure 4-19. A back-to-back bend is two stub bends on the same length of conduit.

Offset Bend

The *offset bend* is used when the conduit must go around an obstruction or when the plane of the conduit must change slightly. Generally, offsets may be done at almost any angle, but shallow bends (those at smaller angles) reduce the force required to pull the wires through the conduit. Deeper bends will bring the

offset bend: Two bends of equal angle a short distance apart to allow a conduit run to clear an obstacle.

offset closer to the obstruction, but will make it more difficult to pull the wires. See **Figure 4-20**.

Another important factor when bending conduit is shrink. *Shrink* is the amount of shortening in a length of conduit caused by adding one or more bends. See **Figure 4-21**. The angle and the distance between the two bends in an offset will influence the amount of shrink. Fortunately, this amount has been calculated and is available in the offset bend table. If the offset bend is going to occur after the obstruction, shrink does not have to be added into the bend location. Regardless of whether you create the offset before or after an obstruction, the bends will be made on the side of the mark that points away from the obstruction. See **Figure 4-22**. Review the following procedures and compare the steps for creating an offset bend before and after an obstruction. In all types of bends, the amount of shrink depends on the size of the conduit. Shrink varies with bend radius, and each size of conduit must be bent to the proper radius.

Offset Bend before an Obstruction

1. Measure the height of the offset.
2. Measure the distance between the connection point and the offset.
3. Look at the offset bend chart to determine which angle you would like to use for the offset bends.
4. Look at the offset bend chart to determine the shrink and the distance between the bends.
5. Add the shrink amount to the distance you measured in step 2.
6. Place a mark on the conduit at this calculated distance.
7. Take the distance between bends found in step 4 and mark the conduit back from the first mark.
8. Place the conduit bender handle on the floor and secure it in place with your foot.
9. Place the conduit in the bender so that the first mark is aligned with the arrow.
10. Bend the conduit to the angle determined in step 3, being careful not to kink it.

11. Without removing the conduit from the bender, rotate the conduit 180° and slide it until the second mark is aligned with the arrow.
12. Bend the conduit to the angle determined in step 3, being careful not to kink it.

Offset Bend after an Obstruction

1. Measure the height of the offset.
2. Measure the distance between the connection point and the offset.
3. Mark the conduit at this distance.
4. Look at the offset bend chart to determine which angle you would like to use for the offset bends.
5. Look at the offset bend chart to determine the distance between the bends.
6. Take the distance between the bends and mark the conduit forward from the first mark.
7. Place the conduit bender handle on the floor and secure it in place with your foot.
8. Place the conduit in the bender so that the first mark is aligned with the arrow.
9. Bend the conduit to the angle determined in step 4, being careful not to kink it.
10. Without removing the conduit from the bender, rotate the conduit 180° and slide it until the second mark is aligned with the arrow.
11. Bend the conduit to the angle determined in step 4, being careful not to kink it.

Pro Tip

Keeping Bends Aligned

When putting two bends in a piece of conduit, they must be in perfect alignment so the conduit will lay flat against the wall. If one bend veers to the left and the other veers to the right, the conduit will not lay flat. To maintain alignment, find a seam in the concrete or tile floor. Line up the first bend and the bender with the seam to keep the second bend properly aligned.

---

shrink: The effective shortening of the overall length of a piece of conduit due to bending.

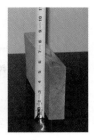

Step 1
Measure the distance to the obstruction.

Step 2
Measure the height of the obstruction.

Step 3
Review the offset bend chart to determine the angle of the offset, the distance between bends, and the shrink.

Step 4
Add the distance to the obstruction and the shrink. Mark this distance from the end of the conduit.

Step 5
The next mark you will make is the distance between bends. Mark this measurement from the first mark back to the starting end of the conduit.

Step 6
Place the conduit in the bender with the first mark aligned with the arrow.

Step 7
Bend the conduit 45°.

Step 8
Without removing the conduit, slide and rotate it 180° so that the second mark is aligned with the arrow.

Step 9
Bend the conduit 45°.

Step 10
Install.

Figure 4-20. An offset bend is used to route the conduit over an obstruction.

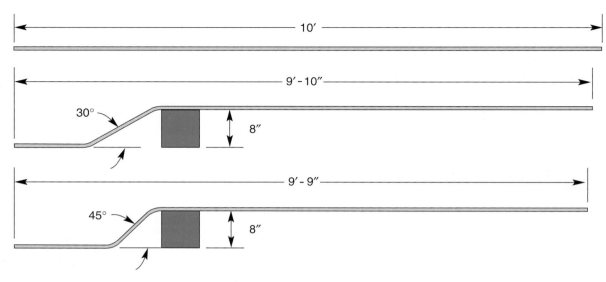

Figure 4-21. How offset angles affect the shrink amount.

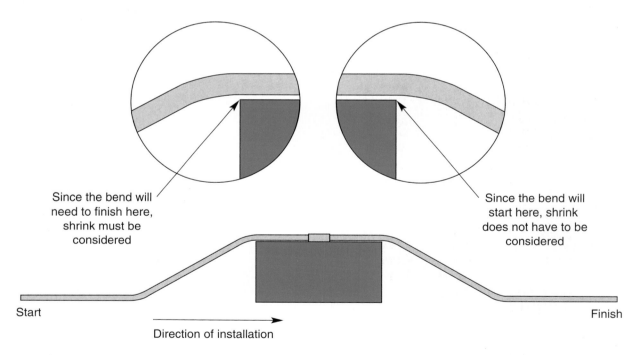

Figure 4-22. If the offset is to occur before the obstruction, shrink will affect the location of the bend. When the offset occurs after the obstruction, shrink will not affect the location of the bend.

Box Offset

An offset that is used frequently is called a **box offset**. The box offset brings the conduit off the mounting surface so that it can fit into a knockout hole of an electrical box. See **Figure 4-23**.

1. Place one mark 2″ and another 8″ away from the end of the conduit.
2. Place the conduit bender handle on the floor and secure it in place with your foot.
3. Place the conduit in the bender so that the 2″ mark is aligned with the arrow.
4. Bend the conduit to a 5° angle.
5. Without removing the conduit from the bender, rotate the conduit 180° and slide it forward (away from you) until the second mark is aligned with the arrow.
6. Bend the conduit (now in the opposite direction) to a 5° angle.

Saddle Bend

The **saddle bend** goes around an obstruction and, unlike the offset bend, returns to the same level after passing the obstruction. The most common saddle consists of one 45° center bend and two 22 1/2° lateral bends. See **Figure 4-24**.

1. Measure the height of the offset and the distance between the connection point and the offset.
2. For every 1″ of obstruction height, move the center mark forward 3/16″ (assuming 1/2″ conduit is being used). Mark the conduit with this new center mark.
3. Lateral marks are placed 2 1/2″ away from the center mark for every 1″ of obstruction height. Place one mark on each side of the center mark.
4. Place the conduit bender handle on the floor and secure it in place with your foot.
5. Place the conduit in the bender so that the center mark is aligned with the rim notch (or the teardrop mark).
6. Bend the conduit to 45°, being careful not to kink it.
7. Without removing the conduit from the bender, rotate the conduit 180° and slide it forward (slide the first bend away from you) until the lateral mark closest to you is aligned with the arrow.
8. Bend the conduit to 22 1/2°.

9. Remove the conduit and flip it end-for-end Place it back in the bender with the second lateral mark closest to you.
10. Line up the second lateral mark with the arrow and bend to 22 1/2°.

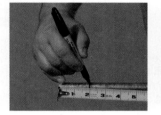

Step 1
Mark the conduit at 2″.

Step 2
Mark the conduit at 8″.

Step 3
Place the 2″ mark at the arrow, and bend the conduit 5°.

Step 4
Place the 8″ mark at the arrow, and rotate the conduit 180°, and bend it 5°.

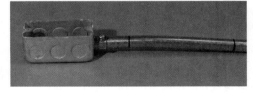

Step 5
Install.

Figure 4-23. A box offset is used to bring the conduit away from the mounting surface so that it fits into a box.

box offset: The small offset, or "kick," needed in the end of a piece of conduit so it can enter a knockout in a junction box or a device box.

saddle bend: Most commonly a bend made of three bends close together used when the conduit has to leave its surface to go over an obstruction then return to the same surface. There is also a four-bend saddle, which consists of two offsets back-to-back or a short distance apart.

Step 1
Measure the height of the obstruction. This duct is 4″ tall.

Step 2
Measure the distance from the conduit to the obstruction. The distance from the center of the duct to the center of the coupling is 20″.

Step 3
Calculate the placement of the center mark. For every 1″ of obstruction height, move the center mark forward 3/16″. The center mark in this example is 20 3/4″ from the end of the conduit.

Step 4
Lateral marks are placed 2 1/2″ away from the center mark for every 1″ of obstruction height. Place one mark on each side of the center mark. This example requires the lateral marks to be 10″ from the center mark.

Step 5
Place the conduit bender handle on the floor and secure it in place with your foot. Place the conduit in the bender so that the center mark is aligned with the rim notch (or the teardrop mark). Bend the conduit to 45°, being careful not to kink it.

Step 6
Without removing the conduit from the bender, rotate the conduit 180° and slide it forward (slide the first bend away from you) until the lateral mark closest to you is aligned with the arrow. Bend the conduit to 22 1/2°.

Step 7
Remove the conduit and flip it end-for-end. Place it back in the bender with the second lateral mark closest to you. Line up the second lateral mark with the arrow and bend the conduit to 22 1/2°.

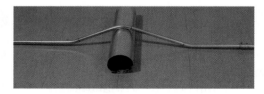

Figure 4-24. The saddle bend consists of one 45° center bend and two 22 1/2° lateral bends.

Electrical Nonmetallic Tubing: Type ENT — *Article 362*		
Locations Allowed	**Sizes**	**Maximum Mounting Distance**
Dry Wet Corrosive	1/2″ through 2″	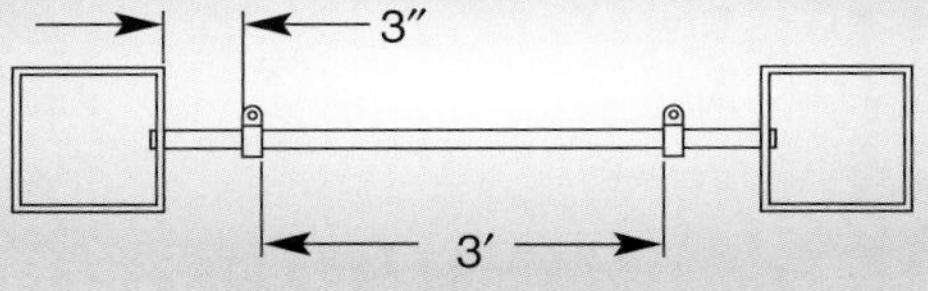 3″ ... 3′

Electrical Nonmetallic Tubing

A newer type of plastic corrugated raceway called *electrical nonmetallic tubing (ENT)* is now recognized for general use by the *NEC* under *Article 362*. It is flame retardant and is resistant to moisture and chemical atmospheres. ENT can be used in almost any building or dwelling regardless of height and can be concealed behind walls, above ceilings, or embedded in concrete. Being lightweight and flexible, ENT is easy to handle. The various connectors, couplings, and fittings are attached with snap-locks or plastic bonding cement. Installation varies and should be performed according to the manufacturer's instructions. See **Figure 4-25**.

There are some restrictions and limitations on the use of ENT:

• Not for hazardous material
• Cannot be left exposed, with some exceptions
• Not to be used as supportive means
• Not permitted for direct burial application
• Not for voltage exceeding 600 V

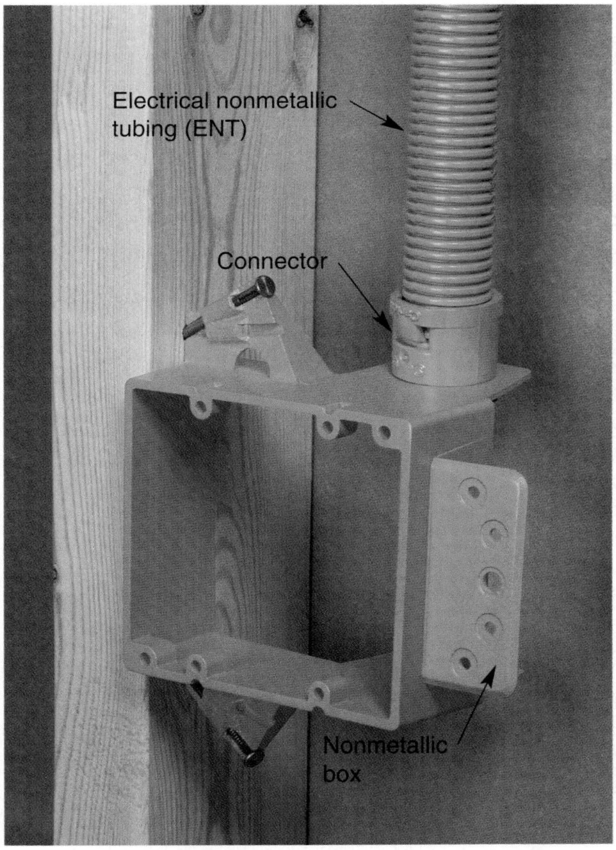

Figure 4-25. Electrical nonmetallic tubing is a corrugated plastic tube that is easy to handle and install. (Carlon, Lamson & Sessions)

electrical nonmetallic tubing (ENT): Plastic corrugated tubing that provides a flexible conduit. Also called smurf because one type of ENT is a bright blue color, like the Smurf cartoon characters.

Rigid Metal Conduit: Type RMC — *Article 344*		
Locations Allowed	**Sizes**	**Maximum Mounting Distance**
Dry Wet Corrosive	1/2" through 6"	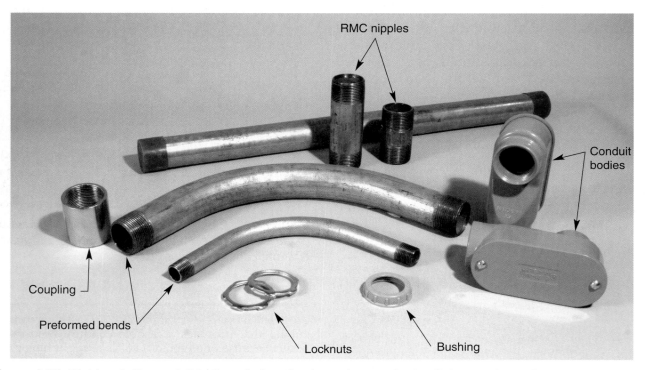

Rigid Metal Conduit

Rigid metal conduit (RMC) is galvanized and somewhat similar to water pipe. It is used for both indoor and outdoor applications. Inside and out, the conduit is smooth and can be cut, threaded, reamed, and bent as necessary for proper installation. To cut RMC with a pipe cutter, follow the cutting procedure demostrated in the previous EMT section RMC must be firmly connected to items such as electrical outlet boxes, and panels with a threaded locknut and bushing. This solid connection is necessary because the conduit itself serves as the grounding conductor. Thus, a separate grounding conductor is not required when using RMC. Fittings should maintain a continuous ground throughout the system. See **Figure 4-26**.

> **Code Alert**
> **Section 344.46**
>
> Where a conduit enters a box, fitting, or other enclosure, a bushing shall be provided to protect the wire from abrasion unless the design of the box, fitting, or enclosure is such as to afford equivalent protection.

Figure 4-26. Rigid metallic conduit is threaded so that it can be attached to fittings and couplings.

rigid metal conduit (RMC): This is the original conduit, used before thin-wall and IMC. RMC, also called *heavy-wall conduit*, has thick walls and provides the greatest protection for the wires inside. Small sizes can be bent by hand with difficulty; larger sizes must be machine-bent.

Threading RMC

1. Clamp the conduit into a pipe vise. See **Figure 4-27**.
2. Place an appropriately sized pipe reamer inside the end of the conduit.
3. Rotate the reamer until all the burrs are removed from the inside of the conduit.
4. Remove any burrs from the outside of the conduit with a file.
5. Mount a threading die inside the head of a hand threader. (See manufacturer's instructions.)
6. Add cutting oil to the end of the conduit to ease the cutting and prevent tool wear.
7. Place the threading die squarely on the end of the conduit.
8. Rotate the hand threader while pressing its head toward the conduit.
9. The die will engage the conduit and start cutting threads.
10. Stop pushing the head and continue rotating the hand threader. Add cutting oil to the conduit after every few rotations.
11. When the end of the conduit is even with the back of the threader die, stop the rotations.
12. Reverse the direction of the hand threader to remove it from the conduit.
13. Clean off the threads with a rag and remove the conduit from the vise.

Manual pipe threader

Powered threading machine

Figure 4-27. Putting threads on RMC requires some specialized tools. (Ridge Tool Co.)

Rigid Nonmetallic Conduit

Rigid nonmetallic conduit (RNC) is constructed of polyvinyl chloride (PVC), a tough, nonconductive plastic. RNC weighs much less than metal conduit and is designed to be used everywhere other types of conduit are used. There are many different fittings available to connect the RNC to metallic and nonmetallic boxes and conduit. See **Figure 4-28**. RNC is only restricted in certain hazardous locations and where it could be physically damaged. Check with your authority having jurisdiction (AHJ) to see if local code permits its use. Do not use to support fixtures.

Rigid Nonmetallic Conduit: Type RNC — *Article 352*		
Locations Allowed	**Sizes**	**Maximum Mounting Distance**
Dry	1/2″	
Wet	through	3′ — See Table 352.30 (B)
Corrosive	6″	

rigid nonmetallic conduit (RNC): A conduit that is constructed of polyvinyl chloride (PVC), a tough, nonconductive plastic.

Figure 4-28. Numerous types of fittings, elbows, and mounting hardware facilitate the installation of rigid nonmetallic conduit. (Kraloy Fittings)

RNC is easily worked. It can be bent using special bending boxes with heating elements to warm the conduit. This allows it to be easily bent by hand, using a simple bending jig. Preformed bends may also be obtained. To connect the RNC and fittings, a special glue and primer are used. See **Figure 4-29**.

Attaching Fittings to RNC

1. Clean the inside of the fitting and the end of the conduit with a rag.
2. Dry-fit the fitting on the conduit to check the final position.
3. Remove the fitting.
4. Apply primer to the inside of the fitting and the outside of the conduit.
5. Apply cement to the primed areas.
6. Push the conduit into the fitting while turning the fitting a quarter turn.
7. Look at the seam for a bead of glue to indicate a proper amount of cement.

Intermediate Metal Conduit

Intermediate metal conduit (IMC) is permitted for use in all atmospheric conditions and in all types of occupancies. Like its counterpart rigid metal conduit, IMC is available in 10′ lengths. Each length or part of a length must be

Step 1
Apply primer to the inside of the fitting.

Step 2
Apply primer to the outside of the conduit.

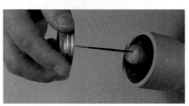

Step 3
Apply glue to the inside of the fitting.

Step 4
Apply glue to the outside of the conduit.

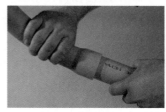

Step 5
Push the conduit into the fitting. Turn the conduit 1/4 turn to spread the glue evenly.

Step 6
This is a cutaway view of the completed assembly.

Figure 4-29. Follow these steps to make the RNC attachments watertight.

properly connected and joined to other lengths or enclosures using the correct fittings. IMC is available with or without threads. Installation is the same as rigid metal conduit.

Intermediate Metal Conduit: Type IMC— *Article 342*		
Locations Allowed	**Sizes**	**Maximum Mounting Distance**
Dry Wet Corrosive	1/2" through 4"	←— 3' ←——— 10' ——→

Intermediate Metal Conduit

The internal diameter (ID) of IMC is larger than that of the equivalent trade size of RMC; therefore, there is more room for pulling wires and calculating conduit fill.

Flexible Metal Conduit (Greenfield)

Flexible metal conduit (FMC) is a spiral-wrapped metal conduit similar to the outer armor in AC. See **Figure 4-30**. FMC is often called *Greenfield* because it was invented by Harry Greenfield. FMC is routed and attached as if it was nonflexible conduit, but it has the advantage of bending without using tools. There are special couplings, locknuts, and bushings for attaching FMC. The wire is fished through as with other conduit.

Code Alert

Section 348.60

Where used to connect equipment where flexibility is required, an equipment grounding conductor shall be installed. Where flexibility is not required, FMC shall be permitted to be used as an equipment grounding conductor when installed in accordance with 250.118(5).

Flexible Metal Conduit: Type FMC— *Article 348*		
Locations Allowed	**Sizes**	**Maximum Mounting Distance**
Dry	1/2" through 4"	←— 12" ←——— 4 1/2' ——→

intermediate metal conduit (IMC): Conduit with walls thicker than EMT but thinner than RMC. Has many advantages over RMC because it is lighter in weight and has more room inside for pulling wires.

flexible metal conduit (FMC): Metal corrugated tubing that provides a flexible conduit.

Greenfield: A common name for FMC.

liquidtight flexible metal conduit (LFMC): This conduit is FMC with a waterproof outer coating and special fittings to maintain its watertight integrity.

Figure 4-30. Flexible metal conduit (Greenfield) is similar to armored cable without the wires.

Frequently, FMC is used with EMT or rigid conduit. It is substituted where bends are needed. Instead of making complicated bends and angles in EMT or rigid conduit, a section of FMC can be inserted. There are special bushings, locknuts, and couplings to connect FMC to the other forms of conduit. There are also length limits as stated in the *NEC*.

Liquidtight Flexible Metal Conduit

Liquidtight flexible metal conduit (LFMC) is similar to FMC, but LFMC is covered with a continuous plastic sheath. This system is easy to install and can be used in most locations.

In residential installations, LFMC is typically used to connect a central air conditioner unit to a disconnect. See **Figure 4-31**. Its extreme flexibility makes LFMC an optimum choice to connect machinery that is portable or may vibrate during normal operation. LFMC is also permitted as a service wiring method up to 6' in length. Use of LFMC requires use of some special fittings and connecting procedures.

Surface-Mount Raceways

Surface-mount raceway is an assembly of two sections, a base and a cover, that is generally rectangular or a flattened oval. Sections are 10' long and range from 3/8" to 3" high and

Liquidtight Flexible Metal Conduit: Type LFMC— *Article 350*		
Locations Allowed	**Sizes**	**Maximum Mounting Distance**
Dry Wet Direct burial (where listed and marked)	1/2" through 4"	12" 4 1/2'

Figure 4-31. This air conditioner is connected to the disconnect with LFMC.

Surface Metal Raceways — *Article 386*		
Locations Allowed	**Sizes**	**Maximum Mounting Distance**
Dry	Unrestricted	See manufacturer's installation instructions

Surface Nonmetallic Raceways — *Article 388*		
Locations Allowed	**Sizes**	**Maximum Mounting Distance**
Dry	Unrestricted	See manufacturer's installation instructions

from 1/2″ to 4″ wide. Surface-mount raceway is constructed of steel, aluminum, or plastic.

Surface-mount raceway is mounted on wall or ceiling surfaces only in dry locations and where it will not be subjected to physical damage. Elbows, connectors, couplings, and boxes are designed to be electrically and mechanically continuous and compatible. It is useful in existing facilities when appearance is important and new wiring cannot be pulled through walls.

Review Questions

Write your answers on a separate sheet of paper. Do not write in this book.

1. Name five key factors that determine the wiring system used for a particular installation.

2. *True or False?* When wiring with rigid metal conduit, a grounding conductor is required.

3. When rigid conduit is cut, it is important that it be _reamed_ to remove any sharp burrs that could damage the _insulation_ during wire installation.

4. A _bushing_ must be added to rigid conduit to protect the wires that are pulled.

5. Intermediate metal conduit is commonly sold in which of the following lengths:
   A. 3′
   B. 6′
   C. 8′
   D. 10′
   E. 12′

6. A _stub_ bend is used when the conduit has to turn 90°.

7. Flexible metal conduit is also called _BX_.

8. LFMC stands for _Liquid Tight Flexible Metal Conduit_.

9. Armored cable is known as AC and _BX_.

10. List three places where armored cable cannot be used. _Commercial garages, Hoistways, elevators, Theatres_

11. *True or False?* Electrical metallic tubing cannot be used as an equipment ground.

12. Which article of the *NEC* outlines rules regarding rigid metal conduit? _344_

13. The following are types of nonmetallic-sheathed cable: NM, NMC, NMS. Where is each used? _Dry   Damp   Dry_

14. Which article of the *NEC* outlines rules regarding rigid nonmetallic conduit? _352_

Know the Code

A copy of the NEC 2005 is required to answer these questions.

1. What is the title of *Section 250.118*?

2. What does the fine print note in *Section 320.10* state?

3. *True or False?* Underground feeder can be used as a service-entrance cable.

This nonmetallic electrical box is large enough for the number of wires required. The electrician has carefully tucked the wires inside to protect them when the sheetrock is installed.

Conductors

Objectives

Information in this chapter will enable you to:

- List the *NEC* rules regarding conductors for general wiring.

- Know the different materials used for conductors.

- Use the *NEC* to select a wire type when given a specific installation.

- Properly specify wire size using the American Wire Gage (AWG) or kcmils.

- Explain the cause of voltage drop.

- Compute voltage drop.

- List the factors that affect conductor ampacity rating.

- Determine the correct conductor size based on the circuit load using the *NEC*.

- Use the *NEC* to adjust conductor ampacity based on ambient temperature and number of conductors.

Technical Terms

Adjustment factor	Circular mil (cmil)
American Wire Gage (AWG)	Correction factor
Ampacity	Derating
	Insulation

Kcmil	Stranded
Marking	Voltage drop
MCM	Wire
Solid	

In this chapter, you will explore the part of the electrical system that provides the pathway and connecting means between the electrical source and the utilization equipment—the conductor. The term *conductor* is used to represent only the metal portion of a wire that conducts electricity. A *wire* is a metal conductor and the insulation that surrounds it. If the conductor normally has no insulation, it too is called a wire. If the conductor is a single solid flexible rod, the wire is called *solid*. If the conductor is made of many thin strands that are bundled together, the wire is called *stranded*. See **Figure 5-1**. Stranded wire is more flexible than solid wire, but the overall diameter of stranded wire is slightly larger.

---

wire: A metal conductor and the insulation that surrounds it. If the conductor normally has no insulation, it too is called a wire.

solid: A conductor that is made of a single, solid, flexible strand.

stranded: A conductor that is made of many thin strands that are bundled together.

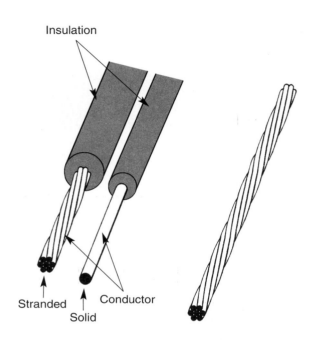

Figure 5-1. The conductor of solid wire is made from a single rod. Stranded wire contains many thin strands to improve flexibility.

Materials

The materials used in wire have a great influence on the wire's ampacity, termination procedure, and environmental restrictions. These factors, along with cost and code limitations, have to be taken into consideration when you are required to select the appropriate wire for a residential installation.

The conductor must be able to transfer the current without generating an unacceptable amount of heat. Resistance to corrosion is another factor that, if not accounted for, can lead to an eroded and unsafe conductor.

The nonconductive component of the wire (insulation) is available in numerous materials. Selecting the right type of insulation may determine if the wiring is a safe and long-lasting installation or one that will cause problems for you and the homeowner.

Conductor

Only copper and aluminum conductors are used in residential wiring. Both materials are flexible, affordable, and have a low resistance to current. Refer to *Articles 300* through *310* in the *National Electrical Code* for general conductor information.

Copper is the most common conductor material for electrical wiring. It is strong and resists oxidation (corrosion). Aluminum also has good conductance. However, it is subject to problems as a result of oxidation and expansion. Proper preparation is critical to the connection's reliability. Before using aluminum you should consult the *NEC*, any local codes, and the manufacturer's installation instructions. Questions about its use should also be directed to the local inspector. Local codes may have restrictions against its use.

Insulation

Conductors that normally carry current must have a nonconductive covering called *insulation*. Acceptable types of insulation are listed in *Table 310.13* of the *NEC*, **Figure 5-2**. The most common insulation used in electrical wiring is plastic or rubber. These materials are excellent nonconductors or insulators of electricity. In addition, these insulated wires are often protected by substances such as braiding, jute, paper, more plastic, or metal. See **Figure 5-3**.

Type THHN is the most common wire used in dry installations, while THHW is frequently used in wet installations. The type of wire used

---

insulation: A nonconductive material that covers a conductor. Various types listed in *Table 310.13* of the *NEC*.

Wire is usually specified by these letters, the gage, and the color of the insulation

Be aware of application restrictions

Table 310.13   *Continued*

Trade Name	Type Letter	Maximum Operating Temperature	Application Provisions	Insulation	Thickness of Insulation			Outer Covering[1]
					AWG or kcmil	mm	mils	
Silicone	SA	90°C 194°F 200°C 392°F	Dry and damp locations For special application[2]	Silicone rubber	14–10 8–2 1–4/0 213–500 501–1000 1001–2000	1.14 1.52 2.03 2.41 2.79 3.18	45 60 80 95 110 125	Glass or other suitable braid material
Thermoset	SIS	90°C 194°F	Switchboard wiring only	Flame-retardant thermoset	14–10 8–2 1–4/0	0.76 1.14 2.41	30 45 95	None
Thermoplastic and fibrous outer braid	TBS	90°C 194°F	Switchboard wiring only	Thermoplastic	14–10 8 6–2 1–4/0	0.76 1.14 1.52 2.03	30 45 60 80	Flame-retardant, nonmetallic covering
Extended polytetra-fluoro-ethylene	TFE	250°C 482°F	Dry locations only. Only for leads within apparatus or within raceways connected to apparatus, or as open wiring (nickel or nickel-coated copper only)	Extruded polytetra-fluoro-ethylene	14–10 8–2 1–4/0	0.51 0.76 1.14	20 30 45	None
Heat-resistant thermoplastic	THHN	90°C 194°F	Dry and damp locations	Flame-retardant, heat-resistant thermoplastic	14–12 10 8–6 4–2 1–4/0 250–500 501–1000	0.38 0.51 0.76 1.02 1.27 1.52 1.78	15 20 30 40 50 60 70	Nylon jacket or equivalent
Moisture- and heat-resistant thermoplastic	THHW	75°C 167°F 90°C 194°F	Wet location Dry location	Flame-retardant, moisture- and heat-resistant thermoplastic	14–10 8 6–2 1–4/0 213–500 501–1000	0.76 1.14 1.52 2.03 2.41 2.79	30 45 60 80 95 110	None
Moisture- and heat-resistant thermoplastic	THW[4]	75°C 167°F 90°C 194°F	Dry and wet locations Special applications within electric discharge lighting equipment. Limited to 1000 open-circuit volts or less. (size 14-8 only as permitted in 410.33)	Flame-retardant, moisture- and heat-resistant thermoplastic	14–10 8 6–2 1–4/0 213–500 501–1000 1001–2000	0.76 1.14 1.52 2.03 2.41 2.79 3.18	30 45 60 80 95 110 125	None
Moisture- and heat-resistant thermoplastic	THWN[4]	75°C 167°F	Dry and wet locations	Flame-retardant, moisture- and heat-resistant	14–12 10 8–6	0.38 0.51 0.76	15 20 30	Nylon jacket or equivalent

Most common in new installations

Always check for footnotes

Figure 5-2. Use the *NEC* to determine the proper wire insulation for the installation. (Reprinted with permission from NFPA 70-2005, *National Electrical Code*®, Copyright © 2004, National Fire Protection Association, Quincy, MA 02169. This reprinted material is not the complete and official position of the NFPA on the referenced subject, which is represented only by the standard in its entirety.)

depends upon the situation and environment where the wire is to be placed. Refer to *Table 310.13* for detailed information regarding insulation properties.

Code Alert

Article 100

Dry location. A location not normally subject to dampness or wetness. A location classified as dry may be temporarily subject to dampness or wetness, as in the case of a building under construction.

Damp location. A location protected from weather and not subject to saturation with water or other liquids but subject to moderate degrees of moisture. Examples of such locations include partially protected locations under canopies, marquees, and roofed porches. Examples of interior locations subject to moderate degrees of moisture include basements, barns, and cold storage warehouses.

Wet location. An installation underground or in concrete slabs or masonry in direct contact with the earth; in locations subject to saturation with water or other liquids, such as vehicle washing areas; and in unprotected locations exposed to weather.

Conductor Size

The size of the conductor to be used depends on the amount of electricity that must be conducted, the length of the conductor, and the type of environment in which the conductor will be used. Our discussion of wire sizes is limited to copper wire. For aluminum, a wire size larger than that for copper is always required. Refer to the *NEC* to determine the correct size.

Caution

Proper Wire Size

Improperly sized wires can be very dangerous. If the wires are too small, they can heat up and destroy the insulation. This could start a fire or create a shock hazard.

Figure 5-4 shows the diameters of copper wires that are typically used in residential wiring. There are two units of measure for designating the sizes of these wires, the first being the *American Wire Gage (AWG)*. The smallest wires in residential wiring are 18 AWG to 1 AWG. The larger the number, the smaller the diameter. After 1 AWG, the wires increase in

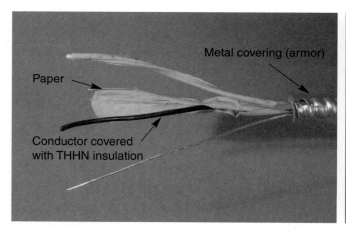
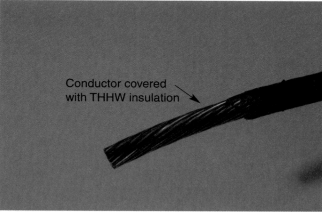

Figure 5-3. Wires may be covered by a variety of materials that protect the conductor and insulation.

American Wire Gage (AWG): A standard unit of measure for wire diameter. The diameter increases as the number decreases for sizes 18 AWG to 1 AWG. Larger wires with an AWG designation range from 1/0 to 4/0 with the diameter increasing as the left digit increases.

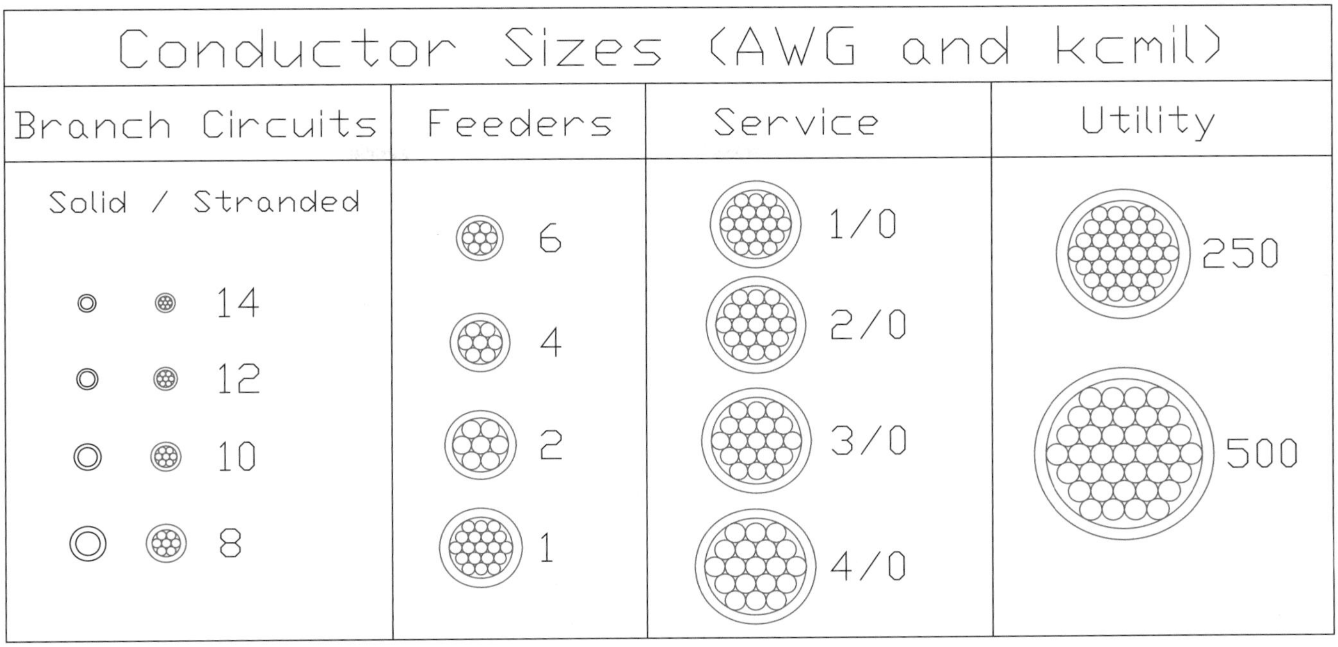

Conductor Sizes (AWG and kcmil)

Branch Circuits	Feeders	Service	Utility
Solid / Stranded	6	1/0	250
14	4	2/0	500
12	2	3/0	
10	1	4/0	
8			

Figure 5-4. These are the sizes of solid and stranded conductors typically used in residential wiring.

size from 1/0 (pronounced "one aught") AWG to 4/0 AWG. Wires larger than 4/0 AWG are designated by the *kcmil* or 1000 cmils (circular mils). A *circular mil (cmil)* is the area of a circle with a diameter of 0.001", **Figure 5-5**.

The reason that larger wires are specified in kcmil instead of diameter is because kcmil is a measurement of the wires cross-sectional area. The area of the wire is important because it is a factor in determining the ampacity of the cable. Doubling the kcmil of a wire roughly doubles its cross-sectional area. See **Figure 5-6**.

History Brief

1,000 – k or M?

When wire sizes are expressed in "thousand circular mils," you may see the designation kcmils or MCM. Why is this? Before the metric system gained popularity, U.S. industry used Roman numerals to express multiples of 1,000. Thus, if a factory wanted to order 5,000 screws, they would put "5M" on the order sheet, since "M" is the Roman numeral for 1,000. If they needed 5 million screws, they might put "5MM." Cable sizes above 4/0 were designated the same way. *"MCM"* stands for "thousand circular mils." So 500 MCM cable is 500 thousand circular mils. Using the metric system, this is expressed as 500 kcmils. Today, both systems of marking cable sizes are in use.

Most branch circuit wires range from 14 AWG to 10 AWG, with 12 AWG being the most common. You may have to use up to 4/0 AWG cables for service entrance wiring. Residential work rarely requires cables larger than 4/0 AWG.

Caution

Stripping Tools and Stranded Conductors

The overall diameter of a stranded conductor is larger than the diameter of a solid conductor of the same nominal size, **Figure 5-7**. Stripping tools that are designed for solid wire cannot be used on stranded wire because the tool will cut too deep and may nick the conductor. Many stripping tools have two wire-size markings for each notch. For example, a notch that is marked to strip a 14 AWG stranded wire is also marked to strip a 12 AWG solid wire.

Selecting the proper wire size is important because it affects voltage drop and ampacity. Voltage drop along the wires may reduce the performance of the electrical equipment.

kcmil: One thousand circular mils; a standard unit of measure for the cross-section of very large conductors.

circular mil (cmil): The area of a circle with a diameter of 0.001" (one mil).

MCM: Abbreviation for "thousand circular mils," from the use of Roman numeral "M" for "thousand."

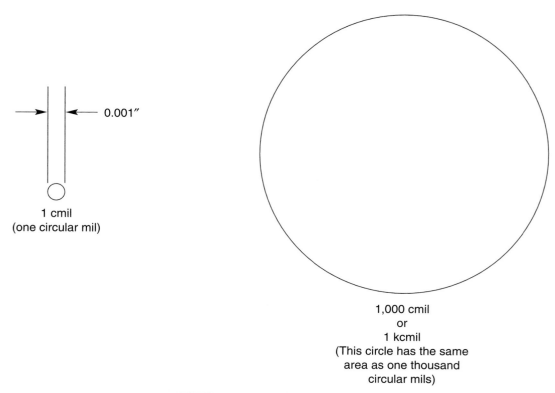

Figure 5-5. A circle with an area of 1 cmil is the base unit for specifying larger wires. A 1 kcmil wire has the same area as 1,000 cmil circles.

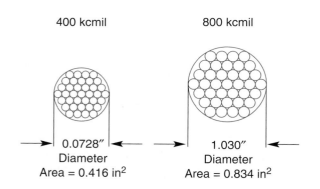

Figure 5-6. Notice that the area of the wire's cross-section increases proportionately as the kcmil designation increases. The diameter, however, increases only slightly.

Voltage Drop

Voltage drop is the loss of electrical pressure (voltage) along a length of a conductor caused by the resistance of the conductor. Resistance increases with longer wires, smaller diameter wires, and temperature increases of the wires. On installations of great length, the voltage drop may be so excessive that a larger diameter wire is needed to compensate.

To compute voltage drop in a single-phase, two- or three-wire system, use the following equation:

$$V_D = \frac{2 \times L \times R \times I}{1000}$$

Where V_D = voltage drop in volts
L = length of conductor in feet
R = resistance of conductor in ohms/1000 ft, from *NEC Chapter 9, Table 8*
I = current in amps

voltage drop: The loss of electrical pressure (voltage) along a length of conductor caused by the resistance of the conductor.

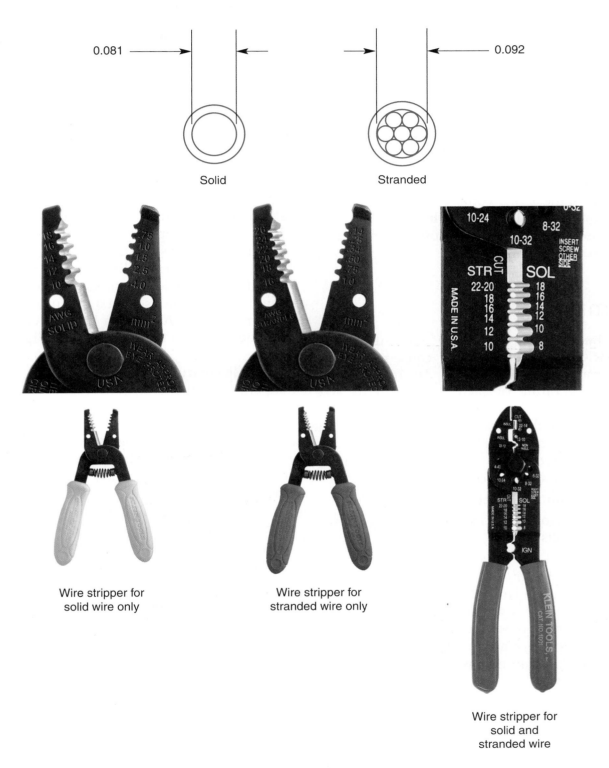

Figure 5-7. Stranded wire has a larger diameter than solid wire. This is why you should use the correct wire strippers for each type of wire.

For example, the voltage drop of 50' of 10 AWG coated copper conductors carrying 30 A would be:

$$V_D = \frac{2 \times L \times R \times I}{1000}$$

$$= \frac{2 \times 50 \times 1.26 \times 30}{1000}$$

$$= 3.78 \text{ volts (approx. 3.1 percent of 120 volts)}$$

Thus, the actual voltage at the device is 120 − 3.78, or roughly 116.22 V. In this respect, not only is wire size (cross section) important, but wire length is as well.

Ampacity

Ampacity is the safe current-carrying capacity of a wire and its consequent heat-dissipation ability. *Table 310.16* lists the ampacity rating of each standard wire size. See **Figure 5-8**. You can select a wire size from this table if the wire will be installed in the following conditions:

- Not more than three current-carrying conductors in a raceway or cable
- Maximum ambient temperature of 86°F
- Conductors with a rating of 0 through 2000 volts

To select the proper size conductor, you will have to know the type of conductor that will be used and the required amperage. You will also have to know how many current-carrying conductors will be adjacent and the maximum ambient temperature. These last two requirements will be explained after this example.

Selecting conductor size

A utility room in a home that you are wiring needs a 20 A receptacle for the washer and dryer. Conduit will be run from the circuit breaker panel to a box in the utility room, without going through the attic. The conduit will be the equipment ground and contain one current-carrying conductor (hot) and one grounded conductor (neutral). All

---

conductors will be THHN copper. Because this situation meets the three criteria listed above, the conductor size can be picked from *Table 310.16*. It appears that 14 AWG is ample, but there is an asterisk next to the *14* in the table. This asterisk directs you to *Section 240.4(D)* where it is stated that a 14 AWG conductor can be used in a circuit rated for a maximum of 15 A. Thus, a 12 AWG conductor is needed in this utility room. See **Figure 5-9**.

Multiple conductor ampacity adjustment factors

The three conditions in *Table 310.16* are required because the ampacity rating of a conductor will decrease as the temperature of the conductor increases. Having multiple current-carrying conductors in one raceway or cable increases the temperature of those conductors.

What if the conduit in the previous example contains a total of seven current-carrying conductors? Since there are more than three current-carrying conductors in the conduit, an adjustment factor from *Table 310.15(B)(2)(a)* has to be included in the calculation. See **Figure 5-10**. An *adjustment factor* is a percentage that is used to reduce the ampacity of a conductor based on the number of current-carrying conductors in a raceway or cable. This percentage is multiplied by the amperage determined in *Table 310.16*. This adjusted ampacity of the conductor is the maximum allowed. If more amperage is required, a larger conductor will have to be used.

---

ampacity: The safe current-carrying capacity of a conductor.

adjustment factor: A percentage that is used to reduce the ampacity of a conductor based on the number of current-carrying conductors in a raceway or cable.

Read and know these restrictions

Table 310.16 Allowable Ampacities of Insulated Conductors Rated 0 Through 2000 Volts, 60°C Through 90°C (140°F Through 194°F), Not More Than Three Current-Carrying Conductors in Raceway, Cable, or Earth (Directly Buried), Based on Ambient Temperature of 30°C (86°F)

Review this table for conductor applications

Size AWG or kcmil	Temperature Rating of Conductor (See Table 310.13.)						Size AWG or kcmil
	60°C (140°F)	75°C (167°F)	90°C (194°F)	60°C (140°F)	75°C (167°F)	90°C (194°F)	
	Types TW, UF	Types RHW, THHW, THW, THWN, XHHW, USE, ZW	Types TBS, SA, SIS, FEP, FEPB, MI, RHH, RHW-2, THHN, THHW, THW-2, THWN-2, USE-2, XHH, XHHW, XHHW-2, ZW-2	Types TW, UF	Types RHW, THHW, THW, THWN, XHHW, USE	Types TBS, SA, SIS, THHN, THHW, THW-2, THWN-2, RHH, RHW-2, USE-2, XHH, XHHW, XHHW-2, ZW-2	
	COPPER			ALUMINUM OR COPPER-CLAD ALUMINUM			
18	—	—	14	—	—	—	—
16	—	—	18	—	—	—	—
14*	20	20	25	—	—	—	—
12*	25	25	30	20	20	25	12*
10*	30	35	40	25	30	35	10*
8	40	50	55	30	40	45	8
6	55	65	75	40	50	60	6
4	70	85	95	55	65	75	4
3	85	100	110	65	75	85	3
2	95	115	130	75	90	100	2
1	110	130	150	85	100	115	1
1/0	125	150	170	100	120	135	1/0
2/0	145	175	195	115	135	150	2/0
3/0	165	200	225	130	155	175	3/0
4/0	195	230	260	150	180	205	4/0
250	215	255	290	170	205	230	250
300	240	285	320	190	230	255	300
350	260	310	350	210	250	280	350

Use these columns for copper conductors

Figure 5-8. *Table 310.16* of the *Code* lists allowable ampacities of insulated conductors. (Reprinted with permission from NFPA 70-2005, *National Electrical Code®*, Copyright © 2004, National Fire Protection Association, Quincy, MA 02169. This reprinted material is not the complete and official position of the NFPA on the referenced subject, which is represented only by the standard in its entirety.)

For example, a run of conduit to a kitchen will contain seven THHN current-carrying conductors, one for a 50 A oven and six for various 20 A appliances and receptacles. According to *Table 310.16*, the 50 A conductor should be 8 AWG and the 20 A conductors should be 12 AWG.

Referencing *Table 310.15(B)(2)(a)*, the adjustment factor for 7–9 conductors is 70 percent. The 8 AWG conductor is rated for 55 A. Multiply this by 0.70 and the conductor is derated to 38.5 A. *Derating* is the reduction in ampacity after calculating adjustment and correction factors. The circuit requires 50 A and after multiplying by the adjustment factor, the 8 AWG wire is too small. You can select each size above 8 AWG and calculate the ampacity to find an adequate conductor.

In this example, the current-carrying conductor for the range was the only one adjusted. The other current-carrying conductors in the raceway should also be adjusted to ensure a safe system.

derating: The reduction in ampacity of a wire after calculating adjustment and correction factors.

the conductors it prov ~~shall be equal to or greater than~~ the rating of the overcurrent device defined in 240.6.

(D) Small Conductors. Unless specifically permitted in 240.4(E) or 240.4(G), the overcurrent protection shall not exceed 15 amperes for 14 AWG, 20 amperes for 12 AWG, and 30 amperes for 10 AWG copper; or 15 amperes for 12 AWG and 25 amperes for 10 AWG aluminum and copper-clad aluminum after any correction factors for ambient temperature and number of conductors have been applied.

(E) Tap Conductors. Tap conductors shall be permitted ~~to be protected against overcurrent in accordance with~~

Figure 5-9. Conductors that are 14, 12, and 10 AWG have maximum ampacities designated in *Section 240.4(D)*. (Reprinted with permission from NFPA 70-2005, *National Electrical Code*®, Copyright © 2004, National Fire Protection Association, Quincy, MA 02169. This reprinted material is not the complete and official position of the NFPA on the referenced subject, which is represented only by the standard in its entirety.)

Three Current-Carrying Conductors in a Raceway or Cab

Number of Current-Carrying Conductors	Percent of Values in Table 310.16 through 310.19 as Adjusted for Ambient Temperature if Necessary
4–6	80
7–9	70
10–20	50
21–30	45
31–40	40

Figure 5-10. When more than three current-carrying conductors will be placed in a raceway or cable, refer to *Table 310.15(B)(2)(a)*. (Reprinted with permission from NFPA 70-2005, *National Electrical Code*®, Copyright © 2004, National Fire Protection Association, Quincy, MA 02169. This reprinted material is not the complete and official position of the NFPA on the referenced subject, which is represented only by the standard in its entirety.)

Ambient temperature correction factors

The ambient temperature surrounding the conductors can also have an effect on the ampacity of the conductors. The bottom section of *Table 310.16* contains **correction factors** that change the ampacity of the conductors based on the ambient temperature. See **Figure 5-11**. If the conduit containing seven current-carrying conductors were routed through the attic of the home, a correction factor would have to be applied to find the proper wire size. Depending on the home's location, attics may reach temperatures of 120°F or higher—far above the 86°F that is allowed in *Table 310.16*.

In the previous example, the current-carrying conductor for the 50 A oven was required to have an ampacity of 71.4 A to handle the 70 percent adjustment factor. Since the conductors will now pass through an attic with an ambient temperature of 125°F, the ampacity will have to be divided by a correction factor to figure the new requirement. Based on the bottom of *Table 310.16*, the correction factor is 0.76. The ampacity of 71.4 A divided by the 0.76 correction factor to reach 93.9 A. According to *Table 310.16*, a 4 AWG conductor, with a standard rating of 95 A, is required to deliver 50 A.

Conductor Identification

The *NEC* requires that all electrical conductors be suitably identified. This is accomplished by having the proper marking and insulation coloring. These two methods ensure the correct wire type is used during the installation and that the conductor's purpose can be identified at any time.

correction factor: A percentage that is used to reduce the ampacity of a conductor based on the ambient temperature.

CORRECTION FACTORS

Ambient Temp. (°C)	For ambient temperatures other than 30°C (86°F), multiply the allowable ampacities shown above by the appropriate factor shown below.						Ambient Temp. (°F)
21–25	1.08	1.05	1.04	1.08	1.05	1.04	70–77
26–30	1.00	1.00	1.00	1.00	1.00	1.00	78–86
31–35	0.91	0.94	0.96	0.91	0.94	0.96	87–95
36–40	0.82	0.88	0.91	0.82	0.88	0.91	96–104
41–45	0.71	0.82	0.87	0.71	0.82	0.87	105–113
46–50	0.58	0.75	0.82	0.58	0.75	0.82	114–122

Figure 5-11. The maximum ambient temperature may change a conductor's ampacity. The correction factors will tell you how much it changes. (Reprinted with permission from NFPA 70-2005, *National Electrical Code®*, Copyright © 2004, National Fire Protection Association, Quincy, MA 02169. This reprinted material is not the complete and official position of the NFPA on the referenced subject, which is represented only by the standard in its entirety.)

Marking

The *marking* is a series of letters, words, trademarks, and numbers that reveals key characteristics about a wire. The marking is usually printed on the outer insulation or jacket of the wire or cable. If the surface is too small to be marked, the required information must appear on an attached tag, a reel, or the smallest unit carton. As shown in **Figure 5-12**, the required marking indicates:

- Voltage rating (maximum).
- Insulation type, indicated by a letter or letters designated in the *Code*.
- The manufacturer's name, trademark, or other distinctive marking by which the organization responsible for the product can be readily identified.
- AWG size or circular mil area.

Cables must also have markings that indicate:

- Number of conductors.
- Outer finish or covering.

Insulation Color

Color-coding of insulation on conductors is also used to identify wiring, **Figure 5-13**. Although the *NEC* does not specify the colors of ungrounded conductors, the preferred colors are black, red, blue, and yellow.

Code Alert

Article 100

Grounded. Connected to earth or to some conducting body that serves in place of the earth.

Grounded Conductor. A system or circuit conductor that is intentionally grounded.

Grounding Conductor. A conductor used to connect equipment or the grounded circuit of a wiring system to a grounding electrode or electrodes.

marking: A series of letters, words, trademarks, and numbers that reveals key characteristics about a wire.

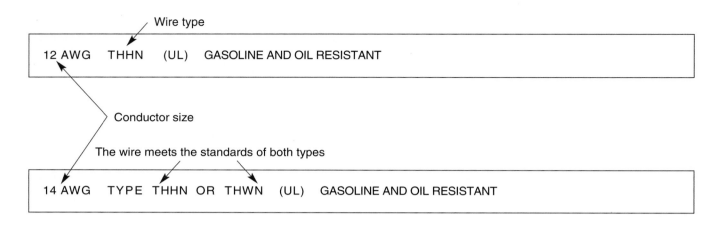

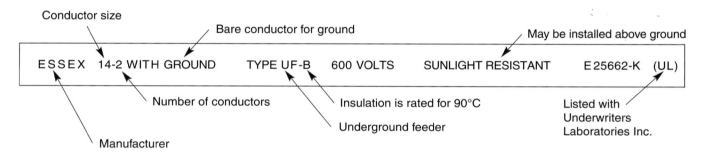

Figure 5-12. Cables and wires are marked on the covering for identification.

Conductor Type	Insulation Color
Ungrounded conductor	Black, red, blue, and yellow are typically used. But, any color other than those listed below can be used to identify an ungrounded conductor.
Grounded conductor, 6 AWG or smaller	Three continuous white stripes along its entire length on other than green insulation.
Grounded conductor, larger than 6 AWG	White Gray Three continuous white stripes along its entire length on other than green insulation.
Grounding conductor, 6 AWG or smaller	Bare Green Green with yellow stripes.
Grounding conductor, larger than 6 AWG	Green

Figure 5-13. Color-coding of insulation indicates the purpose of the conductor.

Review Questions

Write your answers on a separate sheet of paper.
Do not write in this book.

1. What are the two most common metals used in conductors? *Copper aluminum*

2. Conductors that normally carry current must have a nonconductive covering called *insulation*

3. As the AWG number becomes smaller, the wire size becomes *larger* .

4. *True or False?* The notch on a wire stripper that is marked 14 AWG can be used on 14 AWG stranded and solid wire.

5. What is the loss of electrical pressure along a length of a conductor called?

    A. voltage drop.
    B. voltage.
    C. ampacity.
    D. resistance.

6. *True or False?* Between two 12 AWG wires, voltage drop is greater on the longer wire.

7. Determine the voltage drop of 100′ of 12 AWG copper conductors carrying 20 A.

8. *True or False?* Derating is the reduction in ampacity after calculating adjustment and correction factors.

9. What size UF wire is needed to feed a 100 A service subpanel installed in a detached garage? Assume the garage temperature will reach 90°F during the summer.

10. The *Marking* is a series of letters, words, trademarks, and numbers that reveals key characteristics about a wire.

Know the Code

A copy of the NEC 2005 is required to answer these questions.

1. What is the correction factor of a THHN wire in conduit running through an attic with a maximum ambient temperature of 150°F?

2. What type of conductors are referred to in *Section 310.15(B)(4)(a)?*

3. *Section 310.8(B)* describes which locations?

4. List the three types of conductors as defined in *Article 100.*

2 × 100 × ___ × 20

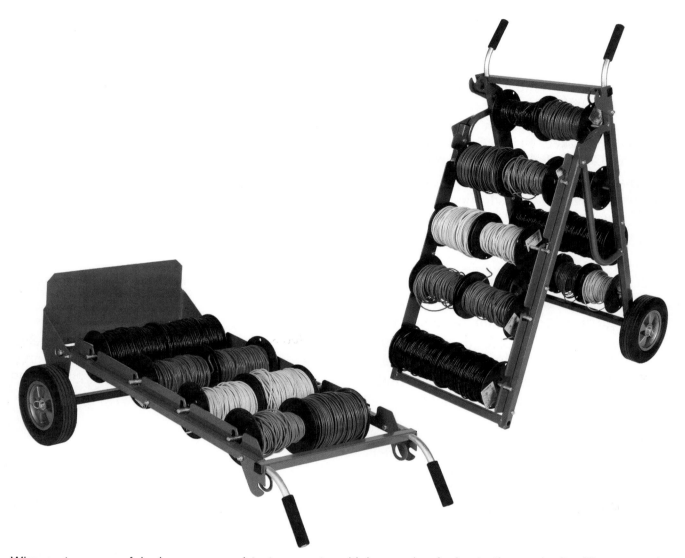

Wire carts are useful when you need to transport multiple spools of wire to the work site. The carts also prevent the wire from twisting by allowing the spools to spin as the wire is removed. Another benefit is the ability to pull more than one wire at a time.
(Sumner Manufacturing Co., Inc.)

Boxes, Fittings, and Covers

Objectives

Information in this chapter will enable you to:

- List the four common box shapes.

- Discuss the four types of boxes.

- Know how to remove a knockout and a pryout.

- Discuss box mounting systems.

- Describe connectors that fasten wiring to boxes.

- Explain the purpose of ground clips and grounding bushings.

- Explain the meaning of fill allotment.

- Identify the purpose of a plaster ring.

Technical Terms

Box cover
Bridge
Ceiling box
Clamps
Conduit bodies
Connectors
Electrical box
Extension rings
Faceplate
Fill allotment
Fittings
Ganging boxes
Ground clip
Handy box
Junction box
Knockout
Nonmetallic boxes
Plaster ring
Pryout
Pull box
Switch box
Wall box

Boxes and covers house and protect electrical conductors and electrical devices. Fittings make tight connections between boxes and conduit or cable assemblies.

Boxes

An *electrical box* is a metallic or nonmetallic enclosure that is used to mount devices, conduit, and cables; <u>protect people from electrical shock</u>; <u>keep exposed conductors away from combustible building materials</u>; and <u>act as a pull point</u>. The *NEC* requires the housing of all joints, connections, and splices inside approved enclosures, **Figure 6-1.** See *Article 314* of the *NEC* for more information.

electrical box: A metallic or nonmetallic container used to mount devices, conduit, and cables; protect people from electrical shock; keep exposed conductors away from combustible building materials; and act as a pull point.

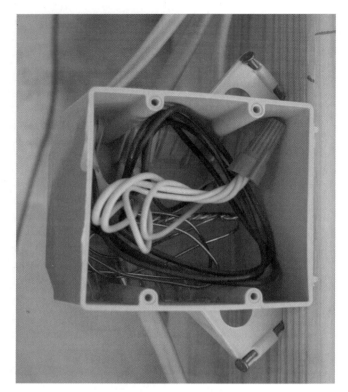

Figure 6-1. Boxes are required by the *NEC* to enclose wire splices and connections to fixtures or devices.

Box Construction

Boxes may be constructed of metal, plastic, or fiberglass. They must be strong enough to withstand the stresses put on them during installation and resist bending or twisting while holding fixtures or devices. Install boxes according to the manufacturer's recommendations and use only *labeled* boxes, covers, and fittings to ensure the integrity and safety of the installation.

Box Shapes

There are four common box shapes in use today, **Figure 6-2**:

- Square
- Octagonal (eight-sided)
- Rectangular
- Round

Each of these shapes is made in various widths, depths, and knockout arrangements. Metal boxes usually have a galvanized (zinc

Square

Octagonal

Rectangular

Round

Figure 6-2. There are four basic shapes for electrical boxes.

coating) finish. They can be used for either concealed or open work where there are no explosive or flammable vapors present. Special types are made weathertight for outdoor applications. Others are produced specifically for hazardous locations.

Types and Uses

Boxes are organized by usage:

- **Ceiling box.** A *ceiling box* is intended for supporting ceiling fixtures and is usually mounted on or between beams or joists. A ceiling box may be square, octagonal, or round. See **Figure 6-3**.

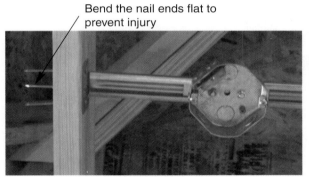

Bend the nail ends flat to prevent injury

Close up view of joist attachment

Ceiling box mounted between joists

Ceiling box mounted to a joist

Figure 6-3. The type of ceiling box and mounting method are dependent on the type of fixture that will be attached.

- **Wall box.** A *wall box* is an electrical box for housing typically a switch or a receptacle. Wall boxes may also be used to contain splices and mount fixtures such as wall sconces. Usually rectangular, a wall box is generally mounted on a stud in a frame building or set into a masonry wall. A special wall box for masonry is shown in **Figure 6-4**. Some wall boxes that are designed only for switches are called *switch boxes*.

- **Junction or pull box.** Unlike the previous boxes, this electrical box is designated by its use and not its location. A *junction box* is installed wherever conductor splices or pulls must be made in a location not appropriate for a switch, receptacle, or fixture. A fish tape is inserted into the conduit at the box and wires are pulled as the fish tape is retrieved. Any type or shape of box is suitable as a pull box. In most cases, splices can be planned where an electrical device will also be installed. It is less expensive to install a larger box for the device and the extra wiring than it is to install a separate box for the junction. Electrical boxes used strictly as junction boxes must be covered with a solid plate of the same material as the box. See **Figure 6-5**.

- **Handy box.** When surface mounting is necessary, a *handy box* is used. These boxes are seamless and have rounded corners to prevent injuries. One is shown in **Figure 6-6**.

---

ceiling box: An electrical box intended for supporting ceiling fixtures.

wall box: An electrical box for housing a switch or a receptacle.

switch box: A wall box designed for switches only.

junction box: An electrical box that is installed wherever conductor splices or pulls must be made in a conduit run that is not appropriate for a switch, receptacle, or fixture. Also called a junction box.

handy box: A seamless electrical box that has rounded corners and is designed to be surface mounted.

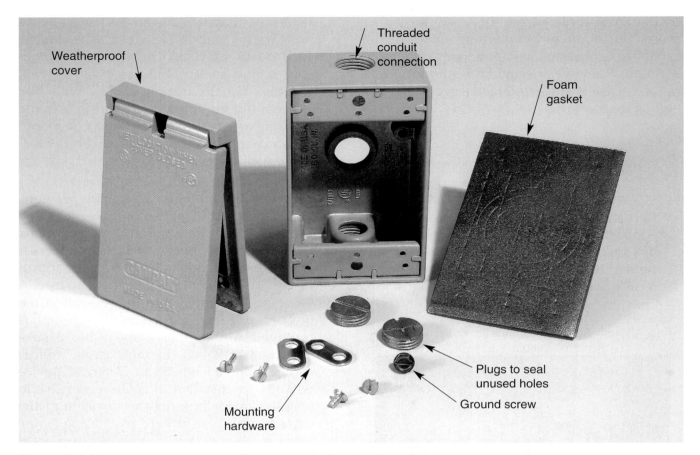

Figure 6-4. Masonry boxes are typically packaged with pieces to aid in mounting.

Cover plate for a square box

Figure 6-5. When a box is used to house only a splice, it must be closed with a solid cover of the same material. The box must also be accessible.

Knockouts and Pryouts

One of the features of electrical boxes that makes them extremely flexible is the number of knockouts each has. A *knockout* is a weakened area on the box that is designed to be easily removed so wires can be brought into the box. A box with many knockouts can have the wires enter the box from many different directions. Some ceiling boxes also contain a knockout that can be removed to receive a lug for mounting fixtures.

There are two basic styles of knockouts. One is made by scoring the material in such a way that only a thin layer holds the knockout in place. A sharp tap with a hammer will remove it or break it loose so it can be grasped and removed with pliers. This type is typical in nonmetallic boxes. In the second type, the knockout is cut all the way through except for one or two spots. These knockouts can be removed by tapping the knockout with a punch until it is bent far enough

Figure 6-6. A handy box, also known as a utility box, is designed for surface mounting. The corners are rounded for better appearance and to avoid injury.

to be grabbed with pliers. A couple of twists with the pliers will break the knockout free.

Some knockouts called *pryouts* have a slot for inserting the blade of a screwdriver. A sharp twist of the screwdriver will remove the pryout. See **Figure 6-7**.

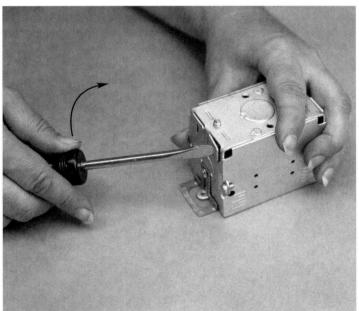

Prying out with a twist of a screwdriver blade inserted in the slot.

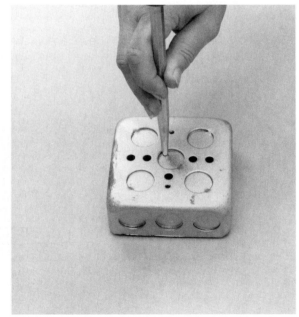

Tapping with a hammer and a punch.

Figure 6-7. Removing a pryout and a knockout.

---

knockout: A weakened area designed to be removed on an electrical box, allowing wires to be brought into the box.

pryout: A knockout removed by inserting the blade of a screwdriver into the pryout's slot.

Any hole created by the removal of a knockout or pryout must be used or the hole will have to be covered. Snap-in seals or special plates are available for covering unused knockout openings, **Figure 6-8**. Refer to *Section 110.12(A)* in the *NEC*.

Ganging Boxes

As shown in **Figure 6-9**, *ganging boxes* is a method of joining small boxes to create one large box that can accommodate multiple devices. To set up a ganged box, remove adjoining sides from two boxes by removing the small screw holding the side plate. Join the boxes and fasten them together by reinstalling the screw.

There are boxes called *multigang boxes* that are designed to handle multiple devices without ganging. It is a good idea to review the electrical plans prior to installation so you know if these special boxes are needed. Multigang boxes are steel or nonmetallic and are not adjustable to other gang sizes. Nonmetallic boxes are one piece and cannot be ganged. **Figure 6-10** shows a variety of metallic and nonmetallic multigang boxes.

Box Mounting Systems

Boxes must be securely fastened to a structural member of the wall, ceiling, or floor of the dwelling. Wall boxes are normally mounted to studs with nails, brackets, or both. There are brackets with built-in fasteners that bite into the wood frame when struck with a hammer. See **Figure 6-11**.

Ceiling boxes are fastened either directly to a joist or to a *bridge*, a wood or metal support that spans two joists. Refer back to Figure 6-3.

Figure 6-8. Knockout seals. These are installed in unused openings of boxes where knockouts have been removed.

These are the two boxes to be joined. Note that in this type, screws and tangs hold the sides together.

Remove one side of each box by loosening the screws.

Join the boxes and tighten the screws over the slotted edge at each end.

Ganging of boxes is completed. The extra sides are discarded.

Figure 6-9. Steps for ganging up two or more single metal electrical boxes.

ganging boxes: A method of joining small boxes to create one large box that can accommodate multiple devices.

bridge: A wood or metal support that spans two joists.

2 gang metal box

4 gang nonmetallic box

Figure 6-10. Various multigang boxes are shown here.

Nonmetallic Boxes

Nonmetallic boxes are either plastic or fiberglass and are particularly popular in areas that allow nonmetallic cable. See **Figure 6-12**. These boxes are rugged, lightweight, and corrosion resistant. Further, their brackets make it easy to position and mount them to wood or metal structural members. Perhaps the greatest

---

nonmetallic box: Electrical boxes that are made from a nonmetallic material such as PVC or fiberglass.

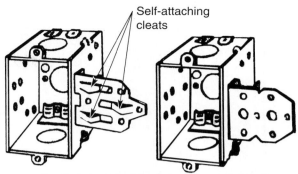

Self-attaching cleats

Bracket designed for mounting on face of stud. Extra length allows offsetting from stud to clear door frame. Type at extreme left has self-attaching cleats.

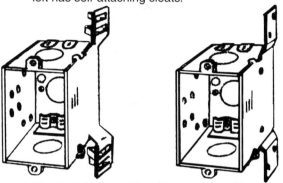

Simple flat bracket for side mounting. Very rigid design, easy to install. Hugs stud.

Bracket angled to fit snugly to face and side of studding. Strongest bracket available when nails driven both ways. Resists strain of marking operations used with drywall.

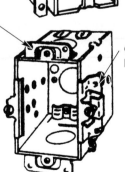

Detachable plaster ears (2)

Grip-tight brackets (2)

Box with detachable plaster ears and griptight brackets are handy for remodeling of old electrical work.

Figure 6-11. Various brackets are designed to make boxes easy to attach to building framing. Some have their own fasteners. (RACO Inc.)

Nails are preset
in the box

The tabs are used
to position the box
for the thickness of
1/2" drywall

Nonmetallic cable

Figure 6-12. Nonmetallic boxes have features that make them easy to position and mount.

advantage is that no grounding connection to the nonmetallic box is needed.

Fittings

Fittings are parts of a wiring system that are designed to interconnect conduit, conductors, or boxes. They include accessories such as box extension rings, clamps, ground clips, connectors, bushings, locknuts, nipples, couplings, conduit bodies, and holding devices. Some of these products are shown in **Figure 6-13**.

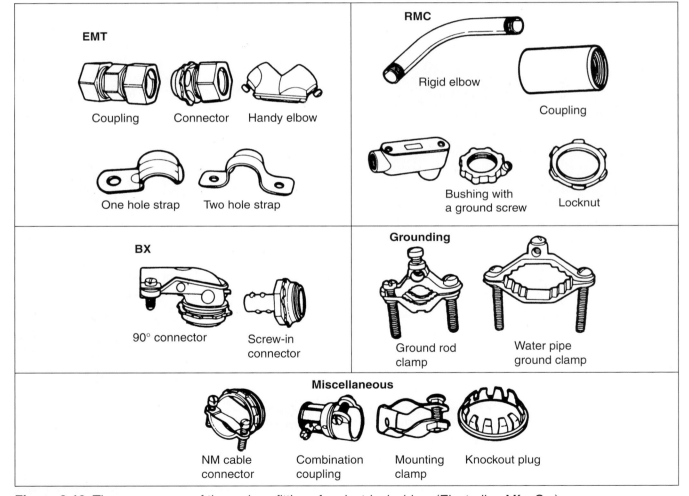

EMT
Coupling   Connector   Handy elbow
One hole strap   Two hole strap

RMC
Rigid elbow   Coupling
Bushing with a ground screw   Locknut

BX
90° connector   Screw-in connector

Grounding
Ground rod clamp   Water pipe ground clamp

Miscellaneous
NM cable connector   Combination coupling   Mounting clamp   Knockout plug

Figure 6-13. These are some of the various fittings for electrical wiring. (Electroline Mfg. Co.)

fittings: Parts of a wiring system designed to interconnect conduit, conductors, or boxes.

Box Extension Rings

Extension rings are actually boxes without bottoms. They are used to:

- Provide additional volume when a box is too crowded with wires
- Bring a box flush to the wall or ceiling surface when the box has been mounted too deep
- Assist in a remodeling job when the electrician wants to add surface wiring to a box that is set in a wall

Flanges on the extension ring provide a method of fastening it to the box. The ring fastens where the cover would go, and the cover fastens to the ring. The ring must be of the same size, shape, and material as the box. See **Figure 6-14**.

Figure 6-14. A box extension ring is attached to an electrical box to add depth and capacity.

Connectors and Clamps

Connectors and *clamps* are fittings that secure cables and conduit to an electrical box. These fittings are available in straight, 45°, and 90° angles. You should select the connector based on the type of conduit or cable that will be attached to the box. EMT can be connected to an electrical box with a setscrew or

Setscrew connector   Clamping connector

Figure 6-15. There are a variety of connectors and clamps to choose from.

extension rings: Boxes without a bottom that are used to provide additional space or bring an existing box flush to a wall or ceiling surface.

connectors: Fittings that secure conduit or the outer covering of armored cable to an electrical box.

clamps: Fittings that secure nonmetallic cable to an electrical box.

compression connector. AC is attached with a setscrew or clamping connector, unless the armor is aluminum. Setscrew connectors are not allowed on aluminum armor. See **Figure 6-15**. Nonmetallic cable is only attached with a clamp to prevent damage to the soft covering. Many boxes have built-in cable clamps to secure armored cable or nonmetallic cable. When such boxes are used, no other connector is needed. See **Figure 6-16**.

Conduit Bodies

Conduit bodies are boxes that are used when a wire pull point is needed. Usually, boxes are used as wire pull points, but conduit bodies are smaller and may be watertight. Conduit bodies come with covers that are removed during the wire pulling. As with boxes, manufacturers must mark bodies for cubic inch capacity. Connections may be threaded, compression, or setscrew. **Figure 6-17** shows a common conduit body.

Ground Clips or Screws

A ground clip or ground screw serves to bond a ground wire to the electrical box. The bonding is required only on metal boxes. The *ground clip* is a spring device that is hooked over the edge of the box and holds the wire in tight electrical contact with the box. The ground screw threads into a tapped hole in the back or the side of the box. **Figure 6-18** shows both types.

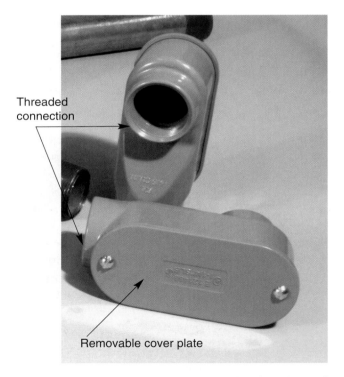

Figure 6-17. These conduit bodies take the place of bends in conduit and allow points for pulling wires.

Threaded connection

Removable cover plate

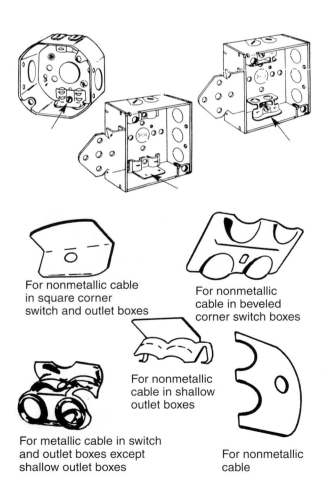

For nonmetallic cable in square corner switch and outlet boxes

For nonmetallic cable in beveled corner switch boxes

For nonmetallic cable in shallow outlet boxes

For metallic cable in switch and outlet boxes except shallow outlet boxes

For nonmetallic cable

Figure 6-16. Some boxes have built-in clamps (arrows) to hold armored cable or nonmetallic cable. (Raco Inc., Electroline Mfg. Co.)

conduit bodies: Boxes designed to be connected to conduit to create a wire pull point.

ground clip: A spring device that is hooked over the edge of a metallic box and holds a grounding wire so that the wire makes electrical contact with the box.

Bushings

The *NEC* requires a grounding bushing wherever conduit enters a nonthreaded opening on a box. The conduit is secured on one side by a locknut and on the other by another locknut and a grounding bushing. Some grounding bushings have a grounding lug where a grounding wire can be attached. **Figure 6-19** shows several types of bushings.

Code Alert

Section 344.46

Bushings. Where a conduit enters a box, fitting, or other enclosure, a bushing shall be provided to protect the wire from abrasion unless the design of the box, fitting, or enclosure is such as to afford equivalent protection.

Fill Allotment

Fill allotment refers to the number of conductors the *NEC* will allow in certain sizes of boxes. *Article 314* of the *NEC* outlines how outlet, switch, and junction boxes are to be used. It is very specific about the number of conductors permitted. **Figure 6-20** summarizes the requirements of *NEC Table 314.16(A)*.

The *NEC* states that electrical boxes shall be of sufficient size to provide free space for all conductors in the box. The table shown in **Figure 6-21** is used to determine correct box size. This table applies where no fittings, devices, or grounding wires are in the box. Additional space allotment must be made when such items are installed.

Items other than conductors (clamps, hickeys, devices, ground wires) are given space in the box equivalent to a certain number of conductors. Internal clamps, no matter how many, are counted as one conductor. A hickey or fixture stud counts as one conductor. Ground wires, no matter how many, count as one conductor. Each strap or yoke with a device (switch or receptacle) counts as two conductors. Clamps that are external to the box (only the

---

fill allotment: The number of conductors the *NEC* will allow in certain sizes of boxes.

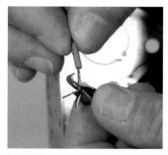

Insert the ground wire into the ground clip.

Use a screwdriver to push the clip on the edge of the box.

The ground wire is folded over the edge of the box and held securely by the ground clip.

Secure a ground wire to the box with this ground screw.

Figure 6-18. A ground clip or a ground screw may be used to connect the ground wire to a box.

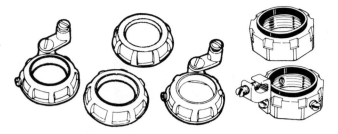

Figure 6-19. Bushings are used to ensure good ground between conduit and boxes. Note that some have lugs for attaching a ground wire. (Electroline Mfg. Co.)

Item	Count
4 conductors, 12 AWG	4
1 or more clamps	1
1 or more grounding conductors	1
1 mounting strap	2
TOTAL	8

threads extend into the box) are not counted. In boxes with multiple conductor sizes, these items are given space equivalent to the largest conductor size.

Example 1: What size box is needed when there are four 12 AWG conductors, two grounding conductors, cable clamps, and a single duplex receptacle to be installed?

Therefore, we would need a box adequate to house the equivalent of eight 12 AWG conductors. Looking at *Table A* under the 12 AWG conductor column, a 4″ × 1 1/4″ square

Conductor Allotment—Metal Boxes						
Box Size	Type	Wire Size			
		14	12	10	8
4 × 1 1/4	round or octagon	6	5	5	5
4 × 1 1/2	round or octagon	7	6	6	5
4 × 2 1/8	round or octagon	10	9	8	7
4 × 1 1/4	square	9	8	7	6
4 × 1 1/2	square	10	9	8	7
4 × 2 1/8	square	15	13	12	10
4 11/16 × 1 1/4	square	12	11	10	8
4 11/16 × 1 1/2	square	14	13	11	9
4 11/16 × 2 1/8	square	21	18	16	14
3 × 2 × 1 1/2	device	3	3	3	2
3 × 2 × 2	device	5	4	4	3
3 × 2 × 2 1/4	device	5	4	4	3
3 × 2 × 2 1/2	device	6	5	5	4
3 × 2 × 2 3/4	device	7	6	5	4
3 × 2 × 3 1/2	device	9	8	7	6
4 × 2 1/8 × 1 1/2	device	5	4	4	3
4 × 2 1/8 × 1 7/8	device	6	5	5	4
4 × 2 1/8 × 2 1/8	device	7	6	5	4

Figure 6-20. This condensed version of *NEC Table 314.16(A)* lists the number of conductors allowed in a box.

Conductor Box Volume	
Conductor Size (AWG)	**Box Volume (in³)**
18	1.5
16	1.75
14	2
12	2.25
10	2.5
8	3
6	5

Figure 6-21. This table contains the box volume required for various conductor sizes. Refer to *NEC Section 314.16* for more information.

or 3″ × 2″ × 3 1/2″ device box with an 18.0 in³ capacity is indicated.

The same results are achieved by using *Table 314.16(B)*. Each 12 AWG conductor requires 2.25 in³ free space and 8 × 2.25 in³ = 18.0 in³. This would lead us to the same minimum size box.

Example 2: What size box is needed to install <u>two</u> 12 AWG conductors, <u>four</u> 14 AWG conductors, <u>two</u> independently mounted devices, <u>four</u> grounding conductors, and <u>three</u> cable clamps?
From *Table 314.16(B)*:

Two 12 AWG	= 2 × 2.25	= 4.5 in³
Four 14 AWG	= 4 × 2.0	= 8.0 in³
Two yokes	= 4 × 2.25	= 9.0 in³
Three clamps	= 1 × 2.25	= 2.25 in³
Four grounds	= 1 × 2.25	= 2.25 in³

TOTAL = 26.0 in³ box minimum needed

In these examples, we used the volume required for the largest conductor in the box

Code Alert

314.16(B)(5)

When computing a volume allowance for grounding conductors, a single volume allowance in accordance with *Table 314.16(B)* shall be made based on the largest equipment grounding conductor or equipment bonding jumper present in the box.

when calculating the fill volume needed for the grounding conductors. In reality, the grounding conductors are often allowed to be smaller than the conductors, and the volume allowance is based on the largest grounding conductor size rather than the largest conductor size.

Covers

Covers are usually used to close a box after the proper terminations are made. Plaster rings are covers that do not completely close a box. There are covers to be used with switches, receptacles, phone and data outlets, surface-mounted boxes, and ganged boxes. Covers may be plastic, metal, ceramic; plain or ornate; white, black, or any color imaginable. The choice depends on the use, cost, and personal preference of the homeowner.

Covers for Switches and Outlets

All switch boxes and outlet boxes must be covered. No wiring can be left exposed. A *box cover*, or *faceplate*, is a flat metallic or nonmetallic plate that is placed over a mounted switch or outlet, and is large enough to cover the wiring and exposed terminals that are in the box. Because there are different sizes and styles of boxes, there are many different kinds of box covers. **Figure 6-22** shows some of them.

Some covers are designed to have the switch or receptacle mounted to them. If you need to install a switch in a surface-mounted 4 × 4 box, you will have to use one of these covers. Terminate the switch, as usual, and attach the switch to the cover. Now the switch and cover assembly can be mounted on the box.

box cover: A flat metallic or nonmetallic plate that is placed over a mounted switch or outlet, and is large enough to cover the wiring and exposed terminals that are in the box; also called a faceplate.

Plaster Rings

A *plaster ring* is an extension for a recessed electrical box which brings the face edge of the box even with the surface of the wall. It compensates for the thickness of the plaster or drywall so a switch or receptacle is flush with the wall surface when installed. If a square box is used as a junction box and as a location for a single-gang device, a plaster ring can be used to provide a mounting point for the device. **Figure 6-23** shows a single-gang and a double-gang plaster ring. Each plaster ring is stamped with the volume the ring adds when calculating fill allotment.

plaster ring: An extension for a recessed electrical box that brings the face edge of the box even with the surface of the wall.

Double-gang   Single-gang

Figure 6-23. Plaster rings are special fittings designed to adapt a box to certain uses. Without these, switches and outlet receptacles cannot be mounted to a square electrical box.

Figure 6-22. All switch and outlet boxes must have a cover. There are many styles and sizes available.

Raised Covers

If a little extra space is required in a box, a raised cover can be used. Normal covers are flat. Raised covers are about 3/8″ deep. They are stamped with the amount of extra volume they provide. They usually offer about 6.25 in^3 of extra space in a box.

Review Questions

Write your answers on a separate sheet of paper.
Do not write in this book.

1. Why must all joints, connections, and splices be contained in a box? *Protect from elec. shock*

2. List the four shapes of boxes. *Sq., Octag., rect., round*

3. Wall boxes house or support _____ *switch, receptacle*.
   A. switches and receptacles
   B. fixtures
   C. splices
   D. all the above

4. A *handy* box is seamless and has rounded corners.

5. Explain the need for knockouts and pryouts.

6. When boxes are joined together they are said to be *gang boxes*

7. Which of the following are advantages of nonmetallic boxes? (Select correct answer or answers.)
   A. Corrosion resistant.
   B. Lightweight.
   C. Not easily broken, even in extreme cold.
   D. Rugged.   *no grounding of box*
   E. Cable clamps are not required.

8. *Fittings* connect cables to boxes in a wiring system.

9. Connectors are available in (select correct answer or answers):
   A. Straight.
   B. 45° angles.
   C. 90° angles.
   D. 15° angles.

10. *True* or False? The *NEC* requires a grounding bushing wherever conduit enters a nonthreaded opening on a box   *wall box ceiling Box*

11. List the four types of boxes (not shapes) and describe what each is used for.   *Junction Box Handy Box*

12. Describe how boxes can be mounted to building components and to each other.

13. *True or False?* It is acceptable to stuff as many wires as possible into a junction box.

14. *True or False?* A plaster ring is used to keep wet plaster from seeping into an electrical box.

Know the Code

A copy of the NEC 2005 is required to answer these questions.

1. How many 14 AWG conductors will fit in a 3″ × 2″ × 3 1/2″ device box?

2. What are the depth dimension requirements of outlet boxes?

3. What thickness must the metal be that is used to make outlet boxes?

This is a sample of the many nonmetallic products available for residential wiring. The boxes shown are designed to accept nonmetallic cable, electrical nonmetallic tubing, and low voltage wiring. Some of these products have features molded in that eliminate the need for connectors.

Device Wiring

Objectives

Information in this chapter will enable you to:

- Discuss the significance of listing or labeling electrical devices and materials.

- Properly prepare conductors for connection.

- Make safe conductor splices.

- Demonstrate the proper method for attaching conductors to devices and fixtures.

- Ground a receptacle.

- Split-wire a receptacle.

- Mount fixtures.

Technical Terms

Break-off fin
Fixture
Grounding-type duplex receptacle
Pigtail
Receptacle
Splicing
Split-wired receptacle
Wire connector

In the finishing stages of a wiring project, the electrician makes the final connection between conductors and switches, receptacles, fixtures, motors, and other devices. The *NEC*, specifically *Article 110*, specifies requirements for the installation of such materials and equipment.

Wiring Methods and Materials

Details on various wiring methods and materials are presented in the articles of *Chapter 3* of the *NEC*. These articles describe, define, limit, and specify the methods and materials of wiring used in the electrical industry today.

> **Code Alert**
>
> **Articles 110 and 300**
>
> Most code violations are items covered in *Article 110* and *Article 300*. If you become knowledgeable in these areas of the *NEC*, your installations will be less likely to suffer the time-consuming, embarrassing, and costly "red-flagging" during an inspection.

Mechanical Considerations

Proper mechanical installation of electrical equipment is important. Electrical equipment must be securely mounted. Further, all materials and equipment must appear orderly. Conductors and cables must be carefully routed and supported to avoid any damage. Conductors must be properly secured to their termination points. Avoid excessive stress or strain on cables and conductors.

Electrical Connections

When electrical wires are terminated or spliced, a suitable connection must be made. This requires a clean and secure physical contact between conductors or conductors and device terminals. All electrical connections must be made inside an electrical box or enclosure. Connections shall not be made between unlike metals unless the electrical devices are suitable for this purpose and are identified as suitable. Splices and connections must be covered with insulation equal to the insulation on the wires. Proper tools must be used so as not to damage cabling or conductors.

Working Clearances

To ensure accessibility and to maintain, service, or operate electrical equipment, the *NEC* insists the work clearances shall not be less than 30″ wide in front of the equipment. Further, these clearances must not be cluttered with any items, including crates or boxes, or in any way used for storage. Storing items in front of electrical equipment would prevent rapid access in an emergency. See **Figure 7-1**.

Identification for Safety

Major electrical equipment components and the disconnecting means for such devices should be clearly identified. Information on voltage, amperage, and the equipment being controlled should be permanently marked on the disconnect means. Panelboard circuit

Figure 7-1. There is not ample working space in front of this electrical equipment. This area should never be used for storage.

directories must be correctly labeled and located at the panelboard. The intent of this rule is safety. Should a circuit or device need to be de-energized, the marking would allow for rapid action. See **Figure 7-2**.

Pro Tip

Labels for circuit identification

Always carry a permanent marker and a number of self-adhesive labels in your tool pouch. Use these labels to clearly identify each circuit at the panel. The permanent marker may be used to mark directly on the panel's surface or on a label.

Preparation of Conductors

Wires conduct electrical energy. They carry this energy from place to place. In this process, they must connect to each other and terminate at various electrical devices. In order for them to move electrons from one place to another, conductors are insulated to eliminate an incorrect or dangerous flow of electricity. However, where connections are made, insulation must be removed for proper contact.

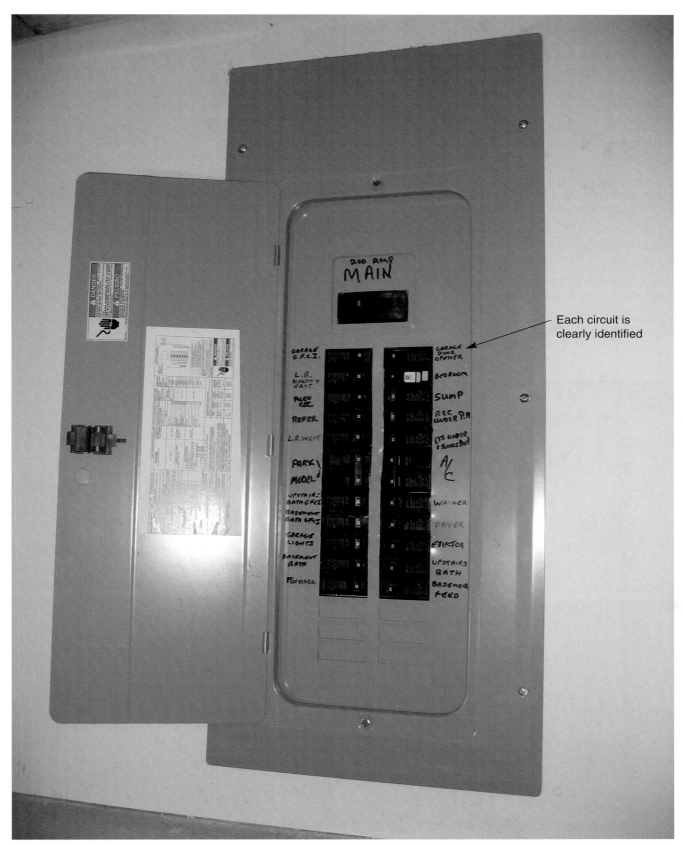

Figure 7-2. Turning the power off to a circuit is much easier when the panel is properly identified. This may save critical time in an emergency.

Stripping Wire

All connections involve stripping some of the insulation from the wire. This exposes the conductor for a good electrical connection. There are many methods for removing the insulation, but the common concern is to not damage either the conductor or the remaining insulation.

Using a stripping knife

You can remove the insulation from a single wire by carefully stripping it away with a sharp pocketknife or electrician's knife designed for this purpose. Do this carefully so that the blade does not nick or cut away any of the conductor. Make sloping cuts toward the wire end and away from your body and hands, as shown in **Figure 7-3**.

Figure 7-3. A large cable is shown for clarity, but the same steps apply when using a knife to strip all sizes of wire.

Do not make a circling cut at a right angle to the insulation. It is almost impossible to control the depth of cut in this way. A nicked conductor will break easily if bent at the point of damage. Also, a nick or groove will reduce the current-carrying ability of the conductor.

After you have cut away the insulation all around the wire using "whittling" cuts, twist the short piece of insulation. As a general rule, a little less than an inch of the conductor should be bared. This allows enough bare wire to make the proper connection. Some electrical devices have gages for determining how much insulation to remove. See **Figure 7-4**.

Using wire strippers

The preferred way to remove insulation is with one of the wire strippers shown in **Figure 7-5**. All of the strippers have circular notches that are sized to cut the insulation without damaging the conductor. Simple wire strippers cut the insulation, but you have to slide the tool to remove the insulation. Automatic wire strippers will cut and separate the insulation with one complete squeeze of the handles.

Attaching Conductors to Device Terminals

When solid conductors are connected to screw type terminals, the ends must be formed in a loop for a proper connection. Use a needle-nose pliers or similar tool to form a curved hook in the conductor as shown in **Figure 7-6**. This must be connected clockwise onto the terminal. When the screw is tightened, the open end of the loop will be pulled inward, making the connection more secure. If the screw turns against the open end of the formed loop (counterclockwise) the loop will tend to open. This results in a poor connection that may be unsafe. See **Figure 7-7**.

Electrical devices are made to connect with wires in many ways:

- A terminal screw is tightened against a loop at the end of the wire

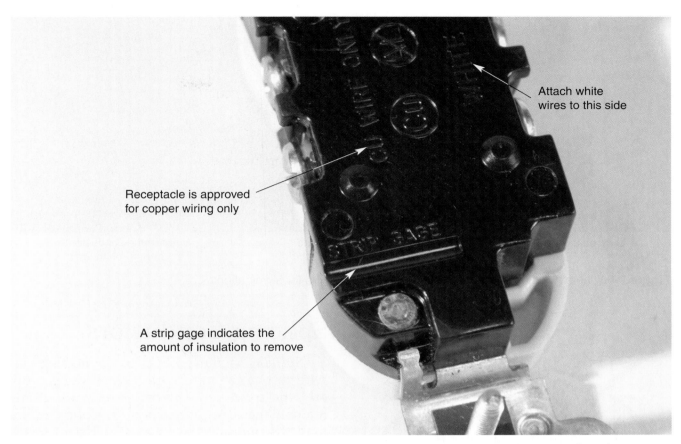

Attach white
wires to this side

Receptacle is approved
for copper wiring only

A strip gage indicates the
amount of insulation to remove

Figure 7-4. Some electrical devices have a strip gage built into them. Place the conductor against the gage to determine how much insulation to cut away.

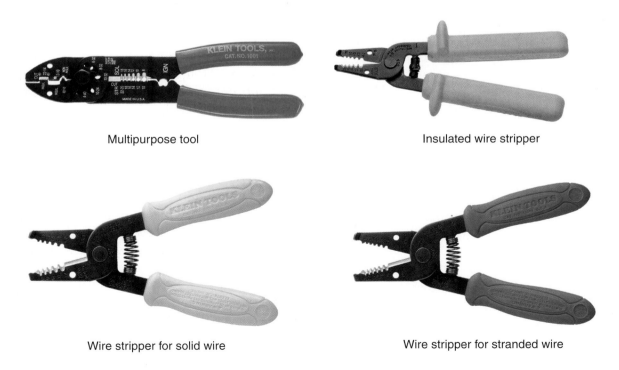

Multipurpose tool

Insulated wire stripper

Wire stripper for solid wire

Wire stripper for stranded wire

Figure 7-5. A wire stripper is the preferred tool for removing insulation quickly and accurately.

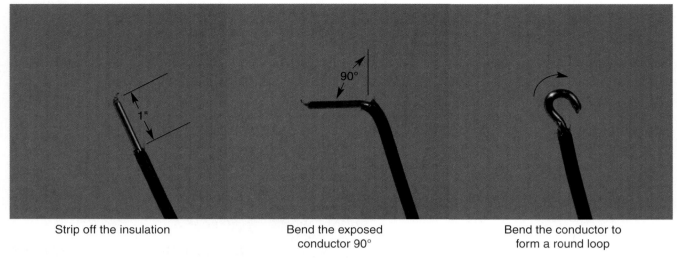

Strip off the insulation   Bend the exposed   Bend the conductor to
                                  conductor 90°   form a round loop

Figure 7-6. Use a needle-nose pliers to form the end of a wire for termination.

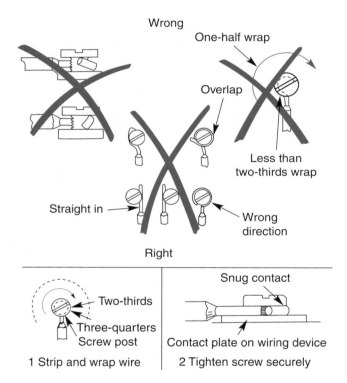

Figure 7-7. Always install the wire loop so that the end is pulled in as the screw is tightened. (GE Wiring Devices Dept.)

- A screw is tightened against a straight section at the end of the wire
- A straight section at the end of the wire is secured by spring tension only

Several of these devices are illustrated in **Figure 7-8**.

Splicing Conductors

Splicing is the process of connecting one wire to one or more wires. When done properly, the splice will last for years without any maintenance. An improper or sloppy splice may disconnect as soon as you let go of the wires or, worse yet, may come apart when the wires are energized. This can cause a fire, injury, or death. The *NEC* requires that all bare wire must be taped with insulation at least equivalent in thickness to that of the conductors' original coverings. See *NEC Section 110.14(B)*. In addition, most connectors are marked CU for copper wire, AL for aluminum wire, or CU/AL for either. This coding must be followed strictly for safety purposes.

Wire connector

A *wire connector* is a device that joins wires together by forcing them into the connector's cone-shaped cavity where a metal coil cuts threads into the wires, **Figure 7-9**. The wires should not be twisted before adding the connector, unless the manufacturer's instructions specify doing so. Some installation

splicing: The process of connecting one wire to one or more wires.

wire connector: A device that joins wires together by forcing them into the connector's cone-shaped cavity where a metal coil cuts threads into the wires.

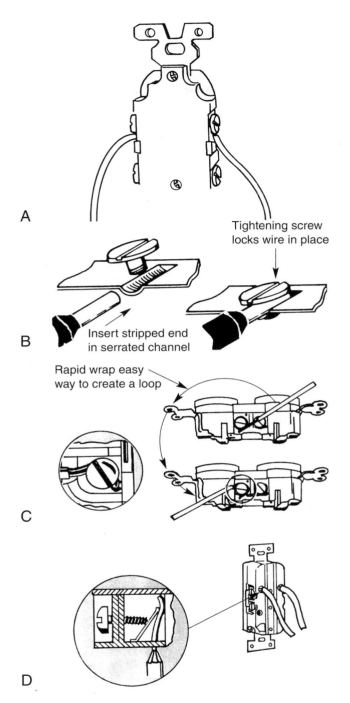

Various wire connectors

Figure 7-9. There are many different manufacturers of wire connectors. Although the colors and shapes may vary, the basic design is very similar.

Figure 7-8. There are several methods of attaching a conductor to a receptacle. A—Receptacle with standard screw-type terminals. B—Pressure type. Bare wire is inserted in groove rather than being wrapped around terminal screw. Tightening screw holds the wire. C—Side-wired receptacle. Conductor is inserted in holes and then snugged around or against screw. (Slater Electric Inc.) D—View of back wired receptacle. Tightening screw wedges wire against spring clip for secure contact.

instructions state that the connector must be tightened enough to cause two twists in the wire. This is a good indicator that the connector is sufficiently tightened. After the wire connector is applied, tug on each wire to verify a complete termination.

To achieve a secure connection using wire connectors, you may want to use one of the special tools that are designed to increase leverage on the connector. There are wrenches, drill-operated sockets, and screwdrivers with a socket in the handle that fit over the wire connectors. See **Figure 7-10**.

Other methods of joining wire

Besides the previously discussed methods of joining wire, joints can be secured with other metal connectors such as bolt-on lugs, split-bolt connectors, compression connectors, and compression lugs, **Figure 7-11**. These types are used to join heavy wires, such as 6 AWG or larger. The compression terminations are made with a special crimping tool. When using any of these items, always wrap all exposed metal with rubber or plastic tape to a thickness equal to the conductor's insulation.

Drill-mounted tools   Hand tools

Figure 7-10. These are a few of the tools available to make the installation of wire connectors easier and quicker.

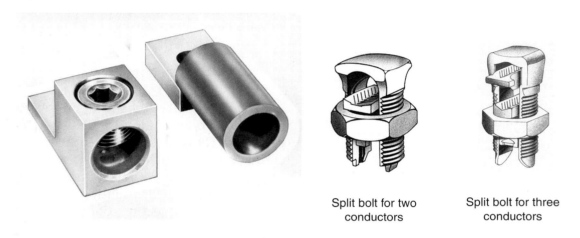

Split bolt for two
conductors

Split bolt for three
conductors

Figure 7-11. Lugs and split-bolt connectors are used on heavy cable.

Wiring Switches, Receptacles, and Fixtures

It is important for you to become familiar with the wiring principles for switches, receptacles, and lamps. This section explains the various devices and how they are to be wired, based on the rules of the *National Electrical Code*.

Switch Wiring

Common switches are generally the same in size and appearance. Their function, of course, is to control the flow of electricity to one or more electrical devices. These devices include receptacles, fixtures, lamps, and heaters.

The most common switches are single-pole, three-way, and four-way. See **Figure 7-12**. A single-pole switch has two terminals and controls a circuit from one position. When the single-pole switch is in the on position, the two terminals are electrically connected.

A three-way switch has three terminals and controls a circuit from two positions. One of the terminals is a color that is different from the other two. This is called the *common* terminal. The other two terminals are called *travelers*.

A four-way switch has four terminals and controls a circuit from three or more positions. All of the terminals of a four-way switch are called *travelers*. Any circuit that is controlled from three or more positions uses a combination of three- and four-way switches.

The switch function, regardless of type, is to interrupt the hot, ungrounded wire only. A

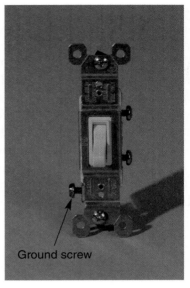
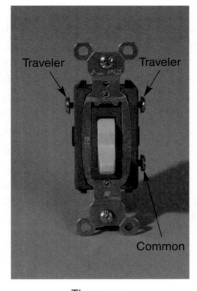

All four terminals are travelers

Traveler   Traveler

Ground screw

Common

Single-pole   Three-way   Four-way

Figure 7-12. These are the most common switches in residential wiring.

switch must never be placed on the grounded neutral (white) wire or the grounding (green) wire. We will explore all types of circuits and how to connect them in Section 3, **Planning**.

Receptacle Wiring

A *receptacle* is a device that is used to transfer electrical energy from conductors to plug-equipped electrical equipment such as lamps, toasters, radios, television sets, blenders, and vacuum cleaners. See **Figure 7-13**. These devices are connected with a flexible service cord that has a two- or three-pronged plug on the end.

receptacle: A device that is used to transfer electrical energy from conductors to plug-equipped electrical equipment.

T-slot allows the insertion of the plug from 20 A equipment

Grounding slot

Non-grounding-type duplex receptacle (can only be used to replace the same type)

20 A duplex grounding-type receptacle

20 A single grounding-type receptacle

Figure 7-13. There are many styles of receptacles available for different purposes.

Makeup of a receptacle

An outlet receptacle's current-carrying and grounding parts are arranged on a yoke or strap that is to be connected to a box with two screws. The parts that conduct current to the appliance cord are enclosed inside nonconducting material. Contacts are made of tough alloys that hold their shape and remain springy, even after years of service. See **Figure 7-14**. When pushed into the slots, the plug's blades push the metal contacts apart. Tension of the metal maintains good electrical connections against the blades. Thus, current may easily flow through the contacts into the plug.

Duplex receptacle

A duplex receptacle accepts two appliance or lamp cord plugs. A **grounding-type duplex receptacle** has five terminals. The two silver-colored screws are for the grounded neutral wires and the two brass-colored screws are for the ungrounded wires. The fifth terminal is a green hex-head screw for connecting the bare or insulated green grounding wire. This terminal is electrically connected to the U-shaped grounding slot on the front of the receptacle. Receptacles with push-in terminals may or may not have screws.

There is a break-off fin between the two neutral terminals and another between the two hot terminals. The **break-off fin** is a removable tab that separates the two outlets on a duplex receptacle. You will learn more about this in the section covering split-circuit wiring.

Receptacles intended for 120 V appliances and other electrical devices have two parallel slots plus the U-shaped ground openings. Other receptacle outlets have different configurations. They are designed to accept only locking plugs or other special plugs. See **Figure 7-15**.

Figure 7-15. Locking-type duplex receptacle. Covers remain closed when the receptacle is not in use. (Harvey Hubbell Inc.)

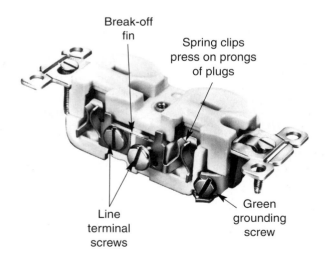

Break-off fin

Spring clips press on prongs of plugs

Line terminal screws

Green grounding screw

Figure 7-14. This is a cutaway of a duplex receptacle. Note that the contacts are shaped like spring clips. They will keep pressure on the blades of the plug to maintain electrical contact. The break-off fin ties the terminals together. (Bryant)

grounding-type duplex receptacle: The most common receptacle, it will accept two grounded plugs at the same time.

break-off fin: A removable tab that separates the two outlets on a duplex receptacle.

Nongrounding receptacle

The nongrounding receptacle shown in Figure 7-13 is installed in older houses that do not have any grounding. You must not install a standard grounding receptacle as a replacement for a nongrounding receptacle unless you are going to upgrade the wiring system to include a grounding path. You should not install a nongrounding receptacle in a house that is grounded. These receptacles do not accept three-pronged plugs, which may limit the receptacle's use to lamps and radios. *Section 406.4(D)(3)* describes the accepted methods of replacing a nongrounding-type receptacle.

Grounding the receptacle

Methods of grounding the receptacles vary. The method selected depends on the type of wiring system and boxes used. In a metal conduit system, the conduit and metal boxes provide a proper equipment ground all the way back to the service entrance panel. In this case, there is no need for a grounding conductor. When the receptacle is attached to the box, grounding contact is made through the receptacle yoke and screws to the box. In addition, local codes may require a bonding jumper to be installed between the receptacle grounding screw and the metal box.

Other wiring systems requiring a ground wire include armored cable (BX), flexible metal conduit (Greenfield), nonmetallic cable, and rigid plastic conduit. There must be continuity from the grounding screw of the receptacle to the ground wire and to the metal box, if present.

Attaching current-carrying conductors

The wiring of receptacles is fairly simple. Connect the white neutral wire to the side of the device that has the silver or light-colored screws. The black or hot wire is then connected to the other side. This side will have brass or dark-colored screws. See **Figure 7-16**.

When more than one receptacle is to be added onto the circuit from the first one, they can be connected as shown in the **Figure 7-17**. It is best to make the connections through a pigtail arrangement. A *pigtail* is a short piece of wire

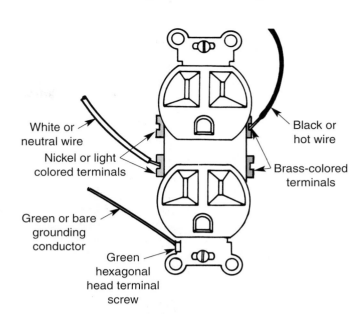

Figure 7-16. Proper termination of a receptacle is critical for a safe installation. (OSHA)

that connects multiple wires to a single termination. The pigtail allows the receptacle to be removed without affecting others in the circuit.

Split-wired receptacles

A *split-wired receptacle* is one in which one of the outlets in a duplex receptacle is controlled by a switch while the other is always energized. One neutral wire can still serve both outlets, however, two hot wires are required. One will go to a switch, the other to the source of current. The break-off fin between the hot-side (dark colored) terminals must be removed. **Figure 7-18** shows a break-off fin as well as a simple schematic of a split-wired receptacle.

Receptacle outlets are manufactured in various configurations. A few of the more common ones are shown in **Figure 7-19**. Other types of locking plug and receptacle configurations are shown in *Appendix C* at the end of this book.

---

pigtail: A short piece of wire that connects multiple wires to a single termination.

split-wired receptacle: A duplex receptacle wired so one of the outlets is controlled by a switch while the other is always energized.

fixture: A permanently mounted lamp, usually attached to a ceiling or a wall.

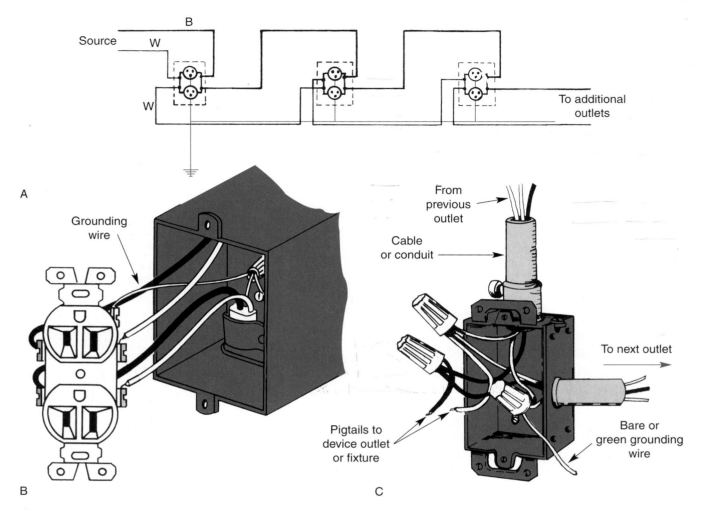

Figure 7-17. Connecting a number of receptacles in a row on the same circuit. A—Schematic shows wiring arrangement. B—One method of running wires to next receptacle. (GE) C—Pigtail method is preferred to direct connection to the other terminals of the receptacle. Grounding wire is required unless metallic conduit is being used.

Fixtures

A *fixture* is a permanently mounted lamp, usually attached to a ceiling or a wall. Fixtures are wired in the same way as outlets. The neutral or white wire of the source is connected to the white or otherwise neutral-indicated wire of the fixture. The black wire (from the source) is connected to the other terminal of the fixture. **Figure 7-20** shows wiring arrangement for a simple pull-chain fixture. This fixture is at the end of a run. A ground wire (bare or green insulated) should be connected between the box and the grounding screw on the fixture. **Figure 7-21** shows the same pull-chain fixture further along a circuit run. Note the symbols and schematics for these hookups.

Figure 7-22 shows a fixture controlled by a switch rather than a pull-chain. If metal conduit is used, the green grounding conductor is not necessary since the conduit itself becomes the grounding means.

Mounting fixtures

It is important to understand how fixtures are safely and securely attached to a wall or ceiling box. Fixtures may be mounted to boxes in a variety of ways depending on the following:

- Type of fixture
- Location of fixture
- Wall or ceiling composition
- Weight of fixture

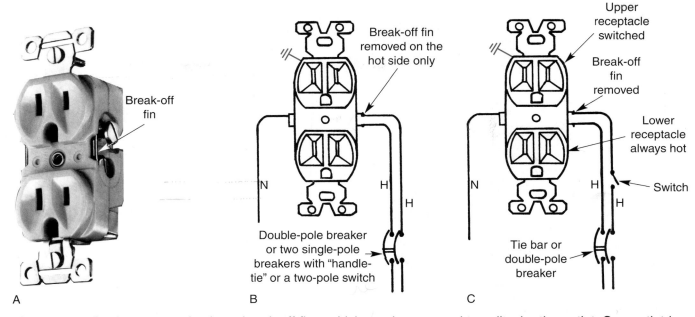

Figure 7-18. Duplex receptacles have break-off fins, which can be removed to split-wire the outlet. One outlet is controlled by a switch while the other is always hot. A—Duplex receptacle showing break-off fin. B—Hot wires of a split-wired receptacle must be on the same double-pole circuit breaker or two single-pole breakers with a tie bar. C—Diagram of a split-wired outlet with one outlet controlled by a switch. (Bryant)

			15 AMPERE		20 AMPERE		30 AMPERE		50 AMPERE	
			RECEPTACLE	PLUG	RECEPTACLE	PLUG	RECEPTACLE	PLUG	RECEPTACLE	PLUG
2-POLE 2-WIRE	125V	1	1-15R	1-15P						
	250V	2		2-15P	2-20R	2-20P	2-30R	2-30P		
	277V	3			(RESERVED FOR FUTURE CONFIGURATIONS)					
	600V	4			(RESERVED FOR FUTURE CONFIGURATIONS)					
2-POLE 3-WIRE GROUNDING	125V	5	5-15R	5-15P	5-20R	5-20P	5-30R	5-30P	5-50R	5-50P
	250V	6	6-15R	6-15P	6-20R	6-20P	6-30R	6-30P	6-50R	6-50P
	277V AC	7	7-15R	7-15P	7-20R	7-20P	7-30R	7-30P	7-50R	7-50P
	347V AC	24	24-15R	24-15P	24-20R	24-20P	24-30R	24-30P	24-50R	24-50P
	480V AC	8			(RESERVED FOR FUTURE CONFIGURATIONS)					
	600V AC	9			(RESERVED FOR FUTURE CONFIGURATIONS)					

Figure 7-19. Receptacles are manufactured for many different purposes. These are a few of the many configurations (shapes to fit special kinds of plugs). (NEMA)

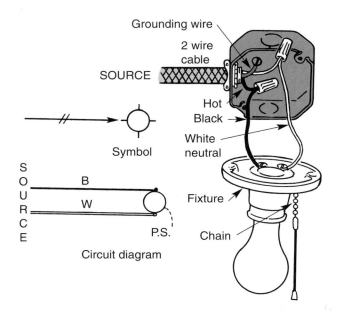

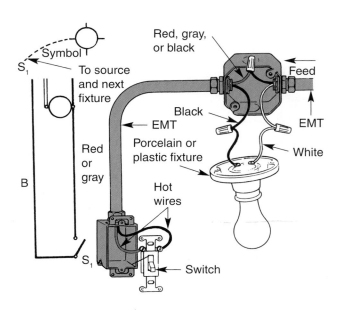

Figure 7-20. Wiring arrangement for a pull chain light fixture. Compare symbol and wiring diagram with actual fixture. Grounding wire (green or bare) must be used with cable conductors.

Figure 7-22. Simple circuit using a switch to control a light. The feed is to a fixture.

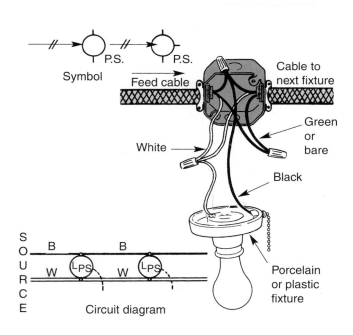

Figure 7-21. Method of wiring a fixture when conductors must go on to another fixture. Note symbol and diagram.

The types of fixtures may range from surface-mount to recessed, chain-supported or not, and small-sized to enormous chandeliers. Regardless of the type, the fixture must be mounted securely to the outlet box.

Where the fixture is to be mounted will affect the manner of supporting it. Usually, wall-mounted fixtures are lightweight and can be directly mounted to the box without special mounting devices. Heavier fixtures require substantial box supports and braces, often referred to as *box hangers*. These attach to joists above the finished ceiling.

If you are mounting a fixture to plaster and lath, wallboard, sheetrock, or any other of the various types of wall finishing, special considerations must be given to the best procedure to follow. Care must be taken to not damage the fixture or finished surface. The illustrations in **Figure 7-23** will serve as a guideline for methods and devices used to mount fixtures. Often, special fittings are supplied with the fixture.

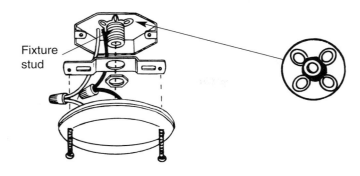

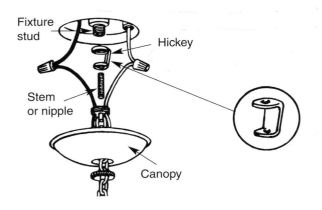

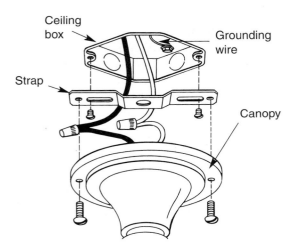

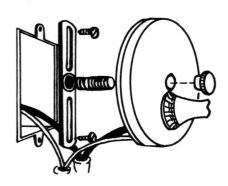

Figure 7-23. Wiring instructions for wiring and hanging ceiling or wall fixtures.

Review Questions

Write your answers on a separate sheet of paper. Do not write in this book.

1. *True or False?* Chapter 3 of the *NEC* goes into considerable detail on methods and materials of wiring used in the electrical industry.

2. Why is storing items in front of electrical equipment against the rules of the *NEC*? *Prevents rapid access*

3. Why should grooving or nicking a wire be avoided during stripping of insulation? *reduce capacity, may break*

4. A splice of two conductors is usually secured with a *wire connector*.

5. When solid conductors are connected to screw type terminals, the ends must be formed in a *loop* for a proper connection.

6. The brass or dark-colored screw on the duplex receptacle is for the _____ conductor.

7. *True or False?* The white, neutral conductor must never be interrupted by a switch.

8. *True or False?* Electrical connections, taps, or splices can be located outside an electrical box or enclosure.

9. Connectors and connecting points are marked CU for *Copper* wire and AL for *Aluminum* wire.

10. Draw a diagram of a circuit containing a split-wired receptacle with one outlet controlled by a switch and the other continuously energized.

11. Explain the purpose of the green hex-head screw on a grounded receptacle.

12. What are the four considerations when deciding on a method to attach a fixture to a box? *Type of fixt. Wall or ceiling location " " composition weight " "*

Know the Code

A copy of the NEC 2005 is required to answer these questions.

1. According to *Article 110.26(A)(2)*, what is the minimum number of degrees that a hinged panel door must be able to swing?

2. What is the maximum size of wire allowed for terminating to a wire-binding screw, according to *Article 110.14(A)*?

3. According to the *NEC*, what is the definition of a device?

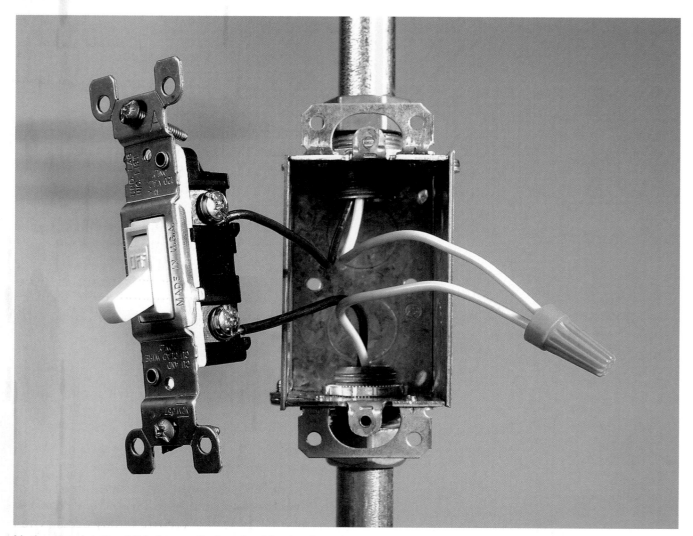

Notice the details of this image that make this simple switch installation professional and safe. The correct amount of insulation has been removed from all of the wires. The conductors in the black wires have been exposed enough for conductivity, but not enough to risk a short circuit. The white wire's insulation ends inside the wire connector without hindering conductivity. Other details include the proper direction of the wire loops on the switch and the orientation of the switch.

Overcurrent Protection

Objectives

Information in this chapter will enable you to:

- Explain the causes of overcurrent.
- List and describe electrical circuit overcurrent protective devices (OCPDs).
- Discuss the rating systems for an OCPD.

Technical Terms

Circuit breaker
Current-limiting fuse
Dual-element fuse
Fuse
Ground fault
Interrupting rating
Overcurrent protection device (OCPD)
Overload
Potential difference
Short circuit
Single-element fuse
Time-delay fuse

All electrical circuits must have an overcurrent protection device installed. An *overcurrent protection device (OCPD)* shuts off power to a circuit when the current in that circuit exceeds the ampacity rating of the OCPD.

Too much current

Causes of Overcurrent

The overcurrent may be a result of overload, short circuit, or ground fault. Any of these conditions, if left unchecked, could cause the conductor to heat up enough to degrade the insulation. This damaged insulation may expose the conductor to other conductors, metallic boxes or conduit, or people.

Overload

An *overload* is a situation where equipment operates beyond the rated ampacity of that equipment or the conductors within the circuit. This type of overcurrent may occur when a motor experiences a large load and draws excessive current for more than a short duration.

---

overcurrent protection device (OCPD): This device shuts off power to a circuit when the current in that circuit exceeds the ampacity rating of the OCPD.

overload: A situation where equipment operates beyond the rated ampacity of that equipment or the conductors within the circuit.

The overload could also be caused by excessive utilization equipment. See **Figure 8-1**. This is a common occurrence during the holidays. Homeowners frequently use outlet adapters to plug multiple decorations into a single outlet. The total amperage requirement of all of these devices may exceed the capability of the circuit.

Short Circuit

A *short circuit* is an overcurrent caused by the connection of an ungrounded conductor to a grounded conductor or the connection of two ungrounded conductors that have a potential difference between them. A *potential difference* occurs when two circuits have differing voltages. The first type of short circuit is more likely in a residential installation.

Ground Fault

A *ground fault* occurs when an ungrounded conductor touches a grounded raceway, box, fitting, or equipment ground conductor. If an energized terminal on a light switch touches the metal box, a ground fault will occur and trip the OCPD. Without the OCPD, a large flow of electricity will cause the conductors to heat up to a dangerous temperature.

Figure 8-1. Too many cords plugged into one circuit may cause an overcurrent. There is also a risk of fire from overheating cords.

Protective Devices

Overcurrent protection devices include fuses and circuit breakers, **Figure 8-2**. Both are manufactured in various shapes and sizes, but all are designed to stop the flow of current should it exceed safe limit. All fuses and breakers are rated in amperes. The rating must not be greater than the overall capacity of the circuit being protected. Never replace fuses or breakers with protective devices of a higher amperage rating than the one intended for that circuit. If you do, you defeat the purpose of the protection device, violate the codes, and create a fire and shock hazard.

Fuses

A *fuse* is a highly reliable and safe overcurrent device. It consists of a resistance-sensitive link encapsulated in a tube. The ends of the fuse are connected to contact terminals of the conductor. The link has very low resistance. If high current occurs, the link melts and opens the circuit.

Two general types of fuses are available: plug and cartridge. Within these two types, fuses can be further classified as the following:

- Single-element or dual-element
- Fast-acting or time-delay
- Renewable or nonrenewable

Single-element fuses have a single element of one or more links that quickly melts in response to an overcurrent. The link melts in approximately three seconds at a 200 percent overload current and usually within thousandths of a

short circuit: An overcurrent caused by the connection of an ungrounded conductor to a grounded conductor or the connection of two ungrounded conductors that have a potential difference between them.

potential difference: The difference in the number of electrons at two points; voltage.

ground fault: A situation when an ungrounded conductor touches a grounded raceway, box, fitting, or equipment ground conductor.

fuse: An overcurrent protection device with a metal conductor that melts during an overcurrent condition.

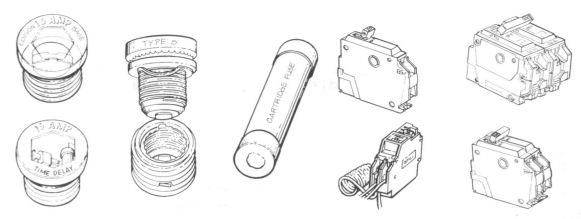

Figure 8-2. These types of fuses and circuit breakers are typical OCPDs in a residential installation. (GE and Leviton Mfg., Inc.)

second (less than a half-cycle of alternating current) for short circuits and ground faults. Since these fuses act rapidly, they are only used in circuits with no transient surge currents or temporary overloads. **Figure 8-3** illustrates a fuse melting and opening a circuit.

A *dual-element fuse* has two elements arranged in series. One element is similar to the element in a single-element fuse, and performs the same function. The other element is designed to allow for low-level overloads of about five times the ampere rating for over ten seconds. This type of fuse is particularly useful in protecting a circuit where temporary surges are normal. A dual-element fuse is shown in **Figure 8-4**. These fuses are marked with a "D."

A time-delay feature is inherent in dual-element fuses. However, not all time-delay fuses are dual-element. The main feature of *time-delay fuses*, regardless of number of elements, is that they allow for momentary overloads.

A *current-limiting fuse* quickly opens the circuit when a specified overcurrent is reached. These fuses clear the circuit of current in a fraction of a second.

How different from regular?

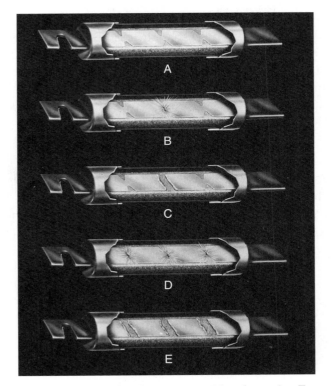

Figure 8-3. A single-element cartridge fuse. A—Fuse in normal working condition. B—An overload melts the fusible element in one location. C—After an overload. D—A short melts all fusible elements. E—After a short circuit. (Bussmann Division of Cooper Industries)

single-element fuse: A fuse that has a single element of one or more links that quickly melts in response to an overcurrent.

dual-element fuse: A fuse that has two elements arranged in series; one element is designed to allow for low-level overloads for a short period of time.

time-delay fuse: A fuse that allows for momentary overloads.

current-limiting fuse: A fuse that quickly opens the circuit when a specified overcurrent is reached.

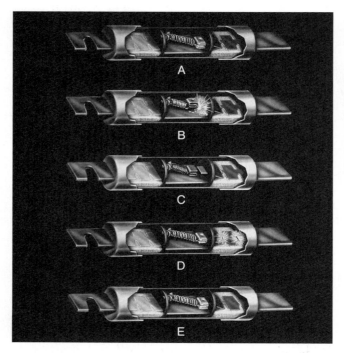

Figure 8-4. A dual-element fuse. A—Normal condition. B—Fuse opens from overload after a brief time delay. C—After an overload. D—Short melts fusible element. E—After a short circuit. (Bussmann Division of Cooper Industries)

Figure 8-5. Type S plug fuses (left) have a thinner stem than Edison-base type fuses (right).

Plug fuses

Plug fuses are available in two varieties: Edison-base and Type S, **Figure 8-5**. Plug fuses have a maximum rating of 30 amps. Fuses rated as 15 amps or less have a hexagonal window, while higher-rated fuses have a circular window, **Figure 8-6**.

Figure 8-6. Fuses rated for 15 amps or less have a hexagonal window.

Plug fuses are limited by the following voltage restrictions:
* Maximum 125 volts between conductors
* Maximum 150 volts between ungrounded conductors and the ground in grounded-neutral systems

Edison-base fuses are interchangeable; fuses of greater current rating can be used in circuits of lesser capacities. This potentially dangerous oversizing problem is eliminated by using a Type S fuse, which uses a screwshell adapter. Type S fuses must be used on all new installations and for replacement installations. There are three classifications of Type S fuses with specific adapters based on their ampere ratings: 0–15 amps, 16–20 amps, and 21–30 amps.

> **Caution**
> **Edison-Base Plug Fuses**
>
> Edison-base plug fuses have no inherent limit to the use of higher ampacities. For example, nothing prevents a 30-amp fuse from being installed in a 15-amp circuit. Using a fuse with an ampere rating higher than that of the circuit is a fire hazard.

Cartridge fuses

Cartridge fuses are used in fused systems over 120 volts or 30 amps. There are two types of cartridge fuse connections: ferrule type and knife-blade type. See **Figure 8-7**.

- **Class H.** These fuses can be renewable or nonrenewable. The nonrenewable types can be time-delay. They have a low interrupting rating of only 10,000 amperes and are not current-limiting. The low interrupting rating restricts their use in new construction.

- **Class J.** Class J fuses are nonrenewable and current limiting with an interrupting rating of 200,000 amperes. They are smaller than Class H fuses and are not interchangeable with any other class. They are rated for 600 volts and up to 600 amperes. These fuses have no time delay. A new "cube" style of Class J fuses is also available, **Figure 8-8**.

- **Class R.** These are nonrenewable, current-limiting fuses with an interrupting rating of 200,000 amperes. These fuses have a rejection feature so no other type of fuse can be installed in the same fuseholder. They may be used as replacements for Class H fuses and are rated for 250 volts and 600 volts and up to 600 amperes.

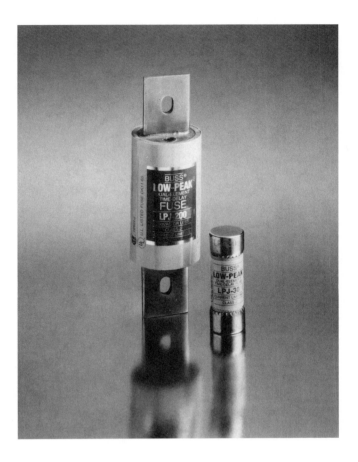

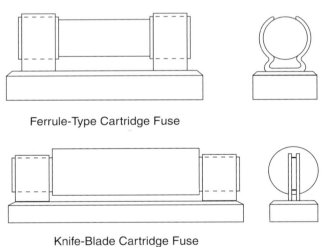

Ferrule-Type Cartridge Fuse

Knife-Blade Cartridge Fuse

Figure 8-7. Knife-blade and ferrule-type cartridge fuses. (Bussmann Division of Cooper Industries)

Underwriters Laboratories classifies different types of cartridge fuses. Most types have unique dimensions. This prevents one class from being replaced by another class in a circuit. Some of the most common types include the following:

Figure 8-8. The CUBEFuse™ is a Class J fuse. It is more compact than other similar fuses. (Bussmann Division of Cooper Industries)

- **Class T.** A nonrenewable, current-limiting fuse with an interrupting rating of 200,000 amperes. There is no time delay with Class T fuses. They are not interchangeable with any other fuse and are rated at 300 volts and 600 volts and up to 1200 amperes.

Procedure for finding the overcurrent source

Before installing the new fuse, there are some steps that should be taken. See **Figure 8-9**.

1. Examine the fuse's window. A clouded window indicates that there was a short circuit or a ground fault. Either condition causes the conductor to rapidly vaporize. An overload will melt the conductor at a much slower rate. You should see a clearer window and less damage to the conductor.

2. Look for the source of the overcurrent condition. If you suspect a short circuit or ground fault, examine the switches and receptacles on that circuit. You may see a black charred area if the short occurred at a device.

3. If the fuse indicates an overload, look for outlets with multiple appliances, overworked motors, or plugged-in machines with an ampacity higher than the circuit's ampacity. If the first condition is the cause, place the higher wattage appliances on separate circuits. Any overworked motors, especially furnace blower motors, may need to be repaired or replaced. Machines with excessive ampacity should be easy to find.

Circuit Breakers

A *circuit breaker* is defined in *NEC Article 100* as "a device designed to open and close a circuit by nonautomatic means and to open the circuit automatically on a predetermined overcurrent without injury to itself when properly applied within its rating." See **Figure 8-10**.

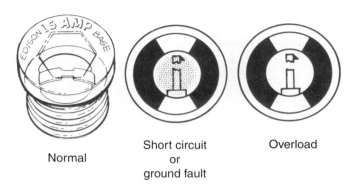

Normal   Short circuit or ground fault   Overload

Figure 8-9. The pattern of a blown fuse can help you identify the cause. (GE Wiring Devices Dept.)

Circuit breaker types

A single-pole breaker serves a 120-volt circuit. A double-pole breaker serves a 240-volt circuit. Typically these breakers are plugged or bolted into the service panel and connected to the ungrounded wire of the particular circuit they are to protect. The neutral conductor of each circuit is not connected to the breaker, but fastens directly to the neutral, grounded bus bar. The amperage rating of each circuit breaker must be matched to the circuit it protects. Information regarding finding the circuit's ampacity is found in Chapter 5, **Conductors**.

Protective Device Rating

Protective devices (fuses or circuit breakers) must be adequate to withstand overcurrents, particularly those created by short circuits. Each device has an *interrupting rating*, which is the maximum amount of current that the OCPD

---

circuit breaker: A resettable device that is designed to open a circuit automatically when a specified ampacity is exceeded.

interrupting rating: This is the maximum ampacity at which an overcurrent protection device will operate without any damage.

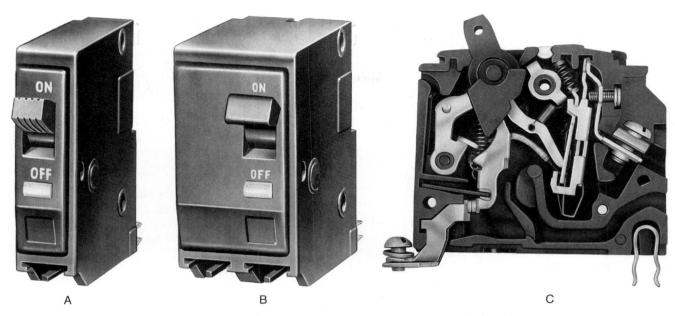

Figure 8-10. Circuit breakers are resettable OCPDs. (Square D Co.)

will reliably function. The interrupting ratings of most circuit breakers range from 10,000 to 20,000 A. Fuse ratings are generally around 200,000 A. See **Figure 8-11**. Naturally, this is much larger than the normal current rating of the fuse or breaker. Normal rating is the current the OCPD is designed to carry under normal operating conditions. All overcurrent protective devices are labeled as to their normal current rating and maximum or interrupting rating. Guides for properly sizing fuses are found in *Article 240* of the *NEC*.

Review Questions

Write your answers on a separate sheet of paper. Do not write in this book.

1. *True or False?* An overload and a short circuit are the same thing.

2. The two types of OCPDs you may find in a residential installation are _fuses_ and _circuit breakers_.

3. *True or False?* A clouded window in a blown fuse indicates that there was a short circuit or a ground fault.

4. A single-pole circuit breaker serves a ___120___ -volt circuit.

5. *True or False?* The amperage interrupting rating of an OCPD is the amperage that will cause it to open the circuit.

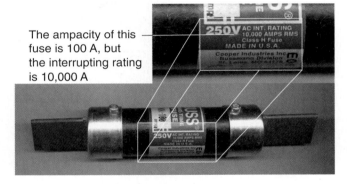

The ampacity of this fuse is 100 A, but the interrupting rating is 10,000 A

Figure 8-11. The amperage interrupting rating of an OCPD is marked on the device or its packaging.

Know the Code

A copy of the NEC 2005 is required to answer these questions.

1. *Section 240.24(E)* prevents the installation of OCPDs in _____ .

2. *Section 240.51* covers _____ fuses.

3. Which section of the *NEC* specifies that circuit breakers used as switches have a marking of SWD or HID?

The International Lineman's Rodeo attracts linemen from around the world to compete in events based on traditional lineman tasks and skills. An exposition of the latest equipment and safety practices takes place along with the rodeo. Notice how many safety related items are on the linemen and the poles.
(Robert Jackson, www.line-man.com)

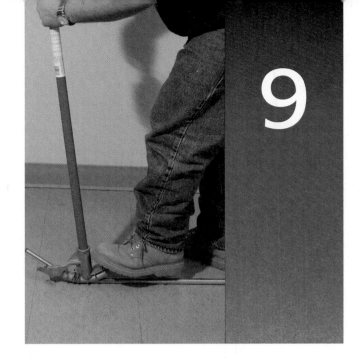

Grounding

Objectives

Information in this chapter will enable you to:

- Cite working principles for electrical grounding.

- Explain equipment grounding and the methods used to install it.

- Explain how system grounding works.

- Define bonding and explain how it is done.

- Explain the operation of a ground-fault circuit interrupter (GFCI) and where it is used.

- Know which branch circuits require an arc-fault circuit interrupter.

- Understand how an AFCI works and the hazards it is designed to prevent.

Technical Terms

Arc-fault circuit interrupter (AFCI)
Bonding
Equipment grounding
Ground-fault circuit interrupter (GFCI)
Grounding
System grounding

Grounding refers to the connection of all parts of a wiring installation to the earth or to other systems that are connected conductively to the earth. This deliberate connecting of the system and the earth provides for the safety and protection of the system itself and the people installing, testing, or using the system.

Grounding Basics

Grounding protects by limiting the possibility of damage to electrical equipment and conductors and by preventing shock to persons contacting electrical equipment.

Electrical systems could receive extremely high voltage from several sources:

- Lightning striking electrical wiring or service wiring, **Figure 9-1**

- Insulation breaking down in the transformer and allowing high voltages

- Accidental contact between the service conductors and high-tension wires

---

grounding: The connection of all parts of a wiring installation to the earth or to other systems that are connected conductively to the earth.

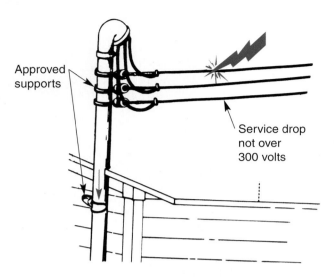

Figure 9-1. Lightning striking supply wiring could send high voltage and overcurrent into an electrical system if it is not grounded. (U.S. Labor Dept.)

In any of these mishaps, very high voltages could enter the electrical system. Voltage could be in excess of several thousand volts. In a system designed to carry no more than several hundred volts, the damage would be substantial. Without proper grounding, the high current related to the high voltage would create so much heat that conductor insulation would melt. Surrounding structural materials could ignite and burn.

With a system properly grounded, this excess voltage and current is directed to earth rapidly. The excess should travel through the grounding conductor and not affect the electrical system at all. See **Figure 9-2**. In the previous chapter, we learned about the dangers of short circuits and ground faults. In either case, without proper grounding, an unwanted electric current could be induced in the system over its exposed portions. Proper equipment grounding would carry this unwanted current back to the service panel. Here it would cause the OCPD to open the circuit. Excess current would go to ground. See **Figure 9-3**.

There are basically two kinds of grounding for electrical wiring. One is system grounding and the other is equipment grounding. They have different purposes and involve two different electrical paths.

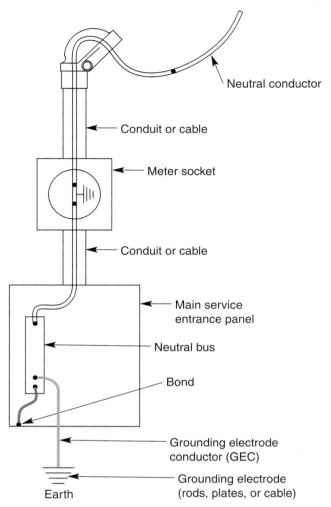

Figure 9-2. In system grounding, the service entrance is connected to earth so that excessive voltage and accompanying overcurrent would be directed to ground. Note in the schematic how the neutral conductor is grounded.

System Grounding

System grounding is the intentional connection of one conductor of the electrical system to the earth. This ground connection is usually to the neutral conductor if one is available in the system. However, it can be a line conductor as in a three-phase, three-wire delta system or a two-wire, 120 V single-phase system.

system grounding: The intentional connection of one conductor of the electrical system to the earth.

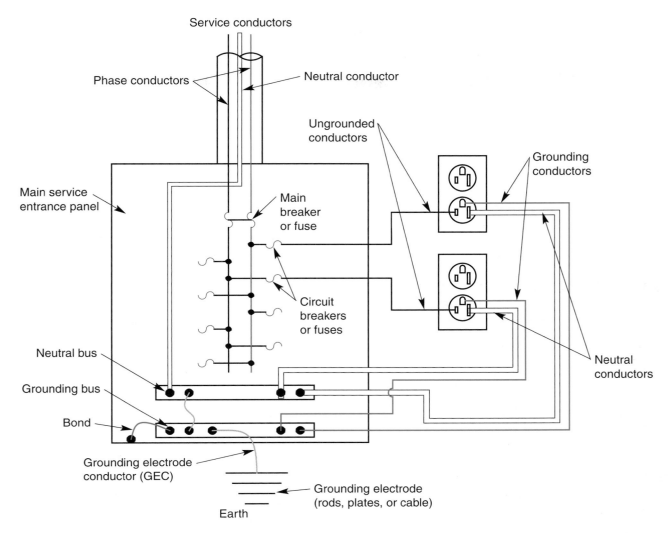

Figure 9-3. Schematic of a system ground. All neutral conductors in the system are connected to ground at service panel. The grounding conductor is continuous from the service panel ground bus to the grounding electrode.

The neutral or line conductor selected to be grounded is connected to a grounding electrode. This may be:

• A driven ground rod that reaches at least 8′ deep into the ground for contact with moist earth

• A metallic water piping system of 10′ or more in length

• A buried ground plate

Other grounding means are outlined in *Section 250.52(A)* of the *National Electrical Code*. Refer also to **Figure 9-4**. Any one of these methods may be used to ground the system. A combination of methods is also acceptable.

Proper grounding of electrical systems is required to:

• Limit the voltage entering the system from surges in power from the supply transformer or from lightning

• Hold all parts of the electrical system (including noncurrent-carrying enclosures) at zero potential to ground

The grounded conductor (neutral or white wire) forms an unbroken path from all the various circuits to the service entrance panel. All the neutral conductors meet in the service panel and connect to a common bus bar called the neutral bus. The neutral bus bar is connected

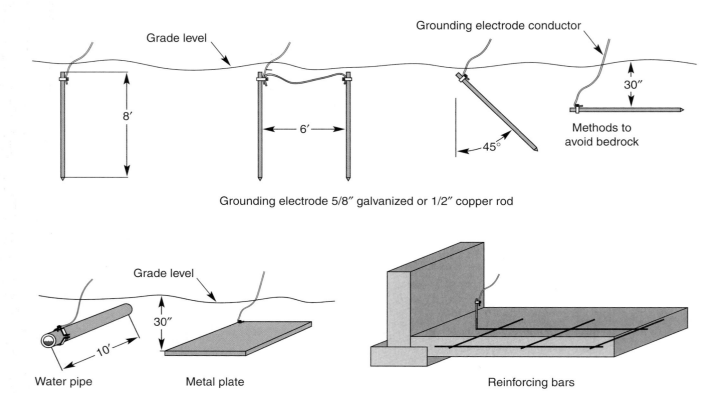

Grounding electrode 5/8″ galvanized or 1/2″ copper rod

Water pipe   Metal plate   Reinforcing bars

Figure 9-4. These are common methods of grounding an electrical system. Check with the local inspector to know which methods are acceptable.

to the ground bus by the main bonding jumper. The ground bus is connected to the grounding electrode by the grounding electrode conductor. Should overcurrent accidentally reach the system, it will be drained off harmlessly into the ground before it can damage any part of the system.

The grounded conductor should never have its continuity interrupted by switches, fuses, or circuit breakers. This would cancel its value as a path to ground. Devices that interrupt the circuit can be used only on hot wires (ungrounded conductors).

The grounding of the neutral wire is done at both the building's service panel and at the power supply pole. See **Figure 9-5**. A commonly accepted method of system grounding is to connect the neutral conductor to one or more ground rods. The rods must be driven to a depth of at least 8′. The depth is important, as the rods must be in contact with moist earth for good grounding.

When multiple rods are used, they should be spaced a minimum of 6′ apart. Ground rods are

one of many types of grounding electrodes. They are connected to the ground bus by a stranded copper conductor no smaller than 8 AWG. This bare wire is known as the grounding electrode conductor (GEC). See **Figure 9-6** for proper sizing of the grounding electrode conductor.

Another method of system grounding is to connect the ground bus to the metal piping of the water supply system in the building. It is a common practice and requirement to use both grounding methods together. It is necessary that the two grounds be interconnected or bonded.

Bonding

Bonding means joining *all* metal parts of the wiring system: boxes, cabinets, enclosures, and conduit. Bonding ensures having good, continuous metallic connections throughout

---

bonding: Creating a continuous electrical connection of the metal parts of the wiring system.

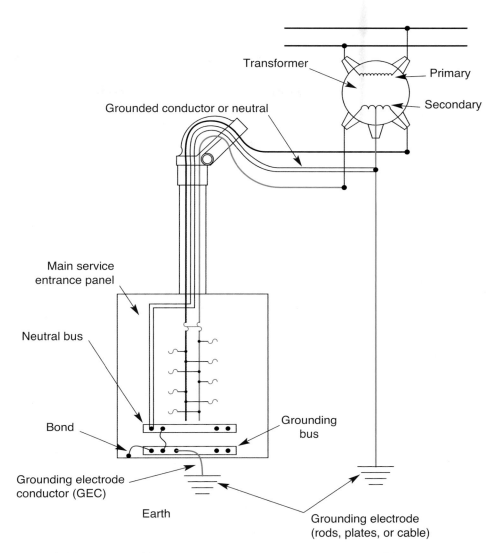

Figure 9-5. A schematic illustration of both system and equipment grounding. The system must be grounded at both the service pole and at the service panel.

Grounding Electrode Conductor for AC Systems

Size of largest service-entrance conductor of equivalent area for parallel conductors		Size of grounding electrode conductor	
Copper	**Aluminum or copper-clad aluminum**	**Copper**	**Aluminum or copper-clad aluminum**
2 or smaller	1/0 or smaller	8	6
1 or 1/0	2/0 or 3/0	6	4
2/0 or 3/0	4/0 or 250 kcmil	4	2
Over 3/0 thru 350 kcmil	Over 250 kcmil thru 500 kcmil	2	1/0
Over 350 kcmil thru 600 kcmil	Over 500 kcmil thru 900 kcmil	1/0	3/0
Over 600 kcmil thru 1100 kcmil	Over 900 kcmil thru 1750 kcmil	2/0	4/0
Over 1100 kcmil	Over 1750 kcmil	3/0	250 kcmil

Figure 9-6. This table lists general sizes for grounding electrode conductors. Refer to *Section 250.66* in the *NEC*.

the grounding system. Refer to *Article 100* of the *National Electrical Code*. Bonding is required at:

- All conduit connections at the electrical service equipment.
- Points where a nonconducting substance is used that might impair continuity. That is, where current may not be able to flow past the nonconductor. Such bonding is done by connecting a jumper around the nonconducting substance.
- All service equipment enclosures whether inside or outside the building.
- All metallic components of the electrical system that normally carry no current.

If a grounding conductor is properly bonded to the metal service equipment, a fault between an ungrounded conductor and any grounded equipment will follow a low-resistance path to the grounded conductor at the transformer. This would allow the OCPD to open the circuit rapidly.

Circuits having conductors enclosed in nonmetallic sheaths or plastic conduit must have an additional grounding wire. This wire must be interconnected between outlets. **Figure 9-7** indicates the size of the grounding wire. This wire ensures a continuous equipment ground.

When metal conduit is used, the conduit itself is the grounding means if the conduit provides an uninterrupted path back to the service entrance. If it does not, an additional grounding conductor must be run in the conduit, **Figure 9-8**.

Sizing Circuit Grounding Conductors		
Rated amperage or amperage setting of automatic overcurrent device	**AWG size**	
	Copper	**Aluminum and copper-clad aluminum**
Not exceeding 15A	14	12
Not exceeding 20A	12	10
Not exceeding 30A	10	8
Not exceeding 40A	10	8
Not exceeding 60A	10	8
Not exceeding 100A	8	6
Not exceeding 200A	6	4
Not exceeding 300A	4	2
Not exceeding 400A	3	1

Figure 9-7. Sizes of grounding conductors to use with various sizes of overcurrent devices. Refer to *NEC Table 250.122* for additional details.

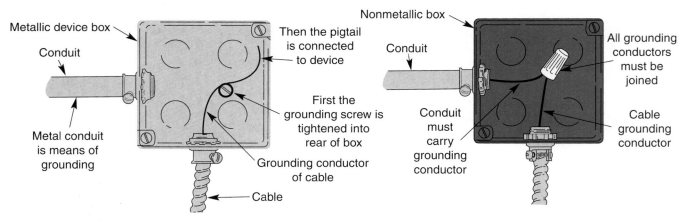

Figure 9-8. This is the proper method of bonding electrical devices to the electrical box and, in turn, the electrical system.

How the System Ground Works

Article 250 of the *NEC* deals with grounding details and should be understood by anyone intending to do electrical work. In fact, a thorough understanding of both system grounding and equipment grounding is essential to completing an electrical installation that is safe to both persons and property. This is the fundamental basis for the creation of the *NEC*.

Equipment Grounding

Equipment grounding is the method that bonds the grounding conductor to equipment enclosures and metallic noncurrent-carrying equipment, **Figure 9-9**. A permanent and unbroken path is formed back to the service neutral and the grounding electrode. If a system does not have a grounded conductor or neutral, one of the line or phase conductors may be intentionally grounded. This is common when there is a three-phase, three-wire delta system or a two-wire, 120 V, single-phase system. One conductor of the system is grounded by connecting it to the grounding electrode.

The equipment ground protects the electrical equipment from damage should a live conductor make contact with the equipment housing or frame. This is known as a *ground fault*. It occurs when conductor insulation fails or when a wire comes loose from its terminal point. Not only is this damaging to the electrical equipment, but it exposes the equipment user to the danger of shock. For this reason, all metal electrical enclosures, frames, wireways, and conduits must have good ground continuity. The relationship between the system ground and the equipment ground is shown in **Figure 9-10**.

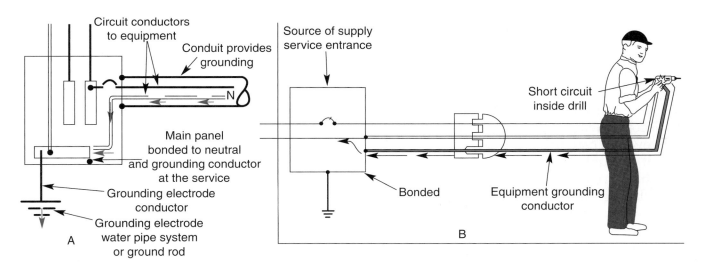

Figure 9-9. Schematic examples of how equipment grounding works. A—Path current will take during a ground fault when there is a proper equipment ground. B—How equipment grounding protects tool use. The current follows grounding conductor back to ground. Otherwise, current could pass through a worker's body to ground. (OSHA)

equipment grounding: Bonding the grounding conductor to equipment enclosures and metallic noncurrent-carrying equipment.

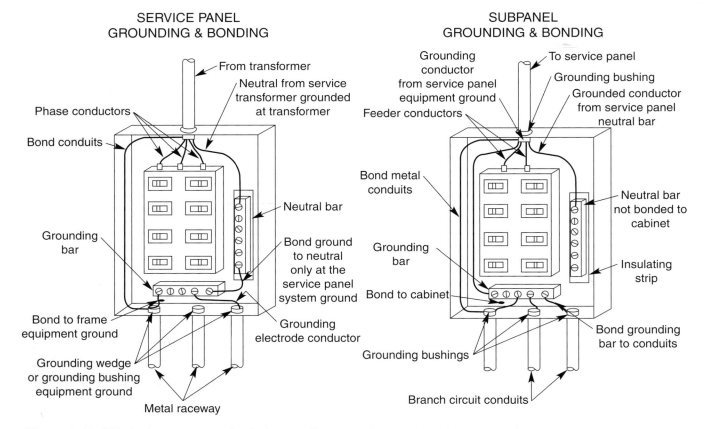

Figure 9-10. This is the proper method of grounding a service panel and a subpanel.

Ground-Fault Circuit Interrupters (GFCI)

The importance of a good grounding system in electrical wiring cannot be overemphasized. However, in certain situations good grounding is not enough. Too many individuals have lost their lives from improperly maintained or imperfect grounding of electrical equipment. Such a situation exists whenever defective, worn, or misused equipment is handled by the operator, especially in damp or wet areas. A *ground-fault circuit interrupter (GFCI)* is a device that opens a circuit if an unusually large current-to-ground is detected. Having this device in the circuit is a way of preventing shock hazards when poorly-grounded equipment is operated. For this reason, the *NEC* requires GFCI protected circuits at the following locations:

• Receptacles in bathrooms and outdoors where there is direct grade access, including bathrooms in motel guest rooms

• Unfinished basement receptacles
• All kitchen countertop receptacles
• Crawl spaces, if at grade or below grade
• Wet bar sinks
• Receptacles in garages unless the receptacles are either not readily accessible or dedicated for a cord-and-plug-connected fixed appliance
• Receptacles that are not part of permanent wiring, such as those used for temporary power during construction

Requirements may be met by installing GFCI breakers or receptacles on the circuits. See **Figure 9-11**.

GFCIs open the circuit if a current leakage or fault-to-ground exceeds 0.006 A (6 mA). Note, a person can be electrocuted by a current of only 2 mA. Normally, the current going to the appliance along the ungrounded wire and the current returning to the source along the white

ground-fault circuit interrupter (GFCI): A device that opens a circuit if a current-to-ground is detected.

Figure 9-11. Ground-fault circuit interrupters are required for extra protection. They are available both as circuit breakers and receptacles. The device shown here is a GFCI receptacle.

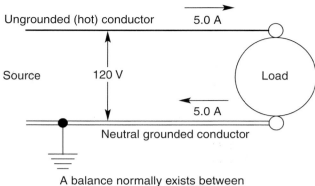

A balance normally exists between the current to and from the load.

or grounded neutral conductor are equal. See **Figure 9-12**. During a ground fault or short circuit, however, an imbalance occurs and the difference represents a dangerous shock hazard. A GFCI monitoring the circuit will sense any imbalance greater than 6 mA and will immediately open the circuit, stopping the dangerous current flow.

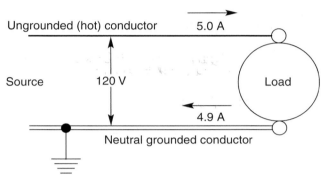

When an imbalance occurs between the ungrounded and the grounded conductor, a serious danger, called a *fault* or *current leak* is present. Contact with such a fault could be fatal.

Figure 9-12. These schematics illustrate the imbalance of current that is detected by a GFCI.

Arc-Fault Circuit Interrupter (AFCI)

Prevents fire - does not prevent shocks

The *NEC* requires that any 125 V, 15 A or 20 A branch circuit that supplies outlet receptacles in bedrooms must be protected by a listed *arc-fault circuit interrupter (AFCI)*. The AFCI opens the circuit when an arc fault is detected. By detecting arc faults, AFCIs will help prevent fires from starting. The breaker form of the AFCI is similar in appearance to a GFCI breaker. See **Figure 9-13**.

The AFCI detects arcing faults that are not detected by standard breakers or GFCIs. Typical conditions that may generate arc faults include the following:
- Damaged wires
- Frayed conductor insulation
- Loose electrical connections
- Overheated or otherwise stressed electrical cords
- Damaged electrical appliances

Figure 9-13. AFCI breakers are required in bedroom circuits. (Cutler-Hammer)

---

arc-fault circuit interrupter (AFCI): A device that opens the circuit when an arc fault is detected.

Review Questions

Write your answers on a separate sheet of paper.
Do not write in this book.

1. *True or False?* Grounding is designed to protect people, not equipment.

2. A ground rod must be ____8____ feet long to make good contact with the earth.

3. *True or False?* A neutral wire can have a switch attached to it.

4. *True or False?* If a system is grounded, it does not need to be bonded.

5. A GFCI breaker or receptacle will open a circuit where there is a current leakage to ground fault greater than _____ A.

6. List three locations where GFCIs are required. *Bathrooms, Kitchen cocenter unfinished basements*

7. All devices in a bedroom must be protected by a(n) *arc fault* circuit interrupter.

8. *True or False?* In general, GFCIs prevent a shock hazard, and AFCIs prevent fires.

Know the Code

A copy of the NEC 2005 is required to answer these questions.

1. *Article* _____ contains most of the information about grounding and bonding.

2. Where does *210.8(A)(1)* require GFCI protection?

3. Which section of *Article 210* covers arc-fault circuit-interrupter protection?

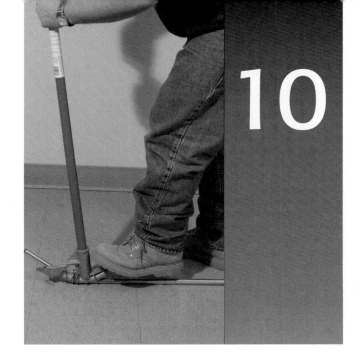

The Service Entrance

Objectives

Information in this chapter will enable you to:

- List the components of the service entrance.
- List service drop clearances specified in the *NEC*.
- List eight basic guidelines when locating a residential service entrance.
- Calculate the size of service entrance needed based on the power needs of the dwelling.
- Select proper conductors and components for the service entrance.
- Size and install conductors between the meter socket, main disconnect, and service panel.
- Provide proper grounding for a service entrance.
- Explain the purpose of a step-down transformer and indicate where it is used.

Technical Terms

Drip loop	Meter socket
Insulator	Service drop
Meter	Service drop mast
Meter enclosure	Service entrance

Service head	Temporary wiring
Service lateral	Transformer rule

The *service entrance* includes all the wires, devices, and fittings that carry electricity from the power company's transformer to the consumer. All electrical energy supplied to power-consuming devices in the building must first pass through the service entrance equipment. The service components protect, meter, and distribute the power to the branch circuits.

Service Entrance Components

The service entrance consists of the following electrical equipment and parts:
- Wires from the utility pole or transformer to the dwelling service point
- Service entrance conductors
- Meter socket, pan, or enclosure

---

service entrance: All of the wires, devices, and fittings that carry electricity from the power company's transformer to the consumer.

- Service entrance panel with breakers or fuses and a main disconnecting means
- Grounding system
- Fittings, fasteners, and other hardware necessary to install the service equipment

> **Pro Tip**
>
> When a piece of equipment is said to be *ahead* of the meter, the equipment is on the transformer side of the meter. Electricians often use this term when describing where to locate disconnects, OCPDs, and service equipment.

Service Location

Service wires brought to the building are run overhead or underground. Those coming in overhead from a utility pole are called the *service drop*. See **Figure 10-1**. Those routed underground, from either a pole or transformer pad, are called the *service lateral*. See **Figure 10-2**. In either type, these service wires will be connected to the service entrance wires at the building.

Most often, the power company will locate the point of attachment of the service entrance for the electrician. In many localities this is required. Check the service specifications of the power supplier to be sure of any additional requirements before installing the service entrance. See **Figure 10-3**.

Where to locate service

When selecting the service entrance location, use the following guidelines:

- Underground service entrance conductors, whether enclosed in cable or conduit, should be installed in a straight path to make finding the buried conductors easier.

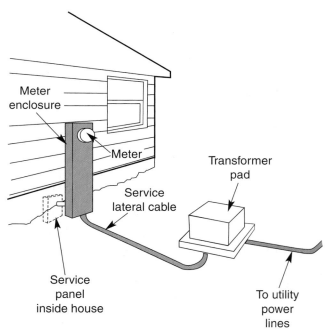

Figure 10-2. This is a typical underground installation for a service entrance.

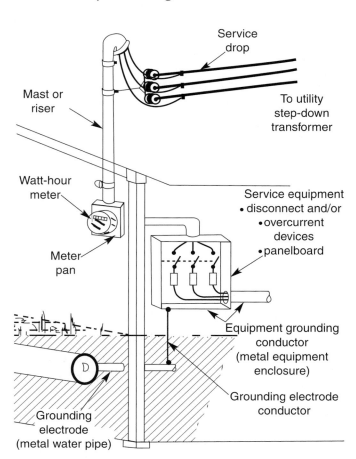

Figure 10-1. This is a typical overhead service drop and service entrance. (OSHA)

service drop: Service wires brought to the building that are run overhead from a pole.

service lateral: Service wires brought to the building that are routed underground, from either a pole or transformer pad.

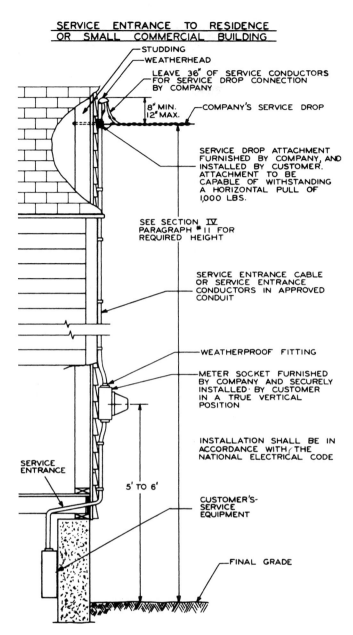

SERVICE ENTRANCE TO RESIDENCE OR SMALL COMMERCIAL BUILDING

STUDDING

WEATHERHEAD

LEAVE 36" OF SERVICE CONDUCTORS FOR SERVICE DROP CONNECTION BY COMPANY

8" MIN. 12" MAX.

COMPANY'S SERVICE DROP

SERVICE DROP ATTACHMENT FURNISHED BY COMPANY, AND INSTALLED BY CUSTOMER. ATTACHMENT TO BE CAPABLE OF WITHSTANDING A HORIZONTAL PULL OF 1,000 LBS.

SEE SECTION IV PARAGRAPH #11 FOR REQUIRED HEIGHT

SERVICE ENTRANCE CABLE OR SERVICE ENTRANCE CONDUCTORS IN APPROVED CONDUIT

WEATHERPROOF FITTING

METER SOCKET FURNISHED BY COMPANY AND SECURELY INSTALLED BY CUSTOMER IN A TRUE VERTICAL POSITION

INSTALLATION SHALL BE IN ACCORDANCE WITH THE NATIONAL ELECTRICAL CODE

SERVICE ENTRANCE

5' TO 6'

CUSTOMER'S SERVICE EQUIPMENT

FINAL GRADE

Figure 10-3. Service entrance specifications like these should be secured from the utility company before the service entrance installation. Refer also to the *NEC* and consult the local electrical inspector whenever necessary. (New York State Electric and Gas Corp.)

- Service conductors should be kept as short as practical to minimize voltage drop.
- Service conductors must enter the building as close as possible to the service panel.
- The service disconnect must be at or very near the point of entry.

- The service panel should be located in a central and accessible area, near the major electrical equipment of the building.
- The service equipment must be protected from physical damage, water, and dust.
- Service equipment cannot be placed in bathrooms, storerooms, closets, or damp cellars.

Number of Services

A structure can have only one service. Thus, each building will have one service drop or one service lateral. While this is the basic rule, there are some practical exceptions. The following exceptions are allowed:

- A completely separate service is permitted to supply a fire pump or other emergency electrical apparatus, such as lights or standby power, **Figure 10-4**.
- If a single service cannot supply a large load demand, another may be added.
- If structures are so large that no single service would allow electrical access to all the tenants of the building, additional services may be provided.
- A generator, driven by an engine or wind, may provide additional service.
- Electric power may be supplied by a solar photovoltaic source in addition to the service provided by the utility.

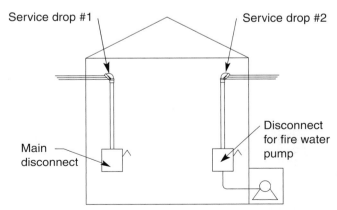

Service drop #1   Service drop #2

Main disconnect

Disconnect for fire water pump

Figure 10-4. A separate service supply is permitted for fire pumps or other emergency electrical equipment.

- If different voltages and phases may be required within the same structure, additional services are allowed.

Number of Service Entrance Conductor Sets

Since the basic rule is that each building will have only one service drop or service lateral, the usual service installation will have only one set of service entrance conductors. Necessary exceptions include multiple occupancies, such as two-family homes, apartment buildings, and commercial establishments with several offices or stores. These occupancies may have any number of service entrance sets tapped from a single service supply, **Figure 10-5**. The *NEC* permits a maximum of six disconnects from any single service drop or service lateral. **Figure 10-6** illustrates a possible installation of this nature.

Regardless of the number of service drops, laterals, or sets of service entrance conductors, the service should be carefully planned so that the service entrance conductors are not routed through the building interior unless encased in concrete. The service entrance conductors should also terminate at the disconnect outside or close to where they enter the structure. See **Figure 10-7**.

Service Load

For new single-family dwellings, the *NEC* requires at least a 100 A service. For homes with electrical heating systems or where future expansion is likely, 150 A or 200 A service is preferred. However, to be sure that the service

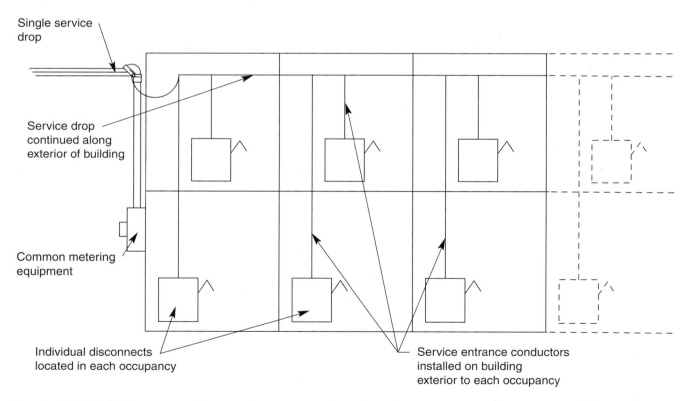

Single service drop

Service drop continued along exterior of building

Common metering equipment

Individual disconnects located in each occupancy

Service entrance conductors installed on building exterior to each occupancy

Figure 10-5. Multiple occupancies may have any number of service entrance conductors tapped from a service drop or service lateral.

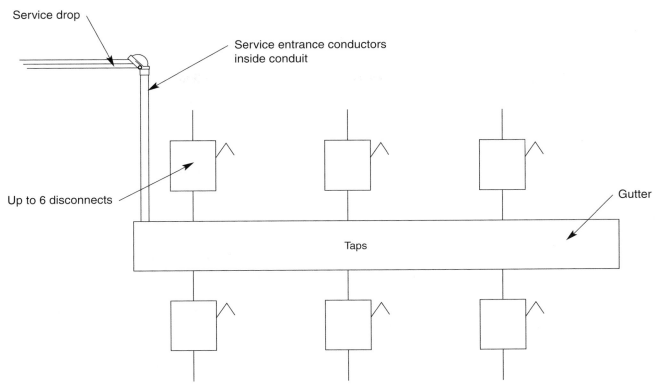

Figure 10-6. A maximum of six disconnects are permitted to be installed at the service entrance. All of these disconnects must be grouped together at a single location.

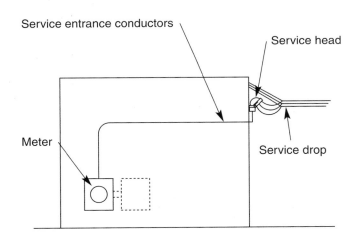

Figure 10-7. Service conductors run along the exterior of a building or are encased in 2″ of concrete within the building. These conductors should terminate at the disconnect or service protection equipment close to where they enter the building or leave the concrete enclosure.

is sized correctly for a residence, the total load should be calculated based on the various circuits of the dwelling. A simple series of calculations can help you find this total load. See **Figure 10-8**. Detailed information on these calculations will be presented in Chapter 12, **Branch-Circuit, Feeder, and Service Design**.

Service Entrance Conductors

Service entrance conductors may be type RHH, THW, THWW, XHHW, or RHW. They can be run through conduit or enclosed in a cable assembly called service entrance cable, **Figure 10-9**. Many service drop installations are made with triplex cable, **Figure 10-10**.

Calculation for Total Load of a One-Family Dwelling

Table 220.12 210.11(C)(1) 210.11(C)(2)		Multiply the total square feet of house by 3 VA.		
	1	This is the total general load.	_1800_ ft² × 3 VA = **5400**	VA
	2	Small appliance loads (two kitchen area circuits at 1500 VA each)	3000	VA
	3	One laundry circuit	1500	VA
	4	Add lines 1 through 3.	Total = **9900**	VA
Table 220.42	5	The first 3000 VA of the total is 100%.	3000	VA
	6	Subtract the first 3000 VA from line 4 to get the remainder. Line 4 – 3000 = **6900**		VA
	7	Multiply the remainder by 35%. × 0.35 Line 6 × 0.35 = **2415**		VA
	8	Add line 5 to line 7 to get the **net load**. Line 5 + line 7 = **5415**		VA
Table 220.53		List the nameplate ratings of each fixed appliance.		
	9	Range	**12,200**	VA
	10	Dryer	**4900**	VA
	11	Dishwasher	**1200**	VA
	12	Water heater		VA
	13	_____		VA
	14	_____ Additional		VA
	15	_____ fixed		VA
	16	_____ appliances		VA
	17	Add lines 9 through 16. This is the **total fixed appliances load**.	**18300**	VA
		Add line 8 to line 17.		
	18	This is the **net calculated load**	Line 8 + line 17 = **23715**	VA
220.82(C)	19	Total heating load	**5000**	VA
	20	Total air conditioning load	**3500**	VA
	21	Enter the larger number between line 19 and line 20.	**5000**	VA
		Multiply line 21 by 40%	× 0.40	
	22	This is the **total heating/air conditioning load**.	Line 21 × 0.40 = **2000**	VA
Total load	23	Add line 18 to line 22 for the **total house load**.	**25715**	VA
	24	Enter the voltage provided (120, 240, or other)	**240**	V
		Divide line 23 by line 24. This is the		
	25	**total amperage required for the house**.	Line 23 ÷ line 24 = **107**	A

Review NEC Sections 230.42(B) and 230.79 for service conductors and disconnecting requirements.

Figure 10-8. Use these steps for calculating the total service load.

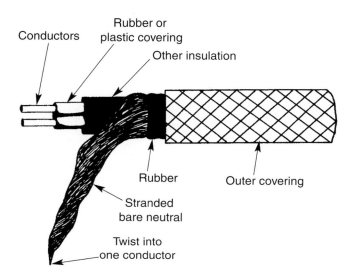

Figure 10-9. Service entrance cable (SEC). Bare, stranded neutral wire must be twisted into a single strand before being connected.

Figure 10-10. Most service drops in new homes are made with triplex cable. It consists of a bare neutral wire around which two insulated cables are loosely wrapped. The neutral wire supports the insulated wires.

When in conduit, all the conductors are insulated. The neutral is white, yellow, or gray. The hot wires are black or red. Service entrance cable is similar, but the neutral is bare.

Whether conduit or cable is used will depend upon customer preference, local codes, building structure, environment, utility specifications, and the electrician's experience. In either case, the conduit or cable must be securely fastened to the building with the proper clamps or supports as shown later in this chapter.

Sizing service entrance conductors

In addition to proper types of service conductors, the right conductor size is essential. As mentioned earlier, *Table 310.16* of the *NEC* establishes the allowable ampacities of insulated conductors. *Note 3* of the table instructs us on proper types and sizes of conductors for three-wire, single-phase dwelling entrance services. See **Figure 10-11**.

Service Drop Mast and Insulator

Very rarely are the service drop mast (or riser) and insulators supplied and installed by the power company. In most situations, the electrician makes the installation. The *service drop mast* is usually a length of rigid metal conduit or, if allowed, rigid nonmetallic conduit. This conduit contains the service entrance cable and is mounted between the service head and the meter.

An *insulator* is a nonconductive device that supports the service drop wires near the service head. It can be clamped to the conduit or attached to the exterior of the building. Insulators are placed approximately 12″ below the service head. See **Figure 10-12**.

Service Head

A *service head* is a fitting installed at the top of the conduit or service entrance cable to prevent water from entering the meter socket and shorting out the conductors. Service heads are designed to be used with either conduit or cable. See **Figure 10-13**. The service conductors should extend through the head for approximately 3′ to provide a suitable drip loop. A *drip loop* is merely a formed curvature of the service conductor to prevent water from entering the service head around the cable or conduit. See **Figure 10-14**.

Metering Equipment

The amount of electrical power used within a residence must be measured, so the utility knows how much to charge the customer. The *meter* is the device that measures and records the amount of electricity used. The *meter socket* is the receptacle that the meter plugs into. This

Conductor Types and Sizes RH—RHH—RHW—THW—THWN—THHN—XHHW		
Copper (AWG)	Aluminum and Copper-Clad Aluminum (AWG)	Service Rating (Amperes)
4	2	100
3	1	110
2	1/0	125
1	2/0	150
1/0	3/0	175
2/0	4/0	200

Figure 10-11. Service entrance cable sizes are specified by the *NEC*.

service drop mast: A length of rigid conduit that contains the service entrance cable and is mounted between the service head and the meter.

insulator: A nonconductive device that supports the service drop wires near the service head.

service head: A fitting installed at the top of the service entrance cable to prevent water from entering the meter socket.

drip loop: A formed curvature of the service conductor to prevent water from entering the service head.

meter: The device that measures and records the amount of electricity used.

meter socket: The receptacle that a meter plugs into.

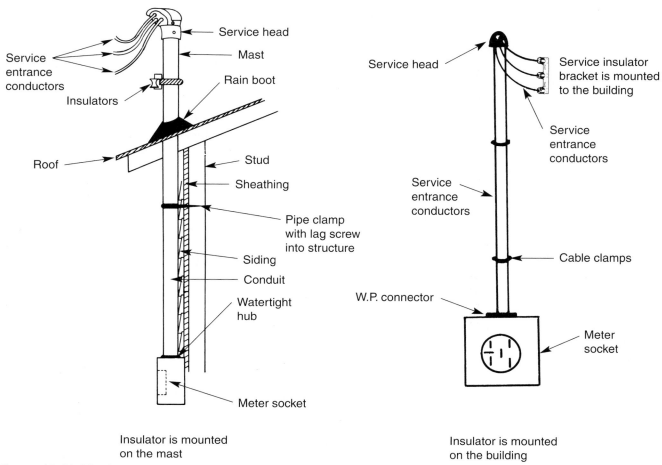

Insulator is mounted
on the mast

Insulator is mounted
on the building

Figure 10-12. The insulator may be mounted on the mast or the building.

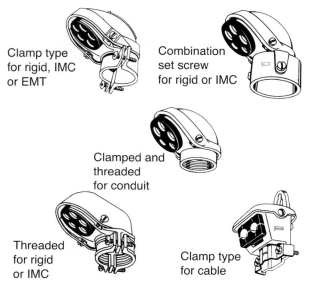

Figure 10-13. Service heads are fittings designed to keep water from entering the service entrance cable or the conduit leading to the meter enclosure. These service heads are designed for specific connections. (Hubbell, Inc.)

allows the utility to remove the meter without having to detach any cables. The meter socket is contained inside the *meter enclosure*, which is the box that attaches to the service conduit. The meter socket and enclosure are usually sold together and referred to as a meter socket. See **Figure 10-15**.

Service conductors enter the enclosure and are secured to the line-side lugs of the socket. Note that the neutral conductor is always connected to the center contact and continues essentially uninterrupted through the meter socket on its journey to the service main disconnect or panel. The meter itself will be installed by the utility when the service drop or lateral is completed.

meter enclosure: A box that attaches to the service conduit.

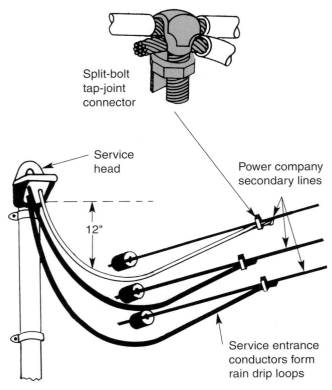

Split-bolt tap-joint connector

Service head

Power company secondary lines

12"

Service entrance conductors form rain drip loops

Figure 10-14. A drip loop prevents water from following the cable into the service head.

Weatherproof Connectors

Fittings called weatherproof connectors are used to connect service entrance cable to the meter enclosure when conduit is not used. One is shown in **Figure 10-16**. The purpose of this fitting is to prevent moisture from entering the meter enclosure.

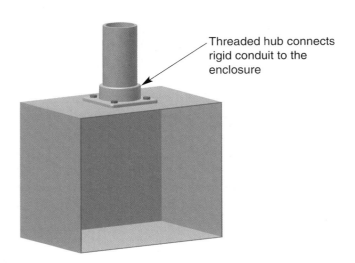

Threaded hub connects rigid conduit to the enclosure

The circuit is completed when the meter is installed in this socket

Grounded neutral

To service panel

From underground service

Figure 10-15. This meter socket is connected to the service cables from the transformer and the cables that connect to the service panel. The grounded neutral is connected, even when the meter is removed.

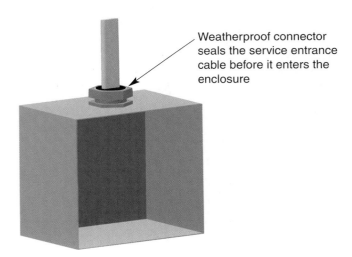

Weatherproof connector seals the service entrance cable before it enters the enclosure

Figure 10-16. Select the proper fittings to prevent water from entering the meter socket enclosure.

Temporary Wiring

Temporary wiring is done to provide electrical power only during construction, remodeling, demolition, repair, or large-scale maintenance of a building. This wiring must be removed when the work is completed. *Article 590* of the *NEC* covers this subject.

Although temporary wiring safety requirements may be less exacting than permanent wiring, most of the same rules apply. However, there are several important differences. Temporary wiring can be used on a construction site during the entire term of construction, regardless of the type of construction, **Figure 10-17**. In addition, temporary power can be brought in for emergency situations, testing, and experimentation.

The key factors for installation of all temporary wiring are:

- All temporary wiring, devices, and equipment should be located in a safe place and should be as neat as possible. Temporary wiring should be kept overhead as much as possible.

- Protect temporary wiring from physical damage.

- Use portable ground-fault circuit interrupter boxes. See **Figure 10-18**.

- Grounding must be in compliance with *Article 250* of the *NEC*.

- All lamps should have protective covers or caging. They should be mounted at heights of 7' or higher.

- All circuits must originate from approved panels or power outlets and must have overcurrent protection.

- Receptacle circuits and lighting circuits must be separated.

- Weatherproof devices and housings should be used wherever there is dampness or exposure to weather.

- Locking type plugs and connectors should be used on power ends.

- Temporary wiring should be inspected frequently for damage.

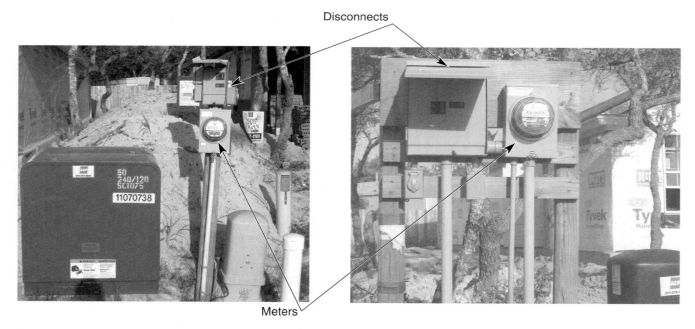

Figure 10-17. These are typical temporary service installations installed at construction sites.

temporary wiring: A method of providing electrical power only during construction, remodeling, demolition, repair, or large-scale maintenance of a building.

GFCI power distribution box

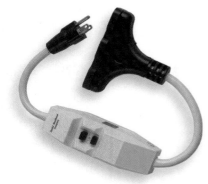

GFCI adapter

Figure 10-18. Use GFCI equipment to protect yourself and other workers. (Coleman Cable, Inc.)

Service Disconnects

Section 230.71(A) of the *NEC* requires that disconnect means or service entrance conductors cannot exceed six switches either in a single enclosure or a group of separate enclosures. Several permissible arrangements are shown in **Figure 10-19**.

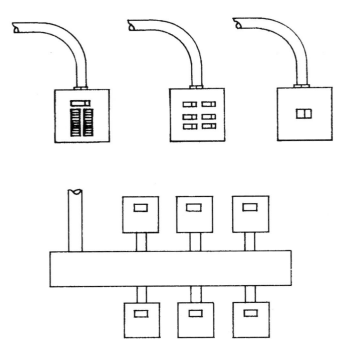

Figure 10-19. Permissible service disconnects.

Main Disconnect and Service Panel

There must be equipment that will disconnect all wiring from the power source. This can be arranged by using a single main disconnect switch or a main circuit breaker that is part of the service panel. See **Figure 10-20**. Regardless of the method used, the disconnect must be located in an accessible place. Further, it must be located as close as possible to the point where the service conductors enter the structure.

Service Grounding

Grounding the service entrance is vital to the safety of the entire electrical system. Careful attention should be given to this section to ensure a thorough understanding of the procedures involved. In addition, you should study all sections of *Article 250* of the *NEC* before undertaking any electrical installation.

Grounding the service entrance involves connecting the neutral or white service conductor with the earth. This is done by means of the grounding conductor. This conductor connects the neutral lug of the meter housing or the neutral bus bar of the service switch (service panel) to the metallic water supply pipe. See **Figure 10-21**.

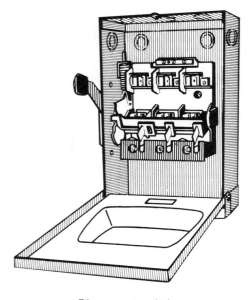

Disconnect switch

Main circuit breaker is
the disconnect switch

Figure 10-20. Within every structure, there must be a means of disconnecting all conductors from the service conductors. These disconnects must be clearly marked and easily accessible. (Wadsworth Electric Mfg. Co., Inc. and Square D Co.)

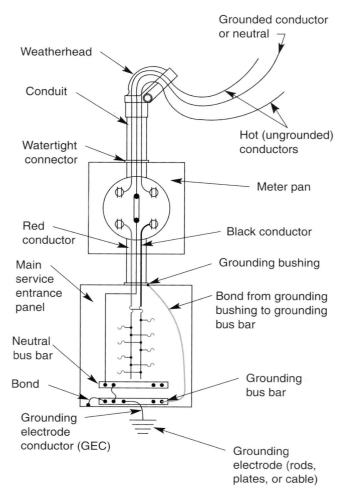

Figure 10-21. The service entrance layout must have continuity of the grounded neutral and grounding electrode through grounding electrode conductor. Metal conduit must also be bonded to grounding means.

In addition to or in place of the water supply pipe, other grounding electrode systems shall be used:

- Metal frames of buildings
- Metal electrodes encased in 2″ of concrete within or near the bottom of a concrete foundation
- 20′ of 2 AWG bare copper wire buried not less than 2 1/2′ below the surface
- Underground metal tanks or other such underground systems or structures

- Rod or pipe electrodes that are at least 8' long, fully driven into the ground or buried not less than 4' below the surface
- Metal plate of no less than 2 ft² surface area

Where two or more grounding electrodes are used, they should be separated by a distance of 6' and bonded (linked with a copper conductor). The resistance between the grounding electrode and the earth must not exceed 25 ohms

Grounding Electrode Conductor

The grounding electrode conductor connects the grounding bus bar to the grounding electrode. This conductor should provide little resistance. For that reason, the conductor is typically copper, aluminum, or copper-clad aluminum. The grounding electrode conductor must also be firmly attached to grounding electrode using approved fittings, **Figure 10-22**. As with all conductors involved in grounding, the grounding electrode conductor must never be interrupted.

Sizing the grounding electrode conductor
Table 250.66 of the *NEC* indicates the proper sizes for the grounding electrode conductor. This is based on the service entrance conductor size. See **Figure 10-23**.

For example, the installation of a 200 A service entrance using 3/0 AWG copper service wires would require a 4 AWG copper grounding electrode conductor.

Figure 10-22. Always firmly attach the grounding electrode conductor to the grounding electrode using approved fittings.

Grounding Electrode Conductor Sizing			
Size of Largest Service-Entrance Conductor (AWG/kcmil)		Size of Grounding Electrode Conductor (AWG/kcmil)	
Copper	Aluminum or Copper-Clad Aluminum	Copper	Aluminum or Copper-Clad Aluminum
2 or smaller	1/0 or smaller	8	6
1 or 1/0	2/0 or 3/0	6	4
2/0 or 3/0	4/0 or 250	4	2
Over 3/0 – 350	Over 250 – 500	2	1/0
Over 350 – 600	Over 500 – 900	1/0	3/0
Over 600 – 1100	Over 900 – 1750	2/0	4/0
Over 1100	Over 1750	3/0	250

Figure 10-23. Refer to *NEC Table 250.66* when determining the size of the grounding electrode conductor.

Service Clearances

Where overhead services are installed, certain regulations concerning clearances must be strictly observed. The *NEC* indicates that clearances for overhead service drop conductors shall be as follows:

* Above roofs, **Figure 10-24**
  A. 8' as measured vertically from all points
  B. 3' if the slope is not less than 4" in 12"
  C. 18" over an overhanging portion of a roof

* Above final grade, **Figure 10-25**
  A. 10' above sidewalks
  B. 12' above residential driveways
  C. 18' above public alleys or thoroughfares subject to truck traffic

* At building openings, **Figure 10-26**
  A. Not less than 10' above a finished surface platform, or other accessible surface
  B. Not less than 3' from a window in any direction (except above the window)

Additional information regarding clearances is found in *Section 230.24* of the *NEC*.

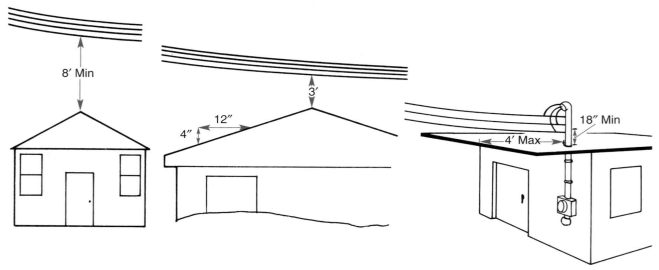

Figure 10-24. Above-roof clearance for overhead conductors. (OSHA)

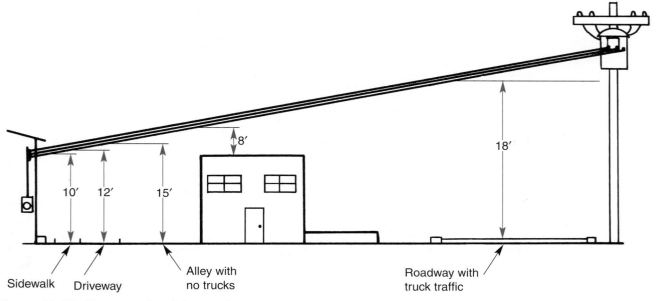

Figure 10-25. Above-grade minimum clearances.

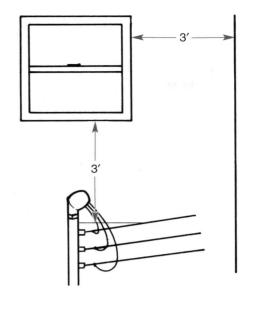

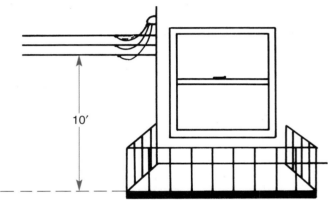

Figure 10-26. Clearances around building platforms and openings.

Service Completion

When the service entrance installation or rough-in is completed, it will be inspected by the electrical inspector. After this, the power company will install the service drop or lateral by connecting the wires from their transformer to the service entrance conductors.

Figure 10-27 shows a typical completed service entrance. Note the drip loops discussed earlier, as well as the positioning of other components in the finished service system.

Transformers

While the residential electrician will not be working on transformers, it is helpful to understand how transformers are made and how they work. Due to the voltages involved, you should be careful when working around this equipment. Transformers are installed and serviced by trained lineworkers employed by the power company.

Transformer Operation

A transformer has a relatively simple structure, **Figure 10-28**. Basically, it contains two coils of wire or *windings* and a common

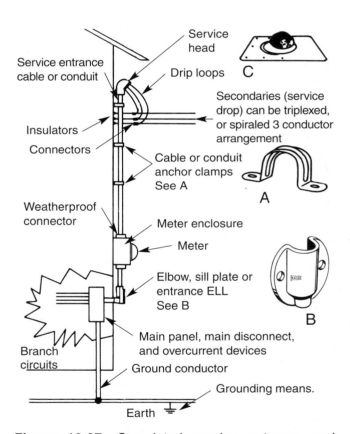

Figure 10-27. Completed service entrance and various fittings. Note relative position of components and special fittings. A—Cable, conduit, or anchor clamps fasten cable and conduit to structure. B—Elbow, sill plate, or entrance ell protect conductors at point where they enter structure. (Hubbell, Inc. and Electroline Mfg. Co.) C—Rain boot (not shown in drawing) is used to protect from leaks when service mast goes through roof.

metal core. When an alternating current is sent through the first coil, the *primary*, it magnetizes the metal core, **Figure 10-29**, causing surges of magnetic flux. These surges are constantly reversing directions. This magnetic flux also moves through the other coil, which is called the

secondary. A current is created there, too. Since the same magnetic flux exists throughout the core, the same voltage per wire turn is created. Therefore, any voltage difference is the direct result of differences in the number of turns in the primary and secondary windings.

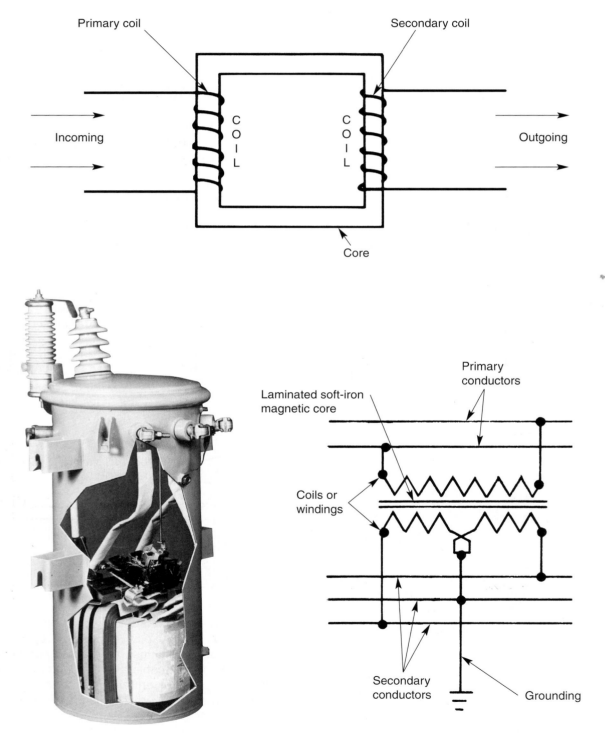

Figure 10-28. Transformers have a simple makeup. They consist of a metal core with windings or turns of wire around opposite sides. Note schematic at right.

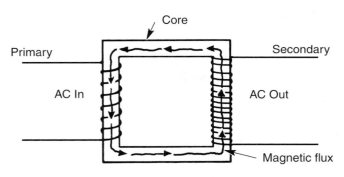

Figure 10-29. Application of alternating current causes a magnetic flux within the transformer core. This magnetic flux creates a current in the secondary side (outgoing) of the transformer.

Transformer Rule

Mathematically stated, the total voltage in the primary coil is to the total voltage in the secondary coil as the number of turns in the primary is to the number of turns in the secondary. This is the **transformer rule** and it can be expressed as:

$$\frac{\text{Voltage of Primary}}{\text{Voltage of Secondary}} = \frac{\text{Turns of Primary}}{\text{Turns of Secondary}}$$

Power into and out of a transformer is (ideally) the same. Since voltage changes within the transformer, so must amperage. Remember, power equals volts × amperes. For this reason, the amperage must change proportionately but inversely, as does the voltage. This can be stated mathematically as:

$$\frac{\text{Primary Voltage}}{\text{Secondary Amperage}} = \frac{\text{Secondary Voltage}}{\text{Primary Amperage}}$$

For example, suppose the primary voltage entering a transformer is 12 volts and the primary amperage is 20 amperes. What will the secondary amperage be if the secondary voltage is 120 volts?

Using the equation just given:

$$\frac{12\text{ V}}{x} = \frac{120\text{ V}}{20\text{ A}}$$

by cross-multiplying

$$\frac{12\text{ V}}{x} = \frac{120\text{ V}}{20\text{ A}}$$

$$120\,x = 240$$
$$x = 240/120$$
$$x = 2 \text{ Amperes}$$

Since a transformer changes voltage, it can either increase or decrease the primary voltage. One that increases the primary voltage is called a *step-up transformer*. One that decreases the primary voltage is called a *step-down transformer*, **Figure 10-30**. Directions for selecting the proper transformer to match the electrical load are found at the end of this chapter.

Service Designation

The power delivered by the power company is routed through a chain of transformers, **Figure 10-31**. The last transformer is near the

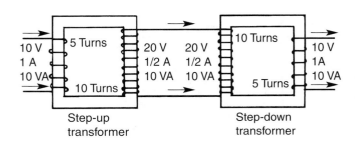

Figure 10-30. Step-up transformers increase the voltage and step-down transformers decrease the voltage.

---

transformer rule: The total voltage in the primary coil is to the total voltage in the secondary coil as the number of turns in the primary is to the number of turns in the secondary.

building that is supplied. See **Figure 10-32**. These transformers are designed to supply the following service ratings:

No. of Wires	Phase	Voltage	Comments
2	Single	120	These installations are no longer made
3	Single	120/240	Most common residential service
4	Three	120/208	
4	Three	120/240	

Phases

Phase refers to the angle between various generated ac currents. The term three-phase indicates three separately derived ac currents that are "out-of-step" from each other by 120 electrical degrees.

Two-phase current occurs when two alternating currents are generated 90° apart. The typical single-phase current exists when one current is produced at regular intervals. **Figure 10-33** illustrates this important variance in electrical power generation.

Single-phase, two-phase, and three-phase are abbreviated as 1φ, 2φ, and 3φ. Single-phase and three-phase current are used commonly in electrical generation. Two-phase has little practical application today.

Three-Wire, Single-Phase System

The most common residential service is a three-wire, single-phase system. This consists of two ungrounded conductors and one grounded conductor. See **Figure 10-34**. One ungrounded conductor is usually black and the other red. The grounded conductor is usually yellow. This system will provide 120 V and 240 V, depending

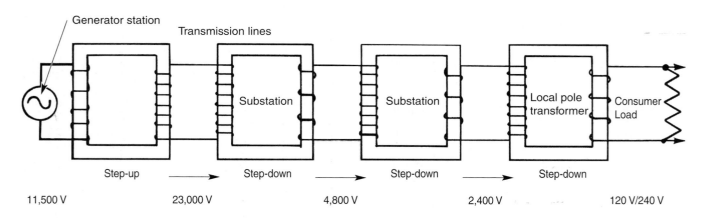

Figure 10-31. Power companies rely on transformers to efficiently transmit electricity over long distances. A chain of transformers links the generating plant with the consumer.

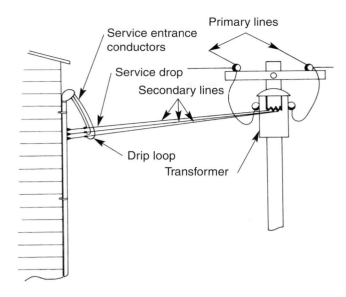

Figure 10-32. The final step-down occurs at the local pole transformer near the structure it serves. Overhead conductors provide the last link to the customer's service wires at the service point.

on how the branch circuit is connected within the distribution panel.

Multiphase Systems

There may be situations where a homeowner requests a system with more than one phase. This is a multiphase system that is usually installed to power heavy-duty or special equipment such as a milling machine or a lathe. Be sure to review local codes for any restrictions regarding installing a multiphase system.

Wye, four-wire, three-phase system

Figure 10-35 illustrates a wye-connected, four-wire, three-phase, 120/208-volt arrangement. Such a system can supply both single-phase 120-volt circuits and three-phase 208-volt circuits.

Study the main-panel wiring diagram shown in **Figure 10-36**. Note particularly the different circuit arrangements that are possible. In this type of panel, there are three hot bus bars. Each has 120 volts to ground when connected to the neutral. For 120-volt circuits, the circuit

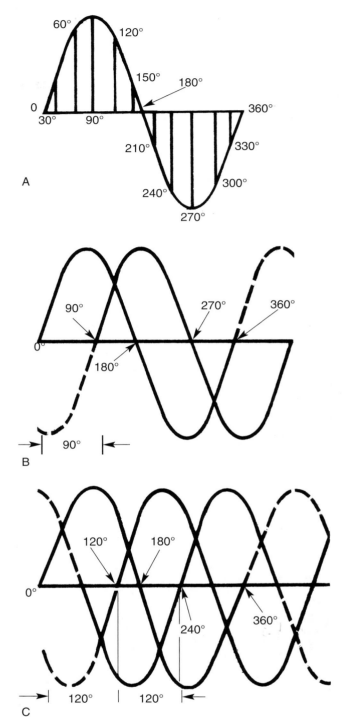

Figure 10-33. The meaning of phase. Electrical energy may be expressed graphically by using sine-wave forms. A—Single-phase electrical energy generation. B—Two-phase current is accomplished by simultaneously generating two single-phase currents 90° apart. C—By generating three, single-phase currents 120° apart, three-phase current is created.

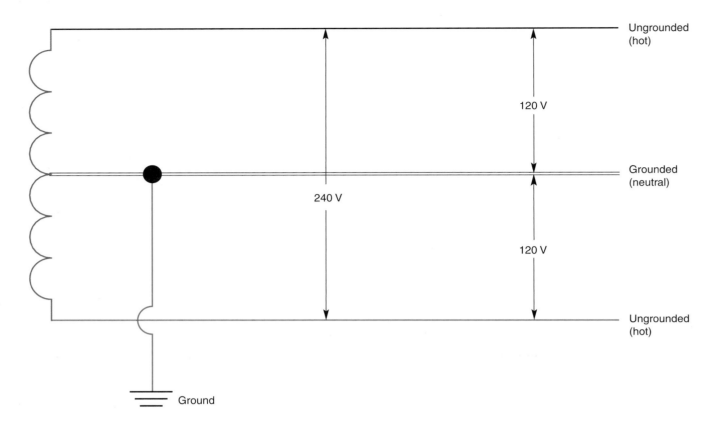

Figure 10-34. Single-phase, three-wire system. By connecting an ungrounded wire and a grounded wire to a load, 120 V service is obtained. Connecting both ungrounded wires to a load will deliver 240 V.

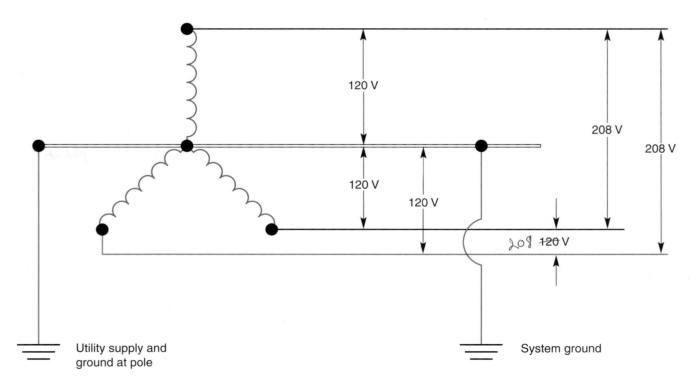

Figure 10-35. A more versatile alternative to single-phase wiring is three-phase wiring. The wye-connected, three-phase, four-wire arrangement provides 120 V/208 V circuits.

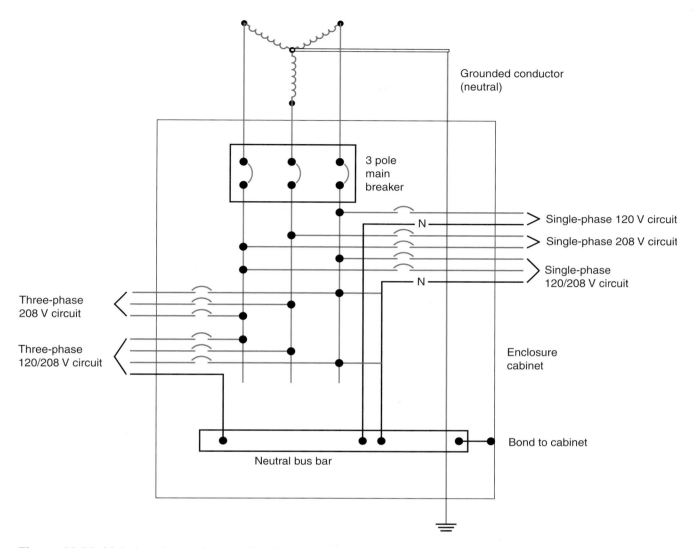

Figure 10-36. Main breaker and panel circuit connections for a wye-connected three-phase, four-wire service. Hot bus bars are marked A, B, and C.

breaker connections are the same as in three-wire, single-phase services.

The black (hot) circuit wire goes to the circuit breaker terminal and the white neutral circuit wire is connected to the neutral bus bar. As with single-phase systems, the 120-volt circuits should be balanced or equally arranged among the three hot buses.

Two-pole circuit breakers are also installed in the same manner as with three-wire, single-phase service panels. That is, the double-pole breaker is attached to any two of the three hot bus bars. Again, carefully balance these between all the buses. These comprise the two-wire, single-phase, 208-volt circuits.

Code Alert

Section 408.3(E)

Phase Arrangement. The phase arrangement on three-phase buses shall be A, B, C from front to back, top to bottom, or left to right, as viewed from the front of the switchboard or panelboard. The B phase shall be that phase having the higher voltage to ground on three-phase, four-wire, delta-connected systems. (See the *NEC* for the complete section)

Delta, four-wire, three-phase system

Another service alternative is the delta-connected, four-wire, three-phase, 120/240-volt system. A schematic for this type is illustrated in **Figure 10-37**. It can provide 120-volt single-phase 240-volt single-phase, and 240-volt three-phase power.

The panel connections, as shown in **Figure 10-38**, are made as follows:

1. For 120-volt single-phase circuits, connect one circuit wire (white) to the neutral and the other (black) to an ordinary single-pole breaker attached to phase A or C only. Note: the breaker must not be attached to phase B for this type of circuit since this would provide 208 volts. Equipment designed for 120-volt operation would be ruined.

   The phase B wire of this system is often called the "high leg" or "wild leg" and must be identified as such at all accessible points with an orange-colored indicator. See *NEC, Section 110.15*. At the panel, wire B is connected to the center bus bar.

2. To derive power at 240-volt single-phase, you simply connect both circuit wires to a double-pole circuit breaker attached to any two phases. Do not include a neutral grounded wire in this circuit.

3. For 240-volt three-phase circuits, run three circuit wires to a three-pole breaker attached to all three phases. Again, ignore the neutral for this type of circuit.

Other variations of multiphase service systems are possible and, in fact, available in many locations:

- Four-wire, wye-connected, three-phase, 277/480-volt systems are very similar to the 120/208-volt system already discussed. The major difference is that the transformer secondary supplying such a system has a higher voltage. Since most major appliances, lighting fixtures, and heating units do not operate at more than 240 volts, this system has limited use.

- Three-wire, delta-connected, three-phase, 240-volt systems have severe limitations. It may supply 240-volt three-phase or 240-volt single-phase circuits only.

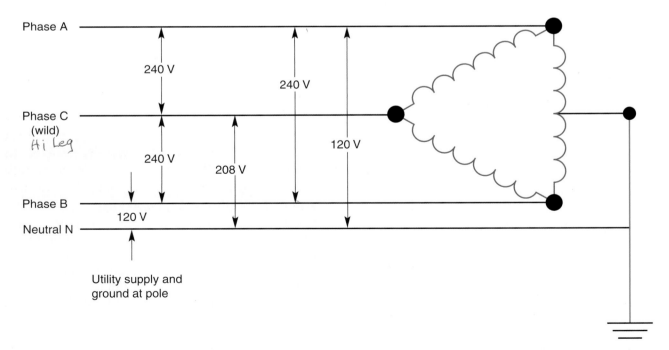

Figure 10-37. Popular delta-connected, three-phase, four-wire service supplies 120 V single-phase, 240 V single-phase, and 240 V three-phase circuits. The "wild" phase C must always be identified at all terminations and accessible points. Usually it is indicated by the color orange.

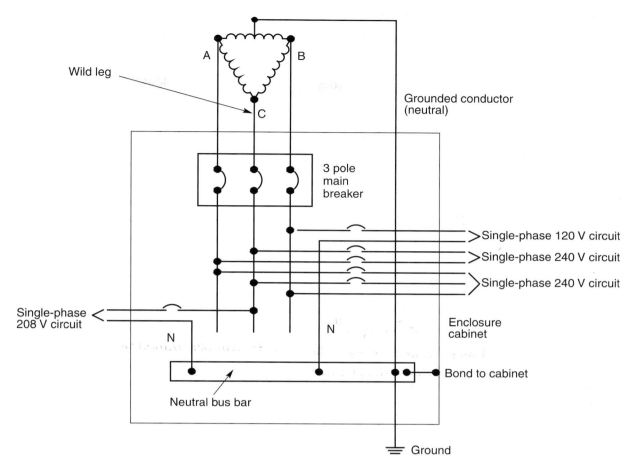

Figure 10-38. Main breaker and panel circuit connections for a wye-connected three-phase, four-wire service. Hot bus bars are marked A, B, and C.

Making a Single-Phase Connection on a Three-Phase System

A more versatile three-wire, 120/208 volt, single-phase circuit can be formed by connecting two circuit wires to a double-pole breaker as previously described and adding a grounded conductor to the circuit. A circuit such as this can be used for 120-volt receptacles and lighting outlets. It can also supply 120/240 volts for electric ranges, counter cooktops, and other devices designed for that purpose.

Three-phase, three-wire 208-volt circuits are derived by connecting the circuit wires to a three-pole circuit breaker. These circuits are specifically designed to operate special three-phase devices such as heaters and various heavy-duty motor-driven equipment.

Last, but not least, a four-wire, three-phase, 120/208-volt circuit is connected in the same manner as the three-wire, 208-volt circuit with the addition of a grounded wire connected to the neutral bus. This type of circuit is extremely useful when extending an electrical system to other circuit panels.

Review Questions

Write your answers on a separate sheet of paper. Do not write in this book.

1. List five major components of a service entrance.

2. The minimum service entrance rating for new buildings is ___100___ amperes.

2. 2/0 copper
4/0 alum or co clad al

3. The proper size service for 200 ampere service is _____ AWG copper wire.

4. Explain what is meant by:

   A. Service drop.

   B. Service lateral.

5. The neutral bus bar at the service entrance panel provides an interconnection means for the _____ conductor(s) and _____ conductor.

6. The minimum clearance of service wires above a sidewalk is _*10*_ feet.

7. The minimum size grounding electrode conductor is _*8*_ AWG.

8. Describe, in your own words, the purpose and location of the following service entrance components:

   A. Meter enclosure. *box containing meter*

   B. Service head. *Fitting installed at top of conduit to prevent moisture*

   C. Main disconnect. *usually - circuit breaker*

Know the Code

A copy of the NEC 2005 is required to answer these questions.

1. Which temporary installations have a 90-day limit?

2. Which part of the grounding system is covered in *Section 250.52*?

3. *Table 310.13* refers to *Article* _____ for the application provisions of underground service entrance cable.

Installing underground service cable requires a trench of sufficient depth. The depth is mandated by local codes, but is usually 18" to 24". A trencher is able to dig 2' to 5' without destroying the nearby grass. (Bobcat Company)

Section 3 Planning

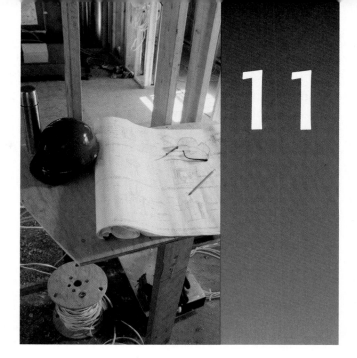

Electrical Prints and Specifications

Objectives

Information in this chapter will enable you to:

- Identify the types of prints that an electrician may read.
- List the standard parts of a drawing.
- Recognize and use standard electrical symbols.
- Understand the schedules that are found on prints.
- Describe the two types of notes.
- Read an electrical print.
- Recognize specifications and understand their importance.
- Draw a circuit layout on a floor plan.
- Plan and install electrical components, including three-way and four-way switches, according to circuit layouts.

Technical Terms

Drawing	Local notes
Electrical print	Plot print
Electrical schedules	Plumbing print
Foundation print	Print
Framing print	Revision block
General notes	Scale
Home run	Specifications
Legend	Title block

Any successful project starts with a plan. An electrician's plan may include prints, schedules, and specifications that show the type and location of all devices, panels, and wiring. There are specific symbols and terminology on these plans that the electrician must know to correctly install the proper products.

Prints

A *print* is a copy of a drawing that illustrates the materials, locations, and methods that must be used during construction. Prints may be called drawings, plans, or blueprints—a term that was popular when the printmaking process created white lines on a blue background. For clarity, a *drawing* in this text will refer to the original document that is created, revised, and approved. A print is a copy of the drawing.

Each group of workers on a project will receive a set of prints that were made specifically for that group. The excavators use a plot

---

print: A copy of a drawing that illustrates the materials, locations, and methods that must be used during construction.

drawing: The original document that is created, revised, and approved.

print when shaping the land, the masons have a foundation print to locate the concrete and bricks, the plumbers have a plumbing print to locate fixtures and piping, the carpenters have a framing print to locate walls, and the electricians have an electrical print to locate devices and calculate circuits. Each group needs access to all of the prints so everyone understands where the other groups' materials will be installed.

Plot Prints

A *plot print* will show the major land-based features such as a swimming pool or garage. Often, this print describes the slope of the land. When appropriate, plot prints will also designate property lines, fences, and easements.

Electricians use an accurate and scalable plot print to locate the service cables, panel, and meter outside of the house. The amount of cable required for a service can be accurately calculated and ordered if the plot print is accurate. The items and features described in a plot print often control the location of underground wiring. The local AHJ will be able to tell you if these items and features can be traversed when running the service cable.

Foundation Prints

Foundation prints show the location and construction of the foundation walls, footings, and other parts of the house that require concrete. The footings and foundation walls support the entire house. Features such as fireplaces, patios, and driveways may also appear on a foundation print.

In situations when service cables may have to pass through a poured concrete or block wall, the foundation print will show the mason and

---

plot print: A copy of the drawing that excavators use when shaping the land.

foundation print: A copy of the drawing that masons use to locate concrete and bricks.

plumbing print: A copy of the drawing that plumbers use to locate fixtures and piping.

framing print: A copy of the drawing that carpenters have when installing the structure of a house.

the electrician where this will occur. A length of conduit can then be placed in the concrete wall before the pour to create a hole. Otherwise, the hole will need to be drilled after the concrete sets. Any cables that will be located under a driveway should pass through conduit. The driveway will not need to be removed if the cables are replaced.

Plumbing Prints

A *plumbing print* contains the locations of all fixtures such as toilets, sinks, showers, tubs, water heaters, and anything else that is connected to the water supply or the sewage lines. The location of the piping that connects these items may be shown on the drawing, but not in most residential projects. You may be able to determine the most likely route for the piping by looking at the locations of the fixtures and the structure around them. A better method is to contact the plumber and ask about the probable route of the piping.

At first, this may seem to be a type of print that an electrician would not have to review. After all, water and electricity are supposed to be separated at all times. Actually, this is a good reason to have a plumbing print; it is easier to avoid the plumbing lines and fixtures when you know where they will be installed. Another reason to review the plumbing print is to locate electrical devices for items such as hot tubs, water heaters, washing machines, and even yard sprinklers.

Framing Prints

There are usually many *framing prints* in a set for a construction project. These prints will illustrate features from the overall shape of the house to the small details of trimming out a window. The beams, joists, and other supporting features of the house will be dimensioned on the framing print. Carpenters also use a floor plan to locate walls, doorways, stairs, and windows.

The structural details will help you determine where to run the cable and conduit in a manner that reduces the number of holes in the joists. Drilling these holes takes time, and the holes may reduce the strength of the joists. The floor plan is a useful print when you must locate outlet receptacles and switches within the rules of the *NEC*.

Electrical Prints

Symbols that represent lighting fixtures, outlet receptacles, switches, panels, and the circuits that connect them are shown on an *electrical print*. The general location of this equipment is shown, but the exact position may not be dimensioned. The electrical print should contain details that describe the types of equipment that you are required to install.

You must be able to understand the symbols, dimensions, notes, and lists on an electrical print in order to complete the job accurately and within all relative codes. The electrical print is used to order the equipment, determine the length of the cables and wires needed, and inform the local inspector about the proposed layout. Since this print is usually created directly from the floor plan, you can foresee most of the structure and adjust the cable and conduit routing.

Understanding Electrical Prints

To many people, an electrical print may look like a drawing that someone covered with hieroglyphics and curved lines. You will soon see the circuits, devices, and wiring that are represented in a well-made electrical print.

Basic Print Components

Before focusing on the specifics of a print, there are some basic components that you will need to understand. These components are present on all drawings and should be easily recognized. The style, size, and even location of the components will vary on drawings created by different schools and companies. However, the information in each must be understandable and complete.

Title blocks

The *title block* is the area on a print that contains basic information for identification purposes. You will find items in the title block such as the drawing name, names of people who worked on the original drawing, drawing number, and drawing scale. This is the first place to look to verify that you have the correct drawing for the job. See **Figure 11-1**.

---

electrical print: A copy of the drawing that electricians have to locate devices and fixtures.

title block: This is the area on a print that contains basic information such as the drawing name, names of people that worked on the original drawing, drawing number, and drawing scale.

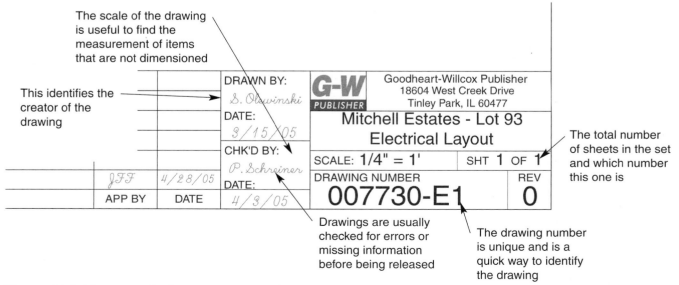

The scale of the drawing is useful to find the measurement of items that are not dimensioned

This identifies the creator of the drawing

Drawings are usually checked for errors or missing information before being released

The drawing number is unique and is a quick way to identify the drawing

The total number of sheets in the set and which number this one is

Figure 11-1. These are the key components of a title block.

Revision blocks

A drawing may require corrections or changes throughout its lifetime. A *revision block* is an area on a drawing where the changes and corrections are recorded. There may be lettered or numbered symbols next to each revision in the revision block. Look for a similar symbol on the drawing area to find the related revision. The revision block is a good place to look if the print appears to be different from the way it did when the job was first started. See **Figure 11-2**.

revision block: This is an area on a drawing where the changes and corrections are recorded.

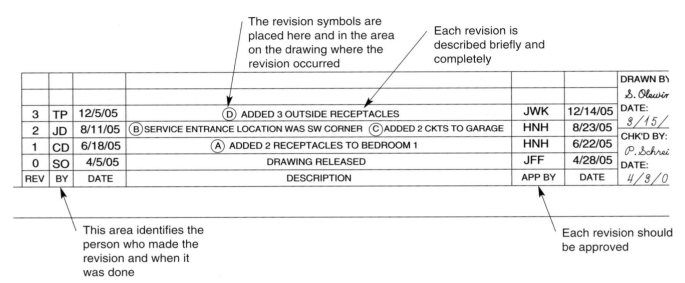

The revision symbols are placed here and in the area on the drawing where the revision occurred

Each revision is described briefly and completely

REV	BY	DATE	DESCRIPTION	APP BY	DATE	
						DRAWN BY S. Olewin
3	TP	12/5/05	Ⓓ ADDED 3 OUTSIDE RECEPTACLES	JWK	12/14/05	DATE: 3/15/
2	JD	8/11/05	ⒷSERVICE ENTRANCE LOCATION WAS SW CORNER ⒸADDED 2 CKTS TO GARAGE	HNH	8/23/05	CHK'D BY: P. Schrei
1	CD	6/18/05	Ⓐ ADDED 2 RECEPTACLES TO BEDROOM 1	HNH	6/22/05	DATE: 4/3/0
0	SO	4/5/05	DRAWING RELEASED	JFF	4/28/05	
REV	BY	DATE	DESCRIPTION	APP BY	DATE	

This area identifies the person who made the revision and when it was done

Each revision should be approved

Figure 11-2. A well-written revision block will help you track the changes that have been made to a drawing.

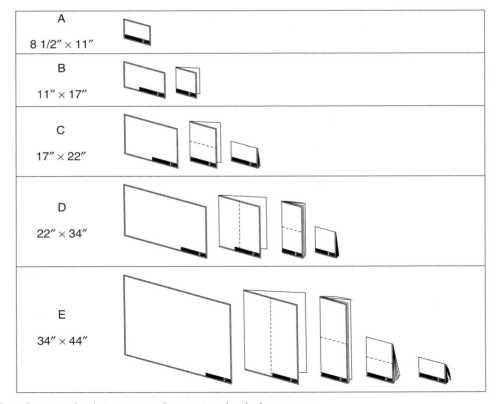

A
8 1/2″ × 11″

B
11″ × 17″

C
17″ × 22″

D
22″ × 34″

E
34″ × 44″

Figure 11-3. Drawings and prints are made on standard-size paper.

Print sizes

The print must be large enough to be legible, yet small enough to handle on the work site. Standard sizes are shown in **Figure 11-3**. Most electrical prints are C, D, or E size. Also, notice the proper way to fold a print to a manageable size. You will have to do this if the print is not rolled up.

Scale

The *scale* of the drawing is the ratio of the size of the object to the size that the object was reduced or enlarged in the drawing. A simple example is a 30′ × 40′ house that measures 7 1/2″× 10″ on a drawing. The scale is 1/4″ = 1′. Every 1/4″ measured on the drawing equals 1′. This means that the drawing is 1/48th the size of the actual house. If a wall drawn on this print measures 3 3/4″, and you know that *NEC* requires no point on a wall be more than 6′ away from a receptacle, you can calculate that there should be at least two receptacles on this wall. See **Figure 11-4**.

The scale is 1/4″ = 1′ or 1/48.

Wall length measured on
the drawing   = 3 3/4″
Actual wall length   = 3 3/4″ × 48
                     = 180″
                     = 15′

Symbols

Most symbols used on electrical plans have been approved by the American National Standards Institute (ANSI). These should be understood by every electrician and committed to memory. A misunderstood symbol may cause the installation of an incorrect device. Not only does this make extra work, this mistake may create an unsafe installation. **Figure 11-5** shows the commonly used symbols you will need to

scale: The ratio of the size of an object to the size that the object was reduced or enlarged in the drawing.

legend: The part of the print, plan, or specification that defines each symbol.

remember. The section at the end of this chapter will illustrate these symbols and the types of devices and circuits they represent.

Other less-common symbols may be used if they are defined in a legend. A *legend* is a part of the print, plan, or specifications that defines each symbol. Normally, a small letter (a, b, c, or d) will accompany any special or unusual symbol, **Figure 11-6**.

Lines

Circuits are represented by curved lines drawn from one device to another. The lines are curved to prevent any confusion with the architectural lines. Most of these lines will be solid, the designation for wires that are concealed

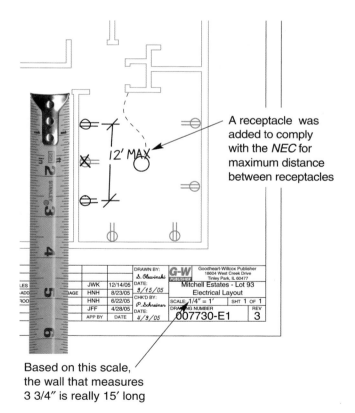

A receptacle was added to comply with the *NEC* for maximum distance between receptacles

Based on this scale, the wall that measures 3 3/4″ is really 15′ long

Figure 11-4. Always check the scale of a print to understand the required length of a cable run.

Electrical Symbols

General outlets

Ceiling Wall

○   —○   Outlet

Ⓔ   —Ⓔ   Electrical Outlet—for use only when a circle used alone might be confused with columns or other geometry

Ⓕ   —Ⓕ   Fan Outlet

Ⓛ   —Ⓛ   Lamp holder

Ⓛ$_{PS}$ —Ⓛ$_{PS}$ Lamp holder with a pull switch

Ⓒ   —Ⓒ   Clock outlet (specify voltage)

Receptacles

⊜   Duplex receptacle

⊜$_3$ Triplex receptacle

⊜$_{WP}$ Weatherproof receptacle

⊜   240 V receptacle

⊜$_R$ Range receptacle

⊜$_S$ Switch and duplex receptacle

⊜$_{GFCI}$ Ground-fault circuit interrupter receptacle

⊜   Split-wired receptacle

◉   Special purpose receptacle

⊟   Floor receptacle

Switches

S   Single pole switch

S$_2$ Double pole switch

S$_3$ Three-way switch

S$_4$ Four-way switch

S$_K$ Key operated switch

S$_P$ Switch and pilot lamp

S$_{CB}$ Circuit breaker

S$_{WCB}$ Weatherproof circuit breaker

S$_{MC}$ Momentary contact switch

S$_{WP}$ Weatherproof switch

S$_T$ Timer switch

Miscellaneous

▬   Flush-mount panel

▬   Surface-mount panel

Ⓣ   Transformer

▭○▭   Surface-mount fluorescent fixture

▭○R▭   Recessed fluorescent fixture

◁   Telephone outlet

—◁   Wall mounted telephone outlet

Figure 11-5. ANSI electrical symbols. These standard symbols should be studied so they become familiar and instantly recognizable. (ANSI)

Any Standard Symbol as given above with the addition of a lowercase subscript letter may be used to designate some special variation of Standard Equipment of particular interest in a specific set of architectural plans.

Figure 11-6. Special symbols carry a lowercase letter alongside. An electrician must know where to look for an explanation. (ANSI)

in a ceiling or wall. Circuit lines made from long dashes represent wiring that is concealed in a floor and short dashes represent exposed

wiring. Any service or feed runs should be indicated with a heavy line. See **Figure 11-7**.

If every circuit were drawn as installed, the lines would continue to the circuit breaker panel. To prevent this buildup of lines near the panel, the circuit line is not drawn all the way back to the panel. Instead, the circuit line stops at the point where the run back to the panel begins; this is called the ***home run***. The branch

home run: The length of conductors from a circuit back to the service panel.

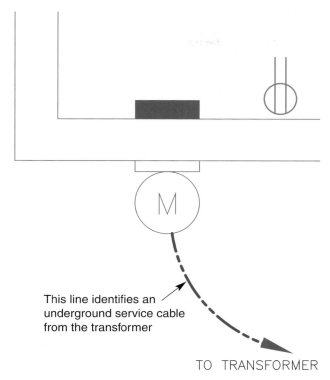

Figure 11-7. Use a heavy lineweight to identify service or feeder runs.

This line identifies an underground service cable from the transformer

TO TRANSFORMER

circuit home run to the panel is then identified with an arrow. There is one arrowhead for each circuit in that run. Often, the circuit is labeled with a number for clarity. See **Figure 11-8**.

Notice the hash marks that cut across the circuit lines. These indicate the number of wires required. The long hash marks indicate the ungrounded wires and the short hash marks indicate the grounded wires.

Schedules

Electrical schedules are tables that list items such as fixtures, power requirements, panel-board information, receptacles, and switches. See **Figure 11-9**. Schedules save print reading time by placing information in one easy-to-find

---

electrical schedules: Tables that list items such as fixtures, power requirements, panelboard information, receptacles, and switches.

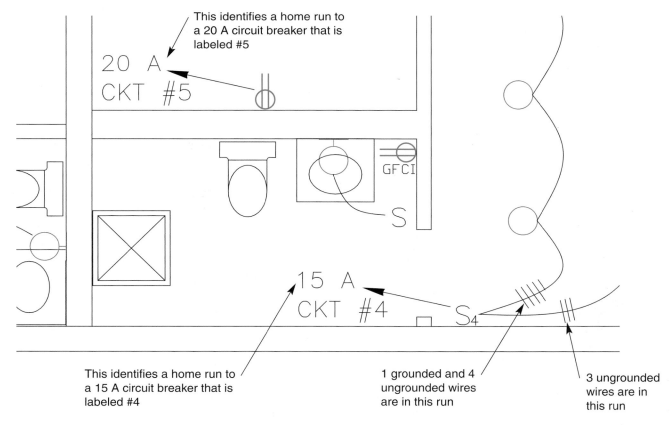

This identifies a home run to a 20 A circuit breaker that is labeled #5

20 A CKT #5

This identifies a home run to a 15 A circuit breaker that is labeled #4

15 A CKT #4

1 grounded and 4 ungrounded wires are in this run

3 ungrounded wires are in this run

Figure 11-8. Branch circuit home runs are indicated with an arrow and, occasionally, a circuit number.

Lighting Fixture Schedule						
Item	Description	Lamps		Mounting	Total	Comments
		No.	Type			
①	HALO H71CT IC Recessed 7" Housing	1	40W A191	Ceiling	14	Halo 170P Albalite Lens with Reflector Cone
②	PFL -2192 22W Fluorescent Circline ceiling mount fixture with SATIN NICKEL finished stainless steel trim	1	22W F	Ceiling	6	Closet fixtures
③	Savoy House #67109	2	50W I	Wall	4	

Figure 11-9. This schedule describes the lighting fixtures that will be installed.

location. This helps with project estimating, purchasing, and construction. The following are some examples of schedules:

- **Lighting fixture schedule.** This type of schedule lists the lighting fixtures used in the project. Each row in the schedule lists basic information for a single type of fixture. The information typically includes the number of fixtures required, the manufacturer, model number, and number and type of lamps. Each type of lighting fixture also has a unique mark (normally identified as a letter). The marks, which are included on the lighting plan, identify the locations of the fixtures.

- **Equipment schedule.** An equipment schedule lists the large electrical equipment being installed. The information provided in this schedule varies depending on the specific type of equipment listed. Equipment schedules may include the voltage provided to the equipment, size and type of overcurrent protection, and the number and sizes of conductors feeding the equipment. Motors, heating units, and cooling units are often listed in equipment schedules.

- **Panel schedule.** A panel schedule lists the basic characteristics of a lighting or power panel. The information normally includes the panel voltage, the panel amperage rating, and a chart listing the circuits, circuit breakers, and equipment served by each circuit.

- **Miscellaneous schedules.** The number and size of schedules is a good way to determine the size of the project. For large projects, schedules may be included to aid estimating

and purchasing. A receptacle schedule and a switch schedule may be included. These schedules are similar to a lighting fixture schedule.

Notes

Often, there will be information that is too difficult or confusing to describe with a dimension or symbol. That is when a note should be added to the drawing. *General notes*, those that contain information regarding the entire installation, should be grouped together at the bottom or side of the drawing. Notes that cover a specific location are called *local notes* and may be moved to the area of the drawing under control. See **Figure 11-10**.

Pro Tip

Using the Print as a Checklist

During the rough-in process, it is common to use the floor plan as a record of work completed. When a run has been completed, a highlighter or colored pencil may be drawn over the run on the floor plan. This practice prevents runs from being overlooked. When two or more electricians are working on the same job, this process is necessary to keep track of work completed.

---

general notes: Notes that contain information that applies to the entire drawing.

local notes: Notes that cover a specific area of a drawing.

NOTES:
1.   CENTER OF ALL RECEPTACLES TO BE 15"
     FROM FLOOR.
2.   CENTER OF ALL SWITCHES TO BE 44"
     FROM FLOOR.
3.   ALL CEILING BOXES TO BE BE SECURELY
     MOUNTED WITH A SUPPORT BAR.

General notes

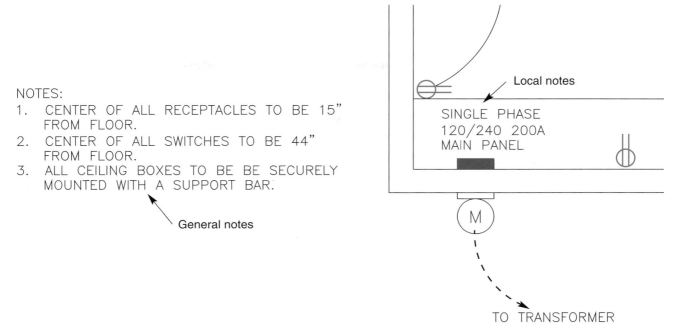

Local notes

SINGLE PHASE
120/240 200A
MAIN PANEL

M

TO TRANSFORMER

Figure 11-10. Most drawings will have general and local notes to clarify various issues.

Specifications

Specifications are documents that list the items of a schedule, the local code requirements not found in the *NEC*, and designations of those responsible for supplying the materials. Specifications, or specs, are included with the prints to clearly define what is to be done, how it is to be done, and who is responsible for doing it.

Although the prints have lists of materials to be purchased, the specifications will also have a similar list. If the lists do not match, the specifications are typically followed. This is because a print may be used for multiple projects, but the specifications are the documents that are created for a specific project.

Often, the local building commission or other AHJ uses the *NEC* as a starting point and adds or modifies some rules. To make sure the electrician and the homeowner are aware of these changes, these specific rules are usually listed in the specifications.

To avoid confusion and lost time, the specifications stipulate who is responsible for purchasing the materials. Most installations require the electrician's company to purchase all of the materials, but some installations may not be so clearly defined. For example, if one company is installing the electrical wiring and another is installing the phone and network cabling, which company purchases the multifunction box where both systems terminate? Specifications should be thorough and clear so that everyone involved is completely informed.

Wiring Circuits

We will now look at the actual wiring of circuits by comparing print and pictorial drawings. These types of drawings cover common circuits found in residential construction.

Compare the circuit in each print with the pictorial. Metallic conduit, flexible metallic

specifications: Documents that list the items of a schedule, the local code requirements not found in the *NEC*, and designations of those responsible for supplying the materials.

conduit, and nonmetallic cable will be drawn as shown in **Figure 11-11**. As you study the circuits shown in **Figures 11-12** through **11-27**, note the wiring method used. Trace the different wires in the pictured drawings until you become familiar with the symbols in the circuit layouts.

No grounding wire is shown in pictorial drawings for metallic conduit. None is required. The conduit itself serves as the grounding conductor. Prints do not show the grounding conductor regardless of the wiring method used.

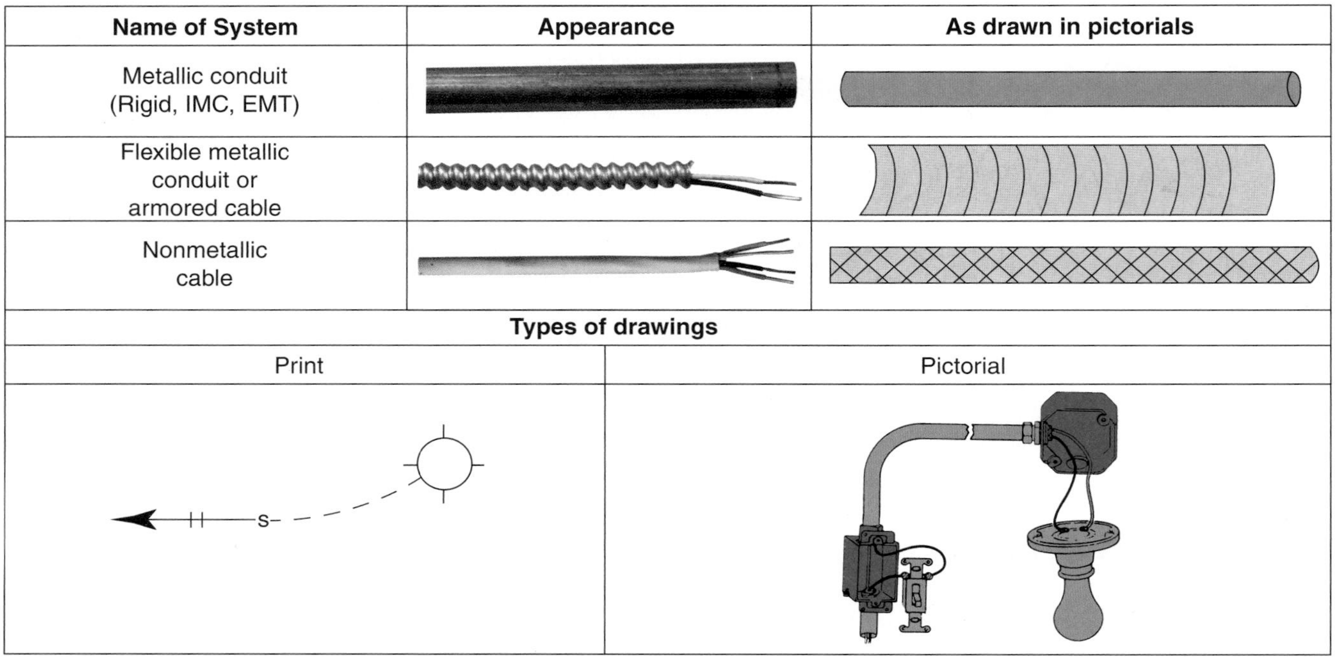

Name of System	Appearance	As drawn in pictorials
Metallic conduit (Rigid, IMC, EMT)		
Flexible metallic conduit or armored cable		
Nonmetallic cable		

Types of drawings	
Print	Pictorial

Figure 11-11. This key will help you to read the circuit drawings in this chapter.

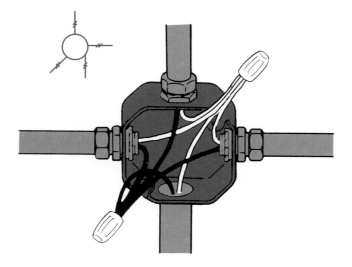

Figure 11-12. Junction boxes serve the purpose of dividing a circuit into several directions. Study the circuit layout and the schematic and compare them with actual wiring method shown in the pictorial drawing.

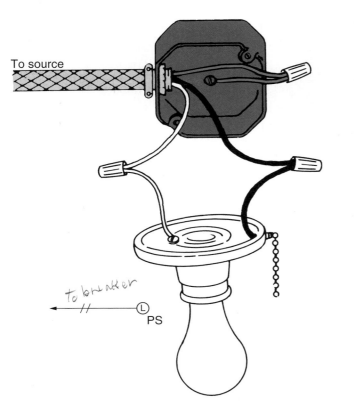

To source

to breaker
L
PS

Figure 11-13. Simple pull-chain fixture at the end of a circuit run. Switch is in the fixture itself.

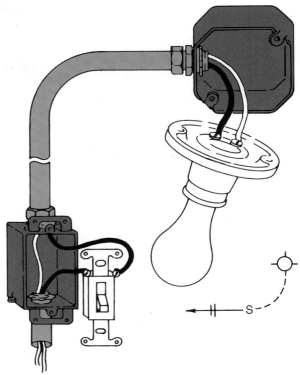

S

Figure 11-14. A single light controlled by a wall switch. Feed is to switch. Switch never interrupts the neutral conductor.

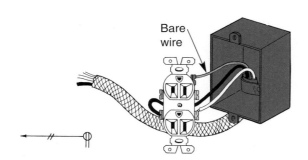

Bare wire

Figure 11-15. Continuously live duplex, grounding-type, receptacle. Both parts of duplex are served by the circuit wires. (GE Wiring Devices Dept.)

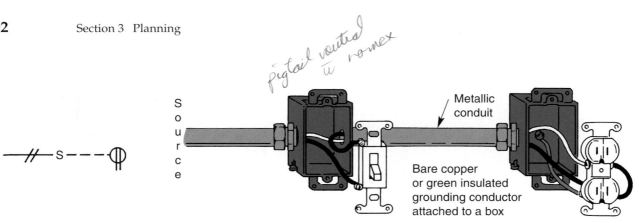

Handwritten: pigtail routed in romex

Handwritten label: Metallic conduit

Bare copper
or green insulated
grounding conductor
attached to a box

Figure 11-16. Switched duplex, grounding-type, receptacles are used in rooms where overhead lighting is not desired. One or both sides of receptacle are controlled by the switch.

Handwritten note: ground to light box but not outlets ?

Handwritten note: Could I use green grounding wire ned?

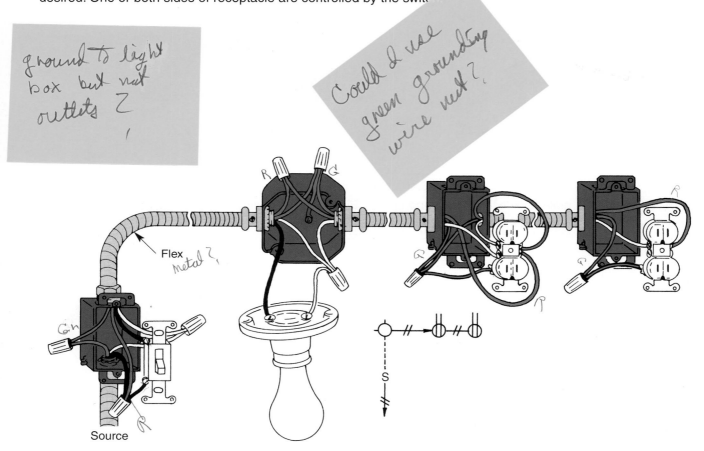

Handwritten label: Flex metal ?

Figure 11-17. Light controlled by a single-pole switch has outlets beyond it that are always live. Source or feed is to switch.

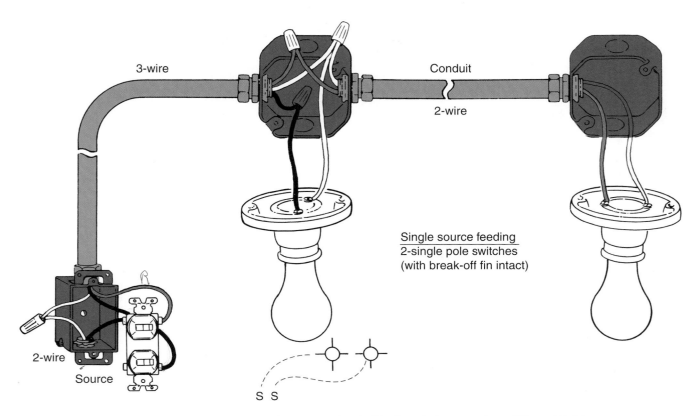

Figure 11-18. Two single-pole switches on the same circuit. Each switch controls a different light.

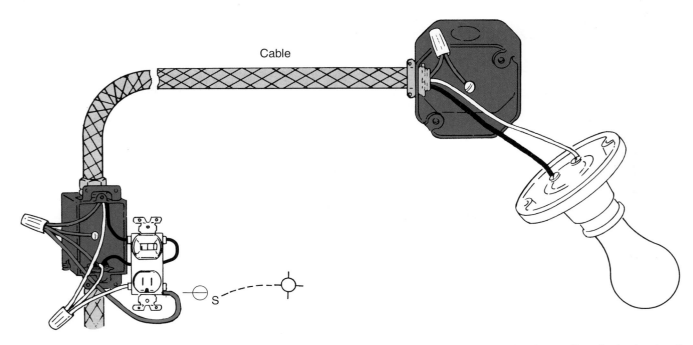

Figure 11-19. Switch/receptacle combination. Switch controls light while receptacle is always live. A single circuit supplies both the switch and the receptacle outlet.

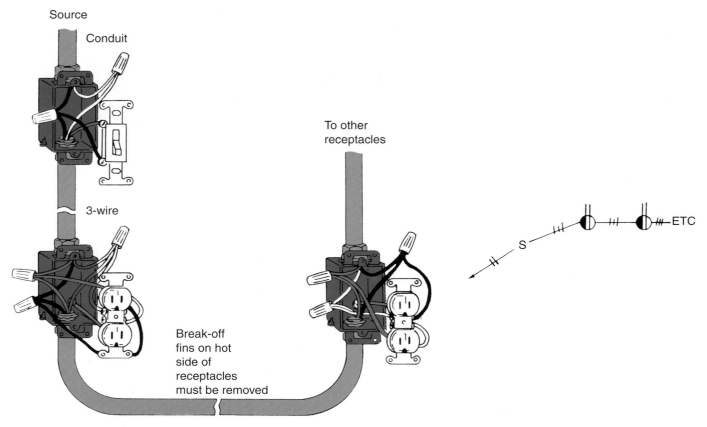

Figure 11-20. Split-wired receptacles. Top half is always hot; bottom half is controlled by single-pole switch.

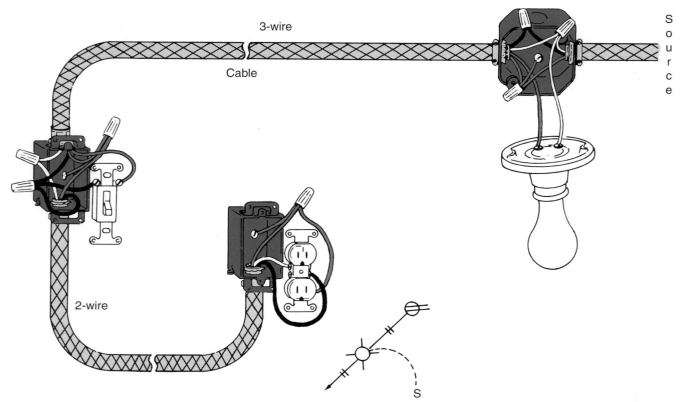

Figure 11-21. Light controlled by a switch. Receptacle beyond the switch is live. Source is at the light.

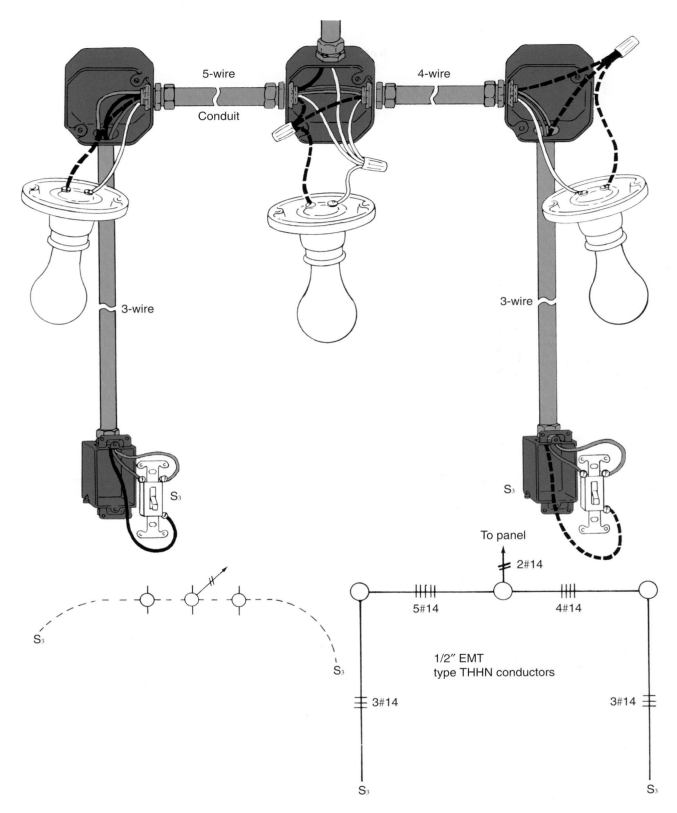

Figure 11-22. Several light fixtures are controlled simultaneously by a pair of three-way switches.

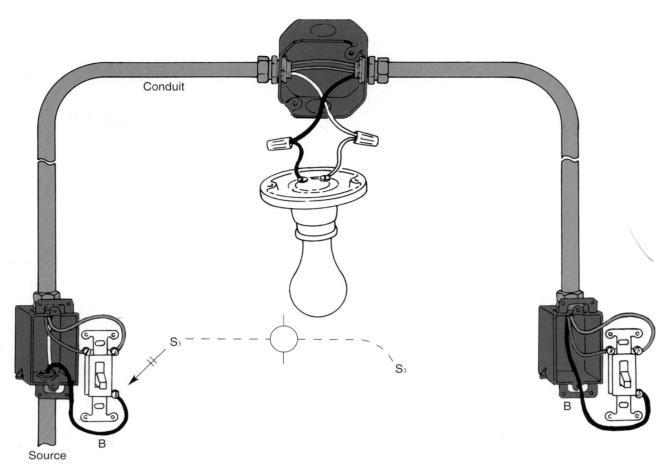

Conduit

S₃

S₃

B

B

Source

Figure 11-23. A pair of three-way switches controlling a single light fixture. Source is to one of the three-way switches.

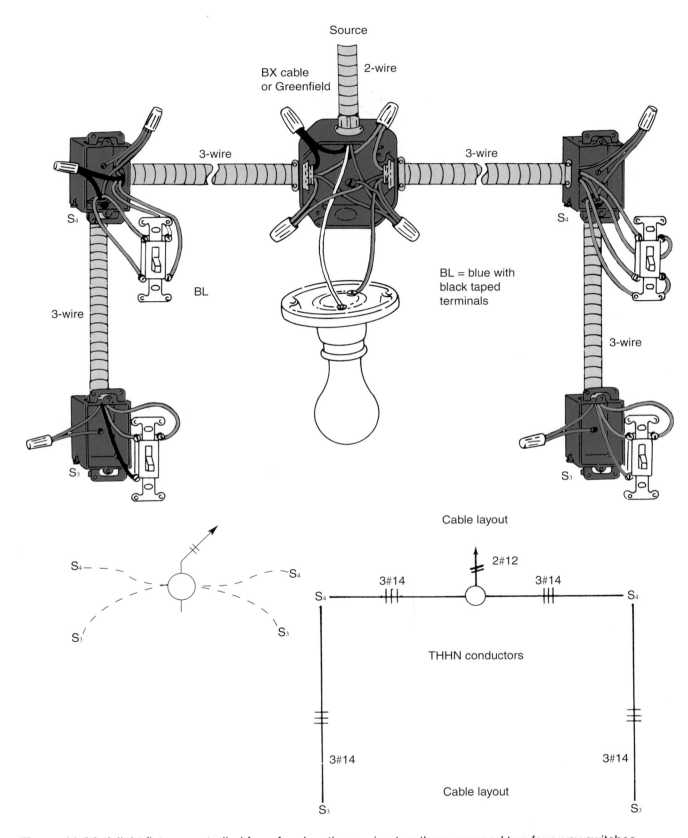

Figure 11-24. A light fixture controlled from four locations using two three-way and two four-way switches.

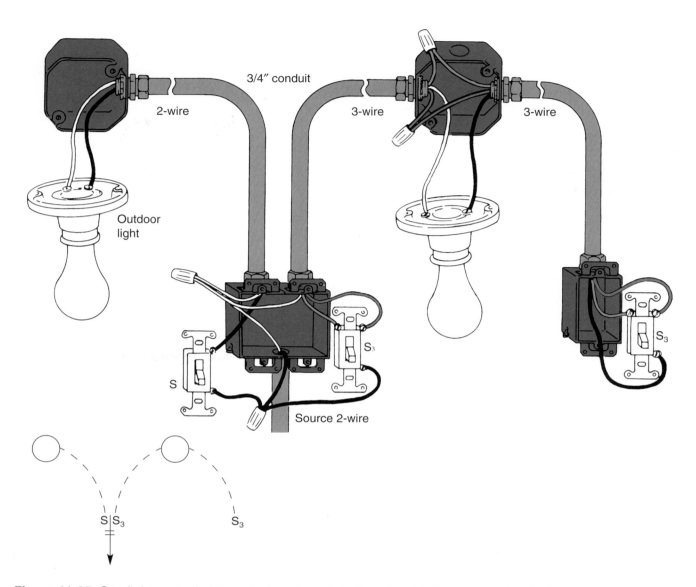

Figure 11-25. One light controlled by a single-pole switch. One circuit is the source, the single-pole and one three-way switch are housed together.

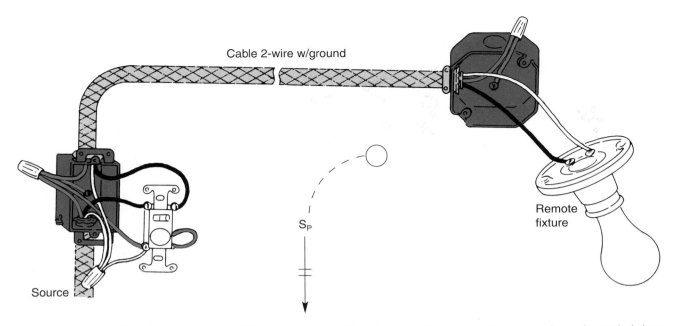

Figure 11-26. Single-pole switch controlling a remote lighting fixture, which cannot be seen from the switch location. Pilot light is on when fixture is on. There are also switches available with red handles that light up when the switch is on. Source is at switch. There are different methods of wiring such as a switch. Refer to manufacturer's instructions.

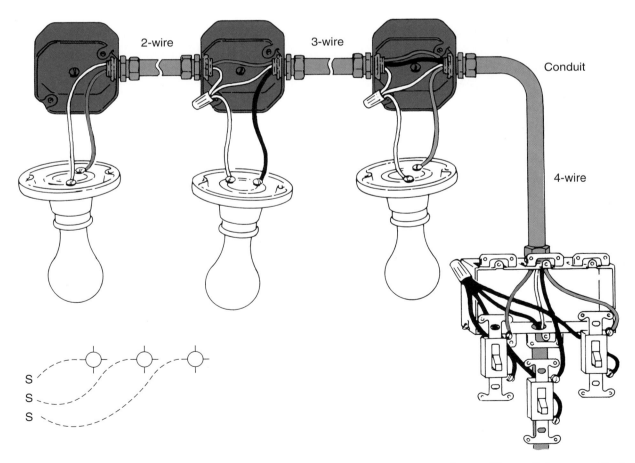

Figure 11-27. Three switches on one circuit. Each controls a separate lighting fixture. The switches are all at one location in a multi-gang box. The source is at the switch.

Review Questions

Write your answers on a separate sheet of paper.
Do not write in this book.

1. Indicate the meaning of each of the following electrical symbols:

(handwritten labels: Lamp holder, Duplex Receptacle, Special purpose receptacle, Single pole switch, 4 way switch, Surface Mount florescent)

2. If you see a standard symbol used on an electrical plan with a small letter alongside, where would you look for an explanation of its meaning? *legend*

3. An electrical plan that shows the size and number of conductors in cable runs is known as a(n) _____.

4. Explain the value of an electrical plan during a rough-in. *equipment location*

Create sketches for the following installations as you would when drawing on a floor plan. Include the proper symbols and lines.

5. A single-pole switch controlling three light fixtures.

6. A single-pole switch controlling a light fixture with two receptacles always live on the same circuit.

7. A pair of three-way switches controlling a light fixture.

8. On a separate sheet, draw and complete the following diagram:

Load

Source

Switches

Know the Code

A copy of the NEC 2005 is required to answer these questions.

1. *Section 90.8(A)* states that plans and specifications that provide ample space in raceways, spare raceways, and addition spaces allow for _____.

2. Which units of measurement appear first throughout the *NEC*, metric or U.S. Customary?

3. According to *Section 210.70(A)(1)*, which rooms require at least one wall switch-controlled lighting outlet?

Branch-Circuit, Feeder, and Service Design

Objectives

Information in this chapter will enable you to:

- Calculate branch circuit loads.
- Determine the number of branch circuits for a house.
- Explain noncoincident loads.
- Calculate feeder and service loads.
- Balance the loads in a three-wire system.

Technical Terms

Branch circuit
Demand factor
Electrical load
Feeders
Noncoincident loads
Service load

Designing a safe and efficient electrical system is a responsibility that an electrician cannot take lightly. The system must be large enough to handle the loads that will be placed on it when the home is new, as well as twenty years from installation. To ensure a quality electrical system, you must calculate the loads, determine a safe number of circuits to install, and select the proper conductors and equipment.

Branch Circuit Design

Just as a tree has many branches growing from its main trunk, a well-designed electrical system has many branch circuits growing from the main service panel. To divide the load, the electricity entering a building is distributed into branch circuits. A *branch circuit* is a separate electrical path, independent of other electrical paths in the building. It draws its current from the main service panel and is protected by its own OCPD. It serves one or more outlets for receptacles, switches, or fixtures. **Figure 12-1** is a schematic of a main service panel with branch circuits radiating outward. The result is an electrical service that is divided. A failure of any one circuit does not disable any other part of the system.

Branch Circuit Load Calculations

An *electrical load* is the amount of power required for a branch circuit, feeder, or service. The load requirement of each of these segments

branch circuit: A separate electrical path, independent of other electrical paths in the building.

electrical load: The amount of power required for a branch circuit, feeder, or service.

211

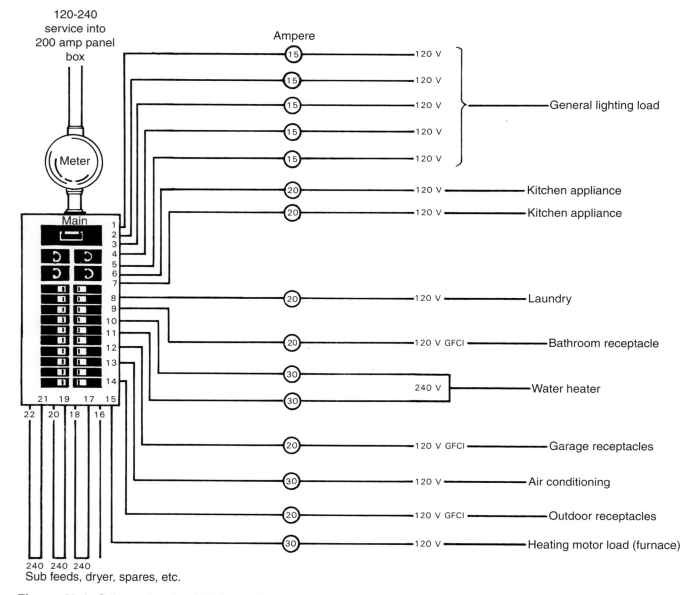

Figure 12-1. Schematic of a 200 A service entrance. The 22 branch circuits will meet minimum standards and provide for future expansion. Note that each branch has its own circuit breaker.

of an electrical system must be calculated before determining the number of circuits and the size of the conductors, OCPDs, and devices to install in a residence.

Many branch circuits and feeders have utilization equipment that will not be used at the same time. Therefore, the total load on these circuits may be reduced by a percentage called the **demand factor** to create a lower electrical load. Throughout this chapter, you will see examples of how and when the demand factor may be applied.

The total of all branch circuit loads can be calculated after you know the square footage of the living space, the number and size of any large appliances, and the largest size of any noncoincident loads. The following sections will explain how you can use this information and the rules of the *NEC* to quickly calculate the

demand factor: A percentage that the total load on a circuit may be reduced to create a lower electrical load.

various types of loads that may be found on a branch circuit.

General lighting load calculations

Although the *NEC* refers to this calculation as a general lighting load calculation, this load also covers small appliances, laundry units, bathroom requirements, and most receptacles throughout the home. The *NEC Table 220.12* specifies the number of volt-amperes for each square foot of building. This table relieves you from having to account for each light fixture, kitchen appliance, and piece of audiovisual equipment. For dwelling units, that number is 3 VA for each square foot of living space. See **Figure 12-2**.

To calculate the general lighting load, first take the outside dimensions and calculate the square footage of the living space of the home. Multiply this total by 3 volt-amperes. This is the total general lighting load for the home. Here is an example that uses the drawing in **Figure 12-3**:

$$\text{Total area} = 2100 \text{ ft}^2$$

Multiply by 3 (from *Table 220.12*)

Total volt-amperes required by general lighting and receptacles = 6300 VA

The *NEC* requires two small-appliance circuits, each having a load of 1500 volt-amperes for a total of 3000 VA.

Two 1500 VA small-appliance loads = 3000 VA

A separate laundry circuit of at least 1500 VA is required by the *NEC*. If the rating on the equipment's nameplate is higher, use that number instead of the 1500 VA.

Load for one laundry circuit = 1500 VA

The laundry load and small-appliance load may be added to the general lighting load prior to applying the demand factor. The demand factor is taken from *Table 220.42* and reduces the load as follows:

General lighting load + small-appliance load + laundry load = 10,800 VA

First 3000 VA is applied at 100% = 3000 VA

Table 220.12 General Lighting Loads by Occupancy

Type of Occupancy	Unit Load	
	Volt-Amperes per Square Meter	Volt-Amperes per Square Foot
Armories and auditoriums	11	1
Banks	39[b]	3½[b]
Barber shops and beauty parlors	33	3
Churches	11	1
Clubs	22	2
Court rooms	22	2
Dwelling units[a]	33	3
Garages — commercial (storage)	6	½
Hospitals	22	2
Hotels and motels, including apartment houses without provision for cooking by tenants[a]	22	2
Industrial commercial (loft) buildings	22	2
Lodge rooms	17	1½
Office buildings	39[b]	3½[b]
Restaurants	22	2
Schools	33	3
Stores	33	3
Warehouses (storage)	3	¼
In any of the preceding occupancies except one-family dwellings and individual dwelling units of two-family and multifamily dwellings:		
Assembly halls and auditoriums	11	1
Halls, corridors, closets, stairways	6	½
Storage spaces	3	¼

[a]See 220.14(J).
[b]See 220.14(K).

Figure 12-2. This table contains the number of volt-amperes (watts) for each square foot. Residential calculations will use the dwelling unit load of 3 VA per ft².

The remainder is applied at 35%: 7800 × .35 = 2730 VA

Total general lighting load = 5730 VA

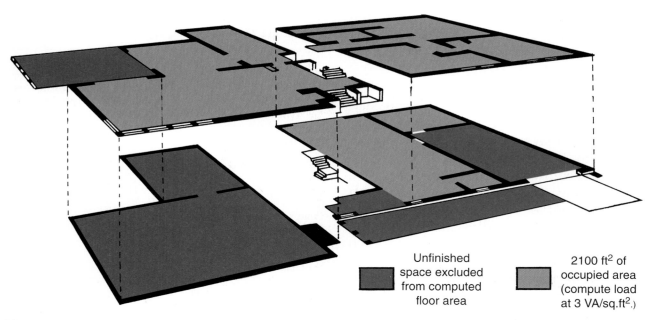

Unfinished space excluded from computed floor area

2100 ft² of occupied area (compute load at 3 VA/sq.ft².)

Figure 12-3. Use the outside dimensions to calculate the number of square feet in a house. You can then find the total general lighting load for that house.

Appliances

The load for specific appliances is based on the ampere rating specified on the nameplate of the appliance. The demand factor of 75 percent can be applied only if there are four or more of these appliances on one feeder or service. This category of appliances does not include electric ranges, clothes dryers, space-heating equipment, or air-conditioning equipment.

$$\begin{aligned}
\text{Dishwasher} &= 1800 \text{ VA} \\
\text{Water heater} &= 3800 \text{ VA} \\
\text{Garbage disposal} &= 972 \text{ VA} \\
\text{Total appliance load} &= 6572 \text{ VA}
\end{aligned}$$

Clothes dryer

Find the load of the clothes dryer by looking at the nameplate. If this rating is less than 5000 volt-amperes, you must use 5000 in the calculations. If the load on the nameplate is higher, use that number. Unless there is more than one electric dryer installed in the home, a demand factor cannot be used, *Table 220.54*. This dryer is a 240-volt, 27-ampere unit.

$$\begin{aligned}
240 \text{ V} \times 27 \text{ A} &= 6480 \text{ VA} \\
\text{Total load for the clothes dryer} &= 6480 \text{ VA}
\end{aligned}$$

Determining the Number of Branch Circuits

Having the proper number of branch circuits on a system will prevent unsafe overloading of the circuits and the nuisance of tripping breakers. Now that you are able to calculate the branch circuit load, it is time to divide the loads into safe and convenient circuits.

Article 210 of the *NEC* outlines the rules regarding the general provisions and specific requirements for branch circuits. These rules, when followed, will certainly provide the safe wiring of the branch circuits.

Bathroom Circuit

Due to the temperature and moisture changes that often occur in bathrooms, circuitry for this area warrants special consideration and discussion. The *NEC* requires that the bathroom be equipped with a switch-controlled lighting fixture and a GFCI-protected receptacle outlet adjacent to the basin.

Figure 12-4 shows a typical floor plan of a bathroom indicating the electrical fixtures. Each vanity is equipped with a soffit-type fluorescent light to illuminate the mirror and a GFCI receptacle for shaving and hair blow-drying.

In addition, recessed lighting fixtures are installed in certain locations to ensure adequate lighting throughout the bathroom. The heater-fan-light device is another convenient, efficient, and practical item worth consideration.

Small Appliances

There must be a minimum of two 20-ampere circuits dedicated to receptacles for small appliances. This circuit load can be included with the general lighting load as stated in *Section 220.52(A)*. These receptacles are located on walls and floors and are used primarily for kitchen appliances.

In addition to the lighting load, the *NEC* requires at least two 20 A, 120 V small appliance circuits. These appliance circuits shall feed receptacles in the kitchen, pantry, dining room, and breakfast room, **Figure 12-5**. Also required is at least one 20 A, 120 V outlet in the laundry area.

Refer to *Article 220* of the *NEC* for specific rules on these circuits. Also, review the tables and examples in *Chapter 9* of the *NEC*.

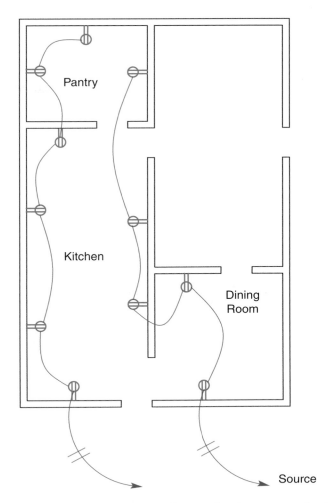

Figure 12-5. Two 20 A appliance circuits are required for receptacle outlets in the kitchen area. These circuits are for plug-in appliances only. Lighting outlets or switched receptacles must be fed by general lighting circuits.

Laundry

The laundry equipment will use a 20-ampere circuit that has no other receptacles. This circuit load can be included with the general lighting load as stated in *Section 220.52(B)*.

Wire Capacity

Although the *NEC* specifies 14 AWG as a minimum wire size, it would indeed be unwise to use anything smaller than 12 AWG in homes built today. Lighting and receptacle outlets wired with 14 AWG will almost certainly be inadequate

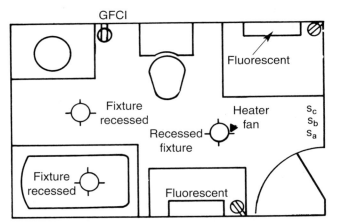

Figure 12-4. Bathroom floor plan. Note the GFCI location.

in 10 to 20 years. Keep this in mind, not only for lighting and receptacle load considerations, but also for *all* feeder calculations. For proper wire ampacities, refer to *NEC Table 310.16*.

Wall Switches

All lights should be controlled by a switch located near each entrance to a room. Wall switches should be placed in locations that are accessible and at a height suitable for all occupants. Generally, wall switches are 48" to 52" above the floor level and on the latch side of a doorway, **Figure 12-6**. *Article 404* of the *NEC* describes additional installation requirements. The Americans with Disabilities Act (ADA), a comprehensive civil rights law for people with disabilities, stipulates that the height of wall switches follow these rules: If the clear floor space allows parallel approach by a person in

a wheelchair, the maximum high side reach allowed shall be 54". If the wall switch must be accessed by reaching forward, the maximum height shall be 48".

Outlet Receptacles

The *NEC* requires that outlets be provided in the kitchen, family room, dining room, living room, parlor, library, den, sunroom, breakfast room, bedroom, recreation room, and other similar rooms in a dwelling. These outlets must be located so that no point along any wall will be more than 6' (183 mm) from a receptacle. This rule applies to wall spaces 2' (61 cm) or wider. Included are outside wall spaces occupied by sliding panels. Where fixed room dividers or freestanding counters add to the wall space, the same 6' rule applies. See **Figure 12-7** and refer to *Section 210.52* of the *NEC*.

Locate the receptacles close to the ends of large wall spaces to avoid concealment by sofas or other large pieces of furniture. Receptacle outlets should be placed 12" to 15" above the floor line. Placing the receptacles at a height of 15" allows for easier access.

A receptacle outlet must be installed at each island or peninsular-type counter top that is 24" or more in length and 12" wide. It may be installed along the side, but it must be within 12" of the counter top.

Receptacle outlets are required in the following places as illustrated in **Figure 12-8**:
- Above any counter space that is wider than 12" in the kitchen and dining areas

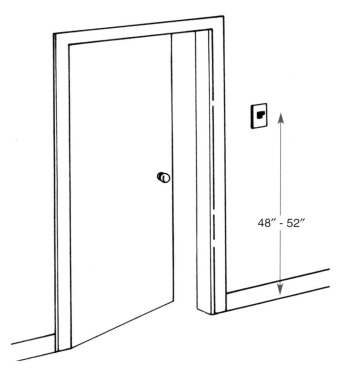

48" - 52"

Figure 12-6. Wall switches must be located at convenient heights. The preferred height for most installations is 48" to 52" above floor level. Locate the switch on the latch side of the doorway.

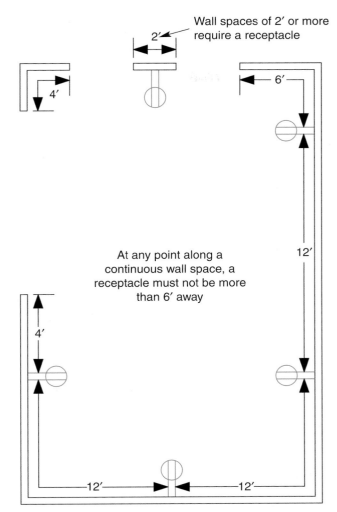

Figure 12-7. Receptacles must be no further than 12' apart along any continuous wall space.

- Next to a bathroom basin, with a GFCI (ground-fault circuit interrupter)
- Outdoors, with a GFCI
- Laundry area
- Basement area, with a GFCI
- Garage, with a GFCI
- Any wall space in excess of 2' and along fixed room dividers
- Hallways
- Crawl spaces at or below grade, where serviceable equipment exists

Maximum number of outlets

The *NEC* does not formally specify the maximum number of outlets permitted for the entire building or even for each circuit. However, the continuous load on any branch circuit is not to be greater than 80 percent of the circuit rating. The maximum wattage for each circuit (CKT) is found as follows:

CKT amperage × CKT voltage × .80 = CKT volt-ampere (VA)

A 20 A branch circuit, for example, can have a maximum continuous load of:

20 A × 120 V × .80 = 1920 VA

While this is clear-cut as far as the total wattage per circuit is concerned, some other considerations must be included in order to determine the number of outlets for each circuit. The load for each lighting outlet can vary considerably. Although some lighting fixtures, like fluorescents, draw a constant load, others do not. Most lighting fixtures can accommodate 25, 40, 60, 75, 100, or 150 W bulbs.

The receptacle outlet load is also variable. Some outlets are rarely used. Others may have no more than a small night-light connected to them. Still others may operate a 100 W table lamp, floor lamp, or portable heater.

Split-wiring

Often, duplex receptacles are split-wired so one outlet may be controlled by a switch. The upper half of the receptacle is always hot while the bottom half is switched. This method of wiring is most frequently used in rooms that do not have a ceiling-mounted fixture, **Figure 12-9**.

Lighting

The *NEC* clearly points out that there are certain lighting outlets that are required in dwelling occupancies. Essentially every room, hallway, stairway, attached garage, detached garage (with power supplied to it), and every entranceway must have at least one

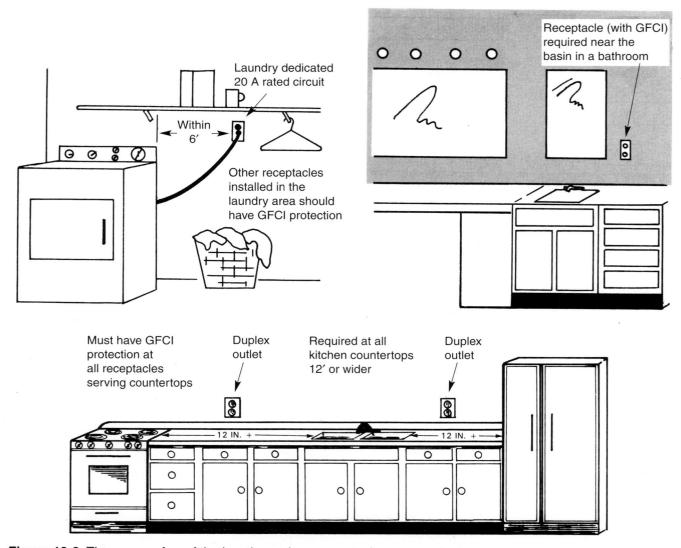

Figure 12-8. These are a few of the locations where receptacles are required.

wall-switched lighting outlet. In addition, the attic, utility room, basement, and below-floor crawl spaces, if used to store items, must have at least one lighting outlet that must be wall switched.

There are exceptions to these basic requirements:

- A wall-switched receptacle is permitted in rooms other than the kitchen or bathroom where a lamp may provide lighting instead of a wall or ceiling fixture.

- A remote-controlled switch may be used for hallways and stairs.

These basic requirements are shown in

Figure 12-10. The quality of lighting and types of lighting fixtures available are beyond the scope of this book. However, good lighting is essential to personal well-being and should be carefully considered.

Good lighting should provide an adequate amount of light where it is needed. Lighting should not create shadows or glare. You must be familiar with the criteria that go into creating good lighting in order to understand it. Terms such as candlepower, lumens, foot-candles, as well as others, must be understood to get a real insight into the proper quality of lighting for the home.

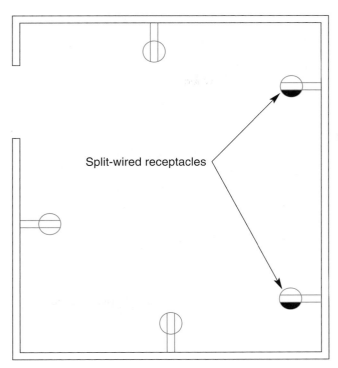

Figure 12-9. Receptacles may be split-wired. That is, the upper half of the receptacle is always "hot," while the bottom portion is switch controlled from each entrance. Thus, floor and table lamps plugged into the bottom half can be switch activated.

Lighting fixture installation rules

Article 410 of the *NEC* deals with:

- Fixtures
- Pendants
- Arc lamps
- Discharge lamps
- Incandescent filament lamps
- Lampholders
- The wiring and equipment forming the above lighting and its installation

Noncoincident Loads

There are loads that will not be operated at the same time; these are called ***noncoincident loads***. An example is the load created when the air conditioner or furnace is running. These two units would never be on at the same time. In this situation, you would calculate the load to be the higher of the two units. The following example compares a central air conditioner to an electric forced-air furnace.

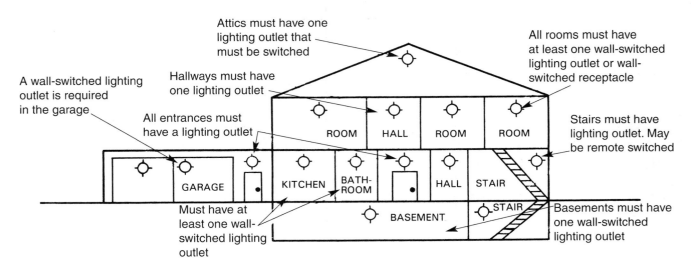

Figure 12-10. These are the basic residential lighting outlet requirements.

noncoincident loads: Loads that will not be placed on a system at the same time.

According to the nameplate on the central air conditioner, 960 VA of power is required to cool the house. The electric furnace requires 13,200 VA of power. Since these loads are noncoincident, you need to use only the higher of the two loads (13,200 VA) when calculating the total load of the house.

Another example of a noncoincident load may take place in a residential garage or workshop. Most power tools in this situation would only be used one at a time. The tool with the largest load would be used to calculate the volt-ampere requirement.

Feeder and Service Load Calculations

A feeder is recognizable by the presence of an OCPD away from the main service panel. See **Figure 12-11**. A detached garage with its own main breaker is connected to the home service panel by a feeder. A kitchen that is located a great distance from the main service panel may

have its own feeder. This method reduces the number of conductors that run this distance from many 12 AWG to a few 3 AWG or 4 AWG. The total of all branch circuit loads and feeder loads is the *service load*.

> **Code Alert**
> **Section 100**
>
> All circuit conductors between the service equipment, the source of a separately derived system, or other power supply source and the final branch-circuit overcurrent device are called *feeders*.

This example requires a feeder to be sent out to the load center in a garage. This feeder will supply 240 V at 60 A from two breakers in the main panel. This would provide enough power for lights, receptacles, power tools, and most welding equipment.

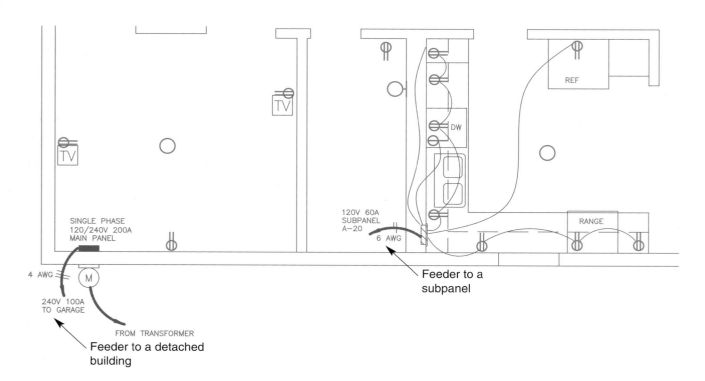

Figure 12-11. A feeder load may serve an outdoor building or a section of a house's interior.

240 V × 60 A = 14400 VA

Feeder for the garage = 14400 VA

Now that all branch circuit loads and feeder loads have been calculated, you can determine the service load. This is done by adding all branch circuit loads and feeder loads.

Total general lighting load =   5730 VA

Total air conditioning load =   3380 VA

Total appliance load =   6572 VA

Total load for the clothes dryer =   6480 VA

Feeder for the garage = 14400 VA

Total service load = 36562 VA

The service to this home will be supplied by a 240 V single-phase, three-wire system. Divide the total service load by the voltage to calculate the amperage required by this home.

36562 VA ÷ 240 V = 152 A

This home will need a minimum of 152 A to operate safely. Round this up to the next standard size main breaker and you would install a 175 A panel. Before settling on this size, you may want to consider other factors such as:

- Is there a good chance that the home could be expanded?

- Will the homeowner build a workshop in the future?

- What size service is installed in the neighborhood homes?

- Is the service large enough to handle the addition of a pool or hydromassage bathtub?

With these possibilities in mind, it may be a good idea to upgrade the service to 200 A. This will leave plenty of power available for the future.

Optional Feeder and Service Load Calculations

Part IV of *Article 220* contains rules for using an optional method that requires fewer calculations to determine feeder and service loads.

This easier method may be used if the residence is serviced by a 120/240-volt or 208Y/120-volt set of 3-wire service or feeder conductors with an ampacity of 100 or more. Since this situation covers many new-home installations, the optional method is frequently used.

The examples above will be used for the optional calculations so that ease-of-use and service load results may be compared.

General loads (optional method)

Each of the following four categories must be calculated and then added together. Subtract 10,000 VA from this total before multiplying it by 40 percent. Add the 10,000 VA back to that product to arrive at the total general load.

1. General lighting and general-use receptacles. Multiply the total square feet of living space by 3 VA/ft² (from *Section 220.82(B)(1)*).

2100 ft² × 3 VA/ft² = 6300 VA

Total volt-amperes required by general lighting and receptacles = 6300 VA

2. Small-appliance branch circuits (two minimum) and a laundry branch circuit. Each 20 A branch circuit requires 1500 VA.

3 × 1500 VA   = 4500 VA

Total small-appliance and laundry circuits = 4500 VA

3. Permanently connected appliances. Total the nameplate ratings of all appliances described in *Section 220.82(B)(3)*.

Dishwasher =   1800 VA

Water heater =   3800 VA

Garbage disposal =   972 VA

Electric clothes dryer =   6480 VA

Total permanent appliance load = 13052 VA

---

service load: The total of all branch circuit loads and feeder loads.

feeder: The circuit conductors between the service equipment and the final branch-circuit OCPD.

The total general load is calculated as follows:

General lighting and receptacles	6300 VA
Small-appliance and laundry circuits	4500 VA
Permanent appliance load	+13052 VA
General load	=23852 VA
Subtract 10,000 VA	− 10000 VA
	=13852 VA
Multiply remainder by 40 percent ×	.40
	= 5541 VA
Add 10,000 VA to the product	+10000 VA
Answer is the total general load	=15541 VA

Heating and air-conditioning load (optional method)

Select the largest of the following six calculations to use for the heating and air-conditioning load:

- 100 percent of the nameplate rating of the air-conditioner

- 100 percent of the nameplate rating of the heating when a heat pump is used without any supplemental electric heating

- 100 percent of the nameplate ratings of electric thermal storage and other heating systems where the usual load is expected to be continuous at the full nameplate value

- 100 percent of the nameplate rating of the heat pump compressor and 65 percent of the supplemental electric heating for central electric space heating systems if the heat pump can operate at the same time as the supplementary heat

- 65 percent of the nameplate rating of electric space heating if less than four separately controlled units

- 40 percent of the nameplate rating of electric space heating if four or more separately controlled units

The air conditioner in the example qualifies for the first calculation in the above list.

Add the air conditioning load, the general load, and the garage feeder load to determine the service load.

$$15541 \text{ VA} + 3380 \text{ VA} + 14400 \text{ VA} = 33321 \text{ VA}$$

$$\text{Service load} = 33321 \text{ VA}$$

The service to this home will be supplied by a 240 V single-phase, three-wire system. Divide the total service load by the voltage to calculate the amperage required by this home.

$$33321 \text{ VA} \div 240 \text{ V} = 138 \text{ A}$$

Based on the optional method, a 150 A service is all that is necessary for this residence. Again, review the previous factors that may justify upgrading the service to a higher amperage before settling on the calculated service.

Balancing Circuit Loads

When planning the hookup of branch circuits and feeders to the main service panel, it is important to keep a balance in the load between the two hot wires in a three-wire system. Remember that the neutral wire in this system is carrying the unbalanced electrical load from both hot wires.

Figure 12-12 helps explain what is happening as current flows through the system. The

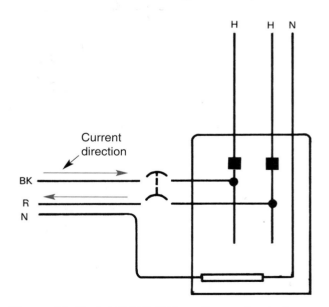

Figure 12-12. A 120 V/240 V appliance circuit. Currents in the two hot wires are always flowing in opposite directions. Thus, opposing currents in the neutral wire cancel each other out.

alternating current in the two hot wires does not flow in the same direction at the same time. At the instant it flows one way in the red wire, it is flowing the opposite direction in the black wire. At the same time the flow for each wire will change in the neutral wire. The two currents flowing in opposite directions through the neutral wire tend to cancel each other's inductance. As long as the current in each direction is nearly equal there is no problem. However, when the current differences are great, there may be trouble. The neutral wire will heat up and the insulation could melt.

This situation can arise with appliances that operate on both 120 and 240 volts. These appliances must be evenly balanced between the two hot wires to reduce the likelihood of overloading the single neutral conductor. **Figure 12-13** shows a system properly balanced at the entrance panel. If you add up the ampere rating of all the circuits on each side, you can see that the ratings add up to nearly the same total. Also, the same number of large appliance circuits is found on each hot wire.

Figure 12-14 shows a typical entrance and hallway. We shall see if the fixtures and receptacles for these areas can be placed on a single 15 A branch circuit. The following outlets and fixtures are needed:

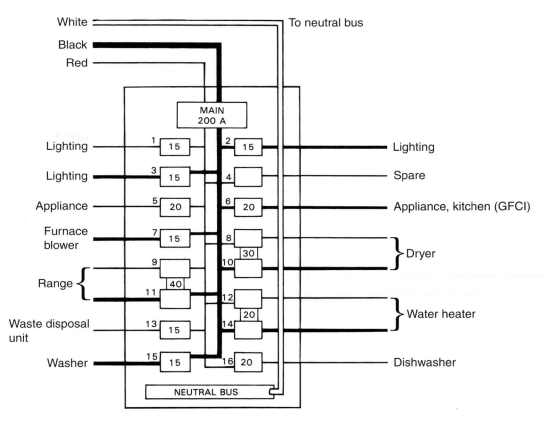

Figure 12-13. Be careful to balance 120 V circuits on both hot wires of a three-wire service. Just add up the total of the rated amperage of each circuit breaker controlling the 120 V circuits.

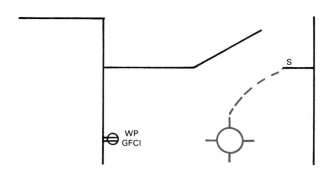

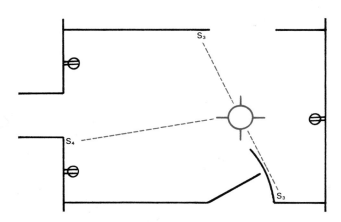

Figure 12-14. Before placing two areas on one circuit, find the load of each area and add them together.

Outlet	Assumed Load (maximum)
1 ceiling fixture (hallway)	150 VA
1 ceiling fixture (entrance)	150 VA
3 receptacles (halfway)	540 VA
1 receptacle (entrance)	180 VA
TOTAL	1020 VA

This total does not exceed the maximum allowable load for a 15 A branch circuit (15 A × 120 V × .80 = 1440 VA). The hallway and entrance can be placed on one circuit with a 15 A overcurrent protection device.

Review Questions

Write your answers on a separate sheet of paper.
Do not write in this book.

1. The _elec. load_ must be calculated before determining the number of circuits for a house.
2. The _____ load covers small appliances, laundry units, bathroom requirements, and most receptacles throughout the home.
3. The *NEC* requires at least __2__ small-appliance circuits.
4. Loads that will not be placed on the system at the same time are called _____ loads.
5. Where should you look to find the ampere rating of an appliance? _nameplate_
6. A group of two 4 AWG wires, one black and one white, running from a main service panel to a smaller service panel near the kitchen is a _____ .
7. *True or False?* The receptacles in the laundry room can be placed on the same circuit as the kitchen.
8. It is important to _calculate_ the loads when connecting the circuits to the service panel.
9. List three locations where GFCIs are required. _Bath Garage Kitchen_
10. Counter spaces in kitchens wider than __2__ feet require a receptacle outlet.
11. *True or False?* If a garage has electricity, it must have a ground-fault circuit interrupter.

Know the Code

A copy of the NEC 2005 is required to answer these questions.

1. What section requires at least one receptacle outlet in the laundry area and how many exceptions are in this section?
2. Where in the *NEC* can you find examples of branch circuit load calculations?
3. Which article covers feeders?

Appliance Wiring and Special Outlets

Objectives

Information in this chapter will enable you to:

- Discuss *NEC* regulations for appliance circuits and other special circuits.

- Discuss installation practices for various appliances and special circuits.

- Describe the various methods of heating.

Technical Terms

Conduction
Convection
Heater circuit
Pigtail plug
Radiation

Wiring for large appliances, such as dishwashers, clothes washers, clothes dryers, garbage disposal units, and water heaters requires special consideration. Often, these units need individual circuits and higher amperage OCPDs. Most issues regarding appliances are covered in *Article 422* of the *NEC*.

General Considerations

A separate appliance circuit may be designed and connected to supply both 120 and 240 volts for devices such as electric ranges and clothes dryers. These appliances may have differing voltage needs at certain times during their operation. For example, clothes dryer circuits are varied and may be split, so that high heat is supplied at 240 volts while low heat is supplied at 120 volts. **Figure 13-1** is a schematic for such a circuit.

With only rare exceptions, the appliance is connected directly to the power panel. It is protected by the branch circuit breaker that also may serve as a disconnecting means. Most

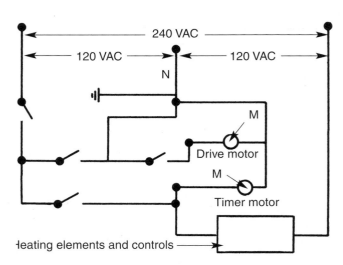

Figure 13-1. Electric clothes dryers are wired for 120 and 240 V. Motors and lights operate on 120 V, while heating elements operate at 240 V.

hookups are made with a *pigtail plug*, a short cord and plug combination that is attached to an appliance, and a receptacle. This is a common practice with clothes dryers and electric ranges, **Figure 13-2**. The pigtail-receptacle method involves running the conductors from the service panel to the receptacle. Then, through the use of the pigtail plug, the circuit is completed to the appliance.

Still another method used is the system illustrated by **Figure 13-3**. Here, provided the appliances are close to one another, a high-amperage appliance power panel is installed. The various appliance circuits are run from this subpanel at 20 A each. This works well in kitchens with built-in units or in utility rooms.

In general, the hookup for a range is a three- or four-wire pigtail plugged into a 50 A heavy-duty receptacle. The fourth terminal is for the equipment ground. Appliances should be placed on a separate circuit if, as in the case of washers, dryers, ranges, garbage disposals, dishwashers, pumps, motors, and the like, they are rated at or above 12 amperes, 1/8 horsepower, or 240 volts. See **Figure 13-4**.

Appliance Classification

In *Article 550*, the *NEC* separates appliances into three types; fixed, portable, and stationary. Since this article only covers mobile homes,

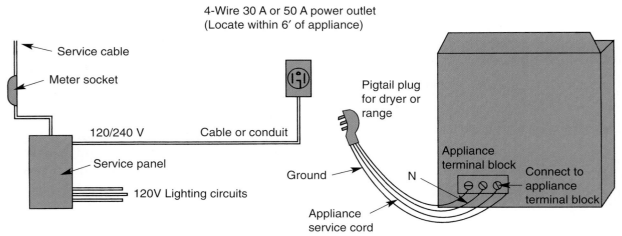

Figure 13-2. Pigtail receptacle hookups commonly used on dryers and ranges. Most ranges and dryers have a terminal block, the place where the pigtail plug or circuit conductors are connected.

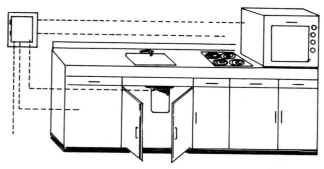

Figure 13-3. Appliance power distribution method is particularly useful when appliances are close to each other.

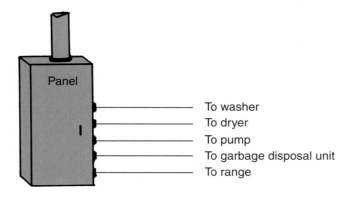

Figure 13-4. Large stationary appliances require separate circuits.

pigtail plug: A cord and plug combination that is attached to an appliance.

these definitions do not apply anywhere else in the *NEC*. Although it may be helpful to read and understand *Article 550*, refer to *Article 422* for most appliance issues.

Kitchen Appliances

There are two concerns when wiring for kitchen appliances: these units typically have larger amperage requirements, and the appliances may be used with or near water. When installed correctly, these appliances can make many kitchen chores easier while maintaining a proper level of safety.

Garbage Disposal Unit

Garbage disposal units, such as the one pictured in **Figure 13-5**, may be controlled directly from the panel circuit breaker, from a plug and cord connection, or most often, with an on-off switch. They are rated at approximately 5–10 A and 120 V. Since garbage disposals must

have overcurrent protection not exceeding 125 percent of their motor's full-load current rating, a 15 A or 20 A breaker is usually sufficient.

Dishwashers

Most dishwashers have a cord and plug that may be connected to one of the 20 A kitchen appliance receptacles. Like garbage disposal units, they carry a rating within the range of 5–10 A at 120 V. In fact, if location permits, the dishwasher and garbage disposal unit can be connected to the same kitchen duplex outlet.

Refrigerator and Freezers

Refrigerators and freezers should have dedicated receptacles. Both are motor-type appliances and, as mentioned earlier, should have overcurrent protection, fuses, or breakers rated at not more than 125 percent of their nameplate current. Connection is almost always by cord and plug. If there is a nearby light that is used frequently, add that light to the circuit for the refrigerator or freezer. This way, you will be alerted of a tripped breaker before the food warms up and spoils.

Cooking Tops and Wall-Mounted Cooking Units

Counter cooking tops and wall-mounted cooking units are each rated at approximately 7.5 kW (7.5 kVA) and 120/240 volts. These types of units require special circuits and overcurrent protection in the form of fuses or breakers, usually 30 or 40 A. They are connected in the same manner as ranges or dryers discussed earlier. Service entrance cable, 8–10 AWG, is often the method of connection, originating from the main panel or subpanel, directly to the unit. In instances where the units are close, it is permitted to connect the pair to a single circuit, providing the overcurrent protection is suitable for the combined load, **Figure 13-6**.

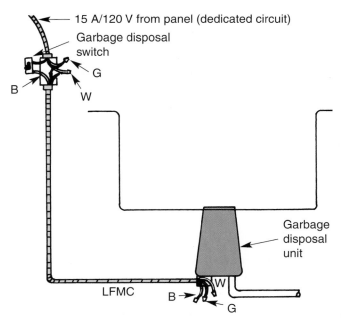

15 A/120 V from panel (dedicated circuit)

Garbage disposal switch

G

B

W

Garbage disposal unit

LFMC

B

W

G

Figure 13-5. Garbage disposal units are installed with a switch control nearby.

Room Air Conditioner Units

Air conditioners are connected for either 120 or 240 volts and generally are rated between 4 and 10 amperes. For example, a typical air conditioner might be rated 1.5 kVA (240 V × 6.25 A). This air conditioner could be placed on a 15 A double-pole breaker or plugged into a receptacle like the one shown in **Figure 13-7**. Other air conditioners, which operate on 120 V, can be plugged into any regular duplex receptacle outlet.

Air conditioners can often be connected to the same circuit as heating units, since they would not be operating at the same time. In these situations, only the larger load is considered, as explained in the section on noncoincident loads from the previous chapter .

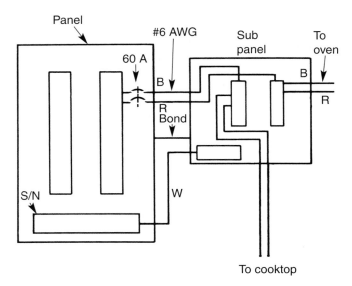

Figure 13-6. Due to their close location, two or more appliances may be placed on a single, properly rated subpanel.

Miscellaneous Special Outlet Units

There are several other devices that should have dedicated receptacles and circuits. These devices are merely listed since they are connected in a manner similar to large appliance outlets.

- Central heating/cooling system
- Attic fans
- Well pump
- Sump pump
- Large shop tools

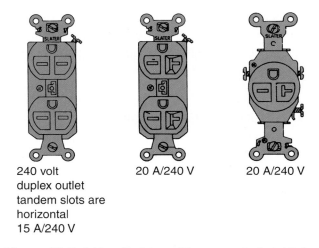

240 volt duplex outlet tandem slots are horizontal 15 A/240 V

20 A/240 V

20 A/240 V

Figure 13-7. 240-volt air conditioners, rated at 16 A or less, most often are simply plugged into special outlets such as these.

Water Heaters

A single-family home or small commercial enterprise will usually have a 30, 40, or 50 gallon water heater. Electric water heaters require a separate 240-volt circuit.

In most instances, the water heater is connected to a two-pole 20 A or 30 A breaker at the main panel or a nearby subpanel. A 20 A circuit should be used for heaters up to 4 kW (4 kVA), while a 30 A circuit is appropriate for those up to about 6 kW (6 kVA). These would be wired with 12 AWG or 10 AWG conductors respectively, **Figure 13-8**. This manner of connecting the water heater will provide 24-hour heating.

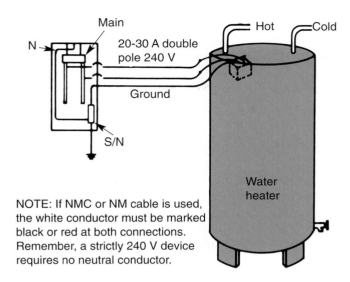

NOTE: If NMC or NM cable is used, the white conductor must be marked black or red at both connections. Remember, a strictly 240 V device requires no neutral conductor.

Figure 13-8. Typical connection for a 240 V water heater.

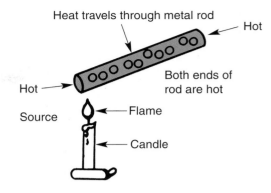

Figure 13-9. Conduction of heat. This is how heat travels through solids.

Water heaters, like most electrical equipment, must be properly grounded. This is accomplished by bonding the water heater unit casing to the equipment grounding conductor of the cable or to the conduit, if supplied in that manner. Additional bonding to the metal cold water supply pipe is recommended.

Heaters

A frequent installation or repair performed by electricians involves electric heaters. These heaters are devices containing resistors through which an electric current passes to produce heat. This heat is subsequently given off to the surrounding area by conduction, convection, or radiation. These are the three methods by which heat travels.

Conduction is the method by which heat passes through a substance by the contact of its molecules. That is, the heat energy is transferred from point to point within the substance by molecules touching each other. Due to the nature of this type of heat transfer, it takes place almost exclusively in solid substances. See **Figure 13-9**.

Convection is the process by which heat is transferred through fluids, liquids, and gases,

by the movement of masses having unequal temperatures. Warm fluid masses rise because they are less dense than the surrounding fluid. Cool fluids sink because they have greater density than their warmer surroundings. See **Figure 13-10**.

Radiation is the primary method by which heat is transferred through energy waves. The waves come out from the source in straight lines,

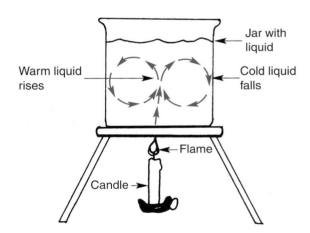

Figure 13-10. Convection of heat. Heated fluids, being lighter, rise. Cooler fluids drop. Both liquids and air circulate this way.

conduction: The means by which heat passes through a substance by the contact of its molecules.

convection: The process by which heat is transferred through fluids, liquids, and gases, by the movement of masses having unequal temperatures.

radiation: The primary method by which heat is transferred through energy waves.

and move in all directions from the source. It is the method by which the sun's energy reaches earth. See **Figure 13-11.**

Heater Installation

Typical home heaters are usually built into floors, ceilings, and walls or are surface mounted. These heaters are almost always automatically controlled by thermostats that are located close to the heating unit or built into it. Some are

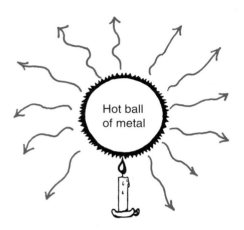

Figure 13-11. Radiation of heat. This is how heat travels through air.

provided with circulating fans to help force the warm air away from the unit while drawing in cooler air to be warmed. Many heating units are designed to be completely portable so they can be easily relocated.

Types of Heaters

Home heating units are available in a great variety of shapes, sizes, and power ratings. Units may be square, rectangular, or circular. The heater's size has traditionally been given in watts or kilowatts of power used. The *NEC* specifies that heaters have a nameplate that states the size of the heater in either volts and watts or volts and amperes.

The units may range in size from 750 W (750 VA) to more than 7500 W. Floor heaters and baseboard units are varied. The size and type chosen depends mostly on room size and comfort needs. **Figure 13-12** illustrates additional types of heater units.

Wall units

Wall units are common. They can have ratings in excess of 6 kW (6 kVA). They may be flush mounted, recessed, or surface installed. Various

Small wall-mount

Toe-kick mount

Portable

Register mount

Large wall-mount

Figure 13-12. Electric heating units are available in a variety of sizes, shapes, styles, and power ratings. (Cadetco, Inc.)

styles of wall units are available. They can operate on the radiation principle (called radiant heaters) or they can be fan assisted. Control may be a wall-mounted or integral thermostat.

Floor units

Floor heating units are primarily of two types:

- Floor heating cable
- Floor duct or drop-in units

These units have general ratings of 120 to 240 volts. The floor heating cables require special installation procedures. Consult the *NEC*, the local inspector, and the manufacturer.

Floor duct units are simple to install. The procedure should be explained and illustrated by the manufacturer. Heat is moved in these units by natural convection or a fan. Thermostats are generally wall mounted.

Baseboard units

Perhaps the most common residential and small commercial-type heaters are baseboard units. Again, these operate at 120, 240, or 208 volts, and have a load rating ranging from 35 W (35 VA) to about 4.5 kW (4.5 kVA), depending on size and construction. Thermostat control is possible from either a wall-mount or integral positions (on the appliance).

Other units

Although only a few specific types of heater units are discussed here, there are many other types available. The choice depends on many factors:

- Size of area to be heated
- Heat loss factors
- Amount of insulation present
- Climatic conditions
- Desired temperature of area to be heated
- Style preference

Other types of electric heaters marketed today are:

- Heat pumps
- Electric furnaces
- Electric fireplaces
- Ceiling heaters
- Outdoor roof-mount central heating

Heater Circuits

A *heater circuit* is a schematic drawing showing how the heater operates and the proper way to connect it to the electrical system. Because of the variations in types, makes, and models of heaters, it would be impossible to describe all the heater circuits possible. However, the common types of heaters available for home or office installation are fairly similar.

Figure 13-13 shows the circuitry commonly found in baseboard units. Generally, these may be wired for 120, 208, or 240 volts. Circuits must be properly grounded.

Figure 13-14 shows a typical wall or ceiling heater circuit. Note the similarity in circuitry of the two units. The relay, in each case, is used because of the time-delay needed to compensate for the slow moving contact points within the thermostat. Most units have built-in relay switches so there is no need for auxiliary wiring. **Figure 13-15** shows a wiring schematic for a heater with fan-assisted circulation.

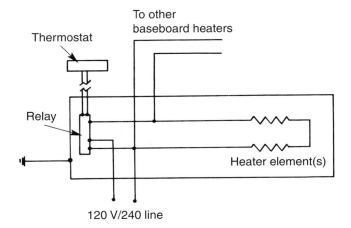

Figure 13-13. Baseboard heater circuit. Baseboards are perhaps the most common heaters used in both residential and light commercial application.

---

heater circuit: A schematic drawing showing how a heater operates and the proper way to connect it to the electrical system.

To thermostat

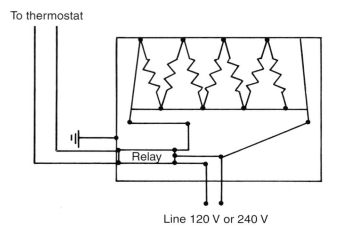

Line 120 V or 240 V

Figure 13-14. Wall or ceiling heater circuit. Note circuitry for relay.

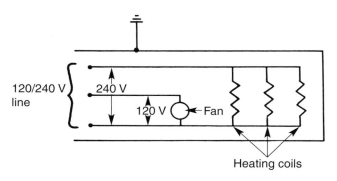

120/240 V line

240 V

120 V — Fan

Heating coils

Figure 13-15. Typical circuit for a heater with fan-assisted circulation.

Review Questions

Write your answers on a separate sheet of paper. Do not write in this book.

1. List five appliances that require special circuits or outlets.

2. Name the three methods by which heat is transferred from place to place.

3. Motor-operated appliances such as garbage disposal units should have overcurrent protection in the form of fuses or breakers that will not exceed _____ percent of their full load rating.

4. A counter cooktop unit rated at 8 kVA and 120/240 V, should be on a separate circuit having a double-pole circuit breaker of_____ A.

5. *True or False?* Heaters may be on the same circuit as room air conditioner units.

Know the Code

A copy of the NEC 2005 is required to answer these questions.

1. *Section 422.16(B)(2)* covers the cord application for which two types of appliances?

2. *True or False?* Is the term *counter-mounted cooking unit* defined in the *NEC*?

3. What is the voltage limit for room air conditioners covered under *Section 440.60*?

Electricians are often called upon to install photovoltaic cells that provide clean renewable energy. The electricians shown are installing a panel as part of a 38.1 kW power supply on top of the 911 Emergency Communications Center in Chicago. An additional 10 kW system with batteries for backup was installed as an uninterruptible power supply. (Bill Lyons, Spire Solar Chicago)

Section 4
Specialized Installations

Farm Wiring

Objectives

Information in this chapter will enable you to:

- Design and install an electrical power distribution system for a farm.

- Describe an appropriate grounding system.

- Select materials and components for corrosive and damp conditions found on farms.

- Install farm wiring.

- Compute loads and design adequate circuits for various farm buildings and operations.

Technical Terms

Connected load
Demand load
NEMA 4X
Yard pole

The sizes of farms and their production capabilities are increasing at a rapid rate. Accordingly, these electrical demands must be met with good quality and high capacity electrical systems. *NEC* requirements for wiring methods used in agricultural buildings are detailed in *Article 547*. You should be familiar with these requirements before attempting farm wiring.

Farms are complex operations requiring careful planning and layout considerations prior to the actual installation of electrical equipment. A farm should be thought of as a small industrial plant that has several buildings. Operating toward that end, each unit or building requires electrical power.

Power Distribution

The electrical power is brought to the farm by the power company. The service drop, in this case, ends not at the dwelling, but rather at a centrally located *yard pole*. Power is subsequently distributed from the pole to the individual buildings. Farm buildings may include a dairy or stock barn, equipment shed, hog barn, poultry house, machine shed, granary, garage, and farmhouse. **Figure 14-1** illustrates electrical power distribution on a typical farm.

Farm Equipment

As with any electrical installation, the total electrical demand should be calculated before beginning actual wiring. Farmers, by necessity,

yard pole: A centrally located distribution point consisting of a large pole, meter, and power lines.

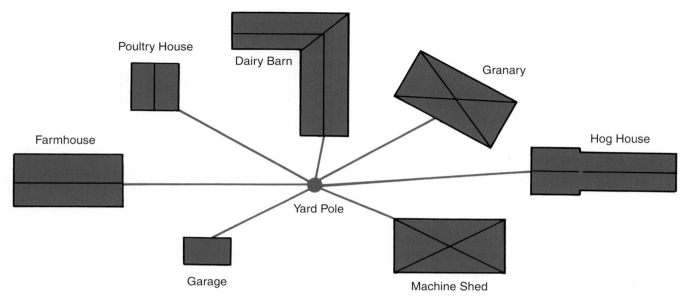

Figure 14-1. The farm power central distribution layout. Power is directed to the various buildings from the farm-yard pole.

have great electrical needs and these must be accurately calculated. For example, devices such as milking machines, coolers, silo unloaders, feed conveyors, barn cleaners, fans, feed mixers, and other motor-driven equipment are typically found on modern farms, **Figure 14-2**. Each of these devices, as well as many others, must be properly wired and connected for safe and efficient operation. Almost all modern farms require a 200 A to 400 A service entrance.

The Yard Pole Service Drop

Although each building will have its own service panel containing fuses or breakers for overcurrent protection, the service drop and meter will be located at the yard pole. This will serve as a power center and overall disconnecting means for the farm. A yard pole is shown in **Figure 14-3**. A fire-pump disconnect and emergency power transfer switch may also be located here.

Grounding

Farm electrical systems often have many grounds. There may be ground rods driven throughout the property to reduce grounding conductor length. Buildings with concrete floors may have the electrical system grounded to the reinforcing rods. If copper piping is used for a water supply, the system may be grounded to the water pipe.

A reliable grounding system is crucial in farm buildings because of the dampness. For this reason, metallic sheathed cable and metal conduit are not suitable for farm wiring systems. Too often the metal corrodes and weakens the ground, creating a hazardous situation. To ensure proper grounding and safe wiring in farm buildings, metal equipment is used as little as is practical. Nonmetallic cable, such as NMC and UF, and nonmetallic outlet boxes, **Figure 14-4**, are preferred.

The ground is established through a ground wire within the nonmetallic conduit or cable, as shown in Chapter 9, **Grounding**. This ground

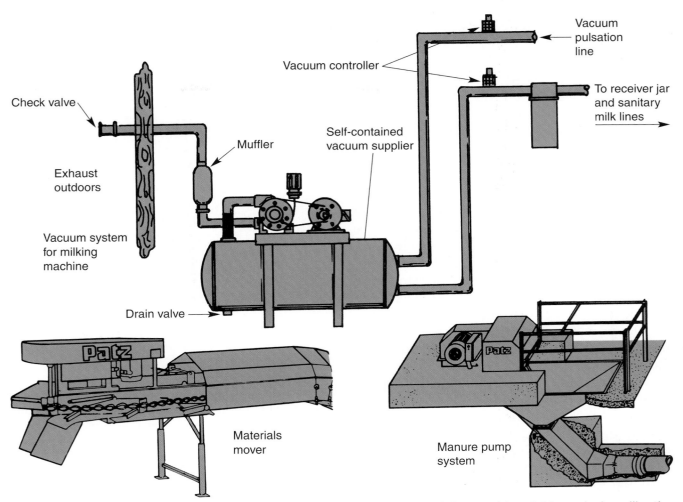

Check valve

Exhaust
outdoors

Vacuum system
for milking
machine

Muffler

Drain valve

Self-contained
vacuum supplier

Vacuum controller

Vacuum
pulsation
line

To receiver jar
and sanitary
milk lines

Materials
mover

Manure pump
system

Figure 14-2. Farms have great electrical demands, which must be carefully considered. Many devices like the ones shown here are common farm necessities. (Patz Co. and DeLaval Agricultural Div.)

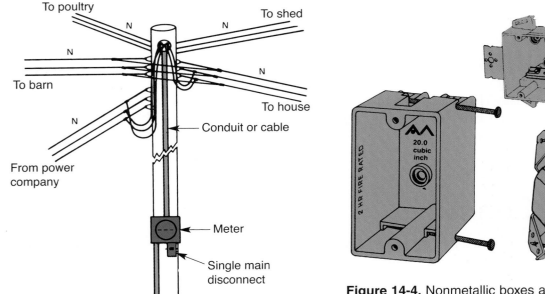

To poultry

To shed

To barn

To house

Conduit or cable

From power
company

Meter

Single main
disconnect

Figure 14-3. The yard pole is the farm's central "hub" of power distribution.

Figure 14-4. Nonmetallic boxes are particularly useful in damp and wet locations. (Raco Inc. and Allied Moulded Products, Inc.)

20.0
cubic
inch

2 HR FIRE RATED

wire is made continuous from the ground at the service entrance to all parts of the system. Sometimes, additional ground rods are located near and connected to motor-driven devices such as large fans and conveyors. Metal equipment and structures, such as metal stanchions, and floor grating should be grounded as well.

Special Devices

On many farms, surface-mounted nonmetallic units are used in place of metal outlet boxes. These nonmetallic units are preferable in damp locations. These units are self-contained, being combinations of box and switch, box and lamp holder, or box and receptacle. These devices are connected with the NMC, LFMC, or UF cable.

Other special devices and equipment used on farms may include vapor-proof light fixtures, timer switches, waterproof (reflector) yard lights, lightning arrestors, weatherproof (outdoor) switches, and outlet boxes. See **Figure 14-5**. Motor disconnects and controllers should be housed in NEMA 4X enclosures, especially in damp/wet areas. *NEMA 4X* is a standard for electrical enclosures set by the National Electrical Manufacturers Association. When a manufacturer states that an enclosure meets the NEMA 4X standards, the enclosure is designed for outdoor use.

Dairy Barn

The dairy barn requires the most electrical power of any building on the farm. Indeed, it is the center of the farm. The numerous motor-driven machines must be carefully considered when calculating feeder load requirements.

Cable or Conduit

Running of cable or raceways in barns and outbuildings should be done with the same care as residential wiring. Make your parallel runs

Figure 14-5. Vapor-proof light fixture. Because of the excessive damp and dusty conditions in farm buildings, these units are installed as another safety measure. The bulb is encased in a glass dome, around which is a strong, protective cage. These units are essential in areas like the haymow. (Appleton Electric Co.)

along the sides rather than the bottoms of beams and joists. Make cross runs through drilled holes rather than over edges. If runs must be made across the surface, protect the cable with 1 × 4 boards. Place wiring where it will be protected from weather wherever possible.

Electrical outlets should be plentiful. One outlet every 12' or closer is best. Receptacles may be located along the walls behind the stanchions. The receptacles should be mounted no lower than 60" (1.5 m) above the floor. Higher is even better as it prevents them from being damaged by animals or tools.

Lights should be located both to the front and rear of the stanchions. A 60-watt porcelain or plastic fixture placed every 15' (4.6 m) is sufficient. Dustproof lights should be installed in the feed-storage, silo, and haymow areas. These lights should be controlled by a wall switch at every entrance to the area. Open feeding areas as well as calf pens should be provided with similar outlets and lighting circuits.

NEMA 4X: A standard for electrical enclosures set by the National Electrical Manufacturers Association.

Locating Lights

Place lights at all alley crossings, stairs, ladders, and chutes in the dairy barn. If ceilings are dark, use reflectors so light is directed downward rather than to the ceiling. Place the lights where joists, beams, and posts will not obstruct the light from a fixture.

Place switches so that lighting can be controlled at all entrances to the building. Use three-way switches. As with residential wiring, pilot lights are advisable when switches control lights that cannot be seen from the switch location.

The milkhouse and milking parlor should have similar lighting and receptacle arrangements as the dairy barn. Again, lighting should be plentiful with outlets mounted high enough to avoid damage. Special branch circuits will be required where the facility includes bulk tank storage or motors for running vacuum pumps for milking machines.

Poultry House, Hog Barn, Sheep House, Horse Barn

These buildings must be well electrified, although the electrical demand for these buildings is much less than that of the dairy barn. Lighting should be plentiful. One light for every 150 ft² of floor area is suitable. Wall-switched lights are advisable. Timer switches to increase egg production should be a part of the lighting circuits of the poultry house. Receptacles should be located every 12' to 15' along the walls and mounted no lower than 5' above the floor.

Computing Farm Power Requirements

Each building's electrical needs must be computed carefully to determine the total farm load. The farmhouse power requirements are calculated using methods that are the same as any residence. The other buildings—barns, sheds, and shops—are computed differently. The farm buildings, having more motors, heating devices, and lighting circuits, will often require more power than the farmhouse.

The procedure for computing such demands begins with a list of the buildings. Include the farmhouse since it will also be connected to the yard pole service drop. The list might appear something like this:

- Farmhouse
- Barn
- Equipment/toolshed
- Poultry house
- Hog barn

Barn Electrical Requirements

Start with the barn, since it probably will have the greatest electrical demand. List the number of lighting circuits, special appliances, motors, and other equipment that it will need. For example:

- 15 lighting circuits 120 V at 15 A or 20 A
- 6 motors with the following horsepower: 1/2, 1, 2, and three with 4 hp
- 1 water heater
- 1 sterilizer

Next, determine volt-amperage requirements. A good rule of thumb for general lighting circuits is about 400 VA each. For motors, see Chapter 18, **Motors**. For heaters, sterilizers, and various other pieces of equipment, use nameplate ratings stamped on the equipment housing. Also, consult Chapter 13, **Appliance Wiring and Special Outlets** and tables under *Article 430* of the *NEC*. See **Figure 14-6**.

Add up the total power needed by the building:

$$
\begin{aligned}
\text{lighting circuits} &= 6000 \text{ VA} \\
\text{*motors, total} \times .50 &= 8600 \text{ VA} \\
\text{heater} &= 5000 \text{ VA} \\
\text{sterilizer} &= 7000 \text{ VA} \\
\text{Total} &= 26{,}600 \text{ VA or } 26.6 \text{ kVA.}
\end{aligned}
$$

*The 50 percent factor may be used when not all motors will be operating at any given time.

The same procedure is followed for each of the other farm buildings. (The home is not included.

Motor Horsepower	Power Rating (Watts)
1/4	250
1/2	500
1	1200
2	2000
3	3000
4	4500

Figure 14-6. Power ratings of electric motors of different sizes (horsepower). These must be known to figure motor's load demand on an electrical circuit.

It must be calculated separately using requirements covered in Chapter 12, **Branch-Circuit, Feeder, and Service Design**.) Add up the totals. The figures may look something like this:

$$\text{farmhouse} = 25.6 \text{ kVA}$$
$$\text{barn} = 26.6 \text{ kVA}$$
$$\text{equip./toolshed} = 7.5 \text{ kVA}$$
$$\text{poultry house} = 6.3 \text{ kVA}$$
$$\text{hog barn} = 3.0 \text{ kVA}$$
$$\text{Total farm power needed} = 69 \text{ kVA}$$

This total, 69 kVA, is called the **connected load**. It represents the amount of power needed if all of the equipment were operating at the same time.

A more conservative figure called the **demand load** represents the amount of power that would most probably be needed at any given time. Generally, the minimum demand load is considered to be about 35 percent of the connected load. Based on this figure, the wire sizes and overcurrent protection at the yard pole are determined. In our example, 69 kVA × .35 = 24.15 kVA (24,150 VA). At 240 V, we arrive at 100 A as our current needed for the farm. Do not forget to consider the future growth, which would demand an increase in power conditions. Thus, sizes of service conductors should be at least one size larger than calculated. In this case, 4 AWG would be minimum, but a wiser choice would be 2 AWG or 1 AWG. Without a doubt, this would be a very small farm.

Use the same methods to determine the wire sizes for the feeders interconnecting the various buildings to the yard pole. **Figure 14-7** may serve as a general guide for average farm

connected load: The amount of power needed if all of the equipment was operating at the same time.

demand load: The amount of power which would most probably be needed at any given time.

Farm Building Loads Summary (Excluding Farmhouse)		
Farm building	**Special equipment (other than lighting and receptacles)**	**Average connected load**
Main barn (dairy barn) including milkhouse, milking parlor, silos, haymows, feeding pens. stanchion area, and calf pens	Gutter cleaners, milking machine pump's compressor motor, refrigeration, water heater(s), silo unloaders, feed conveyors, material movers, heat lamps, calf brooders, circulating fans, and water pumps	79 kVA +
Poultry house including egg packing and feed storage areas	Feed conveyor, candling equipment, chick brooders, egg washers, water heater, and fans	18 kVA
Hog barn	Hog brooders, water heater, fan, and feed conveyor	10 kVA
Sheep barn	Feed conveyor, water heater, and fan	8 kVA
Machinery shed (includes storage and repair areas)	Compressor, heater units, welding equipment, lathe, hoists, lifts, water heater, gas pump, and water pump	20 kVA
Garage and toolshed (may be separate or as one)	Compressor, heating, welder, table saws, drill stands, battery charger, and water heater	12 kVA

Figure 14-7. A chart like this is helpful when figuring electrical loads for the farm.

structures equipped with typical devices, however, these ratings should be verified when the farm equipment is selected.

Review Questions

Write your answers on a separate sheet of paper.
Do not write in this book.

1. Generally, the farm service drop ends at a centrally located distribution point called the _____ .

2. List three common farm buildings, other than the farmhouse, that require electrical service equipment.

3. Most up-to-date farms require a _____ ampere service as a minimum.

4. Indicate which of the following wiring systems is recommended for farm buildings:

   A. Metal conduit.

   B. Nonmetallic conduit (PVC).

   C. BX or armored cable.

   D. Flexible metal conduit.

Know the Code

A copy of the NEC 2005 is required to answer these questions.

1. According to *Table 220.103*, the second largest load will have a demand factor of _____ %.

2. The three phrases that are defined in *Article 547.2* are _____ , _____ , and _____ .

3. *Article 547.9(D)* requires the grounding conductor to be _____ or _____ copper.

A typical farm has many different buildings. Each one is designed for a specific task and has specific electrical requirements. The development of motorized equipment to make the farmer's job easier has necessitated the development of low-cost, safe, and reliable electrical devices and boxes.

Mobile Home Wiring

Objectives

Information in this chapter will enable you to:

- Demonstrate familiarity with *NEC* requirements for mobile home electric service and wiring.

- Compute loads for mobile home circuits.

- Define terms applying specifically to mobile home electrical systems.

Technical Terms

Distribution panelboard
Feeder assembly
Mobile home service equipment
Mobile home

Article 550 of the *NEC* applies to all mobile homes. A **mobile home** is a residential structure that is transportable in one or more sections and is intended to be used without a permanent foundation. A permanent chassis supports the home before, during, and after installation. The basic electrical service components of a traditional house are adapted to meet the temporary requirements of a mobile home. See **Figure 15-1**.

Distribution Panelboard

The **distribution panelboard** corresponds to the service electrical panel in a permanent structure. It must be securely fastened to a structural member of the home either directly or by using a substantial brace. See **Figure 15-2**. The mobile home distribution panelboard receives its power supply through the feeder assembly. An electrician will rarely install this distribution panelboard since the manufacturer of the mobile home almost always supplies it.

---

mobile home: A residential structure that is transportable in one or more sections and is intended to be used without a permanent foundation.

distribution panelboard: An assembly within a cabinet or cutout box that includes bus bars, automatic overcurrent protection devices, and sometimes switches.

Figure 15-1. Typical mobile home electrical installation. A—Pad transformer. B—Pedestal for 100-ampere service. C—Main disconnect in pedestal. D—Under chassis feeder assembly is protected by conduit.

Feeder Assembly

The *feeder assembly* includes the conductors, with their fittings, that carry electrical current from the mobile home service equipment to the distribution panelboard inside the mobile home. See **Figure 15-3**. The feeder assembly must have four conductors. Three must be insulated circuit conductors (two ungrounded and one grounded). The fourth is the insulated green grounding conductor. Depending primarily on

the calculated electrical load of the mobile home and any additional requests of the owner, the electrical feed can be supplied by any of three different ways:

- **A mobile home power supply cord.** This is permitted if the load is 50 A or less. However, if the mobile home has factory-equipped gas or oil heating and cooking equipment, a 40 A cord is permitted. **Figure 15-4** shows a typical installation. The cord, which must always be approved and labeled for mobile home use, must be no shorter than 21' and no longer than 36 1/2' from end to end. The plug must be of the molded type. The opposite end of the cord must be permanently attached to the distribution panelboard in the mobile home. A clamp should

feeder assembly: The conductors, with their fittings and equipment, that carry electrical current from the mobile home service equipment to the distribution panelboard.

Figure 15-2. The NEC requires that the distribution panelboard be securely mounted inside the mobile home.

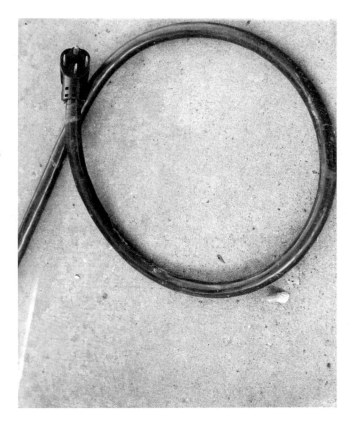

Figure 15-3. A single power cord with a molded plug meets NEC requirements for a mobile home when the electrical load does not exceed 50 amperes. There must be four conductors, all insulated.

be provided at the panelboard knockout to prevent strain on the cord from damaging the cord or its connections to the terminals, **Figure 15-5.** Only one cord per mobile home unit is permitted. See the *NEC, Section 550.10.*

- **An overhead installation consisting of a mast and a weatherhead.** This type is for permanent installations or where the load exceeds 50 A, **Figure 15-6.**

- **An underground lateral service using cable or conduit.** This is an alternative to an overhead permanent installation. It is the most common method used. See **Figure 15-7.** The underground lateral service must follow typical depth requirements based on the materials used. See **Figure 15-8.**

Mobile Home Service Equipment

Mobile home service equipment is all of the equipment, including a main disconnecting means, overcurrent protective devices, and receptacles or other arrangements, for connecting the supply end of a mobile home feeder assembly. The meter may be regarded as part of the service equipment.

mobile home service equipment: All of the equipment, including a main disconnecting means, overcurrent protective devices, and receptacles or other arrangements, for connecting the supply end of a mobile home feeder assembly. The meter may be regarded as part of the service equipment.

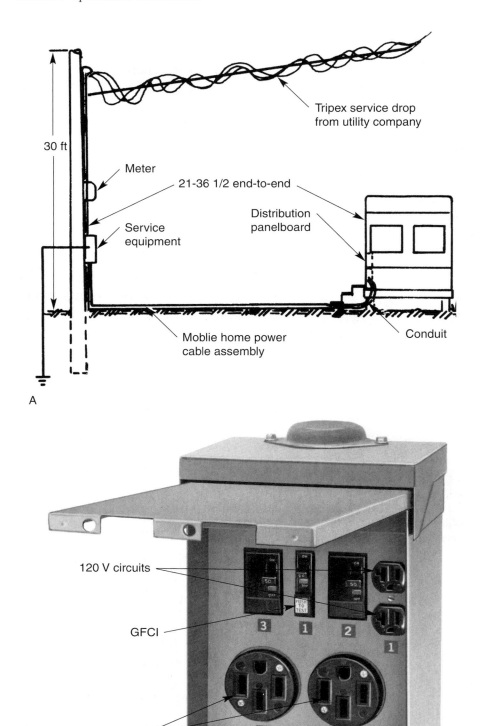

Tripex service drop
from utility company

30 ft

Meter

21-36 1/2 end-to-end

Distribution
panelboard

Service
equipment

Conduit

Moblie home power
cable assembly

A

120 V circuits

GFCI

240 V circuits

B

Figure 15-4. One common hookup for 40 A or 50 A mobile homes uses the power cord. One end of the cord is permanently wired into the distribution panelboard in the mobile unit. The other end will plug into a 120/240 V grounding type receptacle. A—Sketch of complete hookup. B—A power panel designed to supply two mobile homes with a 50 A circuit to each. A 20 A circuit is also available for other purposes, protected by a GFCI.

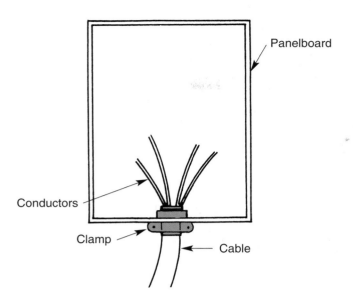

Figure 15-5. When a feeder cord is used to supply electricity to a mobile home, a clamp must be provided at the panelboard knockout to prevent any strain on the cord connections inside the cabinet.

Service equipment should not be mounted on the mobile home. The *NEC* requires that the service equipment be within sight and located a specific distance from the home, usually between 20′ and 30′ away. The equipment must be supported by a pole or a pedestal arrangement. Sometimes the main disconnect, breaker, and meter are mounted together. In other cases, the meter is mounted on a pole and the overcurrent protective devices are on a pedestal.

Overhead Installation

The mast and weatherhead installation must have four continuous conductors that are color-coded. One of the conductors must be an equipment ground. Refer to *Article 230* of the *NEC* for the proper conductors to be used. See also *Article 550.10*.

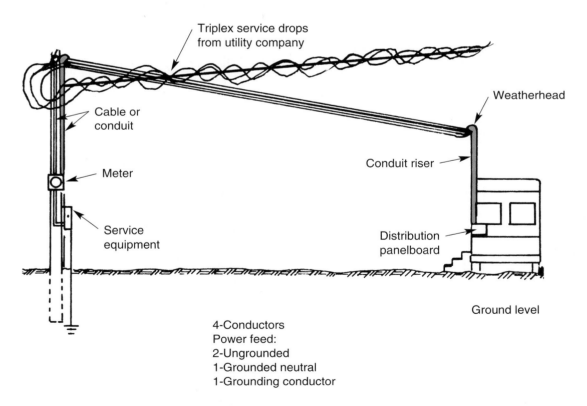

Figure 15-6. This is an overhead feeder hookup. The mast and weatherhead can be attached to the mobile home, but the main disconnect, meter, and breakers are to be located on a pole no more than 30′ away.

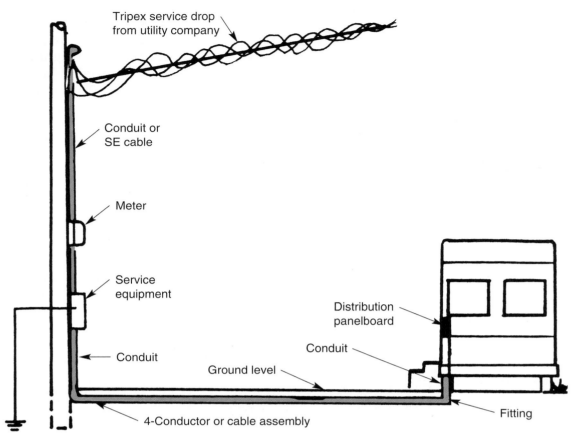

Figure 15-7. Underground feeder hookup for a mobile home is also permitted for permanent installation. This illustration shows cable being used; however, metallic or nonmetallic (PVC) conduit protection can be used as well.

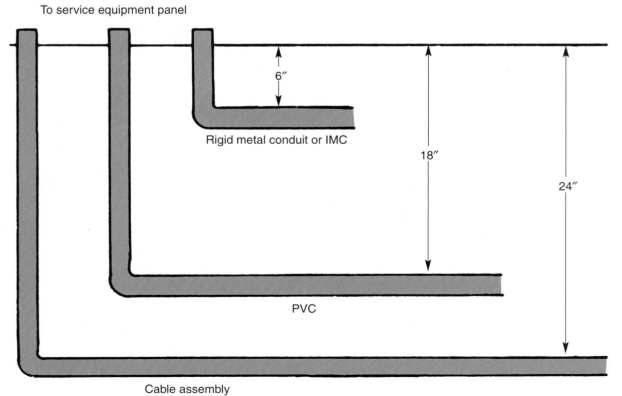

Figure 15-8. Depths are prescribed for direct-buried cable and conduit.

Service Lateral

For a lateral installation, the mobile home must be fitted with a metal or rigid nonmetal raceway that connects to the distribution panel inside the unit and extends to the underside of the chassis. The raceway must have a provision for attaching a junction box. The manufacturer may or may not have provided the raceway with conductors. Refer to *NEC, Section 550.10(B)*.

The electric utility company usually installs the necessary service drop and transformer. The customer must supply the service pole and components as well as the meter pedestal (for underground supply). Both pole and pedestal are permanent installations. The pedestal must be rigidly mounted so that it cannot be easily knocked over. **Figure 15-9** illustrates a typical pedestal arrangement.

Devices and Outlets

The various electrical devices and equipment are almost always installed by the manufacturer and must meet minimum *NEC* requirements. These are checked by the electrician and the electrical inspector for proper polarity and grounding.

Distribution Panel Hookup

The distribution panel, along with a main breaker for branch circuit disconnect purposes, is usually installed by the manufacturer. To connect the power-supply feeder assembly to this panel, carefully study **Figure 15-10**.

Note, particularly, that the neutral conductor is completely *insulated and isolated* from the grounding conductor as well as the equipment enclosure. In addition, the mobile home chassis must be securely bonded to the grounding bus or grounding conductor, as must all metal, non-current-carrying equipment inside the mobile home. This grounding continuity is essential and will be checked by the inspector.

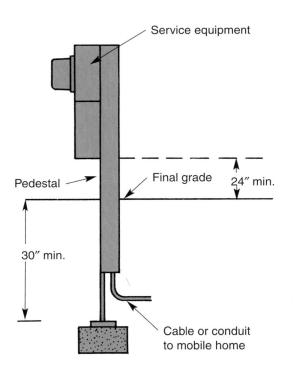

Figure 15-9. Notice the dimensions on this drawing of a pedestal arrangement for supporting the service equipment.

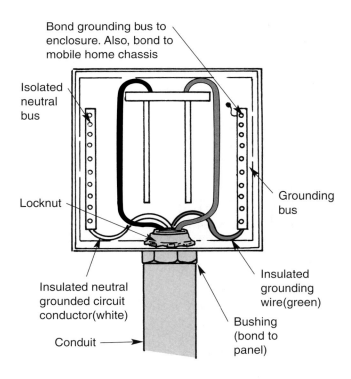

Figure 15-10. Proper connections at the mobile home's distribution panelboard are crucial to the equipment grounding. It is not permissible to connect the frame of the mobile home or any appliance frame to the grounded (neutral) circuit conductor.

Calculating Panelboard Load

The distribution panel load of the mobile home is computed using methods that are similar to those used for a standard residential load, with some minor differences.

Lighting and small appliance requirements are determined similarly to other one- or two-family residences. The 3 VA/ft², two small-appliance circuits, and one laundry circuit rules are used. Add to this the nameplate ratings for motors and the loads for heater, garbage disposal, dishwasher, water heater, clothes dryer, wall-mounted oven, cooking units, and similar appliances.

Free-standing ranges, unlike wall-mounted ovens or cooktops, are rated at 80 percent of their volt amperage, up to 10,000 VA. Beyond that, figure 8000 VA for those loads between 10,000 and 12,500. Add 400 VA for every 1000 VA increase above 12,500. The smaller of the heating and cooling loads can be omitted from the load calculation.

Here is an example of how to apply these rules for a mobile home. Find the total electrical load for a 65′ by 12′ mobile home. It has two small appliance circuits, a laundry circuit, a 2500 VA space heater, a 100 VA fan, a 500 VA dishwasher, an 800 VA air conditioner, 8000 VA range, and a 5 kVA water heater.

Find the general lighting and small appliance load as follows:

1. Find the area.

   $65′ \times 12′ = 780 \ ft^2$

2. Multiply 3 VA for each square foot.

   $780 \ ft^2 \times 3 \ VA/ft^2 = 2340 \ VA$

3. Add two small appliance circuits at 1500 VA each.

   $3000 \ VA + 2340 \ VA = 5340 \ VA$

4. Add one laundry circuit at 1500 VA.

   $1500 \ VA + 5340 \ VA = 6840 \ VA$

5. The first 3000 VA is retained at 100%.

   $3000 \ VA \ at \ 100\% = 3000 \ VA$

6. The remainder (6840−3000 = 3840) is reduced by 35%.

   $3840 \times 35\% = 1344 \ VA$

7. Add the two previous answers to find the net lighting and small appliance requirement.

   $3000 \ VA + 1344 \ VA = 4344 \ VA$

8. Divide the previous answer by the voltage to get the lighting and small appliance amperage.

   $4344 \div 240 \ V = 18.10 \ A$

9. Find the amperage of the space heater.

   $2500 \ VA \div 240 \ V = 10.42 \ A$

10. Find the amperage of the fan.

    $100 \ VA \div 120 \ V = 0.83 \ A$

11. Find the amperage of the dishwasher.

    $500 \ VA \div 120 \ V = 4.17 \ A$

12. Omit the air conditioner (only heating or air conditioning is computed, whichever is larger).

13. Find the amperage of the range.

    $8000 \ VA \div 240 \ V = 33.3 \ A$

14. Reduce by 80%.

    $33.3 \ A \times 80\% = 26.64 \ A$

15. Find the amperage of the water heater.

    $5000 \ VA \div 240 \ V = 20.83 \ A$

16. Add the answers for 8, 9, 10, 11, 14, and 15.

    $17.10 \ A + 10.42 \ A + 0.83 \ A + 4.17 \ A + 26.64 \ A + 20.83 \ A = 80.99 \ A$

Total load is about 81 A. Therefore, a 100 A service is needed. This is considered the minimum for a mobile home.

Mobile Home Parks

The *NEC*, in *Article 550*, outlines the various requirements for mobile home parks. The general demand factors to be considered are shown in **Figure 15-11**.

The application of these demand factors may best be illustrated through the use of an example. If a particular mobile home park is to accommodate 25 mobile homes, we would use the demand factor of 24 percent. This is the minimum. For example, assume that the largest mobile home that will fit in the park has a calculated load, following *Section 550.18*, that is less

Demand Factors for Feeders and Service Entrance Conductors	
Number of Mobile Homes	Demand Factor (Percent)
1	100
2	55
3	44
4	39
5	33
6	29
7-9	28
10-12	27
13-15	26
16-21	25
22-40	24
41-60	23
61 and over	22

Figure 15-11. The size of service needed for a mobile home park can be based on this chart.

than 16,000 VA. *Section 550.31* requires you to use at least 16,000 VA for each mobile home lot.

$$16,000 \text{ VA} \times 25 = 400,000 \text{ VA}$$

According to *Table 550.31*, the demand factor for mobile home parks with 22 to 40 lots is 24 percent.

$$400,000 \text{ VA} \times 0.24 = 96,000 \text{ VA}$$

The mobile home park will be supplied with 240 V service.

$$96,000 \text{ VA} \div 240 \text{ V} = 400 \text{ A}$$

The mobile home park will need at least 400 A to supply power to the mobile homes. In addition to this load consideration, the electrical requirements of common park facilities and equipment (such as security lighting) must

be added onto the overall total service demand. Refer also to the *NEC, Article 550.30*.

Review Questions

Write your answers on a separate sheet of paper. Do not write in this book.

1. List two factors that distinguish mobile homes from ordinary one- or two-family residences.
2. Where must the service equipment (main disconnect and meter) be placed for mobile homes?
   A. on the mobile home.
   B. in the mobile home.
   C. on a pole or pedestal separated from the mobile home.
   D. All of the above.
3. Mobile home power cords must be no less than _____ and no more than _____ feet long.
4. The grounded neutral conductor must be _____ and _____ from the grounding conductor within the mobile home distribution panel.
5. The lighting load of a mobile home is based on the _____ volt-amperes/ft^2 rule.
6. The minimum service rating of a 20-unit mobile home park would be _____ amperes.

Know the Code

A copy of the NEC 2005 is required to answer these questions.

1. Which section of the *NEC* lists definitions for mobile homes?
2. How many requirements for receptacle outlets are listed in *Article 550* of the *NEC*?
3. Which section of the *NEC* covers wiring methods for mobile homes?

This mobile home park has two pedestal-mount meters located between adjoining lots. The lot on the right will have a new mobile home installed and require a qualified electrician to connect the service.

Swimming Pool Wiring

Objectives

Information in this chapter will enable you to:

- List in detail the rules for bonding metal fixtures and parts around a swimming pool.

- Explain grounding requirements for swimming pool wiring.

- Give the *NEC* requirements for wiring underwater light fixtures.

- Name the fixture types used in pools.

- Cite *NEC* rules for overhead conductor clearance around the pool area.

Technical Terms

Dry-niche fixture
Forming shell
Stray currents
Wet-niche fixture

Installation of electrical wiring in and around swimming pools, indoor and outdoor, is of much concern to the *NEC*. The requirements for such installations provide rules that will ensure safety.

Bonding

The specific installation requirements for swimming pool wiring methods are found in *Article 680* of the *Code*. Due to the presence of water, the possible pathways of electrical current must be strictly controlled. Any **stray currents**, those currents that do not follow the intended path, moving between metal parts in and around the pool can be extremely dangerous. These stray currents must be kept at earth potential, which is zero. The bonding of *all* the metal parts accomplishes this and is, therefore, essential. See **Figure 16-1**. Specifically, the following must be bonded using an 8 AWG solid copper conductor:

- metal parts within 5' horizontally of the pool walls, including fencing

- metal parts within the pool walls, including the shells for wet-niche fixtures

- metal parts of the pool structure, including the reinforcing steel, steel decking, ladders, and diving board supports

---

stray currents: Currents that do not follow the intended path.

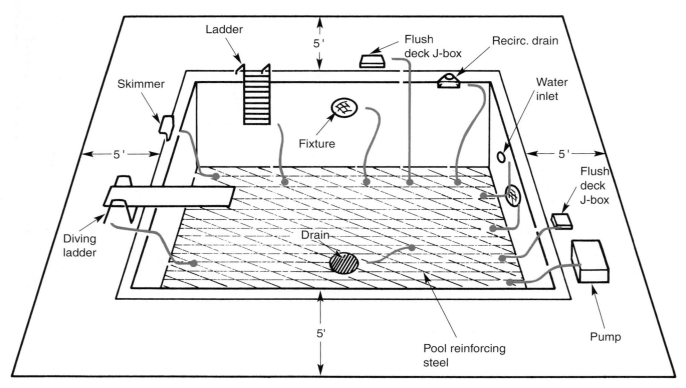

Figure 16-1. Bond all metal parts within the pool and within 5′ of the pool walls using an 8 AWG bare or insulated copper conductor.

- accessory equipment including pump motors, fittings, conduits, piping, and skimmer components

The only job of the bonding conductor is to interconnect the metal parts. This conductor can be bare or insulated. It may be run to a panelboard or service panel ground block, but this is only required if that equipment is within the parameters specified above.

Grounding

In addition to bonding, all electrical equipment related to the pool and within 5′ of the interior pool walls must be properly grounded. This creates a low-resistance pathway for fault-related current to get back to the neutral so that fuses or circuit breakers will operate correctly.

The grounding conductor must be properly sized for the particular circuit, as listed in *NEC Table 250.122*. It cannot be smaller than 12 AWG

copper. Also, the grounding conductor must be insulated and run in conduit with the circuit conductors all the way back to the supply panel grounding terminal block. **Figure 16-2** shows the correct way to ground electrical equipment in and around the swimming pool.

Receptacles

The only receptacle permitted by the *NEC* to be located within 10′ of a pool wall is a receptacle for a cord-connected swimming pool pump. The pool pump receptacle must not be any closer than 5′ from the pool wall. Further, the *NEC* requires that a minimum of one 120 V GFCI-protected receptacle be located between 10′ and 20′ of the pool wall for use of cord-connected devices. This requirement is intended to eliminate the possible use of extension cords originating from inside the home. Any additional outdoor receptacles within 20′ of the pool wall must also be GFCI protected.

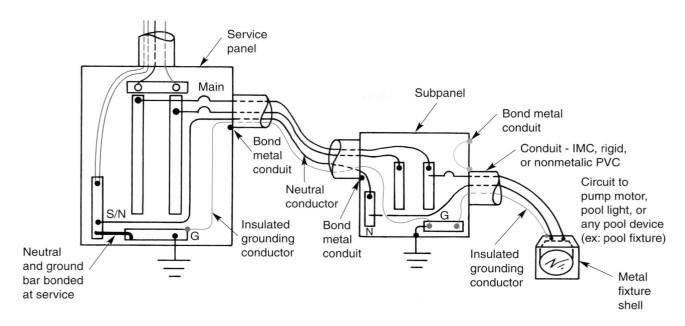

Figure 16-2. The grounding conductor for pool electrical equipment is run with the circuit conductors and is connected at the equipment subpanel ground bar and back to the service grounded (and bonded) neutral bar.

Of course, all receptacles installed outdoors for residential buildings must have GFCI protection. **Figure 16-3** shows basic rules and requirements associated with receptacles around the pool.

Switches

All switches or switching devices of any type must be set back at least 5′ from the pool edge. If not, there must be some type of fixed, permanent wall or barrier between it and the pool.

Lighting

Pool lighting may be viewed as falling into one of three categories for all practical purposes.
- Lighting that existed around the pool area prior to the pool installation will remain there after installation.
- Newly installed lighting is associated with the pool area.

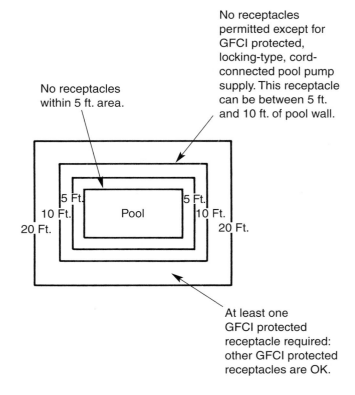

Figure 16-3. Basic poolside receptacle rules.

• Lighting is installed within the pool structure itself.

Looking at each of these categories will provide a general scope of installation methods.

The *NEC* allows existing lighting fixtures to remain as they are, even if the fixtures fall within the otherwise prohibited 5' perimeter of the poolside. This is allowed only if the fixtures are rigidly attached to a structure and GFCI protected. Remember, however, that switching of these lights must be located at a point beyond the 5' area. This important safety factor should not be overlooked.

New lighting fixtures may be installed not less than 5' horizontally from the pool edge and will require GFCI protection. Lights may also be installed above the pool and should be no less than 12' above the waterline for outdoor pools or not less than 7'–6" above the waterline for indoor pools. Indoor lights and fans above the pool must be GFCI protected and totally enclosed. The basic requirements for poolside and above-pool lighting are illustrated in **Figure 16-4**. Refer to *Sections 680.8* and *680.22*.

Underwater Lighting

The installation of underwater lighting fixtures is a subject requiring careful attention. Due to their location, these fixtures can initiate severe electric shock if not installed properly. For this reason, grounding, bonding, and sealing requirements must be strictly followed. Additional requirements include the following:

• Only UL or other lab tested and listed lighting fixtures are to be installed.

• Fixtures may not exceed 150 V between their conductors.

• Fixtures that operate above 15 V must be GFCI protected.

• When installed, the fixture's top edge must be more than 18" below the normal water level. Note: Certain fixtures may be installed at a minimum of 4" below the normal water level *only if identified* for that use.

• The fixture shall have some inherent means to protect it against overheating.

• Raceway between the fixture and the junction box or transformer, for low-voltage fixtures, must be either:

  • Rigid or intermediate metal conduit made from brass or other approved corrosion-resistant metal

  • Liquidtight flexible nonmetallic conduit

  • Rigid nonmetallic conduit having an 8 AWG insulated copper conductor to connect between the fixture and junction box or transformer enclosure

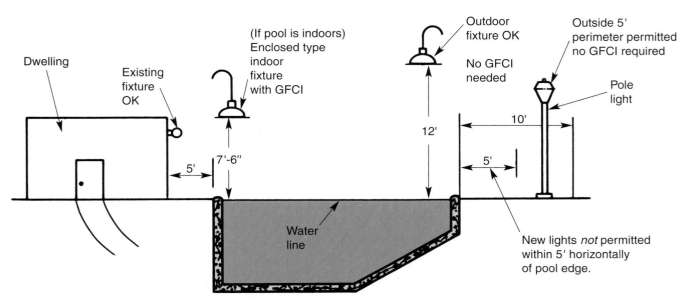

Figure 16-4. Lighting locations above and around the pool are restricted by vertical and horizontal distance.

Wet-niche fixture

The *wet-niche fixture* is made up of a lamp within a housing, a flexible cord, and a sealed lens. The fixture assembly is enclosed in a metal shell called a *forming shell*, which is built into the pool wall. The flexible cord is long enough to allow the fixture, when removed for servicing, to extend out onto the pool deck. Wet-niche fixtures are usually rated at several hundred watts with 12 volts of electricity from a weatherproof, enclosed transformer.

This transformer must be located at least 4' from the pool edge and elevated at least 4"

above the pool deck or ground adjacent to the pool. A flush deck box mounted 4' from the pool edge is permitted if the box is fully sealed with potting compound and only if the fixture is rated at 15 V or less. **Figure 16-5** shows many of the main points concerning wet-niche fixtures and various wiring methods.

wet-niche fixture: An underwater pool light that is designed to get wet and is made up of a lamp within a housing, a flexible cord, and a sealed lens.

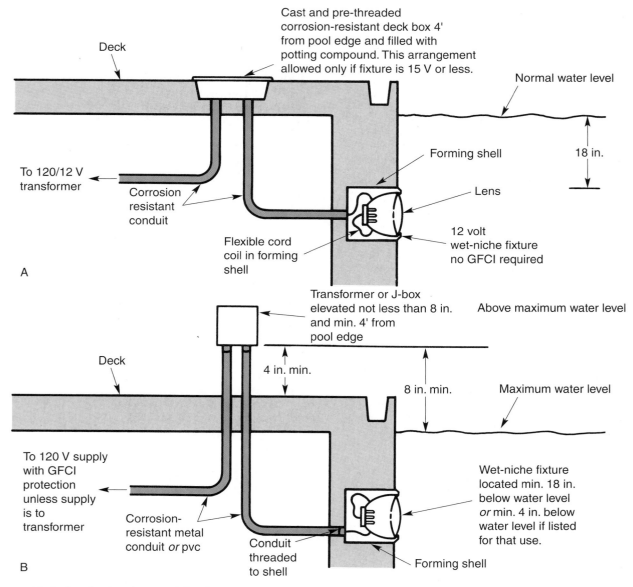

Figure 16-5. A—A 12-volt wet-niche fixture supplied by a remotely located 120 V/12 V transformer with the junction point in a flush deck box completely filled with potting compound. B—Use of an elevated J-box or transformer enclosure. Conduit entry points must be threaded and effectively sealed at the entry point.

Dry-niche fixture

The *dry-niche fixture* is an underwater pool light that is installed inside a watertight enclosure within the pool wall. This type has a drainage pipe provided so that any moisture will be removed. A deck box is required and must be installed flush with the deck surface and a minimum of 4' from the pool edge. This deck box is where the dry-niche fixture is connected to the electrical supply. The dry-niche fixture is illustrated in **Figure 16-6**. Notice the cord-and-plug connection and large deck box for maintenance, repair, and relamping.

Miscellaneous Equipment

Often, pools are equipped with accessories such as heaters, skimmers, audio systems, and automatic pool covers. Manufacturers provide important installation instructions and information that must be understood to ensure a safe environment. As with all electrical items to be wired within or around the swimming pool, care should be taken to ensure proper grounding and bonding as a number one priority. Refer to *Article 680* of the *NEC* and consult with the local electrical inspector when questions arise.

Overhead Conductor Clearance

It should be emphasized that conductors should not be run above a swimming pool. However, for utility company wiring there are some exceptions worth noting. Keep in mind that these exceptions are only for service lines such as telephone, television, or power cables provided by the utility. Further, even within the allowable exception criteria, the conductors must not pass directly over the pool or within 10' horizontally from the inside edge of the pool. **Figure 16-7** shows what is permitted according to the *Section 680.8* and *Table 680.8* of the *NEC*.

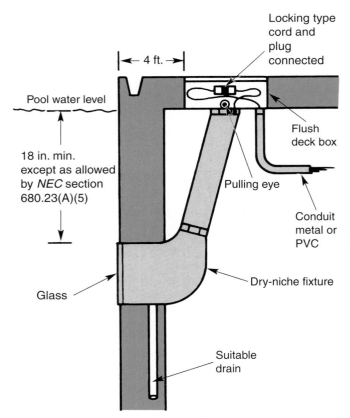

Figure 16-6. Dry-niche fixture is serviceable through a deck box.

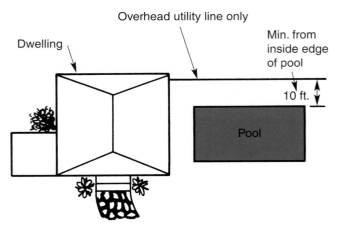

Figure 16-7. Overhead utility conductors must not be within 10' of the horizontal perimeter of the pool.

---

forming shell: The metal shell that is built into a pool wall that will accept a wet-niche lighting fixture.

dry-niche fixture: An underwater pool light that is installed inside a watertight enclosure within the pool wall.

Review Questions

Write your answers on a separate sheet of paper.
Do not write in this book.

1. The two basic types of pool lighting fixtures are_____and_____.

2. All metal structures in and around the pool must be_____.

3. The raceway between a fixture and a junction box or transformer, for low voltage fixtures, must be_____, _____, or_____conduit.

4. Except for the pool pump receptacle, all receptacles around the pool area must be at least_____feet from the pool walls.

5. A grounding conductor to pool electrical equipment devices must never be smaller than number_____ AWG copper.

Know the Code

A copy of the NEC 2005 is required to answer these questions.

1. Which part of the forming shell is covered in *Section 680.23(B)(2)*?

2. Name the section that regulates the motors of electrically operated pool covers.

3. The figure in the *NEC* that illustrates clearances from pool structures is _____.

When properly installed, lighting in a swimming pool is safe, dramatic, and functional. Supervising children is much easier in a well-lit swimming pool.

Telephone and Computer Network Wiring

Objectives

Information in this chapter will enable you to:

- Understand the telephone system from the central office to the telephone.

- Troubleshoot a telephone wiring system.

- Know which cables are used in most residential computer networks.

- Install telephone and computer cabling in a new and existing house.

- Terminate telephone cabling.

Technical Terms

Cable pair
Cable run
Cable termination box
Central office
Crosstalk
Local loop
Patch cable
Protector
Telephone wall plate
Terminal block

Wiring a home for telephone service and connecting computers with a network were two jobs that used to be handled by technicians who specialized in those tasks. Today, the electrician is often called on to install these systems. These are skills that, while not as essential as electrical wiring, will make you a more valuable employee to an electrical company that includes computer network and telephone cabling in new home construction.

Systems Overview

These topics have been combined into one chapter because telephone and network wiring often share the same devices, tools, and installation procedures. In fact, some systems have discarded the traditional phone system entirely, opting to carry voice signals over the Internet.

Telephone

Telephone service receives its power from a local telephone exchange called a *central office*. The telephone connection from the building to the central office is called the *local loop*. The

central office: A building that houses a local telephone exchange where the telephone signals are routed and the power for telephones is generated.

local loop: The telephone connection from the building to the central office.

telephone conductors or *lines* are actually two wires called a **cable pair**. At the central office, the wires are connected to and powered by batteries that supply a direct current to operate the telephone equipment.

As shown in **Figure 17-1**, distribution lines can be run overhead on poles or buried in the ground. Many cable pairs are bundled together in large cables to carry telephone service to area customers.

A **cable termination box** is the enclosure where connections are made for the cable pair coming from each building. It is found in both aboveground and belowground installations. Cable pairs from the building actually terminate at a **protector**. This is a device that protects the cable pair from high voltage should lightning strike the wires.

From the single protector, the cable pair enters the building. They may go:

• Directly through the wall

• Feed through a roof overhang (soffit or rake) into an attic

• Through a wall into a basement

The cable pair usually connects to a terminal block or network interface device inside the building. The **terminal block** is the junction point for all the telephones in the building. It is also called a 42A block, a modular interface, or a modular outlet. All wire pairs for each phone can connect to this terminal. See **Figure 17-2**.

Computer Network

Network wiring is the infrastructure of a network. A network allows personal computers (PCs) to share resources such as files and

cable pair: The two wires that carry the signals and power to a telephone.

cable termination box: The enclosure where connections are made for the cable pair coming from each building.

protector: A device that prevents high voltage from damaging the cable pair.

terminal block: The junction point for all the telephones in the building; also called a 42A block, a modular interface, or a modular outlet.

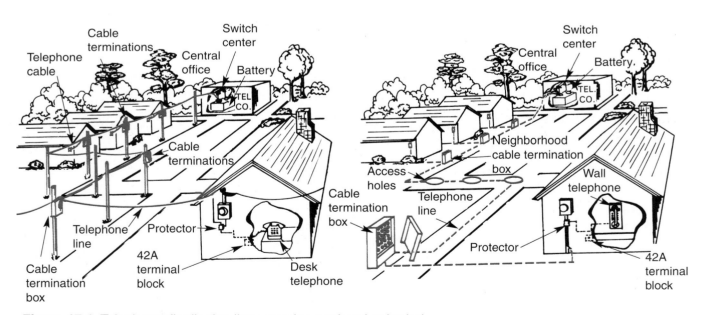

Figure 17-1. Telephone distribution lines may be overhead or buried.

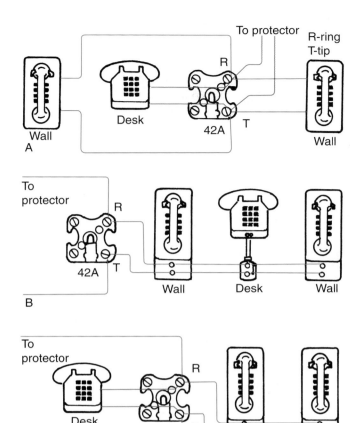

Figure 17-2. Phones are always hooked up in parallel in these patterns. A—All cable pairs start at the same terminal block. B—Additional phones are added by connecting them to the terminals of another phone. C—A combination of A and B.

Installation

Although a high degree of experience is not required to install phone and computer network cabling, the importance of a professional, robust, and accurate installation is no less than any other job you may perform. The phone system is critical in a medical or fire emergency. Also, the time and expense of a callback because of sloppiness may erode any profit or reputation you developed on that job.

Safety

There is little danger of electrical shock from the telephone's own voltage. When the unit is not ringing, 48 V dc is present. Operating the phone signal requires 85 to 90 V ac. This voltage, ac and dc, is supplied by the telephone company. To avoid any shocks, take the receiver off the hook when working on the system.

Regardless of the lower voltages in telephone systems, it is advisable to avoid the possibility of shock by taking these precautions:

- Be sure that the inside wiring is not hooked up to the network interface. This ensures there is no power to the system.

- If for some reason this cannot be done, use screwdrivers, cutters, and strippers with insulated handles. Avoid touching screw terminals or bare conductors with your hands.

Use care in drilling through walls, floors, or ceilings. Avoid areas where there might be electrical wiring, gas pipes, steam pipes, or water pipes. When working on existing telephone wiring, disconnect any transformer that might be supplying step-down voltage for dial lighting.

Keep telephone and network wiring at least 2″ away from power circuits in the building. To avoid high-voltage shock, keep telephone cable pairs away from accidental contact with 120 or 240 V line current.

printers, and to share a common Internet access device. See **Figure 17-3.** Although PCs are often networked to share files and printers, they are typically networked to share a common Internet access device.

Residential networks can use various types of network media, such as copper core cable, radio frequency (wireless), existing phone lines, and existing power lines. This chapter focuses only on copper core cable networks, specifically those that use twisted-pair cable.

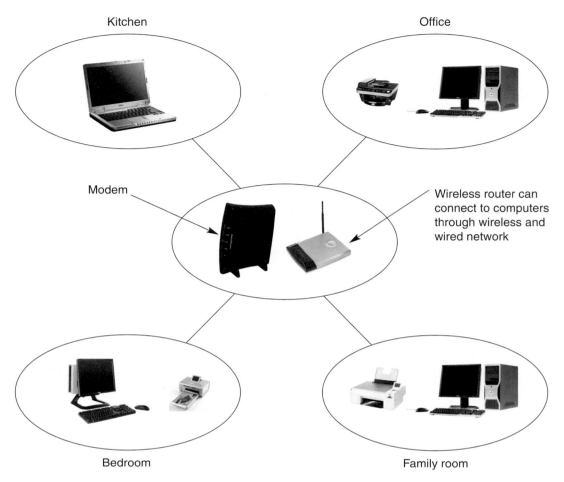

Kitchen

Office

Modem

Wireless router can connect to computers through wireless and wired network

Bedroom

Family room

Figure 17-3. Residential computer networks are designed to share computers, printers, and an Internet connection. (Images courtesy of Dell, Inc.)

Never remove protectors or grounding means placed by the telephone company. Do not modify these installations or make any connection to them.

Keep jacks away from locations such as tubs, showers, swimming pools, and laundry areas. Corded telephones should not be used where the body will be in touch with water.

Tools

There are several tools, such as crimpers, that are designed exclusively for terminating phone and computer network cabling. You will need these to attach an RJ-11 or RJ-45 plug to a twisted-pair cable. However, most of the installation can be accomplished using some of the basic tools that every electrician should have in the tool pouch.

Cable Types

The type of cable you select will depend on the purpose and environment of the finished installation. Always think about the future use of any cabling when comparing its performance and cost.

Telephone cable

Cabling that is designed for telephone use can be divided into indoor and outdoor cable. The indoor cable will be used more than the outdoor cable, since the phone company will probably run the phone line all the way to the house. There are three types of indoor cable: flat, quad, and twisted pair.

Flat cable is generally used to connect the telephone to the wall outlet. This cable is terminated with a plug on each end. Therefore, you must buy the flat cable in the length required.

There are usually two conductors, but some flat cables contain four. See **Figure 17-4**.

The quad cable contains four wires, usually solid, that are bundled together so that they are parallel to each other. This is the lowest grade of cable for telephone systems. However, it has been used reliably in many houses for many years.

Twisted-pair cable contains three pairs of wires with each pair twisted together. The six wires are covered in a jacket for protection. Twisted pair is a better-performing cable for reasons you will learn about in the following section.

Twisted-pair cable

Twisted-pair cable for computer networks contains four twisted pairs of copper conductors. See **Figure 17-5**. Twisting the conductors in each pair helps to reduce crosstalk. *Crosstalk* is the phenomenon of a current-carrying conductor imposing an electrical signal on another conductor. When electrical energy passes through a wire, an electromagnetic field is created around the wire. A current-carrying conductor placed in parallel and in close proximity to another conductor can induce current flow in the other conductor. Twisting the conductors together reduces crosstalk by minimizing the amount of parallel contact between conductors.

An outer jacket covers all four pairs. The conductors in each pair are color-coded. Notice that there is an orange pair, green pair, blue pair, and brown pair. Within each pair, one of the conductors is a solid color and the other is striped. The color-coding plays a role in proper wiring.

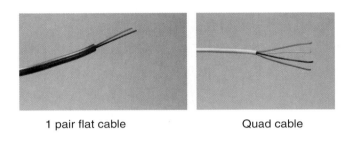

1 pair flat cable   Quad cable

Figure 17-4. These are the most common cables for telephones.

crosstalk: Imposing an electrical signal on another conductor through induction.

Some cables contain a spline to maintain space between the pairs and improve performance

The pairs are twisted to reduce crosstalk

Figure 17-5. The wires are twisted in twisted-pair cabling to prevent crosstalk.

There are two general types of twisted-pair cables: shielded twisted pair (STP) and unshielded twisted pair (UTP). STP has a metallic shield beneath its outer jacket. Some STP cable also shields each twisted pair. UTP does not have a shield. This is the cable that you will use in most telephone and computer installations.

There are seven categories of twisted-pair cable, Category 1 through Category 7. The categories differ in characteristics such as number of twists per foot, wire size, and the rated frequency capacity of the conductors. Category 5, Category 5e, and Category 6 are typically used for residential networks.

Pro Tip

Cat What?

Twisted-pair cabling is often referred to by its category designation. If your supervisor said, "Run some Cat 5e from here to all of the bedrooms," you should install a cable run of Category 5e UTP cabling from your current location in the house to each bedroom.

Twisted-pair cable is available on a spool or in reel-in-box packaging. Reel-in-box packaging makes it easy for one person to run cabling and keeps the cable from kinking and knotting. Using only a spool of cable would require two people for the installation: one to pull the cable and the other to unwind the cable by hand. An alternative is to insert a rod through the spool and have one person hold the ends of the rod while the other person pulls the cable.

A *patch cable* is a length of twisted-pair cable that is terminated on each end with an RJ-45 plug. A patch cable is used for connections between a network device and a computer. Patch cables are available for purchase in various lengths and cable types, such as Category 5e UTP. Patch cables can also be made by hand with the appropriate tools. Making patch cables is rarely an electrician's task.

Cable Installation

These rules should be followed when running cable:
- Do not exceed the pull tension of the cable type.
- Do not bend cables less than the established minimum bend radius of that cable type.
- Do not cinch bundled cables too tightly.
- Use proper wire hangers or straps to secure wire.
- Do not secure wires with plain staples.
- Keep cables away from devices that can cause interference.
- When a cable run must be parallel to electrical wiring there should be at least 5" of space between them.
- When a cable must cross electrical wiring, it should do so at a 90° angle.
- Leave 6" to 8" of extra wire at each cable end.
- Do not exceed maximum home run cable lengths.
- Keep future upgrades and service changes in mind.

The pulling tension of UTP cable is 25 lbs, and the pulling tension of coaxial cable is 35 lbs. Exceeding the pulling tension of either cable can cause physical damage and reduce the quality of the electrical signal. A cable bend should not be *less* than the established minimum bend radius. Doing so will degrade the quality of the electrical signal. The minimum bend radius is usually 4 times the overall diameter of the cable, but be sure to follow the manufacturer's recommendations. See **Figure 17-6**.

There are many products available for securing wire bundles, such as hook-and-loop straps and cable ties. Do not cinch these too tight or the insulation may be damaged.

Cables should be at least 6" away from devices that can cause electromagnetic interference (EMI). This includes fluorescent lighting, motors, and electrical wiring. When a cable

---

patch cable: A length of twisted-pair cable that is terminated on each end with an RJ-45 plug.

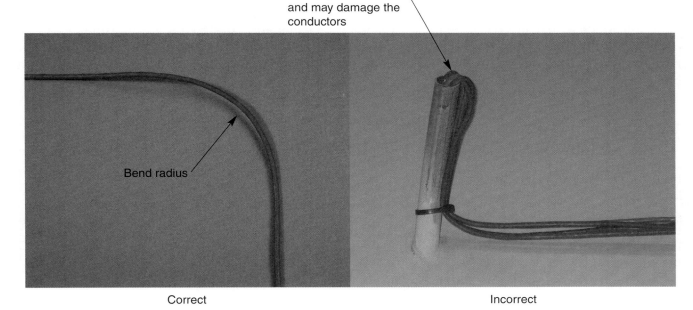

This sharp bend will reduce performance and may damage the conductors

Bend radius

Correct   Incorrect

Figure 17-6. Maintain the minimum bend radius throughout the entire cable run.

crosses over electrical wiring, it should cross at a 90° angle. This prevents the development of crosstalk.

When running cable, always leave an extra 6″ to 8″ of wire at each end of the run. This will allow for ample cable in case the original termination becomes damaged. Also, do not exceed the maximum cable lengths for each home run. The home run for Category 5 and higher cabling should not exceed 295′. RG-59 has a maximum home run of 656′, and RG-6 has a maximum home run of 886′. Remember, satellite and digital cable service uses only RG-6, whereas broadband cable can use either RG-6 or RG-59. The RG-6 cable should be quad-shielded and be able to support a bandwidth of at least 1.8 MHz.

Conduit

Installing conduit is a smart precaution against having obsolete cabling. Electrical and telephone wiring has not changed dramatically within the past few decades. However, manufacturers of computer cabling have consistently developed better-performing conductors every few years. Replacing cables is much easier when conduit is installed.

Electrical nonmetallic tubing

You learned about electrical nonmetallic tubing (ENT) in Chapter 4, **Wiring Systems**. This conduit is typically a corrugated tube with snap-on fittings. Installation requires few tools and limited skills. See **Figure 17-7**. Also, this type of conduit is available in different colors that help identify the purpose for the cabling inside.

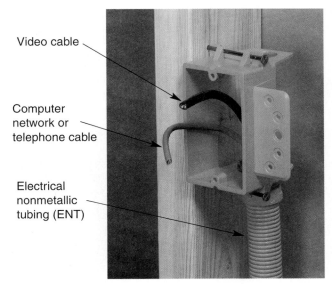

Video cable

Computer network or telephone cable

Electrical nonmetallic tubing (ENT)

Figure 17-7. Electrical nonmetallic tubing is a good choice for containing telephone, network, and video cabling. (Carlon, Lamson & Sessions)

Electrical metallic tubing

For installations that require a stronger conduit or need to guard against electromagnetic interference, use electrical metallic tubing (EMT). Although the installation is more complex than ENT, at this point you should be able to cut, bend, and install EMT fairly quickly.

Boxes

Some installers may use standard electrical boxes for termination points. These may be convenient to use in new construction but are not necessary. There are boxes designed for these low-voltage situations. See **Figure 17-8**. Faceplates with connectors are mounted directly to these boxes.

In new construction, the telephone wiring should be installed before the application of drywall or paneling. Start the wiring at the connection installed near the network interface. If outlet boxes are required by local code, be sure to allow them to extend beyond the stud the thickness of the wall-covering materials. Fasten the telephone wire to a stud only if needed to maintain space between the telephone wire and any electrical wire. Allow about 6″ of wire inside the outlet for your connections.

Locations

It is typically recommended that the kitchen and bedrooms have at least two service locations and that the living room, family room, and office have at least three service locations. The faceplate and jack used will depend on the needed service or services. See **Figure 17-9**.

Jacks and connectors are modular and can be snapped into any of the available openings in the wall plate. For new home installations, the TIA/EIA 570A standard recommends two UTP (Category 5 or Category 5e) and two RG-6 cables be run to each service location. One UTP cable can be used for a network connection and the other for a telephone connection. One RG-6 cable can serve as a CATV connection and the other as a broadband cable Internet access connection or a satellite Internet access connection.

The jack or connector must match the cable type. For example, if the cable run is Category 6, a Category 6 jack must be installed. If the cable run is RG-6, an RG-6 connector must be installed.

Installing Cable in an Existing Home

Installing telephone systems after wall coverings are in place entails more care and usually more work. This is especially true when the wiring is to be concealed. In these cases, use of fish tape and string will help pull wires through wall cavities. Refer to Chapter 20, **Electrical Remodeling**

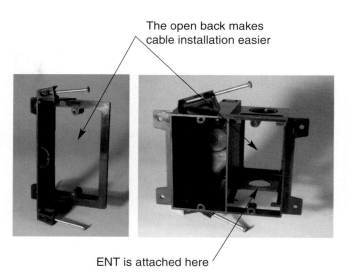

The open back makes cable installation easier

ENT is attached here

Figure 17-8. These boxes are designed to work with low-voltage cabling.

Phone jack

Computer network jack

Video jack

Figure 17-9. Select the proper faceplate and jack when terminating telephone or computer network cabling.

for information on pulling wires through existing construction.

Wires cannot always be run inside walls. They are often mounted on surfaces. Such wire must be supported. Use 1/4″ wide staples made for supporting telephone wire. Insulated staples work well and protect the wire. Ordinary staples are not recommended because they easily damage the insulation on telephone wire. Do not run the wire under carpeting or near traffic areas.

Wires can be made less noticeable if they are placed in areas where moldings, casing, grooves in paneling, or coverings partially or wholly conceal them. Wiring can also be run inside cabinets.

Terminating Cables

Terminal and cable pairs are color-coded. In four-wire cable, the wire colors are usually black, green, red, and yellow. Terminal screws are coded accordingly. Most blocks allow you to run cable pairs for as many as four phones.

A *cable run* is a long length of cable that is typically pulled through walls and the ceiling area. One end of a cable run is terminated at a centrally located patch panel and the other end is terminated at the RJ-45 wall jack connector.

Devices

Terminal blocks should be attached to ceiling or floor joists in the attic or basement. When attaching cable pairs, leave some slack so the wires will not pull loose from the block. A plug is attached to the end of a telephone or network cable to allow the cable to be easily connected to or disconnected from a system. The standard plugs are RJ-11 for telephone and RJ-45 for computer networks. A special crimper is required to attach a plug to a cable. See **Figure 17-10**.

The plug on a cable is inserted into a jack. A jack is attached to the system cabling and is usually mounted on a wall to allow a convenient place to attach a telephone or computer.

---

cable run: A long length of cable that is typically pulled through walls and the ceiling area.

RJ-11 telephone plug

RJ-45 network plug

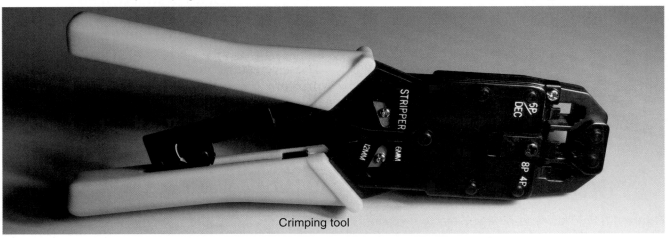
Crimping tool

Figure 17-10. This is a telephone plug, network plug, and the tool that is used to attach them to a cable.

As with electrical wiring, a faceplate for telephone and network wiring hides the cabling and exposed terminations. The faceplate may also support the jack.

A *telephone wall plate* is a special faceplate that has two mounting pegs that fit the slots on the mounting base of a wall-mounted telephone. See **Figure 17-11**. Wall phone outlets should be about 56" from the bottom of the outlet to the floor. Over counters, allow 10" between the bottom of the outlet and the countertop. The pins may be used as ground. If you change plates, you may need to connect a ground wire to the pins.

Other Systems

There are systems other than those covered in this chapter that may be installed by electricians. For now, they are not prevalent enough to justify explanation beyond the introductions below. Product costs, installation complexity, and performance are the reasons these systems are not as popular as copper cabling, Ethernet, and plain old telephone service (POTS) equipment.

Fiber optic

Fiber optic cable is a clear glass or plastic conductor that transmits light signals. Fiber optic cable's outside appearance is very similar to copper cable. Only the marking on the outer jacket and the end of the cable reveal the fragile interior as fiber. Fiber optic cable is unaffected by electromagnetic interference and transmits signals very quickly. The cost of the cable, NICs, and termination equipment have kept fiber optic cable out of most networked homes. This will probably change as the costs decrease.

Structured cabling

There are companies that sell cable management products that work together as a system to protect, manage, and identify all of the nonelectrical cabling in a home. This system, called structured cabling, includes panels, boxes, conduit, and termination devices for the phone, computer network, video, and security cabling in a home. Since these systems are unique to each manufacturer, it is best to rely on the installation instructions and support personnel for the proper installation methods. Connecting the components of these systems is made easier with a composite cable. Composite cable contains coaxial, twisted pair, and sometimes fiber optic cables into one bundle. See **Figure 17-12**. This bundle is run from a central point in the house to each room that requires a computer, telephone, or video connection.

Wireless

Adding a computer network to an existing home has always required fishing cables in walls or hiding the cables in surface-mount raceway. There are products out now that transmit the computer signals using radio frequency and do not need any cabling between computers. These products include NICs, routers, and even printers. The performance is less than cabled networks, but not less than most people's needs. Installation is fairly easy and does not require the skills of an electrician. See **Figure 17-13**.

A wall-mounted telephone has two slots that slide over these studs

Figure 17-11. This type of wall plate is designed to support a telephone conveniently on a wall.

telephone wall plate: A special faceplate that has two mounting pegs that fit the slots on the mounting base of a wall-mount telephone.

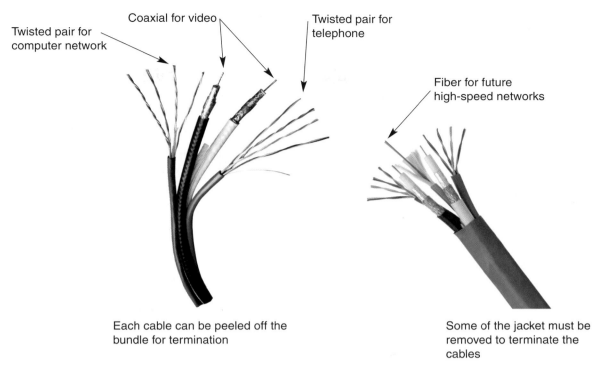

Twisted pair for computer network

Coaxial for video

Twisted pair for telephone

Fiber for future high-speed networks

Each cable can be peeled off the bundle for termination

Some of the jacket must be removed to terminate the cables

Figure 17-12. Composite cabling combines the telephone, video, and computer network cables into one bundle for a complete installation.

Satellite and cable television

These systems bring a television signal into the home from an orbiting satellite or from a coaxial cable that is buried or overhead. The companies that sell these systems have their own trained technicians who handle all aspects of the installation. See **Figure 17-14**.

Figure 17-13. Wireless network products, such as this router, have made it possible for homeowners to install their own computer networks without running any cables. (D-Link Corporation)

Figure 17-14. Satellite and cable television installations are usually handled by the companies that sell these services. (DIRECTV, Inc.)

Review Questions

Write your answers on a separate sheet of paper.
Do not write in this book.

1. The two conductors used to connect a telephone to the system are called a _____.
2. *True or False?* The terminal block can connect all lines in a house to the telephone system.
3. *True or False?* The telephone system in a house must be connected to the electrical system.
4. The wires are twisted in twisted-p0air cabling to prevent ___ .
5. When selecting conduit for telephone and network cabling, which type requires the fewest tools, time, and skill?
6. Which installation does the TIA/EIA 570A standard recommend for each service location?
   A. Two Cat 5 UTP cables and one RG-6 cable.
   B. One Cat 5 UTP cable and one RG-6 cable.
   C. Two Cat 5 UTP cables and two RG-6 cables.
   D. One Cat 5 UTP cable and two RG-6 cables.

Know the Code

A copy of the NEC 2005 is required to answer these questions.

1. Which section contains an exception that removes conduit fill restrictions from raceways for communications wires and cables?
2. According to *Section 800.133(A)(1),* how many types of cable are allowed to be in the same raceway as communication cables?

Motors

Objectives

Information in this chapter will enable you to:

- Interpret data contained on the nameplate of an electric motor.
- Determine permissible voltage drop for an electric motor.
- Properly size circuit conductors for various motors and loads.
- Know the steps for mounting a motor and connecting it to a load.
- Discuss proper procedure for service and repair of motors.

Technical Terms

Continuous duty
Frame number
Limited-duty

Electricians must be familiar with the wiring requirements for electric motors. They also need to know how to order the right replacement when an old motor is no longer serviceable.

Motors operating at 600 V or less are encountered frequently. Motors with higher voltages are found in larger commercial and industrial operations.

Types of Motors

There are several different types of motors based on the method of operation and design. These include:

- DC motors
- Single-phase AC squirrel cage motors
- Polyphase AC motors
- Wound-rotor three-phase motors
- Synchronous motors

Although the specific characteristics of these motors are beyond the scope of this book, electricians dealing with motor-operated machinery will require considerable study and hands-on training before they are able to wire, repair, and maintain motors. The information in this chapter is general and introductory in nature.

Articles 430 and *440* of the *National Electrical Code* should be reviewed carefully before you attempt to install any motor and its associated circuit components. These *NEC* articles deal with the many concerns and variations of motor circuits.

Motor Nameplate

One of the most important aids to installing and wiring a motor correctly is the information found on the motor itself. The nameplate, **Figure 18-1**, provides a wealth of data regarding the characteristics of the motor.

NEC and NEMA (National Electrical Manufacturers Association) requirements state that all motors are to have nameplates providing the following information: name of manufacturer, horsepower rating, type, frame number, time rating, rpm rating, design letter, frequency (in hertz), number of phases, insulation class,

load rating in amperes, locked rotor code letter, voltage, duty, ambient temperature, and service factor. Other information, such as serial number, model number, bearing numbers, and efficiency ratings are often included. This nameplate data should be carefully reviewed before setting and wiring a motor.

Nameplate Data Definitions

Refer to **Figure 18-1** as you read the following names and definitions:

- **Frame and type.** The NEMA designation for frame designation and type.

- **Horsepower.** The power rating of the motor.

- **Motor code.** Designated by a letter indicating the starting current required. The higher the locked-rotor kilovolt ampere (kVa), the higher the starting current surge.

[handwritten: frequency determ speed]

[handwritten: 900 / 1725 / 3500 } common speed]

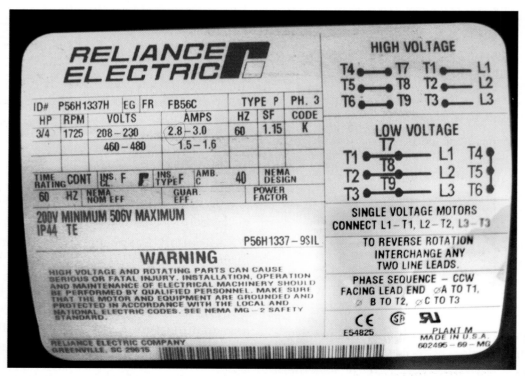

Figure 18-1. The motor nameplate gives motor characteristics. The code designation, service factor, time rating, and ambient temperature are important considerations in selecting a motor for a given job.

- **Cycles (hertz).** The frequency at which the motor is designed to be operated.
- **Phase.** The number of phases on which the motor operates.
- **Revolutions per minute (rpm).** The speed of the motor at full load.
- **Voltage.** The voltage or voltages of operation.
- **Thermal protection.** An indication of thermal protection provided for the motor, if it has any.
- **Amps (A).** The rated current (in amperes) at full load.
- **Time.** Time rating of the motor showing the duty rating as continuous or as specific period of time the motor can be operated.
- **Ambient temperature, or temperature rise.** The maximum ambient temperature at which the motor should be operated, or the permissible temperature rise of the motor above the ambient air at rated load.
- **Service factor.** The amount of overload that the motor can tolerate on a continuous basis at rated voltage and frequency.
- **Insulation class.** A designation of the insulation system used, included primarily for convenience in rewinding.
- **NEMA design.** A letter designation for specifying the motor characteristics.

Frame Number

Motors of a given horsepower rating are built in a certain size of frame or housing. For standardization, NEMA has assigned a *frame number* to the frame size for each integral horsepower motor. This ensures that the shaft heights and dimensions are consistent for motors that are assigned a specific frame number.

Size - Length
      circumference

---

frame number: A number assigned by the National Electrical Manufacturer's Association to categorize the frame size for each integral horsepower motor.

Proper Size of Motor Feeder Conductors

For proper operation of an electric motor, the supply voltage and frequency (cycles per second or hertz) at the motor terminals must match the values specified by the manufacturer as closely as possible. Performance is best over a range of plus or minus 10 percent of rated voltage and 5 percent above or below rated frequency. Frequency is usually no problem since it rarely varies.

However, if applied voltage varies too much from the nameplate specifications, it will produce noticeable changes in the motor torque (turning force). Low voltage from inadequate wiring or any other cause can create severe problems. Motor starting torque may be too low to start the load and keep it moving. The following sections describe and demonstrate how to size wire properly.

Web Site

www.nema.org

The National Electrical Manufacturers Association (NEMA) develops and maintains standards regarding electrical equipment. A description of the frame numbering system is one of the many items within the motor standard available at the NEMA Web site.

Ampere Adjustment and Correction Factors

You learned that the size of a conductor is based on the current rating of the OCPD and may increase if an adjustment factor or a correction factor is required. The adjustment factor is determined by the number of conductors in a raceway or cable and the correction factor is based on the ambient temperature. Motor circuits must include an additional factor to handle the increased load as the motor starts. *Article 430, Section II* describes the situations where a conductor's ampacity would have to be changed. For most AC motor installations, the ampacity requirement of a motor is 125 percent of the motor's full-load current rating. The nameplate should show the full-load current rating, but if it does not refer to *Table 430.250*.

For example, the circuit conductors supplying a 30 hp 460 V three-phase wound rotor motor are found as follows:

1. From the *NEC Table 430.250*, the full-load current rating is shown to be 40 A.

2. The branch-circuit conductors for continuous safe operation must be 125 percent of this rating or 50 A.

3. Thus, the conductors for this circuit must be no smaller than 6 AWG copper (THW, RHW, THHN, RHH, or TW) as shown in *Table 310.16* of the *NEC*.

When aluminum circuit conductors are used, 4 AWG types TW, THW, RHH, THHN, or XHHW would be suitable. Again, refer to *NEC Table 310.16*.

Voltage Drop

Voltage drop, as you recall, is the reduction in voltage along the length of a conductor. This is important to know when you have to wire a circuit for a motor because voltage drop greatly affects the speed and torque of a motor. As specified by NEMA, motors are designed to handle a ten percent fluctuation in voltage above and below the rating on the nameplate. You may not be able to control the typical voltage changes that occur as loads are placed on and off the electrical system, but you can control the amount of voltage drop by installing the proper conductors. Refer to **Figure 18-2** as you determine the proper conductors to install in this example.

1. The *NEC* requires this motor to be supplied by branch circuit conductors having a capacity of 125 percent of the full-load current (20 A).

$$1.25 \times 20 \text{ A} = 25 \text{ A}$$

Copper conductors that are 10 AWG or larger would be required to handle the amperage.

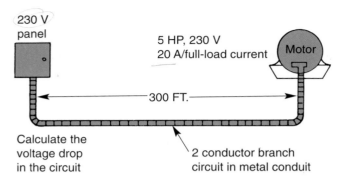

Calculate the voltage drop in the circuit

2 conductor branch circuit in metal conduit

Figure 18-2. Calculation of voltage drop in a circuit is related to the speed and torque of the motor, the length of the branch circuit, and the size of the conductors.

2. The motor is rated at 230 V. Find the amount of voltage drop that the motor can tolerate.

$$230 \text{ V} \times 10\% = 23 \text{ V}$$

3. When the full-load current of 20 A is flowing, find the maximum resistance allowed.

$$23 \text{ V} \div 20 \text{ A} = 1.15 \text{ ohms}$$

4. This maximum resistance is for two wires. Find the maximum resistance for one wire.

$$1.15 \text{ ohms} \div 2 = 0.575 \text{ ohms}$$

5. Find the maximum resistance allowed for each foot of wire.

$$0.575 \text{ ohms} \div 500 \text{ ft} = 0.00115 \text{ ohms per foot}$$

6. The table lists the resistance of conductors in ohms per 1000'.

$$0.00115 \text{ ohms} \times 1000 \text{ ft} = 1.15 \text{ ohms per 1000'}$$

7. *Table 8* lists the resistance of solid 10 AWG conductor as 1.21 ohm/kFT (ohms per 1000'). This resistance is more than the 1.15 that is allowed. The next larger size, solid 8 AWG, has a resistance of 0.764 ohm/kFT.

This example illustrates that although *Table 310.16* allows a 10 AWG conductor for the 25 A adjusted motor circuit, the voltage drop requires a larger conductor, 8 AWG.

The resistances used in the foregoing example are based on an ambient temperature of 167°F (75°C). Higher temperatures will create higher conductor resistance and consequently higher voltage drops. See the notes at the bottom of *NEC Chapter 9, Table 8* to make any necessary adjustments.

Protection of Motor Feeder Conductors

The protection of motor feeder conductors rests primarily on the type of motor circuit involved. For practical purposes, there are four common motor circuits. See **Figure 18-3**.

- **Single motor circuit.** This circuit serves only one motor.
- **Multiple motor circuit.** This circuit serves two or more motors.
- **Motor and other loads circuit.** A circuit that serves one or more motors in addition to other loads such as lighting and appliances.
- **Hermetic compressor motor circuit.** This circuit serves one or more hermetically sealed air conditioner compressor motors.

Circuit Protection

Protection for a motor circuit is provided by an overload relay within the motor starter and with an adequate fuse or circuit breaker at the panel. The overload protection in the starter must have a rating that is not more than 125 percent of the motor's full-load current. Fusing or circuit breaker requirements are found in *Section 430.52* of the *NEC*. The maximum fuse or breaker size permitted for short-circuit or ground-fault protection is 150 percent of the full-load current rating.

For example, look at **Figure 18-4**. Note that the procedure for determining conductor size and protection is the same as for the larger motor used in our previous example. It makes no difference that the motor type and supply voltage are different.

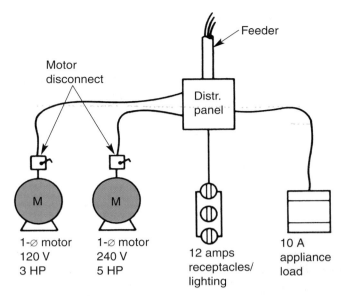

Figure 18-3. Example layout for combination branch circuit having motors, receptacle, lighting, and appliance load.

Dual-element fuses

Dual-element fuses are designed mainly for motor-circuit protection. The fuse blows and opens the circuit when either of two elements inside opens. This occurs during the following circuit faults:

- **Overloads.** A time-delay element made from an alloy melts to open the circuit.
- **Short circuits.** Links on either side or end of the fuse blow in a fraction of an alternating current cycle.

Dual-element fuses have several advantages over single-element fuses. *Time delay breakers*

- They may be used or selected to closely match the actual motor running because they do not blow on harmless momentary overloads. Therefore, there is less nuisance blowing.
- Their low let-through current prevents the fault current from reaching destructive levels in the more vulnerable branch circuits and associated equipment. This would be less possible with ordinary single-element fuses, or where more costly fuses are not justified.

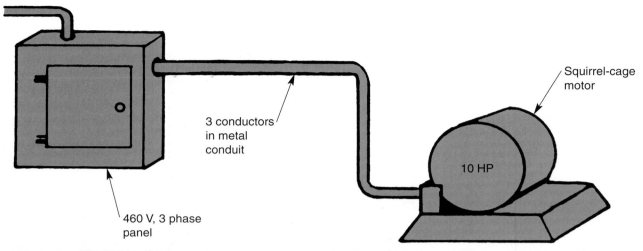

Step	Procedure
1	Full load motor current is 14 A. *(NEC Table 430. 150)*
2	Motor circuit conductors must be capable of carrying at least 18 A. (125% X 14)
3	Conductors must be no smaller than 12 AWG copper or 10 AWG aluminum. Types include TW, THW, THHN, and RHH. *(NEC Table 310.16)*
4	Overload protection in the motor starter must be rated no higher than 125% of the full-load current. This would equal 17.5 A. A 20 A overload device is acceptable since it is the next higher standard rating. *(NEC Table 240. 4(B))*
5	*NEC Table 430.52* shows short-circuit and ground-fault protection is to be 300% of the full-load current. 300% x 14 A = 42A. The next higher standard fuse or breaker is 45 A.

Figure 18-4. Steps for determining adequate overcurrent protection and ground-fault protection for a circuit.

- They can be more closely matched to the protective wiring and equipment because they are not subject to nuisance blowing. Therefore, the equipment used can be more compact and less expensive.
- They are ideally suited for the protection of coils, relays, solenoids, and other magnetic equipment because the time-delay element will not blow on a momentary inrush of current. Yet, they will blow if the overload is sustained.

General Layout

Figure 18-5 shows the general layout acceptable for a single motor branch circuit. This circuit must provide:

- Conductors rated at 125 percent of the motor full-load current
- Circuit overcurrent protection in the form of fuses or breakers
- A motor controller with overload protection
- A means of disconnect

General Purpose Circuit Guide

Follow these general guidelines:
- When each motor is 1 hp or 6 A or less, the circuit will require 20 A/125 V or smaller fuse or breaker; or 10 A/250 V. See **Figure 18-6**.
- Larger motors require a controller and overcurrent protection that is approved for group installation.

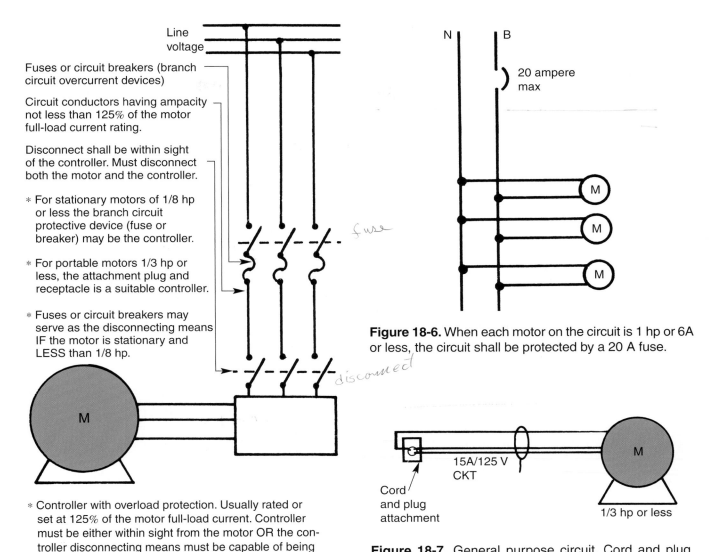

Line voltage

Fuses or circuit breakers (branch circuit overcurrent devices)

Circuit conductors having ampacity not less than 125% of the motor full-load current rating.

Disconnect shall be within sight of the controller. Must disconnect both the motor and the controller.

* For stationary motors of 1/8 hp or less the branch circuit protective device (fuse or breaker) may be the controller.

* For portable motors 1/3 hp or less, the attachment plug and receptacle is a suitable controller.

* Fuses or circuit breakers may serve as the disconnecting means IF the motor is stationary and LESS than 1/8 hp.

fuse

disconnect

M

* Controller with overload protection. Usually rated or set at 125% of the motor full-load current. Controller must be either within sight from the motor OR the controller disconnecting means must be capable of being locked in the open position

Figure 18-5. This layout provides all *NEC* requirements for motor circuit components.

N B

20 ampere max

M

M

M

Figure 18-6. When each motor on the circuit is 1 hp or 6A or less, the circuit shall be protected by a 20 A fuse.

Cord and plug attachment

15A/125 V CKT

M

1/3 hp or less

Figure 18-7. General purpose circuit. Cord and plug are permitted. 15 A fuse or breaker protection is acceptable for motors of 1/3 hp or less.

• Cord and plug connection is permitted. A 15 A circuit with fuse or circuit breaker protection is suitable for motors of 1/3 hp or less, **Figure 18-7**.

Motor Branch Circuit

Each motor needs motor-running overcurrent protection. This protection must not exceed the amperage stamped on the OCPD of the smallest motor on the branch circuit. The OCPD must be approved for group installation in multiple-motor circuits. Each motor

may have an individual disconnect, but it is not necessary.

A single disconnect for a group of motors is permitted if:

• All the motors are part of one machine.

• The disconnect is in sight of all motors.

• Each motor is 6 A or less and less than 300 V. Conductors supplying two or more motors must have a current rating not less than 125 percent of the full-load current rating of the largest motor plus the sum of the full-load current rating of the other motors on the circuit.

Controller Requirements

Motors must be provided with some type of control. The *NEC* defines a motor controller as a switch or other device normally used for starting and stopping a motor. The controller must be protected against short-circuit current damage. There are numerous options available to meet the requirement. The method used depends primarily on the size and type of motor.

Control Methods

On small, single-phase motors, the OCPD may serve as the controller for motors that are rated not more than 1/8 hp, stationary, and normally left running. See **Figure 18-8**. A good example would be a clock motor.

For motors up to and including 2 hp, the controller may be a switch. This switch should be of the general-use type and have a current capacity of at least twice the full-load current rating of the motor. The switch may also serve as the disconnect. **Figure 18-9** shows a suitable switch.

The circuit breaker for a branch circuit may serve as the controller. However, the longer delay prior to opening may permit a fault current to damage the controller or the motor. The circuit breaker may also serve as the disconnect.

A cord and plug arrangement may serve as the controller for motors at or less than 1/3 hp, **Figure 18-10**. The same arrangement may also serve as the disconnect.

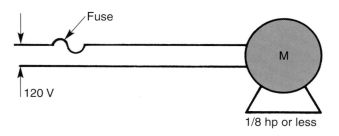

Figure 18-8. On small, single-phase motors, overcurrent device may serve as the controller for motors of 1/8 hp or less.

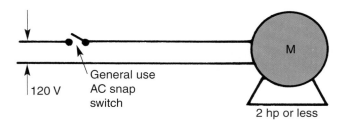

Figure 18-9. A switch may serve as the controller for motors up to 2 hp. Switch should be of the general-use type.

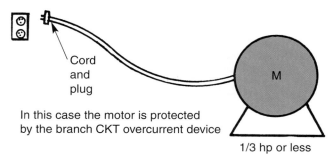

Figure 18-10. Cord and plug may serve as controller of motors having less than 1/3 hp.
at or less

Sealed Hermetic Motors

Motors that are hermetically sealed inside a refrigerating or air conditioning system have low operating temperatures and stay cool during normal operation. They can handle heavier loads than general-purpose motors because of this temperature advantage. Such motors are not rated in horsepower but in terms of full-load current, locked-rotor current, or both.

Controller selection is often determined from *NEC Tables 430.247* through *430.251(B)* by checking the horsepower equivalent. *Tables 430.251(A)* and *(B)* will give the horsepower equivalent for locked-rotor current ratings. The larger of the two values derived from the tables should be used to find the controller rating. Of course, the nameplate provides full-load and locked-rotor current ratings. If exact current values are not given in the charts, then go to the next higher current in the table to find the horsepower rating.

Some controllers are rated in full-load current or locked-rotor current. In such cases, the horsepower equivalent is not needed.

Sample Problem

For example, what is the correct size of the controller for a 230 V three-phase wound-rotor motor that has a nameplate showing 90A locked rotor and full-load current of 25.3 A? Find the full-load current and 90 A locked-rotor current of this motor:

1. Find the full-load amperage from *Table 430.250*. The next full-load amperage above 25.3 is 28. This indicates a horsepower equivalent of 10.
2. The next higher locked rotor amperage shown in *Table 430.251 (B)* is 92. This indicates a 5 hp equivalent. Since the higher hp value is to be used, the controller must be rated for 10 hp.

Motor Duty

Motor design has an influence on the capacities of the controller and fuses used with a motor. All electric motors are designed for either continuous duty or limited duty. Motors designed for **continuous duty** will deliver the rated horsepower for an indefinite period without overheating. General-purpose motors should always be the continuous-duty type. **Limited-duty** motors will deliver rated horsepower for a specified period of time but cannot be operated continuously at the rated load. A limited-duty motor is one used to operate valves, pumps, or elevators. If its operating period is extended, a limited-duty motor will overheat and may burn out prematurely.

Selecting the Proper Size Disconnect

Before discussing proper disconnect sizing, we must first define a few terms.

- **Rated-load current.** The current resulting when a motor is operated at the rated load, rated voltage, and rated frequency of the equipment it serves. The rated-load current is indicated on the nameplate of the motor.

- **Branch-circuit selection current.** The value, in amperes, to be used instead of the rated-load current to determine the size of the branch circuit conductor, disconnecting means, controller ratings, and fault device ratings. This value is always greater than the rated-load current.

The disconnecting means rating for a hermetic motor shall be 115 percent of the nameplate rated-load current or the branch-circuit selection current, whichever is greater. The equivalent horsepower is determined in the same way as described earlier for determining controller horsepower. Again, the larger value is the one used to select the proper disconnect.

Sizing Circuit Components for Combination Loads

The circuit shown in **Figure 18-11** includes two 1 1/2 hp, one 7 1/2 hp, and one 10 hp squirrel-cage motors plus a lighting load of 26,000 VA. The supply consists of a four-wire, three-phase, 230 V delta transformer. In order to properly install this circuit we must determine:

- Conductor ampacities
- Conductor types and sizes
- Conduit sizes and fill
- Switch requirements and sizes
- OCPD capacities

Step-by-Step Method

The procedures that follow illustrate how to find the values needed. Every electrician should master this step-by-step procedure because it is quick and practical. Furthermore, the method can be applied to many power/lighting combination circuits.

---

continuous duty: A motor that is designed to deliver the rated horsepower for an indefinite period without overheating.

limited-duty: A motor that will deliver the rated horsepower for a specified period of time, but cannot be operated continuously at the rated load.

Continue referring to Figure 18-11 as you work through the following steps:

1. From *NEC Table 430.150*, determine the full-load current for each motor.

$$1 \ 1/2 \ \text{hp} = 6 \ \text{A}$$
$$7 \ 1/2 \ \text{hp} = 22 \ \text{A}$$
$$10 \ \text{hp} = 28 \ \text{A}$$

2. Calculate the main motor feeder capacity and conductor size.
(Refer to *NEC Section 430.24*.)

$$(2) \ 1 \ 1/2 \ \text{hp} \ @ \ 6 \ \text{A} = 12 \ \text{A}$$
$$(1) \ 7 \ 1/2 \ \text{hp} \ @ \ 22 \ \text{A} = 22 \ \text{A}$$
$$(1) \ 10 \ \text{hp} \ @ \ 28 \ \text{A} \times 125\% =$$
35 A (This is the largest motor)
$$\text{TOTAL} = 69 \ \text{A}$$

Three 6 AWG (copper) conductors, type THHN, *NEC Table 310.16*, will work well. These should be installed in 1" conduit. See *NEC Annex C, Table C1*.

3. Find the motor feeder protection rating. Refer to *NEC Sections 430.62, 430.24,* and *430.52*.

$$(2) \ 1 \ 1/2 \ \text{hp at } 6 \ \text{A each} = 12 \ \text{A}$$
$$(1) \ 7 \ 1/2 \ \text{hp at } 22 \ \text{A} = 22 \ \text{A}$$
$$(1) \ 10 \ \text{hp at } 28 \ \text{A} \times 250\% = 70 \ \text{A}$$
$$\text{TOTAL} = 104 \ \text{A}$$

The main motor feeder protection should consist of a 100 A switch having 100 A fuses. These fuses should be the time-delay type.

Step 1.   Find full-load current for each motor.
Step 2.   Calculate main motor feeder capacity and conducter size.
Step 3.   Find motor feeder protection rating.
Step 4.   Determine lighting load.
Step 5.   Find combined feeder load.
Step 6.   Size combined feeder switch and overcurrent device rating.

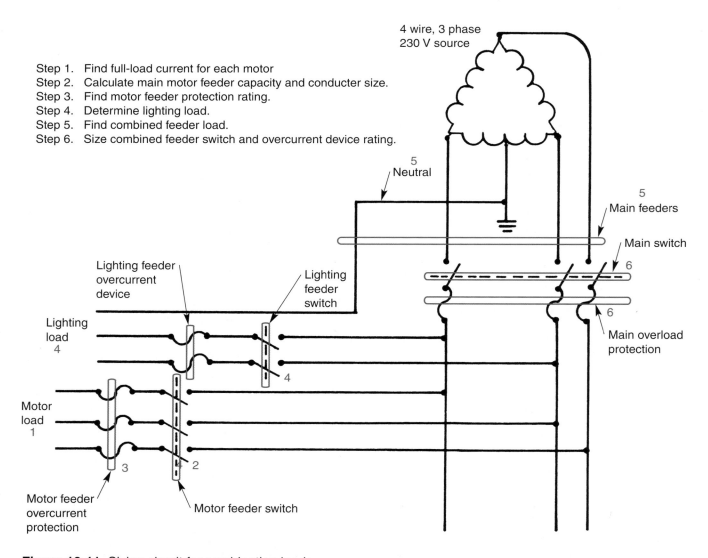

Figure 18-11. Sizing circuit for combination loads.

4. Determine the lighting load.

$$26,000 \text{ VA} / 240 \text{ V} = 108.7 \text{ A}$$

Use three 2 AWG (copper) THW or 3 AWG THHN conductors in 1 1/4″ conduit and provide feeder protection consisting of a 200 A switch with 110 A fuses in each hot leg.

5. Find the combined feeder load.

Note that of the three main feeder conductors, two will carry both the motor and lighting loads while one conductor will carry only a motor load. The two phase conductors carrying the combined motor and lighting load will need a minimum current capacity consisting of:

```
   69.0 A  Motor load
+ 108.7 A  Lighting load
  177.7 A  TOTAL
```

Each of these phase conductors must be adequately sized. 3/0 AWG THW is best suited. The remaining phase conductor serves only the motor load and will need a capacity equal to 69 A. A 4 AWG TW or THW conductor will be adequate.

The neutral, for the lighting load, must be rated to carry the maximum unbalance between it and the hot leg, 108.7 A. Use a 2 AWG THW or 3 AWG THHN conductor, refer to *NEC Table 310.16*.

The four main feeder conductors—two 2/0 AWG THHN, one 4/0 AWG THW, and one 2/0 AWG THW—should be run in 2″ conduit. This is within the *NEC Chapter 9, Table 1* guidelines.

6. Size the combined feeder switch and overcurrent devices. Since two of the phase conductors will carry a 177.7 A load and the other a 69 A load, the main feeder switch should be rated at 200 A.

Overcurrent protection for the phase conductors carrying both the lighting and motor loads will be sized at 225 A, *NEC 430.63*:

```
Motor current draw = 104   A
Light current draw = 108.7 A
      Total draw = 212.7 A
```

The next higher fuse rating is 225 A.

A fuse or breaker supplying 110 A of overcurrent protection must be used for the hot leg that carries only the motor load, 104 A.

Insulation Systems for Small Motors

Four insulation systems are available for small induction motors. They are as follows:

System	Maximum (Hot Spot) Continuous Temperature
Class A	105°C (221°F)
Class B	130°C (266°F)
Class F	155°C (311°F)
Class H	180°C (356°F)

Temperature limits are established by two agencies:

- **Underwriters Laboratories.** This organization protects against fire hazards.
- **National Electrical Manufacturers Association (NEMA).** One of the duties of this association is to create standards to ensure adequate motor life.

Nameplate data generally gives the allowable or maximum temperature rise above the ambient air for motor operation. If these are observed, the hot spot temperature of the motor should remain within the specified value for the insulation system used. Normal maximum ambient temperature is 40°C (104°F) for most motor ratings.

Motor Installation Tips

Proper installation of an electrical motor is essential for satisfactory operation, maximum service, and personal safety. The installation and wiring should conform to the recommendations of the *National Electrical Code* and to any local code.

Causes of Motor Failure

A motor properly selected, installed, and used can give many years of satisfactory service. Failures are most often due to overheating, moisture, bearing failure, or starting mechanism failure. Preventive maintenance and proper motor loading are the best insurance against motor failure. Motor life is prolonged by keeping the motor cool, dry, clean, and lubricated.

Overheating

Heat is one of the most destructive agents and can cause premature motor failure. Overheating occurs because of motor overloading, low voltage at the motor terminals, excessive ambient temperatures, or poor cooling caused by accumulation of dirt or lack of ventilation. If heat is not dissipated, insulation failure can result, ruining the motor.

Moisture

Moisture should be kept from entering a motor. Cover the motor to protect it from the weather, particularly during periods when it is not used.

Bearing failure

Bearings should be kept properly lubricated. Bearings may seize in unused motors that are not rotated for extended periods. Special care in lubrication may be required for these motors.

Starting mechanism failure

Choosing a well-built motor will help solve this problem. The starting mechanism, as well as the bearings and motor windings, must be kept free of dirt and moisture.

Mounting

Secure mounting and correct alignment with the load are essential for proper motor performance. The motor should be positioned where it is readily accessible, but not in the way. If possible, the motor should be located so that it will not be exposed to excessive moisture, dust, or abrasive material.

Mount the motor on a smooth, solid foundation. Fasten the mounting bolts tightly. If mounted on an uneven base or fastened insecurely, the motor may become misaligned with the load during operation. This will exert unnecessary strain on the frame and bearings, causing rapid wear and overheating. Loose mounting also causes vibration and noise.

Connecting to Load

Motors may be connected to the load by direct drive, a chain and sprockets, or a belt and pulleys. A direct drive uses a coupling to connect the shaft of the motor to the driven shaft. In this configuration, the motor and the driven equipment operate at the same speed. The motor shaft and driven shaft should be in near-perfect alignment to prevent excessive wear of the shaft bearings. A flexible coupling is often used to compensate for any misalignment.

A chain drive is used when a high amount of torque is required and the speed of the load must be different than the motor speed. The desired load speed is achieved by selecting the proper combination of sprocket sizes. Maintenance of a chain drive includes lubrication of the chain, adjustment of the chain tension, and inspection of the chain link for wear.

The most common connection between a motor and a load is a belt and pulleys. Using a V belt is the easiest and most common way of connecting a motor to a load.

Proper belt tension must be maintained. If a belt is too loose, it will slip on the drive pulley, overheat, and wear out quickly. If it is too tight, it will cause the belt and bearings to wear excessively.

To properly tension a V-belt drive, measure the length of the belt span, as shown in **Figure 18-12**. The force required to deflect the belt 1/64" for each inch of span should be within the values shown in the table. There are tension gauges available that are designed specifically for tensioning V belts. Follow the manufacturer's instructions that are packaged with the gauge.

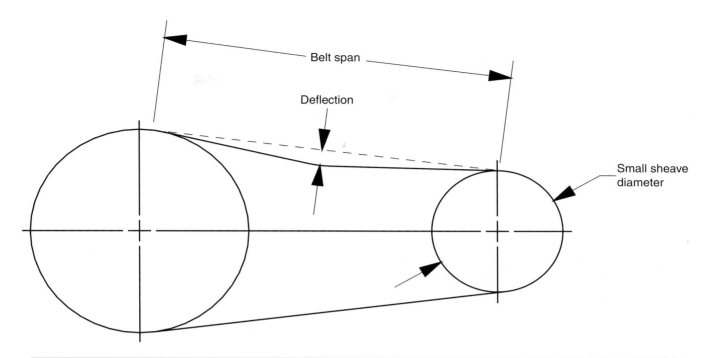

V-belt cross section type	Small sheave diameter range (inches)	Deflection force (lbs)	
		Minimum	**Maximum**
A	3.0 to 3.2	2.3	3.2
	3.4 to 3.6	2.5	3.6
	3.8 to 4.2	2.9	4.2
	4.6 to 7.0	3.5	5.1
B	4.6	4.0	5.9
	5.0 to 5.4	4.5	6.7
	5.6 to 6.4	5.0	7.4
	6.8 to 9.4	5.8	8.6
C	7.0	7.1	10.0
	7.5 to 8.0	7.9	11.0
	8.5 to10.0	9.3	13.0
	10.5 to 16.0	11.0	16.0
D	12.0 to13.0	16.0	24.0
	13.5 to 15.5	18.0	27.0
	16.0 to 22.0	21.0	31.0
E	21.6 to 24.0	33.0	47.0
3V	2.5 to 3.5	3.0	4.3
	3.51 to 4.50	3.5	5.3
	4.51 to 6.0	4.3	6.0
5V	7.0 to 9.0	8.8	13.0
	9.1 to 12.0	9.5	14.0
	12.1 to 16.0	11.0	15.0
8V	12.5 to 17.0	22.0	31.0
	17.1 to 24.0	23.0	34.0

Table title: Recommended Force for 1/64″ Deflection in V-Belt for Each Inch of Span

Figure 18-12. To properly tension a V-belt drive, you must know the V-belt type, diameter of the smaller sheave, and the recommended deflection force.

Service and Repair of Motors

Generally, motors should not be allowed to restart automatically after a loss of power. If automatic operation is necessary, provision should be made for random restarting to prevent the excessive voltage drop in the wiring that would occur if all motors came on at one time. This can be accomplished by including a low-cost time-delay relay in the magnetic motor starter control as shown in **Figure 18-13**. This random restart feature is especially desirable for large horsepower motors.

Figure 18-14 describes a wiring diagram and an elementary diagram. Knowing how to read these diagrams will help you diagnose problems and make the connections correctly.

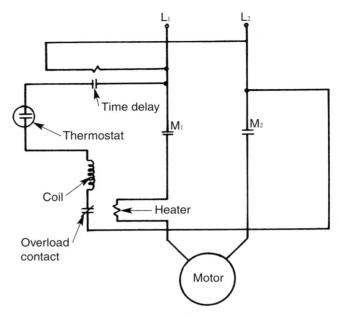

Figure 18-13. Circuit for random restarting of motors under automatic control.

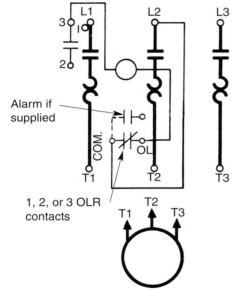

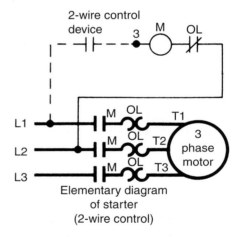

WIRING DIAGRAM

A WIRING DIAGRAM shows, as closely as possible, the actual location of all of the component parts of the device. The open terminals (marked by an open circle) and arrows represent connections made by the user.

Since wiring connections and terminal markings are shown, this type of diagram is helpful when wiring the device, or tracing wires when troubleshooting. Note that bold lines denote the power circuit, and thin lines are used to show the control circuit. Conventionally, in ac magnetic equipment, black wires are used in power circuits and red wiring is used for control circuits.

A wiring diagram, however, is limited in its ability to convey a clear picture of the sequence of operation of a controller. Where an illustration of the circuit in its simplest form is desired, the elementary diagram is used.

ELEMENTARY DIAGRAM

The elementary diagram gives a fast, easily understood picture of the circuit. The devices and components are not shown in their actual positions. All the control circuit components are shown as directly as possible, between a pair of vertical lines, representing the control power supply. The arrangement of the components is designed to show the sequence of operation of the devices, and helps in understanding how the circuit operates. The effect of operating various interlocks, control devices, etc., can be readily seen – this helps in troubleshooting, particularly with the more complex controllers. This form of electrical diagram is sometimes referred to as a "schematic" or "line" diagram.

Figure 18-14. These two diagrams will help you understand the circuit and wiring for an ac magnetic motor starter. (Square D Co.)

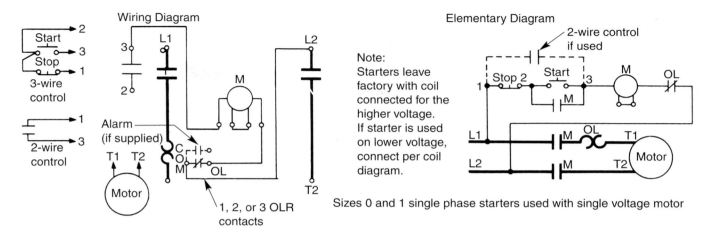

Figure 18-15. Wiring diagrams for starter for single phase voltage. (Square D Co.)

The diagrams for single-phase motors are similar to those created for three-phase motors. Counting the number of terminals on the motor or the number of legs in the power supply will help you determine the phase of the diagram. See **Figure 18-15**. There are many details in the wiring and elementary diagrams as shown in **Figure 18-16**. Various types of starter enclosures and their applications are found in **Figure 18-17**.

A well-made and properly installed electric motor requires less maintenance than many other types of electrical equipment. However, for the best and most economical performance, periodic servicing is required.

The service operations listed should be performed once a year or more often if the motor operates under conditions of severe heat, cold, or dust.

Motor Service Operations

1. Remove dust and dirt from the air passages and cooling surfaces of the motor to ensure proper cooling. Plugged air passages of an open motor, or a coating of dust on a totally enclosed motor, will cause the motor to overheat under normal operation.

2. Check bearings for wear. Excessive side or end play may cause the motor to draw higher-than-normal starting current, develop less starting torque, and, therefore, damage the motor.

3. Make sure the motor shaft turns freely. A tight or misaligned bearing will cause the motor to overheat.

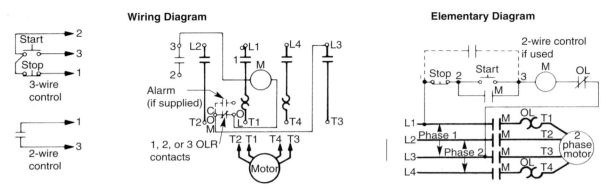

Sizes 3 and 4, 4 pole, 2 phase, 4 wire starters with external 2- or 3-wire control

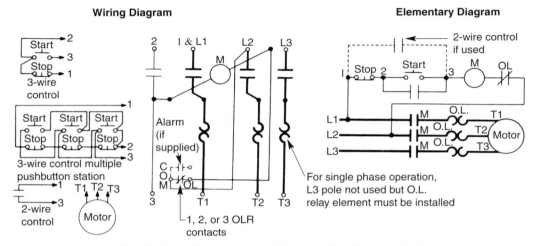

Size 00, 3 pole, 3 phase starter with external 2- or 3-wire control

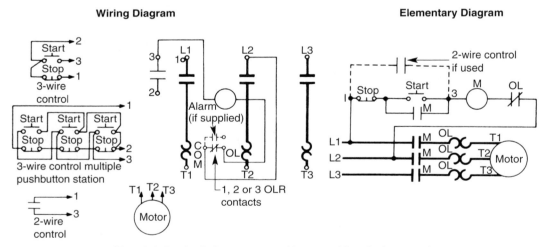

Sizes 0-4, 3 pole, 3 phase starters with external 2- or 3-wire control

Figure 18-16. Diagrams for wiring of two-phase and three-phase magnetic starters.

A   B   C

Figure 18-17. Motor control units. A—Heavy-duty motor control unit is used primarily in foundries, steel mills, etc. Unit is oil and dust tight. B—Watertight, dust tight, and corrosion resistant manual motor starter enclosure. C—Single motor branch circuit safety switch. (Square D Co.)

4. Lubricate the motor according to the manufacturer's specifications. Do not overlubricate.

5. Check all wiring for frayed or bare spots. Repair or replace as needed.

6. Clean the starting switch contacts of split-phase and capacitor motors and the commutator and brushes in wound-rotor (repulsion-type) motors. Use very fine sandpaper, not emery cloth.

7. Replace worn brushes, and make sure the brush lifting and shorting-ring action works smoothly in wound-rotor motors.

8. Check belt pulleys to be sure they are secure on their shafts. Align the belts and pulleys carefully. Improper alignment causes excessive wear on belts and pulleys. Check and adjust belt tension. Replace belts that are badly worn.

Review Questions

Write your answers on a separate sheet of paper. Do not write in this book.

1. For proper performance, the _____ voltage and frequency at the _____ must match the values specified by the manufacturer as closely as possible.

2. *True or False?* Low voltage from inadequate wiring can cause problems in an electric motor.

3. List the information which usually appears on the nameplate attached to an electric motor.

4. Explain how a frame number of an electric motor helps with the standardization of electric motors.

5. List the four common motor circuits.

6. *NEC* requires that the feeder capacity of a single motor circuit be _____ percent of the full-load _____ rating of the motor.

7. What is the full-load current of each of the following squirrel-cage motors? Refer to tables in *Article 430* of *NEC*.

Horsepower	Single Phase 120V	Single Phase 240V	Single Phase 480V
10			
20			
40			
50			

8. A _____ _____ is a switch or other device normally used for starting and stopping a motor.

9. Study the illustration and determine:

   A. Full-load current of the electric motor.
   _____

   B. Correct size of conductors to keep voltage drop within *NEC*-set limits.
   _____

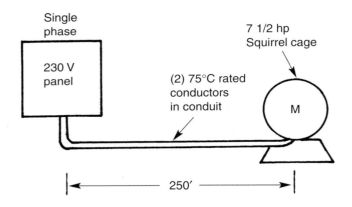

Single phase

230 V panel

(2) 75°C rated conductors in conduit

7 1/2 hp Squirrel cage

M

|← 250′ →|

Note: Max volt. drop
      at motor to be
      3% or 7 V.
      I.E. 223 V. Min.
      at motor
      terminals

10. List all of the following that are causes for overheating in an electric motor.
    A. Lack of insulation.
    B. Excessive ambient temperatures.
    C. Low voltage at motor terminals.
    D. Too high voltage at motor terminals.
    E. Poor cooling from dirt or lack of ventilation.
    F. Overloading of motor.
    G. Lack of lubricant.

11. *True or False?* During periodic motor service, bearings should be lubricated.

12. _____ should not be used to clean contacts of split-phase and capacitor motors and the commutator and brushes of wound-rotor motors.

Know the Code

A copy of the NEC 2005 is required to answer these questions.

1. Name the *NEC* table that lists the code letters for motor input with locked rotor.

2. *Section 430.32* covers _____ motors.

3. According to *Section 430.109(B)*, the OCPD shall be permitted to serve as the _____ .

Problem	Cause(s)	Remedy
Motor overheats	Rotor rubbing on stator –Bent shaft –Worn bearings	Replace shaft or bearings
	Overloading –Binding load	Correct load factor Check current input
	Poor ventilation	Keep motor clean Clear vent holes or venting system
Motor won't start	Power failure –Insufficient voltage	Check the circuit breakers or fuses Replace if necessary
	Improper connections	Check wiring diagram and make necessary corrections
	Overload	Reduce load or use larger motor
	Worn or incorrectly set brushes	Replace brushes or reset them
	Open circuit	Check all connections Clean starting switch contacts Check for short-circuit or ground faults Reset thermal overload
	Too much end play	Add washers to shaft
Rotor or stator burns out	Moisture Corrosive chemicals Dust	Keep motor clean and dry Shield motor if necessary
Brush sparking	Short-circuit or open circuit	Clean, repair, or replace armature
	Sticking or worn brushes	Replace brushes
	Dust	Clean the motor
	Overload	Decrease load or use more powerful motor
	Improperly fit brushes	Refit the brushes to match commutator
	Loose commutator	Replace commutator
Noisy motor	Unbalanced load	Balance the load and pulley
	Loose parts	Tighten motor components and retighten motor mounts
	Faulty alignment	Properly align motor with load
	Bent shaft	Straighten shaft and realign Make sure load is balanced
	Worn bearings	Lubricate or replace bearings
	Dust	Clean motor

Motors are expensive and will last a long time with proper maintenance. This guide is useful should problems arise. Good maintenance is important; without it a motor may have a short life.

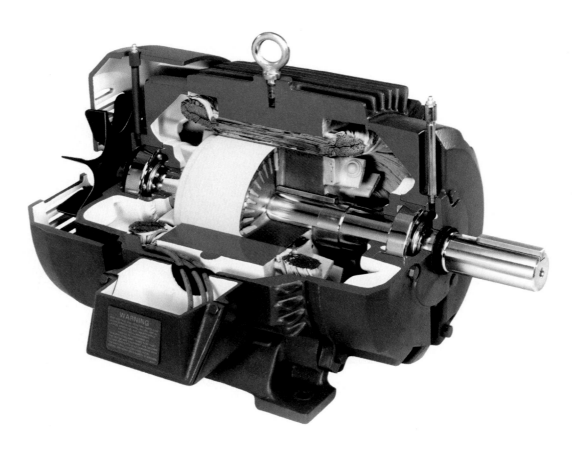

These cutaways reveal the windings, stator, rotor, and bearings that are typical in ac motors. A nameplate is visible on the outside of the variable speed ac motor. (Reliance Electric)

Emergency and Standby Systems

19

Objectives

Information in this chapter will enable you to:

- Discuss installation procedures for standby electrical systems.

- Know when to install a battery-powered uninterruptible power supply.

- Understand the dangers of installing a standby generator without a transfer switch.

Technical Terms

Carbon monoxide
Suicide cord
Transfer switch
Uninterruptible power supply (UPS)

The dependency on electrical equipment for our homes has increased tremendously over the past decade, and this rate will not likely slow down in the near future. This dependency is extremely evident during an extended blackout, when power to a residential area has stopped. Refrigerators cannot keep food from spoiling, sump pumps cannot prevent basements from flooding, and furnaces cannot stop a home's interior temperature from dropping to dangerously low levels. Fortunately, there are systems employing gas-powered generators and battery banks that can continue the supply of electricity throughout these annoying and sometimes dangerous circumstances.

Safety

This chapter will introduce situations that require new safety skills and concerns in addition to the standard electrical hazards you learned about in previous chapters.

Hazardous Fuel

Some standby power equipment requires gasoline, natural gas, or propane. All of these liquids and gases are extremely flammable and may explode if not handled properly. Any sparks, even those caused by turning on a light switch, can ignite the vapors of these chemicals. Always check for leaks immediately after connecting gas supply lines. Never fill a gasoline tank indoors. The vapors expelled during a fill-up quickly travel low to the ground and may find a pilot light in a nearby water heater or furnace.

Carbon Monoxide

The generators used in standby systems rely on an internal combustion engine. These may be as small as a standard lawnmower engine or as large as the engine in your automobile. Regardless of the size, all of these engines produce a deadly gas called *carbon monoxide*. This colorless, odorless, and tasteless gas can accumulate in unventilated areas to a level that causes, at first, headache and nausea. If the person is not immediately moved to fresh air, loss of consciousness and death may occur. To protect yourself and the homeowners, always operate engines outside of the home or garage.

Transfer Switches

When the power to a home is interrupted and a generator is attached to the home's circuit, that circuit must be disconnected from the outside service. Otherwise, electricity can travel out of the home, through the service conductors, and out to the overhead lines or transformer. This situation may injure or kill any worker who believes that the lines are safe to work on. A *transfer switch* disconnects the service conductors from the home's circuit just before connecting the circuit to the generator. You will learn more about the operation and installation of a transfer switch later in this chapter. For now, remember that this device is one of the most important features of a properly installed standby system.

Suicide Cords

A cord that has a male plug on each end is called a *suicide cord*. Although it is possible to plug this type of cord into a generator and an outlet in the home, DO NOT DO IT! This setup presents many possibilities for injury to you, your family, and workers on the power line. The most apparent danger is the possibility of touching the plug while it is energized. You may think that you will connect it and disconnect it in an order that will be safe. In reality, situations that call for emergency power are very physically and mentally demanding. In this type of

hectic environment, it is too easy to disconnect the wrong end and wind up touching a hot plug. See **Figure 19-1**.

Emergency and Standby Systems

The *National Electrical Code* identifies two separate systems, emergency and standby, within *Articles 700, 701,* and *702.* This section will describe the two systems, but the rest of the chapter will concentrate on standby systems, particularly those that are more likely to be used in a residential application.

DO NOT USE!

Figure 19-1. Never use a power cord that has a plug on each end.

---

carbon monoxide: A colorless, odorless, and tasteless gas that can accumulate in unventilated areas to a level that causes headache, nausea, and death if the person is not brought to fresh air.

transfer switch: This device disconnects the service conductors from the home's circuit just before connecting the circuit to a generator.

suicide cord: A cord that has a male plug on each end.

Emergency Systems

Emergency systems are those legally required for emergency power by a municipal, state, or federal governmental agency. Emergency systems are intended to automatically supply enough power to ensure the safety of a building's occupants during a power failure, **Figure 19-2**.

Emergency systems are required mostly in places such as health care facilities, especially hospitals, for fire detection and fire alarm systems, elevator operation, fire pump units, public safety communication systems, essential ventilating systems, and any other building services whose failure to operate could produce a serious threat to life.

Legally Required Standby Systems

These standby systems are discussed in *Article 701* of the *NEC*. They serve loads necessary to the normal operation of vital building systems. Sewage disposal, heating, refrigeration, communication, ventilation and smoke removal, lighting, and other systems, if stopped, could cause great hazards to occupants and could also hamper fire-fighting efforts. In most other respects, the standby system is arranged, controlled, tested, and maintained in a fashion similar to the emergency system.

Optional Standby Power

Many individuals want their residences and commercial properties to have some form of standby power in the event of a power outage. These systems are not legally required since a power failure at a residence or private business location does not represent a life-endangering situation.

Nonetheless, there are situations where loss of heating, refrigeration, data processing, and commercial industrial processing capability could result in great losses. This is particularly true with businesses such as computer processing centers, bakeries, ice cream manufacture or distribution facilities, frozen food packing, or preparation plants and dairy farms.

Generator Size

You have learned in previous chapters how to select the appropriate size service and conductors based on the loads of the home. You will now take this knowledge to calculate the number of watts that must be generated by the standby power supply. **Figure 19-3** lists

Figure 19-2. Large generators, such as this 8.5 kW diesel, are required for buildings that are linked to public safety. (Kohler Co.)

Generator Sizing Estimated Wattage Requirements		
Item	Running	Starting
1/2 HP furnace fan	875	2300
Refrigerator	500	2000
Freezer	500	1000
Lights	75 each	75 each
1/3 HP Well pump	1000	3000
Electric water heater	4000	4000
Heat pump	4669	11672

Figure 19-3. This table lists the estimated wattage requirements of common critical loads.

the approximate wattage of most critical loads, but if the actual wattage is available it should be used instead. Once the required wattage is known, an adequately sized generator can be selected. See **Figure 19-4**.

Portable Generators

A portable generator is a low-cost power supply that operates on gasoline and can generate only enough power to operate a

This residential generator has been installed away from the house to prevent the exhaust gases from entering an open window. Another benefit is the reduction in noise.

Various sizes of residential generators.

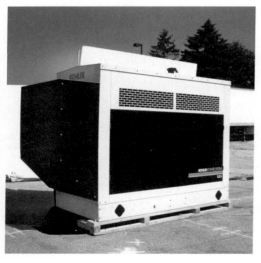

Rooftop and internal commercial generators.

Figure 19-4. Select a generator large enough to supply power to the critical loads.

few critical items, depending on the size of the generator. The utilization equipment that requires electricity may plug directly into the outlet panel of the generator. Another method is to connect the generator directly to the circuit through a transfer switch. The first situation will probably be handled without the aid of an electrician, so we will concentrate on the installation of the second.

Installation

Portable generators are equipped with outlet receptacles that match the generator's power capability. Smaller generators will have one or two 120 V 15 A receptacles while the larger portable generators may have two 120 V 20 A receptacles and one 120/240 V 30 A or 50 A receptacle. The larger receptacles will be used

to connect the generator to the home's circuit through a manual transfer switch.

Manual transfer switch

You learned in the safety section of this chapter that a transfer switch prevents the connection of the generator's circuit and the service. A manual transfer switch accomplishes this transition when the homeowner moves the switch from the utility side to the generator side.

There are manual transfer switches on the market that include circuit breakers, watt meters, and even a receptacle to plug in a work lamp. On the other end of the scale, a simple double-pole double-throw switch can be used as a manual transfer switch, **Figure 19-5**.

Remote power inlet

The installation in the previous section requires a cord that plugs into the generator outside, travels through a window, and plugs

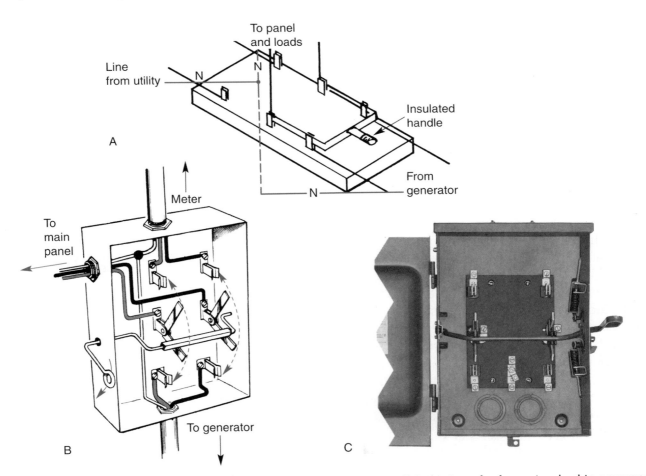

Figure 19-5. A simple double-pole, double-throw switch will accomplish the transfer from standard to emergency supply. Note the continuous, unswitched, neutral conductor. A—Schematic. B—Simplified drawing of a transfer switch mechanism. C—Actual switch. (Wadsworth Electric Mfg. Co., Inc.)

into the transfer switch. With a larger generator, this could be a 240 V 60 A cord that is strung throughout the home. A remote power inlet that is mounted outside the home will allow the generator to be plugged in with a short cord.

Permanent Generators

For homeowners who are looking for a standby power solution that is more convenient and powerful, a permanent generator with an automatic transfer switch is the answer. Permanent generators are usually connected to the home's gas line, natural or propane, for an unlimited supply of fuel. The generator is wired into the main circuit breaker panel through an automatic transfer switch. This eliminates having to plug in a cord and throwing a switch. The homeowner does not even have to be at home during a power outage for the system to work. Maintenance is also automatic on most units. The generator can be programmed to start once a week and run for a short period. This process keeps the engine lubricated and ensures that the system will work when needed. Although the operation and maintenance of a permanent generator is simple, the installation is slightly more complex than that of a portable generator.

Installation

The first step to installing a permanent generator is to calculate the wattage of the circuits that will be protected. Since these generators are larger than portables, you will be able to include noncritical loads such as televisions, computers, and the garage door opener. Once the total wattage is determined, select the proper size generator. Make sure the fuel requirement matches the home's fuel type.

The next issue is the location of the generator. It should be placed close to the gas supply and transfer switch to reduce piping and wiring lengths. The manufacturer's installation instructions will provide the proper clearances from the home, plants, and especially windows. Also, generators of this size usually warrant a concrete mounting pad with anchor bolts.

Grounding the generator

The generator may have to connect to the equipment ground of the main panel or you may have to drive a ground rod near the generator. The installation instructions will describe how to ground the generator, but always check your local codes for any additional regulations.

Automatic transfer switch

The ampere rating of the automatic transfer switch must match the load of the circuit that is protected. If the generator and transfer switch are large enough, the entire home circuit can be protected. Otherwise, the individual circuits that will be protected need to be isolated from the main circuit. The automatic transfer switch should be located near the main service panel.

Uninterruptible Power Supplies

Regardless of how well a standby power supply works, there will always be a delay between the time the utility power stops and the standby power starts. For most utilization equipment, this delay is not noticeable. Plug-in clocks will need to be reset and the lights will go out for a short time, but for the most part everything will proceed as normal. The one exception to this is the personal computer.

Protecting Personal Computers

A power interruption, no matter how slight, can cause a computer to shut down or reset. If this happens, any files that you were working on will be lost, unless you saved the file prior to the power loss. The only way to ensure a constant flow of electricity is to use an **uninterruptible power supply (UPS)**. A UPS

---

uninterruptible power supply (UPS): This device contains a battery and an inverter that immediately supplies power during an outage.

contains a battery and an inverter that immediately supplies power during an outage. The transition from the main power supply to the battery in the UPS is so instantaneous that the computer remains unaffected.

Types of Uninterruptible Power Supplies

Deciding on a UPS is a matter of cost and convenience. A small UPS that will protect one computer for a few minutes can be purchased for fifty dollars. On the expensive end, a whole house UPS can keep the computers, clocks, and refrigerator running until the standby or portable generator starts. These units can cost two thousand dollars or more.

Review Questions

Write your answers on a separate sheet of paper.
Do not write in this book.

1. Explain the difference between emergency, legally required standby, and optional stand-by power systems.
2. An emergency or standby power system is isolated from the regular source of power because of a _____ switch.
3. An _____ keeps electrical equipment working during the time that the normal power supply stops and the emergency power supply starts.

Know the Code

A copy of the NEC 2005 is required to answer these questions.

1. Which article covers the installation of generators?
2. *Article 445.15* refers to which other article?
3. The type of equipment covered in *Article 645.11* is _____

Section 5
The Professional
Electrician

**Chapter 20   Electrical
              Remodeling
Chapter 21   Maintenance and
              Troubleshooting
Chapter 22   Electrical Careers**

Electrical Remodeling

Objectives

Information in this chapter will enable you to:

- Describe the special tools required in remodeling.

- Demonstrate procedures for extending or updating wiring systems.

- Know how to install wiring within finished walls.

- Understand the steps to upgrade the service of a house.

Technical Terms

Extension drill bits
Multioutlet assembly

Updating and extending existing wiring systems should only be undertaken with careful planning and attention to the layout. Familiarity with the building's construction is equally important. This chapter will describe the procedures to complete the job quickly, safely, and properly.

Basic Considerations

Remodeling or modernizing an electrical installation falls under the category known as old work. It is, perhaps, the most difficult kind of wiring to do. Considerable time, effort, and special techniques are needed to bring about a satisfying result.

Portions of finished walls or ceilings may have to be removed or altered during a rewiring job. Wires must often be fished or pulled through blind wall, floor, ceiling, or attic spaces to get from one place to another.

Great care must be used in routing wire cables through walls and similar spaces so as not to damage the conductors and insulation. Also, special effort has to be taken to ensure the continuity and integrity of the grounding conductor when extending or adding to an existing system. The grounding conductor must be continuous from the service panel to all outlets.

There are no set rules concerning the procedures to follow for old work. There is no substitute for experience. However, some basic steps will help you resolve certain difficulties.

Safety

When remodeling wiring, follow the same rules outlined in Chapter 1, **Safety**. Never work on circuits that are electrically hot. Turn off the power to the device or circuit on which you are working. Whether you are absolutely sure or not, always check the circuit with a tester.

Plan a safe installation. Check local codes for your own protection. Use fuses or circuit breakers rated for the amperage in the circuit. Fire or damage to the wiring can result from improper overcurrent ratings. Never touch electrical fixtures when you are wet, standing in water, or on a wet surface.

Use tools with insulated handles. Current is less likely to pass through insulating materials and cause shock.

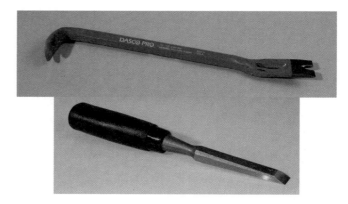

Figure 20-1. Chisels and crowbars are useful for cutting into and prying up floorboards. This allows access to old wiring and to the space where new wiring must be placed.

Special Tools

Certain special tools are needed for old work:

* Chisels and crowbars are needed to pry up floorboards, **Figure 20-1**.
* A keyhole saw is used to cut through floorboards and wall materials, **Figure 20-2**.
* *Extension drill bits* are necessary to drill deep holes through walls, floors, and beams. The length of these bits may be extended through the use of steel shanks with special ends to attach to other steel shanks of similar construction. For example, a simple 2″ brace bit can be extended to lengths of 20′ or more using this method. All of this may be necessary to bore a hole continuously through the first and second floors of a structure.
* A fish tape is used to pull wires through bored holes and wall spaces, **Figure 20-3**.

Figure 20-2. A keyhole saw is designed for use in tight openings. It is used to cut openings into ceilings and walls where new outlets must be installed. It may also be used to cut flooring. (Klein Tools, Inc.)

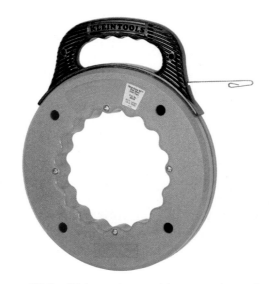

extension drill bits: Drill bits that can be extended to longer lengths for drilling holes through walls, floors, and beams.

Figure 20-3. Old work requiring running of cable through walls is difficult to do without fish tape for pulling the cable. (Klein Tools, Inc.)

Materials

The materials used in old work are essentially the same as those used in new work. However, there are special boxes, box hangers, and extenders made to ease installation. See **Figures 20-4**.

Conduit is out of the question, unless local codes require it. Installation would be virtually impossible without removing large sections of finished walls. Therefore, nonmetallic sheathed cable, Greenfield, or armored cable (BX) are used. These are more readily fished through walls and floors.

Building Construction

The type of building will often dictate the tools and materials used. Walls may be constructed of sheetrock (drywall), wallboard, plaster on lath, brick, or concrete blocks. The type of surface will make enormous differences in the wiring method used.

Wall Openings

Wall openings for switch boxes and outlet boxes, as well as for pulling wire, should be carefully cut. This cannot be overemphasized, especially where the wall is plaster on lath. A switch box opening can easily balloon into a nightmare without careful tracing and cutting.

Make sure that no studs are present at the location where the box will be installed. Use a stud finder or tap with a hammer to locate nearby studs. Trace the box or a template on the wall where the new box is to be located. See **Figure 20-5**. The half circles at the corners are for drilling the holes where you can start cutting with a keyhole saw and the center half circles are for the mounting screws. Drill all four holes. Cut out the opening and slip the outlet box in to check the fit. Trim the wall as needed to adjust the fit. Keep the opening as small as possible.

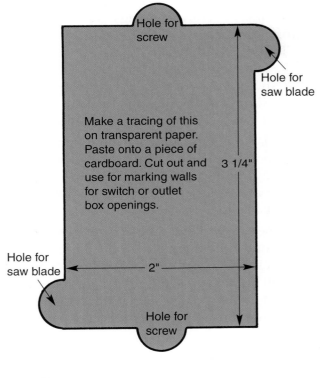

Hole for screw

Hole for saw blade

Make a tracing of this on transparent paper. Paste onto a piece of cardboard. Cut out and use for marking walls for switch or outlet box openings.

3 1/4"

Hole for saw blade

2"

Hole for screw

Figure 20-5. Trace the box or a template on the wall.

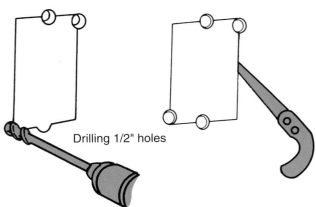

Drilling 1/2" holes

Figure 20-4. Special old-work boxes like this one have expansion devices that grip the wall. (Raco, Inc.)

Installing Cable

Installing cable in old work involves pushing or pulling it through wall openings. If the distance is short and there are no obstacles, this may be accomplished without tools. However, for most cable work, a fish tape must be used to pull the wires through.

Using Fish Tape

A fish tape, whether homemade or purchased, is a practical necessity for running cable in old work. It should be flexible enough to be worked through 90° bends, yet stiff enough to be worked up through narrow openings and within walls without buckling.

To use a fish tape:

1. Feed the tape from the top down, if possible. Usually, you will need to work the tape from one box opening through the wall or a partition to a second opening. See **Figure 20-6**.

2. Twist the tape until it enters the hidden opening, such as a hole drilled in a plate. Continue to push it until it can be seen or felt at the second position to which cable must be fed.

3. If bends prevent a tape from reaching the second opening, a second tape may be inserted through the second hole. Twist and pull on the tapes until they catch each other. Pull on one of the tapes until the other is drawn through the second opening.

4. If a box from old work cannot be removed, insert the fish tape through a knockout as shown in **Figure 20-7**.

5. Secure the cable to the fish tape and pull the cable through the wall to the first opening.

6. Once the cable is brought to the appropriate wall opening, strip back the insulation about 8″ and install the cable connector.

7. Attach the cable to the box and install the box in the wall.

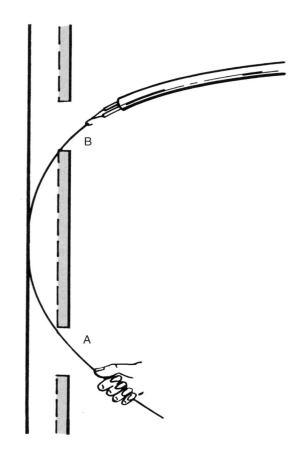

Figure 20-6. Using the fish tape to go from one opening to another in a wall. Tape is fed in at A and is pushed upward until it can be pulled through the opening at B. (GE Wiring Devices Dept.)

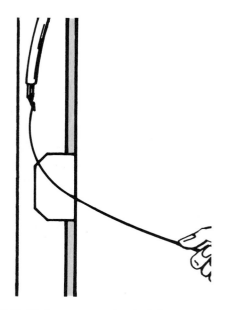

Figure 20-7. Fish tape can be fed through a knockout in an electrical box when going from an existing outlet to a new one.

Wiring behind a Baseboard

Baseboard installations can be done without the use of a fish tape. Before opening up the live outlet, trip the circuit breaker to the off position to deenergize the outlet. Check the outlet with a tester to make sure the power is off. See **Figure 20-8**.

1. Remove the faceplate and unmount the receptacle at point A.

2. With a screwdriver, remove a knockout facing in the direction the new wiring will go. In this case, toward the floor.

3. Locate the new outlet. Use a stud finder or tap on the wall to find the stud locations. Mark the spot where the outlet will be.

4. Put the new box against the wall, or use a template to mark the outline of the new opening.

5. Drill starter holes and cut the wall material with a keyhole saw.

6. Remove the baseboard carefully to avoid damage to either the baseboard or the wall.

7. Drill holes below both points A and B in the area that will be concealed by the baseboard.

8. Cut a groove in the wall and the studs from point A to point B. Make it deep enough so a piece of conduit or cable will fit behind the baseboard. Select wiring according to the circuit ampacity.

9. Install the conduit or cable. (Cable can be installed in conduit if desired. This would protect it from nails driven through the baseboard. If only cable is used, a protective steel plate must be placed over the notch at every stud.)

10. Make connections inside the boxes.

11. Install the new box in the wall.

12. Install receptacles and cover plates.

13. Test the circuit extension.

14. Replace the baseboard.

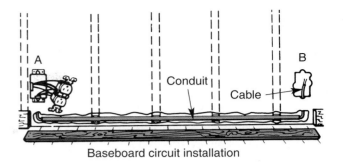

Baseboard circuit installation

Routing wiring where it will be concealed by a baseboard.

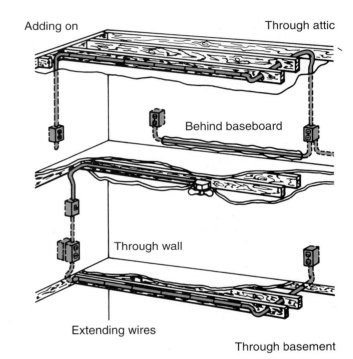

Adding on

Through attic

Behind baseboard

Through wall

Extending wires

Through basement

Figure 20-8. Methods of routing wiring during remodeling. (GE Wiring Devices Dept.)

Box Installation

As in new work, box installation in old work is a simple procedure. However, in old work the technique is different since the boxes are usually not attached to the building studs. For this reason, special boxes and mounting devices are available. See **Figure 20-9**.

Metal Boxes

Whatever devices are used, the box must be prepared and the cable attached to it *before* the box is installed. Simply remove the appropriate knockouts and attach the cable using the connector(s) you have already installed, **Figure 20-10**. Slip the box into the wall opening, secure it, and connect the load device.

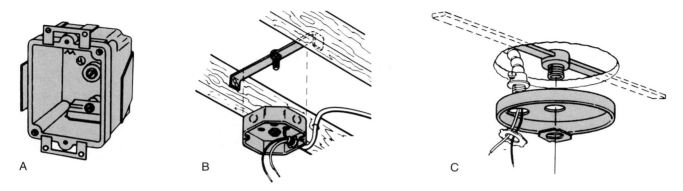

A

B

C

Figure 20-9. Special boxes and devices for clamping boxes in old work. A—Snap-in bracket is part of the box. B—Hanger mount for mounting from ceiling joists in an attic. C—Hanger designed to bridge hole in plaster or drywall.

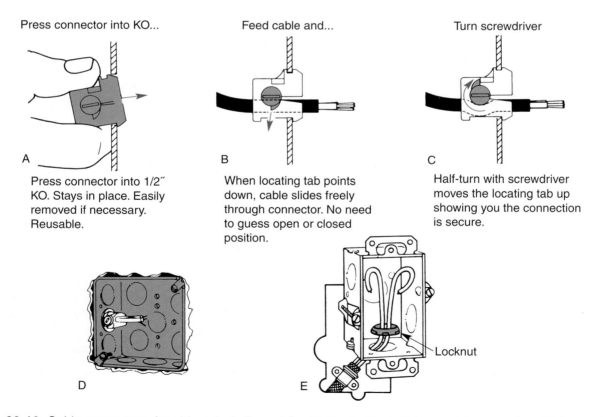

Press connector into KO...

Feed cable and...

Turn screwdriver

A

B

C

Press connector into 1/2″ KO. Stays in place. Easily removed if necessary. Reusable.

When locating tab points down, cable slides freely through connector. No need to guess open or closed position.

Half-turn with screwdriver moves the locating tab up showing you the connection is secure.

D

E

Locknut

Figure 20-10. Cable connectors for old work. A, B, and C—Method of installing special connector which needs no locknut. D—Completed installation with all steps completed inside the box. E—Connector designed for nonmetallic cable. It is fastened to cable before box connection is made. Note locknut. (Raco, Inc.)

Nonmetallic Boxes

Nonmetallic boxes have also been designed for use on old work. Locate the correct knockout, in the direction of the cable, and tap out the thin section as in **Figure 20-11**. Slide the conductors through the knockout and the box clamp. Push through at least 1/4″ of the cable jacket. Using a screwdriver, tighten the cable clamp until the cable is securely fastened in the box.

To install the box, gently guide it with the snap-in bracket attached, through the cutout. Push it into the opening until the "ears" contact the wall. Secure the box by tightening the screw or screws in the bottom of the box, **Figure 20-12**. This will draw the snap-in bracket against the back of the wall.

Modernizing a Service Entrance

More often than not, the electrical demands made on a home built as recently as 15 or 20 years ago, exceed its capacity, **Figure 20-13**. Sometimes a larger service entrance is the best solution.

There are several ways to update a service entrance. The best option will be based on calculating present loads and planning for future loads.

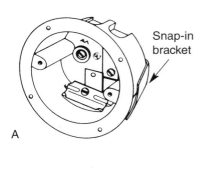
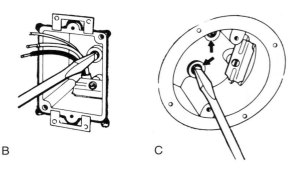

Figure 20-12. A method of securing a box in a wall. A—Snap-in bracket is attached to back of box with adjusting screw. B—When the box is in place with its ears against the front surface of a wall, bring the bracket against the reverse side by tightening the screw. C—Some boxes have two screws for adjusting the snap-in bracket. (Allied Moulded Products, Inc.)

Figure 20-11. Opening up a knockout on a fiberglass or plastic electrical box. The thin section is removed by a sharp tap of a screwdriver.
(Allied Moulded Products, Inc.)

Figure 20-13. Old, outdated electrical equipment is best replaced. Overloaded circuits and extension cords (not shown) are fire hazards. (Scott Harke)

In any case, a minimum of 100 A will be required. In a home where there is electric heating, air conditioning, a range, a clothes dryer, and other 240-volt appliances, a 200 A service is advisable. The updated service entrance must be installed as described for new service entrances. See Chapter 10, **The Service Entrance**. Make sure to provide a breaker panel large enough for all the existing circuits, new circuits, and some spares for future expansion.

Contact the Power Company

Inform the power company before work starts. Certain information, forms, and metering equipment must be obtained before the job begins. In addition, you will need to arrange for a disconnection of the old service and a reconnection of the new or updated one.

After the new service entrance is installed, the old circuits must be connected to it. There are several possibilities:

- If the new panel is to be placed in the same location as the old one, the old circuits may be directly connected to it.

- If the new panel cannot be located in the same position, you must junction the old circuits to the new panel. One way of doing this is to use the old service panel or fuse box as a sub-feed panel, **Figure 20-14**. Use a 50 or 60 A breaker in the new panel to feed it.

- Another possibility is to replace the old fuse box or outdated panel with a new lighting panel and circuit breakers. Then connect old circuits directly to the new panel.

- Still another alternative is to replace the old box or panel with an approved junction box or "J" box, as shown in **Figure 20-15**. Again, connect the old circuits to the new main panel, giving each its own circuit breakers.

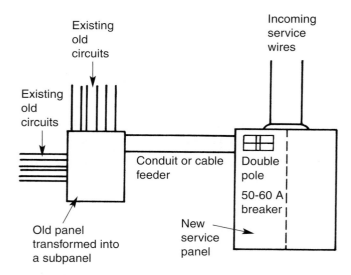

Figure 20-14. Incorporating the old service panel into a new one. The old panel is transformed into a subpanel.

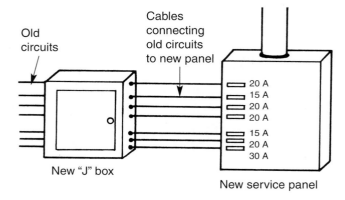

Figure 20-15. Often a junction box is installed to replace the old panel. It offers a connecting means to make the home run to the new service panel.

Adding a Subpanel

The cable feeding the subpanel should match the panel's ampacity. To determine the ampacity needed, refer to the panel rating and the manufacturer's instructions. Be sure to check local codes as well. Also, be sure that the subpanel has sufficient capacity for the number of circuits you wish to add.

To install a subpanel, use two circuit breaker spaces in the main panel. See **Figure 20-16**.

To make the installation:

1. Switch the main circuit breaker to the "off" position or remove the main fuses. Be careful. Remember, the incoming power cable and lineside lugs are still live even though the rest of the panel has been disconnected.

2. The subpanel is usually mounted as near to the main panel as possible.

3. Run cable from the main panel to the subpanel. Make sure that there is extra cable at each end to make the connections.

4. Cut insulated wires long enough to make connections to screw terminals, neutral bar, and equipment ground bar.

5. The two ungrounded conductors, red and black wires, connect to the screw terminal at the top of the new panel. The white wire must be connected to the neutral bar. The green insulated or bare wire goes to the equipment ground bus bar.

6. Make connections inside the main panel. Cut the wires, allowing enough length to make connections to the sub-feed OCPD. As in the subpanel, connect the white wire to the neutral bus bar, and the green or bare wire to the equipment ground bus bar.

7. This completes the wiring of the subpanel. The next step is to add branch circuits and circuit breakers.

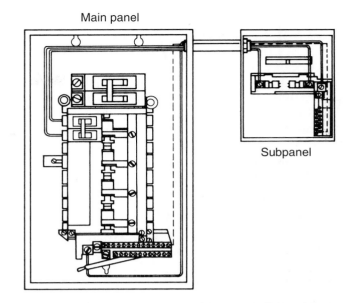

Main panel

Subpanel

Figure 20-16. Hookup for adding a subpanel to a service entrance main panel. It is similar to Figure 20-14 and the hookup is made in the same way. (GE Wiring Devices Dept.)

Grounding Panelboards

All of the equipment grounding conductors must be properly connected to an approved grounding terminal bar, which is located in the panelboard. This grounding bar must not be connected, or bonded, to the neutral bar except at the service panel. **Figure 20-17** shows common violations of this important *NEC* rule.

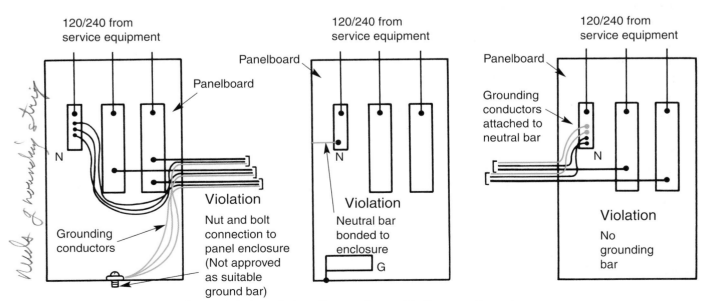

120/240 from service equipment

Panelboard

N

Grounding conductors

Violation
Nut and bolt connection to panel enclosure (Not approved as suitable ground bar)

120/240 from service equipment

Panelboard

N

Violation
Neutral bar bonded to enclosure

G

120/240 from service equipment

Panelboard

Grounding conductors attached to neutral bar

N

Violation
No grounding bar

Figure 20-17. Common Code violations in bonding equipment to the panelboard.

Grounding Remodeled Systems

When installing new panels, or "J" boxes as substitutes for the old fuse box, or when using the old fuse box or panel as a "J" box, the neutral and the ground bus bars must be isolated. That is, *all* neutral or white wires must go to a neutral bus bar and *all* grounding wires must go to a separate ground bus bar. This bus bar must be insulated and isolated from the neutral bus bar. (See *NEC, Section 250.142*) The ground bus must be bonded to the enclosure; the neutral bus must be insulated from the enclosure. This is especially important when using nonmetallic cable. **Figure 20-18** shows the wiring diagram when installing any subpanel.

Surface Raceways and Multioutlet Assemblies

There is a brief section about surface wiring at the end of Chapter 4, **Wiring Systems**. Since surface wiring is used almost exclusively in existing structures, most of the information is saved for this chapter. *Articles 386* and *388* of the *NEC* contain rules for installing surface raceways and *Article 380* covers the use of multioutlet assemblies. A *multioutlet assembly* is similar to surface raceway except it contains prewired receptacles. See **Figure 20-19**. This product usually does not require the skills of an electrician. Remember to always check with your local AHJ to see if these systems are allowed and, if so, what restrictions are in place.

The main benefit of surface wiring systems is that walls, ceilings, and floors do not have to be opened up for installation. So, when time and money are short and the installation area will not subject the raceway to physical damage, surface raceway is a very smart choice.

Installing Surface Wiring

Manufacturers of surface wiring provide detailed instructions on the installation of their systems. A typical installation begins with bringing the line side conductors into the base of the surface assembly. Remove an entrance

---

multioutlet assembly: A prewired unit that makes multiple receptacles available.

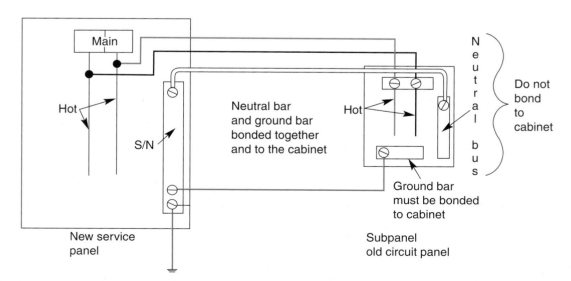

Figure 20-18. Feeder from main panel to subpanel will contain four conductors. Two are hot, one is neutral and one is the grounding conductor. In the subpanel, the grounded and grounding conductors must be insulated from each other. Rules regarding this procedure may be found in Section 250.24 of the NEC.

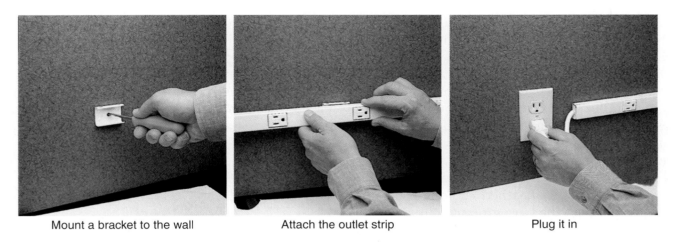

Mount a bracket to the wall   Attach the outlet strip   Plug it in

Figure 20-19. A multioutlet assembly is a simple method of adding receptacles. (The Wiremold Co.)

knockout from the base and attach a suitable connector. If a connector is already attached to the feeder cable, pull the connector and cable through the base. Install a locknut, **Figure 20-20,** and attach the base to the wall with mounting screws provided by the manufacturer.

Receptacles are normally mounted in the cover section of the assembly. Detach one or two receptacles from the cover. Align the cover and receptacles with the base to determine where a connection should be made.

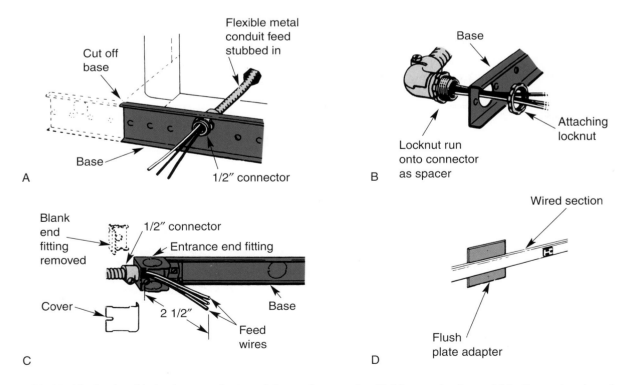

Figure 20-20. Methods of bringing conductors into a wireway. A—Cable can be brought in through a knockout in the base. No box is required in the wall. B—Using a 90° connector. C—Special closure for end feeding. D—Wireway fed from an outlet box using a special cover adapter. (The Wiremold Co.)

Cut and strip the black and neutral wires on both harness and feed as shown in **Figure 20-21**. Connect black and neutral feed wires to black and neutral harness wires. Use solderless connectors or special connectors provided by the manufacturer. Strip away enough insulation from the green insulated grounding conductor in the harness to make an approved connection with the green grounding wire from the feed. **Figure 20-22** shows completed connections.

If nonmetallic-sheathed cable is used for a feeder, connect the bare ground wire as shown in **Figure 20-23**. Use solderless connectors to cap unused leads at the end of the harness, **Figure 20-24**.

When connections are completed, replace the receptacles and harness in the cover. Snap the cover into the base to complete the installation.

To extend surface wiring, attach the new base section to the wall being careful to align and butt the end to the previous section. Remove blank end fittings from the sections. Make an electrical connection between the harnesses in the two sections. Reinstall the covers.

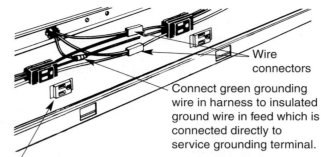

Wire connectors

Connect green grounding wire in harness to insulated ground wire in feed which is connected directly to service grounding terminal.

Orange receptacle cap. Caps must be in place on all receptacles to comply with color identification requirements of UL listing.

Figure 20-22. Making connections from feed to wire harness. Solderless connectors or special connectors supplied by manufacturers can be used.

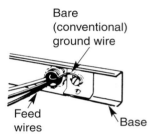

Bare (conventional) ground wire

Feed wires

Base

Figure 20-23. Method of making ground connection when nonmetallic sheathed cable is used. (The Wiremold Co.)

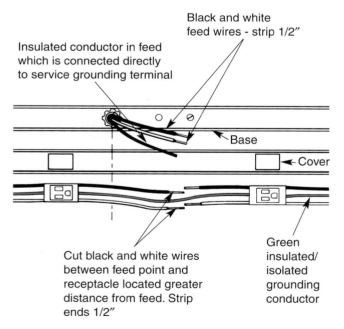

Insulated conductor in feed which is connected directly to service grounding terminal

Black and white feed wires - strip 1/2"

Base

Cover

Cut black and white wires between feed point and receptacle located greater distance from feed. Strip ends 1/2"

Green insulated/ isolated grounding conductor

Figure 20-21. Cutting of wires in harness prior to making connections to feed. Green insulated wire is not cut. (The Wiremold Co.)

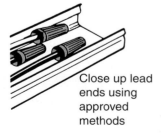

Close up lead ends using approved methods

Figure 20-24. Bare leads at the end of the harness must be capped to prevent short circuits.

Review Questions

Write your answers on a separate sheet of paper.
Do not write in this book.

1. Discuss the major differences between old work and new work.

2. List five special tools needed for remodeling wiring.

3. When extending or remodeling a wiring system, the grounding conductor must be _continuous_ from the service panel to all outlets.

4. The method(s) of wiring used in old work most often is (are):

   A. Nonmetallic sheathed cable.

   B. EMT.

   C. Rigid conduit.

   D. Armored cable (BX).

   E. Greenfield.

   F. None of these.

5. A _____ or the _box_ itself is used to trace the shape of an outlet box on a wall when doing old work.

6. Explain the use of fish tape in electrical remodeling.

7. *True or False?* In old work, boxes are usually attached to studs or joists.

8. Give two common ways that old circuits can be connected to a new service entrance panel.

9. List several benefits of surface wiring.

Know the Code

A copy of the NEC 2005 is required to answer these questions.

1. *Section* _____ of the *NEC* covers the installation of armored cable in accessible attics.

2. Who specifies the maximum conductor size for surface raceway?

3. How many uses are not permitted for multi-outlet assemblies?

Some of the tools shown are required by every electrician, such as the wire strippers, conduit bender, and the steel tape rule. Other tools, such as the mirror, lineman's hammer, and automatic wire strippers, may help you complete some tasks quicker. The pouch should contain the tools that you use most often and the tool bag or toolbox collects the rest. Use a permanent marker, similar to the one shown in the tool pouch, to write your name on all of your tools.

Maintenance and Troubleshooting

Objectives

Information in this chapter will enable you to:

- List safety procedures to follow when troubleshooting electrical circuits.

- List the troubleshooting tools required.

- Explain procedures for testing fuses, receptacles, ground continuity, switches, and fixtures.

- Explain overloaded neutrals and unbalanced currents.

Technical Term

Intermittent shorts

Solving electrical problems in new or existing construction is often the responsibility of the electrician. Proper electrical maintenance should be practiced and may help prevent some of these problems

Safety Considerations

Safety must be uppermost in the electrician's mind, especially during troubleshooting since this aspect of electrical work can be unpredictable and dangerous. In most instances, you will deenergize the device, the circuit, or the entire system in order to correct or repair a malfunction. However, at certain times, it is necessary for the system to remain energized in order to track down the problem. It is during these times that alertness and safety consciousness are essential.

Troubleshooting Tools

Some of the tools of particular importance when troubleshooting are the meters and testers illustrated in Figure 3-2. Review the section in Chapter 3, **Tools for the Electrician** that is titled *Tools for Testing and Measuring Electrical Properties*. These tools will be helpful when looking for excess current.

Diagnosing Problems

Electrical troubles show up as a wide range of symptoms. The common simple problems usually involve faulty receptacles, switches, lighting fixtures, fuses, breakers, and the like. More complex situations may include open circuits, broken conductors, voltage fluctuations, ground-faults, and current leakages. We will limit our discussion to the more commonly encountered and readily solvable troubles.

Solving these problems requires a thought-out, methodical approach. Do not immediately replace random devices because you assume that they are faulty. Use your testers, perform the simplest checks first, and do not skip any steps in the process.

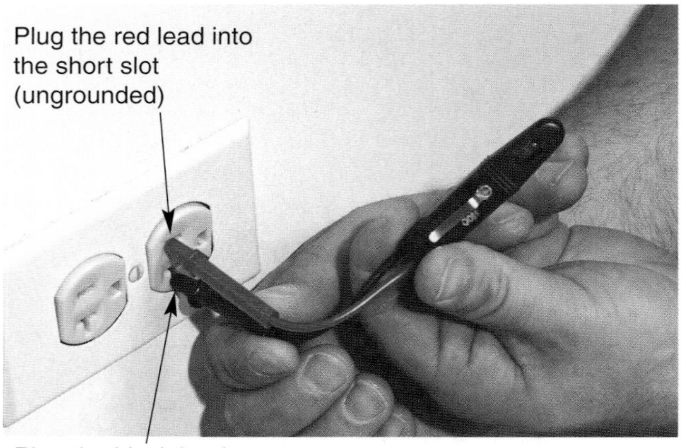

Plug the red lead into the short slot (ungrounded)

Plug the black lead into the long slot (grounded)

Figure 21-1. Checking for power at a receptacle. Insert leads of neon tester into slots of receptacle. If the tester light glows, the circuit and receptacle are functioning.

Testing Receptacles

When receptacles are not performing properly, chances are either the branch circuit or the receptacle itself is at fault. Perform the test illustrated in **Figure 21-1** to determine if the receptacle is operating properly. If the tester does not light, follow **Figure 21-2** to determine if the neutral connection is faulty.

Continuous Ground Check

Too often, improper grounding can result in shocks, which cause discomfort to the user of an outlet or fixture. In some cases, the shock may be serious enough to cause death. The importance and methods of grounding have been continually stressed throughout this text. Checking the grounding system should be routine. Each time a system comes under scrutiny or repair for any reason, a check should be made. The method of checking circuit grounding at the receptacle is shown in Figure 21-2.

To check the ground continuity of receptacles without a ground slot, insert one lead of the tester into the slot for the hot wire. Touch the other lead to the metal mounting screw. The tester will glow brightly if the device is properly grounded. See **Figure 21-3**.

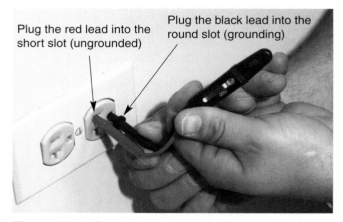

Plug the red lead into the short slot (ungrounded)

Plug the black lead into the round slot (grounding)

Figure 21-2. Check the receptacle for power between the ungrounded slot and the grounding slot. If tester light glows and it did not in the test shown in Figure 21-1, the neutral is open.

Testing Switches

To test a switch, remove the cover plate and determine if there is power to the switch by touching one lead of a tester to the metal box and the other lead to the line side terminal. See **Figure 21-4**. If the tester lights, the circuit is working. Now turn the switch to "on" and

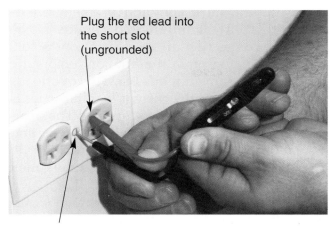

Plug the red lead into the short slot (ungrounded)

Touch the mounting screw with the black lead

Figure 21-3. Check the receptacle for power between the ungrounded slot and the mounting screw (grounding system) of the receptacle. If the tester light glows, the receptacle is connected to the ground.

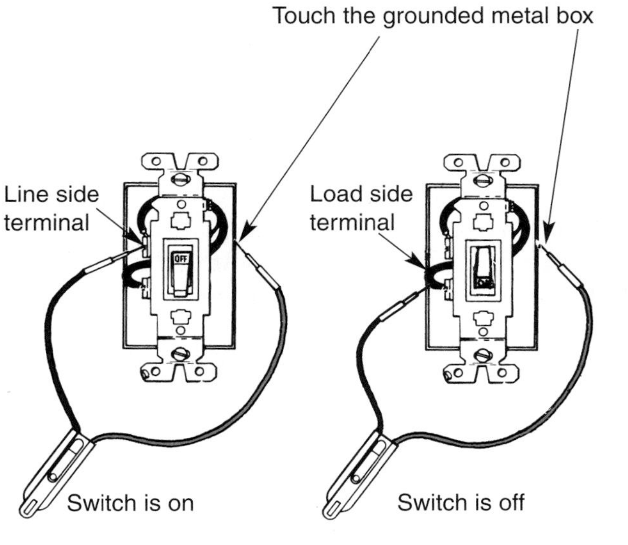

Touch the grounded metal box

Line side terminal

Load side terminal

Switch is on

Switch is off

Figure 21-4. With the switch off, the tester will indicate voltage at the line side terminal screw if the circuit is "live." If the tester does not light, the circuit is faulty. When the switch is on, the neon tester should indicate voltage between the load side switch terminal and the box or neutral conductor. If the tester fails to glow, the switch is faulty. Replace the switch and repeat the test.

touch one lead to the load terminal of the switch while the other lead is touching the metal box. If the test light glows, the switch is functioning and the fixture or wiring to it is faulty. Where nonmetallic boxes are used, one lead of the tester must contact a neutral wire.

Testing Fixtures

The fixture condition can be determined by checking whether power reaches the supply conductors at the fixture outlet. See **Figure 21-5**. If there is voltage indicated at this point, the fixture is not functioning. It needs to be repaired or replaced.

Figure 21-5. If the fixture will not function properly, but the test light indicates that voltage is present at the circuit conductors, the fixture must be repaired or replaced.

Overloaded Neutrals and Unbalanced Currents

It is often more convenient and economical to use one three-wire cable rather than two two-wire circuits. This is particularly true when both circuits would follow the same general direction. Installing two two-wire cables takes more material and time.

The substitution of a single three-wire cable for two two-wire cables constitutes a multiwire branch circuit. The rules regarding such circuits are referenced in *Section 210.4* of the *NEC*. Such a circuit may be used when split-wiring receptacles or when a circuit run consists of many light fixtures. The two circuits formed this way use a common neutral (the white grounded conductor in the cable). That is, both "hot" wires use the same neutral. See **Figure 21-6**.

Current will travel one direction in one hot wire while it is traveling the other direction in the other hot wire. The neutral wire will carry any unbalanced current resulting from differences between the hot wire loads. For example, if one conductor in Figure 21-6 is carrying 5 amperes of electricity, and the other conductor is carrying 7 amperes, the common neutral will conduct the 2-ampere difference.

Improperly Connected Circuits

Some problems do occur with multiwire circuits under certain conditions. With proper troubleshooting, the electrician can detect and correct the problems.

By far the most common problem occurring with split- or multiwired circuits is the improper connection of the circuit conductors at the panel. Too often the hot conductors are placed on the same hot bus bar. This overloads the neutral because the current load it carries is the sum of the two hot wire currents. The overcurrent frequently overheats the conductor and insulation, causing the neutral conductor to short circuit. The insulation may actually melt away from the conductor, **Figure 21-7**.

Further, should the neutral open, an excessive voltage surge may occur along one of the hot conductors. High voltage could damage the loads connected to the circuit.

It is important that you ensure that the loads on each hot conductor are closely matched. They need not be exactly the same, but the closer the better. Remember, the neutral will carry the imbalance or difference. In addition, the *NEC* requires that the two hot conductors have a common disconnect that act simultaneously in case of overcurrent. This rule is important and must not be disregarded. An ordinary double-pole, single-throw breaker will satisfy this requirement.

Fuses

Whenever a fuse "blows," the immediate concern is to determine why it did so. Go back to Figure 8-9 to review the procedure for finding the overcurrent source. Only when the cause is corrected should the fuse be replaced. In addition, never replace a fuse with one having a higher rating. This will only defeat the purpose of the fuse in the first place.

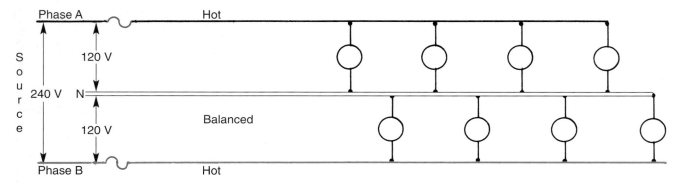

Figure 21-6. Properly constructed split- or multiwire circuit. The neutral will safely carry the unbalanced portion of load.

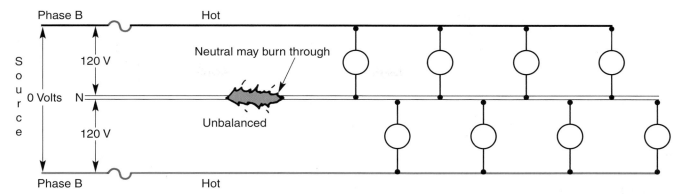

Figure 21-7. One of the most common problems with multiwire or split-circuits is the improper phase division at the lighting panel. In this situation, a serious imbalance can cause overloading and probable damage to the neutral, as well as to the loads.

When plug fuses blow they are easily located and replaced. When cartridge fuses blow we must first identify the blown fuse, since there is often no visible evidence.

You can identify the blown cartridge fuse in one of two ways:

- Remove the cartridge fuse from the panel and test it for electrical continuity. Use a VOM.

- With the cartridge still installed, test it using the circuit tester. This method, **Figure 21-8**, is easier and saves time.

Circuit Breakers

Circuit breakers are treated in much the same way as fuses. Should a circuit breaker trip, there is undoubtedly a cause. Find it before resetting the breaker.

Occasionally, circuit breakers malfunction and will not reset. This is determined using the same method as with a blown cartridge fuse. With the circuit breaker reset, place the neon tester between its terminal and the neutral bus bar. If the results are negative, the circuit breaker is not functioning. See **Figure 21-9**.

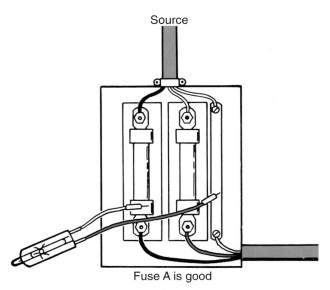

Figure 21-8. Method of testing a fuse. If the fuse is good, the light on a neon tester will glow.

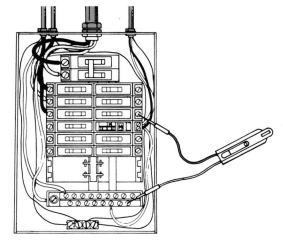

Figure 21-9. Method of testing a circuit breaker. If the light in the tester does not go on, reset the breaker and test again. If the test is still negative, replace the breaker with one of the same rating. If the breaker trips when reset, the problem lies somewhere else in the circuit. (GE Wiring Devices Dept.)

Miscellaneous Problems

Obviously, there are other problems that can arise in electrical systems. Problems originating from electrical equipment can range from *intermittent shorts*, those that occur only at certain times and under certain conditions, to entire system shutdowns because of service equipment failures. These problems, however, are rare in comparison to the minor ones previously discussed. The major service equipment failures are beyond the scope and purpose of this text. However, the key point to keep in mind is that all electrical problems are traceable through safe, careful analysis of the system components and perseverance on the part of the troubleshooting electrician.

---

intermittent shorts: Problems originating with electrical equipment that occur only at certain times and under certain conditions.

Review Questions

Write your answers on a separate sheet of paper. Do not write in this book.

1. List three common testing tools used in troubleshooting an electrical system.
2. Describe the procedure for troubleshooting each of the following:
   A. Receptacle outlets.
   B. Switches.
   C. Fixtures.
3. In a multiwire branch circuit, two different circuits will use a _Common_ _Neuthal_.
4. List the two ways of identifying a blown cartridge fuse.

Know the Code

A copy of the NEC 2005 is required to answer these questions.

1. *Article 700.4(D)* requires a _____ of testing and maintenance on emergency systems.
2. The wiring of a luminaire is required to be tested by which section of *Article 410*?

Electrical Careers

Objectives

Information in this chapter will enable you to:

- Explore the many job titles related to electricity.

- Consider the aspects of business ownership.

- Find groups that can assist you in a successful electrical career.

If you have more than just a casual interest in electrical wiring, perhaps a career in electricity is for you. This chapter will briefly list and explain the various career categories open to you.

Career Categories

The physical and mental skills required for electrical jobs vary greatly. However, all of them require knowledge of electricity and electrical wiring techniques. Following is a partial list of jobs that fall under the general category of electrical construction or maintenance work:

- Power line installer and repairer
- Power line troubleshooter
- Cable splicer
- Construction electrician
- Maintenance electrician
- Electrical inspector

Transmission and Distribution Electrician

One-fourth of the workers in the electric power industry are involved in transmission and distribution jobs. The principal workers in these occupations are those who control the flow of electricity. They are the *load dispatchers* and *substation operators*. Others in this group construct and maintain power lines. Job titles in this category include *line installers and repairers, cable splicers, troubleshooters, ground helpers,* and *laborers.* Line installers and repairers make up the largest single occupation in the industry.

Line installers and repairers construct and maintain the network of power lines that carry electricity from generating plants to consumers, **Figure 22-1.** Their work consists of installation, equipment replacement, repairs, and routine maintenance. When wires, cable, or poles break, it means an emergency call for a line crew. Line

Figure 22-1. The worker in the center is repairing the power line support while the other workers stabilize the line. If the power line moves too much, an arc could jump to the grounded tower, injuring anyone nearby. (Pacific Gas and Electric Company)

repairers splice or replace broken wires and cables, and replace broken insulators or other damaged equipment.

Most installers and repairers work from bucket trucks with hydraulic lifts that take them to the top of the pole at the touch of a lever, **Figure 22-2**. In some power companies, line crew employees specialize in particular types of work.

Troubleshooters are experienced line installers and repairers who are assigned to special crews that handle emergency calls. They move from one job to another, as directed by a central service office who receives reports of line trouble. Often, troubleshooters receive their orders by direct radio communication with the central service office.

These workers must have a thorough knowledge of the company's transmission and distribution network. They first locate and report the source of trouble and then attempt to restore service by making the necessary repairs.

Depending on the nature and extent of the problem, troubleshooters may restore service, or simply disconnect and remove the damaged equipment. They must be familiar with all the circuits and switching points so that they can safely disconnect live circuits.

Cable splicers install and repair insulated cables on utility poles and towers, as well as those buried underground or those installed in underground conduits, **Figure 22-3**. When cables are installed, the cable splicers pull the

Figure 22-2. Power crews work to restore electricity after a hurricane. A line repairer-installer is correcting damaged transmission lines. (Greg Henshall / FEMA)

cable through the conduit and join the cables at connecting points in the transmission and distribution systems. At each connection in the cable, they wrap insulation around the exposed conductors. Cable splicers splice the conductors leading away from each junction of the main cable, insulate the splices, and connect the cable sheathing. Most of the physical work in placing new cables or replacing old ones is done by cable splicers and their assistants.

Cable splicers spend most of their time repairing and maintaining cables and changing the layout of the cable systems. They must know the arrangement of the wiring systems, where the circuits are connected, and where they lead to and come from. When making repairs, they must make sure that the conductors do not become mixed up between the substation and the customer's premises. Cable splicers also periodically check insulation on cables to make sure it is in good condition.

Figure 22-3. Cable splicers are positioning a pad transformer to serve an apartment building. (New York State Electric and Gas Corp.)

Maintenance Electrician

Maintenance electricians keep lighting systems, transformers, generators, and other electrical equipment in good working order. They also may install new electrical equipment.

Duties vary greatly depending on where the electrician is employed. Electricians working in large factories may repair items such as motors and welding machines. Those in office buildings and small plants usually fix all kinds of commercial or industrial electrical equipment. Regardless of location, electricians spend much of their time doing preventive maintenance and making periodic inspection of equipment. This process helps them locate and correct defects before breakdowns occur. See **Figure 22-4**.

When trouble occurs, maintenance electricians must find the cause and make repairs quickly to prevent costly downtime or production losses. In emergencies, they advise management whether continued operation of equipment would be hazardous.

Maintenance electricians make repairs such as replacing fuses, circuit breakers, or switches. Adding and replacing wiring to an existing

This maintenance electrician is inspecting a circuit-breaker panel.

Testing a circuit for proper current is a typical job for a maintenance electrician.

Figure 22-4. Maintenance electricians periodically inspect, repair, and replace many components of an electrical system. (Ideal Industries, Inc.)

building is a common task for a maintenance electrician.

Maintenance electricians sometimes work from blueprints, wiring diagrams, or other specifications. They use meters and other testing devices to locate faulty equipment. To make repairs, they use an array of specialized devices besides pliers, screwdrivers, wire cutters, drills, and other basic tools.

Electrical Inspector

After a number of years as an electrician, you may consider becoming an electrical inspector. An electrical inspector must know the codes that regulate residential and commercial installations within the jurisdiction. Much of this knowledge will come from training and studying the *NEC*, however, you will gain a great deal of information from inspectors during your installations. As an electrical inspector, you will have to recognize incorrect construction and be able to explain the infraction. The electrician may confront the inspector, sometimes angrily, and demand that the inspector approve the work. Electrical inspectors who are fluent in the *NEC* can usually convince the electrician by citing the exact rules that have been violated.

Owning a Business

Many electricians own their own electrical contracting business. They may work alone or lead a crew of electricians. As contractors, they solicit business from customers and bid on jobs, working from plans secured from the potential customer. A contractor generally specializes in a certain field of work and may bid on jobs in industrial electrical maintenance or residential, commercial, or industrial construction.

Advantages of Owning a Business

Working for yourself has certain advantages. There is personal satisfaction in doing what *you* want to do. You are free to put your skills and knowledge to work as you see fit. The rewards of hard, skillful work are yours. You can control your own income. As the owner, you determine how the profit will be spent. If your business is successful, you have job security. Not the least of the advantages is the respect that your efforts might command in the community.

Disadvantages of Ownership

Venturing into your own business has some disadvantages. The following must be weighed against the advantages:

- Should your business fail, you can lose the money invested in it. In addition, you are liable for paying off debts. This could take years.
- Income, especially in the early years, can be uncertain.
- Workdays are considerably longer for the "boss." A 15-hour day, six or seven days a week is common.
- Much of the day will be taken up with routine chores and hard work. Your tasks will include paperwork, maintenance of tools and equipment, bidding jobs, customer relations, selling, organizing your work and that of employees, setting prices, and advertising.

What It Takes

Being your own boss may be just right for you. Or all wrong. It depends on certain characteristics. You should consider your own business if you are:

- **In good health with considerable energy.** You need it because of the long hours and physical labor involved.
- **A good organizer.** You must know what to do and how to schedule the work so it can be done efficiently.
- **Self-motivated.** In other words, you are a "self-starter." You are not afraid to make decisions; you believe in yourself; and you see what needs to be done and do it.
- **An innovator.** You look for ways to improve service to your customers and make your business more competitive.

- **Responsible.** You stand by your decisions. You are willing to shoulder responsibility for bad decisions and for mistakes made by employees. You keep promises and pay your debts.
- **Ready and able to take on a variety of roles.** If you dislike keeping records or supervising others, you may be happier working for someone else.

Advice on Starting a Business

- Gather experience working for another employer first. Observe as much as you can of the business operation.
- Ask others in the business for information. Benefit from their experience.
- Expect suppliers to be wary of extending credit until you prove trustworthy. Be prepared to purchase initial materials and tools with cash.
- If possible, survey potential customers. Try to find out if they would use your services.
- Secure adequate insurance coverage.
- Set up or secure a good accounting and bookkeeping system. This is one of the most important areas of successful management of your business. Yet, many small businessmen keep poor records. This failing often contributes to business failure. Consider taking accounting or bookkeeping courses. Otherwise, seek professional help from an experienced accountant.
- When business expands, hire good help.

Training, Other Qualifications, and Advancement

Most maintenance electricians learn their trade on the job or through formal apprenticeship programs. A relatively small number learn the

trade in the military service. Training authorities generally agree that apprenticeship gives trainees more thorough knowledge of the trade and improves job opportunities during their working life. Because the training is comprehensive, people who complete apprenticeship programs qualify either as maintenance, construction electricians, or technicians. See **Figure 22-5**.

Apprenticeship usually lasts four years, and consists of on-the-job training and related classroom instruction. Subjects such as mathematics, electrical and electronic theory, and print reading are covered in these lessons. Training

Technician uses X-ray machine to rate liquid and solid flame retardant.

Technician carefully checks resistance of product submitted for testing.

Figure 22-5. Some students use the apprenticeship experience to become technicians. (Underwriters Laboratories, Canadian Standards Association)

may include electric motor repair, wire splicing, installation and repair of electronic controls and circuits, and welding and brazing.

Informal Training

Although formal apprenticeship is the preferred method of training, many people learn the trade informally on-the-job by serving as helpers to skilled maintenance electricians. Helpers begin by doing simple jobs, such as replacing circuit breakers and switches. With experience, they advance to more complicated jobs, such as splicing cable and connecting circuit wires. They eventually get enough experience to qualify as electricians.

Selecting Helpful Courses

Persons interested in becoming maintenance electricians can obtain a good background by taking high school or vocational school courses in subjects such as electricity, electronics, physics, algebra, mechanical drawing, shop, and physical sciences. To qualify for an apprenticeship program, an applicant should be at least 18 years old and usually must be a high school or vocational school graduate.

Because the electrician's craft is subject to constant technological change, experienced electricians must continue to learn new skills.

All maintenance electricians must be familiar with the *National Electrical Code* and local building codes. Many cities and counties require maintenance electricians to be licensed. Electricians can obtain a license by passing an examination that tests their knowledge of electrical theory and its application.

Electricians (Construction)

Heat, light, power, air conditioning, and refrigeration components all operate through electrical systems that are assembled, installed, and wired by construction electricians. These workers also install electrical machinery, electronic equipment, controls, and signal and communications systems. Construction electricians follow blueprints and specifications for most installations.

For safety reasons, electricians must follow *National Electrical Code* regulations and, in addition, must fulfill all requirements of state, county, and municipal electrical codes.

Training, Other Qualifications, and Advancement

Most training authorities recommend the completion of a four-year apprenticeship program as the preferred way to learn the trade. As in the electrical maintenance trade, some individuals learn informally by working for many years as electrician's helpers. Many helpers gain additional knowledge through trade school or correspondence courses, or through special training in the military.

Apprenticeship programs are often sponsored through and supervised by local union-management committees. These programs provide 144 hours or more of classroom instruction each year in addition to comprehensive on-the-job training.

In the classroom, apprentices learn print reading, electrical theory, electronics, mathematics, safety, and first-aid practices. On the job, under the supervision of experienced electricians, apprentices must demonstrate mastery of electrical wiring principles.

At first, apprentices drill holes, set anchors, and set up conduit. In time and with experience, they measure, bend, and install conduit, as well as install, connect, and test wiring. They also learn to set up and draw diagrams for entire electrical systems.

To obtain a license, which is necessary for employment in most cities, construction electricians must also pass an examination that requires a thorough knowledge of electrical wiring and of state and local electrical codes.

For more information concerning careers in the electrical trades, contact the following organizations:

International Brotherhood of
Electrical Workers (IBEW)
900 Seventh Street, N.W.
Washington, DC 20001
Telephone: (202) 833-7000
Fax: (202) 728-7676
www.ibew.org

National Electrical Contractors
Association (NECA)
3 Bethesda Metro Center, Suite 1100
Bethesda, MD 20814
Telephone: (301) 657-3110
Fax: (301) 215-4500
www.necanet.org

National Fire Protection Association (NFPA)
1 Batterymarch Park
Quincy, MA 02169-7471
Telephone: (617) 770-3000
Fax: (617) 770-0700
www.nfpa.org

International Association of Electrical
Inspectors (IAEI)
901 Waterfall Way, Ste. 602
Richardson, TX 75080-7702
Telephone: (972) 235-1455
Fax: (972) 235-6858
www.iaei.org

United States Small Business
Administration
409 Third Street, SW
Washington, DC 20416
Telephone: 1-800-U-ASK-SBA (1-800-827-5722)
www.sba.gov

Do not overlook the local power suppliers, trade schools, neighborhood electricians, and electrical inspectors. They are potential employers as well as experienced sources of information.

SkillsUSA and TSA

SkillsUSA and the Technology Student Association are organizations that consist of instructors, students, and sponsoring industries to encourage the advancement of technical training. This is accomplished by researching improved methods of teaching, creating links between industry and education, and organizing competitions to promote and reward outstanding technical aptitude.

All of the aspects listed in the previous paragraph measure equally in importance, but the competitions at SkillsUSA and TSA continue to grab the attention of students and instructors most. See **Figure 22-6**. The requirements for competition may include a written test, conduit bending, device and fixture installation, and an understanding of the *National Electrical Code.*

Figure 22-6. These students show off their wiring skills at a SkillsUSA competition. (Copyright by Lloyd Wolf for SkillsUSA)

More information regarding these organizations can be found at the following:

SkillsUSA
PO Box 3000
Leesburg, VA 20177-0300
Telephone: (703) 777-8810
Fax: (703) 777-8999
www.skillsusa.org

Technology Student Association
1914 Association Drive
Reston, VA 20191-1540
Telephone: (703) 860-9000
Fax: (703) 758-4852
www.tsaweb.org

Review Questions

Write your answers on a separate sheet of paper.
Do not write in this book.

1. List five categories of jobs available to qualified electricians.

2. _____ are experienced line installers and repairers who are assigned to special crews that handle emergency calls.

3. Electricians who keep lighting systems, transformers, generators, and other electrical equipment in good working order are called _____ electricians.

4. *True or False?* Most electricians learn their trade on the job or through formal apprenticeship programs.

5. What must a construction electrician do to get a license to work in most cities?

6. A _____ generally specializes in a certain field of work and may bid on jobs.

7. Apprenticeship programs are often sponsored through and supervised by local _____.

Know the Code

A copy of the NEC 2005 is required to answer these questions.

1. How often does the *National Fire Protection Association* update the *NEC*?

2. How many code-making panels are involved in creating the 2005 edition of the *NEC*?

3. According to *Section 80.13* of *Annex G*, can police assist in the enforcement of the *NEC*?

This electrician is drilling through the framing so nonmetallic cable can be fished into the wall cavity. She has the training and experience to operate many different tools required to install residential wiring in a safe, cost-effective, and professional manner. (Victoria Hamlin, a public works truck driver, and Tradeswomen, Inc.)

Appendix A
Math Review

Every electrician must have a good background in math. This section will review some of the basic math operations needed by the electrician.

Above and beyond the simple addition, subtraction, division, and multiplication skills, an electrician must also be competent in computing or performing the following operations:

- Converting fractions to decimals
- Calculating percentage
- Converting fractions to percentages
- Formula organization
- Circle area and circumference
- Rectangle area and perimeter
- Basic trigonometry

Each of these procedures will be used often by the electrician in such tasks as figuring service entrance capacity, conduit fill, conduit bends, branch and feeder circuits, and wire ampacity. In addition, there are routine business operations to perform on a day-to-day basis. For these reasons, math must be considered an important electrical tool.

Basic Math

There are many aspects of our lives that depend on basic math skills. These skills, including fractions, decimals, percentages, and formulas must be mastered if you want to become a successful electrician. You may not have used any of the following procedures since grade school, or you may use them proficiently everyday. Regardless of your current level, it is a good idea to review the information in this appendix. It is far better to discover a math deficiency now instead of on the worksite.

Converting Fractions to Decimals and Vice Versa

On many occasions, it is necessary to change a fraction into its equivalent decimal. The electrician is constantly making measurements and reading specifications. Many of these figures are in fractions or decimals.

To change a fraction to a decimal, divide the numerator (top part of fraction), by the denominator (lower part of fraction).

Example:

Change $\frac{7}{16}$ to a decimal.

Solution:

$$
\begin{array}{r}
.4375 \\
16\overline{)7.0000} \\
64 \\
\overline{60} \\
48 \\
\overline{120} \\
112 \\
\overline{80} \\
80 \\
\overline{0}
\end{array}
$$

To change a decimal to a fraction, place the decimal number over 10 or 100 or 1000 or 10,000 depending on the number of digits in the decimal. Then reduce to the smallest fraction.

Example:

Change 0.4375 to a fraction.

Solution:

Since the decimal is to the ten thousandths place, we will divide as follows;

$$\frac{4375}{10,000} = \frac{875}{2000} = \frac{175}{400} = \frac{35}{80} = \frac{7}{16}$$

Finding Percentage

It is often necessary to compute the percentage of a given number. This is especially useful when computing conduit fill or discounts on supply items.

To find the percentage one number is of another, simply divide the larger number into the smaller one. Multiply the result by 100%.

What percentage of 87 is 14?

Solution:

$$
\begin{array}{r}
.16 \\
87\overline{)14.00} \\
87 \\
\overline{530} \\
522 \\
\overline{8}
\end{array}
$$

.16 = 16%

A practical application of this follows:

You have just purchased $240 worth of electrical fittings. If you pay the supplier's bill within 10 days, you can take a 5 percent discount. How much can you save by paying early? *Solution:* Multiply the total by 5% (.05) and subtract this result from the total.

$$
\begin{array}{r}
\$240.00 \\
\times \quad .05 \\
\hline
\$12.00
\end{array}
$$

and

$$
\begin{array}{r}
\$240.00 \\
- \ \$12.00 \\
\hline
\$228.00
\end{array}
$$

Converting a Fraction to a Percentage

To convert a fraction to a percentage, divide the numerator by the denominator and move the decimal point two places to the right.

Example:

What percentage is the fraction $\frac{1}{6}$?

Solution:

$$
\begin{array}{r}
.166 \\
6\overline{)1.000}
\end{array}
$$

and

.166 = 16.6%

Formula Organization

Many times the particular unknown in a formula is not isolated. Thus, the formula must be reorganized to separate the unknown from the rest.

Example:

Ohm's law, in formula, is written, $E = I \times R$. Suppose we wish to find R, when E and I are known.

We must rewrite the formula to isolate R.
Solution:
Divide both sides of the equation by I.
$E = I \times R$
to:

$$\frac{E}{I} = \frac{I \times R}{I}$$

result: $\frac{E}{I} = R$

Solve for the unknown (R).

Geometry

Rectangle Area

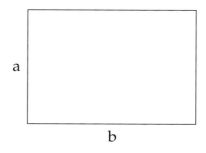

Area $= a \times b$
Example:
The area of a 30′ × 40′ house needs to be known to calculate the general lighting requirements.
Area $= 30' \times 40'$
      $= 1200 \text{ ft}^2$

Rectangle Perimeter

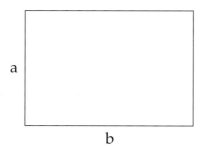

Perimeter $= 2 \times (a + b)$
Example:
The perimeter of a 14′ × 18′ room needs to be known to calculate the number of outlet receptacles required.
Perimeter $= 2 \times (14' + 18')$
           $= 2 \times 32'$
           $= 64'$

Circle Area

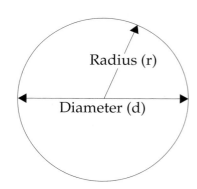

Area $= \pi r^2$
Example:
The area of a 10 AWG (0.049″) conductor needs to be known to calculate conduit fill.
Radius = Diameter ÷ 2
       $= 0.049'' \div 2$
       $= 0.0245''$
Area $= \pi \times 0.0245^2$
      $= \pi \times 0.0006 \text{ in}^2$
      $= 0.0019 \text{ in}^2$

Circle Circumference

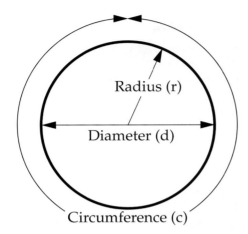

Circumference $= \pi d$

Example:

The circumference of a 30' diameter round room is needed to calculate the length of wire needed to connect all of the outlet receptacles in the room.

Circumference $= \pi \times 30'$

$= 94.25'$ or $94'\ 3''$

Trigonometry

Right Triangle Formulas and Calculator Steps			
To find...	**...and you know...**	**...perform these calculator steps.**	**Formulas**
angle B	sides a & b	b ÷ a [2nd] [SIN⁻¹ SIN]	b/a = Sin B
angle B	sides a & c	c ÷ a [2nd] [COS⁻¹ COS]	c/a = Cos B
angle B	sides b & c	b ÷ c [2nd] [TAN⁻¹ TAN]	b/c = Tan B
angle C	sides a & b	b ÷ a [2nd] [COS]	b/a = Cos C
angle C	sides a & c	c ÷ a [2nd] [SIN]	c/a = Sin C
angle C	sides b & c	c ÷ b [2nd] [TAN⁻¹ TAN]	c/b = Tan C
side a	sides b & c	b [x²] [+] c [x²] [2nd] [√ x²]	$\sqrt{b^2 + c^2}$
side a	side c & angle C	c ÷ [(] C [SIN] [)] [ENTER =]	$\dfrac{c}{\sin C}$
side a	side c & angle B	c ÷ [(] B [COS] [)] [ENTER =]	$\dfrac{c}{\cos B}$
side a	side b & angle B	b ÷ [(] B [SIN] [)] [ENTER =]	$\dfrac{b}{\sin B}$
side a	side b & angle C	b ÷ [(] C [COS] [)] [ENTER =]	$\dfrac{b}{\cos C}$
side b	sides a & c	a [x²] [+] c [x²] [2nd] [x²]	$\sqrt{a^2 + c^2}$
side b	side a & angle B	B [SIN] [×] a	a × Sin B
side b	side a & angle C	C [COS] [×] a	a × Cos C
side b	side c & angle B	B [TAN] [×] c	c × Tan B
side b	side c & angle C	c ÷ [(] C [TAN] [)] [ENTER =]	$\dfrac{c}{\tan C}$
side c	sides a & b	a [x²] [+] b [x²] [2nd] [x²]	$\sqrt{a^2 + b^2}$
side c	side a & angle B	B [COS] [×] a	a × Cos B
side c	side a & angle C	C [SIN] [×] a	a × Sin C
side c	side b & angle B	b ÷ [(] B [TAN] [)] [ENTER =]	$\dfrac{b}{\tan B}$
side c	side b & angle C	C [TAN] [×] b	b × Tan C

Right triangle

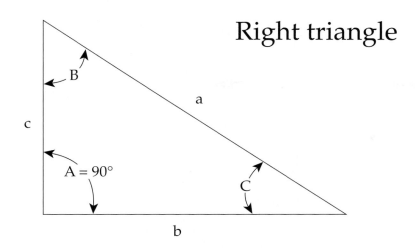

Oblique Triangle Formulas and Calculator Steps

To find...	...and you know...	...perform these calculator steps.	Formulas
angle A	angles B & C	180 — B + C	$180° - (B + C)$
angle B	angles A & C	180 — A + C	$180° - (A + C)$
angle C	angles A & B	180 — A + B	$180° - (A + B)$
side a	side c, angles A & C	C SIN × c ÷ (A SIN) ENTER =	$\dfrac{c \times \sin C}{\sin A}$
side b	side a, angles A & B	B SIN × a ÷ (A SIN) ENTER =	$\dfrac{a \times \sin B}{\sin A}$
side c	side a, angles A & C	C SIN × a ÷ (A SIN) ENTER =	$\dfrac{a \times \sin C}{\sin A}$

Oblique triangle

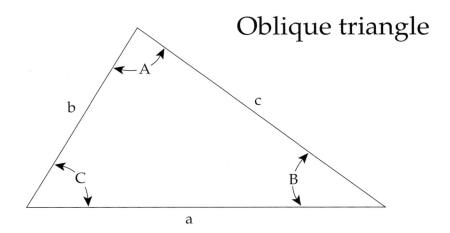

Appendix B
Service and
Feeder Calculation
Methods

This appendix contains blank and completed worksheets for calculating the feeder and service loads of a one-family dwelling.

Calculation for Total Load of a One-Family Dwelling

Table 220.12 210.11(C)(1) 210.11(C)(2)		Multiply the total square feet of house by 3 VA.		
	1	This is the total general load.	_____ ft² × 3 VA = _____	VA
	2	Small appliance loads (two kitchen area circuits at 1500 VA each)	3000	VA
	3	One laundry circuit	1500	VA
	4	Add lines 1 through 3.	Total = _____	VA

Table 220.42	**5**	The first 3000 VA of the total is 100%.	3000	VA
	6	Subtract the first 3000 VA from line 4 to get the remainder. Line 4 − 3000 = _____		VA
	7	Multiply the remainder by 35%. × 0.35 Line 6 × 0.35 = _____		VA
	8	Add line 5 to line 7 to get the **net load**. Line 5 + line 7 = _____		VA

Table 220.53		List the nameplate ratings of each fixed appliance.		
	9	Range	_____	VA
	10	Dryer	_____	VA
	11	Dishwasher	_____	VA
	12	Water heater	_____	VA
	13	_____	_____	VA
	14	_____	Additional	_____	VA
	15	_____	fixed	_____	VA
	16	_____	appliances	_____	VA
	17	Add lines 9 through 16. This is the **total fixed appliances load**.	_____	VA

	18	Add line 8 to line 17. This is the **net calculated load**. Line 8 + line 17 = _____		VA

220.82(C)	**19**	Total heating load	_____	VA
	20	Total air conditioning load	_____	VA
	21	Enter the larger number between line 19 and line 20.	_____	VA
	22	Multiply line 21 by 40%. × 0.40 This is the **total heating/air conditioning load**. Line 21 × 0.40 = _____		VA

Total load	**23**	Add line 18 to line 22 for the **total house load**.	_____	VA
	24	Enter the voltage provided (120, 240, or other)	_____	V
	25	Divide line 23 by line 24. This is the **total amperage required for the house**. Line 23 ÷ line 24 = _____		A

Review NEC Sections 230.42(B) and 230.79 for service conductors and disconnecting requirements.

Optional Calculation Method for Total Load of a One-Family Dwelling

General load NEC 220.82(B)	1	Multiply the total square feet of house by 3 VA.	_____ ft² × 3 VA = _____	VA
	2	Small appliance loads (two kitchen area circuits at 1500 VA each)	3000	VA
	3	One laundry circuit	1500	VA
		List the nameplate ratings of each fixed appliance.		
	4	Range	_____	VA
	5	Dryer	_____	VA
	6	Dishwasher	_____	VA
	7	Water heater	_____	VA
Additional fixed appliances	8	_____	_____	VA
	9	_____	_____	VA
	10	_____	_____	VA
	11	_____	_____	VA

General load NEC 220.82(B)	12	Add lines 1 through 11. This is the **total general load**.	_____	VA
	13	Subtract 10000 from line 12 to get the **remainder**.	Line 12 − 10000 = _____	VA
	14	Multiply line 13 by 40%.	Line 13 × 0.40 = _____	VA
		Add 10000 to line 14 to get the		
	15	**subtotal general load**.	10000 + line 14 = _____	VA

Heating or air conditioning NEC 220.82(C)	16	Total heating load	_____	VA
	17	Total air conditioning load	_____	VA
		Enter the larger number between line 16 and line 17. This is the		
	18	**total heating/air conditioning load**.	_____	VA

Total load	19	Add line 15 to line 18 for the **total house load**.	_____	VA
	20	Enter the voltage provided (120, 240, or other)	_____	V
		Divide line 19 by line 20. This is the		
	21	**total amperage required for the house**.	Line 19 ÷ line 20 = _____	A

Review NEC Sections 230.42(B) and 230.79 for service conductors and disconnecting requirements.

Calculation for Total Load of a One-Family Dwelling

Table 220.12 / 210.11(C)(1) / 210.11(C)(2)	1	Multiply the total square feet of house by 3 VA. This is the total general load.	$\underline{2100}$ ft² × 3 VA = **6300**	VA
	2	Small appliance loads (two kitchen area circuits at 1500 VA each)	3000	VA
	3	One laundry circuit	1500	VA
	4	Add lines 1 through 3.	Total = **10800**	VA

Table 220.42	5	The first 3000 VA of the total is 100%.	3000	VA
	6	Subtract the first 3000 VA from line 4 to get the remainder.	Line 4 − 3000 = **7800**	VA
		Multiply the remainder by 35%.	× 0.35	
	7		Line 6 × 0.35 = **2730**	VA
	8	Add line 5 to line 7 to get the **net load**.	Line 5 + line 7 = **5730**	VA

Copyright by Goodheart-Willcox Co., Inc. Permission granted to reproduce for educational use only.

List the nameplate ratings of each fixed appliance.

Table 220.53	9	Range	**13,000**	VA
	10	Dryer	**5100**	VA
	11	Dishwasher	**1500**	VA
	12	Water heater		VA
	13	_HOT TUB_	**2000**	VA
	14	_____ Additional		VA
	15	_____ fixed		VA
	16	_____ appliances		VA
	17	Add lines 9 through 16. This is the **total fixed appliances load**.	**21,600**	VA

		Add line 8 to line 17.		
	18	This is the **net calculated load**.	Line 8 + line 17 = **27,330**	VA

220.82(C)	19	Total heating load	**5200**	VA
	20	Total air conditioning load	**4000**	VA
	21	Enter the larger number between line 19 and line 20.	**5200**	VA
		Multiply line 21 by 40%.	× 0.40	
	22	This is the **total heating/air conditioning load**.	Line 21 × 0.40 = **2080**	VA

Total load	23	Add line 18 to line 22 for the **total house load**.	**29410**	VA
	24	Enter the voltage provided (120, 240, or other)	**240**	V
		Divide line 23 by line 24. This is the		
	25	**total amperage required for the house**.	Line 23 ÷ line 24 = **123**	A

Review NEC Sections 230.42(B) and 230.79 for service conductors and disconnecting requirements.

Optional Calculation Method for Total Load of a One-Family Dwelling

General load NEC 220.82(B)	1	Multiply the total square feet of house by 3 VA.	2100 ft² × 3 VA = 6300	VA
	2	Small appliance loads (two kitchen area circuits at 1500 VA each)	3000	VA
	3	One laundry circuit	1500	VA
		List the nameplate ratings of each fixed appliance.		
	4	Range	13,000	VA
	5	Dryer	5100	VA
Additional fixed appliances	6	Dishwasher	1500	VA
	7	Water heater		VA
	8	HOT TUB	2000	VA
	9			VA
	10			VA
	11			VA

Copyright by Goodheart-Willcox Co., Inc. Permission granted to reproduce for educational use only.

General load NEC 220.82(B)	12	Add lines 1 through 11. This is the **total general load.**	$27,900$	VA
	13	Subtract 10000 from line 12 to get the **remainder.**	Line 12 − 10000 = $17,900$	VA
	14	Multiply line 13 by 40%.	Line 13 × 0.40 = 7160	VA
	15	Add 10000 to line 14 to get the **subtotal general load.**	10000 + line 14 = 17160	VA

Heating or air conditioning NEC 220.82(C)	16	Total heating load	5200	VA
	17	Total air conditioning load	4000	VA
	18	Enter the larger number between line 16 and line 17. This is the **total heating/air conditioning load.**	5200	VA

Total load	19	Add line 15 to line 18 for the **total house load.**	22360	VA
	20	Enter the voltage provided (120, 240, or other)	240	V
	21	Divide line 19 by line 20. This is the **total amperage required for the house.**	Line 19 ÷ line 20 = 93	A

Review NEC Sections 230.42(B) and 230.79 for service conductors and disconnecting requirements.

Appendix C
NEMA
Receptacle
Configurations

NEMA LINE NO.	WIRES		VOLTS	15 AMP	20 AMP	30 AMP	50 AMP	60 AMP	NEMA LINE NO.
1	2-POLE 2-WIRE	NOT CSA	125V	∅ [ ] W WHITE NEUTRAL					1
2			250V		∅ ∅	∅ ∅			2
5	2-POLE 3-WIRE	GROUNDING	125V	∅ G W WHITE NEUTRAL	∅ G W WHITE NEUTRAL	∅ G W WHITE NEUTRAL	∅ G W WHITE NEUTRAL		5
6			250V	G ∅ ∅	G ∅ ∅	G ∅ ∅	G ∅		6
7			277V AC	G ∅ W WHITE NEUTRAL	G ∅ W WHITE NEUTRAL	G ∅ W WHITE NEUTRAL	G ∅ W WHITE NEUTRAL		7

Straight blade receptacle wiring configurations. Letters ''x,'' ''y,'' and ''z'' refer to ''hot'' terminals. ''W'' indicates the neutral or white grounded wire terminal. ''G'' stands for the equipment ground terminal.   (General Electric Co.)

10	3-POLE 3-WIRE	NOT CSA	125/250V		WHITE NEUTRAL / W / Y / X	WHITE NEUTRAL / W / Y / X	WHITE NEUTRAL / W / Y / X		10
11			3Ø 250V	X / Z / Y	X / Z / Y	X / Z / Y	X / Z / Y		11
14	3-POLE 4-WIRE	GROUNDING	125/250V	G / Y / X / WHITE NEUTRAL / W	G / Y / X / WHITE NEUTRAL / W	G / Y / X / WHITE NEUTRAL / W	G / Y / X / WHITE NEUTRAL	G / Y / X / WHITE NEUTRAL / W	14
15			3Ø 250V	G / Z / X / Y	G / Z / X / Y	G / Z / X / Y	G / Z / X / Y	G / Z / X / Y	15
18	4-P 4-W	NOT CSA	3ØY 120/208V	WHITE NEUTRAL / W / Z / X / Y	WHITE NEUTRAL / W / Z / X / Y	WHITE NEUTRAL / W / X / Y	WHITE NEUTRAL / W / Z / X / Y	WHITE NEUTRAL / W / Z / X / Y	18
24	2-P 3-W	GRND	347 VAC	G / W / WHITE NEUTRAL	G / W / WHITE NEUTRAL	G / W / WHITE NEUTRAL	WHITE NEUTRAL / W		24

Appendix D
National Electrical Code Tables

This appendix contains reproductions of some tables from the *National Electrical Code* that are useful to a residential electrician. These tables are provided to help you become more comfortable with the presentation and location of material in the *NEC*. These tables are not a substitute for the *National Electrical Code*. The information contained in these tables is only a portion of the material you need to know to perform a safe electrical installation. Before using any tables reproduced in this text, be sure to consult the appropriate sections in the *National Electrical Code*.

Tables 110.26(A)(1) and *110.34(A)* provide clear distance requirements for areas around electric equipment. Refer to *Article 110* for additional information.

Table 110.26(A)(1) Working Spaces

Nominal Voltage to Ground	Minimum Clear Distance		
	Condition 1	Condition 2	Condition 3
0–150	900 mm (3 ft)	900 mm (3 ft)	900 mm (3 ft)
151–600	900 mm (3 ft)	1.1 m (3½ ft)	1.2 m (4 ft)

Note: Where the conditions are as follows:
Condition 1 — Exposed live parts on one side of the working space and no live or grounded parts on the other side of the working space, or exposed live parts on both sides of the working space that are effectively guarded by insulating materials.
Condition 2 — Exposed live parts on one side of the working space and grounded parts on the other side of the working space. Concrete, brick, or tile walls shall be considered as grounded.
Condition 3 — Exposed live parts on both sides of the working space.

Table 110.34(A) Minimum Depth of Clear Working Space at Electrical Equipment

Nominal Voltage to Ground	Minimum Clear Distance		
	Condition 1	Condition 2	Condition 3
601–2500 V	900 mm (3 ft)	1.2 m (4 ft)	1.5 m (5 ft)
2501–9000 V	1.2 m (4 ft)	1.5 m (5 ft)	1.8 m (6 ft)
9001–25,000 V	1.5 m (5 ft)	1.8 m (6 ft)	2.8 m (9 ft)
25,001V–75 kV	1.8 m (6 ft)	2.5 m (8 ft)	3.0 m (10 ft)
Above 75 kV	2.5 m (8 ft)	3.0 m (10 ft)	3.7 m (12 ft)

Note: Where the conditions are as follows:
Condition 1 — Exposed live parts on one side of the working space and no live or grounded parts on the other side of the working space, or exposed live parts on both sides of the working space that are effectively guarded by insulating materials.
Condition 2 — Exposed live parts on one side of the working space and grounded parts on the other side of the working space. Concrete, brick, or tile walls shall be considered as grounded.
Condition 3 — Exposed live parts on both sides of the working space.

Table 220.12 provides the general lighting loads for various types of buildings and areas.

Table 220.12 General Lighting Loads by Occupancy

Type of Occupancy	Unit Load	
	Volt-Amperes per Square Meter	Volt-Amperes per Square Foot
Armories and auditoriums	11	1
Banks	39[b]	3½[b]
Barber shops and beauty parlors	33	3
Churches	11	1
Clubs	22	2
Court rooms	22	2
Dwelling units[a]	33	3
Garages — commercial (storage)	6	½
Hospitals	22	2
Hotels and motels, including apartment houses without provision for cooking by tenants[a]	22	2
Industrial commercial (loft) buildings	22	2
Lodge rooms	17	1½
Office buildings	39[b]	3½[b]
Restaurants	22	2
Schools	33	3
Stores	33	3
Warehouses (storage)	3	¼
In any of the preceding occupancies except one-family dwellings and individual dwelling units of two-family and multifamily dwellings:		
Assembly halls and auditoriums	11	1
Halls, corridors, closets, stairways	6	½
Storage spaces	3	¼

[a]See 220.14(J).
[b]See 220.14(K).

Table 310.15(B)(6) provides the required conductor sizes for service and feeder conductors. The size is based on the ampacity of the service or feeder.

Table 250.66 is used to determine the proper size for the grounding electrode conductor. The size is based on the size of the service-entrance conductor.

Table 310.15(B)(2)(a) Adjustment Factors for More Than Three Current-Carrying Conductors in a Raceway or Cable

Number of Current-Carrying Conductors	Percent of Values in Tables 310.16 through 310.19 as Adjusted for Ambient Temperature if Necessary
4–6	80
7–9	70
10–20	50
21–30	45
31–40	40
41 and above	35

Table 250.66 Grounding Electrode Conductor for Alternating-Current Systems

Size of Largest Ungrounded Service-Entrance Conductor or Equivalent Area for Parallel Conductors[a] (AWG/kcmil)		Size of Grounding Electrode Conductor (AWG/kcmil)	
Copper	Aluminum or Copper-Clad Aluminum	Copper	Aluminum or Copper-Clad Aluminum[b]
2 or smaller	1/0 or smaller	8	6
1 or 1/0	2/0 or 3/0	6	4
2/0 or 3/0	4/0 or 250	4	2
Over 3/0 through 350	Over 250 through 500	2	1/0
Over 350 through 600	Over 500 through 900	1/0	3/0
Over 600 through 1100	Over 900 through 1750	2/0	4/0
Over 1100	Over 1750	3/0	250

Notes:
1. Where multiple sets of service-entrance conductors are used as permitted in 230.40, Exception No. 2, the equivalent size of the largest service-entrance conductor shall be determined by the largest sum of the areas of the corresponding conductors of each set.
2. Where there are no service-entrance conductors, the grounding electrode conductor size shall be determined by the equivalent size of the largest service-entrance conductor required for the load to be served.
[a]This table also applies to the derived conductors of separately derived ac systems.
[b]See installation restrictions in 250.64(A).

Table 310.16 provides allowable ampacities for various conductor sizes. This table is used to determine the required conductor size for a known load.

Table 310.16 Allowable Ampacities of Insulated Conductors Rated 0 Through 2000 Volts, 60°C Through 90°C (140°F Through 194°F), Not More Than Three Current-Carrying Conductors in Raceway, Cable, or Earth (Directly Buried), Based on Ambient Temperature of 30°C (86°F)

Size AWG or kcmil	Temperature Rating of Conductor (See Table 310.13.)						Size AWG or kcmil
	60°C (140°F)	75°C (167°F)	90°C (194°F)	60°C (140°F)	75°C (167°F)	90°C (194°F)	
	Types TW, UF	Types RHW, THHW, THW, THWN, XHHW, USE, ZW	Types TBS, SA, SIS, FEP, FEPB, MI, RHH, RHW-2, THHN, THHW, THW-2, THWN-2, USE-2, XHH, XHHW, XHHW-2, ZW-2	Types TW, UF	Types RHW, THHW, THW, THWN, XHHW, USE	Types TBS, SA, SIS, THHN, THHW, THW-2, THWN-2, RHH, RHW-2, USE-2, XHH, XHHW, XHHW-2, ZW-2	
	COPPER			ALUMINUM OR COPPER-CLAD ALUMINUM			
18	—	—	14	—	—	—	—
16	—	—	18	—	—	—	—
14*	20	20	25	—	—	—	—
12*	25	25	30	20	20	25	12*
10*	30	35	40	25	30	35	10*
8	40	50	55	30	40	45	8
6	55	65	75	40	50	60	6
4	70	85	95	55	65	75	4
3	85	100	110	65	75	85	3
2	95	115	130	75	90	100	2
1	110	130	150	85	100	115	1
1/0	125	150	170	100	120	135	1/0
2/0	145	175	195	115	135	150	2/0
3/0	165	200	225	130	155	175	3/0
4/0	195	230	260	150	180	205	4/0
250	215	255	290	170	205	230	250
300	240	285	320	190	230	255	300
350	260	310	350	210	250	280	350
400	280	335	380	225	270	305	400
500	320	380	430	260	310	350	500
600	355	420	475	285	340	385	600
700	385	460	520	310	375	420	700
750	400	475	535	320	385	435	750
800	410	490	555	330	395	450	800
900	435	520	585	355	425	480	900
1000	455	545	615	375	445	500	1000
1250	495	590	665	405	485	545	1250
1500	520	625	705	435	520	585	1500
1750	545	650	735	455	545	615	1750
2000	560	665	750	470	560	630	2000

CORRECTION FACTORS

Ambient Temp. (°C)	For ambient temperatures other than 30°C (86°F), multiply the allowable ampacities shown above by the appropriate factor shown below.						Ambient Temp. (°F)
21–25	1.08	1.05	1.04	1.08	1.05	1.04	70–77
26–30	1.00	1.00	1.00	1.00	1.00	1.00	78–86
31–35	0.91	0.94	0.96	0.91	0.94	0.96	87–95
36–40	0.82	0.88	0.91	0.82	0.88	0.91	96–104
41–45	0.71	0.82	0.87	0.71	0.82	0.87	105–113
46–50	0.58	0.75	0.82	0.58	0.75	0.82	114–122
51–55	0.41	0.67	0.76	0.41	0.67	0.76	123–131
56–60	—	0.58	0.71	—	0.58	0.71	132–140
61–70	—	0.33	0.58	—	0.33	0.58	141–158
71–80	—	—	0.41	—	—	0.41	159–176

* See 240.4(D).

Glossary

A

adjustment factor. A percentage that is used to reduce the ampacity of a conductor based on the number of current-carrying conductors in a raceway or cable.

alternating current (ac). A periodic current that continuously reverses direction.

American Wire Gage (AWG). A standard unit of measure for wire diameter. The diameter increases as the number decreases for sizes 18 AWG to 1 AWG. Larger wires with an AWG designation range from 1/0 to 4/0 with the diameter increasing as the left digit increases.

ampacity. The safe current-carrying capacity of a conductor.

amperage. The measurement of the rate of flow of electrons.

ampere (A). The unit used in measuring amperage or current. Abbreviated as amp (plural amps). Named after André-Marie Ampère.

anode. The positive terminal of a battery.

anti-short bushing. A red, split, plastic sleeve placed between the wires and the rough edge of the armor in AC.

arc flash. An explosion that takes place when electricity short-circuits through the air or across inadequate insulation.

arc-fault circuit interrupter (AFCI). A device that opens the circuit when an arc fault is detected.

armor. The metallic spiral tubing that protects the conductors in armored cable.

armored cable (AC). An assembly of wires contained within a flexible metallic armor for protection.

atom. The smallest particle of an element.

authority having jurisdiction (AHJ). The person or group of people responsible for approving the equipment, materials, an installation, or a procedure.

B

back-to-back bend. Describes two 90° bends in the same piece of conduit, regardless of the distance between bends.

battery. A group of voltaic cells that are connected in series or parallel, usually contained in one case.

blanket heater. A heater to bring nonmetallic electrical conduit up to the proper temperature for bending.

blockout device. A safety device used to stop machinery from moving.

bonding. Creating a continuous electrical connection of the metal parts of the wiring system.

bonding strip. A piece of wire manufactured into AC that runs the length of the armor and is in constant contact with it. It provides the continuous ground necessary in a bonded system.

box cover. A flat metallic or nonmetallic plate that is placed over a mounted switch or outlet, and is large enough to cover the wiring and exposed terminals that are in the box; also called a *faceplate*.

box heater. A device for heating nonmetallic electrical conduit to the proper bending temperature.

box offset. The small offset, or "kick," needed in the end of a piece of conduit so it can enter a knockout in a junction box or a device box.

branch. One of the pathways in a parallel circuit.

branch circuit. A separate electrical path, independent of other electrical paths in the building.

break-off fin. A removable tab that separates the two outlets on a duplex receptacle.

bridge. A wood or metal support that spans two joists.

BX. Another name for armored cable (AC). BX is a trade name attributed to the Sprague Electric division of General Electric.

C

cable. An arrangement of two or more conductors in a protective covering assembled by the manufacturer.

cable pair. The two wires that carry the signals and power to a telephone.

cable ripper. A tool used to cut the outer jacket of a cable for removal.

cable run. A long length of cable that is typically pulled through walls and the ceiling area.

cable termination box. The enclosure where connections are made for the cable pair coming from each building.

carbon monoxide. A colorless, odorless, and tasteless gas that can accumulate in unventilated areas to a level that causes headache, nausea, and death if the person is not brought to fresh air.

cathode. The negative terminal of a battery.

ceiling box. An electrical box intended for supporting ceiling fixtures.

central office. A building that houses a local telephone exchange where the telephone signals are routed and the power for telephones is generated.

circuit. The pathway over which electrons can move.

circuit breaker. A resettable device that is designed to open a circuit automatically when a specified ampacity is exceeded.

circuit tester. A simple light with conductive leads used to determine if a circuit is energized or deenergized.

circular mil (cmil). The area of a circle with a diameter of 0.001″ (one mil).

clamps. Fittings that secure nonmetallic cable to an electrical box.

complex circuit. A combination of series and parallel circuits.

conduction. The means by which heat passes through a substance by the contact of its molecules.

conductor. A substance that allows electrons to flow freely through it; an object having good conductivity.

conduit. Round hollow tubing that is metal or plastic, rigid or flexible, that is used to protect wires from physical damage.

conduit bender. A special tool for bending conduit to the proper bend radius. Contains special markings for making consistent bends at the proper angles.

conduit bodies. Boxes designed to be connected to conduit to create a wire pull point.

connected load. The amount of power needed if all of the equipment was operating at the same time.

connectors. Fittings that secure conduit or the outer covering of armored cable to an electrical box.

continuity tester. Checks for electrical continuity between two objects or devices.

continuous duty. A motor that is designed to deliver the rated horsepower for an indefinite period without overheating.

convection. The process by which heat is transferred through fluids, liquids, and gases, by the movement of masses having unequal temperatures.

correction factor. A percentage that is used to reduce the ampacity of a conductor based on the ambient temperature.

crosstalk. Imposing an electrical signal on another conductor through induction.

current. The flow of electrons.

current-limiting fuse. A fuse that quickly opens the circuit when a specified overcurrent is reached.

cycles. A cycle is one complete repetition of a waveform or signal. The rate at which the signal repeats itself is expressed in cycles per second, or hertz.

D

demand factor. A percentage that the total load on a circuit may be reduced to create a lower electrical load.

demand load. The amount of power which would most probably be needed at any given time.

derating. The reduction in ampacity of a wire after calculating adjustment and correction factors.

diagonal cutter. Pliers with two sharpened jaws for cutting wires.

digital voltage tester. A tool that uses indicator lights or a digital readout to indicate the amount of voltage present.

direct current (dc). A current that always flows in one direction.

distribution panelboard. An assembly within a cabinet or cutout box that includes bus bars, automatic overcurrent protection devices, and sometimes switches.

drawing. The original document that is created, revised, and approved.

drip loop. A formed curvature of the service conductor to prevent water from entering the service head.

dry cell. A battery that uses a chemical paste electrolyte.

dry-niche fixture. An underwater pool light that is installed inside a watertight enclosure within the pool wall.

dual-element fuse. A fuse that has two elements arranged in series; one element is designed to allow for low-level overloads for a short period of time.

E

electric drill. An electric-motor-powered tool for making a round hole.

electrical box. A metallic or nonmetallic container used to mount devices, conduit, and cables; protect people from electrical shock; keep exposed conductors away from combustible building materials; and act as a pull point.

electrical burn. A burn that occurs when electricity passes through the body.

electrical load. The amount of power required for a branch circuit, feeder, or service.

electrical metallic tubing (EMT). Conduit made of aluminum with relatively thin walls; also called *thin-wall conduit*. The smaller sizes can be easily bent with a hand tool.

electrical nonmetallic tubing (ENT). Plastic corrugated tubing that provides a flexible conduit. Also called smurf because one type of ENT is a bright blue color, like the Smurf cartoon characters.

electrical potential. The ability to provide free electrons.

electrical print. A copy of the drawing that the electricians have to locate devices and fixtures.

electrical schedules. Tables that list items such as fixtures, power requirements, panelboard information, receptacles, and switches.

electrical voltage tester. An electronic device that indicates if a voltage is present on a circuit.

electrician's hammer. A specialized hammer with a long neck and a straight claw.

electrician's knife. A single-bladed knife with a curved blade that locks open. Usually used to remove insulation or cable jacket from wire.

electrolyte. The chemical that is a liquid or paste that allows the flow of electrons in a battery.

electromagnetic induction. The process of producing an electromotive force by varying the magnetic field surrounding a conductor.

electromotive force. The force that causes current to flow between two objects with different electrical potential.

electrons. Negatively charged particles that orbit the nucleus of an atom.

energy. The ability to do work.

equilibrium. When two connected bodies have the same number of electrons; a balanced condition.

equipment grounding. Bonding the grounding conductor to equipment enclosures and metallic noncurrent-carrying equipment.

extension drill bits. Drill bits that can be extended to longer lengths for drilling holes through walls, floors, and beams.

extension rings. Boxes without a bottom that are used to provide additional space or bring an existing box flush to a wall or ceiling surface.

F

feeder. The circuit conductors between the service equipment and the final branch-circuit OCPD.

feeder assembly. The conductors, with their fittings and equipment, that carry electrical current from the mobile home service equipment to the distribution panelboard.

field bend. A conduit bend that is made in the field (on the work site).

fill allotment. The number of conductors the *NEC* will allow in certain sizes of boxes.

fish tape. A long tape, either metal or fiberglass, used to pull wires through walls or conduit.

fittings. Parts of a wiring system designed to interconnect conduit, conductors, or boxes.

fixture. A permanently mounted lamp, usually attached to a ceiling or a wall.

flexible metal conduit (FMC). Metal corrugated tubing that provides a flexible conduit.

folding rule. A ruler made of wood, fiberglass, or plastic, that folds into 6″ sections. Usually 6′ total length.

forming shell. The metal shell that is built into a pool wall that will accept a wet-niche lighting fixture.

foundation print. A copy of the drawing that masons use to locate concrete and bricks.

frame number. A number assigned by the National Electrical Manufacturer's Association to catagorize the frame size for each integral horsepower motor.

framing print. A copy of the drawing that the carpenters have when installing the structure of a house.

free electrons. Electrons that are loosely bound to the nucleus of an atom and can easily leave to join other atoms.

fuse. An overcurrent protection device with a metal conductor that melts during an overcurrent condition.

G

ganging boxes. A method of joining small boxes to create one large box that can accommodate multiple devices.

general notes. Notes that contain information that applies to the entire drawing.

generator. A device that uses electromagnetic induction to convert mechanical energy to electrical energy.

Greenfield. A common name for FMC.

grooved-joint pliers. Pliers that allow the jaws to be adjusted to several different spacings.

ground clip. A spring device that is hooked over the edge of a metallic box and holds a grounding wire so that the wire makes electrical contact with the box.

ground fault. A situation when an ungrounded conductor touches a grounded raceway, box, fitting, or equipment ground conductor.

ground-fault circuit interrupter (GFCI). A device that opens a circuit if a current-to-ground is detected.

grounding. The connection of all parts of a wiring installation to the earth or to other systems that are connected conductively to the earth.

grounding-type duplex receptacle. The most common receptacle, it will accept two grounded plugs at the same time.

H

hacksaw. A hand or power saw used to cut metal and PVC pipe. Can create a crooked cut.

hammer drill. An electric hand drill that delivers an impact to the drill bit while drilling. Used for materials such as cinder block and for small diameter holes in concrete.

handy box. A seamless electrical box that has rounded corners and is designed to be surface mounted.

heater circuit. A schematic drawing showing how a heater operates and the proper way to connect it to the electrical system.

Hertz (Hz). A unit of frequency that equals one cycle per second. Named after Heinrich Hertz.

hickey. A tool for bending conduit. It does not have the special markings of a conduit bender.

home run. The length of conductors from a circuit back to the service panel.

hydraulic bender. A conduit bender that uses a hydraulic pump for bending.

I

insulated tools. Tools, with a nonconductive covering, that are designed to prevent the transfer of electricity from the tool to the user.

insulation. A nonconductive material that covers a conductor. Various types listed in *Table 310.13* of the *NEC*.

insulator. A nonconductive device that supports the service drop wires near the service head.

insulators. Substances that prevent electrons from flowing freely.

intermediate metal conduit (IMC). Conduit with walls thicker than EMT but thinner than RMC. Has many advantages over RMC because it is lighter in weight and has more room inside for pulling wires.

intermittent shorts. Problems originating with electrical equipment that occur only at certain times and under certain conditions.

interrupting rating. This is the maximum ampacity at which an overcurrent protection device will operate without any damage.

J

joules. A unit of electrical power. One joule equals one watt-second. Named after James Prescott Joule.

K

kcmil. One thousand circular mils; a standard unit of measure for the cross section of very large conductors.

kilowatt-hours (kWh). A unit of electrical power. One kilowatt-hour is the equivalent of 1000 watts being used for a 1-hour period.

knockout. A weakened area designed to be removed on an electrical box, allowing wires to be brought into the box.

L

left-hand rule. A rule for determining the direction of flow in a conductor caused by electromagnetic induction. Also known as *Fleming's rule.*

legend. The part of the print, plan, or specification that defines each symbol.

level. An essential tool used to make sure conduit and devices are installed plumb (vertical) and level (horizontal).

limited-duty. A motor that will deliver the rated horsepower for a specified period of time, but cannot be operated continuously at the rated load.

lineman's hammer. A heavy hammer, like a mallet, used to drive ground rods into the ground.

lineman's pliers. Pliers with a square nose for pulling wire. Most also have a cutting blade.

liquidtight flexible metal conduit (LFMC). This conduit is FMC with a waterproof outer coating and special fittings to maintain its watertight integrity.

load. Device that converts electricity into another form of energy.

local loop. The telephone connection from the building to the central office.

local notes. Notes that cover a specific area of a drawing.

locking pliers. Pliers that, when squeezed, will remain locked on an object until a release lever is engaged.

lockout device. A safety device that prevents the energizing of a circuit by locking switches, breakers, valves (gas and liquid), or enclosures.

long tape rule. A steel or cloth tape that may be as long as 100′ or 150′.

M

marking. A series of letters, words, trademarks, and numbers that reveals key characteristics about a wire.

MCM. Abbreviation for "thousand circular mils," from the use of Roman numeral "M" for "thousand."

meter. The device that measures and records the amount of electricity used.

meter enclosure. A box that attaches to the service conduit.

meter socket. The receptacle that a meter plugs into.

mobile home. A residential structure that is transportable in one or more sections and is intended to be used without a permanent foundation.

mobile home service equipment. All of the equipment, including a main disconnecting means, overcurrent protective devices, and receptacles or other arrangements, for connecting the supply end of a mobile home feeder assembly. The meter may be regarded as part of the service equipment.

multimeter. A digital or analog meter that measures multiple electrical properties: voltage, resistance, and current. Some will also measure capacitance, temperature, and frequency.

multioutlet assembly. A prewired unit that makes multiple receptacles available. *National Electrical Code (NEC).* The most informative and authoritative body of information concerning electrical wiring installation in the United States.

N

nationally recognized testing laboratory (NRTL). A recognized testing agency that tests materials and equipment submitted to them by electrical material manufacturers to verify that the item is suitable for electrical installation.

needle-nose pliers. Pliers with a long, skinny nose for reaching into crowded spaces.

NEMA 4X. A standard for electrical enclosures set by the National Electrical Manufacturers Association.

neutrons. The particles with no charge in the nucleus of an atom.

noncoincident loads. Loads that will not be placed on a system at the same time.

nonmetallic box. Electrical boxes that are made from a nonmetallic material such as PVC or fiberglass.

nonmetallic sheathed cable (NM). A cable with 2 or more conductors and a ground all within an outer jacket, suitable for use in most residential installations except where conduit is required. NM is called Romex in the trade.

O

Occupational Safety and Health Administration (OSHA). An agency within the United States Department of Labor that is responsible for creating and enforcing health and safety standards to protect persons in all occupations within the U.S.

offset bend. Two bends of equal angle a short distance apart to allow a conduit run to clear an obstacle.

ohms (Ω). The units of measurement used to express resistance. Named after Georg Simon Ohm.

Ohm's law. The law that states the relationship between voltage, resistance, and current.

overcurrent protection device (OCPD). This device shuts off power to a circuit when the current in that circuit exceeds the ampacity rating of the OCPD.

overload. A situation where equipment operates beyond the rated ampacity of that equipment or the conductors within the circuit.

P

parallel circuit. A circuit with multiple paths available for current flow.

patch cable. A length of twisted-pair cable that is terminated on each end with an RJ-45 plug.

personal protective equipment (PPE). The clothing and equipment worn to provide protection from hazards.

pigtail. A short piece of wire that connects multiple wires to a single termination.

pigtail plug. A cord and plug combination that is attached to an appliance.

pipe cutter. A tool that provides a very straight cut, but leaves a large burr.

plaster ring. An extension for a recessed electrical box that brings the face edge of the box even with the surface of the wall.

pliers. A tool used for gripping or cutting.

plot print. A copy of the drawing that excavators use when shaping the land.

plumbing print. A copy of the drawing that the plumbers use to locate fixtures and piping.

potential difference. The difference in the number of electrons at two points; voltage.

power (P). The rate of doing work. Electric power is measured in watts or volt-amperes.

power source. The origin of electrical power.

primary winding. The winding of a transformer that creates a magnetic field and is connected to the power source side.

print. A copy of a drawing that illustrates the materials, locations, and methods that must be used during construction.

protector. A device that prevents high voltage from damaging the cable pair.

protons. The positively charged particles of an atom.

pryout. A knockout removed by inserting the blade of a screwdriver into the pryout's slot.

pull box. An electrical box that is installed wherever conductor splices or pulls must be made in a conduit run that is not appropriate for a switch, receptacle, or fixture. Also called a *junction box*.

R

raceways. A system of conduit, boxes, and fittings through which wires are pulled.

radiation. The primary method by which heat is transferred through energy waves.

reamer. Removes the burrs left behind after cutting metal conduit.

receptacle. A device that is used to transfer electrical energy from conductors to plug-equipped electrical equipment.

receptacle tester. A tester that plugs into an outlet receptacle and indicates the status of the polarity, ground, and sometimes the ground fault capability.

reciprocating saw. A power tool with a cutting blade that moves back and forth to provide the cutting action.

resistance (R). The opposition to the flow of electrons through a conductor.

revision block. This is an area on a drawing where the changes and corrections are recorded.

rigid metal conduit (RMC). The original conduit (before thin-wall and IMC), it is called heavy-wall conduit. It has thick walls and provides the greatest protection for the wires inside. Small sizes can be bent by hand with difficulty; larger sizes must be machine-bent.

rigid nonmetallic conduit (RNC.) A conduit constructed of polyvinyl chloride (PVC), a tough, nonconductive plastic.

Romex. The trade name for NM cable invented by General Cable. It has come into popular use when referring to any brand of NM cable.

rotary hammer drill. A hammer drill that delivers significant impact to the drill bit while turning it. The impact is so strong that special bits must be used.

S

saddle bend. Most commonly a bend made of three bends close together used when the conduit has to leave its surface to go over an obstruction then return to the same surface. There is also a four-bend saddle, which consists of two offsets back-to-back or a short distance apart.

scale. The ratio of the size of an object to the size that the object was reduced or enlarged in the drawing.

secondary winding. The transformer winding connected to the load.

series circuit. A circuit having a single path for current flow.

service drop. Service wires brought to the building that are run overhead from a pole.

service drop mast. A length of rigid conduit that contains the service entrance cable and is mounted between the service head and the meter.

service entrance. All of the wires, devices, and fittings that carry electricity from the power company's transformer to the consumer.

service-entrance cable (SE). The cable used to bring power from the utility pole to the customer's building.

service head. A fitting installed at the top of the service entrance cable to prevent water from entering the meter socket.

service lateral. Service wires brought to the building that are routed underground, from either a pole or transformer pad.

service load. The total of all branch circuit loads and feeder loads.

sharpening stone. A small stone used to sharpen knife blades.

short circuit. An overcurrent caused by the connection of an ungrounded conductor to a grounded conductor or the connection of two ungrounded conductors that have a potential difference between them.

shrink. The effective shortening of the overall length of a piece of conduit due to bending.

single-element fuse. A fuse that has a single element of one or more links that quickly melts in response to an overcurrent.

solder. A metal alloy that melts easily to join wires together. Also used for joining copper water pipe.

soldering gun. An electric tool used to heat solder to its melting point.

soldering paste. A special paste applied to wires prior to soldering.

solenoid voltage tester (Wiggy®). A tester that uses a solenoid to indicate the presence of voltage.

solid. A conductor that is made of a single, solid, flexible strand.

specifications. Documents that list the items of a schedule, the local code requirements not found in the *NEC*, and designations of those responsible for supplying the materials.

splicing. The process of connecting one wire to one or more wires.

split-wired receptacle. A duplex receptacle wired so one of the outlets is controlled by a switch while the other is always energized.

steel tape. A measuring tape with U.S. customary or metric markings (or both) made of flexible steel that rolls up into a case when not in use.

step-down transformer. A transformer that steps down, or decreases, the voltage exiting the transformer.

step-up transformer. A transformer that steps up, or increases, the voltage exiting the transformer.

stranded. A conductor that is made of many thin strands that are bundled together.

stray currents. Currents that do not follow the intended path.

stub bend. A 90° bend used to bring a usually horizontal run of conduit up into a device box. Also called a *stub-up bend*.

substation. A collection of transformers that changes the voltage of the electrical power and redistributes it along another set of conductors.

suicide cord. A cord that has a male plug on each end.

switch box. A wall box designed for switches only.

system grounding. The intentional connection of one conductor of the electrical system to the earth.

T

tagout. The identification procedure that is used to let other workers know who applied a lockout.

telephone wall plate. A special faceplate that has two mounting pegs that fit the slots on the mounting base of a wall-mount telephone.

temporary wiring. A method of providing electrical power only during construction, remodeling, demolition, repair, or large-scale maintenance of a building.

terminal block. The junction point for all the telephones in the building; also called a *42A block*, a *modular interface*, or a *modular outlet*.

time-delay fuse. A fuse that allows for momentary overloads.

title block. This is the area on a print that contains basic information such as the drawing name, names of people that worked on the original drawing, drawing number, and drawing scale.

torpedo level. A special level that is only several inches long, usually not more than a foot. It is handier than an ordinary level since it fits in a toolbox or tool pouch.

transfer switch. This device disconnects the service conductors from the home's circuit just before connecting the circuit to a generator.

transformer. A device that transfers electrical energy from one circuit to another, usually at a different voltage, through electromagnetic induction.

transformer rule. The total voltage in the primary coil is to the total voltage in the secondary coil as the number of turns in the primary is to the number of turns in the secondary.

U

underground feeder and branch-circuit cable (UF). Similar to NM, this cable is suitable for direct burial in the ground. It is used for providing power to detached garages, yard lamps, and outbuildings.

underground service-entrance cable (USE). Service-entrance cable that is approved for direct burial in the ground.

uninterruptible power supply (UPS). This device contains a battery and an inverter that immediately supplies power during an outage.

V

volt (V). The units of measurement of electromotive force caused by the difference in potential between two bodies. Named after Alessandro Volta.

voltage drop. The loss of electrical pressure (voltage) along a length of conductor caused by the resistance of the conductor.

volt-amperes (VA). Very simply, volts multiplied by amps. The amount of power an electric system can provide or the amount of power an electrical device requires. Equivalent to watts in simple systems. Abbreviated as volt-amps.

W

wall box. An electrical box for housing a switch or a receptacle.

Watt's law. The law that states the relationship between power, voltage, and current.

watts (W). The units of measurement used in expressing power delivered to or consumed by an electrical device. Named after James Watt.

wet cell. A battery that uses a liquid electrolyte.

wet-niche fixture. An underwater pool light that is designed to get wet and is made up of a lamp within a housing, a flexible cord, and a sealed lens.

whetstone. A hard, fine-grained stone for sharpening tools

windings. The coils of wire in an electrical device. Windings are used in generators, motors, and transformers.

wire. A metal conductor and the insulation that surrounds it. If the conductor normally has no insulation, it too is called a wire.

wire connector. A device that joins wires together by forcing them into the connector's cone-shaped cavity where a metal coil cuts threads into the wires

wire stripper. A form of pliers with various cutting surfaces for standard wire gages.

wiring. The wires installed in a building that provide the electrical power throughout.

wiring system. In residential construction, the materials and components used to deliver electricity from the service panel to electrical devices. The wiring system includes the wire, its insulating cover, a protective cover, and the connectors that fasten it to an electrical box.

work. The process of changing energy from one form to another, or causing an object too gain or lose energy.

Y

yard pole. A centrally located distribution point consisting of a large pole, meter, and power lines.

Index

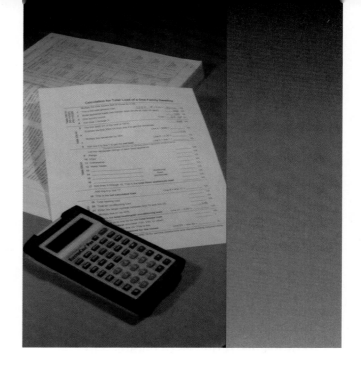